Atlas of the Breeding Birds of Ontario

2001-2005

Editors

Michael D. Cadman, Donald A. Sutherland, Gregor G. Beck, Denis Lepage, Andrew R. Couturier

Publishers

Bird Studies Canada, Environment Canada, Ontario Field Ornithologists,
Ontario Ministry of Natural Resources, Ontario Nature

Library and Archives Canada Cataloguing in Publication

Atlas of the breeding birds of Ontario, 2001-2005 / editors, Michael D. Cadman ... [et al.].

Co-published by: Bird Studies Canada, Environment Canada, Ontario Field Ornithologists, Ontario Ministry of Natural Resources, and Ontario Nature.
Includes bibliographical references and index.
ISBN 978-1-896059-15-0

1. Birds--Ontario. 2. Birds--Ontario--Geographical distribution. 3. Birds--Ontario--Geographical distribution--Maps. 4. Bird populations--Ontario.
I. Cadman, Michael D. (Michael Derrick), 1955- II. Ontario Nature

QL685.5.O5A863 2007 598.09713 C2007-906205-9

This book has been printed on paper harvested from responsibly managed forests that are certified by the FSC (Forest Stewardship Council). The printer of this book, Friesens Corporation, was Canada's first FSC certified book manufacturer, winning Graphic Monthly's 2006 Printer of the Year for blending 100 years of success with social responsibility.

Inks containing soy and linseed oil as well as water-based adhesives were used in the manufacturing of "*Atlas of the Breeding Birds of Ontario, 2001-2005.*"

For more information about the FSC, visit: www.fsc.org

Design: V. John Lee Communication Graphics Inc.
Copy editing: Maureen Garvie
Printed and bound in Canada by Friesens

Published by Bird Studies Canada, Environment Canada, Ontario Field Ornithologists, Ontario Ministry of Natural Resources, and Ontario Nature

For publication and sales information, contact:
Ontario Nature
366 Adelaide Street West, Suite 201
Toronto, Ontario, Canada M5V 1R9
Phone: 416-444-8419 or 1-800-440-2366
www.birdsontario.org or www.ontarionature.org

Suggested citation for this work:

Cadman, M.D., D.A. Sutherland, G.G. Beck, D. Lepage, and A.R. Couturier (eds.). 2007. Atlas of the Breeding Birds of Ontario, 2001-2005. Bird Studies Canada, Environment Canada, Ontario Field Ornithologists, Ontario Ministry of Natural Resources, and Ontario Nature, Toronto, xxii + 706 pp.

Suggested citation for a section of this work:

Cadman, M.D. 2007. Baltimore Oriole, pp. 606-607 in Cadman, M.D., D.A. Sutherland, G.G. Beck, D. Lepage, and A.R. Couturier, eds. Atlas of the Breeding Birds of Ontario, 2001-2005. Bird Studies Canada, Environment Canada, Ontario Field Ornithologists, Ontario Ministry of Natural Resources, and Ontario Nature, Toronto, xxii + 706 pp.

Cover Photographs
Front: John Reaume
Back: Brandon Holden

Additional Photographs
p. xiii: Gregor G. Beck
p. 54: Ethan Meleg
p. 634: Ron Ridout

The *Atlas of the Breeding Birds of Ontario*, 2001-2005

is dedicated to the thousands of volunteer participants
who made this project so successful.

*Net profits from the sale of this book will be used
for bird conservation projects in Ontario.*

For more information about the Ontario Breeding Bird Atlas project,
visit www.birdsontario.org

Atlas Sponsors

(in alphabetical order)

As in the first Ontario Breeding Bird Atlas, **Bird Studies Canada** (formerly Long Point Bird Observatory) is a proud partner in the delivery of the second atlas project. BSC is Canada's largest non-government organization dedicated to the study of wild birds and their habitats, drawing upon the skills and enthusiasm of volunteers who are engaged in meaningful "citizen science."

For more information, contact: Bird Studies Canada, P.O. Box 160, Port Rowan, ON, N0E 1M0. Toll free, 1-888-448-BIRD; fax: 519-586-3532; generalinfo@bsc-eoc.org; Web: www.bsc-eoc.org.

Environment Canada   Environnement Canada

Environment Canada's Canadian Wildlife Service manages wildlife matters that are the responsibility of the federal government. These include protection and management of migratory birds, nationally significant habitat, and species at risk, as well as work on other wildlife issues of national and international importance. The department does research in many fields of wildlife biology and provides incentive programs for wildlife and habitat stewardship. As such, Environment Canada is pleased to support the Ontario Breeding Bird Atlas.

For more information, visit: www.on.ec.gc.ca/wildlife.

The **Ontario Field Ornithologists** (OFO) is the provincial organization dedicated to the study of birds in Ontario. It publishes the journal *Ontario Birds* and the newsletter *OFO News*, operates the listserv *Ontbirds*, hosts field trips, holds an annual convention, oversees the Ontario Bird Records Committee (OBRC), and maintains the official provincial bird checklist. OFO is pleased to be an atlas partner, serving on the Management Board and committees. Its members were active participants as atlassers, species account authors, reviewers, and scientific editors.

For more information, visit: www.ofo.ca.

The **Ontario Ministry of Natural Resources** (OMNR) is responsible for the management and stewardship of Ontario's natural resources. Along with the other atlas partners, OMNR has been actively involved seeking support and collecting data (particularly in Northern Ontario) to deliver a world-class breeding bird atlas. OMNR also played a leadership role through direct involvement on the Management Board and various atlas committees.

For more information on OMNR and its programs, visit: www.mnr.gov.on.ca.

Ontario Nature (formerly Federation of Ontario Naturalists) is very pleased to be a partner in the second Ontario Breeding Bird Atlas, building on the success of the first atlas project in the 1980s. Ontario Nature protects and restores natural habitats through research, education, and conservation action, connecting thousands of individuals and communities with nature. It champions wild areas and wildlife throughout Ontario and preserves essential habitat through its own system of nature reserves. Ontario Nature is a charitable organization representing over 140 member groups and 25,000 individuals across Ontario, many of whom were Ontario Breeding Bird Atlas volunteers.

For more information, contact: Ontario Nature, Suite 201, 366 Adelaide Street West, Toronto, ON, M5V 1R9.
Toll free, 1-800-440-2366; Web: www.ontarionature.org.

About the Editors

General Editors

Michael D. Cadman is a Senior Songbird Biologist, Ontario Region, Canadian Wildlife Service, Environment Canada. He worked "on assignment" for Ontario Nature as coordinator of the second atlas project and was also coordinator of the first atlas project from 1981 to 1987.

Donald A. Sutherland is a Natural Heritage Zoologist with the Natural Heritage Information Centre, Biodiversity Section, Fish & Wildlife Branch, Ontario Ministry of Natural Resources. During the atlas he worked on a number of technical committees, primarily with the Significant Species committee documenting and reviewing records for rare, threatened, endangered, and colonial-nesting species.

Gregor G. Beck is chair of the Atlas Management Board and a member of the Publication, Book and Marketing Committees. During the atlas period, he served as director, Conservation and Science, with Ontario Nature, and director, Avian Science and Conservation, with Bird Studies Canada. He is currently leading consulting projects in conservation, environmental communications, and wildlife ecology research.

Data Management

Dr. Denis Lepage is a Senior Scientist, National Data Centre, with Bird Studies Canada. In addition to maintaining the atlas database, he also created and maintained the Internet data management applications used by volunteers and the various committees. He participated actively in several of the atlas committees and is also involved in other atlas projects elsewhere in Canada.

Spatial Analysis and Maps

Andrew R. Couturier is a GIS analyst with Bird Studies Canada and is closely involved in several atlas projects across Canada. He participated in a number of technical committees including taking lead roles in the design of the Point Count sampling method and in the design and production of maps for the book and web page.

Species Account Editors

Ken Abraham (OMNR) and Ken Ross (CWS) (35 accounts): Waterfowl.

Ted (E.R.) Armstrong (OMNR) (19 accounts): Diurnal raptors and Great Horned Owl, Snowy Owl, Northern Hawk Owl, Great Gray Owl, Long-eared Owl.

Michael D. Cadman (CWS) (12 accounts): Blackbirds.

Bill Crins (OFO) (26 accounts): Shrikes, Vireos, Corvids, Larks, Chickadees, Creeper, Wrens, Starling.

Seabrooke Leckie (Ontario Nature) (98 accounts): all other species.

Margaret McLaren (OMNR) (21 accounts): Kinglets, Gnatcatcher, Thrushes, Mimids, Pipits, Waxwings, Tanagers.

Erica Nol (Trent University) (25 accounts): Shorebirds.

Ron Pittaway (OFO) (8 accounts): Clay-colored Sparrow, Vesper Sparrow, White-crowned Sparrow, Pine Grosbeak, Red Crossbill, White-winged Crossbill, Pine Siskin, Evening Grosbeak.

Al Sandilands (Gray Owl Environmental Inc.) (34 accounts): Gallinaceous birds through Grebes, Bitterns, Turkey Vulture, Rails, Sandhill Crane, Jaeger, Pigeons and Doves, Cuckoos.

Don Sutherland (OMNR) (1 account): Yellow-breasted Chat.

Ron Tozer (26 accounts): Nightjars to Flycatchers.

Chip Weseloh (CWS) (3 accounts): Black Tern, Common Tern, Great Egret.

Table of Contents

Foreword

The *Atlas of the Breeding Birds of Ontario, 2001-2005* is the product of the efforts of more than 3,000 volunteer atlassers and project participants and five project partners over a period of more than eight years. These years span the full breadth of the Ontario Breeding Bird Atlas project, including planning and preliminary field trials in 1999 and 2000, an impressive five years of fieldwork from 2001 to 2005, years of data and geographic information system analyses, extensive cartographic and photographic efforts, and an extraordinary push over the last two years to complete the writing, reviewing, editing, final mapping, and design that now comprise this atlas publication.

Over the course of this monumental undertaking, several themes have emerged, and these reflect the people involved, the tremendous project partnerships, and, of course, innumerable stories about both Ontario's birds and birders. The stories range from personal observations of avian biology and bird courtship to the more scientific and environmental stories now emerging from the results about breeding bird populations, distributions, and changes since the first atlas was completed some twenty years ago.

In a way, the atlas project is *almost* as much about the people who have participated as it is about the birds themselves. Any attempt to summarize or tabulate the extensive contributions of volunteers and staff over this period will be incomplete and underestimated, but some examples may provide an inkling of the magnitude and may begin to express our appreciation to all who participated. Collectively, atlassers contributed over 150,000 field hours to the project, plus about as many hours again compiling results, preparing for fieldwork, and travelling to and from field locations. In addition, much of the book itself was written, reviewed, and edited through volunteer efforts by scores of people, and every one of the photographs was donated. By conservative measures, this incredible volunteer effort translates into an "in-kind" contribution of about $4 million. This, however, does not include the very significant additional in-kind contributions by individuals and organizations toward the cost of travel, equipment, and supplies. The project's field effort was spread across the vast geographic expanse of Ontario's 1.1 million square kilometres, resulting in the successful attainment of one of the project's major objectives – to map the breeding distribution of birds across the entire province. This field effort culminated in the submission of 1.2 million individual bird records, from casual backyard observations to extensive, and often exhaustive, field trips into Ontario's most remote locations. Without the skill and determination of this throng of enthusiastic birders and field biologists, the atlas could neither have been envisioned nor successfully completed. The atlas organizers extend their sincere thanks and appreciation to this dedicated corps of volunteer citizen scientists and project biologists.

The success of the Ontario Breeding Bird Atlas is the result also of the hard work and support of numerous other volunteers and staff. Central to it all was the critical assistance of about four dozen volunteer Regional Coordinators (RCs), who supported, encouraged, organized, and otherwise helped atlassers to complete the planning, fieldwork, and follow-up in regions across the province. RCs were a critical connection between front-line field observers and atlas organizers and helped to ensure complete coverage of atlas squares. These individuals had their fingers on the pulse of the project, and almost invariably put in many extra hours in the field themselves to help complete coverage in various parts of the province. Their names and the regions they coordinated are shown in Table 1.1 and Figure 1.3 in the Methods chapter. Two other volunteers deserve special mention here as they exemplified the spirit of atlassing. Glenn Coady was RC for Toronto and put in innumerable hours both near home and in the far reaches of northern Ontario, literally starting on 1 January 2001 and continuing his fieldwork until 31 December 2005. Reinder Westerhoff volunteered throughout the duration of the project in the atlas office, particularly helping to organize trips to remote northern areas and organizing and leading "square-bashes" in the most difficult-to-cover parts of southern Ontario.

The atlas project benefited from the leadership and support of many staff from several organizations and governmental agencies. These individuals kept us all on track, provided expert (and often around-the-clock) support to atlassers, RCs, and project organizers. Their efforts have gone far beyond the "requirements of the job," and they have been some of the most generous and dedicated volunteers among us. First, special recognition is owed to the project's full-time staff. Mike Cadman was Coordinator for the Ontario Breeding Bird Atlas, and was also Coordinator for the first atlas. From start to finish, Mike provided the atlas with strong and positive leadership, detailed ornithological knowledge, and insightful day-to-day project management. We benefited greatly from his expertise and guidance, his unflappable patience and dedication, and his friendly and good-humoured nature. Without doubt, Mike was the ultimate atlas ambassador! Special thanks go to Environment Canada's Canadian Wildlife Service for so generously assigning him to the atlas project for its duration. The atlas also benefited from the major contributions of our three Assistant Coordinators. Nicole Kopysh worked on the project for five years through virtually the entire fieldwork period, helping with atlassing logistics, volunteer recruitment and training, and data entry. Nicole was the main contact between the project's volunteers and the office, and her charm, energy, and organizational skills contributed greatly to the overall success of the project. Angela Darwin followed capably in her footsteps, helping with the final year of fieldwork and data management and starting the publication process. Rebecca Harrold joined the team for the final year and a half of the project and worked diligently and professionally in dealing with a myriad of details relating to project completion and book preparation.

Special acknowledgment and thanks go to others who contributed enormously through either their work or as volunteers, or frequently both. Andrew Couturier was the atlas's mapping and GIS expert and spatial analyst throughout, producing the majority of maps for the book; Denis Lepage designed and managed the enormous database and the on-line systems for data entry, rare species review, and manuscript management; Donald Sutherland was on several committees, helped coordinate coverage in the far north (and did a lot of the fieldwork himself!), was the primary reviewer of rare species records, edited and wrote numerous species accounts, and was a co-editor of this book; Bill Crins was on almost every atlas committee, including the Management Board, chaired the Volunteer Committee, was a Regional Coordinator and species account editor, wrote many species accounts, and was lead author on the biogeography chapter of this book; Ken Abraham sat on several committees, contributed greatly to the coverage of far northern Ontario, was a species account editor, and wrote several species accounts; Jon McCracken was on the Management Board, acted briefly as a Regional Coordinator, was heavily involved in special fieldwork projects, and wrote and reviewed numerous species accounts; Chris Davies served on the Management Board and provided extensive assistance and insightful advice in numerous areas; Bruce Pond produced the endpaper maps and many of the maps in the introductory chapters of this book, and provided valuable leadership on point count mapping and designing the system used to sample squares in the north; Kevin Middel and Bruce developed and produced the field maps and contributed greatly to the analysis for production of relative abundance maps; Charles Francis chaired the Bird Change Committee, was the person who originally encouraged us to collect abundance data, and played a leading role on the Point Count Committee; Peter Blancher designed and undertook much of the change analyses, calculated population estimates, and co-wrote the change chapter; Erica Dunn played a key role on the Point Count and Bird Change Committees, led the production of the appendix on Point Count data collection, and provided considerable editorial input to technical materials in the book; Ryan Zimmerling led the special boreal bird research project that significantly enhanced the level of field coverage in Ontario's north country; and Pete Read, with Julee Boan's logistical help, led special Northern Boreal projects in collaboration with First Nation communities.

The completion of this book was made possible by the very generous and skilled contributions of scores of individuals who wrote, reviewed, and edited the various chapters and species accounts (see the Acknowledgements and Species Accounts sections). The amount of time spent researching, writing, reviewing, editing, and proofing a book of this scale is great, and we thank all of these individuals very much for contributing their time and knowledge. Special thanks is due to the following species account editors who worked with the authors to review, edit, and revise the species accounts section: Ken Abraham, Ted Armstrong, Mike Cadman, Bill Crins, Seabrooke Leckie, Margaret McLaren, Erica Nol, Ron Pittaway, Ken Ross, Al Sandilands, Don Sutherland, Ron Tozer, and Chip Weseloh. I would also like to extend special thanks to my co-editors of the full book manuscript, Mike Cadman and Donald Sutherland.

The atlas extends its thanks to everyone who donated, or submitted for consideration, photographs to the atlas, helping to make the book more informative and considerably more attractive. More than 6,000 images were submitted for consideration by professional and amateur bird photographers alike, from which more than 400 were selected to illustrate the species, and in some cases breeding habitat and nests.

The atlas team expresses its sincere thanks to John Lee, V. John Lee Communication Graphics Inc., who not only did an exemplary job in the design and layout of the book but also provided helpful and much appreciated input to the publication and printing processes. We extend our appreciation also to Maureen Garvie who copy-edited this large manuscript and helped to bring consistency and unity to a complex, multi-authored initiative. We also thank the printing team at Friesens for their assistance with production of the book. The Faculty of Environmental Science at the University of Guelph contributed substantially to the project by providing a home for the atlas office for its duration. Special thanks are due to Michael Moss, Josef Ackerman, Stewart Hilts, and Joy Steele for their support throughout. The University of Guelph also hosted the listserv, which provided an invaluable link between the office and atlassers.

The Ontario Breeding Bird Atlas illustrates one of the most successful and positive project partnerships imaginable. Through the years of planning, fieldwork, and publication preparation, the atlas has benefited from the contributions and tremendous support of the five sponsoring groups: Bird Studies Canada, Environment Canada's Canadian Wildlife Service, Ontario Field Ornithologists, Ontario Ministry of Natural Resources, and Ontario Nature. Each partner played a vital role and contributed greatly through the provision of expertise, time, and organizational support. Nowhere is this dedication better reflected than in the skilful efforts and collaboration of the atlas's organizing framework of Management Board and committees. Members of these groups have provided direction and leadership for all aspects of the project, including designing field methods, planning, budgeting and fundraising, data analysis and management, reviewing significant species records, publication planning, and general project oversight, to name just a few areas of involvement. Despite the enormity and complexity of this project, the Ontario Breeding Bird Atlas has proceeded in an effective and efficient fashion throughout to achieve its critical milestones. That this has been accomplished professionally and with good spirits is a testament to the tremendous commitment and contributions of the project partners, and to the individual members of the Management Board and atlas committees whose names are listed in the Acknowledgements. Sincere thanks to the project partners and the members of these organizing groups.

The atlas organizers are committed to conservation, and the results of the project will benefit birds and bird habitat and inform sustainable resource management for years to come. To help demonstrate this commitment to conservation, the Atlas Management Board has made two very important publication decisions in this regard. First, the *Atlas of the Breeding Birds of Ontario, 2001-2005* is being printed and produced in accordance with standards developed by the Forest Stewardship Council Canada (www.fsccanada.org). The paper stock and printing process selected by the Atlas Management Board and Publication Committee reflect the project's commitment to sustainable forestry and to conservation while at the same time maintaining a commitment to publication excellence. The application of the FSC logo illustrates the commitment of the paper producer, the book's printer, and the atlas project itself to the FSC mission "to promote environmentally appropriate, socially beneficial and economically viable management of the world's forests." Second, the Atlas Management Board has adopted the policy that any net profits from the sale of this book will be used to further bird conservation projects in Ontario.

In the following pages, you will discover some of the stories that the atlas has to share about birds and bird distribution and status in Ontario. The efforts of volunteers and staff have been compiled into this single volume that we hope will be a valuable reference for conservation planning, resource management, species at risk recovery, environmental assessments, and educational and research applications. The combined efforts of atlassers across the province tell both good news and bad: from the encouraging recovery of many birds of prey, such as the Bald Eagle and Peregrine Falcon, and the expansion of breeding ranges of many northern birds into areas south of the Canadian Shield, to worrying trends for other species such as grassland birds like the Henslow's Sparrow and Loggerhead Shrike and aerial-foraging species including most swallows, the Chimney Swift and the Common Nighthawk.

There are, of course, a lot more stories from the Ontario Breeding Bird Atlas than those that appear in this book. These are the more personal ones – ones that any of the individual atlas contributors could share based on their experiences in the field. Some stories may come from casual observations, perhaps a backyard birding ritual over coffee spent observing a pair of Baltimore Orioles first in courtship, then nest building, and ultimately feeding and fledging young through the course of the breeding season. Or, perhaps, a chance, opportunistic sighting from a car window of a Red-shouldered Hawk carrying food to a nest in the forest. Other atlassers may fondly recall early morning trips to a particular square and the challenge of conducting point counts amidst insects or threatening weather. For many, the stories will be of time spent happily with friends and family on trips far from home – perhaps on canoe or camping trips in Ontario's Boreal Forest, where a glimpse of a pair of Sandhill Cranes or of Olive-sided Flycatchers feeding young provided unforgettable images of life along a meandering boreal stream.... All atlassers will have personal recollections and anecdotes, and it is heartening to think that each of these is now part of the larger, collective atlas story. These personal stories complement the stories yet to come from researchers and conservationists who are now beginning to analyze and use the results for the benefit of birds and bird habitats.

On behalf the project's organizers, I extend the most sincere thanks to everyone involved and trust that the *Atlas of the Breeding Birds of Ontario, 2001-2005* will inspire increased interest and respect for birds and heightened effectiveness for bird conservation and research efforts in Ontario and beyond.

Gregor G. Beck
Chair, Atlas Management Board
October 2007

Acknowledgements

The sponsors of the Ontario Breeding Bird Atlas extend their sincere thanks to the numerous supporters, contributors, and volunteers of this enormous and important bird research and conservation project. The following listing of atlas friends and collaborators illustrates the extent of participation and the strength of the partnerships involved.

The Ontario Breeding Bird Atlas thanks the following for their financial support:

Environment Canada

METCALF FOUNDATION

Ontario Ministry of Natural Resources

The Ontario Trillium Foundation is an agency of the Government of Ontario. For 25 years, it has supported the growth and vitality of communities across the province. OTF continues to strengthen the capacity of the volunteer sector through investments in community-based initiatives.

James L. Baillie Memorial Fund of Bird Studies Canada, with funds raised through the annual Baillie Birdathon

Canadian **Boreal** Initiative
Edwards Charitable Foundation
Human Resources and Skills Development Canada's
Summer Career Placement Program
The McLean Foundation

De Beers Canada Inc.
Eagle Optics.ca

The Ontario Breeding Bird Atlas thanks the following for providing in-kind support:

Environment Canada
Ontario Ministry of Natural Resources

Abitibi-Consolidated Company of Canada Limited
Algonquin Forestry Authority
Air Creebec Inc.
Bearskin Airlines
Bird Studies Canada
Bowater Canada Incorporated
Canadian Forest Service
Canoe Frontier Expeditions
De Beers Canada Inc.
Domtar Incorporated
Ducks Unlimited Canada
ESRI Canada
Kanipahow Kamps and Adams Lake Outfitters
Kimberly-Clark Incorporated
LGL Limited
Musselwhite Mine (Goldcorp Canada Ltd.)
Nature and Outdoor Tourism Ontario
Northern Ontario Native Tourism Association
North Star Air Ltd.
OMNR Aviation Services
Ontario Field Ornithologists
Ontario Nature
Pine Portage Lodge
Spruce Shores Lodge
Tembec Incorporated
University of Guelph, Faculty
of Environmental Sciences
Viking Island Lodge
Wasaya Airways
Weyerhaeuser Company of Canada
Wildlife Habitat Canada

The Ontario Breeding Bird Atlas thanks the following First Nation communities and organizations for their participation and support of the project:

Attawapiskat
Cat Lake
Fort Albany
Fort Severn
Moose Factory
Mushkegowuk Council
Nabinamik
North Caribou
North Spirit Lake
Peawanuck
Pikangikum
Six Nations
Slate Falls
Walpole Island

The Ontario Breeding Bird Atlas extends its sincere thanks to the following people who contributed to the project:

Committee Members

Atlas Management Board
Chair: L.R.L. (Ric) Symmes (2000-2001), Ontario Nature
Chair: Gregor G. Beck (2001-2007, Member 2000-2007), Ontario Nature and BSC
Michael Bradstreet (2000-2003), BSC
Bill Crins (2000-2007), OFO
Chris Davies (2000-2007), OMNR
Wendy Francis (2005-2007), Ontario Nature
Jean Iron (2000-2007), OFO
Jon McCracken (2000-2007), BSC
Rick Pratt (2000-2005), CWS
Caroline Schultz (2007), Ontario Nature
Eleanor Zurbrigg (2005-2007), CWS

Technical/Bird Change Committee
Chair: Mike Cadman (2000-2005)
Chair: Charles Francis (2005-2007, Member 2000-2007), BSC and CWS

Ken Abraham (2000-2007), OMNR
Peter Blancher (2005-2007), Environment Canada
Edward Cheskey (2000-2002)
Andrew Couturier (2000-2007), BSC
Bill Crins (2000-2007) RC, Peterborough
Erica Dunn (2000-2007), Environment Canada
Steve Holmes (2000-2005), Canadian Forest Service
Denis Lepage (2000-2007), BSC
Jon McCracken (2000-2005), BSC
Mark Peck (2000-2005), Royal Ontario Museum
Bruce Pond (2005-2007), OMNR
Rob Rempel (2005-2007), OMNR
Chris Risley (2000-2005), OMNR
Al Sandilands (2000-2005), Gray Owl Environmental Inc.

Point Count Committee
Chair: Mike Cadman (2000-2004)
Co-chair: Andrew Couturier (2004-2007), Member (2000-2007), BSC
Co-chair: Bruce Pond (2004-2007), Member (2000-2007), OMNR
Charles Francis (2000-2007), BSC and CWS
Erica Dunn (2000-2007), Environment Canada
Pilar Hernandez (2002-2003), University of Toronto
Pat Hodgson (2004-2007), University of Toronto
Steve Holmes (2000), Canadian Forest Service
Denis Lepage (2002-2007), BSC
Jock McKay (2000-2001), University of Waterloo
Stephanie Melles (2002-2007), University of Toronto
Kevin Middel (2004-2007), OMNR
Rob Rempel (2004-2007), OMNR
Adam Smith (2004), Carleton University
Lisa Venier (2000-2007), Canadian Forest Service
Ryan Zimmerling (2004-2007), BSC

Significant Species Committee
Chair: Edward Cheskey (2000-2007)
Bill Crins, (2000-2007), OFO
Bob Curry (2000-2007)
Ross James (2000-2007)
Denis Lepage (2000-2007), BSC
Jon McCracken (2000-2007), BSC
Margaret McLaren (2003-2007), OMNR
Mark Peck (2000-2007), Royal Ontario Museum
Chris Risley (2005-2007), OMNR
Al Sandilands (2000-2007), Gray Owl Environmental Inc.
Don Sutherland (2000-2007), OMNR
Chip Weseloh (2004-2007), CWS

Volunteer Committee
Chair: Bill Crins (2001-2005), RC, Peterborough
Debra Badzinski (2001-2005), BSC
Jennifer Baker (2003-2005), Ontario Nature
Bob Bowles (2001-2005), RC, Simcoe
Christine Hanrahan (2001-2005), RC, Ottawa
Andrea Kettle (2001-2003), Ontario Nature
Dave Martin (2001-2005), RC, London
Chris Risley (2001-2005), RC, Peterborough
Ron Tozer (2001-2005), RC, Algonquin

Publication Committee
Chair: Al Sandilands (2005-2007), Gray Owl Environmental Inc.
Ken Abraham (2005-2007), OMNR
Gregor Beck (2005-2007), BSC
Edward Cheskey (2005-2007)
Andrew Couturier (2005-2007), BSC
Bill Crins (2005-2007) RC, Peterborough
Wendy Francis (2005-2007), Ontario Nature
Denis Lepage (2005-2007), BSC
Don Sutherland (2005-2007), OMNR

Book Sub-Committee
Chair: Gregor G. Beck (2005 -2007), BSC
Andrew Couturier (2005-2007), BSC
L. Rebecca Harrold (2006-2007), Ontario Nature
V. John Lee (2005-2007), V. John Lee Communication Graphics Inc.

Marketing Sub-Committee
Gregor G. Beck (2007), BSC
Bob Curry (2007)
Lesley Marshall (2007), Ontario Nature
Elaine Secord (2007), BSC
Glenda Slessor (2007)
April White (2007), CWS

Production of the "Bluebird" and "Nuthatch" CD-ROMs
Antonio Salvadori
Charles Francis

Data Analysis
Peter Blancher, Environment Canada

Staff
Coordinator: Michael D. Cadman (2000-2007), CWS/Ontario Nature

Assistant Coordinators:
Nicole Kopysh (2000-2005), Ontario Nature
Angela Darwin (2005-2006), Ontario Nature
L. Rebecca Harrold (2006-2007), Ontario Nature

Database and Website Management: Denis Lepage, BSC

Spatial Analysis and Mapping: Andrew Couturier, BSC

Data Scanning:
John Gorniak (2001-2002), Ontario Nature
Susan Debreceni (2002-2006), BSC

Boreal Forest Bird Project, BSC:
Scientist: J. Ryan Zimmerling
Assistant Coordinators: Fergus Nicoll and Doug Tozer
Field Survey Team Leaders: Martha Allen, Kevin Cowcill

Northern Boreal Project, Ontario Nature:
Pete Read, Dan Schuurman, Josh Shook

Field Survey Coordinators, Ontario Nature:
John Haselmayer, Joel Kits, Bill McLeish, Doug Tozer

Editorial Assistants, Ontario Nature:
Charles Cecile, Seabrooke Leckie, Joseph Muise, Doug Tozer, Lisa Westerhoff

Office Volunteers:
Franziska Boerlin, John Burger, Garth Casbourn, Nadia Cicco, John and Marlene Hart, Bruce and Carol Koenig, Allyson Parker, Mary Ellen Pyear, Larry Staniforth, Reinder Westerhoff

Regional Coordinators
See Table 1.1 in Methods chapter.

Authors
Species account authors are credited at the end of each species account. Authors of other sections are credited at the beginning of each section, as appropriate.

Reviewers of Species Accounts
Ken Abraham (OMNR), Dave Ankney, Ted (E.R.) Armstrong, Madeline Austen, Debra S. Badzinski (BSC), Shannon S. Badzinski (Long Point Waterfowl and Wetlands Research Fund), Margaret J.C. Bain, Jim Baker (OMNR), Kim Baker, Gregor G. Beck, Peter Blancher, Chris Blomme (Laurentian University), Jacques Bouvier, Jeff Bowman, David Brewer, Serge Brodeur, Rodney W. Brook (OMNR), Christine Trudeau-Brunet, Dawn Burke (OMNR), Peter G Bush, Michael D. Cadman (CWS), Geoff Carpentier, Cindy E.J. Cartwright, Karen Cedar, Allen T. Chartier, Rosalind Chaundy-Smart, Edward Cheskey, Glenn Coady, Daryl Coulson (OMNR), Shawn R. Craik (McGill University), William J. Crins, Kathryn Dickson, Sandy Dobbyn, Rob Dobos, David H. Elder, Christopher G. Harris, Nicholas G. Escott, David Euler (Birch Point Enterprises), J. Bruce Falls, Nancy Flood, Sarah Fraser, Barbara Frei, Marcel A. Gahbauer (Migration Research Foundation), Jean Gauthier (CWS), Mark Gawn, Michel Gendron (CWS), Dr. Alan G. Gordon (Canadian Forest Service), Stew Hamill, Allan G. Harris (Northern Bioscience Ecological Consulting), John Haselmayer (Parks Canada), Audrey Heagy (BSC), Fred Helleiner, Leo E. Heyens (OMNR), Tyler Hoar, Steve Holmes (Natural Resources Canada), Patrick Hubert, Marie-Anne Hudson, Jack Hughes (CWS), David J.T. Hussell, Ross James, Andrew P. Jobes (OMNR), Marc Johnson (OMNR), Paul Jones, James Kamstra, Karl R. Konze, Nicole C. Kopysh, Anthony L. Lang, Jim Leafloor, Seabrooke Leckie, Sheridan Leckie, Harry G. Lumsden, Mark Mallory (CWS), Julia Marko Dunn, Dave Martin, Pam Martin, Pamela Martin, Jon McCracken (BSC), Margaret A. McLaren (OMNR), Peter L. McLaren, Bob Montgomerie (Queen's University), Dave Moore (CWS), François Morneau, Ralph D. Morris, Brian Naylor (OMNR), Linh P. Nguyen, Mark A.J. O'Connor, Stephen O'Donnell, Kathy Parker, Martin Parker, Jennie L. Pearce, George K. Peck, Mark K. Peck (ROM), Ron Pittaway, Paul D. Pratt (Ojibway Nature Centre), Bill Read, Peter Read, Michel Robert (CWS), Carrie Sadowski (OMNR), Al Sandilands (Gray Owl Environmental Inc.), Jean-Pierre L. Savard (Environment Canada), Carl Savignac, Laird Shutt, Julie Simard, Darren J.H. Sleep (National Council for Air and Stream Improvement), Lyndsay A. Smith, Bernt Solymár (EarthTramper Consulting Inc.), Mark Stabb, Dan Strickland, Donald A. Sutherland, Kandyd Szuba (Domtar Inc.), Ian D. Thompson (Canadian Forest Service), Steven T. A. Timmermans (BSC), Rodger Titman (McGill University), Douglas C. Tozer (Trent University), Ron Tozer, Ken Tuininga, Merilyn Twiss (OMNR), Rachel Vallender (Cornell Lab of Ornithology), Christine Vance, Lisa Venier (Canadian Forest Service), Chip Weseloh (CWS), William G. Wilson, P. Allen Woodliffe, Valerie Wyatt, J. Ryan Zimmerling (BSC)

Editors of Species Accounts
Ken Abraham (OMNR), Ted (E.R.) Armstrong (OMNR), Michael D. Cadman (CWS), William J. Crins, Seabrooke Leckie, Margaret A. McLaren (OMNR), Erica Nol (Trent University), Ron Pittaway, Ken Ross (CWS), Al Sandilands (Gray Owl Environmental Inc.), Donald A. Sutherland (OMNR), Ron Tozer, Chip Weseloh (CWS)

General Editors
Gregor G. Beck (Ontario Nature and BSC), Michael D. Cadman (CWS), Donald A. Sutherland (OMNR)

Copy Editor
Maureen Garvie

Photographers
Credited below photograph. Photos are copyright protected by the individual photographers.

Graphic Design
V. John Lee Communication Graphics Inc.

Map Production
Andrew Couturier (BSC), Bruce Pond (OMNR)

Project Advisor
Peter Gilchrist

Logistical Assistance with Northern Coverage
Frank Aquino, Cliff Bennett, Cory Burella, Joel Cooper, Don Filliter, Dean Gill, Trevor Griffin, Mike Hunter, Brian Iwama, Marc Johnson, Peter Kapashesit, Rob Lamont, George Linklater, Maurice Mack, Jay McMacklin, Rod Mitchell, Kevin Mulcair, Mel Orecklin, Mary-Ellen Pauli, Doug Payne, Eddie Reuben, Gord Ross, Dan Steckly, Lyle Walton, Reinder Westerhoff.

Technical Input and/or Data for Introductory Chapters or Appendices
John Cecile, Phil Kor, Dan McKenney, Kevin Middel, Brian Naylor, Pia Papadopol, Elizabeth Snell, Kandyd Szuba, Larry Watkins.

Atlas Participants
James Abbott, Kenneth F. Abraham, Cliff Acton, Alfred L. Adamo, Anne Adams, Crane Adams, Kim Adams, Rita J. Adams, Edward M. Addison, Charis Agnello, David Agro, Brian Ahara, Jim Aikenhead, Bruce F. Aikins, Kathleen P. Aikins, Stephen T. Aikins, Euan G. Aitken, Vic Alberts, Joy Albrecht, Samara Alexander, Glen Alford, Melanie Alkins, Jody Allair, Brad Allan, Doug Allan, T. Allaway, Gary M. Allen, Jeremiah Allen, Martha Allen, Esther Allin, Faye E. Allin, Lance Allin, Robert Allin, Brad Allison, Ken Allison, Ruth Allison, Tim Allison, Rob Alvo, Leslie D. Ambedian, Ambrose Pilon, Judith Amesbury, Charlene Anderson, Clarke Anderson, David John Anderson, Bud Andress, Jill Anderson, Jim Anderson, Lil J. Anderson, Meaghan Anderson, Mike Anderson, Peter Anderson, Rosemary Anderson, Muriel Andreae, Bob Andrews, John Ankenman, Robert Ansell, Anne E.M. Anthony, Lindsay E. Anthony, Jessie Antoniak, Carol Apperson, Doris Applebaum, Maris Apse, Judy Arai, Josette Arassus, Betty Ariss, Lindsay Armer, Andrew Armitage, Erling Armson, Audrey Armstrong, Kim Armstrong, Mark Armstrong, Mark L. Armstrong, Ted (E.R.) Armstrong, Thomas Edward Armstrong, Tracy Armstrong, Martin Arnett, Ron Arsenault, Sandra Arseneau, Sheila Arthur, Colleen Arvisais-Petzold, Tom Ashby, Alicia Ashton, Ken Ashton, Jerry A. Asling, Robert Atkinson, Sabine Attelyn, Peter Attfield, Yousif Attia, Ian Attridge, Phill Atwood, Martin Aubé, Allan Aubin, Randy Aubrey, Danielle Audet, Lionel Audet, Madeline Austen, Mervin Austin, Rick Avery, Faith Avis, Alice Avison, Rae Axford, Bob Aylesworth

Geoff Bacon, Kevin Bacon, Mark Bacro, Vic Badenhorst, Debbie Badzinski, Anna Baggio, Doreen Bailey, Alan Bain, Jill Bain, Margaret Bain, Cheryl Baker, Garnet Baker, Garth N. Baker, King Baker, Linda Baker, Loni Baker, Millie Baker, Seth Baker, Tania Baker, Wasyl D. Bakowsky, Betsy Baldwin, Ken Baldwin, Ted Baldwin, Bill Balkwill, Dorothy Balkwill, Gary Balkwill, Helen Ball, Jerry Ball, David Ballak, Ann Balmer, Kathryn Balmer, Jeff Balsdon, George Bangham, Doug Bannister, Nelson Banting, Aileen Barclay, Allen Barcley, Rosalind Barden, Mike Barker, Peter Barker, Richard Barkman, Lesley Barnes, Barnie Barnett, Bob Barnett, Don W. Barnett, Henry J.M. Barnett, Ian Barnett, Ted Barney, David Barnim, Amanda Barnstaple, Naomi Barratt, Glenn Barrett, Harry Barrett, Kim Barrett, Martin Barrett, Dennis Barry, John Bartley, Mary Bartley, Nick Bartok, Daniel Bartol, Joan Barton, M. Barton, Ed Bartram, Erwin Batalla, Wendy Bateman, David Bates, David Bathe, Bill Baughan, Mike Bauman, Ron Bauman, Kata Bavrlic, Bryan Baxter, Louise Baxter, Eleanor T. Beagan, David Beamer, Jean Beasley, Terry Beasley, Karen Beaton, Leeanne Beaudin, Simon Beaver, Floyd Bebee, Gregor Beck, Tony Beck, Don Beckett, James Beckett, Adam Beckwith, Ron Bedford, Trudy Bedford, Marilyn Beecroft, David Beeston, David Beimers, Thérèse Bélanger-Dunsmore, Nicole Belanger-Smith, Steve Belfry, Christopher Bell, J. Tyler Bell, Joan Bell, Robert Bell, Diana Bellerby, Gordon Bellerby, Tim Bellhouse, Gordon Belyea, Betty M. Bender, Keith F. Bender, Lisa Benedetti, Bernard Beneteau, Gord Benner, Barb Heffernan, Brent Bennett, Cliff Bennett, Donna Bennett, Lorne Bennett, Lynda C. Bennett, Peter Bennett, Susan Bennett, Wayne Bennett, Jerry Bensen, Margaret Benson, Wil Berforce, Maaike Berg-Nonnekes, Jon Bergquist, Pat Beringer, Vicki Bernstein, Angie Berrios-Gawn, Rob Berry, Danielle Berube, Rob Best, Steve Bethell, Greg Betteridge, Craig Betts, Bree Beverage, Joe Bevk, John Bick, Liz Bieniek, Dan Bierworth, Nathan Big Canoe, Anthony C. T. Bigg, Bob Bignall, Lynn Billings, Scott Billings, Mr. Biloski, Gerry Binsfeld, Gwen Binsfeld, Clarke Birchard, Caroline Biribauer, Sylvia M. Biribauer, Christine Birkett, Michael A. Biro, Bob Bish, Mary Bish, Darren Bishop, Dave Bishop, Val Bishop, Genny Bittner, Laura Bjorgan, Ann Black, John E. Black, Joyce

Blaikie, Pam Torlina, Shannon Blanchard, Peter Blancher, Natalie Blanchette, Dave Bland, Donna Blandin, John Blaney, Sean Blaney, Sharron Blaney, Susan Blayney, Valeri Blazeski, Christopher G. Blomme, Lisa Blomme, Robin Bloom, Ray Blower, Susan Blue, Chris Blythe, Siegmar Bodach, Celia Bodnar, Mark Bodnar, Fred Bodsworth, Chris Boettger, Dian Bogie, Richard H. Bogie, Mike Bohm, Albert Boisvert, Bob Bolton, Peter Bondy, Dan Bone, David Bone, Kellie Bonicci, Hugues W. Bonin, Dennis Bonner, Peter Boon, Spencer Bootsma, R. Borger, Ludmilla Borshevsky, Marc Bosc, David Bostock, Andrew Boughen, Mike Bouman, Raymonde Bourgeois, Susan Bourne, Courtenay Bournon, Jacques Bouvier, Brian Bowen, Colin & Pat Bowen, Kelly Bowen, Narda Bowers, Bob Bowles, Jane M. Bowles, Wanda Bowles, Maggie Bowman, Martin Bowman, Rob Bowyer, Greg Boxwell, Jane Boyce, Jeff Boyce, Alex Boyd, Freeman Boyd, Marion Boyd, Melanie Boyd, Mike Boyd, Marian Boys, Dorothy Brace, Bob Bracken, Jim Bradley, Linda Bradley, Peter Bradley, Sharon Bradley, Steve Bradley, Michael Bradstreet, William Terry Bradt, Chuck Brady, Jim Brady, Matt Brady, Bob Braley, Nancy Jane Braley, Reg Brand, Nancy Bray, Don Brazier, Corina Brdar, Aaron Bree, David Bree, Yvette Bree, Calvin Brennan, Al Brethour, Frances Brethour, David Brewer, Paul Bridges, T.S. Bridges, Art Briggs-Jude, Wendy Briggs-Jude, John Bright, Rhea G. Bringeman, Samuel R. Brinker, Jeff Brinsmead, Paul Bristow, John Brittain, David Britton, Holly Britton, Matt J. Brock, Kara Brodribb, Hugh Brody, Ron Brooks, Tim Brophy, Richard Brouillet, Steph Brousseau, Bart Brown, Dave Brown, Doug Brown, Duane Brown, Evelyn Brown, Gilbert Brown, Kevin Brown, Lorraine Brown, Ralph Brown, Rod Brown, Rusty Brown, Vicki Brown, P.W.P. Browne, Liz Bruder, Gerhard Bruins, Frances Brumell-Nijhowne, Christine Brunet, Mélisa Brunet, Stephanie Brunet, Daniel F. Brunton, Andrew Bryan, Jeremy Bryan, Mike Bryan, Rachel Bryan, Susan Bryan, George Bryant, Bruce Brydon, Catherine Brydon, Meredith Brydon, Peter W. Brydon, Judith Bryson, John Brzustowski, Angelo Bucciarelli, Stephen Bucciarelli, Ian Buchanan, Terry Buchanan, Carole Buck, Wayne Buck, Art Buckland, Alan Buckle, Don Bucknell, Robert Budd, Judy Buehler, Remi Buisse, Gert Bujold, Murray Bullied, Geof H. Burbidge, Joanne Burditt, Cory Burgener, Jim Burk, Keith J. Burk, Sue Burk, Dawn Burke, Jennifer Burke, Peter Burke, Peter Burkhardt, Kirsten Elizabeth Burling, Beth Burns, Chris Burns, Claudia Burns, Colin J. Burns, Ian Burns, Joan I. Burns, Kathleen M. Burns, Rebecca Burns, Sally Burns, Linda Burr, James Burrell, Ken Burrell, Mike Burrell, Frank G. Burrows, Sonja Burrows, Lisa Burt, Kathleen Burtch, Bob Burton, Daniel Burton, Emily Burton, Dan Busby, Peter Bush, Mary Butchart, Frank Butson, Creg Buxton, Reid Byer, Dan Byers, Daniel Byers, Marshall Byle, Phil Bywater

Ismael Caamal Angulo, Gaston Cadieux, Mike Cadman, Bert Cain, Mary-Ann Cain, Todd A. Cairns, Clarence Calder, Margaret Calder, Peggi Calder, Doug Caldwell, Carolyn J. Callaghan, Fred Caloren, Gordon B. Cameron, Graham Cameron, Mark Cameron, Phil Cameron, Barbara Campbell, Bob Campbell, Brian Campbell, David Campbell, Doug Campbell, Drew Campbell, Glenn Campbell, Heather Anne Campbell, Howard Campbell, Jane-Anne Campbell, Kip Campbell, Lesley Campbell, Liz Campbell, Robert Campbell, Rodney Campbell, Roy Campbell, Ian Cannell, Jerry Capon, Jane Card, Rick Card, Phillip Careless, Bill Carey, Gladys Carey, Neil Carleton, John Carley, Victoria Carley, Beverly Carlisle, Michael E. Carlson, Ken Carmichael, Mary Carnahan, Michele Carnerie, Margaret Carney, Geoff Carpentier, Richard Carr, Terry Carr, James Carrick, Margie Carroll, Jennifer Carson, Peter Carson, Colin Carswell, Janet Carswell, Brenda Carter, Paul Carter, Devon Cartwright, John Cartwright, Sarah Cartwright, Robert S. Carwell, Erin Casasola, B. Casbourn, Garth Casbourn, Hugh Casbourn, Andre Casey, Martha Caskey, Donna Cassidy, Gary Cassidy, Gord Cassidy, Albion Castle, Alice Castle, Janet M. Castle, Jennifer Castonguay, Jason Caswell, D. Cathcart, Gillian Catto, John Catto, Margaret J. Catto, David M. Cattrall, John Cavanagh, Stewart Cavanagh, Anita Caveney, Stan Caveney, Michele Cawley, Charles P. Cecile, Robert Cecile, Karen Cedar, Alberto Cen Caamal, Bob Cermak, Amy Chabot, Jasmine Chabot, Howie Chaboyer, Pat Chadwick, Laura Diane Challen, D. Champ, Nick Chapman, Pete Chapman, W. Chapman, Aaron Charbonneau, Caroline Charbonneau, Steve Charbonneau, Barb N. Charlton, Barbara Charlton, John E. Charlton, Ted Chatterton, Tom Chatterton, Rosalind Chaundy-Smart, Christopher Chenier, Dee Cherrie, Barry Cherriere, Edward Cheskey, Eric Chipp, Tamara Chipperfield, Karen Chisholme, Mark Chojnacki, Gary Chowns, Laura Chowns, Luanne Chowns, Rose-Marie Chrétien, Bently Christie, Rita Christie, Kit Chubb, Murray Citron, Al Clare, Brenda L. Clark, Marianne Clark, Michael Clark, Michelle Clark, Roger Clark, Tom Clark, Dr. Ken Clarke, Rob Clavering, Glenda Clayton, Jon Clayton, Brad Clements, Mark Clements, Dan Cliffen, William S. Climie, Mark Clock, Kevin Clute, Glenn Coady, Robert D. Cohen, Patricia Cole, Valerie Cole, James Coleman, Jim Coleman, Kerry Coleman, Graham Coles, Jim Coles, Marie Anne Collier, Bruce Collins, John Collins, Mary Collins, Merrill Collins, Norma Collins, Lorie Colvin, Bob Comfort, Mark Conboy, Mark Conlon, C. Thomas Connell, Carrie Connell, George E. Connell, Kim Connell, Tomi-Carmella Connell, Derek Connelly, Floyd Connor, Mark Conrad, Laurie Consaul, Leslie Conway, Peter Coo, Cynthia Cook, Ian Cook, Laura Cook, Minerva Cook, Steve Coombes, Bruce Cooper, Donald Cooper, Joel Cooper, Mary Lois Cooper, Wendy Cooper, Dave Copeland, Devon A. Copeland, Robert R.J. Copeland, William Copeland, Larry Cornelis, Jeremy L. Cornish, Tom W. Cosburn, Floyd Cosby, Fran Coté, Sarah Coulber, Daryl Coulson, Marjorie Coulson, Paul Coulson, Sabine Coulson, Tyler Coulson, Erica L. Couperus, John Couperus, Paula Couperus, Betty Coutu, Denis Coutu, Andrew Couturier, Kevan Cowcill, Beth Cowieson, Dawn Cowling, Murray Cowling, Cindy Cox, Terry Crabe, Don Craighead, Mark Cranford, Amanda Crawford, Dan M. Crawford, Jim Crawford, Rob Crawford, Kathryn Creek, Michael Creek, Agnes Crins, William J. Crins, Melanie Croft, Dale Crook, Thomas Crooks, Barb Crosbie, Joan Crossing, John Crossing, Lawrence Crossing, Erin Crowe, David Crowley, Joe Crowley, Dorothy Crysler, Robert Cubitt, Donald Cuddy, Gwen L. Culter, John Cummings, Ruth Anne Cummings, Tom Cummings, Robin Cunningham, Hugh G. Currie, Jason Currier, Bob Curry, Norma Curry, Lesley Curthoys, Bruce Curtis, Ron Curtis, Michael Czerewko, Ed Czerwinski.

Judith Dacosta, Joseph Dafoe, Shirley Daisley, Drew Dalgleish, Jan Dalgleish, Mary Dalgleish, Phyllis Dalgleish, Robert Dalgleish, Dale D'Allaire, Eva M. D'Amico, Michael D'Amico, Janet Damude, Martin Damus, Janet Dance, Ken Dance, Kevin Dance, Leslie Dandy, Sarah Daniher, Amy Darker, David Darker, Angela Darwin, Sharon David, Anne Davidson, Caroline Davidson, Andrew R. Davis, Bill Davis, Christina L.M. Davis, Eric Davis, Jason G.M. Davis, Peter Davis, Sheldon L. Davis, Sr., Robin Dawes, Heather Dawkins, Penny Dawkins-Whelan, John Dawson, Peter Dawson, Brian Day, James Day, Tim Day, Wayne Day, Joan K.M. Daynard, Kip Daynard, Paul De Biasi, Lynda De Caire, Margy de Gruchy, Tina De Kuiper, Paulette A. de la Barre, Serge de Sousa, Gene De St. Croix, Ron Dean, Tracey Dean, Joyce DeBoer, Susan Debreceni, Melisse DeDobbeleer, Mary R. Deer, Roch Delorme, Miguel Demeulemeester, Marie Deneau, Leslie Dennis, Paul Dennis, Charlene Denzel, Gene Denzel, Daniel Derbyshire, Carol Dersch, Vince Deschamps, Guy Deschenes, Janette Desharnais, Marc Desjardins, Paul DesJardins, Danielle Desrochers, Glenn Desy, Bonnie Devillers, Irene Dewar, Lyle Dewar, Kee Dewdney, Pat Dewdney, Patricia Dewdney, Joanne Dewey, Matthew Dewey, Sarah Dewey, Alan Dextrase, David D'hondt, Bruce M. Di Labio, Luke Dickerson, John Dickson, John Diebolt, Mary Dillon, Don Dimond, Elaine Dimond, Laura Dixon, Marilyn Dobbyn, Sandy Dobbyn, Theresa Dobko, Rob Dobos, Rebecca Dodd, Simon Dodsworth, Phil Dodwell, Georgina J. Doe, Gerry Doekes, Mark Dojczman, Jason J. Dombroskie, David Don, Richard (Teddy) Dong, Rhonda Donley, Joan Donnelly, Herman Doornbos, Angela Dorie, Martin Dorie, Sandra Dosser, Jennifer Doubt, Richard Doucette, Cathy Douglas, Vincent Doulas, Sandra Dowds, Connie Downes, Reg Downie, Eleanor Dowson, Angela Doxsee, Larry Drew, S. Drouillard, Helen Dubeau, Andrée DuBois-Laviolette, Dan Dufour, Germain Dufour, Marc Harvey Dufresne, Ted Duke, Mike Dumouchel, Bruce Duncan, Hugh Duncan, James Duncan, Trudy Dunham, Warren Dunlop, Christopher J. Dunn, Erica Dunn, Keith Dunn, Tammy Dupuis, Lou Durante, Wendy Durante, Brian Durell, Gloria Durell, Linda Dutka, Liz Dykstra, Leslie Dyment, Tim Dyson, Cheryl Dzida

Jim Eadie, Sandra Eadie, Carolle Eady, Gavin Eady, Jasper Eady, Jeremiah Eady, Tim Eady, Paul F.J. Eagles, Chris G. Earley, Al Earnshaw, Deborah Easson, Robert Eberly, Gillian Eccles, Cheryl Edgecombe, Anita Edmunds,

Bill Edmunds, R. Ken F. Edwards, Tony Edwards, Karl Egressy, Darren Elder, David Elder, Tony Elders, Don Eldershaw, Phiip Eldershaw, Chris Ellingwood, Alison Elliott, Bob Elliott, Derek Elliott, Ken A. Elliott, Rhonda Elliott, Stephen Elliott, Jake Ellis, Joel Ellis, Kathy Ellis, Marian Ellis, Rob Elmhurst, Sandra Elvin, Alan Emery, Gord Emmerson, Lucy Emmott, Gary Emms, Margaret Eng, Michael Enright, Daniel Entz, Gerry Ernest, Aarre Ertolahti, Nicholas G. Escott, Bill Essey, J. Essey, John Etches, Tracey Etwell, David Euler, Gary Eustace, Brian Evans, Lois Evans, Ross S. Evans, Russ Evans, Karla Everard, Larry Evon, Kathleen Evoy, James Ewart, Joanne Ewart, Spencer P. Ewart, Vince Ewing

Steven D. Faccio, Scott Fairbairn, Jim Fairchild, Stan Fairchild, Myles Falconer, Bert Falk, Karla Falk, Shari Falkenham, Ann Falls, Bruce Falls, Stephen Falls, Blayne Farnan, Bob Farnan, Jean Farnan, Todd Farrell, Brenda Farrow, Don Farwell, Shari Faulkenham, John Fautley, Kristen M. Fawdry, Michael Fazackerley, Luke Fazio, Xavier Fazio, Keith Feasey, Lorne C. Featherston, David Featherstone, Merv Fediuk, Denise Fell, Todd Fell, Richard Felsman, Andrea Fennell, Carole Ferguson, Larry Ferguson, Peter Ferguson, Ronald Ferguson, John Fernandes, Kim Fernie, Evan Ferrari, Rick Feurer, David Fewster, Sharon Fewster, Bert French, Betty French, Cynthia Fiber, Barbara Fidler, David Fidler, John Field, Marshall Field, Robert Fielding, Don Fillman, George Finney, Janis Fischer, Lucy Fischer, Martha Fischer, George Fisher, Robert Fisher, Susan Fisher, Myria Fitterer, Lynda Fitzpatrick, Sherri Flegel, Judy Fleguel, Manson Fleguel, Karen Scott, Ron Fleming, Andy Fletcher, Donald Fletcher, Kareen Fleury-Frenette, Tom Flinn, Robin Flockton, Christel Floegel, Joachim W. Floegel, Jean Flynn, Stephan Foerster, Emma Followes, Roz Ford, Thomas Ford, Robert Forgie, Roy Forrester, Ray Fortune, Rob Foster, Robert Foster, Evelyn Fotheringham, Ron Fotheringham, Renée Fountain, George Fournier, Dave Fowler, Deborah Fowler, Randy Fowler, Ronald Fox, Philippe Fragnier, Jonathan France, Charles M. Francis, Fiona Francis, George Francis, Dorothy Frank, John Frank, Richard Frank, Joan Frantschuk, Donald M. Fraser, Erin Fraser, Ken Fraser, Kevin Fraser, Pep Fraser, Richard Fraser, Lorne Frederick, Nancy Fredericks, Lisa Freer, Barbara Frei, Patti Freier, Jonathan Gavin French, Louis Frenette, Sylvia Frenette, Lyle Friesen, Paul Frigon, Christian Friis, Kurt Fristrup, Kristine Fritz, Roger Frost, Philip Fry, Rodney Fuentes, Lois Fuller, Mark Fuller, Mary Fuller, Peter Fuller, Cecilia Fung, Mike Furber, Nancy Furber, Michael Furino, Steven Furino, Anne-Marie Fyfe, Bill Fyfe, Janet Fytche

Chris Gaebel, Barbara Gaertner, Noah Gaetz, S.R. (Sandy) Gage, Marcel Gahbauer, Dee Gaiger, Debbie A. Galama, Paul Galpern, Elizabeth Gammell, Henri G. Garand, Margaret E. Garber, Nathan Garber, Patrick Garcia, Denys Gardiner, Jim Gardner, Cathy Gartley, Harold Garton, Geoffrey Gartshore, Mary Gartshore, David M. Gascoigne, Colin Gaskell, Joy Gaskin, Bruce Gates, Sarah M. Gates, Gail Gault, Mick Gauthier, Jessica Gawn, Mark Gawn, Simon Gawn, Stephen Gawn, David Geale, John Geale, Andrea Geboers, Kate Gee, Martin Geleynse, Alan Gemmell, Maymar Gemmell, Benoit Gendreau, Alan German, Carol German, John Gerrath, Bill Gerrie, Morris Gervais, Yvan Gervais, Wendy Gibbs, Brian Gibson, Danny Gibson, Fraser Gibson, Graeme C.A. Gibson, Jim Gibson, Sally E. Gibson, Shawn Giilck, Allan Gilbert, Sharon Gilbert, Wesley Gilbert, D.T. Gildner, Ernie A. Giles, Lori Gilkes, David Gill, Jim J. Gillick, Marjorie Gillick, Steve Gillis, Les Gills, Doug Gilmore, Bill Gilmour, Douglas E. Gilpin, Hilda Gilpin, Cece Girard, Frances Girling, Reuben Girling, Barb Glass, Nicholas W. Godfrey, William Godsoe, Peter L.E. Goering, Bob Gollinger, Clara Ivonne Gomez Rivera, Peter J. Good, Neil Goodenough, Geoffrey T. Gooding, Sheila Gooding, Anita Goodman, Clive E. Goodwin, Grant Goodwin, Joy E. Goodwin, Judith Goodwin, Don Gordon, Rob Gordon, Jon Gorniak, Elaine Gosnell, Lionel Gould, Alain Goulet, Duncan Gow, Greg Grabas, Al Graham, C. Graham, Don Graham, Geraldine Graham, Julie Graham, Sophia Graine, Lynn Granatier, Janet Grand, Jon Grandfield, Mitch Grant, Paul Grant, Wendy Grava, Marc Gravel, Bob Gray, Russell Gray, Tim Gray, Phyllis Graydon, Ethel Green, Liz Green, Bobbi Greenleese, Adrian Greenwood, Allan Greer, Tracy Greer, F. Gregory, Fred Gregory, Steve Greidanus, Stewart Greig, Tim Grey, Bridget Grice, Ann Griffin, Brete Griffin, Jean Griffin, Jennifer S. Griffin, Jim Griffin, Ryan Griffin, Sabrina Griffin, Trevor Griffin, Barry Griffith, Fred Grodde, Maric Grodde, Terri Groh, Dick Grolman, Nick Gromoff, JoAnn Grondin, Shirley Grondin, Patti Groome, Chris J. Grooms, Brett Groves, Gay Gruner, Chester Gryski, Jerry Guenther, Doreen Guerriero, Angela Guest, Eric Guest, Jane Guest, Patrick Guest, Brian Guilbeault, Alexandria Marie Guitard, Stephen Gullage, Cristel Gunn, D. Guthrie, Rob W. Guthrie, Don Gutoski, Chris Gynan, Michael Gyokery, Patti Gysel

Anne J. Hackston, Ada Haddlesey, Larry Hadenko, Bill Hadfield, Dorothy Hadlington, Sidney Hadlington, John Haeberlin, Ingrid Hafemann, Peter Hafemann, Erik Hagberg, Ingrid Hagberg, Sarah Hagey, John G. Haggeman, Jamie Haig, John Haig, Stephen Haig, Charlene Haley, Roy Halfaday, Adam Hall, Brenda Hall, C. Hall, Don Hall, Jackie Hall, Marjorie Hall, Rosalie Hall, Steve Hall, Tyler Hall, Vivian Hall, Jean Hall-Armstrong, Bob Hall-Brooks, Hank Halliday, Stephen Halls, Sylvia Halton, Carl W. Hamann, Hannah Hamel, Peter Hamel, Richard Hamel, Woody Hamel, Bruce Hamill, Carman Hamill, Jim Hamill, Katie Hamill, Mary-Lou Hamill, Stew Hamill, Ted Hamill, Brenda Hamilton, Heather Hamilton, Keith Hamilton, Mr. and Ms. Hamilton, Jane Hampson, Liza Hancock, Debbie Hanks, Sandra Hannah, Christine Hanrahan, Terry Hansberger, Paul R. Hansen, Stacie Harder, Bert Harding, Jo Hardy, Lynn Hardy, Roger Hardy, Marianne Harkema, Anne Harkonen, Colin Harper, Dorothy Harper, Lee Harper, Debra Harpley, Janet Harpley, Paul J. Harpley, Allan Harris, Becky Gaunt (Harris), Christopher G. Harris, Cory Harris, Gordon Harris, Jim Harris, Marie Harris, Ross Harris, Trevor Harris, Barry Harrison, Jeff Harrison, Jim Harrison, Tom Harrison, Valerie Harrison, Gregory Harrold, L. Rebecca Harrold, Ramsey Hart, Karen Hartley, Mary Hartley, Rosemary Hartley, Pat Hartwell McLean, David Harvey, George T. Harvey, John Harvey, Lisa Harvey, Roberta M. Harvey, Thora Harvey, Sharon Harwood, Diane Haselmayer, John Haselmayer, Diane Hasley, Jeremy Hatt, Judy Hatton, Tania Havelka, David Hawke, William F. Hawryluk, Christine Haxell, Colin Haxell, Bill Hay, Carolyn Hay, Rebecca Hay, Barbara Hayes, Susan Hayes, Rick Hayman, Tom Hayman, Crystal Hayton, Alyson Hazlett, Audrey Heagy, Bob Healey, Carl Hearn, Marion Hearn, Sharon Heath-Trottier, Mark Heaton, Mary Ellen Hebb, Paul Hector, Kerstin Hedgecock, Catherine Hedrich, Chris T. Heffernan, Tom Heffernan, Allison Hegarty, Dieter Hegger, Natalie Helferty, Fred Helleiner, Michelle Hemsworth, Gill Henderson, Mark A. Hendrick, George Hendrickson, Lisa Hendrickson, Ian P. Hendry, Eileen Hennemann, Kurt Hennige, Jack Henry, Randy Hepburn, C.A. Herriot, James E. Heslop, Trevor Heuvel, Wendy Heuvel, Grace Hewitt, Leo Heyens, Sue Hibbard, Lee Ann Hickerson, Brian Hickey, Ralph Hill, Steve Hill, Walter Hill, Catherine Hilton, Irving Himel, Tom Hince, Gerree Hind, Matt Hindle, Chris Hines, Ross Hirning, Shelley Hirstwood, Nancy Hiscock, Ted Hiscock, Bob Hitchcox, June Hitchcox, Tyler Hoar, Brian Hobbs, Shannon Hobbs, Wally Hobbs, Pauline M. Hockey, Nick Hodges, Pat Hodgson, Meryl Hodnett, Roy Hoffman, Doris T. Hofmann, Theo Hofmann, Peter Hogenbirk, Catherine Hogg, Sarah Hogg, George Holborn, Matt Holder, Phill Holder, James A. Holdsworth, Julian Holenstein, Gillian Holloway, Steve Holmes, Stig Holmstedt, Stewart Holohan, Margo Holt, Cheryl Homeyer, Bruce Hood, Helen Hoogsteen, Dot Hooker, Ken Hooles, Jim Hopkins, Gillian Horgan, Louise Horne, Tom Horne, Lee Horning, Blain Horsley, Marjorie Horsley, Randy Horvath, Steve Hosking, Jessica Hoskins, Ross Hotchkiss, Joe Houle, Ron Houlihan, Janice House, Mark Hovorka, Jeff Howard, Jennifer Howard, Mark Howard, Elmar Harry Howarth, Daniel Howe, Susan Howlett, Penelope Hubbard, Larry Hubble, Tom Huber, Robert Hubert, Grant Hudolin, Michelle Hudolin, Jack Hughes, Jean Hughes, Lynda Hughes, Ken Hulls, Marg Hulls, Scott C. Hulme, Douglas Hume, D.J.P. Humphrey, Lori Humphrey, Jean Humphries, Barb Hunt, James Hunt, Jim Hunt, Karen Hunt, Leslie Hunt, Murray Hunt, Thomas Huntley, Jack Hurley, June Hurley, Peggy Hurley, Thomas P. Hurst, Brian Husband, David Hussell, Jeremy Hussell, Wendy Hutchings, Helen Hutchinson, Richard Hutchinson, Carrie Hutchison, Terry Huzarski, Betty Hyland

Ed Ignataviciny, Marion Ingerbrigtson, Henry G. Ingersoll, James Ingles, Jeremy Inglis, Joel Ingram, Kathy Innes, Gilbert Inwood, Doreen Ireland, Jean Iron, S. Ironmonger, Bill Ironside, Nancy Ironside, Tim Irvin, George Irvine, Lois Irvine, Steve Irvine, Katharine Irwin, Cynthia Isber, Anna Ives, Natalie Iwanycki

Michael Jaber, Linda Jack, Marcie Jacklin, Thomas Jackman, Brian Jackson, Hilary Jackson, Jessica Jackson, Clint Jacobs, Darren Jacobs, Valerie Jacobs,

Anita Jacobsen, Larry Jago, Lorraine Jago, Cindy E.J. Cartwright, Reiner Jakubowski, Jarmo Jalava, Bonnie James, Carol James, Mac James, Ross D. James, Kirsten Janke, Andrew Jano, Henk Jansen, Kathleen Jansen, Elizabeth Janssen, Kay Janssens, Joyce H. Jaques, Michael J. Jaques, Kerry Jarvis, Taryn A. Jarvis, Greg Jaski, Kim Jaxa-Debicki, Fred Jazvac, Eric Jefferies, Liz Jefferies, Roy Jeffery, Bob Jeffrey, Jean Jeffrey, Roy Jenkins, Barry Jennings, Jack Jennings, Heather Jeramaz, Robert Jerrard, Mark Jessop, Alcides Jesus, N. Adrienne Jex, Jisuo Jin, Andrew P. Jobes, Julius Joe, Ahlan Johanson, Judith Johanson, Roy John, Becky L. Johnson, Carl E. Johnson, Clarence Johnson, Dallas Johnson, David Johnson, Jean Johnson, Joseph W. Johnson, Julia Johnson, June Johnson, Kennon Johnson, Lesley Claire Johnson, Lynn Marie Johnson, Marc Johnson, Marc T.J. Johnson, Lynn M. Johnson & family, Alan Johnston, Don Johnston, Jim Johnston, Keith Johnston, Leslie Johnston, Mike Johnston, Sheryl Johnston, Susan Johnston, Teddy Johnston, Pauline Joicey, Dave Jolly, Annette Jones, Barry Jones, Colin D. Jones, Jason Jones, Livia Jones, Mike Jones, Paul Jones, Rosita A. Jones, Russ Jones, Richard Joos, Kabir Joshi-Vijayan

Dan Kaczynski, Michael Kahn, Christopher Kaloudas, Barbara Kalthoff, Lo Kamp, James Kamstra, Doris Kanter, Jennipher Karst, Kevin Kavanagh, Shawn Kavanagh, Terry Kawulia, Mason Keall, Andrew Keaveney, John G. Keenleyside, Nathan Keeshig, Anthony Keith, Bruce Kellett, Andrew Kellman, Elizabeth Kellogg, Bill Kelly, Harold Kelly, J. Kelly, Janet M. Kelly, Keith Kelly, Allison Kennedy, Don Kennedy, Judith A. Kennedy, William A. Kennett, Darren Kenny, Denise Kent, Betty Ker, Larry Ker, Bruno Kern, Donald J. Kerr, Elizabeth Kerr, Steve Kerr, John Kerr-Wilson, M. Kershaw, Leo Van Kessel, Frank Kessler, Randy Ketterling, Ken Kettley, Sam Kewaquedo, Prabha Khosla, Sylwester Kiepek, Tobi Kiesewalter, Tobias Kiesewalter, Ray Kiff, Richard Killeen, Pat Kilty, Barry Kinch, Anne King, Gordon King, Jeff King, Judith King, Len King, Steven King, Wayne R. King, Beverly A. Kingdon, Ray Kingdon, Dorothy Kings, Andrea Kingsley, Steve Kingston, Ron Kingswood, Donald Kirk, Doreen Kirkland, Jane Kirkpatrick, Ursula Kirkpatrick, Val Kirkwood, Larry Kissau, Ute Kissau, Hugo Kitching, Harry Kits, Joel Kits, Lyndon Kivi, Donna Kleinjam, Brendan Klick, Rebecca Klody, Ralph Knowles, Bob Knudsen, Rudolf F. Koes, Don Komarechka, Igor Konikow, Karl R. Konze, Kathryn M. Konze, Maryanne Koot, Nicole C. Kopysh, Burke Korol, Peter M. Kotanen, Philip Kotanen, Daniel Kott, Esther Kovacs, Mary Kowaltschuk, Stan Kozak, Jim M. Krasovec, Patricia E. Krasovec, David Kraus, Marlene Krebs, Rod Krick, Ruth I. Kroft, Paul Kron, Kathy Krug, Ted Krug, Mark Kubisz, Robert Kuenzlen, Therese Kuenzlen, Ben Kulon, Brenda E. Kulon, Maggie Kurcz, Helen Kwan

Elaine La Ronde, Gloria Labbe, Larry Labelle, Sandra Lachance, Michael Ladarski, Yvette Ladarski, Bernie Ladouceur, Sylvia Lafond, Carol Lafontaine, Kim Laframboise, Dawn Laing, Jim Laird, Colin Lake, Russell J. Lake, Wendy Lalouette, Austin Lamarche, Roland Lamarche, Dan Lambert, Garth Lambert, Thom Lambert, Wilma Lambert, Dave Lamble, Bill Lamond, Rob Lamont, Terry Land, Alexis Landon, Lynn Landriault, Meg Lane, Alexander Lang, Anthony L. Lang, David S. Langford, Adriana Langille, Gerry Lannan, Marlene Lannan, B. Lansdowne, Skye Lantinga, Conrad Laplante, Ellen Larsen, Guy Latimer, Marc Latremouille, Jennifer Lau, Jocelyn Lauber, Ray C. Laughlen, Lys Laurence, Bakiss Laurent, Rick Lauzon, Colleen Lavender, Fulton Lavender, Lance Laviolette, Lindsay Law, David Lawrence, Karen Laws, Diann Lawton, Ruth Lazier, Dale A. Leadbeater, Jim Leafloor, Betty Learmouth, Vince Lebano, Elsa Leblanc, Louise Leblanc-Mazur, Jim LeCain, Joyce LeChasseur, Seabrooke Leckie, Valerie Lecours, Susan Lederman, Dan Lee, Dave Lee, Heddie Lee, Rob Lee, Rod Lee, Dennis J. LeFeuvre, Mary LeFeuvre, Dennis LeFeuvre, Roy Lefneski, Susan Legeza, Jeff Leggo, Reino Lehtisaari, Raymond Leistner, Rodger Leith, Chris Lemieux, John G. Lemon, Robert E. Lemon, Kim Lendvay, Graham Leonard, Denis Lepage, Michael Lepage, Norman Leppan, Jen Leung, Mary Levitan, Gordon Lewer, Dennis W. Lewington, Gwen M. Lewington, Anne Lewis, Chris Lewis, Jackie Lewis, Lesley Lewis, Chris Leys, Marc Lichtenberg, Erik Liddell, Bill Lindley, Kathryn Lindsay, Isaac Linklater, George Linklatter, Ray Lipinski, Catherine Lipsett-Moore, Geoff Lipsett-Moore, Markus J. Lise, Carmen Lishman, William Lishman, Alf Lisk, Jim Little, Nancy Little, Nadine Litwin, Alan Liversage, Donald L. Lloyd, Myron Loback, Thomas J. Lobb, Douglas Lockrey, Steve Logan, Rosalind Logue, Ron Lohr, Pat Lohrenz, Darci Lombard, Dan Loncke, Bill Loney, Tobin Long, Brenda Longhurst, Gord Longhurst, Dave Lord, Mary Lord, Jack Lorimer, Shirley Lorimer, Mary M. Loucks, C. Lougheed, Kelly Lougheed, Ann Love, Joan Love, Laurel Lowndes, Derek Ludkin, Rick Ludkin, Wolfgang Luft, Judy Luginbuhl, Harry G. Lumsden, Sue Lumsden, Mary Lund, Heather Lunn, Simon Lunn, Jennifer Lupton-Holod, Raymond C. Lush, Greg Lutick, Don Lycett, Susan Lynett, D. Barry Lyons

Bonnie Mabee, Dick Mabee, Tara MacEachern, Ian Macauley, Christy MacDonald, Erin MacDonald, Graham Macdonald, Jean MacDonald, Julie E. MacDonald, Liz M. MacDonald, Margaret MacDonald, Mike MacDonald, Sandra MacDonald, Shirley MacDonald, Stuart MacDonald, Barb MacDonell, Gus MacDonell, Kim MacDougall, Neil Macdougall, James Macey, Lauren Macey, Myrna Macey, Sean Macey, Jocelyn MacGregor, Eric Machell, Ian MacIsaac, Rob Maciver, Nick Mack, Jock MacKay, Rory MacKay, Alistair Stuart MacKenzie, Bruce Mackenzie, Jim MacKenzie, Joyce MacKenzie, Paul Mackenzie, Stuart Mackenzie, Carolyn Mackie, Shirley Mackie, Ross Mackintosh, Sandra Mackintosh, John MacLachlan, Dave MacLachlin, Briane Maclaurin, Clifford MacLean, Heather MacLean, Katharine MacLeod, Michael MacPherson, Sheila Madahbee, Jo Maddeford, Ted Maddeford, William R. Maddeford, Mark Maftei, Roswitha Mafuscheh, Jim Maguire, Nelson Maher, Sarah Mainguy, Judy Makin, Arlette Malcolm, John Malcolmson, Ken Malkin, Stuart Mallany, Barbara Mann, Blake Mann, Judy Mann, Matt Mann, Deborah Manners, Dan Mansell, Nora M. Mansfield, Peter J. Mansfield, Craig Mantle, Delores Maples, Bryan M. March, Anne D. Marchand, Jean Paul Marentette, Randy Marinelli, Dan Marinigh, Franco Mariotti, Adrianne Markell, Carolyn Markell, Julia Marko, Cindy, Bobby, and Eric Marr, David Marsh, Lou Marsh, Eve Marshall, Steven M. Marshall, Marty Martelle, Tim E. Martens, Angela Martin, Barbara Martin, Carol Martin, Chris Martin, Dave Martin, Doug Martin, Gordon Martin, James Martin, Luciano Martin, Michelle Martin, Pam Martin, Pamela Martin, Patrick Martin, Paul M. Martin, Scott Martin, Virgil Martin, Bob Martindale, Jenny Martindale, Barb Martinovic, Larry Martyn, Angela Massey, Bruce Massey, Joanne Massig, Brenda Masson, Eric Matheson, Janice Matheson, Sandra Maxwell, Blake Maybank, Ann Mayos, Jack Mayos, Michael Mazur, Amy E. McAndrews, Gord McArthur, Hugh McArthur, Scott McAughey, Bev McBride, William A. McBride, Albert McCallum, Dorothy McCallum, Jack McCallum, Rod McCallum, Cam McCauley, Shaunna McCauley, Patricia McClellan, Darryl McCleod, Wade McClinchey, Jessica McCloskey, Anne McConnell, Will McConnell, Myra McCormick, Shirley McCormick, Grace McCoy, Roxanne McCoy, Jon McCracken, Cathy McCrae, Lorraine McCready, Steve McCready, Brian McCudden, Vicki McCudden, Gary McCullough, Susan McCullough, Diane McCurdy, Allan McDermott, Carol McDermott, Corina McDonald, John McDonald, Dan McDonell, Jan McDonnell, Bill McDowell, Michael McEvoy, Kent McFarland, Betsy McFarlane, Anna McFaul, Bob and Dorothy McGee, Denis McGee, William McGee, Bill McGie, Joy McGiffin, Ralph McGiffin, Sherrill McGrath, Owen McGregor, Sheldon McGregor, Spencer McGregor, Jason McGuire, Kim McGuire, Naish McHugh, Irene McIlveen, William D. McIlveen, Keith McIlwaine, Ken McIlwrick, Marie McInnis, Susan McIntosh, Ronald H. McKay, Vicki McKay, Andy Mckee, Sandra McKee, John McKeeman, Gord McKendry, Bill McKenna, John McKenzie, Joyce McKenzie, Theresa McKenzie, Grant McKercher, Robin McKinley, Eunice McKishnie, John McKishnie, Margaret McKone, Linda A. McLaren, Margaret McLaren, Peter McLaren, Kevin McLaughlin, Lisa McLaughlin, John McLean, Meagan McLean, Dorothy McLeer, William J. McLeish, Brad T. McLeod, Darryl McLeod, Dave McLeod, Marion R. McLeod, Jay McMacklin, Bea McMahan, Jay McMahan, Dan McMahon, Ian McMahon, Candy McManiman, Michael McMurtry, Cindy McNamara, John McNamara, Charlene McNaughton, Gerard McNaughton, Kim McNaughton, Keith McNeely, Ed McNeil, Gail C. McNeil, Don McNicol, Betty McNie, Bill McNie, Doug McRae, Letitia McRitchie, Sharon Meawasige, Neil Meehan, Laura Meilmann, Peter Meisenheimer, Annie Meissner, Erwin Meissner, Ethan Meleg, Stephanie J. Melles, Linda Melnyk-Ferguson, George I. Melvin, Mr. Menie, Stéphane Menu, Stephanie Menu, Reg Mercer, Barbara Merchant, Simone Merey, Aileen Merriam, Doug Merry, Linda Merry, Annette Mess, David Mess, C.

Metcalfe, Raymond Metcalfe, Mary Lynn Metras, Shawn Meyer, Chris Meyers, Don Meyers, Jeanette Meyers, Chris Michener, Mary Elizabeth Mick, John Micucci, Trevor Middel, Tanya Middlebro', Alexander Middleton, Peter Middleton, Sandy Middleton, Karen Mikolieu, Ann Miles, Dawn Miles, John Miles, Steven Miles, Mike Milks, David Millar, Brad Millen, Anthony Miller, Gavin Miller, Henry Miller, James Miller, Jason Miller, Karen Miller, Marilyn Miller, Mary Anne Miller, Richard G. Miller, Robert J. Miller, W.O.C. Miller, Lynn Milligan, Jeff Milloy, Alex Mills, Donald N. Mills, Gisele Mills, Jeff Mills, Ken Mills, Matthew J. Mills, Stephen Mills, Rob Milne, David Milsom, Elizabeth Milsom, Kirk Miner, Brian Mishell, Corinne Mitchell, Daniele Mitchell, George Mitchell, Ray Mitchell, Barbara Mockford, Glenn Mockford, Cathryn Moffett, Ronna Mogelon, Adam Moir, Martin Moir, Judith Moline, Jim Molnar, Denis Monette, Byron Monk, Drew Monkman, Julia Monkman, Rose Mary Montgomery, Louise Montminy, Mary Montsch, Aldon Moore, Brian Moore, Danny Moore, Dave Moore, Dave Moore, Laura Moore, Levi Cameron Moore, Linda Moore, Marlene Moore, Michael Moore, Patrick J. Moore, Richard Moore, Tracy Moore, Daisy E. Moores, Renee Moran, Cheryl M. Moratz, Kyra Moratz, Randy Moratz, Tegan Moratz, William Morden, John Morgan, Paul Morgan, Shelley D. Morgan, Bill Morgenstern, Richard Morlan, Frank Morley, Natasha Morrill, Bob Morris, Ed Morris, Margaret Morris, Ralph Morris, Jim Morrison, Lena Morrison, Kelly Morrissey, Erin Mosley, Marion Mosolf, Linda Mosquin, Ted Mosquin, Cheryl Mound, Robert Mound, Aaron Mountain, Jim Mountain, Kaija Mountain, Laura Mousseau, Loretta Mousseau, Jan Mowbray, James H. Mucklow, David Mudd, Helmut Mueller, N. Mueller, Tyler Muhly, Anne Muir, M. Muir, Ron Muir, Dave Mulhall, Susan L. Mullarky, Molly Mulloy, Andrea Munk, Russ Munro, Sue Munro, Brian Murphy, Bruce Murphy, Carolyn Murphy, Chris Murphy, Glenn B. Murphy, Thomas Murphy, Norman C. Murr, Ben Murray, Laura Murray, Leah Murray, Lesia Huk, Lois Murray, Roderick Murray, Shaunacey Murray, Tom Murray, Anna Muss, Barry Myler

Joanne Na, Graham Nancekivell, Mark Nash, Tom Nash, Vicki Naumenko, Brian J. Naylor, George Naylor, Rob Neale, Dusan Nedelko, Arthur Needles, Frederick Neegan, Mae Neel, Tim Neidenbach, Rick Neilson, Claire Nelson, Michael Nelson, Nancy Newman, Lorien Nesbitt, Paul Nesbitt, Rob Nesbitt, Karen L. Ness, Barbara Neufeld, Dwight Neufeld, Larissa Neumann, Kate Neville, Shannon Neville, Ken Newcombe, Bill Newell, Jason Newman, Lawrence Newman, Wes Newman, Dean Newton, Lois Newton, Lesley Ng, Linh Nguyen, P. Niblet, R. Nicholas, Jen Nickason, Fergus I. Nicoll, Gary Nielsen, Rob Nisbet, Eric Niskanen, Jean M. Niskanen, Heather Niven, Keith J. Nixon, Ron Nixon, Peter Nobes, Bob Noble, Carl Noble, Erica Nol, Joanne Nonnekes, Joe Norman, Lionel A. Normand, Louise Norne, Lorraine Norris, Todd Norris, Norm North, Sandra Northey, Axel Nowak, Linda J. Nuttall

Pamela O, Martyn E. Obbard, Bill O'Borne, Terry O'Brien, Michael O'Connor, M. O'Dell, Mike O'Dell, Joan O'Donnell, Stephen O'Donnell, Evan Ohler, Marilyn Ohler, David Okines, Mark Olacke, Frank Oland, Jon P. Oldham, Michael J. Oldham, Brian Oliver, Dale Ollerhead, Beverly Olmstead, John L. Olmsted, James Ombash, John O'Neill, Meghan O'Neill, B. Onifrichuk, P. Onifrichuk, Larry Onisto, Larry Onysko, Ruth Orr, Victor L. Orr, Rick Orton, Calvin J. Osborne, D. Osborne, Harold Osborne, Terry Osborne, Brian Ostroskie, Cathy Ostroskie, James Oswald, Klaas Oswald, Matt Oswald, Gard Otis, Kenton Otterbein, Barb Outhwaite, Lynn Ovenden, Vicki Owen, Helmut Ozolins

Monique Paajanen, Tapio Paajanen, Prue Packwood, Rod Packwood, Bill Page, Rosie Page, Lynn Paibomesai, Calla Paleczny, Dan Paleczny, Eva Paleczny, Jake Paleczny, Suzanne Paleczny, Jason Palframan, Steve Pallet, Manmohan Panesar, Nancy Parish, Randy Parisien, Alex Parker, Allyson Parker, Andrew Parker, Bruce Parker, Doug Parker, Jim Parker, Kathy Parker, Lucie Parker, Martin Parker, Robert S. Parker, Bruce Parks, Lorie Parrott, Darrell Parsons, Sandra Parsons, Carl A. Pascoe, Jack Patch, Michael Patrikev, Doug Patterson, Harvey Patterson, Heather Patterson, Marianne Patterson, Steve J. Patterson, Dennis W. Paul, Gerald W. Paul, Shirley F. Paul, Mary-Ellen Pauli, Mario Payeur, Daphne Payne, Glen Pearce, Harry Pearce, Bruce Peart, Nancy Peavoy, Cheryl Pechette, George Peck, Mark Peck, Karen Peckover, Karen Pedersen, Ann Pedlar, John Pedlar, Wendy Peebles, Ruth Peever, Victoria Peever, Treava Pegg, Cynthia Pekarik, Carol A. McKnight, Jean E. Pendziwol, Bill Peneston, A. Penfold, Mike Penfold, Andy Penikett, Graham Penner, Mike Penner, Tracy Penner, Shannon Pennington, Todd Pepper, John Pepperell, Myles Perchuk, Joe Percy, Guillermo Perez, Satu Pernanen, Carol Perron, Anthony Perreault, Robin R. Perron, Janice Perry, Vanessa Perry, Diane Peter, Otto Peter, Beverley M. Peterkin, John H. Peters, Bruce Petersen, Ken Petherick, Dianna Pethick, Cole T. Petsche, Don Peuramaki, Barry Peyton, Brian Pfrimmer, Frank Phelan, Gerard Phillips, Judith Phillips, Karin Philp, Paul Philp, Alma Phippen, Andrea Phippen, Stan Phippen, Diana Piché, Ch. Pichette, Roger Pichette, Bob Pick, Kevin Pickard, John Pickles, Mike Pickup, Robin F. Picotte, Mike Pidwerbecki, Gary T. Pieterse, Debbi Pietracupa, Terry Pilgrim, Sue Pilling, Tom Pillish, Adam C. Pinch, Geoff Pincott, Cindy Pine, Ron Pine, Frank A. Pinilla, Elena Pintilie, Marita Pinto, Steve Pitkanen, Ron Pittaway, Robert Scott Placier, Barry Platford, Diana L. MacKenzie, Ian Platt, Elaine Playfair, Jay Playfair, Joanne Playford, Pauline Plooard, M. Pobrislo, Helena Podstawka, W. Frank Pointner, Jeff Poklen, Oriana Pokorny, Reinhold Pokraka, Brian Pomfret, George Pond, Wilf Pond, Mary Beth Pongrac, Winnie Poon, Richard Pope, Ed Poropat, Kieran Poropat, Tamara Poropat, Fred Post, Ginny Post, Sandy Post, Ben Postance, Kathleen Postance, Gerry Postma, Brian Potter, Craig Potter, Denise Potter, Marnie Potter, Penelope Potter, Rod Potter, Reg Potts, Al Potvin, Royden Potvin, Cindy Poulin, Remy Poulin, Helen Poulis, Bob Poulsen, Rachel Powless, Paul Pratt, Jim Prendergast, Tom Preney, Blaine Prentice, L. Robert Prentice, Maxine Prentice, Sue Prentice, Don Presant, Ted Presant, John Prescott, Paul Prevett, James Price, Karl Price, Magda Price, Maria Price, Steven D. Price, Bill Prieksaitis, George W. Prieksaitis, Marjorie Prieksaitis, W. Prieksams, John Pries, Paul Prior, Dave Probert, Judy Probst, Marco Prosdocimo, Gilbert Provost, Kirby Punt, Sandra Purchase, Carey Purdon, Gwen Purdon, Sylvia Purdon, Kelly Purves, Sandra Pusey, Donald Pye, Rayfield Pye, Jason Pyke

Ken Quanz, Thomas Quequish, Guy Quesnel, Nick A. Quickert, Jim Quinn, Norm Quinn, Paul Quinn, Peter Quinney, Evan Quirk-Garvin

Alfred Raab, Gerry Racey, Bill Radix, Karin Radtke, Wolfgang Radtke, Jean Raffin, Radha Rajagopalan, John Ralston, Mary Ramotar, Alan T. Rand, Loreen Randall, Bruce Ranta, Brian Ratcliff, Vivienne Rattray-Eaton, David Ratz, Joyce Ratz, Bill Raynard, David Rayner, William J. Rayner, Bill Read, Pete Read, Sue Read, Jason Reaume, John Reaume, Denis Reavie, Shay Redmond, Chris Reed, Glenn Reed, Corey Robert Reeves, Dustin Reeves, Michael Rehner, Clem Reid, Elva Reid, Fiona A. Reid, Jamie Reid, Marianne Bonnie Reid, Ron Reid, Wayne Reid, Bambi Reilly, Brad Reive, Joanne V. Reive, Michael Reive, W. Rendell, Ed Reynolds, Andrea Rhodenizer, Tammy Richard, Ian Richards, Jim Richards, Benita Richardson, Lynne Richardson, Peter Richardson, Sarah Richer, Audrey Richmond, Jan Richmond, Slee Rick, Terry Ricker, Alf Rider, Eric C. Ridgen, Lois Ridgen, Mark Ridgway, Rob Ridley, Anne Marie Ridout, Ron Ridout, Margaret Ried, Maureen Riggs, Christa L. Rigney, Debra Riley, Garth Riley, Colleen Ringelberg, Bruce Ripley, James Rising, Chris Risley, Tony Roach, Bud Roberts, Phil Roberts, Anne Robertson, Collette A. Robertson, W. Robertson, Andrea Robinson, Barry Robinson, Chris Robinson, Daryle Robinson, David J. Robinson, Jeff Robinson, Margaret Robinson, Martha A. Robinson, Michelle Robinson, Nadine Robinson, Nathalie Rockhill, Leslie Rockwell, Jeff Roddick, Lindsay Rodger, Wendy Rodgers, Bruce Rodrigues, Cliff Rogers, Mitzi Rogers, Pan Rogerson, Allan Roitner, Derrick Romain, Luci Romain, Stephen Romaniuk, Taras Romaniuk, Jack Romanow, Martin J. Roncetti, Jim Ronson, Dieter Ropke, Sam Rosa, Melissa Rose, Darwin Rosien, Andrew Ross, Bob Ross, Bonnie Ross, Doreen Ross, Ken Ross, Su Ross, Thecla Ross, Matthew Rossi, Art Rotenberg, Marlene Rothenbury, Joe Rothermund, Carl Rothfels, Mary Rothfels, Anne-Marie Roussy, Arthur K. Rowe, Jennifer Rowe, Richard Rowe, Sarah Rowe, David Rowell, Kayo J. Roy, Michel Roy, Vic Rozio, Ghislaine Rozon, Dale Rudd, David Rudkin, Tyler Rudolph, Jim W. Rule, Marg Rule, Michael Runtz, Scott Rush, Arthur Rusnell, Margaret Rusnell, Brian Rusnick, Richard Russell, Linda M. Ryan, Heather Ryder, Vicki Ryder, Carla Rydholm

Bob Sachs, Robert M. Sachs, Doug Sadler, Carrie Sadowski, Greg Sadowski, James T. Saigeon, Larry Sales, Dan Salisbury, Rick Salmon, Darlene Salter, Greg Salter, Antonio Salvadori, Elaine Samis, Will Samis, Chris Sanders, Catherine Sanderson, Al Sandilands, Bob Sanford, Cameron Sangster, Teresa Isabel Santos, Marc Sardi, Barry Sargent, Linda Sargent, Victor Sartor, Trevor Satchwill, Jim Sauer, Mark Saunders, David Scallen, Don Scallen, Don Scanlan, John Scarratt, Adam Schizkoske, John B. Schmelefske, Ember Schmelzle, Louise Schmidt, Ted Schmidt, Karin Schneider, Wolf Schneider, Dieter Schoenefeld, Marlies Schoenefeld, Paul Schoening, Stephen J. Scholten, Ray Schott, Jack Schreader, Nadean Schryer, Frederick W. Schueler, Mary Schuster, Dan Schuurman, Burney Schwab, Terry Schwan, Pat Schwartz, John Schwindt, Alex Scott, Beverley A. Scott, Erica Scott, John Scott, Mark Scott, Suzy Scott, T. Ronald Scovell, Christina A. Scrivens, David Seburn, Tim Seburn, Jill Secord, Sue Cornish, René Séguin, D. Seim, Erik Sein, Patricia Sein, Rod Sein, Marily Seitz, Pat Semach, Geoffrey Semark, Andrew Semple, Doug Servage, Kevin Seymour, Christine Shackleton, Kevin Shackleton, Francois Shaffer, Don Shanahan, Ian Shanahan, Betty Shannon, Ronald D. Shannon, Fred Shantz, Howard Shapiro, Chris Sharp, Mirek Sharp, Alan Shaw, Nigel Shaw, Paul Shaw, Mathew Shetler, David Shepherd, Rodney Shepherd, Anna Sheppard, Donna Sheppard, Tiffany Sherratt, David M. Shilman, David Shirley, Kathleen Shirley, Gloria Shoebridge, Tome Shoebridge, Josh Shook, Bob Short, Kimberley Short, Marguerite Short, Brian J. Shulist, Jennifer Shuter, Laird Shutt, George Sikorski, John Sills, Julie Simard, Roger M. Simms, Ron Simons, Arnie Simpson, Barbara Simpson, Chris Simpson, Dan Simpson, Geoff Simpson, George Simpson, Kim Simpson, Shawn Simpson, Tracy Simpson, Al Sinclair, Regena Sinclair, Sarah Sinclair, Trevor D. Sinclair, Marcia Singh, Elaine Sinnott, Janet K. Sippel, Rob Sippel, Langis Sirois, Rod E. Sjoberg, Jen Skelton, Alexander Skevington, Angela Skevington, Jeff Skevington, Richard Skevington, Sharron Skevington, Peter Skierszkan, Dave Skinner, Linda Slade, Mark Slade, Francine Slee, Jim Slee, Rick Slee, Darren J.H. Sleep, Glenda Slessor, Peter Slothower, Roger Slothower, Jan Slumkoski, Evelyn Smeethe, Maggie Smiley, Adam C. Smith, Alan J. Smith, Andrew Smith, Ann Smith, Anna-Marie Smith, Bill Smith, Bronwen Smith, Carol Smith, Catherine Smith, D. Smith, Donald A. Smith, Dorothy Smith, Doug Smith, Elizabeth W. Smith, Gayle Smith, George Smith, Glenn Smith, James A. Smith, John C. Smith, Judy Smith, Ken Smith, Lorraine C. Smith, Lyndsay Smith, Maureen Smith, Nancy Smith, Nicole Smith, Patricia Smith, Patti Smith, Paul D. Smith, Roy B.H. Smith, Shelia L. Smith, Silvia Smith, Stewart Smith, Ted Smith, Terrie Smith, Thelma Smith, Wayne Smith, Melitta Smole, Paul H.P. Shylie, Paul Smylie, Lou Smyrlis, Jake Smythe, William D. Smythe, Janet Snaith, Elizabeth Snell, Les Snell, Peter Snell, Barry Snider, Rick Snider, Rick Snider, Ross Snider, Eric Snyder, Tom Snyder, Mark Sobchuck, Kirk Sobey, Lisa Solomon, Michael Solomon, Nancy V. Sont, Andrew J. Sorensen, Patrick Sorensen, Heddy Sorour, Nancy Spanton, Lloyd Sparks, John S. Speakman, P. Spears, John Spellman, Rosalind Spencer, Sydney Spencer, Lorne Spicer, John Spielbergs, Carol Spittles, Leah Sprague, Paul Sprague, Terry Sprague, Terry Spratt, Jim Spruce, Liz Squires, Melodie Squires, Roxanne St Martin, Jeremy St. Onge, Helga St. Pierre, Mark A. Stabb, Ron Stager, Katherine M. Stainton, Susanne K. Stam, Robert Stamp, Lorraine Standing, Larry Staniforth, Richard W. Stankiewicz, Ian P. Stanley, Andalyne Stapley, T. Starke, Richard Starkey, Dan Steckly, Bruce Steedman, Roslyn Steels, Rod Steinacher, Andrew E. Steinberg, Andy Steinberg, Brad Steinberg, David Stephenson, Patrick S. Stepien-Scanlon, Blair Stevens, Clarence Stevens, Edward Stevens, Jeanine Stevens, John R. Stevens, Bart Stevenson, Andrew M. Stewart, Doug Stewart, Nalini Stewart, Robert B. Stewart, Tim Stewart, Daniel St-Hilaire, P. Stinneson, John Stirrat, Harold Stiver, Rick Stockton, Katherine Stoltz, Michael J. Stone, Irene Stoneman, Noel Storey, George Strampel, Donna Strang, Melissa A. Straus, Mike Street, Dan Strickland, Gus Stringel, Jim Strong, Stella Strong, Kelly Stronks, Rick Stronks, Dwayne Struthers, John Stuart, Dan Stuckey, Ian Sturdee, Jim Sudds, Alissa Sugar, Tanya Suggitt, Cynthia Suhay, Mike Sukava, Janice Sukhiani, Werner Sukstorf, Paul Summerskill, Ainslie Surette, Donald A. Sutherland, Marty Sutinen, Brian Sutton, David Sutton, Peter Swain, Valerie Swain, Rob Swainson, Robert Swainson, Gordon Sweeney, Robert C. Swim, Kern Swope, Trevor Sword, Timothy M. Sykes, Caroline Syme, Abby Symmes, Ric Symmes, Sandy Symmes, Wanda Szabo, David Szmyr, Kandyd Szuba, Cathy Szubba

Richard Tafel, Astrid Taim, Harry Taim, Lee Talbot, Tom Tammi, David R. Tannahill, Collin Tanner, Nancy E. Tar, George Tardiff, James Tasker, Mary Tasker, Ronald R. Tasker, Danielle Tassie, Michael Tate, Austin Taverner, Andrew Taylor, Dave Taylor, Donna Taylor, James A.L. Taylor, Jim Taylor, Joan Taylor, Kevin C. Taylor, Lynn Taylor, Maria Taylor, Marion Taylor, Mark E. Taylor, Neil Taylor, Pat Taylor, Peter Taylor, Roger Taylor, Sheri I. Taylor, Damelda Taynen, Glen Teal, Paula Teal, Ken Teasdale, Jim Tedford, Jacqueline Teeling, Elizabeth Tenhoeve, Anne Tesluk, Nathalie Tétrault, Joe Tetreault, Défrid Théoret, Jerome Thibeault, Sandra Thibeault, Peter Thoem, Tom Thomas, Wynne Thomas, Kevin Thomason, Bruce Thompson, Donald Thomson, Doug Thompson, Ian Thompson, Jim Thompson, John E. Thompson, Karen Thompson, Lyn Thompson, Lynne Thompson, Rodney Thompson, Shaun Thompson, Alison Thomson, Eleanor Thomson, George Thomson, Sylvia Thomson, Bernice Thornborrow, Glenn Thornborrow, Keith Thornborrow, I.G. Thorne, Rick Thornton, Steve Thorpe, Alan Thrower, Linda Thrower, Eve Ticknor, Harry Tiem, Russ Tilt, Karen Timm, Art Timmerman, Steve Timmermans, Matthew Timpf, Douglas Todd, Jennifer Todd, Richard Harley Tofflemire, John Tomins, Michelle Tomins, David W. Tomlinson, Cathy Toole, Steve Toole, Jeannie Torrance, Norah Toth, Tom Tough, Ken Towle, Alex Towns, Douglas C. Tozer, Laura Tozer, Patricia Tozer, Ron Tozer, Christopher W. Traynor, Alan Tregenza, Shirley Tregenza, Cameron Trembalt, Paul Tremblay, Phyllis Tremblay, Bob Trennum, John Triffo, Gayle Trivers, Jim Trottier, Katie Trottier, Maddie Trottier, Robert Trottier, Lauren Trute, Brett Tryon, Judy Tucker, Lisa Tuerk, Ken Tuininga, Ada Tuite, Janet Tuite, Blair Tully, Kim Tully, Tim Tully, Brent Turcotte, Michael Turisk, Mike Turk, David Turner, Michael D. Turner, Ron Turtle, Brian D. Tuttle, Don Tyerman, Ray Tyhuis, Robert Tymstra

George Underhill, Todd Underwood, Jim Ungrin, Rosemary Ungrin, Fred Urie, Ken Ursic

Ian Vaithilingam, Antii Valitalo, Rachel Vallender, Kari Van Allen, Leo Van Arragon, Herman van Barneveld, Joan Van Damme, John Vandenbroeck, Milton van der Veen, Bert Vanderzon, Norma Vanderzon, Jennifer van der Zweep, Johannes van der Zweep, Madeline van der Zweep, Mary Frances van der Zweep, Anton van Eerd, Kees Van Frankenhuyzen, Remi Van Horik, Rhoda Van Horik, Hank Van Luit, John C. van Nostrand, Julie van Ossenbruggen, Marina Van Twest, Rohan Van Twest, Sylvia M. Van Twest, Theo van Twest, Bill Van Vugt, Carol Van Vugt, Bert Van Wout, Robert K. Van Wyck, Christine C. Vance, George F. Vance, Marilyn Vance, Rachel Vanden Berg, Bernie VanDenBelt, Mike Van den Tillaart, Sandra Vanderbrug, Jay VanderGaast, Sonja Vandermeer, Tony Vangaien, Cara Vanness, James P. Vanos, Mary Vansleenwen, Brenda Vansleeuweh, Clayton Vardy, Regina M. Varrin, Stan Vasiliauskas, Angela Vaughan, Owen Vaughan, Liz Vavasour, Al Veal, Jake Veerman, Judson M. Venier, Lisa Venier, Henriette Verhoef, Rich Vickers, Joseph Victor, Christaine Vie, Paolo Viola, Mary Vise, Christel Von Richter, Franziska Von Rosen, Hans Von Rosen, Mr. and Ms. Vujnovich

Brian Waddell, Keith Wade, Mr. Waffle, Mrs. Waffle, Van Waffle, Kerrie Wainio-Keizer, David Wake, Margie Wake, Winifred Wake, Fred Wakefull, Mary Wakil, Rob Waldhuber, Colin Walke, Geoffrey Walker, Jake Walker, Philip Walker, Ruth Walker, Tony Walker, Wes Walker, Dan Wallace, Jean Wallace, Michael J. Waller, Robert Walroth, David J. Walsh, Ben Walters, Katharina Walton, Lyle R. Walton, Margaret Walton, Margaret Wanless, Ray Wanzer, Terry Warcholak, Roger Ward, Stan Ward, Dean Ware, Jeannie Warmington, Kathryn E. Warner, William A. Waterton, A. Watson, David Watson, Hugh Watson, John Watson, Katherine Watson, Meghan Watson, Sloan Watters, Bruce Weaver, Elizabeth Webster, I. Bruce Webster, Chris Wedeles, Russ Weeber, G. Weeks, Claire Wehrle, John Weil, Vi Weil, Paddy Weir, Ron Weir, Arnie Weisbrot, Elly Weisbrot, David Welbourne, Maeda Welch, Colin Weldon, Deborah Weldon, Eleanor Wellman, Alexandra Wendt, Jeff M. Wendt, Stephen Wendt, Bill Wensley, Lori Wensley, Martin Wernaart, Chip Weseloh, Jerry Wesley, Mike Wesno, Martin West, Michael M. West, Lisa Westerhoff, Reinder Westerhoff, Barry Westhead, Darla-Marie Whelan, Ann White, Bob White, Glenn G. White, John White, Marcia White, Mary White, Rick White, Samuel White, Charlie Whitelaw, Becky Whittam, Bob Whittam, Dan Whittam, Marion Whittam, Terry Whittam, Gerry Whyte, Erin Wiancko, Gordon Wichert, Bob Wickett, Cheryl Widdifield, Lauren Wiens, Mark Wiercinski, Betty Wight, Harvey J. Wightman, Bev Wigney, Al Wilcox, Betsy Wilcox, Steve Wilcox, Peter Wilhelm, Heather Wilkerson, Don Wilkes, Angie C. Williams, George

Williams, Ken Williams, Kim Williams, Marsha Williams, Stuart Williams, Ken Willis, Rod Willis, Dave Willison, Lillian Willison, Gerald Willmott, Ian Willmott, Mary S. Willmott, Don Wills, Marianne Willson, Jim Willwerth, Don Wilshere, Karen Wilshere, Audrey E. Wilson, Heather G. Wilson, Jim Wilson, Kayla Wilson, Kirsly Wilson, Linda Wilson, Margaret Wilson, Mary Wilson, May W. Wilson, Mr. and Ms. Wilson, Nancy C. Wilson, Pam Wilson, Randy Wilson, Reid Wilson, William G. Wilson, William J.F. Wilson, Jeff Wiltshire, Joan Winearls, Glen Winegarden, Robert Winter, Teri Winter, Al Winters, Philippa Winters, Margaret Withers, Linda Wladarski, Norbert Woerns, Bonnie Wolfenden, Mike Wong, Arlene Wood, Bob Wood, Dian Wood, Lauren A. Wood, Laurie L. Wood, Myrna Wood, Ross Wood, Paul Woodard, Hannah Woodcock, John Michael Woodcock, Maureen Woodcock, Jim Woodford, Pat Woodford, Allan Woodhouse, Gwen Woodhouse, R. Woodhouse, Allen Woodliffe, Brett Woodman, Taryn A. Woodnote Saberwing, Alan Woods, Doug Woods, Dylan Woods, Irene Woods, John Woods, Nicole Woolnough, Alan Wormington, Willa V. Worsley, David Worthington, Gary Worthington, Sarah Wren, Dave Wright, David Wright, Jeff Wright, King Wright, Laurie Wright, Nancy Fox, Liu Wu, Peter Wukasch, Bryan K. Wyatt, C. W. Wyatt, Valerie Wyatt, Brian K. Wylie, R. Campbell Wyndham, Sarah Wyshynski, Karl Wysotski, Phyllis Wysotski

Marianne Yake, Jim Yaki, Joe Yaraskavitch, Barbara Yeo, Ahlan Yohanson, Bart Young, Bob and Barbara Young, Dora Young, George Young, Mr. and Ms. Young, Peter Young, Rick J.B. Young, Sophie Young, Stephanie Yuill, Bob Yukich, Wilfred Yusek

Dan Zabelishensky, Reto Zach, Eillie Zajc, Christopher Zakrzewski, Anthony E. Zammit, Kim Zbitnew, Sheila Ziman, J. Ryan Zimmerling, Julie Zimmerling, Colleen Zouhar, Fred Zroback, Eleanor Zurbrigg

Institutions Contributing Data to the Second Atlas Project

Bonnechere Provincial Park, Bring Back the Don, Bruce Peninsula & Fathom Five National Parks, Conservation Halton, Ducks Unlimited Canada, EarthQuest Canada, Irish Lake Conservation Club, MacNamara Field Naturalists, Mississippi Valley Field Naturalists, Muskoka Field Naturalists, Northern Bioscience Ecological Consulting, Ontario Natural Heritage Information Centre (OMNR), Ontario Nest Records Scheme (Royal Ontario Museum), Rideau Valley Field Naturalists, Severn Sound Environmental Association, Six Mile Lake Provincial Park, Toronto and Region Conservation Authority, Trent University, Woodland Caribou Provincial Park, Wye Marsh Wildlife Centre.

The sponsors of the Ontario Breeding Bird Atlas have made every effort to acknowledge and include the names of all contributors and project supporters, but should any names have been inadvertently omitted, please accept our sincere apologies and notify us immediately so that corrections can be made on the website and in other materials.

Introduction

This book summarizes the results of Ontario's second breeding bird atlas project. A second breeding bird atlas is quite a different undertaking from a first atlas. The second brings with it the built-in excitement of comparing the distribution of every nesting species to a standard data set collected using the same methodology employed 20 years earlier. The results not only provide a fully up-to-date assessment of the distribution and status of every species that nests in the province but also allow scientists to assess changes that have occurred over the intervening period. Both results are of great value to conservationists and researchers interested in the province's birds and the ecosystems that support them.

But the second Ontario atlas project brought more. We decided not only to repeat the first atlas but to follow the lead of Maryland, Britain, Switzerland, Holland, and others, adding in a system of counting birds that would allow us to produce maps of the relative abundance of many species. This was a big decision, requiring extra preparation and work by the province's birders, but they rose to the occasion splendidly and the results speak for themselves, as you will see throughout this book.

The point count data have allowed us to map the relative abundance of many species throughout the province for the first time, so we can see where each species is most abundant and can assess how its abundance varies with environmental features. The point count data also provide an invaluable base of comparison for future atlases. Repeating these point counts in 20 years' time during the third atlas will allow an assessment of how the relative abundance of each species has changed across the province and of the importance of various factors that might have contributed to those changes.

The point count data also allowed us to produce estimates of the population size of many species in Ontario. The estimates and the methodology used to produce them are provided in Appendix 5.

The overall goals of the second atlas were to:

1. Repeat the 1981-1985 atlas to provide detailed maps of each species' distribution in Ontario and to compare those with the first atlas to show changes in distribution.
2. Collect abundance data to allow contour mapping of the relative abundance of many species and to provide a baseline for comparison with future atlases.
3. Record information on the location of breeding sites of significant species.
4. Get people out into the field to enjoy themselves birding while contributing to an important conservation project.
5. Produce a book and a database available for research and conservation purposes.

Field data collection was carried out during the five-year period of 2001-2005. Data were collected throughout the province. In addition, as in the first atlas, data were collected on several islands in James and Hudson Bay that are part of Nunavut, particularly Akimiski Island in James Bay where the OMNR has a field station and actively collects data annually. Coverage on Akimiski Island was more extensive during the second atlas than during the first. Because of the close biogeographic relationship of these islands with the Hudson Bay Lowlands, the results were combined with those from the Hudson Bay Lowlands region throughout the book.

The "Methods" chapter of this book provides details of how the data were collected. Briefly, volunteer participants were asked to spend time in at least one 10 kilometre (km) by 10 km square ("10-km square"), listing bird species present and recording evidence for breeding on a standard data form. Those able to identify birds by song and call were also given the option of collecting information on the relative abundance of species by doing point count surveys.

Generally, the atlas project met its coverage goals, which is a great credit to the 3,417 participants listed in the Acknowledgements section of this book and to the atlas' sponsoring and supporting organizations.

Ontario is a very large tract of bird habitat (1,068,587 km^2), stretching from Middle Island in Lake Erie (at about the same latitude as Rome and northern California) to the northern hemisphere's most southerly tundra habitat on the subarctic shores of Hudson Bay. The chapter "Biogeography of Ontario" explains more about the ecological and land-use characteristics of the province, providing background for understanding the distribution and abundance patterns shown on the atlas maps.

"Coverage and Results – An Overview" summarizes the coverage obtained and key results. The chapter entitled "Changes in Bird Distribution between Atlases" compares the results of the two atlas projects and assesses why some of the changes revealed might have taken place.

Prior to reading species accounts and viewing the species maps and tables, we recommend that you read the chapter entitled "Interpreting Species Accounts," which explains the various maps and graphs and the format and structure of the written species accounts.

Of course, the species accounts, with the maps of distribution and relative abundance for each species, are the heart of the book. Each of the 286 species (plus two hybrids, Brewster's and Lawrence's Warblers) for which breeding evidence was reported during the second atlas is given a two-page account. At the end of the section is a brief accounting of the other species for which breeding evidence has been reported in Ontario at some time other than during the second atlas – primarily historical breeders.

Following the species accounts are various appendices providing more detail on other aspects of atlassing and of the book itself.

Both the Ontario Breeding Bird Atlas project and this book were made possible through the support and involvement of the province's birders. We trust that all readers, and particularly those who contributed data, will enjoy the fruits of their labour as portrayed here. Additional information about the atlas project is available on the atlas web site, www.birdsontario.org.

Methods

Breeding Evidence

The methods used for collecting breeding evidence in the second atlas were the same as during the first (Cadman et al. 1987), which in turn were based on the methods devised for the first British atlas (Sharrock 1976). The province was divided into the 10-km squares and 100-km blocks of the Universal Transverse Mercator (UTM) grid (Figure 1.1), and all data collected were recorded by 10-km square.

The UTM grid

The atlas employs the UTM-based Military Grid Reference System to identify locations on the earth based on unique combinations of alphanumeric codes. The UTM grid lies within a series of "zones" (Figure 1.1), which are bounded by zone lines at 6° intervals. Within these zones are "blocks" of 100 km per side, each having a two-letter designation. For example, the enlarged inset on Figure 1.1 is a 100-km block in zone 17 and is designated NU. Each 100-km block consists of 100 10-km "squares" referenced by numbers 0 to 9 on the horizontal and vertical axes of the map (Figure 1.1, inset). Each 10-km square is given the coordinates of the lower left-hand (southwest) corner of the square. Thus, the hatched square on the inset is square 41. The 4 comes from the horizontal axis coordinate (the "easting"), and the 1 is from the vertical axis coordinate (the "northing"). The complete reference for this square is 17-NU-41. The first two digits (17) identify the zone within which the square is found; the letters (NU) indicate the 100-km block in which the square is found; and the last two digits (41) identify the specific 10-km square.

Partial squares and blocks occur along zone lines. For mapping and data summary purposes in this book, partial zone line squares or northern blocks containing more than 66.7% of a square or block are treated as normal 10-km squares or 100-km blocks; those containing between 33.3% and 66.7% of a square or block are joined across the zone line into a single square or block; those containing less than 33.3% of a square or block are combined with the adjacent square or block on the same side of the zone line.

The reference parameters (datum) used to align the UTM grid to the real world on the ground has changed since the first atlas, from North American Datum (NAD) 27 to NAD 83, causing an average shift in squares in Ontario of about 200 m to the south and 20 m to the west. This shift should have made very little difference in the species reported in each square, except perhaps in some marginal squares around the shoreline of the Great Lakes and the coasts of James and Hudson Bays. The change in NAD also brought about a change in the two-letter codes used to label 100-km blocks. The new codes are shown in Figure 1.1.

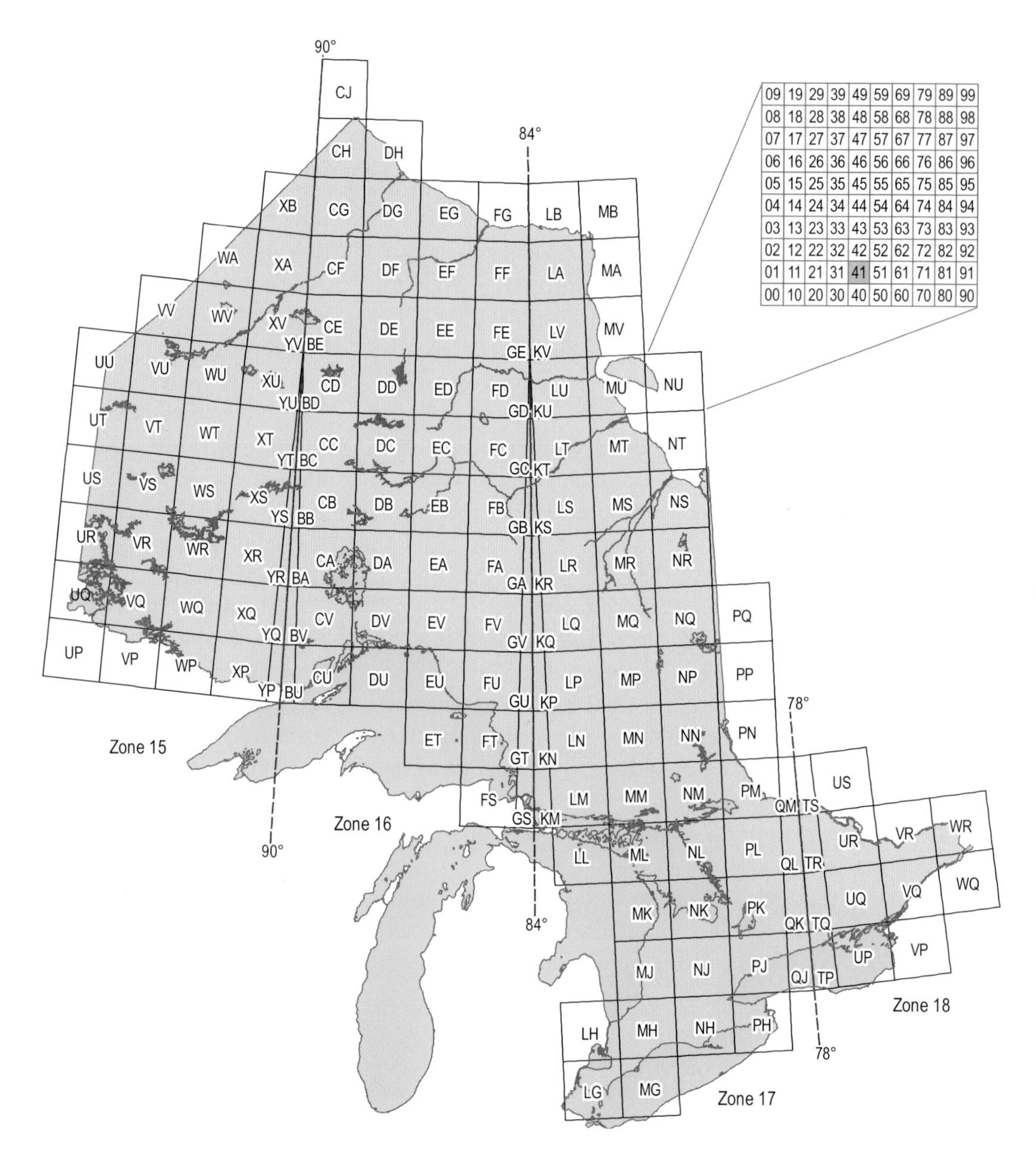

Figure 1.1. UTM zones and 100-km blocks in Ontario used in the second atlas (NAD 83).

The shift in the UTM grid meant that the topographic maps owned by many atlassers were out of date, so the OMNR kindly produced a customized topographic map (Figure 1.2a) for each 10-km square in southern Ontario and for squares to be covered in northern Ontario. These maps provided atlassers with an overview of vegetation types and prominent physiographic features within their square. The maps were available for downloading or printing from the atlas web site. As well as the topographic features of a square, maps showed the 50 on-road point count stations in each square (see below for an explanation of point count methodology), and listed the precise UTM easting and northing for each station. They also showed the 500 m and 1 km UTM grid, and used hash marks on the map border to indicate 100 m intervals. This allowed atlassers to estimate location to within 100 m. In the far north, where large-scale topographic data were not available for producing maps, the OMNR produced photomaps, in which a colour infrared LANDSAT satellite image, with a 30 m pixel size, replaced the conventional topographic information (Figure 1.2b).

To enhance the precision of locations reported to the project (and future citizen science projects), the atlas offered a $50 subsidy to atlassers purchasing a Global Positioning System (GPS) device. Over 200 atlassers took advantage of the offer.

Administrative regions and Regional Coordinators

The province was divided into 47 administrative regions (Figure 1.3) that very roughly corresponded to municipal boundaries. Each region had a volunteer Regional Coordinator (RC). RCs played a vital role, helping to ensure that coverage was complete, that the correct methods were used by atlassers, and that data from each region were accurate. RCs are listed in Table 1.1.

Squares added to southern Ontario for second atlas

Atlassers in administrative regions 34 and 35 requested that certain squares in their regions be added to the area of contiguous 10-km square coverage in southern Ontario for the second atlas. These squares were not covered well enough for inclusion in the area of contiguous 10-km square coverage for the first atlas, but coverage was more complete during the second atlas, and they have been included in the area of contiguous coverage for the second atlas. Figure 1.3 shows the location of the 49 additional squares that were added in regions 34 and 35. The newly added squares are included as part of the Southern Shield region in analyses throughout the book.

Coverage goals

As in the first atlas, a goal was set of obtaining at least 20 hours of fieldwork in every 10-km square in southern Ontario. In the road-accessible areas of northern Ontario, the goal was to obtain 20 hours of coverage in five squares in each 100-km block. In the far north, beyond the road system, the goal was to obtain 20 hours of coverage in at least two squares in each block, and to obtain a minimum of 50 hours of coverage in each block. In the first atlas, the coverage goal for northern Ontario blocks was 50 hours.

To help maximize species coverage in each square in southern Ontario, a target was set with the assistance of RCs for the numbers of species expected in each square. Targets were based on the number of species reported in that square during the first atlas, the habitats in the square, and the level of effort expected in each administrative region. Atlassers made an effort to find the target number of species, and help was provided if the species total was well below expectation. A similar process of target setting was used during the first atlas.

Selection of squares in the far north

In the road-accessible 100-km blocks of northern Ontario, atlassers were not directed to cover any specific squares in each block. In the far north, where access is more limited, much of the coverage was coordinated directly from the atlas office, and atlassers were provided with a short list of squares they were to choose among once in the field. The list of squares was chosen based on accessibility and the representativeness of the habitats in the entire block, as well as whether or not the square had been covered during the first atlas. Once in the field, atlassers chose among the squares on the short list, based on the above factors and whether or not they could find adequate camping or other accommodation in or near the square.

Field methods

Atlas participants were provided with a "Guide for Participants" summarizing the goals and methods of the atlas project, along with data forms and the additional materials described below. A copy of each of these items is available on the atlas web site.

Surveying a square

Atlassers were asked to familiarize themselves with the 10-km square by studying the square map and noting the different habitat types before starting fieldwork. They were encouraged to sample a variety of habitats if they could not cover the entire square.

Fieldwork was carried out primarily during the main breeding season of late May to early July, but also outside of this period for early and late nesting species. Trips later into July and early August were used to help confirm breeding. Atlassers were also encouraged to make dusk and night visits to find twilight and nocturnal species.

Regional differences in access to squares

South of the Shield, almost all squares are accessible by road, with the exception of a few on the Great Lakes or St. Lawrence River that are accessible only by boat. On the Southern Shield, most squares are road accessible, with only a few requiring access by canoe or, in the case of Georgian Bay and northern Lake Huron, by boat. Approximately 60% of the 100-km blocks in the Northern Shield have roads in them, and varying numbers of squares have roads. Generally, more squares in the southern part of the Northern Shield region have road access.

FIGURE 1.2a

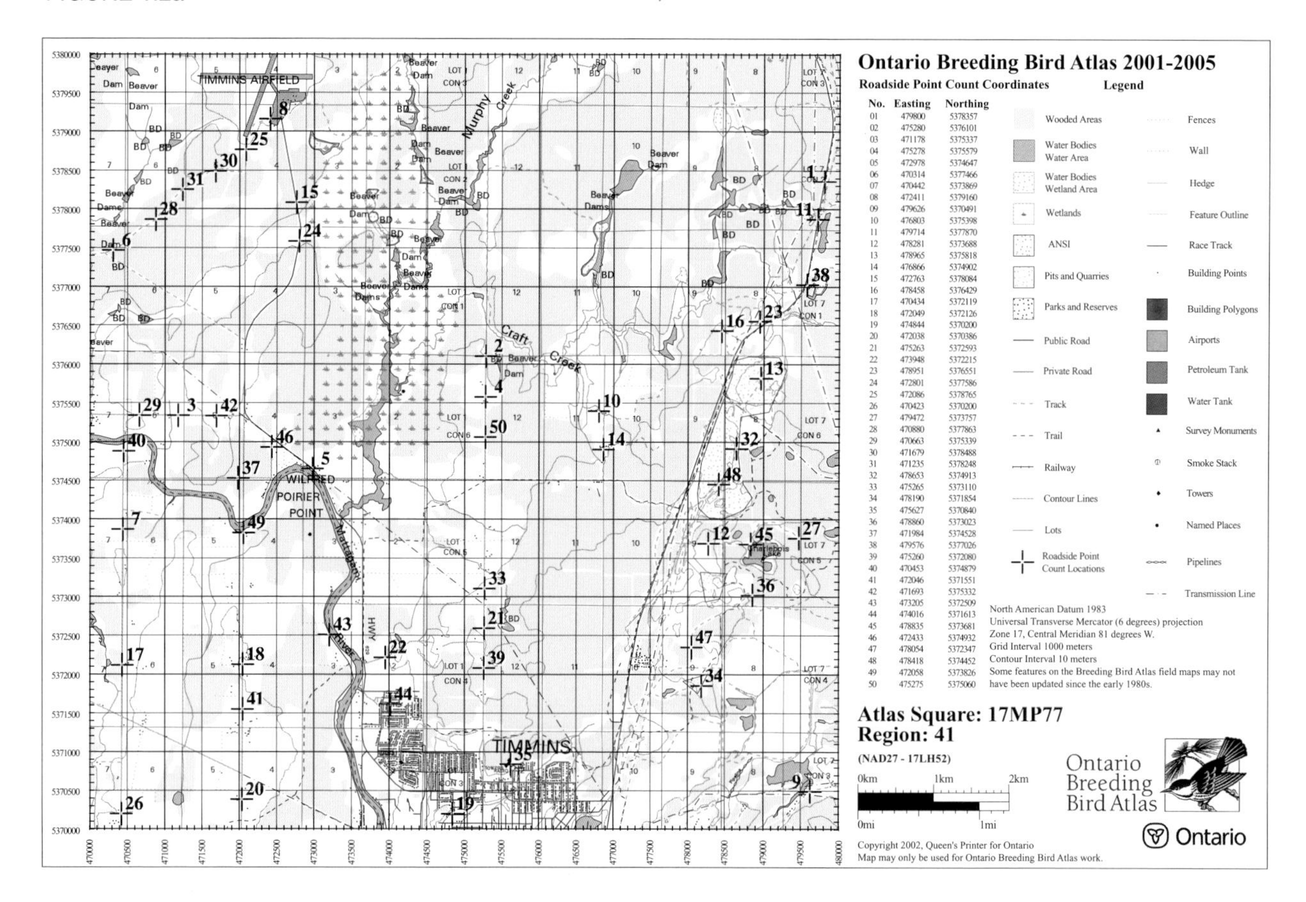

FIGURE 1.2b

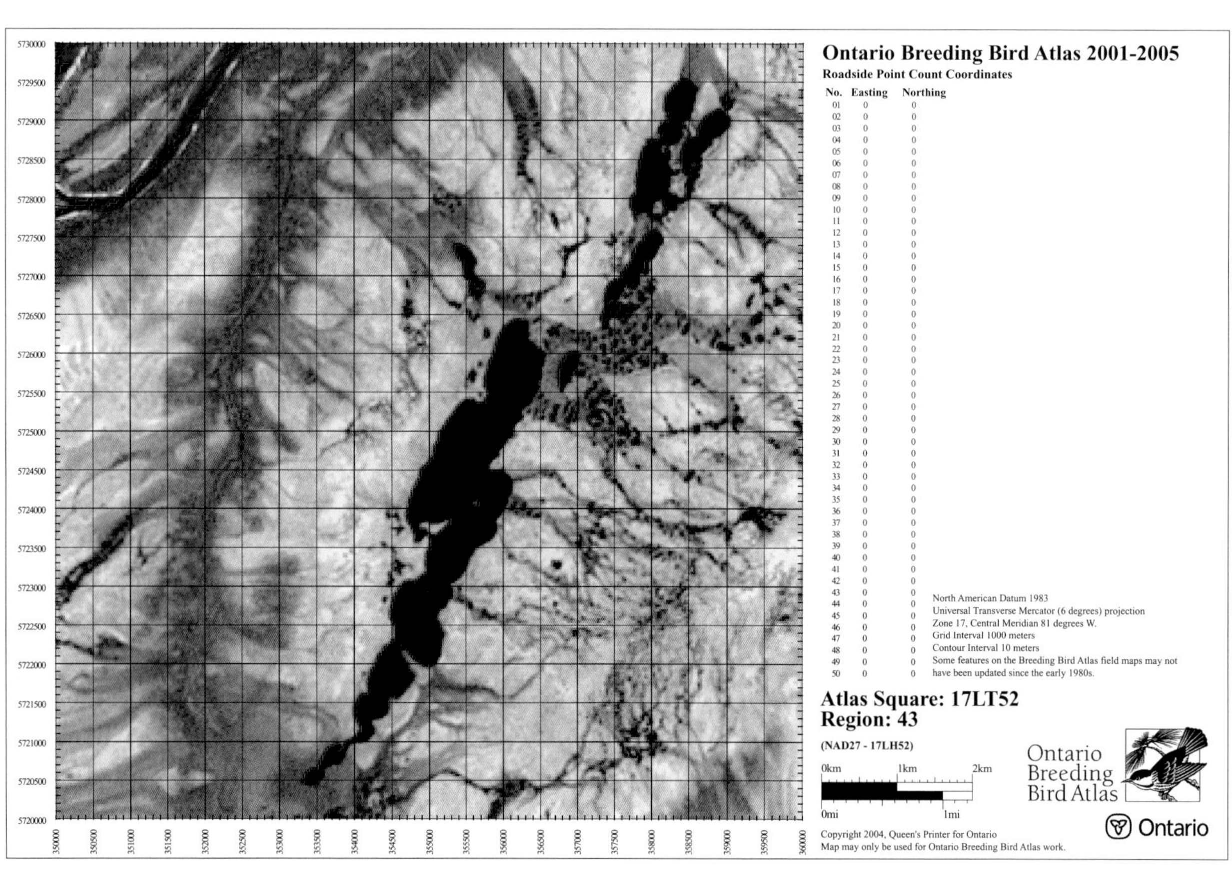

Figure 1.2a. Example of a 10-km square map.
Figure 1.2b. Example of a photomap from a colour infrared LANDSAT satellite image.
Some major habitats are as follows: shrub-rich bog (rosy colour); predominantly spruce (purple tinge); lichen-rich bog (light blue colour); very wet open fen (brownish); and lake or river (black).

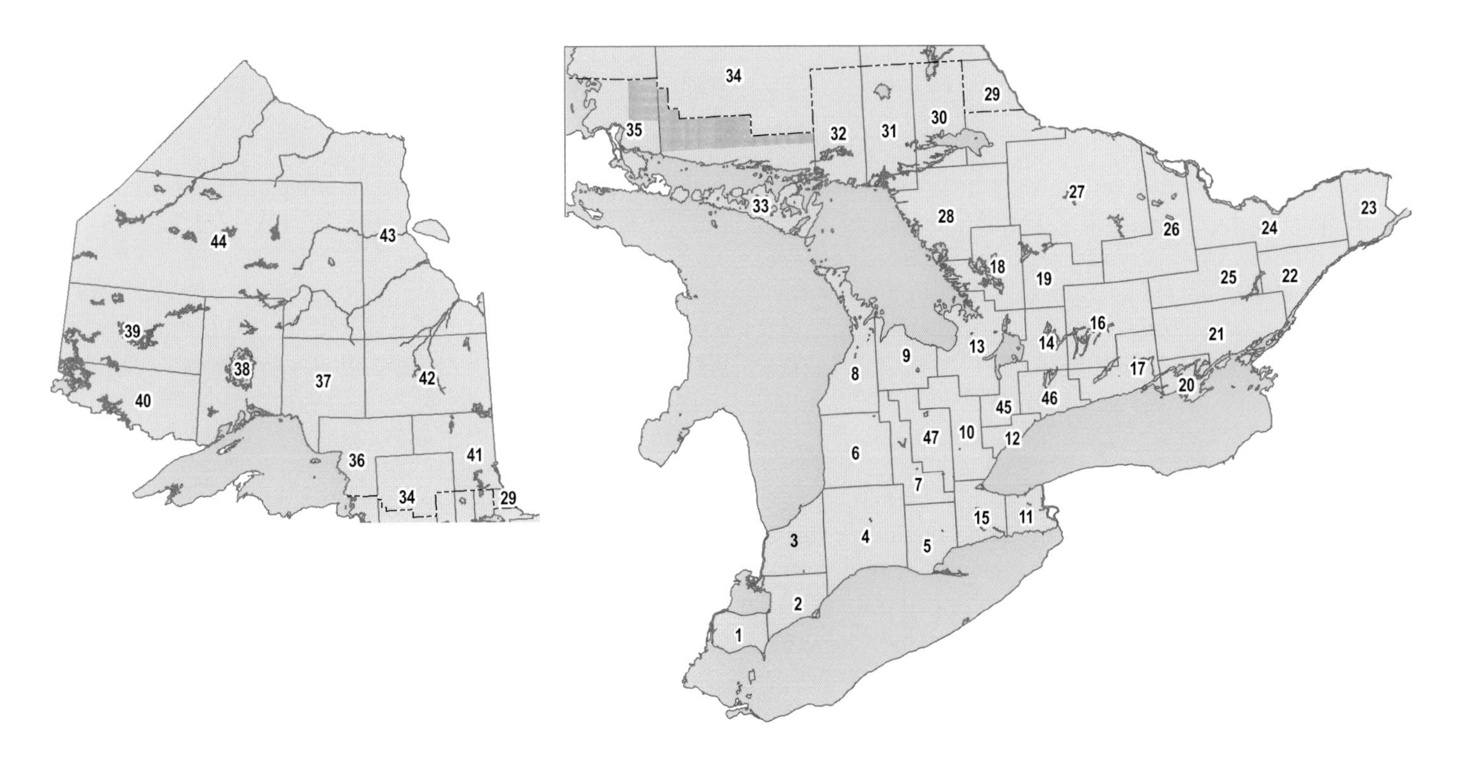

Figure 1.3. Atlas administrative regions in southern and northern Ontario.The squares shaded grey in regions 34 and 35 were added to “southern Ontario” during the second atlas. See text for more details.

Admin. Region	Regional Coordinator
1	Paul D. Pratt (2001-2005)
	Karen Cedar (2001-2005)
2	P. Allen Woodliffe (2001-2005)
3	Terry Crabe (2001-2003)
	Alf Rider (2001-2003)
	Diane Haselmayer (2003-2004)
	Larry Cornelis (2004-2005)
4	Dave Martin (2001-2005)
	Assistants: Pete Read, Ann White, Ian Platt
5	Jon McCracken (2001, 2005)
	Don Graham (2001-2004)
	Audrey Heagy (2004-2005)
6	Rob Ridley (2001-2003)
	Anita Jacobsen (2003-2005)
7	William G. Wilson (2001-2005)
	Assistant: Heather Wilson
8	Cindy E.J. Cartwright (2001-2005)
	Assistants: Mike Pickup, Joe Johnson, Fred Jazvac
9	Lynne Richardson (2001-2005)
	Mike Cadman (2004-2005)
	Assistant: Mark Wiercinski
10	W.D. McIlveen (2001-2005)
11	John Black (2001-2005)
12	Glenn Coady (2001-2005)
	Assistant: Roy B.H. Smith
13	Bob Bowles (2001-2005)
	Assistants: Alex Mills, Rick Miller
14	Chris Ellingwood (2001-2005)
15	Wolfgang Luft (2001)
	Rob Dobos (2001-2005)
16	William J. Crins (2001-2005)
	Chris Risley (2001-2005)
	Tony Bigg (2001-2005)
17	Margaret J.C. Bain (2001-2005)
	Assistants: Clive Goodwin, Roger Frost, Don Shanahan
18	Al Sinclair (2001-2005)
19	Ed Poropat (2001-2005)
	Dennis Barry (2001-2005)
	Thom Lambert (2001-2005)
20	Joanne Dewey (2001-2005)
21	Ron Weir (2001-2005)
22	Stew Hamill (2001-2005)
	Gary Nielsen (2001-2005)
	Laurie Consaul (2001-2002)
23	M. Brian C. Hickey (2001)
	Jacques Bouvier (2002-2005)
	Christine Trudeau-Brunet (2002-2005)
24	Christine Hanrahan (2001-2005)
	Assistants: Mark Gawn, Paul Jones, Chris Harris, Mick Panesar
25	Jean Griffen (2001-2003)
	Don Cuddy (2004-2005)
26	Chris Michener (2001-2005)
	Assistant: Manson Fleguel
27	Ron Tozer (2001-2005)
	Doug Tozer (2005)
28	Martin Parker (2001-2005)
29	Dick Tafel (2001-2005)
	Stephen Romaniuk (2004-2005)
30	Kathy Parker (2001-2005)
31	Floyd Cosby (2001-2005)
32	Charlie Whitelaw (2001-2005)
	Chris Blomme (2005)
33	John C. Smith (2001-2005)
34	Nicole C. Kopysh (2001-2004)
	David Euler (2005)
35	Chris Sanders (2001-2005)
	John Scarratt (2005)
	Assistants: Klaas Oswald, Lisa Venier
36	Carol Dersch (2001-2005)
37	Nicholas G. Escott (2001-2005)
38	Nicholas G. Escott (2001-2005)
39	Leo E. Heyens (2001-2005)
40	David H. Elder (2001-2005)
41	Bruce Murphy (2001-2005)
42	Chris Chenier (2001-2003)
	Leeanne Beaudin (2001-2003)
	Marc Johnson (2002-2003)
	Bruce Mighton (2003-2004)
	Eric Prevost (2005)
43	Ken Abraham (2001-2005)
	Donald A. Sutherland (2001-2005)
44	Mike Cadman (2001-2005)
45	Theo Hofmann (2001-2005)
	Assistant: Bill Edmunds
46	Geoff Carpentier (2001-2005)
	Rayfield Pye (2004-2005)
47	Bryan K. Wyatt (2001-2005)

Table 1.1. Regional Coordinators of the second Ontario Breeding Bird Atlas.

However, some are private or limited-access logging roads inaccessible to atlassers. A larger but unknown proportion of squares in the Northern Shield were accessed by canoe.

In the far north, in inland areas north of the road system, coverage required that atlassers be flown into settlements or directly to a lake or river. As a result, coverage is often highest near these small communities or is concentrated along lakes and large rivers that were accessed by canoe. Although access was by water, atlassers made a concerted effort in the squares targeted for adequate coverage to cover all habitats in the square. Maps based on satellite imagery were used to identify different habitats and were provided to atlassers working in remote northern areas.

On the Hudson and James Bay coasts, coverage was again somewhat focused around settlements, which were a major point of access. Special effort was directed to obtaining coverage in remote squares away from settlements. These were accessed either by helicopter or specially-equipped planes that can land on beach ridges on the tundra or by freighter canoe from remote settlements. Base camps were established in these areas, and one or more squares were covered from that camp on foot or, in some cases, by helicopter.

Other coverage in the far north was obtained by MNR and CWS staff who undertook atlas surveys while doing other work. These included aerial surveys for waterfowl, or other flights at low altitude, on which all species identifiable from the air were recorded. In most cases, the effort in each square was rather small.

Recording effort

Effort data were important for assessing when a square was adequately covered and for making comparisons between the two atlases. For each field visit, atlassers reported the date, start and end time (to the nearest 10 minutes), and total group hours. At the end of the season, atlassers added up the total party hours spent in the square that year.

Atlassers also recorded the number of the visit to the square within each breeding season during which breeding evidence for each species was first observed. These data can be used to assess how the species total increases with effort within each square, for comparison among squares within and between atlases.

Recording breeding evidence

Atlassers were asked to find breeding evidence for as many species as possible within each square. The same levels, criteria, and codes were used as in the first Ontario atlas (Figure 1.4). These codes and categories are compatible with but not identical to the North American standards established by the North American Ornithological Atlas Committee (Laughlin et al. 1990)

As in the first atlas, the category "Nest building" (coded "N") was upgraded from probable to confirmed breeding for most species at the end of the project. Exceptions were those species that are known to construct nests or cavities in which eggs may not be laid, or to use nest materials in performing displays that are not necessarily directly involved in nest construction. Records of falcons, woodpeckers, and wrens were treated in this manner, as were those of the Common Raven and the American Crow. Records of species not known to build nests, such as the shorebirds (Charadriidae and Scolopacidae), owls, and Brown-headed Cowbirds, were downgraded to "H" unless these was evidence for a higher breeding category.

Although atlassers were encouraged to upgrade their records from "possible" to "probable" or "confirmed" breeding for each species, this aspect of atlassing was not emphasized as much during the second atlas as during the first. This was because atlassers were being asked to do additional atlassing work, particularly point counts, and because most researchers treat the atlas data as presence/absence data and do not differentiate among the various levels of breeding evidence. Therefore, it was considered more useful to put additional effort into finding additional species than into upgrading breeding evidence.

Breeding evidence forms with different species lists were used for three different regions of the province: southern Ontario, northern Ontario (essentially the Northern Shield region), and the Hudson Bay Lowlands. Atlassers could choose between entering their data onto scannable forms for scanning into a computer, or entering their data on-line. See Appendix 1 for more information on the scanning and data-entry systems.

Rare and colonial species

Atlassers were asked to complete a Rare/Colonial Species Report Form for all breeding evidence records of provincially and regionally rare species, and for colony locations of colonial species. (The exceptions were Cliff and Bank Swallows, for which only colonies of over eight or over 100 nests, respectively, were to be documented.) More than one location for a species in a square could be documented on the same form.

The Significant Species Committee attempted to ensure that as many rare and colonial species records as possible were documented, especially those indicating unusual numbers or records outside of a species' usual range. Regional Coordinators and the committee reviewed approximately 11,000 documented records and an additional 11,000 undocumented records for which only basic information (date, square, observer) was available. The records shown in the atlas are those accepted by the committee. These records represent a large and invaluable bank of data on species that are of special interest. The data have been provided to the Canadian Wildlife Service and to the OMNR's Natural Heritage Information Centre.

Birds that were considered to be captive, including pinioned waterfowl, were classified as "Captive" by the committee, and those records are not included in this book. Released or escaped Mute Swans, Trumpeter Swans, Wild Turkeys, Ring-necked Pheasants, Northern Bobwhite, and Gray Partridge were classified as "Escaped" or "Released" by the committee and are included.

OBSERVED

X Species observed in its breeding season (no evidence of breeding)

Possible, Probable, or Confirmed breeding were reported only during the species' breeding season and in breeding habitat

POSSIBLE BREEDING

H Species observed in its breeding season in suitable nesting habitat.
S Single male present, or breeding calls heard, in its breeding season in suitable nesting habitat.

PROBABLE BREEDING

P Pair observed in their breeding season in suitable nesting habitat.
T Permanent territory presumed through registration of territorial song, or occurrence of an adult bird on at least 2 days, a week or more apart, at the same place.
D Courtship or display between a male and a female or 2 males, including courtship feeding or copulation.
V Visiting probable nest site.
A Agitated behaviour or anxiety calls of an adult.
B Brood patch on adult female or cloacal protuberance on adult male.
N Nest-building or excavation of nest hole.

CONFIRMED BREEDING

DD Distraction display or injury feigning.
NU Used nest or egg shell found (occupied or laid within the period of the study).
FY Recently fledged young or downy young, including young incapable of sustained flight.
AE Adults leaving or entering nest site in circumstances indicating occupied nest.
FS Adult carrying faecal sac.
CF Adult carrying food for young.
NE Nest containing eggs.
NY Nest with young seen or heard.

Figure 1.4. Breeding evidence levels, categories, and codes

Colonial species data from CWS and OMNR

CWS undertakes extensive surveys of colonial birds on the Great Lakes once per decade, including in 1999-2000. The species involved are: Great Egret, Black-crowned Night-Heron, Double-crested Cormorant, Ring-billed Gull, Herring Gull, Great Black-backed Gull, Caspian Tern, Common Tern, and Forster's Tern. The data from CWS surveys were incorporated into the second atlas database (the only data from outside the 2001-2005 period) and are presented in this book along with 2001-2005 data from atlas participants. Using the CWS data meant that atlassers did not have to undertake potentially hazardous boat trips to islands in the Great Lakes, and they did not have to disturb birds to get accurate counts of nests.

The OMNR provided data from its survey of Double-crested Cormorant colonies away from the Great Lakes in 2004 and 2005.

Additional sources of breeding evidence data

Data from over 50 other field projects underway during the atlas period (2001-2005) were incorporated into the atlas database. These projects were run primarily by BSC, CWS, and OMNR, but numerous other organizations and projects also contributed. Both the effort and breeding evidence data from these projects are included in the database and in the atlas coverage statistics provided in this book.

Additional materials provided to atlassers

For each square, atlas participants were provided with a list of the reported species and their level of breeding evidence during the first atlas; the percentage of squares in the administrative region in which each species had been reported; and a list of "migration dates" and approximate breeding season periods for all species. Migration dates were based on data from Long Point Bird Observatory and adjusted for administrative region, showing when 95% of migration was complete for all migratory species. Breeding seasons were based on data from the Ontario Nest Records Scheme, again adjusted for region. This information provided guidelines for dates during which evidence of breeding could safely be recorded for each species.

These additional materials encouraged atlassers to attain at least as much coverage as in the first atlas and may have had a small (but unquantifiable) effect on the comparison between atlases. It was felt that atlassers could, and many probably would, obtain the same information from the previous atlas anyway, so making it readily available to all atlassers reduced the potential for bias among atlassers or regions. Of course, more complete coverage allows more accurate assessment of the current distribution and abundance of each species, which was one of this project's main goals, and the same materials can be made available in the third atlas to encourage similar levels of coverage.

Method of effort adjustment

Thanks to the tremendous dedication of atlas participants, the effort that went into data collection in the second atlas (152,263 hours) was about 25% higher than in the first (121,684 hours). The amount of effort was not distributed equally among squares and regions. Therefore, several analyses were done to minimize the effect that variable effort might otherwise have on our ability to make legitimate comparisons between the two atlas periods.

The following steps were used to develop standardized comparisons between the two atlases.

We selected a data set consisting of squares that had at least 10 hours of effort recorded in each of the two atlas periods. For each square, we identified the atlas period (first or second) that had the lowest amount of effort (hours of field work). Data for the other atlas period were then selected to match the effort level as closely as possible (that is, using only the species detected within a number of hours that came close to the hours in the other atlas period). Squares without close matches were excluded.

Using the matched-effort data set, we used logistic regression to calculate the probability of finding breeding evidence for a given species (possible, probable, and confirmed breeding combined), according to amount of effort.

From the logistic regressions, we could determine the probability that a species would be found in an atlas square after 20 hours of effort. The result (probability of observation of species X, adjusted to 20 hours of effort) is a standardized measure that allows for direct comparison between the first and second atlases for each species.

Differences were tested for statistical significance. For example, a species could have a probability of observation of 40% in the first atlas (adjusted to 20 hours of effort) compared to 30% in the second atlas (adjusted to 20 hours of effort), with a statistically significant decrease between the two atlases. Tests of statistical significance were carried out with Proc Logistic (SAS V. 8 software), which produces a maximum likelihood estimate of the magnitude of the effect of atlas (first vs. second), and uses Wald's Chi-square for estimating the probability that the effect is zero. A p-value (alpha) < 0.1 was used to signify a statistically significant difference between atlases.

The 20-hour standard was chosen because many squares received at least this amount of effort, and sample size dropped off quickly at higher levels of effort. Twenty hours was also the minimum effort required for "adequate coverage" of a 10-km square.

This standardization method worked well for southern Ontario, where nearly all squares were covered in both atlases and the number of matched squares was very high. For northern Ontario, however, the number was much lower. Logistic regressions to estimate probability of observation at 20 hours in the north were therefore conducted using all squares with at least 10 hours of effort in either atlas, without matching squares by effort. Measures of habitat and latitude and longitude of squares were included in the regressions, to adjust for differences in which squares were covered in each atlas, and to ensure the probability of finding a species was representative of the full region (Figure 1.5), not just those squares sampled.

Subsequently, habitat and lat/long were also included in logistic regressions of matched squares in southern Ontario. This had very little effect on change between atlases, since southern Ontario squares were already matched for effort, but it did in some cases alter the probability of finding a species in both atlases to be more representative of the region as a whole.

In the histograms of standardized change results, shown in each species account, figures for southern Ontario are based on the matched-effort squares. For northern Ontario, the figures are based on all squares with at least 10 hours of effort. In both cases, figures have been adjusted by habitat and lat/long to be representative of the region as a whole. Figures for all of Ontario were calculated by weighting regional figures by the proportion of land area in each region, as follows: Hudson Bay Lowlands 26.6%; Northern Shield 56.5%; Southern Shield 7.7%; Lake Simcoe-Rideau 6.8% and Carolinian 2.5%. Readers should be aware that these analyses correct for differences in the amount of effort in each atlas, but not in quality of effort. There is some risk that changes detected between atlases could reflect a change in how efficiently squares were covered.

Analyses were undertaken to assess directional shifts in the edge and centre of each species' range in southern Ontario. The methodology for this analysis is described in the chapter entitled "Changes in bird distributions between atlases", in the section on climate change.

Figure 1.5. Regions used in analyses.

Point Counts

Field methods

One of the objectives of the atlas was to collect data to allow contour mapping of the relative abundance of as many species as possible. Abundance data provide a means of comparing a species' abundance in different parts of Ontario, and will provide a baseline for understanding population and distribution change when compared with future atlases. After considering the various methods used by other atlases around the world to collect abundance data, and after testing methods during a pilot season in 2000, we settled on point counts. More details on the methods and the reason for choosing them are provided in Appendix 4.

A point count is perhaps the simplest bird survey technique. It basically involves standing still at a prescribed location for a specified time period (five minutes for the atlas) and recording all the birds seen and heard during that interval. The majority of birds are usually heard rather than seen, especially in forested sites, so people doing point counts needed to know the songs of most birds likely to occur in their square. As many atlas participants would not be experienced in doing point counts and therefore might be initially intimidated by them, the conducting of point counts was optional.

Observers willing to do so were expected to be limited, and concentrated in heavily populated areas. We therefore set regional targets for the proportion of squares to be sampled by point counts, and the target number of squares in which point counts were required declined generally from south to north (Figure 1.6). The goal was to have 25 point counts done in 100% of squares in the "Golden Horseshoe" area of highest Ontario population density; in at least 50% of the squares in the rest of the area south of the Canadian Shield (the Lake Simcoe-Rideau region, except for Manitoulin Island), preferably in a checkerboard pattern to ensure even coverage; and in at least 25% of the squares in the Southern Shield region and Manitoulin Island, again preferably in an expanded checkerboard pattern of one in every four squares. In road-accessible 100-km blocks of the Northern Shield, the goal was to attain 25 point counts in at least five squares per block, and in the area north of the road network, the goal was to have 25 point counts done in two squares per block. (See Appendix 4 for more detail on northern point counts.)

The minimum number of point counts required for a square to be considered adequately covered was established as 25, although in the final year of the project, based on additional research, it was decided that any square with 10 or more point counts could be used in point count analyses. Atlassers were asked to spread out the 25 point counts over the season

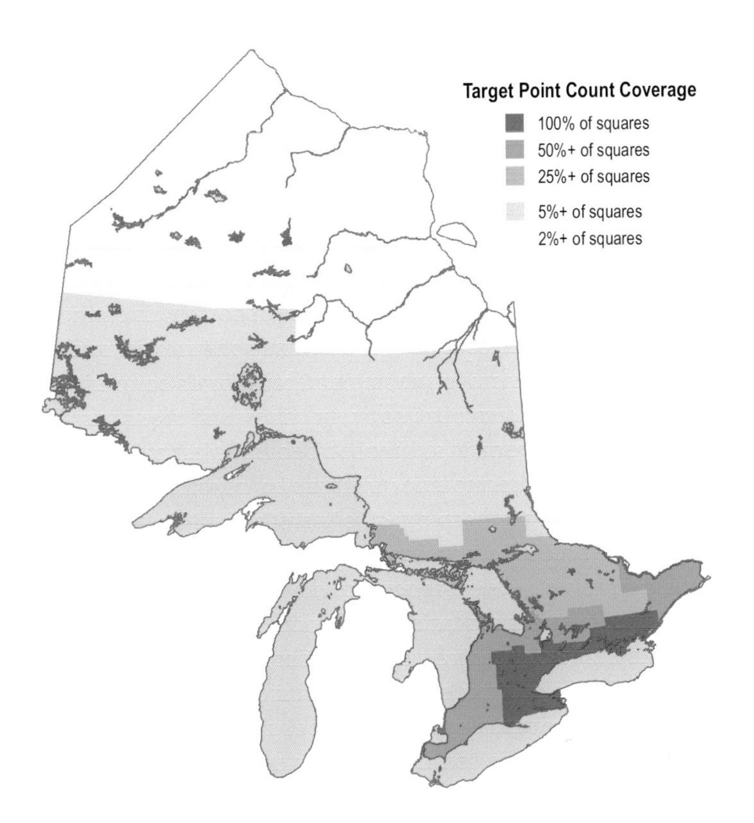

Figure 1.6. The target number of point counts in different areas of Ontario

and even over the years if they were going to keep returning to a square. However, it was quite acceptable to do all the point counts in a square on one day or two consecutive days.

For each square, atlassers were provided with the 10-km square atlas map showing 50 points, each labelled with a number from 1 to 50, randomly placed on roadsides (after exclusion of provincial highways and ensuring that all points were separated by at least 500 m). To avoid bias in which points were covered, atlassers were to cover points 1 to 25. If any points were on busy roads or otherwise unusable, those points were dropped, and the atlasser covered points 26, 27, etc., as required. Once selected, the points could be visited in any order.

Off-road point counts

Off-road point counts were requested when necessary to ensure that the habitats sampled on the point counts in each square were proportionally representative of the habitats in the square. A GIS analysis was undertaken to determine the type of habitat within a 100 m buffer around all the eligible roads in each square (provincial highways excluded). If any habitat making up at least 5% of the area of the square was underrepresented in the roadside buffer area, then enough off-road point counts were assigned to be done in those habitats to ensure proportional representation. The number of off-road counts was subtracted from the number to be conducted on-road, so that the required total remained at 25. Once the minimum required on- and off-road counts were completed, atlassers were free to undertake additional counts.

Because we had no computerized information on land ownership or access, atlassers were asked to find appropriate habitat for off-road counts, and to select the exact spots for these counts on their own. The off-road counts were to be done at least 100 m from the edge of a road, and at least 300 m apart. Atlassers were asked to place points arbitrarily within a habitat, and not to place them at locations known to have "good" birds.

How point counts were to be done

Weather: Point counts were to be done in weather good for bird surveys, i.e., winds less than 19km/hr (<3 on the Beaufort scale); no thick fog or precipitation.

Season: Point counts were to be done in the peak breeding season for the bulk of species. This was largely June in southern Ontario, but counts were acceptable between May 24 and July 10 in southern Ontario, between June 1 and July 10 in northern Ontario as far north as the Hudson Bay Lowlands, and between June 1 and July 17 for the Hudson Bay Lowlands.

Time of day: Instructions called for counting anytime between dawn and five hours after dawn.

Duration: Each point count was of five-minutes duration. The point count consisted of standing at the designated location (known as a "station") and counting all birds seen and heard during the five-minute period.

Distance categories: Birds were recorded separately within two distance categories: less than 100 m, and greater than 100 m from the point count station.

What to count: To reduce the need for judgment calls, atlassers were asked to count all birds observed during the point count, including fledged young, birds flying over or observed flying in the distance, and probable migrants. Obvious migrants and other outliers were removed by the atlas office prior to data analysis and mapping.

Recording data: Counts within and beyond 100 m from the point count station were recorded on special field forms, along with location, date, and start time.

Recording habitat: A standard habitat key was used to report habitat at off-road point count stations. Habitat could also be reported for on-road sites, but this was optional. The habitat key is available on the atlas web site.

UTM designation: Numbered locations of prescribed roadside point counts were printed on the atlas map for each square. The UTM of each roadside station was provided in a table on the map so that participants with GPS units could get very close to the specified station location. Other atlassers used their 10-km map to help find on-road stations, and to estimate UTMs for off-road locations. Atlassers recorded whether UTMs were derived from GPS units or maps.

Institutional data

In addition to including data from atlassers, the atlas also compiled information from other individuals and projects that used compatible point count methods. Most of these counts were conducted off-road. Major sources of institutional data were:

- Ontario Forest Bird Monitoring Program, Environment Canada's Canadian Wildlife Service, WILDSPACE;
- Wildlife Assessment Program, Ontario Ministry of Natural Resources;
- Boreal Forest Bird Project, Bird Studies Canada;
- Ontario Parks, Ontario Ministry of Natural Resources.

Data preparation

To prepare the relative abundance maps, point count data were first verified. Questionable records (out of range or unusually large numbers) were checked by Regional Coordinators and atlas staff in conjunction with the atlasser. Data found to be erroneous were removed from the database. In addition, the following records were flagged and omitted from analysis:

- records from outside the acceptable time of day and season parameters mentioned above;
- records of birds well outside of their known breeding range, or not known or suspected of breeding in the square as determined from the breeding evidence data;
- records from all squares with less than 10 point counts.

In addition, to reduce the impact of flocks of birds, counts that exceeded nine birds of any species on any one count were rounded down to nine.

Data analysis and mapping

For the purposes of the atlas book, birds recorded inside and outside the 100 m radius of each point count station were combined and multiple counts from the same location were averaged. The average number of each species on point counts in each square was determined, and the result was converted to its natural logarithm using the formula $\ln(x + 1)$. This was done to moderate the effect of high counts. These values were assigned to the centre point of each square and were then analysed using Geographic Information Systems tools and a method called Ordinary Kriging. Kriging smoothes out the data from the individual squares and interpolates among neighbouring squares, creating an averaged surface. The resulting surface was divided into six abundance categories and mapped. The highest abundance category contained the highest 10% of records, while the lowest category contained records of 0.001 or fewer birds per point. Essentially, these near-zero values were treated as zero and were labeled as such in the map legend. The remaining records were divided into four equal classes based on the range of abundance values remaining between the highest and lowest categories. To aid interpretation, map legend values were then converted to "birds per 25 point counts" and displayed in the map legend. Since the class breaks were determined against the original logarithmic values, the class breaks may not seem intuitive (or consistent) to the reader. Darker areas on the maps show areas of higher relative abundance.

Maps of relative abundance for all species based on the point count data were produced initially using a batch, unsupervised routine in which the software automatically made decisions regarding model parameters. The Point Count and Significant Species Committees reviewed the maps (and the accompanying statistics provided by the mapping program) for each species to assess whether the map should be included in the book, rejected, or whether additional, customized analysis should be undertaken. This assessment confirmed that kriging was not an appropriate tool for mapping approximately half of the species in question because of low numbers, low detectability on point counts, or restricted geographic coverage, e.g., waterfowl, nocturnal birds, rare species, and most colonial species. A final review determined that 130 species should receive a relative abundance map in the book, 104 of which were created using a supervised, manual kriging approach.

A more detailed explanation of the methods used in analyzing the point count data is provided in Appendix 4.

The Biogeography of Ontario, with Special Reference to Birds

William J. Crins, Bruce A. Pond,
Michael D. Cadman, and Paul A. Gray

At 107 million hectares, Ontario is Canada's second largest province, with over 250,000 lakes making up over 15% of the province's area. It extends from the lower Great Lakes in the south (42° N) to the Hudson Bay coast in the north (57° N), and from the Ottawa-St. Lawrence River drainage in the east (75° W) to Lake of the Woods and the Winnipeg-Hudson Bay drainage in the west (95° W). The substantial geological, climatic, physiographic, and biotic diversity of this large area helps to explain the diversity of breeding birds found within it. The combination of geology, climate, physiography, and hydrology determines the types of natural vegetation that can exist in an area, and hence determines the habitat, including shelter and food, that can support the life processes of the birds found in that area. Ontario's ecosystem diversity is defined by these factors and by the effects of human activity upon them. This chapter describes some broad biogeographic patterns in order to assist the reader in understanding the distribution of the province's breeding birds.

Ecosystems within Ontario have been classified at several scales. Each of these scales is subdivided into smaller units based on important defining factors or characteristics (Crins et al. 2007). In terms of understanding the patterns of breeding bird distribution, the two broadest levels of this classification system, known as ecozones and ecoregions, are most important.

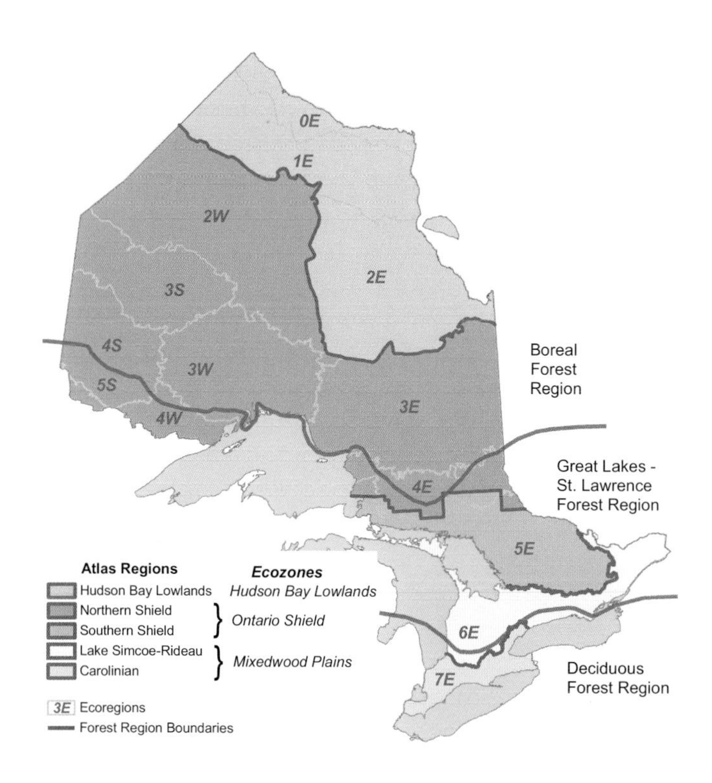

Figure 2.1. Ecoregionalization of Ontario

Ecozones are very large areas of land and water characterized by distinctive bedrock domains. Each one differs from the adjacent ecozone in the origin, age, and chemistry of its bedrock. The characteristic bedrock domain, in concert with long-term continental climatic patterns, has a major influence on the ecosystem processes and biota. Ecozones are resilient to short- and medium-term change, and respond to global or continental cycles and processes operating on the order of thousands to millions of years. Ontario has three ecozones: the Hudson Bay Lowlands, the Ontario Shield, and the Mixedwood Plains (Figure 2.1). The relationship among these ecologically defined zones and the five regions used in this atlas to describe bird distribution and abundance patterns is as follows: the Hudson Bay Lowlands is fairly similar in both schemes; the Ontario Shield contains both the Northern Shield and Southern Shield regions; the Mixedwood Plains contains both the Lake Simcoe-Rideau and Carolinian regions.

Ecoregions are nested within the ecozones and are defined by a characteristic range and pattern in climatic variables, including temperature, precipitation, and humidity. The climate within an ecoregion has a profound influence on vegetation types, soil formation, and other ecosystem processes, and the associated biota that occur there. There are fourteen ecoregions in Ontario (Figure 2.1).

Bedrock geology

Three broad bands of bedrock are found in Ontario. In the far north, a zone composed of Ordovician, Silurian, Devonian (and to a much lesser extent, Cretaceous and Jurassic) dolomite, limestone, siltstone, sandstone, and shale bedrock defines the Hudson Bay Lowlands Ecozone. Except for an inlier of older Precambrian rock comprising the Sutton Ridges, the Hudson Bay Lowlands Ecozone is underlain almost entirely by calcareous bedrock.

South of this, the central three-fifths of the province is dominated by Precambrian gneiss, granite, metasedimentary, and metavolcanic bedrock. This region often is referred to as the Precambrian Shield or the Canadian Shield, and in Ontario it is called the Ontario Shield Ecozone. This broad zone of Precambrian bedrock is further divided into three subzones based on the age and origin of the rocks. The oldest rocks in Ontario, at 2.5 billion years or more, are found within the part of the Precambrian Shield known as the Superior Province, which occupies a substantial part of the northern Ontario Shield Ecozone south and east to Sudbury. A band of rocks between 1.8 and 2.4 billion years old, known as the Southern Province, occurs from Sault Ste. Marie to Kirkland Lake. The youngest Precambrian rocks are found on the southern Precambrian Shield, south of Sudbury and Kirkland Lake to the Frontenac Axis east of Kingston. These rocks are 1.0 to 1.6 billion years old (Thurston 1991). The Precambrian rocks in Ontario generally are acidic, but there are scattered areas where these rocks are circumneutral or even slightly basic (greenstone belts, basalt formations).

The southernmost part of the province, south of the Precambrian Shield, is underlain by Paleozoic limestone and related rocks of Ordovician, Silurian, and Devonian ages. This area, along with the highly complex area known as the Frontenac Axis (a mixture of Precambrian and Ordovician rocks), is called the Mixedwood Plains Ecozone. Except for parts of the Frontenac Axis, the bedrock in this ecozone is calcareous. One of its most prominent bedrock features, aside from the Frontenac Axis, is the Niagara Escarpment. Because of the variety of exposures, moisture regimes, elevations, and outliers provided by the escarpment face, tablelands, and talus along its length, this feature has a significant impact on the vegetation that occurs along it, and as a result, on the avifauna associated with it.

Climate

The climate of Ontario varies widely from north to south and from east to west. The north-south gradient is mainly a temperature gradient, whereas the east-west gradient is mainly one of precipitation and humidity. Temperature bands are moderated by Hudson and James Bays in the north and by the Great Lakes farther south (Figures 2.2a, 2.2b). The Great Lakes also influence precipitation patterns, particularly in the early winter, when increased amounts of precipitation fall in the "snow belts" east of Lakes Superior and Huron (Figure 2.2c). Local relief influences temperature and precipitation patterns in several parts of the province, particularly on the western side of the Algonquin Dome, the Algoma Highlands, the Dundalk uplands, and the highlands northwest of Thunder Bay (Baldwin et al. 2000).

Three major air masses affect Ontario's climate. The cold, dry polar air mass is dominant in winter. The Pacific polar air mass traverses the mountains and prairies before arriving in Ontario. The warm, moist Gulf air mass is most influential during the summer. The day-to-day interactions between these major air masses and the jet stream result in the weather patterns that affect the specific timing of bird migration and nesting, and sometimes, the success of nesting efforts. (For example, late spring or early summer protracted cold spells can have serious effects on the productivity of birds such as the Tree Swallow and Eastern Bluebird.)

In the far north, winters are cold and long, with January mean daily temperatures between -20°C and -24°C (Figure 2.2a), and the summers are short and cool, with July mean daily temperatures from 13.8°C to 15°C (Figure 2.2b). The growing season here is less than 160 days (Figure 2.2d). Average annual precipitation ranges between 430 mm and 550 mm (Figure 2.2c). This part of the province is within the High Subarctic Ecoclimatic Zone (Ecoregions Working Group 1989). The Hudson Bay Lowlands Ecozone contains areas of continuous and discontinuous permafrost, with the band of continuous permafrost being found immediately adjacent to the Hudson Bay coast and inland for a variable distance of up to about 85 kilometres (coinciding with Ecoregion 0E on Figure 2.1). The presence of permafrost affects summer climate, since it prevents moisture penetration into the soil, and

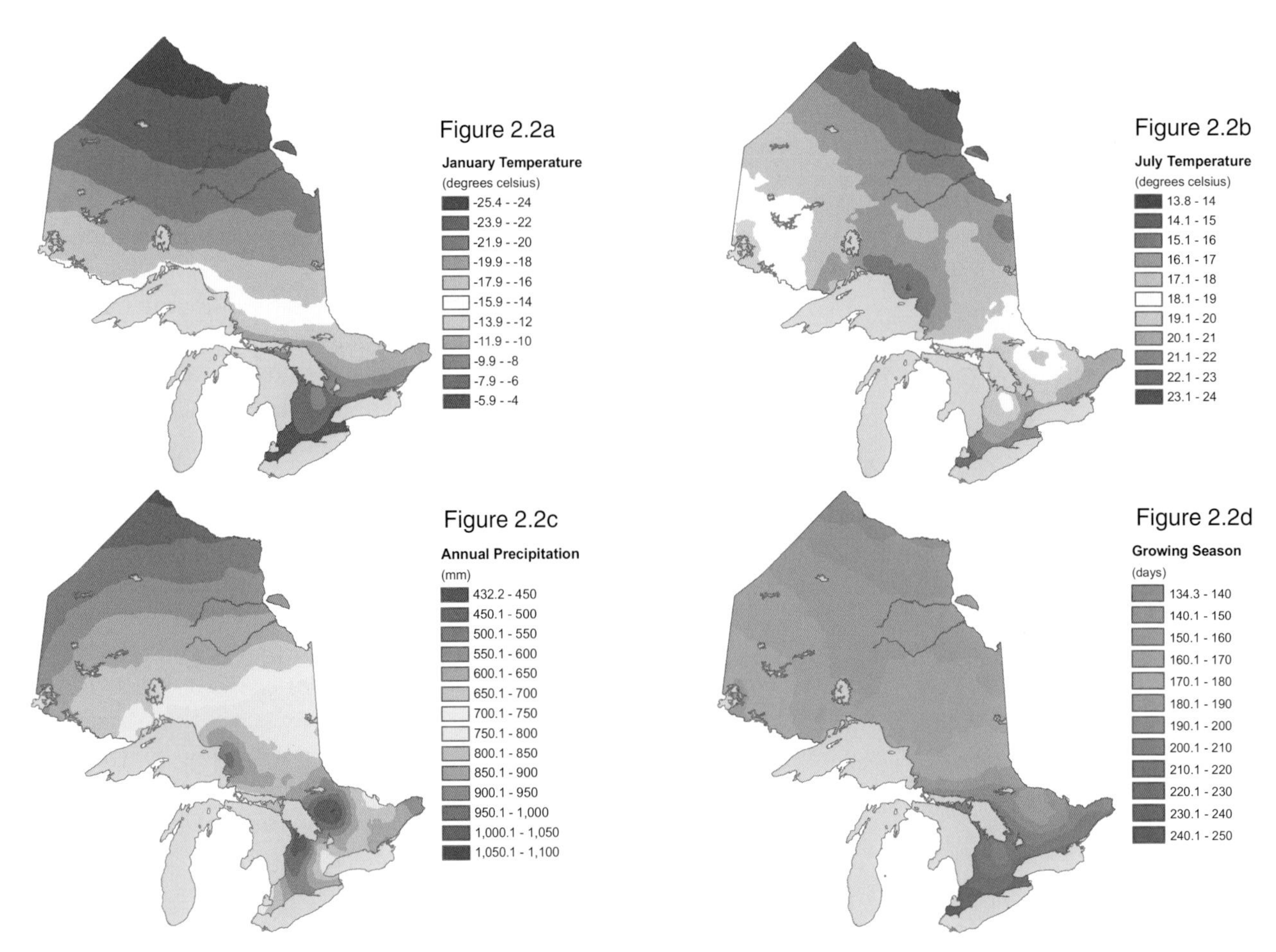

Figure 2.2. Climate means, 1985-2005: a) daily January temperature; b) daily July temperature; c) annual precipitation; d) growing season length (McKenney et al. 2006).

energy is expended evaporating that moisture rather than increasing air temperatures (Stewart and Lockhart 2005).

At the other extreme, in the southwestern part of the province, the climate is among the mildest in Canada. The winters are cool and the summers are long, hot, and humid. The mean annual temperature ranges between 6.3°C and 9.4°C. The mean length of the growing season is more than 230 days. The average annual precipitation is between 800 mm and 1050 mm, with average summer rainfall between 196 mm and 257 mm.

Clear evidence of climate change exists in the form of decreasing duration of sea-ice cover in portions of Hudson and James Bays over the past few decades (Stewart and Lockhart 2005) and increases in average air temperatures of about 1°C since the 1920s (Lemieux et al. 2007). Effects of climate are evident in plants, with the alien invasive Perennial Sow-thistle and Common Dandelion observed in the Hudson Bay Lowlands (K. Abraham, pers. comm.); in birds, with population declines in Gray Jays in Algonquin Park attributed to increased perishability of hoarded food (Waite and Strickland 2006); and in fire disturbance regimes with longer fire seasons and more frequent and intense wildfire outbreaks (McAlpine 1998; Wotton et al. 2005). The effects of climate change on birds in Ontario are dealt with in more detail in the chapter on changes between atlases.

Surficial geology and topography

The following brief summary is based on the information found in Chapman and Putnam (1984), Barnett et al. (1991a, b, c), Barnett (1992), Pala et al. (1991), and Sado and Carswell (1987). A digital terrain model showing altitude across the province is provided in Figure 2.3.

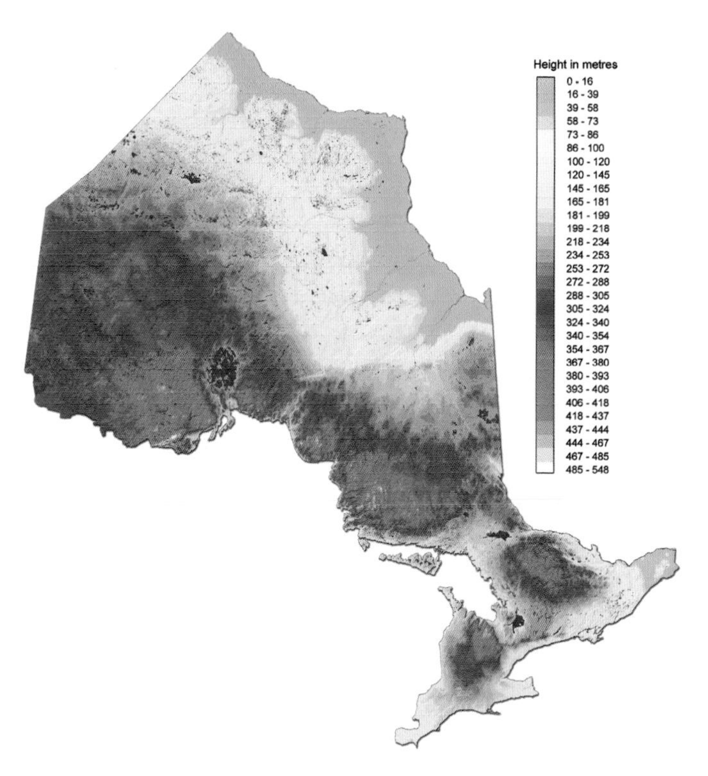

Figure 2.3. Digital terrain model for Ontario. Reproduced with permission from Forest Resources of Ontario (Ontario Ministry of Natural Resources 2006b).

Patterns in surficial geology and topography are important in determining some of the finer-scale patterns seen in the vegetation within each ecoregion. There is a moderate range of variation in topography within Ontario because of its varied bedrock geology and overlying glacial landforms. Elevation ranges between 0 m above sea level along the Hudson and James Bay coasts and 693 m above sea level along the Ishpatina Ridge west of Temagami.

Along the subarctic Hudson Bay coast, a narrow band of continuous permafrost controls soil formation, hydrological dynamics, and vegetation development. Soil development is limited here (Ecoregion 0E on Figure 2.1). This is the area in which tundra develops. Discontinuous permafrost is found just inland from the Hudson Bay coast region, and south along the James Bay coast. Soils are very poorly drained, with peatlands and small lakes occurring frequently across the entire landscape, overlying glacio-marine deposits. In poorly drained areas influenced by permafrost, peaty soils predominate. Although forest vegetation develops, it is often relatively open (taiga).

All of Ontario has been subjected to glaciation. In the far north, the effects of relatively recent de-glaciation (the Laurentide Ice Sheet disappeared about 6,500 years before present) and inundation under a post-glacial sea can be seen in the extremely flat topography, with small depressions being filled with shallow lakes and ponds, and low rises created by successive beach ridges or levees developed along river systems. The land along the Hudson and James Bay coasts is rising at a rate of about 1 m per century due to isostatic rebound following the retreat of the ice sheet (Stewart and Lockhart 2005). The larger river systems have cut deep channels, or in some cases, gorges, into the calcareous clay deposits and bedrock. The most prominent exception to the relatively flat topography is the Sutton Ridges, a series of acidic Precambrian rock cuestas that rise up to 300 m above the surrounding lowlands.

Throughout the province, the effects of glaciation are visible in surficial geological features such as moraines, drumlins, eskers, post-glacial shorelines, post-glacial lake and river deposits, and dune fields associated with post-glacial lakes. Depending on location within the province and the source of the materials that were carried by the glaciers, these surficial deposits may be either acidic or basic. The chemistry of the deposits has a considerable influence on the composition of the vegetation that grows on them.

Moraines of several types are found in the province. The undifferentiated soil-forming parent material that was deposited over the bedrock in a veneer rather than in hills or mounds is known as ground moraine or till. The least distinctive type of moraine in terms of its form, it is by far the most common. More spectacular moraines are those deposited when one or more ice sheets stopped receding for a time. At such locations, material carried along with the ice was deposited in large, often linear or lobed mounds that can now be seen as hills. These are aligned perpendicular to the direction in which the ice sheet was receding. Some prominent examples of such terminal (end) and interlobate moraines in Ontario include the Agutua and Trout Lake Moraines in northwestern Ontario north and east of Red Lake, the Chapleau Moraine running east-west just south of Chapleau in east-central Ontario, the Cartier Moraine north of Sudbury, and the Oak Ridges Moraine running parallel to the Lake Ontario shore from northwest of Toronto to Rice Lake. These moraines usually support vegetation varying from that of the surrounding landscapes because of differing moisture regimes or differing land-use patterns.

Post-glacial lake and sea deposits generally result in relatively flat landscapes, as noted above for the glacio-marine deposits of the Hudson Bay Lowlands. The only other significant glacio-marine deposit in Ontario was deposited in the once-extant Champlain Sea, in the Ottawa River valley from Pembroke east to the Québec border. Ontario has several extensive post-glacial lake deposits, including those underlying the Clay Belt and the Little Clay Belt in northeastern Ontario; those that resulted in the Dryden clay plain, the clay plain from Rainy River to Fort Frances, and many other smaller deposits of clay and sand scattered throughout northwestern Ontario; those in south-central Ontario; and those that created the Norfolk Sand Plain in southwestern Ontario. These features often support species that are substantially different from those of surrounding areas. This is particularly evident on the clay plain near Rainy River.

Sand and gravel deposited by post-glacial rivers are found in the valleys of many existing rivers as well as in locations where no rivers exist today. In extant river valleys, such deposits often are referred to as valley trains or glacio-fluvial deposits; outwash plains and deltas are other types of features in this category. The locations of former rivers can be seen by the presence of eskers, prominent throughout the province. In areas such as the Clay Belt, they provide well drained, raised areas where upland forests grow, in otherwise wet peatland landscapes.

Post-glacial dune fields created by the movement of sand by wind (aeolian deposits) can be found in several areas. These dune fields may provide upland habitat where the surrounding landscape otherwise is predominantly low and wet. Examples of such deposits are scattered through northern Ontario, such as the one near Foleyet. Several major drumlin fields exist in the province north of Sioux Lookout, and in the Guelph and Peterborough areas. These elongate, rounded hills generally are well drained and support upland vegetation.

Vegetation

The vegetation that develops in response to climate, bedrock, surficial deposits and associated soil development processes, and topography has a major influence on the avifauna of an area, as vegetation is an important component of habitat for most species. At a coarse scale, the vegetation of Canada has been subdivided by Rowe (1972) into forest regions, which in Ontario comprise three broad regions: Boreal, Great Lakes-St. Lawrence, and Deciduous (Figure 2.1).

By far the largest region of the three is the Boreal Forest Region. It includes almost all of Ontario north from New Liskeard and Wawa in the east, and from Nipigon and Kenora in the west, north to the Hudson and James Bay coasts. The Hudson Bay Lowlands Ecozone and a substantial proportion of the Ontario Shield Ecozone are included in this forest region (Rowe 1972). In terms of this atlas, the Boreal Forest Region includes the Hudson Bay Lowlands and Northern Shield regions. At its northern limit, it contains sparse forest, extensive peatlands, and tundra. A mixture of arctic and boreal elements grow here, including tree species with boreal affinities, such as Black Spruce, White Spruce, and Tamarack, although these species occur in stunted form in more exposed sites and close to the coast (Riley 2003).

Farther south in the Boreal Forest Region, the vegetation grades from open boreal forest (spruce-lichen woodland, taiga) to closed boreal forest dominated by Black Spruce (upland and lowland), White Spruce, Tamarack, Jack Pine, Balsam Fir, Trembling Aspen, Balsam Poplar, and White Birch. Farther south still, approaching the Great Lakes-St. Lawrence Forest Region, the diversity of forest species increases, and intermixing of species characteristic of each of these regions becomes more frequent. Thus, in the southern parts of the Boreal Forest Region, species such as Eastern White Pine, Red Pine, and Red Maple occur in localized areas, especially in locations with warmer than normal microclimates.

South of the Boreal Forest Region, the number of forest tree species increases substantially. The Great Lakes-St. Lawrence Forest Region extends from the southern edge of the Boreal Forest Region to the Deciduous Forest Region. It includes portions of the Precambrian Shield in east-central and northwestern Ontario, as well as the band of Paleozoic rocks in southern Ontario immediately south of the Shield from the Québec border west to the shore of Lake Huron near the Maitland River. The northern part of this forest region is similar to the southern part of the Boreal Forest Region, in that there is a strong mixture of species from both regions. However, the prominence of species such as Eastern White Pine, Red Pine, Red Maple, Sugar Maple, and Yellow Birch increases substantially. Around Sault Ste. Marie and North Bay, species with more southern affinities, such as Eastern Hemlock, American Beech, Red Oak, Black Cherry, White Ash, and American Basswood become important forest components. Additional species appear as one moves south, especially south of the Precambrian Shield, where White Oak, Shagbark Hickory, Hackberry, Butternut, and other southern tree species are found.

The most species-rich or diverse forest region in the province is the Deciduous Forest Region in the southernmost part of Ontario, from about Grand Bend to Toronto and Kingston (Rowe 1972). The diversity of tree species here is considerably higher than elsewhere in the province, with several species of ash, hickory, and oak as well as Tulip Tree, Black Gum, and Sycamore being added to the species found in the Great Lakes-St. Lawrence Forest Region. The only trees absent here as native species are strictly boreal species such as Jack Pine. The Deciduous Forest Region has often been called the Carolinian Zone (Thaler and Plowright 1973) and has similar boundaries to the atlas's Carolinian region.

Watersheds and riverine systems

Ontario has two major drainage basins. The Great Lakes basin and St. Lawrence River drain eastward to the Atlantic Ocean. The rest of the province drains northward to the Arctic Ocean, by way of Hudson and James Bays. The Arctic watershed often is subdivided into two sub-units. Most of the north drains directly to Hudson or James Bay by way of rivers whose courses flow through the province. These river systems include the Black Duck, Severn, Shagamu, Winisk, Sutton, Brant, Ekwan, Attawapiskat, Albany, Moose, and Harricanaw Rivers and their tributaries. However, in northwestern Ontario, several river systems including the Rainy and Berens Rivers form part of the Winnipeg-Hudson Bay rivers system and flow westward into Manitoba before veering north to Hudson Bay. These numerous and extensive river systems serve as local migratory corridors as well as providing breeding habitat for waterfowl, some shorebirds such as Spotted Sandpiper, and the many songbirds associated with riparian forest and wetland habitats.

Shorelines: Hudson and James Bays

The shores and associated mudflats of Hudson and James Bays provide the only tidal saltwater habitats in the province (Abraham and Keddy 2005; Stewart and Lockhart 2005). These habitats are extremely important for migrating shorebirds and waterfowl, many of which nest farther north in the arctic parts of Canada. For example, the coastal subtidal areas and marshes support a large proportion of the Atlantic Brant (ssp. *hrota*) population during its northward migration, and they also serve as staging grounds for millions of Snow Geese and hundreds of thousands of Canada Geese (Thomas and Prevett 1982). The tidal flats along both Hudson and James Bays in Ontario are of hemispheric importance as staging areas for migrant arctic-nesting shorebirds, particularly in summer and fall. Although the full extent of shorebird passage through northern Ontario remains undetermined, it is likely that several million shorebirds use the coastal mudflats annually; major concentrations of 14 species and considerable numbers of an additional nine species have been documented.

The Ontario coasts and adjacent James Bay islands are known to be of hemispheric importance to migrating Red Knots (ssp. *rufa*) and Hudsonian Godwits (Morrison et al. 1995; Ross et al. 2003). Additionally, they are important as nesting habitat for island nesting gulls, terns, and eiders, as brood-provisioning habitat for the thousands of Snow and Canada Geese that nest in nearby saltwater and freshwater habitats, forests, or tundra, and moulting habitat for tens of thousands of prairie and boreal nesting ducks and temperate nesting Canada Geese. The Ontario breeding distributions of several species are concentrated in the coastal marshes, including populations of the Nelson's Sharp-tailed Sparrow, LeConte's Sparrow, Yellow Rail, Marbled Godwit, and others.

Shorelines: the Great Lakes

The shores and waters of the Great Lakes provide important feeding and staging habitat for migrating birds, and certain shoreline features also provide important breeding habitat. The Piping Plover (Endangered), for example, has relied upon undisturbed beach-dune ecosystems on Lakes Huron and Erie in the past, and may do so again as it begins to recover in adjacent Michigan (Roche 2007). The Great Lakes Basin is large and diverse, spanning portions of two ecozones and seven ecoregions. Migration monitoring stations along the shores of each of Ontario's Great Lakes have shown the importance of coastal sites for migrants. Late fall and winter bird counts have corroborated this pattern.

With the exceptions of coastal marshes and islands, the Great Lakes are less important for nesting birds than for migrating birds. However, evidence provided by this atlas suggests that the shorelines of the southern Great Lakes might be of particular importance to some aerial insectivores such as the Purple Martin and Bank Swallow. This might be related to the populations of flying insects in these areas, and/or the concentration of suitable nesting locations.

Coastal marshes, especially along Lakes Ontario, Erie, Huron, and St. Clair, are important habitats for nesting waterfowl and rails, including endangered species such as the King Rail. Although there are still large marshes at some locations along the shores of Lakes Erie and St. Clair, they are much reduced and altered from their pre-settlement state.

Islands in the Great Lakes provide important nesting places for colonial waterbirds such as the Double-crested Cormorant, Caspian Tern, Common Tern, Herring Gull, and Ring-billed Gull. The extensive archipelago of Georgian Bay, the North Channel, and adjacent Lake Huron and the eastern end of Lake Ontario support significant concentrations of colonial nesting waterbirds.

Disturbance regimes: natural

In Ecoregion 0E (Figure 2.1), water, fog, ice, and wind are the predominant natural forces affecting the vegetation. This area is largely treeless, with the exception of small islands and fingers of trees extending toward the coast on river levees and old beach ridges. The forces of ice and wind ensure that soil development is extremely slow, and the permafrost leads to regular frost heaving and exposure of soil parent materials, resulting in a harsh environment for tree establishment. Although major fires are infrequent, as would be expected in this kind of tundra environment, small fires do occur in treed patches from time to time. Elsewhere in the Hudson Bay Lowlands, fire frequency and size are variable, but the trends probably are similar to those farther south in the Boreal Forest Region; on wetter sites to the east, few fires occur. Also, in the northernmost boreal forests (taiga, lichen-woodland), the spacing between trees prevents fire from propagating well across the landscape. However, there have been several large fires this far north in areas where the canopy is more closed.

In the heart of the Boreal Forest, fire is a dominant force in forest dynamics. Fire patch size and intensity are correlated with the east-west precipitation gradient. Large sections of the western part of the Boreal Forest in Ontario have developed on better drained soils or on bedrock, leading to conditions where fuel can build up and become quite dry during the summer, leading to large, hot fires. The landscapes in the eastern part of the Boreal Forest, at least in areas such as the Clay Belt and the southern part of the Hudson Bay Lowlands, are much wetter, and as a result, fires tend to be smaller, less frequent, and less intense (van Sleeuwen 2006). Fire provides early successional habitat suitable for many species such as the Chestnut-sided Warbler, American Kestrel, and Sharp-tailed Grouse. Of Ontario's productive forest, 3.8% of the area has been burned in the past 10 years, and an additional 2.2% burned between 10 and 25 years ago (Ontario Ministry of Natural Resources 2006b).

Another important force of change and renewal in boreal forest is defoliation by native insects. Major defoliators include Spruce Budworm, Jack Pine Budworm, and Forest Tent Caterpillar. Outbreaks of such species make available to birds an immediate source of food in the form of caterpillars. Species such as the Tennessee Warbler, Bay-breasted Warbler, and Cape May Warbler take advantage of budworms, while the Black-billed Cuckoo utilizes tent caterpillars. Larvae can also have an important effect on forest regeneration, especially when the outbreak is of several years' duration and tree death occurs. This can lead to fuel build-up, increasing the probability of fire, especially in coniferous stands.

In the Great Lakes-St. Lawrence Forest, particularly on the Precambrian Shield, fire plays an important role in forest regeneration, particularly for pines and oaks. Fires here are highly variable in size, intensity, and frequency. Formerly, fire was a more pervasive force in this forest region, but fire suppression has altered ecosystem dynamics. In ecosystems such as tolerant hardwood forests dominated by Sugar Maple and American Beech, although fire was present, other disturbance regimes were equally or more important. The predominant disturbance regime leading to regeneration is now gap-phase dynamics, in which small patches (often less than 1 ha in size; e.g., Krasny and Whitmore 1992) are created in the forest matrix by wind, drought, or other stresses on tree growth. Those tree species capable of taking advantage of small gaps in the canopy grow to occupy the open space and available light. In the absence of larger-scale disturbance, species such as Sugar Maple and Eastern Hemlock, both very shade tolerant, tend to become dominant. However, even in such ecosystems, major disturbances occur occasionally in the form of large blowdowns, fires, or extensive insect defoliations, and in these circumstances, other tree species such as shade-intolerant and semi-tolerant hardwoods (e.g. White Birch, Trembling Aspen) and pines perpetuate themselves.

In the extreme south, forest ecosystems renew themselves in much the same way as in the Great Lakes-St. Lawrence Forest, except that gap-phase dynamics are even more prevalent. However, in the rarer ecosystems such as prairies and savannahs, fire is again the major perpetuating force.

Except in the southwest part of the province, the beaver is an extremely important force in aquatic ecosystem dynamics in riparian ecosystems. It can affect local hydrology, and hence habitat conditions, for long periods of time. Wetland habitats as well as adjacent upland tree composition can be affected for decades. Where beavers are present, a shifting mosaic of habitat types predominates. The ponds are important for nesting waterfowl such as the Hooded Merganser and American Black Duck. Beaver meadows, created after dams have gone out, are important for species such as the Sedge Wren and prior to settlement likely provided much of the habitat available to grassland-nesting species. The alder thickets that often grow as the meadows undergo succession are inhabited by species such as the Golden-winged Warbler, Alder Flycatcher, and Wilson's Warbler.

Disturbance regimes: anthropogenic

During recent geological time, probably the most significant disturbance of Ontario's natural ecosystems, in extent, frequency, and intensity, is the human imprint on the land. The primary disturbance is to vegetation, through settlement, agriculture, transportation and forestry; in some areas, landform disturbance due to mineral extraction, particularly pits and quarries, is extensive enough to warrant concern as well. This alteration or removal of vegetation affects the supply of suitable habitat for wildlife, including birds. Even the simple presence of humans may disrupt the normal animal behaviour patterns necessary for successful breeding and maintenance of sustainable populations.

The following summary of the history and extent of land use change south of the Canadian Shield (Figure 2.4) is based on Larson et al. (1999). Before 1700, the expanse of forest south of the Shield was interrupted by prairie, savannah, alvar, open wetlands, and, on easily worked soils, by areas of aboriginal agriculture. One of the most densely settled areas of aboriginal Canada was Simcoe Co., where Huron agriculture and fallow areas in the early 1600s may have used about 200 square kilometres. Upland areas were almost all woodland with about 1.3% as alvar, prairie, or savannah. Wetlands with some exceptions were dominated by wooded swamp in most areas, with very small areas of scrubland and marsh. Following clearing by European settlers, the low point for woodland extent was around 1920 at approximately 10.6% (including wooded swamp); 94% of the upland woodland/scrub south of the Shield had been cleared. Of the remaining 6%, Larson et al. (1999) were unable to find any true old growth. J. Riley (pers. comm.) estimates that of that 6%, about 1% may be older-growth woodlands, 1% old-pioneer woodlands, and the remaining 4% working native upland forest. Since the 1920s, the spread of replacement woodland and other natural areas has expanded the woodland area to about 29% (including wooded swamp) (Ontario Ministry of Natural Resources 2006b).

Human effect on wetlands south of the Shield has also been substantial, with an estimated loss of 68% of the original existing wetlands (Snell 1987). The highest concentration of wetland was originally in southeastern and southwestern Ontario, where 40-80% of the total area in the various counties was wetland. Wetland decline, primarily through clearing and drainage for agricultural purposes, has been greatest in the Carolinian region, with wetland losses ranging from about 50% in Oxford and Brant Counties to 96% in Essex Co. The

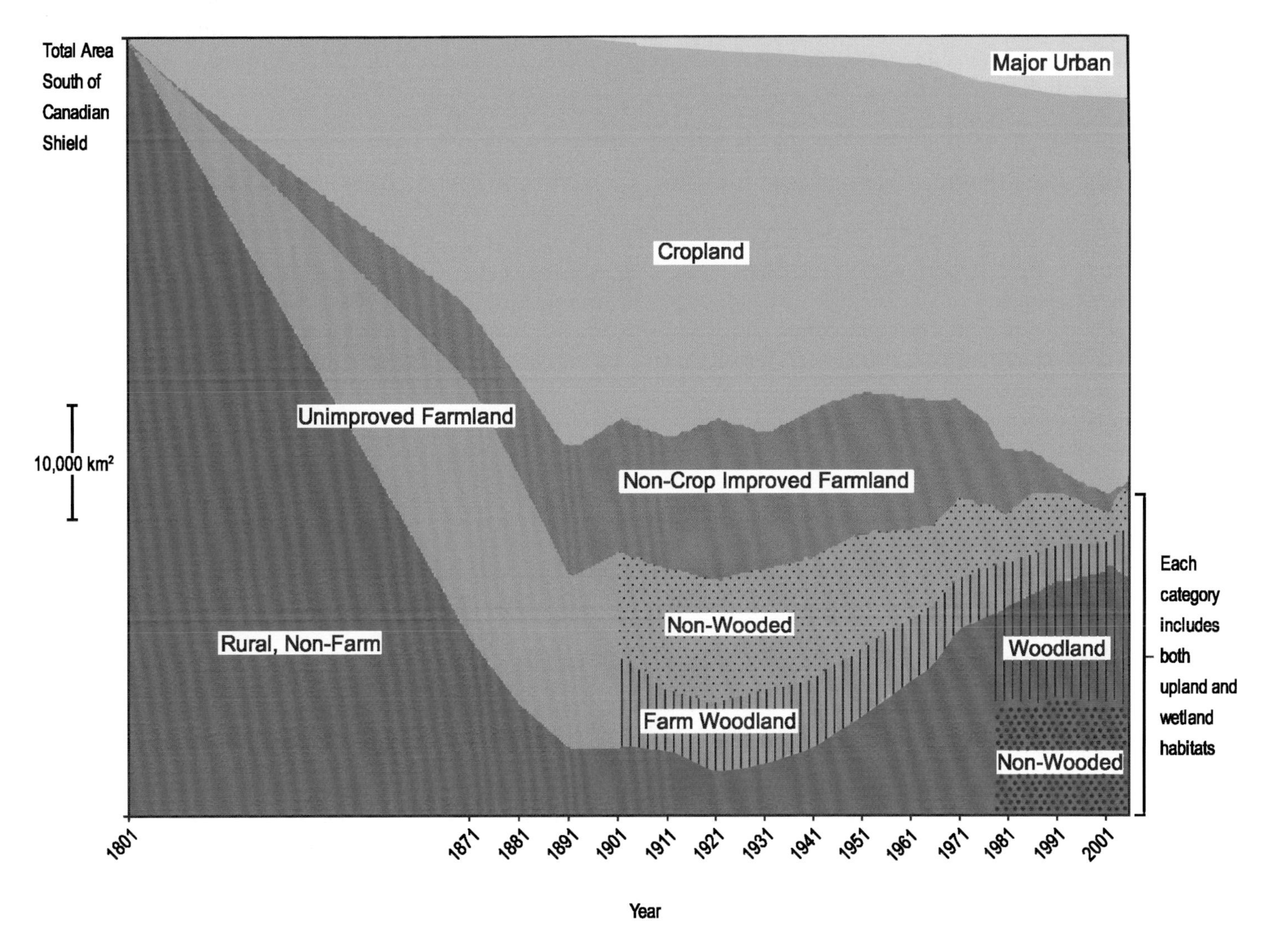

Figure 2.4. Land use change 1801 to 2006 south of the Canadian Shield. Adapted from Larson et al. 1999 by E. Snell.

Major Urban indicates census cities and towns: 2001. Urban (5,629 km²) is area of census units with populations over 1000 and over 400 people/km² according to Statistics Canada, Census Division, Census of Population for 1996, 2001, 2006. Estimates for 1981, 1971, 1951, and 1921 were pro-rated from 2001 using Yeates' (1985) rates of change of urban extent in southern Ontario. Other dates are interpolated.

Cropland: From Census of Agriculture for 1871, 1881, 1891, 1901, 1911, 1921, 1931, 1941, 1951, 1966, 1971, 1981, 1986, 1991, 1996, 2001, 2006 (Statistics Canada, Census Division). Other years are interpolated.

Non-Crop Improved Farmland includes seeded grazing land and summer fallow. From Census of Agriculture for the same years as Cropland, above. Other years are interpolated.

Unimproved Farmland is natural pasture, woodland, and marsh. From Census of Agriculture for the same years as Cropland. From 1901 to 1986 and for 2006, the census separated **Farm Woodland** from **Non-Wooded**. Other years are interpolated.

Rural, Non-Farm is all the remaining area based on the total area of 67,587 km² for counties/regions* south of the Canadian Shield (2006 Census). In the 1800s, it was largely original woodland. Since early 1900s, most Rural, Non-Farm is either replacement woodland or land uses such as villages, scattered and strip development, rural residential, roads, pits, landfills, and abandoned farms. **Woodland** is separated out after 1978 using total woodland from the Forest Resource Inventory for 1978 (from Larson et al. 1999) and SOLRIS for 2002 (Steve Voros, pers. comm.), in each case subtracting interpolated farm woodland. Other dates are interpolated. The remaining land is **Non-Wooded.**

* Counties/Regions are: Brant, Bruce, Chatham-Kent, Dufferin, Durham, Elgin, Essex, Grey, Haldimand-Norfolk, Halton, Hamilton, Huron, Lambton, Leeds and Grenville, Middlesex, Niagara, Northumberland, Ottawa, Oxford, Peel, Perth, Prescott and Russell, Prince Edward, Simcoe, Stormont-Dundas and Glengarry, Toronto, Waterloo, Wellington and York (or corresponding jurisdictions depending on the date).

nature of the remaining marshes has also changed. For example, the marsh around Point Pelee, which declined in area by 71% between 1880 and the mid-1970s (Rutherford 1979) and was once dominated by wild rice (Dore 1969), is now predominantly cattail and Common Reed. There were also considerable losses in the more agricultural parts of the Lake Simcoe-Rideau region, with losses of original wetlands over 80% in Perth Co. and 70-80% in Huron Co. and the United Counties of Prescott and Russell. On the Shield, losses have been far less severe, with less than 20% of the original wetland area converted to other uses.

Disturbance arising from human settlement is clearly indicated on a map of the population ecumene (Figure 2.5). In Ontario 91% of people live south of the Canadian Shield (Ontario Ministry of Natural Resources 2006b). All of southern Ontario is considered inhabited except for Algonquin Park, a small patch of the Ontario Shield in the Madawaska Highlands, and parts of the northern Georgian Bay shoreline. Most of northern Ontario has population densities well below 0.4 persons per square kilometre, except for the Highway 11 corridor through the clay belts, the Thunder Bay area, and the Rainy River-Fort Frances, Kenora, and Dryden areas in northwestern Ontario.

Within this ecumene, the intensity of settlement disturbance varies considerably from sparsely populated recreational areas to major urban centres. The extent of disturbance is conveyed most readily with measures of human population density. In Figure 2.5, densities greater than 400 persons per square kilometre are considered urban, and areas with less than 5 persons per square kilometre are considered sparsely populated rural areas. These thresholds do not appear on the map as sharp discontinuities in the southern Ontario landscape but are rather ends of a continuum of settlement intensity and disturbance. The "Greater Golden Horseshoe" is clearly evident, stretching from Oshawa around to Fort Erie, reaching west to Kitchener-Waterloo, and extending north to Barrie and Lake Simcoe. A number of other urban-centred regions with high population density are Ottawa, London, Windsor, and Sudbury. While none of these is continuously built up, the high population and accompanying structure densities substantially change the character of the landscape and the habitat for birds. There are many fewer natural areas here than where

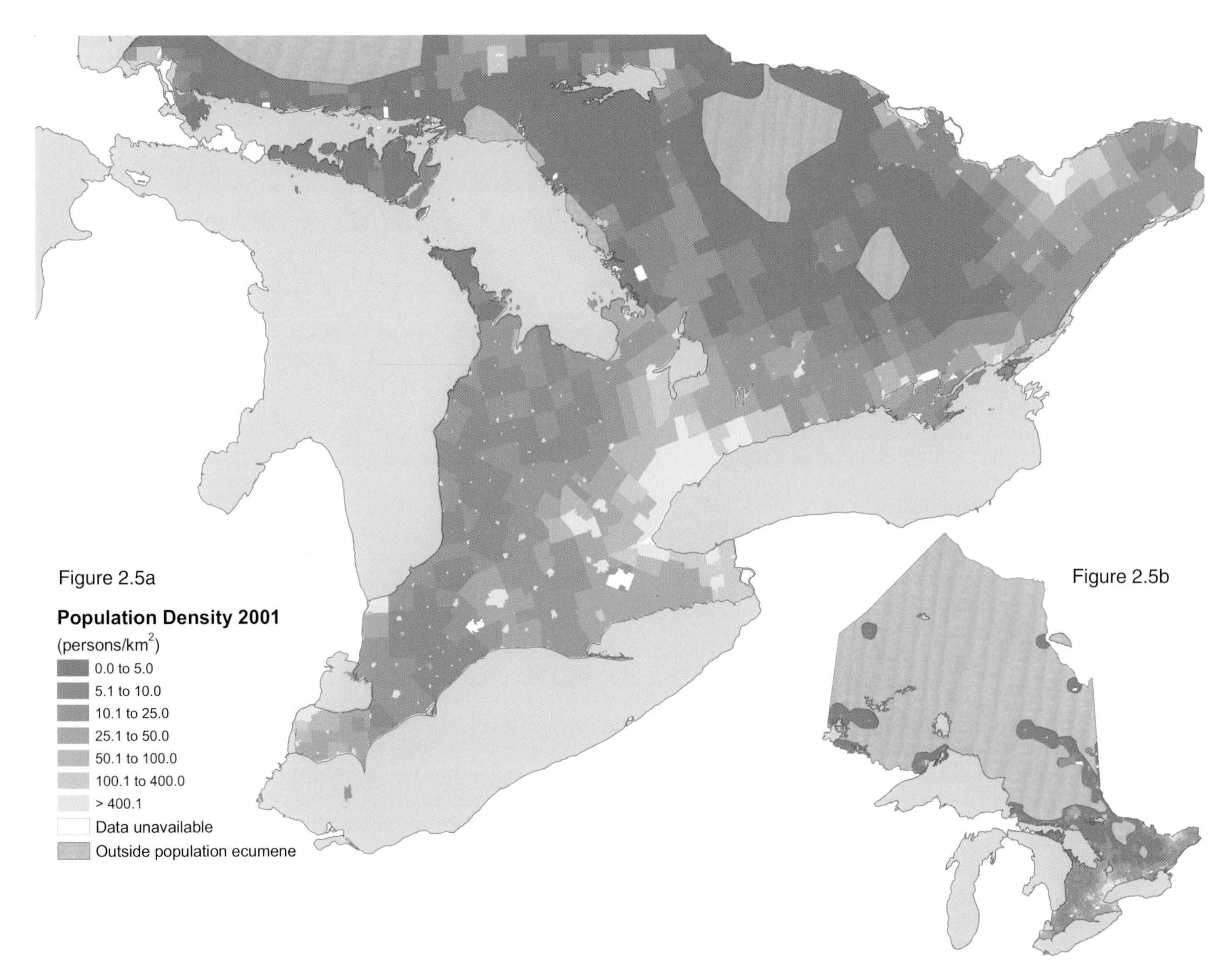

Figure 2.5. Population density in 2001 (Statistics Canada 2002a): a) Population density in southern Ontario; b) Population density in all of Ontario, showing population ecumene.

human population density is lower, and those areas considered natural are usually heavily used for recreation. Even "passive" recreational activities such as nature viewing will at high rates disturb vegetation, changing habitat quality, and disturb fauna, forcing changes in behaviours. Habitat patches that remain relatively undisturbed, such as woodlands or grasslands, are smaller and more widely separated from each other than in less densely settled areas. This reduced size and increased fragmentation reduces both the total available habitat and the likelihood of a patch being recolonized, should resident bird species become extirpated.

Also associated with human activity is the introduction of numerous invasive species, many of which have detrimental effects on native birds directly or (more frequently) on their habitats. Diseases such as Chestnut Blight, Dutch Elm Disease, and recently Beech Bark Disease, Butternut Canker, and Dogwood Anthracnose are affecting the composition of forests. Non-native insects such as the Gypsy Moth can cause heavy defoliation, and wood-boring insects such as the Emerald Ash Borer are beginning to cause tree mortality in the province.

In settled areas, many structures such as office buildings, communication towers, and electrical transmission lines impose significant mortality pressure on birds, particularly migratory species. "An estimated minimum of one million migratory birds die each year in Toronto due to collision with buildings" (City of Toronto 2007). Motor vehicle collisions and predation by house cats are both considered to cause substantial bird mortality, each estimated to be in the order of 100 million deaths annually in the US (cf. Winter and Wallace 2006; FLAP 2007).

Agricultural land use has a number of direct impacts on birds; the most significant is simply the loss and fragmentation of natural habitats through land clearing, draining, and regular and frequent land disturbance caused by cultivation and cropping. Other effects include the reduction of insect populations through use of insecticides and the toxic effects of some pesticides, for example, fungicides on seed grain. On the other hand, for some species, agriculture provides significant food subsidies: the consumption of waste grain by Wild Turkeys provides additional energy, enabling them to survive harsher winters than natural foods alone allow. Figure 2.6 shows both the agricultural ecumene and the percentage of

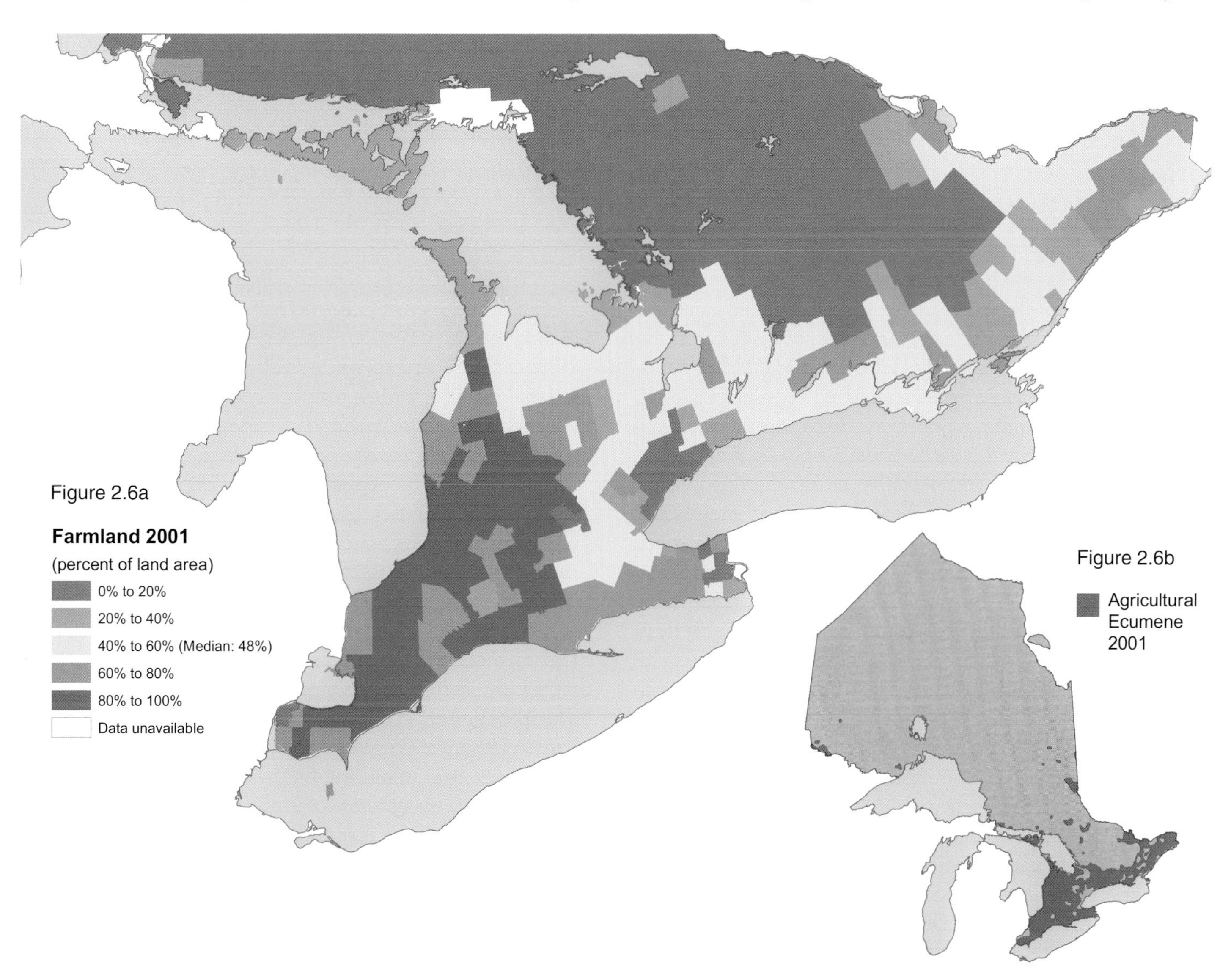

Figure 2.6. Agricultural land use in 2001 (Statistics Canada 2006b): a) farmland as a percentage of land area; b) the agricultural ecumene.

land occupied by farms as an indicator of agricultural intensity. Agriculture is a significant land use in the Mixedwood Plains Ecozone; in the north, there are two relatively small pockets: the Clay Belt near the Québec border, and the Rainy River-Fort Frances area. Within the agricultural ecumene, the most intense agricultural use is in southwestern Ontario, where in many areas cropland comprises more than 80% of the land; much of this is in corn, soybeans, and other intensely farmed row crops. Moving north and east from this region, cropland as a percentage of land area drops significantly, in some areas due to urbanization, in others due to unsuitable land. The effect of the Precambrian Shield in constraining agricultural land use is clear; farther east agricultural intensity increases on the flatter, more fertile and easily tilled clay plains in the Ottawa and St. Lawrence River valleys.

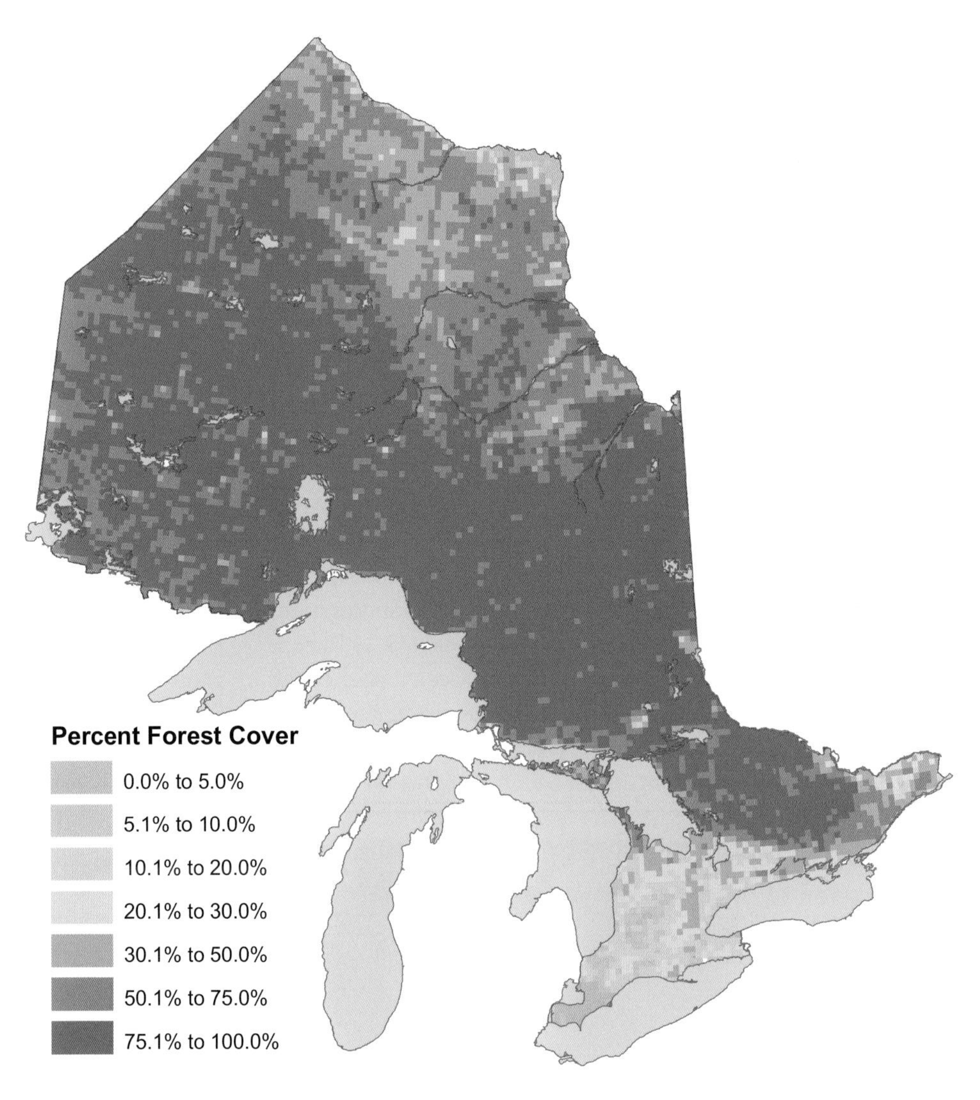

Figure 2.7. Percentage of forest cover circa 2000, excluding recent cuts and burns (Spectranalysis 2004).

Both settlement and agriculture have had an effect on the amount of wooded land remaining in Ontario. Figure 2.7 shows that the distribution of woodland as a percentage of land area is almost a negative image of settlement and agriculture. This measure is an index of the effect of human disturbance on natural heritage features. Forest cover south of the Shield is currently 29% and ranges from less than 3% in parts of Essex Co. and Chatham-Kent to over 60% on the Bruce Peninsula and in parts of Lanark Co. in eastern Ontario. Much of the forest cover south of the Shield is highly fragmented into small, widely dispersed woodlots that do not support full or viable communities of area-sensitive birds or forest interior birds (Freemark and Collins 1992). As shown in Figure 2.7, forest cover south of the Shield is higher in areas near the Shield's southern edge, as well as along the length of the Niagara Escarpment south to about Hamilton, and near Long Point. These areas are often evident on the maps of forest birds in this atlas.

Forest covers 68% of land area on the Precambrian Shield in the Great Lakes-St. Lawrence Forest region and 83% in the Boreal Forest region (Ontario Ministry of Natural Resources 2006b). Forestry in Ontario dates back to the square-timber trade in the Ottawa Valley beginning in the first decade of the 19th century (Epp 2000). Forest management is now the primary land use activity affecting birds and their habitats across approximately 30 million hectares of forested Crown land in the Southern and Northern Shield regions. About 87% of the area harvested in Ontario, primarily in the Boreal Forest, is done using the clearcut system; 13% of forest harvesting uses selection or shelterwood systems, primarily in the Great Lakes-St. Lawrence Forest Region. Roughly 1% of forested land is disturbed by forest management each year (Ontario Ministry of Natural Resources 2004), mostly outside the nesting season.

The contemporary effects of forestry are arguably less dramatic in altering ecosystems and habitats, because the recurrence interval for disturbance is much longer than the annual cycle of agricultural cropping systems or the continuous investment of energy in maintaining built environments. However, forestry, through fire suppression, logging, and forest regeneration activities, has significant impacts on habitat. Logging and forest regeneration activities change the forest structure both within stands and across the landscape and change the tree species and age composition of the forest (Carleton 2000).

Since 1950, the success of fire suppression programs in the Boreal Forest has shifted the balance of disturbance from the natural wildfire disturbance regime to one dominated by logging. While one of the goals of current forest management in Ontario is to emulate natural disturbance processes, it is clear that forestry cannot entirely mimic those processes. Though they may be similar in the spatial configuration of disturbance on the land, they differ substantially in that logging is a physical process involving the removal of biomass, while fire is a chemical process that transforms the biomass in place and causes transport of some elements (Thompson 2000a). Logging and fire suppression have changed species composition, favouring shade and fire intolerant tree species such as poplars and aspens, Balsam Fir, Sugar Maple, Red Maple, and American Beech. This shift has been accompanied by declines in Eastern White Pine, Red Pine, Black Spruce, White Spruce, Eastern Hemlock, Yellow Birch, White Birch, and Red Spruce (Thompson 2000). Fire suppression has the additional effect of extending the return period for disturbance, which has an impact on successional pathways and ultimately on species composition (van Sleeuwen 2006).

New forest management guidelines focus on retaining more structure in cutovers to minimize the differences between cuts and burns (see Ontario Ministry of Natural Resources 2001). Despite the differences between cuts and burns, bird communities in cut and burned habitats begin to converge about 10 years after disturbance and are very similar after 60 years (Schieck and Song 2006).

Aggregate extraction and mining is another significant disturbance of natural ecosystems. Although these activities are considered by some proponents to be simply interim land uses, they remove and substantially alter natural habitats. The chief land-use contention with aggregate resource use is that many deposits are located near markets in parts of the province where natural heritage features are already relatively rare and are threatened by land development and agriculture. On the other hand, extraction of these mineral resources near the market has both economic and environmental benefits, primarily in reduced transportation costs and reduced vehicle emissions. Unfortunately, many of the aggregate deposits are located under and, in fact, form the basis for a number of unique physical and natural environments, prime among them the Niagara Escarpment, the Oak Ridges Moraine, and the Carden Plain. While post-extraction rehabilitation of pits and quarries has the potential to return the land to a relatively natural state, suitable at first for early successional species and eventually for forest birds, the original value of these features at a site level will be irrevocably changed. In addition, pit rehabilitation often removes anthropogenic sandbanks that provide nesting habitat for Bank and Northern Rough-winged Swallows and the Belted Kingfisher.

Mining of mineral resources typically consumes less land and directly alters less habitat than aggregate extraction; however, the secondary effects of mining developments are often substantial. For example, acid precipitation and historic forest harvesting for fuel associated with sintering and smelting activites in the Sudbury area have resulted in 175 km^2 of unvegetated land and 700 km^2 of semi-barren land (Winterhalder 1995); this land is slowly recovering. Current satellite images clearly show a 40 km long "kill zone" northeast of Wawa (Northwatch 2001). The associated development of roads through remote areas fragment habitat and provide inexpensive access for other resource activities such as foresty and hunting which may alter habitats and populations.

Interest in mining exploration and development has increased dramatically in the Hudson Bay Lowlands since the first atlas, particularly during the period of the current atlas. One mine is in development, and numerous claims indicate that others will follow. Mining in this remote area will require road building of some kind (winter roads certainly, and all-weather roads depending on the locations of finds) with their attendant issues of increased access. Where open pits are employed, as in the case of diamond mining, it is anticipated that beyond the relatively small footprint of the mine and processing infrastructure, there will be dewatering of substantial surrounding areas of muskeg, potentially producing changes to wetland and forest habitats.

One final anthropogenic disturbance with far-reaching effects on all ecosystems of Ontario is climate change. Although the average annual global temperature warmed about 0.74°C during the past century (IPCC 2007), warming in Canada was double the world average. However, this warming was not uniform across the country. For example, the average annual temperature increased about 2.0°C in northwestern British Columbia and the Kluane region of the Yukon Territory and 1.2°C in south-central Canada including Ontario, but did not change in Atlantic Canada over the same period (Environment Canada 2006).

Climate (i.e., temperature, precipitation, and wind) is an important factor in the distribution and abundance of birds. Given that Ontario's climate is expected to warm throughout the 21st century (Colombo et al. 2007, IPCC 2007), the life cycle (e.g., migration, reproduction, fledging, and feeding) and/or habitat patterns of most, if not all, birds will be affected. An analysis of the effects of climate change in birds in southern Ontario is described in the chapter entitled "Changes in Bird Distributions between Atlases."

Avifaunal affinities

The immense longitudinal and latitudinal spread of Ontario has resulted in a very diverse biota with multiple geographic affinities. In the far north, subarctic species and ecosystems have developed. Extensive fens, narrow tongues of taiga, and a narrow band of wet and dry tundra are found near the Hudson Bay coast. These areas provide habitat for northern species such as the Pacific Loon, Red-throated Loon, Tundra Swan, Snow Goose, Ross's Goose, Long-tailed Duck, Hudsonian Godwit, Stilt Sandpiper, Short-billed Dowitcher, American Golden Plover, Parasitic Jaeger, Arctic Tern, Willow Ptarmigan, American Pipit, American Tree Sparrow, Harris's Sparrow, Lapland Longspur, Smith's Longspur, and Hoary Redpoll.

The extensive tidal marshes and associated graminoid fens of the lower James Bay coast are known to support populations of a number of species with distinctly western affinities (Todd 1943), including the Clay-colored Sparrow, LeConte's Sparrow, Marbled Godwit, Nelson's Sharp-tailed Sparrow, Wilson's Phalarope, and, at least occasionally, the Sedge Wren.

Inland areas of the Hudson Bay Lowlands are made up primarily of open bogs and fens, with narrow strips of heavier forest on well-drained riverbanks. Conifers dominate on the taiga and on riverbanks, but aspen stands occur following fires. Species such as the Solitary Sandpiper, Greater Yellowlegs,

Blackpoll and Palm Warbler, and Rusty Blackbird occur widely.

Farther south, on entering the more continuous Boreal Forest, the widespread boreal fauna becomes evident. Many bird species characteristic of boreal forests are widespread from east to west, among them the Common Loon, Merlin, Spruce Grouse, Gray Jay, Common Raven, Philadelphia Vireo, Tennessee Warbler, Yellow-rumped Warbler, Lincoln's Sparrow, White-throated Sparrow, Purple Finch, and Pine Siskin. South of the Boreal Forest Region, in the Great Lakes-St. Lawrence Forest Region, species diversity increases. There is a mixture of elements from south and north. On the Precambrian Shield, spruce, Balsam Fir, and Jack Pine-dominated habitat supports boreal species such as the Gray Jay, Boreal Chickadee, Spruce Grouse, and Black-backed Woodpecker. The tolerant hardwood forests support populations of the Red-shouldered Hawk, Eastern Wood-Pewee, Scarlet Tanager, Black-throated Blue Warbler, Blackburnian Warbler, Wood Thrush, and Rose-breasted Grosbeak.

South of the Shield, agricultural habitats predominate. Pastures and meadows provide suitable habitat for many grassland-nesting species such as the Savannah Sparrow and Upland Sandpiper. Rare habitats south of the Precambrian Shield, such as certain kinds of alvars, are important for grassland birds including the Loggerhead Shrike. The Carden Alvar, part of the Carden Plain physiographic region, is particularly noteworthy in this respect. Formerly farmed areas abandoned to natural succession provide habitat for early successional, scrub, and forest edge species such as the Brown Thrasher and Field Sparrow. Row-cropped areas provide habitat for fewer species but are used extensively by the Horned Lark, Vesper Sparrow, and Killdeer.

The southern edge of the Canadian Shield forms an important dividing line between bird communities and has a particularly diverse bird fauna. The area has a great variety of habitats because the forested lands of the Shield are interspersed with the agricultural lands of the Lake Simcoe-Rideau region (Ecoregion 6E in Figure 2.1). Many birds of agricultural lands, such as the Grasshopper Sparrow, Eastern Meadowlark, and Bobolink, are far less common on the Shield than they are to the south. Similarly, many birds of forested habitats, such as the Swainson's Thrush and Blackburnian Warbler, are common to the north of the Shield edge but far less so south of the Shield. As much former agricultural land near the Shield edge has been abandoned, the area is rich in scrubby habitats suitable for the Yellow Warbler and Eastern Towhee. The area is also rich in wetlands, so Black Terns, Virginia Rails, and Marsh Wrens, among others, are relatively common here. A few species such as the Cerulean Warbler and Yellow-throated Vireo are found more frequently near the edge of the Shield than elsewhere in the province, presumably because of preferred forest habitat, while others like the Common Nighthawk and Whip-poor-will are found in good numbers perhaps because of the right mix of forest and rocky openings here.

In the vicinity of Lake of the Woods, at the extreme western edge of Ontario adjacent to Manitoba, is an area of very mixed biotic affinities. Here, a mixture of boreal, southern, and western species occur together. The area is prairie-like in some places but also has extensive peatlands, intolerant hardwood forests, and small patches of tolerant and semi-tolerant hardwoods. This makes the southern Lake of the Woods region (Ecoregion 5S on Figure 2.1) highly valued as a birding location. The mixture of vegetation types is reflected in the fauna, with prairie bird species such as the American White Pelican, Black-billed Magpie, Brewer's Blackbird, Eared Grebe, Marbled Godwit, Sharp-tailed Grouse, Yellow-headed Blackbird, and Western Meadowlark intermingling with species of more southern or eastern affinity, such as the Golden-winged Warbler, Red-headed Woodpecker, Yellow-throated Vireo, and Orchard Oriole and boreal species such as the Boreal Chickadee and Gray Jay.

The biota in the Deciduous Forest Region is the most diverse in Canada. It also is the most imperilled, because of the amount of natural habitat that has been drained, cut, and converted into agricultural and suburban and urban land uses. Some of the remaining remnants of the Carolinian forests still support populations of birds at risk, such as the Acadian Flycatcher and Prothonotary Warbler.

The Deciduous Forest Region once contained most of the original prairie and savannah in southern Ontario, 97% of which has now been lost (Bakowsky 1999), primarily through conversion to agriculture. The Northern Bobwhite, which inhabited the savannah, is now on the verge of extirpation from the province, and the Greater Prairie-Chicken, which inhabited the prairie, has been extirpated. Many grassland-dependent species including the Northern Bobwhite, Bobolink, Upland Sandpiper, and Henslow's Sparrow expanded with the clearing of the forest and the creation of extensive areas of pasture and meadow, but are now in decline in the province as grassland is lost to natural succession in some areas and intensified agricultural practices and urbanization in others.

Summary

Underlying geology, geological history (e.g., glaciation), and climate provide the framework that determines the province's bird fauna. The current biota is much affected, positively for some species, negatively for others, by human effects on the landscape and on the climate, as shown in the results of this atlas project. As human population continues to grow, as the effect on climate increases, and as changes to the landscape continue to occur, it is evident that changes will continue in the province's bird fauna; but at this time, it is impossible to predict what those changes will be. Atlas projects provide a rich data source to pursue in-depth analysis of the issues these changes raise. The chapter entitled "Changes in Bird Distributions between Atlases" looks more closely at changes over the past 20 years and how they have affected the province's birds.

Coverage and Results – An Overview

Effort

One of the main coverage goals of the atlas was to obtain 50 hours of coverage in all 100-km blocks in the province and 20 hours of coverage in all 10-km squares in southern Ontario. The project met its goal in 125 (93%) of the province's 135 full 100-km blocks, and in 1,678 (89%) of the 1,890 10-km squares in southern Ontario. Figure 3.1 shows the number of hours of fieldwork reported in each 10-km square and 100-km block in the province. Judging from the number of species reported (see below), some of the other squares and blocks were probably adequately covered, but effort was not always reported completely.

The pattern of coverage is similar to that obtained during the first atlas, with coverage decreasing markedly from south to north. In the south, almost every 10-km square was covered, while in far northern Ontario north of the road system, an average of only 3% of 10-km squares were adequately covered per 100-km block (range of 0% to 33%).

As in the first atlas, coverage was noticeably higher in the heavily populated area within 50-100 km of Lake Ontario from about Kingston through Toronto to Niagara Falls. Coverage was also high between Ottawa and Kingston, near Windsor, and generally throughout the Carolinian and Lake Simcoe-Rideau regions.

On the Southern Shield, high coverage is evident around population centres such as Sudbury and Parry Sound, and in parts of "cottage country" such as Muskoka and Haliburton Districts. On the Northern Shield, there was some concentration of coverage near communities. The main provincial highway system and other major roads are evident on the map, marked by squares with coverage.

North of the road system, atlassers submitted data from most squares in which they spent time, so the routes taken by atlassers along river systems are often apparent on the coverage maps. Some well-covered squares contain or are near remote communities that provided points of access for atlas work. Also, close to Hudson Bay, a large number of squares show a low level of coverage. This area is frequently flown by OMNR and CWS crews who recorded observations of a few, primarily large species identifiable from the air, particularly waterfowl.

Overall, 152,263 hours of effort were reported during the second atlas, 25% higher than the 121,684 hours reported during the first atlas (Table 3.1). More extensive coverage was attained in all regions during this atlas, but the difference is particularly large in the Northern Shield and Carolinian regions. Much of the additional effort in the Northern Shield was the result of Bird Studies Canada's Boreal Forest Bird Project (BFBP), which involved a large paid crew collecting atlas data in southern and central parts of the Boreal Forest using the atlas methodology. The additional effort in the Carolinian region resulted both from a larger number of atlassers and from more hours of coverage per square (Table 3.2).

	First atlas	Second atlas	Difference	
Region	Total hours	Total hours	Total hours	% Total hours
Hudson Bay Lowlands	4210	5037	827	20%
Northern Shield	13079	19820	6741	52%
Southern Shield	32796	36611	3815	12%
Lake Simcoe-Rideau	49800	59403	9603	19%
Carolinian	21799	31392	9593	44%
Ontario	**121684**	**152263**	**30579**	**25%**

Table 3.1. Total number of hours of fieldwork reported in each region and for all of Ontario for both atlas projects.

The greater effort devoted to fieldwork in the second atlas meant that direct comparison between atlases would give biased results. The comparisons between atlases shown in this book thus incorporate an adjustment to correct for the additional effort. This is explained in the Methods chapter, and it included the removal of the BFBP data from the change analysis.

Table 3.2 shows that 1,900 people contributed data to the atlas. That is, 1,900 people (or, in a few cases, institutions) were listed as the primary atlasser on one or more atlas data forms submitted to the project. An additional 1,517 people were listed on atlas data forms as assistants. The names of all participants are listed in the Acknowledgements. These numbers are well up from those in the first atlas.

The number of atlassers was highest in the Lake Simcoe-Rideau region, but the hours of coverage per square were highest in the Carolinian region, which is smaller. Hours of coverage per square generally decreased with increasing latitude, but were lowest in the very large Northern Shield region.

Considering only squares that had more than 20 hours of coverage (this removes some partial squares and the many northern squares with partial coverage), squares in the Carolinian and Lake Simcoe-Rideau regions had more hours of effort during the second atlas than during the first; the Southern Shield and Hudson Bay Lowlands had about the same; and the Northern Shield had fewer hours. However, considerably more squares were covered during the second atlas than the first in the Northern Shield and Hudson

	First atlas				Second atlas			
Region	Atlassers (including institutions)	Squares with data	Squares with >20 hours	Average hours in squares with >20 hours	Atlassers (including institutions)	Squares with data	Squares with >20 hours	Average hours in squares with >20 hours
Hudson Bay Lowlands	51	351	52	50	81	827	82	49
Northern Shield	223	1441	169	53	386	2252	417	35
Southern Shield	514	816	630	47	685	836	719	48
Lake Simcoe-Rideau	699	756	659	67	1045	762	698	81
Carolinian	314	285	238	79	465	287	261	96
Ontario	**1317**	**3649**	**1748**	**56**	**1900**	**4964**	**2177**	**50**

Table 3.2. The number of atlassers, squares with data, and hours of coverage by square in the first and second atlas projects.

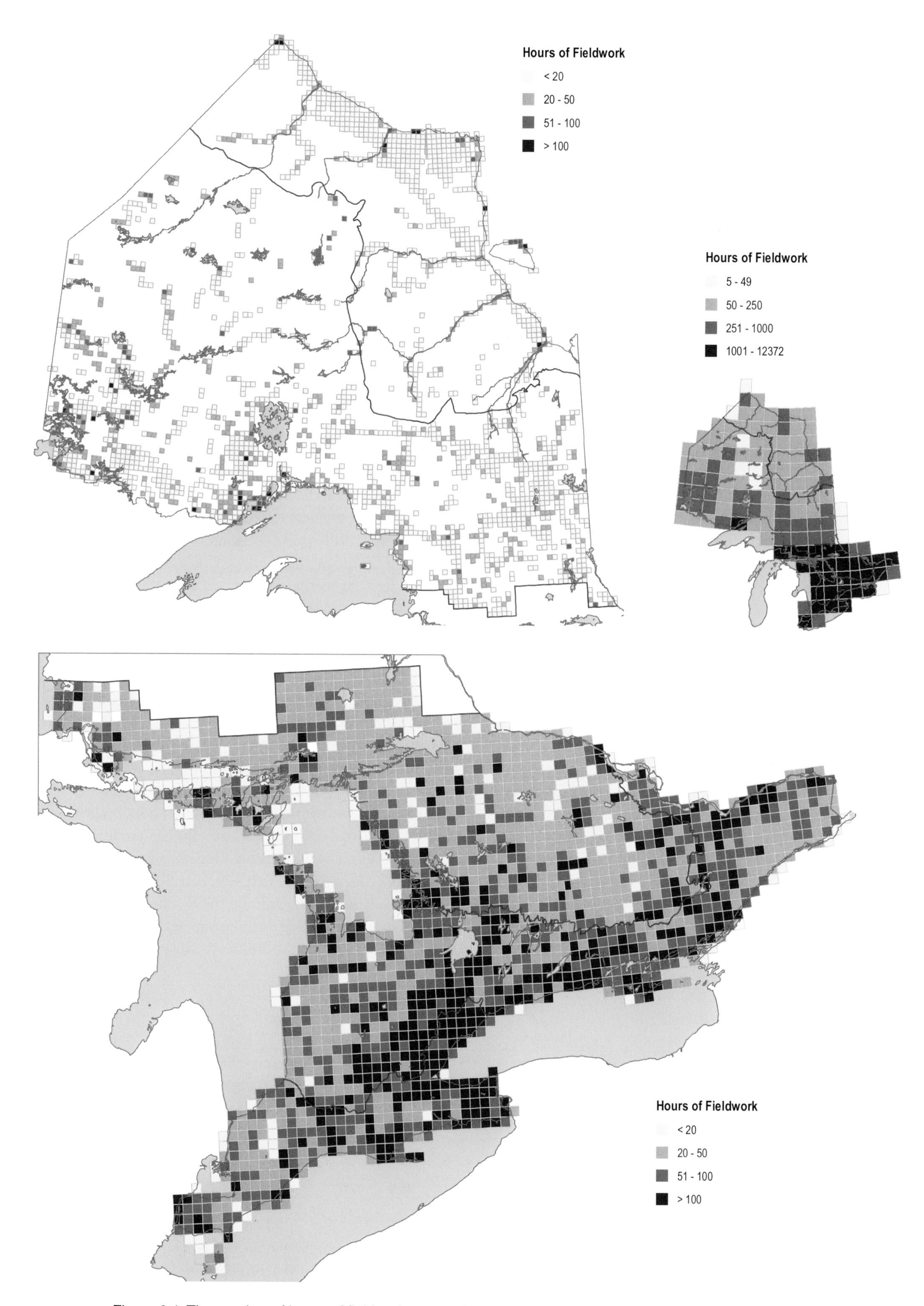

Figure 3.1. The number of hours of fieldwork reported in each 10-km square and 100-km block in the province.

Bay Lowlands regions, in part because of the BFBP and more extensive aerial surveys by CWS and OMNR, but also because of greater effort by regular atlassers.

Over 90% of atlassing took place in May through July, and almost half of all atlassing hours were reported in June, the month when most species are breeding (Figure 3.2). Part of the standardized Eastern Screech-Owl Survey ran during November-December, and that survey probably provided a major portion of the effort reported in those months. Breeding evidence for Great Horned Owls could also be reported starting in December.

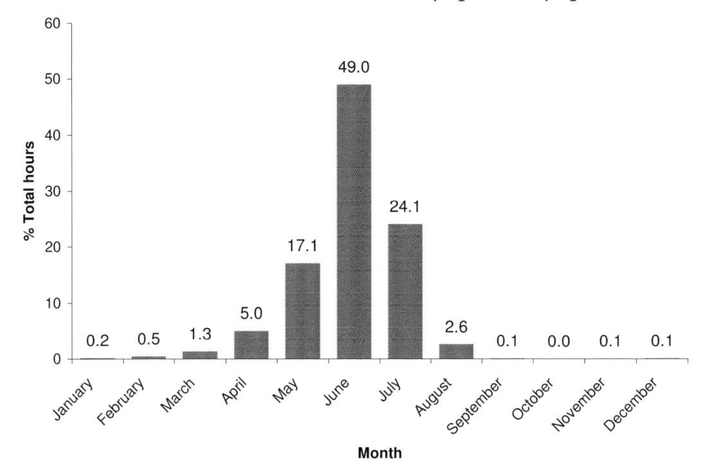

Figure 3.2. Distribution of hours of fieldwork reported by atlassers by month.

Although the dates of all field visits are available for the second atlas, only the dates of the first visit reported on each data form are available for the first atlas. A comparison between atlases showed that first visits reported on data forms were on average six days earlier in the second atlas than in the first in the Hudson Bay Lowlands, and a surprising 20 days later in the second atlas than the first in the Carolinian region (Table 3.3). The difference in the Carolinian region is likely the result, at least in part, of atlassers doing point counts in squares being covered by other atlassers and completing new breeding evidence data forms, including the new first-visit information. However, the result in the Hudson Bay Lowlands (where most point counts were done on the same visits as regular atlassing) suggests that the average dates of fieldwork in the Hudson Bay Lowlands during the first atlas were indeed somewhat later than during the second atlas, and this may have affected results, as discussed below.

Region	Mean start date per card		
	First atlas	Second atlas	Difference (days)
Hudson Bay Lowlands	July 2	June 26	-6.2
Northern Shield	June 15	June 15	0.4
Southern Shield	June 5	June 6	0.2
Lake Simcoe-Rideau	May 27	May 29	2.1
Carolinian	May 26	June 15	19.9
Ontario	**June 3**	**June 7**	**3.2**

Table 3.3. Mean start date per breeding evidence form in both atlases.

Species reported

Breeding evidence was reported for a total of 286 species (Table 3.4) and two hybrids (Brewster's and Lawrence's Warblers). This is down from 292 species (plus the same two hybrids) reported for the first atlas. Breeding evidence was reported for the following 14 species during the first atlas but not the second:

Cinnamon Teal
King Eider
Cattle Egret
Yellow-crowned Night-Heron
Purple Gallinule
American Avocet
Purple Sandpiper
California Gull
Glaucous Gull
Snowy Owl
Mountain Bluebird
Kirtland's Warbler
Lark Sparrow
Snow Bunting

Region	First atlas		Second atlas	
	No. total species	No. species confirmed breeding	No. total species	No. species confirmed breeding
Hudson Bay Lowlands	197	163	199	140
Northern Shield	211	170	220	192
Southern Shield	204	183	210	193
Lake Simcoe-Rideau	220	199	223	199
Carolinian	200	179	199	184
Ontario	**292**	**270**	**286**	**270**

Table 3.4. The number of species reported with breeding evidence and confirmed breeding in each region and overall.

These species are all either extremely rare breeding birds in the province, or were well outside of their usual breeding ranges, or have never been confirmed as breeders in Ontario. Details on the historical breeding records for these species are provided following the species accounts.

The number of species confirmed breeding in each region was as high or higher in each region in the second atlas, except in the Hudson Bay Lowlands where it dropped quite considerably from 163 species to 140. The reasons for this decline despite 53% more hours of fieldwork in this region are unknown; it may be that the generally later fieldwork in the first atlas in the Lowlands (Table 3.3) was more conducive to confirming breeding.

Breeding evidence was reported for the following species during the second atlas but not during the first:

Cackling Goose
Trumpeter Swan
Black Scoter
Eared Grebe
Black-necked Stilt
Eurasian Collared-Dove
Sprague's Pipit
Worm-eating Warbler

Details of these records are provided in full species accounts. The Trumpeter Swan and the Black-necked Stilt were the only species for which breeding was confirmed for the first time during the second atlas, but the Cackling Goose and Black Scoter were both confirmed breeding for the first time in the province in 2006, as described in their species accounts.

The following species were confirmed breeders during the first atlas but not the second:

Cinnamon Teal
King Eider
Surf Scoter
White-winged Scoter
Little Gull
California Gull
Mountain Bluebird
Henslow's Sparrow
Harris's Sparrow
Snow Bunting

The following species were confirmed breeders during the second atlas but not the first:

Trumpeter Swan
Eared Grebe
Black-necked Stilt
Marbled Godwit
Stilt Sandpiper
Western Kingbird
Dickcissel
Hoary Redpoll

More details for these species are provided in their species accounts.

Although breeding had been confirmed previously in Ontario for the following five northern species, actual nests had not been documented in the province until the second atlas:

Ross's Goose
Stilt Sandpiper
Bohemian Waxwing
Pine Grosbeak
Hoary Redpoll

The number of species for which breeding evidence was reported in each square in southern Ontario and each 100-km block in the province is shown in Figure 3.3. These maps are based on the raw breeding evidence data and therefore reflect to some extent the amount of effort that went into data collection in each square. As explained in the Methods chapter, effort varied considerably between atlases, among adjacent squares, and across the province, so analyses were undertaken to standardize effort to 20 hours. Figure 3.4 maps the number of species per square adjusted to 20 hours of effort.

The raw data (Figure 3.3) and effort-adjusted data (Figure 3.4) show a similar overall pattern, with high species richness in the central and northern parts of the Lake Simcoe-Rideau region and the southern part of the Southern Shield region. The effort-adjusted data (Figure 3.4) show the highest numbers of species occurring along the southern edge of the Canadian Shield, the Frontenac Axis, the Bruce Peninsula, the South River-Burk's Falls area west of Algonquin Prov. Park, and areas to the west of Lake Nipissing and east of Sault Ste. Marie. South of the Shield, an area of relatively high species richness extends down the Niagara Escarpment to about Hamilton and Cambridge, and there is another rich area on the Norfolk Sand Plain north of Long Point. In the southwestern part of the Carolinian region, Walpole Island and Rondeau Prov. Park stand out as islands of species richness. These are the same general areas with the highest species richness in the first atlas. The great diversity of habitat in these areas, with fairly extensive cover of primarily mixed forest interspersed with open agricultural land (much of it still grassland or pasture), lakes, and numerous wetlands, and with relatively low density human settlement, presumably leads to the high diversity of birds. The edge of the Shield represents the edge of the contiguous range of many northerly breeding forest birds and more southerly birds of open agricultural land, and the presence of both of these groups contributes to the high species diversity.

Although relatively high numbers of species were reported in parts of the Toronto area (Figure 3.3), those numbers are based on high levels of effort (Figure 3.1). The effort-adjusted data (Figure 3.4) show that the urban Toronto area has relatively low species richness when adjusted to 20 hours of effort.

The average number of species reported in a 10-km square increased between atlases in three of five regions but not in the Southern or Northern Shield regions (Table 3.5). The increase in the Lake Simcoe-Rideau and Carolinian regions is probably due in large part to more effort, but the increase in the Hudson Bay Lowlands occurred despite having about the same number of hours in both atlases (Table 3.2).

	First atlas		Second atlas	
Region	Average no. species	Average no. species in 20 hours	Average no. species	Average no. species in 20 hours
Hudson Bay Lowlands	50	40	57	48
Northern Shield	68	48	68	56
Southern Shield	94	81	92	80
Lake Simcoe-Rideau	96	79	104	80
Carolinian	86	69	90	68
Ontario	**90**	**51**	**90**	**58**

Table 3.5. The average number of species per square in each region and overall for both raw and effort-adjusted data.

The number of species adjusted to 20 hours of effort changed very little between atlases in each of the three southern regions but increased substantially in the Northern Shield and Hudson Bay Lowlands regions. The increases in the north might be due to real increases in species richness but could also result from greater atlassing efficiency in the second atlas. It seems likely that atlassers were on average more skilled in bird identification, particularly by song, during the second atlas, which would presumably make them more efficient in

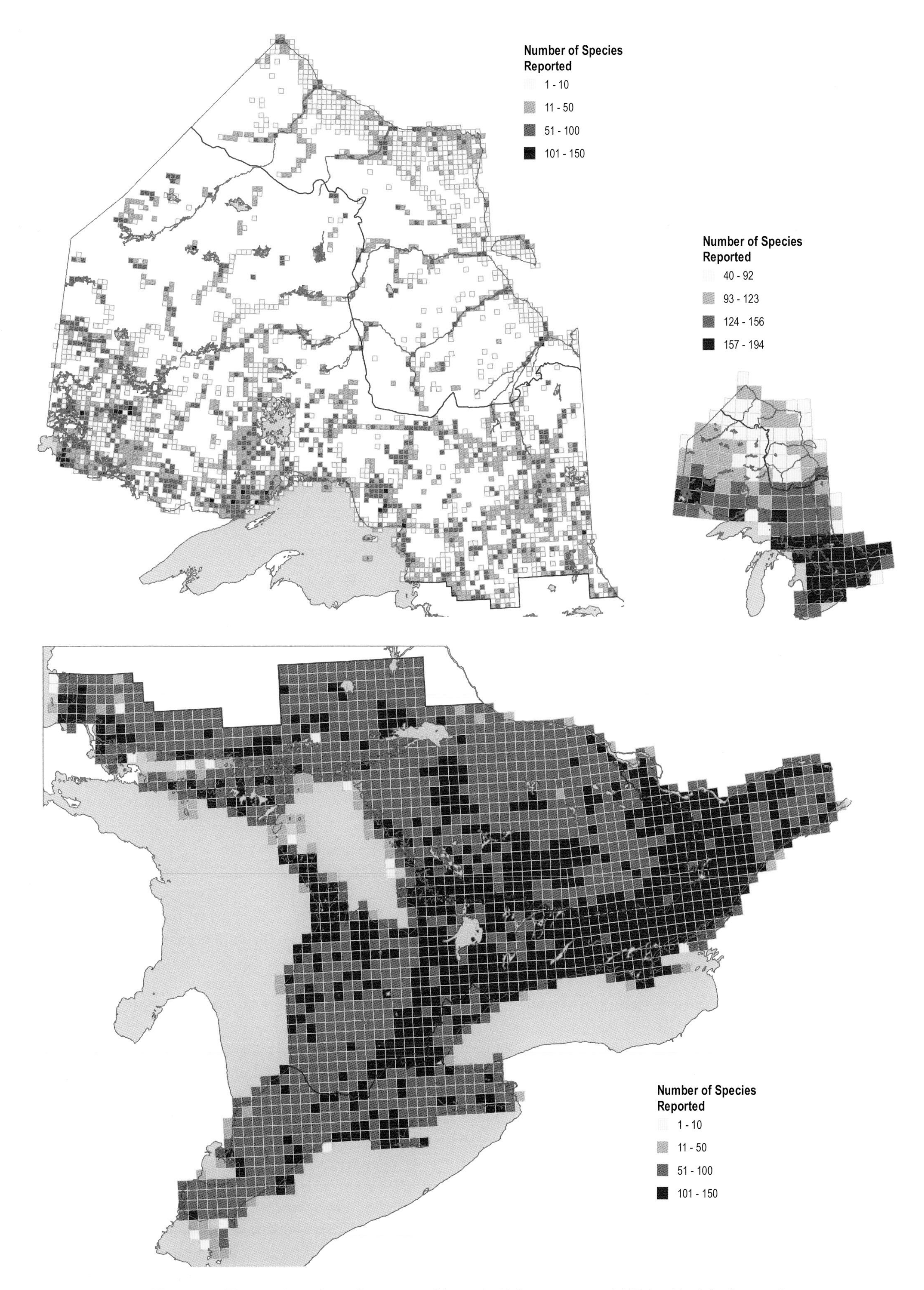

Figure 3.3. The number of species reported in each 10-km square and 100-km block in the province.

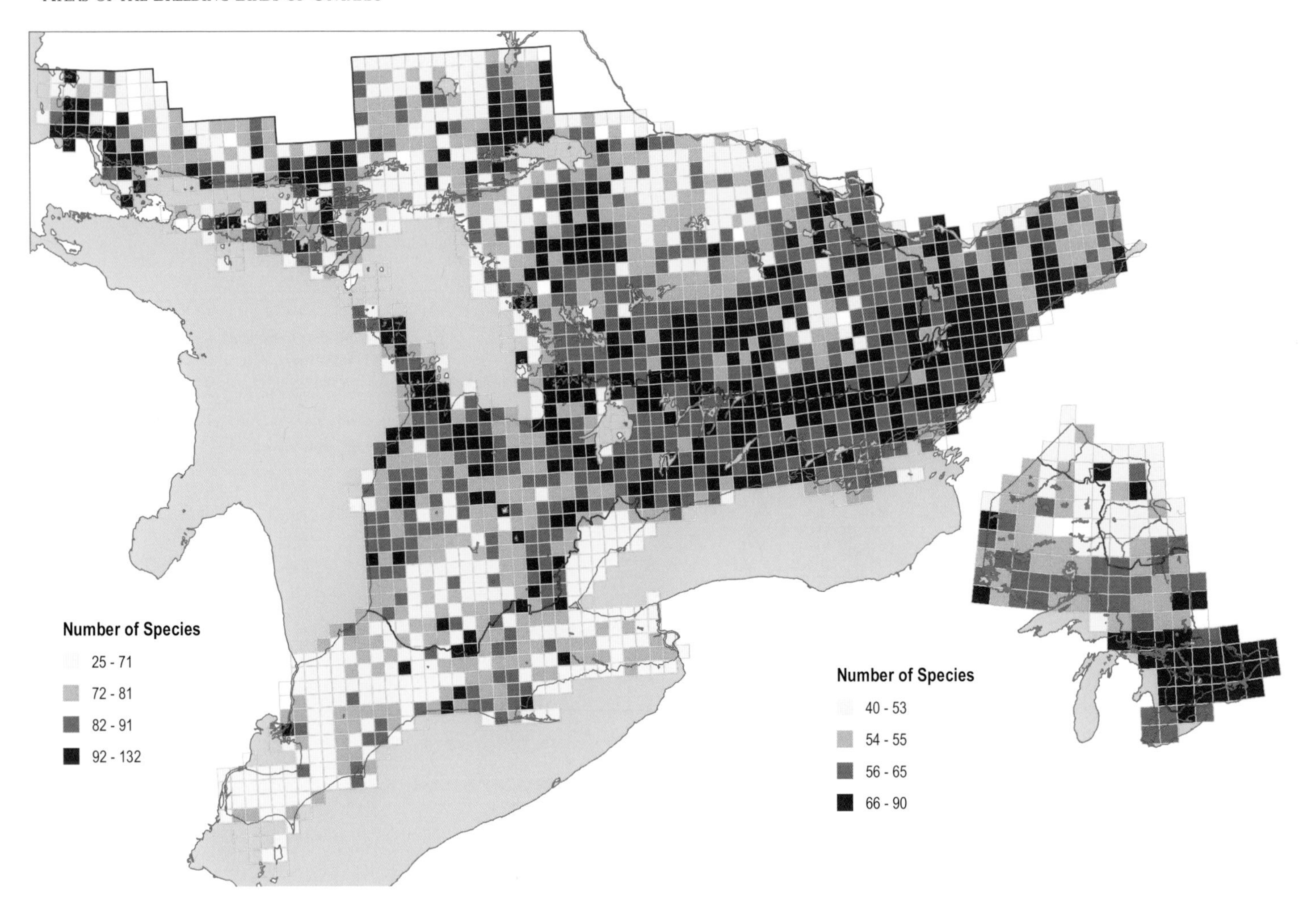

Figure 3.4. The number of species in each square with at least 10 hours of effort in southern Ontario, adjusted to 20 hours of effort, and the average per 10-km square by 100-km block throughout the province.

finding additional species. (Potential differences in atlasser efficiency are discussed further in the "Changes in Bird Distributions between Atlases" chapter.) This effect might have been more pronounced during the second atlas in the north, where much of the data was collected by highly skilled individuals. In addition, the level of song declines noticeably in the Hudson Bay Lowlands by early July, so the six-day difference in the average date of atlassing in the two atlases in that region (Table 3.3) might have facilitated increased atlassing efficiency in the Lowlands during the second atlas, at least for songbirds.

As explained in the Methods chapter, the likelihood that a species was observed in 20 hours of fieldwork is termed the "probability of observation" of that species. Not surprisingly, given that Ontario is primarily forested, northern forest birds dominate the list of the 10 species with the highest probability of observation in the second atlas (Table 3.6).

Additional considerations on coverage and species representation

Generally, as in most bird surveys, less conspicuous or distinctive species and those less familiar to the field surveyor are likely to be recorded less frequently. Nocturnal and crepuscular species such as owls and nightjars, and those such as rails and owls requiring special playback to elicit responses, are likely to be under-represented on the atlas maps. Some atlassers did expend considerable effort to find owls and rails, aided by special recordings of the calls of these species provided by the atlas and from other sources. However, use of these methods was not comprehensive, so atlas results will to some extent reflect where these techniques were used.

Point counts

In total, 68,639 point counts were reported to the atlas (Figures 3.5, 3.6, Table 3.7). Only point counts from within acceptable dates and times of day (see Methods chapter for definitions) and only those from squares with 10 or more acceptable point counts were used in the analyses below and in the relative abundance maps, for a total of 61,877 point counts. The excluded point counts are being retained and may be used in future analyses.

As is evident in Figure 3.6, point count coverage, like general atlassing, was most concentrated in the south and decreased with increasing latitude. With the exception of the extreme southwest, parts of Grey and Simcoe Counties, and the Madawaska Highlands, almost all squares south of Muskoka District and Arnprior had at least 10 point counts completed. As with general atlas coverage, point count coverage dropped off sharply at the northern edge of the Southern Shield region and again at the southern edge of the Hudson Bay Lowlands, with only 3% of

Region	Rank	Species	Probability of observation
Hudson Bay Lowlands	1	White-throated Sparrow	90.4%
	2	Ruby-crowned Kinglet	86.4%
	3	Yellow Warbler	86.4%
	4	Northern Waterthrush	84.8%
	5	Yellow-rumped Warbler	83.9%
	6	Dark-eyed Junco	83.6%
	7	Gray Jay	83.2%
	8	Common Raven	83.1%
	9	American Robin	82.5%
	10	Spotted Sandpiper	79.6%
Northern Shield	1	White-throated Sparrow	98.2%
	2	Red-eyed Vireo	92.7%
	3	Yellow-rumped Warbler	91.7%
	4	Swainson's Thrush	91.4%
	5	Winter Wren	91.2%
	6	Common Raven	89.5%
	7	Northern Flicker	89.4%
	8	Magnolia Warbler	88.8%
	9	Ruby-crowned Kinglet	83.5%
	10	Ovenbird	81.9%
Southern Shield	1	Red-eyed Vireo	98.9%
	2	Black-capped Chickadee	98.0%
	3	White-throated Sparrow	97.6%
	4	Chestnut-sided Warbler	97.3%
	5	American Robin	97.3%
	6	Ovenbird	97.2%
	7	Common Yellowthroat	96.9%
	8	Blue Jay	96.7%
	9	Veery	96.2%
	10	Song Sparrow	96.2%
Lake Simcoe-Rideau	1	American Robin	98.2%
	2	Song Sparrow	97.9%
	3	American Crow	97.7%
	4	Common Grackle	97.0%
	5	Red-winged Blackbird	96.4%
	6	American Goldfinch	96.0%
	7	Chipping Sparrow	95.9%
	8	Blue Jay	95.4%
	9	Tree Swallow	95.4%
	10	Northern Flicker	95.4%
Carolinian	1	American Robin	100.0%
	2	Common Grackle	98.4%
	3	Red-winged Blackbird	98.2%
	4	Song Sparrow	97.7%
	5	Blue Jay	97.5%
	6	House Sparrow	97.2%
	7	Mourning Dove	97.0%
	8	European Starling	96.8%
	9	Yellow Warbler	96.7%
	10	Brown-headed Cowbird	96.6%
Ontario	1	White-throated Sparrow	91.9%
	2	Yellow-rumped Warbler	85.1%
	3	Northern Flicker	85.0%
	4	Common Raven	82.5%
	5	American Robin	81.6%
	6	Red-eyed Vireo	80.5%
	7	Winter Wren	80.3%
	8	Magnolia Warbler	77.3%
	9	Hermit Thrush	76.0%
	10	Swainson's Thrush	75.6%

Table 3.6. The 10 species with the highest probability of observation overall in Ontario and in each region. The table shows the probability that the species was reported during 20 hours of atlas fieldwork in a randomly selected square.

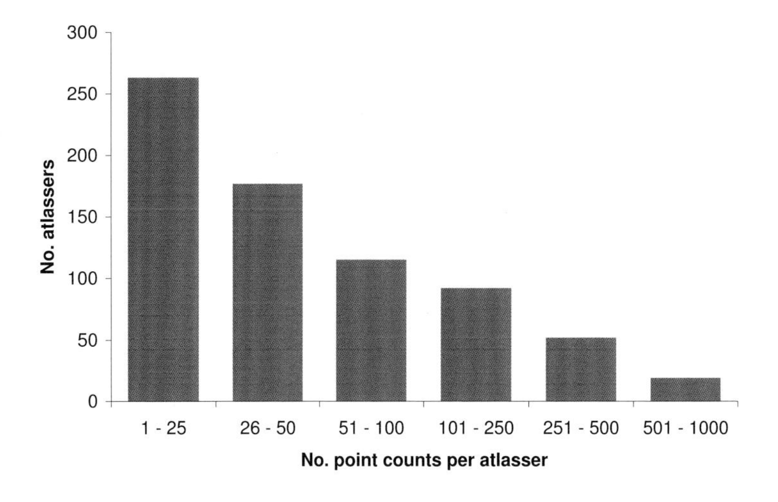

Figure 3.5. Number of point counts per atlasser.

squares in the Hudson Bay Lowlands having 10 or more point counts.

Doing point counts proved to be popular with atlassers. A total of 718 people (38% of all primary atlassers) provided point count data for the atlas. Most people provided fewer than 50 counts each. However, 70 people provided more than 250 counts each, amounting to 49.6% of all counts contributed to the atlas. Twenty-six of those 70 people were paid summer field crew members or atlas staff, and several of the remainder were employed by CWS, OMNR, or BSC to do point count surveys.

Region	No. point counts (all squares)	No. point counts used in analysis	No. squares with at least 10 acceptable point counts	% squares with at least 10 acceptable point counts	No. atlassers who contributed point counts
Hudson Bay Lowlands	2217	1752	78	3%	48
Northern Shield	16911	13452	536	9%	109
Southern Shield	17869	16890	618	73%	239
Lake Simcoe-Rideau	23098	21657	655	85%	403
Carolinian	8544	8126	232	79%	178
Ontario	**68639**	**61877**	**2119**	**20%**	**718**

Table 3.7. The number of point counts in each region and overall.

Population estimates

Appendix 5 lists provincial population estimates of species well represented on atlas point counts, and explains the methods by which the totals were derived using atlas point counts. Table 3.8 lists the 10 most common species in the province and each region and their estimated populations. As explained in Appendix 5, the population estimates, though based on a very large number of point counts distributed throughout the province, are still only rough estimates. Because of rounding, the estimates for each region do not necessarily sum to the provincial total.

The 10 most common species in Ontario, according to these estimates, are entirely or largely forest-dependent, though several prefer forest edges or young forest. Nine of these species have the bulk of their provincial population in the huge expanse of the Boreal Forest in northern

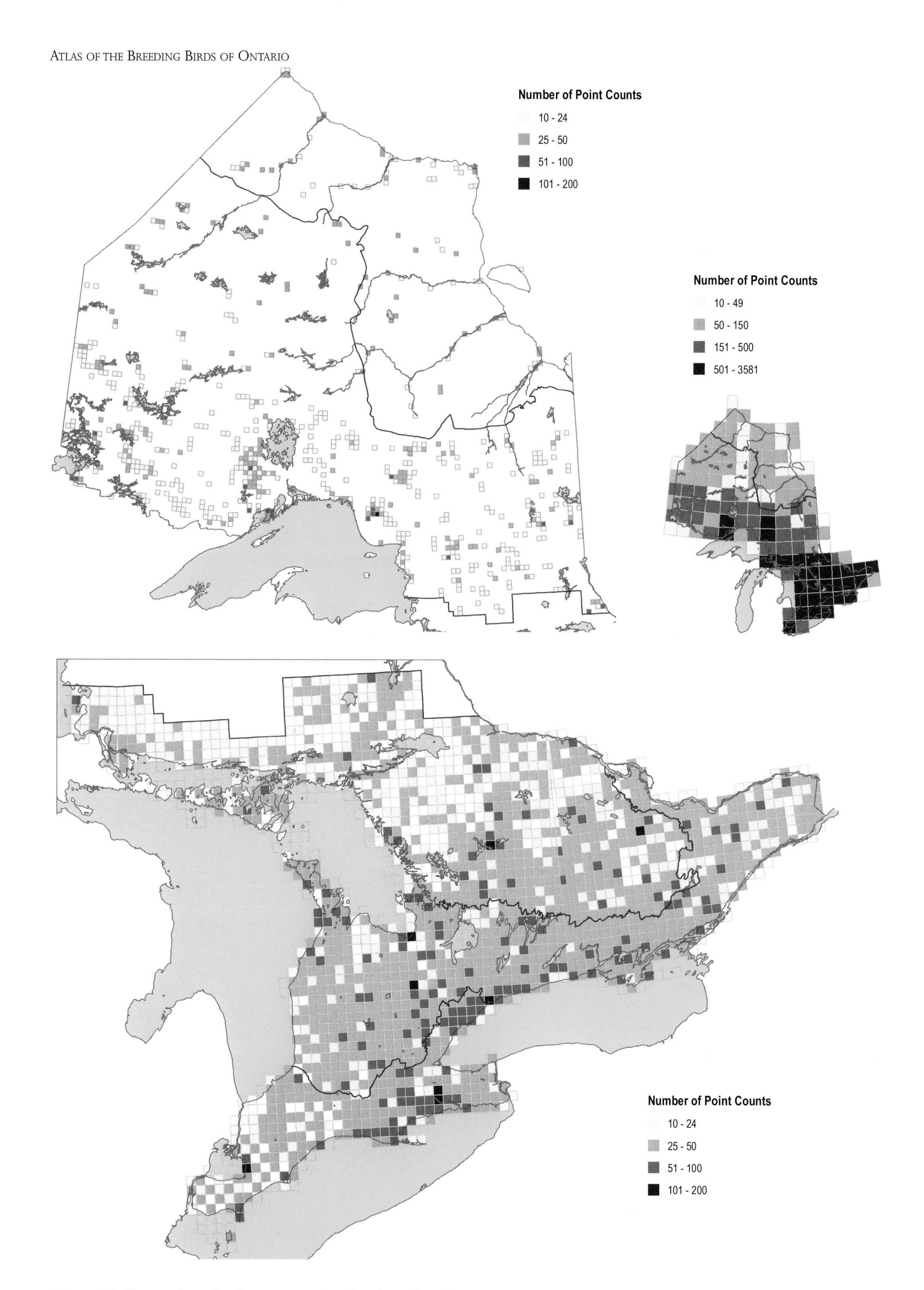

Figure 3.6. The number of point counts undertaken in each 10-km square and 100-km block. Data are shown only for squares with 10 or more point counts, and totals show the number of points surveyed during the acceptable dates and times of day.

Region	Rank	Species	Population estimate
Hudson Bay Lowlands	1	Dark-eyed Junco	7,000,000
	2	Palm Warbler	4,000,000
	3	Yellow-rumped Warbler	3,000,000
	4	Blackpoll Warbler	3,000,000
	5	White-throated Sparrow	2,500,000
	6	Savannah Sparrow	2,500,000
	7	Magnolia Warbler	2,000,000
	8	American Robin	2,000,000
	9	Swainson's Thrush	2,000,000
	10	Ruby-crowned Kinglet	2,000,000
Northern Shield	1	Nashville Warbler	12,000,000
	2	White-throated Sparrow	10,000,000
	3	Golden-crowned Kinglet	10,000,000
	4	Yellow-rumped Warbler	9,000,000
	5	Magnolia Warbler	9,000,000
	6	Chipping Sparrow	7,000,000
	7	Swainson's Thrush	6,000,000
	8	Red-eyed Vireo	6,000,000
	9	Dark-eyed Junco	5,000,000
	10	Winter Wren	5,000,000
Southern Shield	1	Red-eyed Vireo	2,000,000
	2	Chestnut-sided Warbler	1,500,000
	3	Nashville Warbler	1,200,000
	4	Ovenbird	1,200,000
	5	Blackburnian Warbler	1,200,000
	6	Black-capped Chickadee	1,200,000
	7	American Robin	1,000,000
	8	Black-throated Green Warbler	900,000
	9	Magnolia Warbler	800,000
	10	Chipping Sparrow	800,000
Lake Simcoe-Rideau	1	American Robin	3,000,000
	2	American Goldfinch	2,500,000
	3	European Starling	2,500,000
	4	Red-winged Blackbird	2,000,000
	5	Chipping Sparrow	1,500,000
	6	Common Grackle	1,500,000
	7	Song Sparrow	1,200,000
	8	Black-capped Chickadee	1,000,000
	9	House Sparrow	900,000
	10	Cedar Waxwing	800,000
Carolinian	1	European Starling	1,500,000
	2	American Robin	1,200,000
	3	Common Grackle	1,200,000
	4	House Sparrow	1,200,000
	5	Red-winged Blackbird	900,000
	6	American Goldfinch	800,000
	7	Chipping Sparrow	700,000
	8	Song Sparrow	500,000
	9	Mourning Dove	500,000
	10	Brown-headed Cowbird	400,000
Ontario	1	Nashville Warbler	15,000,000
	2	Chipping Sparrow	12,000,000
	3	Dark-eyed Junco	12,000,000
	4	Golden-crowned Kinglet	12,000,000
	5	Magnolia Warbler	12,000,000
	6	White-throated Sparrow	12,000,000
	7	Yellow-rumped Warbler	12,000,000
	8	American Robin	10,000,000
	9	Red-eyed Vireo	9,000,000
	10	Swainson's Thrush	8,000,000

Table 3.8. The 10 most common species and their estimated populations in each region and the province as a whole based on atlas point count data.

Ontario. The exception is the American Robin, which is more evenly distributed across the whole province. Many of the birds most familiar to southern Ontario residents, such as the European Starling and Common Grackle, do not make the top 10 list for the province, because their highest densities occur in developed areas and they are somewhat restricted across much of northern Ontario.

Changes in Bird Distributions between Atlases

Peter Blancher, Michael D. Cadman, Bruce A. Pond,
Andrew R. Couturier, Erica H. Dunn, Charles M. Francis,
and Robert S. Rempel

Comparing the results of the second atlas with those from the first allows an unprecedented opportunity to assess changes in the distribution, and to some extent relative abundance, of all of Ontario's breeding birds. Each of the 306 species reported on in the atlas has its individual pattern of occurrence and change as described in the individual species accounts. Grouping the species, however, reveals some overall patterns that are useful in interpreting changes between the atlases and the possible reasons behind them. As well as describing the changes, we provide some tentative explanations of contributing factors, but these should be considered hypotheses rather than firm answers. Focused research to further investigate the relationships outlined below is now underway and will be continued in the future, using the atlas database and other sources of information. An example of an application of atlas data, in this case looking at the possible effects of climate change in Ontario, is provided at the end of the chapter.

Atlas breeding evidence data essentially record presence/absence. (In fact, the data are "presence/not reported" rather than "presence/absence," as we cannot say for certain that a species was absent if it was not found.) As described in the Methods chapter of the book, our measure of change, common to both the first and second atlases, is an estimate of "probability of observation" after 20 hours of atlassing effort, based on presence/absence data, and it is important to understand that this does not necessarily correspond to population change. An average decrease of, for example, 30% in the probability of observation may reflect a change in population considerably higher or lower than 30%, depending on the dispersion of the species, magnitude of change in different squares, and detectability of the species at different densities.

Uncommon species are more likely to show changes in their presence/absence status in a given square than are more abundant species. Generally speaking, a species with a small population spread across many squares is more likely to show a large change in the number of squares in which it is detected than is a common species for the same change in population size. A common species could decline by 90% in a square and still be found quite readily in it, while that is less likely to be true of an uncommon species. Conversely, when a species is expanding its range, the atlas presence/absence data may indicate a broad expansion, but cannot differentiate between a large and a small number of birds in the squares where they have been newly detected. Moreover, assuming that numbers are lower towards the periphery of a species' range, species are likely to show more change at the edge of their range than at the centre where numbers are higher, even if abundance has changed by the same proportion across all squares.

Additional research using the atlas data should provide more insight into the importance of these factors in understanding population and distribution change, and the extent to which both increasing and decreasing species are affected by these factors. The shortcomings of presence/absence data are one of the reasons that relative abundance data were collected during the second atlas. The point count data collected during the second atlas will allow for much more powerful and quantitative comparisons with future atlases. Nevertheless, the analyses of changes in detection probabilities reveal many interesting and instructive patterns.

Because 25% more effort was put into field data collection during the second atlas, the results discussed below on changes between atlases were all calculated using an adjustment for effort, described in the Methods chapter. In addition, all data collected by the Boreal Forest Bird Project (BFBP) were omitted from change analyses, because the different sampling system (see Appendix 4) was likely to bias results. The regions referred to throughout this chapter are those shown in Figure 1.5 in the Methods chapter.

It is important to understand the meaning of "significant" when we talk about population change both in this chapter and in the individual species accounts. This term is used solely in the statistical sense. The term significant ($p<0.1$) means that the observed difference between the two atlases was so great that there is less than a 10% chance that such a big difference (or even bigger differences) could be found by chance alone if the population had actually been stable. It is quite possible that many populations may have experienced biologically significant changes (e.g., large increases or decreases) that are not statistically significant because our estimates are imprecise.

Overall Changes

One of the more surprising results of the atlas is the extent to which species distributions can change over a period as short as that between the two atlases. Figure 4.1 shows the 50 species with the largest increases and decreases between atlases. Many of the changes shown are very substantial, involving the gain or loss of many hundreds of squares. Possible reasons behind the changes shown are discussed below and in the individual species accounts in the book.

Bird populations are rarely stable, so it is not surprising that most species (209) increased or decreased significantly in probability of observation since the first atlas in at least one region. Among the 157 species that showed significant changes in more than one atlas region, most (127 or 81%) had significant changes all in the same direction; 74 species (such as the Black-and-white Warbler, see Appendix 3) increased significantly in more than one region, and 53 (such as the Eastern Kingbird, see Appendix 3) decreased significantly in more than one region. This consistency among regions suggests that reasons for change often acted at regional or larger scales. Thirty species (such as the Cooper's Hawk, see Appendix 3) showed both a significant increase in one or more regions and a significant decrease in one or more regions. This could

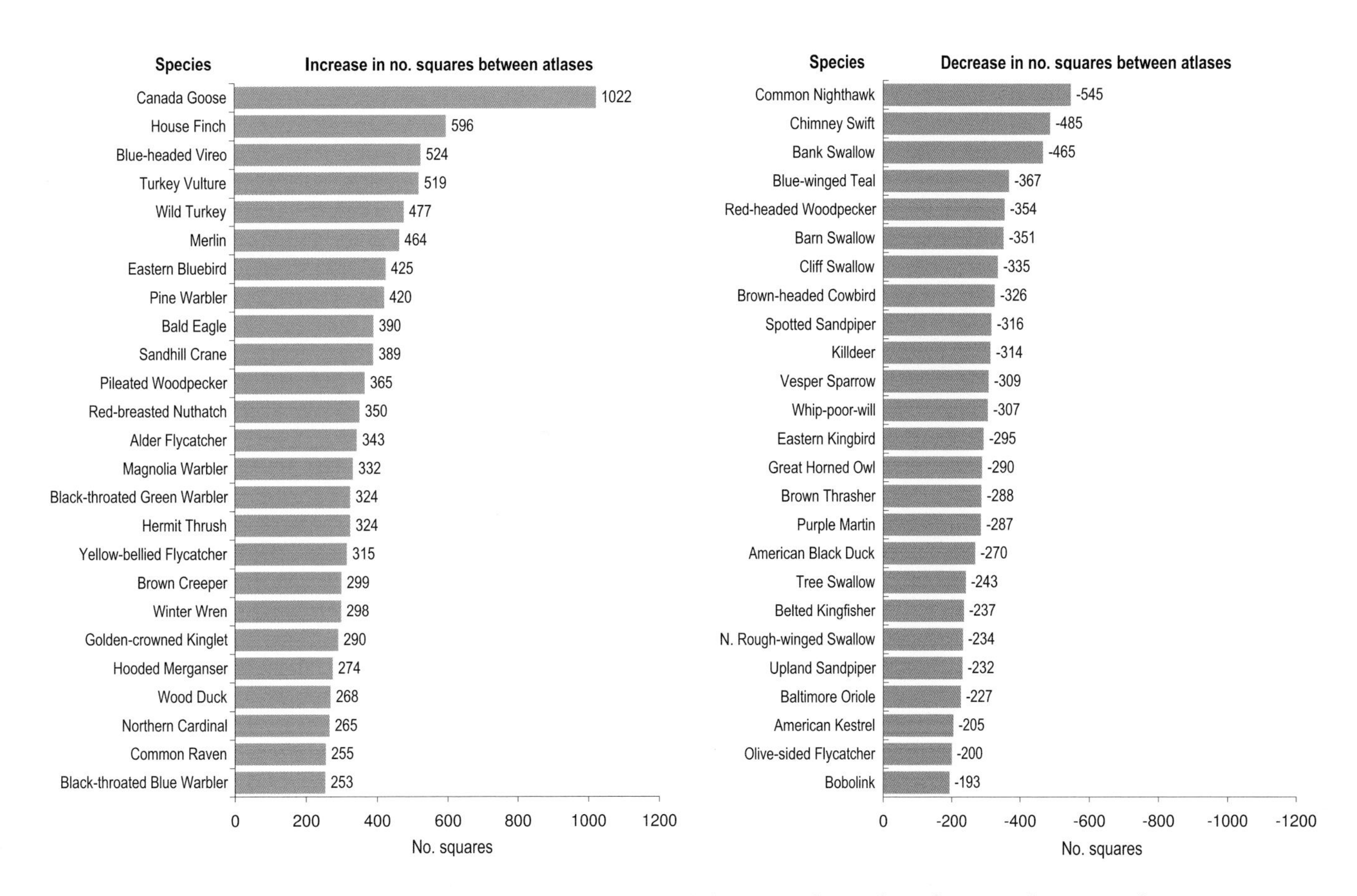

Figure 4.1. Species showing the largest increases and decreases in number of squares between atlases. Only squares with a minimum of 10 hours of effort were used in this analysis.

Region		Woods and Forest	Grassland, Agricultural, Open	Shrub and Early Succession	Wetland	Tundra	Urban and Suburban	All Species
Hudson Bay Lowlands	Increases	41 (16)	9 (3)	14 (8)	46 (17)	12 (3)	6 (1)	128 (48)
	Decreases	22 (5)	7 (0)	5 (0)	23 (2)	15 (1)	1 (0)	73 (8)
Northern Shield	Increases	61 (39)	6 (3)	17 (5)	50 (24)	0	7 (5)	142 (77)
	Decreases	17 (5)	21 (10)	6 (2)	19 (5)	4 (0)	3 (0)	70 (22)
Southern Shield	Increases	47 (28)	5 (3)	15 (9)	39 (21)		6 (3)	113 (65)
	Decreases	35 (23)	23 (18)	14 (10)	21 (12)		4 (3)	97 (66)
Lake Simcoe-Rideau	Increases	45 (31)	5 (2)	12 (8)	38 (17)		4 (2)	105 (61)
	Decreases	39 (19)	27 (19)	18 (8)	32 (15)		7 (2)	123 (63)
Carolinian	Increases	32 (22)	7 (4)	11 (4)	22 (8)		6 (2)	79 (41)
	Decreases	38 (15)	27 (17)	18 (6)	43 (13)		5 (2)	131 (53)
Ontario	Increases	68 (36)	7 (4)	18 (8)	62 (20)	12 (3)	8 (2)	176 (74)
	Decreases	26 (7)	28 (20)	16 (3)	34 (6)	15 (1)	3 (2)	122 (39)

Table 4.1. The number of species that increased or decreased between the first and second atlas, corrected for effort, overall and according to habitat association. Numbers of species with statistically significant increases or decreases are shown in parentheses. Cases where increases and decreases differ by five or more species are highlighted in blue (more increases) or red (more decreases).

indicate shifts in the species' ranges or the influence of different factors within different parts of Ontario, although some of these could simply be statistical artifacts.

Table 4.1 shows that overall in Ontario more species increased than decreased, and that this is largely due to a disproportionate number of species increasing in the two northern regions. Generally, the percentage of species that increased in each region between atlases increases from south to north. The Carolinian region has substantially more species decreasing than increasing; the Lake Simcoe-Rideau and Southern Shield regions have about the same number of species increasing and decreasing; and the two northern regions have substantially more species increasing than decreasing. The relatively large number of declining species in the Carolinian region results from declines in several groups of birds and is discussed below.

Figure 4.2 shows that human population increased substantially in the Carolinian and Lake Simcoe-Rideau regions between atlases. There is no obvious indication in Figure 4.3 that increasing human population has had a direct effect on species' numbers, but more detailed square by square analysis will help reveal whether such a relationship exists.

The reasons for the disproportionately large number of species increasing in the two northern regions are not known. Figure 2.5 in the Biogeography chapter shows that relatively few people live in the north, and that they are mostly restricted to road-accessible parts of the Northern Shield region. Figure 4.2 shows that there was little human population change between 1981 and 2001 in the north, so change in human population in these regions is probably not responsible for the increase in birds. However, although there has been little apparent change in habitat in the Hudson Bay Lowlands and remote parts of the Northern Shield region between atlases, some changes are evident, driven by natural processes. For example, there has been an increase in shrubs in coastal areas since the first atlas period, perhaps due to isostatic rebound (Ken Abraham, pers. comm.), and a similar increase has been detected in nearby Québec (von Mörs and Bégin 1993). Also, fires in the Boreal Forest and Hudson Bay Lowlands combined burned an average of 170,000 ha annually from 1981 to 1985 but only 96,000 ha annually from 2001 to 2005.

Other changes have occurred within road-accessible parts of the Northern Shield. For example, between 1981 and 1985, an average of 165,000 ha (0.6% of the area) was harvested annually. In 1993, that increased to over 200,000 ha annually and from 2001 to 2005 averaged 214,000 ha (0.8% of the area) annually. Furthermore, timber harvesting has been evolving towards emulation of natural disturbance in recent years; there has been an increase in the variation of size, shape, and complexity of cuts, and an increase in edge and standing trees remaining in cuts. As well, more attention has been paid to wildlife habitat requirements in management practices. There has also been a slight increase of poplar, Balsam Fir, and other conifer growing stock (Larry Watkins, pers. comm.; Ontario Ministry of Natural Resources 2006b). The area of defoliation by Spruce Budworm, Jack Pine Budworm and other pests like Forest Tent Caterpillar averaged over 4.8 million hectares annually but decreased considerably from the mid-1980s to today (see Figure 4.12, below).

Changes in climate might also have contributed to the changes in northern bird distributions. Although the average annual global temperature warmed about 0.74°C during the past century (IPCC 2007), the warming trend in Canada was double the world average. South-central Canada, including Ontario, warmed by 1.2°C over the same period (Environment Canada 2006). Between completion of the first atlas in 1985 and 2005, Ontario experienced some of the warmest years on record, which likely continued to influence the temporal and spatial distribution of birds in northern Ontario. As a general rule (from which there are exceptions), species whose range limits occur in the southern parts of Ontario (or south of Ontario) are expected to move north with their climate envelopes as climates and habitats become suitable (Varrin et al. 2007). Many of these species will become established north of their current ranges (Hampe and Petit 2005). Similarly, species whose southern range limits currently occur in Ontario will likely experience northward contractions of their southern boundaries.

Changes in breeding bird distribution in relation to climate change in northern Ontario have not yet been assessed using the atlas data because too few northern squares are "matched" and covered well in both atlases. However, an analysis for southern Ontario is summarized below.

While many factors have contributed to bird population change in the north, there is also a possibility that some of these changes were due to changes in sampling technique or atlasser efficiency. The number and magnitude of these changes seem disproportionately large. There are several ways in which atlassers may have been more efficient during the second atlas, particularly in the north. An increase in the number of forest access roads in the Northern Shield region could have improved atlasser efficiency and increased the probability of observation of some species. Unfortunately, we do not have data that allow comparison of road networks in the north between atlases. Forest access roads, particularly small ones, are often abandoned or actively rehabilitated after use, so even knowing how much road is available at any particular time does not necessarily reflect usability. Nonetheless, it is known that commercial forestry extended farther north over the past few decades, so access was certainly easier in some squares and 100-km blocks.

Another possible explanation is that atlassers working in the north during the second atlas were more skilled in bird identification and/or more experienced in atlas data collection, both of which could easily increase their efficiency. These atlassers also generally knew more about which species to expect in a particular square or region because of the data from the first atlas. Other types of improved efficiency such as our greater emphasis on covering all habitats in a square, and the inclusion of point counts, which often sampled a wide variety of habitats and many parts of the square, may have increased the probability of detecting species' presence.

As mentioned in the Results chapter, in the Hudson Bay Lowlands region atlassing began an average of six days earlier in this atlas than in the first. As song declines notably in early July in the Lowlands, it is possible that the difference in dates of atlassing visits contributed to a higher efficiency in the second atlas in this region; birds may have been more actively singing and thus more conspicuous during an average visit, increasing the probability of detection.

If atlassers were indeed on average more efficient in northern Ontario in the second atlas, then the declines reported from the north are presumably larger and of more potential concern than reported in this book.

In the sections below, species are grouped by habitat or into other guilds to explore some of the patterns in change among species.

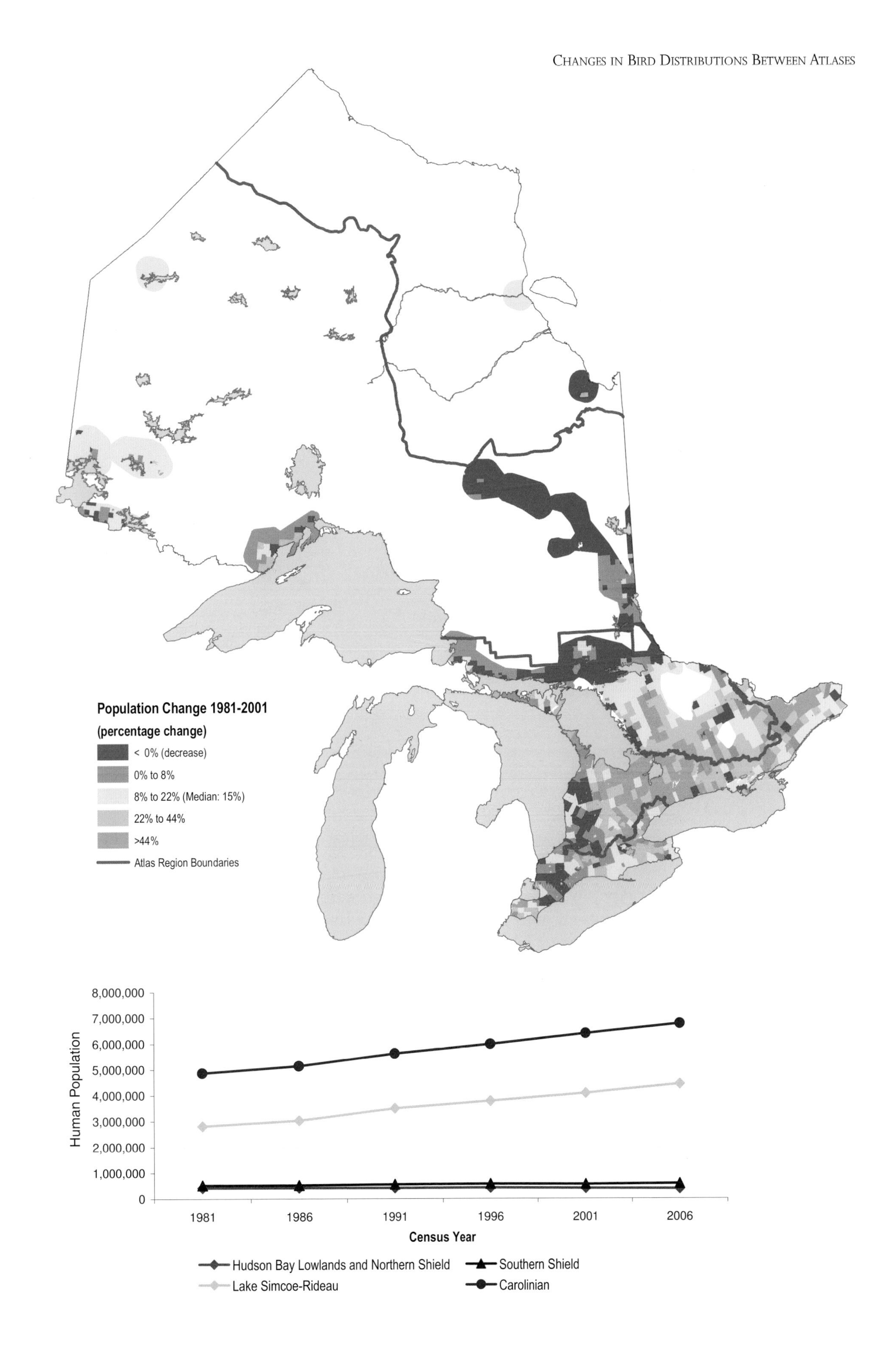

Figure 4.2. Human population change in Ontario from 1981 to 2001. Adapted from Statistics Canada, Census of Canada, 1981-2006.

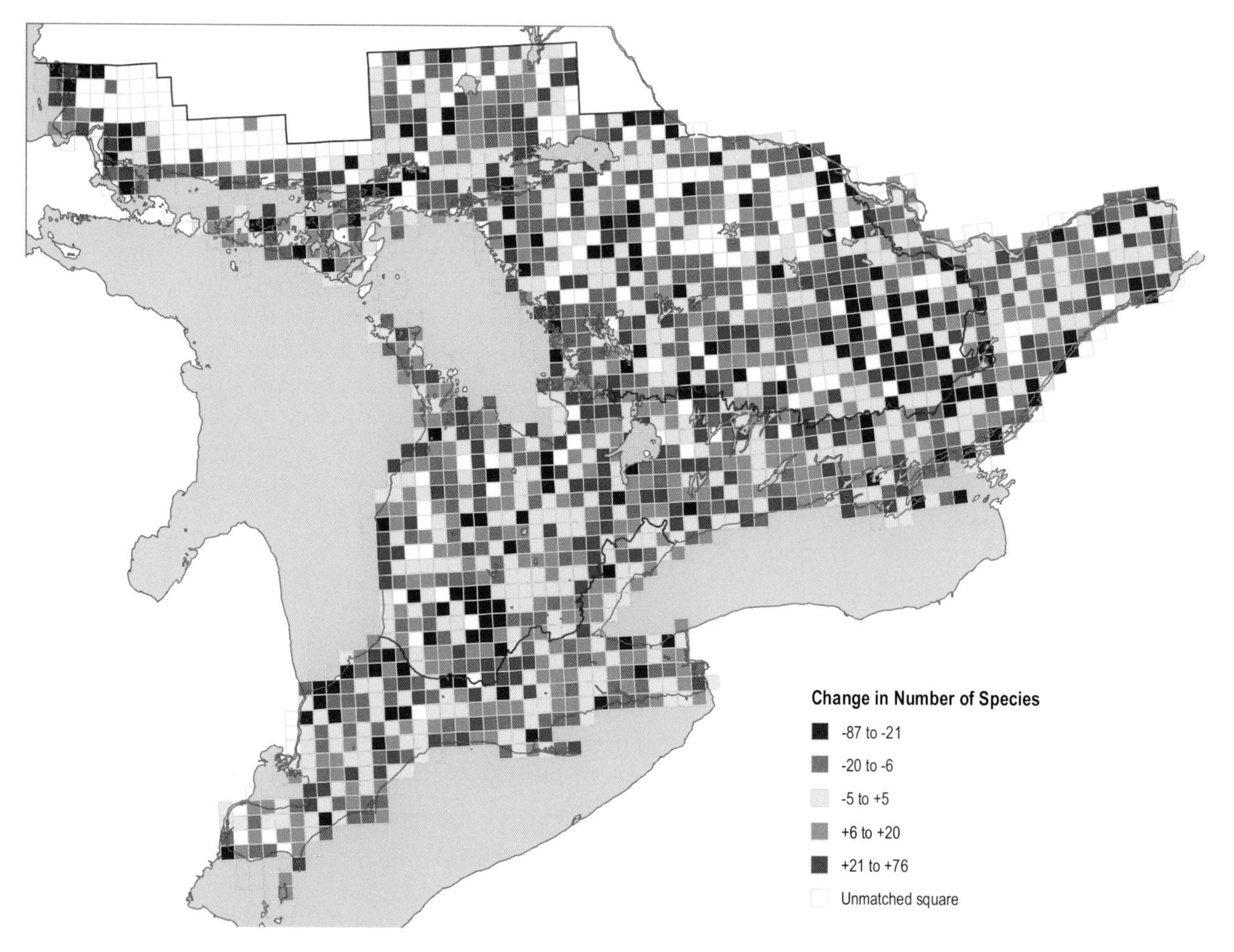

Figure 4.3. Change in overall species richness in squares matched for effort in each atlas (minimum 10 hours of effort in each atlas). Because the methods of atlassing were not strictly standardized, the timing and efficiency of atlassing varied from atlas to atlas and square to square. Therefore, focus is on the overall pattern of change rather than on individual square results.

Changes in Birds by Habitat Preference

The following analysis groups species by habitat preference, with each species being assigned to only one group. This approach is somewhat simplistic, since many birds could fit into more than one category, but is sufficient for looking at overarching patterns. Table 4.1 shows how many species in the province as a whole and in each habitat preference group increased and decreased. Appendix 3 lists the species that showed significant change in the province as a whole and in each region by habitat group. These results suggest that habitat change in Ontario has been a primary factor in changing bird populations.

Forest birds

Substantially more forest bird species increased than decreased in Ontario as a whole and in all regions except the Carolinian (Table 4.1; Appendix 3). The provincial result was again driven largely by the changes in the Northern Shield and Hudson Bay Lowlands regions, in each of which considerably more species increased than decreased. As above, the reasons for these changes are unknown. There were also substantially more forest bird species increasing than decreasing in both the Southern Shield and Lake Simcoe-Rideau regions, though the differences were not as large as those in the north. These results for southern Ontario are in agreement with BBS data. The atlas results from the Carolinian are somewhat contradictory; more woodland species overall declined between atlases, but of the species changing significantly between atlases, more increased than decreased (Table 4.1). The reasons for this discrepancy are unknown. However, the fact that the overall trend for forest birds in the Carolinian region is negative, while those from the rest of the province are positive, suggests that conservation of forest birds in the Carolinian region should be a priority.

Historical data indicate a considerable increase in forest cover in southern Ontario since the 1920s to the present, but at the time of writing little information is available on the extent and pattern of change in forest cover between the two atlas periods. Nevertheless, various studies in southern Ontario indicate the general pattern of increasing forest cover in recent decades, and we outline some of those here and point out some general correlations.

As discussed in the Biogeography chapter, forest cover south of the Shield increased from a low of about 10% in 1920 (Larson et al. 1999) to a current level of 28.8% (Ontario Ministry of Natural Resources 2006b). Figure 4.4 shows the areas of increasing forest cover south of the Shield by municipality between 1955 and 1978. The map indicates that recovery of forest has occurred mostly in the area between Lake Ontario and the southern edge of the Shield, in the Hamilton-Niagara area and in eastern Ontario east of the Frontenac Axis. In areas studied south and east of the Shield, forest cover increased by about 7% per decade since the 1930s and 8% per decade between 1979 and 1995 (Bruce Pond, unpubl. data). It is also evident from Figure 4.4 that in the years between 1955 and 1978, forest cover declined in the most heavily agricultural areas from the extreme southwest to Perth and Oxford Counties. Forest cover increased in Wainfleet Township (now part of Niagara Region) of the Carolinian region between 1934 and 1979 (Moss and Davies 1994). In 1976, it was estimated that 32.6% of all non-urban land in Niagara Region was undergoing secondary succession (Moss 1976).

There is also evidence of forest cover increasing in the Southern Shield region. In North Kawartha Township (Peterborough Co.) on the southern edge of the Shield, forest cover (along with amount of forest edge) increased between 1934 and 1979 due to farm abandonment and an increase in natural generation stands and plantations (Moss and Davies 1994).

As is evident in Figure 4.5, areas showing the most increase in forest birds occur in the contiguous area containing the southern part of the Southern Shield region to Lake Ontario from about Kingston to the Niagara Escarpment, including the Oak Ridges Moraine. These areas correspond well with those areas mentioned above where forest cover increased prior to the first atlas. Forest birds also increased to the north and west of Lake Nipissing.

The increase in forest cover in the eastern (Askins 2000) and southeastern (NASA 2004) US is providing more wintering habitat for short-distance migrants that breed in Ontario and winter in the US. This might help explain the increase in species such as the Blue-headed Vireo and Yellow-rumped Warbler that winter in the southern and eastern US.

About 75% of the forest south of the Shield is less than 100 years old (Ontario Ministry of Natural Resources 2006b), so trees and ecosystems are still maturing in forested areas, and this is presumably affecting bird communities. Some forest birds such as the Pileated Woodpecker, which prefer larger trees, are increasing. Of course, while overall maturation of forests is continuing, selection logging is occurring throughout much of southern Ontario's forest, which is affecting the maturation and structure of forests and their associated bird communities.

Conifer plantations, prevalent in the Lake Simcoe-Rideau region but also present to a lesser extent in the Carolinian and Southern Shield regions, are maturing, benefiting species that

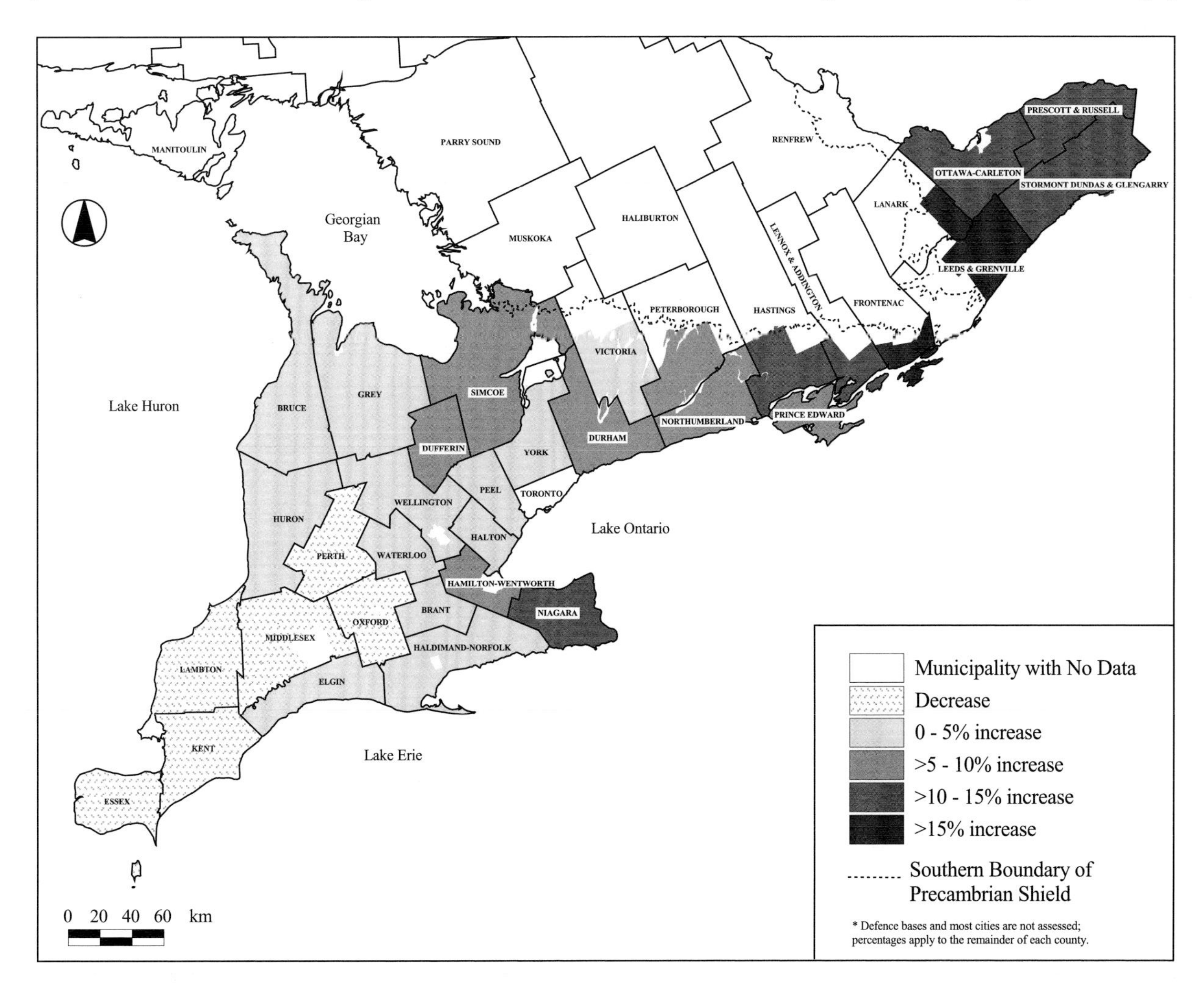

Figure 4.4. Changes in forest cover from 1955 to 1978 by municipality south of the Canadian Shield. The Frontenac Axis is considered part of the Canadian Shield on this map (Larson et al. 1999).

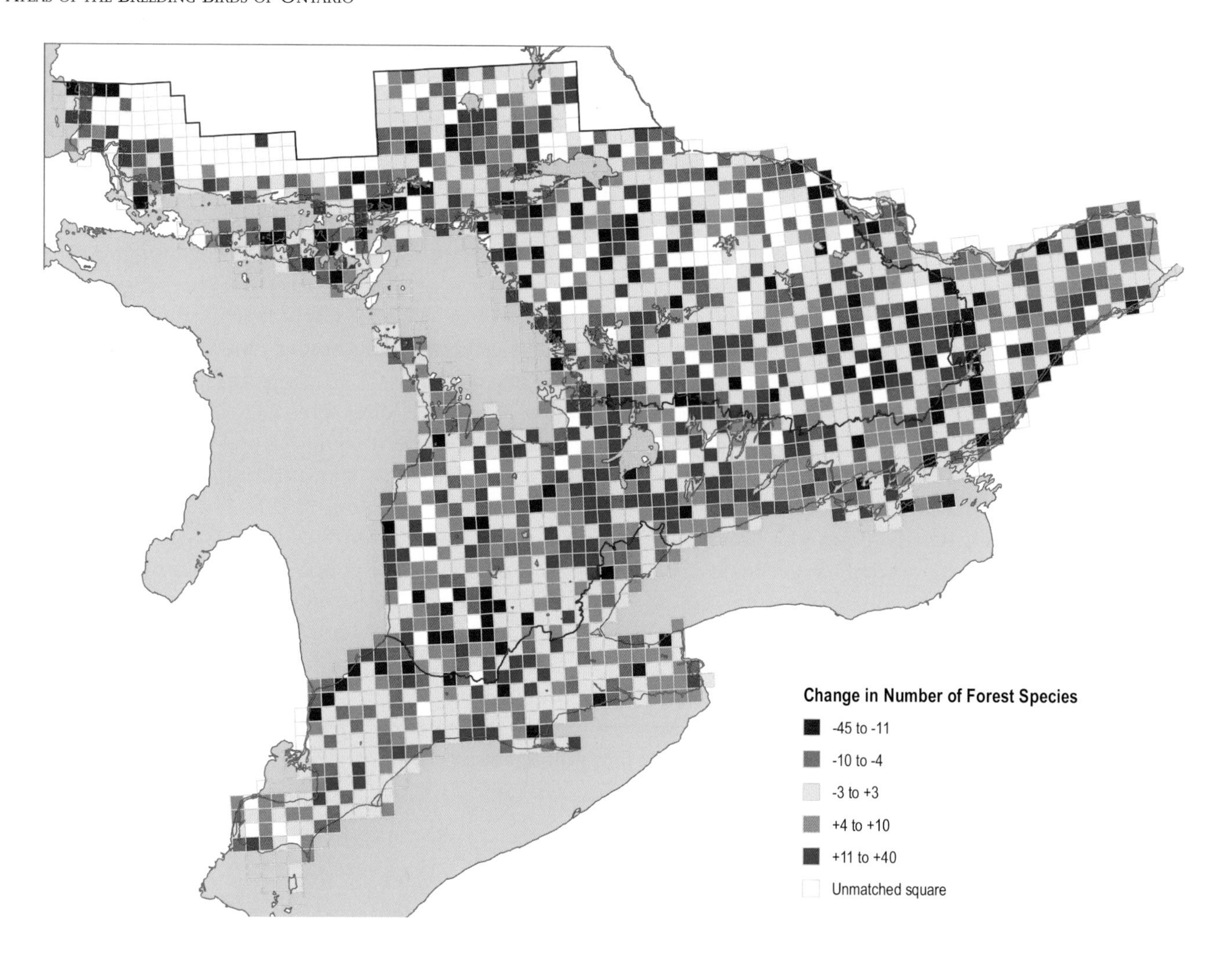

Figure 4.5. Change in forest bird species richness, in squares matched for effort in each atlas (minimum 10 hours of effort in each atlas).

nest in conifer and mixed woods. Many of these tracts were planted in the mid-20th century to help control soil erosion, primarily on sandy soils. As these plantations have matured, they are providing suitable habitat for many birds of coniferous or mixed habitats, including the Black-throated Green Warbler, Magnolia Warbler, and Hermit Thrush. Although these species have expanded considerably in the Lake Simcoe-Rideau region, relative abundance maps in most cases show that their numbers are still very small compared to numbers in the more extensively forested regions on the Shield.

Grassland and open country birds

The decline in grassland birds in North America has been identified as a conservation concern (Brennan and Kuvlesky 2005; McCracken 2005). The atlas results indicate that in Ontario the grassland and open country bird group is showing the most declines between atlases of any habitat-preference group. Substantially more of these species have decreased than have increased in all regions of Ontario (Table 4.1) except for the Hudson Bay Lowlands, where the probable factors causing change are absent. Appendix 3 lists the grassland and open country species showing decreases or increases in each region and in all of Ontario.

As described in the Biogeography chapter, grassland and other open country birds expanded greatly in Ontario with the clearing of forests by Europeans for agriculture and settlement, primarily in the 19th and early 20th centuries. Most species currently present were probably here in small numbers, using natural prairies and savannahs, beaver meadows, flood plains, burns, other naturally occurring open grassy areas, and land cleared by aboriginal people. However, the extensive clearing of forested land and conversion largely to pasture opened the floodgates to grassland and other open country birds in the middle of the 19th century, when many species were reported in Ontario for the first time (McIlwraith 1886). About 94% of upland forest south of the Shield was cleared (Larson et al. 1999), and the southern part of the Shield north to about Algonquin Park was also largely cleared, so that late in the 19th century grassland species such as Loggerhead Shrike were considered common in Muskoka (Campbell 1975). There was also extensive clearing north of Lake Nipissing, near Sudbury, Sault Ste. Marie, and Thunder Bay, and in the Rainy River areas, as well as in both the Little and Great Clay Belts near Englehart and Cochrane, respectively. Figure 2.6 in the Biogeography chapter shows the extent of agricultural land in the province.

Grassland habitat in Ontario appears to be declining for two main reasons, reversion to forest and intensification of agricultural practices, though urban expansion is undoubtedly a factor around built-up areas. As an example of grassland habitat loss, Figure 4.6 shows declines in improved pasture between 1981 and 2001 across the province. Some of the declines in grassland birds (Figure 4.7) correspond to areas with high loss of pasture, such as in Lambton Co., on the southeastern part of the southern Shield, and on the Frontenac Axis.

When farming proved to be economically unsustainable, much of the formerly cleared and farmed land was allowed to revert to forest. Substantial declines in grassland birds are evident throughout southern Ontario (Figure 4.7), but the most evident declines are in the Southern Shield region and the Frontenac Axis, both areas now heavily forested. The first atlas showed that grassland species were fairly restricted in the Southern Shield due to limited suitable grassland habitat (the area was mostly forested, as described above). As reforestation of grassland areas has occurred, further reducing the already restricted grassland habitat, the probability of observation of many grassland species has declined as they have become scarcer and harder to find or no longer occur in some squares.

In the Carolinian region and the southwest and southeast portions of the Lake Simcoe-Rideau region, where agriculture is the major land use, intensification of agricultural practices is probably a major factor in the decline of grassland birds, as fallow and grassy agricultural fields have been converted to row crops. Figure 4.8 shows an increase in cropland in much of this area. As agriculture has intensified, not only is pasture ploughed under but grassy borders of fields and roadside areas are also tilled, so that very little habitat remains for grassland birds, and there is a reduction in the seeds and insects eaten by grassland birds (Vickery et al. 2001). Agricultural pesticides and herbicides are also more extensively used in these more intensively farmed areas and have been shown to reduce the insect prey of farmland birds (Benton et al. 2002). Some pesticides have been shown to affect birds directly (Mineau 2005). Additionally, urban expansion (including sprawl) around urban areas is covering former open space and agricultural land suitable for grassland birds; this might explain, for example, the declines around the periphery of Toronto and along the north shore of the Niagara Peninsula. Grassland birds are declining across the continent (McCracken 2005), probably as a result of these same factors in breeding and wintering grounds and areas used in migration.

Although there is relatively little farmland in northern Ontario (see Biogeography chapter, Figure 2.6), the area of farmland in the north declined 17% from 1981 to 2001, and improved pasture declined by 38% (Figure 4.6). This shift probably contributed to the decline of grassland birds in the Northern Shield region.

Like forest birds, grassland birds show varying degrees of sensitivity to the size of habitat patches: some species such as the Upland Sandpiper, Henslow's Sparrow, and Northern Harrier prefer larger patches of suitable grassland (Walk and Warner 1999). This might explain why some grassland birds are declining more than others, and underscores the impor-

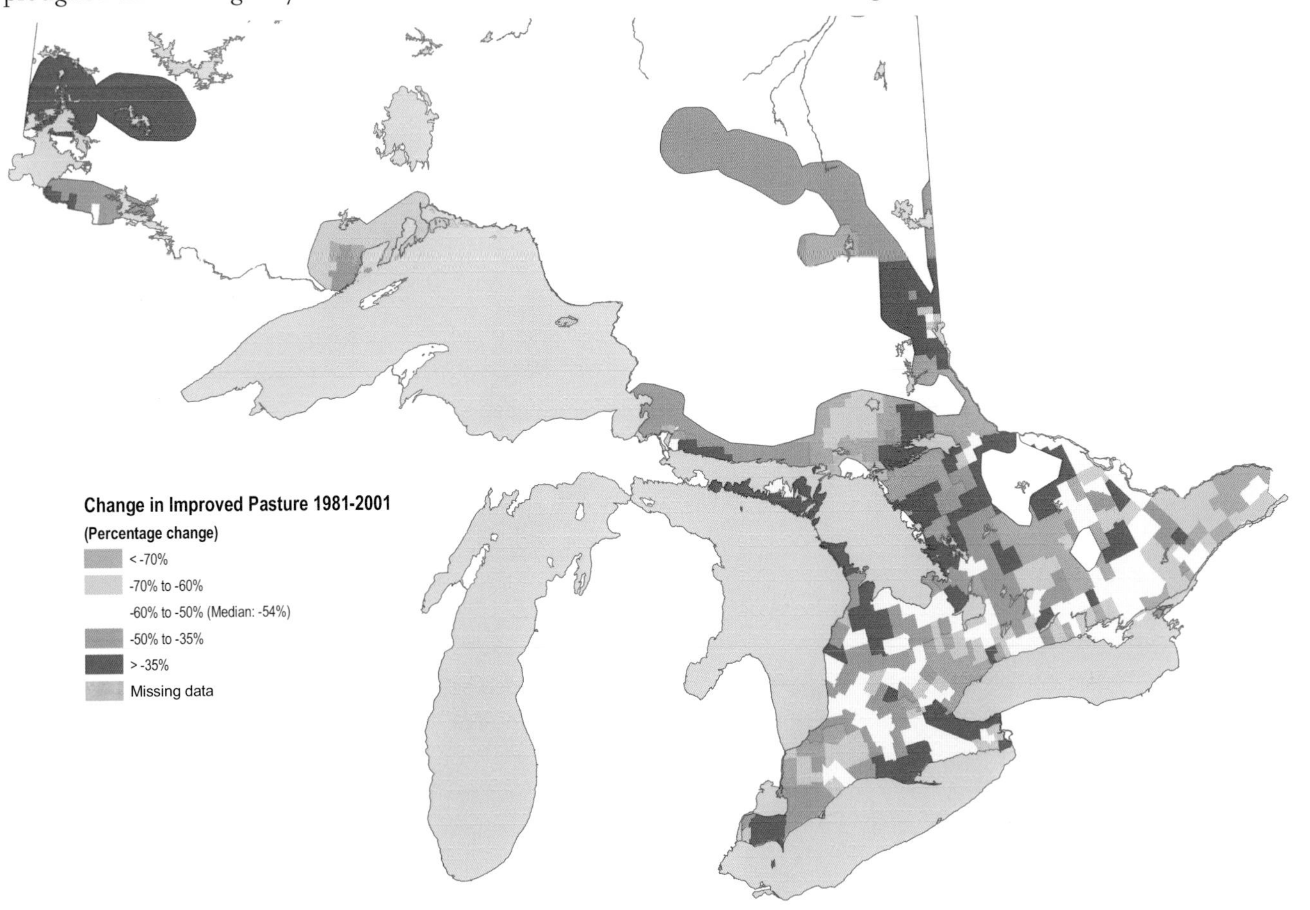

Figure 4.6. The decline in improved pasture between 1981 and 2001. Adapted from Statistics Canada, Census of Agriculture, 1981 and 2001.

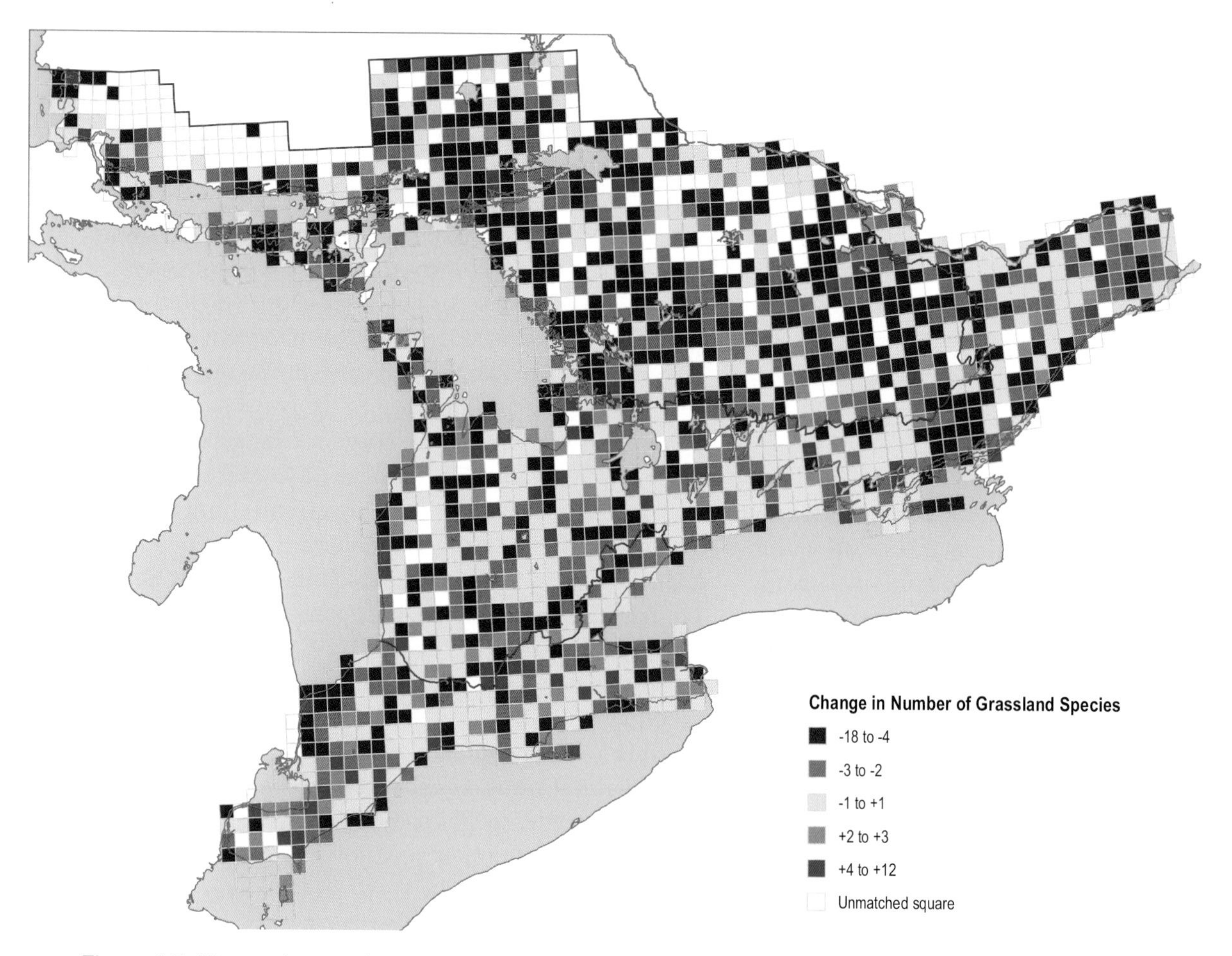

Figure 4.7. Change in grassland bird species richness in squares matched for effort (minimum 10 hours of effort in each atlas).

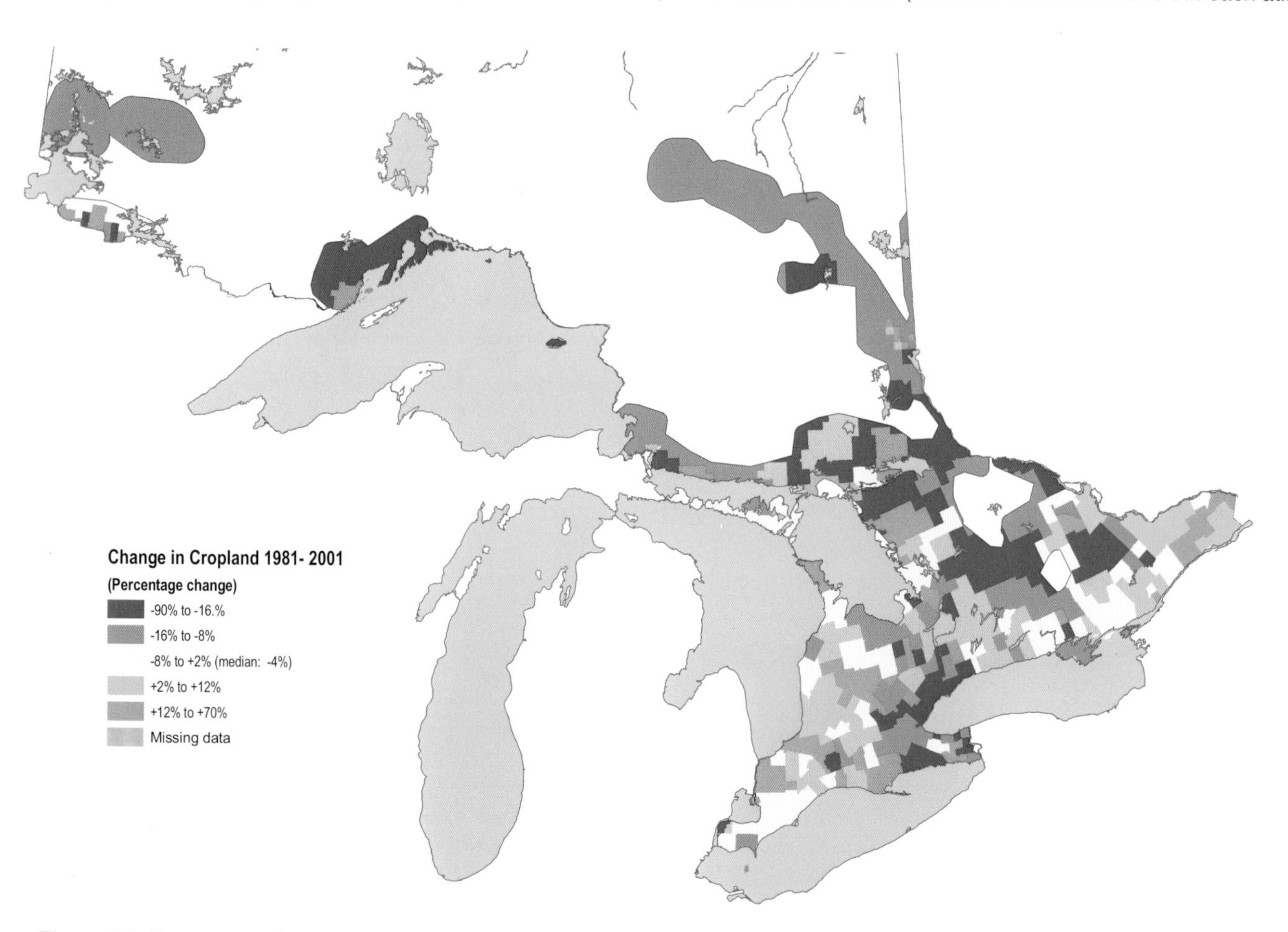

Figure 4.8. Percentage change in cropland from 1981 to 2001. Adapted from Statistics Canada, Census of Agriculture, 1981 and 2001.

tance of extensive areas of grassy habitat like the Carden Plain. Such areas provide not only large patches of habitat but many such patches, providing breeding opportunities to larger populations of area-sensitive birds and thereby increasing the likelihood of maintaining viable populations of these species. Much of the northern part of Lake Simcoe-Rideau region, from southern parts of the Bruce Peninsula east to Kingston just south of the Shield, then just east of the edge of the Shield north to the Pembroke area, stands out on maps (especially relative abundance maps) of many grassland species. Within that area, the Carden Plain and Alvar is particularly evident on maps of several species such as the Loggerhead Shrike, Upland Sandpiper, and Eastern Bluebird.

As well as grassland species, others that we now think of as farmland birds benefited when the clearing of forests created extensive open areas previously unavailable to birds in Ontario. Species such as the Eastern Kingbird, Tree Swallow, Mourning Dove, and Eastern Bluebird began nesting in hedgerows or fence posts. Others such as Barn and Cliff Swallows nested on farm buildings and foraged in the surrounding open habitats. Bank and Northern Rough-winged Swallows took advantage of artificial features such as sand pits and foraged in the open agricultural land nearby. These birds of open country have probably benefited overall from the opening of forests but are now in decline as open spaces are closed in by natural reforestation and farm structures used for nesting are torn down; the intensification of agricultural practices is likely also reducing their food. The decline of swallows is discussed below under "Aerial foragers."

Early successional (shrubland) habitats

This category includes species that breed in early successional habitats such as old fields and other shrubby habitats. Substantially more shrubland species increased than decreased in each of the two northern regions, but in the Lake Simcoe-Rideau and Carolinian regions, somewhat more of these species decreased than increased, although there was little difference considering only significant changes (Table 4.1; Appendix 3).

When large cleared areas of eastern North America, including the Southern Shield and Lake Simcoe-Rideau regions of southern Ontario, began to return to forest, certain early successional species such as the Golden-winged Warbler and Eastern Towhee thrived as grassland birds were declining. By now much of eastern North America, including the Southern Shield region, has returned to forest, so relatively little early successional habitat remains. Early successional bird species have declined accordingly (Askins 2000). However, much of that decline in Ontario appears to have taken place prior to the first atlas, so the effects are not very evident when comparing atlases.

Figure 4.9 shows the most marked increase in shrubland birds in the area along the southern edge of the Shield and adjacent areas south of the Shield edge. Decreases are most evident in the southern part of the Shield, particularly in the southeastern portion. The decline in the shrubland birds in the Carolinian region might be due to agricultural intensification (Figure 4.8), which often reduces shrubby habitats. However, as seen in Figure 4.8, some parts of the Carolinian, particularly around the Niagara Peninsula, and Lake Simcoe-Rideau regions, have lost cropland since the first atlas, which might explain the more equivocal results from these regions.

Of the 19 species in this habitat category in the Hudson Bay Lowlands, eight increased significantly between atlases, and none declined. The increase in shrubby habitats in coastal regions due to isostatic rebound (Ken Abraham, pers. comm.) might be a factor in this result. In the Northern Shield region, the increase in forest area harvested annually between atlas periods (Larry Watkins, pers. comm.) might have influenced this result by creating more early successional habitat.

Wetland birds

Wetland birds show more species decreasing than increasing in the Carolinian region, but more increasing than decreasing in all other regions. Given the overall pattern, the decrease in wetland birds in the Carolinian region is noteworthy. The intensification of agricultural practices, which reduces the amount of grassy or scrubby habitat around wetlands, and the draining of wetlands (presumably small, unprotected ones), along with urban expansion are probably factors in the decline of wetland species in the Carolinian region. The declines of the American Bittern, Common Snipe, Blue-winged Teal, and Mallard may be due to losses of wet meadows and other grassy areas around ponds between atlases due to more intensive farming practices. The decline of the American Coot, Least Bittern, Black Tern, and Common Moorhen suggests that marshes also declined (in size and/or in quality) between atlas periods. Unfortunately, we do not have data on the extent of wetland loss or gain between atlases. Nevertheless, given that so little wetland remained even at the time of the first atlas (Rowntree 1979), the results of the second atlas strongly indicate that conservation measures for wetlands in the Carolinian region should be a high priority.

Maps of several wetland species such as the Wilson's Snipe show that the Kingston area and much of eastern Ontario is particularly important for wetland birds – presumably because of the larger amount of suitable wetland in that area. The area south and east of the southern edge of the Shield is also evidently important to wetland species such as the Least Bittern, Black Tern, and Marsh Wren. The wetland-rich southern area of Grey Co., particularly around Proton Township (known locally as "Float'n Prot'n"), is also evident on relative abundance maps of several wetland species including the Swamp Sparrow.

Tundra

There are about equal numbers of increasing and decreasing species in tundra habitat, with very few species showing significant change between atlases (Table 4.1). Given Ontario's tundra is the most southerly tundra habitat in the northern hemisphere, it might be expected that more dramatic changes would have occurred through climate change. It may be that the atlas data from the north does not provide sufficient precision to detect small changes, that the effects of climate change are not yet affecting Ontario's tundra birds, or that increased atlasser efficiency masked any declines.

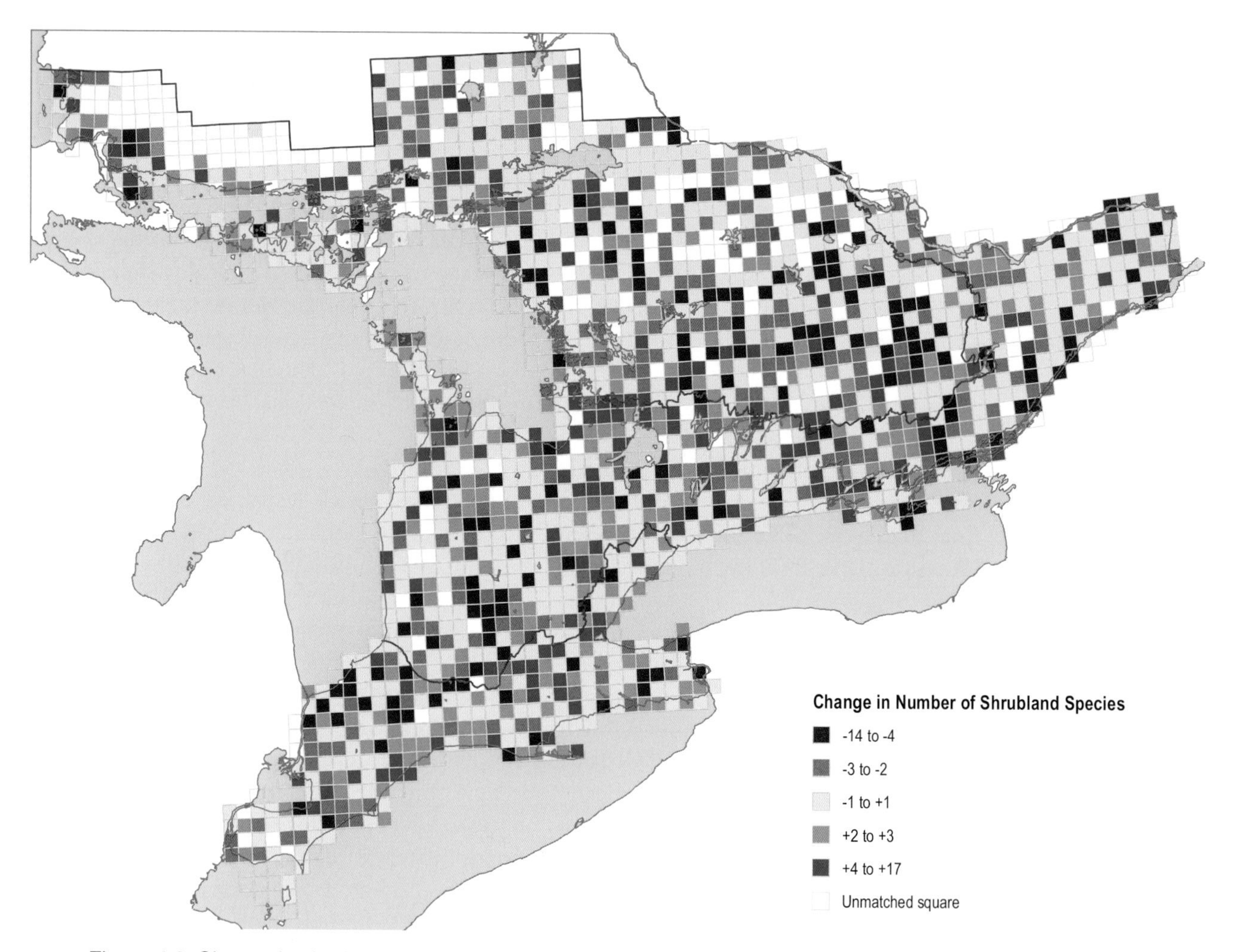

Figure 4.9. Change in shrubland bird species richness in squares matched for effort (minimum 10 hours of effort in each atlas).

Urban habitats

Since urban areas have expanded between atlases, an increase in urban species might be expected, and that is what has been found in the province as a whole (Table 4.1; Appendix 3). Interestingly, there are about equal numbers of increasing and decreasing urban species in all regions except the Hudson Bay Lowlands, where there has been a marked increase in six species. The introduced House Finch, which arrived in Ontario during the first atlas, has increased markedly in all regions. By contrast, the European Starling and House Sparrow, which were introduced over a century ago, are declining in almost every region. The Chimney Swift is also declining, perhaps because old-fashioned chimneys are being modified with caps and flues that render them unusable for nesting and roosting.

Changes in Other Groups

Aerial foragers

The numbers of significantly increasing and decreasing species in selected ecological, taxonomic, and foraging guilds are shown in Table 4.2. The decline of aerial foragers (swallows, nightjars, the Chimney Swift) is an emerging issue North America-wide, particularly in Canada and the northern parts of most species' ranges. In Ontario, all 10 species of aerial foragers declined between atlases, and no species increased. Nine species are listed in Figure 4.1 as among the largest decreases of all species between atlases. More species decreased than increased in all regions.

As swallows and nightjars are primarily birds of open habitats, the natural reforestation of formerly open areas on the Southern Shield is probably a factor in their decline (Figure 4.10). Loss of pasture (Figure 4.6) that provides good foraging habitat might also be a factor. The birds' prey base could have been affected by a whole suite of changes in addition to those in habitat, such as in climate or quality of air and water. The most evident declines on species maps tend to be at the northern parts of species' Ontario ranges, and inland away from the Great Lakes shorelines, although this may be because atlas data are better at detecting changes where numbers are low. BBS data for Ontario show declines for most of the aerial foragers between the two atlas periods, and the confirmatory atlas data help draw attention to this worrying pattern. Seven of Ontario's 10 aerial foragers are declining across their continental breeding ranges (Sauer et al. 2007), suggesting that the causes of decline are not limited to Ontario. See individual species accounts for more details.

Raptors

Substantially more raptors increased than decreased in the province as a whole and in the Carolinian, Lake Simcoe-Rideau, and Northern Shield regions (Table 4.2). This is one of the very good news stories to arise from the second atlas. This extraor-

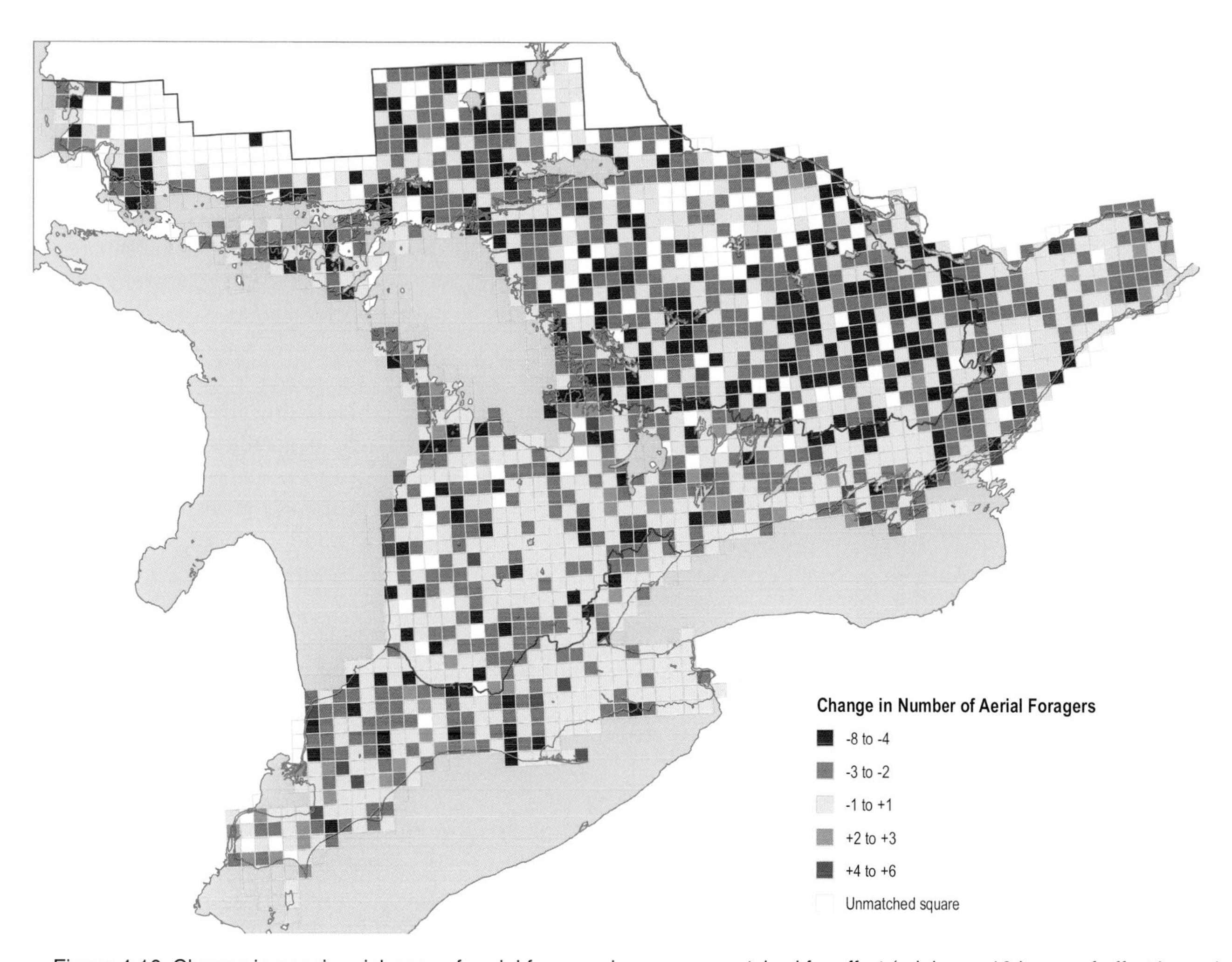

Figure 4.10. Change in species richness of aerial foragers in squares matched for effort (minimum 10 hours of effort in each atlas).

Region		Aerial Foragers	Migration Strategy				Raptors		
			Resident	Nomadic	Short Distance	Neotropical	All Raptors	Diurnal Raptors	Owls
Hudson Bay Lowlands	Increases	1 (0)	16 (4)	2 (1)	74 (31)	35 (12)	9 (5)	6 (3)	3 (2)
	Decreases	4 (0)	13 (1)	6 (2)	29 (3)	25 (2)	9 (0)	5 (0)	4 (0)
Northern Shield	Increases	0	24 (14)	3 (1)	75 (39)	40 (23)	20 (10)	12 (5)	8 (5)
	Decreases	9 (5)	3 (1)	4 (2)	34 (12)	29 (7)	2 (1)	2 (1)	0
Southern Shield	Increases	0	28 (12)	1 (1)	50 (36)	34 (16)	12 (8)	6 (5)	6 (3)
	Decreases	9 (9)	5 (2)	4 (4)	45 (31)	43 (29)	10 (4)	7 (3)	3 (1)
Lake Simcoe-Rideau	Increases	0	20 (14)	2 (1)	50 (30)	33 (16)	14 (9)	10 (7)	4 (2)
	Decreases	10 (8)	14 (7)	3 (3)	54 (25)	52 (28)	8 (5)	3 (2)	5 (3)
Carolinian	Increases	2 (1)	15 (11)	0	38 (16)	26 (14)	12 (8)	10 (7)	2 (1)
	Decreases	8 (6)	12 (7)	3 (1)	63 (21)	53 (24)	8 (3)	3 (1)	5 (2)
Ontario	Increases	0	33 (15)	2 (1)	87 (36)	53 (22)	20 (9)	12 (4)	8 (5)
	Decreases	10 (9)	12 (4)	6 (1)	54 (16)	50 (18)	6 (0)	3 (0)	3 (0)

Table 4.2. The number of species that increased or decreased between the first and second atlas, corrected for effort, according to migration strategy and for selected foraging guilds. Species with statistically significant changes are shown in parentheses. Cases where increases and decreases differ by five or more species are highlighted in blue (more increases) or red (more decreases).

dinary result is presumably due largely to the reduction in DDT and its derivatives in the environment, both in Ontario and in some wintering areas. DDT was banned in the US and Canada in the early 1970s and has continued to decline in the environment since that time (Figure 4.11). The Merlin and Bald Eagle are perhaps the best examples in the atlas of raptor increases probably related to the DDT ban and the reduction in use of other organochlorine contaminants such as PCBs.

Examination of the causes of banded birds being recovered indicates that shooting of raptors declined markedly in the 1960s. Diurnal raptors were formerly shot in large numbers at certain migration concentration spots, such as Hawk Mountain in Pennsylvania. Persecution of raptors in general has probably declined over time, which might also be contributing to these increases.

The expansion and maturation of forests in parts of southern Ontario (and in eastern North America generally) probably helped woodland raptors increase while causing decreases in raptors of open habitats, such as the Red-tailed Hawk and American Kestrel. All three accipiters increased in the Carolinian region, perhaps helped by maturation of conifer plantations and the overall increase of woodland. Moreover, certain raptors such as the Merlin, Cooper's Hawk, and (due to introductions) Peregrine Falcons are appearing more frequently in and around urban environments.

The increase in Ontario's diurnal raptors seems generally consistent with continental patterns. The Bald Eagle and Peregrine Falcon are showing widespread increases across the continent, although American Kestrel numbers are generally down, perhaps because it is a grassland species.

Unlike the situation for diurnal raptors, the apparent increases in probability of observation of nocturnal owls might result from more, or more effective, owl surveys. The availability during the second atlas of better broadcasting equipment (CD and MP3 players in addition to the tape players used during the first atlas), and the inclusion of data from Nocturnal Owl Survey routes and a special Eastern Screech-Owl survey designed for the atlas (see species account), probably meant better coverage of owls. Unfortunately, data on time of day of surveys were not collected during the first atlas, so direct comparisons of owl atlassing effort cannot be made.

Given the increase in owls generally, the decrease in the Great Horned Owl is noteworthy. Natural reforestation of open areas where the owl likes to hunt is probably related to the decline in the Southern Shield and northern parts of the Lake Simcoe-Rideau region, while intensification of agriculture, which probably reduces the owl's prey base, is likely a factor in the rest of the Lake Simcoe-Rideau and parts of the Carolinian regions. The Barred Owl, which prefers more extensive forest cover and mature forest, has increased in the regions where the Great Horned Owl has decreased.

Residents

Note that resident species are resident all year in the province but not necessarily in each region; very few species are resident in the Hudson Bay Lowlands. Of the 45 resident species in Ontario, substantially more have increased than decreased since the first atlas (Table 4.2). The trend is up in all regions,

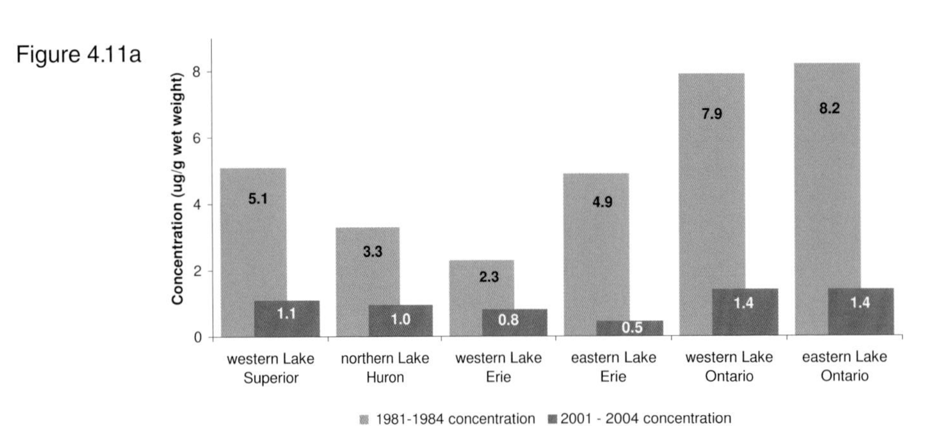

Figure 4.11. Changes in a) DDE, a DDT derivative, and b) PCBs in Great Lakes Herring Gull eggs between the two atlas periods.

and especially in the Lake Simcoe-Rideau and the Southern and Northern Shield regions. Ten of the 15 significantly increasing species are forest birds. This suggests that the forest cover increase discussed above is an important factor. Generally milder winters may also be contributing to better winter survival and thus also fuelling expansion. According to BBS, resident birds in the eastern half of the continent have about the same number of increasing and decreasing species.

Short-distance migrants

Short-distance migrants winter primarily in the US. The atlas data indicate that substantially more short-distance migrants have increased since the first atlas than have decreased. The trend is down in the Carolinian region, up in the Southern and Northern Shield and Hudson Bay Lowlands, and somewhat equivocal in the Lake Simcoe-Rideau region. Continental, Canada-wide, and Ontario-wide BBS guild analyses all show a predominance of decreasing trends among short-distance migrants (Sauer et al. 2005, Downes and Collins 2007), so the increases in Ontario are noteworthy. Short-distance migrants tend to be seed-eating, grassland, or shrubland birds, so as with resident species, habitat may be a primary factor. Again the relatively poor showing of species in the Carolinian region is of concern and may be the result of ongoing habitat deterioration in this region.

Neotropical migrants

Substantially more neotropical migrants have decreased than increased in each of the three most southerly regions, but substantially more species have increased than decreased in each of the two northern regions. About the same number are increasing and decreasing in the province as a whole.

Neotropical migrants are found across all habitat types and foraging guilds, so there are probably a number of factors in their decline in southern Ontario. The inclusion of most of the aerial foragers in this group (eight species), all of which are declining, is undoubtedly an important factor. Continental, Canada-wide, and Ontario-wide BBS guild analyses all show a predominance of decreasing trends among neotropical migrants. However, BBS coverage is not extensive in the Northern Shield region and is non-existent in the Hudson Bay Lowlands.

Re/Introduced species

The Wild Turkey, Peregrine Falcon, Canada Goose, and Trumpeter Swan have expanded considerably since the first atlas, wholly or in large part due to active reintroduction programs aimed at re-establishing these species. The Mute Swan and House Finch have also both increased considerably since the first atlas, though their introductions were not part of organized introduction projects. The Gray Partridge, Ring-necked Pheasant, Rock Pigeon, European Starling, and House Sparrow were all previously introduced to the province. Interestingly, all of these species except the Rock Pigeon have declined since the first atlas either throughout their whole Ontario range or at least in major parts of it, probably related in part to changes in agricultural practices (see individual species accounts for more details). The Rock Pigeon declined in the Carolinian region but increased in much of the rest of the province.

Big birds

Eleven of Ontario's largest 12 birds by weight increased markedly from the first atlas to the second (Table 4.3). A number of factors contribute to these increases. The eagles and fish-eating birds are at or near the top of the food chain, and so likely benefited from the decline in DDT and other contaminants in the environment. Several large species have benefited from release programs. But the fact that such a large proportion of our largest birds have increased may reflect a different societal relationship with these species. Certainly fewer birds are shot nowadays, as noted above for raptors. While shooting of large birds and other "pests" (such as crows and ravens) was formerly commonplace, it is now generally considered less acceptable, especially for non-game species. At the same time, the release programs reflect an interest in re-establishing the pre-settlement wildlife of the province. Species such as the Wild Turkey, Canada Goose, Trumpeter Swan, and possibly Sandhill Crane were greatly reduced or extirpated by early settlers who used them for food. Some of these species are likely more abundant now than they were historically (especially Canada Goose and Wild Turkey), because the habitats into which they have been introduced are dominated by more abundant food sources in the form of cereal grain agriculture (especially corn). In part because of their abundance, some of these species, including the Double-crested Cormorant, Mute Swan, Canada Goose, Sandhill Crane, and Wild Turkey, are now considered pests by some people. Big birds seem to be doing well, with most of these species up across much of their North American breeding ranges.

Species	Weight (g)	% squares 1st atlas (effort adjusted)	% squares 2nd atlas (effort adjusted)	Proportional change (%)
Trumpeter Swan†	10,500	0	109	
Mute Swan	10,000	0**	0.4	+775
American White Pelican*†	7,700	1	4	+300
Tundra Swan	7,000	1.2	2.1	+67
Wild Turkey	5,800	0.1	4.9	+6347
Golden Eagle	4,400	0.6	1.4	+127
Bald Eagle	4,325	9.8	39.1	+300
Sandhill Crane	4,100	11.7	33.4	+186
Canada Goose	3,050	24.8	51.7	+109
Great Blue Heron*	2,400	5.1	3.9	-23
Turkey Vulture	1,830	12.2	27.5	+125
Double-crested Cormorant*	1,700	1.2	2.4	+107

Table 4.3. Change in the number of squares of the 12 largest birds in Ontario between atlases. All numbers are effort-adjusted to 20 hours.

* Only confirmed breeding records used.
† Raw number of squares used instead of effort-adjusted squares.
** Rounded to 0.

Spruce Budworm species

Spruce Budworm outbreaks are known to have a large effect on three classic "budworm warblers," Tennessee, Bay-breasted, and Cape May Warblers. There were moderate to severe levels of infestation in large areas of Ontario during the late 1970s and at the time of the first atlas, with more than 18 million hectares infested in 1981. Since then, areas of infestation have decreased markedly, down to less than 300,000 hectares during the period of the second atlas (Figure 4.12). Each of the "budworm warblers" declined significantly in one or more regions, and other species known to respond to budworm outbreaks, such as the Evening Grosbeak and Purple Finch, also declined between atlases in much of their Ontario range.

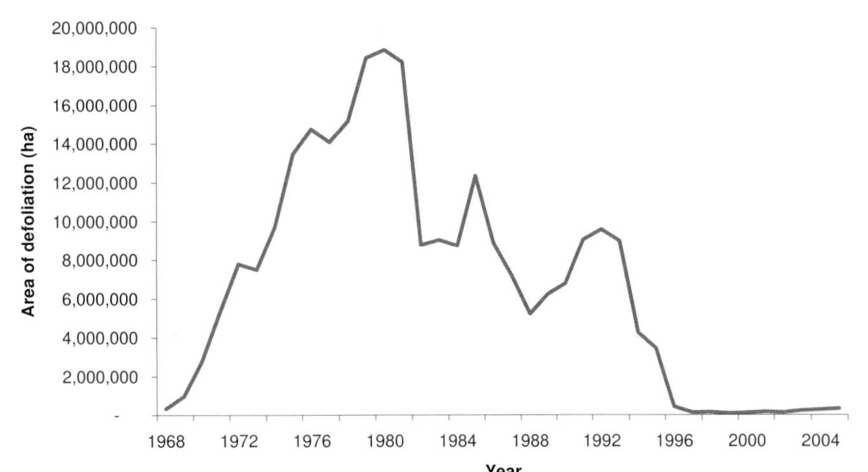

Figure 4.12. Area of Spruce Budworm defoliation in Ontario. Source: Natural Resources Canada, Canadian Forest Service.

More detailed analyses will be undertaken over time using the atlas data to assess the effects of various factors on Ontario's birds. The following is an example, showing an early application of the atlas data.

The Effect of Climate Change on Breeding Bird Distribution in Southern Ontario

The average temperature in southern Ontario was marginally higher during the second atlas compared to the first (0.6°C, Figure 4.13).

Price (2004) used climate models (based on a doubling of CO_2 in the next 75-100 years) in combination with Ontario's first breeding bird atlas to predict quite dramatic changes to southern Ontario's avifauna over the next century, including loss of 35 breeding species, northward contraction of the southern edge of range in another 23 species, expansion of the northern range of 23 southerly-breeding species, and establishment of another seven species as new regular breeders in Ontario. Though these predictions are for the long term, we might expect to see early evidence of these changes in the 20 years between Ontario's first and second atlases.

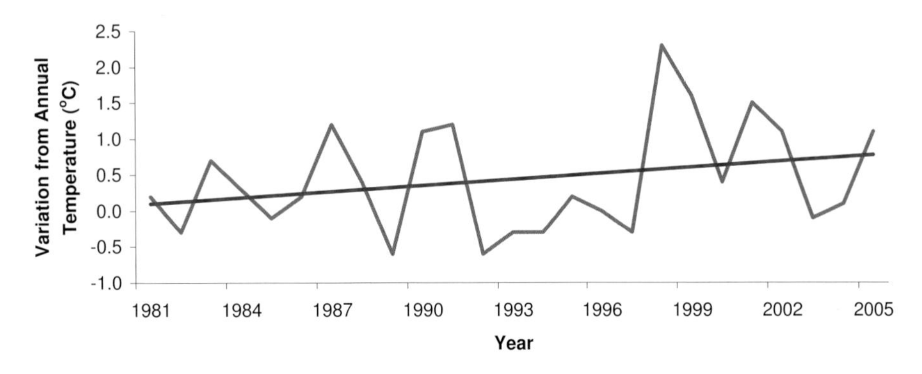

Figure 4.13. Annual temperature departures from the 1951-1980 average, Great Lakes-St. Lawrence Climate Region (Environment Canada 2005).

Statistically significant shifts to the north have been reported in North America using BBS data (Hitch and Leberg 2007) and Christmas Bird Count data (La Sorte and Thompson 2007), and in the United Kingdom (Thomas and Lennon 1999) and Finland (Brommer 2004) where comparisons were based on breeding bird atlases. In all cases, shifts at the northern limits of range were more pronounced than shifts at the centre or southern limits of range. The magnitude of average range shift at the northern edge varied from 0.9 to 2.4 km/yr in the four studies.

Here we examine the evidence for northward range shifts in southern Ontario, using data from atlas squares with comparable effort in the first and second atlases. The following predictions were tested:

1) For 53 species at or near their northern breeding range limit in southern Ontario, we expect:
   a) an average shift northward in the northern edge of their range in southern Ontario;
   b) an increase in the probability of observation within the southern Ontario range of the species.
2) For 62 species at or near their southern breeding range limit in southern Ontario we expect:
   a) an average shift northward in the southern edge of their range in southern Ontario;
   b) a decrease in the probability of observation within the southern Ontario range of the species.
3) We predict a northward shift in centre of range in southern Ontario, on average across all breeding species;
4) For 84 species predicted to show future range changes in southern Ontario (Price 2004), we expect:
   a) contraction of range for species predicted to contract (23) or be extirpated (35);
   b) expansion of range for species predicted to expand (23) or begin breeding (7).

Predictions 3 and 4 are not independent of predictions 1 and 2 since many of the same species are involved; they are included to corroborate results from the initial tests.

All tests were restricted to the 1,636 atlas squares matched for hours of effort in southern Ontario. To test for shifts in northern (or southern) edges of range, we compared the average latitude of occupied squares in the northern (or southern) 1% of occupied squares in each atlas. However, when the number of occupied squares dropped below 1,000, the statistical power to detect change was lower. We therefore compared the average latitude of occupied squares in the most northern (or southern) 5% of squares when the number of occupied squares in southern Ontario averaged between 200 and 1,000; and we compared the most northern (or southern) 10% of occupied squares when the number of occupied squares averaged 50 to 200. Species occupying fewer than 50 squares on average were excluded from analysis.

We also compared the "centre of range" (mean latitude and longitude of all occupied squares in southern Ontario) between atlases. Species were excluded if they were found in fewer than 20 squares on average in each atlas, or in more than 1,500 of the matched squares.

Prediction 1: southern species

Twenty-two species at or near their northern breeding limit in southern Ontario showed evidence consistent with prediction (Table 4.4), 15 with significant range shifts northwards. The other seven expanded their range in southern Ontario as predicted, but without a significant shift northwards. When range in the first atlas was concentrated in or near the Niagara Peninsula, subsequent expansion sometimes occurred to the southwest, as well as the north and northeast (e.g., Northern Mockingbird, Carolina Wren, Tufted Titmouse), so that range in Ontario did not show a significant shift to the north.

In contrast, fifteen species near the north edge of their range in Ontario showed results opposite to predictions, with reduced range in southern Ontario and/or a significant southward shift in range. Many of these species are birds of open habitats (Northern Bobwhite, Upland Sandpiper, Loggerhead Shrike, Eastern Towhee, Field and Grasshopper Sparrows, Eastern Meadowlark), and range shifts to the south likely reflect decreasing availability of suitable habitat at the north edges of their breeding ranges.

Across all southern species, the average shift in northern edge of range was 8.6 km northwards, not significantly different from zero (t-test, $p=0.16$), and smaller in magnitude (0.4 km/yr) than the northward shifts observed for southern species in other studies (0.9 to 2.4 km/yr in the four studies cited above).

Prediction 2: northern species

The predictions for northern breeding species with southern edges of range in or near southern Ontario were that range would contract and/or shift northward. In fact, more species (29) showed results opposite to predictions than supported the predictions (18). Of those showing a showing a statistically significant range shift, 18 shifted south and only eight shifted north. Almost all birds shifting to the south were forest birds, and range change was likely a result of increasing forest cover south of the Shield.

Southern Species	Range Edge Shifted North	Range Centre Shifted North	Expanded Range
Ring-necked Pheasant	Yes		No
Wild Turkey		Yes	Yes
Double-crested Cormorant			Yes
Black-crowned Night-Heron	Yes		
Turkey Vulture	Yes	Yes	Yes
Red-shouldered Hawk	Yes	Yes	Yes
Eastern Screech-Owl			Yes
Red-bellied Woodpecker	Yes	Yes	Yes
Acadian Flycatcher		Yes	
Willow Flycatcher		Yes	
Yellow-throated Vireo	Yes		
Tufted Titmouse			Yes
Carolina Wren			Yes
Marsh Wren	Yes		
Blue-gray Gnatcatcher			Yes
Northern Mockingbird			Yes
Blue-winged Warbler	Yes	Yes	Yes
Golden-winged Warbler	Yes	Yes	No
Hooded Warbler			Yes
Northern Cardinal	Yes	Yes	Yes
Orchard Oriole	Yes		Yes
House Finch	Yes	Yes	Yes

Table 4.4. Range changes in "southern" species.

Overall, there was no significant range shift to the north (average shift = 6.1 km south). A similar lack of a northerly shift in southern range limits was observed in other studies cited above.

Prediction 3: all species

More species showed a significant shift in centre of range southwards (39) than to the north (27). The average shift was 2.3 km northward, not statistically different from zero. It is possible that temperature change would have a greater impact on wintering species than breeding migrants. However, restricting the analysis above to year-round residents made no significant difference to the result.

Predictions from Price (2004) models

Of the 58 species predicted by Price (2004) to be extirpated from southern Ontario or contract in range in the next 75-100 years, 29 did show some contraction in range (14 significant), but the same number expanded range (29 species, 14 significant) in southern Ontario. Of the 23 species predicted to expand range in southern Ontario, only nine expanded range in the past 20 years (seven significant) compared to 14 with reduced range (six significant). None of the seven species predicted to colonize Ontario (Bell's Vireo, Bewick's Wren, Blue Grosbeak, Carolina Chickadee, Great-tailed Grackle, Say's Phoebe, Scissor-tailed Flycatcher) was found breeding during the second Ontario atlas.

Conclusions

Overall, there was little support for a general northward shift in breeding ranges in southern Ontario. This suggests that the modest climate change in Ontario over the past 20 years has not had universal effects on bird ranges over and above any effects on range of other factors (such as reforestation or loss of grassland habitat). This result is in contrast to northward shifts detected in North America in studies by Hitch and Leberg (2007) and La Sorte and Thompson (2007). Those studies were based on slightly longer time periods (31 and 29 years, respectively) and were at a larger geographic scale (eastern North America as covered by BBS, North America to the extent covered by CBC) than the current analysis. Effects of factors such as change in land use may more readily overwhelm climate effects when the geographic scale is small, the time period is short, or there has been relatively little change in climate, all of which were influences in this study.

Summary

Major findings from the atlas include the decline in grassland birds and aerial foragers, which, according to BBS, are declining widely across the continent. Also noteworthy are the overall increases in forest birds, wetland birds, and raptors. The overall increase in northern birds, which is a factor in the increases in these groups, is also noteworthy. However, the possibility that higher atlassing efficiency during the second atlas may have influenced these results must be considered. BBS data for eastern North America including Ontario from 1980 to 2006 show about equal numbers of increasing and decreasing forest birds, and so are not fully in agreement with the atlas data. However, BBS, like the atlas, shows an increase among woodland birds in southern Ontario, and BBS coverage is not extensive in northern Ontario. BBS also shows more wetland bird species increasing than decreasing in eastern North America, which is in agreement with the atlas data.

Fourteen of the species listed among the 20 common species in decline across North America by the Audubon Society (Butcher and Niven 2007) breed in Ontario in sufficient numbers to ascertain a change between atlases using the atlas data: Northern Bobwhite, Evening Grosbeak, Northern Pintail, Eastern Meadowlark, Loggerhead Shrike, Field Sparrow, Grasshopper Sparrow, Snow Bunting, Common Grackle, Whip-poor-will, Horned Lark, American Bittern, Ruffed Grouse, Common Tern, and Boreal Chickadee. According to the atlas data, the first 10 of these species decreased in Ontario. The American Bittern and the Ruffed Grouse decreased in the two southern regions but increased in the Northern Shield; the Common Tern decreased in the Carolinian region but not overall; the Boreal Chickadee increased in the province as a whole and in most atlas regions. The strong agreement between the continental trends and those in Ontario show the tendency for population declines to occur widely across species ranges. The differences indicate that regional changes do not always agree with the continental pattern.

The much larger number of species decreasing than increasing in the Carolinian region is an important finding. About seven million people, almost a quarter of Canada's population, live in this region. The expanding urban footprint and increasing agricultural intensification in parts of the region are likely playing a role in the ongoing decline of many bird species. The atlas results add weight to the calls for focused conservation efforts in this region. The only other region showing more decreasing than increasing species overall is the Lake Simcoe-Rideau region, which is of course the next most populous region and the other region widely affected by urban development and agriculture. Together, the Carolinian and Lake Simcoe-Rideau regions comprise the Ontario portion of North American Bird Conservation Region 13, whose bird conservation plan is currently nearing publication and is indeed timely.

The general pattern resulting from the comparison of the two atlases suggests that human activity, particularly land use change, is the root cause of many of the changes revealed to date by the atlas. Land use changes affect bird populations and distributions indirectly by changing the habitat available to the birds. Some of the largest changes revealed by the atlas, such as the decline of grassland birds, may be brought about by broad-scale economic and social patterns, such as the clearing of southern Ontario's forests for settlement and agricultural purposes, and then the subsequent abandonment of much of that farmland as farming proved to be unsustainable economically. However, the potential for very direct and detrimental effects is apparent, as shown by the decline of many raptors due to the use of DDT and then the expansion of populations after DDT was banned and gradually decreased in the environment. Clearly, very significant changes can also be brought about through reintroduction programs.

It is hoped that further research and application of the atlas results will reveal more about the reasons behind the changes in Ontario's breeding bird populations. The addition of point counts to atlassing procedure should allow us after future atlases to more accurately document change in avian abundance and its geographic patterns, which in turn should provide stronger inference of human effects on bird populations. Such information will be invaluable in helping society work towards a more sustainable relationship with the environment that we share with our birds.

Interpreting Species Accounts

The following species accounts contain information on the status, distribution, and relative abundance of all species for which breeding evidence was reported during the second atlas. Species for which breeding evidence was not reported during the second atlas but for which breeding evidence was reported previously in Ontario are given a brief account under "Historical breeders" immediately following the main species accounts.

The following information will help with interpretation of the species accounts.

Species names

Species names are given in English, Latin, and French, according to the AOU checklist, 7th edition (American Ornithologists Union 1998 and all supplements through 2006). The order of appearance of species also follows the AOU checklist.

Text

The accounts provide background on the Ontario distribution and status of the species and aspects of breeding biology that help to evaluate how well the species is represented on breeding evidence maps. Abundance of the species is also discussed, particularly as portrayed on the relative abundance maps. The author of each account is named at the end of the account.

In the text, the term "southern Ontario" refers to the area shown in Figure 5.1, consisting of three regions: the Carolinian, Lake Simcoe-Rideau, and Southern Shield. "Northern Ontario" (shown in Figure 5.2) is divided into the Northern Shield and Hudson Bay Lowlands regions. The northern edge of the map in Figure 5.1 is the northern edge of the Southern Shield region. The southern edge of the northern Ontario map is the southern edge of the Northern Shield region. A map of the boundaries of all five regions is provided in Figure 1.5 in the Methods chapter. The boundaries between regions are shown on the breeding evidence and the relative abundance maps.

Locations in Ontario mentioned in the text are listed in the Gazetteer (Appendix 7) along with their latitude/longitude, and the most frequently named locations are shown on the maps on the inside of the front and back cover. Physiographic regions are based on Chapman and Putnam (1984). Municipalities are named using the Association of Municipalities of Ontario (2007) nomenclature at the time of publication.

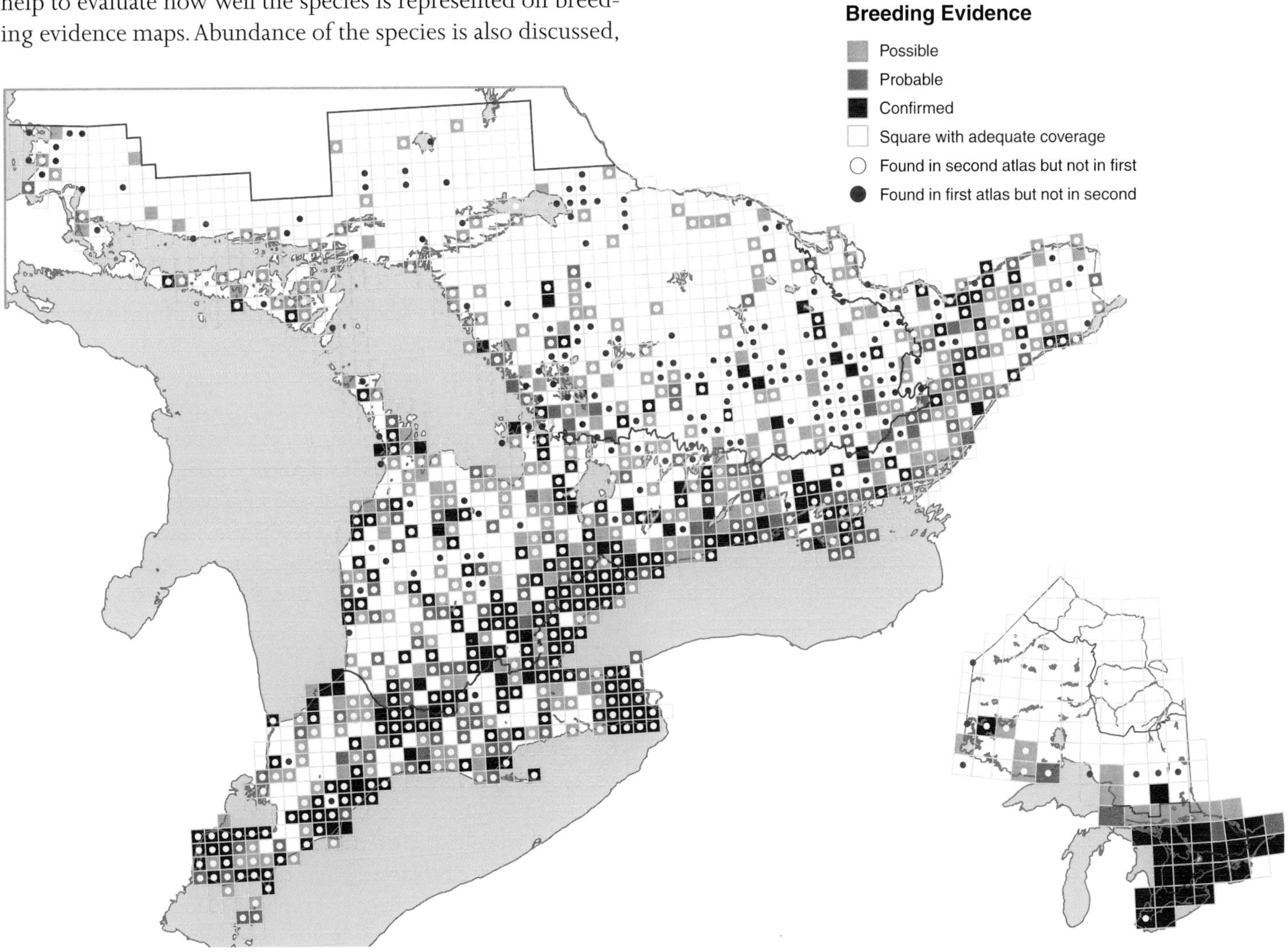

Figure 5.1. Example of a southern Ontario map and an all-Ontario map showing breeding evidence and change between atlases.

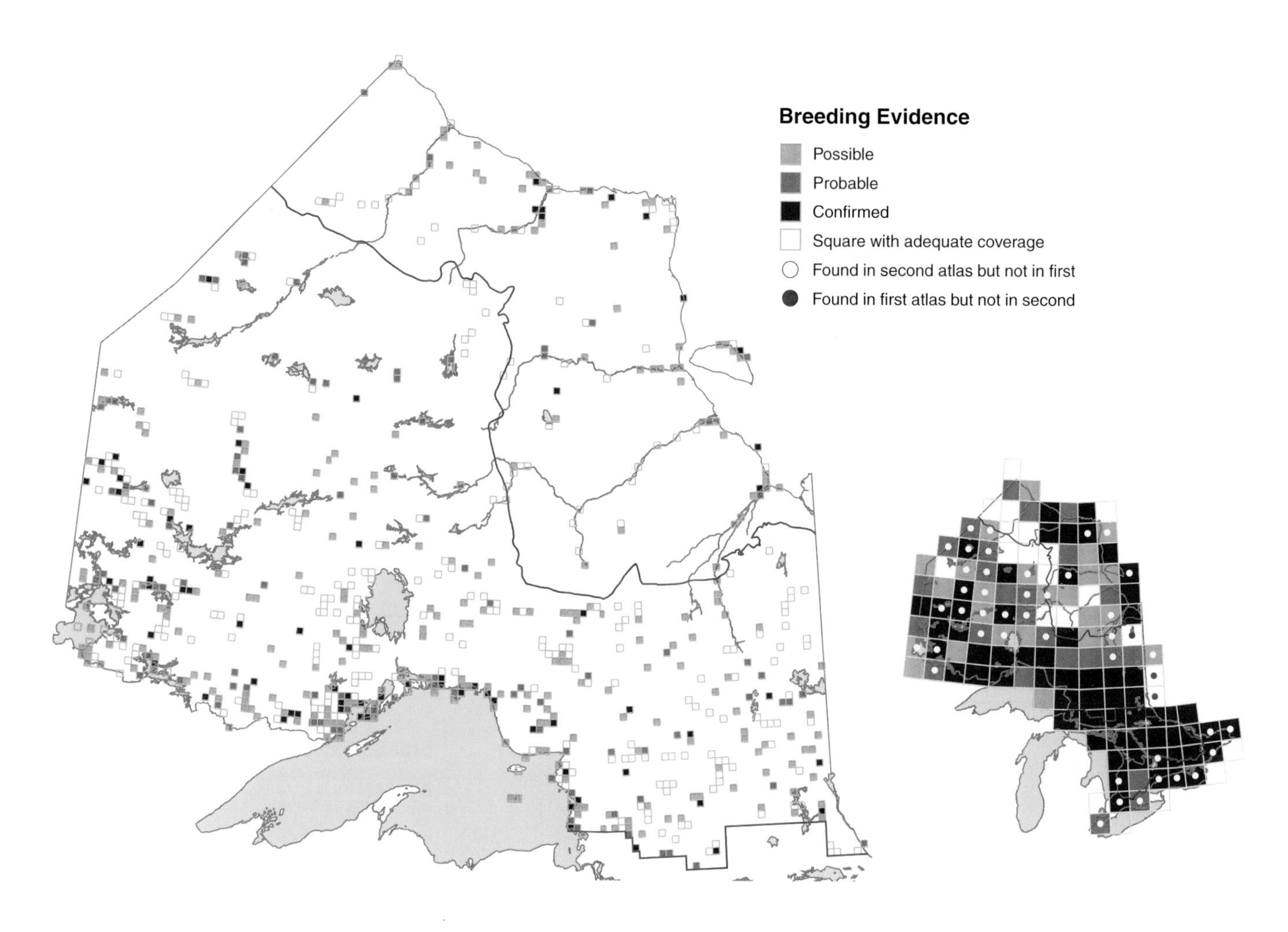

Figure 5.2. Example of a northern Ontario map and an all-Ontario map showing breeding evidence and change between atlases.

In the text, the term "between atlases" is used frequently, and refers to a comparison between the two atlas periods (i.e., 1981-1985 vs. 2001-2005) rather than the period of years between the two atlas periods (1986 to 2000).

The Breeding biology section is intended to provide information pertinent to understanding the breeding evidence and relative abundance maps, but is of secondary importance relative to the Distribution and population status and Abundance sections of each account. As such, the length and content of the Breeding biology section will vary depending on the amount of material in the other two sections; it is not intended to be consistent between accounts, nor is it intended to provide comprehensive information on a species' breeding biology in general. As a result, species for which there is relatively little to say about distribution, change, and abundance will have longer, more detailed Breeding biology sections.

Breeding evidence and change maps

The smaller inset map shows the 100-km blocks in which the species was reported in all of Ontario during the second atlas, and the larger maps show the 10-km squares in which the species was reported in either southern or northern Ontario. On each map, the level of breeding evidence (possible, probable, or confirmed) reported in each square or block is shown using three shades, with darker shades indicating a higher level of breeding evidence.

Coloured dots are used to show changes between the atlases. Black dots indicate that the species was reported in the first atlas but not the second, while yellow dots indicate that the species was reported in the second atlas but not the first. On northern Ontario maps, however, black and yellow dots are not shown at the 10-km square level because the coloured dots are not discernable at this scale. Use the 100-km block map to see the big picture regarding change in the north and across the province.

The breeding evidence and change maps give a sense of whether the species' distribution has expanded or retracted in each part of the province, and the pattern of that change.

Keep in mind when assessing the change information that although there was approximately 25% more effort expended in the second atlas than in the first, no effort adjustment has been used in the production of these maps. Exercise some caution when interpreting yellow dots, which may somewhat over-emphasize increase or expansion, and black dots, which may somewhat underestimate decline or contraction. Authors have tried to alert readers to possible biases in the maps and to highlight those changes that are supported by effort-adjusted data.

On the northern breeding evidence map, the hollow square symbol is used to show squares that were adequately covered but in which the species was not reported during the second atlas. While the species may indeed occur in some of these squares, it was not found during a minimum of 20 hours of fieldwork, so, if present, it probably occurs in small numbers.

Histogram and change

The Methods chapter describes the methods used to adjust for the difference in effort between the two atlas projects. The histogram provided in each species account (Figure 5.3) compares the effort-adjusted breeding evidence data from the first atlas (tan-coloured bars) and the second (green bars). Results are shown for Ontario as a whole and from each of the five regions separately. The length of the bar represents the probability of a species being found in a square after 20 hours of effort, and the specific percentage is printed at the end of the bar. An asterisk (*) following the second atlas percentage figure indicates that there was a statistically significant difference between the first and second atlas results; significance is determined as $p<0.1$.

To simplify the explanation and save space in the text, these values are described as the "probability of observation" of the species rather than the "probability that a species would be found in a square after 20 hours of effort," though the latter is in fact a more accurate depiction of the data.

In the text describing change between atlases, the percentage value given is the proportional change between the two atlases. For example, if the species went from a 20% probability of observation in the first atlas to 30% in the second atlas, the increase is 50%.

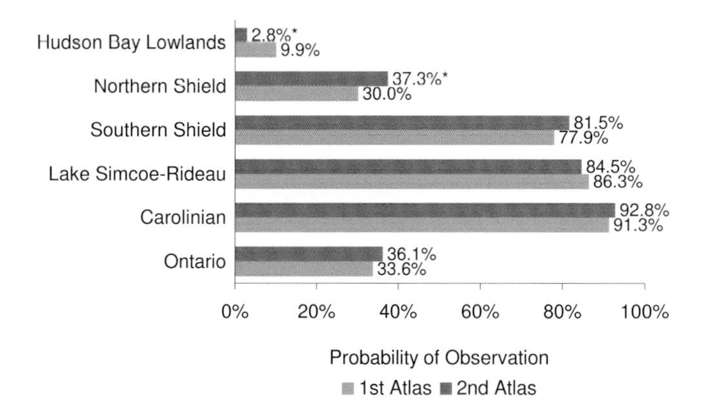

Figure 5.3. Example of a histogram showing the probability of observation of the species in each region and in the province as a whole in both atlases.

For most colonial species, the probability of observation values used in the histogram and the change statistics are based on confirmed breeding records alone. This approach provides the probability of finding a breeding colony in 20 hours of effort, which we think provides a better indication of change than would the probability of finding any breeding evidence for these species; if these species are nesting in a square, confirmed breeding is likely to be recorded. The following colonial species are those for which confirmed breeding records are used to calculate probability of observation: Snow Goose, American White Pelican, Double-crested Cormorant, Great Blue Heron, Great Egret, Black-crowned Night-Heron, Ring-billed Gull, Great Black-backed Gull, Caspian Tern, Common Tern, Arctic Tern, and Forster's Tern. However, for the Bonaparte's Gull, Herring Gull, and Black Tern, as for all the non-colonial species, all breeding evidence records are used to determine the probability of observation because colonies can be hard to find or consist of very few pairs; the species is often actually nesting at localities where unconfirmed breeding records are provided.

Appendix 2 provides the raw number of squares in which each species was reported in each of the five regions and in all of Ontario during each atlas, and shows the number of possible, probable, and confirmed records for each species.

Throughout the species accounts (and other parts of the book), the term "significant" is used only for statistically significant results. For BBS results, "significant" means statistically significant at $p<0.05$, and "marginally significant" or "near-significant" means at $p<0.1$.

Abundance maps

The Methods chapter describes how point count data were collected, analyzed, and mapped. Relative abundance maps (Figure 5.4) are provided for the 130 species whose maps were judged to provide an adequate representation of the species' relative abundance in the province. No maps are shown for species poorly represented on the atlas point counts (e.g., waterfowl and rare or nocturnal birds).

The abundance maps show the pattern of relative abundance of each species in either southern or northern Ontario, and the whole province. Region boundaries are shown on all relative abundance maps. The legend shows the average number of birds per 25 point counts, with darker colours showing higher relative abundance. A value of, for example, 4.0 birds/25 point counts means that an experienced birder stopping for five minutes at each of 25 random locations in a square, during the peak of the breeding season, could expect to hear or see, on average, a total of four birds of that species.

In southern Ontario, where point count coverage was quite comprehensive (see Coverage and Results chapter), the maps provide a fairly accurate portrayal of the relative abundance of each species. However, in northern Ontario, particularly in the far north, squares with point counts were much more widely scattered, so interpolation over great distances with no data between was required. Therefore, when interpreting the data on maps for northern Ontario, look for the broad patterns revealed rather than the specific peaks and valleys in relative abundance. Assessments of relative abundance in the north are best made at the level of the ecoregion (see Figure 2.1 in the Biogeography chapter.)

A different kind of abundance map is provided for six colonial species, Double-crested Cormorant, Great Egret, Black-crowned Night-Heron, Ring-billed Gull, Caspian Tern, and Forster's Tern. Reasonably comprehensive data on colony size

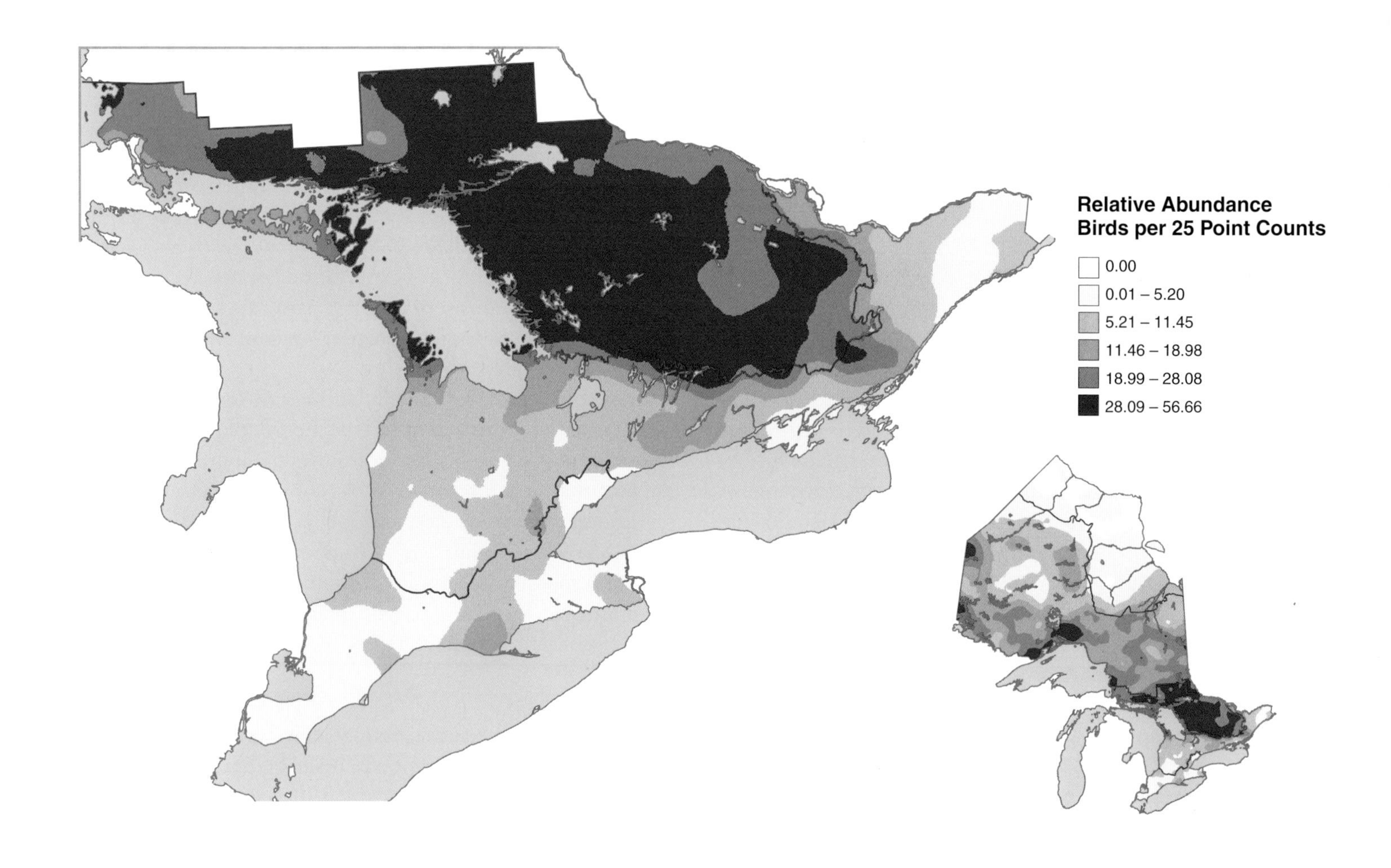

Figure 5.4. Example of a southern Ontario and all-Ontario relative abundance map

for these species were available from the atlas database, and this has allowed us to map the number of breeding pairs of each species per square. The data for these maps were provided largely by CWS, which conducts regular counts of the birds in many of these colonies on the Great Lakes, but some data were provided by volunteers, particularly away from the Great Lakes. The majority of the records mapped are from the atlas period (2001-2005), but if data were not available for 2001-2005, CWS data from 1998-2000 were used for Great Lakes colonies.

Individual treatment of each species

For each species for which breeding evidence was reported during the second atlas, a breeding evidence map for all of Ontario by 100-km block is shown. However, because of limited space and because some species were reported only in southern or northern Ontario, or do not have abundance maps, each species is given one of six standard treatments using the following maps:

1. Breeding evidence and abundance maps for southern Ontario;
2. Breeding evidence map only for southern Ontario;
3. Breeding evidence map only for northern Ontario;
4. Breeding evidence maps for both southern and northern Ontario;
5. Breeding evidence and abundance maps for northern Ontario;
6. Breeding evidence map for southern and northern Ontario and abundance map for all of Ontario.

Generally, because coverage was so much more comprehensive in southern Ontario, the southern maps show the extent of the species' distribution more precisely and completely than do the northern maps. Therefore, if a species occurred in both the north and south, the southern Ontario breeding evidence map is always shown; the northern Ontario breeding evidence map is shown only if there is no abundance map for the species. For species that do occur in the north, but for which no northern breeding evidence map is given, the all-Ontario inset breeding evidence map shows the general distribution in the north.

Similarly, if a relative abundance map is available for both the north and south, the southern Ontario relative abundance map is shown, and the species' relative abundance in northern Ontario can be seen on the all-Ontario map.

The sixth category was used for species occurring in both northern and southern Ontario but whose relative abundance data were best mapped at the all-Ontario scale rather than in either southern or northern Ontario. In these species, the pattern of relative abundance should be interpreted cautiously, and only at a broad regional scale.

Abbreviations used in the text

The following are the standard abbreviations used in the text:

- AOU for American Ornithologists' Union
- BBS for Breeding Bird Survey
- BCR for Bird Conservation Region
- BSC for Bird Studies Canada
- CBC for Christmas Bird Count
- CMMN for Canadian Migration Monitoring Network
- Co. for County
- COSEWIC for the Committee on the Status of Endangered Wildlife in Canada
- COSSARO for the Committee on the Status of Species at Risk in Ontario
- CWS for Environment Canada's Canadian Wildlife Service
- Dist. for District
- GTA for Greater Toronto Area
- LPBO for Long Point Bird Observatory
- MMP for Marsh Monitoring Program
- Nat. Park for National Park
- OBRC for Ontario Bird Records Committee
- OMNR for Ontario Ministry of Natural Resources
- Prov. Park for Provincial Park
- RM for Regional Municipality
- TCBO for Thunder Cape Bird Observatory
- US for United States

The following are brief descriptions of some of the abbreviations used in the text:

The **BBS** is an annual survey of breeding birds conducted primarily by volunteers, who follow a predetermined, roadside route each year during the height of the breeding season. The resultant data are used to determine long-term population trends in North America's breeding birds.

The **CBC** is an annual one-day field count of winter birds undertaken by volunteers between 14 December and 5 January within defined circular areas. The observations have been amassed into a huge database that reflects the distribution and numbers of winter birds over time.

The **CMMN** is a network of bird observatories and monitoring stations in Canada and the northern US that uses a combination of standardized banding and daily counts of migrants to monitor bird populations.

The **LPBO** is comprised of three field stations on Long Point that monitor bird migration. The bird observatory is part of the CMMN.

The **MMP** is an annual survey of marsh birds and amphibians conducted primarily by volunteers in marsh habitats. The MMP provides long-term monitoring of marsh birds and amphibians and their habitats.

The **TCBO** is a CMMN station located at the southern tip of the Sibley Peninsula on Lake Superior's north shore.

ATLAS OF THE BREEDING BIRDS OF ONTARIO, 2001-2005

Species Accounts

Snow Goose

Oie des neiges

Chen caerulescens

Jim Richards

The Snow Goose is the most abundant goose in the world. It breeds from Wrangel Island in the Russian Far East to northwest Greenland, and as far south as James Bay (Mowbray et al. 2000). Although widespread, it nests in relatively few sites in persistent colonies, the largest being in the Canadian Arctic archipelago and on Wrangel Island. It winters from Washington and British Columbia south to Mexico and east to the Mid-Atlantic States. The Lesser Snow Goose (*Chen caerulescens caerulescens*), the form that breeds in Ontario and James Bay, is the more abundant of the two subspecies overall.

Distribution and population status: The Snow Goose breeds on the Hudson Bay and James Bay coasts from the Pen Islands to Cape Henrietta Maria and south to Akimiski Island. Although the distribution of 100-km blocks with breeding evidence was nearly continuous, as in the first atlas, this masks great variation in relative abundance. The majority nest in four discrete colonies established in the late 1940s (Cape Henrietta Maria), 1960s (Akimiski Island), and 1980s (West Pen Island and Shell Brook) (Hanson et al. 1972; Abraham et al. 1999; Kerbes et al. 2006). About 1-2% of Ontario Snow Geese nest outside major colonies, frequently in estuaries with small islands and near small patches of salt marsh brood-rearing habitat along Hudson Bay and northwest James Bay.

The increase of the Snow Goose in North America, including Ontario, over the latter half of the twentieth century is well documented (Abraham and Jefferies 1997; Mowbray et al. 2000). The Cape Henrietta Maria colony grew threefold since the first atlas, and the smaller colonies doubled or increased from their initial establishment to hundreds or several thousands of pairs. However, overall Ontario numbers appear to have stabilized during the current atlas period, which is likely related to population management efforts in the mid-

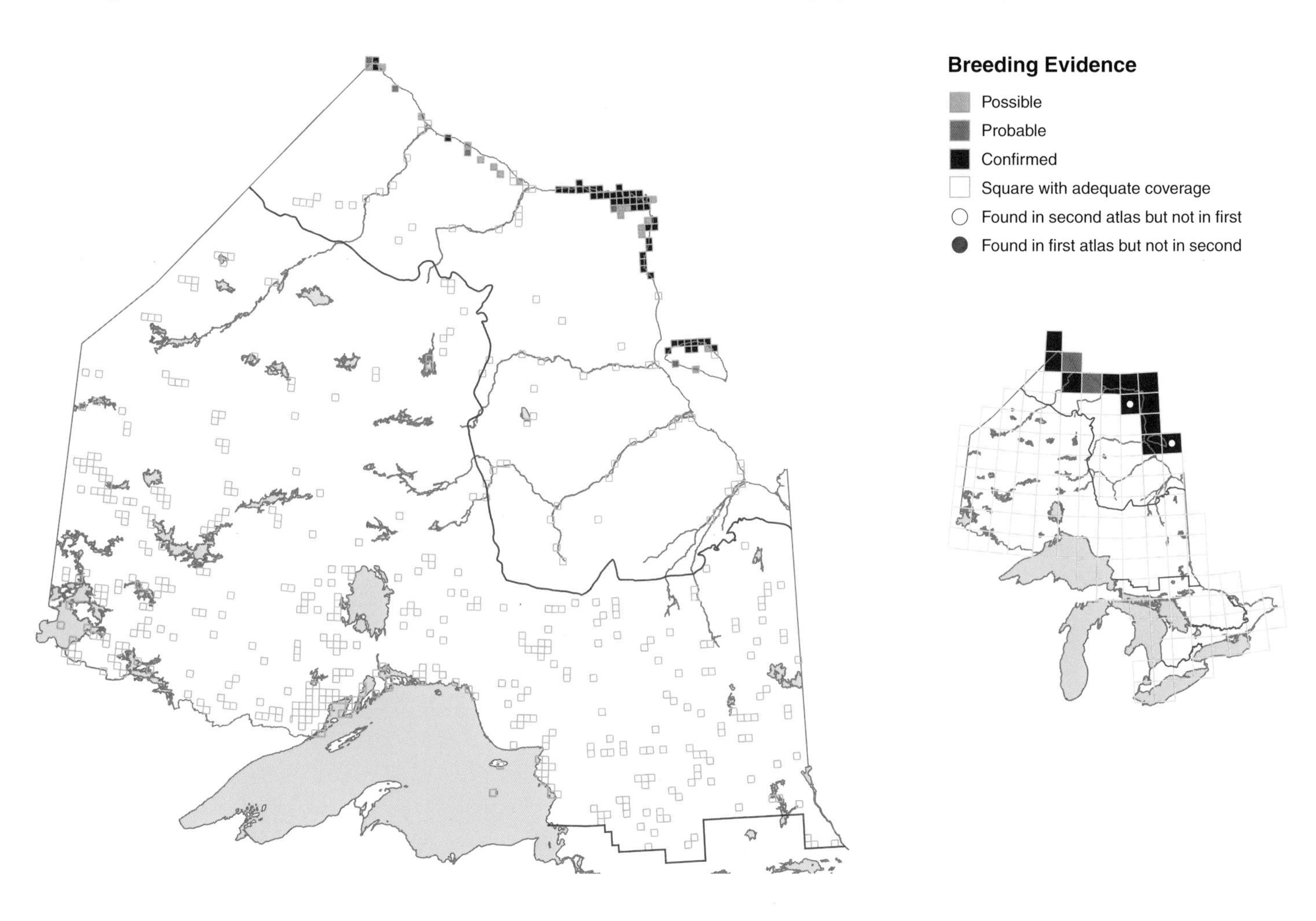

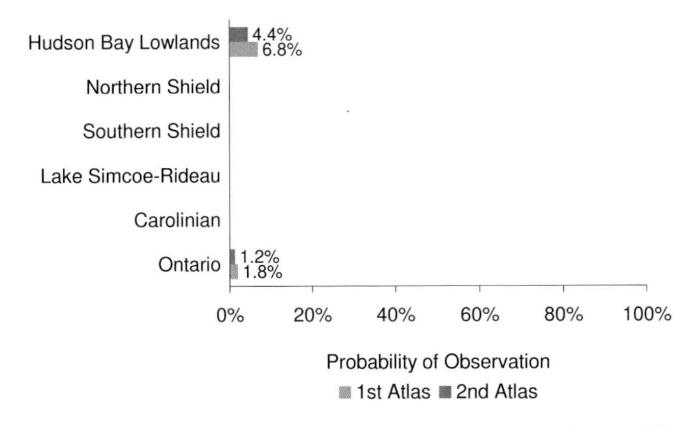

continent migration and wintering areas, and possibly to habitat degradation.

Breeding biology: The Snow Goose forms lifelong pairs while on wintering areas (Mowbray et al. 2000) and can breed into its twenties (Cooke et al. 1995). On migration, the female stores much of the energy required to produce a clutch of three to seven eggs but can continue to do so on breeding areas when conditions permit. This strategy is insurance against poor conditions on the breeding grounds. Annual nest timing is highly correlated with spring weather and can vary annually by up to three weeks due to snow, ice, and melt-water cover conditions. Pairs defend small areas around the nest; spacing of about 5 to 30 m is usual, but can be as little as 1 m. High densities and conspicuous defence behaviour makes atlas breeding confirmation easy. Incubation takes about 24 days from clutch completion, and the goslings hatch synchronously within about a day. Both parents share brood-rearing duties over six weeks until fledging. Amalgamated brood flocks of tens to hundreds of pairs with young also make breeding confirmation simple. A minor complication for determining nesting distribution is the Snow Goose trait of walking tens of kilometres during brood rearing, making an observation of a family with pre-fledged young an inconclusive record of nest location. Strong family bonds are maintained until the next breeding season and sometimes beyond.

Abundance: Aerial surveys of the four Hudson Bay Lowlands colonies were made in 2005 to determine distribution and abundance (CWS and OMNR, unpubl. data). Estimates of colony size and distribution from 1997 surveys and colour morph compositions from banding during all atlas years at Cape Henrietta Maria and Akimiski Island were reported in Kerbes et al. (2006).

The Cape Henrietta Maria colony occupied parts of 24 squares in 2005 over a 100 km stretch of coast from Sutton River to the Cape, with an estimated 130,000 pairs, of which 64% were blue morph geese. In 1997, highest densities were 1,155 adults per km^2. The West Pen Island colony occupied portions of only two squares in 2005 but had 8,500 pairs. In 1997, it had the highest recorded densities of any colony (2,302 adults per km^2). The Shell Brook colony changed substantially between 1997 and 2005. In 1997, it covered 7 km^2 in parts of two squares and contained 2,650 pairs at densities of up to 701 adults per km^2. However, in 2005 it had fewer than 1,000 pairs. The Akimiski Island colony stretched over five atlas squares at low density. There were 1,700 pairs in 1997 at densities up to 340 adults per km^2, but only approximately 1,000 pairs in 2005, with 77% blue morph. – *Ken Abraham*

Goslings within a single clutch hatch relatively synchronously within 24-48 hours of each other. *Photo: George K. Peck*

On the Hudson Bay coast of Ontario, most Snow Goose nests are found within 10 km of the coast in willow-dominated tundra habitats. *Photo: Ken Abraham*

Ross's Goose

Oie de Ross

Chen rossii

Lorraine Norris

Formerly considered the rarest goose in North America, and restricted as a breeder to the central Canadian Arctic and as a wintering bird to California, the Ross's Goose now breeds throughout the central and eastern Arctic and Subarctic south to James Bay in most of the sites where the Lesser Snow Goose breeds. It winters from California, New Mexico, and Mexico to Texas and Louisiana (Ryder and Alisauskas 1995). Although most known colonies (containing 90% of the continental population) are still in the Queen Maud Gulf area, a large Ross's Goose colony became established near Arviat on the west coast of Hudson Bay in the early 1990s. By spring 1998, there was an estimated minimum of 542,000 breeding adults in the central and eastern Arctic and 800,000 of these geese overall (Kelley et al. 2001; Kerbes et al. 2006). During migration and winter, the Ross's Goose is now found wherever the Lesser Snow Goose is found. The majority winters in California, but the number wintering in the mid-continent is estimated at more than 106,000 (Kelley et al. 2001). This eastward range expansion has led to regular occurrences of migrants in the Northern Shield, Lake Simcoe-Rideau, and Carolinian regions in Ontario (Roy 2002), and elsewhere in eastern North America.

Distribution and population status: The Ross's Goose nests in dense colonies in its core breeding areas (Ryder and Alisauskas 1995). Although some colonies are almost exclusively comprised of this species, increasingly it nests in mixed colonies with the Lesser Snow Goose, and this is especially characteristic of the expanded eastern Arctic range, including the Hudson Bay Lowlands. Although the first provincial evidence of breeding was obtained when flightless young were found at Cape Henrietta Maria in 1975 (Prevett and Johnson 1977), the only breeding record in the first atlas was obtained on Akimiski Island. During the second atlas, confirmed breeding evidence was obtained in six squares, all in the Cape Henrietta Maria area of the Hudson

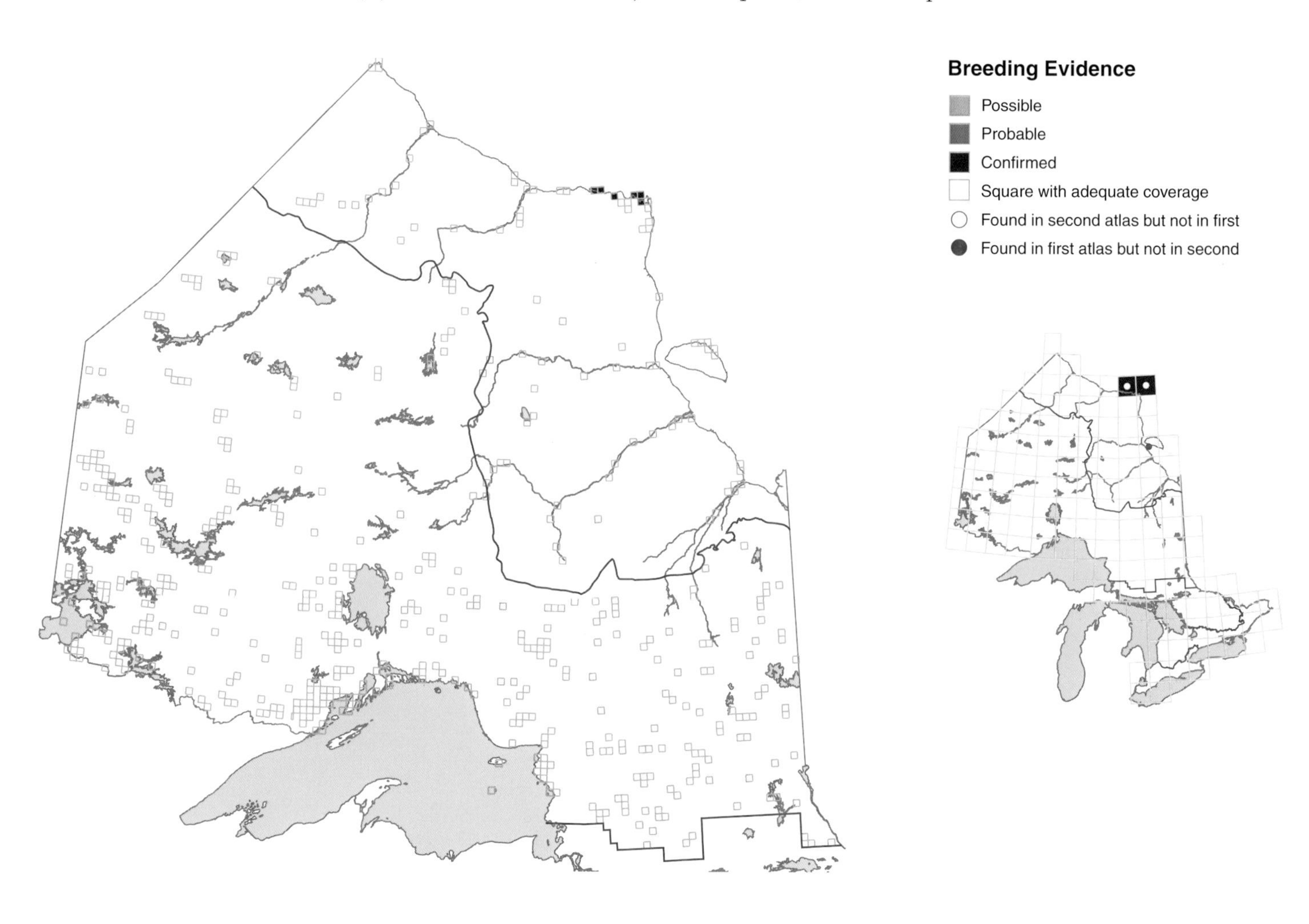

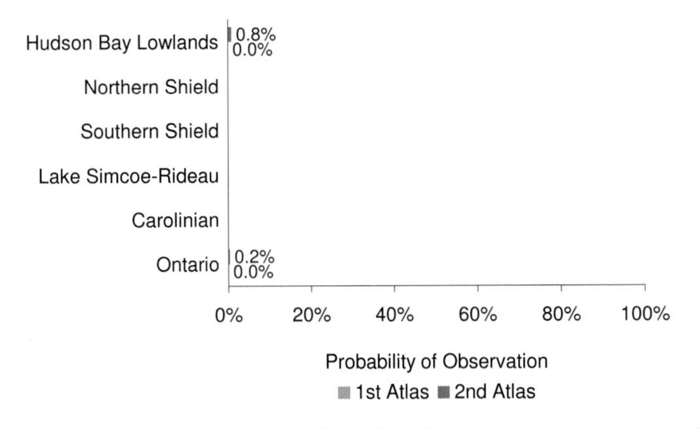

Bay Lowlands. These included the first Ontario nest records (Coady et al. 2007) and several broods of pre-fledged young captured during mass banding drives (Abraham 2002 and unpubl. data). Almost certainly, the Ross's Goose also occurs as a breeder in other Ontario and James Bay Snow Goose colonies. However, the main method of confirmation has been mass banding of flightless broods, which was not conducted at either of the colonies at West Pen Island or Shell Brook during the atlas period. Breeding evidence was not found on Akimiski Island in the second atlas, despite banding there. The numbers of Ross's Goose in Ontario have increased in correspondence with the general population trend in eastern North America. In addition to the breeding evidence reported here, Cree hunters along the Hudson Bay coast have noted the increase during the annual goose hunt.

Breeding biology: Most aspects of Ross's Goose ecology are very similar to those of the Lesser Snow Goose, including clutch size, incubation period, and post-hatch behaviour. The Ross's Goose nests at even higher densities than the Snow Goose, but unlike the Snow Goose (which is strongly associated with coastal salt marshes or near-coast sedge fens), the principal and largest colonies of the species are found on large islands in inland freshwater lakes (Ryder and Alisauskas 1995).

The Ross's Goose reaches fledging approximately one week earlier than the Snow Goose. Several factors coincide to make atlas verification of breeding difficult: the similarity in appearance between these two species (compounded by hybridization); the relative rarity of the Ross's Goose compared to the Lesser Snow Goose in the Ontario colonies; the remote location and difficulty of accessing the breeding colonies; and even annual variation in nesting conditions. An example of the latter was a nearly complete breeding failure related to weather conditions in 2004, the one year when an atlas crew was stationed at the West Pen Islands during nesting.

Abundance: Despite its increase since the first atlas, the Ross's Goose remains a rare breeding bird in Ontario. The best measure of its abundance is a comparison with the more abundant Lesser Snow Goose. Although the Ross's Goose was captured in all atlas years, only 64 adults and 49 goslings (vs. 16,764 Snow Goose adults and 6,686 goslings) were banded, representing less than 1% of captures in relation to the Snow Goose in both age classes. Additionally, the captures were geographically concentrated in a small area of the overall Cape Henrietta Maria Snow Goose range, suggesting a clumped distribution and a relatively small total population of perhaps a few hundred pairs. – *Ken Abraham*

The first nest of the Ross's Goose found in Ontario (Coady et al. 2007). *Photo: Colin D. Jones*

Still rare in Ontario, the Ross's Goose nests in Snow Goose colonies in coastal areas dominated by small ponds, willow thickets, and tundra vegetation. *Photo: Colin D. Jones*

Cackling Goose

Bernache de Hutchins

Branta hutchinsii

Ted (E.R.) Armstrong

In 2004, the AOU assigned the 11 former subspecies of Canada Goose to two species: the Canada Goose and the Cackling Goose (Banks et al. 2004). The Cackling Goose breeds only in North America, from the Aleutian Islands to the arctic islands of eastern Canada (Banks et al. 2004). Three of four currently recognized subspecies breed only in Alaska, while the most abundant subspecies, *hutchinsii*, breeds over most of the Canadian Arctic to west Greenland (Mowbray et al. 2002). It breeds from Banks Island and the Queen Maud Gulf to Southampton Island and Baffin Island, extending southward along Hudson Bay to about 60° N. The Aleutian subspecies *leucopareia* is limited to the Aleutian Islands and consists of about 70,000 birds, based on midwinter counts, having increased from endangered status in the 1970s when fewer than 1,000 remained. The Cackling subspecies *minima* is found in coastal southwest Alaska and now numbers about 160,000 in midwinter after recovering from a severe decline in the 1980s. The *taverneri* subspecies is found in northern Alaska, although its numerical status is unknown. There are two managed units that contain *hutchinsii*: the Short Grass Prairie and the Tall Grass Prairie populations (U.S. Fish and Wildlife Service 2006). The midwinter index of the former is stable at about 200,000, but the latter has been increasing at 6% per year, with a current midwinter index of nearly 500,000. Ontario migrants belong to this population.

Distribution and population status: The Cackling Goose occurs throughout Ontario during migration but is found in abundance only in the Hudson Bay Lowlands. It also regularly occurs in the hundreds as a migrant in the Thunder Bay area and in small groups or as individuals throughout the remainder of the province (Abraham 2005). Its appearance is nearly identical to the Canada Goose, with the principal exception of size. When compared with the common Canada Goose subspecies that occurs in Ontario, the Cackling Goose is distinctly

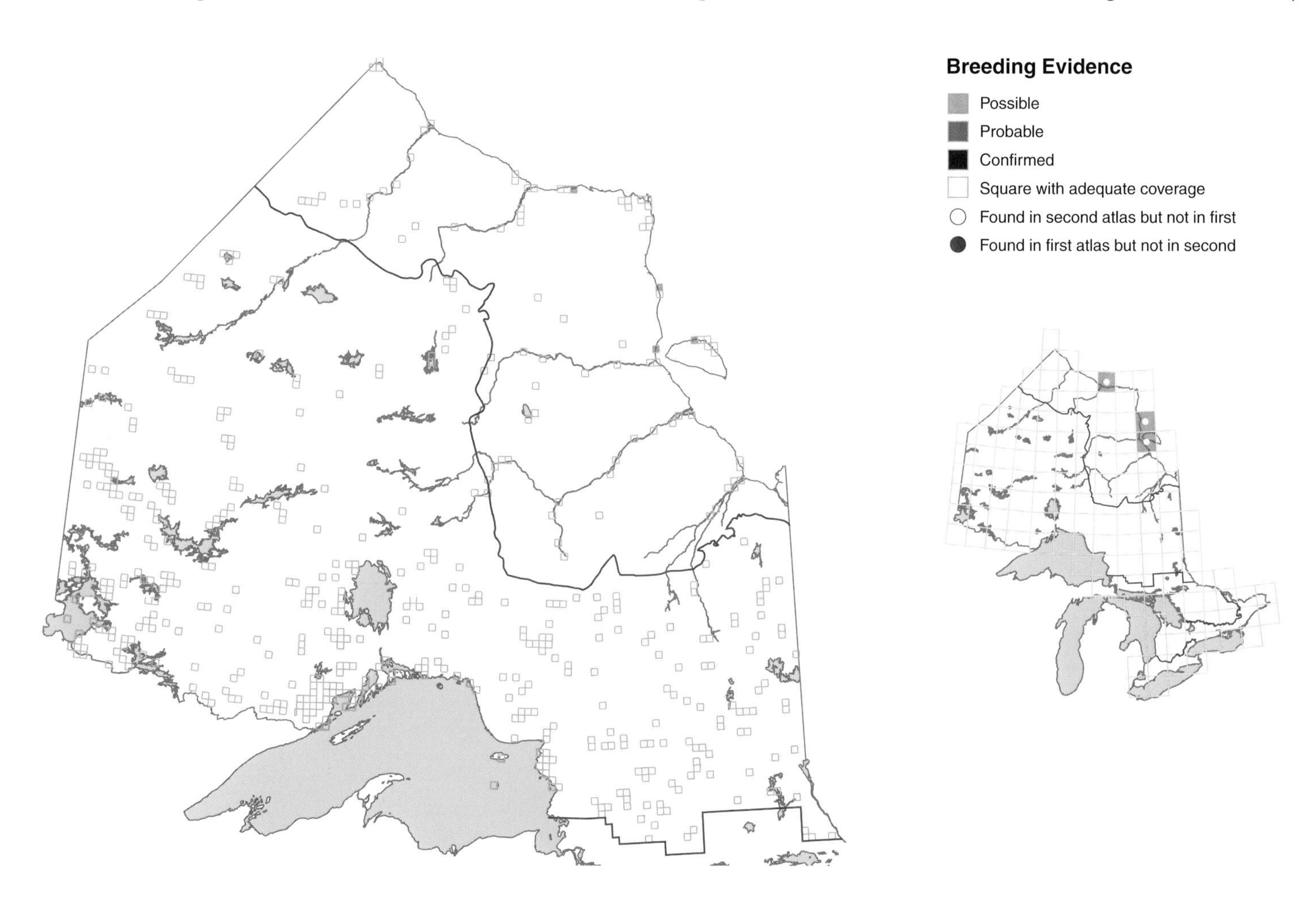

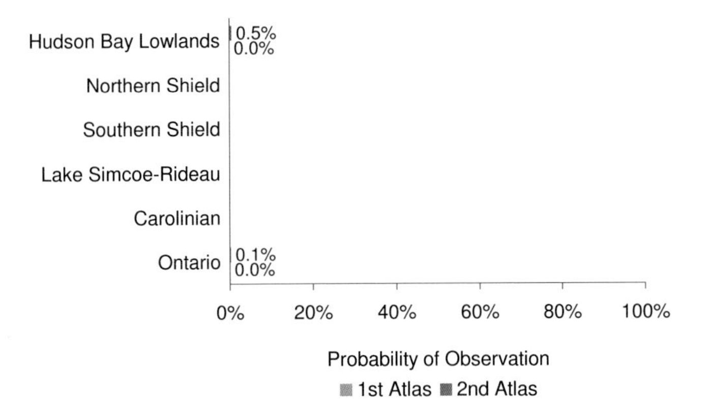

smaller, with a proportionately shorter and more triangular bill, shorter neck, and shorter legs.

During the atlas period, four Cackling Geese were captured along the Hudson Bay and James Bay coasts, each in a separate square (a female in 2003 and a female and two males in 2004). These four birds were flightless and caught with families of non- and failed-breeding Canada Geese in suitable habitat. Neither of the females had brood patches indicative of a breeding attempt. However, they may have been yearlings returning to their natal areas (a common goose behaviour) or adults separated from mates or offspring by the banding operations. These Cackling Geese were deemed to represent evidence of possible breeding; although geese are known for undertaking moult migrations, the principal breeding range is well to the north, and moult migrations rarely occur in a southward direction. Breeding in Ontario was confirmed on 25 July 2006 when a pair and two flightless goslings were captured near Cape Henrietta Maria (Abraham and Armstrong, in prep.).

Breeding biology: The breeding biology of the Cackling Goose is similar in almost all respects to the northern breeding Canada Goose (Mowbray et al. 2002). It is monogamous and maintains year-round, lifelong pair bonds, re-pairing on death of a mate; family structure and cohesiveness are strong, and offspring often associate with parents through spring migration. It nests on tundra in areas with abundant lakes, ponds, and marshes and prefers islands and peninsulas for its nest sites. This is likely an adaptation to the risk of nest loss from ground predators such as the Arctic Fox, but it does not hinder nest finding by atlassers. Clutches consist of three to seven eggs which are laid about 1.5 days apart, the 24-26 day incubation period beginning with the laying of the last egg. Goslings are precocial and mobile within hours of hatch. A grazing herbivore, this goose favours areas with abundant grasses and sedges for brood-rearing and tends to have a coastal distribution, occurring in easily detected multi-family flocks.

Abundance: The Cackling Goose is obviously a rare breeding species in Ontario. In 30 years of banding Canada and Snow Geese along the Hudson Bay coast, and with almost 200,000 birds captured, biologists have only eight records of moulting Cackling Geese before the July 2006 observation and no other evidence of breeding. It is likely to be confined to the general area of Cape Henrietta Maria, where climatic and habitat conditions are most similar to its arctic breeding range. It is unclear whether the 2006 breeding record is exceptional or indicates an expansion of breeding range, or whether its rarity has heretofore masked its presence. – *Ken Abraham*

The female Cackling Goose makes herself as inconspicuous as possible when the nest is approached by mammalian predators. *Photo: Frank B. Baldwin*

A flock of migrant or pre-breeding Cackling Geese in an early-thaw year in Polar Bear Provincial Park; Ontario nesting is exceptional, and the birds are likely part of the northern Hudson Bay population. *Photo: Kim Bennett*

Canada Goose

Bernache du Canada

Branta canadensis

Theodore Smith

The Canada Goose is one of the best known of Ontario's birds, once a harbinger of the changing seasons and a symbol of the northern wilds. In recent years, temperate-breeding populations have grown remarkably throughout Canada and the northern half of the US, and the Canada Goose is now a year-round resident across southern Ontario. It exhibits considerable size variation across its range and inhabits a wide variety of habitats including tundra, boreal forest, prairies, agricultural lands, and even urban areas.

Distribution and population status: Across North America, 15 populations of the Canada Goose are recognized (Dickson 2000), and virtually all are stable or growing. The total spring population now exceeds six million (U.S. Fish and Wildlife Service 2006). In Ontario, there are three breeding populations: two in the north – the Mississippi Valley Population (MVP) and the Southern James Bay Population (SJBP), which occupy different parts of the Hudson Bay Lowlands, and one in the south, the temperate-breeding population. Large numbers of geese from other populations occur during spring, fall, and pre-moult migration: the Atlantic Population in eastern Ontario, the Eastern Prairie Population in northwestern Ontario, and birds from temperate-breeding populations in the Atlantic and Mississippi flyways.

Historically, the Canada Goose probably bred in southwestern Ontario in small numbers but was extirpated during the early years of settlement. In the 1920s, aviculturists began to reintroduce it in a few areas, and in the 1960s, OMNR started a formal reintroduction program (Lumsden and Dennis 1998). This program resulted in a thriving breeding population across much of southern Ontario, so much so that during the second atlas virtually all squares in the Carolinian and Lake Simcoe-Rideau regions had evidence of confirmed breeding. Between atlases, significant distribution increases were observed in every atlas region. These were the result of infilling and increasing

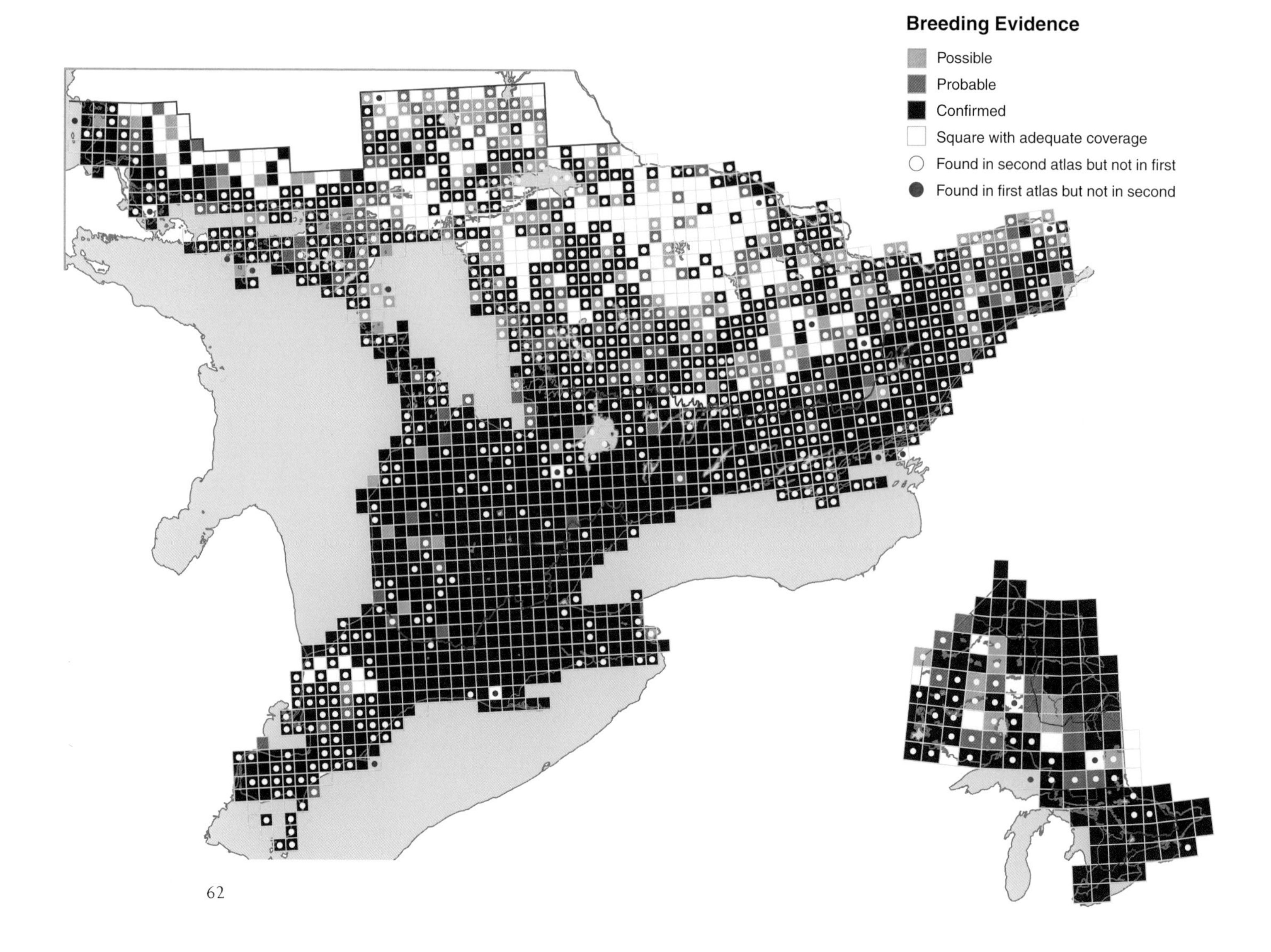

BREEDING EVIDENCE

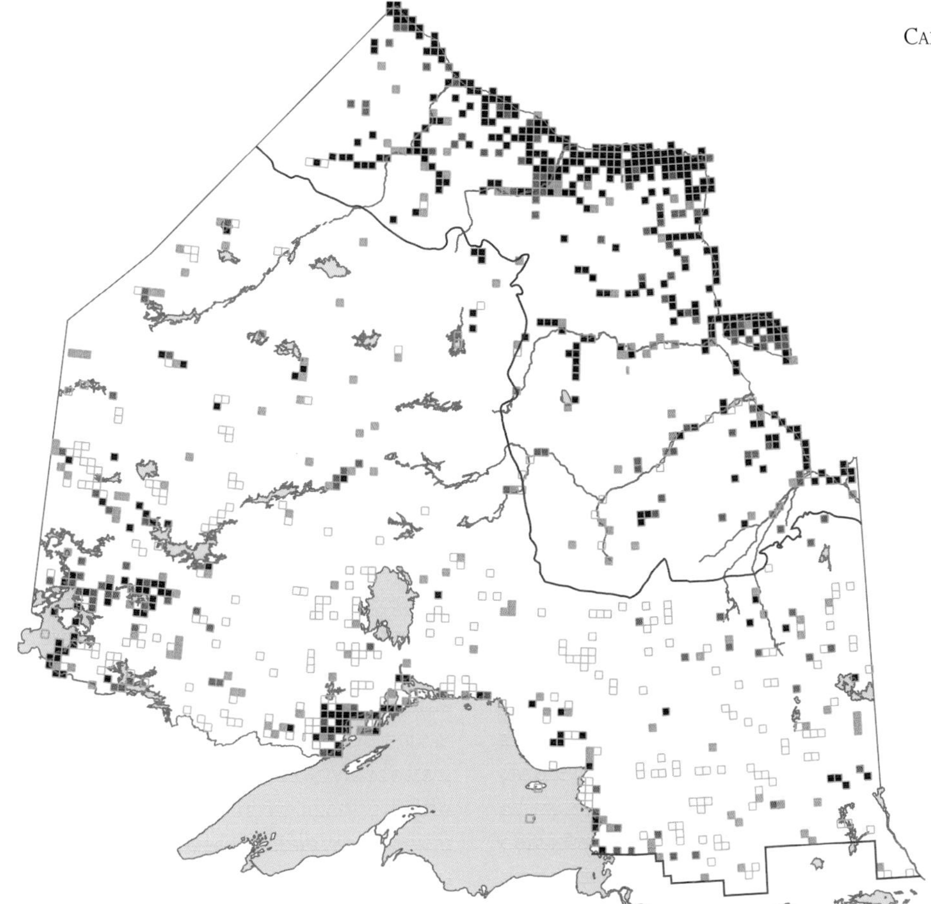

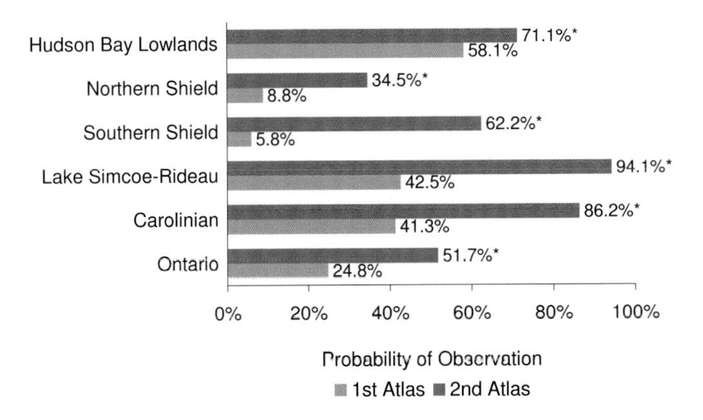

density within the established range. The Northern Shield region historically harboured few if any breeding Canada Geese; however, nesting pairs are now scattered widely, albeit at low density, throughout this region. Where there was formerly a clear separation between the northern and southern populations, the demarcation is slowly becoming less distinct.

Breeding biology: The Canada Goose is a highly adaptable species. On the tundra, it nests near ponds and lakes or in salt marshes and wet meadows; in the muskeg, it nests mainly near ponds and fens; in wooded areas of the Shield regions, it favours beaver ponds and lakeshores; in southern, human-modified landscapes, it nests near lakes, ponds, rivers, and farm impoundments, and even in city parks. It generally prefers to nest on small islands or along shorelines but will occasionally use elevated sites such as hummocks, the fork of a large tree, or a rooftop. Nests are constructed of whatever materials are close at hand such as grasses, mosses, or small twigs and are lined with down from the female's breast. Females typically lay four to six eggs at a rate of about one every 1.5 days. Goslings hatch after about 28 days of incubation, and within one to two days following hatch, the two parents lead them away from the nest to feeding areas where they can find tender young grasses and sedges and usually have quick access to water for protection from predators (Mowbray et al. 2002).

Abundance: Breeding density varies widely. Two areas of concentration occur: in the northern Hudson Bay Lowlands and in the Carolinian and Lake Simcoe-Rideau regions of southern Ontario. The highest densities occur in the north in coastal areas and along river drainages. In coastal areas where the Canada Goose nests semi-colonially, densities can reach 5-9 nests/km^2 over large areas (Bruggink et al. 1994). In the south, the highest densities occur in areas that are dominated by a mix of agriculture and forest. The largest high-density areas are in the upper watersheds of the Grand, Thames, Maitland, and Saugeen Rivers. Other important breeding areas in southern Ontario include the Severn Sound, Toronto, St. Lawrence River valley, and Ottawa areas. Elsewhere, breeding densities are much lower.

Ground surveys of breeding waterfowl in southern Ontario south of the French and Mattawa Rivers estimated the 2006 temperate-breeding Canada Goose population at 182,000 nesting adults (CWS unpubl. data). Surveys of the SJBP and MVP between 2001 and 2005 resulted in combined average estimates of 420,000 nesting adults. Geese in the Northern Shield are not routinely surveyed due to their relatively low numbers. However, adding estimates of non-breeders and failed breeders to the northern and southern survey results puts the total Ontario spring population at about 1,000,000 individuals. *– Jack Hughes and Ken Abraham*

Mute Swan

Cygne tuberculé

Cygnus olor

Mark Peck

The Mute Swan is among the largest of the world's waterfowl and is readily distinguished from other Ontario swans by its long curved neck, orange bill with black, basal knob, and characteristically subdued grunting, snorting, and whistling vocalizations. The species is native to Eurasia, but feral populations became established in eastern North America during the late 1800s following escapes or intentional releases from captive flocks (Ciaranca et al. 1997). The Mute Swan has a discontinuous breeding distribution across the continent. Small populations occur in the Pacific Northwest on Vancouver Island and at other locales within the Georgia Basin (Campbell et al. 1990). The largest resident population is located along the US Atlantic coast from Maine to South Carolina (Ciaranca et al. 1997). During the mid-1900s, the Mute Swan established semi-resident populations within coastal and inland marshes in the Great Lakes region of the US and Canada (Lumsden in Cadman et al. 1987; Ciaranca et al. 1997), where numbers are now rapidly increasing (Petrie and Francis 2003). The first nest in Ontario was documented at Georgetown, Halton Co., in 1958 (Peck 1966).

Distribution and population status: As in the first atlas, the Mute Swan breeding distribution is confined almost exclusively to the Carolinian and Lake Simcoe-Rideau regions of southern Ontario. The second atlas, however, shows this species is now more broadly distributed within those regions along the coasts of Lake St. Clair, Lake Erie, and Lake Ontario, with some breeding reported at inland wetlands and lakes. The probability of observation of the Mute Swan increased significantly in both the Lake Simcoe-Rideau and Carolinian regions, which resulted in an overall increase within the province between the first and second atlases. The species also was detected in more squares east of Toronto during the current atlas, resulting in a 134 km range expansion eastward.

These results are consistent with the rapid increases in Mute

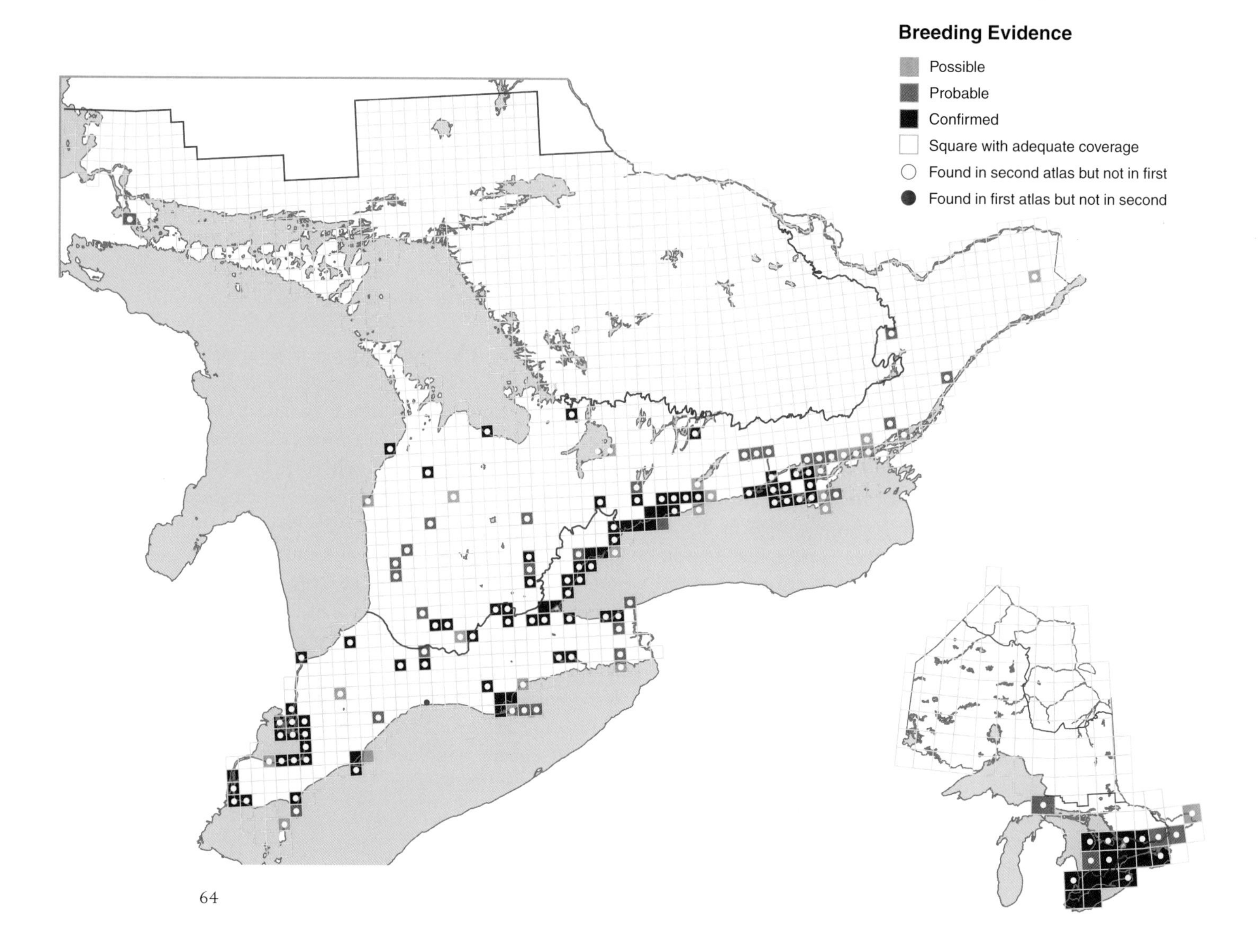

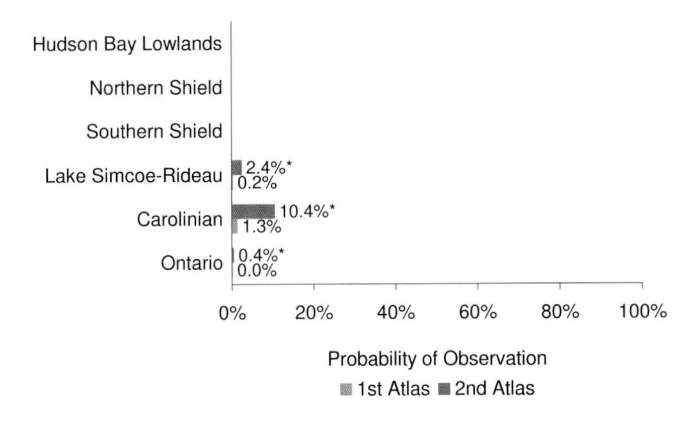

Swan numbers that have occurred on both the US and Canadian sides of the lower Great Lakes since the early to mid-1980s (Petrie and Francis 2003). The increase and range expansion in the Mute Swan population in Ontario can be attributed to several factors, including mild climatic conditions that are similar to those of its native Eurasian range, combined with long-term increasing winter temperatures; high annual reproductive output because of high rates of nest and cygnet survival; and high adult survival rates due to lack of predators and other natural mortality factors. This swan can aggressively displace other native species and, due to its sedentary habits, eat sufficient submerged aquatic plants to degrade breeding and staging habitat for waterfowl and other marsh-dependent wildlife.

Breeding biology: Pairs return early in spring (March) to territories once they are ice-free. Males prominently display on territory during the breeding season and can be aggressive toward other species, even people. Both sexes take part in building very large platform nests, using residual plants, in dense cover along shorelines, on peninsulas and islands, and atop muskrat houses within marshes. Nests containing about five to eight (range: one to 11) large eggs are highly visible at first but become obscured by new plant growth later in the season (Ciaranca et al. 1997). After eggs hatch, parents and cygnets are often visible feeding in open water on submerged aquatic vegetation. Many of these life-history features, along with the species' general conspicuousness, facilitate detection and breeding confirmation (breeding confirmed in 60% of occupied squares).

Abundance: Point count data indicate that Mute Swan abundance is greatest along the lower Great Lakes shorelines and associated coastal marsh habitats. Two general areas show relatively high Mute Swan densities: southwestern Ontario (St. Clair River, Lake St. Clair, and Detroit River to western Lake Erie, including Rondeau Bay); and the western end of Lake Ontario (notably from Grimsby to Oshawa). Lower densities were found in marsh habitats at Long Point Bay in Lake Erie and in the Prince Edward Co. - Bay of Quinte area of eastern Lake Ontario. In 2005, the Ontario lower Great Lakes population was estimated at 2,737 individuals, nearly twice the number counted in 2002 (Mid-summer Mute Swan Survey, unpubl. data). It is suspected that the species has not yet reached carrying capacity of its habitat within southern Ontario (Petrie and Francis 2003). Thus, the Mute Swan's abundance and distribution in southern Ontario likely will continue to increase. – *Shannon S. Badzinski*

Pairs usually return to the female's natal area for nesting. The male may start several nests before the female accepts the site (Ciaranca et al. 1997). *Photo: Jim Richards*

The Mute Swan nests readily in urban marshes. Preferred nest sites have easy access to water and are not readily flooded (Ciaranca et al. 1997). *Photo: George K. Peck*

Trumpeter Swan

Cygne trompette

Cygnus buccinator

George K. Peck

Formerly greatly reduced in numbers, the Trumpeter Swan now breeds in many scattered populations from Alaska to Ontario. In 2005, the continental population was estimated at 34,803 birds (Moser 2006). The Trumpeter Swan was extirpated from Ontario more than a century ago, but restoration was started in 1982 and has since involved the release of 584 captive-reared birds at 54 sites in southern and eastern Ontario.

In Ontario, the Trumpeter Swan might be confused with two other swans. It can be distinguished from the native Tundra Swan by its larger size, absence of a yellow spot on the beak in front of the eye, V-shaped feathering on the forehead projecting onto the upper mandible, and its loud, trumpeting calls. It could be confused with the non-native Mute Swan that as an adult has an orange beak with a black knob at its base. The Mute Swan also swims with its secondary feathers raised and spread over the back in aggression, which the Trumpeter never does.

Distribution and population status: Restoration of the Trumpeter Swan in Ontario was not sufficiently advanced to warrant a distribution map in the first atlas. As of 2005, there are four discrete population centres in Ontario: in northwestern Ontario in Rainy River, Kenora, and Cochrane Districts; in the Sault Ste. Marie area; in southern Ontario from Georgian Bay (Sudbury) south to Lake Erie; and, in extreme southeastern Ontario. In the northwest, swans from the restoration effort in Minnesota have expanded north into the Kenora area where the first known breeding took place in 1989 in the vicinity of Oak Lake, 85 km northeast of Kenora. During the second atlas, the species was detected in 12 squares, with breeding confirmed in six. About half the broods and nests recorded were concentrated in two squares; however, this population is otherwise very scattered, extending from western Rainy River Dist. north to Little Sachigo Lake, Kenora Dist. There have been three observations from the air of pairs in the Lowlands well south of the known distribution of the Tundra Swan. There is no certainty on the

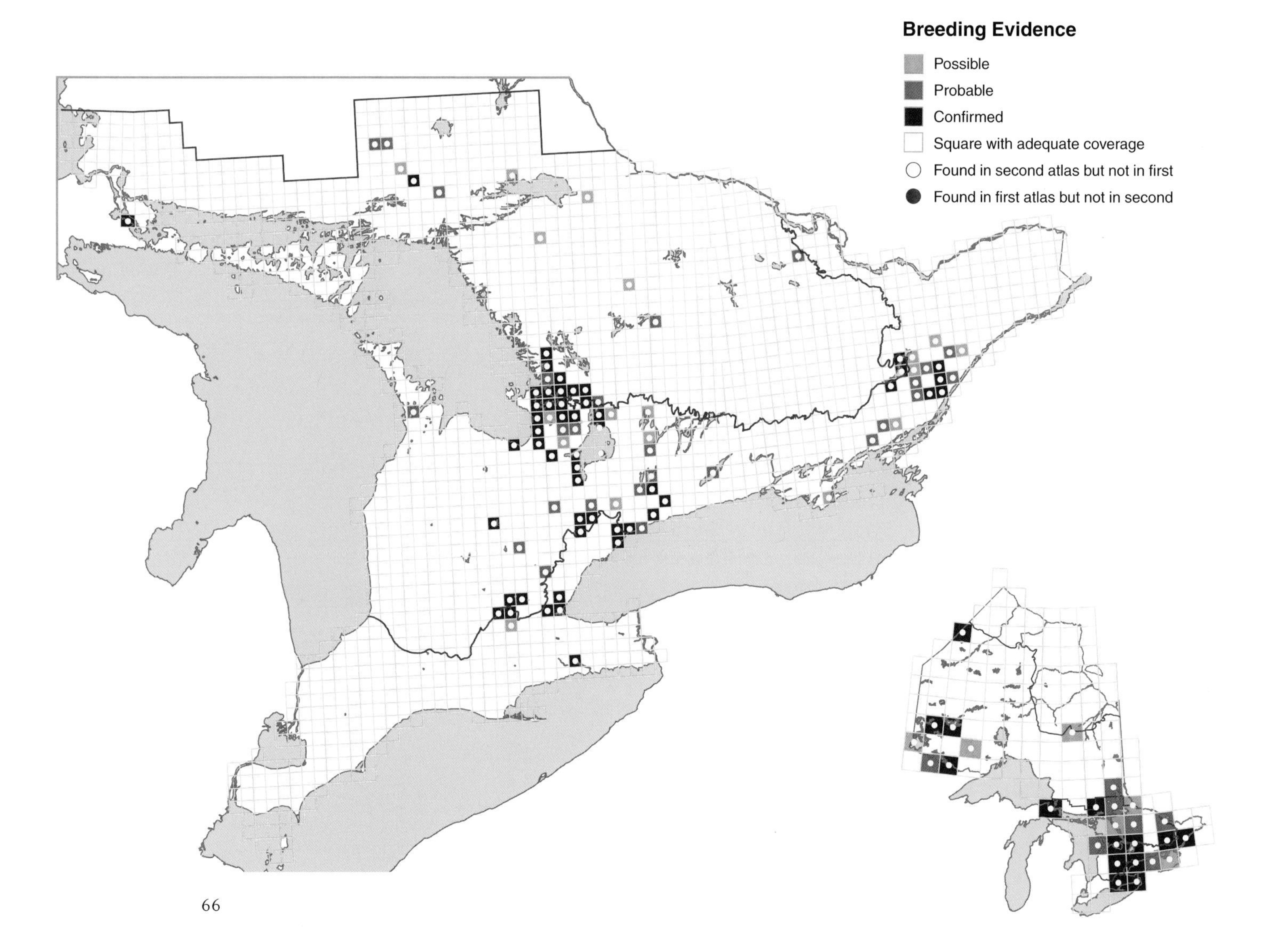

BREEDING EVIDENCE

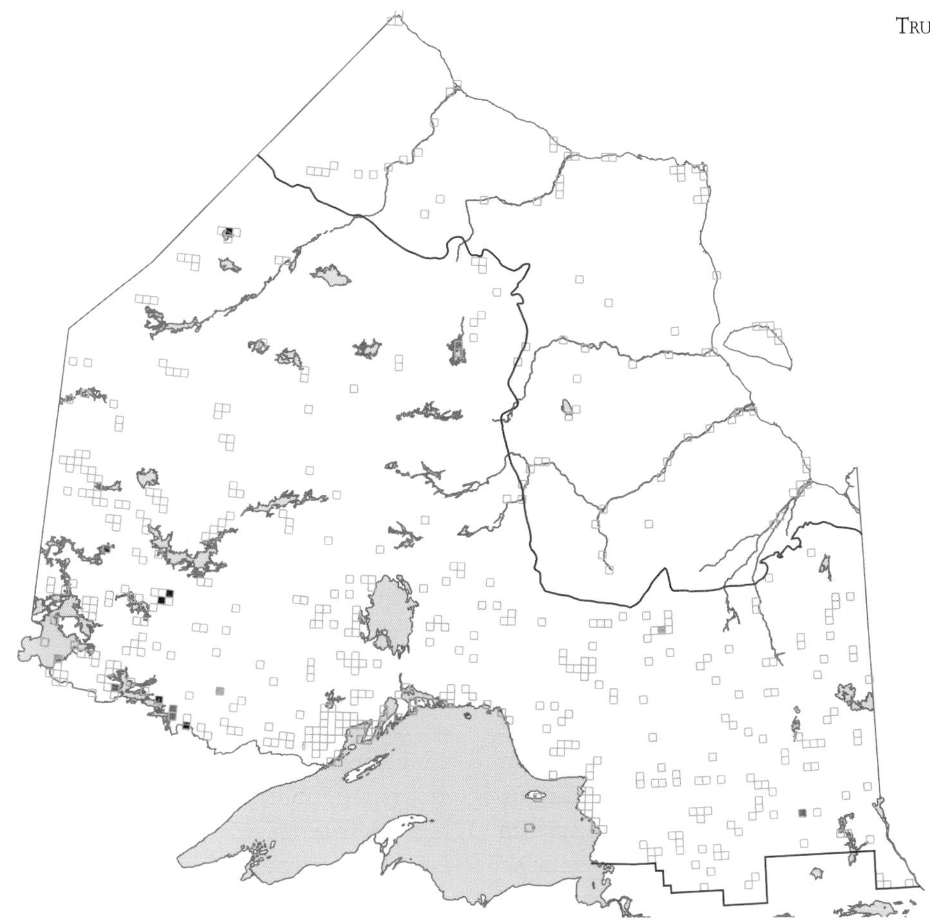

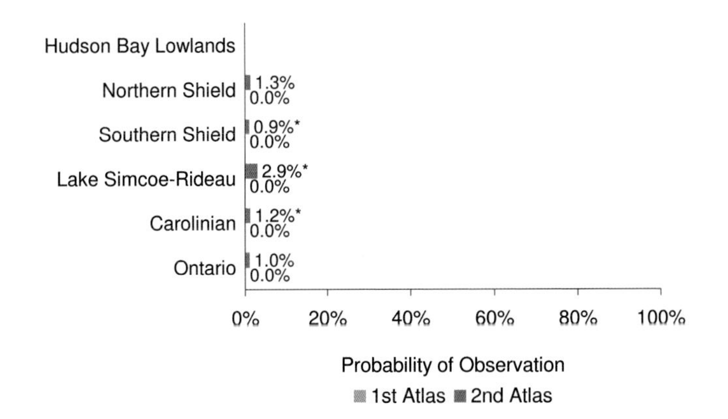

identity of one pair, but a photograph suggests Trumpeter Swans for one record, and the presence of wing tags gives certainty for the other. There were at least 65 swans in this population in 2005.

In the Sault Ste. Marie area, birds have spread north from the expanding Michigan population. In 2005, two broods were found on St. Joseph Island.

The largest Ontario population is distributed from the area around Sudbury to the east of Georgian Bay to Lake Erie. The highest density is found between Lake Simcoe and Huntsville, with birds scattered in a few locations in the GTA and south and west to Hamilton and Cambridge. This southern Ontario population has been increasing at an annual rate of about 8% and is expanding to new locations every year. Breeding was confirmed in 44 squares, probable in 19, and possible in 12. In September 2005, it was estimated that there were 552 Trumpeter Swans in this population (H. G. Lumsden, unpubl. data).

In southeastern Ontario, the Trumpeter Swan has spread from New York State, arriving on Lower Beverley Lake about 1996 and breeding on Big Rideau Lake in 1997. Releases of captive-raised birds were made at Portland and the Mac Johnston Wildlife Area at Brockville and on Little Cataraqui Creek at Kingston to aid establishment of this population. The atlas shows seven squares with confirmed breeding, seven with probable breeding, and six with possible breeding. There are at least 40 Trumpeter Swans in the southeastern Ontario population.

The overall status of this swan in Ontario can only be described as rapidly expanding. None of the four populations has yet occupied all of its available range. At present, these populations remain discrete, and there is no evidence of interchange.

Breeding biology: The Trumpeter Swan builds its nest in marshes or floodplains of creeks, using old muskrat or beaver houses, islands, or stumps and logs in drowned forest as a base. The nest may be as much as 2.5 m in diameter at the base.

Abundance: As of the second atlas, there were a minimum 672 Trumpeter Swans in the wild in Ontario. About 84% of the population is concentrated in the Southern Shield, Lake Simcoe-Rideau and Carolinian regions, and this group is considered self-sustaining. Populations in the northwestern portion of the Southern Shield (Sault Ste. Marie) and Northern Shield regions are small but rapidly expanding. – *Harry G. Lumsden*

Tundra Swan

Cygne siffleur

Cygnus columbianus

George K. Peck

The Tundra Swan has a circumpolar distribution, breeding on wetlands in coastal tundra habitats of the Arctic and Subarctic (Limpert and Earnst 1994). The North American subspecies (*columbianus*) is the most numerous native North American swan, breeding from the Aleutian Islands northward and eastward along Alaska's coasts and continuously along Canadian Arctic coasts and islands between 60° and 70° N to southern Baffin Island and northwestern Ungava Peninsula. Its breeding range extends along the west coast of Hudson Bay as far south as the Ontario coast, where the southernmost extensive tundra in North America is found. The Tundra Swan winters on the Pacific (Western population) and Atlantic coasts (Eastern population). Midwinter surveys estimate the Western and Eastern populations at about 107,000 and 80,000 birds, respectively (U.S. Fish and Wildlife Service 2006; Fronczak 2006). Both populations have increased substantially, almost doubling over the past three decades, due in part to a shift from a diet of mostly aquatic vegetation to one containing more waste grains and other agricultural foods on migration and during the winter.

The Tundra Swan is widespread during migration across Ontario (Sandilands 2005) and particularly abundant during the spring in southwestern Ontario from Lake St. Clair to Long Point (Petrie et al. 2002). It has also increased around Lake Ontario in the past decade (Sandilands 2005). An increasing number of swans stay on the lower Great Lakes through December and into mid-January or longer. This trend towards wintering in the lower Great Lakes will likely persist, given the increasing frequency of mild winters and the species' usual high fidelity to wintering areas. Interestingly, the satellite tracking studies of the Tundra Swan staging at Long Point (Petrie and Wilcox 2003) did not include any Ontario breeding swans. Limited banding data indicate that some of Ontario's breeding swans winter in North Carolina.

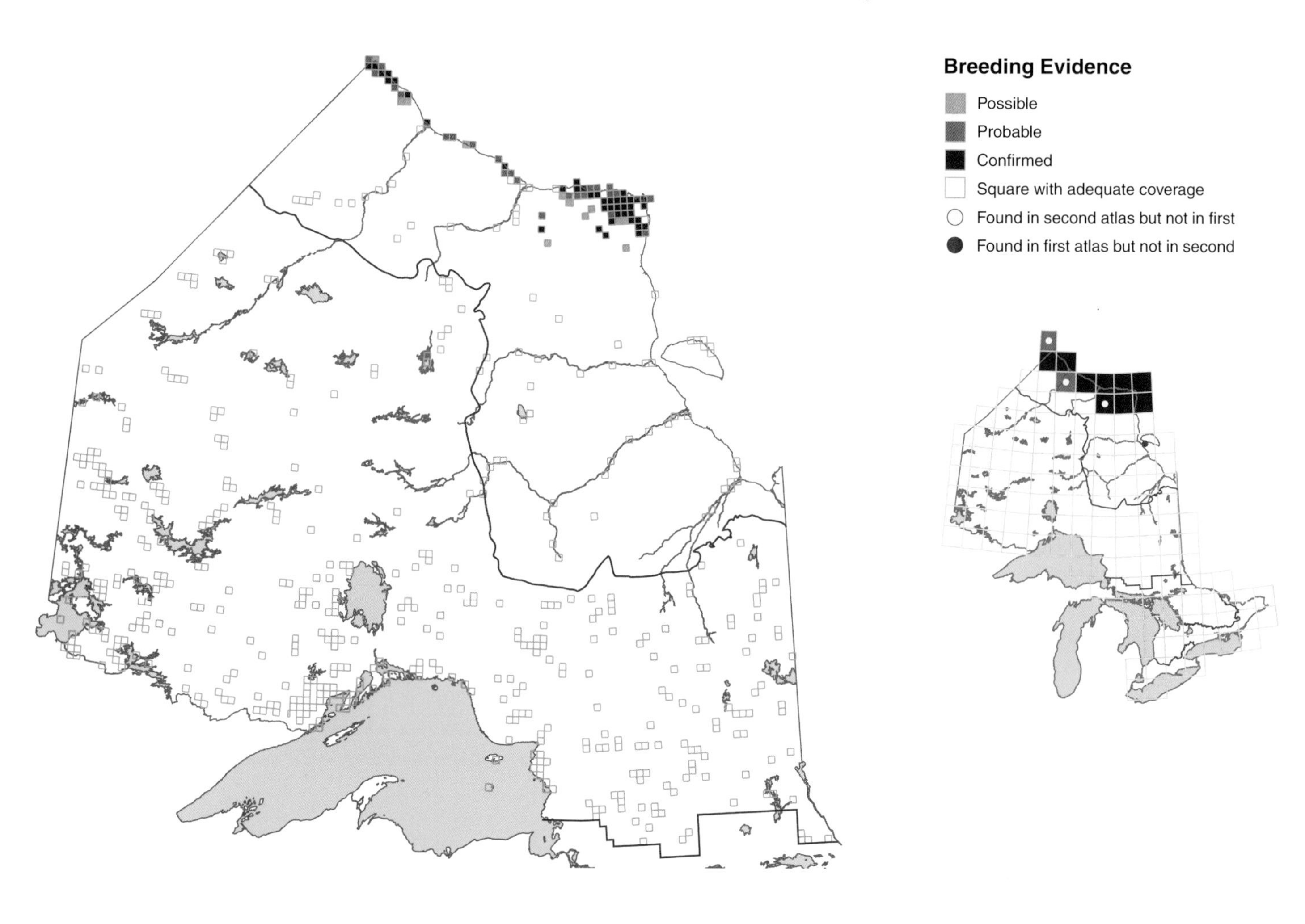

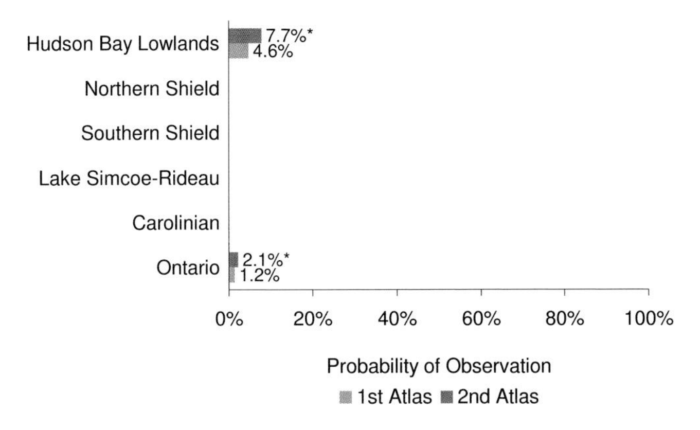

Distribution and population status: The Tundra Swan was extirpated from Ontario during the height of the fur trade when it was heavily hunted for food and feathers (Lumsden 1984b). After a long absence, the Ontario range was reoccupied by breeding swans in the mid-1970s (Lumsden 1976), and numbers have increased since and will likely continue to do so (Lumsden 1984a).

Breeding evidence for the Tundra Swan was reported from 78 squares in 11 100-km blocks in the Hudson Bay Lowlands, compared to 32 squares in nine 100-km blocks in the first atlas. The probability of observation increased significantly by 67% between atlases. Confirmation of breeding was obtained in about half of the squares (41 of 79). Breeding swans are now found along the entire Hudson Bay coast of Ontario in suitable habitat. The tundra lakes and ponds in the area from the Sutton River to Cape Henrietta Maria host most of the breeding Tundra Swans in Ontario. A second area of relatively high density is the tundra area between Fort Severn and the Pen Islands.

Breeding biology: The Tundra Swan is long-lived and monogamous, forming life-long pairs. Breeding begins at about three years of age on average. Nests are large mounds made of material pulled from 2-3 m surrounding the nest and may be built up over several years, as about 50% of Tundra Swan pairs reuse the same nesting site in consecutive years. Breeders maintain territories of 100-200 ha from egg laying through brood rearing. A single clutch of three to seven large, off-white eggs is produced annually.

The Tundra Swan is conspicuous because of its large size, white colour, and distinctive vocalizations, from its arrival on the breeding grounds in late April to its departure in September and October. Birds on nests are easily noticeable from the air and on the ground (17 records, 11% of observations) and rarely flush as aircraft pass over. Single birds in suitable habitat made up 20% of observations and pairs 40% of observations. However, caution is required in documenting both categories because the previous two years' young return as non-breeders to the natal range. Yearlings gather in groups, but these may be groups of two, resembling pairs. As well, sub-adult pairs (two to three years old) may establish territories in the summer before they first nest (Limpert and Earnst 1994). Broods (29% of observations) are easily seen by both air and ground surveyors, and because they are usually reared within the defended territory, are a good index of breeding distribution.

Nests may be substantial mounds of material accumulated over several years of use. About 50% of pairs reuse nest sites over successive years. *Photo: Donald A. Sutherland*

The principal breeding habitat of Tundra Swan in Ontario is open wet tundra with numerous small lakes, ponds, or rivers. Near Radar Site 415, Polar Bear Prov. Park. *Photo: Mark Peck*

Abundance: Only one quantitative estimate of the breeding population and density in Ontario has been made, and it was shortly after the species reoccupied the Hudson Bay Lowlands (Lumsden 1984a). A population of 20-25 breeding pairs was reported. Based on the number and distribution of atlas records and unpublished OMNR data, the current population is likely over 200 pairs. – *Ken Abraham*

Wood Duck

Canard branchu

Aix sponsa

John Reaume

The Wood Duck, so named because it favours flooded forests and nests in trees, is widely regarded as one of the most striking birds in North America. It is the only North American duck that regularly perches in trees. Its breeding range includes southern Canada and most of the US. Where suitable nesting cavities exist, it is found in wooded swamps and woodlands near ponds, streams, and rivers, and also in created wetlands.

Until the 1800s, the Wood Duck was among the most abundant waterfowl breeding in eastern North America, but unregulated market hunting, deforestation, and drainage of wetlands decimated populations to the point where some ornithologists feared it would become extinct (Bellrose and Holm 1994). The Migratory Birds Convention of 1916 enabled the US and Canada to implement legal protection through legislation. Since then, the Wood Duck has made a remarkable comeback in numbers and range and is now the second most numerous duck species harvested in the Atlantic and Mississippi flyways (Hepp and Bellrose 1995).

Distribution and population status: The Wood Duck was virtually absent in Ontario in the early 1900s but is now one of the province's most common duck species. It is absent from the Hudson Bay Lowlands, is sparse but widely distributed in the Northern Shield, but occurs in most squares in the Southern Shield, Lake Simcoe-Rideau, and Carolinian regions. Throughout the Northern Shield, the Wood Duck's sparse distribution may be influenced by the relatively low productivity of wetlands, especially those with insufficient plant and invertebrate food bases, which are essential components of its breeding habitat, and its presence may be related to artificial wetlands. However, the Wood Duck was found in 17 more 100-km blocks in the Northern Shield than in the first atlas, perhaps due in part to additional effort.

Between atlases, there was a significant 53% increase in the probability of observation in the province as a whole and all

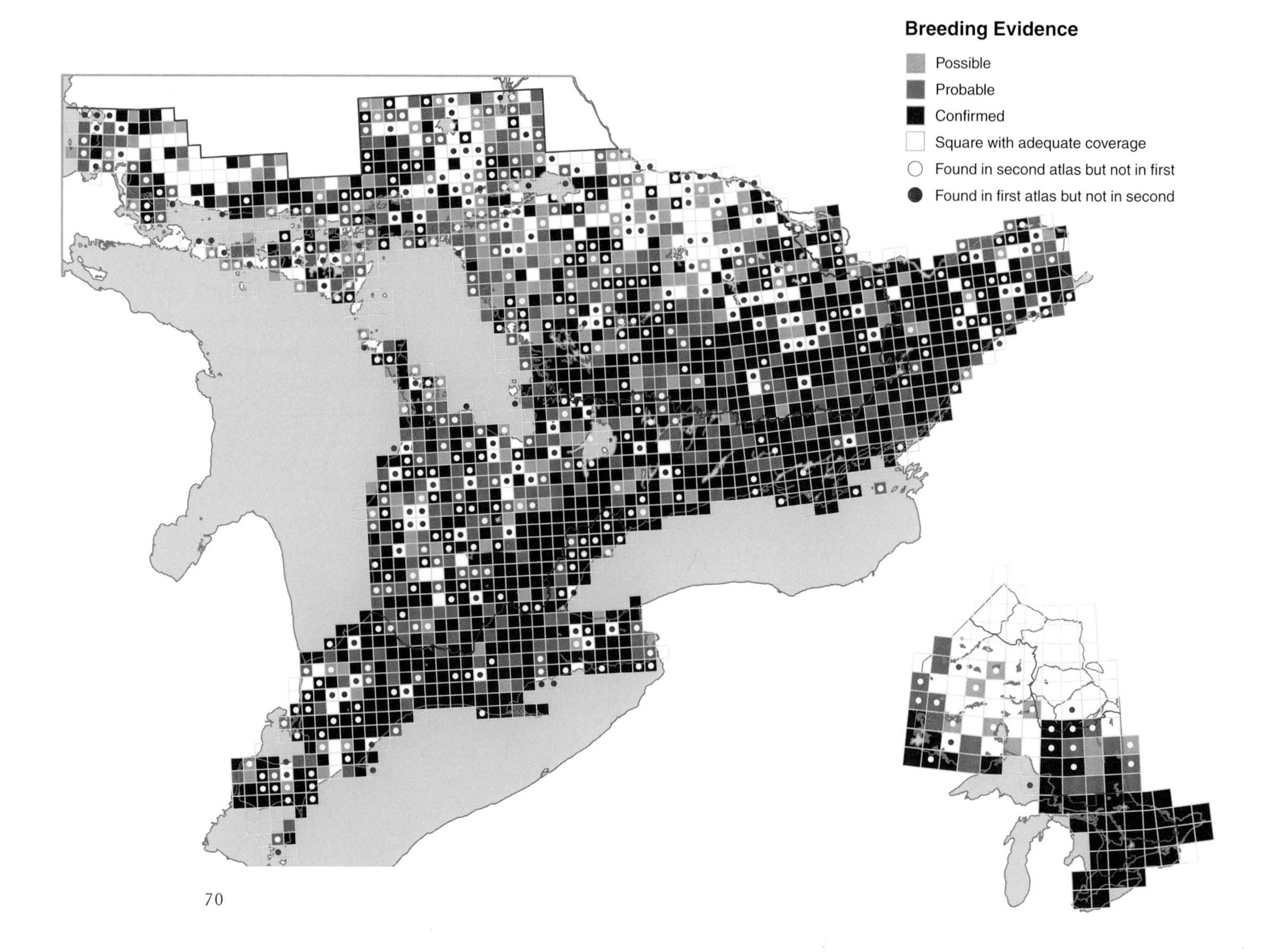

BREEDING EVIDENCE

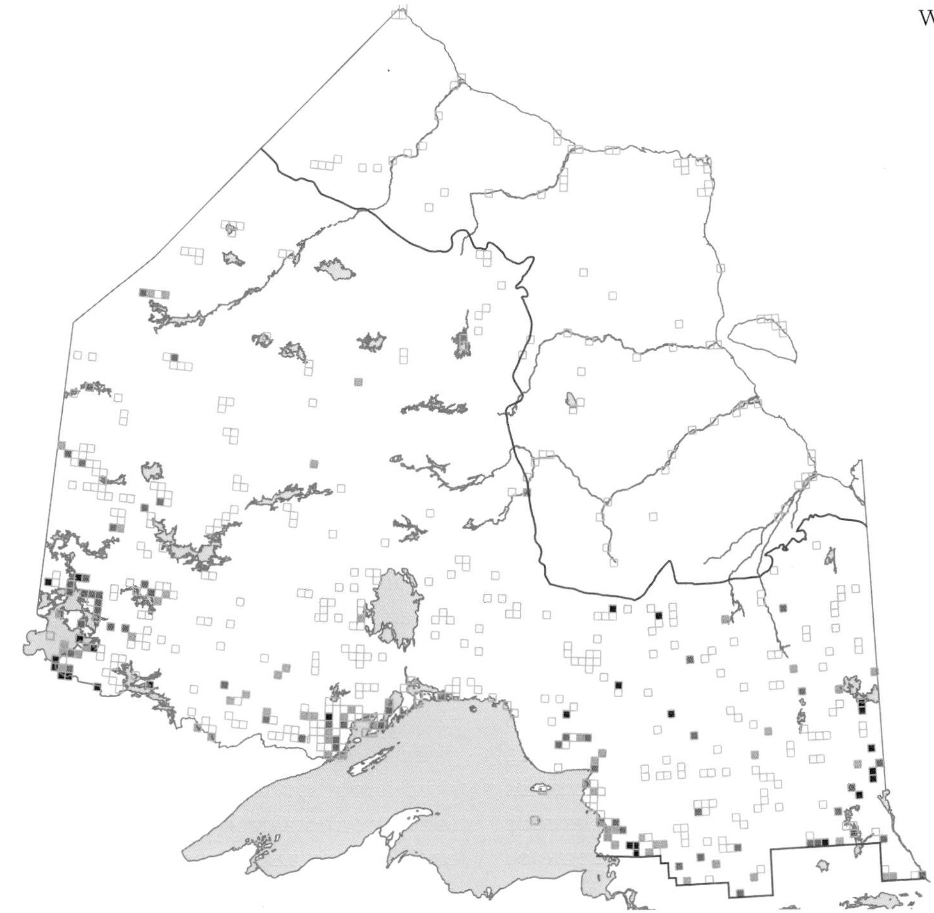

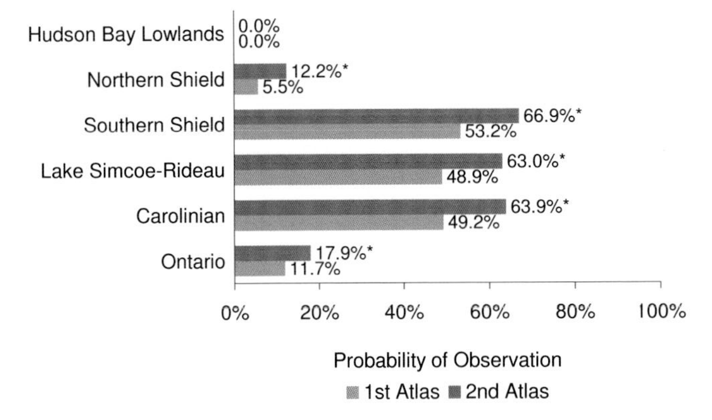

regions where it occurs. The increase was between 26% and 30% in each of the three southern regions but over 100% in the Northern Shield. Part of the increase is undoubtedly due to the large number of nest boxes that have been erected throughout the province since the first atlas and their ready use by the Wood Duck, coupled with the species' high fecundity. The atlas data confirm BBS data for Ontario, which indicate a significant increase of 11% per year in Wood Duck occurrence since the first atlas. Overall, the distribution and breeding evidence map is similar to that of the first atlas and represents this species well.

Breeding biology: The Wood Duck is a cavity nester of woodland streams and ponds, but it does not excavate its own hole. Rather, it uses natural cavities and those created by other species (e.g., Pileated Woodpecker). It will also readily use artificial nesting structures, and females exhibit strong nest site fidelity to these. Research suggests that in Ontario the Wood Duck prefers beaver ponds, especially recently created ones, to all other wetland habitats (Merendino et al. 1995). Nest initiation begins in late March or early April and the cryptically coloured female incubates the eggs and raises the young alone. Within 24 hours of hatching, the young climb out of the cavity and leap down from as high as 20 m to the female waiting below. Locating natural nesting cavities is a difficult task, as they can be more than 750 m from water (Hepp and Bellrose 1995). Breeding was confirmed in 56% of squares overall and all but the two most northerly atlas administrative regions. Broods are relatively easy to observe; 44% of all records and 78% of confirmed records were of fledged young.

Abundance: Waterfowl are poorly sampled using point counts because they breed earlier and vocalize less than do songbirds (Zimmerling 2005); thus detections were insufficient to produce a reliable relative abundance map. Given that cavity availability and suitable brood-rearing wetlands likely limit the local abundance of the Wood Duck, the highest breeding densities are apt to be in a broad band south of the Southern Shield from Ottawa to Georgian Bay where active beaver ponds, natural cavities, and nest boxes are likely most numerous. In the Ottawa Valley, almost 1,000 nesting boxes were erected by researchers and various organizations since the first atlas, resulting in a substantial increase in local Wood Duck abundance (Zimmerling, unpubl. data); similar activity has occurred elsewhere. – *J. Ryan Zimmerling*

Gadwall

Canard chipeau

Anas strepera

This handsome dabbling duck has undergone a dramatic range expansion in North America over the last 50 years and large increases in the continental population size more recently (LeSchack et al. 1997). Interestingly, palearctic populations of the Gadwall have undergone similar range expansion and population increases (Curry 1994). The situation in Ontario mirrors the general pattern in North America. Until the mid-20th century, the Gadwall was a relatively rare transient in Ontario. After the discovery of the first nests at Walpole Island and Luther Marsh in 1955 (Baillie 1963), it gradually increased in the southwest and, beginning in the 1960s, underwent an explosive increase in the southeastern portions of the province (Curry 1994).

Distribution and population status: Results from the first atlas showed the Gadwall to be a scattered breeder throughout southern Ontario north to about Manitoulin Island, and a scattered breeder across northern Ontario north to the Hudson Bay Lowlands. The core concentrations occurred along the north shores of the lower Great Lakes and the St. Lawrence River.

Between atlases, the probability of observation increased significantly in the Southern Shield region, more than doubling. There was a noticeable increase in a band north of Georgian Bay from North Bay to Sault Ste. Marie, including Manitoulin Island. These increases are in the more settled areas west of North Bay and along the road network but not in the undeveloped Algonquin Highlands. Sewage lagoons and other suitable wetlands may have provided breeding habitat for the expanding population. No significant changes occurred in other regions, but there were positive trends in the probability of observation in the Northern Shield and Hudson Bay Lowlands, and negative trends in the Lake Simcoe-Rideau and Carolinian regions. Overall, although the number of occupied squares was the same in both atlases, there was a substantial turnover in the specific squares occupied, especially south of the Shield. In recent years, many sewage lagoons have been

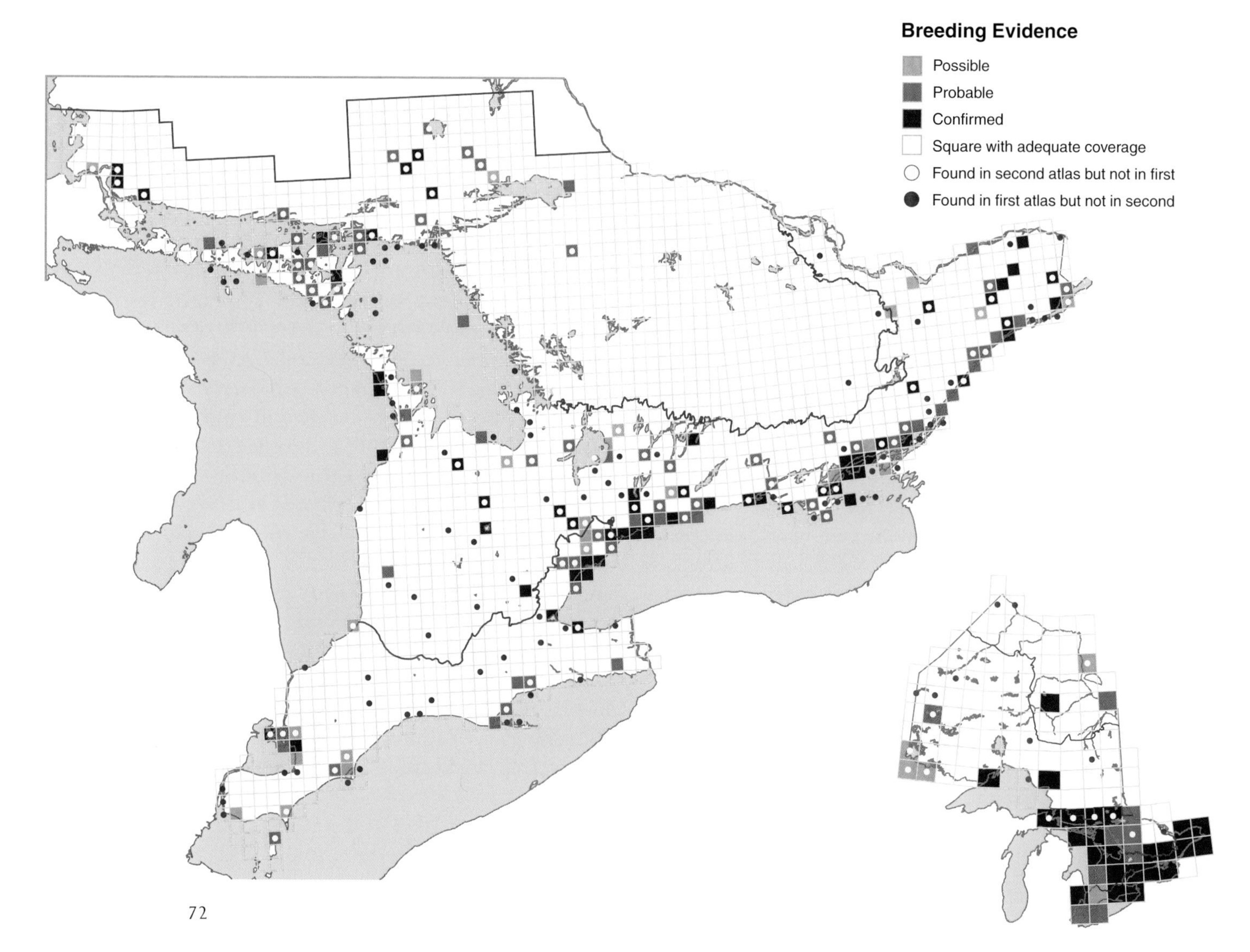

BREEDING EVIDENCE

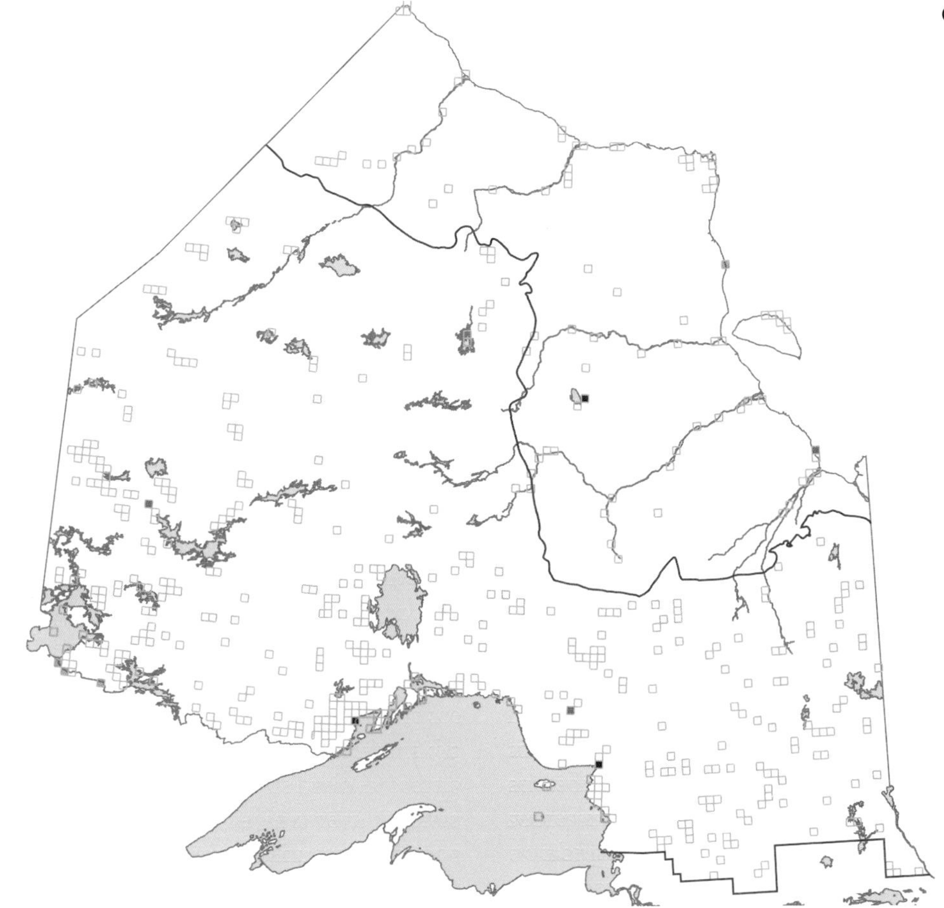

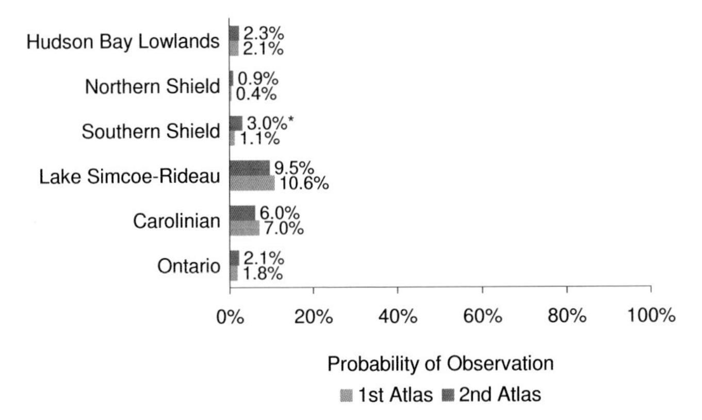

armoured with stone or decommissioned, thus eliminating some Gadwall nest sites, and industrial intensification has destroyed sites in Hamilton Harbour (Curry 2006) and likely other sites as well. Along the north shore of Lake Ontario, there were many newly occupied squares, and in the St. Lawrence Valley, the same turnover in squares as noted earlier has taken place. Clearly, the Gadwall is expanding its Ontario breeding distribution, as the northern edge of the southern Ontario range has shifted 59 km northward and the centre of the range has shifted 30 km north.

Breeding biology: The Gadwall begins to breed relatively early (mid-April in Ontario), and pairs are conspicuous during the pre-nesting period. Females are persistent if nests are depredated, and breeding may continue into July, offering a long period for confirmation of breeding. The species prefers marsh and wetland habitats with tall, emergent vegetation or open water greater than 1 m deep (LeSchack et al. 1997). Primarily vegetarian, it feeds on the emergent vegetation and filamentous green algae that are typically abundant in such locations (Bellrose 1980; LeSchack et al. 1997). Birds nest in relatively high densities where there are islands, and nests are placed in dry areas with dense, tall grasses or shrubs. In addition to large Great Lakes shoreline marshes and managed wetlands, sewage lagoons, reservoirs, and other impoundments have provided ideal Gadwall breeding habitat. Females with broods remain at these sites, helping atlassers to obtain a fairly high confirmation rate of 38%. The Gadwall's affinity for artificial sites that are accessible and frequently visited by atlassers means that the species' distribution is probably well represented on the atlas map.

Abundance: Although it was not possible to generate an abundance map for the Gadwall from atlas point counts, Regional Coordinators report increasing numbers from Toronto eastwards. The north shore of Lake Ontario and the St. Lawrence River likely have the highest Gadwall breeding densities in the province. The area of population growth on Manitoulin Island and adjacent mainland areas of the Southern Shield likely now supports the second-highest Gadwall densities.

The Lake Ontario Mid-Winter Waterfowl Inventory may provide an index of the species' abundance in the province. It is possible that a substantial proportion of Ontario's breeding Gadwalls winter along the Lake Ontario shoreline where they benefit from warm water outflows and sheltered harbours, although this conjecture has not been supported by physical evidence such as banding. Gadwall numbers for the Toronto section (Bronte to Whitby harbours) showed dramatic increases from the mid-1960s to a peak of 1,404 birds in 2002 (Toronto Ornithologists Club, unpubl. data). – *Bob Curry*

American Wigeon

Canard d'Amérique

Anas americana

John Reaume

The American Wigeon is widely distributed throughout much of North America, from Alaska to Nova Scotia. Its core breeding range is in the Canadian Prairie-Parklands, the Old Crow Flats of the Yukon, and the Mackenzie Delta of the Northwest Territories (Mowbray 1999). Sometimes called "Baldpate," the male has a characteristic pale patch on its forehead that, along with its sibilant whistle, makes it easily recognizable. The species is an aggressive and opportunistic forager known to steal food from Redheads and coots. Unlike other dabblers, it has a bill morphology that facilitates grazing (Mowbray 1999) like geese on land.

Distribution and population status: The American Wigeon's highest breeding abundance occurs farther north than that of other dabbling ducks (Mowbray 1999), with highest densities usually being found around northern river deltas (Bellrose 1980). In Ontario, it is most common in the Hudson Bay Lowlands, but it also occurs in low numbers in other parts of the province. It is most often associated with shallow bays and marshes of estuaries (Mowbray 1999) such as along the coasts of Hudson and James Bays, large permanent marshes with open water in the Boreal Forest (Dennis and North 1984), and lake estuary marshes in the Great Clay Belt (Rempel et al. 1997). In southern Ontario, the sparse population of the species has likely benefited from the creation of inland impoundments and especially sewage lagoons, where it is regularly observed.

The wigeon's probability of observation was 17% in the Hudson Bay Lowlands and 8% or less in all other regions. However, the probability of observation for the Hudson Bay Lowlands decreased non-significantly by 32% since the first atlas. Estimates generated from USFWS aerial surveys in areas such as northern Manitoba (Roetker 2005) and northwestern Ontario (Bollinger 2005) surrounding the Hudson Bay Lowlands also suggest that species numbers have declined

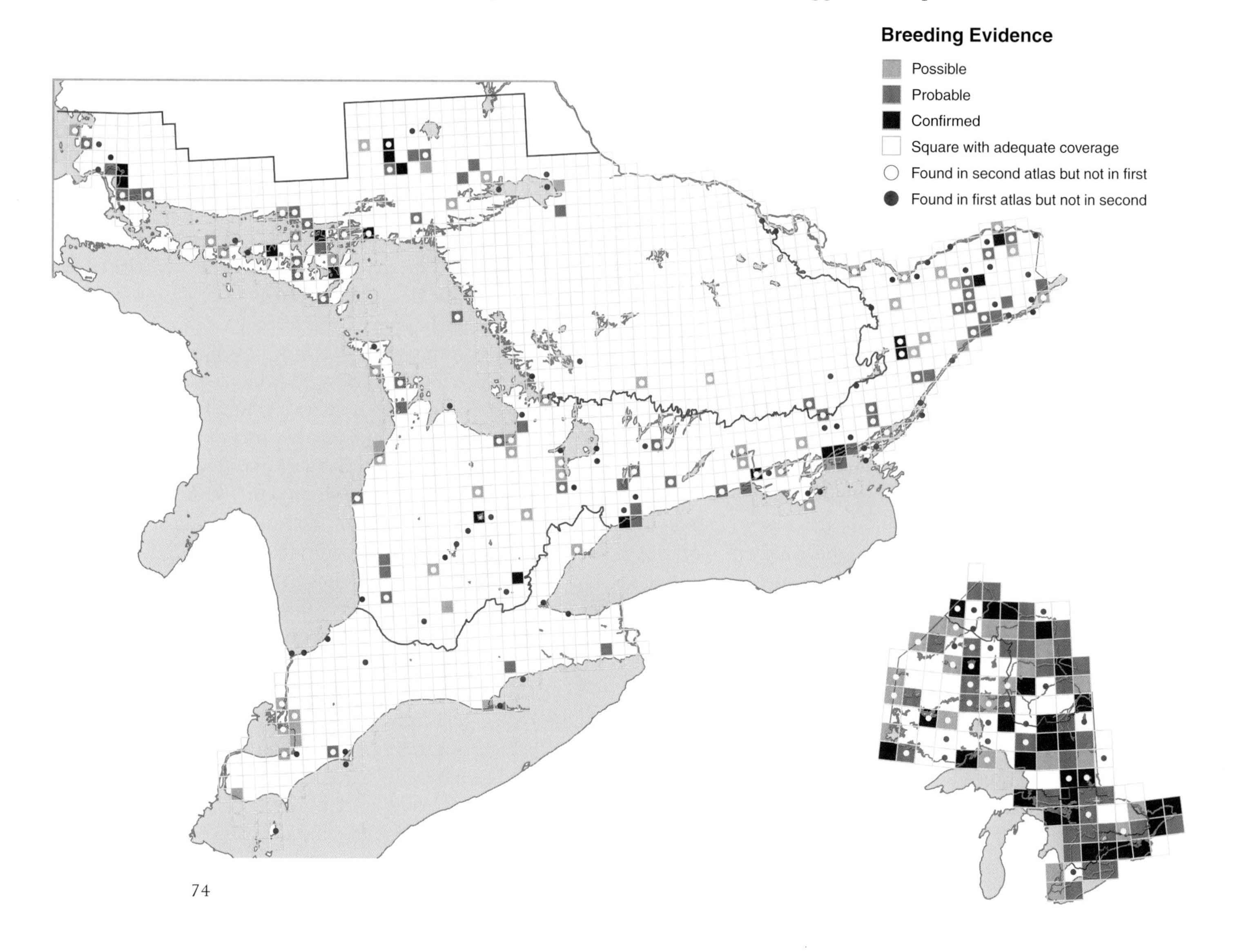

BREEDING EVIDENCE

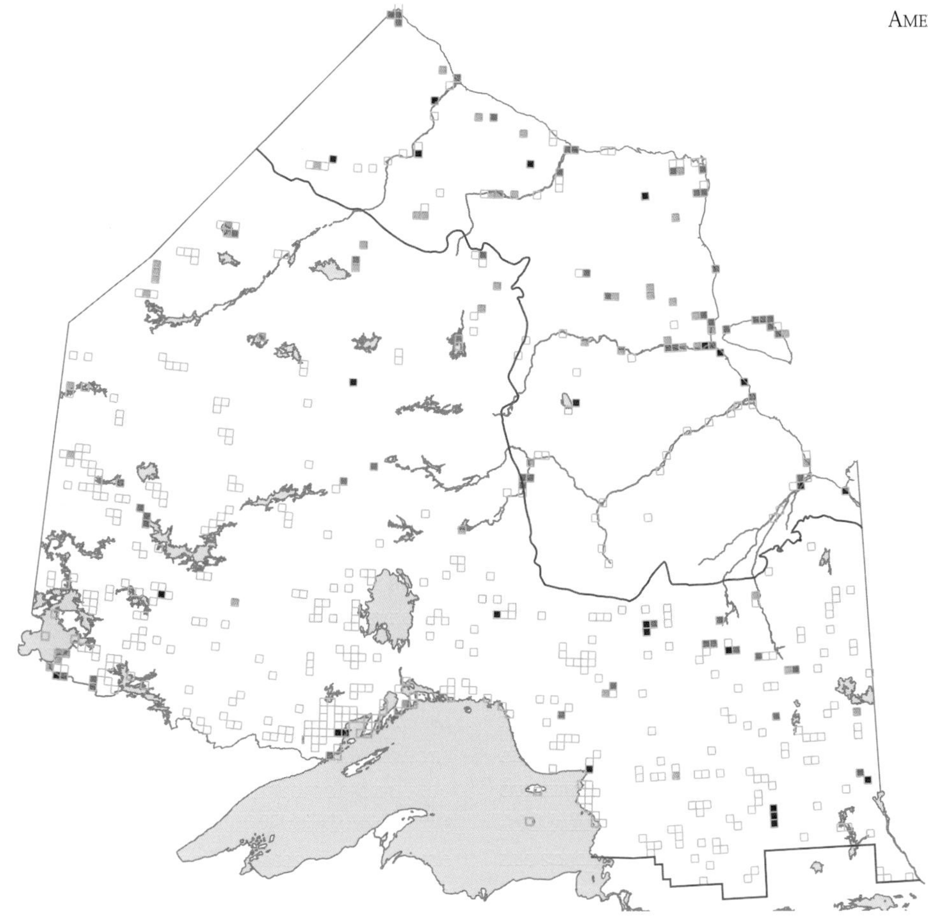

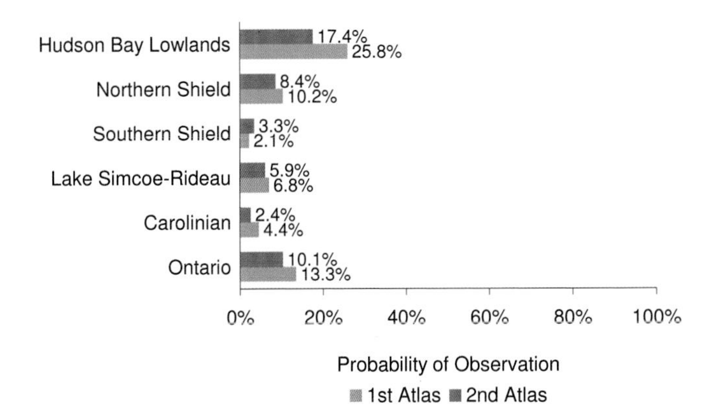

since the first atlas.

The American Wigeon is a relatively new breeding species in southern Ontario, as it is for much of eastern Canada (Mowbray 1999). The first nest in the south was only documented in 1934 (Baillie 1960). Its sparse distribution through most of the province is similar to that in the first atlas, with no significant change in the probability of observation in any region or in the province as a whole. However, there was a large turnover in the particular squares that reported the species, possibly due to the small population spread over a large area. The centre of its range in southern Ontario has shifted north significantly (43 km), likely due to a noticeable increase in observations in the Manitoulin Island and Sudbury areas.

Breeding biology: The pair bond of the American Wigeon, formed primarily on the wintering grounds, is strong and persists well into incubation. At this point, the male abandons the female and joins other males at moulting sites that may be some distance away (Mowbray 1999). Thus, males seen in mid-summer may not actually be breeding in the immediate area. The female shows strong site fidelity, often returning to the same breeding area in subsequent years (Arnold and Clark 1996). The species will nest in a variety of habitats but is usually found in upland sites characterized by tall grass, mixed herbaceous cover, brush, or low shrubs (Mowbray 1999). It begins nesting relatively late compared to other dabbling ducks, and females often re-nest if the first attempt fails (Mowbray 1999). The average clutch is eight to nine eggs. Although nests may be difficult to locate, broods are relatively conspicuous and the female is easy to identify, making June and July the best months to confirm breeding. Accordingly, brood observations were by far the most frequently recorded evidence of confirmed breeding.

As the species is distinctive in both appearance and call and generally fairly conspicuous, the distribution map probably provides a fairly accurate picture of the extent of distribution in Ontario, although breeding evidence level may be underestimated.

Abundance: While point count data from the atlas detected the species in insufficient numbers to produce a map of abundance, other surveys have provided some insight. Fixed-winged surveys conducted by the USFWS for much of northwestern Ontario calculated the 10-year average density as 1.04 pairs / 100 km^2 (Bollinger 2005). Farther east in the Great Clay Belt, Ross et al. (2002) reported 3.0 pairs / 100 km^2 from intense helicopter surveys between 1988 and 1990. *– Michel Gendron*

American Black Duck

Canard noir

Anas rubripes

Ethan Meleg

The American Black Duck is very closely related to the Mallard, with which it routinely interbreeds. It is the only waterfowl species whose breeding range is centred solely in northeastern North America, and although it is still common in eastern Canada, it has declined substantially since the 1950s, leading to its designation as a Species of Concern under the North American Waterfowl Management Plan. The North American breeding range of the Black Duck extends south from the tree-line in subarctic regions, with highest concentrations in the boreal and mixed-wood forests from northeastern Ontario to Newfoundland and Labrador, and south to New England and along the Atlantic Seaboard to Maryland. Low densities occur west through the Great Lakes states, extending into Manitoba.

Distribution and population status: The extent of the Black Duck's range in Ontario has changed little between atlases. It was recorded throughout much of the province, with highest levels of occurrence in the Southern Shield region of central and northeastern Ontario. Numbers are much lower in the Hudson Bay Lowlands, where large concentrations found along the coast are likely composed of moult-migrant males of unknown origins (K. Ross, unpubl. data). Low numbers also occur in the Northern Shield region of northwestern Ontario. Occurrence in the Carolinian and Lake Simcoe-Rideau regions is considerably lower now than in the early 1970s, when southern Ontario had much higher numbers (Dennis 1974a). As in the first atlas, a cluster of 100-km blocks in the Big Trout Lake and upper Severn River area is the only locale where the species was not recorded.

The probability of observation of the Black Duck declined significantly province-wide and in all atlas regions except the Hudson Bay Lowlands. This represents a continuation of the decline observed in the Carolinian and Lake Simcoe-Rideau regions since the early 1970s (Dennis et al. 1989). Potential reasons for the decline include the reduction in wetland and

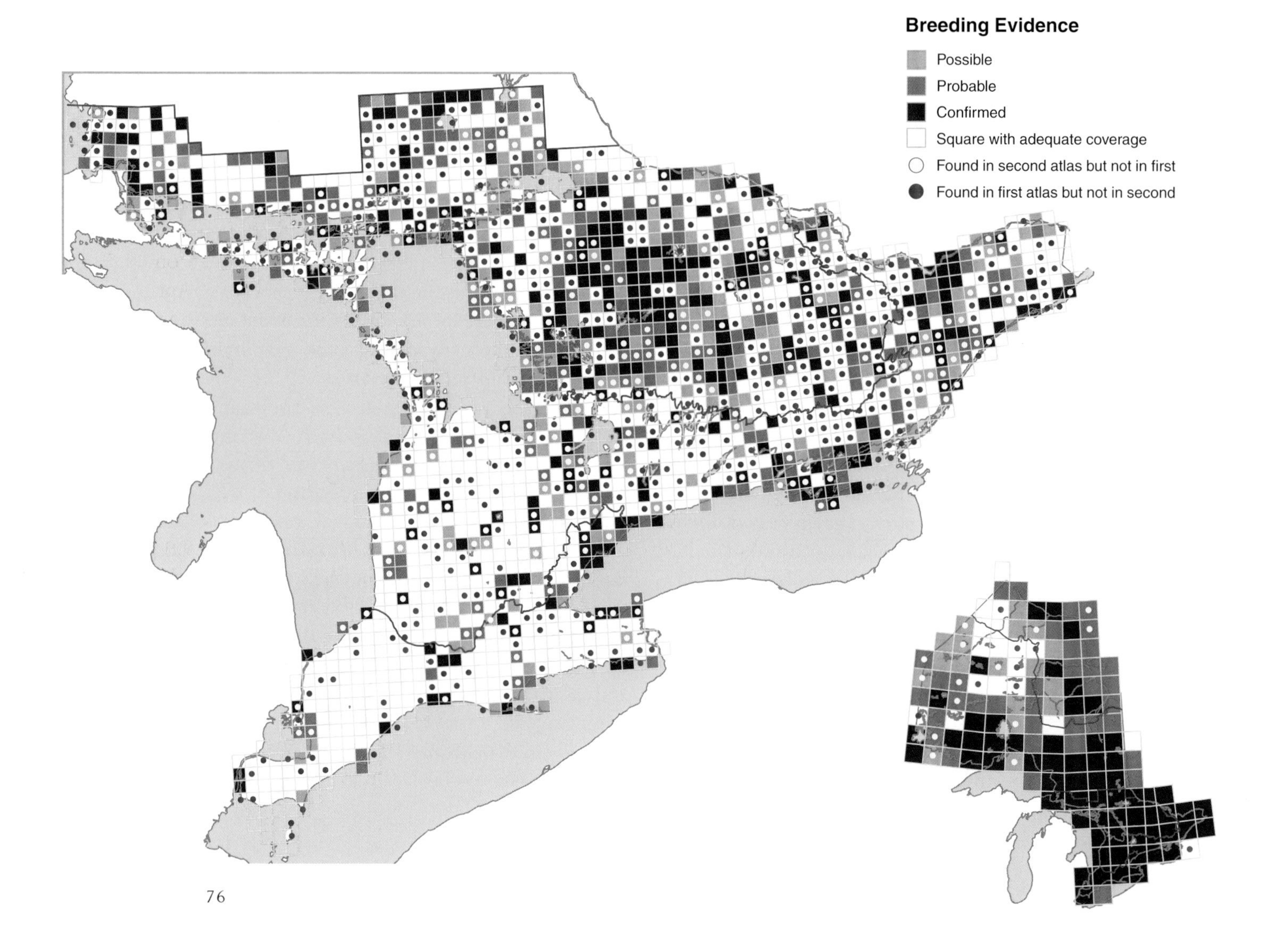

BREEDING EVIDENCE

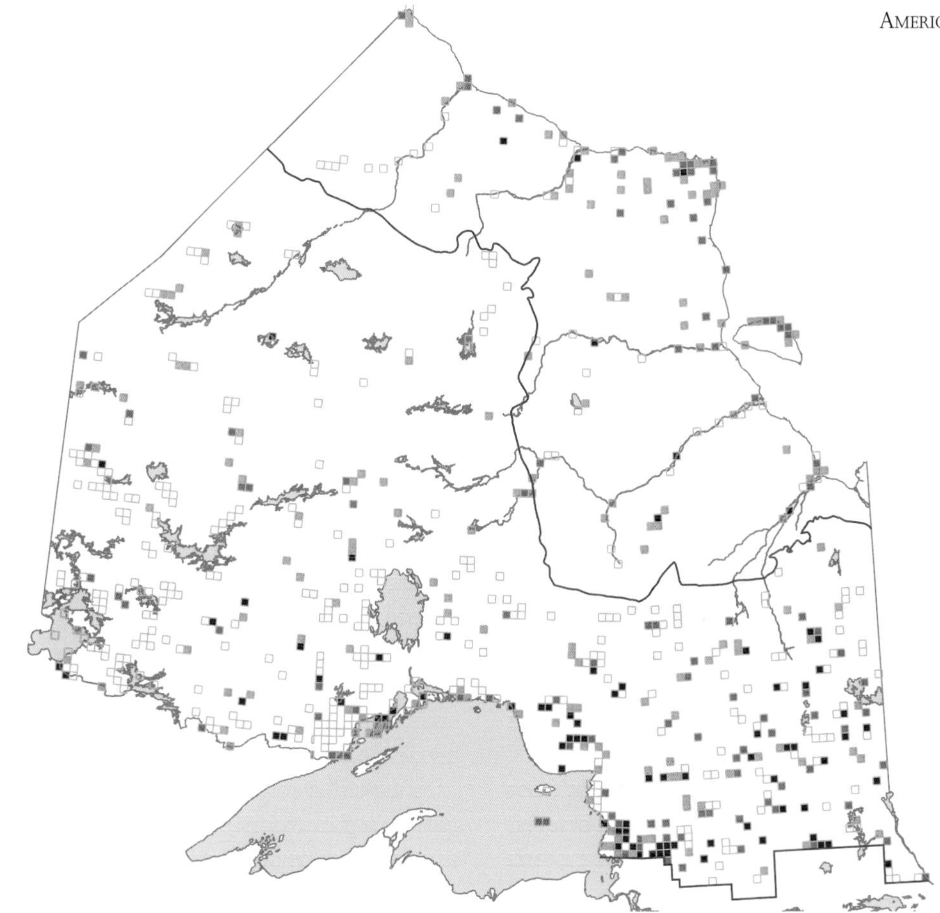

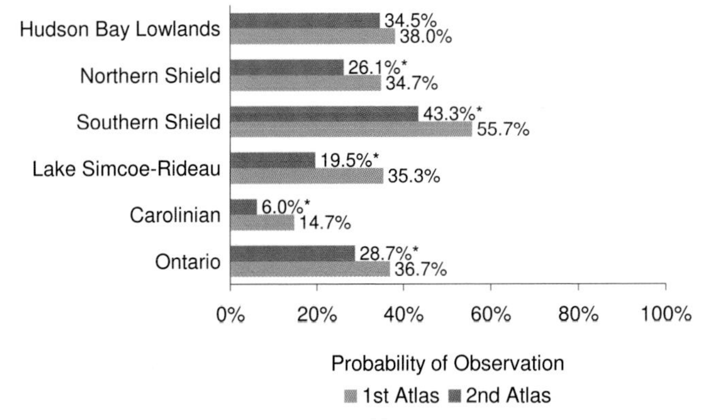

the likely role of the burgeoning Mallard population in displacing the species through competitive exclusion and possibly introgression (Ankney et al. 1987). Decreases in the Southern Shield, which is part of the heart of the species' range in Ontario, were concentrated in the far eastern part and the area immediately contiguous to the Lake Simcoe-Rideau region. Reasons for decline in this area are not clear but may reflect succession in beaver pond habitats and possibly increased human disturbance, to which the Black Duck may be quite susceptible (Longcore et al. 2000). The Northern Shield region also shows a substantial decline in occurrence between atlases. This may be due to a drop in the lower-density western part of the region, as breeding densities in the eastern portion show little change between atlas periods (Ross and Fillman 1990; CWS unpubl. data).

Breeding biology: In Ontario, the Black Duck can be found during the breeding period in a wide variety of habitats including beaver flowages, riverine marshes, alder-covered streams, wooded swamps, and bog ponds surrounded by Leatherleaf and Sweet Gale. Nests are well hidden in grass or reed clumps or under trees or shrubs, and are constructed of vegetation gathered on site such as grass, leaves, and twigs; the nest bowl is lined with down and feathers. Occasionally, a nest can be found in an abandoned nest of other species such as herons or raptors. Nesting in cavities is also known to occur. Nests can be up to 0.8 km from water (Sandilands 2005) but are usually much closer.

Pairs or just drakes can be fairly easily seen on wetlands within their territories during nest initiation (April to early June). The Black Duck is among the earliest nesting waterfowl, and broods are present during the usual peak of atlassing activity. Locating nests is often difficult, due to the heavy cover where they are placed. Caution is required when recording two birds as pairs, given the lack of obvious sexual dimorphism in this species.

Abundance: Aerial surveys of breeding pairs conducted by the CWS in the Shield areas of central and northeastern Ontario indicated a mean breeding density of 19.9 pairs/100 km² during the second atlas period, compared with an average of 19.8 pairs/100 km² in 1991-94. Unpublished CWS data from the ground plot survey in southern Ontario (described in Dennis 1974a) illustrate the steep decline in the Carolinian and Lake Simcoe-Rideau regions plus a narrow strip of contiguous Southern Shield: 1971, 11.7 pairs/100 km²; 1985 (first atlas period), 6.7/100 km²; 1995, 6.9/100 km²; 2003 (second atlas period), 0/100 km². – *Ken Ross*

Mallard

Canard colvert

Anas platyrhynchos

Theodore Smith

The male Mallard's striking green head makes it one of the most readily identified species. Its distribution includes most of the Northern Hemisphere. In North America, it is the most widely distributed and abundant species of dabbling duck, with the highest breeding densities occurring in the prairie pothole region. Although there is considerable annual variation, the continental Mallard population is estimated to be around 10.5 million birds (Drilling et al. 2002). This highly adaptable species occurs in almost every habitat type where fresh water is available, and it is remarkably tolerant of human activities. Its wintering range, which includes southern Ontario, is limited by open water and access to food. The Mallard is prized as a game bird, and more are harvested in North America than any other duck species.

Distribution and population status: Before the 1950s, the Mallard was virtually absent in Ontario, but it is now the most widely distributed duck in the province, occurring in most squares in the south and 100-km blocks in the north, a testament to its recent success. Its distribution has not changed noticeably between atlases, and there were no shifts in either the edge or the core of the Mallard's southern Ontario range between atlases. The male's striking colouration, the female's persistence in nesting when nests are destroyed by predators, and the species' relatively high abundance make breeding evidence relatively easy to obtain; thus distribution gaps at the square level are likely real. Breeding evidence was confirmed in all 47 atlas administrative regions, and the overall probability of observation was 63%.

Between atlases, the probability of observation did not change significantly in the province as a whole, but there were significant increases in the Southern and Northern Shield regions, of 12% and 20%, respectively. However, there was a significant 20% decrease in the probability of observation in the Carolinian region. A number of factors may affect Mallard

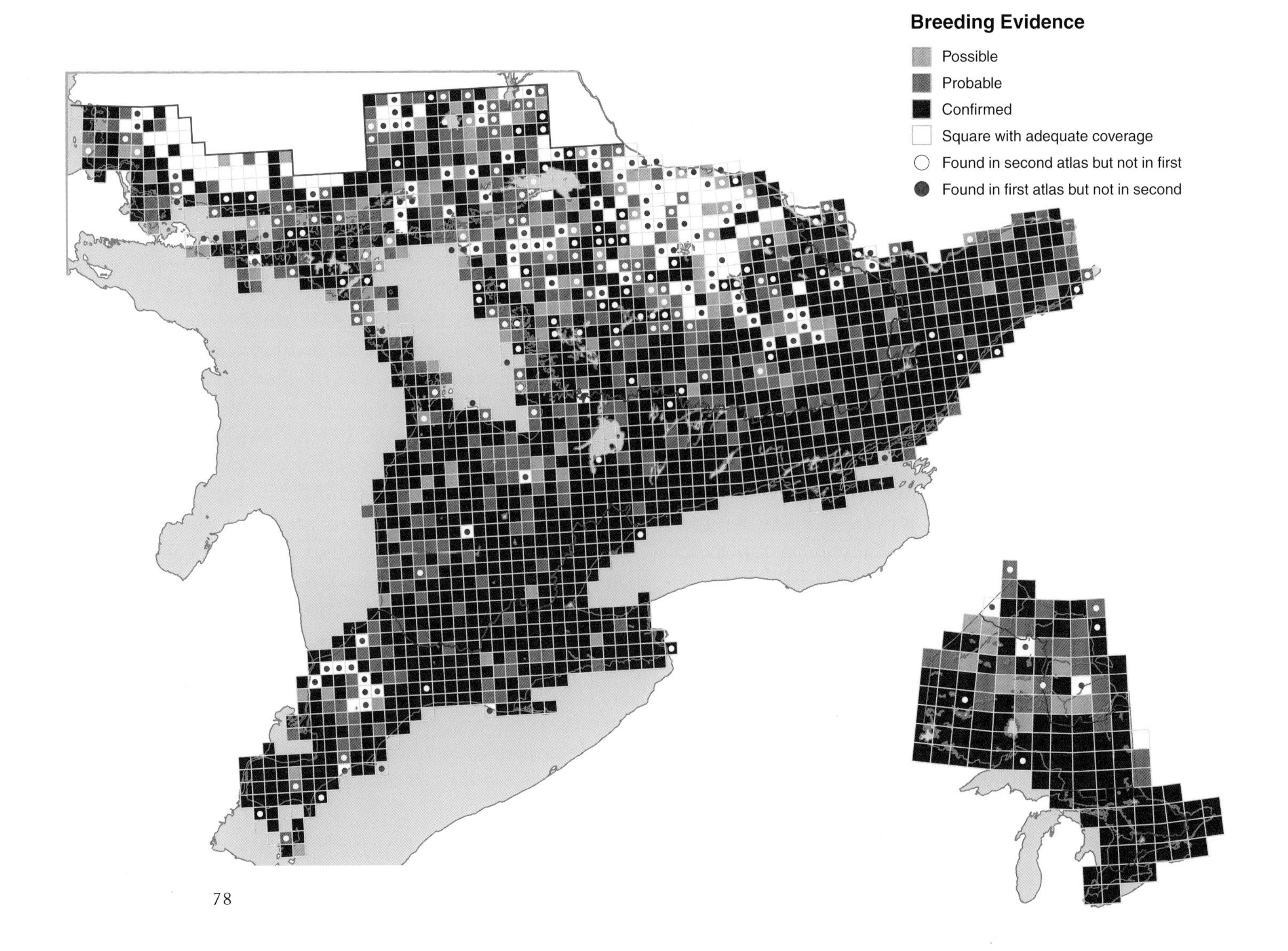

BREEDING EVIDENCE

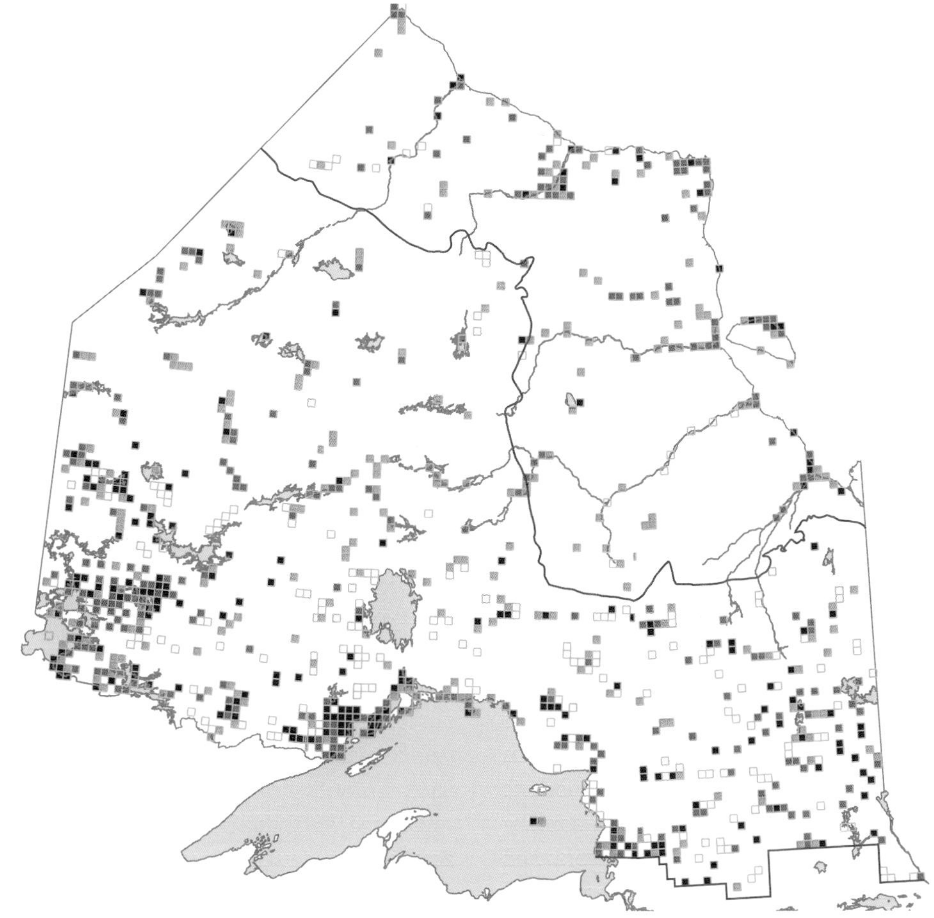

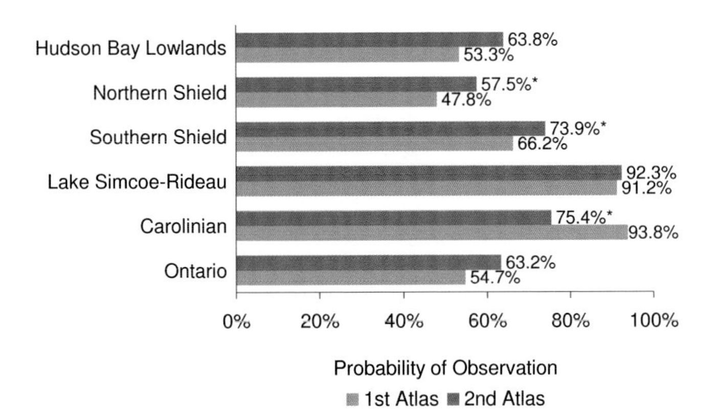

occurrence there, including continued disappearance and decline of productive wetlands due to continued intensification of agriculture and urbanization. In the Southern and Northern Shield regions, Mallards may be benefiting from recent forest-management practices that may be altering the nature of existing wetlands to more marsh-like conditions better suited to waterfowl (Nicoll and Zimmerling 2006). MMP population indices from 1995 to 2004 show a significant Great Lakes basin-wide increase for the species (Crewe et al. 2006).

Breeding biology: In the prairie pothole region, the reproductive success of the Mallard is highly correlated with the number of May ponds (i.e., ephemeral wetlands). On highly productive wetlands (e.g., sewage lagoons), nest density may exceed 2 females/ha (Zimmerling et al. 2006). Predominantly a ground-nesting species, the Mallard is one of the most adaptable ducks in its choice of nesting habitat, provided it has access to fresh water. However, its preferred breeding habitat consists of highly productive wetlands with moderate open water, high shoreline irregularity, and small size (Merendino and Ankney 1994). Nests may be a considerable distance from water and in a wide variety of settings that afford good cover. Occasionally they are found in unusual spots such as in tree roots, urban gardens, or a variety of artificial structures.

Nest initiation in the central portion of the province begins in early April. The Mallard female is cryptically coloured and is well concealed on the nest, often sitting within emergent vegetation during brood rearing. Although nests are not easily found, broods can be fairly evident and made up 38% of all records and 82% of confirmed breeding records.

Abundance: Waterfowl are poorly sampled using point counts because they breed earlier and vocalize less than songbirds. However, the Mallard is common enough that it was recorded at reasonable densities on point counts in all regions except the Northern and Southern Shield. The species is most abundant south of the Shield (throughout southwestern Ontario north through Cornwall and the Ottawa Valley), where nesting habitat and food resources in agricultural fields and wetlands are plentiful. It is also relatively abundant in near-coastal areas in the Hudson Bay Lowlands. Mallard abundance, as is the case with many waterfowl species, is influenced by wetland productivity, and some of the highest densities occur on insect-rich sewage lagoons (Zimmerling et al. 2006). Although wetlands and lakes are common in the interior Northern Shield region where the species is sparse, wetlands in this region are generally less productive and shorelines may provide poor nesting as they are often steep and rocky and suronded by forest. – *J. Ryan Zimmerling*

Blue-winged Teal

Sarcelle à ailes bleues

Anas discors

John Reaume

This teal is a bird of open country and is usually associated with highly productive habitat including marshes, sloughs, and river margins. Its breeding range (Rohwer et al. 2002) forms a triangle centred on the Great Plains, bounded to the west by the Rocky Mountains, to the north by the limit of trees, tapering southeastward through Ontario and southern Québec to the Maritime Provinces, and to the south by the limit of grasslands, tapering northeastward from Texas to New England. It is one of the most abundant duck species on the continent, although its population is regularly subject to great shifts in size. It is the only North American breeding waterfowl species that winters predominantly in South and Central America, with large numbers found as far south as Colombia and Venezuela.

Distribution and population status: Comparison of the maps from the two atlases shows that the species' distribution has changed little in the intervening period. It is found throughout Ontario, with highest numbers concentrated in the agriculture-dominated areas in the south. This teal occurs at very low levels over much of the Northern Shield and Hudson Bay Lowlands, where there are fewer of the preferred highly productive, cattail-dominated marshes. Locally, greater densities occur at the western edge of the province, likely a zone of influence from the Prairies where the species is much more common, and in the relatively rich habitats of the Great Clay Belt and southern James Bay coast.

Although the species' general range in Ontario has not changed, the probability of observation has declined significantly overall (36%), including losses in the Carolinian (63%), Lake Simcoe-Rideau (50%), and Southern Shield (53%) regions. This is in contrast to the first atlas, when numbers were thought to be increasing in response to expansion of agriculture and a rising beaver population. The current decrease likely is caused primarily by habitat changes due to shifting agricultural practices. In the intensively cultivated

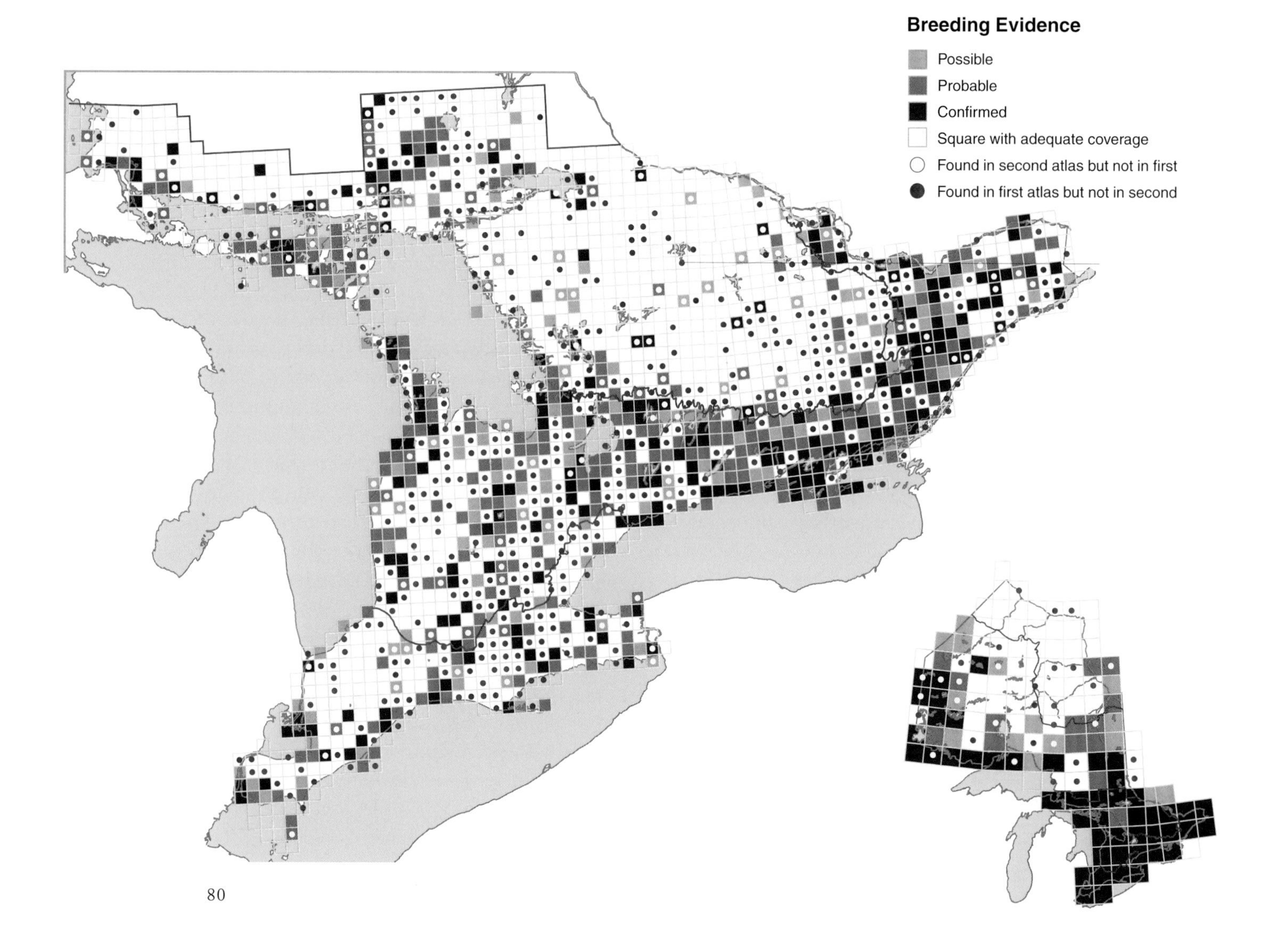

BREEDING EVIDENCE

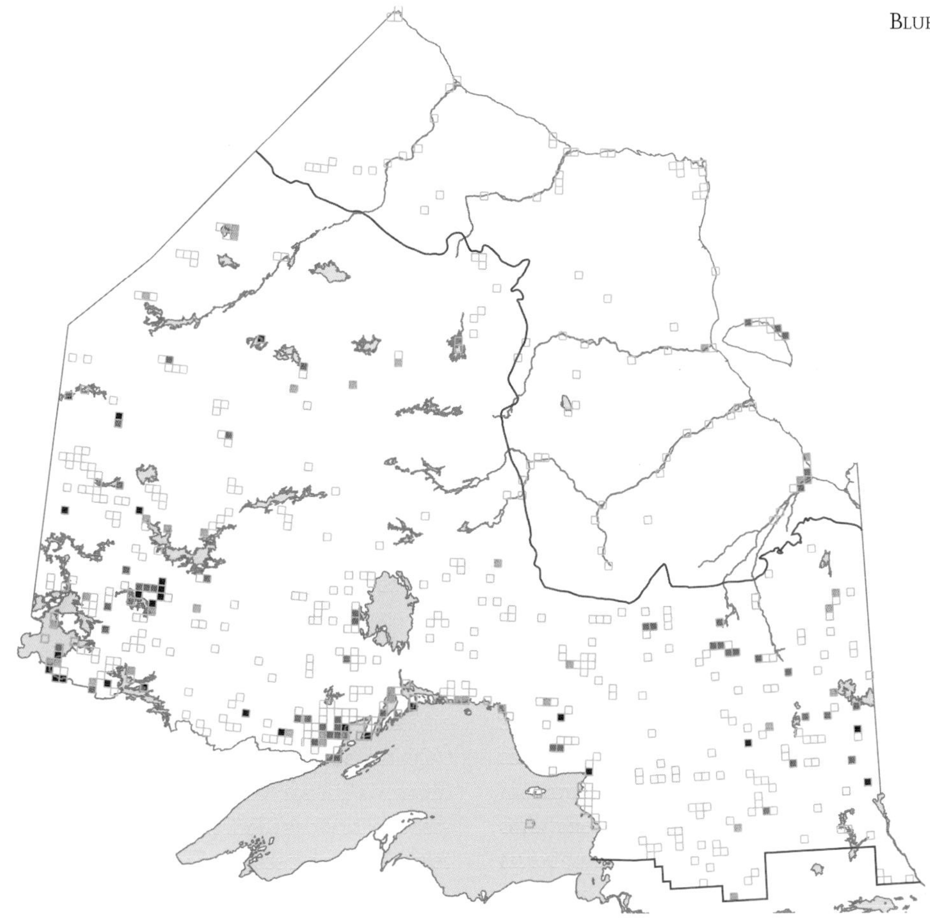

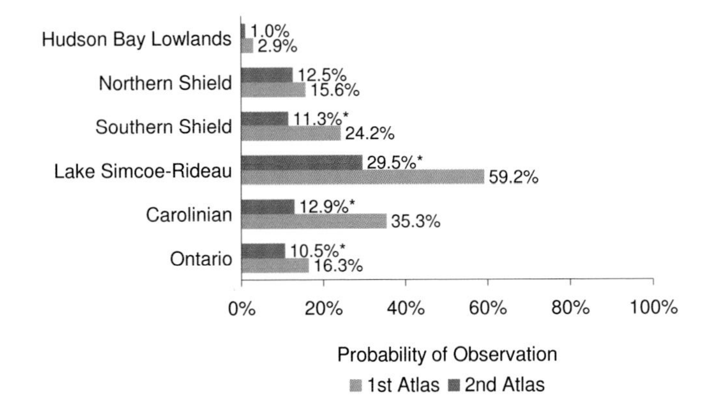

southwest, the decline of teal is probably related to the loss of suitable shallow emergent wetlands to tile drainage.

Similar declines are also seen in the highly urbanized areas west of Toronto. Decreases along the eastern part of the Southern Shield, where farmland is less productive, may be due to both decreases in the amount of pasture land and the natural succession of marginal farmland to forest. Further, beaver ponds may be decreasing in productivity with succession, reducing nesting habitat, and beaver control activities may be reducing creation of new ponds.

Breeding biology: The Blue-winged Teal tends to nest in open areas with well-developed grassy cover, often meadows or farm fields, around shallow, rich wetlands. On the Prairies, the nest is usually placed within 150 m of a wetland (Rohwer et al. 2002). The species has little tendency to philopatry and will move from year to year in response to habitat quality and availability (Lokemoen et al. 1990). The nest is constructed of vegetation such as grasses, reeds, and other monocots from the immediate area. The nest bowl is lined with leaves, moss, and feathers, and as the clutch nears completion, down (Peck and James 1983).

During nest initiation, the territorial drake is conspicuous on the wetland, and because of the species' preference for open, grassy nesting areas, nests are relatively easily found. Although the Blue-winged Teal is one of the latest nesting dabblers, young still hatch during prime atlassing activity, and broods can be located fairly readily. Given the relatively high detection probability, the atlas map is likely a good representation of the breeding range.

Abundance: Breeding density of this species is not effectively determined through point counts, but the general pattern is quite clearly indicated by the breeding evidence map, which suggests highest concentrations in the Lake Simcoe-Rideau region. The Carolinian region has a slightly lower proportion of squares with breeding evidence, probably a result of the relative lack of wetlands. The Northern and Southern Shield have generally much lower breeding densities, with local, minor concentrations in relatively richer, more open agricultural areas (Great Clay Belt, North Bay-Sudbury, Thunder Bay, Lake of the Woods). Spring breeding pair surveys by CWS yielded densities in the area south of the Shield of 3.3 pairs/100 km^2 in 2003 compared with 26.1/100 km^2 in 1985 during the first atlas. None were recorded in the Southern Shield in 2003, compared with 16.0/100 km^2 in 1985. These values confirm the magnitude of the population decline. Average density in northeastern Ontario during the second atlas was 0.7 pairs/100 km^2, and it has been in that general range since the start of aerial surveys in 1990. – *Ken Ross*

Northern Shoveler

Canard souchet

Anas clypeata

Larry Kirtley

With its large, broad bill and striking plumage, the male Northern Shoveler is unmistakable and always a welcome sight. Females and males in eclipse plumage are nondescript and can be easily mistaken for teal, but the distinctive bill is characteristic. The bill is used to sieve small crustaceans from near the surface of the water, so this species tips up to feed much less than other dabblers.

The Northern Shoveler breeds in Eurasia as well as North America. In North America, its main breeding range is from the northwest US to the prairies and north through the Canadian prairies to the Yukon and Alaska. In Canada, it also breeds in the east on Prince Edward Island, in southern New Brunswick, along the St. Lawrence River through southwestern Québec, and in Ontario.

Distribution and population status: The shoveler may be a relatively recent addition to Ontario's breeding avifauna, but it is possible that early ornithologists were unaware of the population along the northern coasts. McIlwraith (1894) did not believe that it nested in the province, and Baillie and Harrington (1936) had only one breeding record for southern Ontario. It has increased in southern Ontario due to nesting at sewage lagoons. During the first atlas, the shoveler was confirmed breeding in northwestern Ontario, documented as breeding sparingly in marshes and tundra ponds along the northern coasts (Ross and North 1983); it nested sporadically in the Southern Shield and southward.

The second atlas revealed a non-significant increase in the probability of observation of the species overall; however, there was a significant increase in the Northern Shield. The general distribution of this species was similar during both atlases. The most continuous distribution is along the Hudson and James Bay coasts. Lesser numbers occur in scattered locations in the Lake Simcoe-Rideau region, near Sudbury, and in

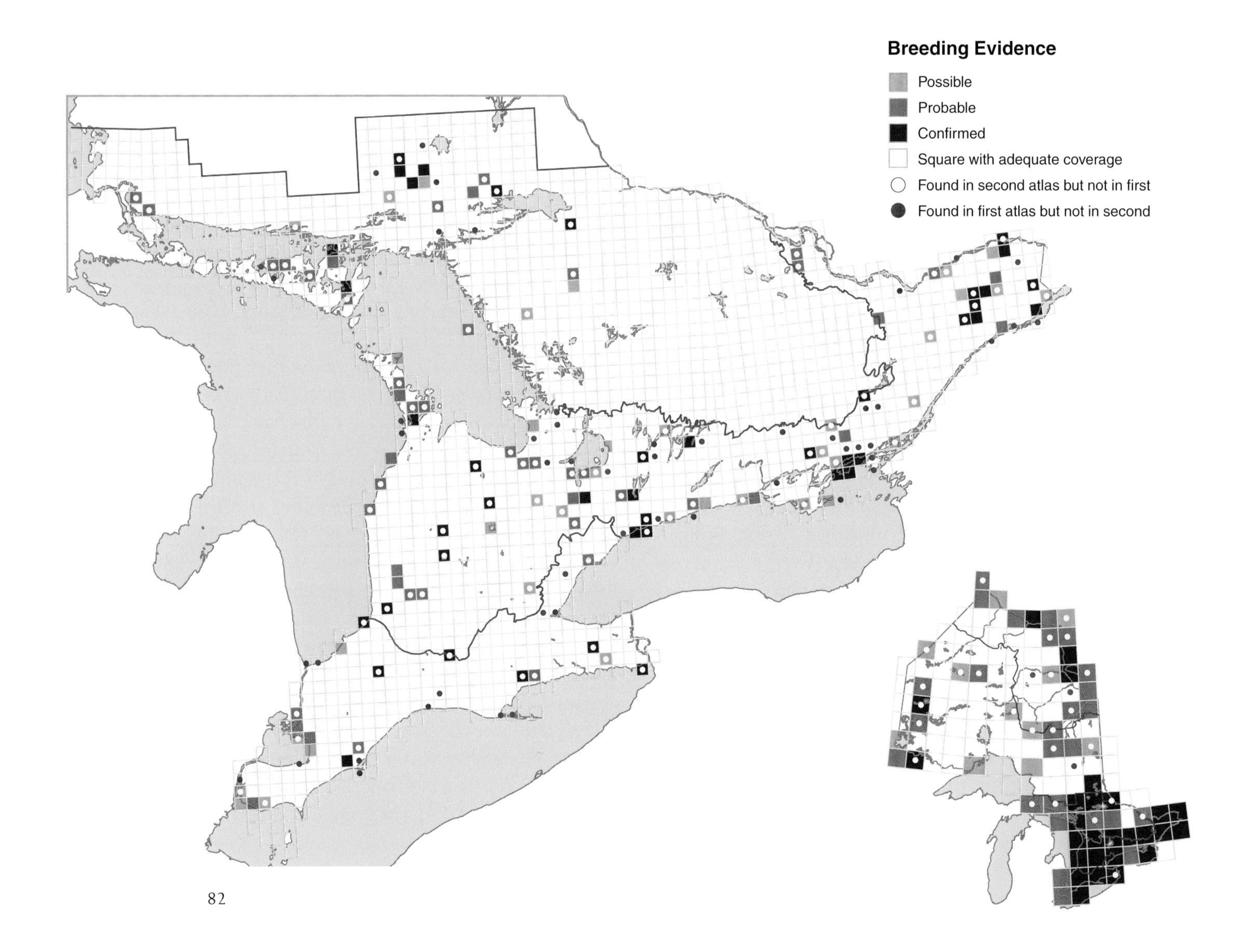

BREEDING EVIDENCE

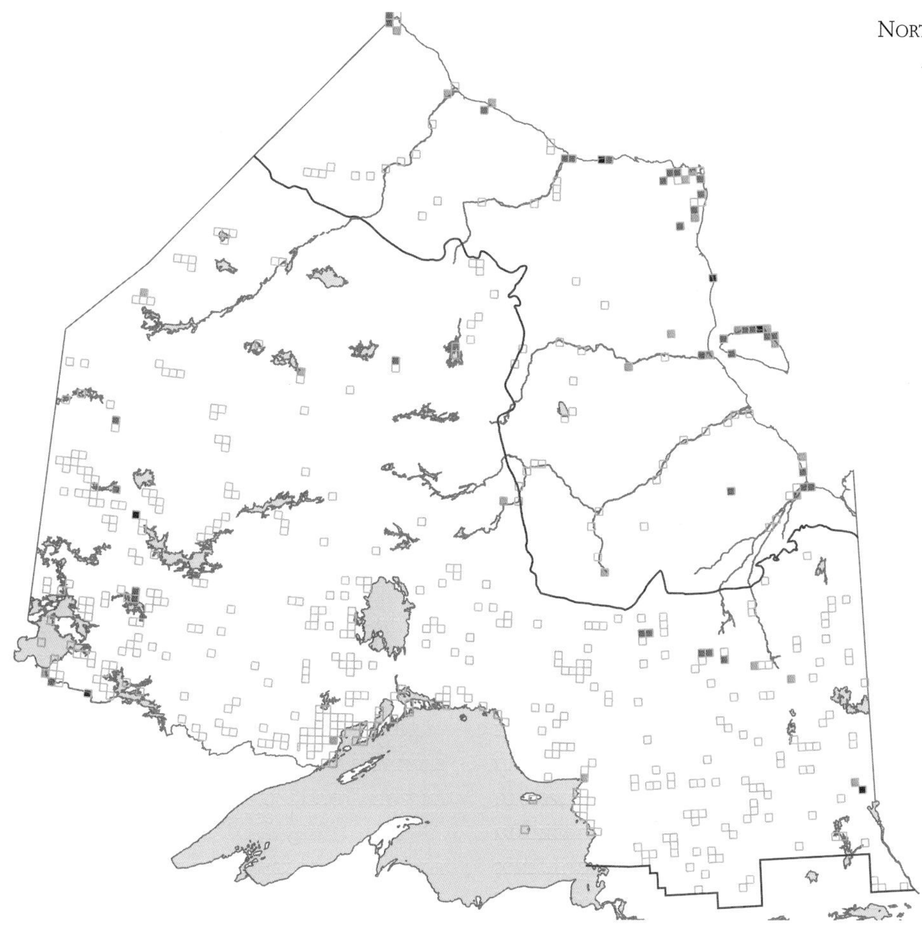

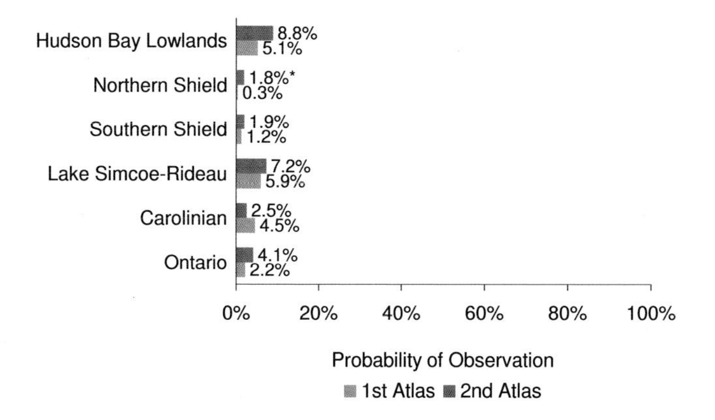

marshes along shorelines of the lower Great Lakes. Many southern inland records are associated with sewage lagoons, but the Northern Shoveler also nests in natural wetlands and impoundments. Although the general distribution south of the Shield remained approximately the same, few locations support it regularly. It was observed during both atlases in certain Great Lakes marshes (Lake St. Clair, Rondeau, and the Kingston area), Lake Simcoe, large inland impoundments such as Hullett and Luther marshes, and some sewage lagoons.

Waterfowl surveys indicate that the Northern Shoveler has increased significantly from the early 1990s to 2005, from about 2,000,000 to 3,500,000 birds, primarily in the prairie pothole region (Canadian Wildlife Service Waterfowl Committee 2005). It was not reported on enough Ontario BBS routes to determine a trend, but it experienced a marginally significant annual increase of 2.7% in Canada from 1981 to 2005.

Breeding biology: The Northern Shoveler prefers to nest in areas with grasses up to 60 cm tall. Nests are typically on the ground within 90 m of water, but occasionally they are on floating mats of cattails (DuBowy 1996). This species prefers to nest near permanent ponds or marshes, and sewage lagoons often provide suitable nesting habitat. Nests are well hidden and difficult to find. Broods, however, are relatively easy to spot, and this is the easiest method of confirming this species. The brood remains with the female near the natal area for six to seven weeks, provided the habitat is suitable; otherwise, she may lead the young to another pond as much as 1-2 km away (Poston 1974; Peck and James 1983; DuBowy 1996). The presence of broods or a female is usually indicative of nesting within the square. Males, however, generally abandon the female before the eggs hatch and move to large water bodies. Thus, males seen after late June may not be in the square where breeding occurred. The optimal periods for detecting breeding evidence for the species are in May when the male is likely to accompany the female and from mid-June to early August when broods are feeding in open water.

Abundance: The Northern Shoveler was not detected on sufficient point counts to generate an abundance map. Nonetheless, point count data indicate that it is most abundant in the Hudson Bay Lowlands. It occurs primarily along the coast where there are numerous shallow marshes and ponds surrounded by short grasses and sedges. Even within this area, it is only locally rare to uncommon and was recorded on less than 1% of point counts. It is almost absent in the Northern Shield and its status in the interior of the Hudson Bay Lowlands is unknown. South of the northern coasts, the species is rare and local in abundance. – *Al Sandilands*

Northern Pintail

Canard pilet

Anas acuta

Larry Kirtley

The Northern Pintail is widely distributed across North America and Eurasia. The core portions of its North American breeding range are Alaska and the prairie pothole region, but it is found throughout northern Canada (Austin and Miller 1995). Although it was once among the most abundant waterfowl species in North America, its continental population has declined greatly since the 1970s (Canadian Wildlife Service Waterfowl Committee 2005). Its favoured breeding habitats consist of shallow wetlands dispersed throughout prairie grasslands and arctic tundra (Austin and Miller 1995).

Distribution and population status: The Northern Pintail was likely a common nester historically in Ontario's north (Manning 1952). In southern Ontario, by contrast, the first documented nesting record for the species was from Chatham-Kent in 1890 (Baillie and Harrington 1936). In the Kingston area, where some of the larger southern Ontario concentrations occur, it was first reported nesting only in 1949 (Quilliam 1973). Since then, it has apparently become more common south of the Shield, though it is unclear if this represents a real range expansion or incomplete historical surveys (Austin and Miller 1995). The species shows an interesting, slightly discontinuous distribution in Ontario, with two nearly separate northern and southern ranges separated by the Boreal Forest.

During the second atlas, the probability of observation for this duck was greatest in the Hudson Bay Lowlands (18%) and Lake Simcoe-Rideau regions (4%) and less than 2% in all other regions. The importance of Ontario's Hudson Bay Lowlands as a breeding area for the species is confirmed by a recent study of pintails marked during winter from New Jersey to northern Florida. Thirteen of 14 birds that summered in Ontario were located in the Hudson Bay Lowlands, the exception being a bird found in the Kingston area (Malecki et al. 2006).

The data collected for this atlas is representative of the previously documented distribution of this species in Ontario,

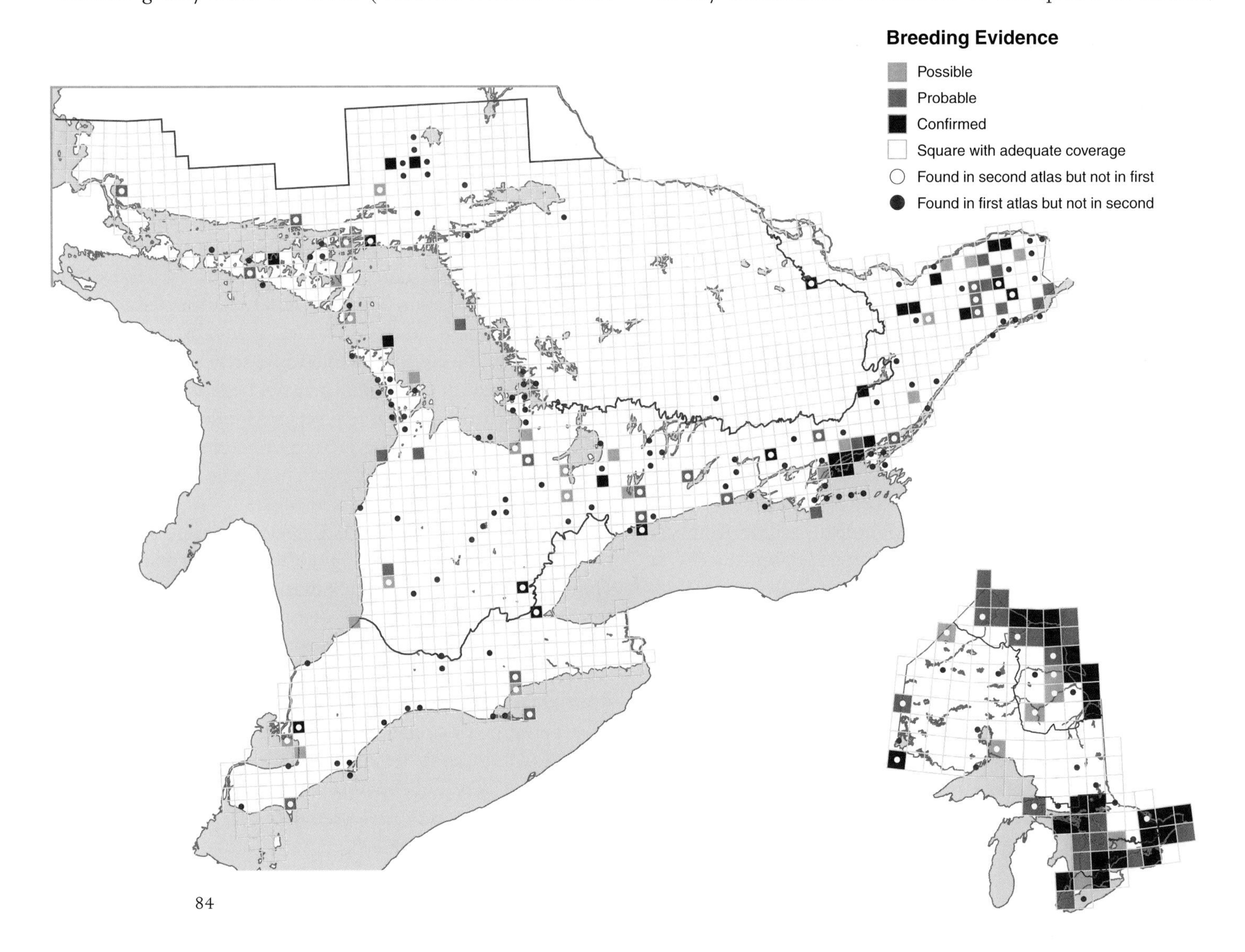

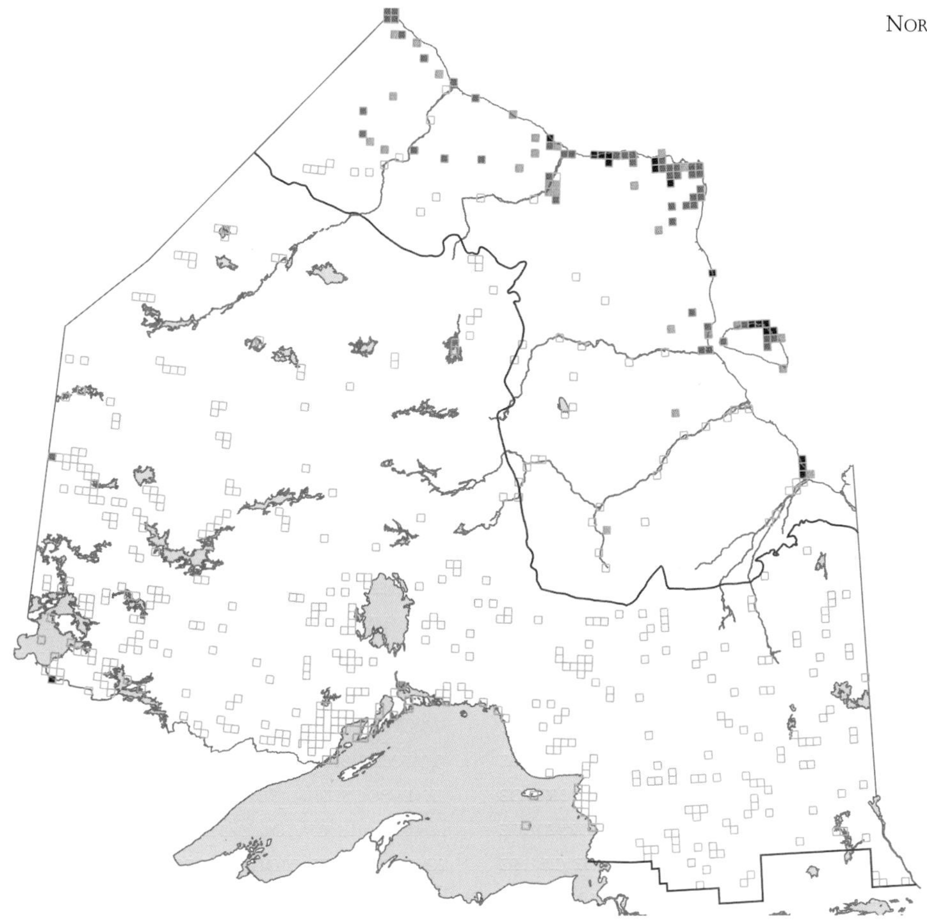

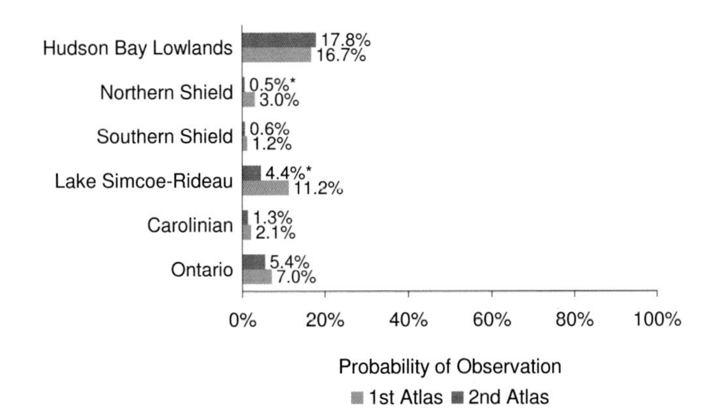

with little change in either the range or relative distribution of squares with breeding evidence since the first atlas. However, the probability of observation declined in four of five regions, although significantly only in the Lake Simcoe-Rideau (61%) and Northern Shield (82%) regions. Only in the Hudson Bay Lowlands did the probability of observation increase, though not significantly. Also, there was a high level of turnover in occupied squares in southern Ontario and through the Boreal Forest, with few squares having pintails in both atlases. Both situations may reflect changing local habitat conditions and bird responses to those changes. However, they may also indicate sampling variability when a small breeding population is spread over a very large area.

Breeding biology: The Northern Pintail begins nesting earlier than most North American ducks, shortly after ice-out, as early as April in the south and about mid-May in the north (Austin and Miller 1995). Individuals form new pair bonds each winter, but males are promiscuous, engaging in extra-pair copulations, particularly during the laying period. Mated and unmated males are often involved in intense pursuit flights (Austin and Miller 1995). The nest is on the ground, frequently a long distance from water and characteristically in an open site with low vegetative cover, including tilled cropland. Males attend females until soon after onset of incubation, after which they join other males in large post-breeding aggregations before flying considerable distances to moulting areas. As pair dissolution likely occurs prior to the peak of most atlassing activity, and incubating females are very inconspicuous, spending up to 80% of the day on the nest, the species was probably overlooked in some squares, particularly in the south. However, pintail females with broods are relatively conspicuous and the hen is easy to identify, making June and July the best months to confirm breeding. Accordingly, broods were by far the most frequently recorded evidence of confirmed breeding.

Abundance: As is the case with most waterfowl, the timing and methods of point counts are not effective for quantifying the abundance of this species. However, the probability of observation does show the relative importance of each region. Density estimates generated from the CWS spring breeding pair surveys (K. Ross, unpubl. data) suggest 13.1 pairs /100 km^2 within the Hudson Bay Lowlands. In contrast, observations in other regions across the province suggest very low pair densities. Although the Northern Pintail has declined considerably since the 1970s across much of Canada, there is no indication that its abundance in the Hudson Bay Lowlands, the core of its Ontario range, has changed substantially since the first atlas. – *Michel Gendron*

Green-winged Teal

Sarcelle d'hiver

Anas crecca

John Reaume

The Green-winged Teal, the smallest and one of the fastest flying of North America's dabbling ducks, breeds commonly throughout Canada and Alaska south of the treeline and in all contiguous US states bordering Canada. Its breeding range extends south into the northwestern and north-central US states, and north, at least sporadically, into tundra habitat. Unlike many North American dabbling ducks, however, breeding density is not greatest in the prairie pothole region. It winters primarily in the US and south to Mexico and Cuba but also along the British Columbia coast; a few may even linger in ice-free waters of southern Ontario. A Eurasian subspecies breeds widely across similar latitudes from Greenland to Japan, occurring in Ontario as a rare vagrant.

Distribution and population status: Historically, the Green-winged Teal may have nested mostly, if not entirely, in the far northern parts of the province (Baillie and Harrington 1936). However, Godfrey (1966) showed it as breeding throughout Ontario, except in the southern agricultural areas. By the time of the first atlas, it was a confirmed breeder in all parts of the province, although still most common in the Hudson Bay Lowlands. Since the first atlas, there has been no significant change in the probability of observation in the province as a whole or in any of the regions, nor has the species shown any range extensions or contractions. Its presence in southern Ontario may represent a true range expansion compared to early settlement times, perhaps in response to human modifications to the landscape. In the southern part of the province, two areas stand out as having the highest breeding densities: one in eastern Ontario south of the Shield and the other in a band from Manitoulin Island northeast to the Sturgeon River valley. It is still a sporadic breeder in southwest Ontario and across most of the Precambrian Shield. As with several other waterfowl species, the low productivity of wetlands throughout much of the Northern Shield region may limit its distribution there.

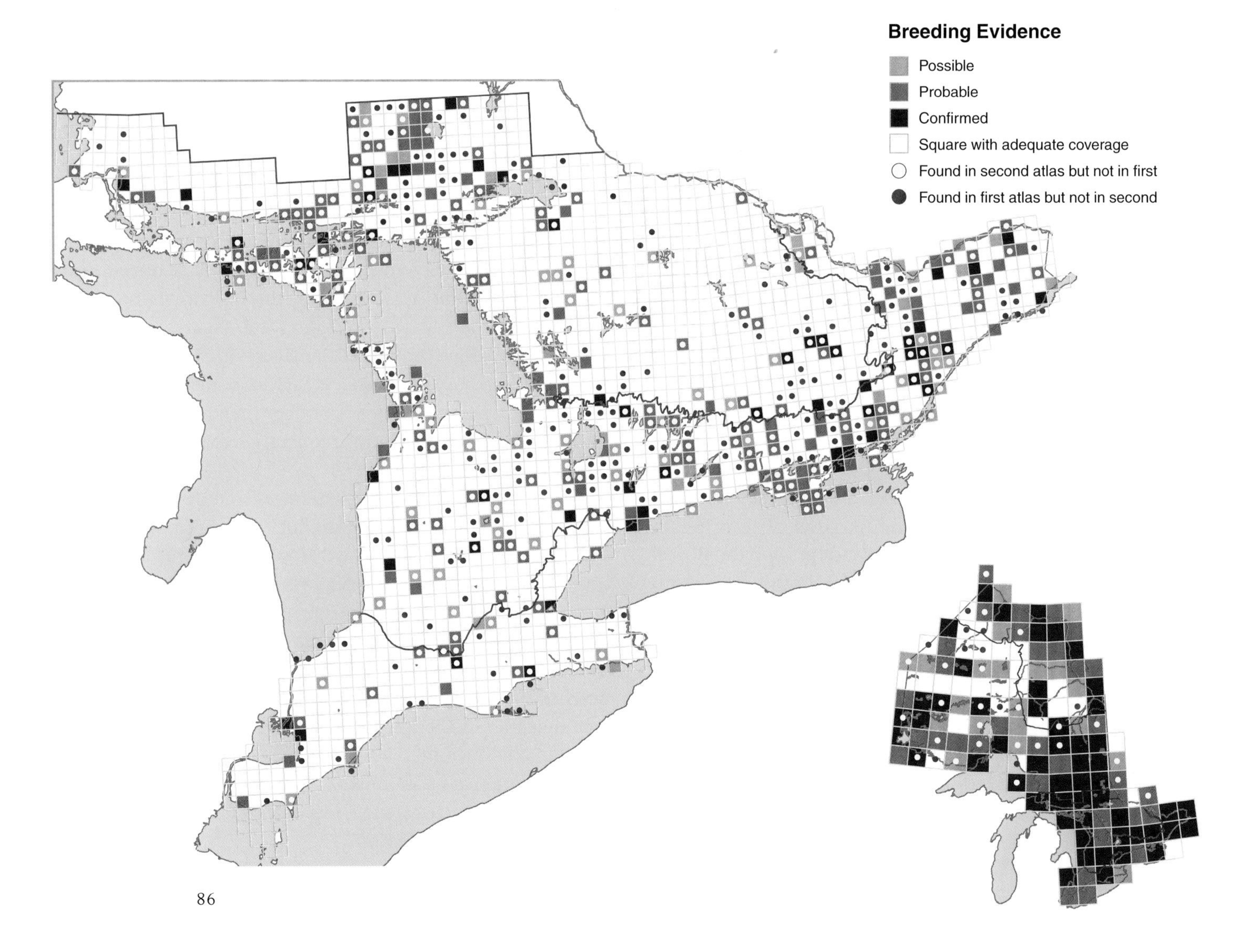

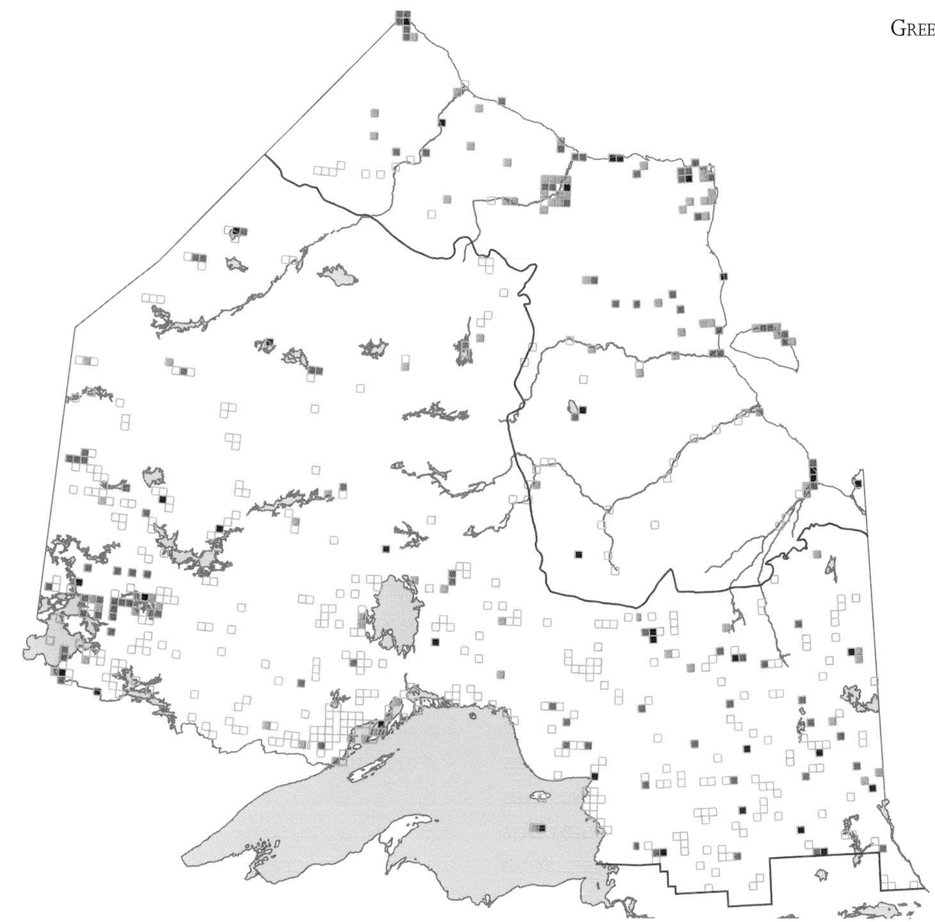

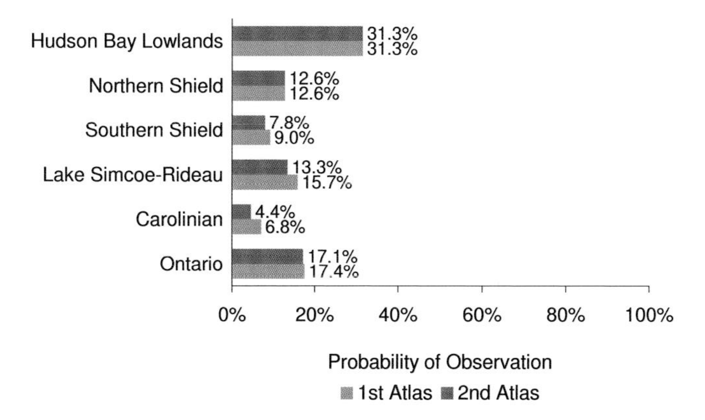

Breeding biology: The widespread distribution of the Green-winged Teal from the Hudson Bay coast to agricultural southern Ontario shows that it is capable of adapting to a variety of habitats for breeding. It generally nests in upland areas with heavy cover of graminoids or brush within 200 m or less of water (Johnson 1995). It also readily nests near anthropogenic wetlands such as sewage lagoons where available. The dense nesting cover typically conceals nests, making them very difficult to detect. Females do not flush from nests unless approached very closely, and their discovery is usually fortuitous. In addition, courtship takes place early in spring, and the male abandons the female shortly after incubation begins, often leaving the area to moult. Thus the presence of a lone drake in suitable habitat in late June or July does not necessarily constitute evidence of local breeding.

Broods are raised on shallow lakes, ponds, bogs, and marshes. The female cares for the brood alone and is generally secretive at this time, usually keeping close to cover, although if pressed she may perform vigorous distraction displays to protect the young (Munro 1949). The confirmation rate for the Green-winged Teal was the lowest of the dabbling ducks (equalled by American Wigeon) at 17% of the squares with breeding evidence. Because of the difficulty of detecting breeding individuals, atlas data may underestimate the true distribution and abundance of this species.

Abundance: The Green-winged Teal population in Ontario appears to be stable in terms of both its distribution and abundance. BBS data show a declining but non-significant trend in Ontario for 1968-2005 (Downes et al. 2005), and data from the Eastern Waterfowl Survey (Canadian Wildlife Service Waterfowl Committee 2006) do not reveal any trend since 1990 when the survey began. Across Canada, BBS data show a non-significant positive trend for 1968-2005 (Downes et al. 2005), and aerial transect surveys of waterfowl in western North America indicate that numbers of this species have grown from an estimated 1.5 million in the 1960s to nearly 2.5 million in recent years (Canadian Wildlife Service Waterfowl Committee 2006).

Point count data are probably unsuitable for evaluating populations of any waterfowl species, particularly a small, cryptic nester like the Green-winged Teal. Nevertheless, the data from the second atlas clearly show that the Hudson Bay Lowlands region remains the part of the province with the highest breeding densities. The tendency to nest mainly in remote northern areas little disturbed by humans, in Ontario and across its range, has probably contributed to the success of this little duck. – *Jack Hughes*

Canvasback

Fuligule à dos blanc

Aythya valisineria

Jim Richards

The Canvasback breeds exclusively in North America and predominantly in the western portion of the continent. Its range extends from subarctic and boreal lakes in Alaska, Yukon, and the Northwest Territories southeast to its core range in wetlands in the aspen parkland from British Columbia to Manitoba and the prairie pothole region of the north-central US (Mowbray 2002). It winters across the southern US and northern Mexico, with the largest concentrations at widely scattered localities such as Puget Sound, San Francisco Bay, the Mississippi River delta, Lake St. Clair, the Detroit and Niagara Rivers, Chesapeake Bay, and coastal North Carolina and Maryland (Mowbray 2002). Much of the variability in the Canvasback population is attributable to annual variation in precipitation, which determines the amount of suitable breeding habitat available. The species has largely recovered from a long period of drought-induced population decline (0.6% annually) from 1955 to 1993 (Bellrose 1980; Kear 2005).

Distribution and population status: Results from the two atlases are quite similar. Breeding evidence was recorded for the Canvasback in six squares during the second atlas (three confirmed, two probable, one possible) and seven squares during the first atlas (four confirmed, three probable). Breeding evidence was obtained during both atlases from the Walpole Island marshes. New sites and breeding evidence during the second atlas include nests at the Toronto Islands and Toronto's Leslie St. Spit, Oshawa (female with brood at Second Marsh), and an abandoned iron mine east of Hwy 105 between Ear Falls and Red Lake in northwestern Ontario. Areas where evidence was recorded during the first atlas but not the second (despite adequate coverage) include Luther Marsh, Rondeau Prov. Park, and the Lake St. Clair area. An area of confirmed breeding at Berens Lake in northwestern Ontario in the first atlas was not surveyed during the second.

The Canvasback has long been a rare and localized breeder

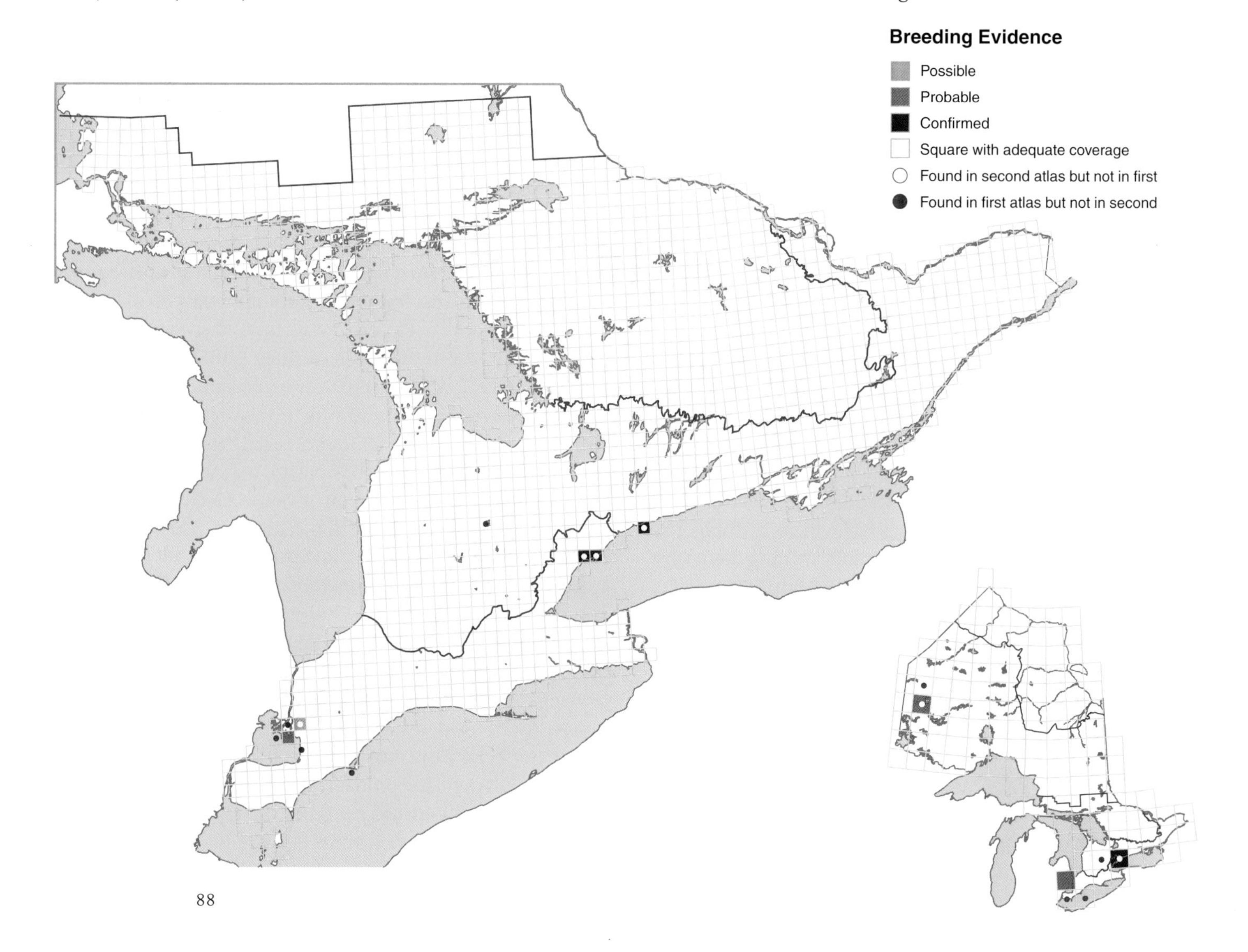

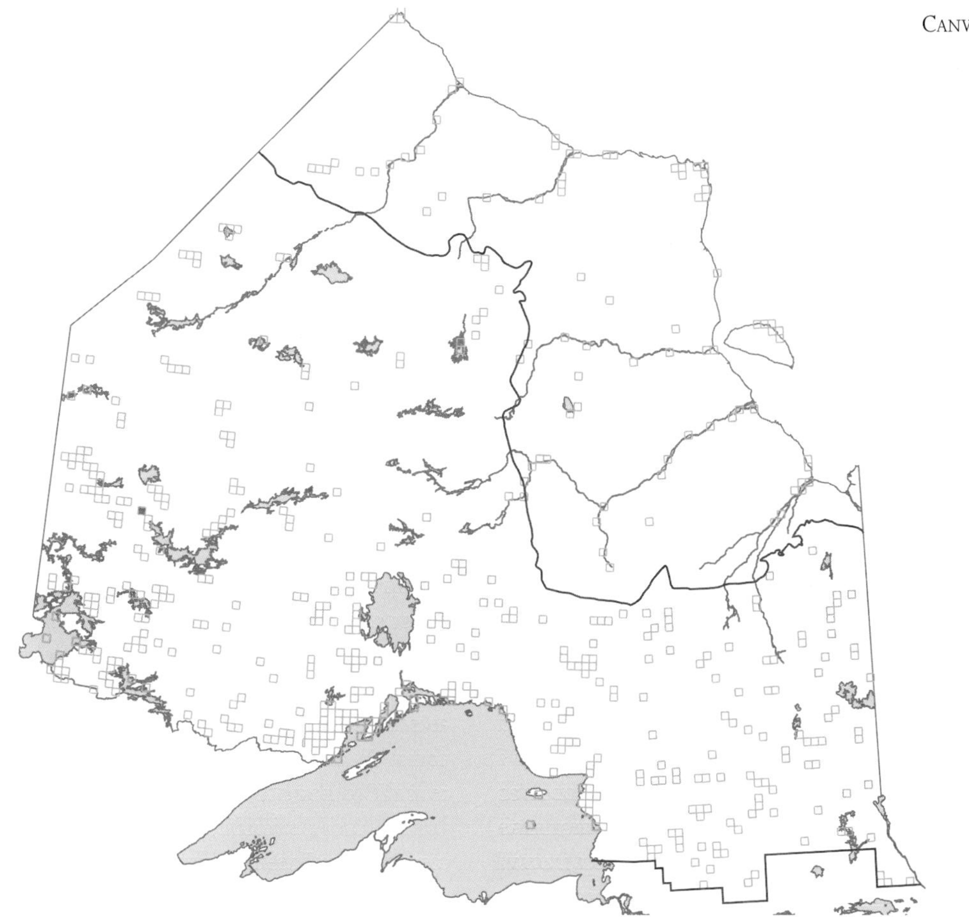

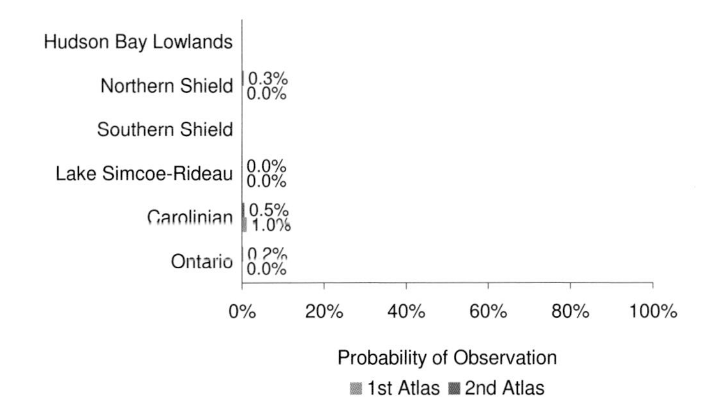

in Ontario. McIlwraith (1894) did not consider it an Ontario breeding bird. Baillie (1962) noted historical records of both nests and broods on Lake St. Clair in 1897, 1948, 1953, and 1954. Peck (1976) and Peck and James (1983) considered it a hypothetical breeder, as previous records lacked material evidence. It was placed on the confirmed list of breeding birds (James 1984a) when a brood was photographed at Luther Marsh in 1983, although breeding likely occurred there annually between 1957 and 1984 (Sandilands 1984). The first documented nests for Ontario were found at the Leslie St. Spit in 2000 (Coady 2000). To date, reports of Canvasback nests or broods have accumulated for Walpole Island, Chatham-Kent (Mitchell's Bay, St. Clair National Wildlife Area), the Counties of Elgin (Port Stanley) and Wellington (Luther Marsh), Toronto (Toronto Islands, Leslie St. Spit), Durham Region (Oshawa Second Marsh), and Kenora Dist. (Berens Lake).

Breeding biology: The Canvasback prefers small lakes, ponds, or marshes with ample emergent vegetation for nesting and an abundance of submergent vegetation (either Sago Pondweed or Wild Celery) for feeding. Many aspects of its breeding biology make it conspicuous and easily confirmed. Pair formation occurs during spring staging and in nesting areas in late April or early May, making courtship behaviour easy to observe. Males are not territorial and do not defend the nest, but do defend a foraging space of 1-3 m around the female early in the nesting season (Mowbray 2002). The breeding home range usually includes several ponds or bays with abundant submergent vegetation for multiple pairs to use as feeding areas. The bulky nests are generally in stands of emergent vegetation in open settings, often close to or over water. Intra- and interspecific nest parasitism is common (especially by the Redhead). Females take regular breaks from incubation to feed, making their presence obvious in the breeding season. Within 24 hours of hatching, the female and young depart the nest pond for larger bays, where their presence is more easily detected. The female stays with early season broods nearly to flight stage and remains two to three weeks with late season broods before undertaking a moult migration. Females and their female offspring are highly philopatric to nesting ponds, facilitating multiple opportunities over successive years to confirm nesting in areas where breeding has been suspected. Atlas results likely present an accurate assessment of breeding status.

Abundance: The Canvasback was not detected on any point counts. It remains a very rare breeder in Ontario, at the extreme eastern edge of its range, with a minimum of eight known pairs and the total number of pairs likely numbering fewer than twenty. – *Glenn Coady*

Redhead

Fuligule à tête rouge

Aythya americana

Ron Ridout

The Redhead is exclusively a North American species, breeding predominantly on the prairies but also through the Northwest Territories into Alaska and in marshes in the western US. Ontario is considered outside its regular breeding range, where Woodin and Michot (2002) described it as breeding very locally and irregularly. It breeds annually within the province in small numbers (Sandilands in Cadman et al. 1987) but is more familiar to Ontarians as a migrant and wintering duck on the Great Lakes.

Distribution and population status: McIlwraith (1894) and Baillie and Harrington (1936) did not think the Redhead nested in Ontario, but there is evidence that it nested on Lake St. Clair as early as 1877 (Peck and James 1983). Lumsden (1951) reported a small population on Lake St. Clair in 1949, and the Redhead pioneered at Luther Marsh shortly after the wetland was created in the 1950s (Boyer and Devitt 1961). The first atlas confirmed that the species was a regular but rare breeder in southern Ontario, and there was one record of a pair from the Red Lake area. Distribution in the south during the first atlas was associated mostly with Great Lakes marshes and large, inland marshes.

The probability of observation of the Redhead did not differ significantly between the two atlases. There were only 13 squares in which the Redhead was observed in both atlases; 12 were in Great Lakes wetlands while the other was at Luther Marsh. Birds were observed in a few more squares in the north, including four in the Northern Shield and two in the Hudson Bay Lowlands. Breeding was confirmed at the Alfred sewage lagoon, but most sewage lagoon records were probably of non-breeders.

The global population of the Redhead has not changed significantly in the past 50 years, but it is relatively low compared with other waterfowl species, averaging only about 0.6 million birds; however, it experienced a high population in the

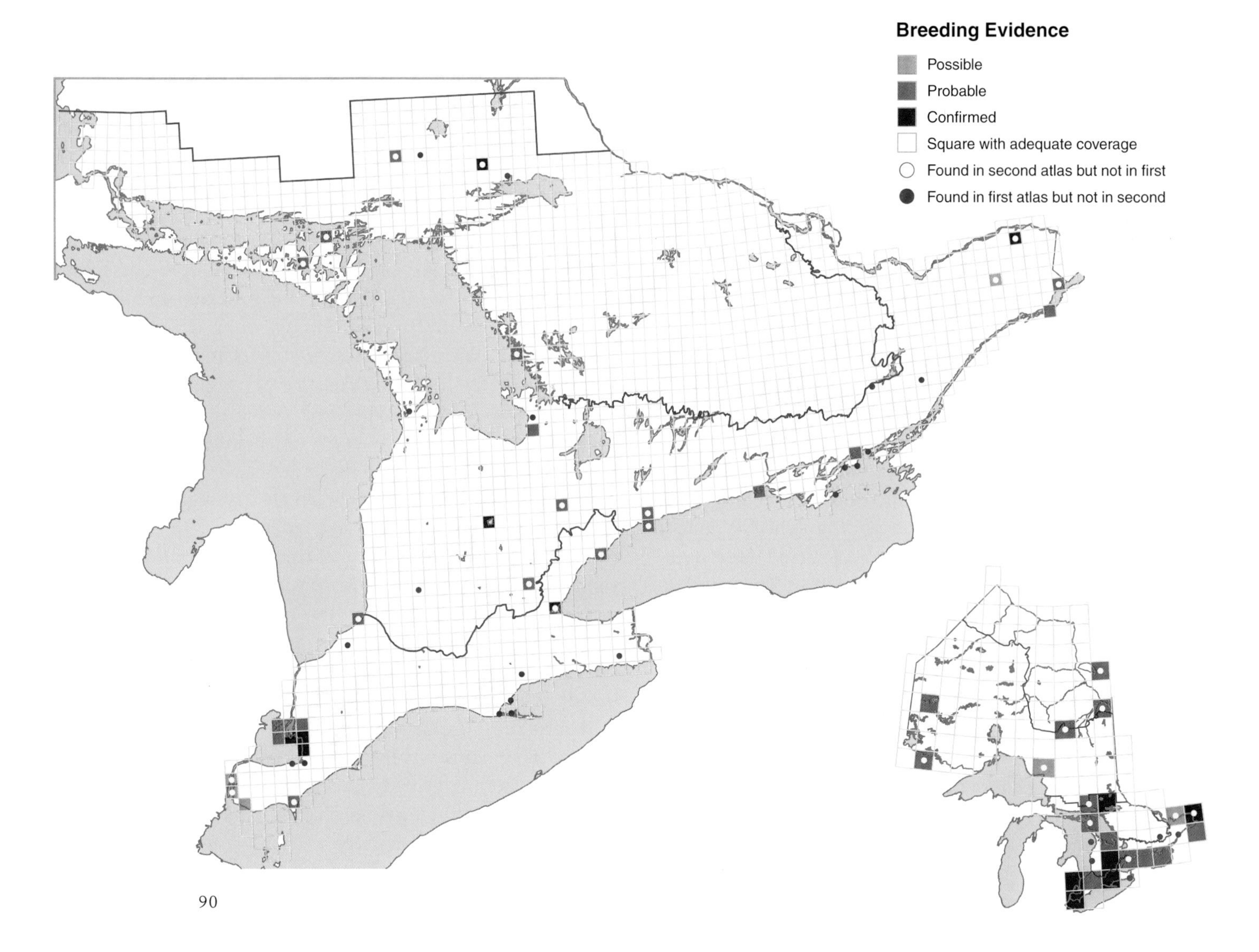

BREEDING EVIDENCE

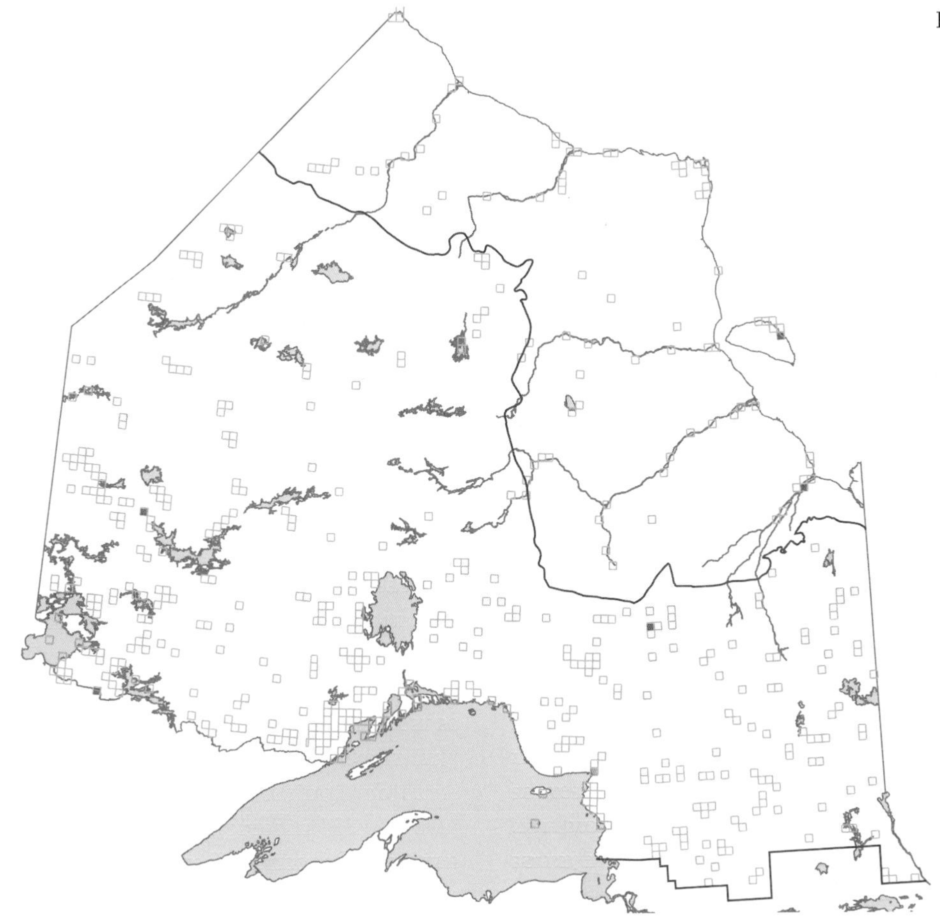

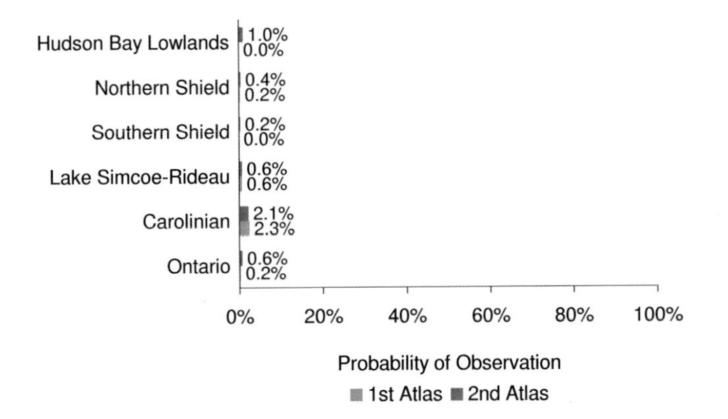

late 1990s (Canadian Wildlife Service Waterfowl Committee 2005; US Fish and Wildlife Service 2005).

Breeding biology: The Redhead is a semi-parasitic species that often lays its eggs in the nests of other waterfowl species. Females use four different nesting strategies to maximize reproductive success: normal egg laying, parasitic egg laying, parasitic egg laying prior to normal egg laying, and non-breeding when conditions are adverse (Sorenson 1991). Thus, in addition to normal atlassing techniques, the Redhead can be confirmed as a breeder by observing Redhead ducklings within broods of other waterfowl species or eggs within other nests. On the other hand, many males do not breed due to the low proportion of females in the population, and each year as many as 50% of adult females do not breed (Woodin and Michot 2002). Consequently, many possible and probable Redhead records may have been of non-breeding birds.

The Redhead typically nests in extensive marshes associated with large water bodies but also occasionally nests in fens and Leatherleaf-dominated peatlands. Cattails and bulrushes are preferred emergent plants for nesting, as is Leatherleaf on shorelines and in peatlands. The nest may be on the ground 1-2 m from the shoreline but is more often within emergents above water (Peck and James 1983; Woodin and Michot 2002). Although nests may be found, checking for broods is the easiest method to confirm breeding. Individual Redhead ducklings should also be sought among broods of other waterfowl species, especially the Ring-necked Duck, Canvasback, and Lesser Scaup in Ontario. The atlas map is a relatively accurate reflection of the Redhead's breeding distribution within the province and demonstrates that there are relatively few sites that regularly support this species. Of the 37 squares in which the Redhead was reported during the second atlas, it was confirmed in only seven, with possible breeding in six squares and probable breeding in 24 squares. As a high proportion of the population does not breed in a given year, the extent of breeding in the province may have been overestimated.

Abundance: The Redhead continues to be a rare but regular breeder in the south and a rare and sporadic breeder in the north. There may be several hundred pairs nesting at Lake St. Clair (Austen et al. 1994), and it continues to be regular but uncommon at Luther Marsh. Outside of Lake St. Clair and Luther Marsh, abundance estimates for all but two squares during the first atlas were of a single pair; estimates in the remaining two squares were of two to 10 pairs. This trend appears to continue, with Lake St. Clair remaining the stronghold for the Redhead in Ontario. – *Al Sandilands*

Ring-necked Duck

Fuligule à collier

Aythya collaris

Ron Ridout

Superficially similar to the more familiar scaup, the Ring-necked Duck is a strikingly plumaged bird of the boreal region. Restricted to north-central North America historically, the species has been expanding its range since the early 20th century and now occurs from the Atlantic Provinces west to British Columbia and the Yukon, locally into Alaska (Hohman and Eberhardt 1998). It favours shallow freshwater marshes, fens, and bogs, feeding primarily on aquatic invertebrates and emergent vegetation.

Distribution and population status: The distribution of the Ring-necked Duck in Ontario changed considerably in the 1900s. Although it may have always been a breeding species in the northwest part of the province, the first documented breeding record for Ontario occurred at Lac Seul in 1919, and nesting was not confirmed in south-central Ontario until the early 1940s (Sandilands 2005). Since then, the species has spread to cover much of the forested region of the Shield. Currently, it breeds from Hudson Bay as far south as Luther Marsh and Prince Edward Co. and east to the Rideau Lakes area.

Since the first atlas, the Ring-necked Duck has shown a dramatic and significant increase in the probability of observation in the province as a whole (58%) and in the Lake Simcoe-Rideau (45%), Southern Shield (70%), and Northern Shield (61%) regions. Surveys by CWS indicate that increases are most evident in the Atlantic Provinces, but populations in the Northern and Southern Shield regions also show a small but positive trend (Canadian Wildlife Service Waterfowl Committee 2006).

The overall extent of the species' range in Ontario has not changed noticeably, and the observed increase largely occurred through infilling of gaps in distribution. Some turnover in particular squares recording the Ring-necked Duck also occurred, perhaps related to changing wetland conditions such as beaver

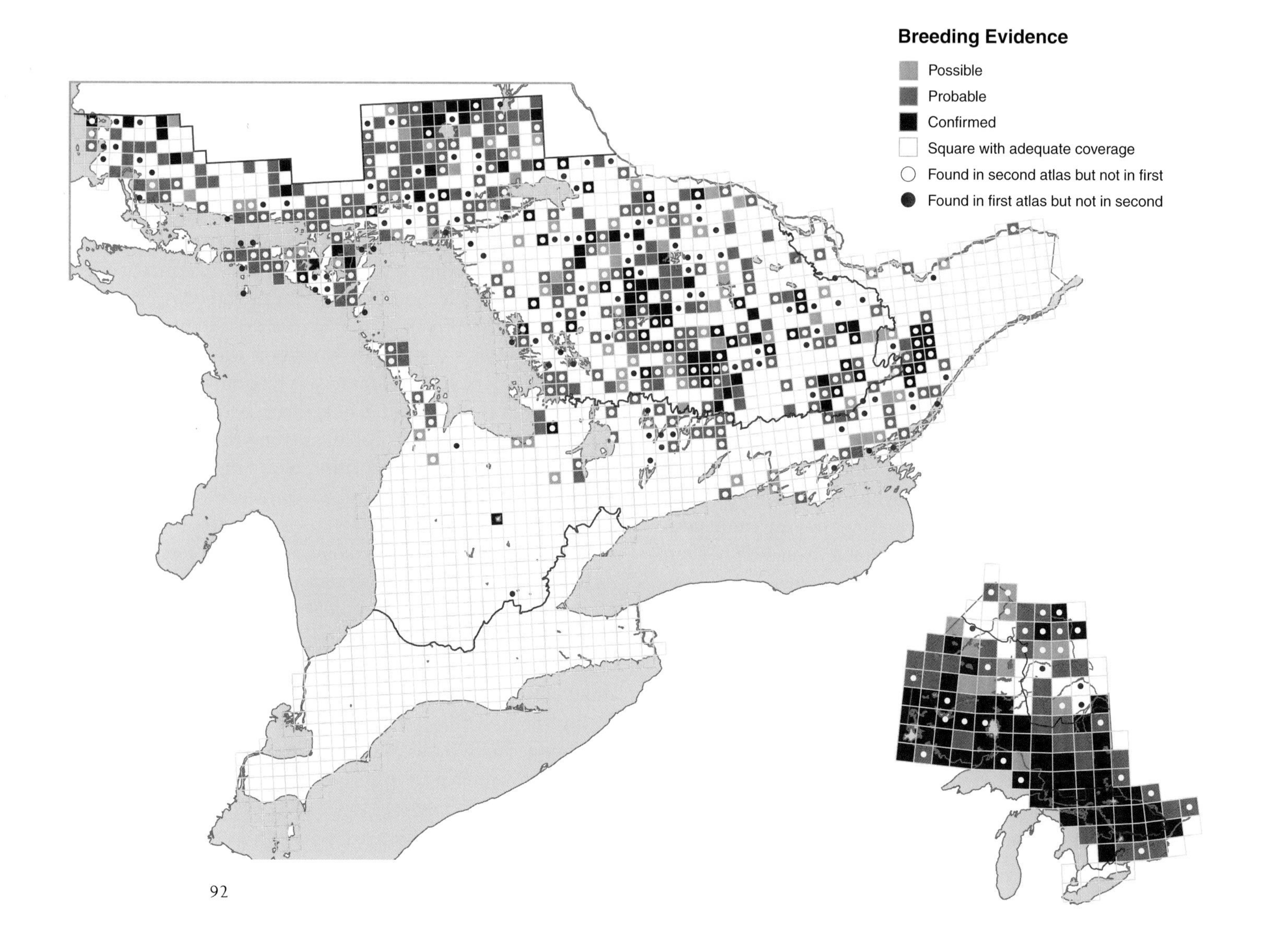

BREEDING EVIDENCE

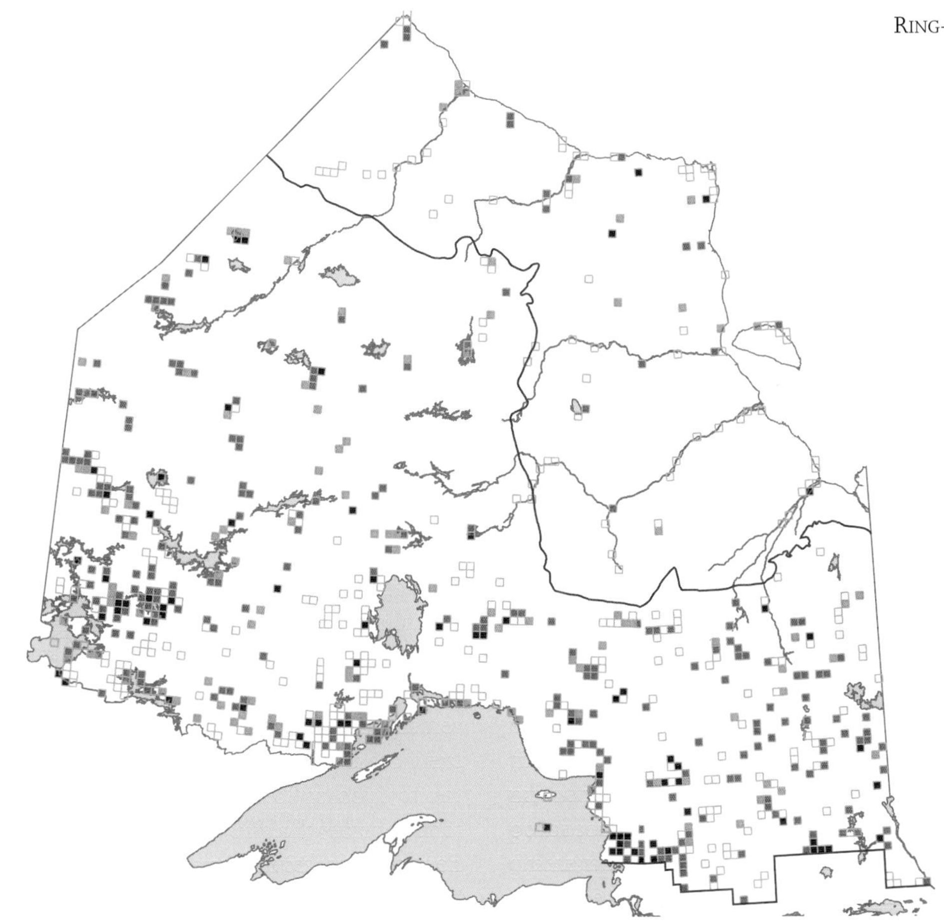

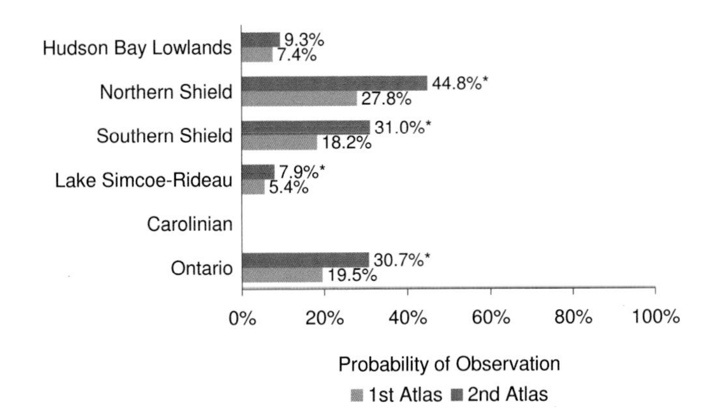

pond and wetland creation and stagnation. Increases were seen especially in the southeastern portion of the Southern Shield and Lake Simcoe-Rideau regions and in the northern Hudson Bay Lowlands.

The population and range expansion exhibited by the species is difficult to explain. Mendall (1958) felt that increases were simply due to eastward pioneering by the western population. However, McNicol (in Cadman et al. 1987) suggested that it might be partly due to an increase in beaver populations, which create good habitat conditions for this duck.

Breeding biology: The Ring-necked Duck forms pairs during migration, occasionally lingering at southern sites into late April or early May. On the breeding grounds, the species is not very territorial, although males may defend mates from others. Nest building takes place shortly after arrival at breeding sites, and eggs are laid as early as mid-May but generally during June, depending on latitude (Peck and James 1983). Males will remain with females until early incubation, at which point they depart, often moving considerable distances to moult (Sandilands 2005). As well, many males may be unpaired during the breeding season, and so single males or those in small groups may not necessarily indicate breeding at the site. The clutch is incubated by the female for 25-29 days, during which time she leaves the nest infrequently and so can be difficult to detect. Young leave the nest shortly after hatching, staying close to the female for seven to eight weeks (Hohman and Eberhardt 1998). During most of this period, the young remain at or near the natal wetland. Outside of the incubation period, foraging pairs and females with broods are both reasonably conspicuous; consequently, they should have been detected in most squares where the species occurs, and indeed most records are of these two types of evidence. Some gaps in distribution may occur farther north where the road network is sparse and preferred habitats are less accessible. Overall, the maps are likely an accurate representation of the duck's distribution and status in Ontario.

Abundance: A reliable abundance map for the species could not be produced due to the difficulty of detecting waterfowl on point counts. However, a study in the region from Huntsville to Cochrane found an average density of about 19 pairs/100 km^2 (McNicol et al. 1987). CWS estimated between 42,000 and 67,000 breeding pairs in the Boreal Shield in northeastern Ontario and western Québec over the atlas period (Canadian Wildlife Service Waterfowl Committee 2005). Data from the first atlas suggested that the Ring-necked Duck was about four times more abundant in the north than the south (Sandilands 2005). Although it was not detected on many point counts, the greatest number of detections occurred in areas between latitudes 45° and 50° N. – *Seabrooke Leckie*

Greater Scaup

Fuligule milouinan

Aythya marila

Barry S. Cherriere

The Greater Scaup is the only diving duck (tribe Aythyini) with a circumpolar breeding distribution. In North America, the species is widely distributed across arctic and subarctic regions from Alaska to Labrador but has a discontinuous breeding distribution (knowledge of which is limited by appropriately timed investigation of remote areas). It mainly nests in coastal tundra but also in taiga habitats. The greatest concentration of breeding birds occurs in western Alaska (Kessel et al. 2002). Breeding observations have been reported from western Hudson Bay south from Rankin Inlet, Nunavut, to the northern Ontario coastline as far east as Cape Henrietta Maria (Peck and James 1983; Kessel et al. 2002). The species also nests in low densities in northern Québec along northeastern James Bay and eastern Hudson Bay east into western Labrador, with scattered breeding in Newfoundland and south to Anticosti Island, Québec, in the Gulf of St. Lawrence (Todd 1963; Godfrey 1986). The Greater Scaup is found on migration throughout the continental interior but winters primarily in coastal waters and on the Great Lakes.

Distribution and population status: In Ontario, the Greater Scaup nests within the Hudson Bay Lowlands. There were a few observations from sewage lagoons at northern aboriginal communities within the Northern Shield but no evidence of confirmed breeding. Both atlases show this species' stronghold in Ontario is the Hudson Bay Lowlands, particularly near Cape Henrietta Maria, with very limited breeding evidence in the interior lowlands. Although the habitat preferred by the species is more extensive in the vicinity of Cape Henrietta Maria, the number of records is in part an artifact of more intensive aerial coverage by OMNR and CWS aerial waterfowl surveys. Suitable habitat occurs all along the coast, and the species was noted breeding in the vicinity of the

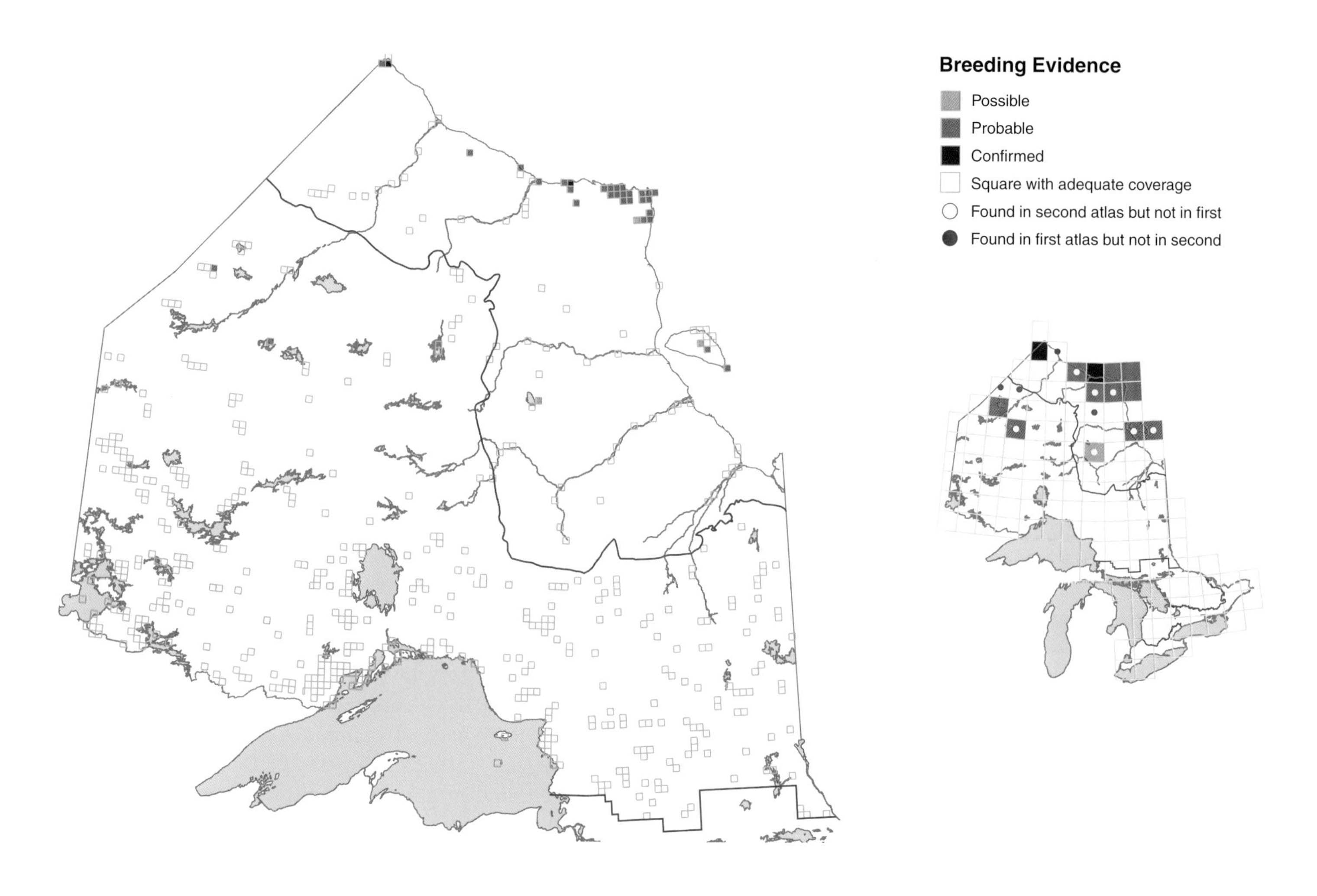

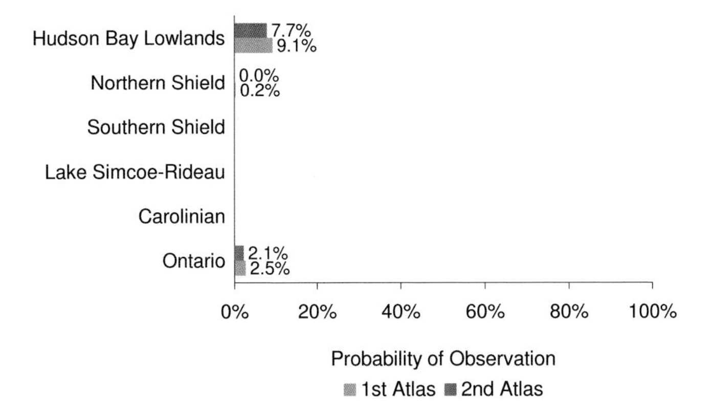

Shagamu River in 1990 (Wilson and McRae 1993). The probability of observation was similar in both atlases. The Greater Scaup did not exhibit any range changes between atlases, probably due to its preference for nesting in the tundra and taiga habitats that are almost exclusively found adjacent to Hudson Bay and northern James Bay.

It is difficult to assess Greater Scaup population status within the province because breeding densities are relatively low and there is no published information regarding its abundance over time. Since the first atlas, however, conservationists have become concerned about the species in North America because relatively little is known about its breeding biology and population dynamics, and there are conflicting population trend estimates between the core breeding areas (i.e., stable numbers of breeders and increasing numbers of non-breeders) and the main Atlantic Flyway wintering area (i.e., declining numbers of birds) (Conant and Groves 2001; Kessel et al. 2002). Further, large proportions of the continental population stage and overwinter in industrialized and urban areas on the Great Lakes and Atlantic coast marine waters, where they are exposed to habitat degradation and various contaminants (Cohen et al. 2000; Petrie et al. 2007).

Breeding biology: Pair formation occurs between February and March. After arriving on the breeding grounds, Greater Scaup pairs typically settle on shallow lakes and ponds surrounded by low vegetation within the tundra or taiga, where they establish territories and nest within about two weeks (Kessel et al. 2002). Females most often nest close to water (less than or equal to 200 m) and on the ground in dry upland areas within standing grasses or sedges remaining from the previous year's growth; some nesting may occur on floating mats of vegetation or on vegetated islands within wetlands or lakes (Kessel et al. 2002). The Greater Scaup has only a single brood per season. Peak nesting in Ontario likely occurs in mid-June, so broods using open water areas of ponds would not be observed until late July or August, after most northern Ontario atlassing was completed (James in Cadman et al. 1987). These characteristics, along with the remoteness and inaccessibility of Greater Scaup breeding habitat, may reduce the number and extent of atlas records for the species, thereby limiting our understanding of its distribution in Ontario.

Abundance: The Greater Scaup was detected too infrequently on point counts to create a relative abundance map; average detection was only 0.7 birds/25 point counts in the Hudson Bay Lowlands. In the first atlas, in certain squares near Cape Henrietta Maria, abundance was estimated to be 11-100 pairs/square or possibly over 100 pairs/square. Data from both atlases suggest that the species may also be relatively abundant on the tundra near the Manitoba border. – *Shannon S. Badzinski*

The female Greater Scaup lines her simple nest with grasses or sedges. Down is added near the completion of clutches, typically 9-13 eggs, suggesting this nest is incomplete. *Photo: Mark Peck*

On tundra ponds selected by the Greater Scaup for breeding activities, the most important feature for nest sites is a substantial amount of the previous year's plant growth (Kessell et al. 2002). *Photo: George K. Peck*

Lesser Scaup

Petit Fuligule

Aythya affinis

Barry S. Cherriere

The Lesser Scaup is the smaller of the two scaup species, both commonly referred to as "bluebills." It is the most abundant and has one of the most extensive breeding ranges of any diving duck in North America. Its core breeding areas are in the western boreal and prairie/parkland regions from central Alaska through Manitoba, but it also nests at lower densities in the east throughout the northern and boreal forests of Ontario, Québec, and Labrador (Austin et al. 1998). In Ontario, highest breeding densities occur in the Hudson Bay Lowlands (Dennis in Cadman et al. 1987). Notably, when the first atlas was undertaken, the North American breeding scaup population (Lesser plus Greater Scaup) was relatively high and stable. Since the early to mid-1980s, however, the population has declined from a high of 7.2 million in 1983 to a near all-time low of 3.3 million in 2006 (U.S. Fish and Wildlife Service 2006). Currently, there is much interest and research to determine causes of the decline and factors inhibiting population recovery (Austin et al. 2000).

Distribution and population status: The Lesser Scaup is widely but sparsely distributed throughout Ontario. It is rarely encountered in the Carolinian region, relatively uncommon throughout the Lake Simcoe-Rideau, Southern Shield, and Northern Shield regions, and most common in the Hudson Bay Lowlands. The distribution of breeding locations was similar during both atlases, and its Ontario breeding range has not changed.

Overall, there was no change in the probability of observation of the Lesser Scaup between atlases, but some regional differences were observed. The probability of observation in the Hudson Bay Lowlands rose from 8% in the first atlas to 15% in the second, a significant 87% increase. These changes may reflect a greater amount of survey effort by CWS and OMNR, an increase in the species' numbers in the region, or perhaps coverage of somewhat different habitats during the second atlas.

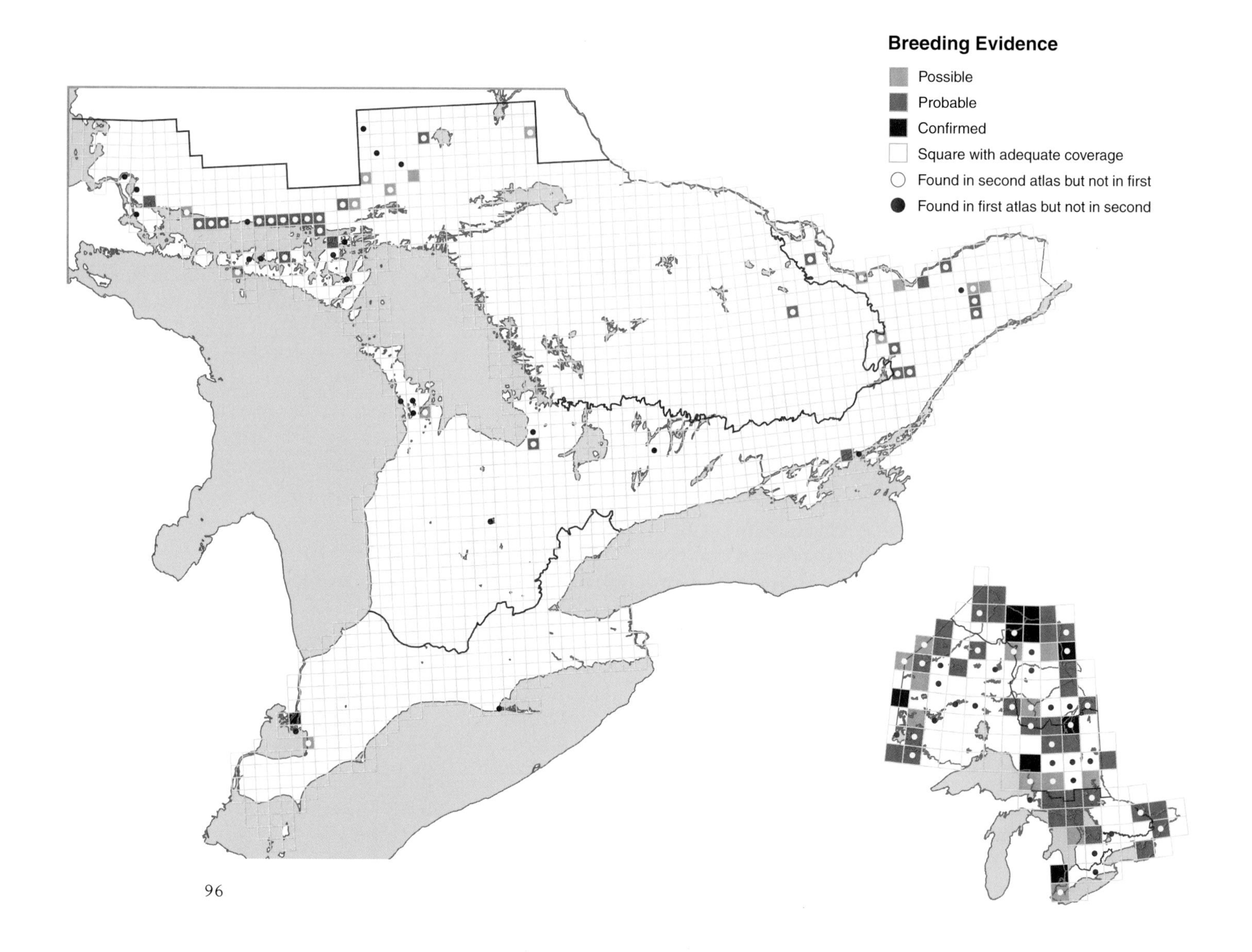

BREEDING EVIDENCE

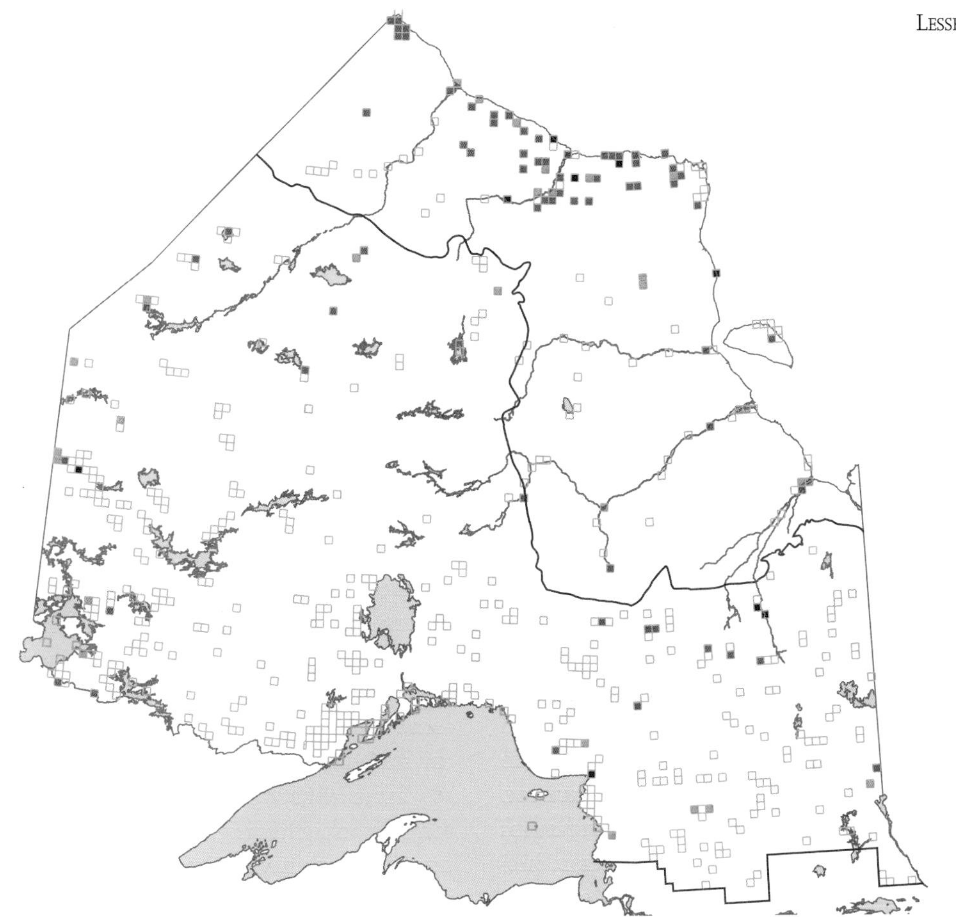

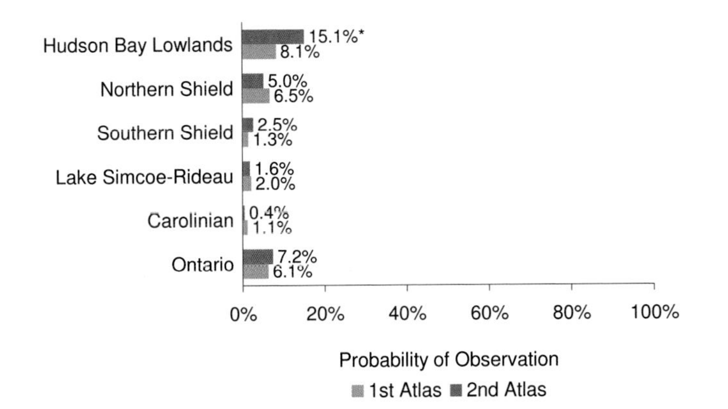

From 1990 to 2006, breeding scaup counted within the eastern region of the Waterfowl Breeding Population and Habitat Survey have generally been stable (U.S. Fish and Wildlife Service 2006). This aerial survey, however, not only includes transects from Ontario's Hudson Bay Lowlands but also those within other parts of scaup breeding range throughout northern Ontario, Québec, and Labrador. Thus, the trend for scaup (the majority of which are Lesser Scaup) in the entire eastern region may not necessarily reflect those within Ontario's Hudson Bay Lowlands.

Breeding biology: Lesser Scaup pairs prefer small seasonal and semi-permanent wetlands and lakes with emergent vegetation for nesting. Nests are frequently located on dry to moist ground in the wet meadow zone adjacent to wetlands, sometimes in sparse shrub patches or on low-lying, vegetated islands within wetlands; over-water nesting occurs but is relatively uncommon (Austin et al. 1998). Once females begin nesting, typically in late May to mid-June across North America (Austin et al. 1998), lone males remain visible on breeding wetlands for several weeks before departing for moulting areas. Females with broods generally use open water areas in wetlands and provide an easy means of confirming breeding.

Several life-history traits of the Lesser Scaup may confound accurate interpretation of breeding status. The species has a very protracted, late spring migration relative to other waterfowl (Austin et al. 1998). The sex ratio in Lesser Scaup also is highly skewed, which results in a surplus of unpaired males during spring (Austin et al. 1998). Further, a substantial proportion (10-30%) of one- and two-year-old females may forgo breeding (Afton 1984), depending on season and wetland conditions. Because of these characteristics, non-breeding birds of both sexes and paired birds may be commonly observed in wetland habitats (e.g., sewage lagoons) in southern Ontario, and staging birds (lone females or males and pairs) may be seen also in suitable breeding habitats farther north during late May to early June.

Abundance: Point count detections were too infrequent to produce a map of relative abundance. However, based on the limited number of point counts, the highest density of birds was recorded in the Hudson Bay Lowlands (0.5 birds/25 point counts), followed by the Northern Shield (0.02 birds/25 point counts). No point count data were available in the remaining regions, likely indicating that point count locations were either in unsuitable breeding habitat and/or that these regions had extremely limited or isolated numbers of breeding scaup. The results further highlight the importance of the Hudson Bay Lowlands for breeding Lesser Scaup in Ontario. – Shannon S. Badzinski

Common Eider

Eider à duvet

Somateria mollissima

Paul Matulonis

The Common Eider is a colourful member of the sea duck tribe and largest of the Arctic ducks. It has a holarctic distribution composed of several geographic subspecies. In North America, it breeds from temperate latitudes on the Atlantic coast to the subarctic and arctic islands and on coastal mainland tundra across Canada to western Alaska (Goudie et al. 2000). The subspecies that breeds in Ontario (*sedentaria*, the Hudson Bay Eider) is so named for its relative lack of movement between its breeding and wintering ranges, which are wholly confined to Hudson and James Bays (Snyder 1941a). It is the largest of the subspecies, likely an adaptation to thermal demands of its winter range. Most information on the Hudson Bay Eider comes from studies in two locations: Belcher Islands, Nunavut (Freeman 1970; Nakashima and Murray 1988), and La Pérouse Bay, Manitoba (Schmutz et al. 1983; Robertson 1995). There is concern about a general decline of eiders over the past two decades in the Canadian Arctic and elsewhere (Goudie et al. 2000). In 1991-92, the Hudson Bay Eider breeding on the Belcher Islands suffered a 75% decline because of unusual sea-ice freezing (Gilchrist and Robertson 1998). Recent surveys indicate up to 100,000 of this subspecies can winter there (G. Gilchrist, unpubl. data).

Distribution and population status: The Common Eider is limited to areas of tundra and offshore islands, notably around the Ontario-Manitoba border, Cape Henrietta Maria, and Akimiski Island. It was recorded in nine squares in six 100-km blocks, compared with eight squares in four 100-km blocks in the first atlas. Confirmation of breeding on Akimiski Island was new but reflected previously known distribution (Abraham and Finney 1986; James 1991). One significant breeding location reported in the first atlas (Little Bear Island) was not visited during the second atlas. The wintering area of the Common Eider breeding in Ontario and James Bay is undescribed but presumably comprises leads and ice-free areas

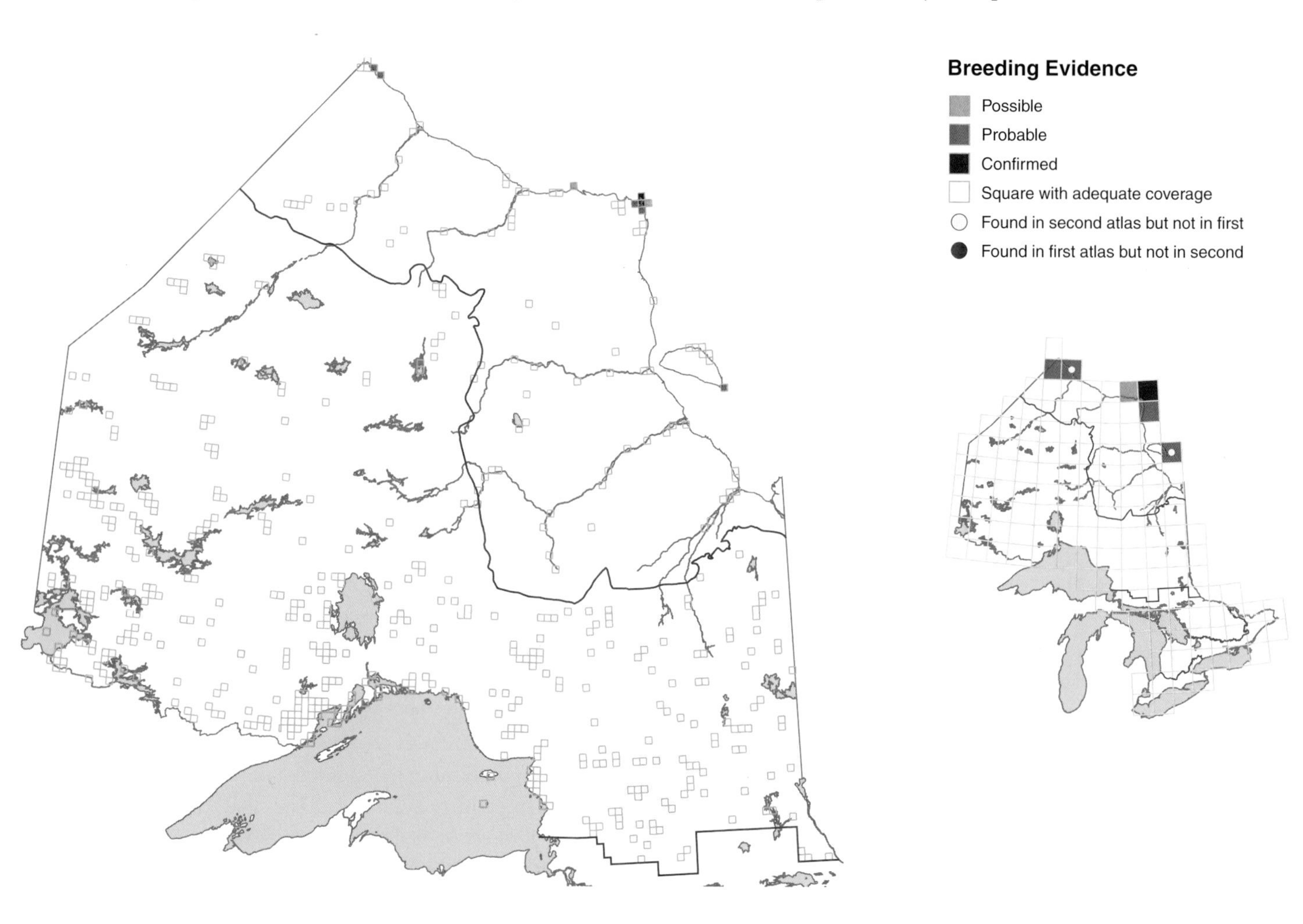

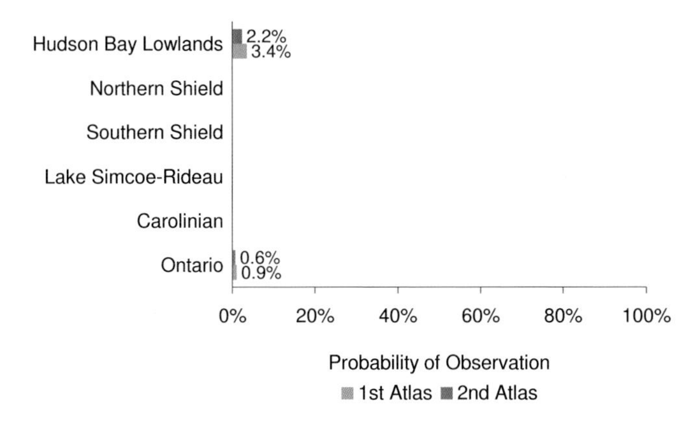

along the Hudson Bay and James Bay coasts, where the birds have been seen in February (pers. obs.). It is possible that some also move to the Belcher Islands, and if so, the Ontario breeding group may have been negatively affected by the winter events of 1991-92.

Breeding biology: The Common Eider is predominantly a colonial nester, and inter-nest distances are often small. Breeding habitat is relatively restricted to marine environments such as offshore islands and coastal tundra lakes and braided rivers, where the species nests primarily on islets. The brightly coloured males accompany females during the pre-laying and egg-laying periods and often sit next to them when they are nest building. At this time, breeding pairs are most conspicuous to atlassers, especially aerial surveyors. Shortly after clutches are complete, males leave for moulting areas. Both the breeding strategy (use of stored protein and fat to fuel reproduction) and average clutch size (three to five relatively large eggs) are goose-like (Goudie et al. 2000). Broods are reared cooperatively among several family groups and almost exclusively in coastal saltwater habitats where bivalves and molluscs are plentiful. Although early brood rearing may occur on fresh water in northern parts of its range, this tundra niche is usually occupied by the closely related King Eider. King Eiders are rare in the Hudson Bay Lowlands, and the Common Eider appears to occupy the freshwater niche to a greater extent there than elsewhere in the Arctic.

On the Hudson Bay coast, the Common Eider has been recorded nesting mostly in river deltas and on small offshore islands. It is recorded occasionally in shallow tundra lakes, usually when the conspicuous males are still present. At other times (e.g., incubation and brood rearing), females are easy to overlook, and use of these habitats has been no doubt underestimated.

Abundance: Common Eider colonies can include thousands of nests, but in the Lowlands, Hudson Bay Eider colonies typically comprise a few dozen to a few hundred on braided river systems, with smaller clusters on lakes. The number of pairs of Common Eider in the atlas area is probably in the low hundreds, but no systematic survey has been conducted, and few nests were found during the atlas. At a known nesting aggregation on the shallow lakes at Cape Henrietta Maria, which were visited repeatedly between atlases and during this atlas, nest numbers have declined from 24 to four. At the same time, nesting Herring Gulls on the same island increased. Whether the decline is because of overall Hudson Bay Eider population decreases or because these females have relocated locally is not known. Overall, the evidence suggests little change in abundance between atlases. – *Ken Abraham*

A typical nest with much down. The variation in egg colour may indicate laying by two females, as individuals lay same-coloured eggs within a clutch (Goudie et al. 2000). *Photo: George K. Peck*

Common Eider breeding records in Ontario are concentrated on islets in tundra lakes and offshore islands near Cape Henrietta Maria. *Photo: Ken Abraham*

Surf Scoter

Macreuse à front blanc

Melanitta perspicillata

Barry S. Cherriere

The male Surf Scoter is the most strikingly marked of the scoters with its multicoloured bill and bright white head patches set off by its glossy black plumage. This is the only scoter endemic to North America, where its breeding range occupies a broad band through Alaska and the Yukon, tapering to a relatively narrow strip in the northern Hudson Bay Lowlands of Ontario and then expanding to a more extensive range in central and northern Québec (Savard et al. 1998). A bird of the Boreal Forest, it is found in habitat ranging from the more closed forest to the transition between open taiga and tundra. In southern Ontario, it occurs on migration on the Great Lakes and larger inland lakes in moderate numbers as it passes to and from its wintering range along the Atlantic shore.

Distribution and population status: The records from this atlas all fall in the northern Hudson Bay Lowlands in habitats ranging from lakes in moderately forested areas to open taiga ponds in the ecotone between taiga and tundra. Records from the two atlases define generally the same range along Hudson Bay, extending partway down James Bay. There were 19 sightings during the second atlas compared to three during the first. Although this might suggest a rising trend, it is likely an artifact of small sample size and the changing nature of the coverage between atlases. During the first atlas, coverage was mostly from the ground, often along rivers or near the shore. After that period, aerial surveys were implemented over much of the Lowlands, and these continued during the present atlas. There was also more use of helicopters to position atlassers in previously inaccessible areas in the second atlas. These changes likely led to improved coverage in the areas more suitable for the Surf Scoter. In addition, the relatively obvious plumage of the male facilitates identification at greater range from aircraft before avoidance behaviour such as diving occurs.

Population trends from wintering ground surveys suggest declines, both on the Atlantic and Pacific. Those data, however,

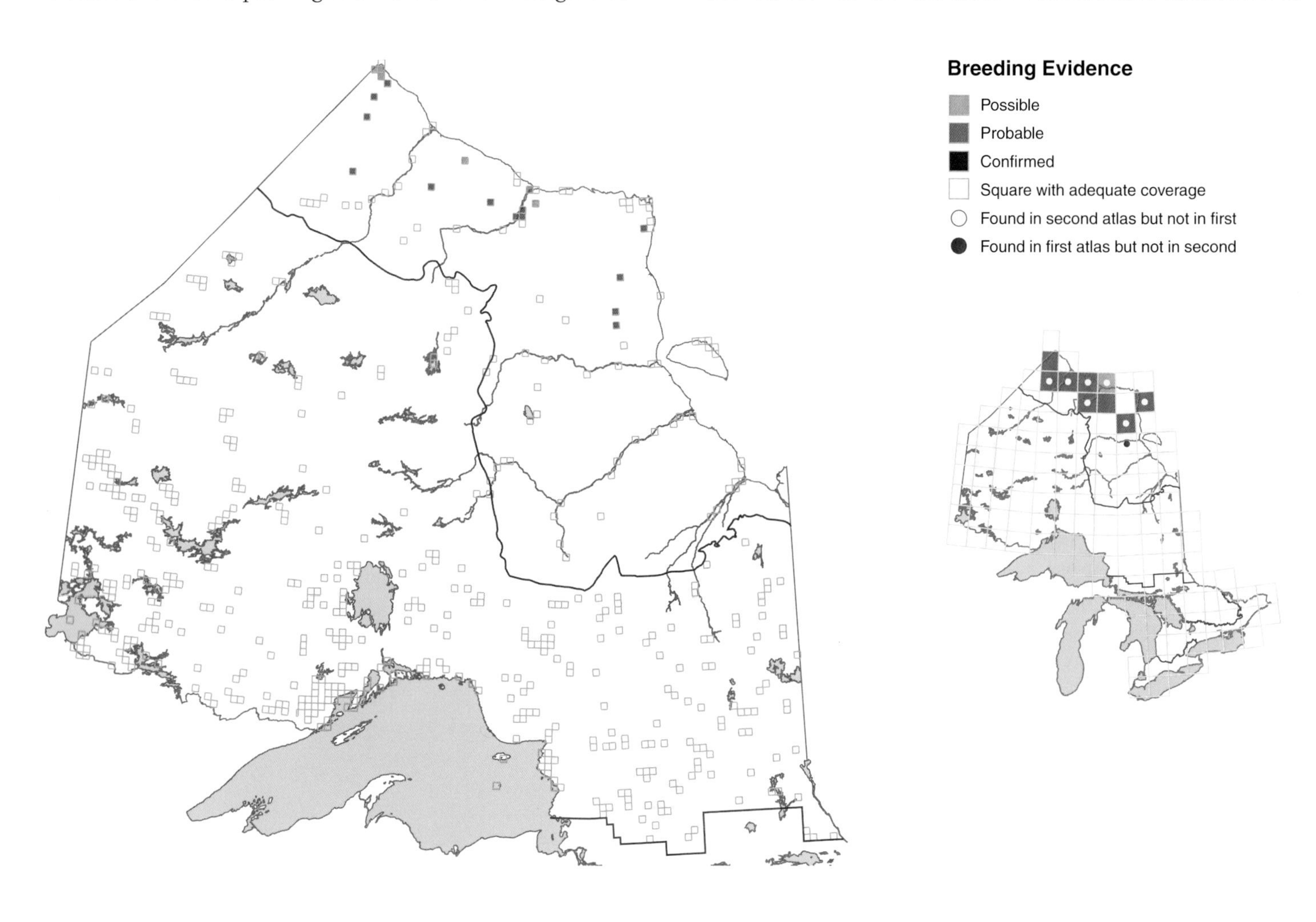

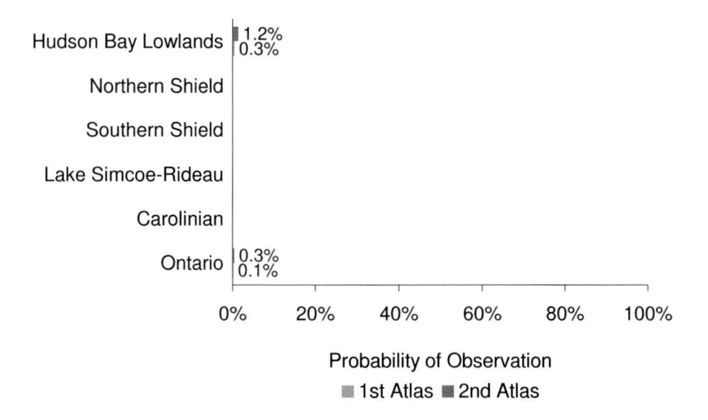

are not definitive, as most winter aerial surveys do not effectively discriminate among scoter species.

Breeding biology: Nest-site habitat and nest characteristics are presently not known in Ontario, although the habitat on which pairs were seen was mostly small to moderate sized lakes (usually less than 10 ha) surrounded by heavy cover, spruce and alders in the more forested areas, and birch and willow in the more open, tundra-influenced areas. There was one sighting on a river, but most occurred in the more poorly drained areas that define the Lowlands. The only extensive studies of breeding ecology have been undertaken in Québec (Morrier et al. 1997), where nests were shallow scrapes lined with vegetation and down and often well hidden under fallen logs. They could be up to 50 m from the water and were often on islands. In northern Québec, this species uses small lakes, mostly those with rocky substrates, and avoids peat and marl-dominated lakes. Rivers and large deep lakes also appear to be avoided (Savard and Lamothe 1991; Gauthier and Aubry 1996). As with the other scoters, this species nests relatively late, which is problematic for atlassing as it reduces the possibility of detecting broods, the only effective means of confirming breeding.

Abundance: Too few records were made to produce a relative abundance map. Breeding pair surveys carried out by the CWS during the mid-1980s yielded estimates of 2.2 pairs/100 km^2, although variance was high; peak estimates of 5.0 pairs/100 km^2 were found in the Sutton Ridges. Breeding densities appeared similar to those of the Black Scoter in the Ontario Hudson Bay Lowlands. Comparable population data are only available from Québec, where breeding densities in the central part of the species' range (drainage areas of Great Whale and Little Whale Rivers) can reach 10 pairs/100 km^2, although 2 pairs/100 km^2 is the average value for the general area (Gauthier and Aubry 1996). Unlike the Black Scoter but similar to the White-winged Scoter, this species does not form large moulting flocks along the Ontario shores of James and Hudson Bays, eliminating a potential alternate population index method. Moulting seems to be more dispersed and may also take place on larger inland lakes, although some moulting flocks have been found along the eastern shore of Hudson Bay (Gauthier and Aubry 1996; Perry et al. 2004), and important moulting areas have been located along the Labrador coast and in the St. Lawrence estuary (Savard et al. 1998). – *Ken Ross*

Like other scoters, the female Surf Scoter usually takes her brood to the safety of open water when threatened because diving is the first escape response. *Photo: Donald A. Sutherland*

Typical breeding habitat of the Surf Scoter consists of shallow lakes and ponds of less than 10 ha with little emergent vegetation (Savard et al. 1998). *Photo: Ken Abraham*

White-winged Scoter

Macreuse brune

Melanitta fusca

Barry S. Cherriere

The White-winged Scoter shares a holarctic distribution with the Black Scoter but is more widely distributed, being found in habitats ranging from low arctic tundra through the Boreal Forest to open prairies. Three subspecies have been described, two in Eurasia (*fusca* and *stejnegeri*) and one in North America (*deglandi*). In North America, the White-winged Scoter's breeding range extends broadly from Alaska through the Yukon, Northwest Territories, and four western provinces to northern Ontario, previously thought to form the eastern extent of its breeding range. Now its breeding range is known to include Québec just east of James Bay (Gauthier and Aubry 1996). It is the most commonly seen scoter in southern Ontario, often occurring in thousands both on migration and in winter on the lower Great Lakes.

Distribution and population status: As in the first atlas, the core of this species' Ontario range is the northern Hudson Bay Lowlands, with most records coming from the more open taiga along Hudson Bay. Unlike the other scoters, this species was also recorded in the more densely treed Boreal Forest of the southern edges of the Lowlands and in Shield areas of northwestern Ontario. In spite of the higher number of records during the second atlas, there is little evidence of changed status or distribution from the first atlas, as low breeding density and surveying effort would combine to obscure any change. There was no confirmed breeding record during the second atlas, in contrast to one in the first atlas. There is general concern that scoter numbers are decreasing, based on winter aerial surveys in the US, which show a general decline in the group; however, species are not differentiated during those surveys. Decreases in the boreal areas of the Northwest Territories and the prairie and parklands in western Canada are evident (Anon. 2003), but the reasons for these declines are not known.

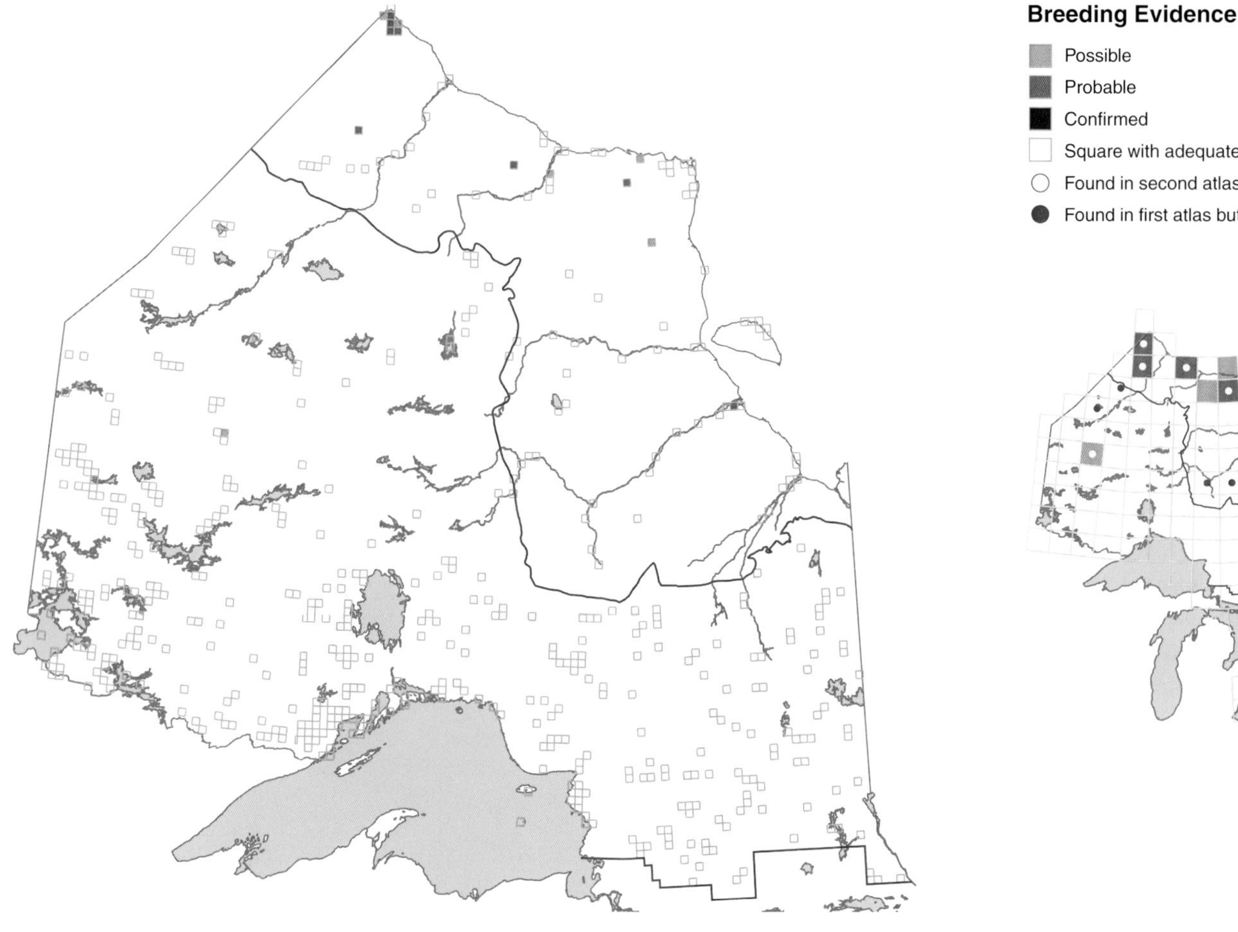

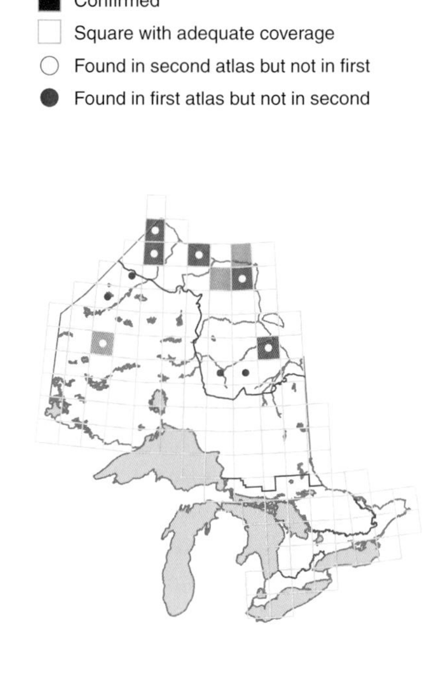

Breeding Evidence
- Possible
- Probable
- Confirmed
- Square with adequate coverage
- Found in second atlas but not in first
- Found in first atlas but not in second

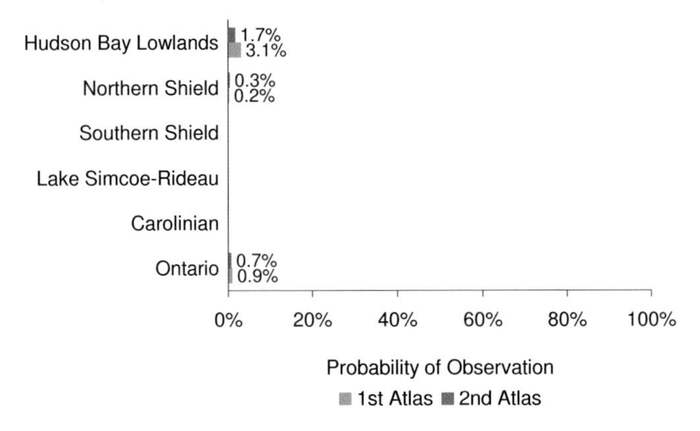

The White-winged Scoter shares with the other scoters a preference for relatively small lakes in spruce and shrub dominated muskeg habitat. *Photo: Ken Abraham*

Breeding biology: Most descriptions of nesting habitat come from the more accessible and better studied part of its range in the western prairies and parklands, where it shows a preference for dense, scrubby cover around lakes, sloughs, and rivers. Island nesting has often been observed, and in these locations, very high breeding densities can be reached (e.g., up to 18 pairs/ha in Europe; Brown and Fredrickson 1997). Also notable is the species' propensity to nest in heavy cover well away from water, making the discovery of nests even more difficult. Much of the breeding habitat is in the taiga; however, nesting in this region is only generally noted and refers to boreal ponds with heavy fringing cover. Actual nests there do not appear to have been described in the literature.

Atlas sightings of potential breeding pairs were often made on ponds in open taiga or tundra habitat with heavy fringing cover of birch and willow or spruce. Sightings were also made on rivers; in one case, a male remained very close to an island on the Winisk River as if on territory. Besides the general inaccessibility of this species' habitat, a further impediment to effective atlassing is its late breeding schedule (nest initiation is probably in mid- to late June), which means that broods are not present during the normal atlassing period. This is compounded by the species' tendency to dive, making it difficult to locate and identify. Its breeding range in Ontario may thus be more extensive than depicted in this atlas.

Abundance: Atlas records are too few to determine an abundance level with confidence. Breeding pair surveys carried out by CWS during the 1980s indicated an average density in the Hudson Bay Lowlands of 0.9 pairs/100 km^2, although with very high variance, which may have been due to earlier than optimal survey timing for scoters. The highest density of 4.2 pairs/100 km^2 was recorded in the Fort Severn area. This contrasts with local breeding densities of up to 80 pairs/100 km^2 in areas just inland of the James Bay coast in Québec (Gauthier and Aubry 1996). There are no records of breeding density in similar boreal and subarctic habitats elsewhere. Also, this species does not form the large moulting concentrations off the Ontario coasts of Hudson and James Bays that the Black Scoter does. Summer occurrence on James and Hudson Bays (Manning 1952) appears to be dispersed. – *Ken Ross*

Black Scoter

Macreuse noire

Melanitta nigra

Brenda Hill

The Black Scoter remains a bird of some mystery in Ontario. It is usually encountered in the south of the province during migration when small groups can be seen well offshore bobbing in the waves, often at the limits of detectability. This sense of mystery continues on the breeding grounds where, until 2006, there was yet to be a confirmed nesting record for Ontario. This species is circumboreal in distribution, although the extent of its range in Canada is only now being understood. Godfrey (1986) could only list a few isolated breeding records, not enough for a range map. We now know that this scoter has two breeding loci (Bordage and Savard 1995), one in Alaska extending into the lower Mackenzie River area and the other in northern Québec, to which subpopulation the Ontario birds likely belong.

Distribution and population status: This scoter was recorded sparsely across the northern Hudson Bay Lowlands. There were also records from Akimiski Island. All these areas are characterized by open taiga with extensive networks of lakes varying widely in size. At present, the extent of the range in Ontario cannot be determined, given the inaccessibility of Ontario's far north, but it is reasonable to conclude that the species is essentially restricted to the Hudson Bay Lowlands and probably the more open area encompassed by the sightings. This scoter was not recorded in the first atlas, which might lead to the conclusion that there has been a range extension into Ontario. However, this is likely an artifact of the limited coverage the Lowlands received and the nature of that coverage during the first atlas. Coverage then was largely restricted to ground surveys in more accessible areas, usually near rivers; aerial survey information, the source of many of the observations, was quite limited. When dedicated waterfowl surveys were initiated in the late 1980s, Black Scoter sightings began to accumulate almost immediately (Ross 1994). These surveys continued during the present atlas peri-

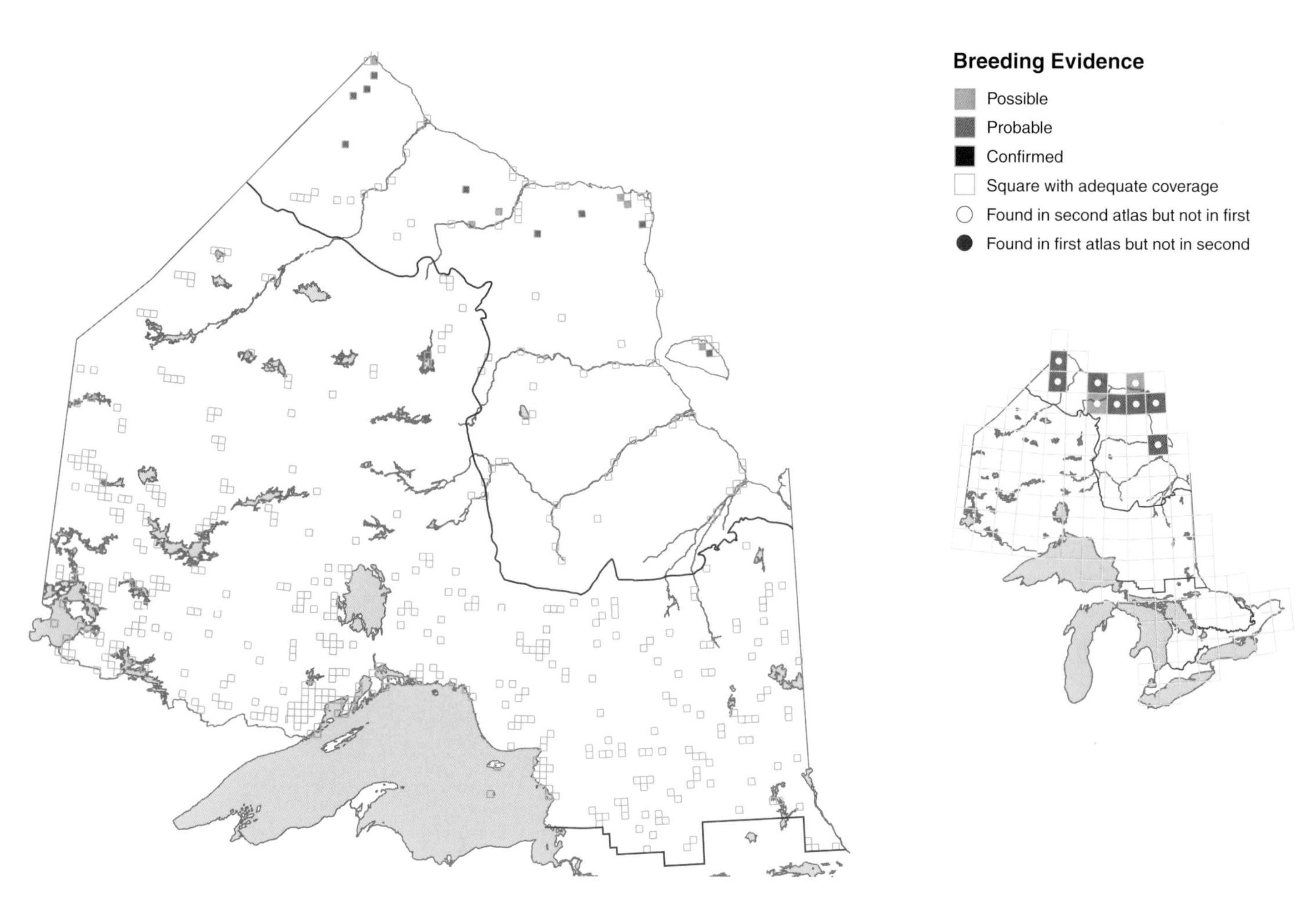

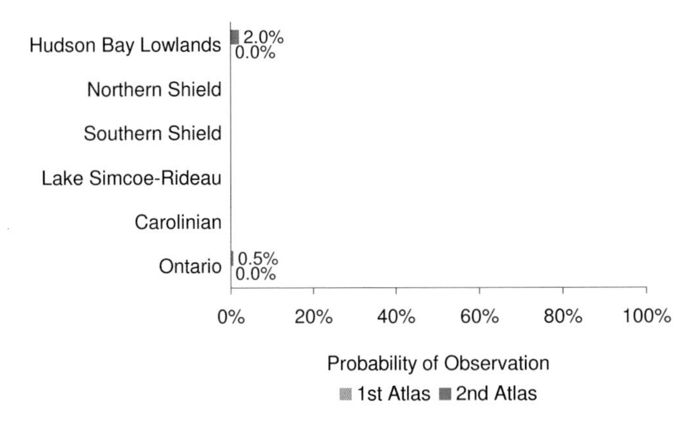

od. Also, large moulting flocks that occur in northern James Bay and at sites along the Hudson Bay coast have long been known (Manning 1952) and likely reflect, in part, nearby breeding activity. These concentrations appear stable in numbers (Ross 1994). The fact that the other scoter species were recorded in the first atlas may indicate that they selected slightly different and more accessible habitat than did the Black Scoter. It may also be significant that in the second atlas the Black Scoter was rarely reported in squares in which the other scoter species were reported.

Breeding was confirmed for the Black Scoter in Ontario on 25 July 2006 when a female with a brood of five small ducklings was observed and photographed about 10 km east of Peawanuck (K. Abraham and D. Filliter, unpubl. data).

Breeding biology: Characteristics of nest sites in Ontario are as yet unavailable; however, potential breeding pairs were often noted on smaller lakes with heavy shrub or conifer-treed shorelines. Elsewhere, nest sites are often hidden in grass or under low shrubs up to 30 m from water's edge (Bordage and Savard 1995); nests have been encountered rarely throughout its range, and there are few descriptions. Open taiga habitat is particularly difficult for atlassers as it is usually very wet and well away from river access. Confirmation of breeding is made more problematic by the relatively late breeding. Egg-laying may not start until mid-June, and broods may not be present until mid-July (Savard and Lamothe 1991) when most atlassing activity has ceased. Brood detection would be the best way to confirm breeding, but this would require helicopter surveys of suitable lakes.

Abundance: Abundance information cannot be derived from atlas data but is available from CWS breeding pair surveys carried out in the Hudson Bay Lowlands during the springs of 1987 and 1988. Survey data indicated a potential breeding density of 2.6 pairs/100 km^2 (K. Ross, unpubl. data) with a peak of 8 pairs/100 km^2 in the Sutton Ridges area. Variance is high, however, and may reflect slightly earlier than optimal survey timing. Peak breeding density in Québec is 12 pairs/100 km^2, with more peripheral areas holding an estimated 2 pairs/100 km^2. The large moulting flocks off the western James Bay coast in July are now known to include Québec breeders (Perry et al. 2004), and thus are not indicative of breeding numbers in Ontario alone. Moulting flocks off Shell Brook and Black Duck River on the Hudson Bay coast are also sizable (est. 33,500 in 1991; Ross 1994) and may hold many Ontario birds. – *Ken Ross*

Black Scoter nests are located on the ground on grassy hummocks or concealed in thick shrubs, usually within 30 m of small tundra or taiga lakes (Bordage and Savard 1995). *Photo: Marnie Shepherd*

Small but relatively productive taiga lakes such as these, where Ontario's first confirmation of breeding occurred, provide brood habitat for the Black Scoter. *Photo: Jean Hall-Armstrong*

Long-tailed Duck

Harelde kakawi

Clangula hyemalis

George K. Peck

The Long-tailed Duck is a small, holarctic sea duck, well known for its bold plumage patterns, distinctive calls, and the long central tail feathers of the breeding male. In North America, it breeds from about 50° N in Labrador northward throughout the Canadian Arctic mainland and archipelago to above 73° N, and westward to coastal southwest Alaska (Robertson and Savard 2002). It winters extensively on the Great Lakes and the Atlantic and Pacific coasts. Its breeding range extends southward through the Hudson Bay coastal regions wherever tundra conditions prevail, as far south as Cape Henrietta Maria, Ontario, Cape Jones, Québec (Robertson and Savard 2002), and the Twin Islands, Nunavut (53° N) in James Bay (Manning 1981). It can occupy ponds and lakes in coastal and inland tundra (Bellrose 1980). Southern James Bay is a major staging area in fall (Abraham and Wilson 1997), but in Ontario it is most accessible to birders on its winter haunts on the southern Great Lakes (Pittaway 1998).

Distribution and population status: The distribution of records in the second atlas is nearly identical to the first, with breeding evidence in the Cape Henrietta Maria and Pen Islands areas, where extensive tundra exists and where breeding has been previously documented. It was found in 25 squares (twice as many squares as in the first atlas). There were only four confirmations (nests and broods) and over half of all observations were of pairs, the remainder being birds in suitable habitat. Broods are relatively conspicuous, but as the Long-tailed Duck is a relatively late nester in Ontario, most atlassing was concluded by the time broods were present. Although a greater percentage of visited squares had breeding evidence in this atlas, the data are insufficient to conclude that the species has increased in Ontario. The more likely explanation is more intensive atlas coverage in areas with suitable habitat, especially in the Cape Henrietta Maria area where ground-based crews had helicopter access to a large area.

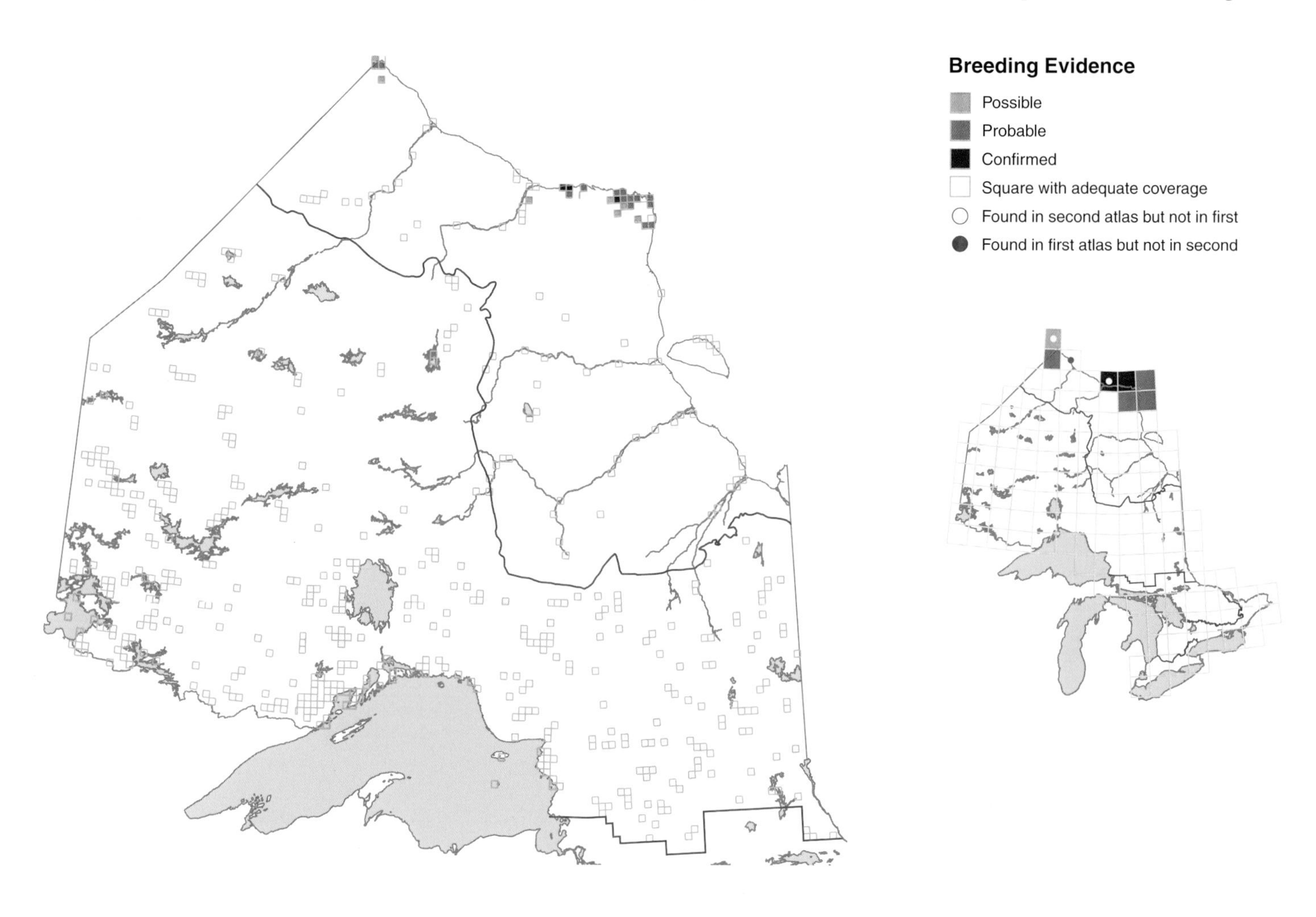

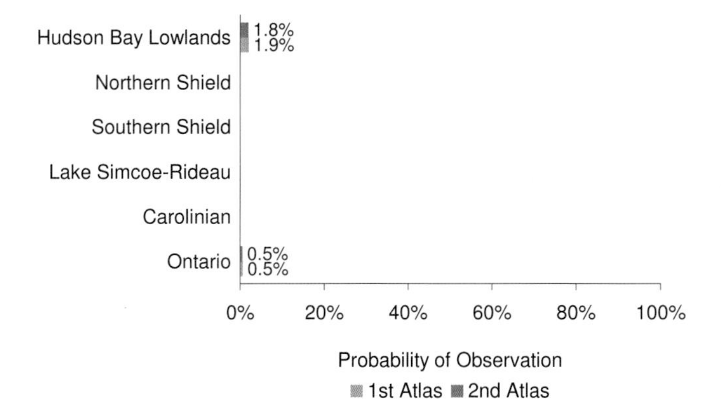

However, given concerns about declining sea duck populations in general, the stability of the species at this southernmost edge of its continental range is heartening.

The Long-tailed Duck probably breeds at low density all along the Ontario Hudson Bay coast. Despite the lack of atlas evidence in the two 100-km blocks between the Winisk River and the Pen Islands, it was reported as a probable nester at Shagamu River (block 16EG) by Wilson and McRae (1993), and there is extensive suitable tundra in block 16DH, especially near the Niskibi River mouth and adjacent coast where no atlassing was done.

Breeding biology: The Long-tailed Duck is gregarious and forms pairs in winter and on spring migration. Soon after arrival on the breeding grounds, pairs disperse to establish territories on small lakes and ponds (Robertson and Savard 2002). Males are highly territorial and guard females while they gather resources for egg production and incubation by eating invertebrates in the ponds of the defended area. Both sexes dive in shallow tundra lakes where larval chironomids are the major source of nutrients. At this time, pairs are conspicuous, and calling is frequent, making probable breeding evidence relatively easy to obtain. Despite the territoriality exhibited during the pre-laying period, nests are not always within the defended area. They are often placed on islands, peninsulas and shores close to water but may be many metres away from water. Nests are usually isolated but can be clustered quite closely together, as on islands or peninsulas. Nests are mostly in depressions, often under dwarf shrubs, and nearby materials are gathered to form the bowl, with abundant down for lining. An average clutch is about seven eggs. Female plumage is highly cryptic, and hens hold tight to the nest during incubation, making it difficult for atlassers to find nests. Both sexes exhibit high fidelity to previous nesting lakes and even specific nest sites (Alison 1975; Bellrose 1980).

Abundance: As with the other coastal sea ducks, there is little quantitative information on abundance of the Long-tailed Duck, but overall it is a scarce breeder in Ontario. In the second atlas, few were heard on point counts, but this may be partly due to the lateness of counts relative to the seasonal timing of territorial defence, when calling might have been expected. In the first atlas, four estimates were 0.02-0.1 pairs per km^2. Elsewhere in its breeding range, densities of 1-2 pairs per km^2 were reported (Robertson and Savard 2002). Territorial behaviour apparently ensures a relatively low pair density, even in suitable habitat. – *Ken Abraham*

A typical Long-tailed Duck nest with abundant down. *Photo: Jim Richards*

Long-tailed Duck nests are often concealed under low shrubs close to the shallow tundra lakes that provide food for hens and broods. This site is at Churchill, Manitoba. *Photo: George K. Peck*

Bufflehead

Petit Garrot

Bucephala albeola

John Reaume

The Bufflehead breeds only in North America and is our smallest sea duck. It has a rapid wing beat, and can take off and land in much shorter distances than other diving waterfowl. The Bufflehead is an obligate cavity-nester, using old Pileated Woodpecker and Northern Flicker holes as well as nest boxes, and is found predominantly in the Boreal Forest from Québec west through British Columbia and north to Alaska, the Yukon, and Northwest Territories. Like its goldeneye relatives, the diminutive Bufflehead prefers small lakes and ponds during the breeding season, where it feeds on aquatic invertebrates (Gauthier 1993). The Bufflehead initiates fall migration earlier than the goldeneyes and tends to winter along ocean coasts in more protected habitats. However, many individuals also spend the winter on the Great Lakes (Bellrose 1980).

Distribution and population status: The probability of observation of the Bufflehead increased several-fold between atlases, with significant increases in the Northern Shield and Hudson Bay Lowlands. It was confirmed breeding as far north as Fort Severn (56° N). Increased observations of the Bufflehead in these northern regions (the expected breeding range) undoubtedly reflect real population increases (Gauthier 1993), with more breeding Bufflehead now being observed both by atlassers and during systematic, regional aerial waterfowl surveys since the early 1980s. In the Southern Shield, new breeding records were reported north of Sudbury and in Haliburton Dist. Both areas have been subject to intensive waterfowl surveys (McNicol et al. 1995) and increased detection opportunities. As part of CWS waterfowl surveys, Bufflehead broods have been observed in several recent years on small headwater lakes southwest of Algonquin Prov. Park, providing the first confirmed breeding in southern Ontario. Separate recent waterfowl surveys have found many Bufflehead pairs in central Ontario (U.S. Fish and Wildlife Service 2003), but those birds are probably late migrants.

Bufflehead populations across North America have been

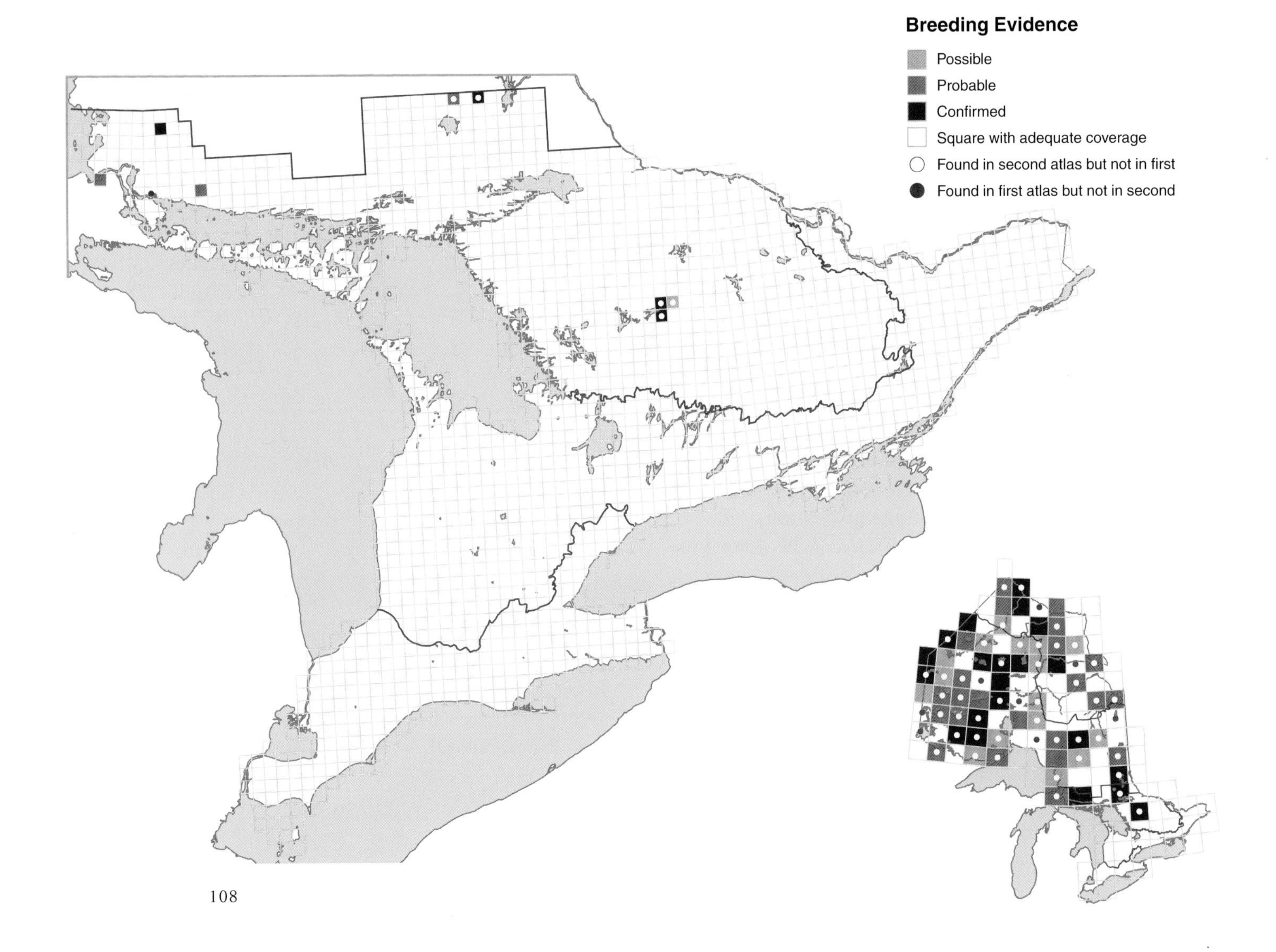

BREEDING EVIDENCE

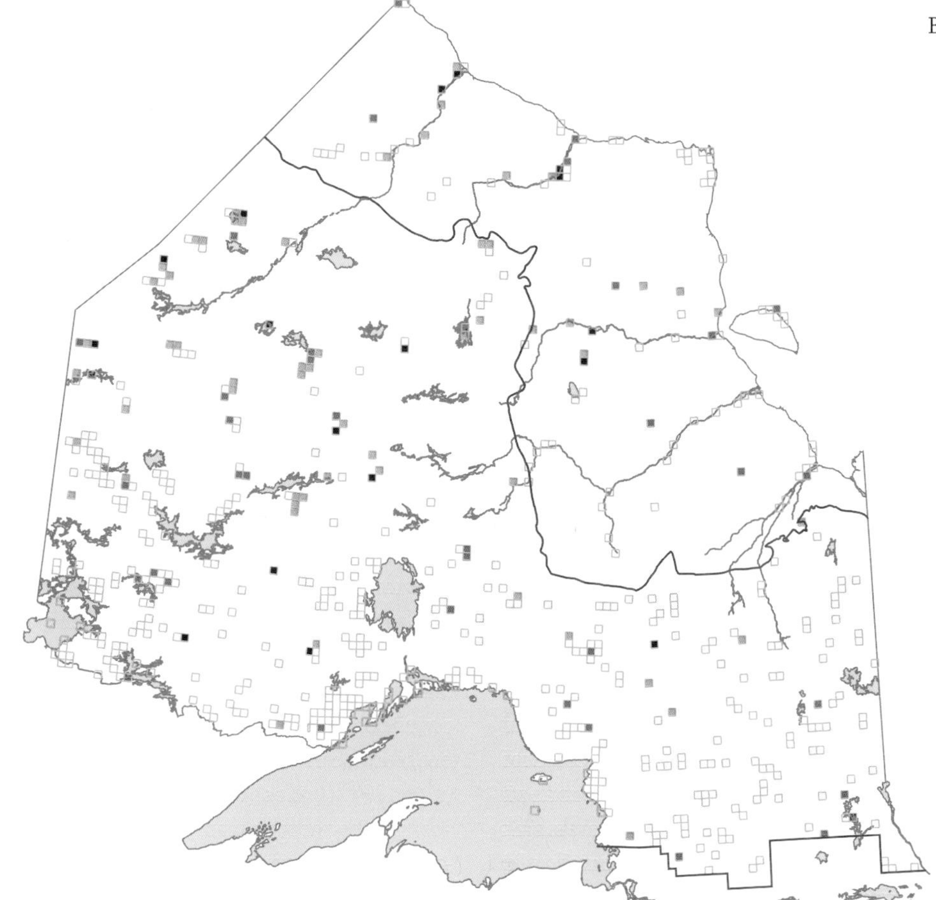

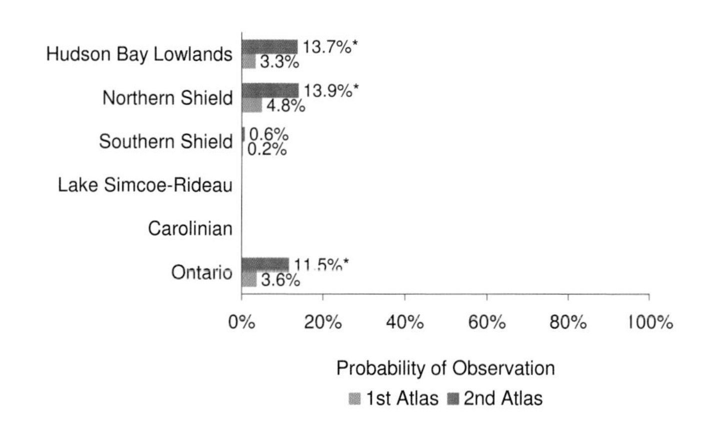

growing since the 1950s, so the increased evidence of breeding in the atlas is consistent with other recent and long-term population monitoring programs (Gauthier 1993; Sauer et al. 2005; Wilkins et al. 2006). Oddly, the Northern Flicker, the Bufflehead's principal nest-site provider, has been declining during this period (Moore 1995), but the Pileated Woodpecker has been increasing (Bull and Jackson 1995). In the southern part of the Bufflehead's range, competition for nest sites may come from Wood Ducks, Hooded Mergansers, and Tree Swallows.

Breeding biology: Spring migration of the Bufflehead tends to be later than that of the Common Goldeneye and mergansers, and paired birds observed in May in the Lake Simcoe-Rideau or Southern Shield regions are likely still moving north to remote breeding lakes.

In spring, paired males are conspicuously aggressive and territorial. This behaviour, along with the availability of natural cavities, may limit breeding densities in some areas (Gauthier 1993). A female will lay six to 11 eggs, at one to three day intervals, typically during early to mid-May. Sometimes, several females will lay eggs in the same nest, resulting in clutches of 12 or more, but this "dump nesting" behaviour is not as common as has been found for goldeneyes. The male departs to moult, possibly to nearby large lakes or reservoirs, while the female incubates the clutch for about one month. Like the goldeneye, a female Bufflehead sits tightly on her nest, usually taking two daily incubation recesses of approximately 80 minutes each to feed, most often during the afternoon (Gauthier 1993). These infrequent trips off the nest mean few opportunities to observe a female entering or exiting a tree cavity, making it difficult to find a nest, particularly if searches are conducted in the morning. During and after incubation, groups of non-breeding Bufflehead may be observed entering cavities to prospect for future nest sites, usually coinciding with late incubation by breeding birds. Thus, seeing a Bufflehead entering a tree cavity in mid-June to early July does not necessarily confirm breeding. The most reliable evidence of breeding comes from observations of broods. After hatch, the female will move her brood to a nursery lake, generally within a few kilometres of the nest site (Gauthier 1993). Like most cavity-nesting waterfowl, Bufflehead exhibit high fidelity to previous nesting lakes, and there is also evidence that the same pair may remain together for several years (Gauthier 1993).

Abundance: Breeding densities are generally low, near 0.05 birds/km^2 (Gauthier 1993). There is no published population size for the Bufflehead in Ontario, but recent CWS helicopter surveys provide a provincial estimate of 13,500 breeding pairs (K. Ross, unpubl. data), consistent with breeding density information. – *Mark Mallory*

Common Goldeneye

Garrot à oeil d'or

Bucephala clangula

George K. Peck

The Common Goldeneye is a medium-sized, holarctic sea duck, known for the bright white face patch of the male and the whistling sound made by its wings during flight. The Common Goldeneye breeds in northern New England, Michigan, and Montana, north through most forested parts of Canada and Alaska (Eadie et al. 1995). This duck nests in cavities of mature trees or in nest boxes and is generally associated with small, clear lakes, ponds, or rivers, where it feeds on aquatic invertebrates during the breeding season. In some areas, such as the acid-stressed Sudbury region, the Common Goldeneye may be observed more commonly on fishless lakes, where it faces less competition for food from insectivorous fish (Mallory et al. 1999). During migration, goldeneyes gather on major lakes, reservoirs, rivers, and coastlines, and then spend the winter in these habitats as far north as open water is available (Bellrose 1980). In Ontario, the lower Great Lakes and St. Lawrence and Ottawa Rivers are important wintering sites (Eadie et al. 1995).

Distribution and population status: The distribution of atlas observations differs little from the first atlas, with evidence of breeding in most 100-km blocks north of 45° N. It is a relatively common boreal species, with a 66% probability of observation in the Northern Shield. It occurs less frequently in other regions, where suitable habitat is scarcer. Between atlases, the probability of observation of the Common Goldeneye increased significantly by 101% and 73% in the Lake Simcoe-Rideau and Southern Shield regions, respectively. A smaller, non-significant increase in the Northern Shield may reflect infilling of the known breeding range in boreal habitats where the species is expected, perhaps attributable in part to intensified, systematic aerial waterfowl surveys since the early 1980s. Increases in observations in the Southern Shield, historically a breeding area (Peck and James 1983), may also result in part from increased effort through recent intensive

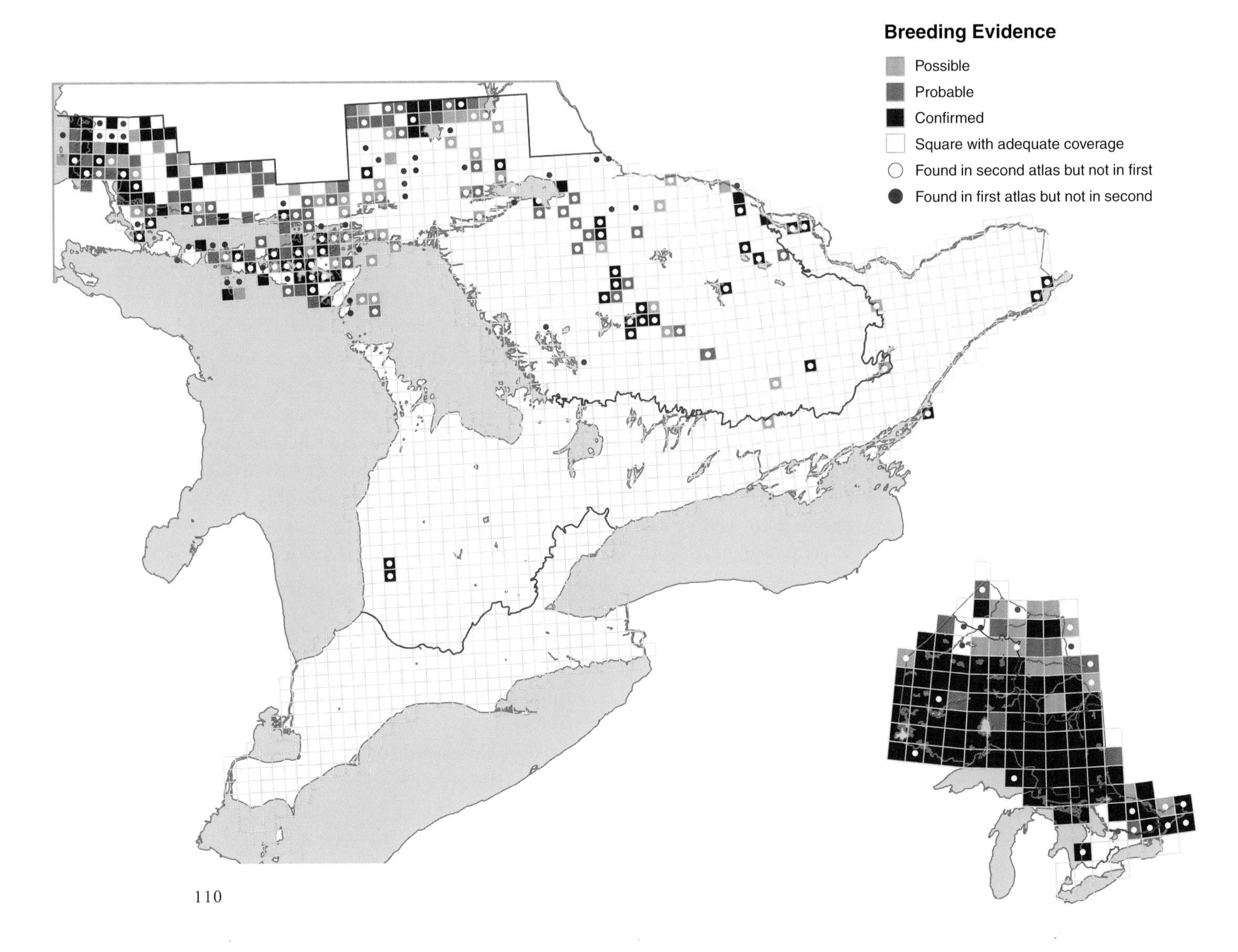

BREEDING EVIDENCE

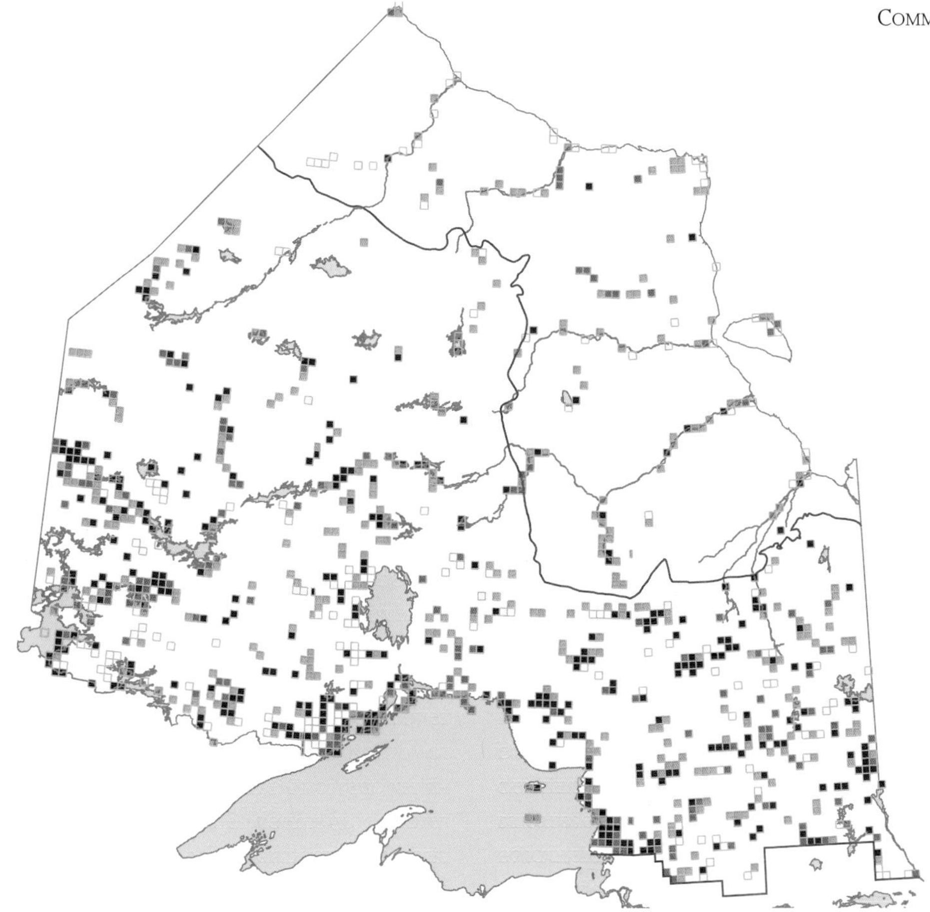

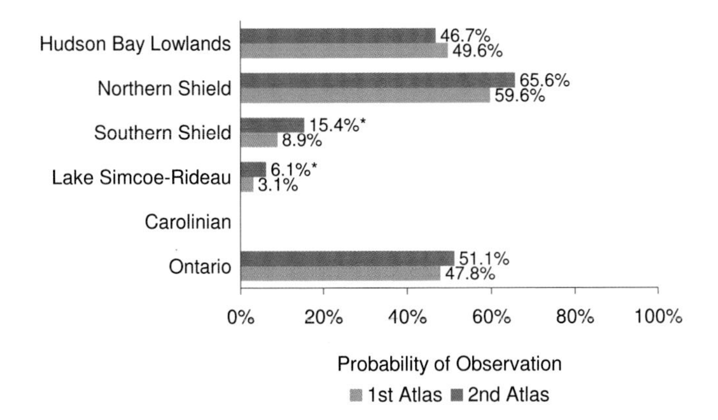

waterfowl surveys (McNicol et al. 1995) and greater road access through expanded cottage development. The increases in the Southern Shield (Algonquin Highlands) and parts of the Lake Simcoe-Rideau region also extend the breeding range south and east. This may be related to increases in forest cover associated with changes in agricultural land use south of Georgian Bay and in east-central Ontario. The two records in the southwest were from Hullett Marsh, where goldeneyes used nest boxes. Interestingly, the Wood Duck (a nest site competitor) and the Pileated Woodpecker (a nest-site provider) populations have increased in Ontario, possibly for similar reasons. While BBS data for these two latter species show increasing population trends, data for goldeneyes show a non-significant decline.

Breeding biology: The Common Goldeneye is highly territorial during the breeding season, with males defending feeding areas for their mates even from some other waterfowl species. Pairs arrive at nesting lakes soon after spring ice-melt. Nest density is dictated by availability of nesting cavities, and nests may be located over 1 km from feeding areas (Eadie et al. 1995). The brilliant white sides of the male make him obvious on lakes and streams during the early breeding season, as do the frequent courtship displays and calling. In April and May, the female lines the nest with down and lays six to nine eggs (Peck and James 1983) at approximately two-day intervals. Other females may "dump" eggs in a nest, resulting in larger clutches of 13 eggs or more. Nest success from large dump-clutches (greater than 16 eggs) is often lower than natural clutches, due to a higher incidence of cracked eggs, less efficient incubation and consequent reduced hatching success, or premature departure of early-hatched ducklings from a crowded nest.

Once incubation starts, the male abandons the female and flies several hundred kilometres north to large moulting lakes in the Boreal Forest or arctic coastal areas of Hudson Bay (Todd 1963); males seen in summer are not indicative of breeding. During incubation, the more cryptic female sits tightly in nest cavities, venturing off for a few short recesses daily to feed. At this time, non- or failed breeders may enter cavities to prospect for future nest sites, making it difficult for observers to confirm breeding until broods are evident. The Common Goldeneye exhibits high rates of fidelity to previously successful nesting lakes and cavities (Eadie et al. 1995).

Abundance: Recent CWS aerial surveys suggest 70,000 pairs breed in the province (K. Ross, unpubl. data). Breeding densities vary substantially, ranging from 1-45 pairs per 100 km², with densities often over 20 pairs per 100 km² north of 47° N, peaking in northwestern Ontario (Dennis 1974a, 1974b; Eadie et al. 1995). – *Mark Mallory*

Hooded Merganser

Harle couronné

Lophodytes cucullatus

John Reaume

The Hooded Merganser is the smallest of the three North American mergansers and the only one found exclusively on this continent. The species is a cavity nester that breeds throughout the eastern half of temperate North America, generally east of the Mississippi River, and in western North America from Oregon and Montana north through southwestern Alberta to north-central British Columbia, but only occasionally elsewhere. It winters mainly to the south of Canada, as far as Mexico.

Distribution and population status: In the early 20th century, the Hooded Merganser had not been confirmed as a breeder in eastern Canada (Macoun and Macoun 1909), which may have been due to ornithologists' unfamiliarity with its distribution. Generally, it occurs now in the same areas it did during the first atlas. In southern Ontario, atlassers recorded it mostly on the Shield. It was also found sporadically in intensively farmed areas of the Lake Simcoe-Rideau and Carolinian regions, but records increased noticeably in areas with less intensive farming. In northern Ontario, the species was found mainly within the Great Lakes-St. Lawrence Forest, extending into the southern section of the Boreal Forest, especially in the Great and Little Clay Belts where breeding was confirmed in most 100-km blocks. There are only a few scattered breeding records north of 51° N, the northernmost confirmed breeding occurring at about 54° N near the Shagamu River in the Hudson Bay Lowlands (D.A. Sutherland, pers. comm.). The species' absence in areas with suitable habitat may be governed partly by competition with the Common Goldeneye in the north and the Wood Duck in the south for trees with cavities of sufficient size to permit nesting.

Between atlases, the probability of observation increased significantly by 80% in the province as a whole, with significant increases in all regions but the Hudson Bay Lowlands. The largest proportional increases occurred in the Carolinian and

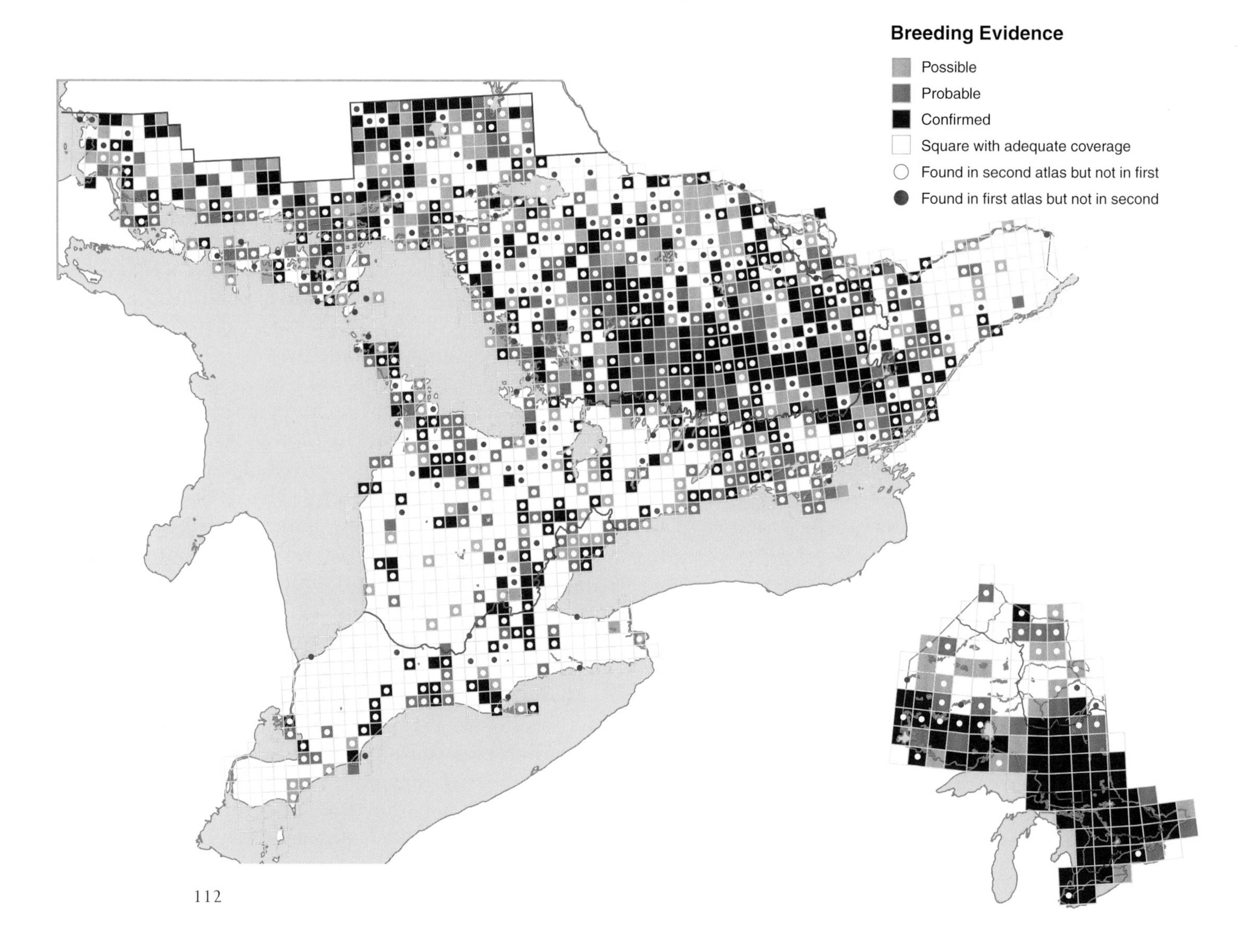

BREEDING EVIDENCE

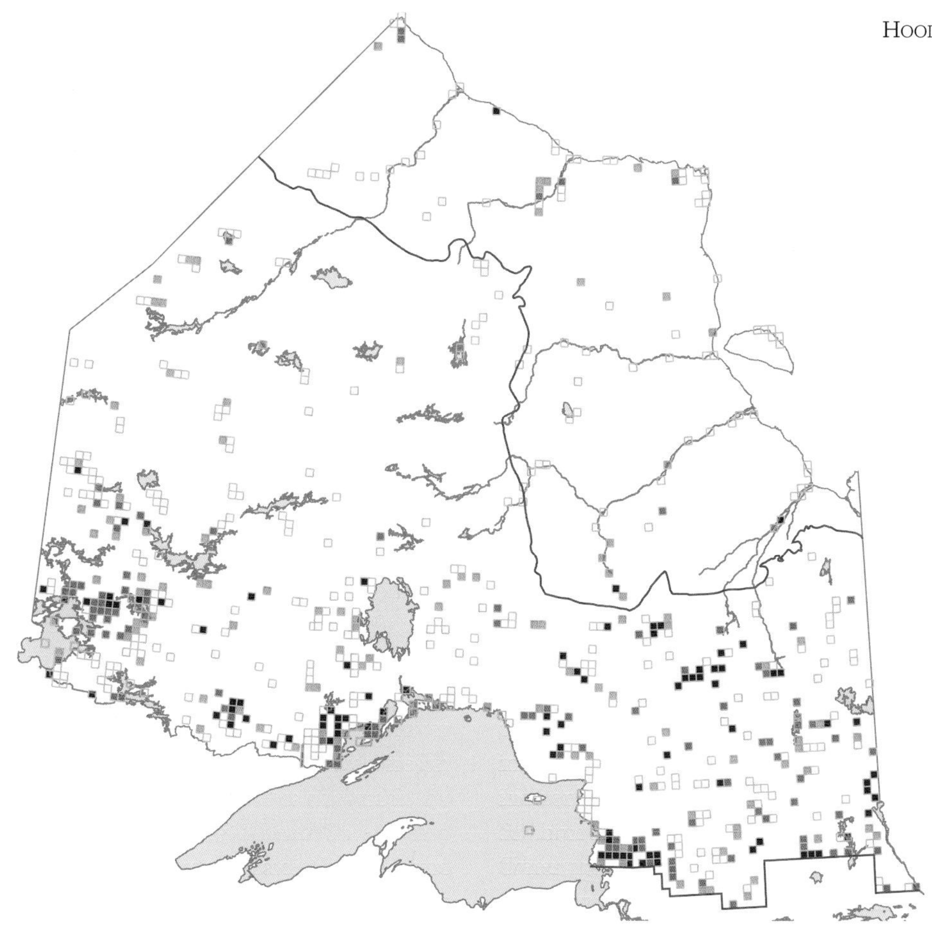

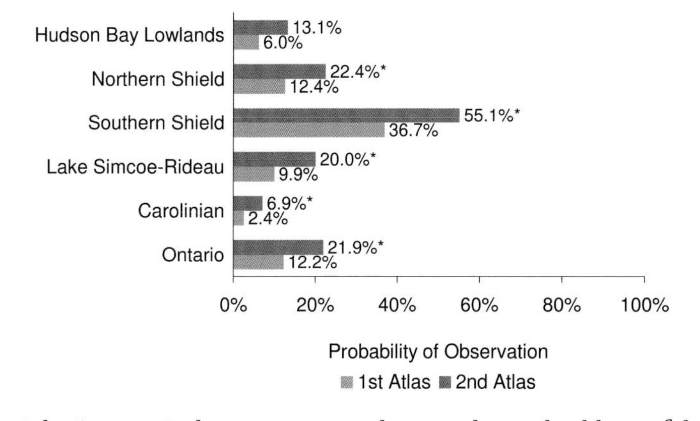

Lake Simcoe-Rideau regions, with more than a doubling of the probability of observation. Within southern Ontario, the northern edge of the range retracted 8 km while the southern edge expanded 33 km, for an overall southward shift of 20 km.

According to BBS data, the Ontario population has shown significant increases of 5.3% per year since 1968 (Downes et al. 2005) and of 9.9% since 1981. CWS surveys show a 2.4% annual increase (1999-2005) in the Southern Shield and parts of the Northern Shield located east of Lake Nipigon and western Québec to a line north from Pembroke (Collins 2005). Reasons for the increase in distribution and numbers since the last atlas are unclear but may be a combination of factors including greater availability of nest boxes and beaver ponds, and provincial guidelines requiring tree harvesters on Crown land to retain a set minimum of live cavity-trees/ha (Naylor et al. 1996).

Breeding biology: The Hooded Merganser is easily overlooked because of its secretive behaviour and habit of nesting on secluded woodland waterways. The pair bond lasts only a few weeks, and the male abandons the female at the onset of incubation (Morse et al. 1969). Females are seldom observed at this time, as nest attentiveness is high (Bouvier 1974). Unless the nest is located in an easily accessible box, breeding is particularly hard to confirm during May and June, at which time the incubating female sits tight in a tree cavity at a height of 6-11 m on the edge of or over water (Peck and James 1983). After young depart a nest cavity, confirmation of breeding continues to be difficult, because the female and her young are very secretive and remain well hidden. The species probably breeds in most squares where only possible and probable breeding was reported.

Abundance: Because Hooded Mergansers are difficult to observe during the breeding season, it is expected that the species is under-recorded by point counts. Nevertheless, point counts suggest that the areas of highest densities are scattered throughout the Southern Shield and the contiguous Lake Simcoe-Rideau region, notably north of Kingston and in the Temagami section of the Great Lakes-St. Lawrence Forest. Other areas of higher density occurred in the Great Lakes-St. Lawrence Forest around Lake of the Woods and in the area east of Lake Nipigon in the Boreal Forest. A few small areas of higher density were also found around Guelph and the area just north of Toronto. CWS aerial surveys in the Southern Shield and northeastern Ontario revealed annual densities of 14.6 to 28.0 pairs/100 km^2 during the atlas period (Ross 2004, unpubl. data). – *Jacques Bouvier*

Common Merganser

Grand Harle

Mergus merganser

George K. Peck

The Common Merganser has a circumpolar range and is among the more widespread and common waterfowl in the Boreal Forest throughout Canada. It is also found in the montane forests of western Canada and the US and in the northern mixed-wood forest of eastern Canada and the Great Lakes and New England states. A minor decrease in the extent of its breeding range along the southern edge of its distribution in the US is generally attributed to habitat loss (Mallory and Metz 1999).

As a primarily fish-eating species, this merganser is associated with rivers and large, clear, low-nutrient lakes. Usually, these are surrounded by forest that affords trees with suitable nest cavities. However, as long as water quality remains good, the Common Merganser is reasonably tolerant of forest disturbance, readily using nest boxes in the absence of natural holes and even nesting occasionally under boulders, in hollow stumps, and in niches among tree roots (Mallory and Metz 1999).

The winter range includes much of the US, but many Canadian birds remain north of the border along the oceanic coasts, Great Lakes, and other freshwater bodies that stay open year-round. Similarly, the species winters as far south as Mexico but is now more likely to remain within the US on reservoirs and dammed lakes (Mallory and Metz 1999).

Distribution and population status: The Ontario breeding range of the Common Merganser includes essentially all of the northern and central parts of the province south regularly to the Lake Simcoe-Rideau region, where there are scattered records of confirmed breeding. However, evidence of breeding in the Carolinian region is extremely scarce, with few, mostly historical records of confirmed breeding (Peck and James 1983). Between atlases, the probability of observation did not change significantly overall, but there was a significant increase of 17% in the Lake Simcoe-Rideau region. This

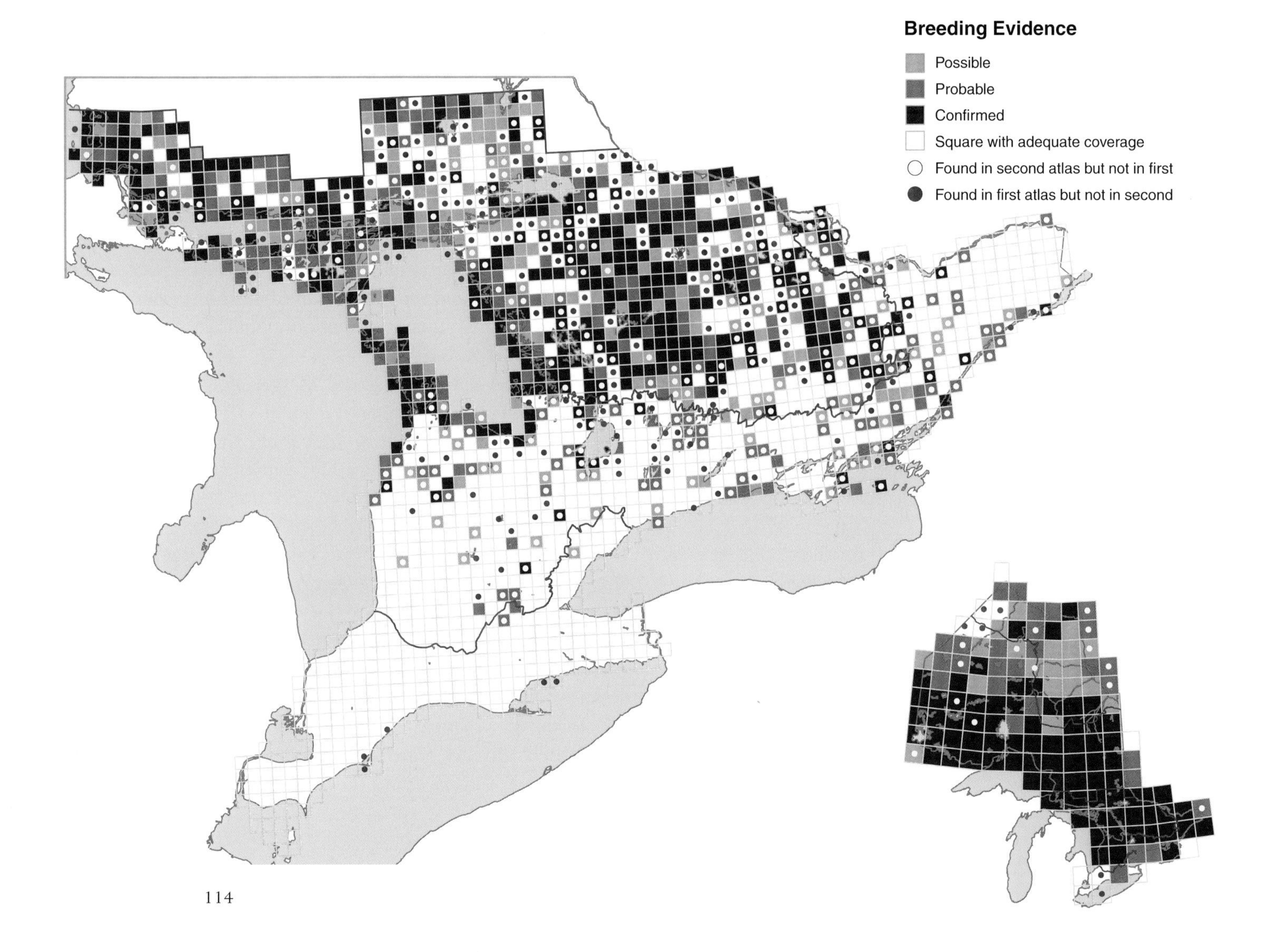

BREEDING EVIDENCE

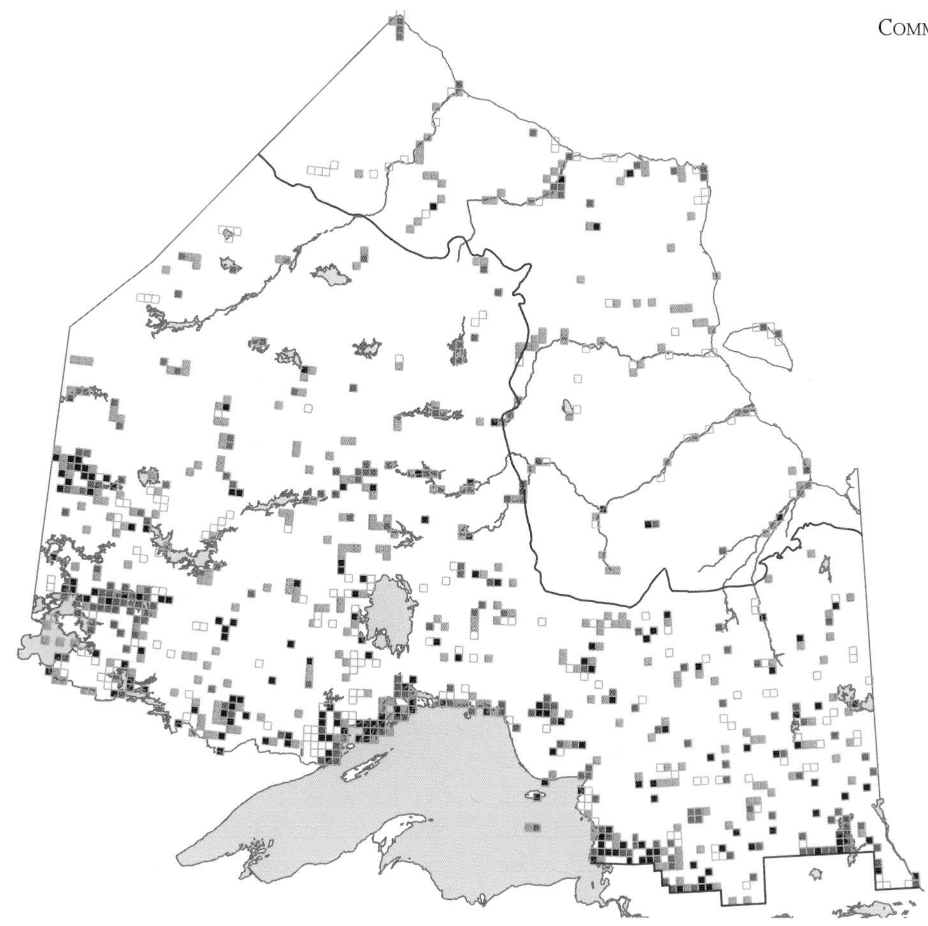

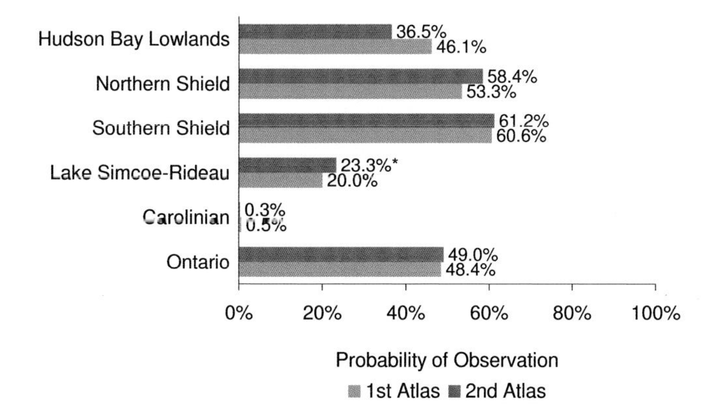

increase led to a slight but significant shift of the centre of distribution in southern Ontario (13 km south and 16 km east). Some records may have involved non-breeding individuals. Although there was a non-significant decline in the Hudson Bay Lowlands, the species was found during the second atlas in five James Bay coastal 100-km blocks from which records were lacking in the first atlas.

Breeding biology: Common Merganser ducklings hatch in June and immediately leave their nest cavities, which are very difficult to find. They are usually led down tributaries to larger water bodies for rearing, where they are conspicuous and readily seen by atlassers. Downy young are attended by single females, but older young may gather in groups of 40 or more (Mallory and Metz 1999). In the first atlas, breeding was confirmed in 41% of squares, 89% of these by observation of broods. In the second atlas, breeding was confirmed in only 36% of squares. Several Regional Coordinators reported that this confirmation rate was lower than expected, and may have reflected differences in effort and timing of visits between the atlases. One must also be cautious in interpreting records, as this species does not breed until two or more years of age, and non-breeders, which resemble females, may be found in spring and summer both on the breeding range and within the wintering range (Mallory and Metz 1999). Even so, this species is likely to have bred in all the squares where it was detected in suitable habitat in the breeding season.

Abundance: As is the case for most waterfowl species, abundance is not well reflected in point counts, which show Common Merganser as being detected in the core of its Ontario range at only about one-sixth the rate of the similarly abundant but more vocal Common Loon. Point count records during the atlas were sparse but nonetheless indicated higher than average density in the Manitoulin Island and Bruce Peninsula areas and along southeastern Georgian Bay. Higher densities also occurred along the border between Ontario and Manitoba. Spring breeding waterfowl surveys in central and northeastern Ontario show no trend for Common Merganser from 1990 to 2005 (K. Ross, unpubl. data), nor do BBS data for Ontario over the past 20 years. Aerial surveys suggest densities of 6-10 pairs/100 km^2 in the core range, with highs of 26-28 pairs/100 km^2 in the Red Lake and Kenora area along the Manitoba border. Densities drop to 2-3 pairs/100km^2 on the Hudson Bay Lowlands (Ross 1987). – *Erica H. Dunn*

Red-breasted Merganser

Harle huppé

Mergus serrator

Glenn Bartley

Among the fastest of birds in level flight (130 km/h), the Red-breasted Merganser is the most northerly breeding of the piscivorous ducks (Titman 1999). It has a holarctic distribution, breeding mostly in tundra and boreal forest zones across Eurasia, Iceland, Greenland, and North America. Within North America, this sea duck breeds from the Aleutian Islands in the west eastward to Newfoundland and from the Arctic coast of the Yukon south to the Great Lakes.

Distribution and population status: Both atlases, as well as historical information, indicate that the Red-breasted Merganser is widely distributed along extensive water bodies at coastal and inland sites throughout Ontario, with the exception of the extreme south (Baillie and Harrington 1936). Breeding evidence was most frequently recorded along major waterways throughout the Hudson Bay Lowlands and farther south, particularly within bays and around islands of several of the Great Lakes. In the Northern Shield region, the species breeds most commonly along the Lake Superior shoreline. Breeding records in the Southern Shield and Lake Simcoe-Rideau regions are most frequent around various-sized vegetated or barren rocky islands of Georgian Bay and Lake Huron, as well as on the shores of Lake Nipissing. Evidence of breeding along Lake Ontario is primarily restricted to the Thousand Islands and Prince Edward Co. areas, and both atlases indicate scarce breeding along Lake Erie, the southern extremity of the bird's continental breeding range. The most southern confirmed breeding record was from Long Point.

There were no significant changes in the distribution or probability of observation between atlases. Non-significant increases in the probability of observation occurred in the Carolinian and Lake Simcoe-Rideau regions, while a decline occurred in the Hudson Bay Lowlands. Reasons for this non-significant decline are not clear but may partially reflect differences in coverage between atlases. Whereas breeding evidence was re-established along most large water bodies, sections of several rivers where breeding evidence was reported in several

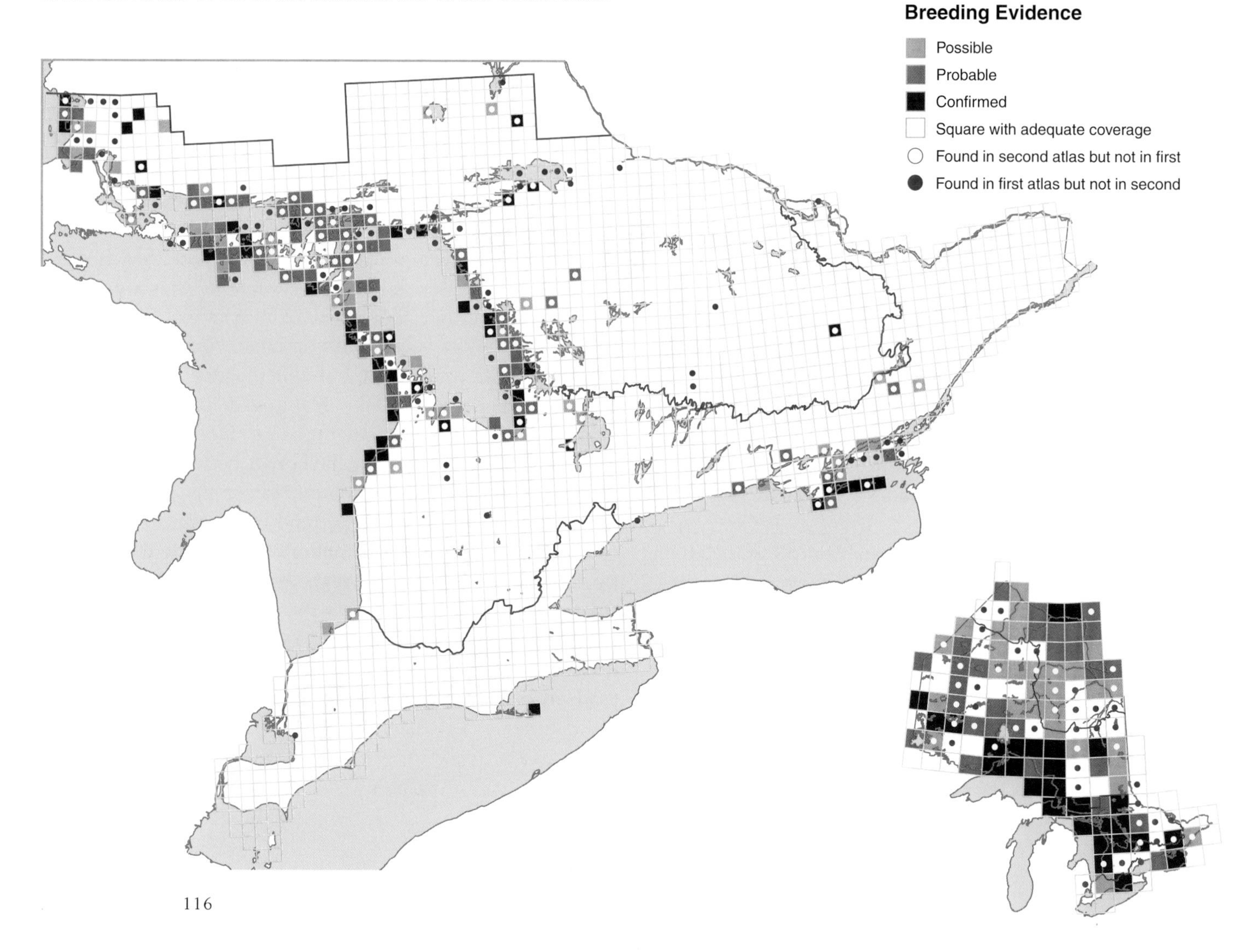

BREEDING EVIDENCE

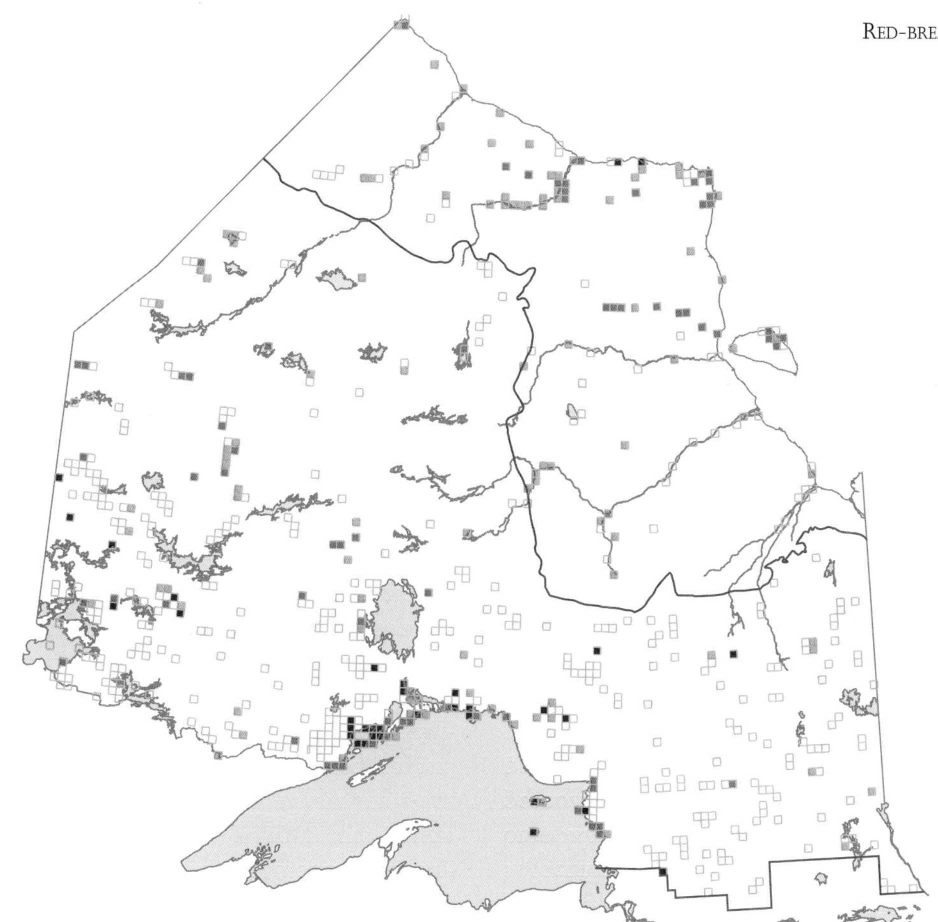

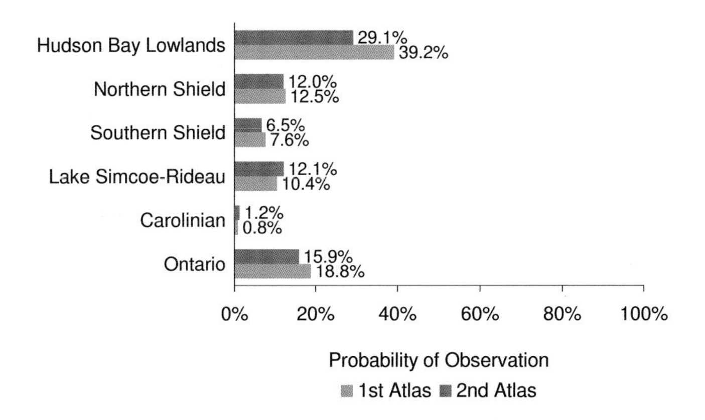

squares in the first atlas, including the Sachigo and Missinaibi Rivers, were not surveyed during the second atlas. Also, the first atlas had a heavy emphasis on areas along the region's major bodies of water, while the present atlas included observations along smaller wetlands that are less preferred by the Red-breasted Merganser. Such differences in coverage resulted in numerous newly surveyed squares lacking breeding evidence for this species. Elsewhere in Canada, from 1990 to 2005, the Eastern Waterfowl Survey reported a 14.8% annual increase in Red-breasted Merganser breeding pairs in the Atlantic Highlands and a 3.6% annual decrease in the Eastern Boreal Shield (Canadian Wildlife Service Waterfowl Committee 2005).

Breeding biology: The Red-breasted Merganser typically nests close to water along lakeshores, forested riverbanks, and marsh edges, and especially on inland and coastal islands (Peck and James 1983), where densities can be high. It occasionally nests in larid colonies. Nests are usually on the ground in a shallow depression or cavity and are typically well concealed under fallen logs, driftwood, or branches of conifer trees, at the base of stumps, or in tall and dense grasses or shrubs (Bengtson 1970). Broods are considerably more conspicuous, as they use shallow open waters, avoid sites with emergent or overhanging shore vegetation, and loaf along open shorelines with short grasses or scattered shrubs (Bengtson 1971). When disturbed, broods often run conspicuously on the water away from the shore. This species is a late breeder, some nests being initiated as late as early July; therefore surveys conducted throughout the peak atlassing period of June and July may take place prior to hatching of some broods. A brood of only two or three weeks of age was observed on 8 September 2003 in Georgian Bay near Parry Sound.

Considerable care must be taken when determining the breeding status of individuals of this species. Males have a female-like plumage into the summer of their second year and only attain breeding maturity and adult plumage that fall. Differentiation of non-breeding second-year female and breeding adult female birds is also difficult. Second-year birds may occur with adults on breeding grounds.

Abundance: Point count data were too sparse to create an abundance map. Both atlases suggest that breeding densities are highest along shorelines of larger bodies of water north of the Carolinian region, most notably northern Lake Superior. Breeding densities are also relatively high around Manitoulin Island, the North Channel, and northeastern Georgian Bay. The Red-breasted Merganser is considerably less common than the Common Merganser, particularly along waterways throughout the Northern and Southern Shield regions. – *Shawn R. Craik*

Ruddy Duck

Érismature rousse

Oxyura jamaicensis

George K. Peck

Perhaps best known for its habit of cocking its long, stiff tail, the Ruddy Duck is one of North America's smallest ducks. The breeding male is striking and unmistakable, and although females and non-breeding birds are more cryptic in plumage, they are unlikely to be confused with other species. The Ruddy Duck is found throughout most of North America, breeding from south-central Northwest Territories south to Mexico and South America. Historically a western breeder, it now occurs regularly, though locally, east to southern Québec, although the great majority (87%) of the population still breeds in the prairie pothole region (Brua 2001). The first reports of nesting attempts in Ontario were from the St. Clair Flats in the 1880s (Baillie 1962), but breeding was not documented in the province until 1949 when downy young were collected from Walpole Island (Lumsden 1951). Since then, the species has expanded its range to include most of southern Ontario south of the Shield, and occurs irregularly farther north.

Distribution and population status: Although the Ruddy Duck was reported in all five regions of Ontario, it generally occurs locally and in small numbers. It is distributed most widely in the Carolinian and Lake Simcoe-Rideau regions. While its range in the south correlates with areas of heavier agricultural use, the majority of records come from sewage lagoons and artificial impoundments. Sewage lagoons are important to its success, likely because midge larvae, one of the primary foods of the Ruddy Duck (Brua 2001), occur in extremely high concentrations in the lagoons due to the high organic content of the water and sediments (Zimmerling 2006). The large number of lagoons associated with the higher human population south of the Shield probably explains the species' more frequent occurrence there than farther north. In northern Ontario, this duck is almost exclusively found in lagoons.

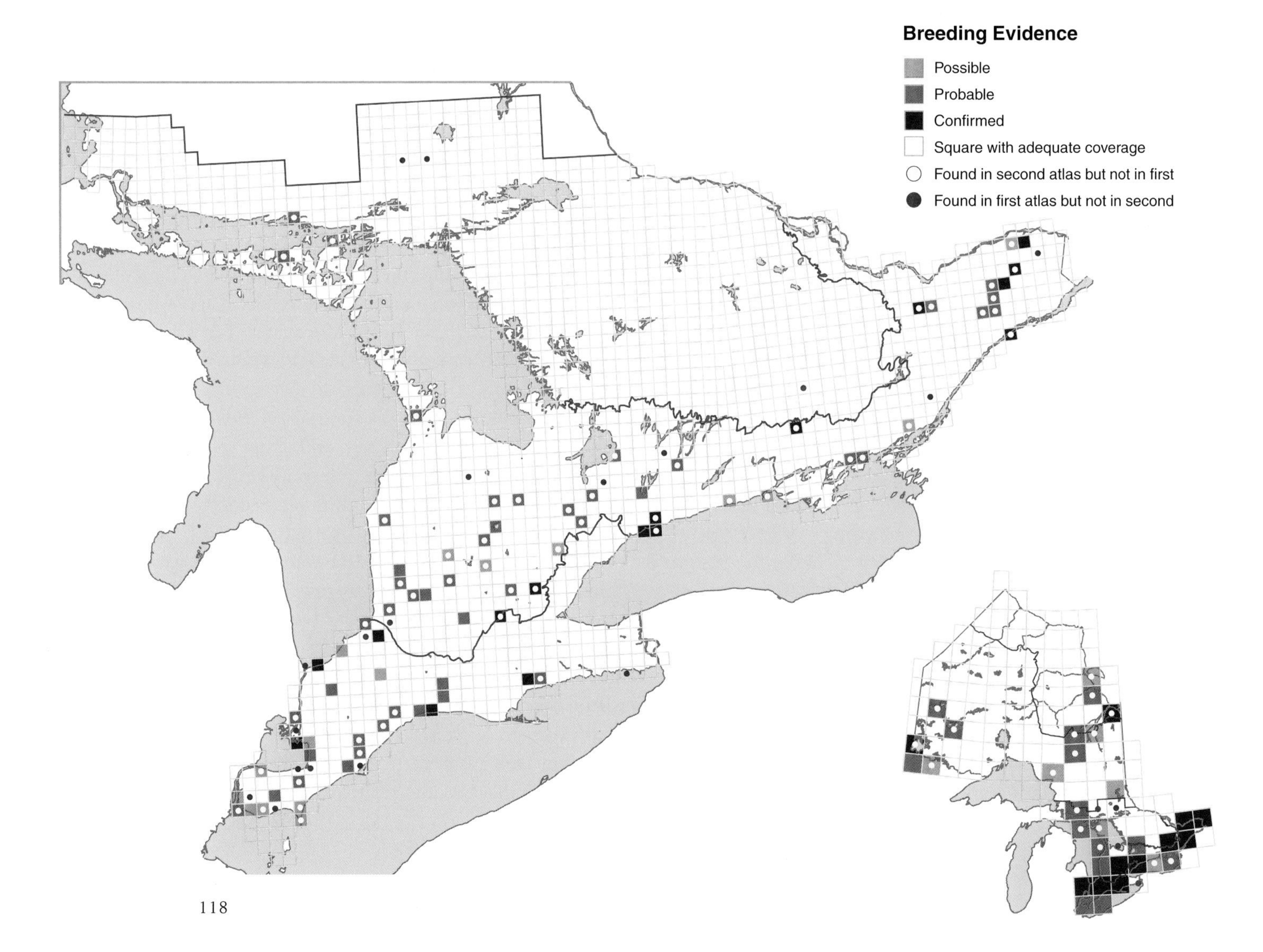

BREEDING EVIDENCE

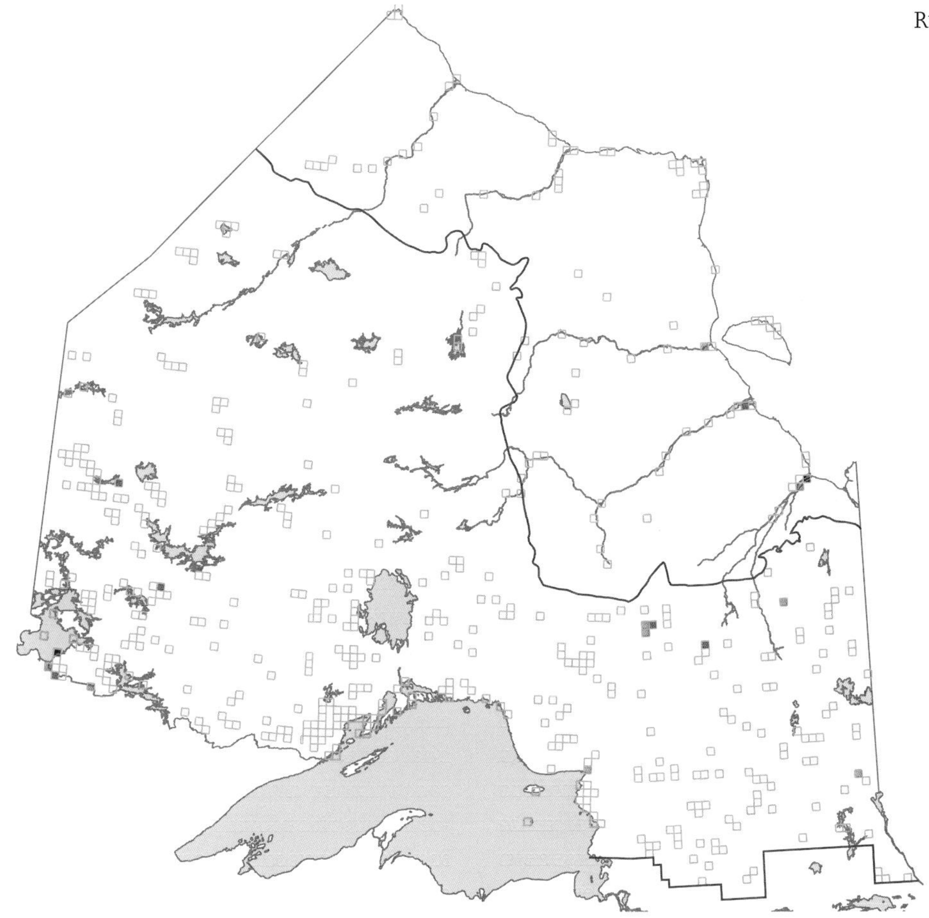

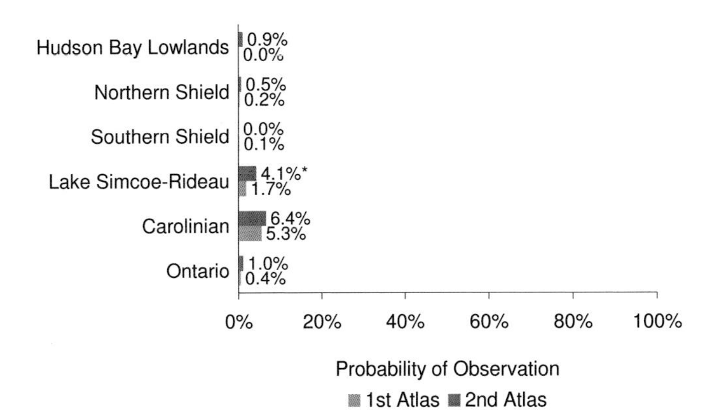

There was no significant difference in the probability of observation of the Ruddy Duck in the province as a whole between atlases, but it increased significantly in the Lake Simcoe-Rideau region, more than doubling its numbers. The species was also reported more widely across the Northern Shield and expanded into the southern part of the Hudson Bay Lowlands, though numbers in the north remain low. While the increase in detections in the north during the second atlas could represent further range expansion by the species, it may simply reflect increased effort by atlassers to survey sewage lagoons.

Breeding biology: The Ruddy Duck is one of only a few duck species to form pairs after arriving on the breeding grounds. Males assemble in conspicuous courtship parties on large ponds, and pairs then disperse to smaller ponds in the area to nest. Pair bonds are short lived, the male usually leaving the female soon after incubation begins. Although nearly all females are paired during the summer, up to 73% of males do not breed in a given year (Brua 2001). For these reasons, individuals or groups of males may not necessarily be breeding or have bred in the square where they were observed. Generally, only one pair nests in a wetland, although multiple nests may occur in more extensive habitat. Incubation takes place primarily in June (Peck and James 1983), during which time the female is secretive and breeding evidence is difficult to obtain. Young can leave the nest within a day of hatching. In the first week, the female will usually lead young to cover when threatened, but as they become older, they increasingly move to open water where they dive for defence (Brua 2001).

While the Ruddy Duck was likely recorded in most squares where it bred, the actual number of breeding individuals may be overrepresented because of the presence of a large proportion of non-breeding males. Breeding was confirmed in only 19% of squares where the species was detected. Observations of females probably represent breeding in that square, due to the very small number of females that remain unpaired. The species is a well-known brood parasite (Brua 2001), occasionally laying its eggs in the nests of other duck and waterbird species, and it is possible that some mixed duck broods containing Ruddy Ducks may have been overlooked.

Abundance: As with most waterfowl, the Ruddy Duck was not detected on sufficient point counts to produce a map of abundance. However, the species occurs most commonly through the more highly populated portion of southern Ontario, outside of major urban centres. The size of Ontario's breeding Ruddy Duck population is likely only a few hundred birds. – *Seabrooke Leckie*

Gray Partridge

Perdrix grise

Perdix perdix

Jean Iron

Previously known as the Hungarian Partridge, the Gray Partridge was introduced to North America from the late 1700s until the early 1900s. In Ontario, it occurs primarily in two disjunct areas, although there are other isolated records. This species prefers agricultural lands and is one of the more difficult species to detect. Its abundance and range were considered under-represented in the first atlas, and this continues to hold true.

Distribution and population status: The Gray Partridge was first introduced in Ontario in 1909, when six birds were released near Brantford. The last releases occurred in 1938 with over 3,800 having been released in 37 counties (Baillie and Harrington 1936; Dawson and Patrick 1960). The areas where it is most abundant are in southeastern Ontario and in Haldimand, Norfolk, and Brant Counties. Ontario populations peaked in the 1950s and 1960s. At this time, density of the Gray Partridge approached 1 bird/4 ha in eastern Ontario, possibly one of the more productive populations in the world. A small population near Thunder Bay was apparently extirpated in the 1980s (Ted Armstrong, pers. comm.).

The probability of observation of the Gray Partridge declined significantly by 44% between atlases in Ontario, with declines of 77% and 33% in the Carolinian and Lake Simcoe-Rideau regions, respectively. The retraction of the Gray Partridge's range was most notable in the southwest. Previously reported from 32 squares in this area, during this atlas it was documented in only nine squares. During the first atlas, this population extended into Niagara Region, but no birds were reported from this area during the second atlas. The eastern population continues to be the stronghold for this species in the province. It was recorded in several new squares in Renfrew Co. and the United Counties of Prescott and Russell. Few records were received from the eastern population west of the United Counties of Stormont, Dundas, and Glengarry, with marked declines in the Kingston area. Due to

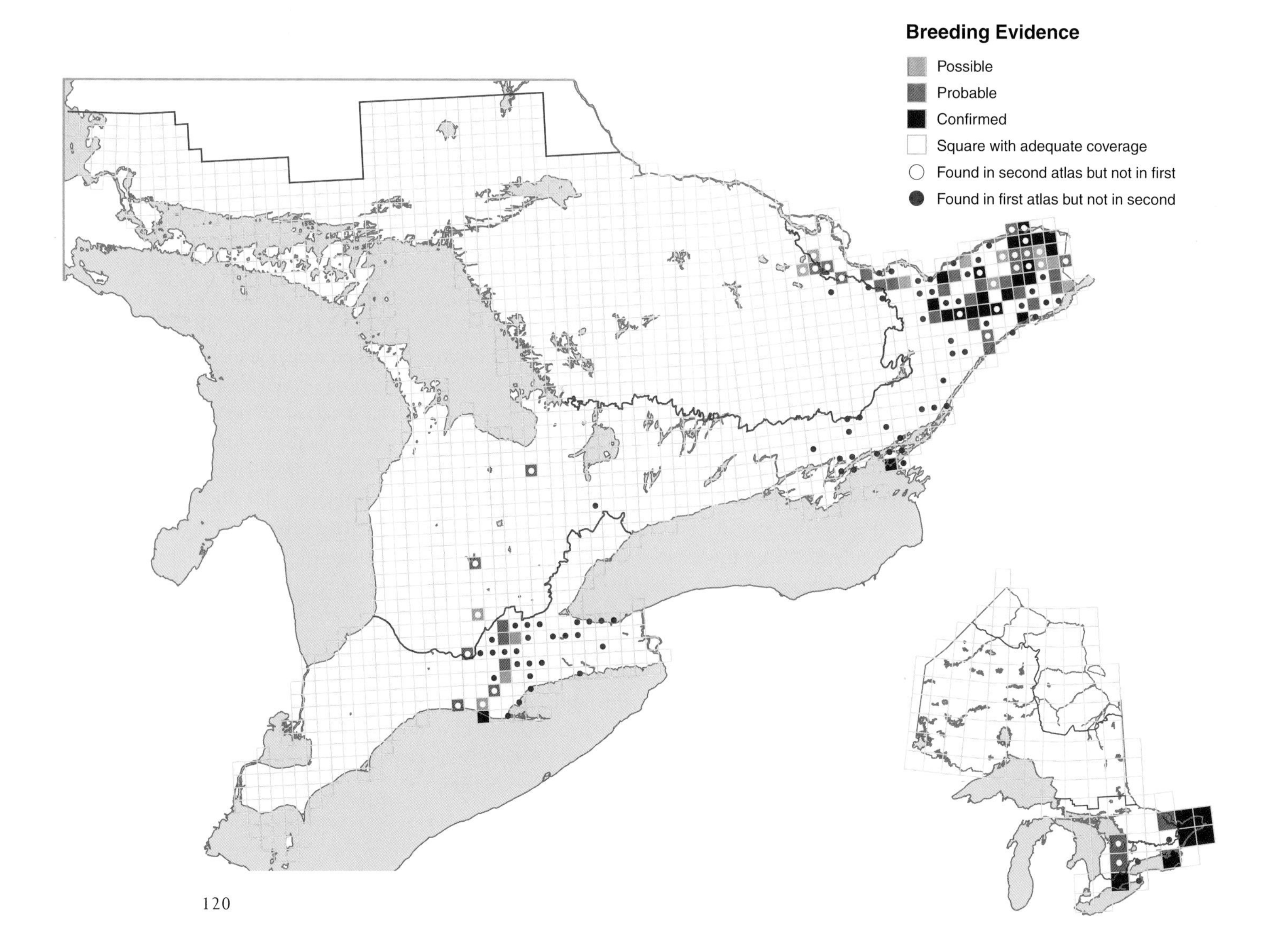

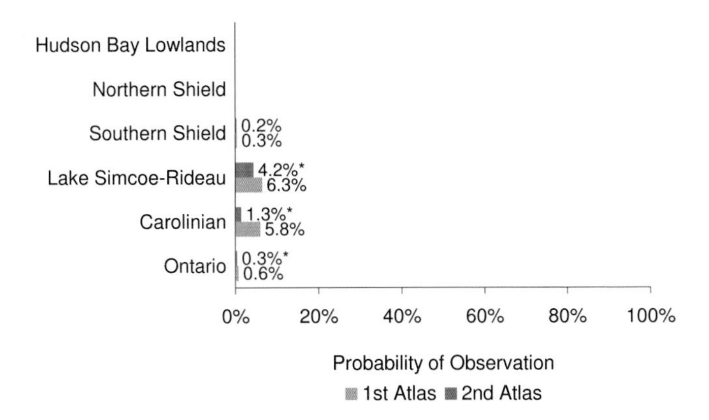

declines in the southwestern population and increases in the eastern population, the average range shifted northward by 41 km between atlases.

The Gray Partridge has been reported on Ontario BBS routes too infrequently for a trend to be calculated, but it has declined on CBC counts since 1981.

Breeding biology: The Gray Partridge is a bird of agricultural landscapes and prefers areas with clay, clay-loam, and sandy loam soils. Highest densities occur where 33-80% of the land is in active agriculture; lowest densities occur when agriculture is 0-11% or 90-100% of the land use (Dawson and Patrick 1960; Allen 1984). It does well in mixed agriculture that includes small cereal grains, corn, soybeans, pasture, and hay.

The first nest is usually in permanent vegetation and almost always in edge habitats such as fencerows, roadsides, drainage ditches, and hayfields; most nests in fields are within 10 m of the edge. Nests are well concealed and very difficult to find, and the female covers the nest when she leaves it. Due to the species' habit of nesting in edge habitats, nest loss due to predation is common, and it is a persistent re-nester; subsequent nests may be in grain fields (Yeatter 1934; Peck and James 1983; Carroll 1993).

Males advertise with a metallic "kee-uck" call in early spring, but it is unlikely that many atlassers are familiar with this call. This species is very difficult to detect during the remainder of the breeding season; it is most evident during the non-breeding season, particularly in winter when birds form coveys and are conspicuous against snow-covered fields. The Gray Partridge is highly sedentary; in Montana, 86% of birds spent their entire lifetime within an area of 115 ha, but home ranges may be as large as 200 ha (Weigand 1980). Birds tend to walk more than they fly, and they are extremely difficult to see in the vegetation. Consequently, finding a Gray Partridge during the breeding season is a combination of knowing where to look, hard work, and luck.

Abundance: Results suggest that the southeastern population is increasing at its northern extent but decreasing in the south, and there has been a marked retraction in the southwestern population. It is probable, however, that the Gray Partridge's distribution and abundance continue to be under-represented. Two new locations were identified during this atlas in Simcoe Co. and Waterloo Region. Due to the species' sedentary nature, it was likely present at these sites during the first atlas but overlooked, and during this atlas, it was probably missed in some squares again. – *Al Sandilands*

Clutch size for the Gray Partridge in Ontario averages 13-24 eggs. In one clutch of 24 eggs, all eggs hatched successfully (Peck and James 1983). *Photo: George K. Peck*

The best habitat for the Gray Partridge appears to be where cereal grains dominate and extensive hedgerows are present (Carroll 1993), but pasture or grassland is often part of the habitat mix. *Photo: Daryl Coulson*

Ring-necked Pheasant

Faisan de Colchide

Phasianus colchicus

Roger Wray

The shape, boldly coloured plumage of the male, and distinctive, harsh call all make the Ring-necked Pheasant difficult to mistake for any other species. The popular upland game bird was introduced to North America from Eurasia in the late 1800s for sport hunting. The species established itself quickly, filling in areas between release points to form its current range by the 1940s (Giudice and Ratti 2001). Its range and population are more limited by habitat availability and winter snow depths than by hunting (Lumsden in Cadman et al. 1987; Giudice and Ratti 2001), although legal hunting of hens may have been a factor in its decline in Ontario (P. Hubert, pers. comm.). Populations are artificially sustained through the release of captive-bred birds.

Distribution and population status: The Ring-necked Pheasant is found in southern Ontario, primarily in the Carolinian and Lake Simcoe-Rideau regions. Most squares in which the species was reported in both atlases were in Essex Co., in the area encompassing the Niagara Peninsula west to London, and the eastern portion of the Greater Toronto Area. In the remainder of the province, there was strong turnover in the squares in which the pheasant was found. It relies heavily on agricultural land for habitat, requiring grassy cover such as hay or alfalfa for nesting and brood-rearing and grain fields for food and cover. During winter, it often inhabits the dense vegetation of marshy areas, or trees and shrubs along field edges, for roosting and cover (Giudice and Ratti 2001). Such varied habitat requirements result in a patchy distribution where all conditions are met, as well as range reductions as land uses change and habitats mature.

In both of its primary regions, as well as for the province as a whole, the probability of observation of the Ring-necked Pheasant declined significantly between atlases. Declines were also documented by CBCs since the first atlas (National Audubon Society 2002) and by BBS data between 1968 and 2005

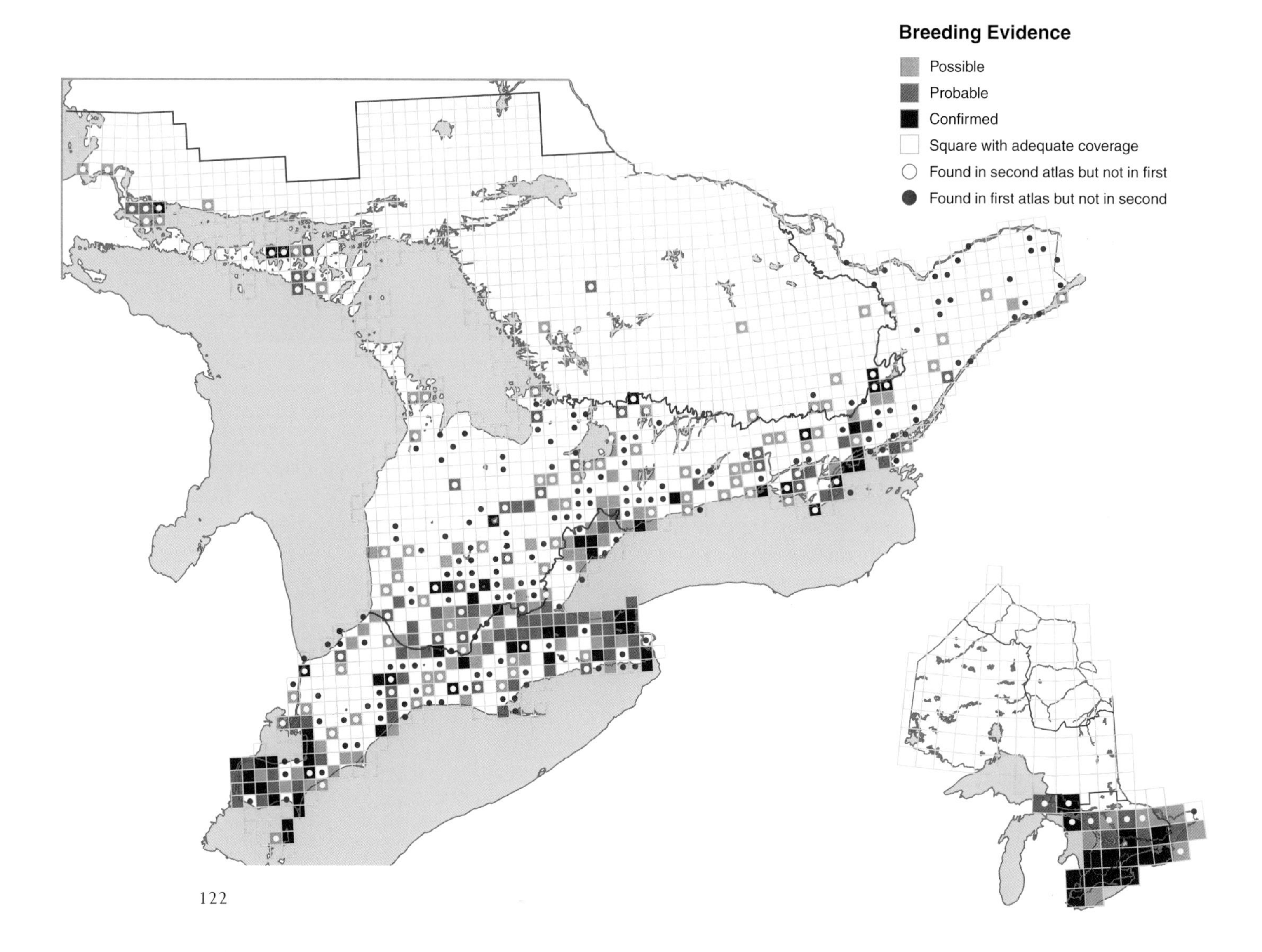

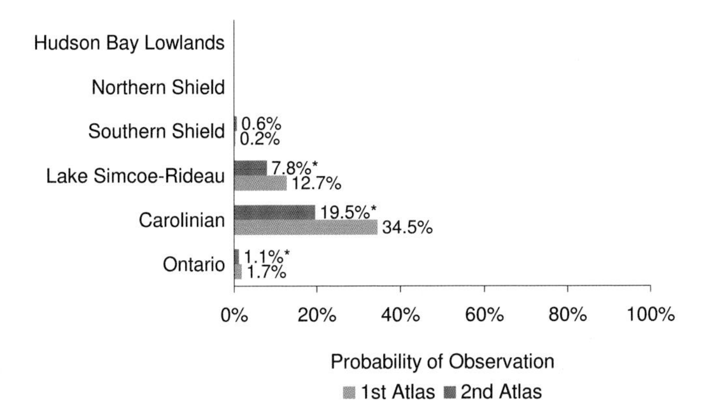

(Downes et al. 2005). Data from both surveys suggest that most of this decline took place prior to the end of the first atlas period and that Ontario populations have been low but relatively stable since 1987. In the rest of Canada, populations have steadily declined. Studies suggest this decline is strongly linked to the loss of suitable habitat as agricultural practices intensify and abandoned fields mature (Giudice and Ratti 2001).

In the first atlas, it was suggested that winter snowfall limited the species' expected natural winter survival to southwestern Ontario and along Lake Ontario (Lumsden in Cadman et al. 1987). The current distribution falls primarily within these approximate boundaries. The species also occurs in the Southern Shield region and areas farther north, probably due to unauthorized releases, as habitat in this area is generally unsuitable. Unauthorized releases confound the true distribution of this species; without releases, it is uncertain if this pheasant would be able to maintain population levels in Ontario.

Breeding biology: The Ring-necked Pheasant is a polygynous species. Females begin forming harems in early April. They nest individually within the territory, but re-form as a group when feeding (Giudice and Ratti 2001). Nests are usually shallow scrapes among the previous year's grasses or forbs. Eggs are laid in May and incubated for about three weeks (Peck and James 1987), during which time the female rarely leaves the nest (Giudice and Ratti 2001). Young are precocial and mobile within hours of hatching. The female and brood usually remain in the general vicinity of the nest site for the first two to three weeks, and young stay with the hen for 70-80 days (Giudice and Ratti 2001). Unless startled, birds usually retreat into cover and hide at the approach of a predator, making them easy to overlook. Most vocalizations are subtle and difficult to detect from a distance (Giudice and Ratti 2001). However, males can easily be heard calling at dawn, and females with broods can often be seen at roadsides or in fields while foraging. It is possible that the species was missed in some squares where it occurs, but the maps likely provide a good representation of its range in Ontario.

Abundance: Ring-necked Pheasant abundance is highest in Essex and Chatham-Kent and eastern Niagara RM below the Niagara Escarpment. High densities also occur through the rest of the Niagara Peninsula and in the Stratford-Aylmer area, where there have been ongoing efforts to re-establish the species. These areas are all milder in winter and likely provide the best mix of habitat for the species. – *Seabrooke Leckie*

Nests are usually shallow scrapes among the previous year's grasses and forbs. Average clutches range from 8-14 eggs (Peck and James 1983). Binbrook, City of Hamilton, 21 May 1969. *Photo: George K. Peck*

Prime breeding habitat for the pheasant includes a mosaic of grassy fields, cereal crops for foraging, and hedgerows for roosting and cover. Pelee Island, Essex Co. *Photo: P. Allen Woodliffe*

Ruffed Grouse

Gélinotte huppée

Bonasa umbellus

George K. Peck

Cryptically coloured and usually quiet, the Ruffed Grouse can be very difficult to spot, but the location of a displaying male is clearly not meant to be a secret. In full display, the fanned tail with its broad, dark sub-terminal band makes an elegant backdrop for the prominent neck ruff and softly coloured body plumage. A territorial male advertises his location by producing an unmistakable drumming sound by rapidly beating his wings in the air while standing on a "drumming log." The species is a year-round resident found south of the treeline from Alaska across Canada to Newfoundland and into the northeastern and northwestern US (Rusch et al. 2000).

Distribution and population status: The Ruffed Grouse is widely distributed in Ontario from the extreme south to throughout the Shield. In the south, it is locally absent in landscapes dominated by agriculture and around major population centres. It is not well established in the Hudson Bay Lowlands, with limited records from this region. The range of the Ruffed Grouse and the probability of observation remained about the same overall between atlases. There were, however, marked regional differences. The probability of observation declined significantly by 53% and 14% in the Carolinian and Lake Simcoe-Rideau regions, respectively. Declines are evident across the Carolinian region, except in Norfolk Co., with the highest forest cover in the region (25%), and there were no records southwest of Rondeau Prov. Park during the second atlas. In the Lake Simcoe-Rideau region, much of the population decline occurred in agricultural areas west of Kitchener-Waterloo and north of London. In the Northern Shield, the probability of observation increased by 27%. This increase could reflect a change in abundance of aspen, a key attribute of Ruffed Grouse habitat (Gullion 1989; Holloway et al. 2004). Carleton (2000) noted that aspen has increased in some parts of northern Ontario.

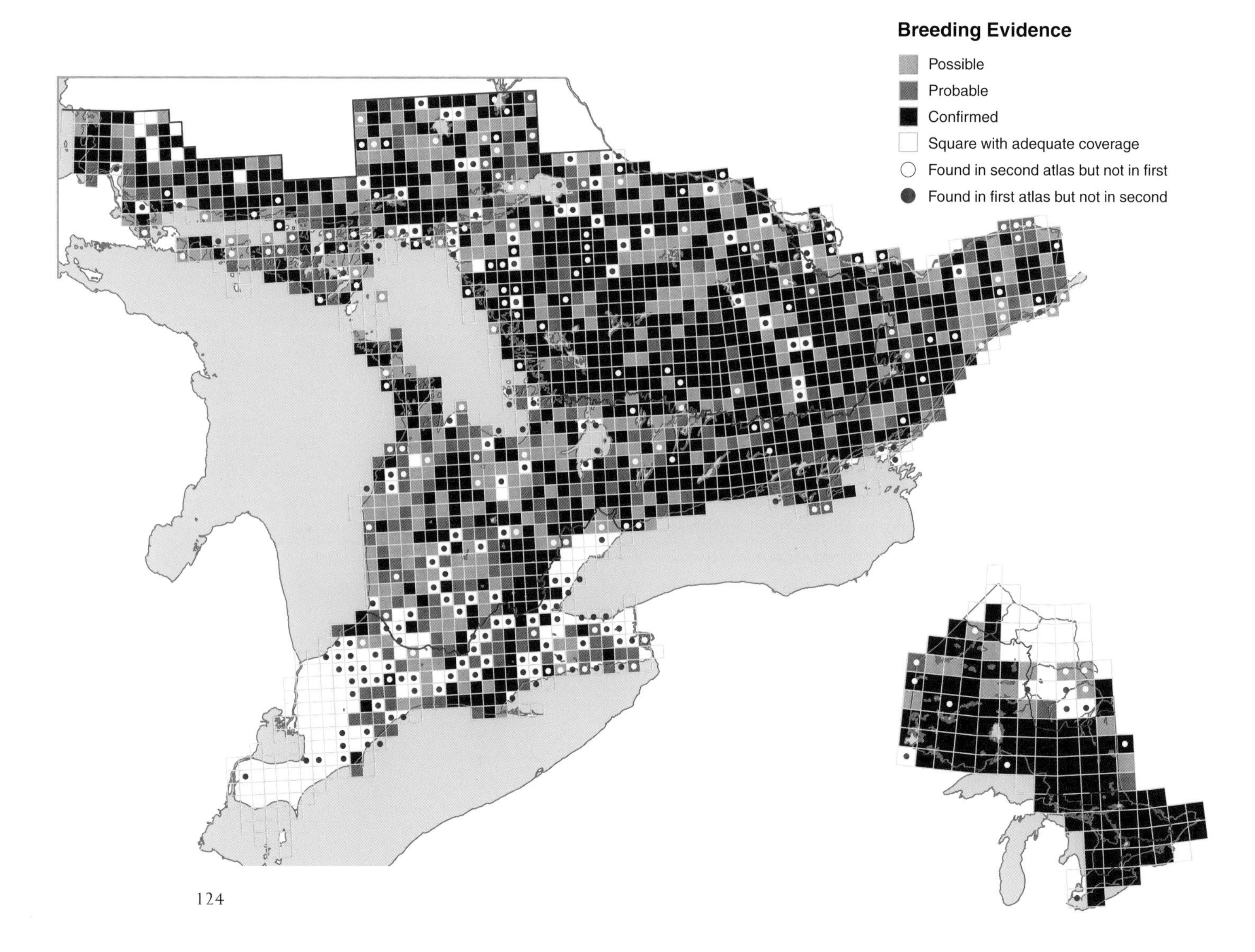

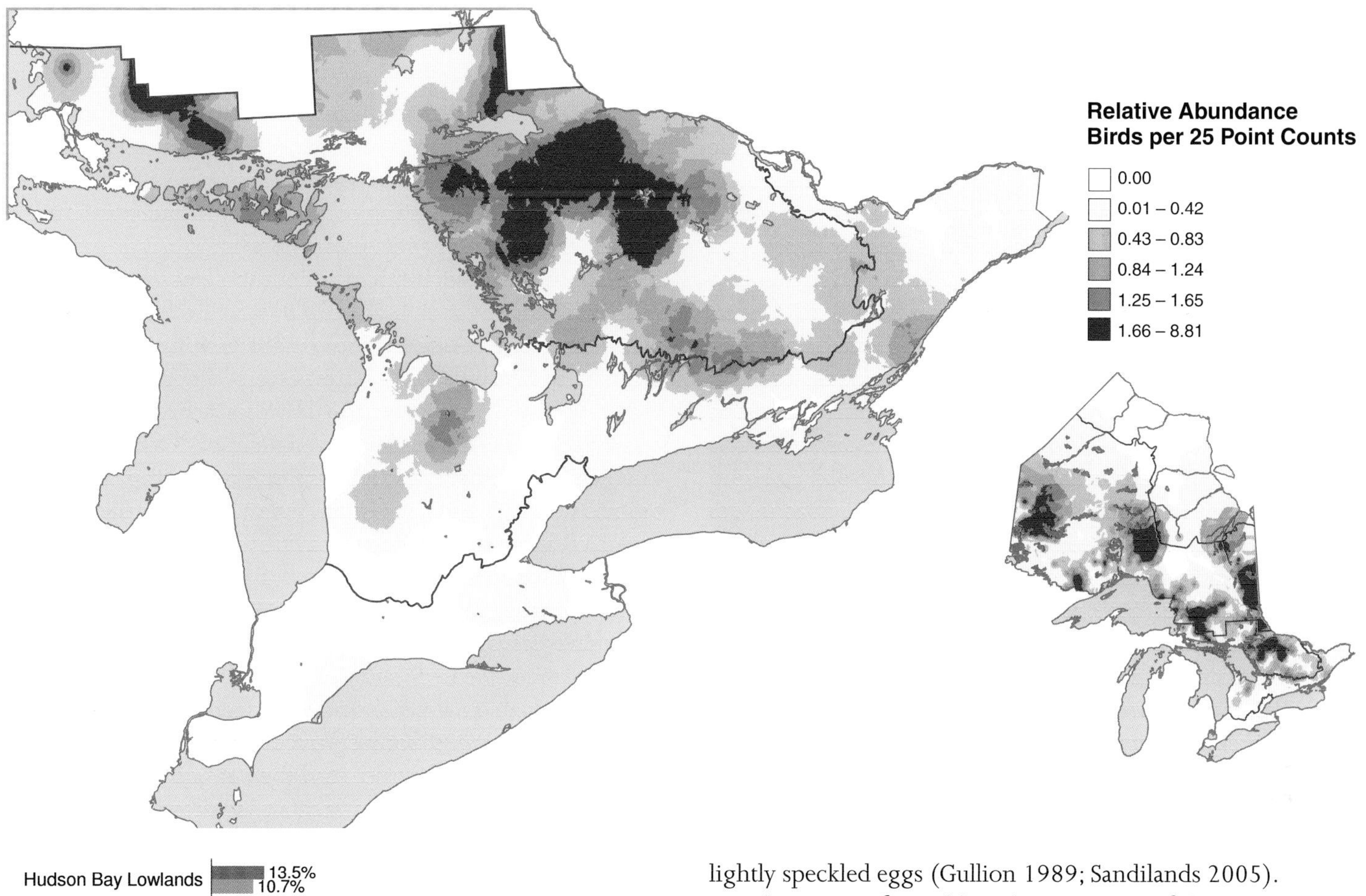

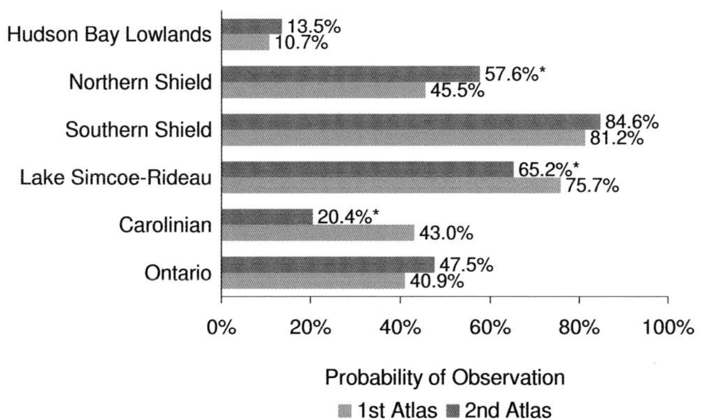

Breeding biology: The Ruffed Grouse is a rather sedentary resident inhabiting a wide variety of forest types including aspen, birch, maple-beech, hardwood, mixed-wood, and even conifer stands, providing there is a hardwood component (James and Peck 1995; Holloway et al. 2004). Territorial males show strong fidelity to drumming sites. Prime sites are young (13-25 years post-disturbance) and dense enough (4,900-14,800 stems/ha; Sandilands 2005) to screen a drumming male from potential predators (Gullion 1989).

Hens establish nests in immature and older forests where the understorey is sparse, affording an unobstructed view (Gullion 1989). The nest is a bowl in the leaves of the forest floor, often adjacent to a tree, stump, log, or boulder. The nest is obvious when the hen is off (infrequently during an average day) but disappears when covered by her cryptic plumage. The hen sits tightly, not flushing until the last moment, and may perform a distraction display. Egg dates range from 15 April to 17 July, with 50% of nests containing eggs between 14 and 28 May (Peck and James 1983). An average clutch consists of 11 buff-coloured, lightly speckled eggs (Gullion 1989; Sandilands 2005).

Atlassers confirmed breeding in 45% of the squares with breeding evidence, likely due to the conspicuousness of hens with precocial chicks, as they wander widely well into summer. Chicks eat invertebrates for the first two weeks of life, followed by fruit and tender leaves, and can fly when less than two weeks old (Gullion 1989). Fleshy fruit, catkins, acorns, and flower buds figure prominently in the autumn diet. In winter and spring, the large flower buds on male aspen trees are a staple food. A Ruffed Grouse "budding" high in a leafless aspen tree cannot be easily missed.

Abundance: Though the most abundant grouse in the province, the Ruffed Grouse is rather sparsely distributed on the landscape. Point counts resulted in an average of only 1 bird/25 points on the Shield where it is most numerous. Most point counts were completed after the peak of drumming, so abundance was likely underestimated. The abundance map probably provides a good indication of local "hotspots" in southern Ontario where a large number of contiguous squares was surveyed, but overstates concentrations in the north.

In portions of its range, populations are cyclic. Not all populations show clear cycles, and for those that do cycle, the time between peaks of abundance may be 2.5-10 years (Sandilands 2005). BBS data for Ontario show recurring peaks of abundance, with the time between peaks being two to six years. It is likely that the atlas period was long enough to provide a good indication of average levels of abundance of the Ruffed Grouse. – *Kandyd Szuba.*

Spruce Grouse

Tétras du Canada

Falcipennis canadensis

Peter Ferguson

The Spruce Grouse, a conifer specialist (Boag and Schroeder 1992), is found in Jack Pine or spruce forest types in Ontario on the Shield and northward, but population densities are greatest in young Jack Pine forests about 4-7 m tall with a thick carpet of blueberries, Trailing Arbutus, and other ericaceous plants (Szuba and Bendell 1983; Naylor 1989; Holloway et al. 2004; pers. obs.). Virtually pure conifer stands created by fire or forest management provide good conditions for this splendid symbol of boreal coniferous forests. Its habit of remaining still rather than flushing likely reduces detection by its principal predator, the Northern Goshawk, but results in an undeserved reputation as the "fool hen" (Robinson 1980). The Spruce Grouse is superbly adapted to life in a species-poor environment where conifer needles are a staple food year round.

Distribution and population status: The Spruce Grouse was plentiful in the vicinity of Orangeville historically, but with relatively few observations on the Southern Shield, generally in the vicinity of Algonquin Park, it is now mainly a bird of the north. It is widely distributed across the Shield and northward where spruce and Jack Pine forests are most abundant (Ontario Ministry of Natural Resources 2002), as was the case in the first atlas. It was observed in almost twice as many squares during the second atlas, but this was largely due to additional coverage in the north, as there was no significant difference when these results were adjusted for effort. It was probably overlooked in many squares where it occurs.

Populations of the Spruce Grouse do not cycle (Sandilands 2005), although a variety of factors influence annual and local reproductive success, including variation in availability of food for hens (Trailing Arbutus flowers, moss capsules); nest predation by Red Squirrels (Naylor 1989); weather conditions affecting the abundance of food for young chicks (insects, berries); and predation on adults (Szuba 1989; Boag and Schroeder 1992).

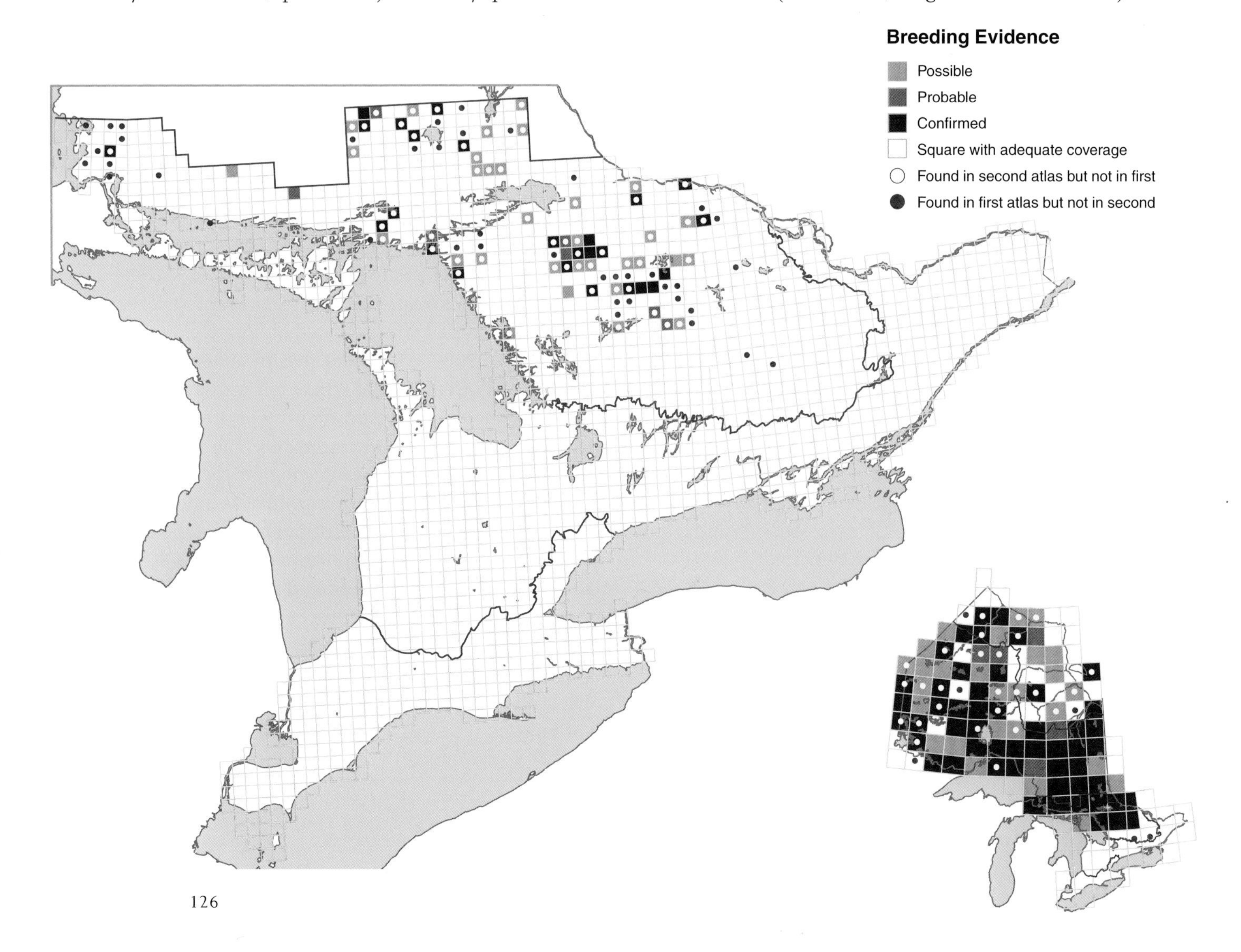

BREEDING EVIDENCE

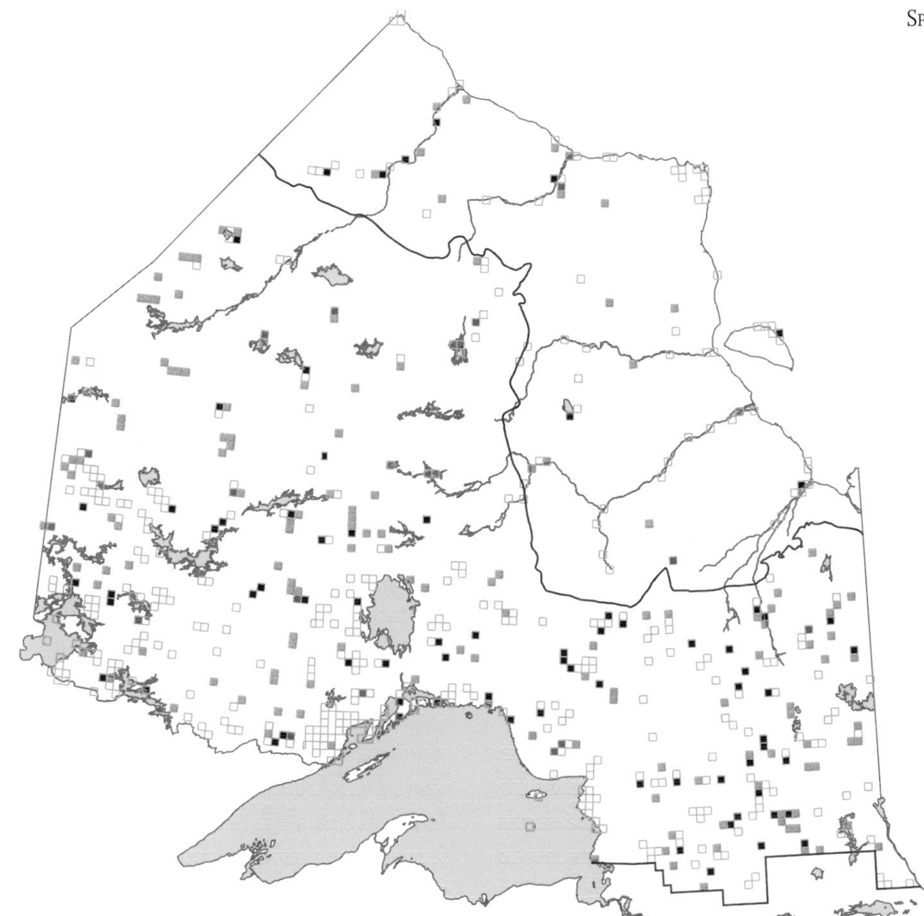

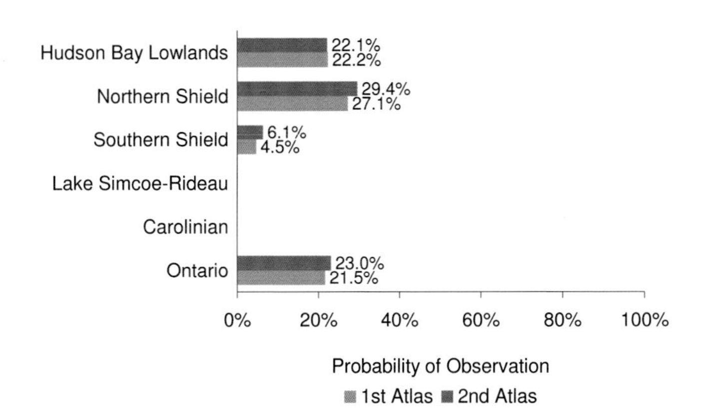

Breeding biology: The Spruce Grouse is a resident species, with occasional short-distance dispersal from relatively open breeding areas to denser conifer cover in winter (Boag and Schroeder 1992). It is usually quiet and well hidden within a dense conifer canopy or among the low shrubs and herbs of the forest floor, making it difficult to find. Both sexes are strongly territorial (Naylor 1989; Boag and Schroeder 1992) and noisy for a brief period in spring. Between mid-April and mid-May, males perform loud "flutter flights" from the ground to a tree and back again in a favourite spot, usually at dawn and dusk, and females periodically give a "cackle" call from treetops. These displays can be elicited and individuals of both sexes attracted by means of broadcasts of the recorded call of a hen. During incubation, birds become very difficult to find.

The male Spruce Grouse is unmistakable with its striking black and white plumage, prominent black chest spot, bright red combs above the eyes, and rusty terminal tail band. A male in full display is a charming and memorable sight (Strickland 1995). Displays include bouts of noisy tail fanning synchronized with slow, purposeful steps. In contrast, hens are cryptically coloured in shades of brown, rust, and white but share the rusty tail band, and, when agitated, show a pinkish patch above the eye. Superficially, a hen resembles a small Ruffed Grouse that lacks a prominent crest. Behaviourally, these two species differ as well, with the Spruce Grouse being more approachable.

The nest of the Spruce Grouse is a bowl in the conifer needles of the forest floor, often adjacent to a tree, stump, log, or boulder. The hen sits tightly, not flushing until the last moment, and may perform a vigorous distraction display. Egg dates range from 9 May to 25 June, with 50% of nests containing eggs between 29 May and 13 June (Peck and James 1983). An average clutch consists of six eggs for adults and five for yearlings, with an overall range of five to eight eggs (Naylor and Bendell 1989). Re-nesting is rare (Naylor 1989; Szuba 1989). The likelihood of confirming breeding increases when the eggs hatch around mid-June. Hens are watchful and fearless in defence of their precocial chicks, which remain together at least until early September.

Abundance: Atlas data probably provide a very good idea of the overall distribution of this bird but most certainly underestimate abundance, which can be as great as 50 birds/km² or more in prime habitat during the nesting season (Szuba and Bendell 1983). The Spruce Grouse continues to be much more common in northern than southern Ontario. – *Kandyd Szuba*

Willow Ptarmigan

Lagopède des saules

Lagopus lagopus

George K. Peck

The Willow Ptarmigan is one of few birds adapted to live year round in Ontario's Hudson Bay Lowlands. A holarctic species, in North America it breeds at or beyond the treeline in arctic, subarctic, and subalpine tundra in Alaska, the mountains of western Canada, and across northern Canada to Newfoundland (Godfrey 1986; Hannon et al. 1998).

Distribution and population status: In Ontario, the Willow Ptarmigan is primarily a species of open tundra, breeding in appropriate habitat along the entire Hudson Bay coast from the Manitoba border to Cape Henrietta Maria and locally along the James Bay coast as far south as Akimiski Island (K. Abraham, pers. comm.). The most southerly confirmed breeding record in Ontario is along the James Bay coast approximately 100 km north of Attawapiskat (Peck and James 1999). It usually winters within its breeding range but is known to travel south of the treeline, occasionally great distances (Hannon et al. 1998).

During the second atlas, the Willow Ptarmigan was recorded in more squares and much farther inland from the coast than during the first atlas. This increase is likely attributable to differences in coverage combined with a period of high population levels. More atlas crews visited the far north compared to the first atlas. Willow Ptarmigan are conspicuous from the air, and increased low-level aerial surveys by CWS and OMNR accounted for significant numbers of detections. During the first atlas, most coverage in the Hudson Bay Lowlands was carried out in 1984 and 1985 when the Willow Ptarmigan was relatively scarce. In contrast, abundance was quite high in most if not all years of the second atlas (K. Abraham, pers. comm.). The number of breeding individuals is known to fluctuate, sometimes dramatically, and the species can vary from rare to common in any given year (James 1991; Hannon et al. 1998). Overall, however, no large-scale changes in numbers have been

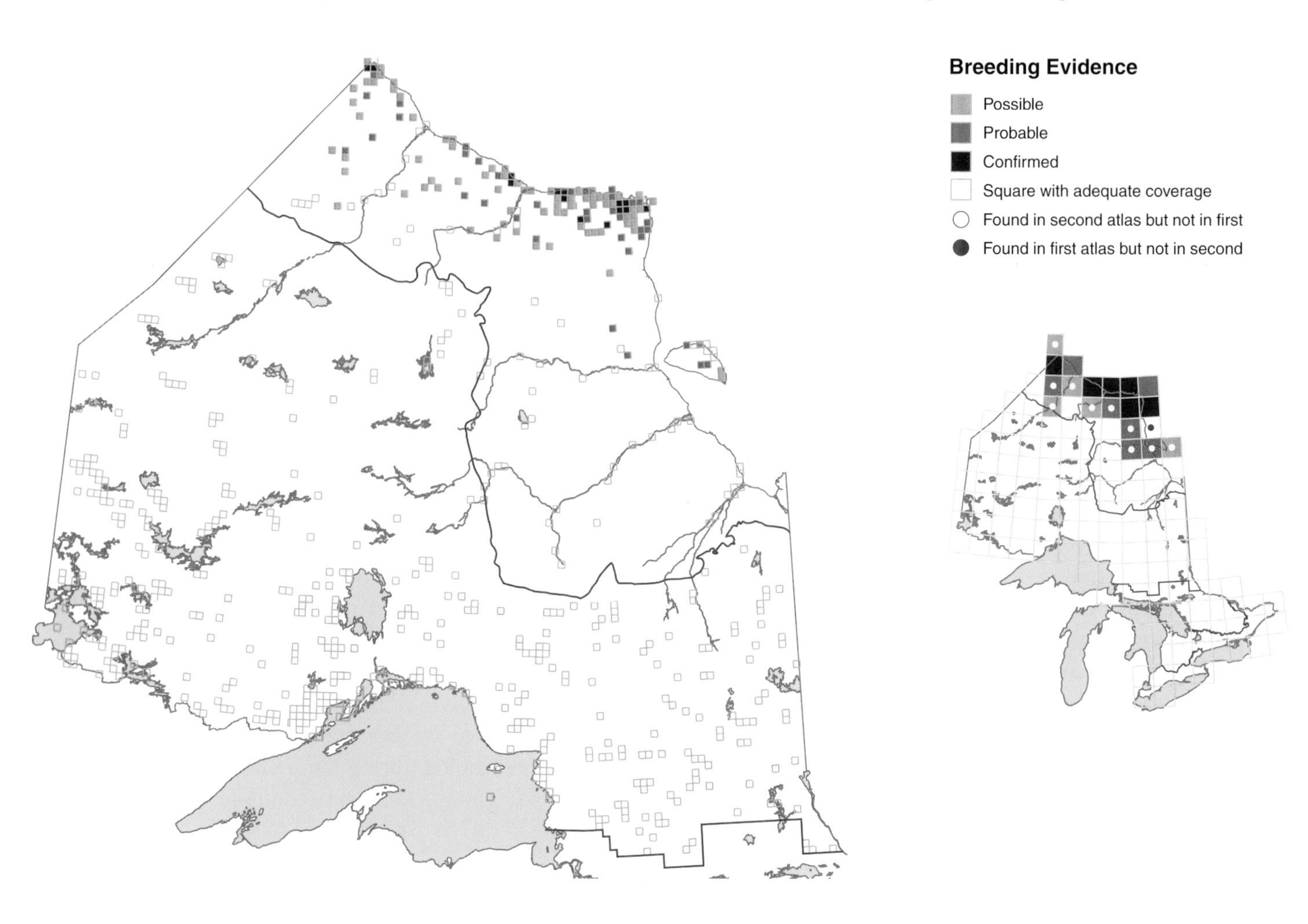

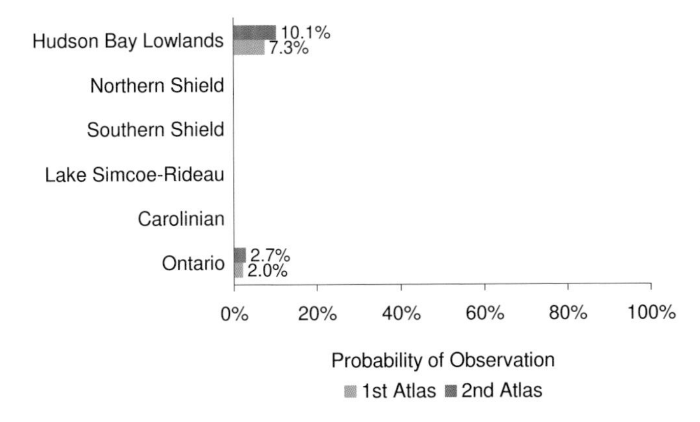

noted over time in North America (Hannon et al. 1998).

Perhaps more difficult to interpret is the increase in inland records between this and the first atlas. The increase is likely a result of improved coverage but could involve lingering, non-breeding birds from winter dispersal; birds that moved south into more marginal but unoccupied territories associated with a period of abundance; a previously undetected sector of the breeding population; or a combination of factors.

Breeding biology: The Willow Ptarmigan is conspicuous and easily detected during the breeding season. In Ontario, it breeds primarily in open tundra above the treeline but also in areas with extensive open palsa plateaus in taiga and the taiga-tundra ecotone (D.A. Sutherland, pers. comm.). The plumage is distinctive, and males are conspicuous patrolling territories along raised beach ridges. A large proportion of birds in successive years occupy the same territory, which males actively defend beginning in late April to early May until the young are out of the nest (Hannon et al. 1998). Early in the breeding season, males are particularly vocal and perform conspicuous display flights. Males are usually monogamous and help to accompany and defend the young until autumn, making the species the only grouse in which the male is regularly involved in parental care (Hannon et al. 1998).

The well-concealed nest is usually on a raised beach ridge or a hummock in a sedge fen (Hannon et al. 1998). It is usually a small depression lined with grass, leaves, moss, and feathers and is frequently placed under a stunted willow or spruce (Bent 1932). Clutch size is typically seven to nine eggs in Ontario (Peck and James 1999) but may range from four to 14 (Hannon et al. 1998). Only one brood is raised per season, but re-nesting may occur if the first clutch fails (Hannon et al. 1998). Due to the female's cryptic coloration and her tendency to sit very tight, nests can be difficult to detect. A total of 30 nests were documented in Ontario prior to 2001 (Peck 2003a), and 20 more were found during this atlas.

Abundance: Detections of the Willow Ptarmigan on point counts were insufficient to produce a relative abundance map. An average of 2.1 birds/25 point counts was calculated in the Hudson Bay Lowlands; densities, however, are known to vary temporally and geographically. Much of the Hudson Bay Lowlands region is unsuitable breeding habitat for this species, so the average for this region greatly underestimates densities within its range. Densities ranging from less than 1 to 30-40 pairs/km^2 were reported from Cape Henrietta Maria in the first atlas. – *Colin D. Jones*

Nests are located on raised beach ridges or on drier hummocks in wet tundra and sedge fens, usually beneath a stunted willow or spruce. Radar Site 415, Polar Bear Prov. Park, 24 June 1970. *Photo: George K. Peck*

In Ontario, the Willow Ptarmigan breeds primarily in open tundra adjacent to Hudson and northern James Bays, but also inland in taiga in areas with extensive palsa plateaus. Radar Site 415, 5 July 1984. *Photo: Mark Peck*

Sharp-tailed Grouse

Tétras à queue fine
Tympanuchus phasianellus

Mark Peck

The Sharp-tailed Grouse is a bird of semi-open country in Canada and the US, ranging from Alaska east to western Québec and south to Idaho, Colorado, and Michigan (Connelly et al. 1998). Two subspecies occur in Ontario, the Prairie Sharp-tailed Grouse (*T. p. campestris*), and the Northern Sharp-tailed Grouse (*T. p. phasianellus*), each occupying different ecological niches and separate geographic areas. This species is not often seen by Ontario birders since, in the case of *T. p. campestris*, it is very local in distribution, and, in the case of *T. p. phasianellus*, it inhabits rarely visited remote peatlands in northern Ontario.

Distribution and population status: The Northern Sharp-tailed Grouse is a permanent resident in the muskegs of northern Ontario. It is widespread in the taiga of the Hudson Bay Lowlands and uncommon and local in the scattered fens of the Canadian Shield. Southward irruptions occasionally occur, the most spectacular in the winter of 1932-33, when birds were seen as far south as Bracebridge and Bancroft. The most recent irruption occurred in the winter of 1967-68 when birds were seen as far south as Chapleau and the north shore of Lake Superior.

The Prairie Sharp-tailed Grouse entered Ontario from the central plains in the early 1900s, colonizing farmlands from Rainy River to Port Arthur and Fort William (now Thunder Bay). From Michigan, it entered Ontario at Sault Ste. Marie and Manitoulin Island. Its numbers peaked in the 1930s, then declined, but several populations still survive. Initially, it hybridized with the Greater Prairie-Chicken and the irruptive northern subspecies, but the prairie-chickens and hybrids have since died out (H. Lumsden 2005). The Prairie Sharp-tailed Grouse was introduced to several locations in southern Ontario, most recently in the 1970s.

Atlas data give an accurate indication of the general distribution of the Sharp tailed Grouse in Ontario. The map shows

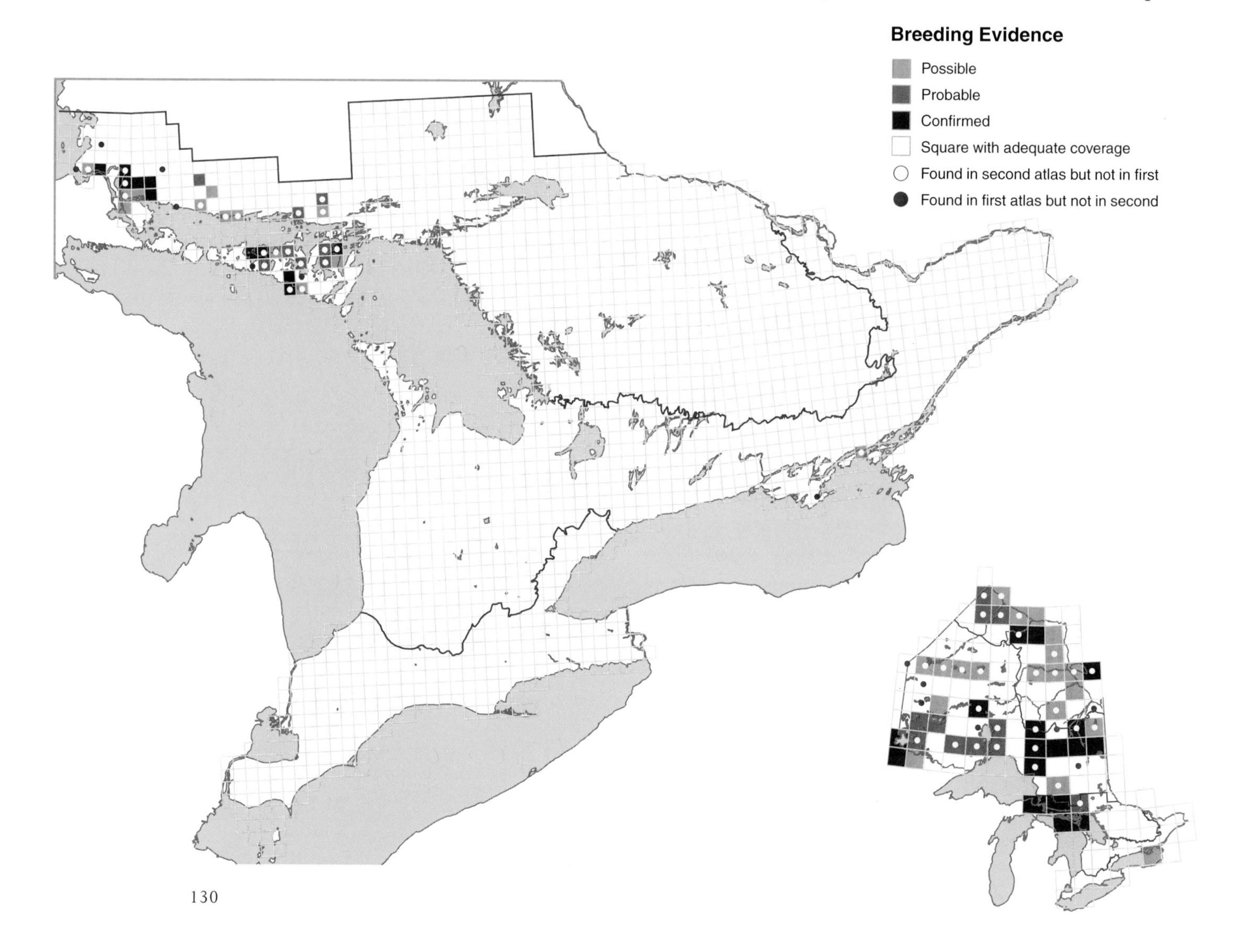

BREEDING EVIDENCE

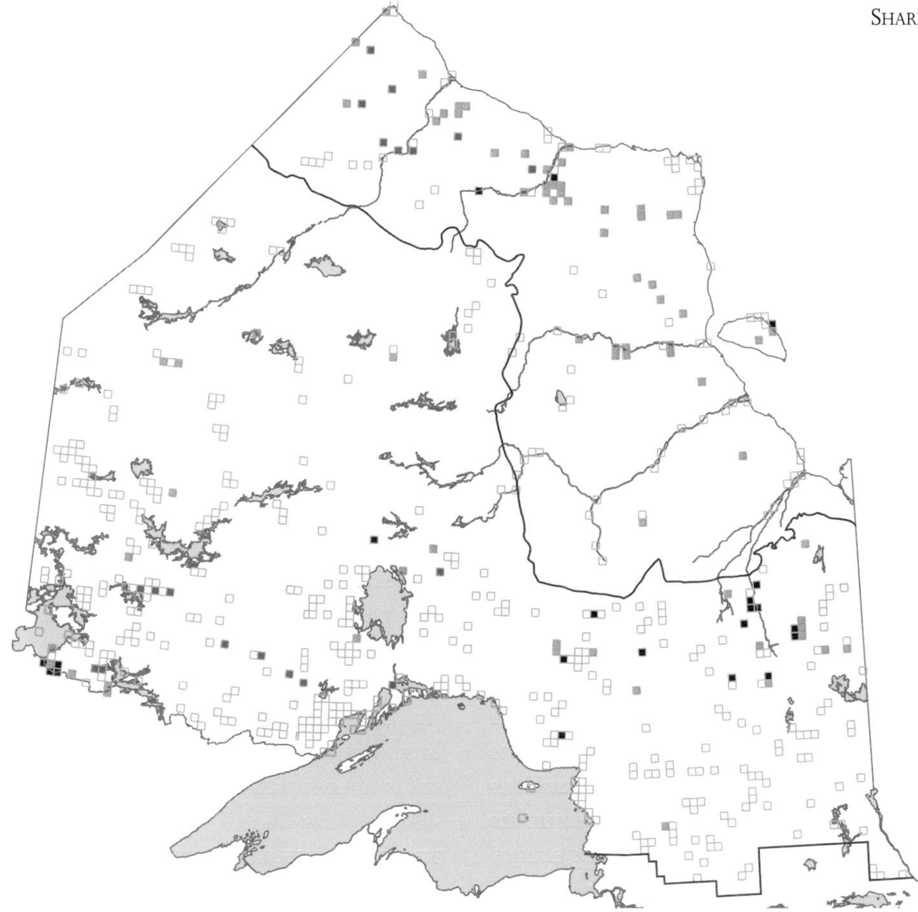

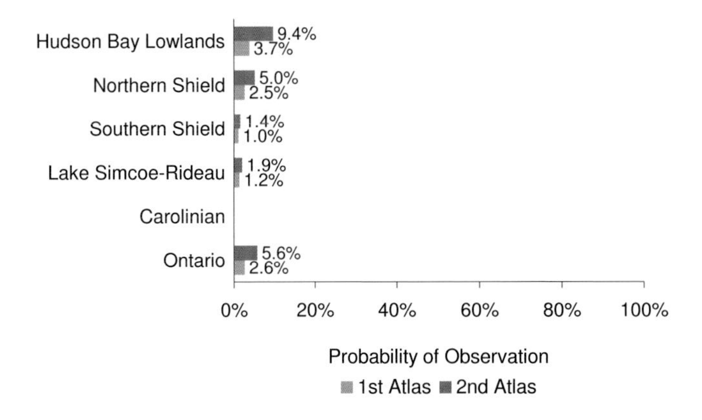

T. p. phasianellus across the Hudson Bay Lowlands extending south into the Canadian Shield. There are two disjunct populations of *T. p. campestris*, one in Rainy River Dist. from Rainy River east to Fort Frances, and the other along the north shore of Lake Huron. One bird was recorded on Simcoe Island, off Wolfe Island, Frontenac Co., on 1 June 2001. The origin of this bird is uncertain; it may have been the result of a recent unauthorized release.

The distribution of the Sharp-tailed Grouse in Ontario has not changed significantly since the first atlas, nor has the probability of observation in the province as a whole or in any region. In the north, it was detected in many more squares than in the first atlas, but this is due to better coverage, primarily through low-level aerial surveys. The species was recorded in several squares in the Thunder Bay and Dryden areas (Escott 2003). These are not new populations but permanent residents in squares that were not fully covered in the first atlas. On the Canadian Shield, it was detected in a few squares in the first atlas but not the second; this may be due to forest regeneration.

The Prairie Sharp-tailed Grouse continues to thrive in agricultural areas around Sault Ste. Marie and appears to have extended its range eastward as far as Webbwood along the north shore of Lake Huron. Several new leks were found on Manitoulin and St. Joseph's Islands as a result of improved coverage. In southern Ontario, the introduced populations have disappeared (H. Lumsden, pers. comm.).

Breeding biology: This is a lek species, most easily detected in the spring when males gather to compete for females on an exposed dancing ground, usually a knoll in a field or open muskeg. In the Boreal Forest, cutovers and burns can provide temporary suitable habitat. The males make various rattling, stomping, and clucking sounds, which carry a long distance. Later, the birds become very secretive. They remain close to the lek area. Females nest in tall grass or shrubbery and stick tight to the nest until the last moment when approached.

Not surprisingly, only two nests were found: a bird was found on a nest at the edge of a hayfield on Manitoulin Island on 7 June 2002, and a nest with seven eggs was discovered in the Hudson Bay Lowlands on 13 June 2004. All other confirmed records are of females with broods. Most atlas records are of adults seen in suitable habitat, or males displaying on leks.

Abundance: This species is not well covered by atlas point counts, so no abundance map is available. It is common in suitable habitat but very local in distribution. – *Nicholas G. Escott*

Wild Turkey

Dindon sauvage

Meleagris gallopavo

Tim Stewart

The Wild Turkey is the largest gallinaceous bird native to North America. It is a familiar bird, having been domesticated for centuries, initially by indigenous peoples (Schorger 1966). Prior to European settlement, the species was common in mixed and temperate forests and savannahs of eastern North America, including southern Ontario, its only Canadian locality (Schorger 1966). Habitat loss and over-hunting led to population declines during the 1800s across its range (Kennamer et al. 1992). The species was extirpated from Ontario by 1909, with the last confirmed sighting in Aurora (Alison 1976). A partnership program led by the OMNR has successfully restored turkey populations in the province. Similarly, the species has recovered across much of North America.

Distribution and population status: The Wild Turkey is common and widespread throughout Ontario south and east of the Canadian Shield. The current distribution is a result of a restoration program that began in 1984 with the release of 74 wild birds imported from Michigan and Missouri. Since then, more birds have been imported from high-density populations in various northern states and Ontario and released in uncolonized suitable habitats. This program has resulted in large population increases across the province during the last two decades.

An experimental release on the Southern Shield near Noëlville, just southwest of Lake Nipissing, took place during the winters of 1999-2000 and 2000-01. Mortality of radio-collared females was very high during 2000-01 due to predation and winter severity (Nguyen et al. 2003). There was some evidence of breeding in 1999 and 2000, but the fate of this population is uncertain. The Noëlville release may have resulted in the birds identified on the breeding evidence map in this area. A similar release was undertaken on St. Joseph Island during winters of 2004 and 2005, and 200 to 250 of these birds were

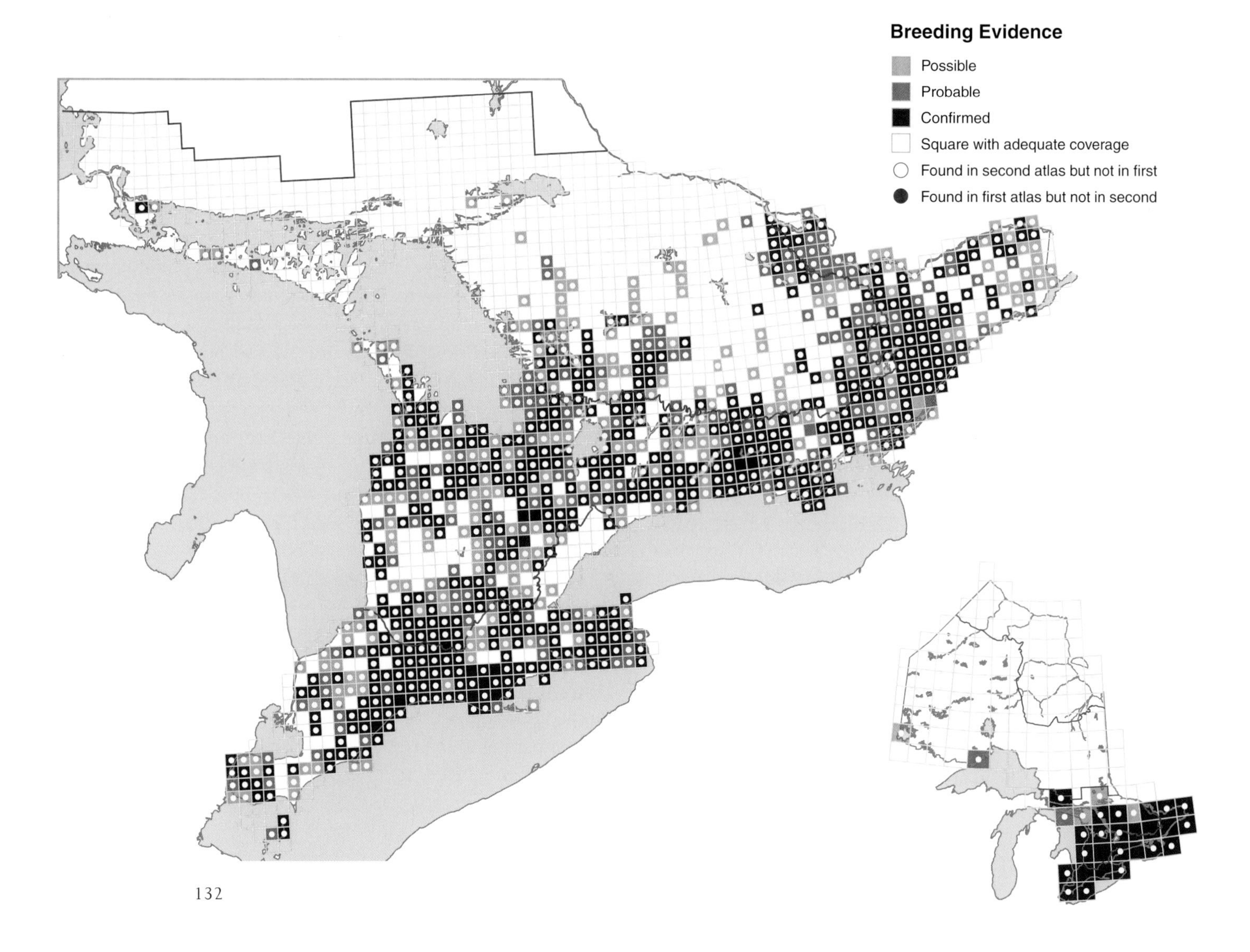

BREEDING EVIDENCE

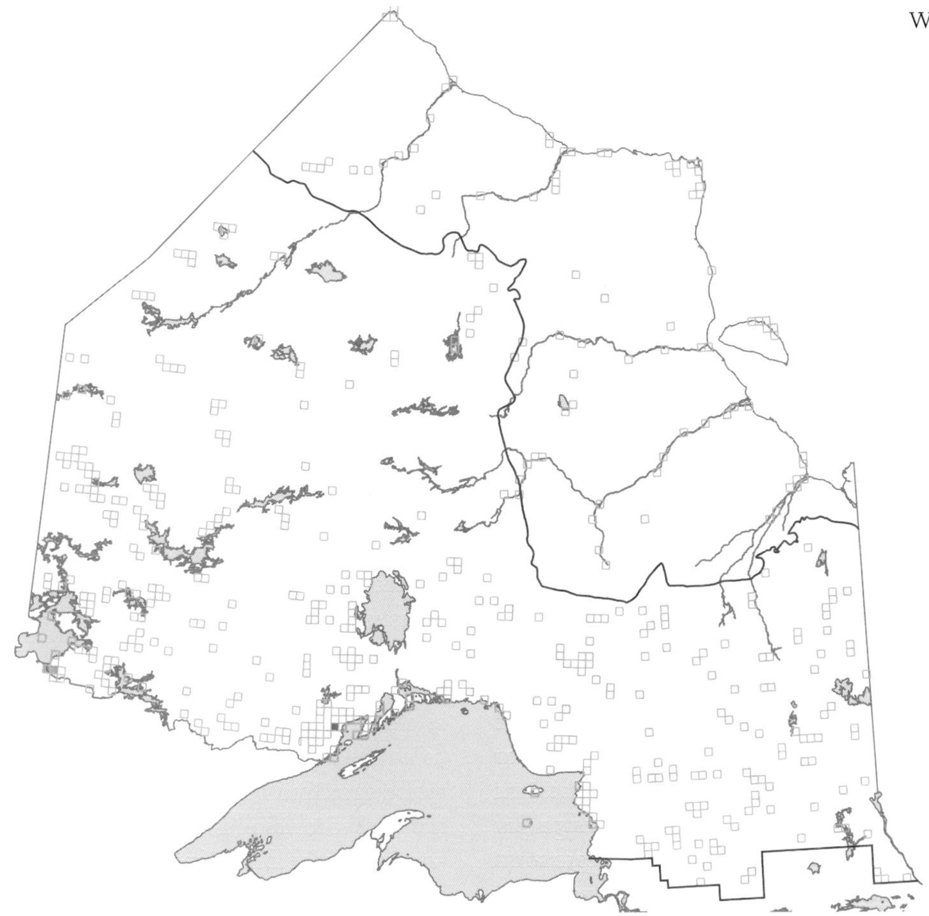

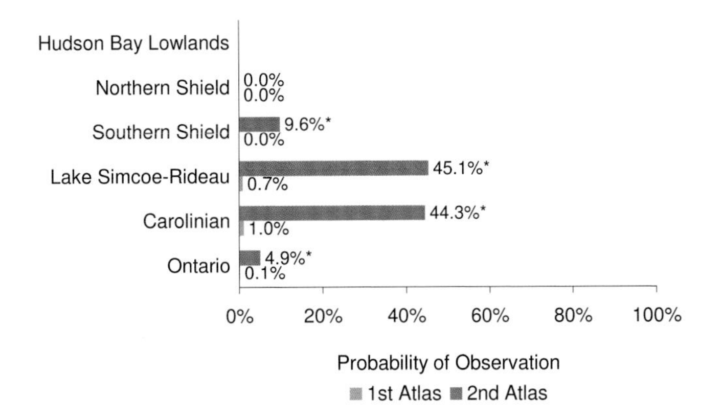

counted in the winter of 2005-06. There is difficulty in assessing the distribution of the Wild Turkey at its range edges because pen-raised birds are occasionally released by private individuals and may be confused with wild birds. Birds observed on Manitoulin Island and in Thunder Bay and western Rainy River districts may be a result of such unofficial releases.

The OMNR ceased to trap and transfer the Wild Turkey after January 2005. Future range expansions within the province will rely on natural processes. The species is limited by deep snow, which interferes with its ability to forage on the ground. Localized starvation may occur where snow depth exceeds 25 cm for more than seven consecutive weeks (Wright et al. 1996).

The current distribution of the Wild Turkey in Ontario is greater than its known historical range. This may be due to release efforts and adaptation to agricultural landscapes offering more productive forage. Healy (1992) concluded that it now uses a wider range of habitats than it did when populations were low.

Breeding biology: The breeding season begins with the breakup of winter flocks into smaller breeding groups after the arrival of warm spring days. Male turkeys are conspicuous at the start of breeding; they begin to make gobbling calls and strut displays in April. Breeding is promiscuous, and dominant males prevent subordinate males from accessing females. Nest initiation occurs April to June (Healy 1992; Nguyen et al. 2003). Median initiation dates near Noëlville were 3 June in 1999 and 17 May in 2000 (Nguyen et al. 2003) and 25 May in southern Ontario (Weaver 1989). Females construct nests by scratching a depression in the ground, and additional nesting materials are not normally used (Healy 1992). However, most nests are well concealed by vegetation and difficult to find; females are secretive and solitary while nesting. Usually 10-12 eggs are laid over two weeks, and incubation requires 28 days. Poults are flightless for two weeks and may experience high mortality due to predation and unfavourable weather until flight is attained (Roberts and Porter 1998; Hubbard et al. 1999). Poults stay with the hen through the summer, providing excellent opportunities for confirmation.

Abundance: At the northern extent of its range, the Wild Turkey is most abundant in landscapes with tall trees for roosting, open fields with lateral cover for nesting, a source of water, and agricultural crops such as corn and soybeans (Porter et al. 1980; Porter 1992). This corresponds to agricultural areas south of the Shield with adequate forest cover. The current abundance pattern in the province is likely still influenced by the legacy of release activities. Greatest abundance occurs near Napanee, Brighton, southern Georgian Bay off the Shield, and in southern Elgin Co. – *Jeff Bowman*

Northern Bobwhite

Colin de Virginie

Colinus virginianus

The Northern Bobwhite is a very rare and declining grassland species found in southwestern Ontario. Its range also includes the eastern and central US and northern Mexico. The species was more widespread in Ontario shortly after European settlement, when newly cleared land interspersed with forest edge and cropland offered ideal habitat. It apparently reached its maximum range in the mid- to late 1800s, when it was found throughout southern Ontario north to southern Muskoka and east to Kingston (Lumsden in Cadman et al. 1987). Since then, the bobwhite's range has declined until the only remaining location for native birds appears to be Walpole Island. The other atlas records scattered across southern Ontario are likely of released or escaped birds from landowners with permits to keep them in captivity or use them for hunting purposes. All observations of bobwhites have been shown on the breeding evidence map because released/escaped birds cannot be differentiated from native birds, thus confounding determination of the precise range and population status of wild birds in Ontario.

The Northern Bobwhite is designated Endangered by both the OMNR and COSEWIC (James and Cannings 2003; Ontario Ministry of Natural Resources 2006a). Several conservation and stewardship groups have created wildlife plantings for the species in southwestern Ontario (MacIntyre 2002).

Distribution and population status: In the first atlas, the Northern Bobwhite was found in 79 squares compared with 34 in this atlas, and there was a 65% decrease in the probability of observation overall. Similar or greater declines have been reported in Michigan, New York, and Ohio (James and Cannings 2003). Known factors affecting its populations are loss of grassland habitat, declining habitat quality, and cold, snowy winters and ice storms (particularly in the 1970s).

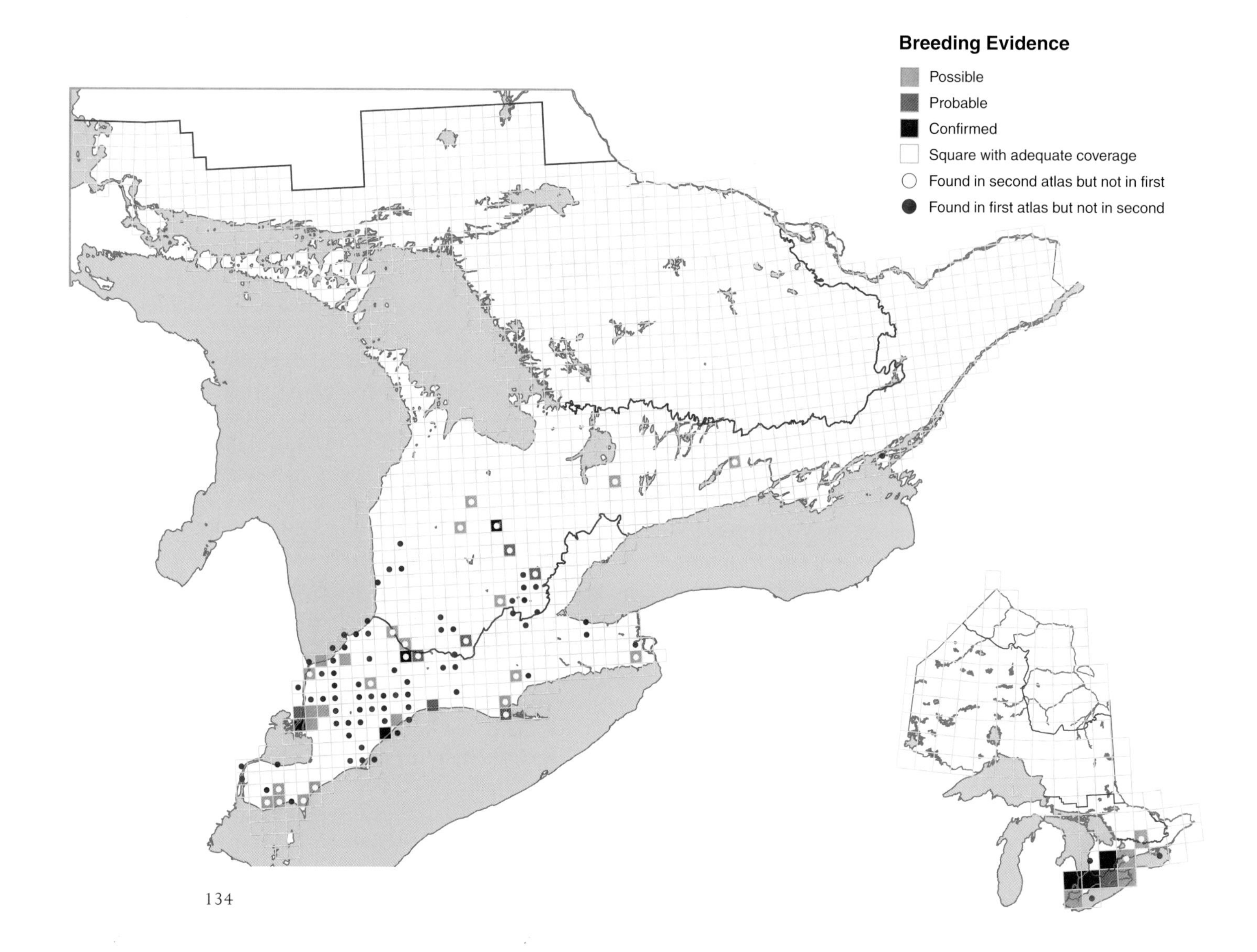

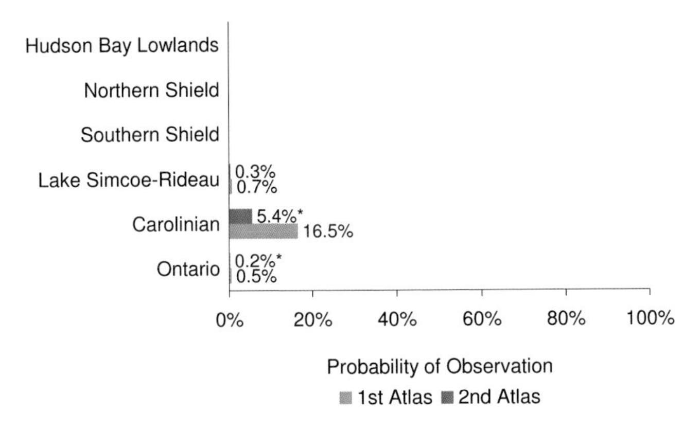

Fragmentation of grassland habitat, fire suppression, and other pressures such as invasive plants and increasing numbers of predators may also have an impact on the population. Several grassland and orchard areas that formerly supported bobwhites have been converted to croplands near Walpole Island during the past 10 years.

The pattern of decline between atlases is clear from the breeding evidence map, with numerous squares in Lambton, Middlesex, and Oxford Counties and in Chatham-Kent having records in the first but not second atlas. The first atlas records represented pockets of native birds such as those along the Thames River in Middlesex Co. and Chatham-Kent, but during the second atlas there were only sporadic single calling birds at these locations, which is more indicative of released bobwhites. Released/escaped birds may breed but seldom persist more than a year. Regional Coordinators from London, Long Point, Essex, and York all considered the birds in their areas to be releases.

Even on Walpole Island, numbers have declined drastically. Surveys done there in 2000 found 92 calling males on roadside "whistling" surveys (MacIntyre 2002). Although no roadside surveys have been done since 2000, fewer than five coveys were found in 2006 after several days of searching bobwhite habitat (E. Nol, pers. comm.).

The best habitat in Ontario for Northern Bobwhite includes the grasslands and savannahs of Walpole Island. There is potential habitat in grassland riparian zones along the Thames River in Middlesex and Elgin Counties and at Kettle Creek in Elgin Co. (MacIntyre 2002). Lambton Stewardship has created habitat at several prairie restoration sites and roadside plantings along Highway 40. Bobwhites have apparently been sighted at these locations, but their long-term survival or breeding status is unknown.

Breeding biology: The male Northern Bobwhite may begin calling its loud and unmistakable "bob-bob-white" in March or April, but nesting does not occur until May in Ontario. Once the coveys break up and pairs form, a well-hidden semi-covered grass nest is made, and normally 12-16 eggs are laid. In late summer, adults and young from several nests join and form a covey of up to 25 birds. Outside the breeding season, bobwhites are generally quiet except when a covey is flushed. Bobwhite remain year-round on territory, although their home range may expand in winter as food supply dictates (Brennan 1999).

Abundance: The Northern Bobwhite is rare and local, and 12 or fewer were found during the second atlas period on the Wallaceburg CBC, which includes much of Walpole Island. The atlas map is not an accurate representation of breeding distribution, as it includes released/escaped birds as well as wild birds. While it is possible that a very few of the records away from Walpole Island are of native birds, most are believed to be non-native. The bobwhite is at risk of being extirpated in southern Ontario unless large areas of grassland and savannah are maintained. – *Chris Risley*

The Northern Bobwhite has a high annual mortality rate but can produce two large broods per year. Nests in Ontario have held eggs as late as 19 September (Peck and James 1983). *Photo: P. Allen Woodliffe*

Oak savannah on Walpole Island is one of the best remaining examples of the Northern Bobwhite's natural habitat in Ontario. *Photo: P. Allen Woodliffe*

Red-throated Loon

Plongeon catmarin

Gavia stellata

The smallest of the world's five loon species, the Red-throated Loon has a circumpolar breeding distribution, preferring arctic and subarctic tundra regions but also breeding in more temperate coastal and montane regions in parts of North America (Campbell et al. 1990). In Canada, it breeds throughout much of the Arctic Archipelago and the coastal plains of western and northern Canada, south to about 52° N in James Bay, the North Shore of the Gulf of St. Lawrence, Anticosti Island, and Newfoundland and Labrador (Barr et al. 2000).

Aside from historical records of extra-limital breeding on Lake Superior at Thunder Cape in 1912 (Baillie and Harrington 1936) and Rossport in 1941 (Baillie and Hope 1943), all subsequent evidence of confirmed breeding for the species in Ontario has been from the Hudson Bay coast near Cape Henrietta Maria (ONRS data).

Distribution and population status: Breeding evidence for the Red-throated Loon during the second atlas was documented in 22 squares in six 100-km blocks along Hudson and northern James Bays near Cape Henrietta Maria and northwest of the Niskibi River. This is similar to the distribution observed during the first atlas, when breeding was reported in 12 squares. There was no significant change in the probability of observation during the second atlas, with the increase in the number of squares in which the species was observed due largely to increased low-level aerial surveys by OMNR and CWS.

Most records of Red-throated Loon during the second atlas were within 20 km of the coast. Observations made farther inland are difficult to interpret and may involve either non-breeding individuals or a previously undetected segment of the breeding population. Not mapped was a record of three individuals on the Winisk River over 100 km inland from Hudson Bay at a site that was considered unsuitable habitat but in the same area where the species was observed during the first atlas. There was no coverage during the second atlas of the

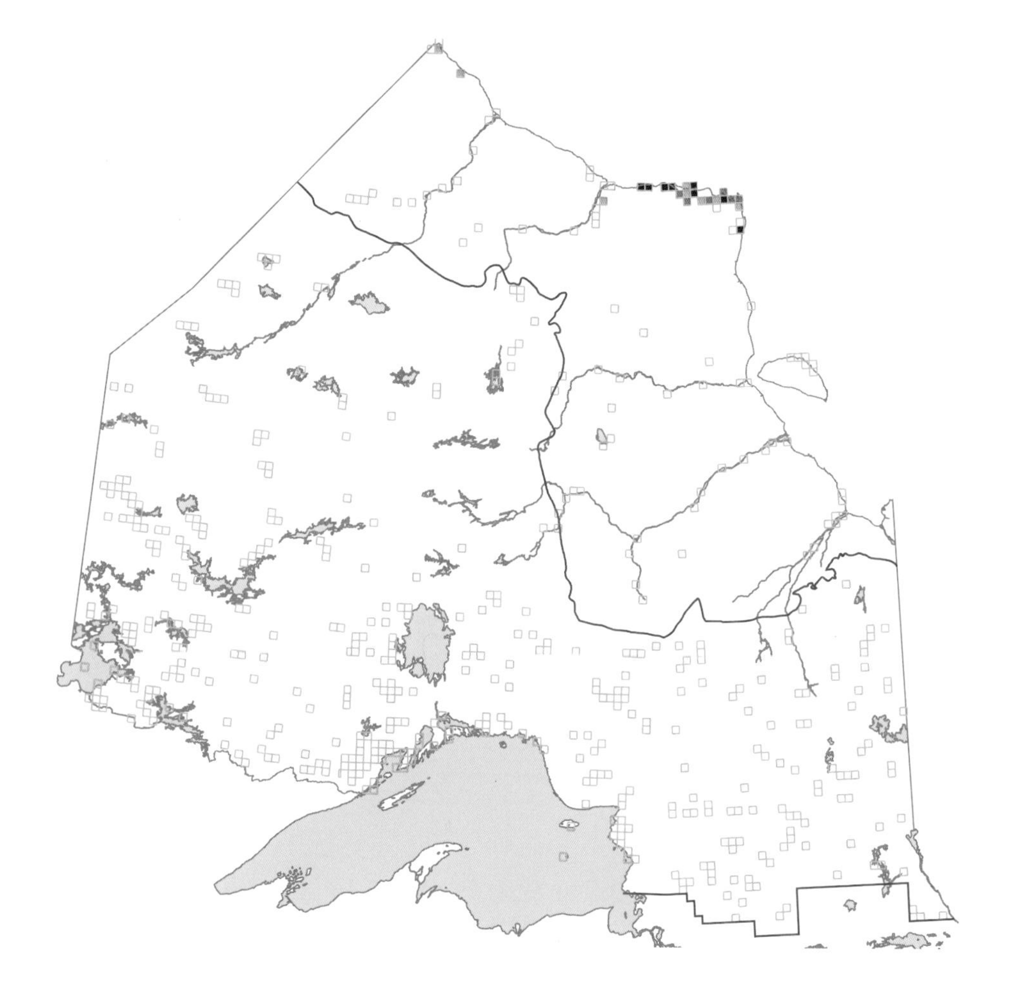

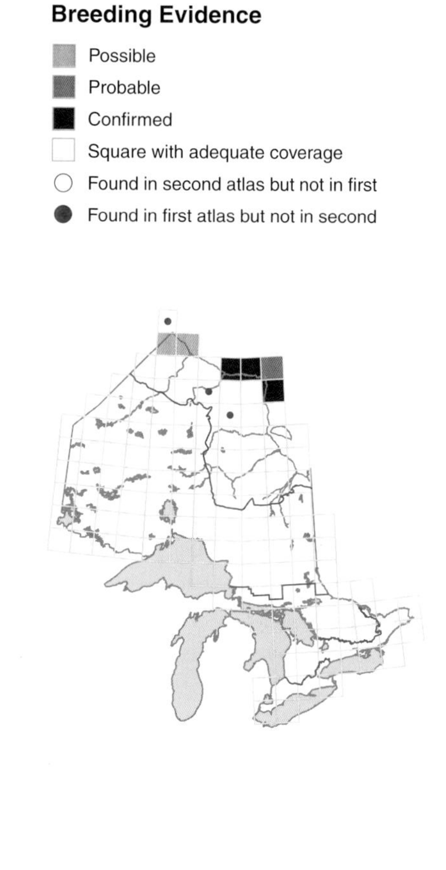

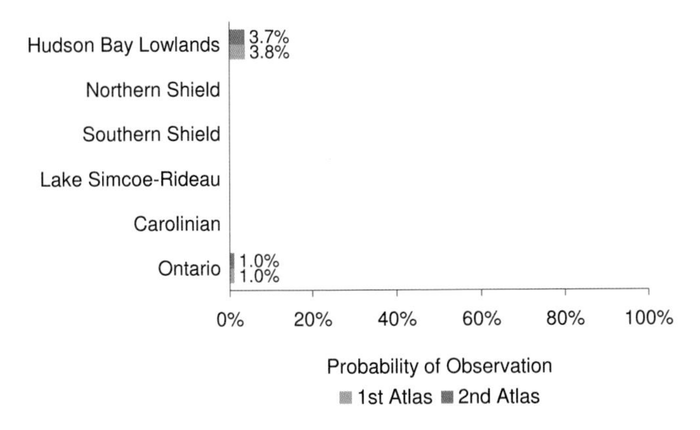

Red-throated Loon clutches usually contain two eggs. Eggs can vary in colour and are laid one to three days apart (Barr et al. 2000). *Photo: George K. Peck*

Islands in small, shallow tundra ponds are often used as nesting sites by the Red-throated Loon; nesting sites are often reused (Barr et al. 2000). *Photo: Andrew Jano*

Opinnagau Lakes area 150 km inland from Hudson and James Bays, where probable breeding was reported during the first atlas. The reasons for the species' apparent absence along the central Hudson Bay coast between the Winisk and Niskibi Rivers are uncertain but may relate to lower densities of suitable nesting ponds.

Breeding biology: The Red-throated Loon returns to breeding areas in northern Ontario by late May. All 15 documented nests in the province have been in either wet or a mixture of wet and dry tundra, mostly on the edges of small, shallow ponds (ONRS data). In areas of sympatry, the Red-throated Loon usually selects smaller ponds over the large lakes preferred by the Pacific Loon for nesting (Barr et al. 2000). In Ontario, small (less than or equal to 0.8 ha), shallow (less than 1 m) tundra ponds are typically used (ONRS data). Areas with single, isolated ponds are seldom occupied, and suitable nesting habitat usually contains several small ponds in close proximity to one another (pers. obs.). The Red-throated Loon is monogamous, and pairs typically occupy ponds and territories isolated from other pairs; however, in areas with higher densities of suitable ponds, pairs may nest as close as 150 m (Barr et al. 2000).

Pair bonds may be established prior to arrival at breeding territories but are regularly reaffirmed during the breeding season through the delivery of far-carrying wails and the "Plesiosaur call," a rhythmically repeated croaking "*gayorworrk*" given by both sexes (Barr et al. 2000). Birds regularly forage away from nesting ponds, often at sea or in larger lakes, travelling up to 20 km, frequently in small groups (Barr et al. 2000). In transit, they elicit vocalizations from other nesting pairs and from mates upon arrival at nest ponds, which aids in detection of both breeding birds and those in transit.

Results from both atlases suggest that the Red-throated Loon is less common and more restricted to coastal habitats in Ontario than the Pacific Loon. However, the Red-throated Loon may be considerably less obvious in nesting areas and more likely to be overlooked. Adults foraging away from nesting ponds commonly leave the semi-precocial young unattended for extended periods. Splash-dive distraction displays, particularly in response to over-flying aircraft, are less demonstrative and conspicuous than those of the more brightly marked Pacific Loon (pers. obs.).

Abundance: Records for the Red-throated Loon remain few, suggesting that it continues to be a rare to uncommon breeder restricted in its distribution to limited suitable habitat directly adjacent to Hudson and northern James Bays, and that the provincial breeding population may be less than 100 pairs.
– Mark K. Peck and Donald A. Sutherland

Pacific Loon

Plongeon du Pacifique
Gavia pacifica

Jim Richards

The Pacific Loon is probably the most abundant of the five North American loons. The majority of its range is in North America, where it nests in predominantly tundra habitat from Alaska east across the Canadian Arctic Archipelago to Baffin Island and Ungava Bay, south to coastal British Columbia in the west, and islands in central James Bay in the east (Russell 2002). It winters on the west coast of North America, primarily off the coast of Mexico. It also breeds in northeast Russia and winters in eastern Asia, where it overlaps with the closely related Arctic Loon with which it was once considered conspecific (Russell 2002).

Distribution and population status: In Ontario, the Pacific Loon nests in tundra areas along the coasts of Hudson Bay and upper James Bay as far south as Hook Point. It was recorded in 28 squares in the first atlas and 37 squares in the second, with no significant difference in the probability of observation. Fewer records during the second atlas between the Winisk River and the Pen Islands, where a sparse but continuous range is expected, reflect lower coverage rather than absence. Many records in the second atlas resulted from aerial surveys by OMNR and CWS, and during both atlases were primarily in the tundra strip near Hudson Bay where surveys were concentrated. The species was rarely recorded inland during the second atlas. Birds were observed 65 km inland on the Winisk River, with no evidence of breeding, and 30-50 km inland on taiga lakes in the vicinity of Peawanuck. During the first atlas, probable breeding was reported 120 km inland on the Black Duck River. The species reaches its southern breeding limit on Akimiski Island, where it has been recorded in eight of 15 years since 1993 (pers. obs.) with confirmed breeding in four years, including 2004.

Breeding biology: The Pacific Loon establishes pair bonds before arriving at nesting areas, facilitating rapid establishment of territories. It shows strong fidelity to nest lakes and sites,

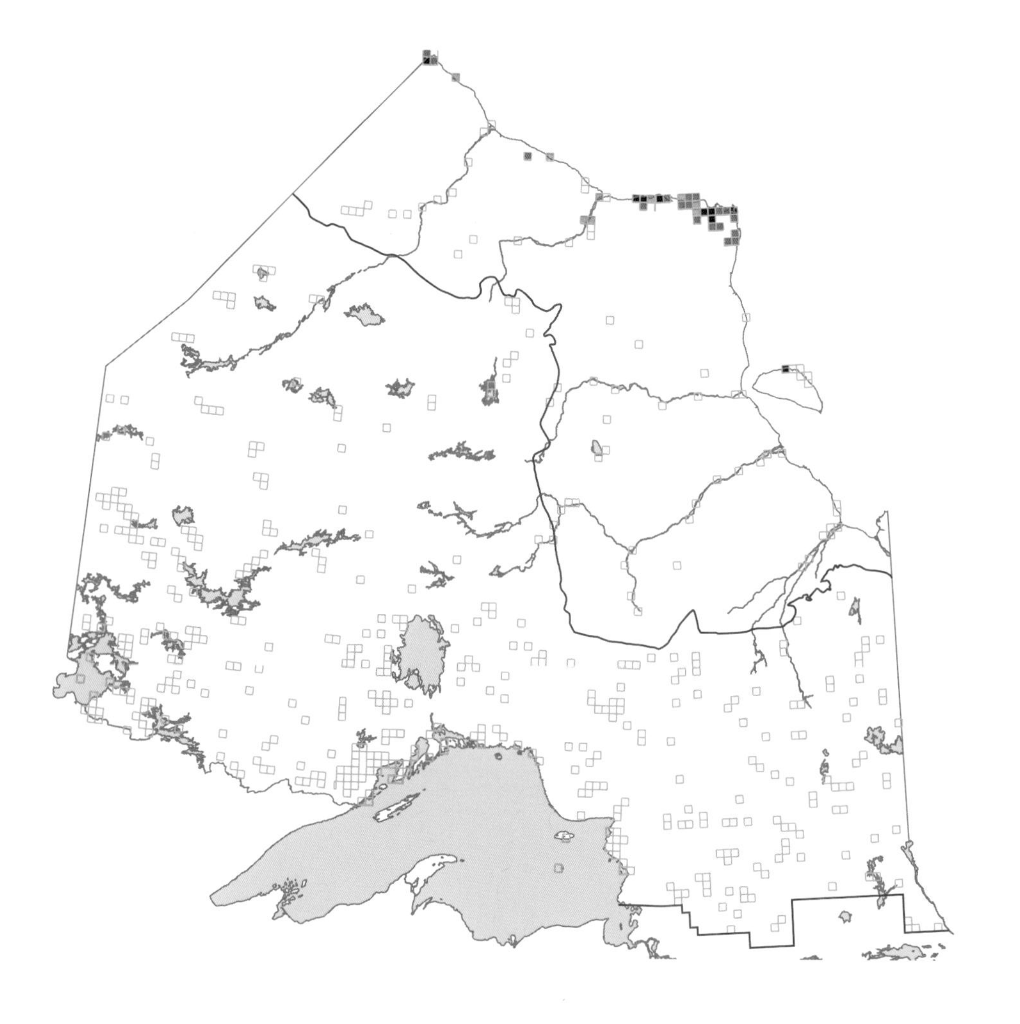

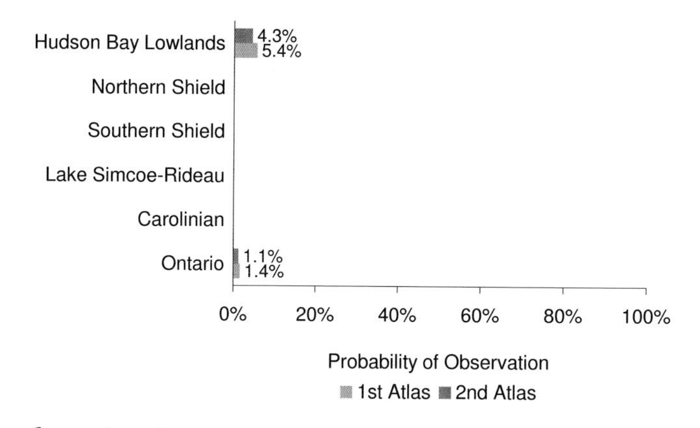

often using the same site over successive years (Russell 2002). Time of arrival is dependent on coastal ice cover and breakup on nesting lakes (Petersen 1989); in Ontario, this occurs in late May or early June, with nest initiation varying annually.

Nesting habitat is freshwater lakes and ponds in tundra and taiga. In Ontario, the species nests more often in areas with clusters of small lakes. It may be rare or absent from areas with few lakes but will nest occasionally on isolated lakes. In years of late spring melt, smaller, ice-free lakes adjacent to larger, ice-covered ones may be selected (Russell 2002). It generally prefers larger, deeper ponds with less emergent vegetation than the Red-throated Loon (Bergman and Derksen 1977). On the Hudson Bay coast during the second atlas, 10 nest lakes averaged 20 ha (pers. obs.). Productive lakes providing nest sites with access to deeper water and fish and large invertebrate prey are preferred. Nests are typically on small islands or islets, often separated from the lakeshore by only a few metres.

The Pacific Loon is distinctive and easily separated from other loons. Its far-carrying calls aid in its detection. Known as the "white-headed loon" to the Cree of James Bay (Smith 1944), its silver-grey head feathers give it a light-headed appearance and make it conspicuous even from the air. It regularly flies to large ponds and marine waters to forage, but rarely provisions young from the sea (Andres 1993; Russell 2002). Such flights make it conspicuous to atlassers. Splash-diving, a reaction to the approach of a potential predator, is a conspicuous display visible from over-flying aircraft. In Ontario, family groups remain intact into late August and early September (pers. obs.), allowing a long period to confirm breeding.

Abundance: The total breeding population of the Pacific Loon in Ontario is unknown but probably comprises several hundred pairs (Sandilands 2005). Although it is likely not abundant in taiga, the extent and density of nesting there is undocumented. Point counts on the tundra indicated 0.49 birds/25 counts, but these were insufficient to provide average densities. Densities vary, depending on the abundance of suitable lakes. Most estimates in the first atlas were 2-10 pairs/100 km^2, but a few were 11-100 (Peck in Cadman et al. 1987); local densities may reach 2.4 pairs/km^2 on the mainland near the Pen Islands (pers. obs.) and in extreme northeastern Ontario, but are generally much lower in most of the species' Ontario range. It is scarce on James Bay islands (Manning 1981; pers. obs.). – *Ken Abraham and Donald A. Sutherland*

Although the precocial, downy young are usually led from the nest in the first two days after hatch, the female may brood them in the nest for up to two weeks (Russell 2002) *Photo: Mark Peck*

Pacific Loon nests are located at the water line on tundra lakes. This typical two-egg nest sits atop a floating mat of Bog Buckbean. *Photo: Mark Peck*

Common Loon

Plongeon huard

Gavia immer

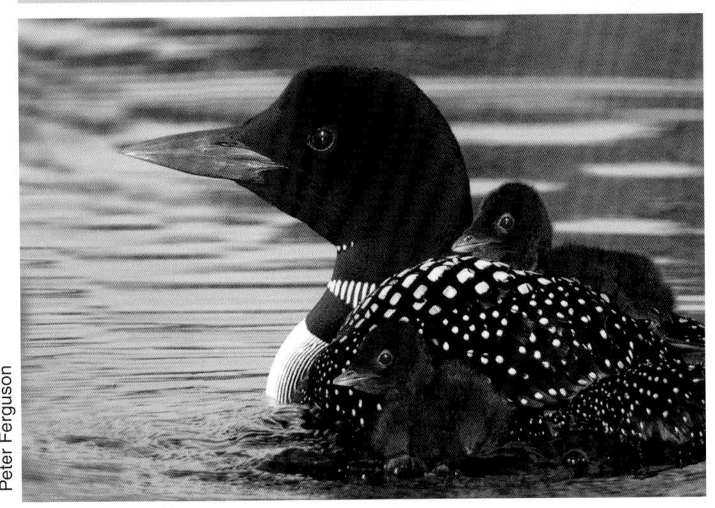

Peter Ferguson

The Common Loon is an icon of Ontario's wildlands, its haunting calls and striking black and white plumage making it one of Ontario's most recognized birds. It breeds in Alaska, the northern continental US, Greenland, and Iceland. However, the majority of the Common Loon population breeds in Canada, with the largest portion distributed throughout boreal ecozones (McIntyre and Barr 1997). Smaller freshwater lakes typically hold only one or two territorial breeding pairs. Lakes greater than 80 ha can support multiple breeding pairs, the numbers ultimately determined by shoreline configuration and the associated geological and physiographic features that form visibility barriers between territorial pairs (McIntyre and Barr 1997).

Distribution and population status: Historically, the Common Loon nested on lakes throughout Ontario, but by the time of the first atlas, the southern extent of its range had receded to largely exclude the Carolinian region (McCracken et al. 1981; Peck and James 1983). In this region, suitable breeding habitat for the species was always limited by the scarcity of large lakes.

Ontario's Common Loon populations are generally stable, and there was no significant change in the probability of observation in the province as a whole between atlases. However, in the Lake Simcoe-Rideau region, the probability of observation did increase significantly by 12% between atlases, with a small expansion of the breeding distribution south of the Shield evident on the map. BBS data show that the Ontario population averaged a significant annual increase of 2.0% between 1968 and 2005 (Downes et al. 2005). The Canadian Lakes Loon Survey recorded a stable breeding success rate from 1981 to 2001 (BSC unpubl. data). In the second atlas, higher survey effort in the north resulted in records from several 100-km blocks where the species was not reported but was probably missed during the first atlas.

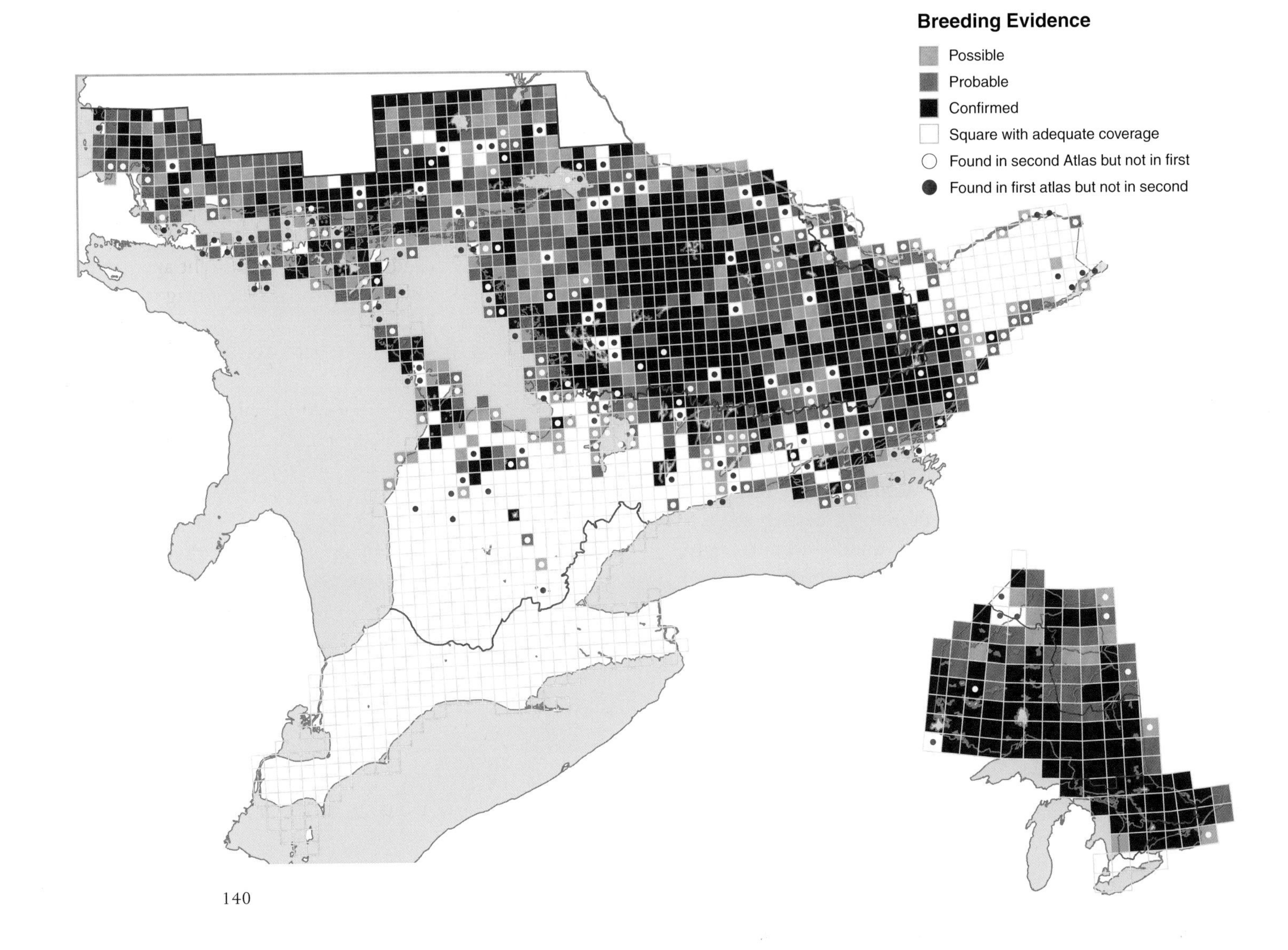

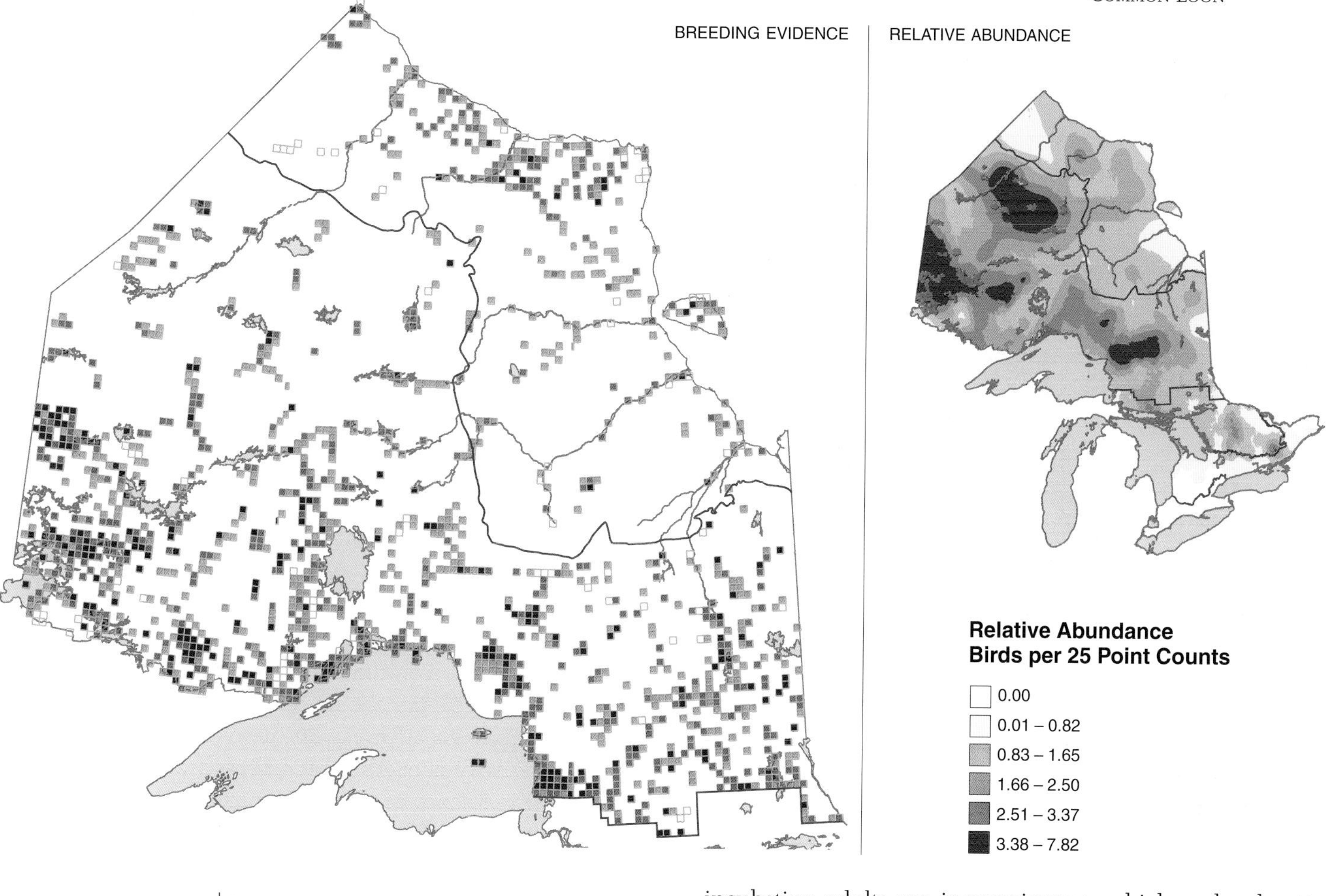

Hudson Bay Lowlands 63.5% 62.0%
Northern Shield 81.1% 80.8%
Southern Shield 88.4% 86.0%
Lake Simcoe-Rideau 36.3%* 32.4%
Carolinian
Ontario 72.0% 70.9%
0% 20% 40% 60% 80% 100%
Probability of Observation
1st Atlas 2nd Atlas

Breeding biology: The Common Loon is diurnal but regularly vocalizes at night. Its wailing and yodelling are heard particularly during the breeding period (Young 1983), with fewer calls of any type occurring after hatch (June-August; McIntyre 1988).

Courtship is subtle and often overlooked. Nest building occurs in May and June, with one to three chicks hatched during late June or early July (McIntyre 1988). While re-nesting occurs if the first nest is lost early (McIntyre 1988; Campbell et al. 1990), pairs rear only one brood each year. Broods of up to four chicks are known, but these occurrences are rare, resulting from abnormally large clutches, nest parasitism, or brood amalgamation (Timmermans et al. 2004). Nests are simple vegetative mats at the water's edge on marshy shorelines or islands. Existing isolated structures such as artificial islands, sedge mats, or muskrat houses are used when available. Both sexes share incubation, alternating between the nest and foraging or roosting areas (McIntyre 1988). Nests and incubating adults are inconspicuous, which makes locating them difficult; it is common to observe only one adult within a territory (BSC unpubl. data), but many single birds reported to the atlas were likely paired.

Breeding Common Loons are territorial and exhibit strong fidelity to nest sites. In spring and early summer, the territory size is similar to the home range, averaging 70 ha in Ontario (7-200 ha; Barr 1973). When nesting on small lakes, loons may forage on nearby lakes as well (McIntyre 1988). Travelling between lakes, they are often quite vocal in flight and easily detected. Loons remain in the vicinity of the nesting territory well into the fall. Adults leave breeding lakes prior to their young, which migrate southward just prior to lake freeze-up (McIntyre and Barr 1997).

Abundance: Point counts revealed the highest abundance of the Common Loon in the Northern Shield region, with lesser concentrations in the southern Hudson Bay Lowlands. Greatest abundance occurred in northwestern Ontario, the area of the province with the highest density of large lakes. Another area of high abundance in the Northern Shield occurred northeast of Wawa. In the Southern Shield, there were no major areas of high abundance, although the species is well distributed within this region. Abundance results from this atlas differ from those of the first atlas, when abundance was estimated instead of calculated from point counts. During the first atlas, highest abundance was estimated to occur in the Great Lakes-St. Lawrence Forest zone. Point count data from the second atlas demonstrate that the highest abundance of the Common Loon occurs in the Northern Shield region in the Boreal Forest zone. – *Kathy E. Jones and Steven T.A. Timmermans*

Pied-billed Grebe

Grèbe à bec bigarré

Podilymbus podiceps

Jim Richards

The Pied-billed Grebe is the most common Ontario grebe, typically found in wetlands with patches of open water. Highly conspicuous early in the breeding season when establishing its territory, it becomes increasingly difficult to find as the nesting season progresses, until the young hatch.

Its Canadian range includes southern British Columbia, the Prairie Provinces north to the southern Northwest Territories, and southern Ontario east through southern Québec and the Maritimes. It breeds throughout the US, the West Indies, and Central America to southern South America (Muller and Storer 1999).

Distribution and population status: Early Ontario ornithologists considered the Pied-billed Grebe a common breeder (McIlwraith 1894; Baillie and Harrington 1936). It undoubtedly declined with European settlement as wetlands were drained. Wetland loss occurs less frequently now but may still affect some small populations, while sewage lagoons with an interspersion of cattails and open water may provide additional habitat. During the first atlas, breeding occurred in scattered locations south of the Shield, with concentrations north of Kingston and south of Ottawa. Farther north, it occurred sparsely to North Bay and Thunder Bay and bred north to Moosonee, with evidence of possible breeding in the Big Trout Lake area.

The distribution of the Pied-billed Grebe did not change substantially between atlases. It continues to breed regularly, but in scattered locations north to a line from Thunder Bay to North Bay. Although it was observed in more 100-km blocks in the northwestern portion of the province, it evidently breeds only sparingly in much of the Northern Shield and Hudson Bay Lowlands regions. Evidence of possible breeding was reported at Peawanuck on the Winisk River in 2001 but not subsequently, and probably involved a non-breeding vagrant. Absences in areas such as the Algonquin Highlands

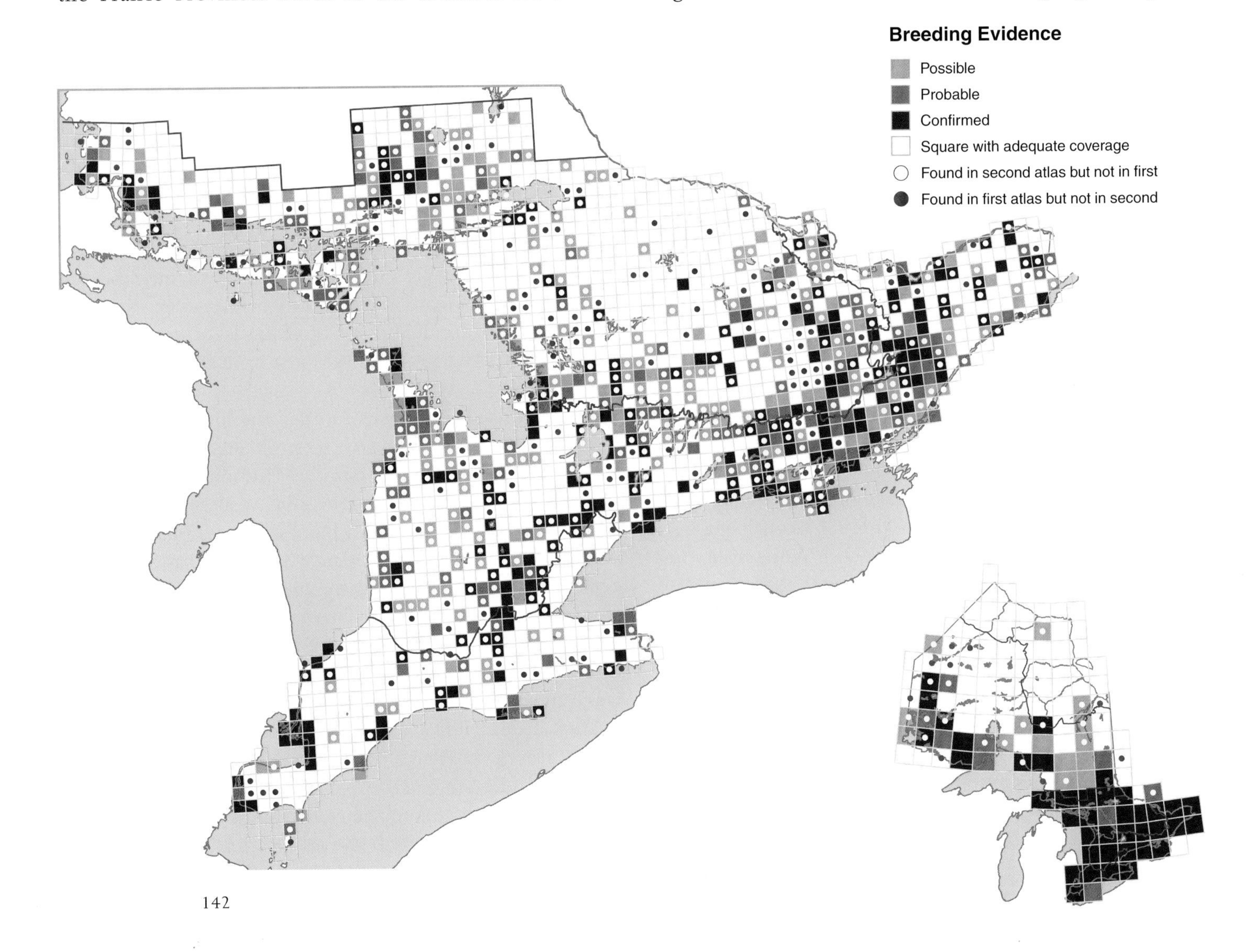

BREEDING EVIDENCE

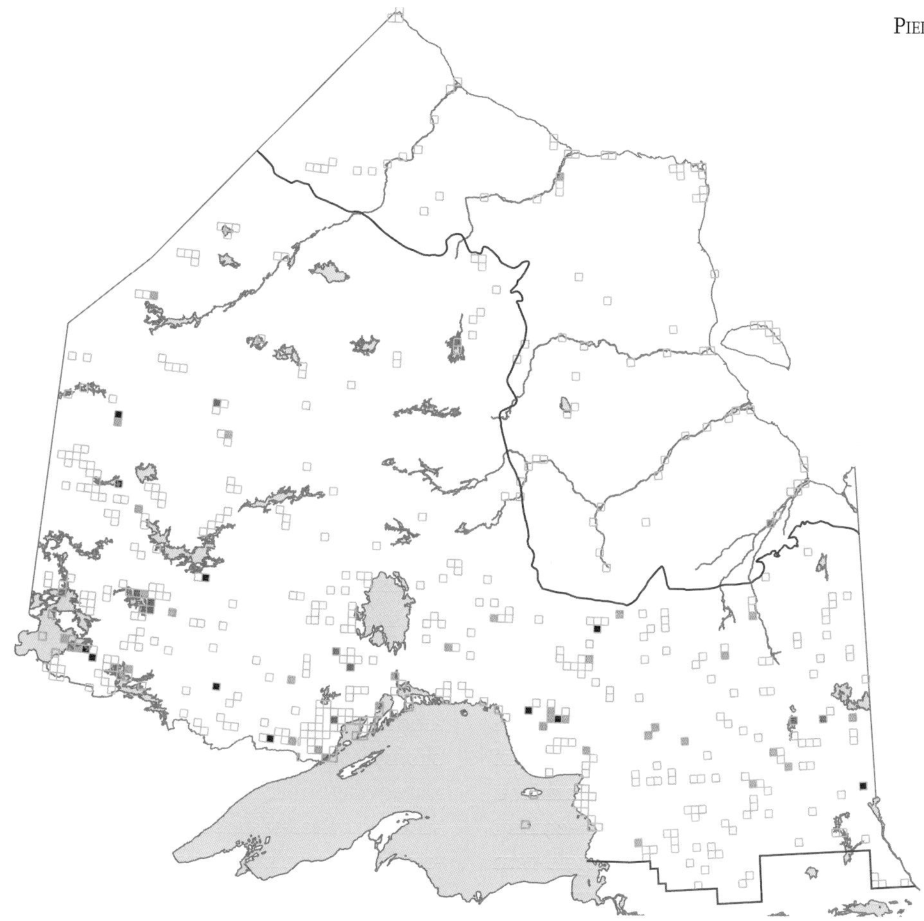

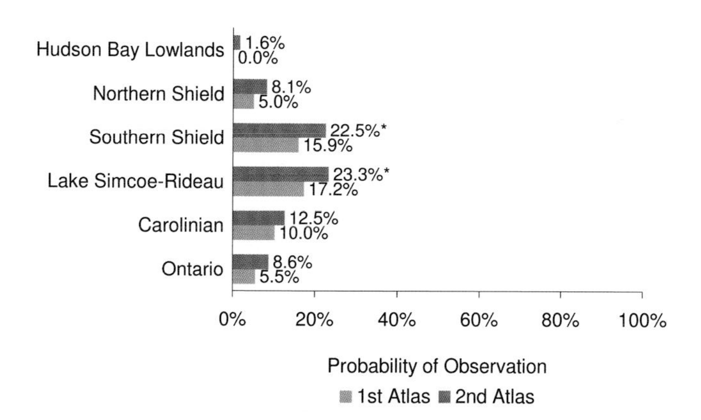

and parts of the Carolinian region are likely due to a lack of suitable wetlands. The overall probability of observation of the Pied-billed Grebe did not change significantly between atlases. There were, however, significant increases of 35% and 42% in the Lake Simcoe-Rideau and Southern Shield regions, respectively, and a non-significant increase of 61% in the Northern Shield. The reason for the increase is not apparent, though it may be due in part to increased use of broadcast-call tapes during the second atlas. Despite this, there is still a high probability that the species was missed in some squares on the Shield.

In contrast to the atlas, MMP data show a significant decline of 7.5% annually from 1995 to 2004 (Timmermans et al. 2006). However, MMP sites are concentrated near the shores of the Great Lakes and so may not be representative of the province as a whole.

Breeding biology: The Pied-billed Grebe typically nests in marshes dominated by cattails or bulrushes and less frequently among burreeds, spike-rushes, and arrowheads. Chabot and Francis (1996) stated that it is predominantly associated with larger marshes with mostly open water. It does, however, nest on small ponds and beaver ponds, including those rimmed with shrubs instead of herbaceous emergent plants, and so may have been overlooked in some smaller wetlands. The nest is usually a floating platform of decaying vegetation among emergent vegetation in 30-100 cm of water (Glover 1953; Peck and James 1983). Unless atlassers canoed or waded into wetlands, they were unlikely to find a nest. Adults frequently cover the eggs with vegetation when they leave the nest, so it is difficult to detect.

The Pied-billed Grebe is usually settled on its territory by mid-April. Until early or mid-May, its distinctive loud calls are obvious, but later in the season it is mostly silent and reclusive. It responds readily to a tape of its song early in the season, but less often in June when most atlassing was done, so some were likely missed. Fortunately, broods are conspicuous and provide the best opportunities for confirming breeding.

Abundance: The Pied-billed Grebe was reported too infrequently on point counts to provide an abundance map. The breeding evidence maps show, as in the first atlas, high concentrations in the Kingston area and south of Ottawa; this area is important for several wetland species, such as the Wilson's Snipe and Black Tern. There are concentrations of records generally near the southern edge of the Shield, on the Bruce Peninsula, and in the Guelph and Sudbury areas. The species is frequently found on the many ponds in the moraines in the Guelph-Cambridge area.

It continues to be locally uncommon north to Thunder Bay and North Bay and rare farther north. – *Al Sandilands*

Horned Grebe

Grèbe esclavon

Podiceps auritus

R. E. Gehlert

The Horned Grebe is an attractive and behaviourally complex species with elaborate courtship displays and a holarctic distribution. In North America, it breeds primarily in the west and largely within Canada, where its range extends from British Columbia eastward to the Ontario-Manitoba border and northwards into the Yukon and Northwest Territories. A small disjunct population occurs on the Magdalen Islands in the Gulf of St. Lawrence in Québec. As a migrant, the Horned Grebe is uncommon in Ontario but is locally common on the Great Lakes.

Distribution and population status: Historically, there is limited evidence of the species breeding in the southwestern and eastern areas of the province (Peck and James 1983). The Horned Grebe was previously believed to breed across southern Ontario and more recently across central Ontario (Godfrey 1986), but most records were based on eggs, which are virtually identical to those of the Pied-billed Grebe. The first atlas demonstrated that the broad range of breeding from northwestern Ontario through to the Lake Nipissing area shown by Godfrey (1986) was largely uninhabited by the Horned Grebe. Before the first atlas, there were no documented breeding records for northern Ontario. In the first atlas, breeding evidence was reported from Fort Severn in the northwest and the St. Clair marshes in the southwest.

During the second atlas, breeding evidence was reported only from northwestern Ontario adjacent to Manitoba, along the edge of the species' known current breeding range (Stedman 2000). Breeding evidence was reported from Opasquia Prov. Park, Pikangikum Lake, and the Rainy River sewage lagoons.

There was no significant change in the probability of observation between atlases. Breeding evidence was reported in only three squares in the first atlas and four in the second atlas. The species was observed in three additional squares in southern Ontario during the second atlas, but without persuasive evi-

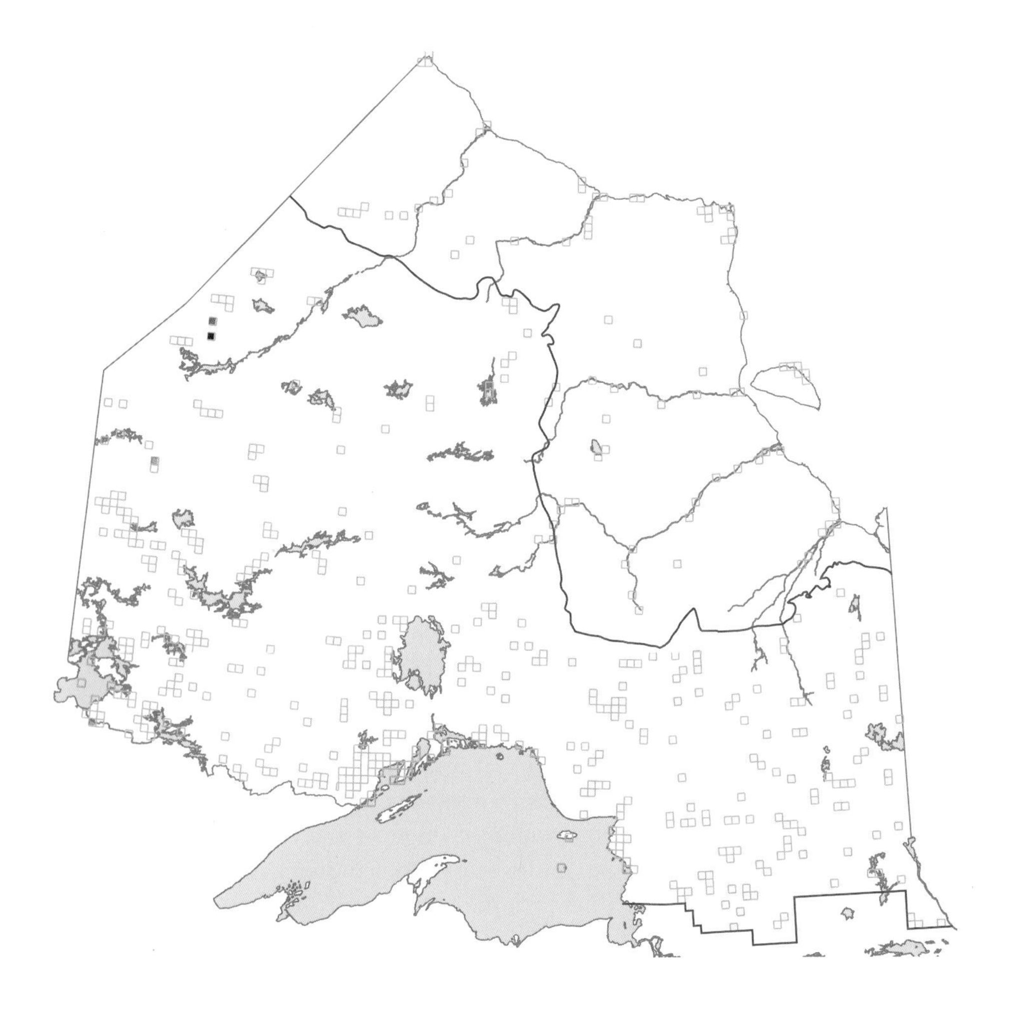

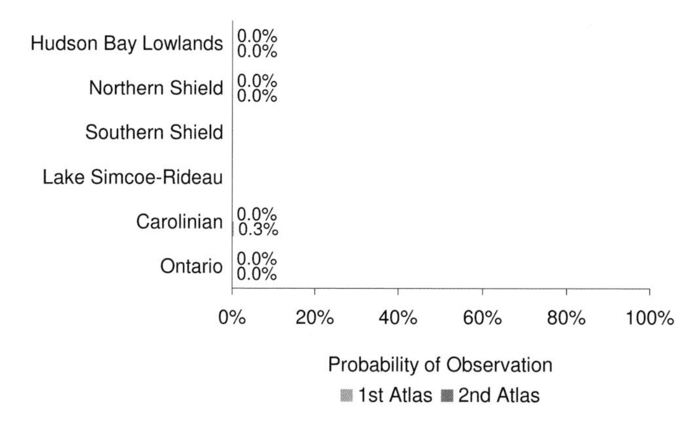

dence of breeding. Canadian BBS data from 1981 to 2005 show a significant 4.4% annual decline and a non-significant annual decline of 0.7% from 1968 to 2005. The North America breeding range of this grebe appears to be shifting to the northwest (Stedman 2000), possibly due to prolonged drought conditions within its core range in the prairie pothole region.

Breeding biology: The Horned Grebe prefers small (less than 10 ha), shallow freshwater ponds with areas of high interspersion of open water and emergent vegetation. Nests are attached to emergent vegetation and are typically within a few metres of open water.

The Horned Grebe is highly territorial. During courtship, pairs engage in various threat displays to defend territories, and fighting among rivals is common (Cramp and Simmons 1977). Territories may be as large as 1 ha. Although the species is typically a solitary nester, loose colonies of 10-20 pairs have been reported (Campbell et al. 1990). It is highly monogamous, with demonstrated sustained fidelity to both its mate and the nest site (Stedman 2000). Nest building takes from a few hours to a couple of days to complete and may be preceded by construction of a copulation platform. The nest is typically built in shallow water averaging 40 cm in depth. Older pairs build nests in more protected patches of vegetation than first-time breeders (Stedman 2000).

Egg dates for Ontario range from 16 May to 1 July (Peck and James 1983). Young hatch in approximately 24 days and usually leave the nest immediately. Parents carry the young on their backs for seven to 10 days and feed them for as long as two weeks.

Establishing evidence of breeding for the Horned Grebe can be difficult, as low-status pairs are excluded from the breeding population so that as much as 10% of the population may be non-breeders (Stedman 2000). Confirmation of breeding is also difficult due to the secretive placement of nests and the similarity of nest and eggs to those of the Pied-billed Grebe (Peck and James 1983). As well, juvenile plumage is retained throughout the first autumn, which may result in birds being mistakenly considered as being in their natal habitat. Many historical records of breeding in Ontario involved birds in juvenile plumage.

Abundance: In Ontario, the number of breeding pairs can be expected to be quite low, as the province is at the periphery of the current range of the Horned Grebe. It is possible that the species may be somewhat more common than either atlas suggests, as most of its range lies in remote areas, but there is currently no evidence to substantiate this hypothesis. – *Tyler Hoar*

Clutch size of the Horned Grebe in Ontario ranges from one to eight eggs, averaging three to six (Peck and James 1983). *Photo: George K. Peck*

A Horned Grebe nest was reported from Lake Mindemoya, Manitoulin Island, in 1938. J.L. Baillie considered all provincial nest records to be questionable due to the similarity of the eggs and co-occurrence with the Pied-billed Grebe. *Photo: George K. Peck*

Red-necked Grebe

Grèbe jougris

Podiceps grisegena

Barry S. Cherriere

The Red-necked Grebe is a familiar migrant on the Great Lakes but is infrequently seen on its breeding range since most nesting occurs in the sparsely populated northwestern part of Ontario. It has a circumpolar distribution, with one subspecies inhabiting Europe and western Asia and the other found in eastern Asia and North America. Its North American nesting range extends from Alaska and the Yukon through the prairies east to Ontario and western Québec and south to northern Washington to Minnesota (Stout and Nuechterlein 1999). East of northwestern Ontario, its nesting range is highly localized.

Distribution and population status: As summarized by Armstrong (in Cadman et al. 1987), the Red-necked Grebe has nested in northwestern Ontario (west of Thunder Bay), Lillabelle Lake in Cochrane Dist. (1960s), Simcoe Co. (1902), Lake Ontario (1940s), and Luther Marsh in Wellington and Dufferin Counties (1950s to 1980s). A population at Whitefish Lake (Thunder Bay Dist.) was not recorded in the first atlas but has been present since 1932 (Dear 1940).

The species is uncommon but widespread in Ontario, occurring from Lake Ontario to the Manitoba border. It was detected in 61 squares, of which 51 are in the Northern Shield region. Most squares with breeding evidence occurred in an area bounded by Cat Lake, Lake St Joseph, Lac Seul, Rainy Lake, and Lake of the Woods. This area has the highest density of large lakes in the province. Elsewhere in northern Ontario, it nests on scattered large lakes from North Spirit Lake (Kenora Dist.) to Kapuskasing. Of the 10 squares with breeding evidence in southern Ontario, six are at the western end of Lake Ontario, three are on Manitoulin Island, and one is near Sudbury. These are all new breeding locations since the first atlas.

The probability of observation of the Red-necked Grebe more than doubled between atlases. The increase was primarily in the Northern Shield region where most of the breeding population occurs. The Whitefish Lake population increased from one to

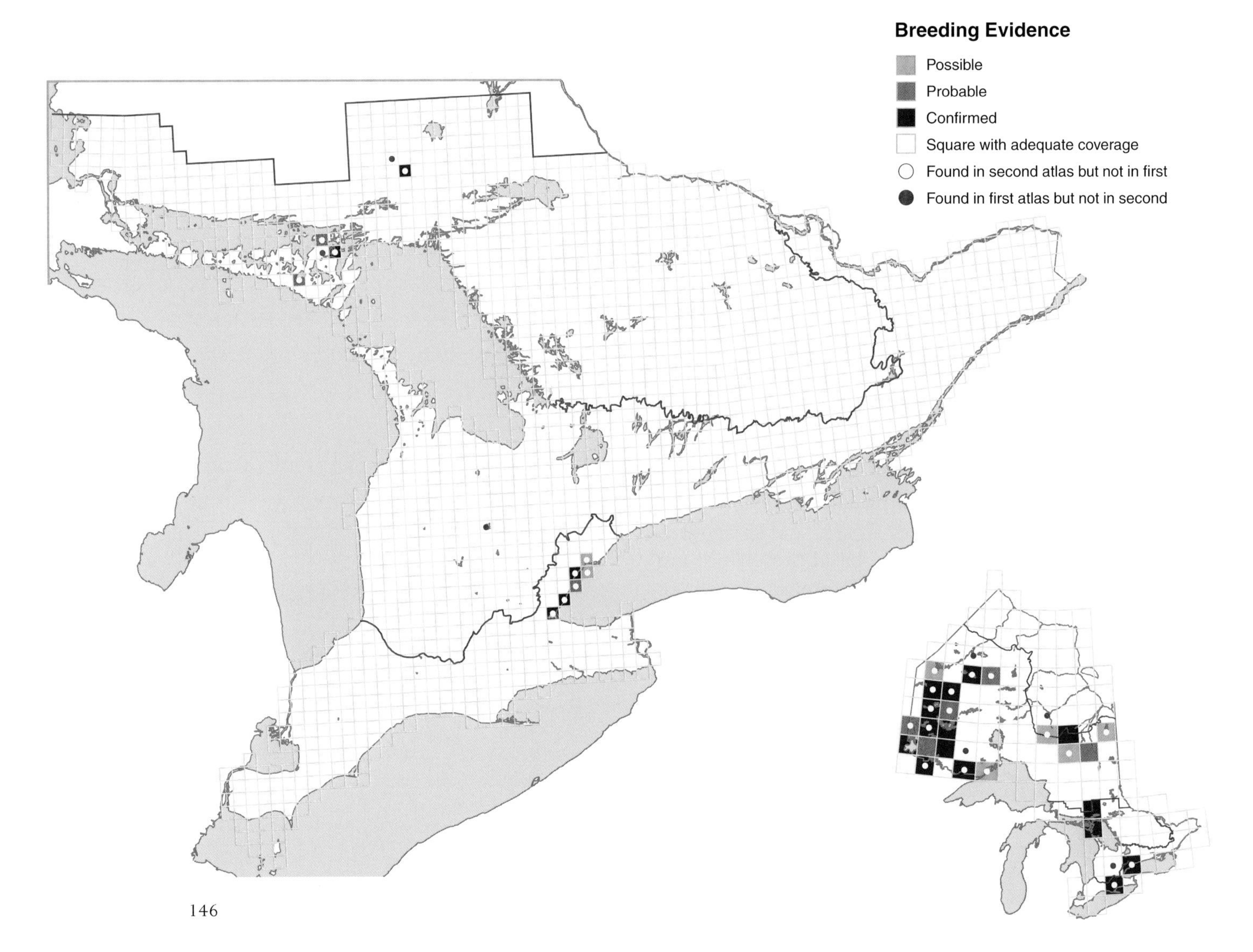

BREEDING EVIDENCE

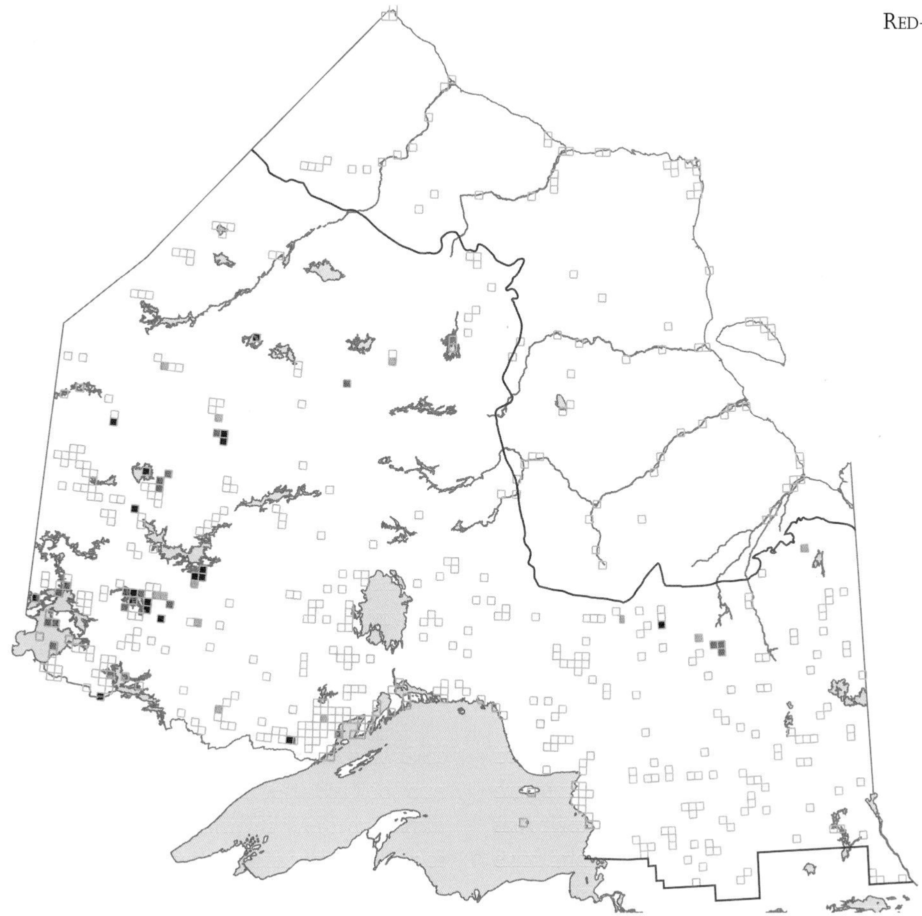

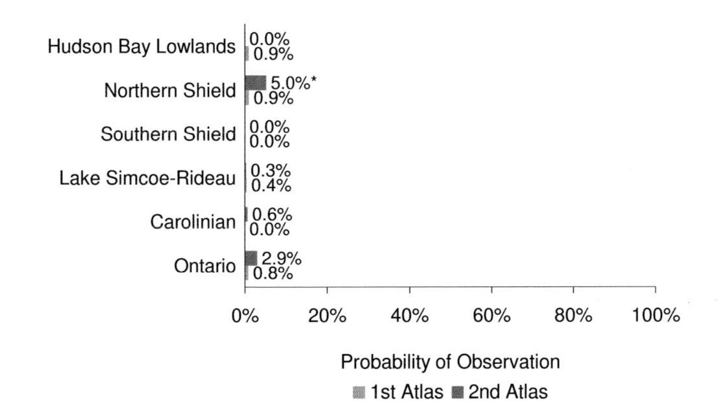

three pairs in the 1930s (Dear 1940) to over 50 pairs from the 1980s to present, possibly due to changes in the fish community (pers. obs.). The North American population is apparently stable, although local declines have been reported in northwestern Canada and Alaska (Stout and Nuechterlein 1999).

No significant range shift occurred between the two atlases, although at least one new population has been established, and another has apparently disappeared. Nesting at Luther Marsh was recorded in the first atlas but not during the second. Nesting occurred at several locations on western Lake Ontario where no breeding evidence was documented in the first atlas, although it nested in this area in the 1940s (Dobos and Edmondstone 1998).

The distribution map generally reflects the true range of the Red-necked Grebe in Ontario, given its conspicuous nesting behaviour. Scattered nesting locations were probably missed in northern Ontario due to the remoteness and inaccessibility of much of its range.

Breeding biology: The Red-necked Grebe arrives on its nesting territory shortly after ice breakup (mid-April to early May in northern Ontario), and nesting begins soon afterwards (Stout and Nuechterlein 1999). Courtship and territorial displays are loud and conspicuous.

Nesting usually occurs in shallow lakes and bays larger than 2 ha, although smaller ponds are used if other water bodies are nearby. Nests are generally sheltered from wind and waves, inaccessible to terrestrial predators, and close to open water. Typically, vegetation around nests consists of bulrushes, cattail, sedges, Wild Rice, or other emergent species. The nest is a floating platform constructed in shallow water from aquatic vegetation. It may be anchored to logs or built on an existing natural or artificial platform. Nests may be quite conspicuous early in the nesting season before emergent vegetation develops.

When disturbed, the incubating adult hides the eggs with nesting material before retreating. Birds nesting near human activity may become accustomed to disturbance and retreat from the nest only when closely approached. Young leave the nest shortly after hatching, often riding on the backs of the parents, and move to open water.

Breeding pairs are usually solitary but may be semicolonial in prime nesting habitat (Nuechterlein et al. 2003). This is the case at Whitefish Lake and other lakes supporting rich marshes.

Abundance: The Red-necked Grebe was rarely detected on point counts. It generally occurs in small numbers, but locally dense populations of as many as 50 pairs occur in rich marshes. It is rare to locally uncommon in Ontario and most abundant in the Lac Seul to Lake of the Woods area. – *Allan G. Harris*

Eared Grebe

Grèbe à cou noir

Podiceps nigricollis

George K. Peck

The Eared Grebe is by far the most numerous and cosmopolitan of the grebes. It breeds throughout much of Eurasia, north and south Africa, and North America. In North America, it is essentially a western species, breeding regularly in interior British Columbia south to California and Arizona and through the Prairie Provinces and states east to Manitoba and Iowa. It has bred sporadically east to Wisconsin, Illinois, central Texas, and possibly Michigan. An isolated population also breeds locally in central Mexico (Cullen et al. 1999).

The preferred habitat of the Eared Grebe is shallow lakes or ponds with mostly open water, some emergent vegetation for nesting, and highly productive macroinvertebrate communities for feeding.

An extremely social species, Eared Grebes nest in colonies that may number in the thousands (Cullen et al. 1999). Adults are strikingly plumaged during the breeding season, with a black head and neck, bold yellow facial plumes, and a bright red eye; the species is unlikely to be confused with anything except perhaps the Horned Grebe.

Distribution and population status: The Eared Grebe was the last species of grebe to be added to the Ontario bird checklist. Ontario's first record involved two birds observed on 28 April 1948 in Hamilton Bay (Baillie 1957). In each subsequent decade post-1950, the number of sightings increased to the point where it is now considered a rare annual migrant in both spring and fall, an occasional winter straggler in the lower Great Lakes, and a rare summer resident at Rainy River (James et al. 1976; James 1991; Coady et al. 2002).

No breeding evidence was detected in Ontario for the Eared Grebe prior to or during the first atlas. However, as early as 1982, breeding season sightings began to occur in the Rainy River area (James 1984c). In 1992, four pairs were noted at the Rainy River sewage lagoons and, although breeding was anticipated, the birds deserted the area when

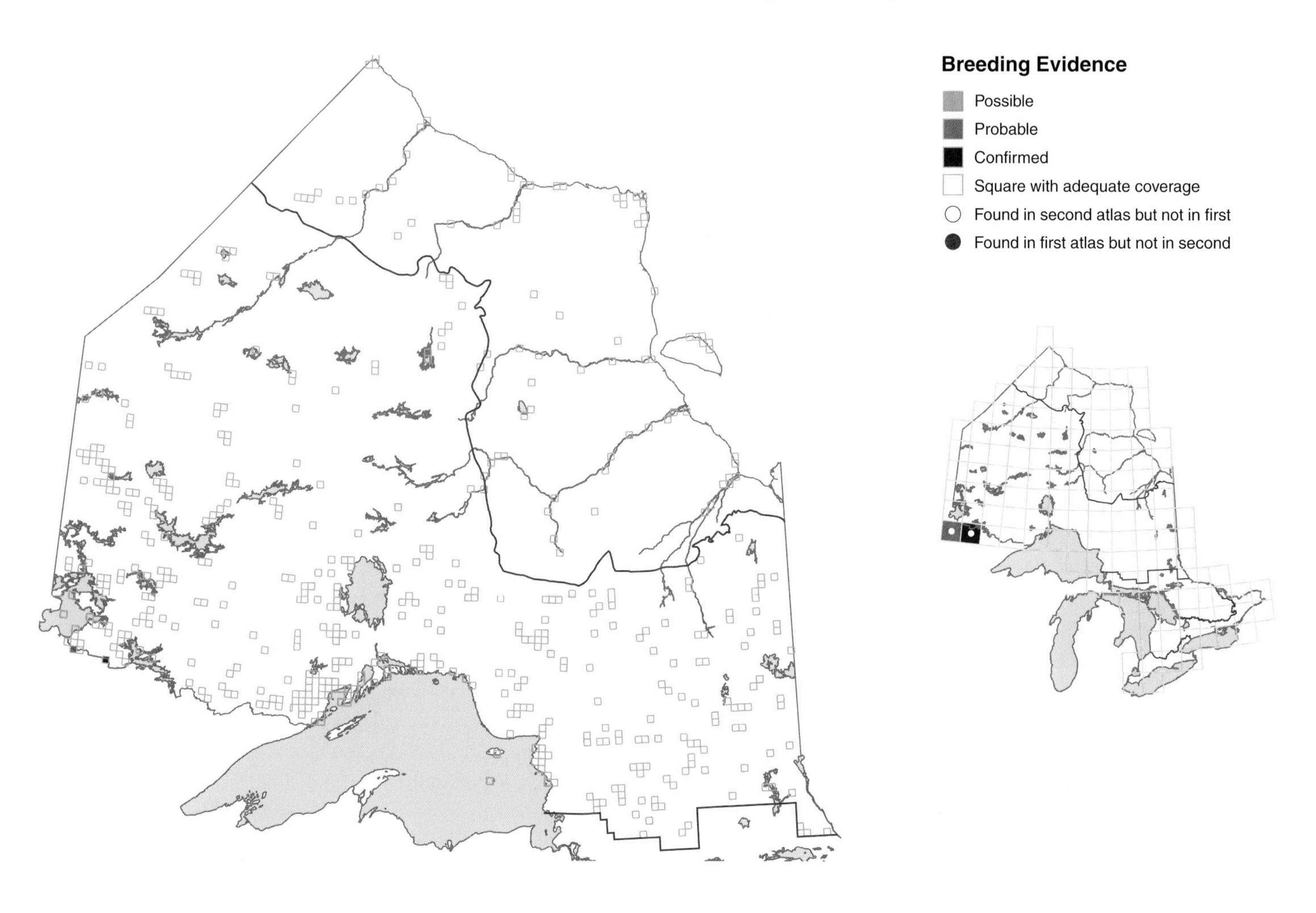

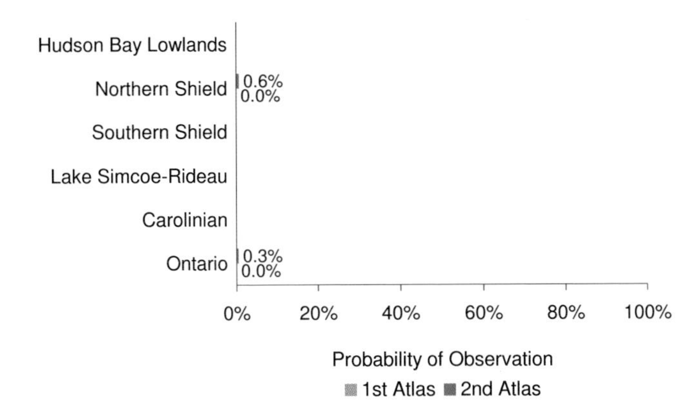

the pond was drained (Bain 1993). A pair of birds observed there in 1996 also failed to nest.

The first known Ontario nesting occurred in 1996 at the Emo sewage lagoons in Rainy River Dist., when a lone pair nested and fledged two young (Elder and Simms 1997), providing material evidence supporting its inclusion on the list of Ontario's breeding species (Dobos 1997). In 1997, two pairs each fledged two young at these lagoons.

In 1996, an adult was observed feeding a large juvenile between 29 August and 12 September at the Thedford sewage lagoons in Lambton Co. (Ridout 1997a). A pair of adults was observed engaging in courtship displays for about a week at this site in 1997 (Ridout 1997b). This represents the only breeding evidence for southern Ontario and is evidently the easternmost breeding record for North America (Cullen et al. 1999).

During the second atlas, breeding evidence was found in two squares. In 2001, a nest with four eggs was discovered at the Emo sewage lagoons. This nest was abandoned when the water level dropped rapidly. Four adults returned to this site in 2002, but no nesting was attempted. Two pairs were observed in 2001 doing courtship displays at the Rainy River sewage lagoons, but no nest initiation was observed (Coady et al. 2002).

Breeding biology: The Eared Grebe selects both small and large shallow open ponds for breeding, preferring those not surrounded by forest. It most commonly nests colonially, often in huge, conspicuous colonies. Courtship displays are very vocal and hard to miss, occurring from late May to early July when atlas coverage is at its peak. Nests are often poorly concealed in small patches of emergent vegetation or completely exposed on floating submergent vegetation. Nest sites are often changed multiple times, allowing many opportunities for detection. Aggression towards the American Coot and Pied-billed Grebe is usually a good indication of local breeding. The adult Eared Grebe has the longest flightless period of any North American bird, remaining so for the majority of time on the breeding territory. As with most grebes, the young are brooded on the parents' backs soon after hatching (Cullen et al. 1999). Since so many aspects of the species' breeding biology render it conspicuous and easily confirmed, atlas results likely present an accurate assessment of its breeding status.

Abundance: The Eared Grebe is a very rare and recent breeder in Ontario at the extreme eastern extent of its range. It probably does not breed annually in the province, and the total number of pairs is likely fewer than five in any given year. *– Glenn Coady*

The nest at the Emo sewage lagoons, Rainy River Dist., 10 June 2001. *Photo: George K. Peck*

Emo sewage lagoons in Rainy River Dist. are the most reliable location for nesting Eared Grebes in Ontario. *Photo: Dave Elder*

American White Pelican

Pélican d'Amérique

Pelecanus erythrorhynchos

Mark Peck

The American White Pelican is one of Ontario's and North America's largest and most spectacular water birds. Its all-white body, black-tipped wings, and huge orange bill with large extensible pouch capable of holding over 11 litres of water (Leahy 2004) all provide an unforgettable image.

This pelican breeds customarily on remote islands in freshwater lakes and occasionally in brackish or saltwater locations. The breeding range includes the western Canadian provinces and some western states between latitudes 27° N and 60° N. Small, non-migratory breeding populations occur in Texas and, sporadically, east-central Mexico (Knopf and Evans 2004). The species generally winters south of its breeding range along the Pacific and Gulf coasts as far south as Guatemala (Knopf and Evans 2004).

Canada supports 50-70% of the North American breeding population, and the Lake of the Woods colony is one of the largest in Canada, amounting to 10% of the Canadian population (Ratcliff 2005). The species is listed currently as Endangered in Ontario. In view of its sensitivity to disturbance, but given its large and expanding population and range in the province, its status in Ontario was recently reassessed and recommended for downgrading to Threatened.

Distribution and population status: In Ontario, the American White Pelican breeds at only two known locations: on islands in Lake of the Woods in Kenora Dist. and in Lake Nipigon in Thunder Bay Dist. (Peck in Cadman et al. 1987; Peck and James 1993a). The colonies in Lake Nipigon became established in 1991 (Bryan 1991) and in 2004 involved three separate sites totalling 638 pairs (Ratcliff 2005). The Lake of the Woods colonies, which in the Ontario portion of the lake have stabilized in recent years, totalled 7,432 pairs in 2004 (Ratcliff 2005). A recently established breeding colony near Garden Island on Big Traverse Bay, Minnesota, indicates the Lake of the Woods population is still expanding, however. On

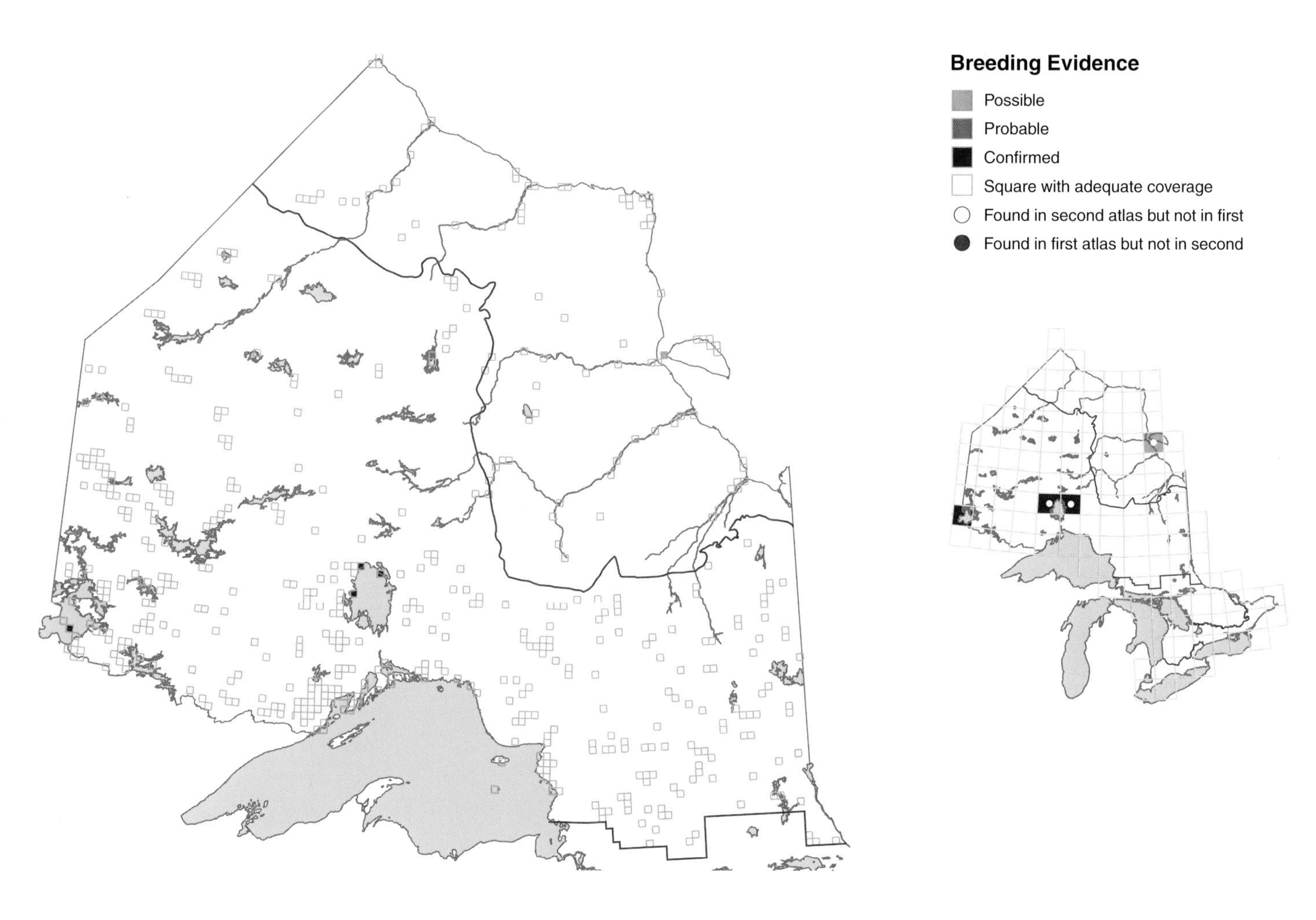

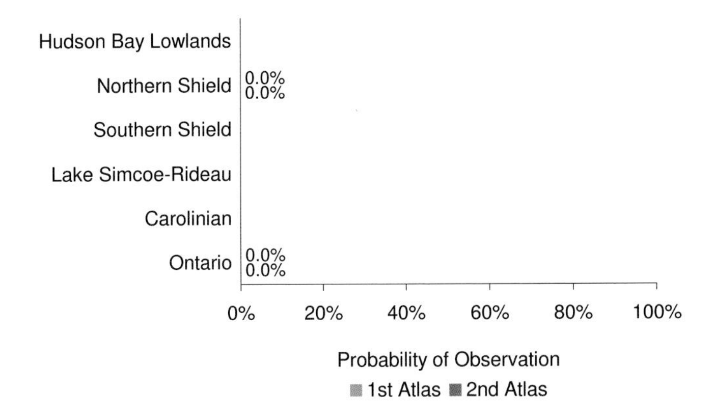

the Great Lakes proper, breeding colonies are currently known to occur only on Lake Michigan, although individuals are frequently observed as non-breeding vagrants in Ontario. Between the initial nesting in 1995 and 2005, the Lake Michigan breeding population increased from six to over 600 at two colony sites (T. Erdman, pers. comm.).

On 28 July 2006, outside the atlas period, approximately 40 adults and two eggs were photographed on an island in the Akimiski Strait, Nunavut (K. Abraham, pers. comm.), indicating an easterly expansion of the species' breeding range. At this location on 3 June 2005, 33 adults in breeding plumage were observed. The histogram is based on confirmed breeding records, so shows no records in the Hudson Bay Lowlands.

Breeding biology: In Ontario, the American White Pelican breeds on small, remote, low bedrock islands in freshwater lakes. It nests colonially, often in company with the Double-crested Cormorant and the Herring Gull. Some of the nesting islands are sparsely vegetated, while others are more thickly covered with shrubs and trees (Peck and James 1983; Peck in Cadman et al. 1987). Currently, the nesting islands in use on Lake of the Woods are barren of tall vegetation (Lockhart and Macins 2001), and on Lake Nipigon the vegetation on the nesting islands is decreasing as colonies increase in size (Ratcliff 2005).

Nests are located on the ground in depressions in the substrate. Composed of soil, sticks, and other vegetation, they are lined with finer sticks, feathers, leaves, and stems. Clutch sizes vary from one to three eggs, two eggs being most common (Peck and James 1983). Egg dates range from 8 May to 27 July, with the height of the season falling between 4 June and 30 June. The incubation period is about 30 days, and the young leave the nest at between 17 and 25 days of age (Knopf and Evans 2004). Fledging occurs at 9 to 10 weeks, and one week or more after their first flights, young leave the colony (Knopf and Evans 2004).

The American White Pelican is known to forage at considerable distances (50-100 km) from breeding colonies. Non-breeding birds (less than three years of age) frequently summer within the breeding range (Knopf and Evans 2004). Observations of foraging and non-breeding pelicans can thus lead to misinterpretations of breeding evidence and may account for other reports of breeding from areas where breeding has not been confirmed (e.g. Rainy Lake, Rainy River Dist., and Onaman Lake, Thunder Bay Dist.; Ratcliff 2005).

Abundance: In 2004, the provincial population of the species was estimated to be 8,070 pairs, the highest population levels on record (Ratcliff 2005). Presently, the population of the Lake of the Woods colonies appears stable, and colonies on Lake Nipigon are increasing. – *George K. Peck*

The altricial young of the American White Pelican are completely dependent on parents for food, warmth, and protection (Klopf and Evans 2004). *Photo: George K. Peck*

Two of The Three Sisters, islands in Lake of the Woods, host nesting pelicans. *Photo: George K. Peck*

Double-crested Cormorant

Cormoran à aigrettes

Phalacrocorax auritus

Jim Richards

The Double-crested Cormorant breeds only in North America, primarily through the central prairies and the Great Lakes. Outside of this range, it can be found on large lakes and water bodies from coast to coast. The species has undergone large-scale population fluctuations over the past century. Persecution led to population declines through the early part of the 1900s; numbers increased from the 1920s until the 1950s, when pesticides such as DDT resulted in reproductive failure and decline. Since the banning of DDT in the 1970s, populations have shown an astronomical increase in breeding numbers (Weseloh et al. 1995, 2002; Hatch and Weseloh 1999). This has led to much controversy regarding the impact of cormorant populations on fisheries, vegetation, and co-occurring species (Cuthbert et al. 2002; Lantry et al. 2002; Hebert et al. 2005). Die-offs of thousands of these birds have occurred due to Newcastle Disease (Glasser et al. 1999) and Type E Botulism (L. Shutt and C. Weseloh, unpubl. data).

Distribution and population status: Cormorants have bred in Lake of the Woods since the 1700s, but the first suspected nesting in other regions of Ontario occurred in 1913 in western Lake Superior (Weseloh et al. 1995). These birds were speculated to have come from colonies at Lake of the Woods (Peck and James 1983). The species continued to spread eastward and reached Lake Ontario in the late 1930s. Ontario populations showed the same pattern of decline and rebounding related to DDT that has been observed elsewhere in its range.

Cormorants now breed abundantly throughout the Great Lakes wherever there are islands. They also nest in smaller numbers at many inland lakes where they were not known previously (Alvo et al. 2002). They occur in greatest numbers on islands along the north and east shores of Georgian Bay, in the North Channel, western Lake Erie, and eastern Lake Ontario, and along the St. Lawrence River. The species is also

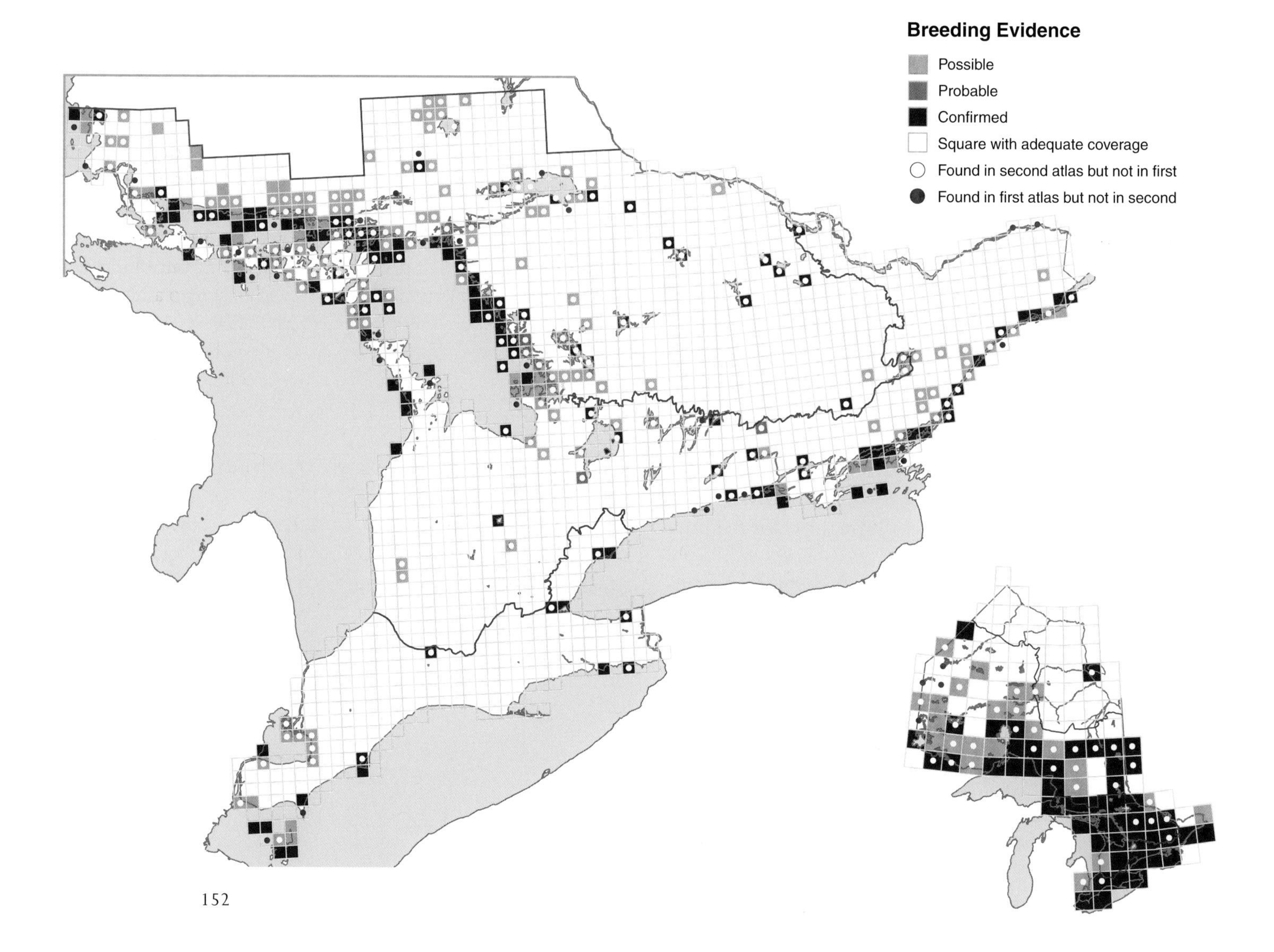

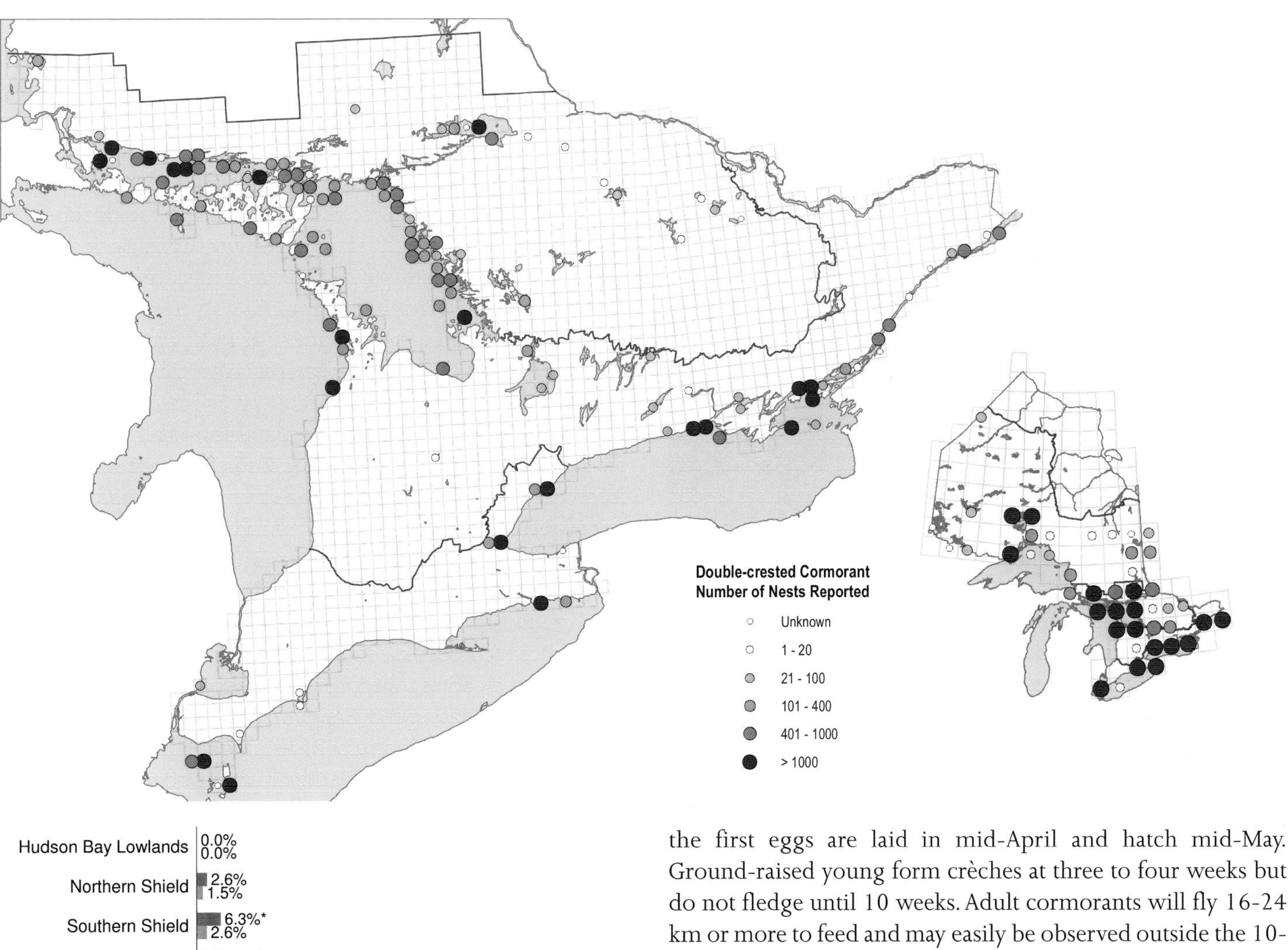

Hudson Bay Lowlands 0.0% 0.0%
Northern Shield 2.6% 1.5%
Southern Shield 6.3%* 2.6%
Lake Simcoe-Rideau 5.6%* 1.3%
Carolinian 1.1% 0.4%
Ontario 2.4%* 1.2%
0% 20% 40% 60% 80% 100%
Probability of Observation
1st Atlas 2nd Atlas

widespread in western Lake Superior. Records elsewhere in the province and inland from the Great Lakes are more scattered. The northernmost confirmed nesting records in the second atlas were from Little Sachigo Lake in northwestern Ontario and Akimiski Strait in James Bay.

While substantial numbers of new records occurred in every region, using only confirmed breeding records (as shown in the histogram) the probability of observation more than doubled in the Lake Simcoe-Rideau and Southern Shield regions and in the province as a whole. Monitoring programs of Great Lakes populations by CWS indicate an annual growth rate of 22% since 1970. These increases are largely due to an abundant food supply and reduced pressures from persecution and environmental contaminants.

Breeding biology: The Double-crested Cormorant appears to prefer to nest in trees but will nest on the ground where trees are limited or have died and fallen. As a colonial tree-nester, its perennial activities usually kill the nest trees within seven to 10 years (Lemmon et al. 1994). In southern Ontario, the first eggs are laid in mid-April and hatch mid-May. Ground-raised young form crèches at three to four weeks but do not fledge until 10 weeks. Adult cormorants will fly 16-24 km or more to feed and may easily be observed outside the 10-km square in which they breed. Immature birds and failed breeders often loaf and roost on islands and shoals away from the breeding colony. In these situations, the paler one-year-old birds are often mistakenly identified as fledglings and assumed to be part of an active breeding colony. Most cormorants (78%) only begin to breed at three years of age (van de Veen 1973). Breeding colonies are usually noisy and can be readily detected downwind by the pungent smell of guano and rotting fish. Colonies of variable size were reported from 181 squares across the province during the second atlas. The average size of Ontario colonies is 228 nests according to ONRS data.

Abundance: In the last 35 years, the Great Lakes cormorant population has increased from 89 nests in eight colonies to approximately 113,000 nests in 210 colonies (Weseloh et al. 1995, 2006). Colonies of over 1,000 nests are located in several areas of Lake Huron, western Lake Erie, and western, central, and eastern Lake Ontario. Cormorant abundance declines more than 16-32 km inland from these areas in southern Ontario and is generally lower in most areas of Lake Superior and northern Ontario. The lower numbers on Lake Superior are probably due to the smaller number of forage fish because of the oligotrophic nature of the lake. – *Chip Weseloh*

American Bittern

Butor d'Amérique

Botaurus lentiginosus

Ethan Meleg

The American Bittern is more often heard than seen, its presence betrayed only by its resounding "*gunk-ker-lunk, gunk-ker-lunk*" call. Its cryptic plumage mimics the surrounding emergent vegetation, and it often waits motionlessly or walks slowly during foraging, relying on stealth. It prefers freshwater wetlands dominated by tall emergent vegetation, although occasionally it nests in brackish wetlands and more rarely in salt marshes (Gibbs et al. 1992a). A widespread North American species, it breeds extensively between about 35° and 60° N and winters primarily in the southern US, Mexico, and Cuba (Gibbs et al. 1992a).

Distribution and population status: Both atlases show that the American Bittern is distributed widely throughout the province, ranging from the extreme southwest to the Hudson Bay coast. Within this broad range, there are gaps, notably in the Carolinian, Northern Shield, and Hudson Bay Lowlands regions. In the agricultural south, these gaps reflect the scattered distribution of suitable breeding habitat, while in the far north the discontinuous distribution is more likely a reflection of uneven coverage. In southwestern Ontario, breeding is primarily restricted to larger inland and especially coastal wetlands, which was also the case during the first atlas. The breeding evidence map shows a relatively high occupancy in the Southern Shield, Manitoulin Island, and the Bruce Peninsula and in the area between Kingston and Ottawa. The probability of observation was greatest in the Southern Shield (52%) and Lake Simcoe-Rideau (41%) regions, as it was during the first atlas.

There was no significant change between atlases in the species' probability of observation in most regions or in the province as a whole. Only in the Carolinian region did the probability of observation decline significantly (37%). Declines in the Carolinian region occurred mostly at inland sites, possibly due to loss or degradation of wetland habitat.

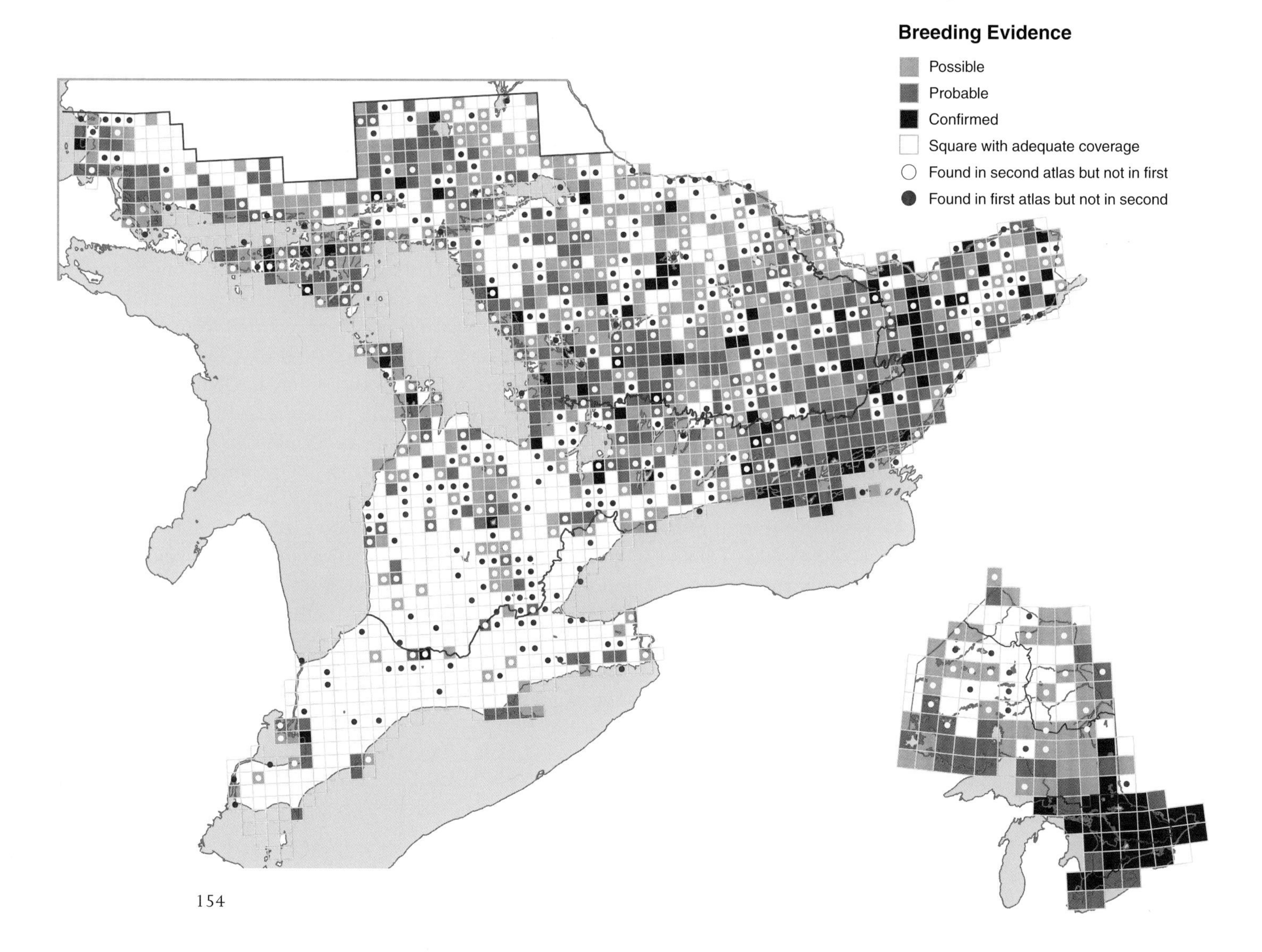

BREEDING EVIDENCE

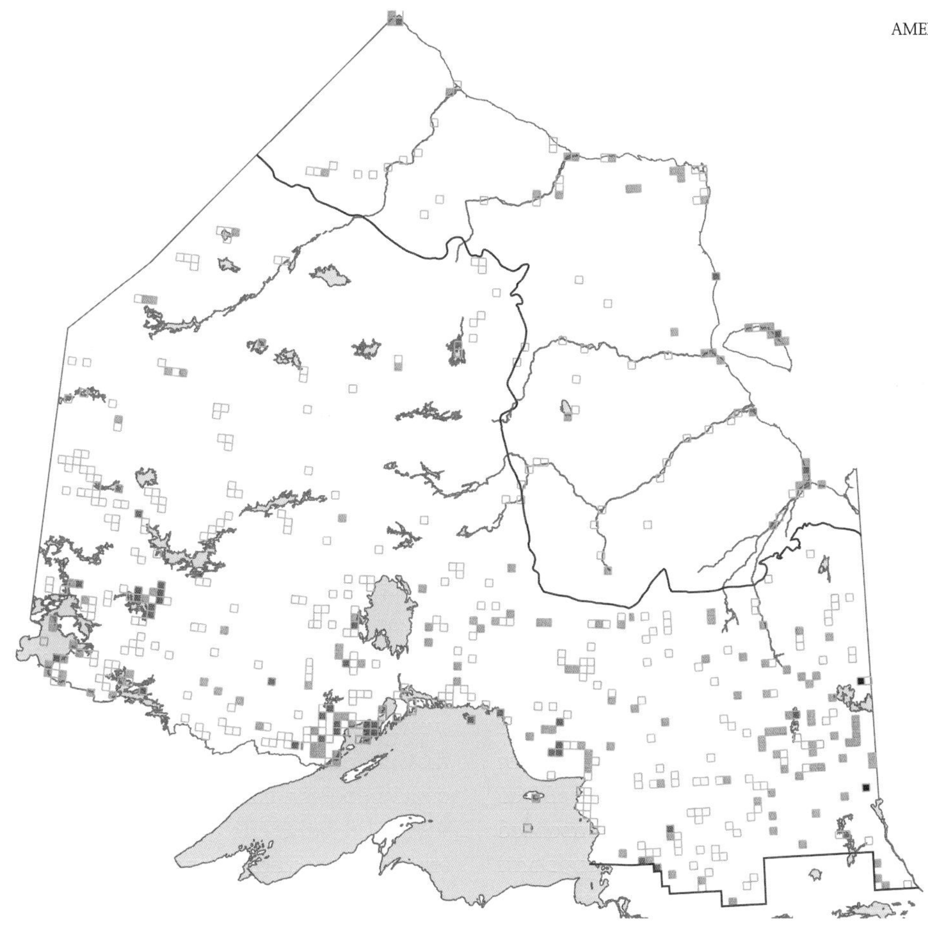

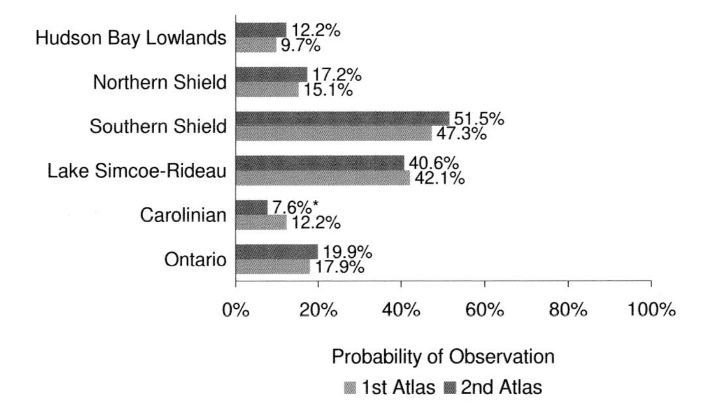

Although there are deficiencies inherent in BBS data for the American Bittern and other marsh birds (Sauer et al. 2005), BBS data for Ontario nonetheless mirror those of the atlas, showing no significant trends for the province on the whole. Consistent with atlas results for the Carolinian region, however, BBS and MMP data for the southern Great Lakes basin both indicate that numbers of the American Bittern have decreased significantly since the mid-1990s.

Breeding biology: In Ontario, this bittern breeds predominantly in freshwater marshes, although it may nest in brackish and saltwater marshes along the coasts of Hudson and James Bays (Peck and James 1983). In addition to nesting in a variety of wetland types, it occasionally nests in dry, upland habitats adjoining wetlands, such as meadows, pastures, and agricultural fields (Peck and James 1983). Most nests in Ontario are over water as deep as 45 cm, but they may also be situated in shrubs or even on the ground in dry fields (Peck and James 1983).

Egg laying can begin in early May, but the peak of nesting in Ontario occurs in the first half of June (Peck and James 1983), coincident with the primary atlassing season. Incubation (by the female only) begins with the laying of the first egg and may take 22-28 days (Peck and James 1983; Gibbs et al. 1992a). Hatching occurs over two to five days, and the young remain in the nest for about two weeks (Bent 1926).

Despite the species' otherwise cryptic and secretive nature, males perform elaborate nuptial courting displays (Bent 1926). Occasional polygyny may occur (Gibbs et al. 1992a). Males do not assist the female during brood rearing, but females – sometimes several of them (Bent 1926; Middleton 1949) – nest within defended male territories (Gibbs et al. 1992a).

The American Bittern is easily detected early in the breeding season when males are vocalizing. The calls can be heard over considerable distances, so the map is likely a good representation of breeding distribution. Nests and young are difficult to find, and consequently only 7% of records were of confirmed breeding.

Abundance: Atlas point count data indicate that the American Bittern has several centres of abundance in Ontario, with a notable concentration in the southern James Bay area. It is also relatively abundant on Manitoulin Island and on the Southern Shield, and in the eastern Lake Simcoe-Rideau region. The pattern of abundance was similar in both atlases, with greatest abundance in the north during the first atlas occurring in the James Bay area. In the south, high abundance was also noted in southeastern Ontario and on the Southern Shield during the first atlas. – *Steven T.A. Timmermans*

Least Bittern

Petit Blongios

Ixobrychus exilis

Jim Flynn

The Least Bittern is a secretive bird that inhabits predominantly cattail marshes. It is the smallest heron breeding in Canada, restricted to the southern parts of Manitoba, Ontario, Québec, New Brunswick, and possibly Nova Scotia (James 1999). Its cryptic behaviour, brief courtship period, and lack of territory defence calls make it difficult to locate. It may therefore be more common than the data indicate. Nevertheless, because of habitat loss and the aggressive nature of vegetation such as Common Reed, the species has been designated Threatened by COSEWIC and OMNR.

Distribution and population status: The Least Bittern appears to have declined from historical levels. Nash (1908) considered it abundant in larger southern Ontario marshes and common throughout its range, while Baillie and Harrington (1936) considered it uncommon overall but locally common in some areas. Historical declines were related to habitat loss, with 68% of the original wetlands south of the Shield in Ontario having been destroyed (Snell 1987). A parallel trend occurred in Michigan and Ohio, where significant declines occurred until the 1950s and early 1960s, with populations being reasonably stable since then (Brewer et al. 1991; Peterjohn and Rice 1991).

The Least Bittern's overall breeding distribution shows little change from the first atlas. In each atlas, only three northern squares reported breeding evidence; those records were from cattail marshes near Dryden and Fort Frances. As in the first atlas, the Least Bittern was infrequently observed, with the overall probability of observation about 1%. There was no significant change in the probability of observation between atlases overall, nor in four of the five atlas regions. There was, however, a 44% decrease in the probability of observation in the Carolinian region.

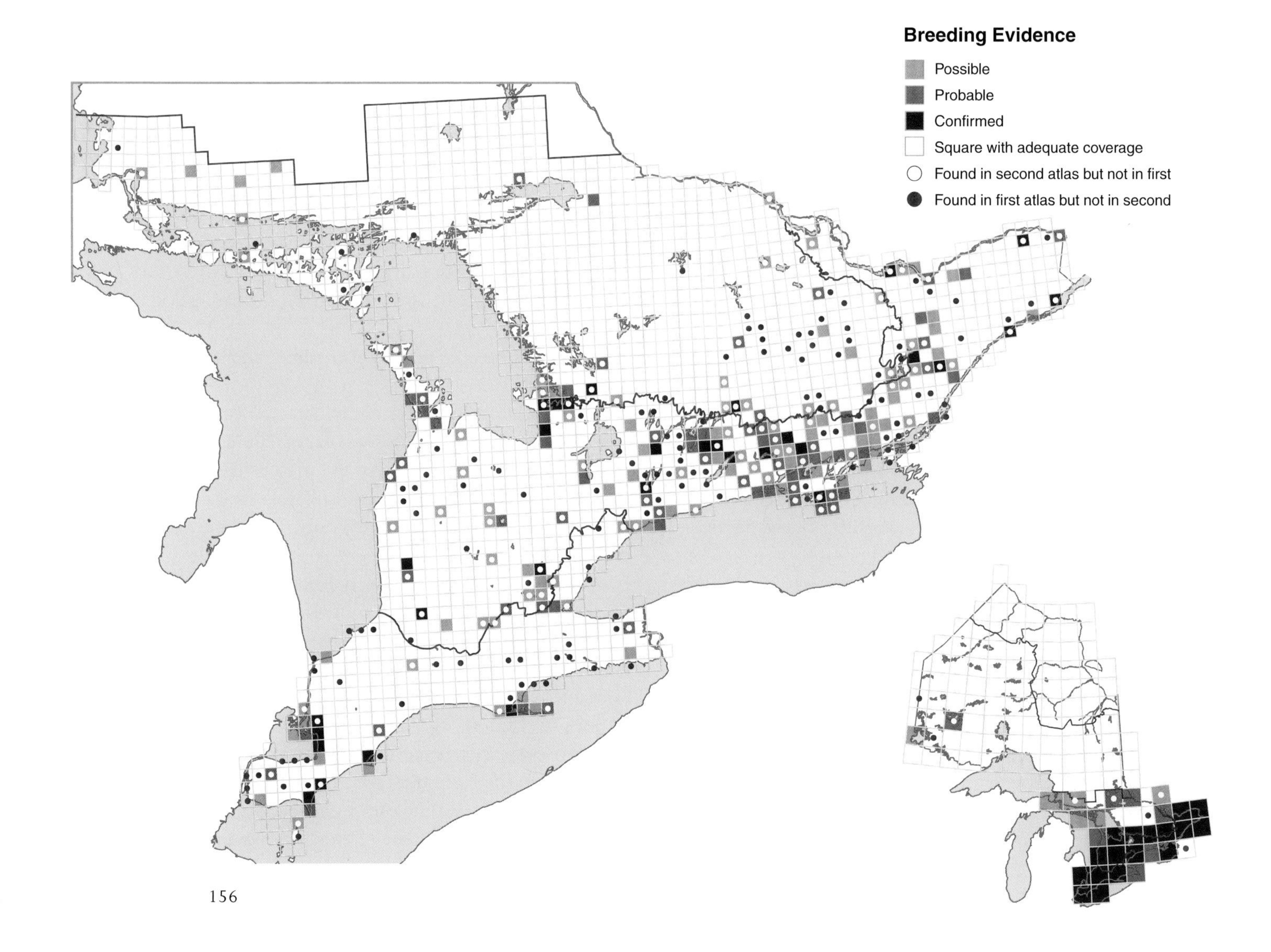

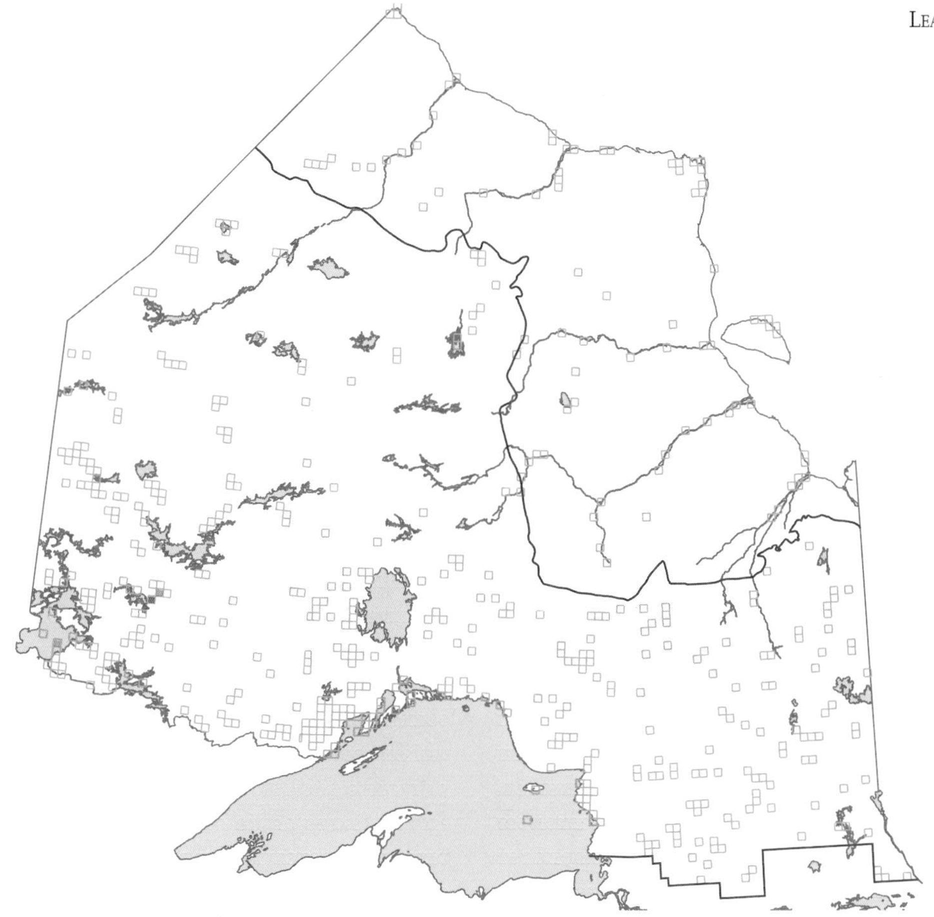

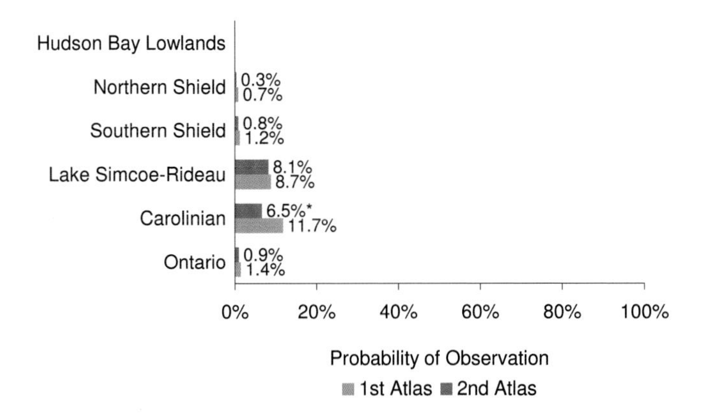

A fairly high turnover of occupied squares occurred between the two atlas periods. Of the 210 squares in which the Least Bittern was recorded in the second atlas, only 31% supported the species in both atlases, and almost half of squares with breeding evidence in the first atlas did not have evidence in the second. Some of these differences may be due to habitat loss. The high turnover may also be related to bitterns moving from Great Lakes coastal marshes inland to higher-quality wetlands (Timmermans 2001), or it could result from differences in survey effort. MMP data from 1995 to 2004 indicate that the Least Bittern has declined significantly at a rate of 11% annually in the southern Great Lakes basin (Timmermans et al. 2006), consistent with atlas results for the Carolinian region.

Breeding biology: The Least Bittern is most frequently found in marshes of at least 5 ha (James 1999), although much smaller marshes, including sites such as cattail stands along creeks and farm ponds partially filled with cattail, may be used occasionally (pers. obs.). Sites such as these may have been missed by atlassers expecting the Least Bittern only in the largest marshes.

In breeding sites, cattail is typically the most dominant vegetation present (Gibbs et al. 1992b), but nests have been found in bulrush, grasses, horsetail, and willow. Nests are usually close to the edge of a stand of vegetation or near openings such as muskrat trails, although they may be as far as 45 m from open water (Peck and James 1983). They are built on a platform of dried vegetation 0.2-0.7 m above water, typically as deep as a metre. In larger marshes, the Least Bittern may nest in loose colonies (Brewer et al. 1991), with nests as close together as 4 m (pers. obs.).

The Least Bittern's courtship display period is only about 10 days. Its soft, low-pitched "*coo-coo-coo*" song is given at dawn or dusk and is difficult to hear except in very calm conditions. The species may be quiet even where it occurs in high density and does not respond well to call broadcasts (Tozer et al. in press), which in turn could affect atlassing efficiency.

Abundance: Detections of the Least Bittern on point counts were insufficient to produce an abundance map. The species' centre of abundance appears to be in the vicinity of Lake St. Clair, Long Point, and an area south of the Shield from about Peterborough to Kingston, including the eastern shoreline marshes of Lake Ontario. The Least Bittern continues to be a rare and local breeder in Ontario and appears to be decreasing in abundance, although difficulty in detection and observer lack of familiarity with its vocalizations may limit its detection in some areas. – *P. Allen Woodliffe*

Great Blue Heron

Grand Héron

Ardea herodias

Ron Ridout

The Great Blue Heron is one of Ontario's largest colonially nesting waterbirds. In North America, it breeds from Cape Breton Island to central Alberta south to Florida and Texas. It also breeds along the Pacific coast from southern Alaska to the Baja Peninsula (Butler 1992).

Distribution and population status: The Great Blue Heron is widely distributed across Ontario from Cornwall to Kenora and Point Pelee to about 51° N, with the northernmost documented colonies near Moosonee and Cat Lake. It is well distributed across the three southern regions, sparsely distributed across the Northern Shield, and occurs sporadically in the Hudson Bay Lowlands.

Considering all breeding evidence, there was a significant 37% decline province-wide in the probability of observation between atlases, and decreases were noted in all regions except the Hudson Bay Lowlands. When only confirmed breeding evidence was included in the analysis (as shown in the histogram), the Southern Shield showed a significant 22% decline, and the Northern Shield showed a large but non-significant 42% decline. This apparent decline may be partly an artifact of differences in survey effort. The first atlas coincided with a detailed province-wide inventory of heronries (Ontario Heronry Inventory, OHI), whereas the second atlas did not. However, a declining trend is consistent with Ontario BBS data (which should be interpreted cautiously for this species) showing a significant 1.9% annual decline from 1981 to 2005. Following the organochlorine pesticide era of the late 1940s to early 1970s, the BBS estimate increased by about 4% each year until about 1990. The OHI estimated over 17,000 breeding pairs in the early 1990s (Collier et al. 1992). The reasons for a potential recent decline are not known. However, since the largest decline appears to have occurred on the Shield, it is unlikely to be a reflection of increasing urban and suburban development and associated habitat loss. Forestry activities are also unlikely to have

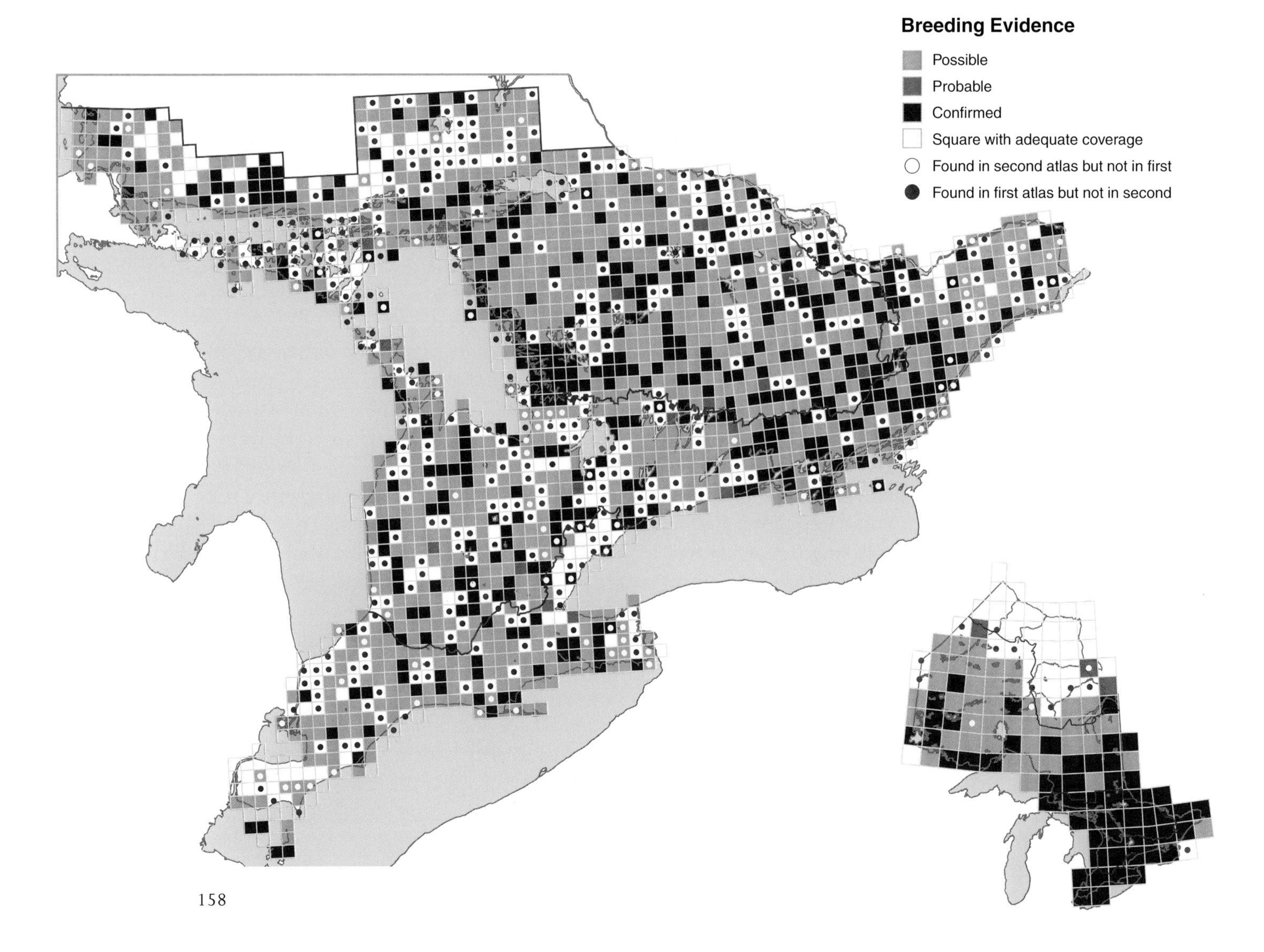

BREEDING EVIDENCE

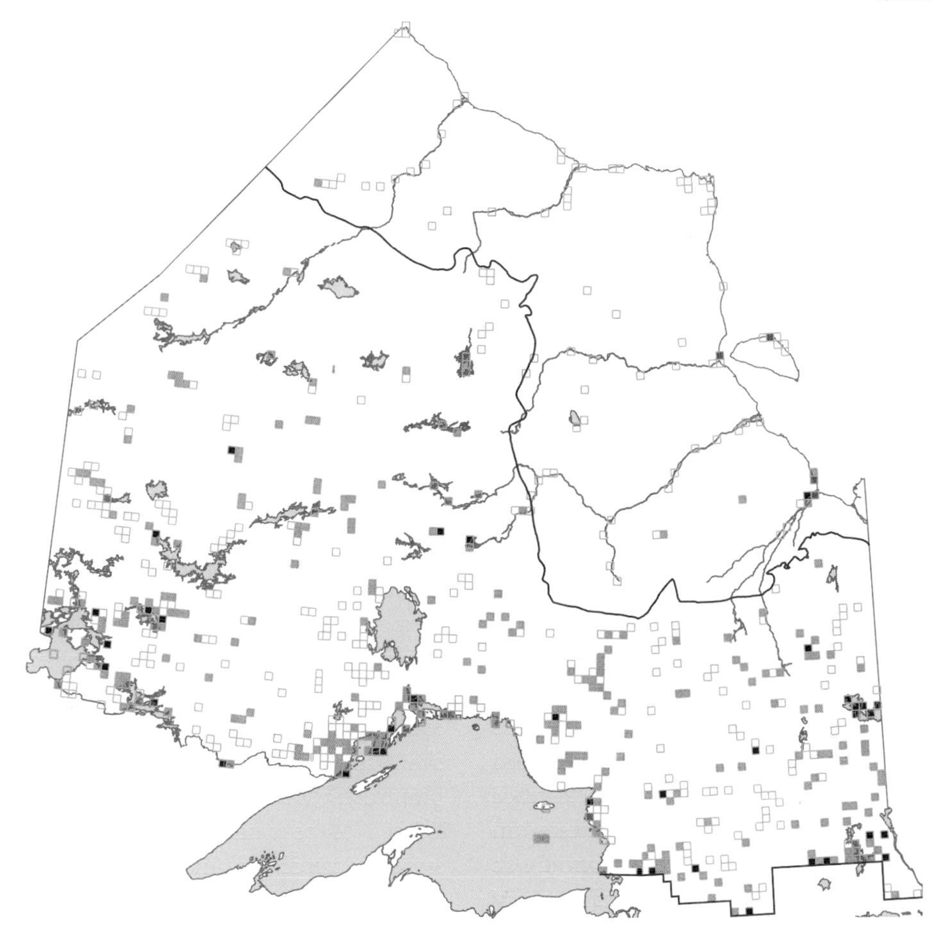

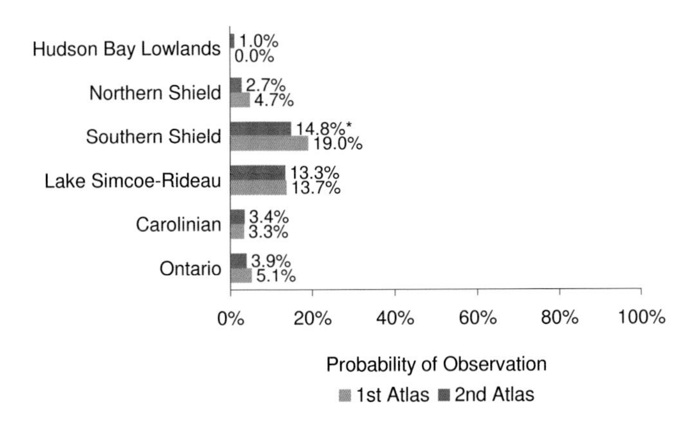

been the cause, because buffers have been used to protect colonies since the mid-1980s (Bowman and Siderius 1984; Ontario Ministry of Natural Resources 1998). The decline may be at least partly related to the overall decrease in many amphibian species such as the Green Frog noted in the Great Lakes basin during the last 10 years (Crewe et al. 2005). Amphibians are important dietary items for the species, and a decline may have had a greater effect on the Shield where productivity of hunting habitat is presumably lower than farther south.

Breeding biology: The Great Blue Heron builds a large bulky stick nest (up to 1 m in diameter) in a living or dead tree, usually over or close to water. Preferred nesting habitat is wet or dry forest, sparsely treed islands, beaver ponds, and marshes (Peck and James 1983). It may nest singly, but greater than 99% of nests in Ontario occur in colonies (Peck and James 1983). Colony size averages about 35 nests, with some colonies exceeding 150 nests (Dunn et al. 1985). Colonies may be very stable and can exist for up to 50 years, but the average heronry lifespan in Ontario is about nine years (Collier et al. 1992).

The Great Blue Heron feeds on small fish, amphibians, rodents, aquatic insects, crayfish, snails, and carrion found in the shallow water of marshes, ponds, and forested wetlands, and along lake and river shorelines (Butler 1992, 1997).

Breeding was confirmed in only 28% of squares with breeding evidence. This is somewhat surprising, given the conspicuous nature of heronries and the timing of nesting relative to the atlas survey window. The species typically returns to its breeding range in Ontario by early April; median egg dates are 3 May to 23 May (Peck and James 1983). Based on an incubation period of 27 days and a nestling period of 53 days (Butler 1992), most fledging occurs by late July. However, while feeding areas are typically within 5 km of colonies, herons may fly up 25 km to feed (Short and Cooper 1985). Thus, squares with possible or probable evidence of breeding do not necessarily contain occupied colonies.

Considering the large size and conspicuous habits of this species, the atlas maps are likely a fairly accurate depiction of its general distribution at the 100-km block level.

Abundance: Data from OMNR's Natural Resources and Values Information System (2007) suggest the highest density of colonies (up to 18 per square) occurs in the Southern Shield. However, the average colony size is larger south of the Shield (Dunn et al. 1985), presumably reflecting a gradient in food supply (*sensu* Gibbs 1991). – *Brian Naylor*

Great Egret

Grande Aigrette

Ardea alba

John Reaume

The Great Egret is a cosmopolitan species with four subspecies. The subspecies of this largest, all-white egret inhabiting North and South America is *Ardea alba egretta*; it ranges south from southern Canada to the West Indies and to Tierra del Fuego in Argentina. In Canada, it breeds in southern Saskatchewan and Manitoba east to southern Ontario and southwestern Québec. The most northerly colony in eastern Canada is on Dickerson Island, Lake St.-François, in Québec, just downstream from Cornwall, Ontario (Gauthier and Aubry 1996).

Distribution and population status: The Great Egret breeds in the southern part of the province. Colony locations tend to change over time, and during the present atlas, confirmed breeding locations were as follows: Chantry Island, Bruce Co.; East Sister, Middle Sister, and Middle Islands in Essex Co.; Walpole Island in Lambton Co.; High Bluff Island in Northumberland Co.; Nottawasaga Island in Simcoe Co.; Bergin Island, Lake St. Lawrence, United Counties of Stormont, Dundas and Glengarry; and the Leslie St. Spit and the marshes of the lower Humber River, both in Toronto. Breeding was reported also on Barrier Island, Georgian Bay, in Bruce Co. in 2003 and 2004, and a probable breeding record was reported in 2004 from Luther Marsh, Wellington Co. (B. Wyatt, pers. comm.). Previous confirmed nestings, prior to 2001, have been on Pelee Island, Essex Co.; in Backus Woods in Norfolk Co.; and on an island in St. Clair National Wildlife Area in Chatham-Kent (Peck in Cadman et al. 1987; Peck and James 1999). The continuing northward expansion of the Great Egret into southern Ontario is evidenced by new nestings since the first atlas. These new confirmed nestings were those reported from Bruce, Norfolk, Chatham-Kent, Northumberland, Toronto, and the United Counties of Stormont, Dundas and Glengarry. The Norfolk record was not reported during the second atlas.

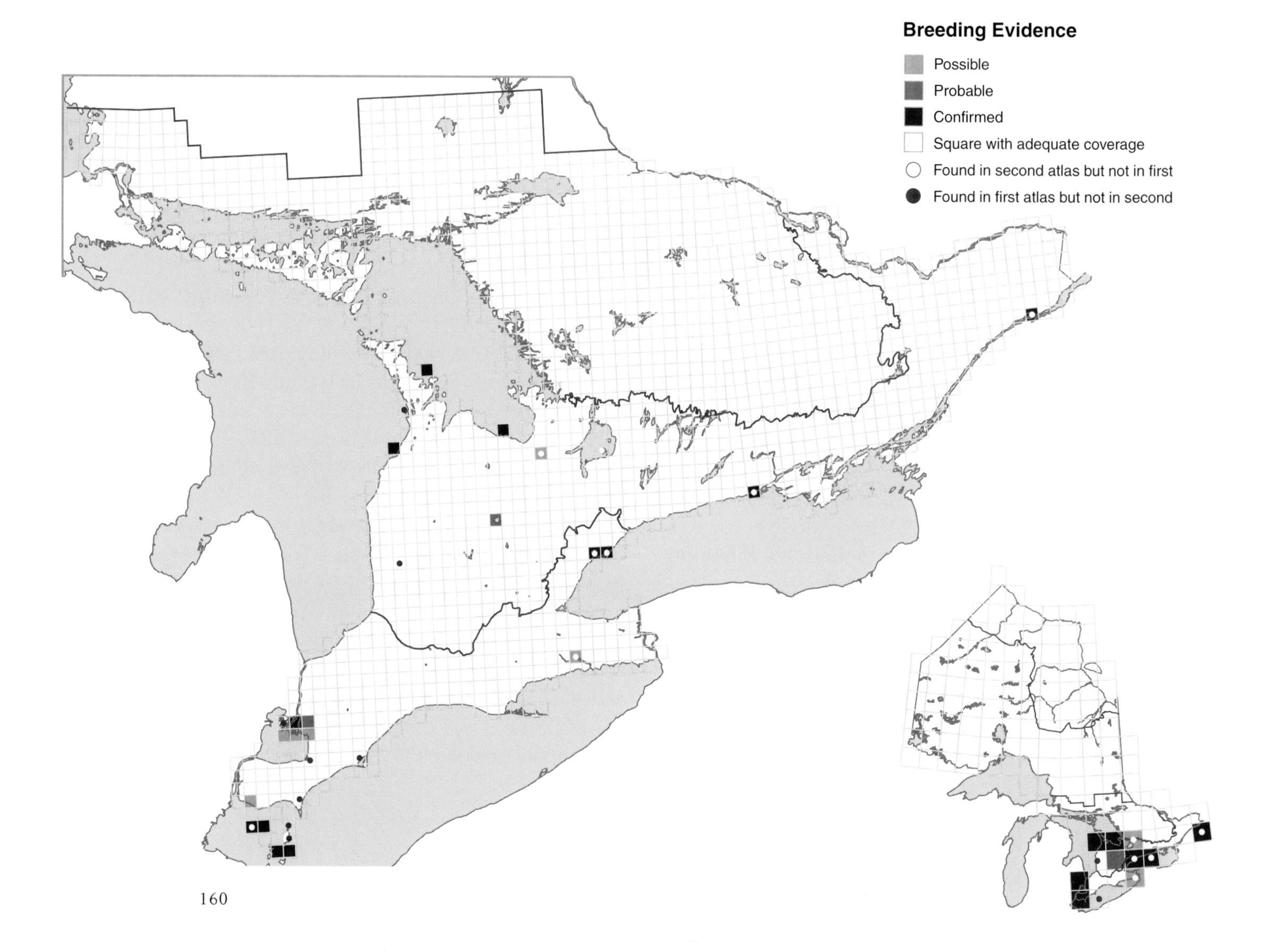

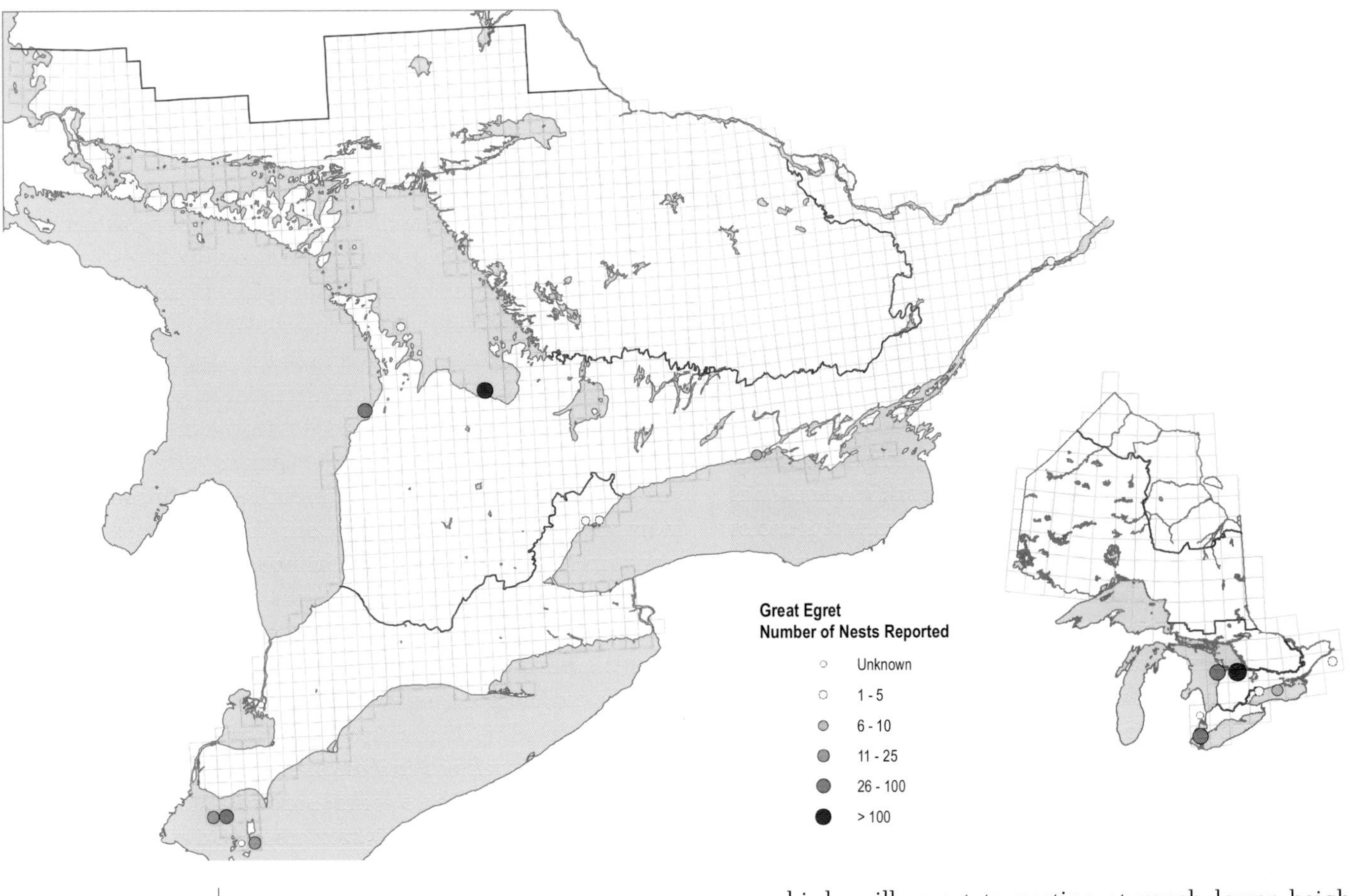

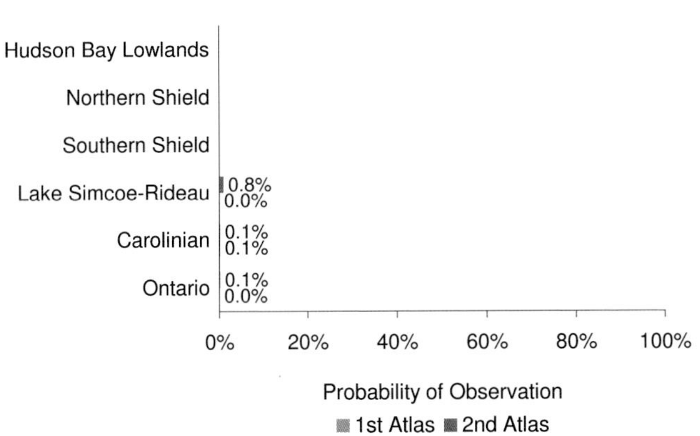

In the second atlas, breeding was confirmed in 12 of the 21 squares in which breeding evidence was reported. Observations of Great Egrets foraging at considerable distances from breeding colonies (up to 40 km; Sandilands 2005) may account for some possible and probable breeding records from some sites where breeding has not been confirmed. Post-breeding dispersal similarly results in observations in non-breeding areas in Ontario.

Breeding biology: The Great Egret is usually a colonially breeding species; its colonies may be homogeneous but more typically are in mixed heronries with the Great Blue Heron and Black-crowned Night-Heron. Other species co-habiting nesting islands include the Double-crested Cormorant, Green Heron, and Ring-billed and Herring Gulls. With the exception of the Toronto and Walpole Island sites, Great Egret colonies have been on treed or shrubby locations. Their bulky stick nests were variously situated in shrubs and trees at heights ranging from 0.6 to 11 m (Peck and James 1983). In marshes and in sites where trees have died or fallen as a result of storm damage, birds will resort to nesting at much lower heights in shrubs or even just above ground or water surface in shrubs or other marsh vegetation.

Egg dates in Ontario range from 28 April to 24 June (Peck and James 1993a). Complete clutch sizes range from three to four eggs, with clutches of four eggs being commonest (Peck and James 1983). Incubation periods range from 23 to 27 days, and variable fledging dates range from 21 to 34 days, with young leaving and returning to the nest to be fed. Young achieve flight ability at seven to eight weeks of age (McCrimmon et al. 2001).

Colony sites may remain occupied for several decades, but as a result of disturbance and vegetation changes, colonies may relocate to more suitable sites. The Nottawasaga Island site has been in use annually since 1985, and the East Sister Island colony has been active since 1953.

Abundance: Twelve squares with confirmed breeding evidence in the present atlas is a considerable increase from six in the first atlas. In the Carolinian region, the number of colonies increased slightly from five to seven, while in the Lake Simcoe-Rideau region there was an increase from one in the first atlas to five in the current atlas.

The provincial population has apparently increased since the first atlas, coinciding with the finding and reporting of new colonies. The colony on Nottawasaga Island has increased from a single nest in 1985 to 100+ nests in 2005, and is currently the largest colony in the province; some similar increases have occurred on Chantry Island and other colonies. By 2004, the average size of colonies reported to the Ontario Nest Records Scheme was 18 nests. – *George K. Peck*

Green Heron

Héron vert

Butorides virescens

George K. Peck

The Green Heron is familiar to many people from its loud squawk as it visits small ponds and wetlands while foraging for fish and amphibians. It is a highly adaptable species and one of the few birds that uses bait to catch its prey (Robinson 1994), luring fish within reach using a crust of bread, mayfly, worm, stick, or other item (Davis and Kushlan 1994). Absent from the prairies, it nests west of the Rocky Mountains from southern British Columbia through Mexico and Central America. It breeds through most of eastern North America east of the prairies north to southern Ontario, southwestern Québec, New Brunswick, and Nova Scotia. Closely related species nest in South America, Africa, Asia, Australia, and the Pacific Islands (Davis and Kushlan 1994). Although the Green Heron typically nests singly in shrubs in or adjacent to wetlands, it may nest in upland shrubby or forested areas at considerable distances from wetlands. Occasionally, it nests colonially, sometimes in wetlands but most often in coniferous plantations (Peck and James 1983; Davis and Kushlan 1994). Despite its versatility, it declined in Ontario between atlases.

Distribution and population status: Historically, the Green Heron was a rare to uncommon breeder in extreme southwestern Ontario. McIlwraith (1894) reported that the shoreline of Lake Erie was the northern extent of its range. Baillie and Harrington (1936) found that it had spread northward and was an uncommon breeder as far north as present-day Middlesex Co., York Region, and the United Counties of Leeds and Grenville. During the first atlas, it was widespread south and east of the Shield and occurred in scattered locations on the Southern Shield north to Lake Nipissing and near Lake of the Woods.

The overall range of the Green Heron did not change substantially between atlases. It was again observed sporadically north to Lake Nipissing, although no records were received from the Lake of the Woods area. There was, however, a significant 29% decline between atlases in the probability of observa-

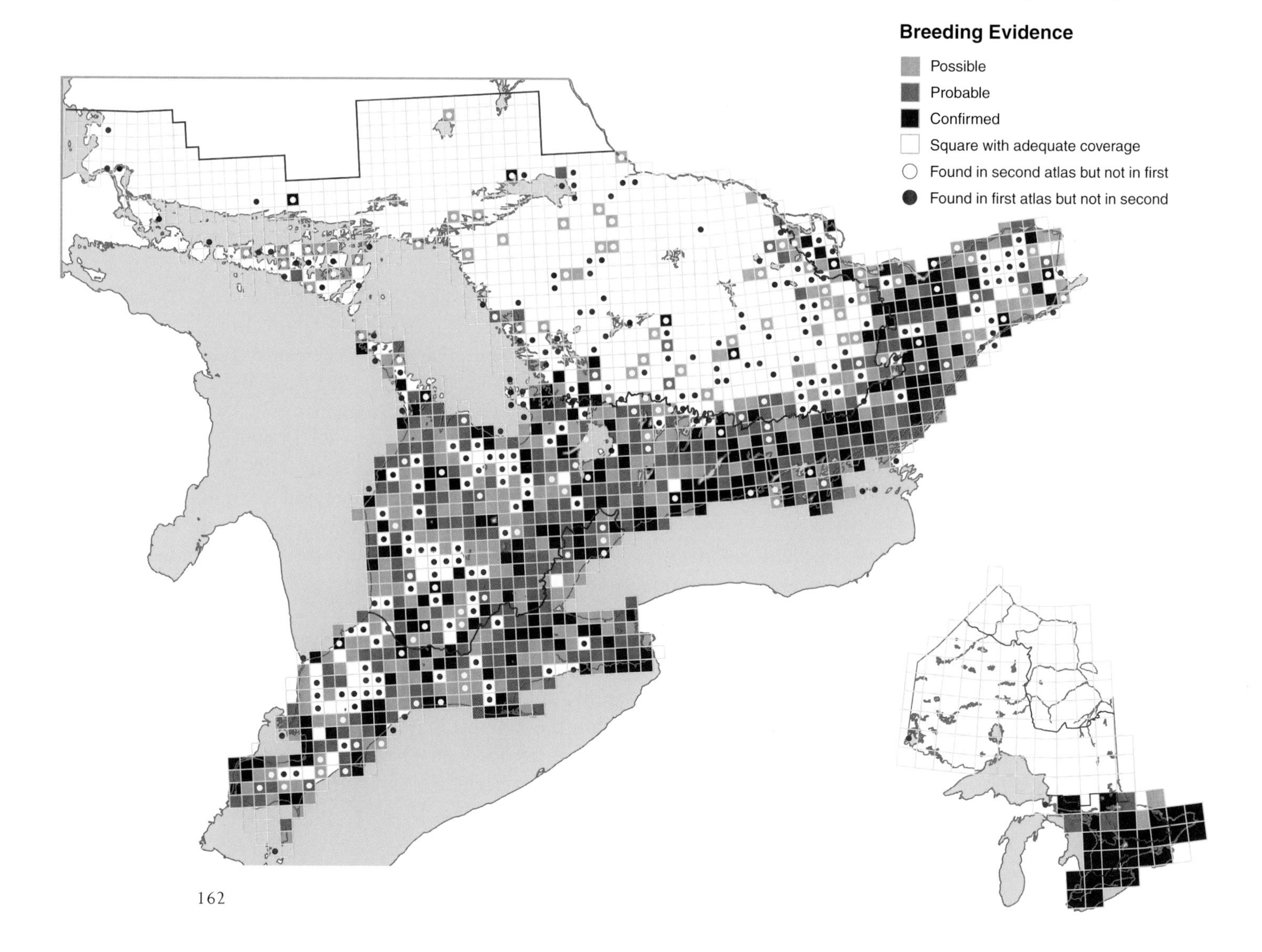

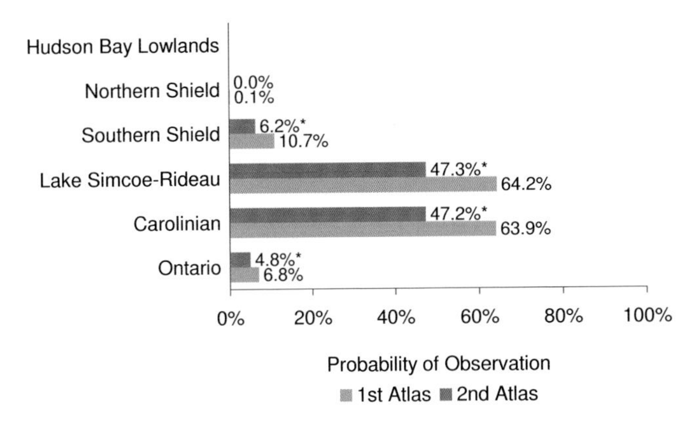

tion in Ontario as a whole. Declines occurred in all regions in which it nested, most notably in the Southern Shield (43%), although declines in the Carolinian (26%) and Lake Simcoe-Rideau regions (26%) were also substantial. Reasons for the decline are uncertain, as much suitable habitat is unoccupied.

BBS data indicate no significant trends for the Green Heron in Ontario, but this survey does not track this species with great precision. The MMP focuses on large Great Lakes wetlands rather than the smaller marshes preferred by the Green Heron, and so this survey has insufficient data to identify any trends in population (Timmermans et al. 2006).

Breeding biology: The Green Heron may initiate nesting in early May in Ontario, but most nesting is in June when most atlassing was undertaken. Nests may be bulky and are usually built of sticks, but in marshes, aquatic emergents are occasionally used. Nests may be placed in deciduous shrubs or trees, less frequently in coniferous trees, and sometimes in emergent vegetation in marshes (Peck and James 1983).

When asked for this atlas to record colonial nesting of the Green Heron, atlassers reported only three multiple nestings. The largest and most unusual was a colony of 14 nests on the ground among raspberries on Indian Island in the Bay of Quinte. Two other colonies with only two nests each were located in a coniferous plantation and a White Cedar-willow swamp.

The Green Heron forages in marshes, ponds, and small water bodies and along drainage ditches and sluggish watercourses. It is relatively conspicuous while foraging or flying to and from feeding areas. Young are conspicuous when foraging, and a high percentage of breeding confirmations were of recently fledged young. Although the species may be retiring around the nest, it is likely that it was found in most squares in which it bred off the Shield; on the Shield, it may have been overlooked in some squares.

Abundance: The Green Heron was not detected on enough point counts to generate a reliable abundance map. Nonetheless, it occurs very sparingly on the Shield, with the greatest numbers south of the Shield. Away from the Great Lakes and major rivers, the predominantly agricultural areas in the southwest support relatively few Green Herons; the species was not observed in many agricultural squares where it occurred during the first atlas. It remains widespread south of the Shield where it is locally common but declining in numbers, and is locally rare to uncommon on the Southern Shield. *– Al Sandilands*

Clutch size is generally three to five eggs. Young leave the nest at 16-17 days. *Photo: Jim Richards*

The nest of the Green Heron is often over water and concealed by overhanging branches. Pelee Island, 8 June 1976. *Photo: George K. Peck*

Black-crowned Night-Heron

Bihoreau gris

Nycticorax nycticorax

George K. Peck

Although often seen during the day, the Black-crowned Night-Heron is primarily nocturnal. In spring, foraging and courtship take place at night. The species roosts during the day, with most birds predictably leaving colony sites after sunset and returning before sunrise (Davis 1993). A cosmopolitan species, it breeds on all continents except Australia and Antarctica.

Distribution and population status: In Ontario, the Black-crowned Night-Heron nests at scattered locations south of a line roughly from Sault Ste. Marie to Cornwall. Breeding colonies are primarily on islands and shores of the Great Lakes and St. Lawrence River, but south of the Shield the species occasionally nests at inland sites. Since the first atlas, the average northern edge of its range has shifted significantly northward by 72 km to islands in the North Channel of Lake Huron and at Sault Ste. Marie. This is the greatest northward expansion in southern Ontario of any bird species except the Red-bellied Woodpecker.

During the second atlas, breeding was confirmed in 35 squares across southern Ontario, compared to 29 during the first atlas. Although, using confirmed records only, no significant changes were observed between atlases, the greatest increase occurred in the Southern Shield region, where breeding was confirmed in six squares, up from one in the first. Well-established night-heron colonies were reported from East Sister and Middle Islands, Lake Erie; Walpole Island, Lake St. Clair; Chantry Island, Lake Huron; Nottawasaga Island, Georgian Bay; near Niagara Falls; Hamilton Harbour; the Leslie Street Spit in Toronto; Gull and High Bluff Islands in Lake Ontario; and McNair and Strachan Islands in the St. Lawrence River (Richards and McRae 1988; Blokpoel and Tessier 1998; Weseloh 2004). Confirmed breeding was reported at only four inland sites: Luther Marsh; southwest of Hamilton on the Grand River; Minesing Swamp, west of Barrie; and near Portland, south of Big Rideau Lake.

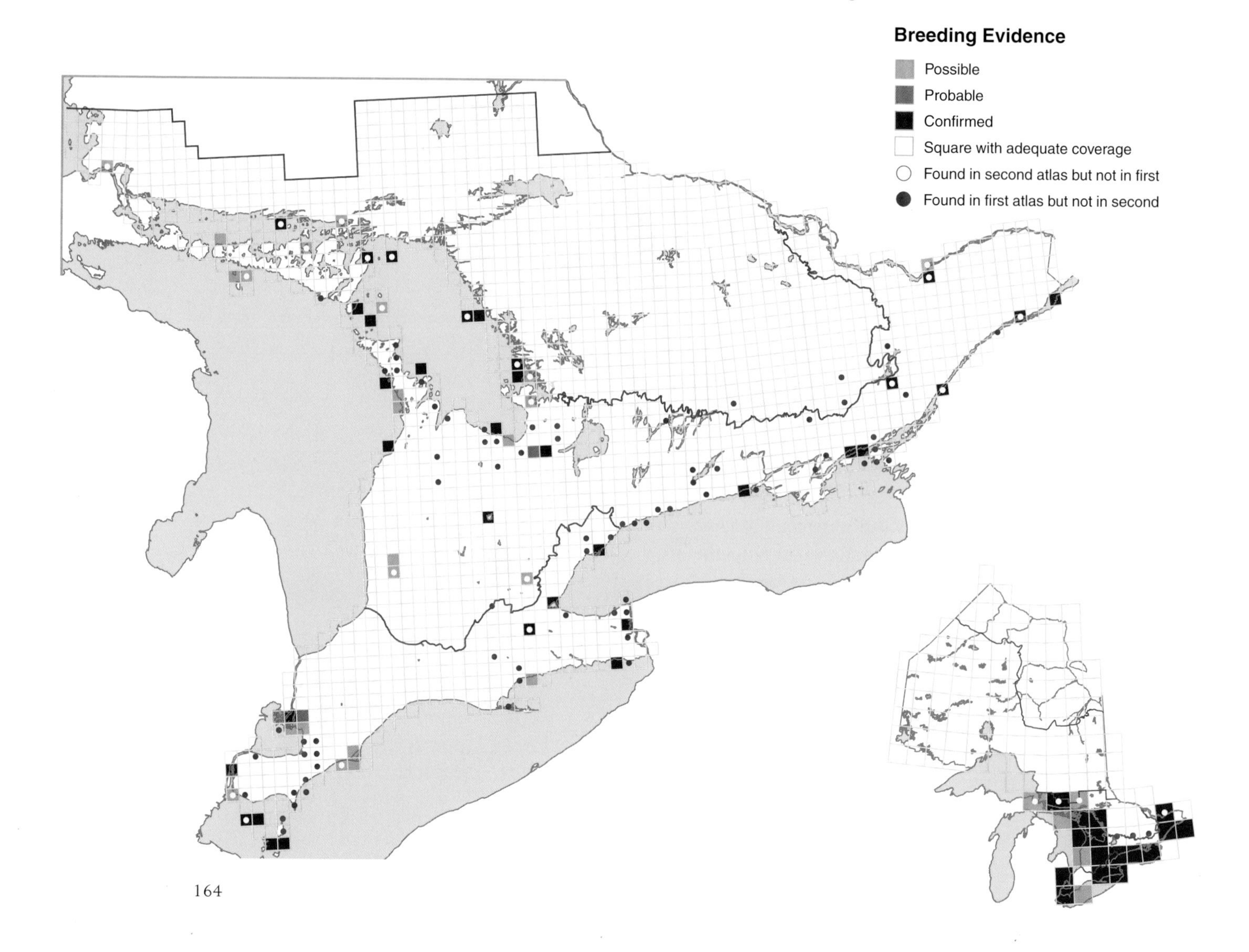

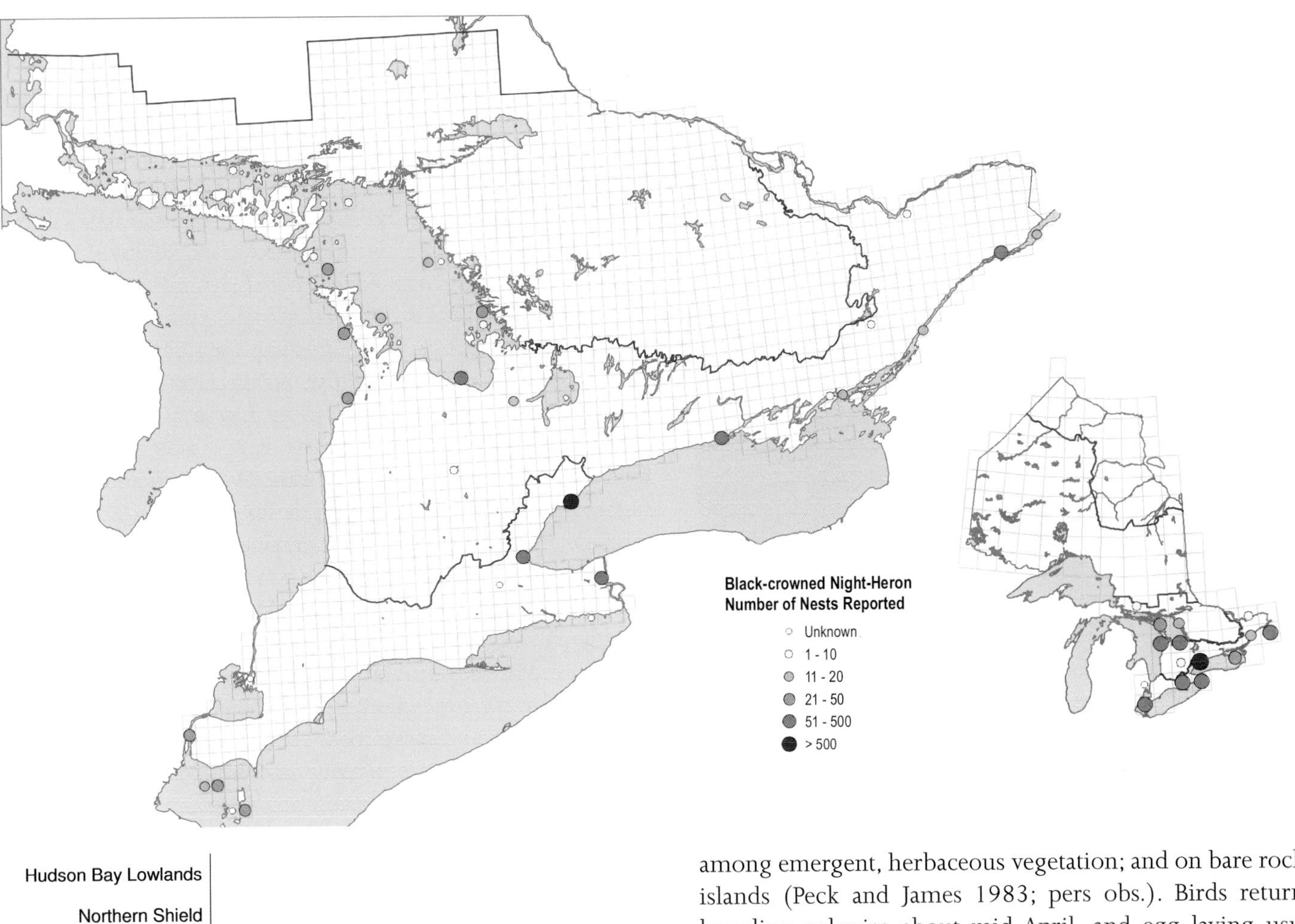

Hudson Bay Lowlands
Northern Shield
Southern Shield 0.3% 0.1%
Lake Simcoe-Rideau 1.7% 1.6%
Carolinian 0.8% 1.0%
Ontario 0.2% 0.1%

0% 20% 40% 60% 80% 100%

Probability of Observation

1st Atlas 2nd Atlas

Several new colonies since the first atlas were reported from Georgian Bay and the North Channel, as well as in eastern Ontario from Prince Edward Co. to Ottawa. However, at several established colonies, night-herons have recently been largely displaced by the Double-crested Cormorant. Some colonies have declined seriously, and many have been abandoned altogether, as cormorant numbers increased (Jarvie et al. 1999; Cuthbert et al. 2002; Weseloh et al. 2002). At the Leslie Street Spit, the number of night-heron nests declined by more than 600 between 2002 and 2006, while cormorant numbers nearly doubled to 6,000 nests (Toronto and Region Conservation Authority, unpubl. data). Although displacement by cormorants may be the primary cause of colony collapse, human disturbance and habitat destruction may be contributing factors.

Breeding biology: In Ontario, this species has been recorded nesting in low shrubs (e.g., elderberry and dogwood); in small trees including White Cedar and Manitoba Maple; in stands of tall, fast-growing trees such as aspen and cottonwood; in large, mature trees; in vine-covered trees; in wetlands among emergent, herbaceous vegetation; and on bare rock on islands (Peck and James 1983; pers obs.). Birds return to breeding colonies about mid-April, and egg laying usually begins in the second week of May. Nests in a colony at Niagara Falls, visited by CWS personnel annually since 1980, have occasionally held young as early as the last week of April, and in 2005 some young were large enough to have been banded (unpubl. data). Back-dating suggests egg laying occurred about the second week of March, nearly two months earlier than average (Peck and James 1983).

Abundance: Night-heron colonies may be small or large; colonies of fewer than five pairs are not uncommon (Weir 1989) and may occur either when a colony is in decline (e.g., Pigeon, Snake, and West Brother Islands in eastern Lake Ontario) or becoming established (e.g., Strachan Island, St. Lawrence River near Cornwall). The largest night-heron colony on record for Ontario is believed to have been one of about 10,000 pairs near Big Sandy Bay on Wolfe Island, Lake Ontario, in the 1950s (Weir 1989). More recently, large colonies of 800-1,200 pairs have been noted on Middle Island in western Lake Erie (Weseloh et al. 1988) and at the Leslie Street Spit (Jarvie et al. 1999). A survey of 44 Canadian night-heron colonies in Lakes Huron, Erie, and Ontario and the St. Lawrence River to below Cornwall in 2003-2004 recorded just over 2,000 nests (Weseloh 2004). Most large colonies are on Lake Ontario, with one on the Niagara River. The only large colony outside of this area, with about 230 nests, is on Nottawasaga Island. The majority of Ontario's colonies contain less than 50 nests. – *Chip Weseloh*

Turkey Vulture

Urubu à tête rouge

Cathartes aura

George K. Peck

With its 1.8 m long wings in their characteristic dihedral position, the Turkey Vulture is one of Ontario's most recognizable birds. A valued and almost exclusive scavenger, it rarely kills small mammals, birds, or other live prey (Palmer 1988; Kirk and Mossman 1998). It is the most widely distributed of the New World vultures and breeds from southern Canada to as far south as the Straits of Magellan in southern Argentina. There are three subspecies recognized in North America, and the one inhabiting Ontario, *C. a. septentrionalis*, breeds in eastern North America west to Minnesota, Kansas, Oklahoma, and eastern Texas (Palmer 1988).

Distribution and population status: Except in the extreme southwest, the Turkey Vulture was rare in Ontario until the late 19th century (McIlwraith 1894). By the 1950s, it occurred sparingly north to the Southern Shield, and its range expansion continued during the first atlas with records from the Sudbury area and northwestern Ontario.

Distribution has increased dramatically since the first atlas, with more than a doubling of the species' probability of observation province-wide. Increases occurred in all regions except the Hudson Bay Lowlands, where it is absent as a breeder. Sightings are particularly prevalent along the 725-km length of the Niagara Escarpment, which attracts the Turkey Vulture with its thermals and ready accessibility of numerous nest sites. The most dramatic increase was in the Northern Shield region where there was a fourfold increase; the northward expansion is evident on the breeding evidence map. Gaps in distribution noted in the first atlas have been filled, notably in eastern Ontario, Prince Edward Co., the area between Toronto and Stratford, and even the heavily forested Algonquin Highlands. Since vultures are wide ranging, some of the observations may have been of non-breeding birds. Nonetheless, the increase is pronounced, and the map is likely an accurate reflection of this species' range in Ontario. Since the first atlas,

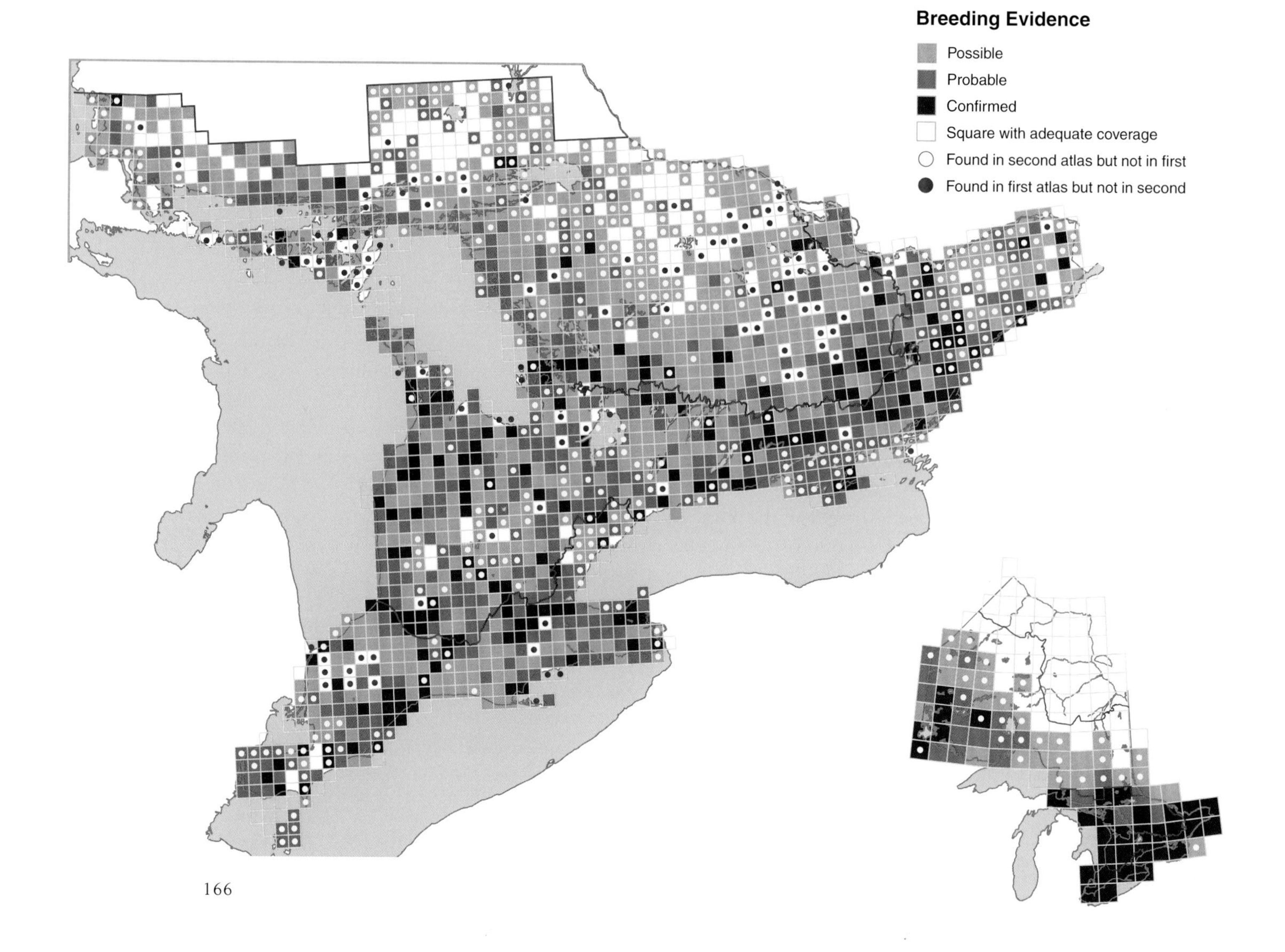

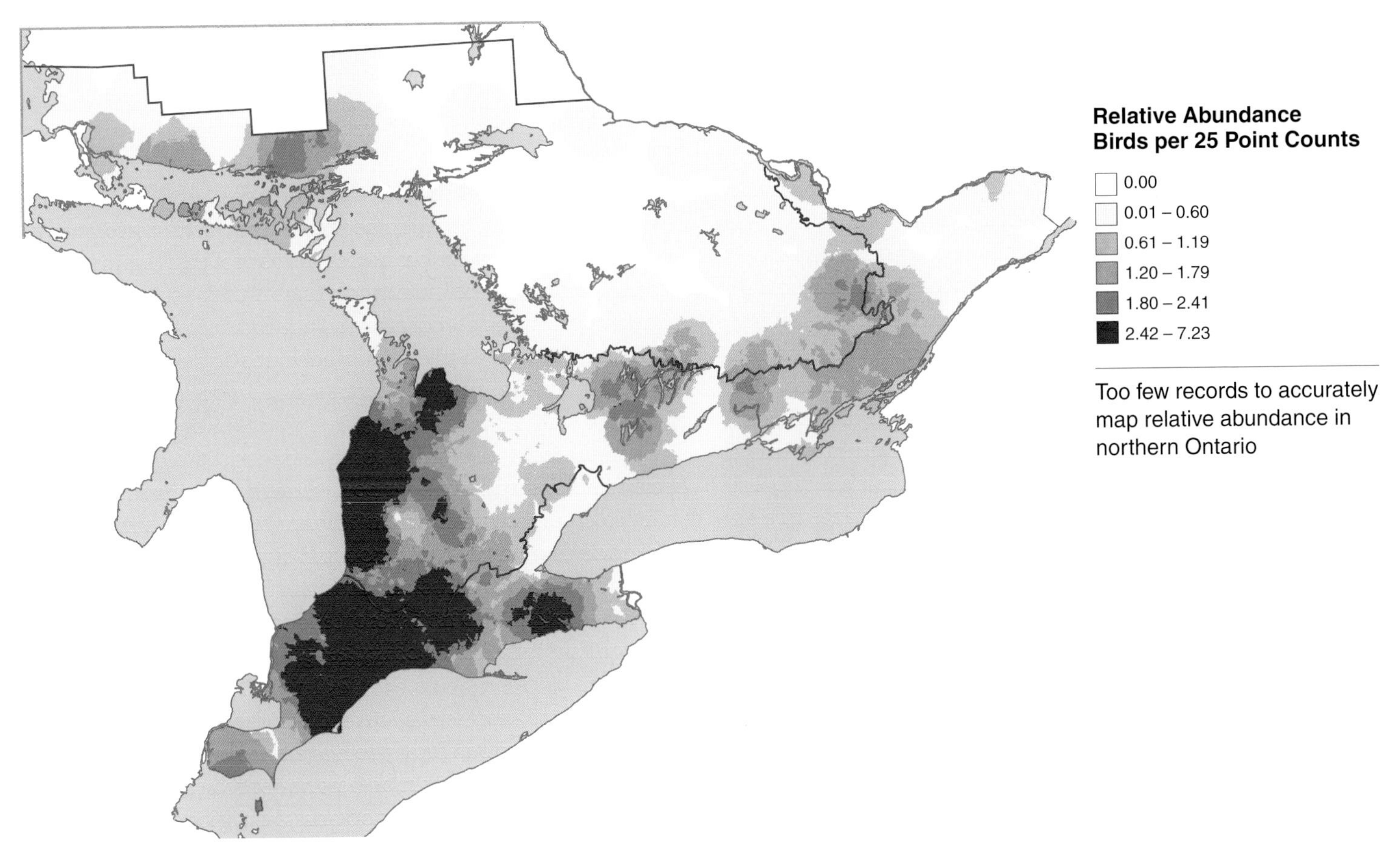

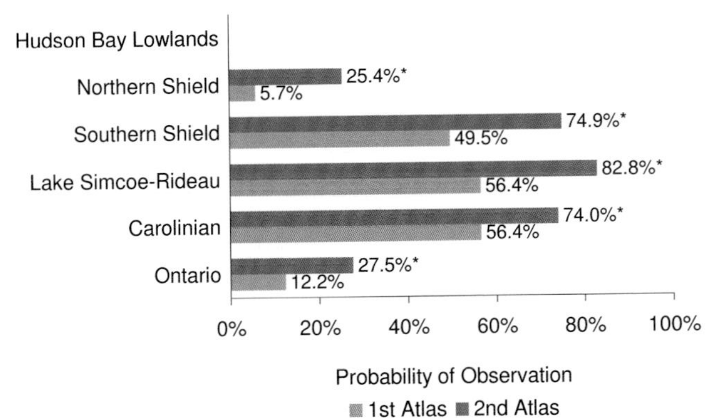

new regional nest records, especially in southeastern Ontario, serve to indicate continuing breeding expansion.

The population increase is occurring throughout northeastern North America and has been attributed to warming trends, increases in deer populations, forest clearing, and, most importantly, more roads with higher traffic volumes, providing more roadkills (Bagg and Parker 1951; Wilbur 1983).

Breeding biology: The Turkey Vulture nests in a wide variety of habitats but prefers agricultural landscapes interspersed with forest to provide sources of carrion and nest sites (Kirk and Mossman 1998). It nests on cliff ledges, in crevices and caves, and among boulders on talus slopes and rocky outcroppings of shield and escarpment areas; in deciduous and mixed woodlands where nests are situated in standing hollow trees and stumps and hollow fallen logs and on the ground beside logs and piled wood; and in abandoned buildings. Although rock sites formerly outnumbered woodland and building sites, since 1989, 46% of reported Ontario nests were in buildings, 35% were in rock sites, and 19% were in logs or stumps in woodlands (ONRS data; Peck 2003b). This species prefers to nest in darkness where there is seclusion from predators and humans (Kirk and Mossman 1998); these criteria are often better realized in abandoned buildings where nests are usually located under floorboards or in dark lofts.

The eggs are placed on bare rock, ground, or boards and occasionally on dead vegetation. Clutch size is most commonly two eggs (Peck 2003b). Ontario egg dates range from 1 May to 20 July, with the height of the season ranging from 20 May to 3 June. The incubation period has been reported as 28-41 days, with the longest estimates most reliable (Jackson 1983). Nestlings remain in or near the nest for at least 52-70 days, and the first flight usually occurs at 60-70 days. Undisturbed nest sites may be used for several years.

Abundance: The highest density occurred in ideal habitat in southwestern Ontario, the warmest area of the province, dominated by agriculture with scattered woodlots. Although the breeding evidence map shows that the species expanded considerably in eastern Ontario between atlases, the abundance map reveals that the species is very thinly distributed there in comparison to the southwest. The same is true in northwestern Ontario, where despite considerable expansion, relative abundance is very low away from the Rainy River area. There is a marked drop in abundance at the southern edge of the Shield, presumably because there is less open agricultural land on the Shield. – *George K. Peck*

Osprey

Balbuzard pêcheur

Pandion haliaetus

John Reaume

Osprey populations declined across much of eastern North America during the organochlorine pesticide era from the mid-1940s to the early 1970s (Ewins 1997). Since then, the species has made an amazing recovery. An Osprey hovering or diving for fish is once again a common sight around lakes, rivers, and ocean coastlines within the forested and subarctic regions of North America from Alaska and northern California to Newfoundland and along the eastern seaboard of the US to Florida (Poole et al. 2002). Outside this continent, migratory breeding populations occur from Scotland to Japan, and resident populations are found in the Middle East and Australasia (Poole et al. 2002).

Distribution and population status: Atlas data suggest a wide distribution across the province, from Cornwall to Kenora and Pelee Island to Polar Bear Prov. Park. The probability of observation of the Osprey is about 30-40% in the Lake Simcoe-Rideau, Southern Shield, and Northern Shield regions, but it is comparatively less widespread in the Carolinian region (2%). The probability of observation is highest in the Hudson Bay Lowlands (47%), where the species is found nesting primarily along rivers emptying into Hudson Bay and James Bay. Within the Southern and Northern Shield regions, it is distributed relatively uniformly. Within the Lake Simcoe-Rideau region, the largest concentration of squares with breeding evidence coincides with the edge of the Shield, from Georgian Bay to Lake Simcoe through the Kawartha Lakes to the Rideau Lakes. In the southwestern and southeastern extremes of the province, distribution may be limited by the supply of shallow, relatively clear water bodies for fishing, available nest sites, and human activity, although the Osprey generally appears to habituate well to the latter.

Between the two atlases, there was no significant change in the probability of observation across the province as a whole, or within the three northern regions. However, a significant

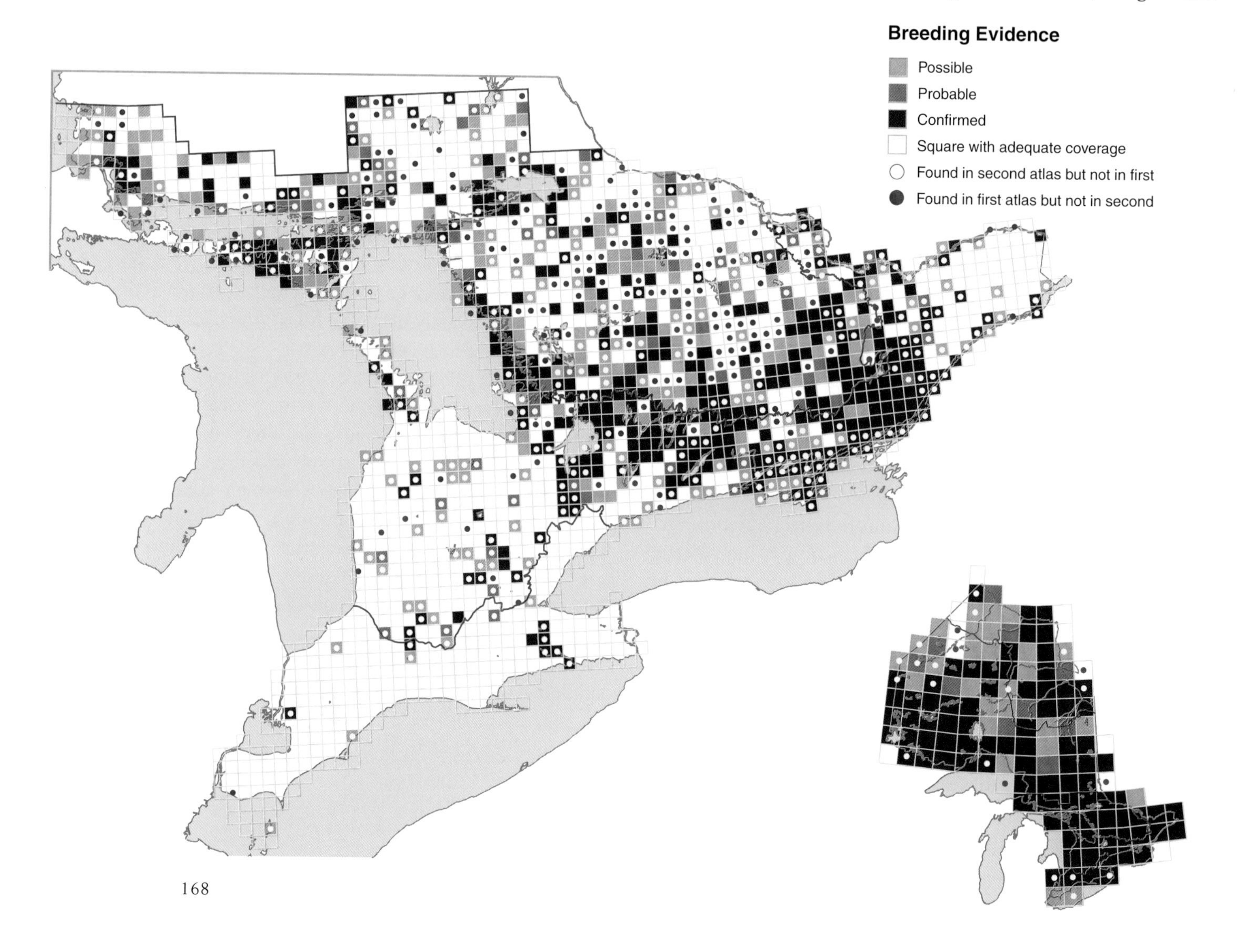

BREEDING EVIDENCE

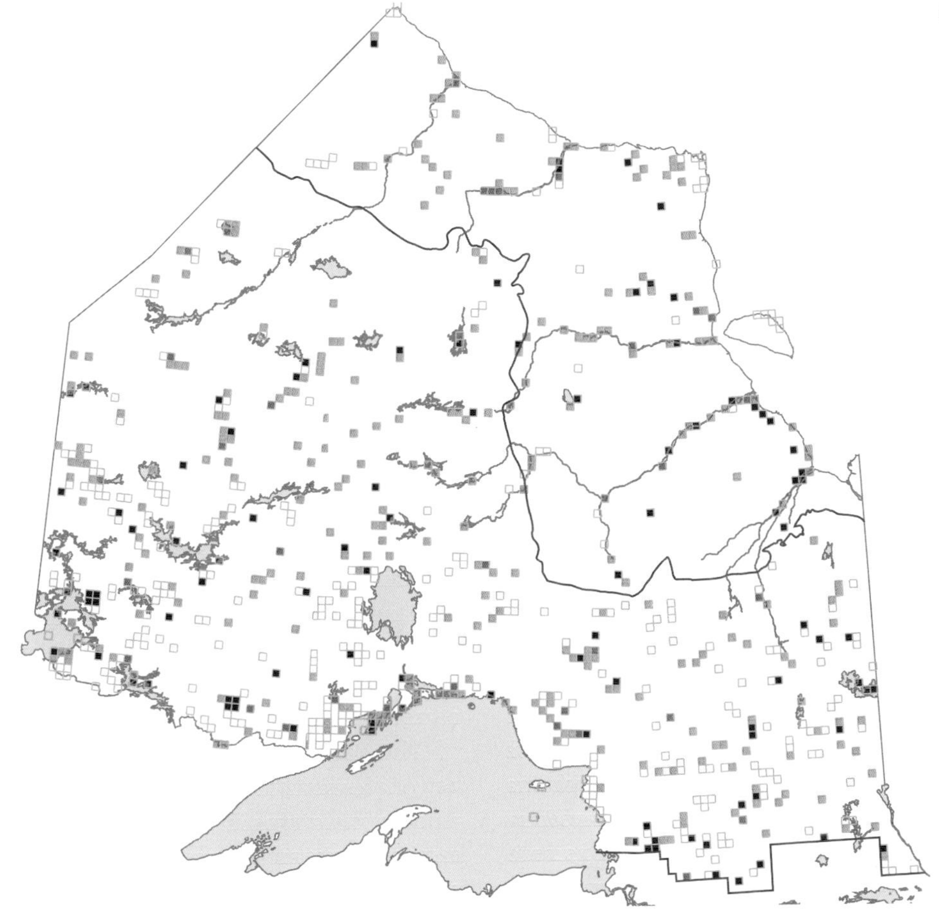

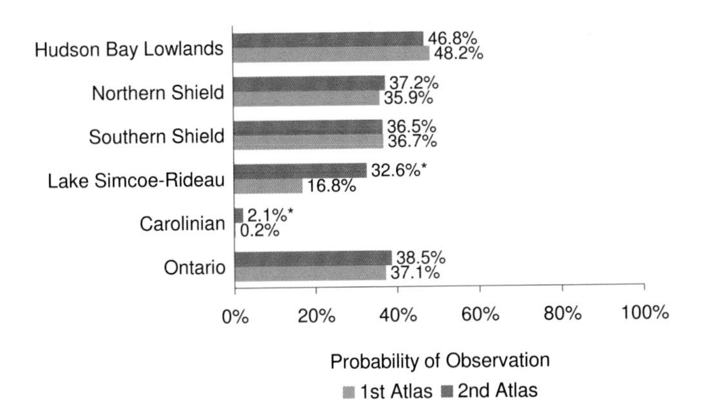

southern and eastern shift in range led to a dramatic increase in probability of observation in both the Carolinian and Lake Simcoe-Rideau regions. This increase may reflect greater availability and use of artificial structures for nesting (e.g., utility poles and towers, nesting platforms) and perhaps increased tolerance of human activities (Ewins 1997).

In the Southern Shield, a large number of squares showed breeding evidence for the first time, but an equivalent number of squares became unoccupied. Forestry activities are unlikely to have been the cause, since buffers have been used routinely to protect nests since the mid-1980s (Szuba and Naylor 1998). Although the Osprey shows high nest-site fidelity, its propensity for nesting in dead trees results in a fairly high turnover rate of nests (Poole 1989). This may be partly responsible for the change in occupancy status of individual squares.

Breeding biology: The Osprey builds a large, bulky nest (1-2.5 m in diameter) of sticks in dead trees, living trees with dead tops, utility poles or towers, or other structures, usually close to or over water in marshes, swamps, bogs, and flooded areas, on islands, or along shorelines of lakes and rivers (Peck and James 1983). It is extremely adaptable, catching a wide variety of fish in large rivers, lakes, reservoirs, estuaries, and ocean coastlines (Poole et al. 2002). The selection of water bodies for fishing may be influenced by proximity to nests, fish productivity, and factors affecting hunting success such as water transparency and depth (Vana-Miller 1987).

Breeding was confirmed in a relatively high proportion of squares (43%). This is not surprising, since nests are very conspicuous due to their size, typical placement on the top of tall structures, and location in open habitats, and the adults' call is loud and distinctive. Moreover, the timing of conspicuous nesting events coincided well with the atlas survey window. The Osprey typically returns to the breeding range in mid- to late April once waterways are almost ice-free (Sandilands 2005). Median egg dates are 22 May-7 June (Peck and James 1983). A 38-day incubation period and 53-day nestling period (Poole et al. 2002) mean most fledging occurs by mid-August.

Considering the large size and conspicuous habits of this species, the atlas is likely a fairly accurate depiction of its general distribution within the province at the 100-km block level. Although the Osprey typically nests close to water, it may fly more than 10 km from the nest to hunt (Vana-Miller 1987). Thus, squares with possible or probable breeding evidence may not necessarily contain occupied nests.

Abundance: Point counts are an imprecise method for surveying abundance of large birds of prey such as the Osprey, and insufficient records were obtained to provide an abundance map. – *Brian Naylor*

Bald Eagle

Pygargue à tête blanche

Haliaeetus leucocephalus

Eleanor Kee Wellman

Catching sight of a Bald Eagle is a highlight of any outdoor trip. Relatively common in northwestern Ontario and more sparsely distributed elsewhere, the species was designated Endangered in Ontario until very recently. Due to its improving status, it is now designated as Special Concern in northern Ontario, while still Endangered in Ontario south of the French-Mattawa Rivers.

The Bald Eagle is broadly distributed across North America, nesting continuously across the northern continent from Alaska to Newfoundland and south along the Rocky Mountain chain in the western US, with a discontinuous distribution within the continental US (Buehler 2000).

In Ontario, nests are typically found near the shorelines of lakes or large rivers, often on forested islands (Peck and James 1983). During the nesting season the Bald Eagle feeds primarily on fish caught directly, scavenged, or stolen from other species such as Osprey (Buehler 2000).

Distribution and population status: Although never extirpated as a breeding bird in Ontario, the species declined substantially during the mid-20th century from chemical contamination (including DDT), habitat loss, and disturbance. Recovery efforts were focused on the lower Great Lakes, where the population collapse was most severe (McKeane and Weseloh 1993; Laing 2006).The Bald Eagle has since increased substantially in Ontario, mirroring trends across North America (Grier et al. 2003). Although not likely well surveyed by the BBS, Canadian data nonetheless show fluctuating but steadily increasing trends from the early 1970s to present.

The Bald Eagle has experienced a substantially expanded range and increased population since the first atlas, with significant increases in the probability of observation in all regions, and an almost fourfold increase across Ontario. In southern Ontario, distribution is primarily along Lakes Erie and Huron, with scattered sites throughout eastern and southern Ontario. Consistent with the historical record, the Lake

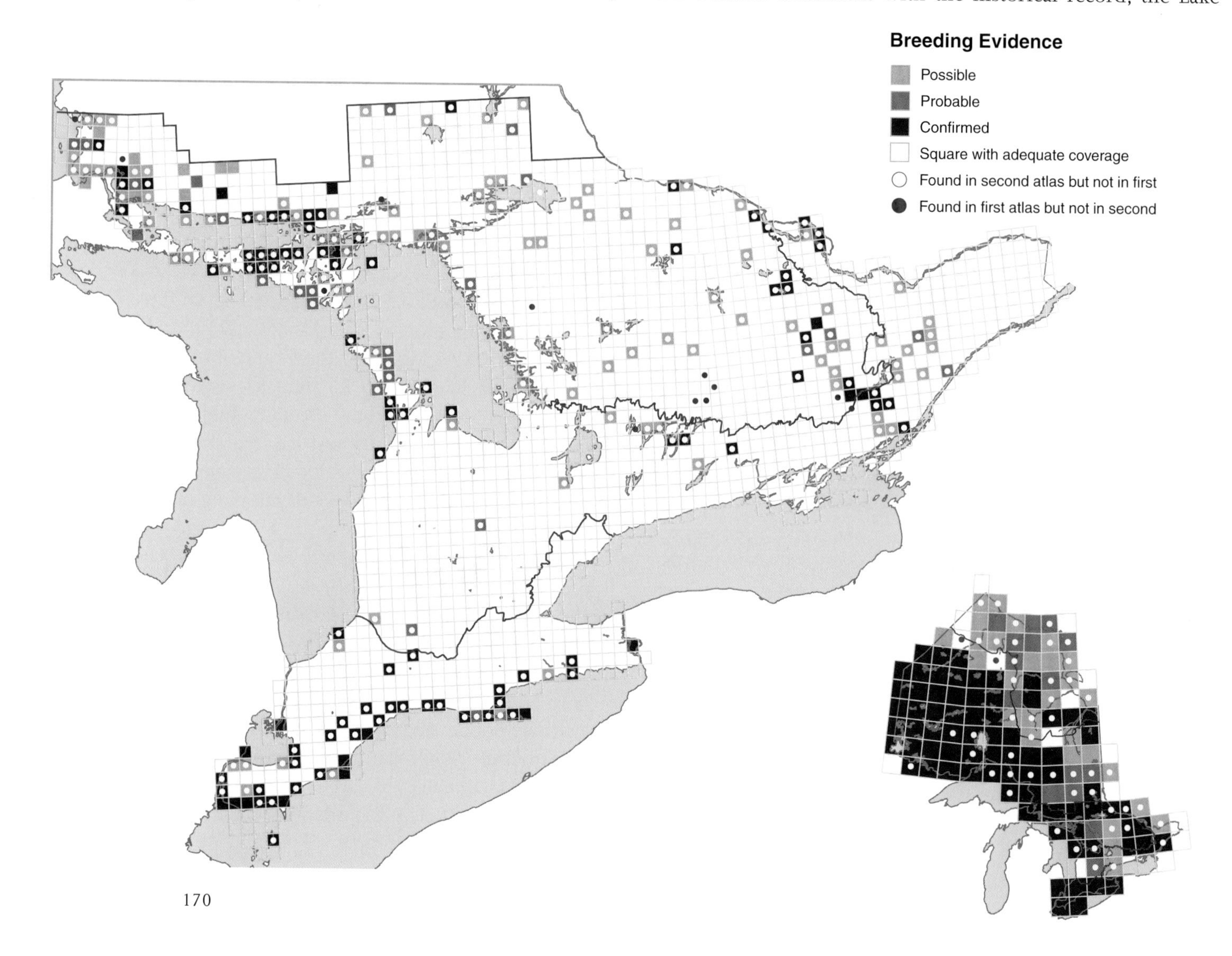

BREEDING EVIDENCE

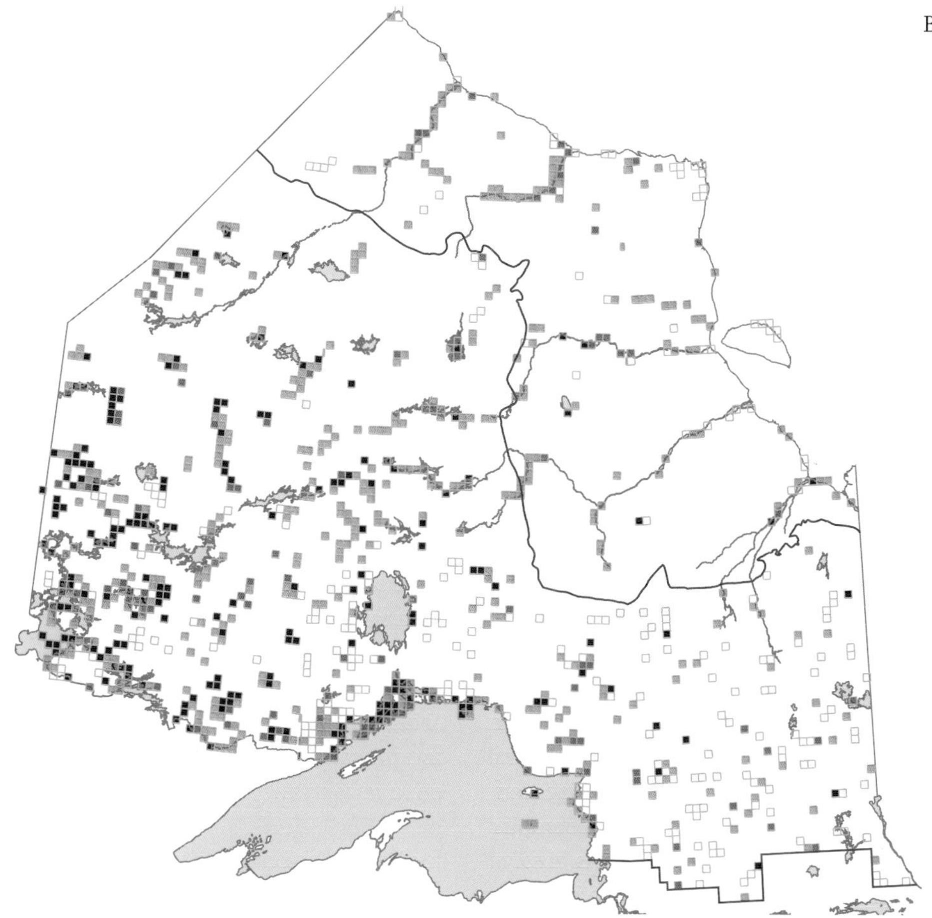

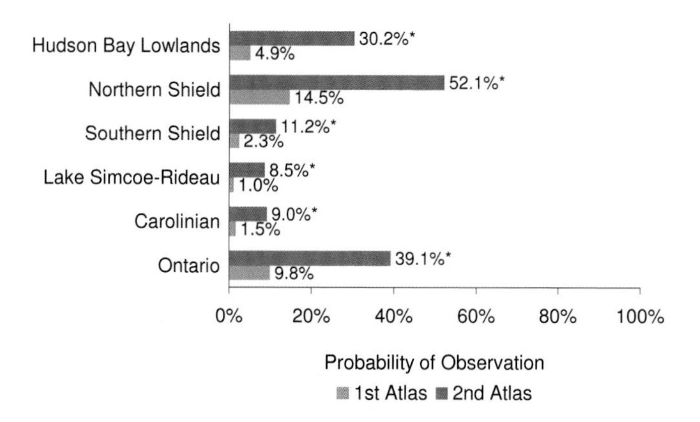

Ontario shoreline remains a major gap in Bald Eagle distribution in southern Ontario. The species is broadly distributed across northern Ontario, with more continuous range in northwestern Ontario coincident with higher populations likely reflecting the higher density of large lakes. Breeding evidence was also reported in many 100-km blocks throughout the Hudson Bay Lowlands, although nesting has never been confirmed in the northern lowlands.

Breeding biology: The large, conspicuous nests of the Bald Eagle, typically in large, "supercanopy" trees along water bodies, are generally easy to locate. Adults are on territory and quite visible from late winter (early February in the south to mid-March in the north) through to late summer. In southern Ontario, many pairs are on territory year-round. Average clutch size is two (range of one to three), and recorded egg dates are from late February to late June (Peck and James 1983, 1993b).

Breeding evidence was reported in almost 1,000 squares. Because this raptor has such a large home range, some observations of birds in suitable habitat may reflect foraging or other territorial movements from adjacent squares, as well as non-breeders. Fledged young may similarly move from the breeding square, although they typically continue to be associated with the nest site until August (Sandilands 2005).

The Bald Eagle shows strong fidelity to nest sites, which are often used from year to year. Nests are refurbished and augmented annually, and there are often both active and alternate nests in the territory (Buehler 2000).

While the Bald Eagle in the northern part of its range typically moves southward in winter, it does not travel along established migratory routes, and birds have a tendency to wander widely after breeding (Sandilands 2005).

Abundance: Atlas data reflect a real increase in both extent of range and populations. Highest densities occur in the Lake of the Woods area in northwestern Ontario, where it appears that the habitat is saturated and at carrying capacity (Grier et al. 2003). The minimum number of active nests in Ontario from 1990 to 1998 rose from 719 to 1,193, an increase of 65% in less than a decade (Grier et al. 2003).

It is clear that the Bald Eagle is still increasing in numbers and range. This increase is most dramatic in the Carolinian and Lake Simcoe-Rideau regions, where the number of squares with breeding evidence increased from 15 to 125. Long-term monitoring of the lower Great Lakes has shown similar trends, with the number of active territories rising from three in 1980 to 43 in 2005 (Laing 2006). Bald Eagle recovery is well advanced in Ontario, and this species is now firmly re-established as a top predator in Ontario's avian community.
– Ted (E.R.) Armstrong

Northern Harrier

Busard Saint-Martin

Circus cyaneus

Mark Peck

The Northern Harrier is the diurnal counterpart of the Short-eared Owl and the only hawk that regularly nests on the ground in Ontario. It is an open-country species, nesting on tundra and in wetlands and grasslands. In Ontario, it typically requires a minimum of 30 ha of suitable nesting habitat (Ontario Ministry of Natural Resources 2000) and may need 250 (Cadman 1993) to 640 ha (Ontario Ministry of Natural Resources 2000) of suitable foraging habitat. Walk and Warner (1999) estimated that it needed 55 ha of nesting habitat in Illinois. The species is highly dependent upon the Meadow Vole for food, and the number of nesting harriers is directly proportional to vole density. When vole populations are low, areas that supported breeding harriers during vole peaks may be devoid of harriers (Clark 1972; Hamerstrom 1979, 1986; Simmons and Smith 1985). The Northern Harrier also breeds in Eurasia. In North America, it breeds from northern Alaska, the Yukon, and all of the provinces south to New England and northern Texas and New Mexico (MacWhirter and Bildstein 1996).

Distribution and population status: This raptor undoubtedly benefited from forest clearing and was considered the most common hawk in Ontario by Baillie and Harrington (1936), who concluded that it bred throughout the province.

The breeding range of the species was similar during both atlases. It is a widespread breeder along the northern coast and in the southern agricultural regions of the province. Breeding also occurs to a lesser extent on the Shield, but it is limited there by the scarcity of large open habitats. There was no significant change in the probability of observation between atlases province-wide. There were, however, significant declines in the Lake Simcoe-Rideau (7%) and Southern Shield (27%) regions. These declines were offset by a significant 37% increase in the Hudson Bay Lowlands. The increase in the north may be a result

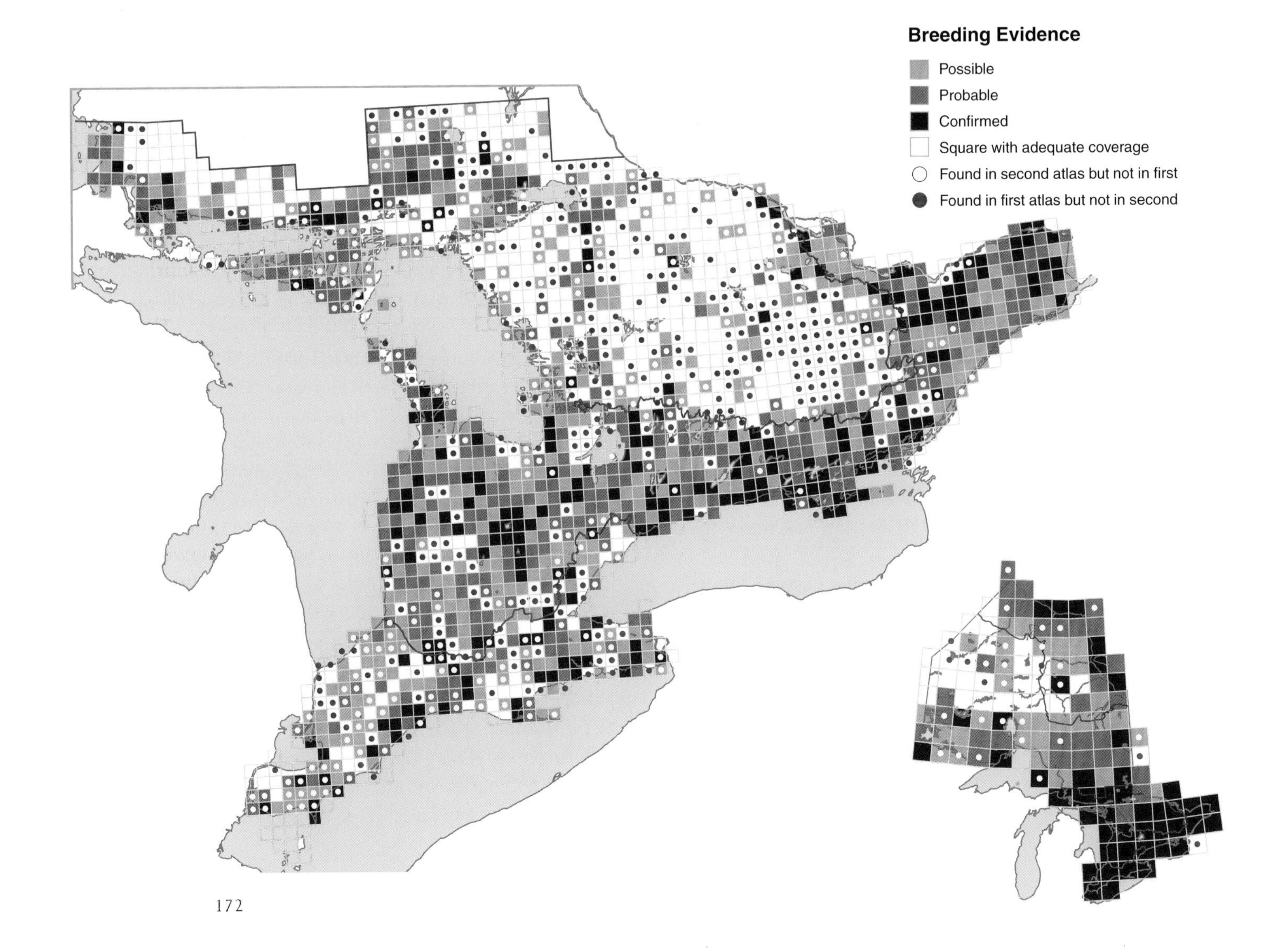

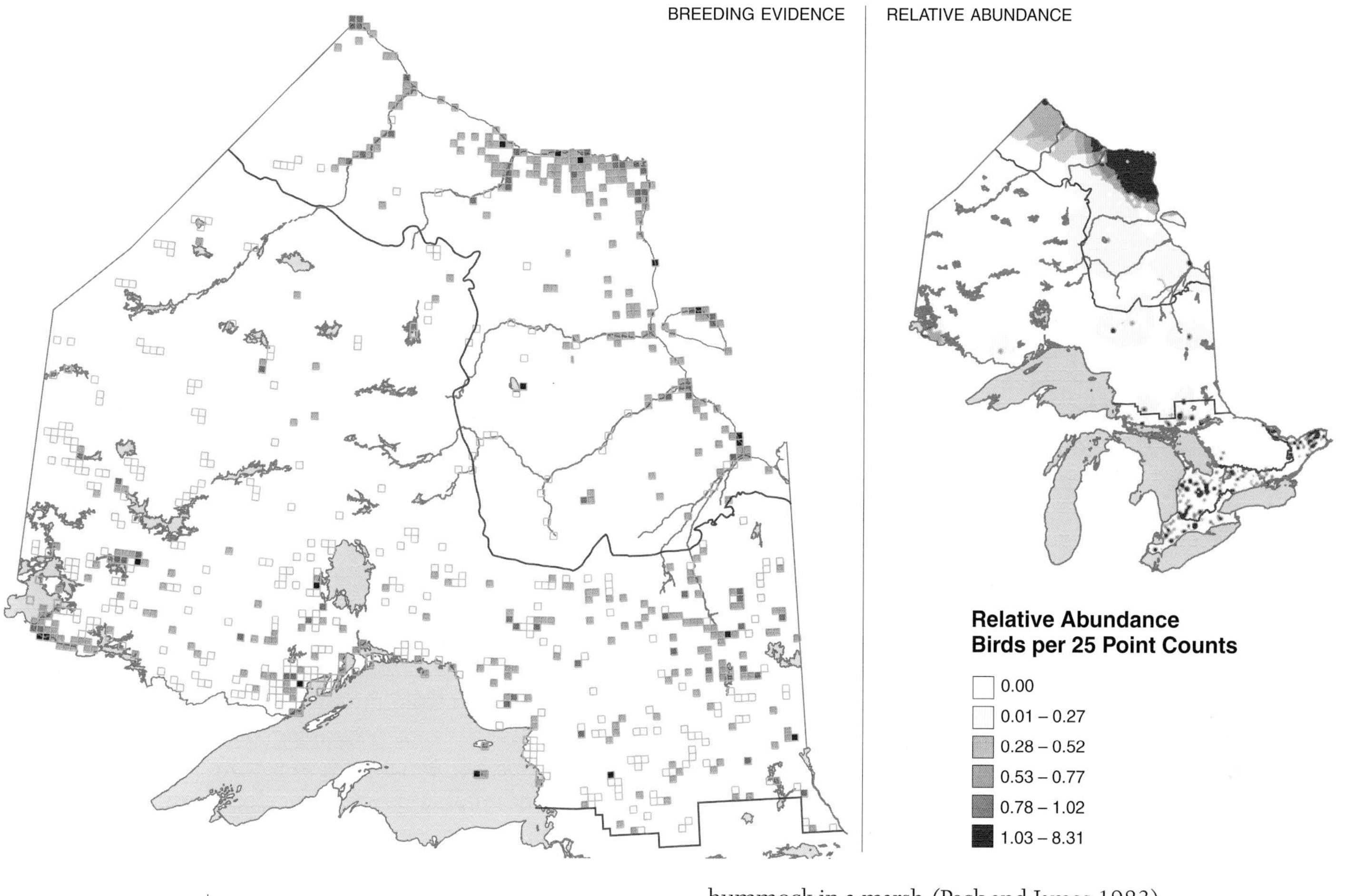

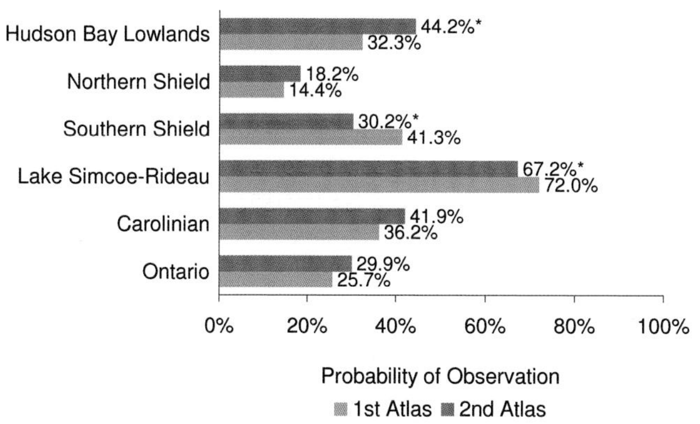

of more efficient coverage during the second atlas, or even a reflection of vole populations. The declines in the Southern Shield and Lake Simcoe-Rideau regions are probably real and may be related to succession of open areas to more shrubby or treed habitat.

BBS data indicate a significant decline in Canada, which has intensified from a rate of 1.8% annually from 1968-2005 to 3.3% from 1981-2005. In Ontario, numbers are erratic from 1981-2005 but show a near-significant annual increase of 3.0% from 1968 to 2005 (Downes et al. 2005).

Breeding biology: Most harriers arrive in Ontario by late April and initiate nesting shortly thereafter. Early in the nesting season, males perform conspicuous aerial displays. The harrier's preferred nesting areas include open wetlands such as marshes, bogs, fens, and open swamps, and large grassy areas such as meadows, pastures, and hayfields. Less frequently, it nests in abandoned gravel pits, hydro rights-of-way, open deciduous woodlands, and young coniferous plantations. Nests are placed on the ground or on a hummock in a marsh (Peck and James 1983).

This species is not strongly territorial and may nest semi-colonially. Cadman (1993) reported four nests in a 0.8-1.2 ha marsh in Niagara Region. Although true colonial nesting occurs, most grouping of nests is due to polygyny. Higher numbers of males are polygynous when prey is abundant (MacWhirter and Bildstein 1996).

Although nests are in open areas, they can be difficult to find, as adults are secretive in approaching them. Eggs may hatch from late May to mid-July. The optimum time to confirm breeding is during the nestling and early fledgling periods, when adults may be observed carrying food to the young. The young remain within the nesting territory until they are about two months old, providing ample time to see recently fledged young or adults carrying food.

Abundance: The most extensive area of high abundance of the Northern Harrier is in the narrow tundra zone along the Hudson Bay coast. In the Northern and Southern Shield regions, there are notable concentrations in the Sudbury and Rainy River areas, reflecting the more open habitat there. Apart from the Sudbury and Sault Ste. Marie areas and the agricultural areas of Rainy River Dist., the species was virtually undetected on point counts on the Shield. South and east of the Shield, highest concentrations are in the less intensively farmed areas of northern Wellington and Dufferin Counties and the United Counties of Prescott and Russell. The harrier appears to be a common breeder along the Hudson Bay coast, locally uncommon on the remainder of the Hudson Bay Lowlands and south and east of the Shield, and absent to locally rare or uncommon on the Shield. *– Al Sandilands*

Sharp-shinned Hawk

Épervier brun

Accipiter striatus

Jim Richards

The smallest of the North American accipiters, the Sharp-shinned Hawk is a fairly common though secretive woodland raptor. Its breeding range extends across most of Canada below the treeline and as far south as northern Argentina (Bildstein and Meyer 2000). In response to significant population declines associated with organochlorine pesticides, it was placed on the Blue List in 1972 (Tate and Tate 1982) but has since rebounded and is no longer considered at risk (Kirk 1997).

Distribution and population status: At the time of the first atlas, the province's Sharp-shinned Hawk population was believed to be stable, but at a lower level than in the 19th century, when it was considered common in southern Ontario (McIlwraith 1894). Historically, there was little evidence of nesting in northern Ontario (Peck and James 1983), but this may have been partly a function of limited search effort.

Although the probability of observation of the Sharp-shinned Hawk did not change as a whole between atlases, it increased significantly in the southernmost two regions and there was a significant range shift to the south. The growth was particularly dramatic in the Carolinian, with an approximately fourfold increase. A significant 68% increase also occurred in Lake Simcoe-Rideau region; however, there were also many squares in this region where the species was recorded only in the first atlas. There was no significant change in the probability of observation for the three northern regions.

The increase in the Sharp-shinned Hawk population is consistent with the pattern for most diurnal raptors. As a group, they have benefited from the ban on DDT in the 1970s and a general increase in concern for their conservation, including a dramatic reduction in shooting since the middle of the 20th century (Bildstein and Meyer 2000). The Sharp-shinned Hawk is also among several raptors that have successfully adapted to living in suburban habitats over the past two decades

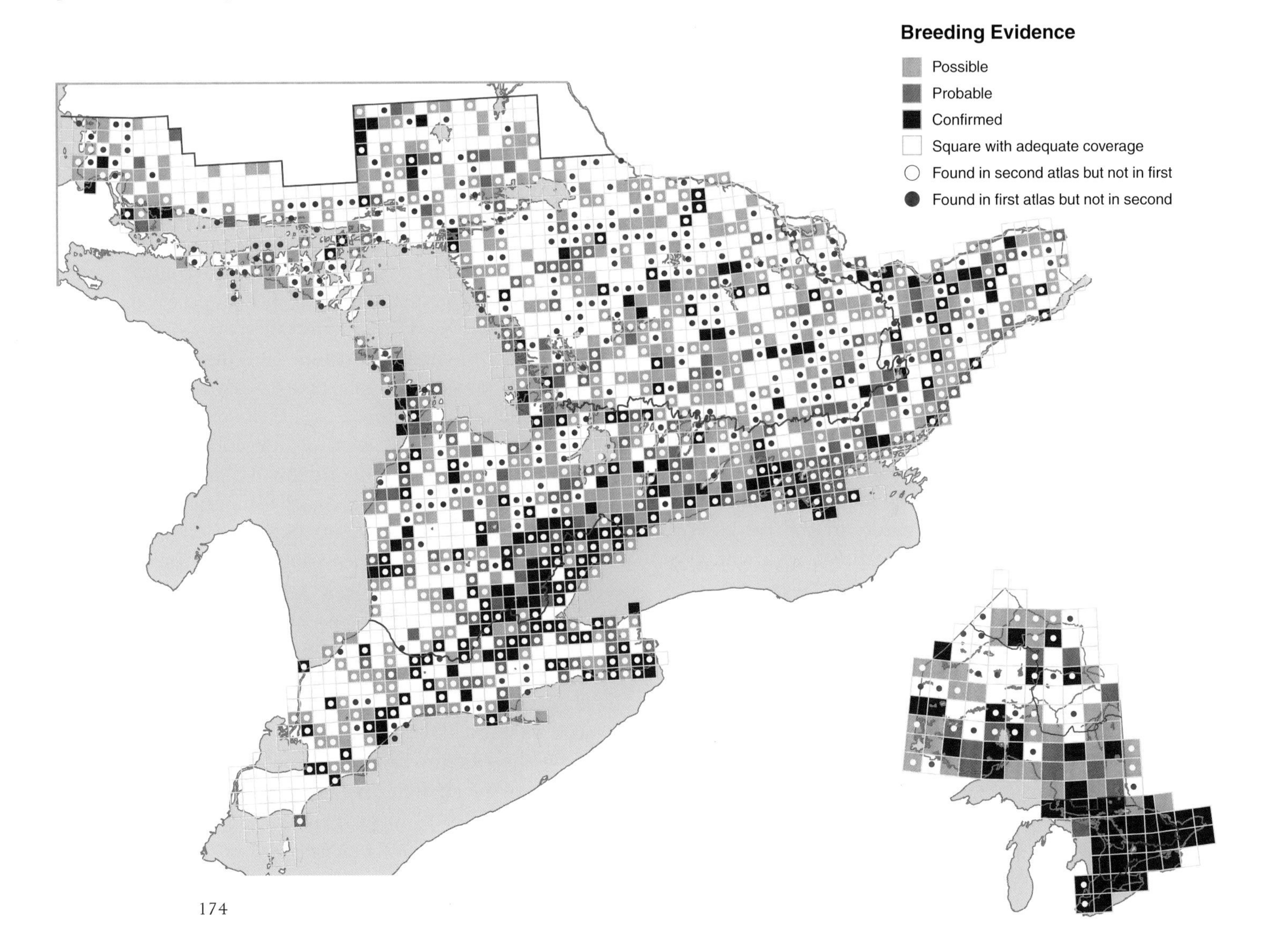

BREEDING EVIDENCE

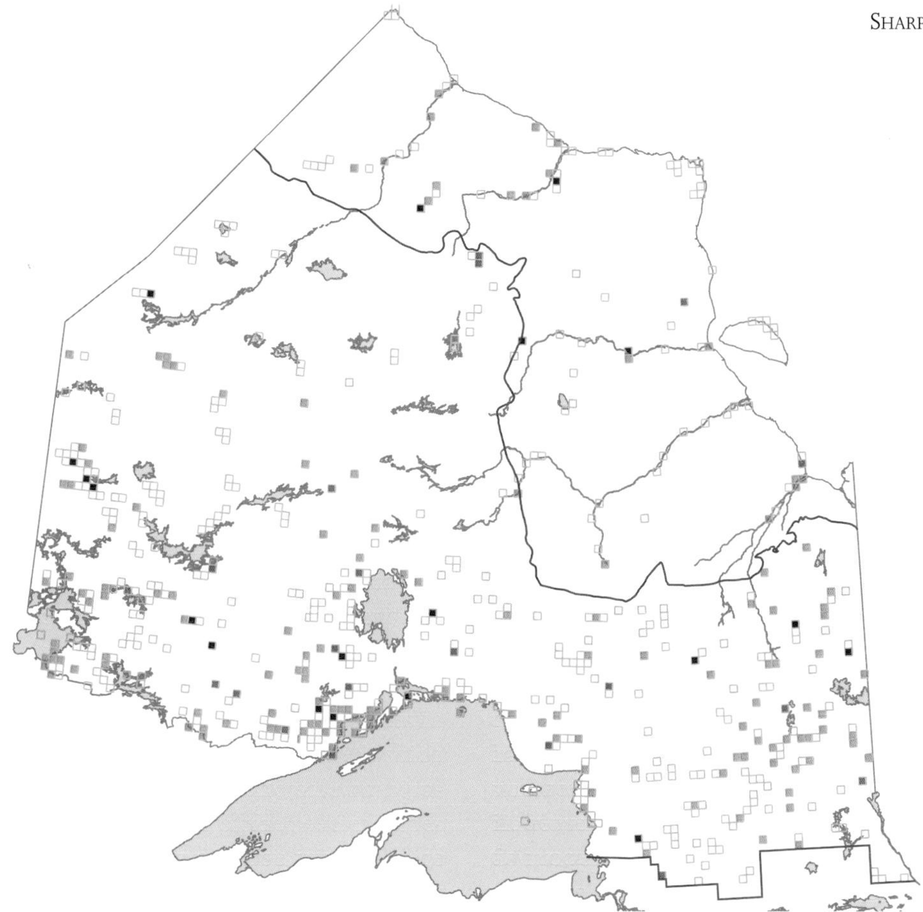

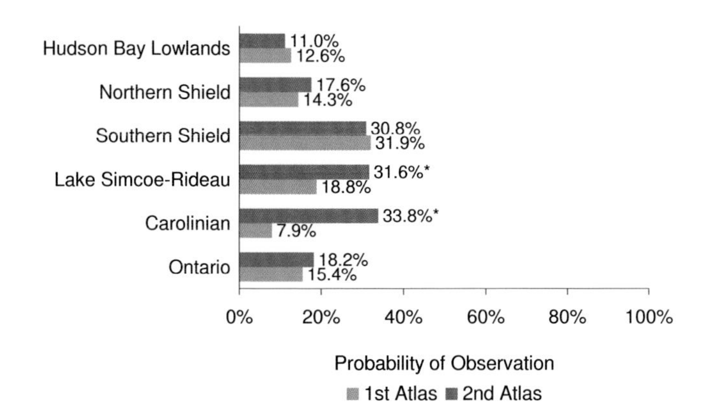

(Coleman et al. 2002). The population expansion in southern Ontario may also be linked to the increase in forest cover since the first atlas, and possibly related to the maturation of coniferous plantations.

Population trends for the Sharp-shinned Hawk are difficult to assess accurately due to its secretive nature, which severely limits the reliability of BBS data. Many raptor migration observatories record large numbers of the species, especially in fall, and their data can provide some indication of overall population trends. However, they do not allow for accurate assessment of specific breeding populations (Bildstein and Meyer 2000). Additional caution must be taken in interpreting migration data, as noticeable declines in numbers of migrants at key migration sites in the 1980s and 1990s were associated with a concurrent increase in birds overwintering in the northern range (Duncan 1996). Rather than declining, the Sharp-shinned Hawk population may be stable or even increasing and simply adjusting its winter distribution in response to the increased affinity for hunting at backyard birdfeeders.

Breeding biology: The Sharp-shinned Hawk usually breeds in dense woods, often favouring conifer stands. Nests are fairly broad, flat, twig platforms, sometimes lined with bits of bark. An inconspicuous species at most times, it is particularly so near its nest. Detecting breeding is easiest in early spring, as the birds are most vocal during nest-building. Once the young fledge, they may be fairly vocal when calling for food. However, the Sharp-shinned Hawk is a relatively late breeder, with young usually fledging in July (Bildstein and Meyer 2000) after the peak of atlassing, and the nest is typically small and located high in a coniferous tree in dense forest and hard to locate. In nearly two-thirds of squares reporting the Sharp-shinned Hawk, it was recorded only as a possible breeder, with confirmation in just 21% of squares. It is therefore likely that the atlas considerably underestimates the distribution and abundance of the species in Ontario. The apparent high rate of turnover in the Southern Shield, where the Sharp-shinned Hawk was documented in many squares on only one of the two atlases, may actually reflect a situation where the species was present but undetected in many squares during both periods, as many atlassers encountered it only fortuitously.

Abundance: Given the species' secretive behaviour, there were insufficient records on point counts to permit an abundance map to be generated. The Sharp-shinned Hawk was considered uncommon in the first atlas. Its extensive breeding distribution suggests that it is now fairly common in southern Ontario and may be relatively common and widespread also in northern Ontario. – *Marcel A. Gahbauer*

Cooper's Hawk

Épervier de Cooper

Accipiter cooperii

Jim Richards

Like other accipiters, the Cooper's Hawk is primarily a forest bird, but in much of its range it has increasingly tended to occupy more open, human-altered habitats. Intermediate in size between the Sharp-shinned Hawk and Northern Goshawk, it is often misidentified. The species has the most southerly distribution of the North American accipiters, breeding across most of southern Canada and as far south as Mexico; it is generally more common in the western part of its range (Curtis et al. 2006). It declined significantly during the middle of the 20th century throughout much of its range as a result of organochlorine pesticide use, becoming classified as at risk in many jurisdictions (Curtis et al. 2006). Placed on the Blue List in 1972, it was already increasing by the early 1980s and is no longer considered at risk (Kirk 1996).

Distribution and population status: Historically, the Cooper's Hawk was a scarce and local breeder in Ontario, considered rare as recently as three decades ago (James et al. 1976). The first atlas revealed a scattered but fairly sizable population, primarily in southern Ontario, with breeding evidence in 345 squares province-wide. This increased to 725 squares in the second atlas, although the overall increase in probability of observation was not significant. The expansion is due to significant increases in the probability of observation within the Carolinian (more than tenfold) and Lake Simcoe-Rideau (nearly fourfold) regions, where the species now occurs in a large number of squares, especially along Lakes Erie and Ontario. However, in the Southern Shield, the probability of observation declined significantly by 35%. There was no significant change in the Northern Shield, where it was observed in only a small number of squares. Both the northern and southern edges of the species' range in Ontario have shifted significantly to the south.

BBS data also indicate a non-significant increase from 1981 to 2005, but do show a sharp upturn since 1990. Other North

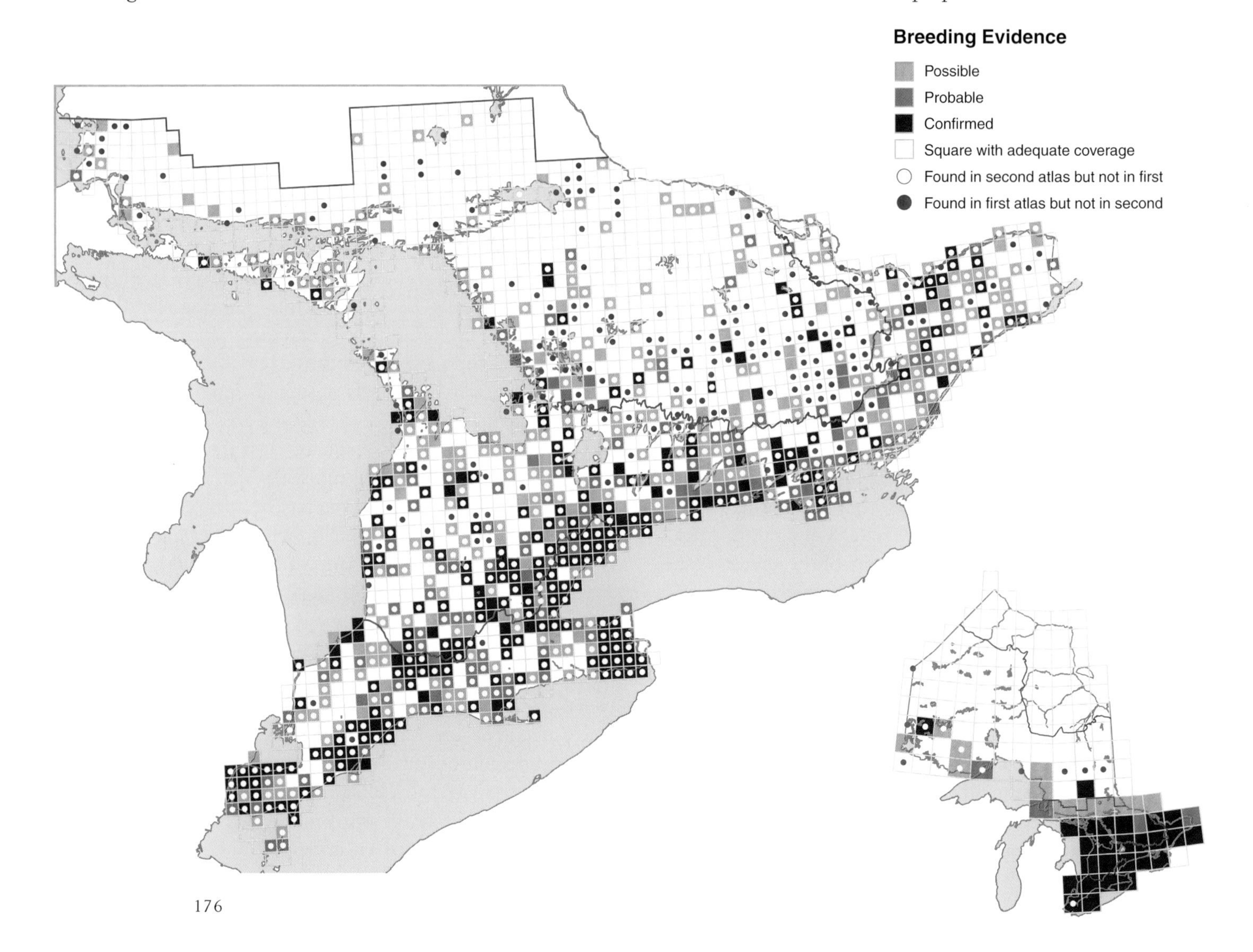

BREEDING EVIDENCE

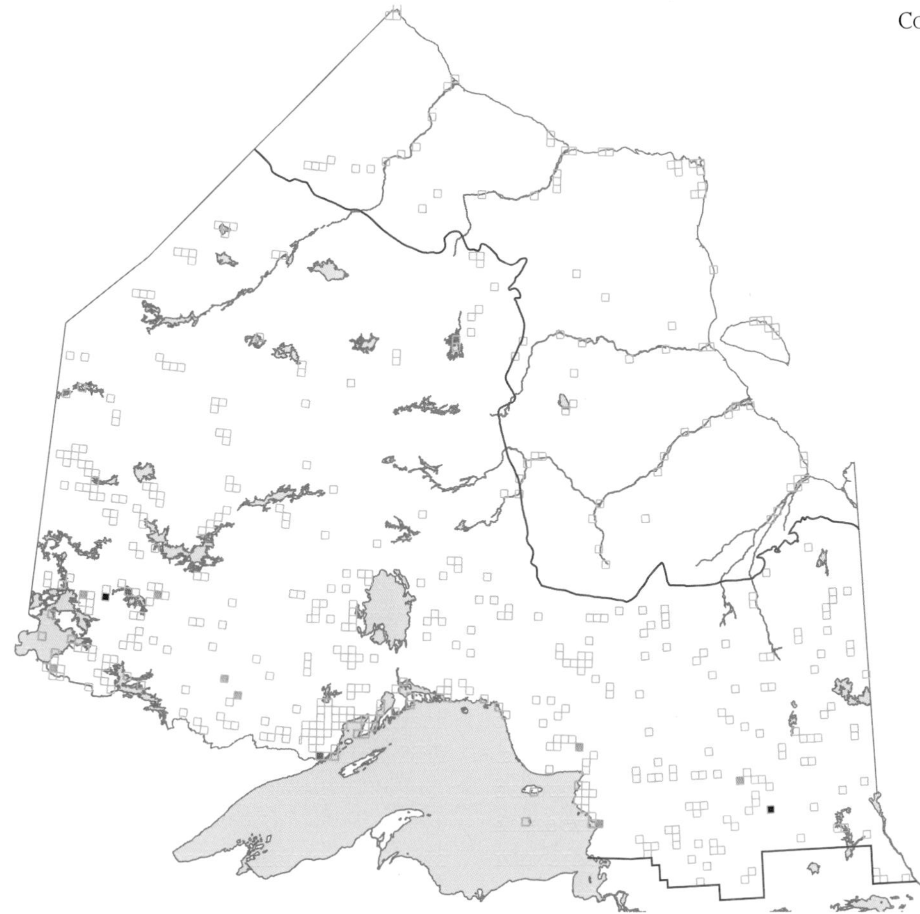

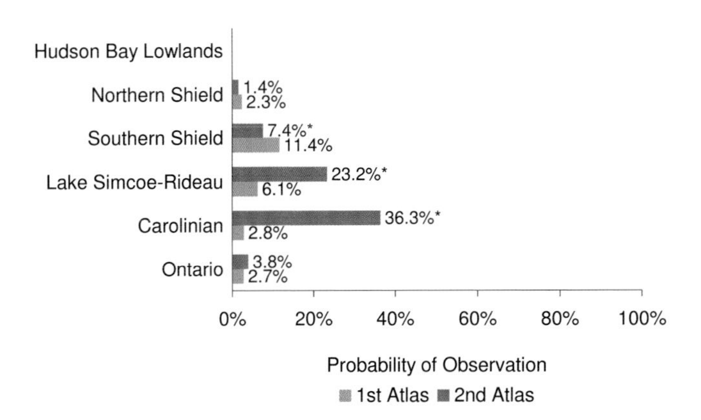

American populations of the Cooper's Hawk have also increased in the last 15 years, in conjunction with its moving into urban areas, where it breeds at higher densities than in natural habitats (Mannan and Boal 2000; Curtis et al. 2006). The earlier stabilization and subsequent rebound of the population was probably rooted at least partly in the ban on DDT imposed in the early 1970s, as well as in a growing interest in protecting raptors.

While several raptor species have moved into urban areas in recent decades, the Cooper's Hawk has been among the most successful. Its range expansion in the Carolinian region has been concentrated around cities, including the Greater Toronto Area, Hamilton, Kitchener-Waterloo, and London. In Windsor and surrounding Essex Co., where forest cover is particularly scarce, the closely related Sharp-shinned Hawk remains virtually absent, while the Cooper's Hawk was recorded in almost every square, despite its absence from the area during the first atlas. Whereas the populations of both species were once limited by the availability of dense forest, the Cooper's Hawk has taken advantage of the abundance of avian prey in cities and adapted its nesting preferences accordingly. The decline of the Southern Shield population may therefore represent a southward shift of birds into more urban and suburban habitats with more abundant prey. Maturing pine plantations have provided additional nesting habitat and probably helped the species to increase south of the Shield outside of urban areas where increases have also been substantial.

Breeding biology: While the Cooper's Hawk is increasingly found in cities, it continues to prefer nesting in relatively dense woods, though these need not be large in area. The nest is a broad, flat platform of twigs, occasionally built atop a smaller old nest. For most of the breeding season, the adults are extremely quiet and secretive in the vicinity of the nest. The species is most easily detected during two relatively vocal periods: April courtship and July fledging. Since both periods are rather brief and fall outside the peak atlassing period, it is likely that this hawk is somewhat under-represented in the atlas.

Abundance: The Cooper's Hawk was considered uncommon in Ontario during the first atlas period. Although point count data reveal notable concentrations around Toronto, central Elgin Co., and Essex Co., point counts are generally an ineffective means of surveying an inconspicuous forest raptor. The breeding evidence data suggest that in southern Ontario the Cooper's Hawk would more accurately be classified as fairly common, and even locally common around some urban centres. – *Marcel A. Gahbauer*

Northern Goshawk

Autour des palombes

Accipiter gentilis

Jim Richards

The Northern Goshawk is the largest of the accipiters or "true hawks," averaging 60 cm in length (Squires and Reynolds 1997). Readily distinguished by size, grey plumage, and prominent white eye-stripe, the adults are imposing birds, aggressive, even fearless, in defence of the nest.

The Northern Goshawk has a holarctic distribution, occurring throughout much of the boreal and temperate forested regions of North America and Europe. In North America, it occurs from Alaska to the US northeast, south in the west, primarily at higher elevations, to Mexico (Squires and Reynolds 1997). It is a permanent resident throughout much of its range, vacating breeding areas in winter only during periods of low prey abundance. Typically only a proportion of the population migrates (primarily sub-adults), but occasional large irruptions, coincident with crashes in the species' principal prey, involve adult males and females (Squires and Reynolds 1997).

Distribution and population status: The Northern Goshawk occurs widely but sparsely in all forested regions of Ontario. In the second atlas, it occurred most frequently in the Lake Simcoe-Rideau and Southern Shield regions where the probability of observation was 10% and 12%, respectively. The species was even more sparsely distributed in the Carolinian, Northern Shield, and Hudson Bay Lowlands regions. The low probability of observation in the province overall is likely a reflection of the species' relatively large home range (up to 3500 ha; Squires and Reynolds 1997) and low densities. The limited distribution in the southwestern portion of the province is due to the more limited forest cover and small forest fragment size.

Across the province, there was a non-significant decline of 40% in the probability of observation for the Northern Goshawk between atlases, with a significant 54% decline in the Northern Shield. While the reasons for the decline are unclear, natural cycles in principal prey species and a reduction in the

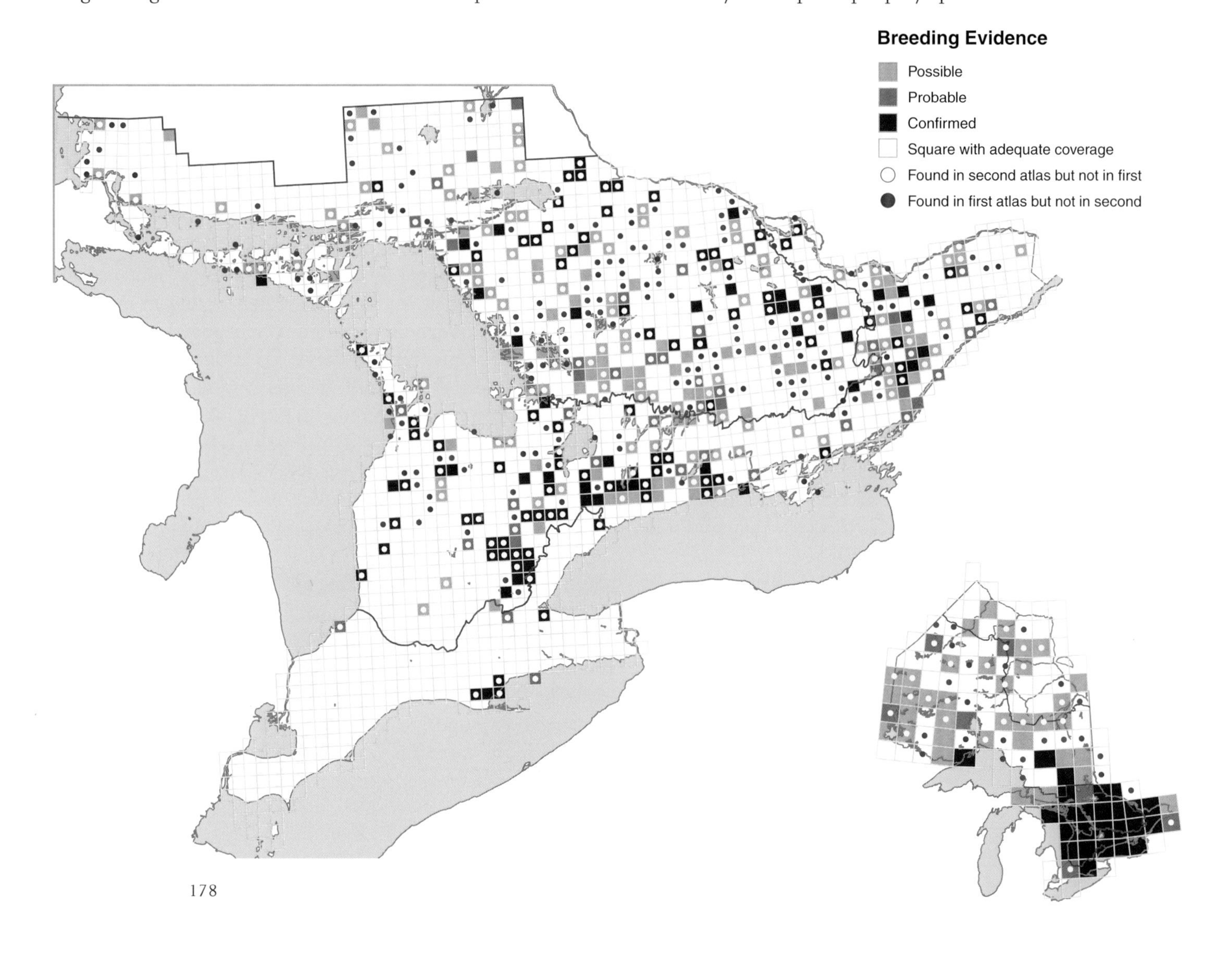

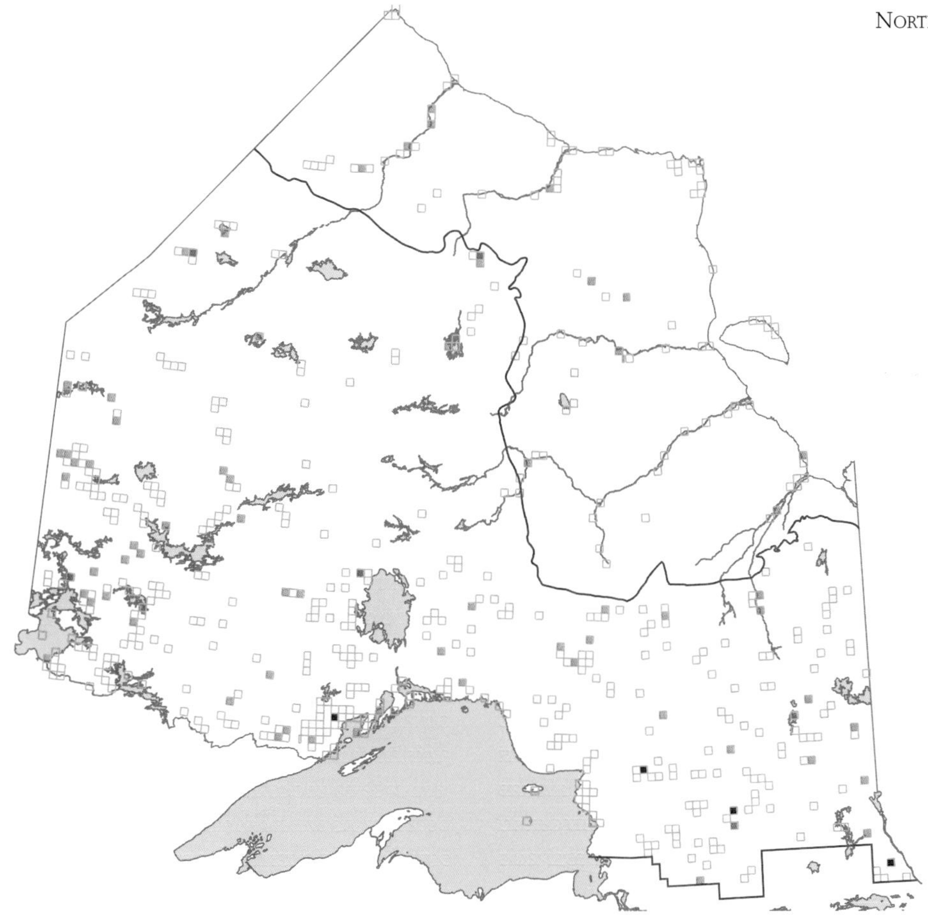

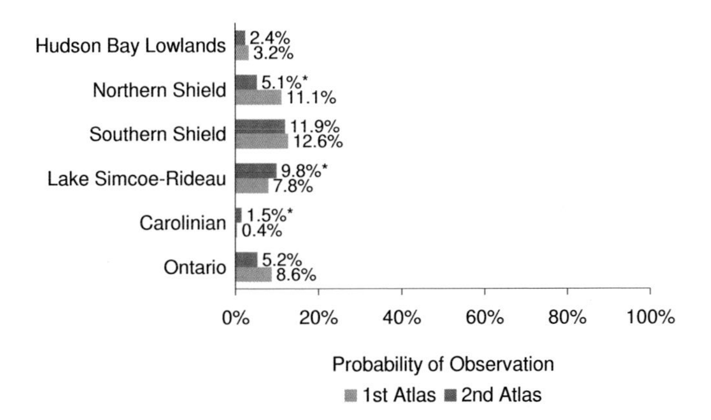

supply of the mature mixed boreal forest habitat offer possible explanations. Significant increases in the probability of observation in both the Carolinian and Lake Simcoe-Rideau regions may be attributable to an expanding source population, and the maturation of forests, including coniferous plantations, in parts of southern Ontario and particularly in the Carolinian where the species is known in only a small number of squares.

Breeding biology: The Northern Goshawk nests in forested areas that are well stocked with larger-diameter trees, fewer smaller-diameter trees, high canopy closure, and generally low ground and shrub cover (Bush 2006). In Ontario, preferred habitat is dominated by White Pine, Red Pine, tolerant hardwoods, and intolerant-mixed woods (Bush 2006), and includes a mosaic of forest types and ages supporting its primary prey (Snowshoe Hare, Ruffed Grouse, Spruce Grouse, and Red Squirrel; pers. obs.). Although larger forest blocks may be preferred for nesting, fragments as small as 12 ha may be suitable (B.J. Naylor, pers. comm.). The species shows strong nest-site fidelity, using the same nest over successive years or alternative nests within 100-300 m of the old nest (Squires and Reynolds 1997; Hautala 2004). In central Ontario, it nests primarily in deciduous trees and seems to prefer aspen (Peck and James 1983).

The Northern Goshawk is secretive and infrequently observed during much of the year. It is most difficult to observe during the early stages of nesting, particularly during egg laying and incubation. Egg laying takes place from mid-April to mid-May and incubation lasts approximately 30-44 days (Kennedy 2003); detection is most difficult during the incubation period. Nonetheless, most records (56%) were of possible breeding, likely reflecting observations of single birds in suitable habitat. Birds aggressively defend the nest site during nest building and rearing of young. Adults may intercept intruders at considerable distances from the nest, and highly agitated, vocal, and increasingly aggressive adults easily reveal nest locations. Breeding was confirmed in 32% of squares in which the species was detected.

Abundance: Estimating population size and trends for the Northern Goshawk in Ontario is difficult in part due to the general inaccessibility of much of its range, the possible cyclic nature of populations, and its partial migratory status. There were too few detections on point counts to produce an abundance map. Based on partial migration data from goshawk invasion years, however, the northern Ontario population was estimated by Duncan and Kirk (1994) at fewer than 5,000 pairs, while Kirk (1995) suggested that the population in central and southern Ontario is possibly in the range of 500-2,000 pairs. – *Peter G. Bush*

Red-shouldered Hawk

Buse à épaulettes

Buteo lineatus

George K. Peck

The Red-shouldered Hawk is a relatively secretive raptor whose presence is often revealed by its loud "*kee-aah*" vocalizations early in the breeding season. The primary range of the eastern North American breeding population extends from Minnesota to New Brunswick and south to Florida, the Gulf States, and eastern Mexico (Crocoll 1994). The majority of the Canadian population is in southern Ontario, but it also occurs in Québec and New Brunswick. The species was designated Special Concern in Canada by COSEWIC in 1983, and was down-listed to Not at Risk in 2006.

Distribution and population status: Although the Red-shouldered Hawk was observed in substantially more squares in the second atlas, its probability of observation did not change significantly across Ontario; there was, however, a significant 83% increase in the Southern Shield. As in the first atlas, it was found primarily in the Southern Shield and Lake Simcoe-Rideau regions. Distribution in the Carolinian region continues to be limited by lack of suitable habitat; the most southerly record consisted of a nest with young at Rondeau Prov. Park. The species is not found in the Hudson Bay Lowlands and is virtually absent from the Northern Shield (three squares).

There was a significant northward shift in the northern edge of range (34 km) but no change in the southern edge, indicating a northward range expansion. In the Parry Sound, Sudbury, North Channel-Manitoulin Island, Sault Ste. Marie, and Lake of the Woods areas, most squares reporting the Red-shouldered Hawk in the second atlas had no records during the first. Both eastern and western range edges shifted significantly to the west, and the species apparently disappeared from many squares in eastern Ontario, particularly in the Cornwall area. Although the range has expanded overall, Regional Coordinators suggested possible declines for the Long Point, Toronto, and Prince Edward Co. atlas administrative regions.

Observed increases in the probability of observation for this

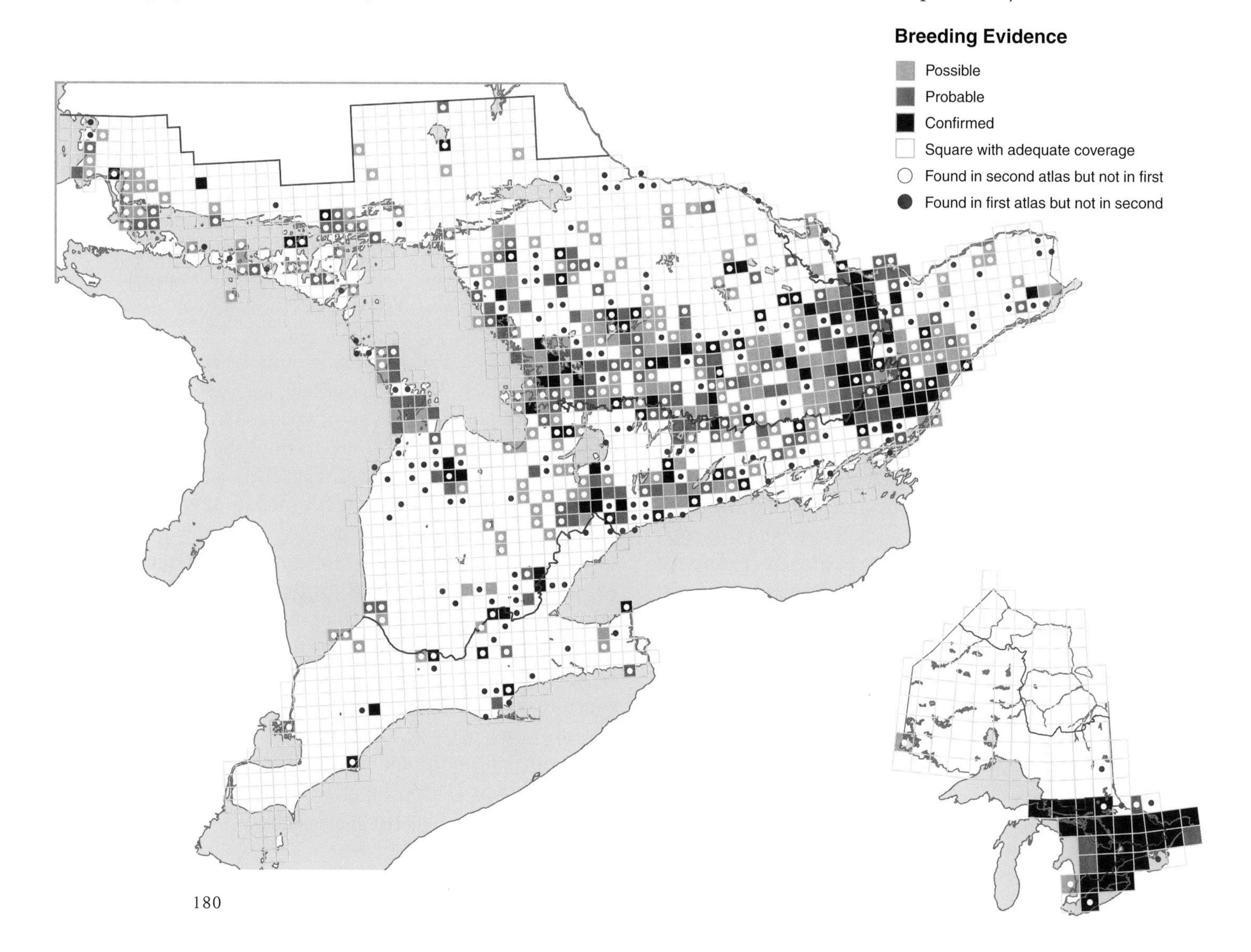

BREEDING EVIDENCE

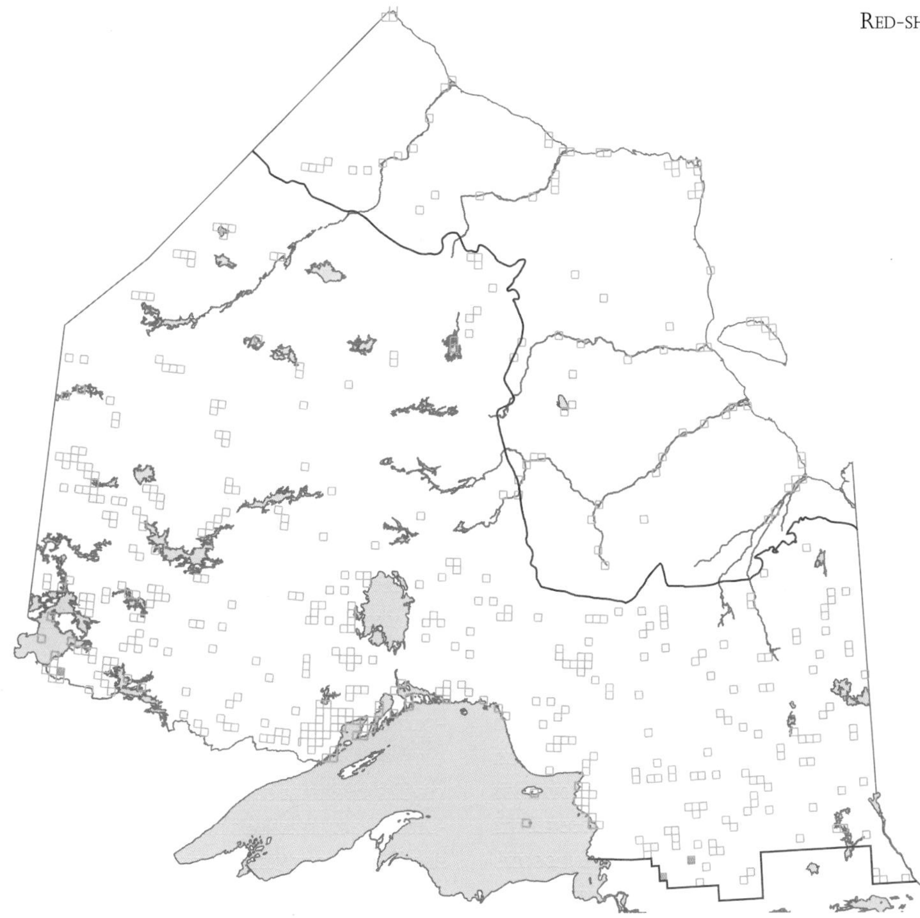

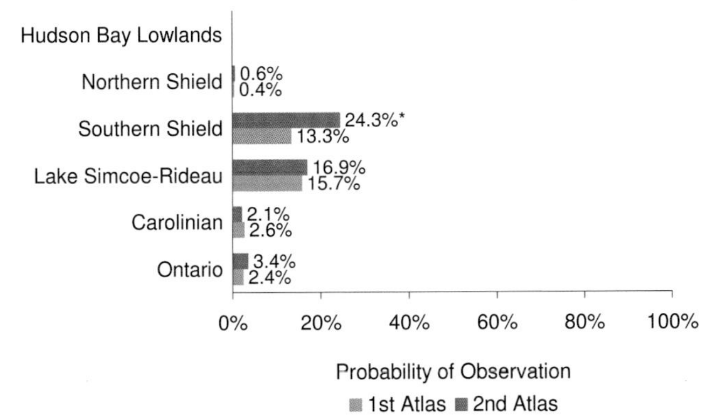

species should be interpreted with caution. A specialized survey for the Red-shouldered Hawk and woodpeckers was implemented in 1991 to monitor this early-breeding raptor (Crewe and Badzinski 2006a). Extensive surveys for nests were conducted on Crown land in the Southern Shield in the late 1980s and early 1990s, with over 100 nests reported, and OMNR and forest companies continue to locate new nests each year to protect habitat and manage long-term habitat supply (Ontario Ministry of Natural Resources 1998; Naylor et al. 1999). Data from these efforts may account for much of the increased detection of breeding evidence for the species. Data from the Red-shouldered Hawk and Spring Woodpecker Survey show that the Red-shouldered Hawk population in Ontario was stable for the period 1991-2005 (Crewe and Badzinski 2006a), and data from migration monitoring stations and checklist programs also suggest a stable or increasing population (COSEWIC 2006b).

A possible range expansion of this hawk in Ontario could be the result of increases in forest cover in some areas and ongoing maturation of existing forest, although overall abundance of the tolerant hardwood forest used by the species has not changed (Ontario Ministry of Natural Resources 2006a). Improved forest management practices may have also benefited this species (Naylor et al. 2004).

Breeding biology: The Red-shouldered Hawk breeds in a broad range of forest types across North America, including bottomland hardwood, riparian areas, flooded deciduous swamps, and upland mixed forest (Sandilands 2005). In Ontario, it is more of a habitat specialist, preferring dense, mature tolerant hardwood forest near wetlands or lakes for nesting (Armstrong and Euler 1983; Naylor and Szuba 1998). Typically area sensitive, it prefers extensive, contiguous, mature to old-growth tracts of upland tolerant hardwoods (Crocoll 1994; Naylor and Szuba 1998; Naylor et al. 2004).

This species has an early breeding season, returning to breeding areas in Ontario in late March, with median egg dates of 20 to 28 April (Peck and James 1983), and thus is poorly monitored by the BBS. Birds are quite vocal and relatively visible during the courtship and pre-incubation period early in spring but relatively inconspicuous thereafter. Nests are typically found in mature forest stands with a wetland or water body nearby (Crocoll 1994). Given these behavioural characteristics and habitat preferences, it is likely that the species was missed by atlassers in many squares.

Abundance: Although this species was detected too infrequently for relative abundance maps to be prepared, data from both the atlas and the Red-shouldered Hawk and Spring Woodpecker Survey suggest it is most abundant in the Southern Shield. Highest abundance appears to be found along the southern edge of the Southern Shield and on the Frontenac Axis. *– Debra S. Badzinski*

Broad-winged Hawk

Petite Buse

Buteo platypterus

Jim Richards

The diminutive Broad-winged Hawk is perhaps more aptly named in French: "little hawk." Smaller in body length than a crow, it is the smallest of the province's buteos. Its size and greater maneuverability make it capable of hunting in denser forest than either the Red-tailed or Red-shouldered Hawk, the other buteos with which it regularly occurs. The combination of broad black-and-white tail bands, white underwings edged with black, bold rust-tipped breast feathers, and shrill whistled call readily distinguishes it from other buteos. It hunts for prey befitting its size, such as frogs, snakes, mice and voles, insects, and small birds, quietly scanning the ground from a perch under the forest canopy, in small forest openings, along wetland edges, or along roadsides (Goodrich et al. 1996).

The Broad-winged Hawk breeds from Alberta to the Maritime Provinces and south to Texas. In autumn, it typically leaves the province in a mass exodus in late September. Incredible numbers pass migration lookouts, particularly along Lake Erie's north shore at sites such as Hawk Cliff and Holiday Beach Conservation Area, where single-day totals in excess of 100,000 individuals have been recorded (Sandilands 2005). The species winters from Mexico and Central America south to Bolivia (Goodrich et al. 1996).

Distribution and population status: In Ontario, the Broad-winged Hawk is primarily a bird of the Shield, where forest cover tends to be dense and relatively continuous. The core of its provincial distribution appears to be the Southern Shield, where the probability of observation was 85%; in the Northern Shield, the probability of observation was somewhat less (46%). Away from the Shield, its distribution is discontinuous or localized. In the Lake Simcoe-Rideau region, the probability of observation was 28% and in the Carolinian, just 8%. In both regions, but especially the Carolinian, this hawk's

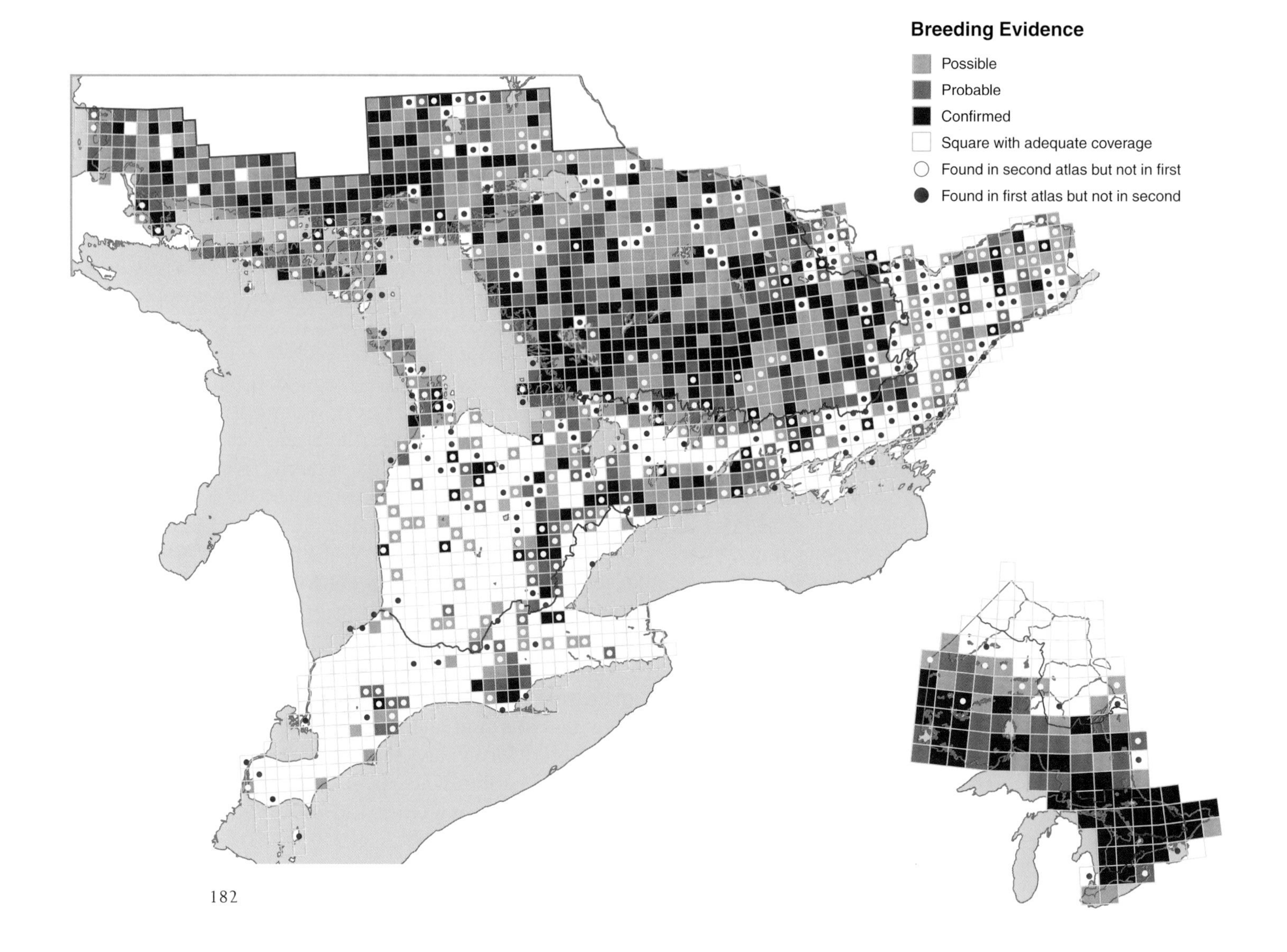

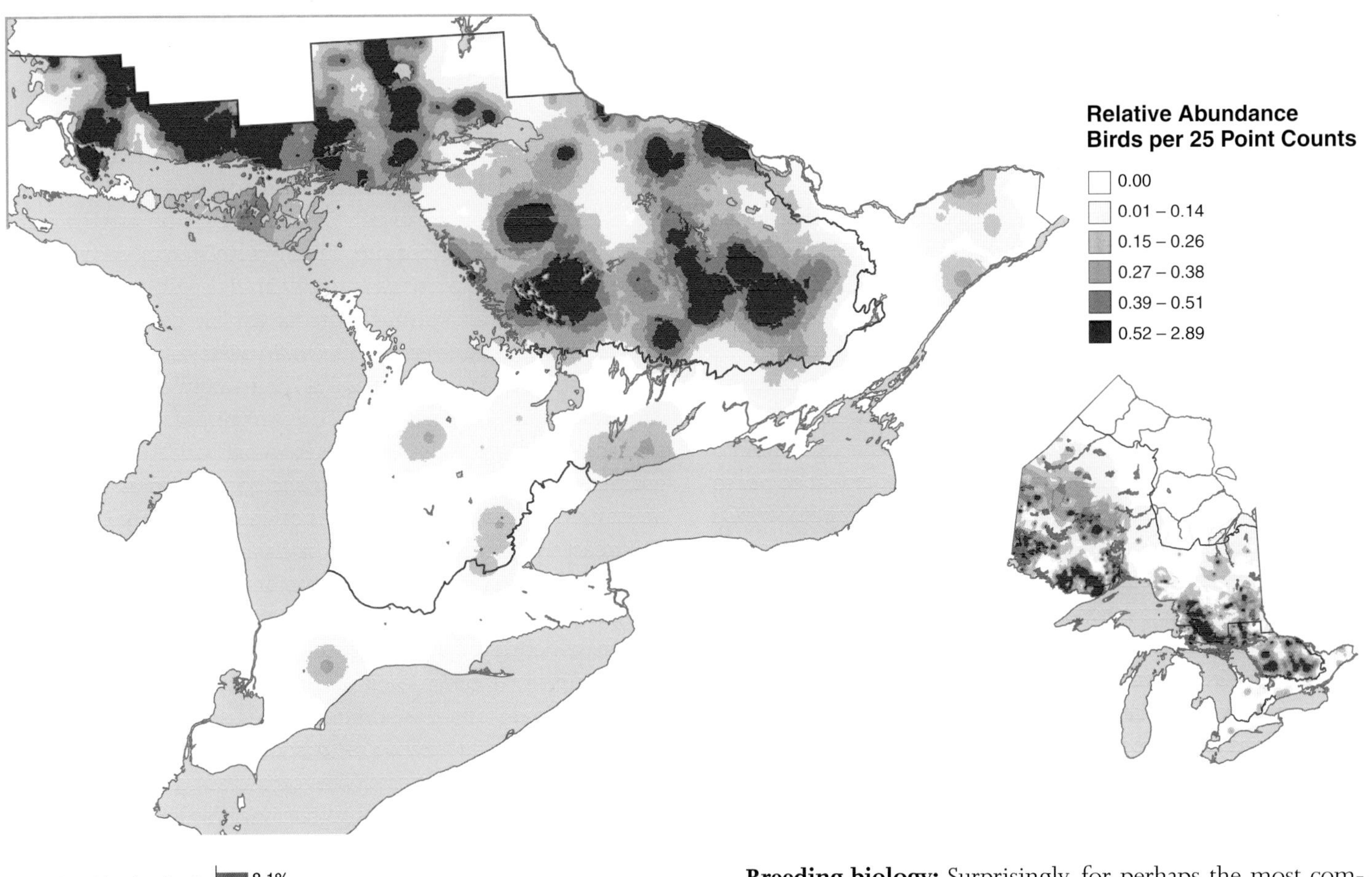

Probability of Observation

Region	1st Atlas	2nd Atlas
Hudson Bay Lowlands	5.5%	8.1%
Northern Shield	39.9%	46.5%
Southern Shield	83.5%	85.1%
Lake Simcoe-Rideau	26.1%	27.7%
Carolinian	6.9%	7.5%
Ontario	32.4%	37.0%

distribution is remarkably well correlated with remaining larger patches of forest cover (Ontario Ministry of Natural Resources 2002). It is virtually absent from the Hudson Bay Lowlands, except for the most southerly reaches. The probability of observation for the province as a whole is among the highest for any raptor at 37%, related no doubt to its habit of perching conspicuously along roadsides and to its distinctive call.

Although Kirk and Hyslop (1998) suggest a possible declining trend across Canada, the distribution of the Broad-winged Hawk in Ontario has not changed appreciably from the first atlas; there was no significant change in the probability of observation in any region or in the province as a whole. Population trends in Ontario from the Red-shouldered Hawk Survey (Crewe and Badzinski 2006a) and BBS were statistically non-significant, although some have questioned the utility of these surveys for the Broad-winged Hawk. A significant annual decline of 5.3%, however, was observed from 1975 to 1990 at the diurnal hawk watch in Grimbsy, Ontario (Hussell and Brown 1992).

Breeding biology: Surprisingly, for perhaps the most common hawk in North America, little is known about aspects of its basic breeding biology and territorial behaviour (Goodrich et al. 1996). The Broad-winged Hawk nests in immature and older hardwood (shade intolerant and tolerant) and mixed forest (Goodrich et al. 1996; Holloway et al. 2004), a broader range of habitat types and ages than those preferred by the Red-shouldered Hawk (Holloway et al. 2004). In Ontario, it arrives and initiates nesting relatively later than other raptors. Egg dates range from 22 April to 2 July, with 50% of the nests containing eggs between 26 May and 10 June (Peck and James 1983).

Although the Broad-winged Hawk may be conspicuous at times, its nest is not. Usually located in the lowest main fork of a hardwood tree, it tends to be rather small and loosely built compared with nests of other buteos (Szuba and Naylor 1998) and is difficult to see when trees are in full leaf, despite the fact that nests are often not far from roads (Rosenfield 1984). Breeding was confirmed in only 19% of the squares surveyed, supporting the contention of Goodrich et al. (1996) that this hawk is secretive when nesting.

Abundance: Atlas maps and point count data suggest the Broad-winged Hawk is widely distributed in forested portions of Ontario but probably most abundant in the Southern Shield region where forest cover and prey abundance are both high (Thompson 2000). The species' relative abundance has probably not changed much since the 1800s, except in the Carolinian region where forest cover has declined greatly. Evidently little has changed since the first atlas, when it was described as "the most common hawk" in various parts of the Northern and Southern Shield regions. – *Kandyd Szuba*

Red-tailed Hawk

Buse à queue rousse
Buteo jamaicensis

Jon Brierley

Many raptors are inconspicuous, but not the Red-tailed Hawk. Its large size, dark belly band, russet tail, unmistakable piercing scream, and habit of perching in the open or soaring high overhead make it one of the most readily observed and identifiable diurnal raptors. This big, handsome bird of the edge prospers where relatively small patches of mature and older forest or fencerows with trees abut large open areas such as fields, meadows, wetlands, burns, or young forest (Preston and Beane 1993; Stout et al. 1998; Sandilands 2005). Tolerant of human development (Bosakowski and Smith 1997), it can be found nesting adjacent to busy highways (Bechard et al. 1990) as well as on power transmission rights-of-way. The species is very broadly distributed across forested and non-forested parts of North and Central America (Preston and Beane 1993), with several recognized subspecies (Preston and Beane 1993).

Distribution and population status: The general distribution of the Red-tailed Hawk in Ontario has not changed perceptibly since the last atlas; it continues to be broadly distributed across all regions. The probability of observation increased by 65% in the Hudson Bay Lowlands, but the difference is not significant. However, there has been a significant 45% increase in the probability of observation in the Northern Shield. In this region, forest management practices that create extensive clearings while retaining residual trees and forest patches (see Watt et al. 1996; Ontario Ministry of Natural Resources 2001) can be expected to benefit edge-loving, perch-hunting raptors such as the Red-tailed Hawk. In the Southern Shield, the probability of observation has remained constant at about 43% but with a striking shift in occupied squares within the region. There are many cases of reverse occupancy (birds found in one atlas but not the other), possibly reflecting the shifting mosaic of early successional forest created by forest management.

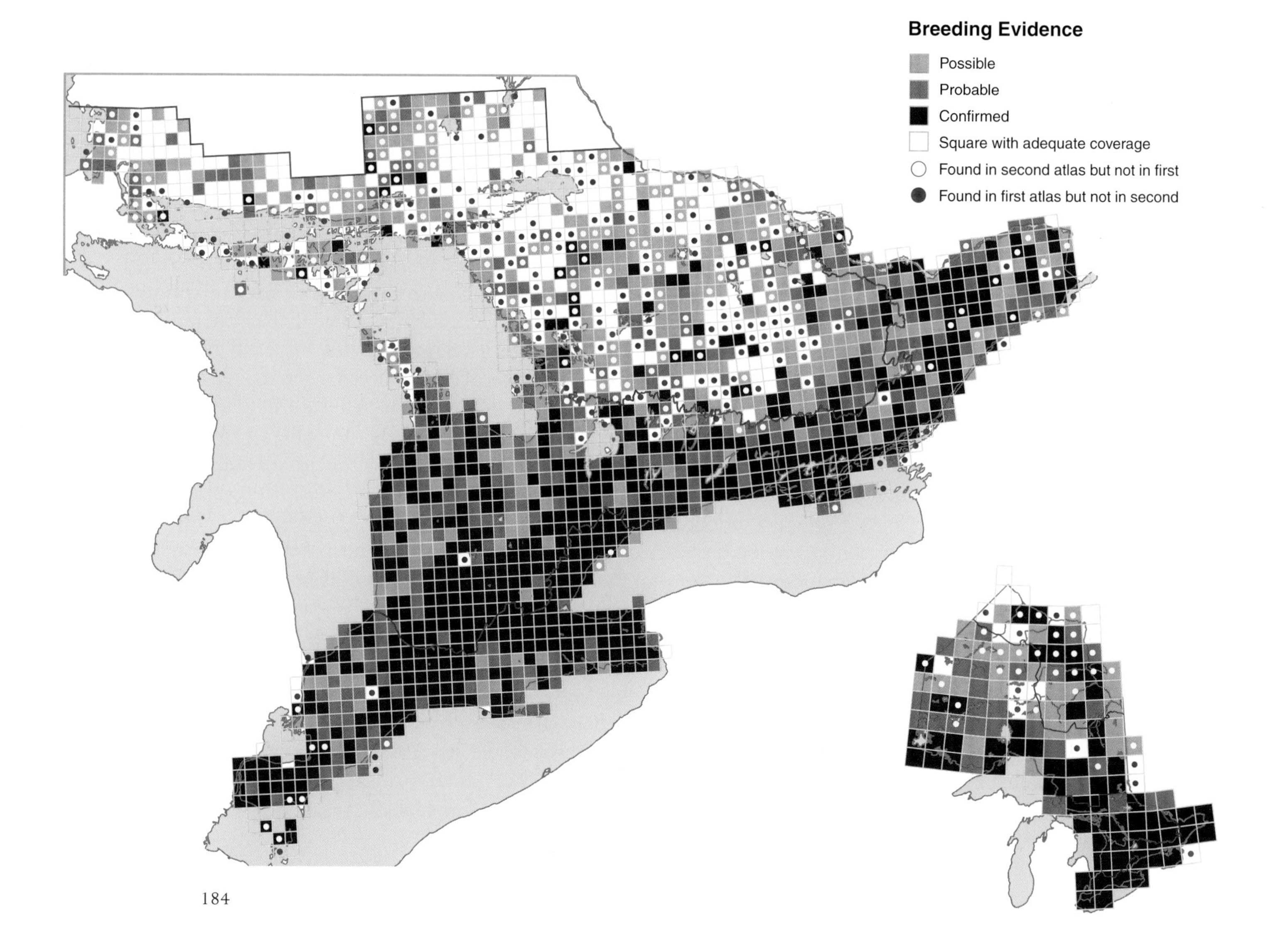

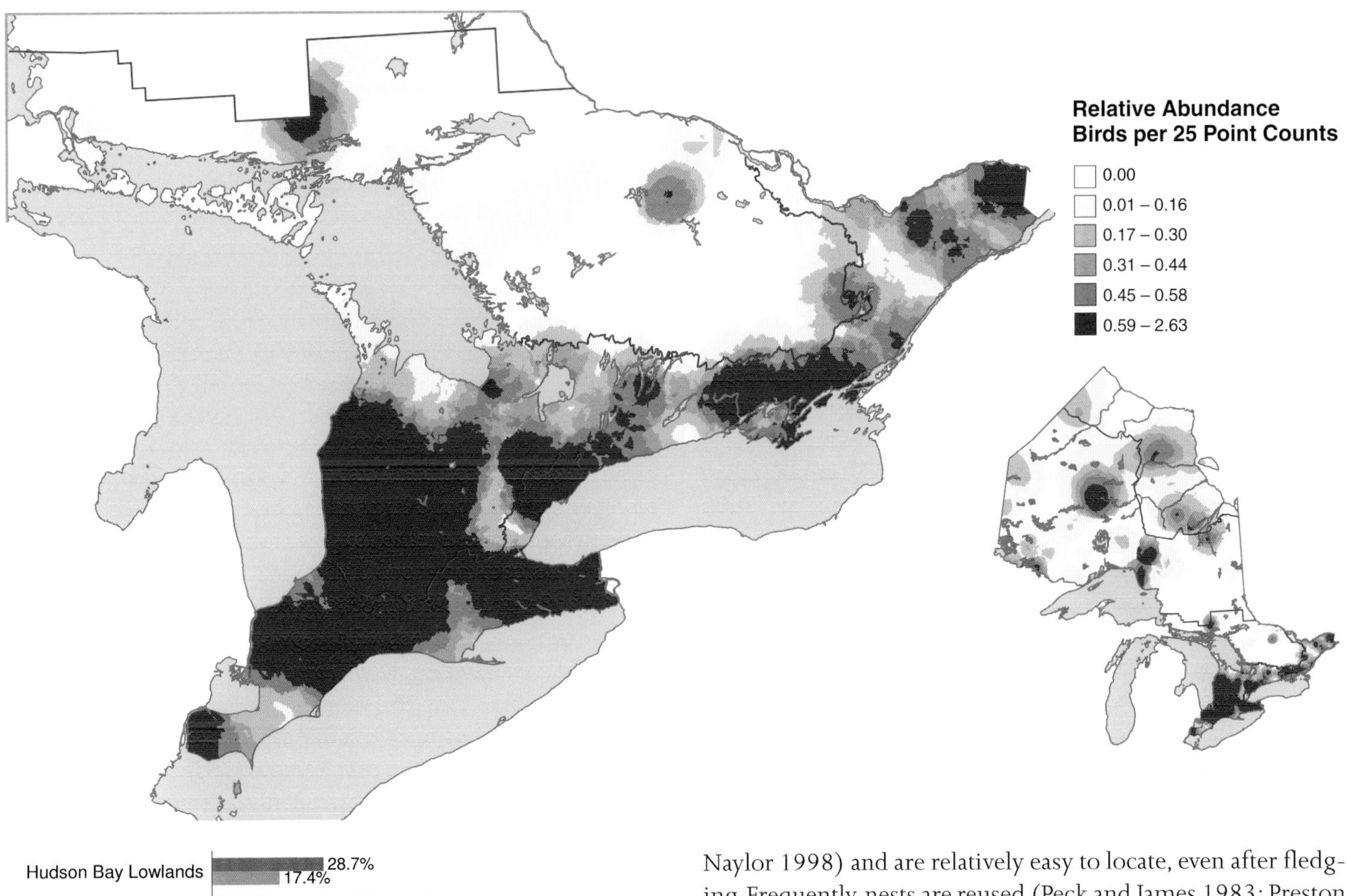

Hudson Bay Lowlands 28.7% 17.4%
Northern Shield 42.4%* 29.2%
Southern Shield 43.1% 44.1%
Lake Simcoe-Rideau 73.8% 77.5%
Carolinian 89.4% 91.0%
Ontario 42.1% 32.0%
0% 20% 40% 60% 80% 100%
Probability of Observation
1st Atlas 2nd Atlas

BBS data indicate no significant change in the Red-tailed Hawk population in Ontario since 1981, although there are only a limited number of BBS routes in the north where the atlas found an increase. Similarly, there is no apparent trend in numbers of Red-tailed Hawks encountered during Red-shouldered Hawk surveys (Crewe and Badzinski 2006a).

Breeding biology: The Red-tailed Hawk nests relatively early. In Ontario, the onset of breeding varies with latitude, beginning as early as late January-February (overwintering birds) in the south and as late as April-May in the north. Pairs are often conspicuous, perching together near prospective nest sites, calling and engaging in aerial courtship displays (Preston and Beane 1993). Egg dates are from 3 March to 15 July, with 50% of nests containing eggs between 5 and 23 April (Peck and James 1983). Adults are often aggressive around the nest (Andersen et al. 1989; Preston and Beane 1993). The birds' large size requires a large nest with good access, usually on or near the forest edge and often high in a prominent tree; these distinctive nests are established well before leaf-out (Szuba and Naylor 1998) and are relatively easy to locate, even after fledging. Frequently, nests are reused (Peck and James 1983; Preston and Beane 1993). Fledged young are easily detected, uttering frequent "*klee-uk*" calls and remaining in the vicinity of the nest for as long as 25 days (Preston and Beane 1993). Because of these attributes and its overall abundance, the Red-tailed Hawk, at 42%, has the highest probability of observation of any raptor in the province as a whole.

This hawk prefers to hunt from a prominent perch in or adjacent to open areas such as old fields, meadows, burns, or cutovers where it can find sufficient room to maneuver (Preston and Beane 1993). Its diet includes small mammals, grouse, small birds, snakes, and even insects (Sandilands 2005). It is a short-distance migrant, with some birds overwintering in extreme southern Ontario (Sandilands 2005) and others in the eastern US (Preston and Beane 1993).

Abundance: The first atlas described an increase of the Red-tailed Hawk in southern Ontario relative to historical numbers, due mainly to loss of forest cover and an increase in agricultural land. Results from the second atlas show that the species is still common across Ontario but is clearly most abundant south of the Shield, where forest cover is still relatively sparse and the interspersion of forest patches and large openings is greatest. A decreasing trend in the probability of observation is apparent from the Carolinian region north to the Hudson Bay Lowlands. Point count data also suggest higher numbers in the southern regions, although such data are not likely precise indicators of Red-tailed Hawk abundance. *– Kandyd Szuba*

Rough-legged Hawk

Buse pattue

Buteo lagopus

Karl Egressy

The Rough-legged Hawk has a holarctic breeding distribution. In North America, it breeds in arctic and subarctic tundra and the tundra-taiga ecotone from Alaska and the Canadian Arctic archipelago, south regularly to 52° N in central Québec and occasionally as far south as 50° N on the North Shore of the Gulf of St. Lawrence (Bechard and Swem 2002; Gauthier and Aubry 1996) and 47° N in Newfoundland (Whitaker et al. 1996). Both the breeding distribution and reproductive output of this prey-based nomad are strongly influenced by the local abundance of small rodents, its principal prey, as well as by the availability of the cliffs it prefers for nesting (Bechard and Swem 2002).

Distribution and population status: The breeding evidence map indicates the only squares in which the species has ever been confirmed breeding in Ontario (Peck and James 1983). All nesting evidence for the Rough-legged Hawk in the province has come from the Mid Canada Line Radar Sites 415 and 416 near Hook Point, south of Cape Henrietta Maria. Although evidence suggestive of breeding was reported as early as 1958 (Baillie 1963), it was not until 1976 that photographic evidence documenting the first nest in the province was obtained (Peck 1976). Prior to the second atlas, only six nests had been reported (ONRS). During the second atlas, breeding was confirmed in 2002 with the discovery of three nests in two squares at the abandoned Radar Sites 415 and 416.

Evidence of possible breeding was mapped during the first atlas in three 100-km blocks along the Hudson Bay coast west of the Winisk River. During the second atlas, the species was reported in 53 squares in the Hudson Bay Lowlands south to Moosonee; however, in all but two squares, these observations were thought to represent non-breeding individuals in habitat unsuitable for nesting, and consequently they were not mapped.

Breeding biology: Throughout its range, the Rough-legged Hawk nests most commonly on exposed bedrock cliffs and

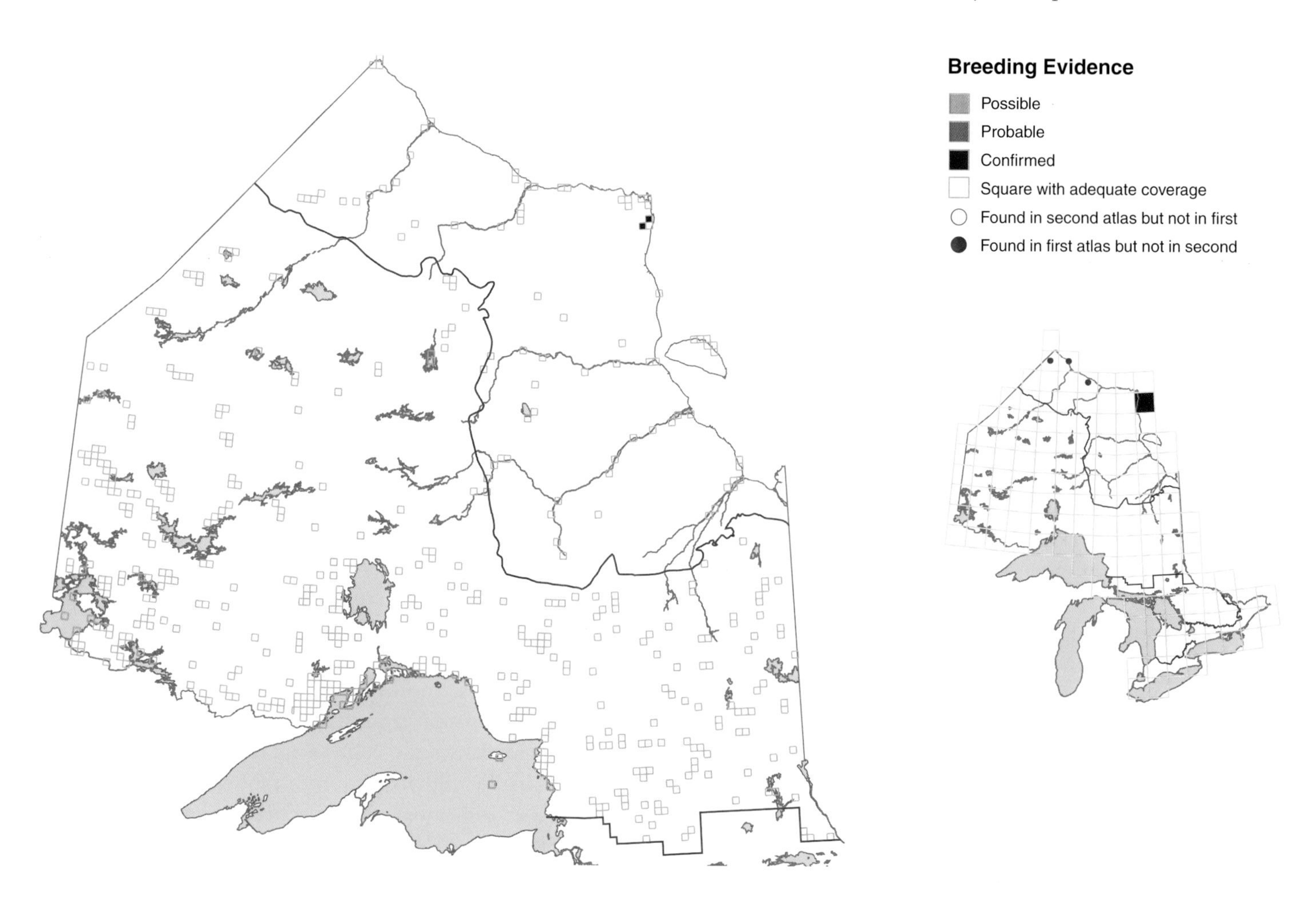

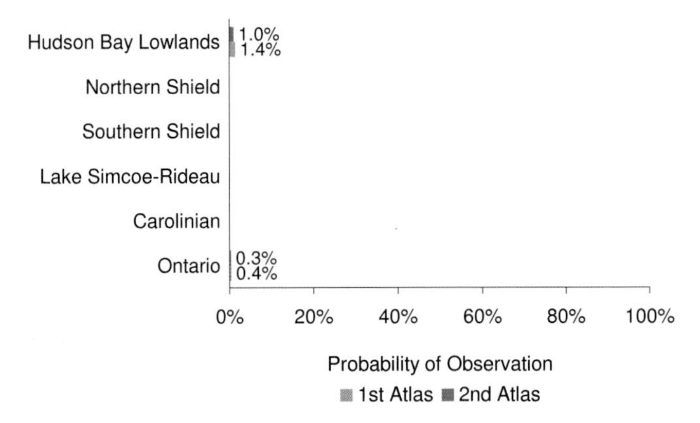

erosion pinnacles of often unstable clay riverine bluffs (Sinclair et al. 2003) and rarely on bedrock crags or boulders in tundra, in trees in taiga, on level ground, and on artificial structures (Bechard and Swem 2002). In Ontario, all nests have been on the structures associated with Radar Sites 415 and 416. Nests discovered during the second atlas were located atop an abandoned building at Radar Site 416 and on a radar dish and a fuel storage tank at Radar Site 415. Nests at Radar Site 415 were separated by less than 300 m and were 5.8 km distant from the nest at site 416.

The Rough-legged Hawk has been described as having a "searching migration" (Bechard and Swem 2002), abandoning areas with scarce prey and locating and nesting in areas with high prey abundance and suitable nest sites. In years of high prey abundance, it may nest south of the tundra in the taiga-tundra ecotone or in taiga (Gauthier and Aubry 1996; Whitaker et al. 1996). Non-breeding sub-adult individuals wander widely, frequently congregating in areas of high prey abundance (Bechard and Swem 2002) including the northern Hudson Bay Lowlands, where suitable nesting sites are limited (Weir in Cadman et al. 1987; Wilson and McRae 1993). Bedrock and riverine cliffs at a number of sites in the northern Hudson Bay Lowlands offer potential breeding habitat. The Precambrian rock cliffs of the Sutton Ridges 70-80 km inland from Hudson Bay, the low (10-15 m) limestone cliffs along the lower Shamattawa and Winisk Rivers, the low (20 m) cliffs on a Precambrian rock inlier 30 km southeast of Winisk, and the 30-40 m clay cliffs along the Severn River 50-60 km south of Fort Severn all offer potentially suitable nesting habitat, although no Rough-legged Hawks have been detected in these areas during aerial surveys for raptor nests by OMNR (Scholten and McRae 1994; pers. obs.).

Abundance: Although the Rough-legged Hawk is a regular summer resident in the northern Hudson Bay Lowlands of Ontario, there is considerable annual variation in its abundance. In years of low prey abundance, it may be essentially absent and nesting may not occur, while during peaks in prey abundance, it may be widely distributed and uncommon, although still nesting only rarely. Some nests may go undetected, but there is currently no evidence to suggest that the annual breeding population in Ontario exceeds three pairs or that the majority of birds occurring in the Hudson Bay Lowlands represent anything other than non-breeding individuals. – *Donald A. Sutherland*

In Ontario, nests are constructed of willow and birch twigs and lined with grasses and other plant material. Most nests are thought to have been former nests of the Common Raven (Peck and James 1983). *Photo: Jim Richards*

All documented nests in Ontario have been on artificial structures associated with abandoned Radar Sites 415/416. Most nests are located on the network of girders on the rear of the radar dishes. Radar Site 415, 9 August 2007. *Photo: Donald A. Sutherland*

Golden Eagle

Aigle royal

Aquila chrysaetos

Mark Peck

The Golden Eagle has a distribution limited to the northern hemisphere, breeding from arctic latitudes south to at least 20° N. In North America, it is primarily of western distribution but historically was more widespread in the eastern US (Kochert et al. 2002). Breeding in eastern North America is currently limited to remote areas of Ontario, Québec, and Maine, as well as Tennessee and Georgia, where it was recently reintroduced. Recent evidence of possible breeding has also been reported in New Brunswick and Nova Scotia (Erskine 1992).

In North America, the Golden Eagle nests most commonly on bedrock cliffs but may also utilize clay cliffs, trees, and occasionally even human structures or the ground. Nests are typically located near extensive open areas, often near water (Kochert et al. 2002).

Distribution and population status: Historical reports of breeding by the Golden Eagle in Ontario are mostly unsubstantiated, and nesting in the province was first documented in 1959 (Peck and James 1983). All documented nests in the province have been found in Kenora Dist. and, with the exception of a nest active in the late 1960s and early 1970s in the upper Severn River drainage, have been located in the far north in the Hudson Bay Lowlands region.

Increased knowledge of the species' breeding distribution is due largely to recent aerial surveys by OMNR of known and potential nest sites (Scholten and McRae 1994; D.A. Sutherland, unpubl. data). The number of squares with breeding evidence increased substantially between atlases, though the probability of observation did not. During the second atlas, most squares with breeding evidence were in the Hudson Bay Lowlands. Aerial surveys of the Sutton Ridges and the lower stretches of the major rivers draining the northern Hudson Bay Lowlands in 2001-2003 documented eight active nests and six additional territories. There were records of adults in suitable habitat south to the Albany River and the upper Severn River drainage at about

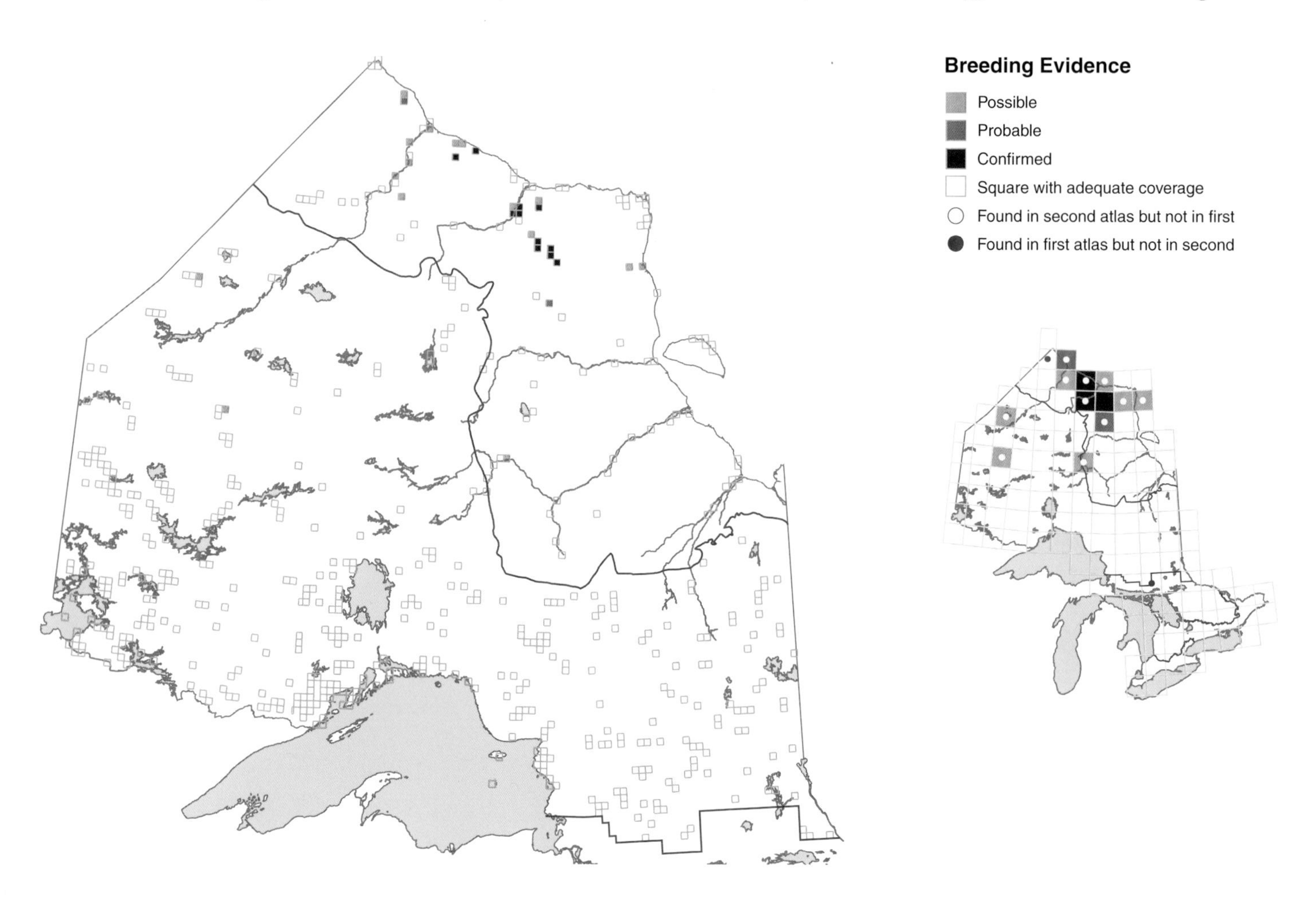

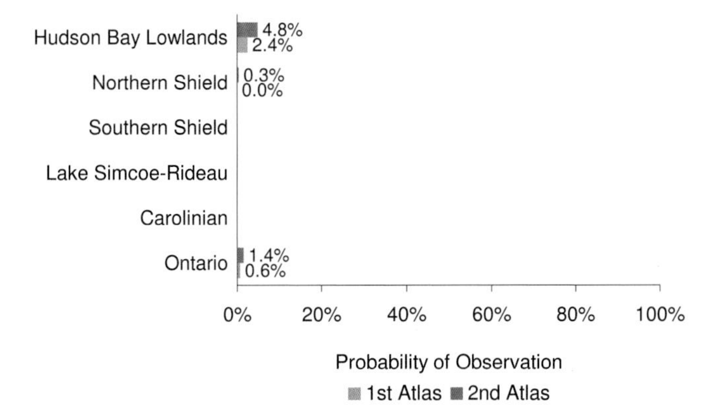

52° N. Despite survey effort, no evidence of breeding was reported from Sudbury Dist. (46° N), where the species was observed in suitable habitat during the first atlas.

Breeding biology: The Golden Eagle is largely monogamous, with pairs maintaining the same territory over successive breeding seasons (Kochert et al. 2002). Pairs may build and maintain between one and 14 alternate nests, though two to three are more typical; alternate nests may be separated by more than 5 km (Kochert et al. 2002). In Ontario, nests are primarily on remote, largely inaccessible bedrock cliffs overlooking large burns, lakes, or tundra. Most nests have been found in the Sutton Ridges, where an extensive series of highly fractured, 40-80 m Precambrian rock cliffs provide numerous suitable ledges. Nests are less commonly located on limestone cliffs, where they are typically saddled on spruce trunks bowed beneath cliff rims, and rarely in tall spruce along riparian corridors in the taiga-tundra ecotone (pers. obs.).

The timing of arrival of pairs at nest sites and the onset of nest refurbishment and courtship have not been documented in Ontario. In adjacent Québec, weather conditions at the beginning of the nesting season are known to constitute a critical factor in nest site location (Morneau et al. 1994). Egg laying is probably initiated in the latter half of April, based on the estimated age of nestlings observed in nests in Ontario and the chronology of nesting in adjacent Québec (F. Morneau, pers. comm.). Adults are wary, and in Ontario often depart the nests with young well in advance of an approaching helicopter or powerboat (pers. obs.).

Most Golden Eagles do not breed until at least their fifth year, and most populations include non-territorial adults or "floaters" and sub-adults (Kochert et al. 2002). Many adult and sub-adult Golden Eagles observed in close proximity to the large Snow Goose colonies along the upper James and Hudson Bay coasts of Ontario during the second atlas were considered to be non-breeders attracted by the large numbers of nesting geese, as has been observed at Churchill (Cooke et al. 1975; Jehl 2004).

Abundance: Due to the difficulty of surveying all cliffs and other potentially suitable habitat, the number of breeding pairs of Golden Eagle in Ontario is currently unknown. Data from recent aerial surveys and the current atlas suggest that 10-20 pairs nest in the Hudson Bay Lowlands and the adjacent Northern Shield regions of Ontario. Although the provincial breeding population may be somewhat higher, breeding densities in Ontario are undoubtedly low, as in adjacent Québec (Morneau et al. 1994). – *Donald A. Sutherland*

Based on the estimated age of nestlings observed in nests, egg laying is probably initiated in the latter half of April in Ontario. Near Sutton Narrows, Sutton Lake. *Photo: Ontario Ministry of Natural Resources*

The highly fractured Precambrian rock cuestas of the Sutton Ridges offer numerous suitable nest sites for the Golden Eagle. Near North Washagami Lake, 14 July 2001. *Photo: Donald A. Sutherland*

American Kestrel

Crécerelle d'Amérique

Falco sparverius

Frank and Sandra Horvath

The American Kestrel, the smallest of Ontario's diurnal raptors, is a common sight along rural roads, perched on poles and wires or hovering above fields in search of prey. Quite tolerant of human activity, the species has also become fairly common in urban settings. It has an extensive breeding range across most of North America south of the treeline, as well as in parts of Central America, the Caribbean, and much of South America (Smallwood and Bird 2002). Northern populations are migratory, but a fair number overwinter in the southern part of Ontario.

Distribution and population status: During both atlas periods, the American Kestrel and Red-tailed Hawk were the most numerous and broadly distributed raptors; however, the probability of observation of the kestrel declined significantly in each of the three southern regions. Although southern Ontario remains the core of the province's population, there were drops of 21%, 15%, and 27% in the Carolinian, Lake Simcoe-Rideau, and Southern Shield regions, respectively. The American Kestrel was already scarce in the Algonquin area during the first atlas, but its absence now extends to many squares southeast to the Frontenac Axis, largely accounting for the 27% decline in the Southern Shield. There was no significant change in the probability of observation in the Northern Shield, where the species has historically been less common than farther south. Breeding evidence was recorded in 12 new 100-km blocks north of Thunder Bay, and the map shows records along the length of Highway 11 between North Bay and Lake Nipigon. The American Kestrel may be taking advantage of grassy roadside verges, clearings from forestry operations, other human and natural disturbances, and scattered agricultural areas. The 39% decrease in the Hudson Bay Lowlands was non-significant, perhaps partially a result of small sample size. The species is of only marginal occurrence there and was rare during both periods. As in the first atlas, there was one confirmed breeding record from

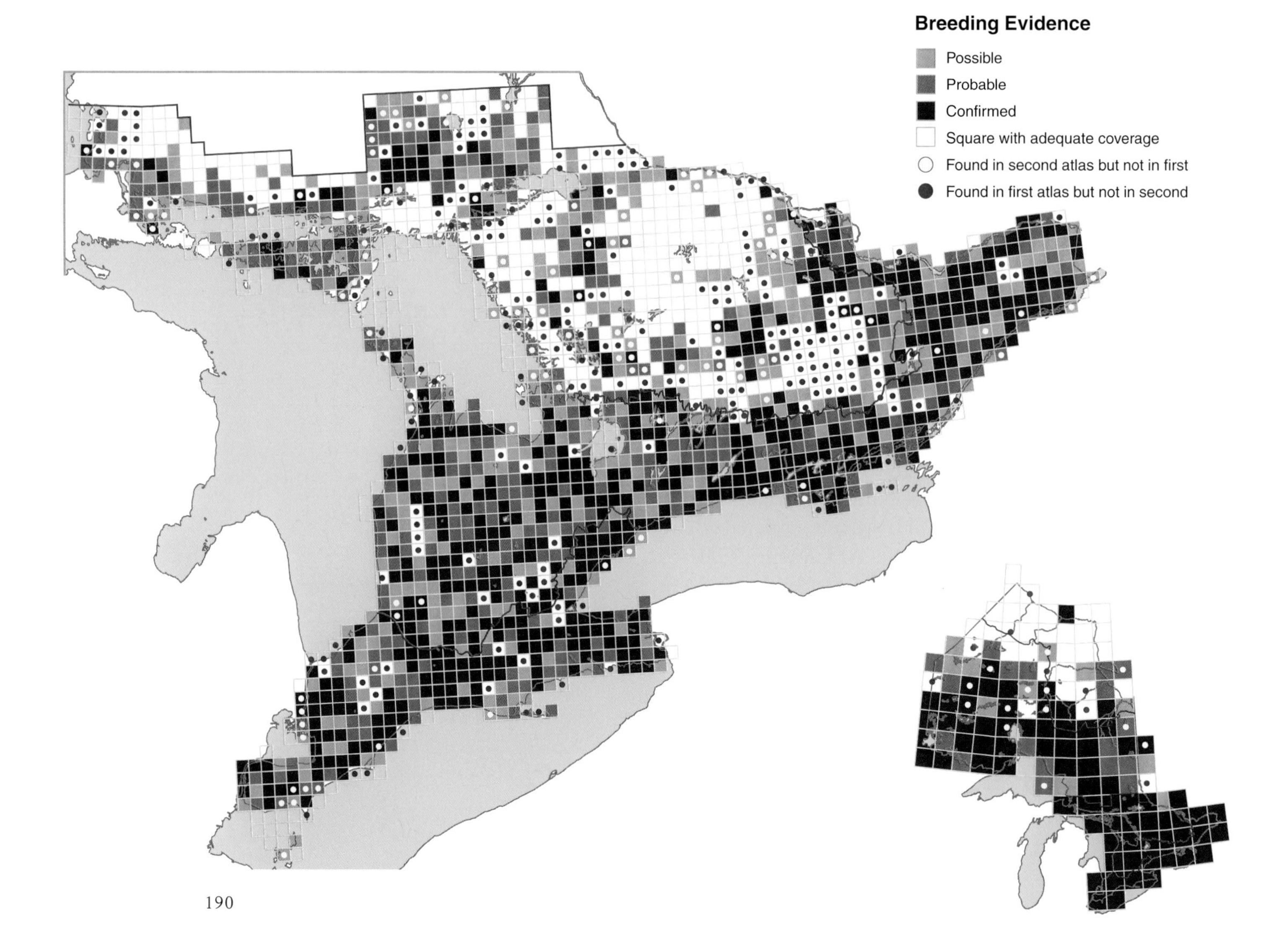

BREEDING EVIDENCE

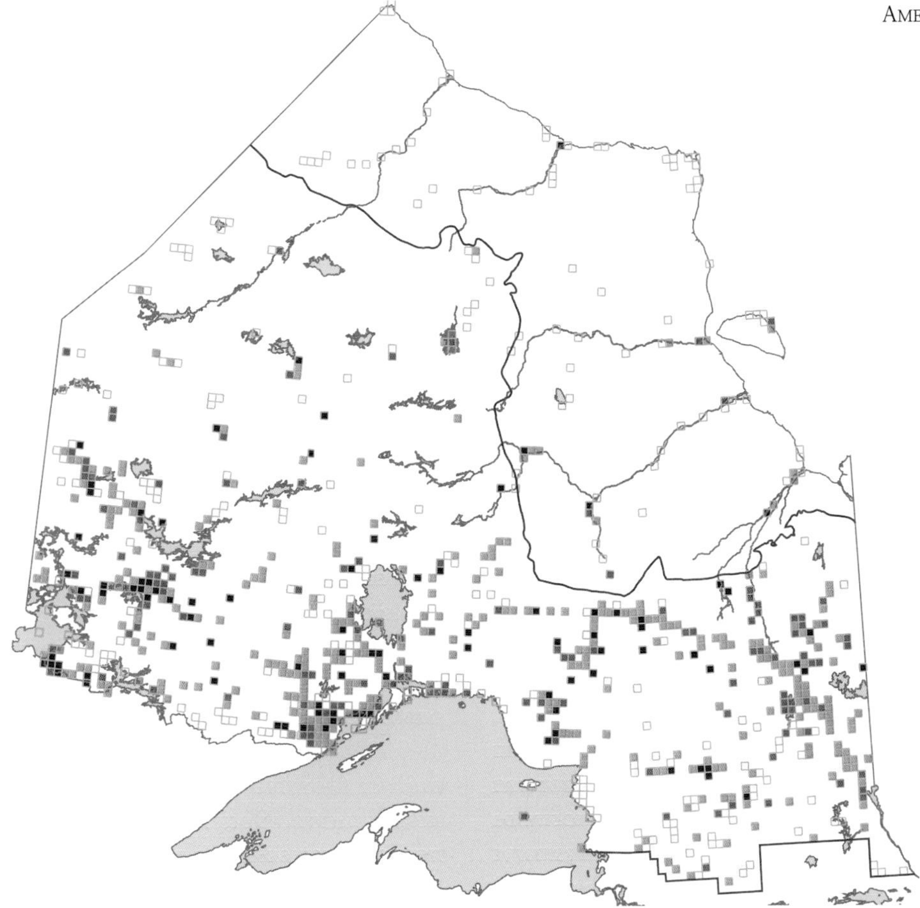

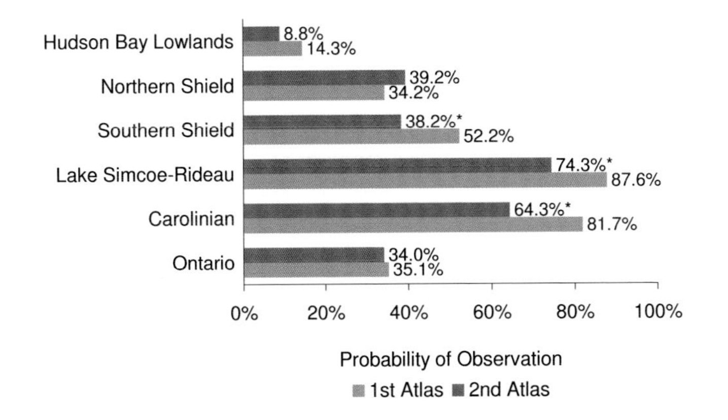

the Hudson Bay coast at the abandoned Winisk airbase hangar.

Cade (1982) estimated a North American population of 1.2 million pairs. Within the past decade, declines have been reported over much of North America; speculated causes include prey declines, environmental contamination, and increased predation by the Cooper's Hawk (Bird et al. 2004). However, BBS trends are inconsistent, with data from 1966 to 2001 showing significant increases in some midwest regions and significant declines in parts of the northeast and the west coast (Sauer et al. 2002). Between 1981 and 2005, BBS data show significant annual decreases of 3.7% and 3.8% for Canada and Ontario, respectively. The decline in Ontario is consistent with that of many other grassland and open country species.

Breeding biology: The typical habitat of the American Kestrel is open country, including grasslands, forest edges, clearings, burns, and extensive clearcuts in which scattered White Birch and aspen have been left standing. In recent decades, the species has increasingly taken to nesting in cities, favouring not only green spaces but also industrial parks. For example, by the late 1990s, there were as many as 50 pairs of American Kestrels in Toronto (Gahbauer 2000). The availability of old woodpecker holes or other suitable nesting cavities can be a limiting factor, although nest boxes can supplement limited natural options (Smallwood and Bird 2002). Sparse or low vegetation is also important for easy location of prey.

Nesting pairs are easily found, as the adults tend to use regular, conspicuous perches and are highly vocal, even near the nest. The male carrying food to the nest is a reliable indicator of success and likely contributed significantly to the 34% of squares with breeding evidence in which breeding was confirmed, a relatively high rate for raptors. Given the ease of detection, it is likely that the distribution of the American Kestrel shown on the maps is accurate.

Abundance: South of 45° N, the American Kestrel is fairly common, with notable concentrations around Toronto, London, Kingston, and Peterborough, reflecting its recent adaptation to urban environments; it is also numerous in the agricultural areas of Haldimand and Elgin Counties. On the Northern Shield, the American Kestrel was the second most frequently encountered raptor on point counts, with peak numbers found around Rainy River, Dryden, and the area from Cochrane to Kapuskasing. In between, on the Southern Shield, it is generally uncommon to rare, except for higher abundance around Sudbury, which is less forested and has a greater road network than adjacent areas. – *Marcel A. Gahbauer*

Merlin

Faucon émerillon

Falco columbarius

Jim Richards

Formerly known as the Pigeon Hawk for its rapid and direct flight, the Merlin is the only Ontario falcon to prefer forest and forest edge habitat. Its circumboreal breeding range includes most of Canada south of the treeline, as well as northernmost US. Of the three recognized North American subspecies, only the Taiga Merlin (*F. c. columbarius*) breeds in Ontario. Most Merlins winter in Mexico and Central America, but some remain in southern Canada and the US, while others migrate as far south as Ecuador (Warkentin et al. 2005).

Distribution and population status: Early records of the Merlin in southern Ontario were primarily of migrants (McIlwraith 1894). However, Macoun and Macoun (1909) considered it an abundant breeder along western James Bay, and Baillie and Harrington (1936) reported it as a regular breeder across central and northern Ontario. Like most raptors, the Merlin declined in the 1950s and 1960s due to DDT and other organochlorine contaminants; by the mid-1970s, it was considered rare to moderately abundant, with a declining or stable population (Fyfe 1976). It was on the Blue List from 1972 to 1981 (Tate and Tate 1982), and by the mid-1980s it still had not recovered to pre-DDT levels (De Smet 1985).

Since the first atlas, Ontario's Merlin population has experienced tremendous growth, with the probability of observation increasing significantly by more than 100%. This trend is opposite that of the American Kestrel which declined in the three southern regions. The Merlin increased significantly in every region except the Carolinian and was found in more squares than the kestrel in both the Southern Shield and Hudson Bay Lowlands. Population growth was most dramatic in the Southern Shield and Lake Simcoe-Rideau regions, where the probability of observation increased approximately threefold and fourfold, respectively. The expansion has been province-wide, with almost three-quarters of newly occupied 100-km blocks being in northern Ontario.

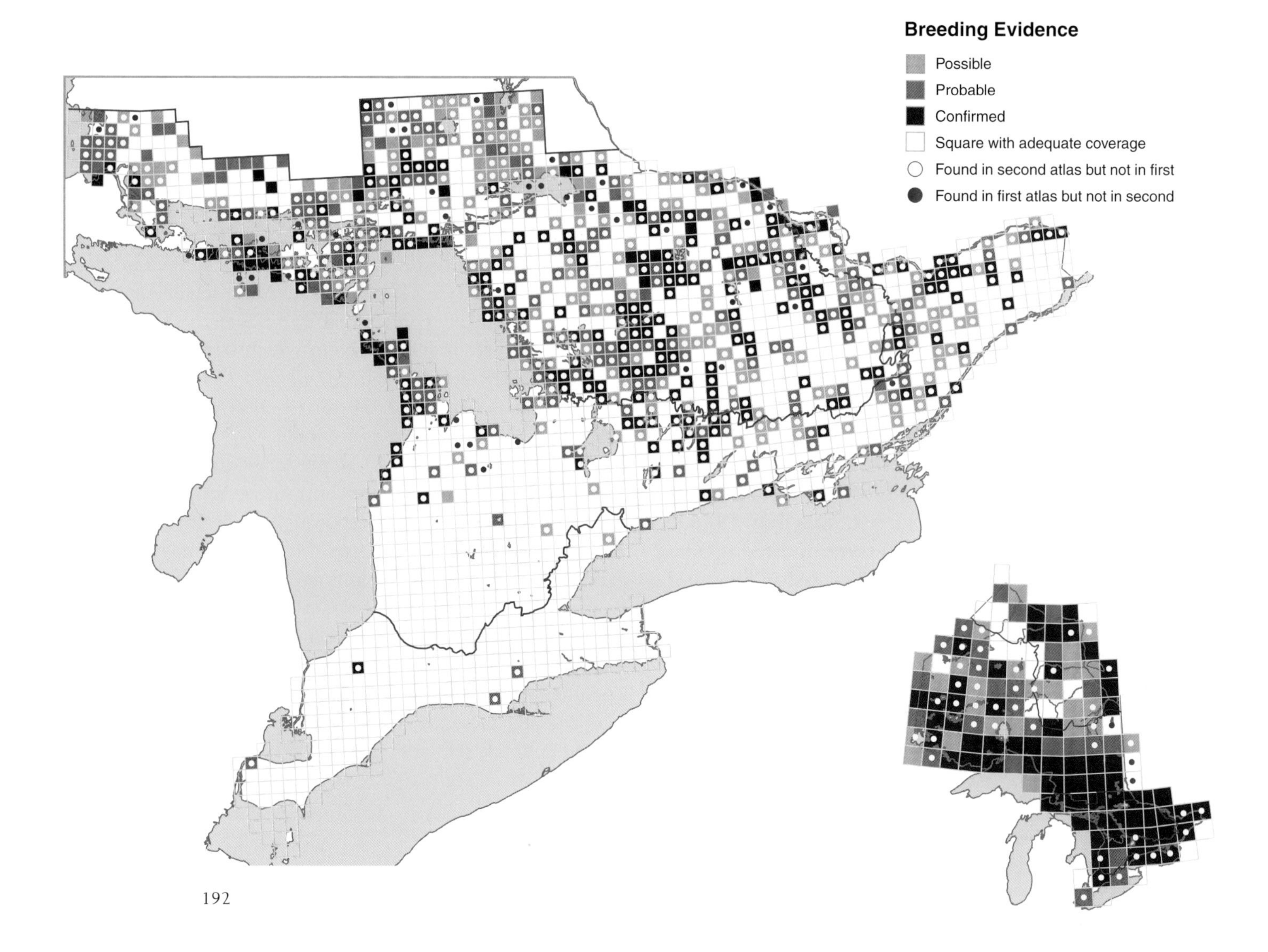

BREEDING EVIDENCE

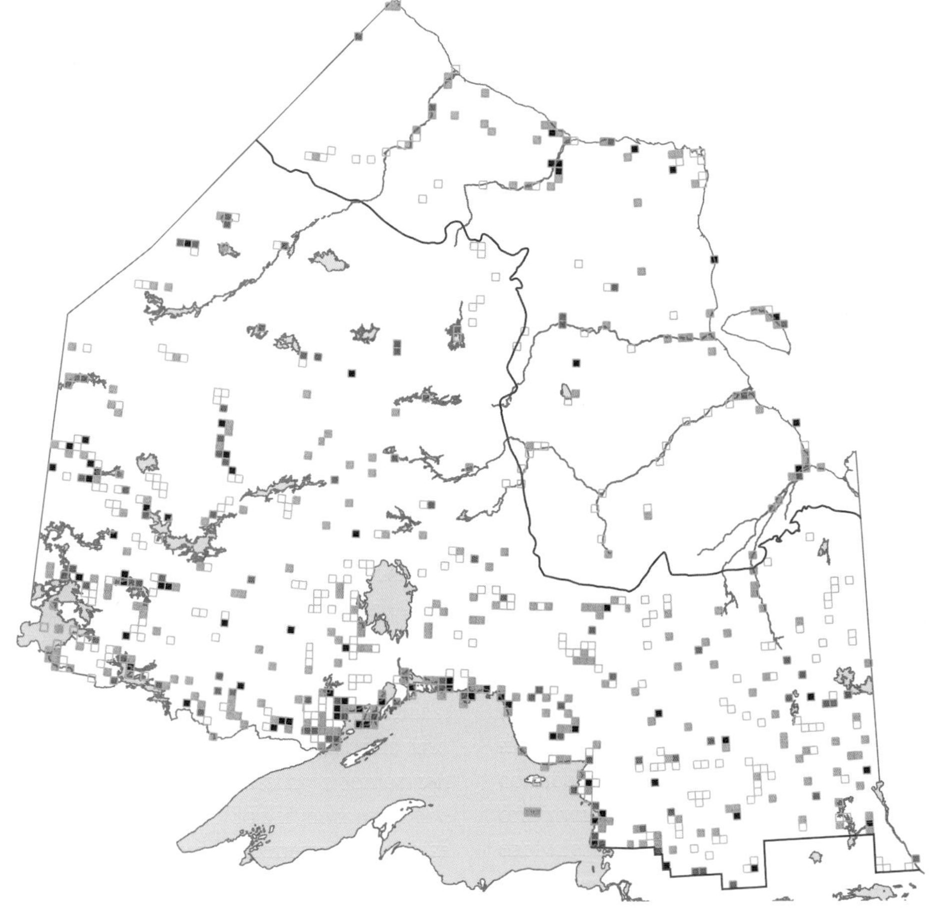

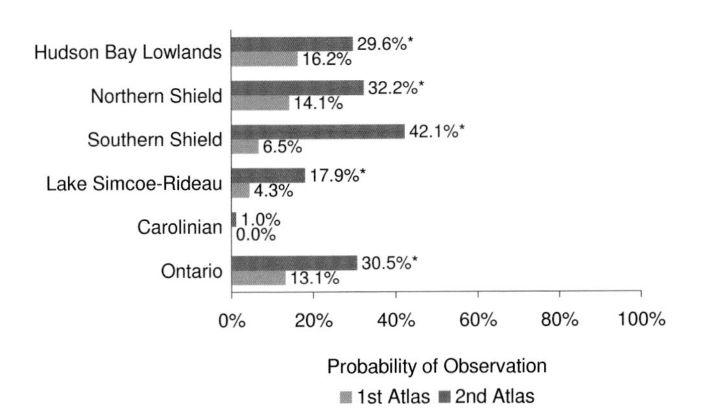

In some areas, the increase is a result of the Merlin colonizing urban areas. While it has bred in cities on the prairies for decades, the only urban record during the first atlas was from Thunder Bay (Escott 1986). Twenty years later, the Merlin is among the most common raptors in some Ontario cities, including Ottawa. Urban areas provide not only abundant prey in the form of House Sparrows and other small songbirds but also a variety of good nesting options (Sodhi et al. 1992). However, the Merlin population has grown tremendously in natural areas too.

Breeding biology: The Merlin prefers open country for hunting, and commonly nests in forests with scattered clearings or adjacent open habitat such as grasslands, wetlands, lakes, or burns. In much of Ontario, it favours islands and peninsulas, where it preys on passerines crossing open water. It typically uses abandoned stick nests of other raptors or the American Crow, mostly in conifers, often preferring those that permit the adults a clear view of the surroundings (Warkentin and James 1988). While adults are often vocal around the nest, it can be well concealed and may require considerable patience and effort to spot. Both the aggressive territoriality of adults and their elaborate courtship flights early in the breeding season are helpful in locating breeding birds. The male brings prey to the brooding female, vocalizing during his approach, and the location of the nest may be identified by tracking her following the food exchange (Warkentin et al. 2005). Detection just prior to and after fledging is aided by the very vocal and conspicuous young. Considering the relative ease of detection, as well as the general awareness among birders during the atlas period about the Merlin's expanding range, the maps likely present an accurate reflection of its current distribution.

Abundance: In the first atlas, the Merlin was considered uncommon to rare, with a noticeably denser population in northern Ontario. Despite its dramatic population expansion since the first atlas, it remains generally uncommon over most of the province. The rate of encounter was three times greater on point counts in the Hudson Bay Lowlands than on the Shield, but this may only be an artifact of coverage along river corridors where the species is apt to concentrate. It can be considered fairly common in a number of other parts of the province, including the Thunder Bay area, the northeastern shore of Georgian Bay, Hearst, Kenora, and Manitoulin Island. *– Marcel A. Gahbauer*

Peregrine Falcon

Faucon pèlerin

Falco peregrinus

Brandon Holden

The Peregrine Falcon is symbolic of the DDT-associated decline in many birds of prey and is the species perhaps most associated in the public's mind with the story of environmental degradation and recovery. Its precipitous decline in North America due to widespread use of DDT (and other organochlorine chemicals) is well established (Peakall 1976). Its history is a reflection of the continent-wide response to its precipitous decline, including the prohibition on DDT in the early 1970s and subsequent large-scale recovery efforts through captive breeding and release.

This cosmopolitan species occurs naturally on all continents except Antarctica, and typically nests on remote cliffs near water bodies. It has recently become an established urban species, nesting on tall buildings, bridges, and smokestacks. Considered endangered for several decades, the species is currently listed as Threatened provincially and of Special Concern nationally.

Distribution and population status: The Peregrine Falcon's status has changed from rapidly declining populations in the 1950s and extirpation as a breeding species in the early 1960s to, more recently, re-establishment and recovery across the province. This mirrors trends across North America (Kiff 1988) and reflects the large-scale efforts to recover the species across its range (White et al. 2002; Cade and Burnham 2003). The Ontario population is now sustained entirely by natural reproduction and immigration rather than releases.

A dramatic increase in distribution and abundance has occurred, from three squares with breeding evidence in the first atlas to 96 in the second. The number of squares with breeding evidence increased from 0 to 49 in the Northern Shield, 0 to 19 in the Southern Shield, 3 to 8 in the Lake Simcoe-Rideau region, and 0 to 20 in the Carolinian region. Urban and cliff-nesting populations are distinct and separate from one another, and birds typically return to the habitat type in which they were raised (Holroyd and

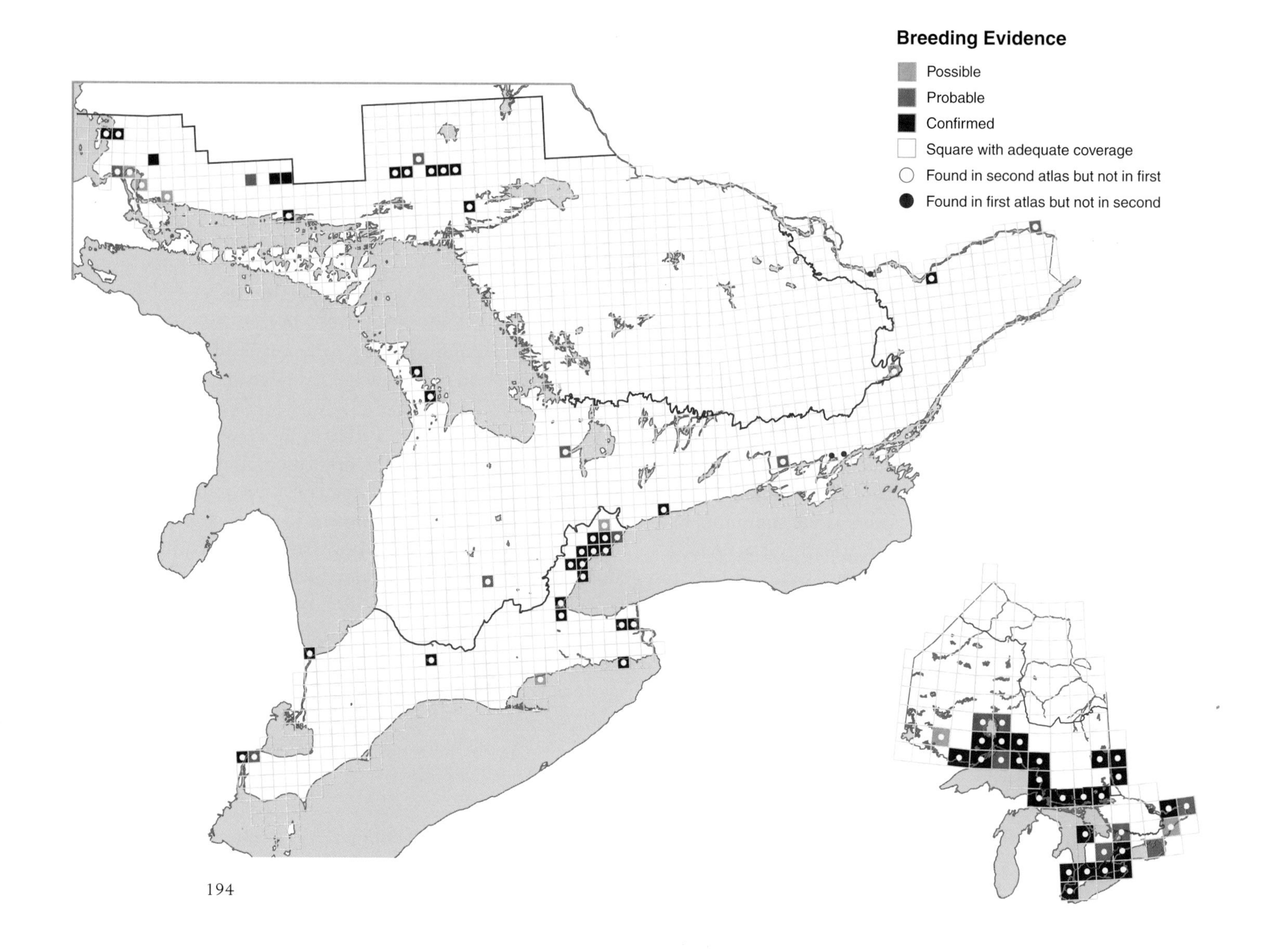

BREEDING EVIDENCE

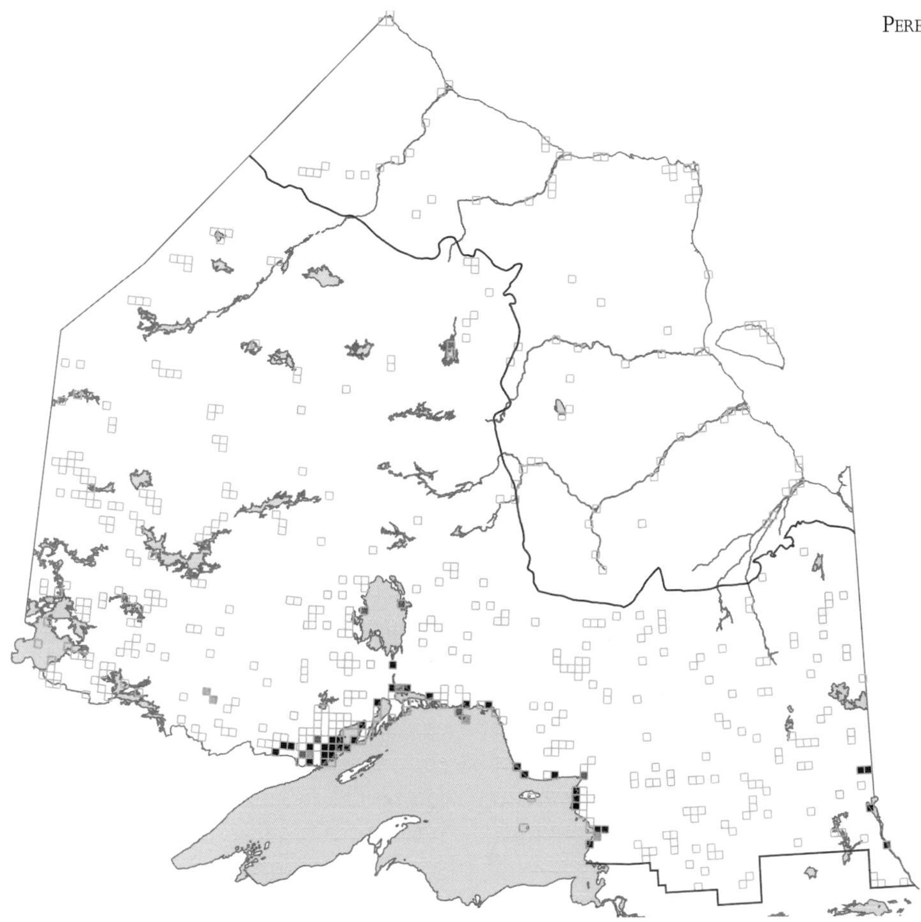

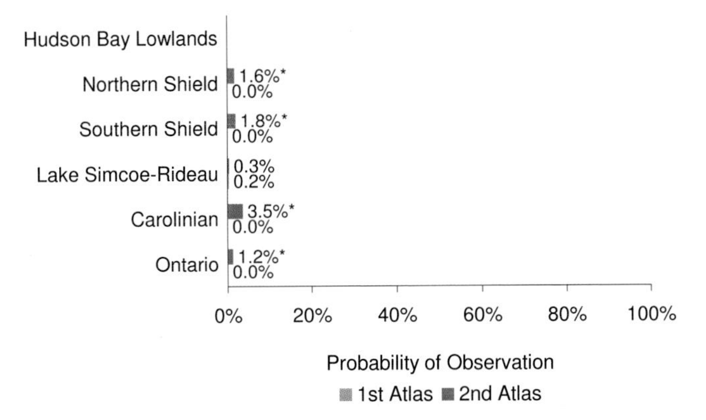

Banasch 1990). The cliff-nesting population is concentrated along shorelines of Lakes Huron and especially Superior, with the urban population found in larger urban centres of southern Ontario. At the atlas 100-km block level, distribution is nearly continuous along the Great Lakes shoreline from western Lake Superior to the St. Lawrence River and along the Ottawa River. The historical range in southern Ontario, particularly in the Southern Shield, has not been reoccupied; this may reflect more marginal cliff habitat relative to other parts of the province.

Breeding biology: The Peregrine Falcon does not build a nest but creates a scrape in the substrate. Typical clutch size is three to four eggs, although five to six are possible but rare (White et al. 2002). While both adults share in incubation and rearing, typically females carry out most of the incubation, and males provide most of the food to the female and young at the nest.

Although cliff-nesting birds are difficult to detect during incubation, this species is highly vocal and visible during courtship, territorial displays, and fledging, and adults and young remain active in the territory for several weeks after fledging. Potential for misidentification by atlassers is limited because of the species' distinctive call and appearance, although many public reports are actually of the smaller Merlin.

Cliff observations are difficult and limited, often requiring strenuous hikes or access by boats or aircraft, and it is likely that some breeding occurrences were missed. Conversely, urban sites are typically highly visible, well known, and occupied year-round, with a much lower probability of missed sites. Territories are often occupied annually through successive generations (Hickey and Anderson 1969).

Although the species is not colonial, territories can be close together in habitats with suitable nesting sites and abundant prey (White et al. 2002), such as the GTA and western Lake Superior. Territories are large enough that some breeding activity may be observed in squares adjacent to squares with nests. Rarely was more than one territory located in any atlas square.

Abundance: Although there are more confirmed breeding sites in Ontario now than the 48 historically documented cliff aeries (Ratcliff and Armstrong 2002), historical documentation was limited, and no doubt the extensive cliffs of northern Ontario held far more nests.

Atlas results parallel those from nation-wide surveys held every five years. No Peregrine Falcon nesting was confirmed in Ontario from 1970 through 1985; the first confirmed nesting after the population collapse was recorded in northeastern Ontario in 1986. Since then, Ontario's Peregrine Falcon population has become firmly re-established and has increased dramatically (Ratcliff and Armstrong 2002), with 78 occupied territories confirmed in 2005 (Ratcliff and Armstrong 2006). Population recovery is expected to continue, with increasing numbers and expanding range in both urban and cliff environments. *– Ted (E.R.) Armstrong*

Yellow Rail

Râle jaune

Coturnicops noveboracensis

George K. Peck

The Yellow Rail's secretive nature makes it one of the least observed birds in North America; it is possible to stand directly above one without seeing it. Luckily, its repetitive, ticking call is distinctive, and territorial males will respond to broadcasts or even stones tapped together in a reasonable imitation. Ninety percent of the species' breeding range is estimated to occur in Canada (Alvo and Robert 1999), and Ontario has significant responsibility for conservation of the Yellow Rail. It breeds at widely scattered sites, primarily sedge-dominated wetlands, in central and southeastern Canada, extreme northern US and southern Oregon, and historically in central Mexico. It is designated Special Concern by COSEWIC and OMNR.

Distribution and population status: As in the first atlas, this species occurred predominantly in three areas: southern and eastern Ontario, in the Rainy River area, and along the coasts of Hudson and James Bays. Both atlases failed to detect it across large areas of interior northern Ontario, perhaps because suitable wetlands are less common there. However, this species was recorded in a few squares between Dryden and Lake Nipigon where it was undetected in the first atlas. These occurrences could be a result of increased coverage in this area but may also reflect the species being present at a location only when water levels and vegetation are suitable. For example, in early July 2005, 157 calling males were present 10 km north of Rainy River, including 56 within 904 ha of flooded meadow adjacent to Wilson Creek. This represents the second highest density (0.06 males/ha) ever recorded (Robert et al. 2004). The high numbers are suspected to be a result of birds forced into the region from wetlands to the south and west when water levels became too high.

The Yellow Rail was not detected at Holland Marsh during the second atlas. A population of unknown size previously occurred there, with at least six males heard calling in the

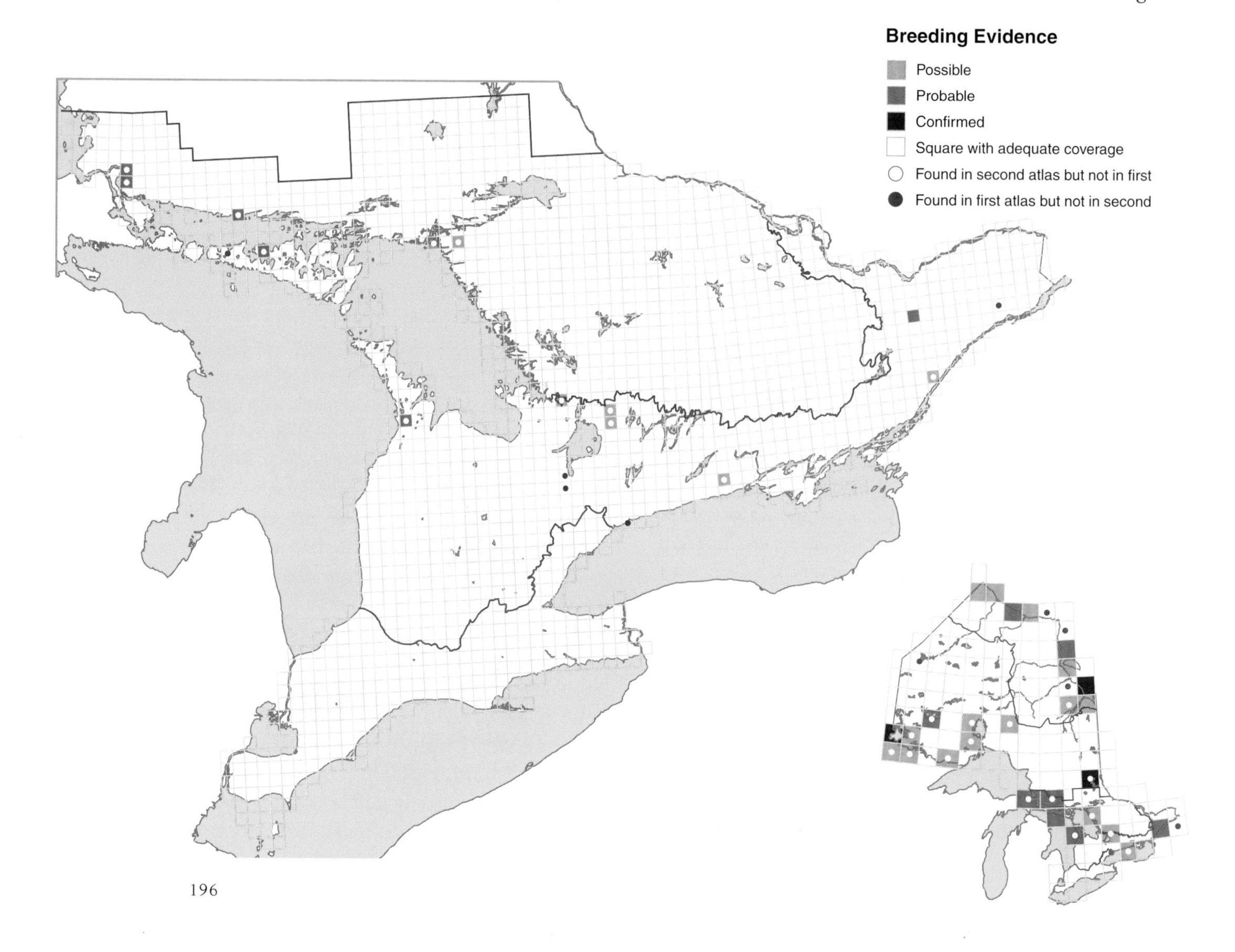

BREEDING EVIDENCE

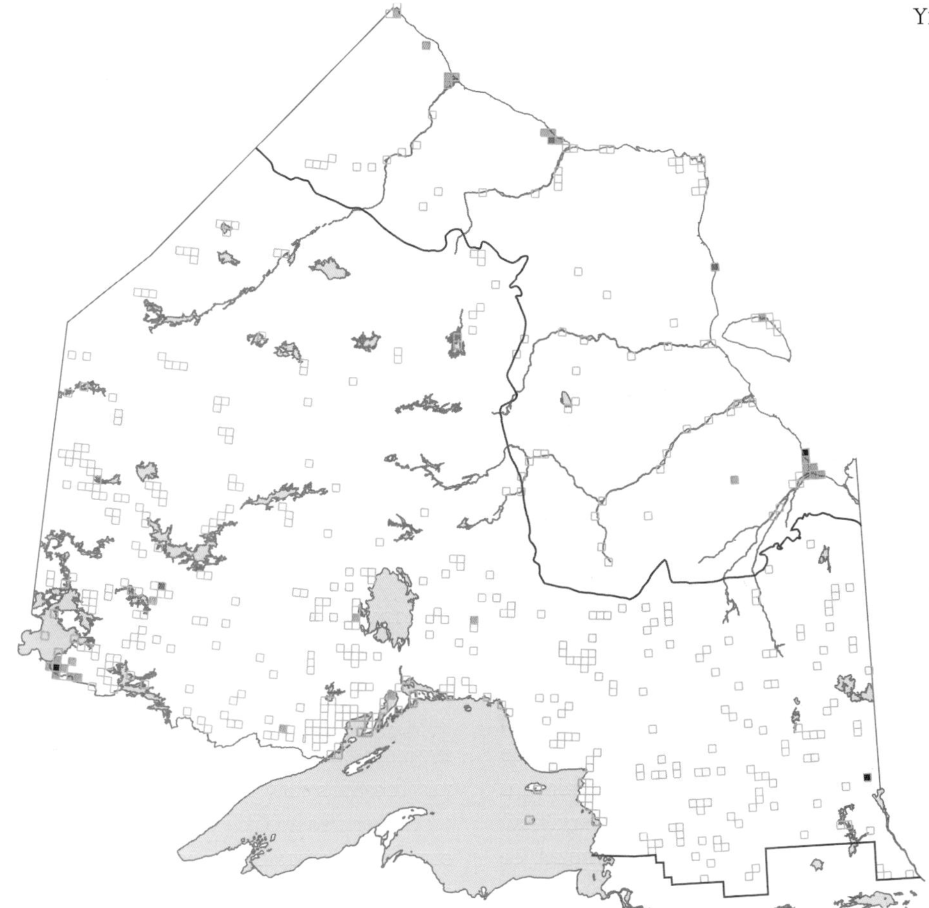

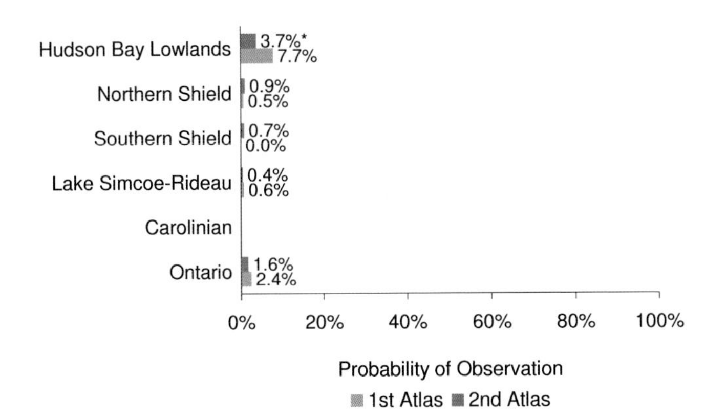

1940s (Devitt 1967). Most of this area was converted to market gardening, but some suitable habitat remained, with the species being present in two squares during the first atlas. The most extensive concentration of this species occurs along the James Bay coast and, to a somewhat lesser degree, along the Hudson Bay coast, where suitable wetlands are less extensive (D. Sutherland, pers. comm.). Atlas data suggest a significant 52% decline in the probability of observation of the Yellow Rail in the Hudson Bay Lowlands. However, it is difficult to assess the validity of this result as no other reliable estimates of population or trends for this species are available anywhere. The fact that different squares were covered during the two atlases may have contributed to this result.

The Yellow Rail was probably under-represented in both atlases due to its elusive nature and difficulty in accessing its primary range in the north.

Breeding biology: The Yellow Rail is most often found breeding in sedge-dominated habitats where the substrate remains damp or has up to 15 cm of standing water throughout the breeding season. Of sites where habitat was recorded in this atlas, 5% were sedge-dominated Great Lakes coastal wetland, 14% hayfield, 16% sedge-dominated inland wetland, 19% sedge-dominated patches within cattail-dominated wetland, and 46% James and Hudson Bay coastal sedge fen and sedge meadow marsh. Nests are built just above the substrate, hidden by a thick canopy of stems and leaves from previous years. Eggs are generally laid in mid- to late June and incubated for 17-18 days; young leave the nest two days after hatching (Bookhout 1995). Jehl (2004) noted that the Yellow Rail was one of the latest arriving birds on the Hudson Bay coast, so its presence may not have coincided with peak atlassing activity. When disturbed, the Yellow Rail escapes quietly by walking or running through low vegetation, making this species especially difficult to confirm.

Prior to 2000, only four nests had been found in Ontario (Peck 2002). One additional nest was found during this atlas: a female was flushed from nine eggs in 2005 near Wilson Creek north of Rainy River.

Abundance: Systematic nocturnal surveys are required for reliable abundance estimates (Bart et al. 1984). At Rainy River, G. Coady estimated that daytime point counts detected 20% of the number of birds heard at night at the same locations. Distributional data suggest that greatest numbers occur in the Hudson Bay Lowlands and Rainy River area. – *Douglas C. Tozer*

King Rail

Râle élégant

Rallus elegans

P. Allen Woodliffe

The King Rail is a species highly sought after by birders. Its rarity, secretive nature, and limited range make it challenging to find. In Canada, it is primarily associated with large marshes in Ontario south of the Canadian Shield. In the US, it occurs from the Atlantic Coast to about the 100th meridian and south to the Gulf States (Poole et al. 2005). It is designated Endangered by COSEWIC and OMNR and has been regulated under Ontario's Endangered Species Act since 1999.

Distribution and population status: During the first atlas, the King Rail was found primarily in larger wetlands in the Lake Erie and Lake St. Clair areas, with a few scattered records across the Lake Simcoe-Rideau region. In the second atlas, there was little change in the breeding distribution for the species in the Carolinian region, but the number of records in the Lake Simcoe-Rideau region increased from five to 10 squares. The increase in the probability of observation, however, was not significant in either region, nor for the province overall. In the second atlas, the greatest concentration of squares with breeding evidence was in the area from Presqu'ile to Kingston. Records in six of these eight squares were from special King Rail surveys conducted for OMNR, so it is unclear whether these new records represent an increase in numbers of the species or are the result of increased search effort. It was reported again from Holland Marsh, Simcoe Co., and a new record was obtained from Sturgeon Bay, Simcoe Co.

The majority of Ontario's King Rail population appears to occur in the marshes associated with Lake St. Clair, and this has apparently been the case for at least 100 years. McIlwraith (1894) and Baillie and Harrington (1936) both noted it as common at the St. Clair flats, an area of extensive cattail marshes along the northern and eastern

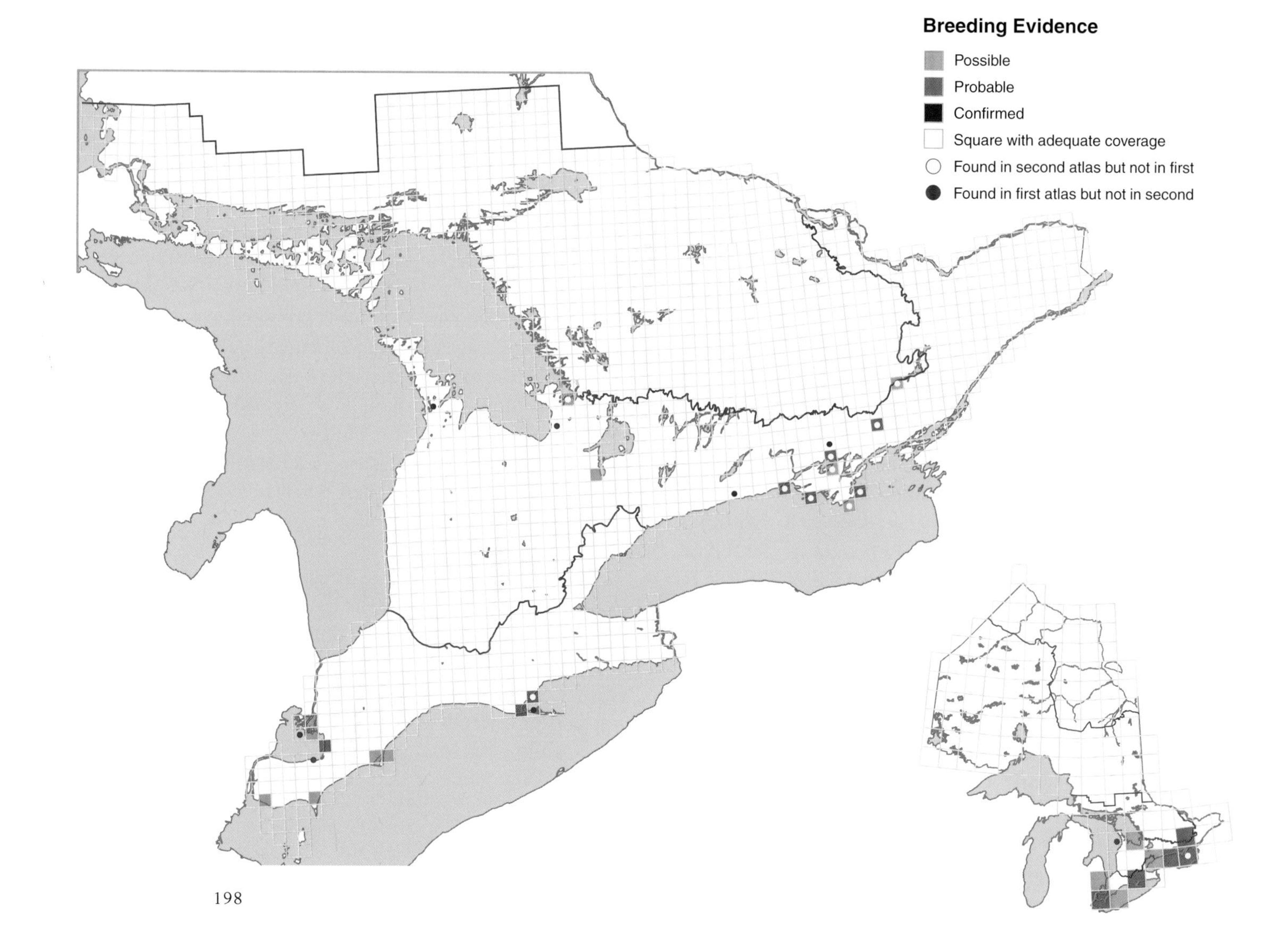

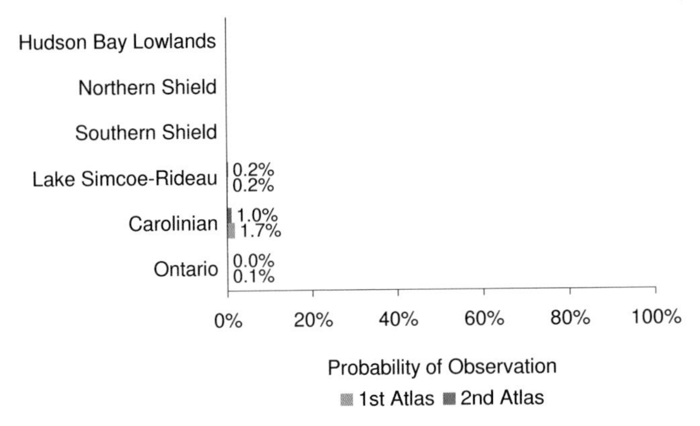

shores of Lake St. Clair. Surveys of the King Rail in known historical locations and areas of potentially suitable habitat in Ontario in 1997 and 1999 detected the greatest number of birds in this area, specifically within the Walpole Island First Nation (Environment Canada 2006b). The vast extent of these and other large wetlands makes detection and documentation of the species difficult, and it is very likely under-reported. BBS data in the US indicate significant range-wide declines averaging 6.6% per year from 1966-2005 (Sauer et al. 2005). It is now the most threatened rail in North America (Poole et al. 2005).

Breeding biology: The King Rail returns to Ontario in mid- to late April. Prime breeding habitat is in cattail marshes, wet meadows, and natural, sometimes shrubby swales where water depths are generally less than 25 cm and there is fairly thick emergent vegetation (Environment Canada 2006b). An interspersion of wet and dry areas is required, with drier areas being frequented by newly hatched broods. Egg dates in Ontario, based on only 12 nests, are between 18 May and 17 July (Peck and James 1983).

The King Rail is notoriously difficult to find and observe because of the heavily vegetated and relatively inaccessible marshes it frequents. Actual sightings are rare, making confirmation of breeding especially difficult. In fact, no confirmed breeding records were documented in the second atlas. Birds may call both day and night, and calls are variable but somewhat similar to those of the much more abundant Virginia Rail. The King Rail does respond to broadcasts of its call, but not consistently (Castrale et al. 1998).

The King Rail is omnivorous, feeding primarily on crustaceans (especially crayfish) and aquatic insects during spring and summer; it also consumes small fish, frogs, and plants (Reid 1989; Poole et al. 2005).

Abundance: The King Rail was reported in only 19 scattered squares during the second atlas and was not detected on point counts. During the first atlas, it was believed that there were about 25 pairs in Ontario but that the population could be greater due to detection difficulties; Austen et al. (1994) concluded there were 20-52 pairs. A directed survey for King Rail in 1997 located 32 territorial birds (Kozlovic 1997), while a 1999 survey located 23 territorial birds, 14 of which occurred in the extreme southwest (Lang 2000). In the two special surveys, it was felt that despite the effort, the species was undoubtedly more numerous since some sites were under-surveyed and other sites were not visited at all. The second atlas confirms that the King Rail is still exceedingly rare in Ontario. – *P. Allen Woodliffe*

This nest was at McGeachy Pond, near Erieau, Chatham-Kent. In Ontario, clutch size varies from two to 13 eggs, averaging eight to 10 (Peck and James 1983). *Photo: P. Allen Woodliffe*

Surveys indicate that the huge expanse of marsh at Walpole Island holds more King Rails than any other site in the province. *Photo: George K. Peck*

Virginia Rail

Râle de Virginie

Rallus limicola

George K. Peck

This secretive bird reveals its presence only to those who watch from a marsh edge or use chest waders or canoes to approach its watery domain. Were it not for its vigorous response to call broadcasts of its peculiar "grunting" calls, the Virginia Rail could easily go undetected. It breeds in the southern half of Canada, the northern half of the US, parts of the American southwest, central Mexico, and parts of South America.

Distribution and population status: With few exceptions, the Virginia Rail's breeding distribution in Ontario shows little or no change from historical accounts (McIlwraith 1894; Baillie and Harrington 1936) or from the first atlas. Both atlases show this species as most common along the edge of the Canadian Shield and south in a broad band with numerous wetlands running from the Bruce Peninsula to Lake Ontario, east to Kingston, and northeast to Ottawa. As noted in the first atlas, the Virginia Rail is absent from many areas in its historical breeding range where wetlands have disappeared, mostly as a result of draining for agriculture and development. This is particularly evident in parts of southwestern Ontario, the Niagara Peninsula, and extreme eastern Ontario. Both atlases show that the species is uncommon in the Algonquin Highlands where there are relatively few productive, emergent wetlands, especially those containing cattails.

The Virginia Rail was found farther north than in the first atlas, at scattered, isolated locations in the Northern Shield, but this is probably a result of increased coverage rather than a range expansion. The northernmost occurrence was near Nabinamik (about 80 km west of Webequie), approximately 250 km north of the northernmost occurrence in the first atlas. Wetland birds as a group have shown significant increases in the Northern Shield from the first atlas to the second.

The probability of observation of the Virginia Rail increased significantly by 72% in the current atlas, with marked increases in the Lake Simcoe-Rideau (24%) and Southern Shield

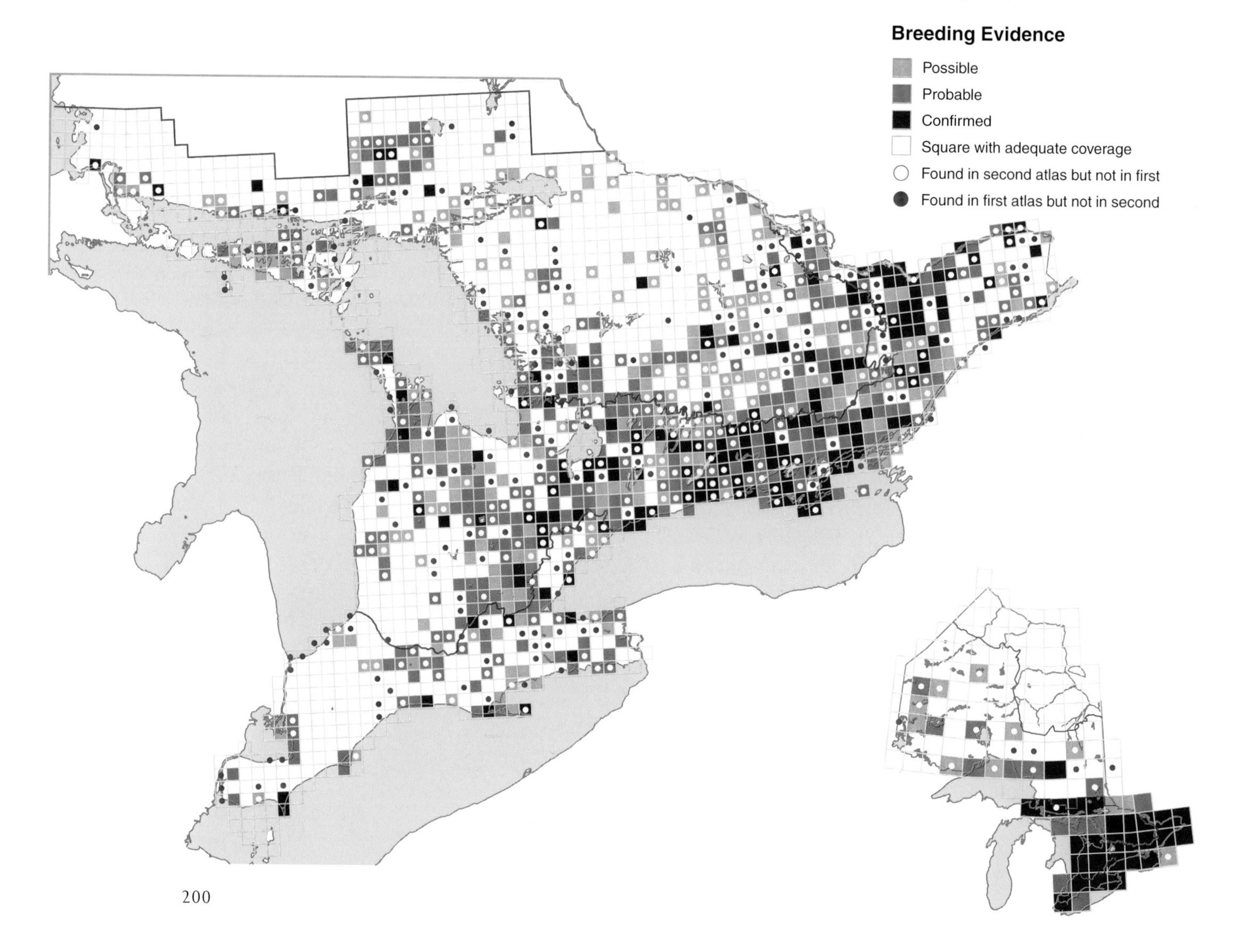

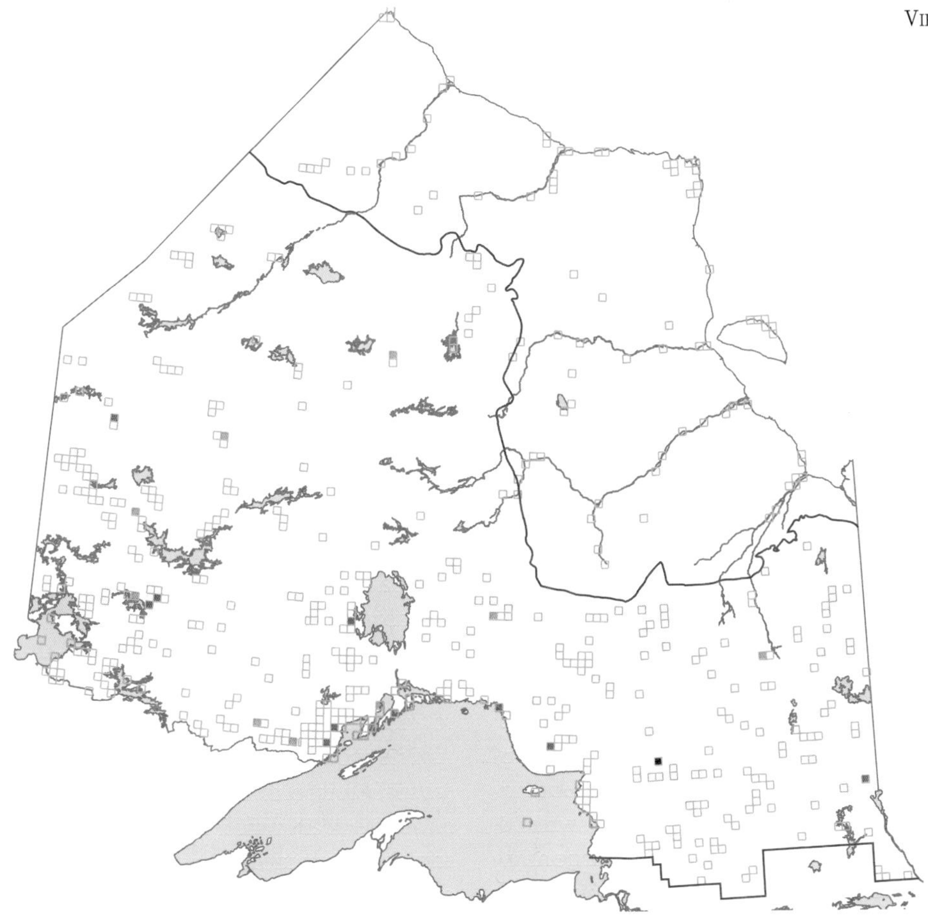

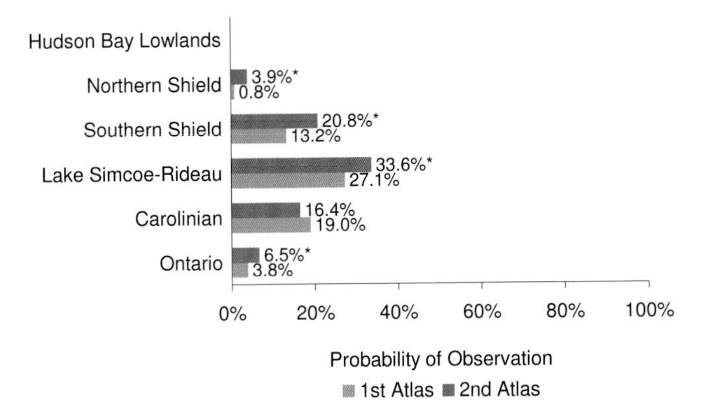

(58%) regions. The probability of observation increased significantly in the Northern Shield also, but numbers there remain quite small. These increases are somewhat unexpected, given that the species is reported to have declined by an average of 4.5% annually at MMP sites across the Great Lakes basin from 1995 to 2003 (Crewe et al. 2005). As well, BBS data suggest that the Virginia Rail population is stable in Ontario and Canada, although this survey is not efficient at detecting this species. The apparent increase indicated by the atlas is probably a result of increased effort by atlassers to find rails, aided by more widespread use of audio equipment for eliciting calls. Atlassers in some regions made special efforts to find rails; in Toronto, for example, an area where an increase in breeding populations of any wetland bird would not have been expected, the Virginia Rail was found in seven squares in which it was undetected in the first atlas. The cluster of squares around Sudbury is likely also a result of special efforts to find rails. Despite such efforts, the species was undoubtedly missed in some squares, considering that suitable wetlands are more common in southern Ontario than the distribution map suggests.

Breeding biology: The Virginia Rail breeds in wetlands that contain moderately dense emergent vegetation interspersed with shallow-water pools and mudflats. Breeding densities are highest and wetland use is most frequent in wetlands larger than 1 ha, but the species occurs in wetlands as small as 0.2 ha.

The Virginia Rail responds to call broadcasts at any time of day or night. A study in the Peterborough region indicated a 60-68% probability that this species would respond to call broadcasts throughout the breeding season (Tozer et al. 2006).

The Virginia Rail is difficult to confirm, and nests are well hidden in vegetation. Young are capable of leaving the nest immediately after hatching, but more commonly leave after three or four days. Adults vigorously defend young and nests that are close to hatching, although intruders must be within about 7 m to elicit a distraction display. Young are dependent on adults for four weeks, and adults with broods occasionally wander to wetlands as far as 3 km from the natal wetland (Conway 1995).

Abundance: Because call broadcasts were not used as part of the atlas point count protocol, point count detections were too infrequent to create an abundance map. However, the highest density probably occurs in a broad band just south of the Canadian Shield, where suitable wetlands are most numerous. – *Douglas C. Tozer*

Sora

Marouette de Caroline

Porzana carolina

George K. Peck

Like most rails, the Sora is adept at hiding in dense marsh vegetation where it breeds; however, its easily recognized, high-pitched calls frequently reveal its presence. The most widespread of any rail in Canada, it breeds in suitable wetlands from coast to coast in southern Canada and the northern US and in the American southwest.

Distribution and population status: There have been few changes in the distribution of the Sora since the first atlas or historically (e.g., McIlwraith 1894; Baillie and Harrington 1936). Both atlases show the species occurring throughout most of Ontario (including the coast of Hudson and James Bays), with the bulk in a broad band along the southern edge of and south of the Canadian Shield. Outside these areas, it occurs at scattered locations where suitable habitat exists. The scarcity of the Sora is particularly noticeable in southwestern Ontario, the Niagara Peninsula, and extreme eastern Ontario, where there is limited suitable wetland habitat. It was detected at only a few widely scattered locations across the interior of the Hudson Bay Lowlands. This might suggest that much of the wetland habitat in the interior of the lowlands is unsuitable for the Sora, but may also reflect minimal effort to find the species there. It is sparsely distributed on the Algonquin Highlands, where suitable wetlands are uncommon.

The probability of observation increased significantly between atlases in the Southern and Northern Shield regions by 33% and over 100%, respectively. Rather than real increases, the higher counts could be a result of increased effort to locate rails using call broadcasts. In the Great Lakes basin, Sora populations declined significantly by 6.2% annually from 1995 to 2003 according to the MMP, which uses call broadcasts to elicit responses from this secretive species (Crewe et al. 2005). Atlas results were similar to those of the MMP, indicating a non-significant decline in the Carolinian and Lake Simcoe-Rideau regions.

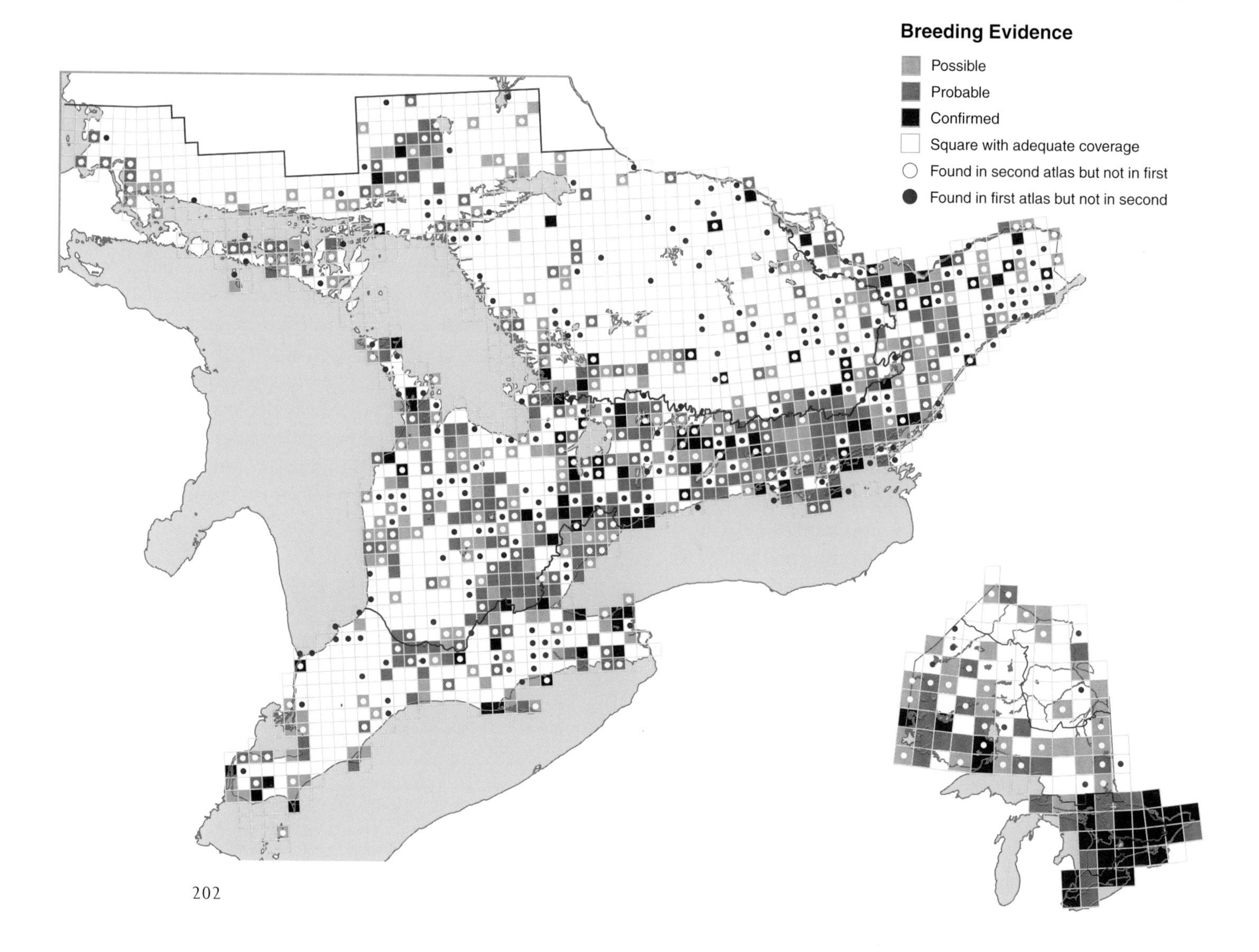

BREEDING EVIDENCE

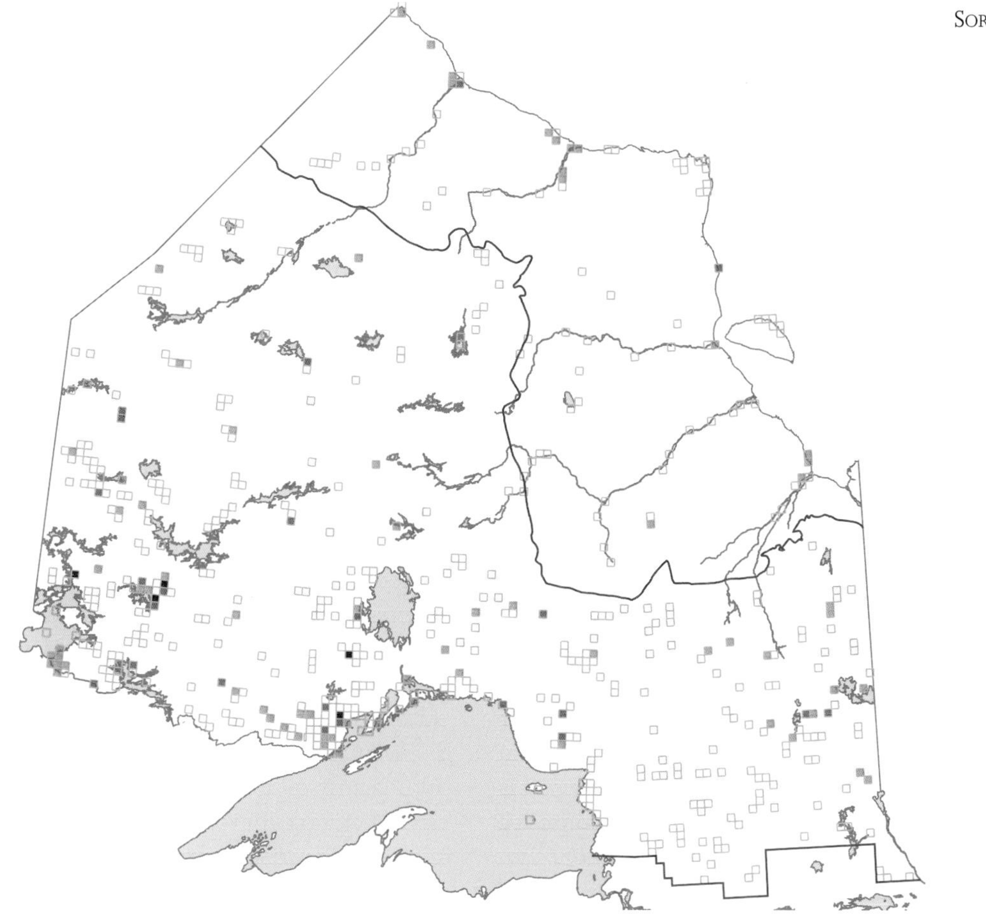

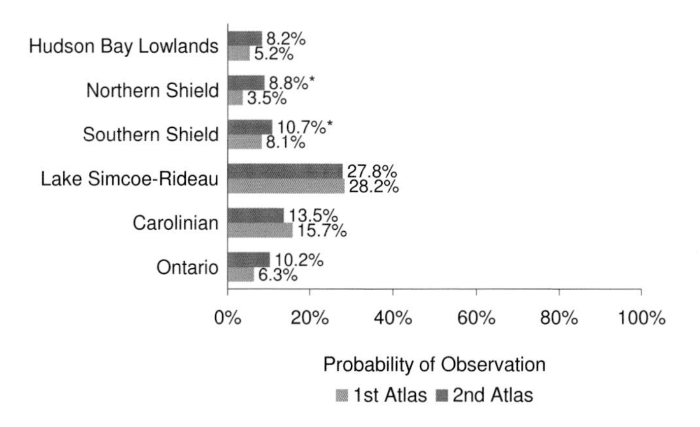

The atlas map is probably an accurate reflection of the distribution of the Sora in Ontario. It is possible that it is more widely distributed in the Hudson Bay Lowlands, as much of this area was not surveyed. Many of the squares in this region were surveyed only by aircraft, and the Sora would not be detected by this method.

Breeding biology: The Sora breeds in emergent marshes of virtually any type, as long as enough exposed, damp substrate is available to adults for gathering invertebrate food for their young. The Sora prefers somewhat greater water depths than the Virginia Rail, and it will breed in wetlands as small as 0.5 ha (Melvin and Gibbs 1996). Given that there are more squares in southern Ontario with suitable habitat than are shown on the map as being inhabited, it was probably missed by atlassers in some areas.

Breeding is difficult to confirm because incubating birds sit tightly on a well-hidden nest in a clump of emergent vegetation, often with a roof of cattail or grass, making nest-finding challenging. Fortunately, confirmation is easier when eggs hatch. At this time, adults vigorously defend the nest area with energetic distraction displays, and they continue to defend the young as broods remain intact within the natal territory for two to three weeks post-hatch. Breeding was confirmed in only 13% of squares in which the Sora was detected.

Abundance: Given that call broadcasts can increase detections of this species by as much as 583% (Gibbs and Melvin 1993), the passive point count protocol used in this atlas yielded too few detections to produce an abundance map. However, the highest abundance probably occurs in a broad band just south of the southern edge of the Canadian Shield, where suitable habitat is most common. A second area of high density probably occurs along the coast of Hudson and James Bays, where numerous suitable wetlands also exist.

The Sora is less abundant than the Virginia Rail on the southern part of the Canadian Shield (especially on the Algonquin Highlands), probably because of its preference for larger marshes with more extensive cattail or sedge, which are uncommon there. It also avoids the smaller and typically shrubbier wetlands commonly occupied by the Virginia Rail. This pattern may be partially attributable to the Sora's relative inefficiency at gathering invertebrate food for its young, as a result of its shorter bill (Kaufmann 1989), and its greater reliance on seeds (Melvin and Gibbs 1996). It may require the largest and most productive patches of emergent vegetation to sustain its young within the relatively unproductive Canadian Shield wetlands. – *Douglas C. Tozer*

Common Moorhen

Gallinule poule-d'eau

Gallinula chloropus

Jim Richards

Although the Common Moorhen is fairly common in Ontario's lower Great Lakes region, this secretive marsh bird is not well studied. Its slate-grey to blackish plumage has hints of purple and chestnut highlights, and its striking red and yellow-tipped bill extends along its forehead to the crown. Although the feet lack any webbing or lobing, it is a good swimmer (Bannor and Kiviat 2002).

The species' breeding range spans the eastern and western hemispheres. In the western hemisphere, its range extends from eastern North America south through much of South America (Bannor and Kiviat 2002). In Ontario, it breeds from Georgian Bay and Lake St. Clair eastward to the Ottawa Valley region.

Distribution and population status: In Ontario, the Common Moorhen occurs only in the south. Most of the gaps shown on the distribution map are probably real, even though apparently suitable marshes exist in unoccupied squares. While the species is found in large coastal marshes, it also occurs in many smaller inland marshes. Its centre of abundance in Ontario appears to lie in the Lake Simcoe-Rideau region within a band between the southern edge of the Southern Shield region and Lake Ontario, where both inland and coastal marshes are relatively widespread. In southwestern Ontario, it is restricted primarily to large coastal marshes.

There was little change in the overall pattern of breeding distribution of the Common Moorhen since the first atlas, although it largely disappeared from the southeast portion of the Southern Shield. Its probability of observation declined significantly by 35% overall between atlases, with declines in all three regions in which it occurred. The decline was greatest in the Southern Shield region where the probability of observation declined by 78%. This pattern is inconsistent with that exhibited by other species of marsh-obligate water birds in Ontario. No other marsh bird declined significantly overall,

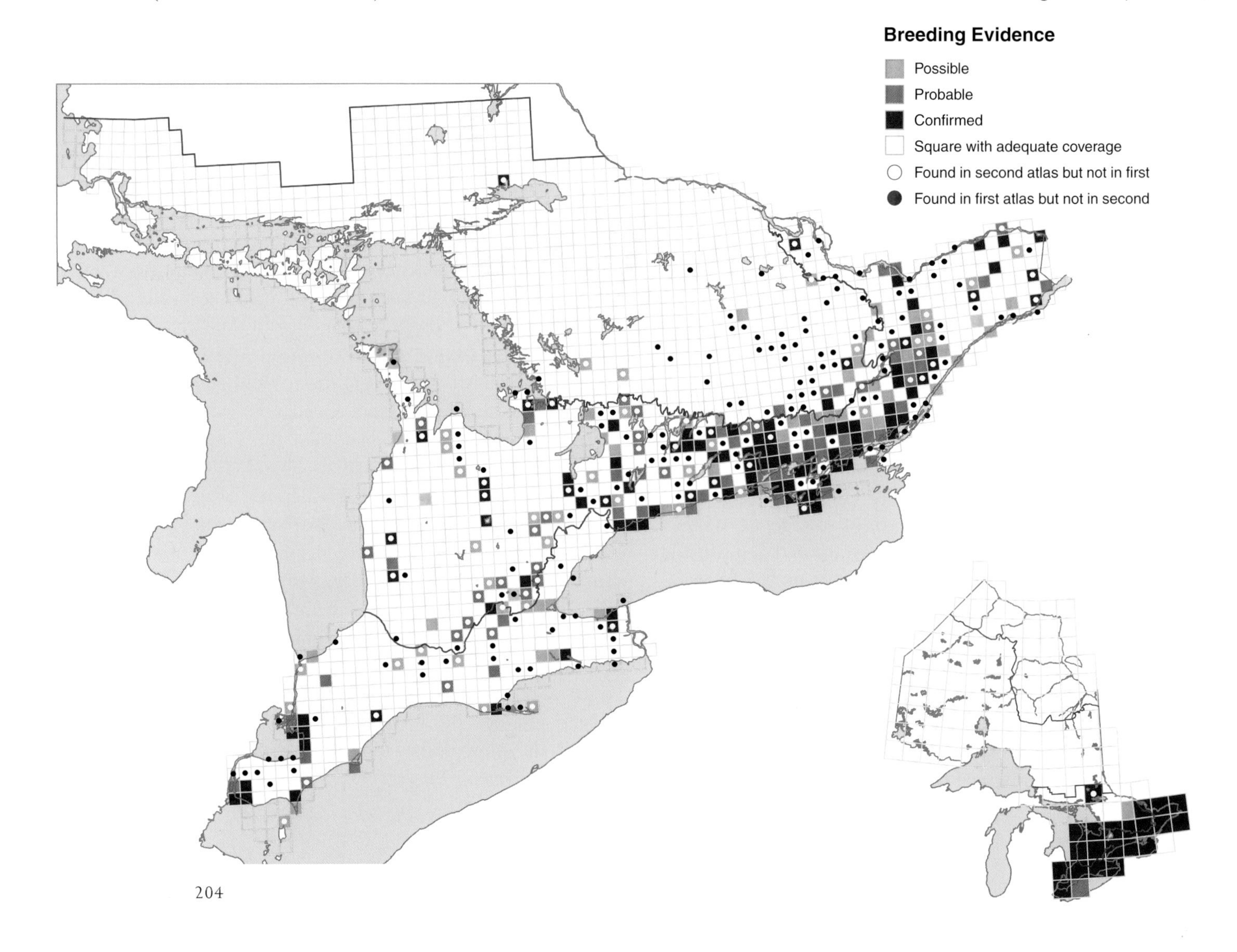

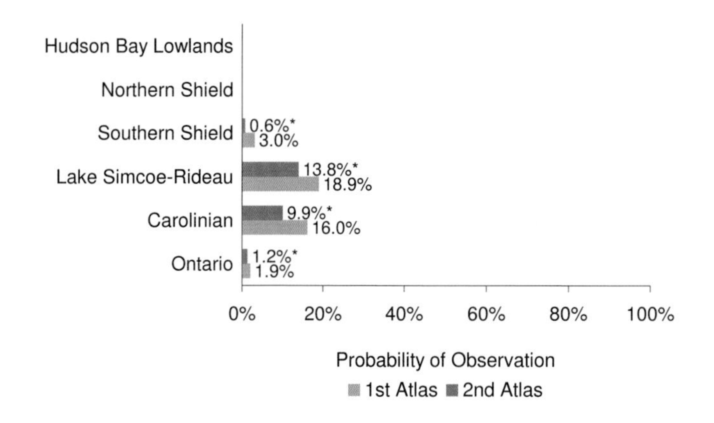

and the Black Tern was the only other marsh species that declined significantly in the Southern Shield. In contrast, the Pied-billed Grebe, Virginia Rail, Sora, and Marsh Wren increased significantly in the Southern Shield, suggesting that habitat loss and degradation are not major problems in this region. Declines in Great Lakes populations may be related to water management practices that result in less interspersion between open water and emergent vegetation.

The Common Moorhen experienced a northward expansion in distribution during the 20th century (Bannor and Kiviat 2002). The decline between atlases may be a result of a retraction by a species that is at the northern extent of its range. MMP data indicate a significant annual decline of about 5% in its relative abundance in the Great Lakes basin for the period 1995-2005 (Crewe et al. 2005). BBS results indicate a non-significant decline in Ontario and a near-significant decline in Canada since 1968.

Breeding biology: The Common Moorhen prefers relatively large, permanent marshes having a more or less equal interspersion of open water and tall emergent vegetation (frequently cattails). It prefers water depths ranging from 15-120 cm. Floating vegetation is usually a prominent feature in the territory, and muskrats are typically present (Bannor and Kiviat 2002). Nests, which are difficult to find, are usually situated close to open water and anchored in stands of robust emergent vegetation (Fredrickson 1971; Bannor and Kiviat 2002).

The moorhen lays six to nine eggs, usually in the first half of June in Ontario (Peck and James 1983). Both sexes assist with the 19-22 day incubation and provide parental care to the young (Siegfried and Frost 1975). Chicks are precocial and are fed by both parents for two to four days (Fredrickson 1971). Chicks begin to feed for themselves at approximately seven days (Bannor and Kiviat 2002).

Although secretive, the species is relatively noisy, responding readily to its neighbours' calls (Bannor and Kiviat 2002). It also responds well to broadcasts of its calls. Many of its vocalizations cannot be distinguished from those of the American Coot, so identification by voice alone is not always reliable. Grey squares on the map are those in which the only evidence for the moorhen during the second atlas was the call of either a moorhen or coot, with no sighting of the bird to verify identification of the species. Later in the season, when family groups move into open water, the moorhen is more conspicuous.

Abundance: The Common Moorhen was not detected on sufficient point counts to produce a map of relative abundance. Based upon its distribution, it is likely most abundant in a band south of the Shield, particularly in the Kingston area.
– Steven T.A. Timmermans

In Ontario, nests are usually in stands of living and dead cattails and made from dead cattails (Peck and James 1983). Eggs of the American Coot are sometimes found in moorhen nests. *Photo: George K. Peck*

The marsh at the north end of the Mountsberg Conservation Area, near Campbellville, is often used for breeding by the Common Moorhen. *Photo: Michael D. Cadman*

American Coot

Foulque d'Amérique

Fulica americana

John Reaume

Although a secretive marsh bird, the American Coot is sometimes seen diving in open water, where it feeds on submerged, aquatic plants. It is highly territorial and frequently reveals its presence through loud vocalizations similar to those of the Common Moorhen. It breeds in southern Canada, the US, Central America, northern South America, and the West Indies (Brisbin et al. 2002). Most of the Canadian population nests in the prairie pothole region (Alisaukas and Arnold 1994).

Distribution and population status: The American Coot's breeding distribution changed very little between the first and second atlases. Baillie and Harrington (1936) considered it irregularly distributed in the south and absent from many areas with apparently suitable habitat, and this pattern continues. There were three isolated observations well north of the northernmost observations in the first atlas: adults with young at the Pikangikum sewage lagoons (90 km north of Red Lake); adults exhibiting nesting behaviour at the Cat Lake sewage lagoons (120 km west of Pickle Lake); and an adult in suitable breeding habitat along the Moose River near Moosonee, where the species has bred in the past (Baillie and Harrington 1936).

The American Coot exhibited an inconsistent pattern of change between the first and second atlases. There was a significant increase (over 100%) in the probability of observation in the Northern Shield region, with significant declines of 32% and 31% in the Lake Simcoe-Rideau and Carolinian regions, respectively, but a non-significant change in the province as a whole. This pattern of change may reflect the transitory nature of the coot and other rallids, generally. The species is highly responsive to changes in marsh water levels (Brisbin et al. 2002) and is able to colonize new wetlands when water levels and vegetation cover become suitable and to leave when conditions deteriorate. Consequently, it tends to be somewhat ephemeral in

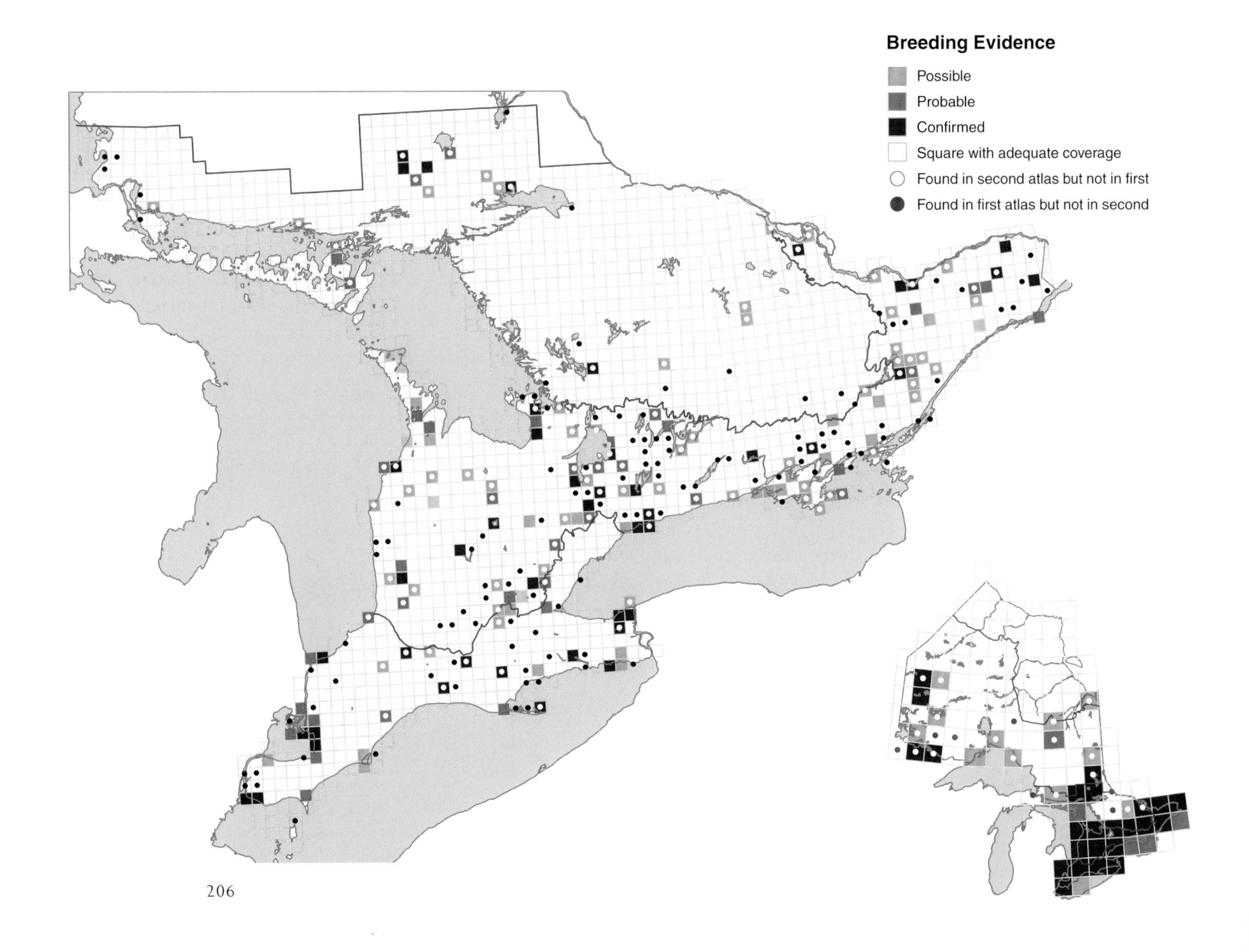

BREEDING EVIDENCE

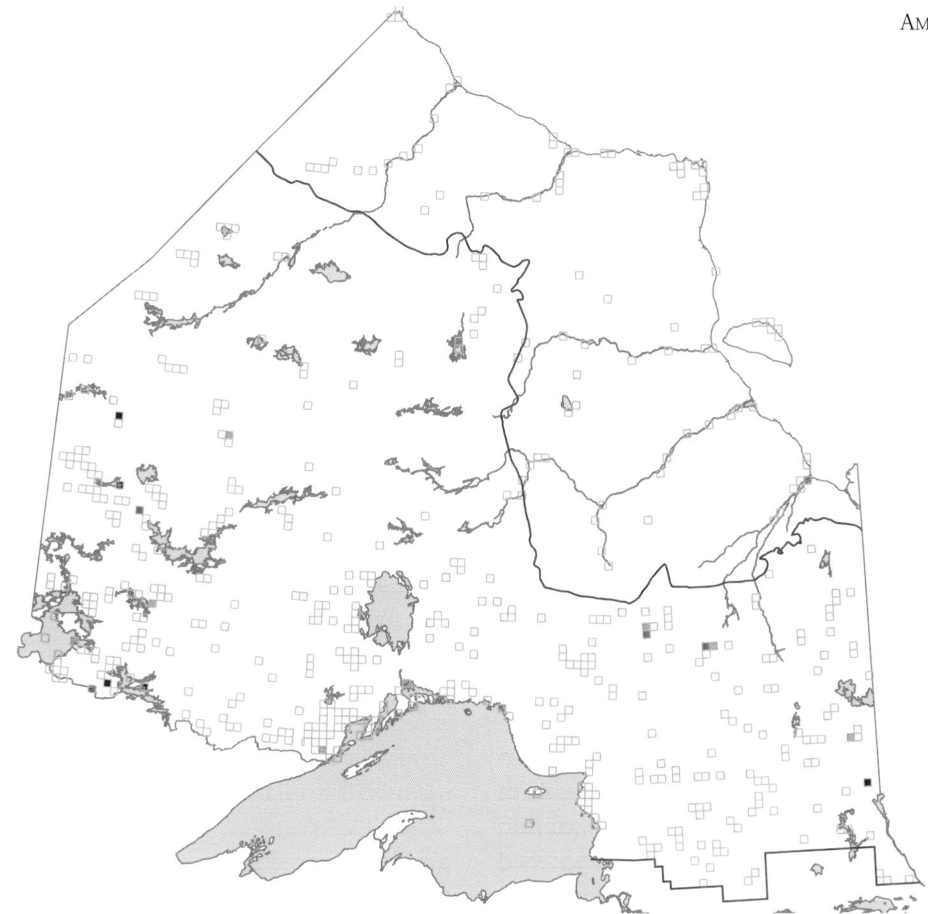

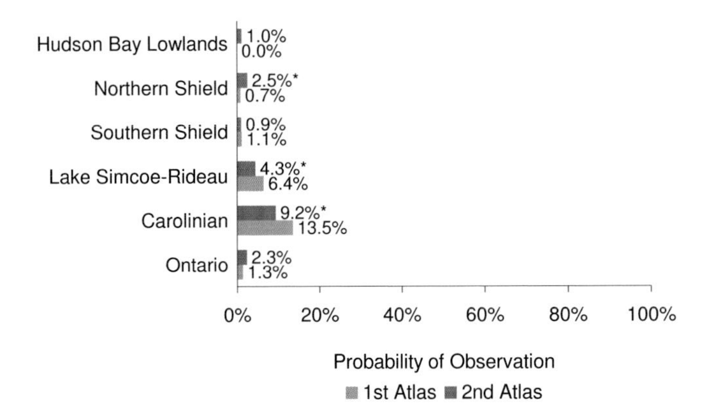

its occupancy of wetlands; it may be present in high numbers in some years and in low numbers or absent in others. The presence of sewage lagoons, with their often dramatic fluctuations in water levels and emergent vegetation, corresponds well with the pattern of occurrence of the coot, particularly in the Northern Shield, where suitable habitat for it is otherwise relatively rare.

Although the species showed a non-significant increase across the province, other evidence suggests that it is decreasing (Sandilands 2005). Lang (1991) concluded that Ontario populations had been declining significantly since 1973, and Austen et al. (1994) noted declines in the Lake St. Clair and Turkey Point-Long Point marshes. MMP data show a non-significant annual decline of 5.2% in the Great Lakes basin from 1995 to 2003 (Crewe et al. 2005). Declines may be related to significant declines that are occurring in the species' core range in western Canada.

Breeding biology: The American Coot breeds in deep-water wetlands where robust, emergent vegetation and open water remain throughout the breeding season. Preferred sites are hemi-marshes, those with a roughly 50:50 ratio of open water and vegetation. Deep-water cattail marshes subject to natural perturbation or with managed water levels are prime habitat. In parts of its range, it regularly breeds in wetlands as small as 1 ha. In Ontario, it prefers larger marshes, but it is noticeably absent from some wetlands with apparently suitable breeding conditions. For example, around Peterborough in 2001, the species was found only in a single 213 ha marsh amongst a randomly selected sample of nine similar wetlands ranging in size from 2.6 to 213 ha; all sites maintained ideal habitat throughout the breeding season and supported breeding Common Moorhen (Tozer 2003). The coot is one of the most easily detected members of the rail family, and given its loud calls, most of the gaps shown on the map are probably real, even though large, apparently suitable marshes may exist in unoccupied squares. Grey squares on the map are those in which the only evidence for the coot during the second atlas was the call of either a coot or moorhen, with no sighting to verify identification of the species.

Abundance: This species was not detected on enough point counts to produce a map of relative abundance. Given its widely scattered pattern of occurrence, a special well-planned survey within and across wetlands would be required to obtain the necessary data. The use of call broadcasts during point counts would likely have improved detections only slightly, given that American Coot does not respond to broadcasts of its call as consistently as most other secretive marsh birds (Conway and Gibbs 2005). – *Douglas C. Tozer*

Sandhill Crane

Grue du Canada

Grus canadensis

The Sandhill Crane is a large, long-lived wader, breeding in extensive open grasslands and freshwater marshes from Alaska to Baffin Island, south to southern British Columbia, the Prairie Provinces, northeastern Minnesota, Wisconsin, Michigan, Ontario, and Québec (Tacha et al. 1992; Gauthier and Aubry 1996). Smaller, disjunct breeding populations, some recognized as distinct subspecies, are found in California, Oregon, Nevada, Utah to Montana, Florida to southern Mississippi and southern Georgia, and western Cuba. Its breeding range formerly was more extensive, reaching south to Arizona, Baja California, northwestern and central Mexico, Illinois, and northern Ohio. Most populations are now stable or increasing (Tacha et al. 1992). Between three and six subspecies have been recognized by various authorities, two of which, *G. c. rowani* (Canadian Sandhill Crane) and *G. c. tabida* (Greater Sandhill Crane), nest in Ontario.

Distribution and population status: Although two subspecies are known to nest in Ontario, atlas data do not distinguish between them. Birds nesting in the Hudson Bay Lowlands and most of the Northern Shield are referable to *G. c. rowani* (Lumsden 1971), while those nesting from the southern edge of the Northern Shield (southern Algoma Dist., western Rainy River Dist.) south to the Lake Simcoe-Rideau and Carolinian regions are *G. c. tabida* (Lumsden 1971; Tebbel and Ankney 1982). The boundary between the two subspecies, however, is unclear.

The range of the Sandhill Crane has expanded substantially since the first atlas, so much so that the species now can be expected almost anywhere in Ontario where suitable extensive open wetland habitat exists. In the Hudson Bay Lowlands and contiguous portions of the Northern Shield, the population is thought to be stable or increasing (Pedlar and Ross 1997), and the increase in the number of squares between atlases may be in part an artifact of increased detection through aerial surveys by

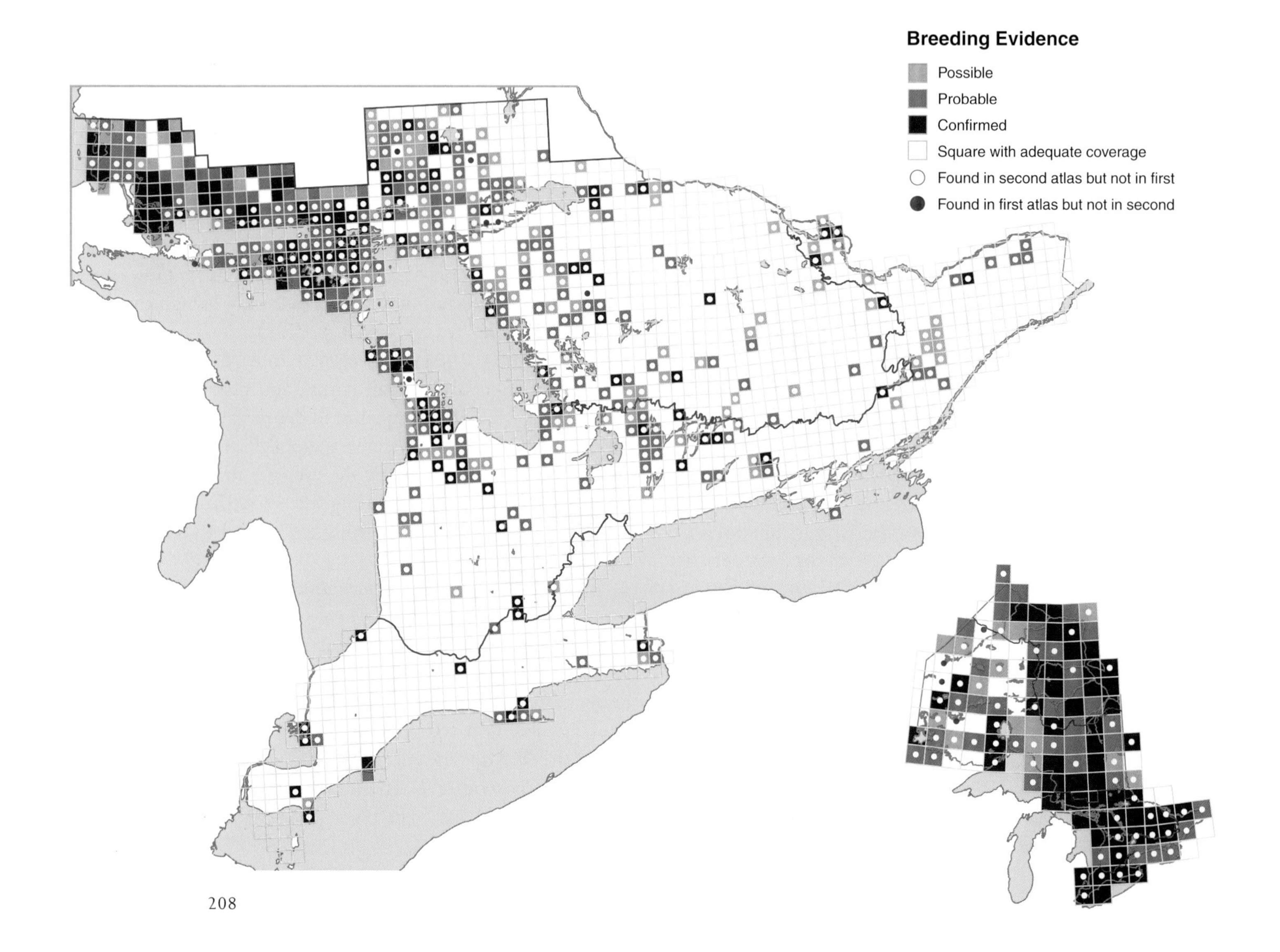

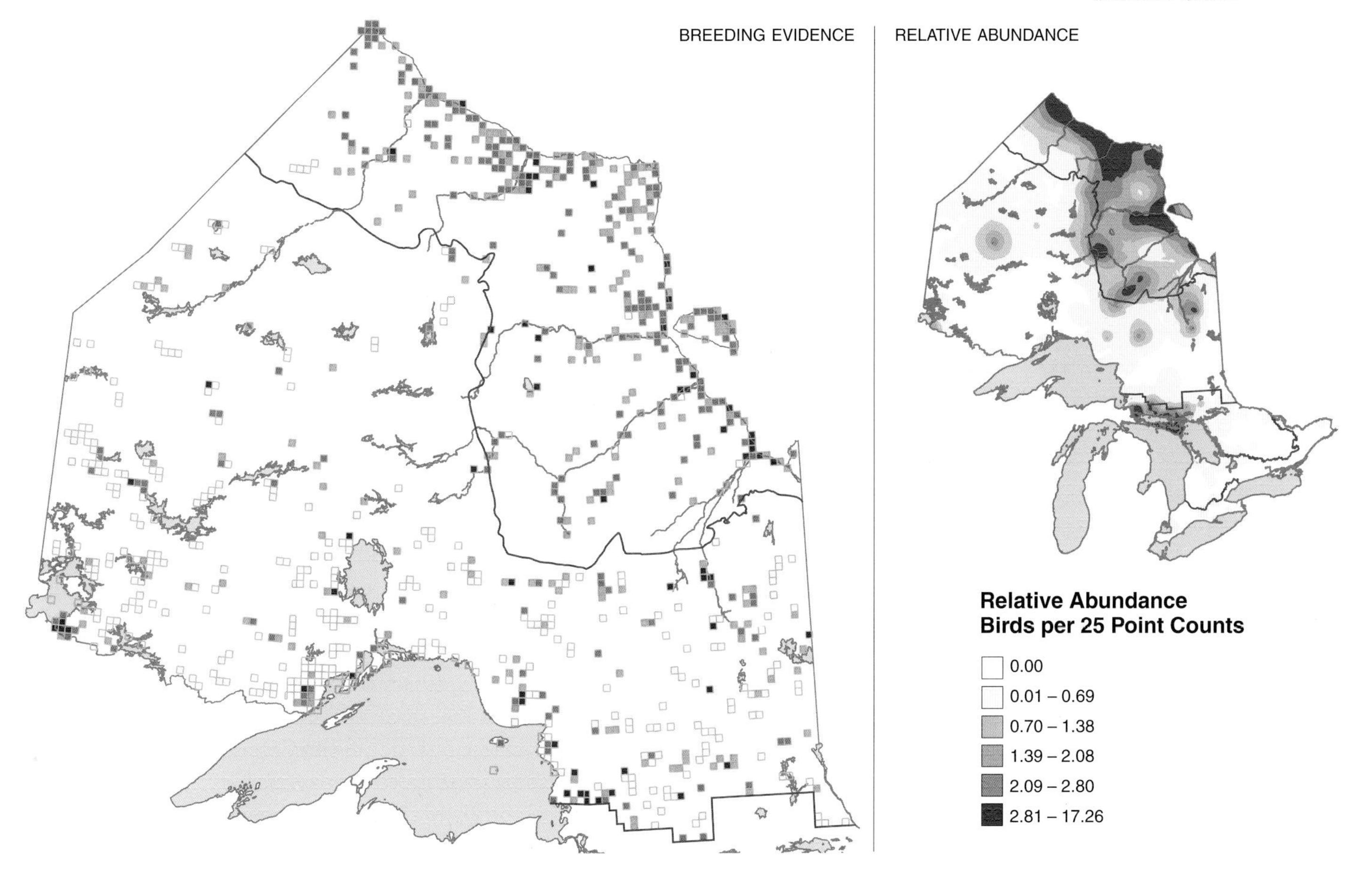

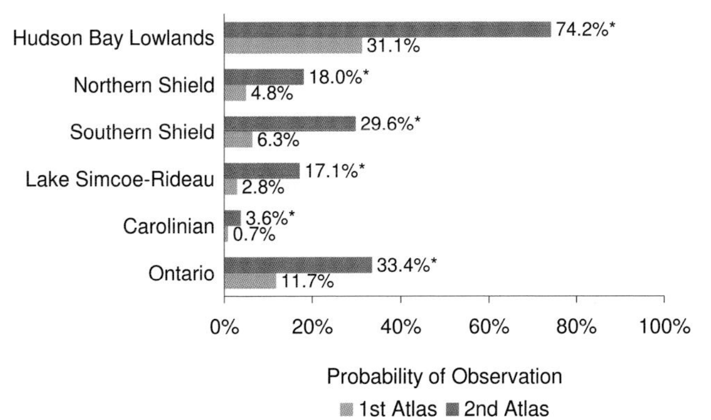

CWS and OMNR. The increase has been most dramatic in southern Ontario, particularly in the Lake Simcoe-Rideau and Carolinian regions. Breeding has been confirmed in all but a few municipalities in southern Ontario since the first atlas.

Breeding biology: The Sandhill Crane is perennially monogamous and exhibits strong fidelity to nesting areas, often occupying the same wetland in successive years. Adults vocalize frequently during the early stages of territorial establishment but less so as the nesting cycle progresses (Tacha et al. 1992). The calls may be heard over substantial distances, facilitating detection. Nests are located in marshes and wet sedge fens and vary from a well-concealed, nearly structureless scrape to a large mound of gathered vegetation (particularly in the south; *G. c. tabida*). The young leave the nest soon after hatching and are initially inconspicuous and difficult to detect, but later forage in adjacent upland areas. Confirmation of breeding through the detection of fledged young is easily achieved during low-level aerial surveys, as the adults often engage in distraction displays (Riley 1982). The adults provide extended parental care, and families remain together until the following breeding season, when yearling birds are forced from breeding territories. Juveniles associate in sub-adult, non-breeding flocks until initial breeding in their fourth to seventh year (Tacha et al. 1992); possible breeding evidence in some squares may have resulted from the observation of non-breeders. Nevertheless, the extent and distribution depicted in the breeding evidence map is probably accurate for the province as a whole.

Abundance: The Sandhill Crane occurs at relatively low densities throughout its breeding range in Ontario. Although the nodes of high density evident on the abundance map are generally unrealistic, likely reflecting accessibility and sampling intensity, the general pattern of overall relative abundance is informative. The map shows areas of highest abundance in the Hudson Bay Lowlands, along the North Channel between Sault Ste. Marie and Sudbury, and on adjacent Manitoulin Island. This pattern of abundance is in general agreement with Pedlar and Ross (1997), who reported densities of 1-5 pairs/100 km^2 over much of the lowlands, with somewhat higher densities in the lower Moose, Albany, and Attawapiskat River drainages in southern James Bay, in the general vicinity of Cape Henrietta Maria, and between the Winisk River and the Pen Islands in the northwest. The Southern Shield, Lake Simcoe-Rideau, and Carolinian regions all support much lower average densities (less than 0.5 birds/25 point counts), consistent with the more localized distribution evident on the breeding evidence map. The lowest average density (0.05 birds/25 point counts) in the Carolinian is expected, given the limited availability of relatively large, isolated wetlands preferred by this species. – *Donald A. Sutherland and William J. Crins*

American Golden-Plover

Pluvier bronzé

Pluvialis dominica

Ron Ridout

Formerly considered a subspecies of the Lesser Golden-Plover, the American Golden-Plover was recognized in 1993 as distinct from the Pacific Golden-Plover (*Pluvialis fulva*) based on breeding vocalizations and nesting habitat (American Ornithologists Union 1993; Johnson and Connors 1996). The American Golden-Plover is a common breeding species from western Alaska (where it occurs sympatrically with Pacific Golden-Plover), east through the Yukon and the northern Northwest Territories to western Nunavut, south along the Hudson Bay coast through Manitoba to the vicinity of Cape Henrietta Maria in Ontario. Ontario represents the most southerly extent of its breeding range. About 78% of the global population is estimated to breed in Canada (Donaldson et al. 2000); the small population in the northern Hudson Bay Lowlands of Ontario constitutes far less than 1% of the total global population. Donaldson et al. (2000) consider the American Golden-Plover to be of high conservation concern in Canada, while Ross et al. (2003) consider it to be of only moderate conservation concern in Ontario due to the peripheral nature of the breeding population in the province.

Distribution and population status: Though the American Golden-Plover has likely always been present as a breeder on the Hudson Bay coast of Ontario, the first nest was not documented until 1970 (Peck 1972). During the first atlas, breeding evidence was reported in five squares between the Sutton River mouth, Cape Henrietta Maria, and the vicinity of Hook Point on the northern James Bay coast; possible breeding was reported in a single square near the Pen Islands. During the second atlas, most occurrences were within a few kilometres of the Hudson Bay coast, but in the Cape Henrietta Maria area the species was reported on relict marine beach ridges as much as 20 km inland. The species probably occurs at least locally elsewhere within the tundra zone along the Hudson Bay coast of Ontario. Suitable breeding habitat occurs in the

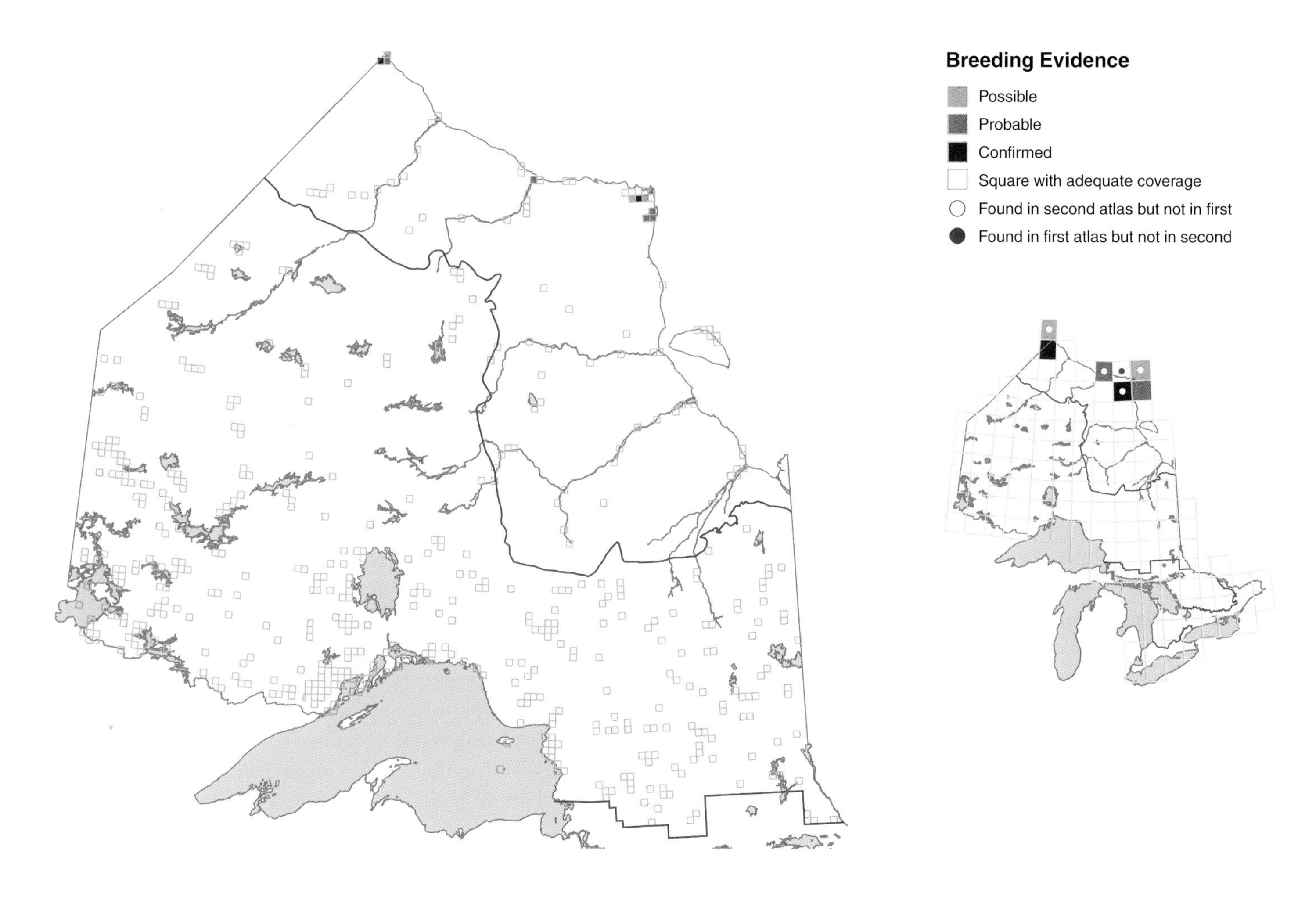

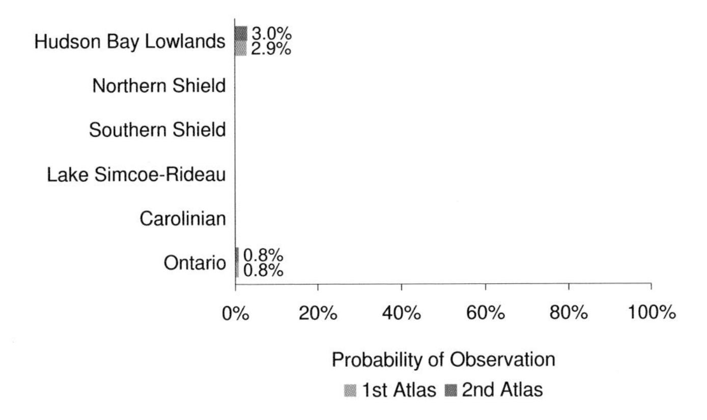

vicinity of the Niskibi River between Fort Severn and the Pen Islands, as well as between the Winisk and Severn Rivers in the vicinity of the Shagamu River, where the species was observed in 1990, though breeding was neither confirmed nor suspected (Wilson and McRae 1993).

Breeding biology: As at Churchill, Manitoba, arrival at breeding areas in Ontario is probably from late May to early June, with the onset of nesting by mid-June (Peck and James 1983, 1993b), later in abnormally cold years (Jehl 2004). In Ontario, breeding habitat may be characterized as relatively dry ridges in a mosaic of wet and dry tundra often interspersed with shallow ponds. Preferred nesting habitat is broad, open, relict marine beach ridges supporting lichen-heath vegetation, which become snow-free earlier than the surrounding landscape. Nesting habitat south of the Pen Islands in 2004 was primarily flat lichen-heath ridges with a micro-relief consisting of frost heaves colonized by lichens and mosses; although scattered, stunted spruce were present, the ridges had few to no shrubs (pers. obs.).

The American Golden-Plover can be overlooked by atlassers, particularly when occurring at low densities. Territories can be large (25 ha) and the intensity of defence and distraction displays tends to be greatest in close proximity to the nest and less so peripherally (Johnson and Connors 1996). The conspicuous "butterfly" display flight accompanied by the rhythmic repetitive call (Johnson and Connors 1996) had probably ceased by the time most atlassing was conducted. Nesting birds are quite approachable and nests are not particularly difficult to find.

Abundance: Detections on point counts were too few to produce a map of relative abundance. The American Golden-Plover was detected on 11 point counts in the vicinity of Hook Point south of Cape Henrietta Maria, near the mouth of the Winisk River, and in the extreme northwest inland from the Pen Islands. Estimated breeding densities (pairs/km^2) for two squares in the vicinity of Cape Henrietta Maria during the first atlas ranged from 0.01 for the square containing the Cape and 0.11 to 1.0 for the square inland from Hook Point. Given the compression of suitable beach ridge habitat in the Cape region, the densities there are probably greater than elsewhere along the Ontario coasts of Hudson and James Bays. During the second atlas, a minimum density of 0.5 pairs/km^2 was found in one square in the vicinity of the Pen Islands. Though a number of areas offering potentially suitable breeding habitat remain relatively under-surveyed, given the limited suitable breeding habitat available and the observed low densities, the provincial breeding population is probably no more than a few hundred pairs, as suggested by Ross et al. (2003). – *Donald A. Sutherland*

Nests are typically located in areas with a micro-relief of frost heaves colonized by lichens, mosses, Mountain Avens, and Lapland Rosebay.
Photo: Jim Richards

Dry, hummocky lichen-heath tundra is the American Golden-Plover's preferred nesting habitat in Ontario. Near Cape Henrietta Maria, Polar Bear Prov. Park, site of the first documented provincial nest, 24 June 1970.
Photo: George K. Peck

Semipalmated Plover

Pluvier semipalmé

Charadrius semipalmatus

Mark Peck

The Semipalmated Plover is a common breeding shorebird in the North American low Arctic from Alaska to the North Shore of the Gulf of St. Lawrence and Newfoundland and Labrador, with occasional unusual breeding records as far south as the lower 48 United States (Nol and Blanken 1999). Locally common in the low Arctic of North America, with breeding densities decreasing with increasing latitude across its range (pers. obs.), the Ontario population could comprise up to 2% (3,000 individuals) of the estimated world population of 150,000 birds (Morrison et al. 2006).

Distribution and population status: Breeding records from the Hudson Bay Lowlands date from as early as a century ago (Hussell in Cadman et al. 1987). The species is easily detectable, and 32 of 53 records in this atlas were of possible or probable breeding. Almost 40% of the records were confirmed, a somewhat lower percentage than the 67% of squares with confirmation of breeding in the first atlas. However, there was a 50% increase in the number of squares with breeding evidence (53 versus 34), due in part to greater effort along the coast during the second atlas. The 37% increase in probability of observation between atlases is not significant. This species ventures inland along the abundant gravel-cobble bars of the Severn, Winisk, and Attawapiskat Rivers up to 160 km from the Hudson Bay coast. It was also reported along the Sachigo River at the confluence of the Severn. Its presence along other major rivers (e.g., Sutton, Black Duck) was not reported, probably due to lack of coverage, although its presence on the Black Duck River about 120 km inland was recorded during the first atlas. The distribution in this atlas is slightly more widespread and suggests a more or less continuous coastal distribution on Hudson and James Bays in suitable habitat to as far south as Northbluff Point. The first atlas reported the species at Moose Factory/Moosonee, but given the dynamic nature of gravel bar habitats, its absence in the

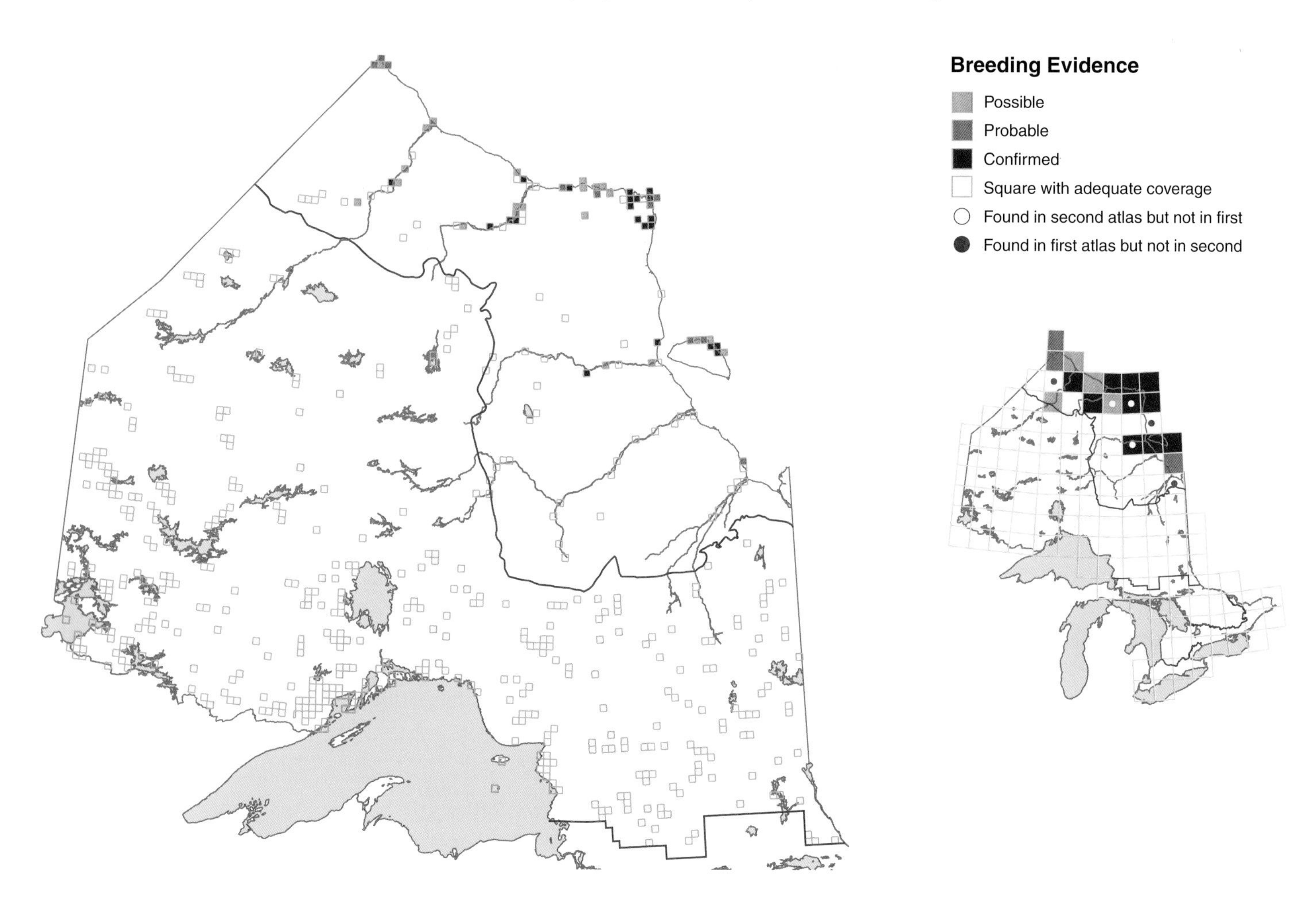

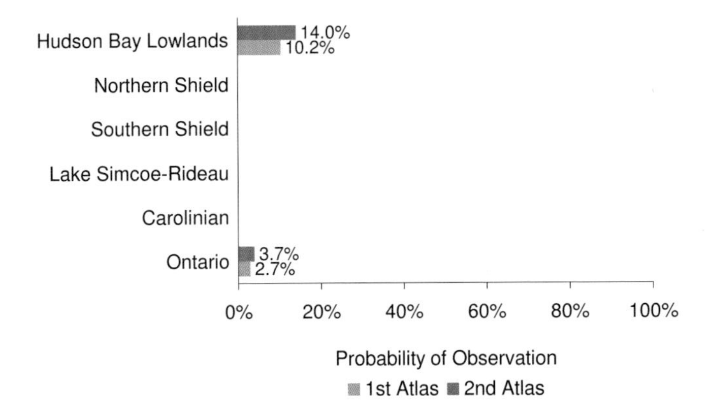

second atlas could be due to changes in the river or to it simply having been overlooked. There were no records from the more northerly Albany River despite abundant, apparently suitable habitat and fairly extensive coverage.

Breeding biology: Breeding is from early June to July (Peck and James 1983). Nests are placed on drier, open habitat with primarily gravel or well-vegetated lichen-heath tundra substrate, on gravel or dry tundra dominated ridges. At least 25 nests with eggs or newly hatched young were reported during the atlas period. Feeding occurs around nest sites and on wet coastal and riparian shores and the edges of small ponds. The long 24-day incubation period (with incubation shared by both sexes) increases the potential time for confirmation of breeding. Both sexes exhibit conspicuous distraction (e.g., "broken-wing") displays when the observer is within 5 m of the nest (pers. obs.). Clutches are comprised of four mottled, cryptic eggs. Males have high breeding-site fidelity (Flynn et al. 1999), and if the territorial male is replaced through death or displacement, the new occupant of the territory often picks a very similar nesting site, suggesting relatively narrow habitat preferences. Nest substrates are stable, relative to those used by many other arctic breeding shorebirds (e.g., wet sedge meadows), so this may help to explain the very similar nesting distribution between the two atlases. There is little evidence of floating, non-breeding individuals.

Abundance: Detections on atlas point counts were too low to produce a map of relative abundance. Estimated breeding densities for 10 squares along the Hudson and James Bay coasts during the first atlas ranged from 0.02 to 10 pairs/km^2. The male display flight, occurring primarily in unmated individuals, is performed over a large territory and is easy to hear, even in wind, making the species easy to detect. Once eggs are present, observers need to be within 5 m of the nest to hear or see this highly cryptic species. Most birds eventually pair and breed (pers. obs.), so individuals heard during the atlas period in the possible breeding evidence category are probably breeding. The species was detected during 36 point counts in 11 squares: about 2% of point counts in the Hudson Bay Lowlands region yielded this species. Breeding densities in the second atlas are probably similar to those obtained during the first. The high rate of breeding confirmation suggests that accurate densities may be obtainable through counts of nests or pairs via transects in low arctic coastal and riparian habitats. – *Erica Nol*

Nests are shallow depressions, frequently lined with lichen or pebbles, with clutches typically comprising four eggs. Cape Henrietta Maria, 18 June 2005. *Photo: Mark Peck*

Relict gravel beach ridges and open, dry lichen-heath tundra are the primary habitats for nesting in Ontario. South of Cape Henrietta Maria, Polar Bear Prov. Park, 18 June 2005. *Photo: Mark Peck*

Piping Plover

Pluvier siffleur

Charadrius melodus

George K. Peck

The plaintive and melodius call of the Piping Plover was once regularly heard at a number of sites on Ontario's lower Great Lakes and on the shores of Lake of the Woods in northwestern Ontario. Historical numbers were liberally estimated at 152 to 162 breeding pairs (Russell 1983). Significant population declines began in the 1930s and continued through the 1960s and 1970s, with the last known breeding in southern Ontario occurring in 1977 at Long Point on Lake Erie (Lambert and Nol 1978).

A small population of the Piping Plover continues to breed in the Lake of the Woods area along the border between Ontario and Minnesota. In Minnesota, the species breeds primarily on two offshore barrier sand islands (Pine and Curry Islands). The Minnesota population has declined from a high of approximately 50 adults during the early 1980s to five adults (one breeding pair) in 2003 (Haws 2005).

The Piping Plover has been listed as Endangered in Ontario since 1977 and in Canada by COSEWIC since 1985. The species, however, has not recovered as a breeding bird in southern Ontario and is on the brink of extirpation in the northwest of the province.

Distribution and population status: During the second atlas, the Piping Plover was reported from two primary locations: shorelines along the southern Great Lakes, and Windy Point on Lake of the Woods. The species was reported from five squares during the current atlas period and three squares during the previous atlas (1981-1985). A courting pair at Wasaga Beach Prov. Park (Jackson 2005) during 2005 was a welcome sign that the species might start to reoccupy former breeding sites in the Ontario Great Lakes area. This pair had been banded as chicks in Michigan's northern Lower Peninsula (Jackson 2005). A pair of Piping Plovers was observed at this same location in 1981 during the first atlas. Fifty-eight breeding pairs were reported in Michigan in 2005, with a self-sustaining rate

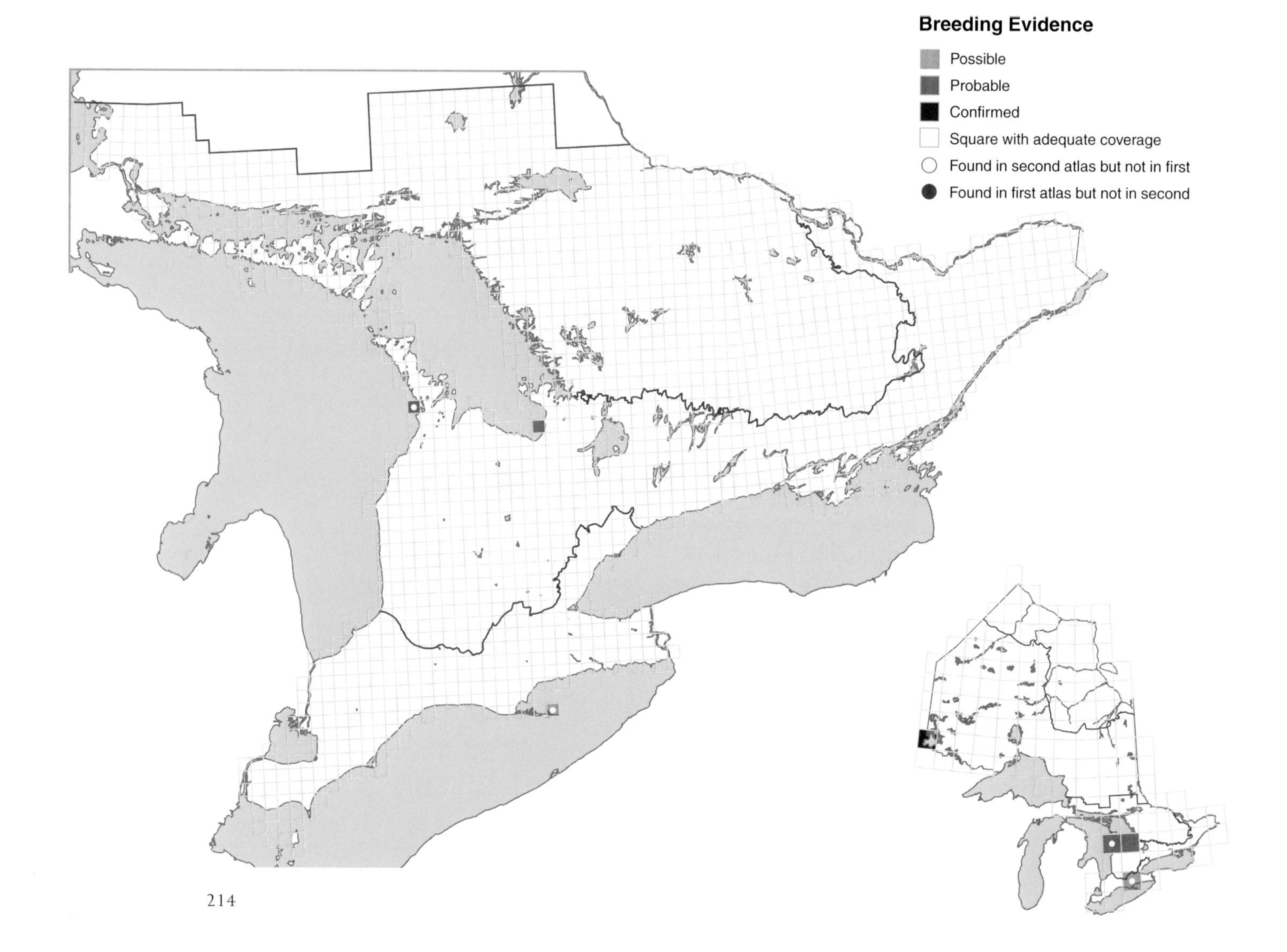

BREEDING EVIDENCE

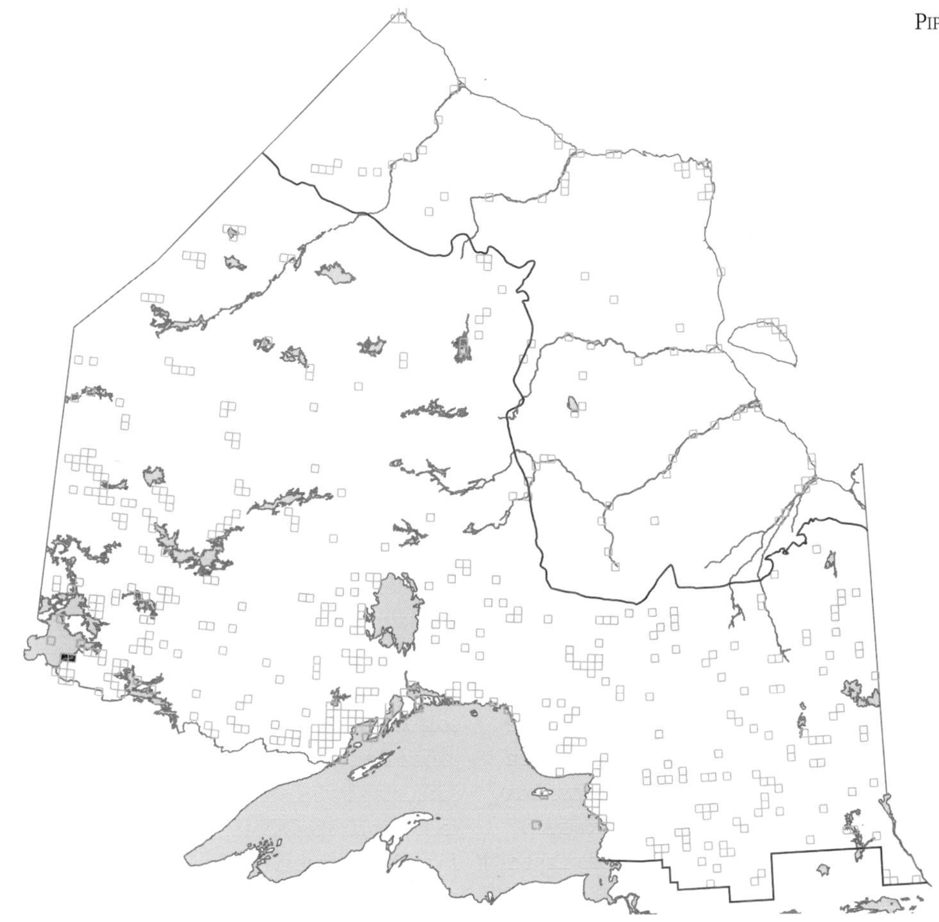

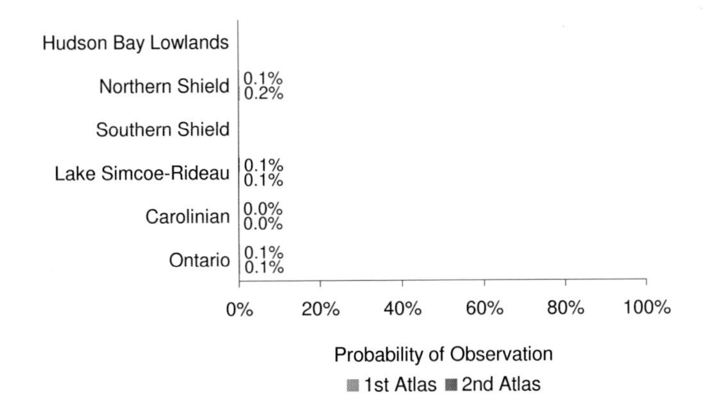

of fledging young (Cuthbert 2006).

A probable breeding pair was reported from Oliphant Beach on the Bruce Peninsula during the 2002 breeding season. However, further monitoring failed to locate this pair, which may have been disturbed by beach users. The species continues to be reported from lower Great Lake shorelines, primarily Long Point, Pelee Island, and Point Pelee on Lake Erie and Presqu'ile Prov. Park on Lake Ontario. While individual birds exhibit breeding behaviour and have been seen for a period of days during the breeding season, no breeding has been confirmed at these former nesting locations.

Breeding biology: Breeding is initiated within a few days of arrival on breeding sites in mid-May in Ontario. The nest site typically includes open sand, gravel, or shell-covered substrates. The male begins nest-scraping and stone tossing as part of courtship activities and pair establishment, and one of a number of scrapes is selected as the nest site. A typical clutch consists of four buff-marked eggs with fine splotches of black or brownish black. Incubation usually lasts about 25-28 days, with both adults sharing incubation duties. Precocial chicks leave the nest area within hours of hatching and begin foraging.

Abundance: In recent years, the Ontario population has been restricted to the Sable Islands Prov. Nature Reserve and to Windy Point. While these plovers continue to be seen on the Sable Islands on an annual basis, the last recorded successful breeding there occurred in 1991. Prior to 1995, birds occasionally attempted to nest on Windy Point, although nesting success was very poor; this is thought to be due primarily to predation by the Red Fox and Ring-billed Gull. The very tip of Windy Point was breached in 1994 by a late fall storm, resulting in the establishment of a small island at the tip of the point. Confirmed breeding occurred at this site in 2000 with three adults and one nest containing eggs, and again in 2002 with five adults and two nests with eggs. Both nests from 2002 were lost due to rising water levels on Lake of the Woods after unusually high June rainfall events (pers. obs.).

Repeated nest failures and the declining status of the neighbouring Minnesota population mean that isolated pairs in northwestern Ontario are extremely vulnerable to extirpation. Recent sightings of the Piping Plover on the Ontario Great Lakes shorelines provide hope that individuals from the growing Michigan population will eventually re-colonize former breeding sites in the Great Lakes Basin. – *Leo E. Heyens*

Killdeer

Pluvier kildir

Charadrius vociferus

Tim Stewart

The Killdeer is one of the most common and familiar of North American shorebirds, breeding in non-mountainous regions from the tropics to the Arctic (Jackson and Jackson 2000). In Ontario, it occurs from the shores of the Great Lakes to the shores of Hudson and James Bays, breeding in open habitats including gravel and sandy beaches, barren raised beach ridges, gravel bars in the braided lower reaches or rivers, islands in lakes, and limestone alvars; now it breeds more commonly in the province in anthropogenic habitats such as gravel parking lots, rooftops, airports, farm fields, road edges, and abandoned building sites.

Although it was mentioned as a common breeding species in the first atlas, BBS data indicate a two-thirds decline in Ontario from 1986 to 2005. The decline noted in Ontario was observed somewhat earlier (by 1980) over all Canadian BBS routes. It is one of the few shorebird species reasonably well surveyed with BBS methodology, and these declines should prompt unease as the cause is not known. The Killdeer is considered a Species of Moderate Concern in Canada (Donaldson et al. 2000), although its large estimated population size in Ontario resulted in a designation of low conservation priority in the Ontario Shorebird Conservation Plan (Ross et al. 2003).

Distribution and population status: Breeding records date from the late 1880s, with early information suggesting that the centre of the species' distribution was in the Prairies and the Great Lakes region. The current atlas indicates that breeding in Ontario is concentrated in the agricultural southwest and other primarily agricultural regions south of the Shield. This species is much less abundant in the Boreal Forest. In the north, the species has a nearly continuous breeding distribution along the Hudson Bay and James Bay coastline, breeding on dry coastal beaches and near human settlements. The Killdeer also breeds up to 100 km inland from these northern coasts along the shores and on gravel bars of major rivers.

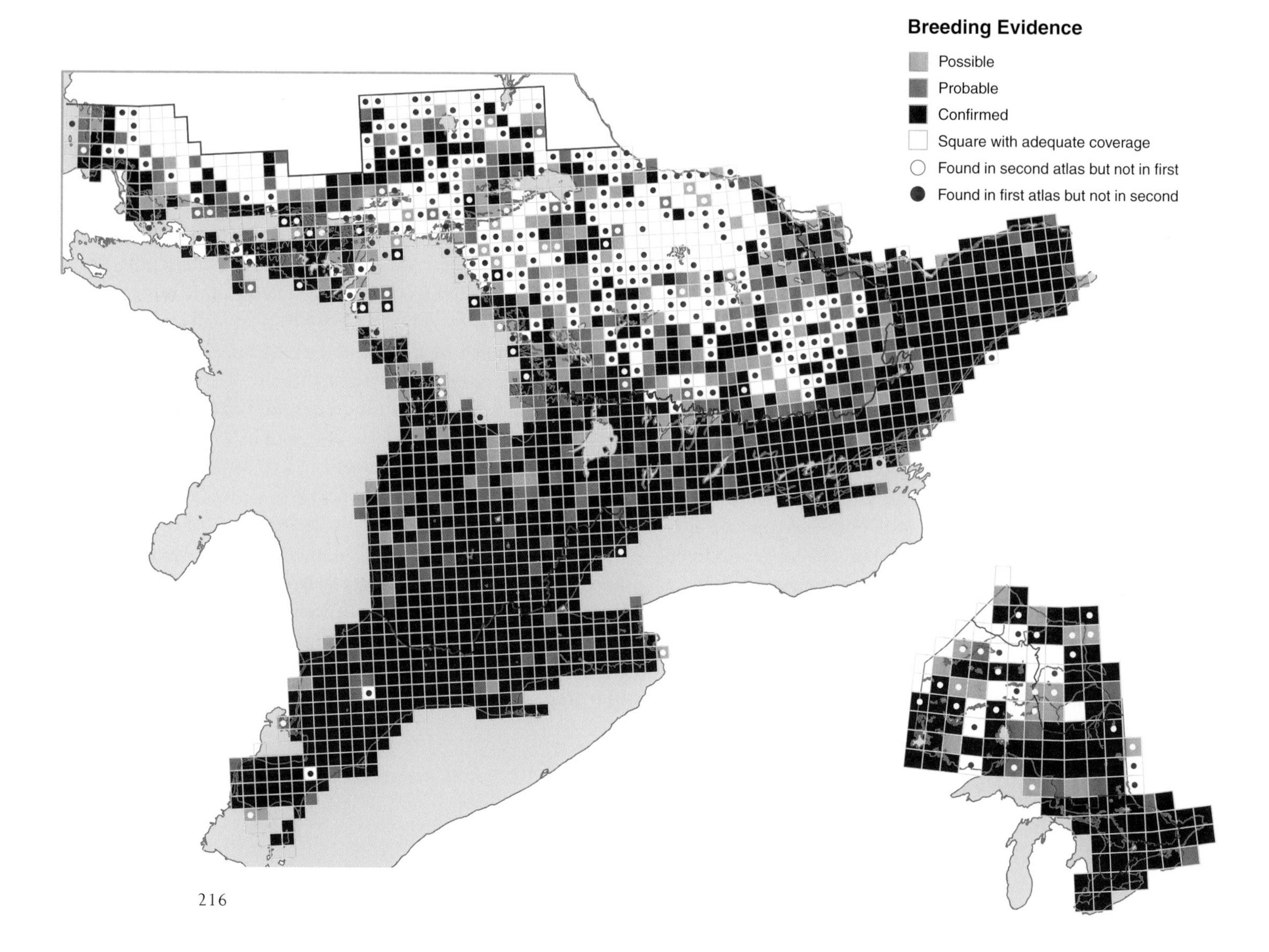

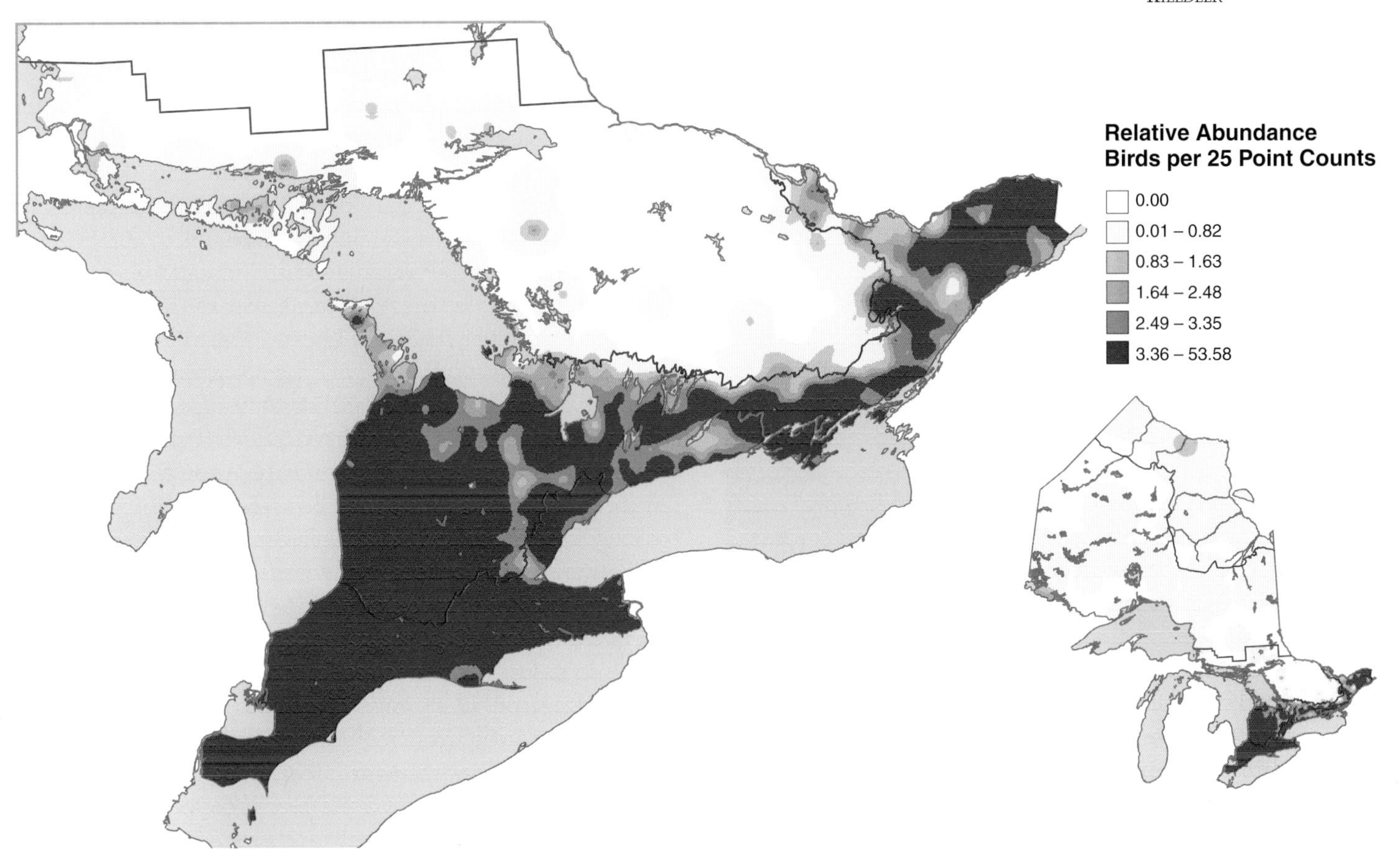

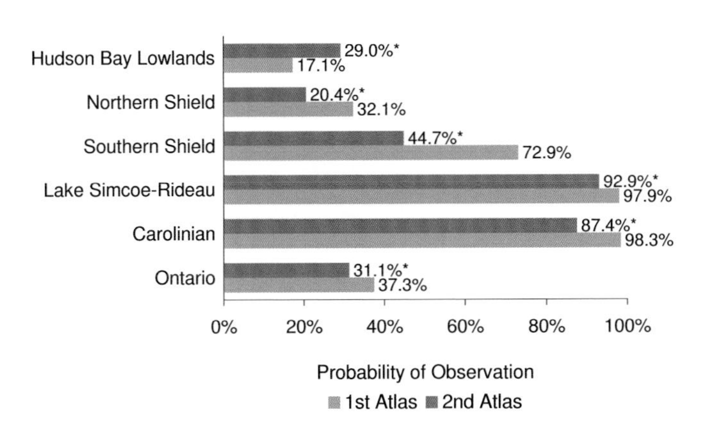

The probability of observation of the Killdeer declined significantly between the first and second atlas overall, with declines of 39% and 36% in the Southern and Northern Shield regions, respectively. Reasons for the losses are unknown but may be attributable in part to loss of nesting habitat due to re-establishment of vegetation in marginal agricultural (mostly pasture) areas. Declines in the agricultural areas of southwestern Ontario may be due to changes in agricultural practices. The Killdeer is still ubiquitous south of the Shield, and the probability of observation increased significantly in the Hudson Bay Lowlands, possibly due to amelioration of spring and summer climate. Killdeer nests in Churchill, Manitoba, often fail through abandonment (pers. obs.), presumably due to the energy stress on adults from low temperatures. Six pairs, by contrast, in the Hudson Bay Lowlands region had fledged young, indicating successful nesting at this latitude. In the first atlas, three of 20 confirmed nests also reported fledged young, so there seems to be little change in the ability of young to be hatched and reared successfully in Ontario's far north.

Breeding biology: Breeding begins early in southern Ontario (April) but not until mid- to late May in the north (later in the far north), extending in all areas through July. Both sexes exhibit conspicuous and noisy distraction ("broken-wing") displays when the observer is within 10-30 m of the nest, displays that can continue long after the observer retreats. In the Subarctic, nesting substrates are quite stable, and distributions appear unchanged, although there was an apparent increase in numbers of breeding birds in the coastal region. In the south, nest-site fidelity is very low with banded adults rarely observed again in subsequent years (pers. obs.). Breeding was confirmed in 63% of the 1,787 squares in which the species was reported and probable in 17%. Killdeer re-nest after nesting failure and have two broods in Ontario, so the probability of confirming breeding is high.

Abundance: The abundance maps indicate a decrease from the southwest through the far north. Abundances are over 3.4 birds/25 point counts throughout the southwest, indicating that this species is still very common in the agricultural and suburban landscape of southern Ontario. From the southern edge of the Shield north, abundances did not exceed 0.8 birds/25 point counts except in the Rainy River area and near Winisk, along the Hudson Bay coast. A new Ontario population estimate of approximately 500,000 birds has been calculated based on the atlas point count data. – *Erica Nol*

Black-necked Stilt

Échasse d'Amérique

Himantopus mexicanus

Mark Peck

The Black-necked Stilt is a conspicuous black and white, medium-sized shorebird with outlandishly long pink legs. Until this atlas period, the species was considered a rare, non-breeding vagrant in Ontario. In the US, it regularly breeds in scattered populations along the east coast from southern Florida to as far north as Delaware Bay, and locally along the Gulf of Mexico from Alabama to extreme southern Texas and through the Great Basin to the Pacific coastal states. It ranges widely, and extra-limital sightings are common after storms or during prolonged periods of drought in its regular breeding areas (Robinson et al. 1999). During a range expansion in 2004, the Black-necked Stilt expanded to the east, nesting in Ontario and in the US Midwest states of Illinois, Wisconsin, and Michigan. In Canada, the Black-necked Stilt is a rare and erratic breeder in southern Alberta and Saskatchewan, although non-breeding birds have been recorded in all 10 provinces (Godfrey 1986; Gauthier and Aubry 1996; Robinson et al. 1999; Manitoba Avian Research Committee 2003). Breeding records in Alberta (Dekker et al. 1979) and Saskatchewan (Salisbury and Salisbury 1989; Smith 1996) have occurred since 1977 and are usually associated with drought in the western US. The earliest breeding record in Canada involves a set of eggs in the National Museum of Canada collected in Fort Qu'appelle, Saskatchewan, on 13 June 1894, a year of widespread drought in the western US (Godfrey 1986; Smith 1996).

Distribution and population status: One breeding record of the Black-necked Stilt was established during the atlas period. What began as an interesting sight record on 18 May 2004 progressed to evidence for the first breeding record of the species in Ontario (Peck et al. 2004). After a pair of Black-necked Stilts was observed at the Jarvis sewage lagoons (Haldimand Co.) 48 km southwest of Hamilton, the birds were seen again the following morning, 19 May 2004, 3.5 km to the west at the Townsend sewage lagoon, before being

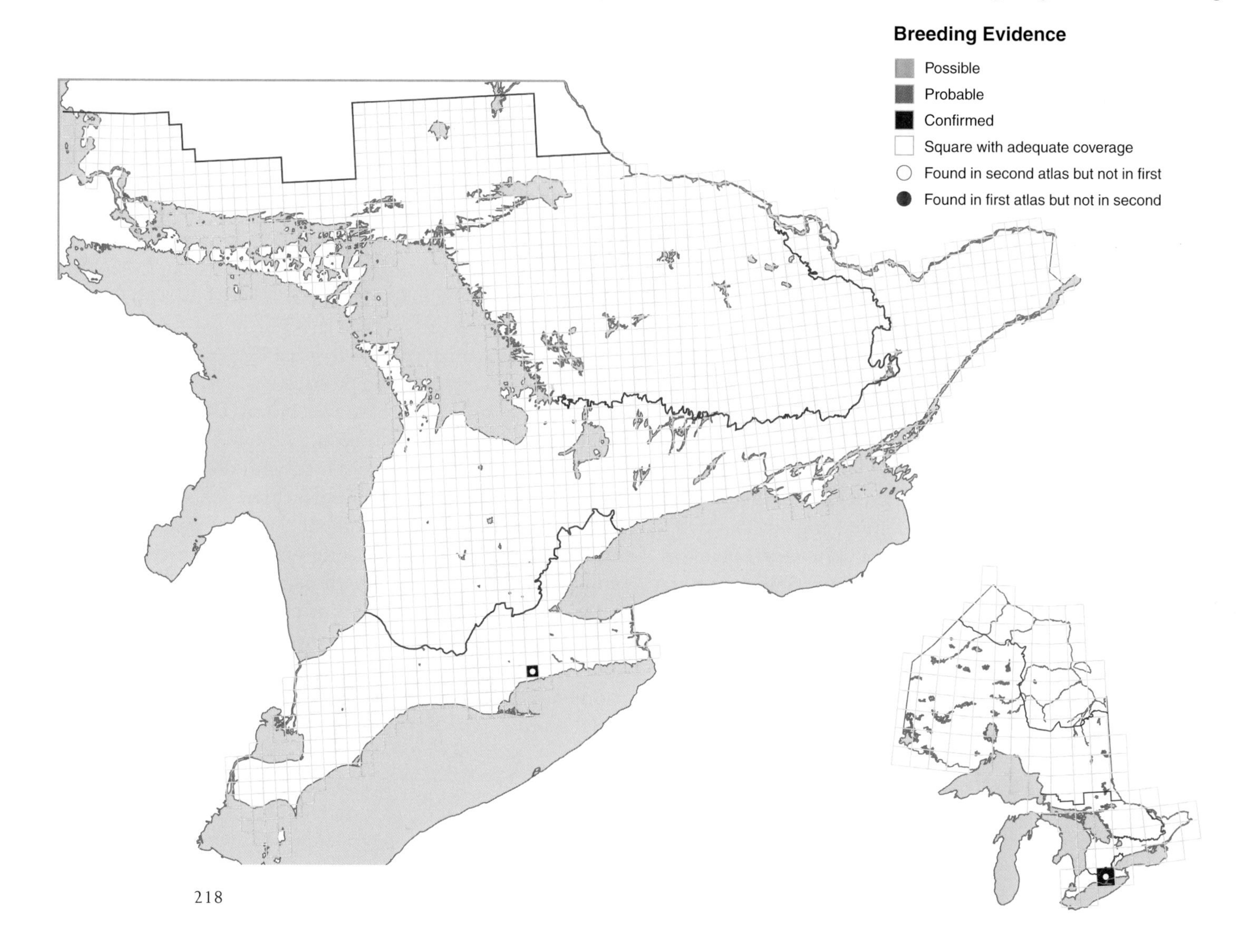

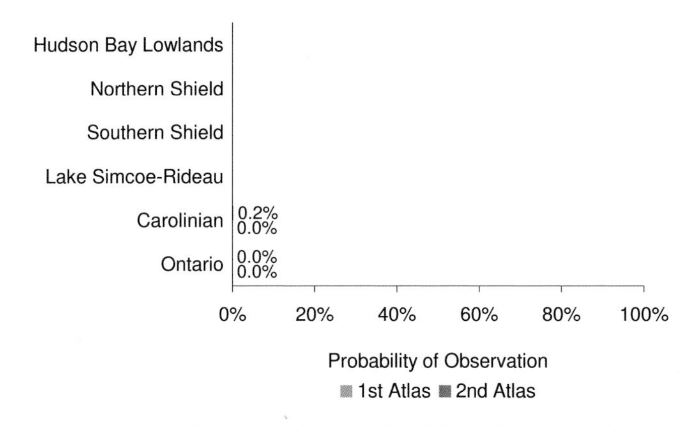

observed copulating and nest building back at the Jarvis lagoons. On 28 May 2004, a nest with eggs was found in a wet, unploughed cornfield approximately 1 ha in size adjacent to the Jarvis lagoons. The last reported sighting was on 5 June 2004, when one of the birds was observed sitting on this nest. The nest was reported as lost to predators on 8 June 2004. This nest represents the easternmost Canadian breeding record. Extra-limital breeding was also reported in 2003 and possibly 2004 in southeastern Michigan. In 2004, breeding evidence was found in Wisconsin and Ohio as well, and there were numerous additional sight records from states in the Mississippi and Ohio River valleys and the Great Lakes Basin (Peck et. al. 2004). The extra-limital sightings around the Great Lakes and evidence of drought conditions throughout much of its western range suggest that the eastern movement resulted from prolonged drought in other parts of the breeding range.

Breeding biology: Black-necked Stilts are monogamous and territorial, with both sexes participating in nest building and incubation. Preferred nest sites throughout the range include tidal impoundments, islands, alkali flats, dikes, and high spots with sparse vegetation. Nests are usually placed in the open, often over water on emergent or dead vegetation (Robinson et al. 1999). The nest found in Ontario was an untidy platform of dead corn stalks, weed stalks, and corn leaves, with no lining. Vocalizations and courtship behaviour in the area allowed the nest to be easily located. Three eggs were found in the nest, with a fourth egg located several metres away a few days later. When approaching or leaving the nest, both parent birds were very vocal while performing wing-flagging and false incubation crouching distraction displays, as described by Robinson et al. (1999).

Abundance: The Black-necked Stilt has not subsequently been reported breeding in Ontario. However, a pair was recorded near Brighton, 145 km east of Toronto, from 10-15 May 2006. Future breeding is anticipated during droughts on the species' principal breeding range and as the climate warms. – *Glenn Coady and Mark K. Peck*

Although four eggs were laid, the usual number for the species, one of the eggs was found several metres from the nest. *Photo: Mark Peck*

Corn stubble field in which the nest was located, adjacent to the Jarvis sewage lagoon, Jarvis, Haldimand Co. *Photo: Mark Peck*

Spotted Sandpiper

Chevalier grivelé

Actitis macularius

Tania & Jim Thomson

The Spotted Sandpiper is one of the most widely distributed and familiar shorebirds in North America. Its characteristic teetering walk and stiff-winged flight are instantly recognizable. A common breeder, it nests in a variety of habitats throughout southern Canada northward to the treeline and slightly beyond. It is most often found nesting and foraging near lakeshores, islands, riverbanks, marshes, bogs, ditches, beaver meadows, and sewage lagoons. Nesting sites may also include drier habitats such as dunes, woodland edges, forest burns, gravel areas, farm fields, orchards, industrial areas, schoolyards, storm-water management ponds, and parking lots (Peck and James 1983; Peck and James 1993b). Although still considered common and widespread in Canada, the Spotted Sandpiper has been designated a species of moderate concern in Canada (Donaldson et al. 2000), based on BBS results that indicate a population decline in Ontario, Québec, and the Maritimes since 1968.

Distribution and population status: Results from the second atlas indicate that the Spotted Sandpiper continues to be widely distributed across the province. Birds were found in all regions, and breeding was confirmed in the majority of 100-km blocks. The distribution in northern Ontario evident in the atlas map was likely strongly influenced by the prevalence of suitable habitat near the canoe routes and fly-in camps used by atlas crews. This sandpiper undoubtedly nests along most if not all of the main rivers and large lakes in the north where open areas exist for foraging and nearby vegetation provides protection for nesting. The lack of observations in some squares in boreal forest and muskeg habitat away from the larger water bodies, including areas with small ponds, streams and extensive sedge wetlands, suggests these areas may not provide ideal foraging and breeding habitat for this species. The more disturbed urban and rural environments of southern Ontario may offer more

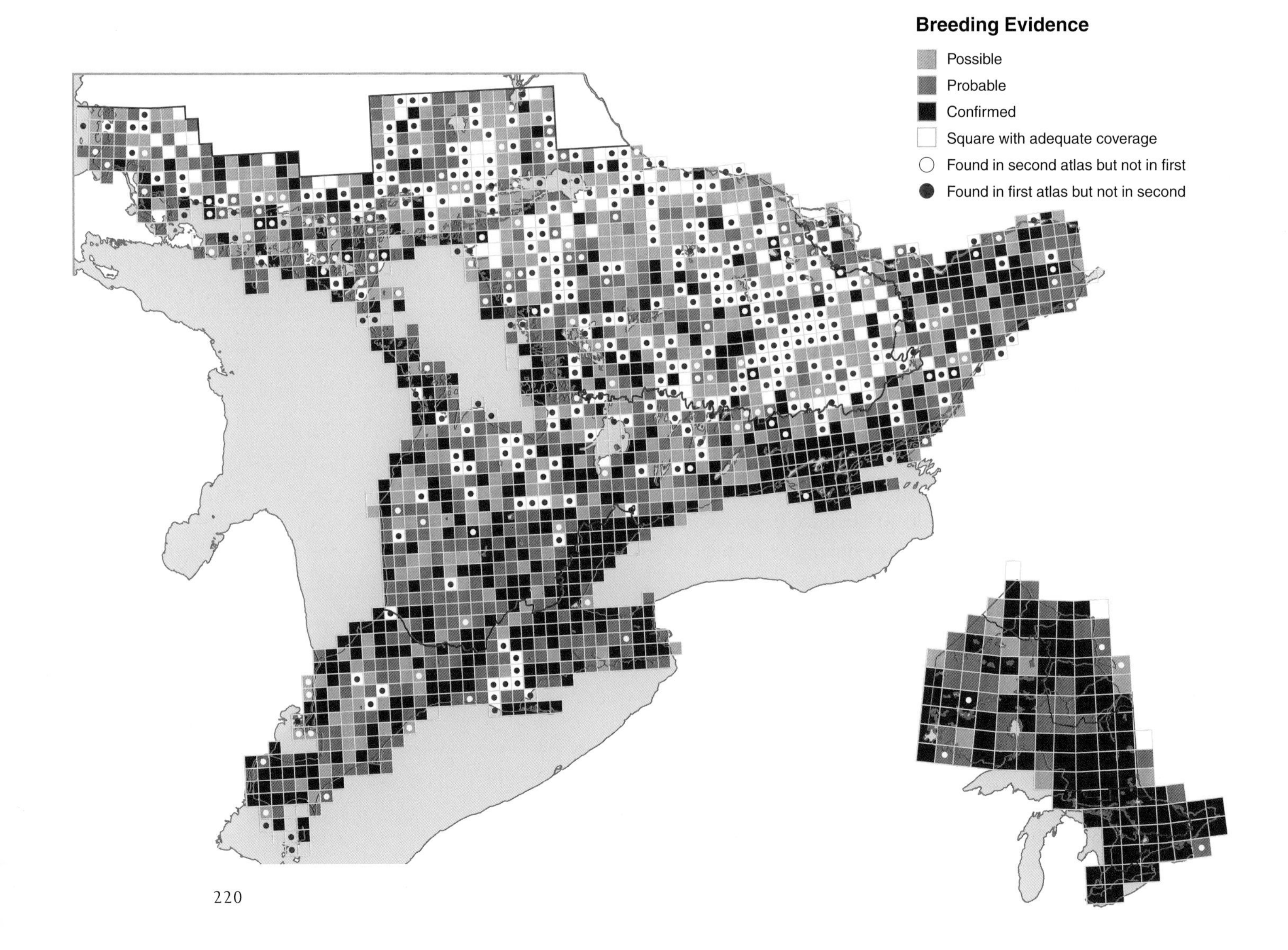

BREEDING EVIDENCE

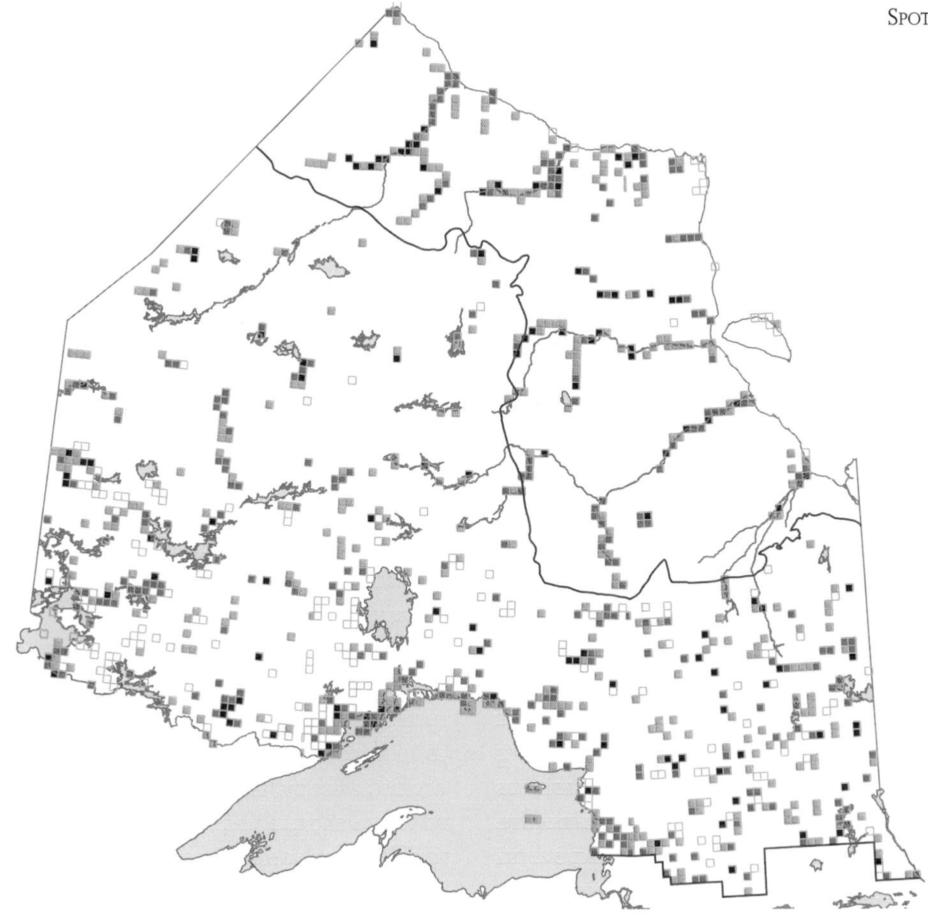

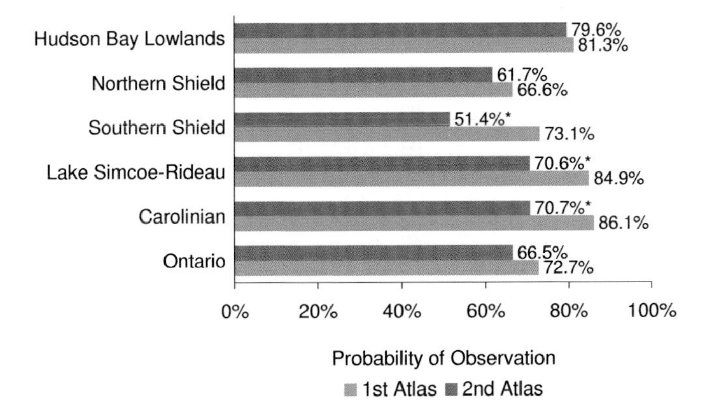

heterogeneous suitable habitats unavailable in the north, albeit with an increase in problems such as human-related disturbance and predation.

Compared to the first atlas, the probability of observation decreased significantly in the Carolinian (18%), Lake Simcoe-Rideau (17%), and Southern Shield (30%) regions, but not in the two northern regions. The population loss across southern Ontario but not in the north suggests decreases may be based on factors within Southern Ontario, though it is not known what those factors might be.

Breeding biology: The Spotted Sandpiper, unlike most other shorebirds, has reversed sex roles and is often polyandrous, with females mating with more than one male in a single season. In late April or early May, the larger, more brightly coloured females migrate into southern Ontario alone or in small groups, four to five days in advance of males. On arrival, they establish territories and attempt to attract males; they may mate monogamously or with as many as four males (Oring et al. 1997). Females assist with incubation duties associated with their initial mating, but if they acquire secondary mates, they leave the first mate to continue his parental duties alone. Parental care of the young is primarily by males, but females will help during the early part of the brood period. In their last mating, females usually play a significant role in incubation and brood rearing (Oring et al. 1997). Small territory size and multiple nestings within a polyandrous female's original territory may cause this species to appear semi-colonial in areas of preferred habitat.

Abundance: There were insufficient data to generate an accurate abundance map, and point count data were considered somewhat misleading; most point counts were done on roadsides, and so the river and lake shorelines that make up the bulk of the Spotted Sandpiper's breeding habitat on the Shield were not well represented. South of the Shield, relative abundance was generally highest near the Great Lakes shorelines, except along Lake Erie southwest of about St. Thomas, where numbers were quite sparse. The Niagara Peninsula had high relative abundance, as did some other urban and rural areas with considerable human development, such as the area along the north shore of Lake Ontario between Hamilton and Port Hope. In southwestern Ontario, high estimates were also found in areas with numerous rivers and streams adjacent to farmland.

Morrison et al. (2006) estimated the total range-wide breeding population of the Spotted Sandpiper at 150,000, which seems conservative given that the estimated Ontario population is in the hundreds of thousands (Ross et al. 2003). Given its wide distribution and the large number of squares with breeding evidence, the Ontario estimate seems reasonable. *– Mark K. Peck*

Solitary Sandpiper
Chevalier solitaire
Tringa solita

Mark Peck

The Solitary Sandpiper is well named, as it usually occurs singly or in small numbers during migration. It is also less noisy and conspicuous during the incubation period than other tringids, but the presence of fledged young can incite it to loud displays of agitation. The Solitary Sandpiper, and the closely related Green and Wood sandpipers of Eurasia, are the only tree-nesting shorebirds, using old nests of other bird species rather than building nests of their own.

Distribution and population status: Evidence of breeding birds was thinly scattered across the Hudson Bay Lowlands and Boreal Forest south to the northern limits of the Great Lakes-St Lawrence Forest. The Solitary Sandpiper showed similar distribution patterns in the first and second atlases and, collectively, has now been reported in almost all northern atlas 100-km blocks. The probability of observation declined significantly by 38% province-wide between atlases, with a 58% decline in the Northern Shield. While this sandpiper shares similar breeding habitat with both the Greater and Lesser Yellowlegs, it is more likely to be overlooked due to its retiring nature, although it will participate with those species in mobbing intruders on its territory. The timing of many northern atlas trips in mid- to late June when the birds are quieter may have precluded finding this species more frequently. Several records of agitated birds or adults with recently fledged young in late June and early July suggest this species may be more conspicuous later in the season.

During the first atlas, this sandpiper was apparently absent from Rainy River Dist., but observations from the second atlas suggest the birds do breed in this area, although they are restricted to more discrete patches of suitable breeding habitat. The southern limit in northeastern Ontario was similar in both atlases, with no indication of a range change. This species is a late spring and early fall migrant, so southern reports were carefully scrutinized to ensure the southern limits of the

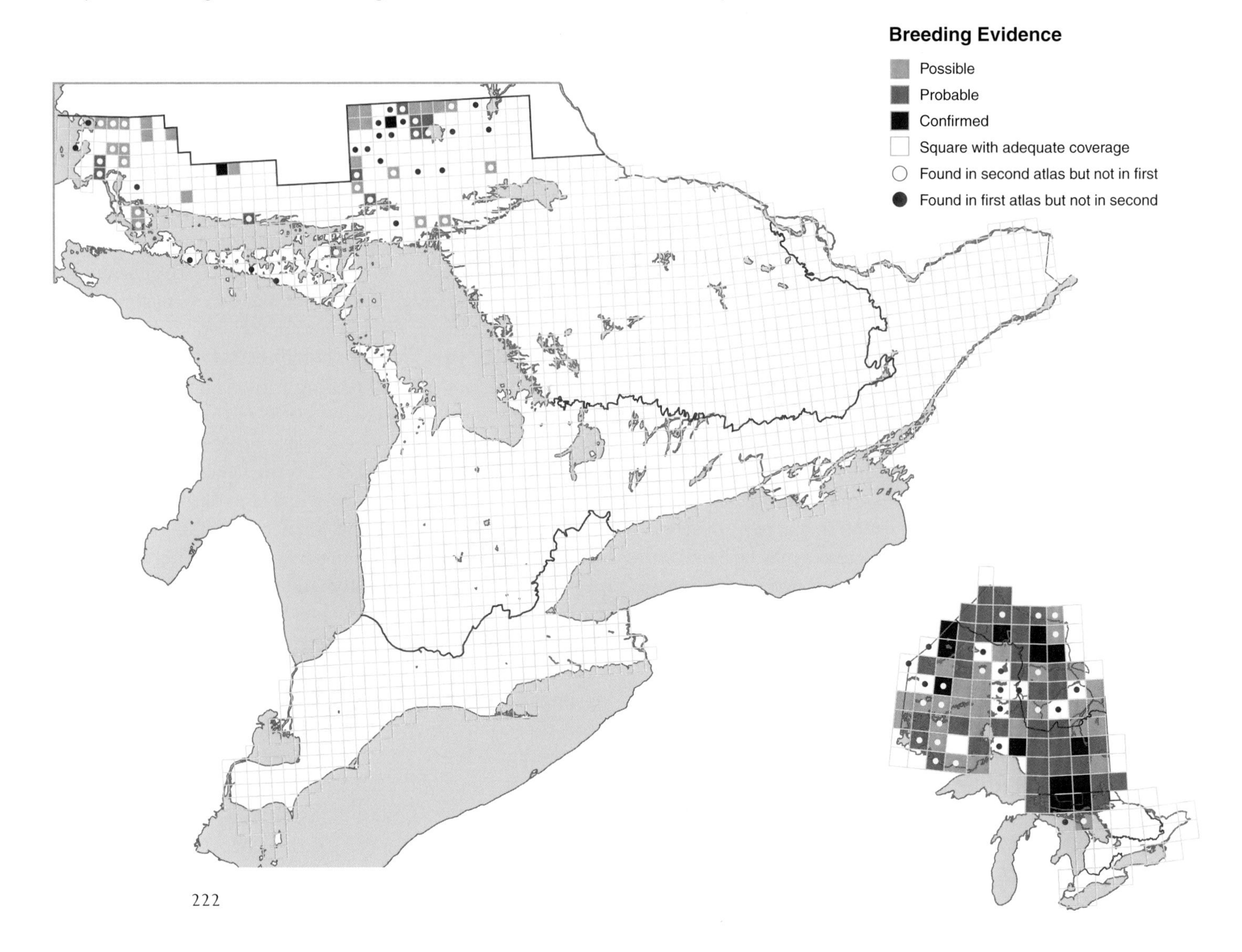

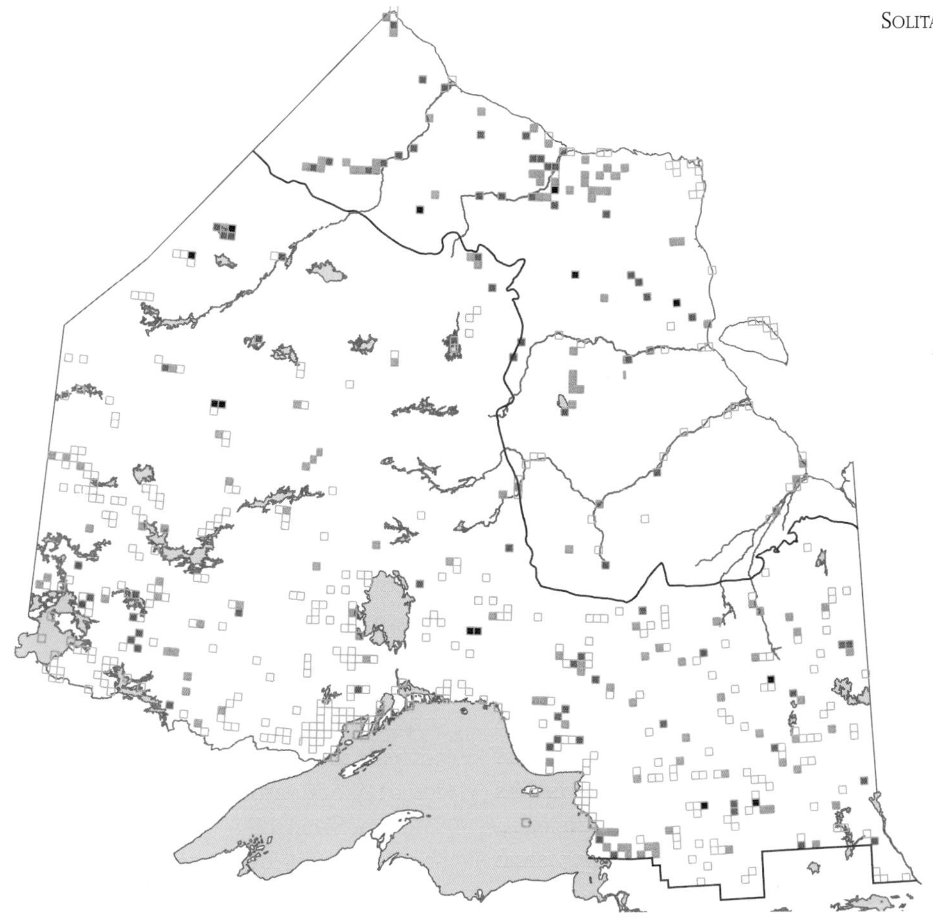

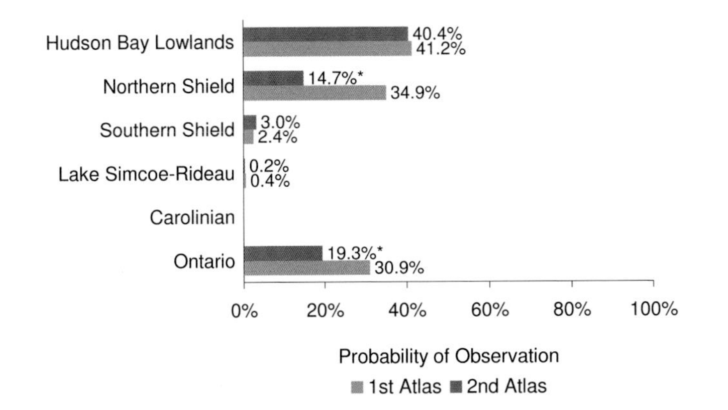

breeding range were accurately established.

Breeding biology: The Solitary Sandpiper is monogamous. Males defend a large nesting territory and may also defend a nearby feeding territory (Oring 1973). In documented atlas records from northern Ontario, observations of the Solitary Sandpiper were always near ponds or wetlands of varying sizes. In the Hudson Bay Lowlands, birds were usually found in areas of open wet muskeg with nearby shallow ponds or sedge wetlands. Small copses of Black Spruce and Tamarack were scattered throughout the area, with a ground cover of lichens, mosses, and Labrador Tea. In the Boreal Forest, birds were associated with beaver ponds or nearby wetlands usually adjacent to spruce forests or pine stands. Several birds including adults with recently fledged young were reported feeding in small pools or ditches along logging roads in wooded areas or roadsides near the margins of the City of Thunder Bay.

Prior to the second atlas, only two nests had been documented for the province (Peck and James 1983, 1999). Three additional nests were found during the atlas (Walker 2004, Peck et al. 2004). The two nests found on 12 June and 23 June 2004, respectively, in open muskeg of the Hudson Bay Lowlands, contained eggs. The former nest contained three fresh eggs and may have been an incomplete clutch. The third nest was found on 10 June 2003 in Wakami Lake Prov. Park, Sudbury Dist., and was positioned over water. The nests were located in either Black Spruce or Tamarack and were thought to be old nests of Rusty Blackbird or American Robin. At the first two nests, prior to the sitting birds flushing, the species had not been observed in the area. Once flushed from the nests, the adults performed distraction displays in the immediate vicinity. The adult did not flush at either visit to the third nest (Walker 2004).

Abundance: The conservative worldwide population estimate of the Solitary Sandpiper, based on extremely limited information, has been placed at 150,000 (Morrison et al. 2006). It appears to occur throughout the Hudson Bay Lowlands and Boreal Forest at low densities, but more extensive surveying is warranted because of the decline observed during this atlas and the uncertainty of population estimates. Given the widespread distribution of suitable habitat in Ontario, the province could have at least 10% of the worldwide population. – *Mark K. Peck*

Greater Yellowlegs

Grand Chevalier

Tringa melanoleuca.

Jon Brierley

The Greater Yellowlegs nests in boreal and subarctic wetlands across North America, primarily between 48° N and 58° N (Elphick and Tibbitts 1998). The species' far-carrying, rhythmically repeated "*whee-odling*" flight song and strident, persistent alarm and "*teu teu teu*" calls are familiar sounds of the Hudson Bay Lowlands. Although populations of Greater Yellowlegs appear to be relatively secure in Canada (Morrison et al. 2006), small but non-significant declines have prompted its recognition as a species of moderate conservation concern in Ontario and Canada (Donaldson et al. 2000; Ross et al. 2003). Interestingly, atlas results suggest the species has expanded in Ontario.

Distribution and population status: Within Ontario, the breeding range of the Greater Yellowlegs is restricted to the northern half of the province in the Hudson Bay Lowlands and Northern Shield regions, where the probability of observation during the second atlas was 74% and 25%, respectively. The probability of observation in the province as a whole was 34%. Results from the second atlas extend the known Ontario breeding limits of the species south to about 49° N, 34 km southwest of Cochrane in the east and 24 km west-northwest of Upsala, Thunder Bay Dist., in the west. The southern limit of breeding in Ontario is thus similar to the southern extent of breeding observed in adjacent Québec (Gauthier and Aubry 1996). The second atlas also shows infilling of gaps in the breeding range shown during the first atlas, particularly in northwestern Ontario.

The breeding distribution of the Greater Yellowlegs increased considerably between atlases. The species was recorded in all 100-km blocks in which it was recorded during the first atlas, and in an additional 33 100-km blocks, many of which were in the Northern Shield region north and west of Lake Superior. The probability of observation increased significantly by 78% between atlases in the province as a whole, with the greatest increase (about fivefold) in the Northern Shield. The reasons for this increase and range expansion are unknown. The expansion

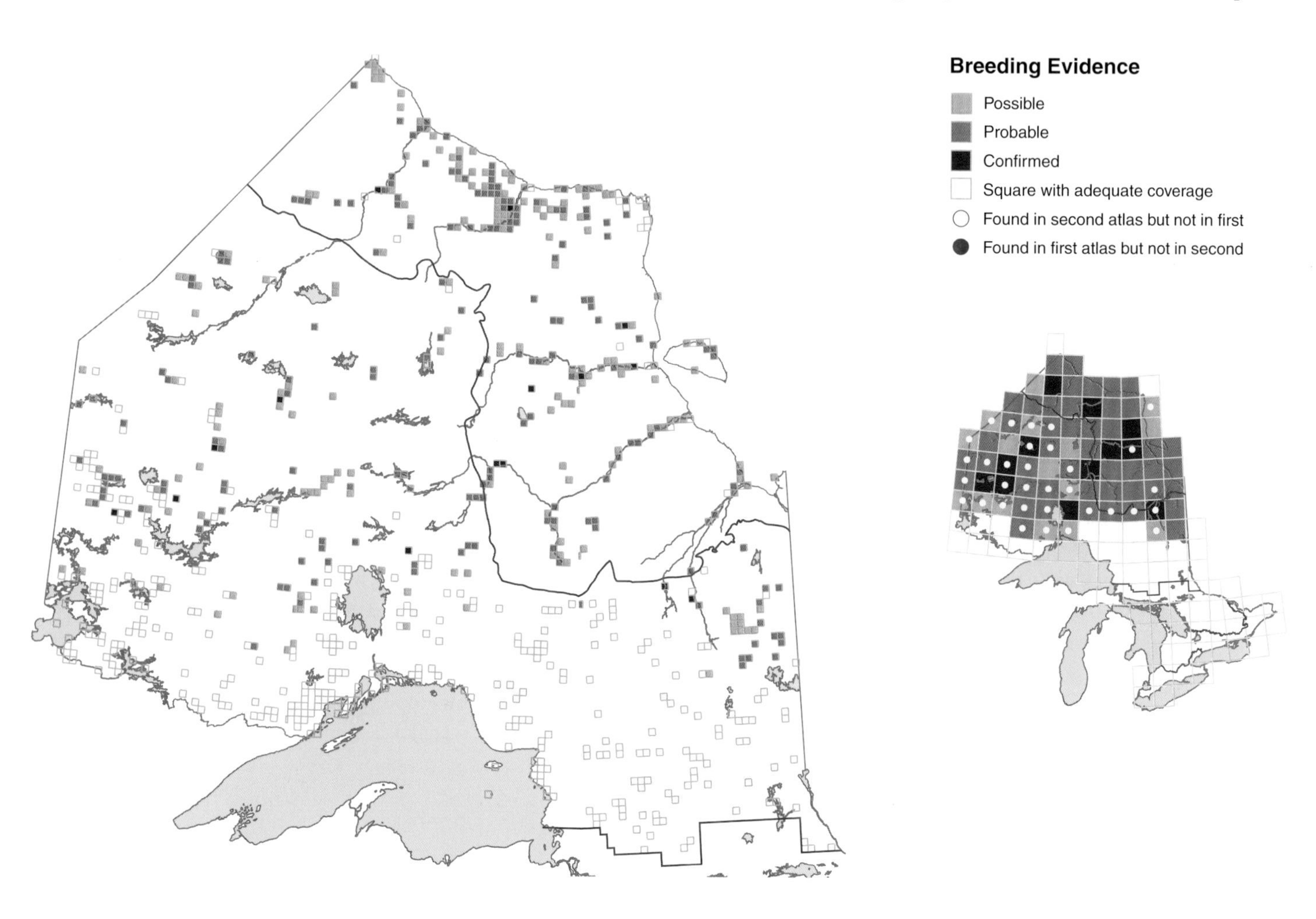

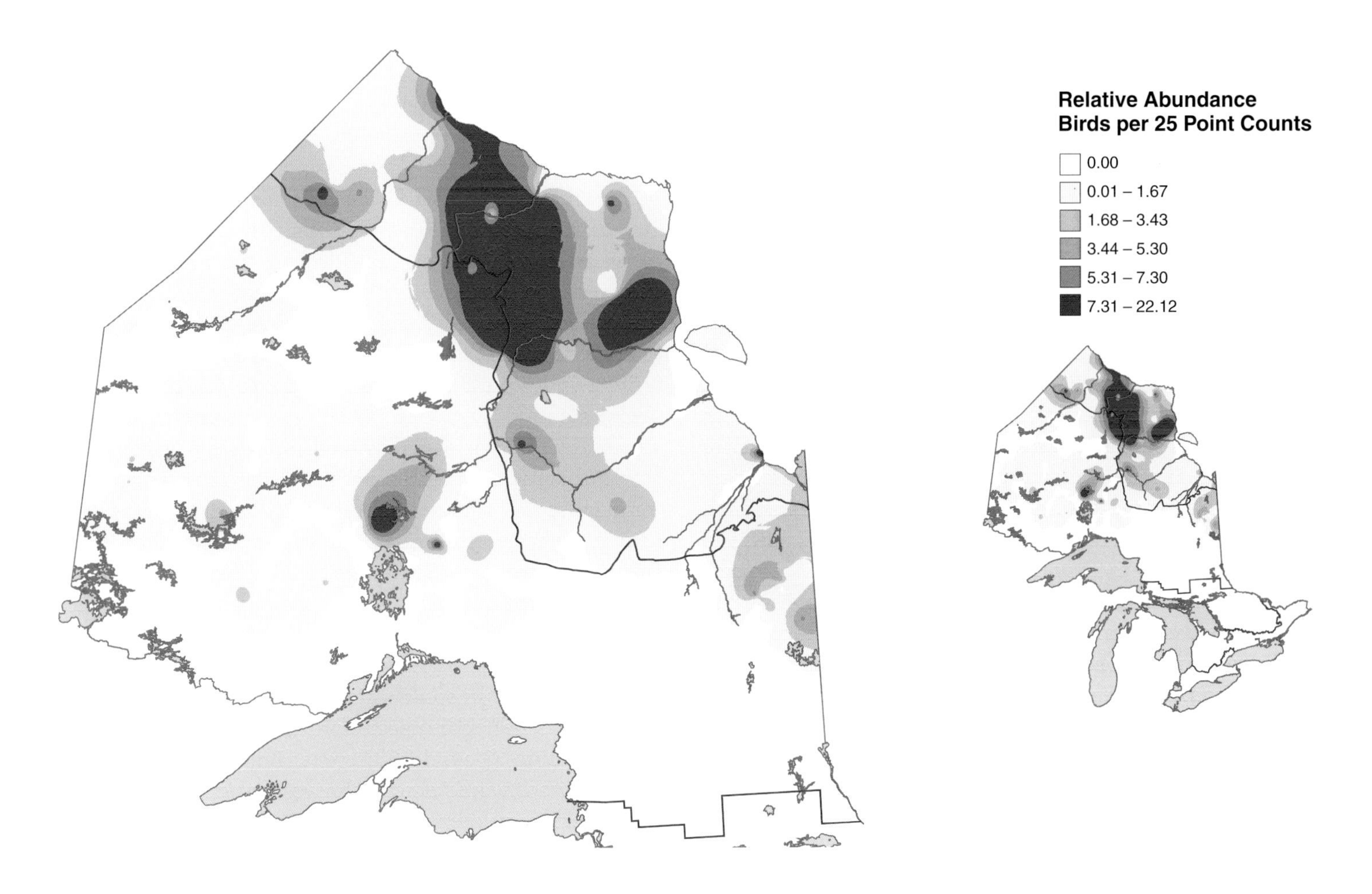

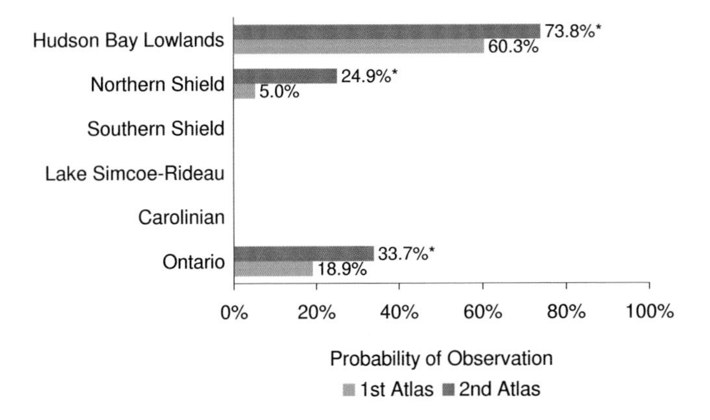

of recently logged areas over this same period, however, may suggest a potential causal relationship between the establishment of large openings in the Boreal Forest and the occurrence of Greater Yellowlegs (E. Nol, pers. comm.); as well, additional forestry access roads may have facilitated atlassing in some areas. The increase in the core breeding range in the Hudson Bay Lowlands, while significant, was considerably less at 22%.

Breeding biology: The breeding biology of the Greater Yellowlegs, like that of the similar Lesser Yellowlegs, is not well known (Elphick and Tibbitts 1998), in large part because it nests in low densities in remote and difficult-to-traverse muskeg habitats. During the nesting season, the species is found in areas with scattered small ponds, lakes, and other wetlands and adjacent drier uplands. Preferred habitats for breeding are usually open graminoid fens and peatlands interspersed with shrubs and trees and adjoining upland burns or palsa plateaus. The wide-ranging, undulating flight displays and songs of the adults are given early in the nesting season, probably before most atlassing effort was undertaken. This relatively large shorebird is well concealed on its ground nest, which is usually placed at the base of a short (1–2 m) coniferous tree and in or next to a moss-lichen or shrub-covered hummock (Peck and James 1983). Adults are presumed to share incubation duties, and allow extremely close approach before flushing from the nest. Both the nest and unfledged young are cryptic and extremely difficult to find. As a result, the number of squares in which breeding was confirmed was low (15 of 375 squares). Prior to the second atlas, only two nests of the Greater Yellowlegs had been reported in Ontario, one at Little Sachigo Lake in 1977 (McLaren and McLaren 1981) and the other near Aquatuk Lake in 1980 (Nash and Dick 1981a). Four additional nests with eggs were discovered during this atlas. Adults are vocal and often surprisingly aggressive in defence of the nest and particularly of fledged young, intercepting and often dive-bombing potential predators at considerable distances from the nest.

Abundance: Point counts are not well suited to providing unbiased abundance estimates of boreal shorebirds, particularly a species like the Greater Yellowlegs that flies to the observer. However, they can provide useful information on relative abundance. The atlas point counts and abundance map indicate that the relative abundance of Greater Yellowlegs is greatest in the Hudson Bay Lowlands, where its preferred wetland habitat is found more extensively than in the more heavily wooded Northern Shield region. – *Ross Harris*

Lesser Yellowlegs

Petit Chevalier

Tringa flavipes

George K. Peck

Most naturalists have never observed the Lesser Yellowlegs on its remote northern breeding grounds in Ontario. For those who have, encounters will doubtless have been with a very agitated bird teetering atop a low tree, incessantly uttering its shrill "*tu tu tu tu*" alarm call. A northern boreal and subarctic breeding shorebird, the Lesser Yellowlegs breeds only in North America, from Alaska east to central Québec and from the limit of trees south to about 51° N (Tibbitts and Moskoff 1999). Its range overlaps extensively with the Greater Yellowlegs but extends farther north and does not include areas east of Québec (Tibbitts and Moskoff 1999).

Distribution and population status: The Lesser Yellowlegs nests across northernmost Ontario. Although the full extent of its breeding distribution in the province remains imperfectly known, it is more abundant and widespread across the Hudson Bay Lowlands region where suitable nesting habitat is most extensive. It appears to be less abundant and more patchily distributed across the Northern Shield, where results from the second atlas suggest that it breeds at lower densities throughout the northern portions of the region, with isolated records of breeding farther south. The Lesser Yellowlegs was recorded in 13 new 100-km blocks in the Northern Shield and Hudson Bay Lowlands during the second atlas, probably due largely to additional effort. The southernmost records during the second atlas involved evidence of possible breeding in squares near Pledger Lake and Moose River Crossing along the southern edge of the Hudson Bay Lowlands.

Although its breeding range in Ontario largely overlaps that of the Greater Yellowlegs, the Lesser Yellowlegs was detected in fewer squares and by contrast exhibited no significant change in distribution or the probability of observation between atlases.

Prior to the second atlas, the few documented records of confirmed breeding for Lesser Yellowlegs in Ontario (Peck and James 1993b) included flightless young at Fort Severn in 1940,

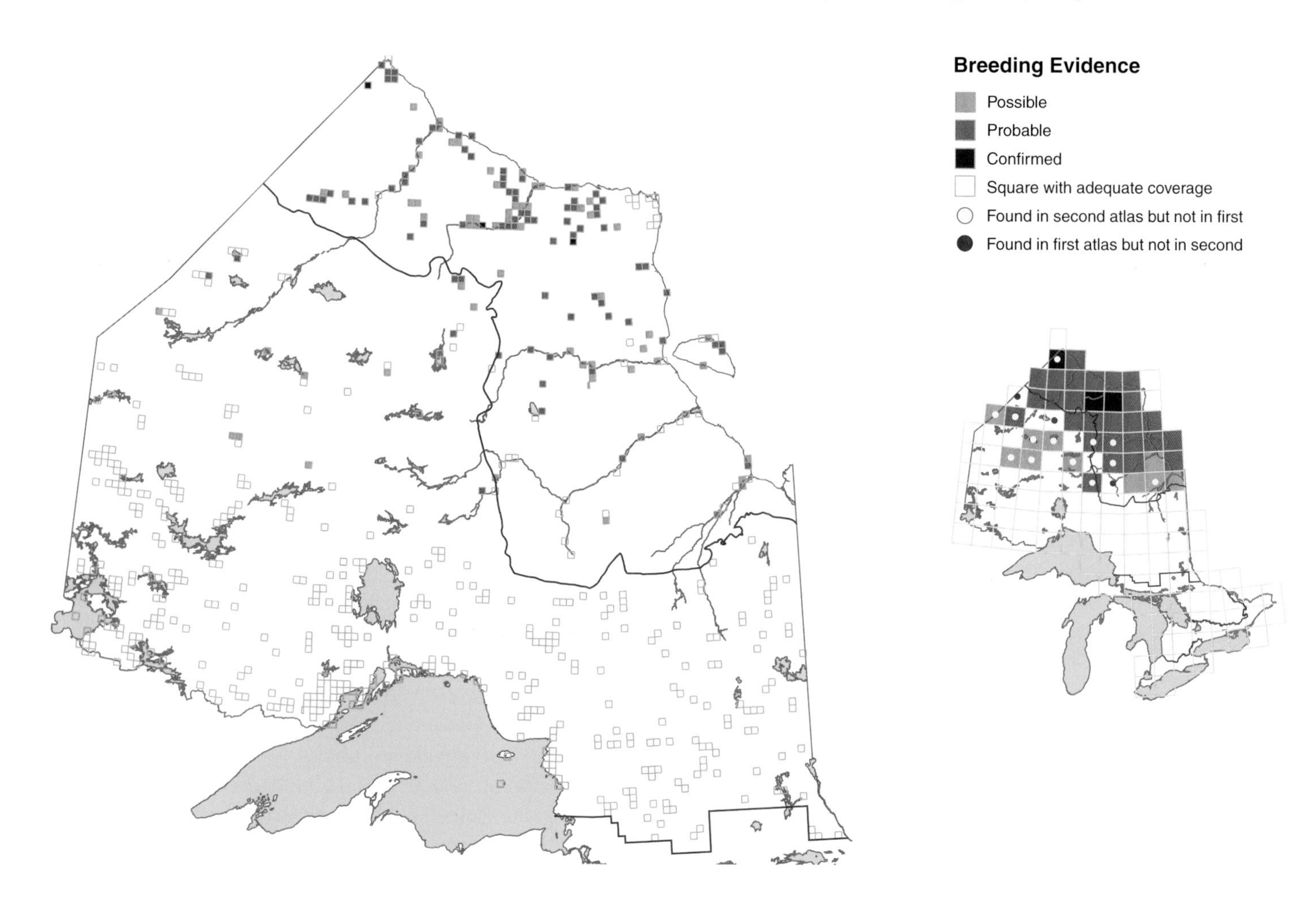

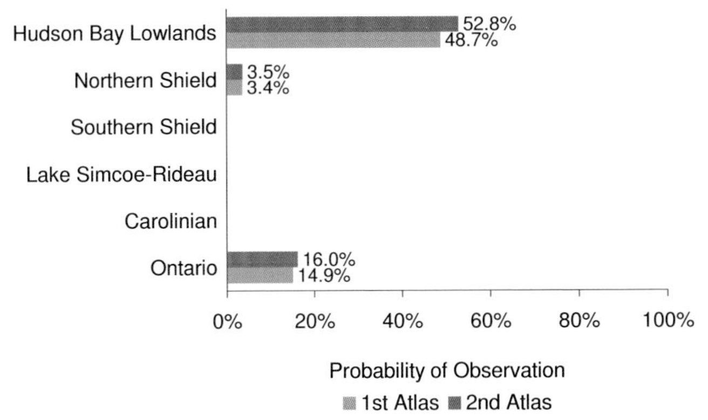

a single nest at the mouth of the Shagamu River in 1990, and two nests near Winisk in 1992, all near the Hudson Bay coast in Kenora Dist. During the second atlas, a fourth provincial nest record was established with the discovery of a nest with eggs near Atik Island on the Winisk River, about 100 km south of Hudson Bay, 5 July 2003. The nest was on exposed peat of a low, mostly unvegetated palsa at the edge of pond in open, hummocky taiga (S.E. McGregor and J. Kits, pers. comm.).

Breeding biology: The breeding biology of the Lesser Yellowlegs is poorly studied (Tibbitts and Moskoff 1999). In Ontario, typical nesting habitat consists of extensive peatlands or muskeg with scattered trees and shrubs, a mosaic of shallow pools, ponds, or small lakes, and raised open areas such as gravel ridges, recent burns, and palsas. Human-altered habitats including seismic lines, pipeline and hydro rights-of-way, road allowances, and mine clearings are occasionally used (Peck and James 1983). Pair formation occurs soon after arrival at breeding areas. From arrival until several days into incubation, males perform conspicuous undulating flight displays accompanied by rhythmically repeated "*pill-e-wee*" songs over nesting and foraging areas (Tibbitts and Moskoff 1999). Based on breeding records from Churchill, Manitoba, most incubation in Ontario probably occurs during June, with the peak of hatch during late June and early July (Peck and James 1983; Peck and James 1993b; Jehl 2004); most brood rearing in northern Ontario probably occurs during July. The species is conspicuous during brood rearing, as adults are easily agitated and intercept potential predators at considerable distances. Most atlassing efforts were likely well timed to coincide with the breeding cycle. Probable breeding evidence was obtained in just over half (54%) of the squares in which the species was detected. Despite its conspicuousness on the breeding grounds, confirmation of breeding is limited, as nests and fledged young are very difficult to find, and only 2% of records were of confirmed breeding.

Abundance: Although point counts are not well suited to providing unbiased density estimates of species like the Lesser Yellowlegs that fly to the observer, they are useful for assessing relative abundance. Atlas point count data suggest that the species is more abundant on the Hudson Bay Lowlands (averaging 3.1 birds/25 point counts) than on the Northern Shield (averaging 0.04 birds/25 point counts). The Lesser Yellowlegs is more restricted to the taiga of the Hudson Bay Lowlands than its close relative the Greater Yellowlegs, which extends more broadly through the Northern Shield region. – *Ross Harris*

Nests are typically located in upland areas adjacent to extensive wetlands, often in regenerating burns on lichen mats at the base of a small tree, stump, or log. Churchill, Manitoba, 24 June 1971. *Photo: George K. Peck*

Sparsely treed taiga with palsa plateaus and numerous small lakes and ponds is breeding habitat for the Lesser Yellowlegs. Near Wood Creek, Polar Bear Prov. Park, 12 July 2003. *Photo: Donald A. Sutherland*

Upland Sandpiper

Maubèche des champs

Bartramia longicauda

Frank and Sandra Horvath

Known for its affinity to grasslands, conspicuous flight display, distinctive "wolf whistle," and habit of perching on fence posts, the Upland Sandpiper is an atypical, monotypic shorebird that spends much of its life away from water. It breeds only in North America, its core breeding range being in the Great Plains, although isolated areas of breeding also occur in Alaska, Yukon, Northwest Territories, and Oregon. In Ontario and much of eastern North America, its range is the result of land clearance in the 18th and early 19th centuries. Nearly decimated by commercial hunting in the 1800s (Bent 1929), the Upland Sandpiper made a moderate recovery by the mid-1900s. Recent BBS data and results from the second atlas suggest its populations are declining again, as are populations of other grassland species. The Upland Sandpiper has not been placed on any lists of imperilled wildlife in Canada; however, it is listed as Endangered or a species of Special Concern in a number of US states, including Ohio, New York, and Wisconsin (Houston and Bowen 2001).

Distribution and population status: Upland Sandpiper distribution in Ontario is similar in both range and pattern to what was reported in the first atlas. It breeds mainly south and east of the Canadian Shield, but a population continues to inhabit the Rainy River/Fort Frances area in the northwest. The small and isolated Thunder Bay population, recorded during the first atlas, has since disappeared (N. Escott, pers. comm.). In 2002, a pair was observed displaying and mating at the Moosonee airport, and a single bird was found in an adjacent square.

Since the first atlas, the core breeding range of the Upland Sandpiper has shifted slightly northwards and eastwards, resulting in a greater proportion of records in south-central and southeastern Ontario. In addition, the probability of observation has declined by a significant 37% in the province as a whole, with reductions of 52%, 40% and 41% occurring

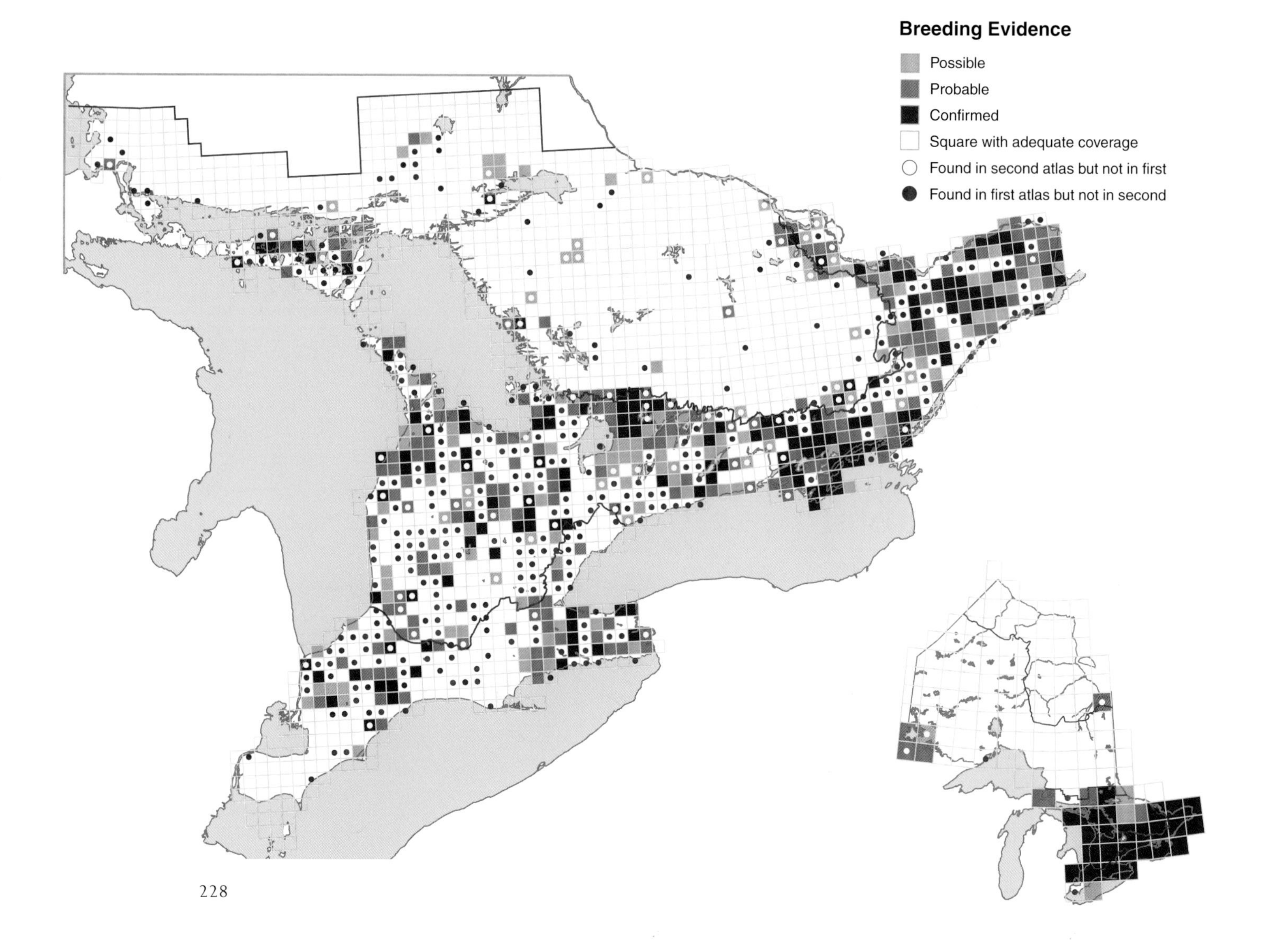

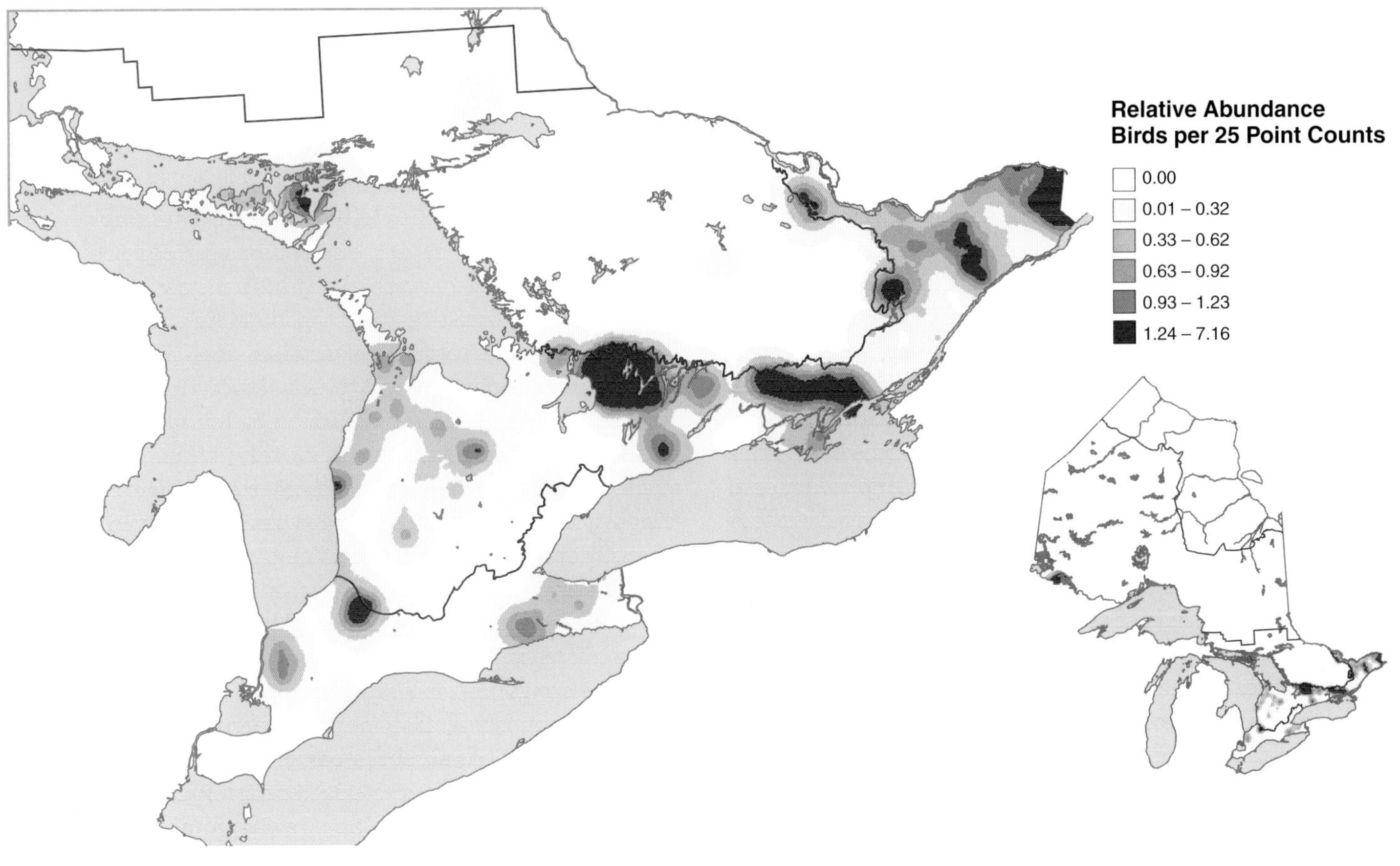

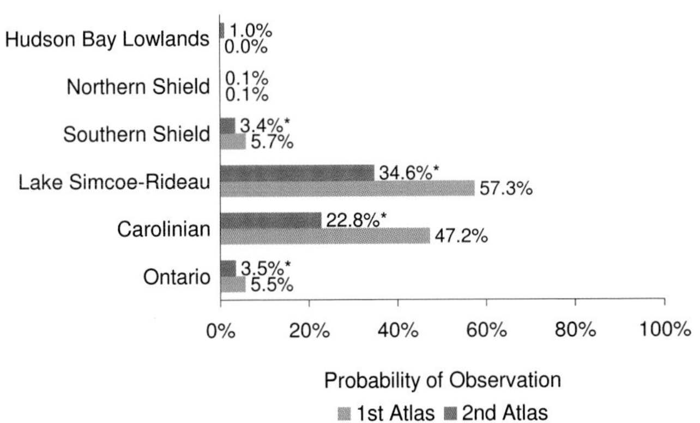

in the Carolinian, Lake Simcoe-Rideau, and Southern Shield regions, respectively. Since 1981, BBS data show a non-significant decline for Ontario and a significant decline for Canada. These declines have probably been influenced by habitat loss and changes in land-use activities on both the breeding and wintering grounds. In Ontario, some grassland habitats have been lost to natural succession, particularly in the Southern Shield and Lake Simcoe-Rideau regions, and to intensification of agricultural practices in the Carolinian region and parts of the Lake Simcoe-Rideau region.

Breeding biology: The Upland Sandpiper typically arrives on territory in early May and begins nest preparation about two weeks later. During courtship, aerial displays incorporate soaring, flutter strokes, a long mellow whistle, and raised wings. This is complemented by a ground display in which the male, with a puffed gular pouch and raised tail, approaches the female uttering a rattle-whistle. Nesting habitat in Ontario includes unused pastures, old fields with scattered hawthorns, hayfields, and airports (Peck and James 1983). As in the northeast US (Houston and Bowen 2001), airports are frequently used by the Upland Sandpiper in northern Ontario, where suitable grassland habitat is limited. Its nest, a shallow depression, may be lined with grass or other vegetation. In Ontario, egg dates range from 7 May to 9 July, average clutch size is four (Peck and James 1993b), and incubation ranges from 20 to 28 days. Adults are well camouflaged and nests are well hidden, but an adult may perform a distraction display if threatened. Young leave the nest 24 hours after hatching and remain with the parents for 27 to 37 days (Houston and Bowen 2001).

Abundance: High concentrations of the Upland Sandpiper occur in several areas: on the Carden, Napanee, and Smiths Falls limestone plains, where there is an abundance of unimproved pasture and juniper or hawthorn shrub alvar, and in extreme southeastern Ontario in the heavy clay areas of the former Champlain Sea which are more suited to pasture than cultivated lands. Other lesser nodes of abundance include: the Haldimand Clay Plain near the eastern end of Lake Erie; pasture lands underlain by clay in northern Lambton, western Middlesex, and southern Huron Counties; the Dundalk uplands; Manitoulin Island; and western Rainy River Dist. – *Ken McIlwrick*

Whimbrel

Courlis corlieu

Numenius phaeopus

Mark Peck

The Whimbrel is a holarctic breeder with six distinct populations recognized, two of which breed in the nearctic region (Engelmoer and Roselaar 1998). In North America, the Whimbrel breeds from the edge of the Boreal Forest to the low Arctic. The western subspecies *rufiventris* breeds from western and northern Alaska and northern Yukon to the northern coast of the Northwest Territories, while the smaller, eastern *hudsonicus* breeds along the western coast of Hudson Bay from southern Nunavut to the vicinity of Cape Henrietta Maria, northern Ontario (Skeel and Mallory 1996), and possibly as far south as 53° N on Akimiski Island in James Bay. The Whimbrel is regarded as a species of conservation concern in Canada (Donaldson et al. 2000) and in Ontario (Ross et al. 2003).

Distribution and population status: The distribution of the Whimbrel in Ontario has changed little since the first provincial breeding record was obtained at Lake River on the northern James Bay coast in 1947 (Manning 1952). As in the first atlas, the species was recorded in most 100-km blocks along the Hudson Bay coast between the Pen Islands and Cape Henrietta Maria. Breeding evidence was not obtained during the second atlas in any mainland squares in the 100-km block south and east of Cape Henrietta Maria, where it was well established in the vicinity of Hook Point between 1948 and 1970 (Peck 1972). Coverage of the northern James Bay coast south of Hook Point during the second atlas was insufficient to confirm the species' presence in the vicinity of Nowashe Creek (45 km south of Lake River) where evidence of possible breeding was reported during the first atlas. However, Whimbrels in suitable habitat were reported throughout the summers of 2004 and 2005 on Akimiski Island, extending by 250 km the southern breeding range limit for the species.

Most squares with breeding evidence during the second atlas were in tundra within 40 km of Hudson Bay, where the Whimbrel appears to occur regularly. However, as near

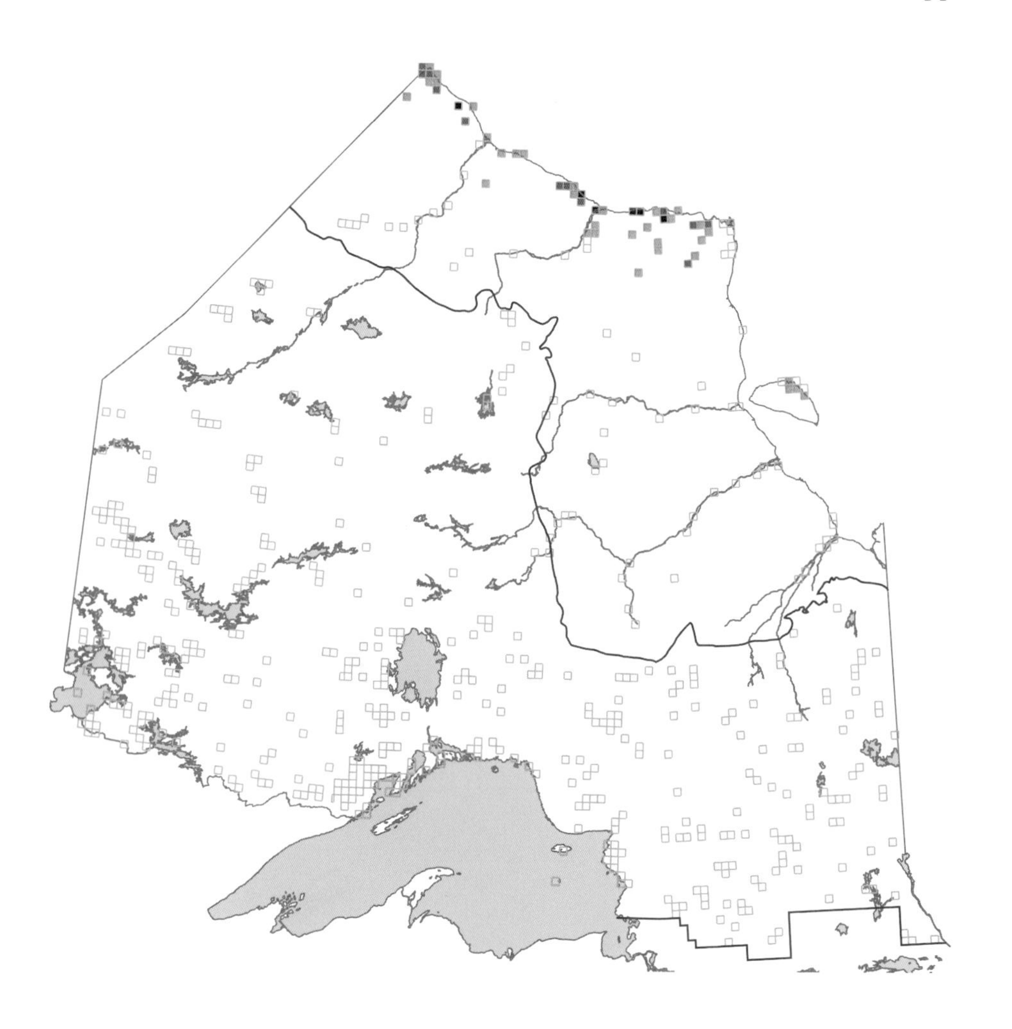

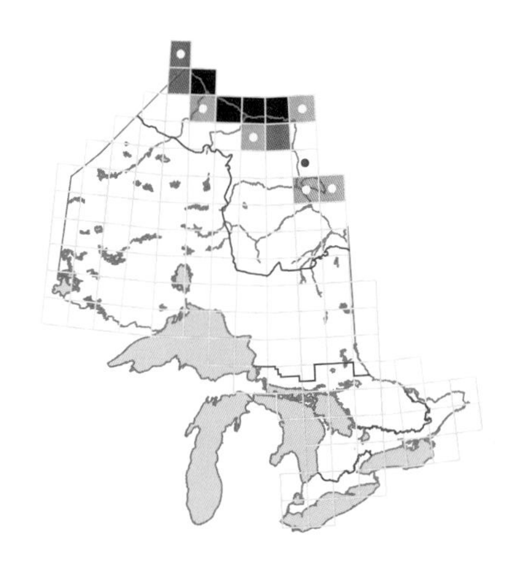

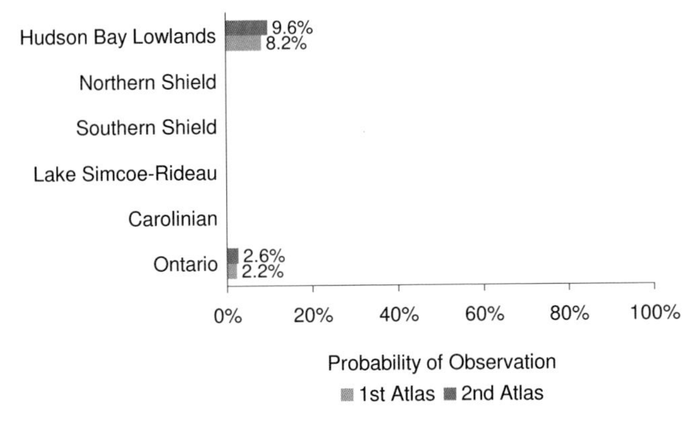

Churchill, Manitoba (Jehl and Lin 2001), the species also appears to breed at low densities considerably farther inland in extensive grass/sedge fens in spruce-Tamarack forest (e.g., 80 km south of Hudson Bay near the Aquatuk River, in the northeast corner of the province).

Breeding biology: In Ontario and other parts of its range, the Whimbrel nests in an array of habitats including subarctic dry heath-lichen tundra, wet willow-birch tundra, vegetated polygonal wetlands, and grass/sedge wetlands (Skeel and Mallory 1996). Northbound Whimbrels arrive at coastal staging areas on James and Hudson Bays by late May. Territories are established and aerial courtship flights are initiated soon after. Migrant Whimbrels may intermix with resident individuals, potentially leading to inflated estimates of local breeding density. During the second atlas, migrant individuals were reported in many squares on Akimiski Island and along the coasts of James and Hudson Bays, often at sites where evidence of breeding had already been confirmed (M. Peck, pers. obs.).

Largely silent for most of the year, the Whimbrel is vociferous and easily detected during the breeding season by its loud, persistent calling throughout aerial displays and during initial contact with aerial and ground predators, including human intruders approaching nesting territories. Both sexes incubate, with off-duty birds frequently found near the nest site (Skeel and Mallory 1996). Incubating birds usually leave the nest while the observer is still a considerable distance away but will return while the observer is in the area. Twelve nests were found during the second atlas period, more than doubling the previous number of nests in the province (ONRS). All nests were north of the treeline in wet sedge meadows or in a mixture of wet and dry tundra, often with nearby standing water.

Abundance: Poor detection on point counts did not allow for the production of a map of relative abundance. Breeding evidence was detected in only 52 squares during the second atlas. However, some Whimbrels were detected in suitable habitat inland from the Hudson Bay coast where surveying was very limited, suggesting that this species may be more widespread and abundant in Ontario than previously thought. Morrison et al. (2006) estimate the eastern Canadian population of the Whimbrel (*N. p. hudsonicus*) at 40,000, while in Ontario Ross et al. (2003) consider it to be an uncommon breeder, with an estimated population in the thousands. – *Mark K. Peck and Donald A. Sutherland*

Nests are shallow depressions on slightly raised hummocks, often in grassy areas, with or without scattered low willow and birch. *Photo: Jim Richards*

In Ontario, the Whimbrel breeds in a variety of open to sparsely treed habitats from large sedge fens in taiga to dry and wet lichen-heath and graminoid tundra. Near Flagstaff Pt., east of the Winisk River. *Photo: Mark Peck*

Hudsonian Godwit

Barge hudsonienne

Limosa haemastica

Ron Ridout

The Hudsonian Godwit is the smallest of the world's four godwit species with a breeding range restricted entirely to North America. This godwit shares with Greater and Lesser Yellowlegs the conspicuous behaviour of alighting on the tops of trees, wings raised, and calling loudly during the breeding season.

The Hudsonian Godwit breeds in several isolated geographic areas across North America. Nesting areas are often associated with major river mouths or coastal flats and are found in western Alaska, northern Yukon, near the mouth of the Mackenzie and Anderson Rivers, and along the southern Hudson Bay coast from Churchill, where the species is considered a fairly common breeder (Manitoba Avian Research Committee 2003), east to Cape Henrietta Maria and south to Akimiski Island, James Bay. Much of the Canadian breeding population, comprising nearly 50% of the global population, stages in large flocks along the western James Bay coast during the fall, prior to its long-distance flight to wintering sites in southern Chile and Argentina (Elphick and Klima 2002). Recent surveys of wintering sites suggest the population has remained relatively stable at 70,000 birds (Morrison et al. 2006.)

Distribution and population status: The breeding distribution of the Hudsonian Godwit in Ontario remains poorly documented. The first evidence of breeding for the province was not established until 1962, when flightless young were discovered near the mouth of the Sutton River (Baillie 1963). The first documented nest was only found in 1992 near Winisk, during an OMNR goose survey (Peck and James 1993b).

The distribution during the second atlas did not differ significantly from that recorded during the first. During the second atlas, birds were found along Hudson Bay from the Pen Islands eastward to Cape Henrietta Maria. Most observations were within 30 km of the coast in large sedge wetlands.

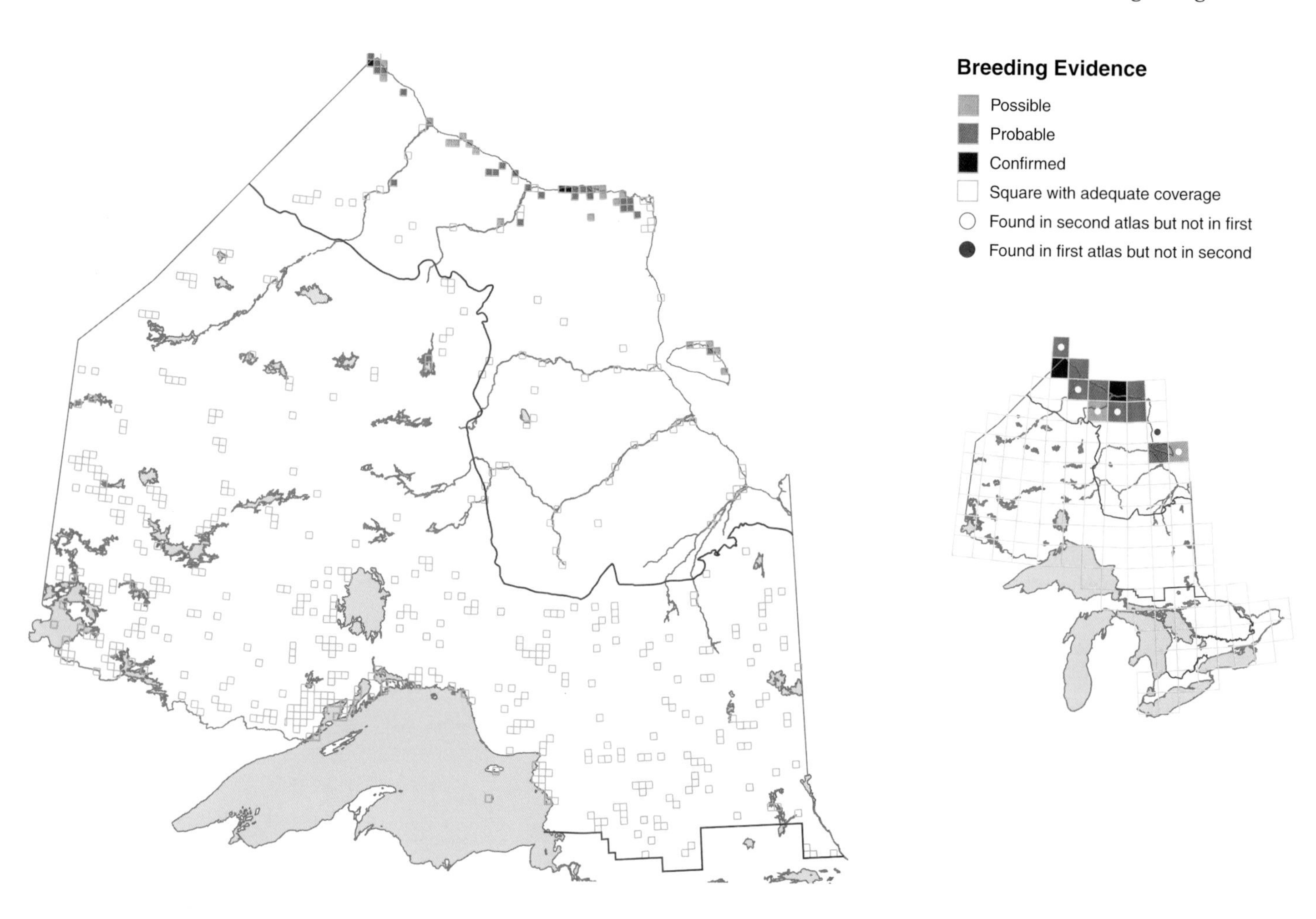

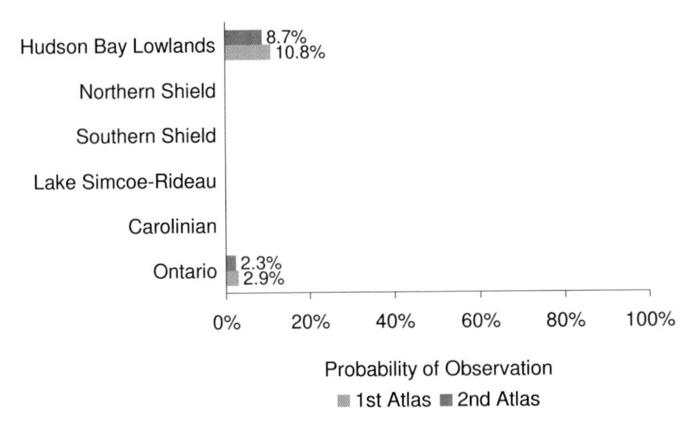

Isolated sightings in extensive taiga fen habitat 75-100 km inland near the Winisk and Fawn Rivers suggest that the provincial breeding range may be more extensive than suspected. The presence of a small population on Akimiski Island (53° N) in habitat shared with Marbled Godwits was established through the observation of individuals and a few pairs in several breeding seasons during the atlas period. This population is nearly 250 km disjunct from populations near Cape Henrietta Maria and suggests a new southern range limit for the species, although breeding was not confirmed.

Breeding biology: The Hudsonian Godwit breeds in wet sedge tundra meadows and in graminoid fens inland in taiga. In Ontario, it is frequently found in areas favoured by the Whimbrel and the Dunlin, usually preferring slightly wetter sites than the former (D. Sutherland and M. Peck, unpubl. data). Breeding godwits are extremely vocal, performing aerial display flights and frequently engaging in vocal chases with conspecifics or other species. Courtship displays, agitation, and distraction displays were noted in 33% of squares. Its relatively large size and conspicuous white rump enable identification even from low-flying aircraft, and the Hudsonian Godwit was detected in a number of squares during aerial surveys by OMNR and CWS personnel. The well-concealed nests are usually located on a dry hummock, generally beneath a small shrub and often near standing water or small ponds (Hagar 1966). Females incubate during the day and are replaced by males in the evening (Elphick and Klima 2002); both sexes care for the young. Four nests were found during the second atlas, three in the vicinity of Burntpoint Creek east of the Winisk River and one south of the Pen Islands. These represent the third through sixth documented nests for the province (ONRS). Migrants, failed breeders, and non-breeding birds congregate on or close to tidal flats and do not provide evidence of breeding. A number of atlas records involved such birds and were accordingly downgraded.

Abundance: The Hudsonian Godwit is almost certainly more widespread and abundant than suggested by atlas data. Detections on point counts were too few to allow for the production of a relative abundance map and the increased number of squares reporting this godwit during the second atlas (46, many previously unsurveyed) compared to the first atlas (21) reinforces the need for additional surveys to accurately reflect this species' true distribution and abundance in the province. Ross et al. (2003) suggest that as much as 50% of the Canadian population may occur in the Hudson Bay Lowlands, with most in Ontario. Given the population estimates of Donaldson et al. (2000) and Morrison et al. (2006), the Ontario breeding population of Hudson Godwit may comprise between 2,500 and 5,000 pairs. – *Donald A. Sutherland and Mark K. Peck*

Both the male and female Hudsonian Godwit incubate the eggs, with females incubating during the day. *Photo: George K. Peck*

Wet-sedge tundra meadow, typical of the breeding habitat of the Hudsonian Godwit in the Hudson Bay Lowlands in Ontario. *Photo: George K. Peck*

Marbled Godwit

Barge marbrée

Limosa fedoa

Ron Ridout

The Marbled Godwit is one of the largest and most imposing shorebirds in North America, breeding and wintering almost entirely on this continent. Its primary breeding population of under 170,000 individuals occurs in the mid-continent prairies, but two small disjunct populations occur in coastal southern Alaska (about 2,000 birds) and in James Bay (about 1,500 birds; Melcher et al. 2006). The Marbled Godwit spends the winter on the Pacific, Gulf, and Atlantic coasts of North America, extending in small numbers to Central America and rarely to South America (Melcher et al. 2006). For breeding, it prefers sparsely vegetated, short grass, or sedge habitats with relatively high wetland densities. Grazed habitats are well used, and there may have been an historic relationship with large ungulates such as bison (Melcher et al. 2006).

Distribution and population status: Distribution has been reasonably assessed by both atlases. The Marbled Godwit can be found breeding in two locations: in the Rainy River area near Manitoba, and in James Bay, with concentrations on Akimiski Island and the southwestern James Bay coast. It occurred in 26 squares in the second atlas, with 22 in the Hudson Bay Lowlands (compared to 15 total squares and 14 in the Lowlands in the first atlas). In James Bay, it was observed from the Québec-Ontario border to just south of Cape Henrietta Maria. The distribution of squares with breeding evidence was patchier in James Bay during this atlas and weighted towards Akimiski Island to the south end of James Bay. A difference in effort is the most likely explanation for the change, and no strong evidence of range contraction exists. Indeed, the range is much the same as it was throughout the latter half of the 20th century (cf. Morrison et al. 1976; Morrison in Cadman et al. 1987). The Rainy River range in Ontario is limited to about 100 km^2 north and east of the town. The mid-continent prairie population with which this group is probably affiliated appears to be stable recently but

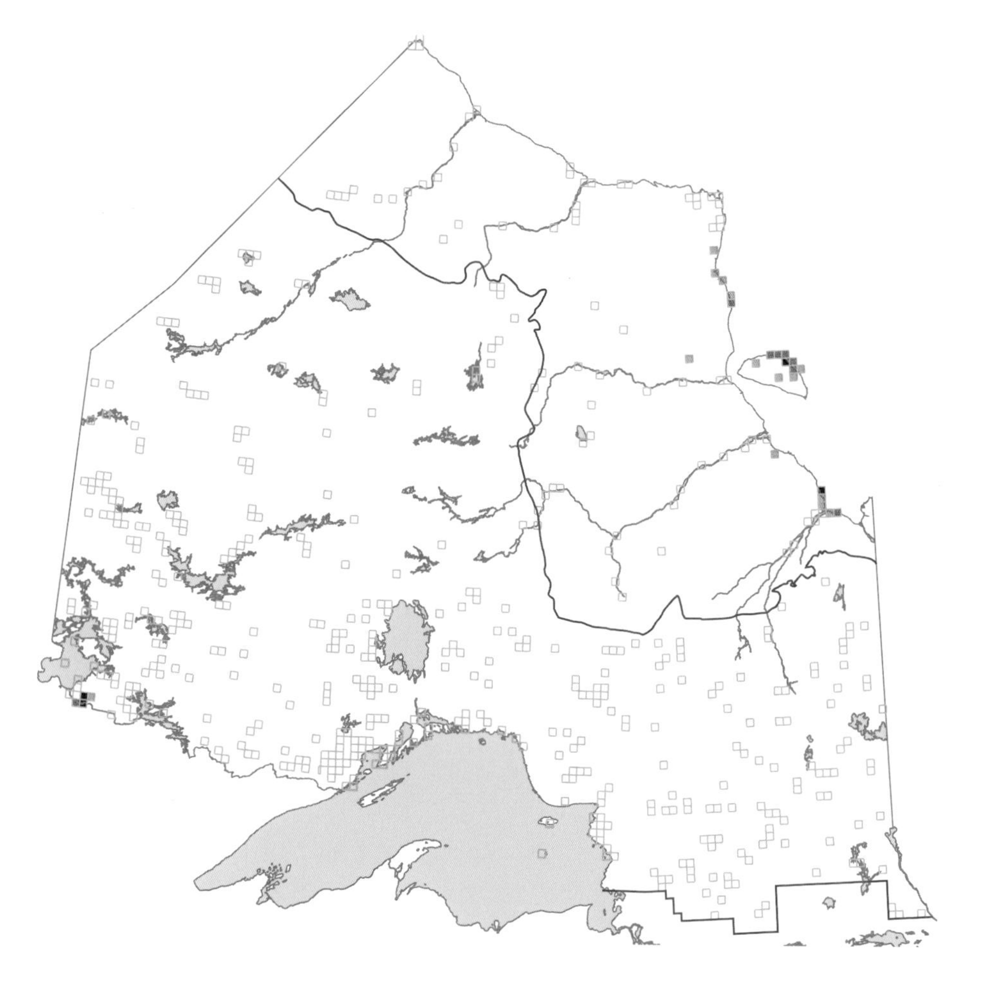

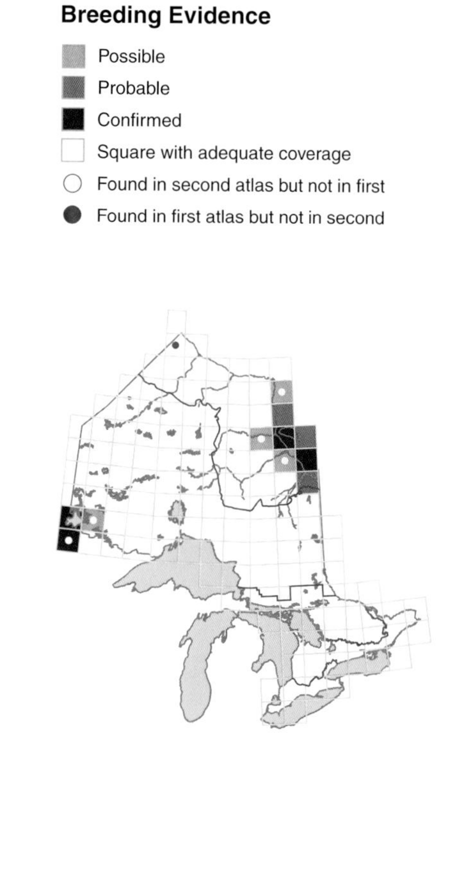

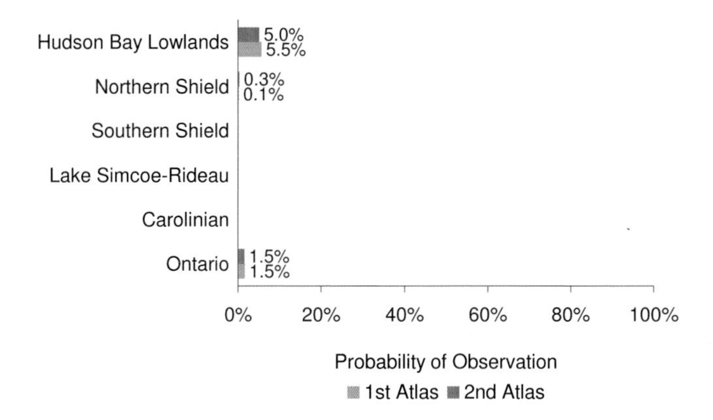

has probably declined over the long term, due mostly to habitat loss (Gratto-Trevor 2000; Melcher et al. 2006).

Breeding biology: The Marbled Godwit maintains large (90-100 ha) territories during breeding; hence pairs are widely spaced at low density (Gratto-Trevor 2000). In James Bay, wetlands suitable for breeding occur in two primary circumstances: the short grass/sedge meadows of the narrow vegetated salt marsh zone and the muskeg-wet tundra zone (which is extensive in parts of the range where godwits were observed). In Rainy River, primary habitats are hayfield and pastures, especially those that have been grazed or cut for hay (D. Elder, pers. comm.). During courtship, territory establishment, and pre-laying, the species is vocally conspicuous and relatively approachable on the ground, making probable and possible evidence easy to obtain. However, nests are extremely difficult to find, and incubating birds must be almost underfoot to be flushed, thus making confirmation via nests extremely rare (one during this atlas period).

Abundance: Although confirmed breeding evidence (nests and young) was sparse, observations were relatively widespread in the two Ontario breeding areas. Occurrence in the muskeg and tundra habitats is so poorly known that no good estimate of abundance can be made, but this habitat type is extensive in the northwest part of James Bay and has potential as breeding habitat for many additional breeding pairs. Highest observed densities occur on Akimiski Island (0.5-1.0 pairs per linear km of coastal habitat, K. Abraham, unpubl. data). The number of birds in the James Bay population is uncertain but is estimated to include about 150 pairs on Akimiski Island. Elsewhere in the Hudson Bay Lowlands, abundance is at best a guess. Limited access made atlas coverage less than desired. A few hundred pairs may occur along the Ontario James Bay coast if densities there are similar to those on Akimiski Island, given that godwits occur along a coastline of over 400 km dominated by suitable coastal meadow marshes and sedge fen habitats with abundant wetlands.

In Rainy River, the Marbled Godwit appeared to have increased from the first atlas. Additional search effort in the second atlas related to knowledge of the godwit's presence and evidence of breeding between atlases (Elder 1994), along with ready access to its hayfield habitats, is the likely cause. However, it was generally scarcer in the last two years of the second atlas period, and there may be as few as 5-10 pairs that return annually to previously used sites in this area (D. Elder, pers. comm.). – *Ken Abraham*

Nests of the Marbled Godwit, generally shallow depressions lined with sedges or grasses, typically contain a clutch of four eggs. *Photo: George K. Peck*

The Marbled Godwit prefers breeding habitat consisting of short grasses and sedges interspersed with shallow wetlands where prey is abundant. *Photo: Jean Iron*

Semipalmated Sandpiper

Bécasseau semipalmé

Calidris pusilla

The Semipalmated Sandpiper may be the most abundant breeding shorebird in Canada, with an estimated population size of 2,000,000 (Morrison et al. 2006). In addition to northern Alaska and far eastern Siberia, this species breeds in arctic and subarctic Canada from northern Yukon and the Northwest Territories across southern Nunavut and along the coastlines of Hudson Bay, Hudson Strait, and northern Labrador (Gratto-Trevor 1992). Despite its numbers, it is now listed as a species of moderate concern in Canada due to significant declines at staging areas in Ontario, Québec, and the Maritimes. Additional declines were also reported along the Pacific coast of North America and, more locally, during the breeding season in Churchill, Manitoba (Donaldson et al. 2000; Jehl 2004).

Distribution and population status: Historically, the Semipalmated Sandpiper was considered an abundant migrant along the west James Bay and southeastern Hudson Bay coasts of Ontario, with breeding records from Cape Henrietta Maria and westward along the coastal tundra areas of southern Hudson Bay (Peck and James 1983). Additional surveys outside of atlas periods indicate that breeding is more common in the northeast and northwest corners of the province (Schueler et al 1974; Wilson and McRae 1993). Results from the first atlas found breeding evidence in 14 squares all within 20 km of Hudson Bay and northern James Bay. During the second atlas, breeding evidence was reported in 33 squares, and between atlases, the probability of observation increased by 76% in the Hudson Bay Lowlands. Whether this difference reflects an actual increase in numbers or is the result of other factors is not immediately clear. Birds were found in coastal squares as expected and, rarely, farther inland and south, including in several squares on Akimiski Island. It is possible that inland observations may have been of late migrants or unpaired individuals, but the display flight observed in one

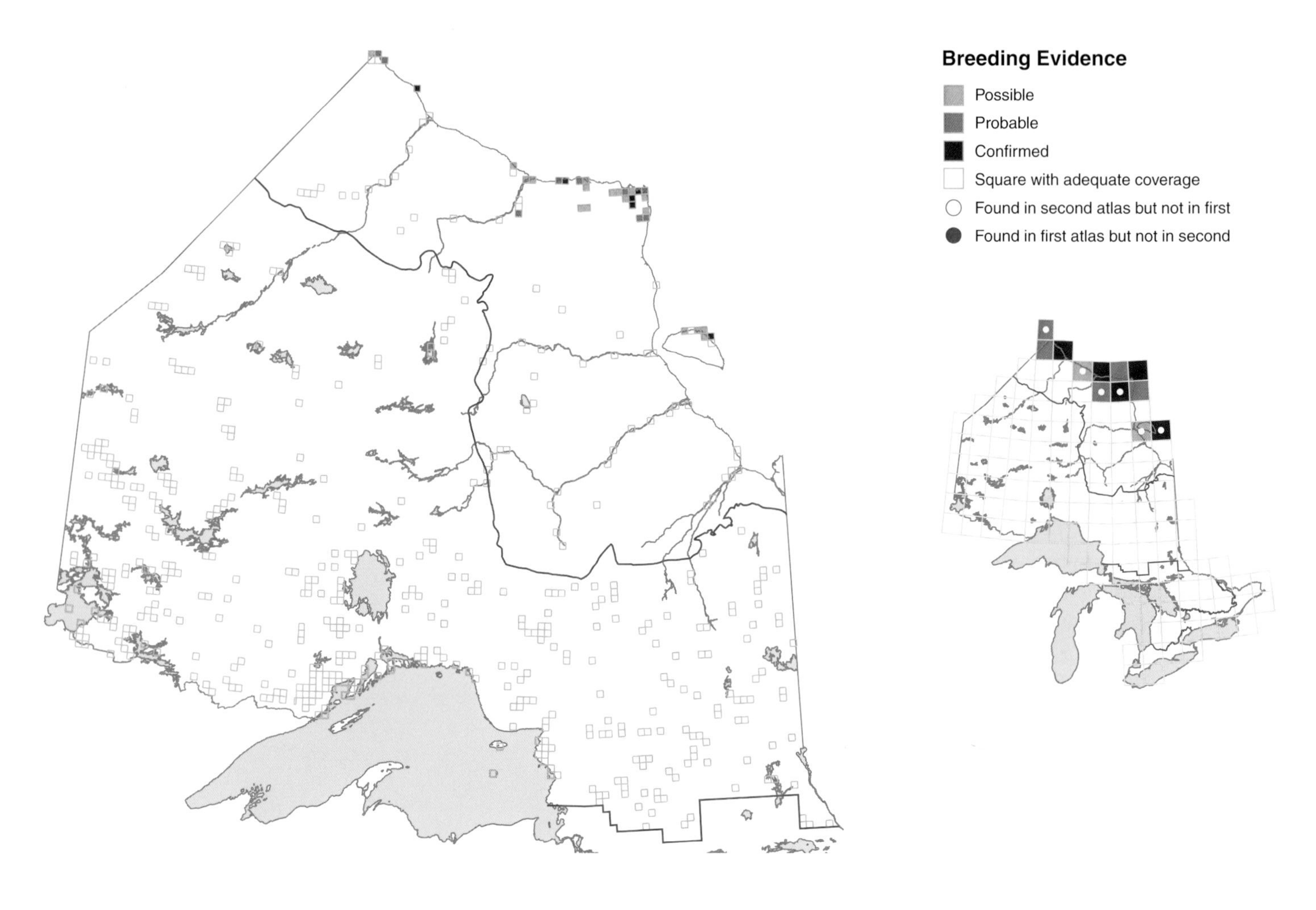

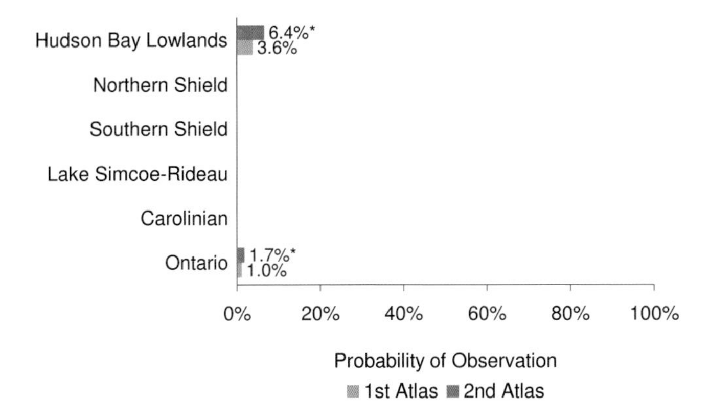

instance suggests breeding is possible (pers. obs.). The species was previously reported breeding on several other adjacent James Bay islands (Manning 1952, 1976, 1981), so the records on Akimiski Island are not unexpected.

Breeding biology: The Semipalmated Sandpiper nests in wet and dry tundra habitat often in association with the Dunlin, Least Sandpiper, and Red-necked Phalarope. It is superficially similar to the Least Sandpiper in size, courtship display, vocalization, and nesting habitat, but it is typically more restricted to coastal tundra areas. Males arrive on breeding grounds in northern Ontario during late May or early June, preceding females by less than a week and establishing territories almost immediately. Unpaired males engage in aerial displays of hovering flight with rapid wing beats accompanied by steady and constant "motorboat " vocalization, differing from the more rhythmically repeated call used by Least Sandpipers (Ashkenazie and Safriel 1979).

The Semipalmated Sandpiper is monogamous and territorial, with both sexes participating in nest building and incubation. Pair bonds remain intact during nesting, but females depart shortly after hatching, leaving the care of young to the males (Gratto-Trevor 1992). ONRS records indicate nests are most often in grassy tussocks in shallow, wet tussock-tundra habitat and occasionally in heath-lichen tundra or on raised beach ridges. Nests are often lined with dead willow leaves or grasses. Incubating birds often leave the nest early when approached by a human intruder but will usually return quickly after a few minutes. Birds flushed from the nest or from brooding young will often use the "rodent run distraction display" with feathers raised on the back and the tail spread, thus clearly indicating breeding. The species defends territories from conspecifics and Least Sandpipers, so territorial disputes also help in detecting this otherwise inconspicuous species.

Abundance: The Semipalmated Sandpiper is considered an uncommon breeding bird in Ontario, with the population estimated in the thousands (Ross et al. 2003). Birds were detected in only 33 squares during this atlas, with few breeding confirmations, despite better coverage in regions where the species was once considered a common to abundant migrant and breeder (Peck 1972; James and Peck 1985). Poor detection on point counts did not allow for the production of a relative abundance map, and it remains unclear whether the Ontario breeding population is increasing or declining. Given that the Semipalmated Sandpiper migrates along the Hudson Bay and James Bay coasts and is known to stage in tundra habitat alongside territorial birds, care must be taken to ensure that relative abundance of Ontario breeding populations is not overestimated during late springs or when failed or non-breeders return early from breeding areas farther north.
– Mark K. Peck

Nests are usually in grassy tussocks and are lined with dead willow leaves or grasses. Radar Site 415, Polar Bear Prov. Park, 25 June 1970. *Photo: George K. Peck*

In Ontario, typical breeding habitat is coastal wet tussock tundra. Heath-lichen tundra or raised beach ridges are occasionally also used. Radar Site 415, Polar Bear Prov. Park, 25 June 1970. *Photo: George K. Peck*

Least Sandpiper

Bécasseau minuscule

Calidris minutilla

Mark Peck

The Least Sandpiper, North America's smallest shorebird, breeds in low arctic and subarctic wetland habitats across North America (Cooper 1994). It is considered a common breeder in Ontario, with estimates in the ten thousands (Ross et al. 2003). Recent declines in Ontario and the Maritimes make it a species of medium conservation priority (Donaldson et al. 2000; Bart et al. 2007).

Distribution and population status: Prior to the first atlas, the distribution of the Least Sandpiper was thought to be largely restricted to tundra and coastal areas along Hudson and James Bays, with scattered numbers slightly inland near major rivers (Manning 1952; Peck and James 1983). During both atlases, breeding was confirmed in most 100-km blocks along Hudson Bay and northern James Bay, with additional breeding evidence reported as much as 250 km inland, indicating a more widespread inland range than suggested by the historical literature. During the second atlas, confirmed breeding evidence was also reported on Akimiski Island and farther south at Northbluff Point, north of the mouth of the Moose River. The latter record was an observation of a young bird incapable of sustained flight, accompanied by an agitated adult, near to coastal beach ridges and saltwater marshes (T. Hoar, pers. comm.) in an area where this species is also known to stage during migration.

Breeding evidence for the province increased from 42 squares in 17 100-km blocks during the first atlas to 69 squares in 21 100-km blocks in this atlas, with a non-significant increase of 18% in the probability of observation in the Hudson Bay Lowlands. Given that inland sites received more limited survey effort and that most northern inland atlas trips took place after the completion of the conspicuous, vocal courtship displays, the Least Sandpiper may be more abundant and have a more extensive breeding range than suggested by the atlas results. A more extensive distribution inland in the

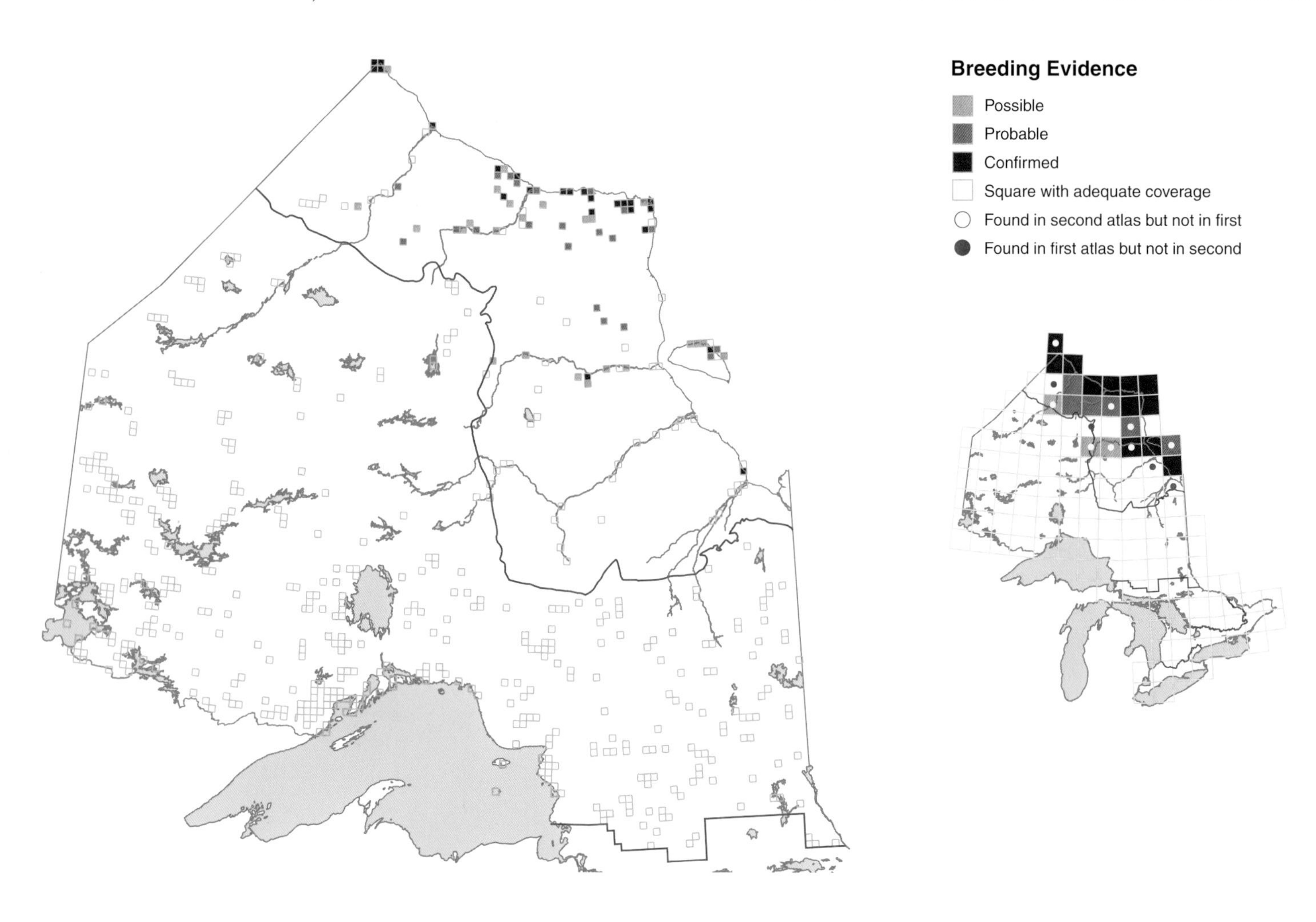

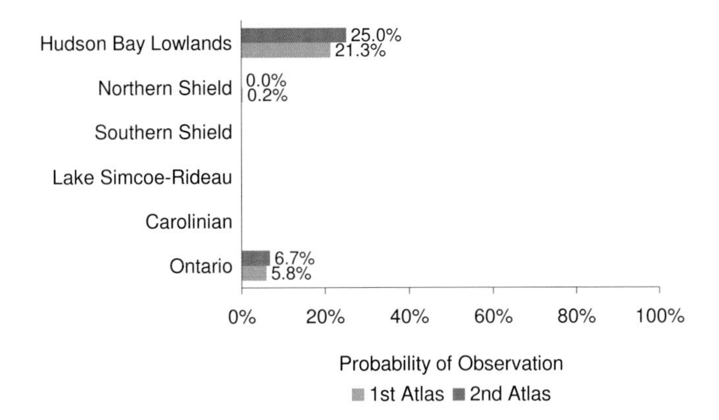

Nests are frequently located on slightly raised frost heaves or ridges, often near pools or small ponds. They are concealed from above by overhanging vegetation and invariably lined with dead leaves of Dwarf Birch and willow. – *Photo: George K. Peck*

Hudson Bay Lowlands of Ontario is consistent with that observed in peatlands and muskeg in the Boreal Forest in central-interior Québec (Gauthier and Aubry 1996). Conversely, more extensive coverage of tundra habitats in coastal squares, where densities are higher and the species is more easily detected, resulted in a more accurate reflection of distribution and abundance.

Breeding biology: Males precede females to the breeding grounds, establish territories, and are very vocal and obvious during aerial displays. Courtship flights involve a rapid ascent to 10-30 m, followed by a hovering flight consisting of alternating bouts of rapid wing beats and gliding, lasting between one and three minutes, while constantly vocalizing (Cooper 1994). The frequency of display flights and territory defence diminishes after egg laying. Least Sandpipers are socially monogamous, with males and females sharing nest building, incubation, and care of young. In Ontario, the species breeds more commonly near the coast in wet or dry graminoid tundra, and apparently less commonly inland in peatlands and sedge fens in taiga. Nests are frequently on slightly raised frost boils or low ridges, often near pools, ponds, or lakes with sparse low shrubs or dwarf trees. Nests are usually concealed from above by an overhanging branch of dwarf birch or willow and lined with dead leaves. Occasionally, eggs are partially or almost completely covered by leaves.

During incubation, birds allow close approach before flushing from the nest, usually fluttering ahead or running away with feathers raised on the back, one or both wings dragging and tail spread. Parents will also fly overhead or perch in nearby trees or bushes when young are present, calling incessantly.

Prior to 2001, only 10 nests had been reported to the ONRS. During the second atlas, an additional 29 nests were documented across the province. Egg dates ranged widely, from 10 June through 23 July during the atlas period.

Abundance: Detection of the Least Sandpiper on point counts was limited, as most atlassing within its breeding range was conducted after the conspicuous aerial courtships display had ceased; consequently, the data were insufficient to generate a relative abundance map. However, available abundance data from both atlases suggest that the greatest densities of breeding birds occur in tundra habitats near the coasts of Hudson Bay and northern James Bay. In coastal tundra habitats, the Least Sandpiper is common and reported in higher densities than other calidridine sandpipers. Densities appear to be considerably lower inland in taiga peatlands. However, as suggested by Ross et al. (2003), additional systematic surveys of inland areas are required in order to better assess the abundance of the species in the interior of the Hudson Bay Lowlands. – *Mark K. Peck*

In Ontario, the Least Sandpiper breeds more commonly in wet or dry graminoid coastal tundra, and apparently less commonly inland in peatlands and sedge fen in taiga. *Photo: George K. Peck*

Pectoral Sandpiper

Bécasseau à poitrine cendrée
Calidris melanotos

George K. Peck

Unusual among calidridine sandpipers, the Pectoral Sandpiper is sexually dimorphic and has a polygamous/promiscuous mating system. It is the one of the earliest shorebirds to return to southern Ontario each spring and has one of the longest annual migration routes of any shorebird. During migration, this species is often found in sewage lagoons, wet grassy meadows, flooded fields, and small marshy ponds.

Distribution and population status: The principal breeding range of the Pectoral Sandpiper is on tundra habitat north and west of Ontario from Baffin Island to central Siberia. Although its summer distribution is extensive, the majority of Pectoral Sandpipers migrate through the interior of North America each spring and fall, wintering in southern and central South America (Holmes and Pitelka 1998). Despite the occasional presence of the species in summer on the Hudson Bay coast, the only confirmed Ontario breeding was recorded in 1948, when two flightless young were collected near Cape Henrietta Maria (Peck and James 1983). This record represents the most southern breeding confirmation for this species. The Pectoral Sandpiper also nests irregularly, and less frequently in years with lower than normal temperatures, near Churchill, Manitoba (Jehl 2004).

The only record of this species during the first atlas was of a lone bird foraging in suitable habitat near Hook Point on the coast of James Bay in early July 1984. Small flocks began arriving days later, including flying juveniles with down still on their heads. Breeding evidence from other species in the area suggested that 1984 had been a very early spring, and it was unclear where the young Pectoral Sandpipers had fledged (James and Peck 1985).

During the second atlas, possible breeding records were accepted from the northwestern and northeastern corners of the province near the Pen Islands and Cape Henrietta Maria, respectively. There were no sightings of this species along the

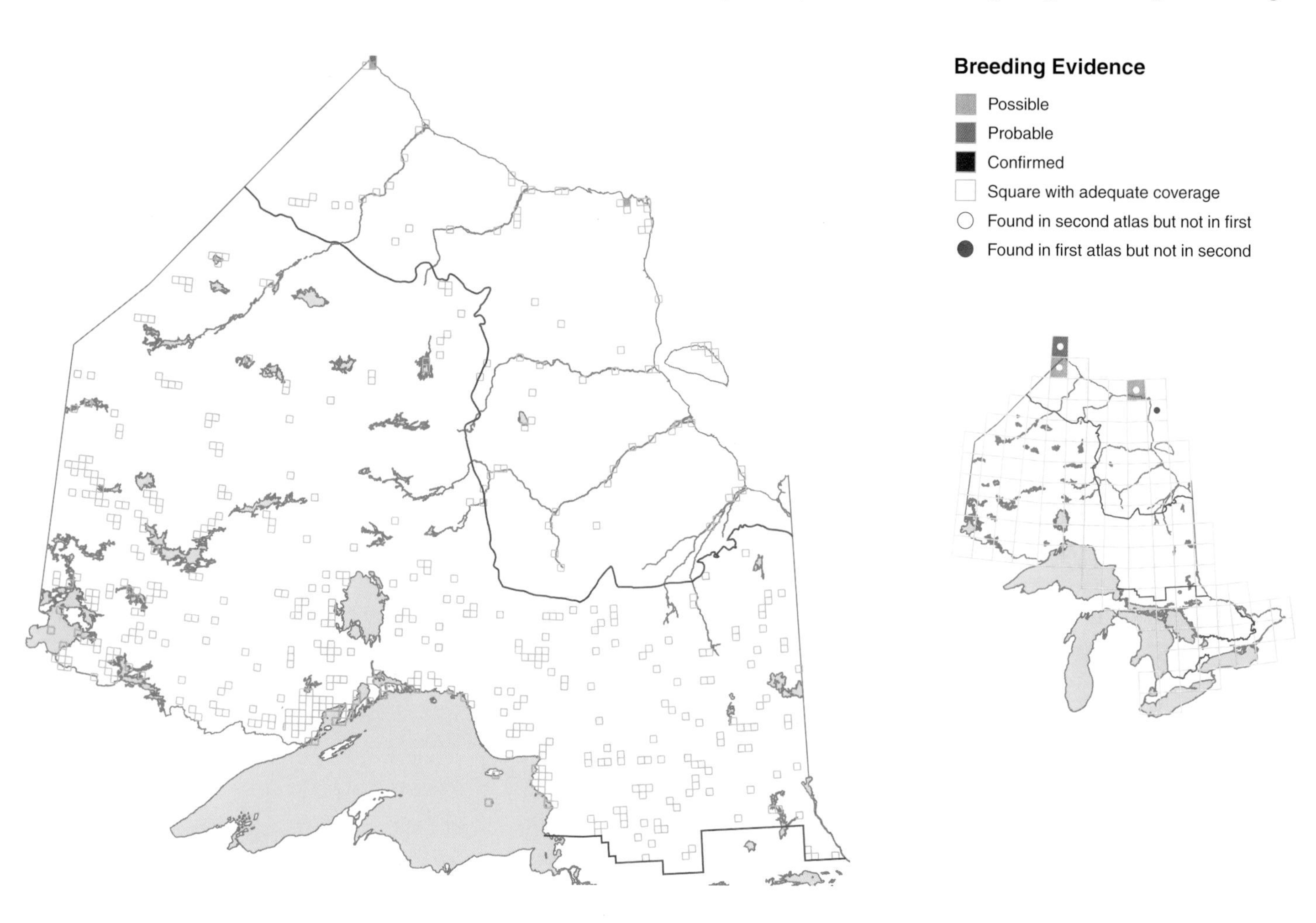

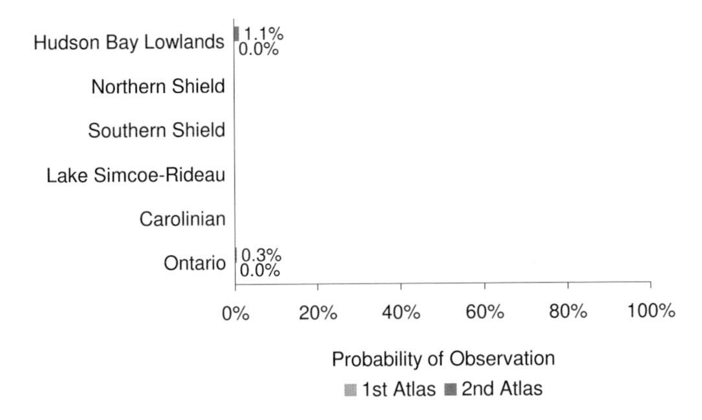

rest of the Hudson Bay coast. A southern observation of a lone bird feeding near Byers Creek on Akimiski Island on 5 July 2005 was designated a probable migrant because it was south of the known breeding range and small flocks were seen nearby shortly thereafter. Numerous July and August records indicate Pectoral Sandpipers regularly stage along James Bay and Hudson Bay coastal areas from the Albany River northward prior to migrating south.

Breeding biology: The courtship display of the male Pectoral Sandpiper is one of the most memorable events of the short arctic summer. In wet grassy tundra, often dotted with hummocks or gravel ridges, the male establishes and defends 4-10 ha territories. During the 150-200 m courtship flights, it flies slowly 1-2 m above the ground, expanding and contracting the large, fatty throat sac and producing loud hooting calls that can be heard from considerable distances (Pitelka 1959). Within its territory, the male frequently stands upright and alert on mounds, surveying the surrounding area. The pendulous bib regularly remains slightly inflated, allowing easy identification.

Both males and females are thought to be promiscuous. Females may visit several territories before choosing a nest site, and male territories may have more than one female nesting in them, although nests are usually well spaced (Holmes and Pitelka 1998). The female selects a nest site in a well-drained area of wet sedge tundra or along the edges of tundra polygons. Nests are substantial and well hidden in sedges or under bushes. The female is wary and often leaves the nest early or flushes when surprised, moving rodent-like, with back feathers ruffled. She alone incubates and cares for the young. The male leaves the breeding grounds first, often prior to the eggs hatching, and joins pre-migratory flocks along the coast.

Abundance: Historically, the Pectoral Sandpiper was one of the most numerous of all North American shorebirds, but its numbers were greatly reduced in the late 1800s, due to habitat changes and market hunting along its migration route (McIlhenny 1943). Today, this species is considered common in Canada, with the worldwide population estimated at approximately 500,000 birds and no clear evidence of population decline (Morrison et al. 2006).

The Ontario breeding distribution appears to be restricted to the northern corners of the province. Given the scarcity of records during the second atlas, the Pectoral Sandpiper should be considered a rare, irregular breeding species in the province. Difficulty in accessing possible nesting habitat, the unpredictability of spring and summer weather patterns during the second atlas, and the potential overlap of breeding birds with staging birds make it difficult to assemble an accurate assessment of this species. – *Mark K. Peck*

Nests are well concealed in sedges, usually sheltered by low willows, on raised areas of open wet sedge tundra. No nest has yet been found in Ontario. *Photo: Jim Richards*

Open wet sedge tundra in the vicinity of Hook Point, south of Cape Henrietta Maria, where the province's only record of confirmed breeding for the Pectoral Sandpiper was established in 1948. *Photo: Donald A. Sutherland*

Dunlin

Bécasseau variable

Calidris alpina

Mark Peck

The Dunlin is a holarctic tundra-breeding shorebird with 10 recognized subspecies based on plumage and morphometric characters (Dickinson 2003), or five subspecies based on genetic analysis (Wenink 1994). In North America, the three accepted subspecies are *C. a. articola* in northern Alaska, *C. a. pacifica* in coastal Alaska, and *C. a. hudsonia* in the central Canadian Arctic from Victoria Island eastward in arctic and subarctic regions. Breeding occurs in Manitoba and Ontario along coastal Hudson Bay and northern James Bay, with a southern localized population on the Twin Islands in James Bay (Manning 1981).

The worldwide population is estimated at nearly 4,000,000 birds, with a maximum North American population estimate of 1,550,000 (Morrison et al. 2001; Morrison et al. 2006). The Dunlin is considered an uncommon breeding species in Ontario with an estimated population in the thousands (Ross et al. 2003).

Distribution and population status: The first confirmed nesting of the Dunlin in Ontario was in the Cape Henrietta Maria region in 1947 (Manning 1952). The few other records prior to the first atlas indicated breeding sites along the coastal tundra of northern James Bay and Hudson Bay (Peck and James 1983). Results from the first and second atlas were similar, indicating that the Dunlin continues to breed along the coastal tundra of Hudson Bay, concentrated in the areas of the Pen Islands in the west and from the Winisk River to the northwest corner of James Bay in the east. The lower number of observations in central coastal areas may be due to either sub-optimal habitat or fewer surveys in those areas. During the second atlas, possible breeding evidence was also obtained on Akimiski Island 250 km south of mainland sites; several documented sightings of birds early in the season in suitable habitat included a singing individual. Several additional pre-atlas

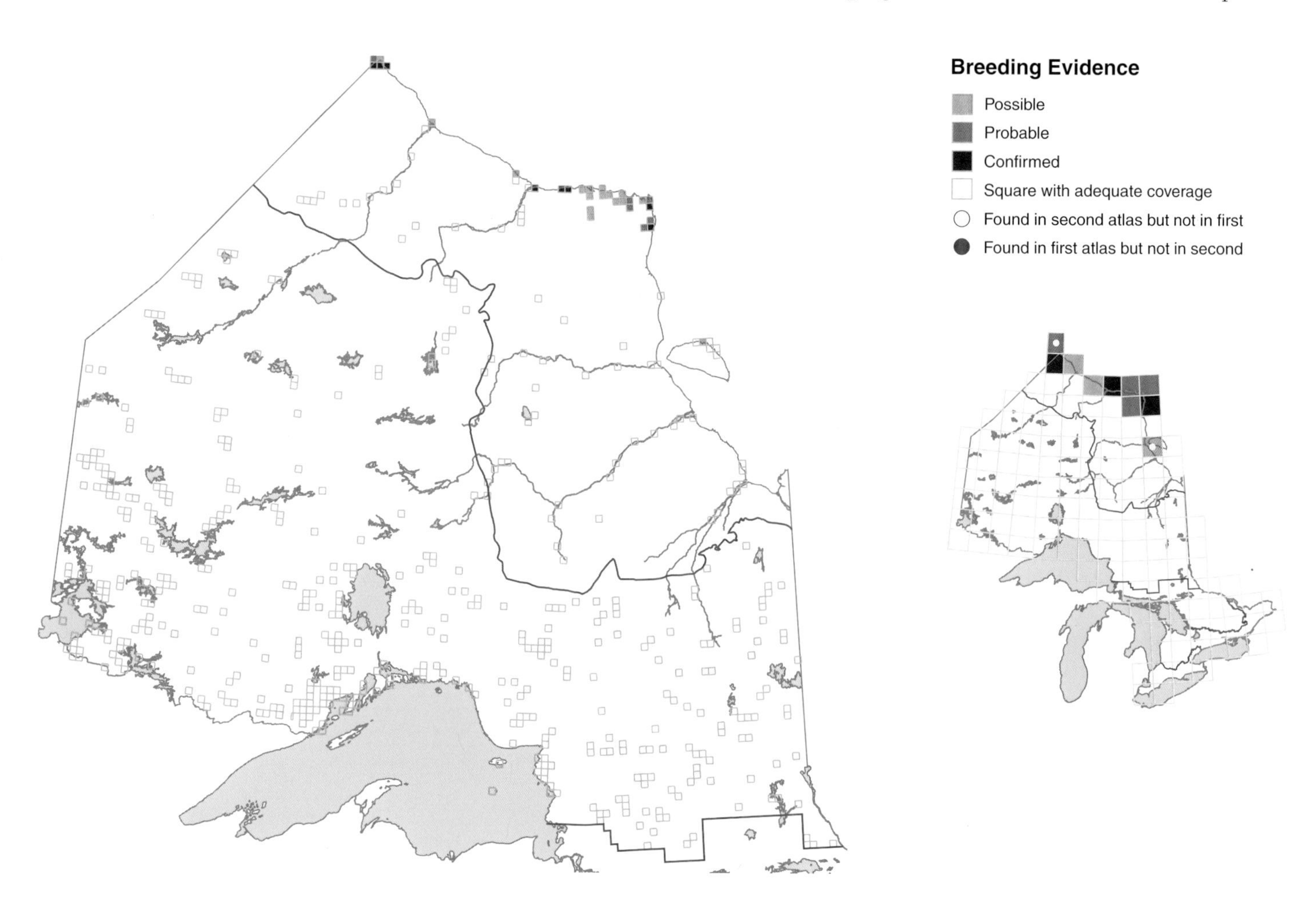

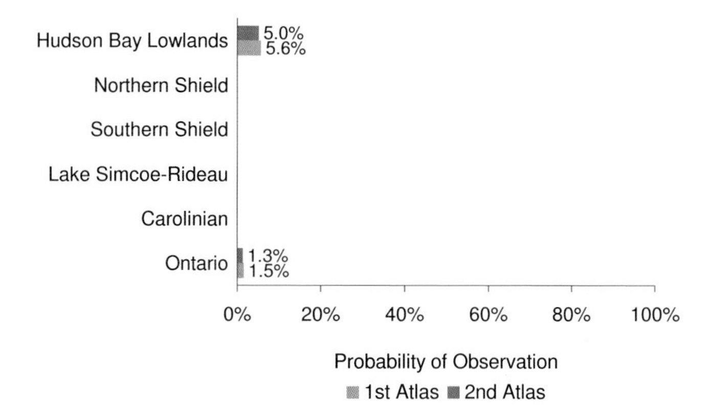

observations of agitated adults suggest breeding on the island is likely (K. Abraham, pers. comm.). Vegetation differences resulting from the harsher climate found on the James Bay islands as compared to the nearby mainland may explain the breeding of the Dunlin and some other tundra-breeding shorebirds on this island.

The Dunlin appears to be more restricted to coastal tundra areas than many other arctic breeding species. During the second atlas, most records were within 20 km of the coast, but the species was also observed in extensive sedge fen near the Aquatuk River, almost 40 km inland from Hudson Bay.

Breeding biology: The Dunlin is a territorial, socially monogamous sandpiper found in arctic and subarctic coastal tundra where it breeds in polygonal wet tussock and peat hummock tundra, often in association with water (Warnock and Gill 1996). It migrates through southern Ontario in large numbers during the latter half of May (Curry 2006), arriving at breeding areas and establishing territories by early June. It is often found sharing habitat with the Semipalmated Sandpiper, Least Sandpiper, Stilt Sandpiper, Red-necked Phalarope, Whimbrel, and Hudsonian Godwit. Males engage in territorial flight displays consisting of short glides with stiff arched wings, interrupted by shallow, rapid flutters and accompanied by the distinctive rhythmically repeated call and song (Miller 1983). Both adults incubate and care for the precocial young and generally stay with the offspring until just before or just after fledging (Holmes 1966). Incubating birds, when flushed, scuttle away in a crouched "rodent-run" posture while the observer is still a considerable distance away, but usually return quickly. Nests are relatively easy to find once the incubating bird has been disturbed.

Twenty-three nests were found during this atlas period, bringing the number of nests documented in the province to 34 (ONRS data). Nest dates ranged from 9 June through 6 July. Nests were found in grass or sedge tussocks or hummocks in areas of wet tundra, with standing water or ponds nearby. In addition, one nest was found on a heath lichen ridge, while another nest was located in a tuft of grass near a tidal pond.

Abundance: Dunlin observations were limited to 30 squares and 10 100-km blocks during the second atlas. The species was reported at a rate of 2.9 birds/25 point counts, higher than any other tundra breeding shorebird with the exception of the Wilson's Snipe. In the Pen Island 100-km blocks, it was detected on 44.3% (54/122) of point counts, while 100-km blocks in the area of Cape Henrietta Maria

Nests are typically located on sedge tussocks or low moss mounds in areas of standing water but may occasionally be located on drier ground on adjacent beach ridges. Near Radar Site 415, 27 June 1970. *Photo: George K. Peck*

In Ontario, preferred nesting habitat is wet tundra with scattered small ponds and standing water with sedge tussocks within 20 km of the Hudson and northern James Bay coasts. Near West Pen Island, 5 July 2004. *Photo: Colin D. Jones*

region reported birds in 31.5% (82/260) of point counts. This suggests that, in favourable habitat, the Dunlin can be quite common. – *Mark K. Peck*

Stilt Sandpiper

Bécasseau à échasses
Calidris himantopus

Mark Peck

The Stilt Sandpiper breeds only in North America, nesting in low arctic and subarctic lowlands from northwestern coastal Alaska east to coastal Nunavut and southern Victoria Island, with a disjunct population along the coasts of western and southern Hudson Bay and northern James Bay (Godfrey 1986). An ongoing decline in the area around Churchill, Manitoba, has raised concerns for the conservation of this sandpiper (Klima and Jehl 1998), and it has been identified as a species of moderate concern in Canada (Donaldson et al. 2000).

Distribution and population status: Breeding by the Stilt Sandpiper in Ontario was first confirmed in 1947 with the collection of a half-grown juvenile at Cape Henrietta Maria (Manning 1952). Numerous observations of summering adults and adults with downy young have since been reported, but no nest had been documented in the province until recently (Burke et al. 2006). During the second atlas, the first provincial nest record was established with documentation of a nest discovered south of West Pen Island on 24 June 2004 (Burke et al. 2006). It was located on a narrow beach ridge 11 m from wet graminoid tundra with standing water and scattered thickets of dwarf birch and willow. Before the nest was lost to predation, neither a non-incubating bird nor an exchange of incubating birds was observed during seven days of close observation. A successful nesting was confirmed on 4 July 2004 in the same area when an adult and two downy young were found near the edge of a small lake 1.2 km from the first nest.

In Ontario, the Stilt Sandpiper has an apparently discontinuous distribution, occurring in isolated areas along the coasts of Hudson Bay and northern James Bay south to the vicinity of Hook Point on the northern James Bay coast (Peck and James 1983). The distribution reported during the second atlas did not differ significantly from the first, with most sightings made within 20 km of Hudson Bay. Observations from both

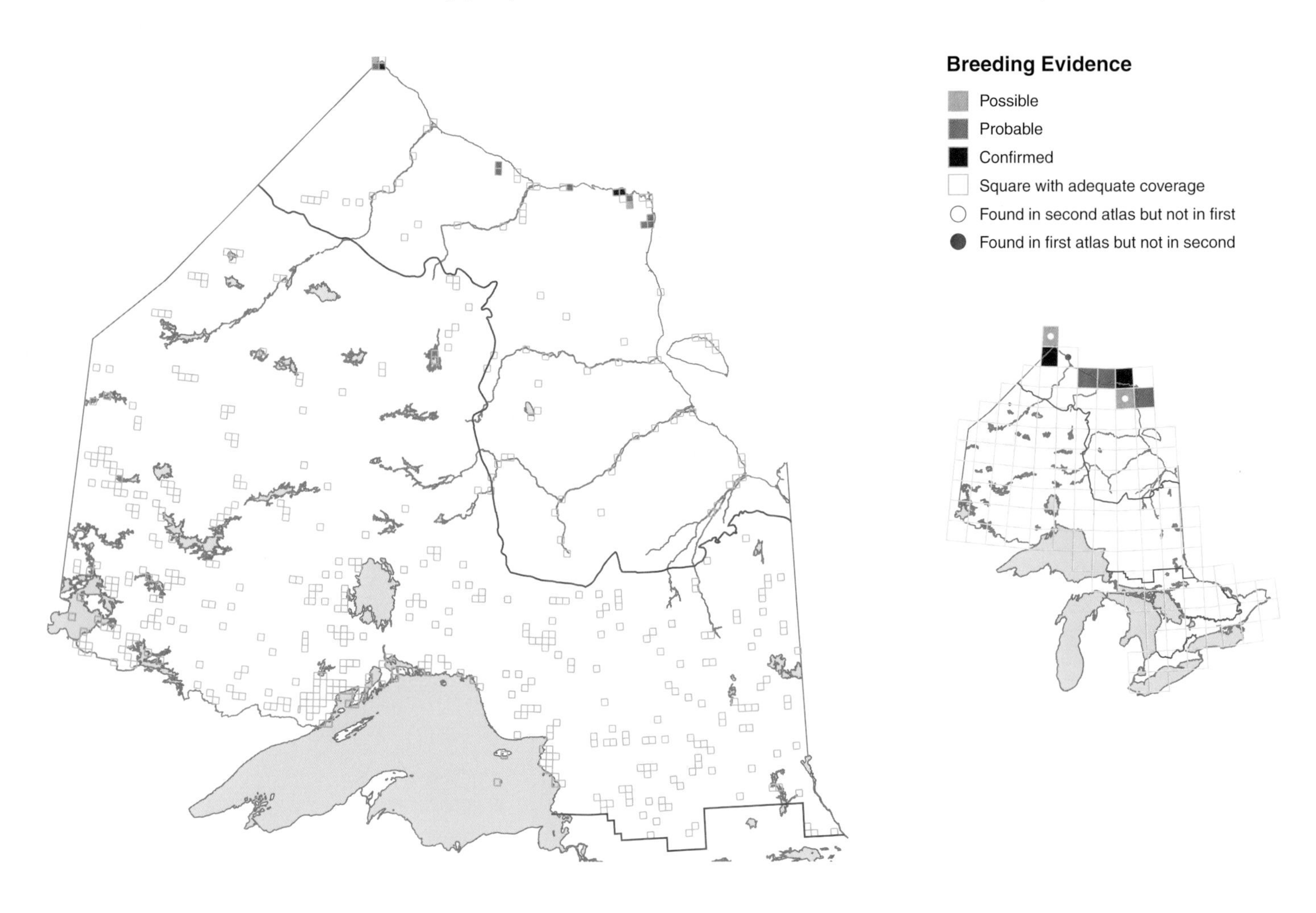

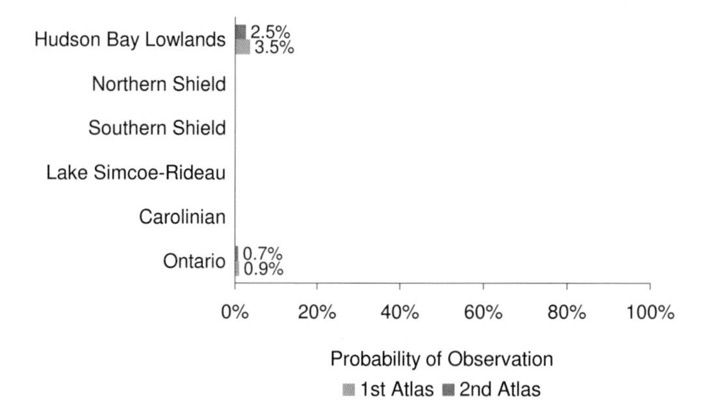

atlases, together with historical breeding records, suggest that the species may be more restricted in its habitat requirements than other northern shorebirds. In the vicinities of the Pen Islands, Cape Henrietta Maria and Hook Point, the Stilt Sandpiper breeds in areas of maritime-subarctic wet tundra consisting of sedge wetlands interspersed with low shrubs, ponds, and shallow lakes, usually adjacent to beach ridges supporting lichen-heath vegetation. However, observations during the second atlas of aerial displays and agitated pairs in extensive taiga fen habitat 30-50 km inland suggest that in Ontario this sandpiper is not exclusively a tundra breeder and may have a wider distribution than previously recognized.

Breeding biology: The Stilt Sandpiper arrives back at breeding areas on the Hudson Bay coast in late May (Jehl 2004), where males immediately establish territories through aerial displays. Older birds may reunite on established territories, reducing or even foregoing courtship and territorial displays and reusing old nest sites (Klima and Jehl 1998). During late May and early June, aerial displays and the accompanying loud donkey-like vocalizations are easily detected. As these displays largely cease with the onset of nesting, birds become harder to detect later in the season when most atlassing occurs. Incubation is by both sexes, typically by the male during the day and the female at night. Pairs usually remain together during territorial establishment and egg laying, but during incubation, off-duty individuals may forage at distances of up to 8 km from the nest (Klima and Jehl 1998). Incubating birds allow close approach, remaining motionless, making nests very difficult to find.

Abundance: Detections of the Stilt Sandpiper on point counts were too few to produce a map of relative abundance, although available data suggest that, at least locally, the species is uncommon. It was detected on 40% (49/121) of the point counts in squares south of West Pen Island and 15% (11/77) of counts in the vicinity of Radar Sites 415 and 416, inland from Hook Point, where as many as 12 individuals were observed daily during the first atlas (James and Peck 1985). Given the difficulty of detection later in the breeding season, increased early-season surveys of coastal squares will probably reveal the species to be more widely distributed and abundant along the Hudson Bay coast than indicated in the breeding evidence map. The Stilt Sandpiper is considered an uncommon breeder in Ontario with the breeding population estimated in the thousands (Ross et al. 2003), representing less than 1% of the total population estimate of Morrison et al. (2006). – *Peter S. Burke, Mark K. Peck and Donald A. Sutherland*

This Stilt Sandpiper incubating a clutch near the Pen Islands in 2004 provided the first nest record for Ontario. *Photo: Ron Ridout*

Wet graminoid tundra with scattered clumps of low shrubs provides breeding habitat for the Stilt Sandpiper. *Photo: Ken Abraham*

Short-billed Dowitcher

Bécassin roux

Limnodromus griseus

George K. Peck

The Short-billed Dowitcher has a distribution confined entirely to the Nearctic, breeding in the transition between the Boreal Forest and subarctic tundra of North America. Three subspecies are recognized, each reputedly with a discrete breeding range (Jehl et al. 2001). Ontario spans the ranges of the "prairie" (*hendersoni*) and the "eastern" (*griseus*) dowitchers, and individuals breeding in Ontario exhibit considerable introgression between the two, making racial distinction difficult. An inhabitant of the remote and largely inaccessible muskeg of the Hudson Bay Lowlands in Ontario, the Short-billed Dowitcher remains one of the least known of the province's boreal-nesting shorebird species. The Ontario Shorebird Conservation Plan (Ross et al. 2003) considers it to be of medium conservation priority due primarily to the unknown size and extent of its provincial breeding population.

Distribution and population status: The Short-billed Dowitcher was only confirmed as a breeder in Ontario in 1963 when recently fledged young were discovered near the Winisk River (Tuck 1968); the first provincial nest was documented as recently as 1992 (Soulliere 1993). Both atlases indicate that in Ontario the breeding distribution of the species is confined to the Hudson Bay Lowlands, primarily north of 53° N. Prior to the second atlas, the scant evidence of breeding had been found mainly in coastal wetlands near the treeline along the Hudson Bay coast, though a record of probable breeding along the Fawn River more than 100 km inland from Hudson Bay during the first atlas raised the possibility of a more extensive inland breeding range. Breeding season records near the Nettichi River south of Fort Albany (Todd 1963), at Longridge Point, (Wilson and McRae 1993), and at Northbluff Point during the first atlas suggested a distribution extending south along the James Bay coast to 51° N.

During the second atlas, the Short-billed Dowitcher was observed in 31 squares in 13 100-km blocks, and there was a large but non-significant increase in the probability of observa-

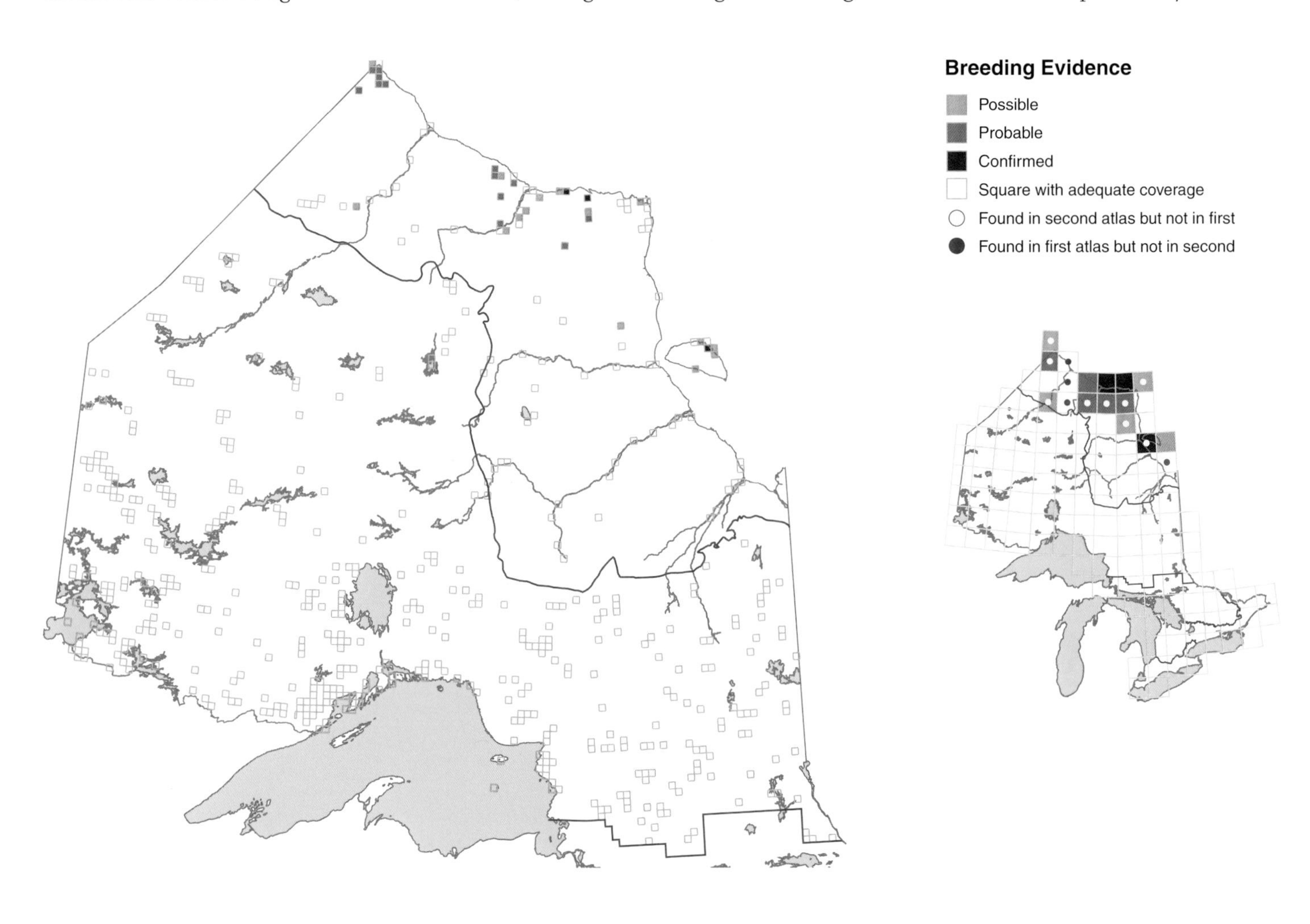

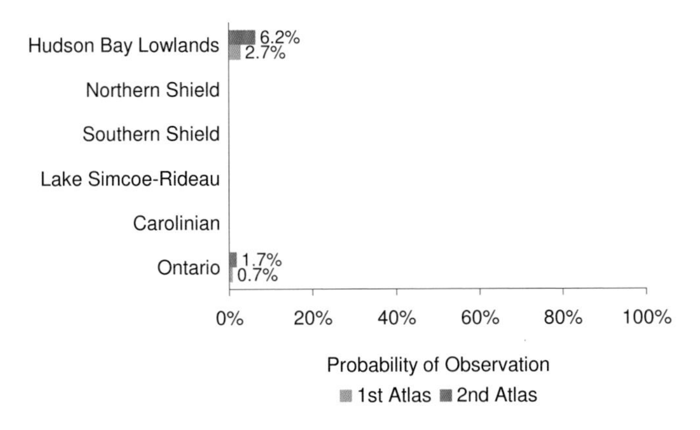

tion between atlases. The increase in detections was largely the result of more extensive low-level aerial surveys by OMNR and CWS. Breeding evidence was found in squares in the boreal-tundra transition between the Sutton, Winisk, and Shagamu Rivers, as well as in squares in the vicinity of the Pen Islands in the extreme northwest. The lack of observations between the Shagamu River and the Pen Islands most likely reflects lower coverage by atlassers as opposed to gaps in distribution. Observations of birds in suitable boreal fen habitat 80-100 km inland on the Aquatuk and Winisk Rivers and 160 km inland near the Sachigo River confirm a more extensive distribution inland. In Ontario, the Short-billed Dowitcher appears to avoid open tundra and is largely absent in the area between the Brant River, Cape Henrietta Maria, and Hook Point on northern James Bay (Wilson and McRae 1993; pers. obs.). With the exception of Akimiski Island (Nunavut), no further evidence of breeding was obtained for the western James Bay coast south of the Attawapiskat River (53° N), though coverage of this area during the second atlas was less extensive than during the first.

Breeding biology: Preferred breeding habitat for the Short-billed Dowitcher includes extensive, sedge-dominated boreal fens with scattered stunted spruce and Tamarack and numerous small ponds and lakes. Breeding also occurs in sedge marshes between relict beach ridges closer to the treeline, as reported at Churchill, Manitoba (Jehl et al. 2001). Arrival at breeding areas in Ontario usually occurs in late May. The intensity of territorial flight displays and aerial pursuits is greatest in the two to three week period prior to the onset of incubation, after which individuals are for the most part silent (Jehl et al. 2001) and opportunities for atlassers to detect displaying birds are diminished. Confirmation of breeding is difficult, and breeding was confirmed in only 10% of squares during the second atlas, a rate marginally lower than in the first. Incubating birds are tight-sitting and highly cryptic, and nest discoveries are largely fortuitous. During the second atlas, only one nest was found, on Akimiski Island in 2005.

Abundance: Point count data gathered during the second atlas are insufficient to confidently assess the abundance of the Short-billed Dowitcher in Ontario, and detections on point counts were too low to produce a map of relative abundance. Ross et al. (2003) suggested a provincial breeding population possibly only in the hundreds, but acknowledged that, given the species' secretive nature and inaccessible breeding habitat, the size of the population is probably underestimated. – *Peter S. Burke and Donald A. Sutherland*

Nesting dowitchers are highly cryptic, and few nests have been found in Ontario. Nests have been located on sedge tussocks in extensive sedge fens. Churchill, Manitoba, 21 June 1972. *Photo: George K. Peck*

Characteristic breeding habitat in Ontario includes taiga sedge fens with numerous ponds and small lakes and sedge marshes between relict beach ridges close to the treeline. Near the Sutton River, Polar Bear Prov. Park, 1 July 2001. *Photo: Donald A. Sutherland*

Wilson's Snipe

Bécassine de Wilson

Gallinago delicata

Mark Peck

In 2002, the Wilson's Snipe was again recognized as a distinct species, distinguished from conspecifics in Europe, Asia, and South America on the basis of winnowing display sounds associated with differences in its outer tail feathers (Banks et al. 2002). One of the most abundant and widespread shorebirds in North America, it breeds throughout most of Canada from just above the treeline southward to the Carolinian region. When not performing its display flights in early spring, it is easily overlooked due to its cryptic colouration, crepuscular habits, and preference for wetlands; however, it may also be found in exposed situations, sitting quietly on fence posts or foraging in the open. Some snipe may overwinter locally in southern Ontario during mild winters, but most migrate south to the southern US and Central America, and as far south as northern Brazil (Mueller 2005).

Distribution and population status: The Wilson's Snipe continues to be a common breeding species throughout most of Ontario, with the exception of the extreme southwest. Essex is the only atlas administrative region in which snipe were not reported in the second atlas, although several adjacent regions similarly show low or decreased levels of occurrence. Between atlases, there was a significant decline in the probability of observation in each of the three southern regions, the largest being a 44% decline in the Carolinian region. However, due to a significant 26% increase in the large Hudson Bay Lowlands region, there was no significant change in the province as a whole. BBS data show a significant 2.7% annual decrease in Ontario from 1981 to 2005, corroborating declines in southern Ontario between atlases. The marked decline in the Carolinian region may reflect the intensification of agriculture in the region, including wetland degradation and loss.

Breeding biology: Male snipe begin arriving in southern Ontario in late March to early April, followed slightly later by females. Territories are established and maintained through dis-

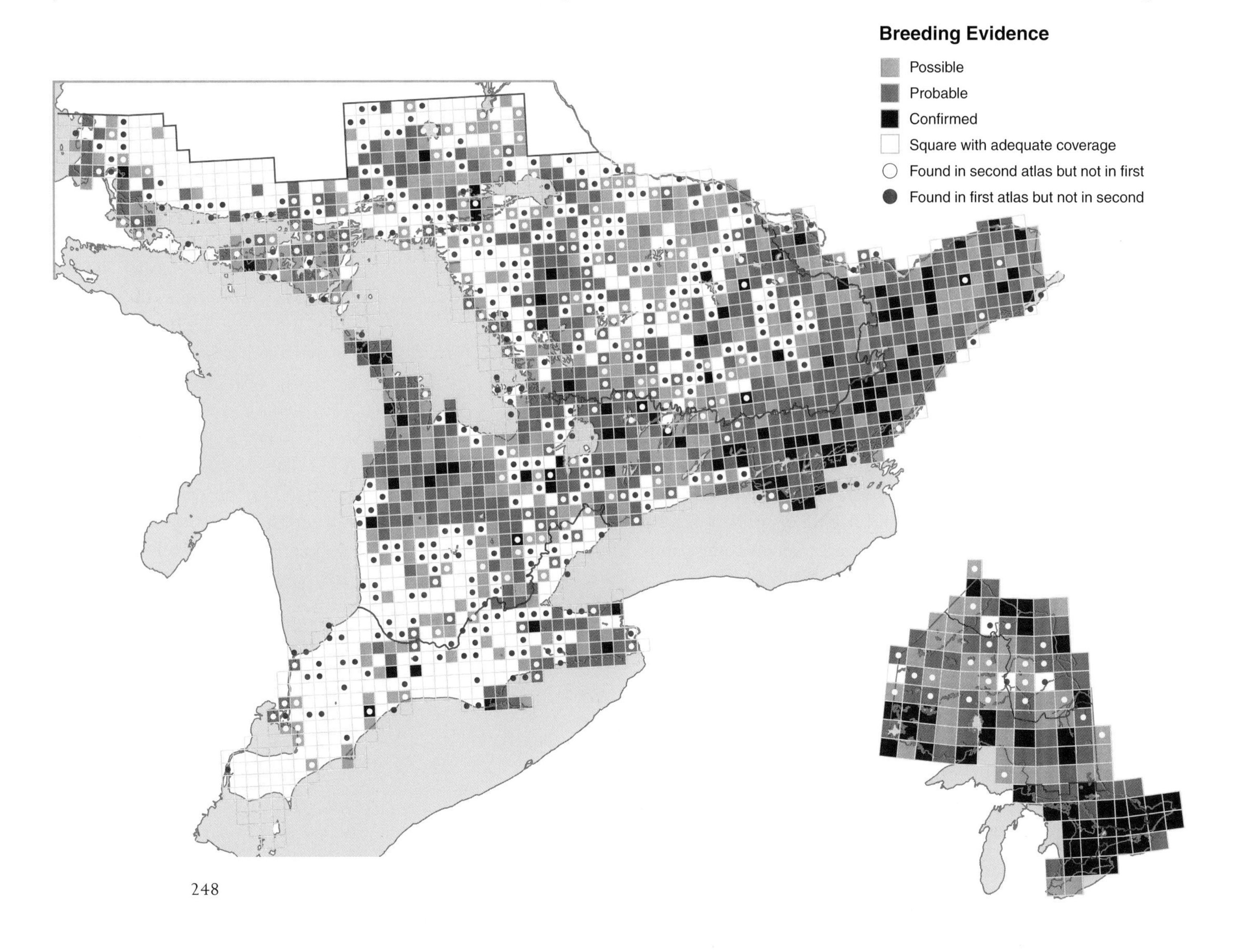

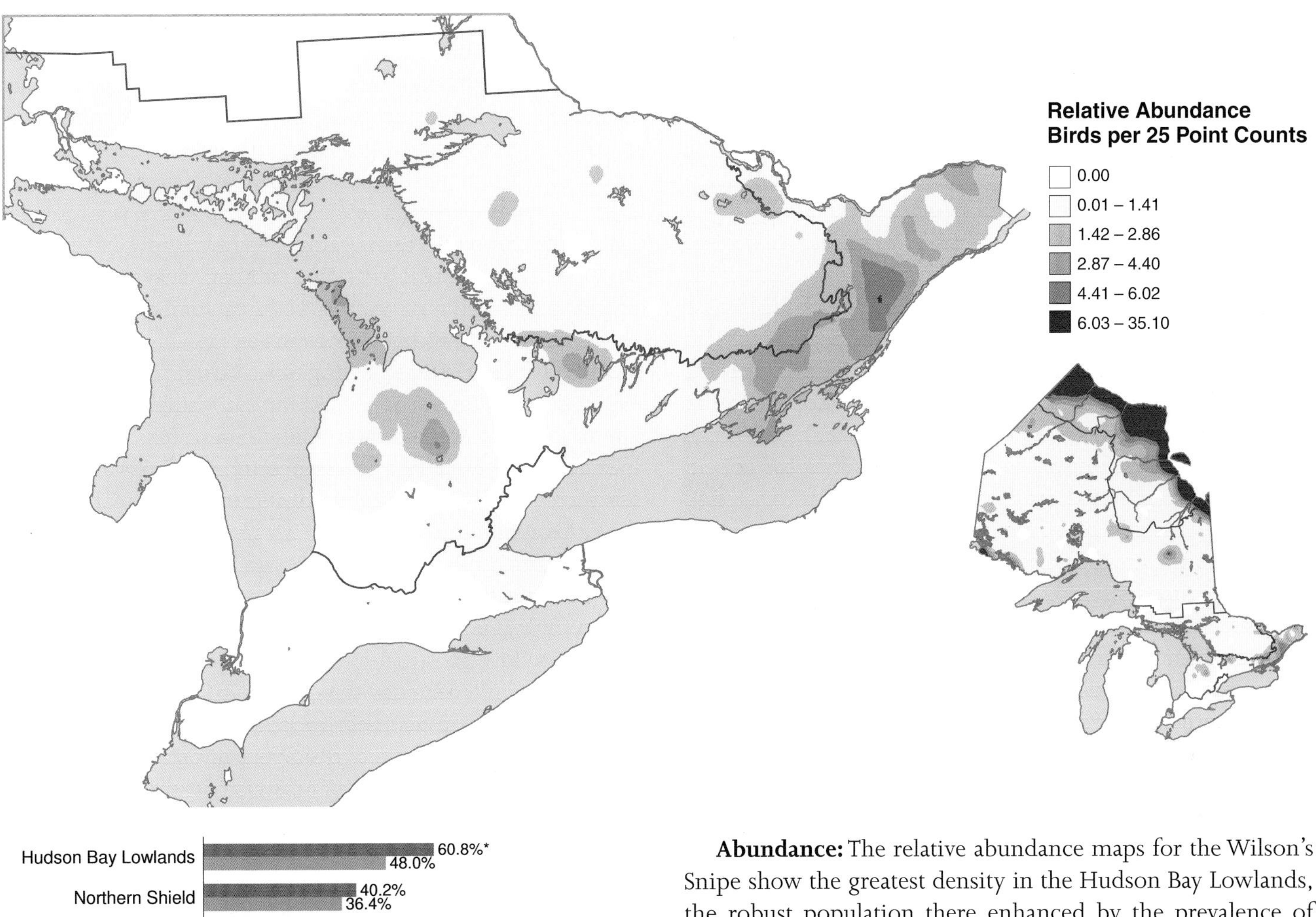

play flights performed predominately by males, with females participating earlier in the season during pair formation. In the south, winnowing display flights are usually restricted to the early evening hours (Tuck 1972). In the Hudson Bay Lowlands, birds arrive by early June and, at least in some coastal areas, the sound of the displaying snipe is almost omnipresent throughout the day and evening (pers. obs.).

The Wilson's Snipe breeds in marshes, fens, bogs, wet meadows, pastures, and tundra. Nests are on the ground, usually well concealed at the base of a small shrub or on a small hummock in wetland habitat. The species is secretive around the nest but performs an injury-feigning distraction display when flushed. Females sit tightly during incubation and brooding, allowing close approach before flushing from the nest. Males rarely attend the nest site but assist with the care of young once they leave the nest (Mueller 2005). Although double-brooding has not been confirmed in Ontario, nests containing eggs have been documented between 24 April and 24 July (Peck and James 1993b).

Abundance: The relative abundance maps for the Wilson's Snipe show the greatest density in the Hudson Bay Lowlands, the robust population there enhanced by the prevalence of suitable wetland habitat and the limited impact of human population. An accurate estimate of abundance may be obtained in the north, owing to frequent diurnal display flights during point count hours. Numbers in the Boreal Forest are lower due to increased forest cover but may also be low due to atlassers' difficulty in accessing suitable breeding habitat early in the season when birds are displaying. Abundance estimates south of the Shield may also be underestimated, because point counts are run no earlier than late May and so miss the peak of display activity. Nevertheless, the Dundalk uplands, the Carden Plain, and a large area of southeastern Ontario stand out as having relatively large numbers of snipe. High survey totals in Manitoba during wet springs suggest that this species may be irruptive in some years (Manitoba Avian Research Committee 2003), which may explain higher than normal densities noted in Rainy River in 2005. It may also explain some of the disparity noted in other areas between the two atlases.

The breeding population has been conservatively estimated at 2,000,000 birds (Morrison et al. 2006) in Canada, and in the hundreds of thousands in Ontario (Ross et al. 2003). Based on the atlas point count data, the Ontario population is estimated at approximately 500,000 birds, 73% in the Hudson Bay Lowlands. – *Mark K. Peck*

American Woodcock

Bécasse d'Amérique

Scolopax minor

Jean Iron

The American Woodcock is a species of young forests and old fields that breeds east of the 98th meridian from southern Manitoba, central Ontario, and southern Québec south to northern Texas and Florida (Keppie and Whiting 1994). Primarily crepuscular, its displays at dawn and dusk are one of the earliest and most familiar signs of spring in Ontario. These displays consist of a series of "*peent*" calls given on the ground, followed by an upwardly spiraling flight display on "twittering" wings, culminating in a rapid descent to the ground (Keppie and Whiting 1994). The plump American Woodcock is exceptionally well camouflaged in mottled earth tones and patterns. Cryptic against the forest floor, it frequently startles observers by irrupting underfoot and zigzagging away through the underbrush in a twittering flight. It is known by a number of colloquial names including timberdoodle, Labrador twister, night partridge, and bog sucker (Keppie and Whiting 1994). It is rarely found far from moist soils that support earthworms, its primary food.

Distribution and population status: The American Woodcock has probably been common historically from the southern Shield southward in Ontario and less common farther north (McIlwraith 1894; Baillie and Harrington 1936). It declined significantly throughout its range around 1900 due to year-round hunting. Numbers increased after hunting regulations were imposed, but the species has experienced a general decline since 1968 (Canadian Wildlife Service Waterfowl Committee 2005), which has been attributed to widespread habitat losses due to natural succession as formerly cleared areas have reverted to forest.

During the first atlas, most squares south of 49° N supported the woodcock, and its distribution was scattered farther north. There was no significant change in its distribution during the second atlas or in the probability of observation in the province as a whole; however, the probability of observation

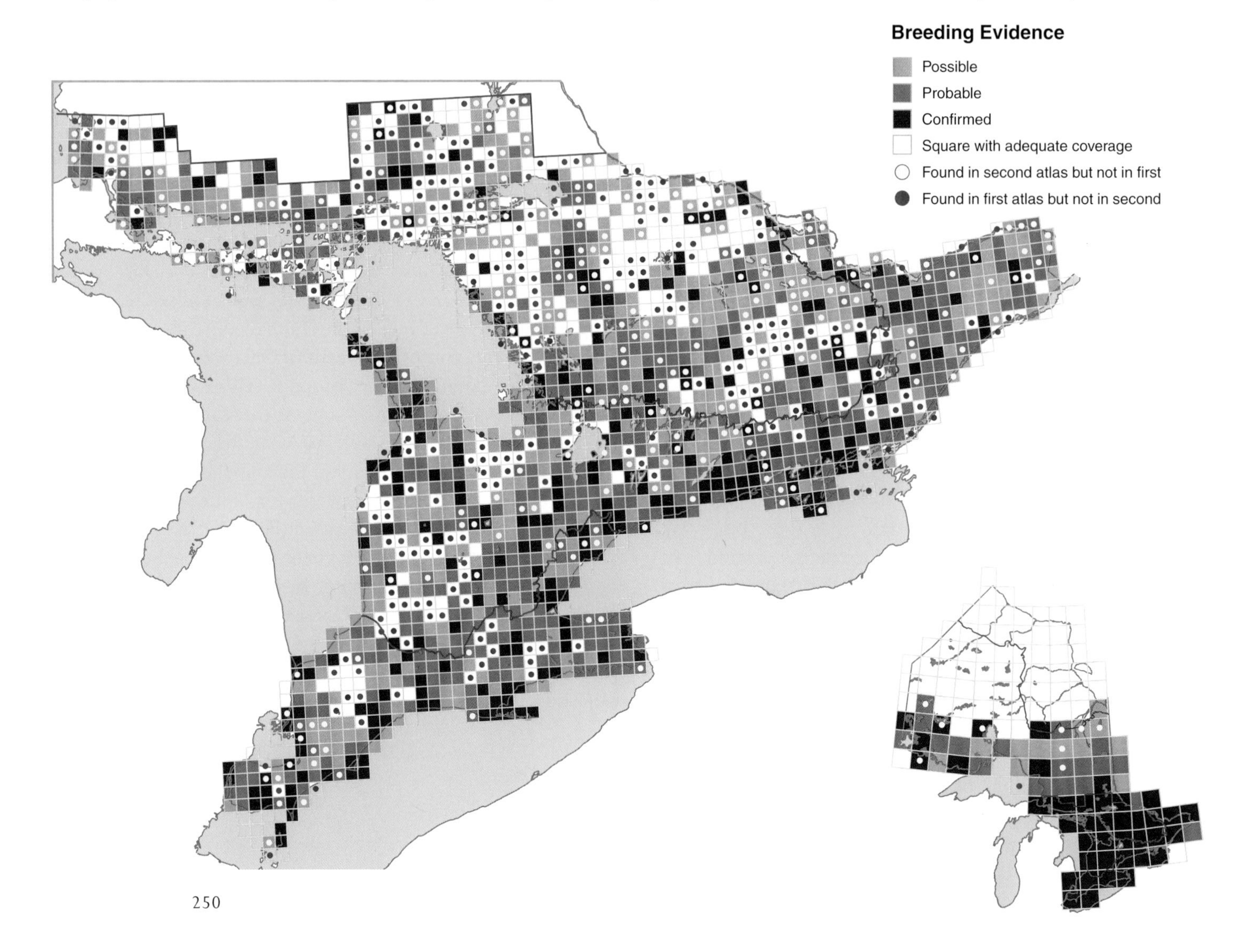

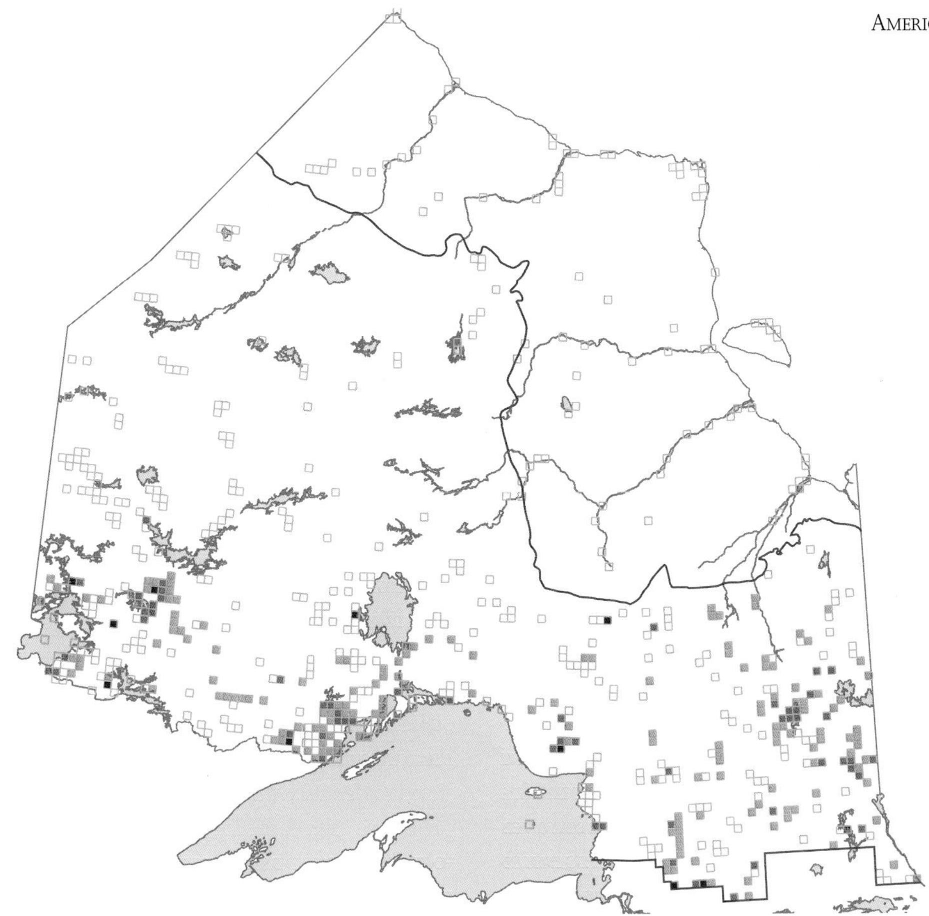

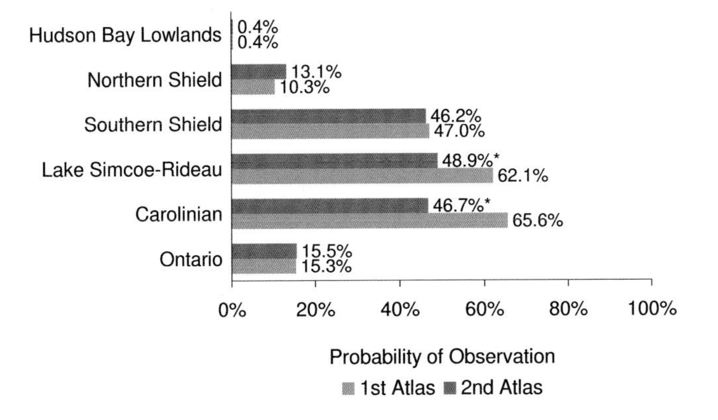

declined significantly in the Carolinian and Lake Simcoe-Rideau regions, by 29% and 21%, respectively. The decline in the Carolinian region may be due to intensification of agricultural practices, leaving fewer of the early successional habitats suitable for the species. Despite the declines, it continues to be common in southern Ontario and uncommon to rare in the Northern Shield and southern Hudson Bay Lowlands where it reaches is northern limit.

The Woodcock Singing-Ground Survey provides a better picture of the status of this species than does the BBS. This survey demonstrates a significant decline of 2.0% per annum in Ontario from 1968 to 2005 (Canadian Wildlife Service Waterfowl Committee 2005). Much of this decline occurred before 1995, as there was no significant trend in numbers in the combined Ontario and Manitoba populations from 1995 to 2005.

Breeding biology: Habitat requirements for breeding American Woodcock include open areas with some shrub or sapling coverage (e.g., upland openings, openings in aspen stands, wet prairies, and pastures) for use by displaying males. Nesting habitat usually includes edges of deciduous upland and lowland forests, coniferous forests and plantations, and mixed forests (Hale and Gregg 1976; Peck and James 1983). The species' northern distribution in Ontario is limited by earthworm distribution.

The woodcock is most conspicuous when the male is performing aerial displays. These occur just before dawn and at dusk, from the birds' arrival in late March or early April, continuing until early June. At other times, this species is very inconspicuous. The nest is a simple depression in the ground, and the cryptically coloured female sits so tightly that she may be touched. Even away from the nest, birds may not flush until they are almost stepped upon, the sudden escape flight startling the unsuspecting observer. The atlas map is an accurate indication of the overall distribution of the American Woodcock, although it is likely that it was overlooked in many squares because atlassers missed this species' most active period.

Abundance: The American Woodcock was detected on too few point counts to generate a reliable abundance map. It continues to be a common breeding species in southern Ontario, although numbers have declined since the first atlas according to surveys conducted specifically for this species. While the rate of decline has leveled off, natural succession and land-use changes may continue to reduce the population in Ontario. Morrison et al. (2001) estimated the Canadian population at 500,000 to 1,000,000 birds (assuming harvest levels are 10-11% of the total, Morrison et al. 2006), and Ross et al. (2003) estimated the Ontario population at tens of thousands of birds.
– Al Sandilands

Wilson's Phalarope

Phalarope de Wilson

Phalaropus tricolor

George K. Peck

Phalaropes are shorebirds known for their sexual role reversal with females larger and more brightly coloured than males. Males perform all parental duties while females mate sequentially within a season with several males. The Wilson's Phalarope, the only strictly New World phalarope, breeds in shallow freshwater marshes and winters largely on saline lakes in south and western South America (Colwell and Jehl 1994).

Distribution and population status: Originally a bird of the prairies, the Wilson's Phalarope has greatly expanded its range westward to British Columbia and eastward to New Brunswick. In Ontario, Baillie and Harrington (1936) listed only two breeding records at Dunnville on the Grand River and in Elgin Co., and considered these extralimital. At Luther Marsh, 90 km northwest of Toronto, Boyer and Devitt (1961) confirmed breeding when they found a colony of six pairs. In southeastern Ontario, Wilson's Phalarope first nested on Amherst Island in 1980 (Weir 1989) and later spread to the Ottawa area. Breeding was confirmed in the Lake of the Woods area in 1988, with perhaps 50 birds breeding annually between 1981 and 1990 (Austen et al. 1994). Morrison and Manning (1976) confirmed breeding at Northbluff Point on the south James Bay coast, and along with Bousfield et al. (1986) concluded that the species probably bred sparingly in the Hudson Bay Lowlands.

Overall, there was no significant difference in the probability of observation of the Wilson's Phalarope between atlases. It was observed in the same number of squares (seven) during both atlases in the Carolinian region, but in fewer squares during the second atlas in all other regions. The decline in the Lake Simcoe-Rideau region was significant at 48%.

As in the first atlas, the Wilson's Phalarope has a spotty distribution in this atlas, with most records from south of the Shield. Nesting-site fidelity appears to be highly variable, and

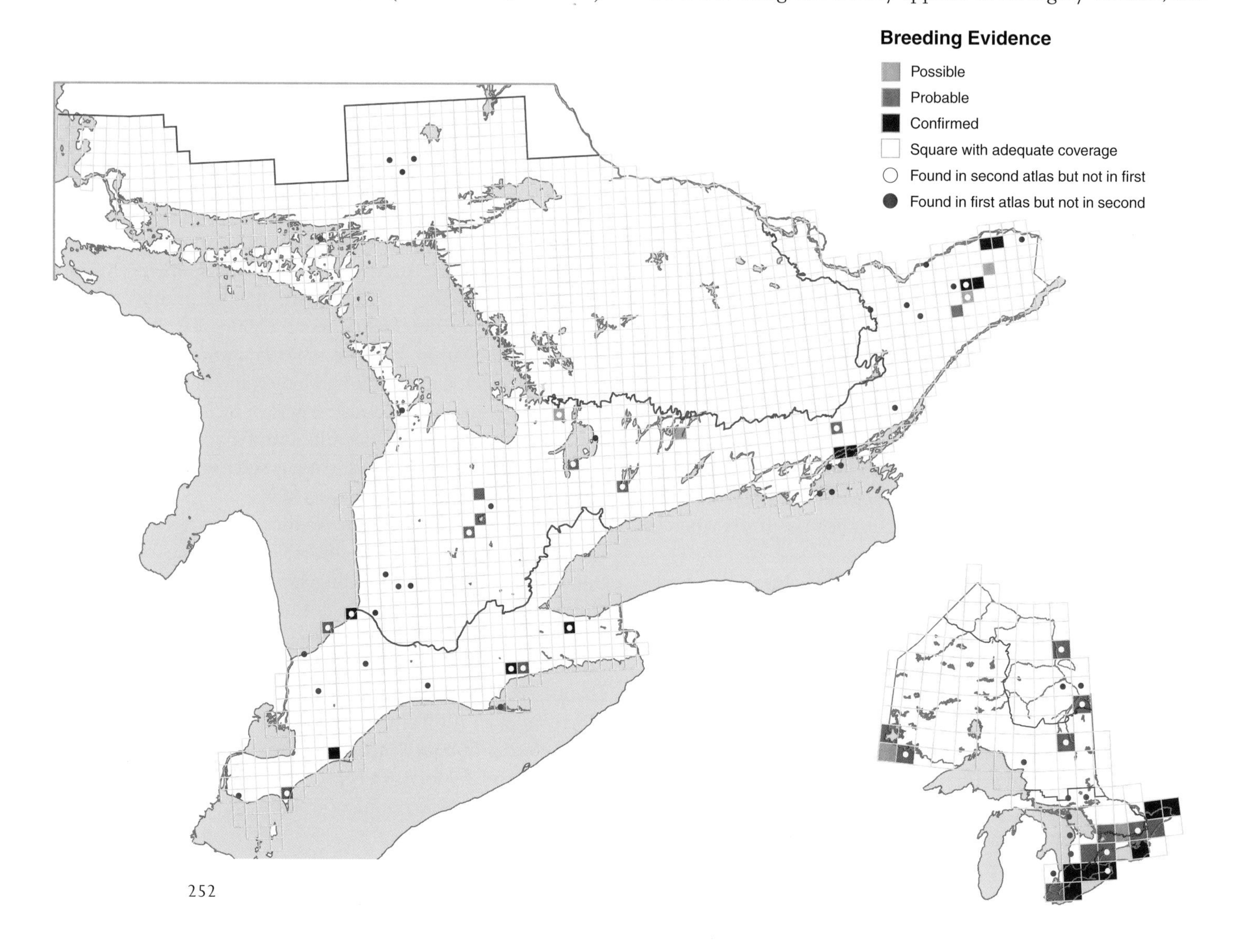

BREEDING EVIDENCE

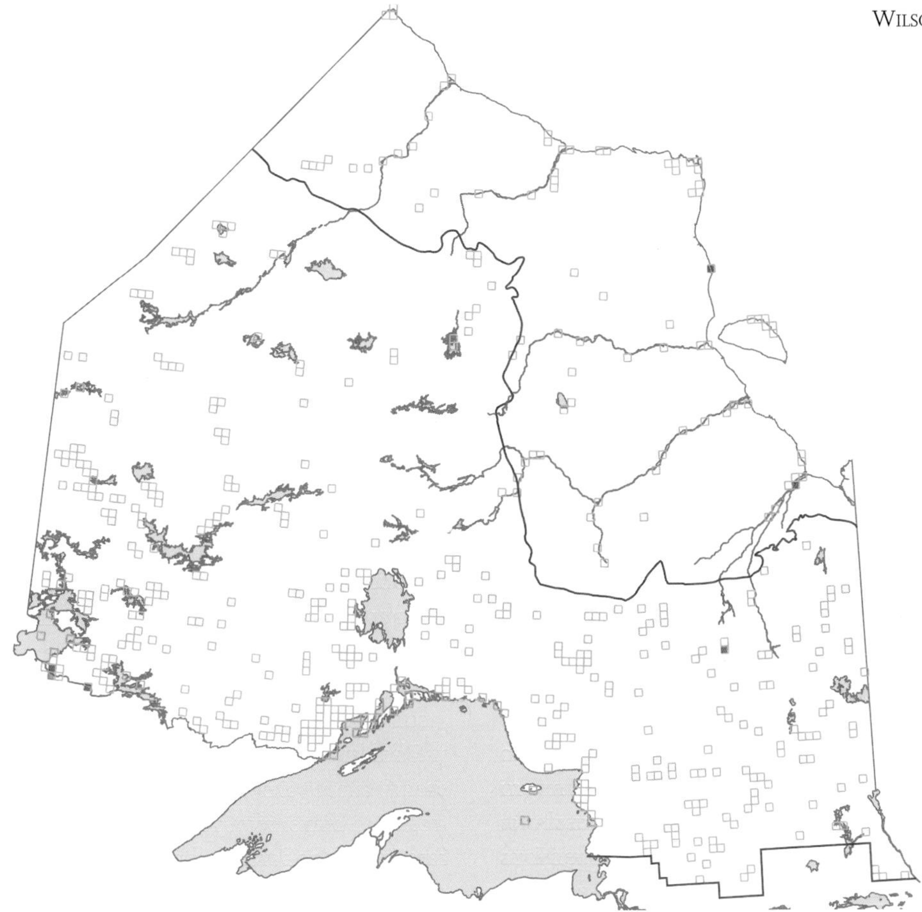

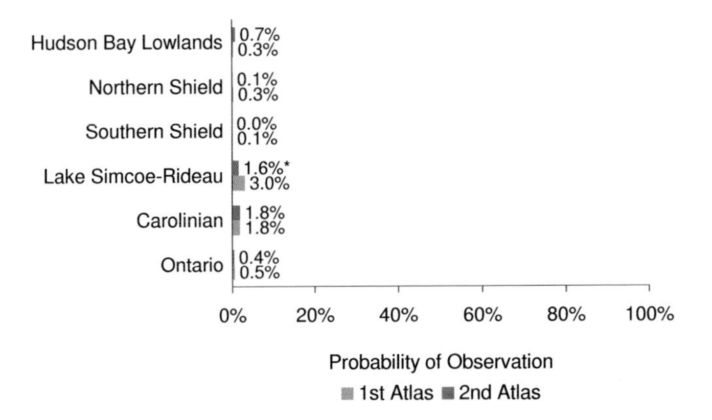

this may be a function of the quality of habitat and the success of previous breeding attempts. The Luther Marsh site has been occupied for over 40 years, although habitat there is marginal now due to natural succession. Many areas used for breeding during the first atlas did not support birds during this atlas, though many new sites were occupied. Along the James Bay coast, no birds were found in the two 100-km blocks where they had previously been reported, but two other 100-km blocks supported birds. The Lake of the Woods area and sewage lagoons in eastern Ontario continued to support populations during this atlas, but no phalaropes were found in the Sandy Lake or Sudbury areas.

Breeding biology: The Wilson's Phalarope nests among grasses and sedges near water, frequently on small islands. It also nests in swales, on muskeg, and at sewage lagoons. Grassy areas with vegetation about 30 cm tall are preferred for nesting; taller grasses are seldom used, and those taller than 60 cm are avoided. Usage by nesting phalaropes declines once woody vegetation cover reaches 25% (Kantrud and Higgins 1992; Naugle et al. 1999). These specific microhabitat requirements may explain why some areas do not support this species for extended periods of time.

The Wilson's Phalarope is easy to detect because of the female's striking plumage and her elaborate aerial courtship displays performed early in the season. Both sexes also forage conspicuously for prey by spinning on the surface of the water to draw up food from the bottom. Females may lay sequential clutches with two to four different males. Females usually desert the first male as soon as the eggs are laid and move to another area to attract and mate with another male (Colwell and Jehl 1994). The male cares for the brood, which remains in the dense, wet vegetation that is usually near the nest site (Colwell and Oring 1988). Adult females commonly leave the province by the first week of July. Due to the conspicuousness of the species, the map is probably a good indication of its distribution, although it may have been overlooked in some areas in the north.

Abundance: The Wilson's Phalarope continues to be a rare breeder in Ontario. Most records are from south of the Shield where it nests predominantly in artificial habitats. It also nests sparingly on the Shield and Hudson Bay Lowlands and perhaps in greatest abundance near Lake of the Woods, the site closest to the centre of its continental distribution. It was observed in only 30 squares during the second atlas, indicating that its distribution is spotty. It appears as though there are few locations in Ontario that support this species in the long term. – *Al Sandilands*

Red-necked Phalarope

Phalarope à bec étroit
Phalaropus lobatus

George K. Peck

The Red-necked Phalarope has a circumpolar breeding distribution across arctic and subarctic sedge-meadow wetlands (Rubega et al. 2000). A small proportion of the North American population (less than 1%) resides in Ontario along the coasts of Hudson and James Bays (Ross et al. 2003). Phalaropes are the only shorebirds that regularly forage while swimming, a characteristic that makes them eye-catching. Unlike many other shorebirds, this species does not defend a territory (Rubega et al. 2000). The Canadian Shorebird Conservation Plan characterizes the Red-necked Phalarope as a species of moderate concern due to significant declines in Québec and unprecedented disappearances from staging grounds in the Bay of Fundy in the mid-1980s (Duncan 1995), believed attributable in part to changes in oceanic temperatures (Brown et al. 2005). Observations at several locations across the breeding range in North America also confirmed local declines (Gratto-Trevor 1994; Jehl and Lin 2001; Schamel, pers. comm.). The Ontario Shorebird Conservation Plan lists this species as one of low conservation priority since Ontario constitutes a small proportion of the species' breeding range (Ross et al. 2003).

Distribution and population status: Confirmed breeding records for this species are scant. The first was in 1947 (Manning 1952), and all subsequent confirmed breeding records came from the Cape Henrietta Maria area (Peck and James 1983), until breeding was confirmed near the Pen Islands during the second atlas. The distribution appears to be discontinuous along the Hudson Bay coast between Cape Henrietta Maria and the Pen Islands, and the only observations in James Bay were within 50 km of Cape Henrietta Maria. Although not indicated by the atlas, there is no reason to expect that the Red-necked Phalarope does not breed more or less continuously between the Cape and the Winisk River mouth, as a number of pairs were found in tundra ponds near

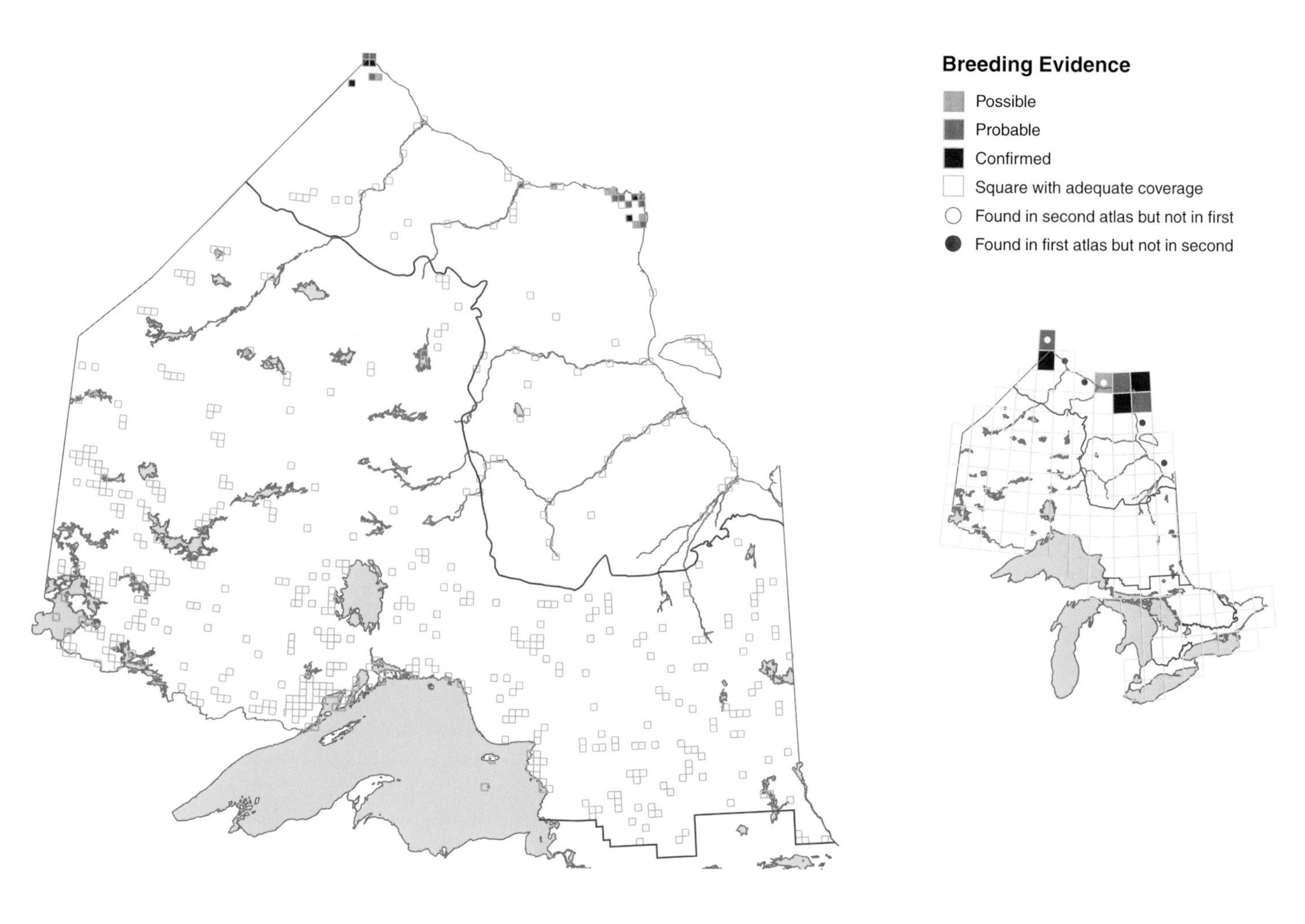

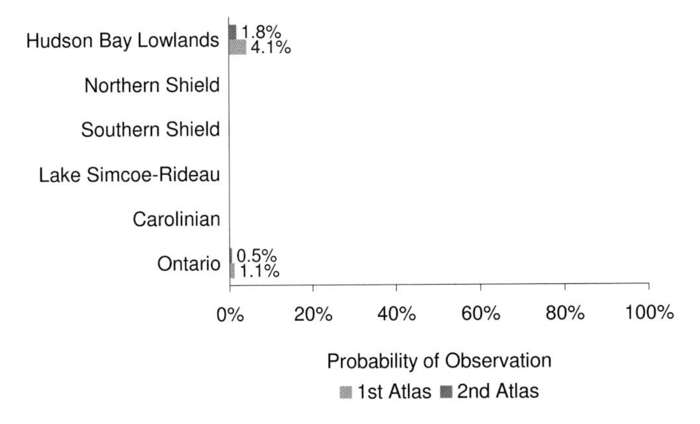

Burntpoint Creek, 125 km west of Cape Henrietta Maria, and south of Wabuk Point at the mouth of the Winisk River. The Red-necked Phalarope was recorded near the Shagamu River, between the Winisk and Severn Rivers in 1990 (Wilson and McRae 1993). Given what is known of the intervening habitat, the species should be expected to occur between the Severn River and the Pen Islands. In the first atlas, few observations and little coverage occurred more than several km from the coast, except on river corridors where the species would not be expected to occur. In this atlas, one observation occurred at the Black Duck River, 46 km inland from the Hudson Bay coast.

The species was seen in 21 squares, up from 18 in the first atlas, but its occurrence was more geographically concentrated, and the probability of observation declined by a non-significant 56%. The direction of change agrees with other sources of evidence for this species.

Breeding biology: Breeding occurs primarily in graminoid and sedge-dominated wetlands where the Red-necked Phalarope feeds on and at the edges of shallow ponds. Females are brighter than males, so in most atlas observations the sexes of the birds were determined. After laying, females move freely among scattered ponds while males incubate the eggs. Of the 21 accepted records, five (24%) confirmed breeding, a proportion similar to that recorded in the first atlas. Two nests were found during the atlas period, and several observers noted parental behaviour by male phalaropes in suitable habitat, although nests were not located. One nest at Cape Henrietta Maria was found in the large Snow Goose colony. Nests are concealed by graminoids, so the small number of nests found is not surprising. Nests were usually less than 5 m from the edges of small ponds. Breeding habitat descriptions included small lakes or tundra ponds surrounded by graminoid meadows, lichen heath, or hummocky sedge tundra with willow, dwarf birch, or moss. The one observation 46 km from the coast was from sedges at the edge of a small shallow lake in quaking peat mat in boreal forest-tundra mosaic. The occurrence of this species in boreal habitat suggests that greater coverage in this large, difficult-to-navigate region might yield a broader distribution and a substantially larger provincial breeding population. The call of the Red-necked Phalarope is quiet and hard to detect, particularly on windy days. However, groups of the birds can be conspicuous early in the breeding season.

Abundance: Detections on atlas point counts were too low to produce a map of relative abundance. This species was heard or seen during 15 point counts. While in most cases the average number of birds per point count was low, the greatest density was found near the Pen Islands. – *Erica Nol and Bree Beveridge*

Nests are usually less than 5 m from the edges of small ponds and are well concealed in dense growths of grasses and sedges. *Photo: George K. Peck*

In Ontario, breeding habitat for this phalarope includes graminoid-bordered ponds and small lakes in tundra and, apparently less commonly, shallow marshy lakes inland in taiga. *Photo: George K. Peck*

Little Gull

Mouette pygmée

Larus minutus

Jim Richards

A holarctic breeding species, the Little Gull is one of North America's rarest larids. Although there are fewer than 100 nest records and only one small breeding colony currently known in North America, it is common in northern Europe and Asia. In Ontario, however, it occurs regularly during migration at stopover sites on the Niagara River (Bellerby et al. 2000), Lake Ontario, and Lake Erie (Joos et al. 2005). Despite low numbers, it currently has no conservation status in Canada or the US. The Little Gull is one of the least understood species on the continent (Ewins and Weseloh 1999).

Distribution and population status: Little Gull records were unpredictable between the species' first discovery in North America on the Saskatchewan River around 1819 (Houston 1984) and 1970. Its resemblance to and association with other small larids probably contributed to historical misidentifications and under-documentation. In Ontario, the first sight record at Port Stanley (Saunders 1930) and the first North American breeding record at Oshawa Second Marsh in 1962 (Scott 1963) have been followed by 32 confirmed nest records. During the first atlas, breeding evidence was reported from 13 squares, including three confirmed breeding records (one each on Georgian, James, and Hudson Bays). The last known Ontario nest was on North Limestone Island (Georgian Bay) in 1989 (Weseloh 1994, 2007).

During this atlas, adults observed at historical breeding sites were reported from two squares at Rondeau Prov. Park, but no confirmed breeding was documented. In one square where possible breeding evidence was obtained during the first atlas, experienced atlassers observed two adult birds engaging in courtship flights and chases over suitable emergent marsh habitat on numerous occasions between 15 May and 4 June 2001. It seems likely that the two adults observed by a different atlasser in the adjacent square on 20 June 2001 involved this same pair. However, there were no subsequent observa-

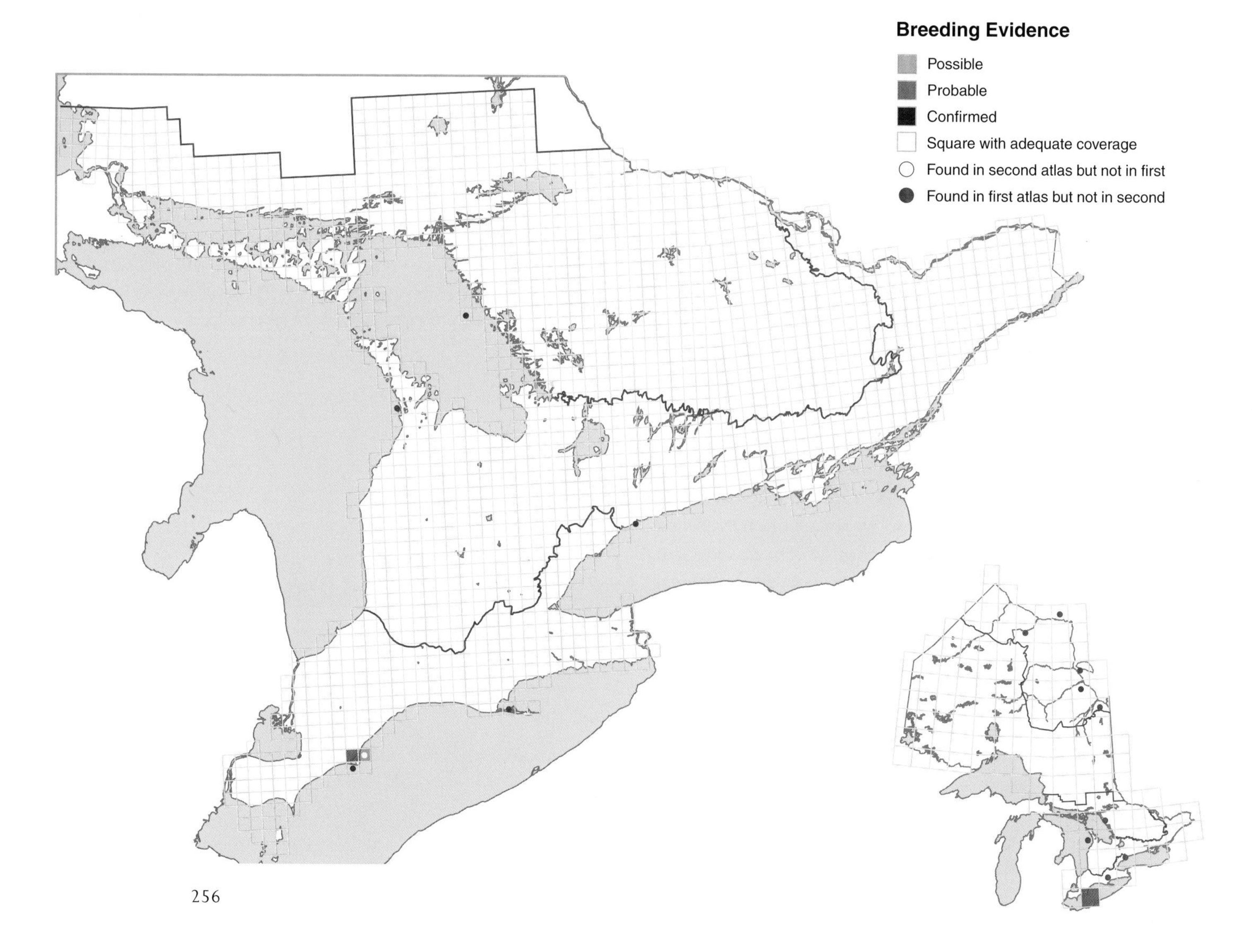

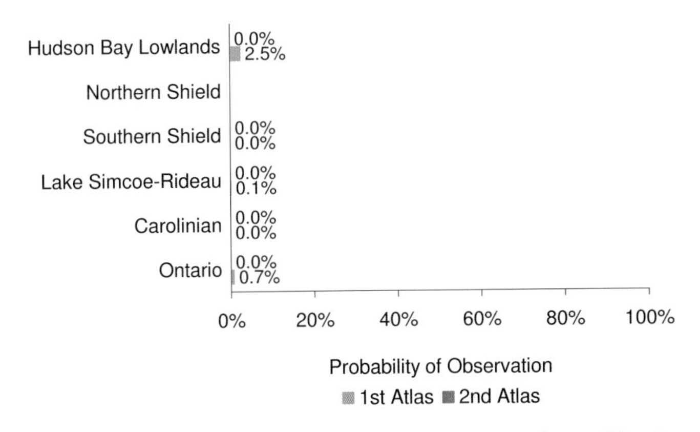

tions or other evidence of breeding. The Little Gull's disappearance as a breeding species on the Great Lakes mirrors a similar northward shift of its breeding range in Europe (Olsen and Larsson 2004).

Although there are breeding records for several areas in northeastern North America over the past 30 years, the only currently known breeding location is in the Hudson Bay Lowlands near Churchill, Manitoba (R. Joos, unpubl. data). Little Gull records from northern Ontario after the first atlas include annual aggregations of more than 15 individuals in the Moose River estuary in the early 1990s, an adult at Shagamu River in July 1991, and adults and young-of-the-year at Longridge Point on James Bay in the same year (Wilson and McRae 1993). Birds were also observed in the Hudson Bay Lowlands interior near Missisa and Kapiskau Lakes in the summer of 1996, but there have been no published breeding season records from northern Ontario in recent years. The Little Gull is distinctive and relatively easily detected from the ground; however, it seems possible that the species is a rare and local breeder in Ontario's Hudson Bay Lowlands and may have been missed in such a vast area.

The regular appearance of juveniles at Port Burwell and Turkey Point on Lake Erie and in Presqu'ile and Sandbanks Prov. Parks on Lake Ontario, plus the northwest to southeast pattern of its autumn movement with Bonaparte's Gulls (Braune 1989), suggests undetected local breeding populations in northern Ontario, but this requires further investigation.

Breeding biology: The Little Gull can be easily overlooked in its breeding season because it tends to nest in remote locations and is relatively quiet around the nest. Pair-bonding behaviour takes place at both staging and colony sites but only sometimes includes aerial displays (Ewins and Weseloh 1999). In the south, nests were located on floating reed mats in emergent marsh vegetation, with Black Terns or Common Terns (Tozer and Richards 1974), but in the north, they are found on ephemeral islets in early successional vegetation adjacent to open water, often with Arctic Terns (McRae 1984). Reported colony size in Ontario has never exceeded five pairs, and the maximum number of pairs documented in North America is eight (R. Joos, unpubl. data). Birds may return to previous nesting areas, but disturbance of the colonies can cause them to relocate.

Abundance: The global Little Gull population is estimated at over 150,000 pairs (Olsen and Larsson 2004). Data collected on migration over the last 30 years suggest that the North American population may number as many as 400 individuals (R. Joos, unpubl. data), although this estimate is based on diverse sampling methodology and data that could include vagrant individuals. – *Richard Joos and Chip Weseloh*

In 1971, the first known Little Gull young produced in the New World were fledged from this nest at Cranberry Marsh, Durham Region. *Photo: George K. Peck*

Little Gull nesting habitat at Cranberry Marsh, Durham Region, on the northern shore of Lake Ontario. *Photo: George K. Peck*

Bonaparte's Gull

Mouette de Bonaparte

Larus philadelphia

The Bonaparte's Gull breeds in boreal, subarctic, and alpine wetlands across North America from Alaska east to central Québec, primarily north of 50° N latitude (Burger and Gochfeld 2002). Its Ontario breeding range is restricted to the Hudson Bay Lowlands and Northern Shield regions, where it breeds from about 48° N north to the limit of trees. It is the only gull that nests almost exclusively in trees.

Distribution and population status: Breeding by the Bonaparte's Gull in Ontario was first confirmed in the late 1930s, when fledged young and nests with eggs were found along the Albany River in southern Kenora Dist. (Dear 1939; Baillie 1939). Its breeding distribution in Ontario remained obscure for another half century, until the first atlas showed its wide distribution in northern Ontario.

The second atlas confirmed that breeding remains confined to the Hudson Bay Lowlands and Northern Shield regions, where the probability of observation is 40% and 30%, respectively. The probability of observation increased between atlases by a significant 53% in the Northern Shield and 40% for the province as a whole. Such increases are likely a reflection of increased coverage of the north through low-level aerial surveys by OMNR and CWS. The Bonaparte's Gull probably breeds in the majority of squares in all 100-km blocks north of 48° N. In the Hudson Bay Lowlands, breeding may occur to within 10 km of Hudson Bay along treed riparian corridors through the tundra strip (Wilson and McRae 1993), and it is evidently absent only from areas of extensive tundra, particularly around Cape Henrietta Maria. On the Northern Shield, the second atlas found a more extensive distribution. The northwest had breeding evidence in 15 additional 100-km blocks with confirmed breeding in Thunder Bay Dist. south to Jordain Lake (48° 58' N), 80 km northwest of Thunder Bay. Reports of probable breeding in two squares near Rainy Lake along the Minnesota boundary were undocumented and may have been non-breed-

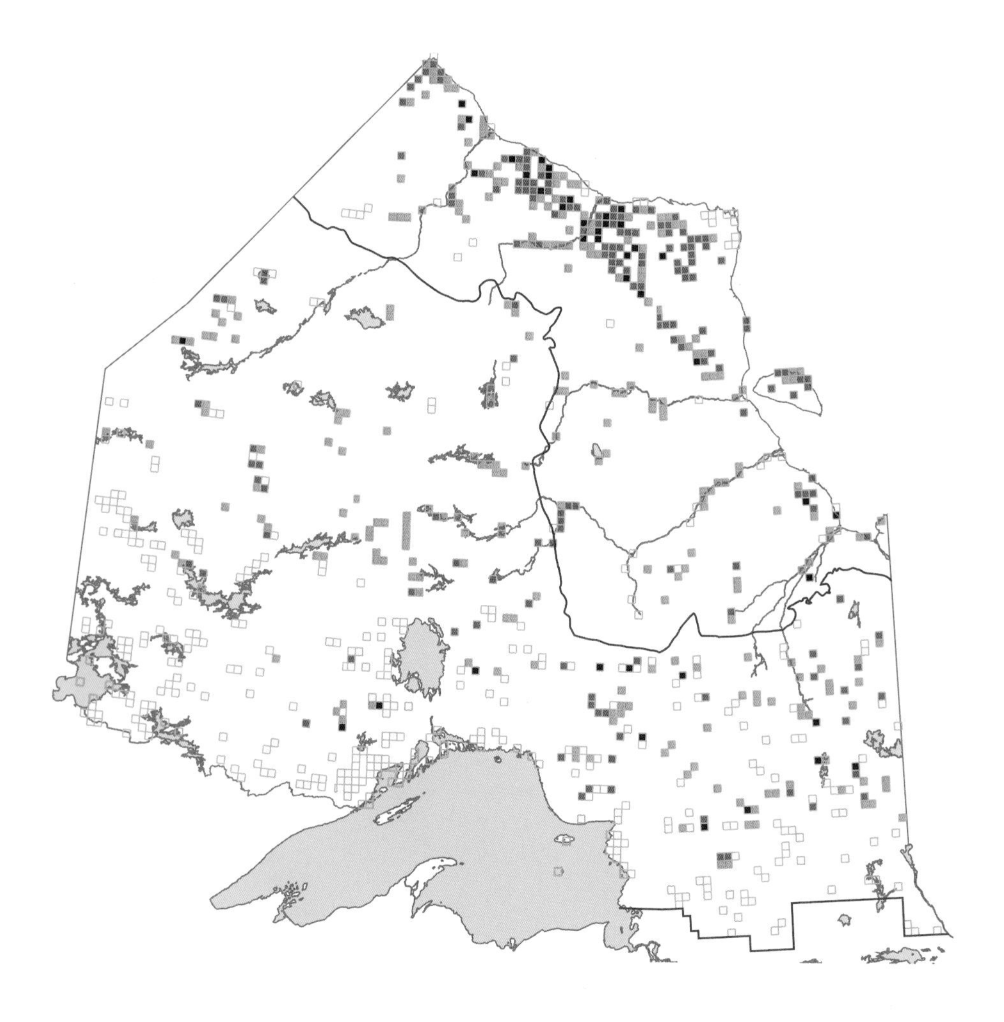

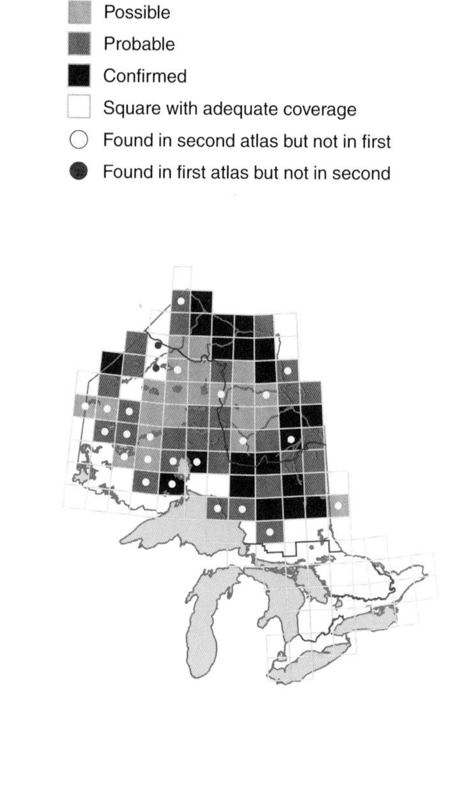

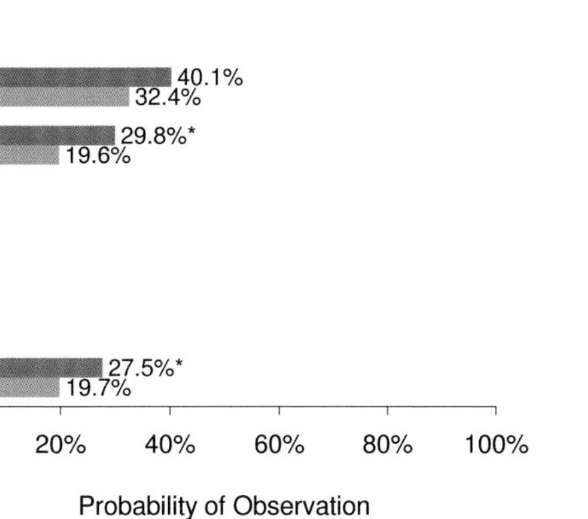

ing birds. In the northeast, breeding was confirmed south to Horwood Lake, Sudbury Dist. (48° N), but the species may breed farther south, as evidence of possible and probable breeding was received for squares near Wakami Lake (47° N), about 190 km northwest of Sudbury.

Non-breeding adults and failed breeders can be encountered at ponds in open tundra, along the Hudson and James Bay coasts, and on larger lakes within the breeding grounds. Few second-year non-breeders appear on the breeding grounds, but hundreds often summer as far north as Lake Simcoe. Most adults depart from breeding areas soon after young have fledged, becoming common in southern Ontario by late July. Young also leave the breeding areas soon after fledging, arriving in southern Ontario beginning in late July and becoming common in August.

Breeding biology: During April and early May, adult Bonaparte's Gulls stage at selected locations in southern Ontario such as the Niagara River and Lakes Erie, Ontario, and Simcoe. Most depart by mid-May, arriving at breeding areas in northern Ontario by late May. In the Hudson Bay Lowlands, adults congregate in estuaries of larger rivers flowing into Hudson and James Bays, moving to inland breeding areas when lakes and ponds are ice-free. Breeding sites are typically at the treed margins of boggy ponds and small lakes but occasionally on treed islands in larger lakes, in oxbow and meander-scar lakes beside larger rivers, and along sluggish rivers through taiga. The species is typically a solitary nester with one pair to a pond or lake, but it may nest in loose colonies of 5 to10 pairs (Blokpoel in Cadman et al. 1987; pers. obs.). Nests are normally in conifers, usually spruce and occasionally Tamarack or White Cedar (Peck and James 1983; pers. obs.).

Sentinel birds perch conspicuously atop spruce spires, often close to nest sites. About 60% of atlas records were of possible breeding. The Bonaparte's Gull reacts aggressively to potential predators in its nesting area. Intruders are intercepted at considerable distances from nests by one or more pairs, and the presence of agitated adults is often the first evidence of probable breeding. Nests and fledgling young are hard to find, and confirmation of breeding is generally difficult to obtain. Breeding was confirmed in only 9% of squares with breeding evidence.

Abundance: The Bonaparte's Gull was recorded on less than 1% of point counts in the Northern Shield and Hudson Bay Lowlands. Point count detections were insufficient to generate a map of relative abundance. However, other atlas results including aerial surveys indicate that it is an uncommon and thinly distributed breeder across the northern half of the province. – *Donald A. Sutherland and Ron Pittaway*

Nests are usually in spruce along the margins of lakes and ponds. The young are semiprecocial, leaving the nest two to seven days after hatching (Burger and Gochfeld 2002). *Photo: George K. Peck*

Spruce-rimmed lakes in the Boreal Forest are the most commonly used habitat for breeding by the Bonaparte's Gull in Ontario. Near Horwood Lake, Sudbury Dist. *Photo: Donald A. Sutherland*

Ring-billed Gull

Goéland à bec cerclé

Larus delawarensis

The Ring-billed Gull is the gull with which most people in southern Ontario are familiar. It is frequently found begging for food at the park, the beach, fast-food outlets, or parking lots. A very adaptable and successful species, it nests in colonies of thousands, often on urban islands and peninsulas and restricted industrial areas. Superficially, it resembles the Herring Gull, also common through much of Ontario, but is smaller, with the characteristic black ring around its bill that gives this gull its name. It breeds only in temperate North America, approximately equidistant on both sides of the Canada-US border (Ryder 1993).

Distribution and population status: The Ring-billed Gull is commonly found along most of Ontario's Great Lakes coastlines, with major breeding colonies on the St. Lawrence, Niagara, and Detroit Rivers, northern Lake Ontario, eastern Lake Erie, eastern Georgian Bay, the North Channel of Lake Huron, and the west shore of the Bruce Peninsula. In most of these coastal areas, it is usually found nesting alongside the Herring Gull. Breeding evidence is much more limited on southern Lake Huron and western and central Lake Erie. Smaller scattered Ring-billed Gull colonies also occur inland on larger water bodies such as Simcoe, Abitibi, and Rice Lakes and at a few other sites south of the Canadian Shield. It nests as well in small numbers inland in northwestern Ontario. Ephemeral, intermittent, and often unsuccessful nestings were noted at Long Point, Rondeau Prov. Park, Middle Island, south of Pelee Island, and occasionally on grassy areas at some sewage lagoons.

Considering all records, the probability of observation increased significantly since the first atlas in the province as a whole and in all regions except the Hudson Bay Lowlands. However, considering only confirmed breeding records (as shown in the histogram), the probability of observation was

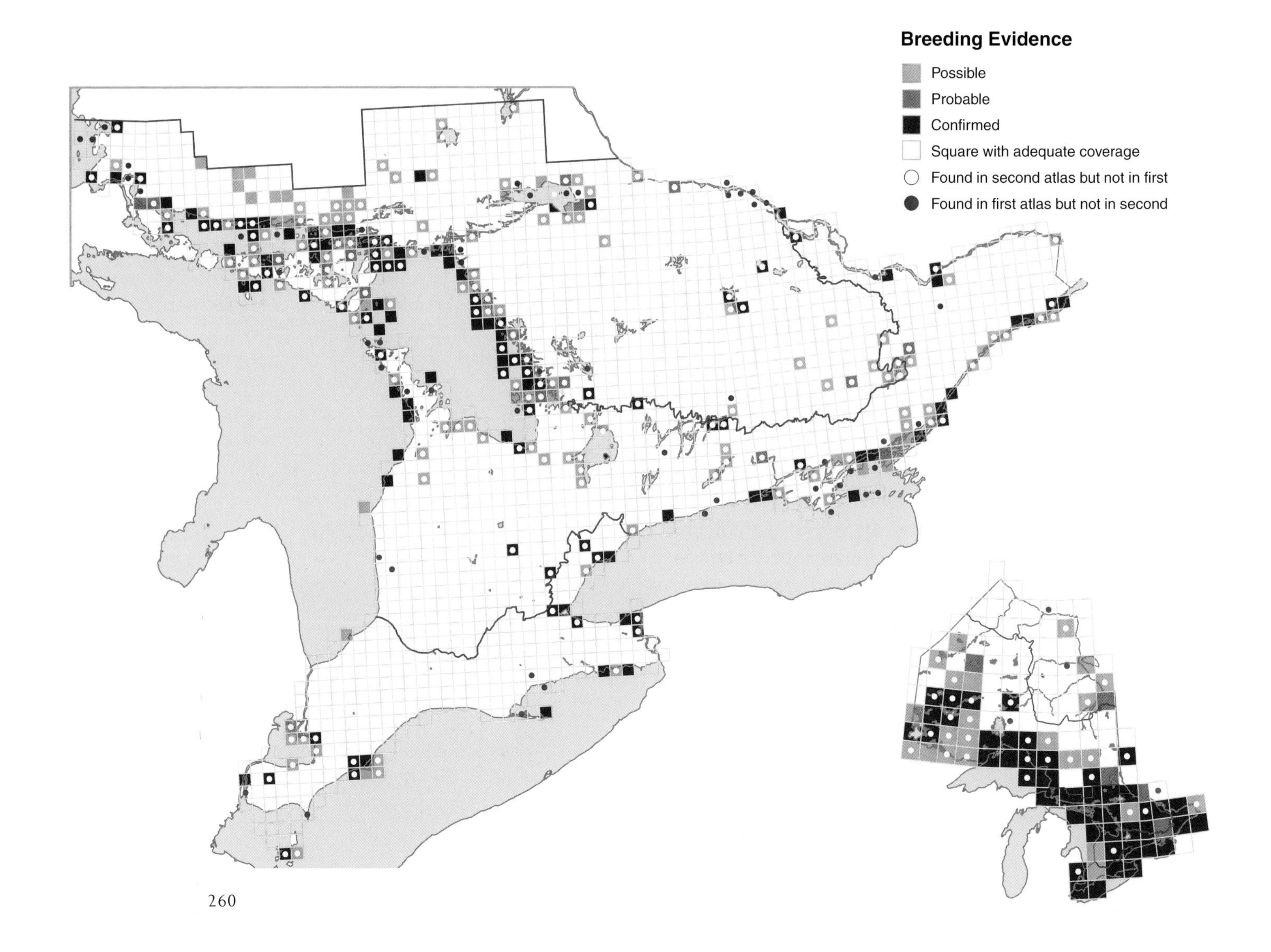

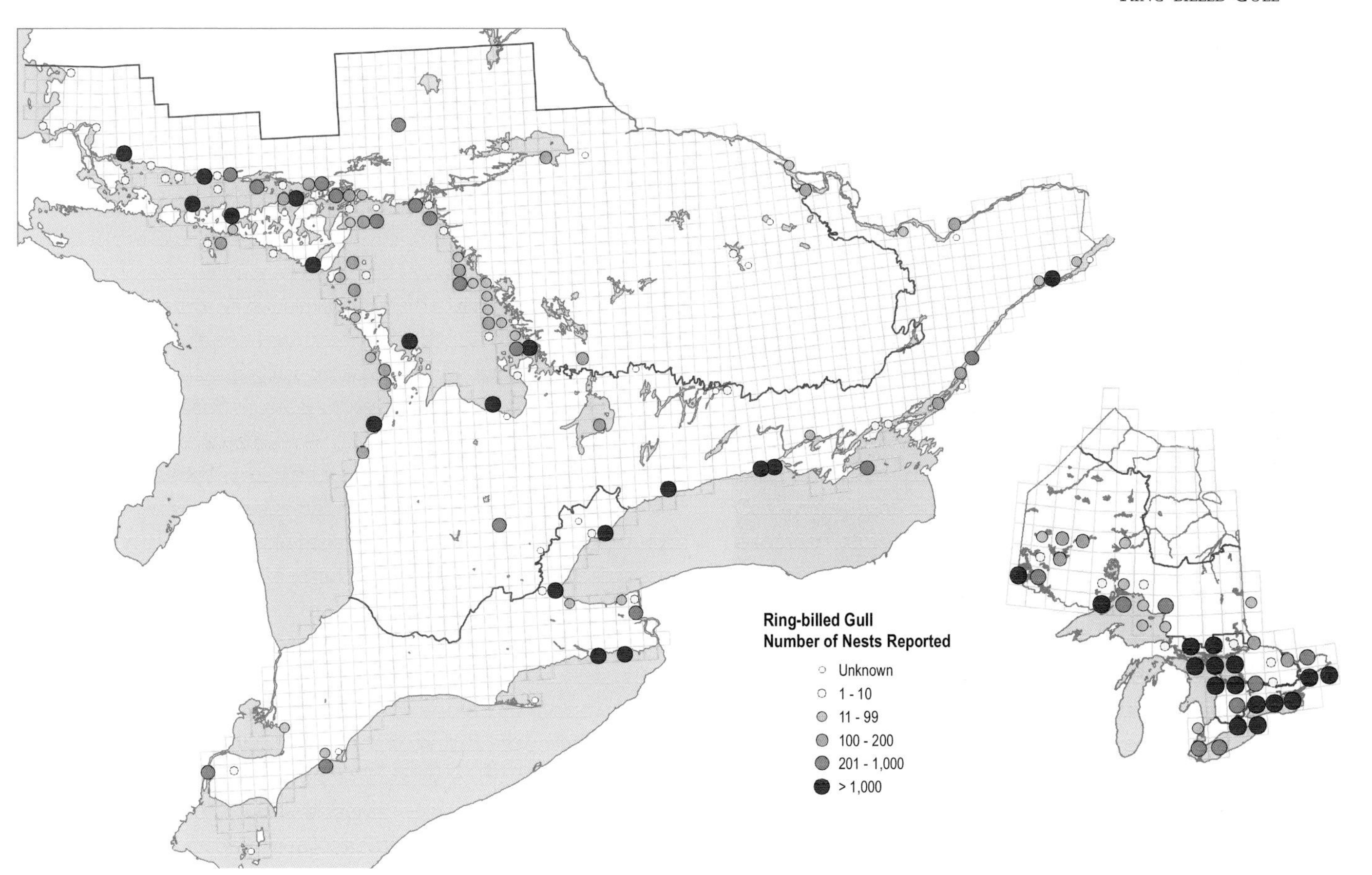

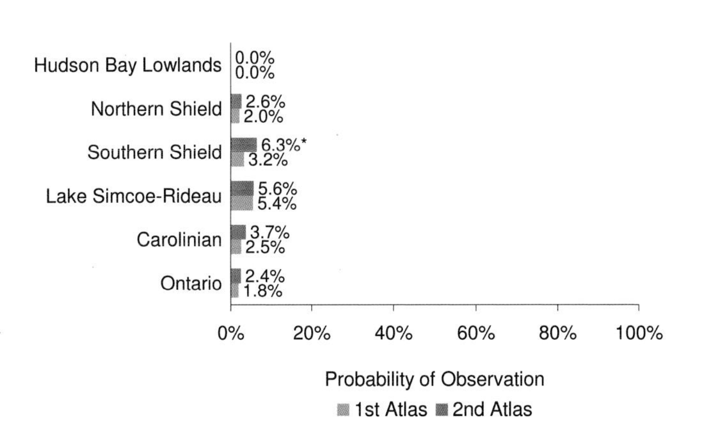

unchanged in the province as a whole but increased significantly in the Southern Shield region. In southern Ontario, increases were especially apparent near Manitoulin Island and along Georgian Bay, and inland from Peterborough to east of Kingston, where population increases were recorded between atlases (Blokpoel and Tessier 1996, 1997). In northern Ontario, much of the increase occurred in the southwestern portion of Kenora and Rainy River Districts as well as in eastern Lake Superior. These increases in numbers are largely due to less persecution than in the past, combined with the species' adaptability. Joint CWS-USFWS surveys indicate that the Great Lakes population more than doubled between 1976/77 and 1989/90. However, from 1989/90 to 1999/2000, populations suffered a 13.1% decline (Cuthbert et al. 2001; CWS unpubl. data), likely a return to equilibrium following the rapid population growth that outstripped the lakes' carrying capacity.

As with most colonial waterbirds, this species often feeds up to 10 km or more from its breeding colony and may be misconstrued as breeding on lakes where it is only foraging and loafing. Hence, although it is an abundant breeding bird in southern Ontario, possible and probable breeding evidence from this atlas probably still overstate the true breeding distribution in Ontario.

Breeding biology: The Ring-billed Gull is very gregarious and nests densely on the ground. Individual territories are usually no more than pecking distance from adjacent incubating birds. The first clutches are laid by mid-April, and young begin flying with parents during late June or early July.

Ring-billed Gull colonies can be very loud and easily detected, although they are often found offshore or at inaccessible locations that make size more difficult to determine. Confirmed breeding was recorded in 40% of squares with breeding evidence. A further 54% recorded only possible breeding, in the form of birds observed in suitable habitat, and many of these may represent foraging birds.

Abundance: The Ring-billed Gull is a very abundant breeding bird along the Great Lakes shorelines, particularly from Sault Ste. Marie east and south along Georgian Bay. Surveys by CWS in 1999-2000 detected the following totals for the Canadian Great Lakes: Lake Ontario, 155,000 pairs; Lake Erie, 44,000; Lake Huron, 99,000; and Lake Superior, 5,900. Just over 300,000 pairs were recorded for the area as a whole (Weseloh et al. 2003; CWS unpubl. data). The largest colonies include Presqu'ile Prov. Park at 58,000 pairs, the Leslie Street Spit at 59,000, Hamilton Harbour at 24,000, Port Colborne at 41,000, and Fighting Island (Detroit River) at 46,000. The species is approximately 10-20 times more abundant in the Carolinian and Lake Simcoe-Rideau regions than elsewhere in Ontario. – *Chip Weseloh*

Herring Gull

Goéland argenté

Larus argentatus

Jim Richards

Along with Ring-billed Gull, the Herring Gull is one of two gull species that breed commonly throughout the Great Lakes. Adults of both species are mainly white with the typical grey back and black wing-tips, and are differentiated primarily by size and bill pattern. While both are found throughout much of the province, the Herring Gull is more widespread in northern Ontario, while the Ring-billed is found mostly in the south.

Distribution and population status: The Herring Gull has been known to breed on the upper Great Lakes and in the northern interior for as long as records have been kept. Langille (1884) noted that fishermen sometimes obtained hundreds of eggs from a colony on Halfmoon Island in Georgian Bay. In southern Ontario, there was a period in the early 20th century when the species did not nest on Lakes Ontario or Erie (Eaton 1910).

In the second atlas, the species was found in all but a few 100-km blocks, primarily at the southern edge of the Hudson Bay Lowlands. Records are sparse through this area, where fewer inland lakes exist. The core of the Herring Gull's distribution is found in the Southern Shield region, where its probability of observation was 61%. Here, it is found in virtually every square along the coasts of Georgian Bay and the North Channel and in the majority of squares inland. It is similarly common throughout the Northern Shield and Hudson Bay Lowlands, with a probability of observation of about 45% and 40%, respectively. The preponderance of small lakes with sheltered, rocky islands through the Boreal Forest provides ample habitat in these regions. Abundance decreases south of the Shield, where it is found primarily at coastal sites. Its probability of observation was 20% in the Lake Simcoe-Rideau region, with most records concentrated on Manitoulin Island and the Bruce Peninsula and along the St. Lawrence River. Probability of observation dropped to just 12% in the Carolinian, where the species was primarily found near

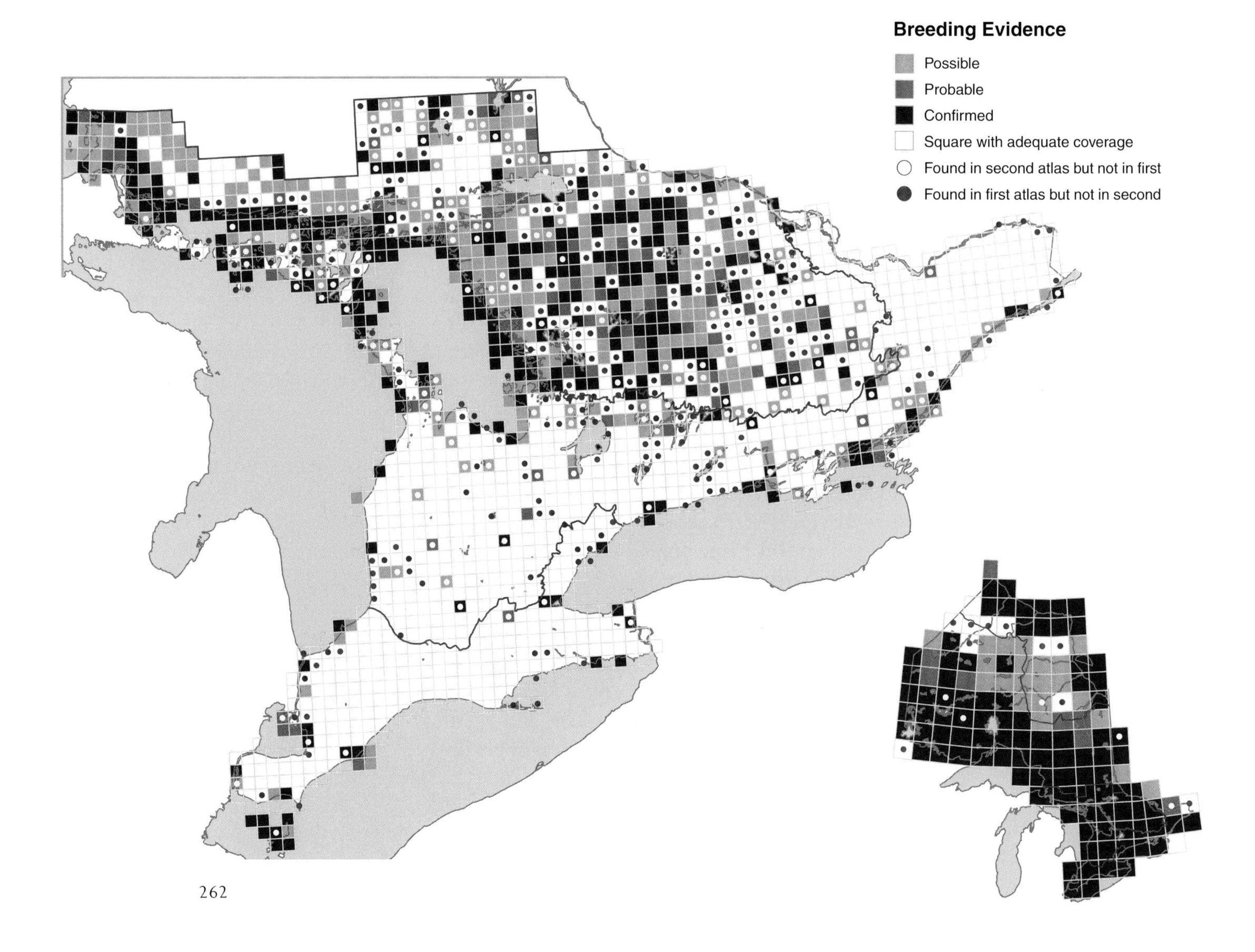

BREEDING EVIDENCE

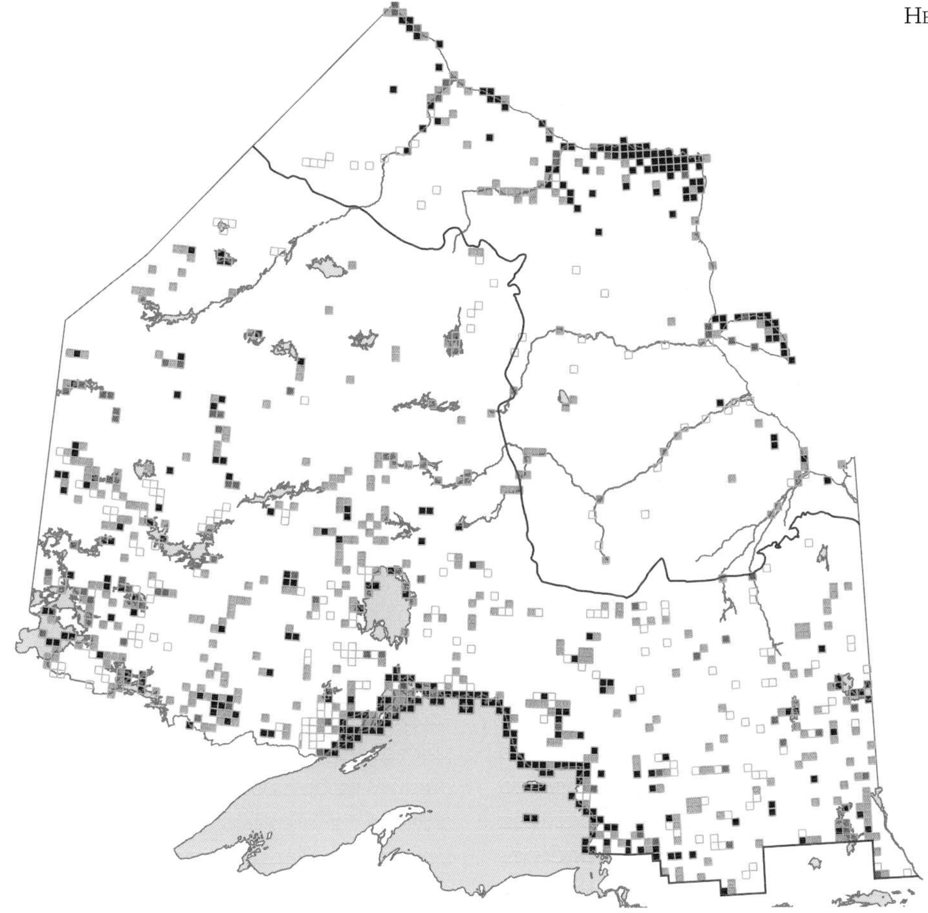

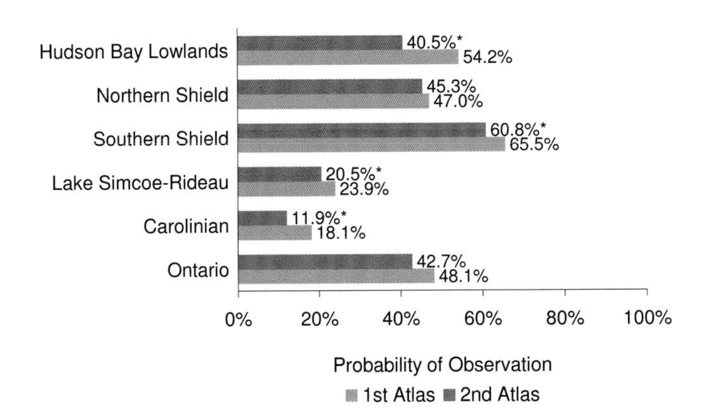

Rondeau, Pelee Island, and northeastern Lake St. Clair. The Herring Gull showed significant declines in all three southern Ontario regions since the first atlas, but this is probably largely a result of more stringent evaluation of breeding evidence records during the second atlas. When only confirmed breeding records were used in the change analysis, there was no significant change in any southern Ontario region between atlases.

Breeding biology: South of the Shield, the Herring Gull breeds in distinct colonies, with the more abundant Ring-billed Gull or in single-species colonies. On inland lakes on the Shield, in Lake Superior, and to some extent in Lake Huron, it more often nests as the most prominent species in mixed-species colonies, including those with Common or Caspian Terns, Double-crested Cormorants, or American White Pelicans; it will also breed solitarily on islands or peninsulas. In the south, eggs are usually laid during the last half of April, but birds will have returned to their colonies six to eight weeks earlier, before the snow and ice have all melted. In the north, the timing can be up to two weeks later. Both parents incubate the eggs, feed the precocial chicks, and vigorously defend the nest and young from predators, including humans (Pierotti and Good 1994).

Nests are often placed in open, barren habitats where they should be easy to locate; however, they can be lost among the sea of nests in a mixed colony. Nesting was confirmed in 41% of squares reporting the species. The highest breeding evidence in an additional 50% of squares was simply individuals observed in suitable habitat, primarily on the Shield where pairs may nest singly.

Abundance: The Herring Gull is a common to very common breeding bird throughout most of its Ontario range. It is very abundant in western Lake Erie and mid-Lake Huron, where the province's largest colony (Chantry Island at Southampton) numbers approximately 2,500 pairs (Blokpoel and Tessier 1997; Morris et al. 2003). In the Canadian waters of the Great Lakes, Morris et al. (2003) noted the following lake totals: Lake Ontario, about 1,300 pairs at 47 sites; Lake Erie, about 3,200 pairs at 28 sites; Lake Huron, about 22,000 pairs at 569 sites; and Lake Superior, about 9,900 pairs at 322 sites. The Canadian Great Lakes population thus totals approximately 36,000 pairs at 966 sites, a 14.3% decline from the 42,000 pairs at 974 sites recorded during 1989-90. The decline is primarily attributed to declining food supply (Morris et al. 2003). Quantitative data on the Herring Gull's nesting population are lacking from most of inland and northern Ontario. – *Chip Weseloh*

Great Black-backed Gull

Goéland marin

Larus marinus

Jim Richards

Although the Great Black-backed Gull is a breeding bird in southern Ontario, it is more common there in the winter than the summer. Worldwide, this species breeds in the Great Lakes, along the Atlantic coast of North America from northern Québec to North Carolina, and in the Palearctic coastally from Greenland and northern Scandinavia south to the British Isles and Spain. It has been used as an indicator of contaminant levels in the Great Lakes (Weseloh et al. 2002; Pekarik-Kress 2004). Its status in Ontario was reviewed by Angehrn et al. (1979), and Blokpoel and Tessier (1996) reported results of the latest survey of all Canadian Great Lakes islands.

Distribution and population status: The Great Black-backed Gull was first recorded breeding in Ontario in 1954 off the west shore of the Bruce Peninsula in Lake Huron (Krug 1956). Single pairs bred sporadically at a few Lake Ontario sites over the following 25 years. In 1983, the first multiple nests at any Great Lakes site were found in eastern Lake Ontario (Weseloh 1984; Richards and McRae 1988).

In Lakes Ontario and Erie, the breeding distribution of this species has remained relatively unchanged between atlases. It was found at only one site on Lake Erie, near Port Colborne. In Lake Ontario, the species was found nesting at the Leslie Street Spit in Toronto, at Presqu'ile Prov. Park and neighbouring islands, at Prince Edward Point, and in the Kingston area. However, elsewhere in the province, the species has undergone a substantial increase since the 1980s. There are now records from five squares along the St. Lawrence River where the species was not reported in the first atlas. Similarly, three squares at Lake Nipissing, one at Lake Simcoe, and all but two squares on Lake Huron and Georgian Bay are new records in the second atlas. In northern Ontario, two records of possible breeding in Lake Superior, one in Nipigon Bay near a multi-species waterbird breeding site, and the other from Caribou Island, as well as three squares in Akimiski Strait in James Bay,

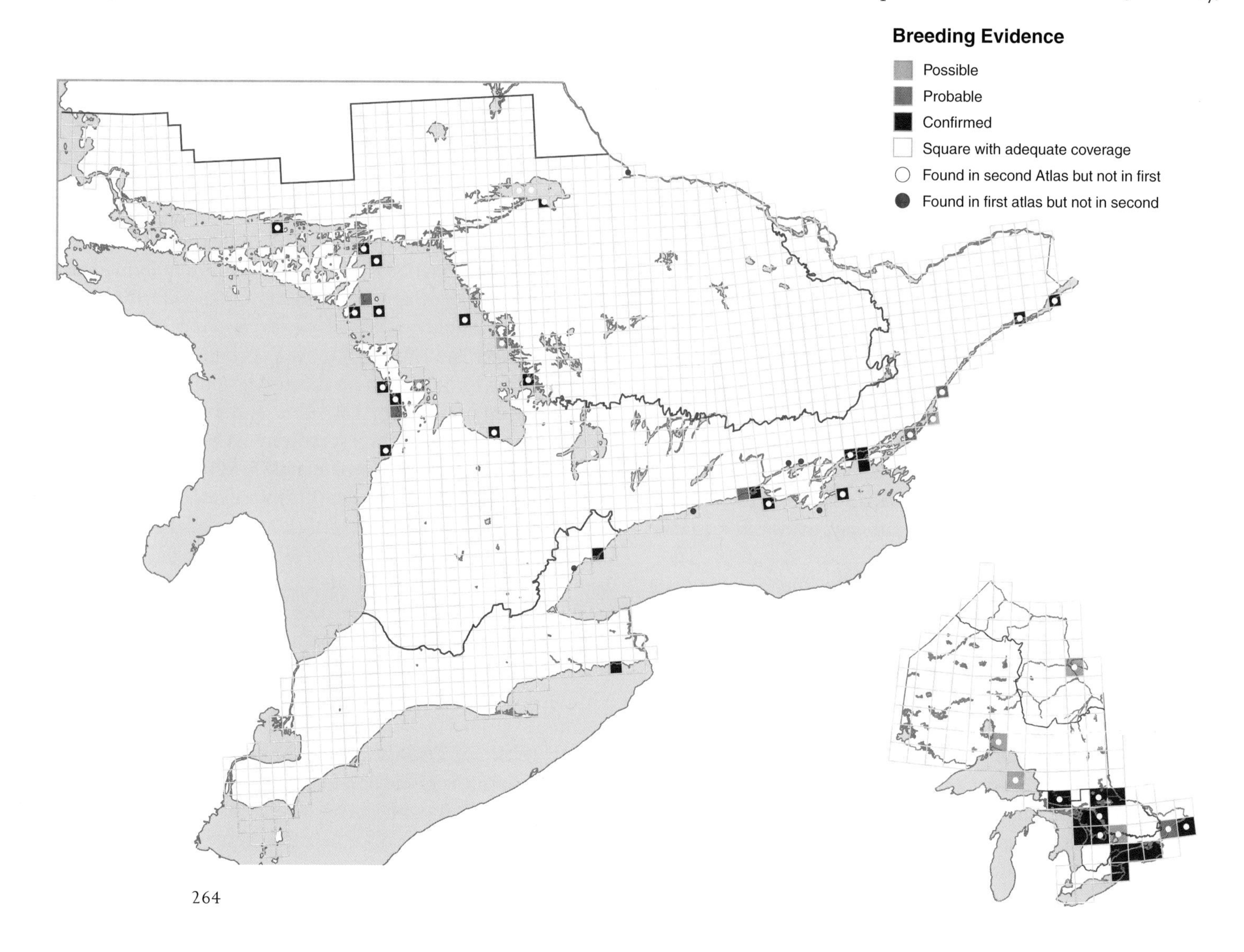

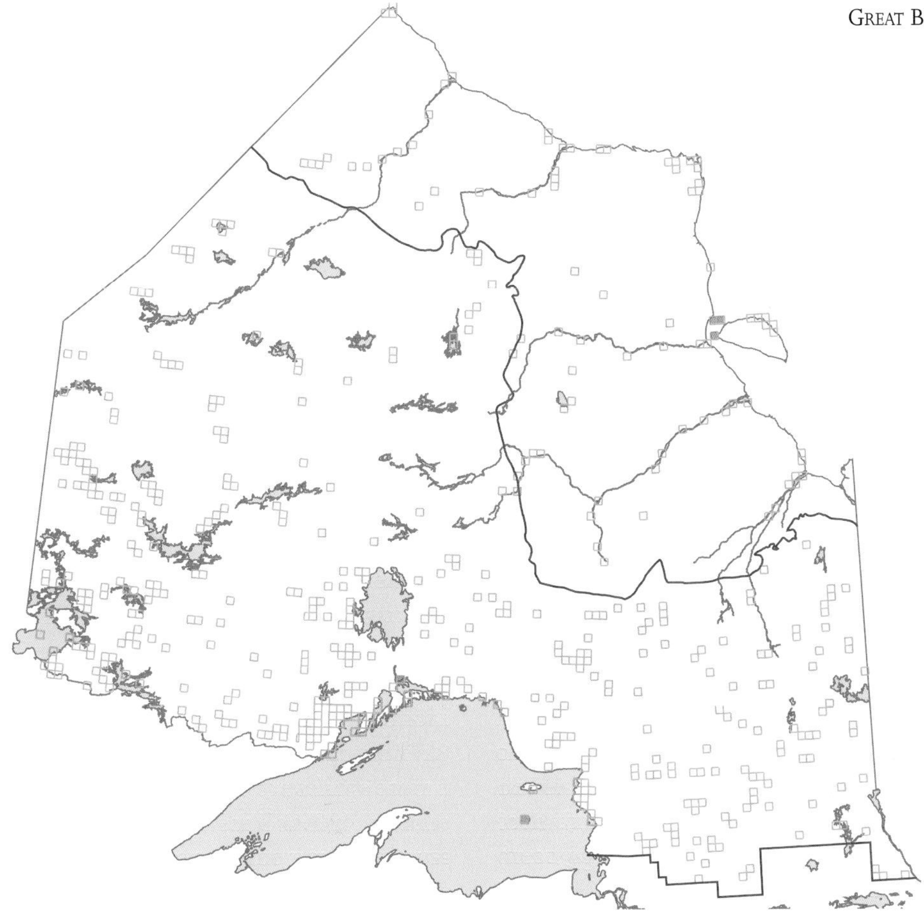

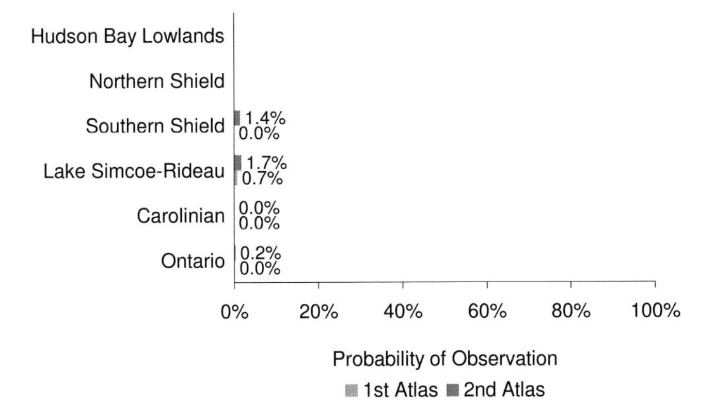

are new for the second atlas and represent the northernmost records of the species in either project. The histogram is based on confirmed breeding records, so shows no rcords in northern Ontario.

Overall, the Great Black-backed Gull was recorded in more than twice as many squares in the second atlas as in the first, up to 38 from 15, and all were at coastal sites or large inland water bodies. In only two squares, one near Cobourg on Lake Ontario, and the other near Mattawa on the Ottawa River, was breeding reported in the first atlas but not the second.

Breeding biology: The breeding biology and chronology of this species on the Great Lakes is much like that of the Herring and Ring-billed Gulls with which it usually nests. It returns to its colony site in early spring, and egg dates are 28 April-29 June (Peck and James 1994). Young are semiprecocial and can fly when about 45 days old (Good 1998), usually about the first of July. This gull requires a relatively large territory, rarely nests more densely than two to three pairs per colony site, and is much less common than its congeners. However, because it usually nests in open sites, often at known gull colonies, and adults are distinctive and conspicuous, breeding is typically easy to confirm, as evidenced by the relatively high 61% of squares reporting confirmed breeding.

Abundance: Point counts and roadside surveys like the BBS are not well suited to detecting waterbirds such as the Great Black-backed Gull. However, CWS has monitored the breeding numbers of colonial waterbirds on the lower Great Lakes since 1976. This species has undergone a gradual increase since then, and by 2002, 15 to 20 pairs nested on both Pigeon Island (near Kingston) and Little Galloo Island (near Henderson Harbor, New York). Up to five additional pairs occurred on each of Scotch Bonnet, Gull (near Presqu'ile), and False Duck (near Prince Edward Point) Islands. Eastern Lake Ontario thus held an all-time high of approximately 50 pairs of nesting Great Black-backed Gulls. However, during 2004-2006, Type E botulism was rampant among colonial waterbirds in eastern Lake Ontario. More than 200 Great Black-backed Gulls died during the epidemic (L. Shutt and C. Weseloh, unpubl. data). In 2006 and 2007, only four and one nesting pairs, respectively, were located, and the population gains made on Lake Ontario between 1980 and 2000 were lost completely.

At present, one to two pairs still breed annually at several sites in Lake Huron. This area could be considered the species' current centre of distribution in the province, particularly following the losses on Lake Ontario. – *Chip Weseloh*

Caspian Tern

Sterne caspienne

Hydroprogne caspia

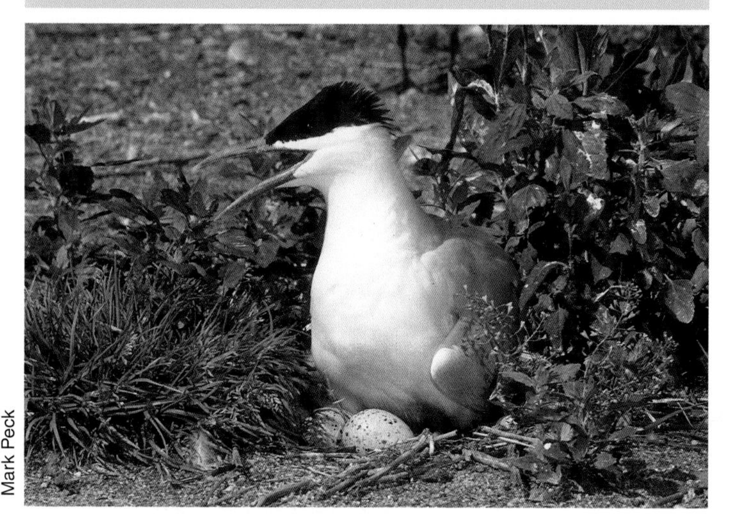

Mark Peck

The Caspian Tern is not only the world's largest tern but it also must have the most raucous and easily discernable call of any larid. Its loud, rasping "*ra-ra-RRRAH*" can be heard at a great distance. It has a cosmopolitan distribution, occurring on all continents except Antarctica (Cuthbert and Wires 1999). It nests in substantial numbers in large, well-established colonies or, less often, in scattered nestings of one to a few pairs, usually persisting for only several years. In Ontario, it almost always nests with the Ring-billed Gull.

Because this species travels up to 50-62 km from its nest site to feed (Cuthbert and Wires 1999), atlas data were carefully reviewed and only records of birds demonstrating acceptable breeding evidence are shown on the maps. Only confirmed breeding records were used in the histogram and analyses presented here.

Distribution and population status: The nesting distribution of this species expanded between atlases. Whereas during the first atlas it nested only on Lake Ontario and Lake Huron, it can now be found on all four Canadian Great Lakes. Lakes Ontario and Huron, however, remain its main area of distribution in the province. In 2001, the species was discovered nesting on Mohawk Island (Lake Erie), near Dunnville. That colony grew to 319 nests in 2006 (D. Moore, pers. comm.). Former nesting sites on Pigeon and False Duck Islands in Lake Ontario have been abandoned (L. Shutt, pers. comm.), but the species has started using other sites (see below). Although it prefers coastal sites, it can also be found using large inland lakes such as Lakes Simcoe or Nipissing or the Kawartha Lakes.

In northern Ontario, the Caspian Tern was found in three 100-km blocks where it was not recorded during the first atlas. In 2003, two single nests were found on two islands, and an apparent pair of birds was reported on another island near Black Bay on Lake Superior east of Thunder Bay. A small colony was discovered on Weagamow Lake about 500 km north of

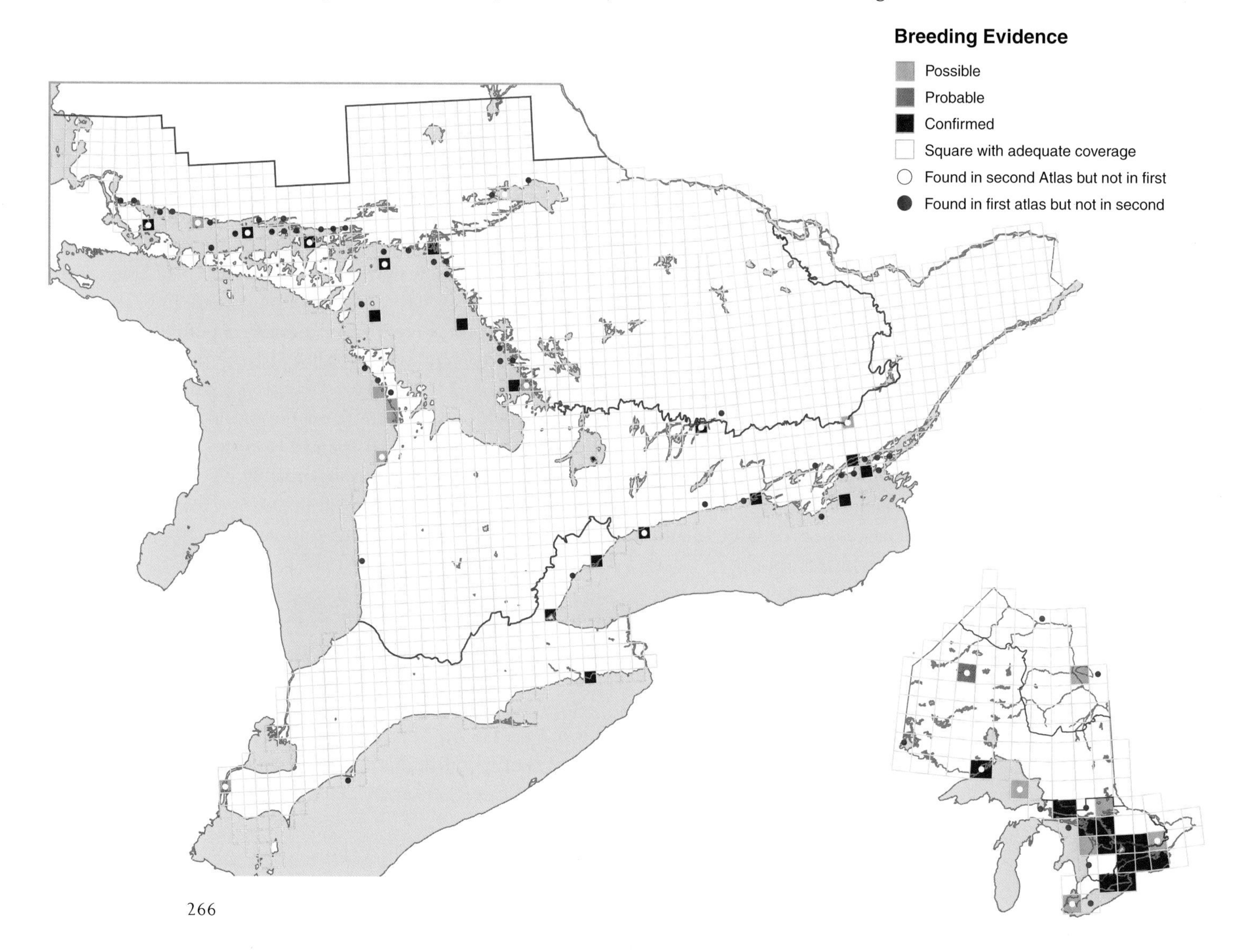

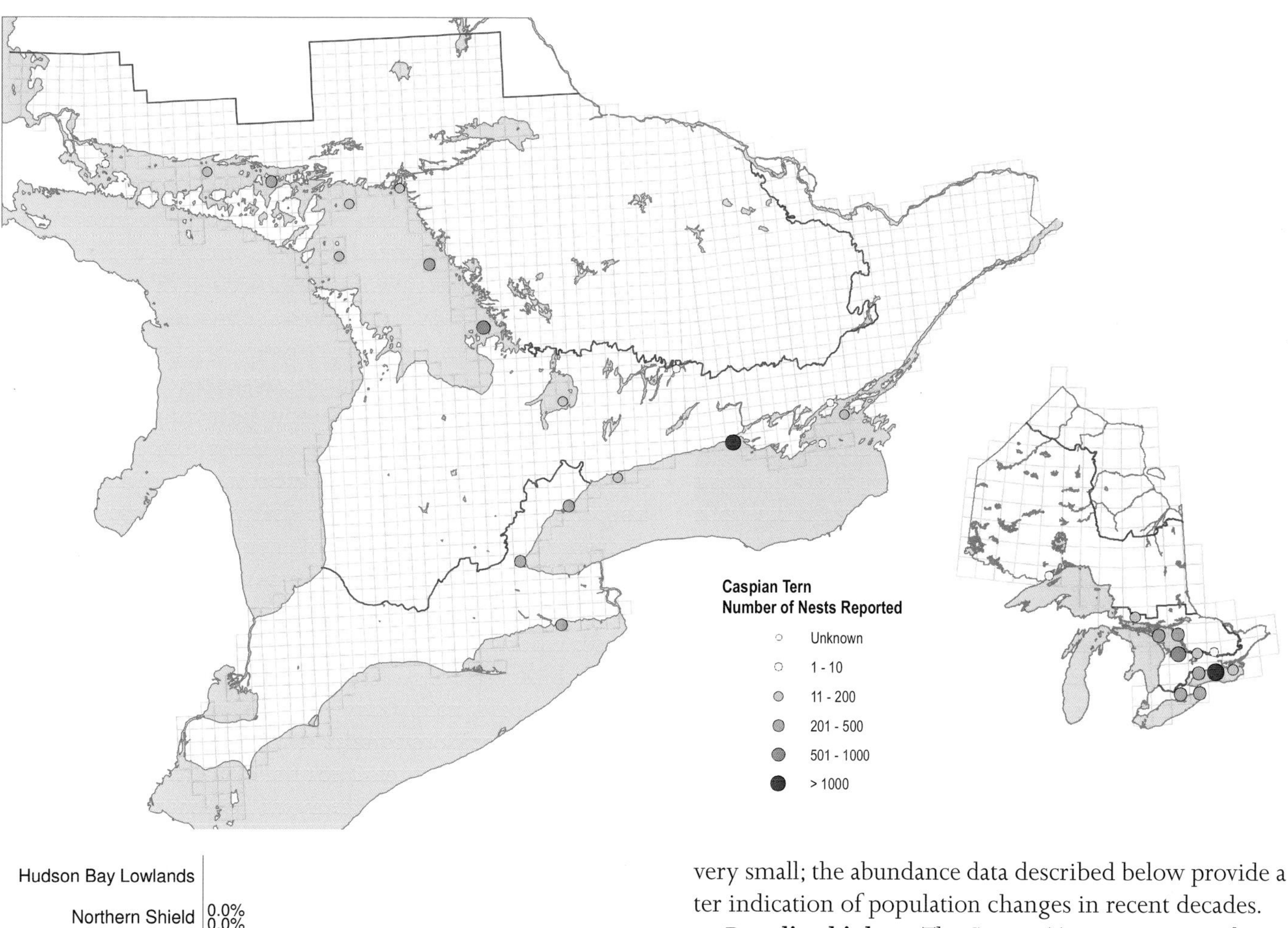

Region	1st Atlas	2nd Atlas
Hudson Bay Lowlands		
Northern Shield	0.0%	0.0%
Southern Shield	0.8%	0.4%
Lake Simcoe-Rideau	0.2%	0.4%
Carolinian	0.0%	0.0%
Ontario	0.1%	0.1%

0% 20% 40% 60% 80% 100%

Probability of Observation

■ 1st Atlas ■ 2nd Atlas

Thunder Bay, and two individuals were observed at Caribou Island in eastern Lake Superior. Nesting was confirmed on islands in Akimiski Strait in James Bay from 1993 to 1996 and again in 2006 (estimated 80 adults observed at nests); 10 adults were observed there during a helicopter overflight in 2005. Possible breeding was reported from an island in a nearby square in 2002.

While the Ring-billed Gull with which this tern usually nests is found in most coastal squares in some areas, squares with confirmed nesting for the Caspian Tern are evenly and more widely spaced on the distribution map. This pattern is likely attributable to the long distances the species will travel from its nesting site to forage. Terns from the colony on South Watcher Island on Georgian Bay were visually tracked to feed in Matchedash Bay, more than 40 km away (unpubl. data).

The confirmed breeding records indicate no significant changes in the probability of observation of the Caspian Tern in the province as a whole or in any region. However, when only confirmed breeding records are used, sample sizes are very small; the abundance data described below provide a better indication of population changes in recent decades.

Breeding biology: The Caspian Tern arrives in early to mid-April in southern Ontario and slightly later in the north. It usually nests on the more elevated areas of islands. Clutches are laid by mid-May, and eggs hatch by early June. In this species more than other terns, the young maintain a bond with the parents well after fledging (Cuthbert and Wires 1999). In August, after juveniles have been flying for a month or more, they can still be seen begging and being fed by adult birds, presumably their parents (Ewins et al. 1994).

Abundance: Data from CWS censuses indicate that from the late 1970s to the late 1990s on the Canadian Great Lakes, the number of Caspian Tern nests increased 11.5% from 2,185 to 2,437. This consisted of a 33.2% decline on Lake Huron and a 20-fold increase on Lake Ontario (Weseloh et al. 2003; unpubl. data). A large colony (1,600 nests in 2005) that has developed on Little Galloo Island, New York, was likely the main contributor to the increase. However, in 2005 and 2006, more than 800 Caspian Terns were found dead in eastern Lake Ontario from Type E botulism (CWS, unpubl. data; W. Stone, pers. comm.), which has reached an epidemic state in the area, putting the fate of colonies there in question. – *Chip Weseloh*

Black Tern

Guifette noire

Chlidonias niger

Jim Richards

Of the two marsh-nesting terns that breed in Ontario, the Black Tern is much more common and widespread than the Forster's Tern. It breeds mainly on the prairies of western North America, but its range extends eastward through much of Ontario and into western Québec (Dunn and Agro 1995). Although it is a freshwater marshbird during the nesting season, from October to April it is highly pelagic, wintering at sea mainly on the Pacific and Caribbean coasts of Central America and northern South America (Dunn and Agro 1995), where it may be the most commonly encountered bird in areas such as the Gulf of Panama (Loftin 1991). A different subspecies breeds in Europe.

Distribution and population status: In southwestern Ontario, there are few areas where the Black Tern was a confirmed or probable nester; these include Long Point, Rondeau, Point Pelee, the northeast section of Lake St. Clair, and Luther Marsh. In south-central Ontario, it was widely reported along the southern edge of the Shield from Matchedash Bay (southeastern Georgian Bay) eastward through Lake Simcoe, Lindsay, and Peterborough to the St. Lawrence River through to the Québec border. It was particularly well reported from Prince Edward Co., and the Kingston and Perth-Smith's Falls vicinities. It was also reported from several squares on the Bruce Peninsula, Manitoulin Island, and the St. Marys River. There are very few reports on the Canadian Shield. On the Southern Shield, colonies include 30 birds reported at Cache Bay on Lake Nipissing, and 16 birds observed over a marsh east of Sudbury. In the Northern Shield, records are very thinly scattered, except in the Lake of the Woods and Dryden areas, where colonies were reported in three and five squares, respectively. Confirmed breeding was reported as far north as Little Sachigo Lake, where a single pair was found nesting in a flooded sedge meadow.

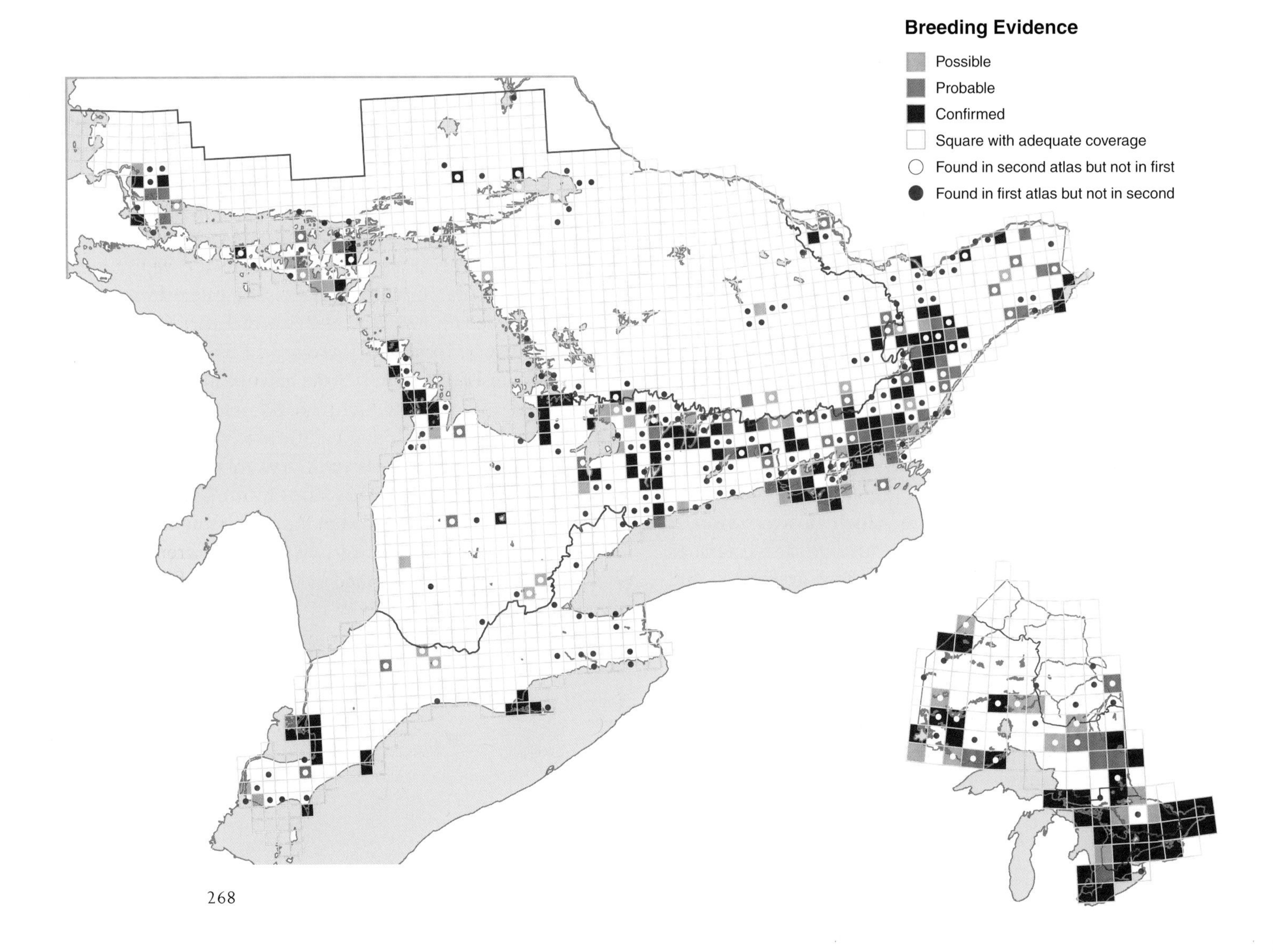

BREEDING EVIDENCE

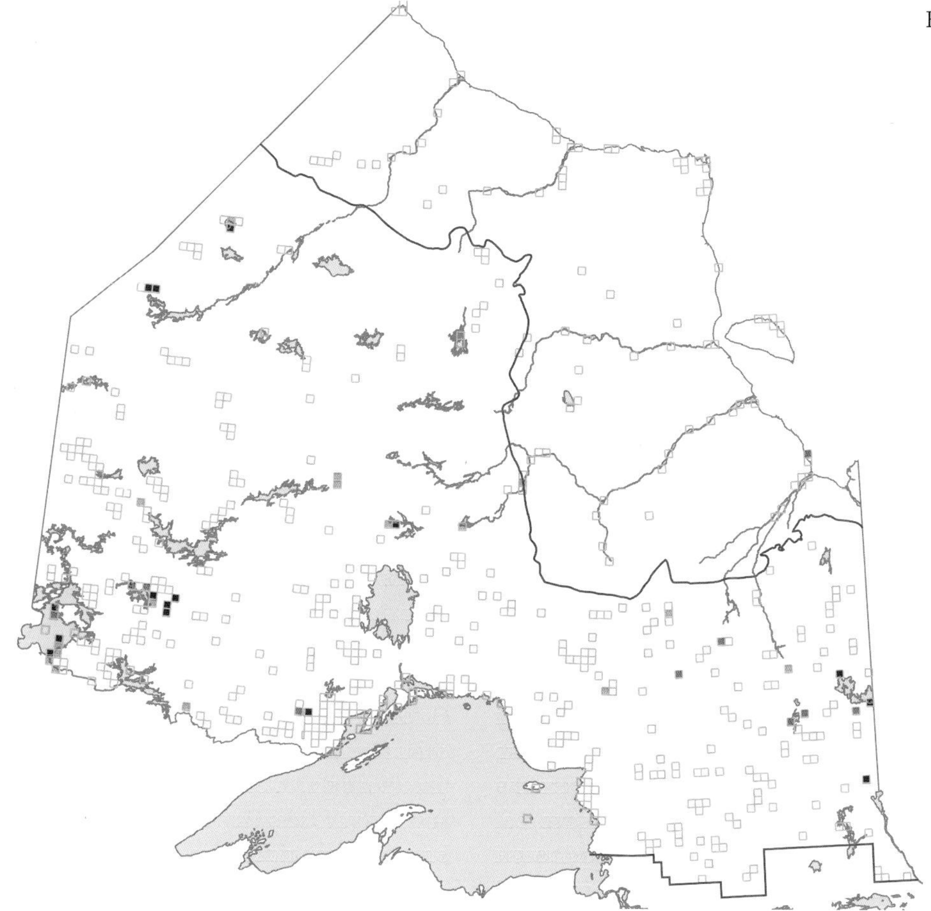

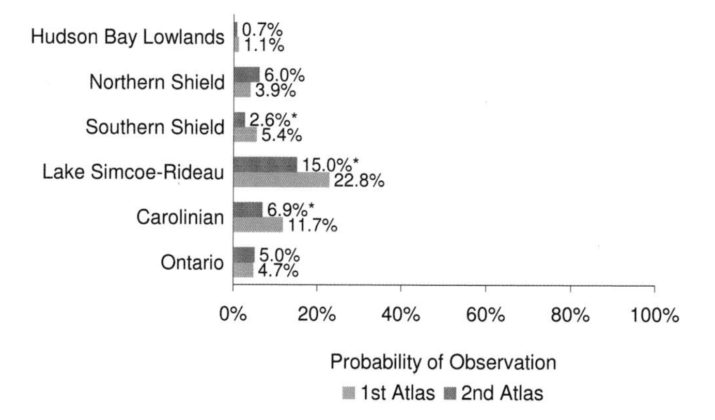

The current distribution is generally similar to that of the first atlas. However, although there was no significant change in the province as a whole, there were significant declines in the probability of observation of 41%, 34%, and 52% in the Carolinian, Lake Simcoe-Rideau, and Southern Shield regions, respectively. The species appears to have disappeared from the Niagara Peninsula and several coastal marshes along the north shore of Lake Ontario (between Toronto and Kingston), including the Bay of Quinte and a few isolated pockets on the Canadian Shield. In adjacent New York, the species is also known to be declining in the state's coastal Lake Ontario marshes (I. Mazzocchi, pers. comm.).

Breeding biology: The Black Tern is loosely colonial or semi-colonial. In Ontario, colonies are typically small, usually consisting of fewer than 20 pairs. Nevertheless, they are well defended against intruders, so nesting is relatively easy to confirm. Unlike most colonial waterbirds, the Black Tern is a relatively late spring migrant, typically arriving in the first 10 days of May. The majority of egg dates occur between 31 May and 21 June, and one egg is usually laid each day until the clutch of three is achieved (Peck and James 1983). Its preferred nesting habitat is a "hemi-marsh" (i.e., a wetland with 50:50 open water and emergent vegetation). The nest is small and very flimsy, nearly flush with the water, and usually built on an upturned cattail root, floating vegetation mat, patch of mud, or even flotsam (e.g., floating plywood; pers. obs.). Incubation is 19-21 days, and the young are semiprecocial. At any sign of danger, young flightless birds flee into aquatic vegetation, where they are very difficult to locate. Chicks are frequently fed by parents for at least two weeks post-hatch (Dunn and Agro 1995) and fledge at 20-24 days.

Abundance: Population surveys of nesting Black Terns along the Great Lakes shoreline were made in 1991 (Austen et al. 1996) and 2001 (Graham et al. 2002). Unfortunately, the two surveys used different protocols, and the data are not directly comparable. In the 1991 survey, more than 545 nests were found in 61 colonies. From 7-25% of the nests were located in each of six water bodies: the St. Lawrence River, Lakes Ontario, Erie, St. Clair, and the main body of Huron and Georgian Bay (Austen et al. 1996). In 2001, 717 individual Black Terns were counted at 40 colonies. Using the same protocol, it was estimated that the 1991 survey would have found 1,094 individual terns at 73 colonies, indicating an overall decline of 35% (3.2% per year, Graham et al. 2002).
– *Chip Weseloh*

Common Tern

Sterne pierregarin

Sterna hirundo

Ron Ridout

The Common Tern is one of five tern species nesting in Ontario. It is often difficult to distinguish from the Forster's Tern or Arctic Tern, which are of similar size and appearance.

The Common Tern has a holarctic breeding distribution mainly south of 65° N (Nisbet 2002) and nests throughout Ontario, but sparsely in the Hudson Bay Lowlands. North American birds winter on both the Pacific coast (Mexico to Chile) and the Atlantic coast (US Gulf Coast, Columbia to Argentina) (Nisbet 2002). The species is listed as Endangered, Threatened, or of Special Concern in all eight US states bordering the Great Lakes, but in Canada it is listed only in Nova Scotia, as Sensitive (Nisbet 2002). Currently, it has no special status under COSEWIC.

Distribution and population status: Major areas of occurrence for the Common Tern during the second atlas were the Northern Shield region west of 85° W; the North Channel and Georgian Bay sections of Lake Huron; Lake Ontario and the Trent-Severn Waterway; and the St. Lawrence, Rideau, and Ottawa River systems. Breeding evidence was largely absent from the Hudson Bay Lowlands except for records on the Severn, Attawapiskat, Albany, and Moose River systems and Missisa Lake, and the Northern Shield region east of 85° W, except for the area surrounding Lake Abitibi.

Using only confirmed breeding evidence, there was no significant change in the probability of observation of the species between the first and second atlases in the province as a whole. However, there was a significant decline of 41% in the Lake Simcoe-Rideau region, which contains all of the Ontario shoreline of Lake Ontario, the St. Lawrence River, Manitoulin Island, and parts of Lake Huron, southern Georgian Bay, and the Ottawa River, as well as the Kawartha and Rideau Lakes. There were no significant changes in the remaining four regions. The most evident decline on the breeding evidence map in southern Ontario is in the Kawartha Lakes and Rice Lake, where confirmed breed-

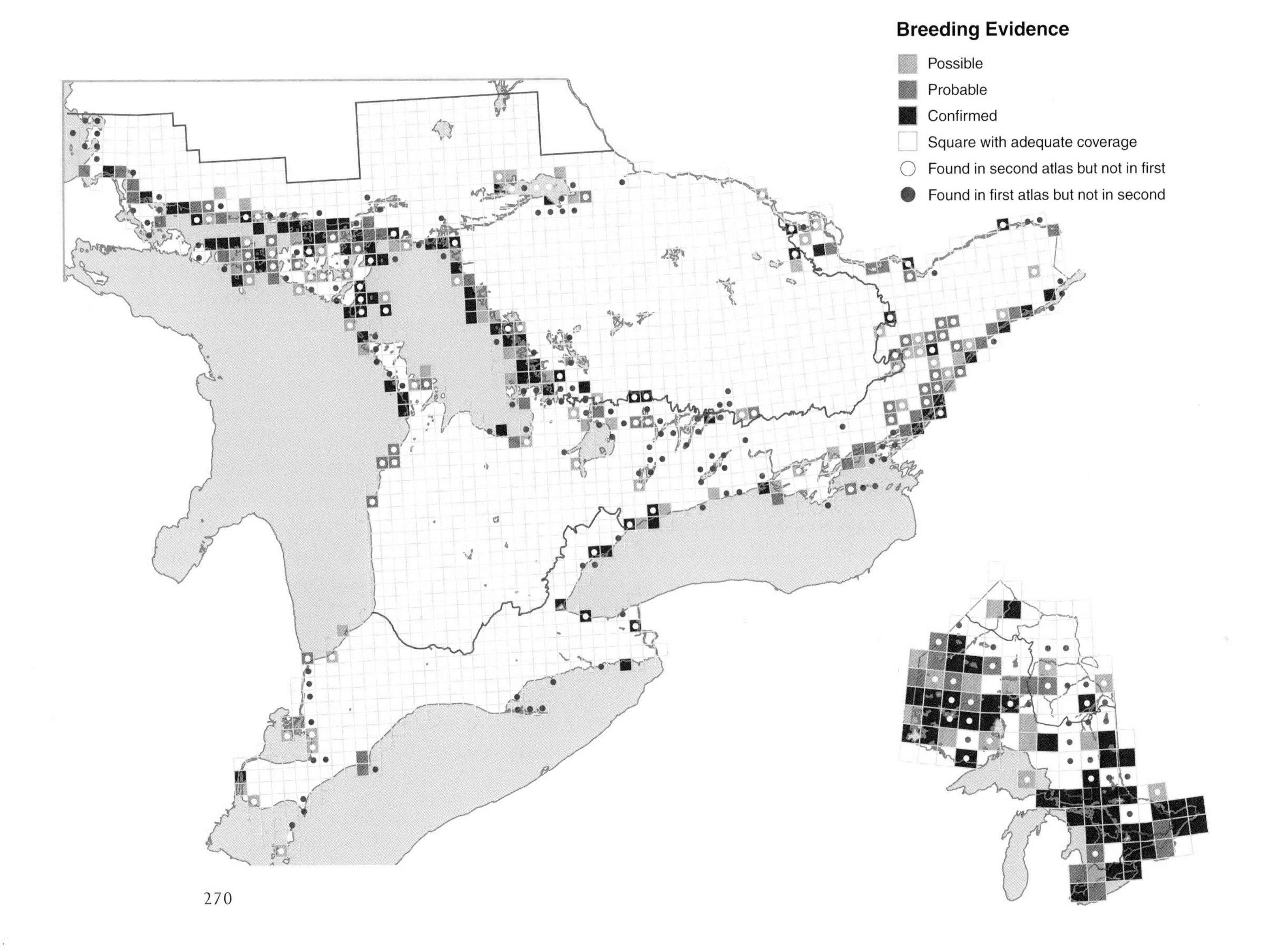

BREEDING EVIDENCE

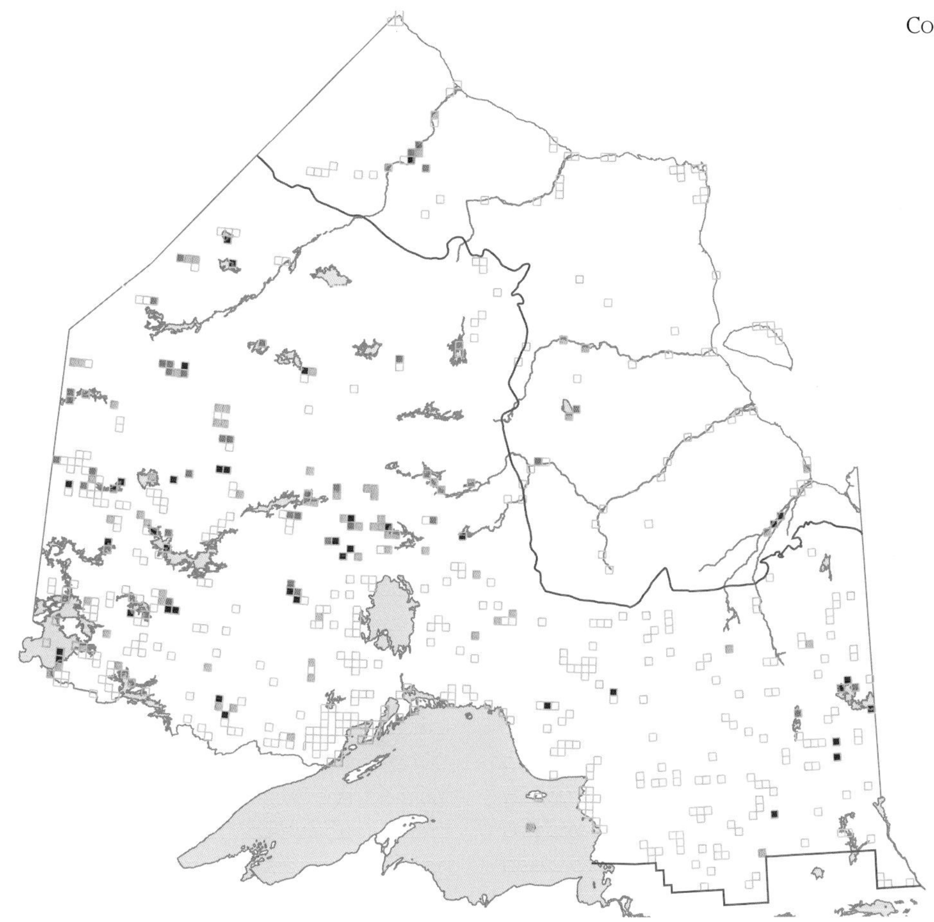

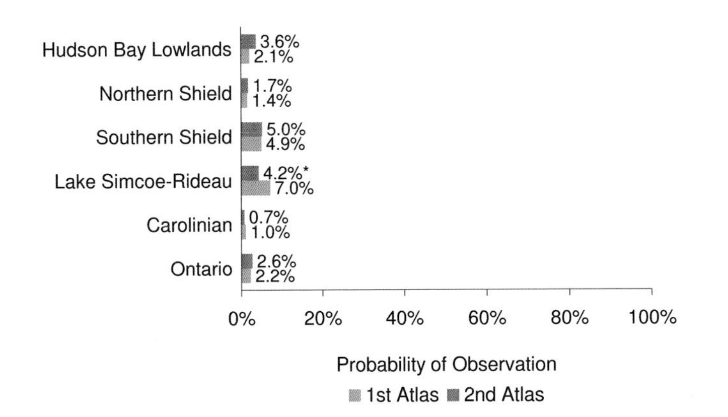

ing was reported in eight squares during the first atlas but only one square during the second atlas.

In Northern Ontario, away from the Great Lakes, atlas data indicate a marked increase in the number of breeding colonies reported in the northwest and a marked decrease in the northeast. The reasons for these changes are unknown.

Breeding biology: The Common Tern usually nests colonially, often with other waterbird species, but occasionally solitarily. In Ontario, it prefers to nest on low-lying islands or peninsulas with sand, gravel, shell, or cobble substrates and scattered vegetation as cover for nestlings. It also nests commonly at managed, artificial sites (e.g., anthropogenic islands and breakwalls, nesting rafts). It is a long-lived, socially monogamous bird; both sexes share parental care of the young (Moore 2002; Nisbet 2002). Terns arrive at breeding sites in Ontario in late April and initiate their three-egg clutches (range two to four) in mid- to late May. Eggs normally hatch 22-27 days after laying, and nestlings fledge 22-29 days after hatching (Nisbet 2002).

In Ontario, this species feeds almost exclusively on small fish captured by plunge-diving into shallow water, generally within 100 m of shore (Burness et al. 1994; Moore 2002). During the breeding season, adults usually forage within 20 km of nesting sites (average distances of 2-4 km, Moore 2002) and deliver single prey items to nestlings.

Abundance: Atlas breeding evidence data allow only a comparison of the number of squares in which the species was reported or confirmed, and point counts are not a good means of collecting data on the abundance of colonial species. However, decadal colonial waterbird nesting surveys conducted across the Canadian Great Lakes by the CWS can be used to track changes in abundance. These data show that the total number of Common Tern nests declined from over 7,600 nests in 1980 to less than 6,500 nests in 1990 (-19%), and to less than 4,100 nests in 1999 (-35%; -48% overall from 1980-1999, -2.4% per year; Blokpoel and Tessier 1993, 1996, 1997; CWS unpubl.). Declines occurred on all water bodies (Lake Huron, -48%; Detroit River, -97%; Lake Erie, -65%; Lake Ontario, -20%; St. Lawrence River, -38%). The population declines demonstrated on the Great Lakes could be indicative of a province-wide decline and are cause for concern. Reasons for nesting declines and colony abandonment include competition for nest space with earlier-breeding Ring-billed Gulls, fluctuating water levels, and changes in vegetation structure at traditional breeding colonies (Morris and Hunter 1976; Morris et al. 1992). – *Dave Moore and Chip Weseloh*

Arctic Tern

Sterne arctique

Sterna paradisaea

Mark Peck

The Arctic Tern has a circumpolar breeding distribution. In North America, it breeds from Alaska and the Canadian Arctic archipelago south in Canada to central James Bay, New Brunswick, and Nova Scotia, reaching the southern extent of breeding at 41° N in Massachusetts (Hatch 2002).

Distribution and population status: Evidence of breeding in Ontario was first established in 1940 at Fort Severn (Baillie 1961; Peck and James 1983) and subsequently in the vicinity of Cape Henrietta Maria, the lower Sutton and Winisk Rivers, and East Pen Island (Peck and James 1983). During the first atlas, the Arctic Tern was reported from 37 squares in 11 100-km blocks, primarily along the coast of Hudson Bay but as much as 80 km inland along the Severn and Winisk Rivers. Between atlases, further reports of nesting were received for the central Hudson Bay coast in the vicinity of the Shagamu and Little Shagamu Rivers (Wilson and McRae 1993) as well as Akimiski Strait, Akimiski Island, and Gullery Island (K.F. Abraham, pers. comm.).

Data from the second atlas indicate that the Arctic Tern is more widespread and abundant in the Hudson Bay Lowlands than suggested by the first atlas. It was reported in 145 squares in 20 100-km blocks, all in the northern Lowlands. This increase is more likely a reflection of increased low-level aerial surveys by OMNR and CWS than an increasing population. Its breeding distribution is now known to extend regularly 80-100 km inland from the Hudson Bay coast and may be more extensive, as documented records were received for the Winiskisis Channel (Winisk River) 250 km south of Hudson Bay and the Attawapiskat River near the Missisa and Muketei Rivers confluence over 200 km inland from James Bay. It reaches its greatest densities along the Hudson Bay coast and in the lower reaches of the major rivers, where it frequently nests in colonies. Densities inland and south along the James Bay coast generally appear to be lower. Evidence of breeding

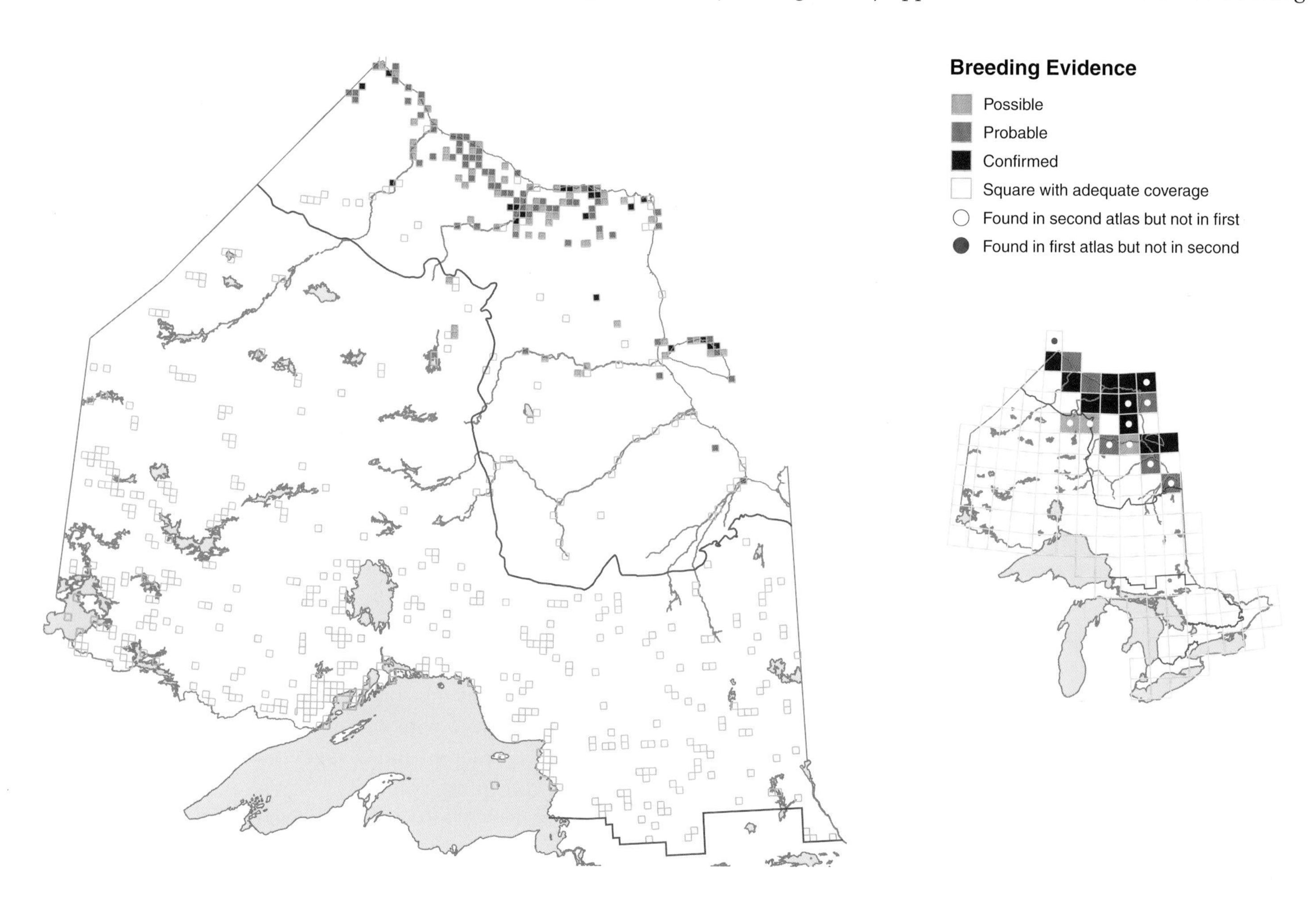

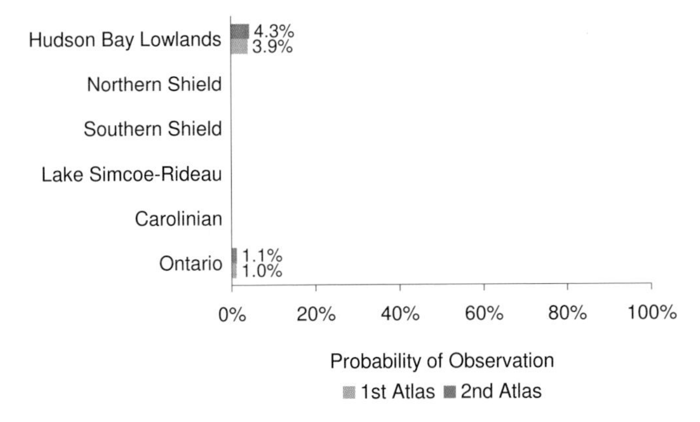

was found in three squares in northern James Bay between Cape Henrietta Maria and Hook Point, where its absence was noted during the first atlas. Aside from Akimiski Island, islands in Akimiski Strait, and Gullery Island, the species was reported in few squares between the Attawapiskat and Moose Rivers, and its status in southwestern James Bay remains unclear.

The Arctic Tern is evidently more prevalent in the northern Hudson Bay Lowlands, while the Common Tern is comparatively rare and local (Manning 1952; Wilson and McRae 1993; Jehl 2004), occurring well inland on larger lakes. In Ontario, the breeding ranges of the two rarely overlap. Both species were noted together during the second atlas in the Moose River estuary, about 200 km inland on the Attawapiskat River, and along the Severn River about 20 km south of the Fawn River confluence.

Breeding biology: The Arctic Tern arrives at breeding sites in the Hudson Bay Lowlands from late May to mid-June (Jehl 2004). Nesting is typically initiated within two weeks of arrival, but timing is largely dependent on the advancement of the season, occurring as early as mid-June or as late as the first week of July (Hatch 2002). In Ontario, it nests both singly and in colonies. In colonies, it nests on gravel-cobble bars in braided sections of larger rivers, on sand-gravel coastal islands and bars, in coastal salt marshes (K. Abraham, pers. comm.), and on grassy or gravel islands in small, near-coastal lakes and shallow tundra ponds. Less commonly, it nests inland from Hudson Bay and away from larger rivers on palsa islands in larger marshy-bordered taiga lakes, typically as isolated pairs but occasionally in loose "colonies" of three to four pairs. During the second atlas, colonies were documented along the lower reaches of the Kinushseo, Sutton, Winisk, Shagamu, and Severn Rivers, as well as in Akimiski Strait and on Akimiski and Gullery Islands.

Abundance: The Arctic Tern probably breeds in many or most squares within 100 km of the Hudson Bay coast and perhaps locally and less commonly farther inland. Its distribution and abundance southward along the James Bay coast is less clear, although it evidently nests locally south to the Moose River estuary. Higher densities and larger colonies (100-300 pairs) are known to occur in the lower Winisk River, on islands in the general vicinity of Cape Henrietta Maria, and on Gullery and other islands in the vicinity of Akimiski Island (pers. obs.; K. Abraham, pers. comm.). The provincial breeding population is likely in the order of several thousand pairs. – *Donald A. Sutherland*

A typical two-egg Arctic Tern clutch in a scrape nest on lichen heath. *Photo: Mark Peck*

Although the Arctic Tern nests predominantly near the coasts of Hudson and James Bays, inland habitats such as this rich wetland provided many scattered breeding records. *Photo: Mark Peck*

Forster's Tern

Sterne de Forster

Sterna forsteri

George K. Peck

One of two marsh-nesting terns that breed in Ontario, the Forster's Tern is generally associated with the large coastal marshes of the southwestern area of the province. Its distinctive hoarse, nasal call and silvery-white primaries and belly separate it from the more widespread Common Tern. The Forster's Tern is the only tern that is restricted almost entirely to North America. It breeds primarily in the Great Basin Desert and prairie potholes region of western North America, with scattered local populations elsewhere.

Distribution and population status: The Forster's Tern has a very limited breeding distribution and population in Ontario. It was reported from one or two squares each at Lake Simcoe, Long Point, and Rondeau Prov. Park, and from nine squares around Lake St. Clair, its main nesting area in Ontario. It was recorded in a single square in northern Ontario, on Lake of the Woods near Rainy River. This breeding distribution has probably not changed much in more than 100 years. In the late 1800s, the St. Clair Flats was the species' stronghold in Ontario (Morden and Saunders 1882; McIlwraith 1894), and that is still the case today. The species has occasionally nested in small numbers at Rondeau Prov. Park and Long Point, and, more recently, on Lake Simcoe, the only confirmed inland nesting area for this species in Ontario.

Within its limited range, the Forster's Tern was recorded in fewer squares in the second atlas than in the first. In the Carolinian region, it was found in just 15 squares in the second atlas, down from 24. Likewise, it was missing from two of the 100-km blocks near the Manitoba border in northwestern Ontario where it was reported in the first atlas. It was also not reported from the Point Pelee Nat. Park and Kettle Point areas where birds were previously recorded. Breeding was confirmed in 12 squares during the first atlas but only in nine in the second. Whether this decrease represents an actual trend is not clear. Although BBS data show no significant population

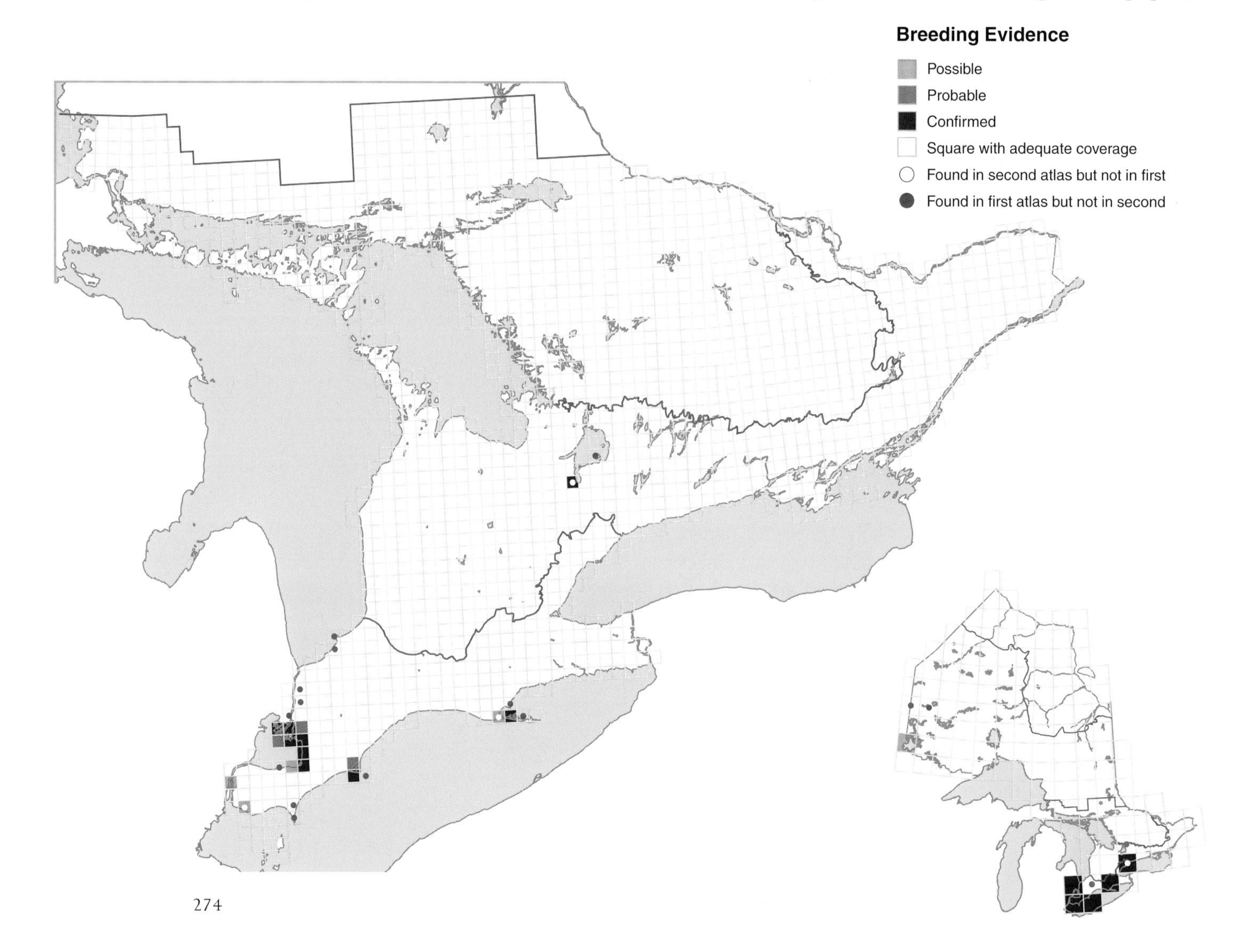

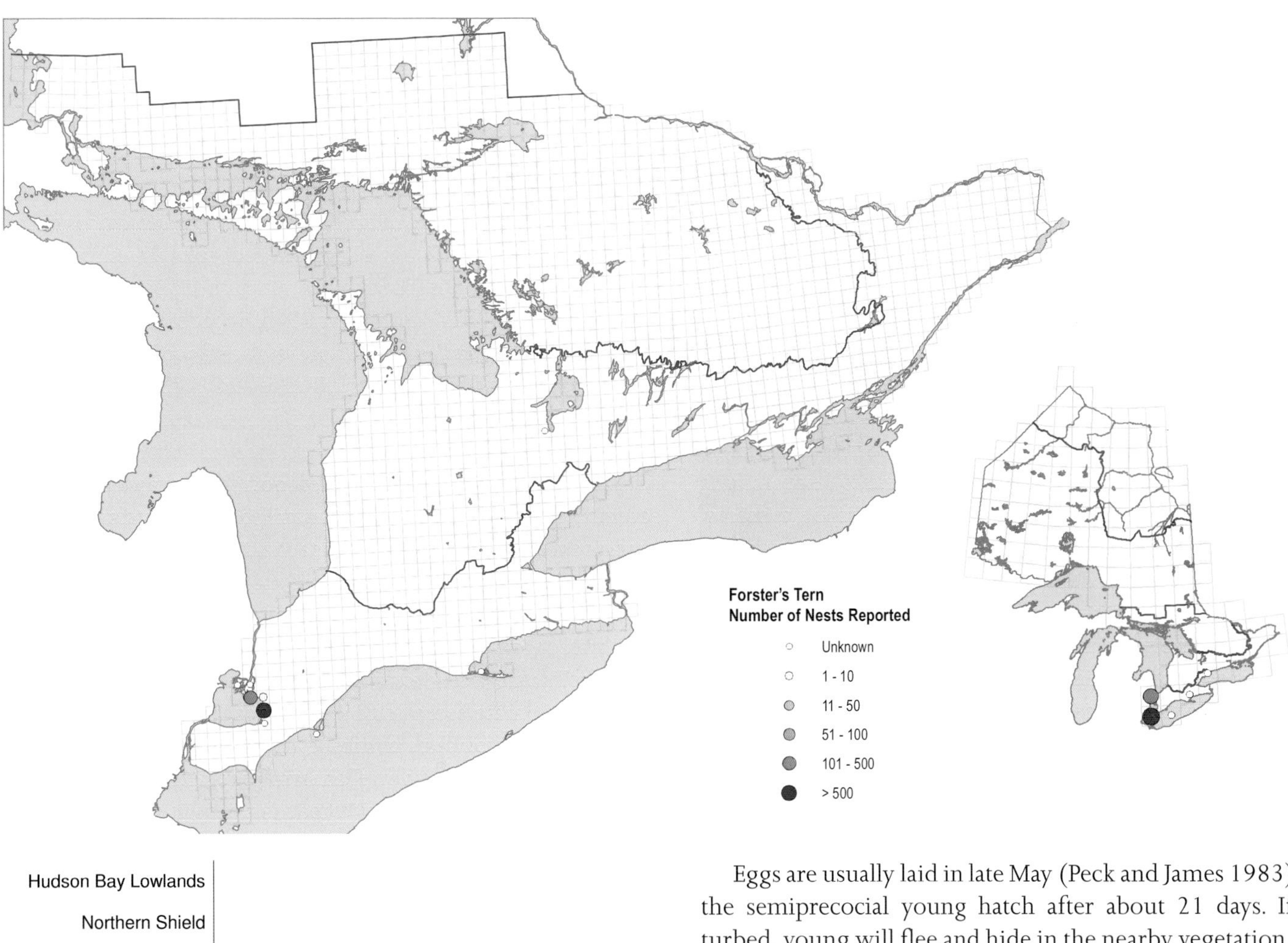

Hudson Bay Lowlands
Northern Shield
Southern Shield
Lake Simcoe-Rideau 0.1% 0.0%
Carolinian 3.8% 4.6%
Ontario 0.1% 0.1%
0% 20% 40% 60% 80% 100%
Probability of Observation
1st Atlas 2nd Atlas

changes, the survey is not well suited to sampling waterbirds. On the Great Lakes, the Forster's Tern has shown some susceptibility to toxic chemicals. A study in Green Bay, Lake Michigan, showed severe reproductive impairment and elevated contaminant levels in eggs and young (Kubiak et al. 1989). However, a more recent CWS survey at Walpole Island (Lake St. Clair) and Lake Simcoe showed that both Forster's and Black Terns had much lower contaminant levels, and there was no suggestion of reproductive impairment (Jermyn and Weseloh 2002). No explanation is currently available for the observed decrease between atlases in the number of squares with the species.

Breeding biology: In Ontario, the Forster's Tern nests in large coastal marshes, almost always in association with the Black Tern. Unlike the Black Tern, which is only loosely colonial, the Forster's Tern nearly always nests in fairly dense colonies, which may consist of 100 or more pairs. Colonies are vigorously defended from predators, including humans, by communal mobbing behaviour.

Eggs are usually laid in late May (Peck and James 1983), and the semiprecocial young hatch after about 21 days. If disturbed, young will flee and hide in the nearby vegetation. They remain in the marsh in the vicinity of the nest until fledged at four to five weeks (Hall 1988, 1989). Of the nine squares in which breeding was confirmed during the second atlas, four documented nests with eggs or young, while the highest evidence in the remainder consisted of adults carrying food or with fledged young.

Abundance: Great Lakes-wide surveys were conducted for Forster's Tern in 1991 and 2001 (Austen et al. 1996; Graham et al. 2002). The 1991 study reported 1,176 terns detected at 24 colonies, while the 2001 study reported 1,647 terns at 22 colonies (Graham et al. 2002). Both studies concluded that Lake St. Clair held nearly all the nesting Forster's Terns in Ontario. CWS surveyed the small colony at Cook's Bay on Lake Simcoe from 1996 to 1999, where the maximum number of nests in any year was nine in 1997 (C. Weseloh, unpubl. data).

As is the case elsewhere in the species' breeding range (McNicholl et al. 2001), colonies in Ontario are relatively unstable and ephemeral. For example, the Long Point colonies, which were first reported in 1976 and increased to over 200 pairs in the early 1980s, largely collapsed following subsequent record-high water levels on Lake Erie (J. McCracken, pers. comm.). – *Chip Weseloh*

Parasitic Jaeger

Labbe parasite

Stercorarius parasiticus

Ron Ridout

The Parasitic Jaeger is most frequently seen in Ontario as a migrant on the Great Lakes, where its aggressiveness and aerial acrobatics in pursuit of prey have awed bird watchers for years. Its plumage is highly variable, with light, dark, and intermediate morphs. The medium-sized species of the three jaegers, it has the most southern breeding range; it is a holarctic breeder extending from the high Arctic south into subarctic regions (Wiley and Lee 1999), extending south to Cape Henrietta Maria in Ontario. Where it coexists with the other jaeger species, it is usually the least numerous. Outside of North America, it may nest colonially, but on this continent it is a solitary nester.

Distribution and population status: The Parasitic Jaeger was first confirmed as a provincial breeding species in 1947 in the Cape Henrietta Maria area (Manning 1952). Peck and James (1983) thought that the species probably bred all along the Hudson Bay coast in small numbers. The first atlas generally supported this belief, as it was found scattered along the Hudson Bay coast between the Pen Islands and Cape Henrietta Maria.

During the second atlas, the Parasitic Jaeger was located only at the two extremes of Ontario's Hudson Bay coast. The primary breeding area is in the eastern portion of Polar Bear Prov. Park, specifically those 100-km blocks in the Cape Henrietta Maria area, with breeding evidence recorded in 17 squares. Breeding evidence was also reported in two squares near the Pen Islands in northwestern Ontario.

Around Cape Henrietta Maria, the frozen expanse of Hudson and James Bays and the associated cold temperatures create one of the most southerly maritime tundra regions in the world. The subarctic tundra, weather conditions and flora typical of more northern arctic regions, and the presence of a large Snow Goose colony provide ideal conditions to support a consistent Parasitic Jaeger population (Manning 1952).

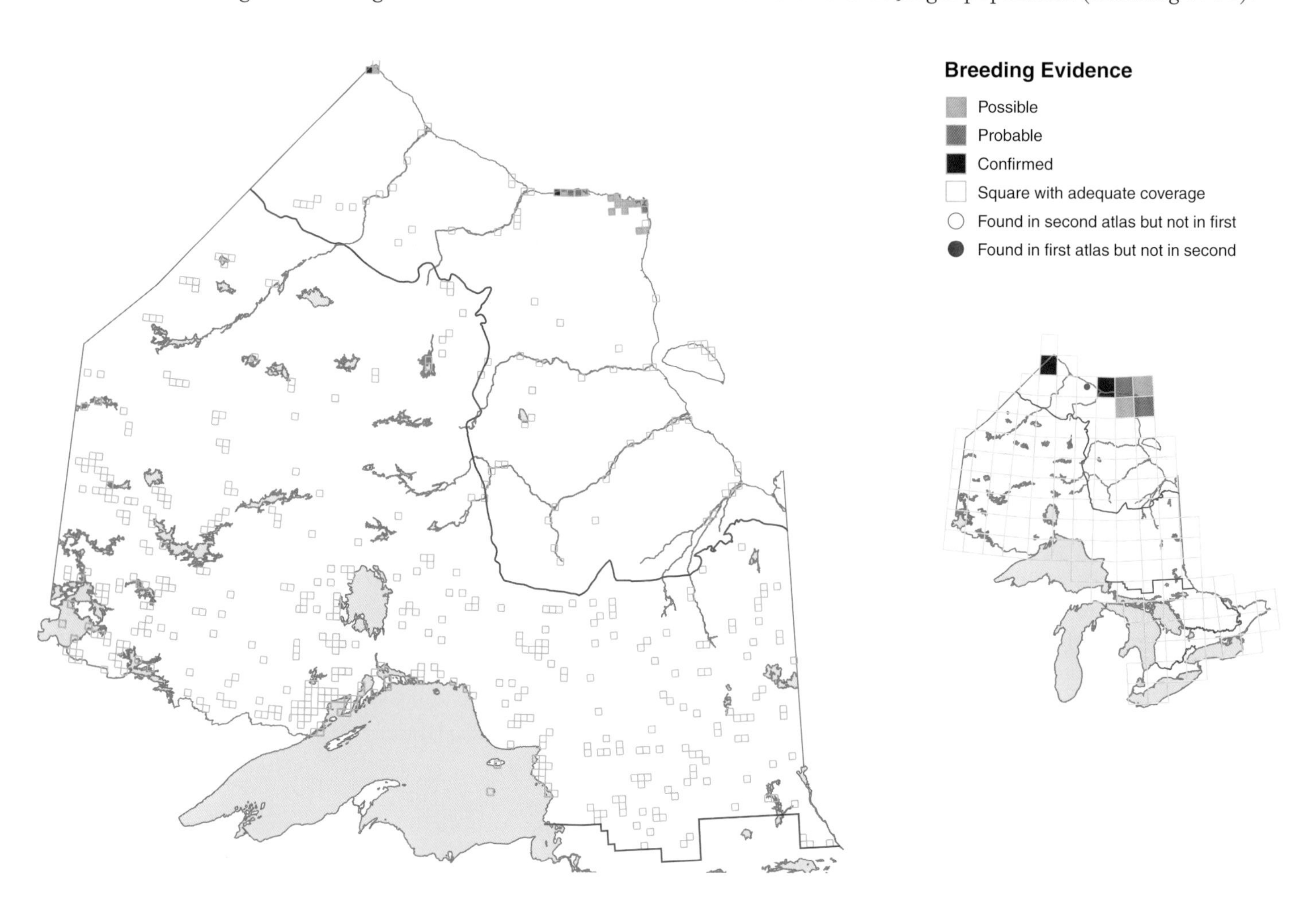

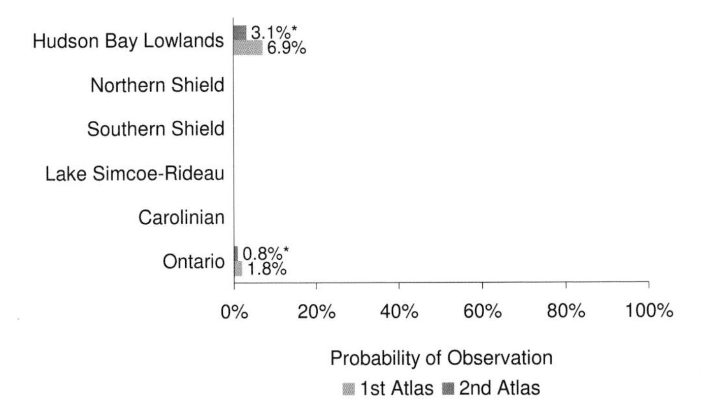

Between atlases, the probability of observation of the species declined significantly by 55% in the Hudson Bay Lowlands. The reason for the decline is unknown.

Breeding biology: Adults return to nesting areas in late May and quickly establish territories. These may be as large as 30 km², making detection difficult. The entire territory is protected from conspecifics, while the area within approximately 100 m of the nest is vigorously defended against all large bird and mammal species. Territories are usually widespread, and spacing between active nests can be 1-7 km (Martin and Barry 1978). Nests are usually on slight rises within areas of wet tundra, often adjacent to water bodies. Nests are regularly attended by one or both adults, and only rarely are both adults absent simultaneously (Wiley and Lee 1999). While hunting, the Parasitic Jaeger often flies only 1–3 m above the tundra in search of prey (Andersson and Götmark 1980), generally confounding detection at a distance. Most hunting takes place on the edge of the territory and can be 3–5 km from an active nest (Parmelee et al. 1967; Maher 1974; Taylor 1974).

The Parasitic Jaeger feeds predominantly on birds, especially passerines, but eggs and young of shorebirds and eggs of many other larger species such as geese, ptarmigan, ducks, and loons are consumed. The Lapland Longspur is the most important species in its diet, and the ranges of the two species overlap extensively. Unlike the other jaeger species, it is not dependent on lemming populations for successful breeding and is unaffected by microtine cycles (Campbell 1990; Wiley and Lee 1999). Studies conducted in the Arctic found Parasitic Jaeger nests to be concentrated near goose colonies (Martin and Barry 1978). Near the Cape, a large Snow Goose colony spreads across the lowland region, and a smaller Snow Goose colony was established in the last 20 years at West Pen Island. Most of the current breeding evidence was obtained near these two colonies.

The Parasitic Jaeger's spacing and foraging behaviours can make locating and confirming this species difficult. However, once an observer approaches within 100 m (Wiley and Lee 1999) of the nest, the adults regularly engage in conspicuous distraction displays, occasionally striking intruders, and so nests are easily located.

Abundance: Detections during point counts (averaging 0.14 birds/25 point counts in the Hudson Bay Lowlands) were too low to construct a relative abundance map. In other locations within the Canadian Arctic, breeding density ranges between 0.03-0.04 pairs/km² (Parmelee et al. 1967; Taylor 1974). The Ontario density is probably lower. The Parasitic Jaeger continues to be a rare breeder confined to tundra habitat along the Hudson Bay coast. – *Tyler Hoar*

Nests are shallow depressions sparsely lined with fine grasses, lichens, or willow leaves. Clutch size is typically one or two eggs, and rarely three. *Photo: Mark Peck*

Nests are typically located on hummocks in areas of flat, wet tundra, often near lakes or other water bodies. Radar Site 415, Polar Bear Prov. Park, 26 June 1970. *Photo: George K. Peck*

Rock Pigeon

Pigeon biset

Columba livia

George K. Peck

The Rock Pigeon is one of our more interesting species because of its history, breeding biology, and extreme familiarity. Native to Eurasia and North Africa, it has been introduced to every continent except Antarctica. Although it has been present in North America for 400 years, ornithologists long refused to acknowledge it. It did not appear on checklists until the 1950s, and was not recorded regularly on CBCs until the 1970s. The Rock Pigeon shuns extensively forested areas (explaining its virtual absence in the Algonquin Highlands) and is most abundant in agricultural and urban areas. Much of its distribution may be explained by its diet, as it feeds almost exclusively on plant seeds. Corn is its most important food item, followed by other cultivated grains.

Distribution and population status: Since its introduction, the Rock Pigeon has probably always been common in urban and agricultural areas of Ontario. During the first atlas, it was nearly ubiquitous in the Carolinian and Lake Simcoe-Rideau regions where there are extensive agricultural and urban areas, and it occurred along major highway corridors and in population centres in the Southern Shield region. In the north, distribution was limited to developed or agricultural areas near highways, the Clay Belt, Sault Ste. Marie and Thunder Bay, and agricultural areas of western Rainy River District.

There was no significant difference in the probability of observation of the Rock Pigeon in the province as a whole between the two atlases. However, there are regional differences, with a significant decline in the Carolinian region and significant increases in the Lake Simcoe-Rideau, Southern Shield, and Northern Shield regions. Notable increases occurred on Manitoulin Island, where the Rock Pigeon was formerly heavily persecuted (Nicholson 1981), and in the Southern Shield except for the Algonquin Highlands. The most northern record was from Moosonee, which appears to be the first record from the Hudson Bay Lowlands (James 1991;

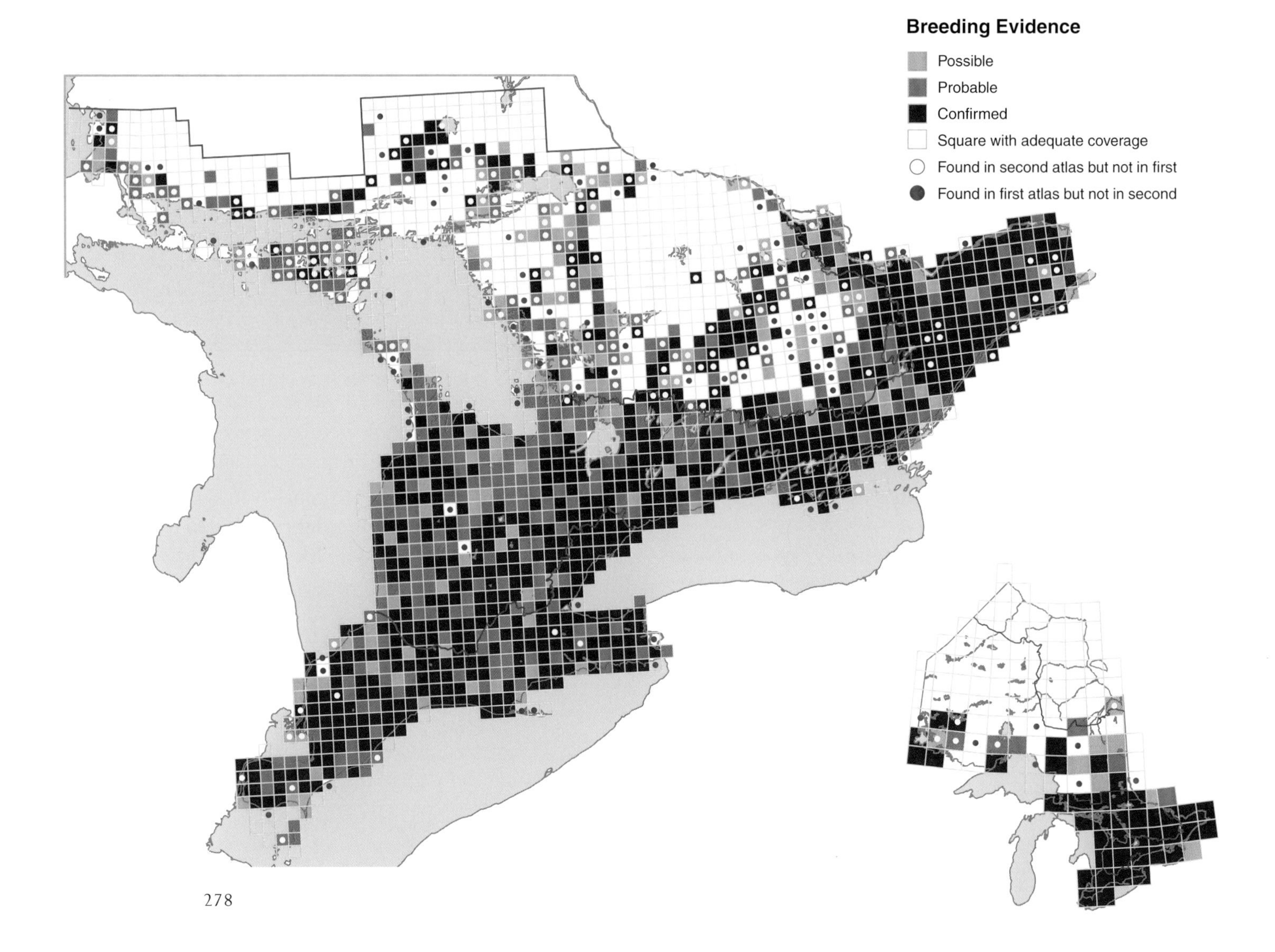

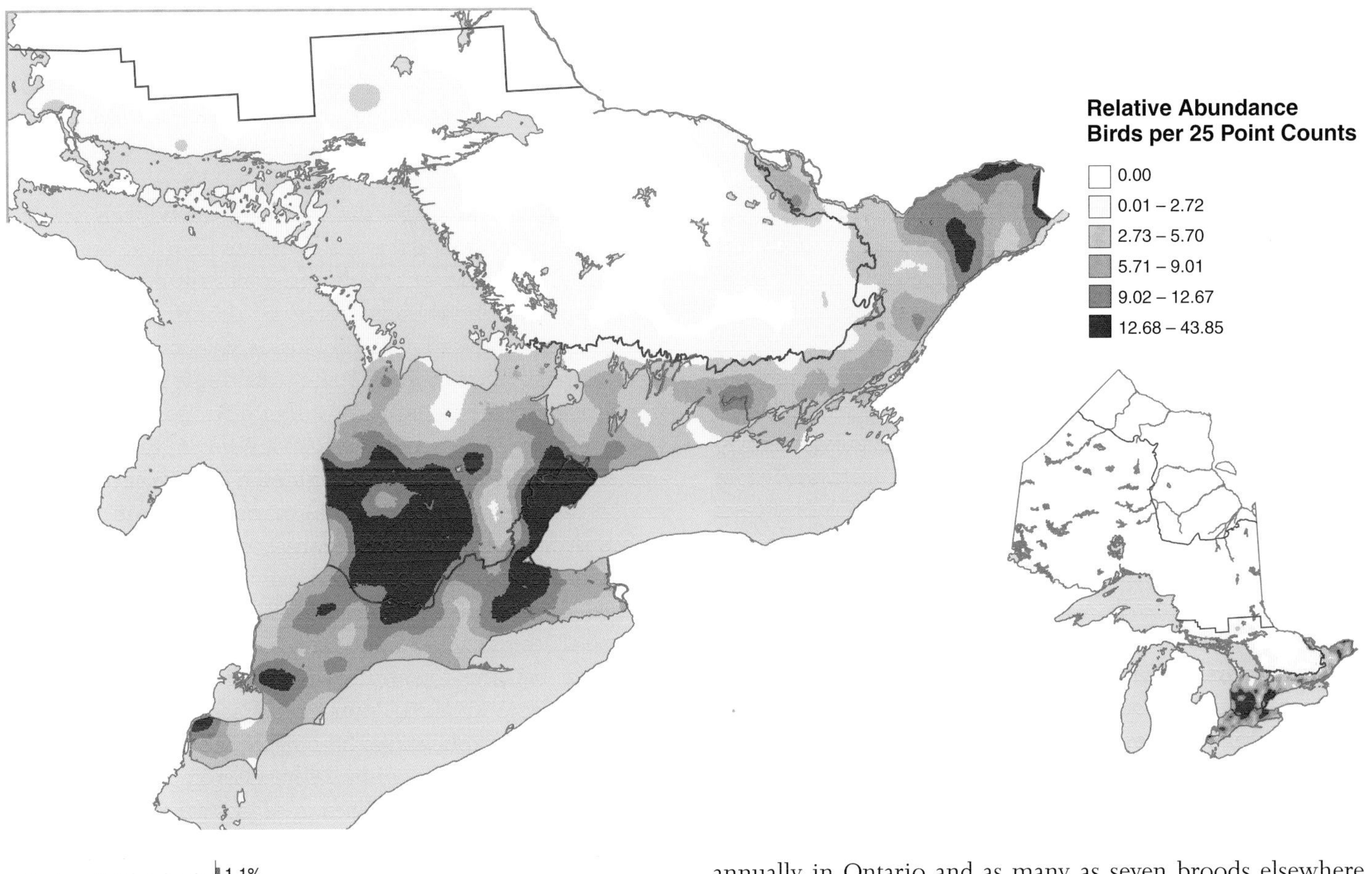

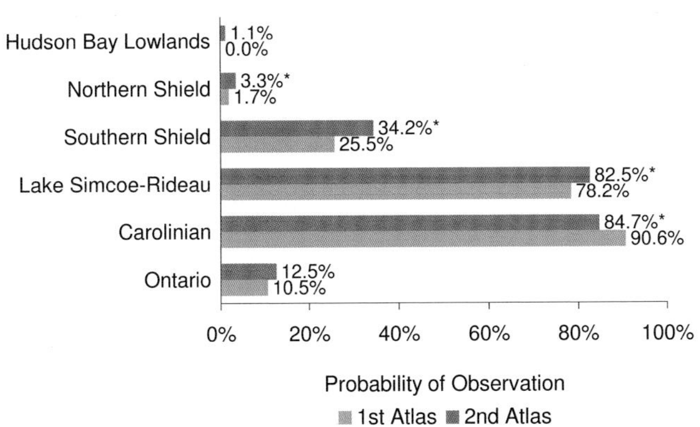

Wilson and McRae 1993). It is likely that this record represents an errant racing pigeon.

Consistent with atlas results, BBS data indicate that southern off-Shield populations are declining, while populations are increasing adjacent to Georgian Bay, in northeastern Ontario, and in the Sault Ste. Marie and Thunder Bay areas. The overall Ontario population is stable, with a nonsignificant increase of 0.9% per year since 1968 (Downes et al. 2005).

Breeding biology: Most nests are in or on buildings or artificial features such as bridges. In cities, this bird nests mainly on buildings with ledges or external ornaments, in steeples, belfries, and parking garages and under bridges. In agricultural areas, it nests in barns and around grain elevators (Peck and James 1983).

Nests are conspicuous and easy to find, but most nesting occurs outside the peak atlassing period. In Toronto, the peak number of nests occurs from December to April (Ewins and Bazely 1995). The species, however, nests throughout the year in Ontario. Pairs have been documented raising four broods annually in Ontario and as many as seven broods elsewhere (Peck and James 1983; Johnston 1992).

Nesting may occur in loose colonies, so the presence of large numbers of birds often leads to the discovery of nests. A high percentage of the population does not breed; in some areas, only 27% of birds nest (Murton et al. 1972). Counts may therefore overestimate numbers of breeding birds.

Urban Rock Pigeons spend their lifetime within a very small area. In Montreal, 90% remained within a radius of 500 m, while in England 90% remained within 100 m (Murton et al. 1972; Lévesque and McNeil 1986). Home ranges of agricultural birds are much larger. Flights of 10 km to feed appear to be common. Birds observed in cities are probably within their breeding square, while agricultural birds may be more wide ranging. Due to the ease of detecting this species, the atlas map is an accurate depiction of its breeding distribution, although the presence of racing pigeons may confound the results somewhat.

Abundance: Point counts revealed that abundance was greatest south of the Shield, but some areas exhibited much higher density than others. These occurred in the urban centres of Toronto and Hamilton and the agricultural landscape from London to Kitchener north to about Goderich and Shelburne. Densities in other agricultural areas, including the extreme southwest, were much lower. The highest densities in agricultural areas correspond primarily to those counties in which corn is the most common crop (cf. Ontario Ministry of Agriculture, Food, and Rural Affairs 2006). The Rock Pigeon continues to be common to very common south of the Shield and locally uncommon to common farther north. – *Al Sandilands*

Eurasian Collared-Dove

Tourterelle turque

Streptopelia decaocto

George K. Peck

The Eurasian Collared-Dove is an Old World species that is among the most recent successful introductions to the North American avifauna. Formerly exclusive to the Indian subcontinent, it expanded into Turkey and the Balkans in the 1600s. In the 20th century, it expanded farther westward through Europe, reaching Britain and Scandinavia by the mid-1950s and Portugal by the mid-1970s. In the last two centuries, its range also expanded eastward with introductions into China and Japan (Romagosa 2002).

It was not known to be present in North America during the first atlas but probably occurred in southern Florida at that time. In the mid-1970s, it was imported by the aviculture trade to the Bahamas and Guadeloupe, where it was soon intentionally released. By the early 1980s, it likely moved unassisted from the Bahamas to south Florida. Since the Eurasian Collared-Dove closely resembles the Ringed Turtle-Dove (a long-domesticated form of the African Collared-Dove), already present in south Florida, it went unnoticed for several years (Banks et. al. 2006). By the mid-1980s, ornithologists realized this rapidly spreading dove was the Eurasian Collared-Dove (Smith and Kale 1986; White 1986).

The species now breeds throughout much of the southeastern US and the northern Caribbean. It is common and uniformly distributed in Florida, Georgia, and the Gulf Coast from Alabama to Texas and is locally common in the Carolinas, Tennessee, Arkansas, Illinois, Missouri, Kansas, Oklahoma, Nebraska, Montana, Colorado, and New Mexico. Small numbers have become established as far north as New Jersey, Pennsylvania, Wisconsin, Minnesota, Saskatchewan, Alberta, and British Columbia, and as far west as California (Romagosa 2002; Hudon 2005; Toochin 2006). It was first confirmed breeding in Canada in the summer of 2002 in both Mortlach and Eastend, Saskatchewan (Houston and Luterbach 2004; R. Smith, pers. comm.), and Red Deer, Alberta (Hudon 2005).

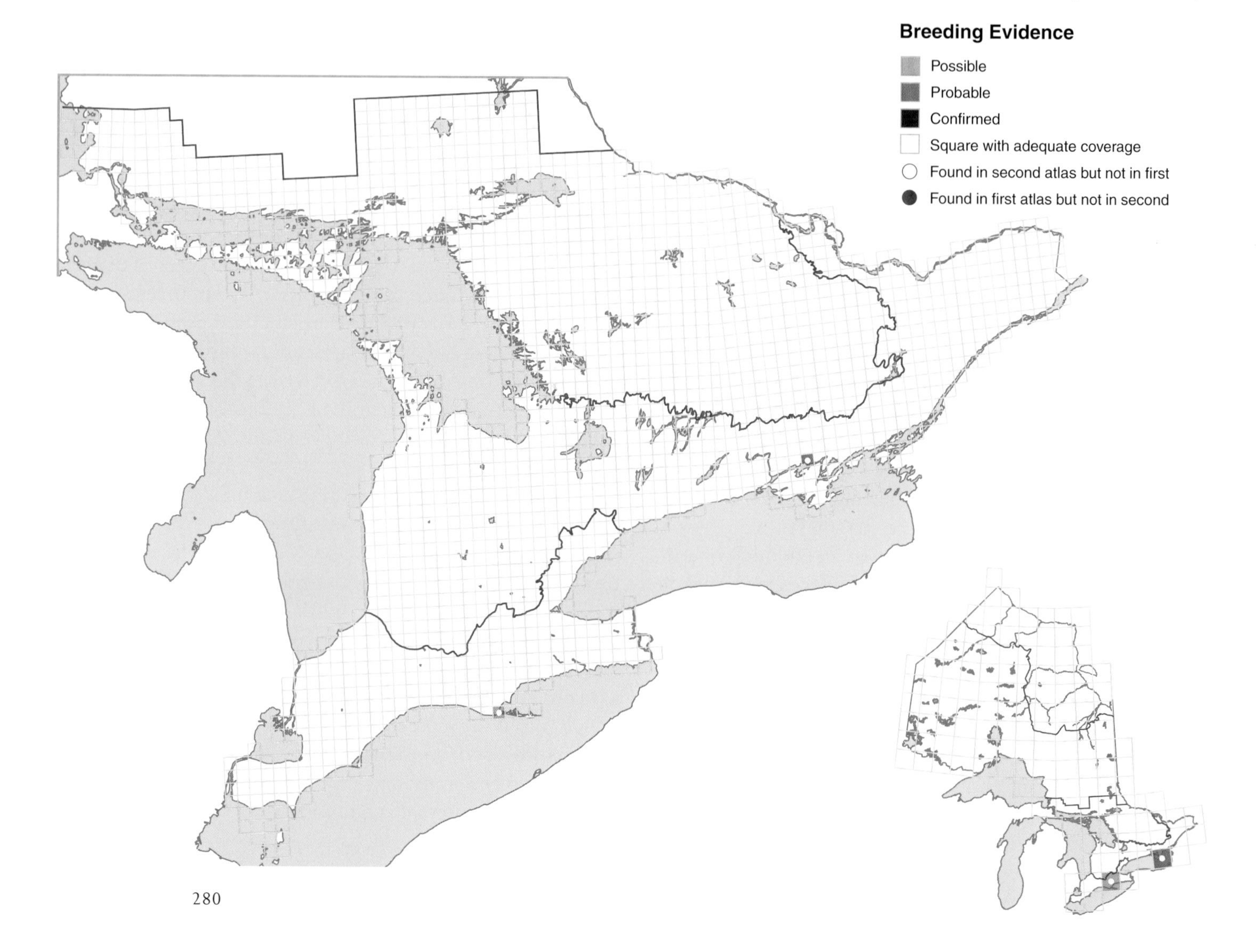

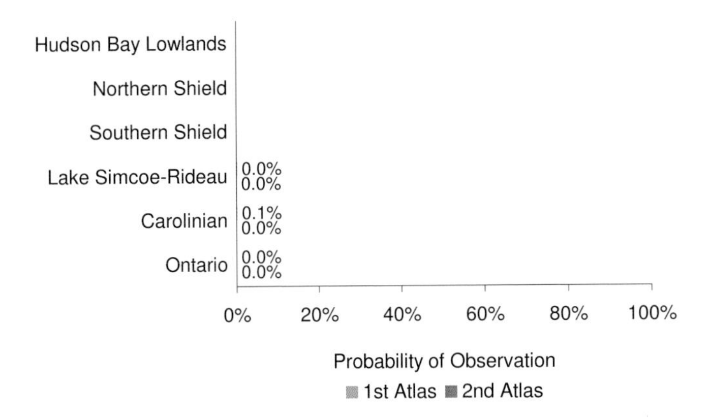

The Eurasian Collared-Dove is primarily found in suburban, urban, and agricultural areas where foraging, roosting, and nesting sites are easily found. It is less abundant in city centres and absent from densely forested areas. It commonly feeds in areas of grain storage or spillage, near livestock yards, and at bird feeders (Romagosa 2002).

Distribution and population status: The first record of the Eurasian Collared-Dove for Ontario and Canada was a single bird found at Pittock Lake in Oxford Co. on 25 July and 4 September 1993 (Dobos 1999). However, subsequent expansion into Ontario has been unusually slow. The Ontario Bird Records Committee (OBRC) accepted only seven records for Ontario by the end of this atlas (Crins 2005, 2006); all of these involved individual birds found in southern Ontario.

Assessment of the Eurasian Collared-Dove's status in Ontario is complicated by its similarity to the highly variable and commonly released Ringed Turtle-Dove, and by the potential for both to hybridize (Smith 1987). The two are readily separated by the colour of the undertail coverts and primaries, tail pattern, and voice (Blackshaw 1988). Although the three-note call of the Eurasian Collared-Dove is easily distinguished from the two-note call of the Ringed Turtle-Dove, hybrids may use both call types, making heard-only records problematic (Romagosa and McEneaney 2000).

Breeding evidence for the Eurasian Collared-Dove was found in only two squares in southern Ontario during this atlas. In the spring of 2002, one was heard calling in suitable habitat near Long Point Prov. Park. Another observed 5-31 May 2003 in Marysville, Hastings Co., was accepted by the OBRC (Crins 2004). Although there was no indication that this presumed male bird had attracted a mate, it gave advertising calls incessantly, frequently performed wing-clapping display flights, and was observed gathering nesting material on 31 May.

Breeding biology: The Eurasian Collared-Dove vigorously defends its territory against rivals and conspecifics. Males tirelessly give advertising calls for prospective mates and perform their wing-clapping display flights from high perches. Pairs perform mutual preening and courtship bowing and pre-copulatory displays, often at the nest site. Nests are commonly located in obvious sites, often on built structures. Nestlings beg noisily and remain dependent near the nest for several weeks after fledging. Pairs may have multiple, overlapping broods, occasionally re-using nests (Romagosa 2002). Most aspects of the species' breeding biology make it easily detected.

The bird reported from Marysville, Hastings Co., often sang and performed display flights from this church steeple (Glenn Coady, pers. comm.). *Photo: Donald A. Sutherland*

Abundance: This exceptionally rare species in Ontario remains on the OBRC Review List throughout the province. It has yet to be confirmed as a breeding species in Ontario. However, with little to limit its spread across North America, it seems likely that it will be a permanent resident bird in Ontario by the time the next atlas begins. – *Glenn Coady*

Mourning Dove

Tourterelle triste

Zenaida macroura

George K. Peck

The repetitive, mournful song of the Mourning Dove is readily identifiable by birders and non-birders alike. A common feeder and garden bird, it is also one of the most popular and widely hunted game birds across much of the US, although it is not hunted in Ontario. Adults feed the nestlings crop milk, a characteristic unique to doves and pigeons.

With a broad North American distribution, the Mourning Dove breeds from British Columbia to the Maritime Provinces and south through the lower 48 US states (Mirarchi and Baskett 1994). It is typically associated with open habitats, where it feeds on seeds on the ground and nests in a variety of coniferous and deciduous trees. Wintering typically occurs throughout the nesting range (Armstrong 1977).

Distribution and population status: The Mourning Dove has been increasing in numbers and expanding its range in Ontario for several decades (Armstrong and Noakes 1983; Kelling 2006). This trend continued between the two atlas periods. Although there were no significant changes in the probability of observation in the province as a whole and in the two most southerly regions, the species increased significantly by 71% in the Southern Shield region. There was a significant northward shift in range from predominantly settled and agricultural areas south of the Shield to include areas in the Southern Shield region. The virtually continuous range of the Mourning Dove includes the Carolinian and Lake Simcoe-Rideau regions and now the southern part of the Southern Shield, but excludes much of the largely forested Algonquin Highlands. Its range also expanded slightly in the northern part of the Southern Shield and the adjacent Northern Shield. It is still very rare in the Hudson Bay Lowlands, where it is primarily a non-breeding vagrant. Most records there of possible and probable breeding were associated with remote communities such as Attawapiskat and Moosonee, where a small pop-

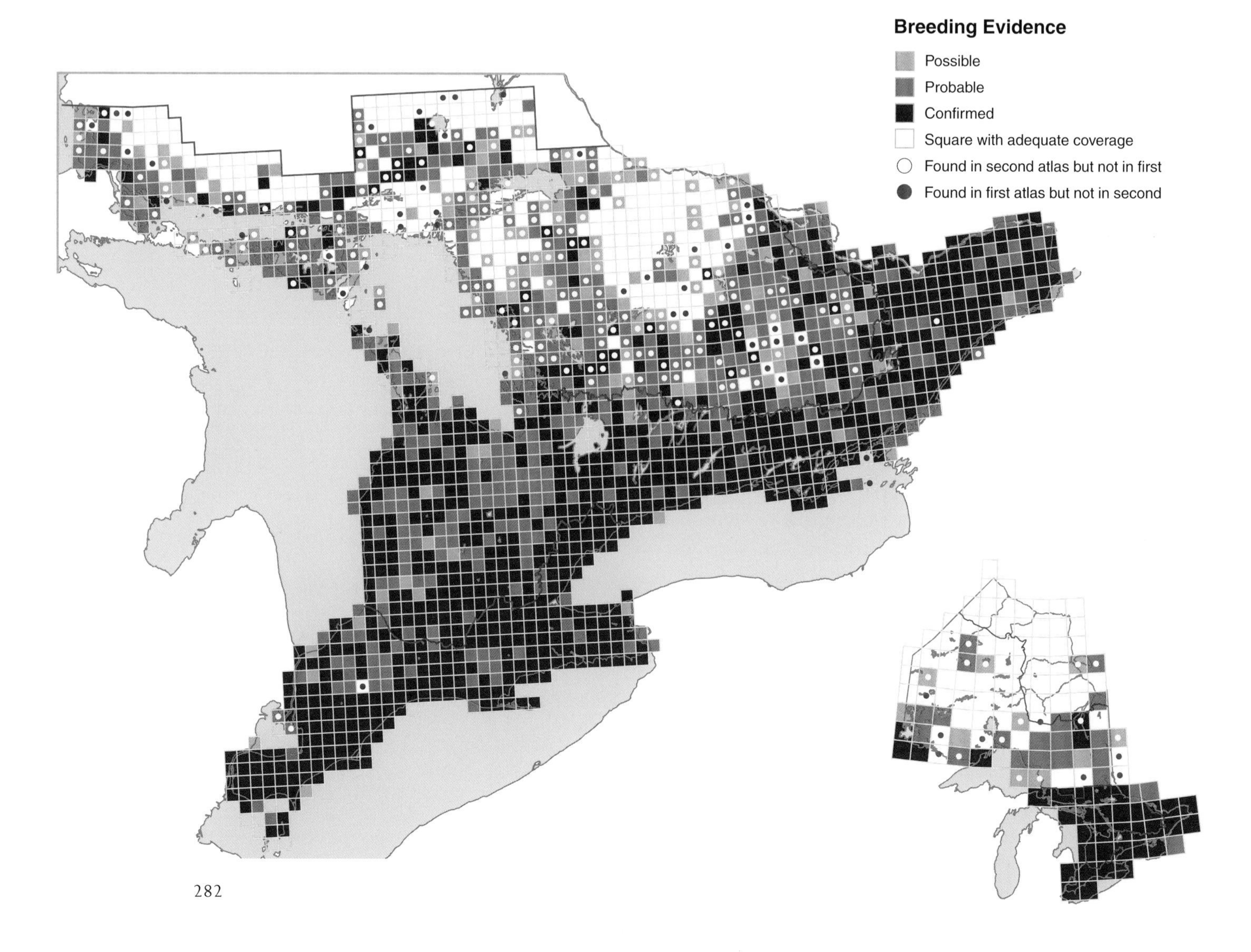

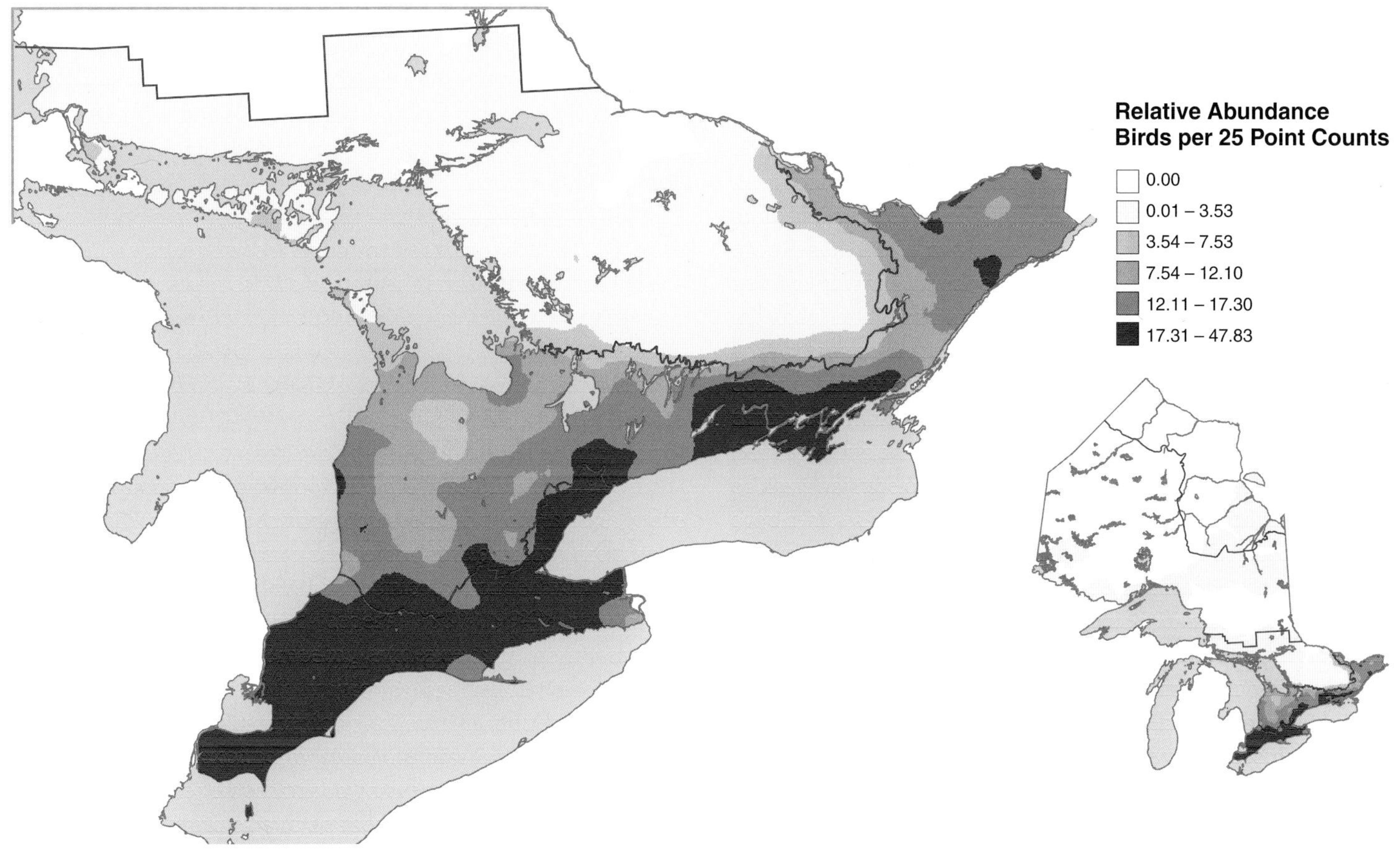

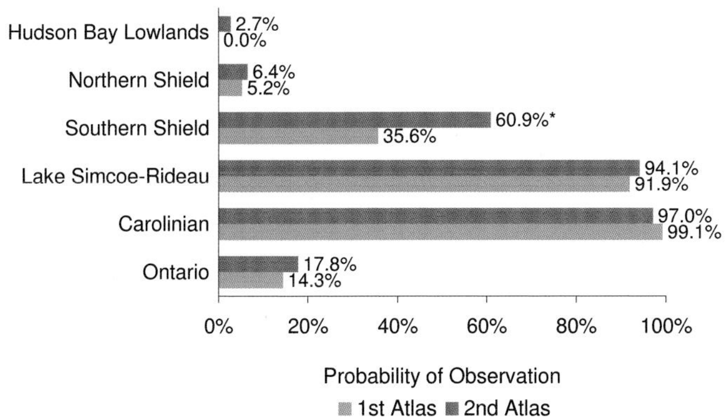

ulation has been expanding since the first atlas.

Typically an open country bird (Peck and James 1983), the Mourning Dove appears to be moving into areas where forested habitat dominates, probably due to milder winters and increasing numbers of bird feeders.

Breeding biology: Breeding evidence is relatively easy to observe, due to the Mourning Dove's readily identifiable breeding song, distinctive long-tailed silhouette, and attraction to open areas such as power transmission wires for perching and roadsides for obtaining gravel. It typically raises more than one brood and often nests several times during the breeding season, which can extend in Ontario from March through early October (Peck and James 1983, 1994), increasing opportunities for observation and breeding confirmation. Fledged young and family groups are quite visible, with fledglings generally remaining within 100 m of the nest until they are about a month old (Mirarchi and Baskett 1994).

The Mourning Dove is not a colonial nester, although it can nest in high densities in traditional nesting areas with abundant nesting habitat (pers. obs.). The flimsy twig nests are often conspicuously located on exposed branches and crotches of trees, making brooding adults quite visible. Verification of nest contents is further aided by the relatively low placement of nests and the often visible clutch of two conspicuous white eggs. The ease of detecting this species resulted in breeding being confirmed for a relatively high 50% of squares, suggesting that the distribution map is likely accurate.

Abundance: Although traditionally a migrant, in recent decades the Mourning Dove has overwintered in increasing numbers in Ontario and expanded its winter range northward (Armstrong and Noakes 1983). These tendencies appear related to the trend towards shorter, milder winters, and increased food availability through increased agricultural acreage in corn and an expanded network of bird feeders. The abundance of the species in Ontario has increased significantly at the rate of approximately 13% annually from 1977 to 2001 (Leblanc et al. 2007). BBS showed similar trends, with an approximately three-fold increase in abundance since the early 1980s, continuing a trend that preceded the first atlas.

Despite its expanded range into the Southern Shield, the Mourning Dove is still most abundant in the Carolinian region, with an average of 26.0 birds/25 point counts, followed by the Lake Simcoe-Rideau region with 13.8 birds/25 point counts. Highest abundance was correlated with the predominantly settled and agricultural landscape of southwestern Ontario and the north shore of Lake Ontario. The Mourning Dove has increased its range and population steadily for the past two decades and longer, and this trend is expected to continue. – *Ted (E.R.) Armstrong*

Yellow-billed Cuckoo

Coulicou à bec jaune
Coccyzus americanus

Tania & Jim Thomson

Ontario's two cuckoo species share several similar traits. They use a wide variety of habitats for breeding because local abundance of their favourite foods may be more important than habitat. Both prefer to eat hairy and spiny caterpillars such as the Fall Webworm, Gypsy Moth, and Forest Tent Caterpillar, prey shunned by most other birds. Both cuckoos are occasionally parasitic when food is abundant, laying their eggs in nests of their own species and others. The most common host is the other cuckoo species, the Black-billed Cuckoo (Preble 1957; Nolan and Thompson 1975; Hughes 1999).

The Yellow-billed Cuckoo breeds in Canada only in southern Ontario and extreme southern Québec. In the US, it breeds mainly from the midwestern states eastward to the Atlantic seaboard, as far south as the Yucatan Peninsula in Mexico and the West Indies (Hughes 1999).

Distribution and population status: The Yellow-billed Cuckoo has never been a common breeder in Ontario. Baillie and Harrington (1936) considered it moderately common, but only in the extreme southwest. At that time, it also ranged north to Parry Sound Dist. and possibly southern Algoma Dist. and Renfrew Co., but it was rare everywhere except in the Lake Erie area. During the first atlas, it was rare to uncommon except south and west of London and in the Kingston vicinity. It was confined primarily to the area south and east of the Shield, with very few records on the southern Shield. During this atlas, there was no substantial change in the distribution of the Yellow-billed Cuckoo in the province. However, despite no overall significant change in the probability of observation between the two atlases in the province as a whole, there were significant regional changes. The probability of observation declined by 28% in the Lake Simcoe-Rideau region but increased by 89% in the Southern Shield. Such regional changes may be a reflection of the irruptive nature of the species in response to outbreaks of the major forest insect pests.

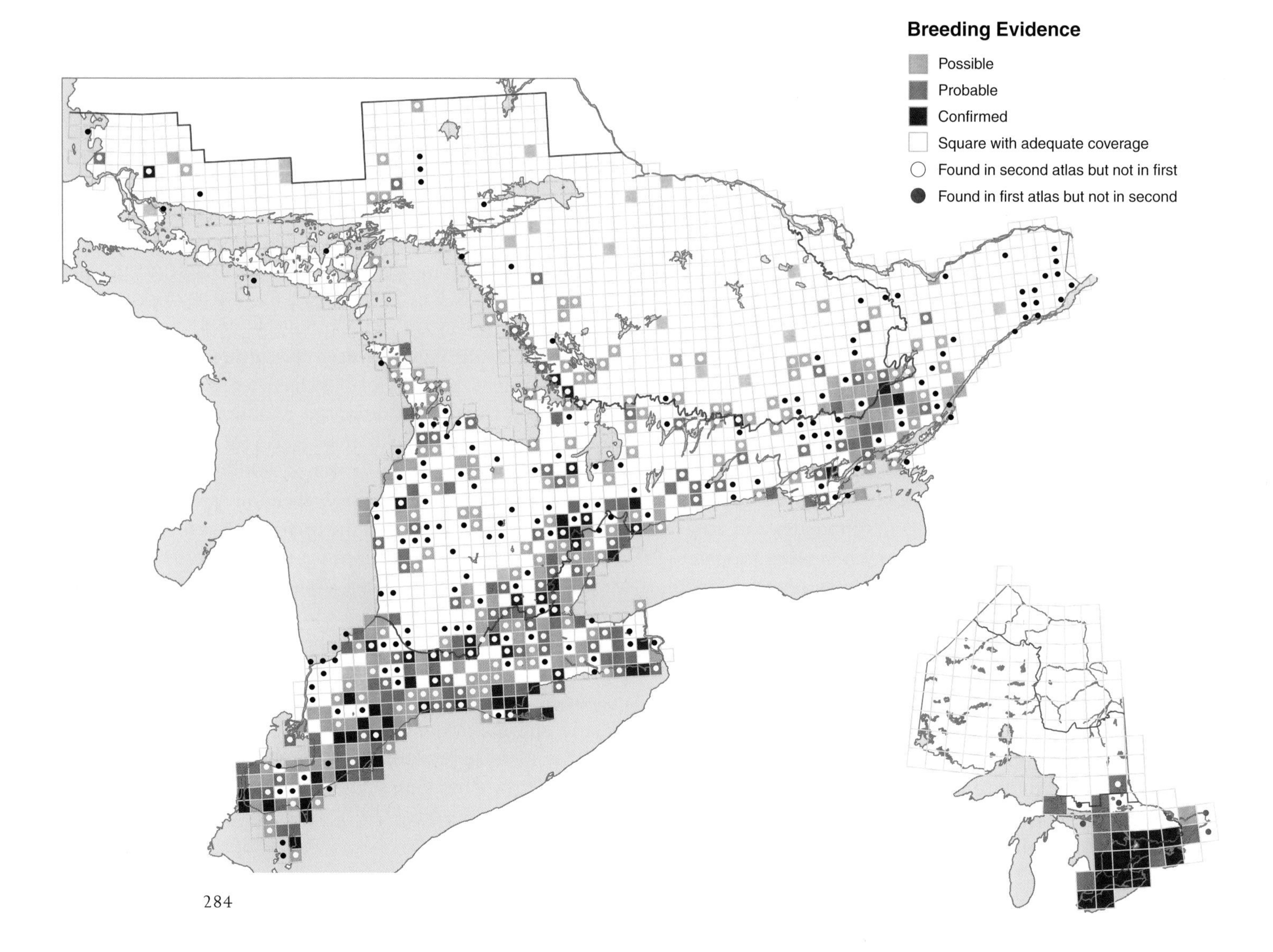

BREEDING EVIDENCE

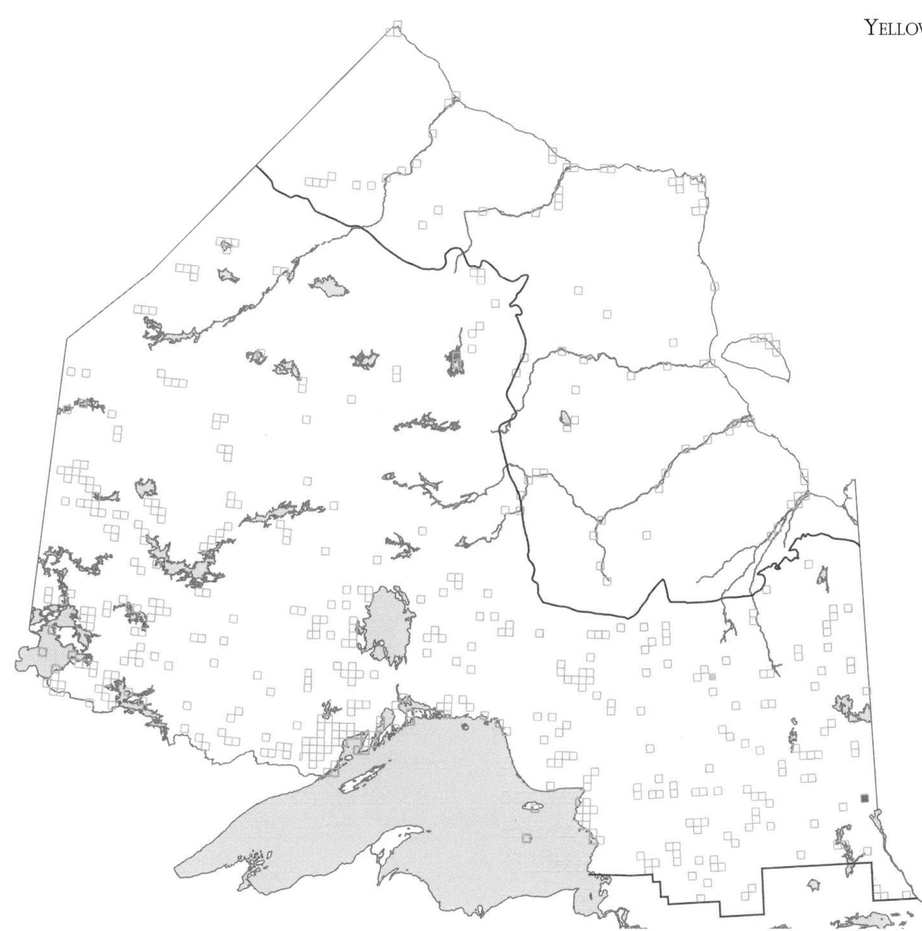

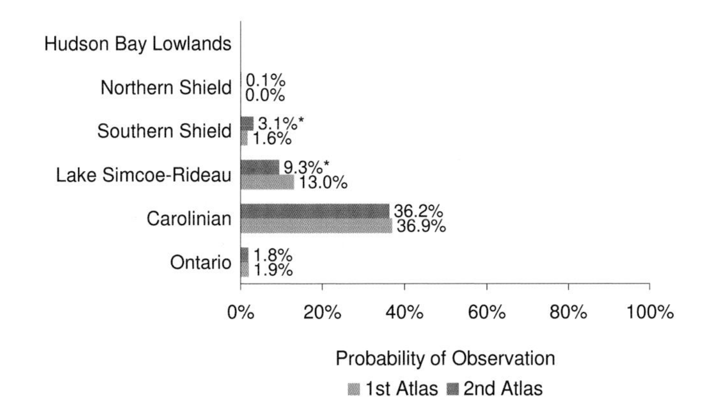

During the second atlas, cuckoos that were heard but not seen were recorded as unidentified cuckoos. Grey squares on the map are those for which the only evidence for the Yellow-billed Cuckoo during the second atlas was the call of a cuckoo with no sighting of the bird to verify identification of the species. Unidentified cuckoos reported in the Northern Shield region were more likely Black-billed Cuckoos.

Breeding biology: The Yellow-billed Cuckoo nests in a variety of open and forested habitats, including old fields dominated by hawthorn, riparian thickets and woodlands, hedgerows and roadsides, deciduous and mixed forests, coniferous plantations, orchards, and cemeteries (Peck and James 1983). It frequently shares these habitats with the Black-billed Cuckoo. Elsewhere in the northeast, the Yellow-billed Cuckoo regularly breeds in forested habitats (Mossman and Hoffman 1989; Robbins et al. 1989), although it is uncertain whether this affinity is as strong in Ontario.

This species is nomadic, even during the breeding season. Abundant food supplies are essential for nesting; it may be common in an area one year and absent another (Nolan and Thompson 1975). The timing of the nesting season is also variable, dependent on food availability. Eggs have been found in Ontario nests from mid-May to early August (Peck and James 1994). Most nesting occurs from mid-June to mid-August throughout its range, but peak nesting dates vary considerably, and populations within a few kilometres of each other may nest at different times (Hughes 1999). Birds seen early in the season that are apparently on territory may move elsewhere to breed if insufficient food is present.

Nests are typically in shrubs, saplings, or vines, and less frequently in larger trees. They are usually close to the ground, with most 1-2 m up, but with a range of 0.6-6 m in Ontario (Peck and James 1983). Although the nests may be relatively easy to find, they are not occupied for long. The incubation period is only 9-11 days, and the young leave the nest by walking out onto adjacent branches when they are only six to nine days old (Hughes 1999).

Abundance: The species was reported on too few point counts to produce a relative abundance map. Nevertheless, point count data indicate that it is still most common in the Carolinian region along the north shore of Lake Erie from Norfolk Co. westward. As in the first atlas, there is a minor area of concentration on the Frontenac Axis. Areas of lower abundance occur in the vicinity of northeastern Georgian Bay and Sudbury, corresponding with documented infestations of several forest defoliators, particularly Forest Tent Caterpillar (Howse and Scarr 2001; Evans et al. 2005). – *Al Sandilands*

Black-billed Cuckoo

Coulicou à bec noir

Coccyzus erythropthalmus

The Black-billed Cuckoo is the more common and widespread of the two cuckoos in Ontario. Fidelity to breeding areas is very low in this species, as local distribution and abundance are highly dependent upon availability of its primary prey. It may be locally abundant in an area some years but rare or absent in others. It feeds primarily on hairy and spiny caterpillars such as the Forest Tent Caterpillar and Fall Webworm and those of the Gypsy Moth. Both cuckoo species are occasionally parasitic, laying their eggs in nests of other species or in other cuckoo nests. This typically occurs only when food resources are very abundant (Hughes 2001).

The Black-billed Cuckoo ranges from southwestern Alberta east through Ontario and southwestern Québec to the Maritime Provinces and south to Oklahoma, North Carolina, and Virginia (Hughes 2001). In Ontario, it is generally uncommon to locally common in the south, becoming increasingly rare northward on the Shield (James 1991).

Distribution and population status: McIlwraith (1894) and Baillie and Harrington (1936) stated that the Black-billed Cuckoo was common and that it nested north to Parry Sound and Thunder Bay Districts and in the Rainy River area. During the first atlas, the Black-billed Cuckoo occurred mostly south of the Shield and in the Southern Shield region.

Although its overall distribution did not change substantially between atlases, there was a significant (24%) increase in the probability of observation in the province as a whole, with the greatest increase (56%) in the Southern Shield region. The increase in the Southern Shield was more an infilling of the previously known range as opposed to a range expansion.

BBS data show the opposite trend to the atlas. Results for Ontario show a downward trend that is not significant. Canada-wide, the Black-billed Cuckoo declined significantly at a rate of 3.0% per year from 1968 to 2005 (Downes et al. 2005). The decline has been more severe recently, with a rate

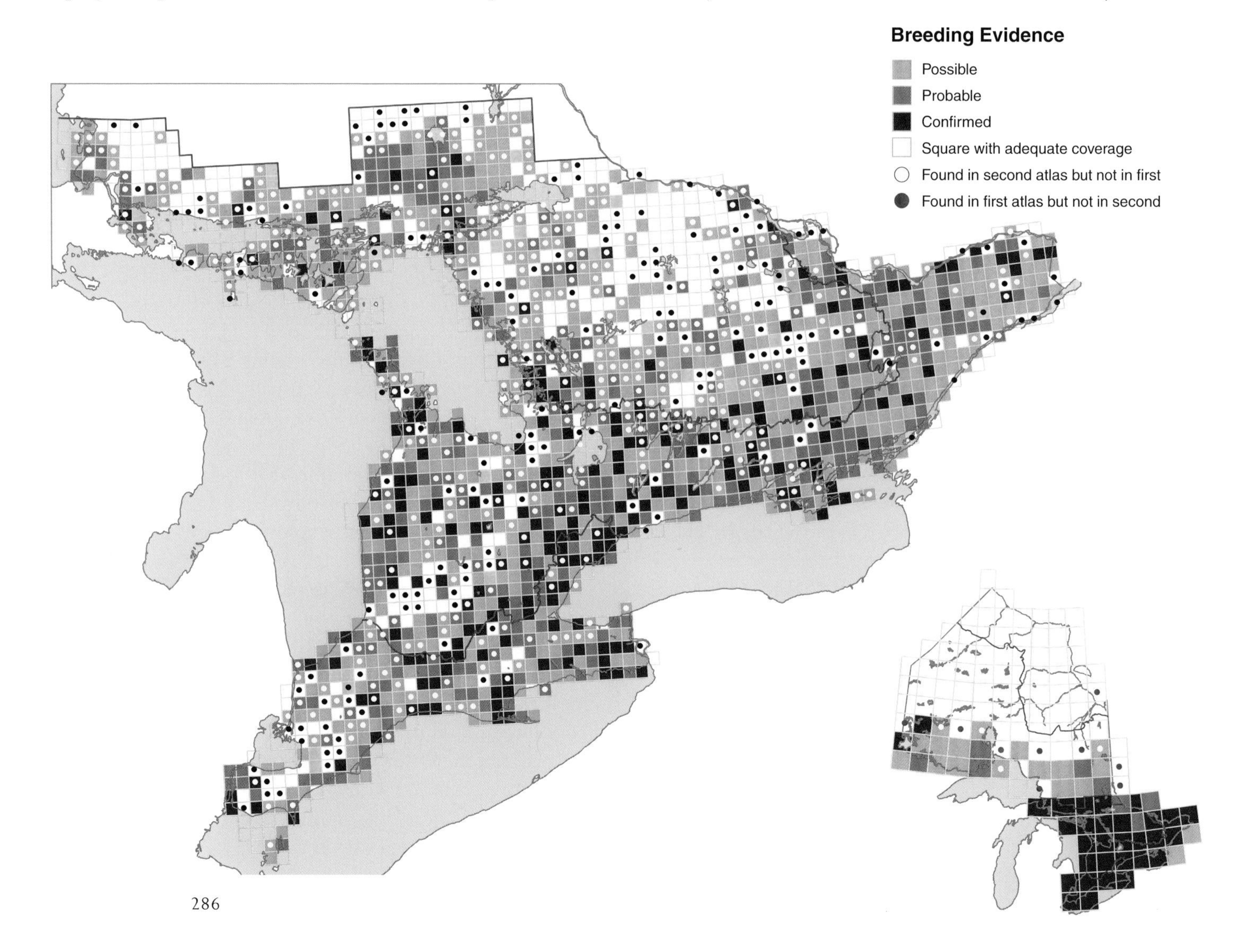

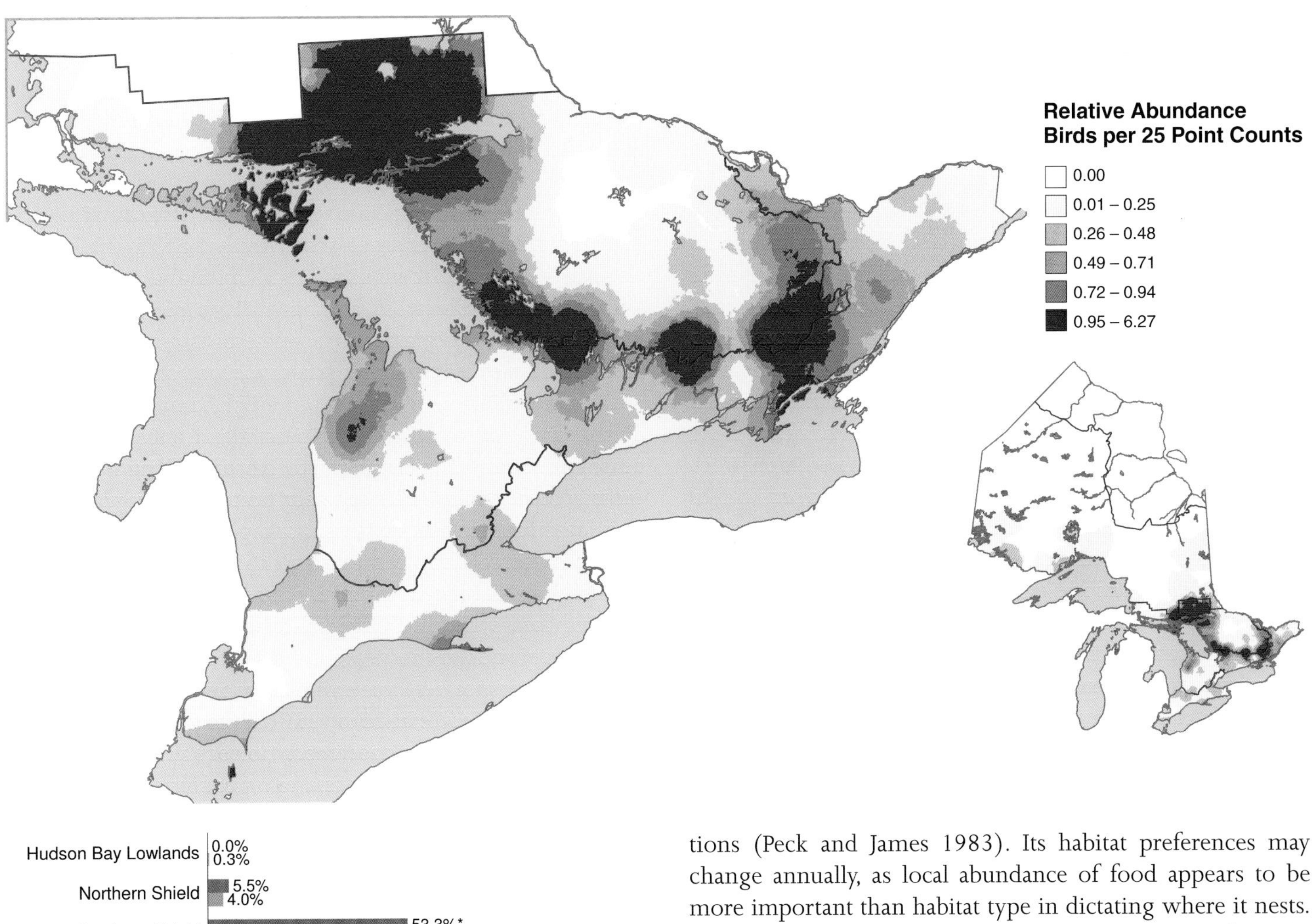

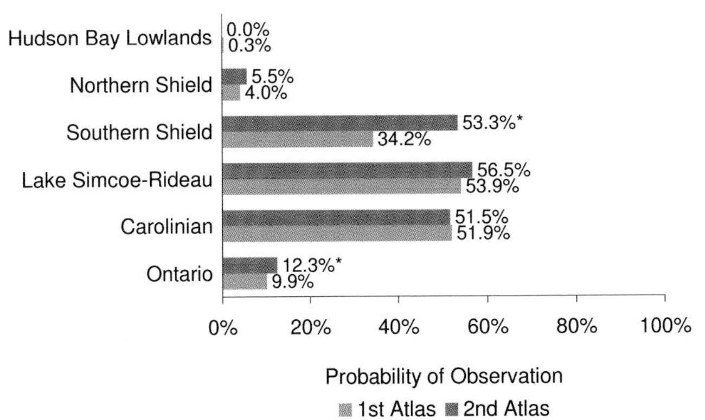

of 5.3% annually from 1981 to 2005. Due to the nomadic behaviour of this species, it is uncertain which survey is more accurate in evaluating the status of this irruptive species. Perhaps the BBS, which samples the same routes annually, would be better at assessing changes in populations than the atlas, which is a composite mapping over a five-year period.

During the second atlas, cuckoos that were heard but not seen were recorded as unidentified cuckoos. Grey squares on the map are those for which the only evidence for the Black-billed Cuckoo during the second atlas was the call of a cuckoo with no sighting of the bird to verify identification of the species.

Breeding biology: The Black-billed Cuckoo nests most frequently in early successional habitats such as shrubby old fields dominated by hawthorn, orchards, hedgerows, riparian thickets and woodlands, and forest edges and openings. In Ontario, as in other areas in the northeastern portion of its range, it is somewhat less likely to nest in forested habitat than the Yellow-billed Cuckoo (pers. obs.) but may nest in deciduous swamps and upland stands as well as coniferous plantations (Peck and James 1983). Its habitat preferences may change annually, as local abundance of food appears to be more important than habitat type in dictating where it nests. Nests are flimsy platforms of twigs typically 1-1.5 m from the ground, although they have been found at heights from 0 to13.5 m in Ontario. Eggs are typically present in Ontario nests in June and early July, but a range of mid-May to early September has been reported. Timing of nesting often depends on local food availability (Peck and James 1983).

Nests are placed low to the ground, but are occupied for a relatively short period of time. The incubation period is 10-14 days, and most young leave the nest when they are only six to seven days old.

Abundance: The areas of greatest abundance are in the Sudbury area, on eastern Manitoulin Island, and along the southern edge of the Shield. These are all areas with considerable amounts of successional thicket and early successional forest habitats. In the north, there were smaller areas of abundance in the Rainy River and Thunder Bay areas, and northern records of unidentified cuckoos were probably of this species.

The abundance map closely mirrors caterpillar abundance during the atlas. In the North Bay-Sudbury area, there were infestations of Spruce Budworm, Gypsy Moth, and Forest Tent Caterpillar. Extensive outbreaks of Forest Tent Caterpillar also occurred near Fort Frances, Lake Nipigon, and Thunder Bay (Howse and Scarr 2001; Evans et al. 2005). – *Al Sandilands*

Barn Owl

Effraie des clochers

Tyto alba

Tania & Jim Thomson

The ghost-like Barn Owl has a nearly cosmopolitan distribution, occurring on every continent except Antarctica. It reaches the northern extent of its range in Canada in southern Ontario and southern British Columbia. The Barn Owl is a species of the open countryside; it typically favours pastures, hayfields, marshes, and other grassy habitats that support adequate populations of mice and voles. Although often undetected, it is closely associated with humans through its use of barns, church steeples, silos, and other structures for nesting. It may also nest in natural cavities in large trees and will readily accept artificial nest boxes. In Canada, the eastern population of the Barn Owl is classified as Endangered by COSEWIC and OMNR.

Distribution and population status: In Ontario, the Barn Owl is restricted to extreme southern Ontario. Its historical status in Ontario is not well known, but before European settlement, it was probably present in small numbers in the tallgrass prairie and oak savannah habitat in the Carolinian region (Solymár and McCracken 2002). Undoubtedly, the Barn Owl benefited from the arrival of European settlers through the clearing of land for agriculture and the construction of barns and other structures. However, many modern agricultural practices, which have switched from livestock operations to more intensive cultivation of cereal crops and viticulture, have reduced foraging habitat and the number of livestock barns suitable for nesting and roosting. Other threats include increases in road mortality and predator populations.

Despite recovery efforts including the erection of over 300 nest boxes in appropriate habitat, the Barn Owl population in the province has changed little since the first atlas. Then, it was confirmed breeding in four squares on the Niagara Peninsula, with possible breeding in another two in Essex Co. and near Kingston. During this atlas, there were only two confirmed

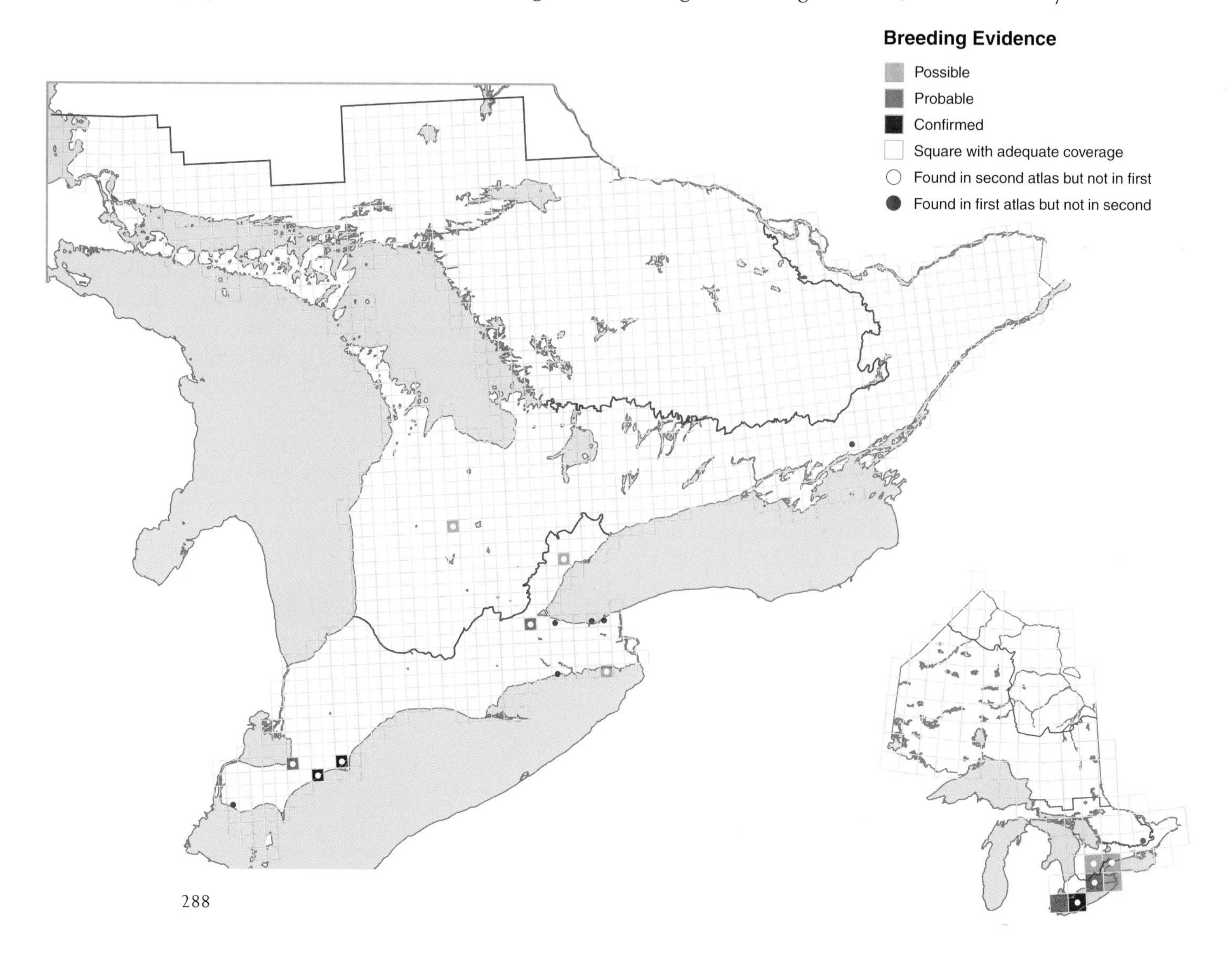

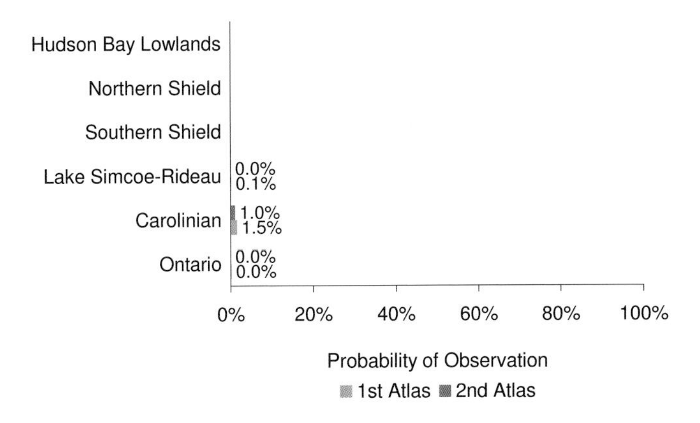

nesting locations, both in Chatham-Kent. An additional two squares reported probable breeding evidence, one also in Chatham-Kent and the other near Hamilton; possible records were reported in three squares, in Wellington Co., Niagara Region, and near Toronto. Unfortunately, the three possible records involved dead birds, two collected as roadkill and one found dead at an airport. Given the species' propensity to disperse over long distances, however, it is difficult to be certain that these three individuals were breeding in the squares where they were found.

In the first atlas, Barn Owl observations were concentrated in the Niagara Region, whereas in the second atlas, more observations came from Chatham-Kent. An increase in viticulture in the Niagara area and a loss of livestock barns are possible reasons for this apparent decline.

Breeding biology: Like most owls, the Barn Owl is very difficult to census because of its nocturnal habits and secretive nature. This difficulty is compounded by a lower rate of vocalization than many other owls, the fact that its call does not carry far, and its general unresponsiveness to call broadcasts. Also, its call – more aptly, a scream – may not be immediately recognizable as that of an owl. The Ontario Barn Owl Recovery Team has found that the distribution of informational materials to rural landowners increases the reporting rate, but the population remains otherwise difficult to census. The presence of a roosting Barn Owl in a barn is often overlooked because it prefers large, dark barns and will typically remain motionless in the highest parts. Trained observers can identify the shed feathers and shiny black pellets. Even so, such detections are difficult, as demonstrated by a dedicated Hamilton naturalist who spent 18 months searching 100+ barns before locating a roost site during the second atlas. The presence of road-killed birds in areas where birds have not been reported further confirms their elusive nature and suggests that breeding Barn Owls may be undetected.

Abundance: This species is too rare to have been detected on point counts. There were 10 definite and eight highly probable sightings of Barn Owls in southern Ontario from 1999 to 2005, five consisting of road-killed individuals (Ontario Barn Owl Recovery Team, unpubl. data). These sightings covered a wide area of southern Ontario, including Pickering, Toronto, Kitchener, Guelph, Haldimand, Norfolk, and Essex Counties, and Chatham-Kent. The highest density of Barn Owls, both from atlas data and road-kill records, appears to be in Chatham-Kent, close to Lake Erie. In Ontario, low population density, the long-distance dispersal of young birds, cold winter weather, and susceptibility to road mortality all render the species vulnerable to local extirpation. The Ontario population is estimated to be five to 10 pairs. – *Debra S. Badzinski*

Clutch size in Ontario has varied from one to 10 eggs, but the average is three to five eggs (Peck and James 1983). *Photo: George K. Peck*

This old barn near Ancaster (City of Hamilton) was occupied by a Barn Owl during the second atlas. The barn has since been destroyed by fire. *Photo: Debra S. Badzinski*

Eastern Screech-Owl

Petit-duc maculé

Megascops asio

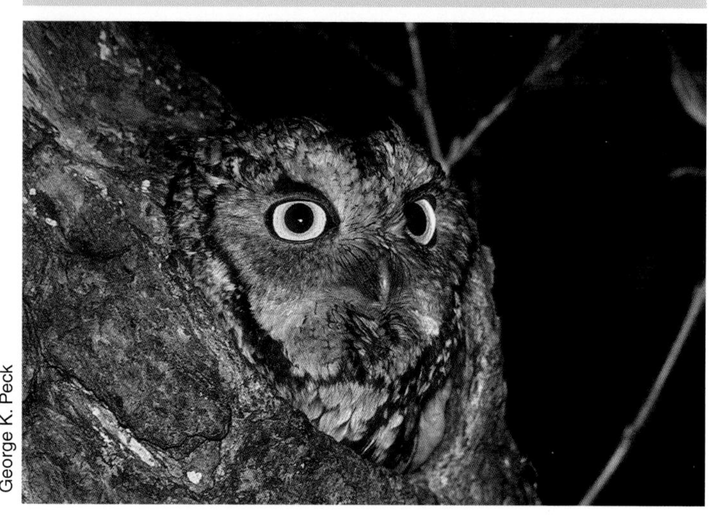

George K. Peck

Since the early 19th century, the Eastern Screech-Owl has been considered one of the most common raptors permanently resident in southern Ontario. Although it was thought to be declining in numbers in the early 1980s (Tate 1981), a 1985 assessment of its status in Canada concluded that it was not at risk (Penak 1986). Its range is restricted to North America, extending from central Mexico north through the central and eastern US into southern Canada (Gehlbach 1995). It occupies rural and urban habitats and can be found in open woodlands, groves, orchards, and shade trees (Gehlbach 1995).

Distribution and population status: In Ontario, the Eastern Screech-Owl was originally thought to occur only in the southwestern part of the province (McIlwraith 1894). However, during the early 20th century, its range was found to be more extensive, occupying southeastern Ontario as well (cf. Macoun and Macoun 1909). Both atlases show it to be a common species south of the Canadian Shield and rare, with scattered occurrences, on the Shield. It was reported in both atlases in most squares throughout southwestern Ontario but was less frequently reported in southeastern Ontario. This distribution pattern may be related to its apparent preference for areas with varied habitats and abundant edge (Belthoff et al. 1993) and to its avoidance of extensive mature forests (Peterjohn and Rice 1991).

The probability of observation of the Eastern Screech-Owl increased significantly between atlases in the province as a whole and in the Carolinian and Lake Simcoe-Rideau regions. The largest increase (35%) occurred in the Carolinian region, the core of the species' historical range, but there was also a marked increase of 18% in the Lake Simcoe-Rideau region. It is likely that the increase in overall records reported in this atlas is a reflection of increased survey effort for owls utilizing call broadcast recordings (often with more sophisticated and powerful playback equipment than

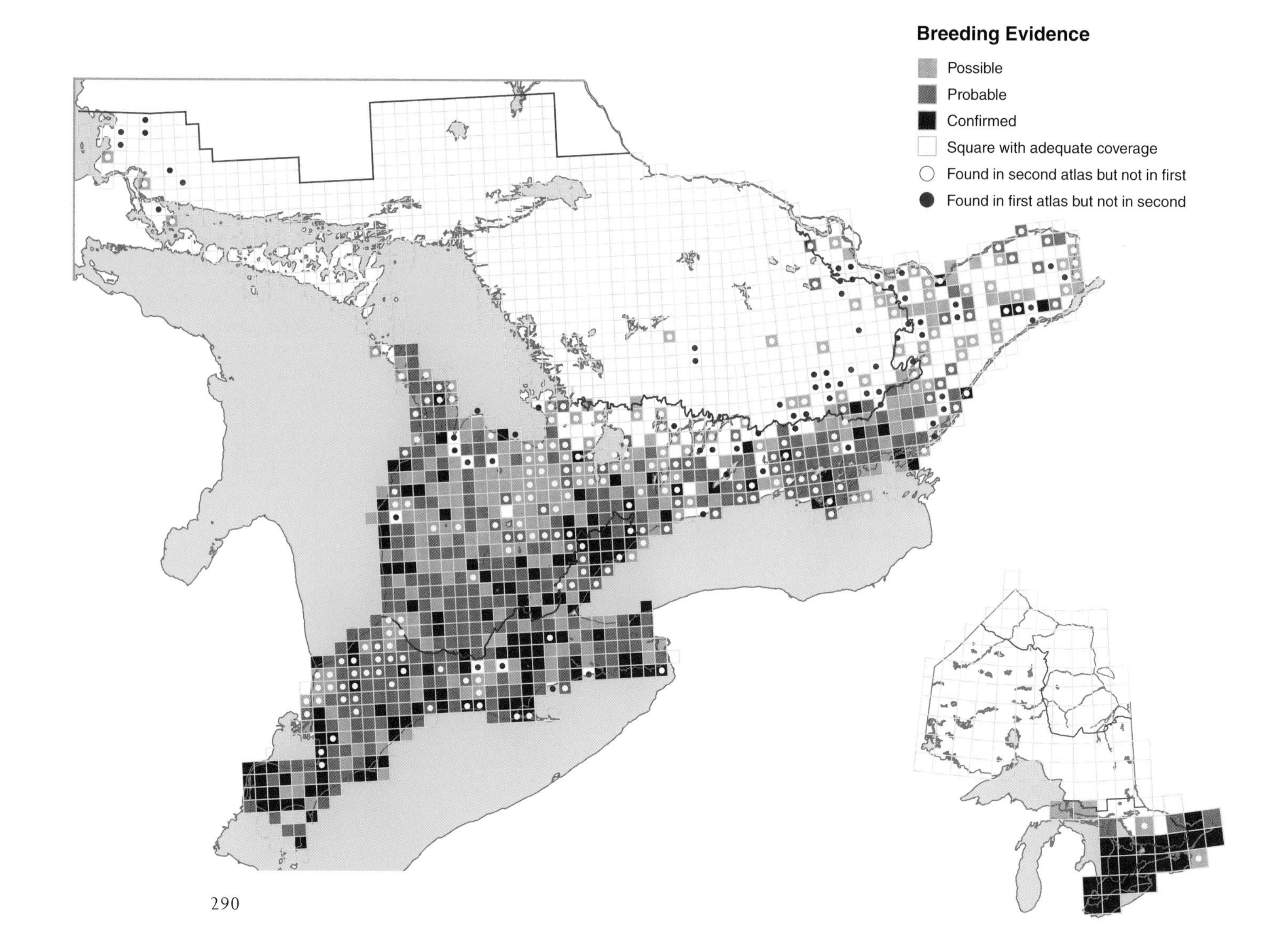

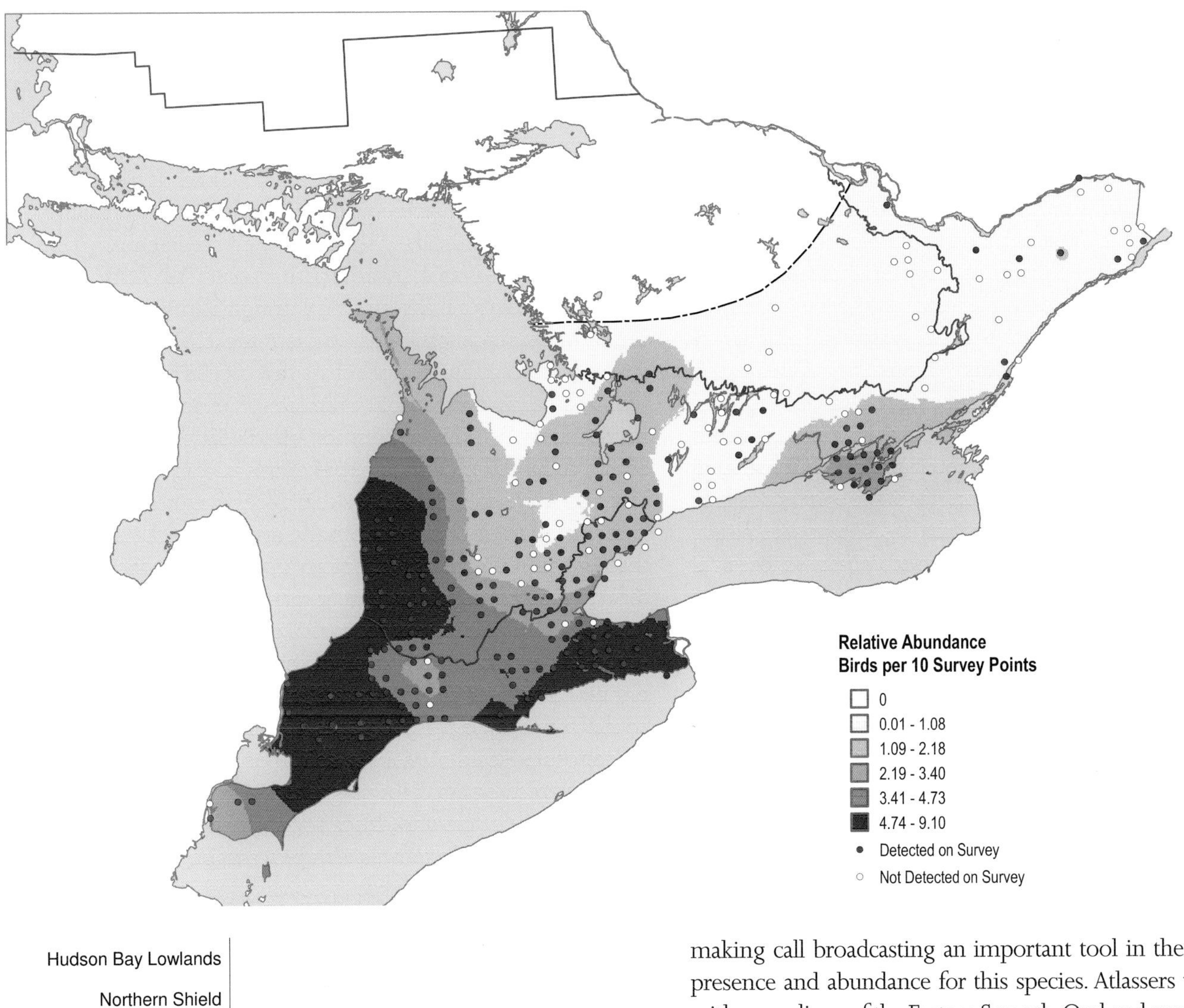

Hudson Bay Lowlands
Northern Shield
Southern Shield 1.9% 1.8%
Lake Simcoe-Rideau 40.9%* 34.8%
Carolinian 64.1%* 47.3%
Ontario 4.5%* 3.7%
0% 20% 40% 60% 80% 100%
Probability of Observation
1st Atlas 2nd Atlas

that used during the first atlas), a special Eastern Screech-Owl survey developed for the atlas, and an extension of the acceptable period for recording breeding evidence for the species.

Breeding biology: An exclusively nocturnal species that occupies cavities during the day, the Eastern Screech-Owl breeds earlier than most species in Ontario. Nesting occurs between mid-March and early June (Peck and James 1983). With the exception of human-made nest boxes, nesting cavities can be hard to locate. Confirmation of breeding is difficult, with only 19% of records confirmed during the atlas period. The young leave their natal area in early fall, and young owls set up territories in late fall and early winter (Shepherd 1992). Acceptable dates for recording breeding evidence were extended during this atlas to include November and December, as in these periods of territorial defence, birds can be quite vocal (Shepherd 1992). The species can respond aggressively to broadcasts of its calls as it establishes and defends its territory, making call broadcasting an important tool in the assessment of presence and abundance for this species. Atlassers were provided with recordings of the Eastern Screech-Owl and encouraged to use them between dusk and dawn from November to April. The resulting records presumably represent breeding birds, as the species is a permanent resident, although there is probably some mortality between the November-December period and the main breeding season. As a result of fairly extensive coverage, the distribution of this owl is likely accurately represented by the atlas map. Small gaps in the distribution map in southwestern Ontario may be due to a lack of coverage rather than an absence of the species.

Abundance: The abundance map shows the results of the Eastern Screech-Owl survey and indicates the squares in which the survey was undertaken. Surveyors used their atlas maps to pick 10 roadside points in suitable habitat, preferably from among the 50 randomly selected point counts in each square, then played a standardized broadcast playback at each stop and counted all birds. Because of the sampling procedure, the map shows the relative abundance of birds in suitable habitat and might over-represent abundance in squares with little suitable habitat. The results of the survey show that more birds were found in southwestern Ontario, particularly in areas adjacent to the Great Lakes. Abundance decreases north and east from this region, with somewhat higher numbers reported in Prince Edward Co. Relatively few birds were found in areas with more natural forest cover and little to no rural or urban land. Areas where more birds were reported may reflect milder winters and the greater variety of habitats found in these parts of the province. – *Nicole C. Kopysh*

Great Horned Owl

Grand-duc d'Amérique

Bubo virginianus

The Great Horned Owl is the largest ear-tufted owl in North America and is readily distinguishable from the similar Long-eared Owl by size alone (Marks et al. 1994; Houston et al. 1998). Throughout its nearctic range, the Great Horned Owl is at home in forest, fen, or pasture but generally prefers fragmented habitats of open, second-growth forests, swamps, and agricultural areas. It breeds from the treeline to central America, and locally to Tierra del Fuego (Houston et al. 1998). It is a permanent resident throughout southern Ontario north to the treeline in the Hudson Bay Lowlands. Due to its heavy weight and broad wings, it is an opportunistic hunter that relies primarily on sit-and-wait hunting tactics, using its formidable talons to capture, subdue, and kill (Houston et al. 1998). It feeds primarily on mammals, from small mammals to hares, and a wide array of birds and invertebrates.

Distribution and population status: In both atlases, breeding evidence was reported throughout Ontario, decreasing in frequency with increasing latitude. There has been little apparent change in the extent of the species' range since the first atlas. However, the probability of observation declined significantly in the Carolinian, Lake Simcoe-Rideau, and Southern Shield regions by 40%, 37%, and 41%, respectively. The increased coverage provided by the Ontario Nocturnal Owl Survey might help explain the non-significant increase in the Northern Shield. Several factors suggest the decline in the three southern regions is likely real rather than the result of different effort. Both the Eastern Screech-Owl and the Barred Owl showed increases in two of these three regions, suggesting that owling effort increased or was at least stable between atlases. Owl surveyors used better broadcasting equipment during the second atlas (CDs vs. tapes), and the "acceptable dates" were expanded for the Great Horned Owl to include December, a period with high vocalization. Also, while effort to locate this owl was not uniform across atlas squares, many

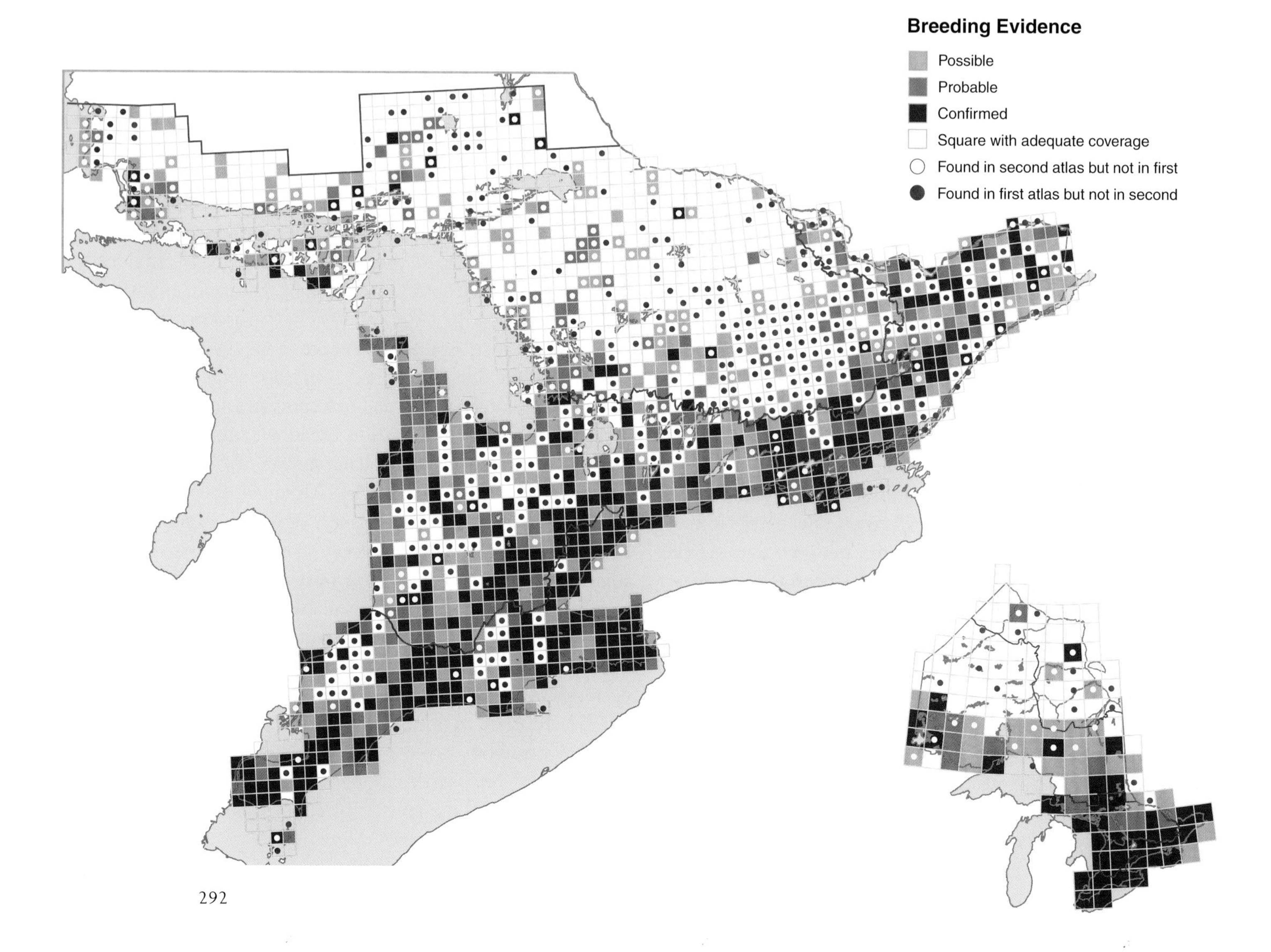

BREEDING EVIDENCE

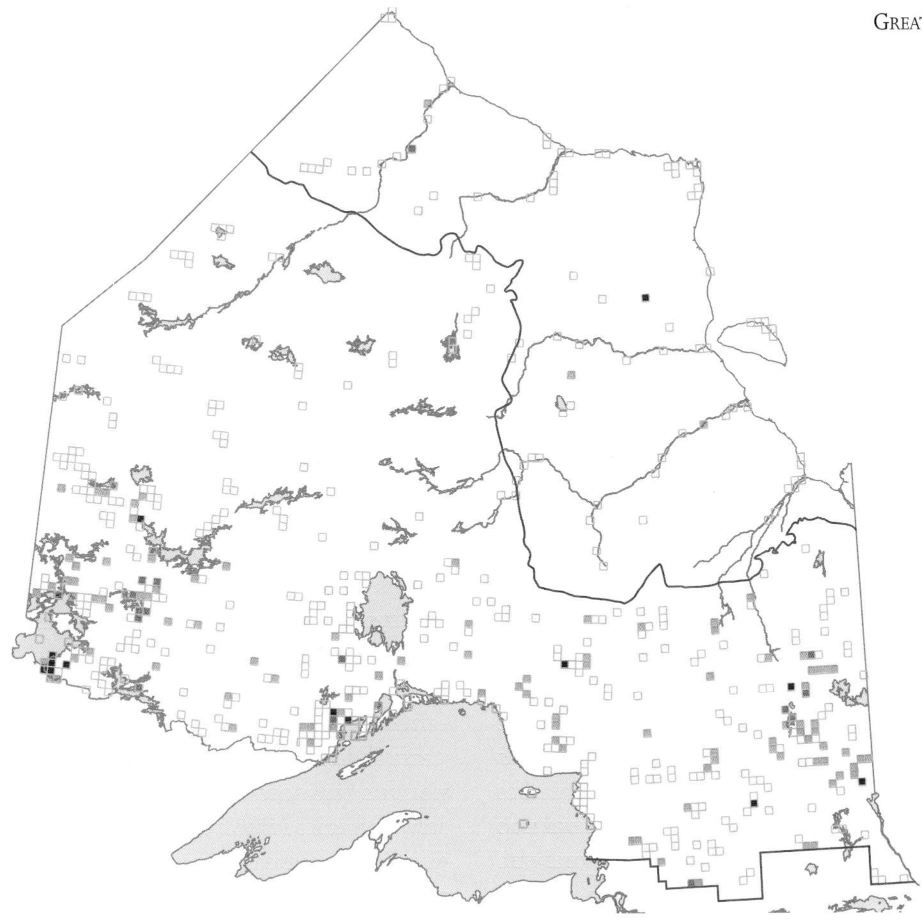

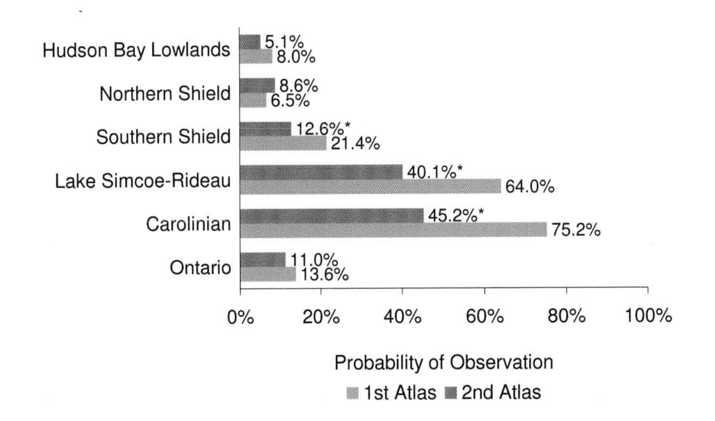

Regional Coordinators suspected declines in their atlas administrative regions.

The reasons for the declines are not clear. However, intensification of agriculture reduces the amount of early successional habitat and grassland that supports higher levels of small mammals and other suitable prey, so this is probably a factor, particularly in southwestern Ontario. The increase in the Barred Owl suggests that as forest cover increases in the Lake Simcoe-Rideau and Southern Shield regions, those areas are becoming more suitable to the Barred Owl and less suitable to the Great Horned Owl (Mazur et al. 1997).

Breeding biology: The Great Horned Owl's tendency to use open, often human-influenced areas (e.g., agricultural areas), combined with its easily identifiable call, makes it relatively conspicuous. Pairs begin to form in mid- to late autumn, with males establishing territories. The species calls regularly during late fall and early winter, and pairs may duet near nest sites during courtship, aiding nest searches. Like most owls, the Great Horned Owl does not construct a nest but uses old nests of the American Crow or other species. Females incubate exclusively, while males provision the female and nestlings. The female generally does not leave the nest except to defecate and cast pellets, or to hunt if male provisioning is insufficient (Rohner and Smith 1996). When prey abundance remains adequate, a pair may reuse territories and nest sites over successive years (Rohner 1996). Both sexes participate in territorial defence through hooting. Family groups may stay together for several weeks into summer, and adults will occasionally provision juveniles. The highly vocal fledged young deliver begging calls which carry over great distances, also aiding detection. Juveniles generally disperse by early fall.

Abundance: Abundance is difficult to estimate for the Great Horned Owl. The species tends to be sparsely distributed and is not well detected by diurnal point counts, so no relative abundance map was produced. Where there was sufficient effort, the breeding evidence maps should represent the bird's occurrence reasonably accurately. However, it may be under-represented in some areas due to low effort.

The probability of observation is highest south of the Shield, where foraging opportunities exist among urban and agricultural landscapes, and with nesting opportunities in small woodlots and escarpments. However, this statistic is probably influenced by the fact that most atlassers live south of the Shield and owling effort was likely considerably higher in that area. – *Darren J.H. Sleep*

Northern Hawk Owl

Chouette épervière

Surnia ulula

George K. Peck

The Northern Hawk Owl is one of the least-studied North American bird species (Duncan and Duncan 1998). It is a permanent resident of the northern forests of both old and new worlds, where it wanders widely in search of its principal prey, mice and voles. It is most often seen in winter during periodic southward irruptions resulting from food shortages in its core range.

In North America, the Northern Hawk Owl is found throughout the Boreal Forest from Alaska and British Columbia to Newfoundland. It nests only sporadically south of the Boreal Forest to southern Ontario and the northern parts of Minnesota, Wisconsin, and Michigan (Duncan and Duncan 1998). The few more southerly nest records typically occur after winter irruptions (Campbell et al. 1998).

Distribution and population status: The Northern Hawk Owl is widely distributed throughout the Hudson Bay Lowlands and Northern Shield regions, with a few exceptional records farther south. The species was recorded in 92 squares and was confirmed in a relatively high 46% of these. The 15 nests found during the atlas period almost tripled the previously known Ontario total (Peck 2002).

Results from the second atlas suggest a dramatic increase in the Ontario population of the Northern Hawk Owl, with the species being found in 39 100-km blocks compared with only 10 in the first atlas. The probability of observation increased significantly in both the Hudson Bay Lowlands and Northern Shield regions, resulting in nearly a fivefold increase provincially. Analysis of atlas data year by year reveals that the first years of this atlas coincided with a large influx of this species into Ontario. This irruption probably started in late 1996 (Campbell et al 1998; Escott 2002) and grew sharply during the winter of 2000-2001. By the summer of 2001, the species was found in 20 squares, and breeding was confirmed in 12.

In 2001, the Northern Hawk Owl was recorded south of

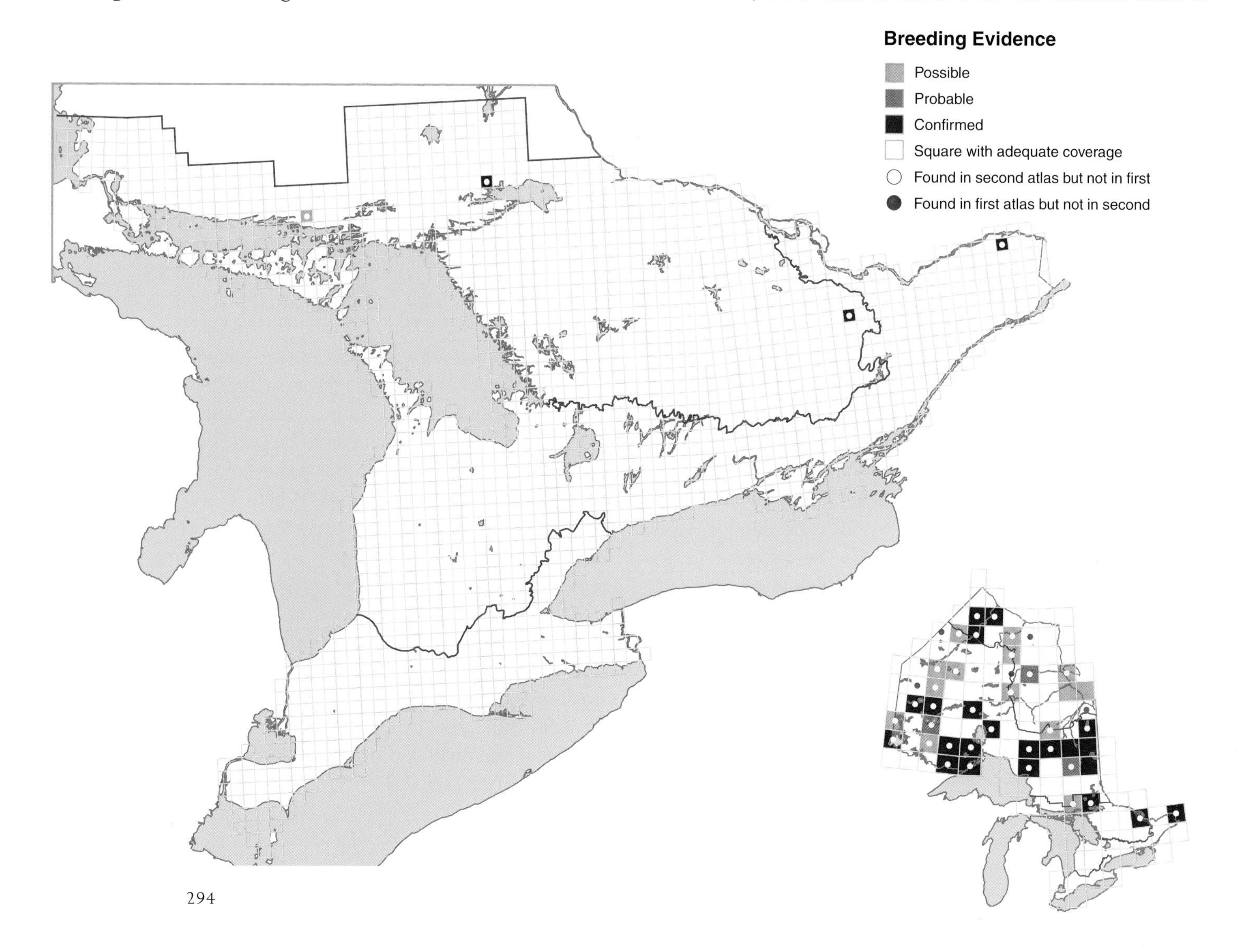

BREEDING EVIDENCE

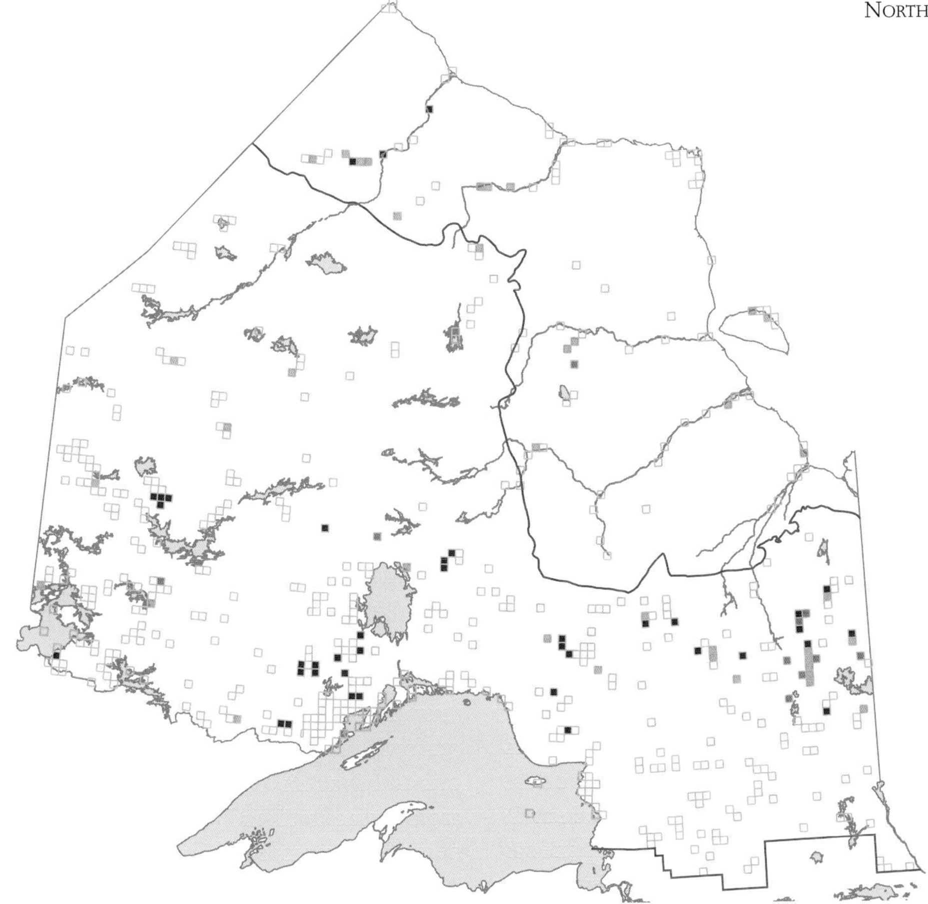

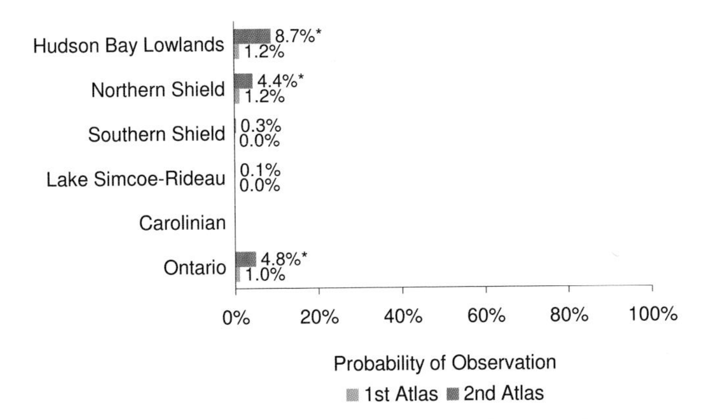

the Boreal Forest at several locations. These included Verner (Nipissing Dist., 46° N), where a pair that had spent the winter nested and fledged young; Rainy River, where two adults with fledged young were found on 2 July; and Massey (Sudbury Dist., 46° N) on the north shore of Lake Huron, where a single adult was seen on 13 April. The most southerly record was near Clayton (Lanark Co.), where one or two adults were seen from 31 March through early June. The easternmost record was at Alfred (United Counties of Prescott and Russell), where an adult was feeding three fledged young on 24 June.

Sightings peaked in 2002 when birds were observed in 39 squares and breeding was confirmed in 22, including seven nests. However, by this time the species had retreated northward, with no records from the Southern Shield. In 2003, it was found in 18 northern squares and confirmed in seven. In 2004 and 2005, there were only five sightings in total, all of single birds and most north of the Albany River. Sightings during the last two years of the atlas were about as frequent as in the first atlas.

Breeding biology: The Northern Hawk Owl is a diurnal hunter that often perches conspicuously on treetops, making it easy to find if present. It is a cavity nester and prefers openings in the Boreal Forest such as fens, burns, and extensive clearcuts, especially those with a graminoid ground cover favoured by voles. Breeding is easy to confirm since paired adults call to each other at the nest, and after the young hatch by late May the male is busy carrying food to the nest, oblivious to human observers. Fledged young are easy to locate by their persistent begging calls as the adult approaches with food.

Abundance: In the first atlas, the probability of observation of the Northern Hawk Owl was 1%, which increased to almost 5% in the second atlas. This significant increase reflects the irruptive influx in the early part of the atlas. Data suggest that irruptions follow a northwest to southeast direction (Duncan and Duncan 1998), and it is likely that by the end of the atlas period the species had retreated back to far-northern Ontario and farther northwest.

The Northern Hawk Owl remains a relatively uncommon Ontario bird, although it may be under-detected, given the extent of its Ontario range. Due to the irruptive fluctuations in numbers, it is not possible to estimate the population in Ontario or to determine an overall change in abundance between atlases. – *Nicholas G. Escott*

Barred Owl

Chouette rayée

Strix varia

Tim Dyson

This denizen of the mixed forests of central Ontario is known for its distinctive call and courtship behaviour. Historically, the Barred Owl bred throughout eastern North America, from northern Ontario east to the Maritimes and south to Florida and Texas, with an additional isolated population in Mexico. In the twentieth century, the species expanded its range northwest through the Boreal Forest and into the Yukon and Northwest Territories to the north, and south through British Columbia and Alberta down to Northern California. It is a year-round resident of large, unfragmented forests, particularly mature and old-growth forests with mixed deciduous-coniferous composition (Mazur and James 2000).

Distribution and population status: Before settlement by Europeans, the Barred Owl probably occurred throughout southern Ontario both on and off the Shield. Clearing of the forests for settlement and agriculture undoubtedly reduced its range and population south of the Shield, particularly in southwestern Ontario. This area was still home to some Barred Owls in the late 1800s (McIlwraith 1894), even though much forest had been cleared, but by the mid-1900s it could only be found in very isolated pockets of suitable habitat (Weir in Cadman et al. 1987).

Currently, the Barred Owl occurs throughout much of the Southern Shield, where its probability of observation is 47%, but it is also found in smaller numbers in the Northern Shield and Lake Simcoe-Rideau regions. It occurs sparsely through much of the Northern Shield north to about 52° N, primarily west of Lake Nipigon. The northernmost record during the second atlas occurred near Weagamow Lake in the Boreal Forest in northwestern Ontario. It was found in only six squares in the Carolinian region, where suitable forest cover is scarce, and the only two confirmed records of that region came from the relatively well-forested Norfolk Sand Plain area.

For the province as a whole, there was a significant 69%

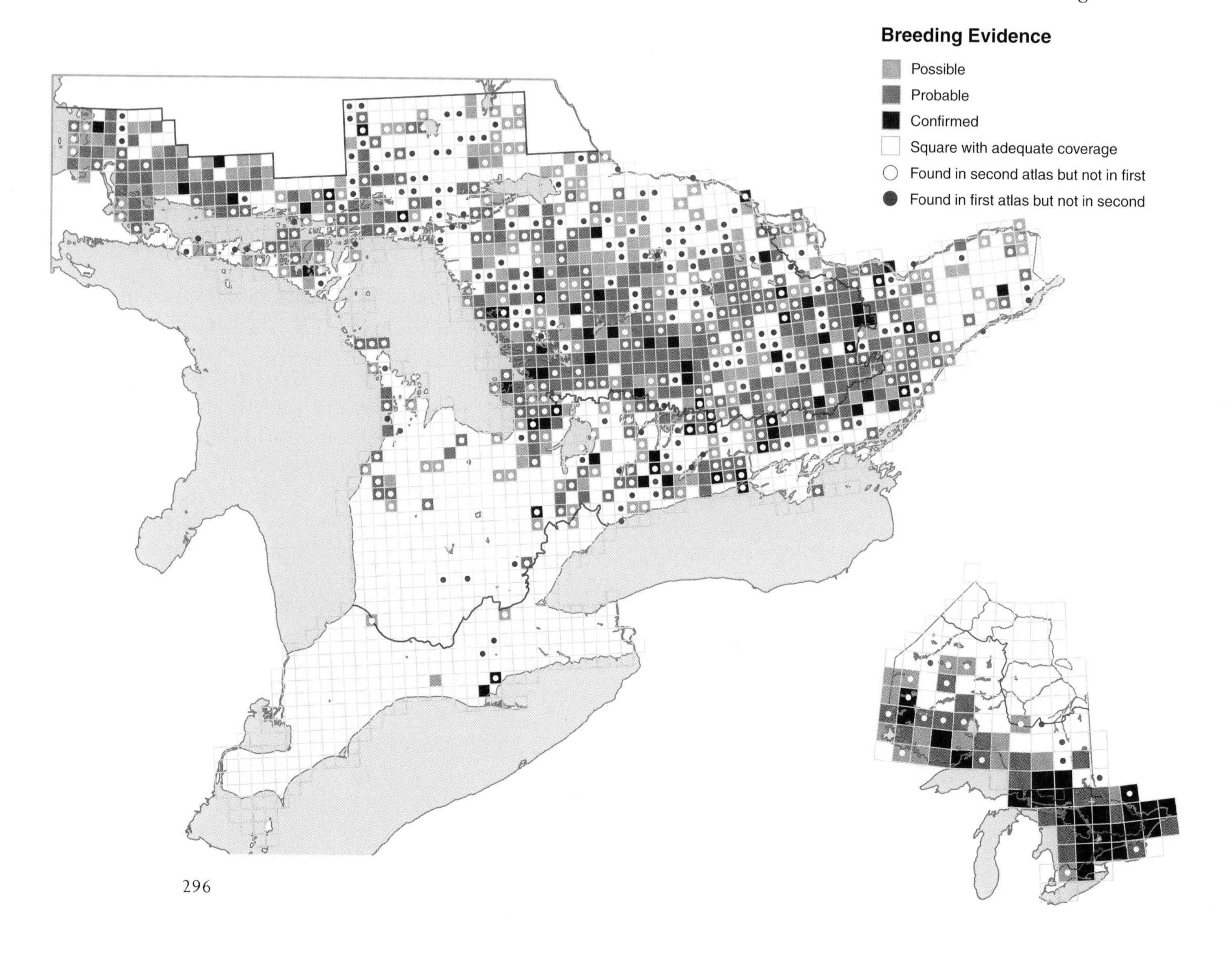

BREEDING EVIDENCE

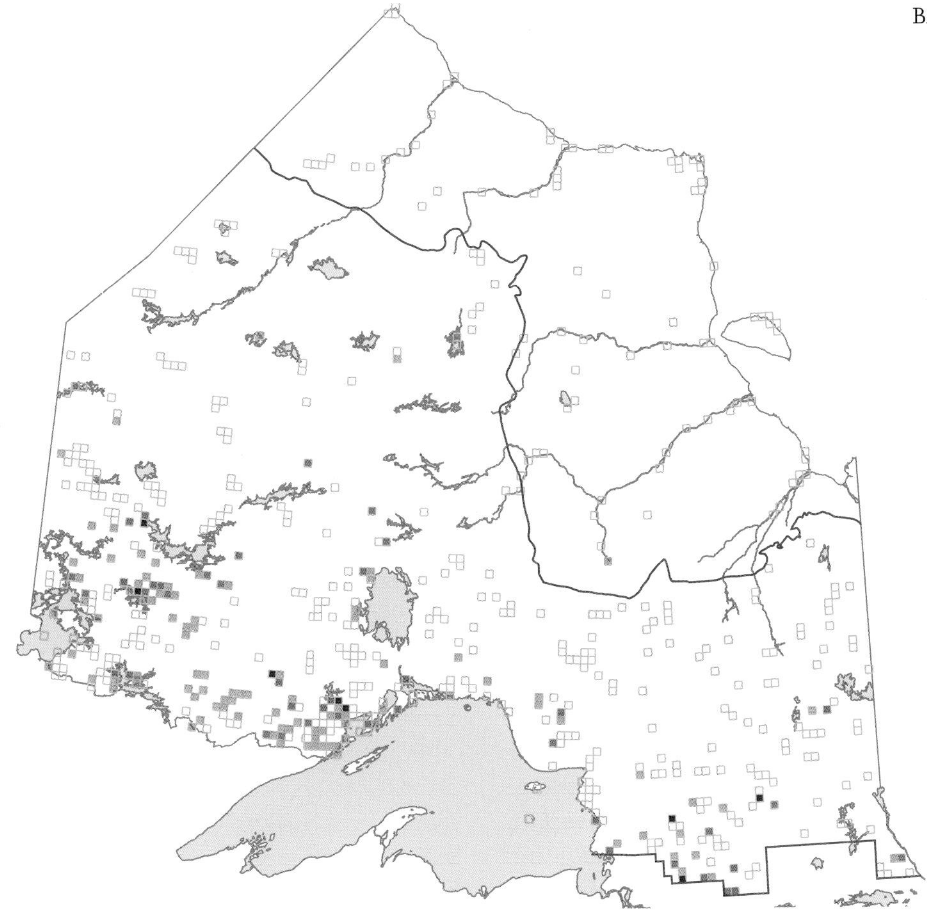

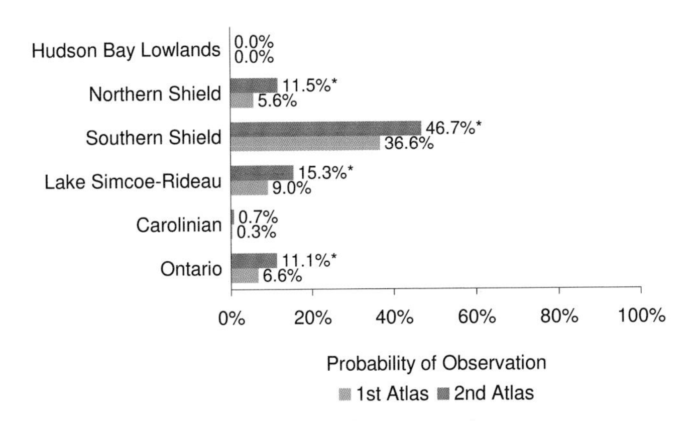

increase in the probability of observation for the Barred Owl compared to the first atlas. The most dramatic increase was seen in the Northern Shield, up about 100% from the first atlas, but both the Lake Simcoe-Rideau and Southern Shield regions also experienced significant increases of 71% and 28%, respectively.

Since the publication of the first atlas, BSC and OMNR initiated the Ontario Nocturnal Owl Survey (ONOS) to track owl populations throughout central and northern Ontario. The increases in atlas data for this species may be partly attributed to more focused nocturnal owl surveying and the inclusion of ONOS data in the current atlas. According to Crewe and Badzinski (2006b), the species has shown evidence of small population growth in central Ontario (on the Shield, south of 47°N) since the survey began in 1995. Its increased detection in the Lake Simcoe-Rideau region, and to a lesser extent in the Southern Shield, could also be the result of maturation of forests in many areas of southern Ontario. Because the ONOS is a roadside survey, gaps in distribution on the Shield and in other heavily forested areas are likely an artifact of uneven coverage and effort due to lack of road access.

Breeding biology: The Barred Owl is generally nocturnal and non-migratory throughout its range (Mazur and James 2000). It nests in cavities in large deciduous trees, but can occasionally be found using abandoned stick nests (Mazur and James 2000). Nests are hard to find, and breeding was confirmed in only 9% of squares, mostly through detection of fledged young.

The Barred Owl is quite vocal, and its distinctive "*Who cooks for you? Who cooks for you all?*" call can be heard throughout the spring. Its calls become even more elaborate during courtship, when pairs perform "a loud series of spectacular dueting vocalizations ... that sound like maniacal laughter" (Mazur and James 2000). It responds readily to call broadcasts, one of the most effective means of locating Barred Owls in the current atlas.

Abundance: The data from the second atlas suggest that the core breeding area for the Barred Owl is the Southern Shield region of southern Ontario, where its probability of observation was highest. ONOS (1995-2005) data also suggest it is more common in the Southern Shield; however, call broadcasts were used only in central Ontario during the ONOS, increasing the probability of detection in this region (Crewe and Badzinski 2006b). The entire Canadian population for this species is estimated to be 10,000-50,000 pairs (Kirk and Hyslop 1998). – *Jody Allair*

Great Gray Owl

Chouette lapone

Strix nebulosa

R. E. Gehlert

Few birds capture the attention of even the most casual of birders as dramatically as the Great Gray Owl. Whether because of its imposing size, almost human-like face, or apparently calm demeanor, this largest of North American owls is difficult not to notice and admire. It has a holarctic distribution, breeding in North America across the Boreal Forest from western Québec to Alaska and south in the west to California, Nevada, and Montana (Bull and Duncan 1993). Only during periodic irruptions when it leaves its usual haunts in search of food do many people see this magnificent bird, nicknamed the "phantom of the north."

It is listed by COSEWIC as Not at Risk and by OMNR as a species of Special Concern.

Distribution and population status: Both atlases indicate that the Great Gray Owl breeds across northern Ontario from Lakes Superior and Huron to Hudson Bay. Irruptions of the species occurred during both atlases (1983-84, 2004-05), probably explaining the sightings of lingering birds in the Southern Shield, along the Bruce Peninsula, and west of Ottawa in the spring of 2005 (Jones 2005). This owl has also been reported breeding occasionally in Algonquin Prov. Park, the Bruce Peninsula, and Manitoulin Island (Forbes 1992; Whitelaw 1998; Turisk 2000).

Between atlases, the probability of observation increased by a non-significant 29% provincially, with a significant increase only in the Southern Shield. It is difficult to assess trends, because occurrence and breeding are closely tied to prey availability, which may be locally high one year but absent or nearly so in subsequent years (Bull and Duncan 1993). Furthermore, the Ontario Nocturnal Owl Survey (ONOS) was underway during the second atlas but not the first and contributed many records from road-accessible areas to the second atlas. The increase in the Southern Shield region probably resulted at least in part from lingering birds following what is arguably the

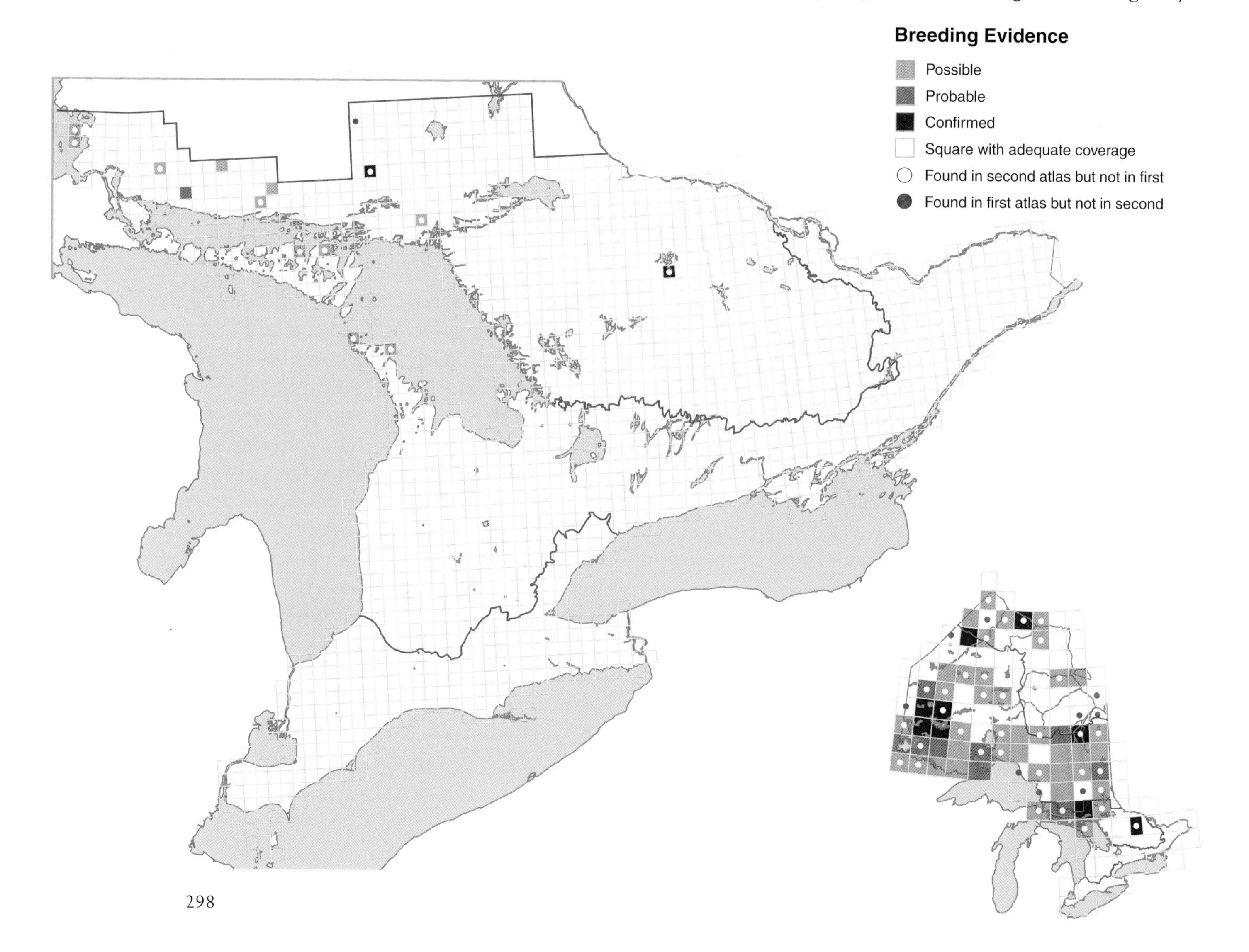

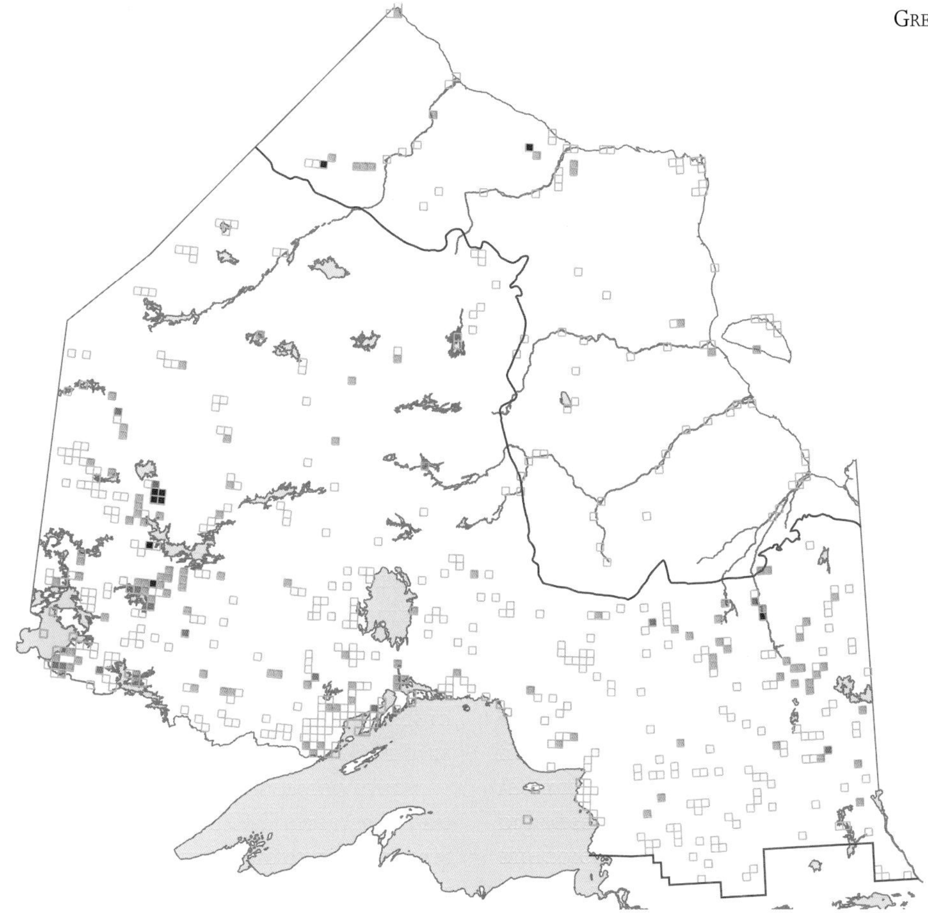

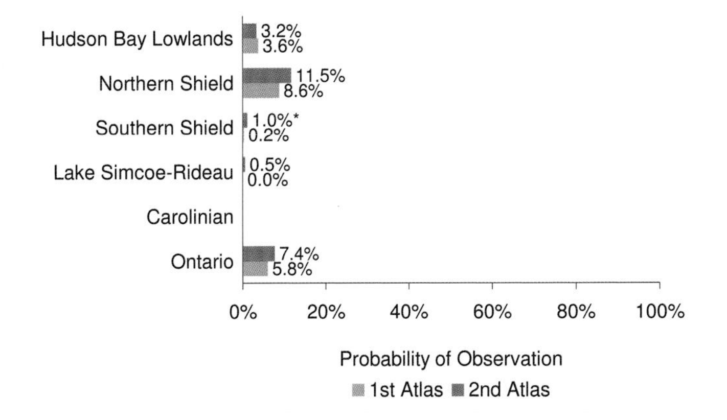

largest irruption yet recorded; large numbers of birds, possibly in the thousands, invaded southern Ontario during the winter of 2004-05 (Jones 2005). The ONOS also suggested a southward extension of the normal breeding range in 2005.

The highest probability of observation (12%) occurred in the Northern Shield, where the increase between atlases was not significant. The density of squares with breeding evidence is highest in northwestern Ontario, where several nests were recently confirmed (Gilmore and MacDonald 1996). However, this is at least in part because of the large number of ONOS routes in the area.

Breeding biology: Breeding is generally confined to the Boreal Forest, where nesting occurs mainly in broken-off dead trees or former Common Raven or raptor nests. In the Red Lake area, nests were located in dead aspen and both dead and living Jack Pine (Gilmore and MacDonald 1996). Prey and nest-site availability appear to be the most important factors determining the species' distribution (Bull and Duncan 1993). This owl will also readily use artificial nesting platforms, even in areas where natural sites exist.

Adults usually pair up in January or February, and the female incubates the two to five eggs through most of March until they hatch, typically near the beginning of April and well before the peak atlassing season. The female leaves the nest only briefly to regurgitate pellets from the young, and can lose up to 30% of body weight during incubation and brooding (Duncan 2003). The male visits the nest every two to three hours, feeding the female and young throughout the day (Duncan 2003). In addition to the Meadow Vole, the primary prey item, the diet includes Red-backed Vole and other microtine rodents, Deer Mouse, Snowshoe Hare, Red Squirrel, birds such as grouse and the Gray Jay, and even the Wood Frog.

Relatively few Great Gray Owl nests have been documented in Ontario (Peck and James 1983; Gilmore and MacDonald 1996), and confirmation of breeding is challenging. Confirmed breeding was relatively low (7%), with most records indicating possible breeding (84%), primarily reflecting observations of individual birds in suitable habitat during the breeding season; many of these records come from the ONOS. Its early breeding season and the fact that it does not respond to broadcasts of its call add to the difficulty of surveying this species.

Abundance: Densities of Great Gray Owl in Ontario are difficult to estimate with the available information. Elsewhere in its range, in areas of high prey abundance, breeding densities have been reported as high as 1.88 pairs/km^2 in Manitoba and Minnesota (Duncan 1987), and 1.72 pairs/km^2 in Oregon. (Bull and Henjum 1990). – *Marc Johnson*

Long-eared Owl

Hibou moyen-duc

Asio otus

George K. Peck

The Long-eared Owl is found throughout the northern hemisphere. Its North American range extends across Canada from the Yukon to the Maritimes south to the northeastern US and southwest to Arizona and New Mexico (Marks et al. 1994). It has a wider distribution than most other Ontario owls, with breeding documented throughout the province. A prey-based nomad, it migrates south in winter in response to vole shortages. Its versatile repertoire when calling may be unfamiliar and confusing. For many birders, it remains one of our most enigmatic owls.

This secretive species typically nests in dense coniferous or mixed forests, coniferous plantations, small woodlots, copses, and hedgerows, usually in close proximity to open foraging habitat such as fields, meadows, open woodlands, and marshes.

Distribution and population status: The Long-eared Owl is among the least known of Ontario owls. Although it has been described by some as an uncommon or even rare breeding species, nests have been documented in more than half of the province's counties and districts (ONRS). Despite clearly being widespread, its breeding distribution is still poorly understood. It was rarely encountered during either atlas, but breeding distribution remained similar in pattern and extent, occurring across all of southern Ontario and ranging north to the Hudson Bay Lowlands. There was, however, a high turnover of atlas squares. In southern Ontario, the species was found in the same square only 6% of the time, perhaps reflecting in part low fidelity to nesting sites in response to cyclical prey populations (Saurola 1997).

Four regions showed significant changes in the probability of observation, with increases in both the Northern and Southern Shield and decreases in the Lake Simcoe-Rideau and Carolinian regions. Changing patterns of farmland, forest cover, and urbanization may be playing a role in these changes.

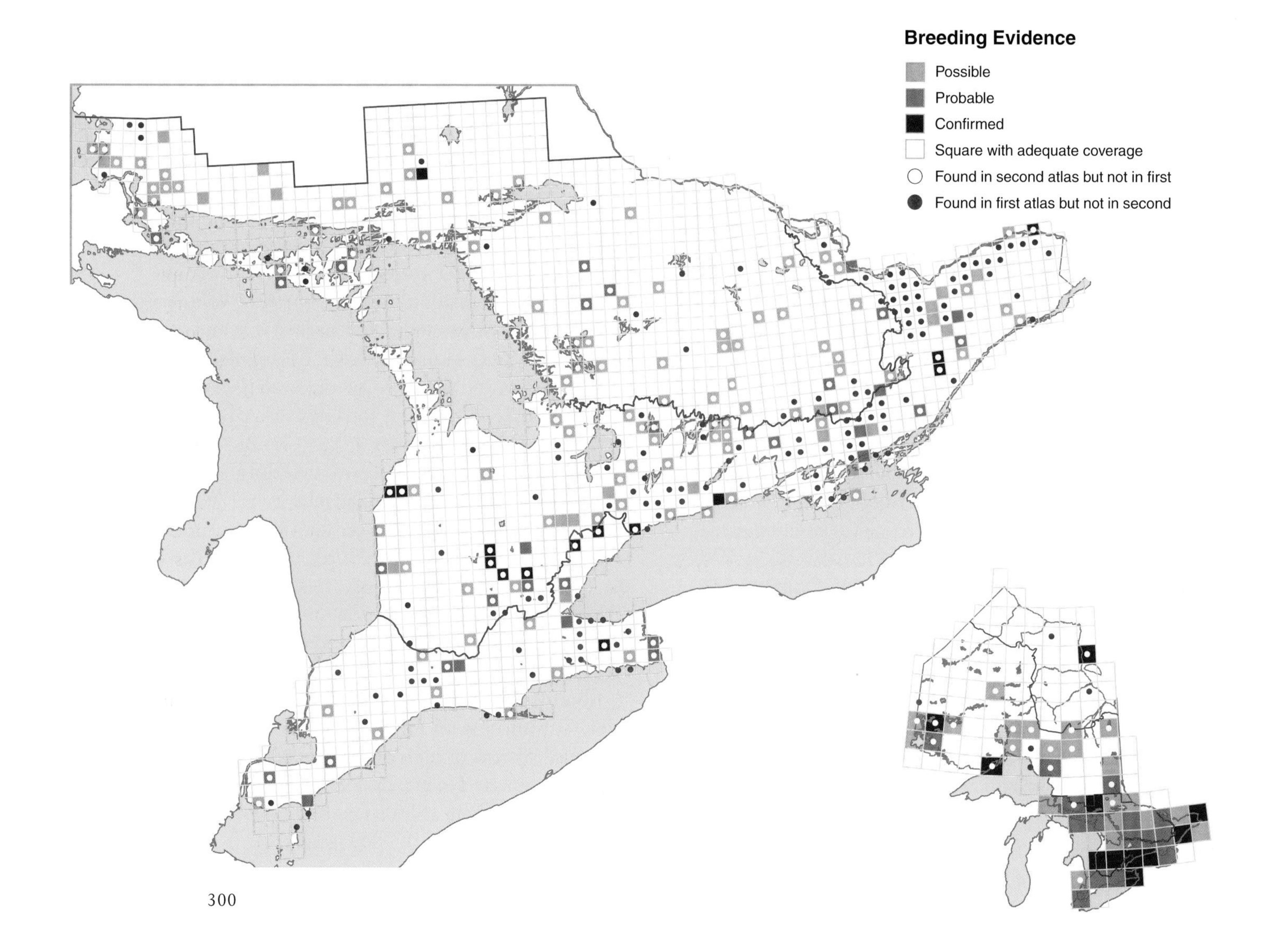

BREEDING EVIDENCE

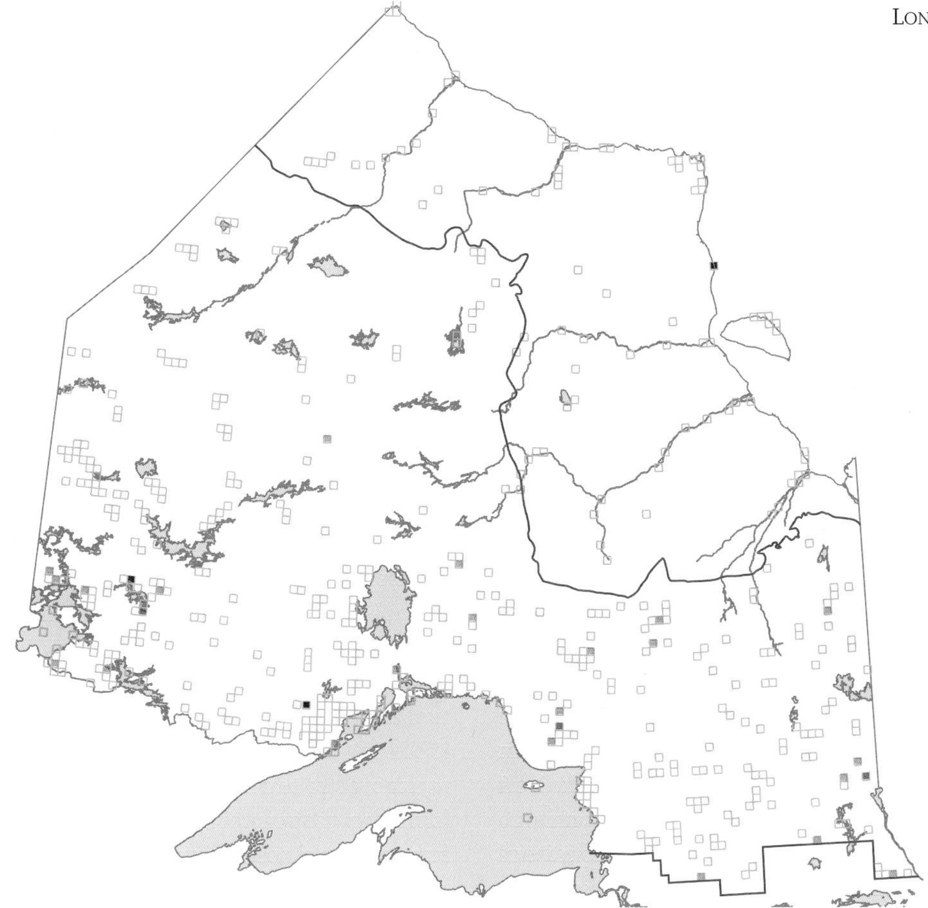

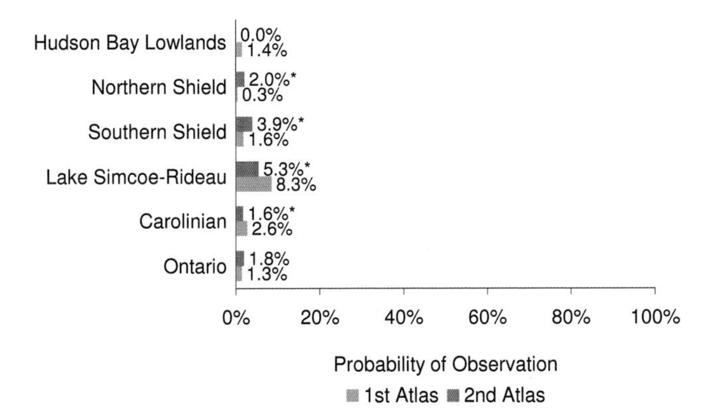

For a cryptic species like the Long-eared Owl, such change may also reflect variation in observer effort and the difficulty of detection. As in the first atlas, approximately three-quarters of all records were documented from the Lake Simcoe-Rideau and Southern Shield regions, where an extensive road network and higher atlasser density likely facilitated detection. The Northern Shield, where plentiful suitable habitat exists but access and atlasser effort are limited, accounted for only 15% of all records. Population trends are unclear due to low numbers, although reports from elsewhere suggest potential declines (Bosakowski et al. 1989; Marks et al. 1994; Kirk and Hyslop 1998). Unfortunately, the Ontario Nocturnal Owl Survey does not monitor this species at a level that provides meaningful trends (Crewe and Badzinski 2006b).

Breeding biology: The Long-eared Owl does not build its own nest but adopts former nests of other raptors, American Crow, or Gray Squirrel. Despite its wide occurrence, locating it during the breeding season is difficult because it is nocturnal and typically roosts in dense cover during the day. Documentation of breeding is complicated by the fact that it is migratory in Ontario. Unless birds are heard calling on territory, they generally cannot be considered possible breeders until April. Parents may also hunt well outside their defended area (Cramp 1985). Documentation is made easier when males perform their nocturnal advertising song, a series of quiet but penetrating "*hoo*" notes. The soft nasal "*shoo-oogh*" nest call of the female is barely audible 60 m away but indicates a nearby nest (Marks et al. 1994). During the fledging period, the food-begging calls of young can be heard up to 1 km and provide the best means of confirming breeding (Dumont 2001). Approximately 70% of atlas observations detected possible breeding only.

Although some Regional Coordinators considered this species under-reported, the atlas map probably reasonably reflects its broad breeding distribution. The true extent of its northern range remains uncertain.

Abundance: Determining the abundance of this nocturnal species is difficult**.** Diurnal surveys such as atlas point counts and the BBS do not successfully detect it. Directed surveys have also proven to be of limited use, likely due to this owl's apparent unresponsiveness to nocturnal call broadcasts (Shepherd 1992); both the atlas and Ontario Nocturnal Owl Survey yielded insufficient data to calculate abundance or trends. Atlas results suggest that while the species breeds across a large range in Ontario, it is apparently sparsely distributed with low abundance where it occurs, although directed surveys have found it to be a more common breeder in the Saguenay and Lac St. Jean region of Québec (Dumont 2001). A better understanding of the abundance and distribution of this little-known species in Ontario may be achieved if future surveys are timed to coincide with the fledgling period. – *Karl R. Konze*

Short-eared Owl

Hibou des marais

Asio flammeus

Mark Peck

The Short-eared Owl is essentially a cosmopolitan species, absent only from Australia and Antarctica. In North America, its breeding range covers most of Canada except for the high Arctic and extends into many northern states. It winters in most of the contiguous US states, usually in small to moderate numbers as far north as southern Ontario and Québec. Despite being widespread, this largely nomadic species is ephemeral and irregular throughout its range, with the location of breeding sites in a given year tightly linked to the population cycles of voles and other small mammals (Clark 1975). It has been classified as of Special Concern in Canada and Ontario by COSEWIC and the OMNR.

Distribution and population status: The Short-eared Owl is generally uncommon in Ontario, the second atlas showing a sparse distribution throughout the province from Windsor to Hudson Bay. The greatest concentration is found within the Hudson Bay Lowlands, where the probability of observation increased significantly, more than doubling between atlases. Much of this increase was due to more extensive low-level aerial surveys by OMNR and CWS personnel. Although widespread in this region, its distribution likely varies relative to prey availability. During the second atlas, the number of detections on aerial surveys gradually increased until 2003, coincident with a peak in small mammal abundance, and correspondingly declined following a crash in microtine populations in 2004 and 2005. Despite apparently ample habitat, there were relatively few detections along the James Bay coast, consistent with results from the first atlas.

Elsewhere in the province, distribution was virtually unchanged from the first atlas, though there was a high rate of turnover in the specific squares occupied, possibly reflecting changing land-use practices. During both periods, areas near Kingston, the lower Ottawa Valley, and the Haldimand Clay Plain were consistently favoured over others. Even in these

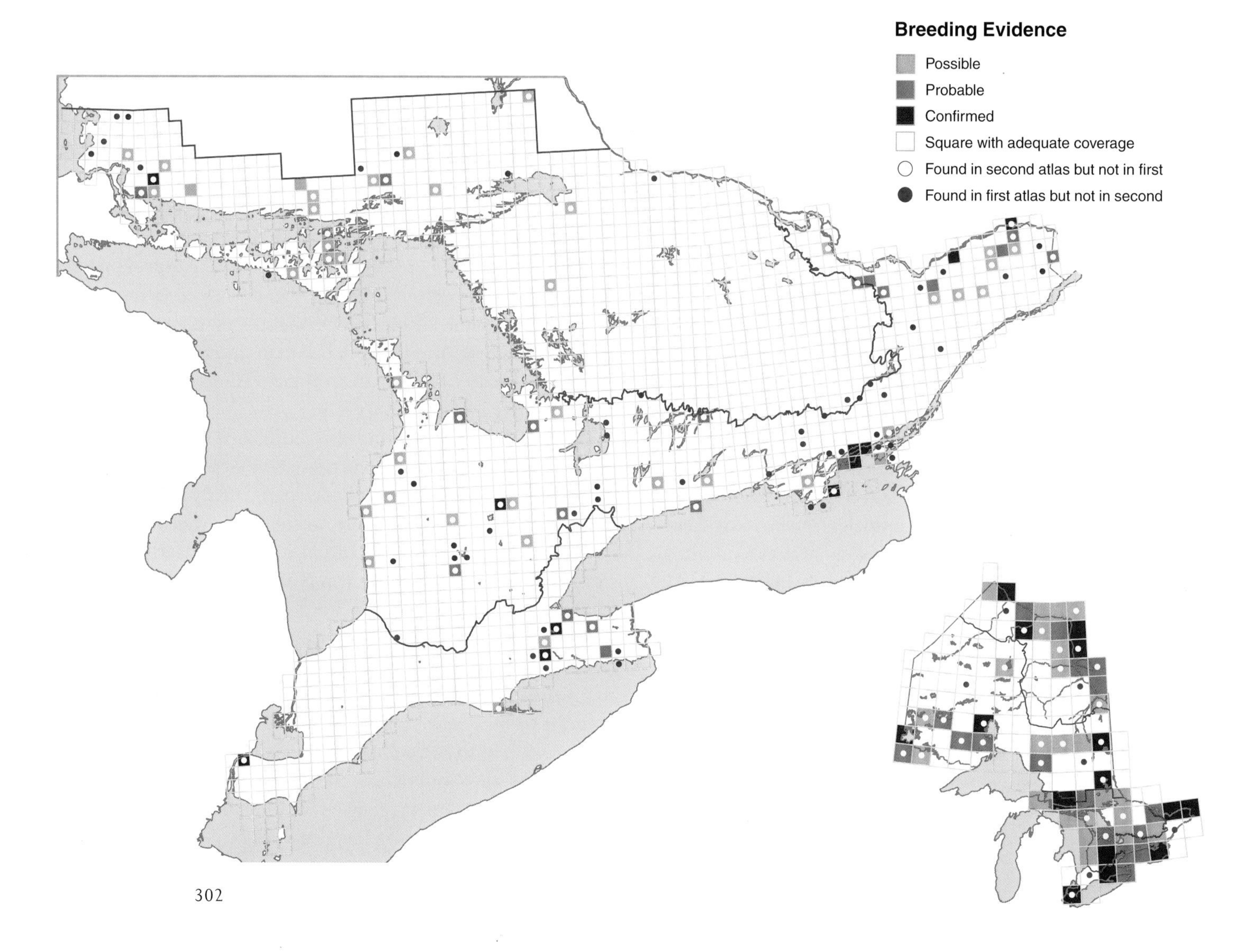

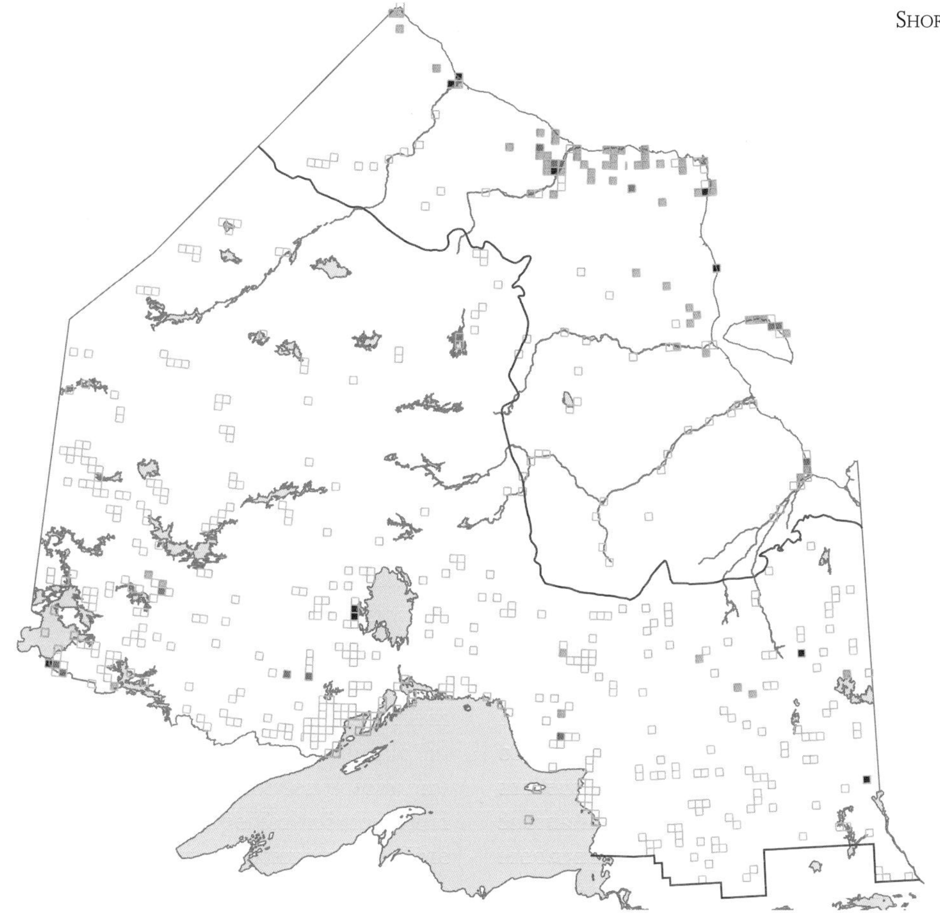

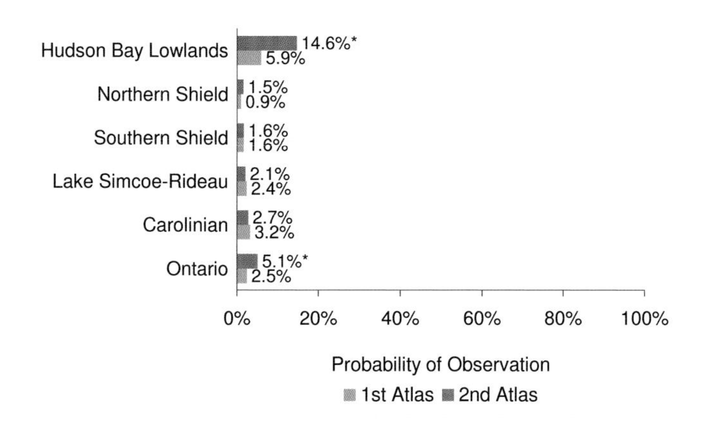

areas, however, it is a very localized and uncommon bird. Both the extensive forest of the Canadian Shield and the highly agricultural southwest generally offer more limited suitable habitat for the species, though it may also use large wetlands or other clearings, including clearcuts and abandoned fields (Wiggins et al. 2006).

Accurate population estimates for the Short-eared Owl are difficult to determine, given the challenges of monitoring a principally nomadic species, and none exist for Ontario. The stable-to-increasing population in Ontario, as suggested by the atlas results, may be somewhat misleading, as aerial surveys in the Hudson Bay Lowlands and targeted searches to locate the species by the Migration Research Foundation in southern Ontario may have resulted in higher detection rates than during the first atlas. This trend is counter to the long-term patterns of decline in the Great Plains and several northeastern states where the species is now considered extirpated (Tate 1992; Wiggins 2004). While a variety of factors may be involved, habitat loss is believed to be at least partly responsible (Wiggins et al. 2006). The Ontario status may be stable to increasing because the core of the species' provincial population is in the extensive and largely unchanged habitat of the Hudson Bay Lowlands.

Breeding biology: The Short-eared Owl prefers open habitats including tundra, grasslands, wetlands, and agricultural lands. The nest is built on the ground, usually adjacent to a clump of tall vegetation that provides some shelter and concealment (Wiggins et al. 2006). Nests are difficult to find, as adults are usually quiet and secretive near them, and although Short-eared Owls are occasionally observed during the day, they are far more active at night. It is not surprising, therefore, that only 13% of breeding records were confirmed, despite fledged young being reliably detected by their food-begging calls. Possible or probable breeding evidence is much easier to record, as the elaborate aerial courtship in April is highly visible and nesting or roosting birds will usually flush if disturbed. However, caution should be used in assuming nesting at areas where early courtship is observed, particularly in areas where migrants concentrate in the winter, as the site may not ultimately be used for breeding (Hunt and Gahbauer 2004).

Abundance: Point counts are poorly suited to assessing the abundance of most raptors, but the occurrence of several Short-eared Owls on Hudson Bay Lowlands counts suggests it is likely a fairly common species in that region. Elsewhere in the province, the species was not recorded on any point counts. Based on the breeding evidence map, it can be considered rare in most regions except the northern Hudson Bay Lowlands. – *Marcel A. Gahbauer*

Boreal Owl

Nyctale de Tengmalm

Aegolius funereus

Soren Bondrup-Nielsen

As its name suggests, the Boreal Owl is a resident of boreal forests throughout the world. In North America, it occurs in the Boreal Forest of Canada and Alaska, south through the Rocky Mountains to Colorado (Hayward and Hayward 1993). Seven subspecies are currently recognized (Hayward and Hayward 1993), six of them restricted to Eurasia where this species is called the Tengmalm's Owl. This small forest owl has been extensively studied in Scandinavia, but in North America, its habits remain relatively poorly understood.

Distribution and population status: Little is known about the historical distribution of the Boreal Owl in Ontario; because of its remote northern range in the province, this species is rarely encountered, and few nesting records exist (Mills in Cadman et al. 1987). Not surprisingly, the majority of Boreal Owl records during the second atlas were from the Northern Shield, although there were three records from the Hudson Bay Lowlands and six from the Southern Shield. Its spotty distribution in the Boreal Forest is in all likelihood largely a reflection of the distribution of the roadside Ontario Nocturnal Owl Survey (ONOS) routes. Areas without road access generally had poor coverage and lower detections rates for this early-breeding species.

Data from the first atlas suggested that the southern limit of the species was north of Georgian Bay in the Sudbury area. The second atlas shows a similar distribution, but with isolated records southeast of Lake Nipissing in the vicinity of South River and Trout Creek in Parry Sound Dist. A number of records of calling Boreal Owls south of Parry Sound were submitted to the atlas by the ONOS, which is conducted in mid-April. However, these records were not accepted as breeding evidence because of uncertainty that these birds were actually on territory. In years when Boreal Owls move nomadically from their northern breeding grounds, it is possible that some individuals may linger in spring south of their typical range.

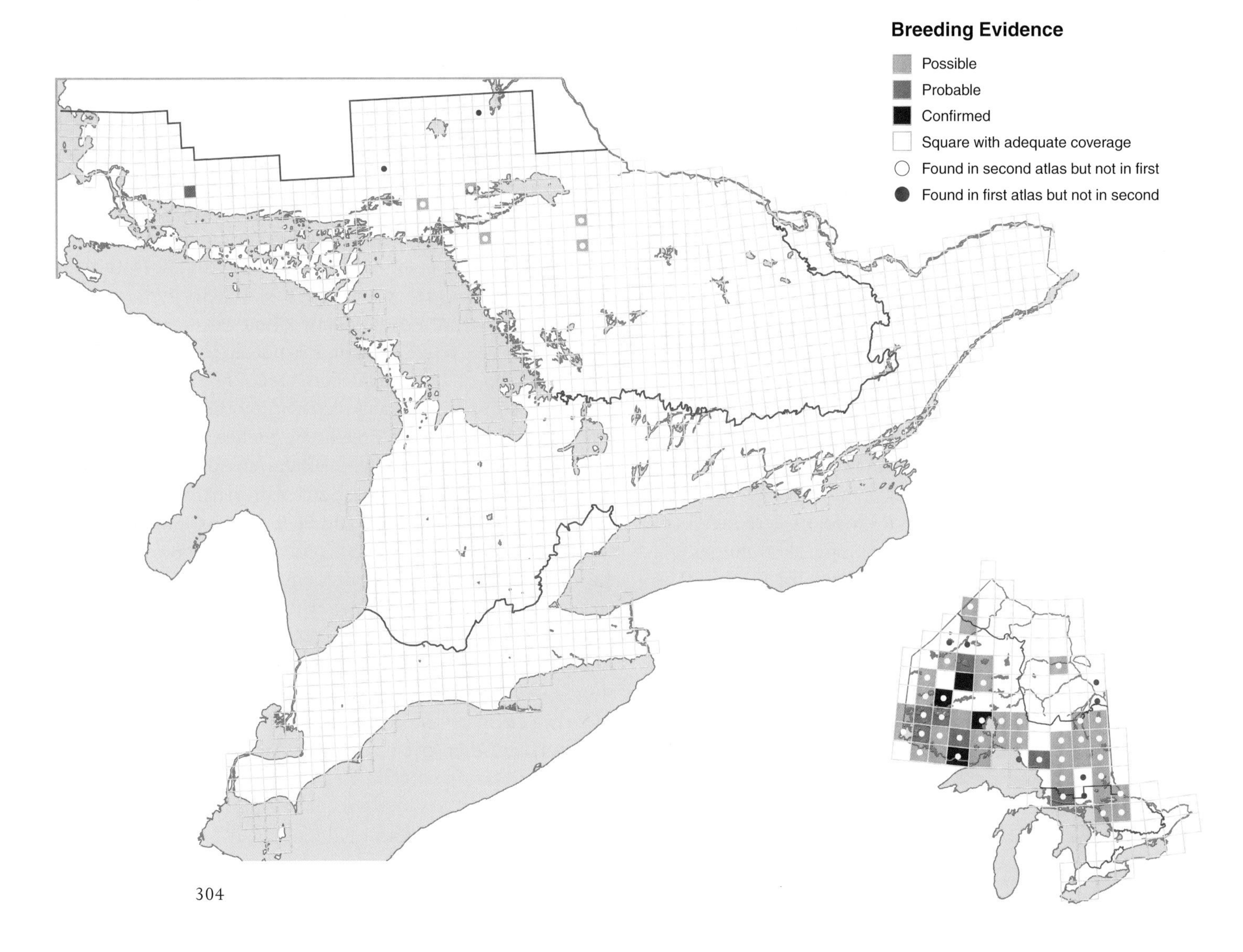

BREEDING EVIDENCE

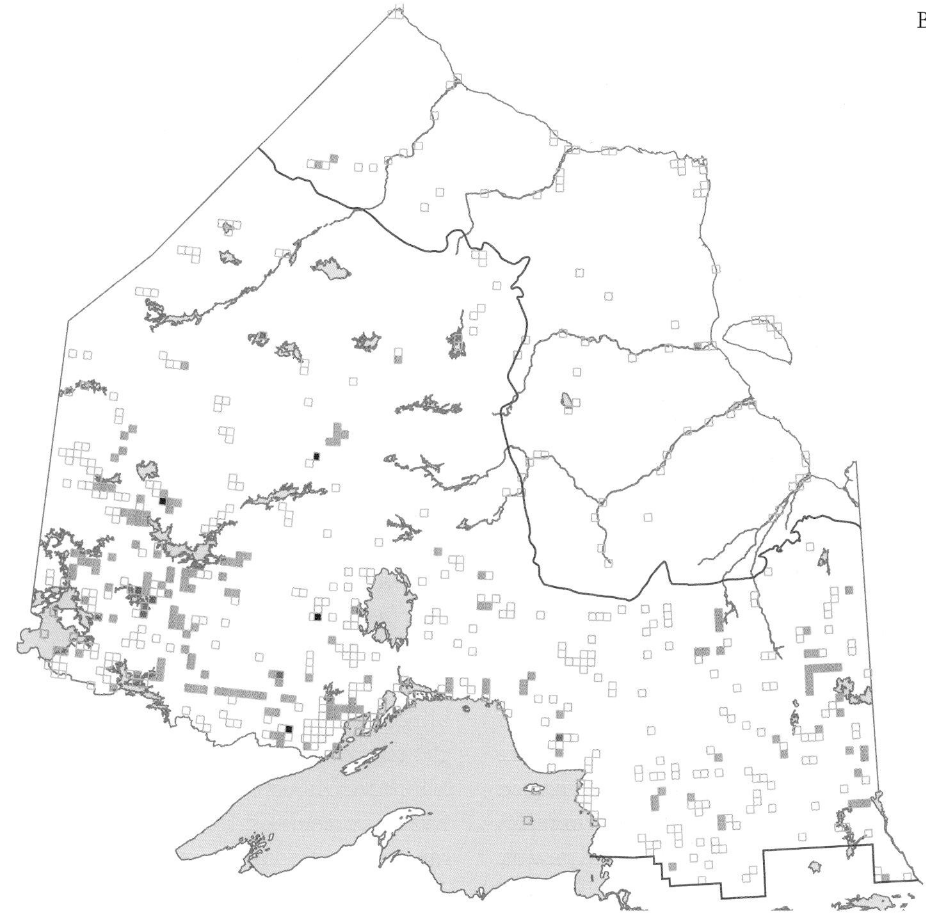

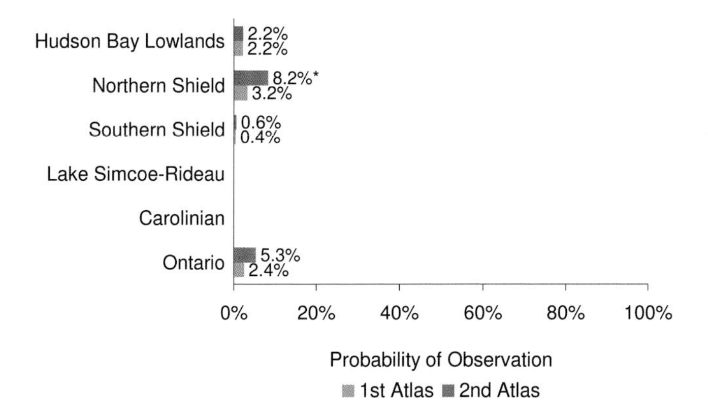

However, the ONOS often records the Boreal Owl south of Parry Sound, so it is possible that its range extends farther south than previously believed.

There was a significant increase in the probability of observation of the Boreal Owl in the Northern Shield between the first and second atlases. However, this is likely attributable to increased effort to locate owl species in the second atlas. During the first atlas, there were no specialized nocturnal owl surveys, and few atlassers undertook surveys of their own in the north. However, in the second atlas, data from ONOS were submitted to the atlas, and atlassers were also encouraged to conduct their own nocturnal owl surveys across the province.

Breeding biology: The Boreal Owl is a nocturnal species that inhabits large tracts of mature mixed forest and roosts in thick coniferous stands (Hayward and Hayward 1993). During the day, it is rarely seen and is typically only recorded on specialized nocturnal surveys during the courtship period (usually February-April; Hayward and Hayward 1993). It responds readily to tape playback of its call. Although this species is a year-round resident, females in particular will move nomadically during periods of food shortage (Korpimaki 1986). In irruption years, the Boreal Owl may winter in southern Ontario, and some individuals may linger into early spring.

Abundance: Atlas point counts were unable to sample the Boreal Owl to determine relative abundance during this period. However, ONOS data suggest that in the road-accessible areas of the province, this owl is most abundant in the northwest, particularly in the vicinity of Red Lake but also through the Clay Belt in northeastern Ontario (Crewe and Badzinski 2006b). Boreal Owl populations tend to be cyclic and track the approximate four-year cycle of its preferred prey species, the Red-backed Vole (Cheveau et al. 2004). Numbers of the Boreal Owl recorded by the ONOS peaked in 1997 and in the first year of the atlas (2001) but were in the low phase of their population cycle for the rest of the atlas period (Crewe and Badzinski 2006b). L'Observatoire d'oiseaux de Tadoussac, Québec, documented relatively large movements of this owl in autumn in 2000 and 2004, with smaller movements in 2001 and 2005 (Savard 2004). Similar movements occurred at Whitefish Point Bird Observatory, Michigan (Whitefish Point Bird Observatory, unpubl. data). These movements suggest that small-mammal numbers in the core of the Boreal Owl's range may have been low during the atlas and that the species' numbers were consequently depressed. – *Debra S. Badzinski*

Northern Saw-whet Owl

Petite Nyctale

Aegolius acadicus

Tim Dyson

The diminutive Northern Saw-whet Owl breeds in a wide variety of forested habitats across southern Canada and the northern US, south through the western mountain ranges to Mexico. Although some individuals remain on territory year round, large numbers (particularly hatch-year birds) move south in fall, some as far as the Gulf of Mexico. There is a marked concentration of migrants on the shores of the Great Lakes.

Distribution and population status: The Northern Saw-whet Owl was found throughout Ontario from about 51° N in the Boreal Forest south to Lakes Erie and Ontario during the second atlas, but the northern extent of its range is not well known. It is widespread but not especially common in any region, with the highest probability of observation, at 20%, in the Southern Shield. It is uncommon in the southwest due to lack of suitable habitat. During the first atlas, breeding evidence was reported in a small number of squares on the north shore of Lake Erie including Point Pelee Nat. Park, Rondeau Prov. Park, and near Long Point. In the second atlas, however, the southernmost records were restricted to one square with possible breeding evidence near Long Point and a fledged young bird caught and banded at Selkirk Prov. Park.

Between atlases, the Northern Saw-whet Owl showed a significant 54% decline in the probability of observation in the Lake Simcoe-Rideau region. Despite increased search effort for owls during the second atlas, declines were noted along the Niagara Escarpment, in areas of eastern Ontario such as Kingston, Cornwall, Ottawa, and Perth, and along the southern edge of the Shield. Compared to the first atlas, the species' southern Ontario range showed a significant shift north and west as a result of these declines, and coincident increases in the area from Manitoulin Island to Sault Ste. Marie.

Data from the Ontario Nocturnal Owl Survey show that the Northern Saw-whet Owl declined in central Ontario (i.e., roughly the Southern Shield region) from 1995-2005. In

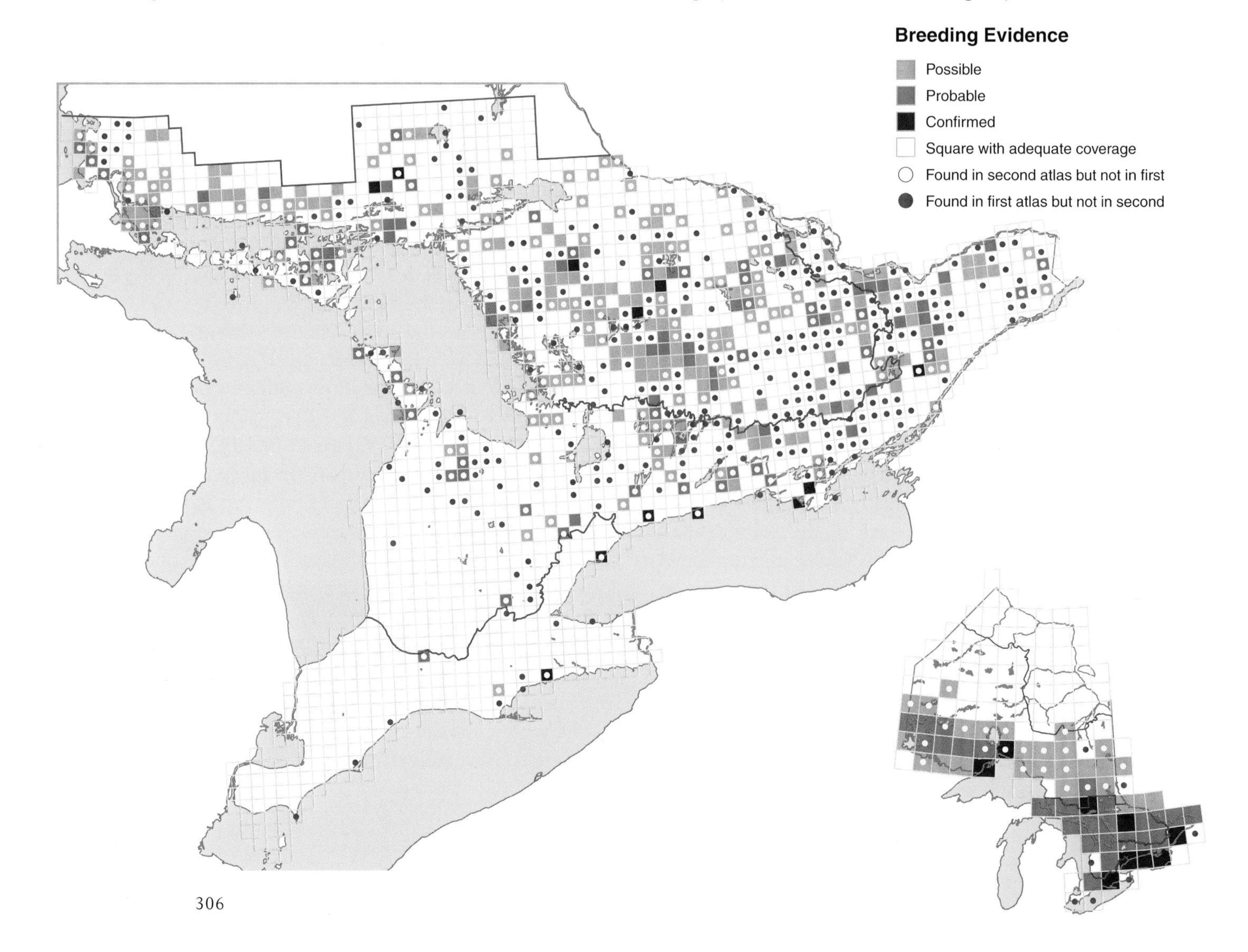

BREEDING EVIDENCE

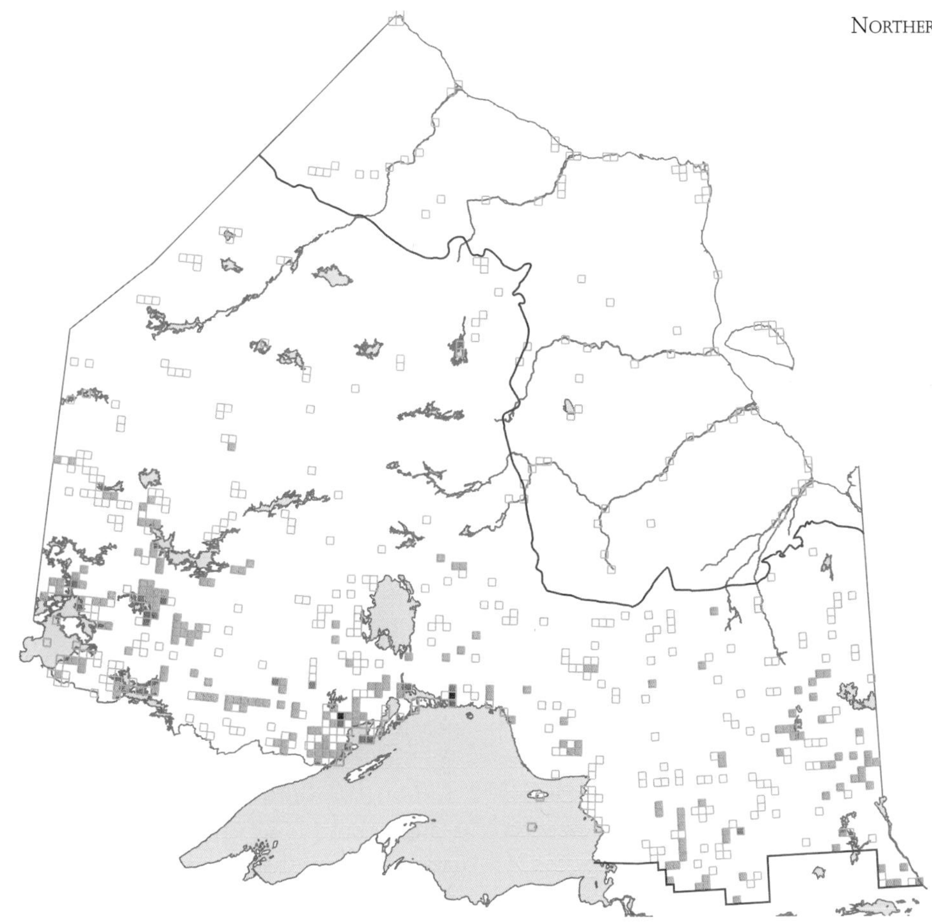

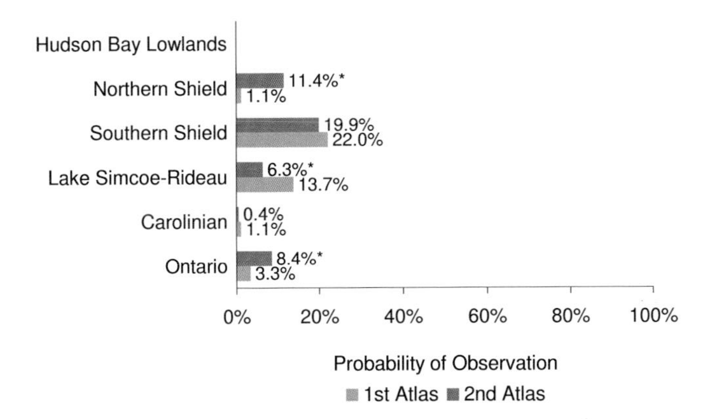

2000, the species showed a significant decline in this region and has remained relatively low since that time, following a pattern of increasing one year and declining the next (Crewe and Badzinski 2006b). Numbers in central Ontario were at low levels for three of the five atlas years (2002, 2004, 2005) and tend to closely track changes in small-mammal abundance (BSC and OMNR, unpubl. data).

In sharp contrast to central Ontario, in the Northern Shield the species showed a significant increase from eight squares in the first atlas to 215 squares in the second. This increase may be largely due to specialized surveys, including the Ontario Nocturnal Owl Survey, which were conducted during the second atlas but not during the first. However, owl survey data also show that in northern Ontario the species reached a peak in abundance in 2002, a year of low numbers in central Ontario, but numbers were also relatively high in most other years of the atlas (Crewe and Badzinski 2006b).

The observed decline in central Ontario, concurrent with the increase in northern Ontario, is difficult to explain but may reflect regional variation in small-mammal abundance. Low prey abundance leading to low breeding success or failure (Cannings 1993) probably results in reduced song frequency and decreased philopatry to breeding sites.

Breeding biology: The Northern Saw-whet Owl breeds in a wide variety of forest types but is most abundant in coniferous forests (Cannings 1993). During the day, it roosts motionless in dense vegetation. It is a cavity-nester that uses abandoned woodpecker holes and nest-boxes. The species is difficult to detect without specialized nocturnal surveys. Although it calls frequently early in its breeding season (March-April), it is typically quiet outside this period, particularly after clutch initiation. Therefore, atlassers searching for the species after April would likely have little success.

Abundance: Because of the difficulty in detecting the species due to its nocturnal habits, no abundance maps were generated. Distribution data indicate that the Northern Saw-whet Owl was recorded most frequently through the Southern Shield and in the area between Thunder Bay and Lake of the Woods, although this may in part reflect higher human populations in these areas and therefore a greater number of nocturnal surveys. Ontario Nocturnal Owl Survey data show that during the atlas period this owl was more abundant in northern Ontario (north of 47° N) than in central Ontario. In northern Ontario, an average of 0.9 owls/route was recorded from 2001-2005, compared to 0.6 owls/route in central Ontario (BSC, unpubl. data). – *Debra S. Badzinski*

Common Nighthawk

Engoulevent d'Amérique

Chordeiles minor

Jim Richards

The Common Nighthawk is most apparent at dusk and dawn when its distinctive call and loud booming can be heard. It is often seen wheeling high over forests or cities or low over water as it feeds on flying insects.

The Common Nighthawk breeds from subarctic regions of Canada throughout the US and less extensively south through much of Central America (Poulin et al. 1996). It is part of the aerial foraging guild, now declining significantly; 9 of 10 species have decreased significantly in Ontario between atlases. The Common Nighthawk appears to be declining significantly throughout its range (Poulin et al. 1996). Suggested contributing factors include filling of gaps in forests through natural reforestation, non-selective spraying for mosquitoes, reduction in numbers of gravelled roofs (Poulin et al. 1996), and nest predation by gulls and crows in cities (Iron and Pittaway 2002).

Distribution and population status: Early Ontario ornithologists considered the Common Nighthawk abundant and widely distributed from the southern boundaries north to the Hudson Bay coast (McIlwraith 1894; Baillie and Harrington 1937). MacLulich (1938) termed it common in Algonquin Park but not as abundant as in the agricultural south, and it was described as common in Niagara by Sheppard et al. (1936). Declines in populations were noted by many Ontario birders as early as the 1970s (Goodwin and Rosche 1974). During the first atlas, the Common Nighthawk was most common along the southern edge of the Shield and in rock barren habitat near Georgian Bay and Lake Huron. Although it occurred in lower densities in the north, a high proportion of the population nested there. During the first atlas, the nighthawk continued to breed in much of the agricultural south, except in areas of intensive farming. Southern concentrations were in cities with numerous flat roofs and on sand plains within extensive forest.

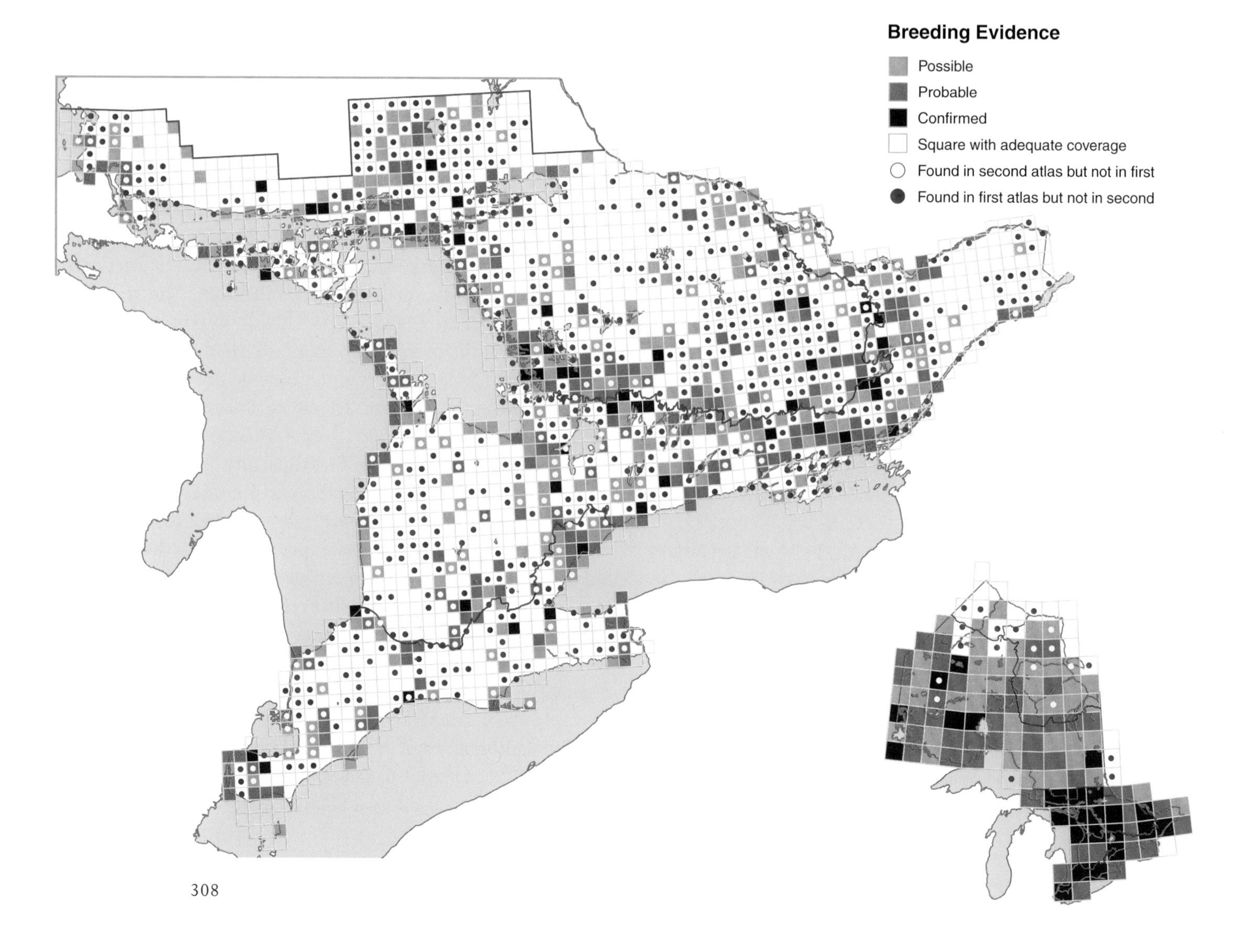

BREEDING EVIDENCE

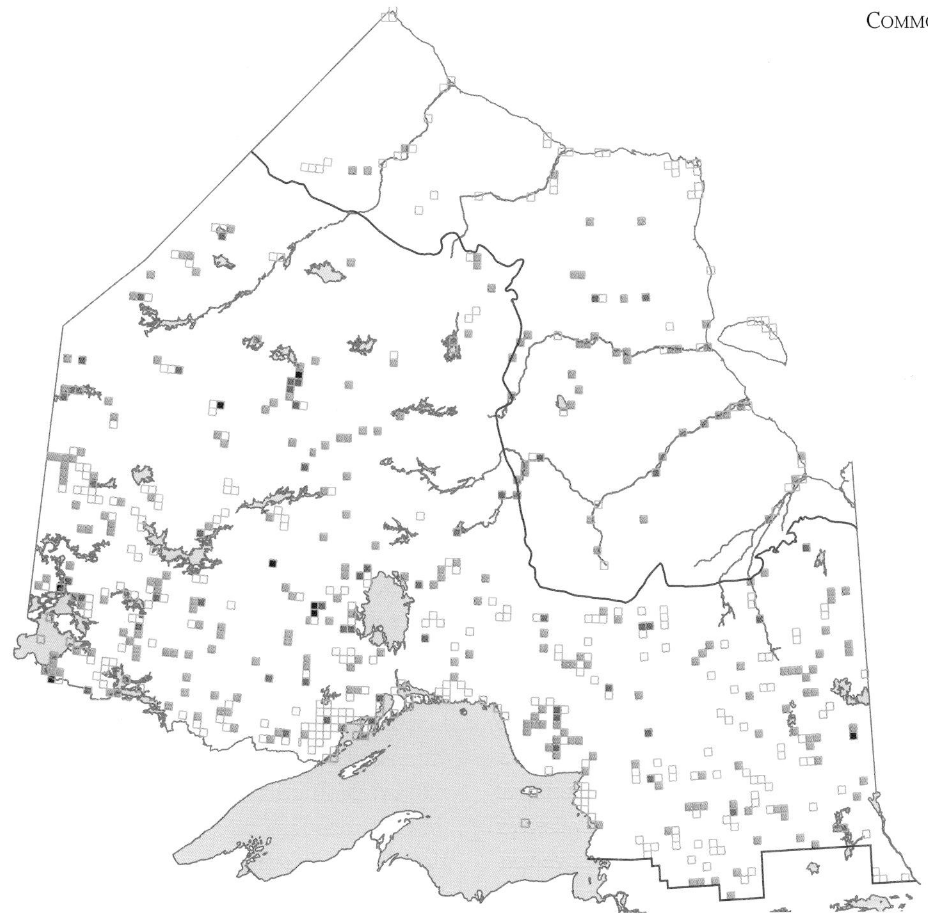

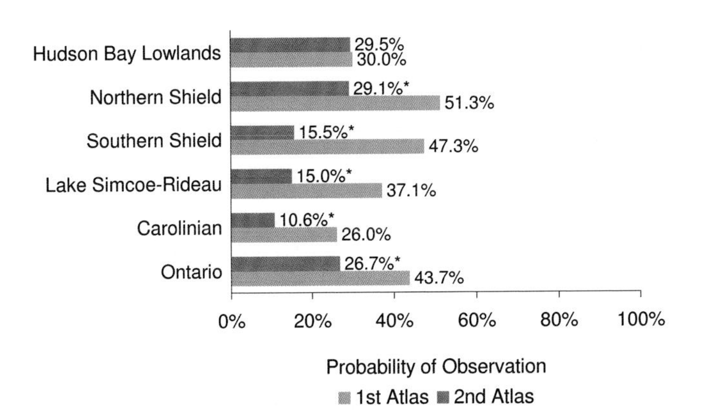

The probability of observation of the Common Nighthawk was 39% lower in the second atlas than in the first. Significant declines occurred in all regions except the Hudson Bay Lowlands. The most precipitous declines occurred in the Southern Shield (67%) and Lake Simcoe-Rideau (60%) regions. During the second atlas, the probability of observation was highest in the Northern Shield and Hudson Bay Lowlands. The most consistent area where it was recorded was again the southern edge of the Shield and the Georgian Bay shoreline, but gaps in distribution occurred there also. Perhaps these areas have the preferred interspersion of open rock barrens and forest cover. Farther south, the nighthawk has virtually disappeared from forested habitats and now occurs primarily in cities, though even there numbers seem much reduced in recent decades.

BBS results reflect the decline noted by the atlas, with significant annual declines of 6.0% and 4.5% since 1968 in Ontario and Canada, respectively (Downes et al. 2005). The decline has been more severe recently, with annual declines of 11% in Ontario and 7.7% in Canada from 1981 to 2005. Anecdotal information suggests that numbers of autumn migrants have also declined (Goodwin and Rosche 1974; Iron and Pittaway 2002).

Breeding biology: The Common Nighthawk nests in open habitats, in forests and in urban areas. It prefers rock outcrops, alvars, sand barrens, bogs, fens, and in forests, openings created by clearcuts and burns. In the agricultural south, it has nested in grasslands, agricultural fields, gravel pits, prairies, and alvars and at airports. In cities, it nests mostly on flat, gravelled roofs but occasionally on railways and footpaths (Peck and James 1983).

In natural areas, nests are in the open on bare or sparsely vegetated rock, sand, or gravel. Given that the nighthawk is predominantly crepuscular or nocturnal, and incubating birds are very well camouflaged and sit tight, this species is difficult to confirm. Young are fed regurgitated food, so confirmation by observation of carrying food is not possible. In cities, most nesting occurs on large gravelled rooftops, almost all of which have walls or other structures on them (Poulin et al. 1996).

Abundance: The Common Nighthawk was not detected on enough point counts to provide a relative abundance map. During the first atlas, 2-10 pairs were estimated for most squares, although there were some estimates of 1 and 11-100. James (1991) considered it common throughout the south and uncommon in the Boreal Forest and Hudson Bay Lowlands. Results of this atlas suggest it is rare to locally uncommon south of the Shield and uncommon on the Shield and in the Hudson Bay Lowlands. – *Al Sandilands*

Chuck-will's-widow

Engoulevent de Caroline

Caprimulgus carolinensis

Alan Wormington

The Chuck-will's-widow is widespread in eastern North America, breeding in deciduous and mixed woodlands at lower elevations. Its breeding range was formerly restricted primarily to the US southeast; however, during the 20th century, its range gradually expanded north and west (Straight and Cooper 2000). From the 1960s to the 1980s, this northward expansion led to extralimital records of possible, probable, or confirmed breeding in Michigan, New York, Pennsylvania, Massachusetts, and Ontario (Straight and Cooper 2000). The Chuck-will's-widow occasionally occurs as a non-breeding spring and fall vagrant north to Québec, New Brunswick, Nova Scotia, and Newfoundland (Godfrey 1986; Straight and Cooper 2000).

Distribution and population status: Since the species was first noted in Ontario at Point Pelee in May 1906 (Fleming 1906), more than 70 records of Chuck-will's-widow have been reported. Most records are from the Carolinian region, but the species has also been found north to Manitoulin Island and Deep River (Renfrew County). Within the Carolinian region, more than 65% of records have come from just four locations: Point Pelee, Rondeau, Long Point, and St. Williams Forest (Norfolk County). Confirmation of breeding in Ontario was established in 1977, when a nest was discovered at Point Pelee; what was presumably the same pair was present there each summer from 1975 to 1979 (Wormington 2002).

In the first atlas, Chuck-will's-widow was reported in six squares. Probable breeding was established in the four squares encompassing Rondeau. In Norfolk County, possible breeding was reported in one square; this record involved as many as three territorial males present in the St. Williams Forest between 1981 and 1984 and represents probable rather than possible breeding status. The other square with possible breed-

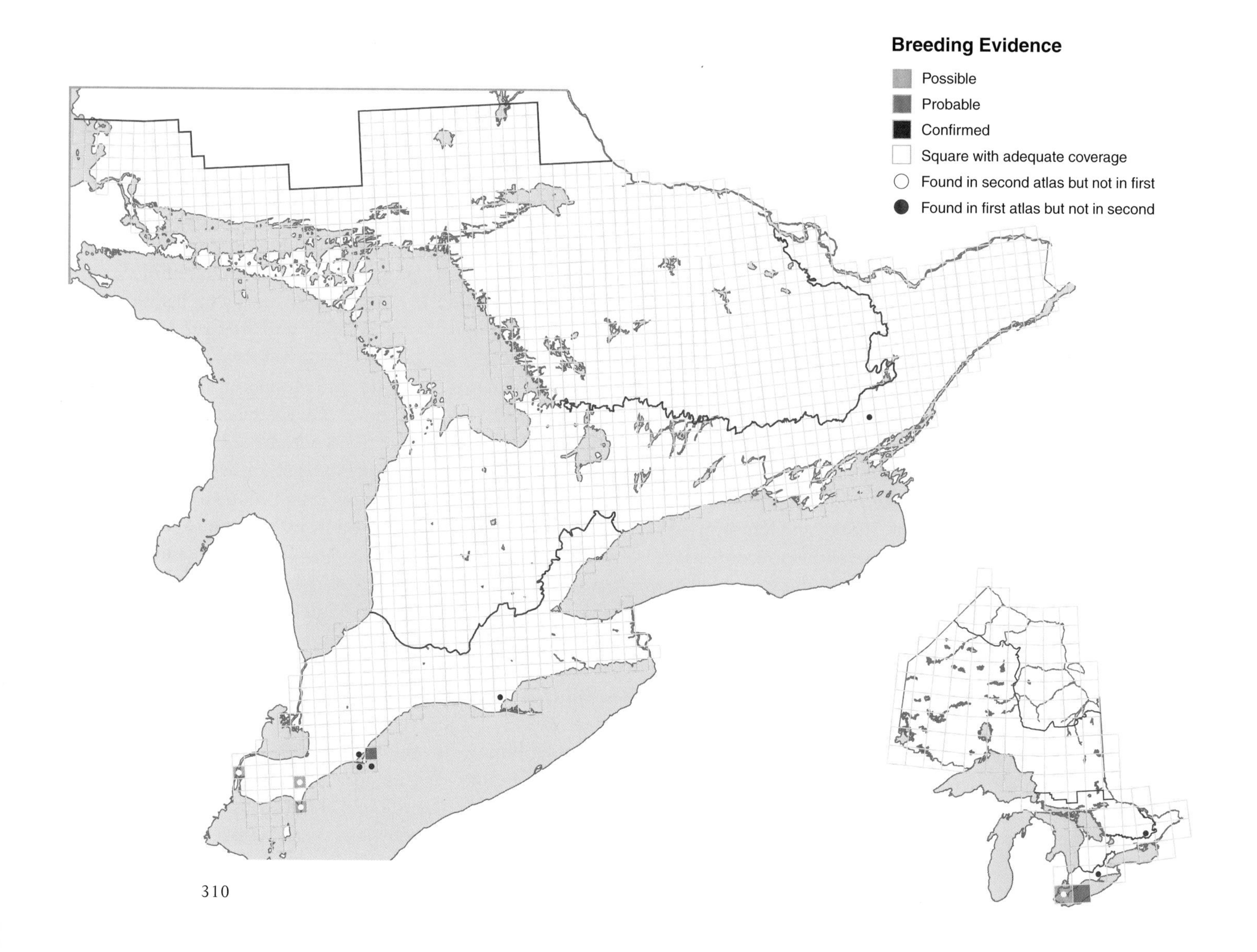

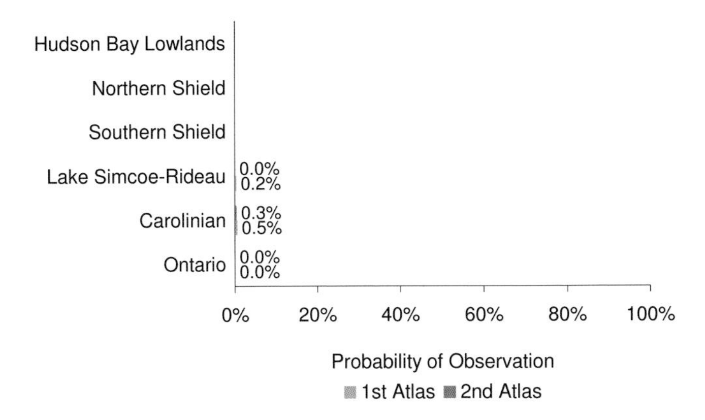

ing evidence involved a singing male at Perth Road (Frontenac County) that was present on only a single date, suggesting a vagrant rather than possible breeding.

Between atlases, evidence of probable breeding occurred at Rondeau (1986, 1988, 1994,1996); South Walsingham Forest, Norfolk County (1986-1988); Long Point (1991-1993, 1995-1996); Burpee Township, Manitoulin District (1992-1995); and Venison Creek, Norfolk County (1995). Also, transient singing males were recorded at Baldwin (York R.M.), Beachville (Oxford County), Point Pelee, Presqu'ile Prov. Park, Spooky Hollow (Norfolk County), and Wheatley Prov. Park.

During the second atlas, the Chuck-will's-widow was reported in four squares. The only square with breeding evidence during both atlases was at Rondeau, where a singing male in the same vicinity in Red Oak-White Pine woodland from 17 May to 18 June 2004 and from 17 May to 27 June 2005 was presumably the same individual. This was the only square with probable breeding evidence. Possible breeding was recorded for three squares. At La Salle (Essex County) and Point Pelee, the birds likely represented late migrants or wandering individuals, as they were recorded on only a single date. A singing male at Wheatley Prov. Park was also recorded on one date, but no follow-up visit was made to confirm its continued presence.

Breeding biology: For breeding, the Chuck-will's-widow prefers oak-dominated deciduous and mixed forest, woodland, and savannah interspersed with abandoned fields (Straight and Cooper 2000). In Ontario, occupied sites are typically sandy, open woodlands or savannahs dominated by White Pine and oak.

The Chuck-will's-widow is a cryptic species unlikely to be detected except by its diagnostic song. The frequency and duration of singing by males is greatest upon arrival at prospective breeding sites but generally declines throughout the nesting cycle with some resurgence prior to migration (Straight and Cooper 2000). Most singing is crepuscular but may continue throughout moonlit nights. Song frequency and duration are also temperature related and are reduced at cooler temperatures (Straight and Cooper 2000). Given its loud, distinctive song, it is unlikely the Chuck-will's-widow was missed in squares where crepuscular surveys were conducted.

The presence of territorial males at sites, occasionally in multiple years, suggests probable breeding, but observations of females and pairs are relatively rare and thus breeding should not necessarily be inferred. Fidelity to breeding areas is unknown, though circumstantial evidence suggests that territories are reoccupied in successive years (Straight and Cooper 2000). Confirmation of breeding is very difficult, as incubating adults and fledged young are highly cryptic.

The two eggs are laid directly on exposed leaf litter in open woodlands. The only documented nest in Ontario was found at Point Pelee Nat. Park in 1977. *Photo: George K. Peck*

In Ontario, occupied sites are typically sandy, open woodlands or savannahs dominated by White Pine and oaks. Rondeau Prov. Park. *Photo: P. Allen Woodliffe*

Abundance: Although the Chuck-will's-widow has occurred in Ontario almost annually since 1975, reports for most years involve only singing males. The nest record for Point Pelee in 1977 remains the only confirmation of breeding in Canada (Wormington 2002). Available data indicate that occupancy of sites is intermittent or transitory and that the Chuck-will's-widow is not yet established as a breeder in Ontario. – *Donald A. Sutherland and Alan Wormington*

Whip-poor-will

Engoulevent bois-pourri

Caprimulgus vociferus

John Reaume

There are many who have heard but never seen a Whip-poor-will. Its "whip-poor-will" song is distinctive, very loud, and often almost endlessly repeated, starting after dusk and continuing long into the night if the moon is bright, then beginning again before dawn. The Whip-poor-will is rarely seen because it becomes active only during twilight and moonlight. During daylight hours, it sits motionless on a branch or the forest floor, well camouflaged by its beautifully intricate but subtle plumage.

The Whip-poor-will occupies two separate breeding ranges, one in eastern North America from South Carolina and Oklahoma northward, and the other in highlands from the US Southwest to Honduras; these populations may represent two separate species (Cink 2002). In Canada, it inhabits open woodlands from the Maritimes (rather sparingly) westward through southern Québec and Ontario to central Saskatchewan. The Whip-poor-will winters from the US Gulf States south to Honduras (Cink 2002).

Distribution and population status: Special surveying effort is needed to detect the presence of the Whip-poor-will, and this species was undoubtedly missed in some squares. Nonetheless, coverage during both atlases was sufficient to demonstrate a continuing dramatic decline in this species' population throughout southern Ontario, consistent with trends noted elsewhere in North America (Cink 2002). The probability of observation declined significantly by 51% between atlases. In Ontario, this trend began in the mid-20th century. Many older atlassers recall days when this species' song could be heard in most parts of southern Ontario, north at least to the Sudbury region. By the first atlas, the Whip-poor-will had withdrawn from most of Ontario's agricultural southwest, although it could still be found reliably in a number of areas in the watersheds of Lakes Erie and Huron. Its disappearance from there is now almost complete, except for

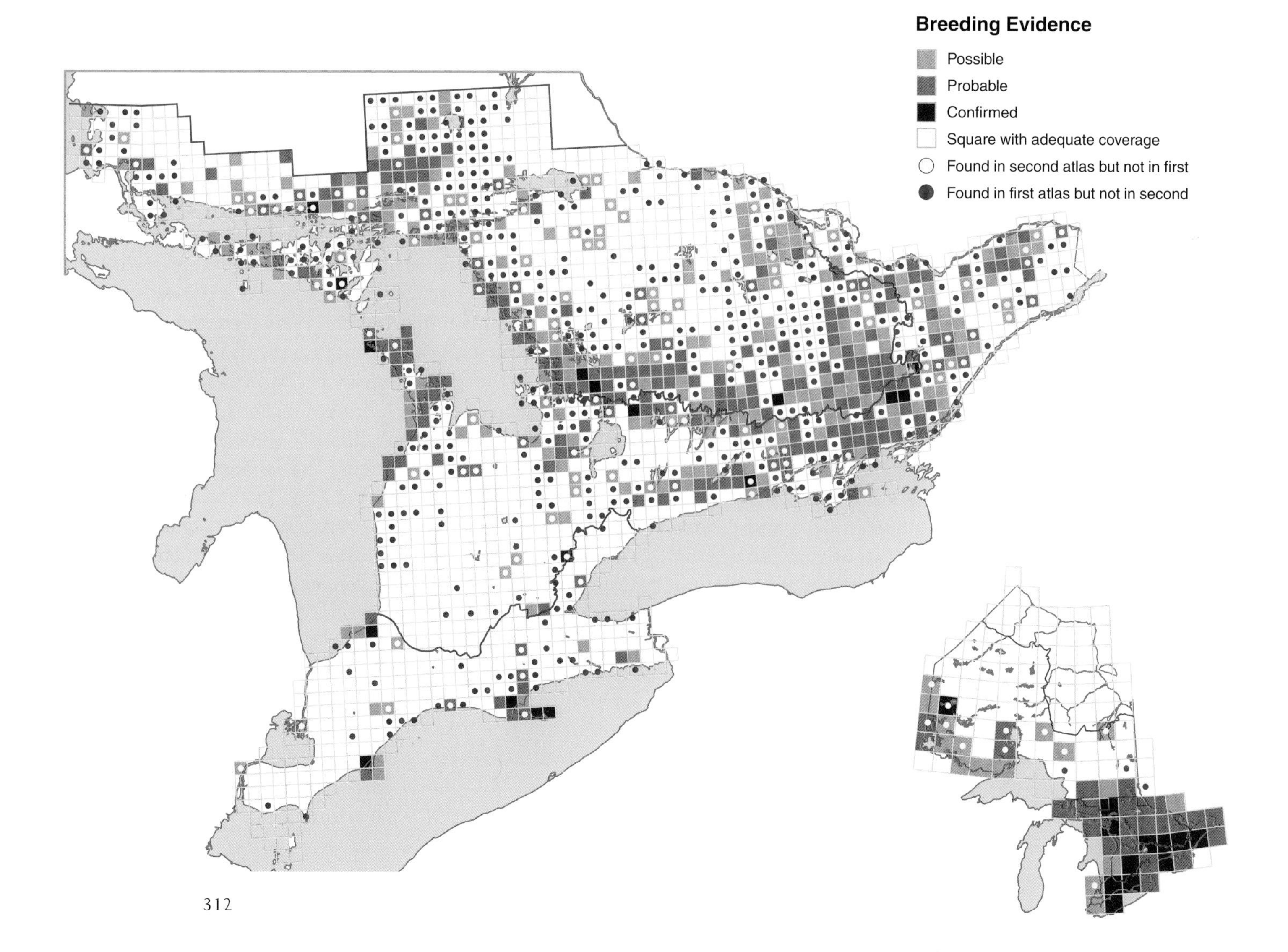

BREEDING EVIDENCE

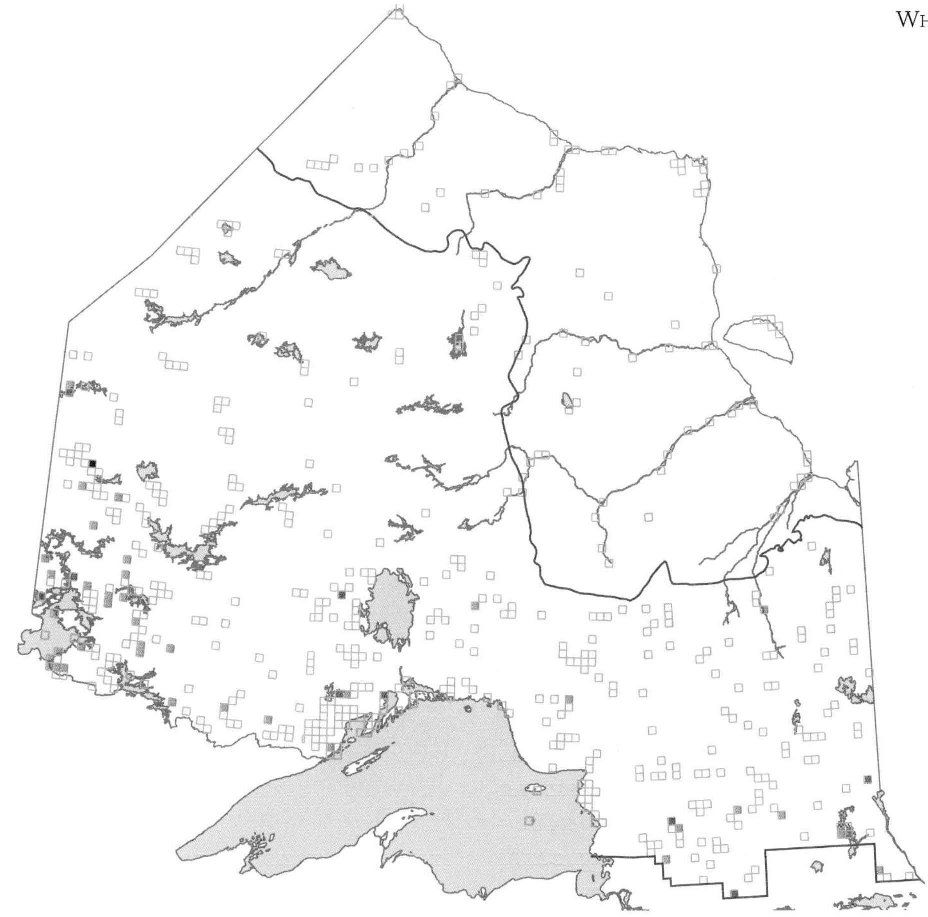

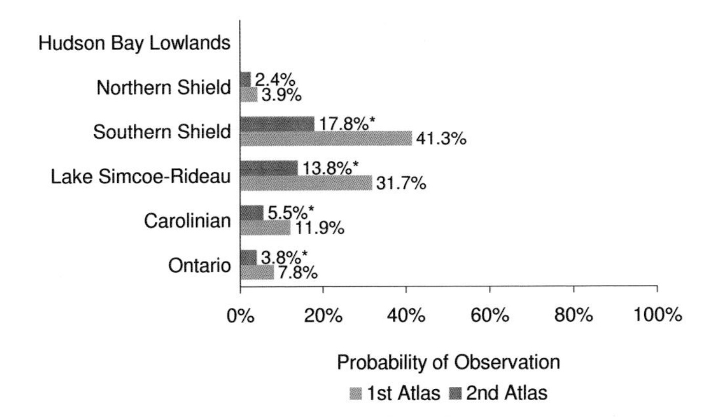

scattered occurrences and isolated populations near The Pinery, Rondeau, and Long Point. Farther north but still south of the Shield, significant populations continue to occur along the Bruce Peninsula, on the Oak Ridges Moraine, and through the Carden Plain.

The Whip-poor-will was widespread through the Southern Shield during the first atlas, although it was scarce in places like the Algonquin Highlands, probably because of extensive mature hardwood forests. Since then, populations appear to have disappeared from large sections of the Southern Shield. In this core area, the squares in which it was found only during the first atlas far outnumber those in which it was recorded only during the second atlas. The main Ontario breeding range currently extends from the Rideau Lakes along the Shield edge south of Algonquin, up the Georgian Bay shoreline (and Bruce Peninsula) to Sudbury. The Whip-poor-will was detected in several 100-km blocks north of Lake Superior, but it is difficult to draw conclusions about the significance of these isolated occurrences.

Breeding biology: This species' habits necessitate special atlassing effort. It sings only when the sun is well below the horizon. Furthermore, if searching is done during non-twilight periods at night, success is unlikely unless there is significant moonlight. Many atlassers made special surveying efforts at night, but in many squares there was little or no nocturnal atlassing. Those searching systematically for owls at night were unlikely to encounter the Whip-poor-will, since owl surveys were generally completed before this bird's arrival in early May. Similarly, the BBS is inadequate to measure the Whip-poor-will's status since it ceases singing at dawn when the survey starts.

The Whip-poor-will shuns both wide-open spaces and deep forest. In Ontario, its preferred habitats include rock or sand barrens with scattered trees, savannahs, old burns in a state of early forest succession, and open conifer plantations. The two eggs are laid directly on the leaf litter, without benefit of a nest, generally at the time of the full moon (Mills 1986). The adult never leaves the nest during daylight and makes relatively few visits even during the night, since the young are fed by regurgitation (Cink 2002). Consequently, it is very difficult to confirm breeding.

Abundance: The diurnal point count surveys yielded no information about the abundance of this species. The decline of the Whip-poor-will is unlikely to have been caused primarily by the same factors behind more recent declines of other aerial-foraging species, although these may be aggravating elements. Declines may be attributable to longer-term, widespread changes in habitat, such as intensive agriculture in the southwest and natural forest succession farther north. The Whip-poor-will is still locally common in ideal habitats such as parts of the Georgian Bay shoreline. – *Alex Mills*

Chimney Swift

Martinet ramoneur

Chaetura pelagica

George K. Peck

The delightful overhead chittering of the "cigar with wings" is heard much less commonly in Ontario than it was 20 years ago, and the demise of the old-fashioned chimney appears to be a large factor in the decline. In April 2007, due largely to rapid population declines, the Chimney Swift was recommended as a Threatened species in Canada by COSEWIC.

The breeding range of the Chimney Swift is restricted to eastern North America. About 25% of its breeding range is in Canada, where it occurs across the Maritimes, southern Québec, southern and central Ontario, southern Manitoba, and east-central Saskatchewan. It breeds throughout the eastern US, with the exception of southern Florida (Cink and Collins 2002).

Distribution and population status: Prior to settlement by Europeans, the Chimney Swift was presumably nesting in large hollow trees, other tree cavities, and cracks in cliffs. However, with the advent of buildings and the decline of forest cover in much of its range, the species moved into settled areas, using the many nesting opportunities provided by these new structures, especially chimneys.

The species has declined markedly over at least the past 40 years. Atlas results indicate a decline between atlases of 46% in the probability of observation in the province as a whole, with the largest declines in the Southern Shield and Lake-Simcoe-Rideau regions, at 58% and 48%, respectively. BBS data show an annual decline of 8.9% in Ontario from 1968 to 2005 (Downes et al. 2005), further emphasizing the dramatic decline of the species.

Atlassers recorded only a few Chimney Swifts in northern Ontario. Its range has retracted southward between atlases; it was not reported at Pickle Lake or Red Lake during the second atlas as it was during the first. However, in both atlases, there

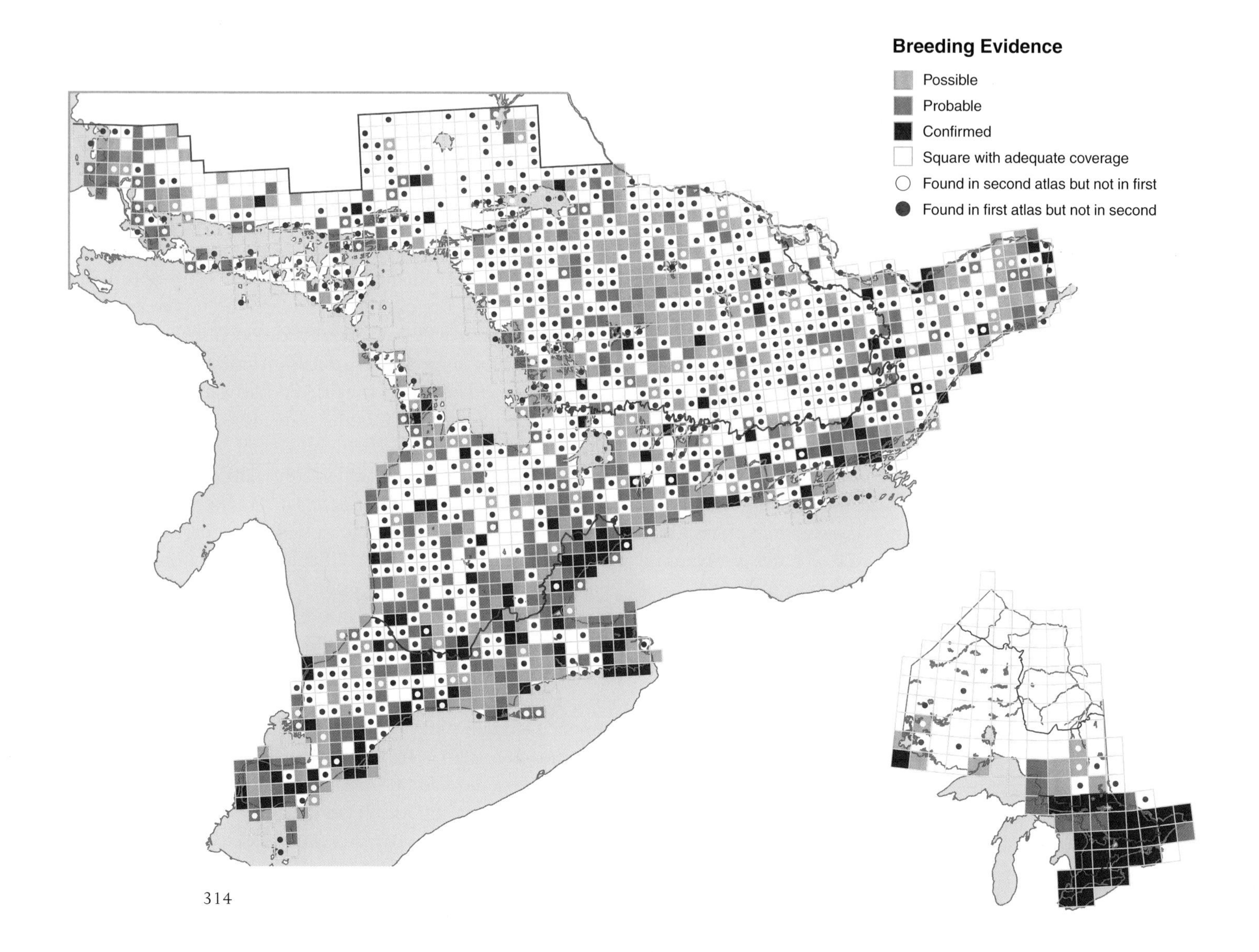

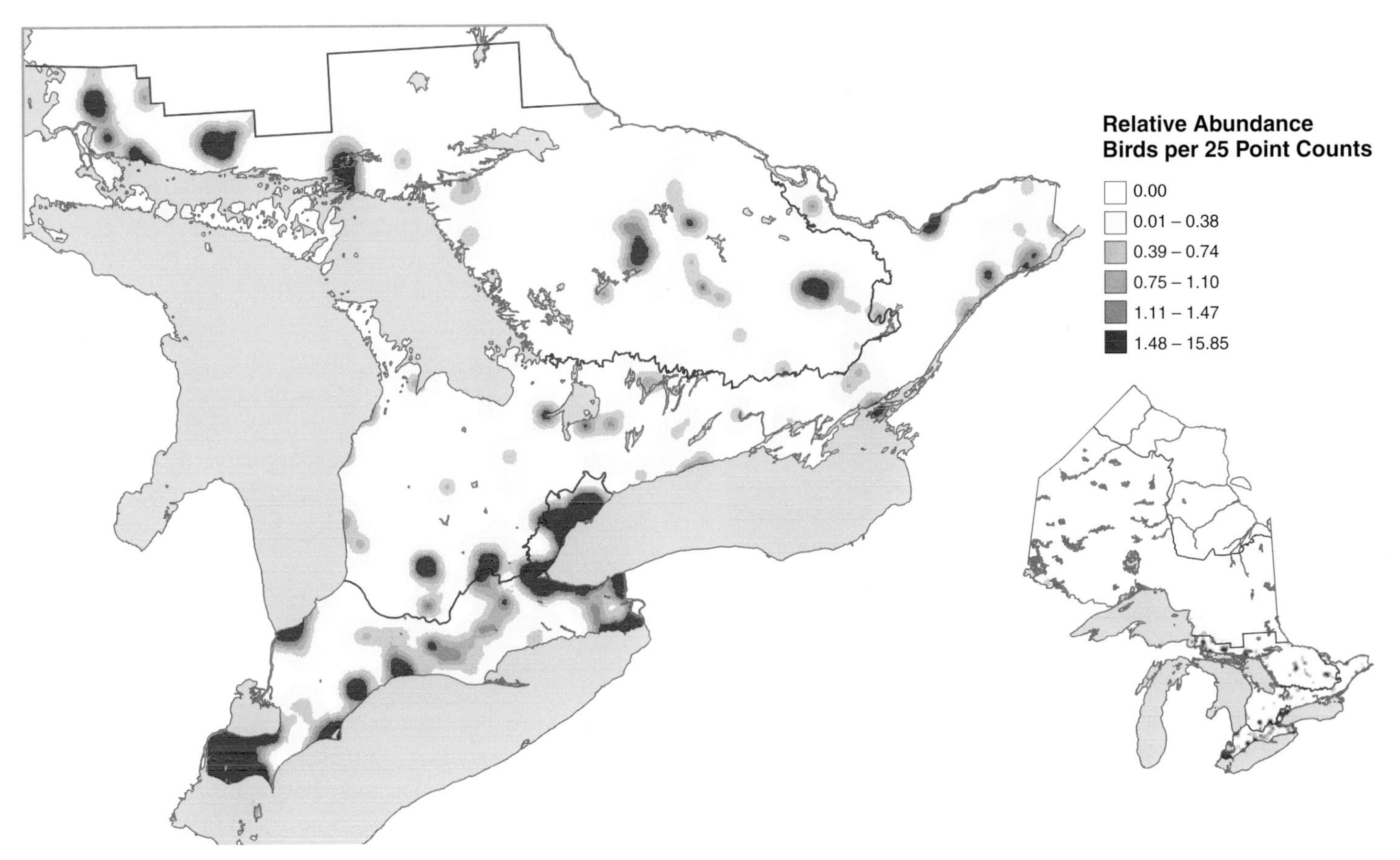

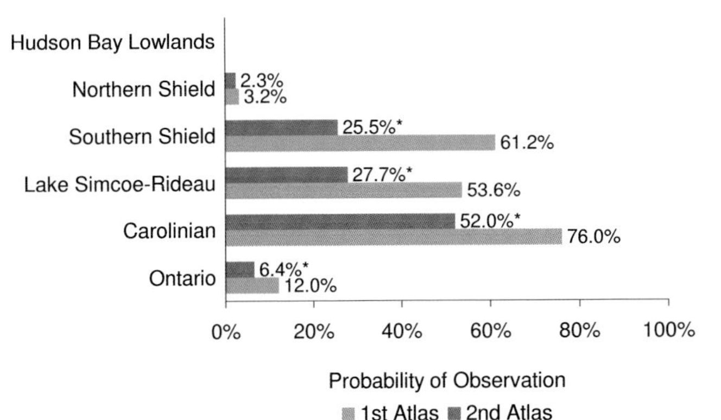

were similar clusters of squares with records in and around Sault Ste. Marie and Rainy River, suggesting that these areas remain particularly suitable for the species.

It is unclear why the Haliburton and southern Algonquin Prov. Park area has maintained a population of swifts while adjacent areas have not, but it could possibly relate to the maturation of the forests in this area. Older forests might be expected to provide more tree cavities and hollow trees suitable for nesting.

The species is most widely distributed in the Carolinian, suggesting that this area is the most suitable for the species in the province. A concentration of records in the Golden Horseshoe, which has the highest population of people and buildings in the province, is evident. However, concentrations of records in rural areas on the Niagara Peninsula, around Long Point, and in Essex County and Chatham-Kent suggest that factors other than the density of chimneys are affecting the species' occurrence. As this same pattern has been found in some swallows, it may be that aerial insectivores benefit from the region's relatively mild climate.

Breeding biology: The Chimney Swift's habit of flying high overhead and twittering frequently make it conspicuous for a bird of its size; if it is breeding in a square, it is quite likely to be reported. It spends 50% of its time foraging within 0.5 km of the nest (Cink and Collins 2002), but some individuals are known to forage at distances of 3-6 km. As birds tend to concentrate in good foraging areas (J. Gauthier, pers. comm.), some records may be of birds nesting in adjacent squares.

The Chimney Swift usually nests with only one pair to a chimney, so a shortage of suitable chimneys is likely to affect numbers. Certainly, the growing use of electric and gas heating, new fire-prevention standards (metal chimney liners, installation of spark arresters, chimney hats, and protective netting against nuisance animals) has reduced the number of traditional chimneys available for swifts (Gauthier et al. 2007). However, about half of nests reported in Ontario by Peck and James (1983) were on walls, rafters, or gables of buildings, though this may reflect the difficulty of observers accessing nests in chimneys.

Abundance: Areas of high abundance occur near shorelines of the Great Lakes, suggesting that the proximity of the lakes contributes to the suitability of the habitat. The highest densities of swifts are in the Golden Horseshoe, along the north shore of Lake Erie between Elgin and Essex Counties, and near Sault Ste. Marie. Smaller concentrations found in the southern part of the Algonquin, Haliburton, and Madawaska Highlands, as well as in the Rainy River area, indicate that there are also populations away from both the Great Lakes and highly urban areas. – *Michael D. Cadman*

Ruby-throated Hummingbird

Colibri à gorge rubis

Archilochus colubris

George K. Peck

The Ruby-throated Hummingbird is the only regularly occurring hummingbird in Ontario. It breeds across eastern North America north to the southern Boreal Forest and across the Canadian prairies to central Alberta. It is well known and appreciated by many, as shown by the abundance of hummingbird feeders.

Everything about the diminutive Ruby-throated Hummingbird is remarkable, including its sparkling iridescence, its ability to hover and fly backwards, and its impressive migration to and from the wintering grounds in Mexico, Central America and extreme southern Florida (Robinson et al. 1996). Weighing a mere 2.5 to 3.5 g, it can complete an 800 km non-stop flight across the Gulf of Mexico (Robinson et al. 1996).

Distribution and population status: The Ruby-throated Hummingbird was reported in most squares in the Carolinian, Lake Simcoe-Rideau, and Southern Shield regions and sparsely throughout the southern part of the Northern Shield. It may always have been a common species throughout this range; however, flower gardens, the opening of forest for cottages, and the widespread popularity of hummingbird feeders, as well as natural succession as some marginal farmland in southern Ontario has returned to shrubland and forest, have all undoubtedly benefited this bird in southern Ontario compared with earlier times.

The overall distribution of this species did not change between atlases. The probability of observation, however, increased significantly in the second atlas by 21% province-wide and by 19% in both the Carolinian and Lake Simcoe-Rideau regions. The largest change in the probability of observation involved a significant 39% increase in the Northern Shield region. This may be due to additional feeders and more suitable habitat now in northern Ontario.

Breeding biology: The Ruby-throated Hummingbird breeds in a wide variety of habitats, including edges and open-

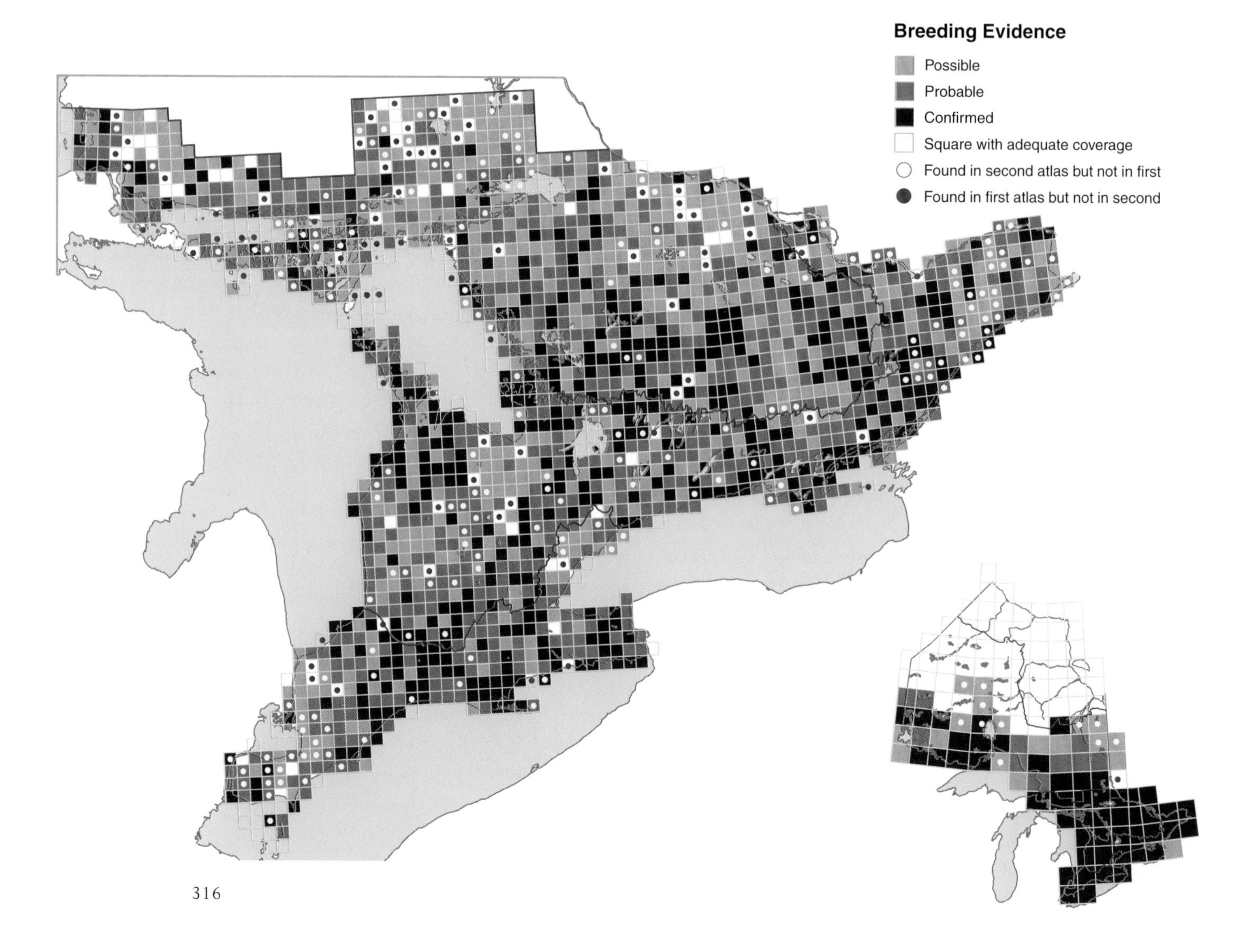

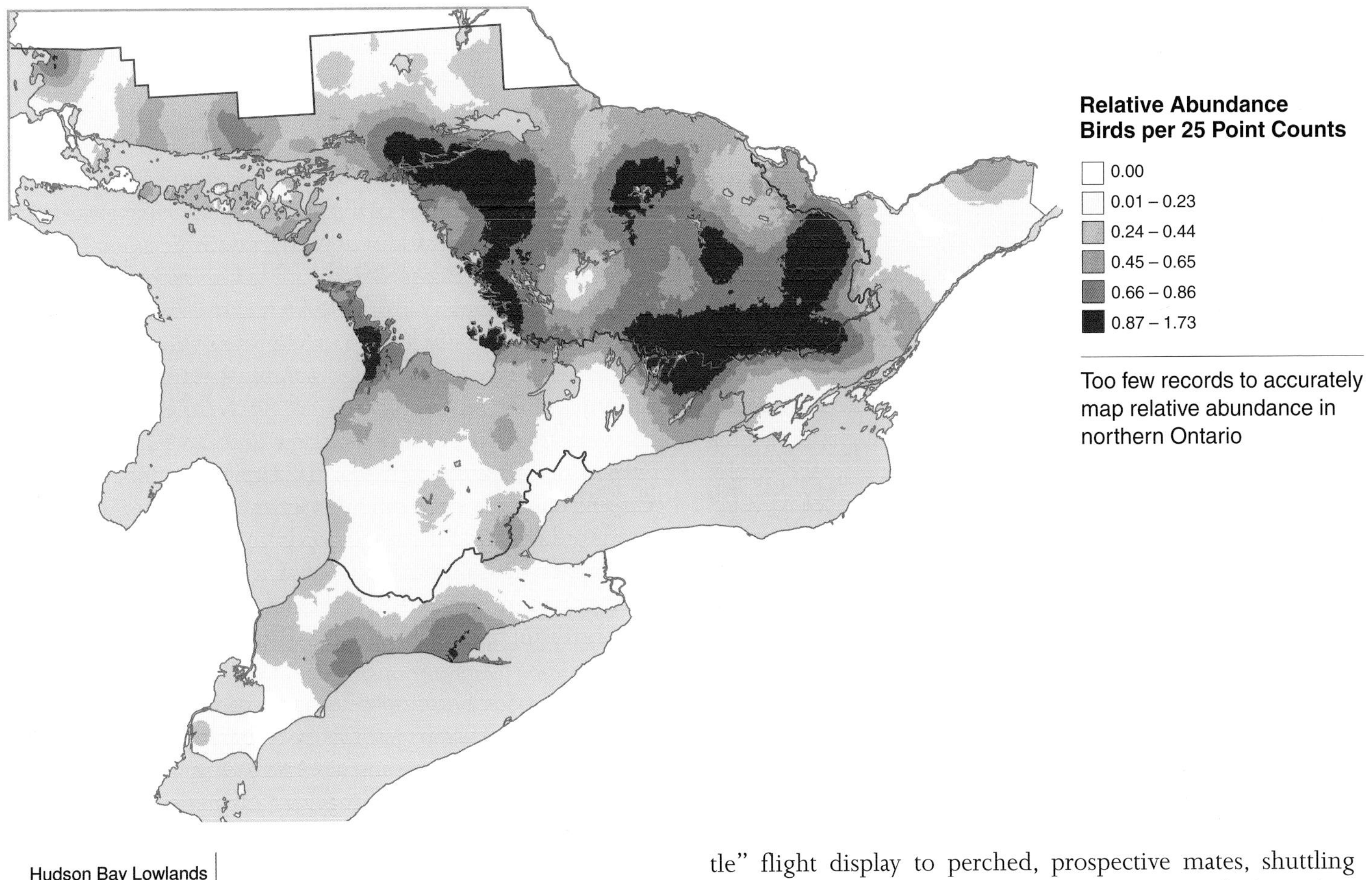

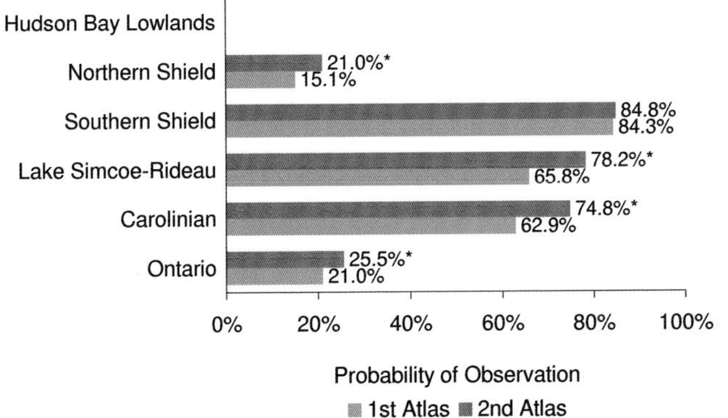

ings in mixed and deciduous forest, orchards, and residential gardens (Robinson et al. 1996). Males arrive on the breeding grounds before females and quickly establish and vigorously defend territories, which are usually centred on an abundant food resource. Breeding density varies based on food availability. Territories are maintained only by breeding males and may be as close together as 15 m (Robinson et al. 1996) but are typically more widely separated and about 0.1 ha in size (Gauthier and Aubry 1996). Banding returns have shown that hummingbirds have strong fidelity to productive breeding sites, often returning in successive years (Sargent 1999).

The male Ruby-throated Hummingbird is aggressive, particularly toward conspecifics, and frequently resorts to physical confrontations with intruding males and prospective mates. Courtship interactions between males and females are often conspicuous and relatively easily detected, involving much vocalizing, chases, and elaborate aerial displays (Robinson et al. 1996). The U-shaped dive display often starts as high as 15 m and descends to within a few centimetres of the female (Robinson et al. 1996). Males also perform a "shuttle" flight display to perched, prospective mates, shuttling from side to side and flashing the brilliant gorget feathers. They also deliver a repetitive, high-pitched but audible "daybreak" song from a high, exposed perch, often countersinging with neighbouring males.

Females alone select nest sites (Robinson et al. 1996). Males do not help with nest building, incubation, or care of the young. Nests are tiny, well camouflaged, and difficult to find. This accounts for the large number of possible and probable reports during the atlas. Of the 24% of squares with confirmed breeding evidence, only 3% involved nests. Confirmation was most often based on the reporting of fledged young, probably at feeders.

Nest construction, incubation, and fledging take 36 to 46 days (Robinson et al. 1996). Egg dates in Ontario range from 25 May to 2 September (Peck and James 1983). Females continue to feed young for four to seven days after fledging, but there is little information available about the post-fledging period (Robinson et al. 1996). Fledged young have been banded as early as 8 July in Ontario (pers. obs.). Sufficient time during the breeding season, late egg dates, and the presence of adult males in late August (pers. obs.) suggest the possibility of second broods here. However, this has not been confirmed.

Abundance: Point count data indicate that the highest abundance (0.7 birds/25 point counts) is in the Southern Shield region, followed by the Lake Simcoe-Rideau and Carolinian regions, both at about 0.3 birds/25 point counts. Areas with the highest abundance include much of cottage country on the southern Shield and Bruce Peninsula. South of the Shield, the most intensively farmed areas generally have low numbers of Ruby-throated Hummingbirds. – *Cindy E.J. Cartwright*

Belted Kingfisher

Martin-pêcheur d'Amérique

Ceryle alcyon

Frank and Sandra Horvath

The only member of its family occurring in Canada, the Belted Kingfisher is easily recognizable with its long, sharply pointed bill, bushy crest, and distinctive rattle call. It is found in the vicinity of streams, rivers, and lakes, where it can often be seen perched on overhanging tree limbs or diving into the water in pursuit of small fish. This species is wide ranging across North America, breeding north to Alaska and northern Québec and south to the southern US. It winters primarily in the US, Mexico, and Central America, and, rarely, as far south as the northern coast of South America (Hamas 1994). While some individuals remain in Ontario throughout the winter near open water, most migrate south.

Distribution and population status: Despite the widespread distribution of the Belted Kingfisher shown by both atlases, the probability of observation decreased in the second atlas in all regions except the Hudson Bay Lowlands. Significant declines of 10-12% were observed in the Lake Simcoe-Rideau and the two Shield regions, with a 32% decline in the Carolinian. BBS trend data for this species indicate a significant annual decline since 1968 of 2.7% in Ontario and 2.2% in Canada as a whole (Downes et al. 2005).

Areas of southern Ontario that showed a greater occurrence of squares with breeding evidence in the first atlas compared to the second included Lambton Co. in the southwest, extreme eastern Ontario, and to a lesser extent, Perth Co. Several other squares in which breeding evidence was detected only during the first atlas were distributed in a broad band extending from Manitoulin Island east to Petawawa. Reasons for reduced evidence of breeding in these areas are not immediately obvious. However, there has been an apparent decline in the availability of nesting sites due to the slumping and rehabilitation of gravel pits and road cuts during the last 20 years in Algonquin Prov. Park, which may have negatively impacted breeding activity there (R. Tozer, pers. comm.). The

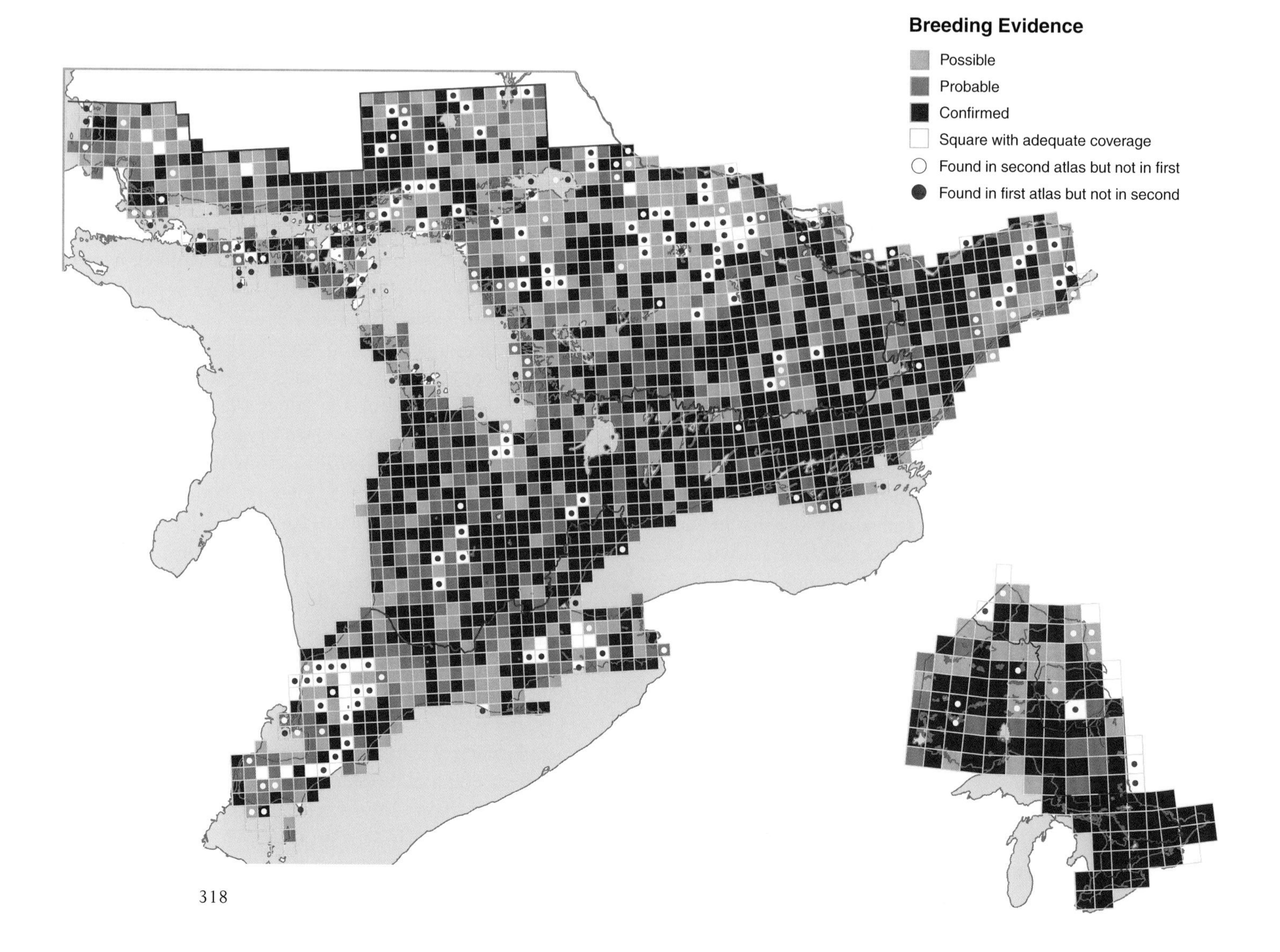

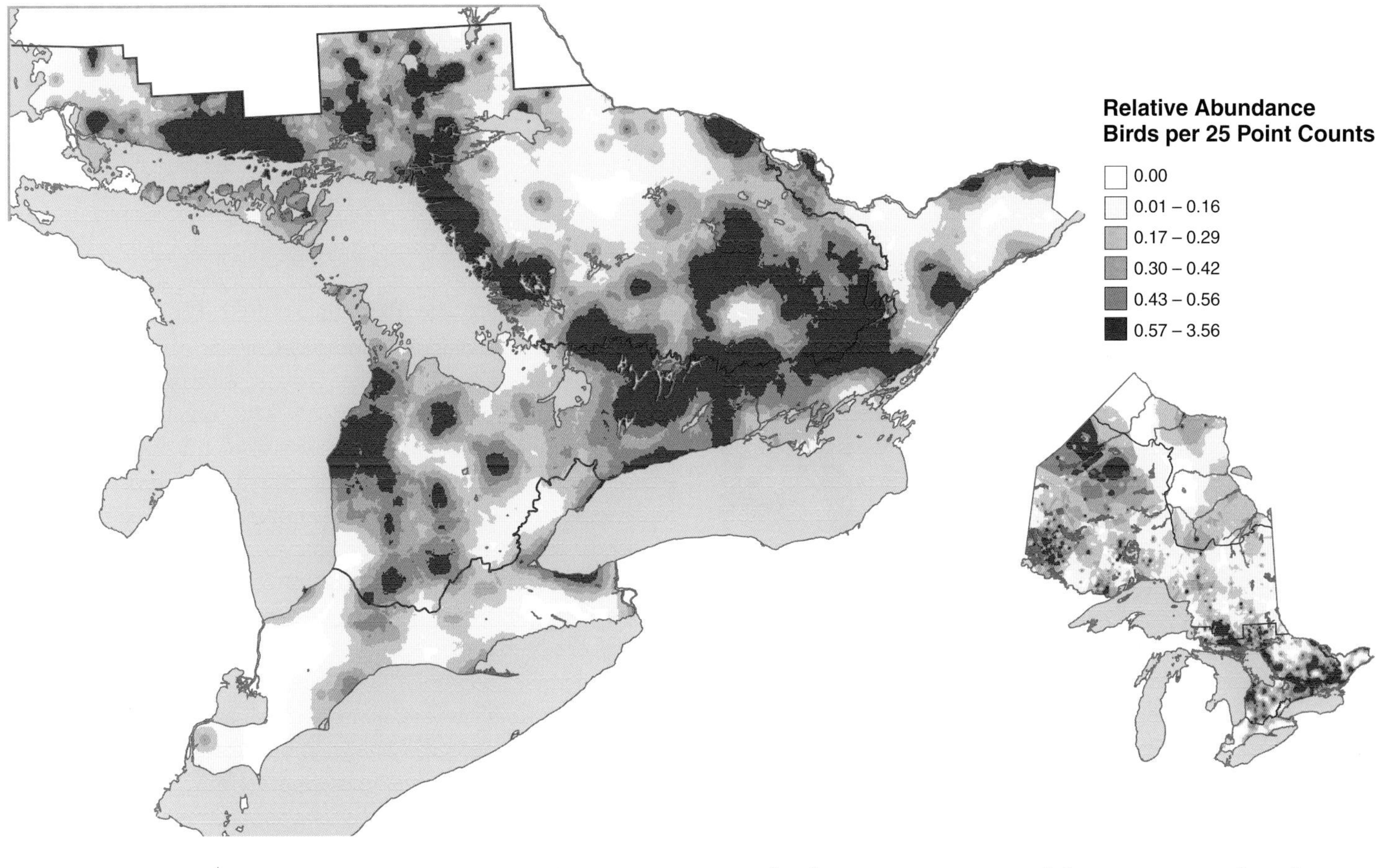

Region	2nd Atlas	1st Atlas
Hudson Bay Lowlands	53.0%	49.7%
Northern Shield	58.3%*	65.7%
Southern Shield	79.8%*	88.5%
Lake Simcoe-Rideau	76.1%*	86.9%
Carolinian	52.0%*	76.1%
Ontario	59.6%	64.9%

0% 20% 40% 60% 80% 100%

Probability of Observation

1st Atlas 2nd Atlas

rehabilitation of pits and quarries by sloping and seeding is a requirement under the Aggregate Resources Act, so the loss of these anthropogenic sites may be a factor across road-accessible parts of the province, though new sites are also being created. The sloping and rehabilitation of sand banks in road cuts is also now evident across much of the province. Other factors that contribute to the Belted Kingfisher's decline may include anthropogenic changes in water quality, turbidity, and depth, which impair kingfisher fishing success; removal and disturbance of trees along waterways; erosion of shorelines and resulting siltation through livestock use of riparian habitat (Popotnik and Giuliano 2000); and a reduction in suitable nest sites due to human disturbance and alteration of shoreline areas (Hamas 1994).

Breeding biology: The Belted Kingfisher forms monogamous pairs during the breeding season from May to July. Breeding and feeding territories, which may be in separate areas, are vigorously defended against conspecifics. Locating nest sites can be difficult, as this species is known to travel up to 8 km between nest sites and foraging areas when these are not available in closer proximity (Gauthier and Aubry 1996).

The Belted Kingfisher nests in a burrow dug into a usually high, vertical bank, typically located along the edge of clear, calm water where fish are readily available. The burrow openings, of an upright oval shape, can also be identified by the presence of two ruts, made by the feet of the adults (Terres 1980). This species usually selects earthen nesting banks high in sand content and free of much plant root penetration, which are better for burrowing than substrates composed of clay or having numerous rocks (Brooks and Davis 1987). Once eggs are laid, generally between May and July, both the male and female can be found in the vicinity of the nest (Bent 1989).

Abundance: The abundance maps indicate that the Belted Kingfisher is most abundant near the southern edge of the Canadian Shield, an area rich in wetlands, and along parts of the shorelines of Lakes Ontario and Huron, and Georgian Bay, including the North Channel. There are also high densities near Kenora, an area with many lakes, and in the far northwest, though this latter area of high abundance is based on very few point counts and so is less certain. Areas of low density are found in intensively farmed areas such as the extreme southwest, parts of the Niagara Peninsula, and southeastern Ontario, where suitable nesting and foraging sites might be in short supply. – *Ryan Archer and Steven T. A. Timmermans*

Red-headed Woodpecker

Pic à tête rouge
Melanerpes erythrocephalus

Tim Stewart

The Red-headed Woodpecker is one of Ontario's most striking birds. Its preference for woodland edges, open parkland, and sparsely treed fencerows makes it much more visible than most other Ontario woodpeckers. In Canada, it breeds across the very southern parts of Saskatchewan, Manitoba, Ontario, and Québec, and in the US from the Great Plains east to New York State, and south to the Gulf States (Smith et al. 2000). BBS data show highest breeding concentrations from the central Great Plains east to about the Mississippi River (Price et al. 1995). The Red-headed Woodpecker is designated Threatened by COSEWIC and Special Concern by OMNR.

Distribution and population status: Overall, the Red-headed Woodpecker declined dramatically in Ontario between atlases, with the probability of observation decreasing provincially by 64%. Significant declines occurred in each of the four regions in which it occurs. As in the first atlas, the majority of records were from the Carolinian and Lake Simcoe-Rideau regions. Notable declines occurred in the Southern Shield and northernmost areas of the Lake Simcoe-Rideau region. In the first atlas, the Red-headed Woodpecker ranged north to the southern Shield, where it was widespread but local in occurrence. The second atlas indicates that its range has receded almost entirely from the Southern Shield and from northernmost areas of the Lake Simcoe-Rideau region. Its distribution remained essentially unchanged in northwestern Ontario near Lake of the Woods, however, where 30-50 pairs are estimated to occur in 10 squares on the Rainy River Clay Plain (L. Heyens pers. comm.). BBS data largely corroborate atlas results, indicating that the Red-headed Woodpecker has experienced a significant annual decline of 5.6% across Canada and a marginally significant annual decline of 4.9% in Ontario since 1981.

In southern Ontario, there has been a significant shift southward in both the northern edge and the core of the species' range, as well as a westward shift of the eastern edge.

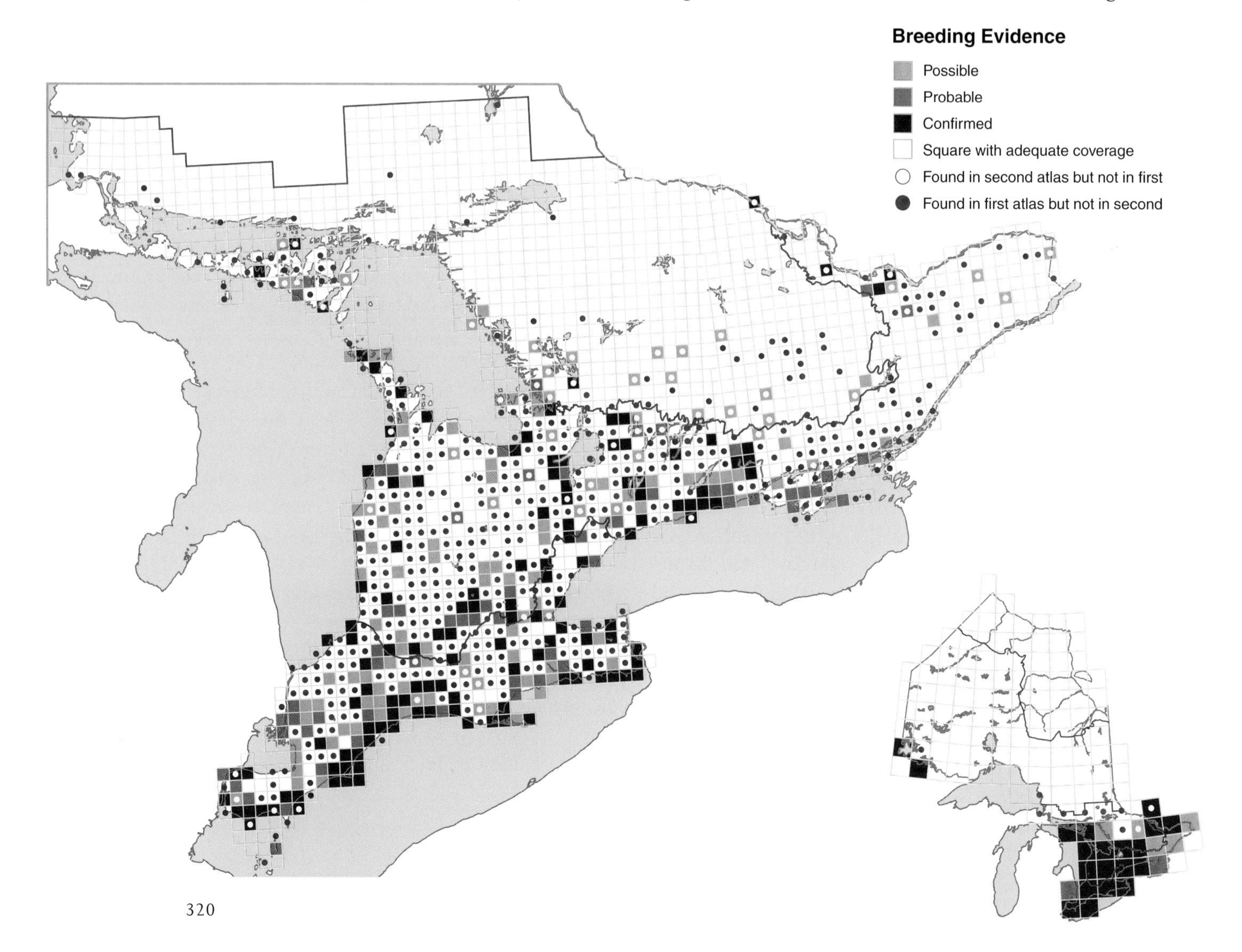

BREEDING EVIDENCE

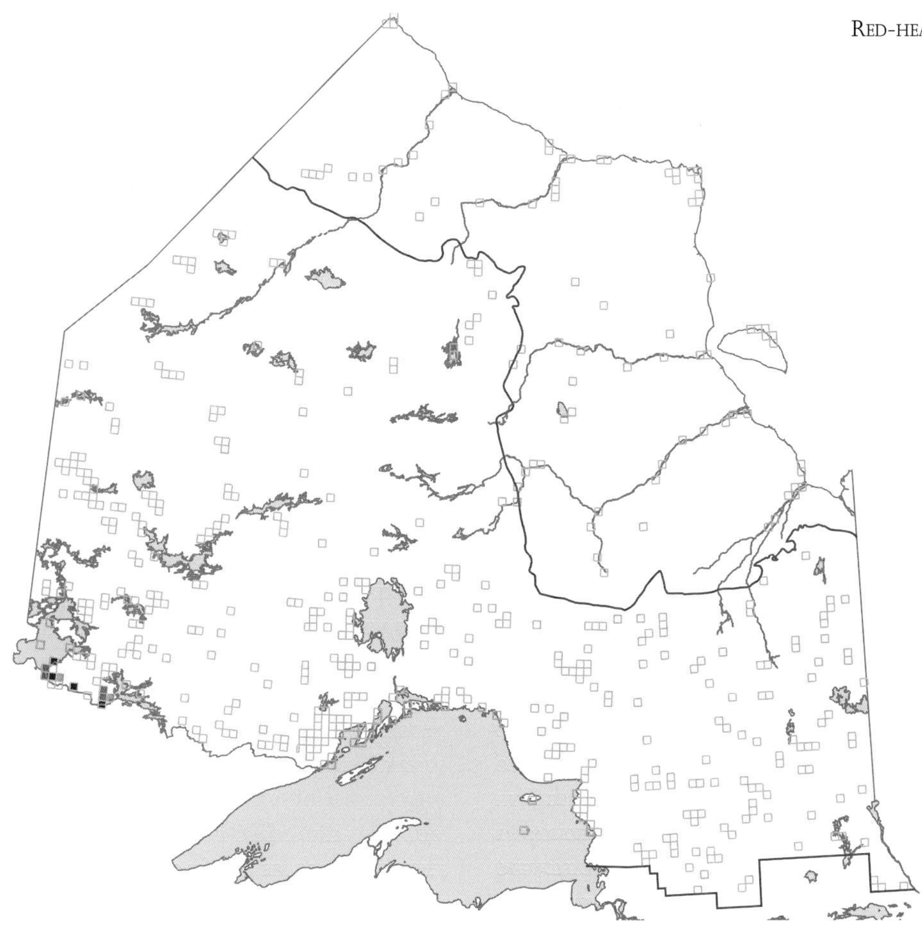

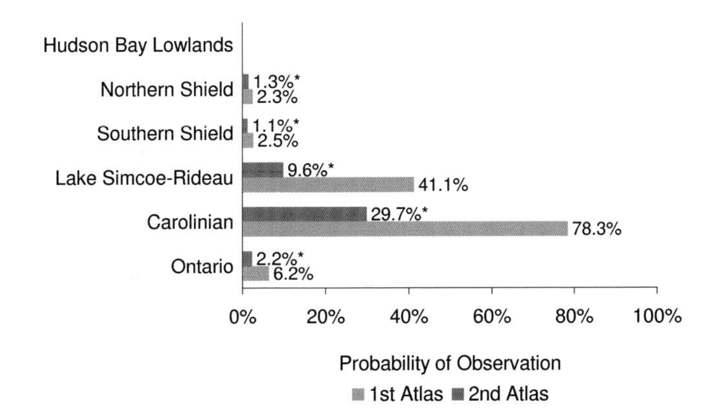

Historically, the Red-headed Woodpecker has always experienced population fluctuations. Populations increased during the first half of the 20th century in response to declines in both American Chestnut and elms, possibly due to an increase in snags for nesting (Smith et al. 2000). A number of factors have been implicated in the recent decline of the species rangewide, including the loss of senescent elm stems and the removal of other snags from forest stands; the rapid spread of Beech Bark Disease and the resultant decrease in American Beech, an important forage species; and increased rates of road mortality (Page 1996; Smith et al. 2000). Competition for nest cavities with the European Starling and the rapidly expanding Red-bellied Woodpecker may also be a factor contributing to the decline of this woodpecker in Ontario, although generally the Red-headed Woodpecker is more aggressive than either species (Smith et al. 2000).

It is unknown whether this downward trend will continue. Perhaps the spread of the Emerald Ash Borer as it attacks ash trees in the Carolinian region and potentially beyond will provide at least a short-lived opportunity for Red-headed Woodpeckers to stabilize or even rebound.

Breeding biology: The Red-headed Woodpecker is a primary excavator and breeds in open woodland and woodland edges, especially oak savannah and riparian forest. These habitats can occur in parks, golf courses, cemeteries, and many private woodlands. An important habitat component is the existence of large, dead, weathered trees or live trees with large dead branches (Kilham 1983).

The Red-headed Woodpecker returns to Ontario beginning in early May. By mid-May, some pairs have established territories and initiated nesting. Egg dates for Ontario range between 14 May and 21 July (Peck and James 1983). Usually only one clutch, averaging four (three to seven) eggs is laid, and both sexes incubate (Smith et al. 2000). During the breeding season, the species is considered to be among the most omnivorous of the woodpeckers, with 34% of its diet being animal matter, most often insects but occasionally bird eggs and young rodents, dead fish, and lizards (Smith et al. 2000).

Abundance: As recently as 1994, estimates of the Ontario population ranged as high as 3,400 pairs (Page 1996). Currently, there may be less than one-third that number, based on an estimate of two to three pairs per square with breeding evidence in this atlas, which equals 660 to 990 pairs. Data were insufficient to generate an accurate abundance map, but point count data show higher nodes of abundance (over 0.16 birds/25 point counts) along the northern shore of Lake Erie from eastern Chatham-Kent through Elgin Co., in eastern Niagara Region, and in eastern Northumberland and southern Hastings Counties. – *P. Allen Woodliffe*

Red-bellied Woodpecker

Pic à ventre roux

Melanerpes carolinus

P. Allen Woodliffe

The Red-bellied Woodpecker has the most restricted range of all Ontario woodpeckers, typically inhabiting hardwood, particularly oak-dominated woodlands and forest in the extreme southern part of the province, especially within the Carolinian region. It occurs in eastern North America from southern Ontario west to the forested portion of the Great Plains and south to the southern tip of Florida (Shackelford et al. 2000).

The Red-bellied Woodpecker is a generalist forager, consuming more vegetable matter (fruit, mast, and seeds) than all other North American woodpeckers, but also feeding on such varied fare as arthropods, sap from Yellow-bellied Sapsucker wells, and bird eggs and nestlings (Shackelford et al. 2000). This opportunistic foraging behaviour allows it to remain in extreme southwestern Ontario throughout the winter, often with frequent visits to bird feeders in the colder months.

Distribution and population status: The breeding distribution of this woodpecker has expanded dramatically since the first atlas. The probability of observation increased significantly in the Carolinian and Lake Simcoe-Rideau regions by about 200% and 600%, respectively. However, the species was detected in only three squares in the Southern Shield region and just one in the Northern Shield. A significant range-edge expansion to the north (112 km) and east (61 km) occurred, with core latitude shifting north by 32 km and core longitude east by 44 km.

The probability of observation of the Red-bellied Woodpecker increased significantly by about 250% in the province as a whole from the first to the second atlas. The BBS reported a non-significant 14% annual increase provincially over the same period. Maturation of forests in northeastern North America, the increasing popularity of backyard bird feeders, and milder winters are all likely factors contributing to the rapid expansion of this woodpecker in the northern part of its range (Shackelford et al. 2000).

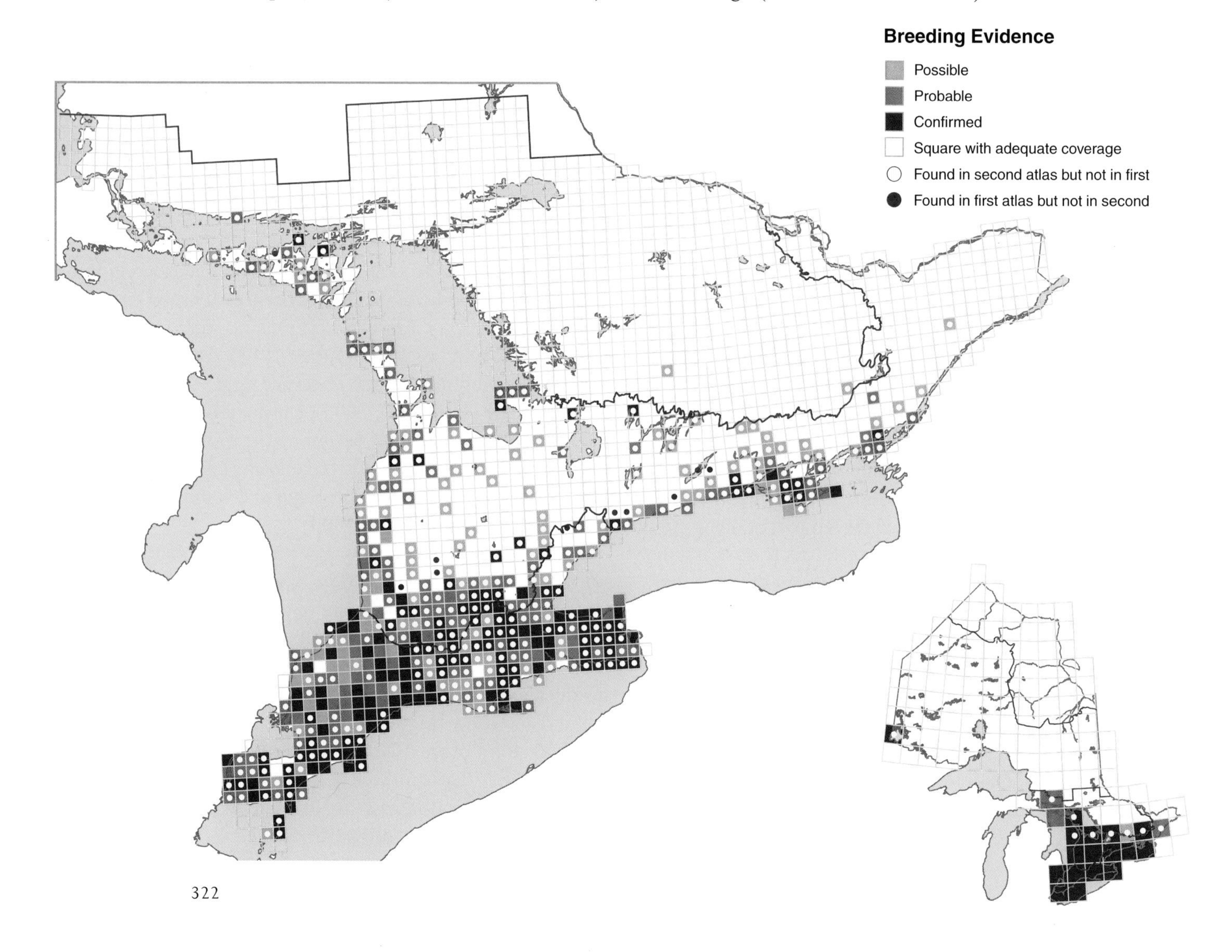

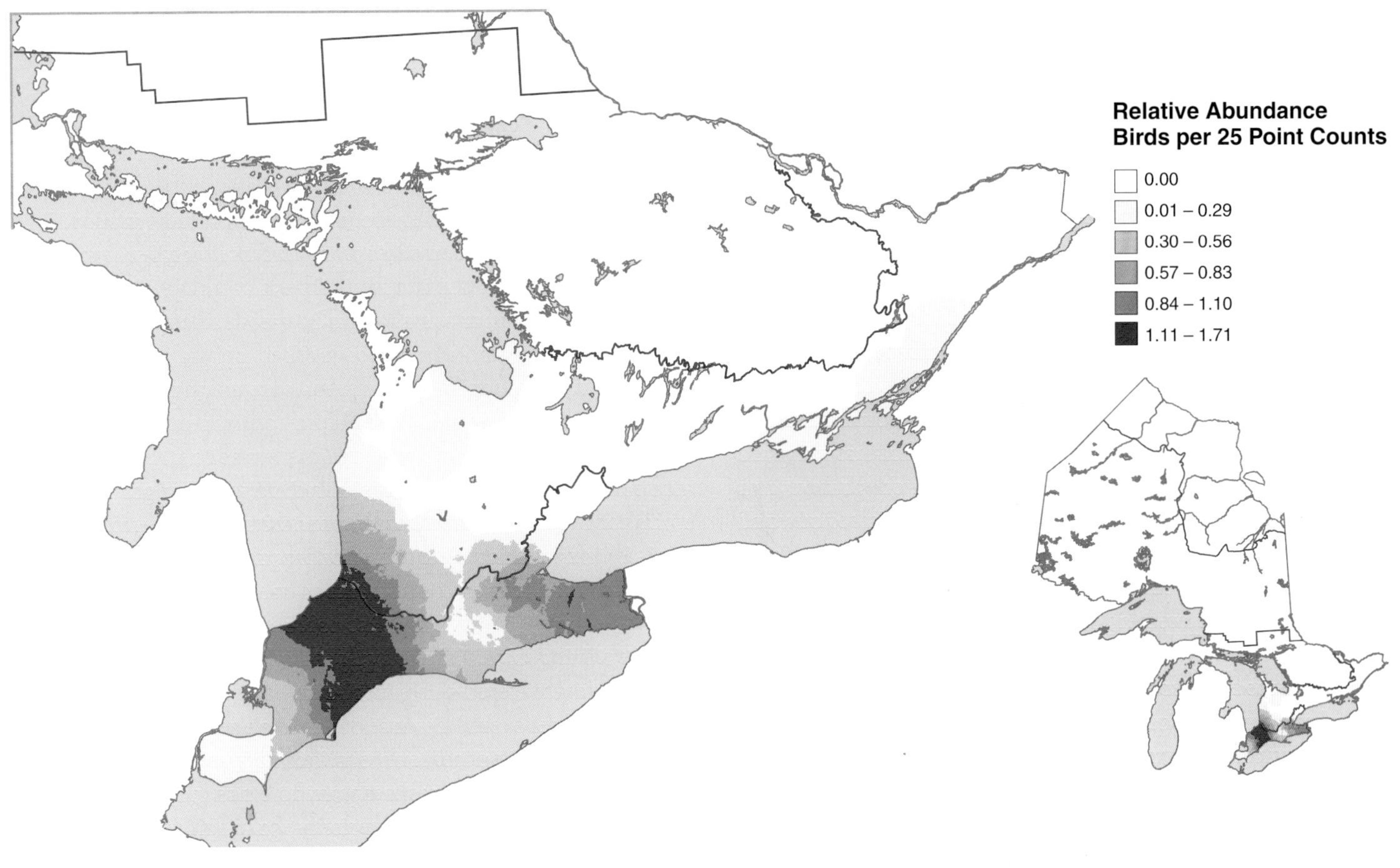

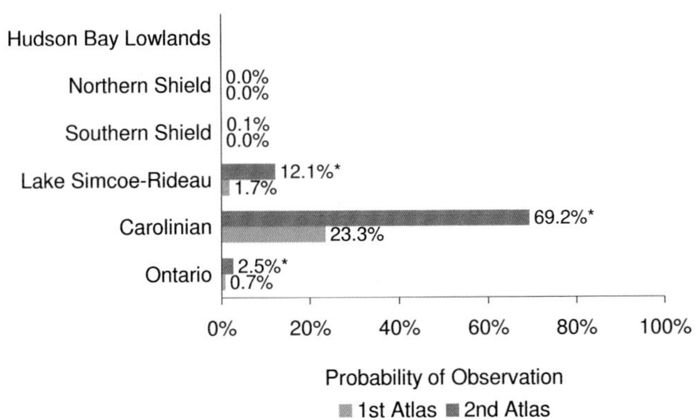

Breeding biology: In Ontario, the Red-bellied Woodpecker prefers to nest in tracts of mature deciduous forest with high basal areas, many large-diameter trees, and snags (James 1984b). It becomes very vocal in late winter during pair formation, and its loud contact calls, drumming, and elaborate courtship displays make it very conspicuous during cavity excavation in early to mid-April. However, its weak nest defence and tendency to nest early in the breeding season result in higher rates of displacement from potential nest cavities by the European Starling than for any other woodpecker (Ingold 1989). Nest competition with starlings has reduced the reproductive success of this species throughout its continental range (Ingold 1989).

Nests are most often placed in a dead limb of a live tree, and less often in the main stem of a live tree at an existing wound or in a snag. Cavities are easily observed before leaf emergence but become very well hidden thereafter. In Ontario, 36 trees used for nesting had an average diameter of 47.6 cm (range 20.7-99.8 cm), an average height of 23.3 m (range 10.8-39.7 m), and an average nest height of 16.0 m (range 7.4-23.1 m; K. Bavrlic, unpubl. data).

The Red-bellied Woodpecker breeds earlier than most Ontario birds, with eggs hatching as early as mid-April. However, the combined egg and nestling period of 36-41 days (Ehrlich et al. 1988), along with later nests and re-nests, allowed atlassers to record some nests. Pairs are highly detectable during the excavation period, when males frequently call to the female from the nest tree. They become more secretive during incubation, but once the two to six young hatch, the nest is a flurry of activity. The constant raspy begging calls of nestlings become progressively louder with age, leading observers directly to the nest cavity and later to fledged young. The young are dependent on the adults for up to 10 weeks, and family groups stay close to their breeding territories. Earlier surveying in the core range would likely have resulted in breeding confirmation in all squares in which the species was detected.

Abundance: Point counts reveal that densities are highest in that part of the Carolinian region occupied during the first atlas, with a high-density band running from Lake Huron to Lake Erie through Lambton, Middlesex, and Elgin Counties. Smaller populations exist in more recently occupied areas along the north shore of Lake Ontario and the eastern shore of Lake Huron. Densities become progressively lower northward. On average, 0.8 birds/25 point counts were detected in the Carolinian and 0.1 birds/25 point counts were noted in the Lake Simcoe-Rideau region. Such a reduction in abundance is expected as the species reaches the northern extent of its distribution. – *Kata Bavrlic*

Yellow-bellied Sapsucker

Pic maculé

Sphyrapicus varius

Mark Peck

The Yellow-bellied Sapsucker is a widespread and familiar species of hardwood forests and mixed forests in the Lake Simcoe-Rideau, Southern Shield, and Northern Shield regions of Ontario. It also occurs less frequently in the Carolinian and Hudson Bay Lowlands regions. It does well in cutover forests where residual birches and poplars have been left, and in gaps where these trees flourish, but it thrives in mature tolerant hardwood forests as well. It breeds from southeastern Alaska to Newfoundland south into the northeastern and north-central US. A short-distance migrant, it winters from the east-central and southeastern US south through Central America and the West Indies to western Panama. Females appear to winter somewhat farther south than males (Walters et al. 2002).

The characteristic rows of small holes known as sap wells that this woodpecker drills in the bark of alders, birches, and other trees are familiar to most naturalists. Sapsuckers defend these wells, but they are often usurped by the Ruby-throated Hummingbird and various mammals and insects. The sapsucker plays an important role in providing this food supply, as well as creating cavities used by many other species of birds and mammals (Kilham 1983; Walters et al. 2002).

Distribution and population status: Between atlases, the probability of observation of the Yellow-bellied Sapsucker did not change significantly in the province as a whole. However, it did increase significantly in the southern three regions, almost doubling in the Carolinian. Local occupation of squares in eastern Ontario and the Carolinian region probably reflects the return of previously agricultural areas to young forest (C. Hanrahan, pers. comm.). The species' distinctive vocalizations and drumming are easily detected, so occurrence patterns observed during the two atlases likely reflect its distribution quite well, at least where adequate atlassing effort occurred.

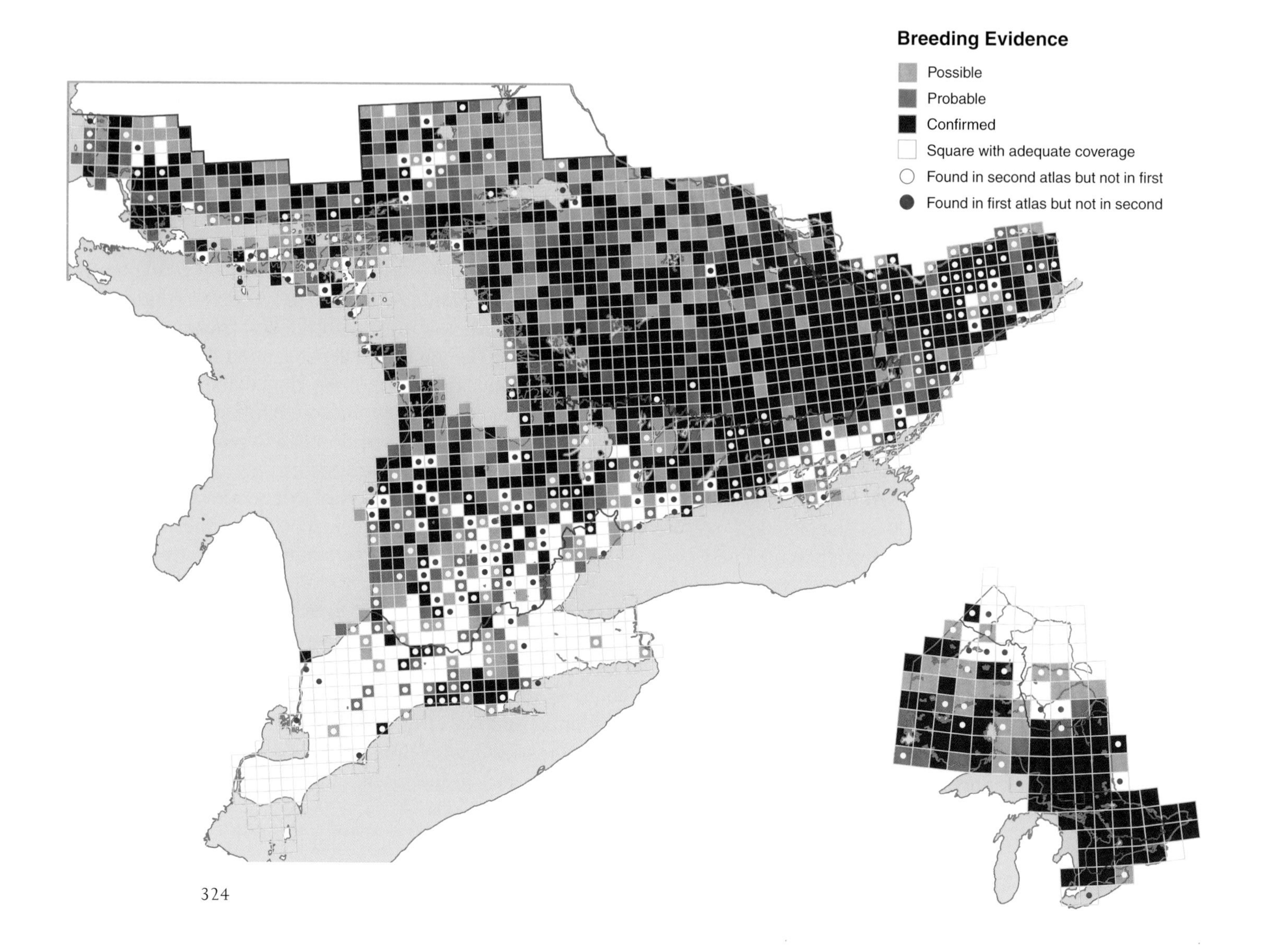

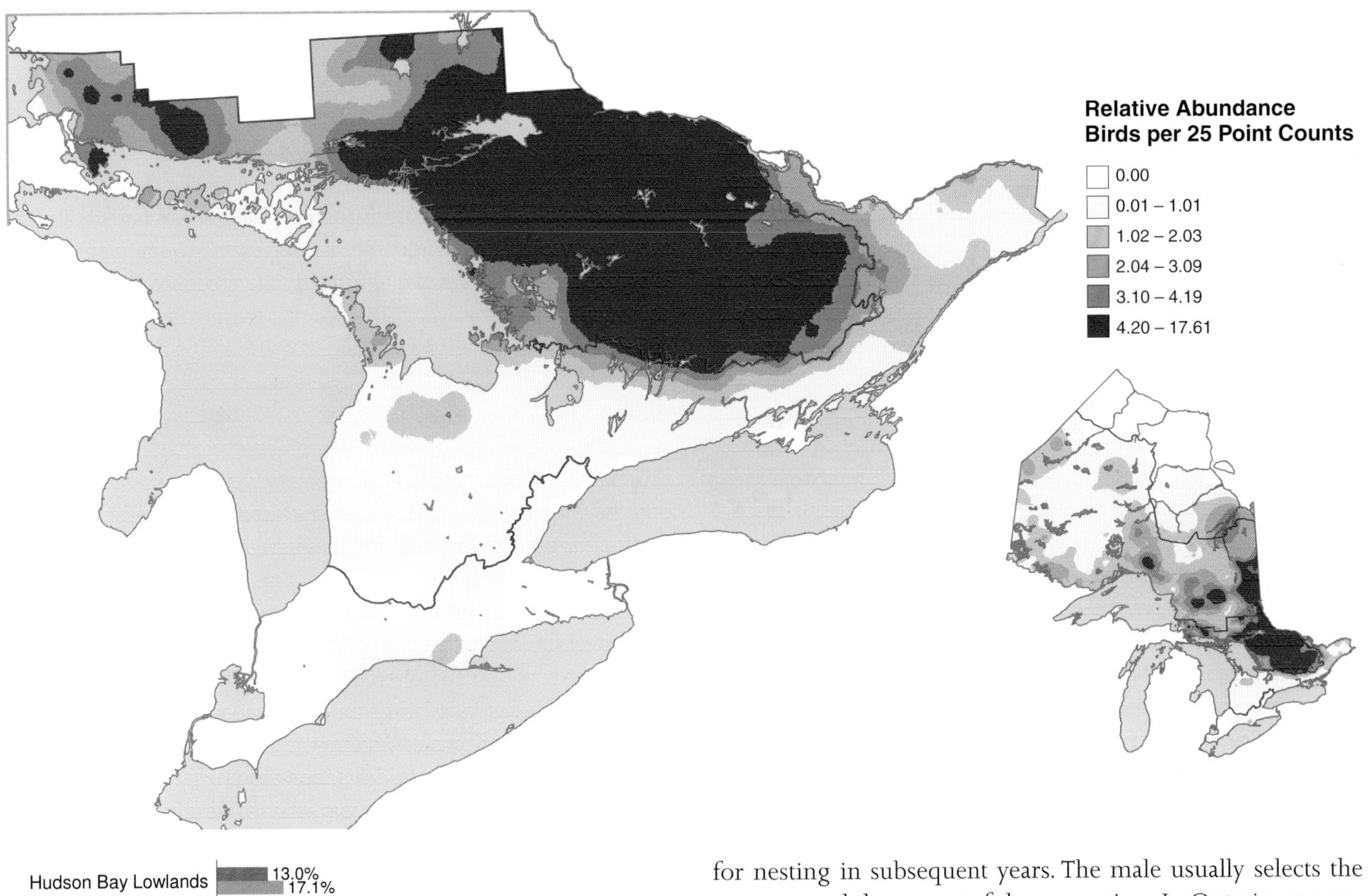

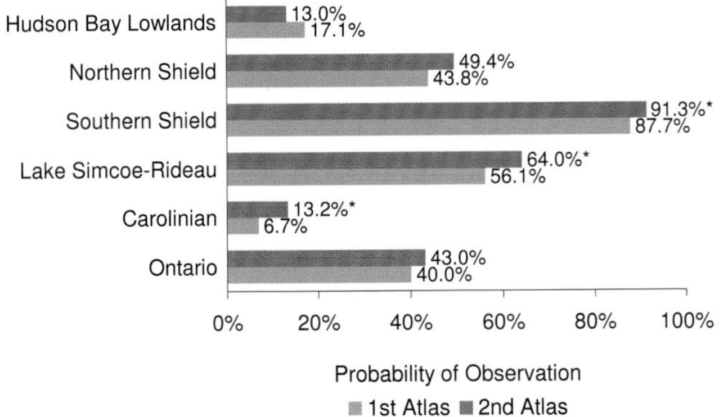

The relatively high level of confirmation of breeding (38%) is also a reflection of this ease of detection. However, two Regional Coordinators in the south felt that the sapsucker was still under-detected there.

There has been no significant change in abundance on BBS routes in Ontario since 1968 (Downes et al. 2005). In adjacent states (Michigan, New York, Pennsylvania, Wisconsin), BBS data suggest positive trends, while in New Brunswick there appears to have been a significant negative trend between 1966 and 2000 (Walters et al. 2002).

Breeding biology: Males arrive at the breeding areas prior to females and immediately begin to establish territories, which may range from 0.65 to 3.1 ha in size (Walters et al. 2002). The characteristic drumming pattern can be heard for relatively long distances since males search for substrates that produce the loudest, most far-reaching sounds (e.g., metal surfaces, resonant hollow logs, and utility poles). Individuals often return to the same territory occupied in previous years and frequently use the same tree – but rarely the same cavity – for nesting in subsequent years. The male usually selects the nest tree and does most of the excavation. In Ontario, excavation of the nesting cavity generally takes 15-28 days from late April to late May (Lawrence 1967). Nest cavities most frequently are excavated in deciduous trees, including Trembling Aspen, White Birch, American Beech, White Elm, and various maples, usually where heartwood or sapwood decay have begun (Walters et al. 2002; pers. obs.).

Females initiate clutches of four to five eggs (Peck and James 1983) about eight days after excavation has been completed. The pair bond remains strong throughout the breeding season, including the fledgling period, and pairs that survive tend to reunite in subsequent years. Although re-nesting may occur if the first brood fails, there are no records of second broods. Incubation lasts 10-13 days, and fledging occurs 23-29 days after hatching when the young are enticed from the cavity by the adults. Both sexes feed the young during the nestling and fledgling stages, although once fledged they may be fed for only a short period. The young birds remain on the territory for six to eight weeks and feed mainly at sap wells.

Abundance: The Yellow-bellied Sapsucker occurs in the greatest densities in an area extending from the southern edge of the Shield northwest to about Sudbury and along the eastern portion of the Northern Shield north to about Timmins. High densities are also found in a few small pockets north and east of Lake Superior. On average, 6.3 birds/25 point counts are found in the Southern Shield and 2.1 in the Northern Shield, with lower densities in the remaining regions. – *William J. Crins*

Downy Woodpecker

Pic mineur

Picoides pubescens

Frank and Sandra Horvath

The Downy Woodpecker is North America's smallest woodpecker, occurring throughout most of the continent from the treeline in Canada to southern California and Florida (Jackson and Ouellet 2002). It is found in a wide variety of habitats from deciduous woodlands and riparian forests to urban parks and residential areas, where it is a frequent visitor to backyard bird feeders (Jackson and Ouellet 2002). Research on the Downy Woodpecker's foraging ecology has revealed sexually distinct feeding strategies across much of the range, with males typically foraging on smaller-diameter branches and weed stems, and females on larger branches and trunks of trees (Jackson and Ouellet 2002).

Distribution and population status: The breeding distribution of the Downy Woodpecker shows little change between the two atlases. It occurs in almost every square in the south, encompassing the Carolinian, Lake Simcoe-Rideau, and Southern Shield regions, and a very few 100-km blocks north of the Great Lakes-St. Lawrence Forest, where deciduous trees used for nesting and foraging become relatively sparse.

The probability of observation of the Downy Woodpecker did not change significantly in the province as a whole between atlases. However, there was a significant 24% increase in the Northern Shield, perhaps due to increases in the amount of mixed woods due to harvest and silvicultural practices in the region (L. Watkins, pers. comm.; Ontario Ministry of Natural Resources 2006b) or to improved access via new forest access roads in many areas of the region. There was also a significant 71% decline in the Hudson Bay Lowlands, though the absolute number of squares reporting the species was low in both atlases, and distribution remained similar. The reason for the decline is unknown. The lack of significant change in atlas results in southern Ontario is consistent with the non-sig-

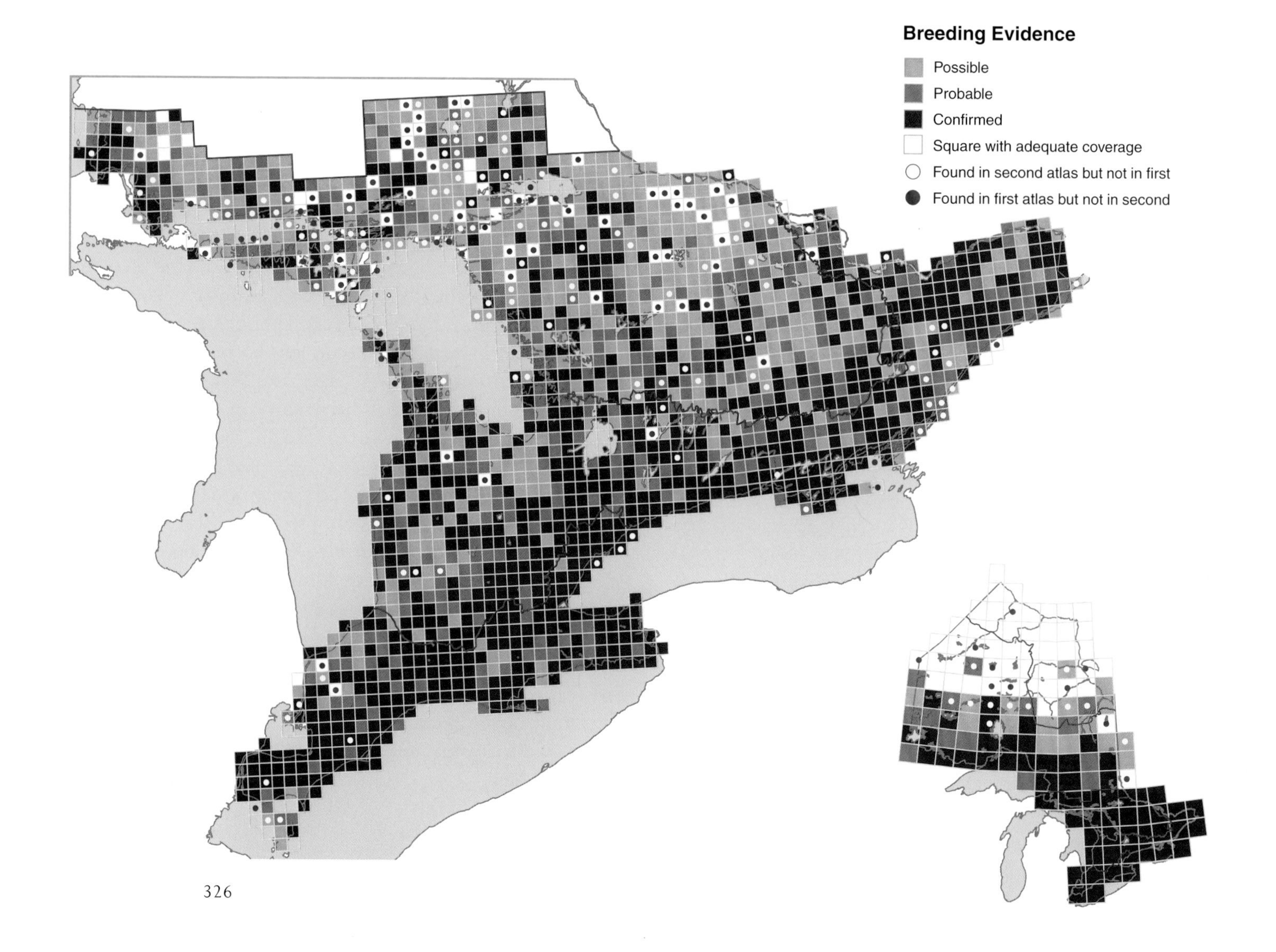

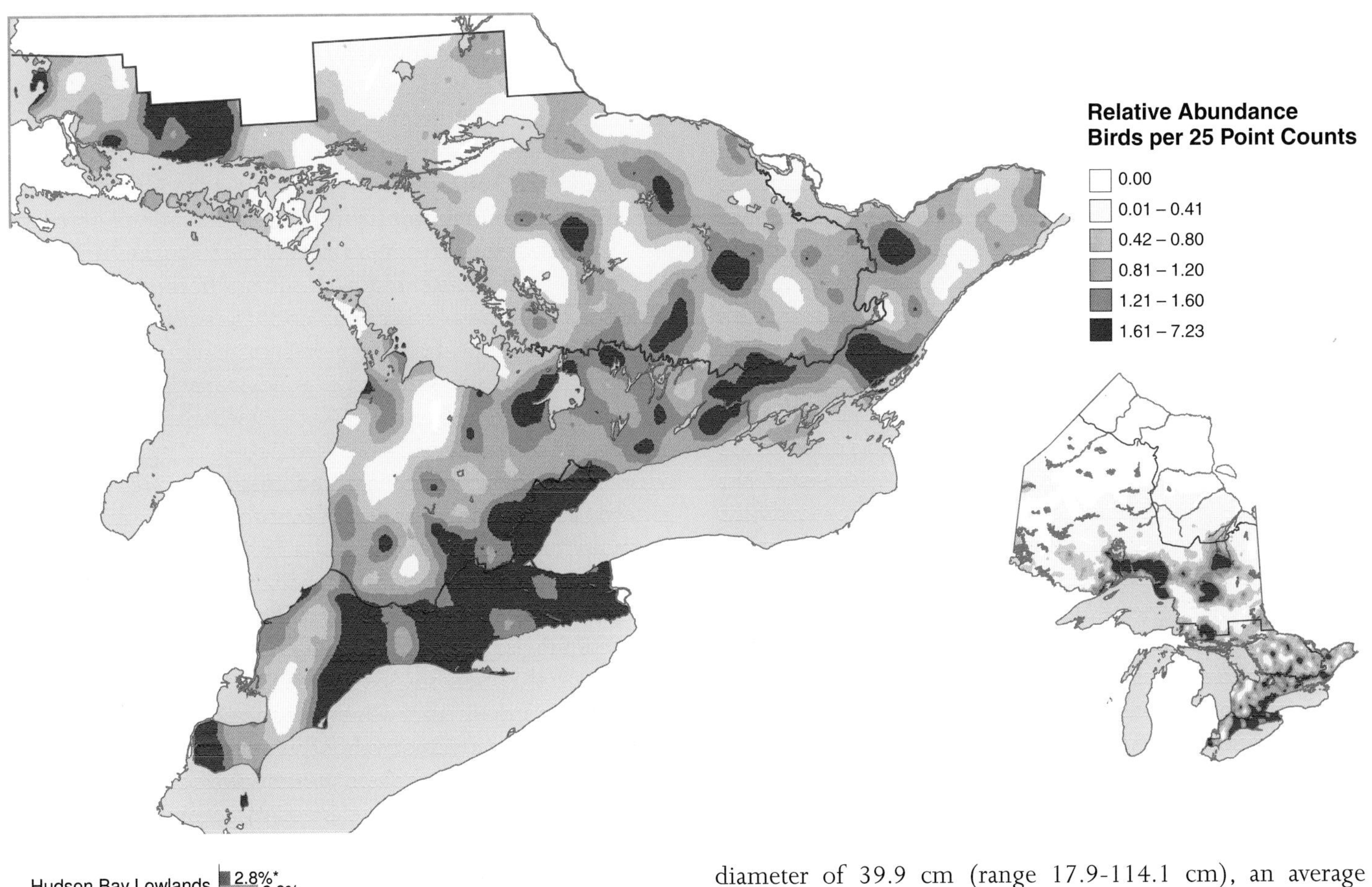

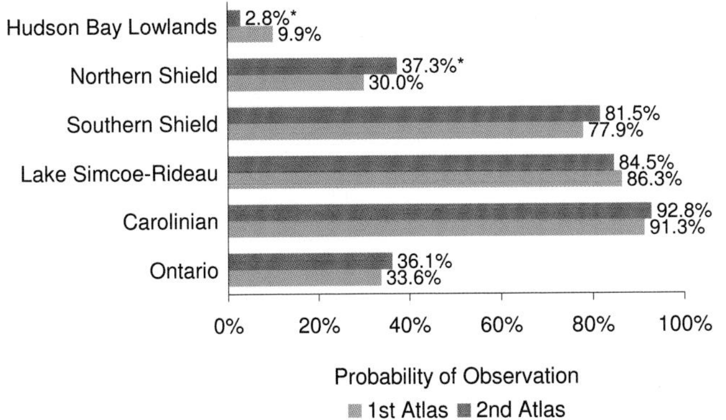

nificant 1.1% increase per year reported by the BBS for the same time period; most BBS routes are in the south.

Breeding biology: The Downy Woodpecker breeds in deciduous woodlands, riparian habitats and, less frequently, coniferous forests with a well-developed deciduous understorey (Jackson and Ouellet 2002). The species prefers more open stands than the Hairy Woodpecker, with early successional habitats, edges, and partially thinned woodlands being ideal nesting sites. Detection of the Downy Woodpecker is high in these habitats except during the incubation stage from mid-May to mid-June, when adults become secretive.

The Downy Woodpecker excavates a new nest cavity every spring (Jackson and Ouellet 2002). Just as in New Hampshire, nest cavities in Ontario are usually in the "broken off, dead top" of a living deciduous tree (Kilham 1974; K. Bavrlic, unpubl. data). The supporting tree must have both sap-rot and heart-rot to weaken the wood enough for the successful completion of cavity excavation (Jackson and Ouellet 2002). In southern Ontario, 33 trees used for nesting had an average diameter of 39.9 cm (range 17.9-114.1 cm), an average height of 20.8 m (range 8.1-35.7 m), and an average nest height of 14.3 m (range 4.0-27.4 m; K. Bavrlic, unpubl. data). Confirmation of breeding can be surprisingly difficult. Nest cavities are often well concealed high in the canopy. Nestlings and family groups can be hard to detect also, because young Downy Woodpeckers are not as noisy as the young of other woodpeckers, and adults are not as vocal when agitated (K. Bavrlic, unpubl. data). Despite these factors, breeding was confirmed in 39% of the squares where the species was found.

Although the Downy Woodpecker breeds earlier than many other forest bird species (egg dates are 2 May to July 1; Peck and James 1983), the longer combined egg and nestling period of 30-33 days (Jackson and Ouellet 2002) results in substantial overlap with the peak atlassing period (June). Once the nestlings have fledged, they are dependent on adults for up to three weeks. Family groups will often travel considerable distances from the nest site, so this woodpecker may be recorded outside of its breeding territory at this time. These factors may not affect the ability to confirm breeding in the south where the Downy Woodpecker is common, but may provide obstacles in the north. Overall, the atlas maps reflect its distribution well in the south, although the northern limit of its breeding range is still poorly defined because of the species' scarcity at higher latitudes.

Abundance: Point counts reveal that abundance is highest in the Carolinian region, where hardwood-dominated forests are common. There is an overall tendency to smaller numbers with increasing latitude, and the Downy Woodpecker is essentially absent from northern parts of the Hudson Bay Lowlands.
– *Kata Bavrlic*

Hairy Woodpecker

Pic chevelu

Picoides villosus

Jon Brierley

The Hairy Woodpecker is one of the most widespread and familiar of North American woodpeckers. Although this permanent resident shows a preference for mature forests, it can also be found in wooded parks and any urban environment that provides it with large-diameter declining trees essential for nesting and foraging (Jackson et al. 2002). The Hairy Woodpecker plays a keystone role in southern Ontario forest ecosystems, providing cavities critical for nesting, denning, and food storage for approximately 15 species of mammals and birds (Bavrlic et al., in press). It breeds throughout most of North America, from the northern limits of Canada's Boreal Forest to the highlands of Panama and the Bahamas (Jackson et al. 2002).

Distribution and population status: The overall breeding distribution of the Hairy Woodpecker has changed little from the first atlas. It occurred in most squares in the south and in almost all 100-km blocks in the north. Compared to the first atlas, it was more widespread in the north, occurring in several new 100-km blocks in the Hudson Bay Lowlands. However, detection there was likely a result of increased coverage rather than range expansion.

Only the Southern Shield and Northern Shield regions showed a significant change in the probability of observation from the first atlas, with a 9% and 16% increase, respectively. While the reason for the change is unknown, recent increases in hardwood-dominated forests and canopy cover in the Southern Shield may account for the change there, as both these components are desirable nesting features. The species was absent from a number of squares in the southwest with low forest cover. Although the probability of observation declined by a non-significant 6% in the Carolinian region, a notable increase in squares with the species was observed in Essex Co.

Across Ontario, the probability of observation increased by

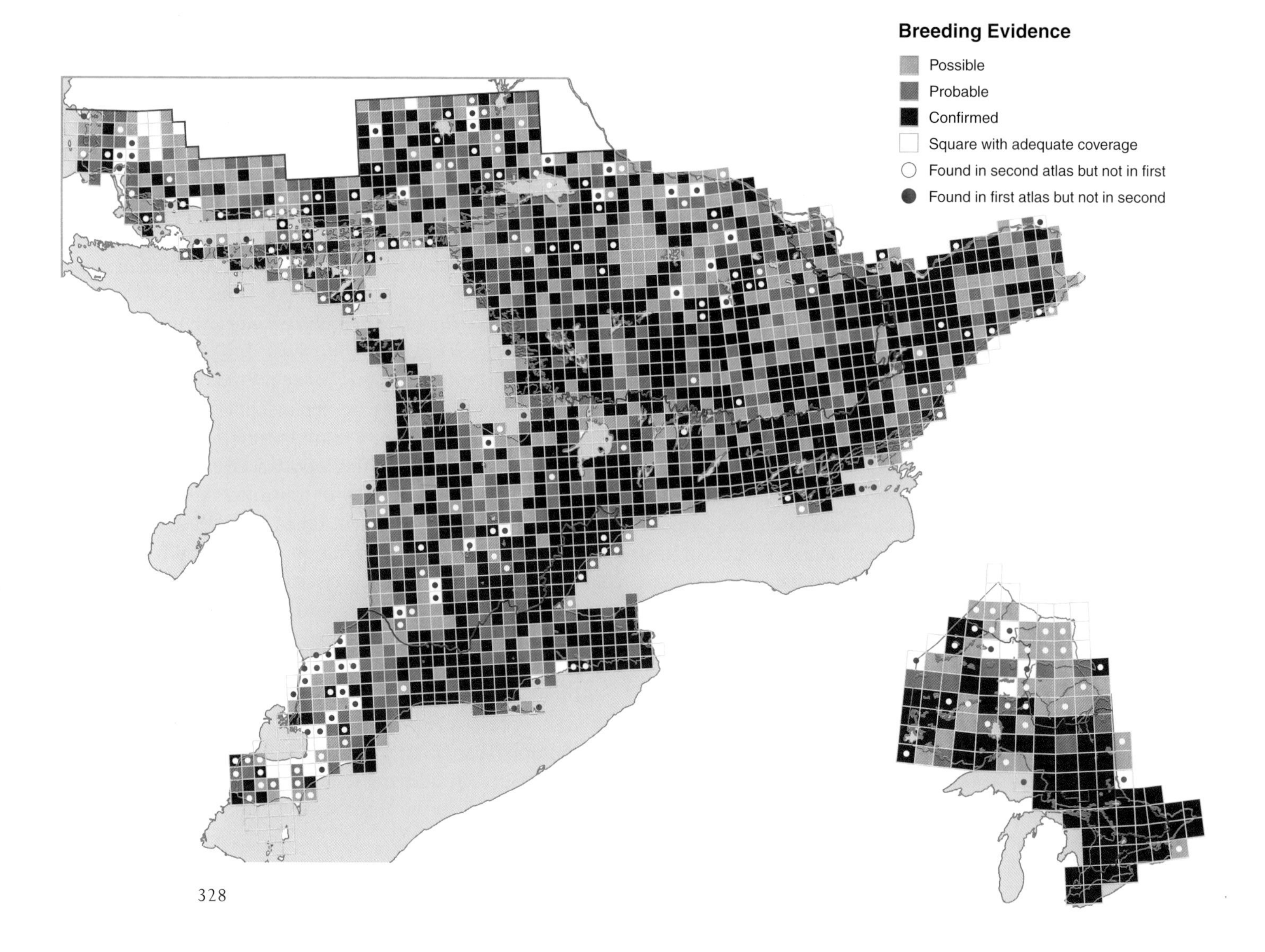

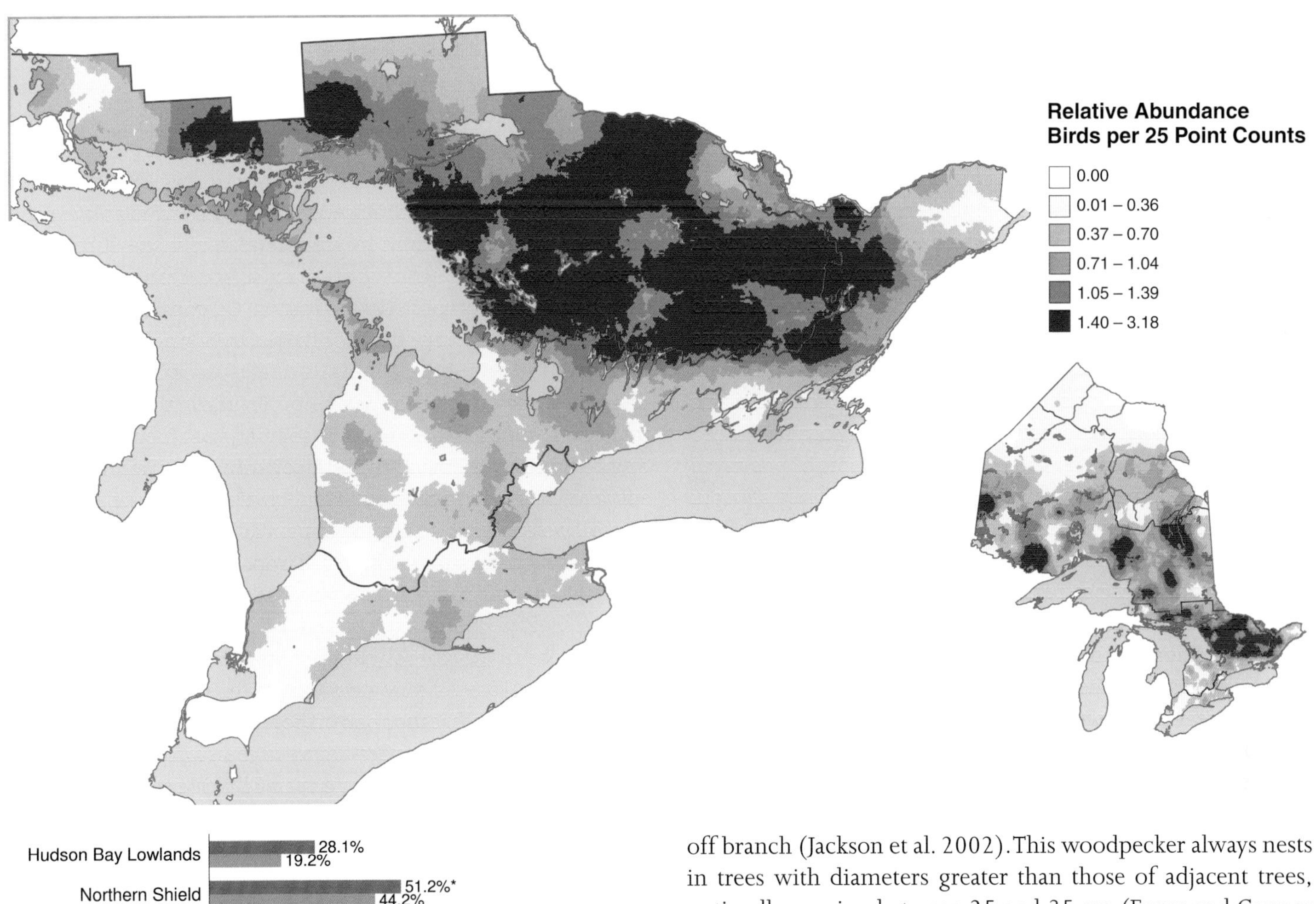

Probability of Observation

Region	1st Atlas	2nd Atlas
Hudson Bay Lowlands	19.2%	28.1%
Northern Shield	44.2%	51.2%*
Southern Shield	83.5%	91.2%*
Lake Simcoe-Rideau	78.9%	78.8%
Carolinian	71.2%	66.9%
Ontario	43.6%	50.4%

a non-significant 16% since the first atlas. This trend parallels the significant increases of 2.1% in Ontario and 1.1% per year in Canada noted in BBS data since 1981. Conversely, Project FeederWatch showed significant declines during winter in roughly the same period (Lepage and Francis 2002).

Breeding biology: The Hairy Woodpecker is found in deciduous, coniferous, and mixed forests but shows a preference for deciduous stands (Jackson et al. 2002). It prefers large blocks of mature forest and becomes uncommon in landscapes dominated by farm, suburban, or urban habitats (Jackson et al. 2002). The many small, isolated woodlots in southwestern Ontario do not provide desirable habitat, and it is not surprising that the Hairy Woodpecker was absent from many squares there.

The breeding pair requires approximately three weeks to excavate a nest cavity, which may be in a dead, declining, or healthy tree. In eastern North America, the species prefers to excavate nest cavities in the main stem of a live deciduous tree with fungal heart rot, or on the underside of a limb or broken-off branch (Jackson et al. 2002). This woodpecker always nests in trees with diameters greater than those of adjacent trees, optimally ranging between 25 and 35 cm (Evans and Conner 1979). Nesting territories are characterized by high canopy cover and high densities of trees with diameters greater than 23 cm at breast height (Anderson and Shugart 1974).

The Hairy Woodpecker breeds earlier than most birds in Ontario, laying eggs in April and May, with young fledging as early as mid-May. After hatching, the nests are a flurry of activity, the young loudly and almost constantly begging for food throughout most of the 28-day nestling period. Adults are very protective of the nest, and an intruder within 30 m of the cavity tree will elicit loud, piercing distress calls. However, breeding was confirmed in only 39% of squares where the species was found, perhaps because atlassers were in the field less often during the Hairy Woodpecker's main nesting period. The distribution maps are likely an accurate representation of the breeding range, despite the low breeding evidence reported in some squares and 100-km blocks.

Abundance: Point counts revealed that densities were highest in the Southern Shield, where forest cover is extensive and many large hardwood trees are available for nesting and foraging. Abundance drops to almost half in the Northern Shield and Lake Simcoe-Rideau regions, with pockets of higher density generally in more heavily wooded sections of the latter. Densities were lowest in the highly fragmented forests of the Carolinian region and in the Hudson Bay Lowlands, where suitable nesting habitat is less common. – *Kata Bavrlic*

American Three-toed Woodpecker

Pic à dos rayé

Picoides dorsalis

Jim Richards

This little-known woodpecker of the northern forests was recently split from its old-world counterpart, the Eurasian Three-toed Woodpecker (*Picoides tridactylus*), all populations having been previously known as the Three-toed Woodpecker (Banks et al. 2003). The American Three-toed Woodpecker is closely related to the larger Black-backed Woodpecker, sharing plumage and anatomical characteristics, range, habitat, and foraging behaviour to an extent, but with some differences.

The American Three-toed Woodpecker is a permanent resident from Alaska and British Columbia to Newfoundland north to the treeline and south to the southern limit of the Boreal Forest. It breeds farther north than any other woodpecker. At higher elevations, its breeding range extends south in the western US to Arizona and New Mexico, with an isolated population in the Adirondack Mountains of New York State. There is sometimes a small southward irruption in the fall to the southern Prairie provinces, northern Great Lakes and New England states, and southern Ontario (Leonard 2001).

Distribution and population status: In Ontario, the American Three-toed Woodpecker occurs regularly as far south as Kenora, Thunder Bay, and Sudbury. Infrequent reports of breeding farther south, including confirmed nesting during the first atlas, are usually in years following significant fall irruptions.

Atlas data give an accurate picture of this woodpecker's general distribution in Ontario. It was found in low densities throughout the Hudson Bay Lowlands and Northern Shield, with the most southerly records north of Iron Bridge, Algoma, and the northeastern Algonquin Prov. Park vicinity and in Killarney Prov. Park. The southernmost records near Algonquin in early May 2001 may have involved late lingering non-breeders (R. Tozer, pers. comm.)

Even though widely distributed in the Boreal Forest, this species is generally uncommon and easily overlooked, having been recorded in only 105 squares in the province. It was confirmed in

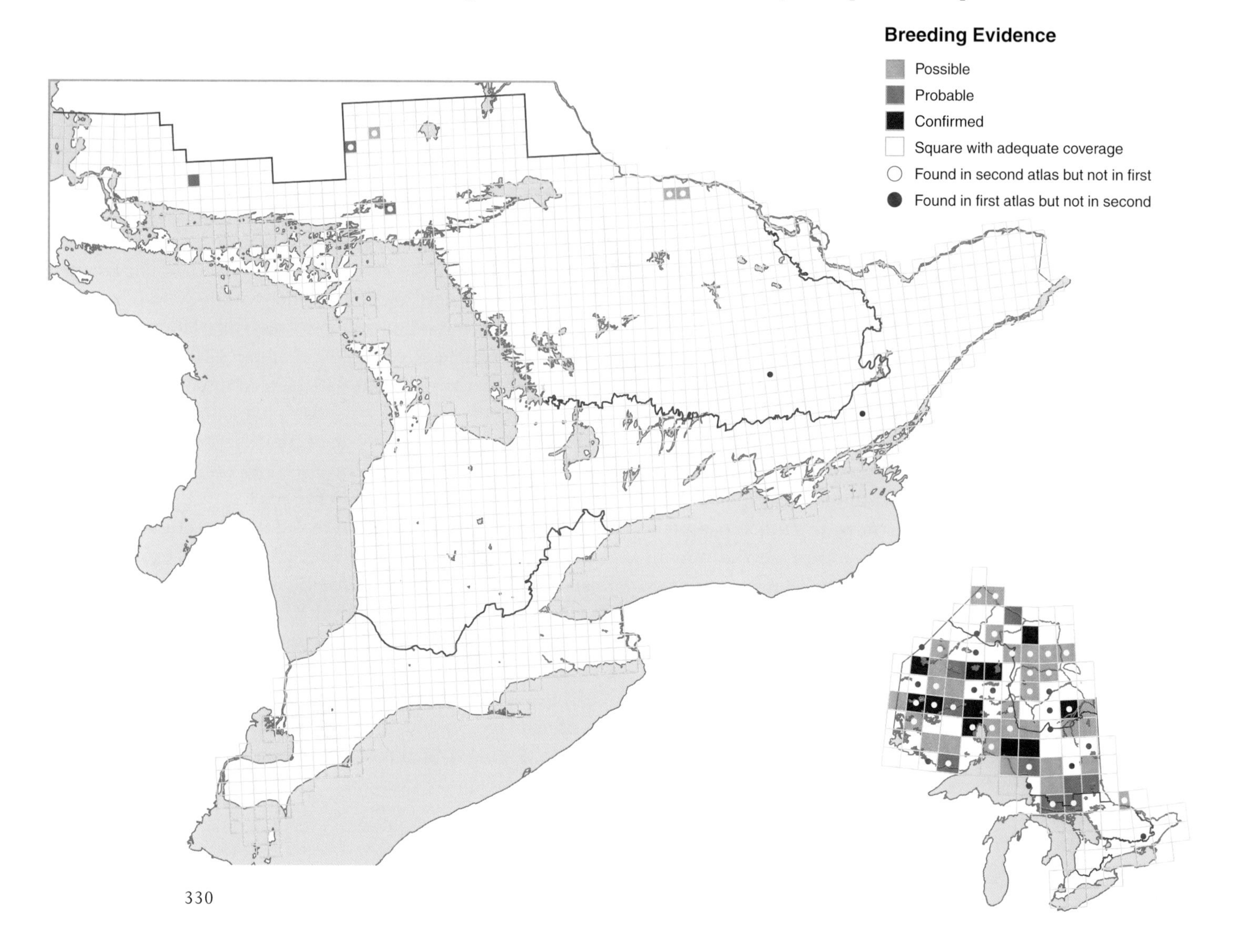

BREEDING EVIDENCE

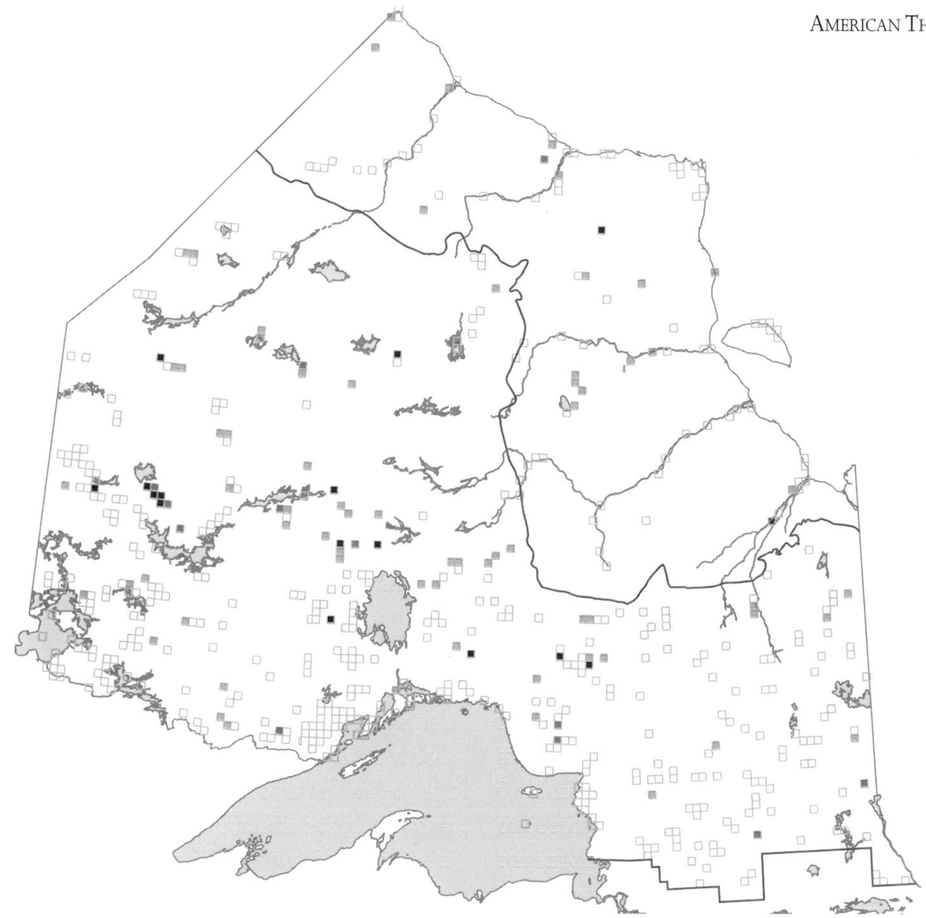

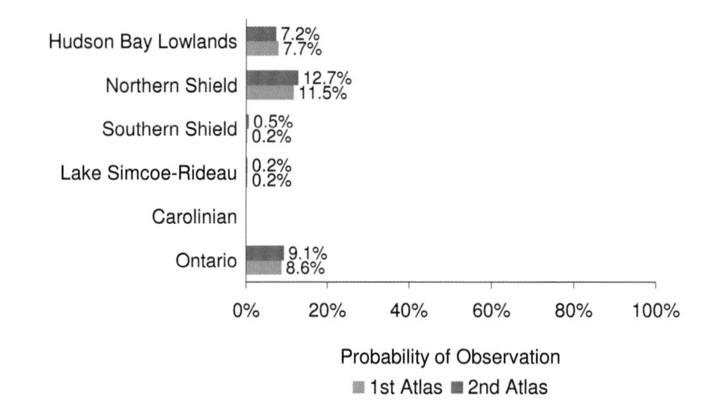

17% of these squares; all confirmed records for which details are available were of nests with young, north of Lake Superior.

There was no appreciable change in the distribution or abundance of the American Three-toed Woodpecker in Ontario since the first atlas. It was not recorded in the vicinity of Lake Opinicon, Frontenac Co., or near Bon Echo Prov. Park, Lennox and Addington Co., where confirmed and possible breeding, respectively, were reported during the first atlas. Such anomalous breeding events probably involved birds that remained after a southward winter irruption.

Breeding biology: The American Three-toed Woodpecker inhabits coniferous and mixed forests in the Hudson Bay Lowlands and Northern Shield regions, particularly where both Black and White Spruce grow, either in wet areas or dry uplands. It requires dead and dying trees on which it forages for insect larvae beneath the bark. It flakes the bark, never drilling into the sapwood as the larger Black-backed Woodpecker does (Elder 2004). Primary food sources are the larvae of bark beetles (Scolytidae, particularly *Ips* species), and the first-instar larvae of wood-boring beetles (Cerambycidae; Leonard 2001).

Compared to the Black-backed Woodpecker, the American Three-toed Woodpecker is more often silent and generally less conspicuous. Its drum, while very distinctive, is probably delivered most frequently prior to the peak of atlassing. Its robin-like call note is more musical and softer than that of the Black-backed Woodpecker, and since it flakes the bark only, its tapping is quieter. It can forage on much smaller trees and on side branches near the tops of trees, making it harder to see. These facts make it more difficult to detect than the Black-backed Woodpecker and contribute to the low probability of observation: only 7% in the Hudson Bay Lowlands, 13% in the Northern Shield, and 0.5% in the Southern Shield.

For those records that were documented, the habitat was described as coniferous or mixed forest, including clearcuts, blowdowns, and recent burns. Often, there was water such a lake or muskeg swamp nearby. This species is not particularly wary of people, and some confirmed records were of nests discovered fortuitously as the adult returned to the nest close to where the atlasser happened to be standing.

Abundance: This species is uncommon throughout its Ontario range, and, where their ranges overlap, is less common than the Black-backed Woodpecker. In the Northern Shield, the probability of observation is 13% compared to 21% for the Black-backed Woodpecker; in the same region, there were only an average of 0.04 birds/25 point counts compared to 0.23 for the Black-backed Woodpecker. Since it is difficult to detect, atlas data may underestimate the population of the American Three-toed Woodpecker in Ontario. – *Nicholas G. Escott*

Black-backed Woodpecker

Pic à dos noir

Picoides arcticus

Barry S. Cherriere

The Black-backed Woodpecker is an uncommon resident species whose range coincides closely with conifer forests across Canada and south into the US along the Rocky Mountains and in a few northern states. In Ontario, this woodpecker is associated predominantly with the Boreal Forest but also occurs in northern areas of the Great Lakes-St. Lawrence Forest. Studies have generally found it in only two broad habitat types: mature and old-growth conifer and mixed-wood forests, and recently burned forests (Hutto 1995; Setterington et al. 2000; Hoyt and Hannon 2002).

The Black-backed Woodpecker forages about 40% of the time on stumps and downed wood and the rest of the time on standing trees (Villard 1994). It often excavates wood to feed on wood-boring larvae of beetles (especially the Scolytidae and Cerambycidae), which lay eggs in the cambium layer of recently dead or dying trees, and particularly on fire-killed conifers (Dixon and Saab 2000). However, it is not unusual to observe this woodpecker flaking off bark with its bill to capture insects or their eggs and larvae. Because large numbers of some wood-boring beetle species (e.g., Whitespotted Sawyer) are attracted to recently burned forests, the Black-backed Woodpecker becomes abundant in these areas soon after a fire. Quantitative assessments of its diet have generally found more than 70% wood-boring beetle larvae (e.g., Bent 1939; Goggans et al. 1988; Murphy and Lehnhausen 1998).

Distribution and population status: In Ontario, the Black-backed Woodpecker can be found throughout the Boreal Forest from the Manitoba border east to Québec and south in Ontario to the Kawartha Lakes. Data from the first and second atlases indicate no change in breeding distribution. BBS data suggest that the species may be declining in Ontario and Canada, but because this woodpecker is so rarely recorded, such an indication is likely to be misleading. Between the two atlases, the probability of observation declined by a non-significant 4% province-wide, with the greatest

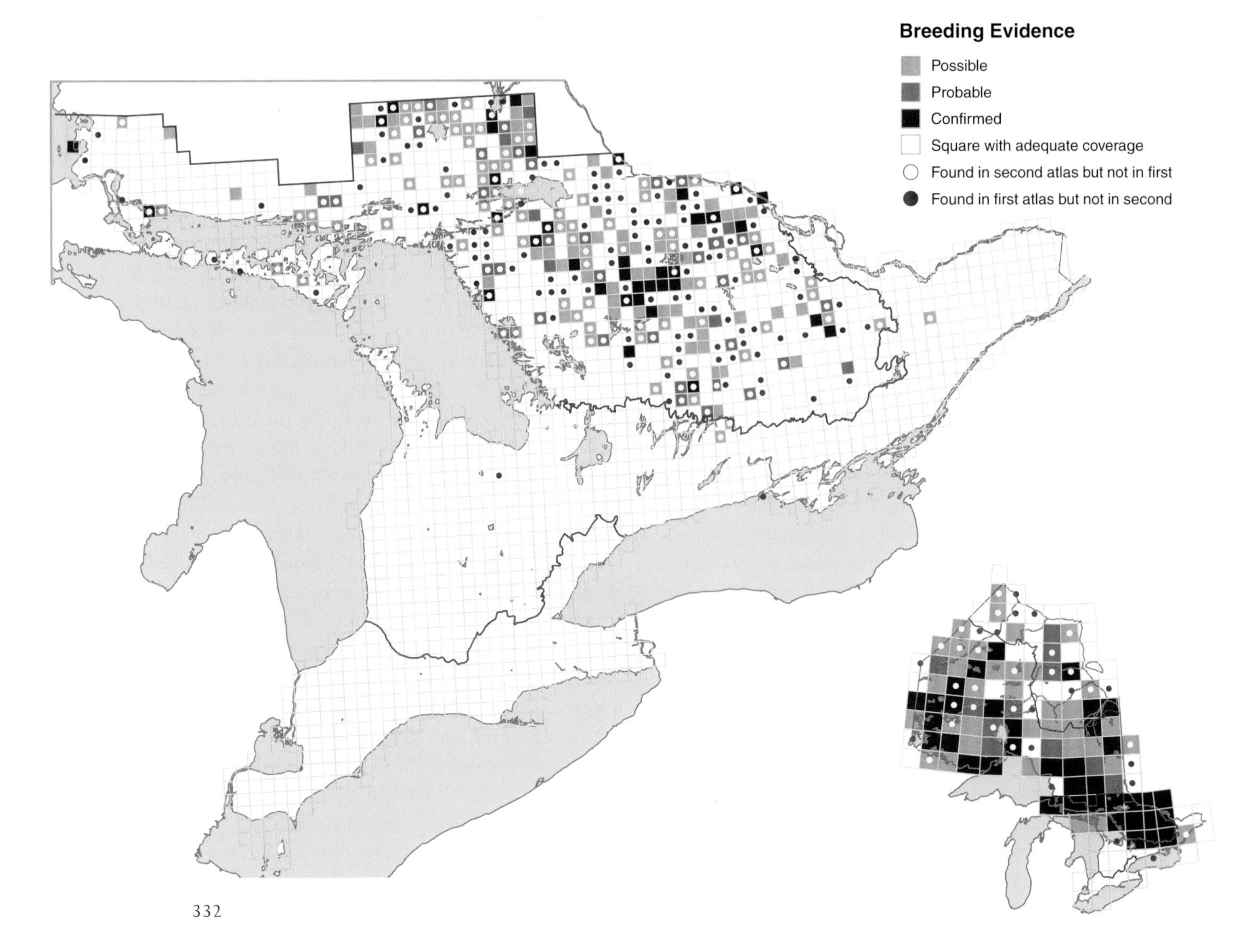

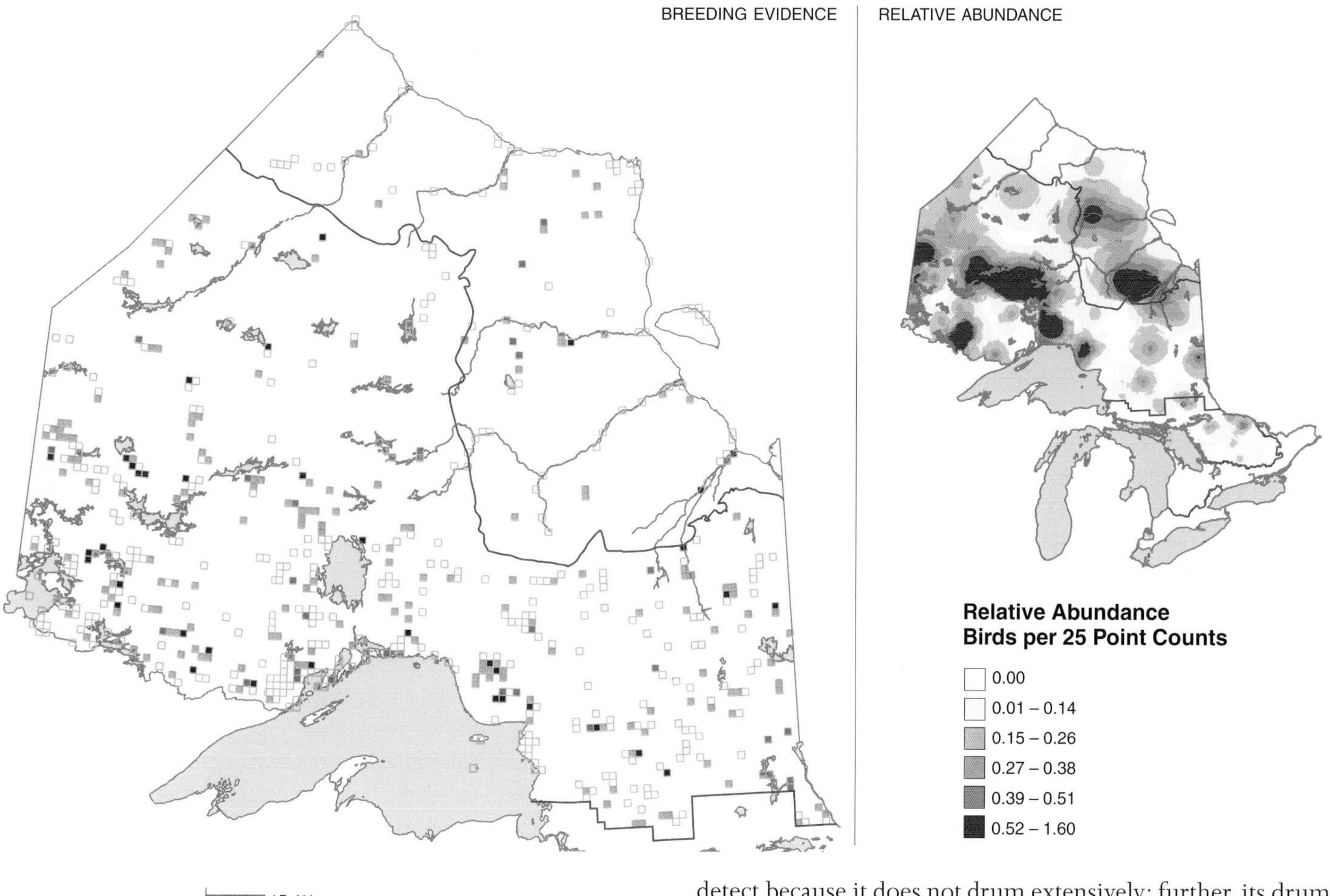

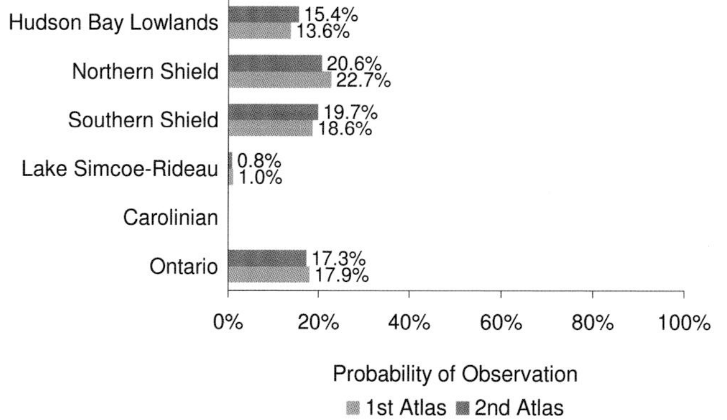

change being a non-significant 17% reduction in the Lake Simcoe-Rideau region.

Breeding biology: The Black-backed Woodpecker nests in live and dead trees both within and away from burned areas. The nest is most often in a dead conifer and is usually associated with edge habitats such as streams, bogs, or logged areas. Trees excavated for nesting by this woodpecker are generally 15-20 cm or larger in diameter (Dixon and Saab 2000). Often the bark is removed from around the cavity entrance in a live conifer, possibly to reduce sap flow at the hole. Both the male and female excavate the nest cavity and incubate and feed the young. Two to six eggs are laid and incubated for 12-14 days, and the young birds fledge at about 24 days. When the parents are absent from the nest, the young call continuously, sounding remarkably like Belted Kingfishers. A new cavity is usually excavated each year, but it is not known if a pair occupies the same site year-round, or whether the birds pair for life.

The Black-backed Woodpecker is generally difficult to detect because it does not drum extensively; further, its drumming is quiet by comparison to the other boreal woodpeckers. However, it may respond aggressively to call playbacks, and this represents the best way to census the species. Hence, in the absence of using playback recordings, it would be common for birds to be present (and breeding) in an atlas square but not be detected. Therefore, the low confirmation rate for breeding (16% of squares) and the relative lack of correspondence between atlases among squares in which the species was detected are not surprising.

Abundance: While generally found in low abundance, the Black-backed Woodpecker can sometimes be observed at relatively high densities from one to six years following a forest fire in older forests (Hutto 1995). Densities in winter of up to 0.8 birds/ha in burned forest have been found near Thunder Bay (Carney 1999; Escott 2001). Comparisons between densities in unburned and burned forests suggest that these woodpeckers are two to 21 times more abundant in the burned areas (Murphy and Lehnhausen 1998; Kreisel and Stein 1999). The birds may also be observed at relatively high breeding densities on sites that have been recently selection-logged and where a considerable amount of recently downed wood still occurs on the sites from one to three years after logging (I. Thompson, unpubl. data). For this atlas, birds were recorded at a density of 0.2 birds/25 point counts in the Hudson Bay Lowlands, 0.2 in the Northern Shield, and 0.1 in the Southern Shield, reflecting the strong preference of this species for boreal conifer forests. – *Ian D. Thompson*

Northern Flicker

Pic flamboyant

Colaptes auratus

Mark Peck

The Northern Flicker is a ground-foraging woodpecker occurring in most wooded areas in North America from the treeline south to Cuba and Nicaragua (Moore 1995). It is a short-distance migrant throughout most of Canada, but a few birds winter in southern Ontario. This ant specialist breeds in open woodlands and savannahs, along forest edges, and in wetlands, as well as in urban, suburban, and rural environments (Moore 1995). The yellow-shafted form is found in Ontario, occurring wherever there is an abundance of large snags or declining trees. The large nest cavities excavated by the flicker are a critical resource to many other cavity-nesting birds and to mammals (Bavrlic et al. in press).

Distribution and population status: The Northern Flicker is the most widely distributed Ontario woodpecker. Its breeding distribution in the province shows relatively little change from the first atlas. However, although the probability of observation did not change significantly overall, there were regional differences. In the Hudson Bay Lowlands, the probability of observation increased by a significant 27%, while there was a significant 7% decline in the Carolinian region. Although the flicker is adapted to human habitats, intensification of agriculture and urban development in the Carolinian region may have reduced the abundance of large-diameter snags and trees and thus the numbers of this woodpecker. Habitat loss may be further exacerbated by competition with the European Starling for nest holes (Moore 1995); atlas data show that starling densities in the Carolinian are nearly double those of other regions.

Although atlas data suggest the Northern Flicker's distribution has remained fairly stable in Ontario overall, BBS results indicate a significant declining trend. Since 1981, flicker populations in Ontario and Canada have declined annually by 1.4% and 1.7%, respectively. There was a 2.4% annual decline on BBS routes throughout North America from 1966 to 2005

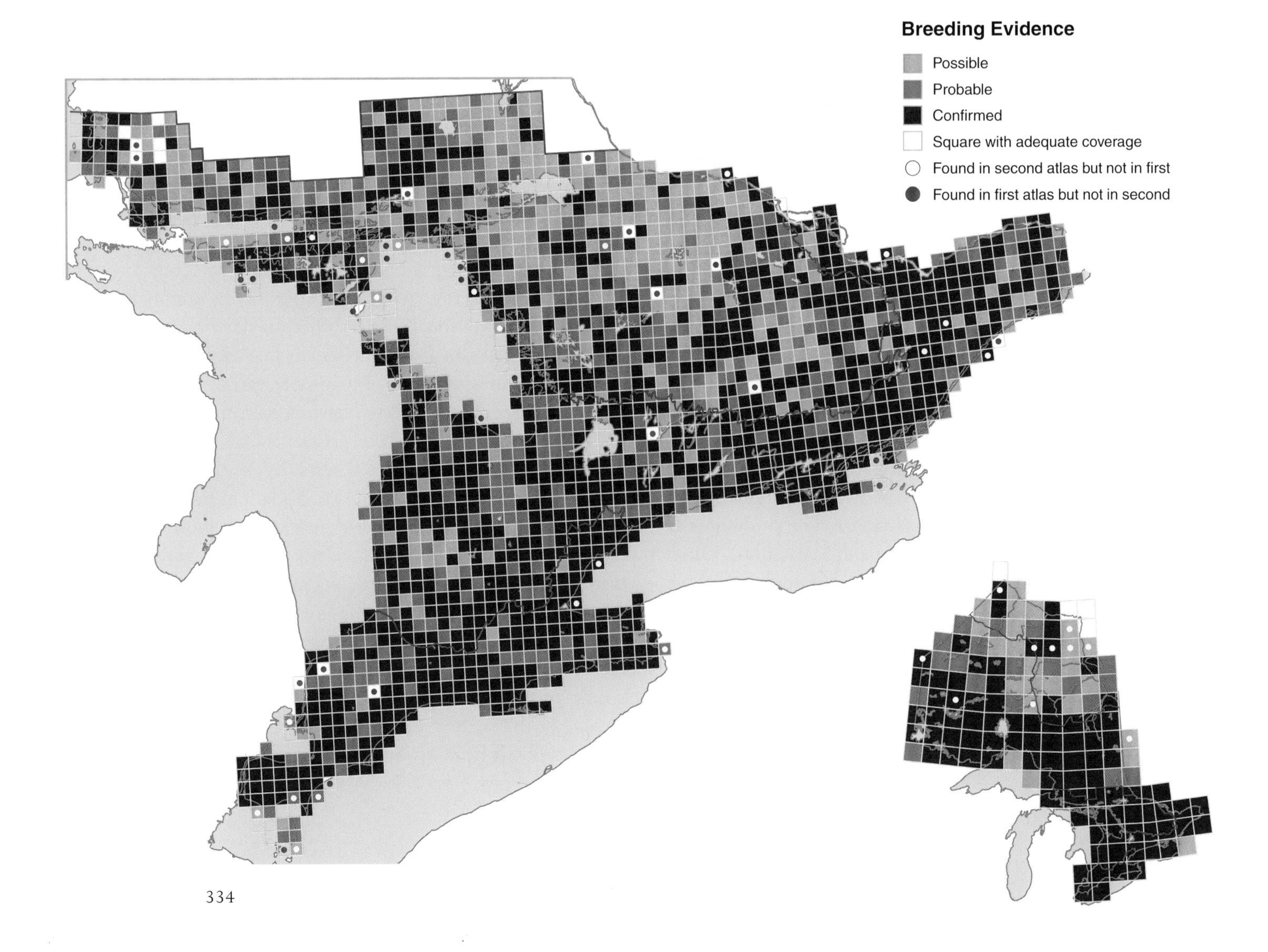

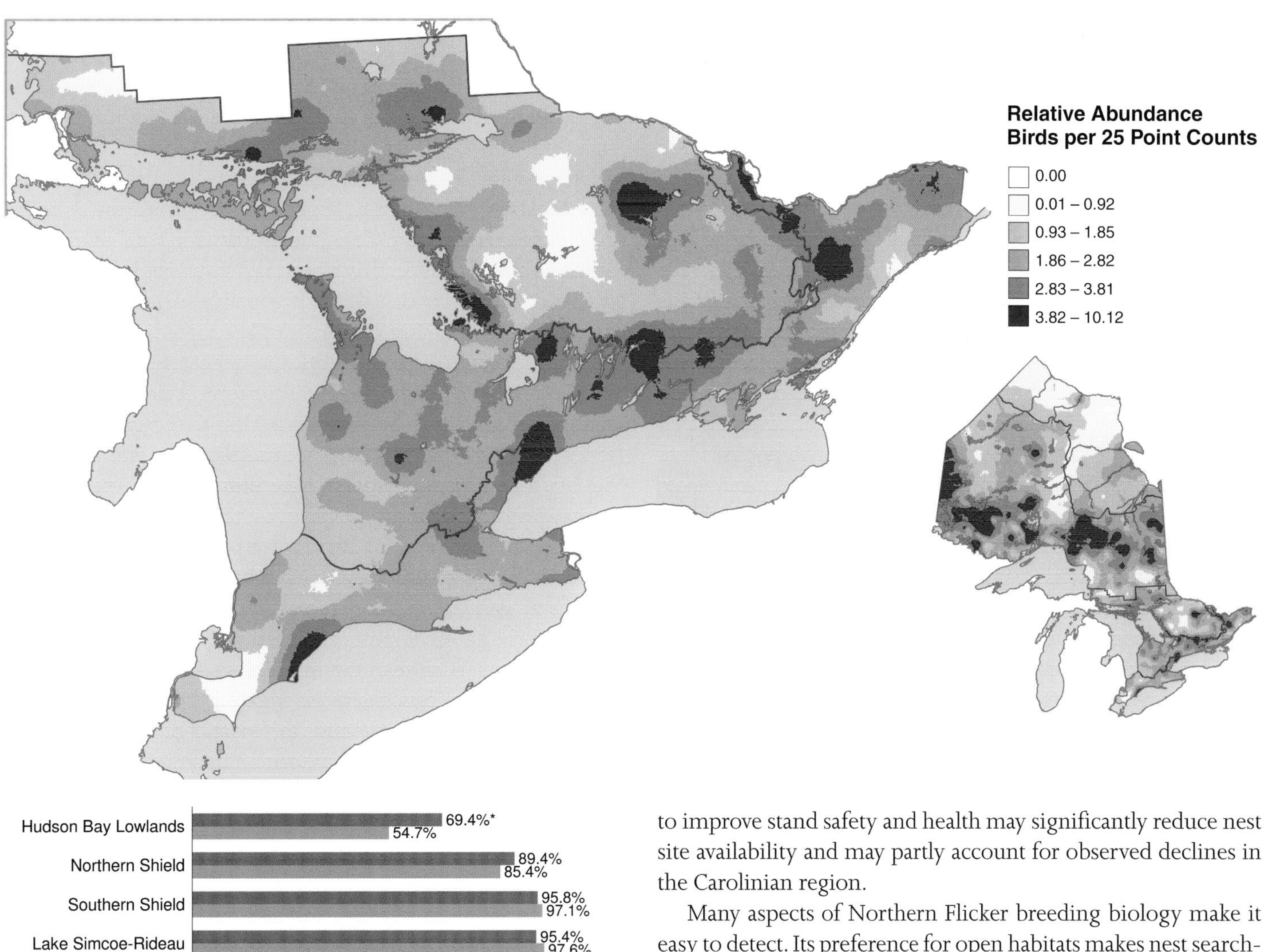

(Sauer et al. 2005). Reasons for the declines include habitat loss, reduction of suitable nest sites (large-diameter snags and declining trees), and competition with starlings (Moore 1995).

Breeding biology: In Ontario, the Northern Flicker is found in openings and edges of deciduous and mixed-hardwood forests and less often in coniferous stands (James 1984b). It is a weak excavator, and cavities are typically made in deciduous snags or live trees with heart rot, usually in the main stem close to a broken top or in large dead limbs. In southern Ontario, 37 trees used for nesting had an average diameter of 47.8 cm (range 25.9-162.1 cm), average height of 19.8 m (range 7.4-36.4 m), and average nest height of 11.1 m (range 3.7-18.6 m; K. Bavrlic, unpubl. data). The species will occasionally use natural cavities, previously excavated cavities (including those of other woodpeckers), and nest boxes. Fidelity to nest trees is strong, and birds will often use the same tree in successive years, with as many as seven old flicker nest cavities in an active nest tree (K. Bavrlic, unpubl. data). The removal of snags and declining trees to improve stand safety and health may significantly reduce nest site availability and may partly account for observed declines in the Carolinian region.

Many aspects of Northern Flicker breeding biology make it easy to detect. Its preference for open habitats makes nest searching easier and breeding confirmation more likely. Territorial and courtship displays in April and May are loud and colourful. Nest excavation can begin as early as mid-April and extend into August. During cavity excavation, adults call frequently, perch by the nest hole, and excavate diligently without much concern for observers. Fresh chips at the base of large snags or declining trees in open areas are reliable signs of cavity occupancy. The combined egg and nestling period of 35-38 days (Moore 1995) results in substantial overlap with the main atlassing period. Although adults are secretive during the incubation and early nestling stage, the *churring* of the young is audible from lower cavities. Also, young about to fledge hang out of the cavity entrance and give repeated, loud contact calls. Fledged young are dependent on adults for up to two weeks.

Abundance: Densities of the flicker are highest across central portions of the Northern Shield region, where extensive burns and clearcuts with standing dead birch and aspen provide abundant nesting habitat. Slightly lower densities (average 2-3 birds/25 point counts) in the Southern Shield, Lake Simcoe-Rideau, and Carolinian regions may be attributable to the more limited availability of snags of suitable diameter for nesting. Low densities in the Hudson Bay Lowlands are probably due to the general absence of large-diameter trees except along major rivers. – *Kata Bavrlic*

Pileated Woodpecker

Grand Pic

Dryocopus pileatus

Ann Cook

The impressive size, dramatic appearance, and laugh-like call of the Pileated Woodpecker make it the most easily identified and memorable of our woodpeckers. It is a permanent resident across the forested portions of southern and central Canada, from Vancouver Island to Cape Breton Island (although absent from Newfoundland and Labrador), and throughout most of the eastern and northwestern US (Bull and Jackson 1995).

Distribution and population status: The atlas data suggest the Pileated Woodpecker is well distributed throughout the predominantly forested regions of Ontario, with the probability of observation 87% in the Southern Shield region, 58% in the Lake Simcoe-Rideau region, and 47% in the Northern Shield region. However, it has a patchy distribution in the Carolinian region, being largely absent from the Niagara Peninsula, Haldimand Clay Plain, Chatham-Kent, and Essex and Lambton Counties. Distribution is also very sparse within the Hudson Bay Lowlands, where suitable habitat occurs only along large rivers.

Comparison of the two atlases indicates almost a 50% increase in the probability of observation in the province as a whole and a 27% to 55% increase within all regions except the Hudson Bay Lowlands. A range expansion is particularly apparent in the southeast end of the Lake Simcoe-Rideau region and in southwestern Ontario.

The increase in overall distribution appears to be part of the steady recovery of this species from historical declines resulting from habitat loss and recreational and market hunting noted throughout southern and central Ontario by 1900 (Dance 1994). With maturation of forests and protection from hunting, populations began to recover by the 1940s. The species may still be increasing in Ontario but at a declining rate; BBS data indicate a significant annual rate of increase of 6.7% since 1968 (Downes et al. 2005) but a non-significant rate of only 2.8% since 1981.

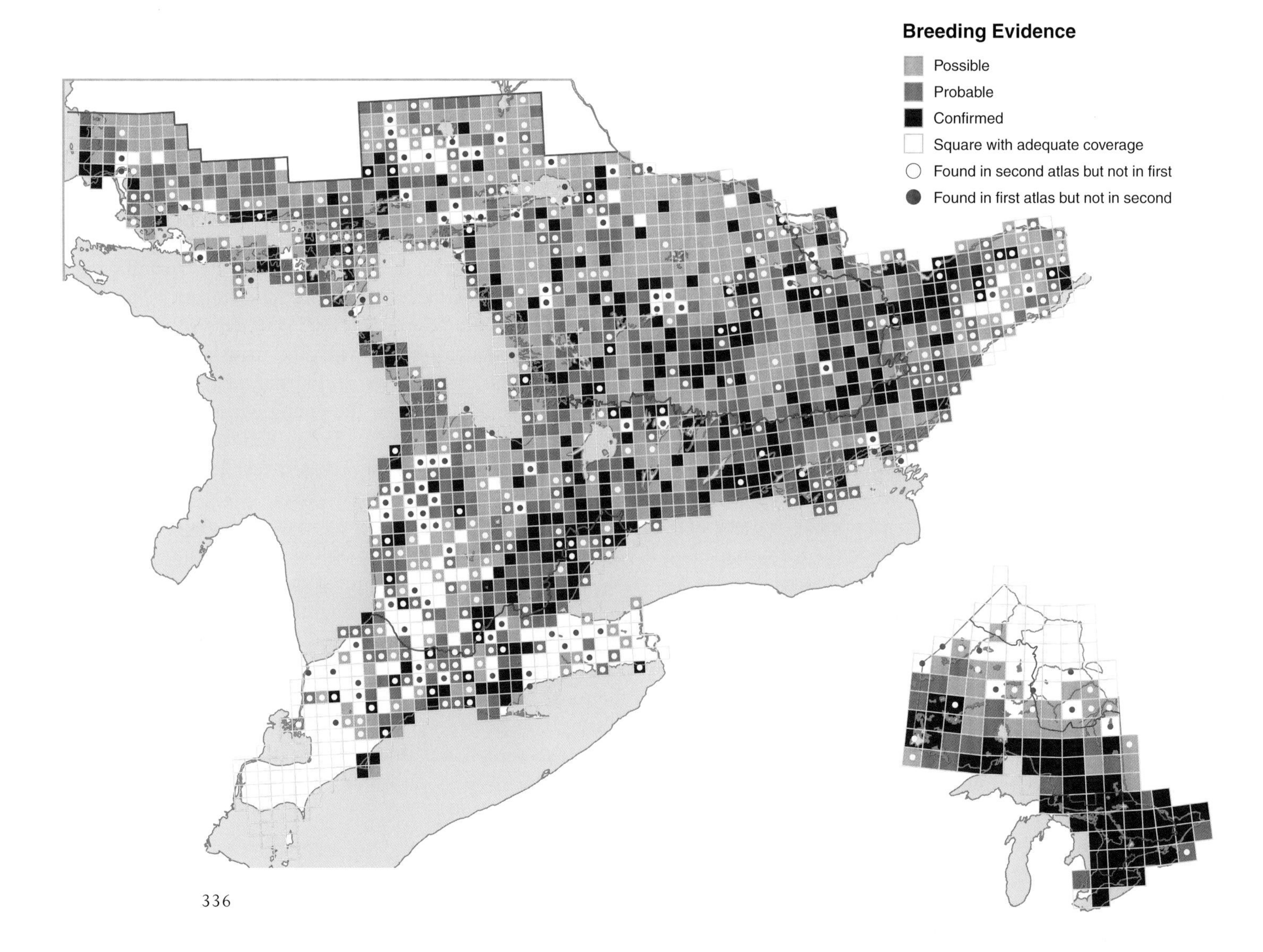

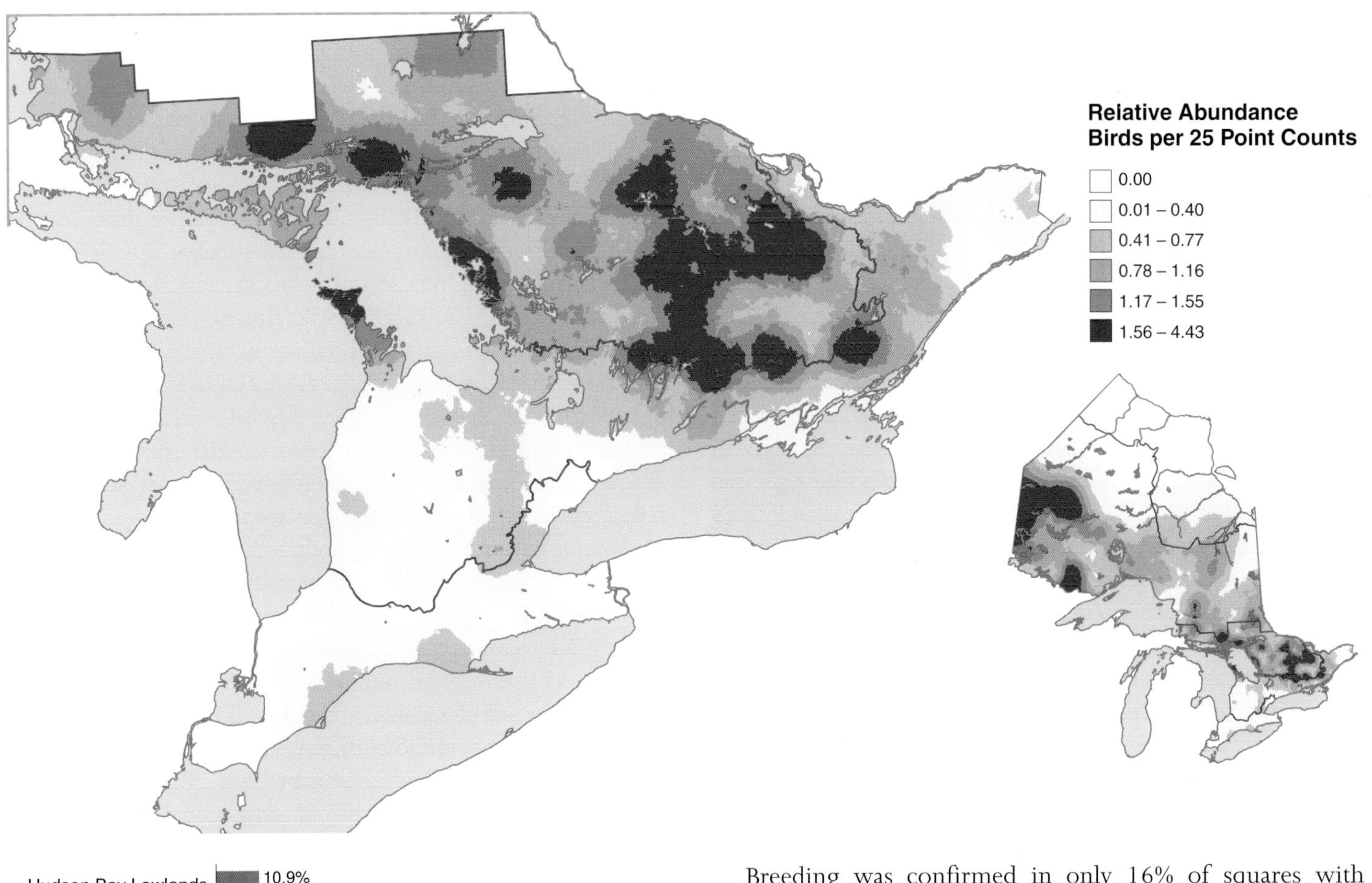

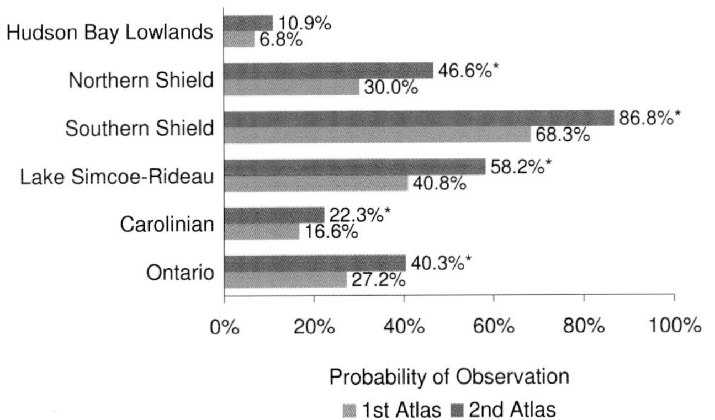

Increases in abundance and distribution since the first atlas may be related to a combination of factors such as increases in the amount of mature forest in the central and eastern portions of the Lake Simcoe-Rideau region, increases in the proportion of hardwood and mixed forest across parts of the Northern Shield, and the focus on providing habitat for this species during forest management activities on Crown land in the Southern Shield and Lake Simcoe-Rideau regions (see Naylor et al. 1996).

Breeding biology: While the Pileated Woodpecker breeds in a wide range of habitats from extensive forest to urban parks, preferred nesting habitat is large patches (greater than 40 ha) of mature and older forest with a mixture of deciduous and coniferous trees (Kirk and Naylor 1996). Nests are usually excavated in large-diameter declining or dead trees. Large declining, dead, and fallen trees are also key components of habitat, providing substrates for the wood-dwelling insects that are the species' principal food (Kirk and Naylor 1996). The low overall probability of observation (40%) may partly reflect habitat availability, especially north and south of the Shield.

Breeding was confirmed in only 16% of squares with breeding evidence. The low rate of confirmation may have been related to breeding chronology. The Pileated Woodpecker defends its territory with loud drumming and calling and excavates nest cavities in mid-March to mid-May (pers. obs.); by the peak of atlas surveying, it would be well into incubation (median eggs dates 9 May to 30 May; Peck and James 1983) and considerably less conspicuous. It can also be difficult to locate and confirm the status of nests because they are generally fairly high in trees, typically about 8 to 12 m (Peck and James 1983).

Considering the large size and conspicuous habits of this species, the atlas is likely a fairly accurate depiction of its general distribution within the province. Moreover, since the species is a permanent resident, squares with possible or probable breeding evidence have a high likelihood of being inhabited by breeding birds.

Abundance: For most resident woodpeckers, which begin nesting well before most songbirds, point count data collected during the atlas likely provide an imprecise estimate of abundance and should be viewed cautiously. However, the general patterns shown are likely valid; abundance is highest in areas where there is a large supply of suitable habitat such as across the central parts of the Southern Shield and Lake Simcoe-Rideau regions and the northwestern portions of the Northern Shield around Quetico and Woodland Caribou Prov. Parks. In southwestern Ontario, highest abundance is associated primarily with the wooded portions of the Niagara Escarpment, especially along the Bruce Peninsula. – *Brian Naylor*

Olive-sided Flycatcher

Moucherolle à côtés olive

Contopus cooperi

Jim Richards

This declining flycatcher utters its loud and distinctively Canadian "*Quick, three beers*" song from atop tall trees in expansive bogs, riparian zones, cutovers, and burns. The Olive-sided Flycatcher is an obligate aerial feeder, capturing bees, wasps, large flies, beetles, and dragonflies on the wing. Breeding only in North America, it nests across Canada in boreal forest from just south of the northern limit of trees south along the Canadian Shield and into the US at higher elevations, south to California in the west. It winters primarily in South America, in the Andes Mountains from Venezuela south through Ecuador to Peru and Bolivia – a remarkably long migration (Altman and Sallabanks 2000).

Distribution and population status: The general distribution of the Olive-sided Flycatcher is relatively unchanged from the first atlas. However, the probability of observation declined significantly by 44% in the Lake Simcoe-Rideau region and 35% in the Southern Shield. Regional Coordinators in Muskoka, Haliburton, and Ottawa noted that this flycatcher has become rarer in these areas in the last 20 years. BBS data show significant declines in Ontario and Canada and across North America within that part of the breeding range accessible by road. Since 1981, this species has declined an astounding 13.9% per year on BBS routes in Ontario. Across North America, its population in 1996 was only 30% of what it was in 1966 (Altman and Sallabanks 2000).

Although the cause of the dramatic decline in Olive-sided Flycatcher populations is unknown, possible contributing factors include loss of wintering habitat, fire suppression, some forest-management practices, potential effects of climatic variations on prey availability, and pesticides (Altman and Sallabanks 2000). The small brood size, short breeding season, fidelity to breeding locations, and long migration may make it particularly vulnerable (Altman and Sallabanks 2000). Research in western North America has indicated that this flycatcher may historically have been dependent on post-fire habitat for breeding (Hutto 1995). However, while both fire suppression and

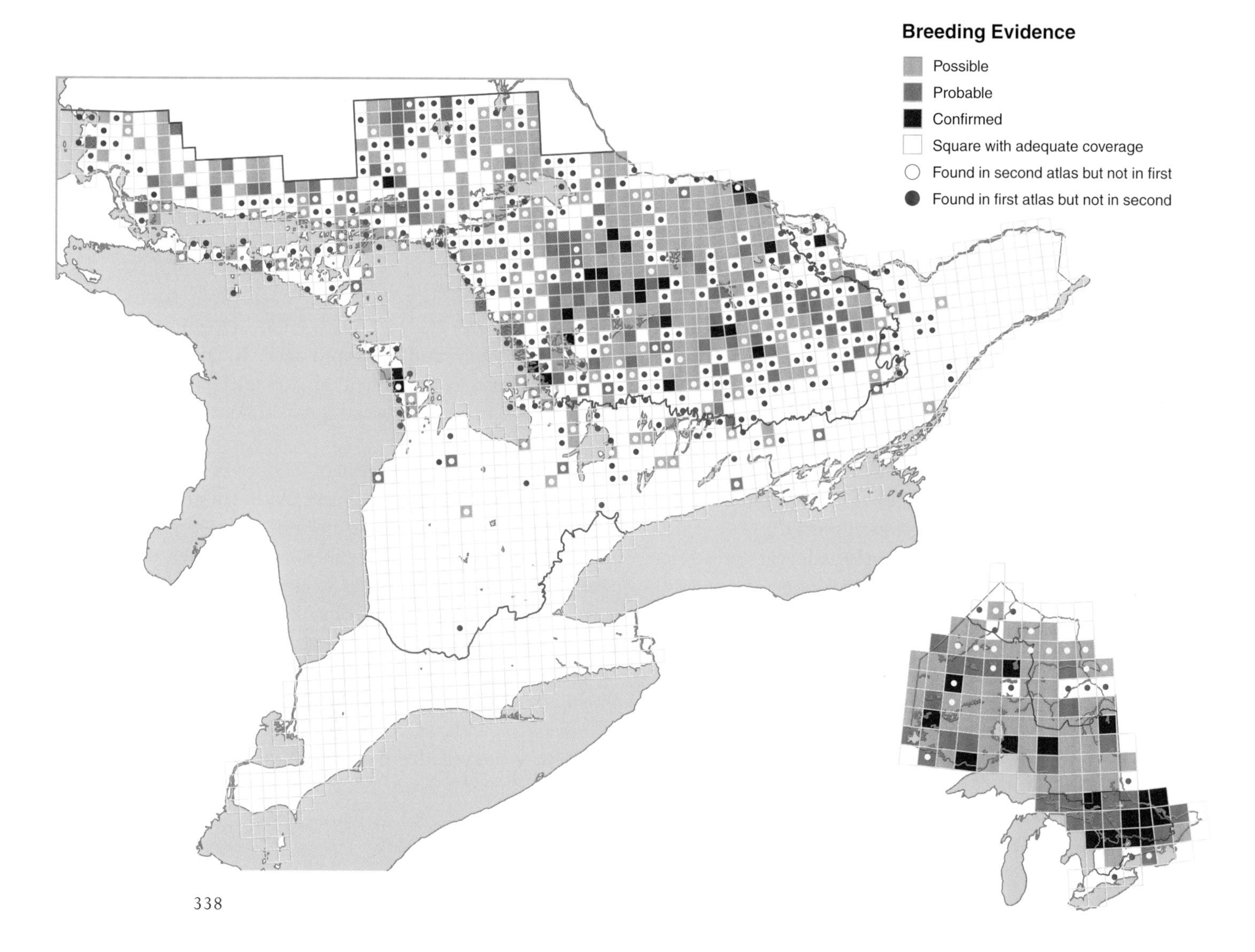

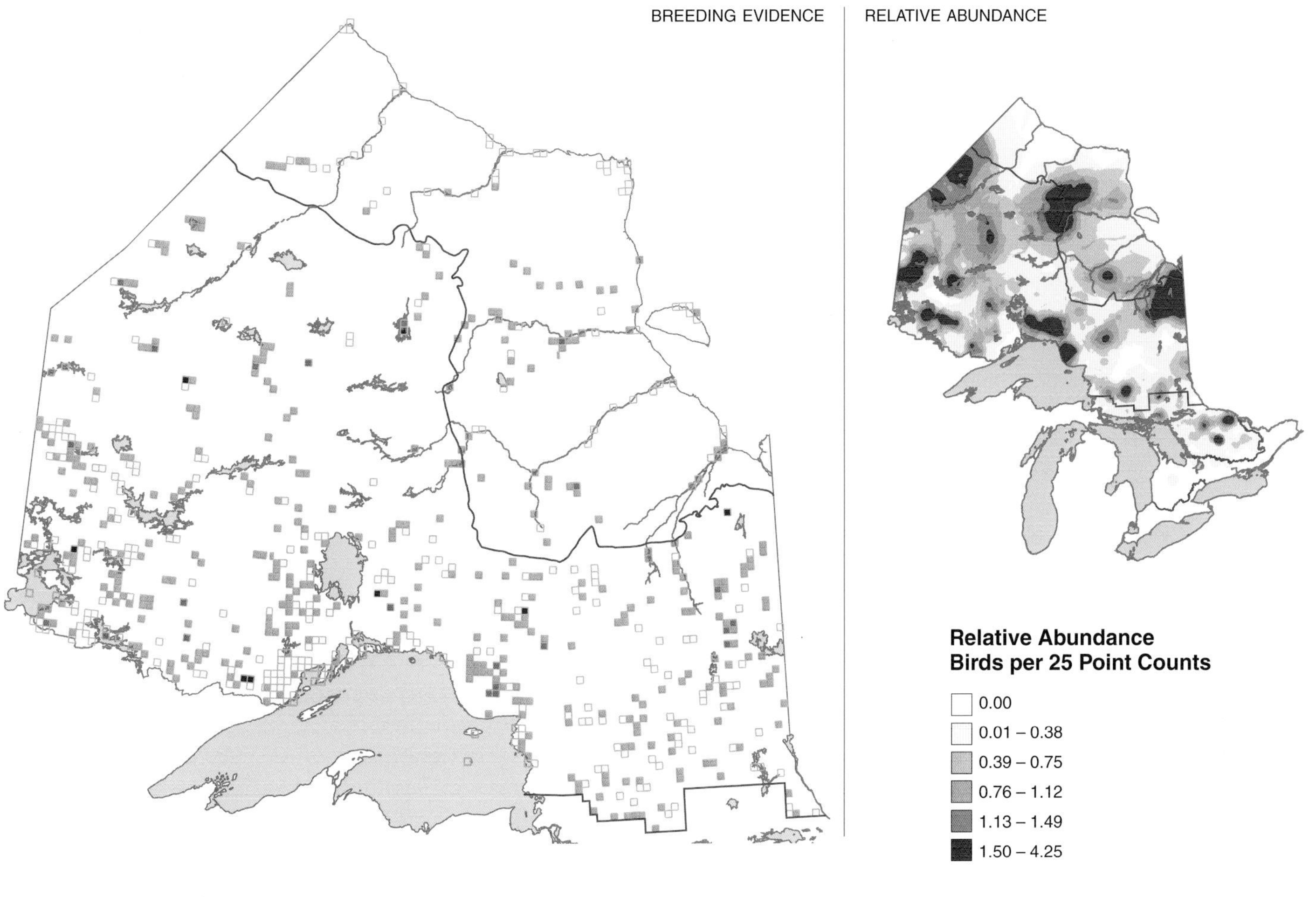

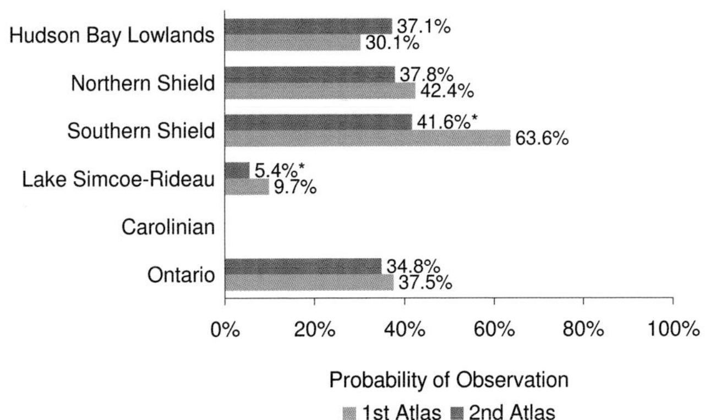

forest management can significantly alter forest composition and structure, the species has been shown to respond positively to a variety of forest harvest prescriptions in western North America, and loss or degradation of wintering habitat has been hypothesized to be a more significant factor in the species' decline, although this has not been studied to date (Altman and Sallabanks 2000).

Breeding biology: The Olive-sided Flycatcher has the longest migration of all flycatchers in the Americas and one of the longest of any passerine. It leaves the wintering grounds in South America from mid-March to May, arriving in Ontario rarely before mid-May and often into mid-June. The extremely late spring migration and the fact that it regularly calls and sings on migration may have resulted in migrants being reported incorrectly as breeding at some locations during the atlas, especially along the southern edge of its nesting range in the Lake Simcoe-Rideau region.

Once on territory, this species is highly conspicuous because of its loud and unmistakable song, its eye-catching behaviour of perching on the highest snags, sallying forth to capture flying insects, and its aggressive defence of its territory and nest site from conspecifics (Altman and Sallabanks 2000). It has the lowest reproductive rate of any Ontario flycatcher, with clutches typically consisting of three eggs, and never more than one brood per year (Altman and Sallabanks 2000). Nests are open cups, usually well hidden and placed at various heights on horizontal limbs of mainly coniferous trees (Peck and James 1987). The young hatch after about 15-19 days and spend about the same amount of time in the nest before fledging (Altman and Sallabanks 2000). Juveniles stay with parents for at least two to three weeks and frequently until the long return flight to the wintering grounds begins (Altman and Sallabanks 2000).

Abundance: Relative abundance is generally highest in the Northern Shield region (averaging 0.7 birds/25 point counts), followed by the Hudson Bay Lowlands and Southern Shield regions, both at about 0.4 birds/25 point counts. The map shows high relative abundance (more than 1.5 birds/25 point counts) as patchy, with most high density locations in the northern Boreal Forest, but this patchiness may be partly due to low numbers of birds and the mapping process. In the south, nodes of high density occur in the upper Ottawa Valley and the Algonquin Highlands. Throughout most of the Olive-sided Flycatcher's range in Ontario, there was less than 1 bird/25 point counts, underscoring the scarcity of this species. – *Edward Cheskey*

Eastern Wood-Pewee

Pioui de l'Est

Contopus virens

George K. Peck

The Eastern Wood-Pewee is a small, greyish-olive, inconspicuous flycatcher. It is best known by its plaintive, whistled "pee-a-wee" song, given from high in the canopy of deciduous trees. Characteristically, the pewee sallies forth to capture flying insects in forest gaps and along woodland edges, returning repeatedly to the same exposed perch. It breeds throughout central and eastern North America from southeastern Saskatchewan east to Nova Scotia, and south to the Gulf Coast (McCarty 1996). Its winter range is in northern South America (McCarty 1996).

Distribution and population status: The Eastern Wood-Pewee was found in all the atlas regions, although it was exceedingly rare in the Hudson Bay Lowlands, where it was reported in only two squares at the extreme southern edge of the region, northeast of Fraserdale and south of Mammamattawa on the Kenogami River. The species was most common in southern Ontario, where its probability of observation was over 80% in both the Carolinian and Lake Simcoe-Rideau regions. Its probability of observation was 62% in the Southern Shield, but distribution was much more sporadic north of the Great Lakes-St. Lawrence Forest. Even in the western portion of the Northern Shield region from Thunder Bay to Kenora, where habitat is similar to that in the Southern Shield, this flycatcher was noted only infrequently.

There was a significant decrease in the probability of observation of the Eastern Wood-Pewee in the Lake Simcoe-Rideau (6%) and Southern Shield (15%) regions in the second atlas compared to the first. Most of the decrease has apparently occurred at the northern edge of the Southern Shield, although, curiously, there was a significant increase in the adjacent Northern Shield region. However, in Ontario as a whole, there was no significant change. These data are similar to the BBS results, which show a near-significant annual decrease of 2.1% in Ontario since 1981. The number of

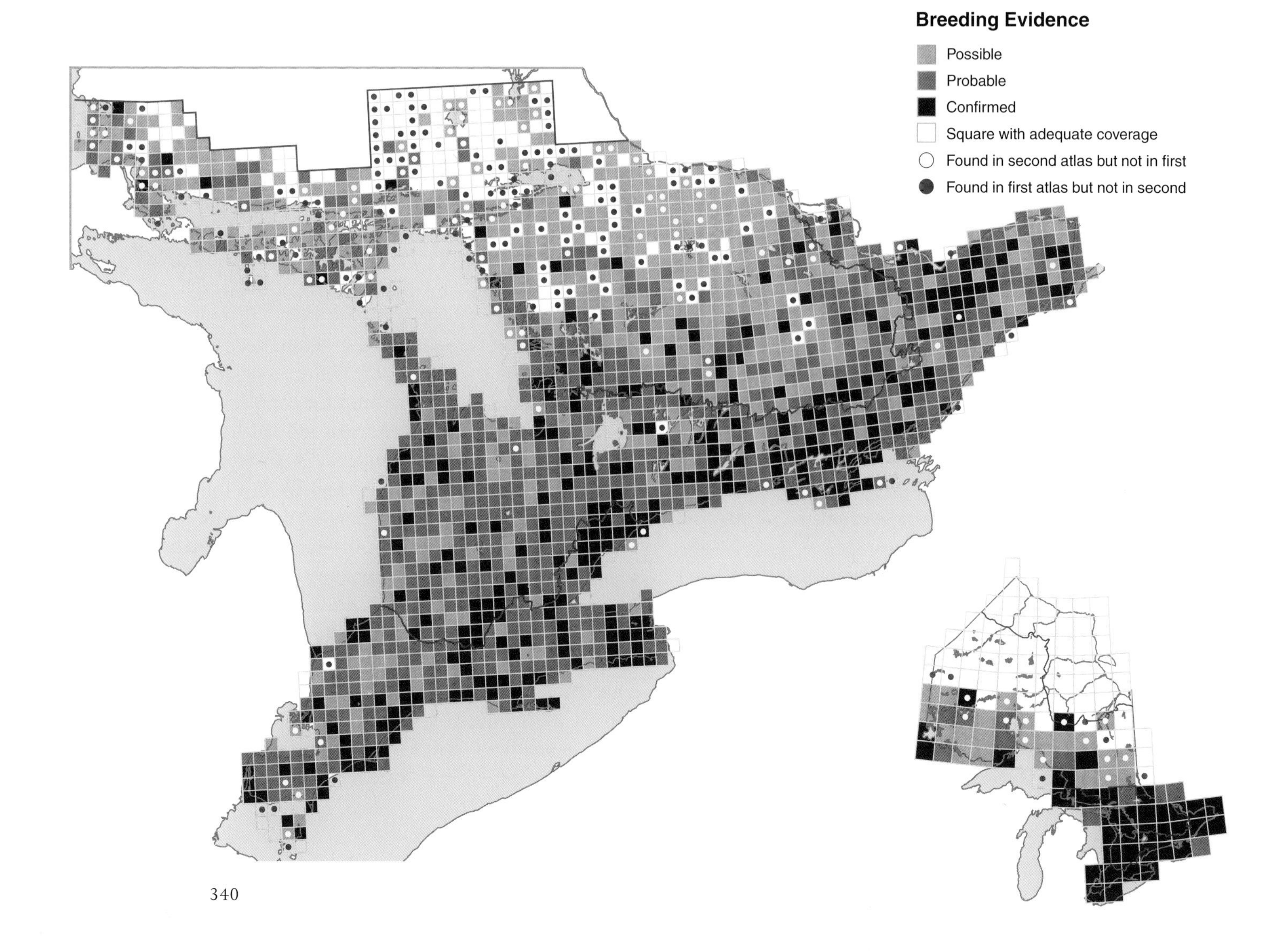

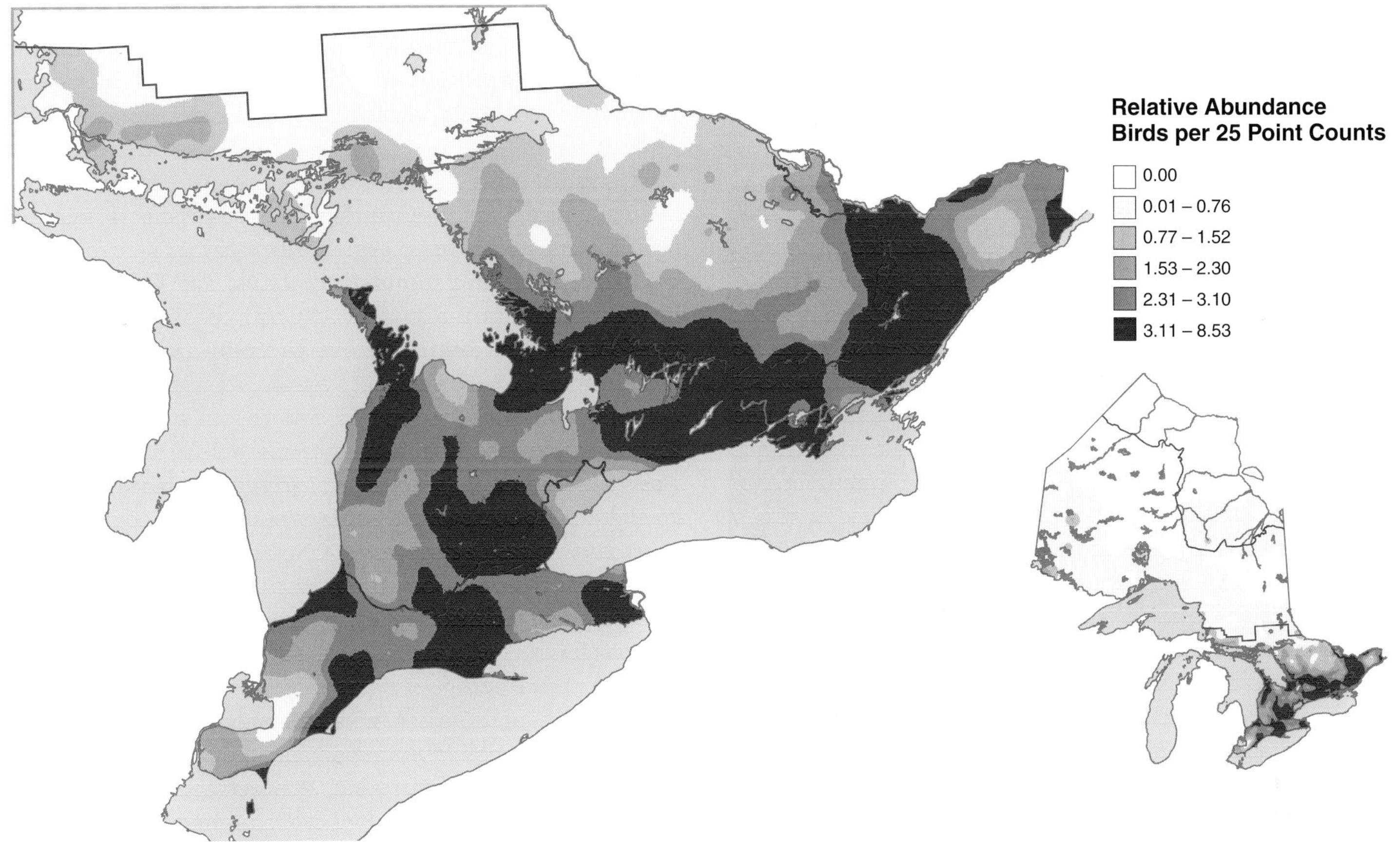

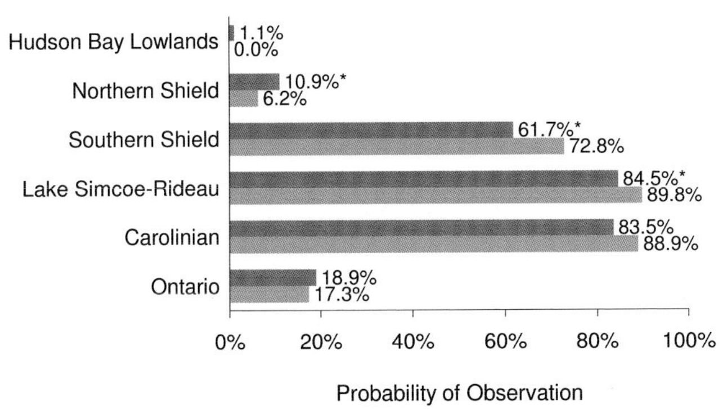

Eastern Wood-Pewees passing through LPBO also showed a slight decline from 1994 to 2004 (Crewe 2006), following a slight increase from 1979 to 1988 (Hussell et al. 1992).

Breeding biology: The Eastern Wood-Pewee is a late spring migrant, with the peak of arrival in northern breeding areas occurring in mid- to late May (McCarty 1996). In Ontario, it typically breeds in deciduous and mixed woods. Its preference for open space near the nest is often provided by forest edges, clearings, roadways, and water (Peck and James 1987). Although it is not a species that requires large areas of woods (Freemark and Collins 1992), it occurs less frequently in woodlots with surrounding development than in those without nearby houses (Friesen et al. 1995). Since it sings regularly throughout the day, and occasionally even at night, it is relatively easy to detect (McCarty 1996).

The cryptic nest of the Eastern Wood-Pewee is usually built on a small branch of a deciduous tree (most commonly elm, oak, maple, birch, or apple), well out from the trunk (averaging 1.5-3 m), and usually fairly high up (averaging 4.5-9 m; Peck and James 1987). The nest is a shallow cup of woven grass, covered with lichens, and often looks like a knot on top of the supporting branch (McCarty 1996). Little is known about the nesting behaviour, but it is believed that only the female Eastern Wood-Pewee incubates the eggs and broods the young in the nest. Both parents feed the nestlings (McCarty 1996). The egg-laying period from early June to mid-August (Peck and James 1987) corresponds well with the period when most atlassing was done. However, overall, the species was confirmed in only 18% of squares where it was recorded, perhaps reflecting the relative inconspicuousness of both nests and fledged young.

Abundance: The Carolinian and Lake Simcoe-Rideau regions comprise the centre of abundance for the Eastern Wood-Pewee in Ontario. In each of these regions, the average abundance is 3.3 birds/25 point counts. The highest densities occur in a wide horseshoe-shaped area extending from Ottawa to Lake Ontario, along the edge of the Shield, and up to southern Georgian Bay. Similar densities are found on the Bruce Peninsula, in a band from Toronto to Wellington Co. and down to Long Point, and in a few other smaller areas in southern Ontario. Densities on the Canadian Shield are much lower, averaging only 1.7 birds/25 point counts in the Southern Shield, and less than 1 bird/25 point counts in the Northern Shield region. – *Margaret A. McLaren*

Yellow-bellied Flycatcher

Moucherolle à ventre jaune

Empidonax flaviventris

Jim Richards

The Yellow-bellied Flycatcher is a characteristic denizen of moist to wet coniferous forests and wooded peatlands on the Precambrian Shield and in the Hudson Bay Lowlands. Because its preferred habitat is moist and mossy, it has been given the apt informal name "Moss Tyrant" (Gross and Lowther 2001). This flycatcher is more often heard than seen on its breeding grounds. It has one of the shortest residence times of any of our neotropical migrants, most birds arriving in late May and departing in August, usually staying only about 66 days on the Ontario breeding grounds (Hussell 1982). Widespread throughout the boreal regions of North America, it extends southward in the breeding season as far as southern Wisconsin, northern Pennsylvania, northern New York, and Maine, with isolated populations in West Virginia. It winters from Mexico to Panama (Gross and Lowther 2001).

Distribution and population status: The Yellow-bellied Flycatcher occurs throughout Ontario from the Southern Shield region northward. On its breeding range, it prefers cool, moist, mossy, coniferous swamps, treed bogs, and treed poor fens dominated by Black Spruce or Balsam Fir, with smaller amounts of deciduous trees such as White Birch, Trembling Aspen, Balsam Poplar, and mountain-ashes. It also breeds on deeply shaded, conifer-dominated, cool, moist, rocky talus slopes (Brunton and Crins 1975), including those below the cliffs on the northern part of the Bruce Peninsula. Generally, its breeding habitats are structurally complex, with evident layers of canopy trees, saplings, shrubs such as Northern Wild Raisin, Speckled Alder, and Mountain Holly, herbs, sedges, and mosses, with the understorey often being quite dense.

Between atlases, the probability of observation of the Yellow-bellied Flycatcher more than doubled in the province as a whole. Significant increases occurred in the three most northerly regions that make up the species' core range in the province.

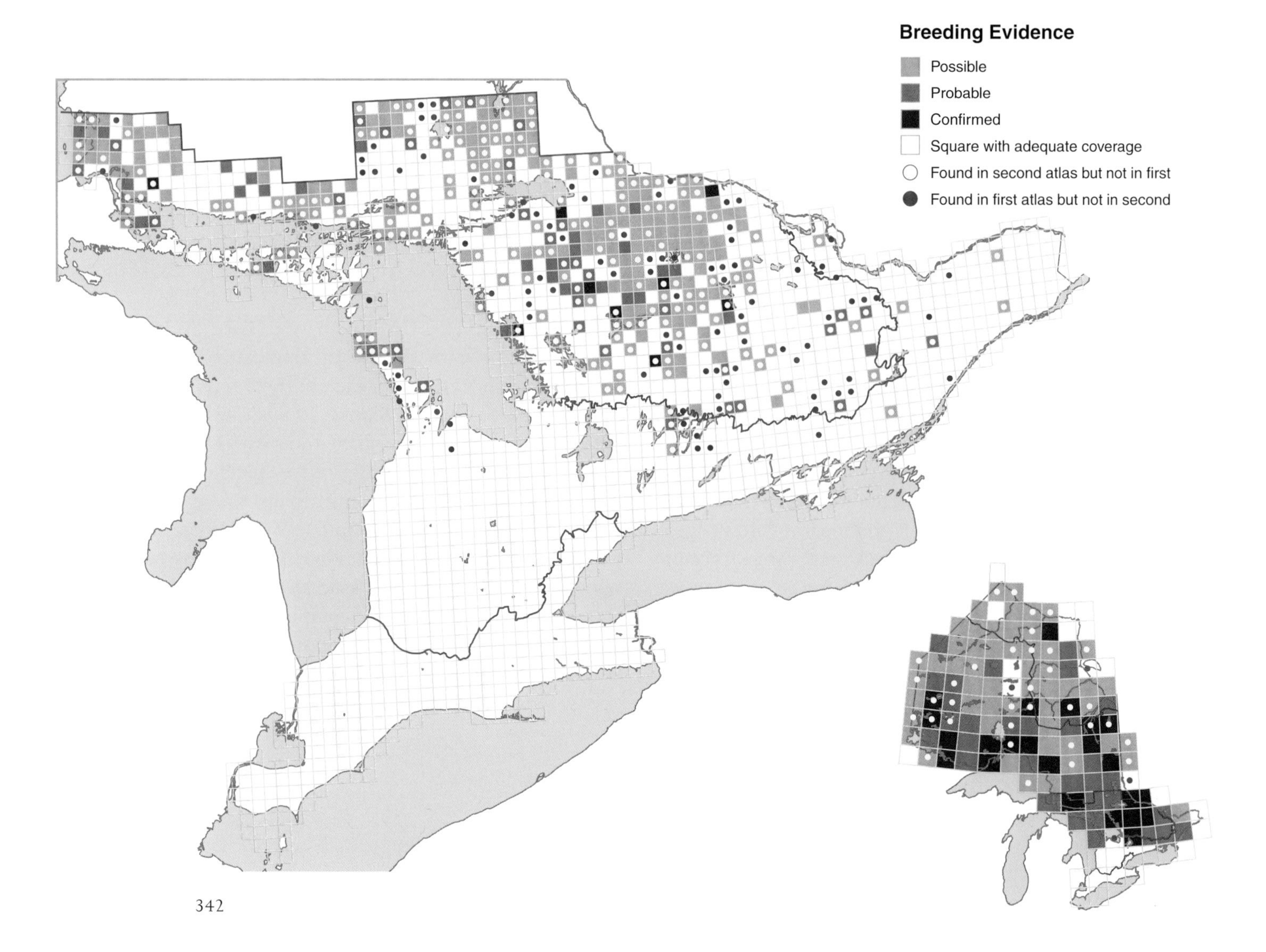

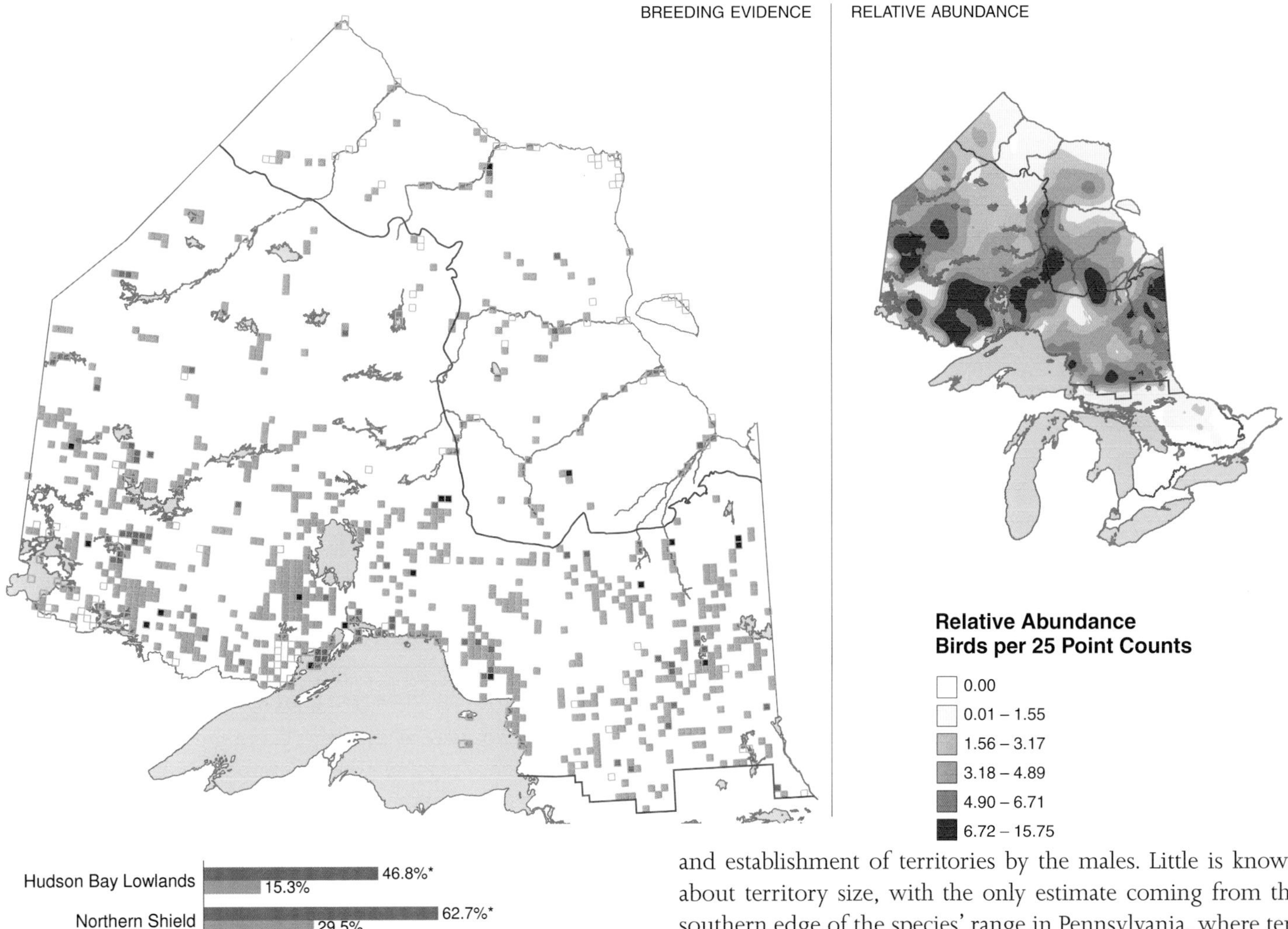

Although it appears that this flycatcher is now somewhat more widespread than it was during the first atlas, this may be an artifact of atlassers' increased familiarity with the songs and calls of the species. At the southern edge of its range near the southern edge of the Shield, the frequency of occurrence remains roughly similar, although there have been shifts among squares.

BBS data show no change in Ontario since 1968 (Downes et al. 2005), but most of the species' range is north of extensive BBS coverage.

Although there appear to be few threats to the Yellow-bellied Flycatcher on its breeding grounds, with the possible exception of slight range retractions due to peatland loss and other land-use changes at its southern limit in Pennsylvania, Wisconsin, and New York, there has been an apparent decline on the wintering grounds in Mexico, due to the loss of rainforest (Gross and Lowther 2001).

Breeding biology: Upon arrival in breeding habitat, males sing repeatedly from high perches. Pairs form soon after arrival and establishment of territories by the males. Little is known about territory size, with the only estimate coming from the southern edge of the species' range in Pennsylvania, where territories were 0.75 to 1 ha in size. On territory, both the male and female respond aggressively to conspecifics, other species of similar size, and potential predators. Females give the "*tu-wee*" call almost constantly when building the nest and when distressed by intruders (Gross and Lowther 2001).

The nest is always on or near the ground, often situated in a cavern-like hole, well hidden by surrounding moss, overhanging vegetation, overarching fallen logs, or roots. Thus, nests are extremely difficult to find. Furthermore, females flush reluctantly from the nest, adding to the difficulty in locating them. This helps explain the relatively low level of confirmations of this species (2% of squares with breeding evidence).

In Ontario, a single clutch is produced, usually of four eggs (Peck and James 1987). Only the female incubates, and the incubation period is 15 days. Young remain in the nest for 13 days. Both parents tend the young, which usually hide as a group in dense vegetation (Gross and Lowther 2001), providing another possible reason for the low level of confirmation.

Abundance: The highest densities of Yellow-bellied Flycatchers are found in the Northern Shield region (average of 5.3 birds/25 point counts). The Hudson Bay Lowlands and the Southern Shield have lower densities at 2.1 and 0.5 birds/25 point counts, respectively. Areas with high densities of over 6.7 birds/25 point counts occur intermittently in a wide band north of Sault Ste. Marie and New Liskeard and south of a line from Moosonee to Red Lake. – *William J. Crins*

Acadian Flycatcher

Moucherolle vert

Empidonax virescens

Jim Richards

A neotropical migrant wintering from Nicaragua south to northwestern South America, the Acadian Flycatcher breeds in forests throughout the eastern US, north to extreme southern Ontario (Whitehead and Taylor 2002). In its core US range, it occurs in mature, mainly deciduous forest, where it may often be as abundant as the Red-eyed Vireo (B. Woolfenden, pers. comm.) In Canada, it breeds only in southern Ontario, where it is generally rare and found primarily within the Carolinian region. Usually unseen in the deep shade of the forest, its presence is best detected by the male's loud and emphatic "*peet-sa*" territorial song. Due to low regional forest cover, woodland fragmentation, and other factors that continue to threaten its remaining habitat, the Acadian Flycatcher is currently listed as Endangered in Canada and Ontario (COSEWIC 2007).

Distribution and population status: The North American distribution of the Acadian Flycatcher likely retracted through the 1800s in response to extensive deforestation (Whitehead and Taylor 2002). In recent decades, however, it appears to have reclaimed much of its former range and expanded slightly to the northeast in New England (Whitehead and Taylor 2002).

In Ontario, its probability of observation increased significantly by 86% between atlases; the species was reported in 50 squares during the second atlas and 29 in the first, with 44 (88%) of the second atlas records coming from the Carolinian region. In neighbouring New York State, the species has also expanded in the last 20 years, from 156 to 236 squares (New York State Breeding Bird Atlas). Much of the Ontario increase may be attributable to directed searches for the species in association with the Acadian Flycatcher/Hooded Warbler Recovery Team efforts since 1997, rather than an actual increase in numbers. The Acadian Flycatcher's distribution is well represented by the atlas maps, especially in the Carolinian where targeted

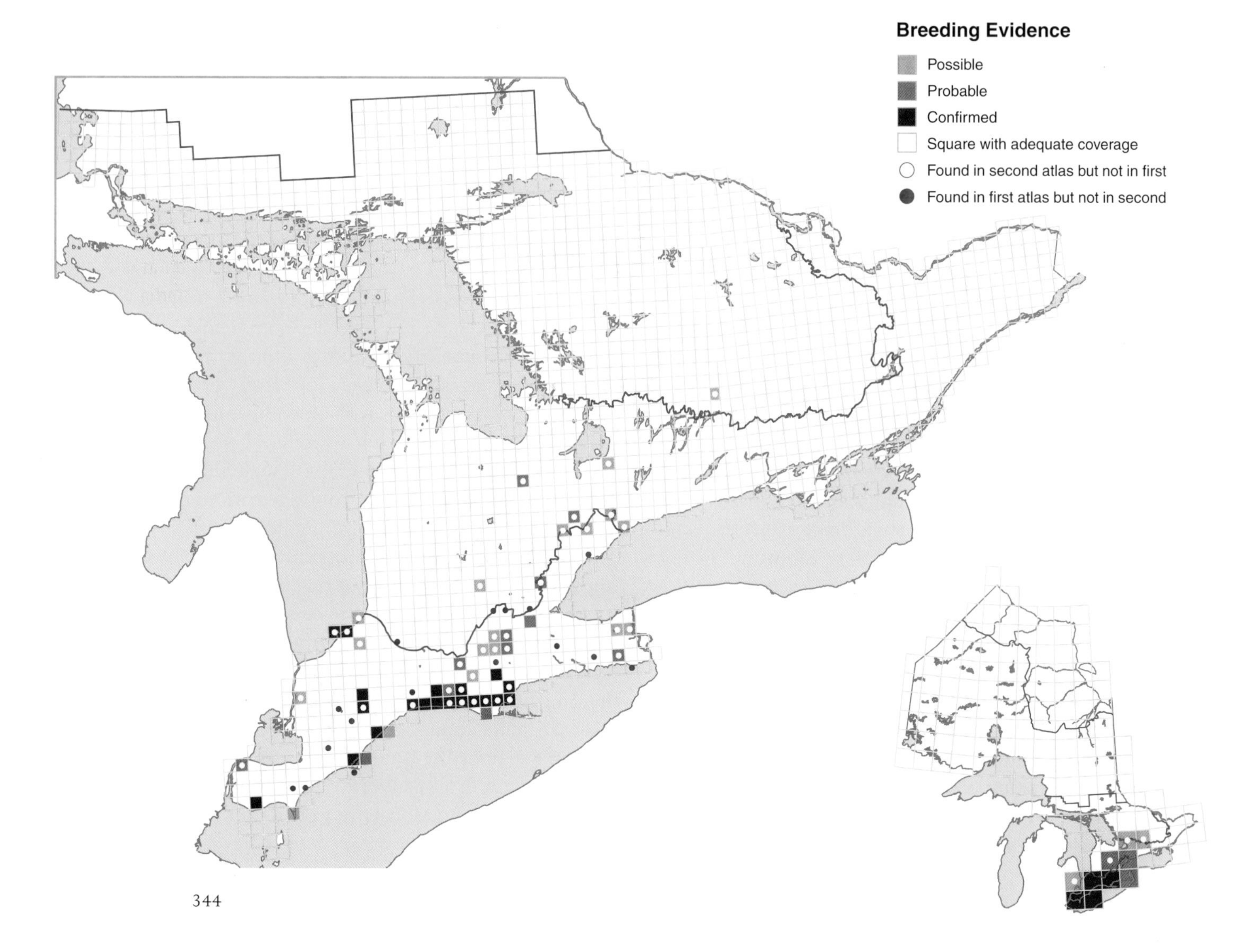

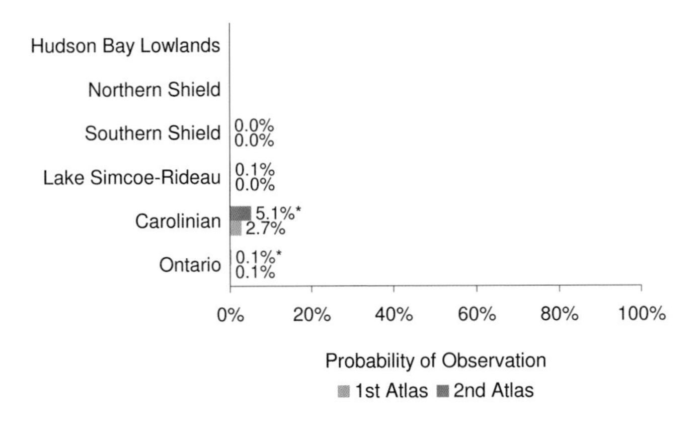

surveys have covered the woodlands where it is most likely to be found. It may be under-represented, though, at the northern edge of its range, where woodland cover is more extensive than in the southwest.

Breeding biology: The Acadian Flycatcher is most commonly encountered in large blocks of mature, primarily deciduous, closed-canopy forest, with an open to sparse understorey and ground layer. Often, territories are located near woodland pools or along streams in heavily wooded ravines. While many nests in upland situations are found in deciduous species such as American Beech, this flycatcher will just as often nest in Eastern Hemlock in ravines. Although many atlassers were not likely to locate the species because of its rarity and its preference for deep woods, it is not usually too difficult to find, as both mated and unmated males vocalize constantly much of the day and late into the breeding season. Finding pairs and confirming breeding vary from easy to difficult, depending on the stage of breeding when a territory is visited, and thus some pairs may have been missed. Nearly 65% of atlas records have probable or confirmed breeding evidence; this is a product no doubt of the concerted effort by Recovery Team members and knowledgeable atlassers able to fully document the presence of this endangered species in the province. Fully 40% of the records were confirmed, and over 100 nest cards were submitted to the ONRS during the atlas period.

Abundance: BBS trends show that the Acadian Flycatcher population remained stable across its North American range from 1966 to 2005, with declines in some areas and increases in others (Sauer et al. 2005). The species has not been detected on Ontario BBS surveys, likely due to its rarity and preference for forest interiors remote from roadsides. As well, it was detected on only 12 atlas point counts. The Acadian Flycatcher/Hooded Warbler Recovery Team (unpubl. data) estimates the Ontario population to be between 27 and 35 pairs in any given year, with concentrations of multiple pairs and unmated males in the larger forest blocks in southwest Middlesex, southeast Elgin, and Norfolk Counties. Many of the smaller sites have only an unmated male, one pair, or perhaps a male with two females. Sites generally flourish for a few to many years, followed by a period with no flycatchers, and then are re-colonized at some later time. Currently, the Ontario population is likely augmented by periodic immigration from the core range in the US. With increasing populations to the south, climate warming, and extensive woodlands with apparently suitable habitat in the Southern Shield region, the Acadian Flycatcher could become more common and widely distributed by the time of the next atlas. – *Dave Martin*

Clutch size for the Acadian Flycatcher is generally three eggs but varies from one to four (Whitehead and Taylor 2002). *Photo: George K. Peck*

Habitat at an Acadian Flycatcher breeding site in Rondeau Prov. Park. *Photo: P. Allen Woodliffe*

Alder Flycatcher

Moucherolle des aulnes

Empidonax alnorum

Eleanor Kee Wellman

For most field observers, the Alder Flycatcher can be reliably distinguished from its close relative, the Willow Flycatcher, only by its territorial song. Casual birders unfamiliar with the song might miss this small, dull green species, despite its broad distribution in Ontario and elsewhere. In the breeding season, this flycatcher is found across North America from Alaska to Newfoundland and south to Tennessee. It winters in South America, but its winter distribution is poorly known because of the difficulty of separating it from the Willow Flycatcher outside of the breeding season (Lowther 1999).

Distribution and population status: The Alder Flycatcher breeds throughout Ontario, except in parts of the Carolinian region. Its historical distribution is not known because the species was considered conspecific with the Willow Flycatcher (as Traill's Flycatcher) until 1973 (American Ornithologists Union 1973).

The probability of observation for this species increased by 26% between atlases in the province as a whole, with significant increases in all regions except the Carolinian. The species was found in a much smaller proportion of squares in the Carolinian region than elsewhere in both atlases. Although the 11% decrease in the Carolinian region between atlases was not statistically significant, it is nevertheless quite substantial and may reflect continuing loss of the species' preferred wet shrubby habitat in this highly agricultural landscape.

The BBS shows a non-significant increase of 0.2% per year for this species in Ontario between 1981 and 2005, but BBS coverage in northern and central Ontario is poor. The many BBS routes in southern Ontario, and especially the Carolinian, may have masked the increase in more northerly areas.

Breeding biology: Although known as a bird of wet thickets (Lowther 1999), the Alder Flycatcher also inhabits drier shrubby areas along roadsides and, especially, regenerating clearcuts (Erskine 1992; McLaren et al. 2006). Nests are well

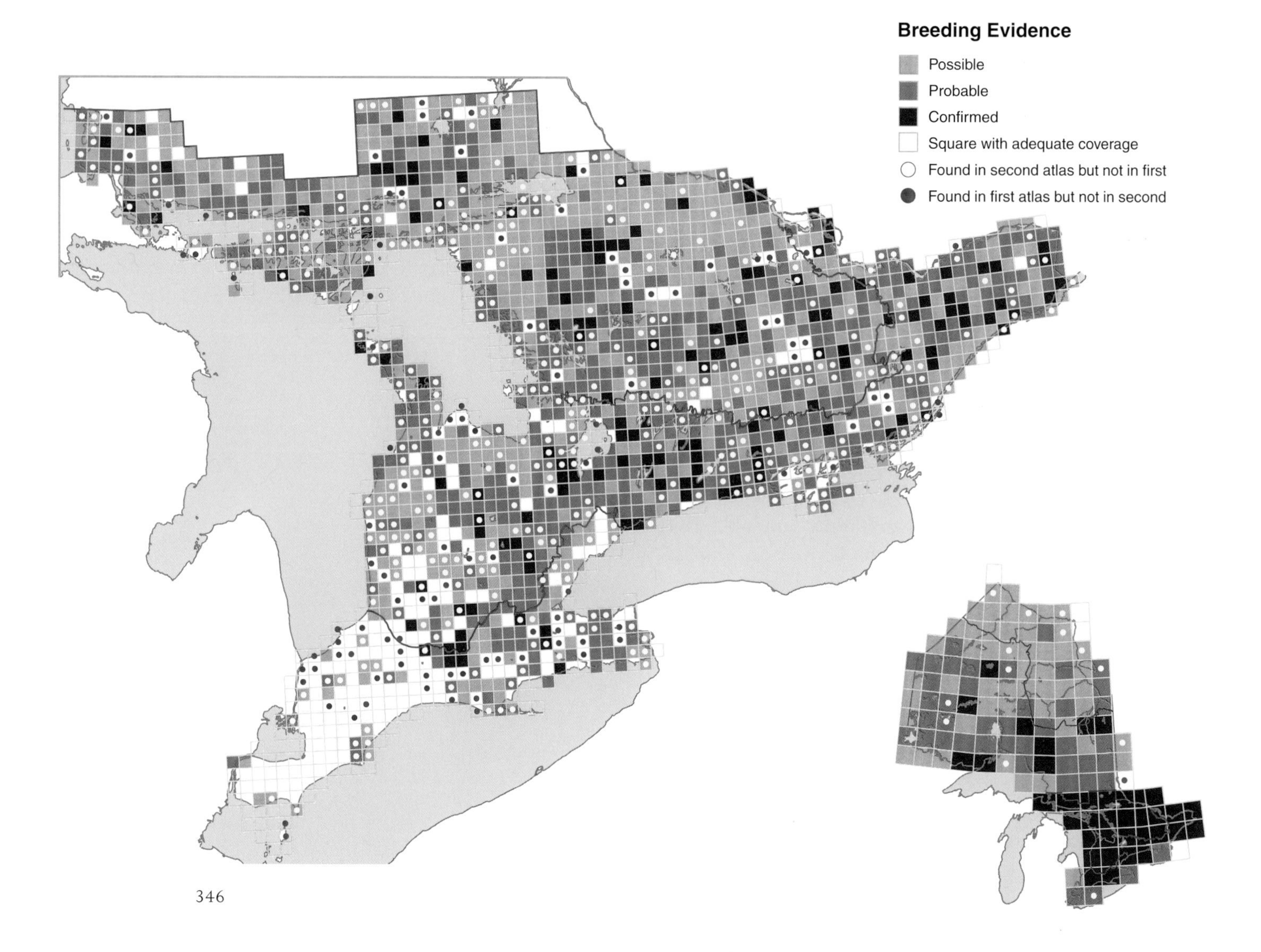

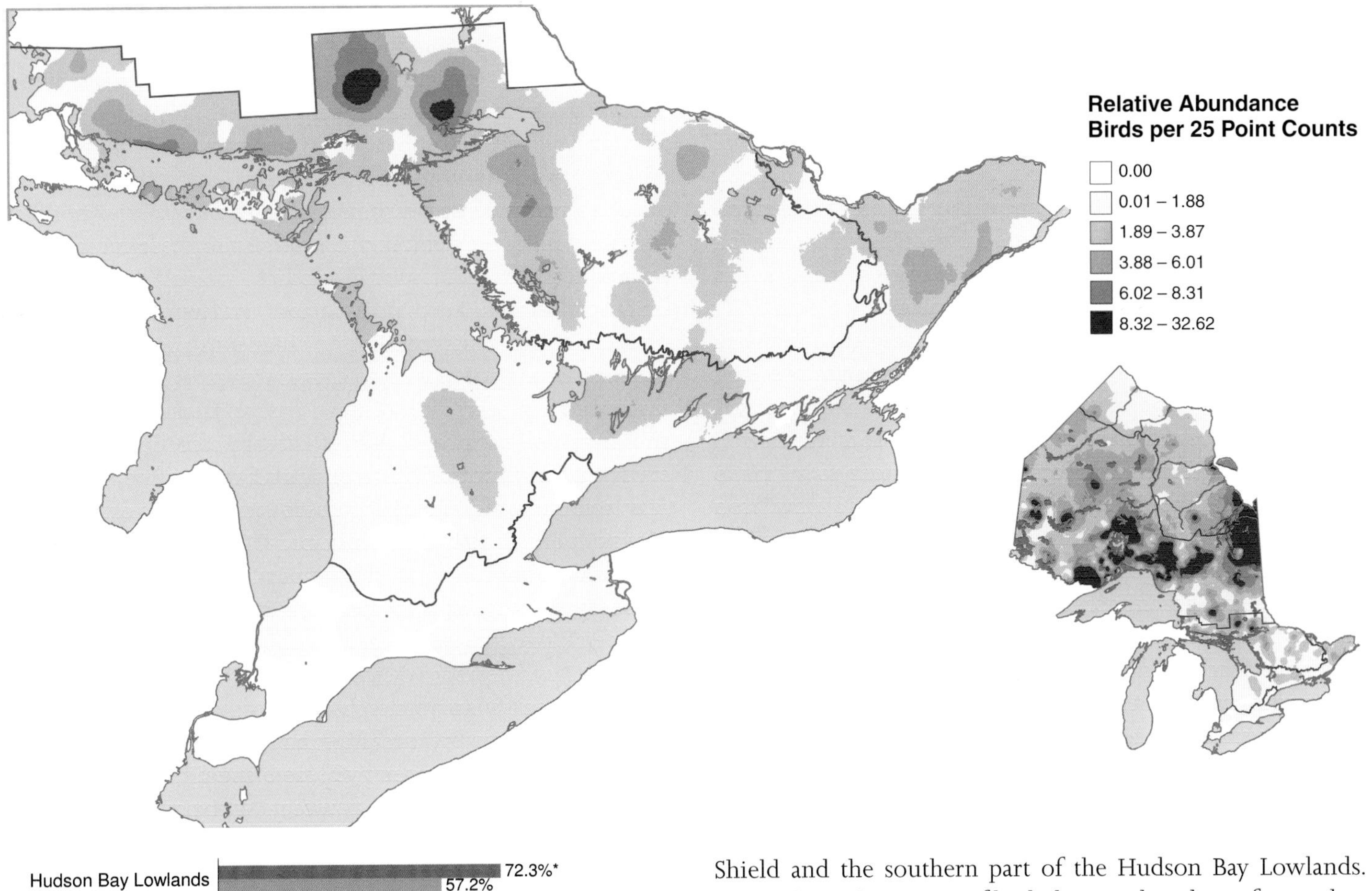

Hudson Bay Lowlands 72.3%* 57.2%
Northern Shield 77.3%* 61.6%
Southern Shield 84.4%* 67.2%
Lake Simcoe-Rideau 64.7%* 47.0%
Carolinian 22.0% 24.8%
Ontario 74.3%* 59.0%
0% 20% 40% 60% 80% 100%
Probability of Observation
1st Atlas 2nd Atlas

hidden in thick shrubs, and the adults are quiet and secretive around the nest (Bent 1942). By the time the young fledge in July, identification is rendered more difficult by lack of singing. Consequently, there were few confirmed breeding records. The most frequently recorded category of breeding evidence (25%) was singing males. In the Northern Shield and Hudson Bay Lowlands regions, the low percentage of squares with even probable breeding evidence may be because many squares were visited only once. It is rather surprising that there were not more probable breeding records in the three southern regions since the species sings actively and territories should have been fairly easy to register. However, the Alder Flycatcher returns late in spring (median arrival on 2 June during the 1960s at Long Point; Hussell 1991a), and the adults leave early, before moulting (median departure on 14 August at Long Point; Hussell 1991b), spending only an estimated 72 days on the Ontario breeding range.

Abundance: The highest densities of the Alder Flycatcher, with over 8.3 birds/25 point counts, occur in the Northern Shield and the southern part of the Hudson Bay Lowlands. Throughout these areas of high density, the edges of meandering, boggy rivers provide excellent habitat for the species; however, it is not likely that this habitat type is sufficiently extensive to explain the pattern of abundance, except possibly near James Bay. Rather, the distribution of young forest regenerating after logging is a more likely explanation for the high abundance in the Northern Shield. All of the areas of very high densities have relatively high proportions of younger forest, where shrubby regeneration may attract the Alder Flycatcher. There are also parts of northwestern Ontario with a high proportion of young forest, but these areas show only moderate densities of the species. Perhaps in the drier climate of the northwest, shrub growth is less dense in regenerating forests. Throughout the Southern Shield region, habitat for the Alder Flycatcher is more restricted to the edges of slow-flowing rivers, the margins of isolated peatlands, and other wetlands where Speckled Alder is prevalent; overall densities are much lower than farther north.

South of the Shield, the density of the Alder Flycatcher is low, but there are several nodes of higher density. These include eastern Ontario, Dufferin, and eastern Grey Counties, and the central and eastern portions of the Oak Ridges Moraine, all areas with higher than average wetland density. – *Margaret A. McLaren*

Willow Flycatcher

Moucherolle des saules

Empidonax traillii

John Reaume

This flycatcher was not recognized as a distinct species until 1973 when the Traill's Flycatcher was split into the Willow Flycatcher and the Alder Flycatcher (American Ornithologists' Union 1973). For most birders, song is the only reliable means of identifying these two species in the field. The songs and particularly the call notes of the Willow and Alder flycatchers are fairly similar, so it takes some expertise to distinguish them. The Willow Flycatcher usually nests in drier habitat than the Alder Flycatcher, but frequently they occur together as well.

The Willow Flycatcher is the most widely distributed species in its genus. It breeds from southern British Columbia to New Brunswick, south to California, Arizona, Tennessee and New England, although there are gaps in its distribution in the Great Plains and the Maritimes (Sedgwick 2000). This flycatcher winters in Central and South America, tending to be farther north than the Alder Flycatcher.

Distribution and population status: The Willow Flycatcher has been expanding its range northward in Ontario. This expansion has possibly been at the expense of the Alder Flycatcher and has likely resulted from wetland drainage and the invasion of abandoned fields by shrubs and trees (Sedgwick 2000). During the first atlas, the Willow Flycatcher was found in most squares south of the Shield and was widely distributed north to Muskoka and Ottawa; there was also a sizable local population in the Sudbury area.

In Ontario as a whole, there was no significant difference between the two atlases in the probability of observation of the Willow Flycatcher; however, there was a significant increase of 79% in the Southern Shield region between atlases, indicative of continued northward range expansion. BBS trends for Ontario are positive although not significant, but data for all of Canada since 1968 show a significant annual increase of 2.4% (Downes et al. 2005). The Willow Flycatcher population in Ontario appears to be increasing as a result of range expansion,

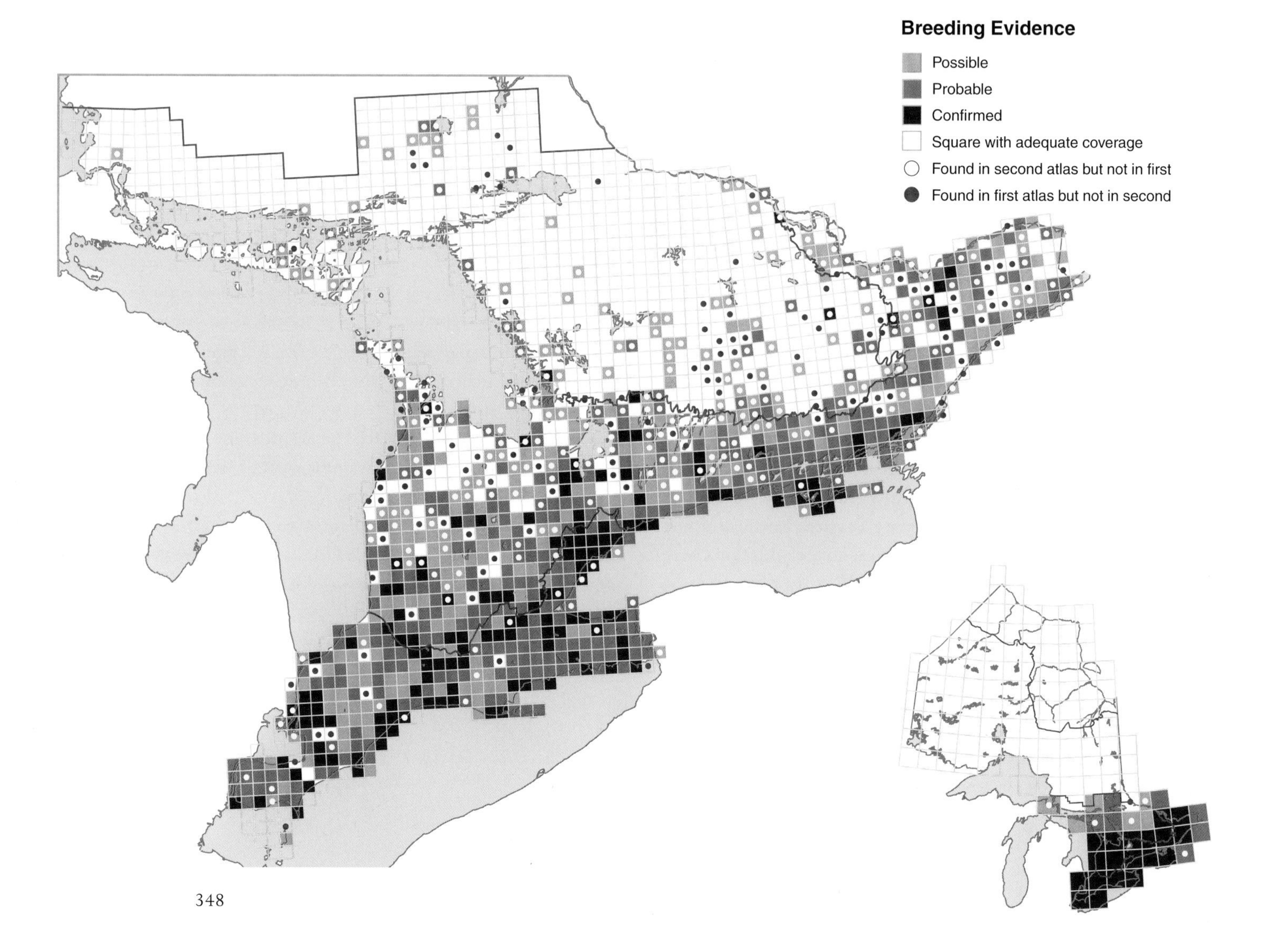

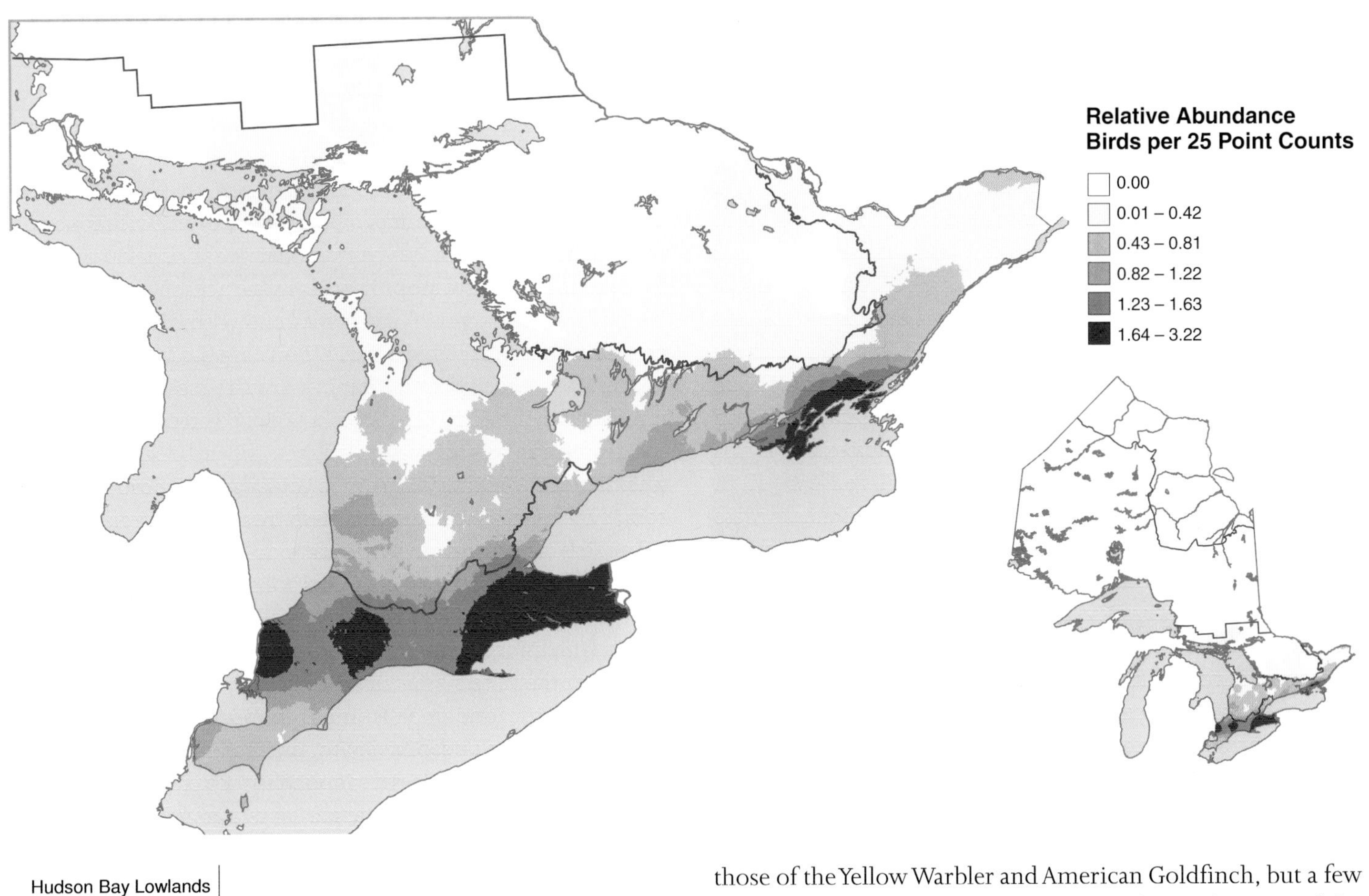

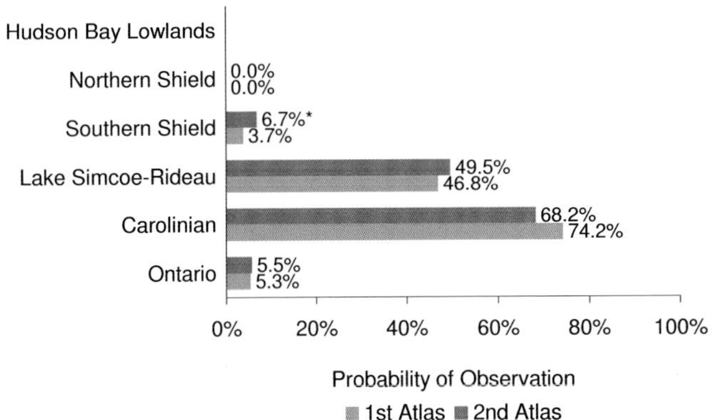

although breeding densities at given locations are not changing substantially. Significant range expansions have also occurred in Québec and British Columbia (Gauthier and Aubry 1996; Campbell et al. 1997).

Breeding biology: The Willow Flycatcher is a shrubland species. The most commonly used breeding habitat is shrubby fields and pastures dominated by hawthorns, often with other species present such as apple, dogwoods, and willow. However, it also nests in willow or willow-dogwood thickets, borders of marshes, and young coniferous plantations with some deciduous trees or shrubs (Peck and James 1987). Snyder (1953) reported that it nested on pastured limestone outcroppings with scattered hawthorns, Fragrant Sumac, and Red Cedar on Pelee Island.

Nests are typically 1-1.5 m from the ground in a deciduous shrub or small tree, although nest heights may range from 0.5 to 3.7 m. Finding nests is not especially difficult, but it is necessary to hear the song of the bird to confirm a nest's identity. Most Willow Flycatcher nests are compact cups that resemble those of the Yellow Warbler and American Goldfinch, but a few have grasses dangling below them, similar to the nest of the Alder Flycatcher (Peck and James 1987), and the presence of adults is thus critical to the identification of nests.

The Willow Flycatcher arrives late in spring and departs early after breeding, providing a very short period for atlassing. It returns to Ontario during late May, before the arrival of the Alder Flycatcher (Hussell 1991a). After nesting is completed, adults depart before moulting, having spent no more than 66 days on the Ontario range (Hussell 1991b). Confirmed breeding evidence was difficult to obtain and was reported in only 17% of squares where the species was found. Still, it is likely that the atlas map is a good representation of its current distribution in Ontario.

Abundance: The Willow Flycatcher reaches its greatest densities in the Kingston and Prince Edward Co. area south of the Shield, from Long Point north to Hamilton and east throughout Niagara Region, and in Lambton and Middlesex Counties. In these areas, it is often associated with old-field habitats, lightly grazed pastures, and riparian thickets. Farther north, there are lesser concentrations near Sudbury and on Manitoulin Island (where it was documented in only one square during the first atlas).

The Willow Flycatcher is still common and widespread south of the Shield. As predicted in the first atlas, it continues to expand its range in the Southern Shield region, but perhaps not as dramatically as anticipated. – *Al Sandilands*

Least Flycatcher

Moucherolle tchébec

Empidonax minimus

Mark Peck

The smallest of Canadian flycatchers is familiar to most birders, but its olive appearance and non-musical "*chebec*" song make it less obvious than many birds. The Least Flycatcher has an extensive breeding range, from southern Yukon to southwest Newfoundland and south to Wyoming and northwest Georgia (Briskie 1994). It is perhaps the first of our songbirds to head south after nesting, with most adults leaving by the end of July, after only about 64 days on the Ontario breeding grounds (Hussell 1981). It spends the winter in Mexico and Central America (Briskie 1994).

The Least Flycatcher is found in a variety of forest types, yet there are many apparently suitable areas from which it is absent. Although territorial like many songbirds, it is found commonly in dense clusters of small territories, with much of the intervening landscape being unoccupied (Briskie 1994).

Distribution and population status: The maps generated by both atlases, which are consistent with what we know about its historical range, clearly show that the Least Flycatcher continues to breed throughout most of the province. In southern Ontario, there has long been a notable gap coinciding with the intensively agricultural Essex County and western Chatham-Kent. Otherwise, the species breeds throughout the south, but there is a recent negative trend in the area between Lakes Erie and Huron, particularly in Lambton Co., where many squares that were occupied during the first atlas now appear to be abandoned, with few gains made in other squares. The populations in this area may have been too small to be stable, given the general decline in species numbers.

The Least Flycatcher was found in most 100-km blocks in the Hudson Bay Lowlands during the second atlas, with a significant 32% increase in the probability of observation since the first atlas. This increase is probably due to differences in coverage rather than a real increase. Evidence from both atlases indicates that the range extends north along the major river

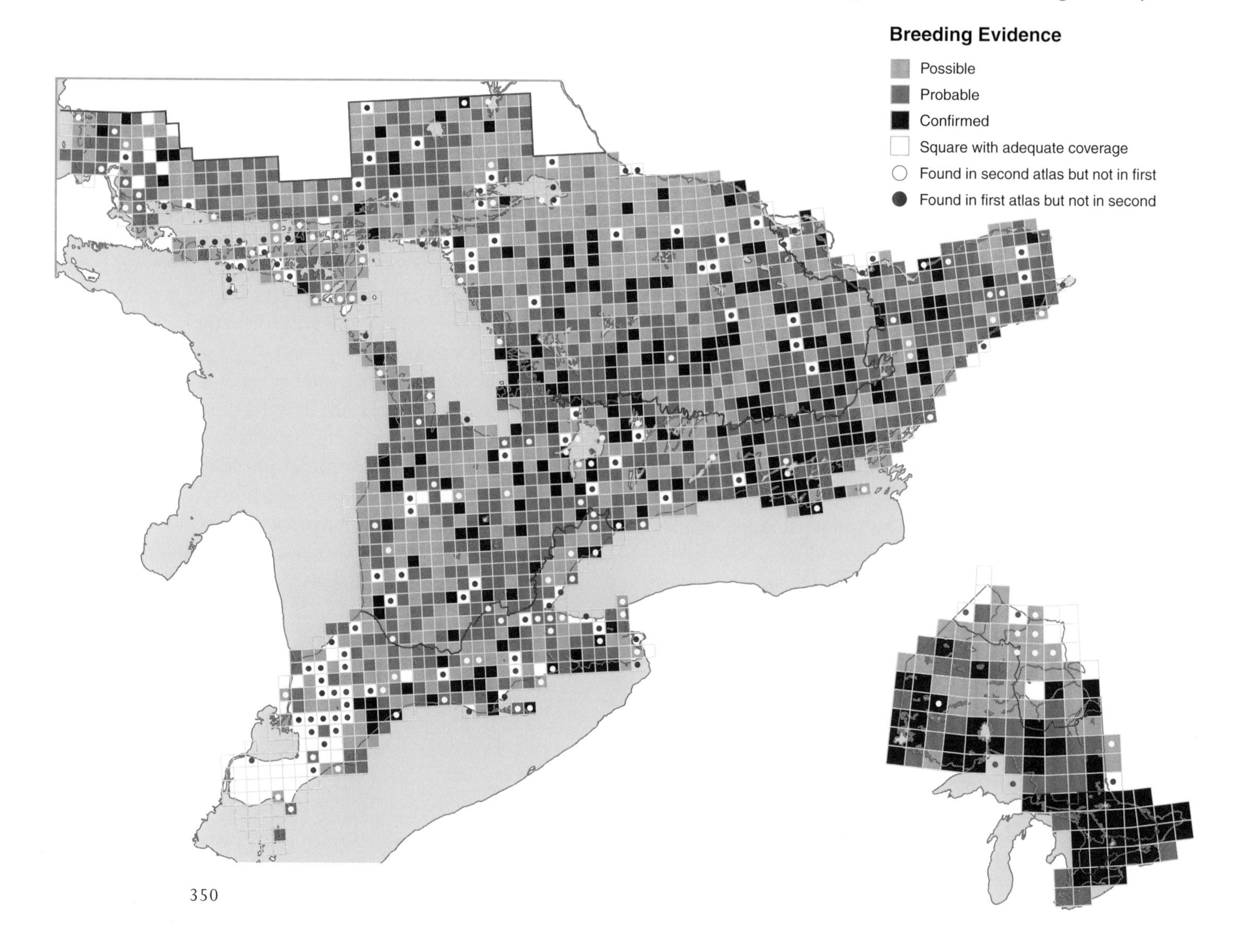

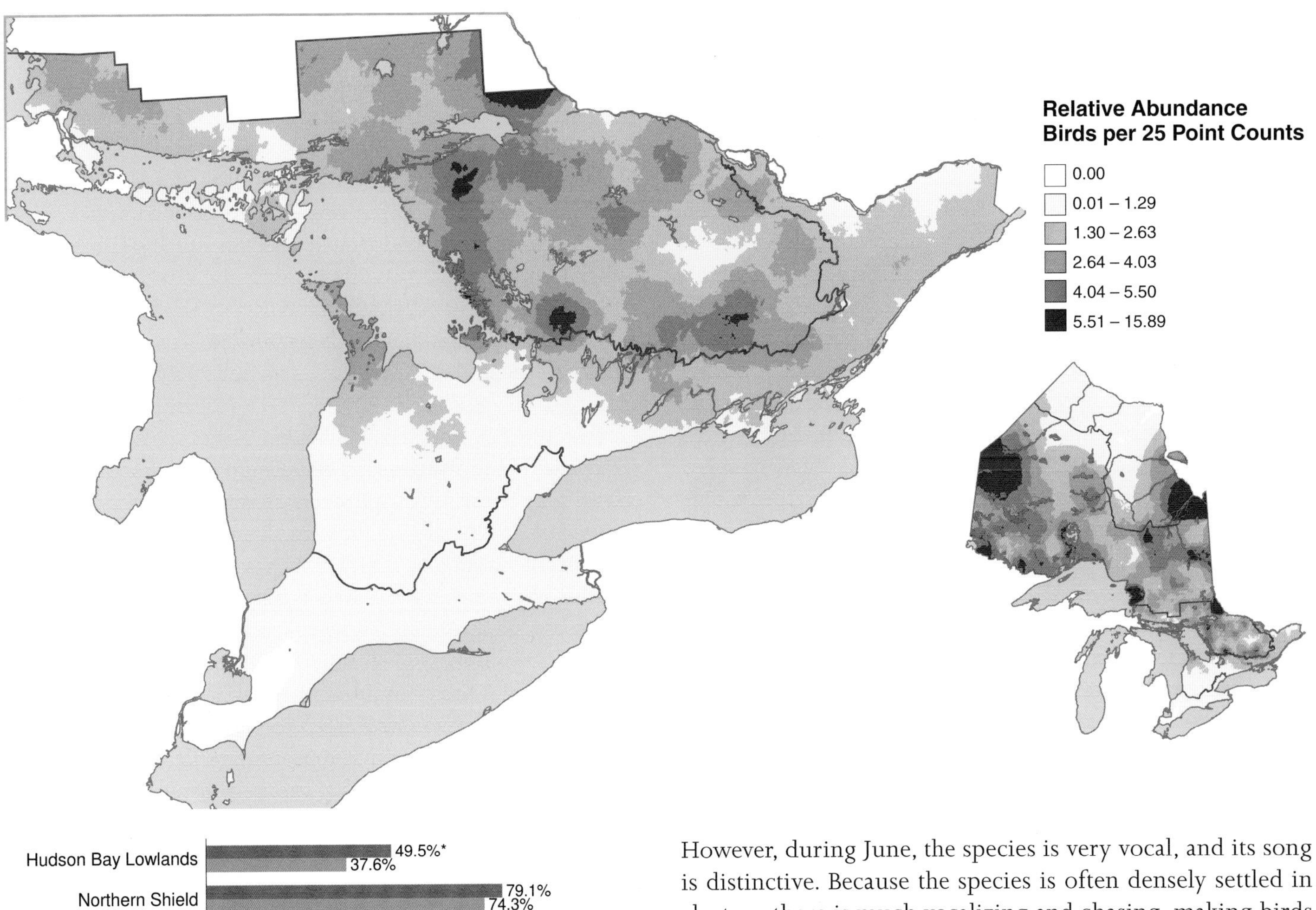

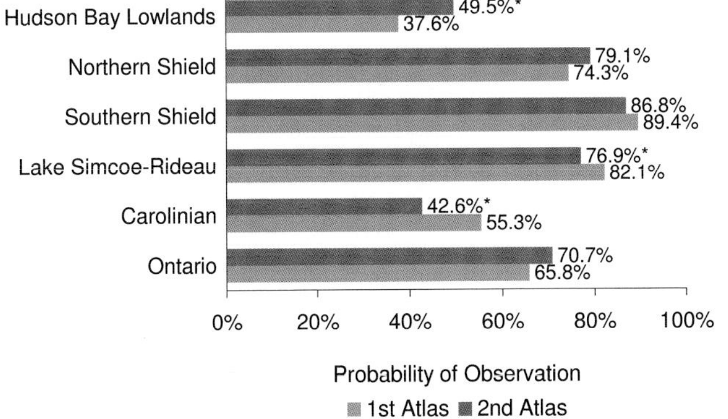

corridors closer to the Hudson Bay coast than shown by Godfrey (1986) or Briskie (1994), but not to the four 100-km blocks around Cape Henrietta Maria.

BBS data show a significant annual decline of 2.5% in Ontario since the first atlas, indicating that population sizes may have been reduced by as much as 50% during that period. This trend may be reflected in the significant declines in the probability of observation in the Carolinian (23%) and Lake Simcoe-Rideau (6%) regions, compared with the first atlas.

Breeding biology: Least Flycatcher territory clusters are commonly found in deciduous forests, but they also occur in mixed forest, rural areas with deciduous copses, and even pine plantations. The species begins nesting soon after returning in May and is single-brooded. Nests are typically placed in a deciduous tree crotch or on a horizontal branch, generally below 8 m (Peck and James 1987). Unlike most temperate zone songbirds, adults moult on the wintering grounds after autumn migration, and so leave immediately after nesting, with the young following a few weeks later. However, during June, the species is very vocal, and its song is distinctive. Because the species is often densely settled in clusters, there is much vocalizing and chasing, making birds conspicuous. Despite this, confirming breeding proved difficult and was achieved in only 11% of squares with breeding evidence in this atlas.

Species with a patchy distribution within the preferred habitat, like the Least Flycatcher, may be more apt to be missed by atlassers who covered squares by visiting representative habitats without visiting multiple areas of that habitat type. However, the abundance of the Least Flycatcher likely offset whatever risk of being missed existed due to its tendency to cluster.

Abundance: Although this flycatcher is found virtually throughout the province, the relative abundance map generated from point counts shows that densities vary dramatically with geography. Relative abundance is low in the far north and in the southwest. The greatest concentrations appear to be around Moosonee and near the Manitoba border. These more northerly sites are based on fewer point counts and consequently may be less reliable. On the other hand, the Least Flycatcher favours aspen forests in some areas, and this may account for its high numbers in those locations. – *Alex Mills*

Eastern Phoebe

Moucherolle phébi

Sayornis phoebe

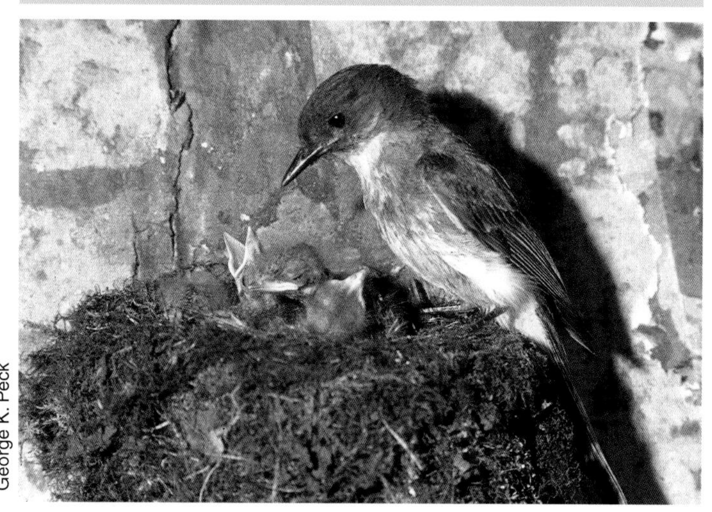

George K. Peck

The Eastern Phoebe is a familiar bird in rural areas. It is the first flycatcher to return in the spring and often builds its mud nest on and around human habitation. Despite its rather drab plumage, it is easily recognized by its distinctive song and its habit of constantly wagging its tail.

The Eastern Phoebe occurs across Canada from the Rocky Mountains to the Atlantic coast and south through the eastern US (Weeks 1994). The species' ready acceptance of artificial structures such as bridges and buildings for nesting has allowed it to expand its range into habitats formerly unsuitable because they lacked the rock outcrops and eroded earthen banks needed for nest support (Weeks 1994).

Distribution and population status: The Eastern Phoebe has been considered a species of woodland edges near water (Bent 1942). However, for birds nesting in natural locations, suitable nesting sites often coincide with stream edges, so it may be difficult to separate preference for streams from presence of suitable nesting sites. Nevertheless, the Eastern Phoebe does require at least some trees and preferably woodlands or forest near its nesting location (Weeks 1994).

In Ontario, the Eastern Phoebe occurs primarily in the Carolinian, Lake Simcoe-Rideau, and Southern Shield regions. There is a noticeable gap in occurrence in the Algonquin Highlands, likely due mainly to the lack of buildings and bridges for nesting. In the first atlas, a major gap in distribution in the extreme southwest of the province was attributed to the lack of flowing streams and bridges. However, there is no lack of buildings for nesting in this region, and the species was found in a larger number of squares there in the second atlas, perhaps due to more systematic coverage. In the north, the Eastern Phoebe occurs sporadically, with noticeable clusters of squares near Thunder Bay and around Lake of the Woods, both areas where human populations with associated artificial structures are more prevalent than in the rest of

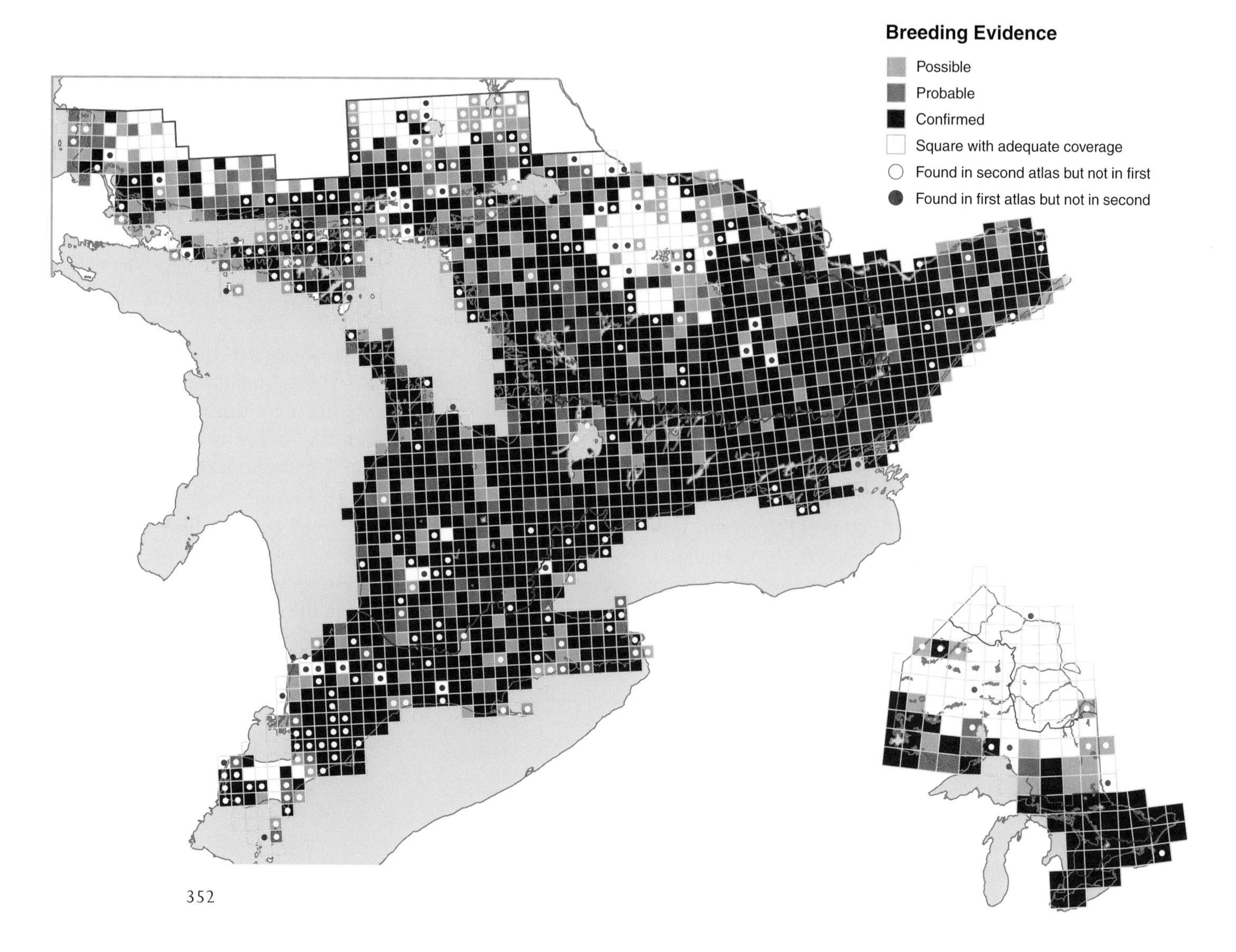

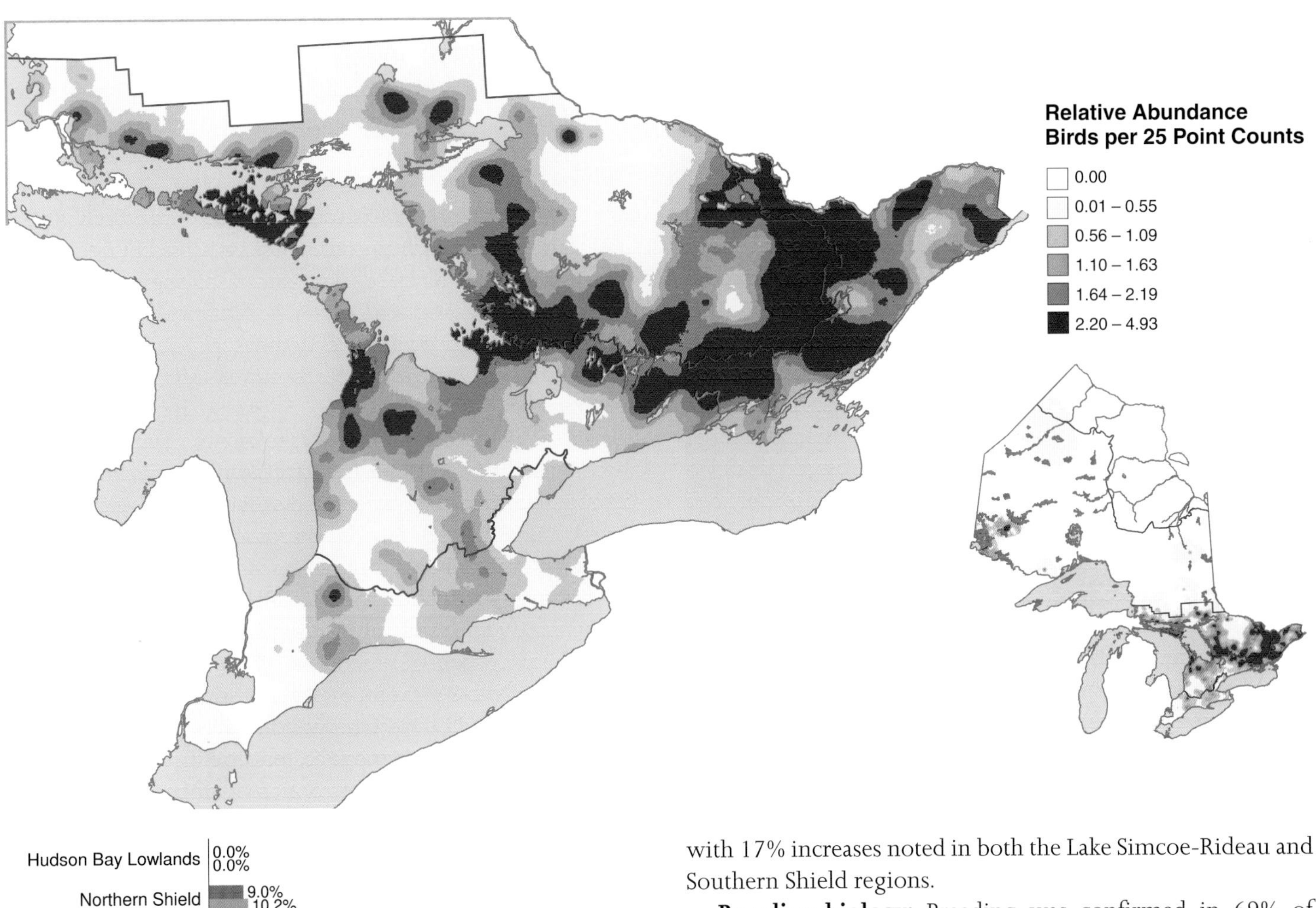

Region	2nd Atlas	1st Atlas
Hudson Bay Lowlands	0.0%	0.0%
Northern Shield	9.0%	10.2%
Southern Shield	80.8%*	69.3%
Lake Simcoe-Rideau	89.1%*	76.3%
Carolinian	69.7%*	48.4%
Ontario	19.0%*	17.4%

Probability of Observation
1st Atlas ■ 2nd Atlas

northern Ontario. The most northerly records in the second atlas occurred at Moosonee, Bearskin Lake, and the Opasquia Prov. Park area on the Manitoba border.

In the early part of the 20th century, the Eastern Phoebe was described as very common and abundant (Macoun and Macoun 1909). In the first atlas, it was stated that such terms "would seem a bit exaggerated today." Although there is evidence that hard winters in the southern US can cause noticeable population declines (James 1960, 1961; Hall 1983), overall, the Eastern Phoebe has shown little change in population since scientific records have been kept. BBS data across Canada indicate little change since 1968, whereas in Ontario there has been a small but significant annual increase of 3% since the first atlas. Migration records from Long Point show a significant increase from 1965 to 2004, with most of the increase occurring between 1965 and 1994 (Crewe 2006). The second atlas reflects these changes, with a significant 9% increase in the probability of observation province-wide. The species increased most significantly in the Carolinian (44%), with 17% increases noted in both the Lake Simcoe-Rideau and Southern Shield regions.

Breeding biology: Breeding was confirmed in 69% of squares where the Eastern Phoebe was recorded, reflecting several aspects of its breeding biology that make confirmation relatively easy. Phoebe nests are fairly obvious, especially when they are placed on buildings. Once the young have hatched, both adults actively feed and regularly sit on branches near the nest. The Eastern Phoebe is often double-brooded, giving atlassers two periods in which to find active nests (Weeks 1994). Even after the young have fledged, used nests are easily identifiable.

Abundance: The Eastern Phoebe has two areas of high abundance. The larger area comprises an arc stretching from Renfrew Co. south along the edge of the Shield to Lake Ontario and sweeping back up to the southern part of Georgian Bay and inland to Muskoka. The second area consists of the Bruce Peninsula and Manitoulin Island. These areas likely provide ideal habitat for phoebes: many buildings and bridges for nesting combined with a landscape with a fairly high proportion of forest cover. Relatively high densities in the Lake of the Woods area probably also reflect the ready availability of nest sites. On the other hand, the suggestion of a broad area of low densities in the far northwest may overstate the situation there. Despite adequate coverage in a considerable number of squares in this area, the Eastern Phoebe was recorded in only five. *– Margaret A. McLaren*

Great Crested Flycatcher

Tyran huppé
Myiarchus crinitus

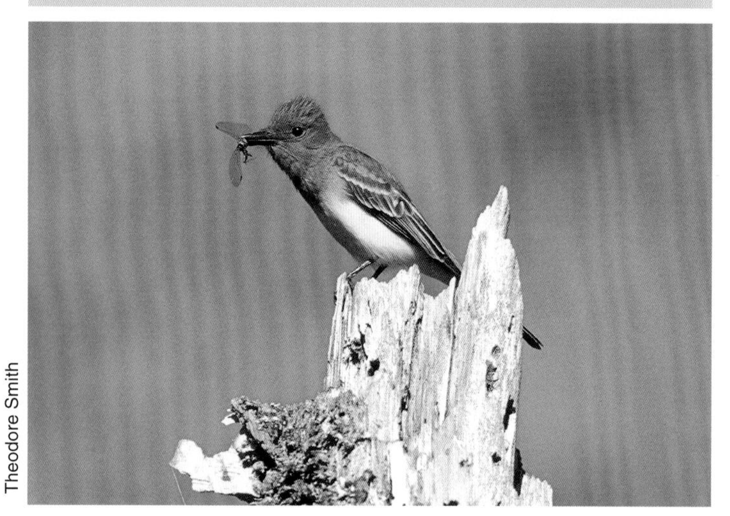
Theodore Smith

The Great Crested Flycatcher occurs throughout the eastern US and northward into southern Canada, in open woodlands, treed fields, and forest edges (Lanyon 1997). In western Canada, the species breeds in the parklands of south-central Alberta and across central Saskatchewan to southern Manitoba. In Ontario, it occurs primarily in the Great Lakes-St. Lawrence and Carolinian Forests. To the east, its range extends across southern Québec into New Brunswick and the southern half of Nova Scotia (Lanyon 1997). The main winter range is from southern Mexico to Panama, where it is found primarily at lower elevations (Lanyon 1997).

The Great Crested Flycatcher is known for its habit of sometimes incorporating shed snake skins into its nesting material, leading to speculation that this is a strategy to frighten predators. Lanyon (1997), however, noted that this is much more likely a response to the crinkly texture of old snake skin. Plastic wrappers, cellophane, and paper, as well as onion skins and birch bark, have all been found in nests.

Distribution and population status: The Great Crested Flycatcher is widely distributed north to the limits of the Southern Shield region in southern Ontario. The species was also detected in a cluster of squares southeast of Lake of the Woods, but records in the rest of northern Ontario were much more scattered. The northernmost record (100 km northwest of Pickle Lake at about 52° N) was considerably farther north than the most northerly record in the first atlas.

The probability of observation of the Great Crested Flycatcher decreased by a significant 8% at the provincial scale between atlases, with the largest decline occurring in the Southern Shield (11%). The probability of observation also decreased significantly in the Lake Simcoe-Rideau region (7%), but since the species was reported in virtually every square, the breeding evidence map shows no pattern to the change. In the Southern Shield, the species was absent from a substantial num-

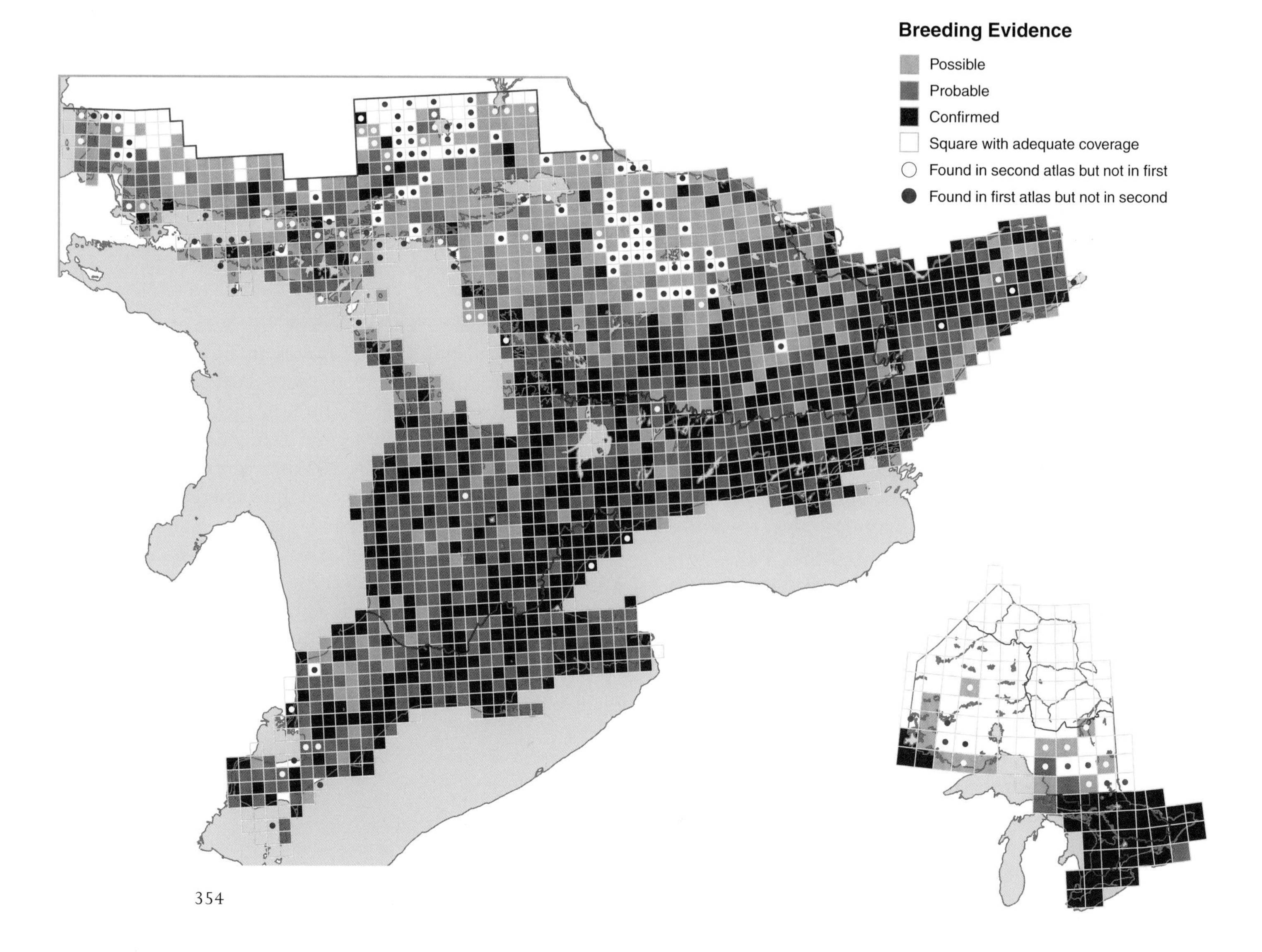

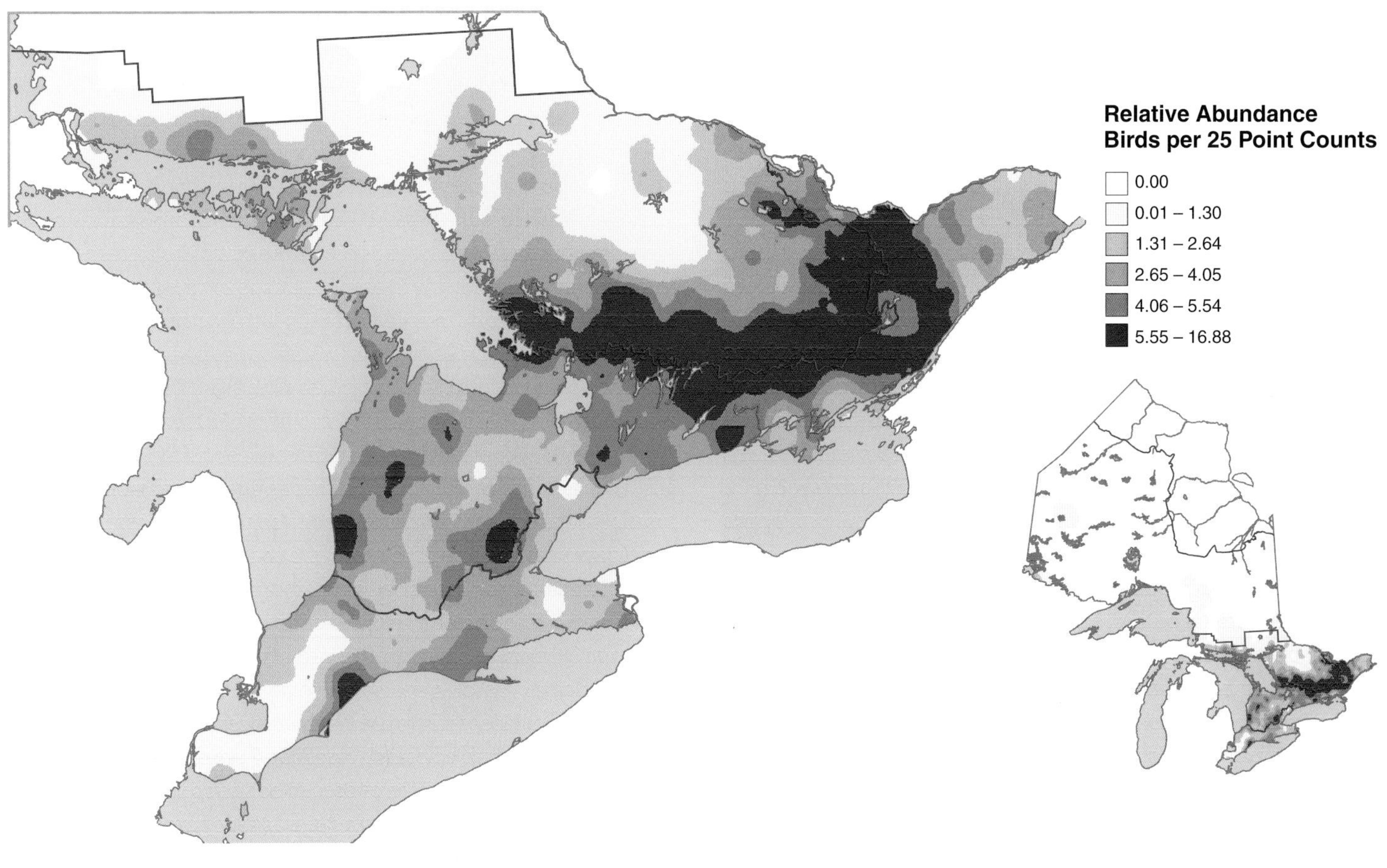

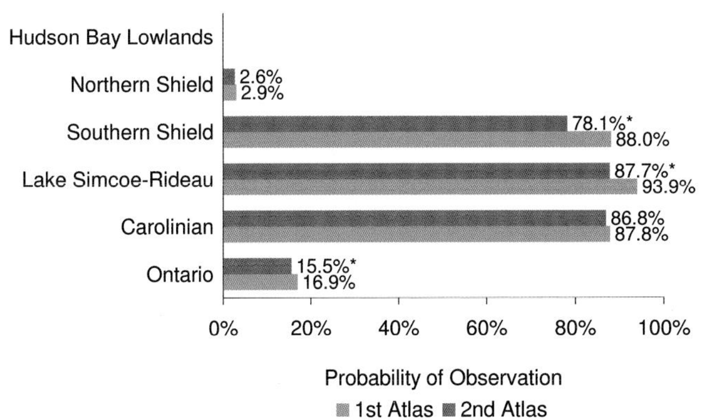

ber of squares in the Algonquin Highlands during this atlas. The decline in this area may be related to maturing forests that do not provide the openings that the Great Crested Flycatcher requires.

BBS data show a near significant decrease across Canada since 1968 for this species, but there is no indication of a change in population size in Ontario during the same period (Downes et al. 2005). Migration monitoring at Long Point similarly shows no significant change since the 1960s (Crewe 2006).

Breeding biology: The Great Crested Flycatcher is the only cavity-nesting flycatcher in eastern North America (Lanyon 1997). It does not excavate its own cavity but uses natural cavities, abandoned woodpecker holes, and a variety of artificial structures. It is found primarily in deciduous and mixed woodlands and has benefited from fragmentation of forests, since it prefers habitats with openings and edges. It also uses suburban habitats readily, including orchards, gardens, golf courses, and fencerows (Lanyon 1997).

The nest is built entirely by the female, who may spend several days filling cavities as deep as 1.8 m with an assortment of nesting material, so that the eggs are laid no deeper than 30 cm from the entrance hole (Lanyon 1997). The female does all of the incubation, although the male often accompanies her to the nest site after she has been foraging. The eggs hatch after 13-15 days of incubation. As with many cavity-nesting birds, the young are quite vocal and audible from shortly after hatching. This behaviour and the ease of accessing this flycatcher's preferred habitat likely contributed to the large number of atlas administrative regions (29 of 39 regions with confirmed breeding) in which nests were found. The family stays together for about three weeks after the young fledge, providing additional opportunities for atlassers to confirm breeding.

Abundance: The Great Crested Flycatcher was most abundant (over 5.5 birds/25 point counts) in a broad band along the boundary between the Lake Simcoe-Rideau and Southern Shield regions, from Georgian Bay to the Ottawa River. Pockets of higher density are also present on the Niagara Escarpment northwest of Hamilton, and in the Long Point area, where large expanses of mixed forest remain. These areas of highest density likely reflect the presence of suitable habitat in the form of small farms interspersed with hedgerows and many woodlots. Farther north, the forest becomes more extensive with fewer of the edges and openings needed by this species, while farther south, there are usually more open fields and less woodland. – *Margaret A. McLaren*

Western Kingbird

Tyran de l'Ouest

Tyrannus verticalis

R. E. Gehlert

The Western Kingbird is a common and familiar species of open habitats such as grasslands, savannahs, desert scrub, pastures, cultivated fields, and urban areas throughout western North America. Its main breeding range extends from southern interior British Columbia eastward to southern Manitoba and western Minnesota, and south to California, northern Baja California, and Mexico (Gamble and Bergin 1996). It winters primarily in southern Mexico and Central America but is also a regular winter resident in small numbers in southern Florida (Gamble and Bergin 1996). Typical of kingbirds, during the breeding season it undertakes aggressive and vocal aerial pursuits of potential nest predators, including corvids, raptors, and other avian, mammalian, and reptilian species.

Distribution and population status: The Western Kingbird has shown a gradual trend toward range expansion throughout North America. Historical records since the late 1800s indicate that as lands were opened up for agriculture, trees planted, and utility poles erected, the species expanded eastward as foraging and nesting opportunities emerged (Gamble and Bergin 1996). BBS data from 1966 to 1994 indicated a significant annual increase of 0.9% in the US and Canada (Gamble and Bergin 1996) and a near-significant annual increase of 1.7% on BBS routes in Canada from 1968 to 2005 (Downes et al. 2005).

The Western Kingbird is a rare but regular spring and fall vagrant to Ontario and a regular summer resident and occasional rare breeder in western Rainy River Dist. in the vicinity of the Rainy River. Documented evidence of breeding in Ontario was obtained relatively recently, and just four accepted nest records exist for the province (Peck and Peck 2006). During the first atlas, breeding was suspected when three adults were observed together in a grassy field with suitable nesting habitat just north of Rainy River in 1983 (Carpentier in Cadman et al. 1987); however, nesting was not confirmed

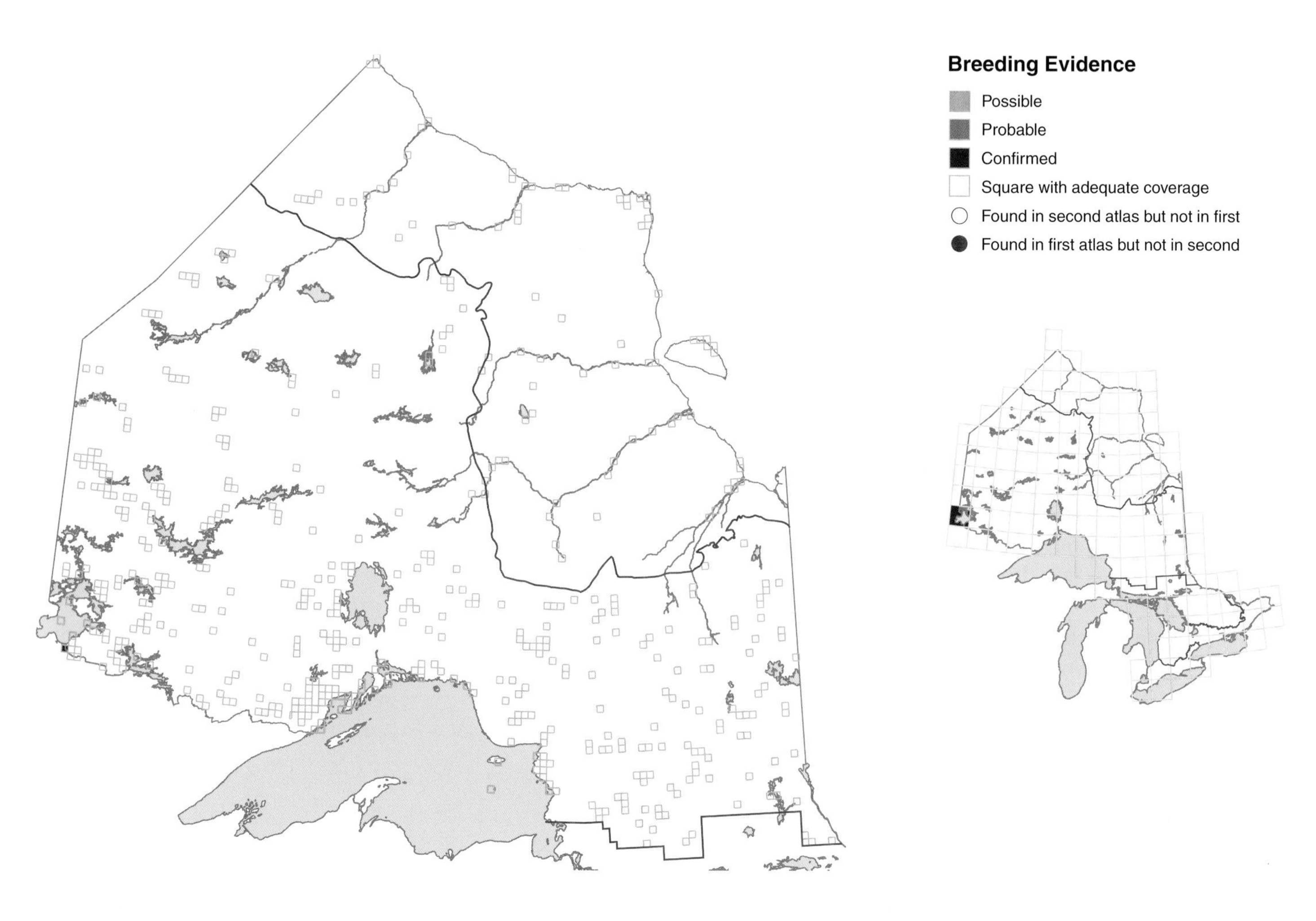

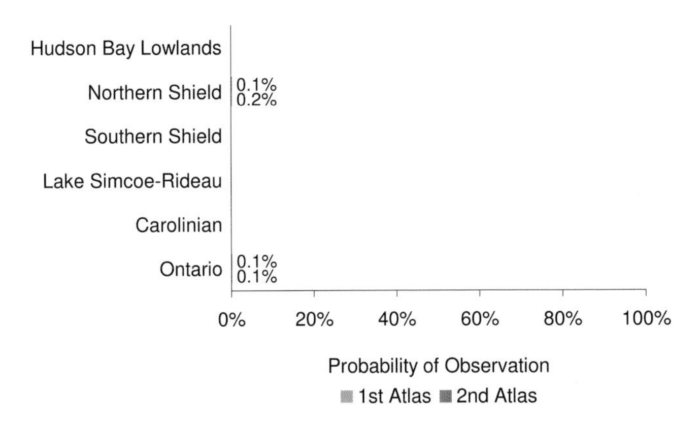

until 1987 (Carpentier 1989). The second and third accepted provincial nest records were established in 1988 and 1991 (Peck and James 1997). A reported nest with eggs, photographed near Port Alma, Chatham-Kent, in 1943 (MacFayden 1945) remains unsubstantiated in the absence of any description of the birds (Peck and James 1987).

During the second atlas, the fourth provincial nest record was established with the discovery of a nest under construction on a microwave transmission tower 12 km northwest of the Town of Rainy River on 12 June 2001. The species was again present at this site in 2005, although only possible breeding evidence was observed.

Breeding biology: Throughout its range, the Western Kingbird utilizes a variety of habitats, including riparian forests and woodlands, scrubland, pastures, and sparsely populated rural areas. Key elements of preferred breeding habitat include open areas with high visibility, an abundance of terrestrial and aerial insect prey, and trees, poles, or other structures to facilitate nesting and perching. Breeding habitat in Ontario consists of scattered copses where medium-height poplar predominates, surrounded by open, low-intensity agricultural lands. The species readily adapts to anthropogenic habitats and human structures for nesting (Gamble and Bergin 1996), as evidenced by the use of a communications tower for nesting during the second atlas. However, other Ontario nests have been situated in willow, Manitoba Maple, and Bur Oak (Peck and James 1997).

Nest construction is by the female alone and takes four to eight days to complete (Gamble and Bergin 1996). Incubation ranges from 12 to 19 days, and fledging occurs at 13 to 19 days (Gamble and Bergin 1996). The Western Kingbird aggressively defends a small territory around the nest site, but despite this, predation of eggs and nestlings is the main factor affecting reproductive success (Gamble and Bergin 1996). Both parents raise the young. The family group stays together for two to three weeks after fledging while the young remain dependent on the parents for food (Gamble and Bergin 1996), which facilitates confirmation of breeding. Interestingly, three adult Western Kingbirds were observed in simultaneous attendance at the nest near Rainy River in 2001. As the males are typically aggressive toward conspecifics, and cooperative breeding in this species is unknown (Gamble and Bergin 1996), the significance of this observation is unclear.

Abundance: The Western Kingbird has occurred as a non-breeding vagrant throughout much of the province. In the period 1978-1997, about three to four records per year were received and accepted by the Ontario Bird Records Committee (Dobos 1998). Most records are in May, June, August, September, or October. The species remains a rare breeder in western Rainy River Dist., with one or at most two pairs present annually. – *Geoff Carpentier*

Nests located in shrubs and trees are usually on a horizontal branch or crotch of an upward-slanting branch (Gamble and Bergin 1996). *Photo: George K. Peck*

Anthropogenic structures are frequently used for nesting. A nest was placed on this radio tower in Rainy River Dist. in 2001. *Photo: George K. Peck*

Eastern Kingbird

Tyran tritri

Tyrannus tyrannus

Bill Rayner

The Eastern Kingbird is a conspicuous bird of open country, well known for its aggressive mobbing of larger birds and its way of appearing to fly on its wingtips. It is the most widespread flycatcher in North America (Murphy 1996), breeding in a variety of open habitats from southern British Columbia to Cape Breton Island, north into the Mackenzie River valley, and across most of the US (Murphy 1996). It is most abundant in the central grasslands of North Dakota south to Kansas (Price et al. 1995; Sauer et al. 2005).

Though it remains a common and widespread breeder in North America, the Eastern Kingbird has been declining in abundance range-wide over the past two decades (Sauer et al. 2005). In this respect, it appears to be similar to many other birds of open habitats, and has been identified as a priority species for conservation in several regions of eastern North America (Partners in Flight 2005), including in southern Ontario (Ontario Partners in Flight 2006b).

Distribution and population status: Historically, this species was probably found in low numbers throughout its current Ontario range, making use of forest clearings, beaver ponds, swamps, and borders of lakes and rivers, as well as the edges of whatever meadows existed prior to European settlement. Population size likely increased greatly in southern Ontario when forests were cleared for farming.

The atlas reflects well its current distribution: ubiquitous across southern Ontario, widespread but less consistently found in the southern Boreal Forest, with scattered records farther north. As in the first atlas, it appears to breed at least occasionally in Ontario as far north as the Hudson Bay coast.

Since the first atlas, there has been a reduction in the probability of observation in all regions but particularly in the Northern and Southern Shield, where significant decreases of 34% and 27%, respectively, were observed. The result is a significant southward shift in the centre of the species' Ontario

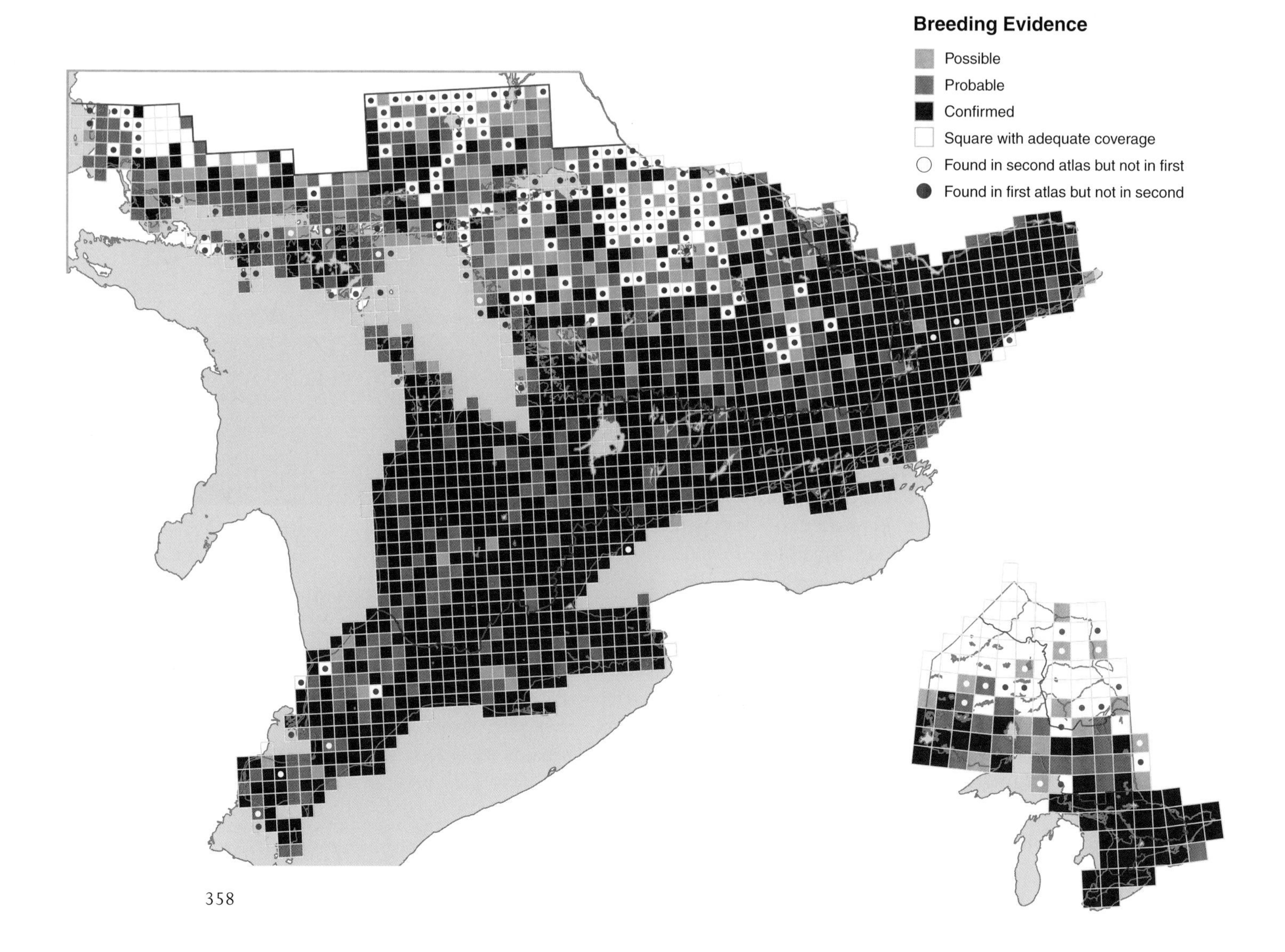

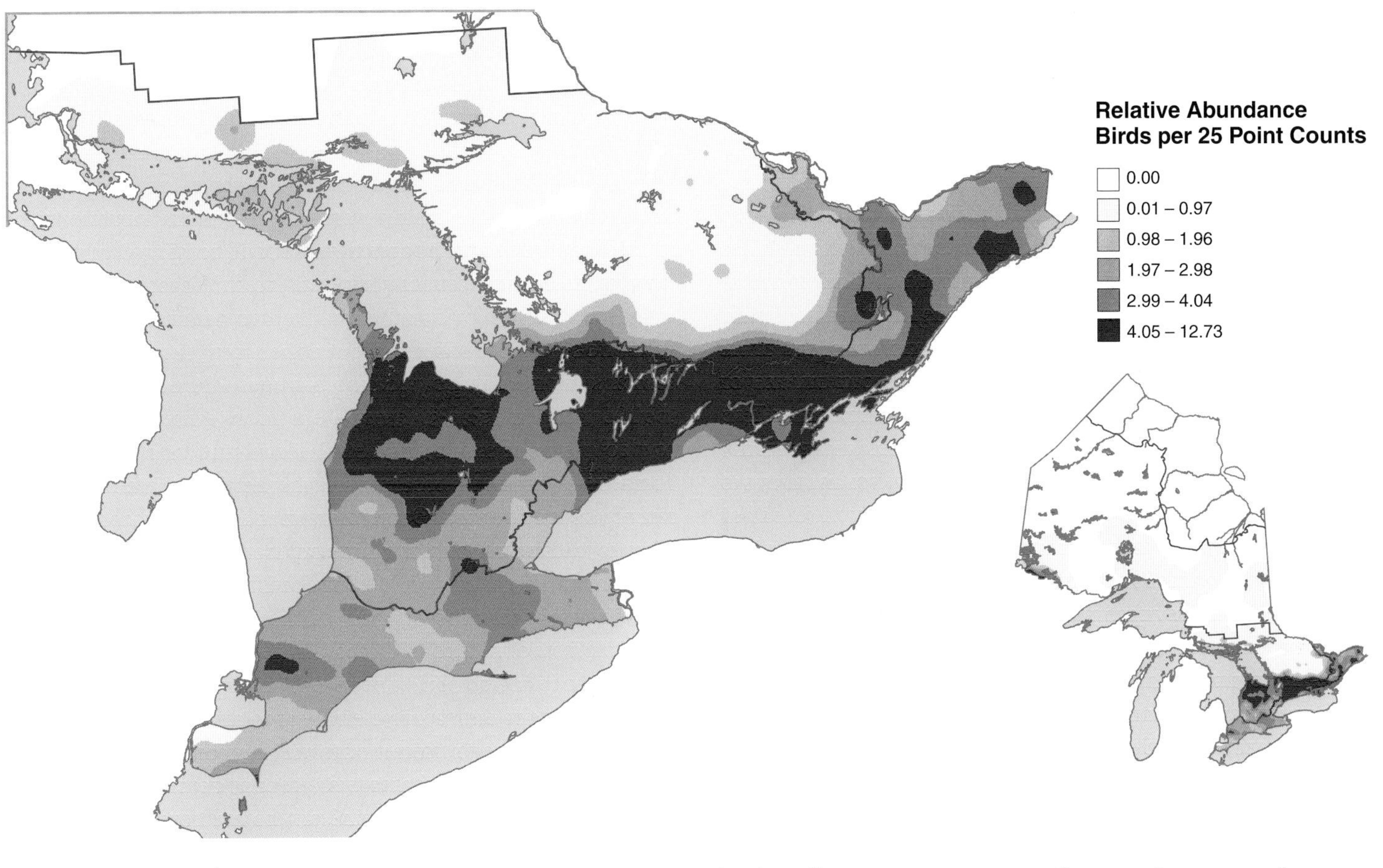

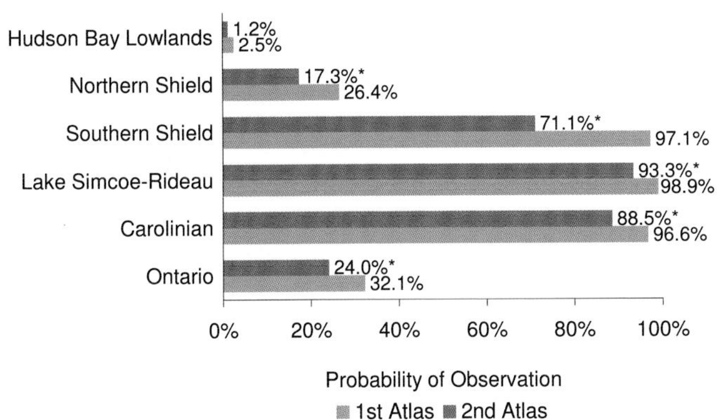

distribution, although the northern limit of its range does not appear to have changed. In southern Ontario, the loss is most prominent on the Shield, especially in and around Algonquin Prov. Park and north of Sudbury.

This decrease parallels a gradual decline in abundance detected by the BBS over the past 20 years in Ontario, across Canada, and throughout the eastern US (Sauer et al. 2005). Recent declines south of the Shield and in the southern part of the Southern Shield region may reflect a reduction in small farms and other open areas, but reasons for the more drastic changes farther north on the Shield are less apparent.

Breeding biology: The Eastern Kingbird is one of the easier birds to detect and confirm as a breeder. In addition to its aggressive nature, it perches conspicuously along roadsides, catches flying insects in the open, builds poorly concealed, bulky nests, and usually feeds fledglings near the nest for two to five weeks after fledging. As a result, it was confirmed in over 1,000 squares. Ease of detection is somewhat reduced in northern squares, where breeding may be confined to wetlands or forest openings remote from road access, so that some squares with breeding birds may have been missed.

The Eastern Kingbird arrives on its Ontario breeding grounds in May. It may re-nest as many as three times following nest failure, with some nests active into August (Blancher 1978). Following breeding, birds begin to drift south in loose flocks, losing the typical aggressiveness shown by breeding birds. It is unlikely that many breeding records were attributable to non-breeders or to movements by birds breeding in other squares.

The species shows a preference for nesting over water where available, often feeding large flying insects such as dragonflies to its young (Holroyd 1983; pers. obs.). Factors reducing flying insect abundance (e.g., pesticide use, wetland drainage) would negatively affect this bird.

Abundance: Highest abundance in Ontario is in the Lake Simcoe-Rideau region, which has a relatively high proportion of pasture and other low-intensity agriculture. Relative abundance in southern Ontario is near the peak for Eastern Kingbirds in eastern North America, according to BBS data, though it is only about half that observed in central grasslands in the US.

Point counts revealed a sharp drop in breeding density north of the Shield edge, where forest cover is greater and wetlands are less productive. This low density on the Shield helps to explain why reductions in the probability of observation were most apparent there, since where density is low, loss of relatively few birds will result in a lack of breeding evidence.
– Peter Blancher

Loggerhead Shrike

Pie-grièche migratrice

Lanius ludovicianus

Jean Iron

Referred to as a "passerine raptor," the Loggerhead Shrike lacks the strong talons of a true raptor, so it often impales its prey on thorns, sharp branches, or barbed wire. The species is widespread in North America, although declines have been noted continent-wide. It breeds currently in the Canadian prairies and southern Ontario, and primarily in the Great Plains and southern portions of the US. COSEWIC listed the Loggerhead Shrike as Threatened in Canada in 1986, and uplisted the eastern subspecies (*L.l. migrans*) to Endangered in 1991. In Ontario, it also was listed as Endangered in 1991. Many factors may be contributing to its decline, including loss of habitat on the breeding and wintering grounds, pesticides, road-associated mortality, adverse weather, and interspecific competition (Cadman 1986).

Distribution and population status: The first record of the Loggerhead Shrike in Ontario was from Hamilton in 1860 (McIlwraith 1886). The species likely expanded into Ontario and much of the rest of northeastern North America with the clearing of land for agriculture (Cadman 1986). At its peak in the mid-1900s, it bred in agricultural areas throughout southern Ontario, in Rainy River Dist., near Thunder Bay, and from Sault Ste. Marie to North Bay (Peck and James 1987). Since then, population declines have been documented throughout its range in North America, and BBS data indicate a significant continental decline since 1966 (Sauer et al. 2005). Between atlases, the probability of observation declined significantly by 63% in Ontario.

The Loggerhead Shrike has bred consistently during both atlases only on and around the Napanee and Carden Plains. Elsewhere in the province, it now occurs sporadically, reflecting its high dispersal capacity. Records of possible breeding evidence may reflect the presence of single, unmated birds that do not remain on territory for long.

Although the Loggerhead Shrike was found in several squares

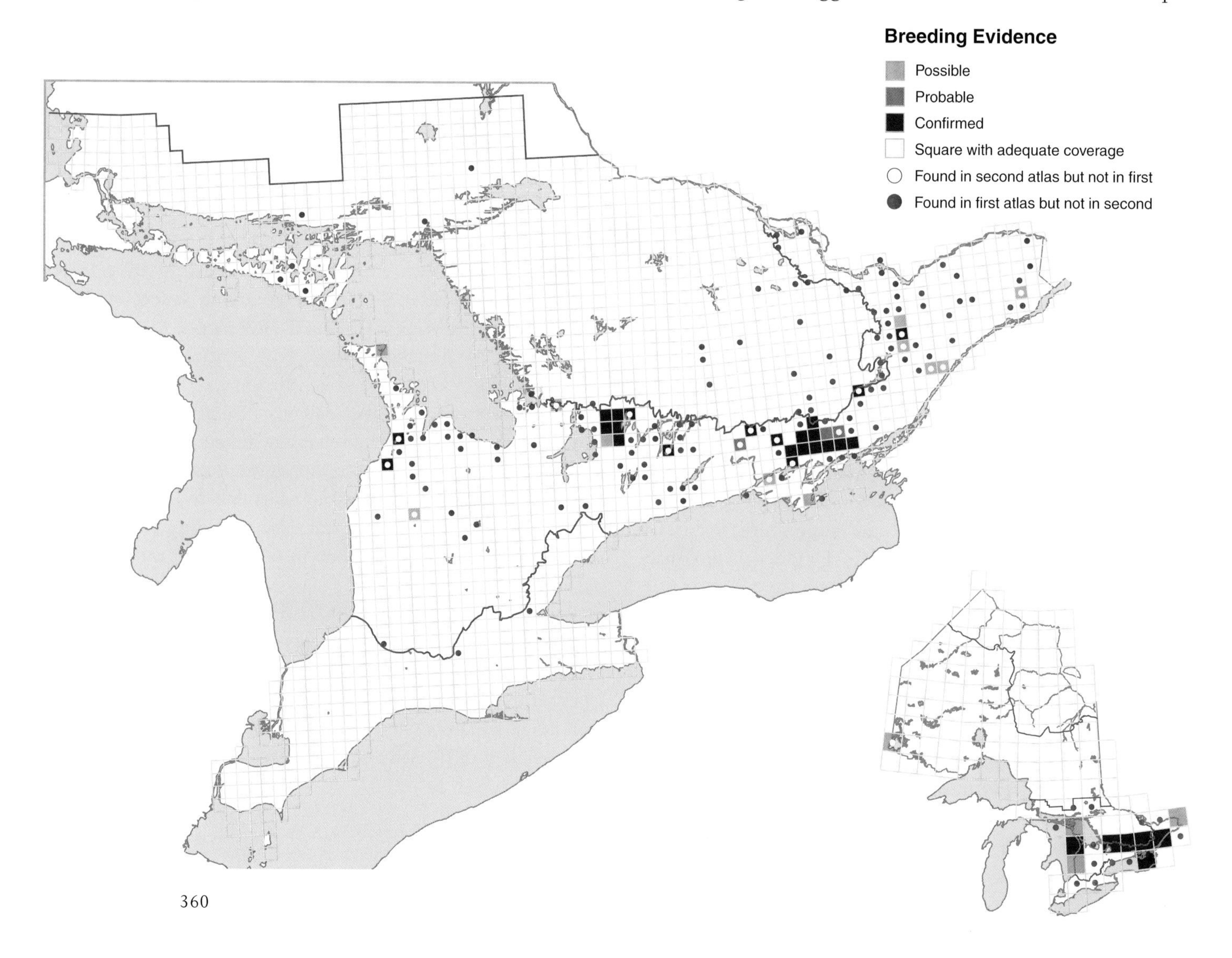

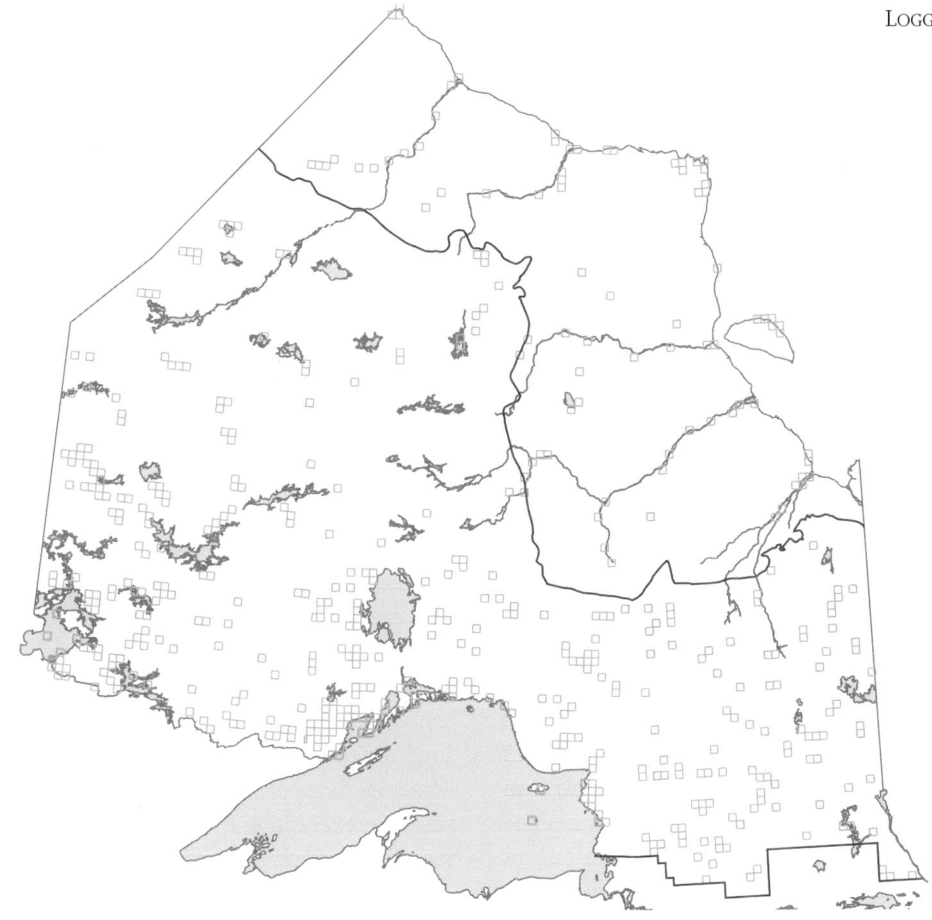

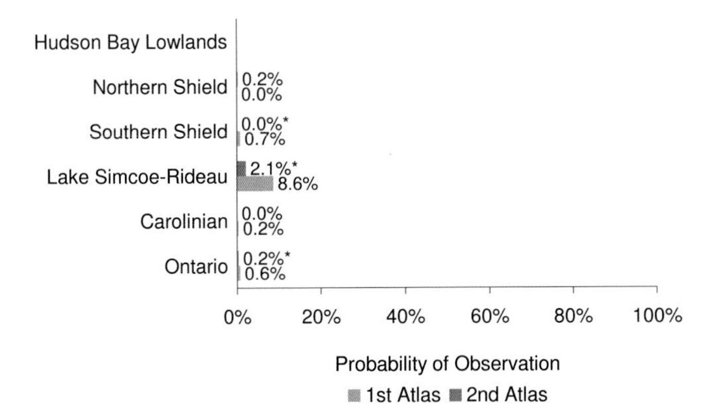

where it was not recorded in the first atlas, the northern edge of its Ontario range has retracted significantly by 80 km south (the largest retraction of any species in the province), and the eastern edge has contracted 50 km west. Most notable are its absence on Manitoulin Island and its limited occurrence in Grey and Bruce Counties and in the Smith's Falls area, all once considered core breeding areas. Atlas data also indicate retraction of its range within the Carden and Napanee core breeding areas, with most of the remaining birds at Carden occurring in areas of heavily grazed pasture on shallow soil over limestone. Declines in the northern portions of its range and elsewhere in the Lake Simcoe-Rideau region may be due to natural succession; however, apparently suitable but unoccupied habitat is present elsewhere, which may indicate that factors other than habitat loss are contributing to its decline.

Breeding biology: In Ontario, the Loggerhead Shrike prefers early successional shrubland habitat, including unimproved pasture. The male defends a territory that typically is about 50 ha in size, much larger than elsewhere in its range (Cuddy 1995). Reuse of sites is fairly strong, increasing the chance of locating birds, but territories are usually reoccupied by different birds in consecutive years (Okines and McCracken 2003).

The Loggerhead Shrike is an early nester, with egg dates in Ontario from 1 April to 5 August (Peck and James 1987) and the peak of incubation in mid-May. Early nesting attempts may fail, but overall reproductive success is high, and two broods are occasionally produced (Chabot et al. 2001a). Foliage density appears to be important in nest-site selection, with isolated hawthorns and Red Cedar preferred (Chabot et al. 2001b). Hedgerows are used less often (Chabot et al. 2001b), and nests in them may be more susceptible to predation (Yosef 1994). Monitoring by the recovery team may have resulted in the large proportion of confirmed breeding records (61%).

Abundance: Concern for the status of the Loggerhead Shrike following the first atlas resulted in a two-year survey in 1987 and 1988, and the species was included in the Ontario Rare Breeding Bird Program (Austen et al. 1994), which included field surveys from 1989 through 1991. A National Recovery Plan was approved in 1993, with a recovery goal of 500 pairs in Ontario and Québec. Recovery activities include annual monitoring efforts in core breeding areas. Since 1991, the population has gone from a high of 55 pairs in 1992 to a low of 18 pairs in 1997, when a captive breeding colony was established. The population rebounded to 40 pairs in 1999, but by 2006 had again declined to 18 pairs. – *Amy A. Chabot*

Northern Shrike

Pie-grièche grise

Lanius excubitor

George K. Peck

The Northern Shrike is the North American member of a holarctic species complex of which the palearctic representatives are known collectively as the Great Grey Shrike. The taxonomic disposition of the two described nearctic subspecies is unresolved, and North American birds may represent a single variable race (Cade and Atkinson 2002).

In North America, the Northern Shrike breeds from Alaska southeast to coastal Labrador, reaching the southern limit of its breeding range at about 51° N in southern James Bay. Its preferred breeding habitats include sparsely treed open muskeg and spruce-lichen woodland patches within open peatlands, extensive regenerating burns, and riparian thickets of willow and alder in the taiga-tundra ecotone.

Distribution and population status: Although undoubtedly it has been a summer resident in the Hudson Bay Lowlands historically, records of the Northern Shrike from the region are few, and Ontario was not included in the breeding range by Godfrey (1966). Schueler et al. (1974) collected a female with enlarged ova at Moosonee in May 1972, the first evidence suggestive of breeding. The observation of a family group of five young at Northbluff Point, James Bay, in 1975 (Manning 1981) and an individual collected from a group of four fledged young near Kiruna Lake in the Sutton Ridges in July 1981 (James 1981) provided the first documented confirmation of breeding provincially. Additional confirmations during the first atlas included the observation of adults with fledged young on the Sachigo River, 65 km from its confluence with the Severn River, and an adult carrying food to fledged young on the Fawn River at the Pitticow River. The only other confirmation of breeding prior to the second atlas involved two adults and five begging young at Fort Severn on 28 June 1993 (Peck and James 1999; K.F. Abraham, pers. comm.).

Distribution of the Northern Shrike has not changed appreciably between atlases. During the second atlas, 15 observations were documented in 14 squares, south to Opapimiskan Lake (52° N) in

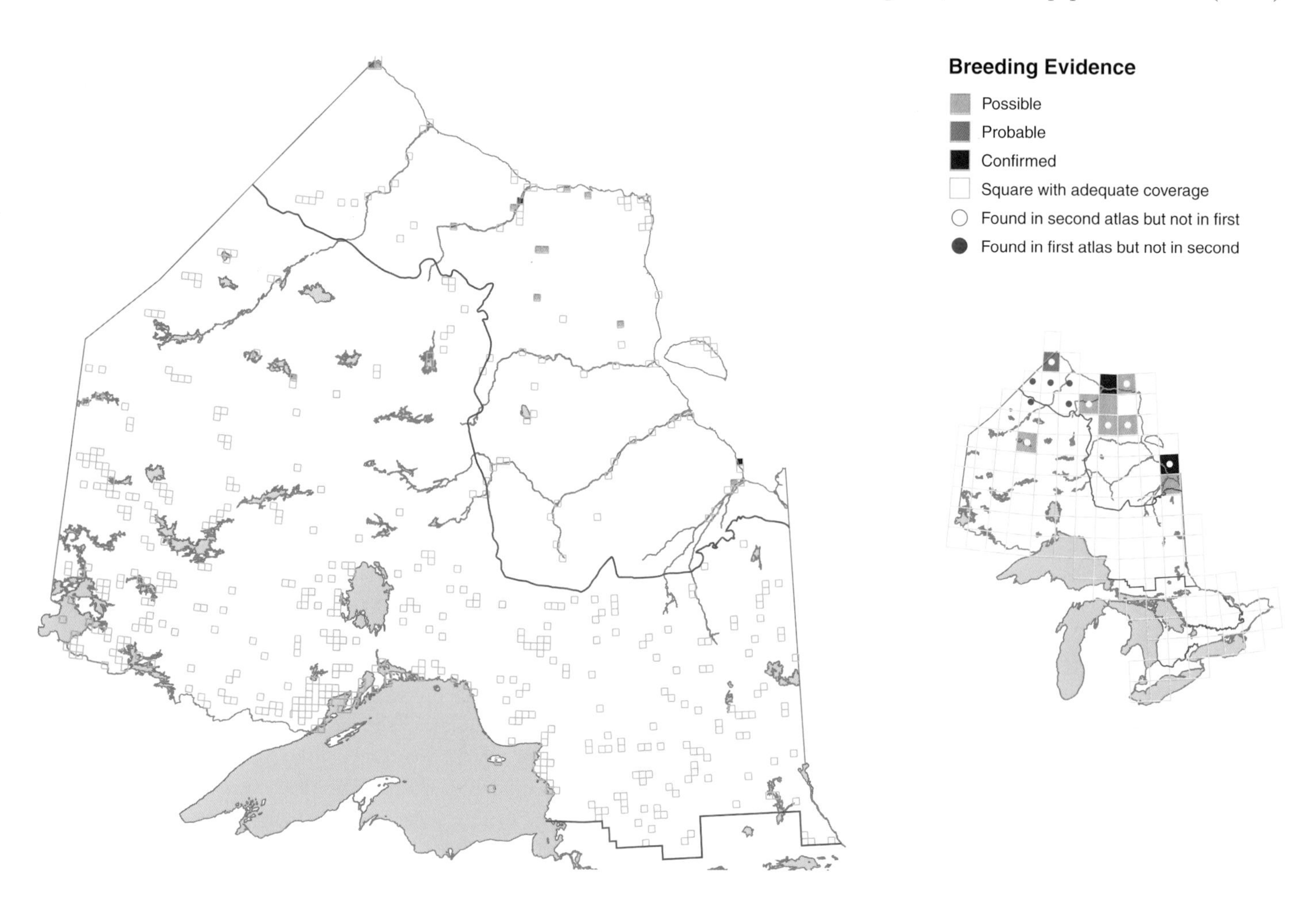

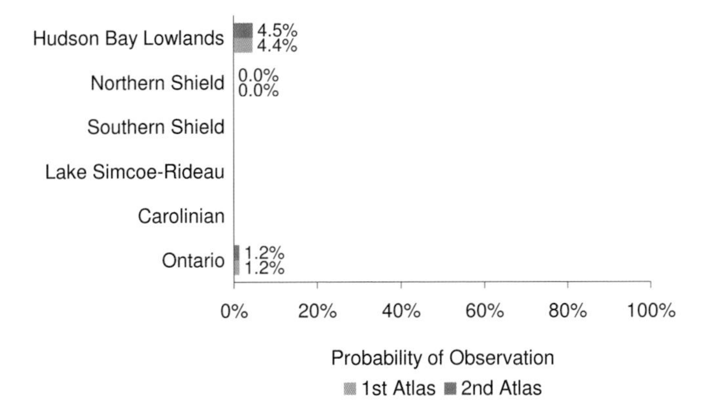

the western portion of the Northern Shield region and in the east to Moosonee (51° N) in the Hudson Bay Lowlands. A shift in the 100-km blocks in which breeding evidence was obtained between atlases likely is an artifact of changes in coverage, and difficulty of detection is due to its sparse population, not a reflection of real distributional change.

Breeding biology: Arrival at breeding areas in Ontario is undocumented but probably occurs in early to mid-May, as at Churchill, Manitoba (Jehl 2004). Pair formation likely takes place in wintering areas, as males and females appear to arrive at breeding areas simultaneously (Cade and Atkinson 2002). While both sexes may sing at any time of the year, singing is most frequent by males, particularly between late winter and the onset of egg laying (Cade and Atkinson 2002). The primary song is a mimid-like, formless series of low-amplitude notes unlikely to be heard by atlassers. Few documented atlas records reported vocalizations, and none involved a singing bird. Most (87%) documented records during the second atlas involved observations of individuals in suitable habitat.

Nests usually are well concealed and difficult to find (Cade and Atkinson 2002). No nest has yet been found in Ontario (Peck and Peck 2006). However, a comparison of published incubation and nestling periods (Cade and Atkinson 2002) with documented observations of family groups suggest that clutches probably would be initiated in Ontario by late May or early June. Breeding is most easily confirmed through the observation of family groups. During the second atlas, breeding was confirmed in only two squares, both involving fledged young: a family group of five begging young in riparian willow thickets along the Winisk River just north of Peawanuck on 8 July 2003, and a juvenile in coastal willow thickets near Shegogau Creek, 30 km north of Moosonee, on 5 August 2005. Family groups may remain intact into early September (Cade and Atkinson 2002).

Territories and inter-pair distances generally are large, and inter-pair aggression is high (Cade 1967), perhaps contributing to the low likelihood of detection.

Abundance: The Northern Shrike exhibits generally low fidelity to breeding areas, probably related to annual variations in prey abundance and snow cover (Cade and Atkinson 2002), which confounds estimates of abundance. Densities of breeding pairs in subarctic North America, although variable, generally appear to be low (e.g., 1-8 pairs/100 km^2; Cade and Atkinson 2002). During the second atlas, it was not detected on any point counts, and observations were too few to allow for a population estimate. – *Donald A. Sutherland*

Although no nest has been found in Ontario, nests are placed in a dense spruce, willow, or alder in open spruce woodlands or riparian shrub thickets. Churchill, Manitoba, 30 June 1972. *Photo: George K. Peck*

Sparsely treed open peatlands, spruce-lichen woodlands, extensive regenerating burns, and willow and alder riparian thickets are all breeding habitats for this species in Ontario. *Photo: Mark Peck*

White-eyed Vireo

Viréo aux yeux blancs

Vireo griseus

Frank and Sandra Horvath

Were it not for its energetic bursts of song from the dense shrubbery of woodland edges, streamside bushes, or overgrown fields, the White-eyed Vireo would be detected much less often. Its breeding range extends over most of the eastern half of the US south to the Atlantic slope of northeastern Mexico, but only a very few birds range north into southern Ontario. One of a handful of species in Ontario with a pale iris, it is the only vireo in Ontario that prefers shrub thickets to forests, and is a noted mimic of other species, making it an interesting member of the province's avifauna.

Distribution and population status: Historical reports of nesting by the White-eyed Vireo in Ontario near Niagara Falls (Beardslee and Mitchell 1965) and in Toronto (Macoun and Macoun 1909) were unsubstantiated and probably erroneous (James 1991). Following a retraction in its breeding range during the early part of the 20th century (Hopp et al. 1995), the species showed a highly significant population increase and northward expansion of its breeding range beginning about 1950 (Robbins et al. 1986). Nesting was first confirmed in Michigan in 1960 (Brewer et al. 1991) and in Ontario in 1971 (Peck 1976; Rayner 1988). Since the first nesting record, small numbers continue to occur, with nesting likely in most years.

At the time of the first atlas, small populations had become regular, at least at Point Pelee Nat. Park and Rondeau Prov. Park, and the range expansion was expected to continue. However, there has been little change in distribution in the past 20 years, and the species is still largely confined to the southwest along Lake Erie. It is found in a few other places in the southern part of the Carolinian region each year but generally is not reliable apart from the two aforementioned places and the Long Point area. It often wanders north of its usual breeding range, particularly in spring (Hopp et al. 1995), and has been seen in many areas of southern Ontario north of the Carolinian region, but nesting is unlikely outside of the Carolinian.

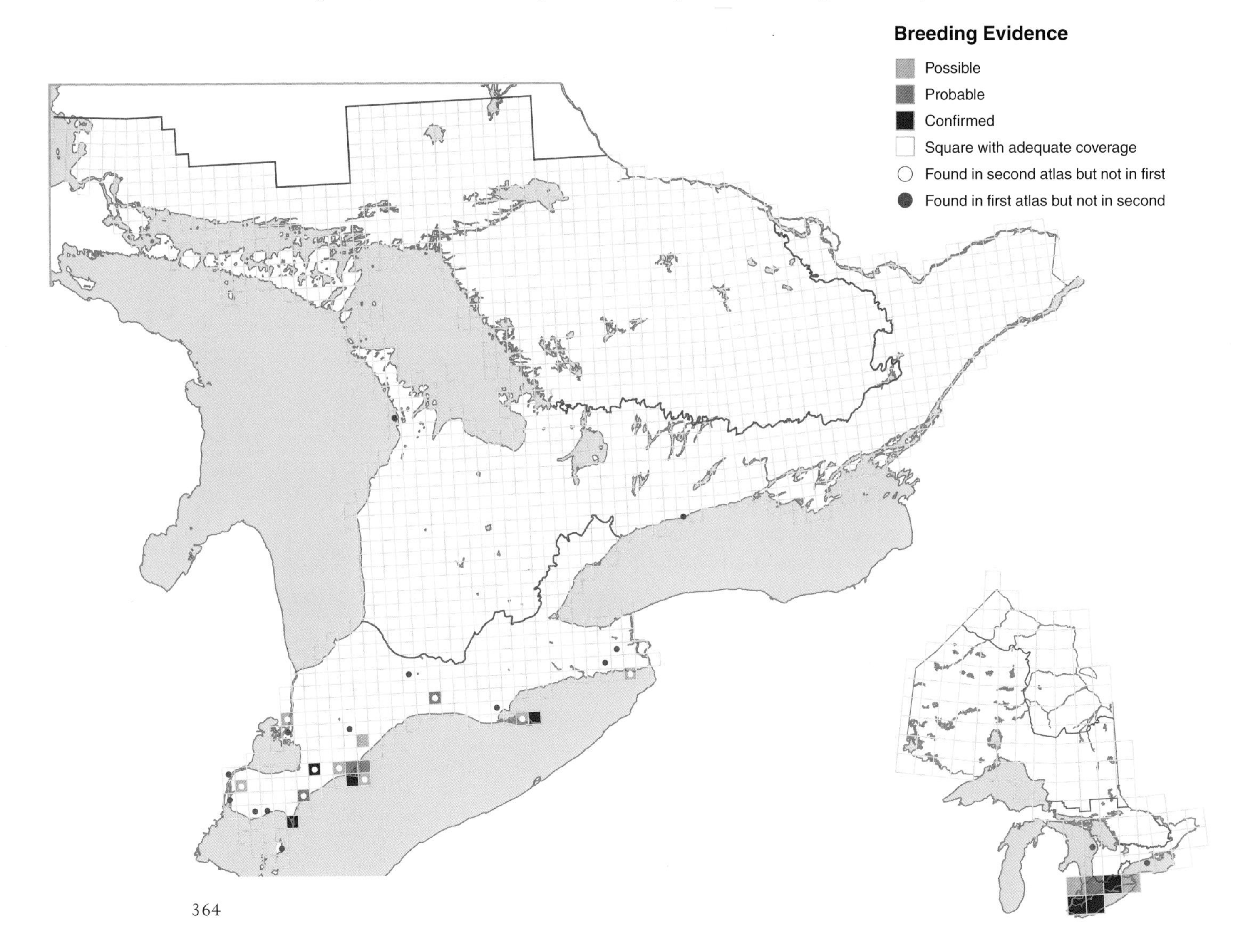

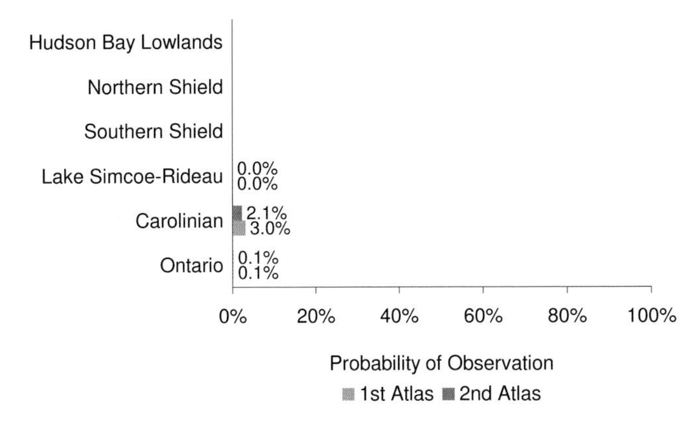

The White-eyed Vireo exploits early successional habitats, including those resulting from human activities, and to some extent has probably benefited from the highly altered landscape of southern Ontario. At the same time, reduction of the supply of early successional scrub habitat through intensive agriculture in much of southwestern Ontario and urbanization in many other areas will tend to limit opportunities for this species in the future. Habitat supply is likely not the only factor limiting range expansion, however, as the species is inexplicably absent from some areas with otherwise suitable or adequate habitat. BBS data from the Eastern BBS Region (which includes Ontario) indicate a significant increase since 1966 but a relatively stable population since 1980. Areas with increases include Ohio and Pennsylvania, but despite this growth nearby, the species does not appear to be expanding its range, suggesting there is little chance of any notable increase occurring in Ontario at this time.

Breeding biology: The loud, distinctive, nearly incessant song, usually beginning and ending with clear chip notes and consisting of various warbles and scolding notes, makes locating and identifying the male White-eyed Vireo relatively easy early in the breeding season. The extent of singing diminishes progressively through the nesting period; this, in combination with the incorporation of other species' call notes (Hopp et al. 1995), the lack of specific song perches, and the habit of wandering about in the territory, could make its detection difficult later in the season. Confirmation of breeding is more difficult as this vireo can be very secretive in thick vegetation. Nests typically are well concealed in low, dense vegetation, and the nest can usually be closely approached before scolding by agitated adults betrays its presence.

Nevertheless, the distribution map likely provides an accurate representation of the breeding distribution of White-eyed Vireo in Ontario. Nesting is likely to be irregular or sporadic anywhere other than Pelee, Rondeau, and Long Point, and no nesting should be expected north of the Carolinian region at present.

Abundance: The White-eyed Vireo continues to be a rare species in Ontario with a very limited distribution. Its main stronghold is along Lake Erie, especially at Point Pelee, Rondeau, and Long Point, where it occurred during both atlases. Optimism about continued expansion in the first atlas has not been borne out. However, given the relatively small population, it is premature to draw conclusions. – *Ross James*

Clutch size is usually four eggs but ranges from three to five. Young leave the nest nine to 11 days after hatching (Hopp et al. 1995). *Photo: George K. Peck*

This shrub thicket in Point Pelee Nat. Park, Essex Co., was used for nesting during the first atlas. *Photo: George K. Peck*

Yellow-throated Vireo

Viréo à gorge jaune

Vireo flavifrons

Bill Rayner

The Yellow-throated Vireo often occurs in the same forests as the Red-eyed Vireo but generally prefers more open woodlands with tall, mature trees with spreading canopies. It is particularly fond of upland Red Oak woods and lowland maple swamps. It breeds across most of the eastern US and ranges north into Canada in southeastern Saskatchewan and southern Manitoba, Ontario, and Québec (Godfrey 1986). Areas with a high percentage of regional forest cover with large mature deciduous trees are required to sustain populations of this species (Robbins et al. 1989).

Distribution and population status: The Yellow-throated Vireo probably has experienced widespread declines coincident with extensive land clearing in southern Ontario. It also declines noticeably where coniferous trees begin to dominate the forests in the Southern Shield region.

In Ontario, the Yellow-throated Vireo is found primarily in the three southern atlas regions. There are two main areas of concentration, one in the Carolinian region, and the other across the southern edge of the Precambrian Shield and west to the Bruce Peninsula. These concentrations probably represent areas with adequate amounts of suitable deciduous or mixed forest cover. Gaps in distribution in these areas likely are due to the absence or fragmentation of forests, especially in Essex Co. and Chatham-Kent, which are almost entirely comprised of agricultural land. This vireo's absence from much of the Lake Simcoe-Rideau region is harder to explain, although it is likely that many areas of this region have insufficient forest cover of the size and composition necessary to support the species. Small numbers occur in the Rainy River area, where Great Lakes-St. Lawrence Forest also occurs.

There has been substantial turnover between the two atlases in the specific squares in which the Yellow-throated Vireo was recorded. Some of this shift may be due to changes in forest cover in the intervening years, but it also likely is related to the

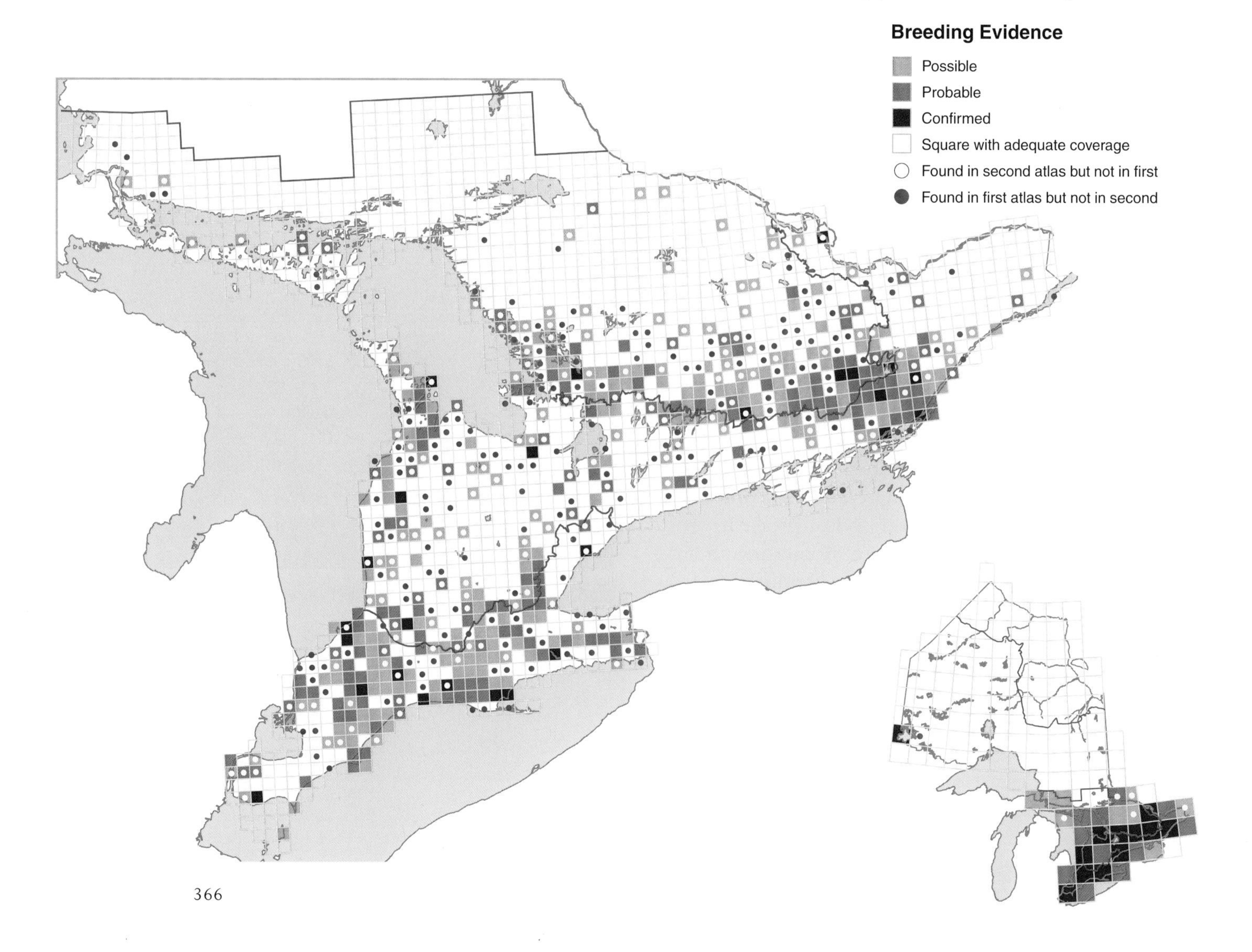

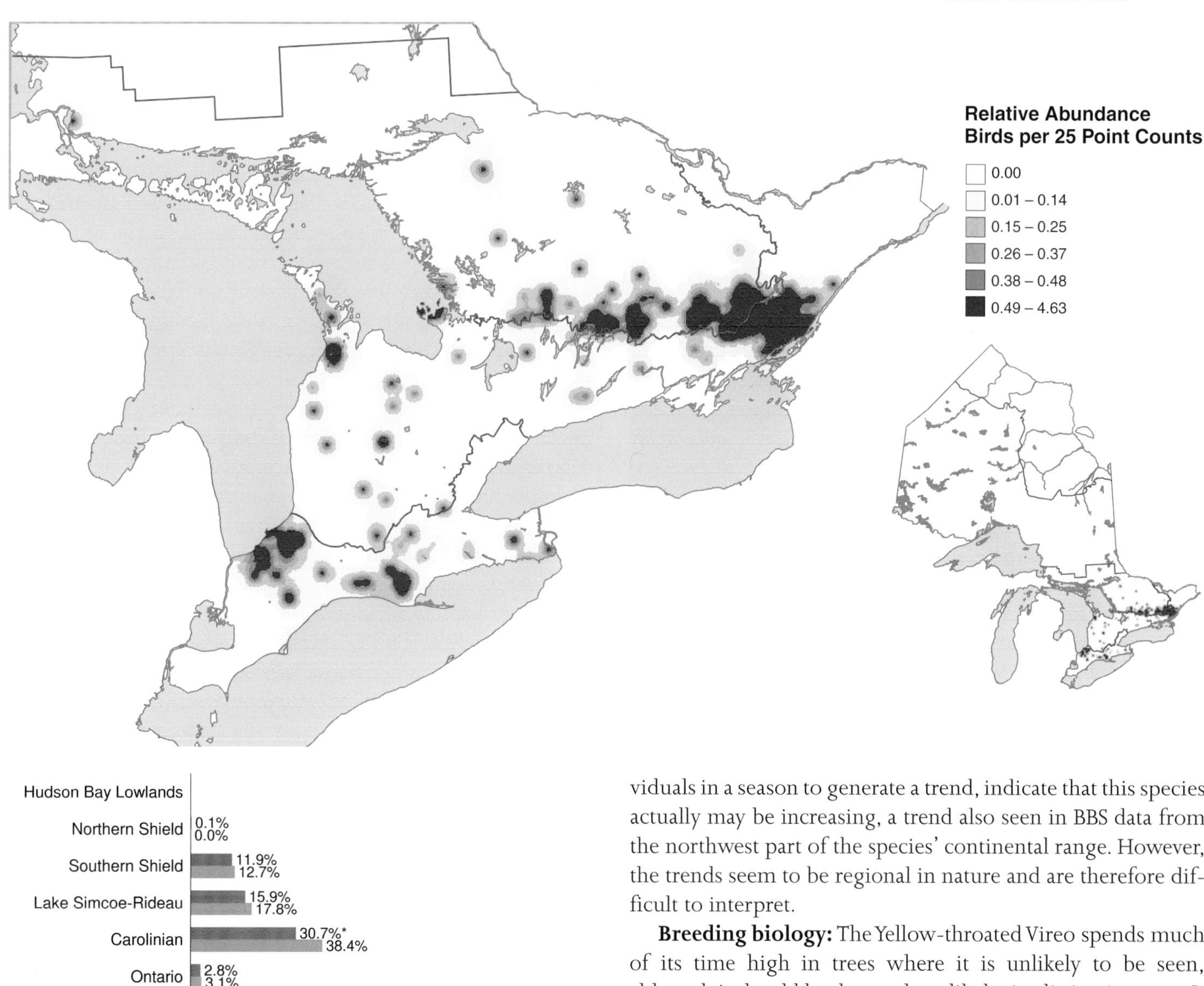

relatively small and dispersed population shifting about in a highly fragmented environment, attempting to find suitable habitat and mates.

BBS data indicate that numbers in Ontario overall have remained relatively stable over the past 25 years, and atlas data indicate no significant change in Ontario as a whole between atlases. However, there has been a significant 20% decrease in the probability of observation in the Carolinian region.

The breeding evidence map shows records farther north in the Southern Shield region than during the first atlas and a significant northward shift in range in southern Ontario. Many of the most northerly records likely involve singing or territorial males, easily detected by sustained singing but likely unmated and so not currently contributing to the population. The northern expansion may be temporary and obscuring an overall decline, suggested by the trend in the Carolinian region, but could also represent a real range expansion. In fact, migration monitoring data from Haldimand Bird Observatory's Ruthven station, the only station in Ontario that detects enough individuals in a season to generate a trend, indicate that this species actually may be increasing, a trend also seen in BBS data from the northwest part of the species' continental range. However, the trends seem to be regional in nature and are therefore difficult to interpret.

Breeding biology: The Yellow-throated Vireo spends much of its time high in trees where it is unlikely to be seen, although it should be detected readily by its distinctive song. It is most vocal when unmated but does sing through the nesting season. Confirmation of nesting is difficult, as the few confirmations even in areas of relatively high density indicate. Nests typically are high in the forest canopy and obscured by foliage. Both adults feed the young, but an adult at the nest will leave just as the other arrives; unless the exchange is seen, it may appear as if a single bird passed through the tree without stopping, not revealing the presence of a nest (Rodewald and James 1996). During the second atlas, not a single nest was reported; most confirmed breeding evidence involved adults carrying food. However, while breeding status may be underestimated, the documented distribution in Ontario probably is relatively accurate.

Abundance: The Frontenac Axis stands out as the largest area of high abundance, with patches of abundance across the southern edge of the Shield. In the Carolinian region, the northern part of Lambton Co. is evidently of particular importance to the species, as is Norfolk Co. Without the maintenance of larger and contiguous areas of mature deciduous forest, this species likely will remain relatively rare or may even decline in the province. – *Ross James*

Blue-headed Vireo

Viréo à tête bleue

Vireo solitarius

George K. Peck

The Blue-headed Vireo is the only vireo in Canada to make extensive use of coniferous trees, breeding from eastern British Columbia to southwestern Newfoundland and south into the highlands of the eastern US (James 1998). Although it prefers a mix of coniferous and deciduous trees, it may be found in pure coniferous forest and less often where deciduous trees dominate. Formerly called the Solitary Vireo (which has now been split into three species), it was well named, as pairs often are widely spaced.

Distribution and population status: The Blue-headed Vireo probably bred at one time throughout most of southern Ontario. Clearing of forests would largely have eliminated it south of the Precambrian Shield and reduced its numbers farther north. During the first atlas, it was found in only 66 squares south of the Shield, where remnant forests were large enough or extensive conifer plantations had matured. Between atlases, its probability of observation for the province increased significantly by 85%, with the greatest increase, nearly 300%, occurring in the Lake Simcoe-Rideau region; the increase is particularly evident along the Niagara Escarpment and on the Oak Ridges Moraine. A similar increase has also occurred in several other birds of coniferous forests (e.g., the Magnolia Warbler and Black-throated Green Warbler) and is probably related to ongoing maturation of conifer plantations. The species has increased significantly by 94% in the Southern Shield. In the Carolinian region, little change is evident as intensive agriculture continues to dominate.

The probability of observation has also increased significantly in the Northern Shield and Hudson Bay Lowlands regions, possibly suggesting a northward range expansion. In the Hudson Bay Lowlands, virtually all occupied squares are located along major rivers supporting suitable riparian coniferous and mixed forest habitat. During the first atlas, two of these river corridors, the Attawapiskat and Ekwan, were not

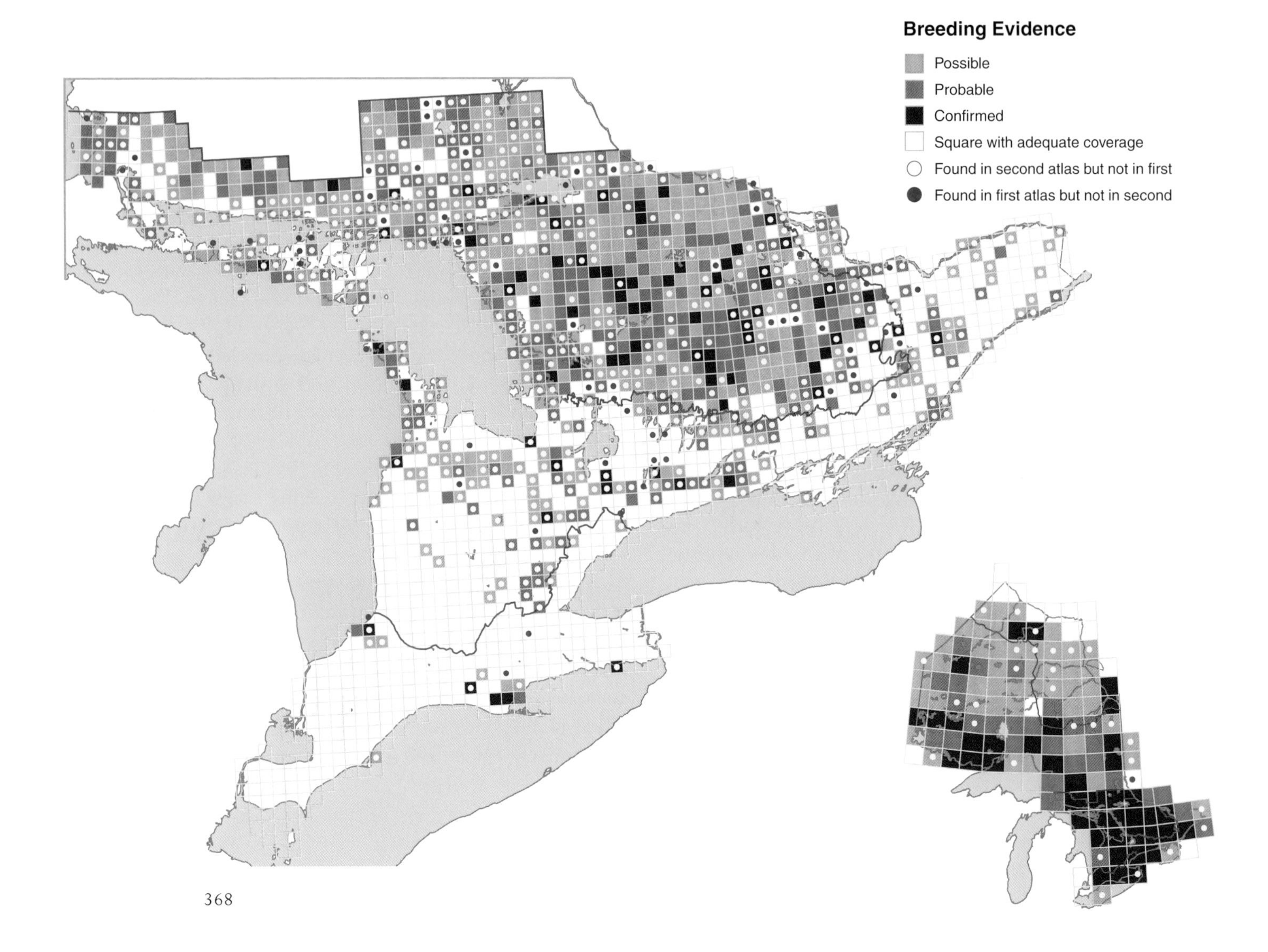

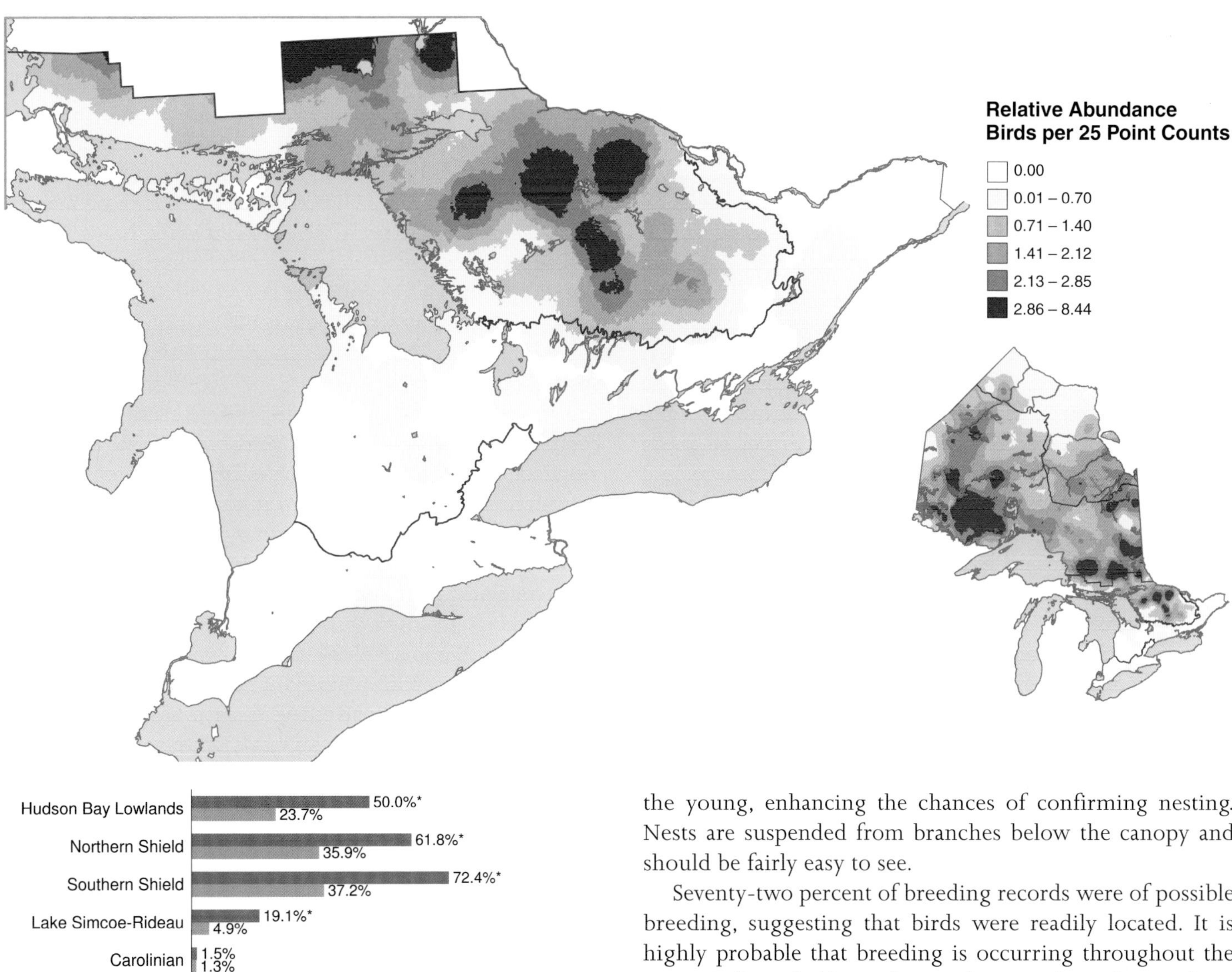

covered. Results from the BBS across Canada and in Ontario show a significant increase over the past 25 years. Reasons for the increase in the north are unclear. However, maturation of forests in the wintering grounds in the southern US may be a factor in all the increases between atlases.

The distribution map for this species reflects the overall distribution pattern well. It likely occurs in virtually every square in the Southern and Northern Shield regions, although the probability of observation is only 72% and 62%, respectively. It is quite possible that the species, if present in low densities, could be overlooked. However, south of the Shield and in the far north, many of the gaps probably are real.

Breeding biology: The loud song of the Blue-headed Vireo should make location and identification easy for experienced atlassers. However, only unmated males are persistent singers. Males may wander widely, even when mated, which could make breeding more difficult to confirm, but should increase the chances of encountering birds. Males sing through most of the summer, and both parent birds feed the young, enhancing the chances of confirming nesting. Nests are suspended from branches below the canopy and should be fairly easy to see.

Seventy-two percent of breeding records were of possible breeding, suggesting that birds were readily located. It is highly probable that breeding is occurring throughout the range indicated. Along the northern and southern edges, there may have been some unmated birds, but the general increase in population makes it likely that most reports represent breeding birds.

Abundance: The relative abundance map indicates that highest densities are on the Precambrian Shield. The areas of greatest abundance correspond roughly with areas of continuous forest cover. Lower densities would be expected in the Great Clay Belt and Little Clay Belt and along the Hwy. 17 corridor between Lake Nipissing and Sault Ste. Marie, areas with more extensive agriculture and more fragmented forests, as well as in the Hudson Bay Lowlands region, where extensive wetlands become more frequent. In the Lake Simcoe-Rideau region, forest fragmentation and land clearing are factors limiting abundance, as they are in the Rainy River and Lake of the Woods areas. However, north of Rainy River, low abundance may be an artifact of fewer point counts, as forest cover should be sufficient to support higher densities there.

Given that this is a widespread species increasing in numbers, the pattern of abundance suggests that the Blue-headed Vireo benefits from extensive and continuous areas of forest and will decrease wherever forests become fragmented. While it may be able to occupy outlying plantations and more fragmented woodlands, its productivity may be very low in such places. – *Ross James*

Warbling Vireo

Viréo mélodieux

Vireo gilvus

John Reaume

While it ought to be a familiar bird of rural roadsides, parks, small towns, and streamsides, the Warbling Vireo probably would go unnoticed if it were not for the persistent warbling song that betrays its presence. It breeds across most of southern Canada, more extensively in the western highlands, and throughout most of the US, south at higher elevations to southern Mexico. It prefers deciduous woodlands with less than 75% canopy closure but also occurs in hedgerows, narrow riparian strips, and landscape plantings, especially around wet areas (Gardali and Ballard 2000). It shuns conifer-dominated stands and continuous, closed-canopy forest.

Distribution and population status: The Warbling Vireo benefited from forest clearing, evidently extending its range northward during the 1800s and early 1900s (e.g., western Rainy River Dist.; Snyder 1938) and becoming more numerous in areas where it was formerly scarce (e.g., eastern Ontario; Baillie and Harrington 1937). Although the species has generally continued to increase in Ontario since that time, there are indications that this trend has stabilized in recent years. BBS data show a steady and significant increase in Ontario since the survey began in 1968 (Downes et al. 2005), but only a near-significant increase since 1981. Migration monitoring data from LPBO (Crewe 2006) also show significant increases since 1980, but with no significant increase in 1995 to 2005. Province-wide, there was no significant change in the probability of observation between atlases, and in the Southern Shield there was actually a 15% decline. This decline may be due to increases in forest cover in that region and the related reduction in farmland.

The species is still essentially absent from the Algonquin Highlands. It is present in many squares near the southern edge of the Precambrian Shield, where preferred habitats such as human habitations, maple swamps, and aspen stands are more frequent. Its distribution extends up the Hwy. 11 corri-

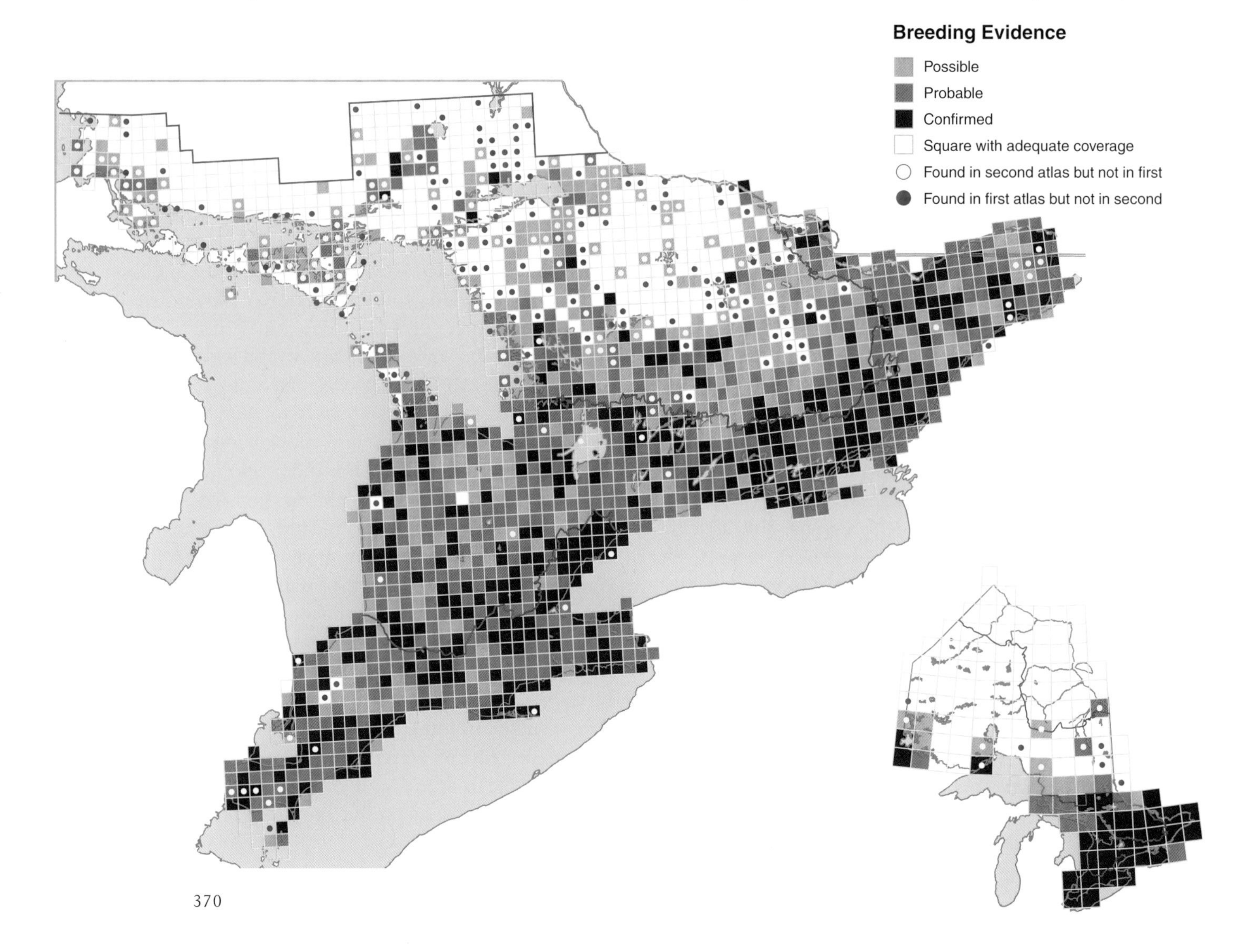

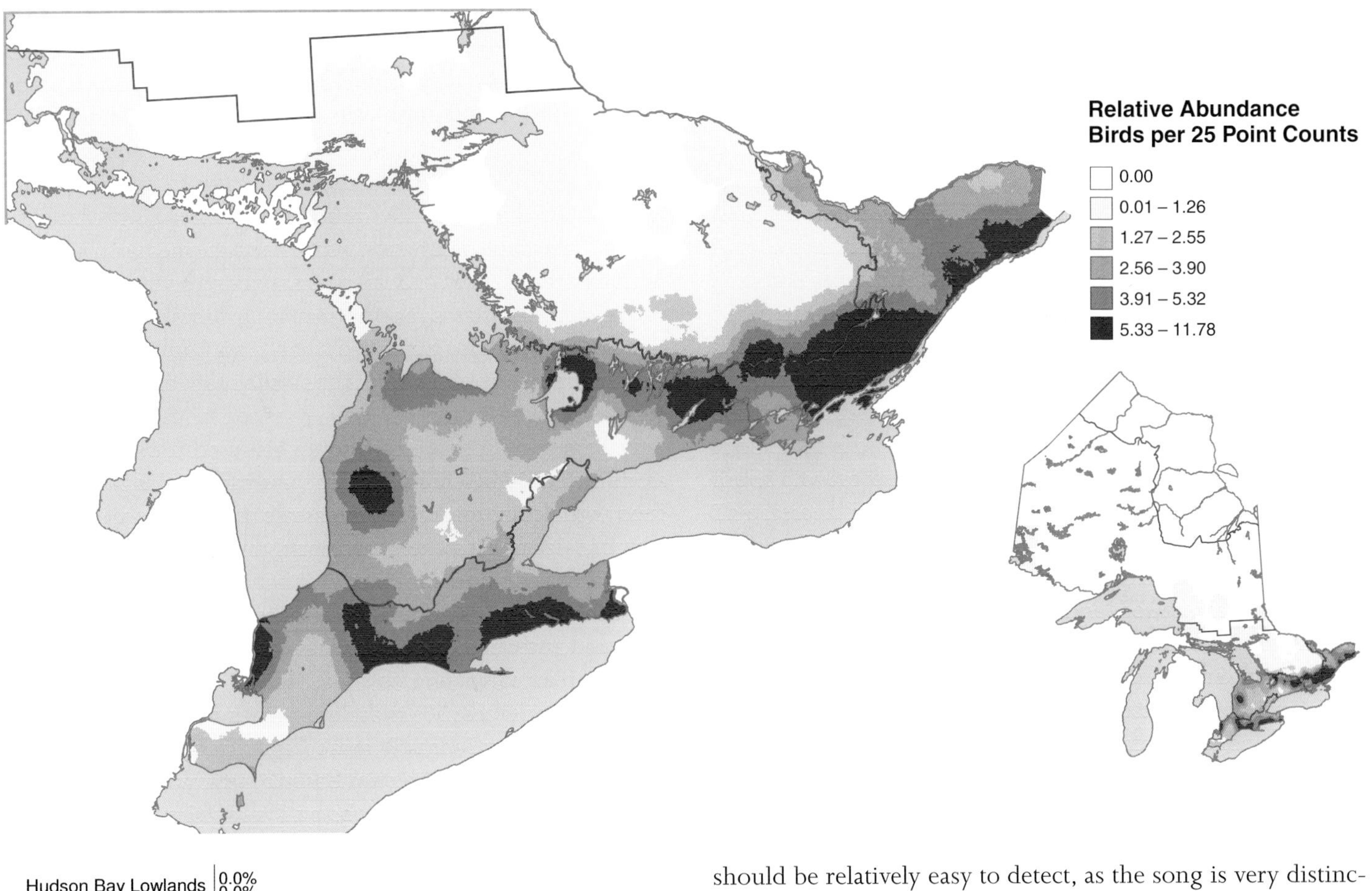

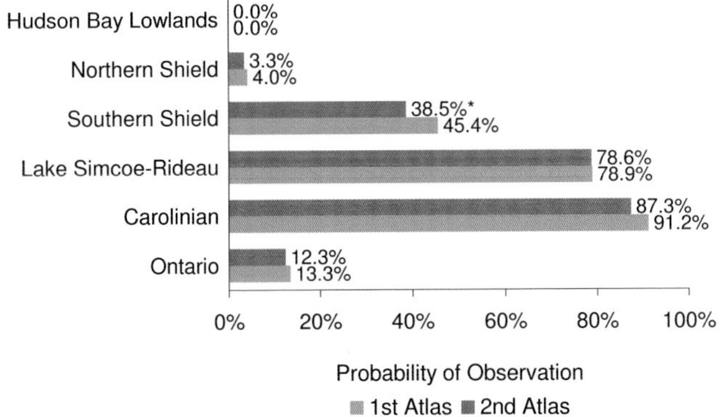

dor through Muskoka and Parry Sound Districts, where it occurs in rural areas and small towns. Clusters of occurrence also exist in the Sudbury and Sault Ste. Marie areas. In northern Ontario, it was found in a few squares where it was not found during the first atlas, most notably in the Hudson Bay Lowlands. There is now a small population established in Moosonee (D.A. Sutherland, pers. comm.). Occurrences have been reported from as far north as the Albany River since the first atlas (D.A. Welsh, pers. comm.), and because occurrences are so widely spaced and remote, others may have been missed. However, given limited suitable habitat, any further expansion in northern Ontario is unlikely to be extensive. In the Carolinian and Lake Simcoe-Rideau regions, the species' distribution has remained unchanged between atlases, and it is found in almost every square.

Breeding biology: Pairs of Warbling Vireos tend to be thinly spread, taking advantage of small patches and narrow strips of habitat, which may increase the difficulty in finding birds, particularly in more northern areas. However, if present, they should be relatively easy to detect, as the song is very distinctive and is given through the nesting season (Gardali and Ballard 2000). The male often sings on the nest. Because of the species' ability to use small habitat patches, it is frequently found close to areas of human activity where it should be readily detected. Finding nests may be difficult, as they tend to be high and well concealed by foliage. However, confirmation of breeding should be fairly easy, as both parents feed the young and seem little concerned by the presence of observers.

Abundance: The abundance map indicates that the highest densities of the Warbling Vireo are found along the shore of eastern Lake Erie, south of the edge of the Precambrian Shield, along the St. Lawrence River, and in a small area east of Lake Huron. This is not surprising, as there is considerable suitable habitat in these areas. Densities were lower in the more intensively farmed and urbanized areas of the Greater Toronto Area and extreme southwestern Ontario. Although point count coverage was good on Manitoulin Island, lower abundance was recorded there. On the Shield and to the north, the density of birds is considerably lower, and the relatively low number of point counts in the north probably biases the abundance patterns to some extent. The areas of higher density along eastern Lake Superior, in the Kenora-Rainy River area, and west of Lake Timiskaming are based on detections in very few squares. – *Ross James*

Philadelphia Vireo

Viréo de Philadelphie

Vireo philadelphicus

Jim Richards

The Philadelphia Vireo's song is so similar to that of the slightly larger Red-eyed Vireo that it can often use it to exclude its congener from an occupied territory – a fine example of interspecific territoriality (Rice 1978a, 1978b). The Philadelphia Vireo is widely distributed across the Boreal Forest of Canada and into the extreme northern US. It is a bird of open, early successional woodlands, particularly where Trembling Aspen is found, often with an interspersion of alder or birch (Moskoff and Robinson 1996).

Distribution and population status: The Philadelphia Vireo has been present in Ontario probably as long as boreal forests have existed here. Forest clearing and logging may have had a positive effect on the species, since mature closed forests are not a favoured habitat. However, there has been a notable change in its range during the past 20 years, most evident on the atlas maps along both the southern and northern edges. In the Southern Shield, this vireo is relatively uncommon and absent in most squares; however, the probability of observation increased significantly by 29% between atlases. In the Lake Simcoe-Rideau region, including Manitoulin Island, it was newly reported in a considerable number of squares, although there was no significant change in the probability of observation in this region as a whole. Along the northern edge of its range, it was found in several 100-km blocks farther north than during the first atlas, particularly along the major river corridors, but increases of the species in the Northern Shield and Hudson Bay Lowlands are not significant. Better coverage and/or more familiarity with the song among atlassers can perhaps account for these increases. However, it should be noted that the Philadelphia Vireo was found to be common in parts of the James Bay lowlands during the 1970s (S. O'Donnell, pers. comm.). BBS data have shown a steady increase in numbers

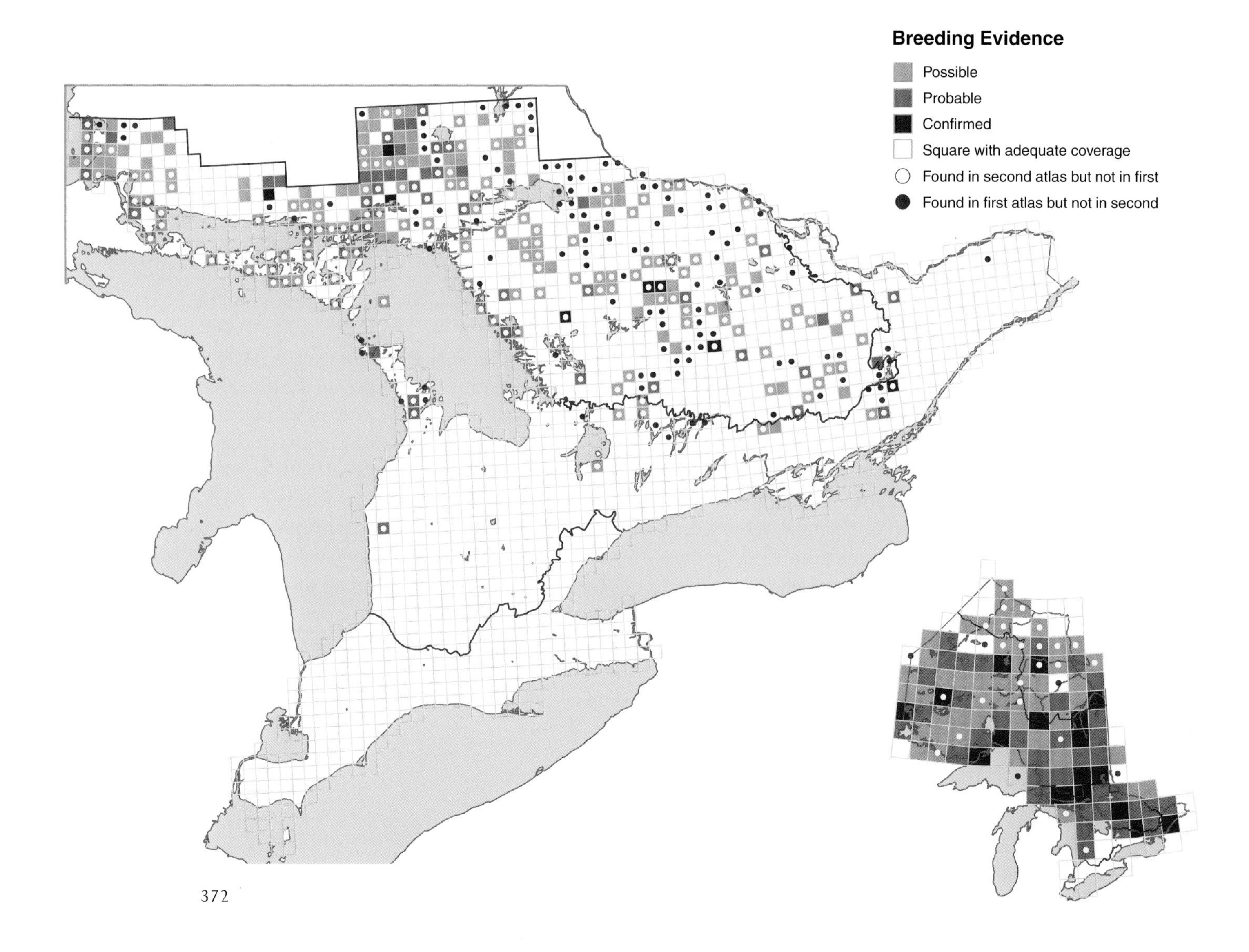

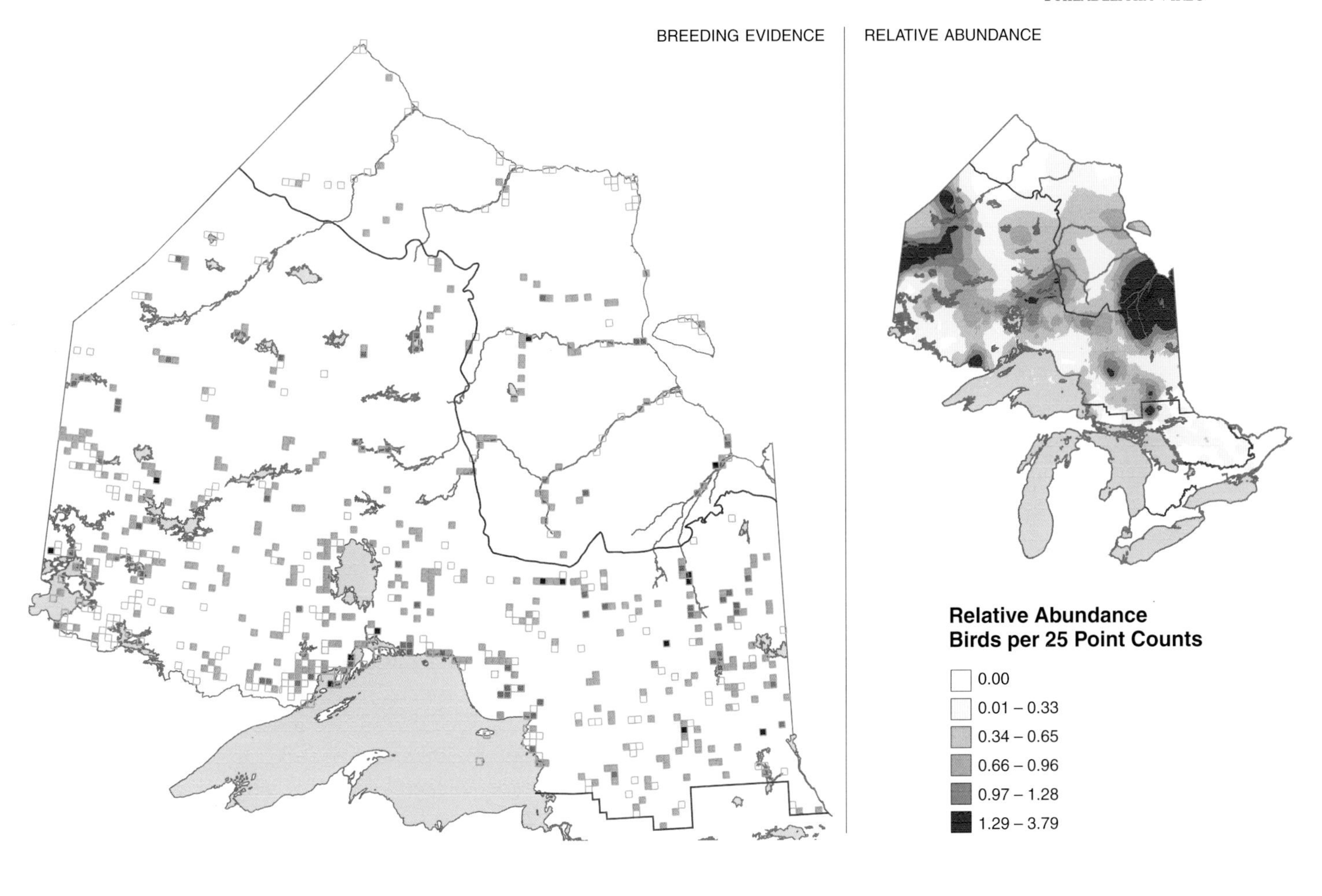

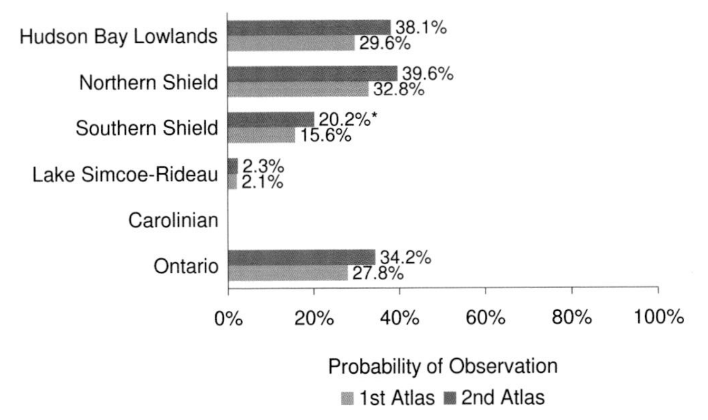

across Canada since 1968 (Downes et al. 2005). In Ontario, numbers have fluctuated considerably in recent years, and there has been no significant change since 1968.

The reasons for the increase shown by the atlas data in Ontario are unclear. Logging, the most extensive factor in habitat alteration in the Boreal Forest (along with fire), may be part of the answer, because of the Philadelphia Vireo's preference for younger and more deciduous forests, although it cannot account for change north of 51° N. The modest increase in southern Ontario in recent years may be related to increasing amounts of poplar on abandoned farmland and in old conifer plantations that have been thinned and are reverting to deciduous species. As tolerant hardwoods come to dominate these southern forests, however, the Philadelphia Vireo's expansion likely will end, and it could then retract to its former range.

The distribution map represents the actual distribution of this species fairly well. In northern Ontario, searches of more squares certainly would have filled in some apparent distributional gaps. The species is thinly scattered in much of the northern Hudson Bay Lowlands and Southern Shield regions, and it is rare farther south.

Breeding biology: The Philadelphia Vireo is not nearly as persistent a singer as the Red-eyed Vireo and could go unnoticed in the presence of its more vocal relative. However, once detected, it should be easier to confirm as a breeder. Both members of a pair regularly visit the nest during construction, share incubation duties, and feed the young. The male will sing on the nest. Some nests are high and difficult to detect, but others are lower, sometimes even located in shrubs. Nevertheless, few probable and confirmed records were obtained, since much of the species' range is in remote areas where atlassers had relatively little time to spend searching or to make repeat visits.

Abundance: The abundance map indicates highly variable concentrations, with multiple peaks of abundance across northern Ontario. It seems likely that this is an artifact of the relatively few and widely dispersed point counts in the north rather than an accurate portrayal of abundance. However, the maps do indicate that the main area of abundance occurs in a band running diagonally across the province, between 49° N and 53° N, from south of James Bay to the angle of the western border with Manitoba. If deciduous softwoods such as poplars and birches become dominant in the Boreal Forest in the future due to changing climate, increasing numbers of Philadelphia Vireo may be expected. – *Ross James*

Red-eyed Vireo

Viréo aux yeux rouge

Vireo olivaceus

George K. Peck

Noted more for its singing than for the colour of its eyes, the Red-eyed Vireo is an indefatigable singer capable of delivering more than 20,000 songs in a day (Lawrence 1953). It occurs in a wide variety of deciduous and mixed forest types with understoreys of shrubs and saplings where nests often are placed. It is found across most of the forested parts of North America but seems to avoid conifer-dominated stands. Although it has been characterized as a species of woodland interiors, it occurs wherever tree canopy closure is at or above 25%, and also in more open areas containing mature trees, such as city parks, savannahs, and rural gardens.

Distribution and population status: The Red-eyed Vireo is found virtually everywhere in the woodlands of southern Ontario. In all but the Hudson Bay Lowlands region, it was detected in most squares with adequate coverage. The few places where it was not found were likely water-dominated squares or squares with little suitable habitat.

In the Northern Shield and Hudson Bay Lowlands, overall distribution has remained nearly the same, with the species being found in virtually every 100-km block, except for a few in the most northerly areas close to the Hudson Bay coast. The Hudson Bay Lowlands has shown no significant changes, but this is an area where the species is relatively thinly distributed along the major rivers in Balsam Poplar and poplar-alder stands. The probability of observation increased significantly by 15% in the Northern Shield region and by 2% in the Southern Shield. BBS data show a small but significant increase in numbers in Canada and in Ontario since 1968 (Downes et al. 2005). Reasons for the increase are unclear. It is possible that in the north the opening of extensive areas of coniferous forest through logging activity may have encouraged the growth of more aspen and birch, to the benefit of this species.

Breeding biology: The Red-eyed Vireo is easily located and identified, as it is a loud, persistent singer. Confirmation of

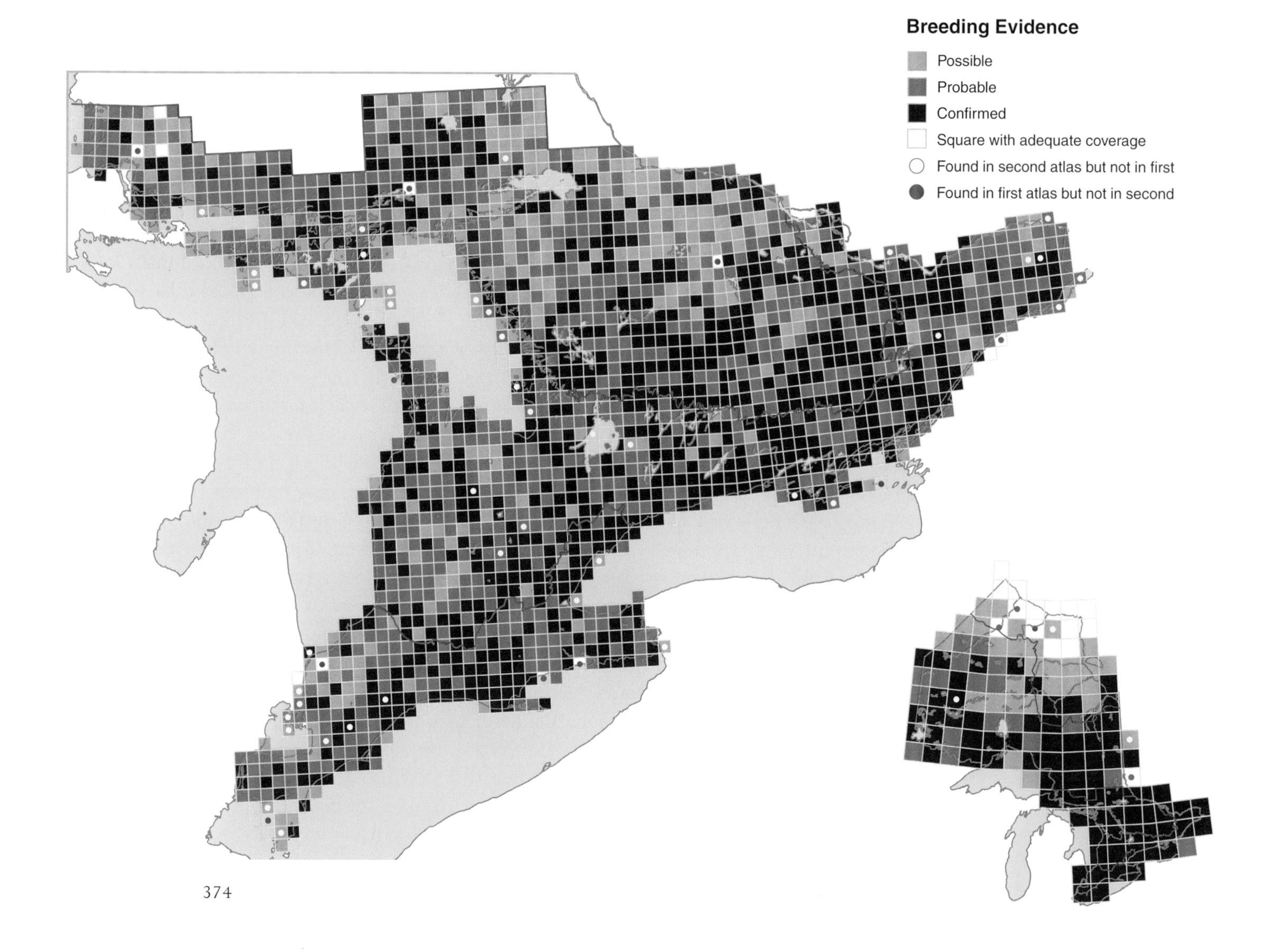

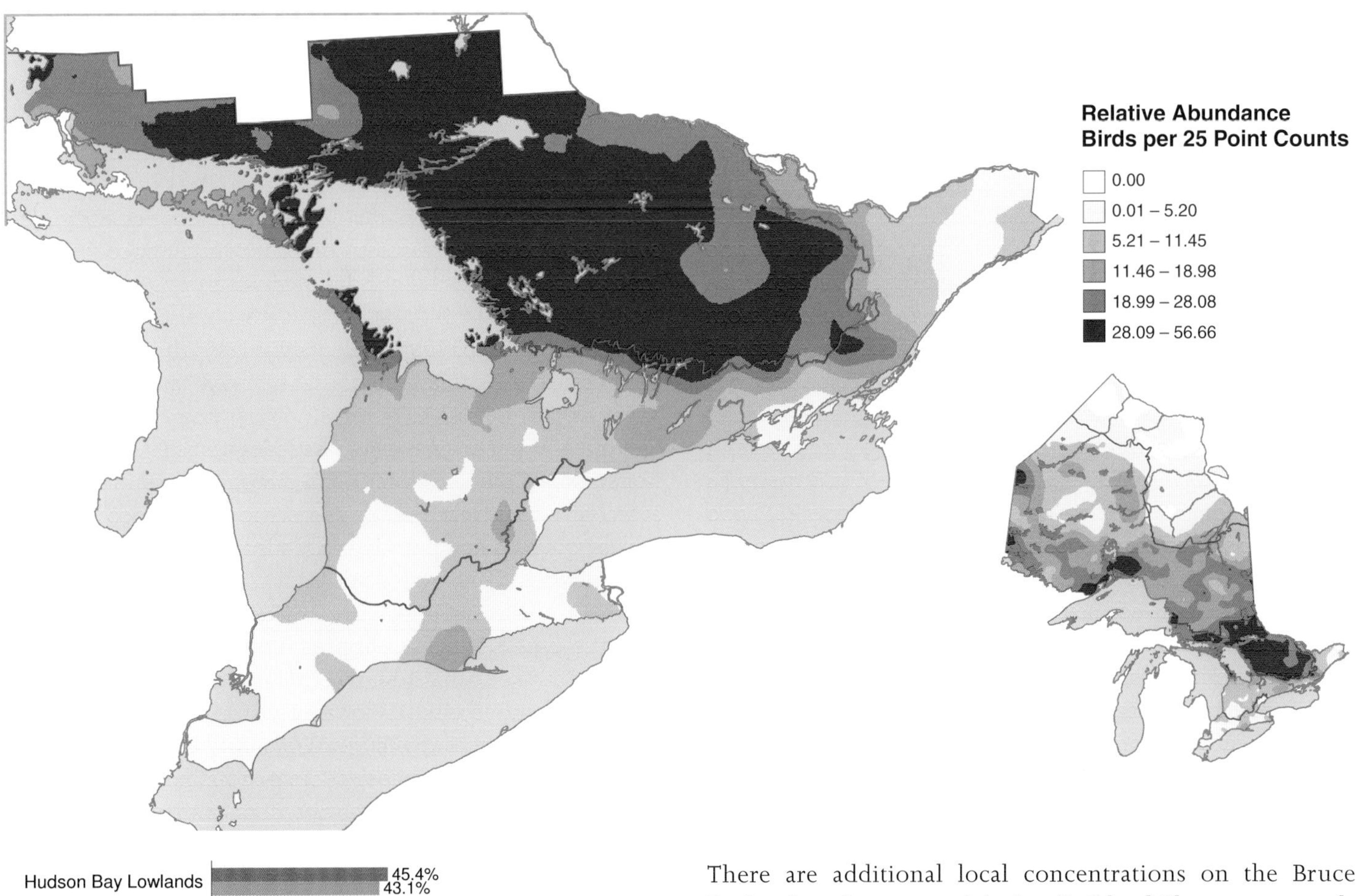

Region	1st Atlas	2nd Atlas
Hudson Bay Lowlands	43.1%	45.4%
Northern Shield	80.7%	92.7%*
Southern Shield	97.1%	98.9%*
Lake Simcoe-Rideau	91.9%	93.1%
Carolinian	88.5%	87.4%
Ontario	72.9%	80.5%*

0% 20% 40% 60% 80% 100%

Probability of Observation

1st Atlas 2nd Atlas

breeding is more difficult. The male does not assist in nest building or incubation. Nests typically are placed fairly low, but the female tends to sit very still, even on close approach, and will slip quietly from the nest to avoid revealing its location. Confirmation is easier during the nestling and post-fledging periods, when both parents can be seen carrying food. Nests persist through the winter and can be used to confirm breeding. For all these reasons, the range map gives a very good indication of the breeding distribution of this species. The few probable and confirmed records in the north are more an indication of lack of time for searching or repeat visits than an absence of breeding.

Abundance: The abundance maps indicate that the most extensive area of high concentration of the Red-eyed Vireo extends across most of the Southern Shield region, and that abundance generally declines with latitude north of this region. To the east and southwest of the Precambrian Shield, numbers drop off, as would be expected, as the land becomes more extensively cleared for agriculture and urbanization. There are additional local concentrations on the Bruce Peninsula and on eastern Manitoulin Island. These areas are relatively densely forested with deciduous and mixed forest, a good match for the habitat preferences of the species. In the Southern Shield region, there was an average of about 35 birds/25 point counts.

Across the Northern Shield, the abundance map indicates a mosaic of density. In general, the areas of highest abundance are in areas of deciduous and mixed forests in the southern part of the region, with numbers diminishing northward. There was an average of 18.1 birds/25 point counts across the Northern Shield region. The species is scarce or absent in the northern part of the Hudson Bay Lowlands, with an average of only 1.6 birds/25 point counts across the region as a whole. As a highly vocal species, this vireo is easily detected, and with more even and extensive coverage, the pattern of abundance across the north probably would be more uniform.

Based on atlas point count data, the Red-eyed Vireo population is estimated at 9,000,000 birds, making it among the commonest birds in the province. Although the Boreal Forest is the core of the range for most species having the highest populations in the province, the highest densities of the Red-eyed Vireo occur in the Great Lakes-St. Lawrence Forest. – *Ross James*

Gray Jay

Mésangeai du Canada

Perisoreus canadensis

Dan Strickland

The Gray Jay stands out among Ontario's avifauna: its inquisitive behaviour, attractive appearance, and widespread distribution in the Boreal Forest combine to make it one of the best known and most endearing of northern birds. Moreover, the species is biologically unique in relying on stored food to live on permanent territories despite apparently foodless boreal winter conditions, and in breeding in late winter, with young fledging before most boreal migrants have even returned. It also has an unusual juvenile dispersal system in which one brood member forces its siblings to leave the natal territory in June, thereby consigning them to a much greater first-summer mortality rate (Strickland 1991). As well, the Gray Jay is one of only two bird species in Ontario that regularly breeds cooperatively (the other being the American Crow) – but with the further unusual feature that breeders prevent non-breeders from feeding nestlings, although allowing them to feed fledglings (Waite and Strickland 1997; Strickland and Waite 2001). The species' range comprises the boreal and subalpine forests of North America from Newfoundland to Alaska and from the treeline south to the limits of significant spruce stands: northern California in the Coast ranges, New Mexico and Arizona in the Rocky Mountains, and northern New England in the east (Strickland and Ouellet 1993).

Distribution and population status: In Ontario, the southern limits of the Gray Jay's range are largely contained within the Southern Shield, although the species does occur sparingly within the Lake Simcoe-Rideau region on the south shore of Manitoulin Island, in the Kawartha Lakes area, and in large, off-Shield peatlands in eastern Ontario (Alfred Bog and Mer Bleue), where nesting has been attempted or suspected. Although there were a number of new records of Gray Jay in the Southern Shield during the second atlas, the probability of observation did not change significantly in that region. This finding contradicts a 30-

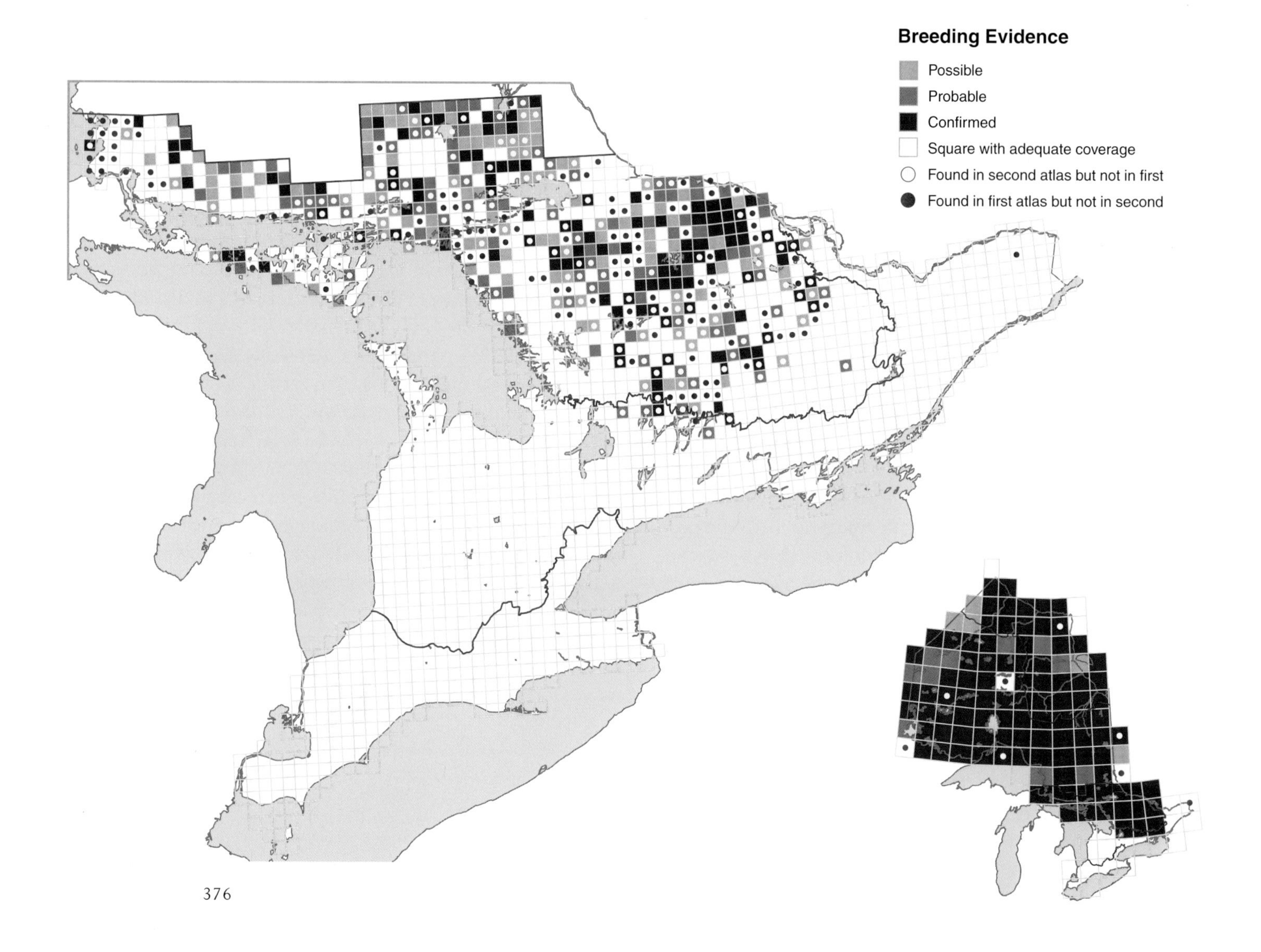

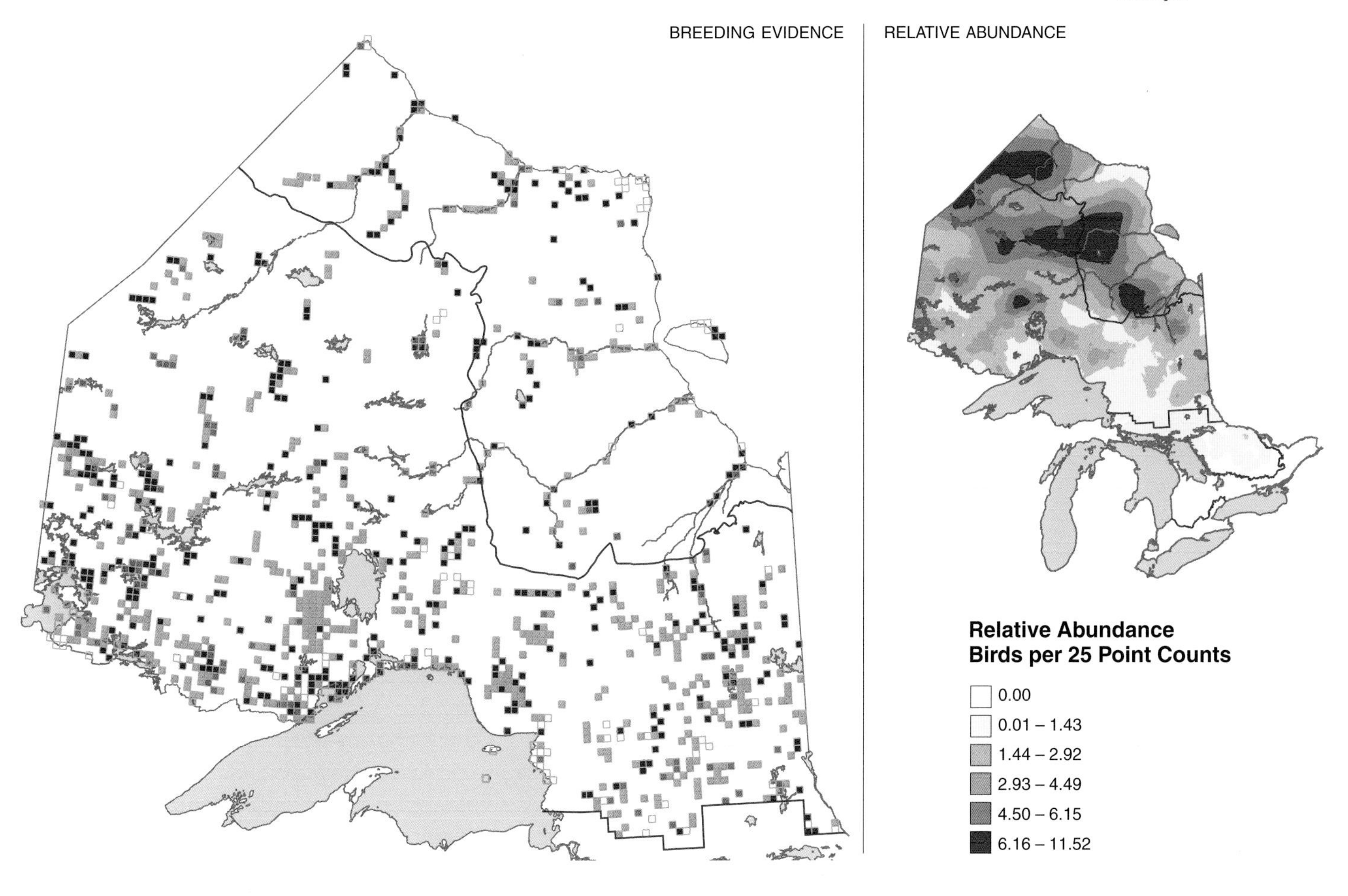

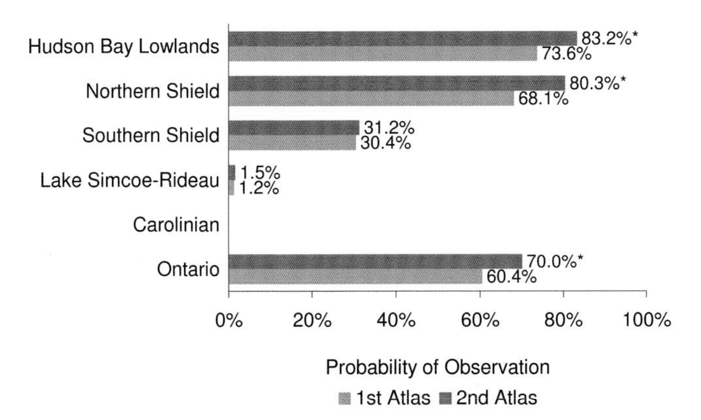

year study of a colour-banded population in Algonquin Prov. Park, which indicates a decrease in occupied territories of over 60% and suggests that a decline is underway in the southern part of the range. The Algonquin losses have been plausibly linked to an erosion of reproductive success best predicted by warm weather in the previous fall (Waite and Strickland 2006). The Gray Jay, dependent for winter survival and nesting on supplies of seemingly perishable stored food, may thus be suffering from the effects of climate warming, at least near the southern edge of its range. If so, one would eventually expect to observe a northward shift of the southern limit of the species. That the atlas did not detect the Algonquin Park decline may result from the fact that breeding evidence data collected on a 10-km square basis are less sensitive for detecting population changes than are local surveys of abundance.

Breeding biology: Except for nest-building in February and early March, breeding activity is extremely inconspicuous in the Gray Jay. Females sit tightly throughout the egg-laying and incubation periods and may be fed by their mates as infrequently as once a day. Even in the nestling period, visitation rates seldom exceed once an hour. This strategy of maximizing food loads and consequently minimizing nest visits is believed to help conceal the nest from Red Squirrels, but it also adds to atlassers' difficulties in detecting nests. Fledged young, being immune to squirrel attacks, are fed more often by their parents, and any non-breeder on the territory may be allowed to participate (Strickland and Waite 2001). Even these behaviours occur well before most atlassing activity, however, and the timing of Gray Jay breeding and the tendency of even habituated birds to ignore humans in the warmer months led most Regional Coordinators in the Southern Shield region to suspect that both presence and breeding confirmation were underestimated in this atlas.

Abundance: The second atlas suggests that the Gray Jay is more abundant near the centre of its continental range (i.e., in spruce-dominated northern Ontario) than near its southern limit on the much less coniferous Southern Shield. Between atlases, the probability of observation of the Gray Jay increased significantly by 16% in the province as a whole, and by 18% and 13% in the Northern Shield and Hudson Bay Lowlands regions, respectively. The increases in the north are again somewhat contrary to expectation because the density of this sedentary, long-lived, food-storing species is believed to vary very little (Strickland and Ouellet 1993). Increased efficiency of northern observers during the second atlas may have contributed to this result. – *Dan Strickland*

Blue Jay

Geai bleu

Cyanocitta cristata

Bill Rayner

The combination of unmistakable bright blue plumage, easily recognizable voice, raucous behaviour, and adaptation to most human-altered landscapes makes the Blue Jay one of Ontario's most conspicuous and well-known birds. It breeds exclusively in North America, where it is a permanent resident east of the Rocky Mountains, across the southern portion of the Boreal Forest from British Columbia to Newfoundland, and south to the Gulf of Mexico from Texas to southern Florida.

The Blue Jay breeds primarily in forests, where it is associated more with edges than forest interior. It also frequents river valleys, regenerating scrub habitats, and orchards, and favours both rural and residential areas, especially those with ornamental conifers and mature oaks, maples, and other mast-producing trees (Tarvin and Woolfenden 1999).

Distribution and population status: The status of the Blue Jay in the Ontario portion of its range has remained relatively constant. McIlwraith (1894) considered it to be a common resident species throughout Ontario, while recognizing that part of the population was migratory. Baillie and Harrington (1937) described it as common in southern Ontario north to central Sudbury Dist. and Thunder Bay, and much less common north to southern Kenora Dist. and the Missinaibi River in Cochrane Dist. Speirs (1985) considered it to be common in the deciduous and mixed forest areas of southern Ontario and Rainy River Dist., uncommon in the southern Boreal Forest, and rare north of 50° N.

This distribution was confirmed in the first atlas. The Blue Jay was confirmed throughout southern Ontario and also throughout the southern portion of the Boreal Forest of northern Ontario, where its abundance declined, to a well-defined northern limit extending from about Sioux Lookout to Fraserdale. Breeding was confirmed in northwestern Ontario as far north as the Red Lake area, and evi-

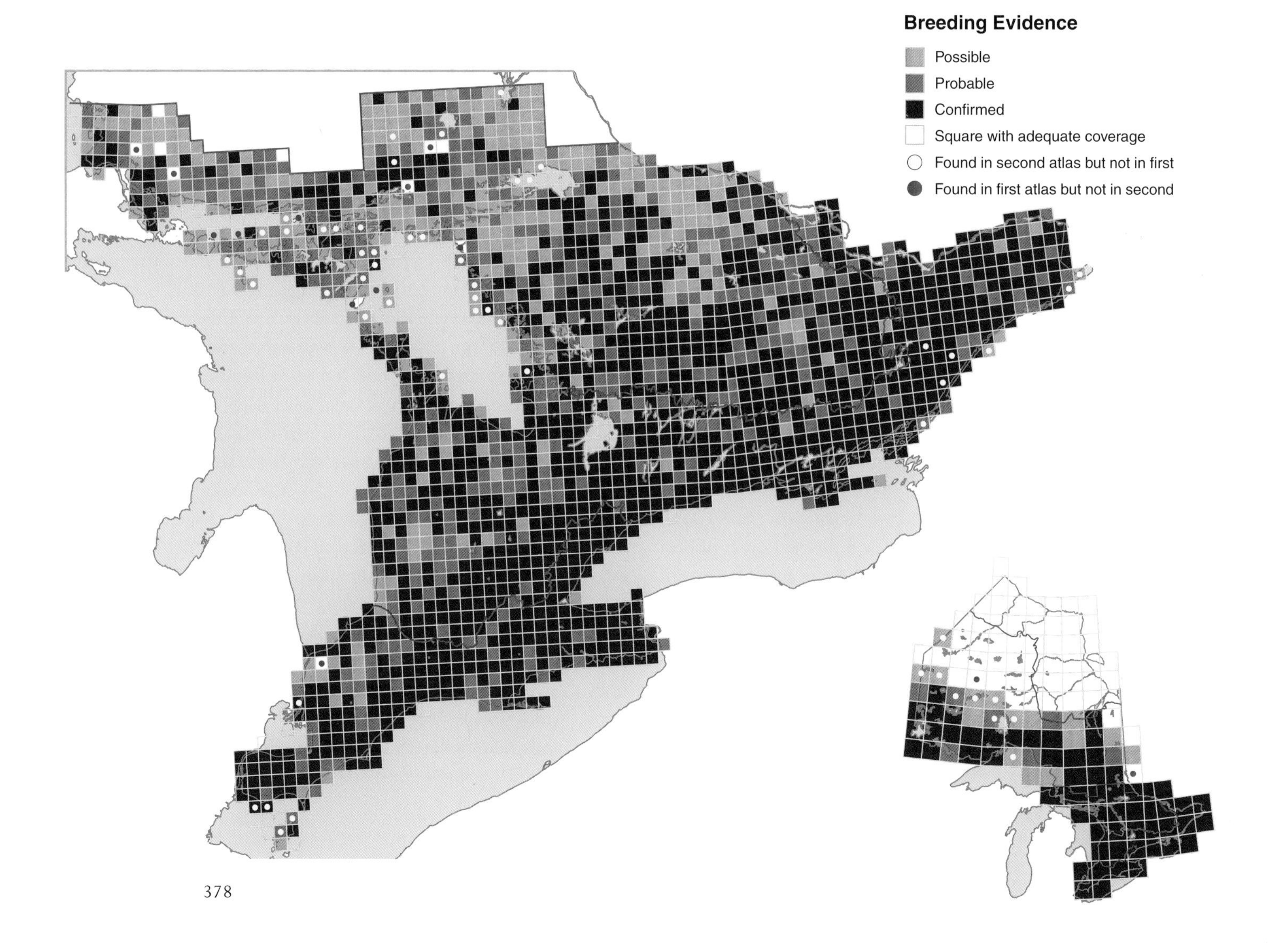

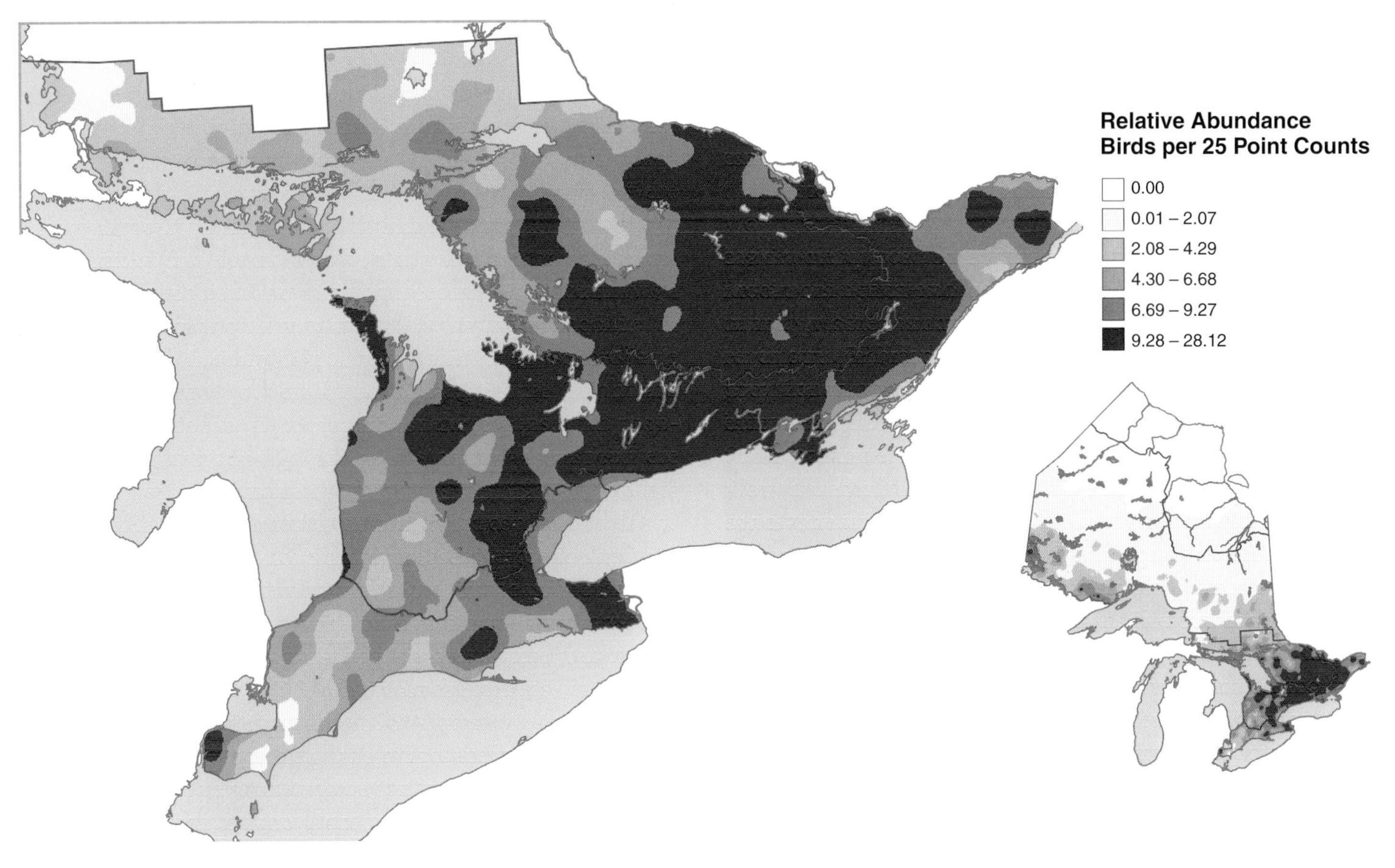

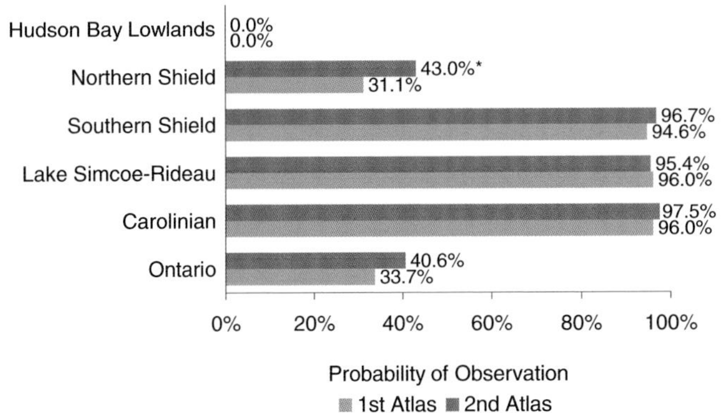

dence of possible breeding was found about 90 km west of Pickle Lake.

In the second atlas, the map of breeding evidence shows a remarkably similar pattern to that in the first atlas. The Blue Jay is a common breeding bird, with confirmed or probable breeding evidence found in most squares in the Carolinian, Lake Simcoe-Rideau, and Southern Shield regions, with probabilities of observation of 98%, 95%, and 97%, respectively. Breeding likely takes place in all squares in these regions. It is less common and less likely to be confirmed as a breeder in the southern portion of the Northern Shield region, although there was a significant increase (38%) in the probability of observation in that region compared with the first atlas, and records from new 100-km blocks suggest a small northward extension of the range. The reason for the increase and possible range expansion is unknown. It is nearly absent from the Hudson Bay Lowlands and the northwestern portion of the Northern Shield regions, although it was recorded as a possible breeder north of Sandy Lake in Opasquia Prov. Park.

Ontario BBS data for the period 1968-2005 show the Blue Jay population to be stable, with a non-significant annual increase of 0.3% during that period (Downes et al. 2005).

Breeding biology: The boisterous Blue Jay of most of the year often becomes stealthy and silent as the start of its breeding season approaches in April. A monogamous and a solitary nester, it defends only a small area around the nest, so inter-pair aggression is limited to this small area. Its large vocal repertoire, including mimicry, makes it difficult to associate vocalization with breeding activity, since it does not sing in defence of a territory. It does exhibit courtship feeding, and males routinely feed incubating females (Tarvin and Woolfenden 1999). Fledged young are raucous, providing the easiest method of confirmation along with adults carrying food, both activities occurring during peak atlassing periods. In areas where abundance is low, repeated visits may be needed to achieve breeding confirmation. The breeding evidence map likely is an accurate reflection of distribution but underestimates confirmed breeding in the north.

Abundance: The abundance map shows the Blue Jay to be most abundant in southern Ontario, primarily in the more heavily deciduous and mixed forest areas of the Lake Simcoe-Rideau and Southern Shield regions. High abundance is maintained in older urban and suburban areas such as Toronto, Hamilton, Kingston, and Ottawa. The large orchard areas in Grey Co. and Niagara Region show high abundance, but the intensive agricultural areas in the southwestern part of the Carolinian region, with greatly diminished forest cover, have lower abundance. In the Northern Shield region, abundance is considerably lower, especially in areas where coniferous forest dominates. – *Glenn Coady*

Black-billed Magpie

Pie d'Amérique

Pica hudsonia

Roger Wray

The Black-billed Magpie is a conspicuous and vocal corvid with bold black and white plumage and a long tail that make it unmistakable. Long associated with humans, it is known to have lived off the refuse of native bison hunting (Houston 1977); two centuries ago explorers Lewis and Clark described its bold opportunism in entering tents to steal meat (Ryser 1985).

Until recently, the Black-billed Magpie and Eurasian Magpie (*Pica pica*) were considered to be conspecific. Following studies that indicated distinct morphological, behavioural, and genetic differences (Birkhead 1991; Enggist-Dublin and Birkhead 1992; Zink et. al. 1995), the American Ornithologists' Union (2000) recognized the Black-billed Magpie of North America as a distinct species.

This magpie is a resident of open country with scattered trees, riparian corridors, open woodland, forest edge, farmland, and suburban clearings. It occurs from southern Alaska, southern Yukon, eastern British Columbia, Alberta, central Saskatchewan and Manitoba, extreme western Ontario, and northwestern Minnesota south to eastern California, Nevada, Utah, northern Arizona and New Mexico, western Kansas, and Nebraska (Trost 1999).

Distribution and population status: Remarkably, the first record of the Black-billed Magpie in Ontario involved one collected in 1771 at Fort Albany, near the James Bay coast, well east of its breeding range (Forster 1772). Speirs (1985) detailed a long list of occurrences from all seasons across much of Ontario dating back to the late 1800s. Birds are often kept in captivity, and instances of probable escapes in southern Ontario are well documented. However, the species' post-breeding and winter movements are extensive (Speirs 1985), and it is possible that some southern Ontario records may involve genuine vagrants, although this remains unproven. A large irruption involving at least 40 reports was

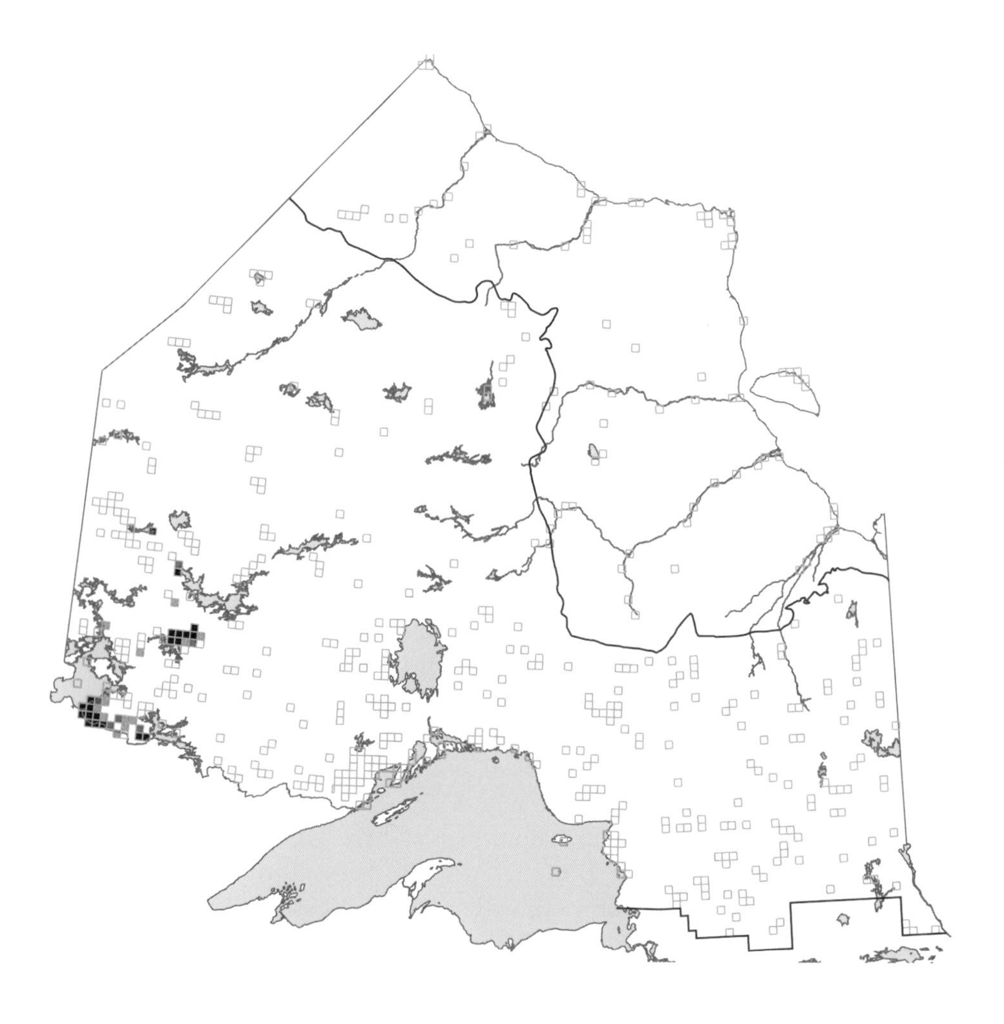

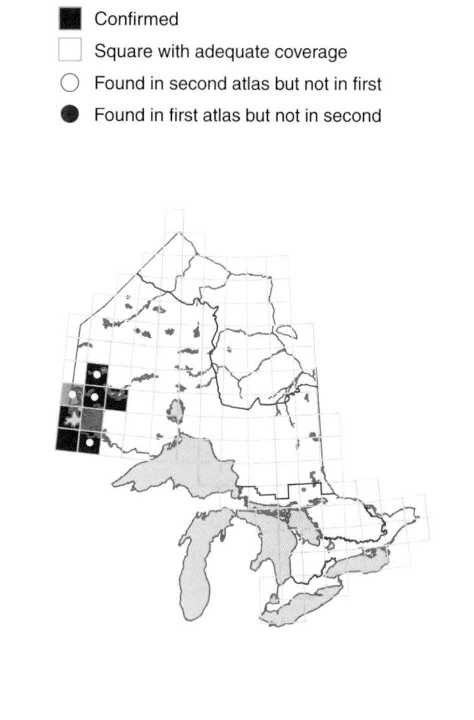

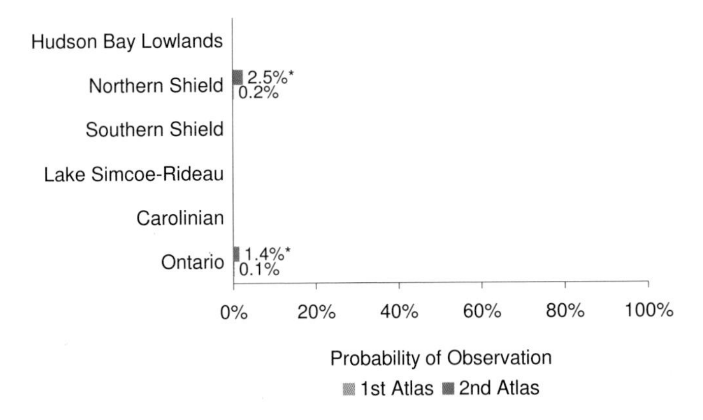

noted in north-central Ontario from Sioux Lookout and Nakina south to Atikokan and Terrace Bay in 1972 (Speirs 1985). In northwestern Ontario, the Black-billed Magpie is a relatively recent arrival in the areas in which it now breeds (Elder 2006). It was first noted in Kenora in 1947, Thunder Bay in 1958, Atikokan in 1959, Rainy River in 1975, Pickle Lake in 1977, and Dryden in 1983 (Speirs 1985). Nesting in Ontario was first confirmed when four nests were found near Rainy River in 1980 (Lamey 1981).

The Black-billed Magpie is intolerant of heat and humidity (Bock and Lepthien 1975; Hayworth and Weathers 1984), and the direct physiological consequences of climate may limit its potential range in the province to northwestern Ontario (Pittaway 1997). It will be interesting to monitor future range changes as temperature and humidity patterns change.

During the first atlas, breeding evidence was found in six squares in four 100-km blocks in the Northern Shield region (four in the Rainy River area, one near Kenora, and one in Dryden). In the second atlas, breeding evidence was found in 39 squares in eight 100-km blocks (23 in the Rainy River-Fort Frances area, 10 in the Dryden-Vermillion Bay area, two in the Kenora area, and four in the Ear Falls, Perrault Falls, and Red Lake areas of Hwy. 105). Breeding was confirmed in 20 squares during this atlas, compared to only one square in the first atlas. Canadian BBS data for the period 1968-2005 show a significant 1.6% annual increase (Downes et al. 2005), which may be providing a source of birds for the range and population expansion in northwestern Ontario.

Breeding biology: The Black-billed Magpie is easily detected on its breeding territory. It is very noisy and tends to nest in association with human settlement. It constructs bulky domed nests over a six-week period. Incubation is completed exclusively by the female, and she calls loudly for food from the male while on the nest. Young also call raucously for food. They stay near the nest for three to four weeks after hatching and remain dependent on adults for food for about eight weeks. During that period, they tend to remain close to the nest site. All these factors make confirmation of breeding relatively easy. The map of breeding evidence thus provides an accurate assessment of breeding distribution.

Abundance: Detections of the species on point counts were not sufficient to map relative abundance. However, breeding evidence was obtained in 39 squares, and birds were reported from 58 discrete point count locations. As many as 50-75 birds have been seen at single communal roosts in the Rainy River area. Since the first atlas, it appears that the Ontario population has experienced a ten-fold increase, with an estimated 200-250 breeding pairs now present. – *Glenn Coady*

Black-billed Magpie nest in a small willow. Note the characteristic "barrel" shape and side entrance. *Photo: Dave Elder*

Typical Black-billed Magpie habitat in the Rainy River area comprising farm fields and scattered stands of Trembling Aspen with a willow understorey. *Photo: Dave Elder*

American Crow

Corneille d'Amérique

Corvus brachyrhynchos

Ron Ridout

Almost everyone in Ontario is familiar with the American Crow and its distinctive calls. Although it is found over much of the province, it is most abundant in settled landscapes. Its breeding distribution is extensive in North America south of 60° N and east of the Rocky Mountains, extending north to the vicinity of Great Slave Lake in the Northwest Territories and east through central Québec to southern Labrador (Verbeek and Caffrey 2002). Many individual crows are non-breeding auxiliaries associated with territorial pairs, and this probably leads to overestimation of the number of breeders.

Distribution and population status: The American Crow breeds almost throughout Ontario, from Fort Severn to Pelee Island. While it has been found in nearly every square in southern Ontario, its frequency of occurrence diminishes farther north, especially in the Northern Shield and Hudson Bay Lowlands regions. Between atlases, the probability of observation increased significantly in the province as a whole by 28%. This overall increase is based largely on a significant increase of 46% in the Northern Shield and a non-significant 30% increase in the Hudson Bay Lowlands, indicating an expansion in the northern part of the species' Ontario range.

The American Crow has a history of range expansion in the province. McIlwraith (1894) noted that it preferred cultivated areas and increased in numbers as the province became settled. Baillie and Harrington (1937) concluded that it was one of the most common and widespread breeding species in Ontario. BBS data also show a significant increase in Ontario since 1981, but show a small but non-significant decline nationwide.

Breeding biology: The American Crow nests early, with eggs being laid as early as March but more typically near the end of April in southern Ontario. Nesting may occur in almost every habitat in the province except treeless tundra. Nests typically are in trees, with about 54% of Ontario nests in conifers (Peck and James 1987). Nests in deciduous trees are easy to

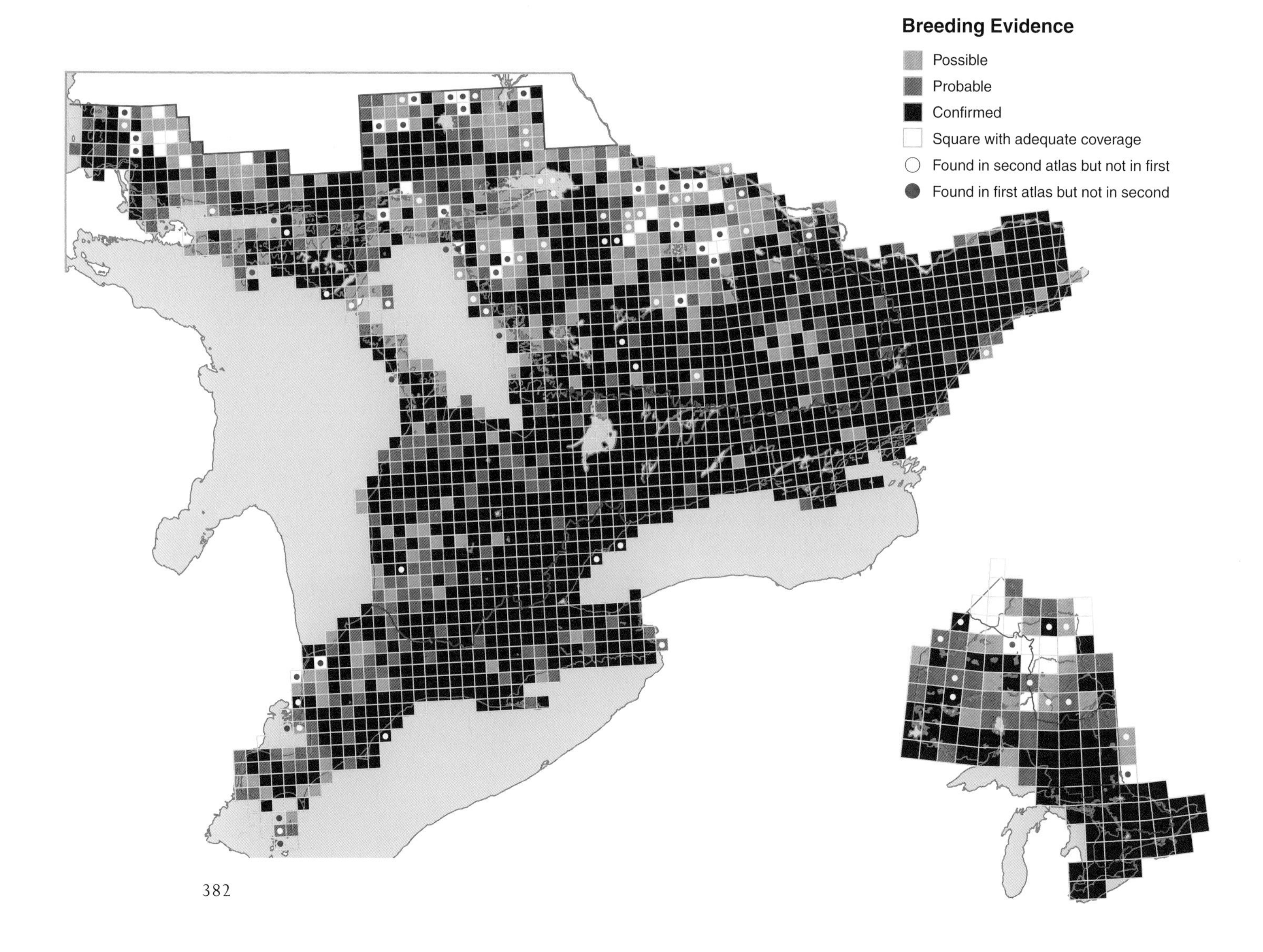

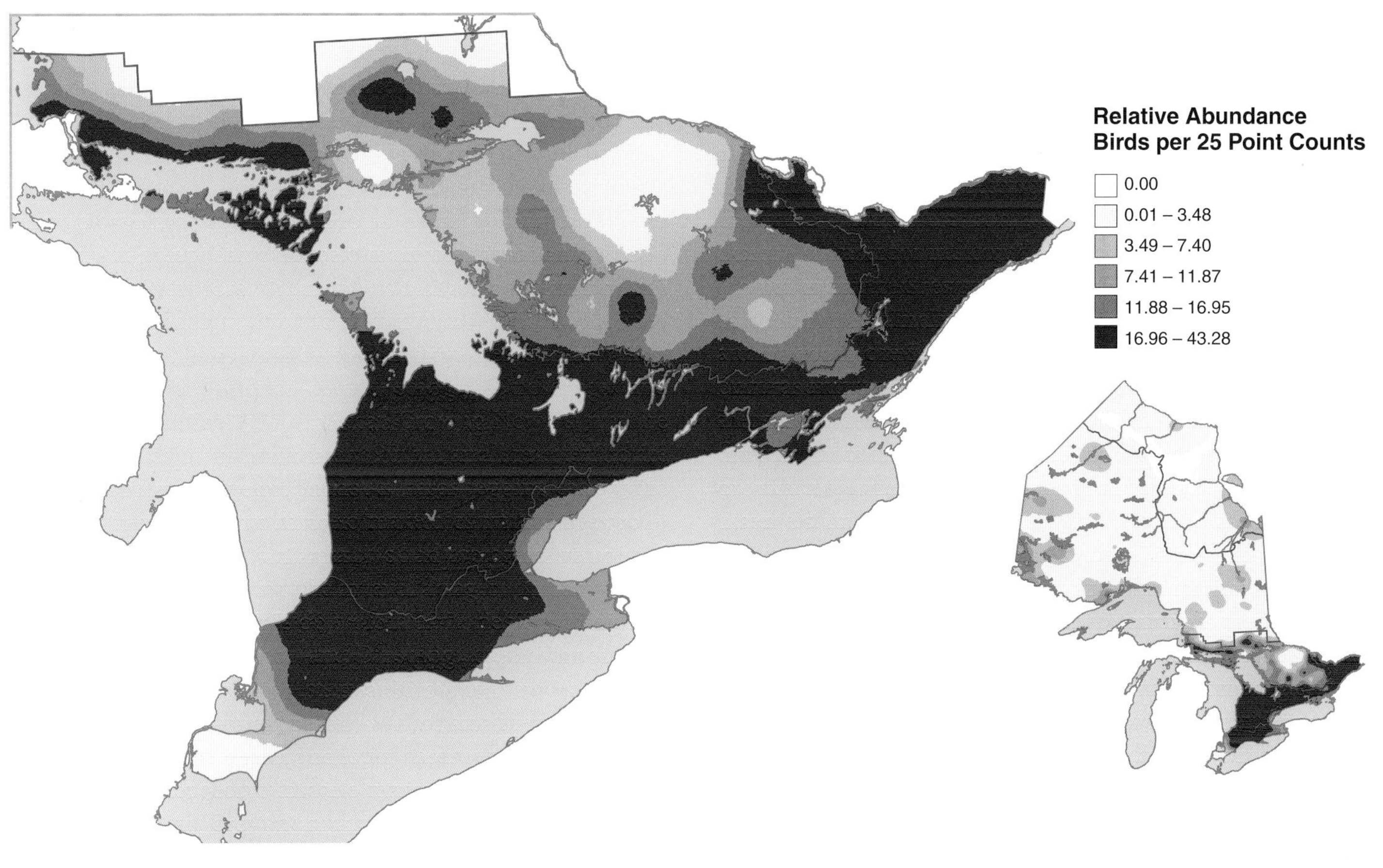

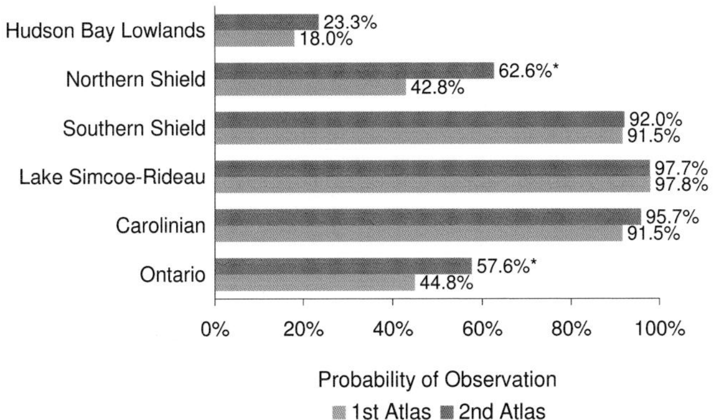

find before leaves develop. The loud, nasal begging calls of the nestlings and fledged young also make confirmation easy.

The American Crow normally does not breed before the age of two, and 25% may delay even longer (Kilham 1989; Caffrey 1992). Pairs of crows often have helpers that assist with territorial defence and feeding of nestlings and fledglings. Groups of the American Crow in New Hampshire had territories of approximately 90 ha, and these territories may be defended year round. As birds within the group mature, they may form discrete territories within the group territory. In New York, urban crows had average territories of 8.7 ha compared with 37.7 ha in rural areas, but in more open habitat in Manitoba, birds defended territories averaging 260 ha (Kilham 1989; Sullivan and Dinsmore 1992; Verbeek and Caffrey 2002). This suggests that, although crows may be abundant in a given area, perhaps only a small proportion are territory-holding breeding pairs.

The American Crow forages in open habitats and usually does not feed in forested areas. It is an opportunistic omnivore, feeding on whatever is most abundant. It is mostly vegetarian, eating primarily cultivated grains but also fruits. It eats all types of animal matter, and carrion may form a significant portion of the diet. The intensification of agriculture and higher traffic volumes that result in roadkills undoubtedly have benefited the crow and contributed to its increase.

Abundance: As expected, the abundance map indicates that the American Crow is most abundant in the Carolinian and Lake Simcoe-Rideau regions. It flourishes in these agricultural and urban landscapes where there is plenty of food. Densities are lower in the extreme southwest, probably due to the scarcity of trees for nesting, along with the territoriality of the species. Even the GTA has a higher density of crows than Essex Co. In the north, nodes of higher abundance occur around urban centres such as Kenora-Dryden, Thunder Bay, Sault Ste. Marie, Timmins, and Sudbury, and in the agricultural and more open areas of Rainy River and the Clay Belt. Records of crows in the north tend to be concentrated along the major highways, though they were absent from adjacent forested areas that also received atlassing coverage. Highways provide a source of carrion as well as openings in the forest that are suitable for nesting.

The American Crow continues to be an abundant breeder south and east of the Precambrian Shield, uncommon to locally common in the Southern Shield region, and scarce and local farther north to Hudson Bay. – *Al Sandilands*

Common Raven

Grand Corbeau

Corvus corax

Theodore Smith

The Common Raven, a widespread holarctic species, is the largest North American passerine and, arguably, the world's most intelligent bird. It is a permanent resident (although non-breeders wander widely) in habitats as diverse as desert, tundra, alpine peaks, sea coasts, prairies, tropical and temperate forests, and even busy urban areas (Boarman and Heinrich 1999). Except for the southern portions of the Prairie Provinces, and, until recently, most of southern Ontario south of the Precambrian Shield, it breeds throughout Canada as far north as the high arctic islands (Godfrey 1986).

Distribution and population status: Early reports of the Common Raven suggested that it was more common in southern Ontario prior to extensive land clearing (Wilson 1814; Saunders and Dale 1933). Later, because of habitat destruction, human persecution, and the use of poison baits and trapping to reduce wolf populations, ravens became rare in the southern and settled parts of the province until well into the 20th century, when a recovery became apparent (Blomme in Cadman et al. 1987). Since the first atlas, the raven has continued its dramatic southward range expansion into southeastern and south-central Ontario. This breeding range expansion may be due at least in part to development and urbanization, with its resultant increase in roads and roadkills, landfill garbage, and nest-site availability on buildings, towers, and other human structures (Peck 2005). During the second atlas, breeding was confirmed in 36 atlas administrative regions representing most of Ontario's counties, districts, and regional municipalities, with the exception of some counties lying south of the Precambrian Shield in extreme southwestern Ontario.

Between atlases, there was no significant change in the probability of observation of the raven in the province as a whole, or in the heart of its Ontario range, the Northern Shield

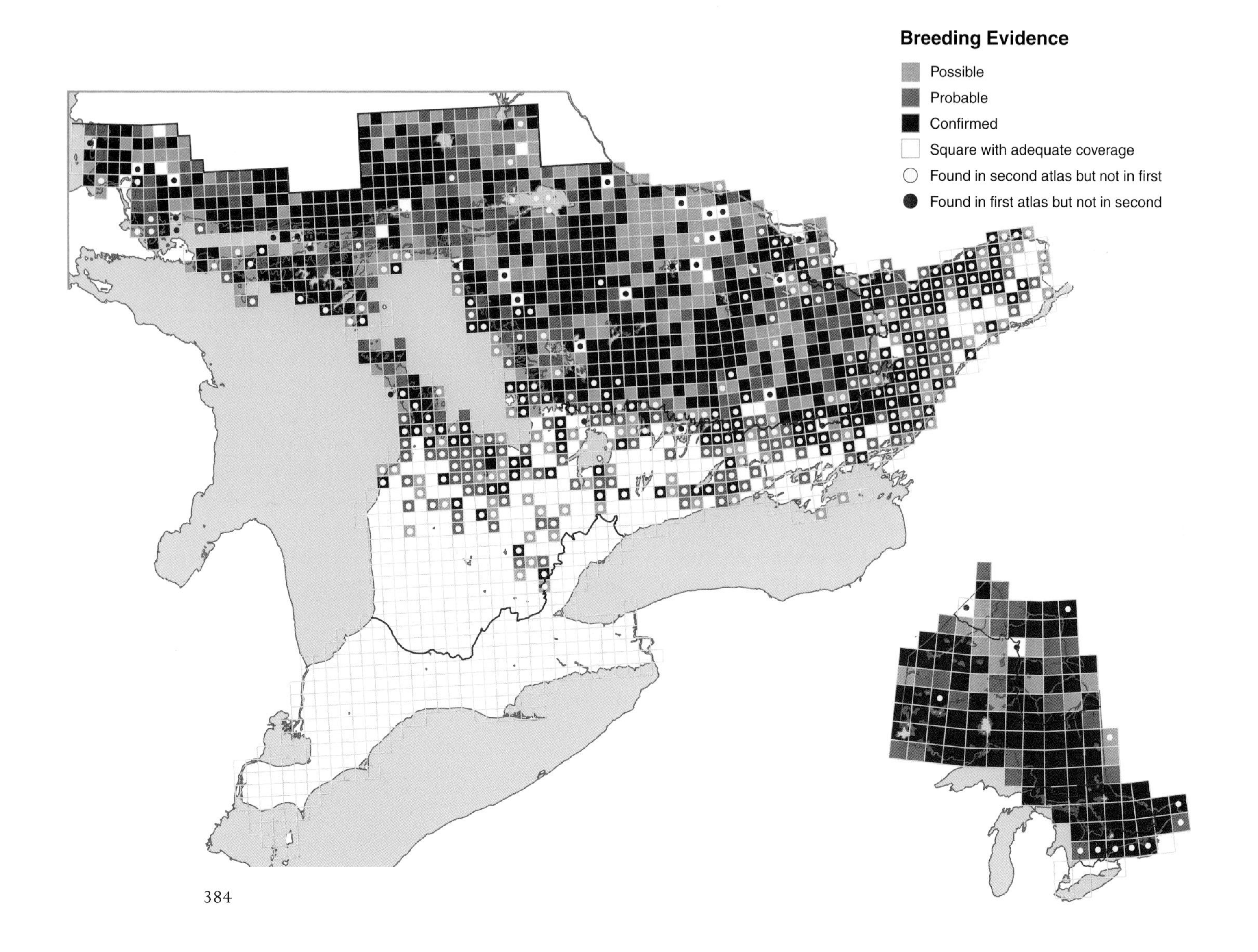

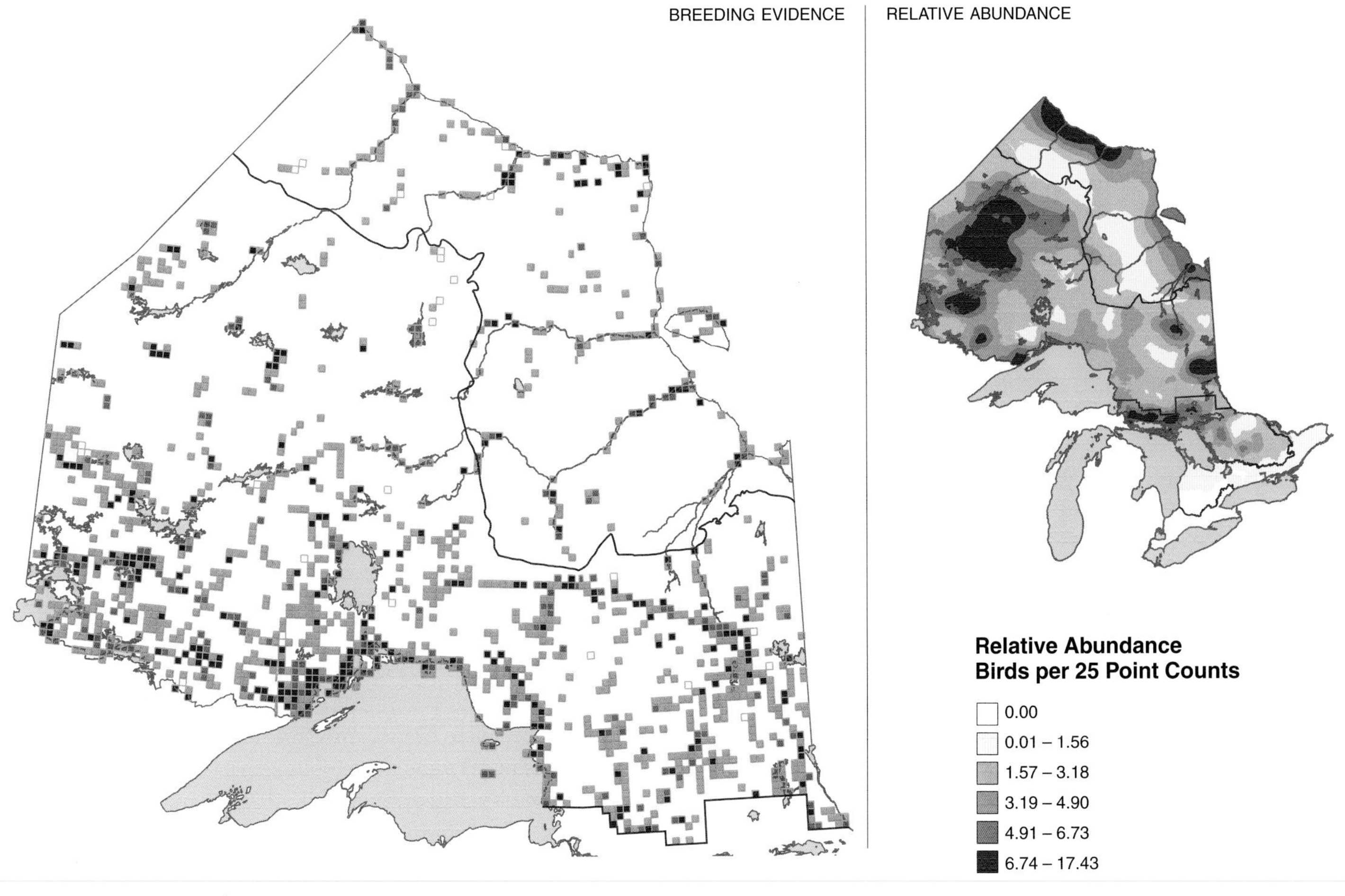

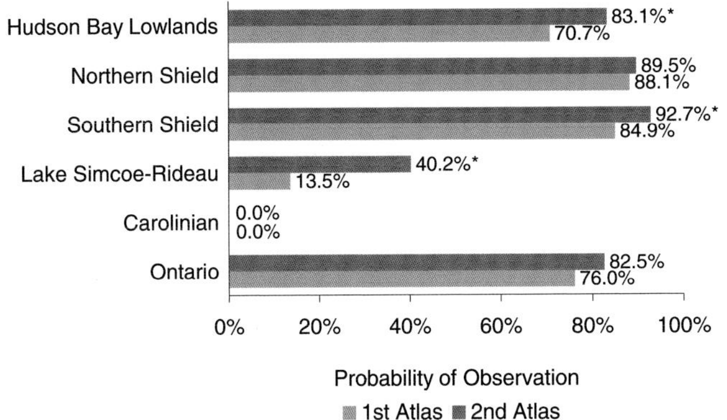

region. However, there were significant increases in three regions. The greatest increase, approximately threefold, occurred in the Lake Simcoe-Rideau region, followed by the Hudson Bay Lowlands (18%) and the Southern Shield (9%).

Areas in northern Ontario without breeding evidence almost certainly indicate lack of coverage rather than a real lack of breeding activity.

Breeding biology: The Common Raven breeds in a wide variety of habitats, including ledges and crevices of natural cliffs, as well as on similar anthropogenic cliffs in quarries, open-pit mines, and railway and highway rock cuts. It also nests in trees in forested areas, in open and shrubby grassland and agricultural areas, in or on human structures in rural and urban areas, and in tundra (Peck and James 1987; Peck 2005). Of 432 nest records in the ONRS, 40% were on cliffs and rock faces, 38% were in trees, and 22% were on human structures. In the Lake Simcoe-Rideau region, the use of structures is considerably higher. The species' stick nests are large and often quite visible, and this, combined with the frequent loud vocalizations of the adults, makes nest-finding relatively easy.

The Common Raven is an early nesting species. Egg dates in Ontario range from 2 March to 16 May, with 50% (height of season) of laying from 20 March to 2 April (Peck 2005). Incubation periods range from 20 to 25 days, and the young fledge at four to seven weeks of age (Boarman and Heinrich 1999), making the nesting period quite protracted and raising the likelihood of confirming breeding.

Specific nest sites, if secure and undisturbed, are reused annually or sometimes intermittently for considerable periods. One nest in Algonquin Prov. Park had 21 years of use between 1970 and 1999 (R. Tozer, pers. comm.). In the ONRS database, of 102 nests with known outcomes, 78 nests (76%) successfully fledged young, an unusually high percentage when compared with other passerine species. However, ravens appear to be much more vulnerable to human persecution than are some other Corvidae (Goodwin 1976).

Abundance: As expected, the average number of birds/25 point counts decreased from north to south, with 4.7 birds in the Hudson Bay Lowlands, 4.0 in the Northern Shield, 3.8 in the Southern Shield, and 0.6 in the Lake Simcoe-Rideau region. The abundance maps reveal that the raven is more common along the western portion of the Hudson Bay coast and the southern portion of the James Bay coast than in inland areas of the Hudson Bay Lowlands, and that in Algonquin Park densities are lower north of the Hwy 60 corridor. These patterns suggest that ravens occur in higher numbers around pockets of development in otherwise undeveloped areas. – *George K. Peck*

Horned Lark

Alouette hausse-col

Eremophila alpestris

George K. Peck

Larks constitute an Old World family of which only the Horned Lark is native to the Americas. It is widely distributed in hot and cold deserts, prairies, and agricultural land in the Northern Hemisphere. In the Americas, its range extends from 75° N in the Canadian Arctic south to Mexico, with a disjunct population at 5° N in Colombia. As many as 40 subspecies have been distinguished, 21 of them occurring in North America (Cramp 1988; Beason 1995). Plumage colour and size vary geographically. The dorsal surface tends to match the colour of the local nesting substrate, and larger subspecies occur in colder climates.

Four subspecies occur in Ontario. The smallest, the Prairie Horned Lark (*E. a. praticola*), breeds in the south and in the Clay Belt. Records in Rainy River Dist. presumably refer to *E. a. enthymia*, which breeds in adjacent areas in Manitoba and Minnesota. The Northern Horned Lark (*E. a. alpestris*) breeds on Akimiski Island, along the coast of James Bay, and westward along the Hudson Bay coast. Between Winisk and Fort Severn, it is replaced by or intergrades with Hoyt's Horned Lark (*E. a. hoyti*; Snyder 1957).

Breeding habitat in Ontario includes pastures and arable land, sparsely vegetated fields, and raised beach ridges on tundra. It is absent from heavily forested regions, except for isolated breeding occurrences in large anthropogenic clearings such as airfields.

Distribution and population status: Prior to European settlement, the Horned Lark was probably absent from Ontario as a breeding bird, except along the Hudson Bay and James Bay coasts. Following clearing of forests, the Prairie Horned Lark spread into eastern North America from the west. It first appeared in southern Ontario about 1868 (McIlwraith 1894), probably from Michigan (Pickwell 1931; Pickwell 1942), and subsequently spread throughout southern and northeastern Ontario. Recently, its range has contracted in south-central

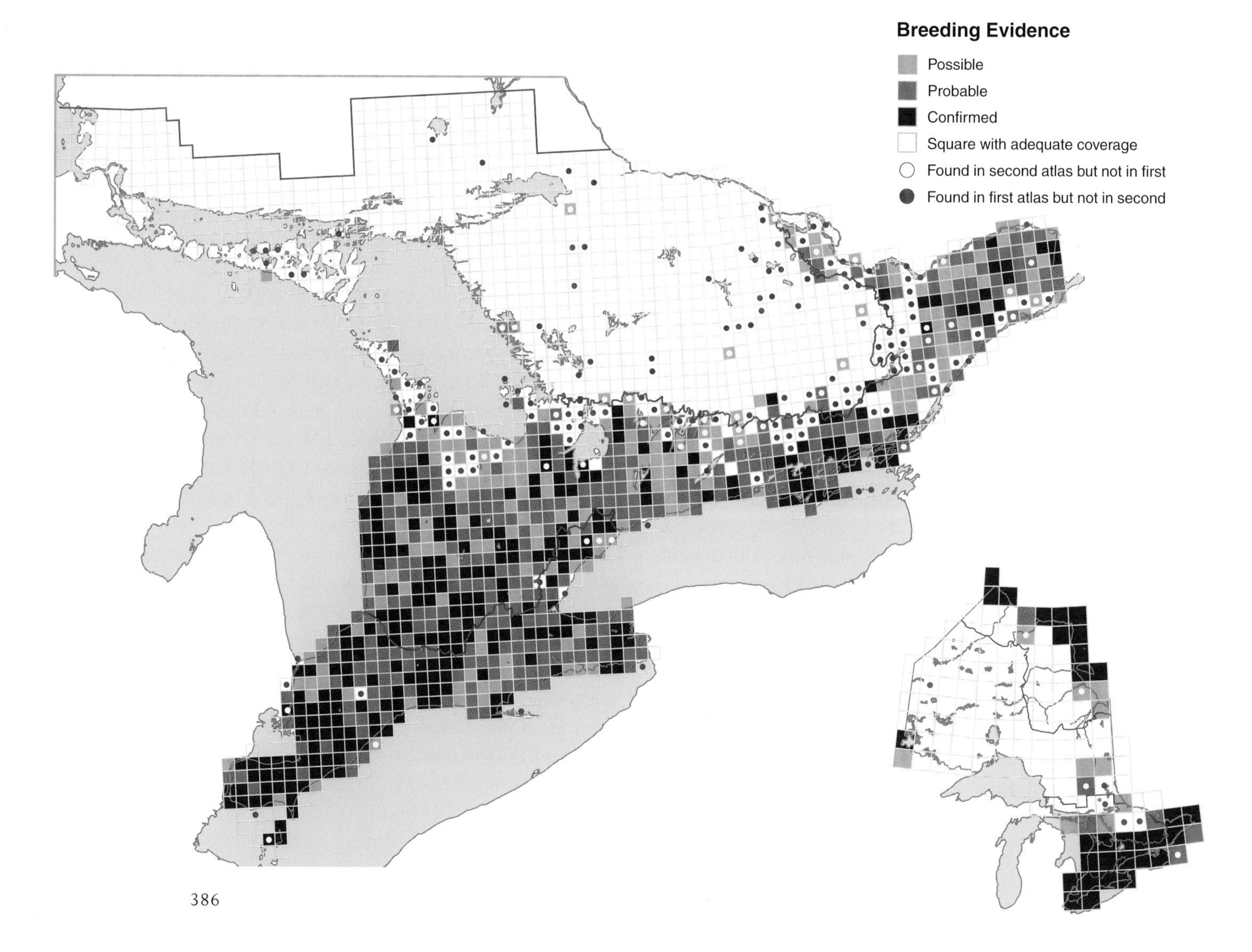

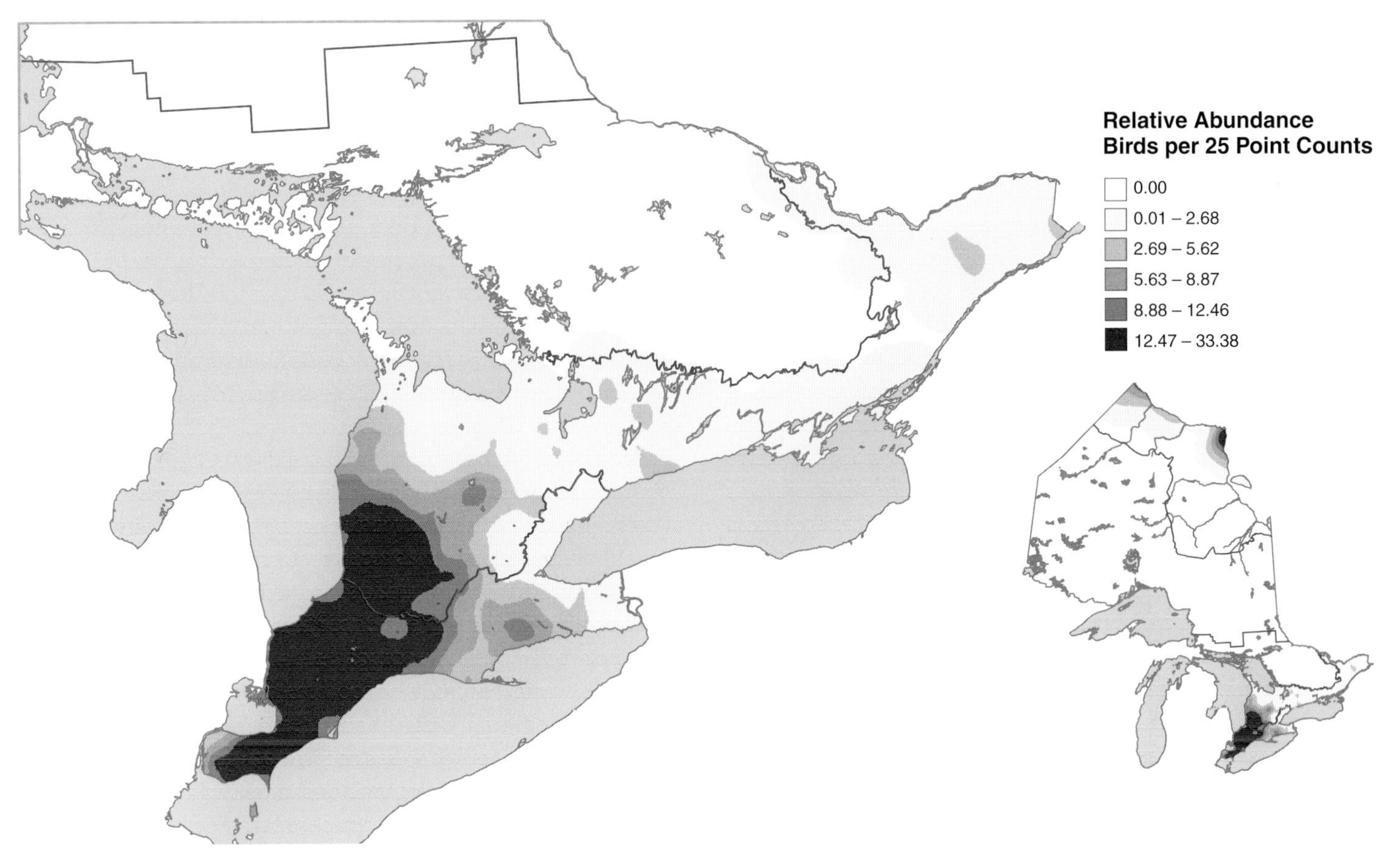

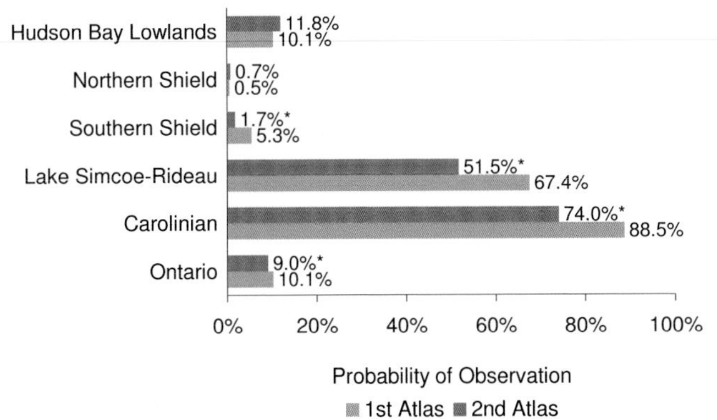

Ontario. Fleming (1901) described it as "an abundant breeding resident" in Muskoka and Parry Sound Districts, but now there are only a few scattered records for those areas.

Between atlases, the probability of observation of the Horned Lark declined significantly in the province as a whole and in the Carolinian, Lake Simcoe-Rideau, and Southern Shield regions. The greatest decline occurred in the Southern Shield region (68%). The Horned Lark is now almost completely absent from its former range on Manitoulin Island, much of the Bruce Peninsula, and the Southern Shield, and it has withdrawn from many squares along the southern margin of the Precambrian Shield and in southeastern Ontario. This is a continuation of a trend noted in the first atlas and is due primarily to the loss of suitable habitat related to reforestation of marginal farmland. Scattered occurrences in Rainy River Dist. and the Clay Belt of northeastern Ontario, and the distribution of subarctic nesting populations along the Hudson Bay and James Bay coasts, are unchanged from the first atlas.

Breeding biology: The Horned Lark is an early nester in the south, with eggs often reported in April. By mid-summer, it becomes inconspicuous and may be missed easily by a casual observer. The song, given from the ground or in flight, is distinctive and repeated often. The species is found frequently along roadsides, so it is unlikely to be missed in squares that were covered early. Subarctic nesters favour poorly vegetated, well-drained ridges and raised beaches, also favoured as travel routes by atlassers.

However, confirmation of breeding is difficult. Nests are situated on the ground and are surprisingly inconspicuous, even when on unvegetated ground such as ploughed fields, and are most easily found by watching females during nest building or by observing either sex carrying food to the nestlings. The young leave the nest before they can fly and are fed by their parents for several more days. Consequently, the maps accurately reflect the distribution and abundance of the species, but breeding likely occurred in many more squares than those in which it was confirmed, particularly in the core of the range in southern Ontario.

Abundance: The abundance map clearly indicates that the Horned Lark is much more abundant in southwestern Ontario than elsewhere in southern Ontario, presumably because of the greater availability of suitable agricultural habitat. The high concentration in the far northeast results from a few point counts near Cape Henrietta Maria and likely reflects a substantial population, but estimates farther inland are artifacts of the map contouring method; the Horned Lark is confined to a relatively narrow strip adjacent to the coasts of Hudson Bay and James Bay. – *David J.T. Hussell*

Purple Martin

Hirondelle noire

Progne subis

Eleanor Kee Wellman

The Purple Martin is North America's largest swallow. Because of its habit of nesting socially in artificial nest boxes, it is well known, especially to those living near larger water bodies in southern Ontario. It breeds throughout eastern North America north to the Boreal Forest and locally in the west, but is absent from much of the Great Plains.

Distribution and population status: There is evidence that the Purple Martin withdrew from the northern edge of its range in the last century, as the species no longer occurs in the Northwest Territories and its occurrence in British Columbia has contracted southward (Brown 1997). In Ontario, since the first atlas, the northern edge of the range has withdrawn from Lake Temagami, Thunder Bay, and Dryden and now occurs in the Rainy River area, near Sault Ste. Marie, and just north of North Bay. The second atlas shows a marked reduction throughout much of the species' Ontario range, with the most evident decreases in northern and inland areas. Overall, the probability of observation declined 46% between atlases.

Within southern Ontario, the northern edge of the Purple Martin's range shifted a significant 56 km south between atlases, which is the third-largest retraction of any species, exceeded only by the Cooper's Hawk (57 km) and Loggerhead Shrike (80 km). The largest decline was in the Southern Shield region, where the probability of observation declined by 80% between atlases. The species was not found breeding around Sudbury or Lake Nipissing during the second atlas. Regional Coordinators indicated that the Purple Martin has been extirpated from the Haliburton region, and that the nesting box of the last known colony in Muskoka was destroyed in a storm in 2005.

South of the Shield, the most evident declines are in inland areas and on the Bruce Peninsula. The Purple Martin was

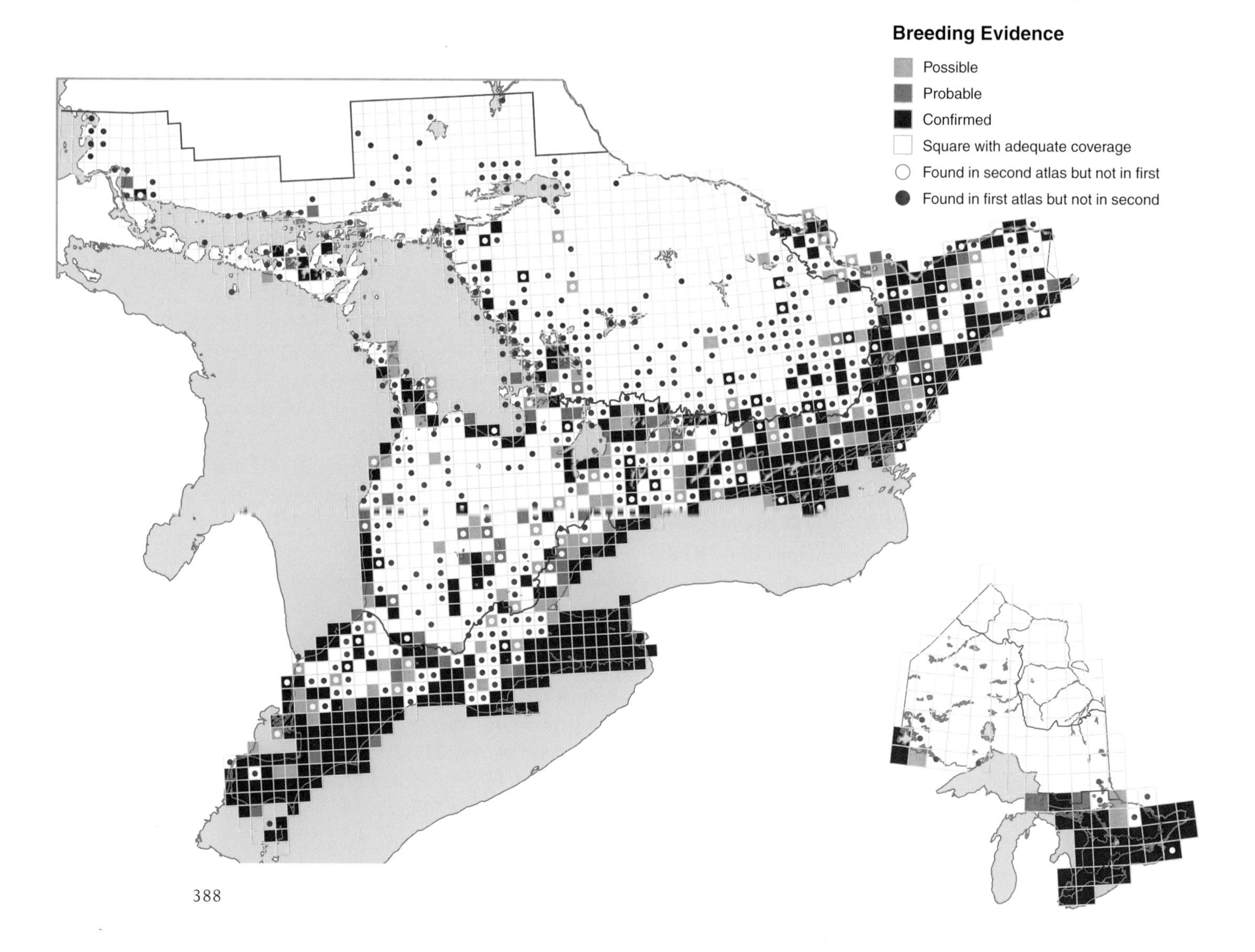

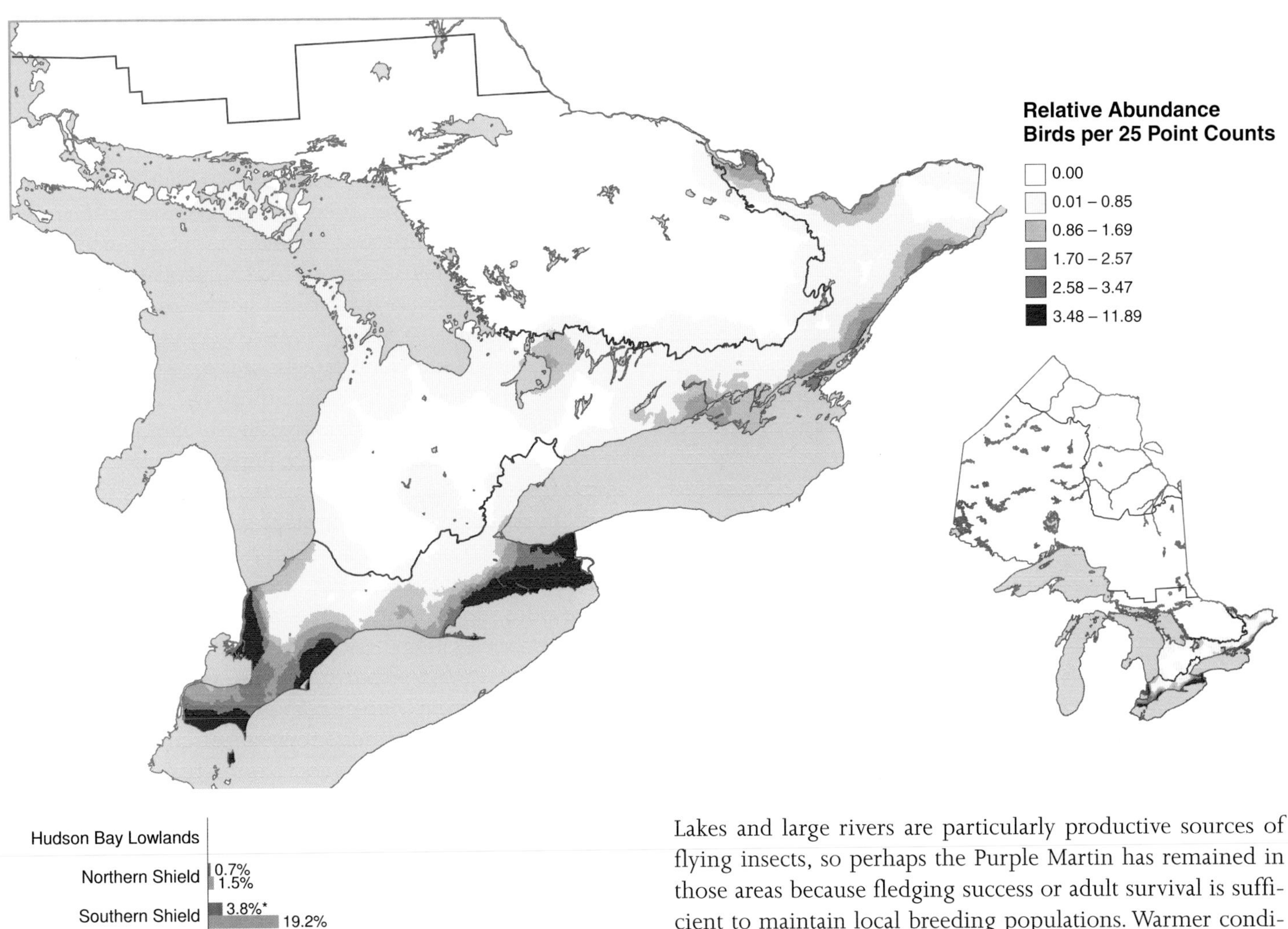

reported in almost every square along the major shorelines, south along Lake Huron from about Goderich, east across Lakes Erie and Ontario, and along the St. Lawrence and Ottawa Rivers. It was also ubiquitous on the Niagara Peninsula, in Chatham-Kent, and in Essex and Prince Edward Counties, and was reported in most squares around Lake Simcoe and the Kawartha Lakes.

The reasons for the disproportionate decline of the Purple Martin in inland areas, and the decline farther north even near large bodies of water, are unclear. Taverner (1922) indicates that the species arrives very early in the spring and that at times they "suffer severely from late frosts and cold rains which stop the flights of insects and deprive the birds of the necessary large and constant supply of food." If such episodes have happened more frequently in recent years, or if the birds are arriving earlier due to generally warmer springs, this could be contributing to the species' decline in Ontario and elsewhere in the northern part of its range. There is some evidence to suggest that the shores of the large water bodies such as the Great Lakes and large rivers are particularly productive sources of flying insects, so perhaps the Purple Martin has remained in those areas because fledging success or adult survival is sufficient to maintain local breeding populations. Warmer conditions in the south may also be more conducive to Purple Martins. The highest densities range-wide occur in the southeastern US (Sauer et al. 2005).

BBS data (1966-2003) indicate that the species is increasing in the Canadian Prairies and in much of the southeast US, but decreasing in much of the midwest and the northeastern part of its range, including Ontario (Sauer et al. 2005).

Breeding biology: In Ontario, the Purple Martin breeds almost exclusively in nest boxes or other artificial structures and is quite conspicuous, so was undoubtedly well represented on breeding evidence maps in both atlases. In western and Mexican populations, pairs often nest solitarily and use natural cavities in trees and cliffs more frequently (Brown 1997). European Starlings and House Sparrows will usurp nesting boxes from Purple Martins, but both species are declining in Ontario, so this may not be a major factor in the Ontario decline.

Abundance: The abundance map shows a pattern similar to that of the distribution map, and further demonstrates the importance of certain southern areas and large water bodies to Ontario's Purple Martin population. The Niagara Peninsula stands out as an area of high abundance, as do Chatham-Kent and Essex and Lambton Counties, particularly in shoreline areas. Other areas of moderately high numbers are around Lake Simcoe, in Prince Edward Co., and along the shores of the Ottawa and St. Lawrence Rivers. – *Michael D. Cadman*

Tree Swallow

Hirondelle bicolore

Tachycineta bicolor

Tim Stewart

This attractive swallow, which owes its Latin name to the striking contrast of its iridescent blue back and its pure white belly, is familiar to many because of its regular use of nest boxes placed around human habitations. It is typically found in open areas including fields, marshes, and shorelines, as well as in wooded swamps, throughout most of central and northern North America, approximately north to the treeline (Robertson et al. 1992).

Distribution and population status: During both atlases, this species was found and breeding was confirmed in virtually every square surveyed in southern Ontario, where there is ample open habitat for foraging and nest boxes are common. During the second atlas, the probability of observation was highest south of the Shield at circa 95% and generally declined northward. Between atlases, the results show a significant decline in the probability of observation in Ontario overall (17%), largely because of significant declines in the Southern and Northern Shield regions (18% and 28%, respectively). Although the overall distribution has remained largely unchanged, there was a small but significant southward shift in the average latitude and northern edge of the species' range in southern Ontario, largely due to a sparser presence in the Southern Shield region during the second atlas.

While earlier BBS data suggested that the population had increased in the eastern and central portion of the continent between 1966 and 1979 (Robbins et al. 1986), they now suggest the opposite trend in Canada, with a significant annual decline of 2.1% between 1981 and 2005. The decline was slightly larger in Ontario over the same period, with a significant annual decline of 2.6%, representing an estimated loss of about half of the population in the last 25 years. BBS data are predominantly collected in the southern part of the province, but it is almost certain that the population decline is affecting the species throughout its Ontario range.

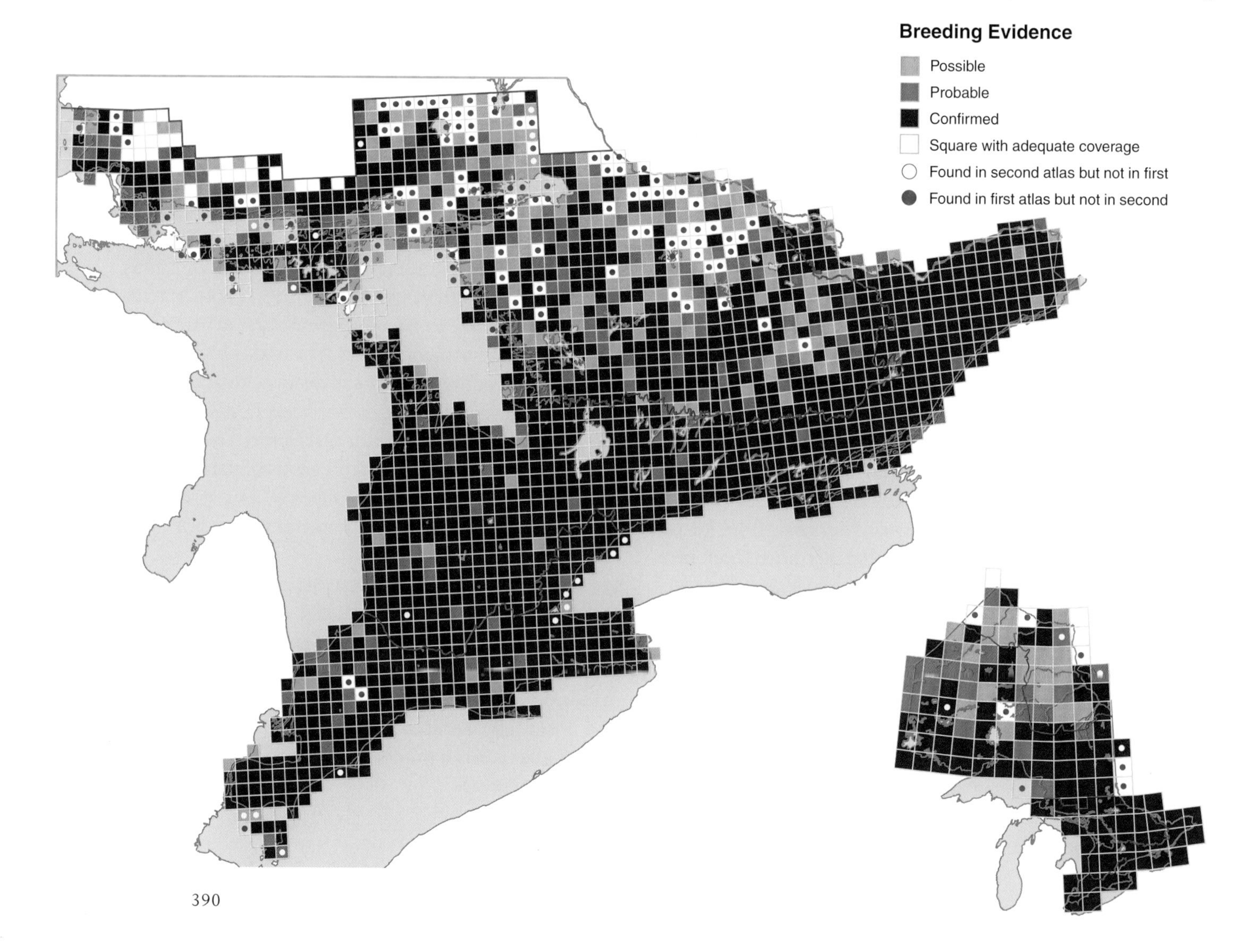

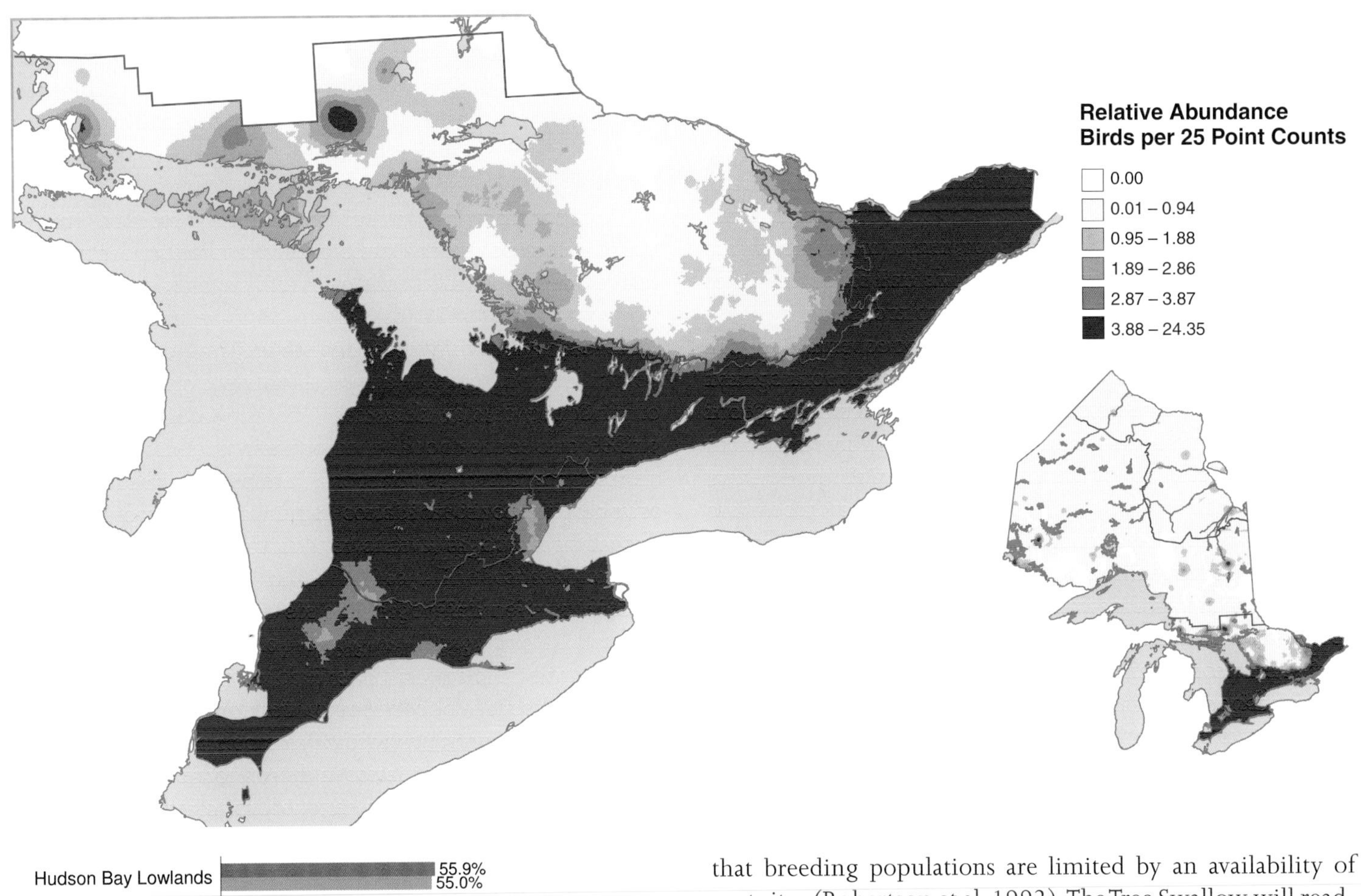

Probability of Observation

Region	2nd Atlas	1st Atlas
Hudson Bay Lowlands	55.9%	55.0%
Northern Shield	52.2%*	72.1%
Southern Shield	79.5%*	96.8%
Lake Simcoe-Rideau	95.4%	97.5%
Carolinian	93.6%	88.6%
Ontario	59.2%*	71.6%

The observed decline is consistent with the pattern observed for almost all other aerial insectivores in Ontario since the first atlas, including swallows, nightjars, and swifts (Ontario Partners in Flight 2006a). The causes for this decline in aerial foragers are still largely unknown at present and probably have multiple origins (Heagy and McCracken 2004, 2005). However, they are likely related primarily to phenomena affecting their common food source or breeding habitat, such as the intensification of agricultural practices, grassland conversions, and decreases in insect populations due to a number of causes. Like other swallows, this species occasionally suffers from severe mortality events following extreme spring weather conditions, which may potentially impact population levels.

Breeding biology: Most Tree Swallows arrive in Ontario in April from their wintering grounds in the southern US and Central America, and timing of nesting appears to be largely determined by environmental conditions encountered early in the breeding season (Nooker et al. 2005). Studies suggest that breeding populations are limited by an availability of nest sites (Robertson et al. 1992). The Tree Swallow will readily use artificial nest boxes installed in rural and urban areas, making breeding confirmation relatively easy around human populations. Pairs may also use natural cavities excavated by woodpeckers or other species. Adults will usually defend their nest aggressively against intruders such as humans, potential predators, or other birds that may compete for nesting sites, such as other Tree Swallows, House Sparrows, and Eastern Bluebirds. The ease in locating nests and confirming breeding in this species is reflected in the relatively high 61% of squares with confirmed evidence. All but one atlas administrative region reported nests with young, the highest level of breeding confirmation.

Abundance: The abundance map clearly shows that the species is most abundant south of the Shield, in the Carolinian and Lake Simcoe-Rideau regions, where recorded densities average about 8 and 10 birds/25 point counts, respectively. It is much less common in the other regions, which is expected for a bird that mostly lives in open areas. On the Shield, the presence of the species is mostly linked to wetlands, where it can find suitable nesting and foraging habitat. It is also less common in the Hudson Bay Lowlands, probably owing to a scarcity of trees with nesting cavities. Pockets of intermediate density can be found in areas of northern Ontario, particularly near human populations such as Kenora, Dryden, Moosonee, and Cochrane, as well as at the southern fringe of the Shield near Sault Ste. Marie and Sudbury and south along Georgian Bay. – *Denis Lepage*

Northern Rough-winged Swallow

Hirondelle à ailes hérissées

Stelgidopteryx serripennis

Jim Richards

The Northern Rough-winged Swallow historically nested in earthen banks, and populations apparently increased after European settlement by adapting to nesting in artificial sites such as sand and gravel pits and pipes underneath concrete bridges. Unlike the Bank Swallow, it does not ordinarily excavate its own nest burrows. Consequently, it is dependent upon burrows constructed previously by Bank Swallows or Belted Kingfishers, or upon other cavities. It usually nests solitarily, although 2-25 pairs may nest colonially (Peck and James 1987), often at the periphery of active Bank Swallow colonies. Due to the similarity of these two species, the Northern Rough-winged Swallow may easily be overlooked in Bank Swallow colonies.

In Canada, the species breeds from southwestern Québec across southern Ontario and the southern Prairie Provinces to British Columbia. Its breeding range extends southward to Costa Rica (DeJong 1996).

Distribution and population status: The Northern Rough-winged Swallow appears to be a relatively recent breeder in Ontario. McIlwraith (1894) knew of only a single record from London, and Fleming (1907) considered it rare in the Toronto area. Baillie and Harrington (1937) stated that it was not particularly numerous and that its distribution was patchy. The first record of breeding in the Kingston area was in 1925 (Weir 1989). This species generally benefited from increased human populations, which resulted in an increase in nest sites. It was scarce in the northeastern US until the last third of the 19th century. A major northward range expansion occurred between 1950 and 1970 (Lunk 1962; DeJong 1996).

The Northern Rough-winged Swallow is common and widespread south of the Shield, becoming uncommon in the Southern Shield. Distribution on the Shield during both atlases is correlated with major highway corridors where bridges and other human structures provide suitable nesting habitat.

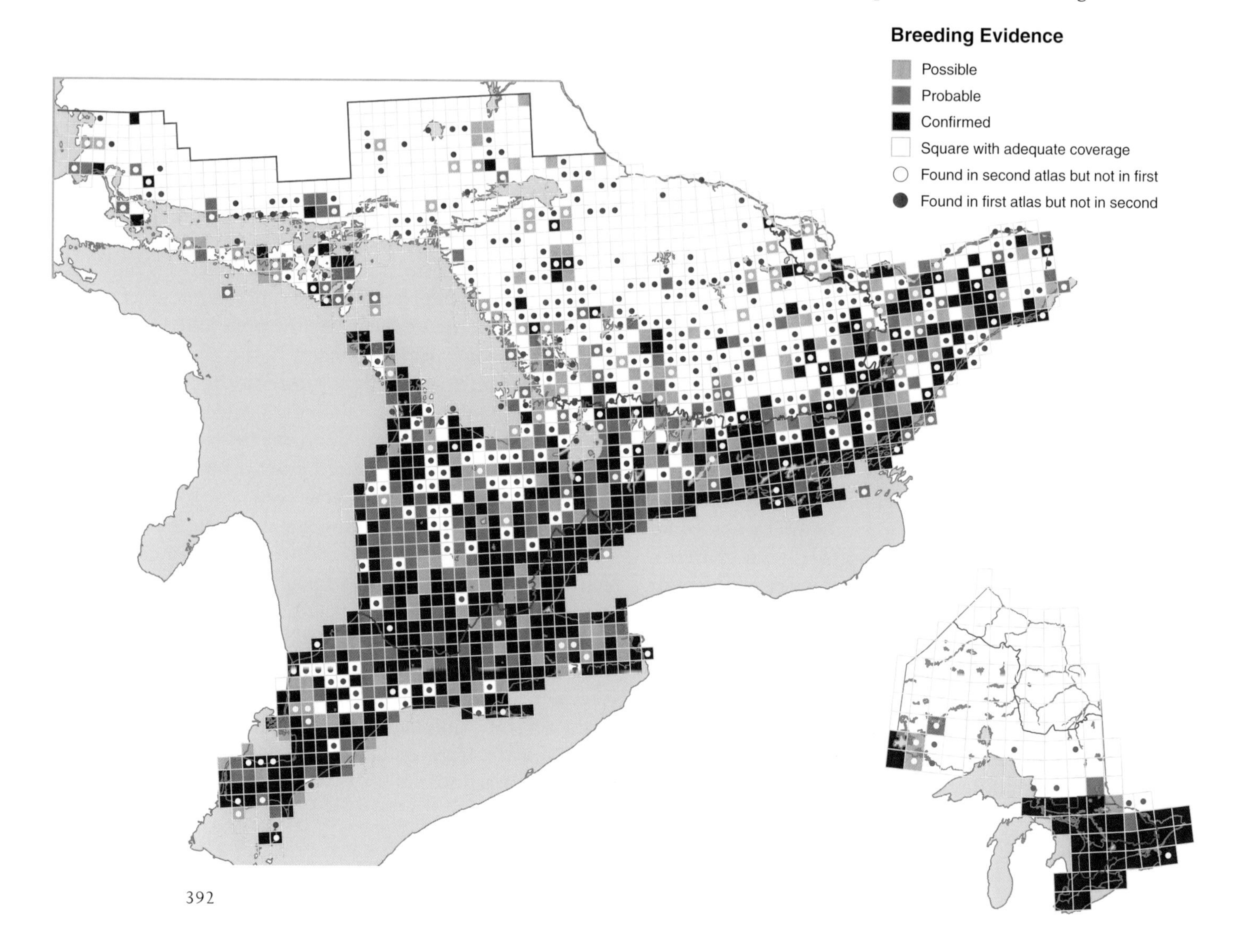

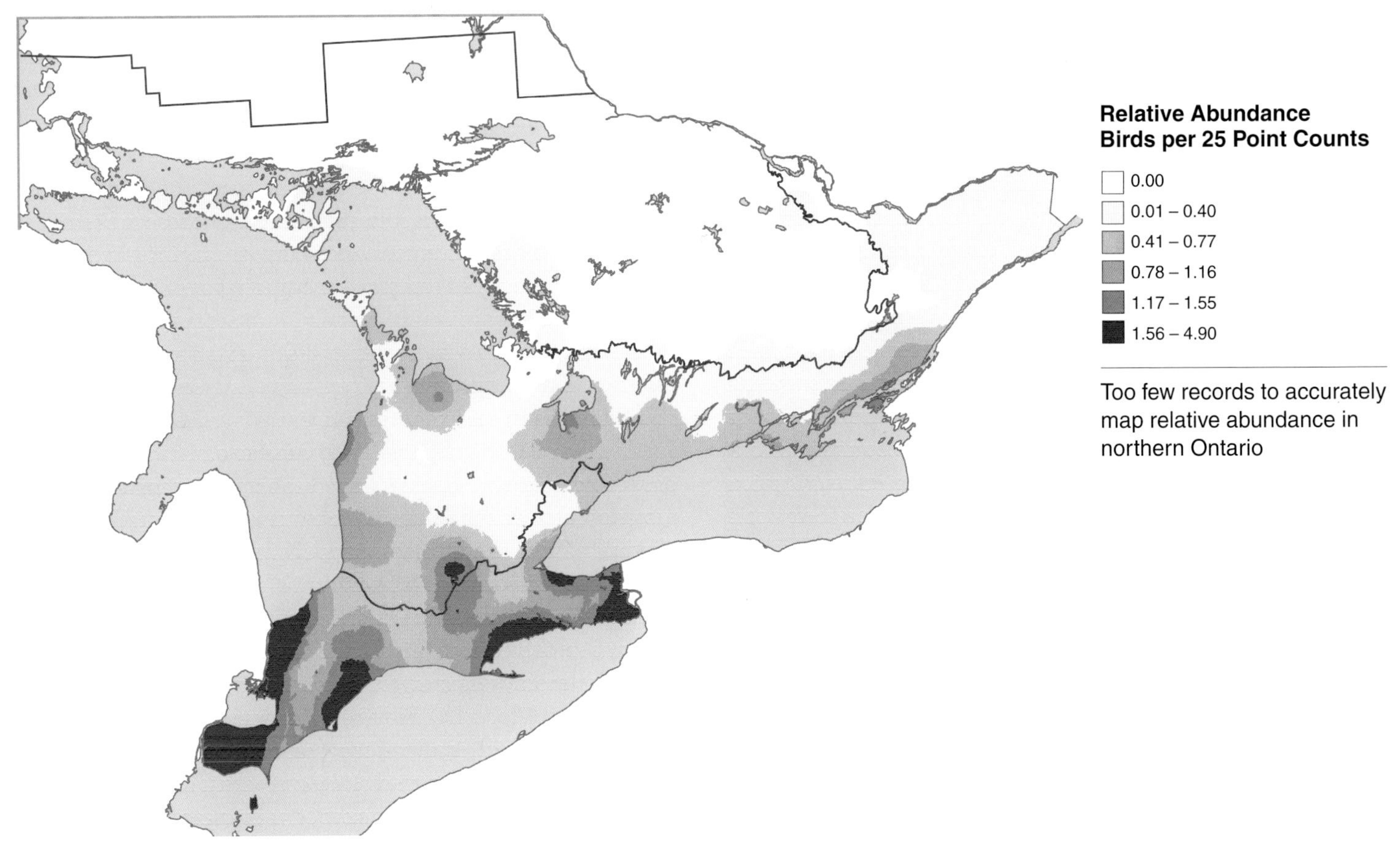

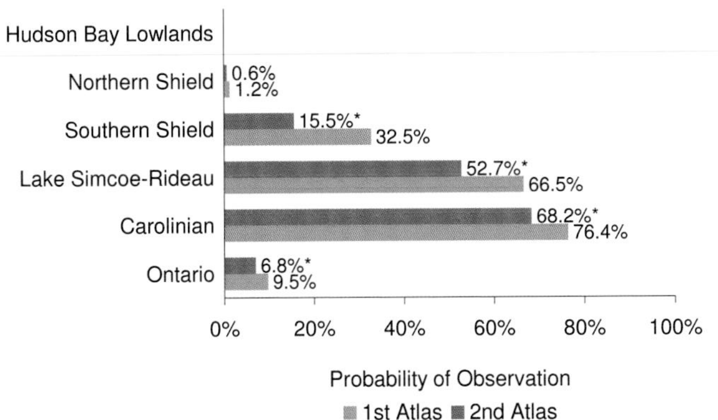

The probability of observation of the species in Ontario declined significantly by 29% between atlases. Significant declines occurred throughout southern Ontario but primarily in the Southern Shield (52%) and Lake Simcoe-Rideau (21%) regions. As a result, the average range of the species in southern Ontario exhibited a significant shift south. Other swallow species have shown similar but generally more dramatic declines and southward range shifts in Ontario. The reasons for declines of insectivorous birds are uncertain (Sauer et al. 1996).

BBS data for the Northern Rough-winged Swallow show no significant changes in Ontario since the first atlas, but the species experienced a significant Canada-wide decline of 3.0% per year during the same period. Its decline may be linked in part to the Bank Swallow's precipitous decline, as fewer nest sites may be available in areas where the Bank Swallow has disappeared.

Breeding biology: The greatest limiting factor for the Northern Rough-winged Swallow in southern Ontario is the availability of nest sites. In areas where there is a scarcity of suitable sites, the individuals present may be non-breeding birds. Nests under bridges are easy to find to confirm this species. Detecting this swallow at large Bank Swallow colonies may be difficult, as there is usually a maximum of one or two pairs within a colony. Broods leave the nesting area shortly after fledging and move around widely over a large area. During this period, they spend considerable time together perched on wires, fences, and trees (Lunk 1962). Some records of fledged young may actually have been from areas other than the natal square. Nonetheless, the atlas map is probably an accurate representation of the species' distribution.

Abundance: The Northern Rough-winged Swallow is most abundant in southwestern Ontario. Highest concentrations are associated with the Great Lakes shorelines, particularly the Lake Erie shoreline east of Long Point and near Rondeau, as well as the St. Clair and Niagara Rivers, and inland in Essex and western Lambton Counties. Higher densities are also found in northern Brant Co. and the southern portion of the Region of Waterloo, likely associated with the Grand River. A small concentration appears to be present in Rainy River Dist., but this is likely an anomaly caused by a small number of records, as the species was reported from very few squares in this area.

The Northern Rough-winged Swallow continues to be a common and widespread breeder south of the Canadian Shield, where gaps in distribution are likely due to lack of nest sites in those areas. It has declined on the Southern Shield and is only locally common in this region, with many gaps in distribution. – *Al Sandilands*

Bank Swallow
Hirondelle de rivage
Riparia riparia

John Reaume

The Bank Swallow has a holarctic distribution, breeding in much of Eurasia and in scattered areas in Africa, where it is known as the Sand Martin. In North America, it breeds from western Newfoundland west to northern Alaska and south to New England and northern California. The Bank Swallow traditionally nested in Ontario in exposed earthen banks created by erosion along watercourses and lakeshores. It continues to nest in these areas but has also adapted to nesting in sand and gravel pits, along roadsides, and in stockpiles of soil and other materials. In some areas, these artificial sites support more breeding Bank Swallows than natural sites and provide habitat where it otherwise would be absent. The shorelines of the lower Great Lakes support the largest populations in the province. Although single nests occur, the vast majority of birds nest in colonies ranging from two to several thousand nests. This species excavates its own nest burrows in exposed soils. It forages aerially on insects and, similar to most species in this foraging guild, is experiencing significant population declines.

Distribution and population status: In Ontario, the Bank Swallow probably increased after European settlement due to provision of artificial nest sites. It was not recorded in the Kingston area in the mid-1800s but was common by the 20th century (Weir 1989). Baillie and Harrington (1937) stated that the Bank Swallow was a common and widespread breeding species throughout Ontario, although there were gaps within its distribution. During the first atlas, its breeding range covered the entire province, but with notable gaps on the Shield and Hudson Bay Lowlands, and also in scattered areas south of the Shield. Availability of nest sites probably limits its breeding range.

The Bank Swallow has declined significantly in Ontario since the first atlas. The probability of observation in the province as a whole declined by 45% between atlases, with the

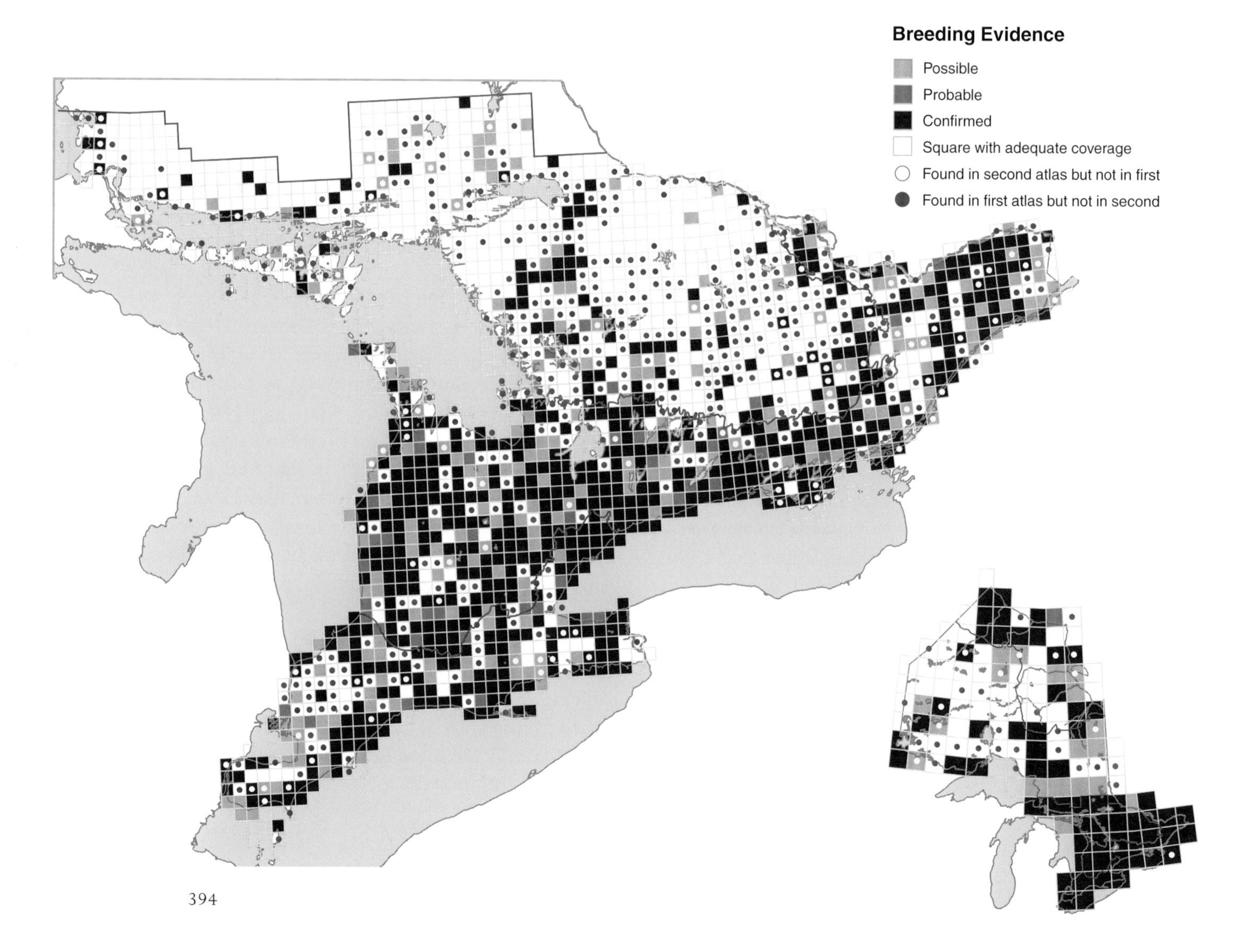

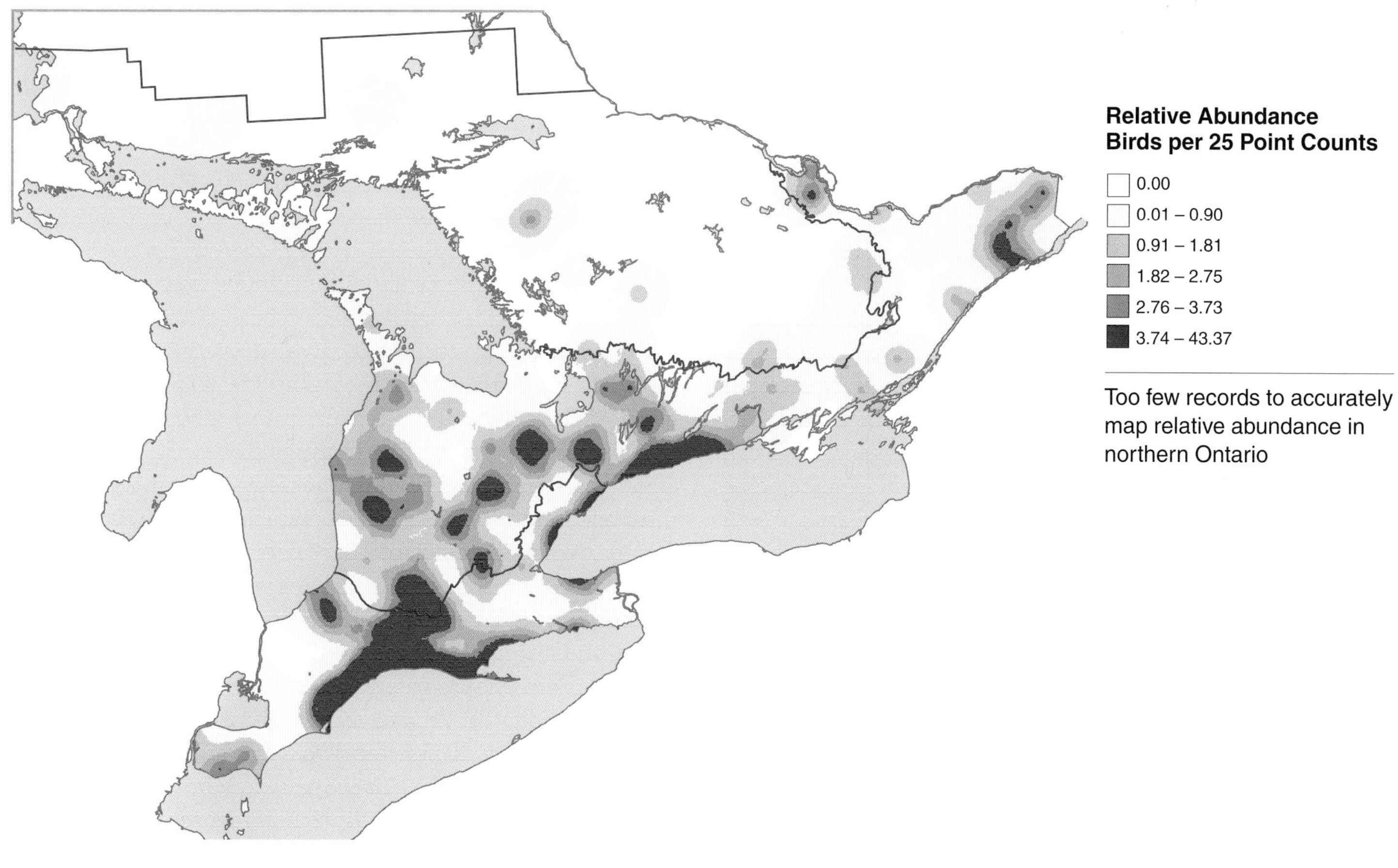

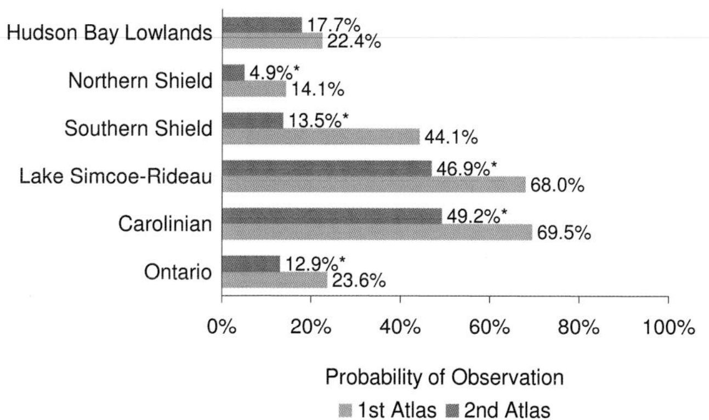

greatest declines in the Southern Shield (69%), Northern Shield (65%), and Lake Simcoe-Rideau (31%) regions. As a result of these declines, there was a significant southward shift in the species' average range in southern Ontario. BBS data also show a significant decline of 6.6% per year in Ontario since 1981. Although many bird species that forage aerially on insects are declining, the reasons for this are uncertain (Sauer et al. 1996). Local extinctions of Bank Swallow colonies have been linked to loss of nearby grasslands and increases in discharge rates in watercourses, which likely affect food availability and bank erosion rates. Small colonies are more likely to become extinct than larger ones (Moffatt et al. 2005).

Breeding biology: The Bank Swallow's habit of nesting colonially in banks along shorelines and in artificial sites such as sand and gravel pits makes it easy to confirm breeding. Long-term colonies are associated with long, tall banks with regular erosion that maintains the vertical face. Shortly after fledging, young move away from the nesting colony with their parents and roost communally. Telephone and hydro lines are used most frequently for diurnal roosting, and this habit also makes it easy to confirm nesting. These roosts, however, may be a considerable distance from the nesting area (Beyer 1938; Garrison 1999), so that it is possible that breeding was confirmed in a few squares where no breeding actually occurred. At 67%, the species has one of the highest rates of confirmation among Ontario's passerines.

Abundance: The highest average relative abundance of Bank Swallows was recorded in the Carolinian region and decreased with latitude through the other regions. Atlassers were requested to report colonies of 100 or more nests. A total of 72 colonies with over 100 nests were reported, but only eight of these were in natural banks. The largest colony of 3,000 nests was reported from the shoreline of Lake Erie. Lancaster et al. (2004) speculated that there were tens or even hundreds of thousands of Bank Swallows nesting along the lakeshore within Elgin Co., and those large numbers are reflected on the relative abundance map. Other areas supporting large natural colonies are the north shore of Lake Ontario and the Saugeen and Albany Rivers. No doubt there are many other colonies that went unreported, as the large colonies along Lake Erie were under-reported. The Bank Swallow continues to be locally common south of the Shield and is locally abundant along the Lake Erie shoreline. On the Shield and in the Hudson Bay Lowlands, it is locally rare to uncommon. If the population declines continue, many of the smaller colonies will probably be abandoned. – *Al Sandilands*

Cliff Swallow

Hirondelle à front blanc
Petrochelidon pyrrhonota

Mark Peck

The Cliff Swallow breeds throughout much of North America north to about the treeline, though it is rare, but increasing, in much of the southeastern US and parts of the northeastern US. Historically, this swallow was primarily a bird of the mountains in western Canada and the US, where cliffs, its natural nesting habitat, are plentiful. It spread east with European settlement and the building of structures suitable for nesting, such as bridges and barns (Brown and Brown 1995).

All six swallow species breeding in Ontario have shown a marked decline since the first atlas, but the Cliff Swallow is unique in that, although it decreased considerably overall, it increased in one region, the Carolinian.

Distribution and population status: The Cliff Swallow was presumably quite rare or absent in Ontario prior to European settlement. However, by the late 19th century, it was already "very numerous" throughout the settled parts of Ontario (McIlwraith 1894). It appears to have been rare and local in the far north as long as records have been kept. Baillie and Harrington (1937) mention a record on the Severn River on Hudson Bay; interestingly, Fort Severn was the location of the northernmost record during the second atlas.

Early 20th century reports that the species was not common and appeared to be in decline (Baillie and Harrington 1937) might be reflective of its dynamic history in the province. BBS data for Ontario show that Cliff Swallow populations increased steadily from 1968 (the first year of the survey in Canada) to a peak in about 1985, and then declined to 2005. This decline coincided with the two atlas projects, and the extent and pattern of the decline is evident in the breeding evidence data and maps.

Between atlases, the probability of observation of the Cliff Swallow declined significantly by 50% in the province as a whole. North of the road system in northern Ontario, there was no evident decline, with about the same number of 100-

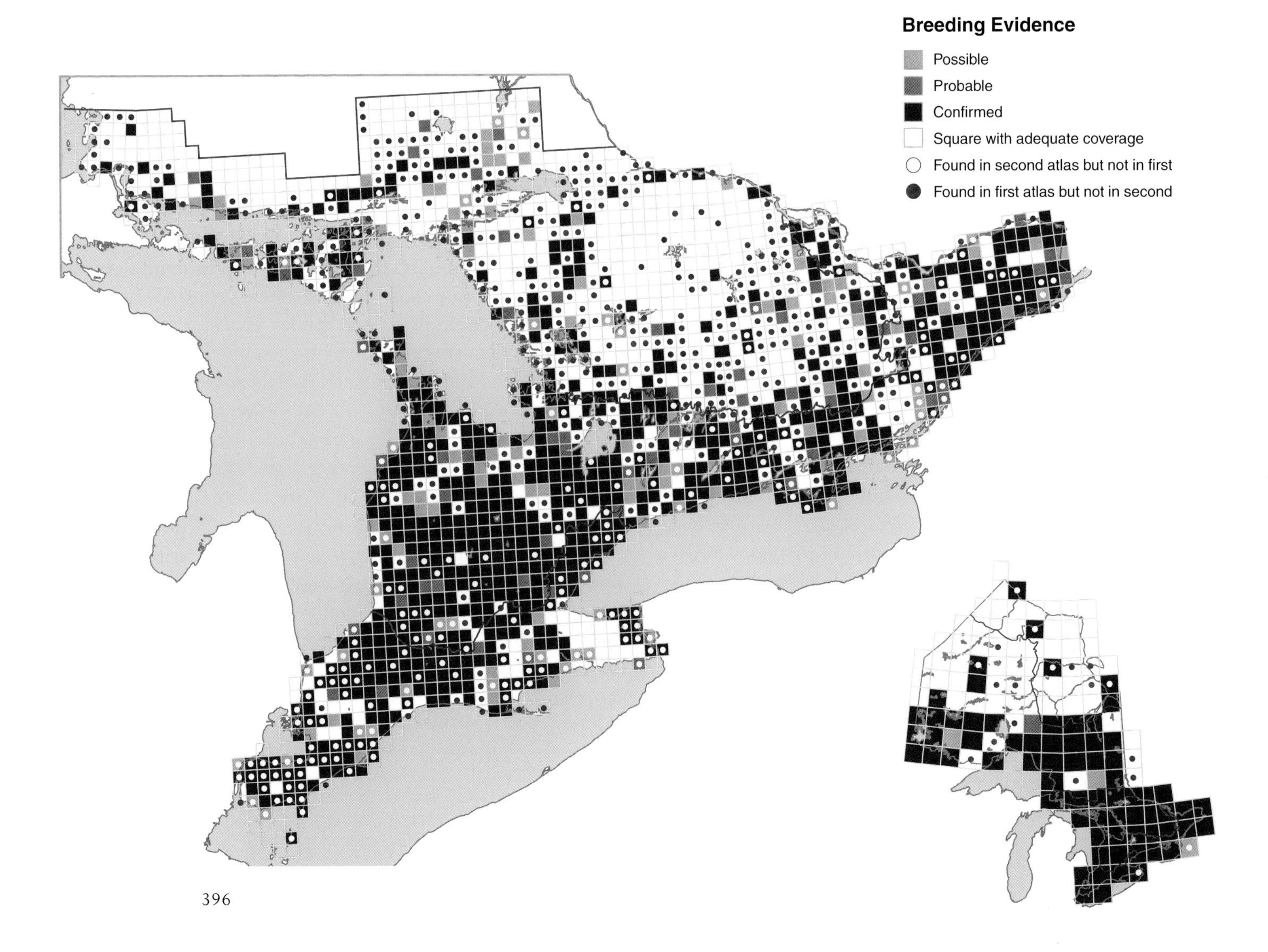

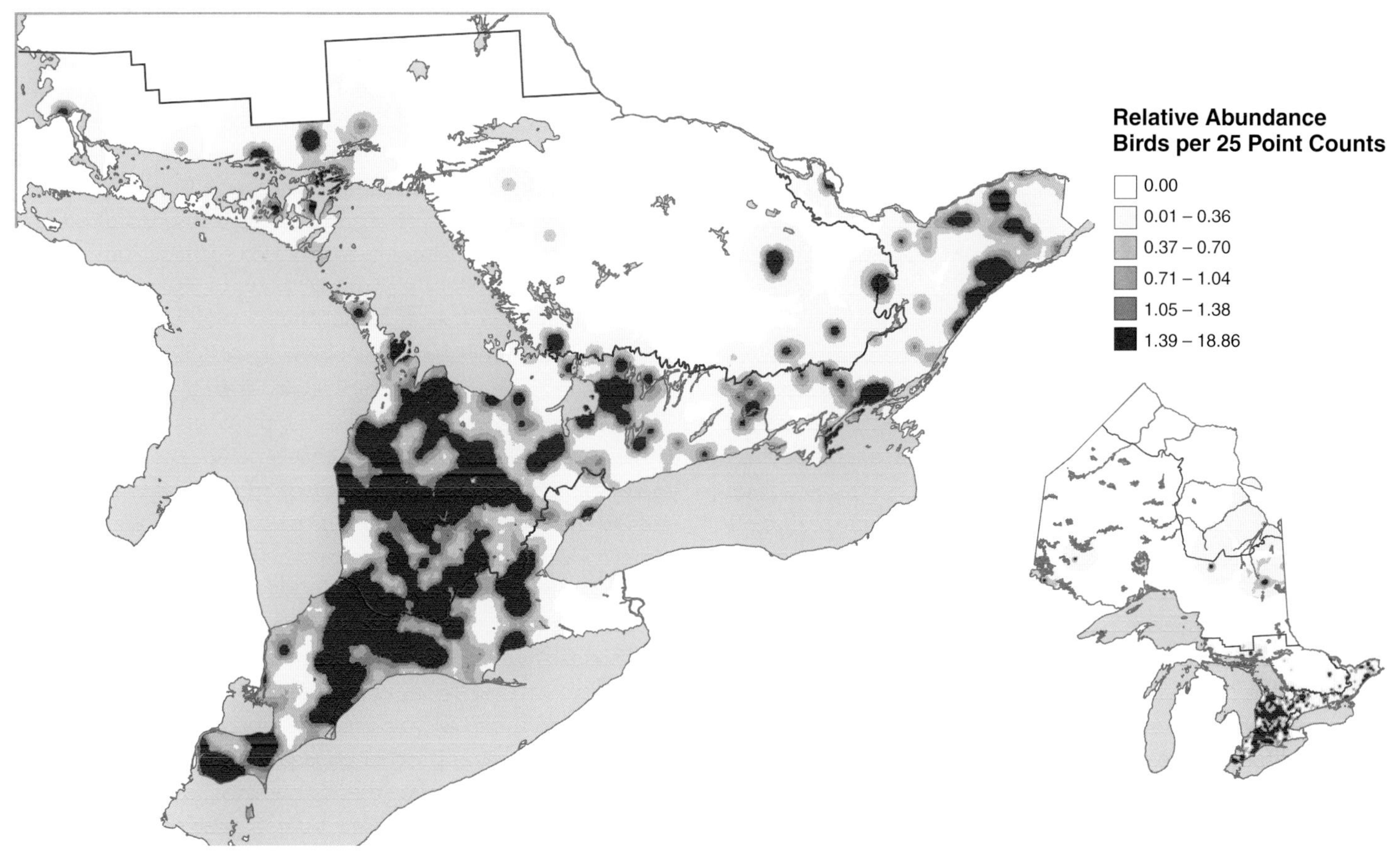

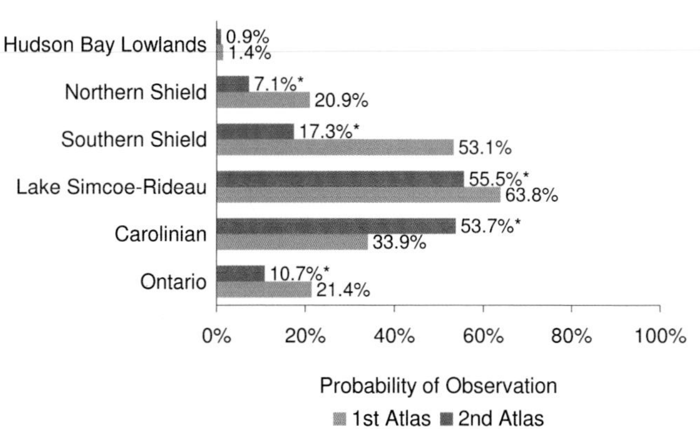

km blocks reporting the species in both atlases. In road-accessible areas of the Northern Shield, however, a marked decline is apparent; in the region as a whole, there was a significant 66% decline in the probability of observation between atlases. The Southern Shield showed a similar significant decline of 67%. There was a smaller decline of 13% in the Lake Simcoe-Rideau region, but a marked increase of 58% in the Carolinian. Due to the increase in the south and the declines farther north, the core of this swallow's southern Ontario distribution shifted 58 km south between atlases, one the largest southerly shifts of any species.

The reasons for the decline in this and other swallow species between atlases are not known. The reduction in the amount of open country in the Southern Shield as abandoned farmland returned to scrub and forest generally parallels the decline in the Cliff Swallow. Similarly, as farms were retired, barns, which were frequently used for nesting, have fallen or been taken down, leaving fewer suitable nesting sites. Alternatively, similar declines have been observed in other swallows and most aerial-foraging avian insectivores in the province since the first atlas, and it is conceivable that some other factor, possibly climate related, is causing long-term changes independent of land-use change. A suspected decline in insect populations generally has been implicated in the overall declines in aerial insectivores. Unfortunately, there are no long-term monitoring data to demonstrate changes in insect populations in Ontario.

Breeding biology: The Cliff Swallow is probably well represented on atlas maps as it is easily found if present. It is colonial, noisy when alarmed, and builds distinctive mud nests on human structures. In Ontario, it nests most frequently under the eaves of buildings, especially barns, and under bridges (Peck and James 1987).

Abundance: The abundance maps show that during the second atlas the Cliff Swallow occurred in relatively high numbers throughout most of southwestern Ontario. During the first atlas, the number of occupied squares in Essex Co. and the Niagara Peninsula was much lower than elsewhere in southwestern Ontario. The current abundance map suggests the density of birds in Essex is now equivalent to much of the rest of the southwest, though it is still low in Niagara. Generally, numbers are lower east of Toronto, except along the north shore of the St. Lawrence River. The area of relatively high abundance near Rainy River is consistent with BBS data, which also show a peak of high abundance in adjacent northern Minnesota and eastern Manitoba (Price et al. 1995). – *Michael D. Cadman*

Barn Swallow

Hirondelle rustique

Hirundo rustica

Bill Rayner

This aerial acrobat, a common sight in virtually any open habitats in much of Ontario during the breeding season, is familiar to many because of its use of human structures for nesting. It is the most widespread swallow in the world, found on every continent except Antarctica. The American race *erythrogaster* breeds in North America from southern Alaska, Hudson Bay, and central Québec to the southern US and Central Mexico, and winters throughout Central and South America.

Distribution and population status: The Barn Swallow was likely uncommon in Ontario prior to human settlement. As human populations expanded, particularly in the first half of the 20th century, Barn Swallows were able to find new suitable breeding sites and move into new areas. In the second atlas, the species was found in almost every square south of the Shield, with a probability of observation of 96% and 90% in the Carolinian and Lake Simcoe-Rideau regions, respectively. Records were much more scattered in the Southern Shield, particularly during the second atlas, with a probability of observation of 59%. This swallow appears to be absent now from large portions of the Algonquin Highlands, as well as from large areas in the northern part of southern Ontario. In both atlases, there were isolated pockets of populations in far western Ontario, particularly around Thunder Bay and Lake of the Woods, and the species was found sporadically throughout northern Ontario, often in association with human settlements and major roads (e.g., the Trans-Canada Highway). Isolated records occurred north to the Hudson Bay Lowlands.

The probability of observation for the Barn Swallow declined significantly between atlases, particularly in the Northern and Southern Shield regions (51% and 32%, respectively), but also in the Lake Simcoe-Rideau region (7%). Overall, a significant decline of 35% was observed throughout Ontario.

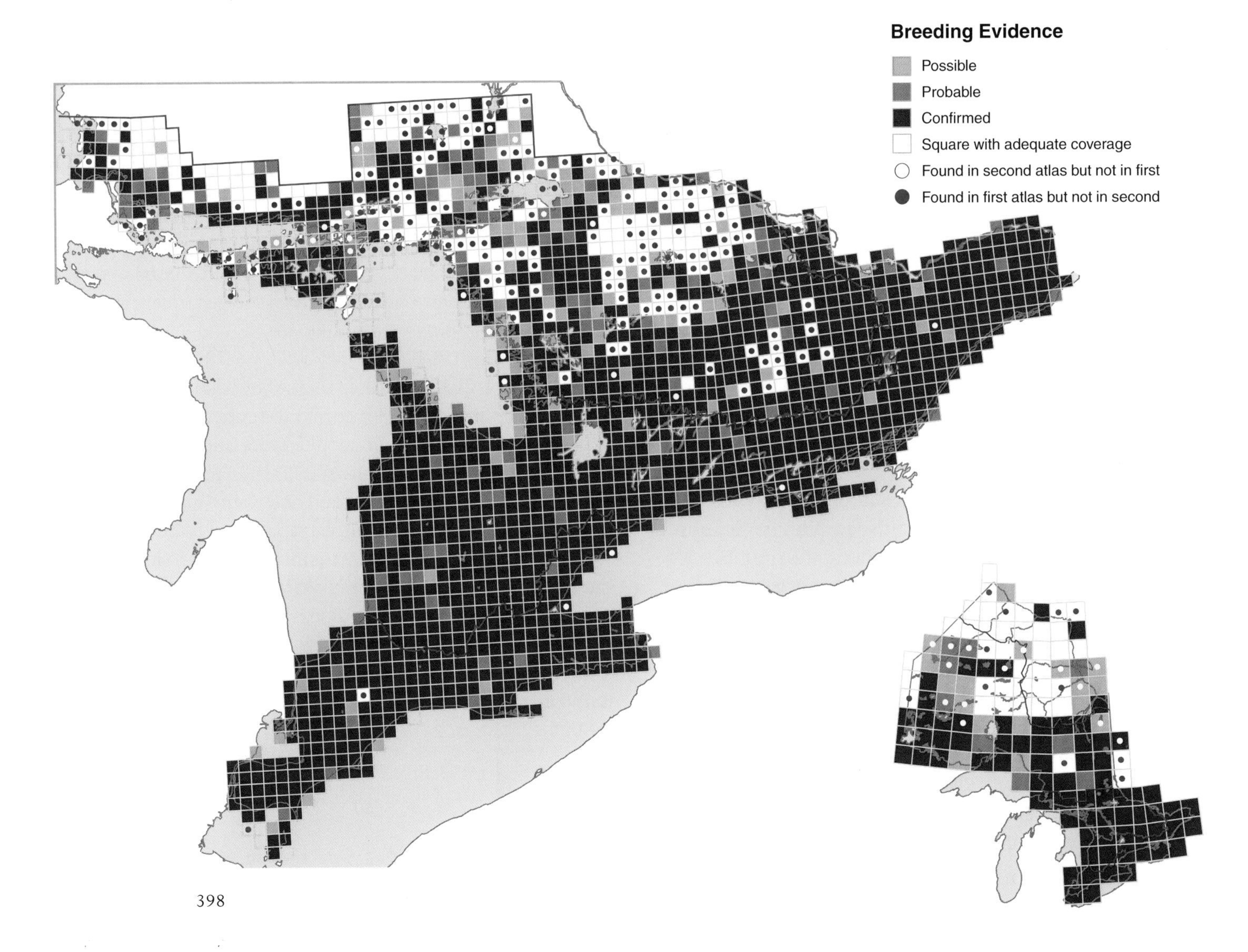

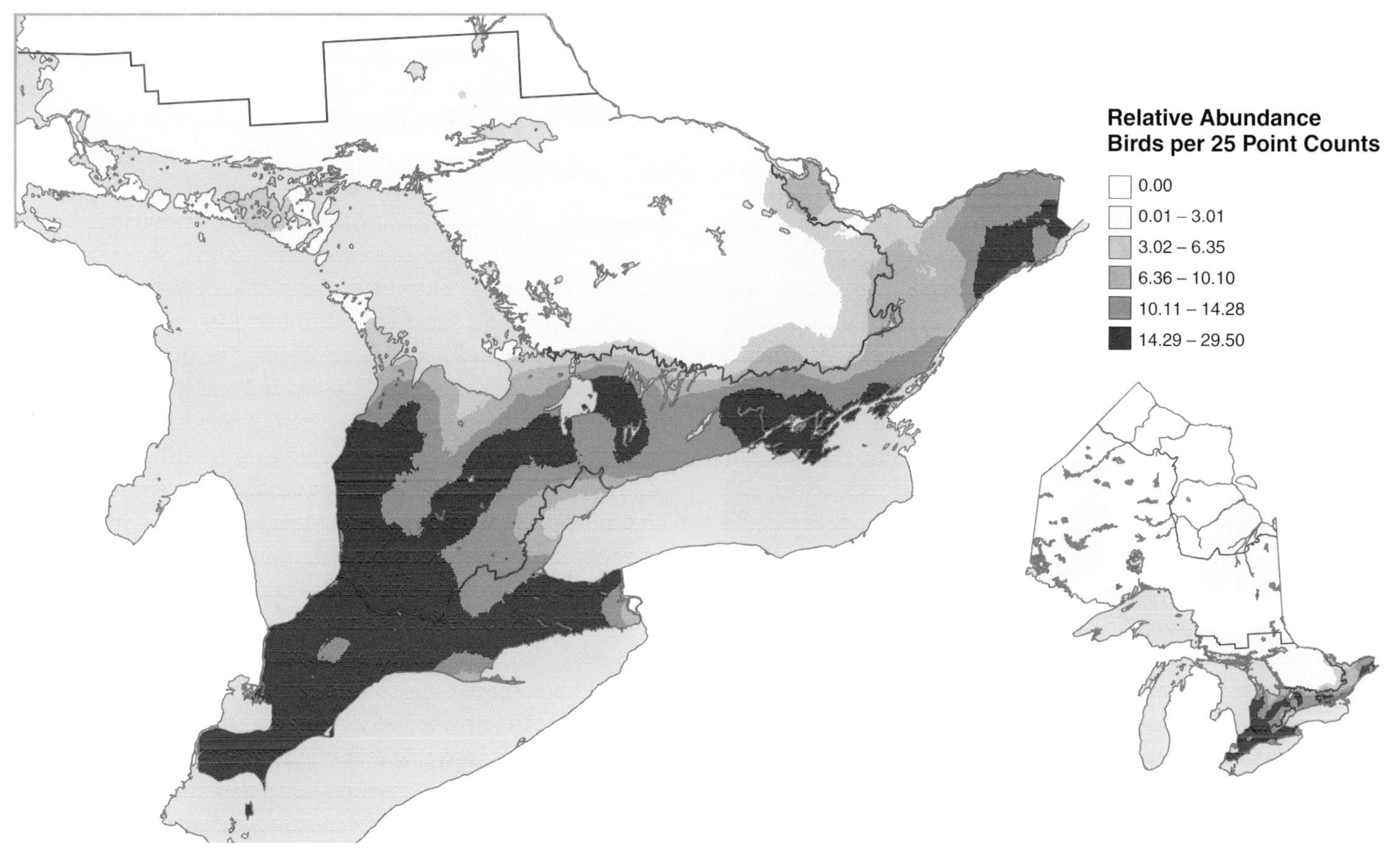

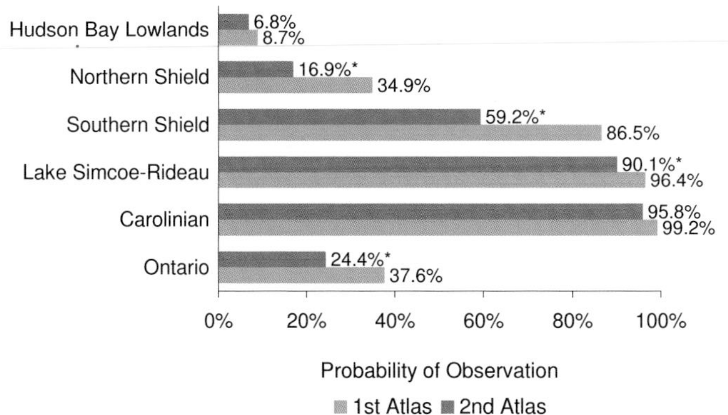

The disappearance of the species was most noticeable in the northern part of the species' core range in southern Ontario. The decline in the Southern Shield appears to be responsible for a small but significant southward shift in range between the two atlases, both of the northern edge and the average latitude of the southern Ontario range. There was also a significant eastward shift of the western edge of the range.

Although the species is still widespread throughout most of its global range, there are many indications that the population level has dropped significantly over the last 25 years in Ontario and elsewhere in the world. BBS data from 1981 to 2005 indicate a steady significant annual decline of 5.4% in Canada and 3.5% in Ontario, which represents a corresponding total estimated decline of 75% and 60% of the species' population between the start of the first atlas and the end of the second atlas. This decline is consistent with that observed for many other aerial insectivores such as other swallows, nighthawks, and swifts; consequently, aerial insectivores have been identified as a priority group of concern for conservation actions by Ontario Partners in Flight (2006a). The causes of the decline are still largely unknown (Heagy and McCracken 2004, 2005), but it is likely related to a decline in aerial insect abundance.

Breeding biology: As its name suggests, the Barn Swallow will usually build its mud nest on ledges or walls in or outside of a barn or another human-made structure, including buildings or bridges. Natural nest sites such as cliffs or caves are now rarely used. The species will often breed in small colonies, occasionally nesting in groups of 50 or more pairs (Peck and James 1987). Adults are usually very vocal, both while foraging and at the nest. Nests are generally conspicuous and easy to detect, reflected by the fact that breeding was confirmed in 78% of squares reporting the species.

Abundance: The Barn Swallow is most abundant south of the Shield. It is most common throughout agricultural areas in the Carolinian and Lake Simcoe-Rideau regions, with average abundances of about 18 and 14 birds/25 point counts for each region, respectively. It is noticeably less common in extensive urban areas, particularly around the Greater Toronto Area and Ottawa and, to a lesser extent, Fort Erie. Areas with higher forest cover such as in the Long Point area also show lower abundance. Throughout the Southern Shield and farther north, this swallow is much less abundant. Not surprisingly, it was virtually undetected from the extensive area of Boreal Forest in northern Ontario. – *Denis Lepage*

Black-capped Chickadee

Mésange a tête noire

Poecile atricapillus

Tim Dyson

"Whoever saw a dejected Chickadee?" asked W. Earl Godfrey (1986), calling this species "the personification of cheerfulness." The Black-capped Chickadee holds a special place for most people with even a casual interest in nature. This inquisitive, gregarious, and at times remarkably tame species has likely graced more hands in exchange for a seed and its familiar "*chickadee*" call has likely put more smiles on faces than any other bird in Ontario. The two-noted, whistled, primary advertising song is one of the most familiar sounds in Ontario woodlands. It is heard most frequently from late winter to late spring. This species has a proven ability to adapt to most treed habitats, including urban woodlots and back yards. Its range extends from Alaska and the southern Yukon to Newfoundland, south to northern California and Nevada in the west, and to Ohio, southern New York, and along the Appalachians to the Carolinas in the east (Smith 1993). It is never far from trees for nesting and foraging.

Distribution and population status: The first atlas indicated that the Black-capped Chickadee occurred in every 100-km block south of the Hudson Bay Lowlands region, and in almost every square across southern Ontario, except in the extreme southwest. In the second atlas, in Essex and Lambton Counties and Chatham-Kent, it was found in 31 squares in which it was not recorded in the first, contributing to a significant 11% increase in its probability of observation in the Carolinian region. The Northern Shield region also had a significant increase of 15% over the first atlas. BBS data show a significant 2.7% average annual increase in Ontario since 1968 but no significant change since 1981.

Breeding biology: The biology of the Black-capped Chickadee is well known, particularly due to the work of Smith (1993). It requires cavities for nesting and roosting but will utilize trees in many habitats, including hedgerows, thickets, suburban and urban areas, and narrow riparian strips as well

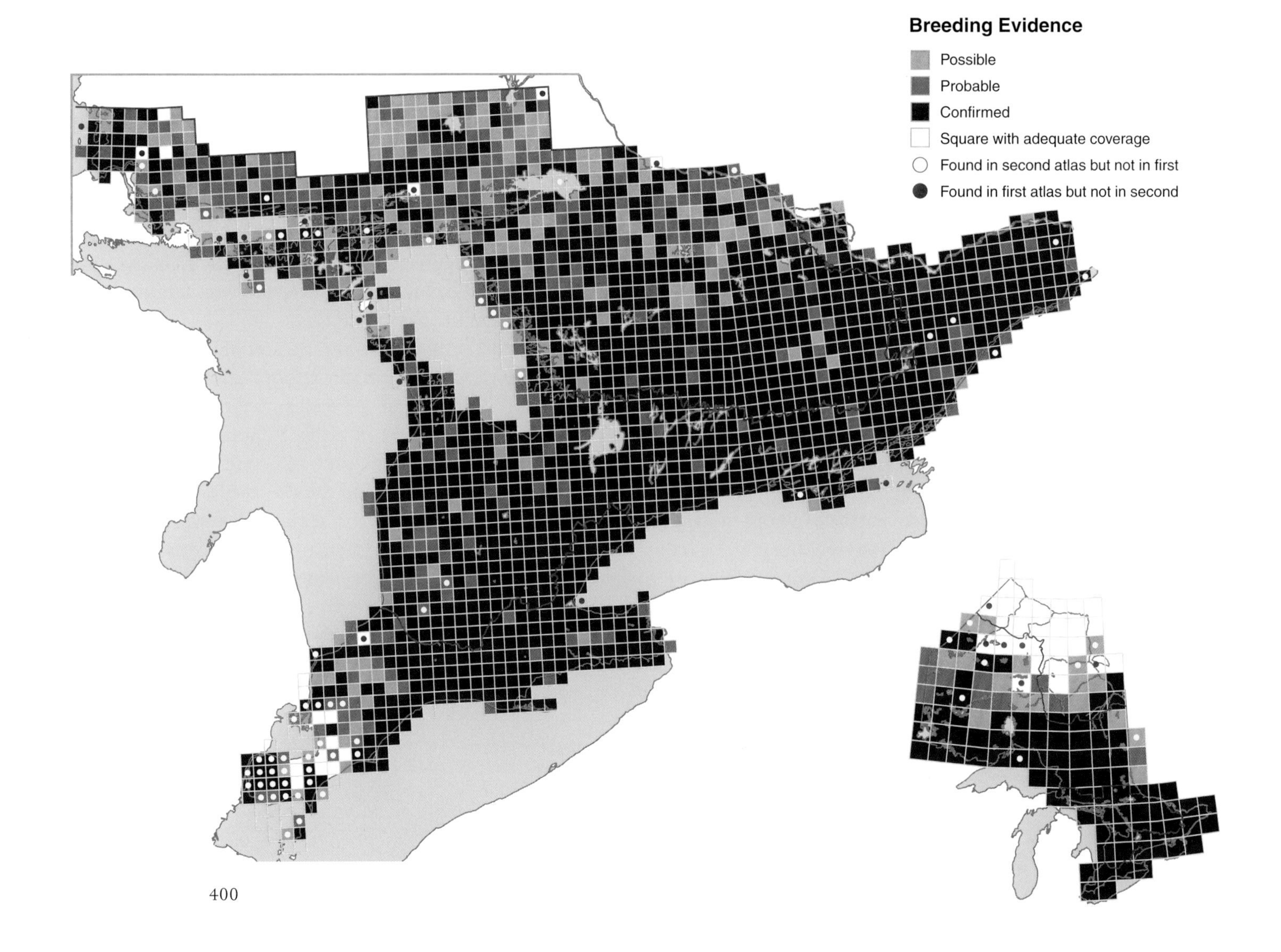

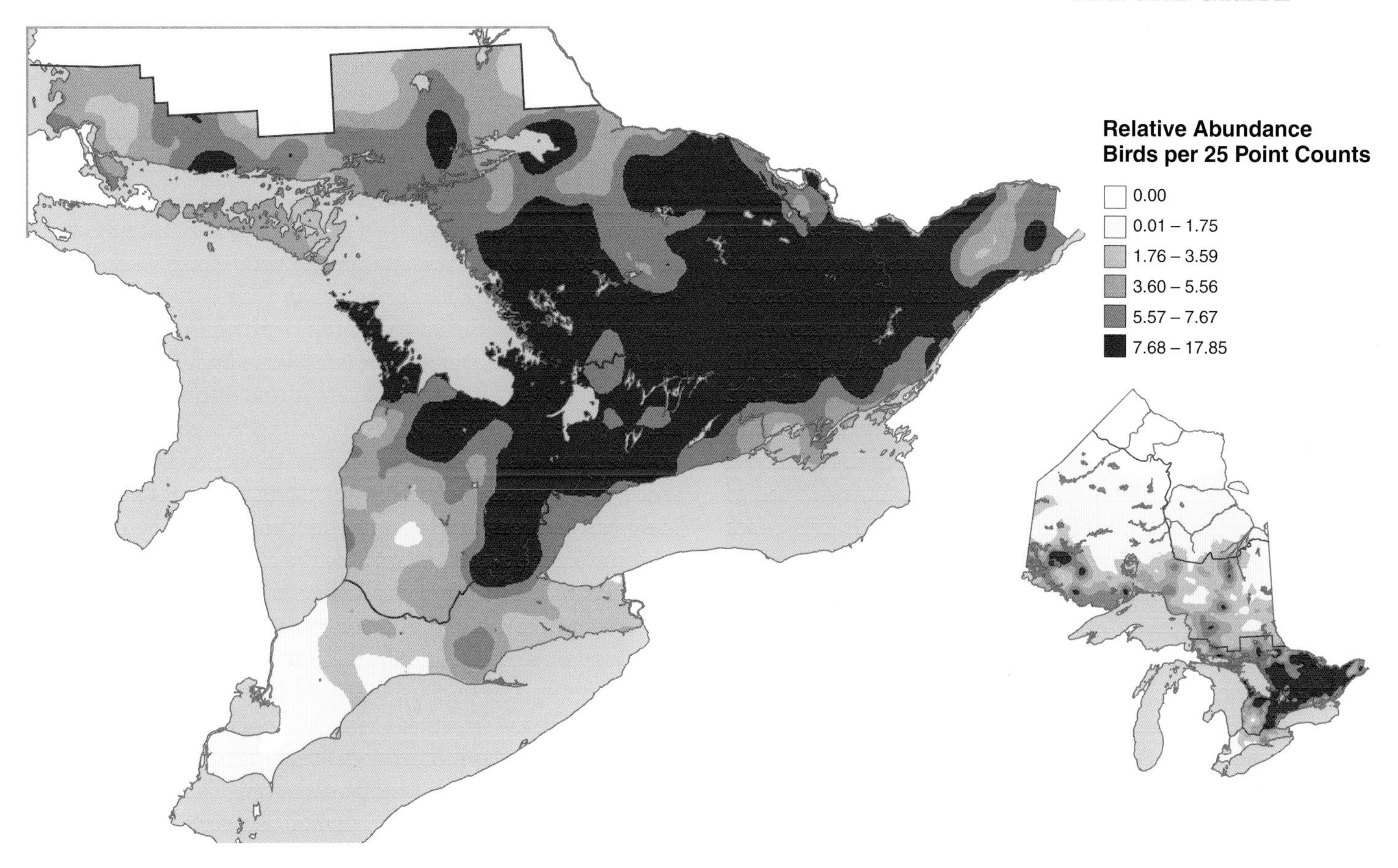

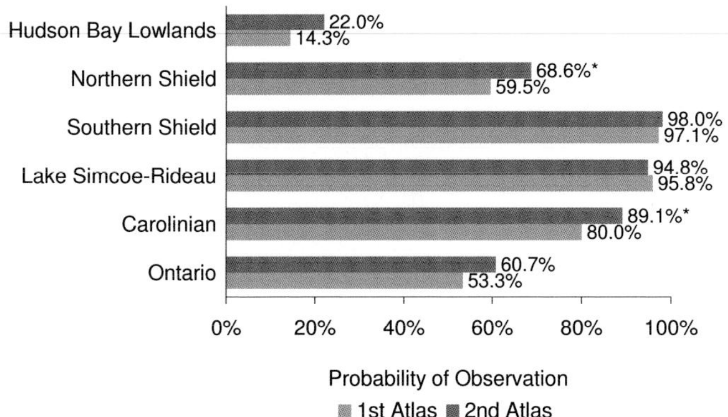

as woodlands. It is omnivorous, consuming mainly arthropods during the warmer months and a much higher percentage of seeds, nuts, and berries in the winter. It is well known for its food-caching behaviour, particularly during the fall and winter, and can remember the locations of its caches several weeks later (Smith 1993).

The Black-capped Chickadee has two contrasting social structures over the course of the year. In the late summer and early fall, flocks comprised of young of the year as well as immigrant adults from other areas form around territorial pairs. Winter flocks disperse in late March and April, with new pair bonds forming between unmated birds. A dominant pair will assume much of the winter flock territory.

Nests are situated in cavities excavated in the soft wood of partially rotten trees or snags, in cavities excavated by other species, and in nest boxes. The female constructs the nest, typically using mosses, usually laying six to seven eggs, sometimes as early as late April but usually in mid- to late May (Peck and James 1987). During this period, the male defends the territory. The Black-capped Chickadee is monogamous, establishing pair bonds either in the early fall or late winter, depending on mortality within the winter flocks. Occasionally, it has a second brood in late June or July (Smith 1993). Family groups remain together for three to four weeks after fledging, before the young disperse. During this period, the begging calls and behaviour of the young make confirmation of breeding relatively easy.

The Black-capped Chickadee is essentially a non-migratory species, vacating northern portions of the breeding range only during periods of food shortage. Large irruptions occur with regularity. About every three to five years, large numbers pass through central and southern Ontario. Banding data suggest that the vast majority of these birds are young of the year (e.g., Bruce Peninsula Bird Observatory, unpubl. data).

Abundance: The highest densities of the Black-capped Chickadee (over 7.7 birds/25 point counts) occur from the Bruce Peninsula and Brantford east to Brockville and Ottawa and north to Mattawa and Port Loring. Another area of high density is situated near Dryden in the Northern Shield region. Southwest of London and in much of the Boreal Forest, it is scarce, with fewer than 1.8 birds/25 point counts. As in the first atlas, it appears to be entirely absent from the northern part of the Hudson Bay Lowlands region north of 53° N. – *Edward Cheskey*

Boreal Chickadee

Mésange à tête brune

Poecile hudsonica

Mark Peck

As its name suggests, the Boreal Chickadee is a bird of northern coniferous forests. It is not nearly as well known as its more southerly cousin, the Black-capped Chickadee, both because of its northern range and its generally quieter nature. The Boreal Chickadee's breeding range matches the distribution of northern coniferous forests, extending from Alaska to Newfoundland and southward to northernmost Washington and Montana in the west and Minnesota, Wisconsin, Michigan, and northern New England in the east. There also is a disjunct population in the Adirondacks in New York State (Ficken et al. 1996). Although the species is for the most part sedentary, wintering throughout its breeding range, there are periodic major irruptions in which substantial numbers of individuals move southwards, occasionally as far as Massachusetts and Ohio (Ficken et al. 1996).

Distribution and population status: In Ontario, the Boreal Chickadee is found from the coast of Hudson Bay south to Algonquin Prov. Park. Its distribution has remained almost identical to that in the first atlas, with the few gaps in 100-km blocks having been filled. However, the species is not very vocal nor very noticeable among the conifer branches and, despite its broad distribution, had a probability of observation of only 46% in the Northern Shield region and 61% in the Hudson Bay Lowlands region in the second atlas. As in the first atlas, there is a cluster of squares containing this species in Algonquin Prov. Park in the Southern Shield region, and then a gap in distribution to north of Lake Nipissing. This distribution may be explained by the cooler climate and the associated types of more northerly forest found in the Algonquin Highlands.

There was no significant change between atlases in the probability of observation of the Boreal Chickadee in either

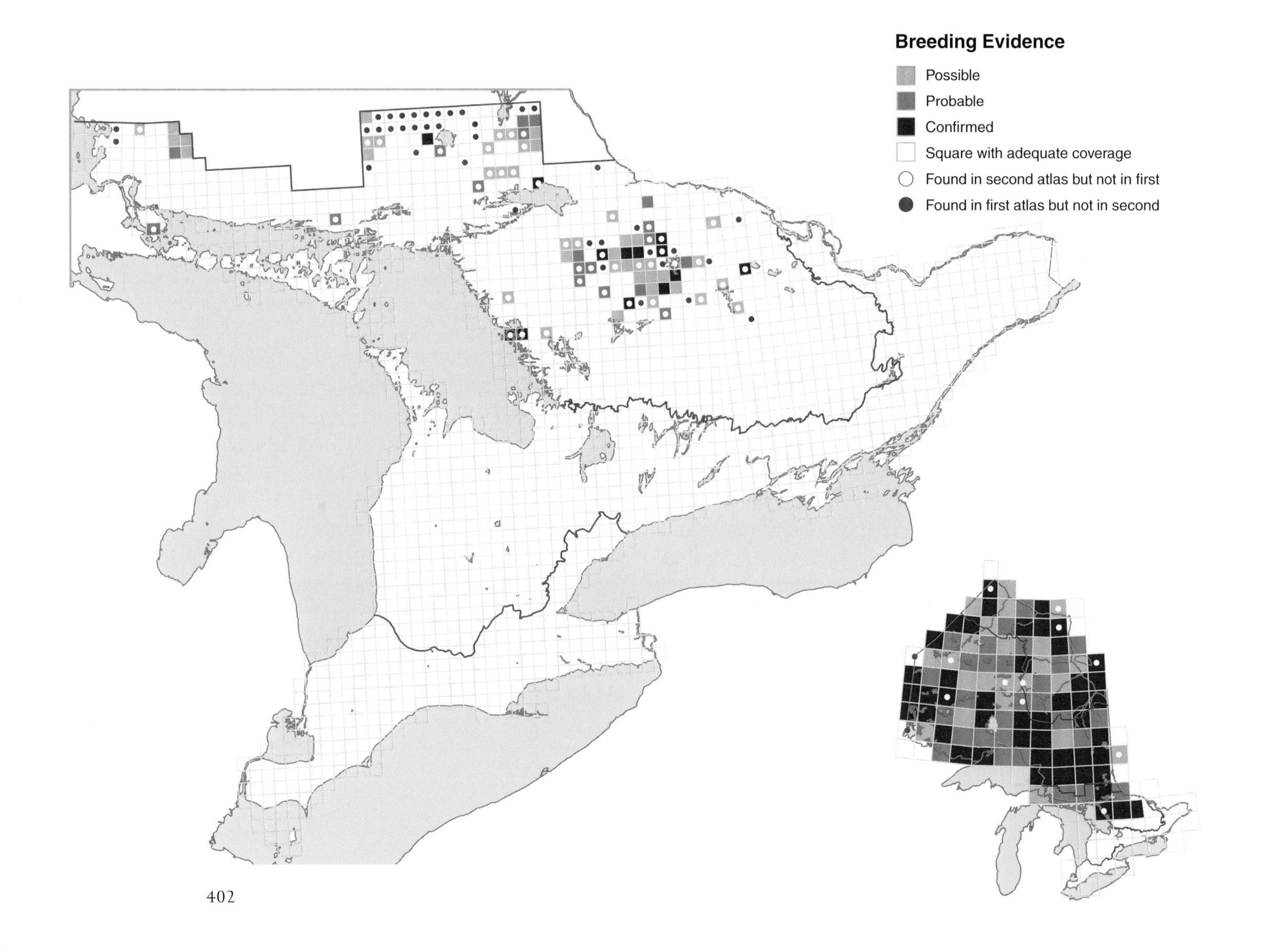

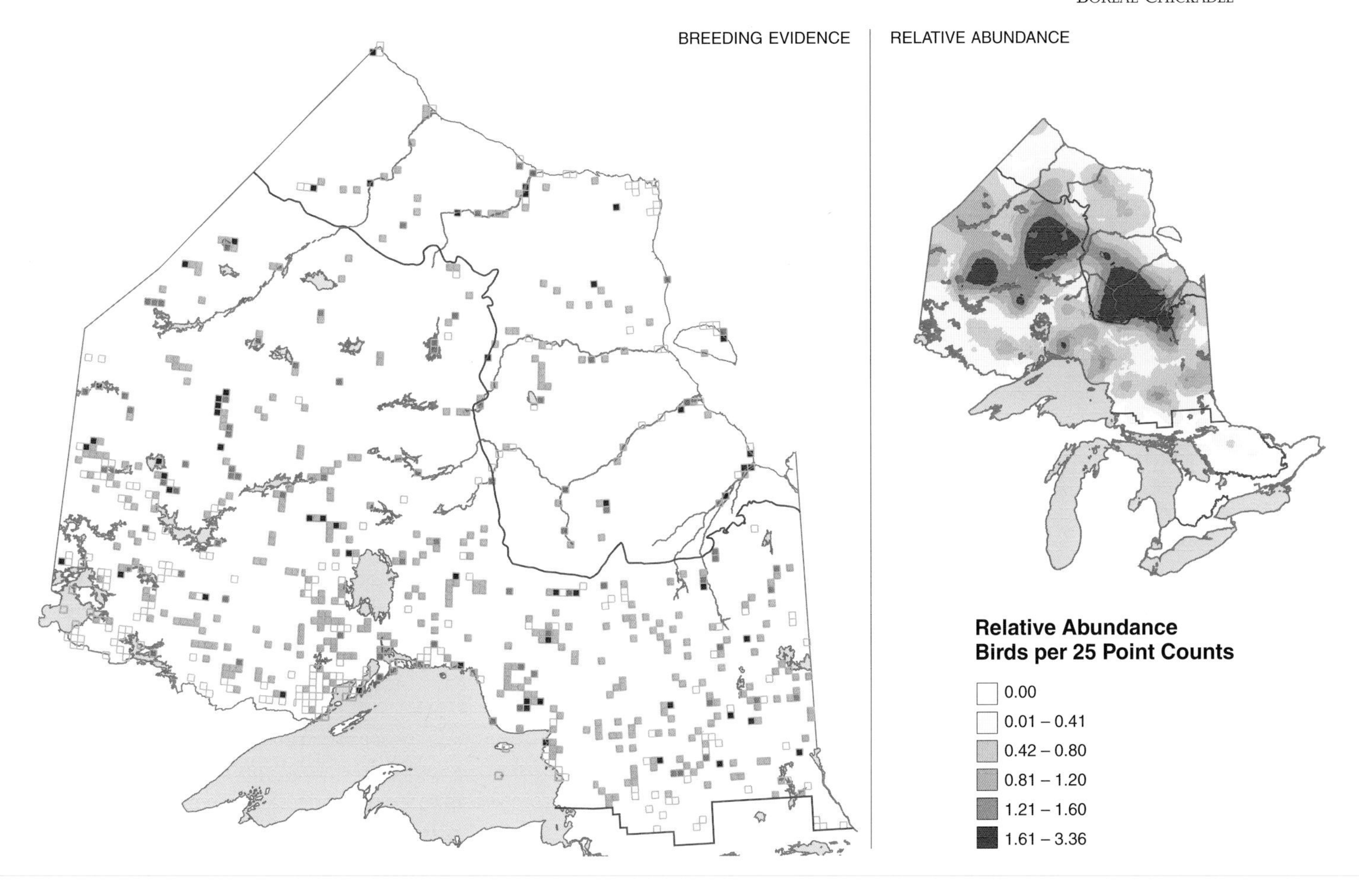

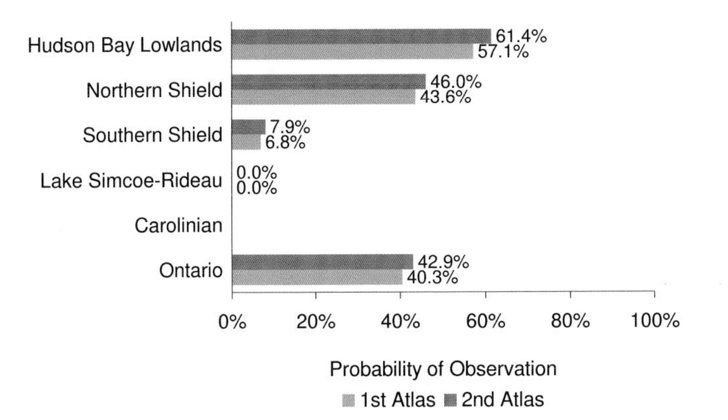

the province as a whole or any of the atlas regions. However, BBS data for both Ontario and Canada show a significant decrease in this species; in Ontario, the decrease has been 11.5% annually since 1981. As the BBS in Ontario covers only a small portion of the Boreal Chickadee's range, the apparent decrease may be an artifact of small sample size. Moreover, the timing of BBS surveys coincides with the period of least vocal activity for the species. It has been suggested that there is a link between Spruce Budworm outbreaks and Boreal Chickadee abundance (Gage et al. 1970; Bolgiano 2004). Thus, lower numbers may be related to the lack of a significant budworm outbreak in the vicinity of BBS routes for 30 or more years (R. Tozer, pers. comm.).

Breeding biology: Although primarily associated with coniferous forests, the Boreal Chickadee may also breed in forests with a deciduous component. It is a cavity nester, excavating its own cavity in dead trees and stumps. The female does most of the excavation, while the male stays nearby (Ficken et al. 1996).

Nests are easiest to find during the excavation period, which occurs in early May before many atlassers were in the field, especially in the more northerly parts of the range. During this period, the male frequently feeds the female in response to her wing-quivering display and "*broken-dee*" call (Ficken et al. 1996). Vocalization is reduced considerably during incubation and occurs primarily when the female solicits food from the male when she leaves the nest.

After the young hatch, they are fed by both parents for about 18 days until fledging. In this period, the adults make frequent trips to the nest but remain relatively quiet. Only after the young fledge does the species become more detectable as the family group travels together through the large breeding territory and the young give frequent begging calls.

Abundance: Although densities of over 1.6 birds/25 point counts were recorded in some areas, the Boreal Chickadee is not often detected on point counts. The average density in both the Hudson Bay Lowlands and Northern Shield regions was less than 1 bird/25 point counts. Areas of high density include the southern part of the Hudson Bay Lowlands and the northern part of the Northern Shield. The higher densities found in these areas reflect the larger proportion of the species' preferred conifer habitat found in more northerly areas. Given the difficulty of detecting this species, the pattern of low abundance shown on the map should be interpreted with caution.
– Margaret A. McLaren

Tufted Titmouse

Mésange bicolore

Baeolophus bicolor

Peter Ferguson

The Tufted Titmouse is a sedentary species found through much of the eastern US and eastern Mexico, ranging as far north as Michigan and southern Ontario. The only eastern titmouse species, it is still uncommon and local in southern Ontario, where it is restricted mostly to areas near the shores of Lakes Erie and Ontario and the larger river valleys in the Carolinian region. It was first recorded in Ontario in 1914 at Point Pelee and has spread northward slowly (Peck and James 1987). Although breeding evidence was noted in 1936, it was not until 1953 that the first nest was discovered (Peck and James 1987). It remains established as a breeder only within the Carolinian region, though it is perhaps making inroads in the vicinity of Kingston in the Lake Simcoe-Rideau region.

Distribution and population status: The core range of the Tufted Titmouse is situated in the Niagara Peninsula, with additional concentrations along Lake Erie and in Chatham-Kent, and Essex and Lambton Counties, where it was not found during the first atlas. Within the Carolinian region, the species showed a significant increase of approximately 300% in the probability of observation between atlases. In addition to infilling of gaps in its previous range, a limited increase occurred to the north and east, including a minor expansion from four to seven squares in the Lake Simcoe-Rideau region. Birds in eastern Ontario likely are originating from the expanding population in adjacent New York.

Between 1980 and 2005, BBS data show an annual increase of about 1% in the US, with greater increases in the states neighbouring Ontario: 4% in Michigan and 10% in New York (Sauer et al. 2005). The species is not common enough to be detected on sufficient Ontario BBS routes for trend analysis.

Numbers increased steadily in the Windsor area beginning in the mid-1980s. The small portion of the Detroit River, Michigan CBC that falls on the Windsor/LaSalle side of the Detroit River had 32 titmice on 1 January 2000 and 35 in

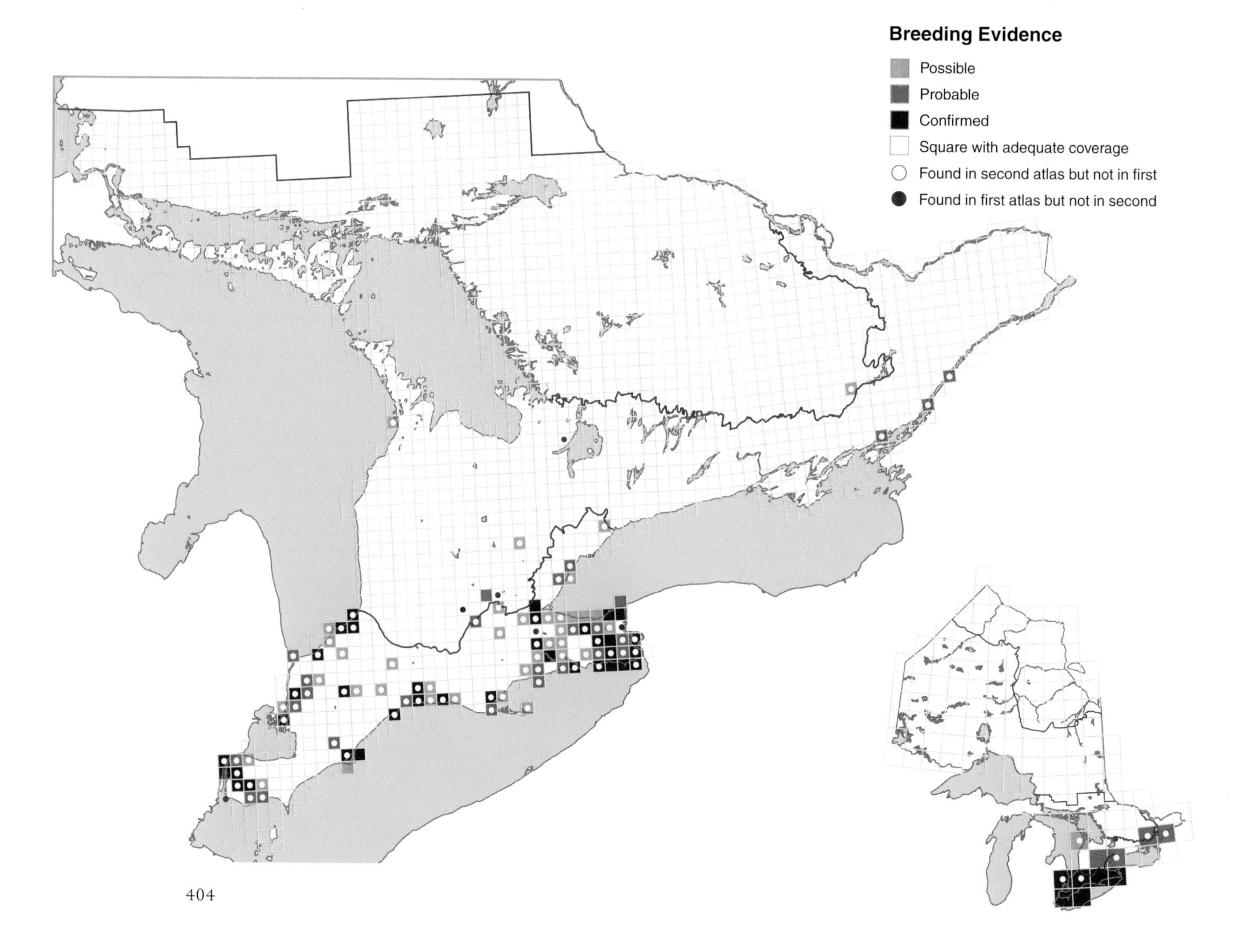

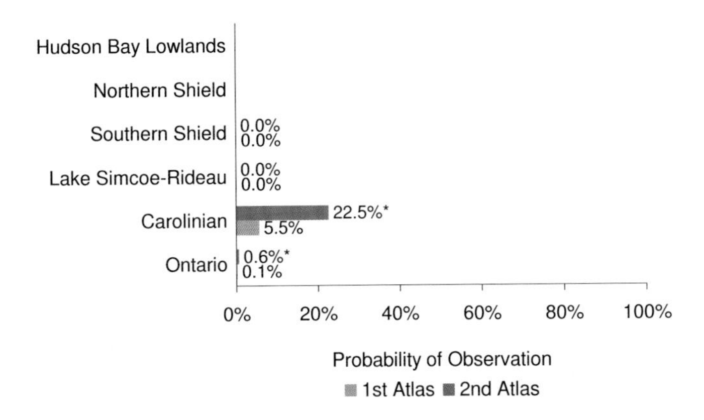

2001. The 2002 West Nile Virus outbreak wiped out close to 80-90% of this population, with a sudden drop in numbers in the latter part of 2002. The population now seems to be slowly recovering, with four birds on the 2006/2007 CBC (P. Pratt, pers. comm.).

The Tufted Titmouse has joined species such as the Red-bellied Woodpecker and Northern Mockingbird whose ranges have expanded northward between atlases. These expansions may be attributable at least in part to climate change (Price 2004). Specific factors relating to the expansion of the Tufted Titmouse include the availability of suitable habitat and food sources and its tendency to wander north in the fall and winter (Grubb and Pravosudov 1994). It prefers woodlands with large trees, especially those producing abundant mast, such as Pin Oak and beech (Grubb and Pravosudov 1994); the current distribution of the Tufted Titmouse in Ontario coincides very closely with that of Pin Oak. Combined factors of milder winters, the species' habit of hoarding food in fall and winter, and widespread availability of bird feeders together allow it to survive winters farther north.

Breeding biology: Often, the Tufted Titmouse forages high in trees, making it somewhat difficult to observe. However, family groups remain together, active and noisy for up to six weeks following fledging (Grubb and Pravosudov 1994), improving detection probability. Because it is sedentary, the species tends to nest in the same area in which it winters. In their first winter, young titmice join flocks, either with their parents or other adults, and remain near the nesting area. In early spring, flocks break up, and birds live in pairs or trios.

Nests are usually located in natural cavities or cavities excavated by woodpeckers, but the Tufted Titmouse also will use nest boxes. Nesting begins in April, with eggs laid during the first or second week of May. It is single-brooded, and young fledge by early June in most areas (Grubb and Pravosudov 1994).

Abundance: The Tufted Titmouse was detected on too few point counts to create an abundance map. The limited data suggest that it is more common in the Niagara area than elsewhere. It occurs in moderate densities in the Lambton Co. area but is found in low densities in the rest of its range. Although it is on the increase and expanding its range, it is still not widespread or common in southern Ontario. If it continues to take advantage of bird feeders and to benefit from milder conditions, there is great potential for continued expansion. – *Peter Read*

Clutch size is three to nine eggs, usually five or six. Nestlings leave the nest on the 15th or 16th day after hatching (Grubb and Pravosudov 1994). *Photo: George K. Peck*

The Tufted Titmouse frequently uses tall, open, oak-dominated forest with a heavy herbaceous layer of grasses and forbs for breeding in Ontario. *Photo: P. Allen Woodliffe*

Red-breasted Nuthatch

Sittelle à poitrine rousse

Sitta canadensis

George K. Peck

Like all nuthatches, the Red-breasted Nuthatch often forages for insects and spiders by moving head first down tree trunks and branches with acrobatic flare. It spends considerable time in the crowns and areas of dense growth on conifers, especially spruce and fir trees. It caches food items in fall and winter for later retrieval, which may be essential to the survival of birds that remain for the winter in the Boreal Forest. The species undergoes irruptive migrations roughly biennially, mirroring the seed-crop cycle in the Boreal Forest.

True to its specific name *canadensis*, the majority of the species' global range is in Canada, from Newfoundland to British Columbia and southern Yukon. This diminutive passerine also occurs across the most northern parts of the continental US, extending as far south as Mexico at high altitudes in the west, and in the east along the Appalachians into North Carolina (Ghalambor and Martin 1999).

Distribution and population status: As predicted by Mills (in Cadman et al.1987) in the first atlas, the Red-breasted Nuthatch has expanded southward in the past 20 years, likely in response to habitat provided by maturing conifer plantations across southern Ontario. Largely absent in southern Ontario a century ago (Macoun and Macoun 1909), the species is only absent today in extreme southwestern Ontario, where conifer plantations and woodlots are scarce in the intensively agricultural landscape, and in the extreme north, perhaps because there are few coniferous forests of adequate stature. The probability of observation of the Red-breasted Nuthatch increased significantly by 38% in the province as a whole. There were significant increases in all five regions, with the greatest increase occurring in the Hudson Bay Lowlands, where the probability of observation more than doubled. As well as this increase in the far north, there was a significant 17 km southward shift of the core range of this species in southern Ontario since the first atlas, caused by large increases in the

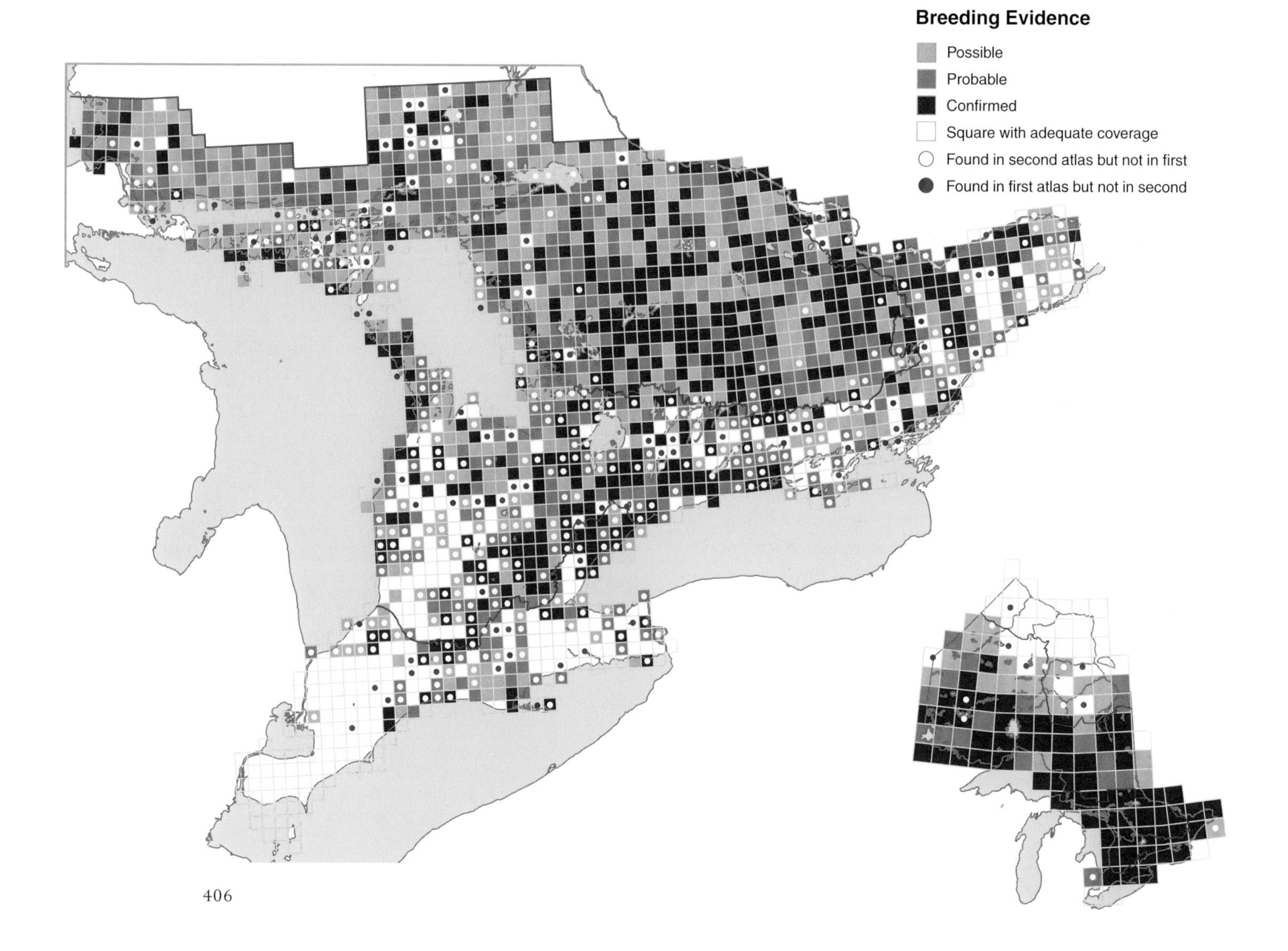

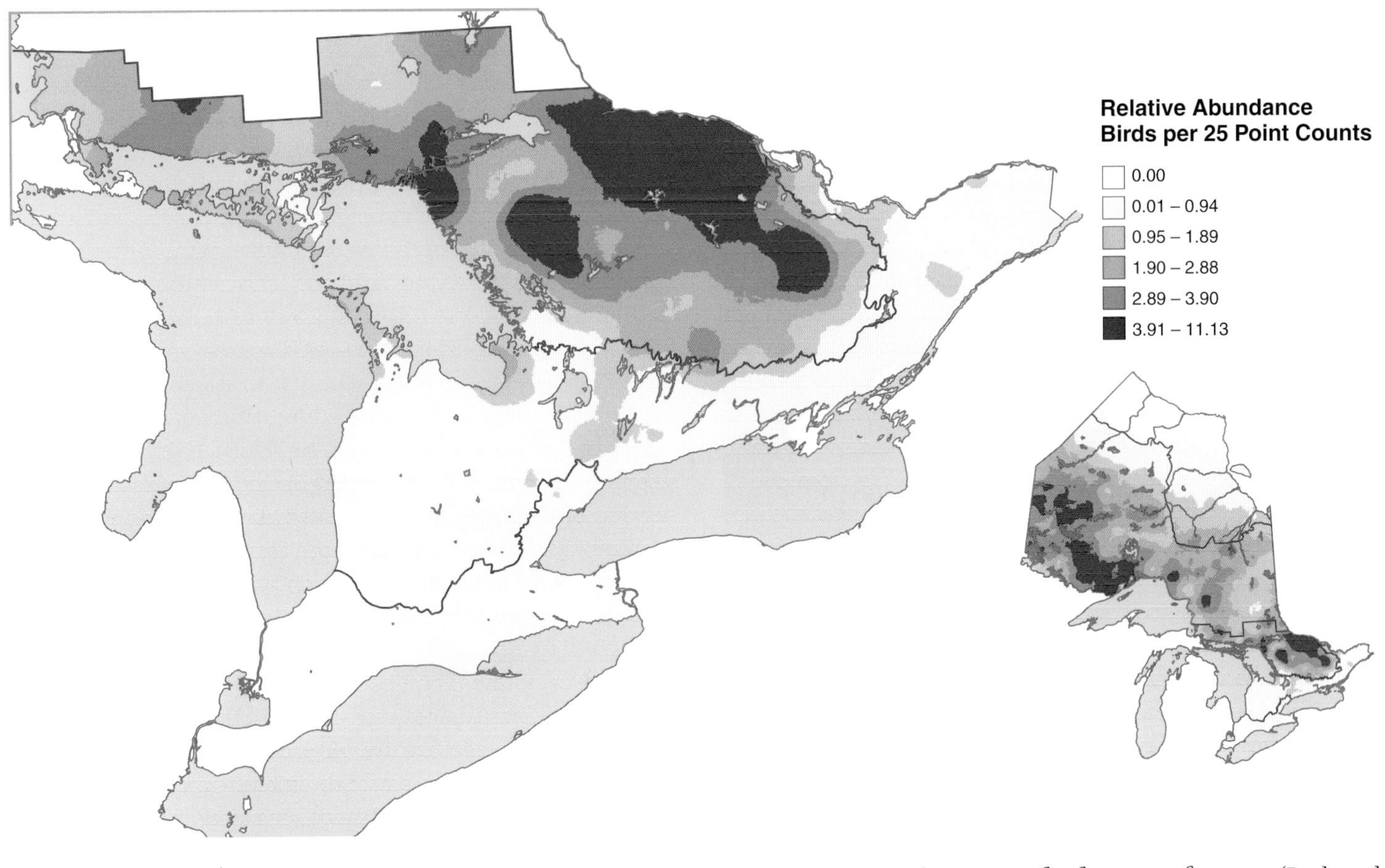

Probability of Observation

Region	1st Atlas	2nd Atlas
Hudson Bay Lowlands	11.4%	27.4%*
Northern Shield	57.1%	74.7%*
Southern Shield	82.5%	92.6%*
Lake Simcoe-Rideau	32.9%	52.6%*
Carolinian	10.6%	19.2%*
Ontario	44.1%	60.6%*

Carolinian and Lake Simcoe-Rideau regions. BBS data suggest a small but significant increase in the species' Ontario population since 1968 (Downes et al. 2005) but with no significant changes since the first atlas. This discrepancy is difficult to explain but may be due to the particular habitat sampled by BBS roadside routes.

The primary reason for the species' expansion south of the Shield over the past half-century is likely the increase and maturation of conifer plantations in many areas, which create attractive breeding habitat for this and other species; the Yellow-rumped Warbler, Hermit Thrush, and Golden-crowned Kinglet have also seen significant increases in these regions. Even small clumps of mature spruce in an urban setting have enticed Red-breasted Nuthatches to nest nearby (Cheskey 1990). The reasons for the increases farther north are unclear.

Breeding biology: The Red-breasted Nuthatch begins nesting in March or early April. Excavation is started by the male but primarily completed by the female while the male aggressively defends the territory. Nests average 3-9 m high in a dead deciduous tree and are never far from conifer trees (Peck and James 1987; Ghalambor and Martin 1999). Unique to cavity-nesting passerines in North America, the Red-breasted Nuthatch smears conifer resin around the cavity opening, apparently a tactic to deter potential nest predators (Ghalambor and Martin 1999).

More nasal than the call of the While-breasted Nuthatch, the loud, high-pitched "*yanks*" and incessant series of "*aih aih aih aih*" notes of the Red-breasted Nuthatch are easily detected. Most possible or probable evidence was of calling or territorial birds, and the species' presence is unlikely to have gone undetected in most squares, except possibly in some in the Lake Simcoe-Rideau and Carolinian regions, where its occurrence may be highly localized or ephemeral. Although confirmed breeding was recorded in 44 of 47 atlas administrative regions, breeding was confirmed in only 22% of the squares in which the species was found. Confirmation was usually in the form of fledged young; while nest holes may be concealed and difficult to spot in dense forest, family groups are quite vocal and relatively easy to locate.

Abundance: The Red-breasted Nuthatch is found in highest abundance in the central and upper Ottawa River valley and the Algonquin Highlands in eastern Ontario, and northwest of Lake Superior to the Berens River and Sandy Lake. Densities are often over 3.9 birds/25 point counts in these areas. This likely reflects the prevalence in these areas of coniferous forest, its preferred habitat. In contrast, north and south of the Shield, less than 1 bird/25 point counts was observed. – *Edward Cheskey*

White-breasted Nuthatch

Sittelle à poitrine blanche

Sitta carolinensis

Peter Ferguson

The White-breasted Nuthatch is a familiar year-round resident of deciduous and mixed forests in North America, from the southern regions of Canada to central Mexico (Pravosudov and Grubb 1993). It is easily identified by its nasal calls and its nuthatch habit of moving down tree trunks head first, and is distinguished from the Red-breasted Nuthatch by its white breast and face. Breeding pairs stay together throughout the year and will often travel with mixed flocks that have entered their permanent territories in the winter. A frequent visitor to backyard bird feeders, this nuthatch will often leave its territory to reach this rich food source in the winter (Pravosudov and Grubb 1993). It hoards food in the cooler months, and takes its name from its tendency to hack open nuts and seeds that it has lodged in tree crevices.

Distribution and population status: The White-breasted Nuthatch is most common in southern Ontario where the deciduous trees it uses for nesting and foraging are abundant. The probability of observation for the species is 77% in both the Carolinian and Lake Simcoe-Rideau regions and 58% in the Southern Shield. It is uncommon in northern Ontario, where its preferred habitat is scarcer. Within southern Ontario, the species' range has expanded to the north by a small but significant amount since the first atlas, possibly due to milder winters and the growing popularity of backyard bird feeders.

Between atlases, the probability of observation for the species increased significantly in the province as a whole by 19%, and in the Lake Simcoe-Rideau and Southern Shield regions by 7% and 28%, respectively. Although it is still somewhat patchy in distribution in the southern Shield, most squares where it was new in the second atlas occurred in the area from Algonquin Prov. Park west to Sault Ste. Marie. Increases in hardwood-dominated forests and canopy cover in this region, as a result of forest succession and maturation,

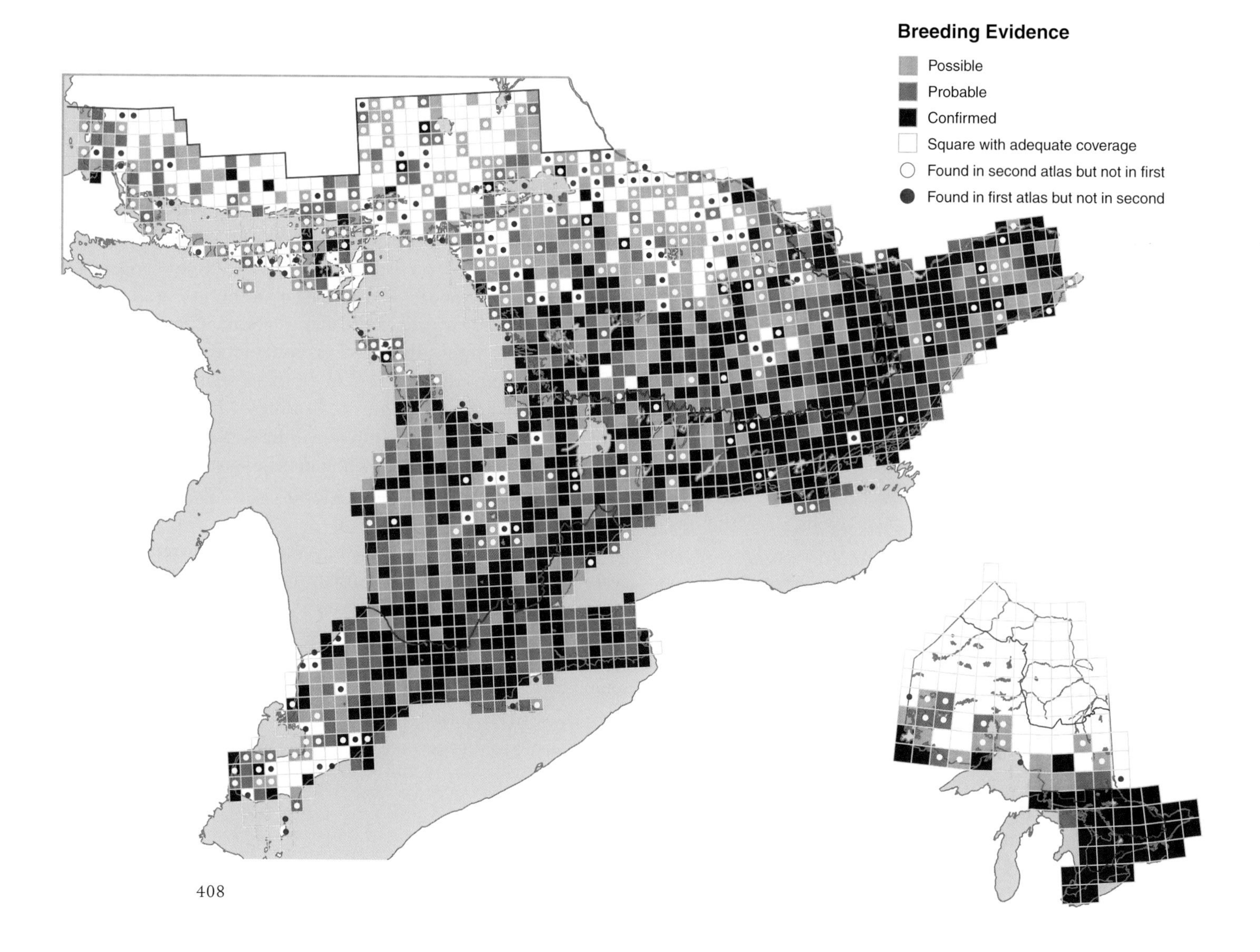

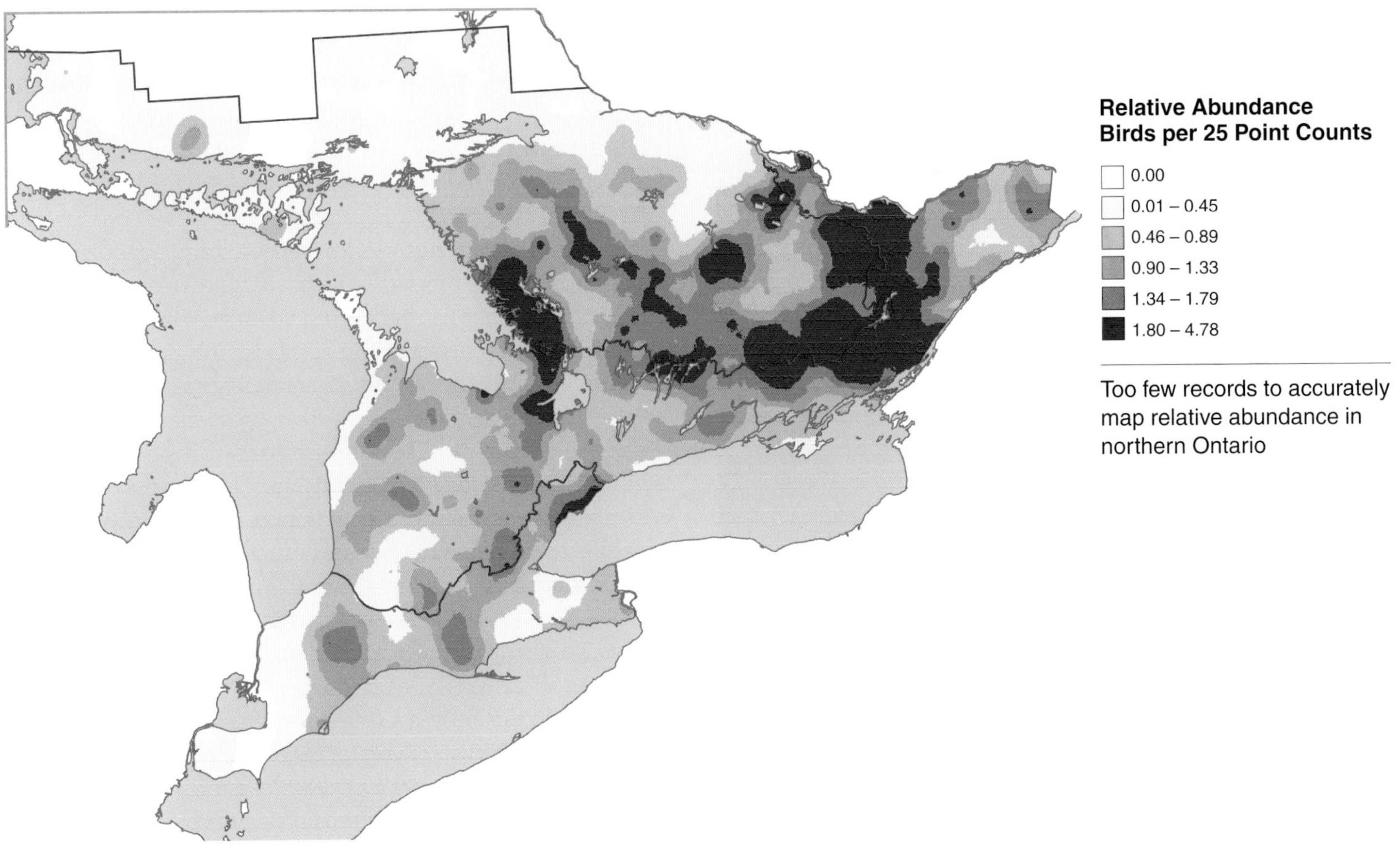

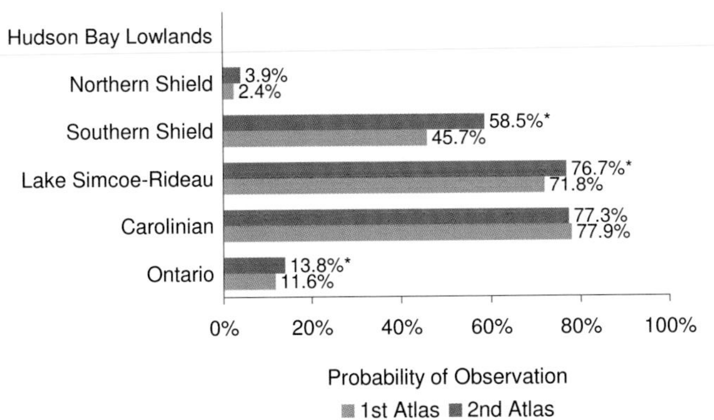

likely have resulted in more favourable environments for this forest associate, and therefore higher occurrence.

The White-breasted Nuthatch was also found locally as far north as Timmins in the east and Lake Nipigon and Lac Seul in the west in areas where it was not recorded in the first atlas. Breeding was confirmed near Rainy River and in the Thunder Bay area, where it was also confirmed in the first atlas.

The increase in populations observed between atlases reflects the BBS annual increases over the same period: a 4.1% near-significant increase in Ontario and a 2.9% significant increase in Canada. Many other resident species have shown similar trends, which can also be attributed largely to milder winters and an increase in bird feeders.

Breeding biology: In Ontario, the White-breasted Nuthatch prefers mature beech-maple forests but will also use mixed-hardwood forests (James 1984b). It generally prefers to nest close to forest edges or canopy gaps (Pravosudov and Grubb 1993). Nests are usually built in natural cavities in the main trunk of large-diameter living trees, and the same cavity is often reused in subsequent years.

The White-breasted Nuthatch begins inspecting cavities in early April, starting incubation between late April and mid-May. Although the adults stop singing during breeding and are inconspicuous early in the season, the young can be heard peeping from lower cavities within days of hatching, their begging calls getting progressively louder with age. Shortly before fledging, the nest becomes a flurry of activity, as feeding trips by the adults are frequent and continuous. Although the nests are difficult to inspect, behavioural cues can often confirm breeding status. Fledged young remain with adults in the pair's territory close to the nest for several weeks, further aiding in the detection of breeding pairs. The species' distinctive, nasal calls are usually readily detected, and breeding can be reasonably easy to confirm, as shown by the relatively high 38% of squares that received this status. The atlas maps are therefore accurate reflections of breeding distribution.

Abundance: Densities of the White-breasted Nuthatch are highest from Kingston north to Ottawa and west to Georgian Bay, with more than 1.8 birds/25 point counts across much of this area. This region has an abundance of suitable deciduous forest ideal for this species. Densities in the Carolinian region are lower and more localized, likely a result of less available habitat within the highly fragmented agricultural and urban landscape. Abundance is lowest in the north where the large hardwoods necessary for foraging and nesting are rare. – *Kata Bavrlic*

Brown Creeper

Grimpereau brun

Certhia americana

George K. Peck

One of the smallest and most inconspicuous of songbirds, the Brown Creeper breeds from Alaska to Newfoundland and south to the mid-Atlantic states in the east and to Central America in the west. It is a permanent resident throughout much of its range, withdrawing only from the northernmost areas of the breeding range in winter (Hejl et al. 2002). Its preferred habitat is mature and older coniferous and mixed forests containing large-diameter (over 30 cm dbh) trunks. Trees with strongly furrowed bark are preferred for foraging (Hejl et al. 2002). The Brown Creeper's characteristic foraging method consists of a spiral search up the trunk as it gleans insects and spiders from the bark of one tree, followed by a flight to the base of another tree where the spiral search pattern begins again.

Distribution and population status: The Brown Creeper is widely distributed throughout Ontario but is uncommon in the Carolinian region where forest cover is sparse, with only a 9% probability of observation. The probability of observation was similar in the three most northerly regions, at 55% in the Southern Shield, 52% in the Northern Shield, and 48% in the Hudson Bay Lowlands. The probability of observation in the Hudson Bay Lowlands likely overstates the actual distribution of the species in much of this region. It prefers large trees, which, in the Hudson Bay Lowlands, are largely restricted to riparian areas that support narrow strips of spruce forest. These habitats were likely over-represented, since many of the squares with data in this region were covered by canoeists.

The probability of observation of the Brown Creeper increased significantly in the three most northerly regions between the two atlases. The increase is particularly noteworthy in the Northern Shield and Hudson Bay Lowlands regions, where the probability of observation doubled and tripled, respectively, compared to the first atlas. This may reflect the participation of more skilled observers better able to detect the

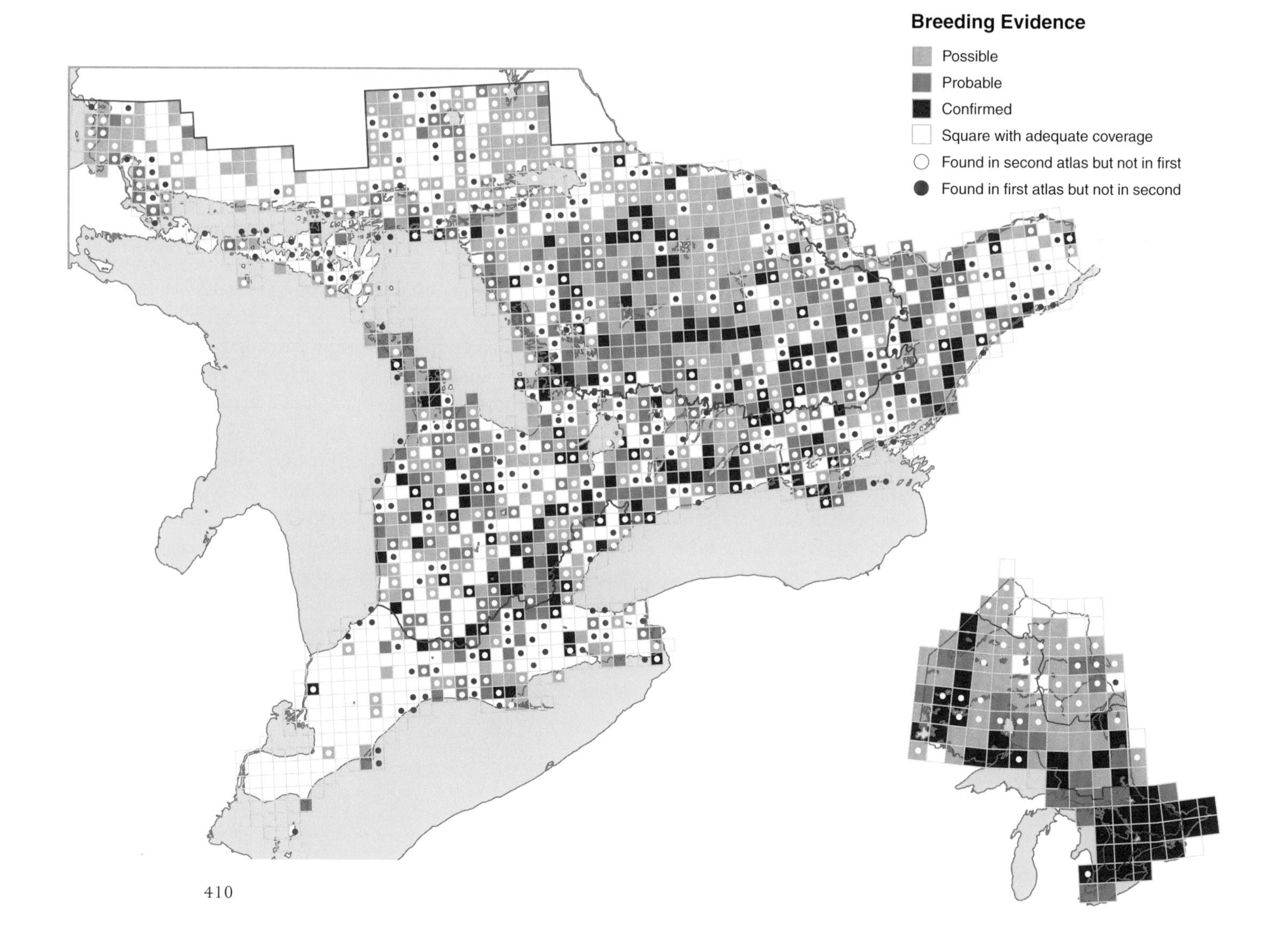

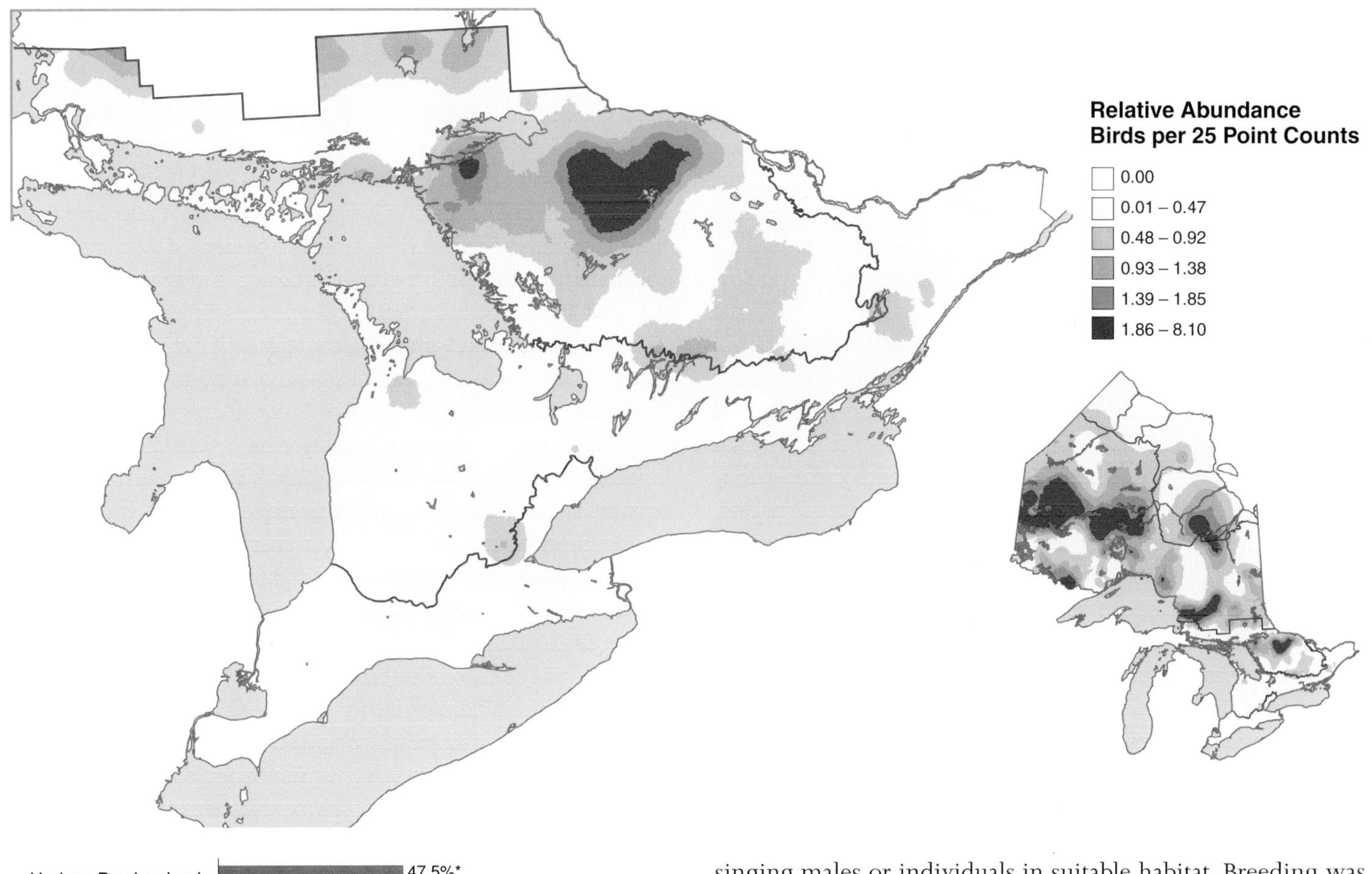

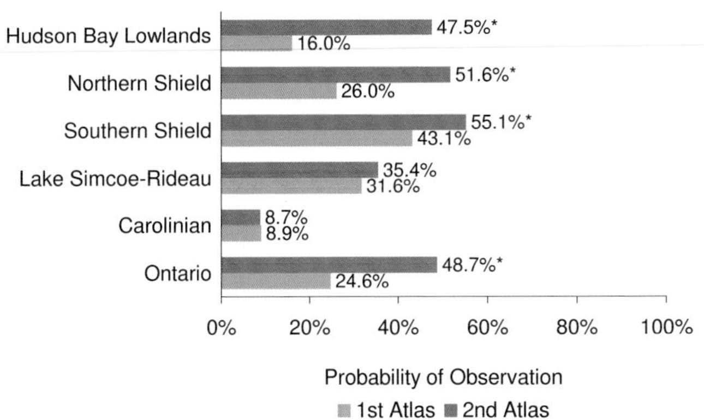

species in this atlas. The BBS shows no change in abundance between the two atlas periods, but an increase in the two northern regions would not likely be picked up by the BBS since most routes are in southern and central Ontario.

Breeding biology: Pair formation in the Brown Creeper apparently occurs during late winter (Hejl et al. 2002), and males sing most actively early in the spring. The song, though musical, is thin and does not carry long distances. The female builds the nest, typically between the trunk and a flap of bark on a dead tree. Both deciduous and coniferous trees are used, the most important feature being the presence of loose plates of bark under which to hide the nest. The female is quite inconspicuous during incubation but becomes more obvious when the adults are feeding young in the nest. The species is probably most conspicuous once the young fledge. The family group travels through the trees together, with both adults and young frequently giving trilling call notes.

In 67% of the squares in which the Brown Creeper was detected, the highest breeding evidence was in the form of singing males or individuals in suitable habitat. Breeding was confirmed in only 13% of squares. Despite the difficulty of locating nests of this species, nests with eggs or young were recorded in 11 of the 47 atlas administrative regions.

Abundance: In the areas of highest abundance, the Brown Creeper was recorded at densities of over 1.9 birds/25 point counts. Areas reporting high abundance include Algonquin and Quetico Prov. Parks and the Algoma Highlands. The proportion of older forests preferred by the species may be higher in these areas than on the rest of the landscape, which consists of a mosaic of forest of different age classes. The abundance map also suggests a very large area of high density in northwestern Ontario, from Woodland Caribou to Wabakimi Prov. Parks. Most of the point counts in this area were in the parks or north of the area where logging occurs, and the method used to create the abundance maps may therefore overestimate the density in the intervening landscape.

In southern Ontario, the Brown Creeper was recorded in relatively low numbers, averaging less than 1 bird/25 point counts in each of the three regions. The species was not recorded on point counts in most of the Carolinian region and southeastern Ontario east of Cornwall, areas with intensive agriculture and generally low forest cover. – *Margaret A. McLaren*

Carolina Wren

Troglodyte de Caroline

Thryothorus ludovicianus

John Reaume

First noted in Ontario by Thomas McIlwraith in 1891 (McIlwraith 1894), the Carolina Wren has since become a resident breeding species in the southern part of the province. Its expansion into and across southern Ontario has probably been due to the creation of new habitats following the clearing of the forests in the 18th and 19th centuries, and to changing climatic conditions. It is vulnerable to deep snow and severe cold periods when mean daily minimum temperatures fall below -12°C (Haggerty and Morton 1995).

The Carolina Wren appeared on the National Audubon Society's Blue List in the 1980s (Tate and Tate 1982; Tate 1986) because populations were considered to be low in Ontario, the mid-western prairies, and the southern Great Plains regions. It remains an uncommon permanent resident in Ontario. Its loud song continues to ring out in its preferred habitats in the southern part of the province, although it suffers occasional setbacks in survival during harsh winters.

Distribution and population status: Between atlases, the species expanded considerably, with a significant, more than five-fold increase in its probability of observation in the Carolinian region and the province as a whole. In the Lake Simcoe-Rideau region, the species has expanded from seven squares with breeding evidence in the first atlas to 65 squares in the second atlas. The distribution map indicates a clear affinity for southern Ontario south of the Shield, particularly near the lower Great Lakes shorelines. The distribution also follows major river valleys, such as the Thames and Grand Rivers, due to habitat preferences. Scattered locations occur farther inland, suggesting possible continued expansion of range. However, the species is limited in its potential northward expansion by snow depth and the severity of winter cold (Haggerty and Morton 1995).

The Carolina Wren is reported too infrequently on BBS in Ontario to be analysed for trends. However, BBS data indicate

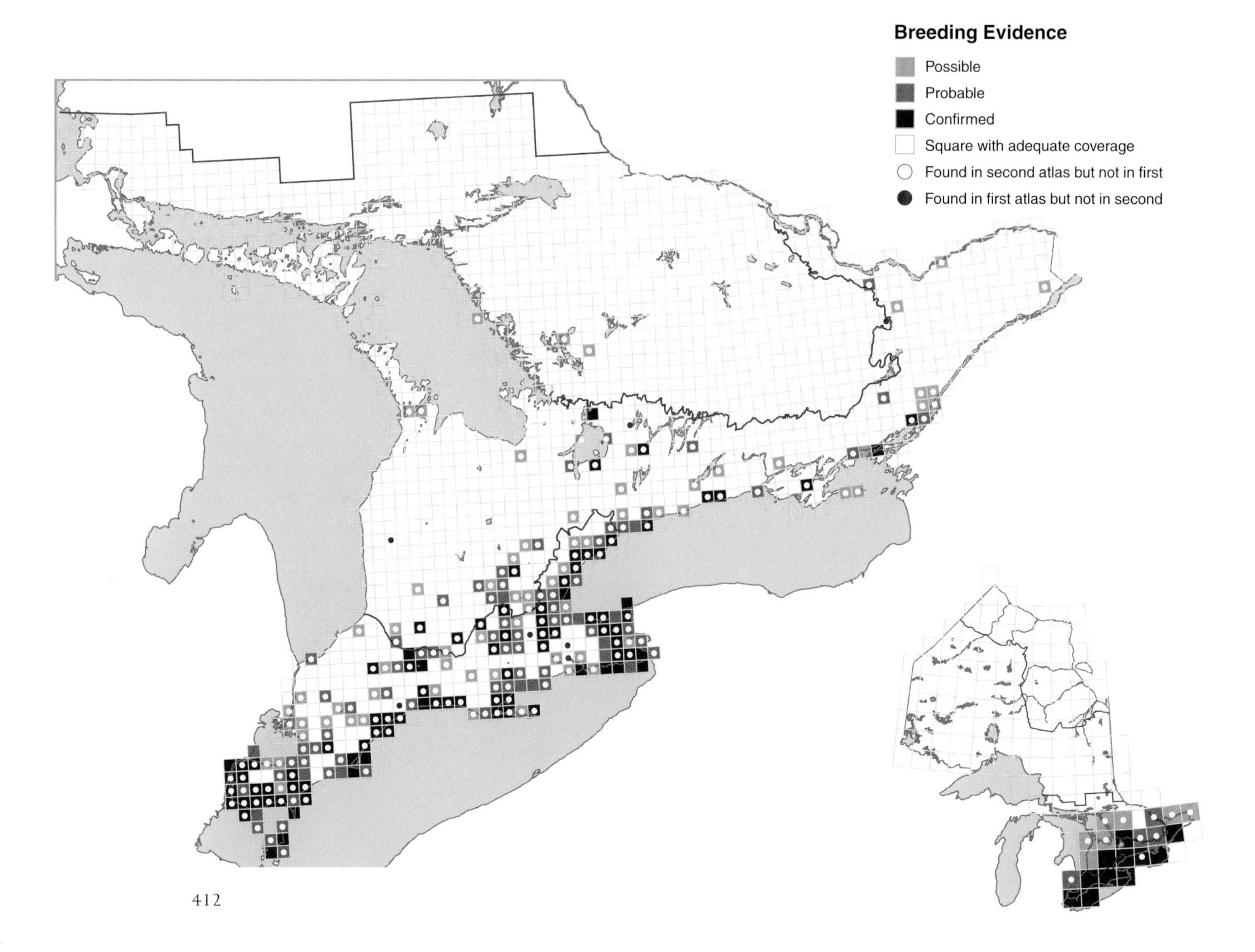

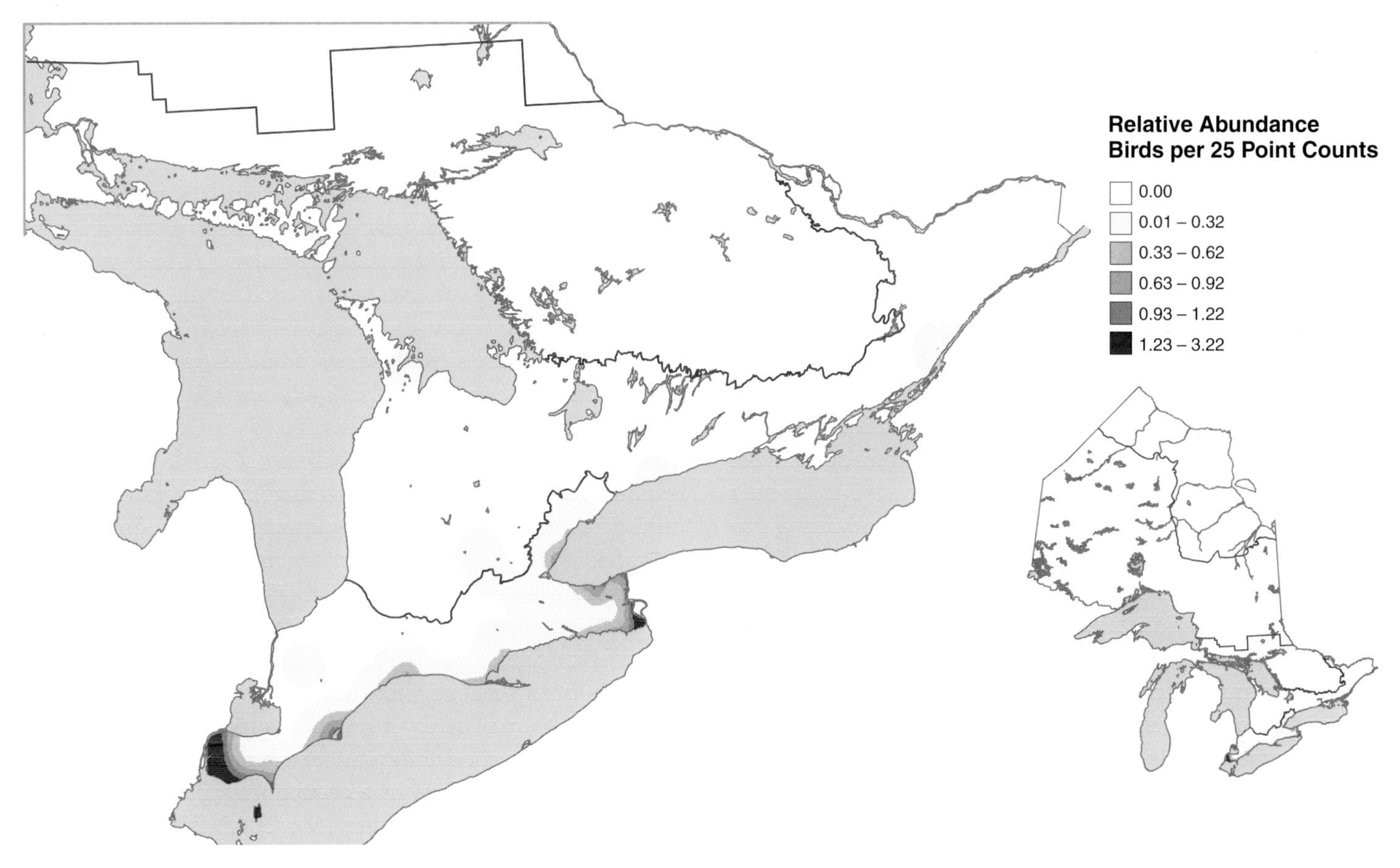

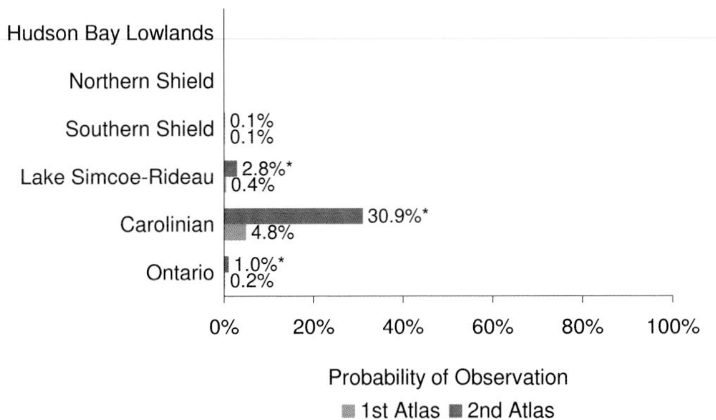

that populations have grown substantially in nearby US states, with significant annual increases in New York (22%) and Ohio (4%) (Sauer et al. 2005).

Breeding biology: The Carolina Wren is non-migratory, and territories and pair bonds are maintained all year (Haggerty and Morton 1995). It begins nesting early in the season and is at least occasionally double-brooded in Ontario, with egg dates ranging from early April to early August (Peck and James 1987). Males are very vocal prior to nest building, and often select high singing perches. The species also occurs quite frequently in urban areas with suitable habitat. It responds readily to "pishing" and similar inducements. All these behavioural aspects contribute to the ease and high probability of detection, and suggest that the map is a good representation of this wren's current distribution in the province. However, once nesting begins, song frequency declines. Song frequency is also dependent on population density, which in turn is dependent on habitat quality. In most of the species' range in Ontario, population densities are low, resulting in relatively low song frequency.

The Carolina Wren prefers moist or bottomland woods rather than dry upland woods. It usually builds its hidden nest in tangles of vegetation, shrubs, holes, and crevices. The cup-shaped nest is made from a varied assortment of materials and is more haphazardly built than that of other wren species (Haggerty and Morton 1995). In the northern part of its range (including Ontario), nest volumes are greater, presumably providing greater insulation, and often they are located in or around human habitations. Several "dummy" nests may be built within a territory. Only females brood, and they sit tightly on the nest (Haggerty and Morton 1995); males deliver food to the female. Since both parents feed the nestlings, careful observation may reveal the nest once the young hatch. Even though parents are secretive around the nest site, there was a very high level of breeding confirmation at 38% of the squares with breeding evidence, reflecting the relative ease of finding fledged young or adults carrying food. Dispersing hatch-year males sing regularly in the autumn (Haggerty and Morton 1995).

Abundance: The abundance maps suggest that densities of the Carolina Wren are low in southern Ontario, and show the areas of highest abundance to be in Niagara RM and Essex Co. The Carolina Wren population in Ontario likely will remain variable in abundance in the near future, due to its susceptibility to adverse winter conditions, even though it can adapt to various habitats and benefits from feeding stations. – *Peter Read*

House Wren

Troglodyte familier

Troglodytes aedon

Despite being small, brown, and lacking in conspicuous plumage, the House Wren is surely one of the most familiar birds in southern Ontario. Its ability to adapt to such anthropogenic habitats as suburban gardens, its tendency to use artificial structures as nest sites and, above all, its irrepressible singing make it difficult to overlook. The taxonomy of the House Wren complex is a matter of some dispute among ornithologists, with anywhere between one and 10 species being recognized. With the exception of the introduced House Sparrow, the House Wren superspecies occupies a greater latitudinal range in the Americas than any other passerine, occurring from northeastern British Columbia to Tierra del Fuego (Brewer and MacKay 2001). In eastern North America, its breeding range encompasses a broad swath of territory between approximately 36° N and 46° N. This range has expanded substantially, especially southward, in historical times, due to the creation of suitable habitat through forest clearing and the availability of nest sites in artificial situations (Johnson 1998).

Distribution and population status: In Ontario, the distribution of the House Wren did not change significantly between atlases. Comparison with the first atlas shows no significant change in the probability of observation in the province as a whole. In both atlases, the species was almost universally present in the Carolinian and Lake Simcoe-Rideau regions, but it drops off sharply on the Precambrian Shield. In the Southern Shield region, it is infrequent along the southern fringe from Lanark Co. west to Muskoka Dist., and is absent from large areas of Nipissing (Algonquin Dome) and Parry Sound Districts. Nevertheless, there was a significant 18% increase in the probability of observation for the species in this region. BBS data for Ontario between 1981 and 2005 indicate a modest population increase.

The House Wren was also found in a significant proportion

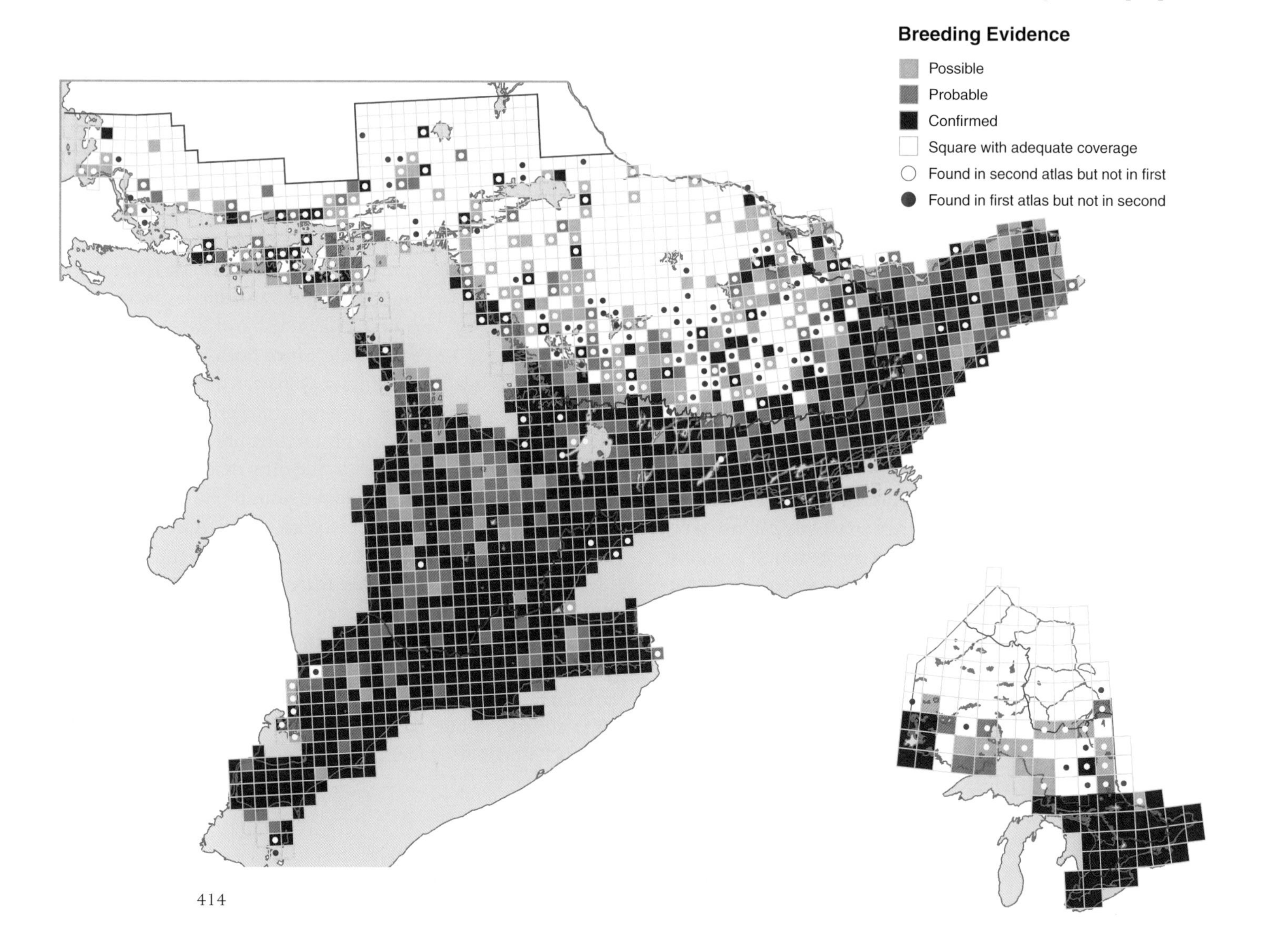

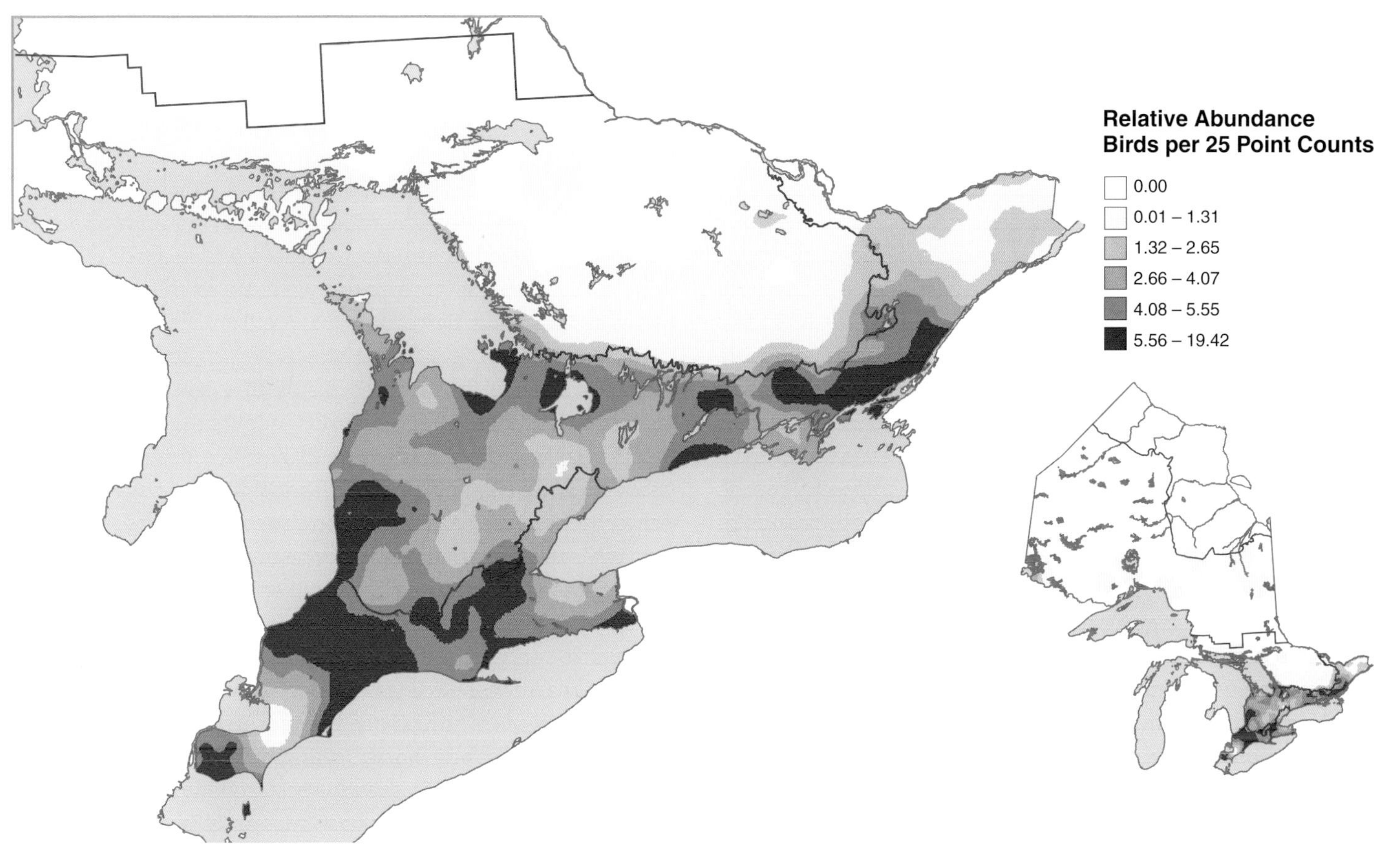

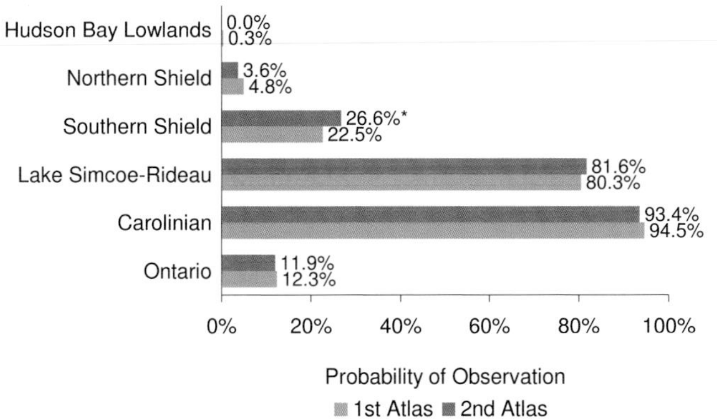

of the squares on Manitoulin Island and along the North Channel. Farther north, in Algoma Dist. and north of the French River, it becomes increasingly infrequent. In the Northern Shield, it is extremely sparse, with only a 4% probability of observation, and even this is due to a concentration in the Lake of the Woods area. This pattern of distribution reflects the species' preferred habitat, which includes areas with scattered shrubs such as abandoned farmland, open suburban areas, and field edges. It is associated with deciduous vegetation, so it is absent from the predominantly coniferous northern regions, despite patches of apparently suitable habitat.

Breeding biology: The House Wren is a cavity nester, readily using artificial nest boxes. This has resulted in its being studied as intensively as any North American passerine (Johnson 1998). A corollary of the use of nest boxes, as well as its ability to thrive in modified habitats, is the very high proportion of squares with confirmed breeding (59%) in contrast to most other wrens. The young are fed insects by both parents, and confirmation of breeding is often facilitated by their conspicuous forays for food. A small proportion of males are polygamous, in which case the second female tends to receive less assistance in feeding the young (Johnson 1998).

The presence of the House Wren frequently is detrimental to other species in its territory. Many wrens are known to attack the eggs of other species. Indeed, two large neotropical wrens have received the local name of "egg-sucker," doubtless due to their depredations in hen-houses, but this tendency seems to be especially prevalent in the House Wren, giving rise to a vitriolic attack on them in a 1925 article entitled "Down with the House Wren boxes" (Sherman 1925). This wren can have a significant effect on the breeding success of species such as the Prothonotary Warbler, and the decline of Bewick's Wren in eastern North America is correlated suspiciously with the appearance of the House Wren in the same areas (Kennedy and White 1997).

Abundance: The abundance maps for the House Wren give a clear picture of the influence of habitat. The highest densities are in areas with scattered deciduous woodland and shrubs, from Huron to Haldimand Counties and from southern Georgian Bay to Brockville. The most intensively agricultural areas of southwestern Ontario have lower densities, as do the most densely urban areas in the GTA.

The House Wren is highly migratory and winters in the southern US and Mexico, almost entirely south of the breeding range (Brewer et al. 2000). Thus, it is less likely than the Winter Wren to be affected negatively by severe winters. *– David Brewer*

Winter Wren

Troglodyte mignon

Troglodytes troglodytes

David Welbourne

The Winter Wren is unique in its family in having a very wide geographic distribution; an ancestral population in North America colonized the Old World, probably via the Bering land bridge, and is now widely distributed in Europe, Asia, and North Africa. In some parts of its Eurasian range, this wren has been very successful in colonizing diverse habitats and has become one of the most abundant species (Brewer and MacKay 2001). In North America, it is somewhat more specific in its habitat requirements; this and its more northerly distribution result in it being less familiar to the general public than the House Wren.

Distribution and population status: In Ontario, the Winter Wren is predominantly a species of conifer-dominated forests (Hejl et al. 2002). It is found sporadically and in small numbers in the Carolinian region, with only a 7% probability of observation. It occurs in the rather rare patches of suitable habitat in the Carolinian, including, for example, those of the Norfolk Sand Plain and Niagara Peninsula. As in the first atlas, the southernmost breeding outpost of the species was at Rondeau Prov. Park. In the Lake Simcoe-Rideau region, it is much more widely distributed, with a 49% probability of observation, but with evident gaps in the heavily agricultural areas of Perth and Huron Counties and in extreme eastern Ontario. In the northernmost areas of the Lake Simcoe-Rideau region, its presence is almost universal, and in both the Southern and Northern Shield regions, it occurs in almost every square. It becomes more sparsely distributed in the Hudson Bay Lowlands, where the probability of observation is 69%.

The Winter Wren is highly migratory, with only very small numbers overwintering. Sedentary populations in western Europe are frequently reduced catastrophically by severe winters (Brewer and MacKay 2001). Although the migratory pop-

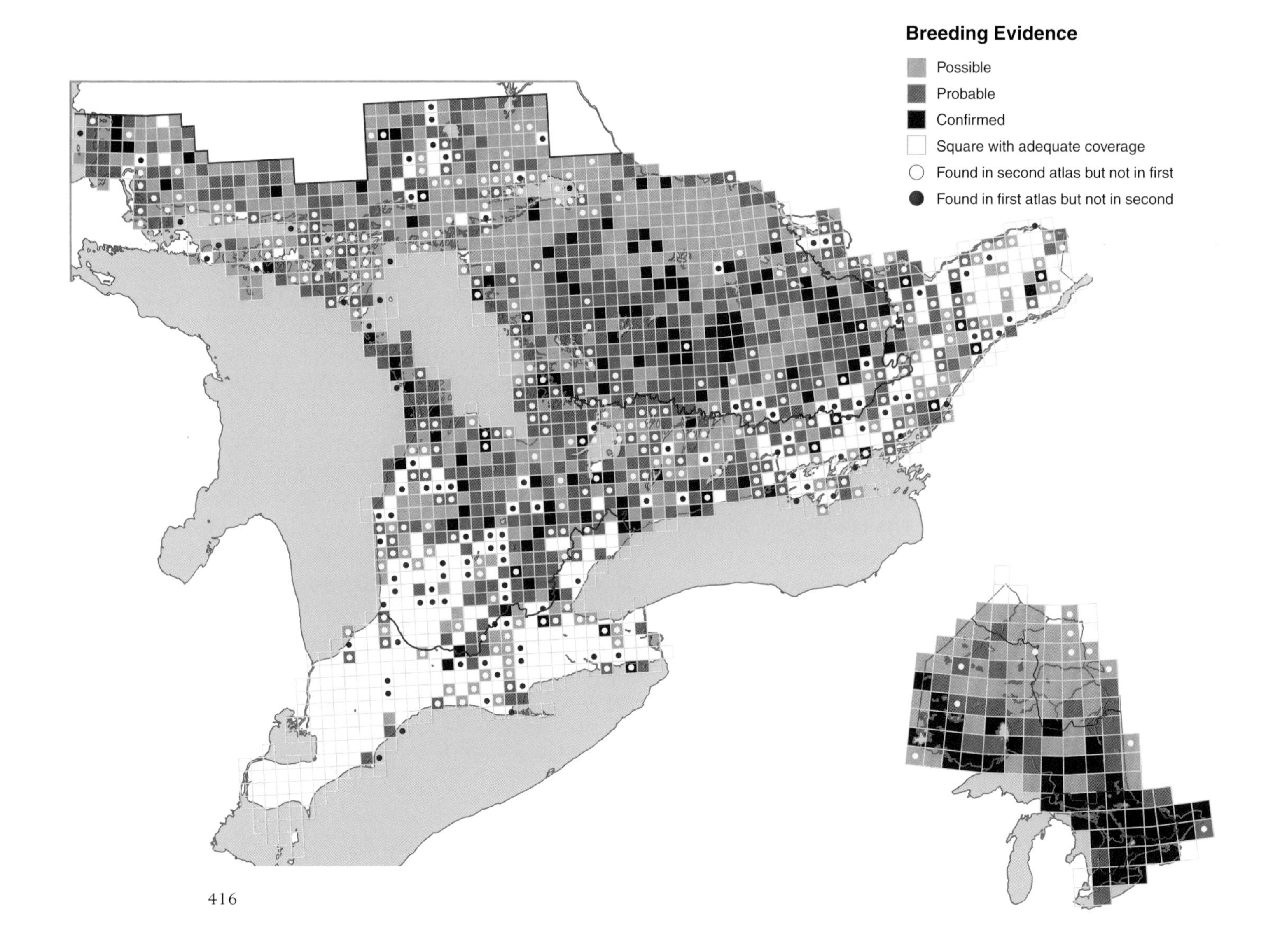

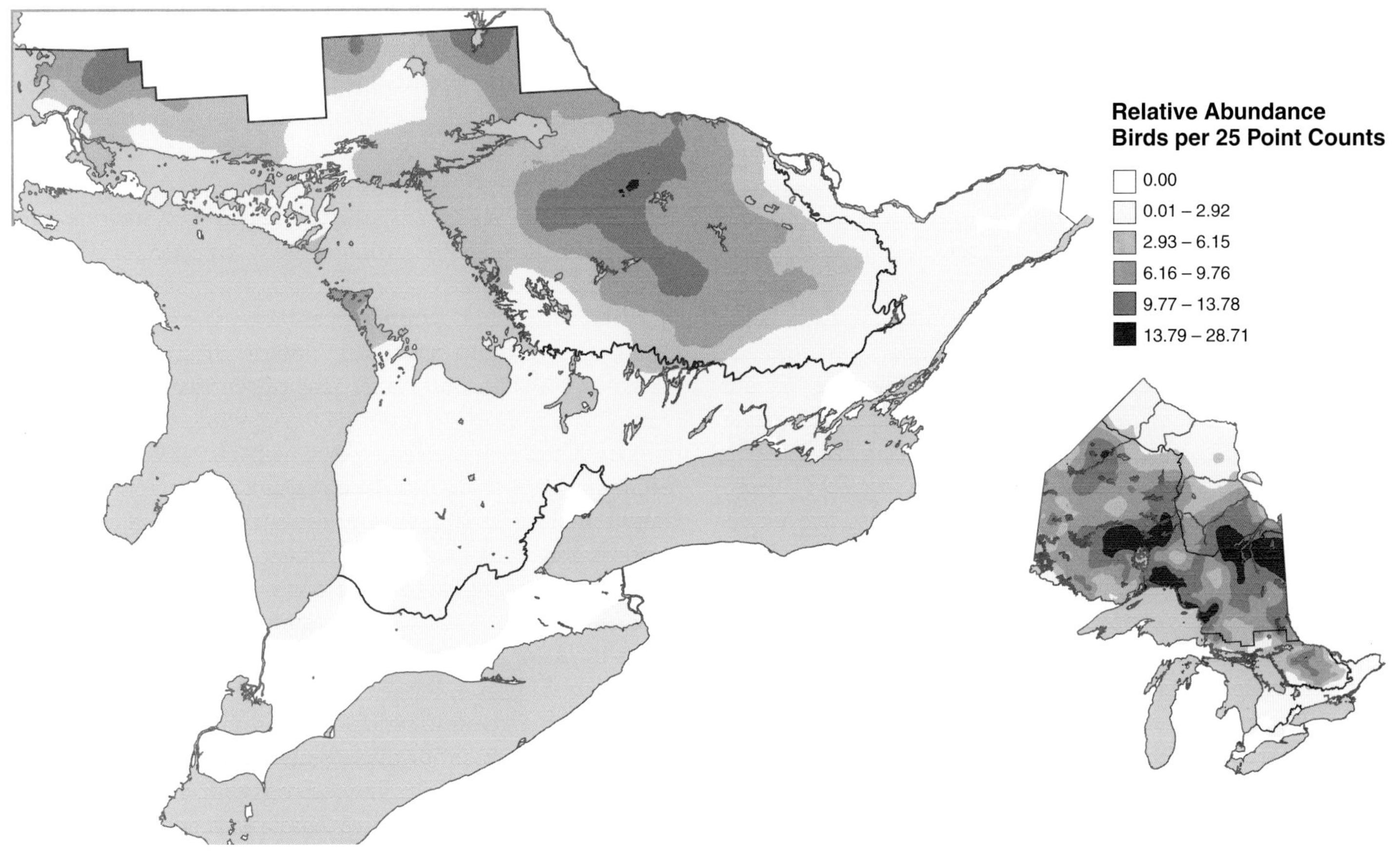

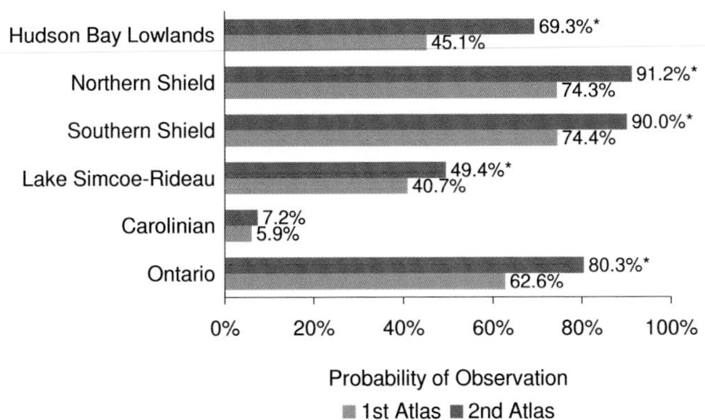

ulations of Ontario might be anticipated to be less vulnerable, prolonged heavy snow in the wintering area, which extends through much of the eastern US south to the Gulf Coast, might be expected to cause high mortality as well. Overall, the probability of observation of the Winter Wren increased between atlases by 28%, with significant increases of 21% to 54% in four of the five atlas regions. Similarly, BBS data show significant 5.5% annual increases in Ontario since 1981. It is tempting to attribute this increase, which is almost certainly real, to the recent tendency to shorter and milder winters on the wintering grounds, although maturation of conifer plantations, changing forestry practices, or other factors may also have contributed to the increase.

Breeding biology: The food of the Winter Wren is comprised largely of invertebrates encompassing a wide variety of arthropods, but it also consumes a small amount of vegetable matter. In Ontario, the prime breeding habitat is coniferous woodland, especially wetter woodlands, swampy areas, and streamside forests. The presence of fallen rotting logs appears to correlate with high population density. Studies in western North America suggest that very intensive forest management, with clear-cutting and monoculture replanting, generally is deleterious to the species, although the presence of disintegrating tree stumps seems to be helpful (Hejl et al. 2002).

The song of the Winter Wren is loud, persistent, and far carrying. Thus, its detection rate by atlassers on the breeding territory is probably very high. It makes multiple nests, but these usually are extremely well concealed. Confirmation of breeding is difficult and was achieved in only 6% of occupied squares.

Abundance: The abundance maps give a clear picture of the breeding density of the Winter Wren in Ontario, and its relation to habitat can be inferred from them. It is totally absent from the intensively agricultural areas of the Carolinian and is present only in selected habitats in much of the Lake Simcoe-Rideau region. Since these habitat patches are uncommon, its overall density in the latter region is low, even though it may be quite abundant locally. The only areas with somewhat higher densities in this region are the northern tip of the Bruce Peninsula and the northern Kawartha Lakes. By contrast, on the Precambrian Shield, its density is comparatively high, and much higher than for any other wren species in the province. Highest densities are found in the Northern Shield, especially in Thunder Bay and Cochrane Districts. Abundance drops off sharply in the Hudson Bay Lowlands, and the species is found in few squares at low density in the subarctic conditions close to the Hudson Bay coast. – *David Brewer*

Sedge Wren

Troglodyte à bec court

Cistothorus platensis

John Reaume

The name of the Sedge Wren accurately reflects its habitat preference of wet sedge meadows. A secretive bird most readily detected by its song, it is enigmatically inconsistent and variable as well as somewhat nomadic, with a demonstrable change in range between the first and second broods (Herkert et al. 2001). In North America, it nests from east-central Alberta to Ontario, Kansas, Illinois, New York, and Vermont. However, in May and June, it is confined largely to the western and northern parts of its range, from the Prairie Provinces and Ontario to North Dakota, Minnesota, and Wisconsin. Only after July does it expand eastward and southward to rear a second brood (Herkert et al. 2001). This breeding strategy, probably unique among North American passerines, undoubtedly complicates the picture in interpreting the species' Ontario breeding population.

Distribution and population status: The Sedge Wren is confined largely to southern Ontario from Algoma and Nipissing Districts south, and to the extreme west in the Rainy River and Kenora areas. It occurs infrequently and sporadically in the Carolinian region, where its probability of observation is only 4%, concentrated especially around Windsor and Hamilton. In the Lake Simcoe-Rideau and Southern Shield regions, it is more widely distributed, with a probability of observation of 12% and 10%, respectively. Some minor concentrations occur along the Niagara Escarpment from the southern Bruce Peninsula to western Lake Ontario, and from Ottawa to Kingston, with absences in heavily agricultural regions such as Huron and Perth Counties. In the Northern Shield, it had a 5% probability of observation, with the densest populations found in Rainy River and southern Kenora Districts. In the Hudson Bay Lowlands, it was detected in only two squares, north to Attawapiskat and the Ekwan River on the

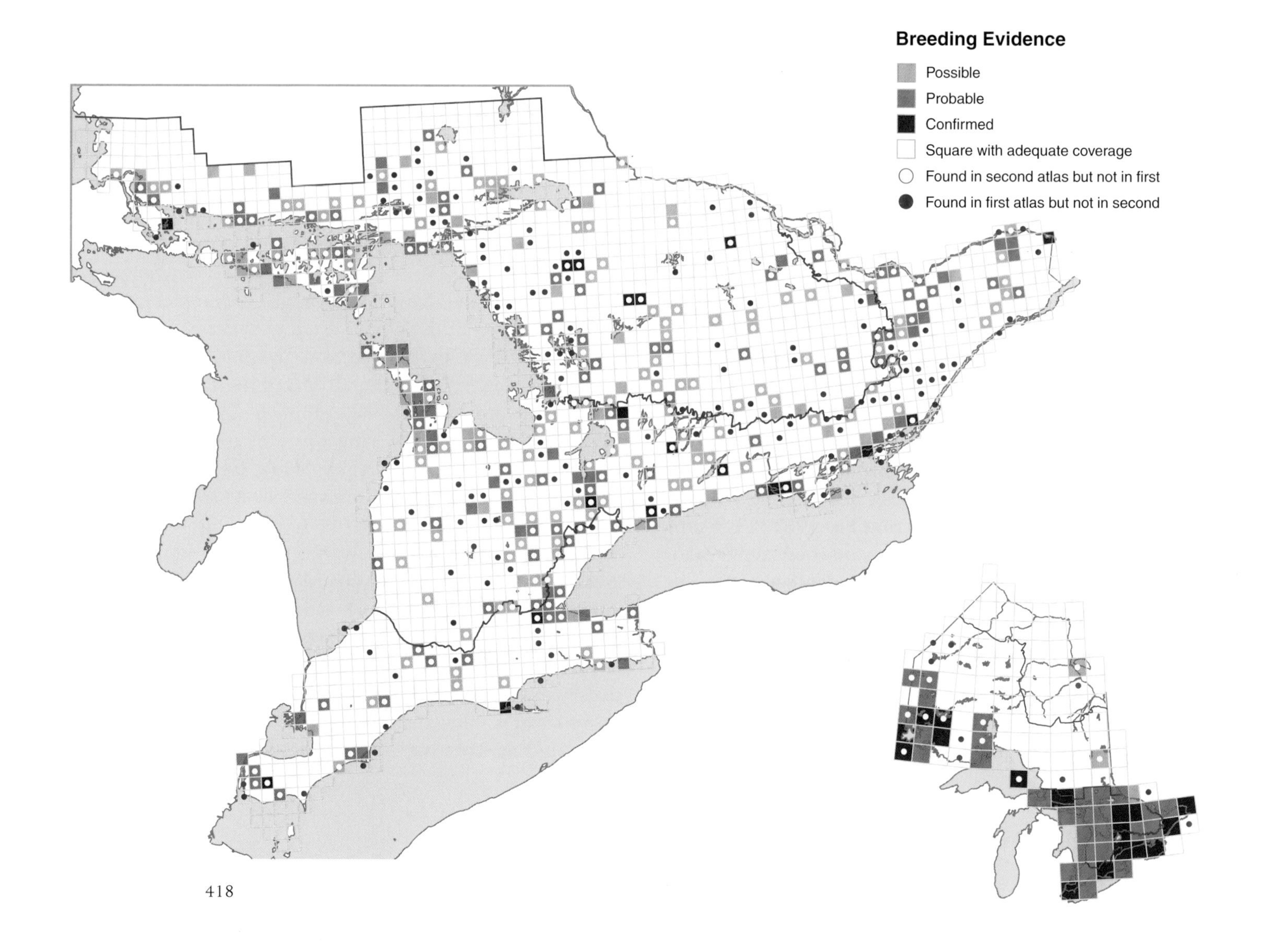

BREEDING EVIDENCE

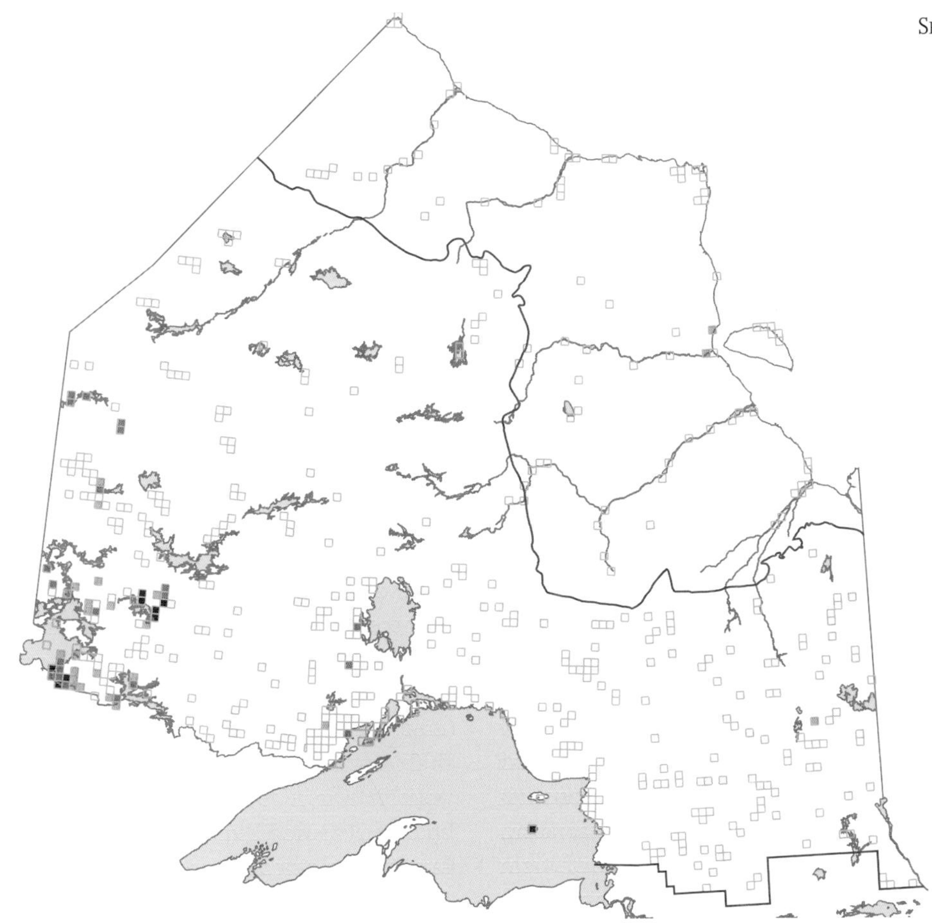

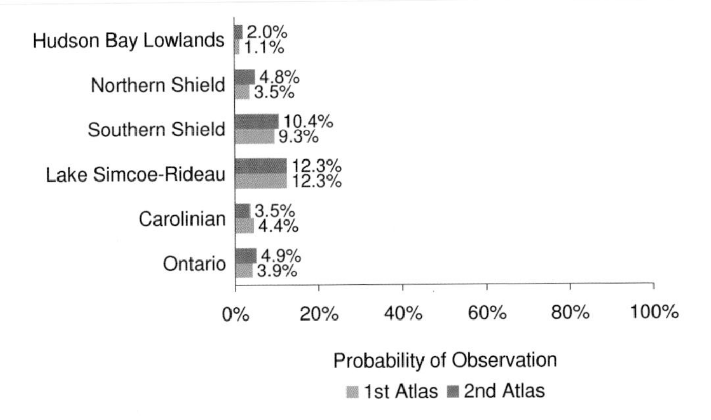

James Bay coast. It is possible that its nomadic nature may lead to overestimation of the population overall, if some squares are colonized and others abandoned by the same individuals within a breeding season. On the other hand, some breeding locations were likely missed, since the species is elusive and its song does not carry far.

Breeding biology: The habitat of the Sedge Wren is primarily wet sedge meadows, often with scattered shrubs. It avoids marshes with standing water and cattails. It seems to be very susceptible to ephemeral changes in habitat caused by seasonal variation in rainfall, flooding, and desiccation, often leading to high mobility and low site fidelity. However, in some large sedge meadows, it occupies territories consistently from year to year. It builds multiple nests and polygamy is quite frequent, though to a lesser degree than in the Marsh Wren (Brewer and MacKay 2001). The young are fed mostly by the female, often with little or no help from the male. After rearing a brood, birds frequently desert a nesting area and settle elsewhere.

Abundance: Over most of its Ontario range the Sedge Wren occurs in low numbers. Even in those parts of southern Ontario with the highest proportion of occupied squares, birds were detected on only 2% of point counts. There was insufficient data to produce an abundance map, with year-to-year variations in distribution complicating efforts to map the species' breeding range. In fact, the breeding evidence map provides a somewhat misleading impression of its apparently very high breeding concentration in the Rainy River area (about 50% of squares in some areas). This is deceptive, since it is based almost entirely on one season of data in 2005, a year that was exceptionally wet, with singing Sedge Wrens found in many areas where they had been absent during the previous four years. Between 2001 and 2004, more than 2,000 point counts in Rainy River Dist. yielded only four counts with the Sedge Wren. In 2005, 316 point counts resulted in 43 counts with one or more Sedge Wrens detected. In one square in 2001, 11 point counts had no Sedge Wrens, while in the same square in 2005 it was present on 16 of 59 counts (27%). This extraordinary surge is much too great to be explained by reproductive success, and must have been due to immigration from other areas, possibly from Manitoba, Wisconsin, and Minnesota where, according to the BBS (Price et al. 1995), there are large populations of the species. Emigration from these regions may have been caused by flooding of traditional breeding sites. The Sedge Wren's breeding biology and distribution represents a complex picture, but it remains a sparse and uncommon breeding bird in Ontario. – *David Brewer*

Marsh Wren

Troglodyte des Marais

Cistothorus palustris

John Reaume

Birders who spend time at cattail marshes frequently find themselves captivated by the tiny Marsh Wren. This inquisitive species advertises its presence by belting out its loud song across its territory. It breeds across much of southern Canada but is absent from the western mountains and most areas in the Maritime Provinces; it also breeds in the northeastern US, the Atlantic and Gulf coasts, and patches throughout the northern and western contiguous states. There is an isolated population in central Mexico.

Distribution and population status: The breeding distribution of the Marsh Wren remains similar to that recorded in the first atlas and historical accounts (cf. Baillie and Harrington 1937). During the second atlas, it was recorded in every region except the Hudson Bay Lowlands, with the greatest probability of observation occurring in the Lake Simcoe-Rideau region (27%). Although widespread south of the Shield, its abundance is limited by the availability of suitable habitat. In southwestern and eastern Ontario, wetland drainage associated with agriculture and urbanization has reduced the amount of habitat available to the species.

There was no significant change in the probability of observation of the Marsh Wren in the province as a whole, but there was a significant 68% increase in the Southern Shield. The reason for the increase in the Southern Shield is unclear. As a result of this increase, there has been a significant northward shift of the northern edge of the species' southern Ontario range by 24 km. In the first atlas, it was noted that a slight northward expansion had occurred relative to previous information (cf. Baillie and Harrington 1937; Godfrey 1986), but this was thought to be the result of increased coverage in the north rather than a range expansion. The MMP detected a significant annual decline of 6.7% in the Lake Erie basin between 1995 and 2003 but no significant changes in any other basin (Crewe et al. 2006).

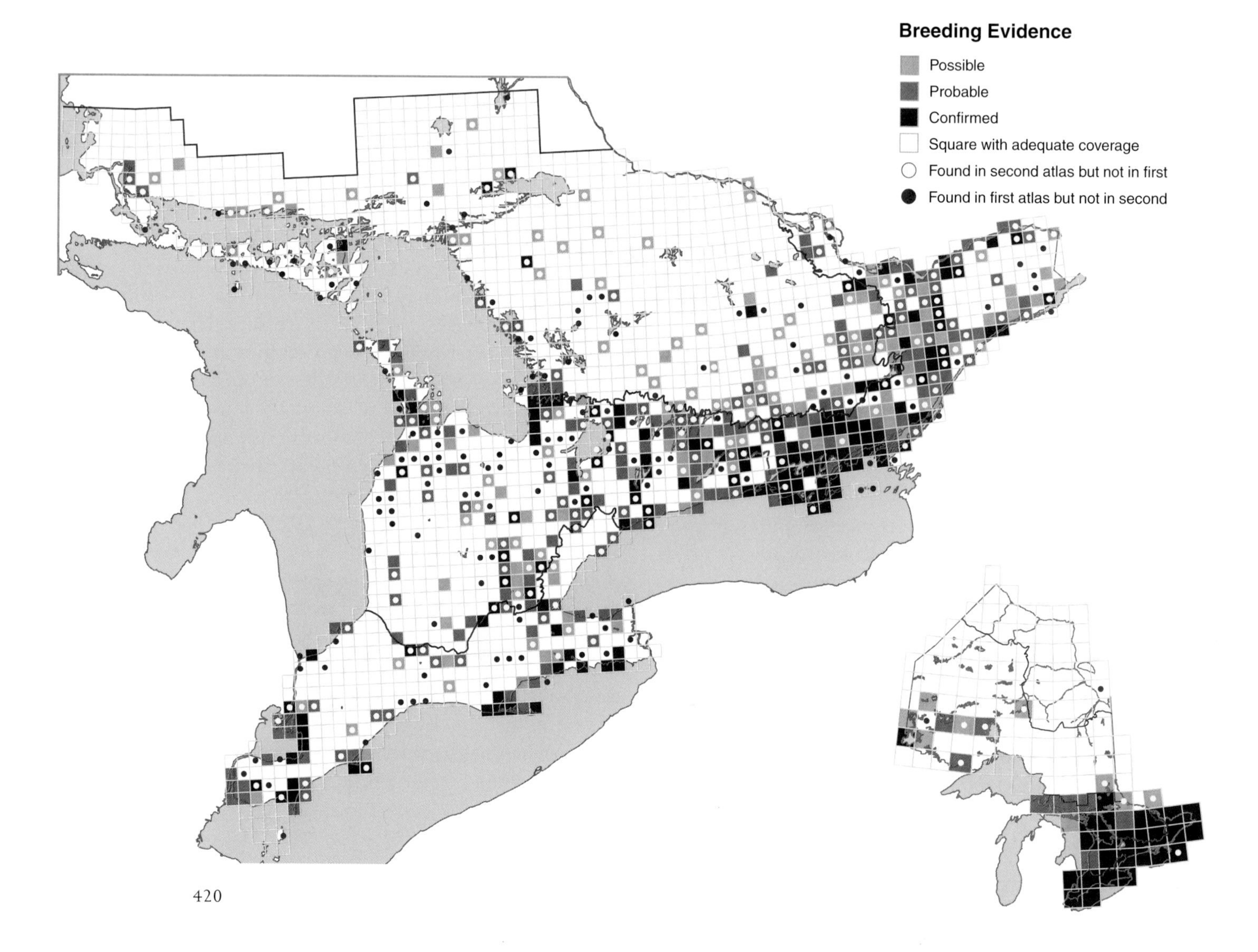

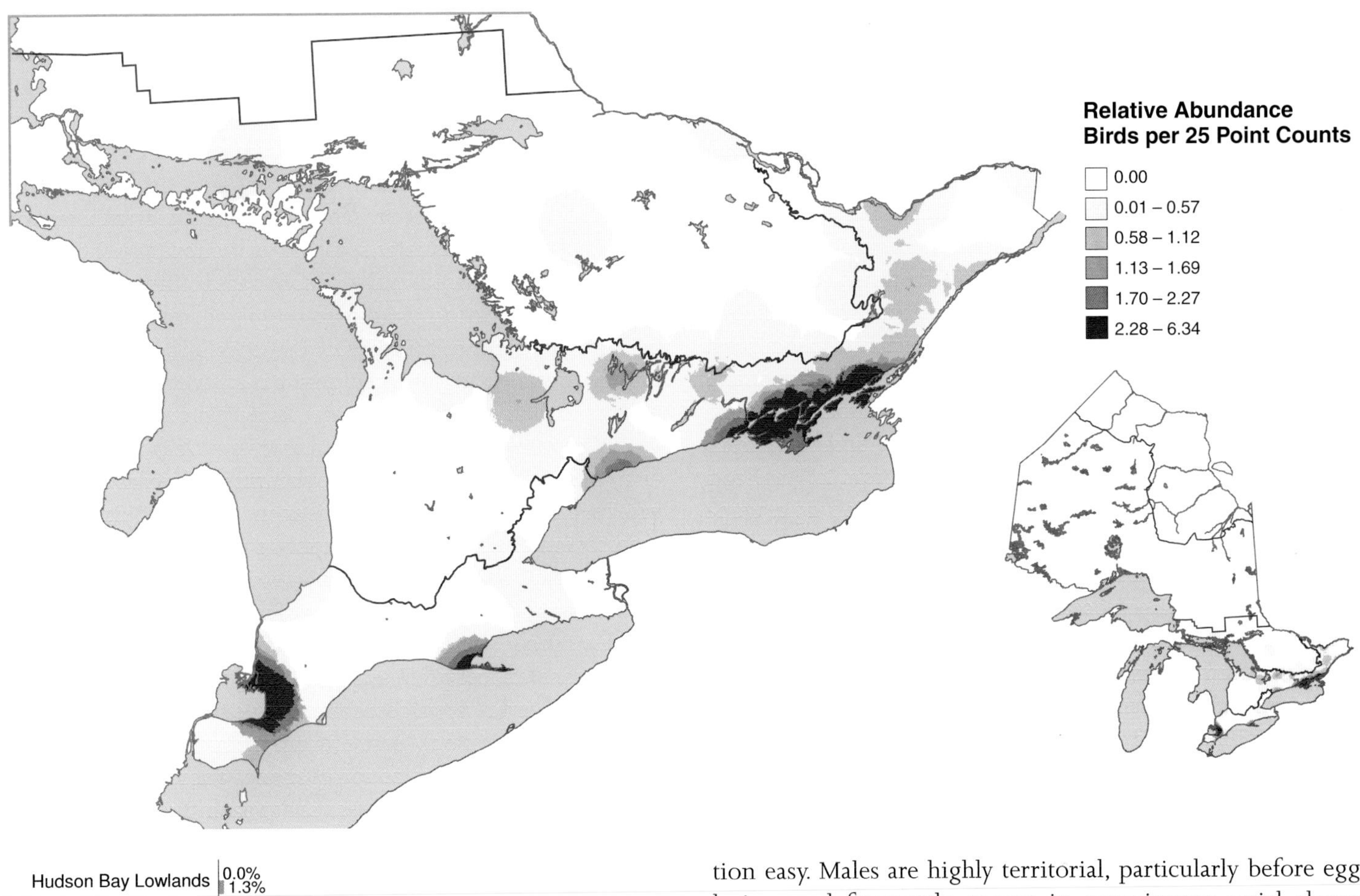

	2nd Atlas	1st Atlas
Hudson Bay Lowlands	0.0%	1.3%
Northern Shield	1.3%	1.0%
Southern Shield	5.9%*	3.5%
Lake Simcoe-Rideau	27.1%	25.7%
Carolinian	16.3%	18.8%
Ontario	3.4%	3.4%

0% 20% 40% 60% 80% 100%

Probability of Observation

1st Atlas 2nd Atlas

Breeding biology: In Ontario, the Marsh Wren breeds predominantly in shallow to deep-water cattail marshes. Territory size and breeding density vary with habitat, and large patches of shallow-water emergent marsh with good interspersion generally support larger populations. Territory size may be small (60 m^2; Kroodsma and Verner 1997); however, the species may exploit small patches of optimal habitat. The Marsh Wren has a polygynous breeding system, with up to half of all males attracting more than one female. Males construct 7-22 "dummy" nests (Kroodsma and Verner 1997) in their territories. The significance of these nests is unresolved, although they may serve both as indicators of male fitness (Verner 1964) and decoys to predators (Leonard and Picman 1987). Nests are domed structures of tightly woven vegetation, spherical or elliptic in shape. Conspicuous early in the season, they quickly become obscured by emergent vegetation and more difficult to detect.

The Marsh Wren's song is loud and distinctive, and the male sings throughout most of the breeding season, making detection easy. Males are highly territorial, particularly before egg laying, and frequently engage in conspicuous aerial chases with neighbouring males. Singing or territorial males were the highest breeding evidence in most squares, and evidence of possible and probable breeding was achieved in 72% of squares in which the species was detected.

Abundance: As a persistent singer, the Marsh Wren is well suited to detection on point counts, but its marsh habitat may not be very well represented on roadside surveys. The abundance map generally gives a reasonable overview of the species' relative abundance in southern Ontario. However, there are some anomalies, perhaps artifacts of the mapping process. The area between Lake St. Clair and Lake Erie should show high density only in a narrow strip along the shore of Lake St. Clair and in the Pelee and Rondeau areas, where extensive cattail marshes exist, but not inland where some of the most intensive agriculture in the province has eliminated over 90% of all wetland habitat, including virtually all suitable wetlands for breeding Marsh Wrens. The same is true to a lesser extent inland from the base of Long Point. The Marsh Wren is also fairly common in a broad strip south of the Precambrian Shield and along its southern edge, where numerous cattail-dominated wetlands provide ideal habitat for breeding. As well, it is abundant along Lake Ontario from Cobourg to Gananoque, where cattail marshes are particularly plentiful. There is a notable gap in extreme eastern Ontario, where many wetlands have disappeared. – *Douglas C. Tozer*

Golden-crowned Kinglet

Roitelet à couronne dorée

Regulus satrapa

Frank and Sandra Horvath

The Golden-crowned Kinglet breeds in coniferous forests across North America from Alaska to Newfoundland and south along both the Appalachians in the east and the mountains of the western US (Godfrey 1986). Interestingly, a disjunct resident population also breeds in the mountains of Mexico and Guatemala (Ingold and Galati 1997). In winter, the Golden-crowned Kinglet may be found in appropriate habitat through much of the US and in southern British Columbia, Ontario, Québec, and the Maritimes. In Ontario, it winters as far north as Sault Ste. Marie, North Bay, and Mattawa (Root 1988).

Distribution and population status: In Ontario, the Golden-crowned Kinglet is absent as a breeding bird only in tundra and taiga areas of the far north, the agricultural habitats of the extreme southwest, and with the exception of one square, the Niagara Peninsula. The species is most widely distributed in the Northern and Southern Shield regions, where it was detected in the majority of squares. The probability of observation was considerably lower in the Lake Simcoe-Rideau region; in the Carolinian region, the species was found primarily in a few squares north of Long Point.

Although the overall distribution of the Golden-crowned Kinglet has changed little since the first atlas, between atlases there was a significant 47% increase in the probability of observation in the province as a whole, and significant increases of 40%, 17%, and 68% in the Lake Simcoe-Rideau, Southern Shield, and Northern Shield regions, respectively. In the Lake Simcoe-Rideau region, maturing conifer plantations may have contributed to the increase by providing additional habitat. In the core of the species' range in the Northern Shield region, the availability of suitable habitat is unlikely to have changed substantially between atlases. Increases there, and in the Southern Shield, may be due in part to differences in coverage

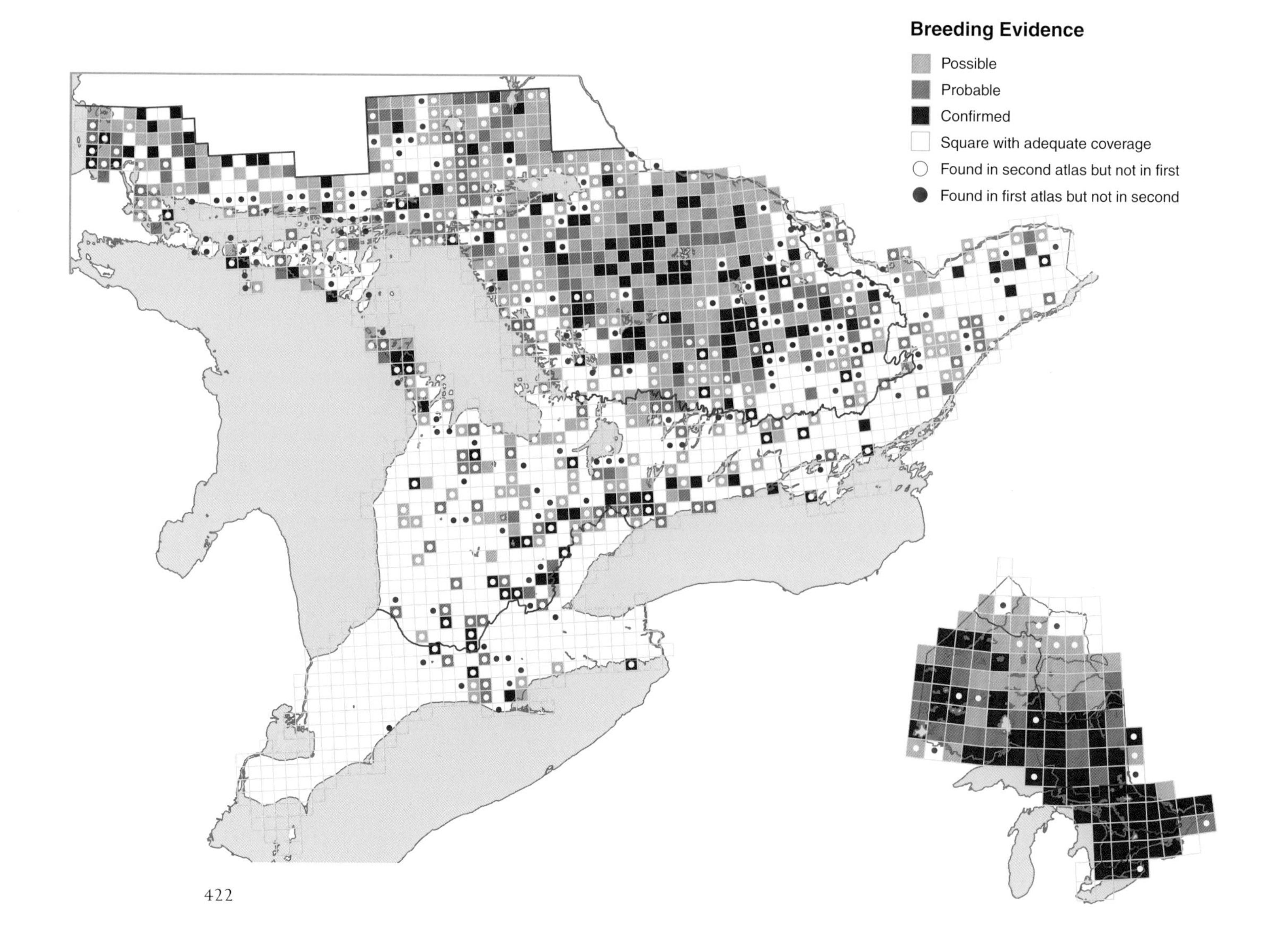

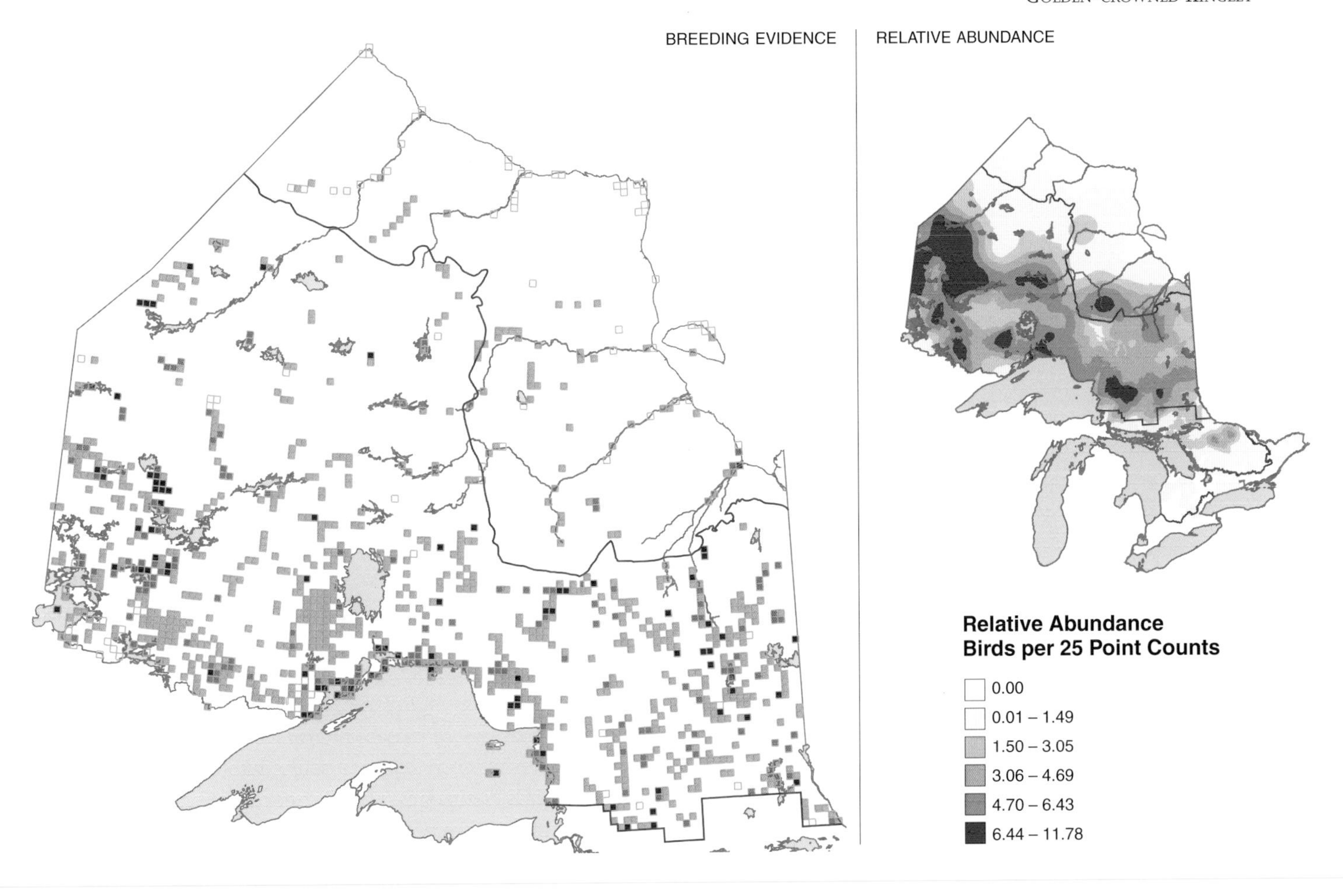

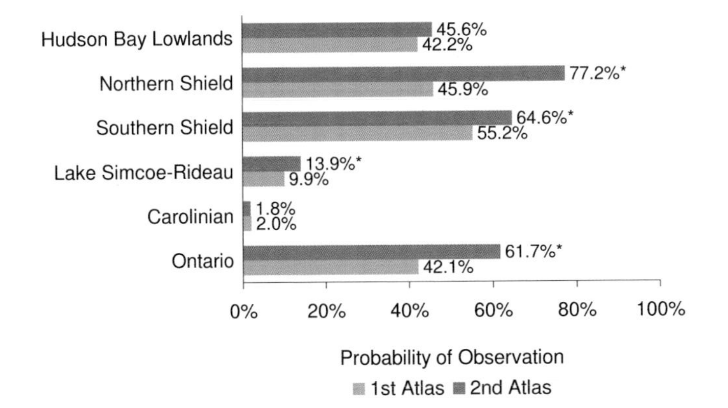

by more experienced observers during this atlas. The Golden-crowned Kinglet's high-pitched, weak song and calls may have been missed more often during the first atlas.

The BBS shows a small but non-significant increase in numbers of this species in Ontario since the previous atlas. Migration data from LPBO are equivocal, showing no change in spring and a significant increase in fall during the last 10 years compared to earlier years.

Breeding biology: The Golden-crowned Kinglet prefers mature Balsam Fir and spruce forests for breeding but may also be found in other conifers as well as in mixed forests dominated by conifers (Ingold and Galati 1997). Even though this species has two broods per season and builds a separate nest for each, it is not easy for atlassers to obtain even probable breeding records. Not only are its song and call notes easily overlooked but its nest is very difficult to locate. Prior to the atlas period, only 19 nests had been reported in Ontario (Peck 2001), and atlas observers added only three more (Peck and Peck 2006). Overall, breeding was confirmed in just 13% of squares.

The nest is usually placed in the upper crown of a spruce or Balsam Fir near the trunk and well hidden from view. Although both adults bring food to the nest, the nestlings do not call loudly, and even after fledging they tend to stay high in the trees where they are difficult to see. The female begins to build her second nest before the first brood has fledged. Because she is incubating the second set of eggs very shortly after the first young fledge, the male does most of the feeding of the fledglings (Ingold and Galati 1997). In the majority of atlas regions, the highest confirmed breeding evidence consisted of adults carrying food.

Abundance: The Golden-crowned Kinglet shows a pattern of abundance rather similar to that of the Brown Creeper, another species that prefers mature conifer forests. The highest densities were found in northwestern Ontario, including Woodland Caribou Prov. Park and a substantial area north and east of Red Lake. Over 6.4 birds/25 point counts were found in this area. Across the Northern Shield, densities averaged 4.9 birds/25 point counts, considerably higher than the 1.3 birds/25 point counts recorded in the Southern Shield. In the latter region, the highest densities occurred in the Algonquin Highlands, where conifer-dominated habitats resemble those found farther north. Despite its fairly wide distribution in the Lake Simcoe-Rideau region, the Golden-crowned Kinglet was uncommon there, being recorded at a rate of only 0.05 birds/25 point counts. – *Margaret A. McLaren*

Ruby-crowned Kinglet

Roitelet à couronne rubis

Regulus calendula

Larry Kirtley

The Ruby-crowned Kinglet is widespread in the northern and central regions of the province. It breeds throughout boreal and montane North America, from the treeline south to northeastern Minnesota, northern Wisconsin, the Adirondacks of New York, and southern Vermont, and in the west to the Rocky Mountains and the higher peaks of the Cascades and Sierra Nevada (Ingold and Wallace 1994). In the east, it prefers to nest near water in open Black Spruce peatlands, where it achieves its highest densities, but it may occur in drier, open woodlands with a coniferous component. It is a short-distance migrant, wintering from southern New England and British Columbia to southern Mexico and Guatemala (Ingold and Wallace 1994).

Distribution and population status: As in the first atlas, the Ruby-crowned Kinglet is widespread in the three northern regions. Documented breeding records are infrequent south of the Southern Shield, and the scattered records in both atlases of possible breeding in the Lake Simcoe-Rideau region may have involved late migrants.

Between atlases, there were significant declines in the probability of observation in both the Lake Simcoe-Rideau and Southern Shield regions, but a significant increase in the Northern Shield and Hudson Bay Lowlands. Although the population of the Ruby-crowned Kinglet is stable across Canada, BBS data for Ontario indicate a significant decline of about 5% per year since 1968 (Downes et al. 2005). This decline is reflected in the reduction in the probability of observation of the species in the Southern Shield. Broad-scale habitat changes may be responsible for the decrease; there is now considerably less suitable habitat in several areas where there were clusters of squares with the species during the first atlas. Near Sault Ste. Marie, there is much more young forest than was the case in the first atlas, and east of Georgian Bay and south of Lake Nipissing, there is much more hard-

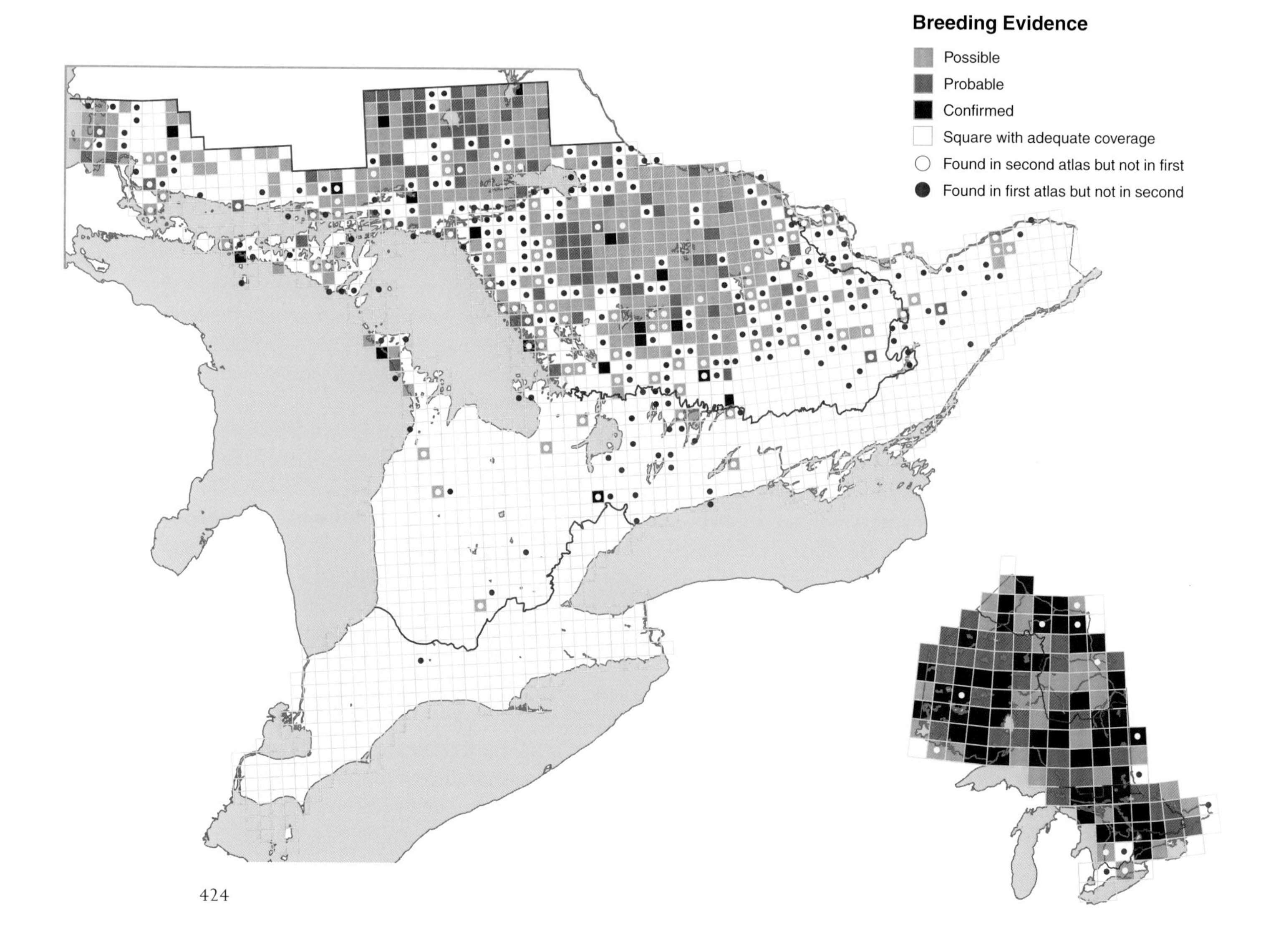

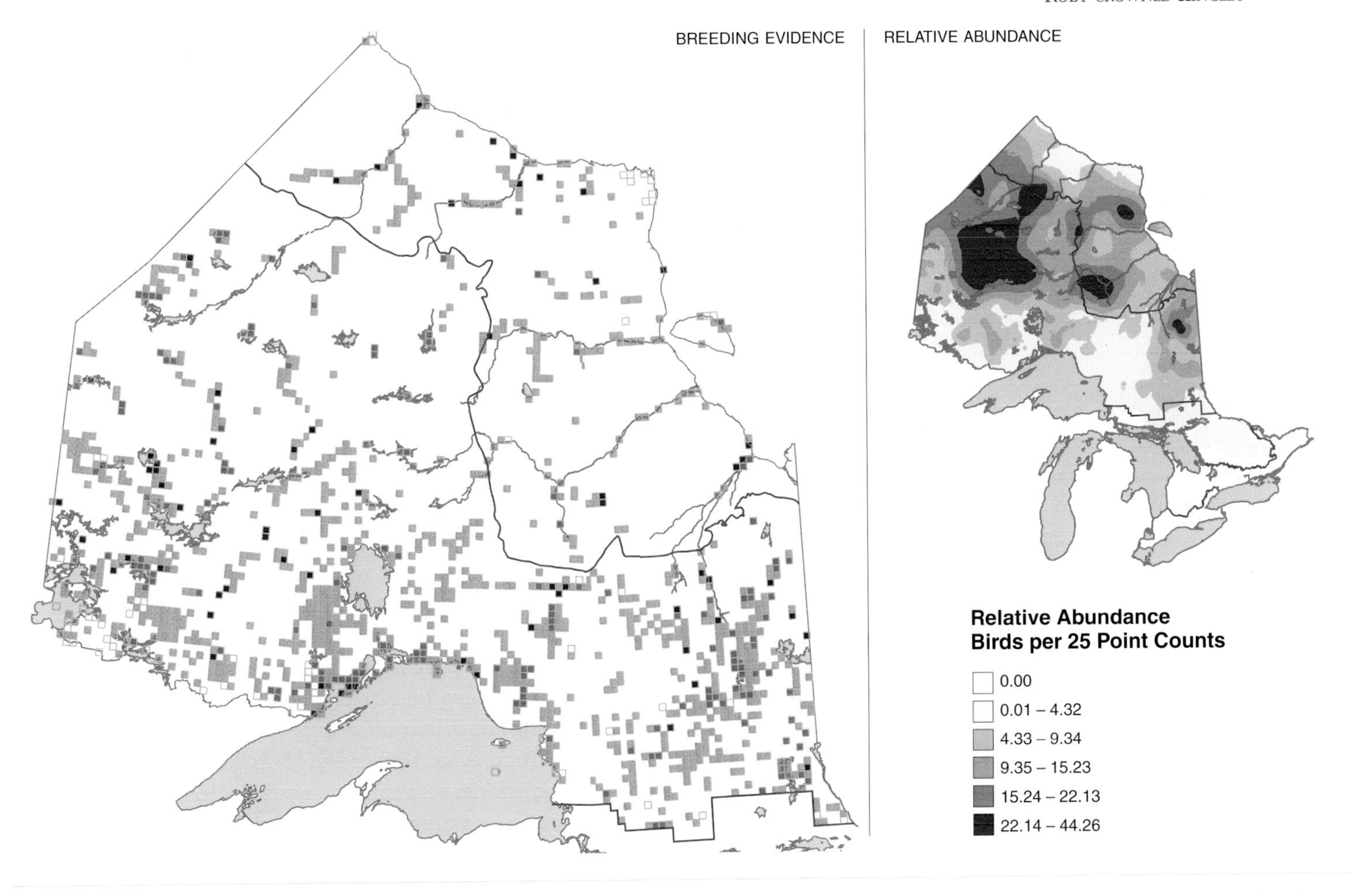

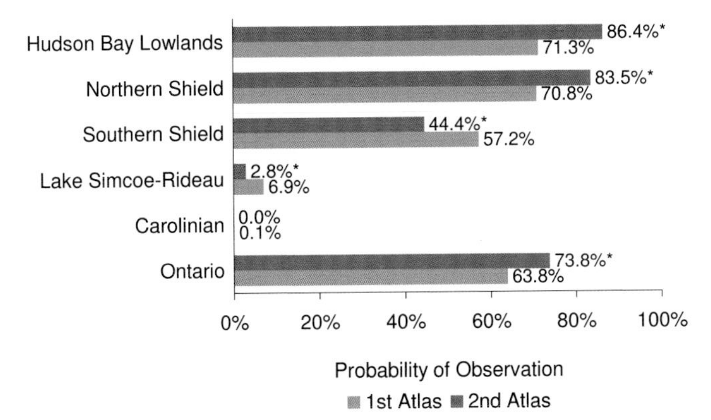

wood forest. Few BBS routes are situated in the northern core of the species' range, so it is not possible to compare atlas results with BBS trends there.

Breeding biology: The male Ruby-crowned Kinglet returns to the breeding grounds earlier than the female and immediately establishes a territory. Monogamous pair formation occurs as soon as females arrive. Territories range in size from 1.1 to 6 ha, quite large for such a small bird. Territories are larger in mixed coniferous-deciduous woodlands than in the preferred conifer-dominated peatlands. Males sing from high perches, often in the upper branches of a spruce, but they also can sing while flutter-gleaning for insects or even while consuming prey. Females also sing, generally during incubation and chick rearing but sometimes during nest building as well.

The female Ruby-crowned Kinglet builds the nest on her own, in about five days. The nest is well hidden, suspended from dense clumps of thin branches 1 or 2 m from the top of a Black or White Spruce (6 to 17 m above ground level in Algonquin Prov. Park). The round or elongated open cup is formed with mosses supplemented with feathers, lichens, and webs, and lined with feathers and other fine materials (Peck and James 1987; Ingold and Wallace 1994).

The female lays a clutch of up to 12 eggs (in Ontario, the average clutch is eight), the largest clutch of any small North American songbird (Peck and James 1987; Ingold and Wallace 1994). She incubates the eggs for 13 to 16 days, beginning before the clutch is completed. Fledging takes 16 to 18 days. Second broods are never produced, but if the first nesting attempt fails, re-nesting may be attempted (Ingold and Wallace 1994).

Although the loud, characteristic song of the Ruby-crowned Kinglet allows it to be detected readily, the rate of breeding confirmation was very low (5%). This reflects the difficulty in locating nests, as well as the small size of food captured, making observations of adults carrying food difficult.

Abundance: The Ruby-crowned Kinglet shows a pattern of declining abundance from north to south. On average, 11.0 birds/25 point counts were recorded in the Hudson Bay Lowlands, 7.7 birds in the Northern Shield, and 0.5 birds in the Southern Shield region. The relative abundance map suggests that much of the area with the highest density, over 22.1 birds/25 point counts, is in the northwestern part of the Northern Shield region, though density is generally high in northern parts of the Northern Shield region and the southern part of the Hudson Bay Lowlands. – *William J. Crins*

Blue-gray Gnatcatcher

Gobemoucheron gris-bleu

Polioptila caerulea

George K. Peck

The Blue-gray Gnatcatcher is one of Canada's smallest songbirds. This perky little bird can often be seen cocking its long tail, wren-like, as it forages in the tree canopy for tiny insects. Compared to other gnatcatchers, it has a large breeding range in North America, extending from southern Ontario and southwestern Québec through much of the US and south through Mexico to Central America (Ellison 1992).

Distribution and population status: Since the late 1940s, the Blue-gray Gnatcatcher's breeding range has expanded northward dramatically across northeastern North America (Ellison 1992). Formerly rare or absent, the species is now quite well established across much of southern Ontario south of the Shield. During the atlas period, it was recorded as far north as Manitoulin Island, where in 2005 a pair built but later abandoned a nest.

Much of the change between the two atlases consisted of consolidation of the range in the Carolinian region, where the probability of observation increased significantly by 48%. A statistically significant increase (40%) was also observed in the Lake Simcoe-Rideau region. A similar range consolidation in adjacent western New York has been documented by the New York Breeding Bird Atlas.

As with several other "southern" species that have pushed northwards into Ontario over the past century, the Blue-gray Gnatcatcher's range expansion may be a result of recent climate changes, perhaps coupled with regional increases in forest cover.

Because it is still uncommon in Ontario, the Blue-gray Gnatcatcher is not recorded frequently enough on BBS routes to detect statistically valid population trends for the province; however, BBS trends for eastern North America indicate that gnatcatcher populations increased significantly, by an average rate of 0.6% annually, from 1966 to 2005 (Sauer et al. 2005). Based on data collected during migration at LPBO, there has

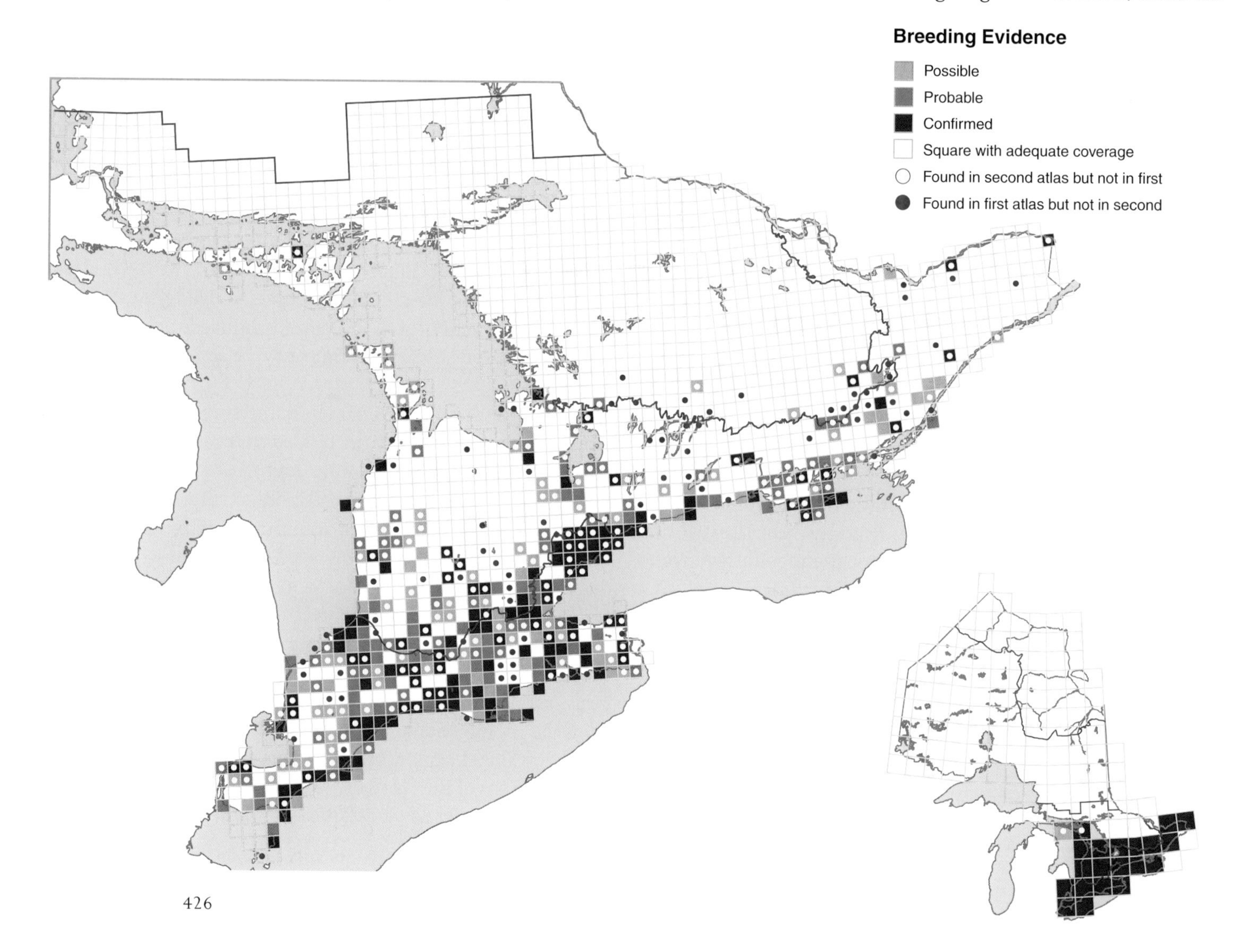

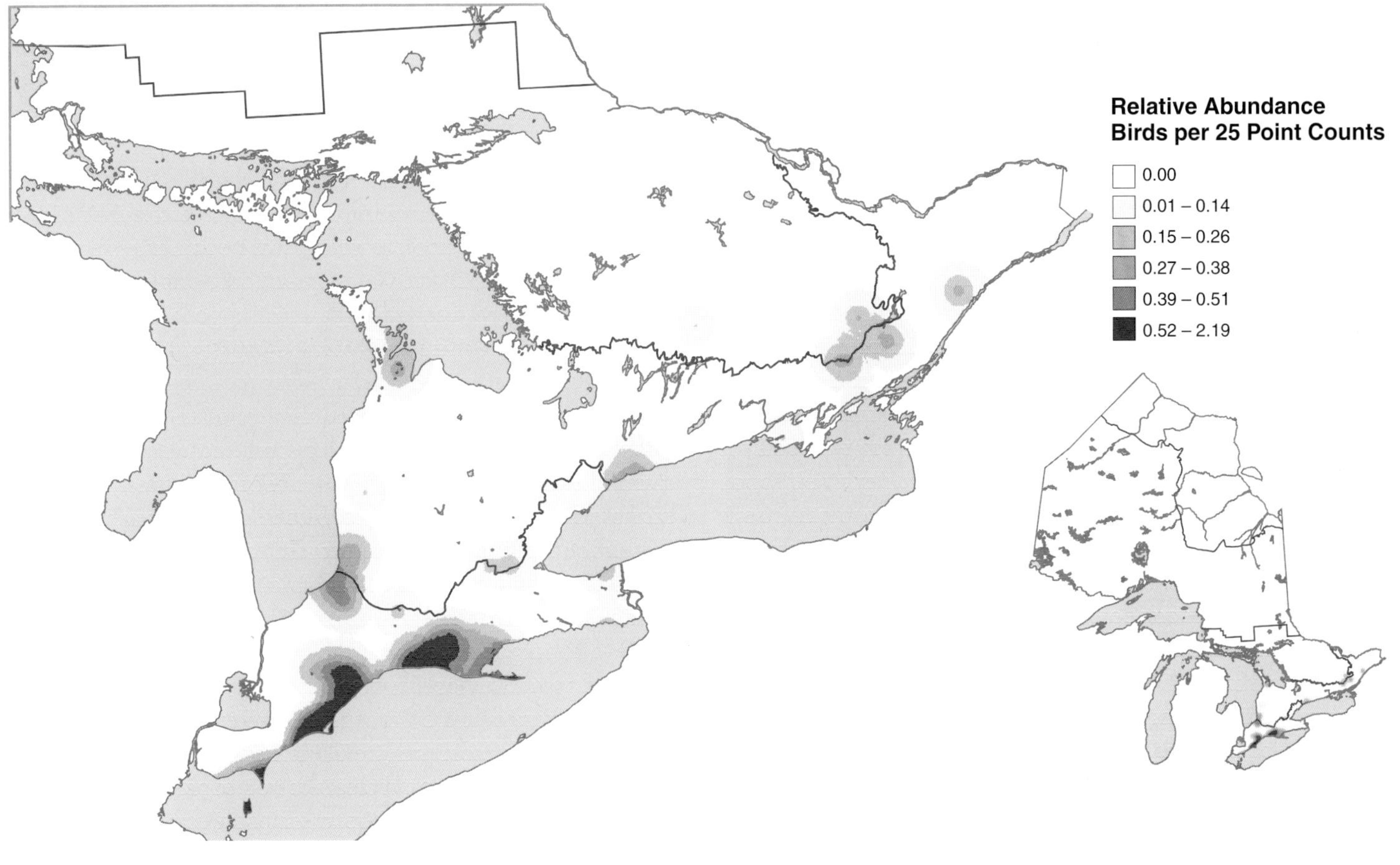

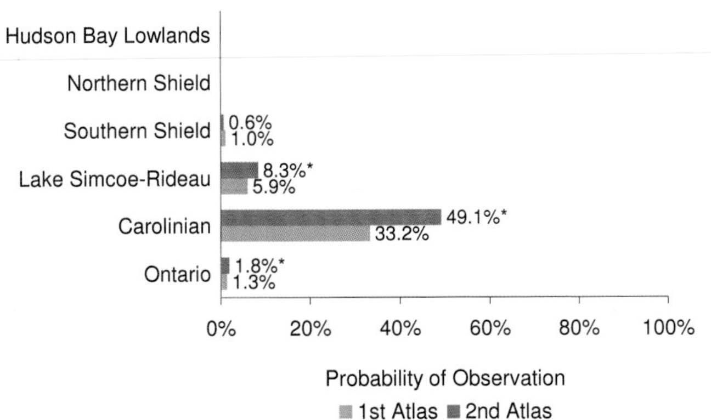

been a statistically significant average annual increase of nearly 5% per year since 1961, with the greatest rate of increase having taken place since the late 1970s (Crewe 2006).

Breeding biology: For a small insectivore, the Blue-gray Gnatcatcher is surprisingly hardy. An early spring migrant, it typically arrives in southern Ontario beginning in mid-April. Nesting begins earlier than in many other small migrant songbirds, with nest-building evidently often commencing by mid-May (Peck and James 1997; Curry 2006), a time when it is apt to be overlooked by atlassers who concentrate their field efforts in June and July. The species nests in a variety of deciduous woodlands, often in close proximity to water and at the edges of openings. In Ontario, it seems to favour open-canopied, deciduous swamp and floodplain forests.

Gnatcatcher nests are very difficult to find. Not only are they tiny, but they are placed fairly high up on small horizontal tree limbs and camouflaged with a decoration of lichens. Nests are most easily detected during the construction phase (Peck and James 1997), as mated pairs are quite vocal and active and readily located by careful observation. Breeding was confirmed in 37% of the squares where the species was recorded.

The Blue-gray Gnatcatcher's tiny size makes it fairly difficult to locate visually. Likewise, its wheezy song and call notes are weak, high-pitched, and uttered most frequently during the early part of the breeding season, earlier than many atlassers are apt to be concentrating their field efforts. Thus, the species was likely overlooked to some extent during both atlas periods. Nevertheless, the range map probably reflects its true breeding distribution in the province.

Abundance: The atlas distribution and abundance maps show that the Blue-gray Gnatcatcher has an affinity for the Carolinian region. It is most numerous in the vicinity of the lower Great Lakes, particularly around the north shore of Lake Erie. This and other areas of at least moderate density (i.e., near Grand Bend on Lake Huron, along the shore of Lake Ontario, and on the Frontenac Axis) are all within the zone of mean daily June temperatures in excess of 18°C and are centred on areas with concentrations of occupied squares. The southern Bruce Peninsula and the Peterborough area are both outside the 18°C temperature zone and have only a scattering of occupied squares. In these areas, the maps may over-estimate actual densities.

This species can be expected to continue strengthening its foothold in southern Ontario over the next 20 years and may continue to expand its range northwards if climate warming continues. – *Jon McCracken*

Northern Wheatear

Traquet motteux

Oenanthe oenanthe

Mark Suomala

In Ontario, watching the Northern Wheatear perform its song flight is an extremely rare event. Although this small, ground-dwelling passerine has a relatively wide global breeding range, only two records of possible breeding exist for Ontario, both in suitable open tundra habitat in the Hudson Bay Lowlands. Most of the breeding range is in northern Europe and Asia south to the Middle East and North Africa. The nominate subspecies breeds mainly in the Old World but extends its range from eastern Asia into Alaska and Yukon, while the "Greenland" race (*O. o. leucorhoa*) breeds in Iceland, Greenland and the eastern Canadian Arctic. Breeding habitat is almost exclusively open, rocky terrain, where it nests in crevices under rock piles and boulders, on cliffs, and in ruined buildings (Sutton and Parmelee 1954; Kren and Zoerb 1997). All Northern Wheatear populations winter in sub-Saharan Africa. It is the only North American breeding passerine that winters in Africa (Kren and Zoerb 1997).

Distribution and population status: In Canada, the Greenland race of the Northern Wheatear breeds primarily in northern Labrador, Québec, Baffin Island, and Ellesmere Island, with isolated records from both the east and west sides of northern Hudson Bay as far west as Rankin Inlet, Nunavut (Godfrey 1986; Gauthier and Aubry 1996), and more recently, Churchill, Manitoba (R. Koes, pers. comm.). There is some evidence that the species may breed, at least occasionally, in the Hudson Bay Lowlands of Ontario. Several autumn records in the region indicate that it may also be a regular but rare migrant in the Hudson Bay Lowlands (Wilson and McRae 1993). Elsewhere in Ontario, it is considered a rare transient, mainly in the autumn (James 1991).

Prior to the first atlas, there was no documented evidence of the Northern Wheatear breeding in Ontario, nor were there any known summer records from the coastal tundra of Hudson Bay. During the first atlas, however, a single male was

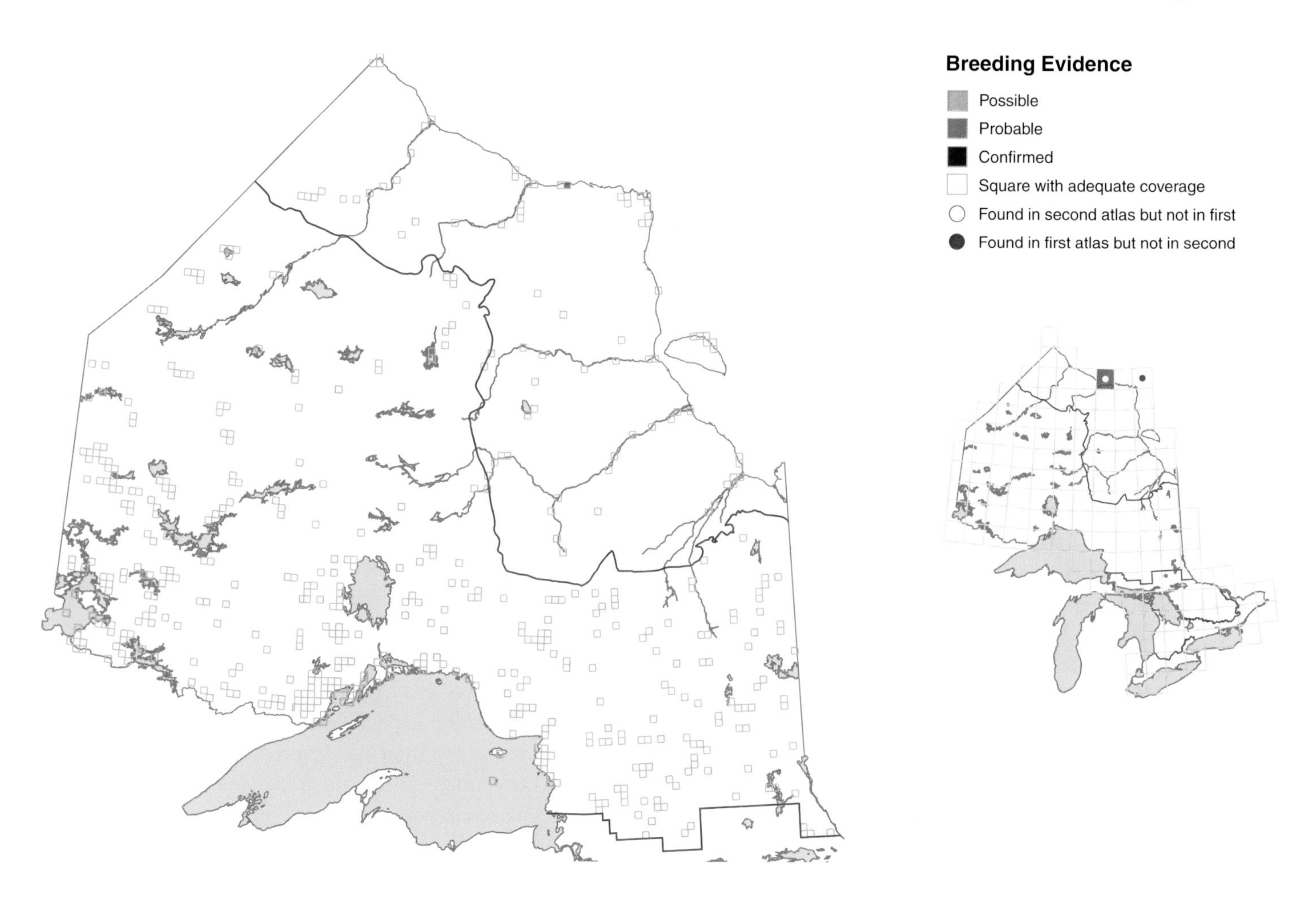

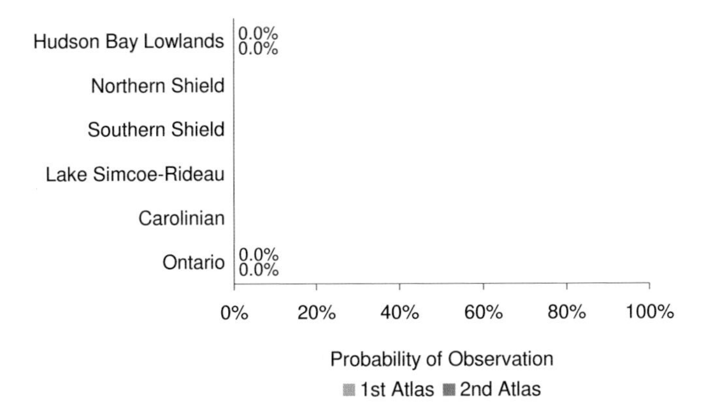

Relict beach-ridge habitat near Burntpoint Creek, Polar Bear Prov. Park, where a territorial male Northern Wheatear was observed performing aerial song flights, 8-15 July 2005. *Photo: Colin D. Jones*

observed in suitable nesting habitat (an area of dry, grassy ground with large, scattered boulders) on the barren outer ridges of Cape Henrietta Maria on 2 July 1985. In addition, there were two records of female Northern Wheatears from the Hudson Bay Lowlands, one at Winisk on 2 June 1981 and another at Northbluff Point on 4 June 1982 (James 1984c). These records were not submitted to the atlas, perhaps because the birds were considered to be migrants.

On 8 June 2005, a male Northern Wheatear was observed performing song flights near Burntpoint Creek, approximately 85 km east-northeast of Peawanuk. The habitat was a raised, relict beach-ridge, with lichen-heath vegetation and large boulders along its northern edge. Crevices beneath and between many of the boulders offered suitable sites for nesting. The five-person atlas crew searched the area for signs of a female or nest (by examining crevices under boulders), but without success. Regular visits to the site in the following days revealed that the male was still present and singing until at least 15 June. On at least three subsequent visits, the last on 19 June, atlassers did not detect the bird. Although no confirmed breeding records exist in Ontario, this evidence suggests that this species may at least occasionally breed in appropriate habitat in the Hudson Bay Lowlands. Much of this area is extremely remote and, apart from annual waterfowl surveys and goose research, is infrequently visited by ornithologists. Moreover, much of the Hudson Bay Lowlands lacks the rocky outcrops and boulders to provide suitable nesting habitat. Therefore, it is likely that if this species does breed in Ontario, it does so irregularly and sparsely.

Breeding biology: In eastern North America, breeding is confined to open tundra with suitable crevices for nesting. The female builds the nest and incubates between five and eight eggs, with both parents (mainly the female) caring for the young (Cramp 1988). Although it is a small bird, the Northern Wheatear's song flight, combined with its tendency to stand atop rocks and boulders, makes it relatively conspicuous. In addition, it shows strong site fidelity, returning to specific breeding sites for multiple years (Kren and Zoerb 1997). Despite the under-surveyed status of the Hudson Bay Lowlands, if the species does breed regularly, one would expect that it would have been recorded more frequently than it has, given that Cape Henrietta Maria and especially the Burntpoint Creek area are visited relatively frequently by biologists.

Abundance: With only a single record during this atlas period, abundance estimates cannot be calculated for this species. – *Colin D. Jones and David J. T. Hussell*

Eastern Bluebird

Merlebleu de l'Est

Sialia sialis

Kelly Dodge

The Eastern Bluebird is a cherished sight for birdwatchers across Ontario. It held a special place in the folklore of our early settlers, who welcomed it as a true harbinger of spring with its colourful appearance and easily recognizable calls. The species was designated Rare by COSEWIC and OMNR based on its low population following the severe winters of 1976 to 1978 (Risley 1981). Since then, the population has increased significantly to a point where it was de-listed in 1996 (Read and Alvo 1996).

The Eastern Bluebird breeds across eastern North America from southeastern Alberta east to the Atlantic and south into Mexico and Central America. It is found in a variety of habitats from apple orchards to boreal forest and will nest in almost any area with short vegetation as long as suitable nest cavities are available (Gowaty and Plissner 1998). Although it is considered to be an uncommon winter resident in southern Ontario, small numbers of bluebirds are recorded on CBCs each year.

Distribution and population status: The Eastern Bluebird breeds in all areas of the province except the Hudson Bay Lowlands. During the first atlas, the major concentration of the species occurred along the southern edge of the Canadian Shield. The second atlas showed significant increases in the province as a whole and in all four regions in which it breeds. Although proportionally large, the increase in the Northern Shield region is based on relatively few squares. The species now occurs across northern Ontario as far north as Red Lake, with outlying records near Sachigo Lake along the northwestern border with Manitoba. Particularly in southern Ontario, the atlas map is an accurate depiction of its breeding distribution.

Gowaty and Plissner (1998) suggest that burned areas in the Boreal Forest may have been ancestral habitat for bluebirds. The apparent northward expansion of the species' range

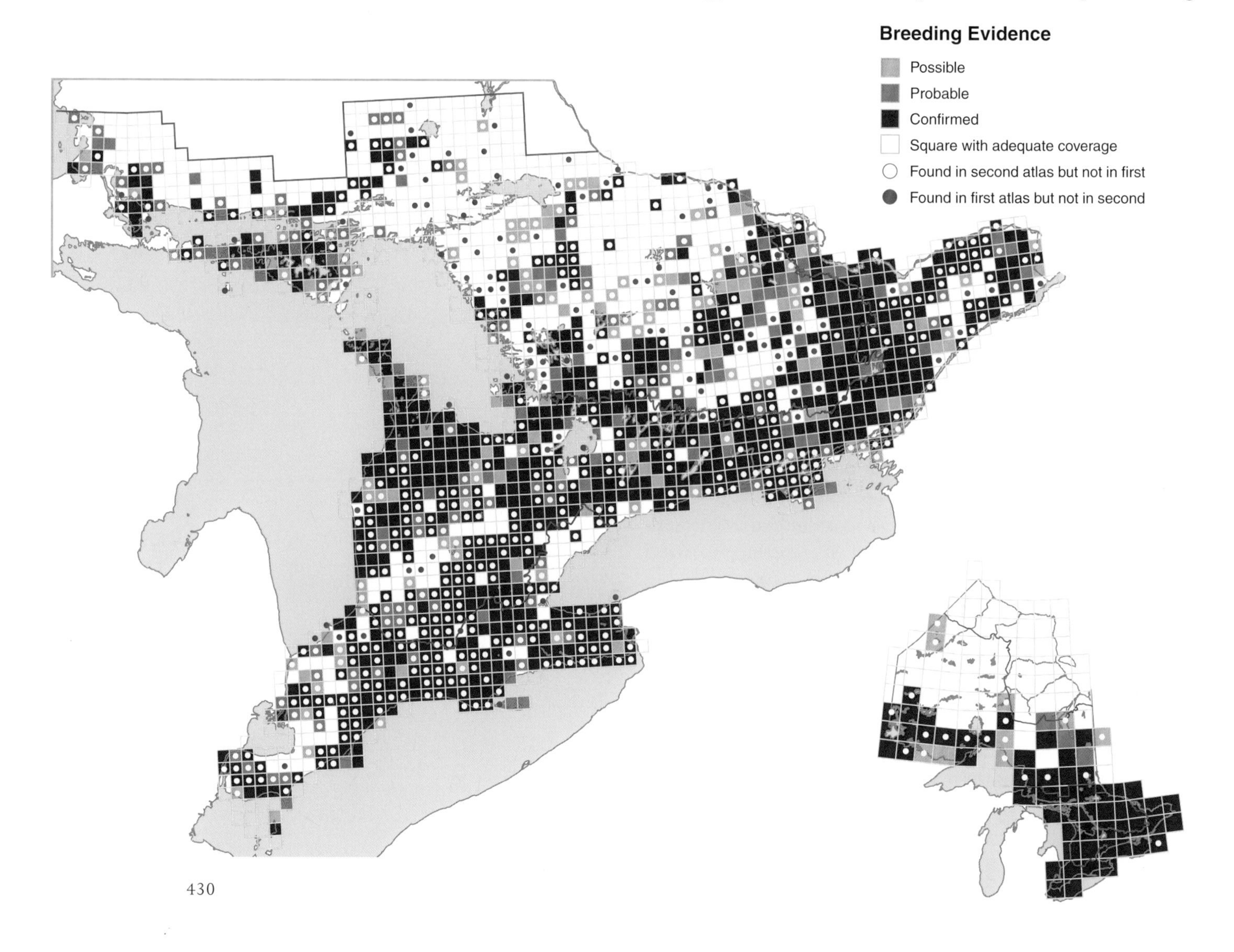

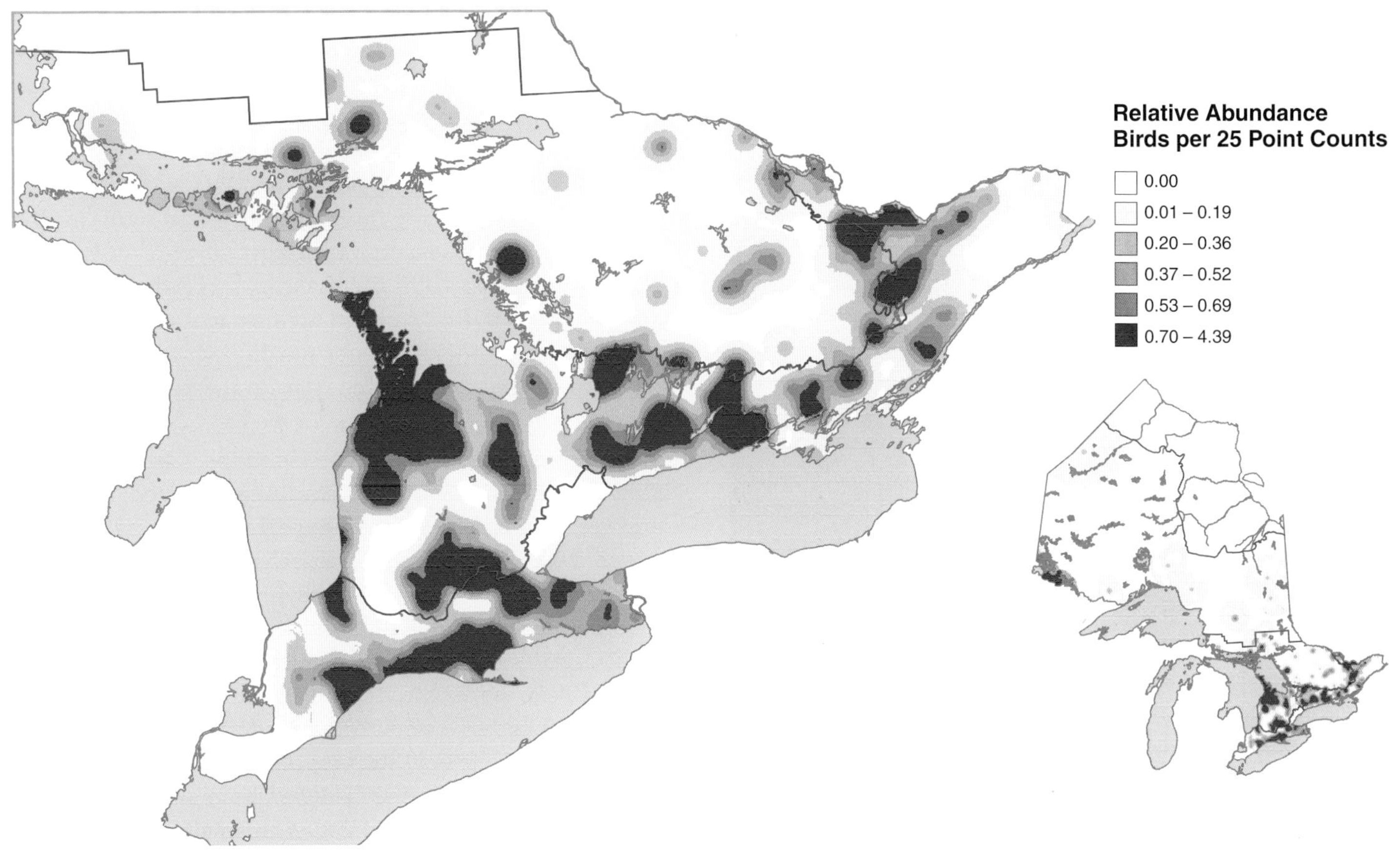

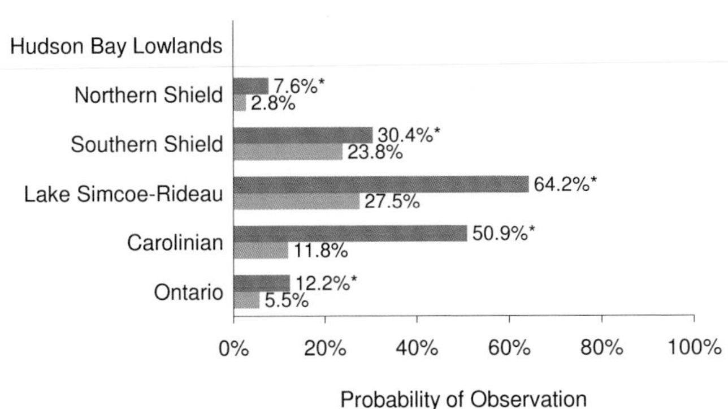

detected in this atlas may be related to better coverage, but increased population levels may also have allowed bluebirds to reoccupy suitable but unused habitat in the north.

Weather is the primary factor influencing bluebird population fluctuations. Cold, wet springs cause nest failures, and extreme weather events, such as the ice storm of April 2003, can have devastating consequences for adult bluebirds. Warmer winters over the past 20 years have assisted this species to recover from the low population levels of the late 1970s. The formation of the North American Bluebird Society in 1978 and the Ontario Eastern Bluebird Society in 1988 encouraged thousands of individuals and groups across North America to erect nest boxes for bluebirds. Well-managed, predator-proof nest box trails now contribute substantially to annual production and are largely responsible for the considerable increase in the Carolinian region.

The Eastern Bluebird is one of the few grassland species that has shown a population increase since the first atlas, largely as a result of human intervention. Between 1981 and 2005, BBS data indicated an annual increase of 8.0% in Ontario.

Breeding biology: The Eastern Bluebird nests individually or in loose colonies where suitable habitat and nesting cavities coexist. Most nests in Ontario are found in nest boxes or in natural cavities in old fence posts and branch stubs. Nests are relatively easy to find. Parent birds frequently make distress calls when a nest site is approached and often search for food from nearby overhead perches. Egg dates are from 27 March (Risley 1981) to 2 September (Peck and James 1987). Fledged young stay nearby while the adults raise a second brood.

Abundance: The relative abundance map shows numerous nodes of high density of the Eastern Bluebird in southern Ontario, with much lower densities in the Southern and Northern Shield regions. Higher densities almost always correlate with areas that have well-managed, predator-proof nest box trails. Many areas of southern Ontario have suitable grassland habitat, but a lack of nest cavities may prevent the species from reaching high densities in these areas. The area of high density in northwestern Ontario is associated with extensive suitable pasture lands in western Rainy River District. The patchy abundance across the north reflects a scarcity of suitable habitat, although bluebirds nesting in clearcuts and burned areas might have been missed because of lack of atlas coverage. Bluebirds were found in these habitats during atlases in the Maritimes and Québec (Erskine 1992; Cyr and Larivée 1995).

Volatile weather attributed to climate change will likely continue to affect the Ontario Eastern Bluebird population in the future. – *Bill Read*

Veery

Grive fauve

Catharus fuscescens

Jim Richards

The presence of this shy woodland bird is usually detected by its breezy, cascading song or its distinctive call notes. The rusty-backed Veery has the faintest, most indistinct breast spots of all the brown thrushes. Its breeding range covers moist and swampy woodlands in the southern third of Canada and the northern US and extends south in the Appalachian and Rocky Mountains (Bevier et al. 2004).

Distribution and population status: The breeding range of the Veery in Ontario appears unchanged since the last atlas. With notable gaps in areas of intensive agriculture and urbanization, the species occurs broadly across the three southern atlas regions. The probability of observation was highest in the Southern Shield at 96%. The breeding range extends into areas of young deciduous growth in the Northern Shield, where the probability of observation was 34%. The northern edge of the Veery's breeding range is almost identical to that noted in the first atlas and, excepting several isolated outliers, extends north to about Red Lake in the northwest and around Fraserdale in the east.

The probability of observation of the Veery declined significantly between atlases in the Carolinian and Lake Simcoe-Rideau regions, by 27% and 12%, respectively. The decline in the Carolinian region may reflect continued degradation of swamp forests through the large existing system of municipal drains utilized for agricultural purposes (McCracken 2006) or pressure from high densities of nest predators and nest parasites (Brown-headed Cowbirds) associated with fragmented landscapes (Askins 2002). Increased browsing of ground vegetation by ever-growing numbers of deer may also decrease nesting habitat (Bevier et al. 2004). In the Lake Simcoe-Rideau region, the decrease may be due to maturation of forests combined with drier conditions during recent years of low rainfall.

In the Northern Shield region, the probability of observation for the Veery increased significantly by 22% between

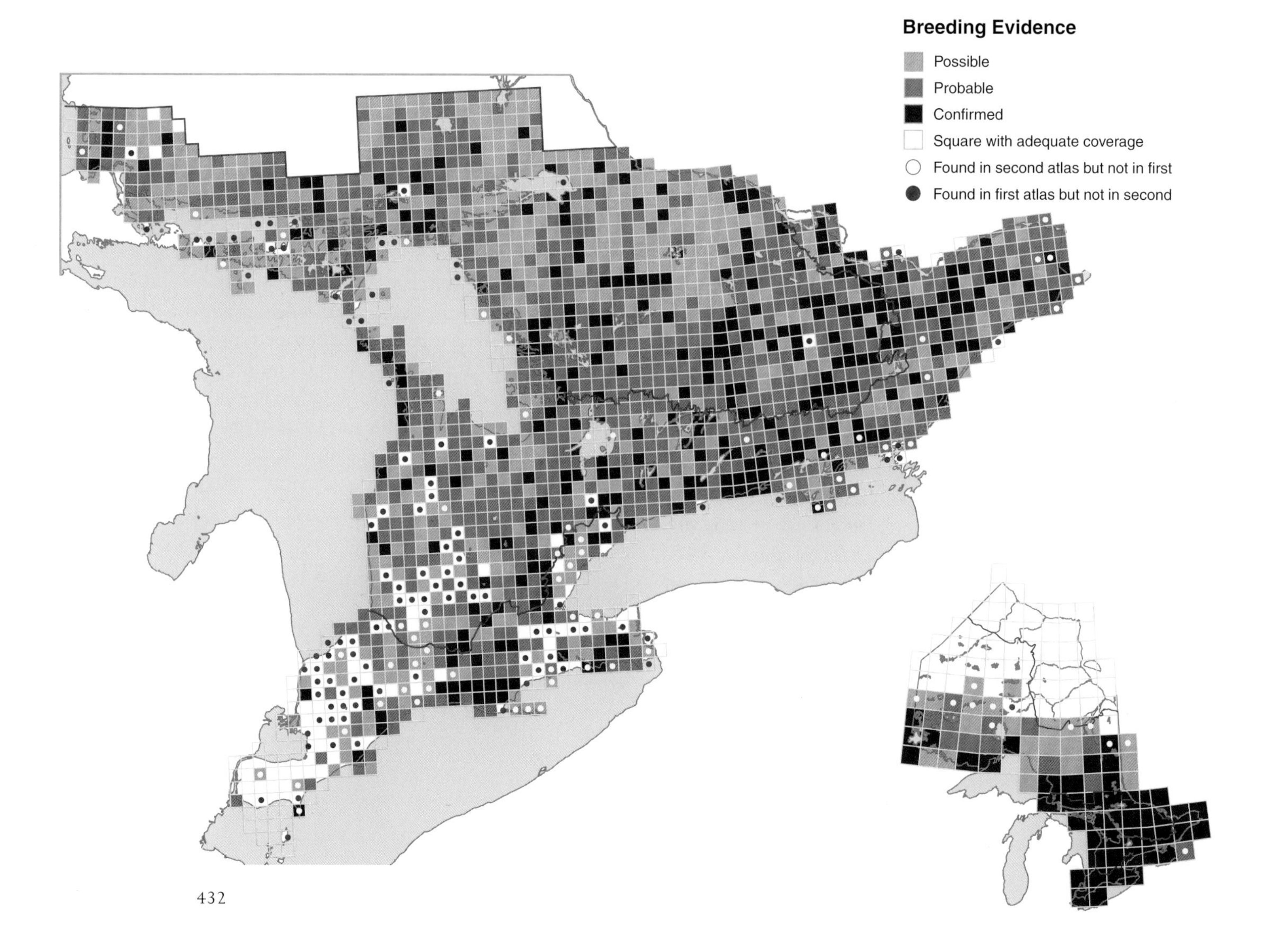

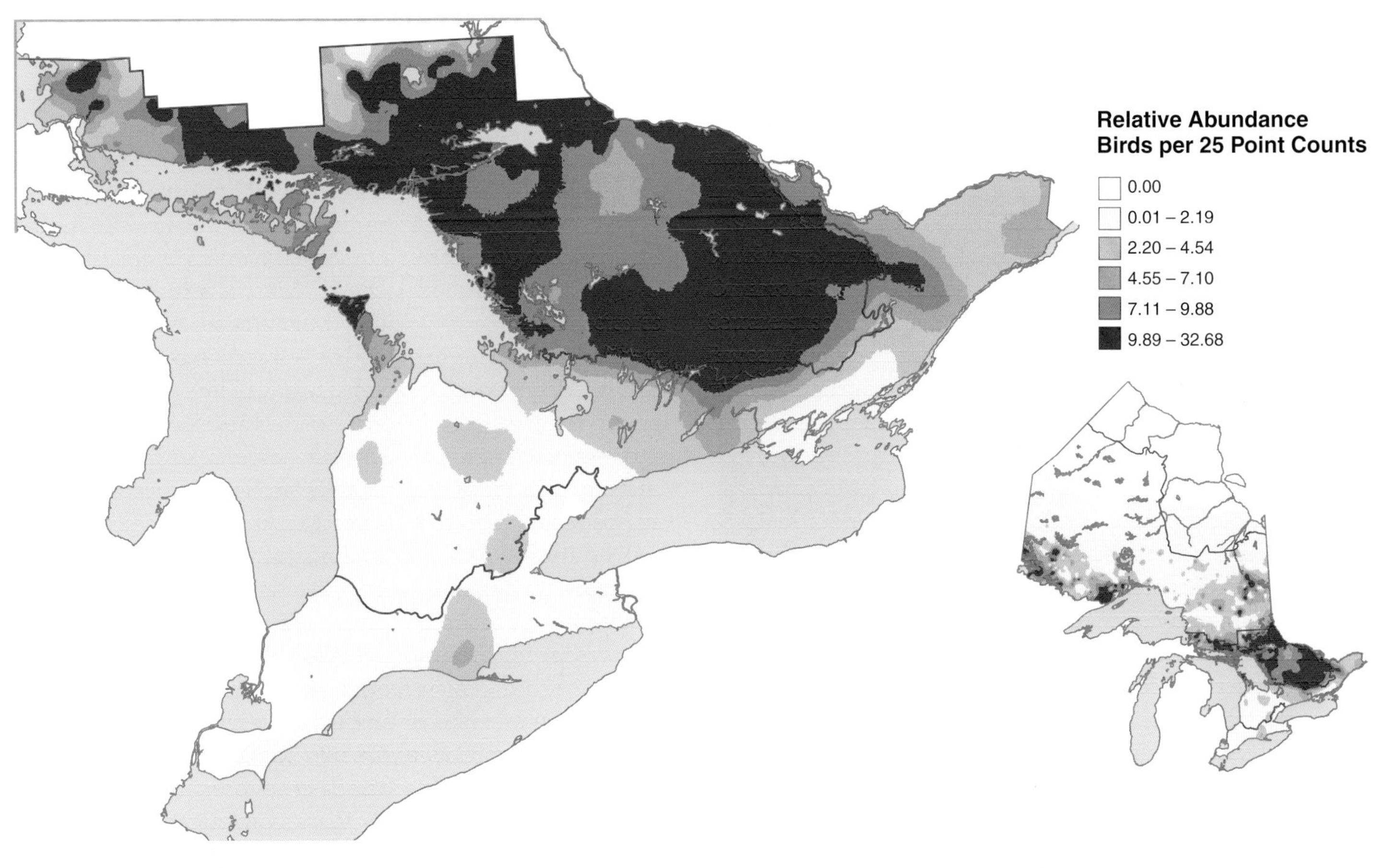

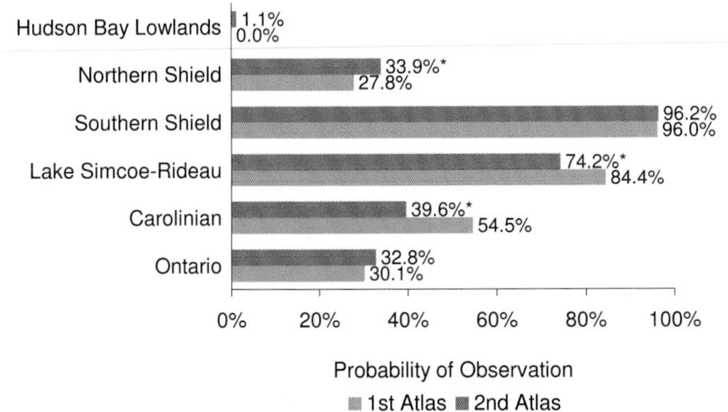

atlases. This may reflect improved atlasser effort and expertise, but the proportion of young forest preferred by the Veery has also increased across most of this region.

Although the Veery is clearly still an abundant species in Ontario, BBS trends indicate a significant decline of 1.9% per year since 1981. Breeding habitat supply does not appear to be a limiting factor, given the extent of logging in the Southern and Northern Shield regions and the proliferation of early successional habitat that follows. Rather, the decline might reflect rapid deforestation on the species' wintering grounds in southern Brazil (Sibley 2001).

Breeding biology: The Veery is area sensitive and occupies a variety of woodland types (Bevier et al. 2004), favouring moist, second-growth woods with dense shrubbery and ground cover. It prefers deciduous and mixed associations and occurs less frequently in stands dominated by coniferous species. Disturbed forests resulting from logging or forest fires are particularly attractive, presumably because of the profuse understorey associated with early successional stands. Where its range overlaps with that of the Wood Thrush, the Veery is typically found in younger, wetter wooded areas (Bevier et al. 2004). Its preference for brushy undergrowth may be related to the use of low perches to make short aerial forays to catch insects or to watch for prey in the leaf litter (Kaufman 1996).

Nests are typically placed on or near the ground at the bases of shrubs, saplings, and trees (Peck and James 1987). The female sits very tightly (C. Vance, pers. comm.), and the placement of the nest in low, dense foliage often limits detection, as evidenced by the fact that breeding was confirmed in just 15% of the recorded squares. However, the species is likely breeding in most of the squares in which it was present.

Abundance: The relative abundance map clearly depicts the Southern Shield region as the Veery's focal breeding area in Ontario. High densities were practically uniform from the southern edge of the Shield north to the southern edge of the Boreal Forest, with the exception of the Algonquin Highlands where abundance was considerably lower. This anomaly may relate to silvicultural practices in Algonquin Prov. Park, where the carefully controlled selection system of cutting may create less suitable Veery habitat than is found in adjacent areas (R. Tozer, pers. comm.) The Veery also occurred in high numbers in parts of the Great Lakes-St. Lawrence Forest in northwestern Ontario. In southwestern Ontario, the Veery population remains sparse due to the lack of preferred young damp forest habitat. Based on point count data, the provincial population is estimated at approximately 2,000,000 birds. – *Lyle Friesen*

Gray-cheeked Thrush

Grive à joues grises

Catharus minimus

The Gray-cheeked Thrush is the least studied thrush species in North America owing to the inaccessibility of its remote, subarctic breeding range, where it inhabits brushy willow-alder thickets and low coniferous forests with dense undergrowth (Lowther et el. 2001). On the breeding grounds, it is the least vocal of the Ontario thrushes, with singing activity typically concentrated in the early and late daylight hours, but not necessarily for prolonged periods (Wilson and McRae 1993).

The Gray-cheeked Thrush is virtually indistinguishable in appearance from the Bicknell's Thrush (*C. bicknelli*), and the two were only recently split. Among the other *Catharus* thrushes, and despite being more closely related to the Veery (Lowther et al. 2001), the Gray-cheeked most resembles the Swainson's, from which it can be distinguished by the absence of a buffy eye-ring. The breeding range is the most northerly of all the spotted thrushes, extending broadly from Newfoundland to eastern Siberia (Godfrey 1986). The Gray-cheeked Thrush is one of the few American bird species that regularly breeds outside of North America and winters in the American tropics, primarily in South America east of the Andes (Lowther et al. 2001).

Distribution and population status: Data from the second atlas did little to clarify the status of this species in Ontario. The Ontario breeding range extends from just inland from the Hudson Bay coast south to about 53° N in the vicinity of the Attawapiskat River. The species was reported in three new 100-km blocks in the second atlas, but was not reported from five 100-km blocks in which it was reported during the first atlas. (No data were submitted this time from the sixth 100-km block where it occurred in the first atlas.) The paucity of breeding evidence – records from eight squares in both the first and second atlases – makes it

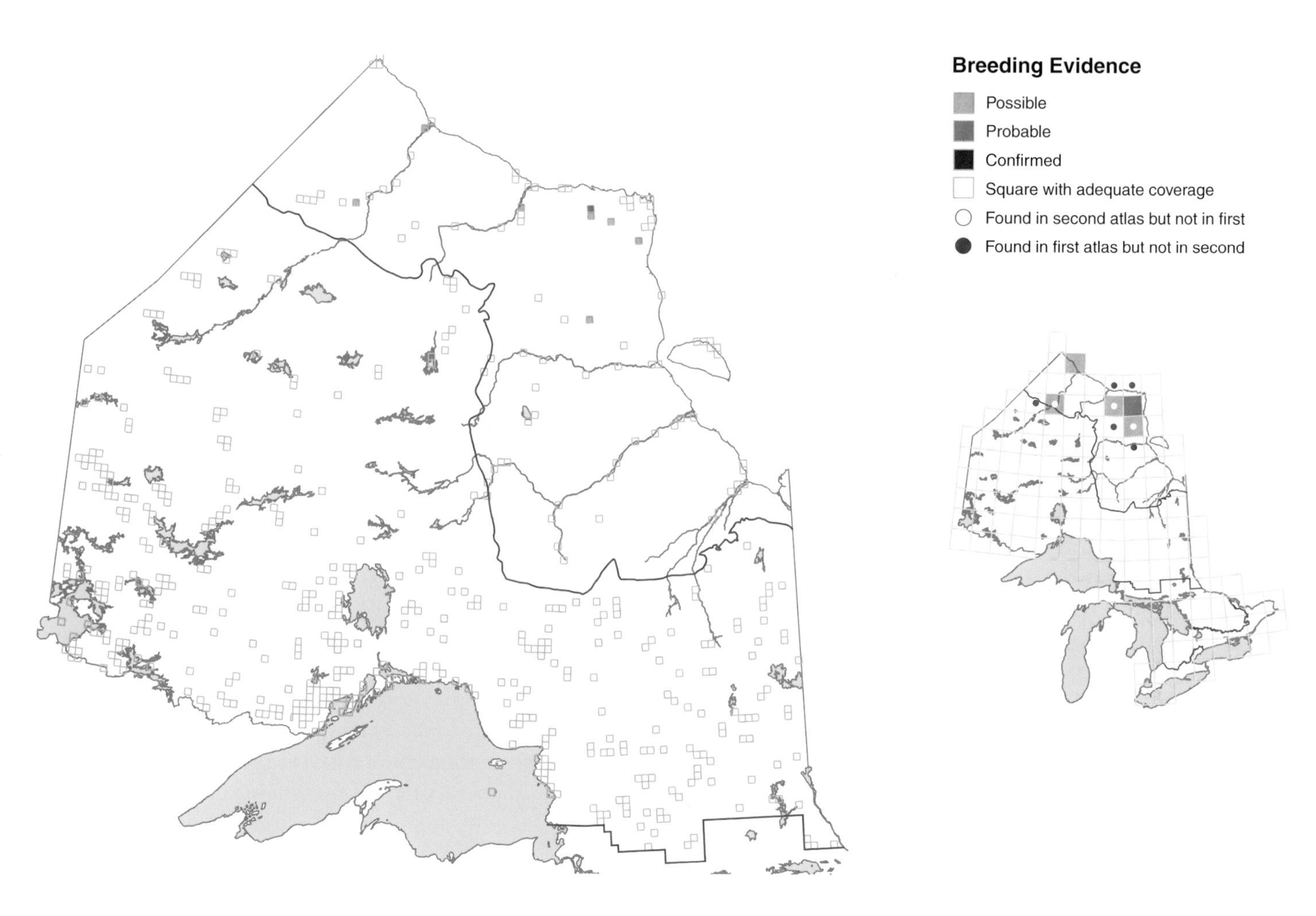

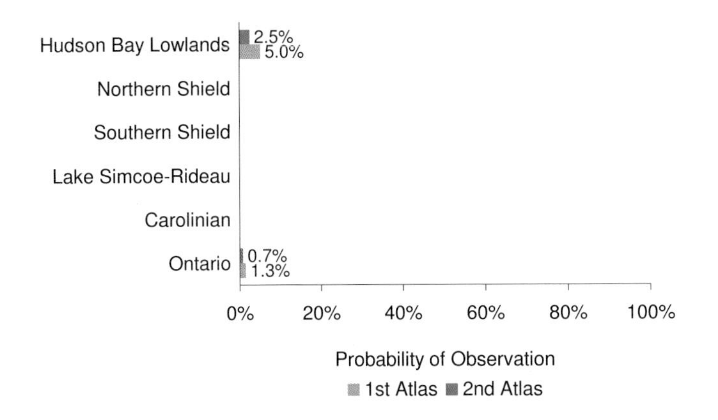

impossible to judge whether any distributional changes have occurred or even to gauge more precisely the extent of its range, particularly at the more southerly latitudes.

The scarcity of breeding records in the Hudson Bay Lowlands is surprising given the abundance of apparently suitable habitat. This thrush may have been overlooked because of its relatively weak song, which often is delivered for only short periods during the day, because survey crews visited areas after peak singing dates in the breeding cycle, or because it was difficult for surveyors to be in optimum habitat promptly at dusk and dawn when the species is most active vocally. Nevertheless, intensive atlas work was conducted throughout the region by experienced observers, and it seems unlikely that the species could have been consistently missed if it were present. In the future, targeted surveys using song broadcasts might provide a more accurate index of distribution. The results from the second atlas, however limited, are consistent with those from the first, namely, that the species appears to be a rare but regular breeder within a relatively short distance of the Hudson and northern James Bay coastlines, and that it becomes even rarer and more isolated farther inland.

Breeding biology: In Ontario, the Gray-cheeked Thrush is found in riparian willow-poplar-alder thickets, along the edges of extensive burns having dense spruce-willow-birch-Green Alder regeneration, and in open, stunted spruce woodland with willow-birch understorey, which is sometimes interspersed with wet willow and alder thickets (D. Sutherland, pers. comm.). This thrush also occurs along rivers and streams bordered by open spruce woodlands and mature aspen stands.

Only two nests have ever been found in Ontario, and none since 1964 (Peck and James 1987; Peck and Peck 2006). Compact affairs (for a thrush), nests are usually placed on the ground or low in a tree. Information on the species' breeding biology is extremely limited (Lowther et al. 2001).

Abundance: Population estimates indicate that, except for the Bicknell's Thrush, the Gray-cheeked Thrush is likely the least abundant (circa 12,000,000 individuals) of the spotted thrushes in North America (Rich et al. 2004). The low overall population size combined with the expansive continental breeding range suggests that breeding densities are probably low in most areas where it occurs. In Ontario, all the breeding records during the second atlas were of single birds. Indeed, there is scant information on the species' continental population trend, because its isolated breeding range lies well to the north of most BBS routes (Lowther et al. 2001). The Gray-cheeked Thrush remains a scientific enigma, certainly deserving of more extensive research and attention throughout its range. – *Lyle Friesen*

Nests are usually on the ground or low in a small tree. Only two nests have been found in Ontario and none since 1964. Churchill, Manitoba, 21 June 1971. *Photo: George K. Peck*

In Ontario, preferred breeding habitat includes dense, low spruce-alder-aspen-willow riparian thickets and woodlands, regenerating burns, and taiga in the Hudson Bay Lowlands. *Photo: John Reaume*

Swainson's Thrush

Grive à dos olive

Catharus ustulatus

Eleanor Kee Wellman

The upwardly spiralling song of the Swainson's Thrush resonates throughout northern forests. Primarily a reclusive denizen of mature coniferous and mixed wood forests, the Swainson's Thrush also inhabits pure hardwood stands in the southern portion of its Ontario range. Its broad breeding range spans North America from Alaska to Newfoundland and extends in forested landscapes from northern Minnesota and Wisconsin to the treeline. At higher elevations, the range extends south into the mountains of both the eastern and western US (Godfrey 1986; Evans Mack and Yong 2000). The species winters mostly in primary and secondary forests from southern Mexico to northern Argentina (Evans Mack and Yong 2000).

Distribution and population status: The Swainson's Thrush is found throughout Ontario except for the extreme north, where trees are naturally absent, and the southwest, where it has apparently never occurred in any numbers during the breeding season (McIlwraith 1894). It is practically ubiquitous in the coniferous-dominated Northern Shield region and is likely breeding wherever it is found. Distribution is less uniform but still prominent across the two adjacent regions, namely the Hudson Bay Lowlands and the Southern Shield. Within the Southern Shield region, the species was consistently found in both atlases across the Algonquin Highlands and in the northern part of the region; south and east of the Algonquin Highlands, it was widely distributed in both atlases but frequently was found in different squares. The Lake Simcoe-Rideau region represents the southern extreme of its breeding range within the province; here, it is well established on the Bruce Peninsula, particularly the north end, on Manitoulin Island, and in pockets within Simcoe Co. north of Orillia and in the Kawartha Lakes region. The species' breeding range in Ontario thus closely approximates the geographical extent of its preferred coniferous and mixed forest habitat.

The Swainson's Thrush is one of the most common birds

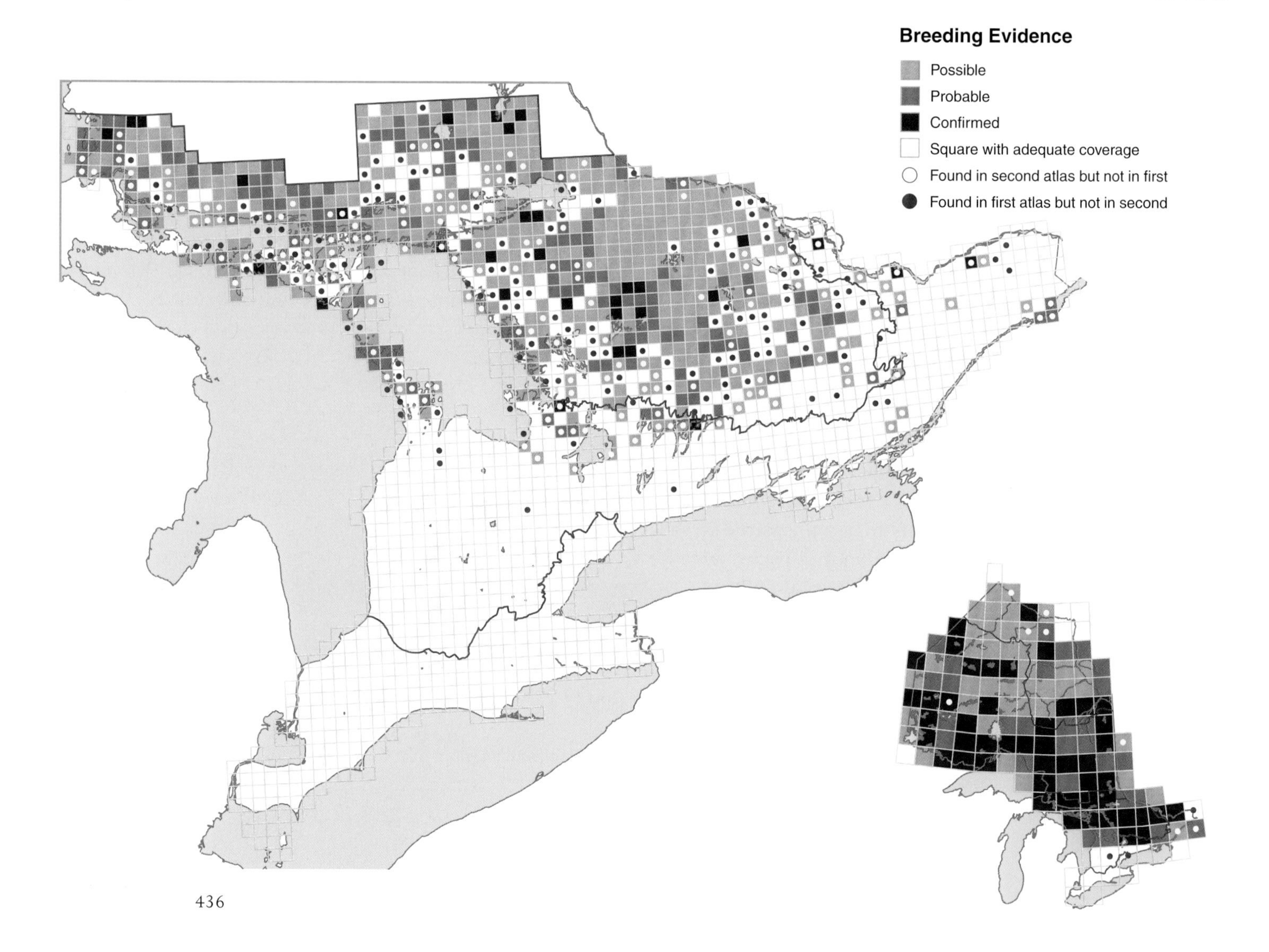

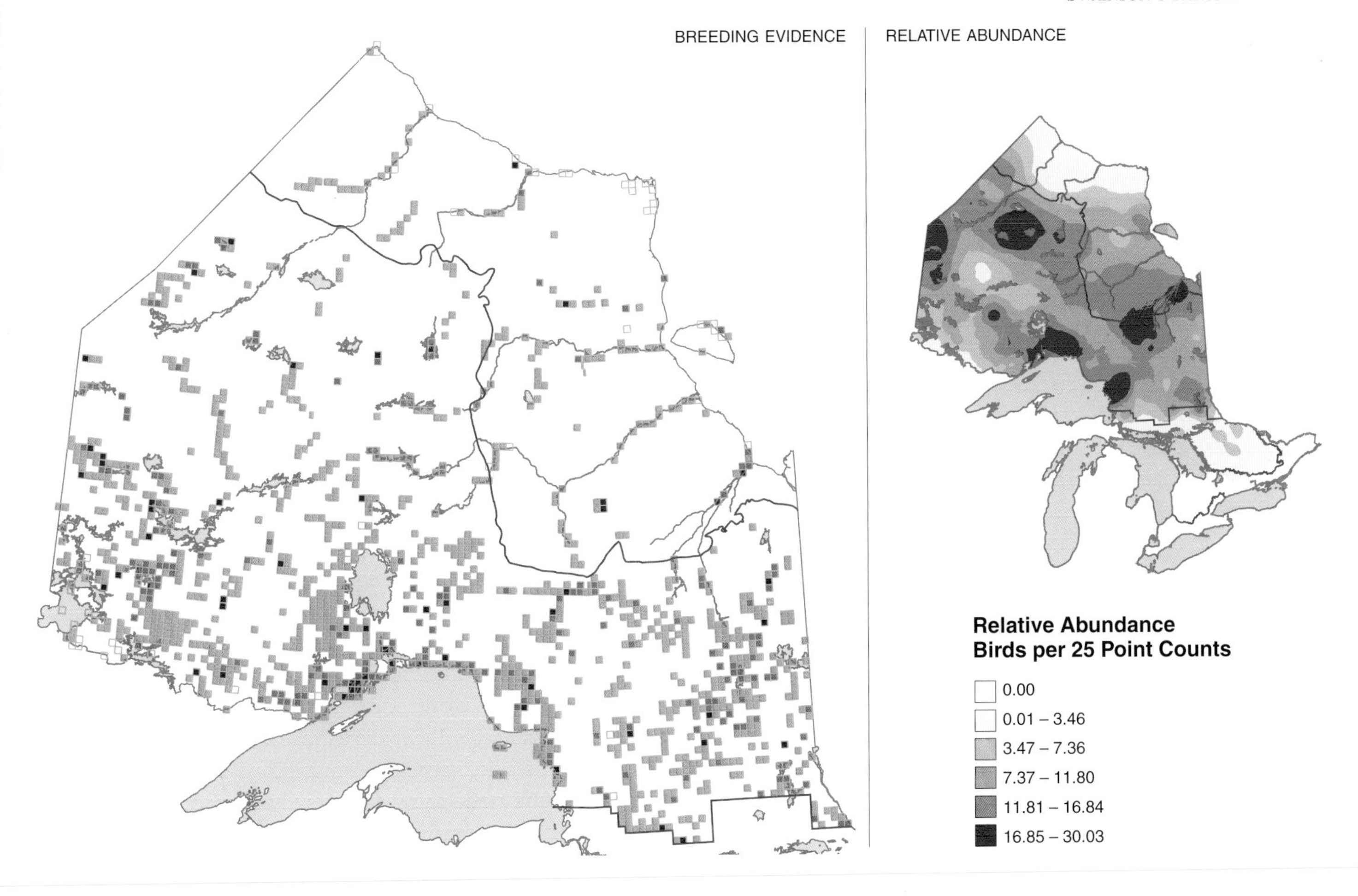

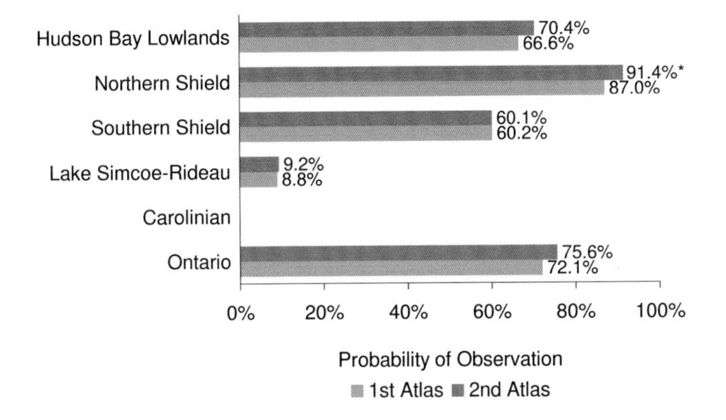

in Ontario's northern forests and has shown a significant increase of 5% in the probability of observation in the Northern Shield region between atlases. However, BBS data suggest the species has undergone a near-significant population decline of 1.7% per year in Ontario since 1981. The apparent contradiction between the two trends is difficult to explain; BBS coverage is not strong where roads are scarce, as is the case in the Northern Shield region, and might not be providing an accurate index of this northern species' status. However, population declines are occurring elsewhere in the species' range where it is abundant, such as in Alaska and in the Northeastern US (Evans Mack and Yong 2000). Breeding-ground changes, such as shorter cutting rotations in the Boreal Forest, resulting in less optimal younger forests, may be contributing to the declines in some areas (Erskine 1992). Deforestation on the wintering grounds may also be a factor in population changes (Evans Mack and Yong 2000).

Breeding biology: The Swainson's Thrush sings primarily very early in the morning and late in the evening. The amount of singing can vary substantially from day to day with no apparent relationship to weather conditions (Evans Mack and Yong 2000). These characteristics may have reduced the opportunities for atlassers to detect this species or to record territories if squares were visited only during periods of less singing.

Confirmation of breeding may also be difficult. The bulky nest of twigs, moss, bark, and leaves (Harrison 1975) is placed in trees and shrubs, usually at heights of 0.9 to 2.4 m (Peck and James 1987). Nests are well concealed, especially when placed in conifer saplings. The protracted period of egg dates in Ontario suggests double-brooding, but this has not been confirmed

The female is very cautious while incubating, and the young may not be very vocal in begging for food (Evans Mack and Yong 2000). Both parents feed the young, but the northerly distribution of the species likely reduced the opportunity for many atlassers to observe fledged young or adults carrying food. Overall, breeding was confirmed in only 5% of squares.

Abundance: The Swainson's Thrush is by far the most abundant of the spotted thrushes in North America (Rich et al. 2004). The abundance maps show that the population stronghold in Ontario is within the Northern Shield region, and to a lesser extent, in the southern part of the Hudson Bay Lowlands. Based on atlas point count data, the Ontario population is estimated at 8,000,000 birds, 6,000,000 of which are found in the Northern Shield region, and only 5,000 of which are found in the Lake Simcoe-Rideau region. – *Lyle Friesen*

Hermit Thrush

Grive solitaire

Catharus guttatus

George K. Peck

The Hermit Thrush is arguably the finest singer of all the brown-backed thrushes. Its clear, pensive song, each phrase beginning on a different pitch, is distinctive and far carrying. Occasionally, this thrush will carol throughout the day, although vocal activity usually peaks at dawn and dusk. It is also readily distinguished from Ontario's other brown thrushes by its reddish tail, which is often slowly raised and lowered (Sibley 2000). It is the most widely distributed of the brown thrushes (although the Swainson's Thrush is more abundant; Rich et al. 2004), breeding in much of forested Canada south to the northern US and extending farther south in the Rocky Mountains and Appalachians (Jones and Donovan 1996). It is the only woodland thrush that routinely winters in the southern US.

Distribution and population status: The Hermit Thrush has significantly increased its distribution from the first to second atlas in all regions of Ontario excepting the Carolinian region. During the second atlas, the probability of observation was 95% in the Southern Shield and 81% and 78% in the Northern Shield and Hudson Bay Lowland regions, respectively. Given the high density of birds detected on point counts in the Northern Shield, it is probable that the species is present in virtually every square and that distribution gaps reflect inadequate effort in many squares.

In southern Ontario, the Hermit Thrush's breeding range has expanded south and east since the first atlas. It is one of the few avian species to thrive in monoculture pine plantations (Manitoba Avian Research Committee 2003), and the maturation of Red and White Pine reforestation stands on the Oak Ridges Moraine from Dufferin Co. and Peel RM to Northumberland Co. has widened its habitat opportunities. In this atlas, it also occurred in many additional squares in which it was not reported in the first, in the Bruce Peninsula and southern Grey Co. and the southern Frontenac Axis eastward to Cornwall. Forest cover in southern Ontario increased threefold

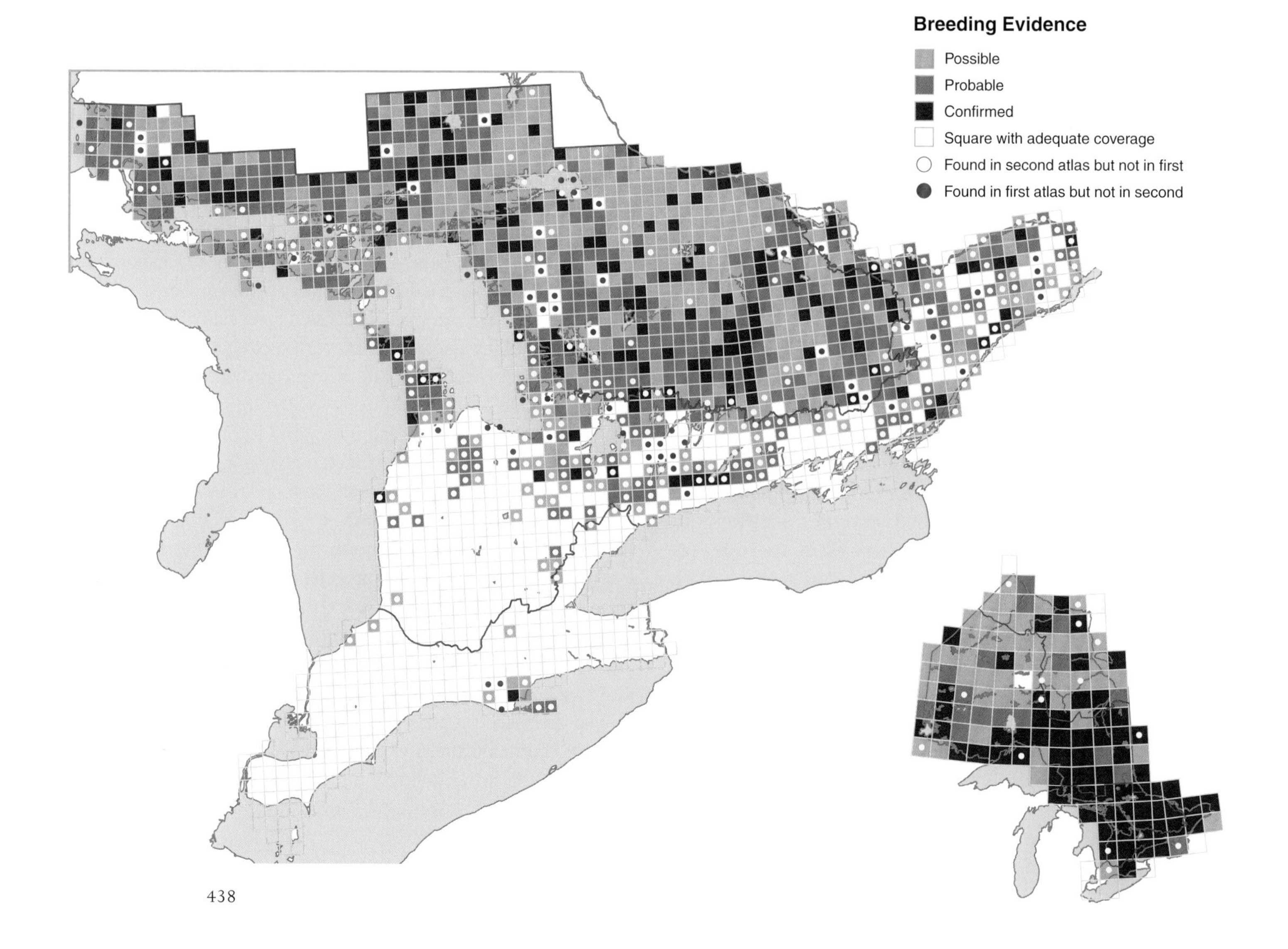

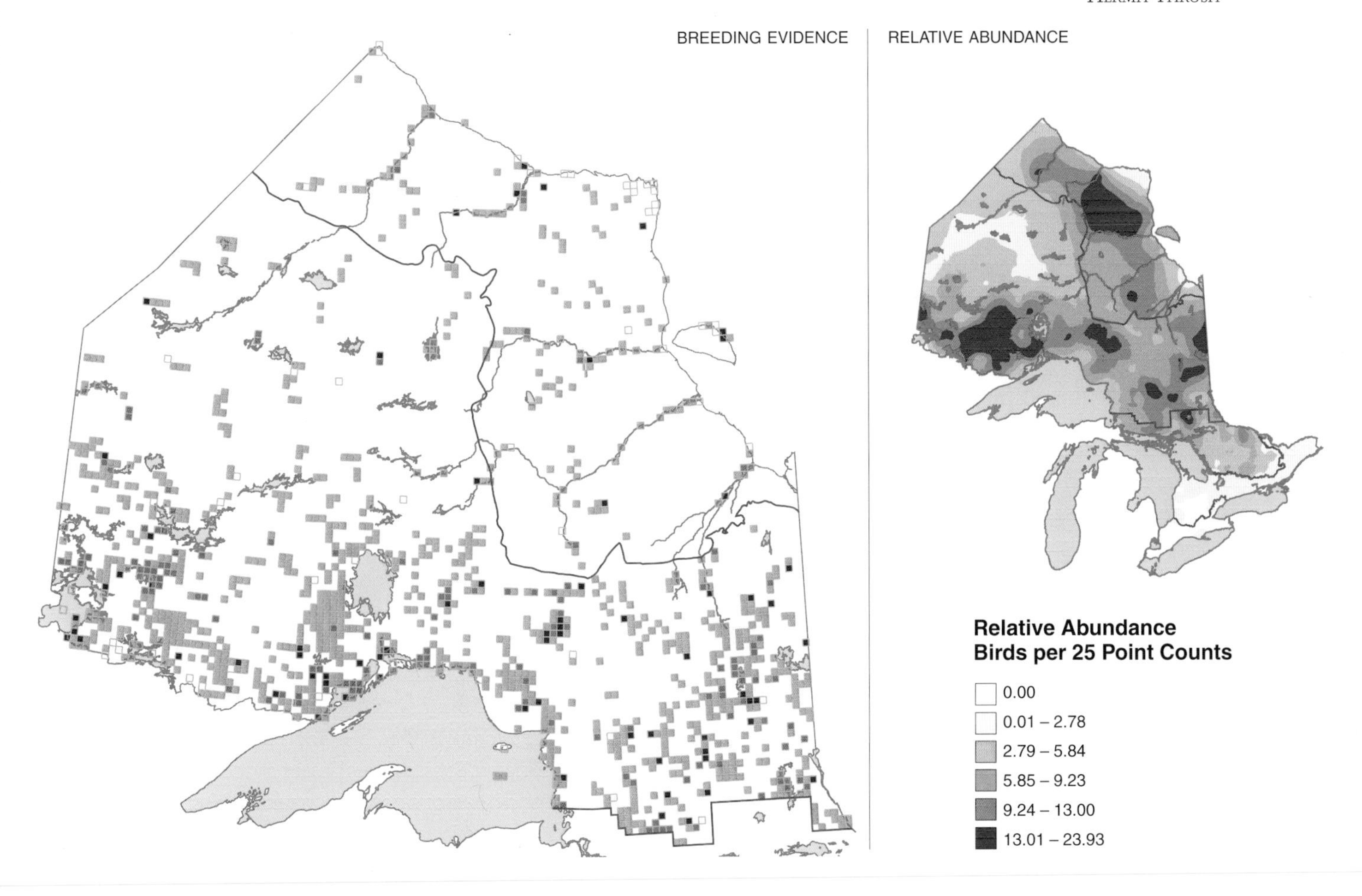

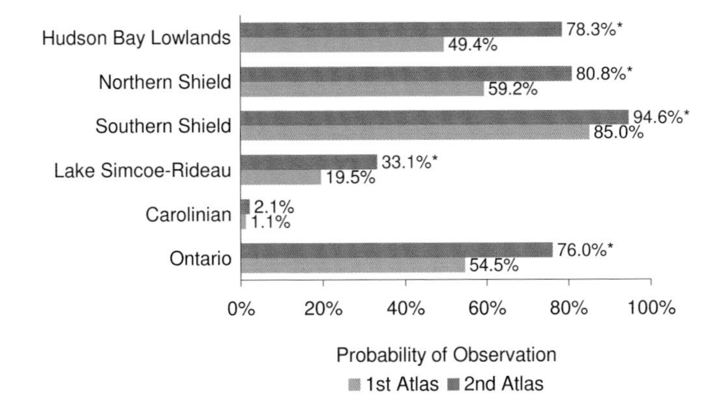

from 1920 to 1990 as abandoned, marginal farmland reverted back to forest (Larson et al. 1999). Rates of forest gain increased eastward, and the range expansion of the Hermit Thrush mirrors this pattern.

The species remains scarce and extremely local in southwestern Ontario from Grey Co. to the Lake Erie shoreline. Not coincidentally, this is the portion of the province where forest fragmentation is most acute. The Hermit Thrush is area sensitive (Freemark and Collins 1992), and forests in this region are generally too small and regional forest cover is too low to support the species.

BBS data for Ontario show a stable population trend from 1981 to 2005, suggesting that the quality and supply of breeding habitat are being maintained. The population stability may also reflect the fact that the Hermit Thrush winters farther north than other brown thrushes and is less vulnerable to the effects of tropical deforestation (Kaufman 1996).

Breeding biology: The Hermit Thrush uses a broader array of forested habitats than any of the other brown thrushes, which in part accounts for its extensive breeding range (Jones and Donovan 1996). In Ontario, it occupies both wet and dry coniferous, mixed, and deciduous woods, Tamarack-spruce peatlands, barrens, savannahs, and forests regenerating after fire or logging. Jack Pine forests on sand or rocky ridges are a preferred habitat within the Boreal Forest (Manitoba Avian Research Committee 2003). Territories are often established along internal forest edges such as the margins of a pond or a beaver meadow and edges associated with disturbances such as logging, road-building, and utility lines.

Nests are bulky but usually well concealed by dense vegetation and are typically placed on the ground, often at the base of shrubs and small trees. Only 11% of breeding records were of confirmed breeding (the same percentage as in the first atlas), testifying to the difficulties of locating nests. Double broods are probable in Ontario, given the records of late egg dates (Peck and James 1987), but this remains to be confirmed.

Abundance: The species' population core rests within the Northern Shield and the Hudson Bay Lowlands, where 10.1 and 8.4 birds/25 point counts, respectively, were reported. Although range expansion has occurred in eastern Ontario, the density of the species remains low there. The low abundance levels in the Lake Simcoe-Rideau region suggest habitat conditions are less than optimum, and perhaps also reflect interspecific tension with the Wood Thrush, which dominates the Hermit Thrush (Jones and Donovan 1996). – *Lyle Friesen*

Wood Thrush

Grive des bois

Hylocichla mustelina

George K. Peck

Famed for its lyrical, liquid song delivered especially at twilight, the Wood Thrush is widely distributed in deciduous and mixed forests across southern Ontario. Were it not for its loud, distinctive vocalizing, it might go undetected, given its retiring nature and earthy coloration, matching the forest floor where it typically forages. Its breeding range extends across the eastern half of the continent from southeastern Canada to the Gulf States and west to the Great Plains (Roth et al. 1996).

Distribution and population status: The Wood Thrush's breeding distribution in Ontario has not changed significantly since the first atlas. The species' core range in the province closely mirrors the distribution of its preferred deciduous and mixed forest habitats. Now as in the first atlas, it is almost uniformly blanketed across the Carolinian and Lake Simcoe-Rideau regions. Here, any gaps in the recorded distribution are likely attributable to an acute shortage of habitat in intensively agricultural areas or to urbanization; the species usually shuns woodlots surrounded by houses (Friesen et al. 1995).

The Wood Thrush occurs throughout the Great Lakes-St. Lawrence Forest, where suitable habitat exists. Its distribution extends north through the Southern Shield almost continuously to about Lake Nipissing. It is spread thinly to New Liskeard in the northeast and along the shores of northern Georgian Bay and eastern Lake Superior, north to Wawa. A small, isolated population also occurs in Great Lakes-St. Lawrence Forest in western Rainy River Dist. near Lake of the Woods. Despite its apparent absence from this area during the first atlas, there is no indication that this is the result of a recent range extension. It remains a rare summer visitor in neighbouring Manitoba (Manitoba Avian Research Committee 2003).

The Wood Thrush has experienced severe population declines in many parts of its North American breeding range. BBS data for Ontario, however, indicate a significant annual

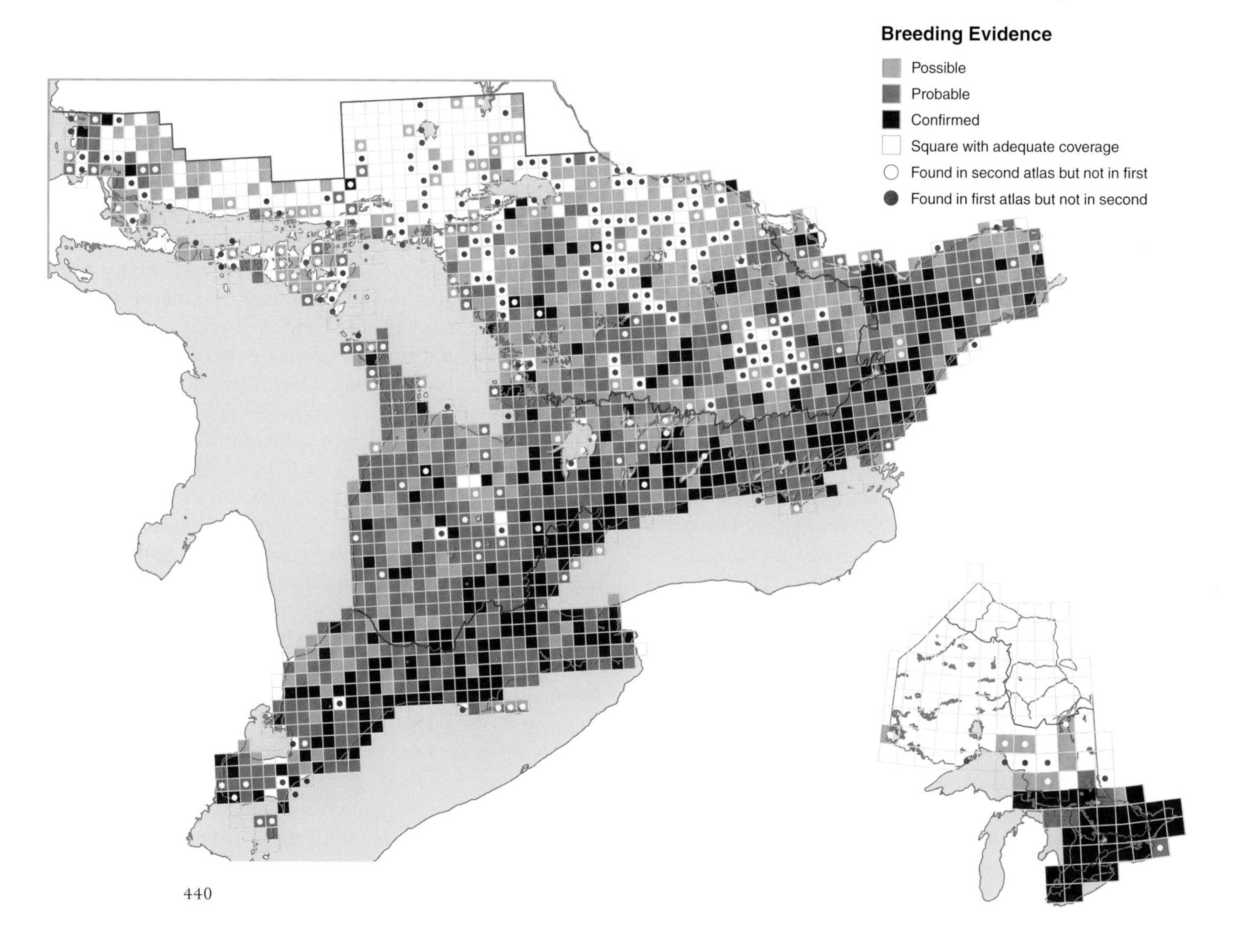

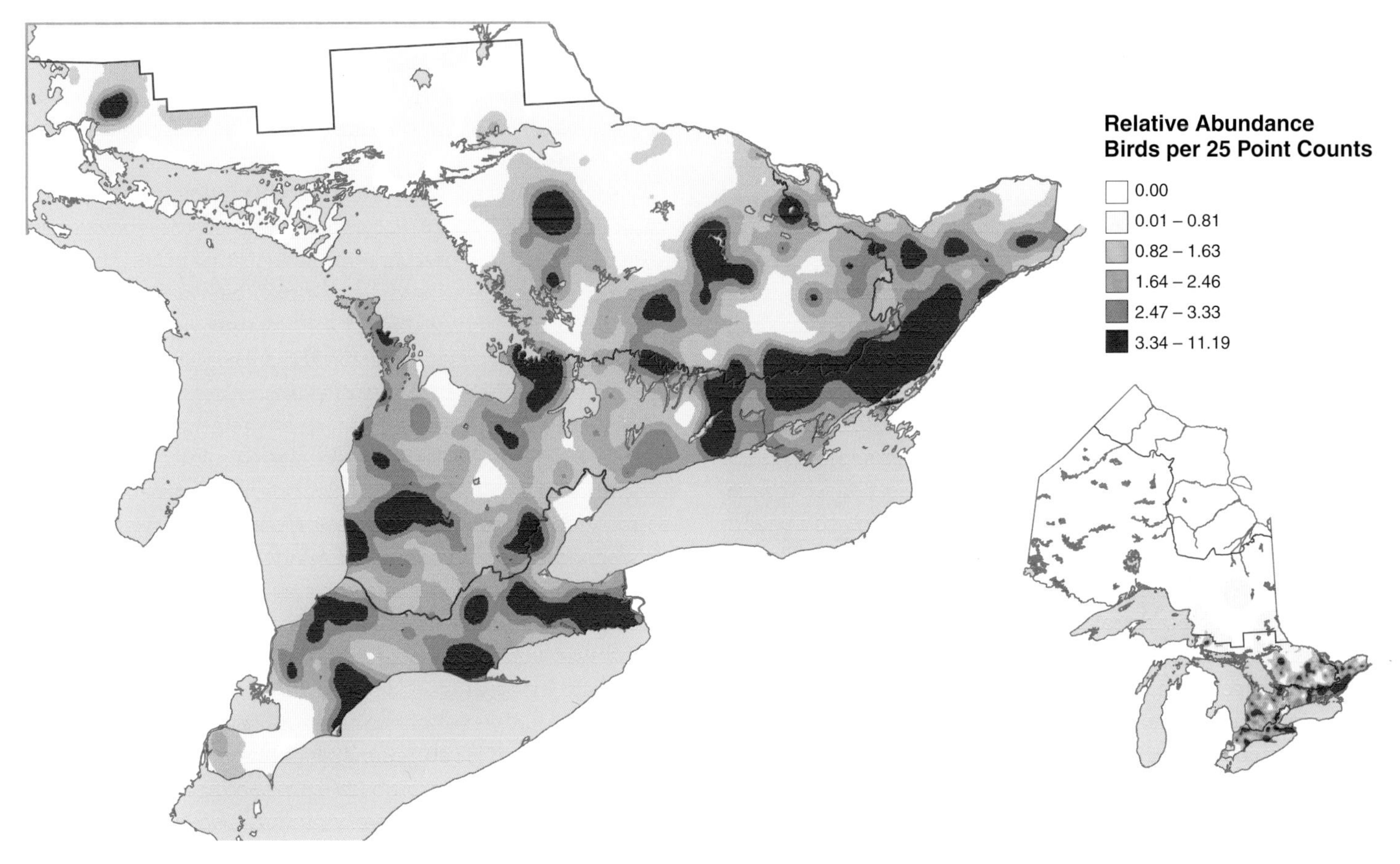

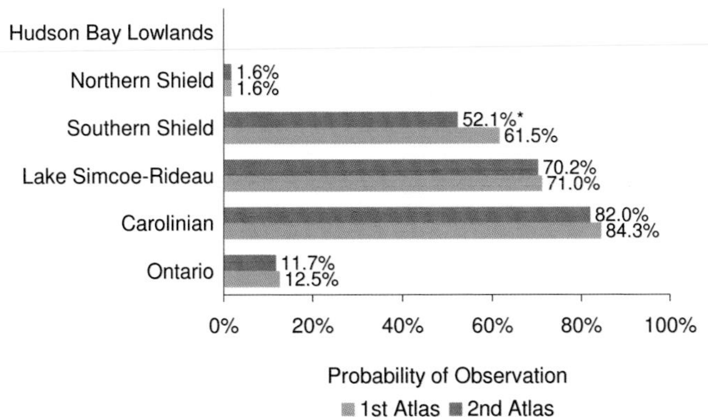

increase of 4.4% between 1981 and 2005. This increase is not reflected in an increase in the probability of observation between atlases for the two southern regions, possibly because the species was already using available suitable habitat during the first atlas. The three-fold increase in woodland cover south of the Shield since the 1920s has been especially dramatic in areas of eastern Ontario and the Niagara Escarpment (Larson et al. 1999), and this reforestation has likely helped fuel the population surge. In the Southern Shield region, the probability of observation declined significantly by 15% between atlases. The decline may be linked to the effects of acid rain (Strickland 2006), which has been implicated in the Wood Thrush's reduced reproductive success (Hames et al. 2002). Increasingly mature forests with less of the dense understorey needed by this species (Ahlering and Faaborg 2006) may also be an important factor.

Breeding biology: Although the Wood Thrush has been reported to be area sensitive throughout its breeding range (Roth et al. 1996), in Ontario it inhabits woodlands ranging from small (3 ha) and isolated to large and contiguous (Friesen et al. 1999a). The presence of tall trees (used for singing perches) and a thick understorey are usually prerequisites for site occupancy. Two, and rarely three, broods are produced per season (Friesen et al. 2001). The species is less affected by cowbird parasitism in Ontario than in some other portions of its breeding range (Friesen et al. 1999a).

Nests are typically located 2 to 5 m above the ground and usually concealed within a thicket or sapling stand but may also be placed in a large tree (usually Sugar Maple), sometimes in a very exposed manner. The nest resembles that of the American Robin but is lined with dark rootlets rather than grass. Wood Thrush nests tend to be more conspicuous than those of other forest birds, being relatively large and embroidered with beech leaves, with pale, desiccated plant stalks and sometimes even long strips of plastic hanging down. However, despite their apparent visibility, nests can be difficult to find, and confirmed nesting was reported in only 21% of the occupied squares. Most singing birds are paired (Friesen et al. 1999b), and the species is likely breeding in almost all squares for which there are records, particularly in the south.

Abundance: The Wood Thrush is most abundant in the Lake Simcoe-Rideau and Carolinian regions. A massive ice storm that devastated forests in eastern Ontario in 1998 resulted in huge swaths of regenerating forest, and this region now boasts the most extensive area of high-density Wood Thrush habitat in the province. – *Lyle Friesen*

American Robin

Merle d'Amérique

Turdus migratorius

Karl Egressy

The American Robin is the largest, most abundant, and most widespread thrush in North America (Sallabanks and James 1999). Familiar to many as the harbinger of spring, this conspicuous and easily recognized backyard bird has a loud, musical voice that makes it difficult to overlook or mistake for another species. Outside the settled areas of the province, however, birds that breed in woodlands are much more secretive and easier to miss. Overall, few species rival the robin in its ability to thrive in both suburban and natural habitats.

Distribution and population status: The size of the breeding range of the American Robin has increased in the last two centuries, particularly in the prairies and the southern US, with the establishment of farmlands and homesteads and the increasing availability of suburban parkland (Sallabanks and James 1999). In Ontario, both atlases indicate that the American Robin is virtually ubiquitous in the south, but less so in the north. Though its overall breeding distribution has not changed appreciably since the first atlas, the probability of observation increased significantly by 19% in the Northern Shield and 93% in the Hudson Bay Lowlands. The reason for such a substantial increase in the latter region is unknown; however, as the effect of differences in coverage between atlases is removed by the change analysis, the increase may be real. The substantial increase in the latter region is more likely a function of differences in coverage and effort between atlases than a true change in distribution or numbers. Furthermore, availability of habitat is unlikely to have changed in that region. The somewhat smaller increase in the Northern Shield may reflect both an increase in edge habitats and greater accessibility associated with forestry. Small declines in the probability of observation in the Lake Simcoe-Rideau and Southern Shield region are non-significant.

BBS data tend to confirm that American Robin populations in Ontario and Canada are stable or slightly increasing. BBS

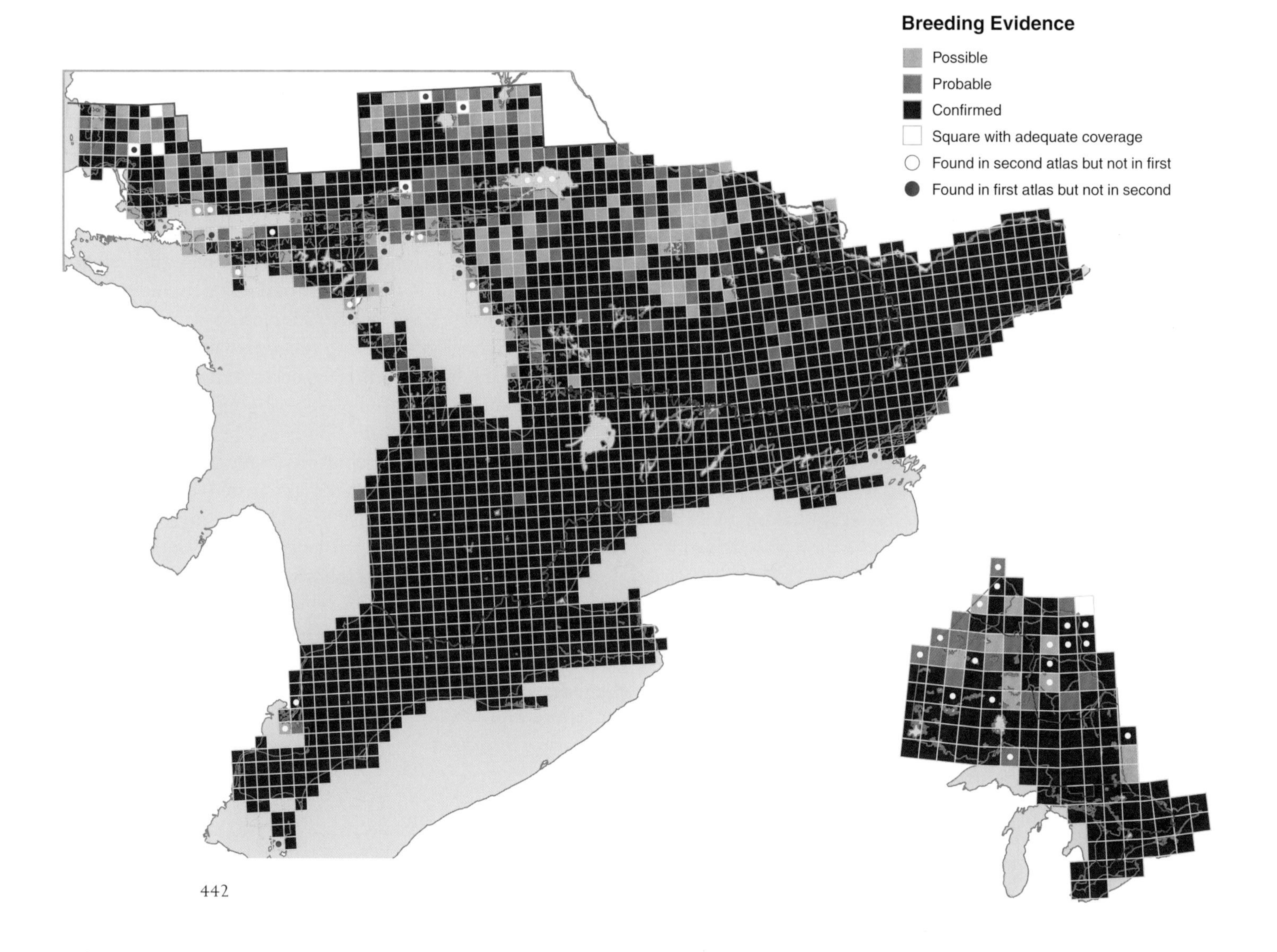

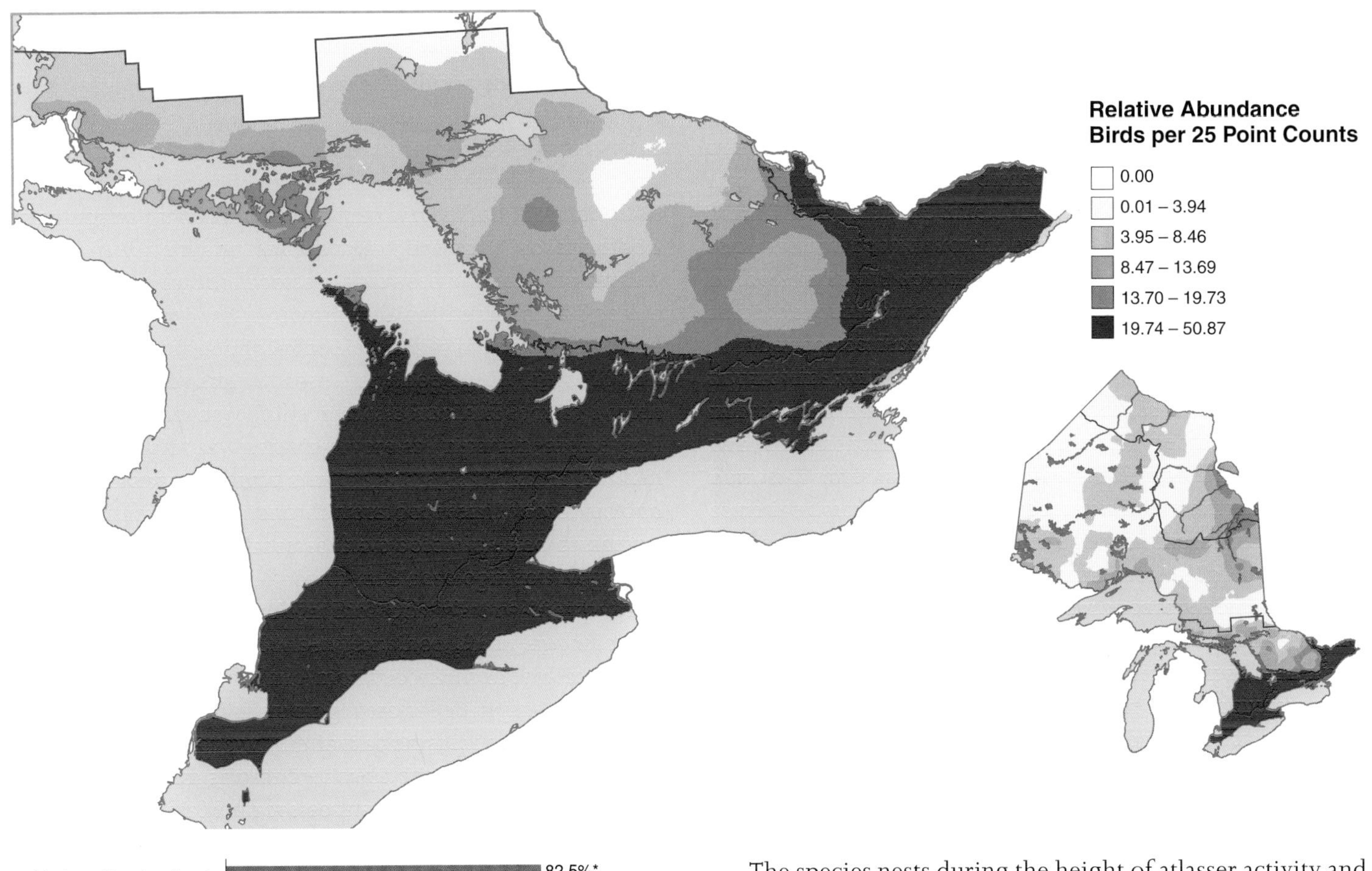

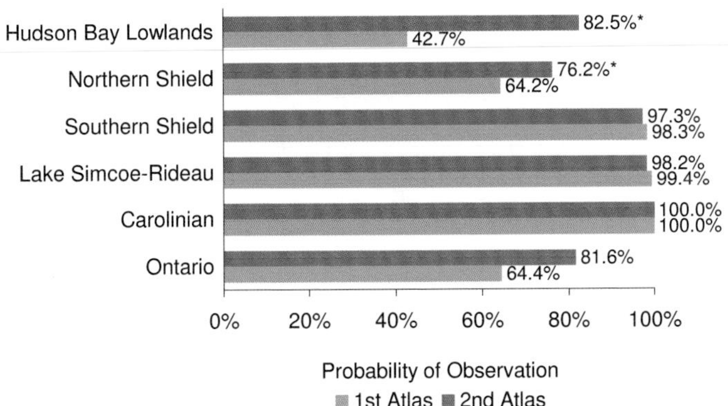

data indicate small but significant annual increases of 0.7% and 0.5% for Ontario and Canada between 1968 and 2005 (Downes et al. 2005). Increases have been especially noticeable in regions of suburban growth and development. Migration monitoring data at Long Point Bird Observatory show population increases of nearly 3% per year since 1961 (Crewe 2006).

Breeding biology: The American Robin breeds in a wide variety of habitats including forests, riparian areas, golf courses, and gardens where lawns and areas of short grass are interspersed with shrubs and trees. In urban, suburban, and agricultural areas, the species is conspicuous, and confirmation of breeding is easily obtained. Birds begin to sing before dawn, sing actively through the early part of the day, and continue to sing after sunset. They hop about in the open, forage on lawns, and build highly conspicuous nests, often on or in buildings. When observers are near a nest, the parents usually scold loudly. Nestlings are quite audible when begging for food, and fledged young are easily observed and readily distinguished from adults by their spotted breasts.

The species nests during the height of atlasser activity and usually has two broods per season, allowing atlassers multiple opportunities to confirm breeding. However, the robin that inhabits unsettled landscapes of the province seems almost a different species. In areas of greater natural cover, such as forest ecosystems, nests can be very difficult to find because they are so well concealed and the birds are more secretive (James and Long in Cadman et al. 1987).

The American Robin was a confirmed breeder in 58% of squares in which it was detected. In southern Ontario and much of the Southern Shield region, breeding was confirmed in nearly every square. In the northern regions, however, confirmation rates were much lower, reflecting both the more secretive nature of northern robins and lower effort in many of these squares. Nevertheless, the species likely bred in nearly all of the squares where it was reported.

Abundance: The American Robin is most abundant in the populated Lake Simcoe-Rideau and Carolinian regions where only the Common Grackle, European Starling, and Red-winged Blackbird were detected more frequently on atlas point counts. On the Shield and farther north, where forest cover is high, densities of the American Robin are much lower. In the Southern Shield region, the Algonquin Highlands is an area of particularly low density for this species. Throughout the north, there is a tendency for higher densities to be centred on towns, cities, and farming areas. However, the patch of considerably higher density in and around Moosonee is probably an artifact of sampling and the methods used to produce the abundance maps. – *Dawn Burke*

Gray Catbird

Moqueur chat

Dumetella carolinensis

Tim Stewart

The Gray Catbird breeds widely across southern Canada and south through most of the US except for the dry Southwest (American Ornithologists Union 1998). In Ontario across the southern half of the province, it is a familiar summer sight and sound. In addition to its recognizable cat-like mew, its intricate song, punctuated by imitations of numerous other species, emanates from thickets and tangled shrubbery in forest clearings, woodland edges, and overgrown gardens. Any brush or scrubby habitat, such as is found in ravines and valleys in farming country, in abandoned fields or hedgerows, is likely to support catbirds.

Distribution and population status: The Gray Catbird no doubt benefited from the clearing of the eastern forests by Europeans and has been a very common resident of southern Ontario at least since the second half of the 19th century (McIlwraith 1894). It breeds north continuously to about Sudbury in the Southern Shield region, but only sparingly in the Northern Shield region, except in the vicinity of Thunder Bay and in western Rainy River District near Lake of the Woods. The northernmost evidence of breeding was a male in suitable habitat at Moosonee, where the species was recorded during the first atlas and breeding has been confirmed on at least one previous occasion (Wilson and McRae 1993). Compared to the first atlas, there was no significant change in the probability of observation in the province as a whole, but there were significant declines of 26% in the Southern Shield region and 4% in the Lake Simcoe-Rideau region. There was no significant change in the Carolinian region, the catbird's stronghold in the province. Ontario BBS data show no significant trend since 1968, but there has been a small, statistically significant decline of 1.9% per year across the Canadian range since 1968 (Downes et al. 2005). The continental range is essentially stable, with declines in the southeastern United States and along the northeastern periphery of the range (Sauer et al. 2005);

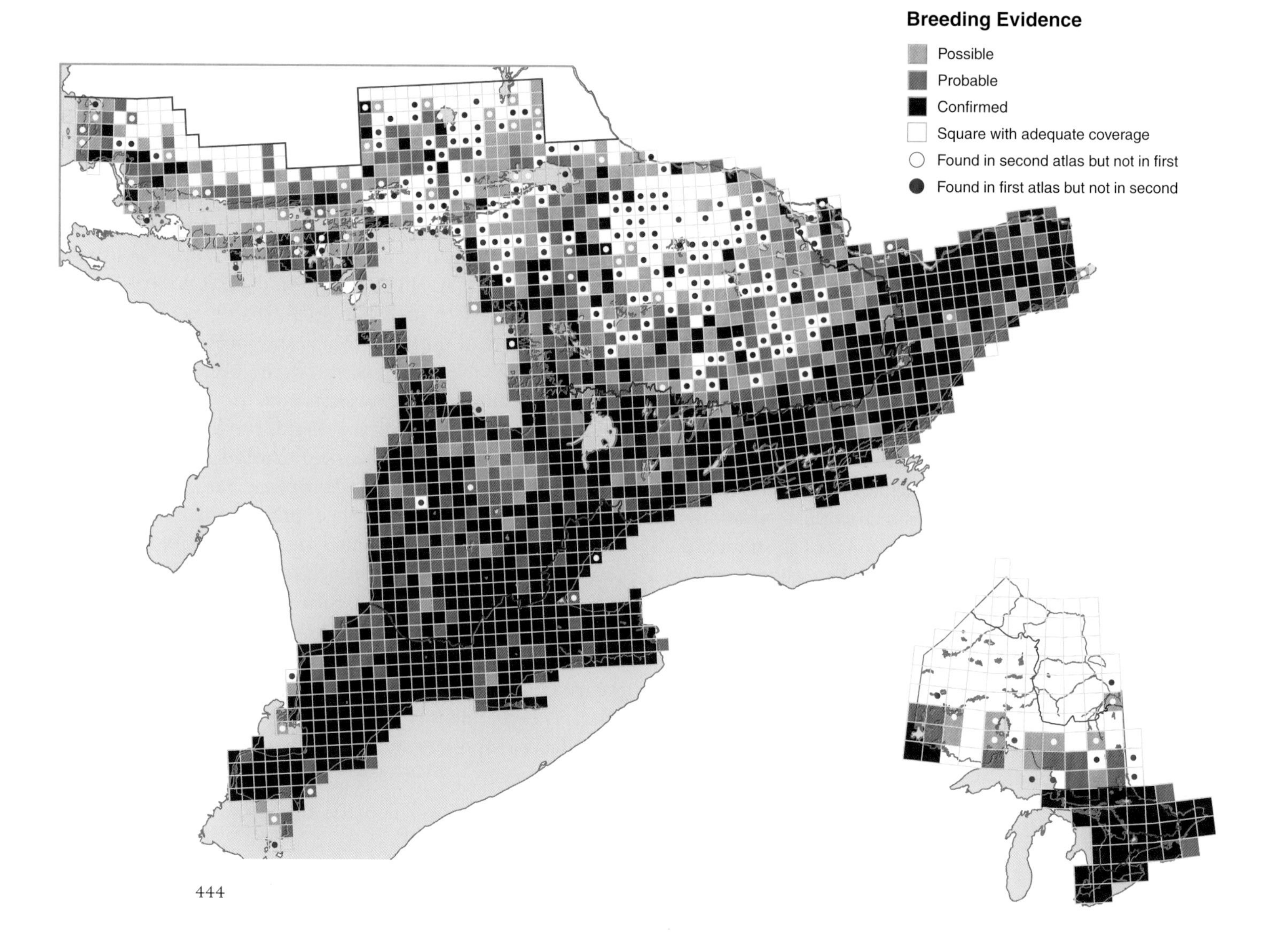

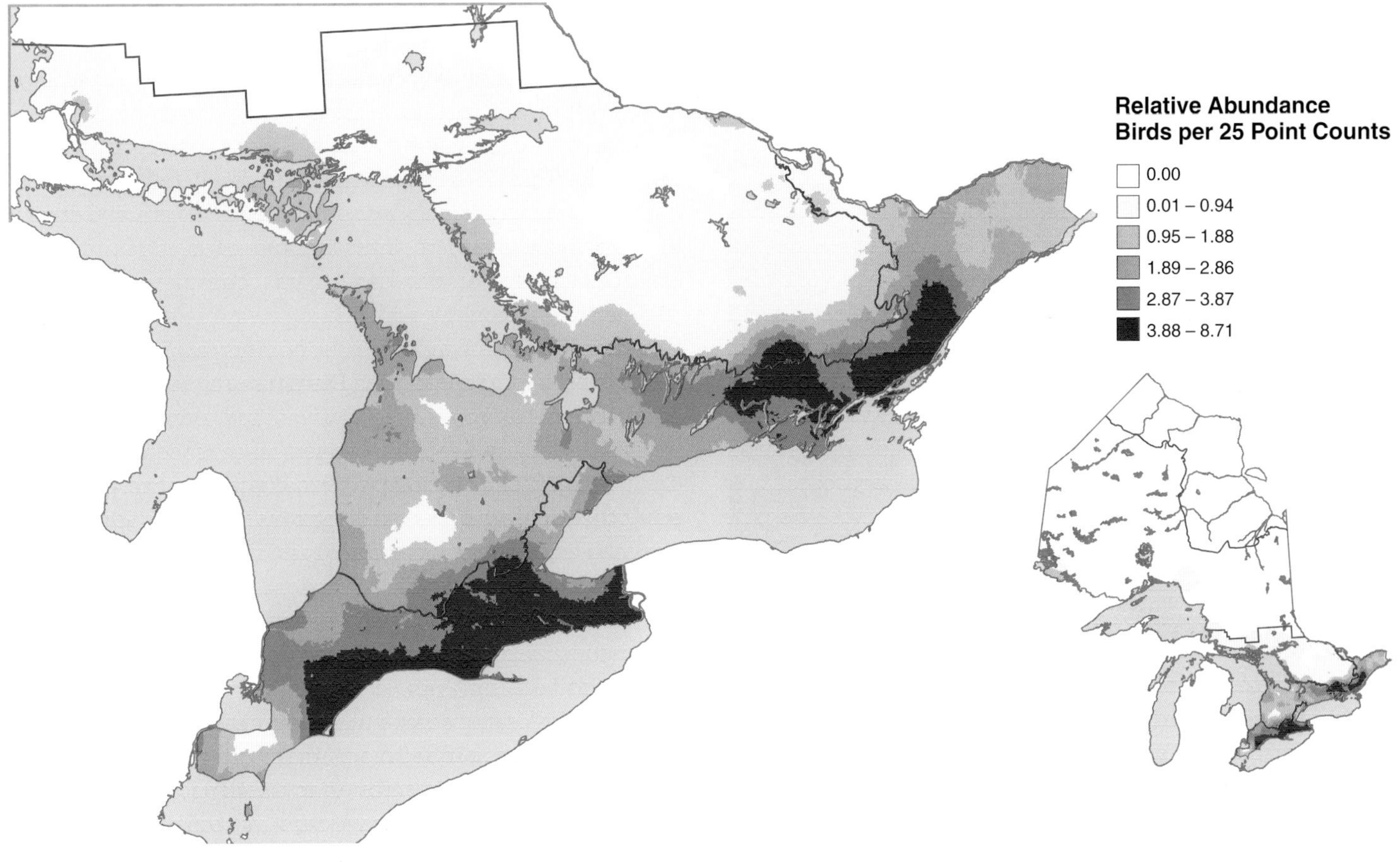

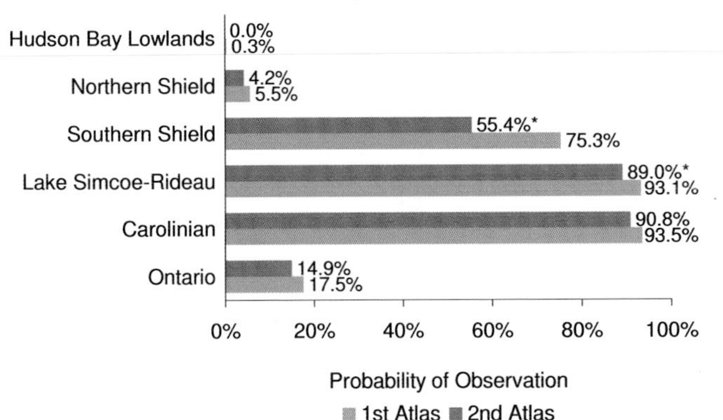

the latter situation is confirmed by Ontario atlas results.

Declines on the Shield may result from a reduction in the availability of scrubby, early successional habitats through forest maturation. An apparent range increase along the northern edge of the range, north of Lake Superior and Sudbury, may be due to increased accessibility along forest access and logging roads. Small declines south of the Shield may be due to a combination of urbanization and more intensive farming methods, both of which result in the reduction of hedgerows and thickets. The declines on the Shield have resulted in an 11 km shift to the south of the species' average southern Ontario range.

Breeding biology: The Gray Catbird is a fairly conspicuous summer resident of southern Ontario. It is a persistent singer from dawn until late morning and again in the evening; thus breeding evidence is fairly easily obtained. It has a protracted breeding season, often raising two broods each summer, with fledged young apparent until early August (Cimprich and Moore 1995).

Egg dates in Ontario extend from 2 May to 18 August (Peck and James 1987). Parents respond quickly to approaches to nests or young, scolding the intruder persistently, which allows for probable breeding status designation. However, only 47% of records are of confirmed breeding, compared to 52% in the first atlas. This drop is difficult to explain but may be the result of a slightly lower emphasis on confirming breeding during the second atlas. Nevertheless, the atlas maps are an accurate representation of the catbird's breeding distribution in the province.

Abundance: Highest breeding densities occurred in two areas. A band of high abundance extends from southern Lake Huron along the counties bordering Lake Erie and through the Niagara Peninsula. The other high-density area is in southeastern Ontario from east of Peterborough along the shores of Lake Ontario and the St. Lawrence River and inland about 30 km to the southern edge of the Shield. The Lake Erie counties have a richer mix of fields and edge habitat compared to the more intensively cultivated areas of extreme southwestern Ontario and the farm country between London and Kitchener and the southern shores of Georgian Bay. The high densities in the southeastern counties occur on marginal and abandoned farmland; such densities may not be maintained as forest cover returns. On the Canadian Shield, nesting is likely linked to shrubby habitats in scattered urban settlements, and densities are thus much lower. – *Bob Curry*

Northern Mockingbird

Moqueur polyglotte

Mimus polyglottos

Winnie Poon

Known for its incredible song repertoire, the Northern Mockingbird was historically captured and sold as a caged bird, leading to localized population depletion in parts of the eastern US. Today, the species is found throughout most of the US, Mexico, and the Caribbean but reaches its highest densities in the shrublands of south Texas (Price et al. 1995). Canada lies at the northern limit of its range, but during the 20th and early 21st centuries the species has expanded its range north and west on a broad front across the continent.

Distribution and population status: The Northern Mockingbird was first recorded in Ontario in 1860, but only three records exist prior to 1900. The first breeding reports came from Essex Co. between 1906 and 1919. By the 1930s, isolated occurrences had been documented north and east to Middlesex and Durham Counties and even as far north as Moose Factory, but the species was considered very rare (Baillie and Harrington 1937).

By the time of the first atlas, the Northern Mockingbird was well established in the Niagara Peninsula and was described as "a fairly common bird in gardens and orchards" on the Iroquois Plain below the Niagara Escarpment (Curry in Cadman et al. 1987). Otherwise, and with the exception of a small cluster of squares near Kingston, the distribution in the early 1980s consisted of scattered and isolated records, few of which were confirmed.

Since then, the Northern Mockingbird has extended its continuously occupied range around the western end of Lake Ontario to encompass the entire urbanized area south of the Oak Ridges Moraine as far east as Bowmanville. Some consolidation of the range has also occurred from Prince Edward Co. east to Kingston and north almost to the edge of the Shield and the Ottawa Valley. In extreme southwestern Ontario, the species has established a foothold in Chatham-Kent, and there has been limited westward expansion into Haldimand Co., but

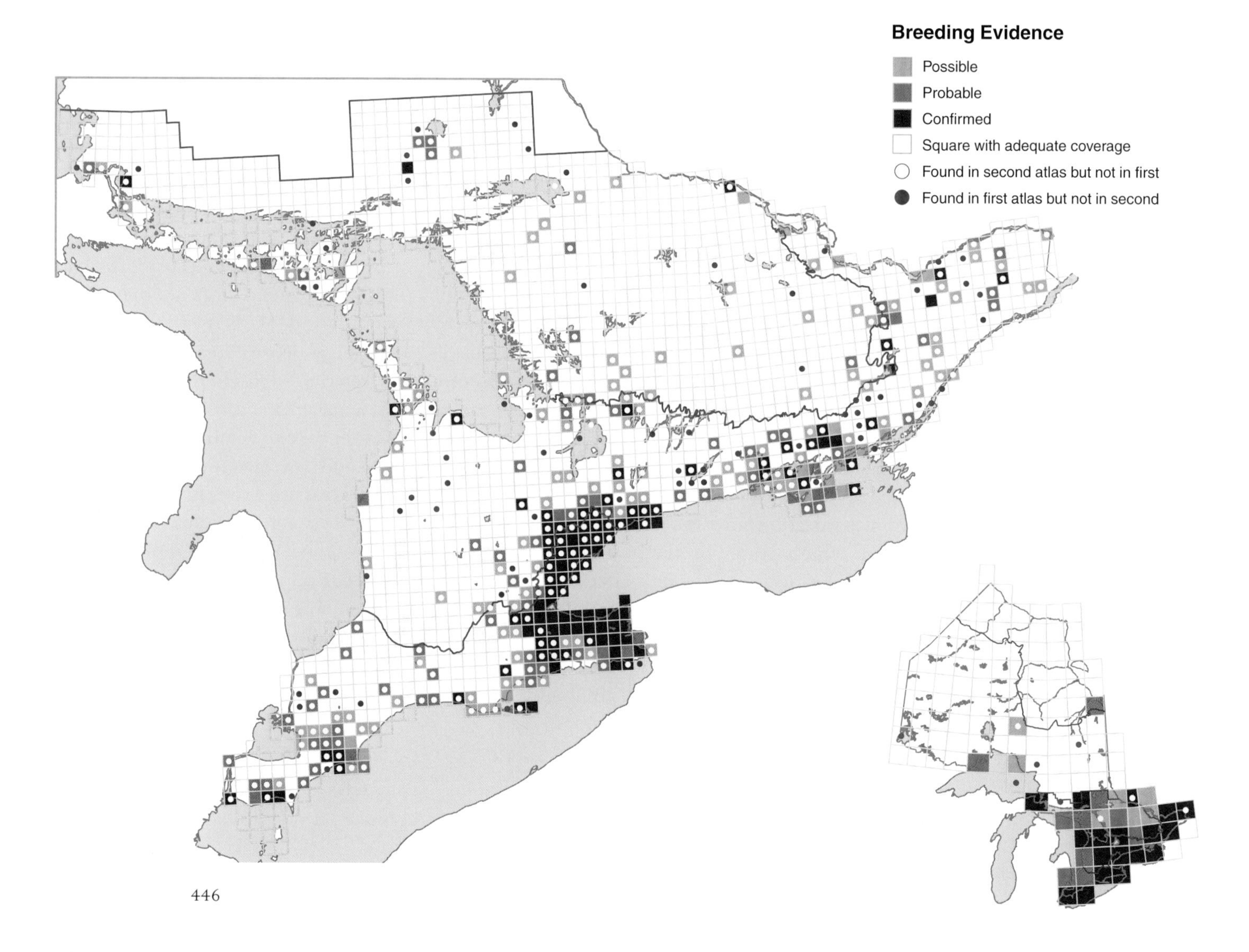

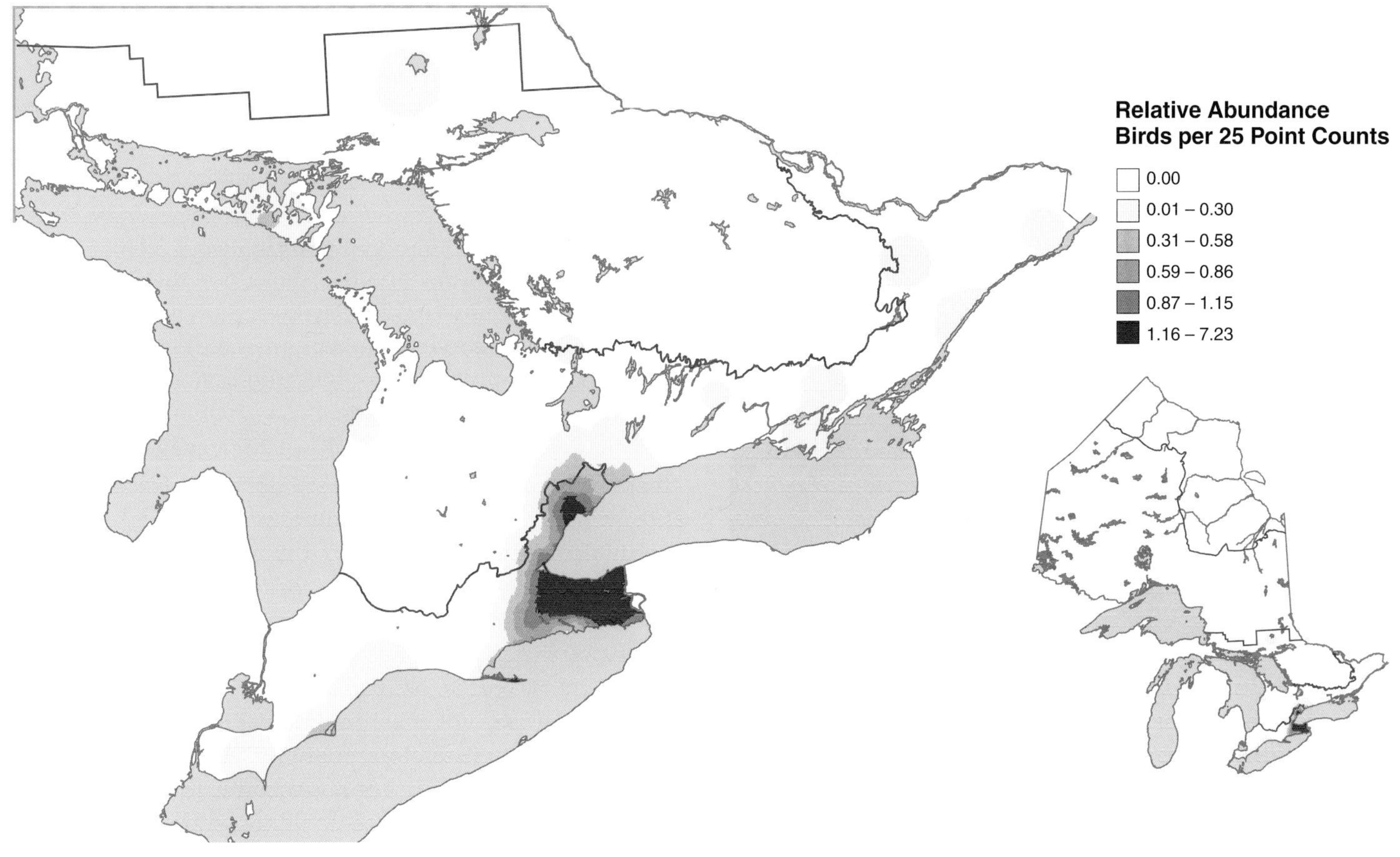

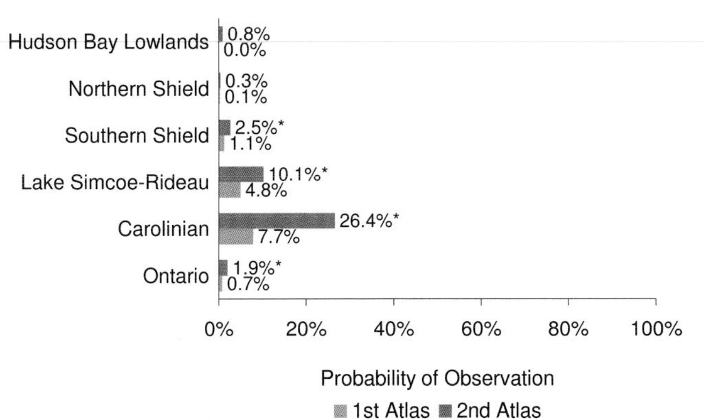

the distribution elsewhere remains sparse.

During the second atlas period, breeding was confirmed as far north as Sudbury, with non-confirmed outliers east of Lake Nipigon and at Moosonee. A pattern of scattered occurrences well north of the continuous range has been characteristic of the mockingbird's spread northwards, with isolated first breeding records (Curry in Cadman et al.1987; ONRS data) for Manitoulin (1955), Ottawa (1971), Sudbury (1972), and even Moosonee (1979). Wandering pioneers may follow railway and hydro corridors, which could explain multiple records of birds reaching Moosonee and even Churchill, Manitoba (Manitoba Avian Research Committee 2003).

For Ontario as a whole, the number of squares with breeding evidence has more than doubled since the first atlas. These changes were predicted by Curry (in Cadman et al. 1987), and based on current trends, we may expect more consolidation of the range south of the Shield. Some mockingbirds in northern parts of the range are believed to be migratory, but the ability to establish winter territories is probably a key factor in expansion into new areas (Wright 1921). Conditions on or north of the Shield are usually too severe for regular winter survival, but the species is predicted to benefit from global warming (Price 2004).

Breeding biology: The Northern Mockingbird is conspicuous and relatively easy to confirm. It has a long breeding season in Ontario, with the first territories established in late March or early April. Active nests have been found between mid-April and late August, with a first egg date recorded as early as 14 April 2004 (Poon and Smith 2005). Successful pairs typically make two or three (rarely four) nesting attempts per season in southern Ontario, giving atlassers many chances to locate nests and young. Nesting cycles may overlap, with the male building a new nest while still feeding dependent young (Derrickson and Breitswich 1992). Nests are typically placed low in a small tree or shrub, with small spruces preferred in the Greater Toronto Area, although vine-covered fences and hawthorns are also used frequently (ONRS data).

Abundance: Based on point counts, the Northern Mockingbird remains most abundant in the Niagara Peninsula. Nevertheless, it can reach high densities in the Greater Toronto Area where particularly rich squares may have 20-40 territories, and intensive surveys estimated that about 400 territories were occupied annually during the second atlas period (Smith and Poon 2006). There are no similar data for the Niagara Peninsula or Hamilton, but outside these core areas, there may be only one or two territories per square. Hence, the abundance maps exaggerate the situation around Sudbury, on Manitoulin, and along parts of the north shore of Lake Erie. *– Roy Smith and Winnie Poon*

Brown Thrasher

Moqueur roux

Toxostoma rufum

R. E. Gehlert

The Brown Thrasher breeds in the eastern two-thirds of North America from southeastern Alberta to Nova Scotia and south to the Gulf Coast (American Ornithologists Union 1998). The breeding and wintering ranges overlap extensively in the southeastern US, with northern breeding individuals spending the winter primarily in the southeastern states. With one of the largest vocal repertoires of any North American passerine (Cavitt and Haas 2000), the Brown Thrasher can be heard in scrubby overgrown pastures, alvars, hedgerows, and shrubby thickets across southern Ontario.

Distribution and population status: The Brown Thrasher breeds regularly from southernmost Ontario north to about the latitude of Sudbury and Sault Ste. Marie, but locally and perhaps irregularly northward. It was absent in both atlases from most squares in the Algonquin Highlands, where shrubby habitat is rare. A provincially disjunct population occurs in the farm country in western Rainy River Dist. near Lake of the Woods. This population is an extension of the range from adjacent Minnesota and southeastern Manitoba. In the Hudson Bay Lowlands, where it occurs annually in small numbers, particularly in spring (Wilson and McRae 1993), evidence of possible breeding was found near Burntpoint Creek (2001, 2002), Peawanuck (2001), and near Winisk (2004).

Although the Brown Thrasher originally benefited from the clearing of forests for settlement, the species is now in steep decline in Ontario. Atlas results show a 24% overall decline in the probability of observation since the first atlas. Significant declines occurred in all regions except the Hudson Bay Lowlands. The decline was greatest in the Northern Shield (55%), Carolinian (32%), and Southern Shield (29%) regions, but was also high (14%) in the Lake Simcoe-Rideau region. BBS trends for the period 1968-2005 show statistically significant annual declines of 2.3% in Ontario and 2.8% in Canada (Downes et al. 2005). This species has also declined consider-

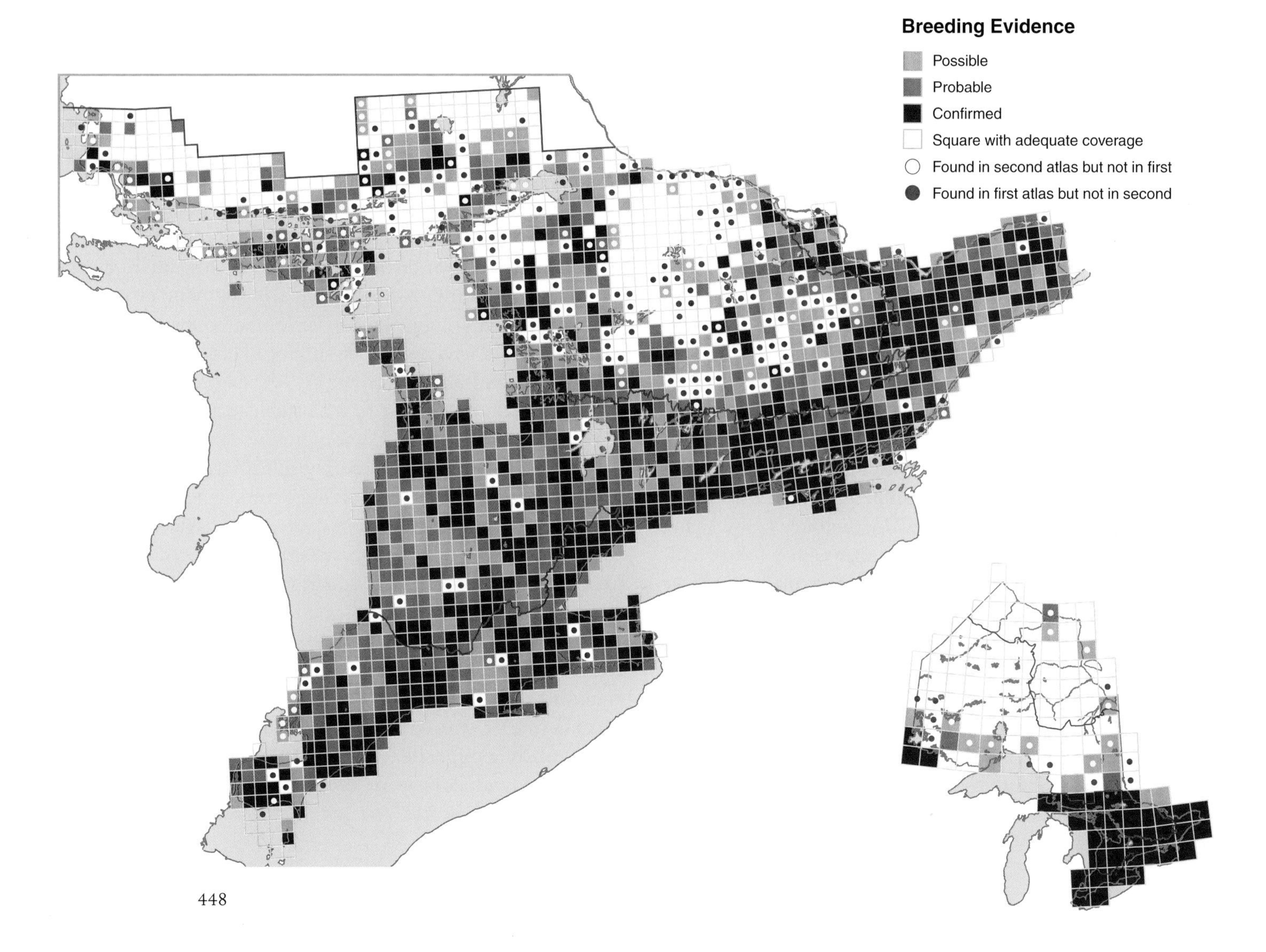

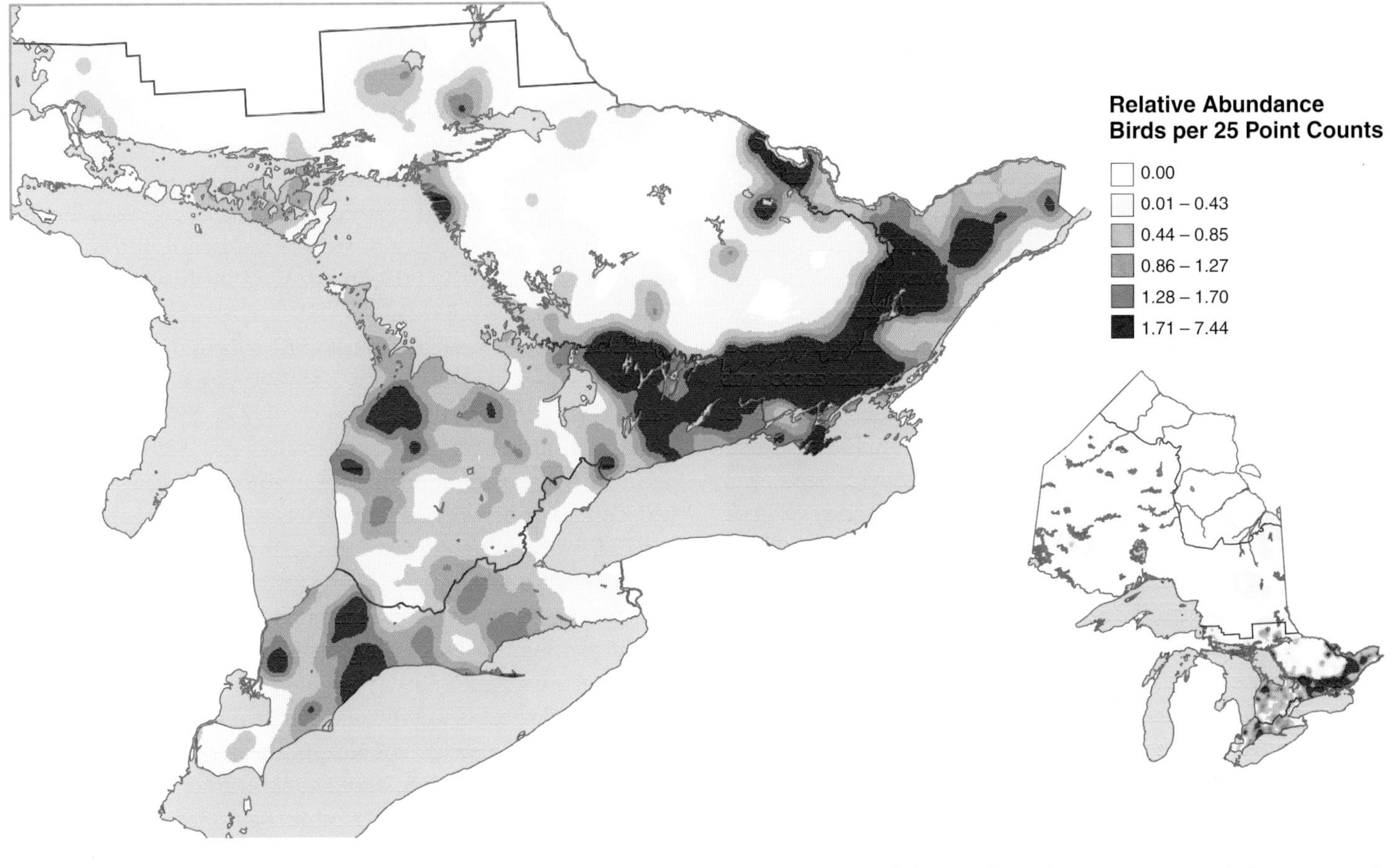

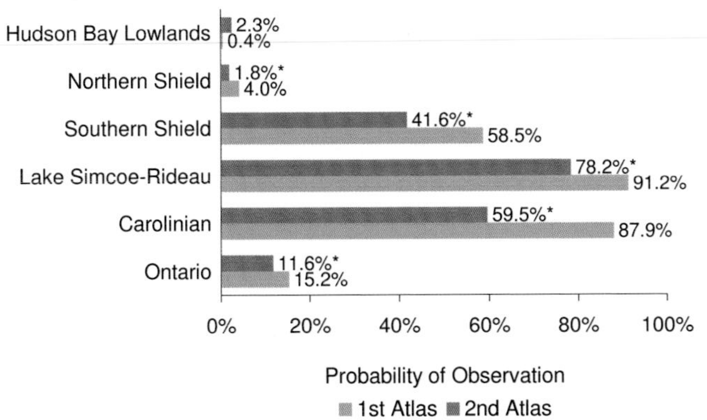

ably in adjacent US states. Results from the second New York State Breeding Bird Atlas, 2000-2005, show many fewer squares occupied than in the first. BBS results for BCR13, which includes the Carolinian and Lake Simcoe-Rideau region in Ontario and parts of adjacent states, show a 3.7% annual decline since 1968, representing a decrease in the total population of 61% (Partners in Flight 2004). This trend is consistent with the continental picture in which the annual decline has been 1.2% since 1966 (Sauer at al. 2005).

The decline in the Southern Shield region is probably attributable to forest succession. Abandonment of marginal farmland and changes in logging practices have allowed forest to replace scrub habitats that were available to thrashers during the first atlas. North of Sudbury, squares where the Brown Thrasher was found in this atlas but not the first may be the result of recent logging as well as increased access by atlassers. The declines in the two southern regions are likely attributable to loss of suitable habitat as scrubland has been cleared for housing, changing agricultural practices have removed hedgerows, and landholders have encouraged forest growth and conifer plantations.

Breeding biology: The map is a fairly accurate representation of the distribution of the Brown Thrasher. The species is conspicuous when announcing its territory during the first half of the breeding season, allowing probable breeding to be relatively easily established. The species usually rears two broods per season, with Ontario egg dates extending from 20 April to 20 July (Peck and James 1987). Although the nest is concealed in thick tangles, thrashers are often aggressive and noisy in defence of their nests or young. Some Regional Coordinators in the south suggested that the species was sometimes missed; while this may be the case, the continental and provincial picture of decline suggests that in some squares thrashers may simply be no longer present.

Abundance: Point count data indicate that thrasher densities are very uneven across southern Ontario. Clusters of higher density occur as follows: in a band from Elgin Co. northwest towards Lake Huron; in southern Grey and Bruce Counties; in Haldimand Co.; in a broad swath south of the Shield from Lake Simcoe east beyond Ottawa; and along the Ottawa River east of the Algonquin Highlands. These core areas still have the requisite brushy second-growth habitat required by this species. Intensively cultivated areas such as Essex Co. in the extreme southwest, the Niagara Peninsula, and the largely agricultural landscapes between London, Kitchener, and Shelburne harbour fewer thrashers. Increased urban sprawl near the west end of Lake Ontario since the first atlas has eliminated habitat, resulting in reduced numbers on point counts in that area. – *Bob Curry*

European Starling

Étourneau sansonnet

Sturnus vulgaris

John Reaume

The European Starling is one of the most familiar, and most disliked, birds in Ontario. Its unpopularity is in part related to its being a non-native species that often out-competes native birds for nesting cavities in trees. It also frequently nests in buildings, sometimes in locations inconvenient to the other occupants. The species breeds throughout much of Eurasia and North America, south of the Arctic. It is closely associated with human development, especially urban areas, buildings, and farmland. It often forages in short grass, so it is found commonly on urban lawns and in areas of pasture. The marked decline in pasture in Ontario has probably contributed to its decline in the province in recent decades.

Distribution and population status: The release of about 100 European Starlings in New York City's Central Park during 1890 and 1891 was one of the most successful introductions on the continent. The North American population is estimated to exceed 200,000,000 (Cabe 1993). It spread rapidly across the continent, reaching southern Ontario in 1914 (Gauthier and Aubry 1996), and the first known Ontario nesting was reported in 1922 (Baillie and Harrington 1937). Expansion continued until some time in the mid-20th century, but the species has declined steadily, at 3.2% per year in Canada and 1.9% per year in Ontario, since the beginning of the BBS in 1968 (Downes et al. 2005).

The overall distribution of the European Starling in Ontario is similar in both atlases and reflects its close association with human development and agriculture. It was reported in most squares south and east of the Shield in both atlases. The significant 13% decline in the probability of observation between atlases in the Southern Shield appears to correlate with the decline in open and agricultural habitats and perhaps older buildings. As forests have filled in former farmland and other open areas, the total area of land suitable for starlings in the region has been reduced. For example, there are fewer open,

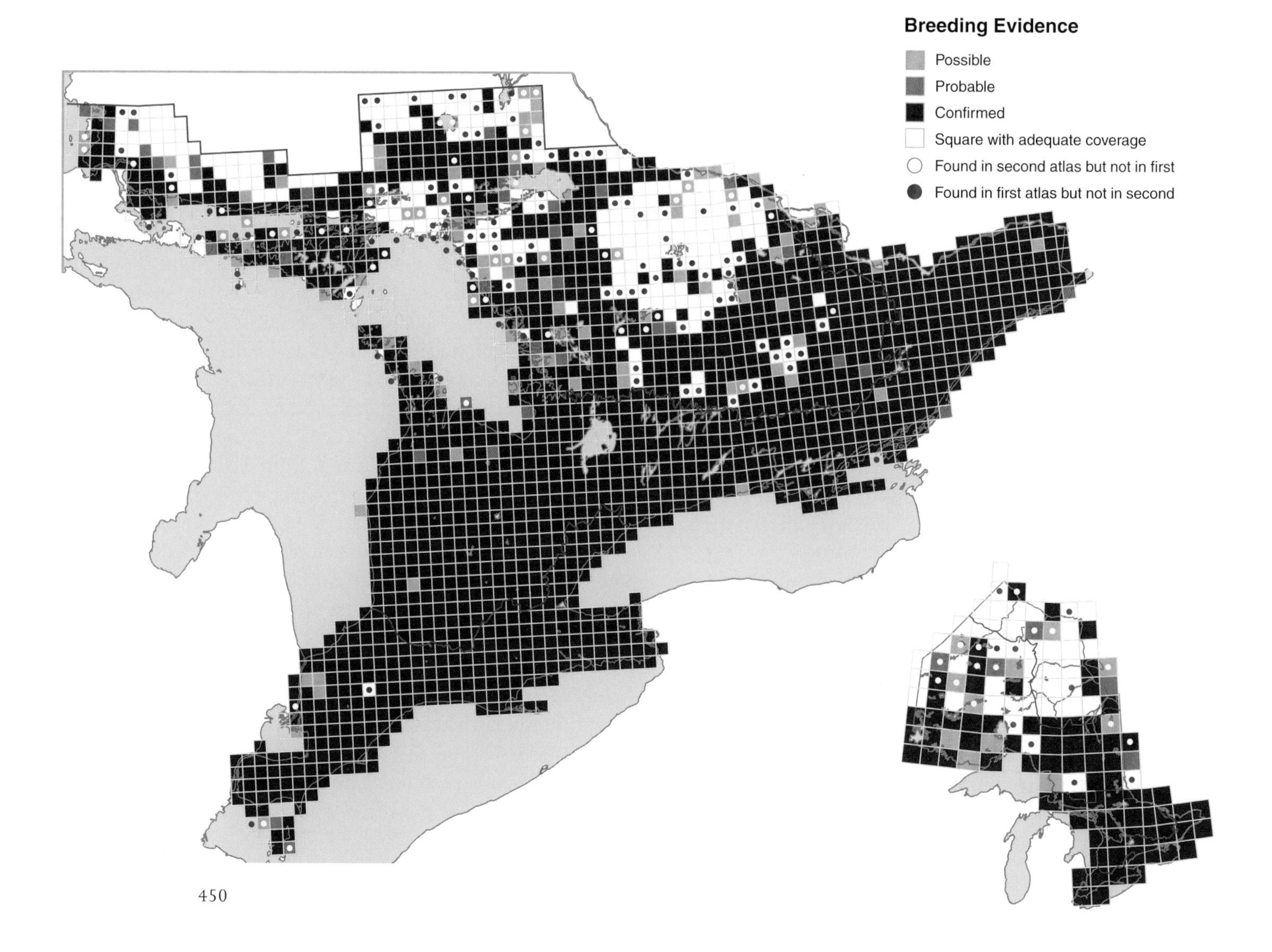

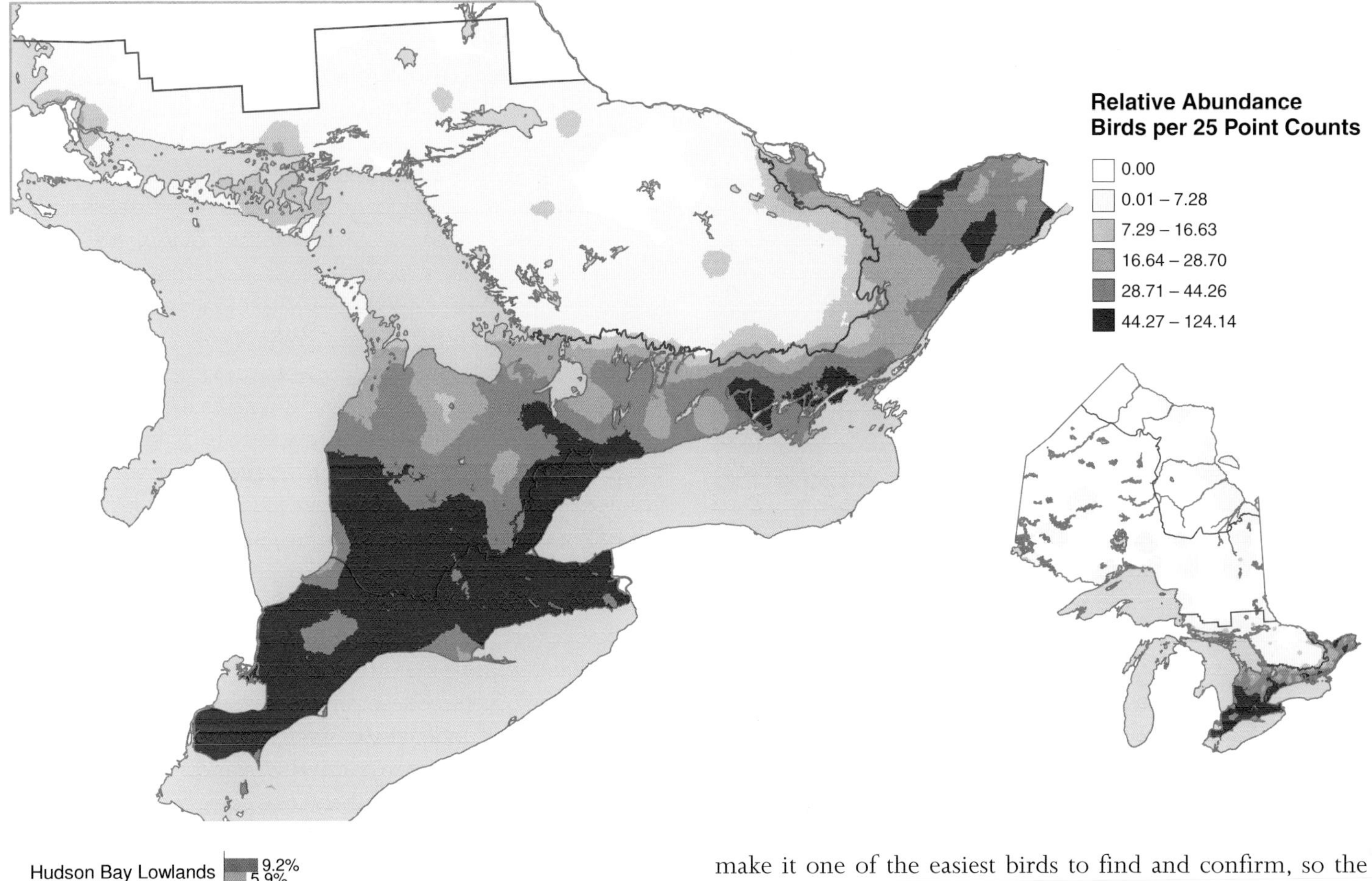

Region	2nd Atlas	1st Atlas
Hudson Bay Lowlands	9.2%	5.9%
Northern Shield	14.5%	19.1%
Southern Shield	63.0%*	72.0%
Lake Simcoe-Rideau	94.9%	97.2%
Carolinian	96.8%	100.0%
Ontario	24.3%	26.9%

0% 20% 40% 60% 80% 100%

Probability of Observation

1st Atlas ■ 2nd Atlas

grassy areas adjacent to suitable nesting sites (e.g., openings in buildings) now compared with 20 years ago along Highway 60 in Algonquin Prov. Park (R. Tozer, pers. comm.), and the decline is evident on the breeding evidence map. The starling was reported in every 100-km block in road-accessible areas of northern Ontario. North of the road network, it was reported in scattered 100-km blocks north to Hudson Bay, usually but not exclusively where settlements are found, including several 100-km blocks in which it was not reported during the first atlas. The new records may be the result of more extensive coverage in the second atlas in and around the northern settlements. As in the first atlas, breeding evidence was obtained at the abandoned Mid-Canada Line Radar Site 415 near Cape Henrietta Maria, and at nearby Radar Site 416 in an adjacent square. As these old radar facilities are scheduled for demolition, the starling presumably will lose some of its most remote breeding sites, roughly 200 km from the nearest community.

Breeding biology: The association of the starling with human development and agriculture, and its conspicuousness, make it one of the easiest birds to find and confirm, so the breeding evidence map accurately reflects its pattern of occurrence. Unlike many cavity-nesting birds, it builds its own nest inside the cavity, and frequently is seen carrying long lengths of material into nest holes. It is identified readily in flight by its distinctive shape and direct flight pattern and has a habit of flying across open areas with a bill full of food for its young. It is not at all shy around its nest, coming and going in full view, especially when feeding young.

Abundance: BBS data reveal that an area encompassing Ontario south of the Shield and much of the US Midwest, Pennsylvania, and New York has the highest densities of European Starling on the continent (Price et al. 1995; Sauer et al. 2005). Atlas data indicate that in Ontario south of the Shield, the highest densities occur in the southwest and along Lake Ontario into the lower Ottawa River valley, coinciding generally with the area of intensive farming and urban development. Abundance declines substantially northward, away from these highly developed areas, to the Shield, which is largely forested. The lowest densities, and often complete absences on point counts, are found in remote parts of Algonquin Prov. Park and in far northern Ontario remote from settlements. Based on point count data, the Ontario population is estimated at approximately 4,000,000 birds. – *Michael D. Cadman*

American Pipit
Pipit d'Amérique
Anthus rubescens

George K. Peck

Formerly included in the Water Pipit (*A. spinoletta*) complex of the Palearctic, the American Pipit is now recognized as a distinct species. The American Pipit is represented in North America by three subspecies, of which the nominate subspecies (*rubescens*) breeds east of the Rocky Mountains in the Arctic and Subarctic south to northern Ontario, Québec, and Newfoundland and locally farther south in alpine meadows above 1200 m at Mt. Katahdin, Maine, and Mt. Washington, New Hampshire (Verbeek and Hendricks 1994; Palmer and Taber 1946).

Distribution and population status: In Ontario, the American Pipit breeds only in the northern Hudson Bay Lowlands, primarily on coastal tundra, usually within a few kilometres of the coast. Documentation of breeding was first obtained in the 1940s in Ontario at Fort Severn and in the vicinity of Cape Henrietta Maria (Peck and James 1987). Most subsequent breeding evidence has been gathered in the latter region, primarily in the vicinity of Radar Sites 415 and 416, southwest of Hook Point.

The distribution of the American Pipit has not changed appreciably since the first atlas. Breeding evidence was reported from 30 squares primarily east of the Sutton River and north of Hook Point in the general vicinity of Cape Henrietta Maria. The species was also detected in four squares in the vicinity of the Pen Islands, where its occurrence was reported during the first atlas. It was not reported from any squares at Fort Severn from which breeding evidence was obtained during the first atlas and where breeding was first confirmed in 1940. Notable also is the absence of breeding evidence for any squares between the Winisk and Severn Rivers, where in 1990 it was reported to be present near the Little Shagamu River (Wilson and McRae 1993), or between the Severn River and the Pen Islands where, particularly in the vicinity of the Niskibi River, extensive suitable habitat

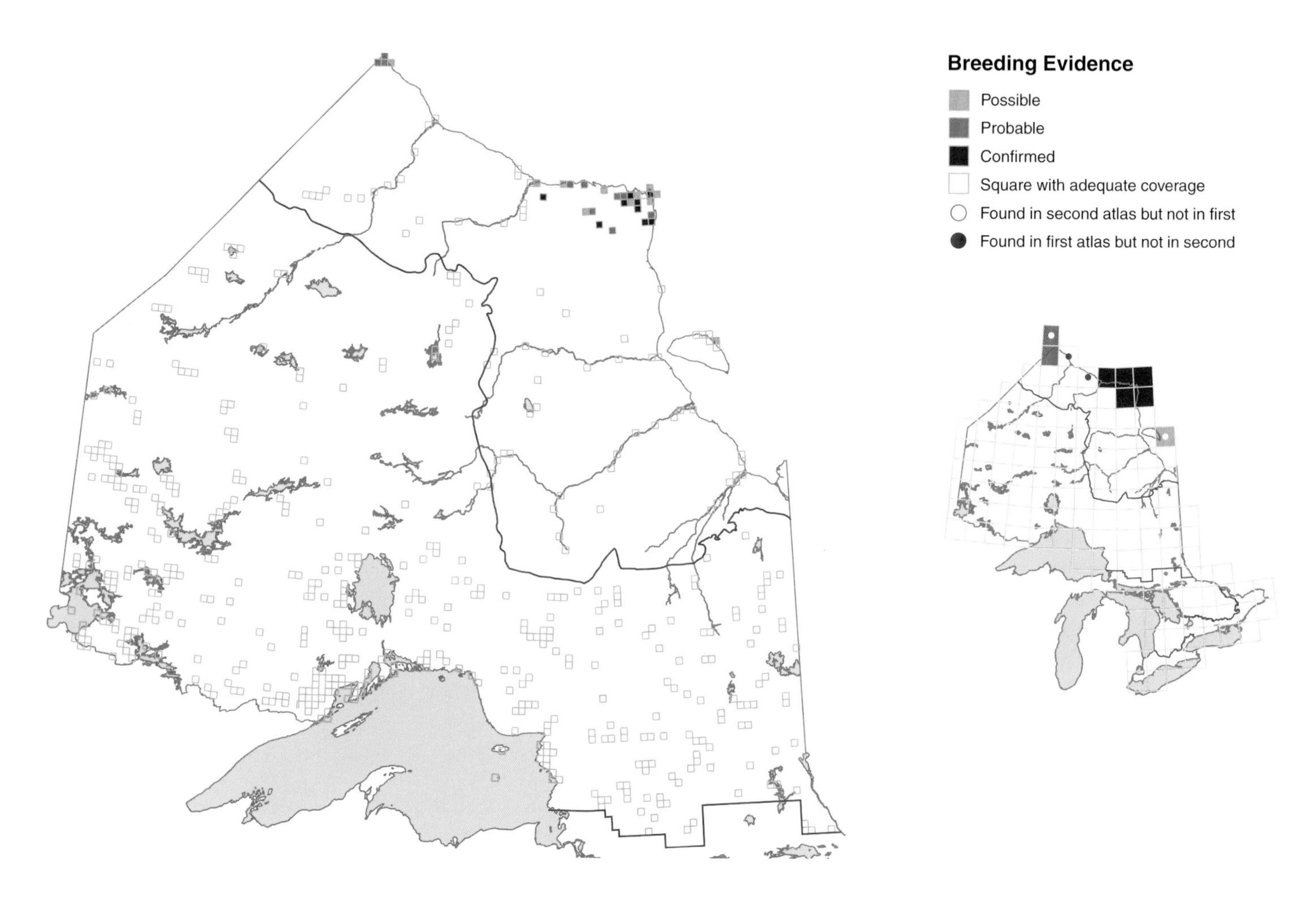

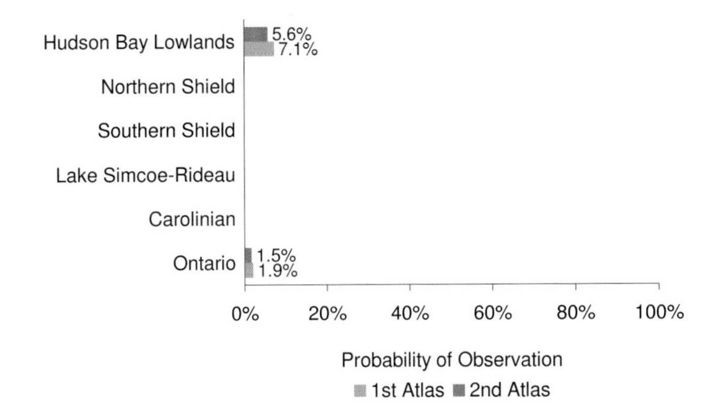

exists. More extensive coverage of these areas would likely have revealed the presence of the species.

In Ontario, the American Pipit typically occupies relict gravel and boulder-strewn marine beach ridges within 20 km of the coast. However, during the second atlas, breeding evidence was reported in four squares more than 30 km inland from Hudson Bay, in one of which breeding was confirmed. Pipits were encountered in areas of open or very sparsely treed graminoid tundra with scattered, coalescent palsa plateaus in two squares east of the Aquatuk River 38 km inland, as well as in squares near the Kinushseo River and the headwaters of the Lakitusaki River, 53 and 65 km inland, respectively, from Hudson Bay, indicating that breeding can occur well inland from the coast, at least locally.

Breeding biology: The American Pipit is an early migrant but a late nester. As has been reported for Churchill, Manitoba (Jehl 2004), most individuals probably arrive at breeding sites in Ontario by late May or early June, but nesting is not initiated until late June or early July. The male delivers the song, typically in flight in an aerial display culminating in a parachute-like descent to the ground, but occasionally also from a perch upon alighting. Although distinctive, the song does not carry far, and under the normally windy conditions encountered on the Hudson Bay coast, it may have been missed by some atlassers. Pipits are highly territorial and regularly engage in prolonged aerial chases of both conspecifics and other species such as the Horned Lark (Verbeek and Hendricks 1994); consequently, there was some opportunity to establish probable breeding. Nests are difficult to find, and confirmation of breeding is more likely to involve observations of adults carrying food.

While the map indicates the general extent of the distribution of American Pipit along the northern James and Hudson Bay coasts, it is likely that the species breeds in many more squares than the few in which it was detected. Suitable habitat is present along the entire Hudson Bay coast and along the northern James Bay coast south to about 54° N in the vicinity of the Lakitusaki River, and breeding distribution of the American Pipit is likely nearly continuous.

Abundance: Given the patchiness of its preferred habitat, the American Pipit is probably less numerous than might be inferred from point count data. Detections on 31 point counts yielded an average 0.4 birds/25 point counts; however, 90% of detections were from seven squares in three 100-km blocks in the general vicinity of Cape Henrietta Maria. As was suggested in the first atlas, the extent of suitable beach ridge habitat there likely supports higher densities of the species. – *Donald A. Sutherland*

Nests are typically located on the sides of lichen-heath hummocks, usually sheltered from above by overhanging moss or sod and often near water. *Photo: Jim Richards*

Preferred habitat of the American Pipit in Ontario is relict gravel and boulder-strewn beach ridges within 20 km of the Hudson Bay coast. It also occurs locally inland on extensive, open palsa plateaus. *Photo: George K. Peck*

Sprague's Pipit
Pipit de Sprague
Anthus spragueii

R. E. Gehlert

The Sprague's Pipit is a breeding species of the mixed and short-grass prairies of the Great Plains of southern Canada and the adjacent US, wintering from the southwest US south to central Mexico (Robbins and Dale 1999). Formerly more widespread and abundant, it is now considerably reduced, particularly along the periphery of its range. Conversion of native grasslands for agriculture, intensive livestock grazing, and periods of extended drought have severely limited the species, resulting in reduced breeding densities and local extirpations (Robbins and Dale 1999). Although still common in many areas in its Canadian range, continuing declines and fragmentation of its habitat have led to its designation as Threatened in Canada.

Distribution and population status: During the second atlas, a singing male Sprague's Pipit was observed near Burntpoint Creek, Polar Bear Prov. Park, 76 km east-northeast of Peawanuck on the coast of Hudson Bay. The male was observed performing aerial display flights over extensive, dry to seasonally wet graminoid tundra about 1 km inland from the coast on 15-19 July 2001. Although this bird may have been present prior to and beyond the observation dates, the site was not checked, and thus it is unknown for how long this bird may have been present. Given the abnormally dry year, the expanse of flat, normally wet *Carex*-dominated tundra approximated the dry grassland habitat attractive to the species.

Although breeding has never been confirmed in Ontario, singing male Sprague's Pipits have been reported on three previous occasions in western Rainy River Dist. near Lake of the Woods. In 1980, two singing males and a third, silent bird (possibly a female) were observed in a large pasture about 2 km northeast of the Town of Rainy River, 3-12 July; and a third singing male was discovered at a second site near Pinewood on 7 July (Goodwin 1980; Lamey 1981). Single singing males were present in the same general vicinity, 2-12 June 1990 and

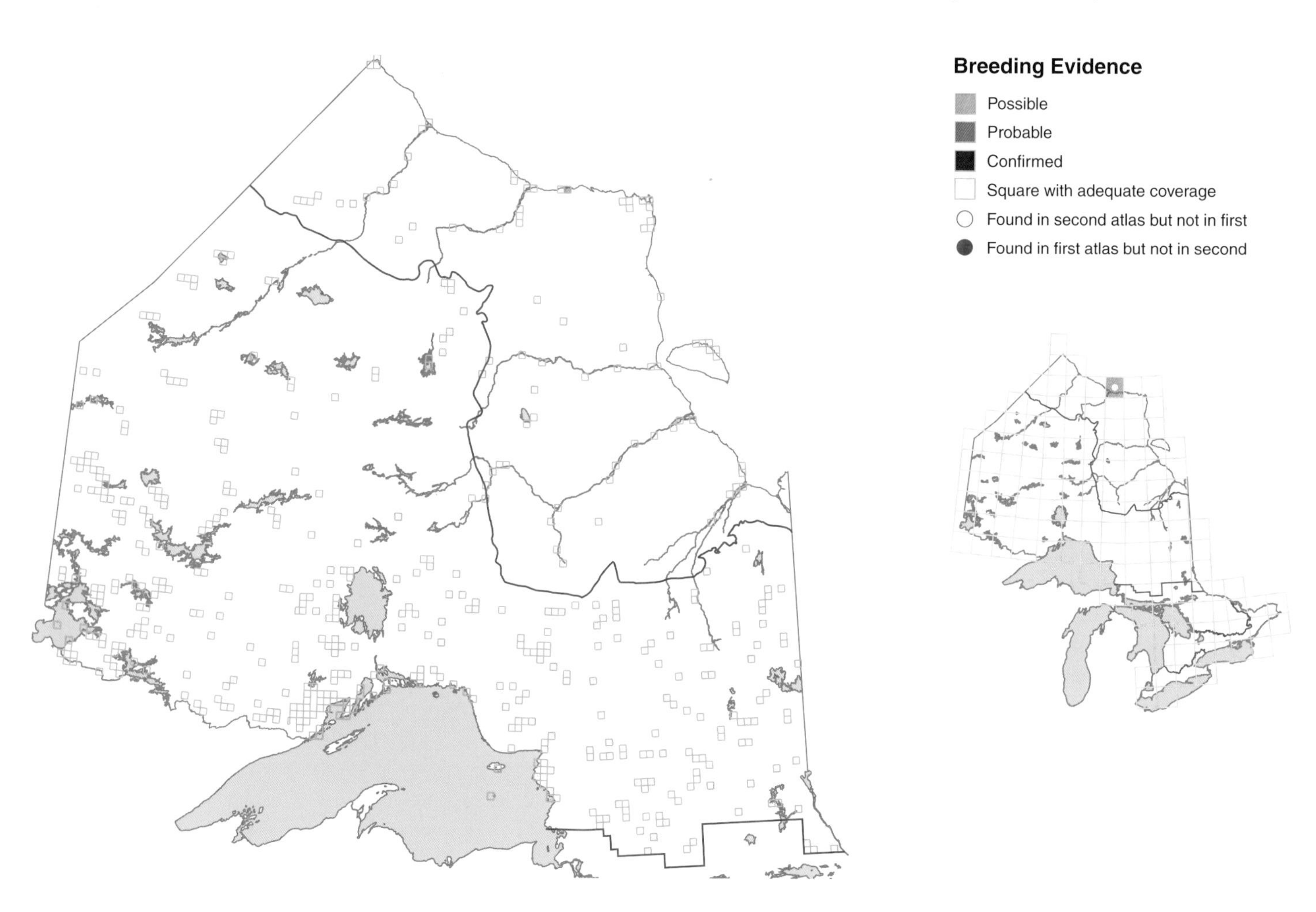

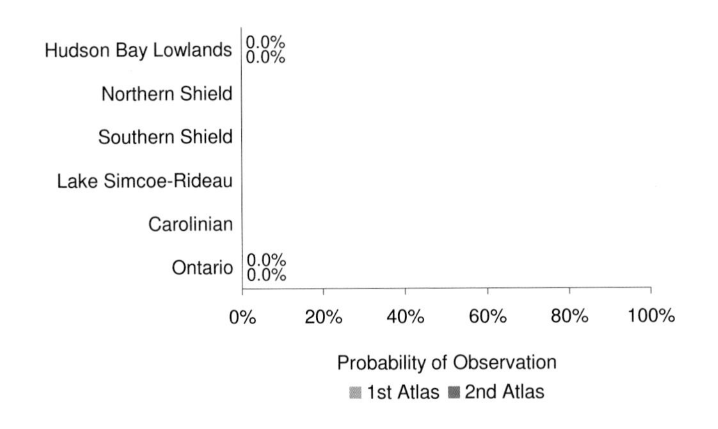

Extensive wet *Carex aquatilis*-dominated tundra near Burntpoint Creek where a territorial male Sprague's Pipit was present during the abnormally hot, dry summer of 2001. *Photo: Ken Abraham*

6-19 July 1998 (Curry 1991; Dobos 1999). During the second atlas, these and other sites in western Rainy River Dist. with potentially suitable habitat were surveyed on a number of occasions in both June and July, 2001 and 2005, but no pipits were found (G. Coady, pers. comm.).

Breeding biology: The Sprague's Pipit prefers well-drained, short and mixed-grass prairies for breeding. Grasslands with low shrub density, grass cover of intermediate height and density, and moderate litter depth offer optimal breeding habitat. Although pastures and other agricultural grasslands may be used, large areas of native grassland are preferred (Robbins and Dale 1999). In the species' core breeding range, establishment of breeding territories and pair formation occur shortly after arrival at the breeding areas from late April to mid-May. The male performs an aerial display comprised of an ascent to heights of 50-100 m followed by a "parachute" descent on fanned wings and tail, during which the brief but distinctive song is delivered. Early in the breeding season, bouts of aerial display are of shorter duration (less than 20 minutes), but by June they become increasingly longer (Robbins and Dale 1999). Detection of the Sprague's Pipit is principally during its conspicuous display flights. The flights terminate with a rapid descent to the ground, after which both sexes are highly cryptic and exceedingly difficult to detect. Nests are well concealed in dense grass, usually at the base of a grass tussock. Incubation, brooding, and feeding of nestlings is primarily or exclusively by the female (Robbins and Dale 1999), probably resulting in fewer opportunities for nest detection.

Extended periods of severe drought within the species' core breeding range are known to result in records of vagrancy, including isolated extra-limital breeding events (Robbins and Dale 1999). Sporadic breeding in southeastern Manitoba appears to correlate with periods of drought (Manitoba Avian Research Committee 2003), and isolated breeding in the southern interior of British Columbia in 1991 (Campbell et al. 1997) coincided with severe drought on the central Great Plains. Sprague's Pipit is a casual summer visitor at Churchill, Manitoba, where singing males have been recorded in areas of open tundra in at least three years since 1981 (Jehl 2004).

Abundance: The Sprague's Pipit is of only rare and sporadic occurrence in the province. Most records have apparently involved only unpaired, singing males. No definitive observations of pairs or other evidence of probable or confirmed breeding have been observed in Ontario. – *Donald A. Sutherland*

Bohemian Waxwing

Jaseur boréal

Bombycilla garrulus

R. E. Gehlert

An irregular winter visitor throughout much of Ontario, the Bohemian Waxwing has a holarctic distribution in summer, breeding in open boreal forests throughout Europe, Asia, and western North America. Within Canada, breeding has previously been confirmed throughout much of the Boreal Forest from the Yukon south and east to northwestern Ontario (Witmer 2002). Summer sightings in Nunavut, eastern Ontario, and Québec (Gauthier and Aubry 1996) and as far east as Nova Scotia (Tufts 1986; Erskine 1992) possibly suggest a more extensive breeding range in eastern Canada. Breeding in Ontario was first confirmed in the early 1960s near the junction of the Sutton and Warchesku Rivers (Schueler et al. 1974). Additional records include observations of family groups in northwestern Ontario during the first atlas and summer sightings near Kapuskasing (Speirs 1985).

Distribution and population status: Records of the Bohemian Waxwing are few and widely distributed across the far northern part of the province. Despite this, observations during the second atlas indicate an eastward expansion in the known breeding range of this species. In the first atlas, evidence of breeding was restricted to nine 100-km blocks in the northwest corner of the province, all in the Hudson Bay Lowlands region. Evidence of breeding in the second atlas was found farther east and south in Ontario in 12 100-km blocks and 16 squares, including four squares in the Northern Shield region.

There were only two confirmations of breeding during the atlas period. The first documented nest in the province was found 12 June 2003 just north of the Swan River, close to the James Bay coast. This nest presently represents the easternmost documented breeding record in North America (Peck et al. 2004b). On 13 July 2003, fledged young were found 50 km southeast of Peawanuck in an extensive burn with bog vegetation. The most southern and eastern observation during this

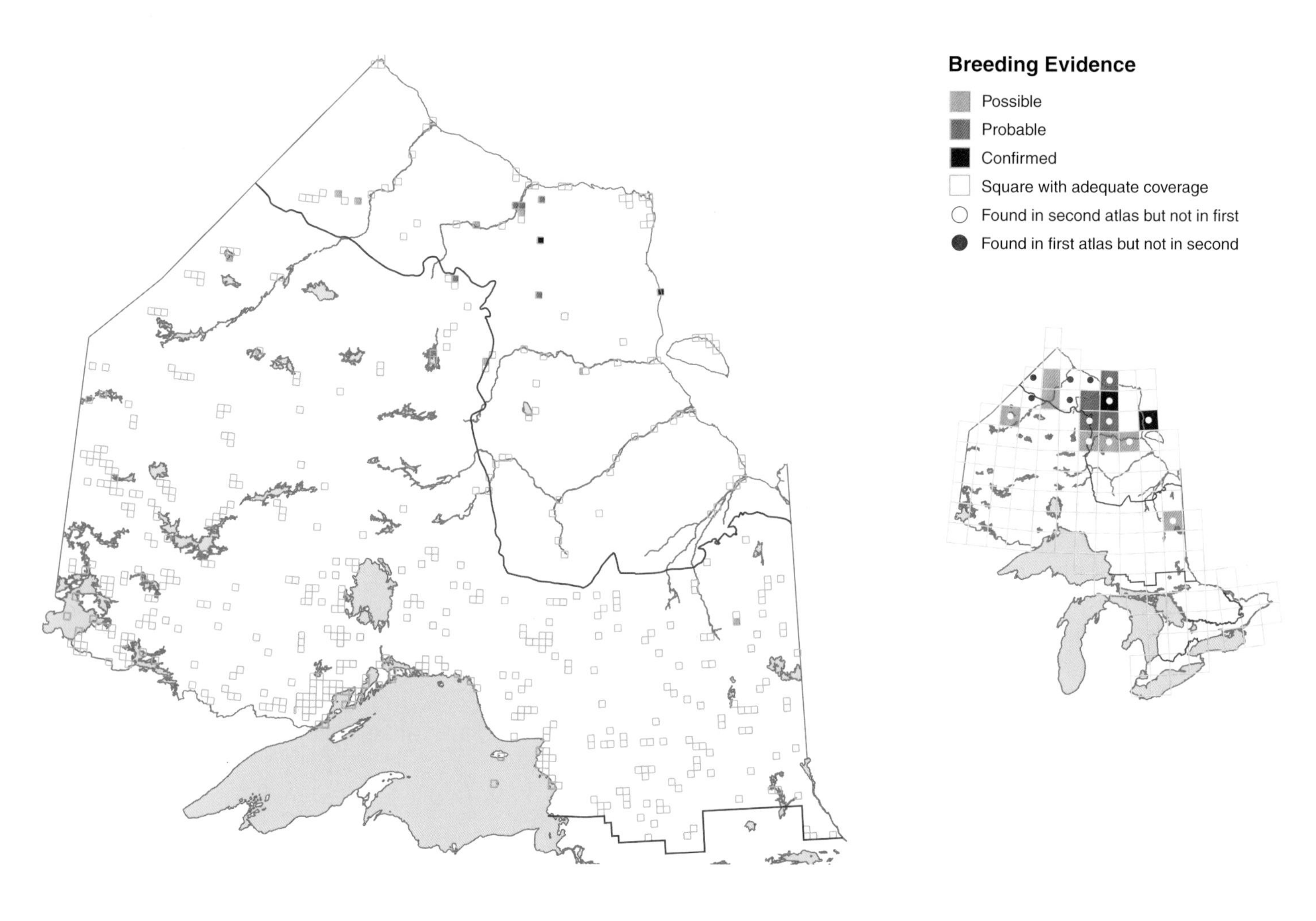

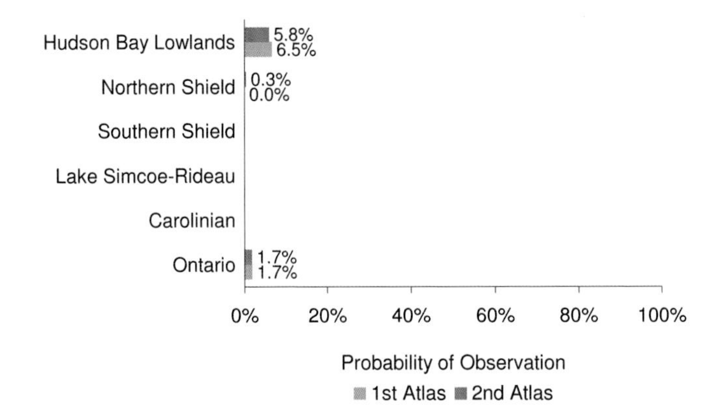

atlas was of a single bird seen on subsequent days in mid-July 2002 in an open Black Spruce clearcut approximately 80 km northeast of Cochrane.

The Bohemian Waxwing is not difficult to detect where it occurs, and it is possible that the species occurs more frequently than is depicted by the map. Results from the Québec atlas (Gauthier and Aubry 1996) and the two Ontario atlases suggest an eastward expansion of the range in the last 20 years. However, given the erratic nature of this species and the limited coverage in northern regions, it is unclear whether recent observations in the east are part of an ongoing eastward expansion or are simply the result of annual shifts in response to regional climatic conditions.

Breeding biology: The Bohemian Waxwing is non-territorial year-round, often allowing conspecifics to approach nest sites (Howell 1973). Courtship behaviour observed in late winter and in spring flocks suggests that pairing occurs prior to arrival at the breeding site (Howell 1973). Like the Cedar Waxwing, the Bohemian Waxwing is thought to breed later than many other birds, timing its nesting with the ripening of fruit. However, based on the date of observation of fledged young and nest records in both atlases, there is no evidence to suggest later nesting in Ontario, and observations from the Yukon suggest that fruit may not be as important in North America as in Eurasia (Sinclair et al.2003). The records of fledged young from the Winisk River in 1984 and the Sutton Ridges in 2003 were both recorded in mid-July, suggesting that nesting began in mid-June, based on a combined 30-day incubation and nestling period (Baicich and Harrison 1997). This is in agreement with the Swan River nest, which had a complete clutch of four eggs on 13 June. Typical of the species, this nest was located 3.2 m above the ground in a 7 m White Spruce with considerable hanging lichen (Cramp 1988). The nest was situated in the middle of open woods with White Spruce, Tamarack, willow, and alder. Breeding sites are usually found on woodland edges, often near lakes, rivers, or streams, or in swampy areas, beaver ponds, and burns (Campbell et al. 1997). In favourable habitat, this species has been observed to be semi-colonial, although such behaviour was not reported during the second atlas. Females alone incubate the eggs; the male usually perches nearby, delivering food to the female during incubation and the early nestling period. Both parents stay with young for at least two weeks after fledging (Campbell et al. 1997).

The first documented Ontario nest of the Bohemian Waxwing was discovered 3.2 m high in a White Spruce in open spruce-Tamarack woods 2 km inland from James Bay, 27 km north of the Swan River, on 12 June 2003. *Photo: Mark Peck*

Open spruce-Tamarack-willow-alder woods with abundant tree lichen bordering wet sedge fen is nesting habitat for the Bohemian Waxwing. North of the Swan River, 12 June 2003. *Photo: Mark Peck*

Abundance: Despite apparent expansion eastward in the second atlas, the limited and sparsely distributed occurrences of this species suggest it remains an uncommon breeder in Ontario. – *Mark K. Peck and Glenn Coady*

Cedar Waxwing

Jaseur d'Amérique

Bombycilla cedrorum

Jim Richards

The Cedar Waxwing is one of Ontario's most familiar songbirds. Found in a variety of habitats from urban parks to boreal forest, it was among the most frequently recorded species during both atlases. Its distinctive appearance readily distinguishes it from all other Ontario birds except the much scarcer Bohemian Waxwing, and its call is equally characteristic. It breeds across the southern half of Canada and the northern half of the US (Witmer et al. 1997).

Distribution and population status: Both atlases show that the Cedar Waxwing ranged across the province and occurred in almost every square in the south and most 100-km blocks in the north. Interestingly, the few gaps in its Ontario range are in the Hudson Bay Lowlands, where its breeding range overlaps that of the Bohemian Waxwing.

Although the Cedar Waxwing is still widespread, its probability of observation declined significantly between atlases in the Lake Simcoe-Rideau and Southern Shield regions, by 3% and 5%, respectively. These decreases may be related to broad declines across the continent in recent years. BBS data indicate that the species increased between 1968 and 1980 but has declined continentally in the period between atlases. Since 1981, it has experienced significant declines of 1.1% per year across North America (Sauer et al. 2005), 1.2% per year in Canada, and 3.3% per year in Ontario.

Reasons for the recent declines are uncertain. They appear to be part of a wide-ranging phenomenon, as many other shrubland species are experiencing declines. Losses in parts of the Southern Shield and the Lake Simcoe-Rideau regions may be due to natural succession from marginal farmland through shrubby old fields to forest; destruction of hedgerows and other shrubby habitat as a result of agricultural intensification may also be a factor. Although the species is still very common in

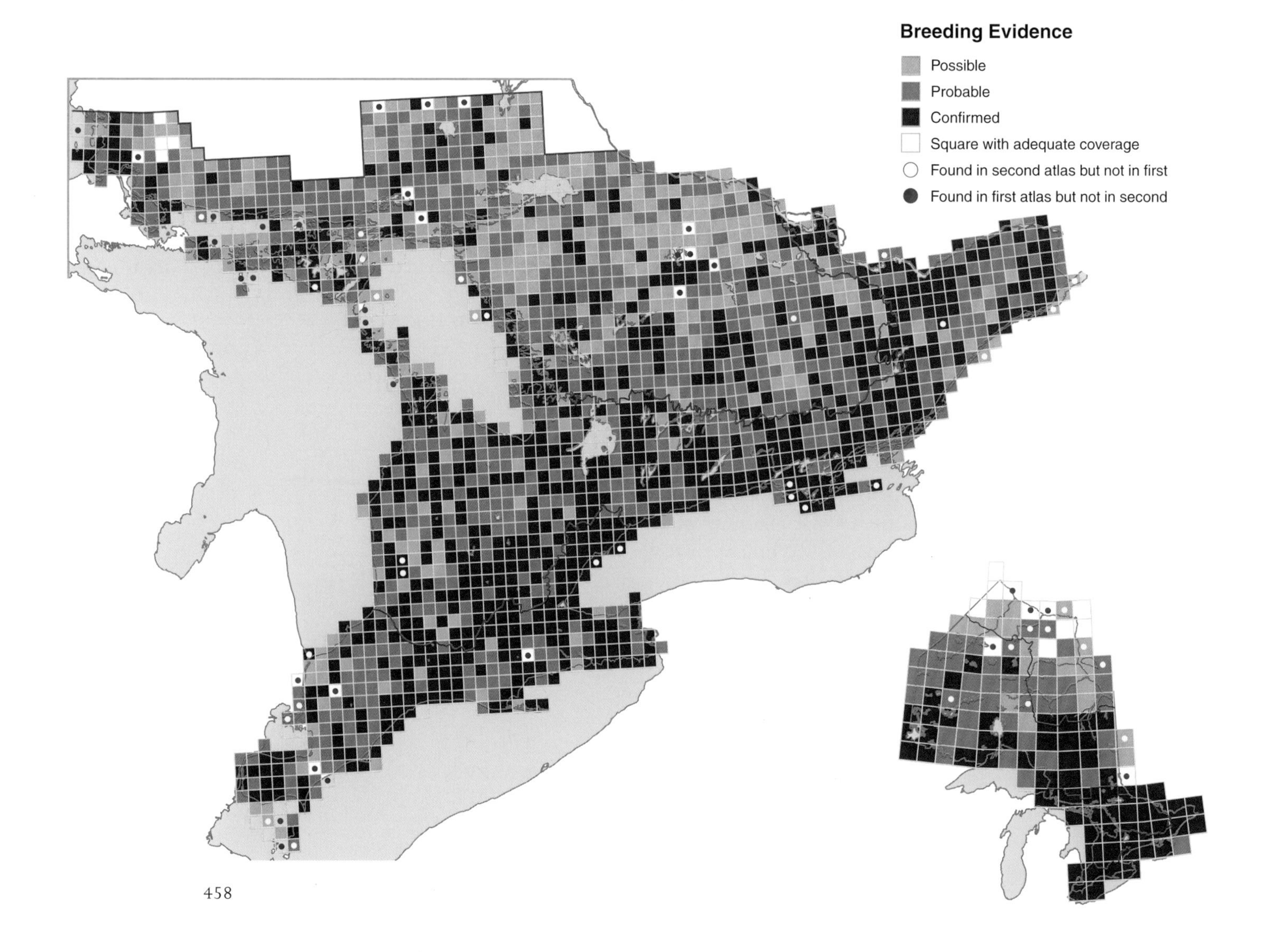

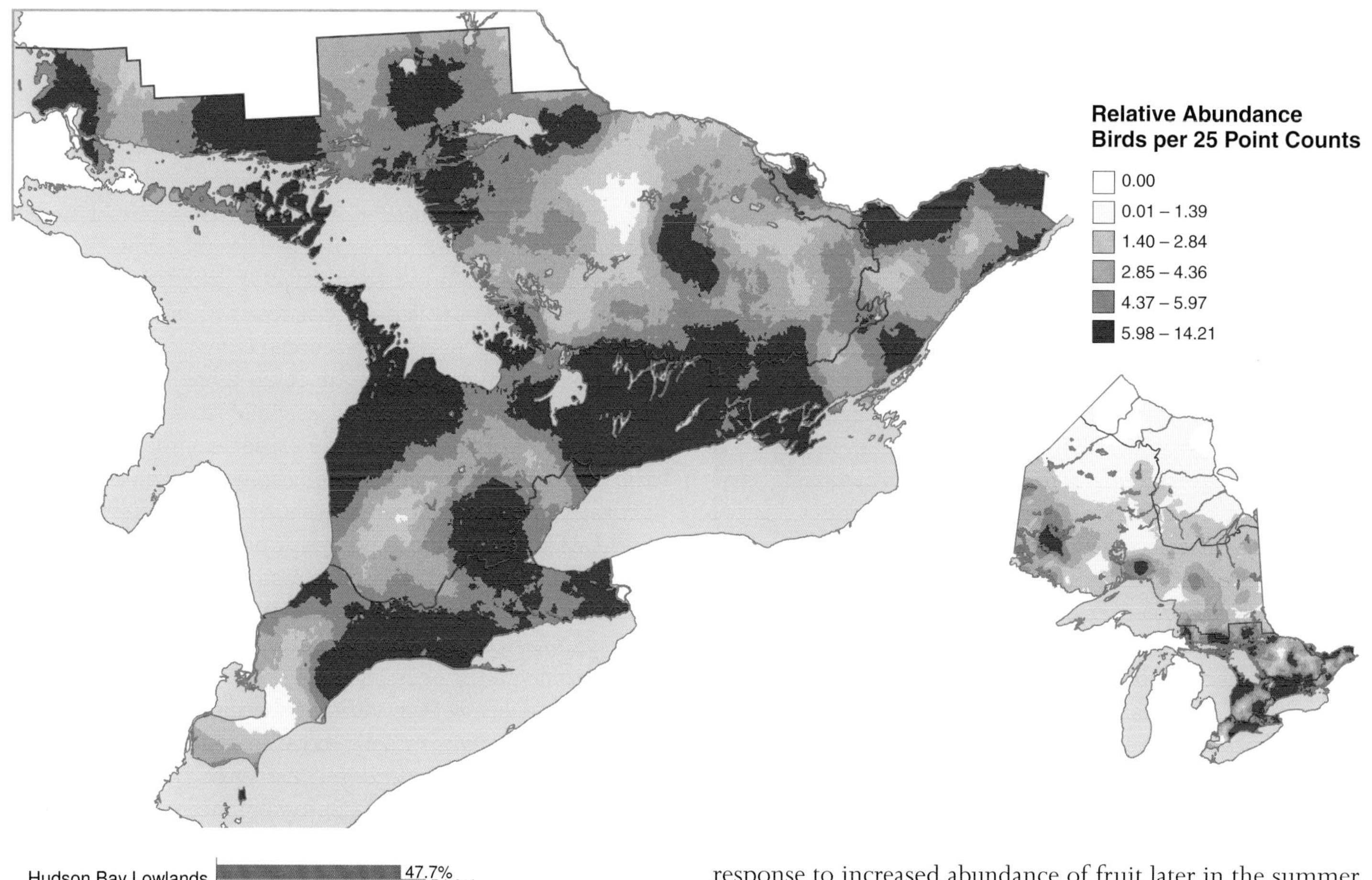

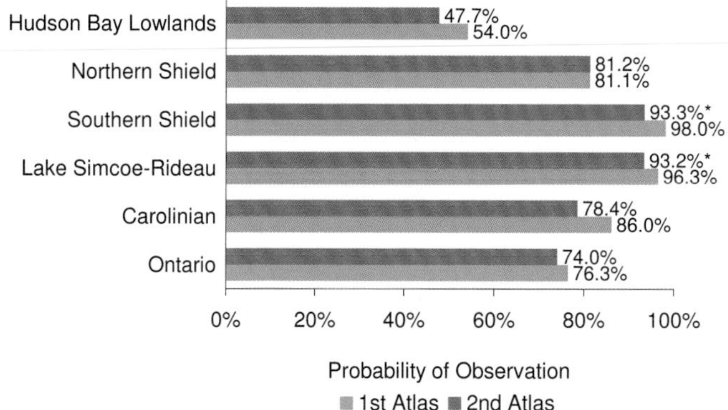

many areas, it may eventually disappear from areas of marginal habitat if the trend continues. A comparison between the southern Ontario data from the two atlases shows no significant shifts in either the edge or the core of the species' range.

Breeding biology: The Cedar Waxwing breeds primarily along woodland edges, in open wooded or park-like settings, and in shrubby old-field habitats. It eats mostly fruit, with insects forming a small portion of the diet (Witmer et al. 1997). This reliance on fruit has led to a number of adaptations that help it to exploit patchy and ephemeral food resources, and these can make atlassing for the species somewhat difficult.

Due to the patchy distribution of its food, it is often found foraging in flocks a considerable distance from the nest site during the breeding season. Birds observed foraging may not indicate breeding in the immediate area, and birds observed together are not necessarily a pair. With the species' protracted migration period, some birds are still migrating during late May and early June. This may have elevated some point count results.

The Cedar Waxwing breeds later than most species, in response to increased abundance of fruit later in the summer. Nesting usually begins in late June. Egg dates for Ontario are 21 May to 16 September, with 50% being found from 25 June to 14 July (Peck and James 1987). Atlassers who spent little time in the field after June may not have had opportunities to confirm this species.

Additionally, adults generally regurgitate food for the young rather than carrying it in their bills, and consume fecal sacs rather than carrying them away from the nest (Witmer et al. 1997). Thus several codes for confirming breeding cannot be used for this species. Nonetheless, it was confirmed in 39% of squares in the south.

Abundance: The relative abundance map for the Cedar Waxwing shows an uneven distribution across the province but a general decrease northward, with the lowest numbers in the far north in the Hudson Bay Lowlands. Local areas with high relative abundance may reflect a high density of fruiting plants, forest insect infestations, or extensive areas of suitable nesting habitat. Two areas in the south with relatively low abundance levels, the Algonquin Highlands and the heavily agricultural southwest, reflect the relative scarcity of suitable nesting habitat. Point count data demonstrate that the Cedar Waxwing is common northward through the Southern Shield, uncommon to common in the Northern Shield, and rare to uncommon in the Hudson Bay Lowlands. – *Joel H. Kits*

Blue-winged Warbler

Paruline à ailes bleues

Vermivora pinus

Barry S. Cherriere

The Blue-winged Warbler is one of many scrubland-reliant species decreasing in population size throughout much of its breeding range. In contrast, its breeding population in Ontario has generally increased over the past few decades as part of a continuing northeastward range expansion, despite significant declines within its core range in the US since the mid-1960s (Sauer et al. 2005). This overall decline is presumed to be associated primarily with natural succession and other losses of early successional habitats.

The Blue-winged Warbler shares much of its northeastern North American range with the closely related Golden-winged Warbler, with which it regularly hybridizes. Introgression with the Blue-winged Warbler is one of several reasons to which the Golden-winged Warbler's recent decline is attributed.

Distribution and population status: First recorded in the province in the early 1900s, by the mid-1950s the Blue-winged Warbler was becoming established as a breeder (McCracken 1994). During the first atlas, it was recorded breeding in most regions south of the Shield, with concentrations around Long Point and Hamilton and isolated records north to the Bruce Peninsula and the vicinity of Bracebridge in central Muskoka Dist. Although the extent of its distribution has not expanded greatly since, there has been considerable in-filling of its range. It now occurs more extensively in the Carolinian region and has colonized several areas of the Oak Ridges Moraine between Orangeville and Trenton as well as areas of southern Hastings, Lennox and Addington, and Frontenac Counties north of Belleville and Kingston. This colonization has resulted in significant northeast shifts in its average latitude and longitude since the first atlas.

The probability of observation of the species in the province increased significantly by 74% between atlases. Changes were greatest in the Lake Simcoe-Rideau and Southern Shield regions, with approximately threefold and fivefold increases, respectively. Significant increases have also been recorded on BBS surveys. The trend is expected to continue as the species' range expansion per-

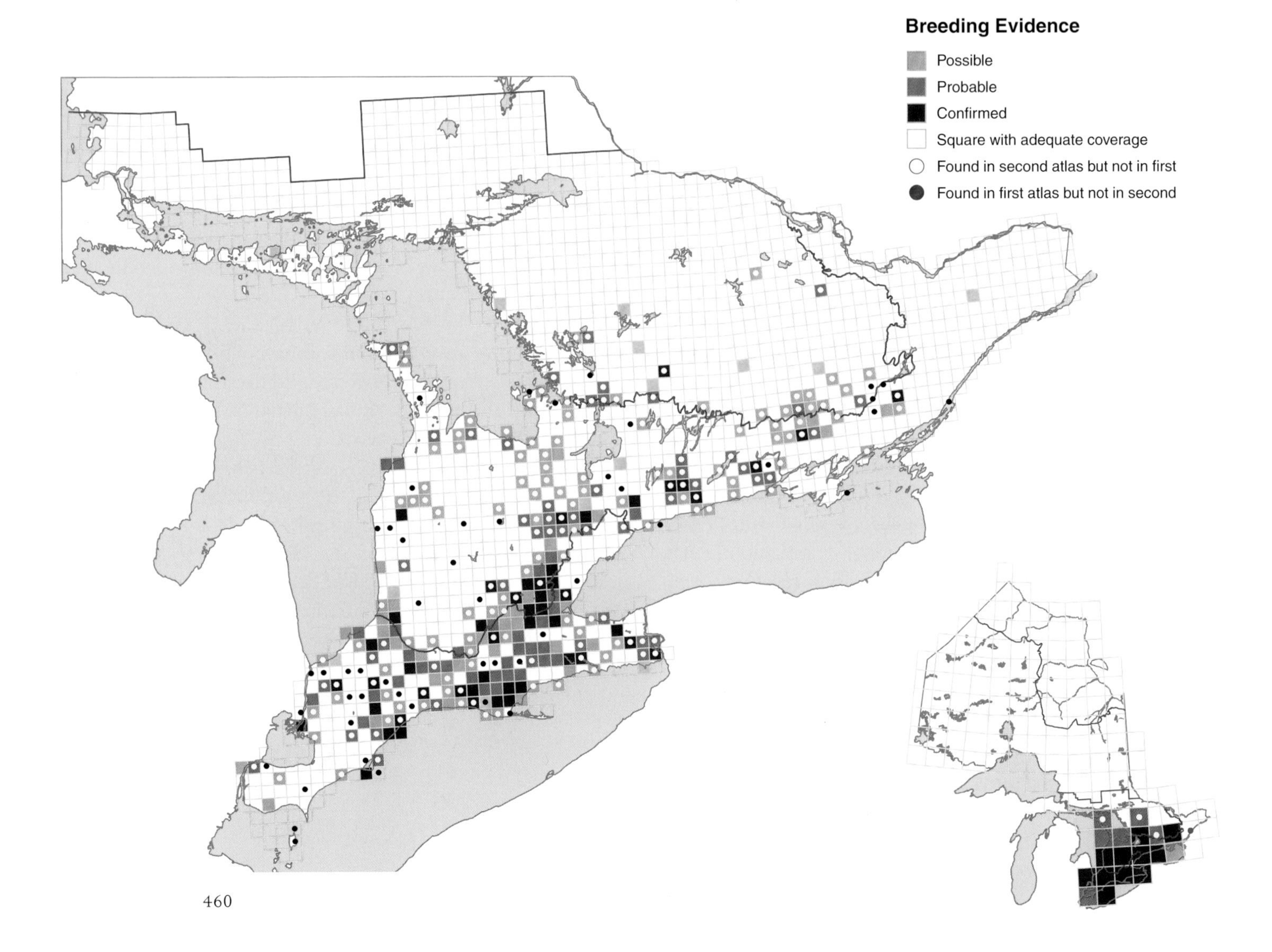

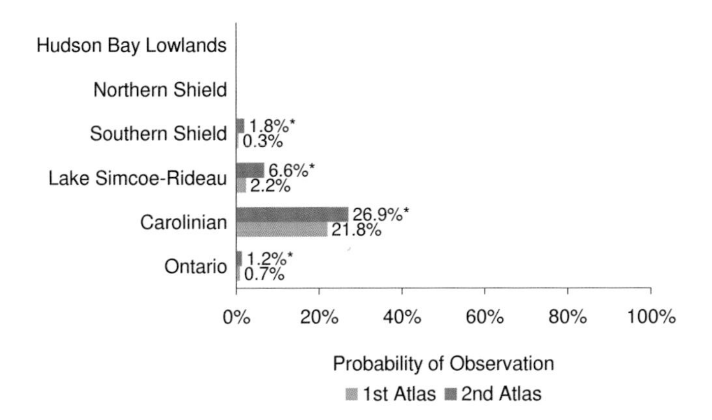

sists. Continued encroachment into areas currently populated by the Golden-winged Warbler means that hybridization between these two species can be expected to increase throughout the province in the future. The disappearance of the Blue-winged Warbler in some areas since the first atlas may be indicative of the maturation of breeding habitat beyond the stage preferred by the species, as has been described in other parts of the species' range (Gill et al. 2001).

Breeding biology: The Blue-winged Warbler prefers areas of dense, early to mid-successional scrub occurring in regenerating old fields and along edges and gaps in mature forest, hydro and railway rights-of-way, and roadsides. Although there is considerable overlap in habitat preferences between the Blue-winged and Golden-winged Warbler, this species generally prefers drier sites (Gill et al. 2001). In Ontario, it appears to shun the wet alder thicket swamps frequently occupied by the Golden-winged Warbler. Nests are located on or very near the ground, at the base of a shrub or clump of goldenrod, usually within 30 m of the forest edge in areas of dense young saplings. Nests are sometimes parasitized by the Brown-headed Cowbird; parasitism rates vary by population but can greatly affect fledging success (Gill et al. 2001).

The difficulty in locating nests in this warbler's dense habitat is reflected by the fact that only 21% of squares confirmed breeding, and most confirmations were by observation of fledged young or adults carrying food. In fact, nests were reported from only two squares during the second atlas period.

Hybrids and some adults may sing Golden-winged Warbler song types. Grey squares on the map are those for which the only evidence for the Blue-winged Warbler during the second atlas was the song of either a Blue-winged or Golden-winged Warbler, with no sighting of the bird to verify identification of the species. Although the breeding evidence map depicts the species' range in the province reasonably accurately, directed surveys using call broadcasts are necessary to further refine the species' distribution and abundance in the province.

Abundance: Abundance of the Blue-winged Warbler in Ontario remains relatively low. Local regions of high density tend to be associated with areas with abundant supplies of early to mid-successional scrub habitats. The species is most common on the Norfolk Sand Plain, particularly in Norfolk Co., where there is extensive forest cover interspersed with open fields, and where the species was reported to be common in the mid-1980s (McCracken 1987). However, even there the species was recorded on average less than once per 50 point counts. – *Rachel Vallender*

The nest of the Blue-winged Warbler is often narrow and deep, supported on a sturdy foundation of dead leaves arranged with their petioles facing outward (Gill et al. 2001). *Photo: Bill Rayner*

This site on the Norfolk Sand Plain near Turkey Point was used by the Blue-winged Warbler for several years during the atlas period. It is fairly typical breeding habitat showing forest edge and old field characteristics. *Photo: Gregor G. Beck*

Golden-winged Warbler

Paruline à ailes doreés

Vermivora chrysoptera

The Golden-winged Warbler breeds in the northeastern US and south-central Canada, from Manitoba east to New Hampshire and south to Kentucky (Confer 1992). Rare in the early 1900s, it underwent an increase in numbers and a dramatic northeastward range expansion beginning in Ontario around 1930 (McCracken 1994). However, the species has recently been experiencing a similarly dramatic range contraction in its core breeding range in the US. It is now one of the most rapidly declining passerine species in North America and is listed as Threatened in Canada (COSEWIC 2005). The primary reasons for declines include loss of breeding and wintering habitat, nest parasitism by the Brown-headed Cowbird, and hybridization with the Blue-winged Warbler (Gill 1980, 1987, 1997; Confer 1992). Hybridization occurs in all areas where Blue-winged and Golden-winged Warblers are in contact and has increased in Ontario in recent years (McCracken 1994; Vallender et al. 2007).

Distribution and population status: The Golden-winged Warbler is currently found primarily in southern Ontario and near Rainy River. It appears to be most common along the southern edge of the Shield, including the Frontenac Axis where the landscape is a mosaic of abandoned and marginal farmland, rock barrens, wetlands, and forest. The species is also concentrated in areas of higher forest cover south of the Shield, primarily along the Niagara Escarpment and Oak Ridges Moraine, where a good supply of suitable old field habitat is available. It is uncommon in all regions, with its highest probability of observation (19%) recorded in the Southern Shield. Although scattered across most areas of this region, it is notably absent from the Algonquin Highlands where its preferred habitat is scarce.

BBS data indicate that Golden-winged Warbler populations in the US decreased significantly by an average annual rate of 3.4% per year between 1966 and 2005 (Sauer et al. 2005). In

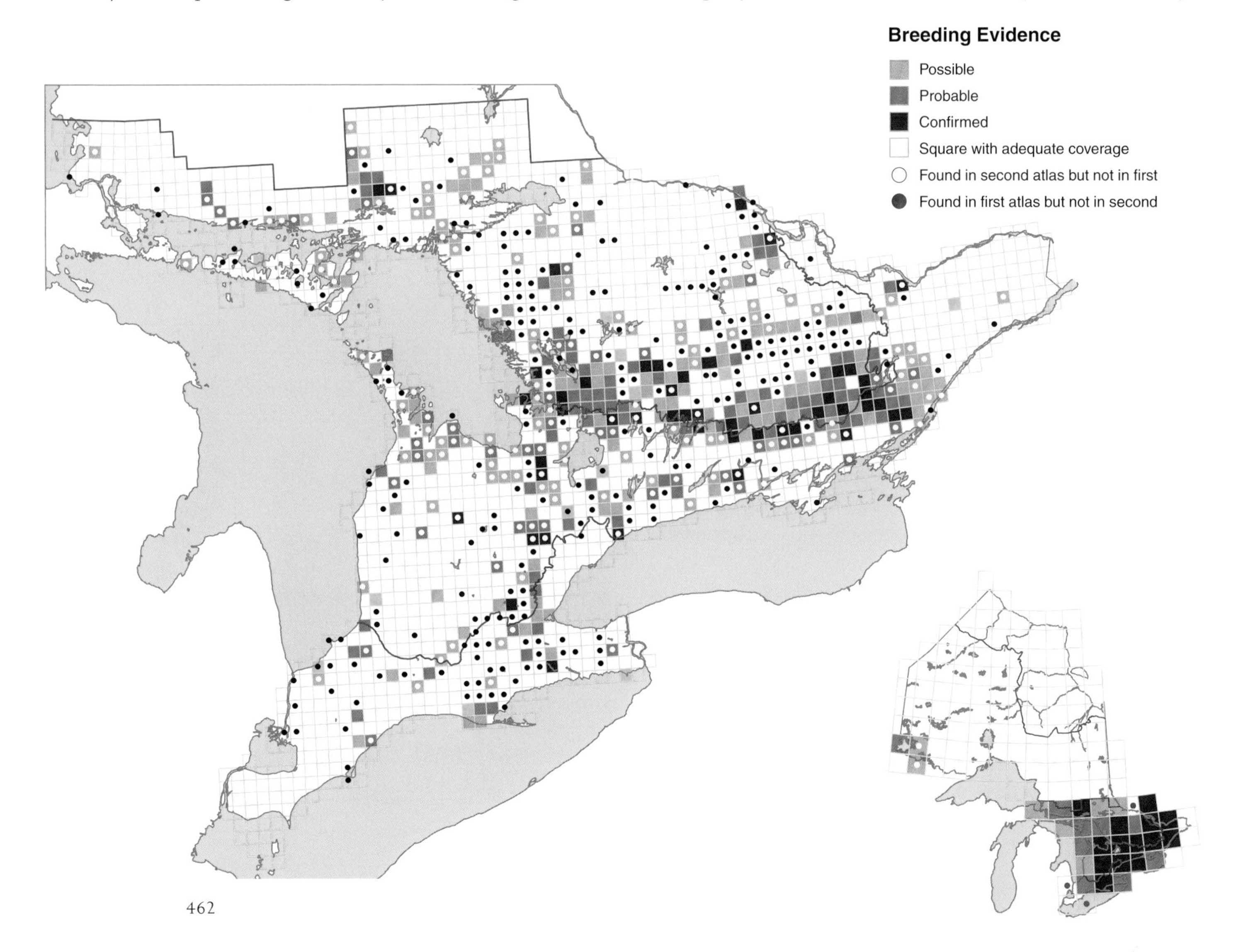

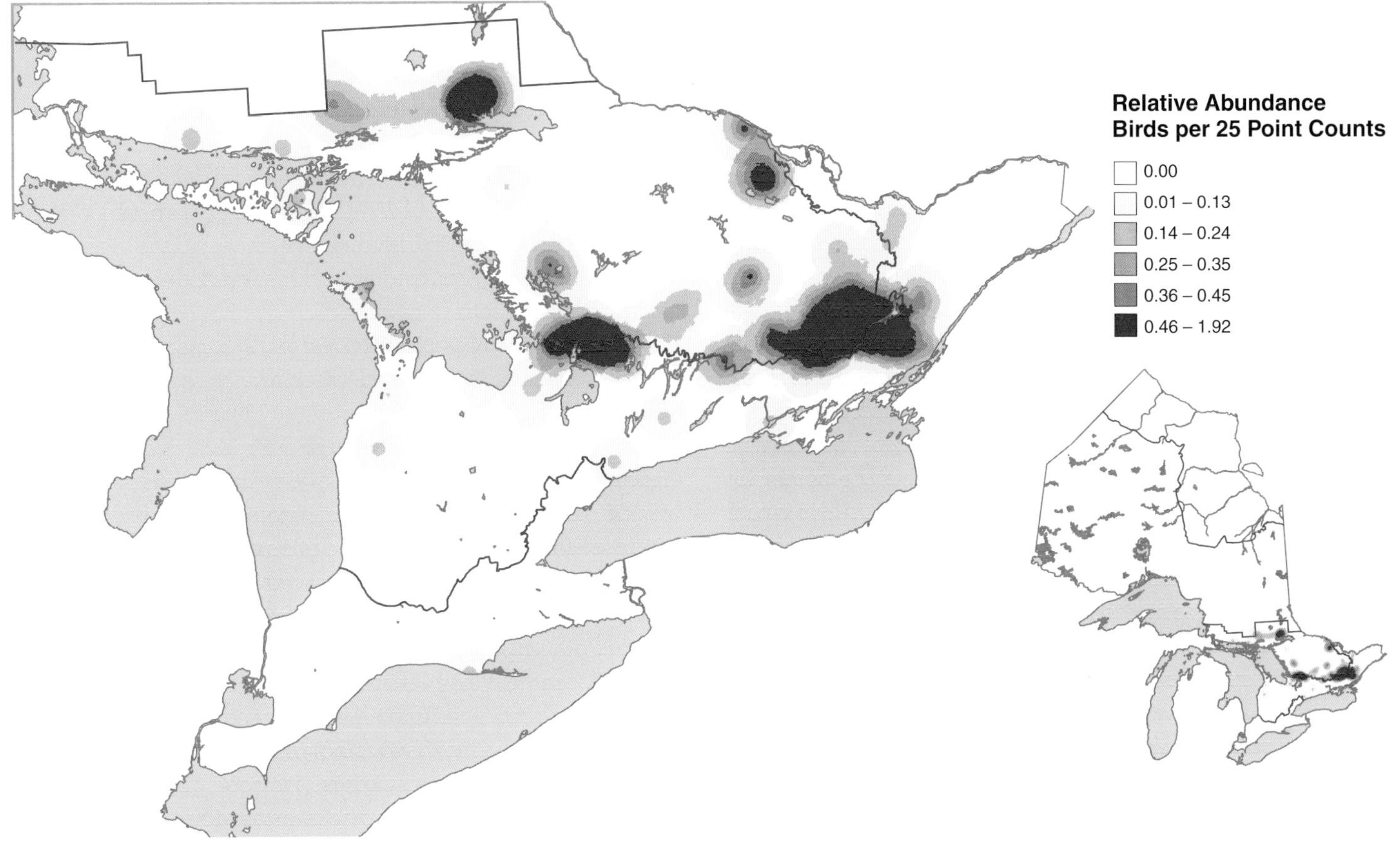

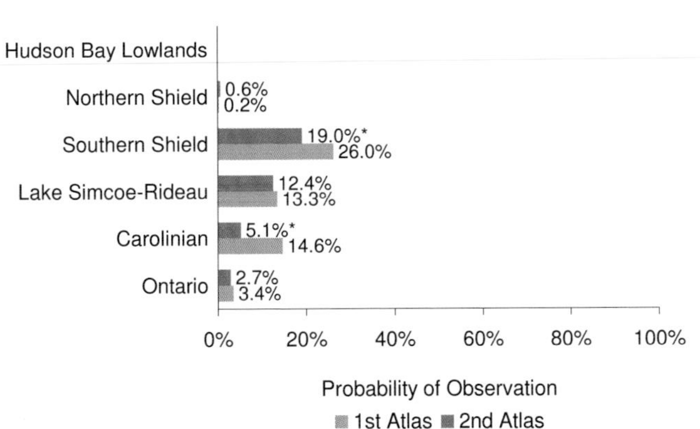

Ontario over the same period, however, the species experienced significant population growth (Downes et al. 2005), likely due to continued northeastward range expansion (McCracken 1994). Then, in the past decade, this expansion nearly ceased, and the species has started to disappear from regions in the southernmost portions of Ontario. Significant declines of 65% and 27%, respectively, in the probability of observation were recorded in the Carolinian and the Southern Shield regions since the first atlas. Declines in the Carolinian, particularly on the Norfolk Sand Plain, are likely due primarily to displacement by the Blue-winged Warbler, while those in the Southern Shield are probably a result of natural succession of habitat, as the range of the Blue-winged Warbler currently does not extend far onto the Shield.

Although the primary advertising song of the Golden-winged Warbler is distinctive, individuals, including hybrids, can sing either parental song type. Grey squares on the map are those for which the only evidence for the Golden-winged Warbler during the second atlas was the song of either a Golden-winged or Blue-winged Warbler, with no sighting of the bird to verify identification of the species.

Breeding biology: The Golden-winged Warbler breeds in successional scrub habitats surrounded by forests that are used for foraging and song posts. Due to the patchy nature of its preferred breeding habitat, pairs are often clustered, although territories are aggressively defended from individuals of the same species. Nests are built entirely by the female and constructed on the ground, often at the base of a shrub. The density of the habitat makes them difficult to locate. Only females incubate the eggs and brood the young, but parental care is otherwise shared by both sexes (Confer 1992).

Breeding was confirmed in only 15% of squares reporting the species, and the difficulty in finding nests is reflected by the fact that only two squares documented nests. Most confirmed evidence was in the form of fledged young or adults carrying food. The highest breeding evidence reported in the majority of squares was the presence of singing or territorial males.

Abundance: The species has one of the lowest global population estimates of any warbler, at 210,000 (Rich et al. 2004), of which 18% is believed to occur in Canada, nearly entirely in Ontario (Sauer et al. 2005). Concentrations are highest along the southern edge of the Shield, especially southeastern Georgian Bay and the Frontenac Axis north of Kingston, near Gravenhurst, and east of Sudbury. These areas have shifted from the previous atlas when concentrations were mostly in the southernmost areas of the province, and represent the highest availability of suitable habitat in areas where the Blue-winged Warbler is not yet established. – *Rachel Vallender*

Brewster's Warbler / Lawrence's Warbler

Paruline de Brewster / Paruline de Lawrence

Vermivora pinus x Vermivora chrysoptera

(L)Tim Stewart (R) Barry S. Cherriere

Hybridization between two species is generally rare in nature. Pairings often involve vagrant individuals, or interbreeding of congeners where ranges overlap. An example of the latter is the hybridization between Blue-winged and Golden-winged Warblers. This pairing produces two recognizable forms, the Brewster's and the Lawrence's Warblers. Their hybrid origin was intermittently disputed until Parkes (1951) suggested a plausible pattern of inheritance for the plumage characters, whereby facial and body plumage patterns were controlled by two independent genes. The hybrid plumages were expected to have one or the other facial and body patterns seen in the parental species (Parkes 1951), with the Brewster's form resulting from the dominant forms of the genes and the much rarer Lawrence's produced by recessive genes. Morphological analyses of hybrids in the field show extensive irregularities in predicted plumage patterns, suggesting a more complex genetic process complicated by the regular back-crossing of hybrids with "pure" forms.

Distribution and population status: Although neither hybrid form is common, the dominant Brewster's form is encountered much more regularly through southern Ontario. It can be found largely throughout the Carolinian and Lake Simcoe-Rideau regions, the primary zone of overlap between the Blue-winged and Golden-winged Warblers. Breeding evidence was recorded in 47 squares in the second atlas, up from 24 in the first, ranging from Windsor north to Lake Rosseau (Muskoka Dist.) and Ottawa. Distribution reflects the occurrence of higher forest cover interspersed with open fields, as the hybrid is primarily found on the Niagara Escarpment and Oak Ridges Moraine, along the southern edge of the Shield, and in the Long Point area, generally in or in close proximity to squares recording the Golden-winged Warbler.

The hybrid's pattern of change between atlases reflects the changes in distribution of the Golden-winged Warbler, which has likewise become scarcer in the Carolinian, particularly on the Norfolk Sand Plain, where it was once relatively common, and the

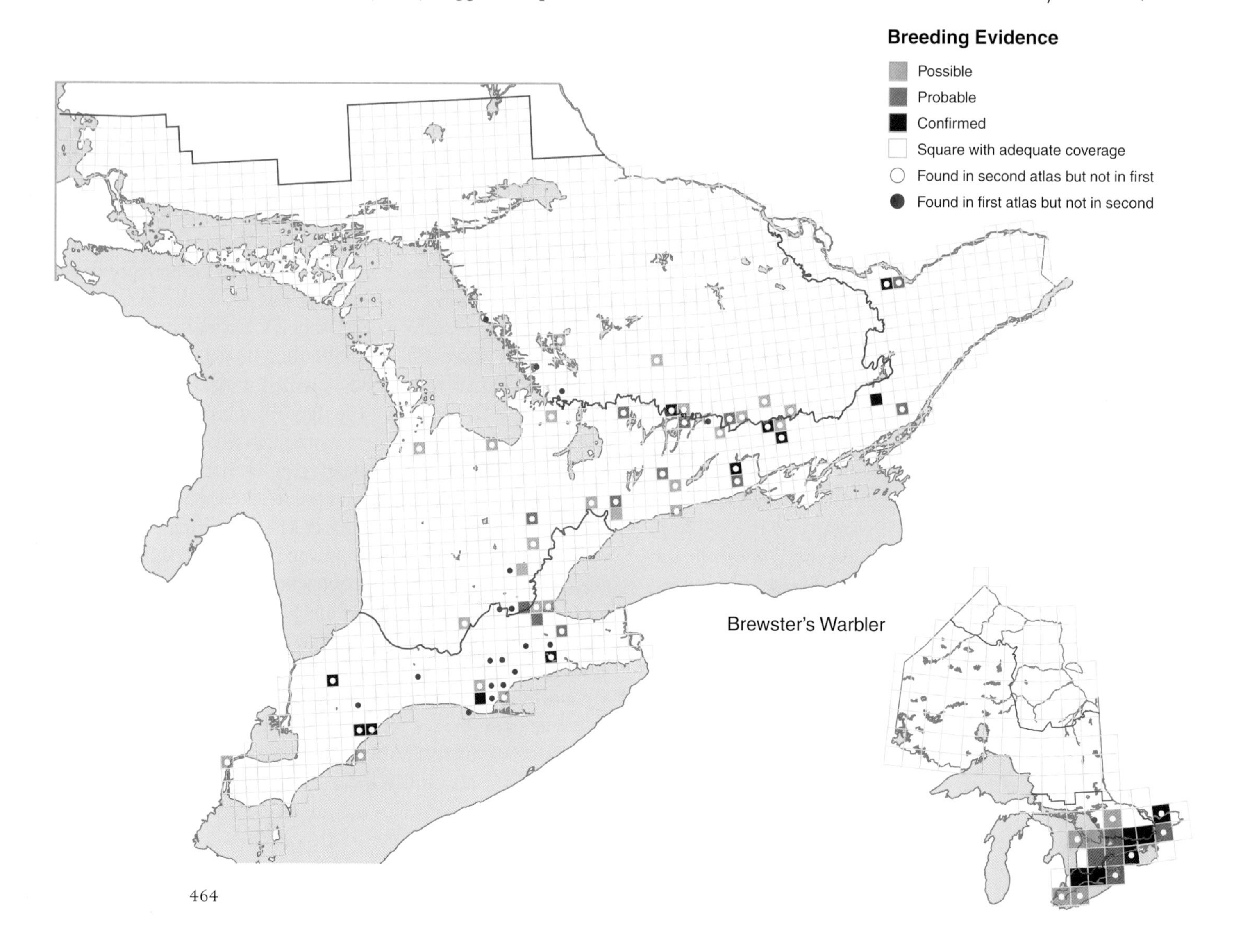

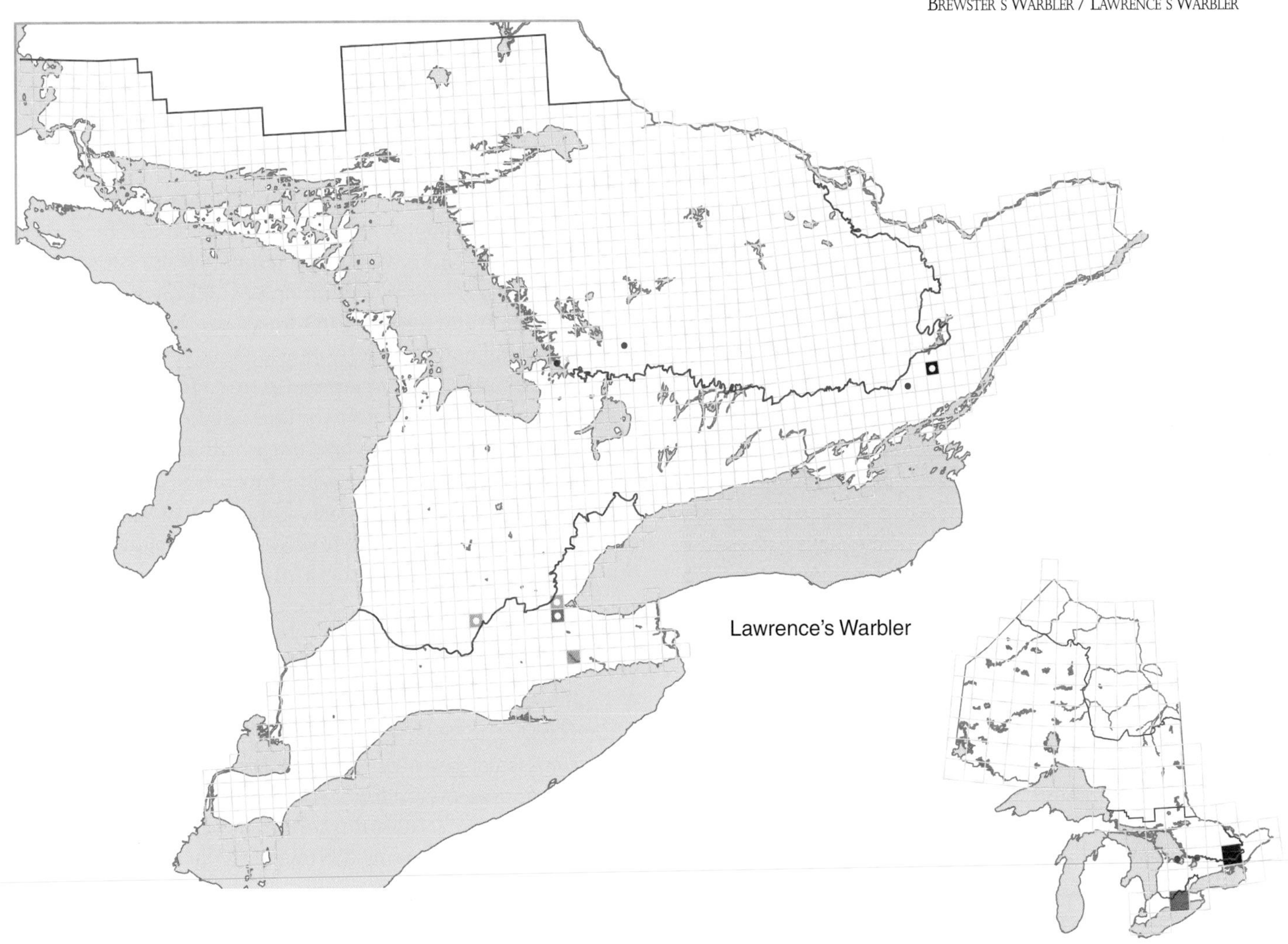

Blue-winged Warbler, which has expanded significantly into the Lake Simcoe-Rideau region and now overlaps more broadly with the Golden-winged Warbler. The probability of observation of the Brewster's Warbler increased significantly in the Lake Simcoe-Rideau region, by about fourfold; it expanded from seven squares in the first atlas to 26 in the second. Conversely, the much rarer Lawrence's Warbler was found in only five squares in the second atlas compared to four in the first. Of the five, in only one square was it also recorded in the first atlas, with no apparent pattern or explanation for the changes. Because hybrids can sing either parental song type, identification relies on visual confirmation, and heard-only birds are not included on distribution maps. It is thus likely that the map under-represents the distribution of these hybrids.

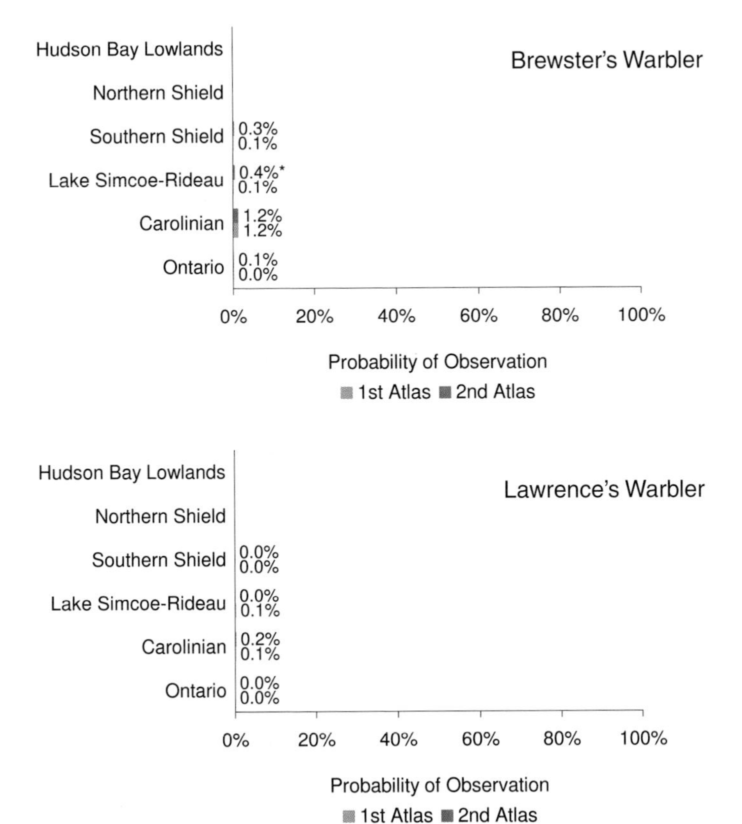

Breeding biology: Like both their parent species, Brewster's and Lawrence's Warblers prefer early successional habitat for breeding and rely on scrubby vegetation for nest sites. Because of their relative rarity, the hybrids are usually found paired with an individual of one or the other parent species. Nests are difficult to locate.

Abundance: The Brewster's Warbler is increasing in Ontario as hybridization between the two parental species continues in areas where their breeding ranges overlap. This trend is expected to continue and potentially increase as the Blue-winged Warbler expands into areas currently inhabited by the Golden-winged Warbler. The decrease in abundance of the Brewster's form in the southernmost regions of Ontario evident between the two atlases is likely associated with the displacement of Golden-winged Warbler populations by Blue-winged Warblers following a brief period of hybridization, during which time the hybrid forms would be present. This process is likely to continue, advancing north with the expansion of the Blue-winged Warbler. – *Rachel Vallender and Seabrooke Leckie*

Tennessee Warbler

Paruline obscure

Vermivora peregrina

Glenn Bartley

The Tennessee Warbler is one of several wood-warblers that specialize in Spruce Budworm. Although it does not feed exclusively on this moth's caterpillar, it responds quickly to outbreaks, and numbers of transients and breeders fluctuate considerably in a given location from year to year. A widespread boreal breeding species, this warbler ranges from southeastern Yukon Territory east to Newfoundland and south to central British Columbia, northern Minnesota, and the Adirondacks in New York (Rimmer and McFarland 1998).

The Tennessee Warbler occupies early successional boreal forests dominated by spruce, Tamarack, and Balsam Fir, containing open, grassy areas, dense shrub thickets of willows and Speckled Alder, and groves of young deciduous trees such as Balsam Poplar, Trembling Aspen, and White Birch. The species uses both upland and lowland forests and will use successional habitats created by logging (Rimmer and McFarland 1998).

Distribution and population status: The overall distribution pattern of the Tennessee Warbler has remained much the same since the first atlas. It is widespread from Algonquin Prov. Park north to Hudson Bay and most common in the Northern Shield and Hudson Bay Lowlands, where the probability of observation was 70% and 71%, respectively. It is much less common in the Southern Shield region and was found in just 12 squares in the Lake Simcoe-Rideau region, primarily on Manitoulin Island, the Bruce Peninsula, and the southern edge of the Canadian Shield, where the spruce forest it prefers is available.

Significant declines of 52% and 27% in the probability of observation since the first atlas were recorded in the Lake Simcoe-Rideau and Southern Shield regions, respectively. BBS data also show a significant decline province-wide since 1981, as do CMMN data from LPBO. The decline probably reflects, at least in part, reductions of Spruce Budworm populations, which have been in decline in Ontario since 1985 (National Forestry Database Program 2007). Caution is needed in assessing BBS trends for this species, since few

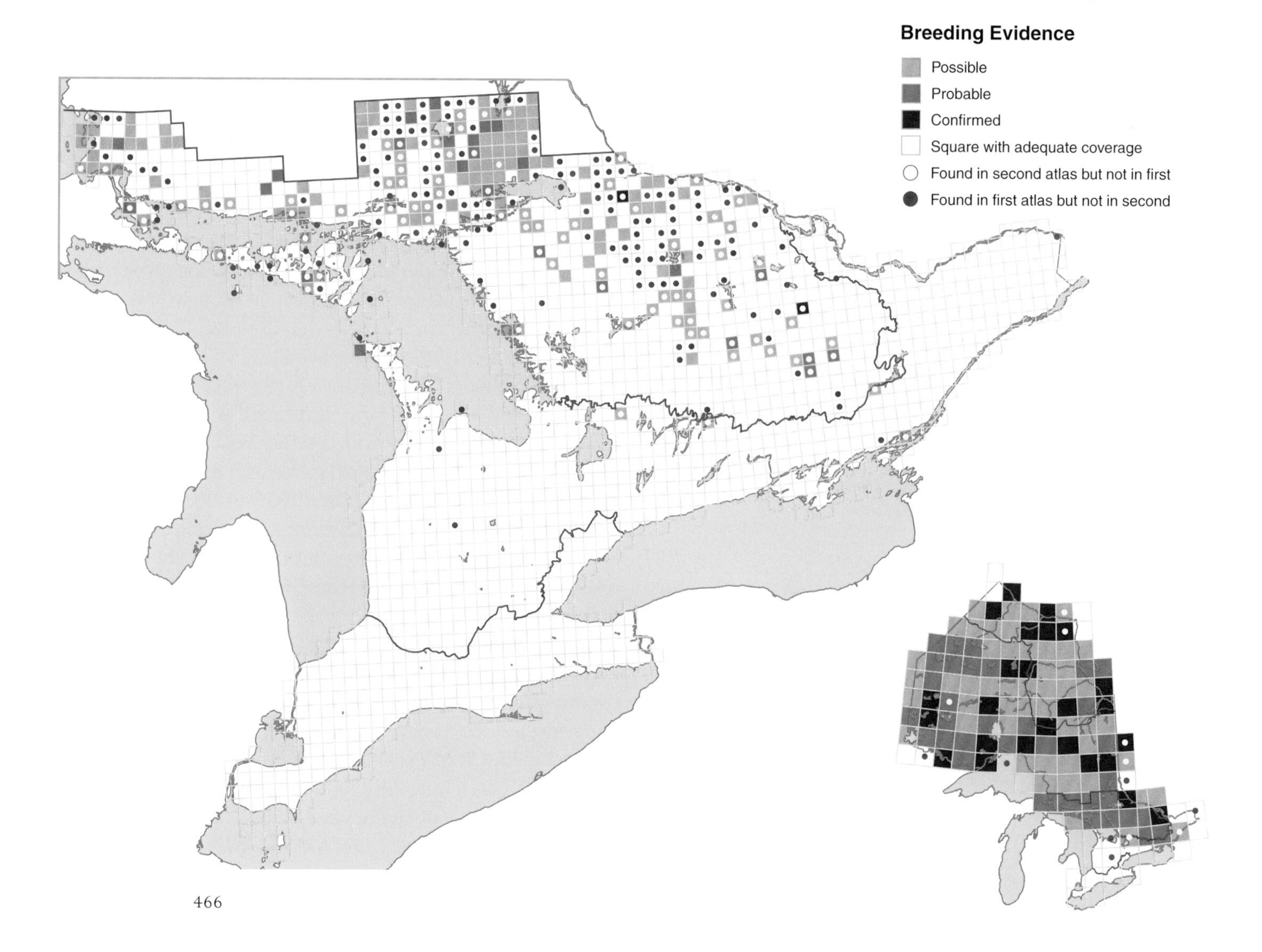

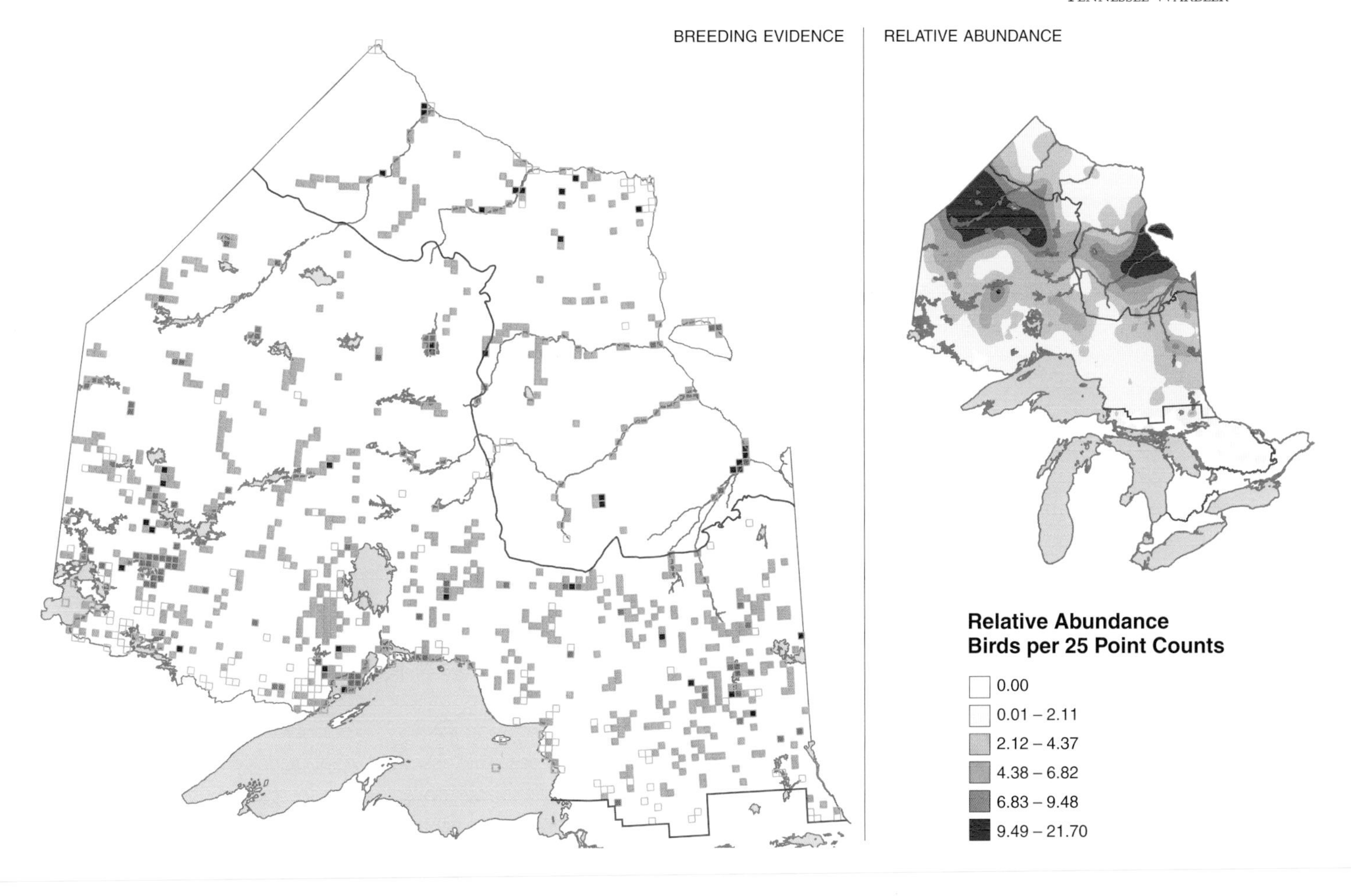

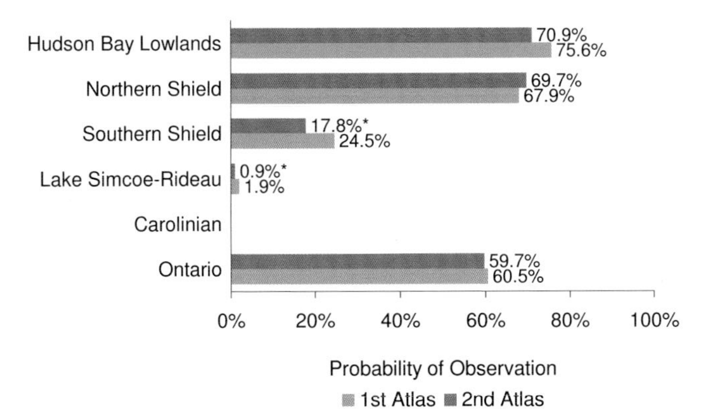

routes sample its core range, and the trend may simply reflect maturation of the forest on the sampled routes.

During this atlas, several Tennessee Warblers were recorded singing south of their usual breeding range up until late June. These birds likely were non-breeding stragglers or late migrants, which are well known throughout the migratory range of the species (Rimmer and McFarland 1998). It also tends to leave the breeding range early if it fails to breed successfully. Several Regional Coordinators noted the problem of determining whether singing birds found in their regions were breeders, late northbound migrants, or early southbound migrants.

Breeding biology: The nest of the Tennessee Warbler is extremely difficult to find. The well-concealed, finely woven cup is situated on the ground, usually embedded in a Sphagnum or lichen hummock at or near the base of a small tree or shrub, often shielded from above by low-hanging branches. The clutch ranges from three to eight eggs, with the larger clutches produced during Spruce Budworm outbreaks. Once the eggs have hatched, both adults feed the nestlings, although the female spends much more time doing so than the male (Holmes 1998). The young fledge after 11 or 12 days in the nest (Rimmer and McFarland 1998). Spraying for budworm control affects female brooding and foraging behaviour but not nestling survival or growth (Holmes 1998).

Only two atlas administrative regions reported confirmed breeding in the form of nests with eggs or young. Breeding was confirmed in just 4% of squares, generally through observation of adults carrying food or with fledged young. In 87% of squares, singing males or individuals observed in suitable habitat constituted the highest breeding evidence reported.

Abundance: The Tennessee Warbler is most abundant in the Hudson Bay Lowlands followed by the Northern Shield region, with averages of 4.4 and 2.3 birds/25 point counts, respectively. Densities exceeding 9.5 birds/25 point counts were found in the general area of Opasquia Prov. Park and Big Trout Lake in northwestern Ontario, and in the vicinity of Fort Albany and on Akimiski Island in James Bay in the northeast.

During outbreaks of Spruce Budworm, densities have been recorded to exceed 5 singing males/ha. In 10-25 year old regenerating coniferous forest cut-overs in Ontario, densities have ranged from 217 to 794 males/100 ha (Rimmer and McFarland 1998). It has been suggested that current populations probably exceed those of pre-settlement forests (Rimmer and McFarland 1998), but data on population trends, as well as knowledge of historical forest dynamics, are equivocal or limited.
– William J. Crins

Orange-crowned Warbler

Paruline verdâtre

Vermivora celata

Mark Peck

The Orange-crowned Warbler is primarily of western distribution, only one of its four subspecies (*V. c. celata*) breeding in eastern North America. It ranges from Alaska across boreal and subarctic Canada, including Ontario, east to Labrador (Sogge et al. 1994). In Ontario, it breeds in the northern third of the province, where its status has been described as uncommon (James 1991).

Throughout its range, the Orange-crowned Warbler utilizes a variety of scrubby, often second-growth deciduous and mixed habitats for breeding. In the east, it breeds in open deciduous and mixed woodlands with a dense, low shrub understorey; in riparian willow, poplar, and alder thickets; in burns regenerating in willow, birch, and alder; and in other open, scrubby areas. Habitats vary from dry to wet, though in Ontario most utilized habitats are wet. It appears to shun pure coniferous stands in Ontario as elsewhere in the east (Gauthier and Aubry 1996).

Distribution and population status: The breeding distribution and status of this warbler in Ontario historically were poorly known. The first provincial nest record was not reported until 1938 (Baillie 1960), and relatively few nesting records have subsequently been documented.

During the second atlas, breeding evidence was reported from most 100-km blocks north of 51° N, with scattered records in squares south to about 48° N in the vicinity of Timmins and the south end of Lake Nipigon, a pattern of distribution similar to that observed during the first atlas. While the geographical extent of its distribution remained essentially unchanged between atlases, there was a significant increase of 48% in the probability of observation of the species in the province as a whole, largely due to an increase of about 100% in the Hudson Bay Lowlands. Such an increase may be the result of northern atlassers being more familiar with the song during the second atlas than the first. No population trend data are available from other surveys, as this warbler's range is north of BBS routes, and it does not occur in

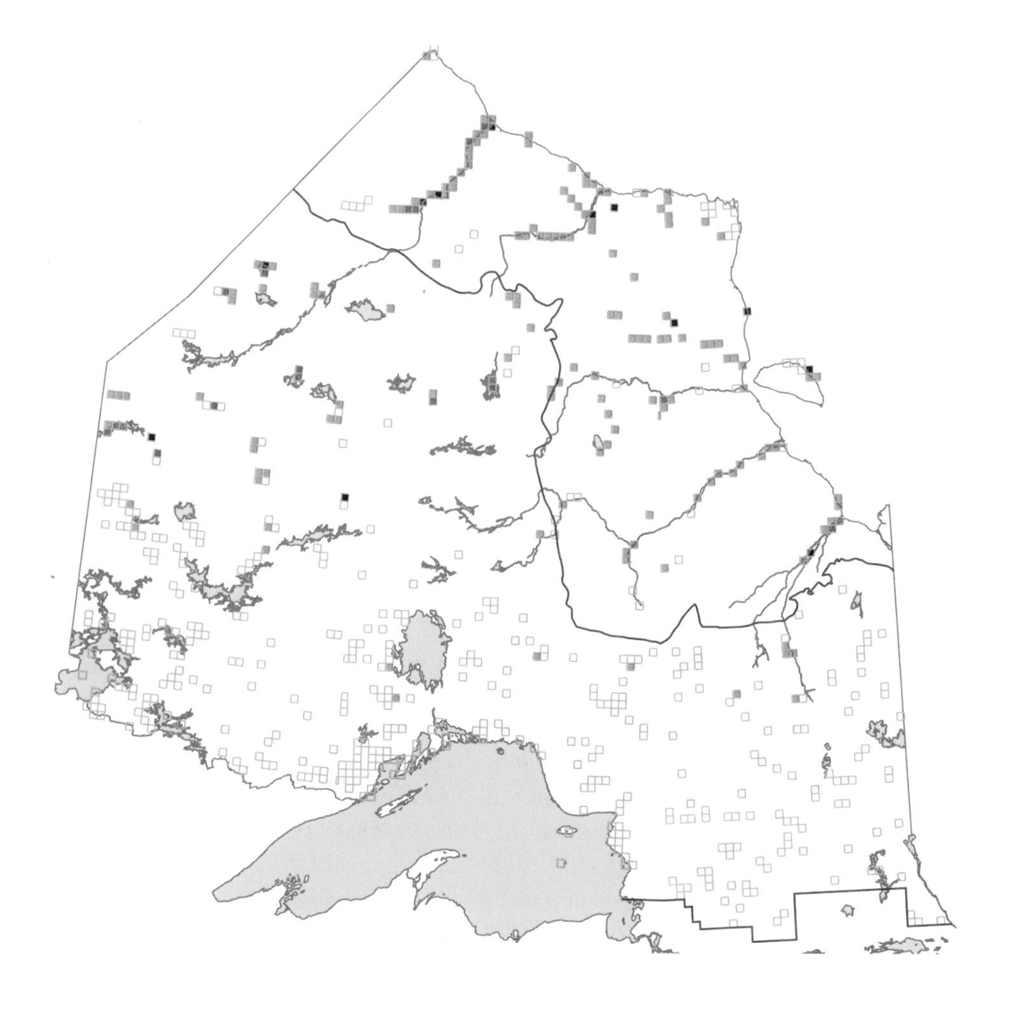

Breeding Evidence

- Possible
- Probable
- Confirmed
- Square with adequate coverage
- Found in second atlas but not in first
- Found in first atlas but not in second

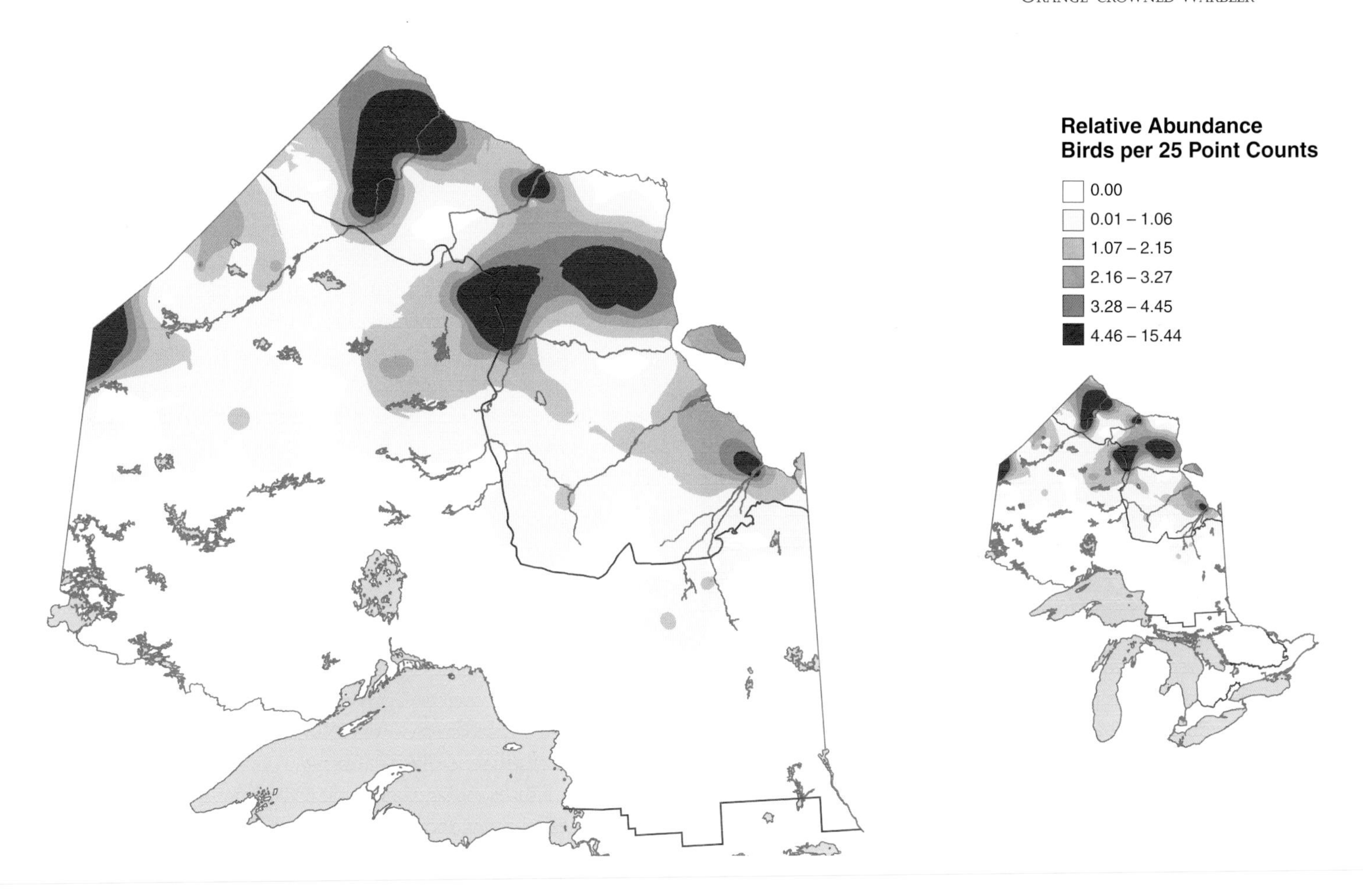

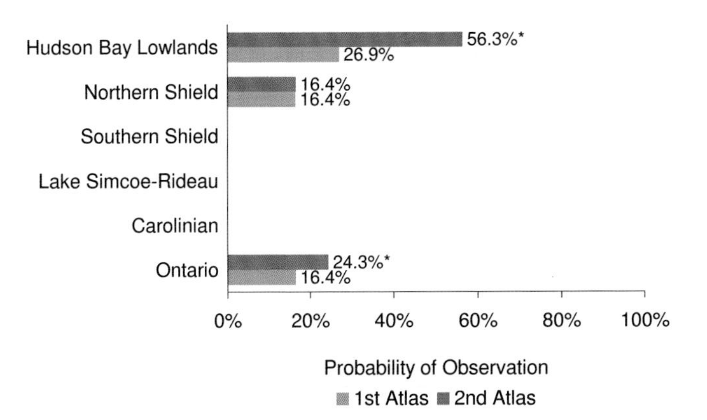

large numbers at Ontario's CMMN stations.

The Orange-crowned Warbler probably breeds in most squares in the Hudson Bay Lowlands north of 51° N. However, the breeding distribution south of 51° N appears to be generally discontinuous and local in nature. During the second atlas, evidence of possible breeding was documented south to Timmins, Longlac, and Little Sturgeon Lake in Thunder Bay Dist., where isolated singing males were recorded in extensive regenerating burns. Such occurrences may represent only transitory breeding events or unmated singing males, as the Orange-crowned Warbler is essentially unknown as a breeding species in the Thunder Bay area (N.G. Escott, pers. comm.).

Breeding biology: Little is known of the breeding biology of the Orange-crowned Warbler in Ontario. As at Churchill, Manitoba (Jehl 2004), arrival on breeding territories in the Hudson Bay Lowlands in Ontario likely occurs during the latter part of May. The song is a rather weak, two-parted trill of down-slurred notes fading at the end, somewhat reminiscent of the songs of the more common Palm Warbler and Dark-eyed Junco, with which it frequently shares its breeding habitat. Males typically sing from inconspicuous perches in the dense tops of trees and tall shrubs; detection of the species is therefore usually dependent on recognition of the song. Song frequency is greatest during territorial establishment prior to courtship and less frequent from the onset of nest building through the remainder of the breeding season (Sogge et al. 1994), so that the species can easily be overlooked. Most breeding evidence (85%) was of possible breeding, primarily through the detection of singing males. Nests, like those of other *Vermivora* warblers, are located on or near the ground, well concealed in moss and by overhanging vegetation and are difficult to find. Breeding was confirmed in just 7% of squares, and evidence mostly consisted of adults carrying food. Prior to the atlas, only two nests had been documented in Ontario. During the second atlas, a third provincial nest record was established at Peawanuck in Kenora Dist. (ONRS data).

Abundance: The Orange-crowned Warbler is found in greatest numbers in Ontario within its core range in the Hudson Bay Lowlands. The abundance map shows areas of highest abundance, above 4.5 birds/25 point counts, along portions of the Severn, Winisk, Ekwan, and Moose Rivers, likely coinciding with extensive areas of the preferred aspen-willow riparian thicket and woodland habitat. Given the relatively infrequent song and the similarity of its song to other more common species, the abundance of Orange-crowned Warbler may be somewhat underestimated. – *Donald A. Sutherland*

Nashville Warbler

Paruline à joues grises

Vermivora ruficapilla

Mark Peck

The Nashville Warbler breeds across much of central and southeastern Canada from Saskatchewan to the Maritime Provinces, south into the northeastern US. A disjunct population of a different subspecies breeds in southern British Columbia south to California. The Nashville Warbler is something of a generalist, with an ability to use a wide variety of habitats. In much of the Canadian Shield, its preferred habitat appears to be open second-growth mixed and coniferous forests, predominantly Black Spruce, and especially those with a shrubby understorey. It has also been known to breed in old-field habitat, cedar-spruce swamps, open peatlands, and wet coniferous woods (Peck and James 1987; Williams 1996a). It winters in Mexico and Guatemala and is one of the earlier wood-warblers to arrive in Ontario in the spring.

Distribution and population status: The Nashville Warbler is a widespread breeding species throughout much of Ontario, with a 67% probability of observation in the province as a whole, a percentage among the highest of all the wood-warblers. Evidence was obtained from the southernmost parts of the Carolinian region north to the coasts of Hudson and James Bays. However, it is rare in the Carolinian region, with a probability of observation of only 2%. Farther north, it becomes progressively more common, with the highest probability of observation in the Southern and Northern Shield regions at 93% and 80%, respectively. In the Hudson Bay Lowlands, the distribution was also widespread but much more sparse at 39%.

Although the overall pattern of distribution is similar between the two atlases, there was a significant 50% increase in the probability of observation. Virtually all of this increase was in the Hudson Bay Lowlands and Northern Shield, where the species was recorded in at least 20 more 100-km blocks

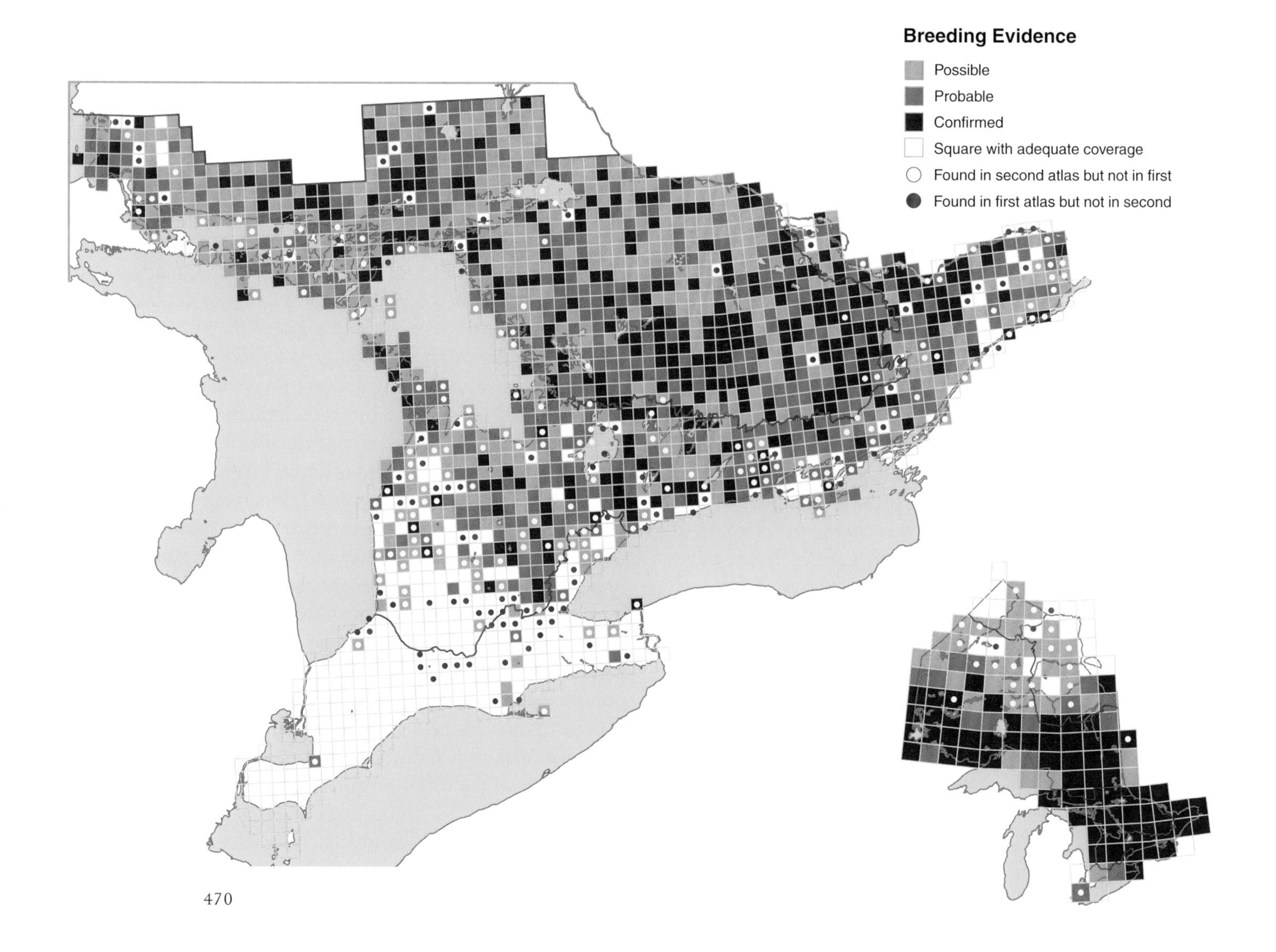

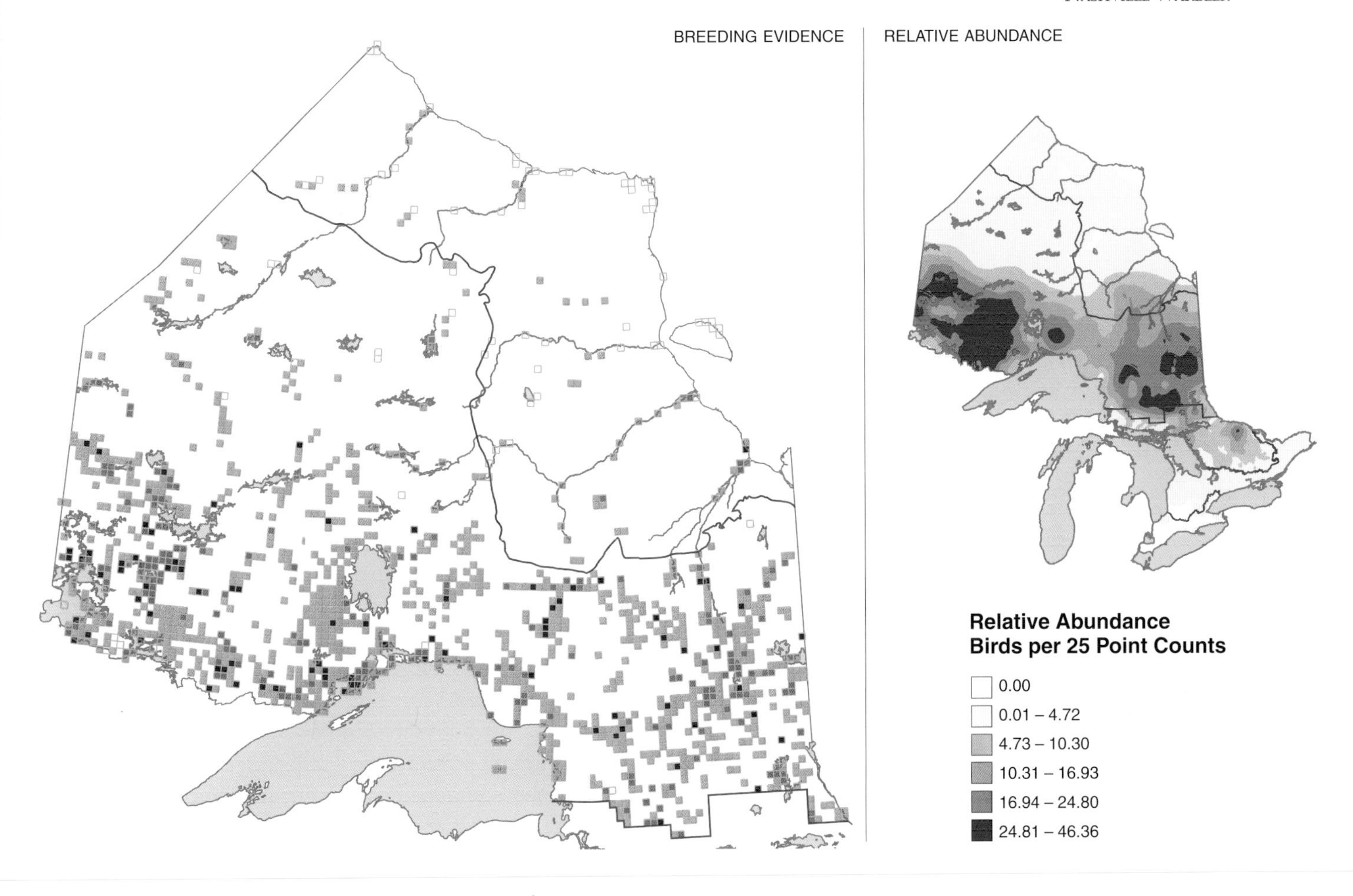

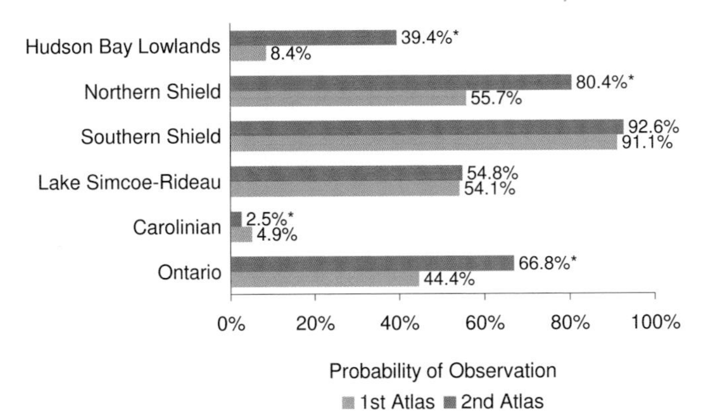

than in the first atlas, most of them in the interior of the province. The reasons for such substantial increases are unclear. In the Northern Shield, an increase in younger forest across most of the region as a result of logging may have increased the amount of available habitat for the species, though this is not a factor in the Hudson Bay Lowlands. Exogenous factors such as climate change or changes in habitat on wintering grounds cannot be excluded.

Numbers of the Nashville Warbler appear to be stable or slightly increasing. BBS data for Ontario show no significant changes; however, BBS coverage is low or non-existent in the area of the province where atlas data suggest the population is increasing. CMMN data for LPBO indicate a small but significant increase in migrants since the start of monitoring in 1961 (Crewe 2006).

Breeding biology: The Nashville Warbler's song is distinctive and carries well. It is fairly easily identified, similar to and likely to be confused only with some dialects of the Yellow-rumped Warbler. Singing males and birds on territory constituted the majority of breeding evidence for this species. Breeding is often difficult to confirm. Nests are built on the ground and are generally well concealed under a shrub or fern, and females tend to be inconspicuous, remaining in the low vegetation near the nest. The difficulty of finding nests is evidenced by the fact that only 28 squares in all of Ontario had evidence in the form of nests. Both parents participate in feeding young, and adults carrying food was the most frequently reported evidence of confirmed breeding.

Abundance: The area of greatest abundance for the Nashville Warbler occurs across a broad band covering the southern half of the Northern Shield region and the northern part of the Southern Shield region, from about 45° N to 50° N. In the Northern Shield, densities averaged almost 20 birds/25 point counts, with over 24.8 birds/25 point counts in southern Thunder Bay, Rainy River, and southern Kenora Districts in northwestern Ontario, as well as in a broad band from eastern Lake Superior east to the Québec border. In the Southern Shield, densities were much lower, with an average of about 8.6 birds/25 point counts. Higher than average densities in this region were noted in the Algonquin Highlands in northeastern Algonquin Prov. Park. South of the Canadian Shield and in the Hudson Bay Lowlands region, average densities were fewer than 2 birds/25 point counts. – *Peter L. McLaren*

Northern Parula

Paruline à collier

Parula americana

Ron Ridout

The Northern Parula is not only one of the smallest of the wood-warblers but is also one of the least studied and least familiar to Ontario birders. It is relatively uncommon and tends to frequent the higher canopy of wet forest habitats that can be difficult to survey. It breeds throughout the eastern half of North America, from Manitoba east to the Maritime Provinces and south through the US to the coast of the Gulf of Mexico. In the northern part of its range, its breeding habitat is typically mature coniferous and mixed swamp and bog forests, particularly those with abundant growth of tree lichens of the genus *Usnea* (Moldenhauer and Regelski 1996). However, in Algonquin Prov. Park and a few other areas, it has also been reported to use dry pine or hemlock forests in which *Usnea* is rare or absent, particularly forests near lakes or other water bodies (R.G. Tozer, S.J. O'Donnell, pers. comm.). The parula winters primarily in areas bordering the Gulf of Mexico, including the Caribbean Islands, the Gulf States, and southern Mexico (Moldenhauer and Regelski 1996).

Distribution and population status: The distribution of the Northern Parula extends generally from about Belleville and Barrie north and west to Kapuskasing and Dryden, with scattered records north to the southern Hudson Bay Lowlands, and in the southern Lake Simcoe-Rideau and Carolinian regions, but only rarely and perhaps irregularly in the latter. Its core distribution comprises the Southern Shield and the southern portions of the Northern Shield, north to about Lake Abitibi through Woodland Caribou Prov. Park. It tends to be patchy in distribution, however, with just a 29% probability of observation in the Southern Shield and 26% in the Northern Shield. It is absent from most of the agricultural areas to the south, and the southernmost confirmed breeding evidence was recorded on the northern Bruce Peninsula and in Muskoka

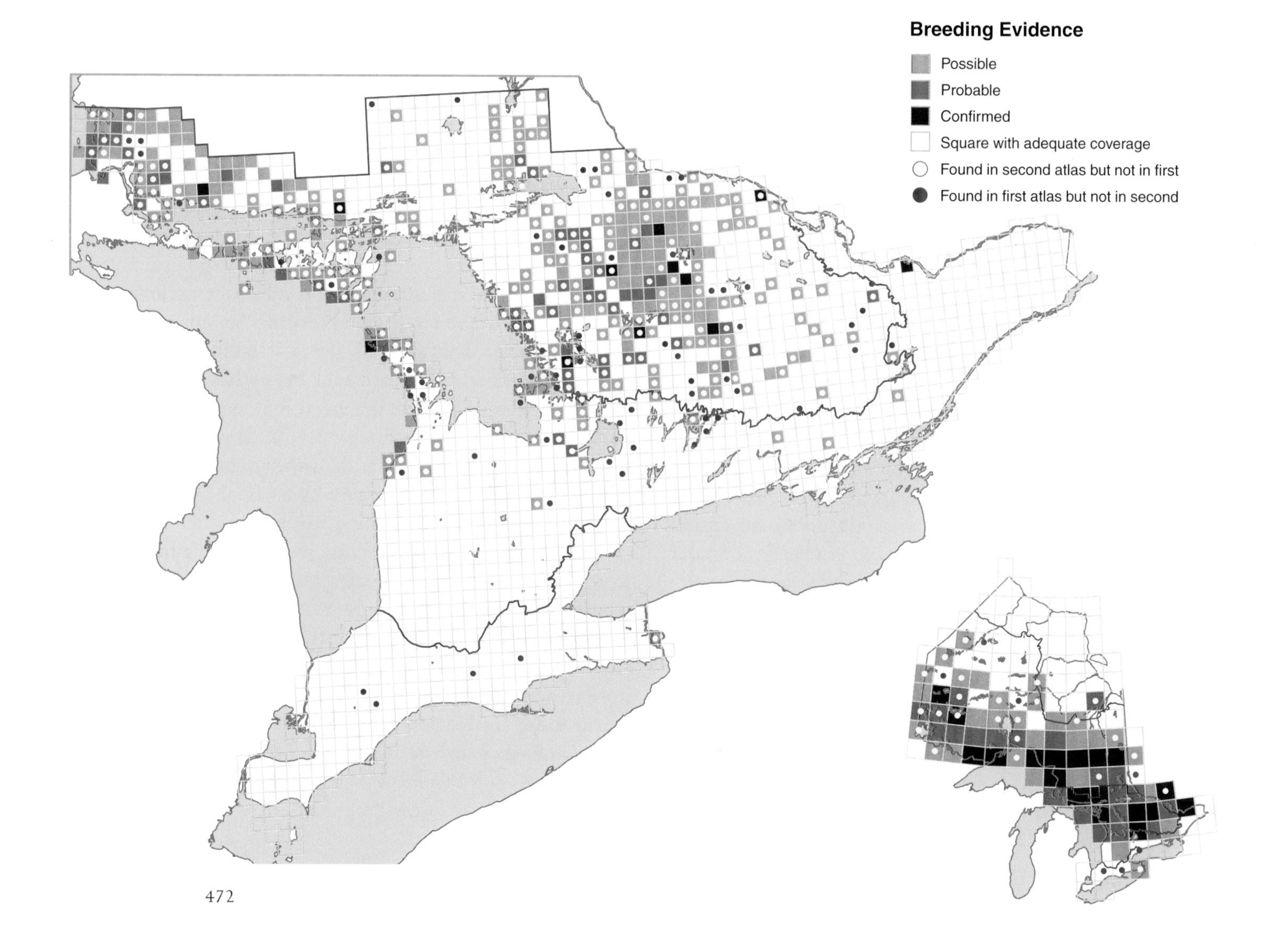

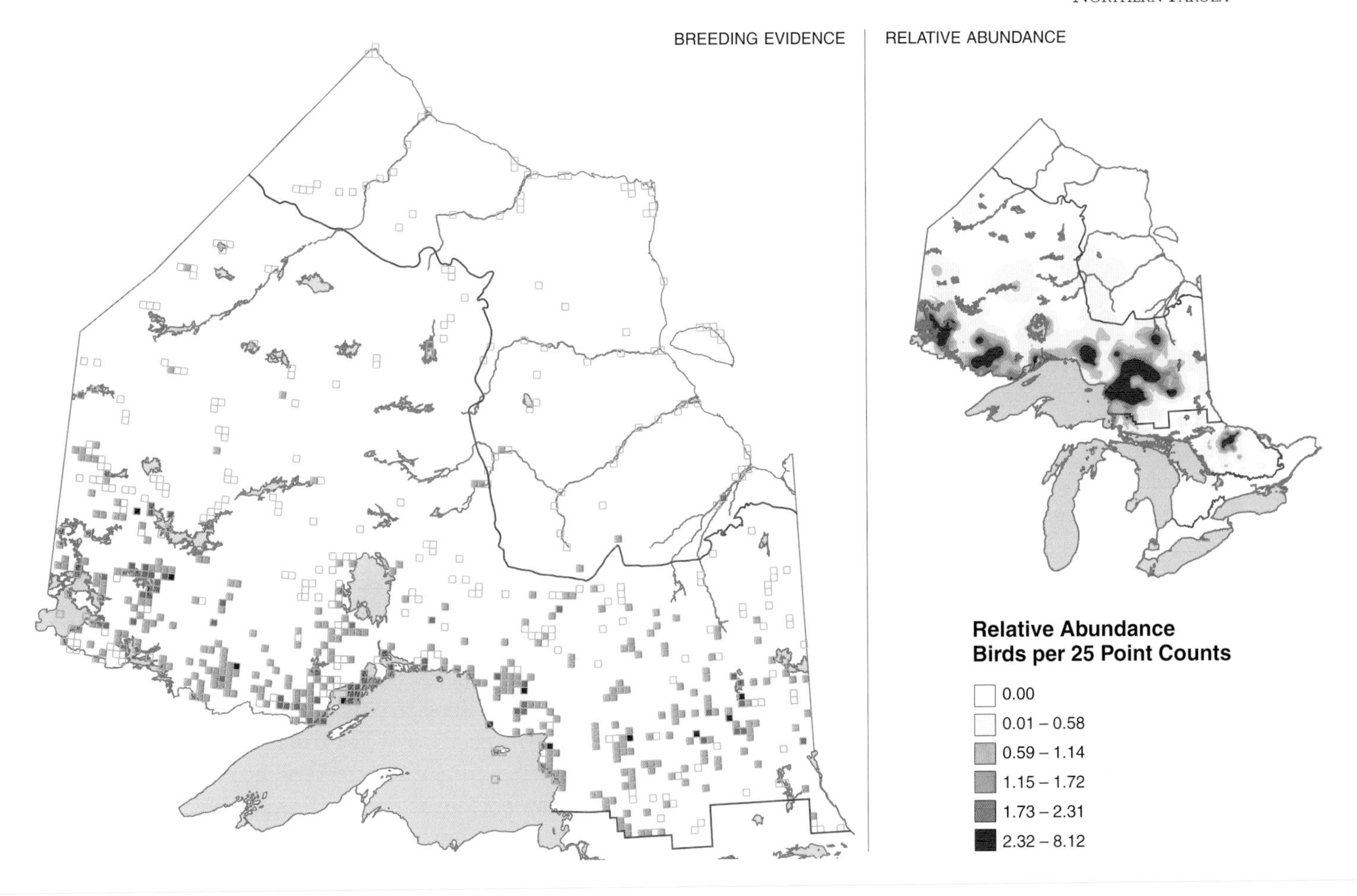

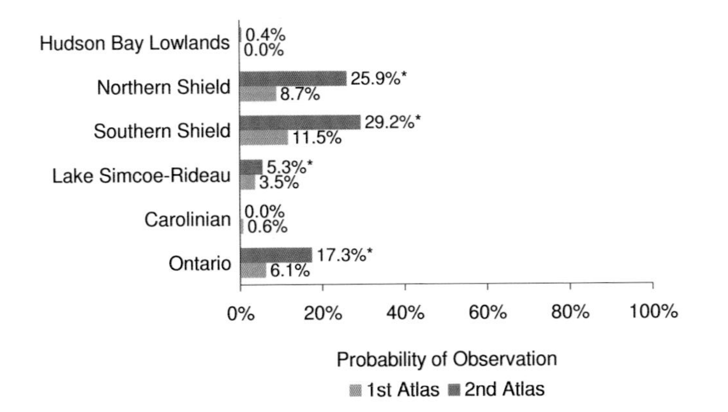

Dist. In the Hudson Bay Lowlands, breeding was not confirmed north of about 50° N, although singing males were heard substantially north of that line.

Although the overall pattern of distribution of the Northern Parula is similar between the two atlases, there were significant increases in the province as a whole and in the Northern and Southern Shield regions, with the probability of observation more than doubling in both regions. Areas where increases were particularly noticeable include Manitoulin Island and the area north of Lake Huron, and the area surrounding Algonquin Prov. Park. However, caution should be used when interpreting these data. Although it is possible that the species is in fact becoming more widespread, local increases may reflect differences in coverage between atlases. BBS data indicate no significant change since 1968 in Ontario (Downes et al. 2005), and neither BBS nor migration monitoring data from TCBO (Crewe 2006) suggest any increase in Northern Parula populations since the first atlas.

Breeding biology: Although it does occur in habitats without tree lichens, the Northern Parula prefers to build its nest in *Usnea*. The nest is usually well hidden in a clump of *Usnea* at the outer end of a branch anywhere from 2 to 30 m above the ground, though usually below 6 m. Only three nests were found, in Algonquin Prov. Park, on the Bruce Peninsula, and on the eastern shore of Lake Superior. In fact, only eight nests have been found in Ontario since the first nest for the province was discovered in 1943.

The Northern Parula was among the most difficult of all species for which to obtain confirmed breeding evidence. Although the young beg actively and loudly after fledging (Moldenhauer and Regelski 1996), few atlassers would have spent much time in the preferred wet coniferous forests. Breeding was confirmed in only 3% of the squares in which the species was found, one of the lowest rates among passerines. Most records (81%) were of possible breeding, mostly singing males.

Abundance: As well as having patchy distribution, the Northern Parula is not particularly common in those areas where it does occur. Even in the centre of its distribution, the Southern Shield region and the southern part of the Northern Shield, densities averaged less than 1 bird/25 point counts. Areas of higher density, over 2.3 birds/25 point counts, were noted in the Algonquin Highlands, east of Lake Superior, and in the Thunder Bay-Kenora area. These areas all contain extensive amounts of mature coniferous forest and conditions suitable for an abundant growth of *Usnea*. – *Peter L. McLaren*

Yellow Warbler

Paruline jaune

Dendroica petechia

George K. Peck

For residents in both town and country, the Yellow Warbler is perhaps the most familiar wood-warbler. It has the most widespread breeding range of all the wood-warblers, nesting across much of North America from Alaska to Newfoundland and south to Mexico. Although typically associated with riparian environments, it nests in a wide variety of habitats, most commonly in moist deciduous thickets and in disturbed and early successional habitats, including suburban yards, overgrown fields and pastures, power transmission corridors, and river edges. It tends to avoid only open grassland and denser forested habitats (Lowther et al. 1999).

Distribution and population status: The Yellow Warbler is one of Ontario's most common and widespread species, with a probability of observation in Ontario of 71%. It has been reported from every 100-km block in the province during one or the other of the atlases and is most widespread in the Carolinian and the Lake Simcoe-Rideau regions, where its probability of observation is 97% and 93%, respectively. It is also common in the Southern Shield region, although it tends to be absent from the squares in the heavily wooded areas in and around Algonquin Prov. Park, and from the squares in the most northerly parts of the region. In northern Ontario, it is found primarily in the vicinity of towns and villages and in the shrub habitat along the coast and rivers, particularly in the Northern Shield region where the habitat is more forested.

Although no significant changes between atlases were noted in most regions of Ontario, the Yellow Warbler did show a significant increase (14%) in the probability of observation in the Hudson Bay Lowlands. The reasons for this increase, if real, are unclear, and it may be an artifact of more efficient surveying in the region. BBS data indicate no significant changes for the species for Ontario since 1968 (Downes et al. 2005), although those data are limited to the portions of the province accessible by road. CMMN data for LPBO show highly signifi-

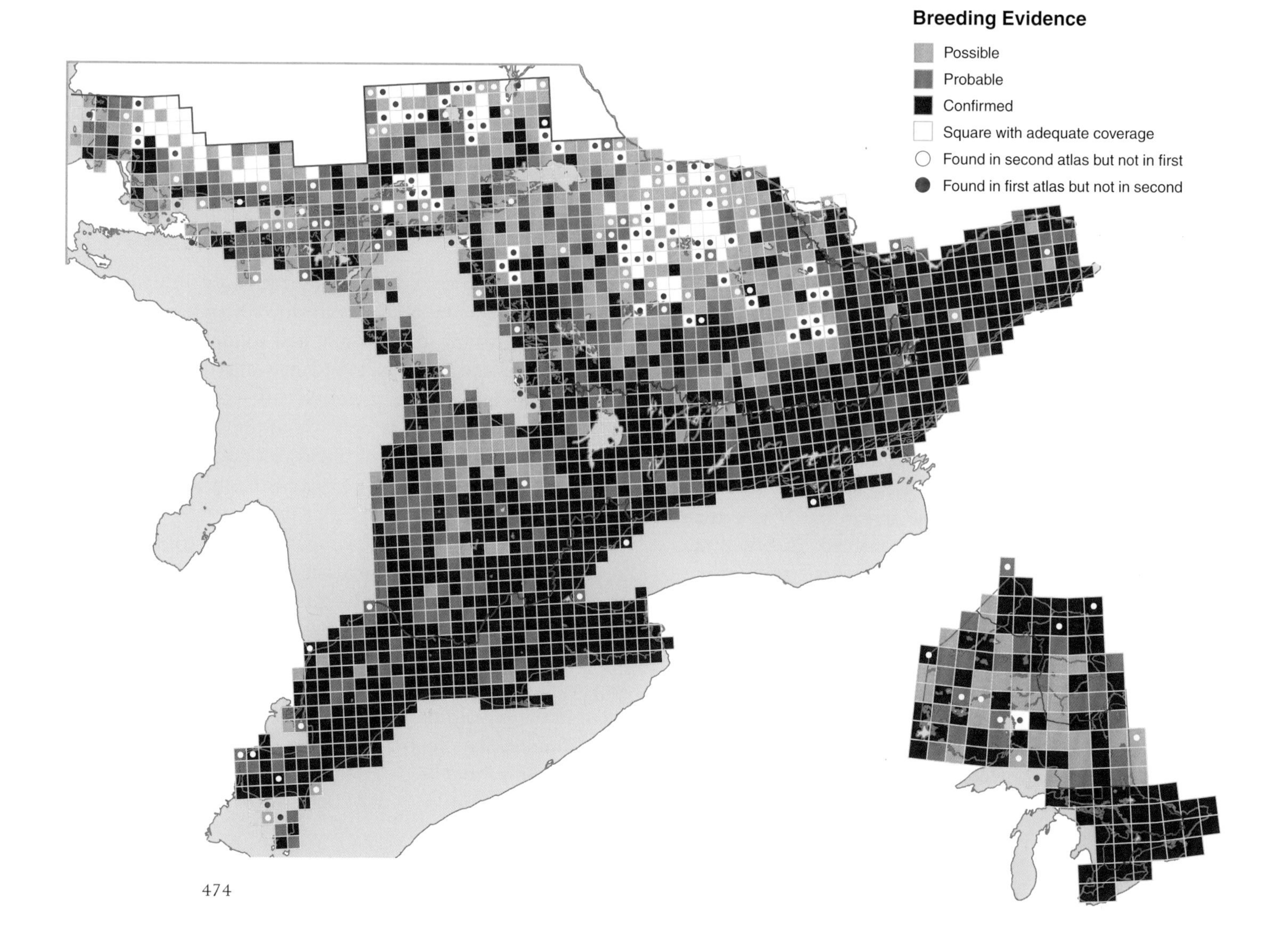

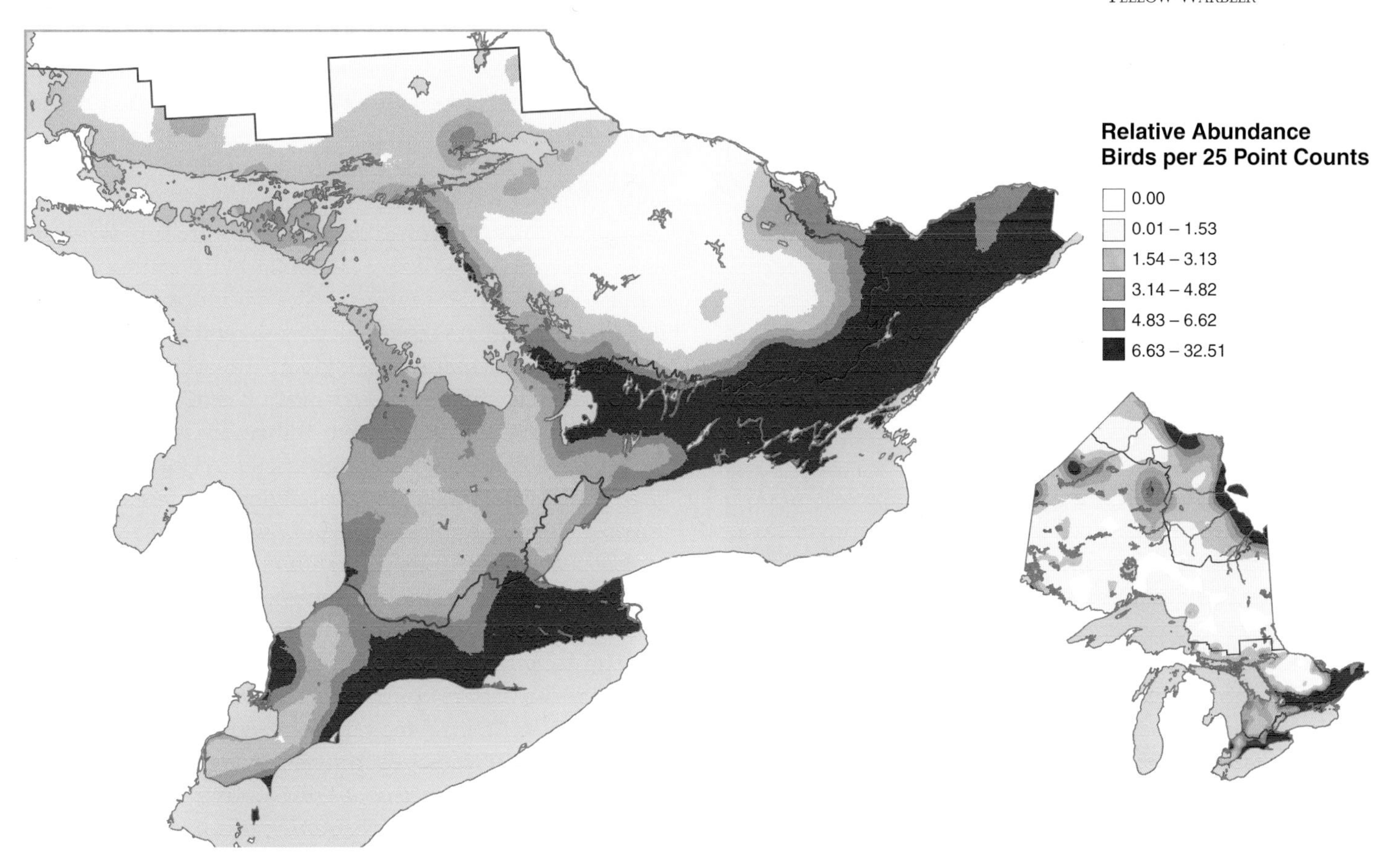

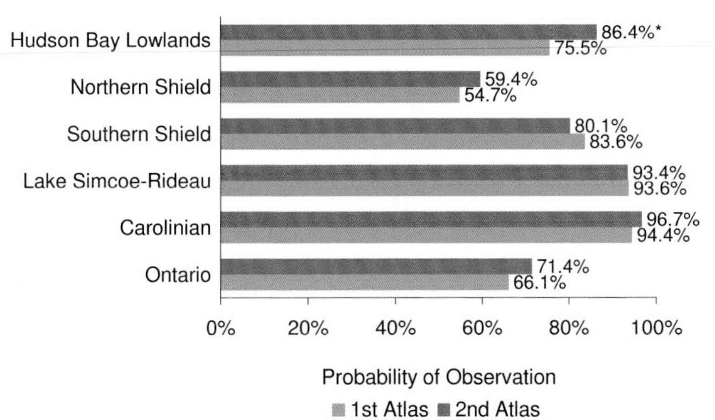

cant increases since monitoring began in 1961, but less so since 1994, and data for TCBO show no significant increases in the last decade (Crewe 2006). In the Haliburton area, the Regional Coordinator felt that numbers had actually declined since the first atlas and that the species was becoming more difficult to find. If this is in fact the case, it may reflect the succession and maturation of abandoned farmland during that period in the Southern Shield region.

Breeding biology: The nest of the Yellow Warbler is generally situated within 2 m of the ground, most often in shrubs or young trees. Both parents make frequent trips to feed the young in the nest and after they fledge. As well, the species is a target of the parasitic Brown-headed Cowbird, and cowbird fledglings can be very vocal, which would draw attention to the family. Consequently, it is relatively easy to confirm nesting, and, indeed, breeding was confirmed in 41% of the squares in which the species was recorded. Nests with eggs or young were found in 40 of the 47 atlas administrative regions, and confirmed breeding was recorded in all 47. These values are among the highest for all the wood-warblers. Probable breeding, primarily in the form of pairs or territorial males, was reported in another 22% of the squares in which the species was reported.

Abundance: The Yellow Warbler is highly visible and sings regularly throughout the day. Thus, it should be easily detected during point counts where present. Densities average over 8 birds/25 point counts in the Carolinian and Lake Simcoe-Rideau regions, where it is the most abundant of the wood-warblers. The species is particularly abundant south of the Shield, with densities of over 6.6 birds/25 point counts from the Niagara Peninsula southwest along Lake Erie to the Rondeau Prov. Park area and from Lake Simcoe east to the Québec border. Lower densities were observed in the more agricultural and urban areas of southwestern Ontario and the more forested Algonquin Highlands. Densities are also very high in the coastal areas of the Hudson Bay Lowlands, with an average density of almost 6 birds/25 point counts for the region as a whole. Although the species was reported in nearly all 100-km blocks in the province, there were large areas across the Northern Shield where no Yellow Warblers were recorded on point counts. This reflects the low densities at which the species occurs in the heavily wooded Boreal Forest.
– Peter L. McLaren

Chestnut-sided Warbler

Paruline à flancs marron

Dendroica pensylvanica

The Chestnut-sided Warbler is a summer resident throughout much of eastern North America, from Alberta east to the Maritime Provinces south through the northeastern US and down through the Appalachian Mountains to northwest Georgia. It winters in Central America from southern Mexico to Panama (Richardson and Brauning 1995).

The Chestnut-sided Warbler is a striking example of the relationship between birds and their environment. Early ornithologists such as Audubon and Wilson rarely saw this species during their collecting in the early 1800s (Bent 1953). However, since then, it has become one of the most common and widespread wood-warblers of the northeast, a product of successional habitat growth following the return of abandoned fields to young forest. Its preferred breeding habitat includes shrubby second-growth deciduous woodlands, including forest edges, abandoned fields, and small clearings. In northern Ontario, it is also regularly found in areas where the forest is in the process of regeneration after fire or logging.

Distribution and population status: The Chestnut-sided Warbler is a widespread breeding resident in Ontario north to about 51° N. The centre of its distribution in the province is the Southern Shield, where it was reported in virtually all of the surveyed squares. It is also a common breeder south of the Shield, particularly in the Lake Simcoe-Rideau region, but is less widespread in the Carolinian, which is reflected by the lower probability of observation in that region. Similarly, the probability of observation for the species decreases as one moves north from the core of its distribution.

The species' pattern of distribution in Ontario is similar to that noted in the first atlas, but with more records in the far north. Between atlases, the probability of observation of the species significantly increased by 14% in the Lake Simcoe-Rideau region. In the Hudson Bay Lowlands, the probability of

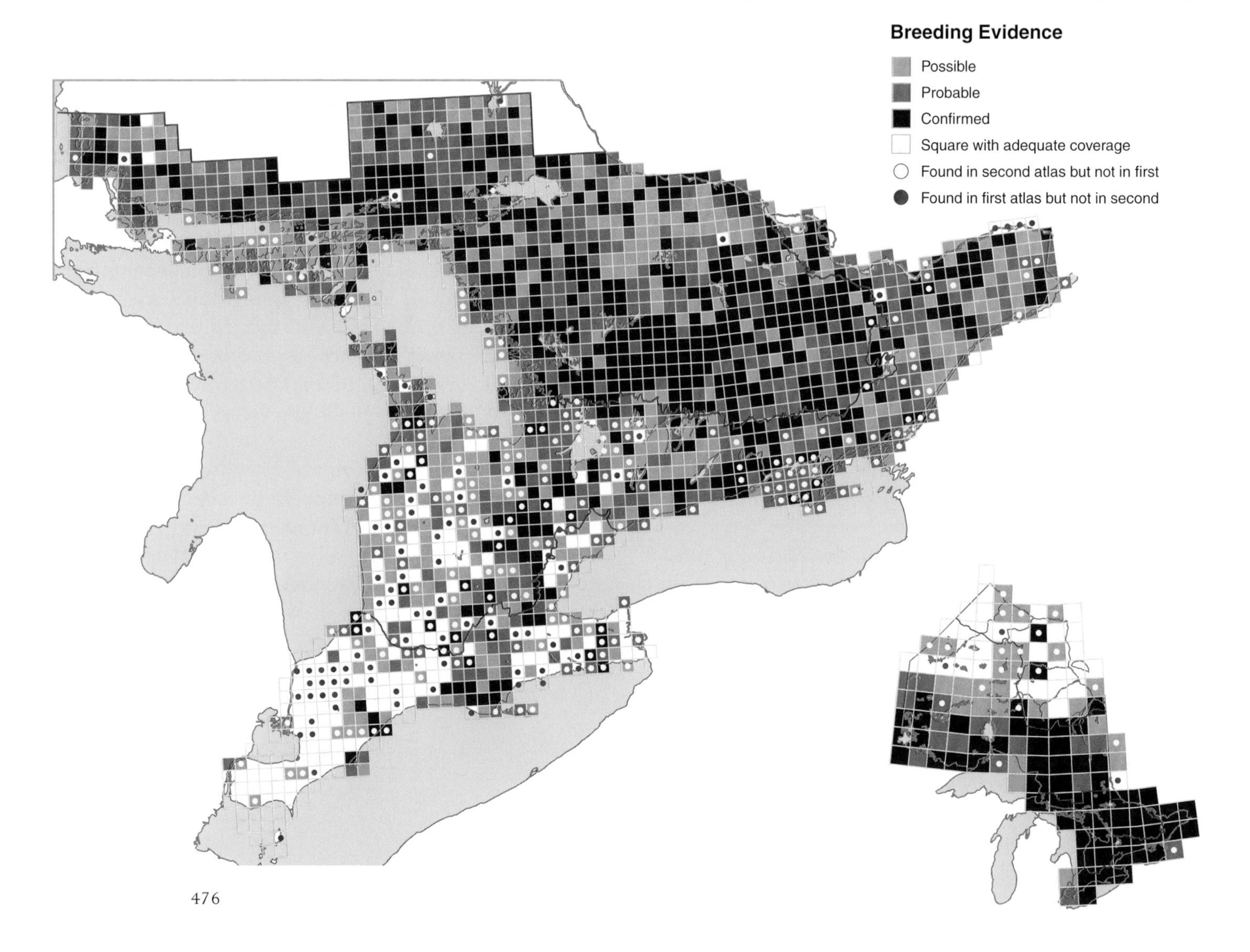

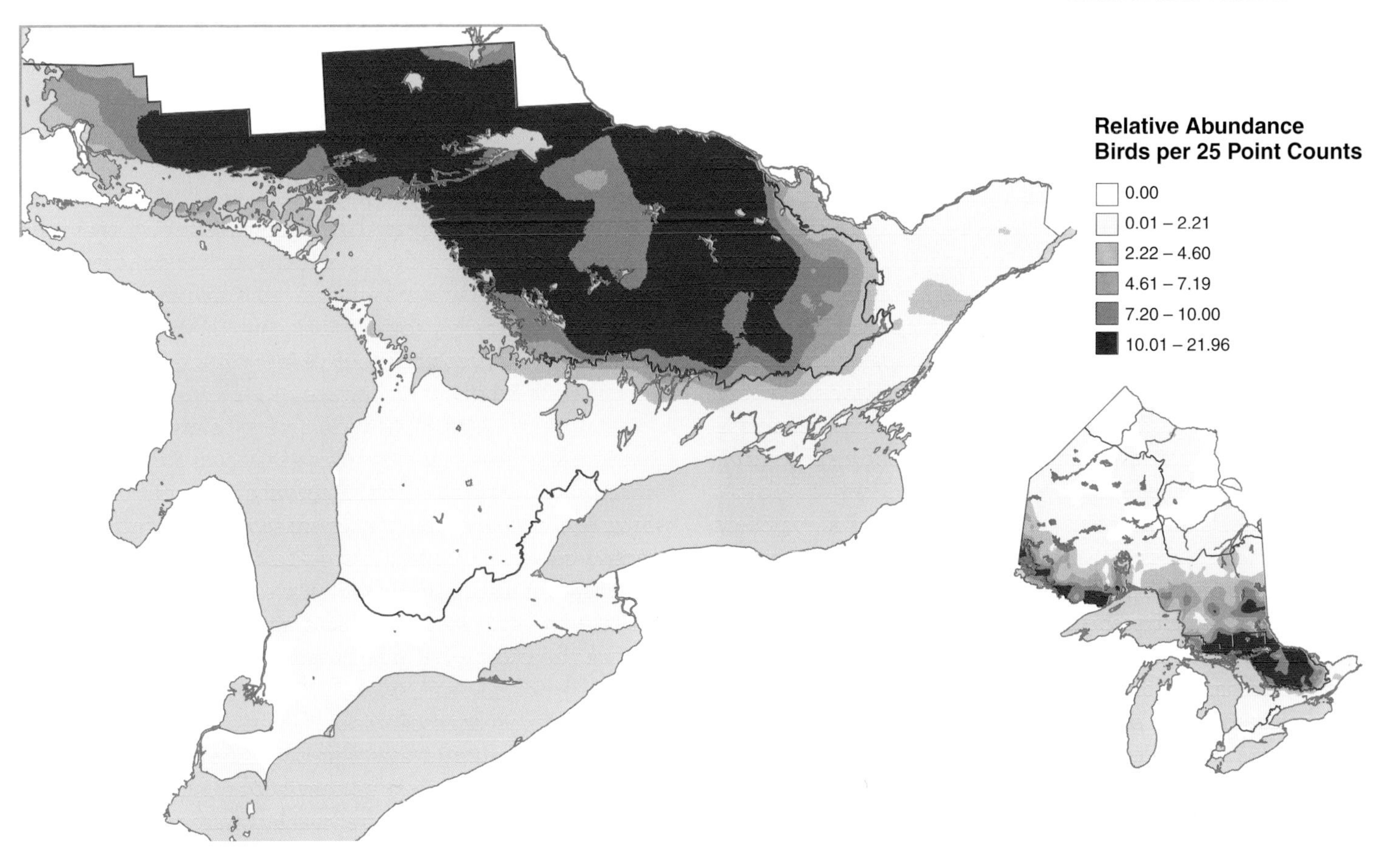

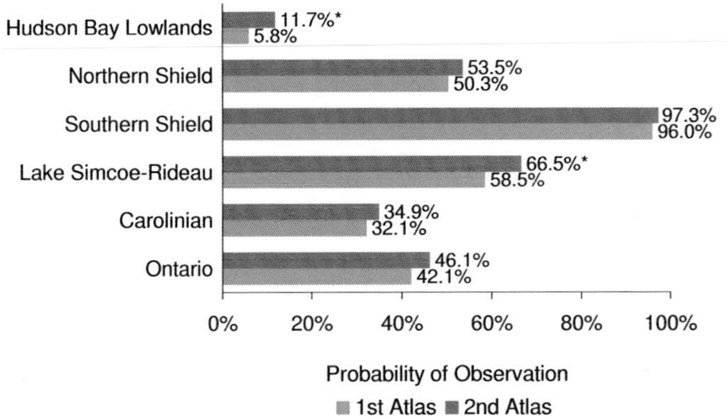

observation doubled between atlases, and breeding evidence was recorded in 11 100-km blocks, compared to one in the first atlas. Given that breeding was confirmed in two of these 100-km blocks, the expansion is probably real, but the extent to which numbers may have been enhanced by greater atlassing effort or efficiency is not known. The species is relatively uncommon north of the road network and human habitation that provide much of the shrubby second growth habitat it requires in the forest-dominated north. This suggests that the species may not be as common in the far north as the breeding evidence map implies, since much of the atlassing in this region took place in the vicinity of communities, roadways, and riverine habitats. It is most likely absent or very thinly distributed away from these habitats in large areas of northern Ontario, as shown on the relative abundance map.

BBS data for Ontario show no significant change from 1968 to 2005 (Downes et al. 2005). However, migration monitoring data from LPBO have shown a significant increase in numbers of Chestnut-sided Warblers since 1961 (Crewe 2006). The succession of abandoned farmland in central parts of southern Ontario and the resulting increase in second-growth and edge habitat may have contributed to this increase.

Breeding biology: The territory of the Chestnut-sided Warbler is quite small, ranging from 0.4 to 1.1 ha (Richardson and Brauning 1995), and its nest is generally located in a shrub within 1-2 metres of the ground (McLaren 1975; Peck and James 1987). Although nests may be difficult to locate in the dense second-growth habitat the species prefers, adults may be observed carrying food, and females will give conspicuous distraction displays upon the approach of a predator. Fledged young can also be quite vocal and easy to locate. These characteristics make the species readily amenable to confirmation of breeding, and indeed, probable or confirmed breeding evidence was recorded in over 51% of squares reporting this species. Confirmed breeding was generally in the form of fledged young or adults carrying food.

Abundance: Densities of the Chestnut-sided Warbler were highest throughout the Southern Shield region and in the Northern Shield region from Rainy River to Thunder Bay, as well as near Kirkland Lake. In the Southern Shield, the average density was 12.3 birds/25 point counts, the second highest of any of the warblers that are common in this region, behind only the Ovenbird. To the north and south of these areas, densities are much lower, presumably due to lower forest cover in the south, a lower deciduous forest component in the north, and the reduction in suitable deciduous edge habitat. – *Peter L. McLaren*

Magnolia Warbler

Paruline à tête cendrée

Dendroica magnolia

Jim Richards

One of the most brilliantly coloured and best-known of the wood-warblers, the Magnolia Warbler is a breeding resident across much of central and southeastern Canada, from Yukon and northern British Columbia east to Newfoundland. It is also found in the northeastern US, east from Minnesota and south through the Appalachian Mountains to Virginia. It winters in Central America and the West Indies (Hall 1994). The Magnolia Warbler is a species of mixed and coniferous forests, particularly favouring edge habitat and natural openings. Its single strongest habitat requirement appears to be young coniferous growth (McLaren 1975). Consequently, it is also regularly found in old fields, hydro rights-of-way, and blowdowns with young regenerating forests.

Distribution and population status: In Ontario, the Magnolia Warbler is a widespread breeding resident. Historical accounts indicate that it was once a common species through much of Ontario (Macoun and Macoun 1909). During the second atlas, the probability of observation was 77% in the province as a whole, and it was reported in all of the atlas administrative regions with the exception of Essex and Chatham-Kent in the intensively agricultural southwest. It is uncommon in much of the Carolinian region, where few young coniferous forests exist, with only a 3% probability of observation and confirmed nesting only in the Long Point area. However, it is more common to the north, especially in the Southern and Northern Shield regions where the probability of observation was 89% in both regions, and also in the Hudson Bay Lowlands and Lake Simcoe-Rideau regions, at 66% and 39%, respectively.

The general pattern of distribution of the Magnolia Warbler documented in this atlas is essentially the same as that found in the first. However, there were significant increases in the probability of observation in all regions except the Hudson Bay Lowlands, with the largest proportional increases in the

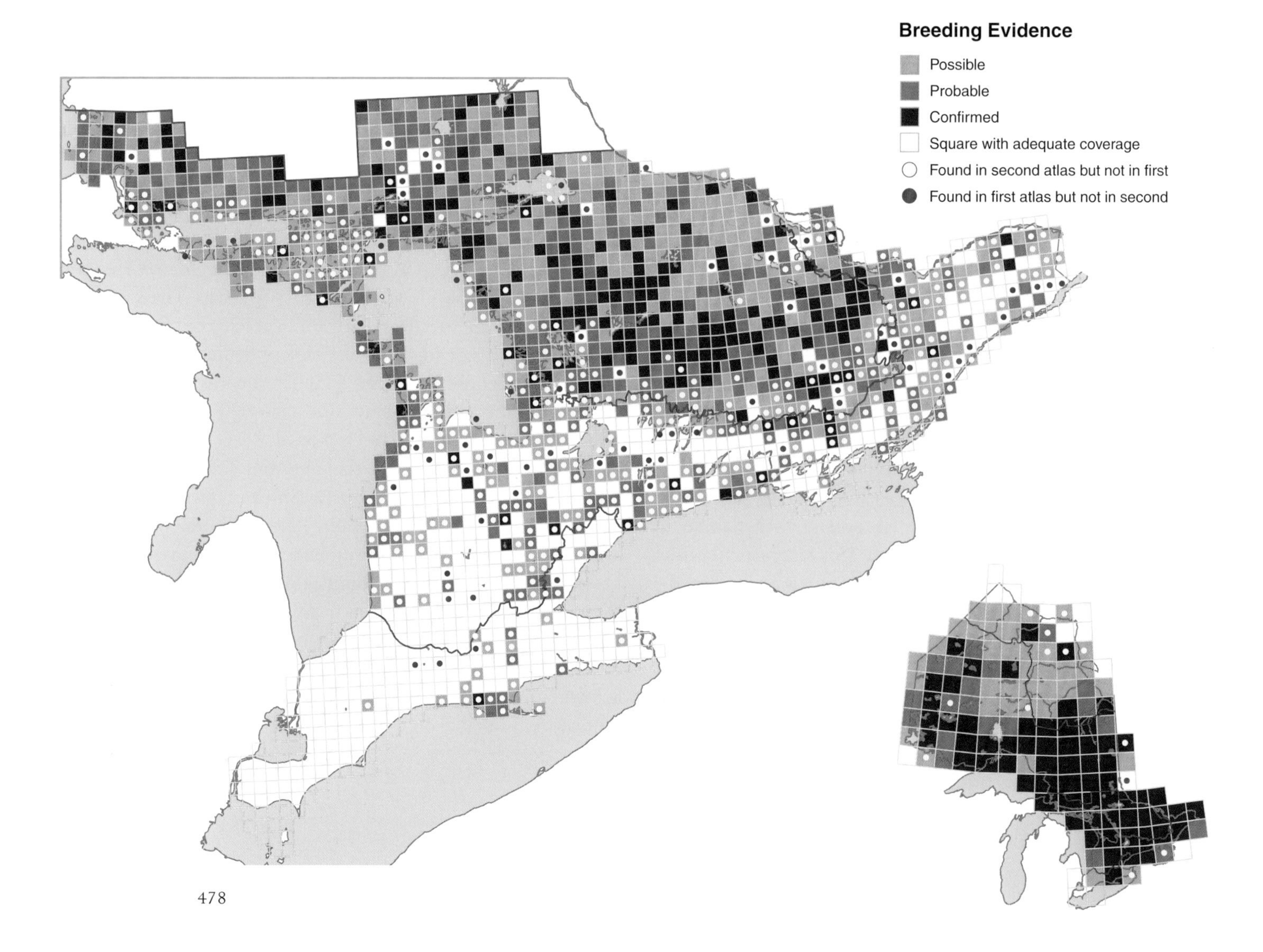

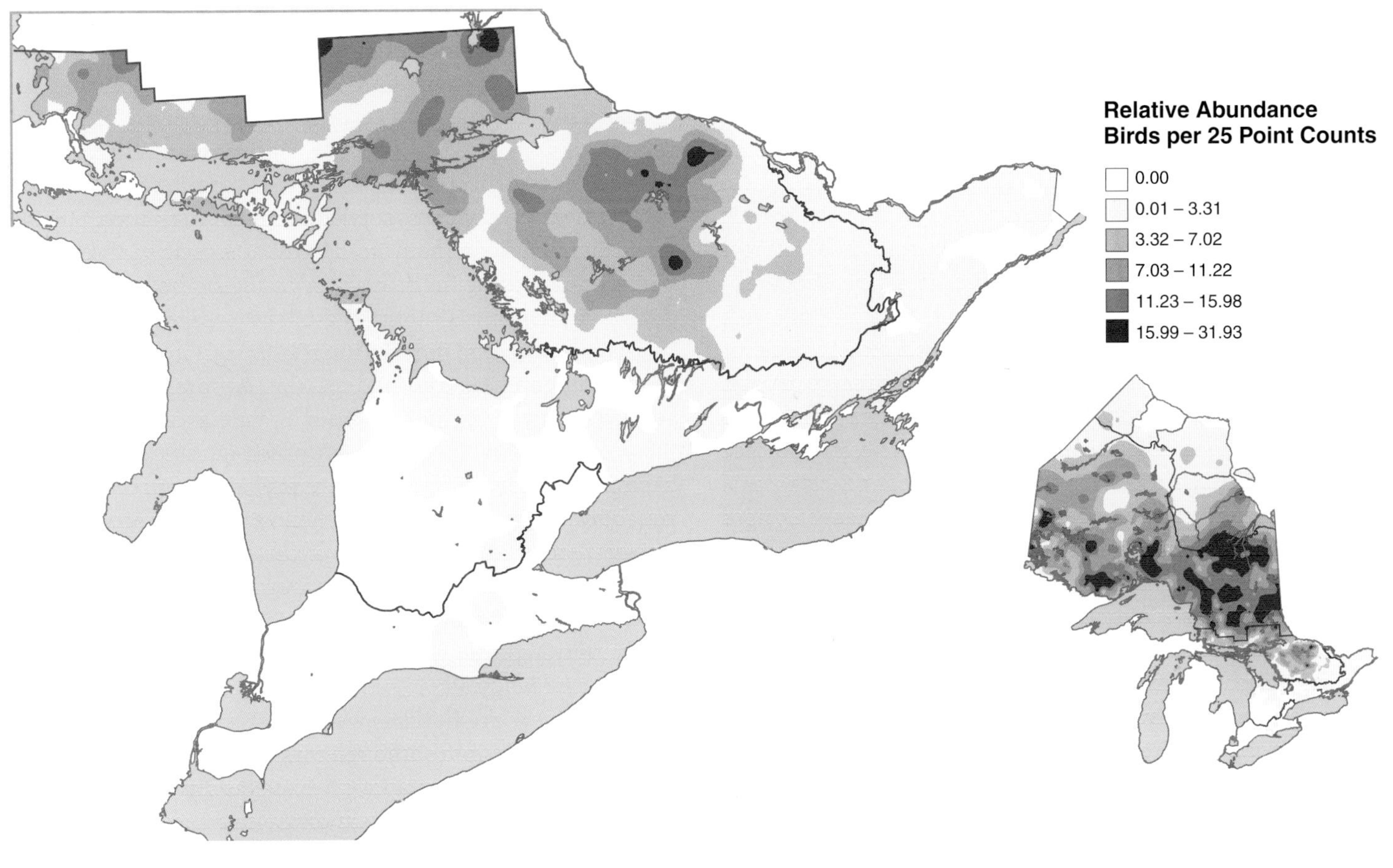

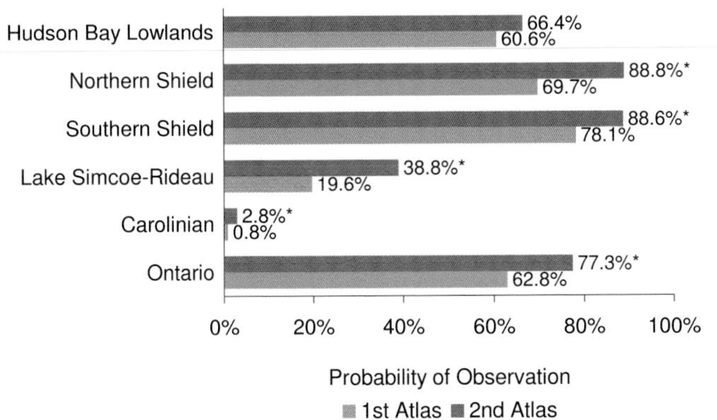

Carolinian and Lake Simcoe-Rideau regions. In southern Ontario, the increase is likely a consequence of retired farmland that has been allowed to succeed to young forest during the 20 years since the first atlas. In the north, increases are likely a result of a greater volume of logging and the regrowth of cut areas. CMMN data (Crewe 2006) and BBS for Ontario both demonstrate a significant increase in abundance of this species in the province since 1981.

The core and average latitudes of the range of the Magnolia Warbler have shifted south significantly by about 25 km between atlases. These shifts are attributable to the species' increased presence in the Lake Simcoe-Rideau region and in the Long Point area of the Carolinian region.

Breeding biology: The Magnolia Warbler tends to concentrate its activities within 6 m of the ground, including building the nest which is usually less than 2 m above the ground, in young conifers rarely exceeding 3 m in height (McLaren 1975; Peck and James 1987). Young are noisy and obvious for the first few days after fledging, as both parents attend to them. Although breeding was confirmed in 36 of 45 atlas administrative regions reporting the species, confirmed breeding evidence was obtained in only 13% of squares, which seems somewhat low for a species that is relatively easy to detect. Nests were found in only eight of the 36 atlas administrative regions where breeding was confirmed; the most frequently observed evidence of confirmed breeding was adults carrying food.

Abundance: The Magnolia Warbler has a loud, distinctive, and thus easily identifiable song. Consequently, it is readily detected during point counts. Point count data reveal that this species is one of the most common birds in Ontario. Its pattern of abundance mirrors its breeding distribution, with an average density of 11.8 birds/25 point counts recorded in the Northern Shield region. The areas of highest densities (over 16 birds/25 point counts) were noted in the forests south of about 51° N, the northern limit of forest currently available for logging and lumber operations. Previous studies have indicated the Magnolia Warbler to be one of the most commonly recorded breeding birds in cutover boreal forest (Welsh and Fillman 1980). Densities in the Southern Shield region averaged almost 6 birds/25 point counts, with a concentration in the Algonquin Highlands area, likely also a result of logging in the area. The limited distribution of the Magnolia Warbler south of the Shield is reflected in the average of less than 1 bird/25 point counts in the Lake Simcoe-Rideau and Carolinian regions. – *Peter L. McLaren*

Cape May Warbler

Paruline tigrée

Dendroica tigrina

Ron Ridout

The Cape May Warbler breeds in boreal coniferous forests from eastern British Columbia and the southern Northwest Territories east to the Maritime Provinces. Its winter range comprises the West Indies and Caribbean coastal areas of Central America.

The male Cape May Warbler is a striking and elegant member of the wood-warbler family. The species is among the most specialized of the Boreal Forest warblers, normally occurring only in tall mature coniferous, and, to a lesser degree, mixed forests. The great majority of its time and activity, including singing, foraging, and nesting, is spent in the upper canopy of trees at least 10 m in height. The Cape May Warbler is considered to be a Spruce Budworm specialist along with, to a lesser extent, the Bay-breasted Warbler. The populations of both of these species fluctuate often quite dramatically with the cycle of the Spruce Budworm, reaching high densities during outbreaks, and then declining (Williams 1996b; Baltz and Latta 1998).

Distribution and population status: The Cape May Warbler is almost entirely confined to the Northern Shield and Southern Shield regions. Although widespread throughout these regions, the species nevertheless appears to be absent from large portions of them. The probability of observation was only about 25% in both of these regions. Most of the records in the Southern Shield were in the northern half of the region, north and west from the Algonquin Highlands. The species was reported rarely in the Hudson Bay Lowlands, where, although the forests are mature, the trees do not have the requisite height.

The Cape May Warbler was also recorded in the Lake Simcoe-Rideau region, although only rarely so. Its distribution there is restricted primarily to the upper Ottawa River valley and Manitoulin Island. Most records in this region were of possible breeders, although breeding was confirmed east of Ottawa and along the upper Ottawa River.

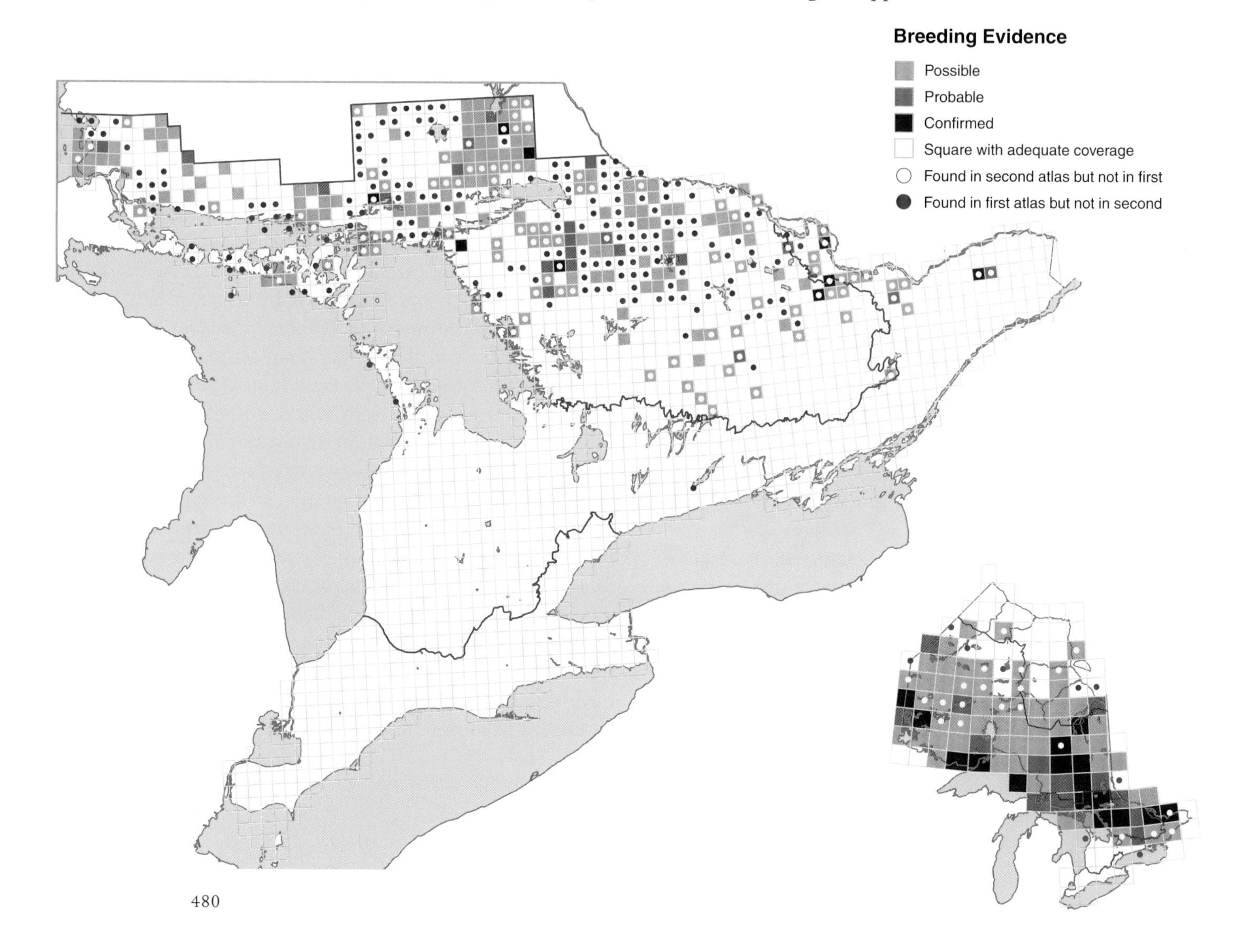

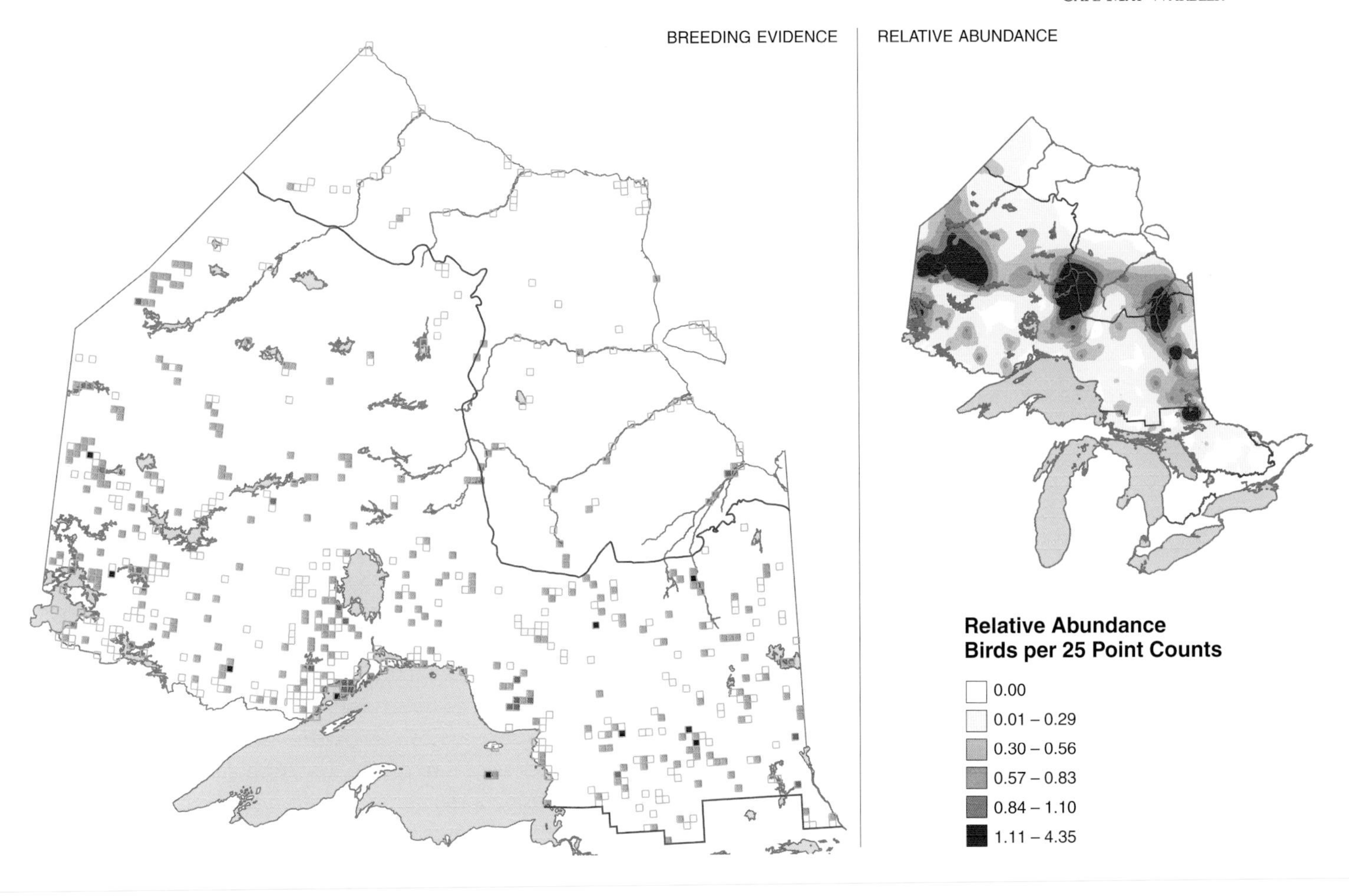

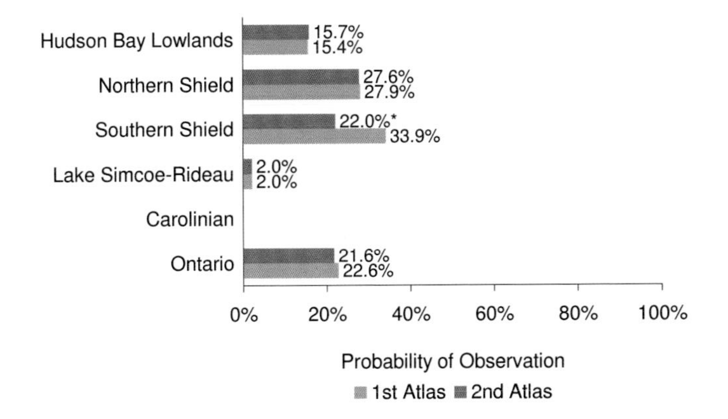

Although there was no significant change in the probability of observation of the Cape May Warbler in the Northern Shield, or in the province as a whole, there was a significant decrease of 35% in the Southern Shield between the two atlases. During the second atlas, many fewer squares in the Algonquin Prov. Park area and in the areas north and west of Sudbury reported the species. This decrease may be due to a decrease in numbers of Spruce Budworm; in Algonquin Park, budworm was about twice as common during the first atlas as it was during the second (R. Tozer, pers. comm.). CMMN data for LPBO indicate that numbers of Cape May Warblers have been declining significantly since the early 1990s (Crewe 2006).

Breeding biology: The Cape May Warbler nests high in mature coniferous trees, generally at heights greater than 12 m and close to or against the trunk. Thus, the nests are extremely difficult to find, and in fact fewer than 10 nests have ever been reported in Ontario (Peck and Peck 2006). Breeding was confirmed in only 4% of the squares in which the species was recorded. Most confirmed breeding records consisted of adults carrying food, although nests with young were found in the Lake of the Woods and English River areas of northwestern Ontario. The highest breeding evidence recorded in fully 88% of the squares was of singing males or individuals in suitable habitat, one of the highest percentages for any songbird.

Abundance: The song of the Cape May Warbler is high and fairly weak and attenuates quite rapidly. Consequently, it may be under-recorded on point counts, resulting in lower than actual densities. Although the species has a widespread distribution across northern and central Ontario, it does not appear to be particularly common anywhere. In all regions, an average relative abundance of fewer than 0.4 birds/25 point counts was recorded. The species appears to be most common across the northern portions of the Northern Shield Region, with several areas exceeding 1.1 birds/25 point counts. Given that there was little Spruce Budworm activity in Ontario during the second atlas period (Canadian Council of Forest Ministers 1998), these densities and distribution may well represent baseline population data for this warbler in the province. As well, most areas of highest abundance for the Cape May Warbler do not correspond to those for the Bay-breasted Warbler, Tennessee Warbler, or Blackburnian Warbler (cf. Kendeigh 1947), other Spruce Budworm feeders, which suggests that the observed densities were not linked to budworm outbreaks. – *Peter L. McLaren*

Black-throated Blue Warbler

Paruline bleue

Dendroica caerulescens

John Reaume

The Black-throated Blue Warbler is a relatively common neotropical migrant that breeds in the mixed forests of southeastern Canada and northeastern US and in the Appalachian Mountains south to Georgia. It nests predominantly in the dense understorey vegetation of mature forests. In Ontario, the core of the species' breeding range is on the Canadian Shield. As some forests in southern Ontario have continued to mature over the last 20 years, this warbler is re-inhabiting areas of the Carolinian and Lake Simcoe-Rideau from which it was recently absent.

Distribution and population status: Historically, the Black-throated Blue Warbler probably bred more extensively across southern Ontario; there are nesting records from Perth and Wellington Counties in the late 1800s and early 1900s (McIlwraith 1894; Macoun and Macoun 1909). The almost complete absence of records south of the Shield or the Bruce Peninsula during the first atlas was attributed to the loss of suitable habitat through widespread forest clearing for agriculture.

The Black-throated Blue Warbler continues to be found most commonly in the Southern Shield (with an 85% probability of observation) and to a lesser extent in the Lake Simcoe-Rideau and Northern Shield regions (23% and 21%, respectively). Within the Northern Shield, isolated occurrences were recorded as far north as Weagamow Lake at 53° N, but most observations were south of 50° N. The species can be found in the Carolinian region as far south as Rondeau Prov. Park, but greatest concentrations are in the more extensive forests of the Norfolk Sand Plain.

The probability of observation for the province as a whole increased significantly by 63%, with significant increases in all four regions where it occurred. The most substantial increases occurred in the Lake Simcoe-Rideau and Northern Shield regions. The probability of observation increased significantly but to a lesser extent (19%) in the Southern Shield. In the

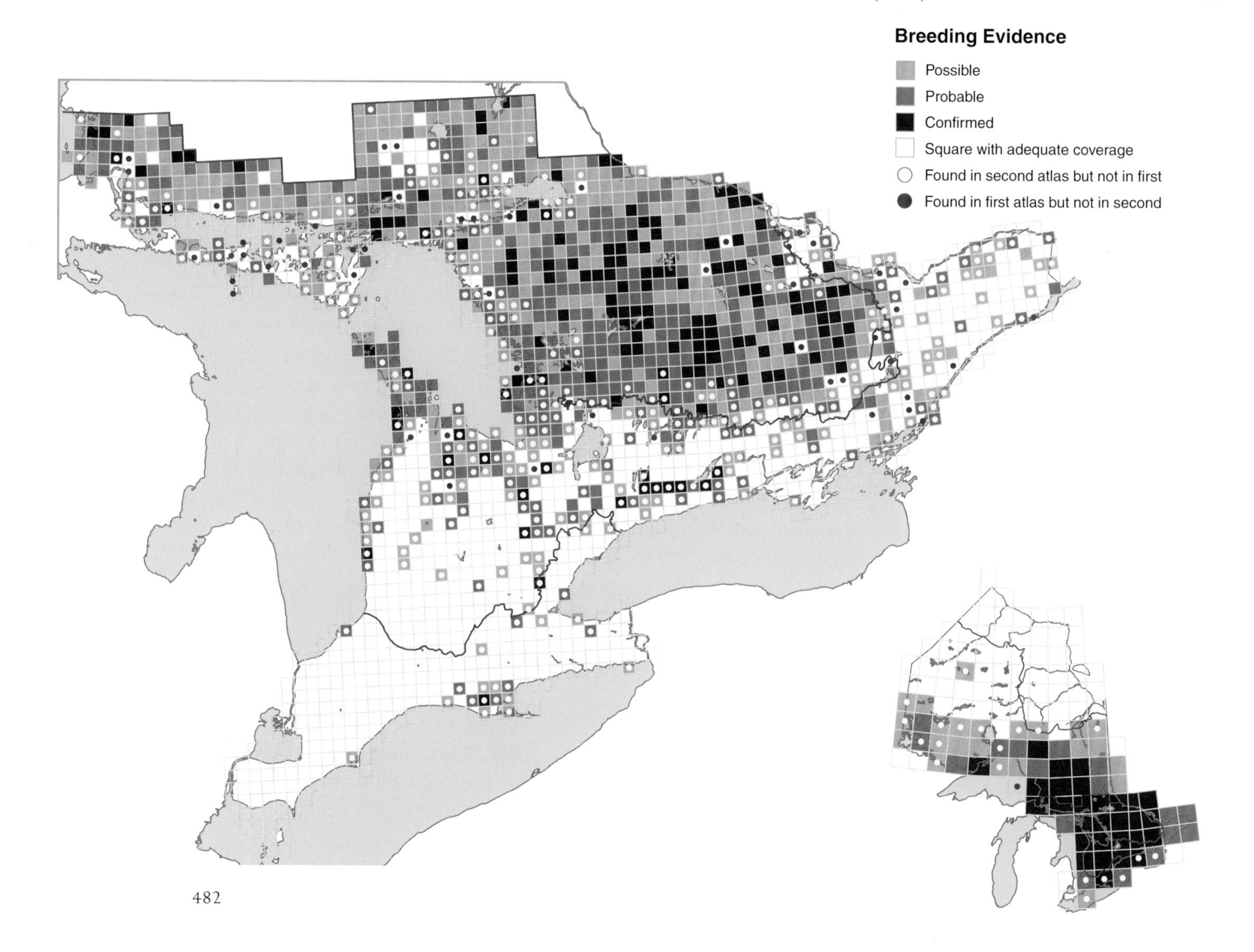

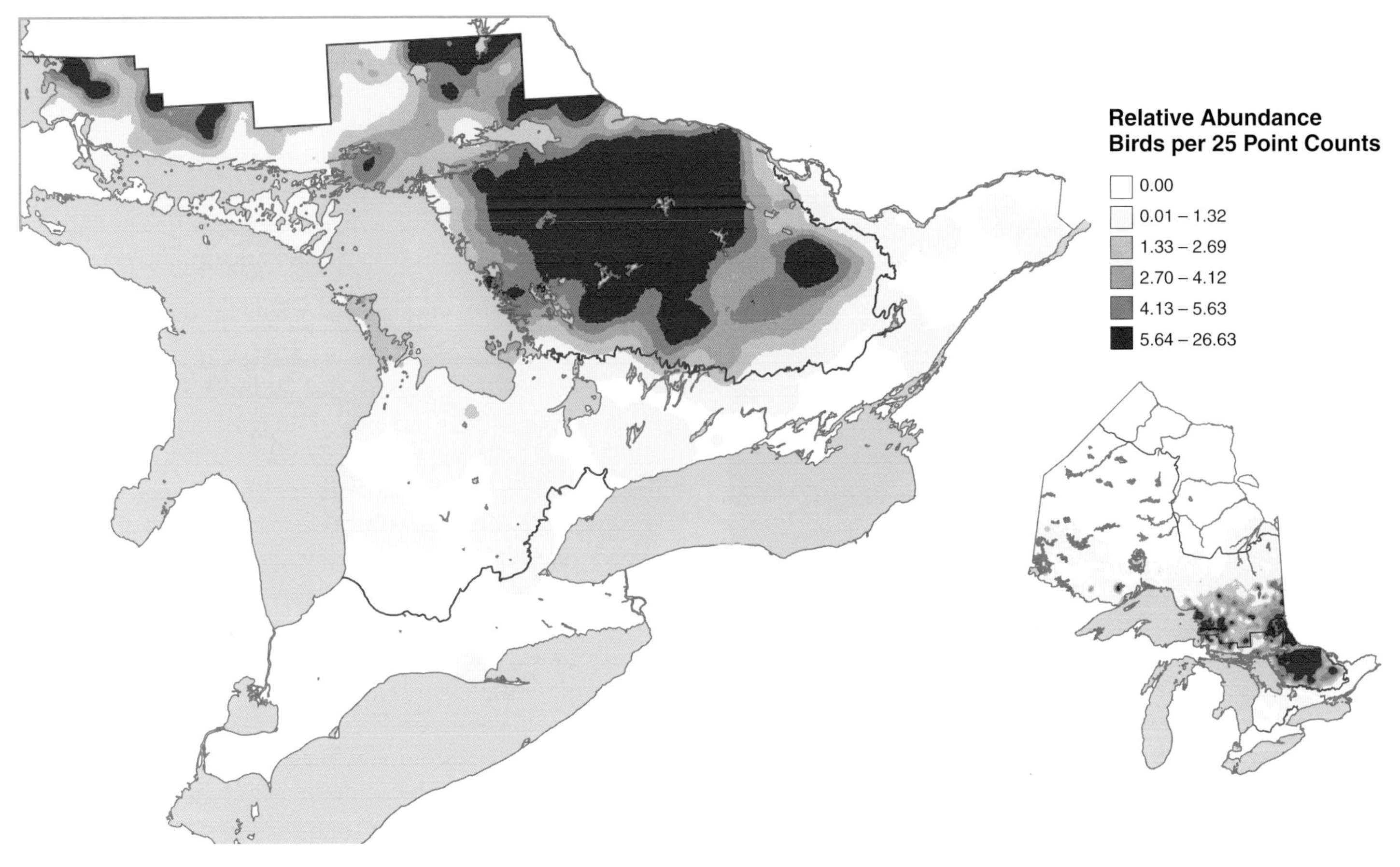

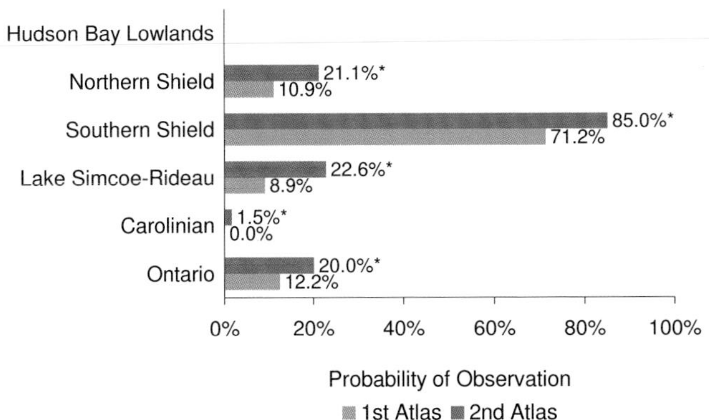

Carolinian region, the species was recorded in 23 squares in this atlas compared to none in the first. BBS data indicate a near-significant annual increase of 4.3% in Ontario populations since 1968 (Downes et al. 2005), although most of the increase occurred in the early 1980s. CMMN data also show a significant increase in numbers of migrants passing through Long Point over the same period, but primarily in the early 1990s (Crewe 2006). The map shows the substantial recolonization along the relatively heavily forested Niagara Escarpment and Oak Ridges Moraine. These increases resulted in a significant 24 km southward shift of the core breeding area in southern Ontario and a significant southward shift of more than 100 km in the southern edge of the species' range.

Breeding biology: The Black-throated Blue Warbler has been identified as a forest-interior and area-sensitive species (Robbins et al. 1989), preferring tracts of relatively undisturbed deciduous and mixed forests with a well-developed shrub understorey (Holmes et al. 2005). In Ontario, it often selects areas of dense sapling regeneration in forest clearings created naturally or through forestry along forest access roads and shorelines (Peck and James 1987). The breeding territory is typically large (1-4 ha) and its size is inversely correlated with shrub density (Steele 1993). The nest is a neat, compact cup located less than 2 m (0.2 to 1.7 m; Peck and James 1987) above the ground, often in dense Hobblebush or a deer- or moose-browsed conifer saplings. Both males and females share in parental care of nestlings. The preference for dense patches of shrubs as nesting substrates (Steele 1993) and the tendency of females to be very secretive close to the nest mean that nests can be difficult to find. Indeed, the number of confirmed breeding records was a relatively low 11%. Most confirmed records were observations of adults carrying food, or with fledged young. However, some males often sing loudly and persistently and also respond to song playback, allowing for relatively easy detection. Evidence of possible breeding was primarily singing males, reported in 57% of squares with breeding evidence.

Abundance: The Black-throated Blue Warbler is most abundant in the Southern Shield region, particularly in and around Algonquin Prov. Park, and in the Northern Shield in the Algoma Highlands and Temagami-Lake Timiskaming area. Densities in these areas exceed 5.6 birds/25 point counts. This may reflect the availability of suitable habitat, as these areas are dominated by large, mature tracts of deciduous and mixed forest. – *Richard Joos*

Yellow-rumped Warbler

Paruline à croupion jaune

Dendroica coronata

George K. Peck

The Yellow-rumped Warbler is one of the most common and widespread wood-warblers in Ontario and North America. The species is comprised of two recognizable morphological types, the Myrtle type (*D. c. coronata*), which is the only subspecies that breeds in Ontario, and the Audubon's type (including *D. c. auduboni*), which is western in distribution. The Myrtle Warbler nests from northern Alaska across the entire Boreal Forest to northern Québec and Newfoundland, south to south-central Alberta in the west and northern New Jersey in the east. It occurs locally in the Appalachian Mountains to West Virginia and Maryland. There is a narrow zone of hybridization between the two subspecies along the British Columbia-Alberta border (Hunt and Flaspohler 1998). However, hybrids and members of the Audubon's type are rare vagrants in Ontario and are not known to have bred here (James 1991).

The Yellow-rumped Warbler prefers mature coniferous and mixed coniferous-deciduous forests, including conifer plantations, but it is a generalist, using whatever conifer species is present. It is tolerant of logging and fire and can maintain near-normal breeding densities after a disturbance, providing some mature conifers remain. Although it nests and forages primarily in conifers, it makes use of a broad range of microhabitats within its territory.

Distribution and population status: The Yellow-rumped Warbler breeds throughout the province, with the exception of most of the Carolinian region. There, it is restricted to the forests of the Norfolk Sand Plain and a few other scattered areas with substantial coniferous forest cover. The core of its distribution is on the Precambrian Shield, with the probability of observation 95% in the Southern Shield and 92% in the Northern Shield. This is not surprising, given the broad expanses of coniferous forest on the Shield. The Hudson Bay Lowlands and Lake Simcoe-Rideau regions also provide ample

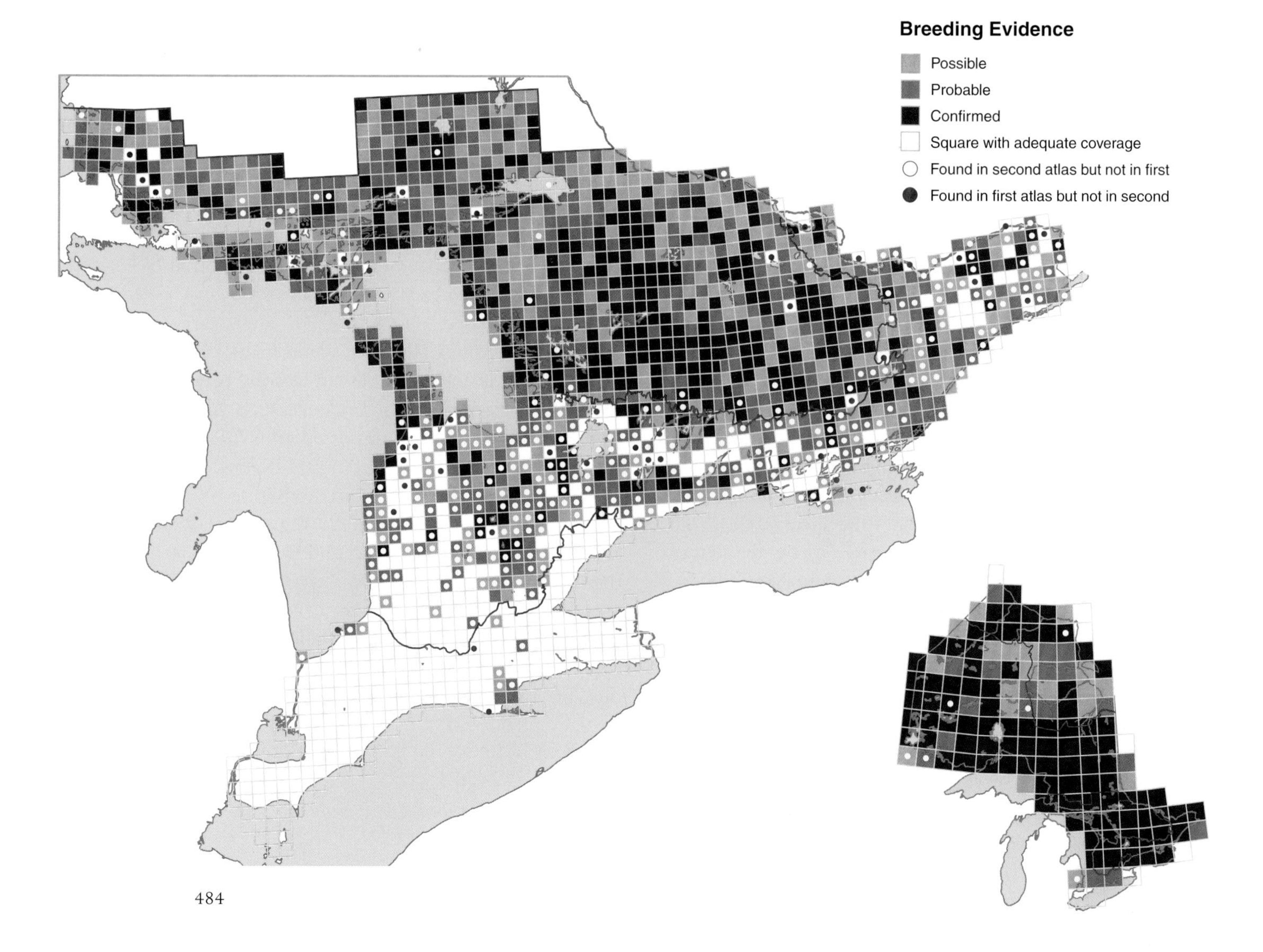

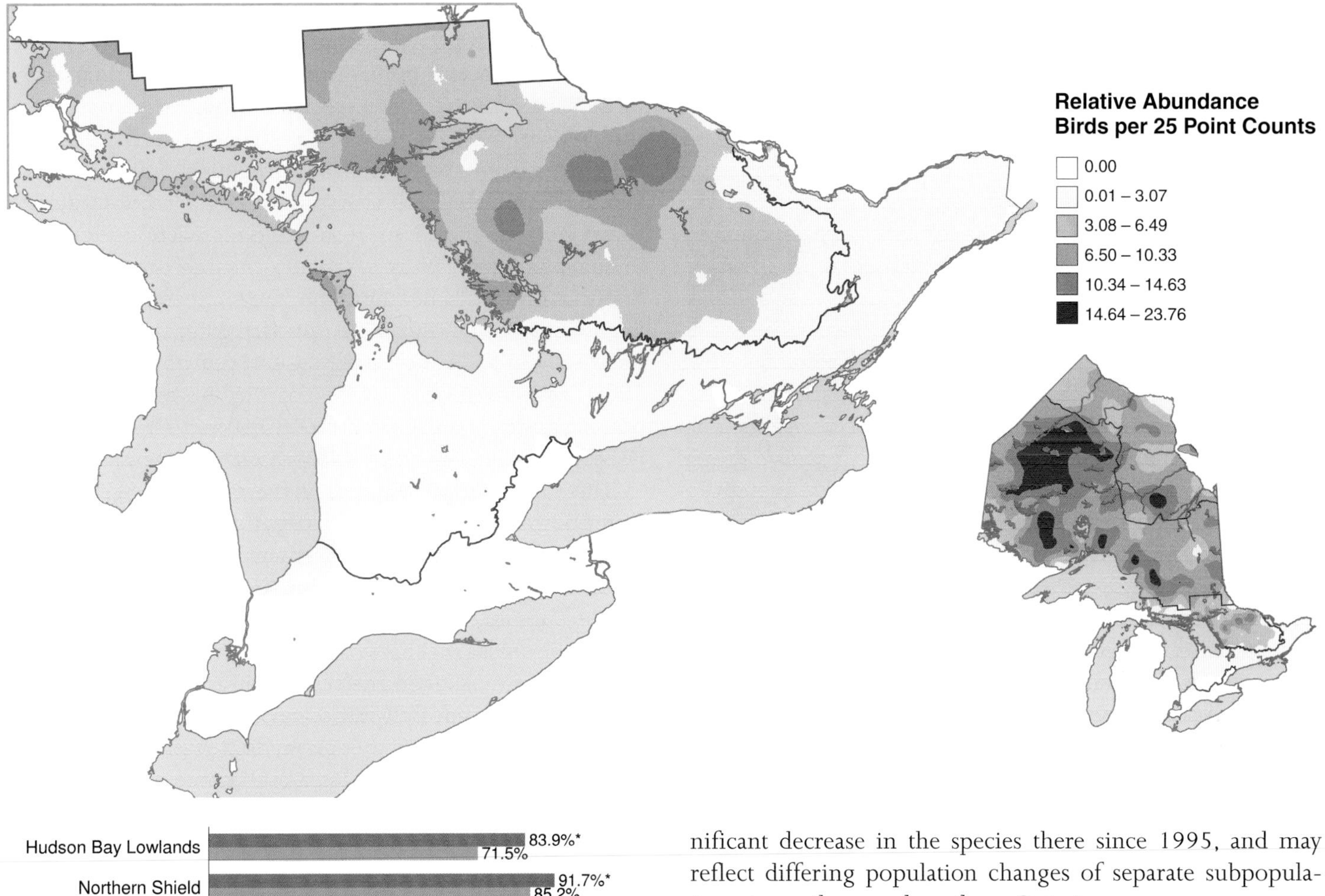

Region	1st Atlas	2nd Atlas
Hudson Bay Lowlands	71.5%	83.9%*
Northern Shield	85.2%	91.7%*
Southern Shield	91.1%	95.0%*
Lake Simcoe-Rideau	37.0%	54.0%*
Carolinian	1.0%	2.6%*
Ontario	76.7%	85.1%*

Probability of Observation (0%–100%)
■ 1st Atlas ■ 2nd Atlas

suitable habitat, and the probability of observation there is 84% and 54%, respectively.

Although the broad pattern of distribution has remained similar to that recorded in the first atlas, there has been a significant increase of 11% in the probability of observation province-wide, and 46% in the Lake Simcoe-Rideau region. This latter increase is primarily a result of the species' colonization of maturing conifer plantations and areas where forests with a coniferous component have regenerated on previously cleared land. This increase and that in the Carolinian region have resulted in a significant southward shift of the core latitude of the Yellow-rumped Warbler's range in southern Ontario. A similar pattern has been observed in other areas outside of Ontario near the southern edge of its range (Hunt and Flaspohler 1998). BBS data show no significant change in Ontario since the first atlas. However, CMMN data for LPBO indicate a significant increase in the number of migrants recorded at the station since 1967 (Crewe 2006). Interestingly, migration monitoring data for TCBO show a significant decrease in the species there since 1995, and may reflect differing population changes of separate subpopulations in northern and southern Ontario.

Breeding biology: Males generally arrive on the breeding grounds a few days earlier than females, and immediately begin to establish territories. The nest, a loose or compact cup of twigs, pine needles, and grasses (Hunt and Flaspohler 1998), typically is situated on a horizontal branch of a conifer, anywhere from 1.2 to 15.2 m above the ground. There is a fairly high incidence of brood parasitism by the Brown-headed Cowbird in Ontario (31% of reported nests in ONRS), likely predominantly south of the Shield where the two species' ranges overlap.

Nests may be difficult to spot due to their height and cryptic nature, but adults carry food to nestlings and will respond conspicuously to the presence of intruders. Young can be vocal and often are easy to locate as a result. Breeding was confirmed in 23% of squares, and the majority of these were records of fledged young or adults carrying food.

Abundance: The areas of highest density for the Yellow-rumped Warbler occur in the Northern Shield, particularly in the northwest, where over 14.6 birds/25 point counts were recorded in several locations. Overall, the Northern Shield region averaged 10.1 birds/25 point counts, while the Hudson Bay Lowlands averaged 6.9 and the Southern Shield 5.2. Previous studies have shown that densities increase as the forest ages, and decrease as the proportion of deciduous trees in the breeding habitat increases (Hunt and Flaspohler 1998). Based on atlas point counts, the Ontario population is estimated to be 12,000,000 birds. – *William J. Crins*

Black-throated Green Warbler

Paruline à gorge noire
Dendroica virens

David Welbourne

The Black-throated Green Warbler can be one of the most common breeding warblers in the forests it inhabits. It breeds in coniferous and mixed forests from northeastern British Columbia to Newfoundland, south to northeastern Minnesota and central Michigan and through the Appalachian Mountains to northern Georgia. It is a foliage-gleaner that prefers to feed on non-hairy caterpillars. During migration, it will feed on the berries of Poison Ivy (Morse and Poole 2005).

Distribution and population status: The breeding range of the Black-throated Green Warbler in Ontario did not change substantially between atlases. It is found in all five regions, with its centre of distribution occurring in the Southern Shield where the probability of observation was 93%. Generally, it is found sparsely in the Carolinian region but is more abundant in the more forested areas of the Norfolk Sand Plain and Rondeau Prov. Park. Its continuous range extends to about 51° N. North of that latitude, it becomes irregular and uncommon to rare and in the second atlas was unrecorded in a number of 100-km blocks in which it was recorded in the first atlas. The northernmost records in the second atlas were from Opasquia Prov. Park in the west and the Ekwan River in the east.

This warbler has become more common in southern Ontario, with significant increases in the probability of observation in all three southern regions, including 94% in the Lake Simcoe-Rideau region, and over 100% in the Carolinian region. This increase is likely due to the regeneration and maturation of forests on abandoned farmland and to the maturation of conifer plantations. A significant increase of 23% was observed in the Northern Shield region, but the reason for that increase is unclear. BBS data show no significant trends for Ontario, but CMMN data for LPBO indicate a significant increase between 1967 and 2004 (Crewe 2006).

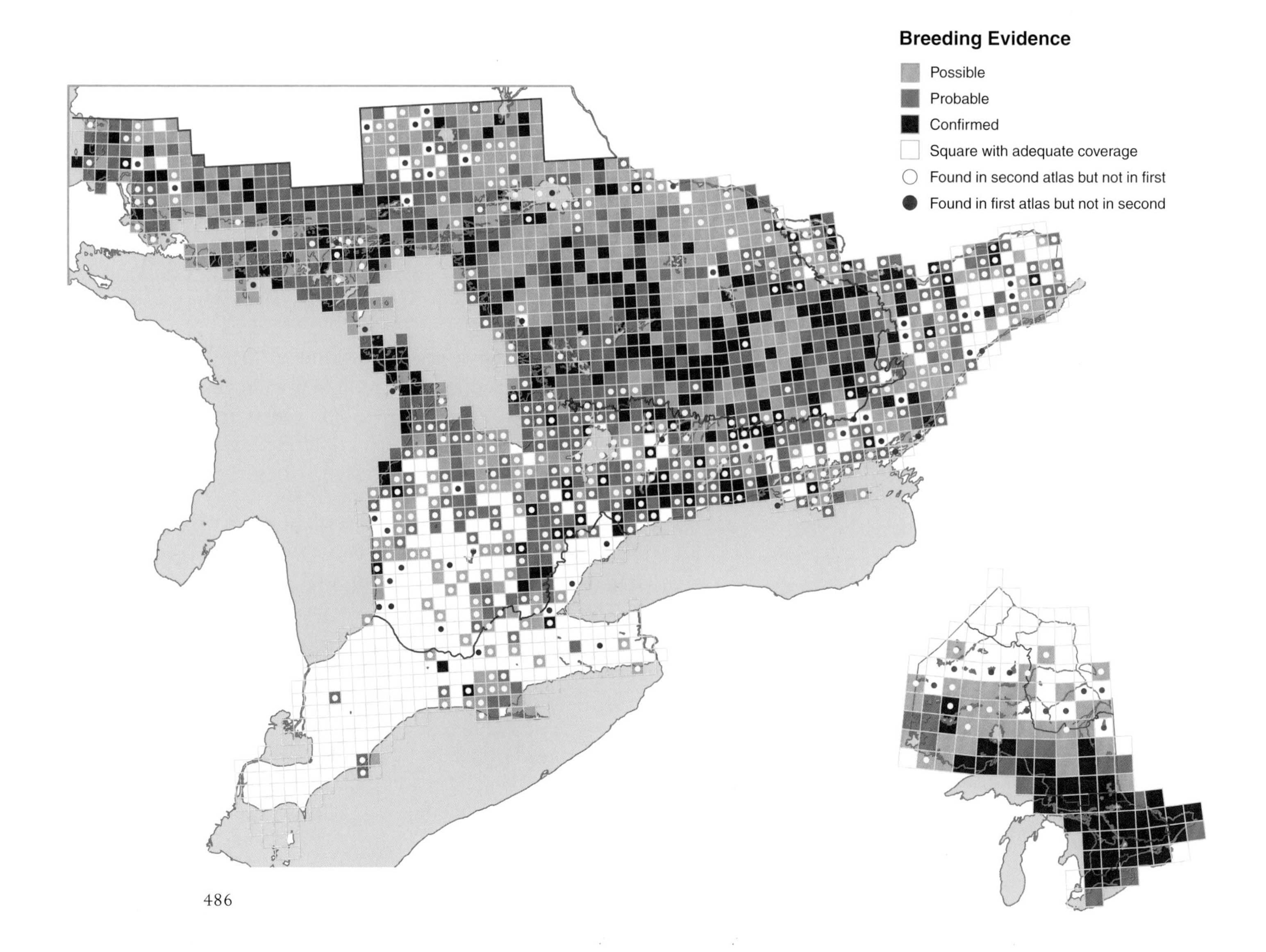

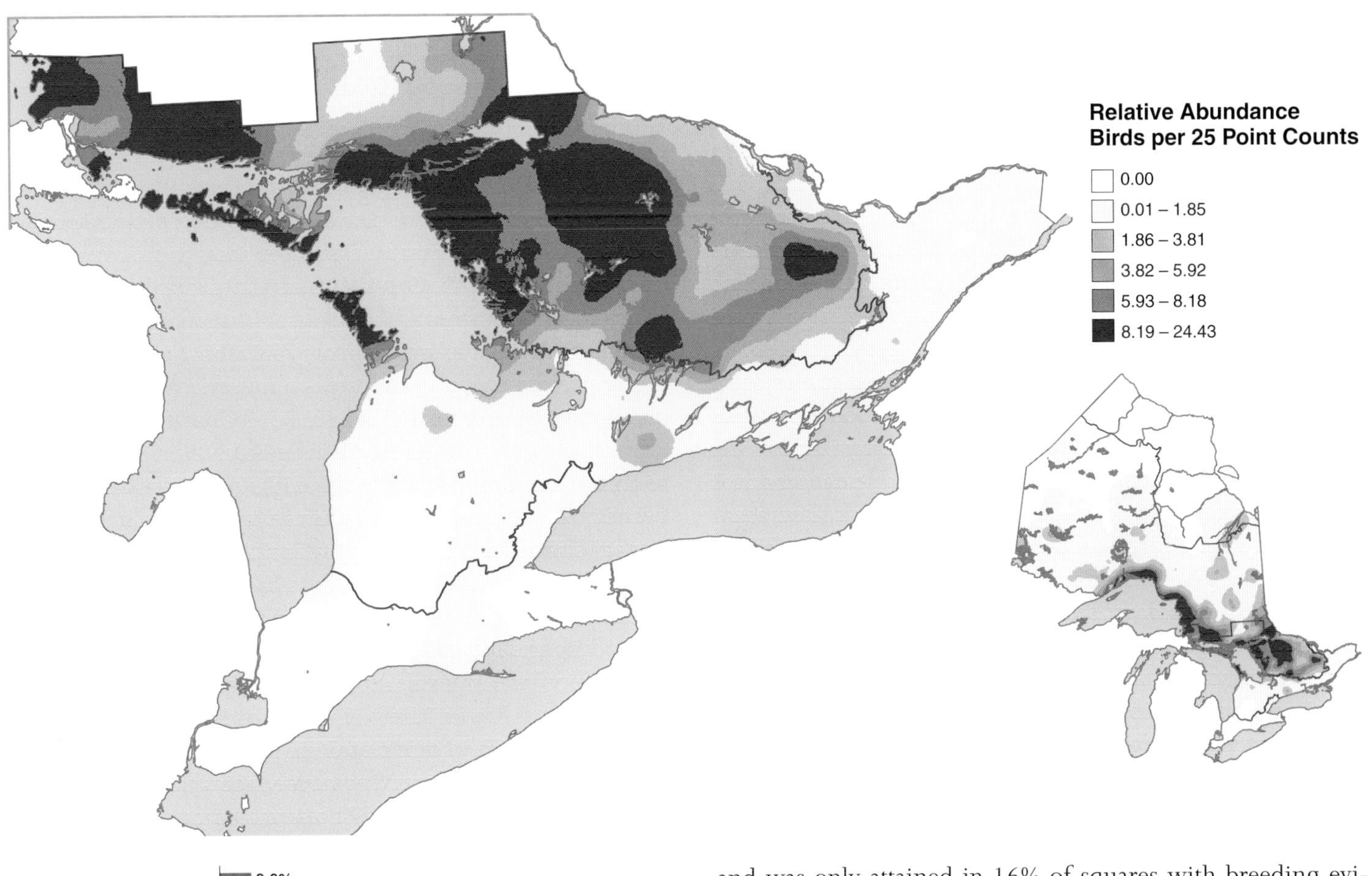

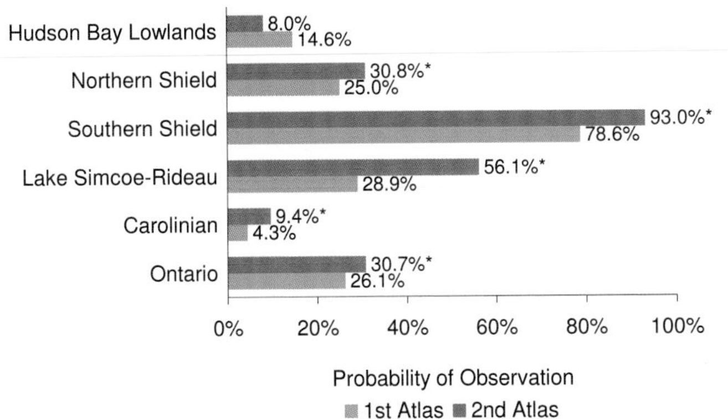

Breeding biology: The Black-throated Green Warbler prefers to nest in middle-aged and mature forests dominated by conifers including spruces, White Pine, Balsam Fir, Eastern Hemlock, and Jack Pine. Males establish territories shortly after arriving on the breeding grounds, usually by mid-May. In western Ontario, territories averaged 0.5 ha, ranging from 0.3 to 0.9 ha. Individuals frequently return to the same territories in successive years (Morse and Poole 2005).

The nest is situated typically in a fork of branches well out from the trunk of a coniferous tree, usually 2.7 to 7.5 m above the ground (Peck and James 1987). Cup-shaped and tightly woven of twigs, plant stems, bark (especially White Birch), and spiderwebs, it is lined with fine plant material, hair, mosses, and feathers. Often it is well concealed (Peck and James 1987), and this, coupled with its height from the ground, may make it difficult to find. The young remain with the parents for up to a month after fledging and can be very loud and conspicuous during this period (Morse and Poole 2005). Confirmation of breeding is difficult to obtain for this species and was only attained in 16% of squares with breeding evidence. Most of these records were of fledged young or adults carrying food. Males have a distinctive song and are particularly vocal, sometimes singing as frequently as once every 10 seconds (Morse and Poole 2005), and so are unlikely to have been missed where they occurred. The highest breeding evidence recorded in 52% of squares was of singing males or individuals in suitable habitat.

Abundance: Although the Black-throated Green Warbler is widespread, there are well defined areas of higher abundance along the north and east shores of Lake Superior, east to Georgian Bay and Algonquin Prov. Park, as well as on the Bruce Peninsula and the southern shore of Manitoulin Island. In these areas, more than 8.2 birds/25 point counts were recorded. These areas coincide with relatively high moisture levels from lake effects or orographic precipitation in upland areas, which supports extensive mixed forest with strong concentrations of coniferous trees, particularly White Pine and Eastern Hemlock. The Southern Shield region had the highest average regional abundance at 7.6 birds/25 point counts, with the Northern Shield region next at 2.3 birds/25 point counts. Based on atlas point count data, the Ontario population is estimated at 2,500,000 birds, with about 90% of those in the two Shield regions. – *William J. Crins*

Blackburnian Warbler

Paruline à gorge orangée

Dendroica fusca

John Reaume

The Blackburnian Warbler is one of several structurally similar wood-warblers that can coexist through niche partitioning (Morse 2004). It specializes in coniferous treetops, where it gleans foliage for Lepidopteran larvae. The species breeds from central Alberta to the Maritimes south to Massachusetts and New York, and in the Appalachian Mountains south to northern Georgia. Range expansions have occurred in New York along the Appalachian Plateau and possibly also in Vermont, where this warbler has colonized reforested areas (Morse 2004). It inhabits mature coniferous and mixed forests, and in places even occupies strictly deciduous forests. In the southern part of its range, it has a particular propensity for Eastern Hemlock. In areas with spruce forests, it often prefers spruces draped with lichens (Morse 2004).

Distribution and population status: The Blackburnian Warbler is widespread throughout the Northern Shield, Southern Shield, and Lake Simcoe-Rideau regions. The centre of its range is the Southern Shield region, where it had an 83% probability of observation. Here, it was recorded in almost every square, except for a small area near Sudbury. It is a relatively rare breeder in the Carolinian region, primarily found in the extensive forests on the Norfolk Sand Plain and in Rondeau Prov. Park, and is found only at the very southern edge of the Hudson Bay Lowlands region. The distribution of the species in the Lake Simcoe-Rideau region reflects the availability of mixed forests, with concentrations of squares occurring on the Bruce Peninsula, Dundalk uplands, Oak Ridges Moraine, and Frontenac Axis.

The probability of observation of the Blackburnian Warbler changed significantly between atlases in the Southern and Northern Shield regions, where there were increases of 6% and 35%, respectively. The reasons for the increases are

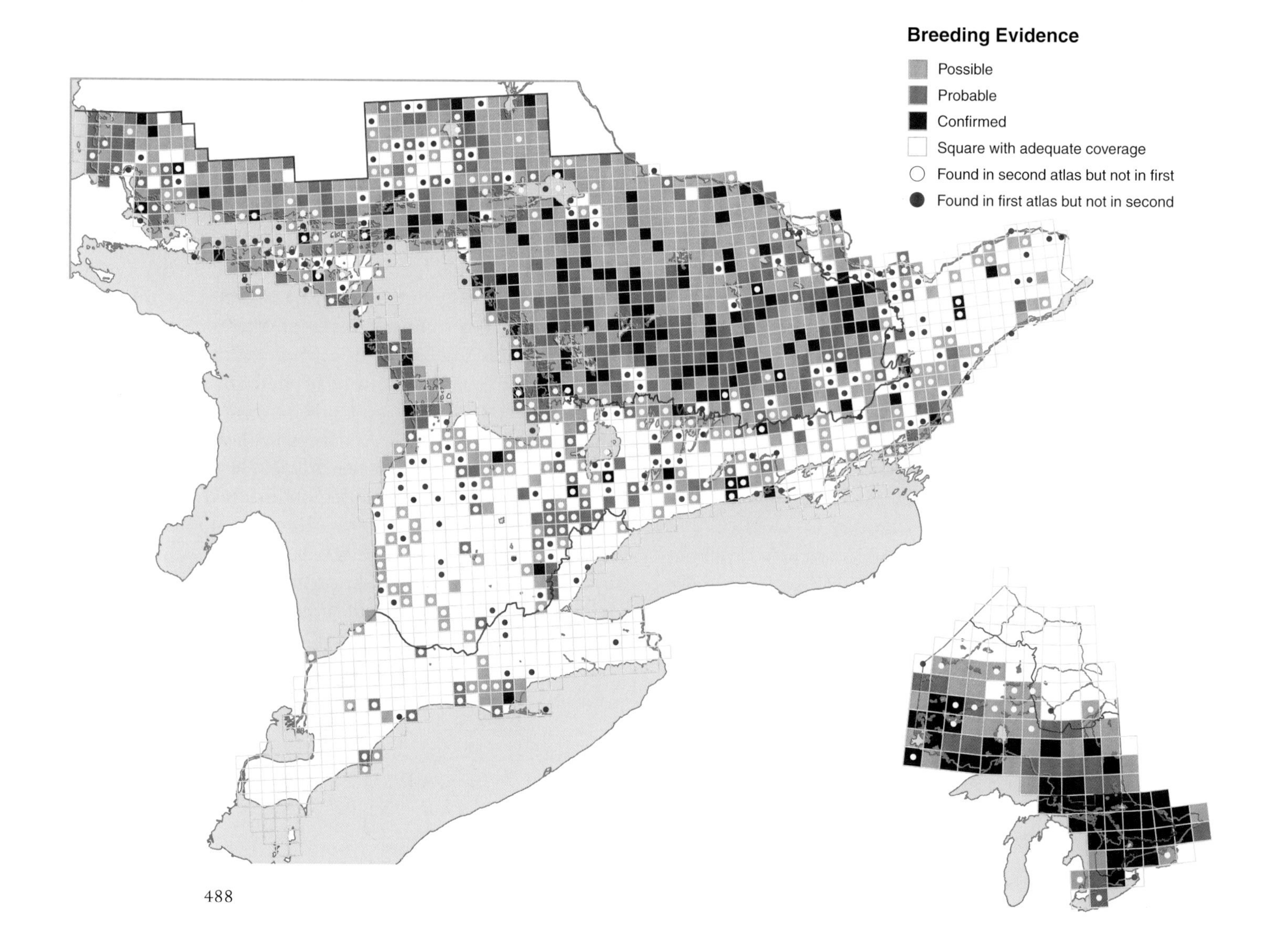

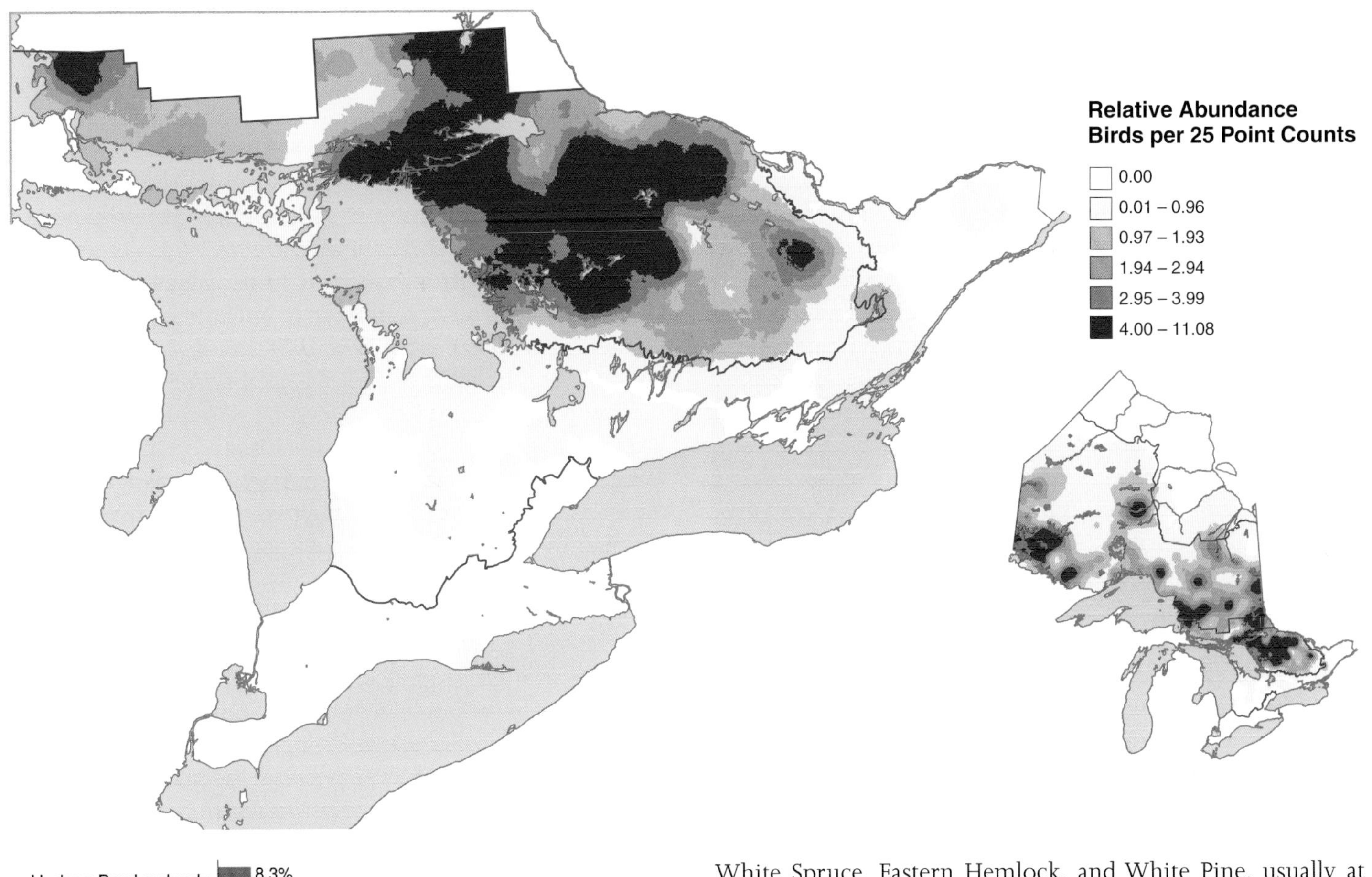

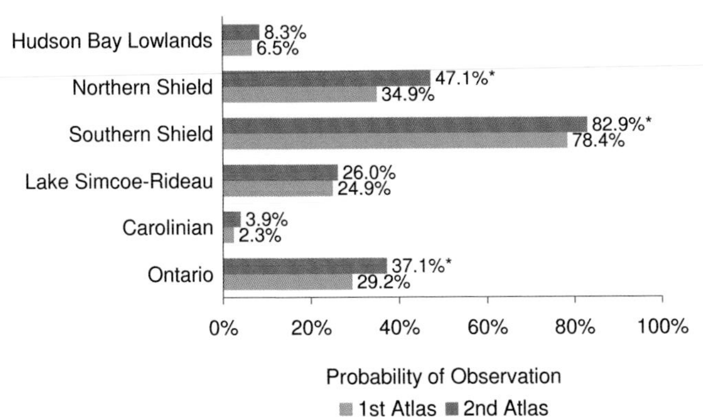

unknown. The distribution map shows a widespread increase in occupied squares in parts of the Lake Simcoe-Rideau region, similar to that shown for several other birds of coniferous forests such as the Yellow-rumped and Black-throated Green Warbler. Some Regional Coordinators indicated that spruce and mixed forest stands were occupied following the first atlas. In some cases, these stands have developed on former farmland. However, the additions were balanced by losses in areas where the species was recorded in the first atlas but not the second, primarily in Huron and Bruce Counties and on Manitoulin Island, resulting in no significant change for this region as a whole.

BBS data for Ontario show a marginally significant annual increase of 2.3% since 1968 (Downes et al. 2005). CMMN data for TCBO and LPBO show no significant change over roughly the same period.

Breeding biology: Relatively little is known of the nesting behaviour of this species, because of the difficulty in observing nests. These are almost always located in conifers such as White Spruce, Eastern Hemlock, and White Pine, usually at heights of 6 to 12 m, often placed well out from the trunk (1.8 to 2.4 m) near the end of a limb and concealed from beneath with stout twigs (Peck and James 1987). The nest is a densely constructed cup well hidden in the foliage. Only the female constructs the nest and incubates the eggs. She sits very tightly on the eggs and spends about 80% of her time incubating. Both parents feed the young in the nest, but after fledging, each parent may care for part of the brood independently (Morse 2004).

Males have a distinctive song, and will sing both from exposed perches and while foraging. The highest level of breeding evidence in 66% of squares was possible breeding, mostly singing males. The fact that only 10% of squares with breeding evidence recorded confirmed breeding reflects the difficulty in finding nests; the majority of confirmations were through the observation of fledged young or adults carrying food.

Abundance: The Blackburnian Warbler is most abundant in the Southern Shield region, with an average of 3.6 birds/25 point counts, followed by the Northern Shield, with 2.2 birds/25 point counts. Abundance was substantially lower in the Lake Simcoe-Rideau region with just 0.2 birds/25 point counts. Centres of highest abundance, over 4.0 birds/25 point counts, are scattered within the Southern Shield and Northern Shield regions and include areas from Kenora to Lac Seul, Quetico Prov. Park, near Fort Hope, Lake Superior Prov. Park, and the Little Clay Belt, and from Killarney Prov. Park east to Algonquin Prov. Park and north to Temagami. These high-density areas reflect the distribution of mixed forests with a strong coniferous component. – *William J. Crins*

Pine Warbler

Paruline des pins

Dendroica pinus

Barry S. Cherriere

The Pine Warbler is a species of upland mature pine forests and mixed hardwood-pine forests, also frequently using pine plantations. It is a common breeder and year-round resident in the southeastern US, but farther north its densities are lower, and it is a short-distance migrant. It is one of the earliest wood-warblers to return in Ontario, usually arriving at the same time as the Yellow-rumped Warbler or shortly after. It breeds from southeastern Manitoba east to southwestern New Brunswick and New England and south to eastern Texas and Florida. However, its distribution is somewhat discontinuous throughout this range (Rodewald et al. 1999).

Distribution and population status: The Pine Warbler is found in all regions of Ontario except the Hudson Bay Lowlands, occurring north to about 51° N. It is also absent from most of the extreme southwest and the Niagara Peninsula, where its preferred pine forest habitat is scarce. The core of its range lies in the Southern Shield region, where the probability of observation was 70%, but it is also relatively common in the Lake Simcoe-Rideau region.

The Pine Warbler has undergone explosive population growth in the province since the first atlas. The probability of observation increased significantly in all four regions where it occurs, with an increase for the province as a whole of over 100%. It has expanded its breeding range northward into the Northern Shield region since the first atlas, resulting in a significant and more than five-fold increase in the probability of observation for the region. It has now been found breeding north to Cochrane, Timmins, Nakina, Armstrong, and Ear Falls, whereas in the first atlas its northern limit was roughly from Temagami to Chapleau and from Thunder Bay to Kenora. However, north of Sault Ste. Marie and Sudbury, the distribution of this species becomes more localized.

Within southern Ontario, a significant southward shift of 20 km in the core range of the Pine Warbler was recorded,

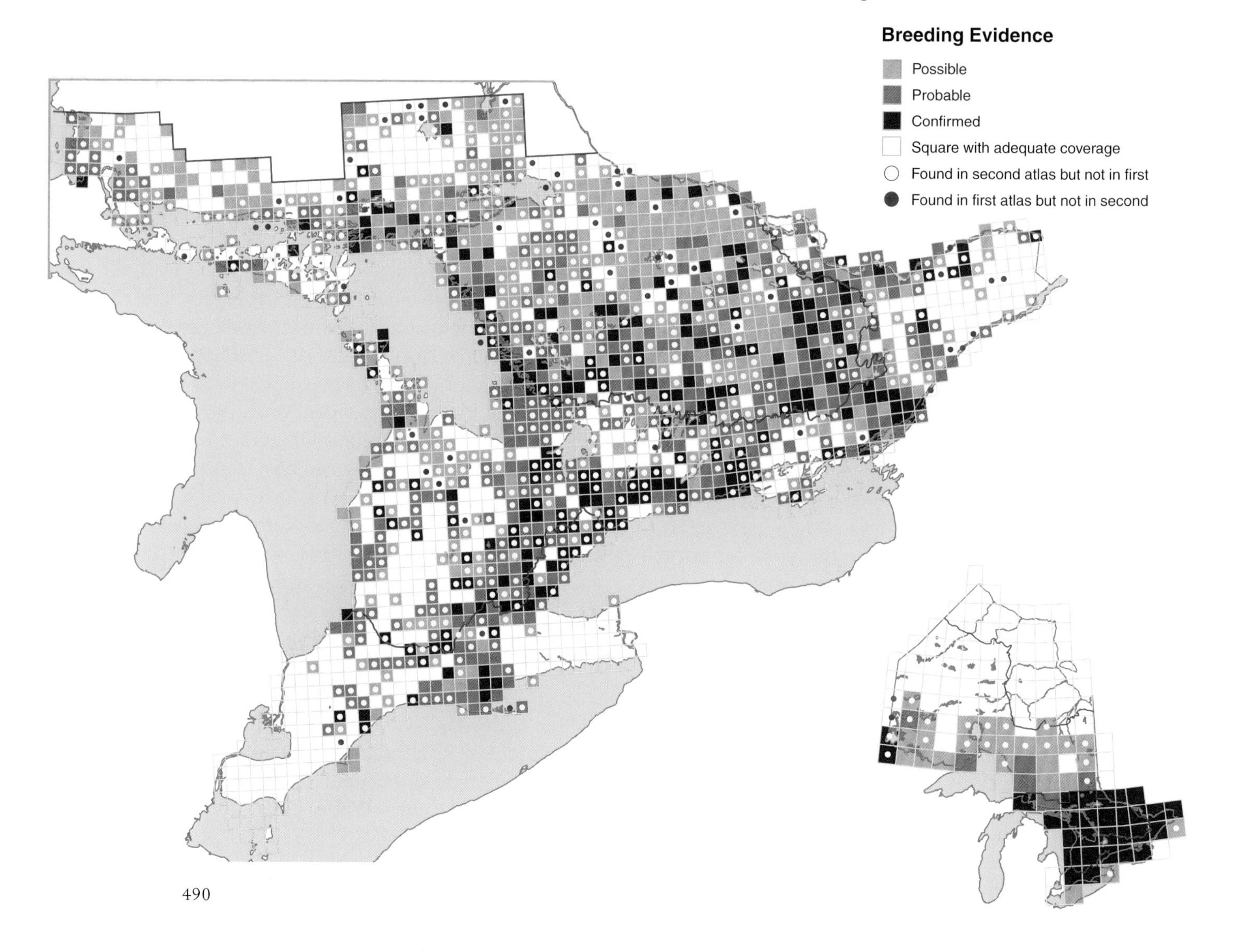

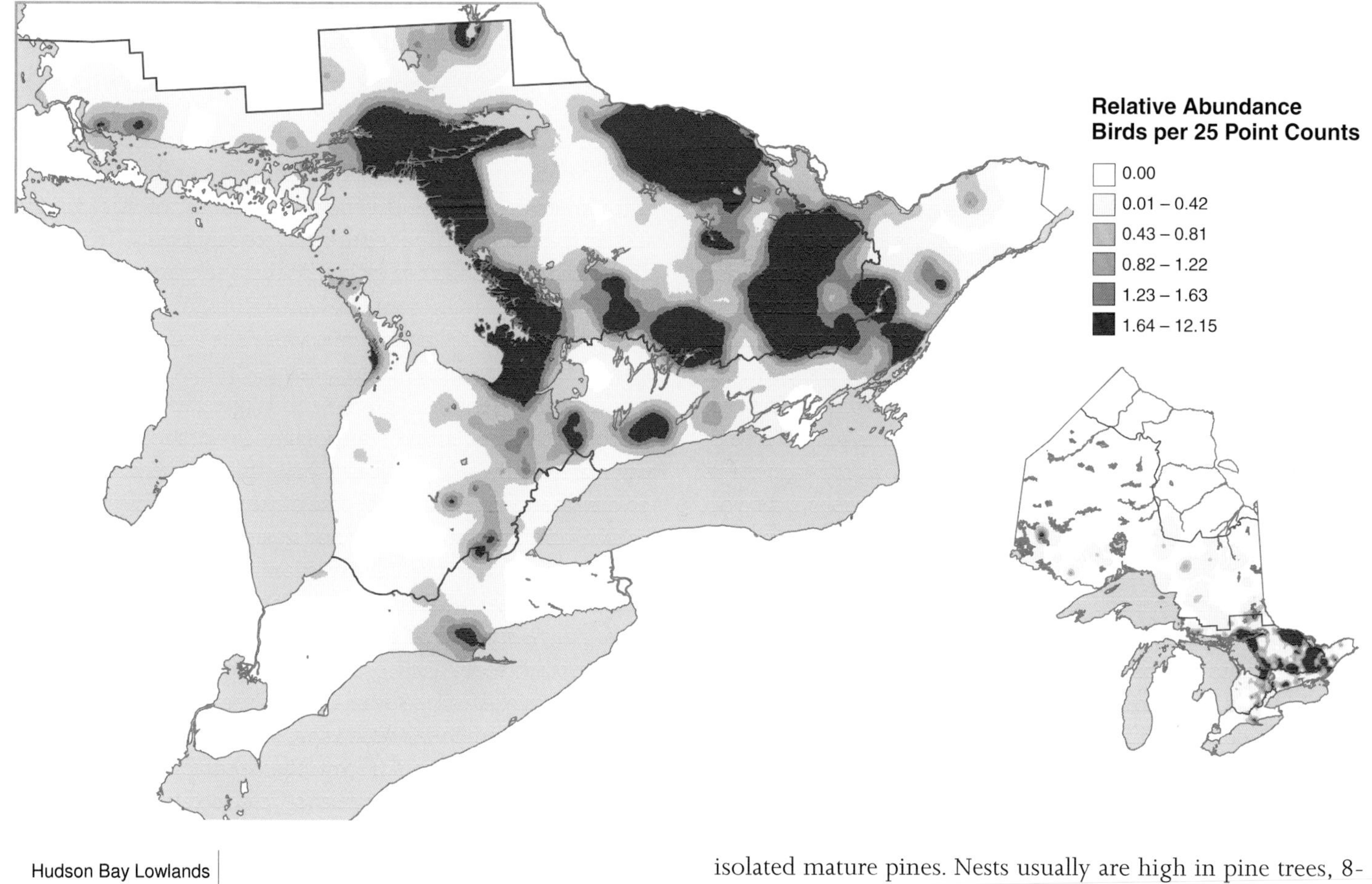

Probability of Observation

Region	1st Atlas	2nd Atlas
Hudson Bay Lowlands		
Northern Shield	1.1%	6.3%*
Southern Shield	39.6%	69.7%*
Lake Simcoe-Rideau	12.2%	34.8%*
Carolinian	9.2%	20.6%*
Ontario	4.7%	11.8%*

probably as a result of the large number of additional squares in which it was found south of the Shield. The greatest increases in the probability of observation in southern Ontario occurred in the Lake Simcoe-Rideau region (almost 200%) and the Carolinian region (over 100%). These increases are likely the result of pine plantations and regenerating farm fields maturing throughout these regions since the first atlas, but some Regional Coordinators have suggested that, especially in the Southern Shield region, the observed increase may be due in part to better recognition of the species by atlassers. BBS data support these observed trends, with a significant 7.3% annual increase in Ontario since 1981.

Breeding biology: Upon arrival on the breeding grounds in April, the male Pine Warbler immediately establishes a territory, singing persistently while foraging. The song is generally easily recognized, although variants of it may be similar to that of several other species, particularly the Chipping Sparrow. Territories generally are less than 1 ha in size, and this warbler regularly makes use of even small patches of suitable habitat or isolated mature pines. Nests usually are high in pine trees, 8-15 m above the ground on a horizontal branch, in a fork, or more often in twigs and needles at the end of a branch, where they are well concealed. Rarely, other conifers are used. The nest consists of a deep, compact, solidly constructed cup, often bound together with the silk of spiders or caterpillars (Peck and James 1987; Rodewald et al. 1999). Once the eggs have hatched, both parents participate in the brooding and feeding of the young (Rodewald et al. 1999). The difficulty in detecting nests is reflected by the fact that the species was confirmed to be breeding in only 19% of the squares in which it was found, and the majority of confirmations were through the observation of adults carrying food or with fledged young. The highest evidence recorded in most unconfirmed squares was of singing males.

Abundance: The Pine Warbler is found in greatest density in the Southern Shield region, where it averaged 1.7 birds/25 point counts, followed by the Lake Simcoe-Rideau region (0.6 birds/25 point counts). Highest concentrations occur in the eastern Georgian Bay area, along the southern edge of the Shield, on the Frontenac Axis, and from eastern Algonquin Prov. Park northeast to the Ottawa River. The high densities in these areas reflect the higher availability of the species' preferred pine forest habitat. – *William J. Crins*

Prairie Warbler

Paruline des prés

Dendroica discolor

John Reaume

The Prairie Warbler breeds throughout eastern North America, wintering in the Caribbean basin. A species of early successional habitats, it is reported to have been rare or absent prior to European settlement in much of its current breeding range in the northeast (Nolan et al. 1999). In Canada, it breeds only in southern Ontario, where the population is quite small. Although now absent from several historical localities, such as along the sand dunes at Nottawasaga Bay (Simcoe Co.) (Devitt 1967), where circa 1948 it once had a significant population, its core breeding range in the province has remained largely unchanged for more than 100 years. Designated Special Concern by both COSEWIC and OMNR in 1985, its national and provincial status was downlisted to Not At Risk in 1999.

In Ontario, most enduring populations of the Prairie Warbler are located in Precambrian rock barrens in which sparse, scrubby Common Juniper, White Pine, and oak vegetation are prevalent. In southeastern Georgian Bay, occupied habitat was characterized by Harris (1998) as 34% exposed rock, 41% shrub, and 25% tree cover. Common Juniper was found to be present at all sites, with White Pine and Red Oak constituting the most important overstorey species. Particularly in the Georgian Bay area, this rock barren habitat is maintained in an extended state of early succession through a combination of periodic fire and austere climatic conditions (Lambert and Smith 1984; Harris 1998).

Distribution and population status: There has been no substantial change in the distribution of the Prairie Warbler in Ontario since the first atlas. Its primary distribution includes the rocky southeastern shore of Georgian Bay between the Pointe au Baril and Port Severn areas, and discontinuously eastward in similar habitats along the southern edge of the Precambrian Shield between Simcoe and Frontenac Counties. It has evidently declined or disappeared from several localities at which it was recorded during the first atlas. It is now extir-

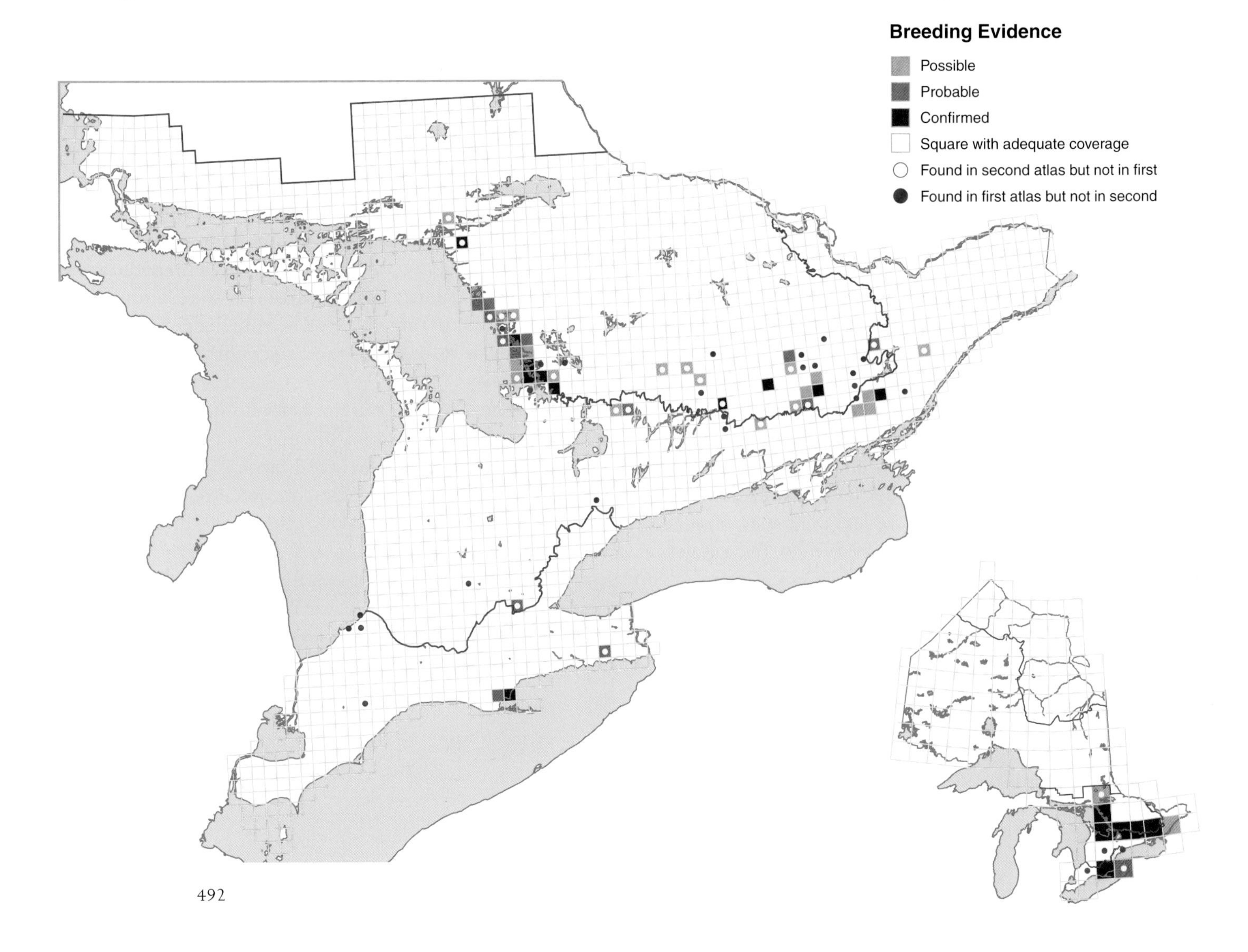

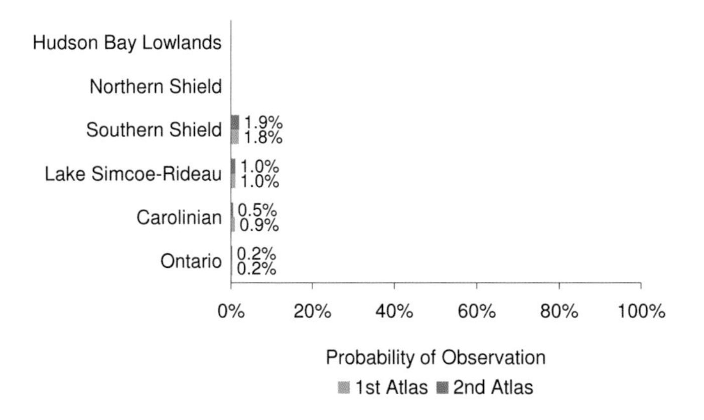

pated at both Grand Bend (Lambton Co.) and Long Lake (Peterborough Co.), where populations of 10 to 15 pairs persisted until 1988. Several smaller but relatively long-standing occurrences (e.g., Mazinaw and Canoe Lakes, Frontenac Co.) have also disappeared or decreased since the first atlas, likely due to gradual successional changes in the rock barren habitat.

Small, isolated populations at Skunk's Misery (Middlesex Co.) and Bamberg (Waterloo RM) no longer appear to be extant. A number of isolated individuals were discovered during the second atlas in limestone shrub alvars and regenerating old fields dominated by Common Juniper, where the species has not been recorded with any regularity, as on the Flamborough, Carden and Napanee limestone plains; these birds were probably only transitory. This is likely also true of apparently anomalous records in Grundy Lake Prov. Park (Parry Sound Dist.) and along the Murdock River (Sudbury Dist.), areas previously uninhabited by the species. Small, isolated populations with limited habitat are prone to extirpation with probably little chance of recolonization. However, the population in the Long Point-Turkey Point area, never larger than eight pairs, has persisted virtually continuously since the 1930s.

Breeding biology: In Ontario, the Prairie Warbler arrives on territories in southeastern Georgian Bay between early and mid-May (Lambert and Smith 1984). Upon arrival, and during the early part of the nesting cycle, it sings frequently, particularly in the early morning (Nolan et al. 1999), facilitating easy detection by atlassers. Song frequency diminishes by early July and has largely ceased by mid-July. In Ontario, nests are usually built in low shrubs, often juniper, at heights of less than 1.5 m (Peck and James 1987). Nests are cryptic and hard to find, and even family groups with dependent young can be difficult to detect. Confirmation of breeding was obtained in only 24% of squares in which the species was found and primarily consisted of fledged young or adults carrying food. In most squares, the highest evidence recorded was of singing or territorial males.

Abundance: Detections on point counts were insufficient to generate an abundance map. At the time of the first atlas, Lambert and Smith (1984) estimated a maximum provincial population of 468 to 709 pairs but believed the lower estimate was more accurate. A recent survey of suitable breeding habitat in southeastern Georgian Bay between Port Severn and Parry Sound (Harris 1998) detected 254 territories and suggested an upper population limit of no more than 270 pairs. Data from the second atlas suggest that away from the Georgian Bay area fewer than 50 pairs occur and that the total provincial population is unlikely to exceed 320 breeding pairs.
– Donald A. Sutherland and Christopher G. Harris

In Ontario, nests are usually in Common Juniper and less commonly in deciduous shrubs such as this nest in an American Hazel. St. Williams Forest, Norfolk Co., 13 June 1987. *Photo: George K. Peck*

White Pine-oak-Common Juniper Precambrian rock barrens are characteristic breeding habitat in eastern Georgian Bay. Near Niblett Island, Moose Bay, Georgian Bay, Muskoka Dist., 13 June 1997. *Photo: Christopher G. Harris*

Palm Warbler

Paruline à couronne rousse

Dendroica palmarum

George K. Peck

This familiar tail-wagging warbler is among the earliest of migrant warblers to pass through southern Ontario in spring. Its breeding habits, however, are generally little known, due to its northerly distribution and the inaccessibility of its peatland habitat. The Palm Warbler breeds across the Boreal Forest of North America from the southern Northwest Territories east across the northern Prairie Provinces, northern Ontario, and southern Québec to Newfoundland and Labrador. As much as 98% of the global population is estimated to breed in Canada (Blancher 2003), with the southern extent of its breeding range just reaching northern portions of Minnesota, Wisconsin, Michigan, New York, and Maine (Wilson 1996). Two subspecies have been described: the "Yellow" Palm Warbler, a strongly yellow and generally more brightly coloured eastern subspecies (*hypochrysea*) occurring from southeastern Ontario eastward, and the "Western" Palm Warbler, the pale-bellied, less brightly marked nominate subspecies (*palmarum*) that occupies the remainder of the range, including northern Ontario.

Distribution and population status: The Palm Warbler is widely distributed throughout northern Ontario, with a 76% probability of observation in the Hudson Bay Lowlands and just 40% in the Northern Shield region. Between atlases, there were significant increases in the probability of observation for both of these regions – 73% and 76%, respectively, resulting in a significant increase of 74% for the province as a whole. These increases could be attributable to greater effort during the second atlas to survey areas of suitable open peatland habitat away from roadsides and densely treed river corridors. CMMN data for LPBO, which likely predominantly involves birds from Ontario, indicate a significant increase in numbers of the Western Palm Warbler passing through on spring migration since 1961, but no significant changes in the last decade.

South of the Clay Belt, the Palm Warbler increasingly becomes locally distributed and is essentially absent from much of the

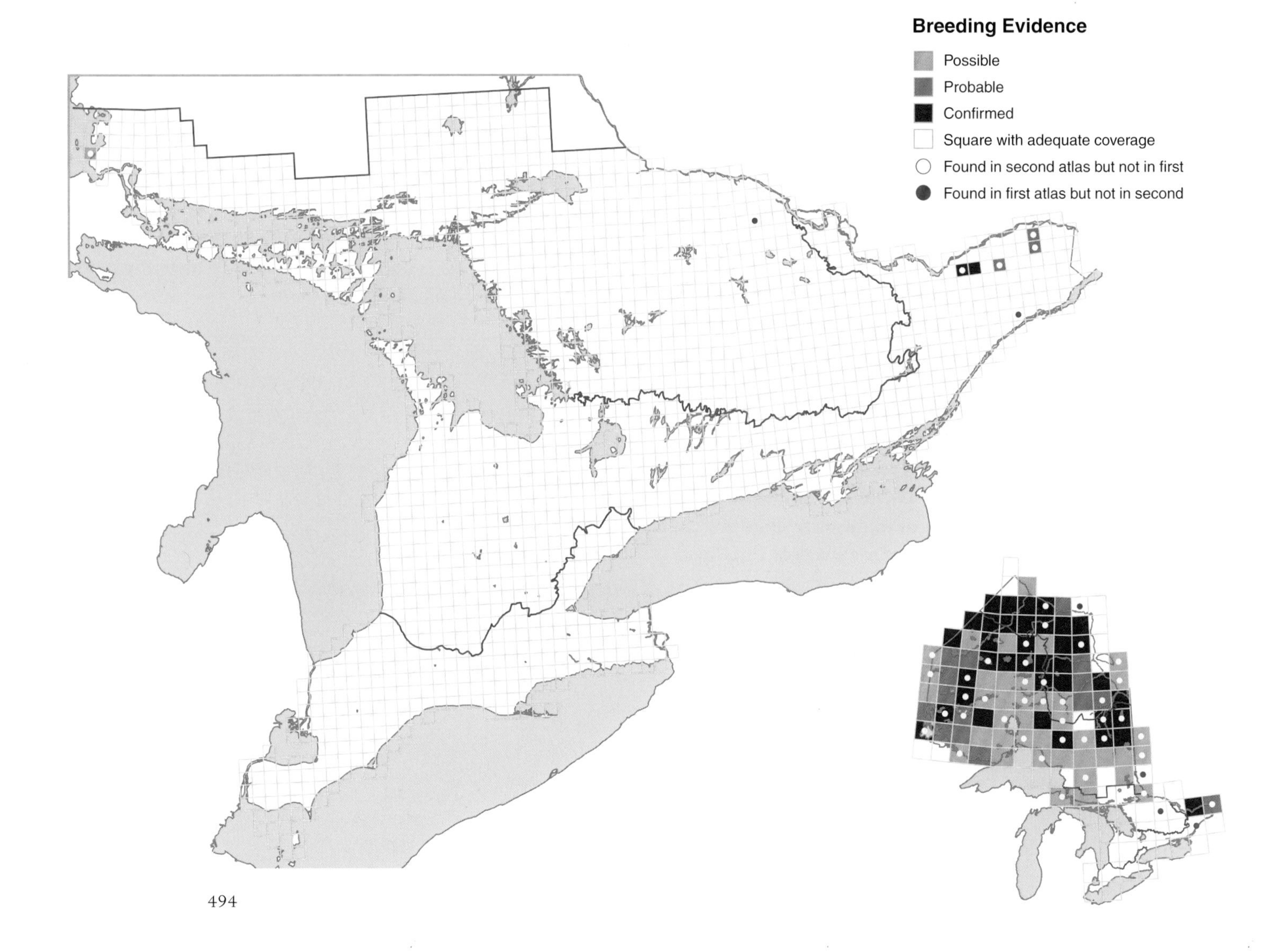

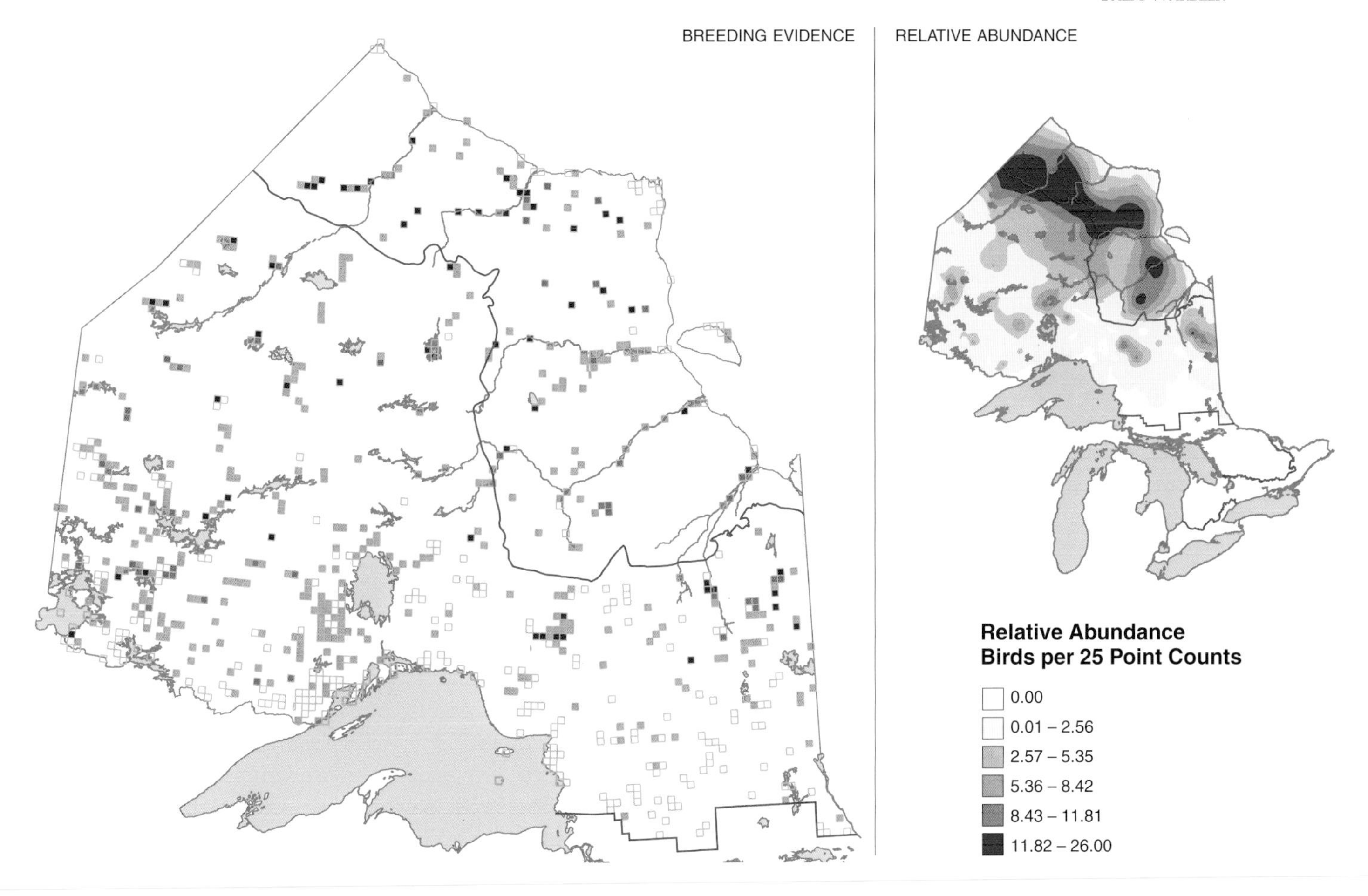

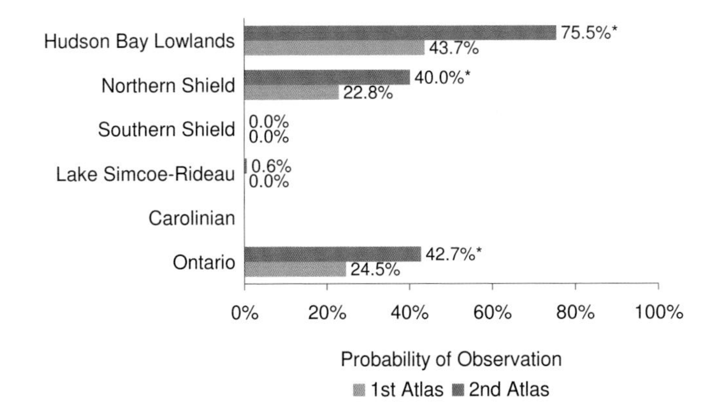

Southern Shield. An isolated breeding population of Yellow Palm Warblers occurs in the Lake Simcoe-Rideau region in southeastern Ontario. The species remains a very locally distributed breeder in a few relict peatlands associated with the Champlain Sea deposits between Ottawa and Cornwall. Its presence was confirmed in the Mer Bleue (City of Ottawa), where a small breeding population has been known for more than 100 years and where birds were documented during the first atlas. In the Alfred Bog, where the species went undetected during the first atlas, a sizeable population is now known to occur. An apparently territorial male discovered in the LaRose Forest north of Casselman (United Counties of Prescott and Russell) in 2002 was not detected subsequently.

Breeding biology: Throughout most of its Ontario breeding range, the Palm Warbler is found in large, open peatlands with scattered, stunted conifers. In the Northern Shield, it occasionally also utilizes areas of dense regeneration resulting from clearcuts or burns in spruce and Jack Pine dominated forest. Mixed shrub thickets of birch, Green Alder, and spruce are used in the northern Hudson Bay Lowlands in addition to the extensive, sparsely treed peatland habitat. Within the latter, more commonly occupied habitat, territories typically incorporate treed margins or "islands" of conifers (Welsh 1971; Wilson 1996).

The Palm Warbler is a ground-nesting species; nests are well concealed in moss hummocks, often beneath the cover of small conifers and dense shrubs (Peck and James 1987) and are consequently difficult to find. Confirmed breeding was reported in just 13% of squares and, as with many passerines, confirmations primarily involved recently fledged young or adults carrying food. The most frequently reported evidence of breeding, in 76% of squares, was singing males and individuals in suitable habitat.

Abundance: The Palm Warbler is evidently widespread and relatively common, but seemingly nowhere abundant throughout much of northern Ontario. It reaches its greatest abundance in the interior of the Hudson Bay Lowlands. Point count data indicated an average density of 7.2 birds/25 point counts in the Hudson Bay Lowlands, but only 1.7 birds/25 point counts in the Northern Shield. Based on atlas point count data, the Palm Warbler is among the commonest birds in the province, with an estimated population of 7,000,000 birds, 4,000,000 of which occur in the Hudson Bay Lowlands. The population in southeastern Ontario, though small, is larger than expected. At least 10-20 pairs are estimated to occur in the Mer Bleue (L. Sirois, pers. comm.), while in the more extensive habitat in the Alfred Bog, a population in excess of 100 pairs is estimated (J. Bouvier, pers. comm.). – *Donald A. Sutherland*

Bay-breasted Warbler

Paruline à poitrine baie

Dendroica castanea

George K. Peck

The Bay-breasted Warbler is a well-known Spruce Budworm specialist. Although it will utilize other prey, a 10-fold increase in local populations may occur in response to budworm outbreaks (Williams 1996b). It is a neotropical migrant, with 90% of its breeding range in the Canadian Boreal Forest from northeastern British Columbia and southeastern Yukon east to southwestern Newfoundland. As a result of this narrow range and apparent recent declines, the species has been placed on the Partners in Flight Watch List (Rich et al. 2004).

Distribution and population status: As much as or more than any other warbler, the Bay-breasted Warbler's distribution and population closely reflect the occurrence of Spruce Budworm outbreaks. Depending on the location, several males per hectare may be recorded during outbreaks, only to be rare or absent from the same area a few years later.

The Bay-breasted Warbler is widely distributed in the Northern Shield but becomes progressively less common and local southward in the Southern Shield and rare south to the northern edge of the Lake Simcoe-Rideau region. The area occupied includes the majority of the Boreal Forest as well as portions of the Great Lakes-St. Lawrence Forest, and corresponds with the distribution of the spruce-fir forests in which the species preferentially breeds. It occurs only sparingly in much of the Hudson Bay Lowlands, with possible breeding evidence recorded north to between 53° N and 55° N on the Fawn and Sachigo Rivers. While there was no significant change in the probability of observation of the species in the province as a whole, there was a significant 22% increase between atlases in the core of its range in the Northern Shield region, where there is a 53% probability of observation. Given that the budworm population has been declining in Ontario since the 1980s (Environment Canada 1999), an increase in this region is some-

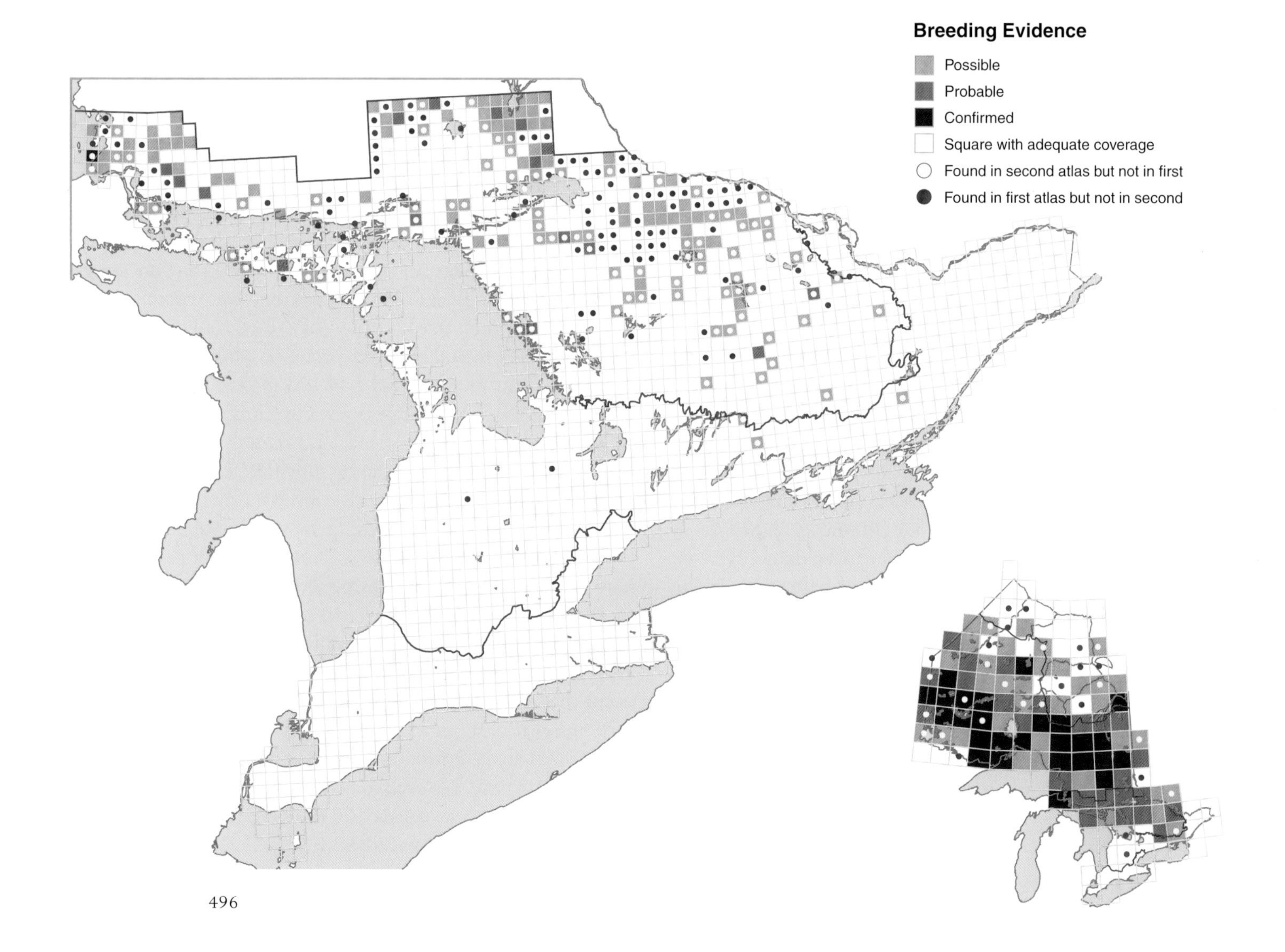

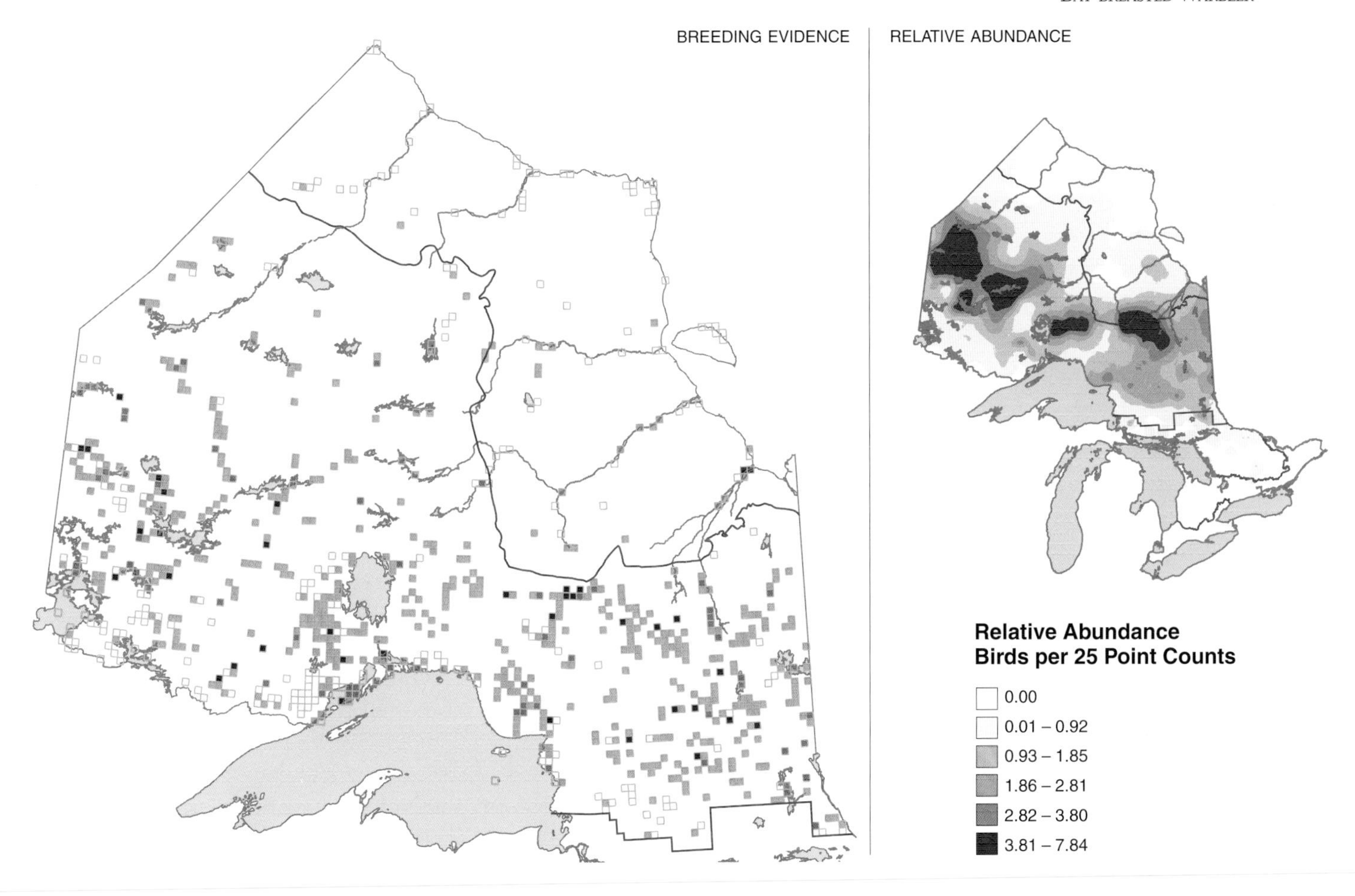

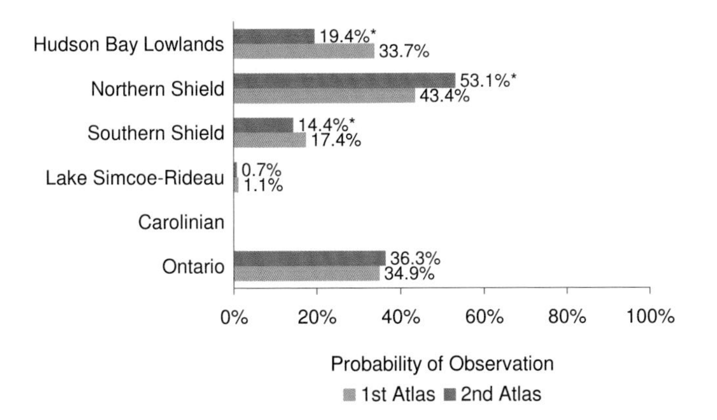

what surprising. More expected is the 17% decline in the Southern Shield region, where the frequency of occurrence and extent of range were predicted to decline (Welsh in Cadman et al. 1987). There was also a significant 42% decline in the probability of observation in the Hudson Bay Lowlands. The reason for this decline is unclear but may reflect changes to the limited available habitat or be related to reduced budworm numbers. No significant change is evident in the Lake Simcoe-Rideau region, where suitable breeding habitat is limited and the species is rare.

Several authors (e.g., Erksine 1992) have suggested that this species may be impacted by current forestry practices in Ontario, particularly the harvest of mature spruce and fir forests and insecticide spray programs to control budworm outbreaks. CMMN data for LPBO and TCBO both indicate significant declines over the last decade in the number of migrants passing through these stations (Crewe 2006). However, the increase in the probability of observation in the Northern Shield in the second atlas suggests that the species' sensitivity to forest management and insecticides on the breeding grounds may have been overstated. In some ecoregions in Ontario, the Bay-breasted Warbler is more common in second-growth forest (20-80 years old) than in mature forest, suggesting that it is not necessarily a mature forest specialist (J.R. Zimmerling, unpubl. data); Holmes (1998) suggests that the indirect effects of forest spraying with lepidoptera-specific insecticides pose little risk to forest songbirds.

Breeding biology: The Bay-breasted Warbler breeds primarily in dense spruce and Balsam Fir forests. Females generally build nests in the middle branches, 2-7 m above the ground (Peck and James 1987), in large conifers. Nests were thus not frequently encountered by atlassers. Indeed, only 5% of the squares in which this species was recorded obtained confirmed breeding evidence of any type. Both adults actively feed the young, and observations of adults carrying food or with fledged young were the most commonly reported confirmed evidence. Fully 85% of evidence was simply in the form of singing males or individuals in suitable habitat.

Abundance: The abundance map appears to accurately reflect the relative abundance of the Bay-breasted Warbler throughout the province and shows that this species is virtually absent from the Hudson Bay Lowlands, Carolinian, and Lake Simcoe-Rideau regions and uncommon in the Southern Shield, where spruce-fir forests are more limited or absent. In the Northern Shield region, it is most common along the northern edge of the Boreal Forest. Particularly high densities are evident around Woodland Caribou Prov. Park, Sioux Lookout, Lake Nipigon, and Kapuskasing. – *J. Ryan Zimmerling and Fergus I. Nicoll*

Blackpoll Warbler

Paruline rayée

Dendroica striata

David Welbourne

The Blackpoll Warbler breeds across boreal and subarctic North America north of about 51° N, but locally farther south, principally at higher elevations in southwestern Québec, Maine, New Hampshire, New York, Massachusetts, and north-central Pennsylvania (Hunt and Eliason 1999). The species has the most northerly breeding distribution of any warbler in the province, breeding from the limit of trees south through the Hudson Bay Lowlands to northern parts of the Northern Shield region.

Distribution and population status: Data from the second atlas indicate a significant increase of 44% since the first atlas in the probability of observation for the species in the province as a whole. This increase was greater in the Hudson Bay Lowlands than the Northern Shield, where the Blackpoll Warbler is evidently far less common and widespread. Though the breeding evidence map accurately depicts the extent of its breeding range in the far north, the probability of observation was just 61% in the Hudson Bay Lowlands region. This lower probability is likely an artifact of lower coverage in the interior of the region, and the species probably occurs in most if not all squares there (pers. obs.). The range limit in the south remains unclear. The southern extent of the continuous breeding range appears to be about 51° N, in the vicinity of Woodland Caribou Prov. Park in the west and Moosonee in the east. Farther south in the Boreal Forest, its distribution becomes discontinuous. It may occur only irregularly at localities near the southern limit of its range in Ontario. During the second atlas, it was recorded in several squares near Moosonee where it had not been detected during surveys between atlases (cf. Wilson and McRae 1993). The reasons for its apparently ephemeral occupancy of some areas within its range are unknown. It has been suggested that the species may be a budworm specialist, although evidence in support of this is lacking or inconclusive (Hunt and Eliason 1999). First-year males

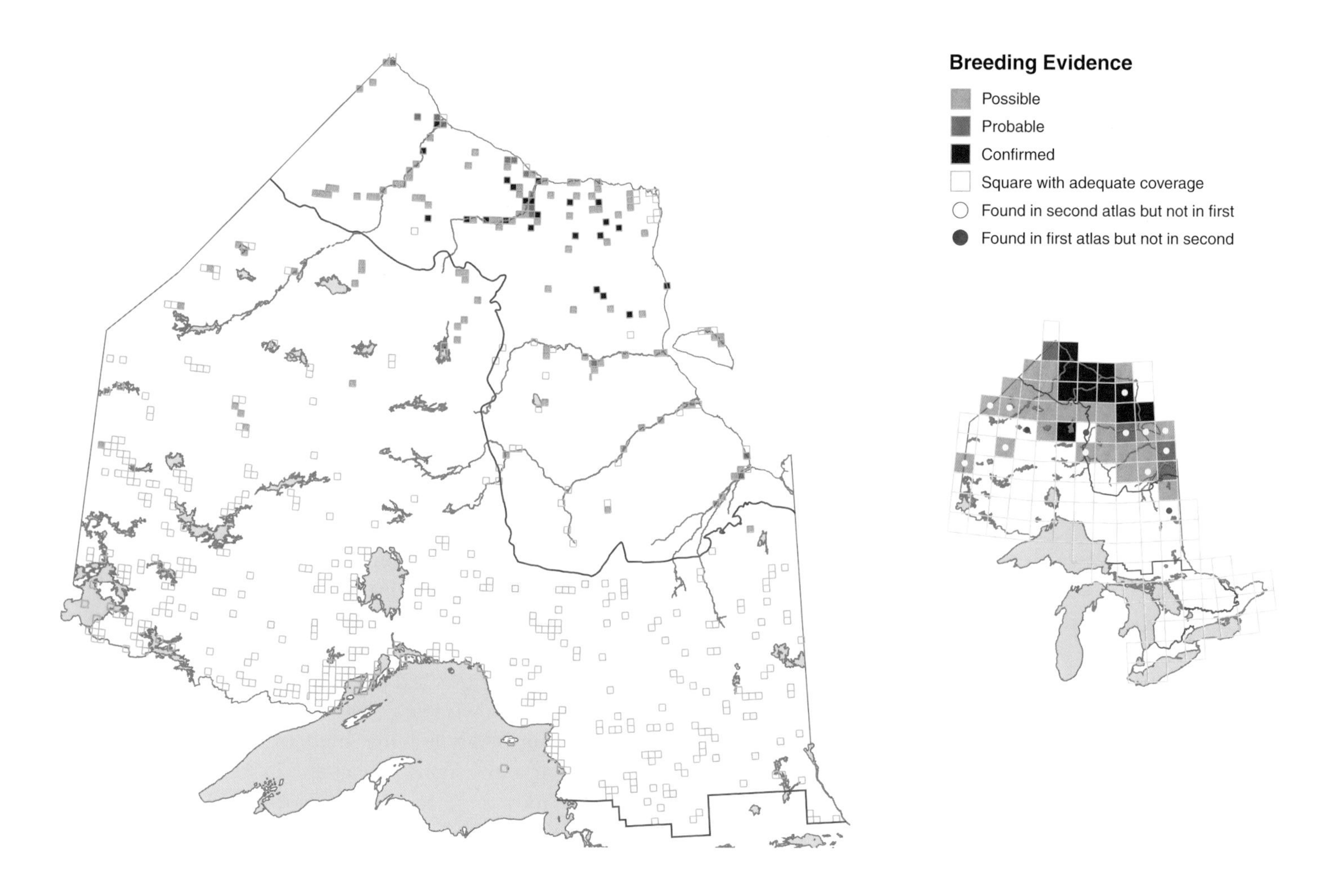

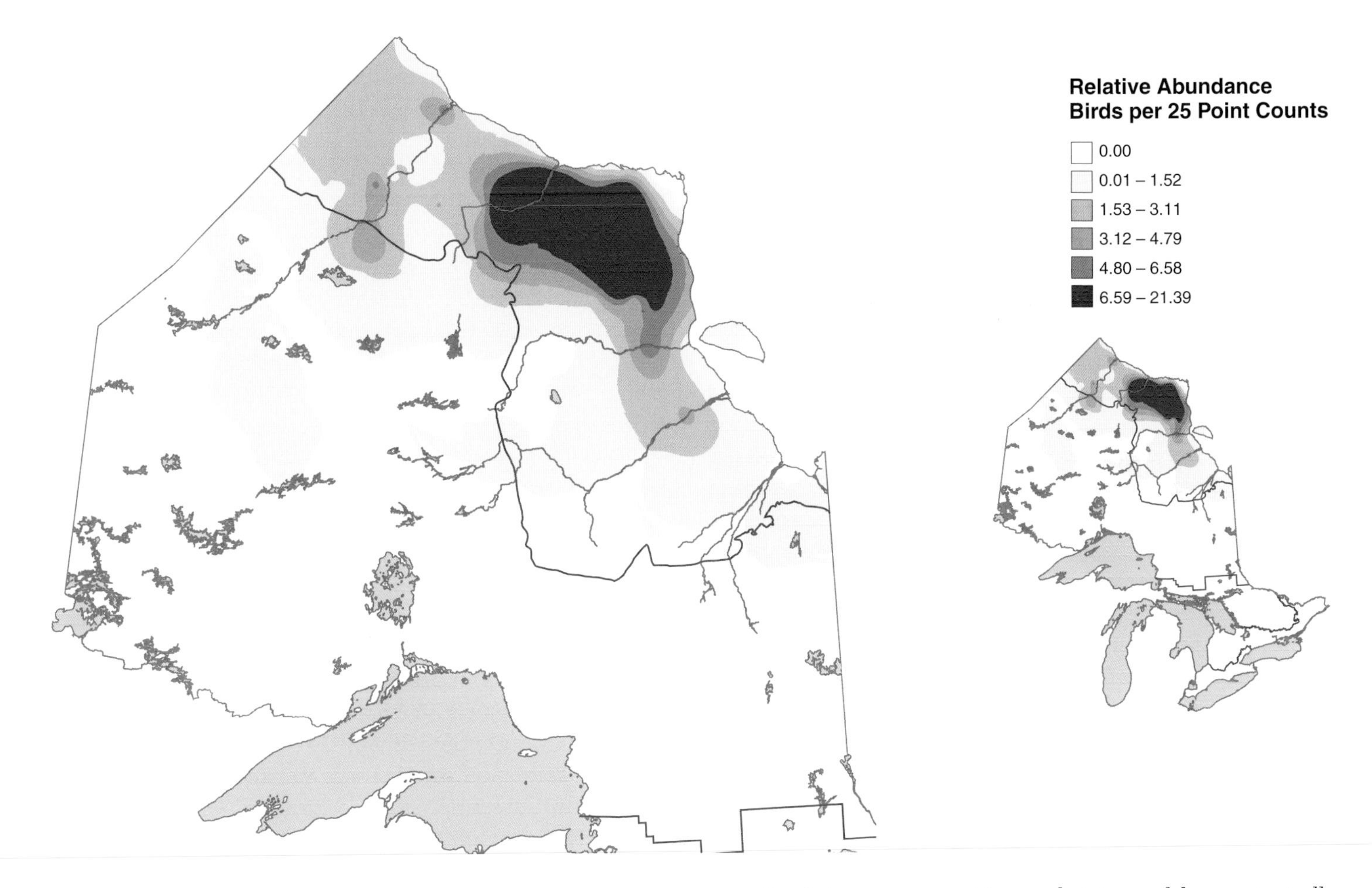

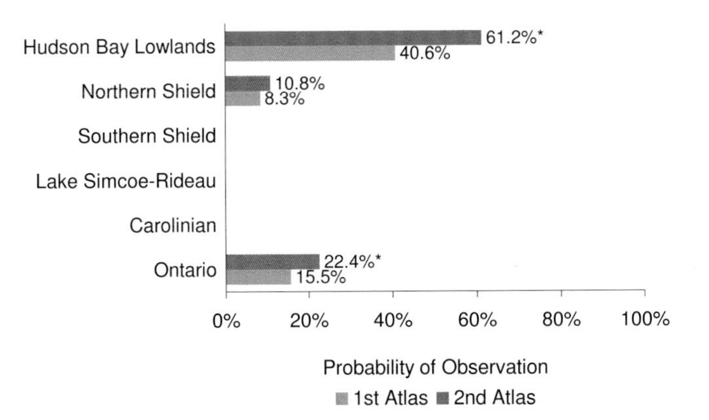

are known to arrive on territory later than older males (Hunt and Eliason 1999) and may account for reports of possible breeding well south of the species' established breeding range during both atlases. There were no reports of occurrences near Little Abitibi Lake (49° N) where it was reported during the first atlas. The southernmost evidence of breeding during the second atlas was from the vicinity of Kesagami Lake (50° N), 100 km south of Moosonee.

Breeding biology: The Blackpoll Warbler is among the last warbler species to arrive on breeding territories in Ontario. Earlier migrants typically arrive in mid-May, but peak arrival occurs in late May and early June. The species' song is very distinctive, and males sing almost continuously during daylight hours (Hunt and Eliason 1999), so that the species is easily detected. Possible breeding evidence, primarily singing males, constituted about 75% of the evidence reported for the species.

Preferred nesting habitat in Ontario is open spruce-lichen woodlands in wet spruce-Tamarack taiga and burns, typically dominated by Black Spruce with a variable low understorey of spruce saplings, alder, willow, birch, and Labrador Tea. This warbler also occurs in isolated groves of stunted spruce in open tundra, around small lakes and ponds, and along drainages in tundra. Less commonly occupied habitats include willow-aspen riparian woodlands (McLaren and McLaren 1981b; Peck and James 1987). It has been reported to also use low willow and willow-birch riparian thickets on tundra, particularly in the northwestern portion of its range (Hunt and Eliason 1999), but there is little or no evidence of use of this habitat in Ontario.

Nests are typically constructed on or near the ground, usually close to the trunk of a small spruce, willow, or Tamarack (Peck and James 1987), and are well concealed and difficult to find. As with many passerines, breeding is most easily confirmed through the observation of fledged young or adults carrying food. Breeding was confirmed in only 17% of squares with breeding evidence, and most confirmations consisted of adults carrying food.

Abundance: The map of relative abundance indicates that the Blackpoll Warbler is most abundant in the northeastern Hudson Bay Lowlands inland from the coast in an area bounded by the Winisk and Attawapiskat Rivers, and less common to uncommon elsewhere. Such a distribution may be an artifact of the uneven distribution of point counts. The species is typically present wherever suitable habitat patches exist (pers. obs.) and is probably relatively uniformly widespread and common in most squares in the northern Hudson Bay Lowlands, becoming progressively less common and discontinuously distributed southward. – *Donald A. Sutherland*

Cerulean Warbler

Paruline azurée

Dendroica cerulea

George K. Peck

The Cerulean Warbler breeds in the canopy of mature deciduous forest where it is difficult to observe and most readily detected by its distinctive buzzy song. Its breeding range is primarily in the eastern US from the Mississippi Valley east to New England, extending north into southern Ontario and southwestern Québec. It winters in the mountains of South America.

Analyses of BBS data from throughout its breeding range indicate a highly significant long-term decline of about 4% per year from 1966 to 2005, one of the largest declines of any warbler (Sauer et al. 2005). Although BBS trend data are not available for Canada, it has been designated a species of Special Concern in Ontario and Canada.

Distribution and population status: The Cerulean Warbler was found in 86 squares during the second atlas, all in southern Ontario, with more than one-quarter in the Frontenac Axis north of Kingston. The other main concentration was in Norfolk Co., north of Long Point, although there were also records along the boundary between the Southern Shield and Lake Simcoe-Rideau regions as far west as Georgian Bay.

The species was reported in 22 fewer squares than in the first atlas, and there was an overall non-significant 30% decline in probability of observation. The only significant decline (47%) was in the Carolinian region. There was little change in the Lake Simcoe-Rideau region but a non-significant 33% drop in the Southern Shield. In both the Kingston and Long Point areas, the species was found in many of the same squares in both atlases; elsewhere, this was only true for a few squares, mainly in areas with long-established populations. Atlassers were provided with information on the history of the species in their square and encouraged to make a special effort to look for it, so many of the absences probably indicate real disappearances.

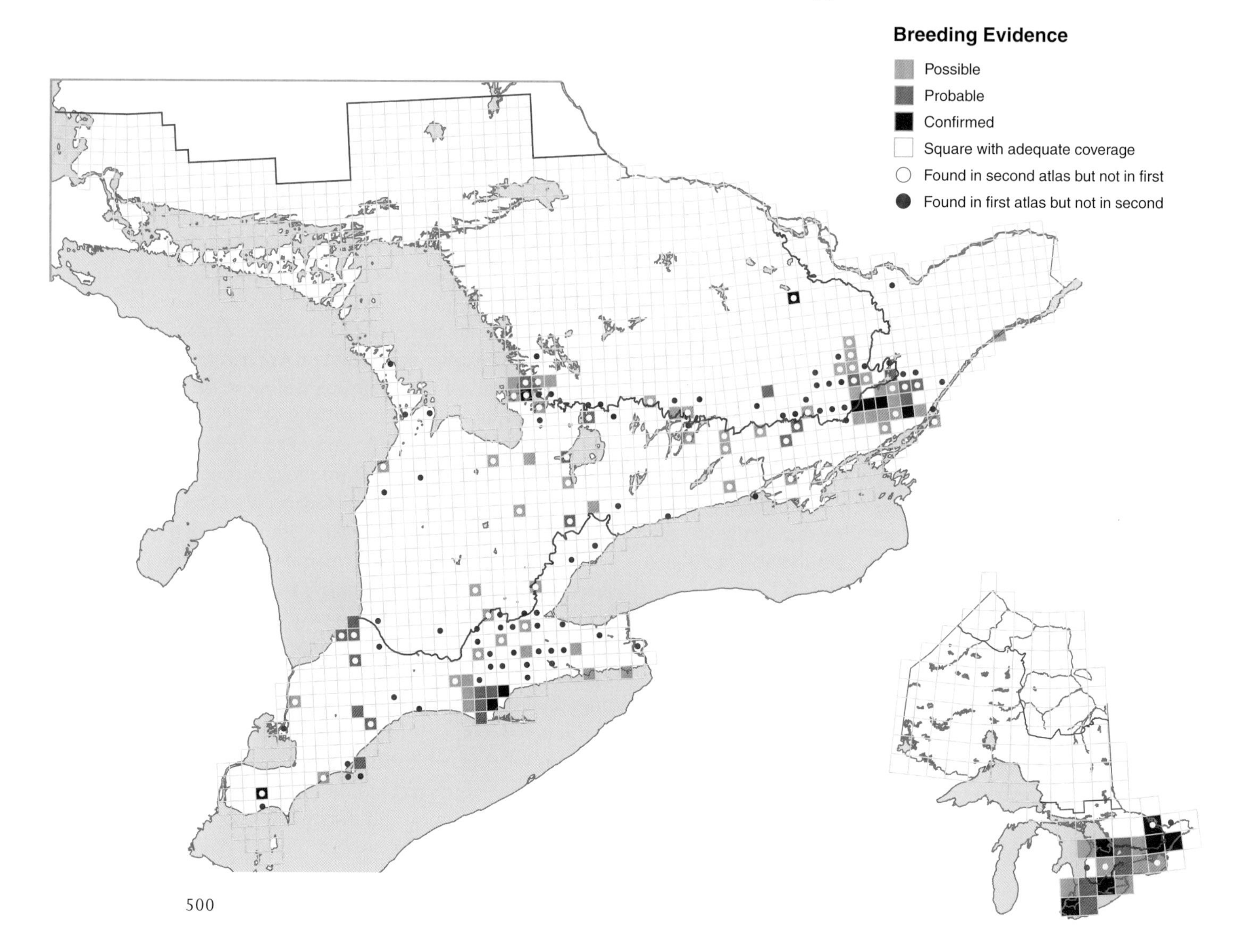

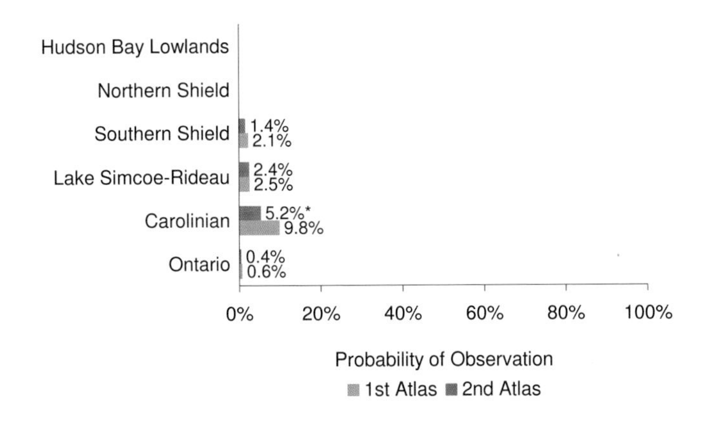

Overall, these results are consistent with the range-wide decline observed in the BBS. Discoveries of previously unknown populations during first-round atlases in New York and Ontario led to suggestions this species may have been expanding in the northeast (Hamel 2000). Whether or not that was the case formerly, it is clearly not true now. Even in its core breeding area near Kingston, Jones et al. (2004) estimated that adult mortality was high enough that the population might not be self-sustaining, although there was no evidence of a decline in their study area.

Breeding biology: The Cerulean Warbler nests mainly in mature deciduous upland or swamp forest with a tall canopy of uneven structure, often with gaps, and a sparse understorey. In Ontario, the core of each territory is usually associated with large oak or Bitternut Hickory trees, which provide good singing perches (Barg et al. 2005). The species is most often associated with large forest tracts with interior forest, although it may occur in woodlots as small as 10 ha (COSEWIC 2003). The nest is built on the outer branch of a large tree, 5-18 m above the ground and an average of 3 m from the main trunk, partly concealed from above by leaves.

Breeding was confirmed in only nine squares; several confirmations were by crews studying the species. This reflects the difficulty of observing the species and finding nests. Nearly all remaining records were of singing males, with very few observations of females outside of confirmed sites. Given the low abundance of this species, it is likely that some records involved unpaired singing males. In several cases, observers noted that they were unable to relocate singing males on subsequent visits in the same breeding season.

Abundance: The Cerulean Warbler was detected on only 55 point counts, of which 38 (69%) were in nine squares on the Frontenac Axis near Kingston. This concentration suggests that the majority of the remaining population of the species in Canada is in this area. The total population of this species in Canada has been estimated at 500-1000 breeding pairs, of which fewer than 40 pairs are in Quebec, and the remainder are in Ontario (COSEWIC 2003). The number of individuals reported on Rare/Colonial Species Report Forms over the five years of the atlas indicates at least 200 different territories. Given that many areas, such as on private land, were not surveyed, this seems consistent with the COSEWIC estimate. As with the point count data, the highest reported densities per square were in the Kingston area, but five or more territories per square were also reported from squares near Skunk's Misery, Pinery Prov. Park, and the Long Point area, and around Awenda Prov. Park, all areas where the species was reported in the first atlas. – *Charles M. Francis*

Nests are typically saddled on a horizontal limb of a large deciduous tree, 5-18 m above the ground. Near Campbellville, Halton Region, 6 June 1964. *Photo: George K. Peck*

Mature Sugar Maple-Beech forest habitat of the Cerulean Warbler near Junetown, United Counties of Leeds and Grenville. A tall canopy of uneven structure, often with gaps, is characteristic of the species' habitat in Ontario. *Photo: Donald A. Sutherland*

Black-and-white Warbler

Paruline noir et blanc

Mniotilta varia

Mark Peck

This aptly named wood-warbler is one of the most distinctive members of its family, both for its striking black and white plumage and its unusual habit (for a warbler) of foraging on tree trunks and thick limbs. Former names for this species include Pied Creeper, Creeping Warbler, and Black-and-white Creeper. It is one of the earliest warblers to return to Ontario in the spring, presumably because it is not dependent on foliage as a substrate for foraging. The Black-and-white Warbler is a common summer resident throughout Canada from the southern Northwest Territories east to Newfoundland and south through the eastern US to Georgia and east Texas. It winters in the West Indies, Central America and northwestern South America (Kricher 1995).

Distribution and population status: The Black-and-white Warbler is found widely throughout Ontario during the nesting season. Its preferred habitat includes both mature and second-growth deciduous and mixed woodlands. The probability of observation is 62% across Ontario as a whole, and it was reported in all of the atlas administrative regions in the province, with the exception of Essex in the far south. It is much less common in southwestern Ontario than in other areas of the province, and the probability of observation is only 10% in the Carolinian region. Although historically the species was reported to be reasonably common through southwestern Ontario, most of the region is now heavily agricultural or urbanized, limiting available habitat. This warbler is substantially more widespread farther north, with the probability of observation a much higher 70% in the Lake Simcoe-Rideau region and 94% in the Southern Shield, where suitable habitat is more common. The species is also widespread throughout northern Ontario, occurring somewhat more sparsely in the Hudson Bay Lowlands primarily in riparian woodlands along major river corridors.

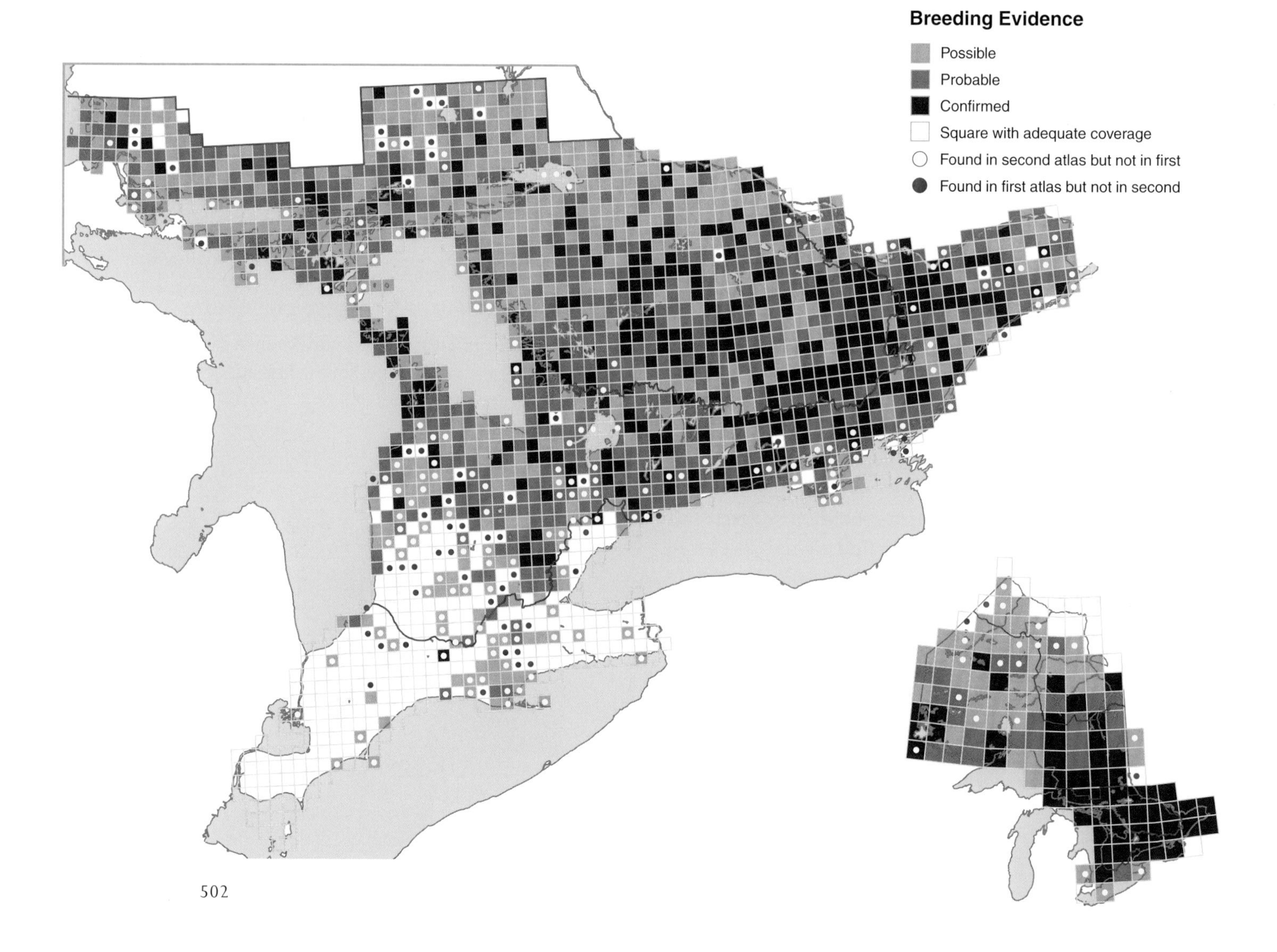

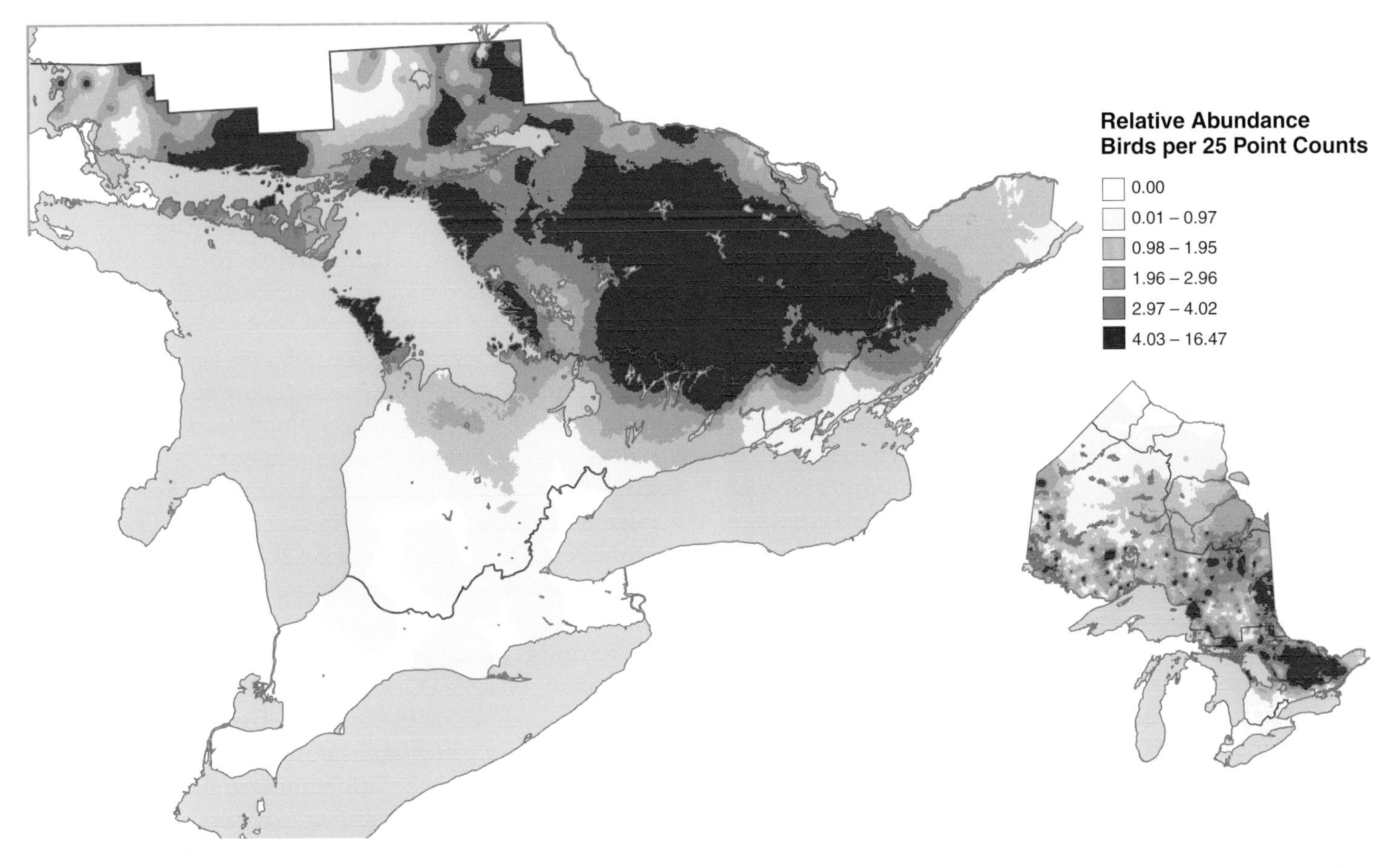

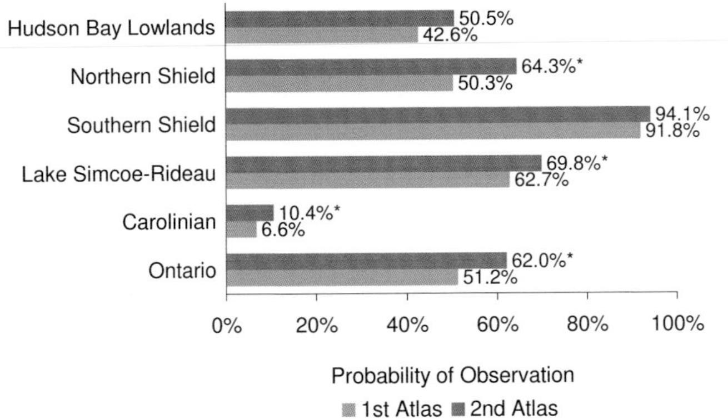

Both atlases demonstrate a similar pattern of distribution in Ontario, but the probability of observation of the species increased significantly by 21% between atlases in the province as a whole. There were significant increases in the Carolinian region (57%) and the Lake Simcoe-Rideau region (11%). These increases are likely due to an increase in suitable breeding habitat as old retired farmland returns to forest through natural succession. A significant increase of 28% in the probability of observation was also seen in the Northern Shield region. This is more difficult to explain but may be due to maturing successional habitat following historical logging or clearing, or could be a result of more efficient coverage during the second atlas.

BBS data have shown a near-significant annual increase of 1.4% in Black-and-white Warbler populations in Ontario since 1968 (Downes et al. 2005). Migration monitoring data from LPBO show a significant increase in numbers between 1961 and 2004 (Crewe 2006). Presumably, the primary cause is the succession of abandoned farmland in central Ontario and the resulting increase in young forest habitat.

Breeding biology: Although the Black-and-white Warbler sings readily and its song is very distinctive, its territory is relatively large for a wood-warbler, which can make it harder to detect. During the breeding season, the male can be quite aggressive toward individuals of the same and other species that enter its territory. Nesting takes place from late May through July, with most eggs laid during June. The nest is typically located on the ground, usually in a depression at the base of a tree, stump, or shrub, or under logs or dead branches. More rarely, nests may be slightly elevated in stump cavities or upturned roots. In general, nests are well hidden and difficult to find. Consequently, confirmed breeding was obtained in only 16% of the squares with data, and the great majority of confirmation was by viewing adults carrying food. Nests were found in only eight of the 38 atlas administrative regions where breeding was confirmed.

Abundance: Densities of the Black-and-white Warbler were highest in the Southern Shield, averaging 4.5 birds/25 point counts. The species was abundant in virtually all parts of this region. It was also common from the eastern shore of Lake Superior to Lake Abitibi, and north to Moosonee, decreasing in density to the west, but with moderate densities in the Rainy River area and west of Lake Nipigon. Although the species was widespread in the Lake Simcoe-Rideau region, densities were only about a third of those recorded in the Southern Shield, and it was rarely recorded on point counts in the southernmost parts of the province. – *Peter L. McLaren*

American Redstart

Paruline flamboyante

Setophaga ruticilla

Elizabeth Gow

The American Redstart is among the more easily detected of the wood-warblers, due to its tendency to flycatch, its conspicuous vocalizations, and the bright orange and black plumage of the male. In its wintering areas, this species is referred to as "*la candelita*," or little candle. The redstart has one of the most widespread breeding ranges of the wood warblers, extending across North America from southern Yukon and British Columbia east to Newfoundland and south through much of the central and eastern US to the Gulf of Mexico. It is primarily a species of deciduous understorey and woodland edges. Its preferred habitat includes open and semi-open deciduous and mixed forests; it tends to avoid fully mature forests. It winters in the West Indies, Central America, and northern South America (Sherry and Holmes 1997).

Distribution and population status: The distribution of the American Redstart in Ontario is essentially the same as that documented in the first atlas and earlier publications (e.g., Godfrey 1986). It is a widespread summer resident throughout the province, north to the latitude of the Attawapiskat River and Big Trout Lake. In the northern and western portions of its breeding range, it is more sparsely distributed, restricted to the pockets of deciduous woodlands within the predominantly coniferous forest. However, it is common in areas of the province south from Wawa and Lake Abitibi. Its distribution is concentrated in the Southern Shield and the Lake Simcoe-Rideau regions, where the probability of observation was 96% and 80%, respectively. The redstart is also relatively common in the Northern Shield and Carolinian regions, with probabilities of observation of 52% in both regions. Gaps in distribution in southern Ontario are primarily due to lack of suitable habitat, especially in the intensively farmed areas of the southwest.

It was suggested in the first atlas that redstarts were declining in Ontario. However, there were significant increases between atlases in the probability of observation in the Lake

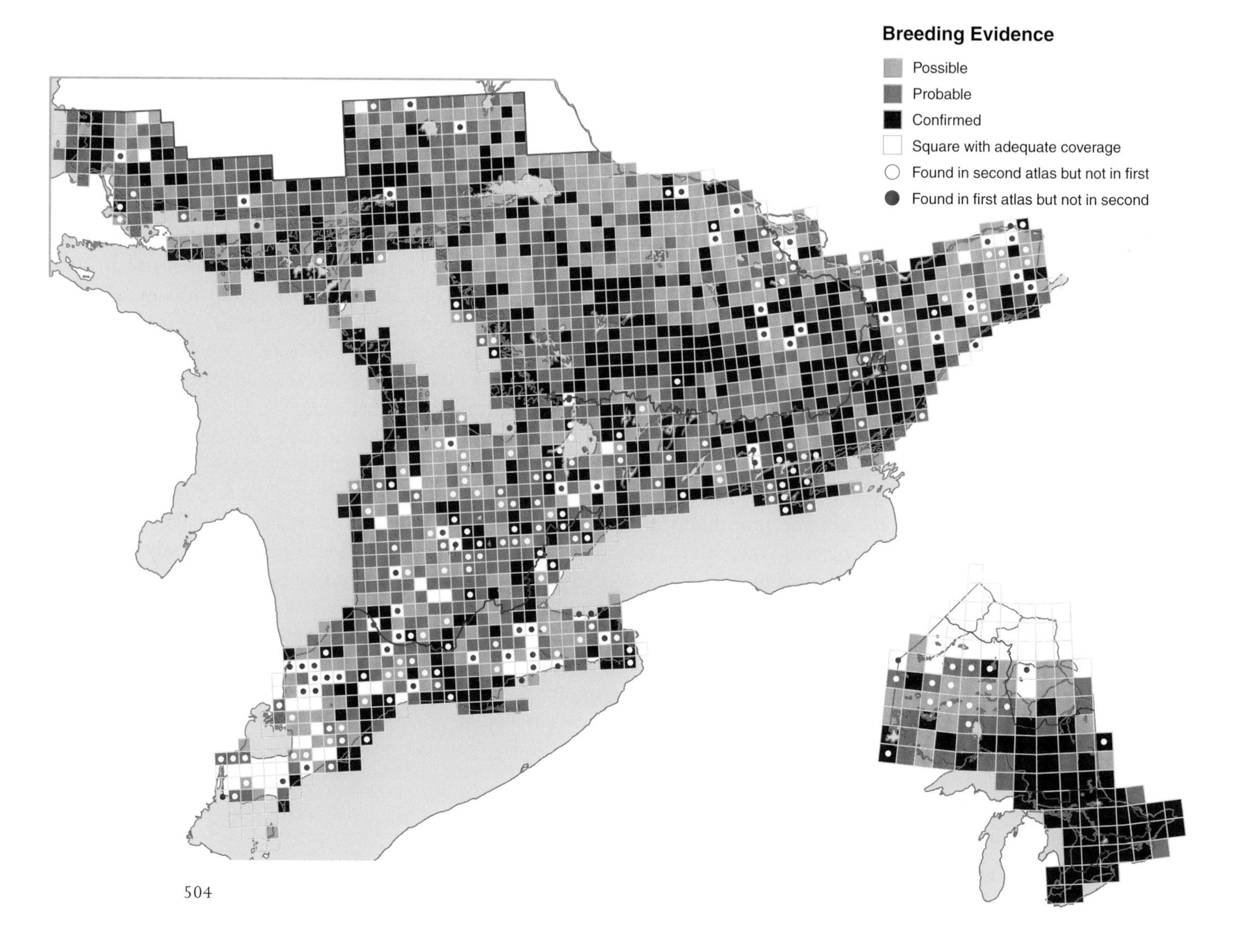

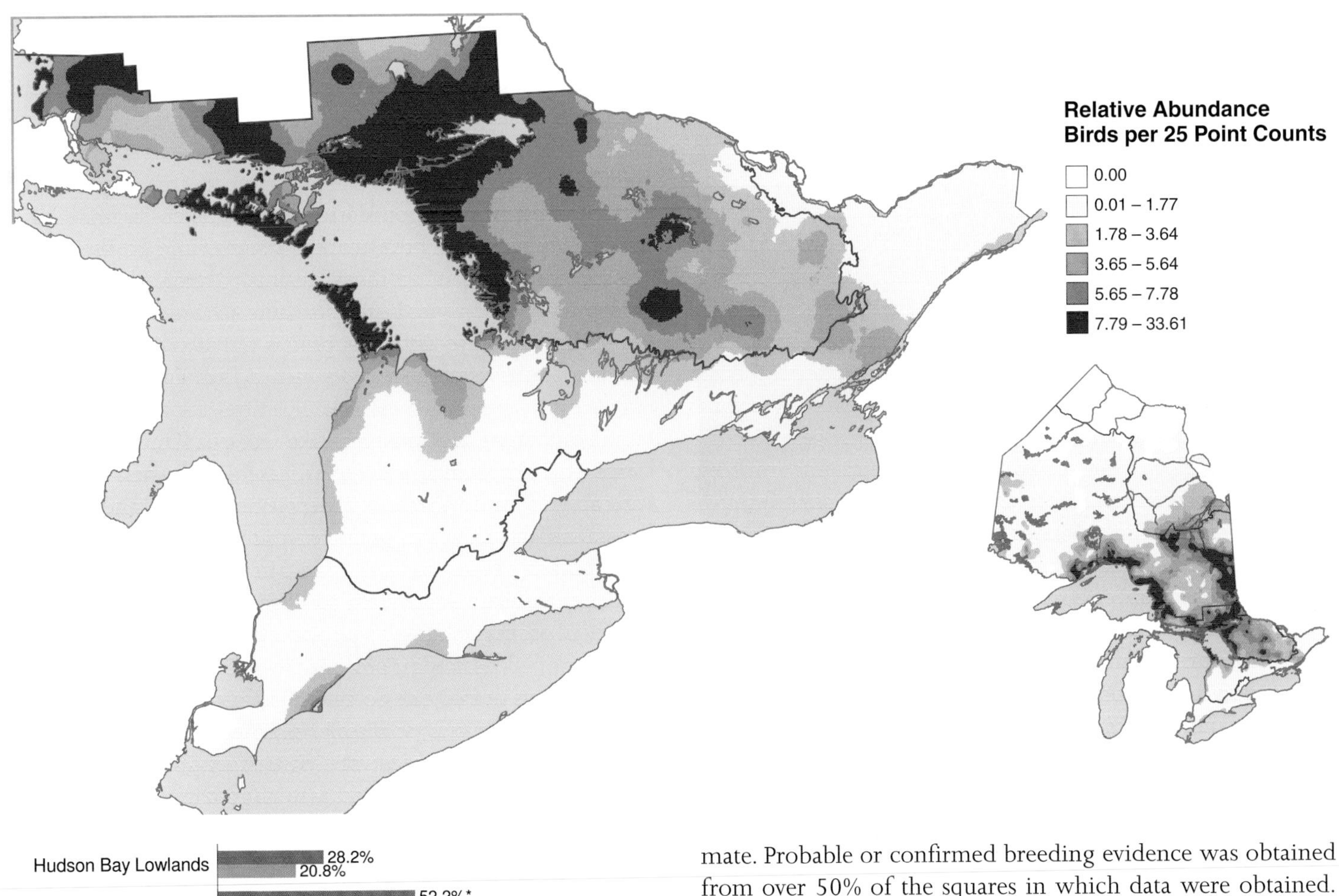

Region	2nd Atlas	1st Atlas
Hudson Bay Lowlands	28.2%	20.8%
Northern Shield	52.2%*	42.1%
Southern Shield	95.8%	96.9%
Lake Simcoe-Rideau	80.2%*	74.0%
Carolinian	51.5%	56.4%
Ontario	51.0%	43.1%

Probability of Observation
■ 1st Atlas ■ 2nd Atlas

Simcoe-Rideau and Northern Shield regions of 8% and 24%, respectively, although no significant change in the province as a whole. BBS data suggest that numbers in Ontario are stable (Downes et al. 2005), and data from migration monitoring studies at LPBO in fact show significant increases in numbers of this species during both spring and fall migration over the period 1961-2004 (Crewe 2006).

Breeding biology: In Ontario, the American Redstart begins nesting in mid-May, with most nests active by early June (Peck and James 1987). The nest is relatively easy to locate, usually built in the crotch of branches of deciduous saplings and shrubs, often along forest edges. The nest is generally within 10 m of the ground but averages about 2 m above the ground (Peck and James 1987). Both parents will mob intruders that approach the nest, and will often perform conspicuous distraction displays. It is one of just a few passerine species in which the male does not attain full breeding plumage until his second breeding season. First-year males may sing and defend small territories, but not all will attract a mate. Probable or confirmed breeding evidence was obtained from over 50% of the squares in which data were obtained. Breeding was confirmed in all atlas administrative regions, with the highest evidence in each region being primarily in the form of nests with eggs or young.

Abundance: Male American Redstarts are strong singers, and the song is for the most part easily identifiable. Thus, this species should be readily noted during point counts. The relative abundance map shows that it is most abundant (over 7.8 birds/25 point counts) north and east of Georgian Bay, along eastern Lake Superior, and in the Clay Belt from Lake Timiskaming to Cochrane. Curiously, relatively low densities were reported in the region from Chapleau to Temagami; it is unclear if this is a function of sub-optimal habitat in this area or a function of lower survey effort away from the main highways and populated areas. Overall, densities in the Southern and Northern Shield regions averaged 6 and 3.5 birds/25 point counts, respectively. Although almost as widespread south of the Shield as it is on the Shield, the American Redstart is a much less abundant bird south of the Shield. The average density in the Lake Simcoe-Rideau region was only about one third of that recorded in the Southern Shield region; in the Carolinian region, it was only about one sixth. – Peter L. McLaren

Prothonotary Warbler

Paruline orangée

Protonotaria citrea

Mark Peck

The Prothonotary Warbler breeds primarily in the southeastern US, where it is common in mature, deciduous swamp forests and forested floodplains. North of the Gulf States and the Carolinas, breeding populations become increasingly less common and more scattered. The northern extent of its breeding range barely reaches into southern Ontario; it is one of Canada's rarest songbirds and designated as Endangered in Ontario and Canada.

In 1997, a national recovery team was established to help reverse the decline of the species in Canada. The team has conducted intensive annual surveys to monitor population size, initiated a nest box program at key breeding sites, and undertaken several habitat creation and restoration projects (McCracken et al. 2006).

Distribution and population status: There is little evidence to suggest that the Canadian range of the Prothonotary Warbler, unlike several other Carolinian birds, has changed substantially over time. It has probably always been very rare in southwestern Ontario, where it is restricted to pockets of suitable habitat near the north shore of Lake Erie (most regularly at Holiday Beach Cons. Area, Rondeau Prov. Park, and the Long Point area), and western Lake Ontario (Dundas Marsh). Despite the presence of suitable habitat inland, especially in the Lake Simcoe-Rideau region, it is very seldom found nesting more than about 30 km inland from the shores of the lower Great Lakes.

The Prothonotary Warbler's breeding distribution in Ontario has not changed significantly since the first atlas. Evidence of confirmed or probable breeding was found at several new sites during the second atlas, including the Holiday Beach-Amherstburg area (Essex Co.), near the St. Clair River (Lambton Co.), and at Dundas Marsh (City of Hamilton). A further occurrence near Caledon (Region of Peel) is the northernmost breeding record in Canada to date. As with nearly all breeding occurrences in Ontario, however, site occupancy is

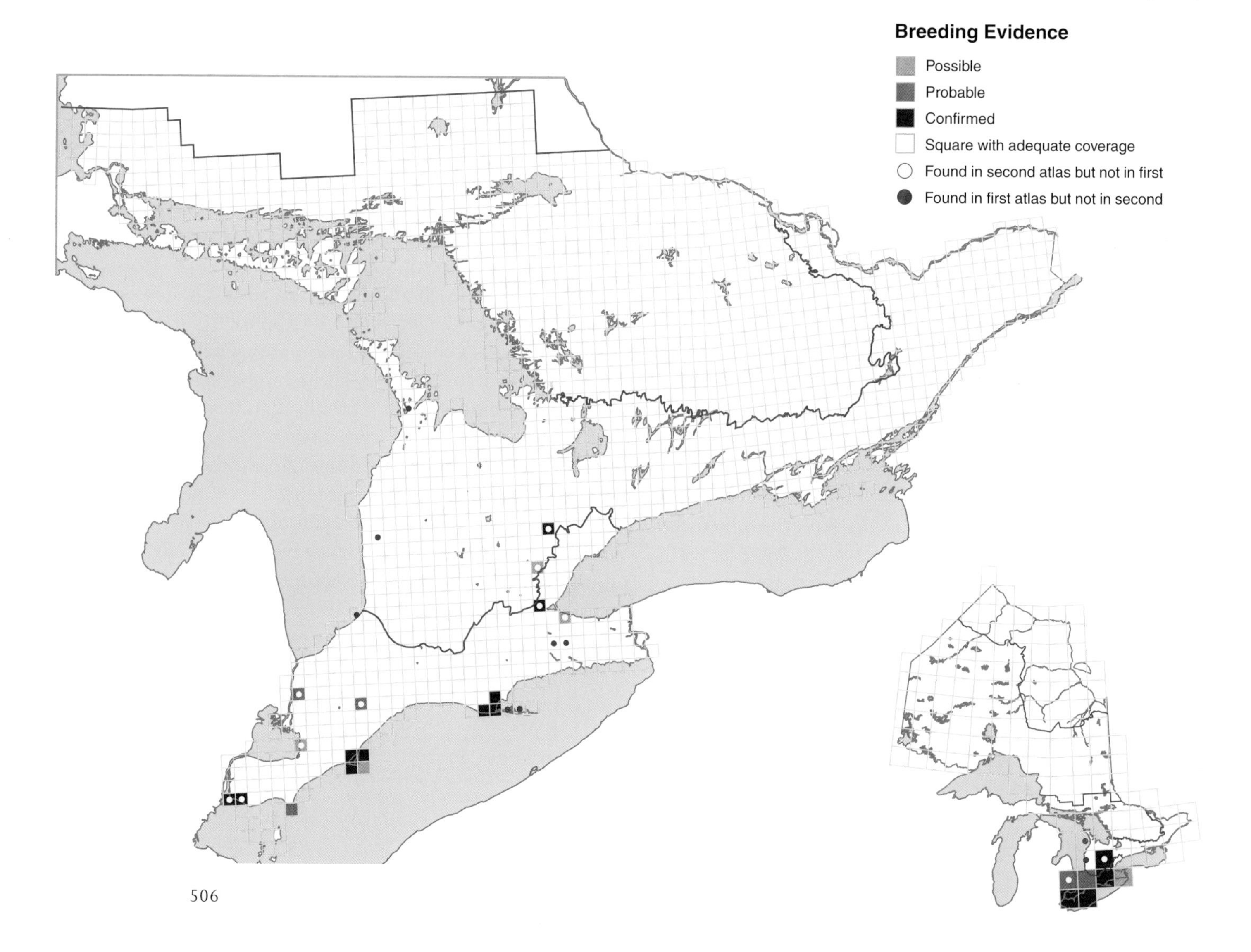

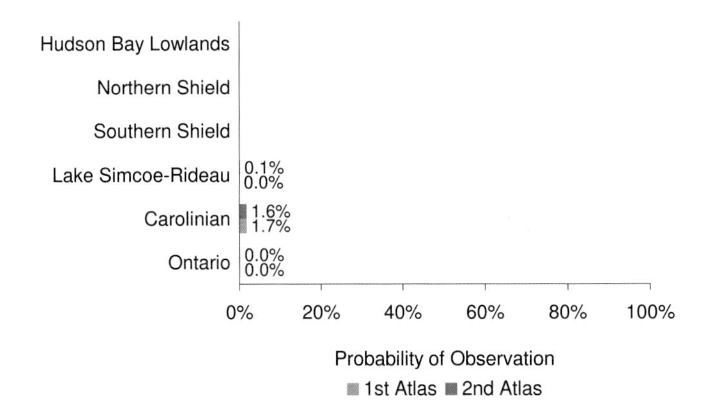

typically quite ephemeral, even when multiple pairs occur in successive years. Indeed, Rondeau is the only site in Ontario known to have been continuously occupied by this warbler over most of the past century. Conversely, Dundas Marsh has a long history of site occupancy dating back to the 1950s but exhibits a pattern of temporary abandonment followed by re-colonization (Curry 2006).

In Ontario, there was little difference in the number of squares where the species occurred in the first and second atlases (15 and 17 squares, respectively). However, North American BBS results indicate that Prothonotary Warbler populations declined significantly by an average rate of 2.1% annually in the period 1981-2005 (Sauer et al. 2005). In neighbouring New York State, the species was found in 50% fewer squares in the second atlas over the same period (New York State Breeding Bird Atlas). This decline is echoed in the findings of recent surveys in Ontario (McCracken et al. 2006).

Breeding biology: The Prothonotary Warbler is very much a habitat specialist, nesting exclusively in suitable tree cavities in deciduous swamp forests and floodplains (Petit 1999). Where present, it is relatively easily detected owing to the male's loud, distinctive "*tsweet-tsweet-tsweet*" territorial song. Because it resides in relatively inaccessible swamp forest, it can be overlooked by atlassers. For those venturing into swamps, however, breeding is easy to confirm, since the species almost always nests at low heights in tree cavities or nest boxes, over open water. Given the above, and with results from annual population surveys for the species in Ontario, the atlas map represents an accurate depiction of the species' occurrence.

Abundance: The atlas distribution map clearly shows the Prothonotary Warbler's affinity for the Carolinian region of Ontario. It is most numerous around the north shore of Lake Erie. Its centre of abundance is closely tied to the availability and extent of suitable swamp forest habitat, coupled with favourable climatic conditions. Annual abundance and occurrence in Ontario are influenced by local conditions, particularly changes in water levels in preferred habitats.

Although the species was recorded in about the same number of squares as in the first atlas, intensive annual surveys since 1997 suggest the current population consists of no more than 10 to 25 pairs annually (McCracken et al. 2006), far lower than the estimate of up to 80 pairs during the first atlas (McCracken in Cadman et al. 1987). Declines have been particularly severe at Rondeau Prov. Park.

The Prothonotary Warbler is aggressive towards female Brown-headed Cowbirds. The species is not known to eject cowbird eggs but often responds by abandoning the nest (Petit 1999). *Photo: George K. Peck*

The sloughs of Rondeau Prov. Park support a large proportion of Ontario's Prothonotary Warblers. *Photo: Frank and Sandra Horvath*

The species' occurrence in Ontario is strongly dependent upon immigration from robust source populations in the US (Tischendorf 2003). Thus, unless the serious decline of its core population in the US is reversed, the Prothonotary Warbler faces extirpation in Ontario. – *Jon McCracken*

Worm-eating Warbler

Paruline vermivore

Helmitheros vermivorum

John Reaume

The Worm-eating Warbler breeds throughout the eastern US, with the core of its breeding range in the Appalachian and Ozark regions (Hanners and Patton 1998). Scattered outlier breeding populations exist beyond the range periphery, including areas of southwestern Michigan, central Ohio, and south-central New York (Hanners and Patton 1998). There is some evidence of a northward expansion of the breeding range in the northeast US, probably due to reforestation (Hanners and Patton 1998).

Although the Worm-eating Warbler is reported annually in southern Ontario during spring migration, most birds are presumed to be transient "overshoots." There are no confirmed breeding records in Ontario or Canada (Godfrey 1986; Peck and Peck 2006). However, the number of records of birds in summer, including several during the second atlas, suggest that the species may occasionally breed in the province.

Distribution and population status: At least 15 breeding season records of the Worm-eating Warbler exist for Ontario. Prior to the second atlas, breeding evidence had been reported in 1971 (singing male, Westdale Ravine, City of Hamilton, 7 June; Curry 2006); 1974 (singing male, Ajax, Durham Region, 1-4 July; A. Wormington, pers. comm.); 1983 (male present, but in habitat considered unsuitable for nesting, Point Pelee, 12 June to 21 July; A. Wormington, pers. comm.); 1988 (hatch-year bird banded, South Walsingham Forest, Norfolk Co., 26 August; J.D. McCracken, pers. comm.; and singing males present there in 1992 and 1994; D.A. Sutherland, unpubl. data); 1993 (singing male, Utica, Durham Region, 11 June; A. Wormington, pers. comm.); 1996 (hatch-year bird banded, Long Point, 22 August; J.D. McCracken, pers. comm.); 1997 (singing male and possibly a female, 14 to at least 22 June, Spooky Hollow, Norfolk Co.; W.G. Lamond and D. Gardiner, pers. comm.); and 1999 (singing male, along a tributary of Big Creek north of

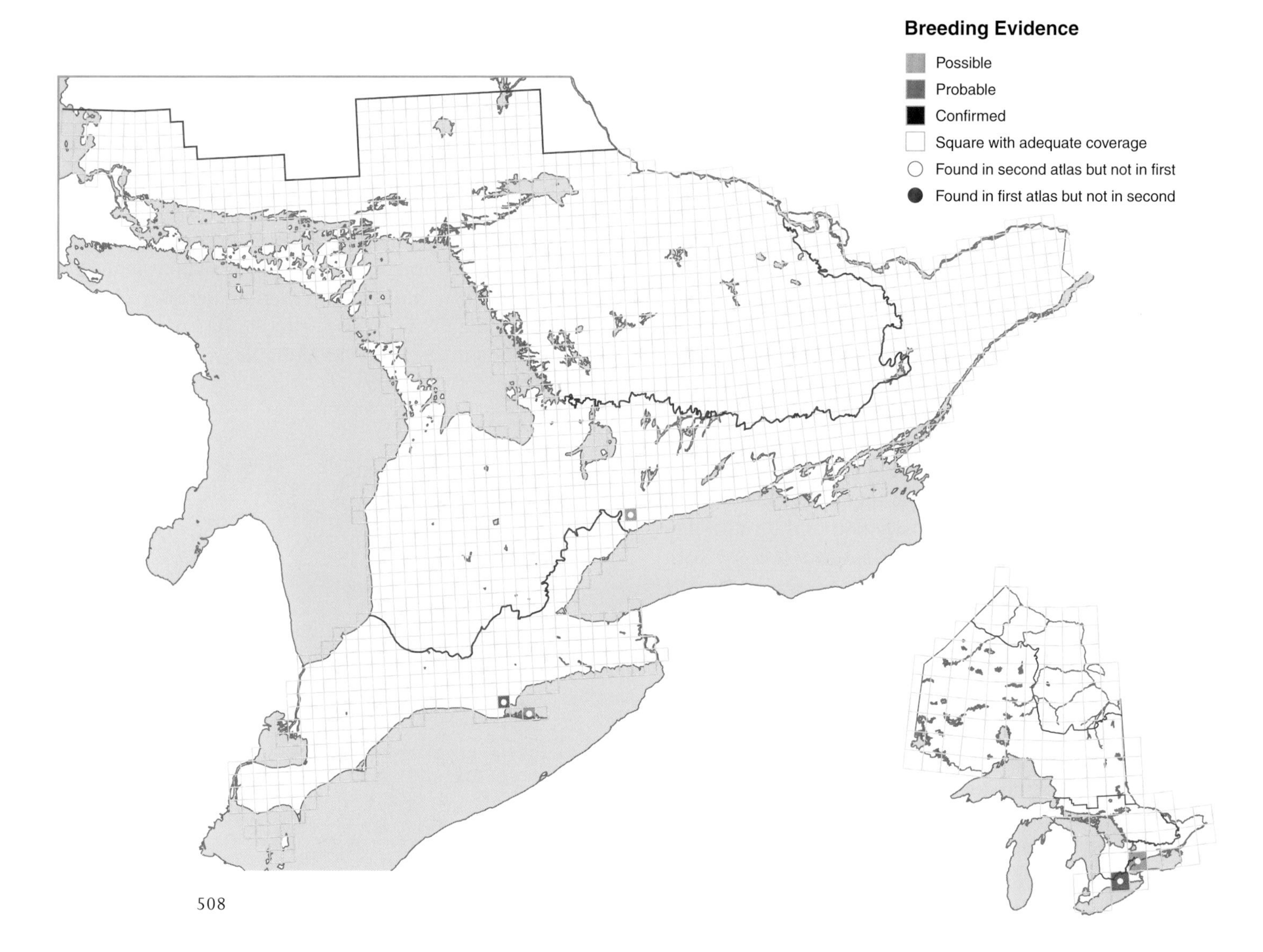

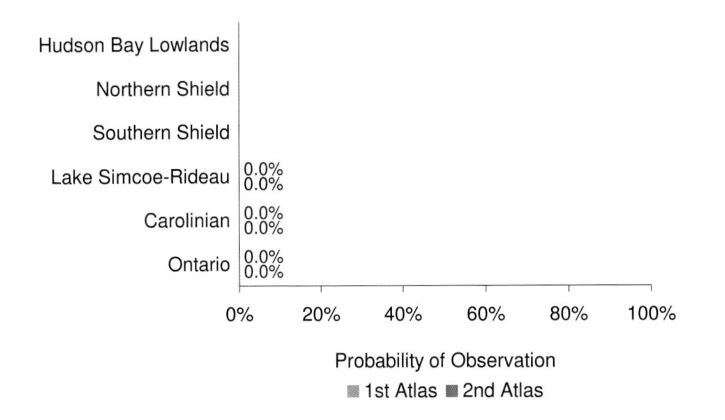

An apparently unmated male was reported on territory at this location in St. Williams Forest Nursery Tract, Norfolk Co., from 27 June to 7 July 2005. *Photo: Gregor G. Beck*

Walsingham, 18 May to 17 June) and again in 2000 (11 May to 17 June; J.D. McCracken, pers. comm.).

During the second atlas, evidence of possible and probable breeding was documented at four sites: a singing male was present in Backus Woods, Norfolk Co., 1 June 2002; an individual in suitable habitat was observed along Urfé Creek near Brock Road, Pickering, Durham Region, 13 June 2002; a singing male was present on Squires Ridge, Long Point, Norfolk Co., 20 June 2004; and a territorial male was present in the St. Williams Forest, Norfolk Co., from 27 June to at least 7 July 2005.

Historically, the Worm-eating Warbler has been regarded primarily as a rare spring transient in the province, with only infrequent, scattered reports of birds heard or seen during the breeding season in southern Ontario (James 1991). Atlas results tend to support this pattern of occurrence. However, while there has been no substantive evidence of breeding in the province, the increasingly regular occurrence of singing males in suitable habitat and the presence of hatch-year individuals, particularly in those forest tracts (e.g., South Walsingham Forest) in which singing males have also been present, suggest that at least occasionally the species may breed in the province.

Breeding biology: The Worm-eating Warbler breeds in large, mature, dry-to-moist forest stands with well-developed shrub and herbaceous understorey layers, characteristically on steep hillsides or deeply incised ravines (Hanners and Patton 1998). It breeds in a variety of deciduous and mixed forest communities, but at its northern range periphery often occurs in forests of maple, beech, and hemlock (Brewer et al. 1991; Hanners and Patton 1998). Nests are on the ground, typically on hillsides with moderate to steep slopes, and are well concealed in a drift of leaves, often beneath a tangle of downed woody debris (Castrale et al. 1998; Hanners and Patton 1998). During territorial establishment, males sing frequently from a perch in the sub-canopy, ceasing almost entirely once mated in late May or early June. However, unmated males may sing regularly into July (Hanners and Patton 1998). The song is a truncated dry trill, very similar to and easily confused with that of the Chipping Sparrow.

Breeding evidence obtained during the second atlas was of individuals, most singing, found in suitable habitat in June. The late dates of singing for these birds suggest unmated individuals, as does the lack of a well-developed cloacal protuberance on the territorial male present in the St. Williams Forest in 2005. However, breeding pairs are difficult to detect as males sing infrequently once mated and females are typically inconspicuous.

Abundance: The Worm-eating Warbler is a rare but increasingly regular breeding season resident in southern Ontario. It is generally inconspicuous and easily overlooked, and is therefore probably somewhat under-detected. Breeding remains unconfirmed in Ontario. – *Audrey Heagy and Donald A. Sutherland*

Ovenbird

Paruline couronnée

Seiurus aurocapilla

Mark Peck

The Ovenbird is a common and widespread neotropical migrant that typically breeds in the interior of larger tracts of mature deciduous and mixed forests across northern and northeastern North America. It is both a ground forager and nester, selecting breeding areas with a closed canopy and deep leaf litter that provide both suitable nesting sites and ground invertebrates. Although the species' density tends to be higher where deciduous trees dominate, it has a broad tolerance for breeding in different plant communities.

Distribution and population status: The Ovenbird is widely distributed across Ontario, occurring in every region of the province. It is most common in the Southern Shield where it has a probability of observation of 97%, but it is also widespread in the Lake Simcoe-Rideau and Northern Shield regions with a probability of observation of 85% and 82%, respectively. It is less common in the Carolinian region where the forested landscape is highly fragmented, and in the Hudson Bay Lowlands where mature forests are less extensive. Here the species is essentially restricted to river corridors where suitable large stands of Balsam Poplar and Trembling Aspen occur; however, away from the rivers, the habitat is for the most part unsuitable. The northernmost records from this atlas came from the Fawn and Ekwan rivers at roughly 54° N.

Although the Ovenbird remains fairly widespread, there was a significant decline of 22% in the probability of observation between atlases in the Carolinian region, likely a reflection of continuing fragmentation of large forest blocks. In most of the extreme southwest, it is virtually absent because woodlots are very small and fragmented. Where forest cover is low and few large source woodlots exist, the species' occupancy of small, poorer quality woodlots will be low and will vary from year to year (Nol et al. 2005). In portions of Huron, Lambton, and Middlesex Counties, heavy logging has likely contributed to the Ovenbird's decline or loss. Though the area from

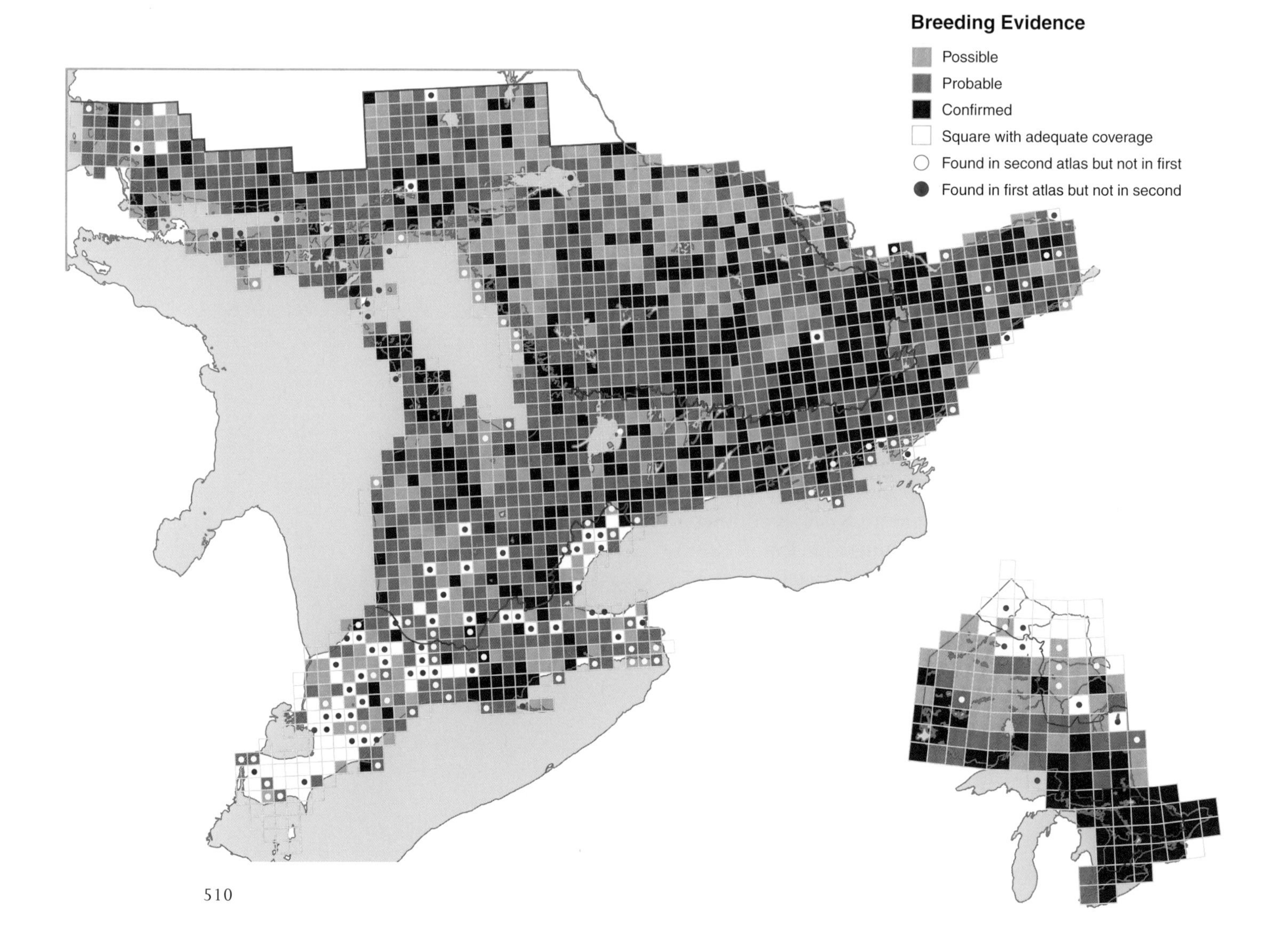

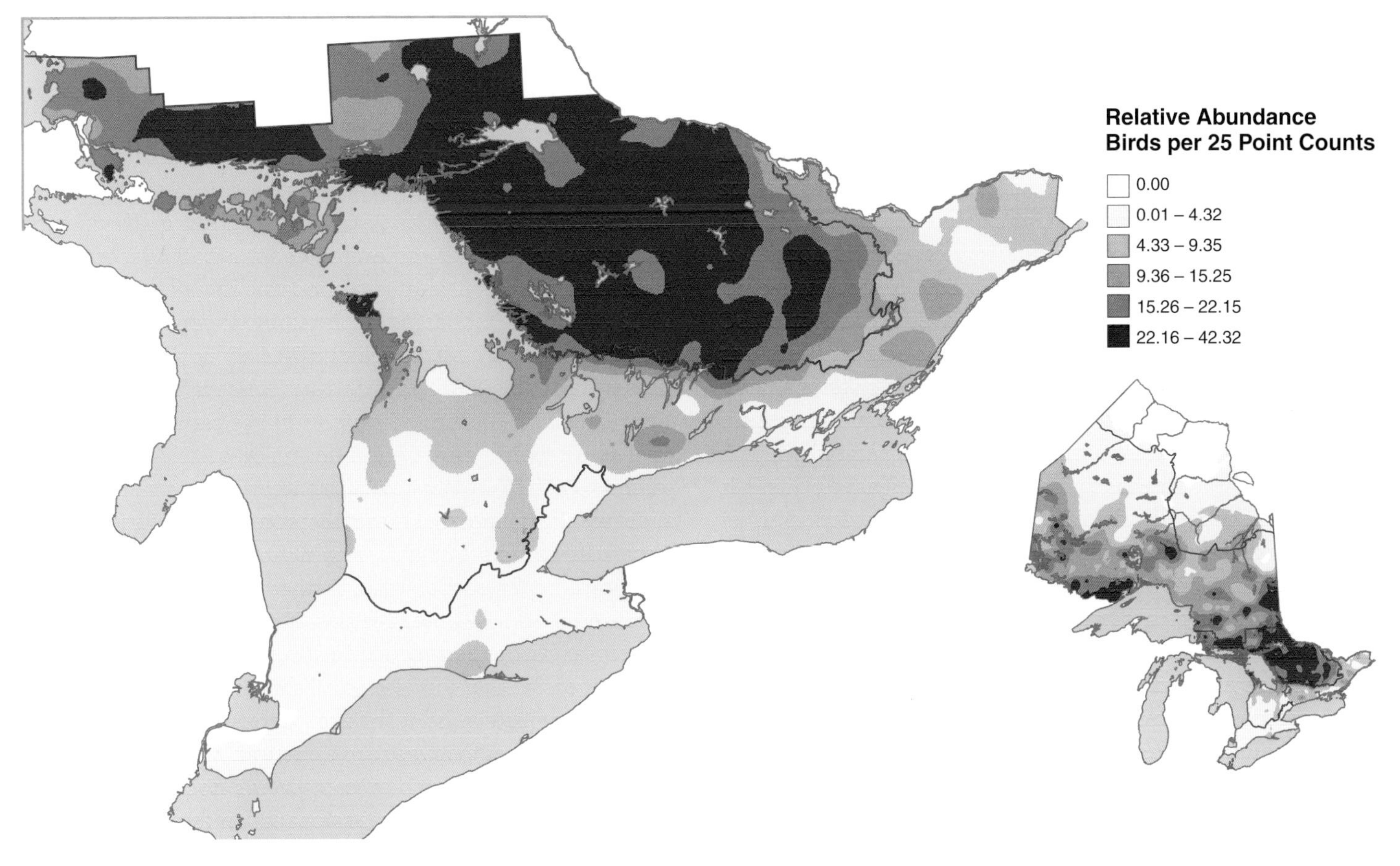

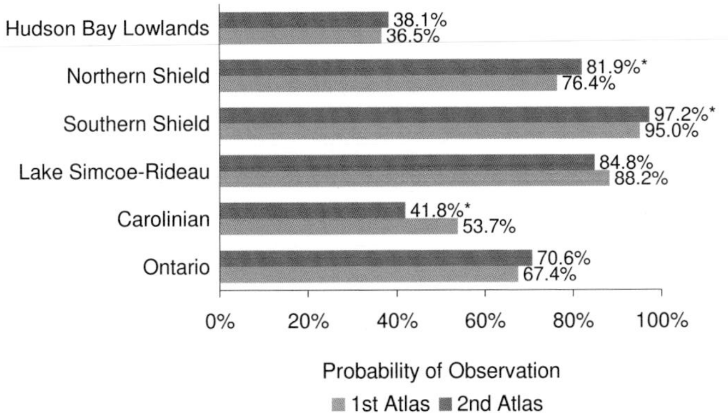

Niagara to Toronto has some squares where forests have recovered and the species now occurs, it generally shows fewer gains than losses to urbanization. BBS data support these observations, showing a significant decline in Ontario since the first atlas, as do CMMN data for LPBO.

In the Southern Shield where the species has its greatest stronghold, the probability of observation increased significantly by 2%. Despite its sensitivity to logging and loss of mature forest habitat, populations remain stable there because forest cover is high and large continuous tracts of deciduous and mixed woods forest provide buffers against smaller-scale local changes in distribution and abundance.

Breeding biology: In Ontario, the Ovenbird breeds from mid-May through early July. Though detection of the highly vocal, territorial males is facilitated by their well-known, loud "*teacher-teacher-teacher*" song, breeding is more difficult to confirm. Females build cryptic, domed nests of leaves and grasses on the ground and are hesitant to flush. Breeding was confirmed in just 17% of the squares with breeding evidence, and the highest evidence reported in the large majority of unconfirmed squares was of singing or territorial males. However, since possible or probable breeding records are relatively easy to obtain, the distribution map accurately depicts the Ovenbird's range.

Although many Regional Coordinators believe the level of breeding evidence for Ovenbird under-represents the actual percentage of confirmed breeders, where forest cover is lower and the landscape is highly fragmented, a portion (sometimes the majority) of territorial males may not be paired (Burke and Nol 1998). These males are often readily detected because they sing frequently and often late into the breeding season, but they are not actually breeding. In contrast, where forest cover is high, densities are high, and so the vast majority of Ovenbirds should be confirmed breeders.

Abundance: The Ovenbird reaches its highest densities in the southern part of the Shield, particularly in forests with a strong deciduous component. It is much less common across the Hudson Bay Lowlands and the Carolinian region. Next to the Red-eyed Vireo, it is the most abundant forest breeding bird in the Southern Shield, where densities over 22 birds/25 point counts were recorded. Areas of higher abundance in the largely urbanized landscape south of the Shield include the Oak Ridges Moraine, Norfolk Sand Plain, Niagara Escarpment, and Frontenac Axis. The Ovenbird is an area-sensitive mature forest specialist, and though it presently remains one of the most abundant forest birds in many squares, its sensitivity to widespread disturbances suggests there will be continued declines or losses in many areas. – *Dawn Burke*

Northern Waterthrush

Paruline des ruisseaux

Seiurus noveboracensis

John Reaume

Superficially resembling a member of the thrush family, this wood-warbler is a common summer resident through much of Canada north to the treeline, absent only in western British Columbia and the southern Prairie Provinces. The range of the Northern Waterthrush extends south into the US in the Rocky Mountains and through the northern Great Lakes states and New England. It winters in the West Indies, Mexico, Central America, and northern South America.

The preferred breeding habitat of the Northern Waterthrush in Ontario is wet mixed and deciduous woodlands, including flooded forests and swamps, lake edges, riverbanks, and wooded ravines. Dense cover near ground level, combined with the presence of water, appear to be the two most important habitat requirements throughout its breeding range (Eaton 1995). An unusual characteristic of this species is its continual tail-bobbing while foraging, a habit it shares with the closely related Louisiana Waterthrush.

Distribution and population status: The Northern Waterthrush breeds throughout most of Ontario, being absent only in the farmland of southern Ontario southwest of Rondeau Prov. Park to Lake St. Clair and in most of the Niagara Peninsula. It has just an 18% probability of observation in the Carolinian region, where it is present primarily in the area north of Long Point. This part of the highly agricultural and urbanized region has the greatest amount of forest cover and likely provides the best habitat for the species.

North of the Carolinian region, the Northern Waterthrush is widespread, likely to be present wherever appropriate habitat exists. The probability of observation was 58-85% in all regions except the Carolinian. Its apparent absence from many of the squares in the Sault Ste. Marie and Sudbury areas is curious. The Regional Coordinator in the former area believed that the species was under-represented by the data, as suitable habi-

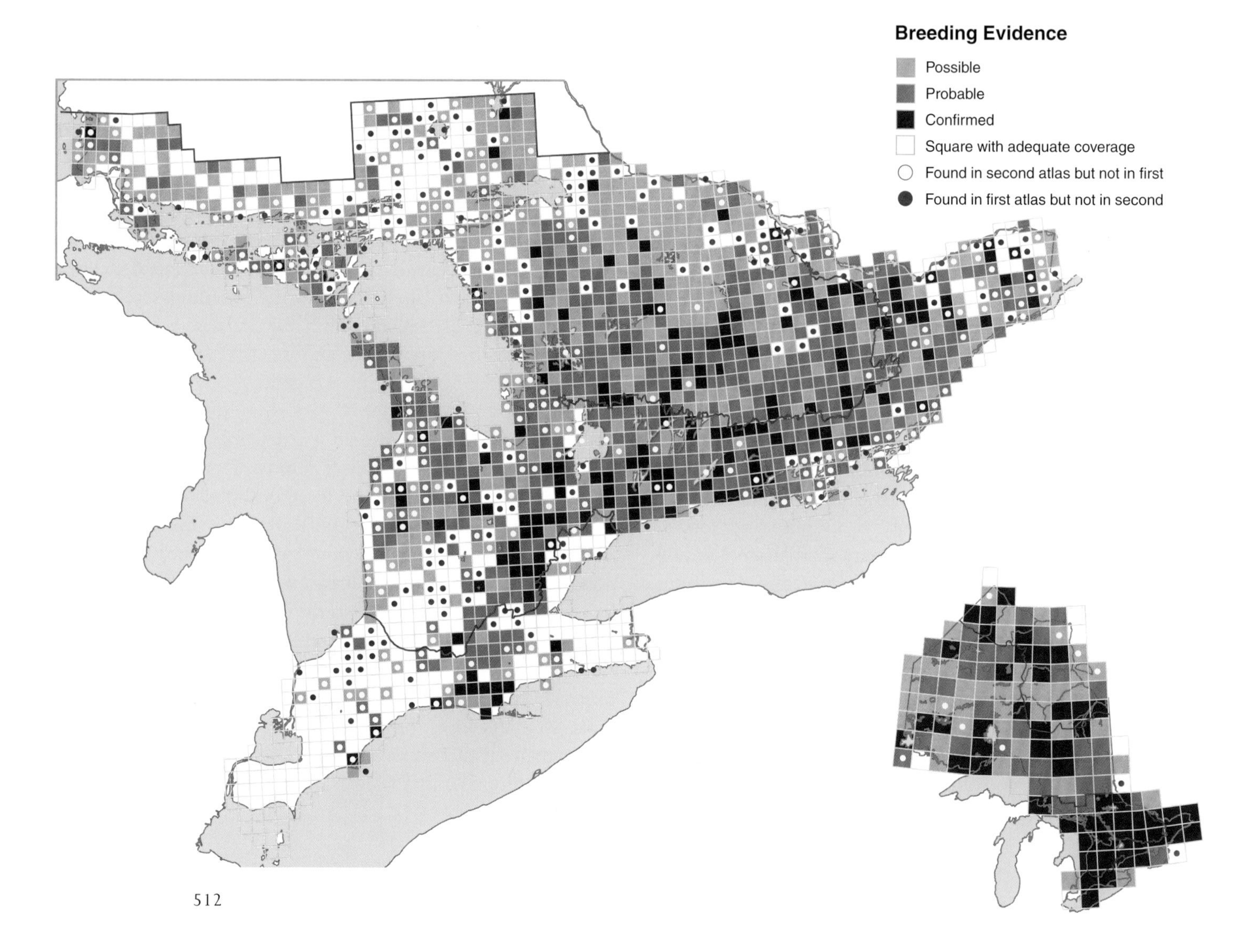

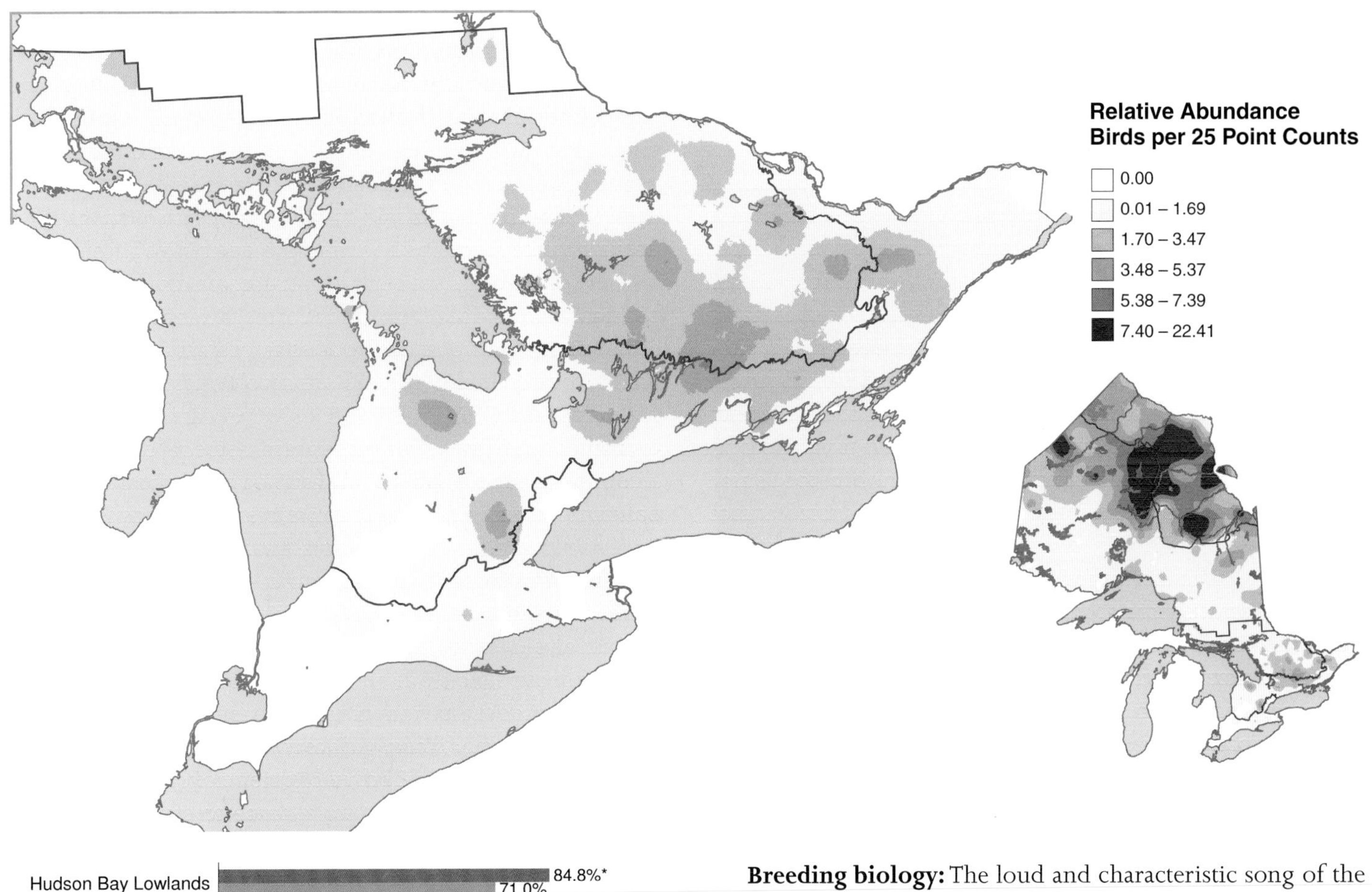

Probability of Observation

Region	1st Atlas	2nd Atlas
Hudson Bay Lowlands	71.0%	84.8%*
Northern Shield	64.2%	70.5%*
Southern Shield	65.3%	69.3%*
Lake Simcoe-Rideau	53.6%	57.5%
Carolinian	15.7%	17.5%
Ontario	64.2%	72.0%*

tat is available in most squares. In general, the observed breeding distribution reflects the distribution of wet forest habitats with dense shrub cover.

Between atlases, the probability of observation increased significantly in the province as a whole (by 12%) and in the Southern Shield, Northern Shield, and Hudson Bay Lowlands regions (by 6%, 10%, and 19%, respectively). Although the species has apparently disappeared from a number of squares in southern Ontario, primarily in the interior of the southwest and in the Sudbury area, it was also found in many new squares on Manitoulin Island, south of the Bruce Peninsula, southwest of London, and east of Ottawa. CMMN data from LPBO show that numbers have not changed significantly over the past 20 years (Crewe 2006), as do BBS data since 1968 (Downes et al. 2005), though much of the species' range is north of BBS coverage. Regional Coordinators from London, Long Point, and Ottawa felt that Northern Waterthrush populations in those areas had in fact increased since the first atlas.

Breeding biology: The loud and characteristic song of the Northern Waterthrush allowed atlassers to record singing males as the highest breeding evidence for this species in 56% of the squares where it was detected. Confirmation, however, was much more difficult. As well as residing in difficult-to-sample habitat, the Northern Waterthrush builds a well-concealed ground nest, generally in upturned tree roots, in moss-covered hummocks, or along riverbanks. The female alone incubates, and when leaving or approaching the nest, moves furtively through the vegetation, although if surprised she will perform a distraction display to attempt to draw a predator away from the nest (Eaton 1995). Evidence of confirmed breeding was obtained in only 10% of the squares with data. Most of these confirmations were in the form of adults carrying food.

Abundance: The Northern Waterthrush is highly vocal, with a loud, distinctive song. Thus, it is fairly easy to detect on point counts where it is present. The highest densities of the species are found in northern Ontario, especially in the Hudson Bay Lowlands, with an average of nearly 6 birds/25 point counts. Concentrations of more than 7 birds/25 point counts occur over a large area of northeastern Ontario, from Akimiski Island west to approximately Fort Hope. To the south, densities are much lower and average 1.2 to 1.5 birds/25 point counts in the Northern Shield, Southern Shield, and Lake Simcoe-Rideau regions. In southern Ontario, the highest densities are found in the Kawartha Lakes area north to Algonquin Prov. Park and east to Perth, along the Niagara Escarpment in Halton Co., and in the Dundalk uplands. – *Peter L. McLaren*

Louisiana Waterthrush

Paruline hochequeue

Seiurus motacilla

George K. Peck

The Louisiana Waterthrush's breeding range extends across much of the eastern US. It is rare in Canada, where it is designated as a species of Special Concern (COSEWIC 2006a). Although it is largely restricted to southern Ontario, a small, somewhat disjunct and perhaps ephemeral population may also exist in southwestern Québec (COSEWIC 2006a).

Distribution and population status: In Ontario, the Louisiana Waterthrush occurs primarily in the Carolinian region and adjacent areas of the Great Lakes-St. Lawrence Forest south of the Canadian Shield. It is largely confined to areas below 300 m in elevation, with the mean annual temperature exceeding 6°C (COSEWIC 2006a). Within these tolerances, the presence of clean, cold-water streams that flow through mature forest is a very important factor. Though it is nowhere common, concentrations are greatest in parts of Norfolk, Elgin, Middlesex, and Oxford Counties and more locally along portions of the Niagara Escarpment and Oak Ridges Moraine and in the Rideau Lakes region.

Over the last century, the species' breeding range has slowly expanded northward in some areas of the northeastern US (Craig 1985; Andrle and Carroll 1988). This expansion may be attributed to re-colonization of formerly held territory that was heavily logged in the 1800s and has since undergone extensive reforestation (Brewer et al. 1991). In Ontario, evidence of a similar range expansion is apparent only for the Rideau Lakes area north of Kingston. Louisiana Waterthrush populations in Ontario have been reduced in regions where loss of forest cover and drainage of swamps have been most severe. Most notably, it has been all but extirpated in Essex Co. and Chatham-Kent (COSEWIC 2006a).

The overall distribution of the Louisiana Waterthrush in Ontario has not changed markedly since the first atlas. However, site occupancy is ephemeral, and as a result the particular

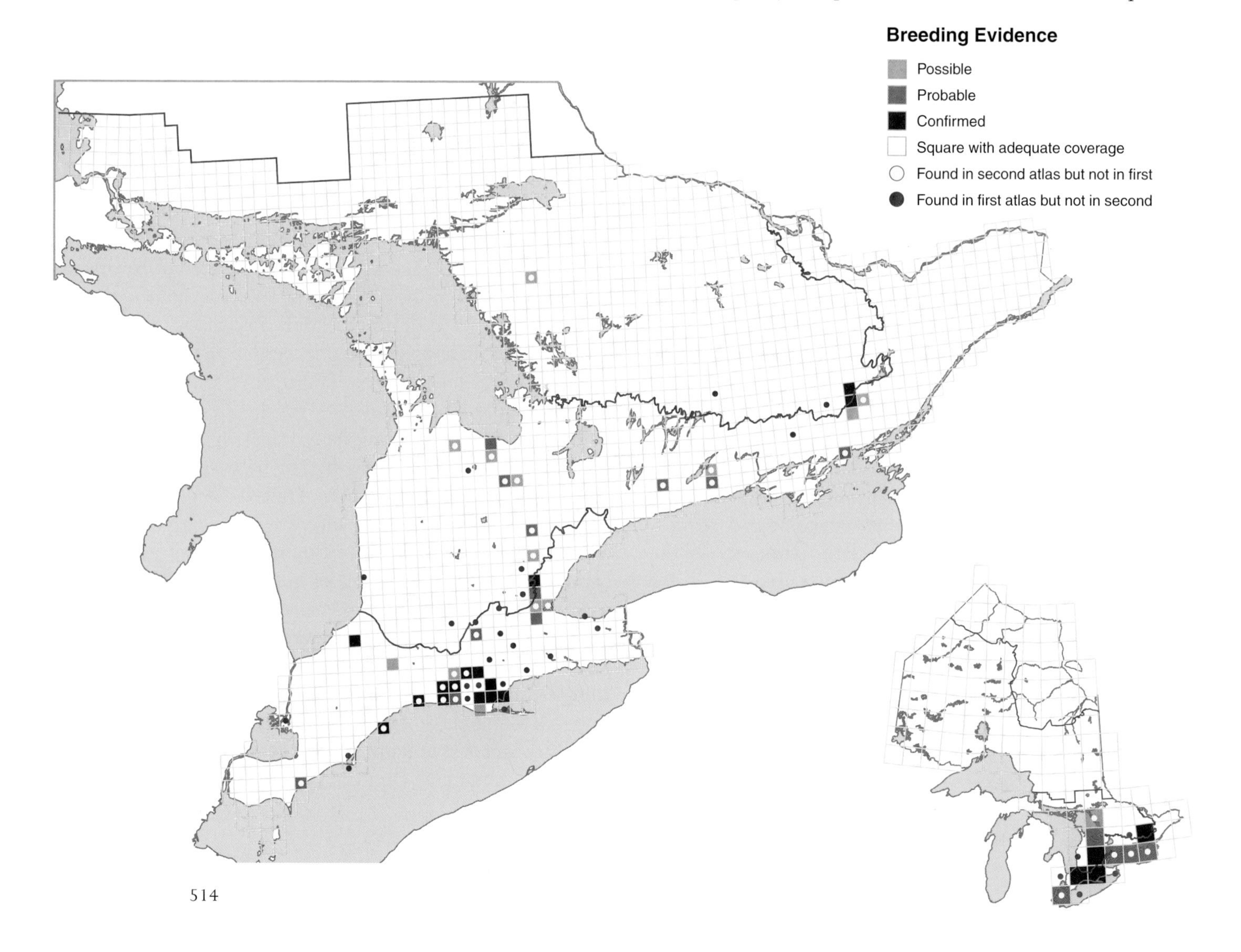

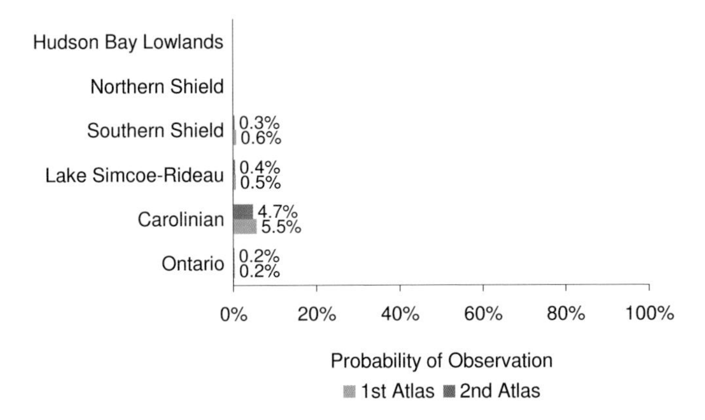

squares recording the species in the first and second atlas differed in many areas. Because populations in Ontario are small and scattered, the species appears subject to local extirpation. Many sites are occupied for several successive years before falling vacant, probably following the death of one or both members of a pair. Sites are frequently reoccupied by different birds, probably through immigration (COSEWIC 2006a).

BBS results indicate that US populations increased significantly by an average rate of 0.9% annually in the period 1966-2005 (Sauer et al. 2005). Although the population is small in Ontario, the species was found in almost the same number of squares in the first and second atlases (40 and 39 squares, respectively). However, in the New York State Breeding Bird Atlas, the species was found in considerably fewer squares during the second atlas than the first.

Breeding biology: The Louisiana Waterthrush shows a strong preference for nesting in tracts of mature forest bordering pristine headwater streams (Buffington et al. 1997; Prosser and Brooks 1998). In Ontario, it favours deciduous and mixed forests with a strong Eastern Hemlock component, in deeply incised ravines (COSEWIC 2006a). It also inhabits large flooded tracts of mature, deciduous swamp forest, sometimes in association with the more common and widespread Northern Waterthrush (Craig 1984, 1985). The two species look very similar, but the Louisiana Waterthrush is easily distinguished by its distinctive song.

An early spring migrant, the Louisiana Waterthrush arrives at breeding territories in April and early May. Males initially sing loudly and profusely, but song frequency diminishes markedly through June, at the time when most atlassing was conducted. Also, favoured habitats tend to be relatively inaccessible, and so the species may have been overlooked in some squares. Nests are concealed in cavities in the roots of tipped trees, in stream banks, and in and under mossy logs (Robinson 1995; Prosser and Brooks 1998) and are difficult to find. However, birds respond readily, often aggressively, to call broadcasts, frequently engaging in distraction displays; thus, with effort, evidence of probable and confirmed breeding may be obtained. Directed surveys of historical, known, and potential breeding sites were made by several atlassers, and so the atlas map should represent a fairly accurate depiction of the species' occurrence in Ontario.

Abundance: Abundance mapping was not possible because of the species' rarity. Nevertheless, its centre of abundance in Ontario clearly lies within the deeply incised ravines associated with the Norfolk Sand Plain (eastern Elgin, southern Oxford, southern Middlesex, and Norfolk Counties). Overall, the Ontario population is believed to have remained essentially stable over the last two decades at an estimated 105-195 breeding pairs (COSEWIC 2006a). – *Jon McCracken*

Nests are well concealed, typically in exposed, tangled root masses of tipped trees and along eroding stream banks, or in and under mossy logs and stumps. *Photo: Bill Rayner*

Meandering stream through mature Sugar Maple-Beech-Yellow Birch forest, breeding habitat for Louisiana Waterthrush, near Arab Lake, Frontenac Prov. Park, Frontenac Co., 31 May 2003. *Photo: Donald A. Sutherland*

Kentucky Warbler

Paruline du Kentucky

Oporornis formosus

John Reaume

The Kentucky Warbler nests in very dense, shrubby understorey vegetation associated with large openings in moist deciduous forests. Its breeding range is centred in the southeastern US, extending north to northern Ohio, central Pennsylvania, southern New York, and southern Michigan (McDonald 1998). It winters in southern Mexico, Central America, and northern South America. Prior to 1945, there were only 10 records for Canada (Stirrett 1945). There appears to have been a weak northward range expansion to Ontario since about 1970 (McCracken 1988). Though still rare, the Kentucky Warbler now occurs regularly in small numbers during migration in southwestern Ontario, mostly around lakeshores. While nesting is strongly suspected to occur on very rare occasions in southern Ontario, breeding still awaits confirmation.

Distribution and population status: The northern edge of the Kentucky Warbler's breeding range is masked by the occurrence of what are believed to be "overshoots" during spring migration. Even so, there are two instances of territorial males persistently returning to southern Ontario for up to four consecutive years to reoccupy exactly the same territories (McCracken 1988; Curry 2006). Male Kentucky Warblers appear to exhibit an exceptionally high level of site fidelity from year to year (McDonald 1998).

During the first Ontario atlas, the Kentucky Warbler was reported in nine squares. There were only three reports of the species in Ontario during the second atlas: a singing male in the St. Williams Forest (Norfolk Co.) on 6 June 2001, a singing male south of Harrow (Essex Co.) on 1 July 2005, and an agitated male that maintained a territory in the Dundas Valley (City of Hamilton) from 12 June to 13 July 2001. Curry (2006) speculated that the Dundas Valley bird might have been paired with a female Hooded Warbler, which was also present and visibly agitated. All the records in the second atlas came

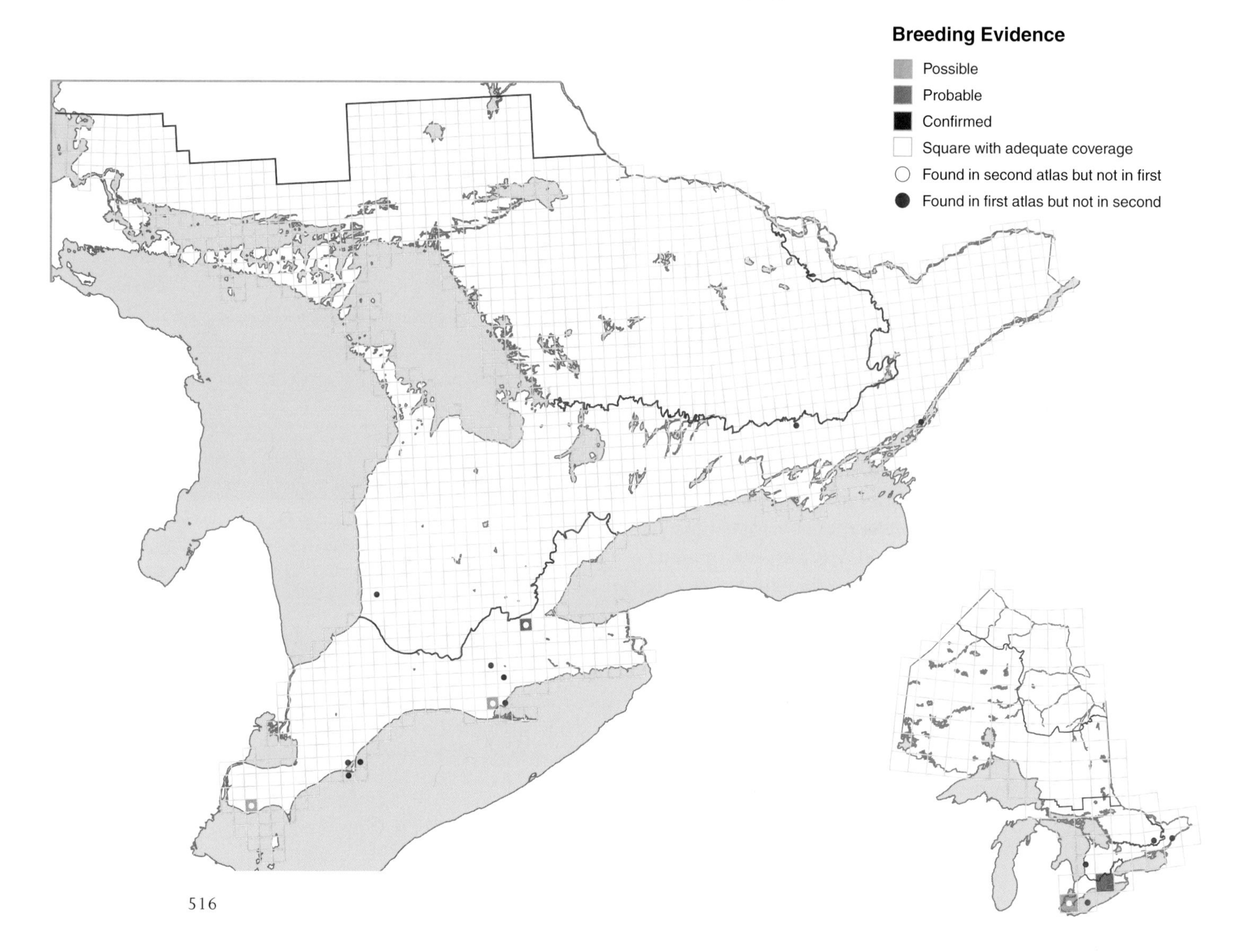

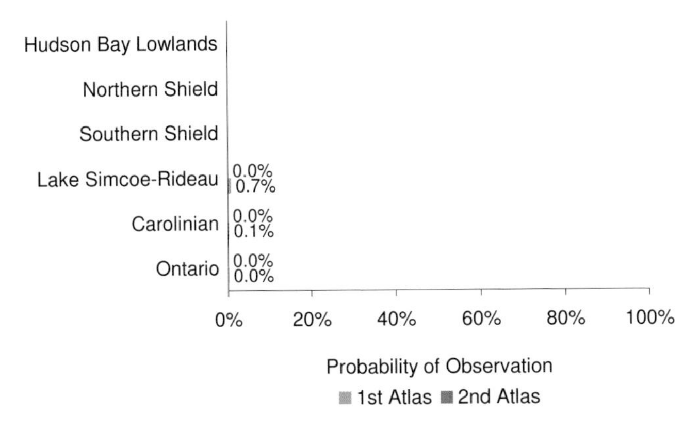

from different squares than those reporting the species in the first atlas. Thus, in Ontario, despite the male's reportedly strong tendency to return to sites for several successive years, site occupancy appears to be more ephemeral.

Although the change in the number of squares occupied in Ontario is probably too small to be meaningful, BBS data indicate that the species has experienced a significant, range-wide population decline of about 1% per year since 1966, particularly evident in the northeast (Sauer et al. 2005). Declines have also been documented in New York State's second atlas.

LPBO banding records furnish additional evidence suggesting that nesting may occur in Canada. From 1961-2005, 42 Kentucky Warblers have been captured at Long Point. As might be expected at the northern limit of a species' range, the majority of records (78%) have been in the spring. Because females accounted for about 40% of the spring records, this suggests that there is indeed potential for territorial males to attract mates in southern Ontario. Moreover, all nine fall records from Long Point have involved hatch-year individuals, though these could include birds dispersing from US breeding sites.

Breeding biology: The Kentucky Warbler is a difficult bird to observe because, like other members of its genus, it frequents dense patches of shrubby understorey and spends much of its time on or near the ground. Although the male's song is very loud, the up-slurred, two-syllable pattern and ringing tonal quality can be quite easily confused with songs of the Carolina Wren as well as the Tufted Titmouse and Ovenbird. Consequently, the Kentucky Warbler is apt to be overlooked by many atlassers. Moreover, its nest is exceptionally well hidden at the base of dense shrubbery and thick ground cover, and the female is notorious for skulking silently around the territory (Chapman 1968; McDonald 1998). Despite this, adults will respond to the intrusion of predators with relatively rapid, loud chip notes and obvious agitation. As parents carry food to young, the observation of agitated parents with food may be the easiest way to confirm breeding. The atlas breeding evidence map is probably a reasonably accurate depiction of the species' occurrence in Ontario.

Abundance: There were far too few occurrences to map relative abundance. At most, only a few pairs occur in the province, although there is likely considerable annual variation; breeding, if it occurs, is likely to be quite irregular. All records in the second atlas involved just a single male per square. However, females are highly cryptic, and it is possible that some pairs were overlooked. – *Jon McCracken*

The site used by the Kentucky Warbler in St. Williams Forest, Norfolk Co. *Photo: Gregor G. Beck*

Connecticut Warbler

Paruline à gorge grise
Oporornis agilis

David Welbourne

The Connecticut Warbler is among the most elusive and infrequently observed of Ontario's wood-warblers. It is a summer resident through a fairly narrow band of central Canada, extending from east-central British Columbia to western Québec, and the northern portions of the central US. It winters in northern South America, primarily east of the Andes. In Ontario, its breeding habitat typically includes wet, fairly open Tamarack-spruce fens, generally with a well-developed understorey. In Rainy River Dist. in Ontario and western portions of its range, it more commonly breeds in open aspen-dominated woodlands, and occasionally in dry Jack Pine stands (Elder 1991; Pitocchelli et al. 1997). Very little is known about the population status of the Connecticut Warbler because of its low abundance on surveys, although there is some evidence that the species may be declining. It has been identified as a Priority Species in Ontario (Ontario Partners in Flight 2006a).

Distribution and population status: The Connecticut Warbler is almost entirely confined to the Northern Shield and southern portions of the Hudson Bay Lowlands. Although widespread, it appears to be absent from a large portion of these regions, though it may simply have been undetected due to lower atlassing effort, difficulty in accessing its preferred habitat, and its shy, retiring nature. Its probability of observation was only 16% in the Northern Shield and 15% in the Hudson Bay Lowlands.

Singing male Connecticut Warblers were also recorded in two squares west of Sudbury in the Southern Shield and in one square on St. Joseph Island in the Lake Simcoe-Rideau region. These sightings may represent the southern edge of the species' Ontario range.

There was a significant increase of 94% in the probability of observation of this species in the province as a whole since the first atlas. The most substantial change was in the Hudson Bay Lowlands, where the probability of observation

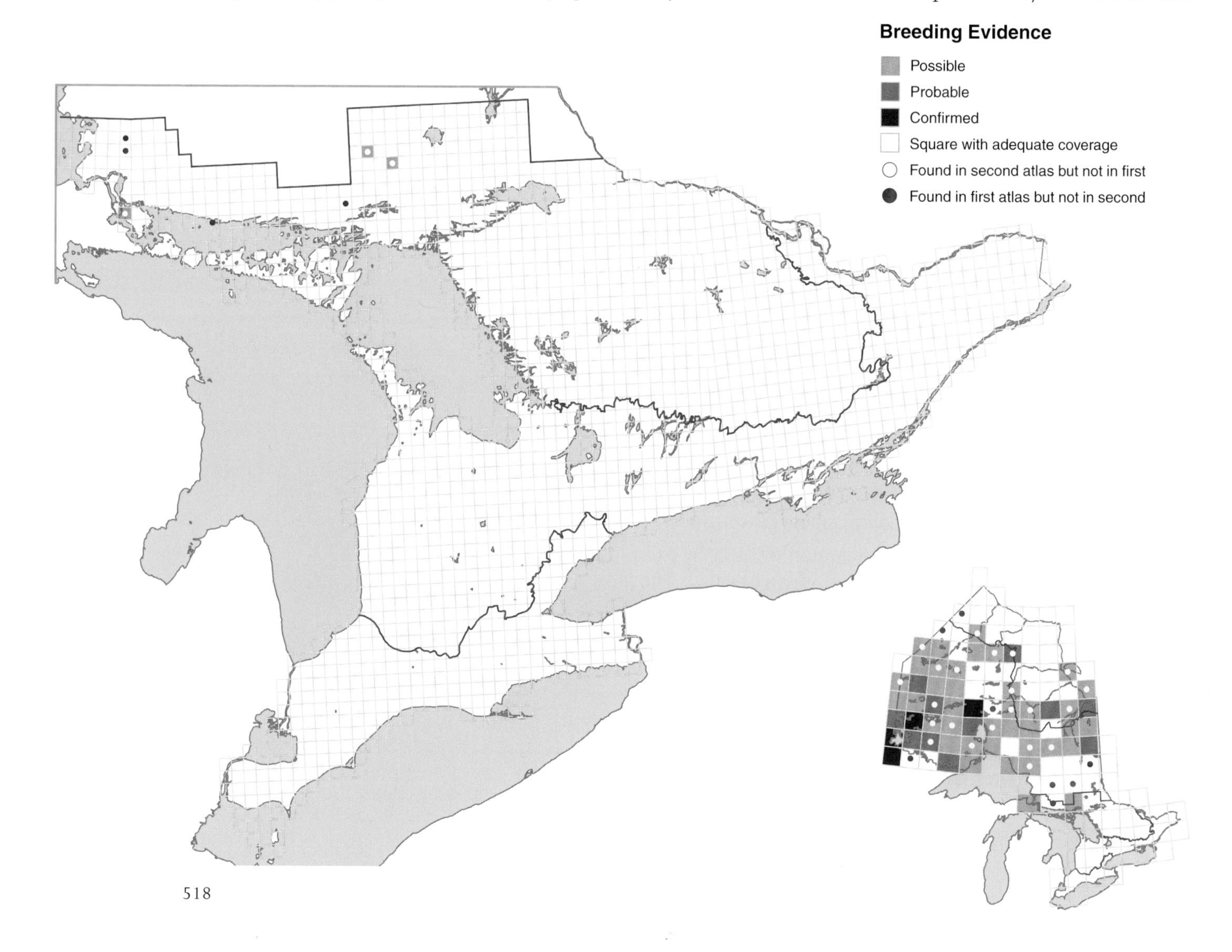

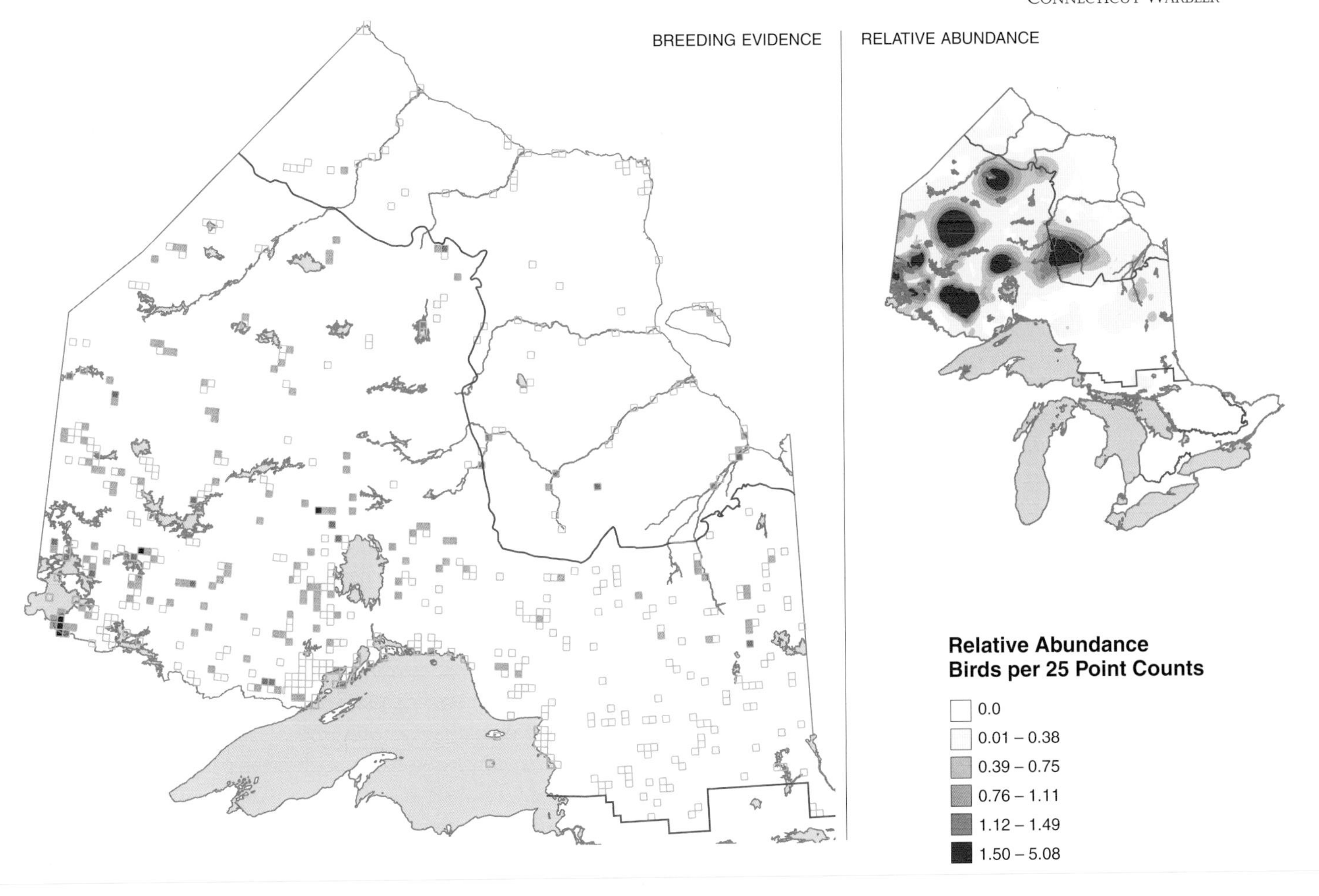

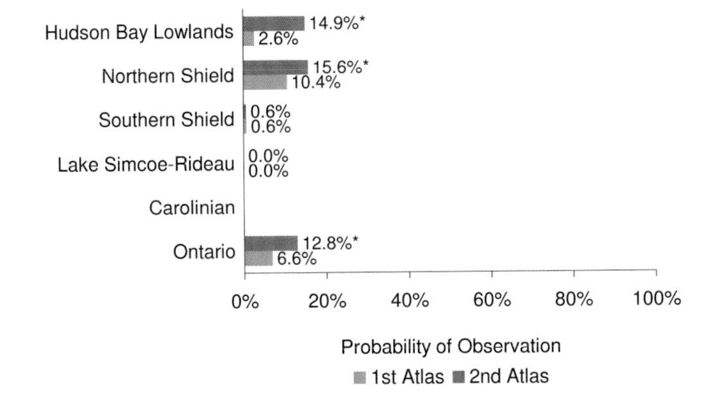

increased several-fold, but there was also a significant 50% increase in the Northern Shield region. It is difficult to say whether this increase is real, a result of enhanced atlas effort, or merely an artifact of a small data set. BBS data indicate that numbers in Ontario have been declining significantly since 1981; however, because of its uncommon nature and the difficulty in surveying the species, this too is likely an artifact of small sample sizes.

Breeding biology: The Connecticut Warbler nests on or near the ground. Nests are extremely difficult to find, hidden in a thick undergrowth of shrubs or saplings or in cavities in moss hummocks and often obscured from view by overhanging vegetation. In fact, only one nest has ever been reported in Ontario (Peck and Peck 2006). However, this species has a powerful and generally unmistakable song and is unlikely to be overlooked if present and singing. In 88% of the squares in which it was found, the highest breeding evidence recorded was possible breeding, primarily singing males.

It is difficult to upgrade breeding evidence for the Connecticut Warbler. Because of its strong song, probable breeding evidence should be achievable on the basis of birds on territory, but due to the difficulty of atlassing in this species' breeding habitat, few if any sites were visited more than once. Breeding was confirmed in only 3% of the squares in which the Connecticut Warbler was reported. All confirmation was in the form of distraction displays, adults carrying food, and fledged young. Confirmed breeding was recorded primarily in northwestern Ontario in four squares in the vicinity of Lake of the Woods, a pattern similar to that reported in the first atlas.

Abundance: Although the species has a widespread distribution across northern and central Ontario, it appears to be generally uncommon. In all regions, the Connecticut Warbler averaged fewer than 0.5 birds/25 point counts. It is most abundant in the western part of the Northern Shield, but in only a few areas did densities exceed 1.5 birds/25 point counts. However, the species can be locally common in its preferred habitat. Wilson and McRae (1993) found it to be the most commonly detected bird on transects through Tamarack-treed fen at Moosonee, with densities of or approaching 60 birds/km^2. – *Peter L. McLaren*

Mourning Warbler

Paruline triste

Oporornis Philadelphia

Ron Ridout

The Mourning Warbler is apparently so named because of its black breast patch resembling the black crape cravat of Victorian men's half-mourning clothing; but the male's loud, cheery song is anything but funereal. Among the latest of all wood-warblers to appear in spring, it normally arrives at breeding areas in the last week of May and first week of June (Pitocchelli 1993). It breeds in recently disturbed and regenerating conifer and mixed forests from northeastern British Columbia to Newfoundland and south marginally to the upper Midwest and New England states (Pitocchelli 1993). Its preference for recently disturbed forests with a dense understorey suggests that this neotropical migrant likely has benefited from anthropogenic disturbances to the landscape. Historically, it may have been less common in Ontario because such disturbances were less pervasive. Prior to European settlement, the species was probably common only locally, where natural disturbance regimes created younger successional habitat.

Distribution and population status: The Mourning Warbler is found in all regions of Ontario but is very uncommon in the far north. The region with the highest probability of observation is the Southern Shield, at 70%. It is also fairly common in both the Lake Simcoe-Rideau and Northern Shield regions, with 49% probability of observation in both. These three regions contain the highest proportion of forest cover, providing ample potential for breeding habitat. The species is somewhat less common in the heavily agricultural and urbanized Carolinian region, with just a 24% probability of observation. There, it is found predominately in areas with more extensive forest cover, primarily Haldimand and Norfolk Counties and Niagara Region. Surprisingly, it is found through most of the highly urban Toronto area, where presumably its small territory size allows it to exploit habitat patches in parks and ravines. In the Lake Simcoe-Rideau region, its absence from the Belleville-Kingston area (where it was also absent in the first atlas)

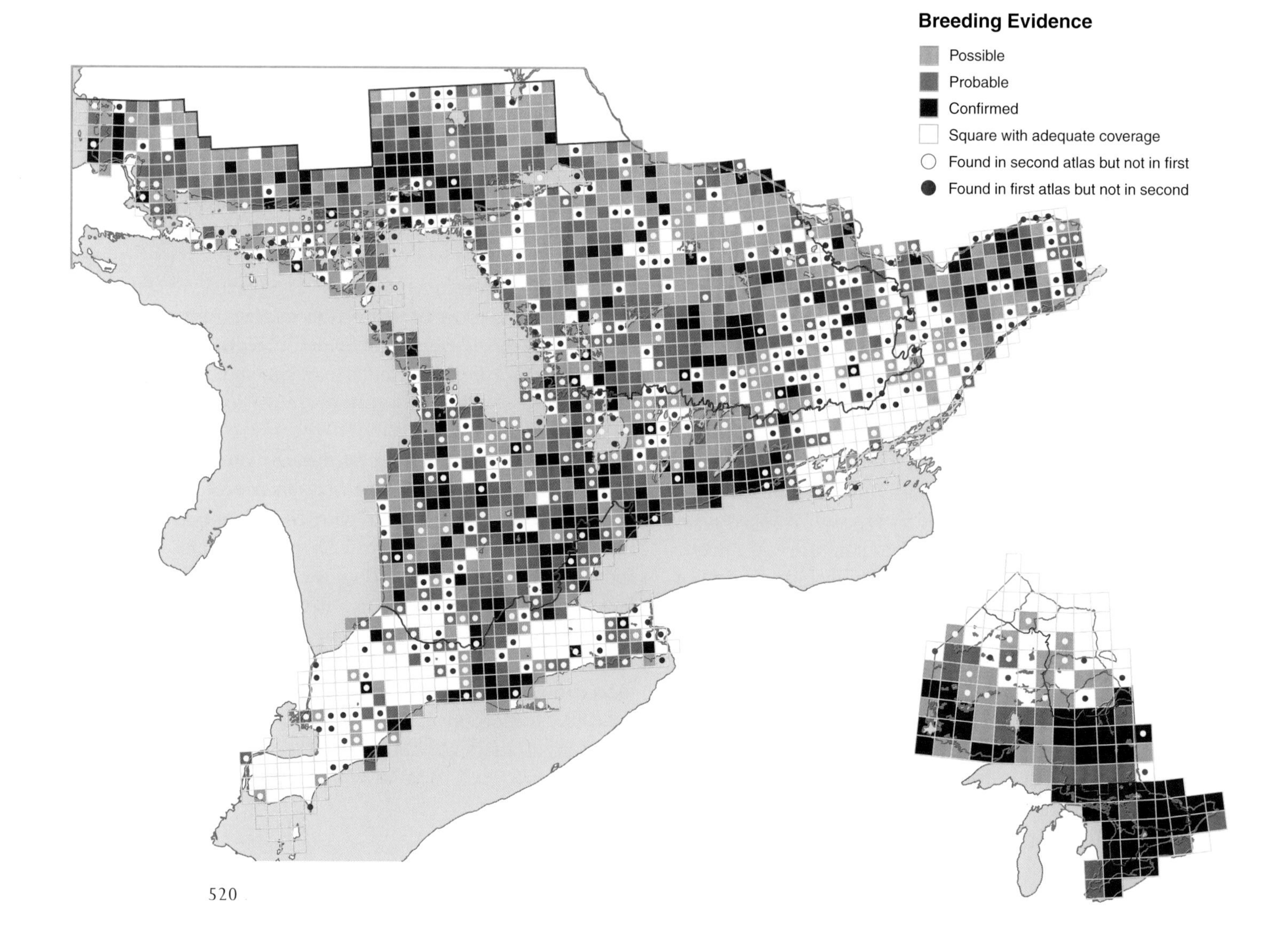

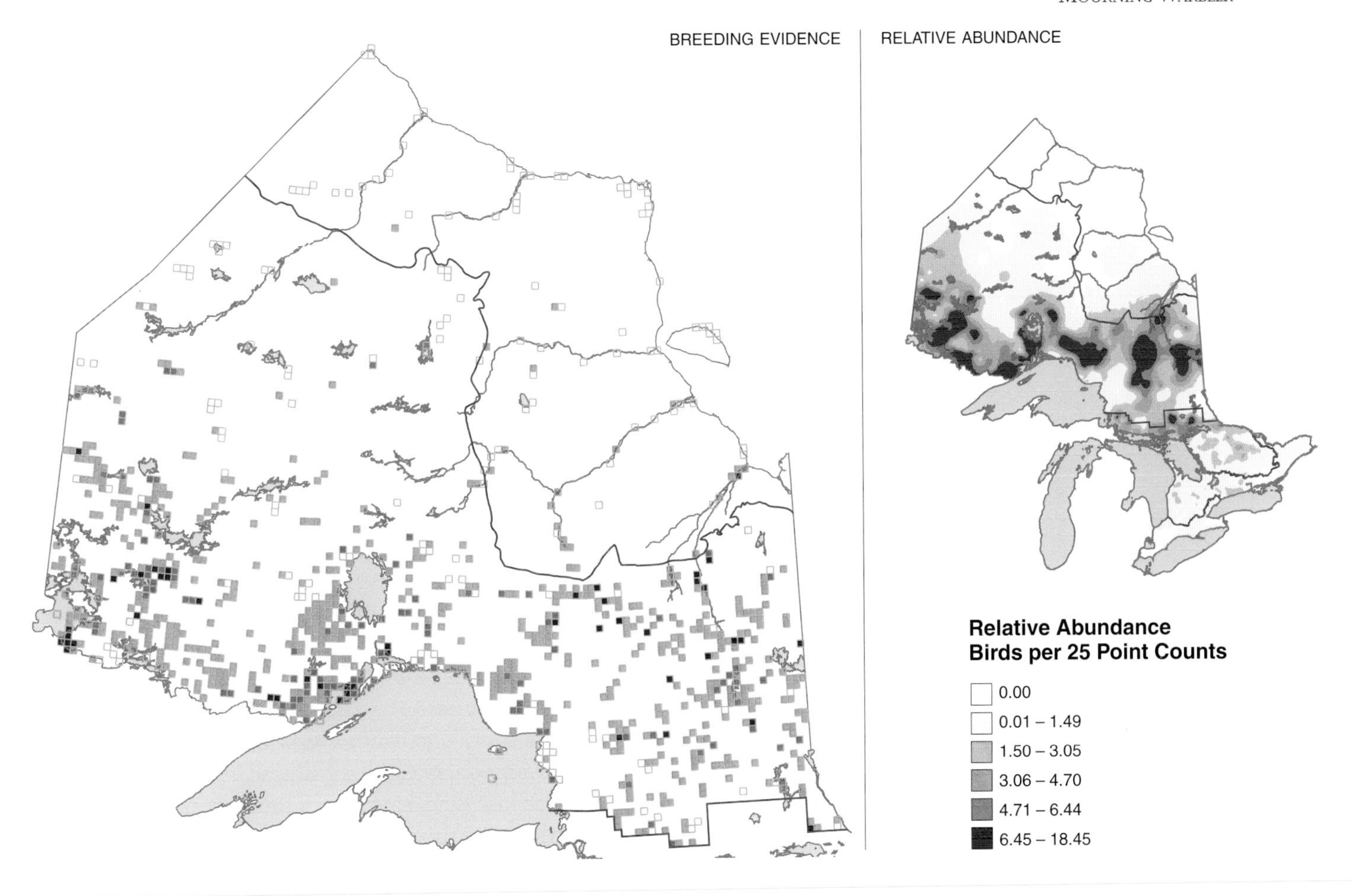

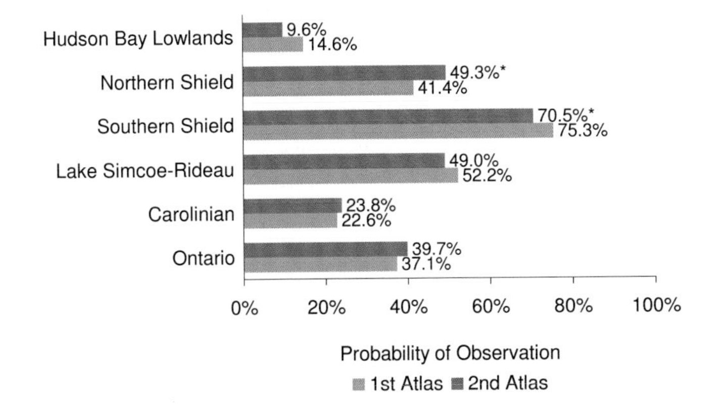

is difficult to explain, as apparently suitable habitat exists interspersed in the primarily agricultural landscape. The species is virtually absent from the Hudson Bay Lowlands, breeding regularly in riparian aspen woodlands north to the Moose and Albany Rivers (James 1991; Wilson and McRae 1993). Records during the second atlas along the Fawn (54° N) and Ekwan (53° N) Rivers may represent isolated breeders or vagrants.

The probability of observation changed significantly between atlases only in the two Shield regions. The species had a 6% lower probability of observation in the Southern Shield in the second atlas, although the reasons for this decline are not clear. The 19% increase in the Northern Shield is doubtless a reflection of increased habitat supply through forest management. BBS data show a significant annual decrease of 3.1% in Mourning Warbler populations in Ontario since 1981, which may be a reflection of the maturation of habitat along static BBS survey routes.

Breeding biology: The Mourning Warbler breeds in early successional habitats including regenerating forests, burns, hydro rights-of-way, and roadsides. It is especially prevalent in 10-15 year old post-harvest spruce forests that have been replaced by aspen and birch with a dense understorey (Pitocchelli 1993). Despite its preference for fairly open, early successional habitats, like other members of its genus it is a skulker and difficult to observe. It is most readily detected by means of its loud, distinctive song. Indeed, the highest breeding evidence in 59% of squares in which it was detected was of possible breeding, primarily singing males. The nest is well concealed on or near the ground in raspberry thickets, fern clumps, sedge, or grass tussocks (Peck and James 1987). Incubation is by the female alone. When approached, she may skulk away from the nest rather than take flight, and nests are consequently difficult to find. However, both parents tend to the young during the nestling and fledgling period, and will usually respond to "pishing." Most confirmed evidence was of adults carrying food.

Abundance: Mourning Warbler abundance was highest in the Northern Shield in a band from Dryden to Lake Abitibi between 48° N and 50° N, where it occurs in densities of over 6.4 birds/25 point counts. Forest management has disturbed a large portion of this forested landscape through the use of clearcut silviculture (pers. obs.), and many of these regenerating forests are now providing ideal breeding habitat. Elsewhere, the species is locally abundant only where regenerating deciduous forests occur and so is rare or absent from much of the Hudson Bay Lowlands and southern Carolinian regions. – *J. Ryan Zimmerling*

Common Yellowthroat

Paruline masqueé
Geothlypis trichas

Tim Stewart

The Common Yellowthroat is an abundant summer resident across North America from Yukon to Newfoundland south throughout the US and much of Mexico. It winters in the southern US, the West Indies, Mexico, and Central America. In Ontario, it may be one of the most familiar warblers. The black mask of the male is an unmistakable field mark, and its distinctive song is easily recognized. It is a common and widespread nesting species, occurring in many habitats with open areas and low, thick vegetation, including dry, second-growth old field, bogs, marshes, swamps, and Black Spruce forest, but it is primarily a bird of wetlands (Guzy and Ritchison 1999).

Distribution and population status: The Common Yellowthroat is one of the most widespread bird species in Ontario, with a 65% probability of observation for the province as a whole. The species is more extensively distributed in the Lake Simcoe-Rideau, Southern Shield, and Carolinian regions, where the probability of observation is 94%, 97%, and 85%, respectively. It becomes progressively less common and more locally distributed northward in the Northern Shield and Hudson Bay Lowlands, where in the latter region the probability of observation is 47%. Although the presence of singing males on the coasts of James and Hudson Bays might suggest the species is more generally distributed in the Hudson Bay Lowlands, it becomes rare to very uncommon and locally distributed northward, and essentially absent within 100 km of Hudson Bay.

Given its ability to use a wide variety of habitats, the Common Yellowthroat has likely always been a widespread species in Ontario. Nonetheless, the probability of observation increased between atlases by a significant 17% and 33% in the Northern Shield and Hudson Bay Lowlands regions, respectively. In the far north of the province, the yellowthroat was recorded in several squares north of the Attawapiskat River

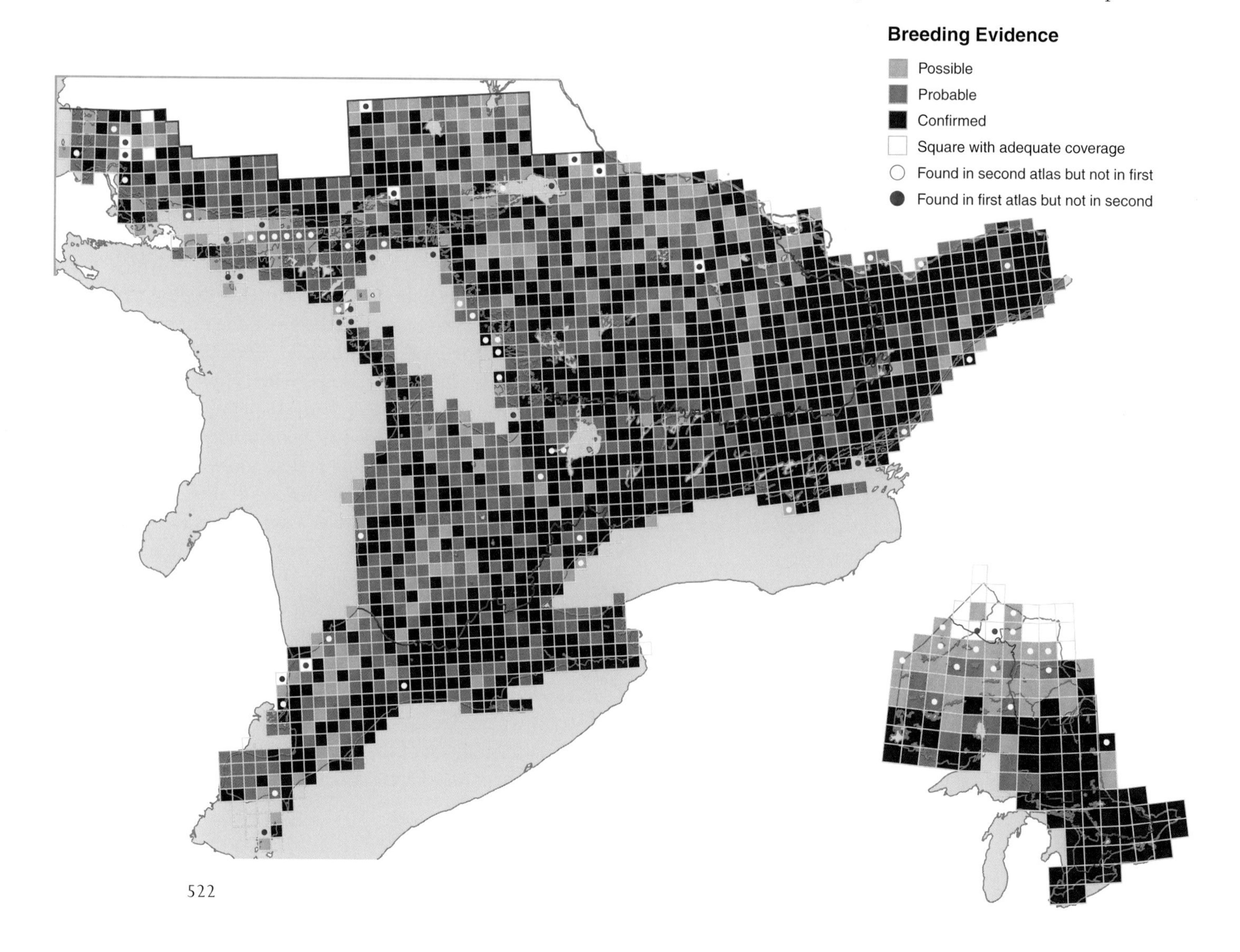

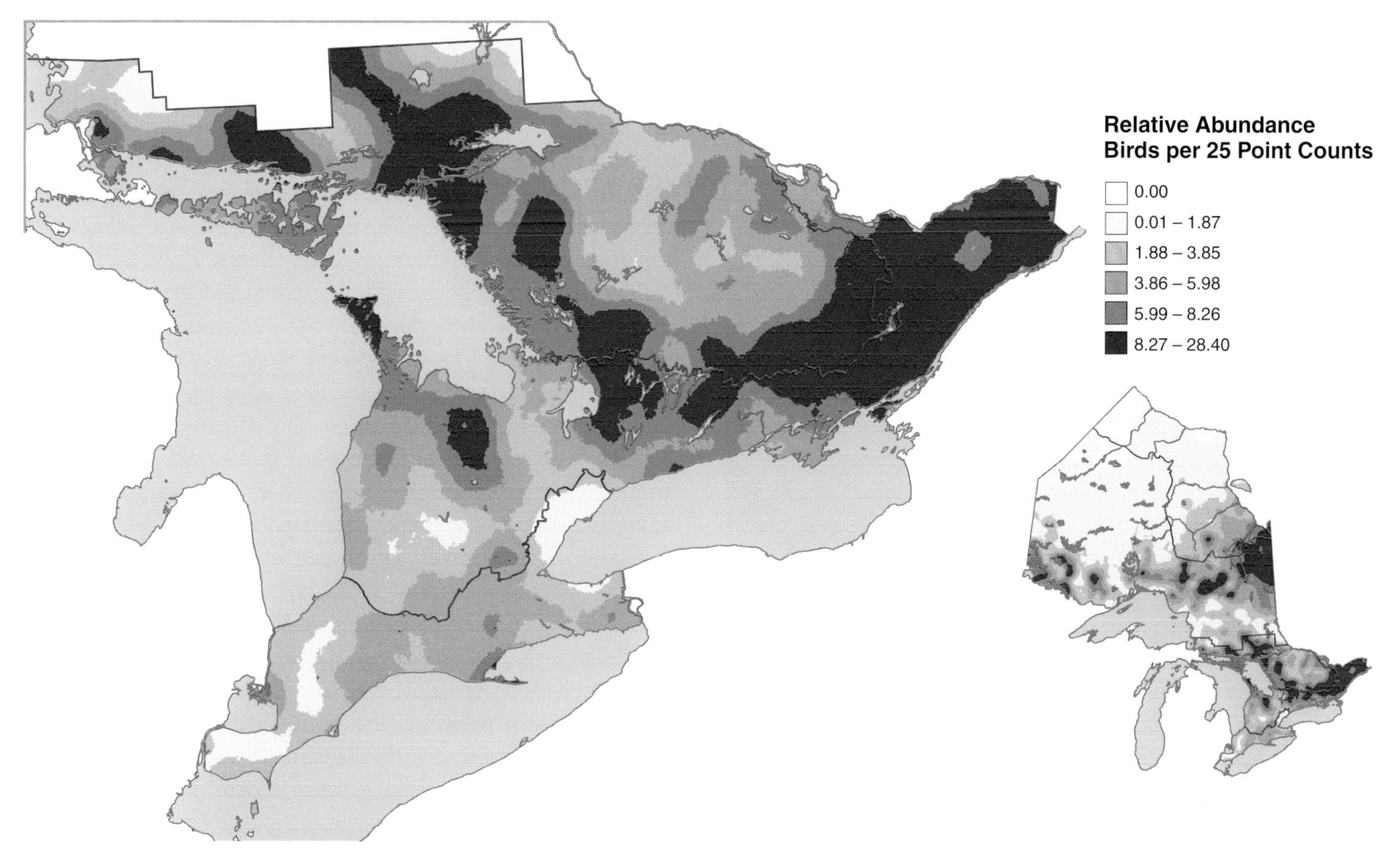

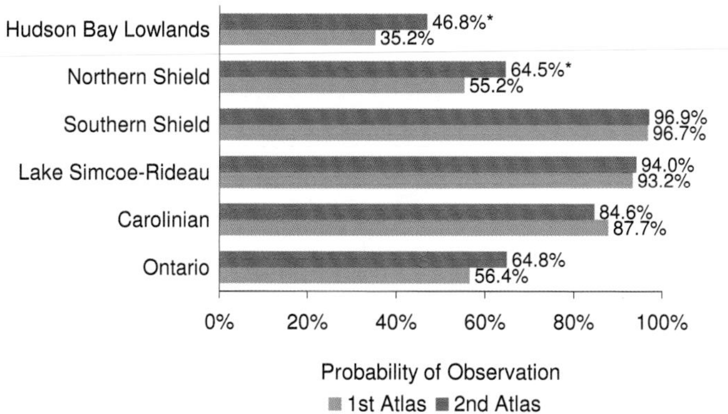

only during the second atlas, and, although these northern records may represent expansion of range, it is possible that they are attributable to increased atlassing effort in that area.

Regional Coordinators considered the Common Yellowthroat to be one of the most common warblers in Ontario. Several felt that the species should have been found in all squares in their atlas administrative regions. BBS data indicate no significant change in Ontario since 1968 (Downes et al. 2005). However, numbers of yellowthroats migrating through the Long Point area have increased significantly over the past 20 years (Crewe 2006), suggesting that the population may be increasing.

Breeding biology: The nest of the Common Yellowthroat is usually constructed on the ground, or a few centimetres above it. Although it is generally well hidden in thick shrubs, the openness of the habitat can facilitate discovery of the nest, usually by flushing the female or following the adults. More typically, however, they leave and enter the nest by moving through the low vegetation rather than flying directly to or from the nest. Both parents participate in feeding the nestlings, and adults carrying food are often seen. These characteristics of the species' behaviour were reflected in the breeding evidence obtained. Evidence of probable and confirmed breeding was obtained in 66% of all squares in which it was recorded, one of the highest percentages among all wood-warblers, aided by its ubiquity and ease of detection. Confirmed breeding evidence was obtained from 46 of the 47 atlas administrative regions. The most commonly reported evidence confirming breeding was of adults carrying food.

Abundance: The song of the Common Yellowthroat is loud and easily identified. During the nesting season, the male can often be seen singing from prominent locations. Thus, it should be readily detectable during point counts, and data should provide a good indication of its abundance. The highest densities were recorded in the Southern Shield and Lake Simcoe-Rideau regions, particularly in easternmost Ontario, as well as the area north and east of Georgian Bay. High densities were also reported in a broad area south and southwest of Moosonee. The reason for this pattern of abundance is unclear, as habitat availability does not appear to be a limiting factor. Although the species is widespread in the Carolinian region, the densities there are only about half of those recorded to the north, presumably reflecting lower availability of wetland habitat in this heavily agricultural and urbanized region. Similarly, although the abundance map indicates that the yellowthroat is found throughout the province, it appears that there are large areas of Boreal Forest and the far north where the species is scarce or absent. – *Peter L. McLaren*

Hooded Warbler

Paruline à capuchon

Wilsonia citrina

Bill Rayner

The strikingly beautiful male Hooded Warbler often reveals its presence through its enthusiastic "*a-wheeta-wheeta-whee-tee-o*" song. The species breeds in the eastern US and winters in Mexico and Central America and typically is found breeding in deciduous and mixed forests in the northeast (Evans Ogden and Stutchbury 1994). It reaches the northern limit of its range in southern Ontario, where most of the population occurs in the Carolinian region. The species is currently designated as Threatened in Canada (COSEWIC 2000).

Distribution and population status: Once a rare breeding bird in Ontario, the Hooded Warbler has increased its population size and rapidly expanded its range in recent years. Data from the second atlas show a dramatic change from its historical distribution, as well as since the first atlas. The species was first documented in Ontario in 1878 (Baillie 1925; Baillie and Harrington 1937), but the first nest was not discovered until 1949 in Elgin Co. It is possible that this warbler was always present in Ontario in low numbers but was either overlooked by naturalists unfamiliar with the species or dismissed as a vagrant (Sutherland and Gartshore in Cadman et al. 1987).

There was a significant increase of about 400% in the probability of observation of the Hooded Warbler in Ontario between atlases. Historically, the majority of the Canadian population was found at only a few breeding sites, with most in Norfolk Co. In the last 20 years, the species has expanded its range north, west, and east. Although still most common in the Carolinian region (62 squares), it was also found in 18 squares in the Lake Simcoe-Rideau region and in one square in the Southern Shield region. During the first atlas, it was only found in 21 squares in the Carolinian region and was not recorded in either the Lake Simcoe-Rideau or the Southern Shield regions.

The New York State Breeding Bird Atlas also shows a large increase in the Hooded Warbler's distribution, particularly in

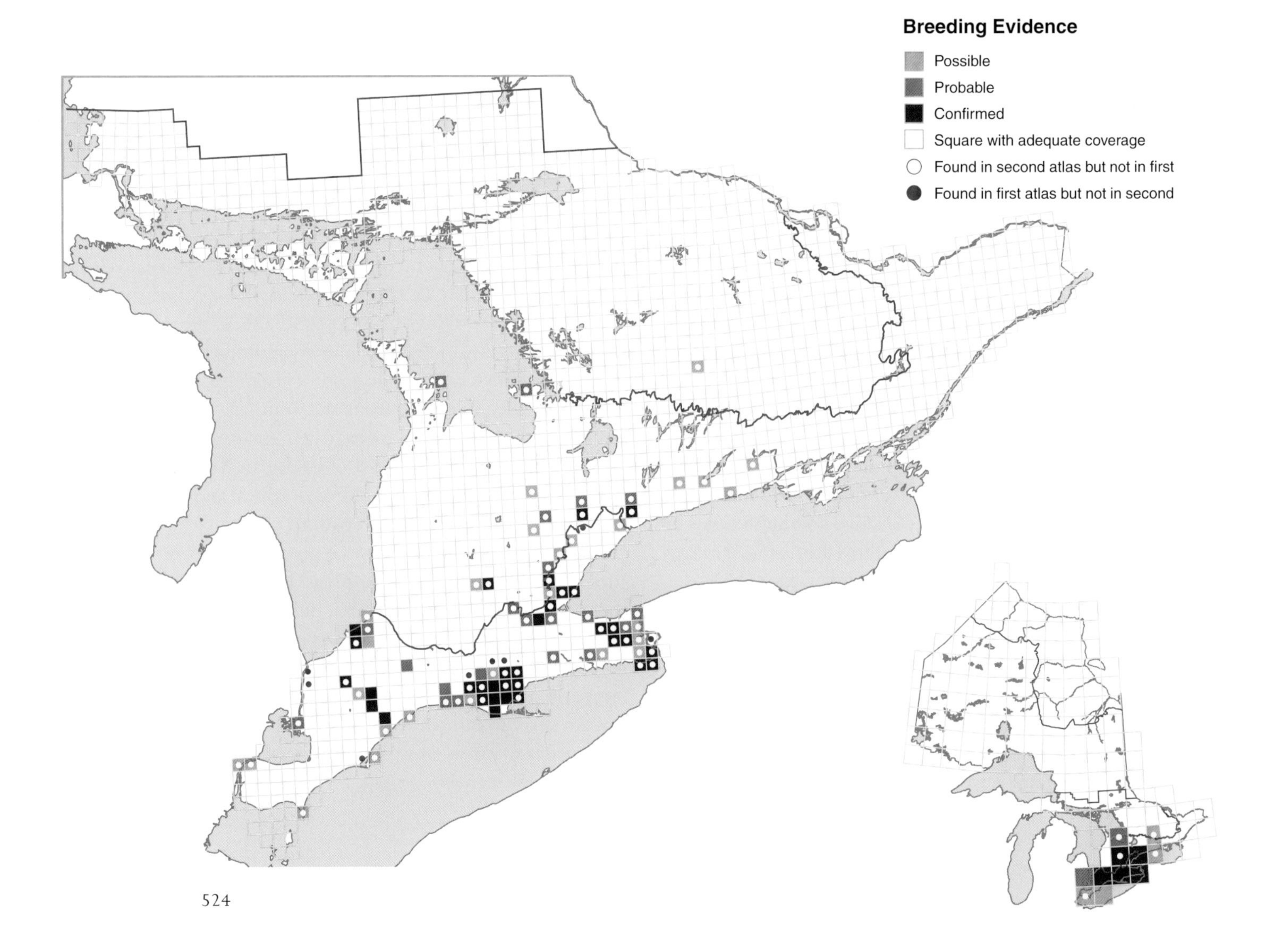

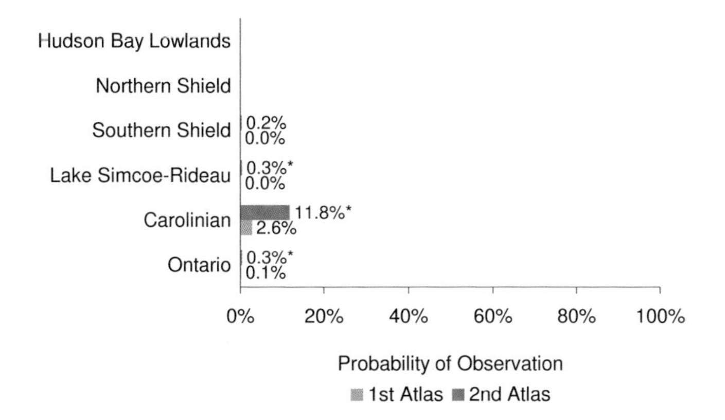

the western part of the state bordering eastern Lake Erie. The increasing population of Hooded Warblers in neighbouring US states is a possible source of immigrants to the Ontario population. BBS trends for the species from 1980 to 2005 show a non-significant increase (0.8%/year) across its North American range (Sauer et al. 2005).

Although there has been little overall change in forest cover in the Carolinian region since the first atlas, increased forest cover across eastern North America may account for some of the species' population expansion. In addition, the maturation of conifer plantations in parts of the Hooded Warbler's range may be another driving factor. The number of extreme weather days in July was found to be an important predictor of Hooded Warbler presence in Ontario (Melles 2007), suggesting that climate change could also be facilitating the northward expansion of the species.

Breeding biology: In Ontario, the Hooded Warbler is usually found in relatively large, mature forests with canopy gaps that have been created either naturally or through selective logging. Birds have been found in woodlots as small as 10 ha, but typically occur in areas with high regional forest cover and in close proximity to larger woodlots (BSC, unpubl. data; Melles 2007). Nests are commonly less than a metre above the ground and are well hidden in the dense, shrubby vegetation that proliferates in forest gaps. The species readily re-nests following a failure and will usually raise more than one brood in a season. Males sing frequently throughout the breeding season and are thus relatively easy to detect in appropriate habitat. Females, on the other hand, are quite cryptic and are typically only detected when feeding young, or by observers who are familiar with this warbler's distinctive chip notes.

In the second atlas, 41% of squares recorded confirmed breeding evidence, compared to only 19% of squares in the first atlas. This increase can be attributed to increased knowledge of the species' biology, greater effort to confirm nesting, and a larger emphasis on Hooded Warbler research since the 1990s.

Abundance: This species was detected too infrequently on point counts to produce a map of relative abundance. However, directed surveys suggest that the Hooded Warbler is most abundant in Norfolk Co., with over 130 recorded territories in the area during the atlas period. The next largest concentration is found in Niagara Region, with 33 recorded territories. The province contains an estimated 300 Hooded Warbler territories (Acadian Flycatcher/Hooded Warbler Recovery Team, unpubl. data). – *Debra S. Badzinski*

Only the female Hooded Warbler builds the nest, typically in five to six days but occasionally in as few as two (Evans Ogden and Stutchbury 1994). *Photo: Yousif S. Attia*

Typical nesting habitat, South Walsingham Forest, Norfolk Co. Some nests are in canopy openings along trails or tracks through mature forest. *Photo: George K. Peck*

Wilson's Warbler

Paruline à calotte noire

Wilsonia pusilla

Frank and Sandra Horvath

The Wilson's Warbler is a summer resident across much of Canada and the US, from western Alaska and British Columbia east to Newfoundland, and more locally south through the western US to southern California and New Mexico. It winters throughout much of Central America and in the extreme southern US along the coast of the Gulf of Mexico (Ammon and Gilbert 1999). Although its range is largely associated with boreal forest, it tends to avoid the forest itself. In Ontario, its preferred nesting habitat includes alder/willow swamps with Black Spruce and Tamarack, and shrubby or grassy riparian or other wet habitats (Peck and James 1987).

Distribution and population status: During migration, the Wilson's Warbler may be encountered in much of Ontario, but the breeding range is generally north and west of Sault Ste. Marie and Lake Nipissing. The species was reported in virtually all 100-km blocks in northern Ontario in either the first or second atlas. Although widespread throughout this zone, it is nonetheless apparently uncommon or absent from substantial portions of it. The probability of observation was just 74% in the Hudson Bay Lowlands and only 41% in the Northern Shield region. These percentages may indicate the lack of appropriate habitat in large parts of northern Ontario, but may just as likely reflect the difficulty in accessing the wet habitat in which the species occurs. Such habitats tend to be under-represented in surveys, and consequently the species may in fact be more widespread than it appears. The observed range is, however, consistent with the distribution of the species noted in the first atlas.

Between atlases, the probability of observation increased significantly in the province as a whole by 41%, and in the Northern Shield and Hudson Bay Lowlands by 52% and 30%, respectively. It is unclear, however, to what degree this represents a real increase and an in-filling of the species' range. It is

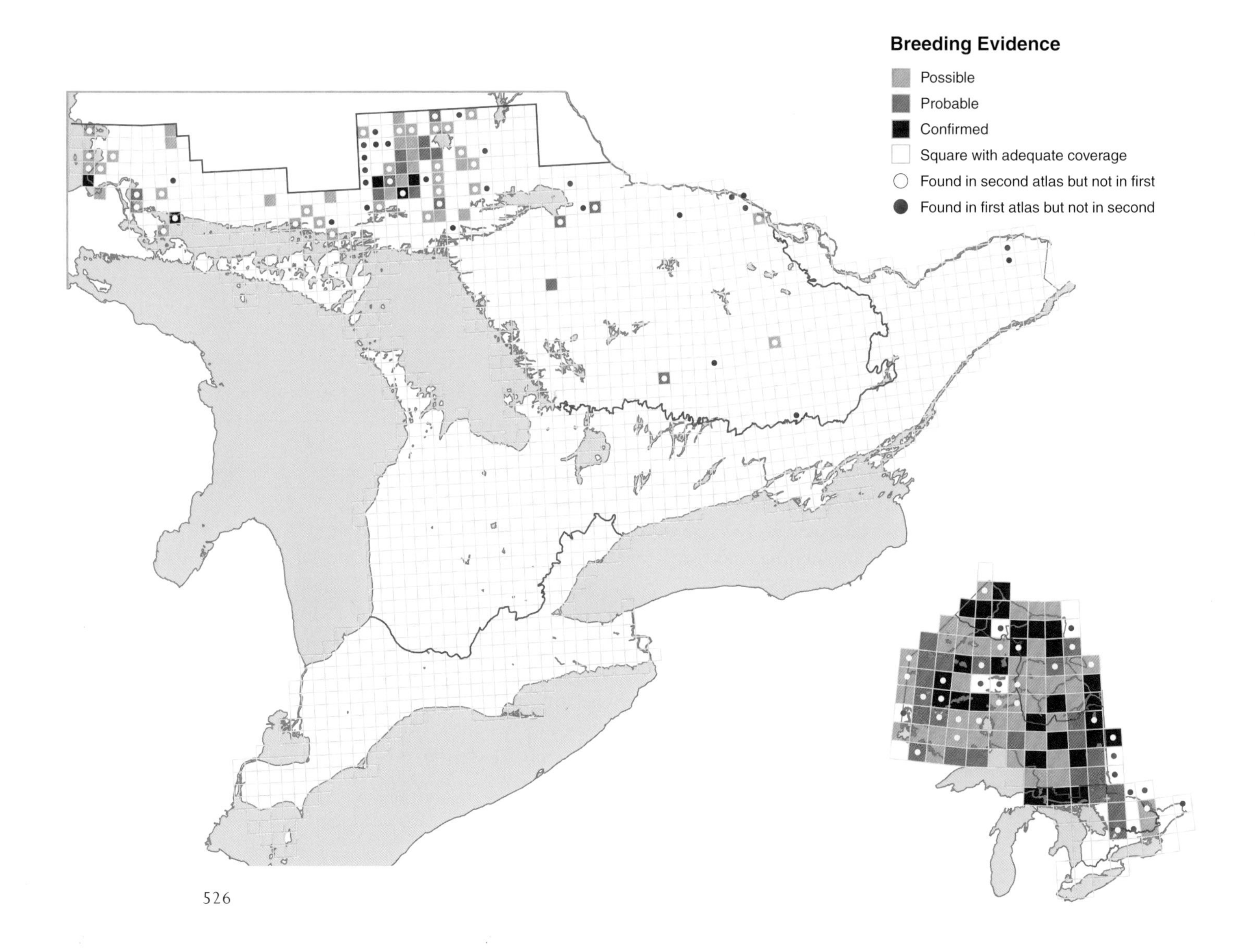

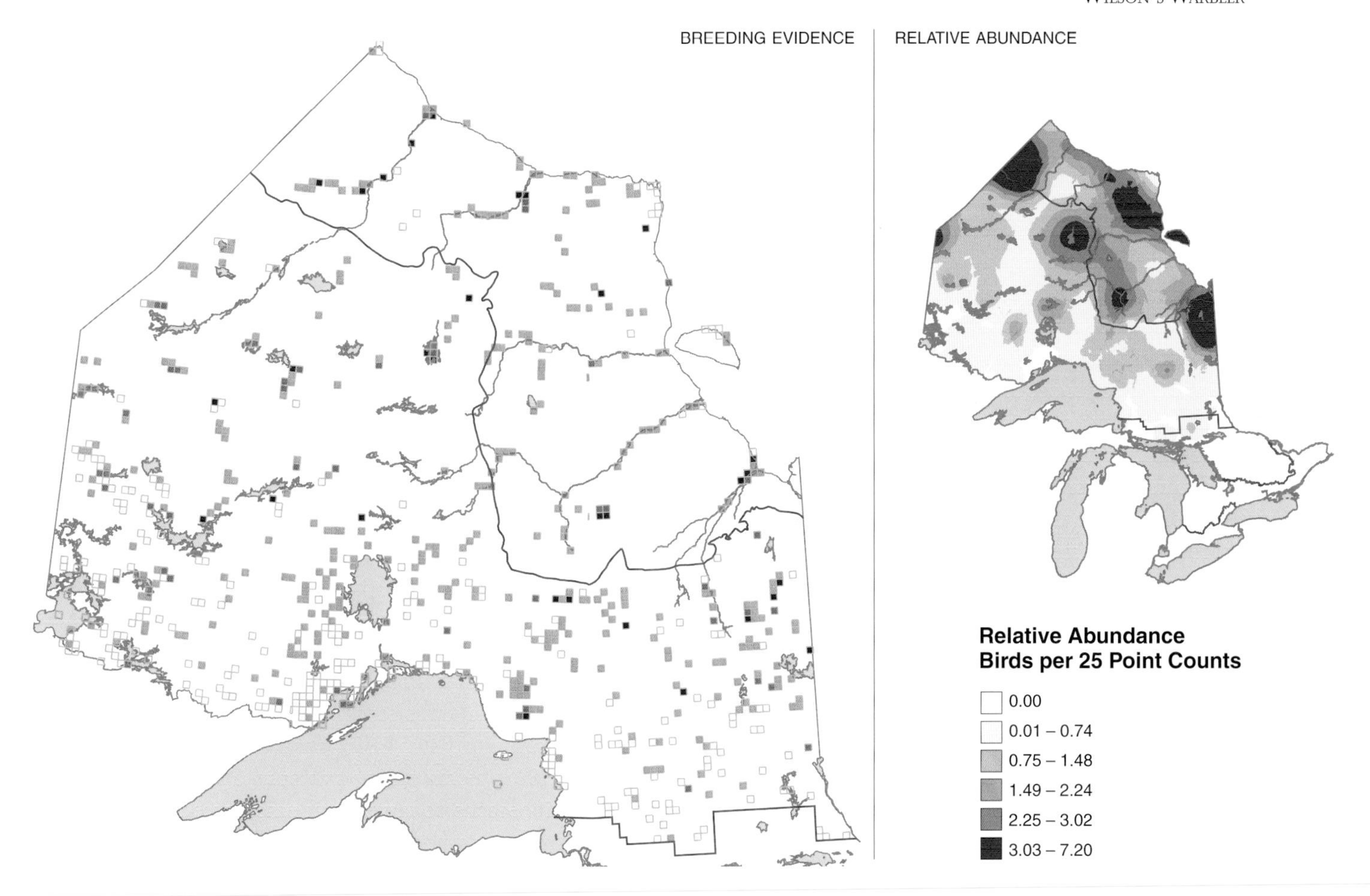

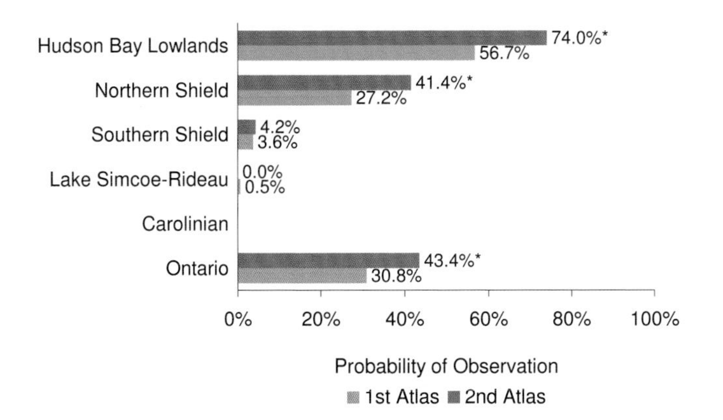

possible that the increase is a result of atlassers in northern Ontario being more familiar with this warbler's song during this atlas than the first, or greater efforts being made to survey the often difficult-to-sample habitat in which the species resides. Neither BBS nor CMMN data indicate that Wilson's Warbler populations have undergone any significant changes in Ontario since the first atlas. BBS data do indicate a significant decline across Canada as a whole since 1968 (Downes et al. 2005), but because much of the species' breeding range is north of the area covered by the survey, the accuracy of this trend is difficult to determine.

Singing male Wilson's Warblers were also recorded south of the main breeding range in the Southern Shield and Lake Simcoe-Rideau regions, as they were in the first atlas. However, nesting in these areas was not confirmed. It is more probable that these individuals were wandering males or short-stopped migrants rather than active breeders.

Breeding biology: Nests of the Wilson's Warbler are very difficult to locate, as they are generally built at ground level, at the base of shrubs or small trees, or under clumps of grass, sedge, or moss. Some nests may even be excavated where the substrate is soft. However, the species can readily be detected by song, by far the easiest way to detect it in dense vegetation. The combination of nest location and difficult-to-sample habitat is reflected in the types of breeding evidence reported. Fully 80% of evidence was in the form of singing males or birds in suitable habitat, and probable or confirmed breeding evidence was obtained in only 20% of the squares in which this warbler was reported. Breeding was actually confirmed in only 7% of the squares, and the large majority of these records were of adults carrying food. In fact, only three squares reported nests with eggs or young during the atlas period. Only 18 nests have ever been documented for this species in Ontario (Peck and Peck 2006).

Abundance: Although found throughout the north, the Wilson's Warbler is more abundant in the Hudson Bay Lowlands than in the adjacent Northern Shield region. Densities averaged about three times higher in the former region than in the latter, likely because the low, wet, shrub thicket habitat the species prefers is found more extensively in the Hudson Bay Lowlands. The apparent pockets of very high densities throughout both regions may be an artifact of sparse point count sampling, but do indicate that the species can be abundant in appropriate habitat. – *Peter L. McLaren*

Canada Warbler

Paruline du Canada

Wilsonia canadensis

David Welbourne

The Canada Warbler is a summer resident across central and southern Canada from northern Alberta to Nova Scotia, and in the northeastern US south through the Appalachian Mountains. It winters in South America, from Colombia to Peru. This species is one of the last of the wood-warblers to arrive on its nesting grounds and also one of the first to depart. It is usually found in moist coniferous-deciduous forests with a well-developed understorey, especially in low-lying areas such as cedar woods or alder swamps (Conway 1999).

Distribution and population status: The Canada Warbler breeds throughout Ontario north to about Moosonee and Opasquia Prov. Park. The centre of its distribution in Ontario lies in the Southern Shield region, where it is widely distributed with a 68% probability of observation. It is much more sparsely distributed to the north and west, with breeding evidence obtained as far north as Sandy Lake and Moosonee. South of the Canadian Shield, the Canada Warbler is also widespread but locally distributed, presumably a consequence of lack of suitable damp wooded habitat. The probability of observation in the Lake Simcoe-Rideau region was 26%, and even lower in the Carolinian region. Evidence of breeding was obtained as far south as the Rondeau and Lake St. Clair areas, with concentrations of records near Long Point and in southwest Middlesex Co. and adjacent western Elgin Co.

The distribution of the Canada Warbler changed little between the two atlas periods. Although the probability of observation did not change significantly in the province as a whole between atlases, it declined significantly by 10% in the core of the species' range in the Southern Shield and by 36% in the Carolinian, the latter being a region in which the species has always been rather rare (James 1991). Areas north and west of Sudbury and between Algonquin Prov. Park and Kingston showed the most evident decrease on the breeding evidence map. Although declines in the Carolinian are most likely due to

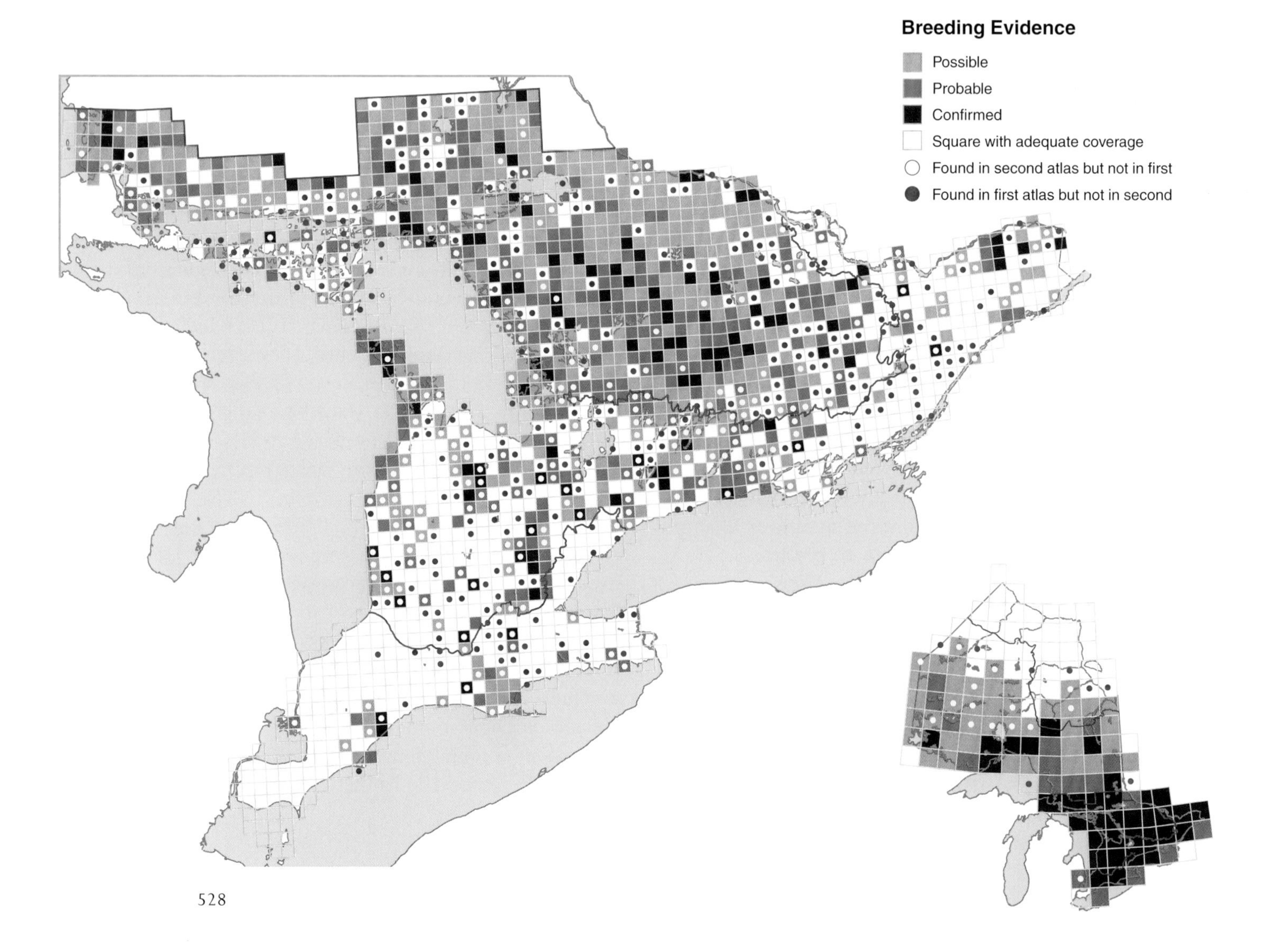

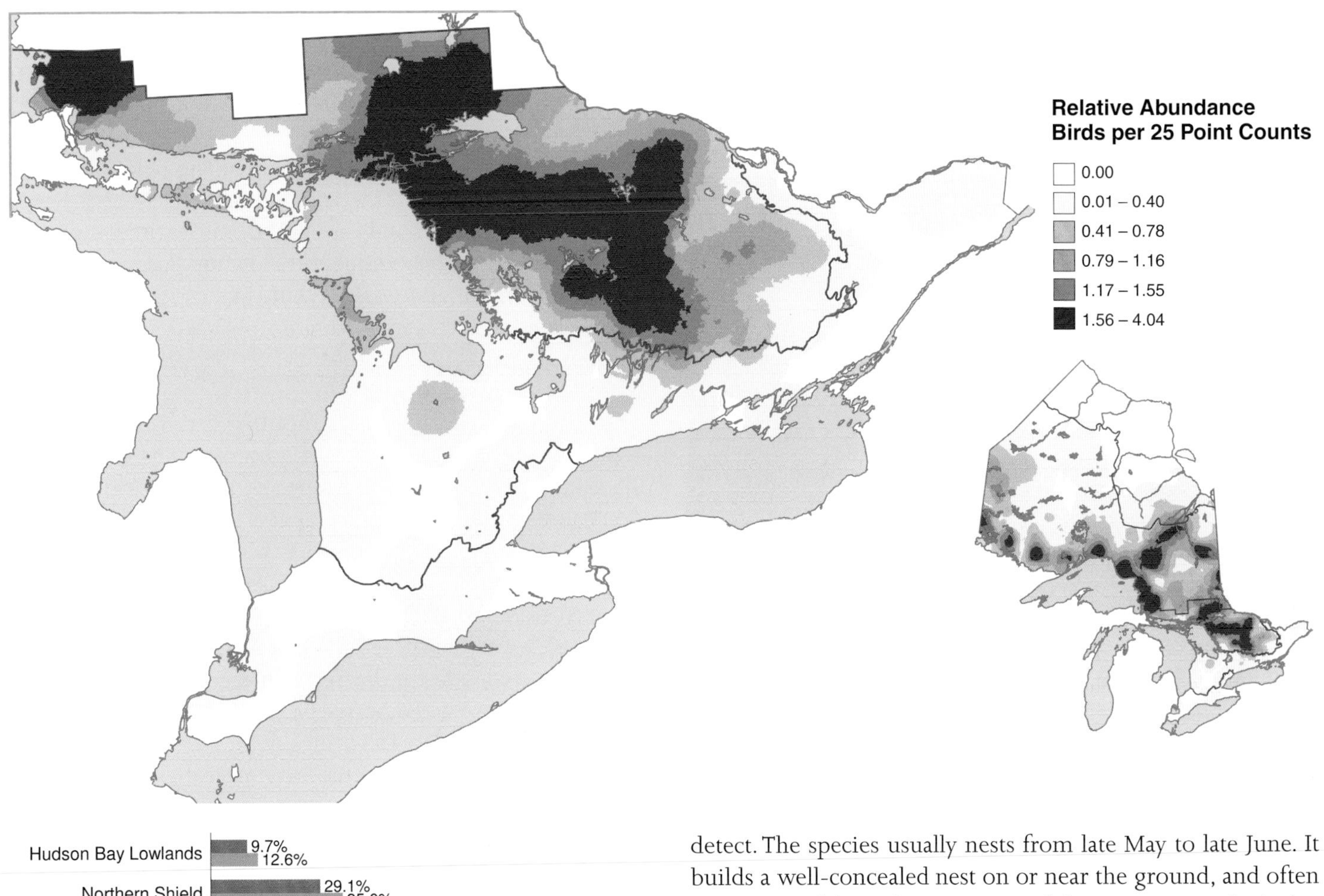

Region	2nd Atlas	1st Atlas
Hudson Bay Lowlands	9.7%	12.6%
Northern Shield	29.1%	35.0%
Southern Shield	67.5%*	74.6%
Lake Simcoe-Rideau	26.0%	26.9%
Carolinian	3.3%*	5.1%
Ontario	26.0%	30.8%

0% 20% 40% 60% 80% 100%

Probability of Observation

1st Atlas ■ 2nd Atlas

loss of swamps and moist woodland, reasons for the decline in the Southern Shield are unclear.

BBS data show no significant changes in Ontario, despite significant annual declines of 4.3% for Canada as a whole for 1968-2005, and 5.1% for 1981-2005. Although CMMN data from TCBO indicate a significant decrease in numbers during spring and fall migrations, this decline was not noted at LPBO (Crewe 2006). Some recent studies, including BBS data for the US, suggest that numbers of Canada Warblers in the northeast US and Ontario decreased substantially in the 1980s and 1990s. It may be that populations in these areas grew in response to increasing habitat with the succession of fields abandoned during the early part of the 20th century, and are decreasing to earlier levels as these forests mature (Conway 1999). Partners in Flight has recognized the decline by placing the species on its Watch List (Rich et al. 2004).

Breeding biology: The Canada Warbler often resides in difficult-to-sample habitat, but its distinctive song is generally loud and given frequently and therefore is relatively easy to detect. The species usually nests from late May to late June. It builds a well-concealed nest on or near the ground, and often in stumps of fallen logs. In 67% of the squares in which this species was recorded, only possible breeding evidence was obtained, most frequently in the form of singing males. Confirmed breeding was reported in only 9% of the squares with data. The large majority of these confirmations were in the form of adults carrying food, as nests containing eggs or young were reported very infrequently.

Abundance: Although nowhere in the province especially abundant, the species is found in highest densities through the Southern and Northern Shield regions. The abundance maps indicate two main areas of abundance: from Sudbury south to Georgian Bay and east to Algonquin Prov. Park, and in a band from Rainy River to Cochrane, extending south along the eastern shore of Lake Superior. In the Southern Shield region, the centre of its provincial distribution, densities averaged fewer than 2 birds/25 point counts. In the other regions, densities averaged fewer than 1 bird/25 point counts. These data are consistent with data from other parts of its breeding range. Conway (1999) considered the Canada Warbler to be uncommon throughout its range. – *Peter L. McLaren*

Yellow-breasted Chat

Paruline Polyglotte

Icteria virens

John Reaume

The largest of the wood-warblers, the Yellow-breasted Chat is notoriously secretive, usually remaining hidden in dense thickets and vine tangles. Were it not for its loud and complex song, it might go largely undetected in the breeding season. It breeds from central Mexico north to southern Canada. Two subspecies have been described: the longer-tailed *auricollis* breeds in the west from southern British Columbia, Alberta, and Saskatchewan south discontinuously to central Mexico; the nominate *virens* breeds extensively east of the 100th meridian, north to extreme southern Ontario (Eckerle and Thompson 2001).

Distribution and population status: The Yellow-breasted Chat probably expanded its breeding range in eastern North America in the late19th and early 20th centuries, in the wake of agricultural land abandonment following European settlement. However, by the early 1960s, loss of its early successional habitats to forest maturation resulted in population declines, particularly along the northern periphery of its range (Eckerle and Thompson 2001).

In Ontario, the extent of its breeding distribution has evidently changed little over that observed historically (cf. Macoun and Macoun 1909; Baillie and Harrington 1937). Its distribution in the province has always been largely limited to the Carolinian region, where it has been regarded as at most locally uncommon (James 1991). During the first atlas, it was reported outside the Carolinian region at only a few sites north to Goderich, Shelburne, and the Kingston area.

The second atlas indicates a major range reduction. Breeding evidence was reported in 27 squares in eight 100-km blocks, compared with 45 squares in 10 100-km blocks during the first atlas. Between atlases, its probability of observation declined significantly by 86% in the Lake Simcoe-Rideau

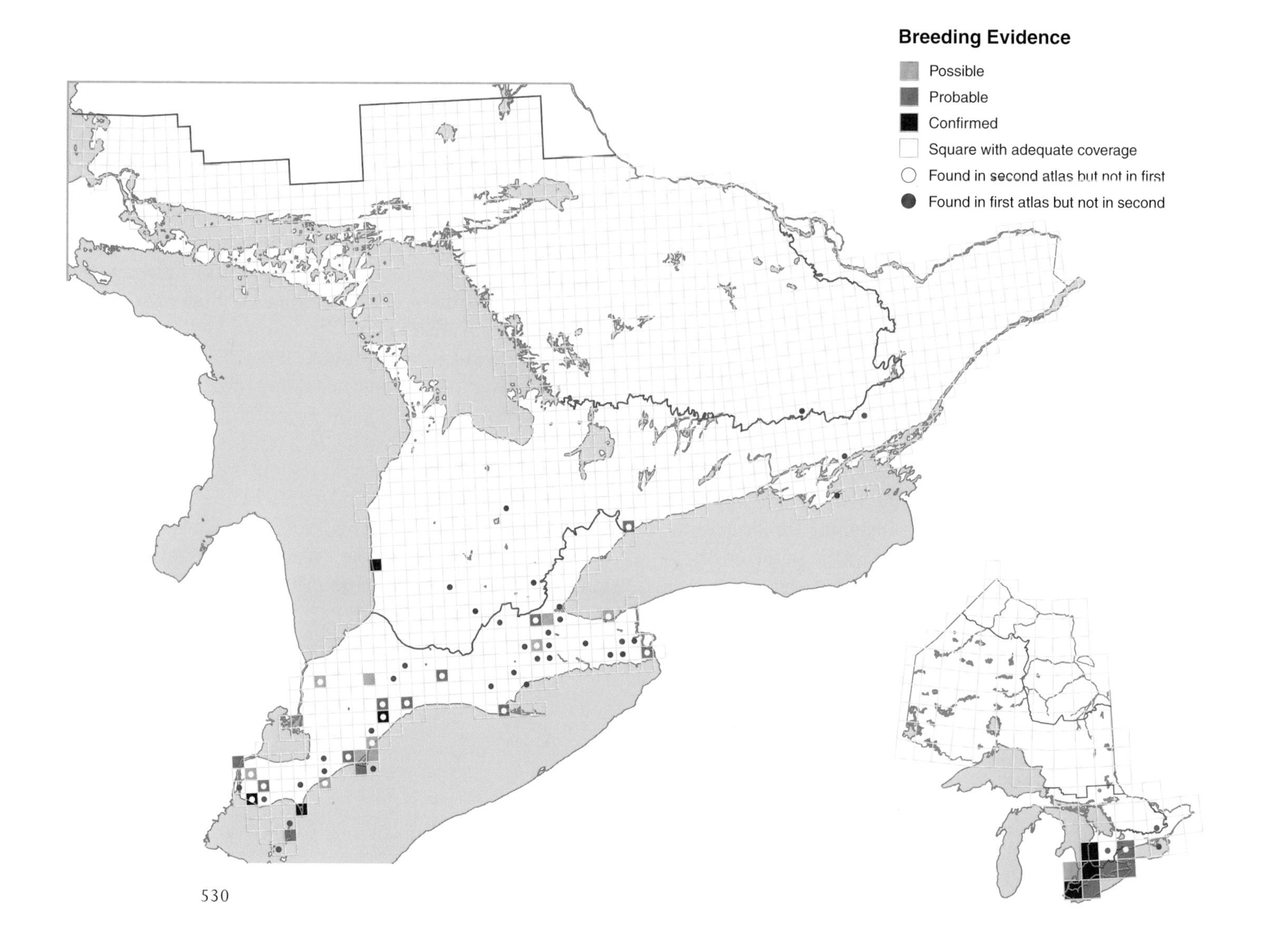

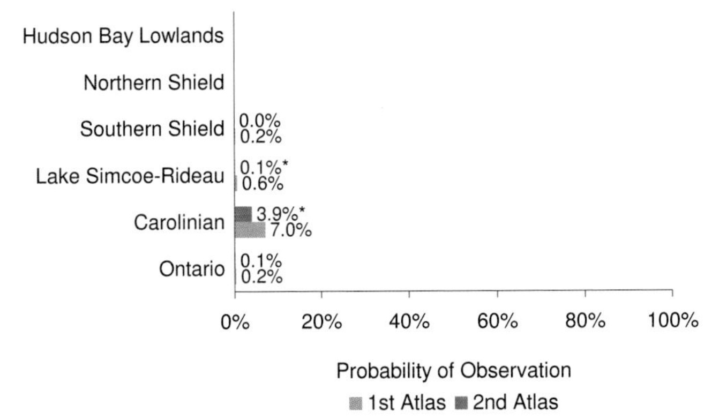

region, and the species is now essentially confined to the Carolinian region. Even in the Carolinian region, the probability of observation declined by a significant 45%. Observed declines are consistent with trends elsewhere at the periphery of the species' range in the northeast.

Breeding biology: The Yellow-breasted Chat breeds in scrubby, early successional habitats. In Ontario, it utilizes regenerating old fields, forest edges, railway and hydro rights-of-way, young coniferous reforestations and, occasionally, wet willow-ash-elm thickets bordering wetlands. Tangles of grape and raspberry are a feature of most breeding sites. Fidelity to breeding sites was low between atlases, as the chat was recorded in only nine (20%) squares in which it was recorded during the first atlas. In Ontario, relatively few sites appear to be occupied for more than a few years, and many sites are not occupied in successive years. Fidelity to breeding sites does not appear to be correlated with changes to breeding habitat, as has been observed elsewhere in the species' range in the east (Eckerle and Thompson 2001).

Chats arrive at breeding sites in Ontario by mid-May. Males sing both morning and evening and often at night. The song is a highly variable, mimid-like series of notes, usually delivered from dense thickets but also from elevated perches and during a distinctive parachute display flight. Song levels drop quickly as the breeding season advances, so that by July singing has largely ceased. Nests are well concealed in dense thickets, and confirming breeding is generally difficult. Only 15% of records were of confirmed breeding, not substantially different from that obtained in the first atlas.

Although the distribution shown in the breeding evidence map is probably accurate, it is possible that the species may have been overlooked in some squares. Its furtive nature, propensity to wander rather widely during the breeding season (Eckerle and Thompson 2001), and the similarity of portions of its song to those of the Gray Catbird and Brown Thrasher may reduce opportunities for its detection by atlassers. As it responds readily and aggressively to call broadcasts and other imitations of its song, call broadcast surveys could substantially increase detection rates, although it is unlikely that many atlassers employed this technique.

Abundance: In Ontario, the Yellow-breasted Chat's ephemeral occupancy of breeding sites tends to confound accurate estimates of its abundance, and its status in the province is somewhat unclear, although densities are very low. Data from the second atlas suggest that most squares support only single territories. The species' tendency toward loose coloniality (Eckerle and Thompson 2001) can result in somewhat higher densities in some squares, such as those containing Point Pelee Nat. Park and Pelee Island, areas currently supporting almost 40% of the provincial population (D.A. Sutherland, pers. comm.). Atlas data and recent NHIC data indicate a minimum population of 42 pairs, and it is unlikely that the provincial population greatly exceeds 50 pairs. – *Paul F.J. Eagles*

Clutch size is usually three to five eggs, but clutches of six have been reported. The incubation period is about 12 days (Eckerle and Thompson 2001). *Photo: George K. Peck*

Yellow-breasted Chat breeding habitat on Pelee Island, Essex Co. *Photo: A. Mathes (Ontario Nature archives)*

Summer Tanager

Tangara vermillon

Piranga rubra

John Reaume

The Summer Tanager is a very distinctive songbird seldom encountered in Ontario. It occurs as a rare spring and fall vagrant to the province, particularly in spring in the south (James 1991). Breeding has not been confirmed in Ontario, although there is some evidence to suggest that it may do so, at least occasionally. It breeds in the southwestern US and northern Mexico, throughout the eastern US, from Florida, Texas, and southeast Nebraska, north and east regularly to central Indiana, Ohio, and southern New Jersey and south to Florida. It winters in Central America and northern South America (Robinson 1996).

Distribution and population status: The Summer Tanager is likely a rare, occasional, or sporadic breeder in the Carolinian region of Ontario, although definitive evidence has not been found. The first evidence of possible breeding involved an individual in Rondeau Prov. Park in June 1965 (Speirs 1985). During the first atlas, the Summer Tanager was recorded in two squares: a singing male was located at the Royal Botanical Gardens, Hamilton, in late May 1983; and a pair was present in Rondeau Prov. Park, 26 May to 30 July 1985, with copulation observed on at least one occasion (Woodliffe in Cadman et al. 1987). Prior to the second atlas, single singing males were present near Turkey Point, Norfolk Co., 15 June 1996 (J.D. McCracken, pers. comm.), and in Point Pelee Nat. Park in June 1997 and again in June 2000 (A. Wormington, unpubl. data).

During the second atlas, the Summer Tanager was found in three squares: at Point Pelee, where single singing males were present during June in three successive years (2003-2005); in the South Walsingham Forest, Norfolk Co., where a male was singing on territory, 12 May to 15 June 2001; and in a woodlot near Glencoe, Middlesex Co., 15 May 2001. In view of the single mid-May date and the fact that the species was not recorded at the site subsequently, the

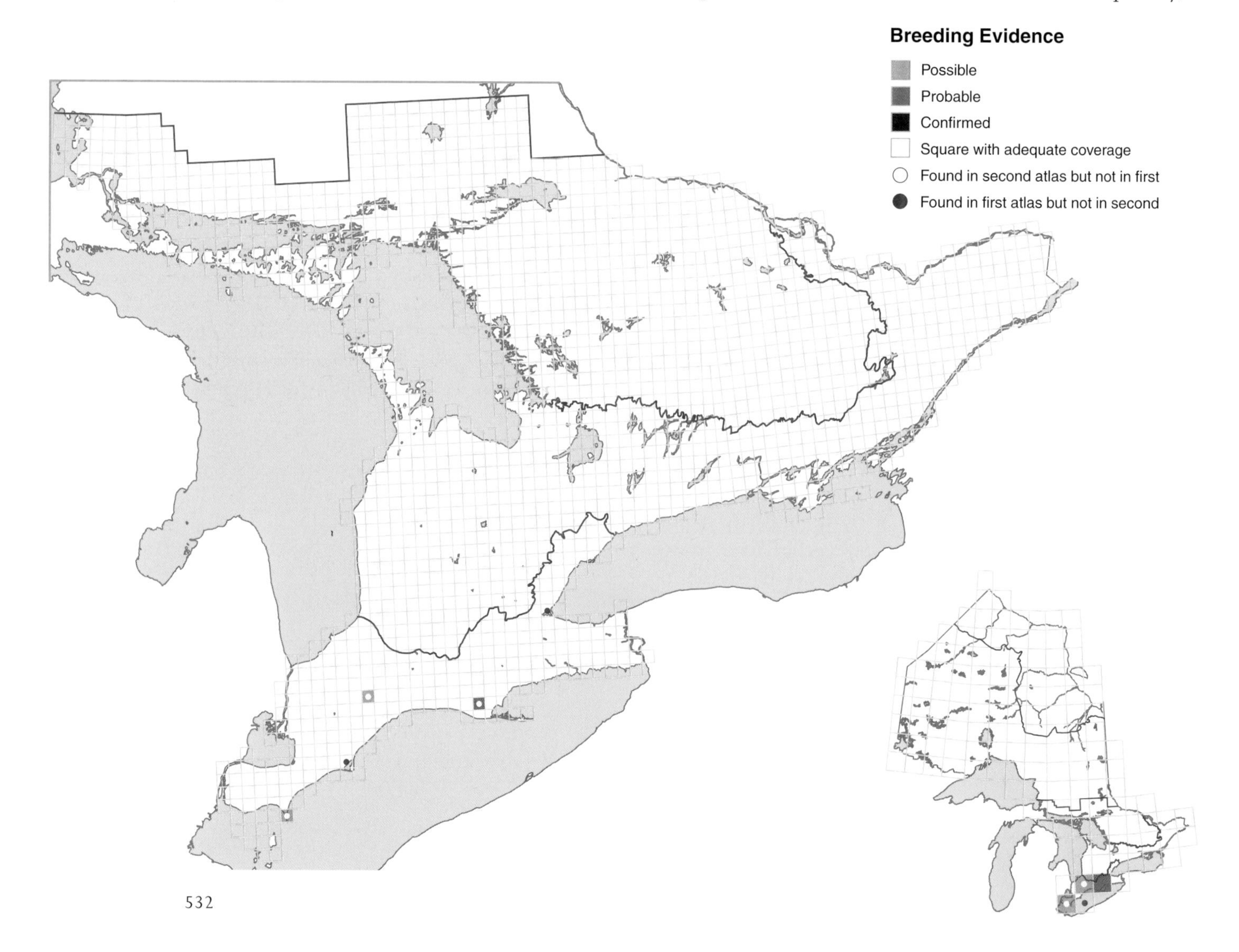

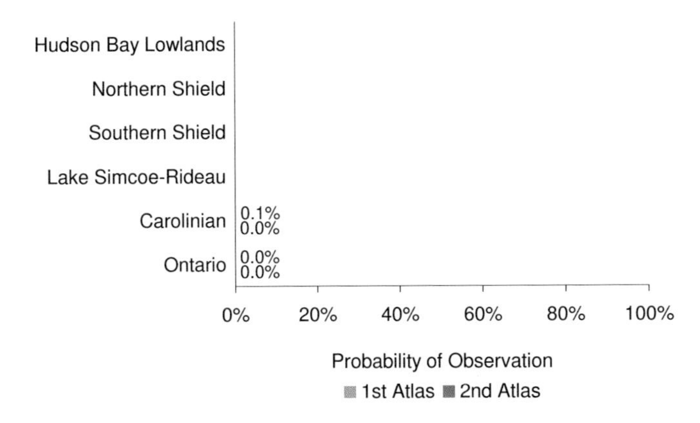

last record more likely involved a vagrant individual. The species may be expanding its range northwards in Ohio and Michigan (Peterjohn 2001; Brewer et al. 1991), but in Ontario it continues to be very rare and local with little change between the atlases.

Breeding biology: In spring, the Summer Tanager reaches the northern limit of its breeding range in early May. However, migration continues through late May (Robinson 1996). Males sing regularly upon arrival at prospective breeding sites, responding vigorously to the songs of conspecifics and those of the Scarlet Tanager (Robinson 1996); both sexes utter a characteristic "*pi-tuk*" or "*pit-i-tuck*" call. Although distinctive, the primary song of the Summer Tanager is sufficiently similar in structure and tempo to those of Scarlet Tanager and American Robin that it can be overlooked (Castrale et al. 1998; Robinson 1996). Calls are uttered throughout the day but primarily at dawn and dusk (Robinson 1996) and may be interspersed with long silent periods during which the species may be inconspicuous and hard to detect (P.A. Woodliffe, pers. comm.).

In the northeastern part of its range, the Summer Tanager prefers fairly mature, open deciduous or mixed woods in which oak and pine are prevalent (Castrale et al. 1998; Peterjohn 2001). Preferred habitats are often drier and more open than those of the Scarlet Tanager, and territories are more frequently near forest openings or at forest edges, rather than in the closed-canopy, interior forest habitats preferred by the Scarlet Tanager. Habitats in which the Summer Tanager was recorded during the second atlas were closed to moderately open deciduous or mixed woodlands on fairly dry upland sites in which both oak and pine were prevalent.

The Summer Tanager may be somewhat prone to vagrancy, and individuals (primarily males) are routinely detected north of the established breeding range during spring migration (Robinson 1996). In Ontario, vagrants have been recorded in spring north to Ottawa, Manitoulin Island, and Thunder Cape (James 1991). At Long Point, 13 of 15 individuals banded in the period 1985-2006 were male; females are rarely encountered. Most captures were during May, but males have been captured as late as 8 June (LPBO data; J.D. McCracken, pers. comm.), suggesting that some or many males observed in southern Ontario early in the breeding season may be late spring vagrants.

Abundance: The Summer Tanager is a rare but regular vagrant to Ontario. Occurrences during the breeding season are rare, and most evidence of breeding is unpersuasive. While undetected nesting may have occurred, breeding remains unconfirmed in the province. – *Fiona A. Reid*

An adult male Summer Tanager sang at this location on the sand road through Wilson Tract in the South Walsingham Forest in May and June 2001. *Photo: Gregor G. Beck*

This location in Rondeau Prov. Park was used by a pair of Summer Tanagers during the first atlas but breeding was not confirmed. *Photo: P. Allen Woodliffe*

Scarlet Tanager

Tangara écarlate

Piranga olivacea

Tim Stewart

Although frequently well hidden in the upper canopy of the forest, the bright red and black male Scarlet Tanager is one of our most colourful songbirds. This species breeds throughout eastern North America from extreme southern Saskatchewan and Manitoba through Ontario, southern Québec, and the Maritime Provinces south to northern Georgia, Alabama, and Mississippi. The winter range stretches from Panama to Bolivia, with most birds wintering in primary or high-canopy secondary forests on the eastern slopes of the Andes (Mowbray 1999).

Distribution and population status: The deciduous and mixed forests of the Carolinian, Lake Simcoe-Rideau, and Southern Shield regions constitute the heart of the Scarlet Tanager's distribution in Ontario. Although there are several gaps in distribution in the Carolinian region, especially in Essex and northern Lambton Counties and Chatham-Kent, where forest cover is low and agriculture more intensive, the probability of observation is over 55%. In the Lake Simcoe-Rideau region, where the probability of observation is also over 55%, gaps in distribution are particularly evident on the Dundalk Till Plain in Dufferin, Grey, and Wellington Counties, and between Lake Simcoe and the Kawartha Lakes, again in areas with a combination of low forest cover and more intensive agriculture.

In the heavily forested Southern Shield region, the probability of observation is close to 70%. The Scarlet Tanager was recorded in most of the squares from Lake Temagami across the North Channel of Georgian Bay to Sault Ste. Marie but was much scarcer farther north. It was also scarce in northwestern Ontario between Thunder Bay and Kenora, even though parts of that area contain a considerable amount of deciduous forest similar to the Southern Shield.

The overall distribution of the Scarlet Tanager has changed little between atlases. There were no significant changes in the

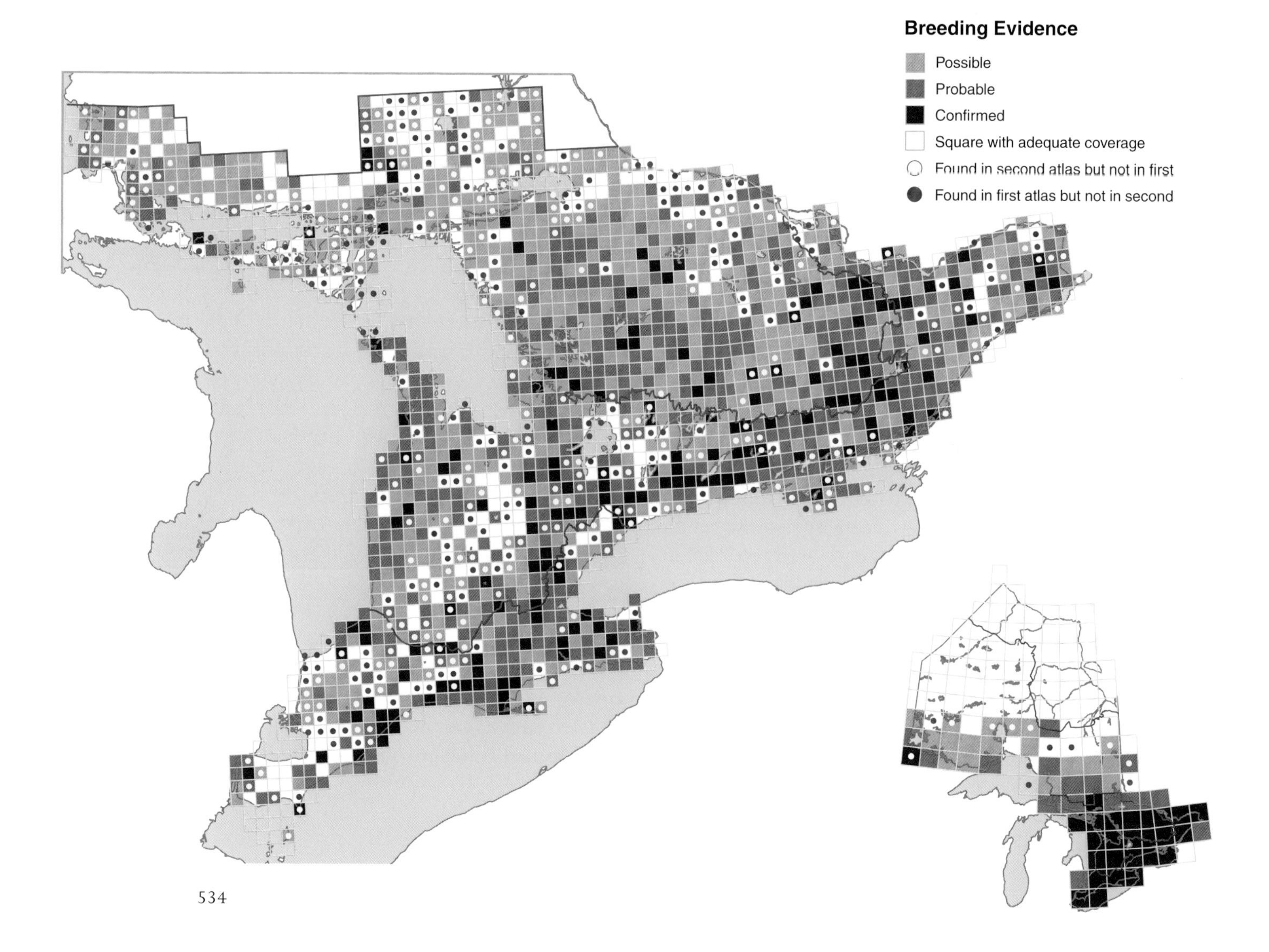

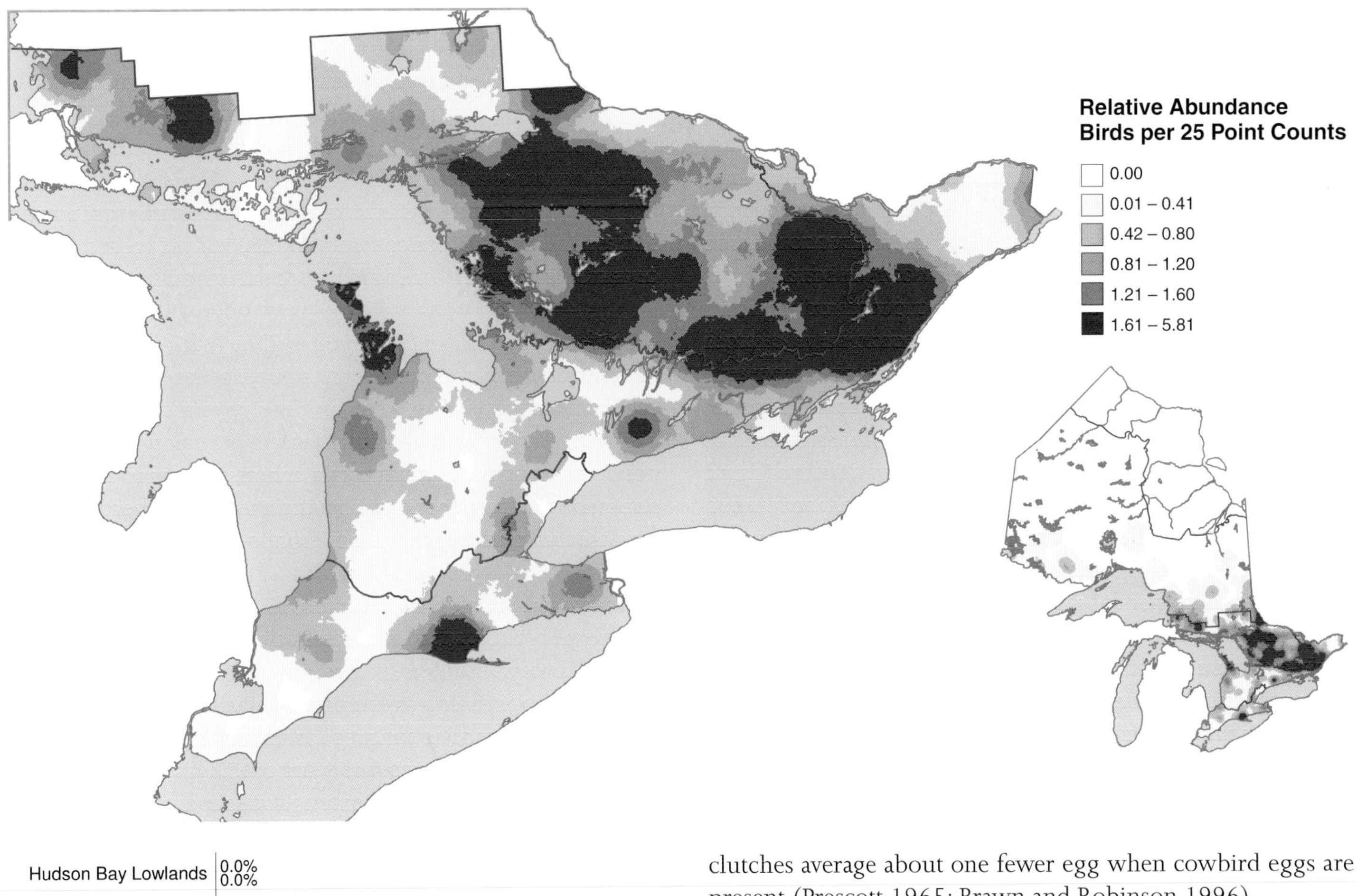

Hudson Bay Lowlands 0.0% 0.0%
Northern Shield 5.5% 5.4%
Southern Shield 68.9% 67.5%
Lake Simcoe-Rideau 55.9% 58.7%
Carolinian 55.7% 57.1%
Ontario 13.6% 13.6%

0% 20% 40% 60% 80% 100%

Probability of Observation
1st Atlas 2nd Atlas

probability of observation in any of the atlas regions. Although BBS data suggest a 3.1% annual decrease Canada-wide since 1968, there has been no significant change in Ontario (Downes et al. 2005).

Breeding biology: The Scarlet Tanager prefers mature deciduous forests, especially those dominated by large trees, but may also occupy mixed forests and younger deciduous habitats (Mowbray 1999). In southern Ontario, the primarily deciduous habitat often has a coniferous component, usually White Pine (D. Sutherland, pers. comm.). At the extreme northern edge of the range, the species uses mature aspen stands with large-diameter trees (Erskine 1977).

The Scarlet Tanager is reported to be an area-sensitive species, and its breeding success is negatively affected by forest fragmentation (Rosenberg et al. 1999). Where small woodlots are interspersed with farmland, as occurs in much of the Carolinian and Lake Simcoe-Rideau regions of southern Ontario, nests are frequently parasitized by Brown-headed Cowbirds (Mowbray 1999). Studies have shown that tanager clutches average about one fewer egg when cowbird eggs are present (Prescott 1965; Brawn and Robinson 1996).

The nest site is chosen by the female, and the nest is usually placed on a horizontal branch well out from the trunk of a large-diameter tree. The greenish-coloured female is much better camouflaged than the brightly coloured male, and she alone incubates (Mowbray 1999). Both parents feed the young during the nestling period and after fledging. Fledged young remain on the natal territory for about two weeks.

Breeding is difficult to confirm in the Scarlet Tanager. Nests tend to be placed high in the canopy of deciduous trees (Peck and James 1987) and are difficult to find. Breeding was confirmed in only 11% of squares, and in most atlas administrative regions where the species was confirmed, adults carrying food was the highest breeding evidence. Fortunately, the male sings his "robin with a sore throat" song quite frequently. The highest level of breeding evidence in 46% of squares was the presence of singing males.

Abundance: The area of greatest abundance for the Scarlet Tanager extends from the St. Lawrence River near Kingston north to the Ottawa River as well as north through the western portion of the Southern Shield region to Lake Nipissing. The lower densities in the eastern Southern Shield region reflect a much higher proportion of coniferous forest there. The Scarlet Tanager is also common on the Bruce Peninsula and in the area just north of Long Point, one of the few areas in extreme southern Ontario with a relatively high proportion of forest cover. The maps show relative abundance diminishing farther north in the Northern Shield region, with very low numbers in the southern Boreal Forest. – *Margaret A. McLaren*

Eastern Towhee

Tohi à flancs roux

Pipilo erythrophthalmus

Jim Richards

A boldly marked, long-tailed member of the sparrow family, the Eastern Towhee was known as the Rufous-sided Towhee until 1995, when genetic evidence established the eastern and western races as separate species. One of several towhee species, it is the only one that breeds in the east, primarily east of the Great Plains, north to southern Manitoba, southern Québec, and Maine, with isolated populations in southeastern Saskatchewan and possibly New Brunswick (Greenlaw 1996).

Distribution and population status: The Eastern Towhee is found predominantly in the Carolinian and Lake Simcoe-Rideau regions, becoming progressively less common northward through the Southern Shield to the latitude of Lake Nipissing and the North Channel of Georgian Bay. It prefers mid- to late successional shrubby habitat, and so is found more sparsely farther north where continuous forest predominates. However, the presence of a disjunct population in western Rainy River Dist. was recorded during the first atlas, and breeding was confirmed there during the second, representing the northernmost breeding record for the species in the province.

There was no significant change in the probability of observation in the province as a whole between atlases, but significant declines of 17% and 19% occurred in the Carolinian and Southern Shield regions, respectively. These declines are probably attributable to the loss of shrubby, successional habitats through natural succession to forest in the Southern Shield, and to intensive agriculture and urbanization in the Carolinian. BBS data show no significant trends for the species in Ontario (Downes et al. 2005), although a significant decline was recorded for the Eastern North American BBS Region as a whole since 1966 (Sauer et al. 2005). Interestingly, migration-monitoring data from LPBO indicate a relatively steady, long-term decline of birds passing through on spring migration since monitoring began in 1961. A study docu-

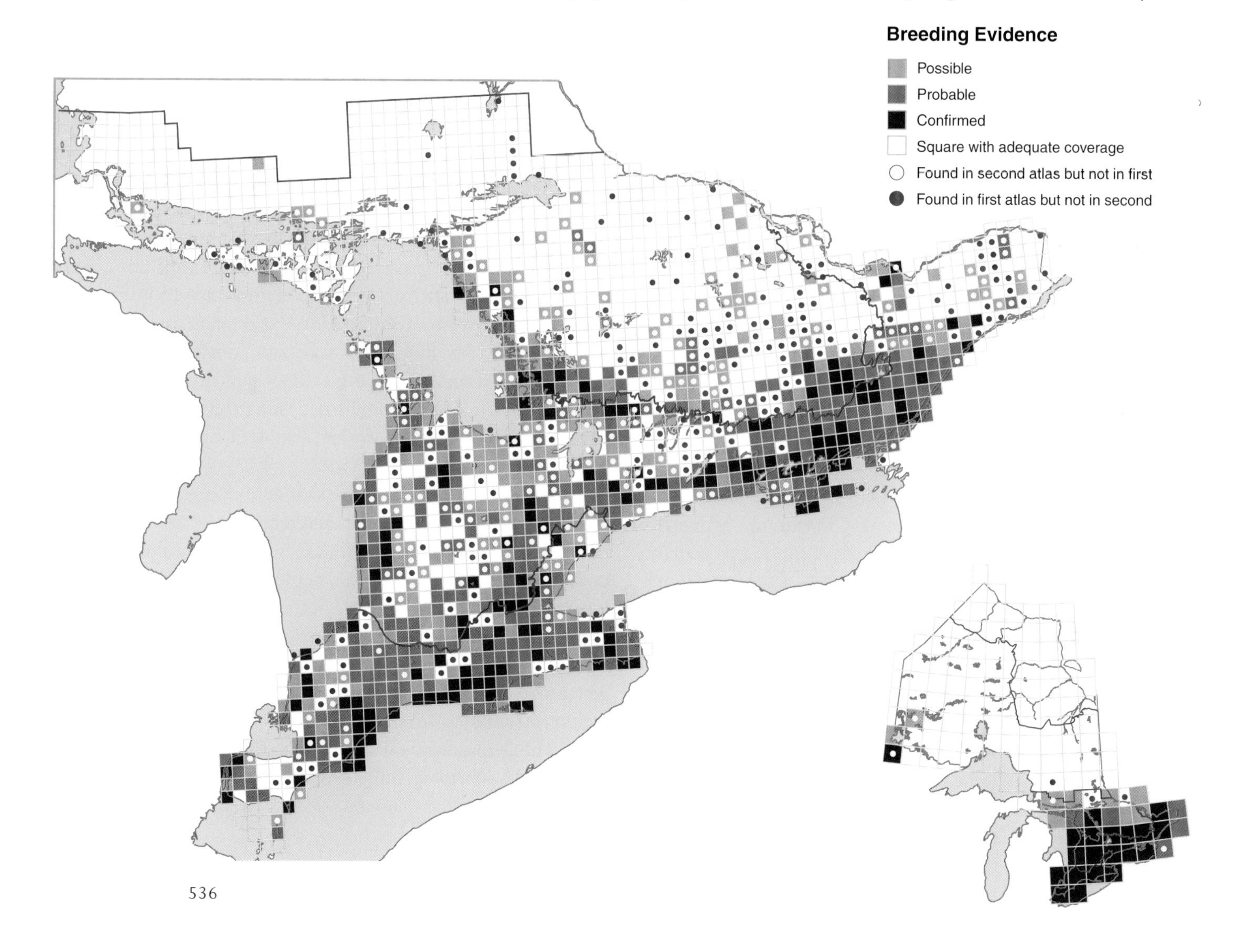

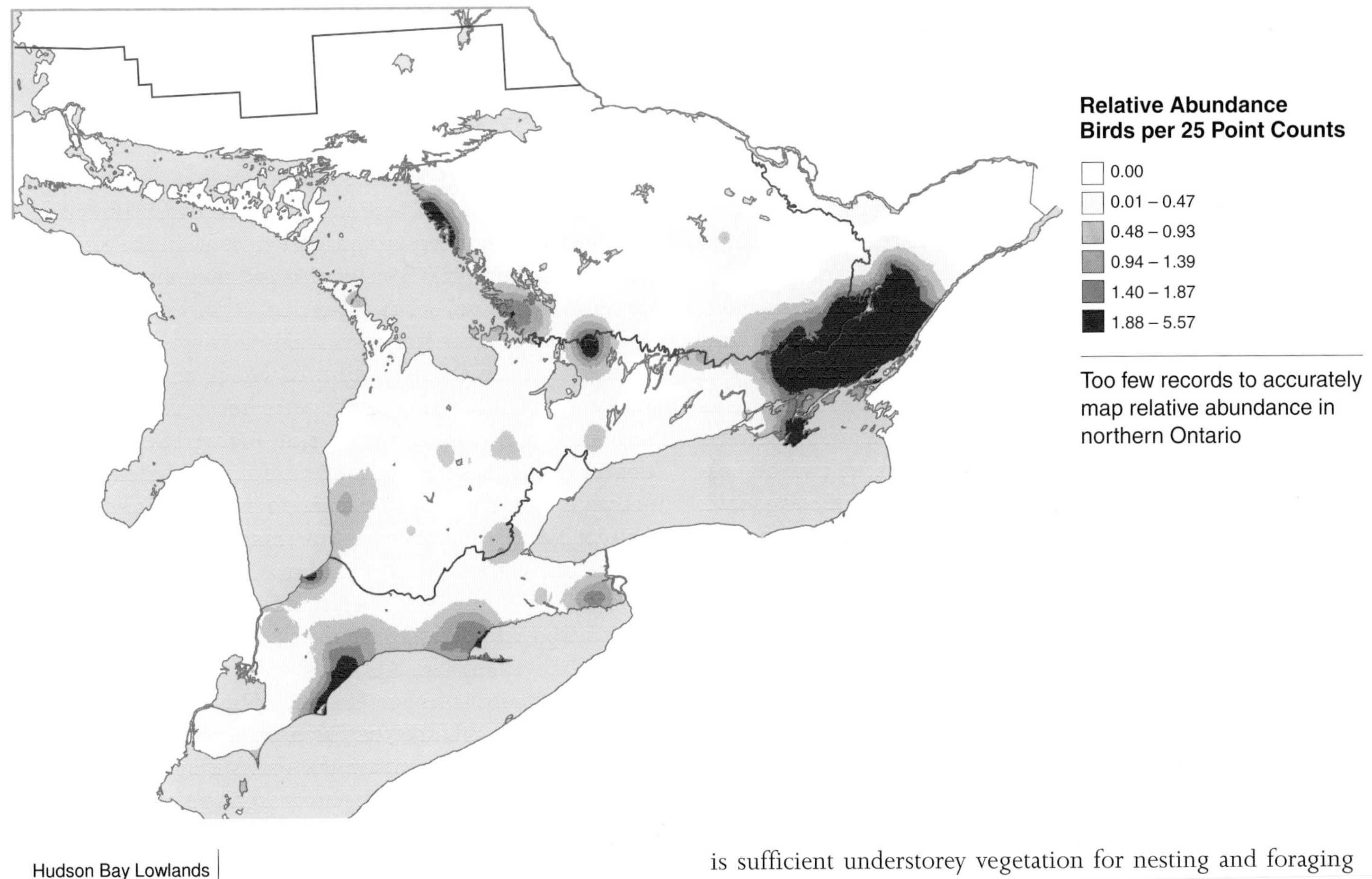

Region	1st Atlas	2nd Atlas
Hudson Bay Lowlands		
Northern Shield	0.3%	0.1%
Southern Shield	15.3%	12.3%*
Lake Simcoe-Rideau	40.6%	38.8%
Carolinian	70.6%	58.9%*
Ontario	5.8%	5.1%

Probability of Observation
1st Atlas 2nd Atlas

menting the decline in the eastern US suggests that natural succession of forests from earlier land-use practices could be the primary cause (Hagan 1993).

The entire Ontario breeding range saw considerable turnover in the squares reporting the species. These changes are likely due to the local availability of suitable breeding habitat. Regional Coordinators suggest maturation of scrubby habitats as a reason for decline in some areas, and pasture succession for increases in others. Changes in the landscape in just a few years can have a large impact on the availability of suitable breeding habitat in a localized area. In the years following a Gypsy Moth outbreak, the density of the towhee population increased significantly due to an increase in understorey cover (Bell and Whitmore 1997). Changes to wintering habitats could also have contributed to the decline.

Breeding biology: The Eastern Towhee is considered to be a habitat generalist, breeding in edge and early successional habitat, including old fields, Precambrian rock barrens, alvars, and sand barrens. It will readily utilize forests, providing there is sufficient understorey vegetation for nesting and foraging (Hagan 1993). The species has a distinctive and easily recognized song, though it is usually given in bouts between other activities. This may mean that it could be missed if atlassers spent only a short time at a site. Singing usually begins once birds reach the breeding grounds, so singing males can be presumed to be breeding at the site (Greenlaw 1996). Nests are usually placed on the ground in dense vegetation, which can make them difficult to find. However, both parents feed the young, which remain with the parents for three to four weeks after fledging (Greenlaw 1996). The readily identifiable characteristics of this species' plumage and vocalizations suggest that its distribution is reflected accurately in the atlas data, although confirmed breeding is probably underestimated due to its ground-dwelling nature.

Abundance: The Eastern Towhee is found in highest abundance in two main areas of the province: from Prince Edward Co. east to the United Counties of Leeds and Grenville, and along the Lake Erie shore in Haldimand, Norfolk, and Elgin Counties and Chatham-Kent. This pattern of occurrence is very similar to that of other species with similar habitat preferences, such as the Field Sparrow. In the east, these areas correspond to the scrubby habitat of the Napanee Plain and the Precambrian rock barrens and abandoned farmland of the Frontenac Axis. In southwestern Ontario, areas of higher abundance are associated with the Norfolk Sand Plain and several scrubby river valleys and sand plains between Grand Bend and the Lake Erie shore. The Eastern Towhee is also relatively abundant on the Carden Plain and the eastern shores of Georgian Bay. – *Matthew Timpf*

American Tree Sparrow

Bruant hudsonien

Spizella arborea

George K. Peck

The American Tree Sparrow is best known to Ontario naturalists as a common migrant and winter resident, frequenting "fields, marshes, hedgerows, gardens and open forests" (Naugler 1993). In winter it is a regular visitor at bird feeders, but the remote nature of its breeding range makes it poorly known in the nesting season. The name "American Tree Sparrow" may have resulted from confusion by early European settlers with the Eurasian Tree Sparrow, rather than an association with forested habitats (Naugler 1993).

Distribution and population status: The American Tree Sparrow breeds across northern Canada and Alaska, preferring open scrubby areas, usually near the treeline (Naugler 1993). In Ontario, it is found in coastal areas of the Hudson Bay Lowlands region where the forest becomes stunted and sparse. Its range is not particularly extensive in the province, as it was found in just 50 squares, and the Ontario population comprises only a small portion of its North American numbers. Most records were concentrated around Polar Bear Prov. Park and the Cape Henrietta Maria area. However, a greater proportion of squares were surveyed in this area compared to elsewhere, leading to higher detection rates. Squares in which breeding evidence for the species was documented range from the Ontario/Manitoba border on Hudson Bay to Akimiski Island in James Bay, the latter representing the southernmost breeding record of the species in either atlas. Few records were more than 100 km from the Hudson and James Bay coasts, likely reflecting the distribution of the scrubby habitat it prefers.

No significant change was noted in the probability of observation for the species between the first and second atlases. Migration monitoring data from spring and fall as well as CBC data from the early winter period suggest that the species' numbers have remained relatively stable in Ontario and the northeast of the US.

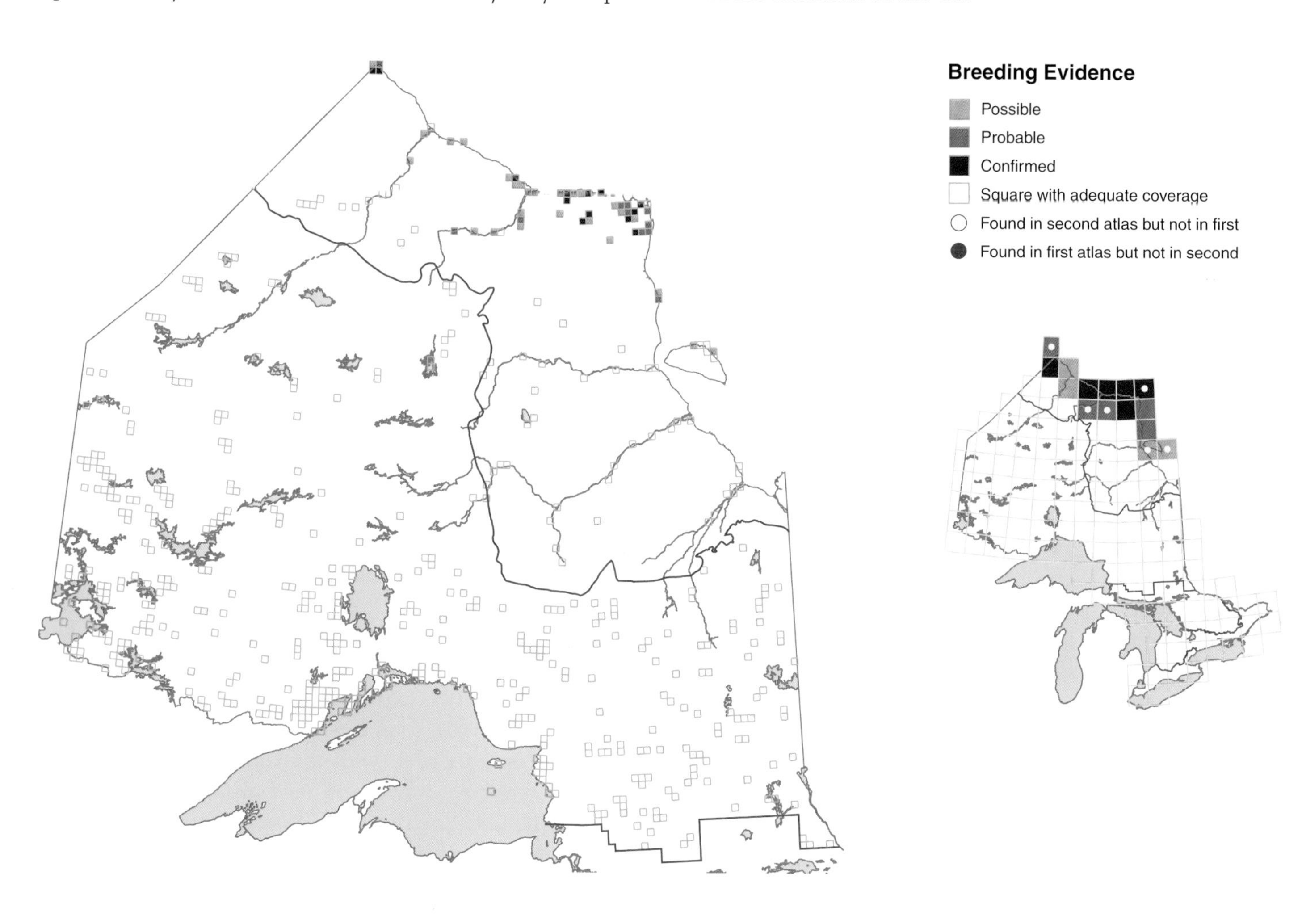

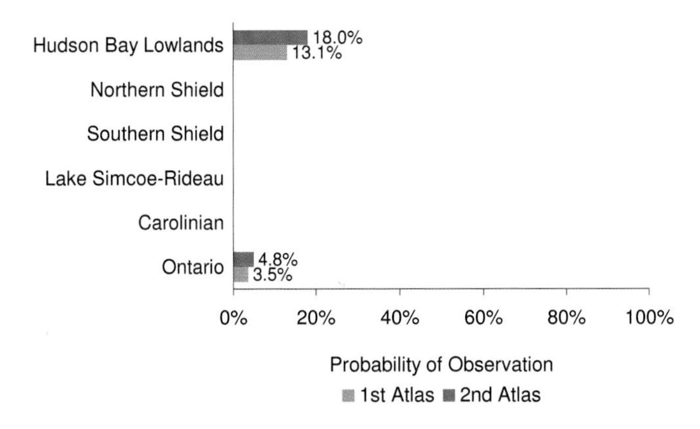

Breeding biology: The American Tree Sparrow nests primarily along the treeline where the Boreal Forest merges with the sweeping tundra. Scrubby areas with willow, birch, and alder thickets, stunted spruces, and open tundra with scattered shrubs and small lakes provide ideal breeding habitat. A typical territory for this species will include small trees for singing posts, with water nearby (Naugler 1993). Territory sizes in Churchill, Manitoba, ranged from 0.5 to 1.5 ha (Heydweiller 1935). Only the male sings, but the song is distinctive, with a series of liquid notes that carry some distance. Singing is most frequent in the first four weeks after males arrive on the breeding grounds, then decreases as the season progresses. Song takes place predominantly during the early morning, with continued but less frequent singing throughout the rest of the day (Naugler 1993). This pattern makes the species relatively easy to detect in the squares where it occurs.

Nests are hard to locate because they are well concealed in tussocks of grass at the base of small trees or shrubs, and their location in muskeg makes human accessibility difficult. As a result, nests were found in only six squares during this atlas period. However, young are fed by both the male and female while in the nest and for two to three weeks after fledging (Naugler 1993) and are quite conspicuous, allowing for easier breeding confirmation during this time. Most confirmed records were from observing fledged young or adults carrying food. The male's frequent song is easily recognizable, so the American Tree Sparrow should be well documented in squares that were visited during the early part of the breeding season. However, visits made later in the summer or only briefly may not have detected the species. Despite this, the map probably reflects the general breeding distribution of the species fairly accurately. Confirmed breeding is likely underestimated due to the difficulty of locating nests and the small amount of time and effort available for atlassing northern regions.

Abundance: Because the American Tree Sparrow has a very restricted geographic range in northern Ontario, it was not detected on sufficient point counts to produce an abundance map. However, the limited point count data collected suggest that abundance may be highest in the squares within 30-40 km of the coast, and decreases farther inland, likely revealing preferred habitat availability. An average of 1.7 birds/25 point counts was reported in the Hudson Bay Lowlands. Most of the squares with high numbers (over 5 birds/25 point counts) are concentrated between Winisk and Cape Henrietta Maria. – *Christopher G. Harris*

In Ontario, nests are usually on the ground, sunken at the base of a small bush, and characteristically lined with feathers, often those of ducks or the Willow Ptarmigan (Peck and James 1987). *Photo: Mark Peck*

American Tree Sparrow nest site on a low palsa in sparsely treed taiga near the Aquatuk River, 35 km south of Hudson Bay, 16 June 2005. *Photo: Mark Peck*

Chipping Sparrow

Bruant familier

Spizella passerina

Ron Ridout

The Chipping Sparrow is one of North America's most common and widely distributed migrant birds. Though many sparrows are associated with grassland communities, this species prefers open woodlands, the borders of forest openings, edges of rivers and lakes, and brushy, weedy fields. Its preferences for nesting in conifers and for foraging in brushy open areas suit this sparrow to human-modified habitats. It is a common summer resident in towns and gardens throughout much of its range, which extends from Atlantic to Pacific oceans and from Central America to the tundra (Middleton 1998).

Distribution and population status: Both atlases show that the Chipping Sparrow is widely distributed across the province, ranging from the Carolinian to the Hudson Bay Lowlands regions. Apart from changes in the level of breeding evidence in a few squares, there were few changes from the first atlas in the Carolinian and Lake Simcoe-Rideau regions. Although the probability of observation did not change significantly between atlases in the province as a whole, it did decline significantly by 6% in the Southern Shield region. The decline is most evident on the map in the Algonquin Prov. Park area and may be related to in-filling of open areas with forest through natural succession.

Conversely, in the Northern Shield, there was a significant increase of 21% in the probability of observation of the species. The reasons for this change in breeding status are not known. Probable or confirmed breeding status is now reported in most 100-km blocks. It is likely that increased effort during the second atlas has resulted in a more accurate picture of breeding in this part of the province.

The probability of observation of the Chipping Sparrow in the Hudson Bay Lowlands is only 33%, largely because much of the region contains unsuitable habitat for the species. In this region, it does occur in some human settlements but is also found in natural habitats along major rivers.

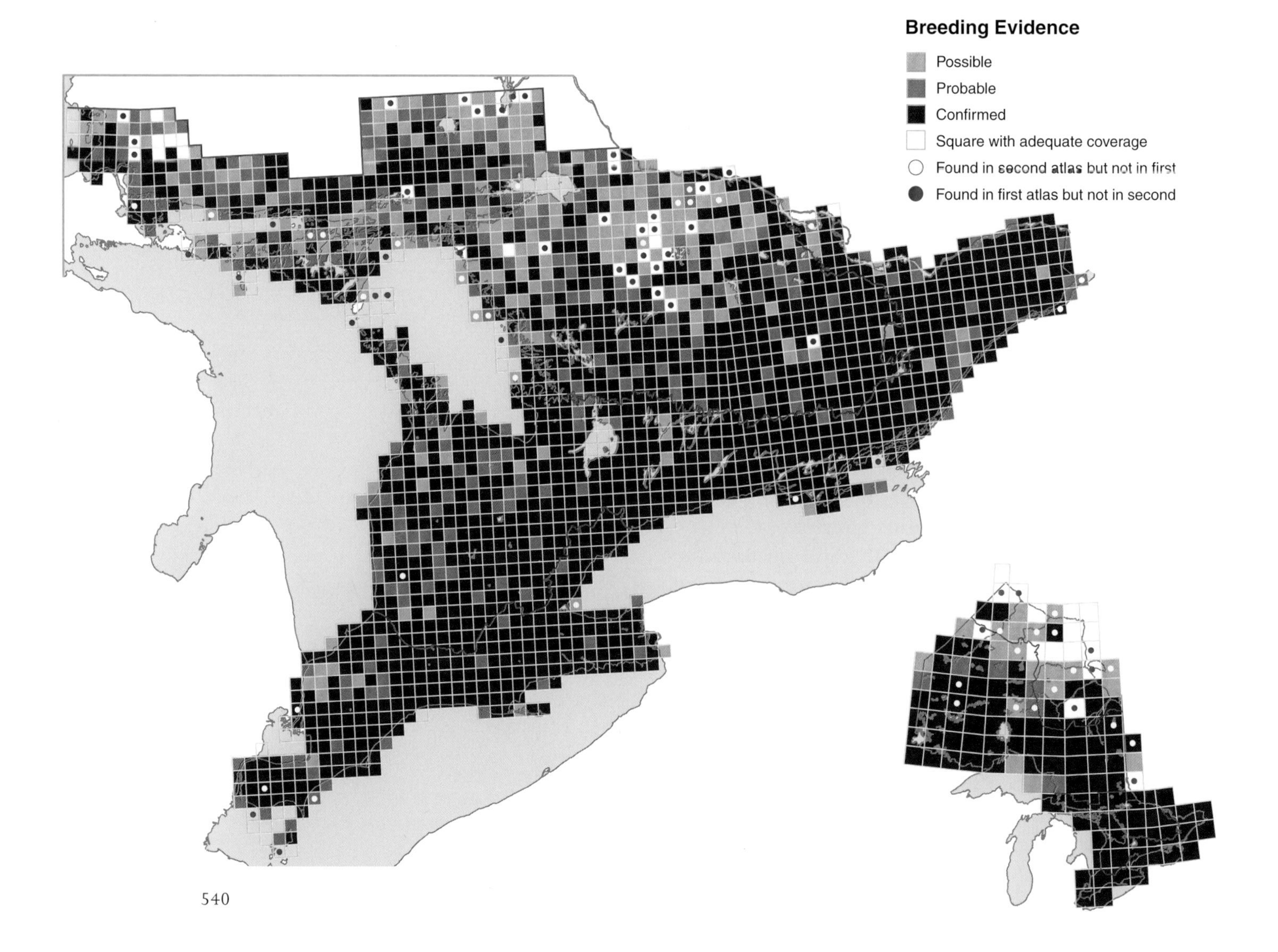

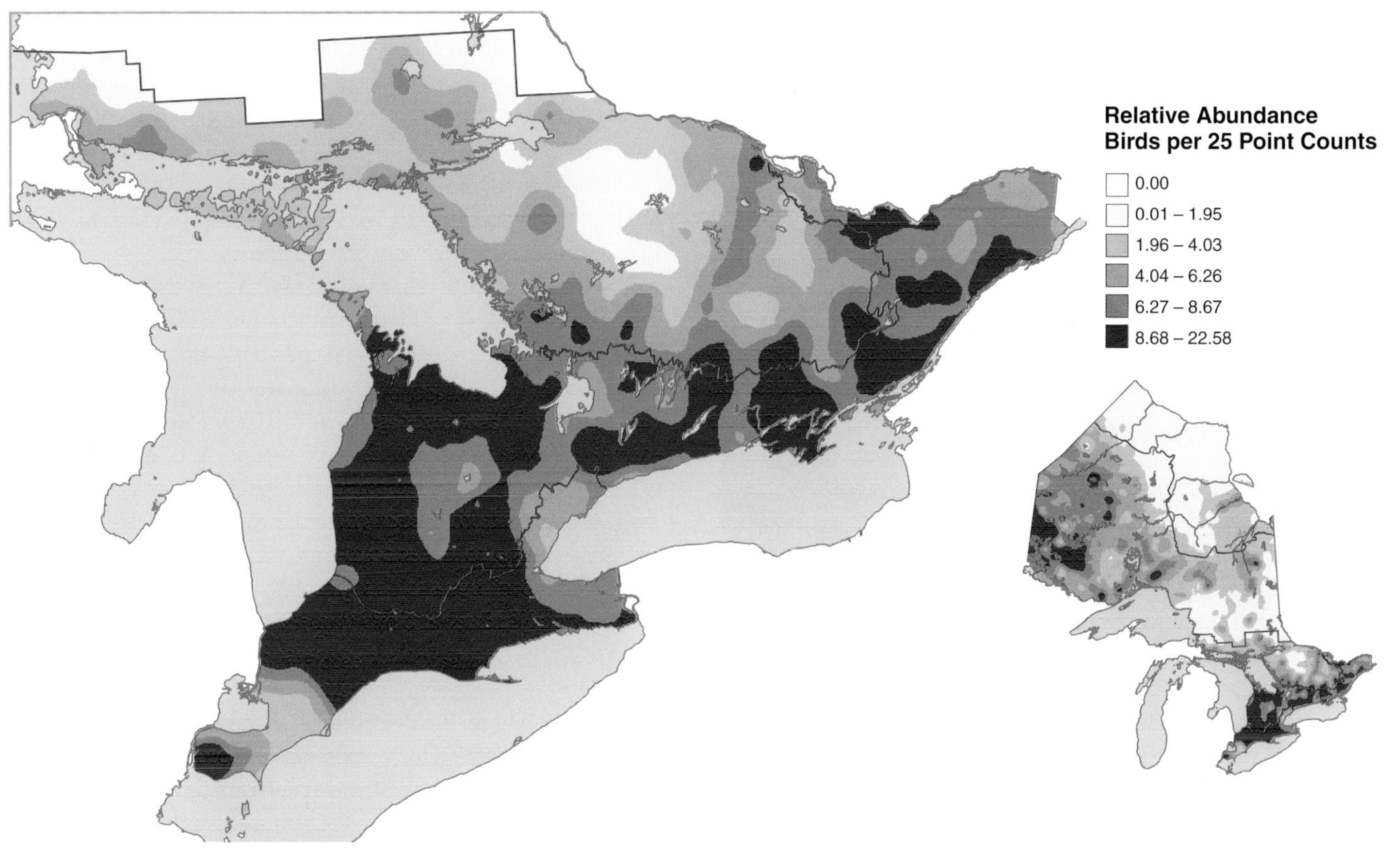

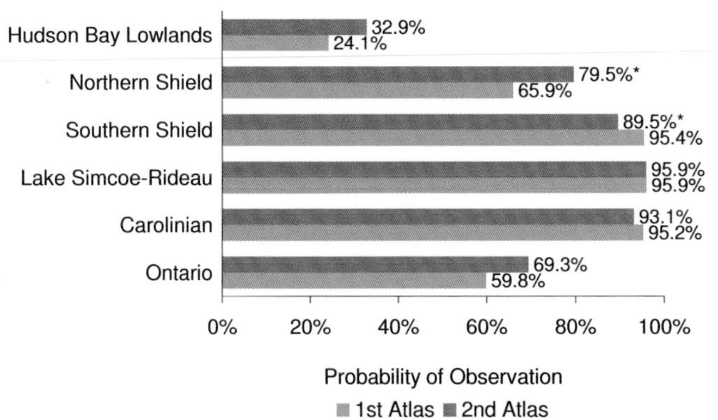

Migration monitoring data from Long Point from 1967 to 2004 indicate that the Chipping Sparrow had among the largest annual increases (4.2%) of all bird species (Crewe 2006). BBS data show no significant change in Ontario since 1968 (Downes et al. 2005); however, most BBS routes are in the south.

Breeding biology: The Chipping Sparrow nests primarily in early successional or low-growth woodlands where shrubby vegetation and conifers are abundant. This adaptable species has clearly benefited from the human occupation of North America. Urbanization and the expansion of agriculture and forestry have created new nesting habitats and provided abundant food (seeds of grasses and various annual plants) well suited to the Chipping Sparrow. It now appears to be more common, and is abundant around rural residences, orchards, and farms than in natural habitats (Middleton 1998).

Territorial defence is by males, largely through song. Nesting usually begins within two weeks of the birds' return to breeding areas, generally mid- to late April in the south. The nest is built by the female, accompanied closely by the male. Nests have been recorded in a wide variety of trees, although conifers are preferred. The flimsy nests, usually located 1 to 3 m above ground in thick clusters of needles or leaves, are constructed from rootlets and dried grasses and often lined with animal hair. In Ontario, egg laying extends from early May to mid-August (Peck and James 1987). Even though the species is secretive around the nest, its familiar trilling song and alarm calls are easily detected clues to nesting (Middleton 1998). The atlas maps therefore probably provide an accurate picture of the species' distribution.

Abundance: Atlas point count data show that the Chipping Sparrow is most abundant south of the Shield, with the exception of the intensively farmed parts of extreme southwestern Ontario, where suitable habitat is restricted, and in the western half of the Northern Shield. Predictably, the lowest counts occurred in the Hudson Bay Lowlands. Numbers generally decrease as latitude increases across the Southern Shield, the eastern portion of the Northern Shield, and the Hudson Bay Lowlands. Within these regions, there is some fluctuation in breeding density, which probably reflects human population distribution, the impact of forestry, and the patchy availability of suitable habitat. Based on atlas point count data, the population of the Chipping Sparrow is about 12,000,000 birds, making it among the most abundant birds in the province. Approximately 7,000,000 birds (or 63% of the Ontario population) are found in the Northern Shield region. – *Michael D. Cadman*

Clay-colored Sparrow

Bruant des plaines

Spizella pallida

George K. Peck

The Clay-colored Sparrow is closely related to the Chipping Sparrow. It breeds from central British Columbia and southern Northwest Territories east to the Great Lakes states and southern Québec and south to Wyoming and Colorado (Knapton 1994). The core of its range is the Canadian prairies, where it breeds in open, uncultivated brushy areas with shrubs interspersed with grassland. It is probably a relative newcomer to most of Ontario. Taverner (1934) reported it as occasional in southern Ontario. It is now generally an uncommon to rare breeding bird in the province, nesting in open deciduous and coniferous habitats such as fields with scattered shrubs and Christmas tree plantations. In the breeding season, it is rather easy to find, as the male sings its distinctive low-pitched, buzzy song from a low exposed perch.

Distribution and population status: During the past 75 years, the Clay-colored Sparrow expanded its range eastward across Ontario to southwestern Québec and western New York. It now breeds primarily in small concentrations at scattered locations in southern Ontario and in northwestern Ontario in the vicinity of Rainy River near the Manitoba border. It occurs more sporadically elsewhere in the north, most frequently in the Hudson Bay Lowlands, particularly adjacent to Hudson and James Bays.

The Clay-colored Sparrow increased substantially in numbers since the first atlas. A similar increase is evident from the New York State Breeding Bird Atlas over the same period, although BBS data from Ontario show no significant trend. In the province as a whole, the probability of observation increased by 80% between atlases. There were significant increases ranging from about 100% to 150% in four of the five atlas regions, with a non-significant increase of 13% in the Hudson Bay Lowlands. These increases could be partly attributable to more available

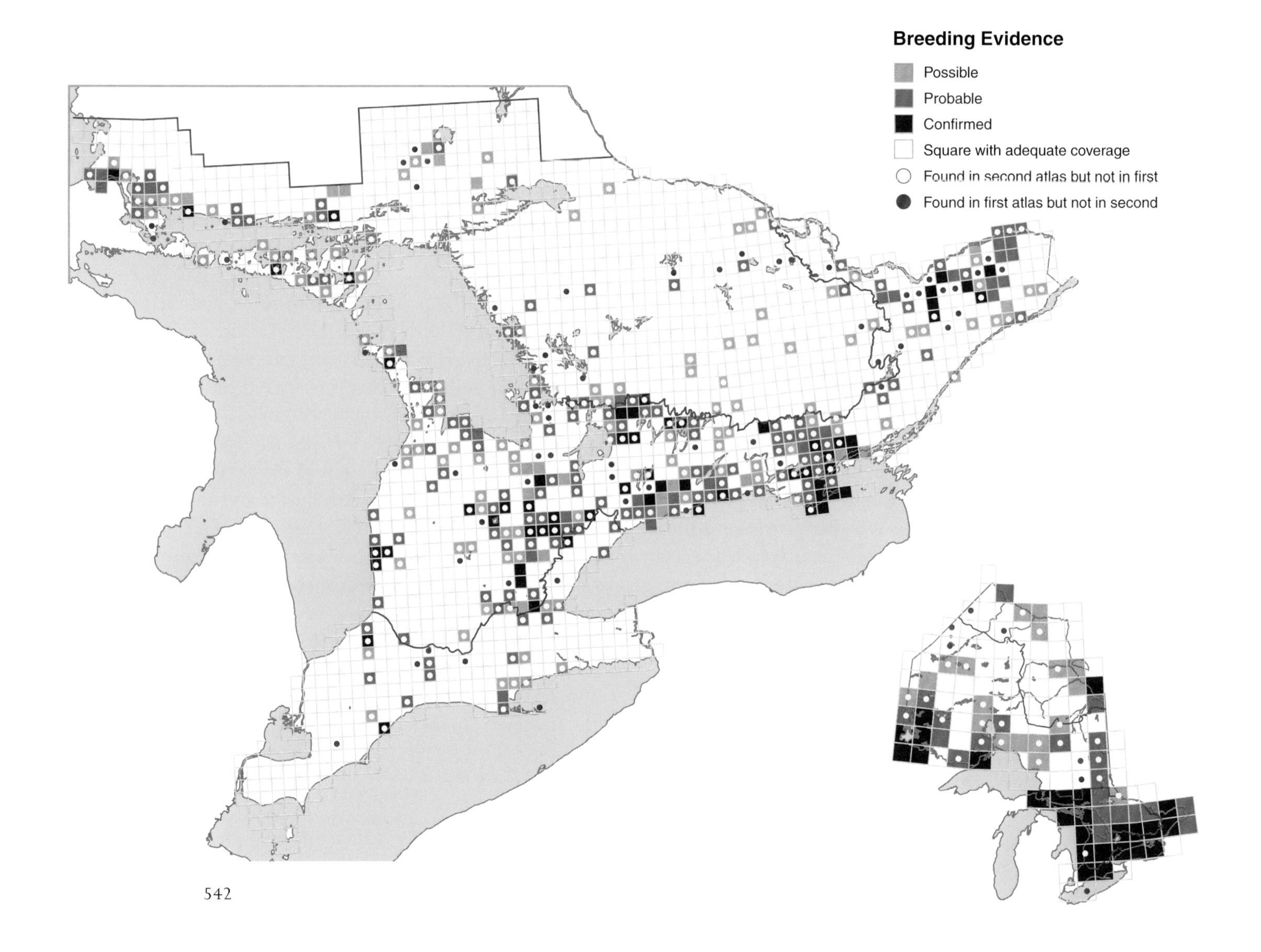

BREEDING EVIDENCE

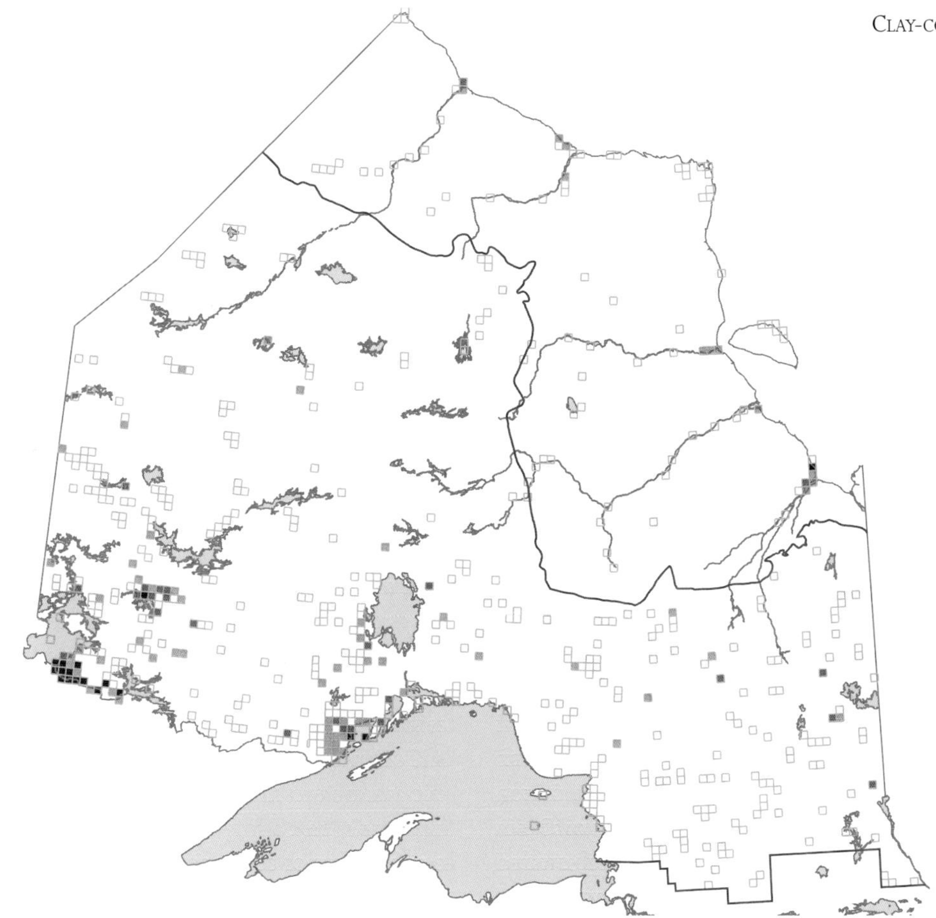

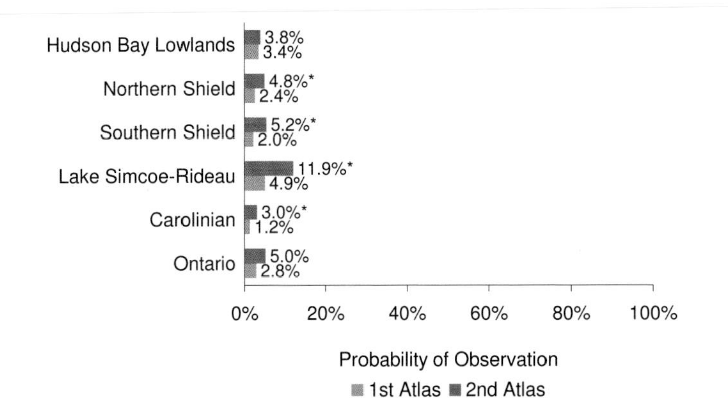

habitat due to regeneration of abandoned fields to early-succession scrub, but may also represent a continuing expansion in the province independent of recent habitat change.

Breeding biology: The Clay-colored Sparrow breeds in both dry and wet uncultivated open shrubby areas interspersed with areas of grasses or sedges. In the Lake Simcoe-Rideau region, it is most commonly found on alvars and in open, previously disturbed areas with young conifers such as small Red Cedars. In the Hudson Bay Lowlands, where it is a rare and local breeder, it is found in open willow and birch thickets.

The song is distinctive, and territorial males sing persistently from conspicuous perches, making them fairly easy to locate. Breeding territories are small, so that individual singing males are restricted to a confined area and a few favourite perches. The nest, a woven cup of grasses and other fibres that resembles the nest of the Chipping Sparrow, is usually well hidden, placed on or near the ground (usually less than 0.3 m) to above 1 m in a small conifer or shrub. The three to five eggs (usually four) are laid from late May through early July, but mostly from late May to early June. In most squares, the highest breeding evidence obtained comprised singing or territorial males; very few nests were found. Breeding was confirmed in only 17% of squares where it occurred, primarily by sightings of fledged young or of adults carrying food.

The Clay-colored Sparrow is socially monogamous. It lays replacement clutches and sometimes is double-brooded. When feeding nestlings, it eats a variety of insects and other invertebrates, and at other times consumes a wide variety of seeds. Occasionally it hybridizes with the closely related Chipping Sparrow, and it is commonly parasitized by the Brown-headed Cowbird.

Abundance: Point count data for the Clay-colored Sparrow were insufficient to produce a relative abundance map, indicating that the species is at best uncommon. However, the data do indicate a discontinuous distribution, with the highest abundance in the Rainy River area where the species occurs in abandoned rough pastures with encroaching low willows. South of the Canadian Shield, it is most common on shrub alvars and in old fields on the Carden Plain and on the Napanee Limestone Plain between Belleville and Kingston; juniper alvars are particularly favoured in the latter location. The Northern Shield has the highest number of birds with 0.3 birds/25 point counts, and the Lake Simcoe-Rideau region is second at 0.1 birds/25 point counts. The Hudson Bay Lowlands and Southern Shield each have 0.03 birds/25 point counts. The lowest density occurs in the Carolinian region (0.01 birds/25 point counts), probably because intensive agricultural practices and urbanization have left little suitable habitat. – *J.D. Rising*

Field Sparrow

Bruant des champs

Spizella pusilla

George K. Peck

The Field Sparrow breeds from central Montana through the Great Plains east to the Atlantic Coast and south to the Gulf Coast. Except for small outlying populations in southern Manitoba and southern New Brunswick, its Canadian range comprises southern Ontario and southwestern Québec. In winter, the species withdraws from the northernmost parts of its range. It may occasionally winter in extreme southwestern Ontario, but the primary winter range is in the US from Lake Erie south to Florida and the Gulf Coast, extending into northern Mexico.

Distribution and population status: In Ontario, the Field Sparrow is most widely distributed in the Carolinian region where it was recorded in the majority of squares. It was also recorded widely through the Lake Simcoe-Rideau region except in the easternmost part of the province, where the species was not reported in numerous squares; a decline between atlases is evident from the map. The Field Sparrow is much more sparsely distributed in the Southern Shield (17% probability of observation), where a largely forested landscape provides much less suitable habitat. Singing males, possibly unpaired individuals, were recorded well beyond the expected range in two relatively northern squares, one near Chapleau and the other even farther north, over 100 km north of Cochrane.

The probability of observation of this species decreased significantly in two regions between atlases, with a 17% decrease in the Carolinian region and a 33% decrease in the Southern Shield region. In the Southern Shield, there has been considerable regeneration of forests since the first atlas, with a concomitant reduction in the amount of old field habitat preferred by the Field Sparrow. The decrease in the Carolinian is similar to that shown by many grassland-dependent species and may be due to intensification of agricultural practices reducing old field habitat and other early successional habitats. BBS data

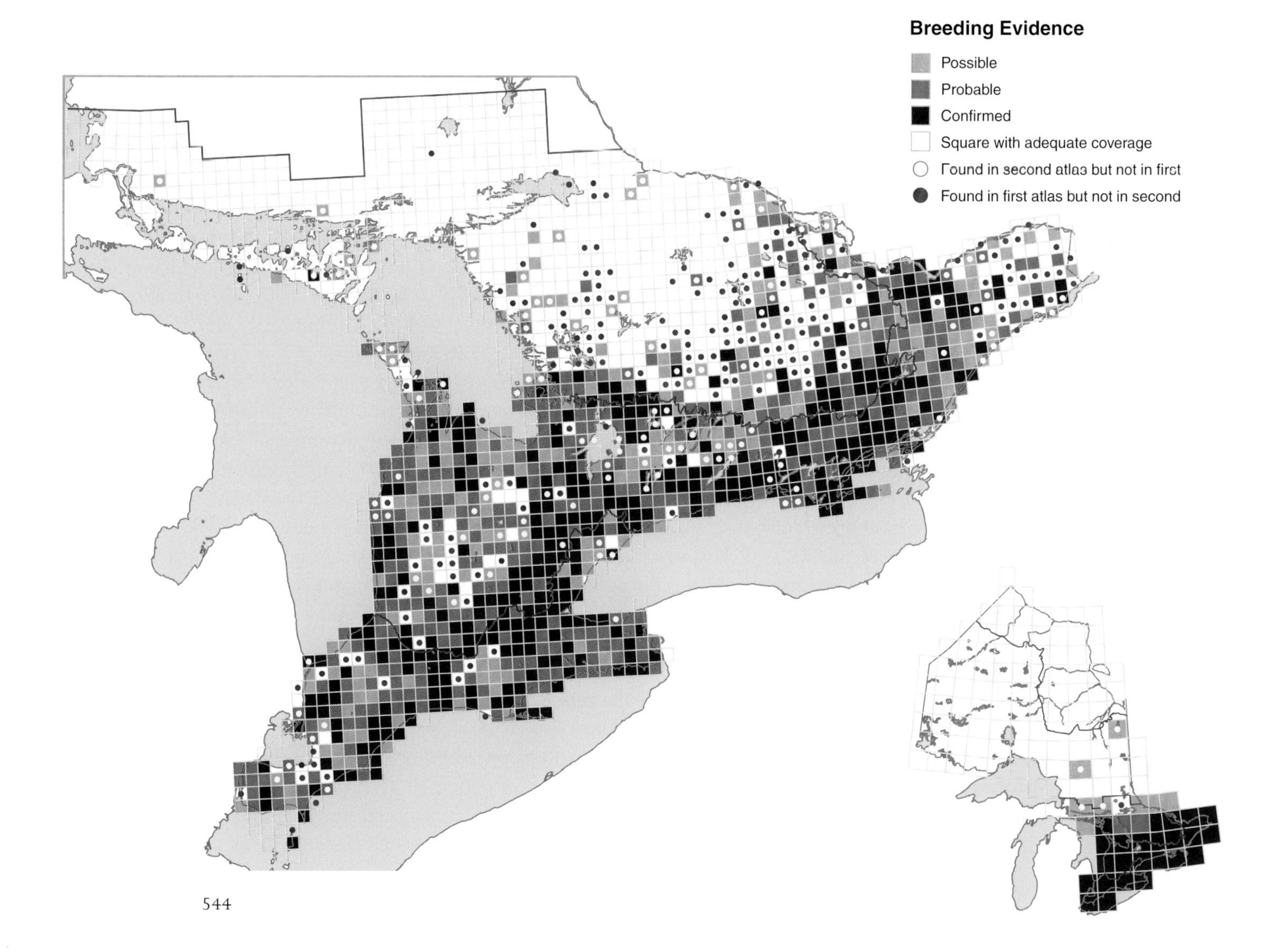

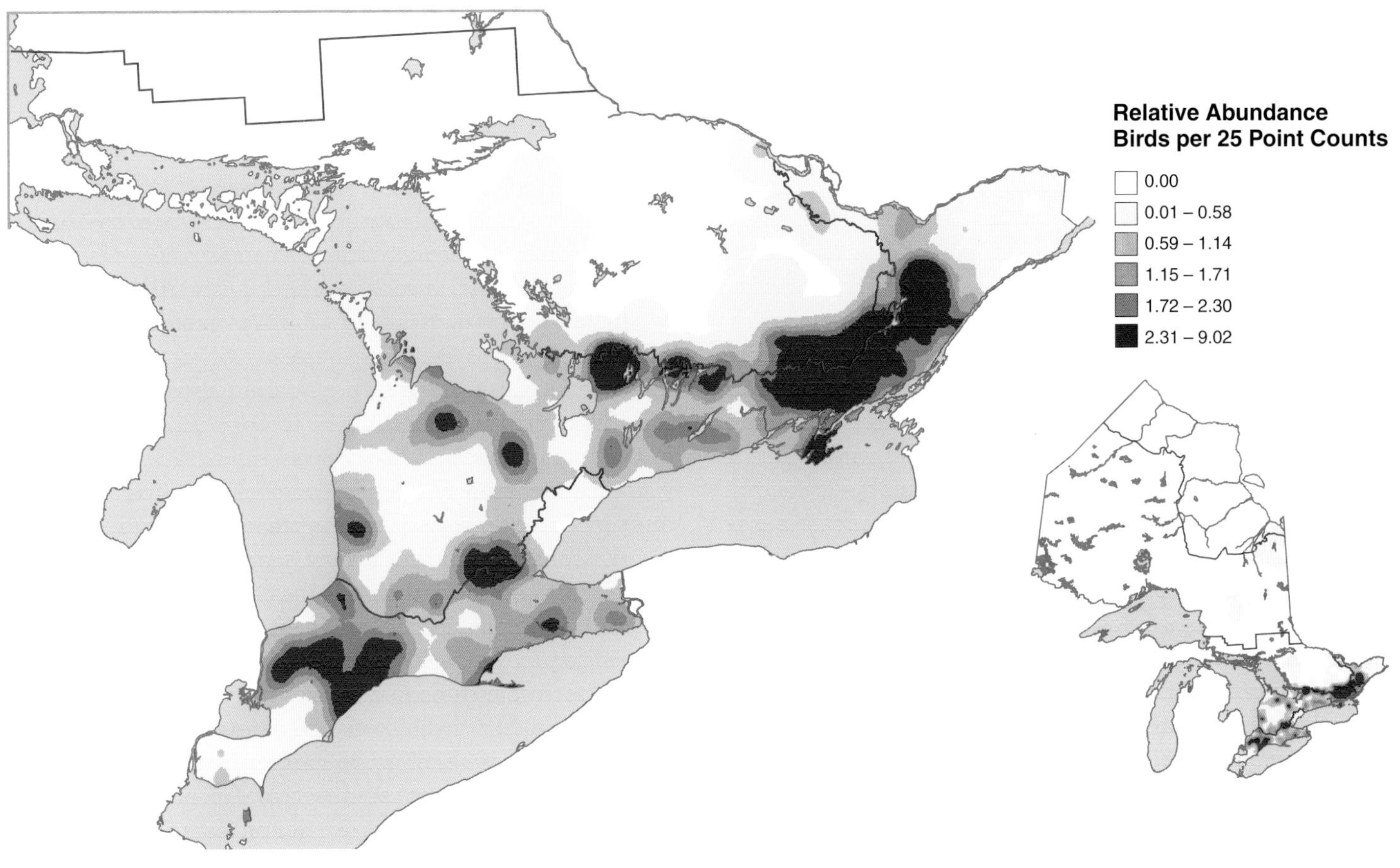

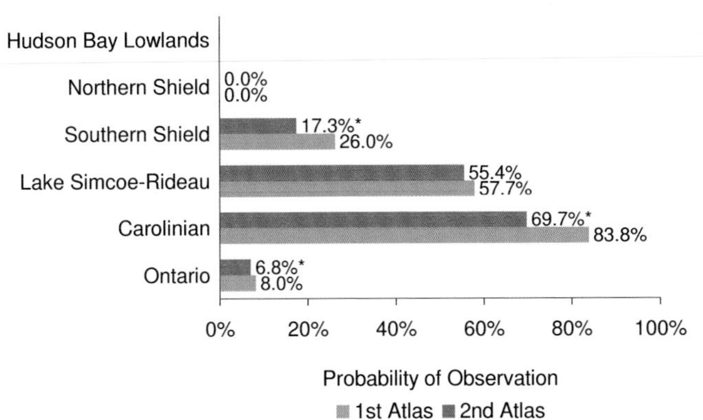

show no change in abundance of the Field Sparrow in Ontario, although there has been a significant decrease of 4.0% per year in Canada as a whole since 1968 (Downes et al. 2005).

Breeding biology: The Field Sparrow's preferred habitat consists of brushy old fields, woodland edges, and brushy roadsides near open fields (Carey et al. 1994). In Ontario, the species is often found on alvars and Precambrian rock barrens where shallow soils prevent growth of dense forest, in Red Cedar savannah, and on brushy sand dunes along the shores of the Great Lakes (pers. obs.; D. Sutherland, pers. comm.).

The Field Sparrow requires at least scattered patches of upright woody vegetation for song perches and usually places the nest fairly close to a shrub or small tree. Early in the season, nests are usually placed on the ground, but later nests may be built in a bush or low in the crotch of a small tree (Carey et al. 1994).

Singing activity peaks early in the breeding season and decreases considerably after pair formation, although this sparrow remains a fairly persistent singer throughout the season, and its distinctive song is easily recognized (Carey et al. 1994). The female alone builds the nest and incubates the eggs. Once the young have hatched, both parents actively feed nestlings and fledglings. Family groups travelling together through the open habitats favoured by this species are noisy and conspicuous, and contributed to the relatively high 38% of squares where breeding was confirmed.

Abundance: The Field Sparrow averaged about 1.2 birds/25 point counts in the Lake Simcoe-Rideau and Carolinian regions. However, over 2.3 birds/25 point counts were recorded in several areas of southern Ontario, most notably along Lake Ontario and the St. Lawrence River from Prince Edward Co. to Morrisburg and north to the edge of the Shield. This area contains extensive Red Cedar savannah on the Napanee Plain, as well as the Precambrian rock barrens and abandoned farmland associated with the Frontenac Axis. The Carden Plain northeast of Lake Simcoe also has extensive suitable habitat that supports a high abundance of the Field Sparrow. The area of high abundance extending from the shore of Lake Erie northwest to the Grand Bend area includes several river valleys and sand plains that provide extensive scrubby edge or old field habitat. The strip of high abundance along the Lake Erie shore is probably a reflection of the availability of scrubby edge habitat associated with the eastern Norfolk Sand Plain. West of Hamilton, the area of high abundance corresponds with the western extent of the Flamborough Plain and with the Galt and Paris moraines, both of which support suitable successional vegetation. – *Margaret A. McLaren*

Vesper Sparrow

Bruant vespéral

Pooecetes gramineus

Jim Richards

The Vesper Sparrow is an attractive, uncommon sparrow showing conspicuous white outer tail feathers in flight. It takes its name from its tendency to sing in the late afternoon and evening. The species prefers short-grass dry fields and heavily grazed pastures usually interspersed with shrubs and small trees used for singing perches. It breeds across southern Canada from central British Columbia east to Nova Scotia and south into the US (Jones and Cornely 2002).

Distribution and population status: Historically, many grassland species including the Vesper Sparrow were primarily prairie birds that spread east when pioneers established openings. If the Vesper Sparrow was present in Ontario before European settlement, it was restricted to scattered natural openings caused by wildfires and to areas where Aboriginal peoples cleared and burned forests for corn fields, making ephemeral pockets of grassland habitat, primarily south of the Canadian Shield. When large numbers of European settlers came to Ontario in the 1800s, grassland sparrows benefited from the clearing and burning of forests for permanent pastures and grain fields.

Both atlases show the Vesper Sparrow as breeding mainly in southern Ontario south of the Canadian Shield and locally in very small numbers in northern Ontario. The probability of observation was highest at 67% in the Carolinian region, where land use is primarily agricultural. The species is also found in the Lake Simcoe-Rideau region, which has considerable agricultural land use. In the Southern and Northern Shield regions, this sparrow is associated with farms and large clearcuts.

Although still widespread, the Vesper Sparrow has declined as a breeding species since the first atlas. The decline was most pronounced in the Southern Shield and Lake Simcoe-Rideau regions, where the probability of observation decreased sig-

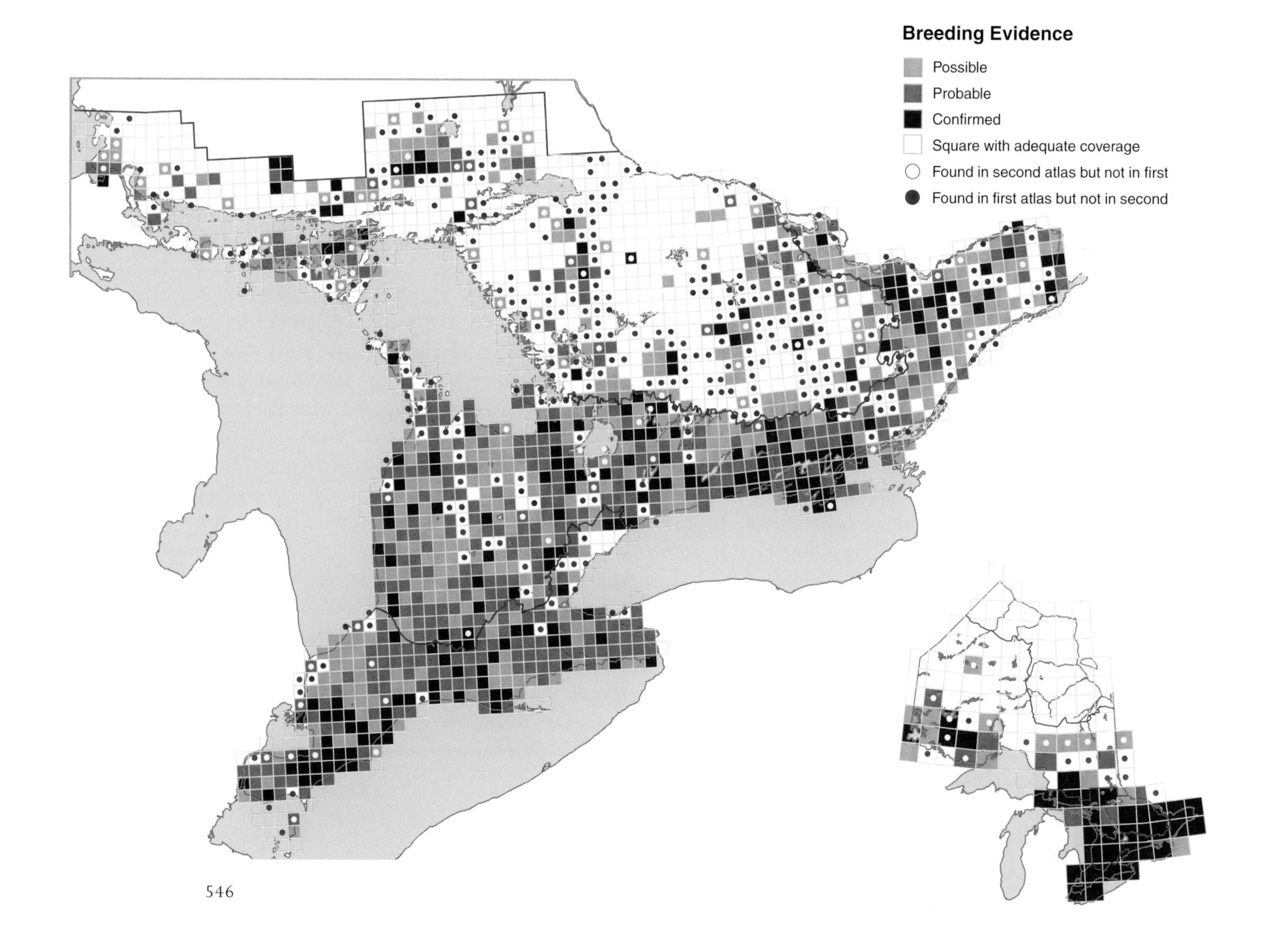

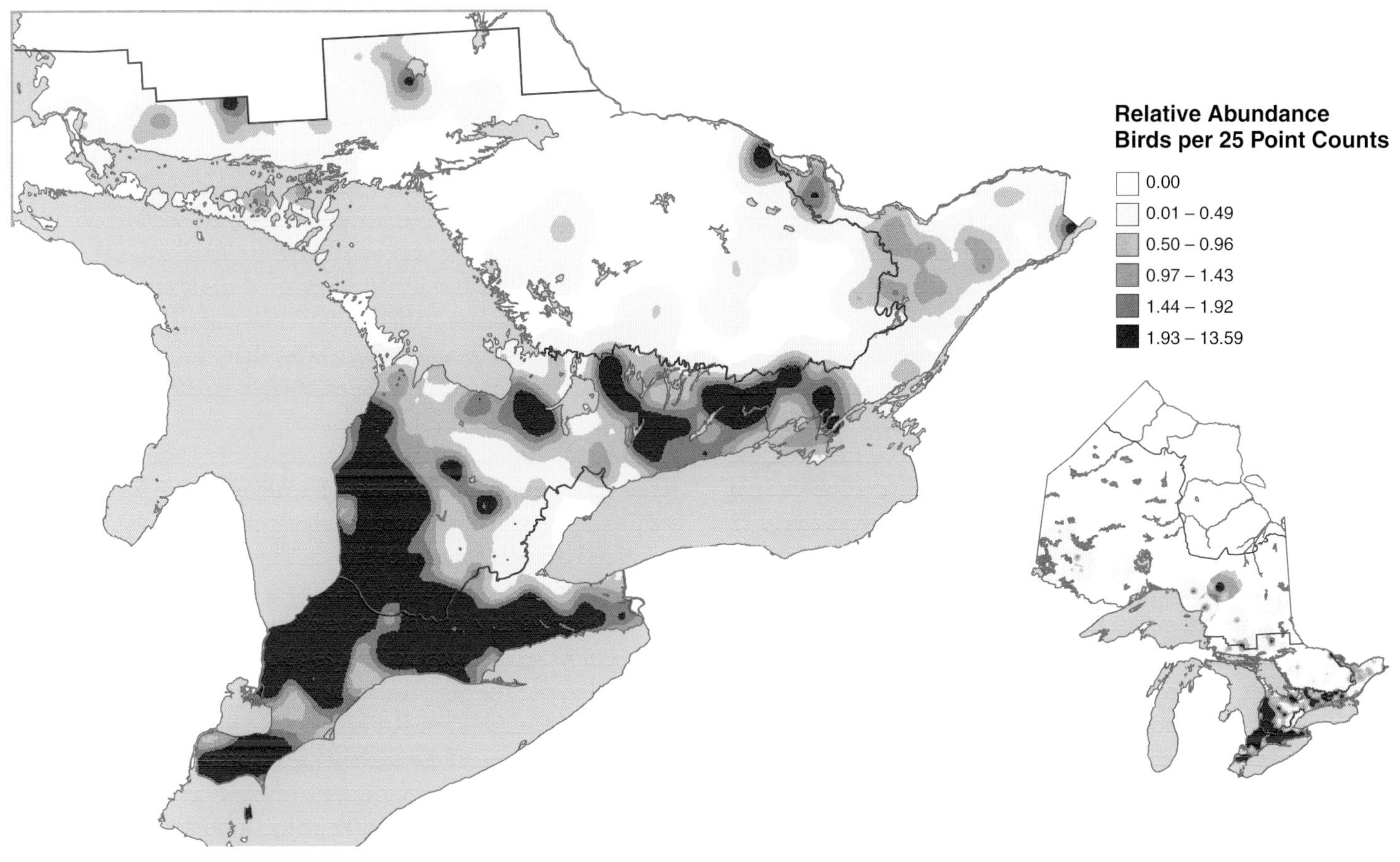

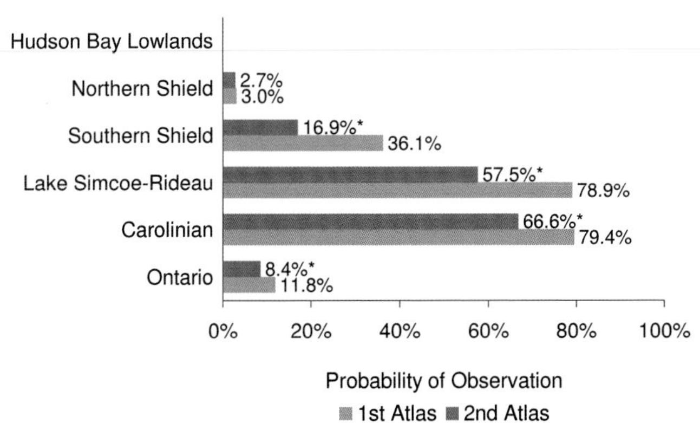

nificantly by 53% and 27%, respectively. There also was a significant 16% decline in the Carolinian region. BBS data show a significant long-term decline in Ontario. Overall, atlas data indicate a province-wide decline of 29% and show that the core breeding range has shifted south and west.

Breeding biology: The Vesper Sparrow prefers to breed in dry, short-grass habitats with scattered perches. It spends much time on or near the ground, but singing perches on its breeding territory are important. Nests are placed on the ground, usually in a depression in short grass on well-drained fields and occasionally even in cultivated fields. The species rarely nests in marshy and moist areas where the Savannah Sparrow is found. In Ontario, the Vesper Sparrow lays an average of four eggs (range two to five). Eggs are laid from late April through early August. Incubation is by the female. The species is socially monogamous, and both adults feed the young. When double-brooded, the male takes primary responsibility for feeding the fledged young from the first brood while the female begins a second nest (Jones and Cornely 2002).

In territorial advertisement, males sing from a conspicuous perch, often on a fence post, shrub, or isolated tree. The song is distinctive, and males are easily observed, but locating them is of little help in finding nests. However, when a predator or human is close to a nest, both adults flutter along the ground in a broken-wing distraction display, sometimes also attacking the predator. About 10% of nests (as high as 34% in Grey Co.) are parasitized by the Brown-headed Cowbird.

The observed distribution of the species is probably accurate. However, the low level of confirmed breeding records (20%) likely underestimates the actual breeding status, as the well-concealed nests are difficult to find and family groups with fledglings are easily missed when they disperse.

Abundance: The Vesper Sparrow is an uncommon breeding bird in Ontario. The abundance map shows it is most common in agricultural areas in southwestern Ontario and between the north shore of Lake Ontario and the southern edge of the Shield from Port Hope to Napanee. In those areas, more than 1.9 birds/25 point counts were recorded. However, the species is rarely found in urban areas, so abundance is very low around cities such as Toronto. As well, numbers are low on the Canadian Shield where forest predominates. Scattered pockets exist in northern Ontario around farms and large forest clearcuts. Most Regional Coordinators believed atlas data accurately represented the breeding distribution and abundance in their regions but felt that numbers have decreased since the first atlas. The Vesper Sparrow will likely continue to decline in Ontario because of spreading urbanization and marginal farmland reverting to woodland, but primarily because of increasingly intensive agricultural practices. – *J.D. Rising*

Savannah Sparrow

Bruant des prés

Passerculus sandwichensis

Tim Stewart

The Savannah Sparrow is one of the most widespread and abundant of North American birds (Rising 1996). In Ontario, it is the most common breeding bird in most meadows and pastures (Rising in Cadman et al. 1987). Although not colourful, it sings persistently from small trees, weeds, fence posts, or wires and is usually not difficult to see. In the east, it breeds from southern Pennsylvania west to central Iowa and north and east to the limit of the mainland; in the west, it is found in montane meadows and moist tundra from Alaska south to central Mexico. A few birds winter as far north as southern Ontario, but most winter in the southern US and Mexico.

Distribution and population status: Both atlases show that the Savannah Sparrow is found across the province, with no overall change in distribution in Ontario. BBS data show that, like most grassland birds in eastern North America, the species is declining. In Ontario, it experienced a significant annual decline of 2.0% since 1981 and a 2.5% annual decline since 1968. Interestingly, atlas data show that the probability of observation of the Savannah Sparrow increased province-wide by a non-significant 12% between the first and second atlases. This overall Ontario increase is mostly due to the significant 40% increase in the Hudson Bay Lowlands, which is not covered by the BBS; other regions show smaller, non-significant changes. The habitat in the Hudson Bay Lowlands has been little affected by human activity, so the reason for the increase is unclear. The non-significant declines in all four regions south of the Hudson Bay Lowlands probably reflect the abundance of the species and the fact that it can use relatively small areas of suitable habitat, so even if the species has declined within a square, there may still be sufficient birds present to be found while atlassing.

Habitat loss doubtless explains the population declines in the east. As European settlers cleared much of the eastern woodland for agricultural purposes, the Savannah Sparrow,

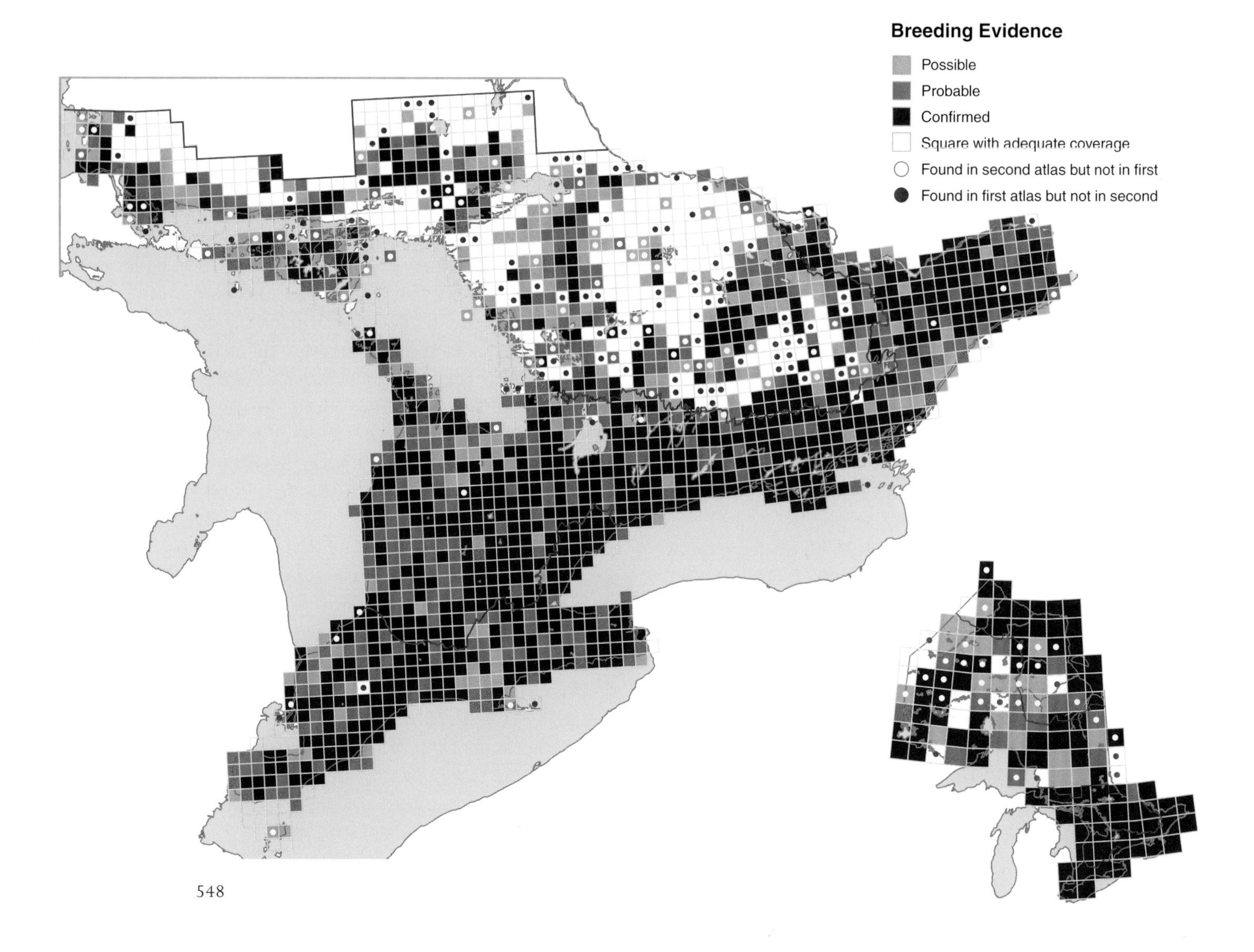

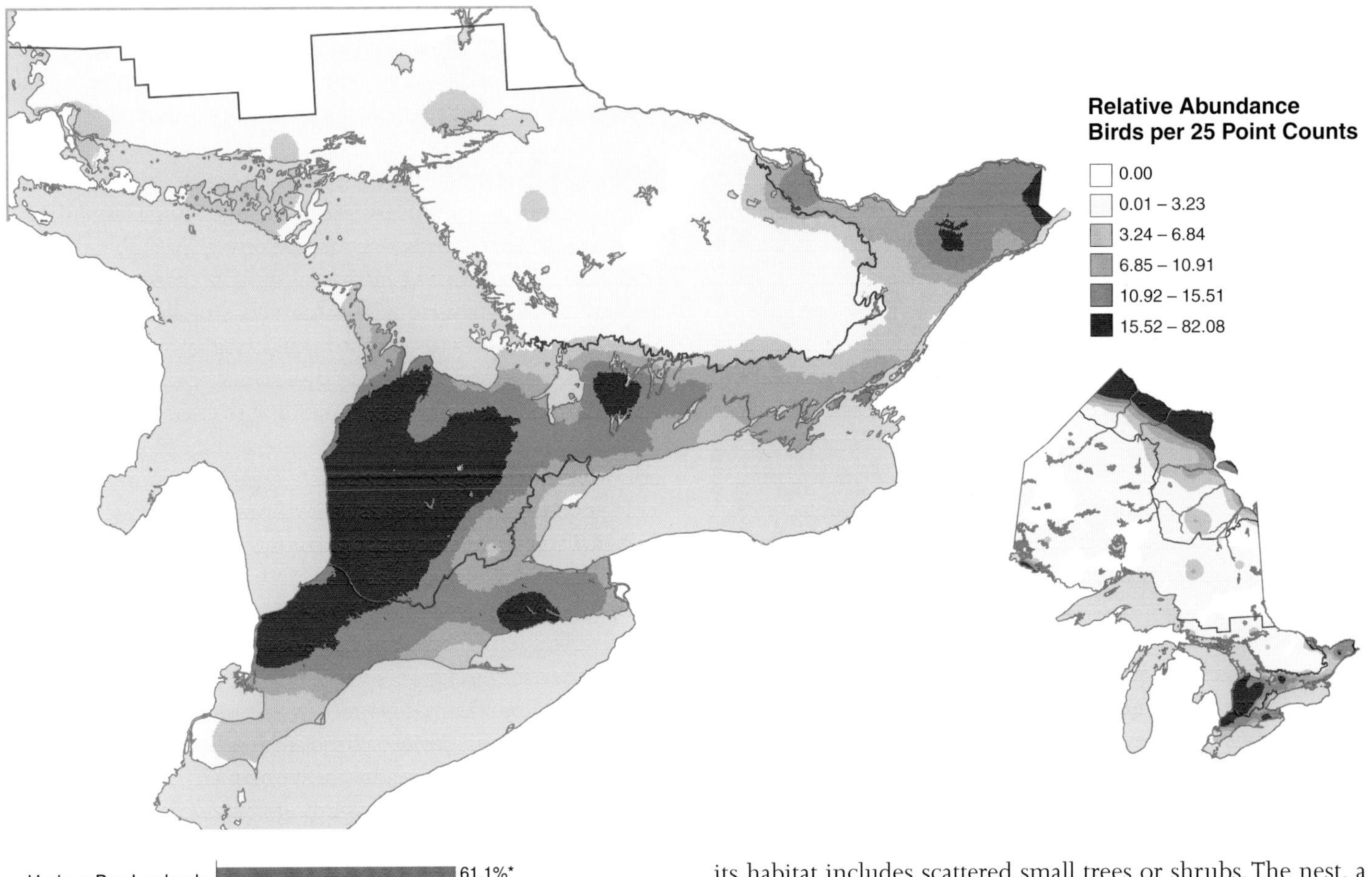

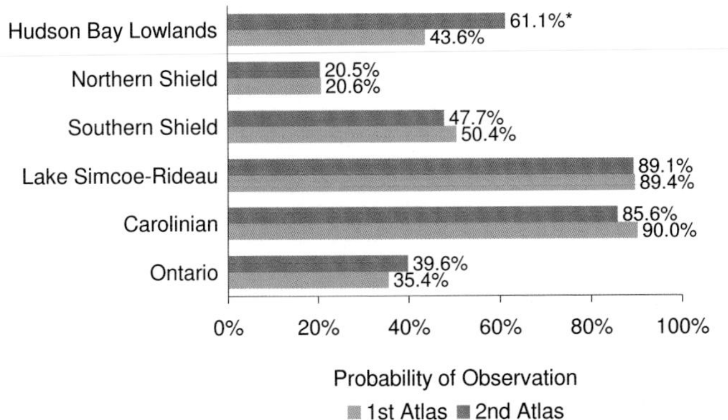

along with many other grassland species, greatly increased in numbers where historically it was found almost exclusively in natural meadows and graminoid marshes. In the 20th century, much of the cleared land was allowed to revert to forest, exposed to more intensive agriculture, or developed to accommodate urbanization, almost certainly explaining the decline in numbers of many species that earlier benefited from the clearing.

The Savannah Sparrow is apparently scarce on the edge of the Southern Shield and nearly absent from the Algonquin Dome. Local pockets of breeding birds occur on the Little Clay Belt near New Liskeard and in the Great Clay Belt of the Cochrane-Timmins area.

Breeding biology: In the southern part of the province, the Savannah Sparrow breeds primarily in grassy meadows, cultivated fields (especially alfalfa), and pastures and along roadsides. In the north, it is most common in beaver meadows and peat lands and in sedge fens, supra-tidal meadows, and graminoid tundra along the coasts and other waterways. Often its habitat includes scattered small trees or shrubs. The nest, a simple cup of woven grass lined with fine grasses, hair, or plant cotton, is placed on or near the ground, often in a hollow scratched into the earth, and is generally well concealed. In Ontario, the clutch-size averages four eggs (usually four to five; average slightly higher in the north); eggs are laid late April through early August (mostly late May and June). During the breeding season, young are fed mostly insects, but at other times of the year the Savannah Sparrow eats mostly small seeds (Wheelwright and Rising 1993).

During the breeding season, males sing frequently and persistently from an exposed perch in or near their breeding territory. Although the song is distinctive, the presence of a singing male is of little help in finding the well-concealed nest, and unmated and migrating birds also sing.

Abundance: The relative abundance maps show that the Savannah Sparrow is most common near the coast of Hudson Bay and northern James Bay and in southwestern Ontario, especially in pastures east of Lake Huron and north of Lake Erie. High numbers also occur on the Carden Plain, on the Haldimand Clay Plain, and locally in far eastern Ontario. On the Shield, it is largely restricted to pastureland and airports and is occasionally found in natural clearings (burns, blowdowns, large bogs, and beaver meadows); high numbers occur in the Rainy River area. – *J.D. Rising*

Grasshopper Sparrow

Bruant sauterelle

Ammodramus savannarum

George K. Peck

Like other members of the genus *Ammodramus*, the Grasshopper Sparrow is generally inconspicuous. Were it not for its distinctive, "sizzling" grasshopper-like song, it would doubtless go largely undetected. Throughout its rather extensive range, it occurs in drier, more open grasslands than most other sparrows, preferring areas of sparse, short grass, often with patches of exposed ground (Vickery 1996). It is most abundant in the Great Plains region of North America, though it breeds locally east to the Atlantic and in isolated areas west of the plains. Southern Ontario is near the northeastern-most extent of its distribution (Sauer et al. 2005; Vickery 1996). BBS data indicate that it has been declining significantly across most of its range (Sauer et al. 2005).

Distribution and population status: The Grasshopper Sparrow, like other western grassland birds, undoubtedly benefited from the clearing of land following European settlement, the initial increase in its range and abundance in Ontario being attributable to agricultural expansion (McCracken 2005). The species is now found across southern Ontario, mostly south of the Canadian Shield, with small, isolated populations north to Sault Ste. Marie and in western Rainy River Dist. near Lake of the Woods.

The Grasshopper Sparrow did not show a significant change in probability of observation in Ontario as a whole between atlases. However, it did decline significantly in the Carolinian region by 48%. The primary reason for this decline is probably intensification of agriculture, including conversion of pastures and other grassy habitats to row crops. However, on the Norfolk Sand Plain, this sparrow uses fields planted in winter cereals such as winter wheat and rye, which produce a grassland-like habitat in the early part of the season. The mature crop is rather sparse as it is growing on sand, and so is suitable for the Grasshopper Sparrow. Areas occupied by the species in much of the Lake Simcoe-Rideau region are on

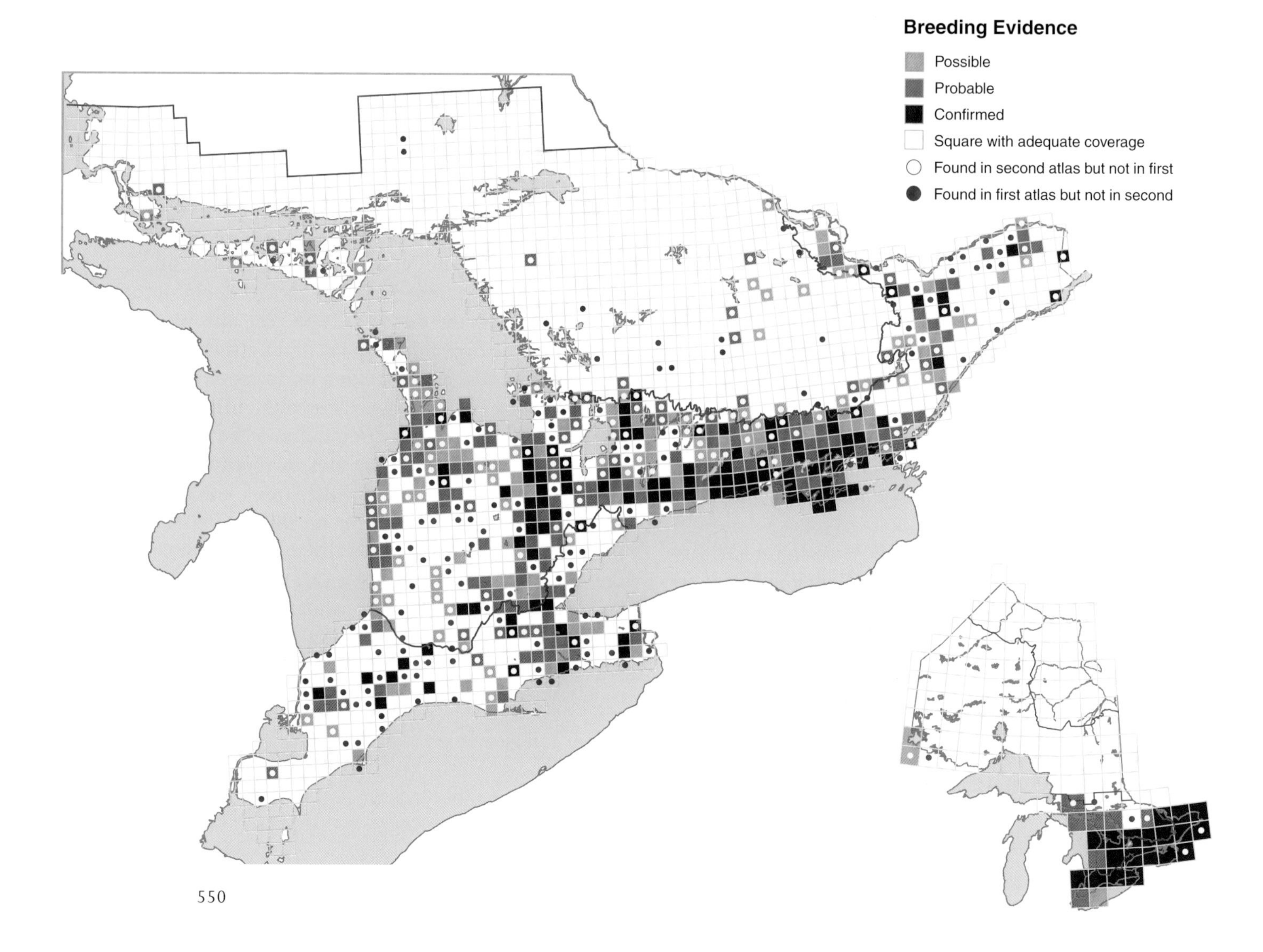

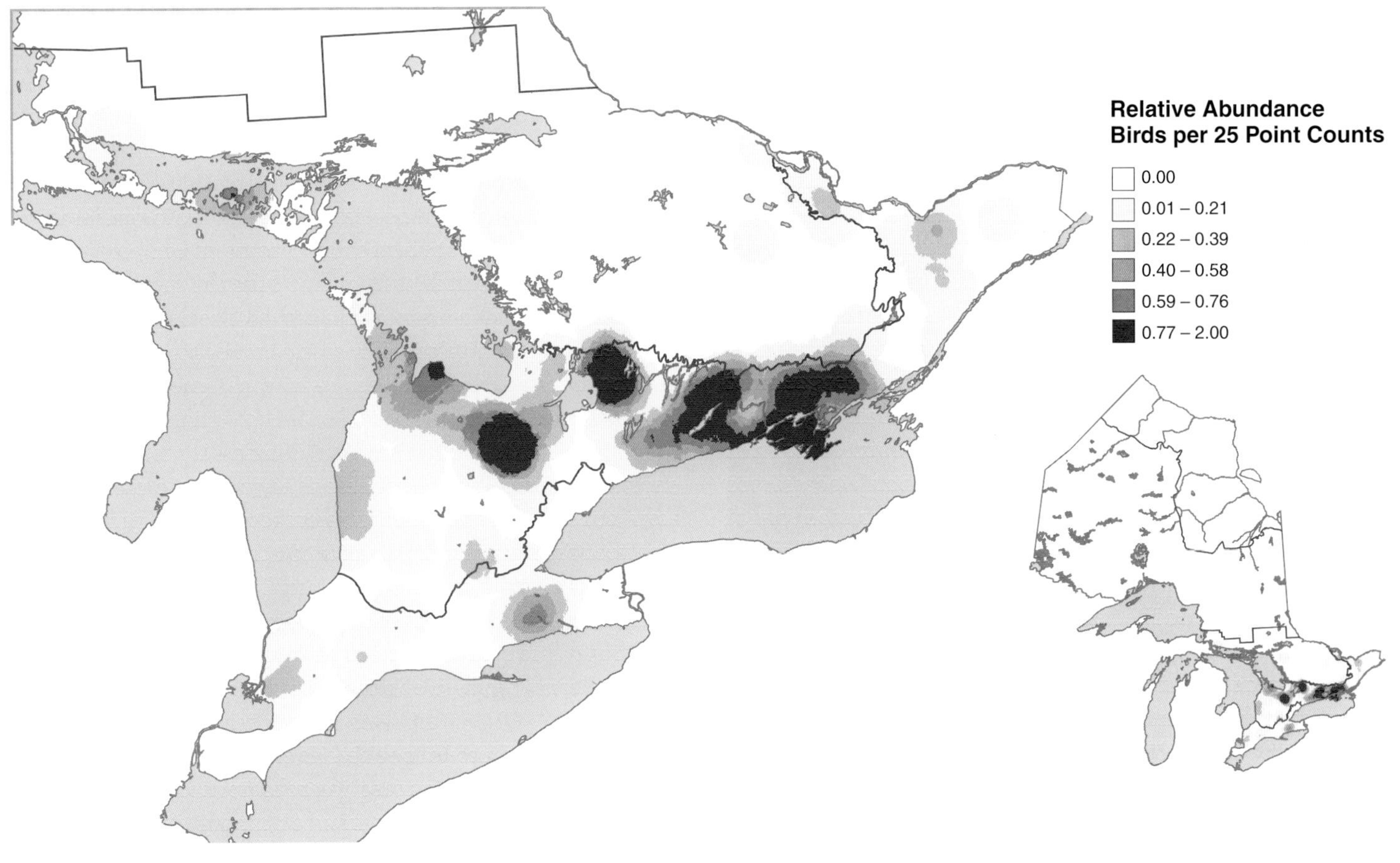

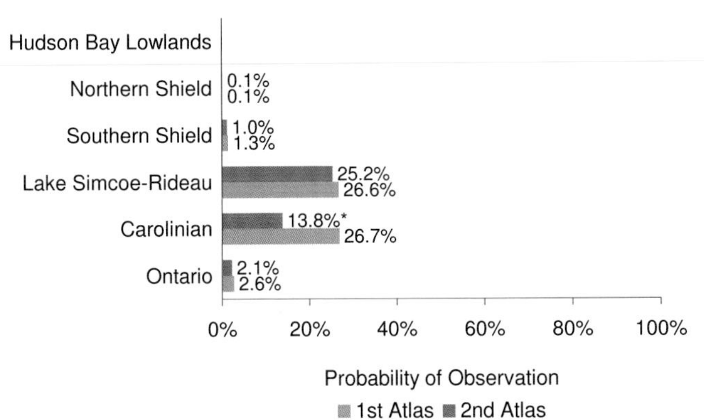

droughty sand, till moraines, and shallow soils over limestone beds, which are often used for pasture. Some ungrazed areas are reverting to forest. So, while agricultural practices first allowed the species to expand in southern Ontario, changing practices may be the cause of its present demise in some areas. The decrease in the Carolinian has contributed to a significant shift 12 km north in the core latitude of the species' population in southern Ontario.

Breeding biology: The Grasshopper Sparrow prefers drier, sparsely vegetated grasslands, particularly rough or unimproved pastures, at least 30 ha in size. Such grasslands support varying amounts of forb and shrub growth. It will occasionally also use cultivated hayfields and cereal crops. Males often sing from a perch such as a mullein stalk, small shrub, or fence-post, anything that might stick out of the grass, but they may also sing while on the ground (Rising 1996).

The distinctive song is the easiest means of detecting the species, and evidence of possible or probable breeding was reported in 74% of atlas squares. Males sing throughout the day and occasionally also at night (Vickery 1996). Nesting females are cryptic, and nests are difficult to locate. However, adults will perform distraction displays to draw predators from nests or fledglings. The species usually nests twice each breeding season (McCracken 2005; Vickery 1996). Where it was found, 26% of squares recorded confirmed breeding evidence. Many of these records were of adults carrying food for nestlings or fledglings.

Although the species' secretive behaviour and insect-like song suggest that it may have been overlooked in some areas, the song is distinctive and when singing the species is reasonably conspicuous. Thus the atlas map probably depicts the breeding distribution fairly accurately.

Abundance: The relative abundance map of the Grasshopper Sparrow shows its highest densities to be in a band from the southern Bruce Peninsula to the Kingston area, including the Mono and Mulmur Hills in Dufferin Co., the Carden Plain northeast of Lake Simcoe, and the eastern extent of the Oak Ridges Moraine in Northumberland Co., the adjacent Napanee Limestone Plain, and Prince Edward Co. As expected, the point counts show that the species is most common south of the Shield, occurring in the north only in a few isolated locations with sufficiently large areas in agriculture. – *Chris G. Earley*

Henslow's Sparrow

Bruant de Henslow

Ammodramus henslowii

John Reaume

The Henslow's Sparrow is one of the least familiar of Ontario's sparrows. Its skulking nature and characteristically soft "*tse-lick*" call – easily overwhelmed by the songs of other species, particularly during the morning chorus – make it easy to overlook. Its often ephemeral occupancy of sites makes locating this sparrow even more of a challenge, even for experienced atlassers familiar with the species. The Henslow's Sparrow is found in the grasslands of eastern Minnesota south to Kansas and east to central New York. In Canada, it is restricted to southern Ontario. It was designated as Endangered in Ontario by OMNR in 1993 and in Canada by COSEWIC in 2000 (Environment Canada 2006a).

Distribution and population status: The Henslow's Sparrow was unknown in the province until 1898, when it was first reported in southwestern Ontario. As elsewhere in the northeast, it evidently expanded its range into the province with the clearing of forests for agriculture. It became locally common in Essex and Lambton Counties in the early 1900s and continued to move north and east over the next several decades. Records of the species have occurred as far north as Manitoulin Island and east to Ottawa (Knapton 1984; Godfrey 1986).

Since its period of greatest abundance in the province in the 1950s and 1960s, the species' range has retracted, in large part due to increasingly intensive agricultural practices. In the first atlas, it was found in 38 squares, concentrated mainly in two areas in the Lake Simcoe-Rideau region: the Dundalk uplands in Wellington, Dufferin, and Grey Counties (nine squares), and the Napanee Plain in the vicinity of Kingston (21 squares). The probability of observation has declined significantly by 86% in this region since the first atlas. The species is apparently now absent from the Dundalk uplands and Napanee Plain and was found in just five squares in this region during the second atlas. These declines are likely the result of changes in agricultural land use. More extensive areas in cultivation and tile

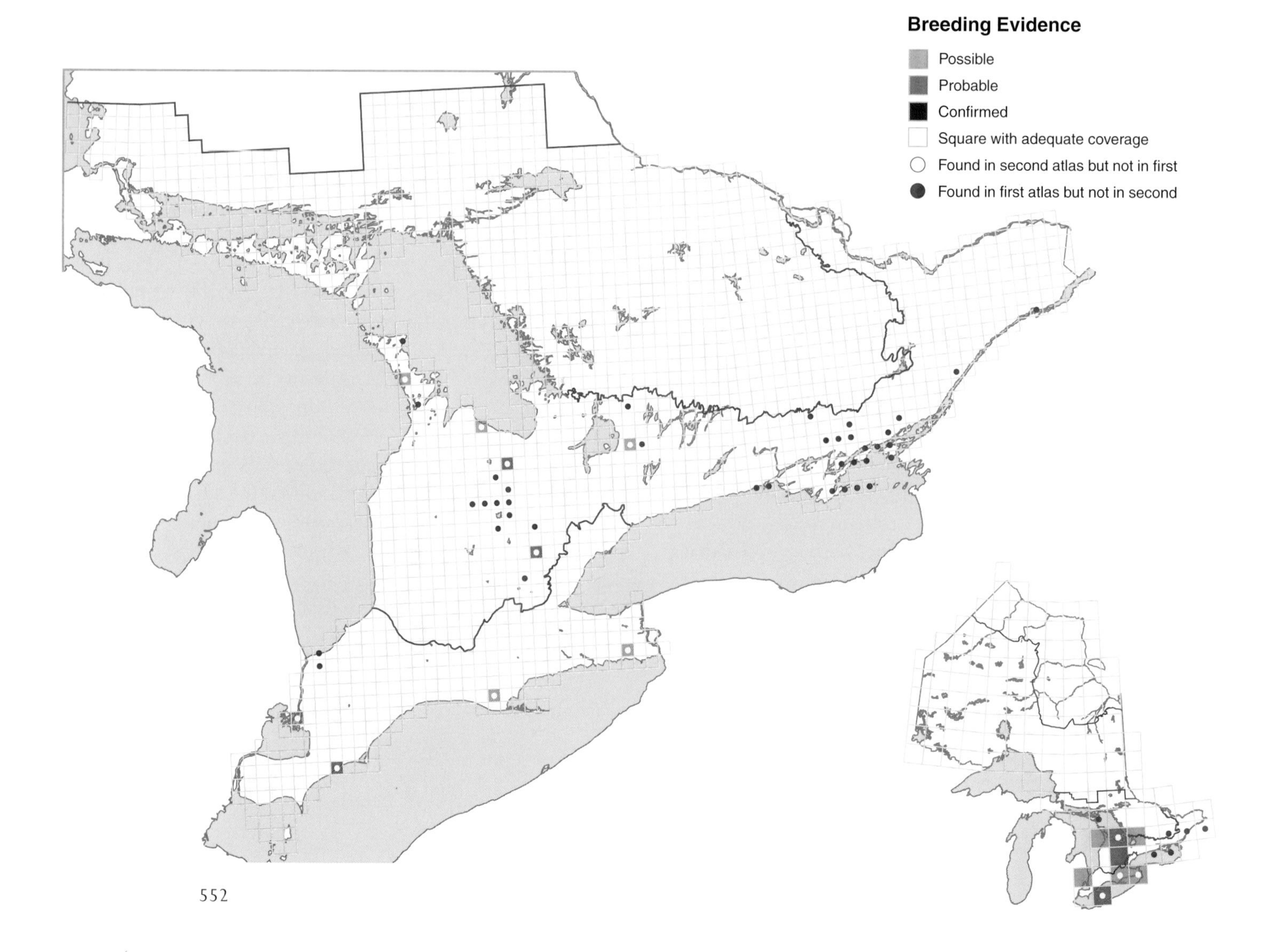

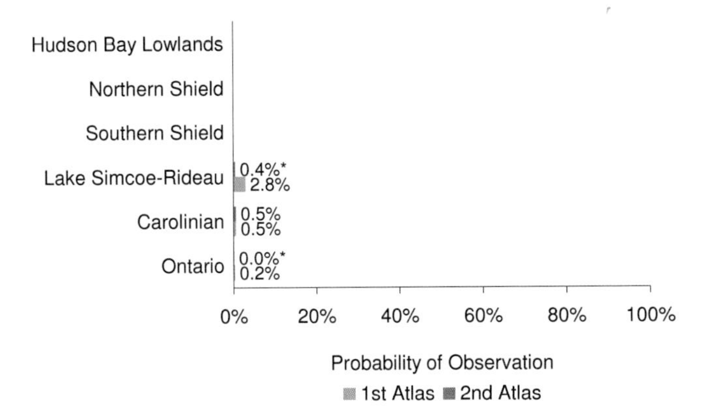

drainage, intensive livestock grazing, and shorter fallow periods have resulted in fewer of the large, moist, idle grasslands preferred by the species. While abandoned fields are not uncommon on the Napanee Plain, many are currently too small and dry or have in some cases succeeded to shrubs and trees. Three of the four sites reported from the Carolinian region during the second atlas were in native tallgrass prairie remnants or restorations.

Six of the nine records during the second atlas involved single singing males, observed on just one or a few subsequent visits. The only evidence of probable breeding was of two birds present at a site near Dealtown, Chatham-Kent, over a three-week period in 2005; a singing male near Badjeros, Grey Co., which remained for at least a week in 2002; and up to four birds recorded at a site south of Acton, Halton RM, in 2001. No confirmed breeding was documented during the second atlas.

The provincial population was estimated at a maximum of 50 pairs during the first atlas. Although a concerted effort was made in the current atlas to locate the species, its inconspicuous song and habits mean it may have been overlooked in some squares. Currently, the Henslow's Sparrow is detected on average at only one or two sites per year in Ontario. Due to its characteristically ephemeral site occupancy, it exhibits considerable annual variation in occurrence in the province. Breeding pairs, if present, are likely to be very few in any year. No known pairs were reported during the second atlas, but females are inconspicuous and easily overlooked.

Breeding biology: The Henslow's Sparrow nests in large, open, usually moist to wet, often flat fields with a high graminoid to forb/shrub ratio. Vegetation must be dense and over 30 cm in height. Most nests are on or near the ground and well concealed from above by clumps of grasses and thick litter. In Ontario, this sparrow has nested in regenerating old fields, lightly used pastures, hayfields, wet meadows, and sedge marshes (Peck and James 1987). It tends to form loose breeding colonies but typically exhibits low breeding site fidelity (Herkert et al. 2002). Fidelity is generally greater in large grasslands supporting larger colonies.

Abundance: Numbers of Henslow's Sparrow in Ontario are extremely low, and its distribution is scattered and somewhat unpredictable. In the first atlas, two to 10 pairs were estimated to be present in 19 (59%) of the squares for which abundance estimates were taken. However, only two squares recorded more than one individual during the second atlas. – *Ken Tuininga*

In Ontario, this sparrow has nested in regenerating old fields, lightly used pastures, hayfields, wet meadows, and sedge marshes (Peck and James 1987). Green Lane, near King City, York Region. *Photo: George K. Peck*

The Henslow's Sparrow nests in large, open, often flat fields, usually moist to wet, with a high graminoid to forb/shrub ratio. Carden Alvar, City of Kawartha Lakes. *Photo: Gregor G. Beck*

Le Conte's Sparrow

Bruant de Le Conte
Ammodramus leconteii

Jean Iron

This elusive denizen of flooded meadows, sedge marshes, and quaking bogs combines mouse-like secrecy with a thin, grasshopper-like buzz of a song to pose a serious challenge to the accurate delineation of its Ontario range. First described in 1790 from a winter specimen taken in Georgia, the Le Conte's Sparrow was not encountered again until the 1830s (Lowther 2005). Its breeding grounds were discovered in North Dakota in 1873 (Coues 1874), and the first nest was found in Manitoba in 1882 (Seton 1890). Scarcely more than 100 nests have ever been documented (Walkinshaw 1968; Winter et al. 2005).

The species breeds from the southern Northwest Territories through Alberta, Saskatchewan, and Manitoba to North Dakota, Minnesota, Michigan, and Wisconsin. Its eastern Canadian distribution is more poorly understood, as it breeds in widely separated areas across northern Ontario and southern Québec (Lowther 2005). It prefers dry wetland borders that include tall grasses, dense litter, and minimal woody vegetation, found optimally in areas with periodic disturbance resulting from fire, flood, tidal surge, hay cropping, and grazing (Dechant et al. 2003).

Distribution and population status: McIlwraith (1894) did not list the Le Conte's Sparrow as occurring in Ontario. The first provincial record occurred at Toronto in 1897 (Fleming 1907), and the first two Ontario nests were found at Fort William in 1924 (Dear 1940). Baillie and Harrington (1937) reported colonies at Baden, Toronto, and Bradford in southern Ontario and at Thunder Bay and Algoma Districts in northern Ontario. The Bradford colony at Holland Marsh was the best-known population in the province before that area was drained for agriculture (Devitt 1967). The species was found along the Ontario coast of James Bay by the 1940s (Manning 1952; Todd 1963).

The Le Conte's Sparrow is found in all atlas regions except the Carolinian, although it is not widespread in any. Its probability of

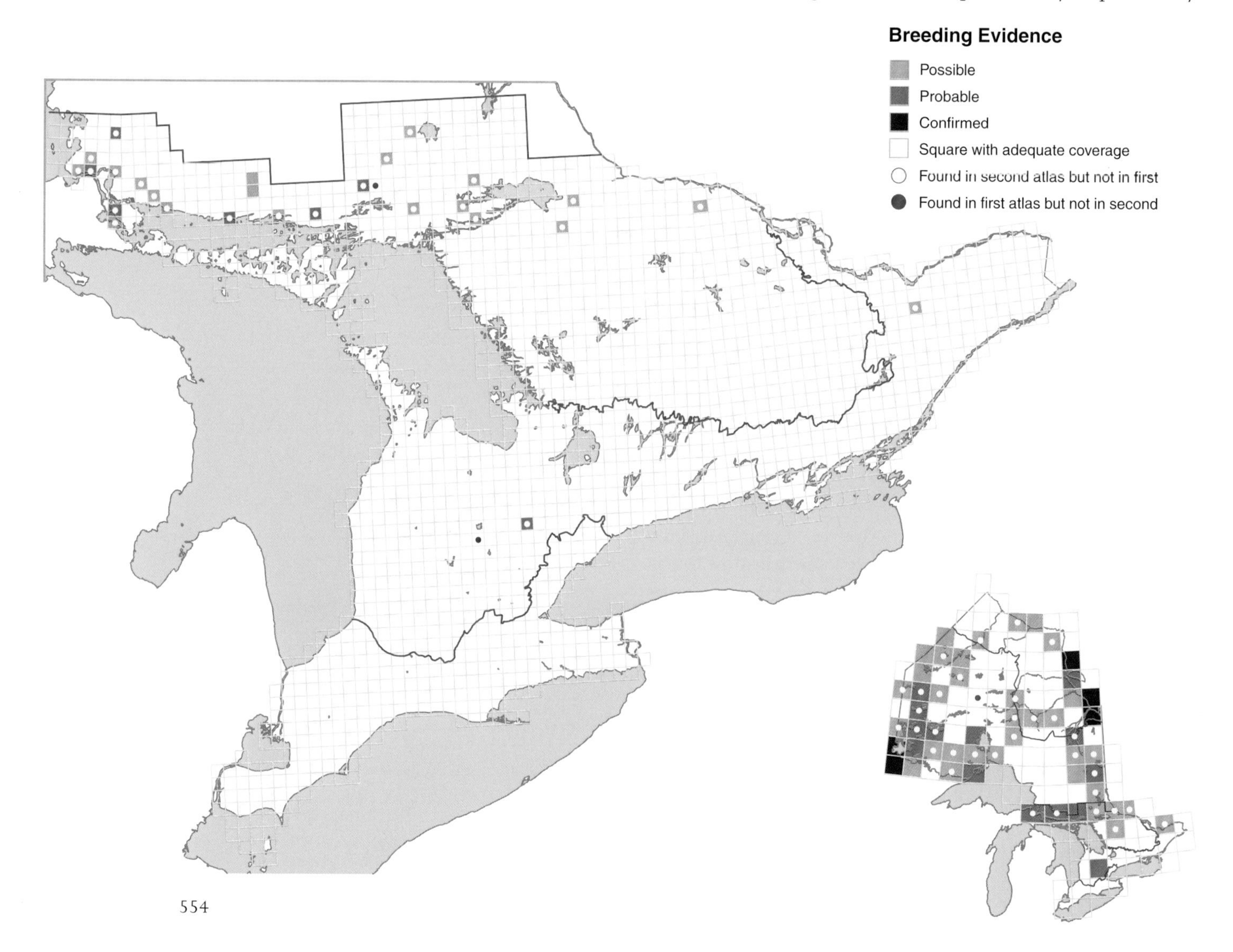

BREEDING EVIDENCE

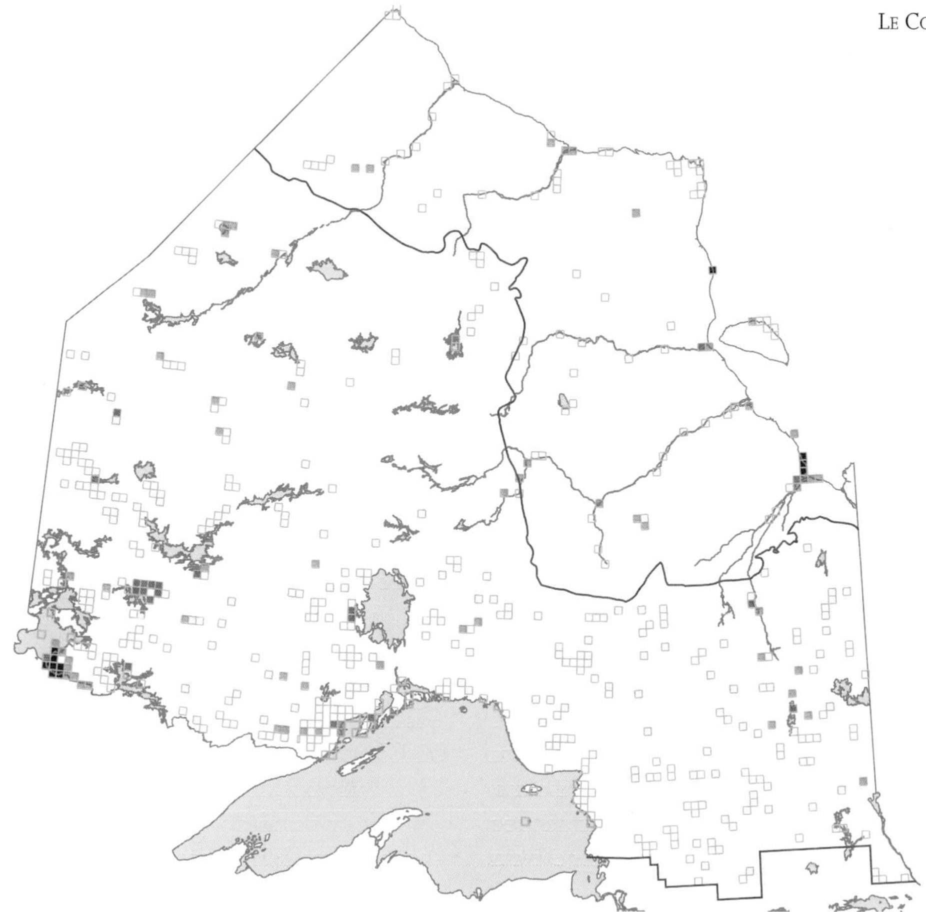

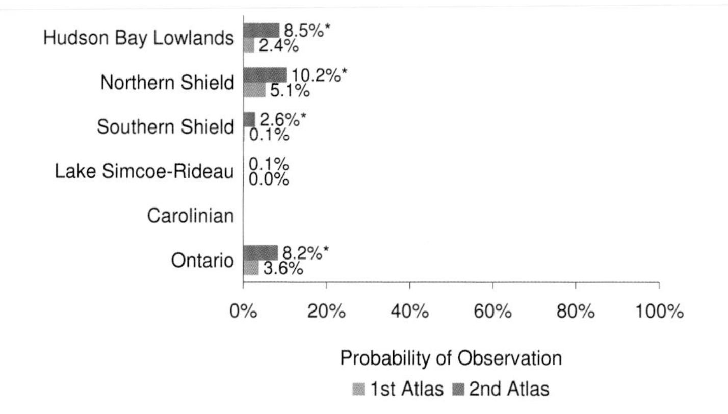

observation is highest in the Northern Shield (10%) and Hudson Bay Lowlands (8%), where it is found at scattered, isolated locations, with clusters of squares in the Rainy River and Dryden areas and Moosonee, respectively. In southern Ontario, it occurred most frequently in a band from Sault Ste. Marie east to the Lake Nipissing area. It was located in only two squares south of the Shield, one east of Orangeville and one south of Ottawa.

Between atlases, the probability of observation of the species for the province as a whole more than doubled, a significant increase. The largest proportional increase, about 20-fold, was in the Southern Shield. Significant increases were also seen in the Northern Shield (98%) and the Hudson Bay Lowlands (approximately threefold). Much of this increase may simply reflect a combination of improved atlasser familiarity with the species and normal population fluctuation in the interval. Canadian BBS data show no significant trends but are likely unrepresentative of the majority of the species' Ontario habitat, which is north of the main road network.

Breeding biology: The Le Conte's Sparrow has an inconspicuous song that is most frequently delivered from concealed perches, easily overwhelmed by the songs of other species and possibly mistaken for insects or overlooked by novice observers. As a result, atlas maps likely underestimate both its range and abundance. It constructs well-concealed nests beneath a thick canopy of dead grasses. Adults enter and leave the nest area after travelling a considerable distance concealed under this thick litter layer (Lowther 2005). Breeding was confirmed in only 9% of the squares in which the species was recorded, with all but one of these squares reporting adults carrying food as the highest evidence. Only 11 nests have ever been found in Ontario (Peck 2004). The two nests found during this atlas were in extensive sedge fens about 25 km north of the Swan River along the James Bay coast, in 2003.

Abundance: The areas of highest abundance correspond to the densest concentrations of occurrences on the distribution map, in the south-central James Bay coast, the western Rainy River Dist., and the Dryden area. High abundance estimates near Thunder Bay in the first atlas were not replicated in this atlas. Local populations of this sparrow have been shown to fluctuate in response to available wet conditions (Knapton 1979). Igl and Johnson (1995) documented a dramatic 500-fold increase in local numbers between drought and wet periods during 1990-95 in the northern Great Plains. Most point counts in the Rainy River area, conducted after a prolonged wet period in 2005, recorded much higher than usual numbers of the Le Conte's Sparrow and the co-occurring Sedge Wren and Yellow Rail. – *Glenn Coady*

Nelson's Sharp-tailed Sparrow

Bruant de Nelson
Ammodramus nelsoni

Jean Iron

Despite its delightfully gaudy pumpkin and grey colouration and its unique buzzing song, reminiscent of a bead of water dropping onto a hot frying pan, the skulking Nelson's Sharp-tailed Sparrow remains one of the most poorly studied of Ontario's birds.

Since the first atlas, the former Sharp-tailed Sparrow, *Ammodramus caudacutus*, has been split into two species based on genetic, morphometric, behavioural, song, and habitat differences (Greenlaw 1993; Rising and Avise 1993; American Ornithologists' Union 1995): Nelson's Sharp-tailed Sparrow, *Ammodramus nelsoni*, and the Saltmarsh Sharp-tailed Sparrow, *Ammodramus caudacutus*, which breeds from Maine to North Carolina. Two disjunct subspecies of the Nelson's Sharp-tailed Sparrow breed in Ontario: the Prairie race, *A. n. nelsoni*, breeds in freshwater sedge marshes and wet meadows, and the James Bay race, *A. n. alterus*, breeds in coastal graminoid marshes (Greenlaw and Rising 1994).

Distribution and population status: The species now called the Nelson's Sharp-tailed Sparrow was unknown as an Ontario breeder by McIlwraith (1894) and Baillie and Harrington (1937). The first breeding evidence for Ontario came from Attawapiskat in 1939, and the first two nests were found in 1942 on 25 June at Fort Albany and 16 July at the mouth of the Nettichi River (Baillie 1960). It was reported subsequently to be most common along the southern James Bay coast, north and west across the Hudson Bay coast as far west as Winisk (Manning 1952; Schueler et. al. 1974).

At least five birds were observed at Rainy River on 30 June 1979 (Speirs 1985). James (1991) classified the species as an "uncommon summer resident along the north coast," with individuals likely being of the subspecies *alterus*. He also described summer records from western Rainy River Dist., where "no birds have been collected, nor proof of breeding established, but they are probably of the *nelsoni* race."

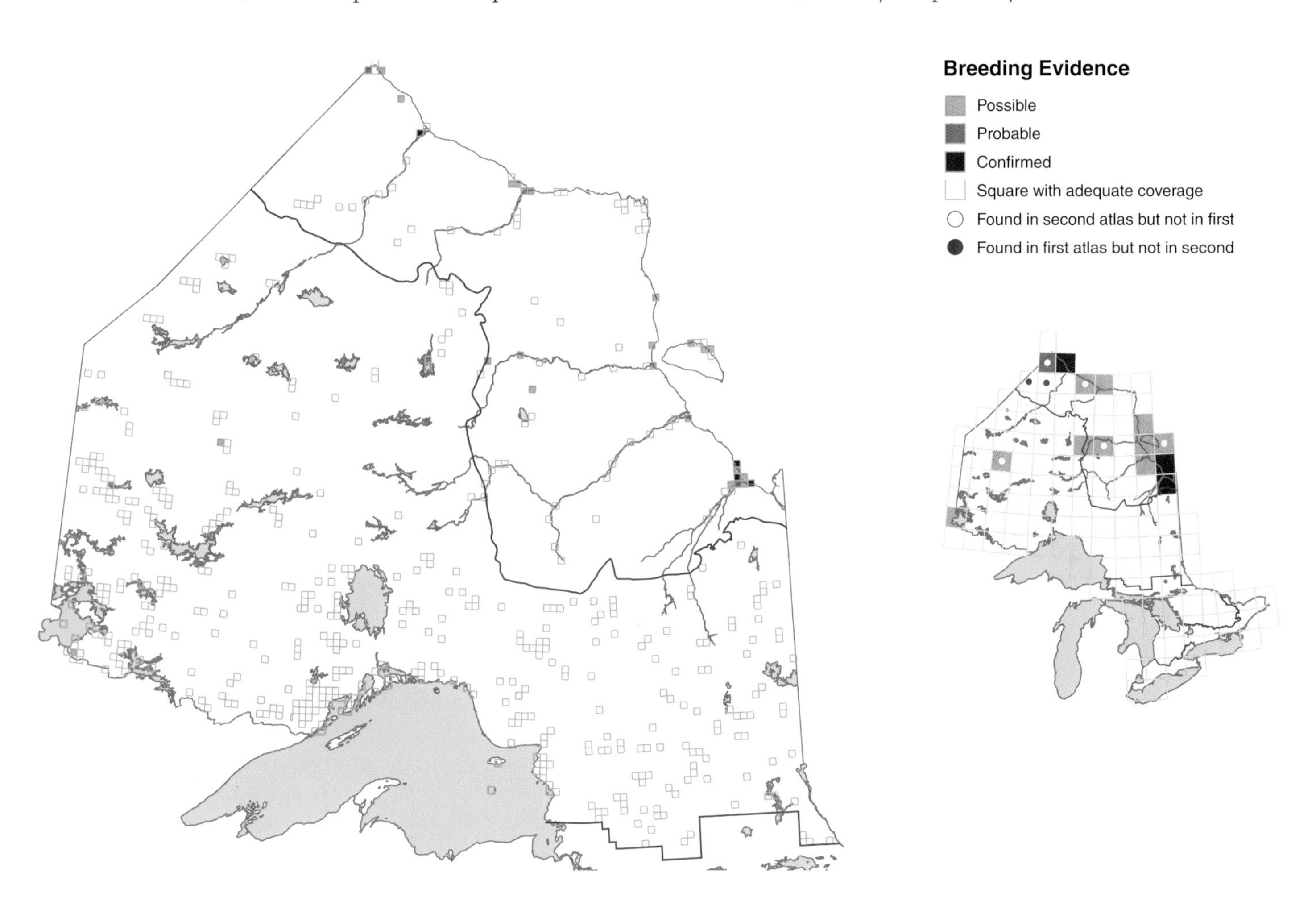

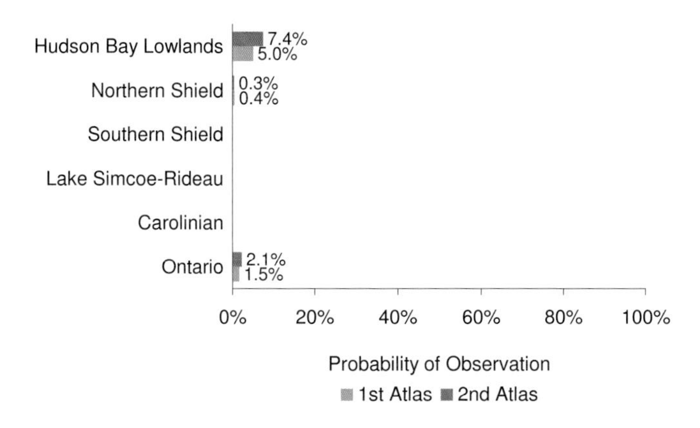

Between atlases, there was no significant difference in the probability of observation in the province as a whole or in either of the two regions in which the species was reported. Breeding is confined to northern Ontario, most commonly along the southern James Bay coast, north to the boundary of Polar Bear Prov. Park, as well as on the west-central Hudson Bay coast near Winisk, Fort Severn, and the Pen Islands. Possible breeding evidence was again found far inland in the Hudson Bay Lowlands in the Attawapiskat River drainage from late June, raising the possibility that the subspecies *alterus* may not be strictly coastal, as previously believed. In both atlases, singing birds were found near Rainy River, presumably of the Prairie subspecies *nelsoni*, but breeding here was not confirmed. New for this atlas was a singing male near Cat Lake on 5 June 2004. This may represent a late migrant *alterus*, or could indicate that the subspecies *nelsoni* may occur farther north and east than western Rainy River Dist.

Breeding biology: The male has a very distinctive song, sung from exposed perches, on the ground, or in flight (Greenlaw and Rising 1994), and frequently all night. Thus, even though it is rarely seen, the species is not difficult to detect by song, so the atlas map likely presents a reasonably accurate representation of its presence or absence within its range. Since it breeds late and sings on migration, care must be taken in interpreting records in early June. Females collected at Attawapiskat in mid-June 1971 were not yet in full breeding condition (Schueler et al. 1974).

The Nelson's Sharp-tailed Sparrow is non-territorial, practising a polygynous mating system. Birds typically forage and copulate inconspicuously below the sedge vegetation layer. Females are notorious skulkers, and they alone build the nest, incubate eggs, and provide all parental care. Females rarely reveal themselves while carrying nest material or food for young, and nests are well hidden below dead sedge or tidal wrack (Greenlaw and Rising 1994). It is therefore a difficult species to confirm, with breeding confirmed in only four squares, and the distribution map likely underestimates breeding status in the province. Only four nests have ever been found in Ontario (Peck 2004). A nest containing four eggs, discovered near Fort Severn on 11 July 2003, was the only one found during this atlas.

Abundance: Accurate population estimates will likely require a targeted census of suitable coastal habitat. High numbers reported include 35 singing males noted in a relatively small area near Shegogau Creek on the James Bay coast north of Moosonee in 2005 (K. Abraham and J. Iron, pers. comm.). Of the limited point counts that detected the species, it was recorded most frequently near Moosonee. Although it was uncommon, the average number of birds/25 point counts (0.5) was higher in the Hudson Bay Lowlands than for the related Le Conte's Sparrow (0.3). – *Glenn Coady*

A Nelson's Sharp-tailed Sparrow stands at the entrance of its well-hidden ground nest. *Photo: George K. Peck*

Extensive coastal graminoid wetlands such as this James Bay site provided many atlas records of the Nelson's Sharp-tailed Sparrow. *Photo: Ken Abraham*

Fox Sparrow

Bruant fauve

Passerella iliaca

George K. Peck

Many people may have seen what appears at first glance to be an overgrown, rusty red Song Sparrow scratching at dropped seeds under a feeder in March or April; fewer will have actually seen an Ontario Fox Sparrow on its northerly breeding grounds. The Fox Sparrow is widely distributed across boreal and subarctic North America from Alaska to Newfoundland, and south in the US to Maine in the east and to Colorado in the western mountains. This species varies dramatically in size and colour across its range. While as many as 18 subspecies have been proposed in the past, more recent research suggests that on the basis of colour, measurements, and genetics, recognition of three or four species-groups is more appropriate (Weckstein et al. 2002). Fox Sparrows breeding in Ontario belong to the eastern *iliaca* (Red Fox Sparrow) group. The Red Fox Sparrow breeds from Alaska east to northern and central Ontario, northern Québec, Newfoundland, and Labrador, through the Maritime Provinces to northwestern Maine. It winters primarily in the eastern US and irregularly and rarely as far north as southern Ontario.

Distribution and population status: The Fox Sparrow is widely distributed in the Hudson Bay Lowlands, where its probability of observation is 70%. In the Northern Shield region, the probability of observation is only 20%, but the majority of this region lies south of the Fox Sparrow's range. In the part of the Northern Shield that lies north of about 52°N, the Fox Sparrow was detected quite regularly. The southernmost records were near the Little Abitibi River, about 70 km north of Cochrane, the same area with the southernmost records in the first atlas.

There was a significant increase between atlases in the probability of observation in both regions where the species occurred. The reasons for this increase are unclear. The habitat is unlikely to have changed significantly in this remote northern part of the province, and in both atlases, northern squares were covered by experienced birders.

No BBS routes in Ontario are located within the Fox Sparrow's range. Across Canada, the species shows no change in abundance during the period covered by the two atlases.

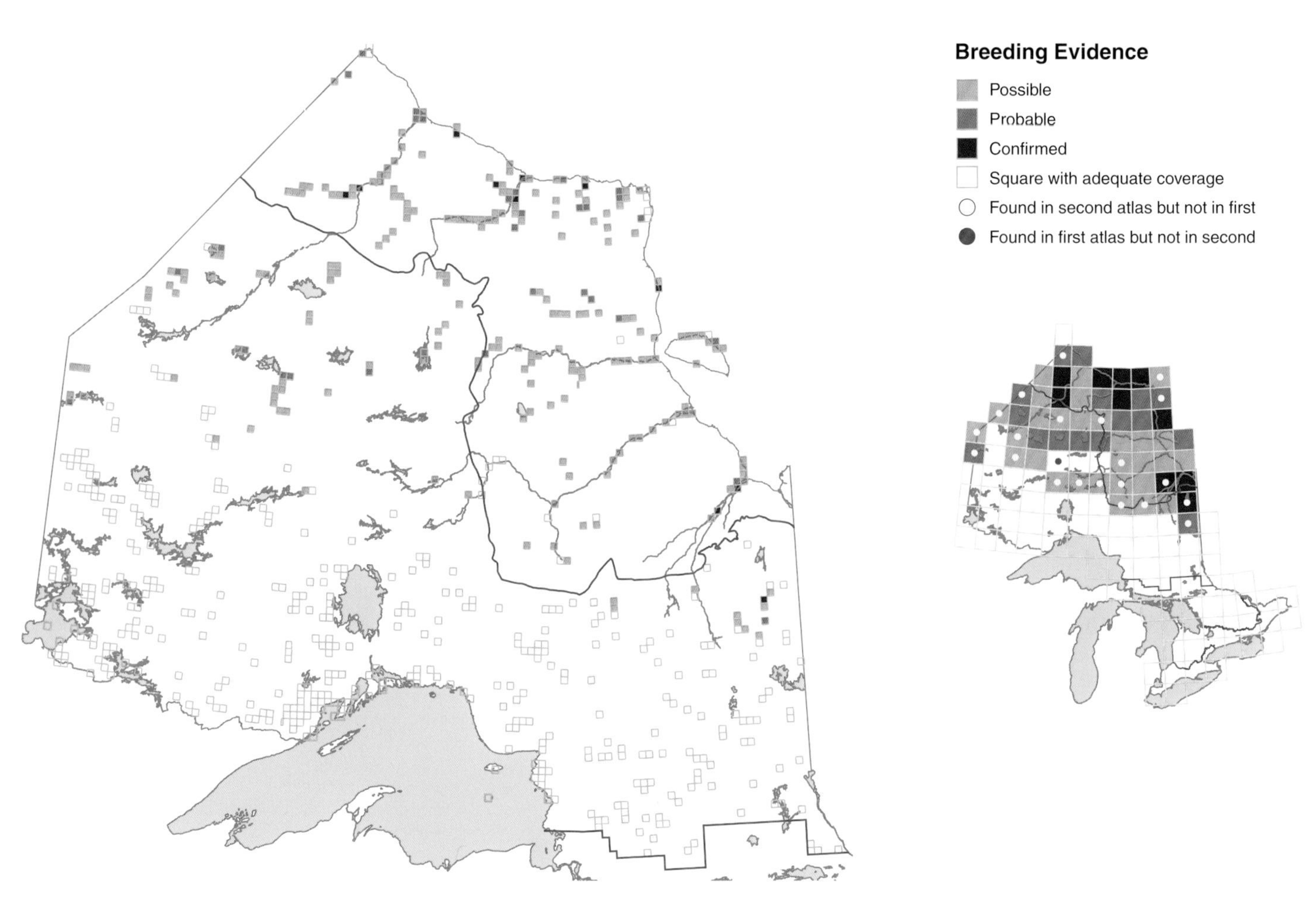

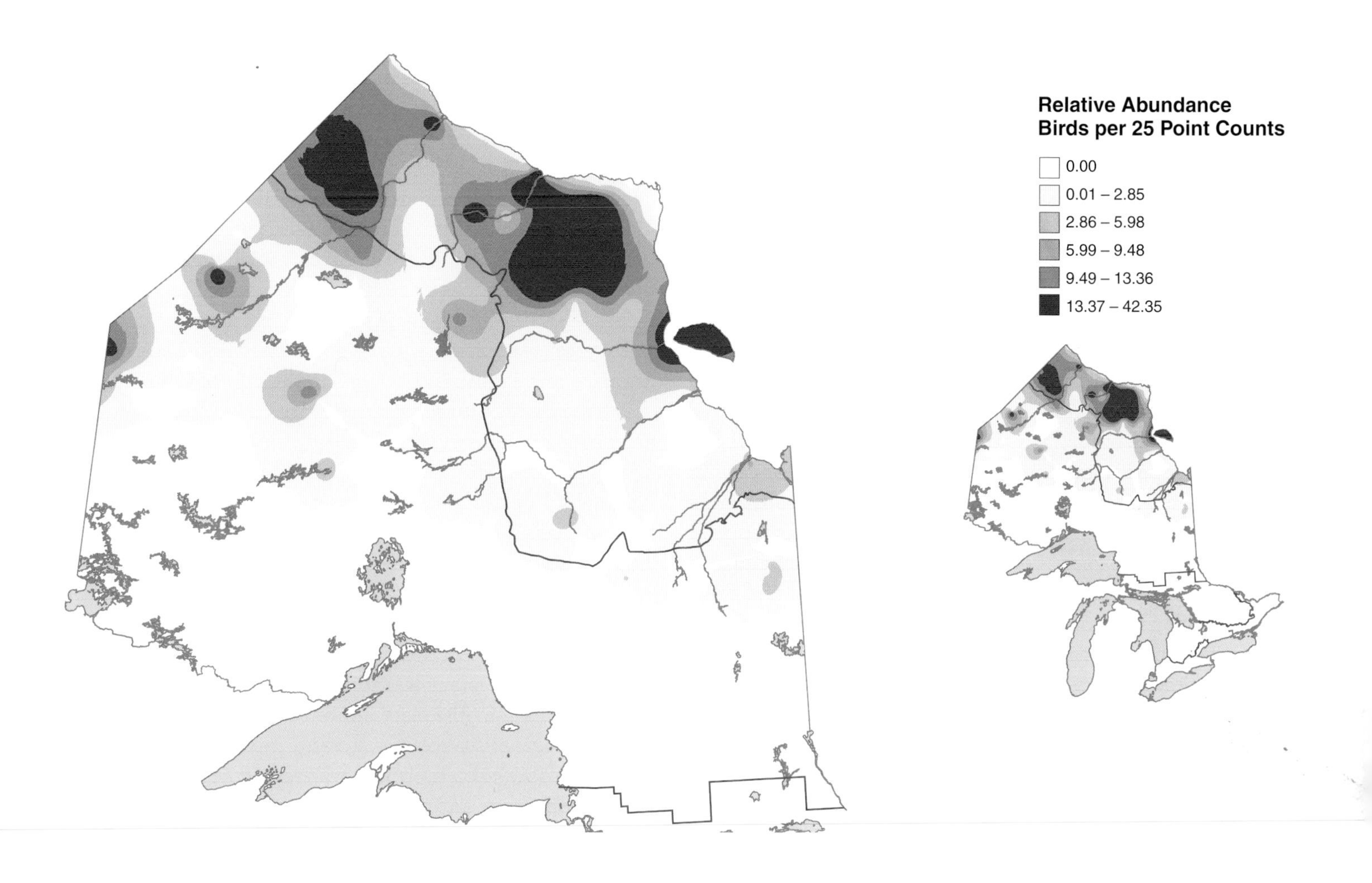

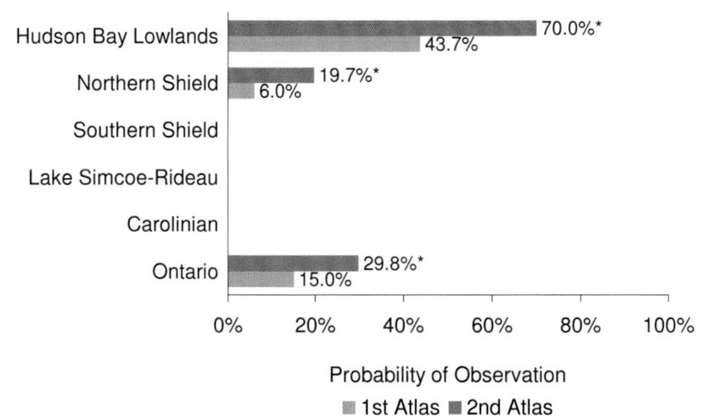

Monitoring of birds passing through Long Point during migration shows contradictory trends, significantly decreasing in spring and significantly increasing in fall (Crewe 2006).

Breeding biology: In Ontario, the Fox Sparrow prefers dense stands of stunted conifers in taiga areas as well as dense thickets of conifers, willows, birches, and alders in regenerating burns and along the shores of lakes, rivers, and streams. It is largely absent from areas of open tundra, occurring only locally in riparian shrub thickets. The nest is probably built entirely by the female and is placed on the ground or, occasionally, the low branches of a bush or small tree. It is well concealed and very difficult to find. The female alone incubates the two to four heavily splotched eggs and provides most of the food for the nestlings. Although the male rarely feeds young in the nest, he does feed them after fledging (Weckstein et al. 2002).

In the majority of squares (83%), only possible breeding, mostly in the form of singing males, was recorded. The Fox Sparrow's whistled song is both distinctive and far carrying and is the easiest means of detecting its presence. Given that many squares in the Hudson Bay Lowlands were covered by atlassers who canoed through them, the low proportion of probable or confirmed squares is not surprising. Probable breeding in the form of agitated adults or pairs of birds was recorded in 13% of squares, but breeding was confirmed in only 11 (4% of squares with records). Despite the difficulty of finding nests of this species, atlassers added another six nests to the five found previously in Ontario (Peck 2001; Peck and Peck 2006).

Abundance: Within its relatively restricted breeding range in Ontario, the Fox Sparrow can be abundant. There were three large areas of high abundance in the northern part of the Hudson Bay Lowlands. Densities of over 13.4 birds/25 point counts were recorded in a large area south of Peawanuck, in an area adjacent to the Ontario-Manitoba border, and also on Akimiski Island (Nunavut). The average density in the Hudson Bay Lowlands was 7.2 birds/25 point counts. South of the Lowlands, abundance is much lower, averaging 0.3 birds/25 point counts in the Northern Shield region. – *Margaret A. McLaren*

Song Sparrow

Bruant chanteur

Melospiza melodia

Jim Richards

The Song Sparrow is one of the most widespread and abundant of North American birds. There is a great deal of geographic variation within the species, as up to 52 subspecies have been named and 24 are commonly considered to be valid (Arcese et al. 2002). There also is a great deal of inter-populational variation in the species' ecology and biology.

At all times of the year, this is an easily found sparrow, with a variable but distinctive song and call note. It commonly sings from conspicuous perches and readily responds to "pishing." In Ontario, it is found in fairly open, shrubby habitats, often along rivers and lakeshores (especially on the Shield), as well as in urban areas where sufficient shrub habitat exists. In eastern North America, the clearing of forests doubtless benefited the Song Sparrow, since it breeds in second growth and edge areas. As marginal agricultural lands have been abandoned, it has moved into the tall second growth, although it generally avoids dense vegetation. Although a few Song Sparrows winter in southern Ontario, most migrate south into the US in the autumn.

Distribution and population status: Both atlases show that the Song Sparrow occurs across the province and was found in nearly every square in the south and most 100-km blocks in the north. The probability of observation was more than 95% in the Carolinian, Lake Simcoe-Rideau, and Southern Shield regions, 74% in the Northern Shield, and 56% in the Hudson Bay Lowlands. Between atlases, there was a non-significant increase in the probability of observation of 12% province-wide, with a significant 37% increase in the Hudson Bay Lowlands and a small but significant decrease of 2% in the Southern Shield. BBS data show a slight decrease in Song Sparrow numbers across Canada and Ontario, with significant annual declines of 1.4% and 0.8%, respectively, from 1968 to 2005 (Downes et al. 2005).

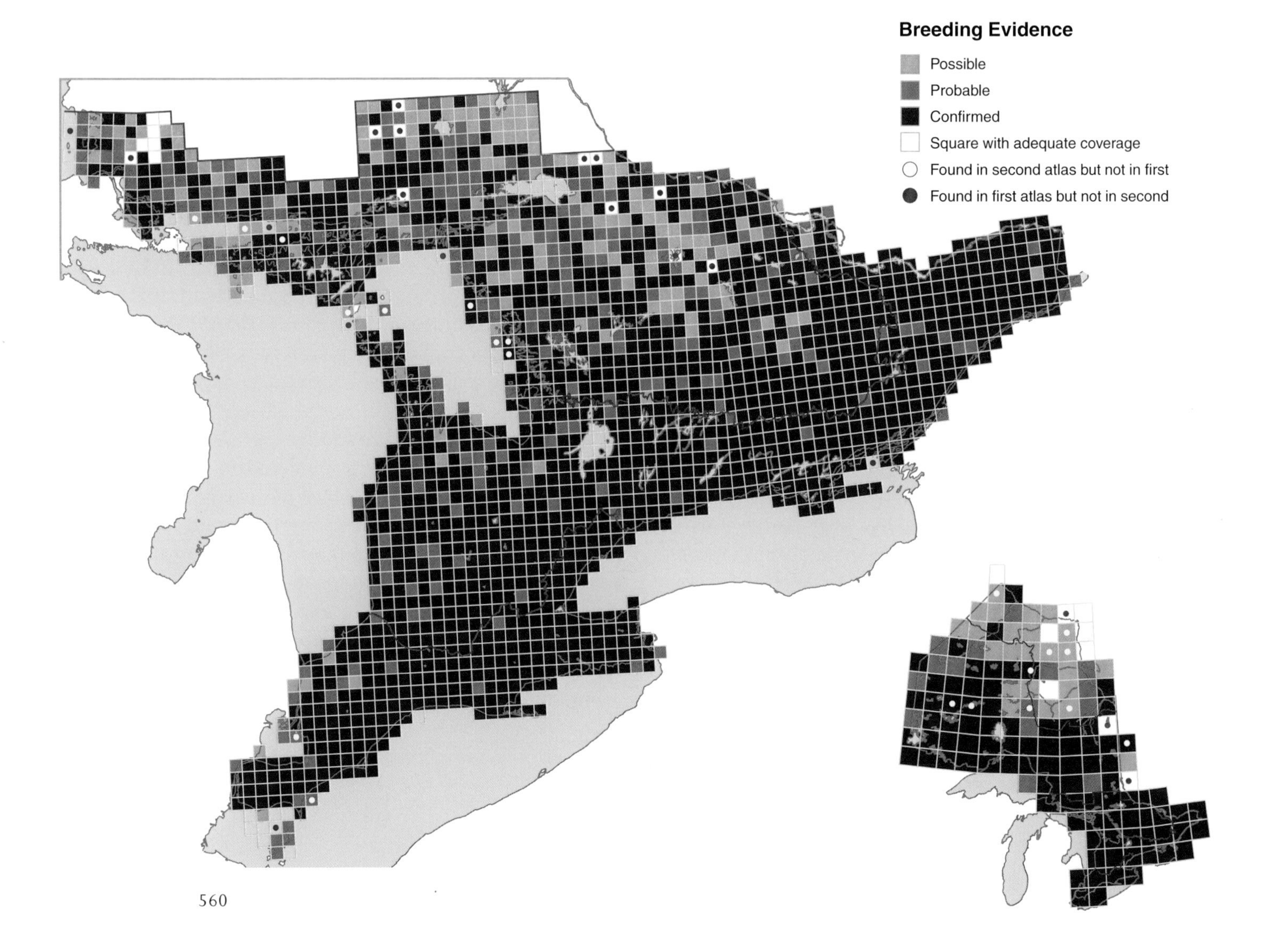

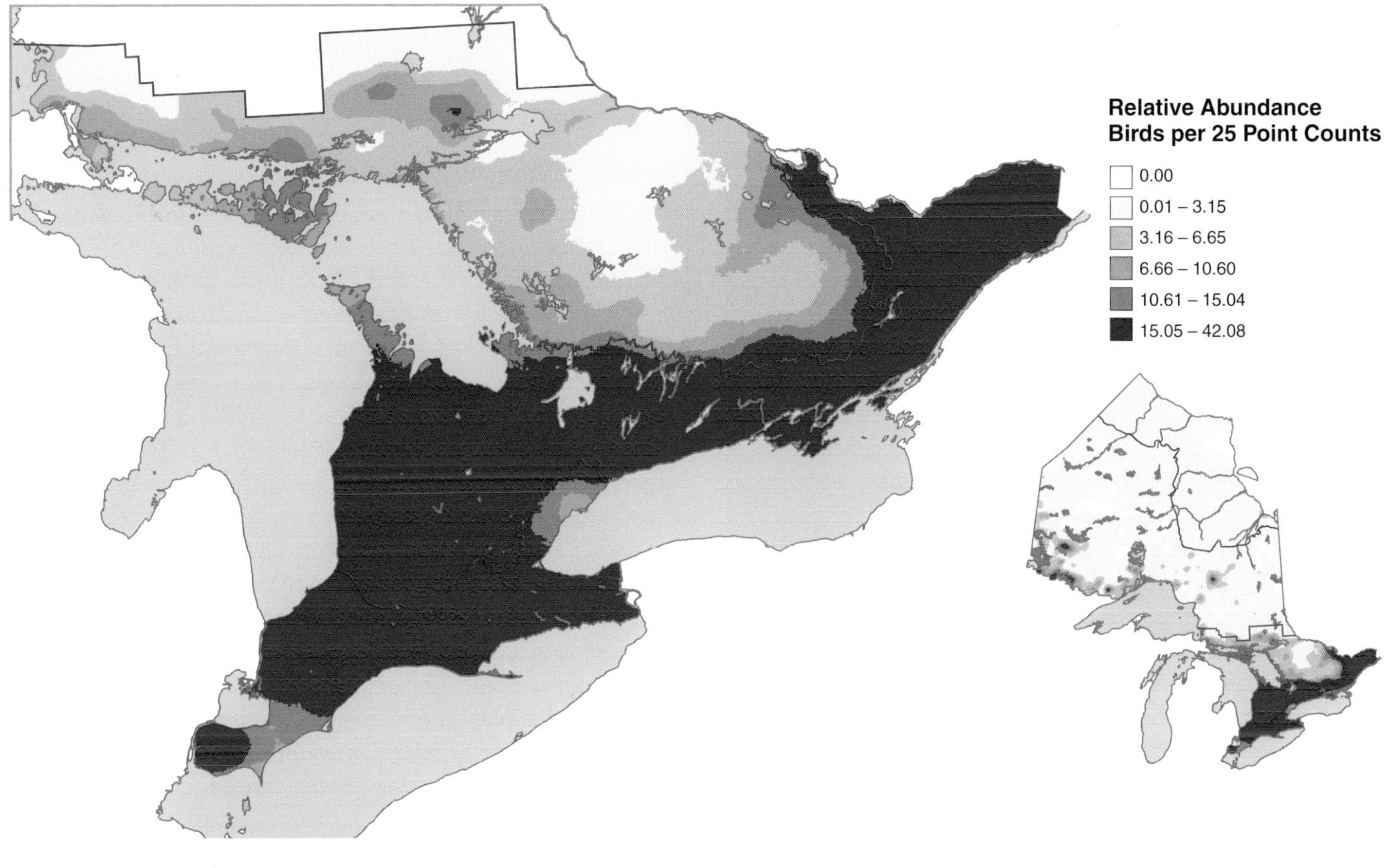

Hudson Bay Lowlands 56.5%* 41.2%
Northern Shield 74.4% 67.8%
Southern Shield 96.2%* 98.2%
Lake Simcoe-Rideau 97.9% 99.0%
Carolinian 97.7% 96.7%
Ontario 73.5% 65.9%
0% 20% 40% 60% 80% 100%
Probability of Observation
1st Atlas 2nd Atlas

Breeding biology: The Song Sparrow's nest consists of a bulky cup of strips of bark, leaves, grass, and weeds, lined with fine grass, hair, and rootlets. Most nests are placed on the ground amidst vegetation such as sedges, grasses, cattails, or small shrubs, but some are built in bushes within a metre of the ground. Generally, nests are inconspicuous and difficult to find (Rising 1996). Clutch size varies from one to eight eggs but is usually four or five. Egg laying begins in mid-April, rarely extending into early September. As many as three broods may be raised in a season, but the Song Sparrow generally is single- or double-brooded in Ontario. Although the male sings persistently, this is little help in finding the nest. Females will sometimes give a rodent-run distraction display, and both parents scold intruders. Both parents feed the young, providing many opportunities for atlassers to witness them carrying food or feeding fledged young. The Song Sparrow is often parasitized by the Brown-headed Cowbird in southern Ontario, where their ranges overlap.

The species is generally monogamous, but in Ohio and British Columbia, a small percentage of males are polygynous. Birds in juvenal plumage closely resemble juvenile Lincoln's and Swamp Sparrows, although the Song Sparrow is larger, with a larger bill. These differences can be determined by sight if the bird is well seen. The Song Sparrow undergoes a partial first prebasic moult before migrating, and thus observations of juvenal-plumaged individuals probably involve birds fledged locally (Rising 1996).

Although many Regional Coordinators noted that breeding was not confirmed in many squares in which it likely bred, it is generally thought that the atlas data accurately represented the breeding distribution.

Abundance: The relative abundance maps show the Song Sparrow is commonest south of the Shield, though there are small pockets of lower abundance in urban Toronto and parts of Essex Co. and Chatham-Kent, where there is presumably less suitable habitat. Generally, relative abundance declines northward across the Southern Shield, and the species is relatively thinly spread across the Northern Shield and Hudson Bay Lowlands. However, it is locally common along the Rainy River in western Rainy River District. On the Shield and in the Hudson Bay Lowlands, it is most commonly found in brush along lakes and rivers, and so may not be fully represented on the abundance map, which is based primarily on roadside point counts in areas with roads; where there are no roads, points were generally located away from river and lake edges. Based on atlas point count data, the Ontario population is estimated to be 3,000,000 birds, with 60% of the population south of the Shield. – *J.D. Rising*

Lincoln's Sparrow

Bruant de Lincoln

Melospiza lincolnii

David Welbourne

The Lincoln's Sparrow is one of the most poorly studied birds in North America. It breeds in sub-boreal, boreal, and subarctic regions of North America from central Alaska east to Newfoundland, and winters primarily in Mexico. Throughout its breeding range, it prefers peatland and shrub wetland habitats, occurring also in upland alder, birch, and willow thickets farther north. As an early successional habitat specialist, it may benefit from large-scale natural and anthropogenic disturbances such as fire, blowdowns, and forest management prescriptions (e.g., clearcutting) that create large gaps and early successional habitats (Ammon 1995).

Distribution and population status: The Lincoln's Sparrow is widely distributed throughout the Hudson Bay Lowlands and the Northern and Southern Shield regions, with breeding evidence recorded as far north as the Black Duck River (56° N). Atlas results suggest a significant 46% increase in the probability of observation of the species for the province as a whole. Increases in the Hudson Bay Lowlands and Lake Simcoe-Rideau regions were greatest (60%), followed by the Southern Shield (51%) and Northern Shield (37%). In the three northernmost regions, the species was recorded in more than 21 100-km blocks in which it was not recorded in the first atlas. The increase in the Lake Simcoe-Rideau region is particularly striking, given the relative lack of preferred peatland habitat, and there is some evidence of use of early successional upland and wet thicket habitats. The species remains exceedingly rare in the Carolinian region, although a small population has persisted for decades in the Wainfleet Bog near Port Colborne.

Regional Coordinators indicate that the increase in the number of squares where the Lincoln's Sparrow was detected is real but may partly reflect increased song recognition on the

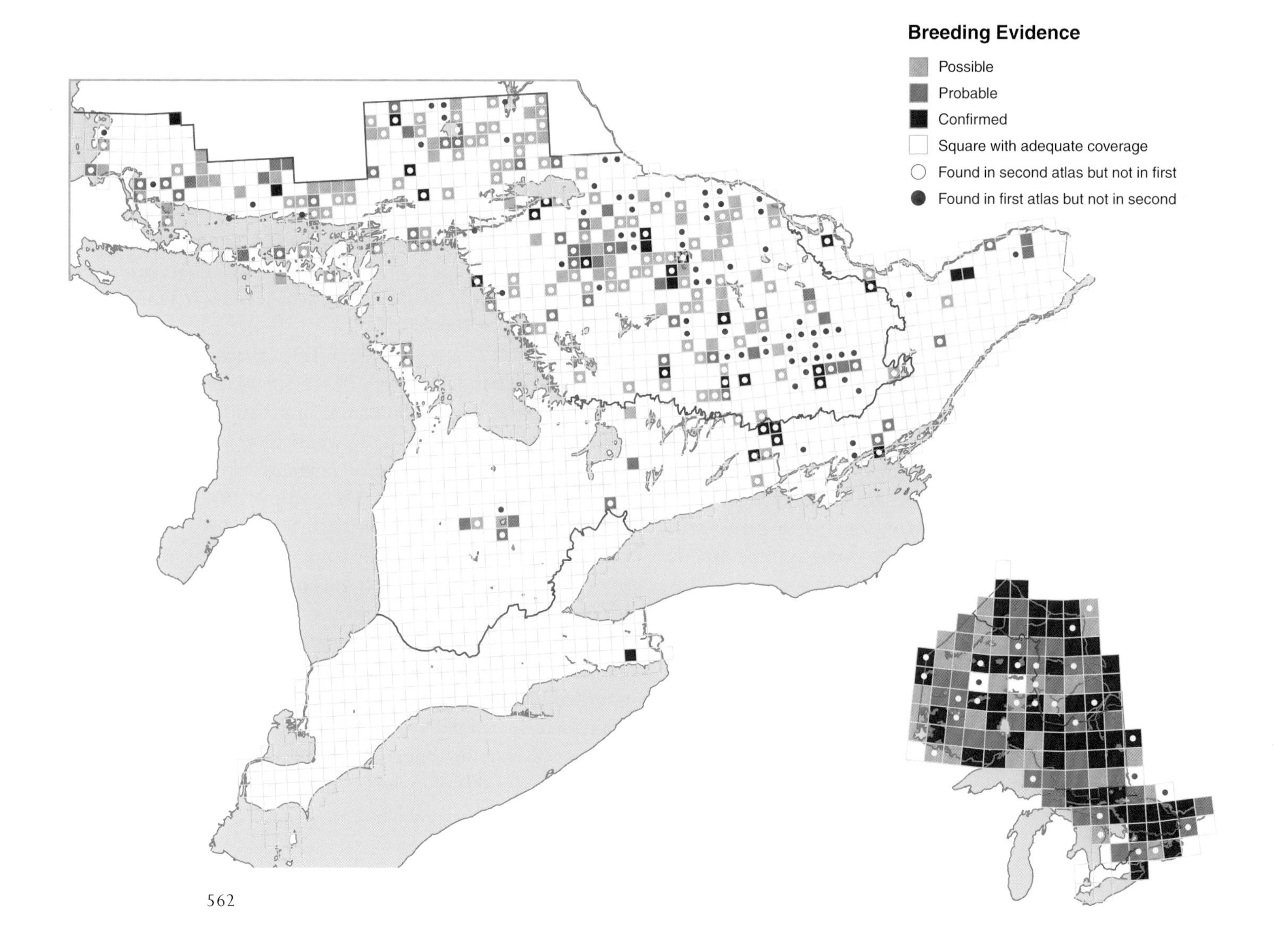

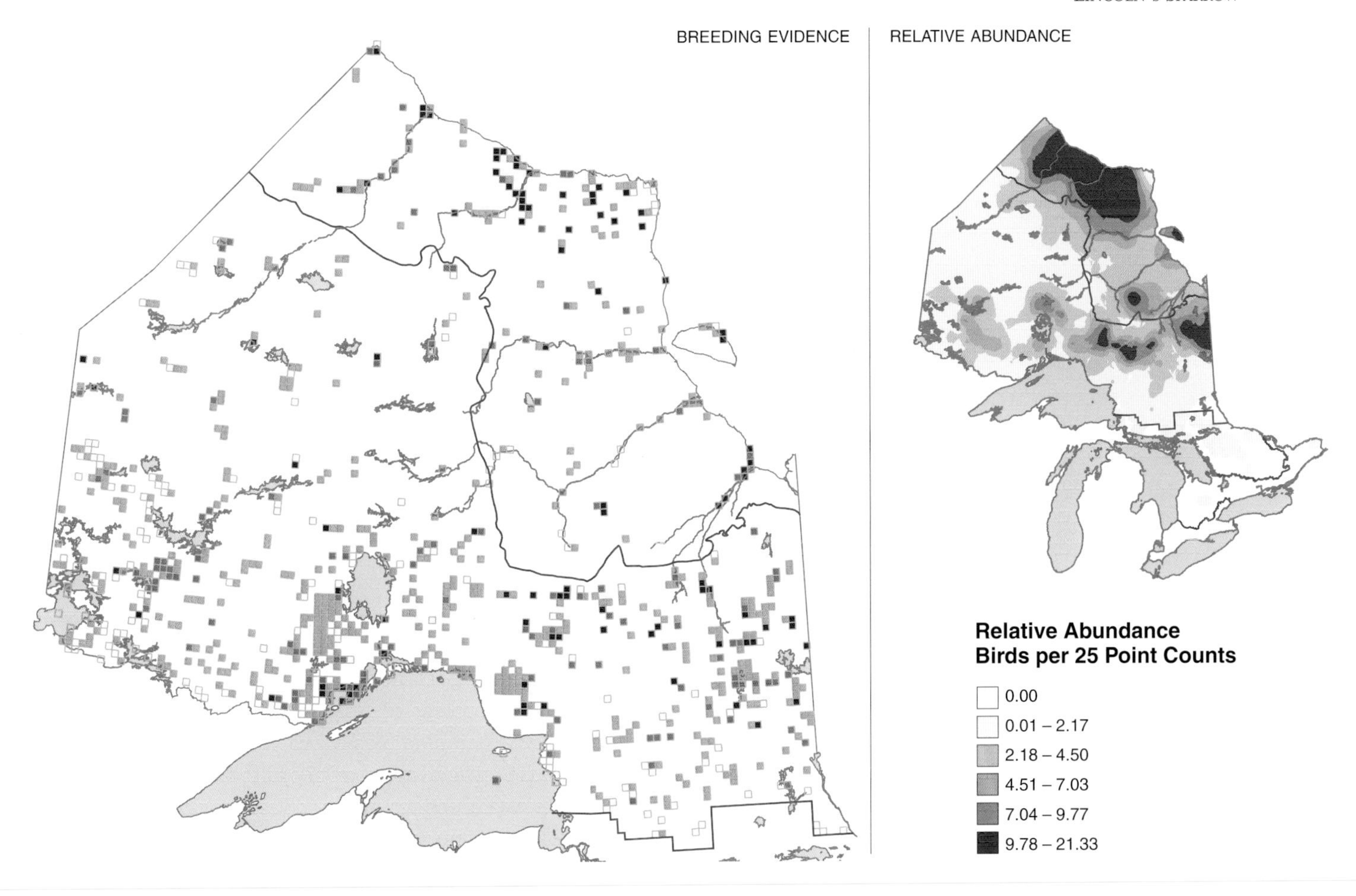

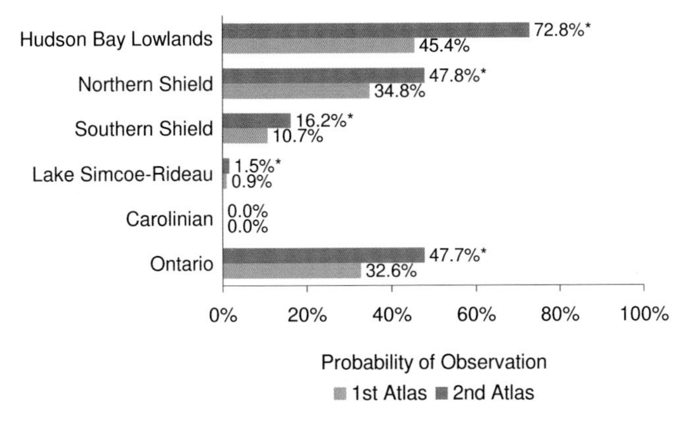

part of field surveyors. This bird can be difficult to observe even for skilled atlassers during the breeding season because, when approached, males may stop singing and skulk away. However, they can often be heard across long distances. In the Southern and Northern Shield regions, the increases may be attributable in part to an increase in the proportion of regenerating forests, resulting in suitable breeding habitat. BBS data show no significant change for the species in Ontario; however, this is likely because much of its range is outside the BBS coverage area. Data from CMMN stations in eastern Canada likewise show no significant population trends. It is therefore difficult to speculate on the cause of the observed increase of the species in atlas data, or even on whether the influencing factor is on the breeding or wintering grounds.

Breeding biology: Because of the Lincoln's Sparrow's elusive nature, relatively little is known about its breeding biology. It is a ground-nester whose nest is usually well concealed with a distinct entrance tunnel through ground vegetation (Ammon 1995). In Ontario, the nest is usually placed in moss or grass/sedge hummocks or at the base of a small tree or shrub (Peck and James 1987); hence, few were found by atlassers. In fact, confirmed breeding evidence was found in only 13% of the squares in which this species was detected. It is usually single-brooded and typically lays a clutch of three to five eggs, with a modal clutch size of four eggs (Peck and James 1987). Incubation is by the female alone, and nest defence behaviour may be subdued, further reducing the probability of locating nests. The male does assist with feeding the young during the nestling and fledgling stages, so it may be possible for a skilled observer to find a nest with young.

Abundance: The relative abundance map indicates that the Lincoln's Sparrow is virtually absent south of Georgian Bay, where suitable habitat is uncommon. It is undoubtedly more common than previously thought and, locally, in many younger clearcuts in the Boreal Forest of Ontario, is amongst the commonest bird species detected (J.R. Zimmerling unpubl. data). In Ontario, its density is highest throughout the Hudson Bay Lowlands, especially in a band from Fort Severn almost to James Bay, where treed bogs and fens dominated by willow, sedge, or moss are abundant. Farther south, in the Northern Shield region, it is particularly common from Red Lake east to Iroquois Falls and south to the northernmost shore of Lake Superior, where forest management activities and, to a lesser extent, wildfires have created young, regenerating forests with the dense shrubs on which this species depends.
– J. Ryan Zimmerling

Swamp Sparrow

Bruant des marais

Melospiza georgiana

Eleanor Kee Wellman

The Swamp Sparrow is the only sparrow that is likely to be encountered as a breeding bird in large cattail marshes in Ontario. It also breeds in a wide variety of wetlands, including sedge marshes, wet sedge fens, shrub thicket swamps, and marshy shorelines. On the Shield, it is often found in leatherleaf-sedge peatlands. It is widespread in eastern North America, breeding from central Northwest Territories and eastern British Columbia east across Canada to Newfoundland, and south in the US to Iowa and the mid-Atlantic states.

Distribution and population status: Post-European settlement, there was extensive draining of marshes south of the Canadian Shield, doubtless decreasing the amount of habitat available for this species; however, most of that habitat loss probably occurred before the 1970s (i.e., before the first atlas). The Swamp Sparrow is frequently found in small wetlands created where roads disturb natural drainage patterns, as well as in sewage lagoons supporting emergent vegetation, so some human activities may benefit the species. It is among the more widespread birds in Ontario, with breeding evidence reported during the second atlas in all but two of the 135 100-km blocks.

Compared to the first atlas, there was a significant 17% increase in the probability of observation of the Swamp Sparrow in the province as a whole. This increase was largely due to a significant increase of 21% in both the Northern Shield and Hudson Bay Lowlands regions and a significant increase of 6% in the Southern Shield. There was a non-significant increase in the Lake Simcoe-Rideau region and a non-significant decrease in the Carolinian region. Probable or confirmed breeding was recorded in most of the squares in southern Ontario, except in the extreme southwest where there is intense agricultural activity and wetlands are much reduced. BBS data show a significant 1.6% annual increase in the species in Ontario from 1981 to 2005. Reasons for the increases are not clear.

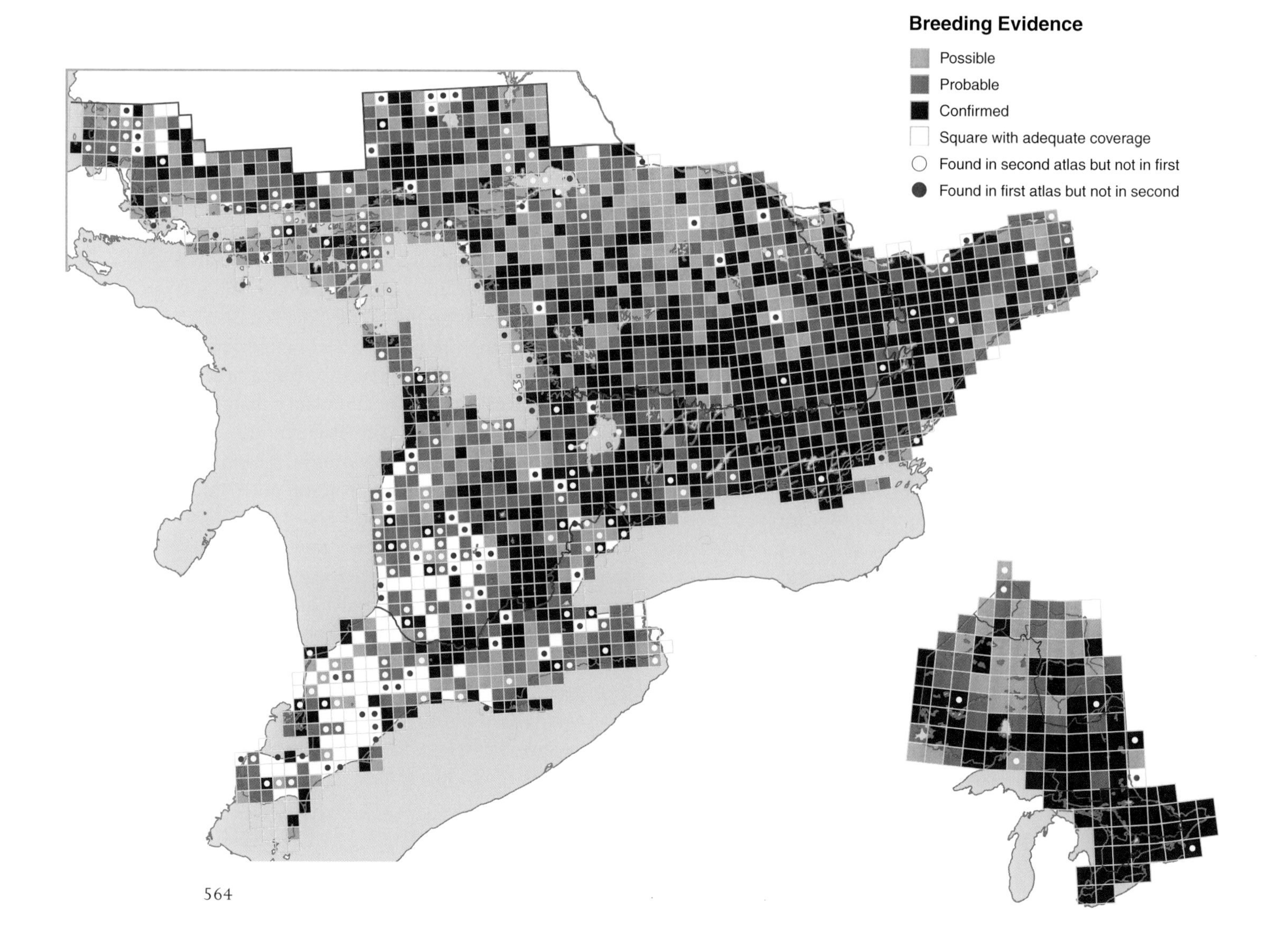

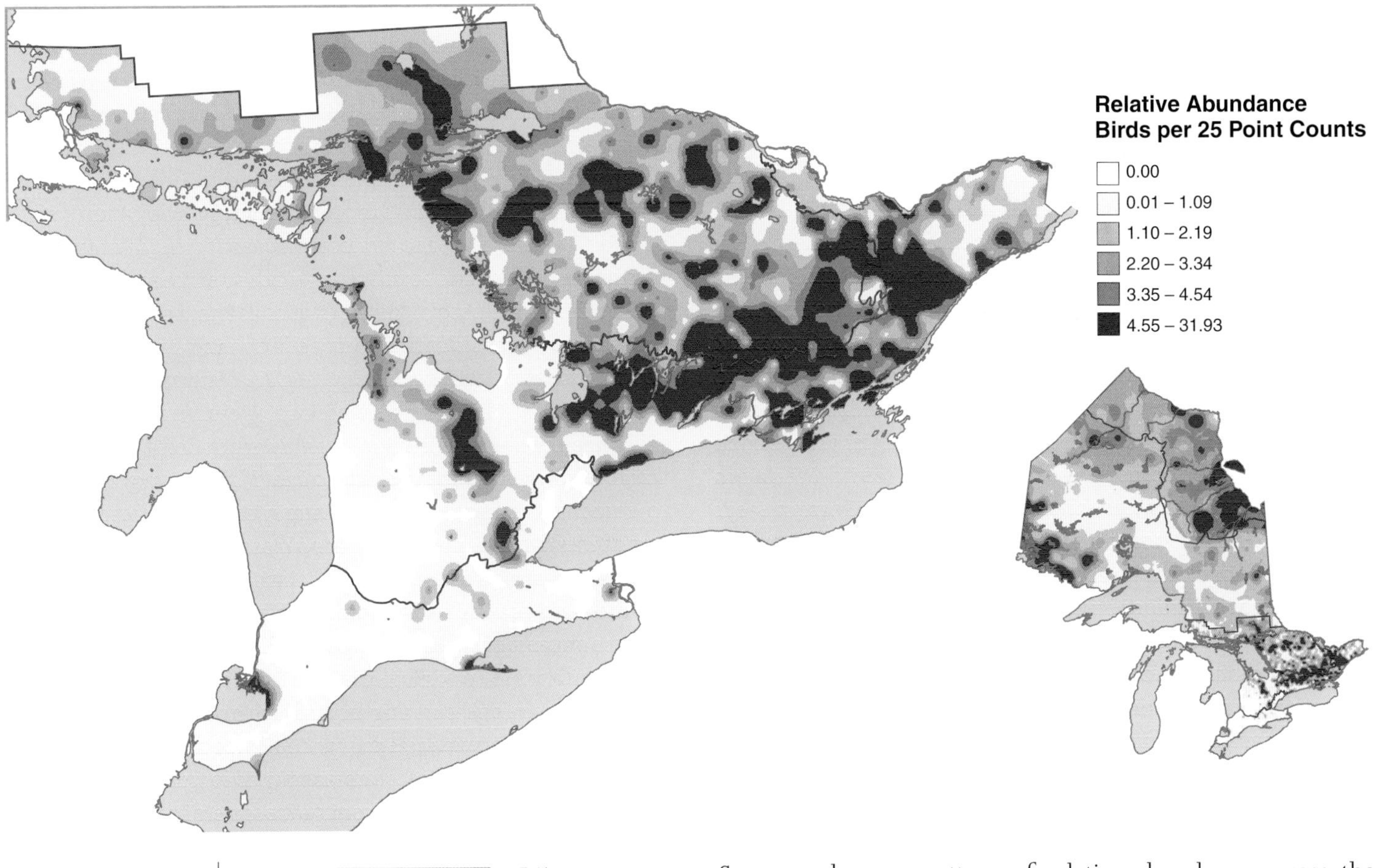

	2nd Atlas	1st Atlas
Hudson Bay Lowlands	69.7%*	57.7%
Northern Shield	75.3%*	62.4%
Southern Shield	92.3%*	87.3%
Lake Simcoe-Rideau	75.2%	72.7%
Carolinian	41.0%	43.5%
Ontario	74.2%*	63.3%

0% 20% 40% 60% 80% 100%

Probability of Observation

1st Atlas 2nd Atlas

Breeding biology: The Swamp Sparrow sings frequently, often from an exposed perch, and consequently evidence of possible or probable breeding is easily established. Nests, however, are hard to find, as they are well concealed in dense vegetation, often just above the water, in marsh habitats that are often difficult to access. The female builds the nest and incubates. When the nest is approached, she quietly slips away, making nest detection even more difficult. The species is parasitized by cowbirds. Nesting takes place from late April through late July, giving atlassers a long season to confirm breeding; sometimes the Swamp Sparrow is double brooded (more commonly so south of Ontario). Some males are polygynous, but both parents feed the young. The adults respond readily to "pishing" (Rising 1996), making it fairly easy to confirm breeding through adults carrying food. Most Regional Coordinators thought that the maps represented the distribution of the species well, but that the species likely bred in all squares in which it was reported.

Abundance: The relative abundance map for the Swamp Sparrow shows a pattern of relative abundance across the province similar in some respects to that of the Wilson's Snipe, probably reflecting the occurrence of suitable wetland habitat. The highest densities for the Swamp Sparrow, above about 4.6 birds/25 point counts, occurred in several areas: the extensive wetlands of the southern and eastern portions of the Hudson Bay Lowlands, including Akimiski Island; in Rainy River and southwestern Kenora Districts and along the Manitoba border near Red Lake, which is perhaps reflective of the influence of prairie-like wetlands in this region; in southeastern Ontario and along the southern edge of the Canadian Shield, where several other wetland species, such as the Marsh Wren, Black Tern, Least Bittern, and Wilson's Snipe are also most abundant; and in the central Southern Shield (Algonquin Prov. Park), though why this area should have high density is unclear. The species is least common in southwestern Ontario, doubtless due to the intensity of agriculture in that region. There is an area of relatively high abundance in the Dundalk uplands and to a lesser extent along the length of the Niagara Escarpment north of about Hamilton, presumably due to the relatively large amount of wetland in those areas. Based on atlas point counts, the Ontario population is estimated to be 2,000,000 birds, with 38% of the population in the Hudson Bay Lowlands and only 16% in the three southern regions combined. – *J.D. Rising*

White-throated Sparrow

Bruant à gorge blanche

Zonotrichia albicollis

David Welbourne

The "*Oh sweet Canada, Canada, Canada*" song of the White-throated Sparrow is one of the quintessential sounds of Ontario's cottage country. The main breeding range of the species occurs east of the Rockies, where it is found from the treeline south to the prairies and east to Newfoundland. The southern edge of its breeding range extends to the southern limit of coniferous and mixed forests in the Great Lakes states and at higher elevations in the Appalachians. It winters primarily in the southeastern US, with a few birds wintering as far north as southern Canada (Falls and Kopachena 1994).

Distribution and population status: The White-throated Sparrow breeds throughout Ontario, although in the Carolinian region, where it was reported in only 33 squares, its distribution is restricted to a few locations with appropriate habitat. The species occurred in the majority of squares in the Lake Simcoe-Rideau, Southern Shield, and Northern Shield regions, with the probability of observation peaking at approximately 98% in both the Southern and Northern Shield regions. Except for the extreme northern tip of the province and the 100-km block including Cape Henrietta Maria, where no suitable habitat occurs, the White-throated Sparrow was also found throughout the Hudson Bay Lowlands region.

There was no significant change between atlases in the probability of observation of the White-throated Sparrow in the province as a whole, but there was a significant decline of 9% in the Lake Simcoe-Rideau region. While this decline has no obvious explanation, loss of early successional habitat due to intensification of agricultural practices, maturation of early successional forests and edges, and urbanization may all play roles in different parts of the region. Neither the BBS (Downes et al. 2005) nor migration monitoring (Crewe 2006) shows a decline in the species in recent years.

Breeding biology: Field guides published before the early 1970s showed the female White-throated Sparrow with a tan-

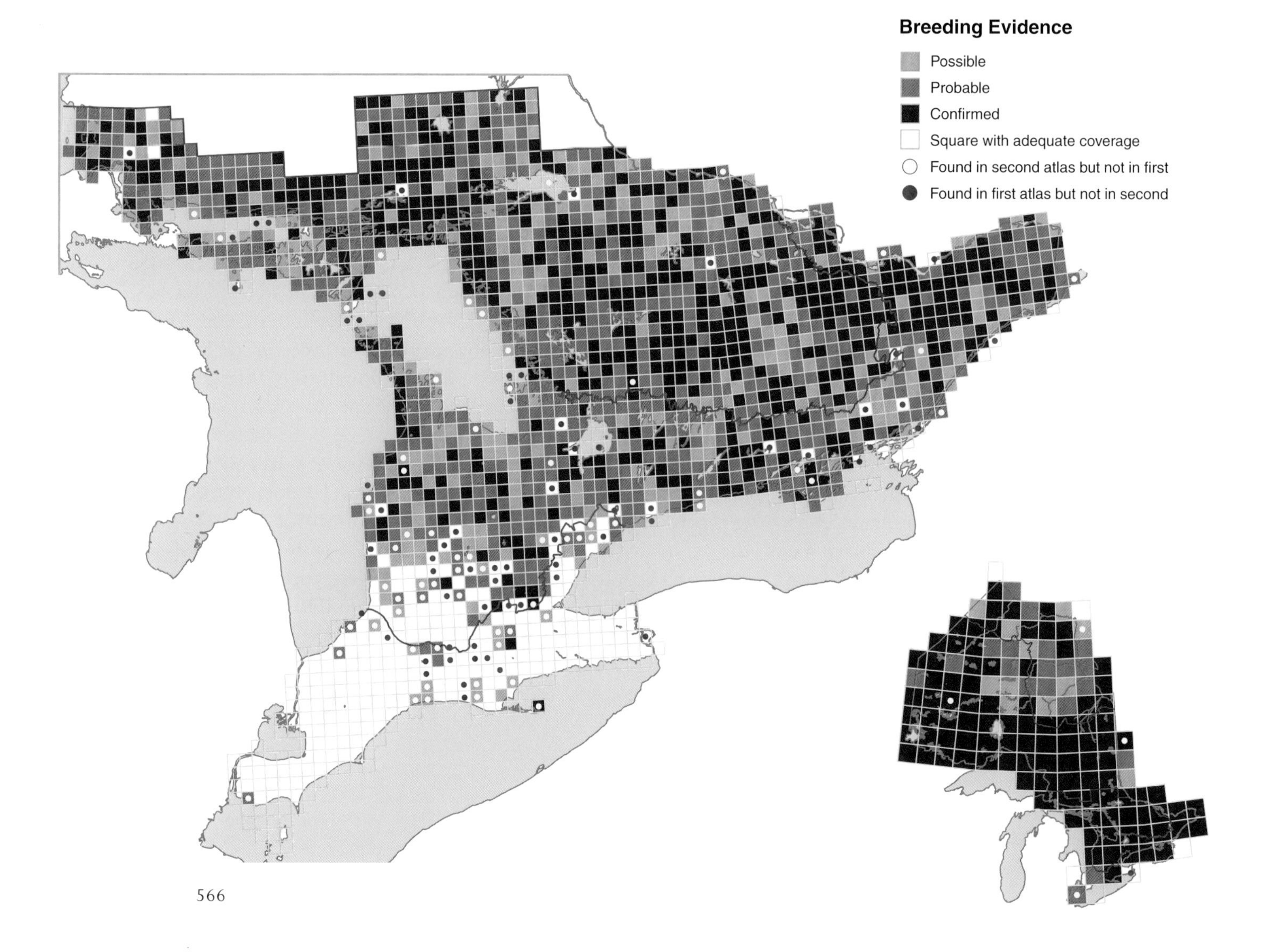

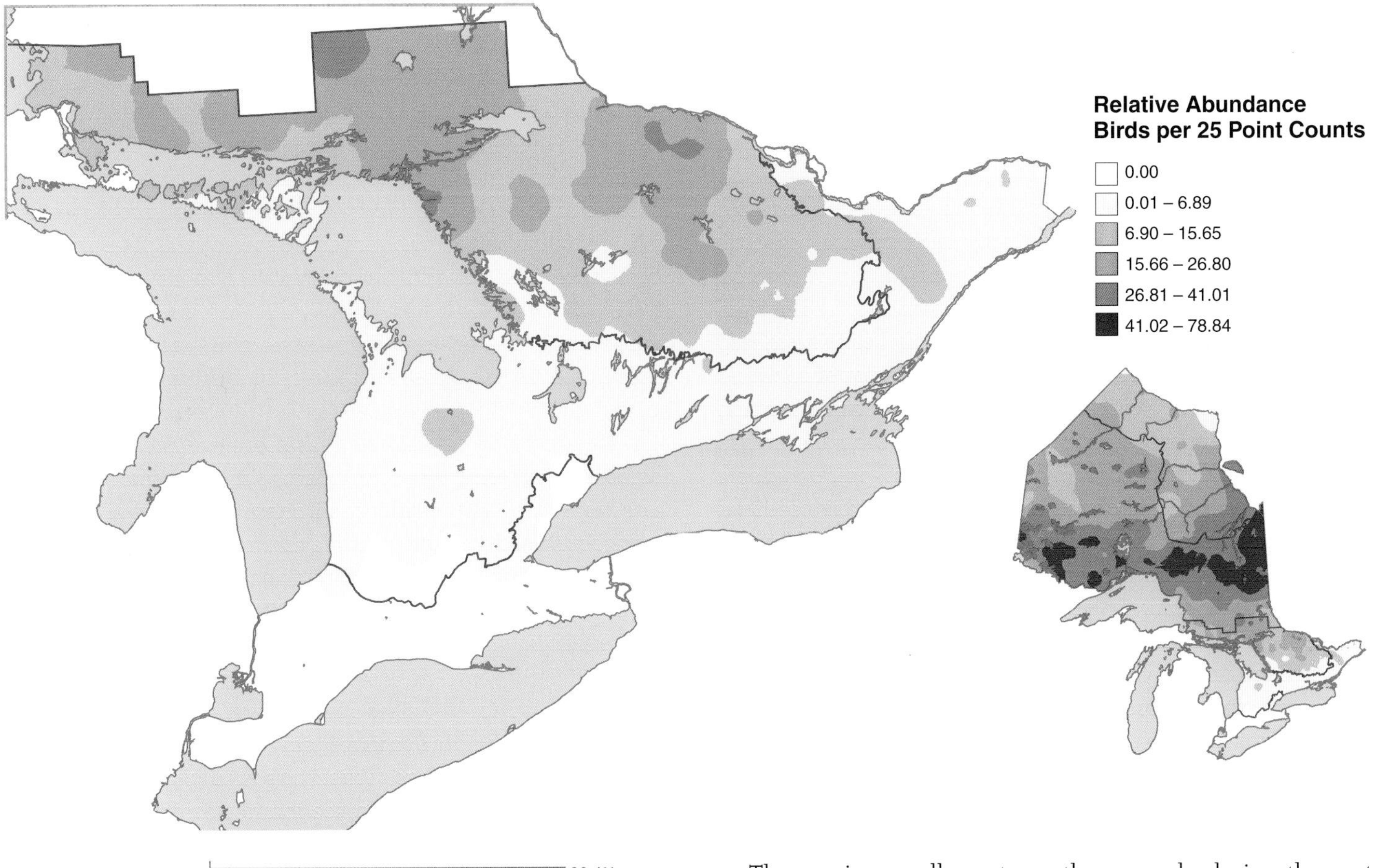

Region	2nd Atlas	1st Atlas
Hudson Bay Lowlands	90.4%	85.4%
Northern Shield	98.2%	98.3%
Southern Shield	97.6%	98.2%
Lake Simcoe-Rideau	69.4%*	75.8%
Carolinian	5.8%	7.3%
Ontario	91.9%	91.1%

0% 20% 40% 60% 80% 100%

Probability of Observation

1st Atlas ■ 2nd Atlas

striped head, and the male with a white-striped head. Subsequently, work done mainly in Algonquin Prov. Park showed that birds of either sex could have either head-stripe colour and that almost inevitably, mated pairs would be one bird of each colour morph. White-striped males sing more often than the more cryptic tan-striped males, which are often overlooked. This is one of the few passerine species in which females may sing as much as males. Tan-striped females rarely sing, but females of the white-striped morph sing as much as tan-striped males (Falls and Kopachena 1994).

Breeding habitat for this sparrow consists of openings and edges in coniferous and mixed forests. Areas of second growth after logging, fires, or insect damage, and edges of beaver ponds, beaver meadows, and open bogs, especially in spruce, Balsam Fir, and Jack Pine forests, are all used. In Algonquin Prov. Park, a mixture of coniferous trees and openings with a dense ground cover of blueberry is used extensively. The White-throated Sparrow is usually common in the early years of forest succession, but it declines in numbers as the forest becomes dense.

The species usually nests on the ground, placing the nest under low vegetation such as dead bracken or a blueberry bush. The female alone incubates the eggs, but both parents actively feed the young once they are hatched. Adults are quite obvious as they carry insects to the young, both in the nest and after fledging. Breeding was confirmed in 27% of the squares where this sparrow was found. The only atlas administrative regions without confirmed breeding were Toronto and those in the extreme southwest.

Abundance: The White-throated Sparrow is a species that benefits immensely from the creation of early successional habitats. Both wildfires and clearcut logging, which provide forest openings and edges, help maintain a supply of preferred breeding habitat. Areas of high abundance (over 41 birds/25 point counts) occur across the Boreal Forest, particularly between 47° N and 51° N, and largely mirror the area where commercial logging occurs. Forest regrowth following fire would have provided habitat prior to the advent of logging and still does throughout the north. It is likely that the areas north of commercial logging with very high abundance have experienced recent fires.

Despite its iconic status as a symbol of the wilderness in central Ontario, the White-throated Sparrow is not nearly as abundant there as it is farther north. In central Ontario, forest cover is extensive and lakeshores, beaver ponds, and artificial openings provide the majority of appropriate habitat. – *Margaret A. McLaren*

Harris's Sparrow

Bruant à face noire

Zonotrichia querula

John Reaume

Harris's Sparrow is North America's largest sparrow (Sibley 2000) and the only passerine to breed endemically in Canada (Norment and Shackleton 1993). It is listed by Partners in Flight as being of Continental Importance and is on its Watch List of widespread and common species that may be "declining and/or threatened throughout their ranges" (Rich et al. 2004). It was listed primarily because it is not well monitored, with few data available to document trends. Its vulnerability is thought to be primarily within its small wintering range, which is mostly in the southern Great Plains.

The Harris's Sparrow breeds in the transition zone between the subarctic taiga and the low arctic tundra of northern Canada. Its breeding habitat consists of patches of stunted coniferous trees with a dense shrub understorey of birch, willow, and alder.

Distribution and population status: The species' breeding range extends from the Arctic Ocean through mainland Nunavut and eastern and northern Northwest Territories, south to northern Manitoba and the Hudson Bay coast of extreme northwest Ontario. Records from the second Ontario atlas as far east as the mouth of the Brant River suggest that breeding may occur more widely than previously suspected.

The only confirmed breeding record in Ontario is from Fort Severn in 1983 during the first atlas, where the species was also reported in 1940 (James et al. 1976). The nest was in a patch of shrubby willows and stunted spruces in a predominantly open area near the town's airport.

The breeding status of Harris's Sparrow in Ontario has not changed since the first atlas. Although poorly known, it is a rare breeding bird in the province. During the second atlas, possible breeding evidence was reported from four different squares; however, there were no records of probable or confirmed breeding. In 2001, two birds were observed in suitable breeding habitat on 23 May at the OMNR's Burntpoint camp,

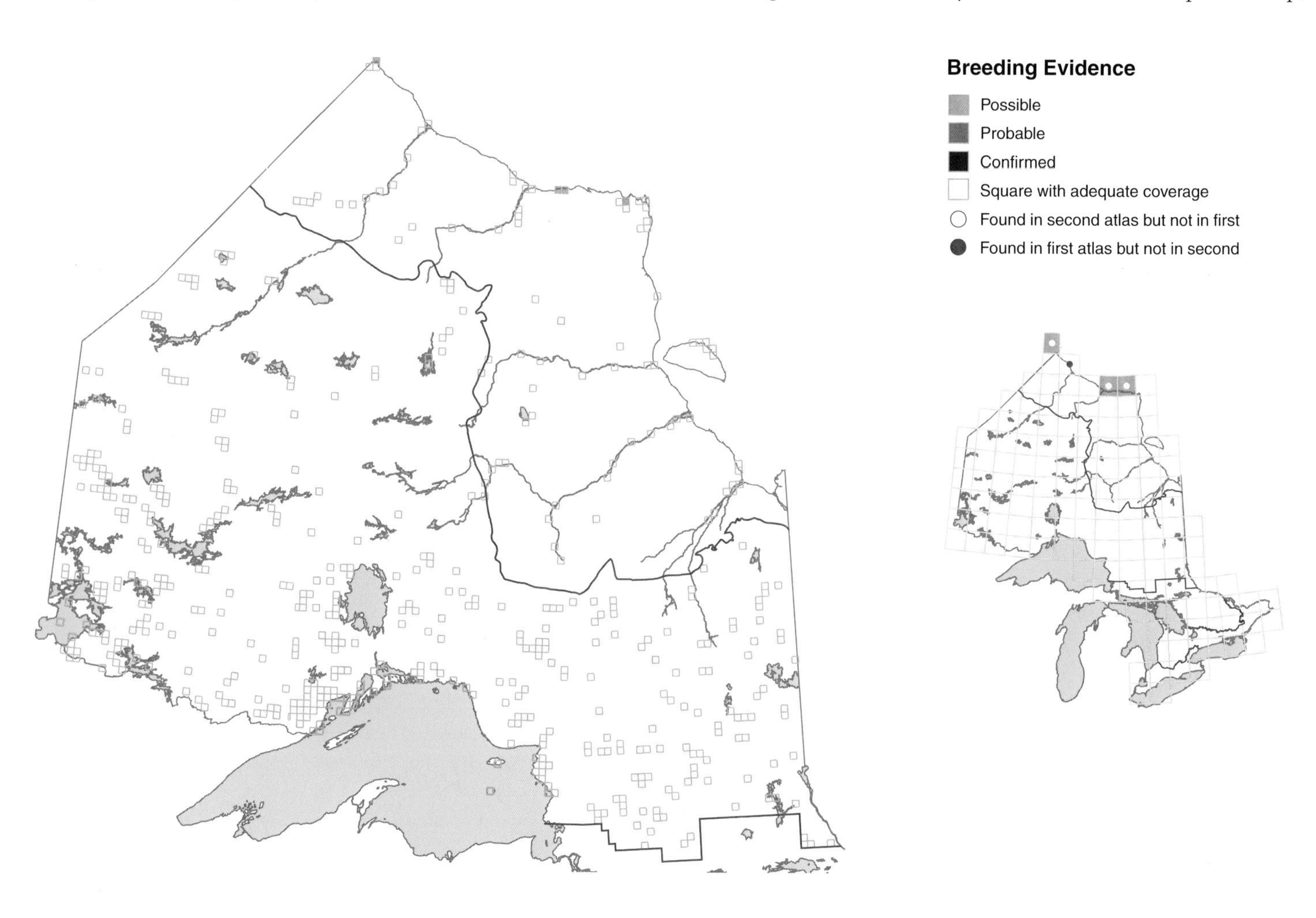

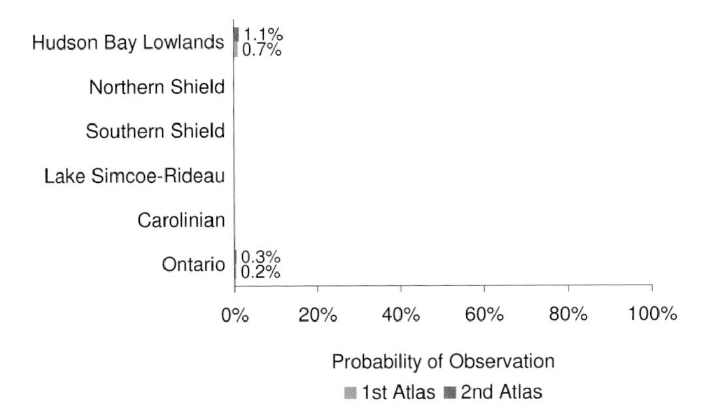

about 120 km west of Cape Henrietta Maria. Two birds were found at the same location on 25 May, and one bird was found on 26 May, but no more birds were observed at this location, even though atlassers were present for at least three subsequent weeks. The species was also not observed in over three weeks at the camp in the 2002 breeding season. A single bird was reported there on 9 June 2003. Interestingly, a single bird was recorded on 9 June 2005 in the square immediately to the west but was also not seen again on subsequent visits.

There were two records for the species in 2004. On 2 July, a single bird was found on the Hudson Bay coast near the Manitoba border. It was observed in willows surrounding a small pond on a dry tundra ridge for approximately 45 minutes, during which time it fed almost continuously and did not sing. A singing bird was discovered near the mouth of the Brant River on 16 and 17 June 2004 in relatively dense willow thickets along the shore of a tundra lake.

Breeding biology: The Harris's Sparrow is a large sparrow with a distinctive though not particularly loud song, so it is fairly conspicuous in its open breeding habitat and is therefore likely well represented in well-covered squares within its narrow Ontario range. However, the period of most intense singing is in the four weeks following arrival on the breeding territory (late May), and singing declines rapidly after hatching (Norment and Shackleton 1993). Thus the peak period of song may not have coincided with some atlas trips. At low densities, it may be overlooked during less extensive atlas surveys. Given that only a small fraction of the squares in the species' range were well covered during both atlases, it is feasible that the species is more widespread than it appears on the map. Because it breeds in such remote areas, it was one of the last passerines in North America to have its nest and eggs described. That nest was found on 16 June 1931 at Churchill, Manitoba (Semple and Sutton 1932).

Abundance: The global population of Harris's Sparrow is estimated at approximately 3,700,000 birds (Rich et al. 2004). As the records described above are all that were reported to the atlas, despite hundreds of hours of fieldwork in potentially suitable breeding habitat, it is apparent that Ontario contains a very small portion of the species' overall population. It may be that the species does not nest in the province every year. – *Michael D. Cadman*

The Harris's Sparrow always nests on the ground, usually beneath low shrubs in moss, lichen, or grass substrates. Churchill, Manitoba, 22 June 1971. *Photo: George K. Peck*

Breeding habitat of the Harris's Sparrow contains abundant shrubs in and near conifer forests, such as this site in Wapusk Nat. Park, Manitoba, with Tamarack and Labrador Tea. *Photo: Rocky Rockwell*

White-crowned Sparrow

Bruant à couronne blanche

Zonotrichia leucophrys

Mark Peck

The White-crowned Sparrow is a large, sleek, handsome sparrow, which is easily observed because it usually stays in the open. It breeds from northern Alaska east across the northern mainland of Canada to northern Newfoundland, and in western North America south to California and New Mexico (Godfrey 1986). It is more common in western North America than in the east, but nonetheless it is a locally common breeder in northern Ontario, mainly near the treeline adjacent to Hudson Bay. Most people see it in Ontario only during migration. The White-crowned Sparrow is divided into several subspecies of differing biology. Those that breed in the north and the western mountains are migratory, whereas those breeding along the Pacific Coast are sedentary. Most research has been done on west coast populations, but information in this account is based primarily on observations in northern Ontario.

Distribution and population status: The White-crowned Sparrow is virtually restricted to the Hudson Bay Lowlands as a breeder, where it is locally common in open areas with dwarf trees, usually spruce, Tamarack, birch, or willow. It is most common near Hudson Bay, becoming less numerous inland and along James Bay. Most squares in which it was found were within 100 km of the Hudson Bay coast, in the area of Polar Bear Prov. Park. This area received more coverage than others due to the presence of regular OMNR and CWS crews. The species was recorded rarely south to the Moose River southwest of Moosonee and inland in the west to Weagamow Lake about 450 km from Hudson Bay.

During the second atlas, breeding evidence was recorded in 123 squares in the Hudson Bay Lowlands compared to 61 squares in the first atlas; there was also a significant increase of 56% in the probability of observation in that region, and a 50% increase in the province as a whole, based largely on the Hudson Bay Lowlands data. Some of the increase is probably due to differences in coverage by atlassers, as there has been lit-

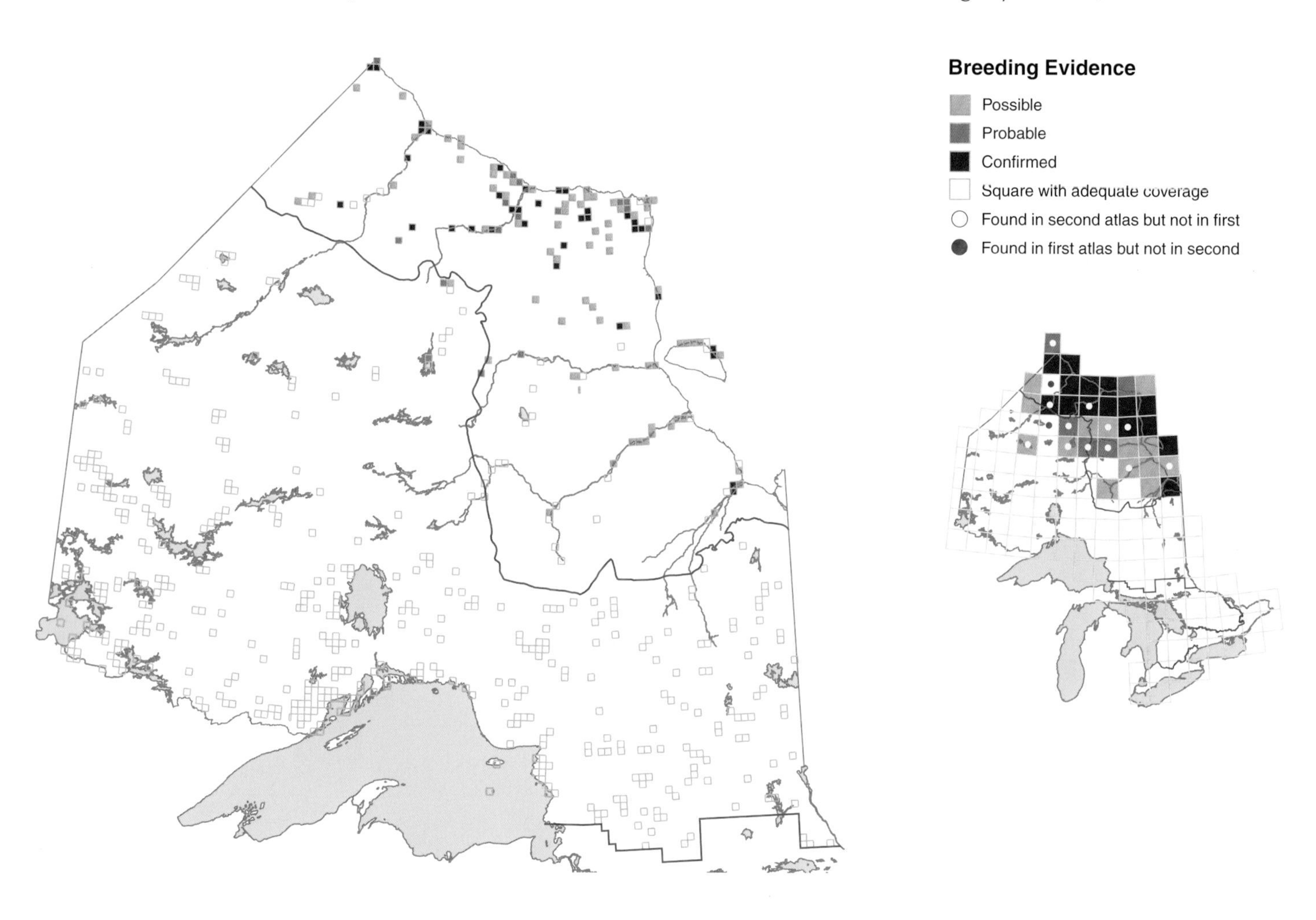

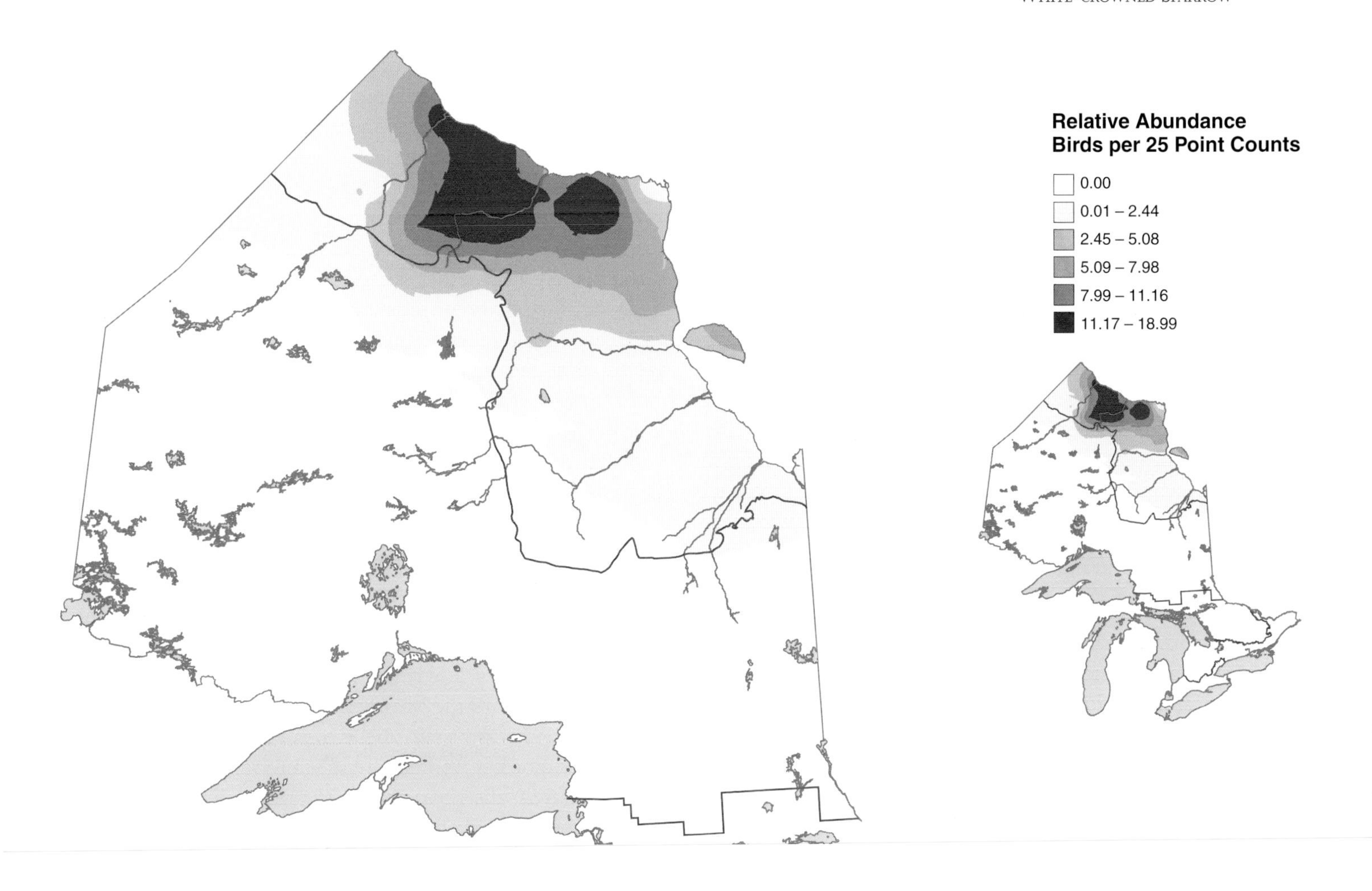

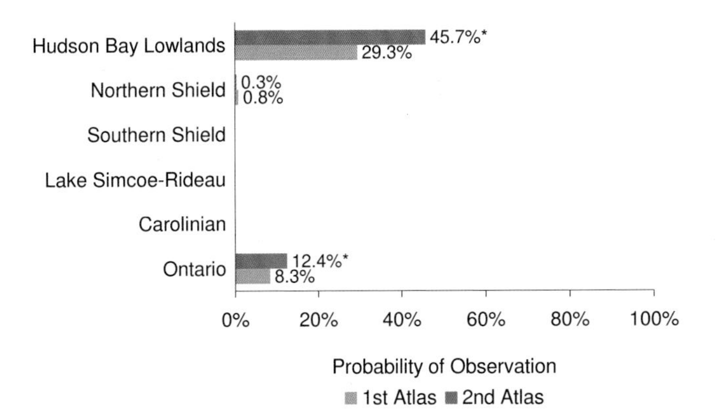

tle change in the breeding habitat since the first atlas, but other factors may be involved. The species is rare in the Northern Shield region, where breeding evidence in the second atlas was reported from just four squares.

BBS data provide no trend estimates for eastern North America because the White-crowned Sparrow breeds north of the survey coverage. However, CMMN data from LPBO show a highly significant increase in the number of migrants (Crewe 2006). Reasons for the increase are not clear. CBC data from Ontario, New York State, and Ohio also indicate an increasing trend over the last 25 years, although this may reflect changes on the wintering grounds or a tendency of the species to winter farther north.

Breeding biology: The White-crowned Sparrow sings persistently during the day and intermittently through the night (Rising 1996), so territories are easily located. When excited, as it often is near the nest, it erects its crown feathers. It nests in June and July in open areas with scattered small trees. The nest is almost always placed on the ground, often at the base of a small willow, spruce, or Tamarack, under Labrador Tea, or rarely, up to 3 m high in shrubs. Well concealed and generally difficult to locate, the nest is a bulky cup of coarse grass, twigs, bark shreds, moss, and lichens. Females run mouse-like and inconspicuously when leaving the nest. Breeding is more easily confirmed through the observation of adults carrying food or with fledged young. Family groups stay together for at least 35 days after fledging (Chilton et al. 1995). The young moult on the breeding grounds before fall migration, so observations of heavily streaked juveniles almost certainly indicate locally raised birds. Breeding was confirmed in 28% of the squares reporting this species, with singing and territorial males comprising most other observations.

Abundance: The White-crowned Sparrow is a relatively common breeder in appropriate habitat close to the Hudson Bay coast. Highest densities are in the northern Hudson Bay Lowlands from Fort Severn east into Polar Bear Prov. Park and inland from Peawanuck along the Winisk and Fawn Rivers, where over 11.2 birds/25 point counts were recorded. Abundance decreases farther inland and in the southern portion of the Hudson Bay Lowlands. The species is uncommon along the west coast of James Bay and a rare breeder in the Northern Shield region. Atlas data may underestimate the breeding abundance in Ontario due to the inaccessibility of much of the species' range. – *J.D. Rising*

Dark-eyed Junco

Junco ardoisé

Junco hyemalis

George K. Peck

As a bird that is primarily grey and white, the Dark-eyed Junco is one of the most distinctive of the sparrows. It is also one of the few sparrows that is sexually dimorphic in coloration, although the differences between the sexes are less striking than in some other dimorphic sparrow species (e.g., longspurs or towhees). The Dark-eyed Junco is a complex of well-marked populations that are at present recognized as separate subspecies but in future may be accepted as different species (Rising 1996). The junco that occurs in Ontario and throughout the east is known as the Slate-colored Junco and is so called in many older books. Not surprisingly for such a widespread and variable species, aspects of its biology vary geographically. In Ontario, it usually breeds in fairly open coniferous or mixed woodlands, although it can be found also in mature hardwood forests with dense ground cover (Nolan et al. 2002).

Distribution and population status: Both atlases show that the Dark-eyed Junco is found across Ontario in most 100-km blocks and squares in the Southern Shield, Northern Shield, and Hudson Bay Lowlands regions. It is uncommon and local as a breeding bird south of the Shield. During this atlas, the probability of observation was 45% in the Southern Shield, 69% in the Northern Shield, and 84% in the Hudson Bay Lowlands. BBS data show that the species has declined significantly both across Canada and in Ontario since 1981, with atlas data showing a significant decrease of 15% in the Southern Shield. However, the probability of observation increased significantly by 24% in the Northern Shield and 20% in the Hudson Bay Lowlands, resulting in a significant 20% increase province-wide. BBS coverage in northern Ontario is not extensive, and much of the area where junco breeding density is highest is well north of the BBS routes, which might help explain the discrepancy between the atlas and BBS results.

In Algonquin Park, the Regional Coordinator noted that the

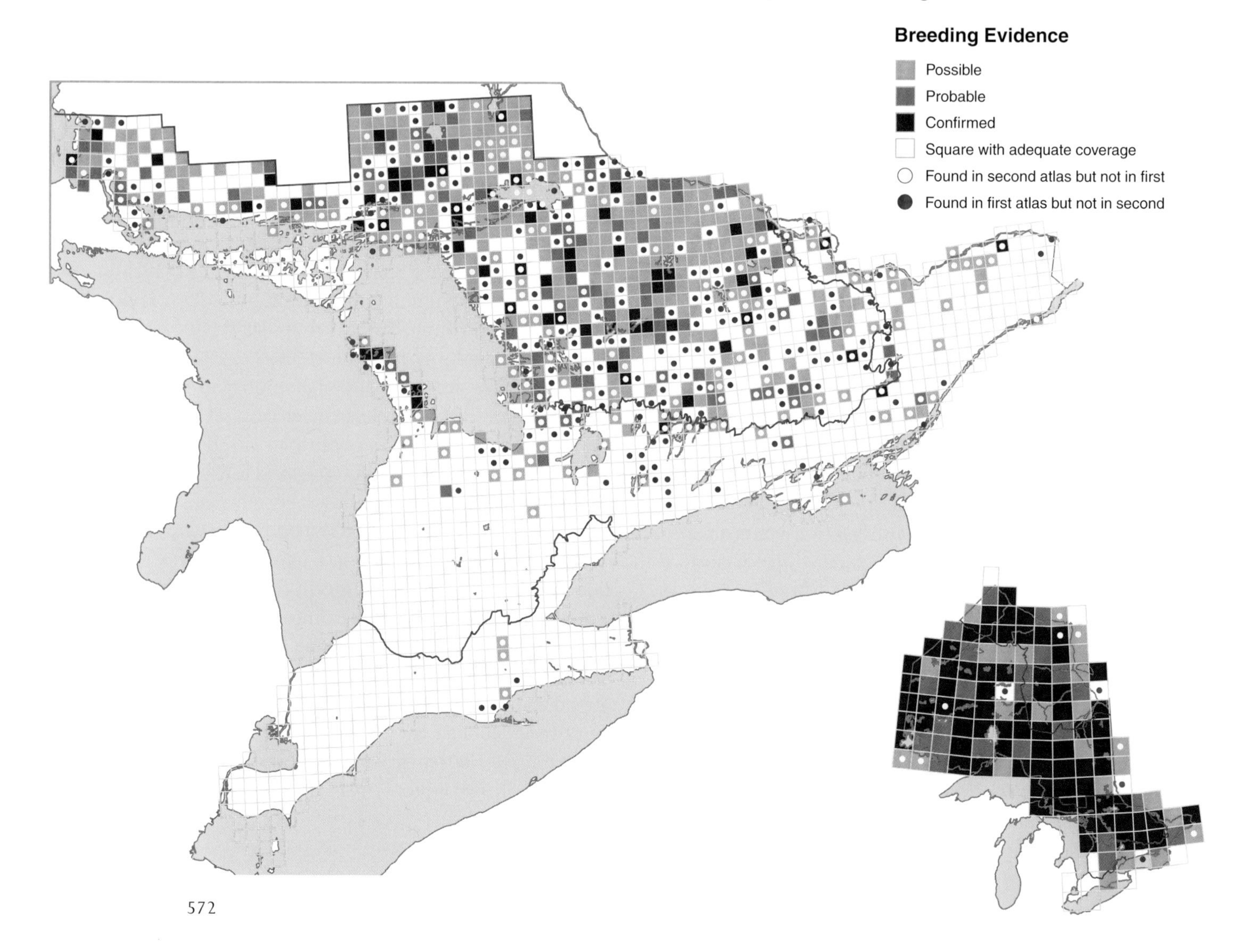

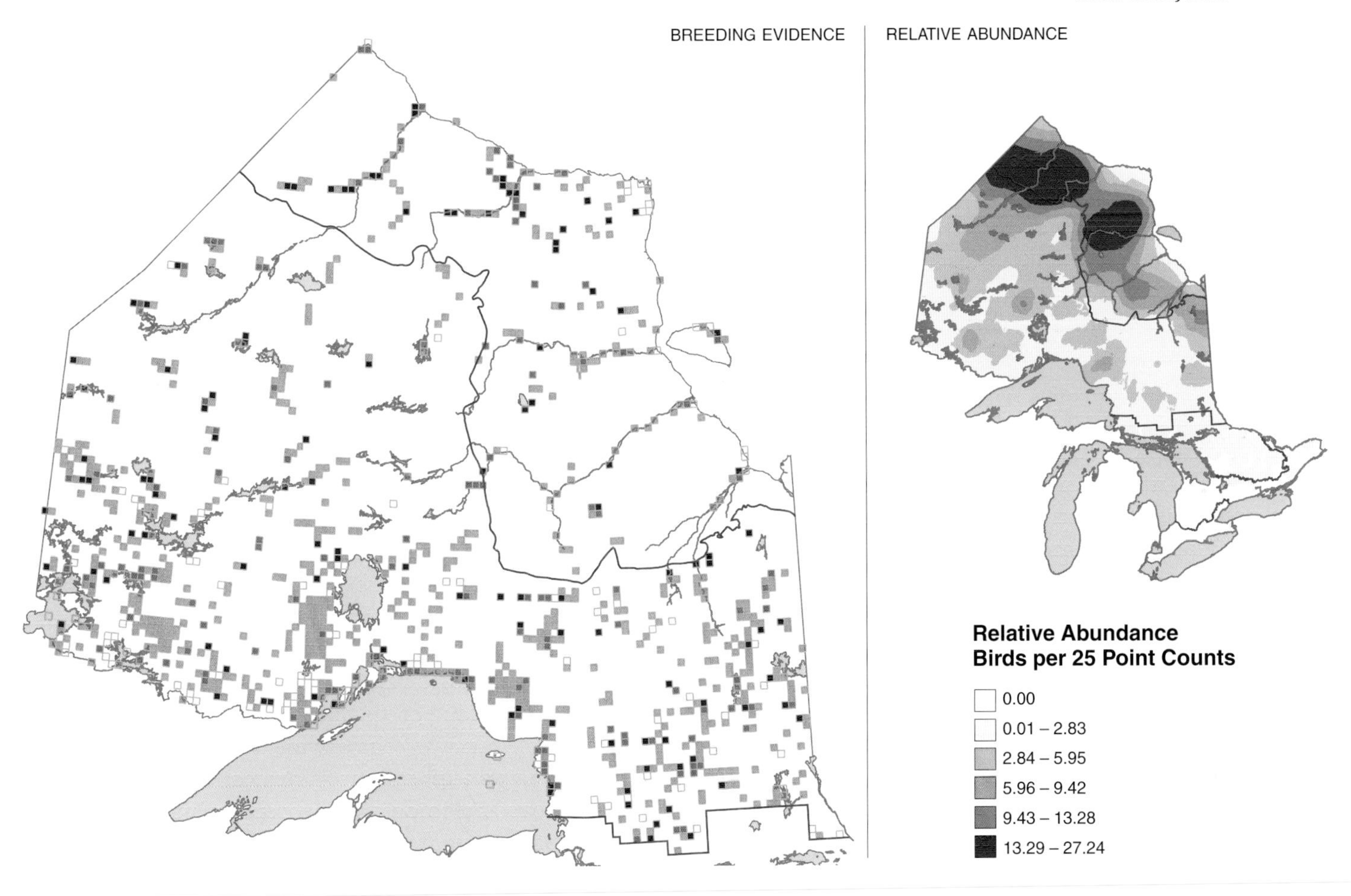

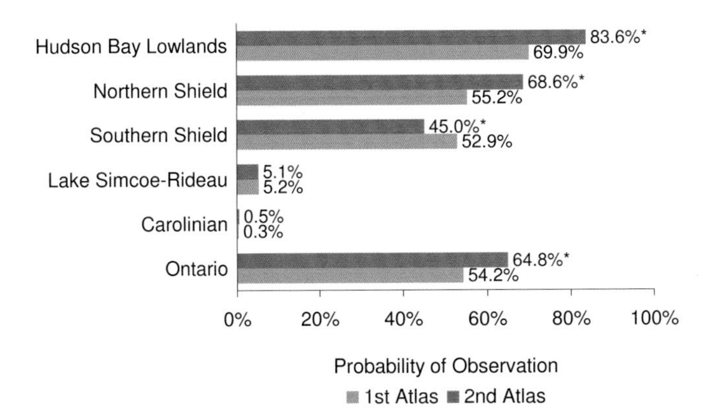

Dark-eyed Junco had decreased in numbers between atlases, perhaps reflecting in-filling of open forest in the park; the same may be true across the Southern Shield region. South of the Shield, the species occurs only sparingly and is nearly entirely absent from the Carolinian region. There were few confirmed nesting records south of the Shield, with four on the Bruce Peninsula where the species can be found at the northern tip of the peninsula and on talus slopes below the cliffs of the Niagara Escarpment. Breeding was also confirmed south of the Shield near Alfred, east of Ottawa. In the south, mature conifer plantations may provide suitable nesting habitat. As in the first atlas, possible breeding records were reported in and around the St. Williams Forest near Long Point.

Breeding biology: The Dark-eyed Junco typically begins nesting in Ontario in the latter half of April, although overwintering and migrant males may begin singing in March, leading to possible misinterpretation of breeding evidence early in the season. The song is sufficiently similar to those of several other "trillers" that potential for misidentification exists, particularly where Chipping Sparrow, Pine Warbler, or Yellow-rumped Warbler are common. Detection of singing males accounted for 71% of all breeding evidence. Nesting takes place from late April (in the south) through early August. Nests are usually placed on the ground, often in existing depressions or under vegetation, logs, rocks, and roots, but occasionally are placed low in trees. As nests are well concealed and generally difficult to find, breeding is more easily confirmed through observation of adults carrying food or feeding fledged young. Both parents feed the young and, when agitated near the nest, conspicuously flit about, flashing their white tail feathers and giving frequent sharp alarm notes. Nesting has been reported as late as August, and there is some evidence that the species may be double-brooded in Ontario (Peck and James 1987). Only 13% of observations were of confirmed breeding.

Abundance: The Dark-eyed Junco is most common in the northern part of the Hudson Bay Lowlands, where numbers exceed 13.3 birds/25 point counts, with an average of 10.4 birds/25 point counts across the whole region. Densities decrease from north to south, averaging about 3.2, 0.5, 0.01, and 0 birds/25 point counts in the Northern Shield, Southern Shield, Lake Simcoe-Rideau, and Carolinian regions, respectively. Overall, breeding abundance and distribution reflect the species' preference for open coniferous and mixed woodlands. – *J.D. Rising*

Lapland Longspur

Bruant lapon

Calcarius lapponicus

Jim Richards

The Lapland Longspur breeds on the arctic tundra and is the only member of its genus that also occurs outside North America. The name "longspur" refers to the unusually long claw on the hind toe. The species has a circumpolar arctic breeding range, except for being absent from northeast Greenland, Iceland, and Spitsbergen. In North America, it breeds from 52° N on the Aleutian Islands to at least 80° N on Ellesmere Island. North American and Greenland populations winter abundantly on the Great Plains of the US (flocks as large as four million have been reported) and more sparsely eastward to the Atlantic seaboard in southeastern Canada and the northern US, and westward to southern British Columbia and California (Hussell and Montgomerie 2002). In Ontario, its breeding range is confined to the tundra along the Hudson and James Bay coasts. Breeding has been reported on the Twin Islands, Nunavut, in James Bay (Godfrey 1986), but not on Akimiski Island.

Distribution and population status: The Lapland Longspur is probably the most numerous arctic-nesting terrestrial bird worldwide. Its North American breeding population was recently estimated to be about 40 million (Hussell and Montgomerie 2002). In most of its range it is common in wet, fresh-water habitats, as well as on drier, well-vegetated ground, but it is relatively scarce at high latitudes and altitudes where these habitats are poorly represented. Hummocky meadows with a good growth of mosses, grasses, sedges, and dwarf shrubs are favoured.

Along the Hudson Bay coast of Ontario, the Lapland Longspur is also found on the numerous relict marine beaches that support sparse vegetation with exposed gravel and cobble and intersect lower-lying, well-vegetated meadows.

Breeding in Ontario was first documented in 1947 at Cape Henrietta Maria (Manning 1952). Subsequent investigation of this extreme northeastern part of Ontario produced addition-

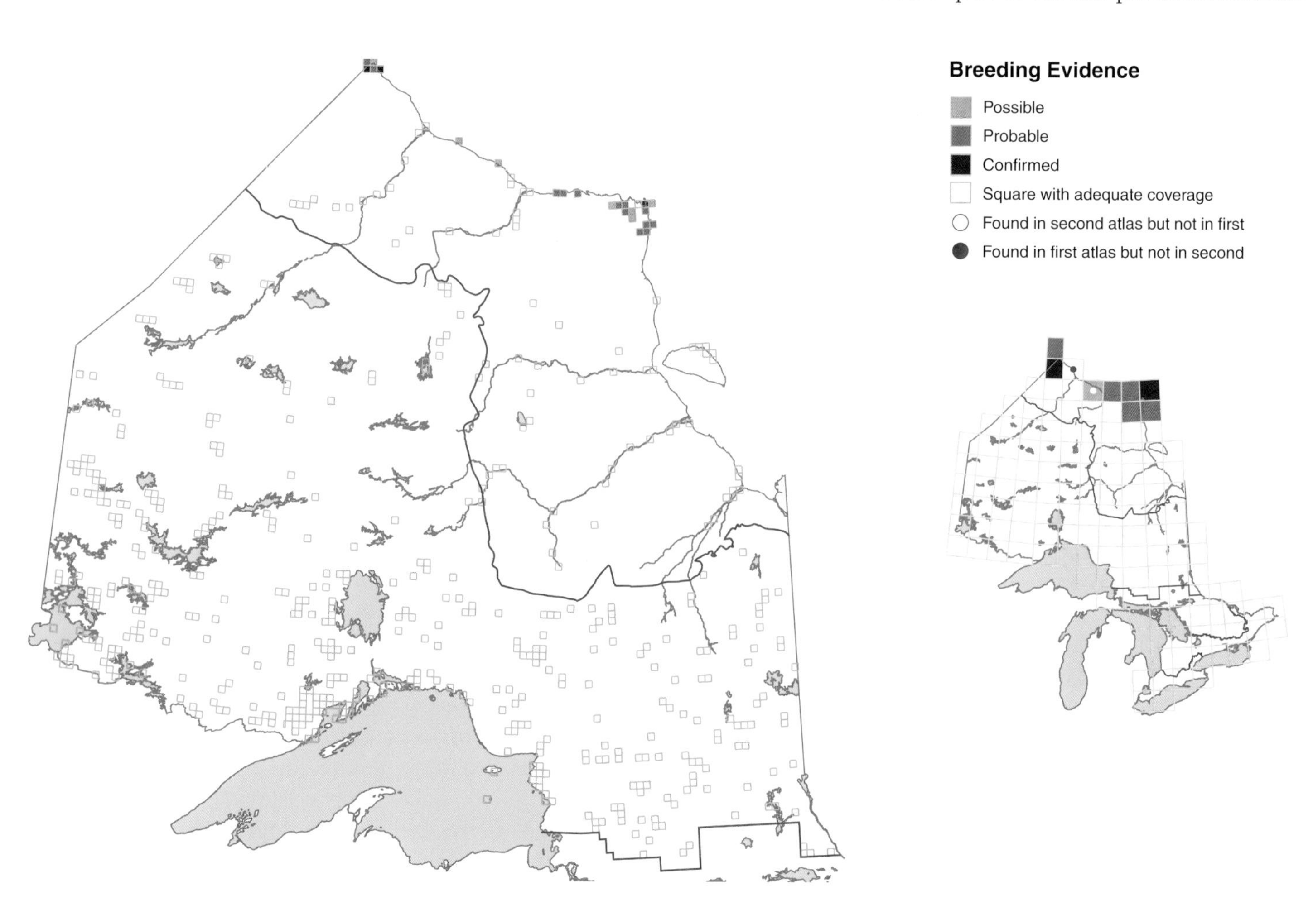

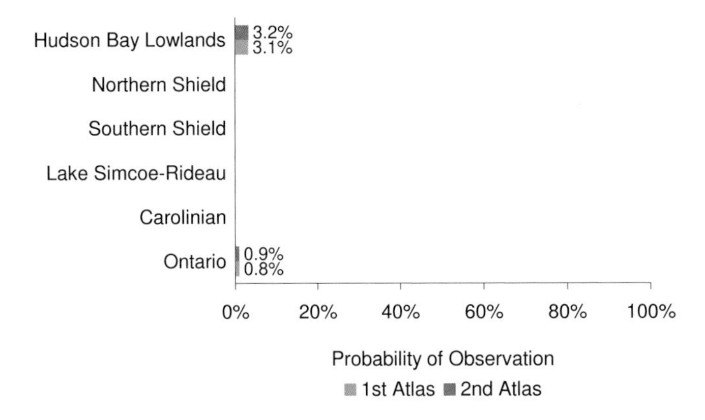

al records (Peck 1972; Peck and James 1987). The first atlas showed that breeding also occurred near the Manitoba border, at the other end of Ontario's Hudson Bay coast, but sparsely, if at all, in between. This atlas shows a similar pattern, with probable and confirmed breeding at the western and eastern ends of the Hudson Bay coast and in the two most northerly 100-km blocks on James Bay, but with only two scattered records of possible breeding on the central Hudson Bay coast.

Breeding evidence was reported in 23 squares in eight 100-km blocks, compared with 18 squares in eight 100-km blocks (one different) in the first atlas. The increase in square records is undoubtedly a consequence of somewhat more extensive coverage in this atlas.

Breeding biology: Early in the breeding season, the male Lapland Longspur advertises its presence with frequent songs given both in aerial displays and from the ground, described by Sutton (1932) as "the loveliest of Arctic bird-music." The inconspicuous female is relatively secretive while nest-building and incubating eggs, but nevertheless easily observed in the species' open habitat. The species is single-brooded, and in Ontario females usually lay four or five and occasionally six eggs. Nests are lined with feathers and usually well hidden under overhanging vegetation in the side of a hummock but occasionally on level ground or on the top of a hummock. Of 12 Ontario nests, 11 were in relatively dry areas with a heath/lichen community, moss, grass, and occasional arctic willows, and one nest was in wet graminoid tundra (Peck and James 1987). The incubation period is about 12 days, and the young leave the nest before they can fly at 8-10 days. The male gives alarm calls conspicuously when an observer enters its territory. Both parents are easily observed carrying food to their nestlings or fledged young, but confirmation may have been difficult during brief visits to squares prior to hatching.

Abundance: The bulk of the distribution and population is concentrated in the relatively wide expanse of tundra in the four 100-km blocks at and adjacent to Cape Henrietta Maria, which accounted for 14 of the squares with records and 10 of the 16 probable and confirmed records. There are insufficient data from point counts to produce a reliable map of relative abundance. During the first atlas, R.D. James and M.K. Peck estimated 13.3 pairs per km^2 in wet tussock tundra 40 km south of Cape Henrietta Maria, and abundance estimates of 101-1,000 pairs were reported for three squares in the same region (Hussell in Cadman et al. 1987). Despite a dramatic contraction of range eastward from Churchill, Manitoba, in the second half of the 20th century (Jehl 2004; Hussell and Montgomerie 2002), there is no evidence of a change in Ontario since the first atlas. – *David J.T. Hussell*

In Ontario, nests are often located on the side of a hummock in drier heath-lichen tundra, usually well concealed from above by overhanging vegetation and lined with feathers. *Photo: Mark Peck*

Typical breeding habitat for the Lapland Longspur in Ontario is wet, hummocky graminoid tundra interspersed with low, sparsely vegetated gravel beach ridges. Near Oosteguanako Creek, south of West Pen Island, 2 July 2004. *Photo: Donald A. Sutherland*

Smith's Longspur

Bruant de Smith

Calcarius pictus

Ron Ridout

In 1832, Smith's Longspur was named the "Painted Bunting" by William Swainson from a specimen collected at Carlton House by John Richardson during Franklin's second expedition. In 1844, it was renamed by John James Audubon in honour of Gideon B. Smith, a wealthy friend and subscriber to Audubon's *Birds of America* (Mearns and Mearns 1992).

In summer, the Smith's Longspur inhabits the more northerly part of the Boreal Forest-treeless tundra ecotone (Jehl 1968). Its subarctic breeding range is confined to North America, stretching in a narrow strip from the west coast of James Bay in Ontario to the Brooks Range in northern Alaska, with a small disjunct population in northwestern BC and southeastern Alaska (Briskie 1993). Its total population is "unlikely to be more than about 75,000 birds" (Briskie 1993). Typical habitat consists of drier sedge meadows and grassy, wet tussock tundra, interrupted by old beach ridges with scattered clumps of spruce and Tamarack (Peck and James 1987; Briskie 1993). Suitable habitat tends to be patchy in distribution.

Distribution and population status: The first evidence of breeding in Ontario was the collection of a juvenile by Manning (1952) at Little Cape on the Hudson Bay coast in 1947. The first Ontario nest was found the following year by a ROM party, about 40 km south of Cape Henrietta Maria (Peck 1972). In the first atlas, Smith's Longspur exhibited a more or less continuous breeding distribution paralleling the Hudson Bay and extreme northern James Bay coasts, with breeding evidence reported from 19 squares in seven 100-km blocks.

This atlas shows a similar distribution, although the number of squares with breeding evidence has increased to 37 in nine 100-km blocks. This increase is likely due mainly to more extensive coverage of suitable squares in the second atlas. The current distribution and point count data strongly suggest that

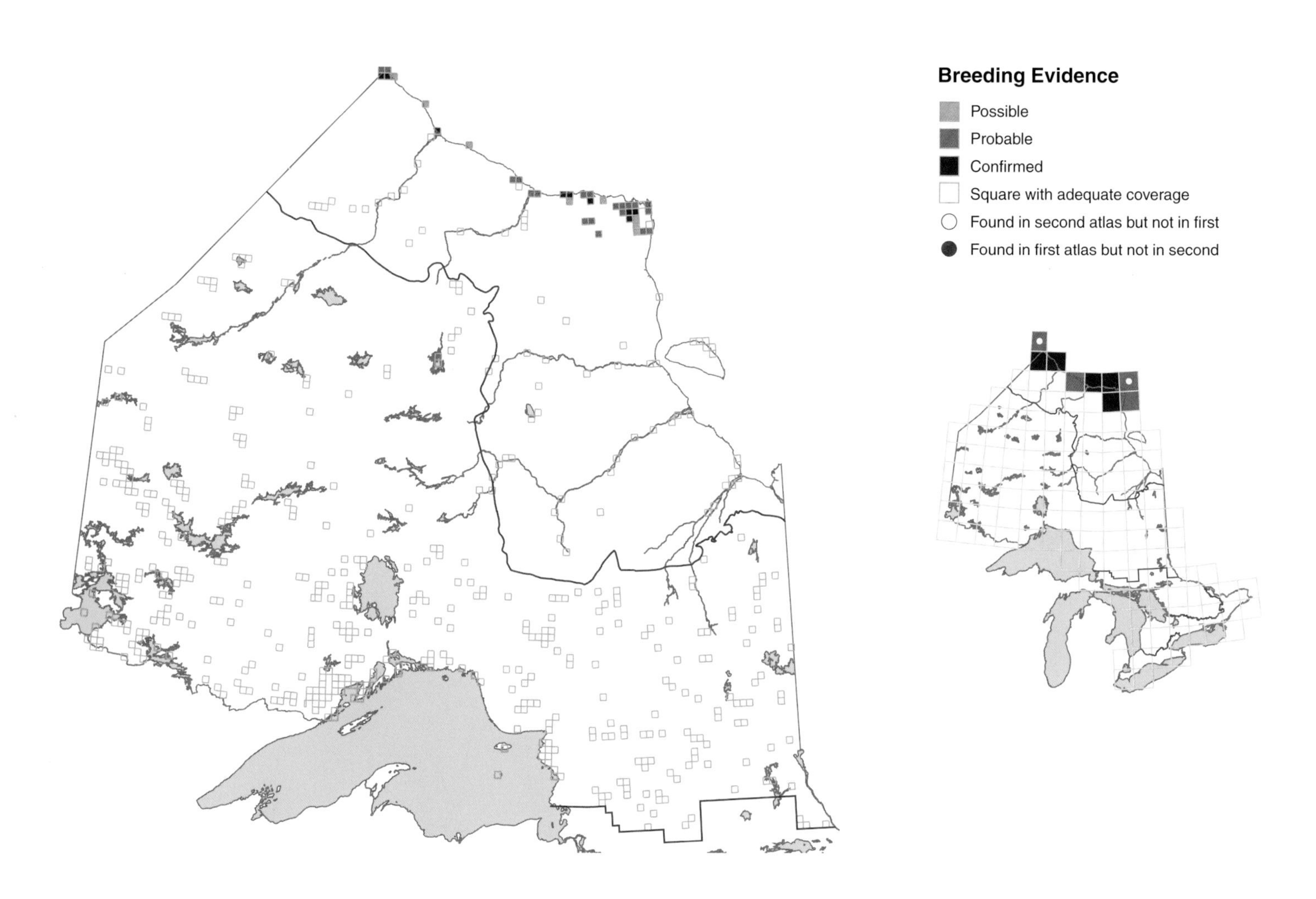

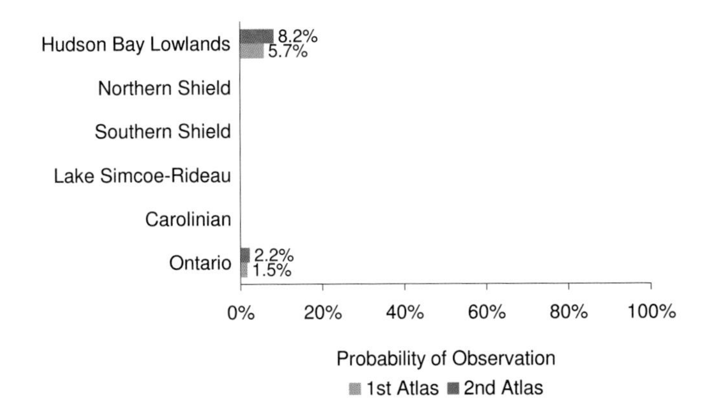

the main population concentrations are near the Manitoba border and particularly near and inland from Cape Henrietta Maria. This distributional pattern is similar to that of the Lapland Longspur and is likely related to the presence of larger expanses of appropriate habitat in those areas. In contrast to the Lapland Longspur, Smith's Longspur may occur in suitable transitional habitat 40-60 km inland but is absent from exposed treeless tundra near the coast.

Breeding biology: Unlike the Lapland Longspur, Smith's Longspur does not have a conspicuous flight song, nor does it defend a clearly defined territory, but it does sing both from the ground and from trees (Jehl 1968). It has an extraordinary mating system called polygynandry: males form short-term pair bonds and mate sequentially with one to three females, and females pair and mate serially with one to three males for a single clutch, usually consisting of three to five eggs (Briskie 1993; Briskie in Jehl 2004). Nests are typically between tufts of grass or other vegetation, in the tops of dry, flat hummocks, occasionally in the side of a low hummock, or sometimes between frost boils (Jehl 1968; Peck and James 1987; D.A. Sutherland, pers comm.); unlike most Lapland Longspur nests, they are unprotected from above, although they may be at the base of a small shrub or tree. Nest-building and incubation are done by the relatively inconspicuous females. Both sexes feed the young, and more than one male may attend each brood. The nestlings leave the nest before they can fly. Confirmation is most easily achieved during the nest-building and brood-rearing stages.

Abundance: Data from Churchill, Manitoba, indicated that densities are low on the breeding grounds, ranging from 0.3 to 0.4 birds per ha in the mid-1960s to a mean of 0.2 birds per ha in 1992 (Briskie 1993). Densities of 0.2 to 0.4 pairs per ha (20 to 40 pairs per km^2) were recorded in wet tussock and dry heath-lichen tundra, respectively, at Radar Site 415, about 40 km south of Cape Henrietta Maria in 1984 (James and Peck 1985). The population in the square encompassing their study area was estimated to be between 1,001 and 10,000 pairs during the first atlas.

Absolute and relative numbers vary from year to year. Peck (1972) described the species as less abundant than the Lapland Longspur in 1970, whereas James and Peck (1985) found it more numerous than the Lapland Longspur in the same area in 1984. At Churchill, numbers varied widely from year to year between 1995 and 2000 (Jehl 2004).

Atlas point count data indicate that Smith's Longspur populations occur in greatest density near the Manitoba border and in the Cape Henrietta Maria region, those areas where they are also most widely distributed. – *David J.T. Hussell*

Nests are located in grass tufts on or beside hummocks or between frost boils. Unlike those of the Lapland Longspur, nests of the Smith's Longspur are unprotected from above. Polar Bear Prov. Park, 1 July 1970. *Photo: George K. Peck*

Hummocky graminoid tundra with scattered stunted spruces interspersed with low gravel ridges is the prime breeding habitat for this species in Ontario. Near Burntpoint Creek, Polar Bear Prov. Park. *Photo: Ken Abraham*

Northern Cardinal

Cardinal rouge

Cardinalis cardinalis

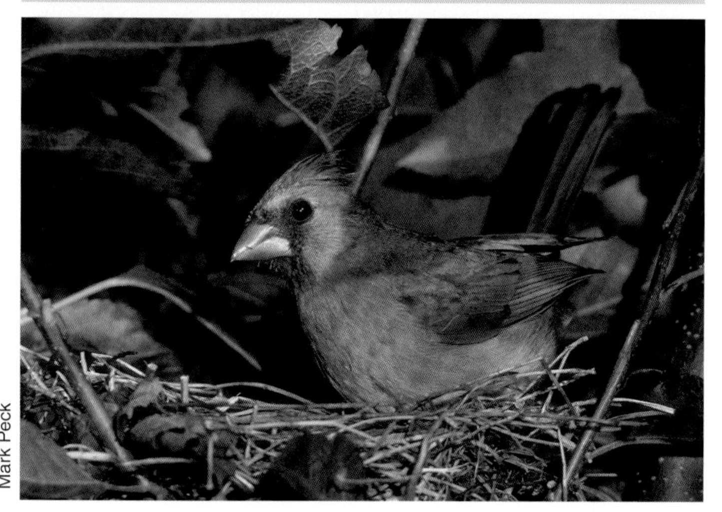

Mark Peck

The bright red plumage of the male Northern Cardinal and its preference for habitats that include urban and suburban landscapes make this species one of the most popular and best-known birds of southern Ontario. Even though the female is not as colourful as the male, both sexes are easily identifiable by sight, even by inexperienced birders. The cardinal is a resident species throughout eastern North America north to about 46° N in central Ontario and southern Québec and south to the Yucatan Peninsula of Mexico and northern Belize (Halkin and Linville 1999). Throughout the 20th century, it gradually expanded its range northwards and appears to be continuing to do so in Ontario.

Distribution and population status: The Northern Cardinal probably did not occur in Ontario when European settlers first arrived. The earliest record for the province is from 1849 when one was collected at Chatham (Snyder 1951). The first Ontario nest was found at Point Pelee in 1901, with subsequent breeding records at London (1915), Brantford (1919), and Toronto (1922) (Snyder 1957). By 1985, at the end of the first atlas period, cardinals were well established throughout the Lake Simcoe-Rideau region, east to Brockville, and north to the central Bruce Peninsula. Squares with records for the species were more scattered but still frequent east to Cornwall and north to Ottawa.

The Northern Cardinal has continued to expand its range in Ontario, with an 8% probability of observation in the second atlas in the province as a whole, compared to 5% during the first atlas. Most of the expansion has occurred in the Lake Simcoe-Rideau region, where the gaps in the east and north noted in the first atlas have been almost completely filled. Cardinals are now nearly ubiquitous east to Cornwall and north to Ottawa. There are also numerous records on Manitoulin Island. In the Southern Shield region, its range has expanded in the urban centres of Bracebridge, Gravenhurst,

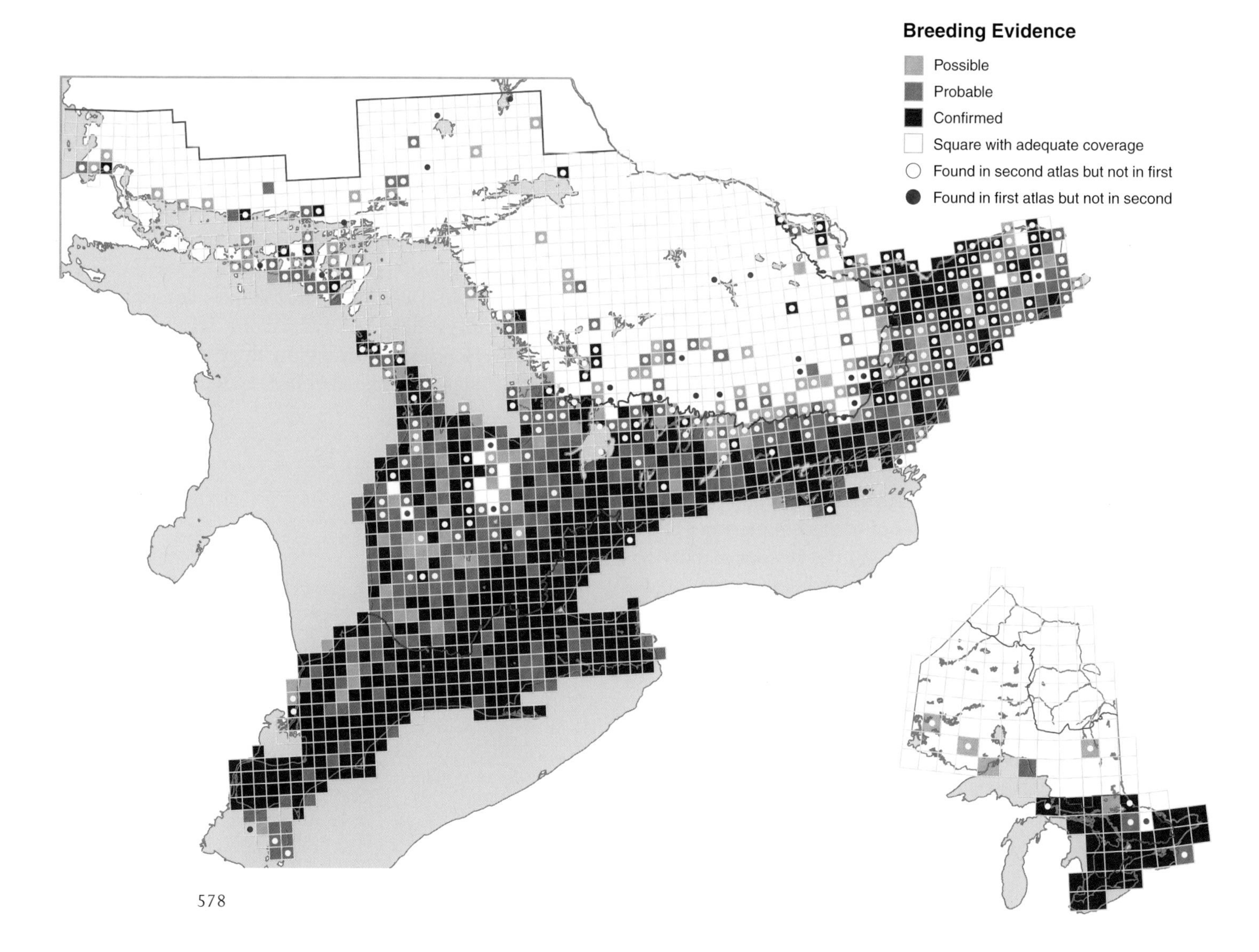

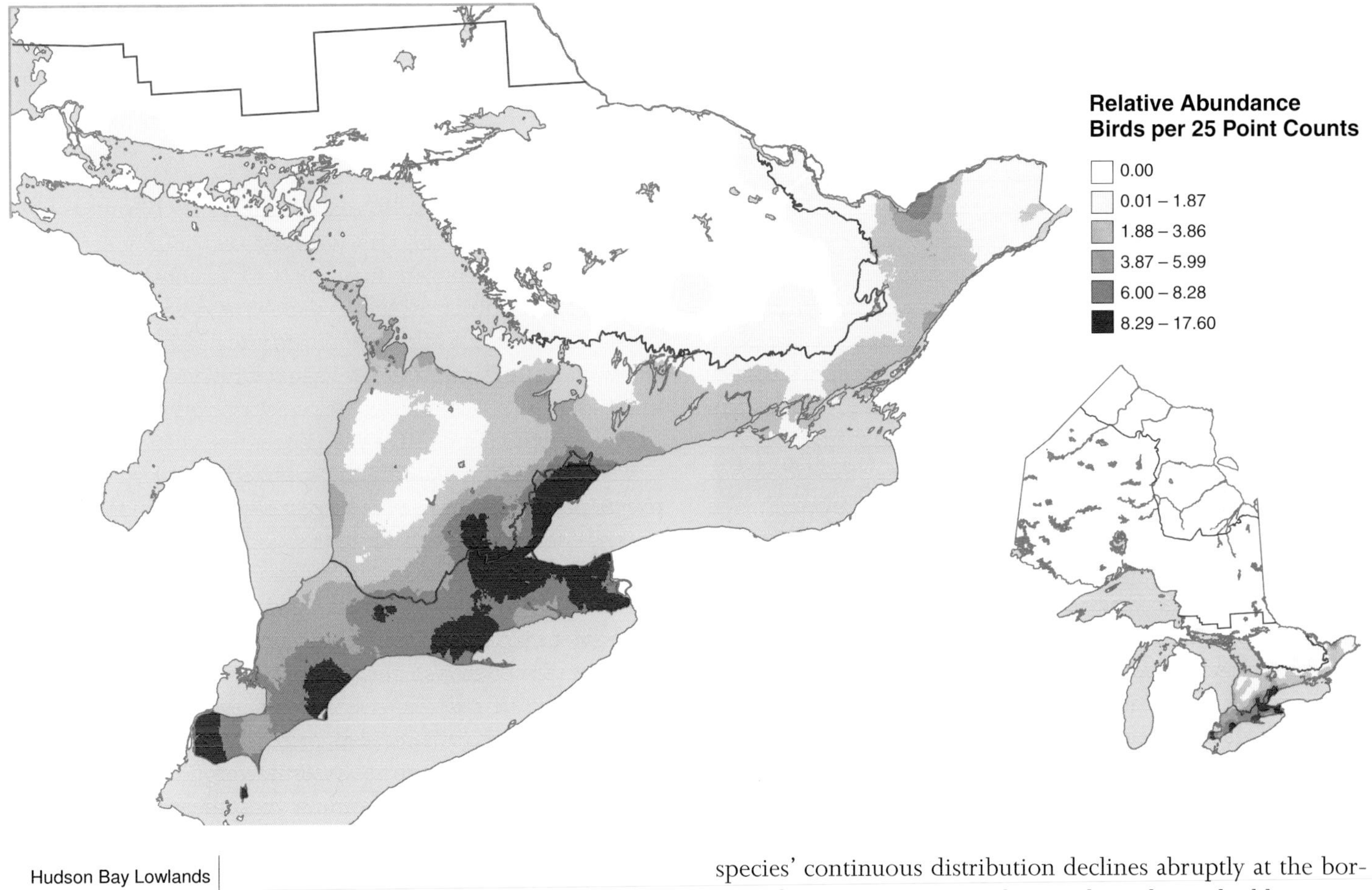

Hudson Bay Lowlands
Northern Shield 0.4% 0.0%
Southern Shield 6.6%* 1.7%
Lake Simcoe-Rideau 77.2%* 42.8%
Carolinian 96.0% 97.2%
Ontario 8.3% 5.4%
0% 20% 40% 60% 80% 100%
Probability of Observation
1st Atlas 2nd Atlas

Huntsville, and Parry Sound, and in Bancroft and Minden in the Haliburton Highlands. Between atlases, the probability of observation increased by 80% in the Lake Simcoe-Rideau region and more than doubled in the Southern Shield, though the species is still uncommon in the latter region. The northward range expansion appears to be continuing. Records from squares near Atikokan, Cochrane, and Kenora represent significant northward movement since the first atlas. Winter survival of cardinals in these northern areas, and probably throughout the province, may be assisted by the increased popularity of bird feeders. BBS data also indicate an increasing cardinal population, with an average annual increase of about 11% in Ontario from 1981 to 2005.

Warming temperatures are likely responsible for the expanding range and increasing population of the Northern Cardinal. The northern edge of the area where cardinals are found regularly approximates the isotherm for the January mean minimum temperature of minus 16°C, and this isotherm has moved east and north since the first atlas. The species' continuous distribution declines abruptly at the border of the Lake Simcoe-Rideau and Southern Shield regions, and given the cardinal's preference for shrubby habitats and forest edges, it may be that a more highly forested landscape on the Shield is restricting expansion there.

Breeding biology: The loud and easily identifiable song is given by both sexes, although much more commonly by the male. Males sing to some extent all year (Halkin and Linville 1999), but increasing song frequency is a sure sign of spring in southern Ontario. Nests are usually placed deep within a brushy tangle and can be difficult to find. Nevertheless, just over 50% of squares with Northern Cardinal had confirmed records. The young are fed for a month or more after fledging (Lemon 1957; Halkin and Linville 1999), providing atlassers with many opportunities to observe fledged young with their parents.

Abundance: The Northern Cardinal is most abundant in the areas along the north shore of Lake Erie and southwestern Lake Ontario, northeast to about Toronto. There is also a higher density in the Ottawa area, perhaps reflecting both the species' preference for suburban shrubbery and also the heat effect of the city, resulting in warmer winter temperatures. Small numbers of cardinals were recorded on point counts as far north as Manitoulin Island and Sault Ste. Marie. Although there are several squares with cardinal records in Muskoka and in the Sudbury area, no cardinals were apparently recorded on point counts, so these clusters are not reflected in the abundance maps. – *Margaret A. McLaren*

Rose-breasted Grosbeak

Cardinal à poitrine rose

Pheucticus ludovicianus

Jim Richards

The Rose-breasted Grosbeak is a common songbird that breeds in the deciduous forests of eastern and central North America. It is found most often in second-growth deciduous woods with relatively open canopies. It also breeds at forest edges and in a wide variety of more disturbed habitats such as well-treed suburban neighbourhoods, parks, and gardens (Wyatt and Francis 2002).

Distribution and population status: In the 20th century, the range of the Rose-breasted Grosbeak appeared to have expanded in Ontario, Québec, and New York State, as its preferred second-growth and edge habitat became more common there. Its use of these habitats may make it less vulnerable to human disturbance than many other species (Wyatt and Francis 2002). However, BBS data suggest a significant annual decline in population of 3.4% in Ontario and 3.7% in Canada since 1981. This appears to be part of a similar significant declining trend observed in BBS data across this species' range (Sauer et al. 2005). CMMN data from Ontario show no significant trends, however, and the decline in BBS numbers may be due in part to successional changes of vegetation along static survey routes.

Both atlases show that the Rose-breasted Grosbeak is ubiquitous throughout most of southern Ontario, with the probability of observation highest in the Lake Simcoe-Rideau region (86%). The species occurs more sporadically in the Boreal Forest of the Northern Shield. Consistent with BBS results, there was a significant 8% decline between atlases in the probability of observation in the province as a whole. Significant declines in the Lake Simcoe-Rideau and Southern Shield regions are likely attributable primarily to corresponding declines in occupied squares in the Manitoulin and Sudbury areas, respectively. Reasons for these declines are not clear, but the result is a significant southward shift in both the core and the northern edge of this grosbeak's southern Ontario range.

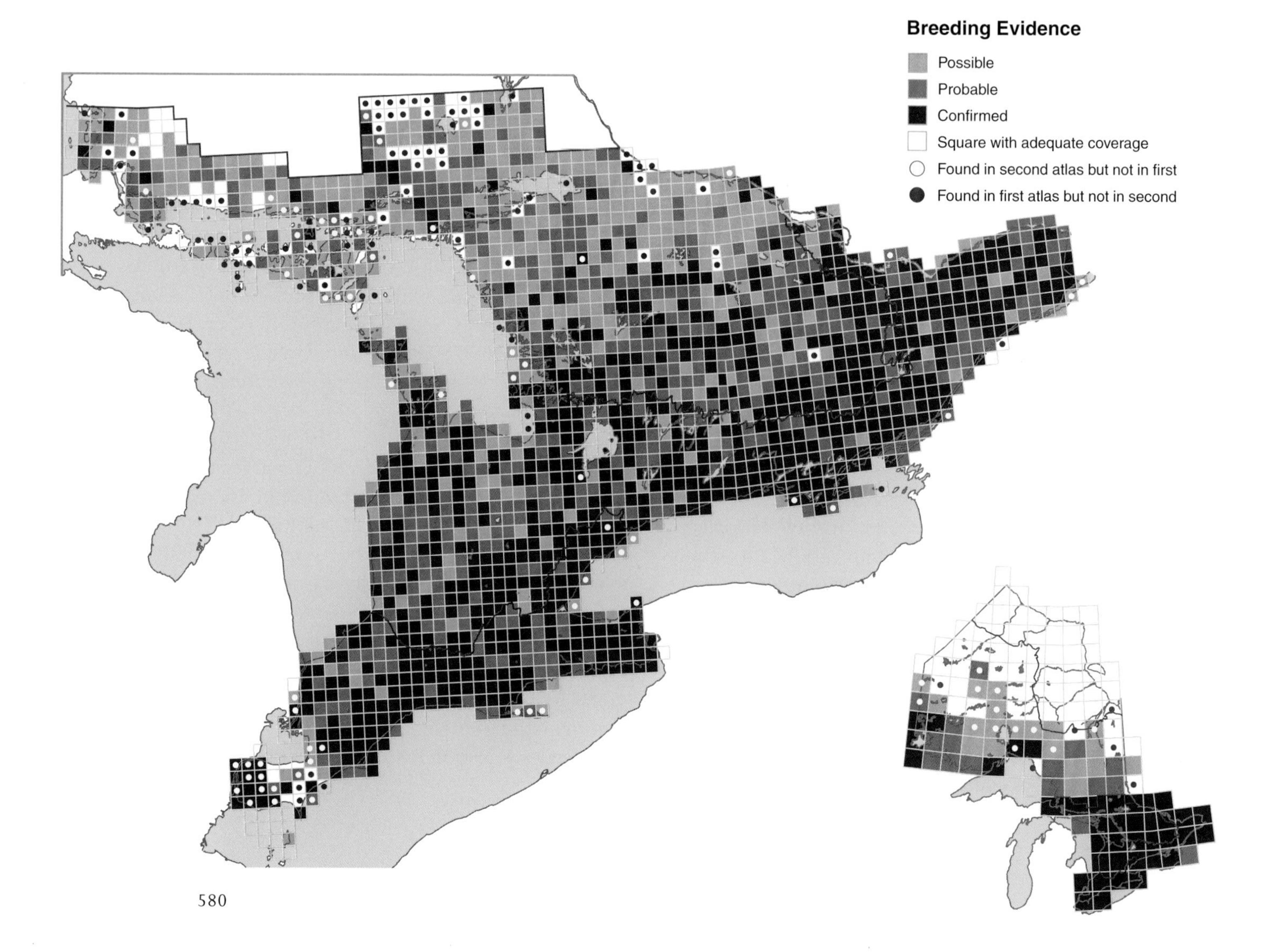

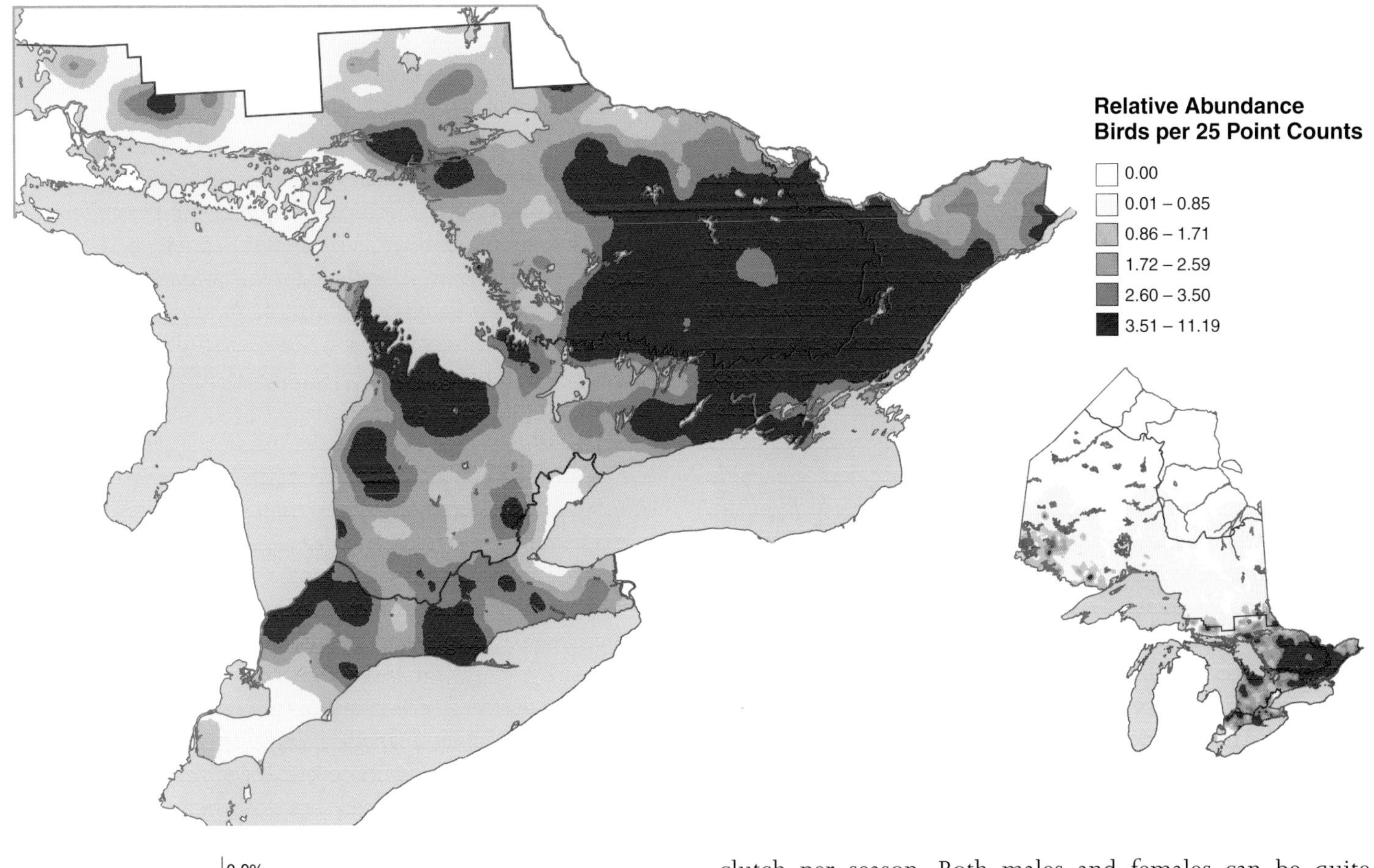

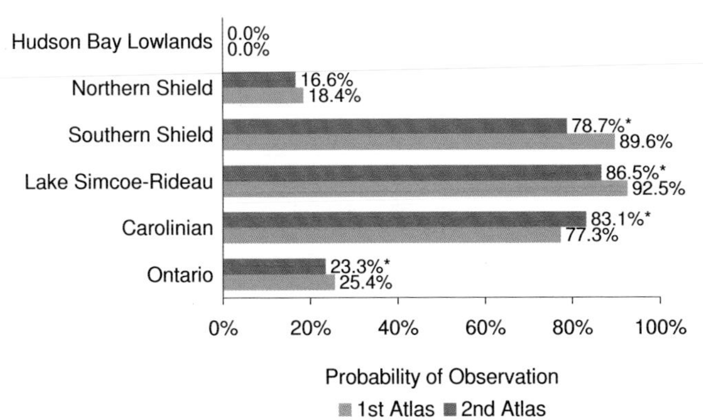

Despite this, these two regions, along with the Carolinian, still appear to serve as the species' stronghold in Ontario.

The first atlas indicated that distribution was more restricted in the intensively agricultural Carolinian region, especially in Essex Co. Although the reason for the subsequent increase in this area is still unclear, it may be that the increase in rural residential housing and associated trees and plantings have provided an expansion of suitable habitat. The second atlas showed a corresponding significant increase in the probability of observation in the Carolinian region as a whole.

Breeding biology: The male Rose-breasted Grosbeak is an ardent defender of its territory early in the breeding season and highly vocal with a melodious song and a distinctive call note, both easily detected. Indeed, the highest breeding evidence in most squares where breeding was not confirmed was singing or territorial males. These activities are somewhat curtailed once the clutch is complete, as both the male and female are involved in incubating the eggs, although males frequently sing from the nest. The species only has one clutch per season. Both males and females can be quite aggressive towards intruders near the nest. Because of these characteristics, it seems likely that breeding birds would be easily detected if present and that the atlas maps accurately reflect distribution. Breeding was confirmed in 38% of squares reporting the species.

Abundance: The Rose-breasted Grosbeak is most abundant in the Lake Simcoe-Rideau and Southern Shield regions, where the average abundance is 3.3 and 3.6 birds/25 point counts, respectively. Densities exceed 3.5 birds/25 point counts in parts of these regions as well as in the Long Point and north Lambton portions of the Carolinian region. The species is much less abundant in the extreme southwest, Manitoulin Island, and Toronto, where there is very little suitable forest habitat. The abundance map also reflects the scarcity of this grosbeak in the Northern Shield region, except in the Rainy River and Dryden areas, which have relatively high proportions of deciduous forest.

Although the Rose-breasted Grosbeak is quite common and easily identified, living in close proximity to humans, historically it has not been well studied. Wyatt and Francis (2002) identified the highest research priority for this species as developing a better understanding of population dynamics and the factors that limit its population. Many studies are now underway or being completed on these issues; the data provided by this atlas, especially when compared with data from the first atlas, offer another excellent source of information on factors affecting its population, distribution, and abundance in Ontario. – *Valerie Wyatt*

Indigo Bunting

Passerin indigo

Passerina cyanea

John Reaume

The male Indigo Bunting is Ontario's only completely blue bird. It can often be seen sitting on roadside wires or tree branches at the edges of woodlots and hedgerows, while the much drabber brown female is frequently overlooked. During the breeding season, the Indigo Bunting is found from southern Manitoba east through southern Ontario and Québec to southern New Brunswick, and south to Colorado, New Mexico, and southern Texas. During the latter part of the 1900s, the species' breeding range expanded to local areas of Utah, Arizona, and California. The species winters from southern Florida through Mexico and Central America (Payne 2006).

Distribution and population status: The Indigo Bunting is widespread in southern Ontario. The probability of observation of the species is over 75% in the Carolinian and Lake Simcoe-Rideau regions. Its distribution is somewhat more scattered from southern Algonquin Prov. Park north to Sudbury and Sault Ste. Marie, but it is still commonly observed to the northern limit of the Great Lakes-St. Lawrence Forest, including in the Kenora-Fort Frances area where farmland again provides suitable habitat. In the Boreal Forest, Indigo Bunting records are very scattered north to Hearst and west to Sioux Lookout.

Between atlases, there was no significant change in the probability of observation of the Indigo Bunting in the province as a whole, but there were significant declines in the Carolinian and Lake Simcoe-Rideau regions of 14% and 11%, respectively. The decline in the Carolinian, where the Brown Thrasher, Eastern Towhee, and Field Sparrow have also declined, suggests that intensification of agricultural practices, which often result in the removal of hedgerows and other early successional and edge habitats, may be a factor. The reasons for the decline in the Lake Simcoe-Rideau region are not clear, as loss of habitat in this region is not as evident.In the

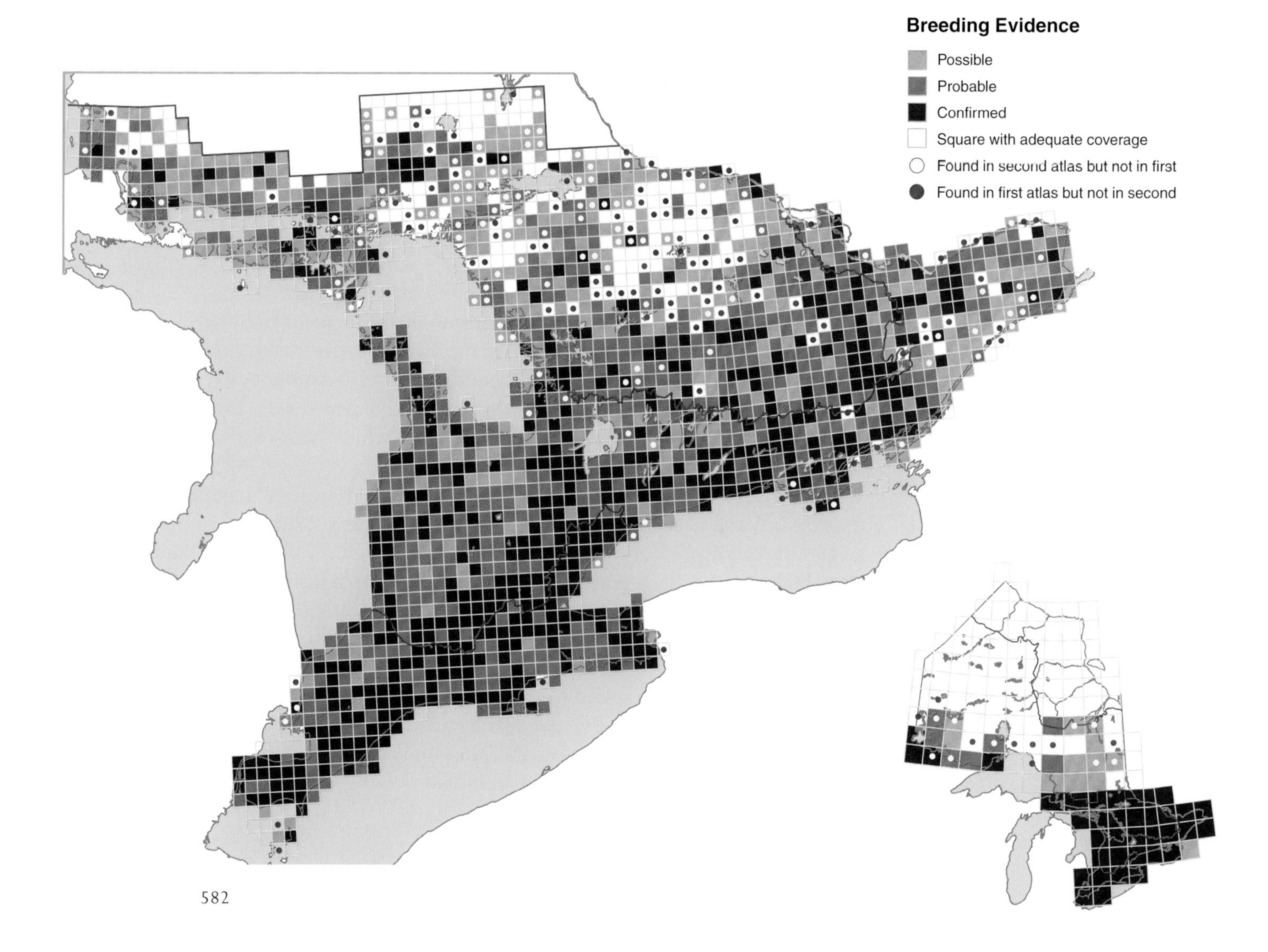

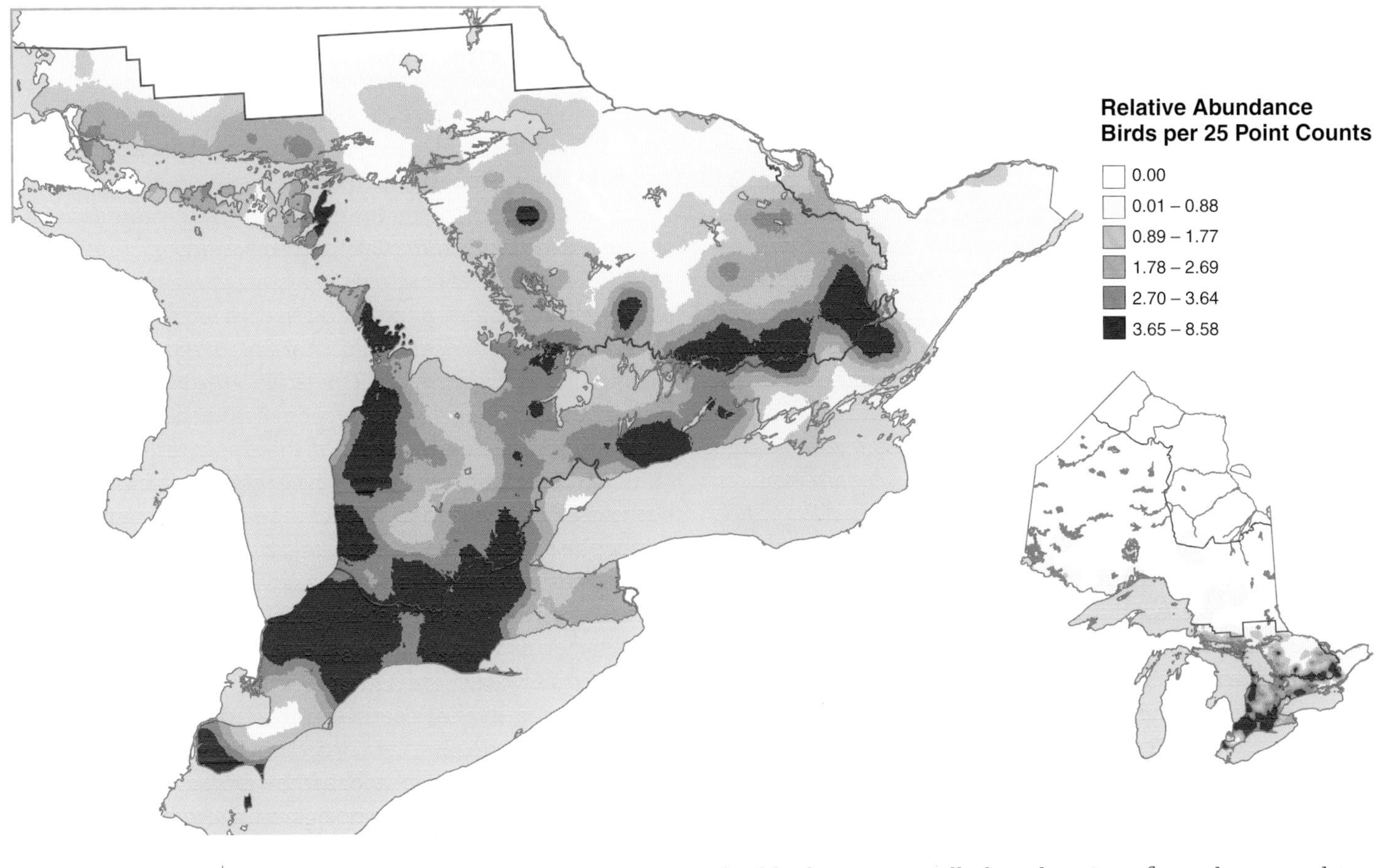

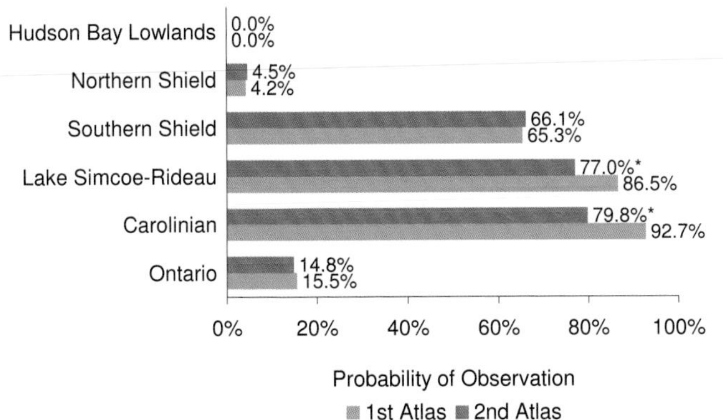

Southern Shield and Northern Shield regions, there was no significant change in the probability of observation. However, as is often the case with range-edge species, the specific locations where buntings are present seem to vary over time, perhaps due to the species' scarcity at the edge of its range. In the second atlas, the Indigo Bunting was found in nine 100-km blocks where it was not found in the first, but it was also found in seven 100-km blocks in the first atlas where it was not found in this atlas.

In contrast to the atlas results for southern Ontario, BBS data for Ontario show a near-significant increase from 1981 to 2005, whereas migration data show a significant increase in passage of the Indigo Bunting in the spring between 1961-1994 and 1995-2004 (Crewe 2006).

Breeding biology: The Indigo Bunting nests in edge habitats where deciduous trees and shrubs are interspersed with tall herbaceous vegetation. Hedgerows, roadsides, railway and hydro rights-of-way, regenerating clearcuts, forest clearings, and shrubby old fields are all acceptable habitats. The female builds the nest, usually less than 1 m from the ground in a branching shrub, or, later in the season, even in herbaceous vegetation such as goldenrod (Payne 2006). The male does not take part in incubation and rarely assists in feeding of the young until they have been fledged for several days. At that point, he may take over most of the feeding, which occurs with decreasing frequency, while the female prepares for a second brood (Payne 2006). Since the male is by far the more easily located of the pair, his general lack of parental care may explain the rather low percentage (31%) of squares with confirmed breeding. However, fledged young are noisy, and females will respond aggressively to "pishing," so dedicated searchers should be able to confirm breeding.

Abundance: The Indigo Bunting is most abundant in the Carolinian region, averaging approximately 3.6 birds/25 point counts. Its abundance decreases with increasing latitude, with averages of 2.3, 1.6, 0.1, and 0 birds/25 point counts in the Lake Simcoe-Rideau, Southern Shield, Northern Shield, and Hudson Bay Lowlands regions, respectively. The main areas of low density south of the Shield include Chatham-Kent, where the landscape is heavily agricultural and forest cover is very low. The areas of lower abundance in Grey Co., eastern Ontario, and Prince Edward Co. are not as easy to explain, since abandonment of farmland in the past 20 years, especially in the east, should provide suitable habitat. The lower densities in the areas around Algonquin Prov. Park are presumably due to higher forest cover reducing the amount of suitable edge habitat available to the species. – *Margaret A. McLaren*

Dickcissel

Dickcissel d'Amérique

Spiza americana

Frank and Sandra Horvath

The Dickcissel is a characteristic and abundant breeding bird of the grasslands of the US Midwest, where its core breeding range includes all or portions of Illinois, Iowa, Kansas, Missouri, Nebraska, Oklahoma, and South Dakota, extending peripherally to Colorado, Indiana, North Dakota, and Texas. Outside this area, it breeds only sporadically, the result of drought-induced dispersal from its core range (Temple 2002). During the 19th century, its range extended farther east in anthropogenic grasslands from New England south to the Carolinas, but by the beginning of the 20th century its breeding range had retracted westward (Temple 2002). The Dickcissel is a neotropical migrant, wintering in northern South America primarily in the Ilanos of central Venezuela. Surveys of its limited wintering range in 1993 suggested a minimum world population of 6,000,000 birds (Temple 2002).

Distribution and population status: The Dickcissel has always been a rather rare and sporadic breeder in Ontario. During the 19th century, coincident with the eastward expansion of its range, it may have been a more regular and not uncommon breeding resident of the southwestern counties (Saunders and Dale 1933). Breeding was first documented in the province in Essex Co. in 1884, and subsequently in the Counties of Elgin (1885) and Middlesex (1895). During the 20th century, evidence of breeding was recorded in 20 different years spanning most decades. Prior to the first atlas, breeding evidence had been reported in 11 counties north and east to Bruce Co. and Ottawa-Carleton RM, but most frequently in the southwestern counties of Essex, Middlesex, and Elgin, respectively.

During the first atlas, evidence of probable and possible breeding was reported in two squares: a territorial male was present near Hope Bay, Bruce Co., 5-20 June 1981, and a singing male was observed in suitable habitat in Lambton Co.,

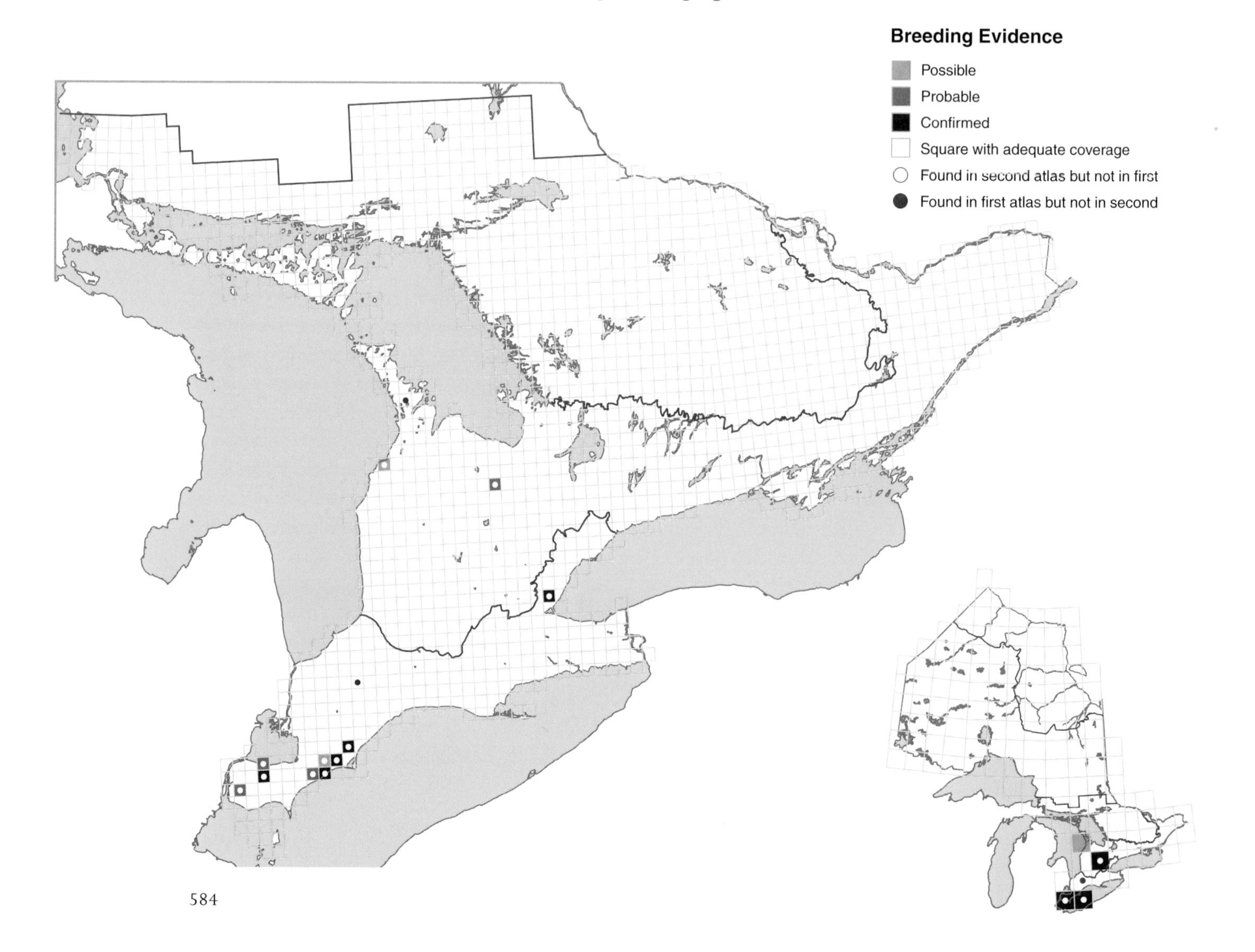

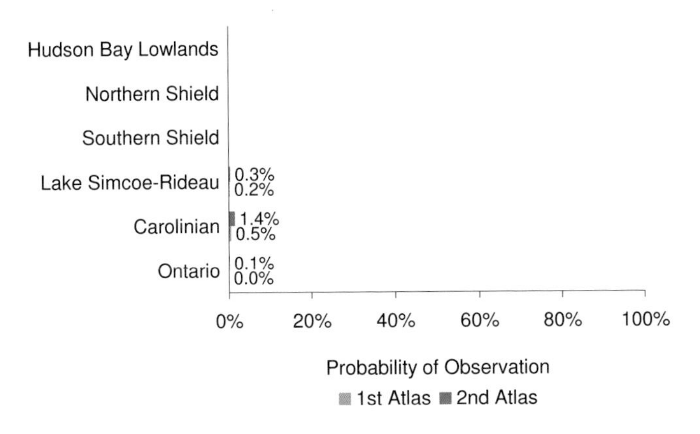

18 June 1985.

Between atlases, breeding evidence for the Dickcissel was detected in five years (1988, 1989, 1990, 1992, and 2000). In 1988, a severe drought in much of the species' Midwest US range precipitated an irruption of unprecedented proportions (Temple 2002). In Ontario, this irruption likely involved hundreds of individuals with breeding evidence (including 29 nest records; ONRS data) reported from at least seven counties, north and east to Bruce Co. and York RM (Weir 1988). A second, smaller irruption occurred in 2000 with breeding evidence reported at isolated localities in Hamilton-Wentworth RM and Elgin and Haldimand Counties, and up to 30 pairs in Chatham-Kent.

During the second atlas, the Dickcissel was reported in 11 squares north and east to Bruce Co. and Halton RM. Breeding was confirmed in five squares, but pairs (some copulating) were observed in four additional squares, and thus nesting probably occurred in at least nine squares. A singing male reported from Bruce Co. was the most northerly breeding evidence reported. Breeding evidence was reported in three of five years during the atlas period. In 2003 and 2004, the species was reported in squares in Bruce Co. and Chatham-Kent, but in 2005 at least 43 individuals were reported from 10 squares in Essex and Dufferin Counties and Halton RM and Chatham-Kent.

Breeding biology: The Dickcissel is an irruptive species, dispersing widely during periods of extended spring drought within its core breeding range. Sporadic breeding in Ontario evidently occurs more commonly coincident with such irruptions, with most breeding occurrences in early summer. During the second atlas, all evidence of breeding occurred during the latter half of June and July. The Dickcissel is polygynous, with rates of multiple pairings varying with habitat quality and season. Higher rates of multiple pairings are more likely in larger habitat patches with dense (90-100%) cover of grasses and a high forb-grass ratio, and later in the season when vegetation is denser (Temple 2002). During territory establishment, males sing for as much as 70% of the day, vigorously defending territories against other males, and thus are easily observed. The species is single-brooded, and all incubation, brooding, and parental care of young is by the female. Females care for fledglings for up to 14 days, often after males have vacated territories.

Abundance: As expected with an irruptive species, there is considerable annual variation in Dickcissel abundance in Ontario. During rare, large irruption years, the species may be widespread and relatively common, but in most years it is evidently either unreported or present in very low numbers in the province. Breeding site fidelity beyond the core range is reported to be low (Temple 2002), and in Ontario there is no evidence of fidelity to sites in consecutive breeding seasons. *– Peter Read and Donald A. Sutherland*

Nests of coarse grasses and weed stems are located on the ground in dense grass cover or low in shrubs. Bronte Creek Prov. Park, Halton Region, 27 June 2005. *Photo: Mark Peck*

Hayfield and hedgerow breeding habitat of the Dickcissel in Bronte Creek Prov. Park, Halton Region, 28 June 2005. *Photo: Mark Peck*

Bobolink

Goglu des prés

Dolichonyx oryzivorus

George K. Peck

The male Bobolink is one of Ontario's most distinctive songbirds, immediately recognizable by its entirely black underparts contrasting with a bold white and yellow pattern above. Conversely, the somewhat smaller and heavily streaked yellowish-brown female resembles a large sparrow. During the breeding season, the Bobolink is restricted to grassland habitats across most of southern Canada and the northern US. An early fall migrant, it begins to assemble in large flocks in July, and is notable for its long migration to Argentina, an annual return distance of approximately 20,000 km (Martin and Gavin 1995).

Distribution and population status: Both atlases show that the Bobolink's distribution is largely restricted to southern Ontario, occurring essentially continuously north to the Highway 17 corridor between North Bay and Sault Ste. Marie. Scattered populations occur locally farther north, especially in the Clay Belt areas in Timiskaming and Cochrane Districts in the northeast and in the Thunder Bay, Rainy River, and Dryden areas in northwestern Ontario.

Between atlases, the probability of observation of the Bobolink declined significantly by 28% in the province overall. The largest declines occurred in the Northern and Southern Shield regions, where the probability of observation declined by 68% and 28%, respectively. In the Southern Shield, decline is particularly evident in the Algonquin, Madawaska, and Haliburton Highlands. Farther south, in the Lake Simcoe-Rideau and Carolinian regions, while the species is still very widespread, the probability of observation declined by 5% and 10%, respectively.

The considerable decline of the Bobolink on the Southern Shield and northerly parts of Lake Simcoe-Rideau regions may be at least partly attributable to the advance of natural succession on abandoned farms in this part of the province, and is similar to patterns observed for other grassland and shrubland

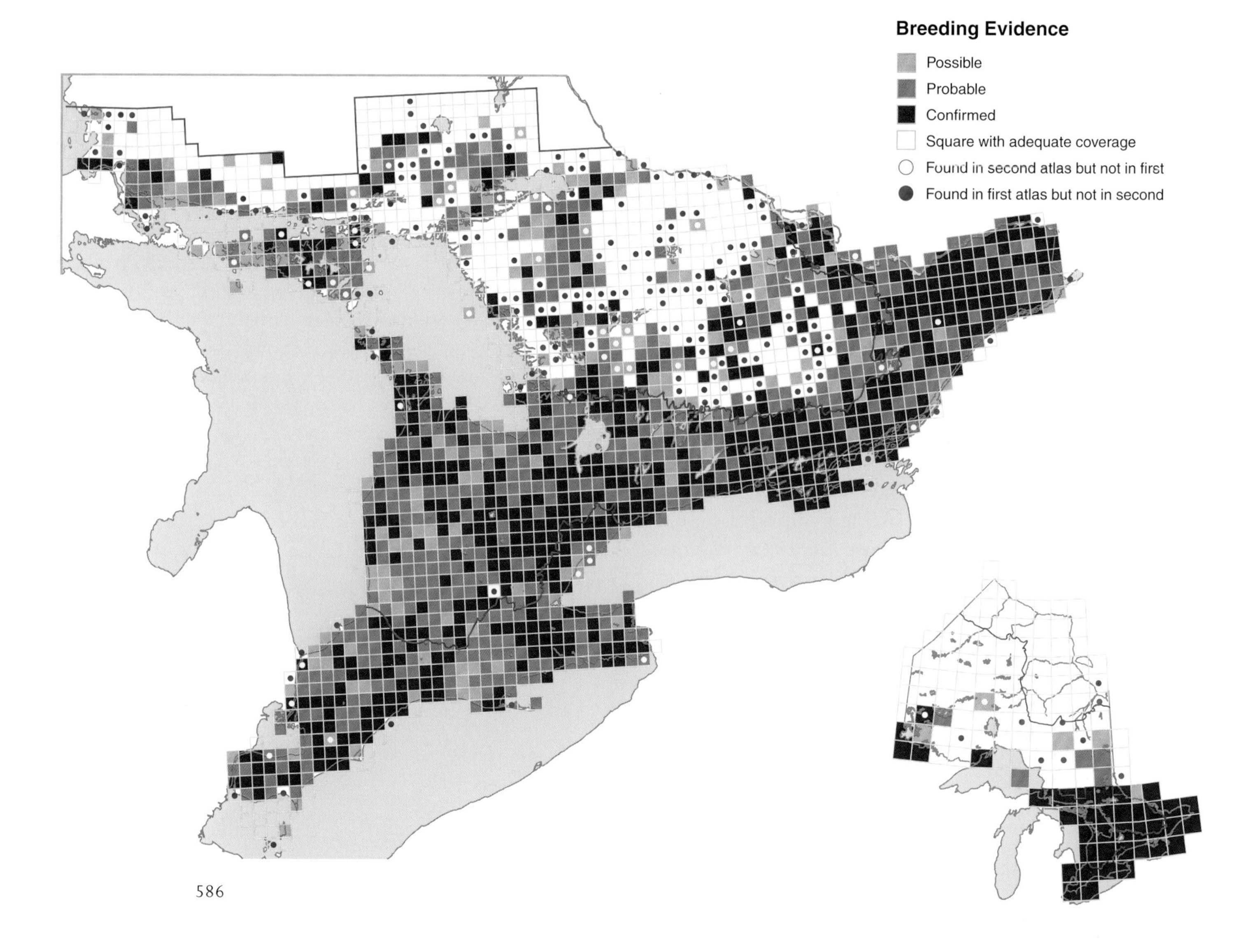

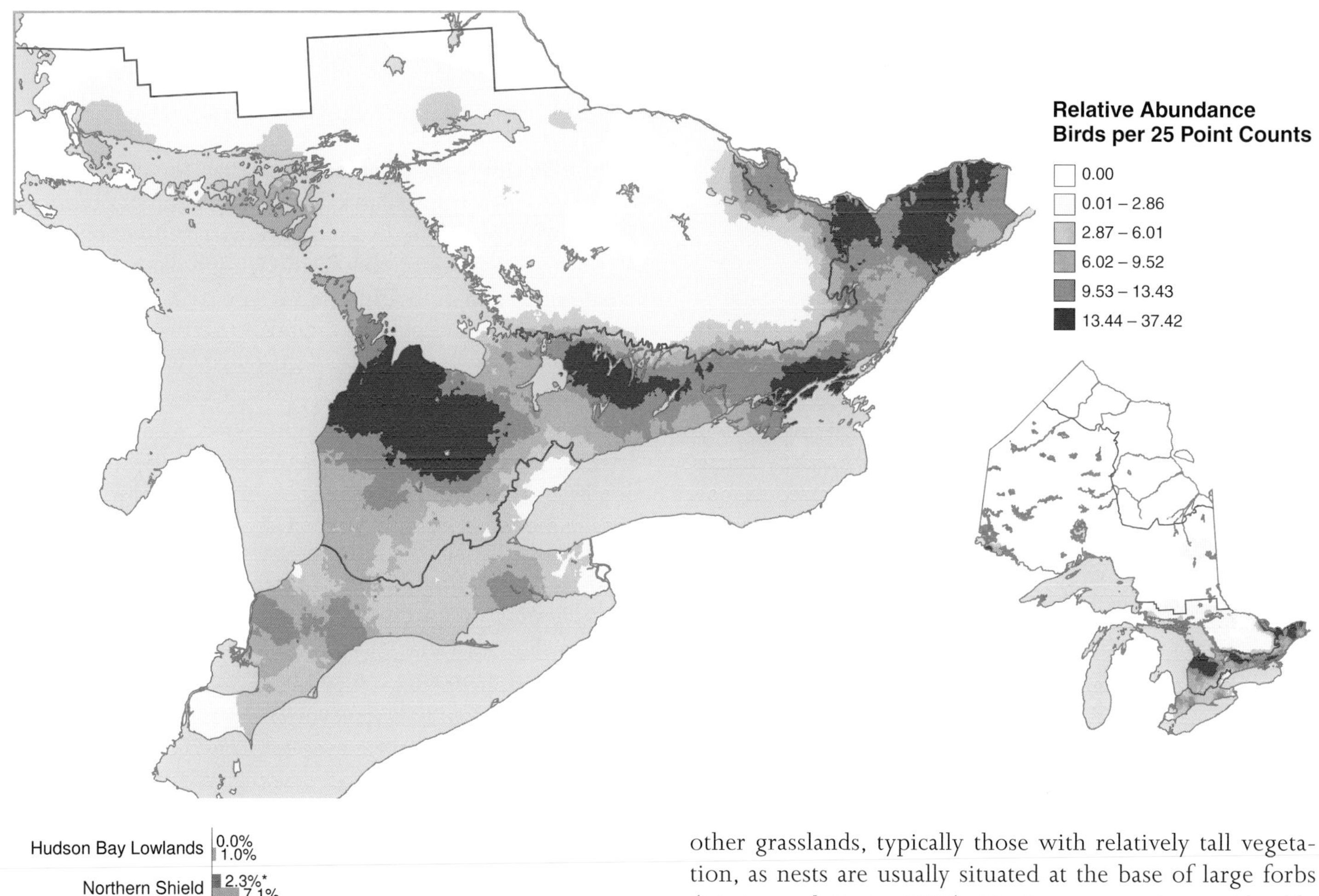

Hudson Bay Lowlands 0.0% 1.0%
Northern Shield 2.3%* 7.1%
Southern Shield 40.5%* 56.4%
Lake Simcoe-Rideau 87.6%* 92.5%
Carolinian 73.2%* 81.2%
Ontario 12.1%* 16.9%
0% 20% 40% 60% 80% 100%
Probability of Observation
1st Atlas 2nd Atlas

species. Elsewhere in southern Ontario, loss of suitable habitat may also be an issue for the species, but more likely is due to intensification of agriculture and urbanization rather than reversion to forest.

In general, the range of the Bobolink in eastern North America increased dramatically with the clearing of forests for agriculture, but the species has more recently undergone a downward trend as such land is lost to natural succession, urbanization, or other changes in land use. BBS data for Canada indicate a sharp decline beginning in the 1980s, with the annual index of abundance during the years of the second atlas only one-quarter of what was observed during the first atlas period. The decline has been much more gradual in Ontario and did not become apparent until the late 1980s. This suggests that the Ontario population is relatively robust, likely due to the large remaining areas of marginal farmland that provide suitable breeding habitat with minimal human disturbance.

Breeding biology: The Bobolink breeds in hayfields and other grasslands, typically those with relatively tall vegetation, as nests are usually situated at the base of large forbs (Martin and Gavin 1995). Nesting success is considerably higher in undisturbed fields and those mown in mid- to late summer, as early haying results in a high rate of juvenile mortality or nest failure.

The conspicuous display flight and loud bubbly song of the male Bobolink make this an easy species to detect, and thus the maps should accurately reflect its distribution. The nest is difficult to find, as the female usually approaches it indirectly, landing some distance away and walking to it out of sight through the grass. However, pairs and agitated behaviour are easy to observe, as are adults carrying food to highly vocal fledged young, allowing the species to be recorded as probable or confirmed in 84% of squares where it was reported.

Abundance: Ontario's core Bobolink populations are tightly linked with areas of relatively low-intensity agriculture. Specifically, the species is most abundant in Grey and Bruce Counties, around Peterborough and Kingston, and between the Ottawa and St. Lawrence Rivers in extreme southeastern Ontario. Despite having declined since the first atlas, the Bobolink remains a very common bird in much of southern Ontario, as it was the 12th most abundant species on point counts in the Lake Simcoe-Rideau region, and 24th most abundant in the Carolinian region. Breeding areas on the Shield and in the Clay Belt are generally less densely populated, averaging fewer than 2.9 birds/25 point counts, but densities in the Rainy River area are similar to those in core areas of southern Ontario. – *Marcel A. Gahbauer*

Red-winged Blackbird

Carouge à épaulettes

Agelaius phoeniceus

Tim Stewart

The Red-winged Blackbird is an abundant and conspicuous component of the avifauna in wetland and upland habitats, including grassy fields, suburban parks, and sewage lagoons. It is among the most numerous bird species in Canada and the US, with an estimated population of 193,000,000 birds (Rich et al. 2004). Its breeding range encompasses most of the southern two-thirds of the North American continent, generally south of the Boreal Forest. On wintering grounds in the US, the Red-winged Blackbird forages in open fields and agricultural areas, where it is considered a "pest" species. It is among the few species not protected under Canada's *Migratory Birds Convention Act*.

Distribution and population status: The Red-winged Blackbird is widely distributed across the province, occurring in most atlas squares in the south and most 100-km blocks in the north, except along the northern edge of the Northern Shield region and in the Hudson Bay Lowlands, where it is of highly localized and generally sporadic occurrence north of 51° N. In the northern portion of its range, the species seems to be limited by the scarcity of fertile wetland habitats with emergent vegetation. Although its range in Ontario has changed little, the population increased in the first part of the 20th century (as it did across the continent), and that was thought to be due to the success of the species at utilizing the waste grain that makes up a substantial part of its diet in Ontario (Weatherhead in Cadman et al. 1987), and its adaptation to nesting in upland habitats (Graber and Graber 1963). BBS data show that the Ontario Red-winged Blackbird population peaked in about 1976 and has been declining since. At first glance, the breeding evidence map does not appear noticeably different between atlases. However, there was a significant (22%) decline in the probability of observation of the species across the province. The largest decline (33%) occurred in the Northern Shield region, with smaller declines of 10%

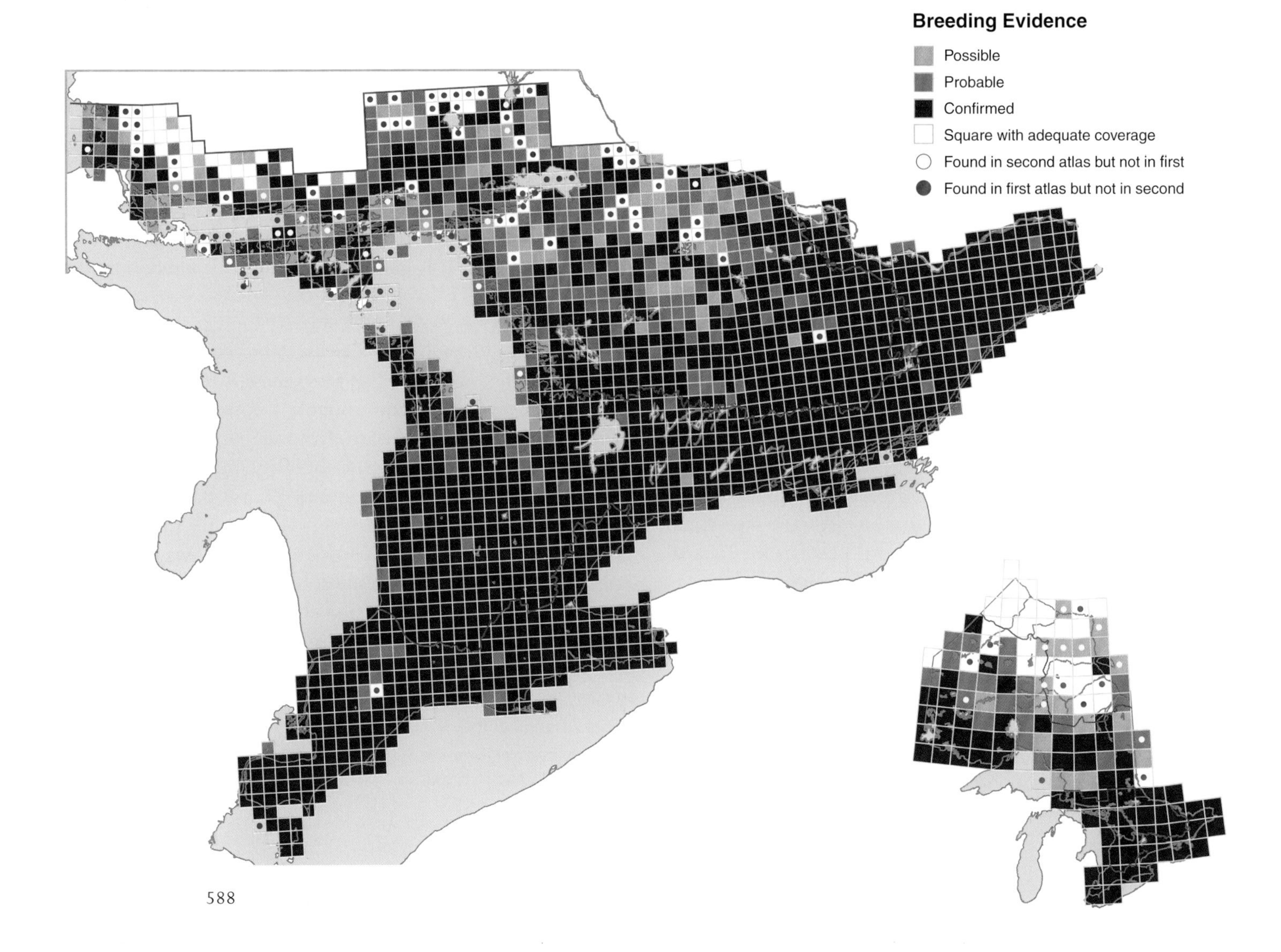

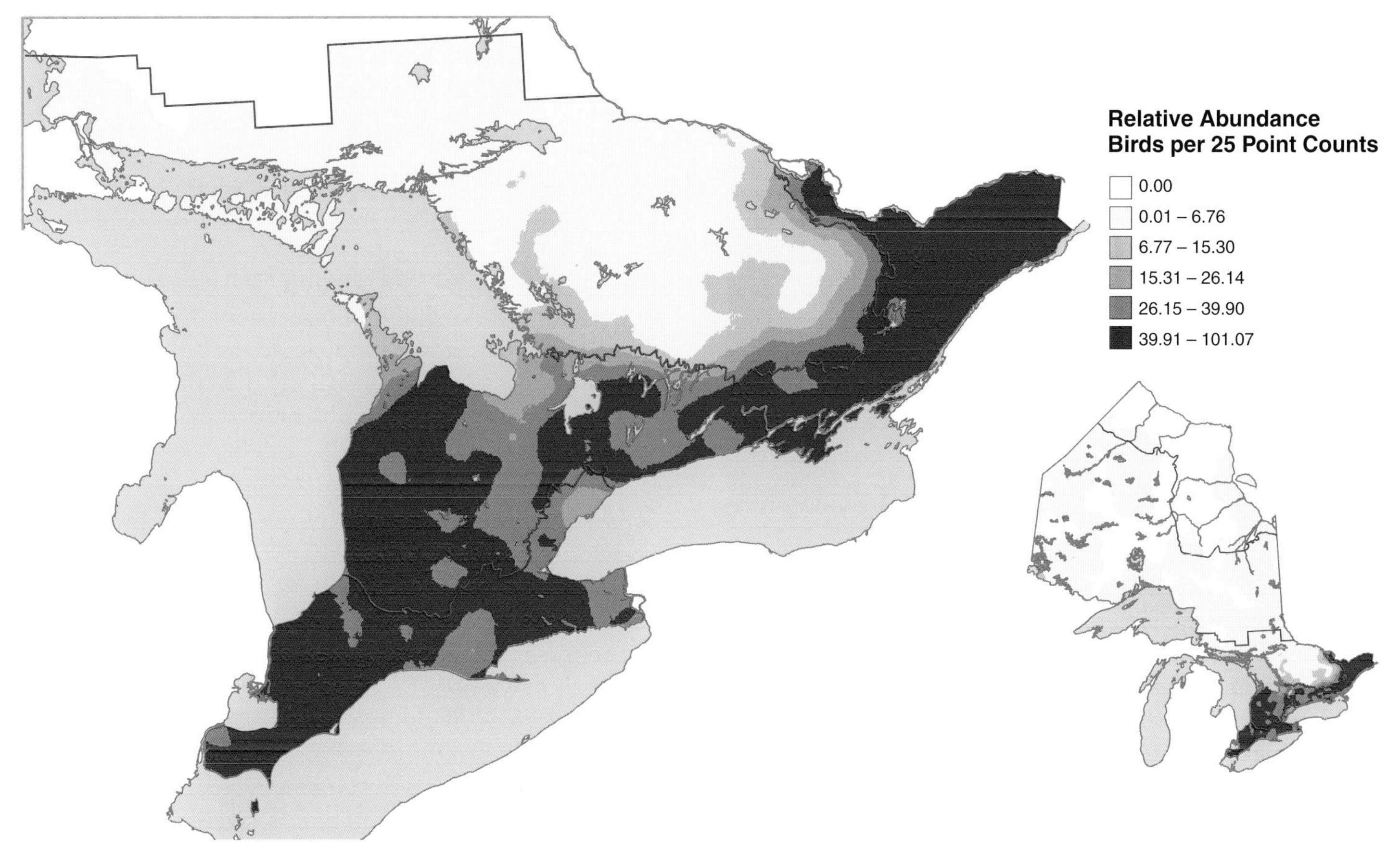

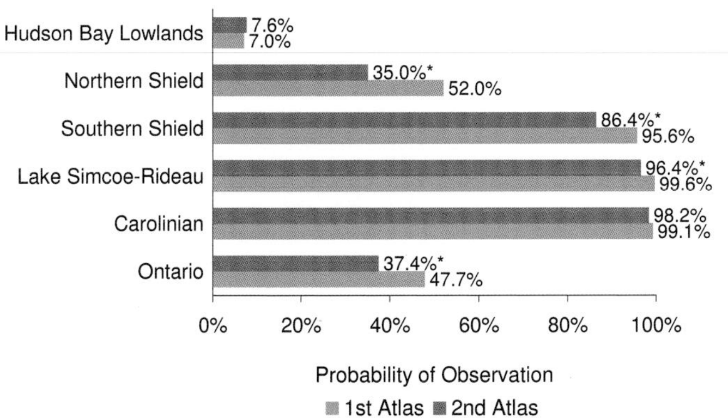

and 3% in the Southern Shield and the Lake Simcoe-Rideau regions, respectively. These declines may be related to reduced survival on wintering grounds in the US (Weatherhead 2005) where control programs periodically spray avicides on large blackbird communal roosts, killing millions of Red-winged Blackbirds. However, the loss of open fields and agricultural areas that has occurred on the Shield, along with increasingly efficient agricultural practices that waste less grain, may also have contributed to the decline.

Breeding biology: Although primarily associated with large, natural freshwater marshes, the Red-winged Blackbird also nests in anthropogenic wetland and upland habitats, including small patches of marsh vegetation in roadside ditches, flood retention ponds, sewage lagoons, hayfields, pastures, and suburban habitats (Peck and James 1987). In the central portion of the province, nest initiation begins in late April to early May (Peck and James 1987). It is among the easiest species to detect; males are highly visible and vocal during territorial displays and will physically attack conspecifics and other intruders, including humans. Males often breed polygynously and may have harems of up to three or more females (Weatherhead 2005). Early in the breeding season, nests are constructed of grasses within the dead emergent vegetation from the previous year, making them relatively easy to locate. Later in the breeding season, nests become more difficult to find as they are concealed by new growth.

Abundance: The relative abundance map for the Red-winged Blackbird shows a general decline with higher latitude, with a sharp drop-off at the edge of the Shield. The species is most abundant from southwestern Ontario north and east through Cornwall and the Ottawa Valley. In this area, nesting habitat, including agricultural fields and wetlands, is abundant, although many of the "wetlands" in the intensively farmed southwest are roadside and drainage ditches. Lower numbers of birds are evident in urban Toronto, where there are few wetlands, and along the Niagara Escarpment, where perhaps there are fewer open marshes due to heavier forest cover. As is true of many wetland-nesting passerines, Red-winged Blackbird abundance is influenced by wetland productivity, and some of the highest densities occur on sewage lagoons because of the high insect availability (Zimmerling 2006). As a result, the relatively low abundance in the Northern Shield and Hudson Bay Lowlands likely reflects lower wetland fertility and shorelines that lack emergent vegetation, providing poor nesting habitat. – *J. Ryan Zimmerling*

Eastern Meadowlark

Sturnelle des prés

Sturnella magna

Ethan Meleg

The Eastern Meadowlark is one of the most recognizable and familiar of Ontario's grassland birds. Its bright yellow breast makes it difficult to mistake for anything but the closely related and much rarer Western Meadowlark. Where the species are found together, the Eastern Meadowlark can be distinguished by its distinctive whistled song. The species is wide ranging, found from the Atlantic coast into the Midwest and from southern Canada to the US Gulf Coast. It is a year-round resident in most of its range, but in Ontario and the northeast, it is primarily a migrant. Although it prefers native grasslands, it will nest in pastures and agricultural fields, especially those in alfalfa and hay. It also uses old fields and meadows, often overgrown with shrubs, and prefers dry habitat to wet and tall grass to short. Occasionally, it will use other areas such as golf courses or sand dunes (Peck and James 1987; Lanyon 1995).

Distribution and population status: The Eastern Meadowlark expanded into northeastern North America, including southern Ontario, with the clearing of the forests for agriculture and settlement (Bent 1958). By the beginning of the 20th century, the species had become common throughout southern Ontario as far north as the southern end of Muskoka Dist. (Mills 1981). It has been known since at least the 1940s in the Blezard Valley between Chelmsford and Sudbury (Baillie and Hope 1947), was called abundant in the Lake Nipissing area by Ricker and Clarke (1939), and was reported north to Englehart by Baillie and Harrington (1937).

The species' Ontario range has not changed significantly since the first atlas. It was found in the majority of squares in the Carolinian and Lake Simcoe-Rideau regions, while on the Shield it was mostly limited to highway corridors and settled areas. However, during the second atlas, its probability of observation was 13% lower in the province as a whole than during the first atlas, with significant declines of 9-17% in the three southern Ontario regions. There was also a decline in the

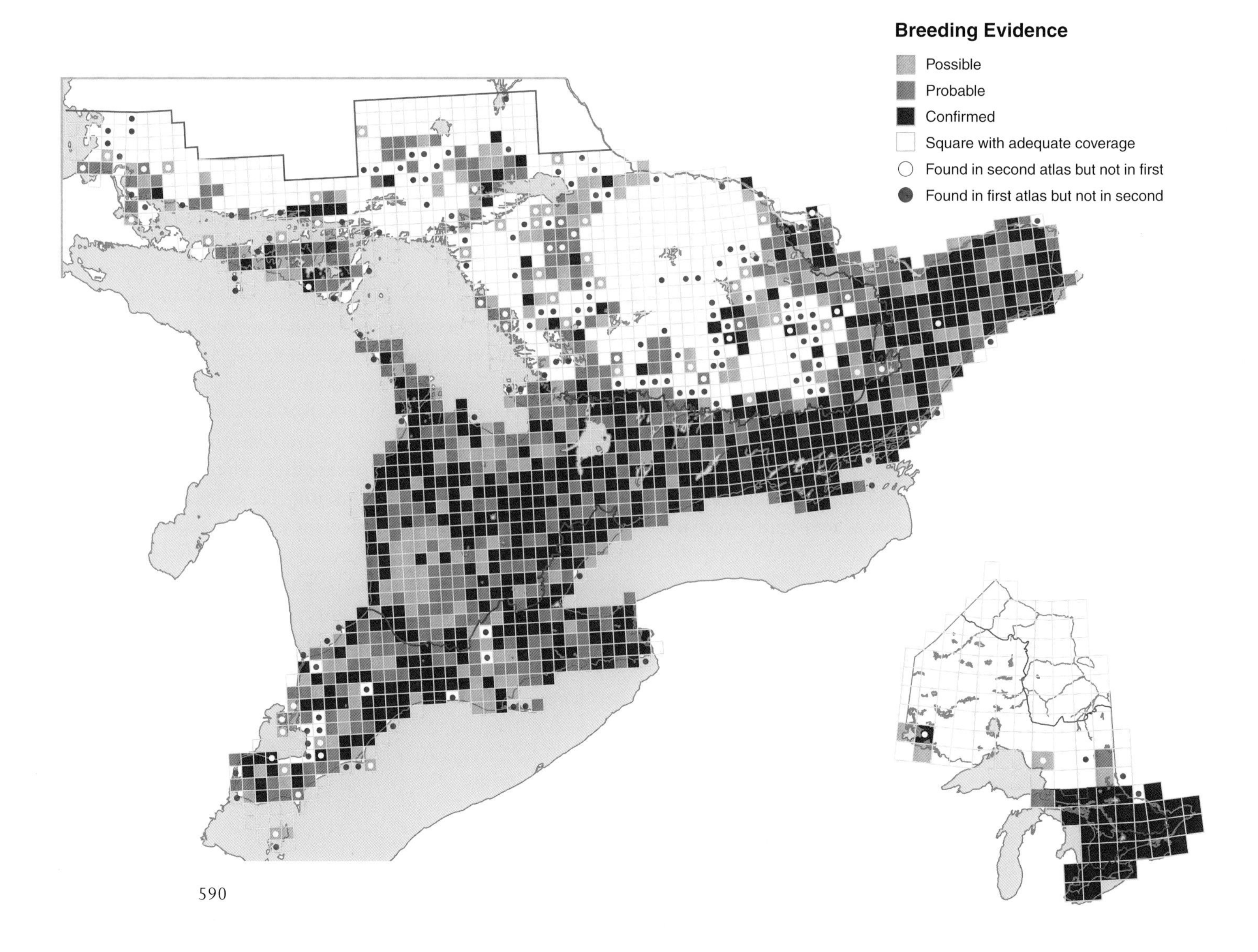

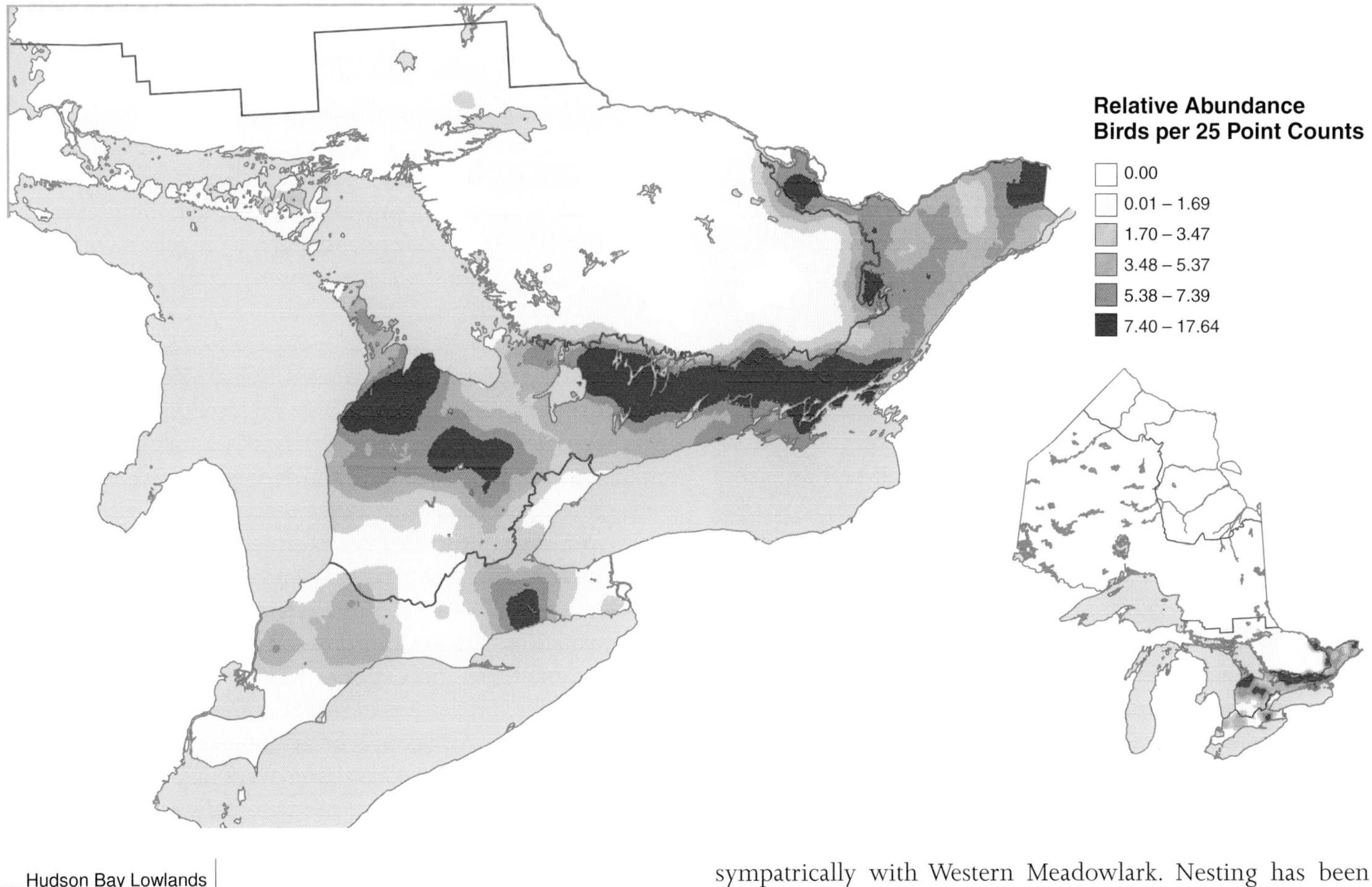

Hudson Bay Lowlands
Northern Shield 0.4% 0.7%
Southern Shield 27.2%* 32.7%
Lake Simcoe-Rideau 83.4%* 92.0%
Carolinian 73.8%* 88.2%
Ontario 9.8%* 11.3%
0% 20% 40% 60% 80% 100%
Probability of Observation
1st Atlas 2nd Atlas

Northern Shield region, but the numbers reported were too small for the change to be statistically significant.

The natural succession of abandoned agricultural fields back to forest on the Shield and the northern portion of the Lake Simcoe-Rideau region, together with more intensive farming practices and expanding urbanization in southwestern and eastern Ontario, has resulted in significant habitat loss for grassland species including the Eastern Meadowlark. BBS data show a near significant 1.5% annual decline in Eastern Meadowlark populations in Ontario since 1968 (Downes et al. 2005) but no change since 1981. No BBS region in North America shows a statistically significant increase in the species since 1981 (Sauer et al. 2005).

The few records in the Little and Great Clay Belts are somewhat surprising, given the amount of apparently suitable habitat. Even within these areas, the species was not recorded in the same squares in both atlases, suggesting that occupancy of sites may be ephemeral and perhaps only by unmated males. It was reported in both atlases in Rainy River Dist., where it occurs sympatrically with Western Meadowlark. Nesting has been confirmed in the Thunder Bay area (Peck and James 1987), but the species was not recorded there in either atlas.

Breeding biology: In Ontario, male Eastern Meadowlarks arrive on breeding territories in April. Females generally arrive two to four weeks later and quickly form pair bonds through courtship displays consisting of relatively conspicuous duets and aerial chases (Lanyon 1995). Eggs may be laid as early as the beginning of May but average late May to mid-June, and the species may be double-brooded (Peck and James 1987), offering additional opportunities to confirm nesting over a season. During nest building and incubation, the female is secretive. Because of the species' distinctive song and habit of singing from prominent perches such as trees or roadside wires, and its association with open, human-modified habitat, it should be detected wherever it occurs, so the distribution maps likely portray a fairly accurate representation of occurrence in Ontario.

Abundance: The Eastern Meadowlark occurs in highest densities through the Lake Simcoe-Rideau region and primarily from Kingston to Lake Simcoe and in Grey, Dufferin and southern Bruce Counties. Fields through this region tend to be less intensively farmed, pasture is relatively extensive, and the dominant crops are the alfalfa and hay preferred by meadowlarks. This mix seems to provide better habitat than the more heavily agricultural soybean and corn dominated regions of southwestern Ontario (Statistics Canada 2001), where Eastern Meadowlark numbers are considerably lower.
– Seabrooke Leckie

Western Meadowlark

Sturnelle de l'Ouest

Sturnella neglecta

R. E. Gehlert

Easily confused with the similarly plumaged Eastern Meadowlark, the Western Meadowlark is best distinguished by voice. Its songs differ from those of the Eastern Meadowlark in being lower-pitched with more dramatic changes, and is flute-like in quality rather than whistled. Call notes are also distinctive. Where the two species overlap in range, both can adopt mixed repertoires that may include songs resembling those of the other species (Lanyon 1994). Primarily a bird of the prairies, the Western Meadowlark is found from the Pacific coast south to Mexico and east regularly to southern Ontario, where it occurs in small and scattered numbers in pastures and hayfields. It breeds occasionally in New England and New Jersey (Lanyon 1994).

Distribution and population status: The Western Meadowlark was first documented in northwestern Ontario in Rainy River Dist. and the Thunder Bay area prior to 1930 (Baillie and Harrington 1937; Snyder 1938), and in southern Ontario in 1932 (Baillie 1960). By the 1950s, it had spread widely, occurring in small isolated breeding colonies, occasionally interbreeding with the Eastern Meadowlark (J.B. Falls, pers. comm.). By the time of the first atlas, a marked decline in abundance had occurred, which has continued until most records are now of widely scattered single males. Only in the southwestern Rainy River Dist., contiguous with Manitoba and Minnesota, is there still a viable population.

Currently, the Western Meadowlark is found locally in the Carolinian and Lake Simcoe-Rideau regions as far east as the Peterborough area. It occurs at scattered sites through the Shield regions, but its stronghold is in the southwestern portion of Rainy River Dist. Interestingly, it was recorded there in more squares in the second atlas than the first (13 vs. 8, perhaps due to greater effort), yet anecdotal evidence (D.A. Sutherland, pers. comm.) suggests that it was more common at the time of the first atlas, certainly outnumbering the

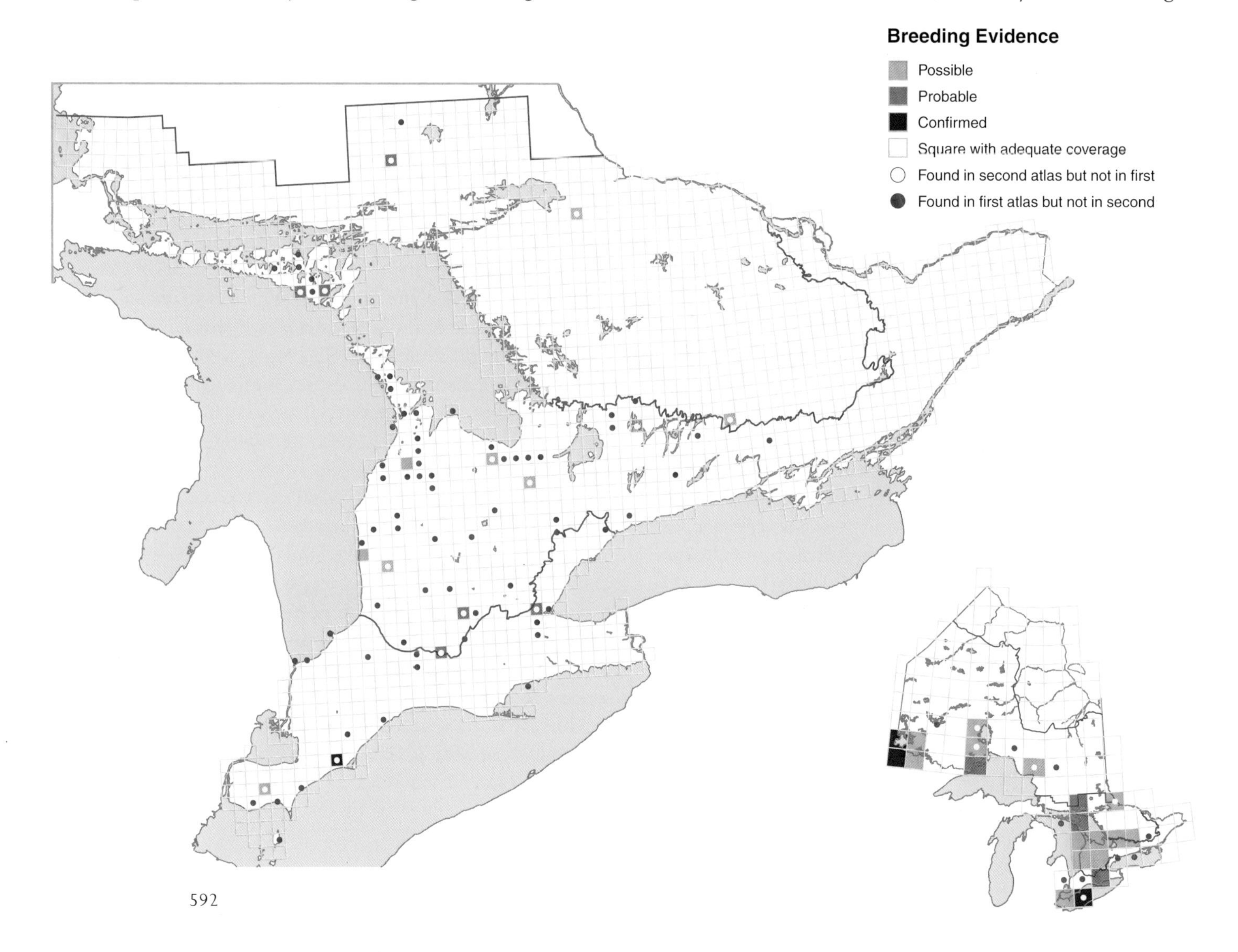

BREEDING EVIDENCE

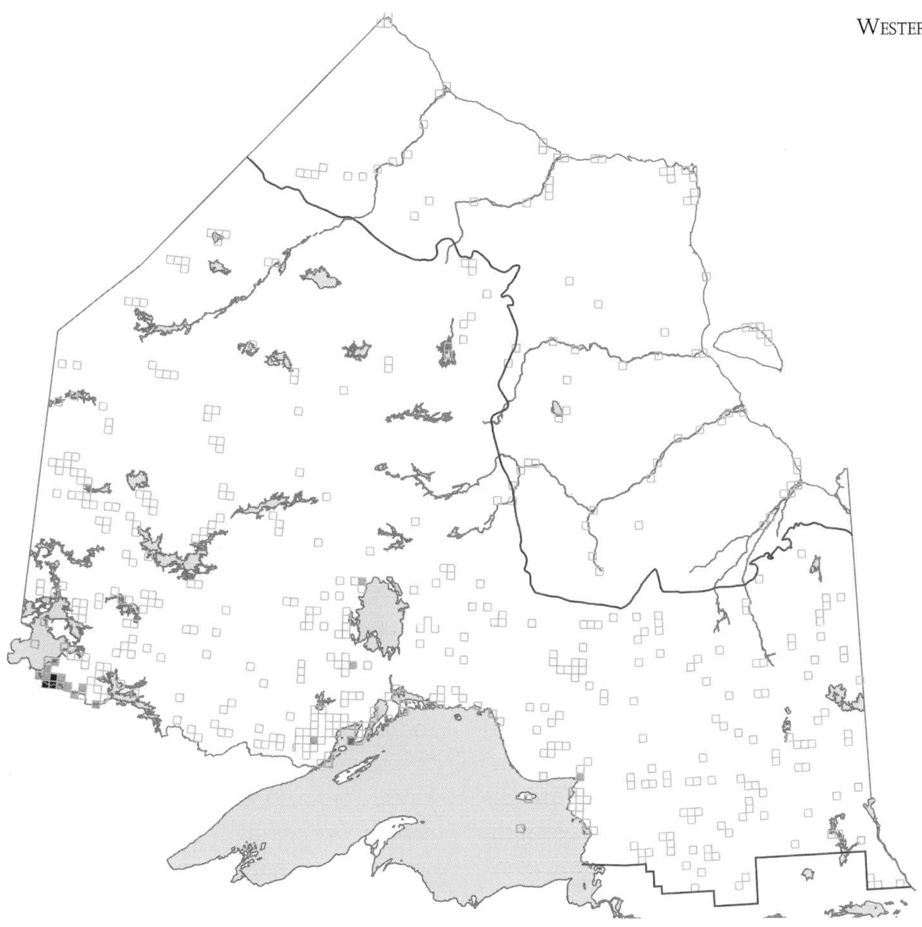

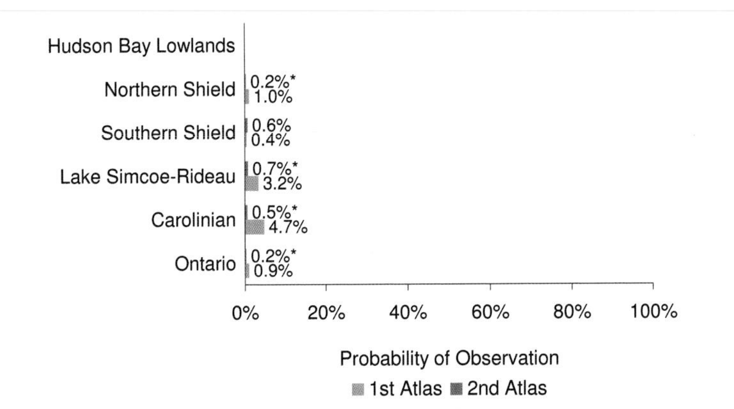

Eastern Meadowlark, and has since declined in abundance.

Between atlases, the probability of observation of the Western Meadowlark declined by 89% in the Carolinian region and 80% in the Lake Simcoe-Rideau region. BBS data show that it has declined significantly by 11% per year within Ontario since 1981, and is in fact declining significantly across the whole of its range. Grassland species are declining from loss of habitat, as the agricultural fields on which they came to depend are lost through land-use change. Abandoned fields maturing through natural succession, increasing urbanization, more intensive farming, and conversion from pasture to row crops and from alfalfa/hay to corn and soybeans have all reduced the amount of available habitat for the species (Askins 2000). Only one square in southern Ontario recorded Western Meadowlark in both the first and second atlases, which is likely a reflection of the changing availability of limited suitable habitat. Western and Eastern Meadowlarks will defend territories against both species in areas where they occur together (Lanyon 1994), which further limits the habitat available to the species.

Breeding biology: Like its eastern counterpart, the Western Meadowlark is migratory in the northern part of its range, including Ontario. Males usually arrive in Ontario in April, females two to four weeks later, and pair bonds are formed immediately. Courtship displays include aerial chases, which are often fairly conspicuous (Lanyon 1994). Eggs are laid and incubated from mid-May to June (Peck and James 1987), during which time the female can be very secretive. Nests are hard to find. Females will usually abandon the nest if disturbed during this period (Lanyon 1994). Of 34 squares in which breeding evidence was reported for the species during the second atlas, only four had breeding confirmed. Observations of fledged young and adults carrying food constituted three of these, and are the easiest criteria by which to confirm meadowlarks. Only one nest was found during this period, and just nine were documented for Ontario prior to 2000 (Peck 2002). Most records during this atlas period were of singing males, and many of those were likely unpaired individuals.

Abundance: The Western Meadowlark is a very uncommon summer resident in the province. In southern Ontario, it is found most often as a single individual, and usually territories are occupied for only a year or two in succession. The species occurs in highest abundance in the southwestern portion of Rainy River Dist. It was detected on point counts in only nine squares during the second atlas and was recorded on more than one point in only three squares, all contiguous, one of them containing the town of Rainy River. – *Seabrooke Leckie*

Yellow-headed Blackbird

Carouge à tête jaune

Xanthocephalus xanthocephalus

George K. Peck

The Yellow-headed Blackbird occurs in Ontario at the extreme eastern edge of its range, which extends west through the Prairie Provinces to eastern British Columbia and south through much of the western US. The winter range covers most of Mexico.

This blackbird is a species of permanent marshes and sloughs, where it nests in emergent vegetation, particularly cattails and Common Reed. Foraging habitat includes cultivated and other open areas that may be far from water. A gregarious and polygynous species, the Yellow-headed Blackbird breeds in colonies of a few to many hundreds of pairs.

Distribution and population status: The Yellow-headed Blackbird is a regular breeder in Ontario only near Lake of the Woods and in the extreme southwest around Lake St. Clair. Nesting was first documented near Rainy River in 1961 (Baillie 1961), and in the Lake St. Clair marshes in 1965 (Sawyer and Dyer 1968).

There is no evidence of important change in distribution within Ontario between the atlases. In northwestern Ontario, the number of squares in which the Yellow-headed Blackbird was found increased from 7 to 13, but this could have resulted from more extensive northern coverage during the second atlas. The most northerly record was of a paired female carrying nesting material at the Pikangikum sewage lagoons, about 90 km north of Red Lake. While it seems likely that complete coverage of squares in northwestern Ontario would have uncovered additional colonies, the overall range indicated by the current map is thought to be accurate.

The Yellow-headed Blackbird prefers to nest over open water, typically at least 0.5 m deep, and water levels must remain sufficiently high to support both adequate edge habitat and overwinter survival of the primarily aquatic insect prey (Twedt and Crawford 1995). Local changes in numbers can be related to fluctuations in water depth (Lederer et al. 1975),

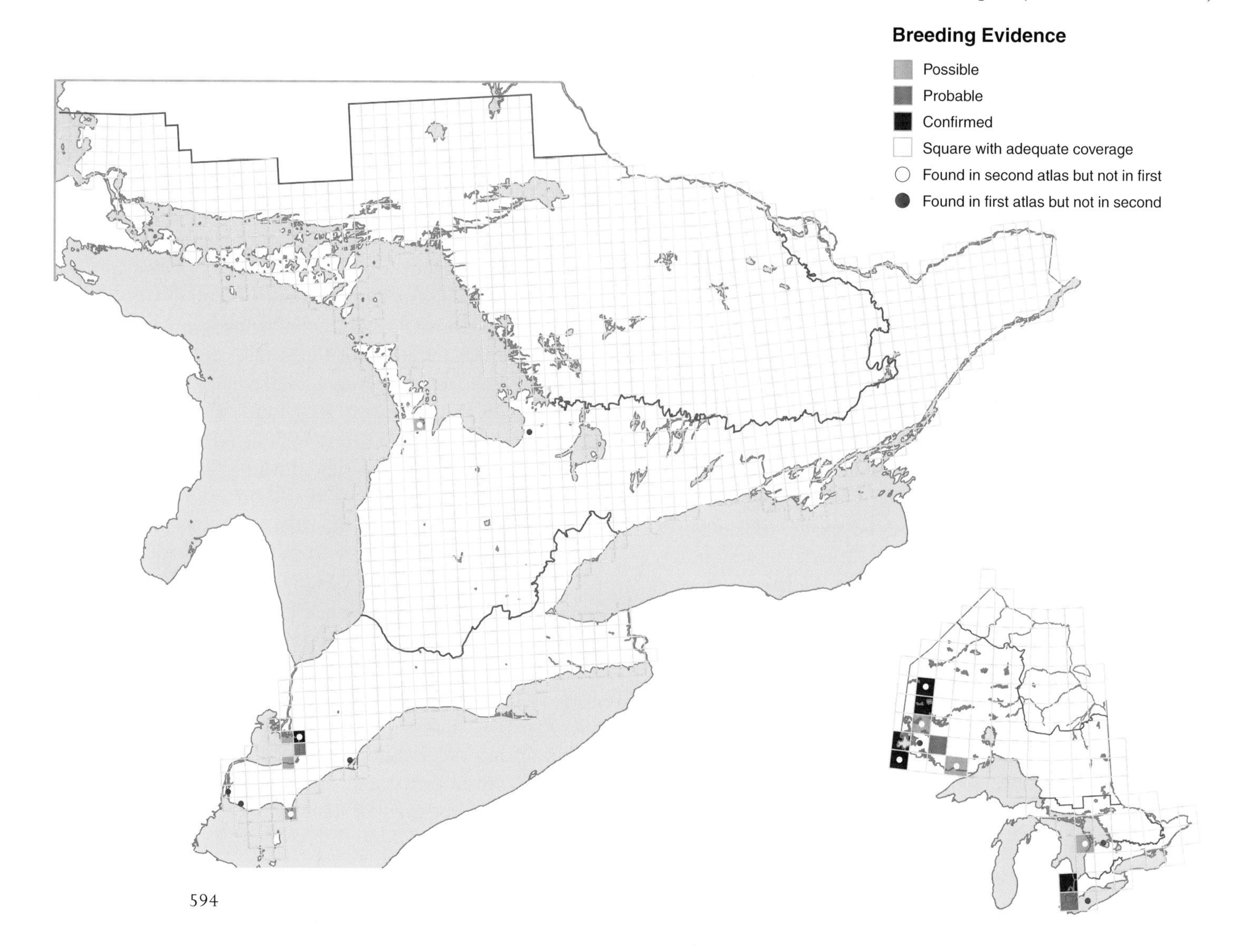

BREEDING EVIDENCE

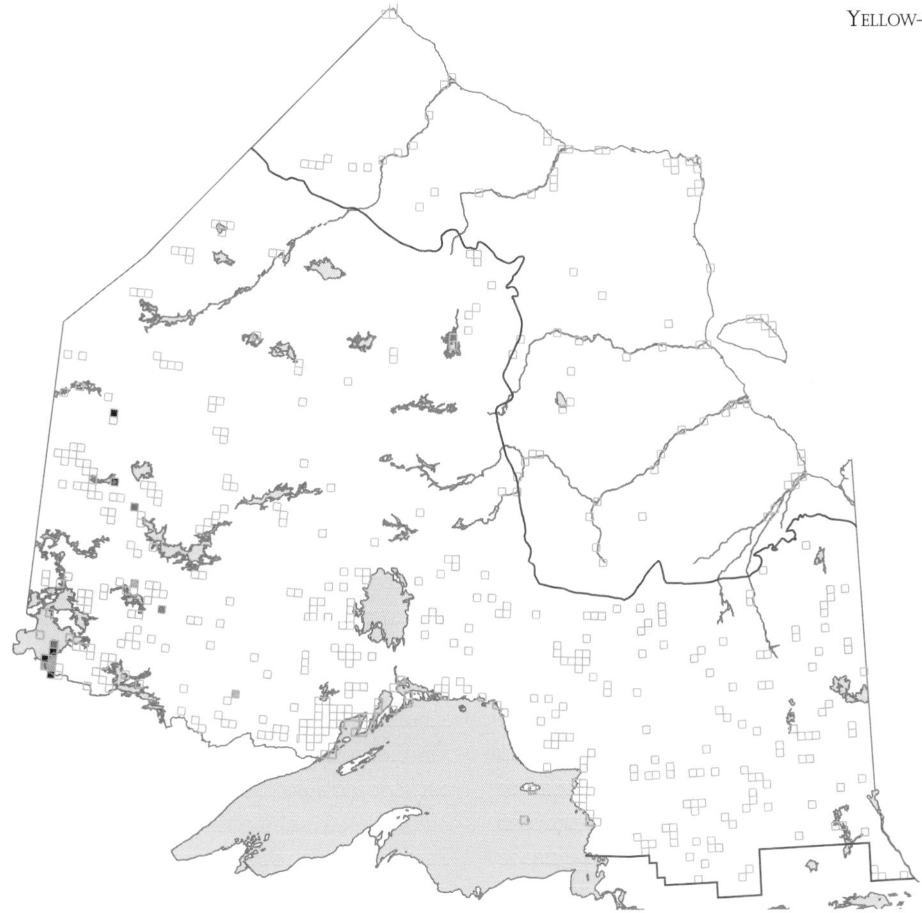

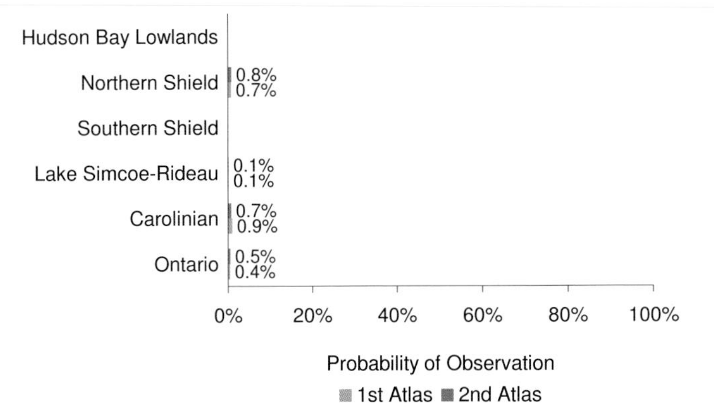

which alter amount of edge habitat preferred for nesting. Small colonies at the species' range periphery are vulnerable to extirpation (McCabe 1985), and colonies at sewage lagoons in Essex Co. at Amherstburg and Essex and in the marsh in Tremblay Beach Conservation Area near Stoney Point, Lake St. Clair, disappeared or declined between atlases due to habitat degradation or loss. Regional population declines also occur when there are sustained droughts (Nelms et al. 1994). BBS data show a significant decline across Canada in the past 20 years, with numbers first increasing, then decreasing. Numbers now appear to have stabilized at a level higher than during the early 1970s.

Breeding biology: Yellow-headed Blackbird colonies are quite conspicuous, as they are often large. The brightly coloured males are aggressive and loud during territorial and courtship displays, and both parents carry food to the young. Given these characteristics, it is somewhat surprising that the species was reported only as a possible breeder in half of the squares in which it was reported. The Rare/Colonial Species Report Forms for these squares indicate that most observations were of single birds, including the isolated square in the Bruce region south of Georgian Bay. Given the colonial nature of this species and relative ease of determining whether more than one individual is present, the probability is low that there was breeding within squares where only single birds were observed.

Only one nest was found during the first atlas, but nests were found in five squares in the second, perhaps due to greater effort. One atlasser reported using waders to reach a colony site, while another used a canoe.

Abundance: The colonial habit of this species concentrates birds into limited portions of marshes, which themselves are patchily distributed in the landscape, and colonies are usually distant from the shallow waters of marsh edges. Thus, Yellow-headed Blackbirds are poorly sampled by point counts, and colony number and size is a better indicator of abundance. In the first atlas, only one estimate of abundance was reported, of 2 to 10 pairs in a square in the Lake of the Woods area. For the second atlas, the Rare/Colonial Species Report Forms available for all records provided some clues as to abundance. For the squares with probable or confirmed breeding, some squares had very small colonies (less than 10 pairs), but three colonies reported from northwestern Ontario had 12, 15, and 25 nests. There were no details for specific colonies in southwestern Ontario provided to the atlas. However, the population in the marshes on the east shore of Lake St. Clair, excluding Walpole Island, during the atlas period is estimated to be 75-100 birds (J. Haggeman, pers. comm.). – *Erica H. Dunn*

Rusty Blackbird

Quiscale rouilleux

Euphagus carolinus

George K. Peck

The Rusty Blackbird breeds largely north of the areas of highest human populations, throughout the Boreal Forest and subarctic regions from Newfoundland, the Maritimes, and northern New England across all the Canadian provinces and territories to Alaska (Avery 1995). It winters mainly in bottomland swamp forests in the southern and eastern US. Despite its extensive distribution, there is evidence from the CBC, BBS, and other sources of a dramatic long-term population decline across the continent over more than a century (Greenberg and Droege 1999). Quantitative analyses indicate a decline of 85%-95% from the 1960s to the present (COSEWIC 2006c). The decline was strongest from the 1960s through the early 1980s, but BBS data indicate a continued decline of the species in Canada at about 5.8% per year since the early 1980s. Despite concerns about CBC data reliability and the fact that BBS covers only the southern portion of the range, it has been designated a species of Special Concern in Canada.

Distribution and population status: In Ontario, the Rusty Blackbird was found from the Southern Shield north to the Hudson Bay Lowlands. In the south, records were concentrated in Algonquin Prov. Park as well as areas north of Lake Huron, in a total of 86 squares. It was recorded in 134 squares throughout the Northern Shield and 140 squares in the Hudson Bay Lowlands.

Change analyses between atlases for the Shield seem to corroborate the long-term declines reported from other surveys. There was a significant drop of about 30% in the probability of observation in the Southern Shield and 32% in the Northern Shield. In Algonquin Prov. Park, the Rusty Blackbird was found in only 25 squares compared with 42 in the first atlas. However, in the Hudson Bay Lowlands, where the species is most abundant, there was a significant increase of 37%. It is possible that across the province the species has not declined but rather shift-

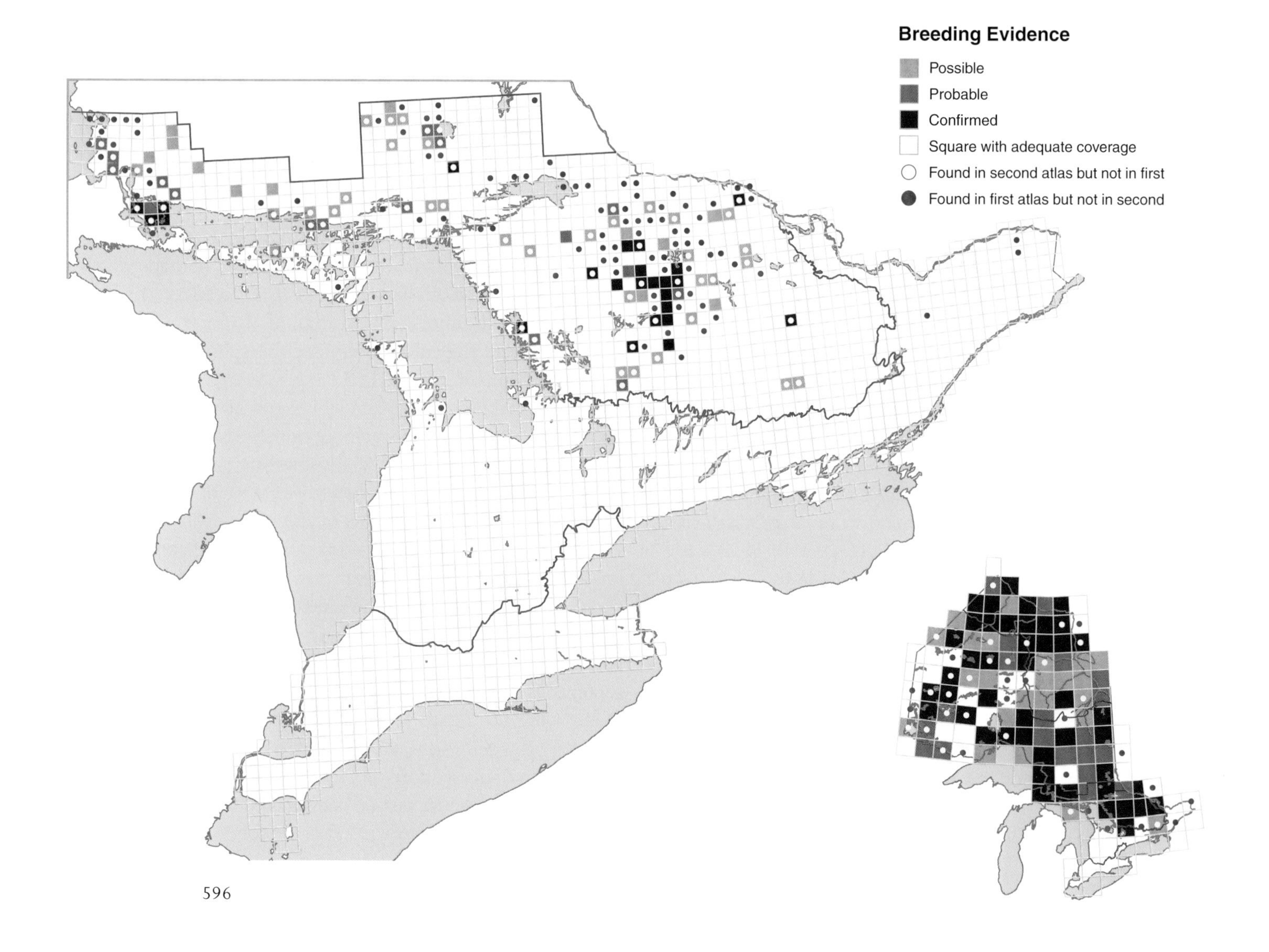

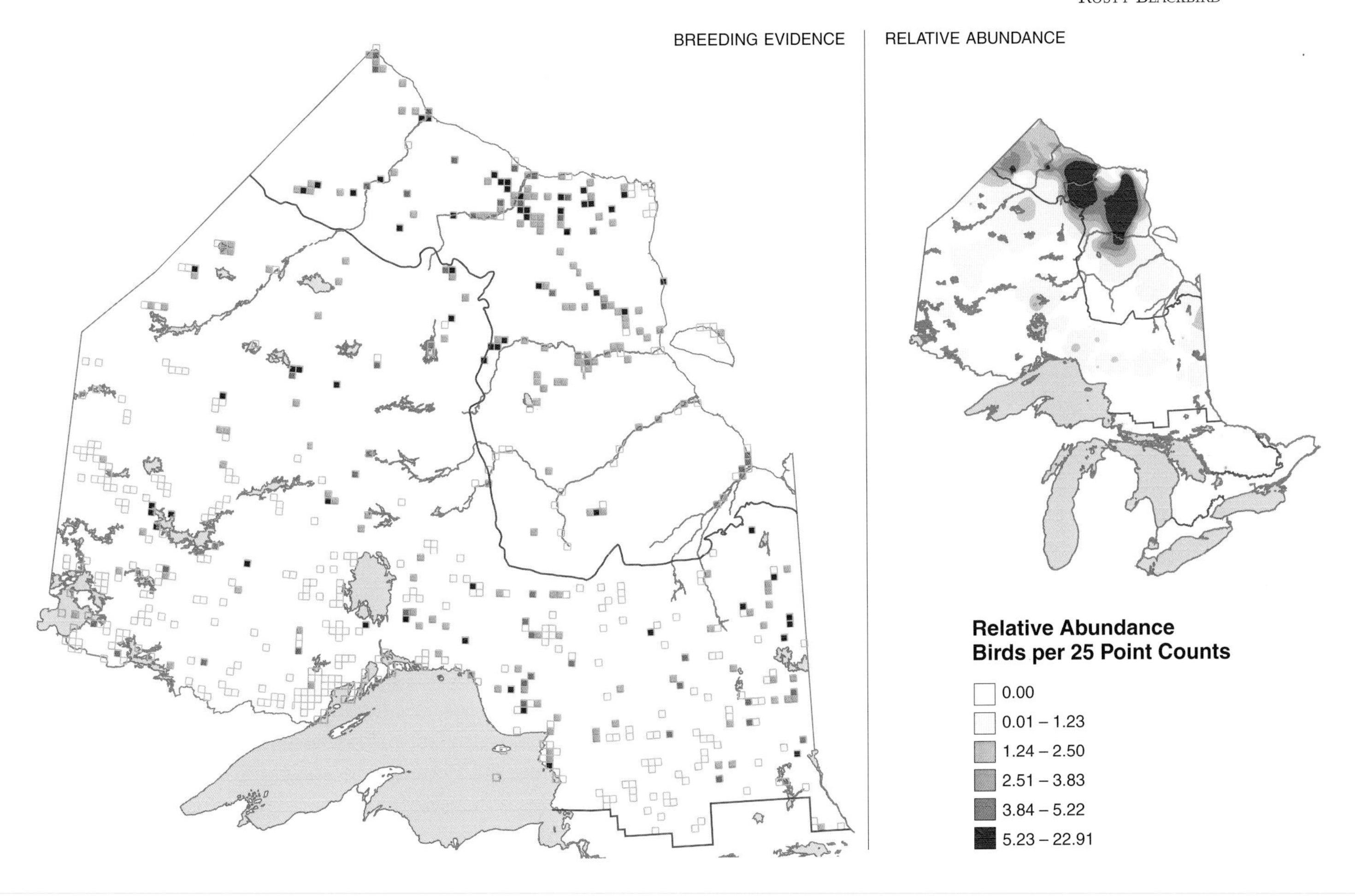

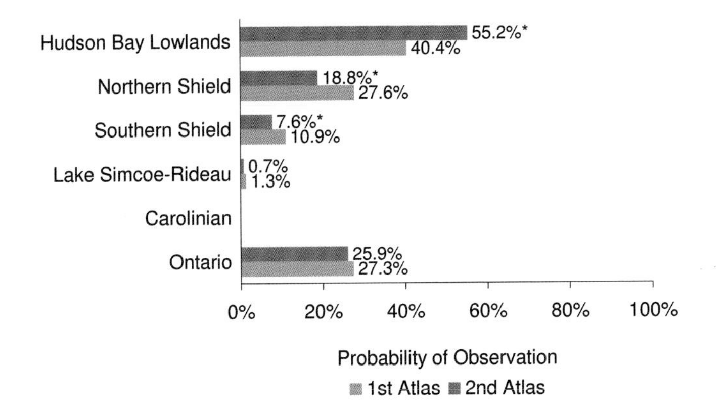

ed its distribution northwards. However, some caution is required, as there were differences in type of effort in the second atlas, especially in the north, with increased emphasis on carrying out point counts and covering more habitats.

Breeding biology: The Rusty Blackbird breeds in forested wetlands and swamps, including fens, bogs, muskeg, beaver ponds, and other wet openings in forest. In the Hudson Bay Lowlands, it occurs in muskegs, mainly along creeks, where it is found near dense vegetation with or without trees, including shrub thickets. The nest is typically built at a height of 0.5-6 m in small trees or shrubs near water (Avery 1995). Birds have been reported nesting at the edges of disturbed areas including remnant riparian forest next to regenerating cutovers or large burns (COSEWIC 2006c).

Abundance: Point count data indicate that the majority of the remaining Rusty Blackbird populations in Ontario are in the Hudson Bay Lowlands. In squares with the highest densities in this region, the species was detected on up to 45% of point counts, with an average of 2.4 birds/25 counts for the region. In contrast, average densities in the Northern Shield were much lower at only 0.1 birds/25 point counts, and even lower in the Southern Shield at 0.02 birds/25 point counts. These patterns are consistent with the distribution of breeding evidence data: overall, 39% of squares where the species was reported were in the Hudson Bay Lowlands, despite the relatively low effort in the region.

The presence of much higher densities in the taiga areas of northern Ontario has not previously been reported, although considerable geographic variation in density has been documented in Québec (COSEWIC 2006c). This raises the question of whether this density gradient has always existed, or whether the dramatic decline in this species over the past several decades has affected populations differently in different parts of Ontario. There is some evidence for this in the strong decline between atlases on the Shield but increases in the Hudson Bay Lowlands. Causes for the apparent decline of the species are not known but may include loss or deterioration of wetland habitat on the breeding or wintering grounds, as well as incidental mortality during blackbird control programs in the US. It seems unlikely that suitable habitat in the Shield regions of Ontario has declined enough to cause declines of 90% in the species without similar declines in other insectivorous wetland birds. This suggests a wintering-ground explanation may be more likely. Research on whether populations from different parts of Ontario winter in different areas may help to clarify this question, and may suggest possible approaches to attempting to restore numbers of this species. – *Charles M. Francis*

Brewer's Blackbird

Quiscale de Brewer

Euphagus cyanocephalus

Jean Iron

In the early 1900s, the Brewer's Blackbird occurred in the western US and southern parts of British Columbia and the Prairie Provinces. As human settlement opened agricultural and transportation corridors over the next half-century, the species expanded its range eastward along both sides of the Canada-US border (Martin 2002). This movement is understandable, given the main elements of the Brewer's Blackbird breeding habitat. These elements include scattered farm buildings; roads and highways with nearby open fields and pastures for foraging; perch sites afforded by scattered trees, shrubs, and fence lines; and sources of slightly to moderately calcareous, non-stagnant water. Iron (1998) has suggested that the Brewer's Blackbird is intolerant of heat and humidity, which may prevent it from breeding farther east in North America, similar to the situation reported for the Black-billed Magpie.

Distribution and population status: The species was first recorded as breeding in Ontario in Thunder Bay in 1945 and reached Sault Ste. Marie in 1953 (Gordon in Cadman et al. 1987). Ultimately, it spread eastward across the province in a discontinuous band north of Lake Huron, as well as settling on Manitoulin Island and in the Bruce Peninsula and the Muskoka area.

The Brewer's Blackbird exhibits an interesting physiographic restriction in the area between Sault Ste. Marie and Lake Nipissing, south to Bracebridge, where there is interspersion of soils derived from both the granitic Canadian Shield and the semi-calcareous floor of the post-glacial Lake Algonquin (Lake Superior and Lake Huron). In this region, the Brewer's Blackbird has a scattered distribution associated with water that is of moderate pH and clear and often moving, in streams, ditches, and ponds. The species does not frequent or breed on sites with moisture derived solely from the granitic Canadian Shield, which covers most of northern Ontario. The local vegetation of these two major physiographic land-types

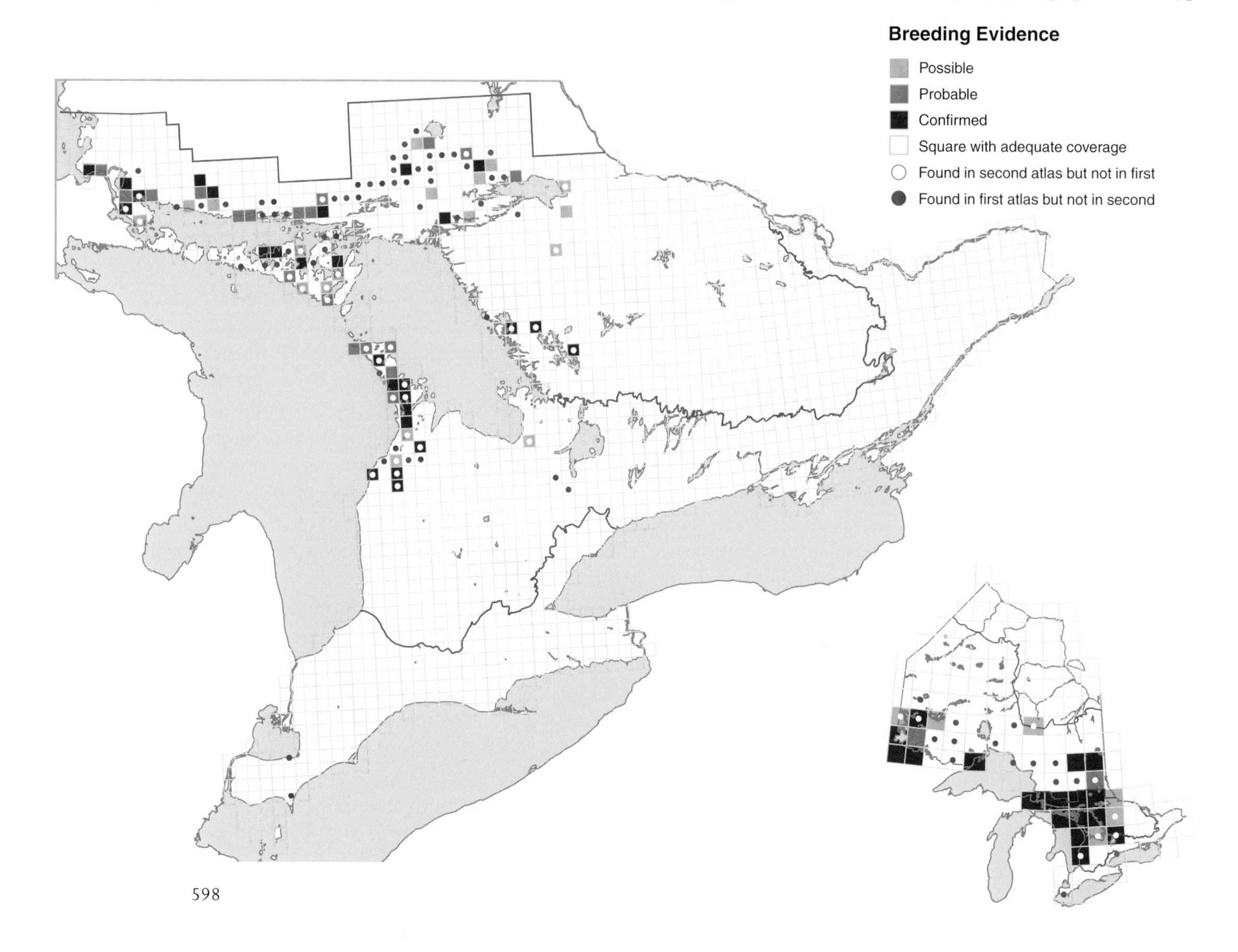

BREEDING EVIDENCE

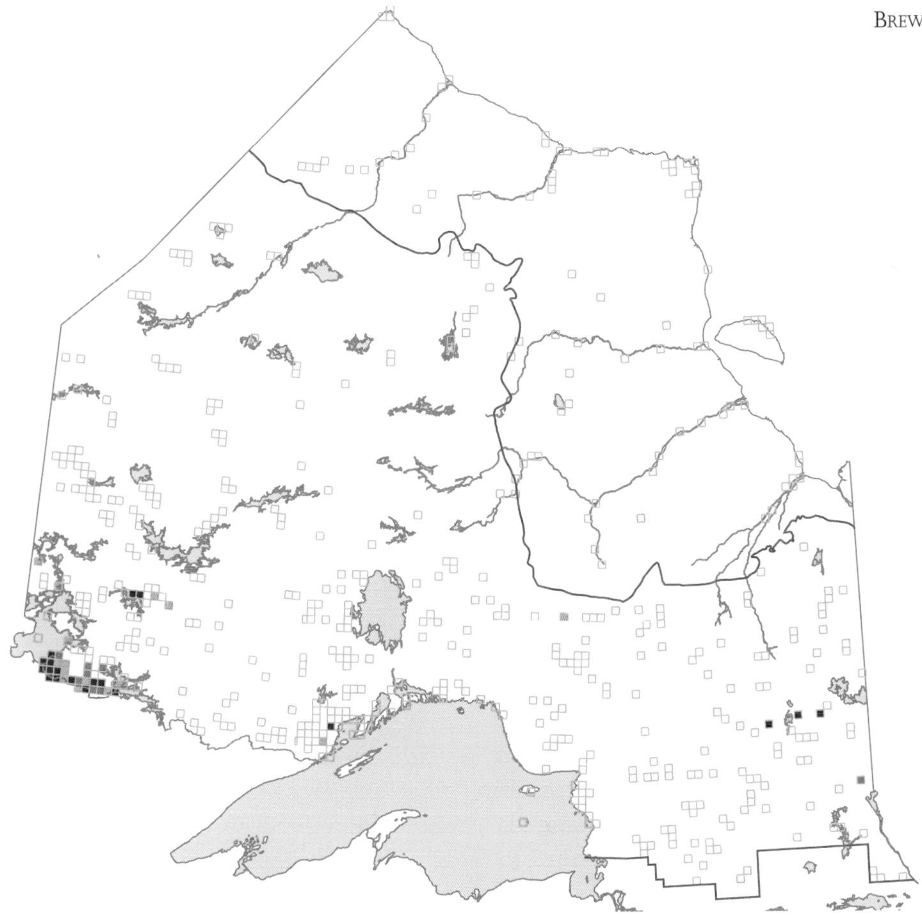

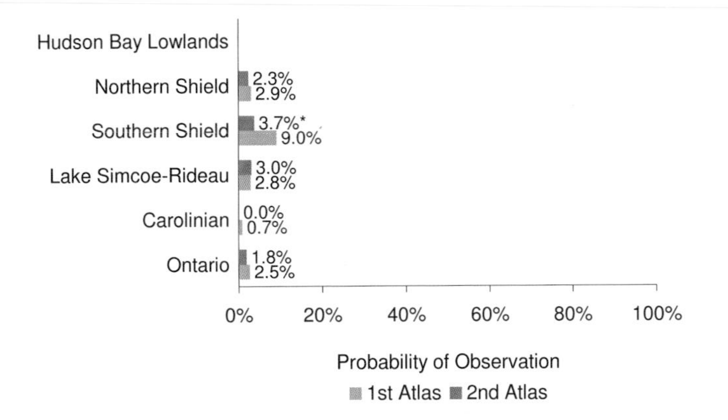

is of course also different, as would be the invertebrate fauna. In southern Ontario, the association of this species with calcareous soils is not apparent, as limestone-derived soils are so widely distributed there.

Data from the second atlas show that in northwestern Ontario the species remains well established in the Rainy River area, and, as in the first atlas, there are scattered records across the Northern Shield to the Québec border. However, there has been a significant decrease of 59% in the probability of observation of the species in the Southern Shield. Most of this decrease was between Sault Ste. Marie and North Bay. Occupancy of these squares during the first atlas does not appear to have been an artifact of especially high effort in squares near roads but instead probably reflects the presence of suitable habitat along the transportation corridor. There was an increase in detections on the Bruce Peninsula and in scattered areas east of Georgian Bay. Breeding records in southern Ontario in the first atlas (Essex and Simcoe Counties) were not replicated during the second atlas. BBS data also show a decrease in the Ontario population, following a peak in the late 1980s, but numbers may now be stabilizing.

Breeding biology: The Brewer's Blackbird is a colonial breeder, nesting in groups of a few to over a hundred pairs. In Ontario, colonies usually comprise fewer than a dozen pairs (Stepney 1979; Gordon in Cadman et al. 1987). Nests are built on a wide variety of substrates and heights but are usually close to or on the ground, particularly in eastern parts of the North American range. In Ontario, nests above ground are at an average height of 1.2-1.8 m to a maximum height of 2.7 m (Peck and James 1987). A common factor in colony sites is proximity to water, usually a stream, ditch, marsh, or other water source. Females are inconspicuous once nesting, and adults forage far from the colony, so small colonies can be overlooked.

Abundance: Point count detections were insufficient to produce an abundance map. The Brewer's Blackbird is probably better sampled by roadside point counts than many other colonial wetland species because of its preference for edge habitats. However, many of Ontario's colonies are adjacent to the Trans-Canada and other large highways, and point counts were not run along these highways for safety reasons, which might help explain the low numbers detected. – *Erica H. Dunn and Alan G. Gordon*

Common Grackle

Quiscale bronzé

Quiscalus quiscula

George K. Peck

A large blackbird with iridescent plumage and yellow eyes, the Common Grackle is abundant throughout much of North America east of the Rocky Mountains. It is found in a variety of habitats, frequenting open areas with scattered trees. The clearing of forested land for agriculture in the 18th and 19th centuries resulted in range expansion and population increase for the species throughout the east. During the 20th century, the Common Grackle greatly expanded its breeding range westward and became one of the most successful and widespread species in North America (Peer and Bollinger 1997). In 1993, it was ranked eleventh in terms of total numbers of birds counted on BBS routes across North America (Peterjohn et al. 1994). Most of the population winters in the US, where it forms very large mixed-species "blackbird" flocks; nocturnal roosts may exceed one million birds (Peer and Bollinger 1997). On its wintering grounds, it forages with other "blackbird" species in open fields and agricultural areas for seeds and grains, causing millions of dollars in damage to sprouting corn. As a result, it is actively controlled as a pest species (Peer and Bollinger 1997).

Distribution and population status: The Common Grackle is widely distributed throughout Ontario, occurring in most atlas squares in the south and most 100-km blocks north to about the Attawapiskat River but absent from the northern Hudson Bay Lowlands. No shift has been demonstrated in either the core or the edge of range limits in southern Ontario since the first atlas. However, even though numbers remain high, there is evidence of decline throughout the province, although only in the Southern Shield region was there a small (3%) but statistically significant decline in the probability of observation. In all other regions, declines were non-significant. BBS data tend to corroborate this modest decline, indicating that since the early 1980s the continental population has been declining at a rate of 1% per year (Sauer et al. 2005a),

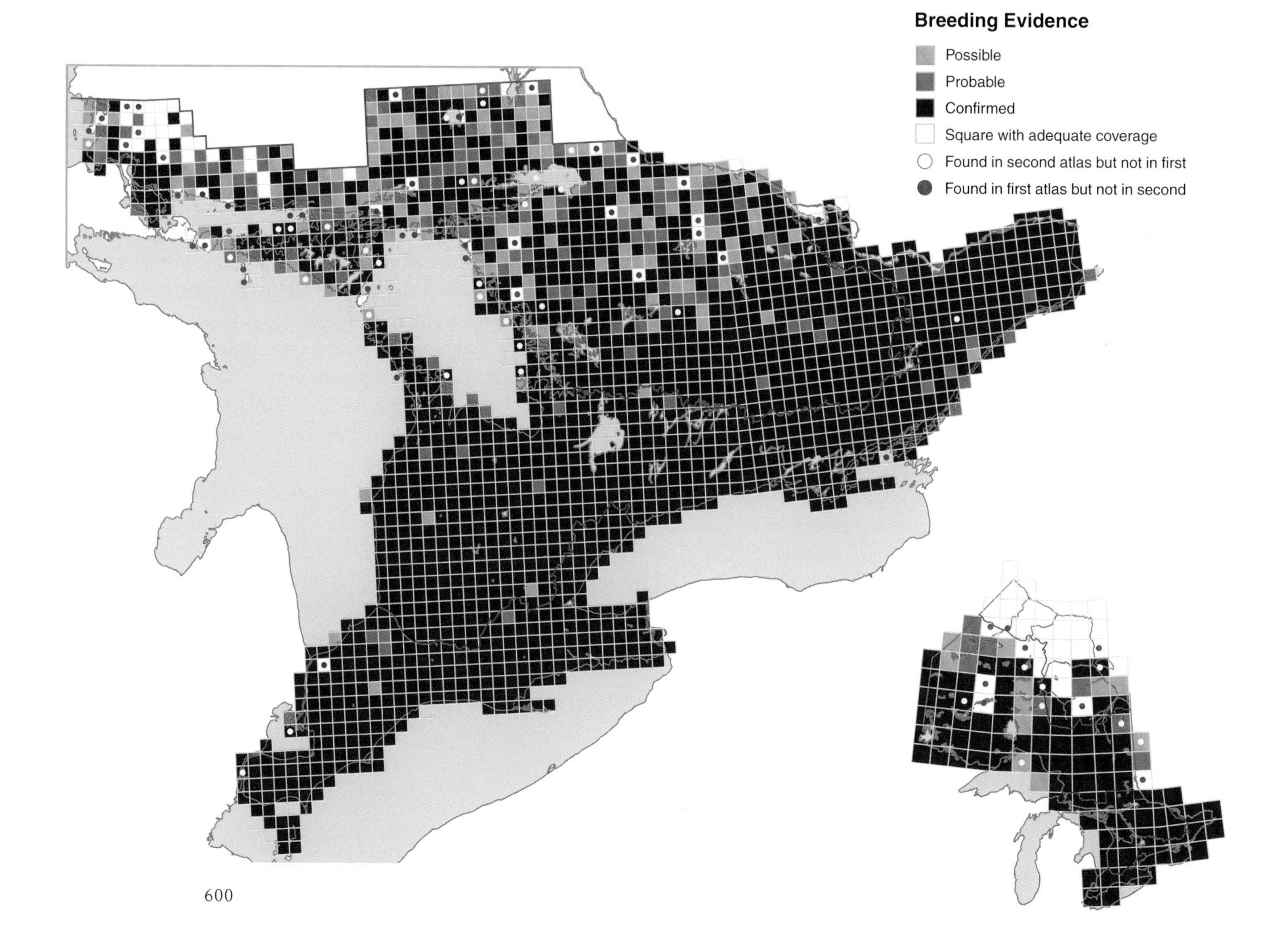

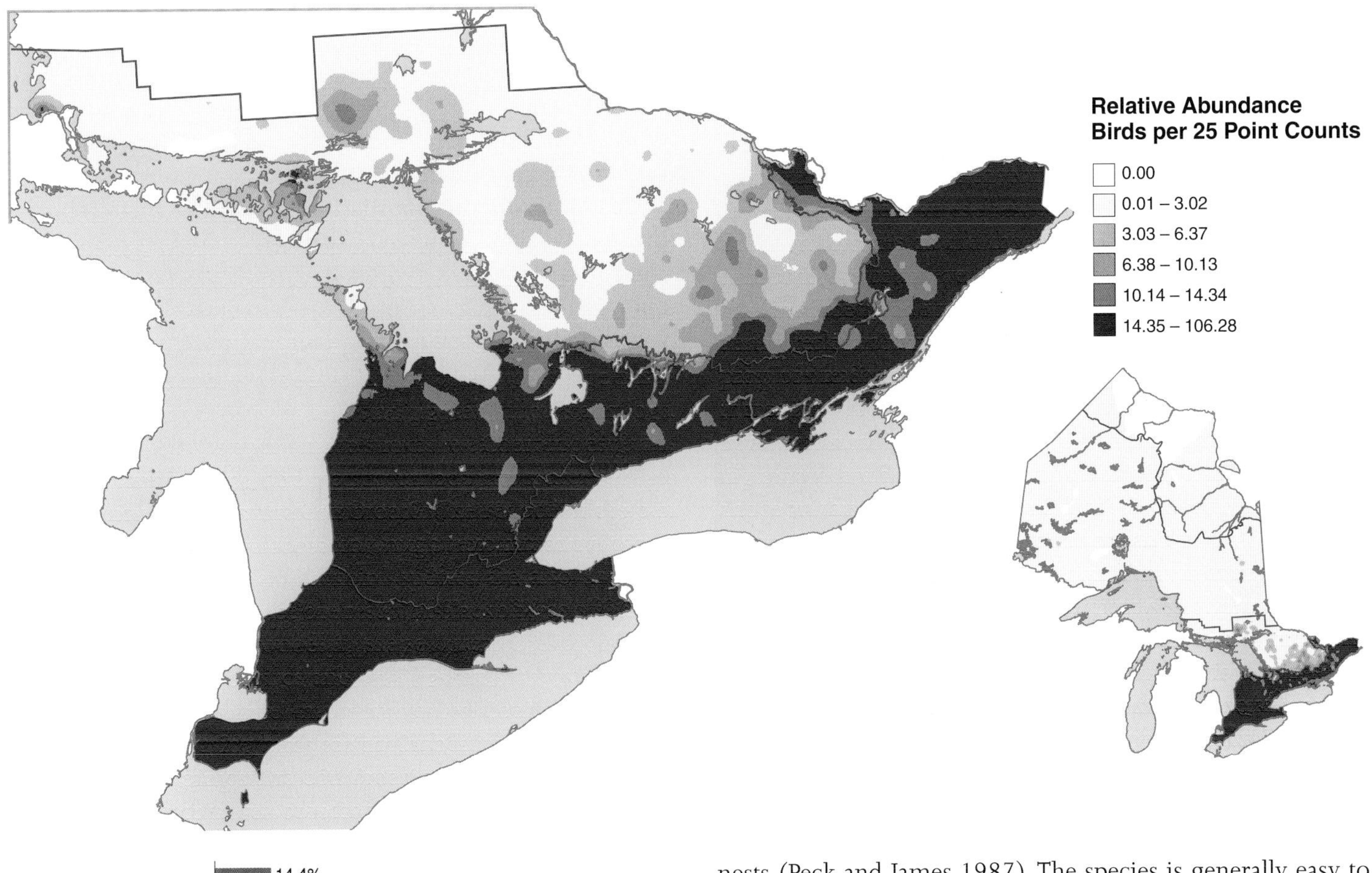

Region	2nd Atlas	1st Atlas
Hudson Bay Lowlands	14.4%	10.3%
Northern Shield	47.4%	54.1%
Southern Shield	91.1%*	94.4%
Lake Simcoe-Rideau	97.0%	98.3%
Carolinian	98.4%	99.2%
Ontario	46.6%	49.6%

0% 20% 40% 60% 80% 100%

Probability of Observation

■ 1st Atlas ■ 2nd Atlas

and at a rate of 1.2% per year in Canada, with at a smaller (0.5%), non-significant rate in Ontario. The reduction of open areas due to natural reforestation might explain some of the decline. However, other blackbird species are also showing declines, and these may be the result of blackbird control programs on wintering grounds in the southern US. Large numbers of roosting blackbirds and starlings are killed, often by a detergent-like substance that removes weatherproofing oils from feathers, causing birds to succumb to exposure.

Breeding biology: The Common Grackle is one of the earliest songbirds to begin breeding, with nest initiation occurring in late March or early April in southern Ontario. Breeding occurs in a wide variety of open habitats, from areas of human habitation to marshes, woodlands, and boreal forest. It nests in trees, shrubs, and vines, cattails and grasses, stumps and logs, and, less typically, human-made structures. Conifers, especially cedar and spruce, are preferred nesting sites, perhaps because of the early start of its breeding season. About half of all nests are located in loose colonies with an average of 10 nests (Peck and James 1987). The species is generally easy to atlas. It is not a secretive bird even while nesting, and is readily recognised. Its gregarious nature and proclivity for colonial behaviour also facilitate detection. The distribution and breeding evidence maps appear to accurately reflect its distribution, although the presence of the bird probably suggests breeding even where breeding was not confirmed.

Abundance: The relative abundance maps appear to accurately reflect Common Grackle densities throughout the province and show a general decrease in abundance with increasing latitude. In the Carolinian region, only the European Starling and Red-winged Blackbird were reported in higher average densities than the Common Grackle. The abundance in this and in the Lake Simcoe-Rideau region is likely related to the high level of agriculture and human settlement and, in some areas, numerous wetlands that provide both food and potential nesting habitat. The density is lower in southern parts of the Southern Shield region, perhaps due to the lower availability of open agricultural land, settlements, and productive wetlands. The relatively low abundance level of the Common Grackle on the rest of the Shield, and its absence in the northern Hudson Bay Lowlands, are perhaps due to increasingly limited availability of suitable habitat, as well as extended periods of snow-cover and subfreezing temperatures, the latter being probably the most significant factor limiting populations (Peer and Bollinger 1997). – *J. Ryan Zimmerling*

Brown-headed Cowbird

Vacher à tête brune

Molothrus ater

John Reaume

The Brown-headed Cowbird is well known as an obligate brood parasite, laying its eggs in the nests of other birds and relying on the host for parental care of its young. Prior to European settlement, its range is thought to have been restricted to grasslands in the central part of the continent; however, forest clearing and the corresponding increase of agriculture led to a considerable expansion of its range during the 20th century. Its breeding range now extends from northern Mexico north throughout southern Canada in the east and to northern British Columbia and Alberta in the west (Godfrey 1986; Lowther 1993). This expansion exposed many additional species and populations to brood parasitism, the implications of which are not yet fully understood.

Distribution and population status: The first reference to the cowbird in southern Ontario is from the 1870s (Peck and James 1987), after which it expanded its range throughout road-accessible areas of the province. The species is restricted to developed and agricultural areas, so is considerably more restricted in the north than in the south. The probability of observation declined by 35% between atlases, with the most evident declines in the north; there were declines of 69% in the Northern Shield region, 48% in the Southern Shield, and 7% in Lake Simcoe-Rideau region. There was no significant change in the Carolinian, the region in which the species is most widespread, with a 97% probability of observation. The downward trend is consistent with BBS data that indicate cowbird populations declined significantly, at a rate of 3.5% per year in Canada and 3.9% per year in Ontario between 1981 and 2005.

The availability and proximity of suitable feeding areas has a strong influence on the presence of the cowbird in a landscape (Goguen and Mathews 2001; Morrison and Hahn 2002), and in combination with the availability of breeding opportunities, this is likely the primary factor responsible for

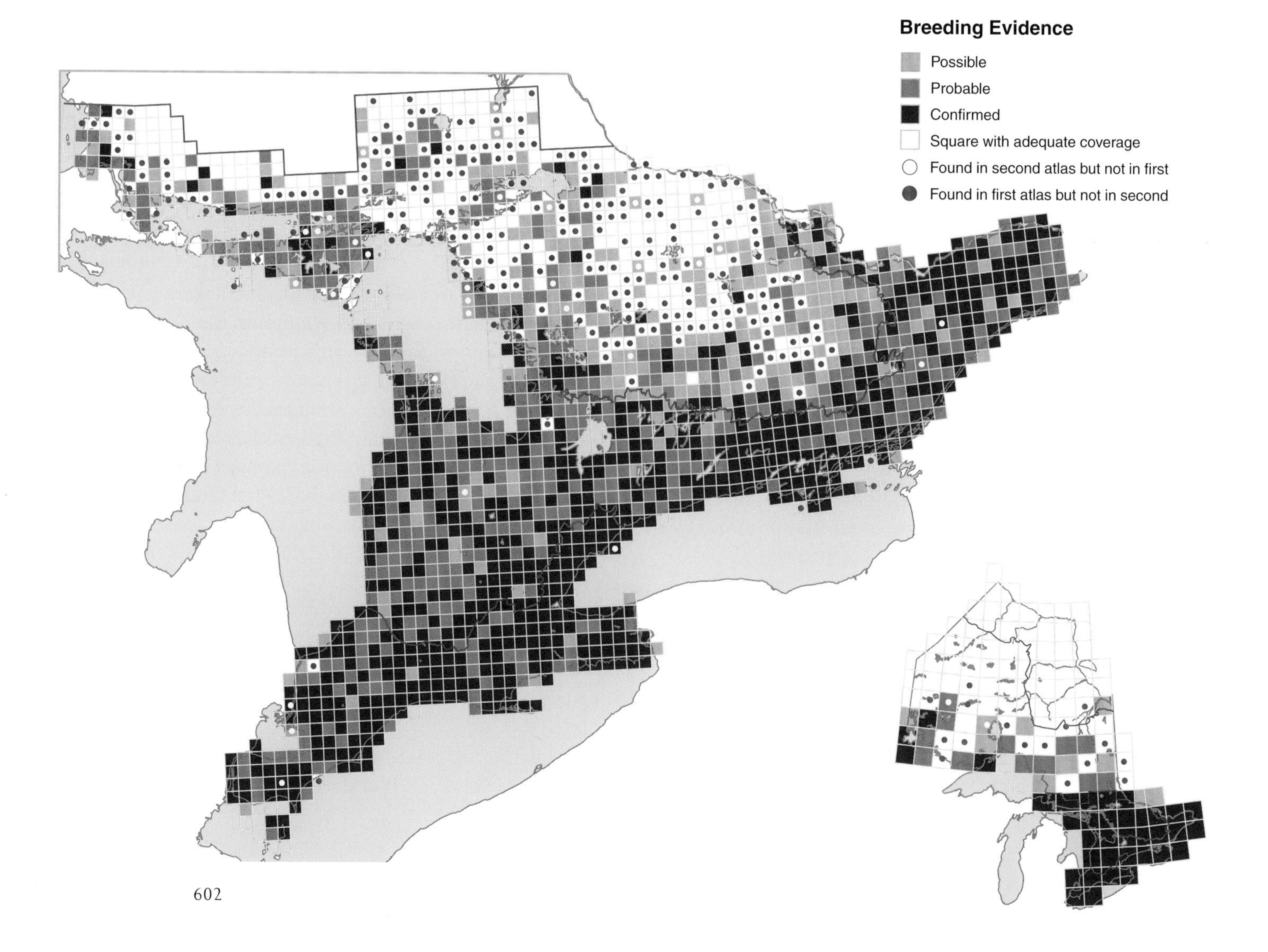

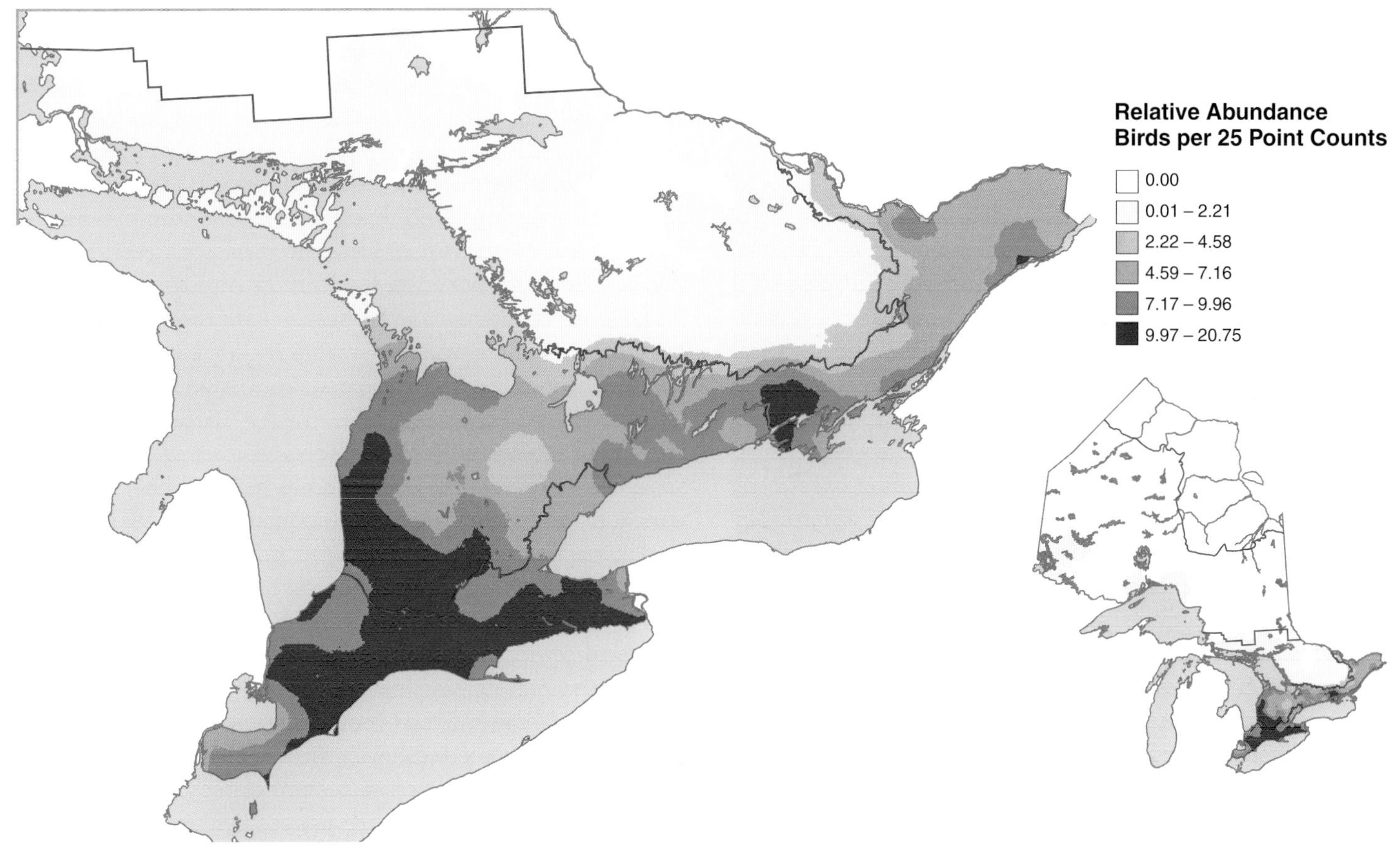

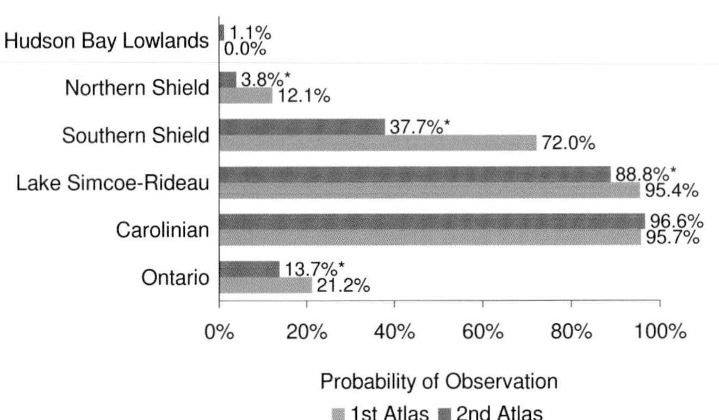

decline of the species in Ontario. The cowbird depends on open fields and crop and pasture lands for foraging on seeds and small invertebrates, preferentially consuming insects stirred up by grazing livestock (Lowther 1993; Goguen and Mathews 2001). Agricultural intensification, which has increased field size, contributed to a loss of pasture, and reduced landscape heterogeneity through the removal of hedgerows, fencerows, woodlots, and wetlands (Boutin et al. 1999), has increased the distance between foraging areas and high-quality breeding habitat (i.e., forest) for cowbirds. Combined with the abandonment and loss of farmland to urbanization in Ontario in the past 20 years (Statistics Canada 2006b), in particular the disappearance of small dairy farms (Jobin et al. 1996), less suitable habitat remains for the cowbird in Ontario. This has likely led to its decline in the Lake Simcoe-Rideau region and the southern part of Southern Shield region. Farther north, high levels of forest cover and limited feeding opportunities have always rendered the habitat as sub-optimal for the cowbird (Morrison and Hahn 2002), and declines in abundance are usually accompanied by significant contractions in range in areas of low abundance (Rodriguez 2002).

Breeding biology: The atlas data reflect the distribution of the Brown-headed Cowbird well. Possible or probable breeding records are easily attained, as breeding males often congregate in the open in small, sometimes mixed sex groups and sing a very distinctive song. Breeding was confirmed in 45% of squares in which the species was reported. However, many Regional Coordinators suggest that breeding was likely occurring wherever the species was detected. Despite fledged young that make loud and persistent begging calls, confirmed breeding is sometimes difficult to establish as no parental cues such as adults carrying food can be used.

Abundance: The abundance of the Brown-headed Cowbird is generally inversely related to the amount of forest cover and strongly correlated with proximity to high-quality foraging areas (Morrison and Hahn 2002). The abundance map thus closely reflects the pattern of farming intensity in Ontario. The highest densities of the cowbird occur in the fragmented agricultural landscape of southwestern Ontario where the mosaic of habitats likely affords the greatest diversity and abundance of feeding opportunities and potential hosts. Abundance evidently declines sharply northward on the Shield, where forest cover is more continuous and the amount of suitable foraging area is correspondingly reduced. Conversely, lower abundance of the cowbird in some regions of Essex and Chatham-Kent and in the Greater Toronto Area probably results from low forest cover combined with intensive farming or urbanization, respectively, resulting in lowered diversity and abundance of potential hosts. – *Karla Falk*

Orchard Oriole

Oriole des vergers

Icterus spurius

Bill Rayner

In Ontario, the Orchard Oriole is typically associated with the Carolinian region. An attractive neotropical migrant that breeds in orchards and open woods, it is the smallest of the orioles native to North America. The species is also found throughout the eastern half of the US and breeds sparingly in southern Saskatchewan and Manitoba (Godfrey 1986).

Distribution and population status: Both McIlwraith (1894) and Baillie and Harrington (1937) noted that the Orchard Oriole was essentially restricted to southwestern Ontario, primarily along Lake Erie. Wood (1948) stated that by the late 1940s it was becoming "a common bird in Kent and Essex and is becoming more so in Middlesex." This coincides with an increase in Ohio that began in 1945 and continues today (Peterjohn 2001). Additionally, there were rare but regular occurrences in Ontario well outside of this early range.

The overall distribution of the Orchard Oriole in Ontario has continued to expand from earlier reports and from the distribution shown in the first atlas. The majority of the 113 squares where it was recorded during the first atlas were in the Carolinian region, with about two dozen records in the Lake Simcoe-Rideau region, largely along Lake Ontario. Between atlases, its probability of observation increased about threefold overall. Increases were observed in both the Carolinian and Lake Simcoe-Rideau regions, with a fourfold increase in the latter. Similar increases have been reported in adjacent Michigan and Ohio (Brewer et al. 1991; Peterjohn 2001). The species now occurs in scattered squares as far north as the base of the Bruce Peninsula and north of Kingston. Two records in the Rainy River area and one in the Southern Shield are also new since the first atlas.

Despite the increase of the species in Ontario and elsewhere, further increases might be limited by the general

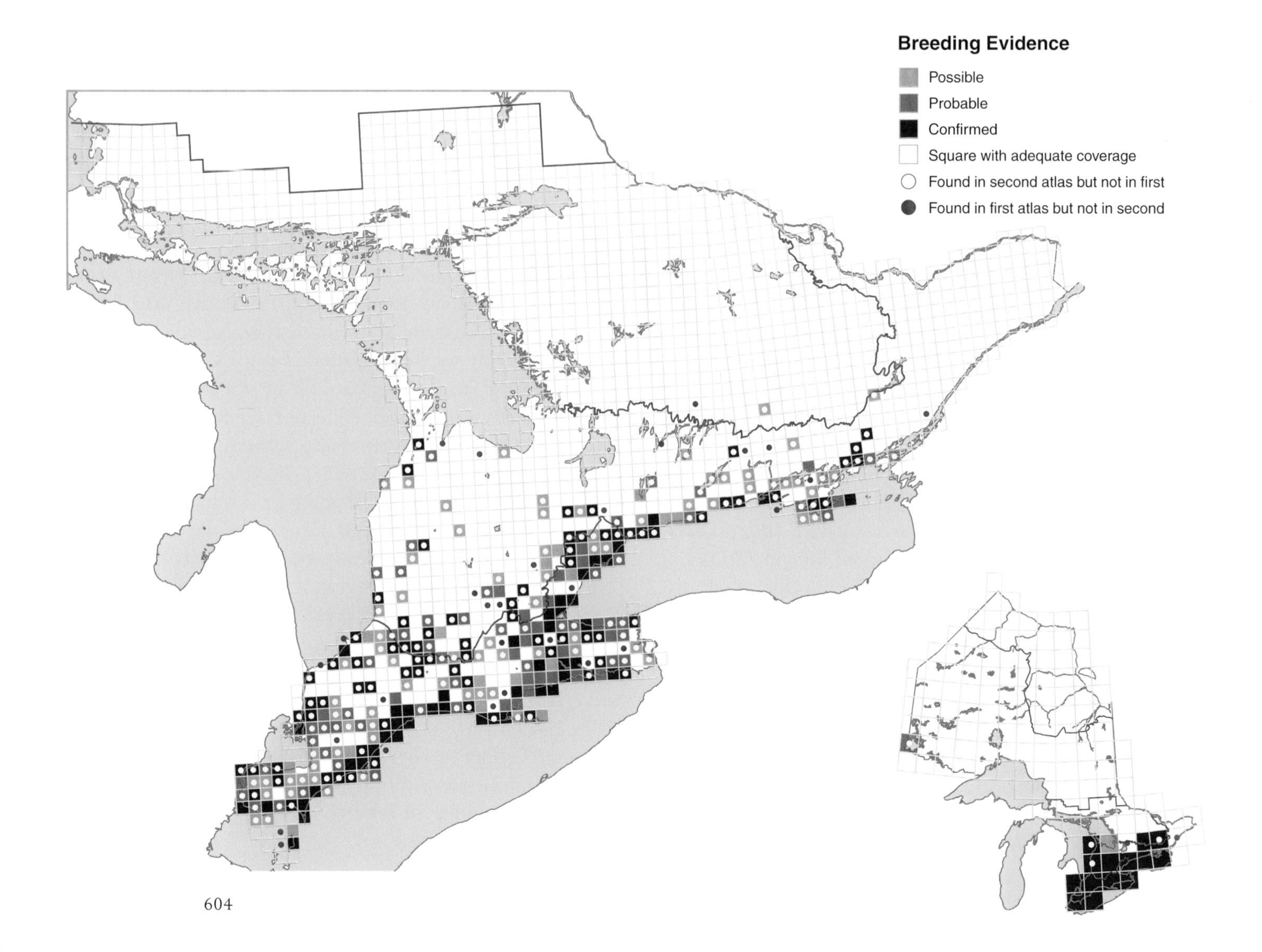

BREEDING EVIDENCE

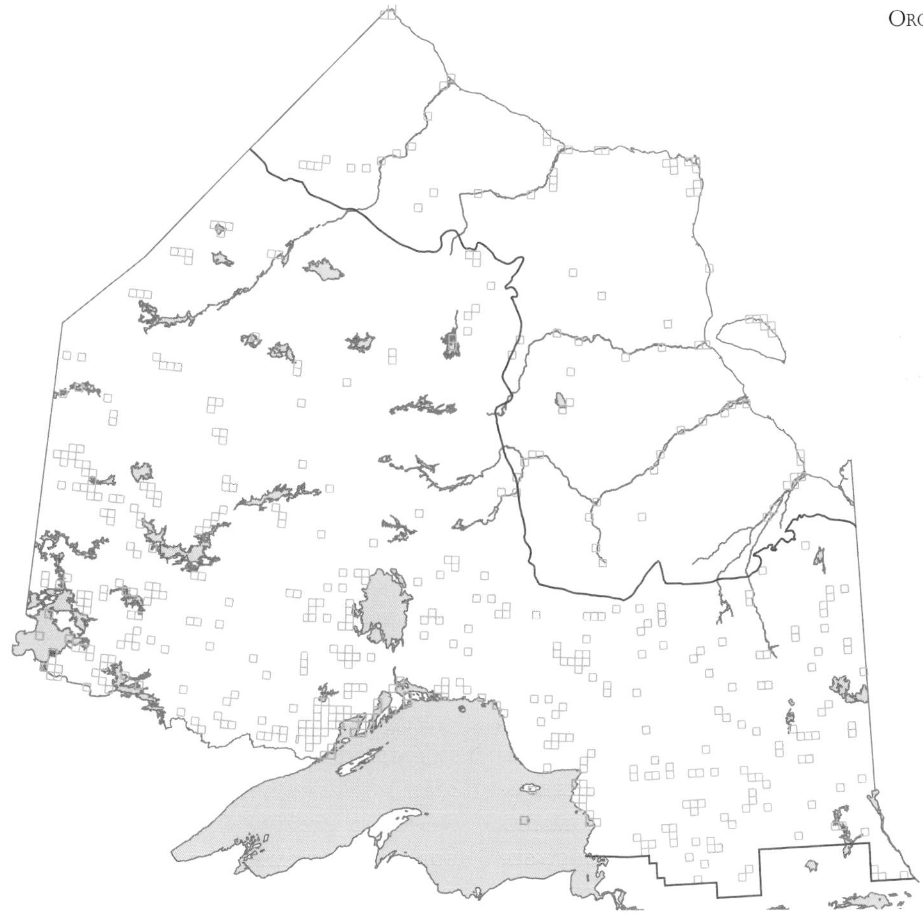

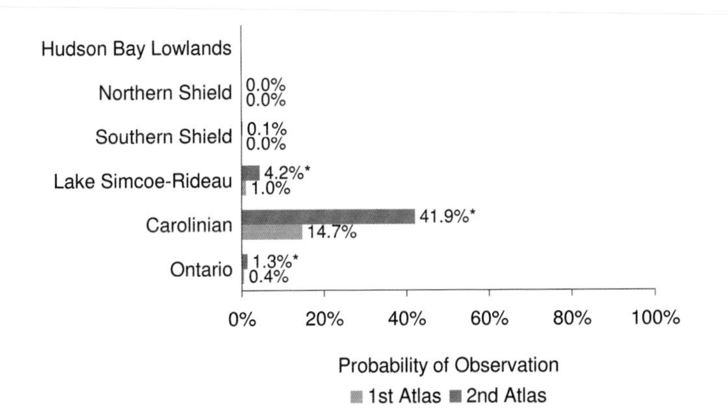

decline in orchards and hedgerows, continued use of pesticides, closing of forest canopy as woodlands mature, and effects of cowbird parasitism (Brewer et al. 1991).

Breeding biology: The Orchard Oriole's vocalizations are fairly distinctive and carry well, although one of its songs is similar to those of the Purple and House Finches, potentially causing it to be overlooked. Additionally, males usually cease singing by late June, making them more difficult to detect. Second-year males have distinctive non-adult plumage and limited reproductive success, but have been known to help adults feed nestlings (Scharf and Kren 1996). Orchards, hedgerows, open woods, cemeteries, golf courses, oak savannahs, and open riparian forests are all used as breeding habitat, especially if water is nearby. The species is known to sometimes nest semi-colonially in southern parts of the US (Scharf and Kren 1996) and in Michigan (Brewer et al. 1991), but in Ontario it is mostly solitary and local in occurrence, except at Point Pelee Nat. Park and Pelee Island, where it occurs at higher densities than elsewhere in the province. Once young birds are able to care for themselves, the adults begin to move south, as early as mid-July in the case of adult males (Scharf and Kren 1996). Thus the species can be missed later in the season, especially due to the close resemblance of young birds to several similarly coloured, nondescript warbler species. However, because of this oriole's generally conspicuous breeding behaviour, it is likely the maps accurately reflect the species' current range.

Abundance: In Ontario, the Orchard Oriole is most abundant along the north shore of Lake Erie, with the greatest concentration in the extreme southwest and in the Long Point area. These areas are characterized by their close proximity to water, abundant hedgerows, rural residential areas and, in the case of the Long Point area, meandering rivers and orchards as well. There is a lower level of abundance adjacent to Lake Ontario east to Prince Edward Co., as well as along the Lake Huron shoreline north to the base of the Bruce Peninsula.

Although the Orchard Oriole has gradually increased in abundance in Ontario over the past two decades, there is considerable annual variation in its abundance throughout much of southern Ontario. In the Long Point area, it may be quite frequent some years and essentially absent others. Away from the Carolinian region, many records involve isolated, unmated males, though the species can and sometimes does nest as far north as the edge of the Southern Shield (e.g., Waubaushene, Simcoe Co., southeastern Georgian Bay, 1976). In adjacent Michigan, local northern populations similarly persist for a few years and then disappear (Brewer et al. 1991). *– P. Allen Woodliffe*

Baltimore Oriole

Oriole de Baltimore

Icterus galbula

Kelly Dodge

The glorious orange and black colours of the adult male Baltimore Oriole make it a favourite with many bird lovers. This oriole's taxonomic status has changed since the first atlas when, along with its western counterpart, the Bullock's Oriole, it was considered a subspecies of the Northern Oriole. The Baltimore Oriole is again considered a full species, its breeding range extending from the Maritime Provinces south of the Boreal Forest across the Prairie Provinces and south to the Gulf States.

The species nests in woodland edges, wooded riparian areas, hedgerows with tall trees, open forest, urban parks, and other areas with tall shady trees. The great majority of nests in Ontario are in deciduous trees, particularly elm, maple, and poplar (Peck and James 1987).

Distribution and population status: Historically, the range of the Baltimore Oriole in Ontario appears to have expanded slightly to the north with the opening of the forest and the creation of suitable habitat in and around northern towns (Flood in Cadman et al. 1987); however, the second atlas documents a withdrawal in most northern parts of its Ontario range. Between atlases, the probability of observation declined significantly by 20% in the province as a whole and in the Southern Shield and Lake Simcoe-Rideau regions by 46% and 4%, respectively.

Although earlier reports (McIlwraith 1894; Baillie and Harrington 1937) mention the species breeding north to Parry Sound and in the Lake of the Woods area, they did not mention it as breeding between these two areas, including the North Bay, Sudbury, Sault Ste. Marie, and Thunder Bay areas. Breeding evidence was reported in five squares in the Thunder Bay area during the first atlas but in only one square during the second atlas. The species was also reported in many squares in the North Bay-Sudbury area during the first atlas (indicating that it had expanded north into that area), but it had clearly

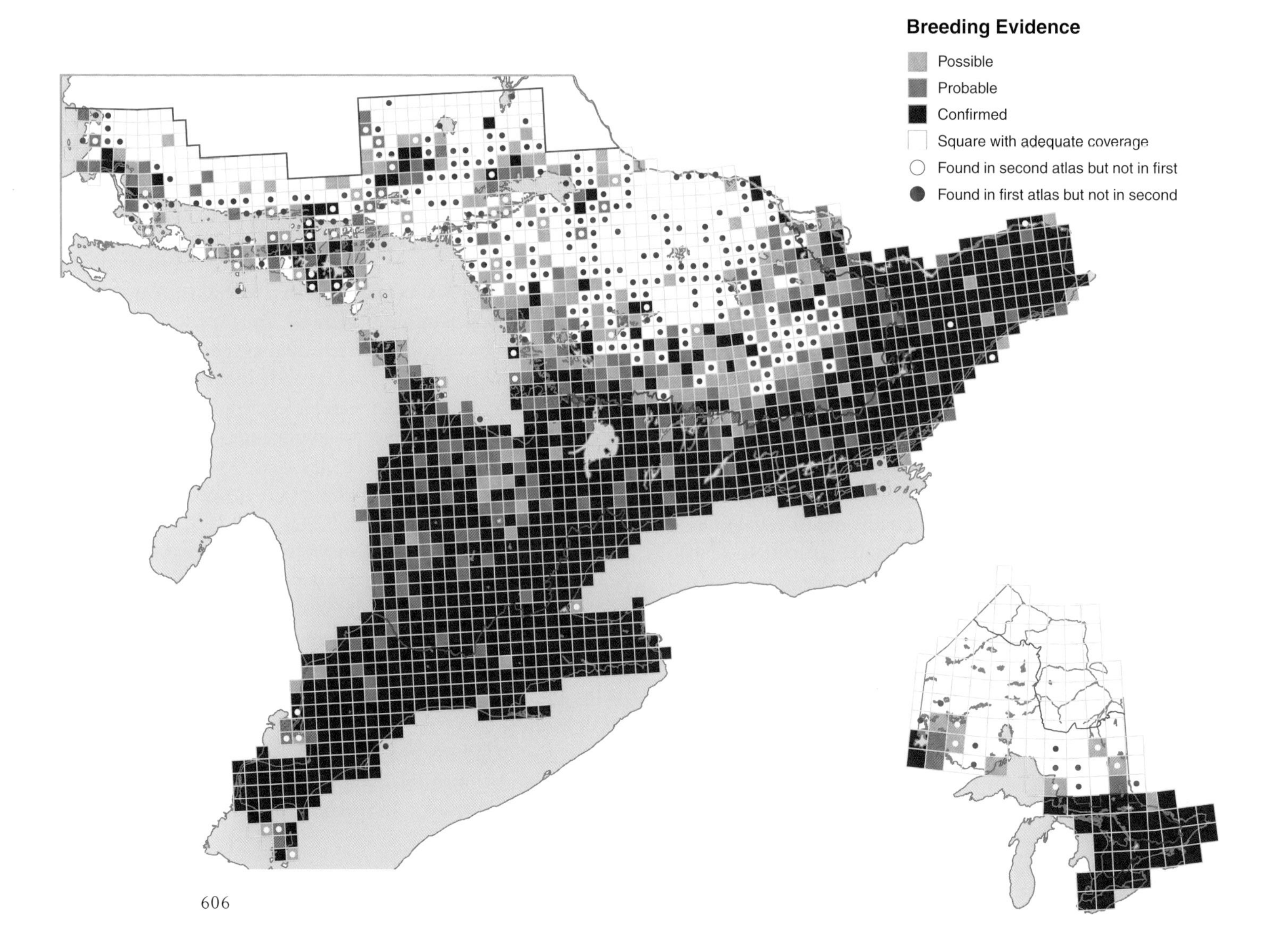

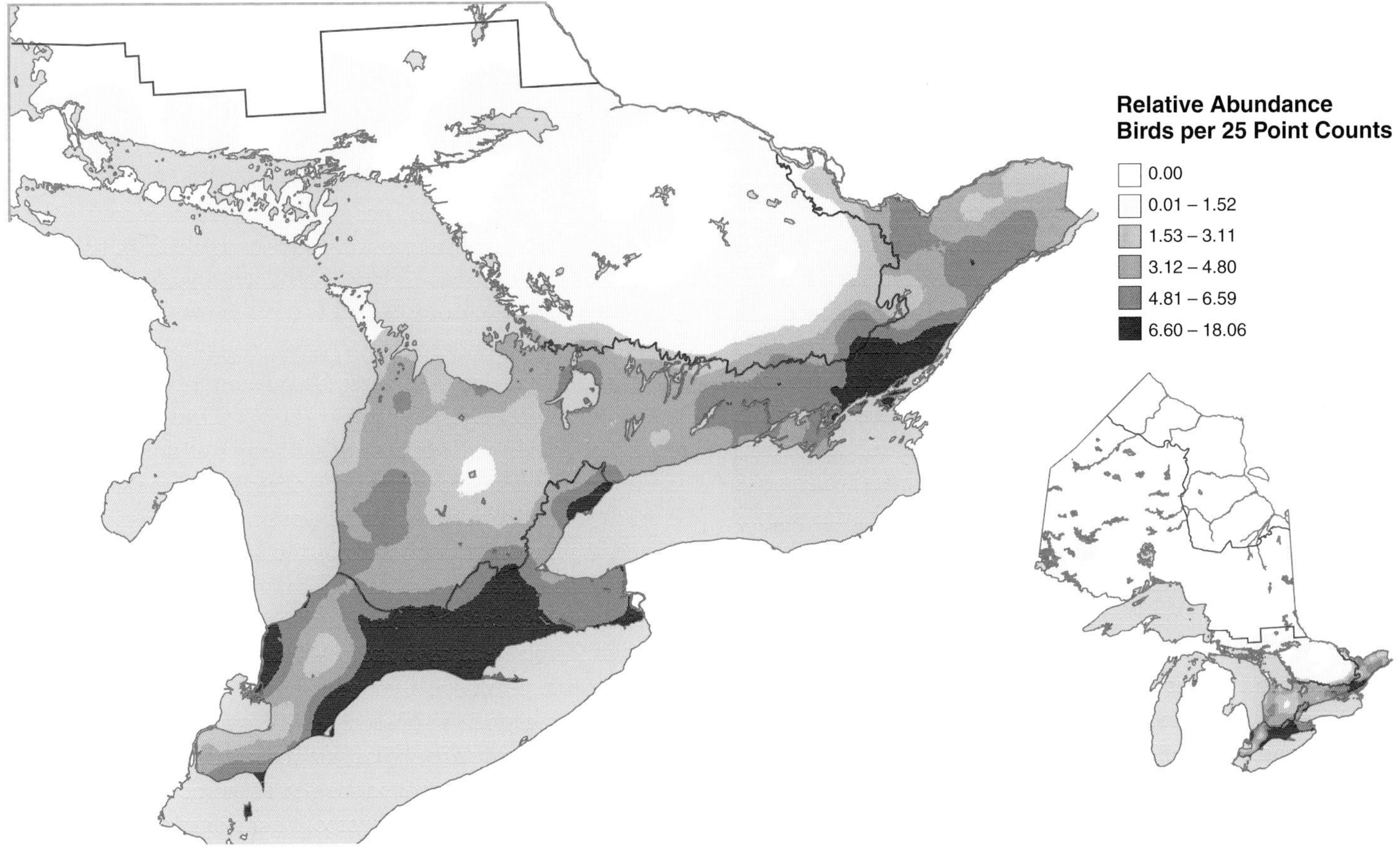

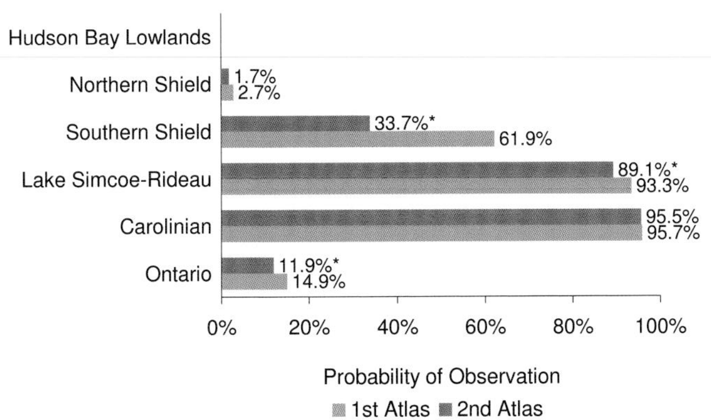

declined there by the second atlas. The pattern of decline is evident across much of the rest of the Southern Shield.

In the Southern Shield, Regional Coordinators reported that the Baltimore Oriole had "virtually disappeared" from Algonquin Prov. Park, and that it had declined steadily over the past 20 years in Haliburton region, even in optimal habitat. In the squares in which it was reported on the Southern Shield, most records are of possible breeding, suggesting relatively small numbers. The relatively low density on the Southern Shield is also evident on the abundance map.

The pattern of decline is consistent with the increase in forest cover and the reduction in the amount of open habitat and therefore forest edge on the Southern Shield. Overall, nine species of "open woodland" birds decreased significantly on the Southern Shield, while only three increased.

Breeding biology: The Baltimore Oriole is probably under-represented on point counts and other atlas work undertaken after late May, because song frequency generally declines following pair establishment (Rising and Flood 1998). The nest is often in the outermost branches of large deciduous trees, so the female can be quite conspicuous during nest building, especially if leaves are not fully out; both adults can be conspicuous when feeding young. The distinctive nest often remains in place after the tree has dropped its leaves, making it easy to confirm breeding for this species even in late fall or winter.

Abundance: The relative abundance maps show that the species is only thinly distributed in the Southern Shield and farther north, including in the Lake of the Woods area. Overall, densities are higher south of the Shield, except in the Dundalk uplands of Grey and Dufferin Counties, on the northern Bruce Peninsula, and on Manitoulin Island. Colder temperatures at higher elevations and in close proximity to Lake Huron may be less conducive to the Baltimore Oriole, as cold or inclement weather commonly results in delays in territorial establishment and mating, or in egg desertion in this species (Rising and Flood 1998).

The areas of highest abundance are around Kingston and throughout much of the Carolinian region, with the exception of inland areas of Essex and Lambton Counties and Chatham-Kent, where forest cover is very low and even single shade trees are infrequent. Toronto stands out as having relatively high densities of Baltimore Orioles, presumably because of the high concentration of mature shade trees in some urban neighbourhoods, parks, and ravines. The area bordering the Southern Shield edge, much of it marginal farmland with numerous hedgerows and large shade trees, also supports relatively high densities of the species. – *Michael D. Cadman*

Pine Grosbeak

Durbec des sapins

Pinicola enucleator

Mark Peck

The Pine Grosbeak is known to most birders only as an uncommon winter visitor when it irrupts irregularly south of the breeding range. It nests in boreal, subarctic, and subalpine regions of North America and Eurasia. In Canada, it breeds in open coniferous and mixed forests (Godfrey 1986). There is little information on its breeding habits because its remote range and secretive nesting behaviour make nests hard to find (Adkisson 1999).

Distribution and population status: The earliest reports of breeding in Ontario were in the mid-1930s and 1940s in Nipissing and Parry Sound Districts at the southern edge of the range. The first documented record of breeding in the province was in 1958 at Hawley Lake, Kenora Dist., based on the collection of a female with an unshelled egg in the oviduct (Baillie 1960).

During the first atlas, the Pine Grosbeak was reported in 76 squares, with most observations in the Southern and Northern Shield regions east of Lake Superior between Sault Ste. Marie and Moosonee. Limited distribution was also noted in northern and western areas of the province. During the second atlas, the species was reported in a similar number of squares (80) but with a generally more northern distribution and many additional records from the Hudson Bay Lowlands. Significant decreases in the probability of observation in the Southern and Northern Shield were offset by a significant increase in the Hudson Bay Lowlands. Additional records during the second atlas were from south of the expected range in Rainy River Dist. The scarcity of records and apparent range gaps evident on the map are difficult to explain. It is possible that this species is thinly distributed across a wide area, or it may reflect the difficulty of atlassing in remote areas and limited survey time.

Breeding biology: The Pine Grosbeak starts pairing in late winter, with courtship behaviour observed while birds are still flocking. It is monogamous and strongly territorial during the

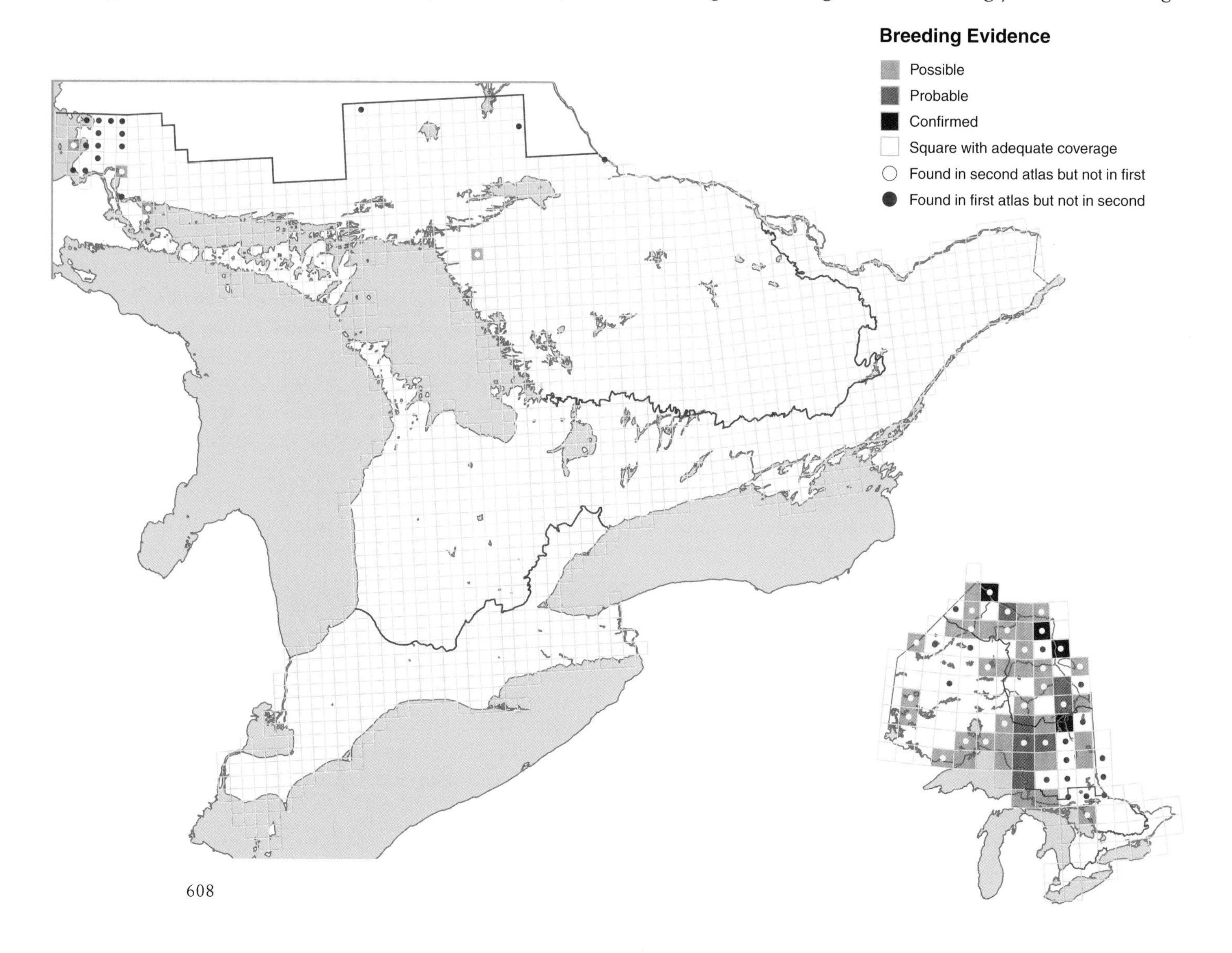

BREEDING EVIDENCE

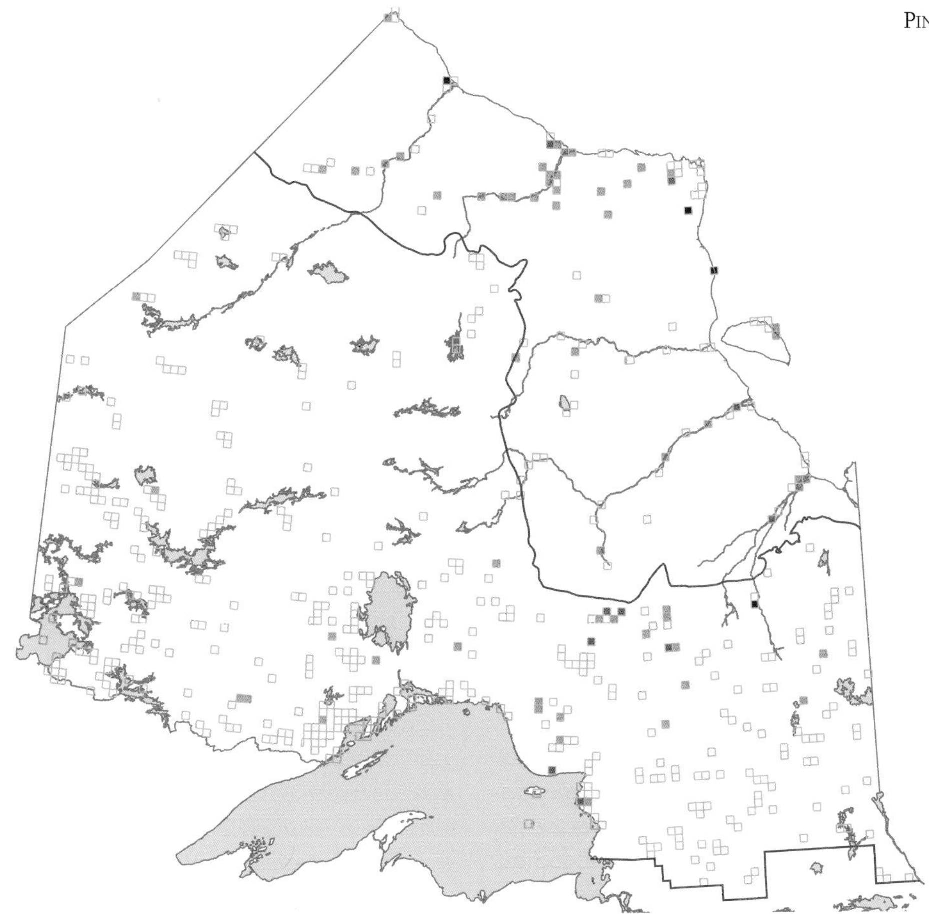

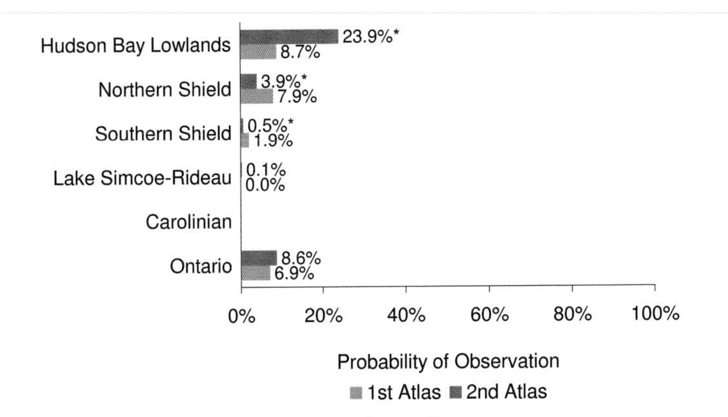

breeding season. The male sings loudly from the tops of conifers, but much singing probably took place before most atlassers were on the breeding grounds. Preferred nesting habitat is moist, open coniferous or mixed forests near water. The female builds the nest beginning in late May, usually 2-4 m above ground and concealed in a dense conifer. Only the female incubates, but the male visits the nest to feed her. Both parents feed the young (Adkisson 1999).

Results from both atlases attest to the difficulty of finding breeding evidence for this species; it is secretive around the nest, which may be an adaptation to avoid nest predators such as the Red Squirrel. During the first atlas, breeding was confirmed in only a single 100-km block when several family groups were observed near the headwaters of the Black Duck River in extreme northwestern Ontario. Results from the second atlas were similar, with only four squares with confirmed breeding. Fledged young were found in three of four squares. The fourth square had the first documented nest in Ontario, located north of the Swan River, 1 km from the James Bay coast (Peck et al. 2004a). Discovered 12 June 2003 on an old beach ridge in open mixed forest of White Spruce, Tamarack, willow, and Speckled Alder, the nest was 2.4 m up in a small White Spruce. The female continued incubating during visits to the nest. A russet-coloured male, probably a second-year bird, fed the female on the nest during one visit.

Abundance: The Pine Grosbeak is an uncommon breeding species in northern Ontario. There was insufficient data to generate an abundance map, but the greatest concentrations for the species appear to be in northeastern Ontario near Kapuskasing, with low abundance and apparent absences throughout the rest of the range in the province. The abundance of this grosbeak, like most boreal finches, varies annually from place to place in association with availability of food resources. It is unclear why the northeast had the highest breeding abundance in both atlases. However, the species prefers moist open habitats, and the northeast receives more precipitation than the northwestern portions of the province. The Kapuskasing area may also have higher abundance because of better observer access throughout the breeding season due to the extensive road and railway network. More extensive open habitat resulting from agricultural practices in the area may also favour this species. The BBS has been showing a significant long-term decline at the southern edge of its range in Canada (Downes et al. 2005). – *Mark K. Peck and Glenn Coady*

Purple Finch

Roselin pourpré

Carpodacus purpureus

Larry Kirtley

The male Purple Finch is often quaintly described as having been "dipped in raspberry juice," as its purplish-red colouration extends throughout its upper body plumage and flanks (Peterson 1980). It can be confused with the House Finch, which is slightly smaller and less stocky. The Purple Finch breeds across much of the Boreal Forest from Québec to British Columbia and the Yukon. In eastern North America, it winters mainly from southern Ontario to the Gulf States. Its winter presence is somewhat cyclical, as its occurrence is closely tied to heavy seed crops and Spruce Budworm outbreaks, which give rise to periodic irruptions (Wootton 1996; Bolgiano 2004).

Distribution and population status: The overall distribution of the Purple Finch in Ontario does not appear to have changed much for as long as records have been kept (McIlwraith 1886; Baillie and Harrington 1937), but there have been changes within its Ontario range and population in recent decades. The probability of observation is highest, at 84%, in the Southern Shield region, where there is more of its preferred open mixed and coniferous woodland. The atlas point count data suggest that it is equally abundant in much the eastern part of the Northern Shield region. The species is thinly spread in the Hudson Bay Lowlands, particularly in the northern part of the region; interestingly, records were obtained in both atlases for the Fort Severn area on the Hudson Bay coast.

The Purple Finch is and probably has always been an uncommon breeder in the Carolinian region, where its distribution is discontinuous and restricted to isolated squares. In the Lake Simcoe-Rideau region, its probability of observation is 48%, a significant increase of 26% since the first atlas. This change is likely a result of succession and maturation of retired farmland and maturation of conifer plantations providing additional habitat for the species, and is similar to increases

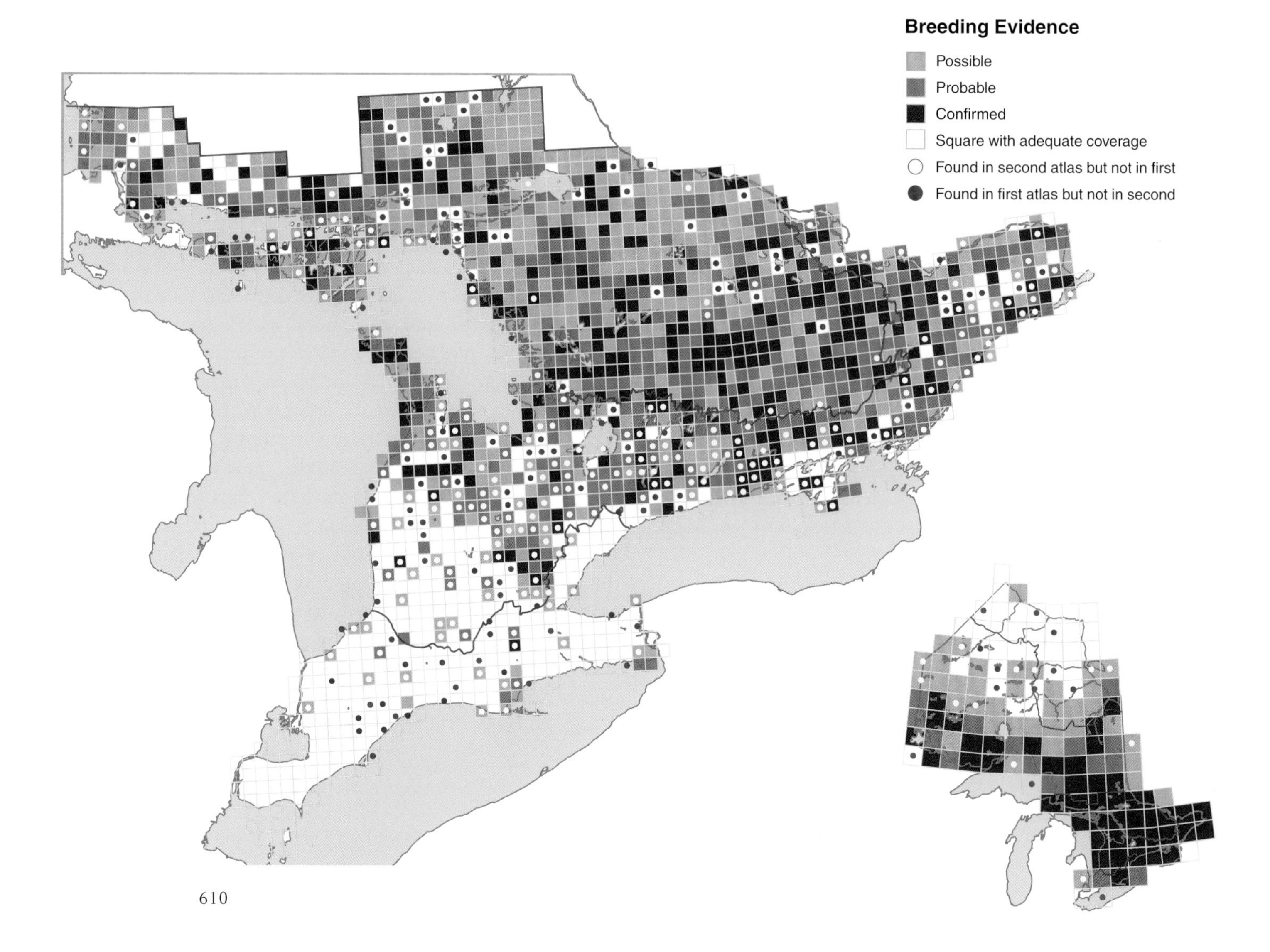

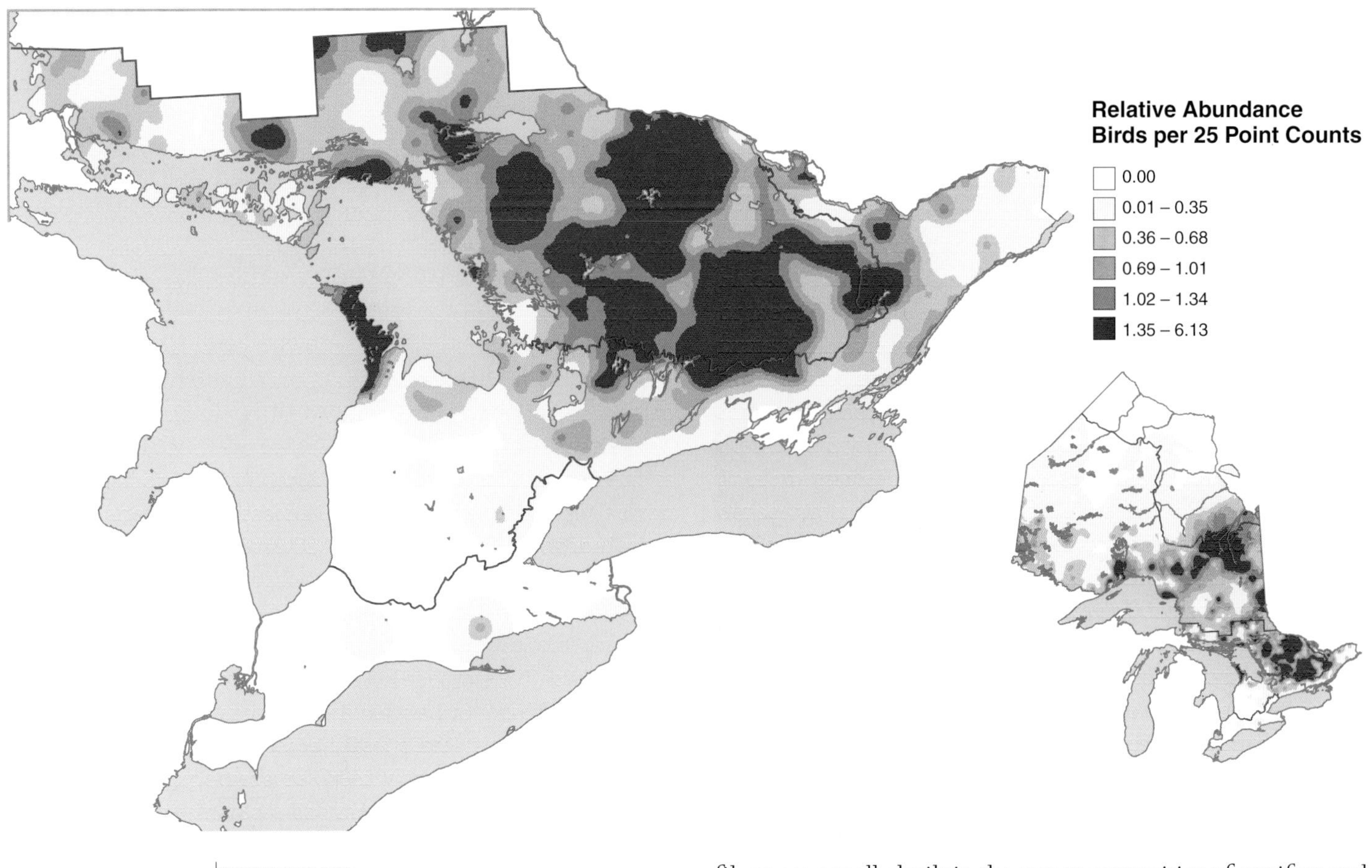

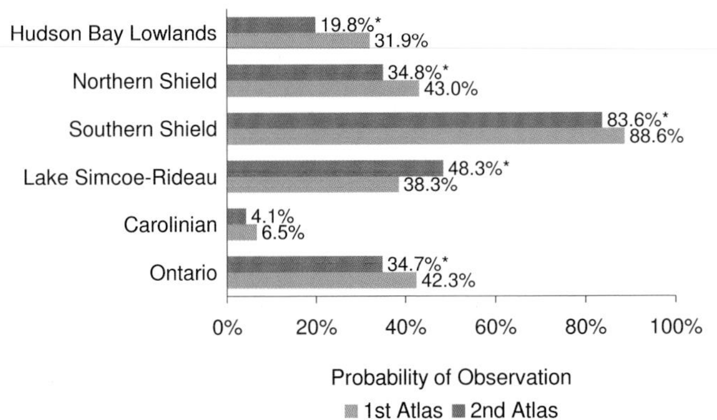

evident for other coniferous forest birds such as the Yellow-rumped and Black-throated Green Warblers.

Despite this increase in the south, the probability of observation of the species declined significantly between atlases by 18% in the province as a whole and by 6%, 19%, and 38% in the Southern and Northern Shield and the Hudson Bay Lowlands regions, respectively. The BBS also shows significant annual declines of 2.6% in Ontario and 3.3% in Canada since 1968 (Downes et al. 2005). Little is known about the reasons behind these trends (Wootton 1996). However, Spruce Budworm populations have declined considerably in Ontario since the major outbreaks during the first atlas (National Forestry Database Program 2007) and may be an important factor.

Breeding biology: The Purple Finch breeds primarily in moist or cool coniferous forests but also in mixed coniferous-deciduous forest and open habitats with scattered conifers. In Ontario, nesting occurs between mid-May and early August (Peck and James 1987). The small nests of twigs and plant fibres are usually built in the upper extremities of conifers and occasionally also in deciduous trees or shrubs. Nest building and incubation are mainly by the female. Young remain in the nest for about 14 days, where they are fed by regurgitation by both parents. Though replacement nesting occurs, second broods are unusual (Wootton 1996).

The species is relatively easy to detect due to its loud, bubbly song, usually delivered from high in a tree; however, confirmation of breeding status is more difficult and was obtained in only 18% of squares. As a result, the distribution map likely reflects the occurrence of the species well, but underestimates the breeding status in many squares.

Abundance: The Purple Finch is sparsely distributed in the densely settled agricultural areas of the south and in the Hudson Bay Lowlands of the north where suitable habitat is limited; it is most abundant where coniferous forest predominates. This pattern is reflected in the abundance maps, which show that the species is most abundant across most of the Southern Shield, where suitable habitat is plentiful, and in the Northern Shield, where the highest abundances are centred around Kapuskasing and extend west to Thunder Bay. Surprisingly, abundance in the western part of the Northern Shield is generally lower. This may reflect some characteristic of the habitat in these areas, such as mean annual precipitation, which decreases farther north and west in the province; this, in turn, may affect availability and density of seed crops. Based on atlas point count data, the provincial population is estimated at 700,000, with about 60% of those birds in the Northern Shield region. – *Seabrooke Leckie and Michael D. Cadman*

House Finch

Roselin familier

Carpodacus mexicanus

Jim Richards

Native to western North America, the House Finch was introduced to the east in 1940 with the release of a handful of individuals on Long Island, New York (Hill 1993). In the years since, it has been enormously successful, expanding its range at a phenomenal rate, and now has a contiguous range across the US and portions of southern Canada (Sibley 2000). Although it uses some undisturbed habitats in the west, in the east it is associated almost exclusively with human settlement (Hill 1993). The increasing urbanization and spread of suburban development has likely aided its expansion through the Midwest by creating suitable habitat in the form of urban parks and yards with trees. The species is a regular visitor to bird feeders, and the male's bright plumage and cheerful song make it a familiar local resident for birders and non-birders alike.

Distribution and population status: The House Finch reached Ontario in the early 1970s, with the first nest documented in 1978 at Niagara-on-the-Lake (James 1978b). During the first atlas, its breeding distribution in the province was still restricted, occurring primarily along Lakes Erie and Ontario. However, even within the first atlas period, the number of confirmed records increased from a handful in the first year to over 100 squares by the end of the period.

The species has continued its expansion northward and is now found in nearly every square of the Carolinian and Lake Simcoe-Rideau regions. Significant increases in the probability of observation were recorded for all three southern Ontario regions and for the province as a whole. Breeding was confirmed in over 400 squares in the second atlas, and a few confirmed breeding records even exist for northern Ontario, in the Thunder Bay and Lake of the Woods areas.

Although the species was found in most squares south of the Canadian Shield, records of breeding evidence decrease abruptly at the edge of the Shield, with only a 6% probability

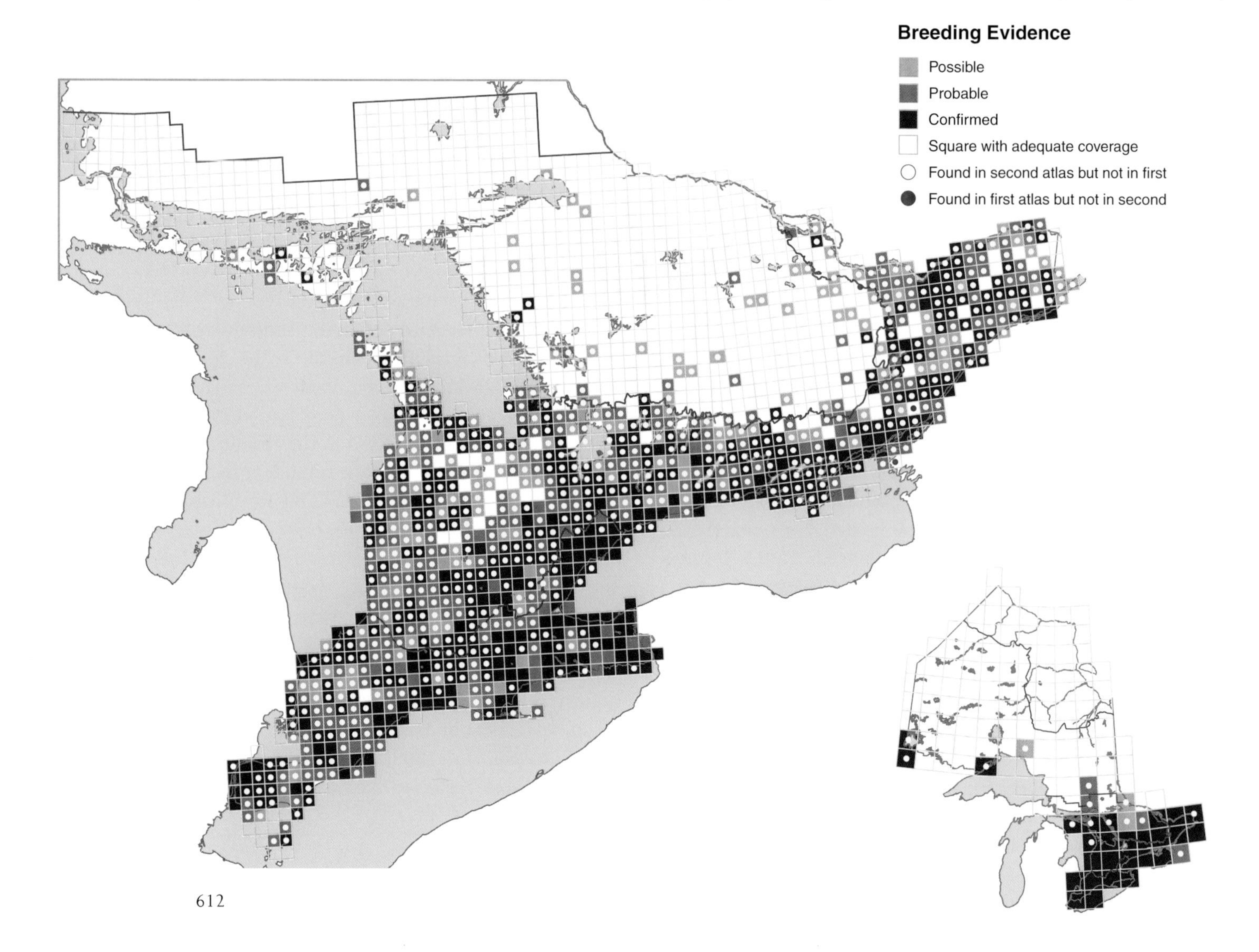

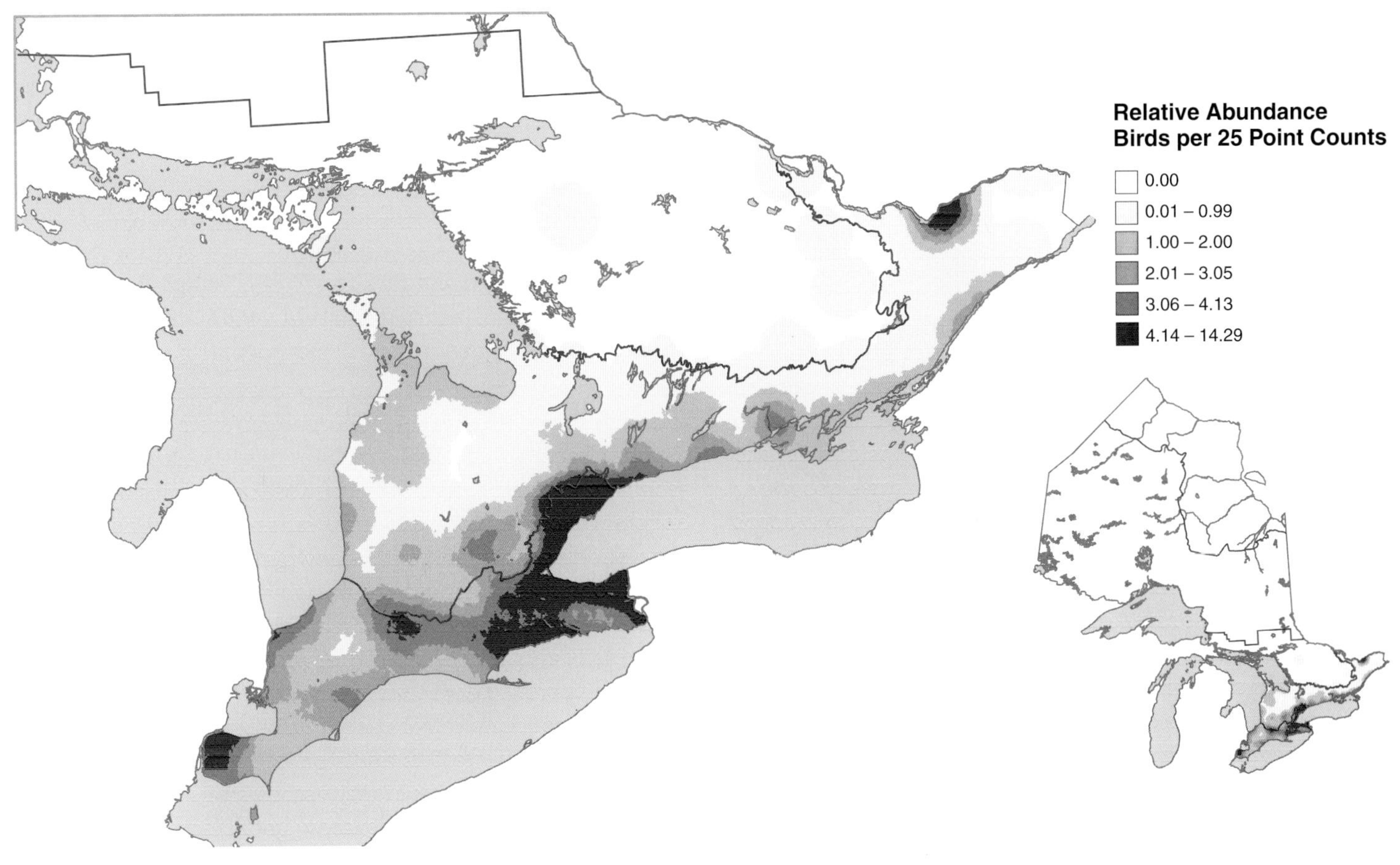

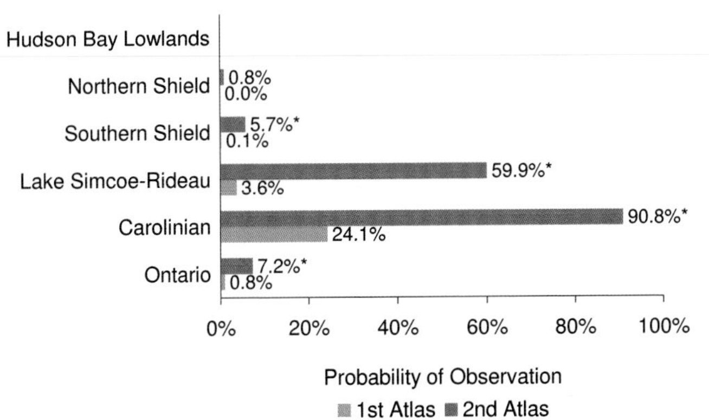

of observation in the Southern Shield. The House Finch's close association with human habitation, which provides the open habitat it prefers, along with an often abundant and easy source of food from winter bird feeders, has undoubtedly helped its spread. It seems likely, therefore, that while it may continue to expand its range northward, numbers will remain lower on the Shield due to the denser forest habitat and sparser human settlements. The House Finch and House Sparrow share similar habitat requirements and often occur sympatrically (Kozlovic in Cadman et al. 1987). Atlas results indicate that the two species now have similar ranges in Ontario, though the House Sparrow's range still extends further north.

Breeding biology: The song of the male House Finch is similar enough to that of the Purple Finch that they are often confused by novice birders, but the House Finch will usually sing from exposed perches, allowing for visual confirmation. Both sexes sing, but the song of females is generally much simplified (Hill 1993). Feeding is by regurgitation, so adults do not visibly carry food, but young can be quite vocal both in the nest and after fledging, helping atlassers to confirm breeding. The House Finch often builds its nest in coniferous trees in gardens, under awnings, and in hanging plant baskets (Peck and James 1987). As nests are generally easy to find and vocal young are hard to miss, the distribution map likely portrays an accurate picture of the species' occurrence in Ontario.

Abundance: Not surprisingly, given the species' close association with humans, House Finch abundance was greatest in the highly urban areas of the GTA and Niagara Peninsula, London, Windsor, and Sarnia, as well as in the Ottawa area. More moderate densities occur through the rest of southwestern Ontario and along the Lake Ontario shore.

Mycoplasmal conjunctivitis appeared in eastern House Finches in the mid-1990s, and has since taken a toll on populations (Dhondt et al. 1998). BBS data indicate that the Ontario population peaked in 1995, then declined sharply over the next six years, where it has levelled off at about one-third of its peak abundance. Although numbers are lower now than before the outbreak, they remain many times higher than during the first atlas. Based on point count data from the second atlas, the provincial population is estimated at approximately 250,000 birds. – *Seabrooke Leckie*

Red Crossbill

Bec-croisé des sapins

Loxia curvirostra

John Reaume

The nomadic and highly variable Red Crossbill breeds in the coniferous forests of North America (Adkisson 1996). Although its movements have been called erratic and unpredictable, it normally occurs in areas in response to large cone crops (Benkman 1990). In Ontario, it is found primarily in the southern Boreal and Great Lakes-St. Lawrence Forests, occurring rarely and perhaps only sporadically elsewhere.

The taxonomy of the Red Crossbill remains largely unresolved. The most recent authority (Parchman et al. 2006) describes nine sibling types in North America that may represent separate species. Types differ slightly in body size, bill size and shape, and flight calls, and each is reproductively isolated and adapted to feed on specific conifer cones (cf. Groth 1993, 1996). Types 2 and 3 (and probably 4) occur in Ontario (C. Benkman, pers. comm.). Distinguishing among the types in the field is very difficult; however, Type 2, which has a larger-sized bill and feeds primarily on White Pine, appears to be the most frequently encountered Red Crossbill in the province. This White Pine-dependent type of eastern Canada and the adjacent US had declined dramatically by the late 1800s, coincident with the loss of mature White Pine to logging, but made a moderate recovery as second-growth pine forests matured (Dickerman 1987). Type 2 also may breed in association with good crops on Red Pine. The smallest-billed Type 3, adapted to small, soft cones, breeds periodically after flight years, often in large numbers linked to large cone crops on Eastern Hemlock and spruces, but is usually absent from the province at other times. There was no evidence of Type 3 breeding in Ontario during this atlas (R. Pittaway, pers. comm.).

Distribution and population status: Consistent with the first atlas, the second atlas confirms that the Red Crossbill is most widespread and common in the Southern Shield region, with a probability of observation of about 6%. Given the species' long history of breeding in the pine-dominated habi-

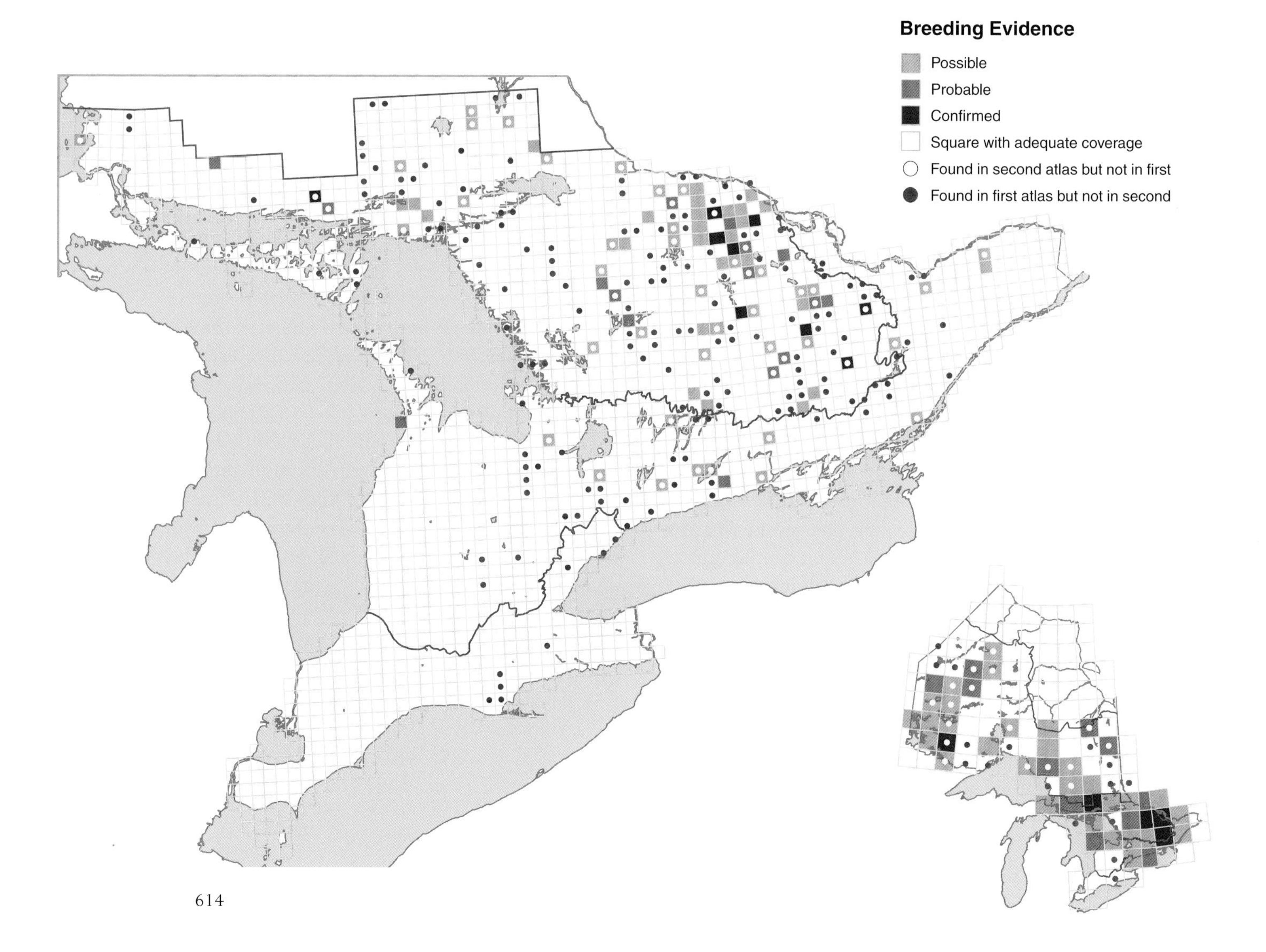

BREEDING EVIDENCE

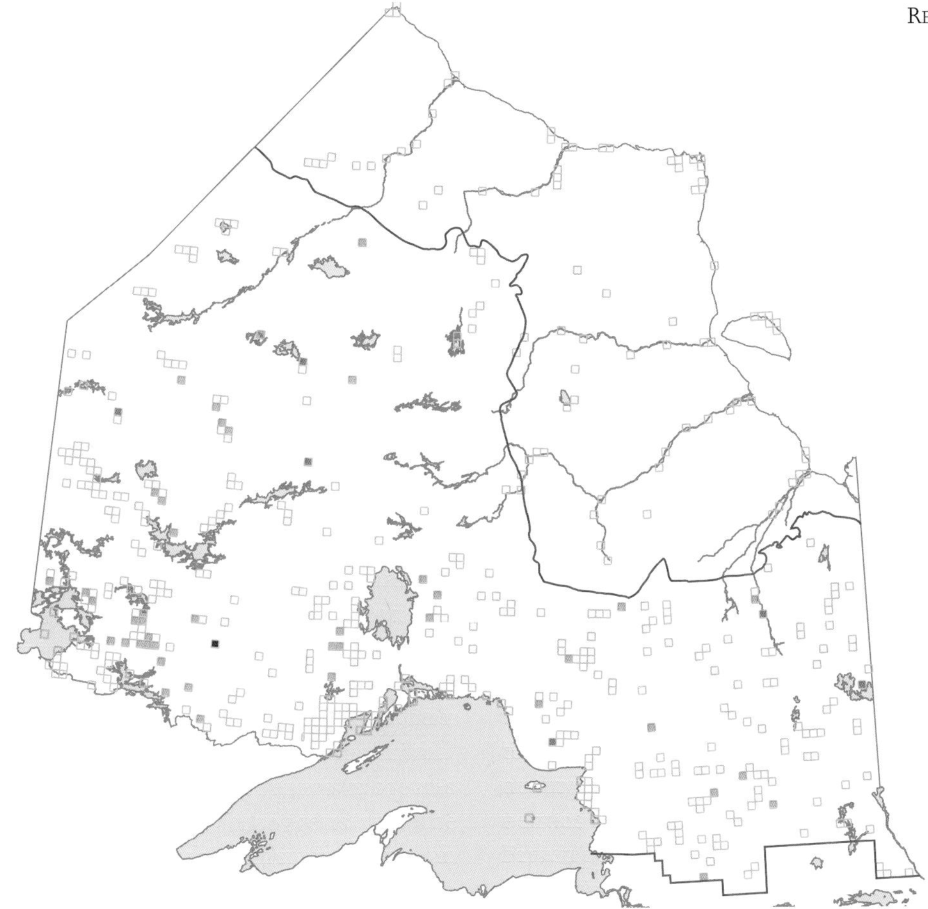

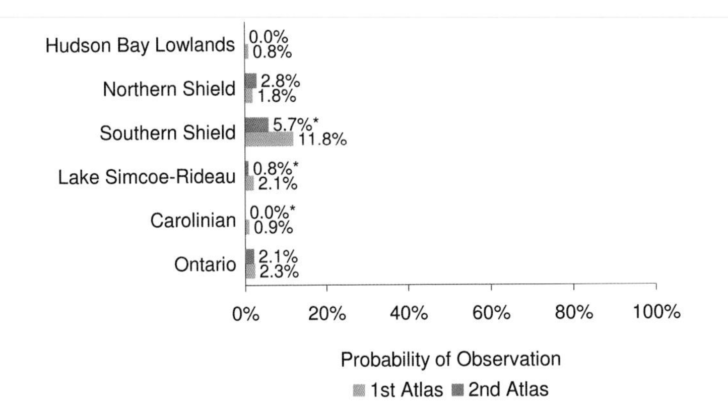

tats common in this area (Lumsden and Smith in Cadman et al. 1987; Simard 2001), this result is not surprising. The Red Crossbill is less widespread and common in the Northern Shield and Lake Simcoe-Rideau regions, where the probability of observation was 3% and 1%, respectively. Province-wide, the probability of observation was 2%, the same as that observed during the first atlas. As most detections in squares presumably involved Type 2 birds, this suggests that the province's pine forests have provided sufficient habitat to maintain the species' population over the last 20 years. However, significant regional differences were found between atlases. The species declined by 63% in the Lake Simcoe-Rideau region and by 51% in the Southern Shield. In the Northern Shield, the probability of observation increased substantially but non-significantly by 56%. There were no reports of the Red Crossbill in the Carolinian region during the second atlas. The reason for such significant regional change is unknown, but may simply reflect the species' irruptive nature in response to variation in food abundance. Its absence from the Carolinian region, where a small population had persisted for years in mature pine plantations on the Norfolk Sand Plain, is noteworthy. The absence appears to be real, as the species has not been reported from the St. Williams Forest since the late 1990s (R. Ridout, pers. comm.).

Breeding biology: In Ontario, the Red Crossbill breeds most often in late summer and early fall in response to maturing cone crops, or in late winter in conjunction with the retention of large seed crops (Benkman 1990; Simard 2001). This nesting chronology does not coincide well with peak atlassing periods and may explain the low rates of probable and confirmed breeding (16% and 7%, respectively). Moreover, nests are very difficult to find, and the presence of independent, streaked young does not necessarily indicate local breeding, as juvenal plumage is prolonged. Except in irruption years, small flocks search for food over broad areas, often making detection difficult. Unlike the first atlas, no large irruptions occurred during the second atlas. However, after the atlas period, numbers of Type 3 increased dramatically in the Algonquin Prov. Park area in 2006-2007 in response to larger cone crops on hemlock and spruces.

Abundance: Due to the Red Crossbill's nomadic breeding behaviour, it did not occur in high enough numbers during the atlas period to generate a relative abundance map. However, the distribution maps appear to accurately represent the true extent of the species' range in the province. *– Julie H. Simard*

White-winged Crossbill

Bec-croisé bifascié

Loxia leucoptera

George K. Peck

The White-winged Crossbill ranges throughout northern coniferous forests in North America and Eurasia. In the New World, it breeds from Alaska to Newfoundland south to the northern US. It wanders back and forth across the expanse of the Boreal Forest in search of cone crops, stopping to breed when it encounters large crops. Its movements and breeding ecology are best understood in relation to this highly variable food resource (Benkman 1992). In Ontario, it prefers to breed in areas with large seed crops, especially on native spruces, but it also utilizes Tamarack, Balsam Fir, and Eastern Hemlock. Periodic major irruptions south of the breeding range are linked to extensive cone crop failures in the Boreal Forest.

Distribution and population status: In both atlases, the White-winged Crossbill was found in many more squares and much farther north than the Red Crossbill. Before the first atlas, the distribution of the White-winged Crossbill in Ontario was poorly known. That atlas showed its widespread distribution in coniferous forests from Lake Ontario to the treeline. The bulk of breeding evidence was found in 1984, a major irruption year in the province. Many of the gaps in the distribution are explainable by limited or no atlassing in those areas during that important breeding year.

During the second atlas period, significant incursions occurred in many parts of Ontario in every year, improving opportunity for widespread detection. It is not surprising that province-wide there was a significant 61% increase in the probability of observation between atlases. The probability of observation nearly tripled in the Lake Simcoe-Rideau region, with new squares near London, the outskirts of the Greater Toronto Area, Northumberland Co., southern Peterborough Co., and the United Counties of Prescott and Russell. Sporadic breeding in the Lake Simcoe-Rideau region, south of the core range, normally coincides with large cone crops in boreal-like patches of spruce and in spruce plantations.

In the Southern Shield region, the probability of observation

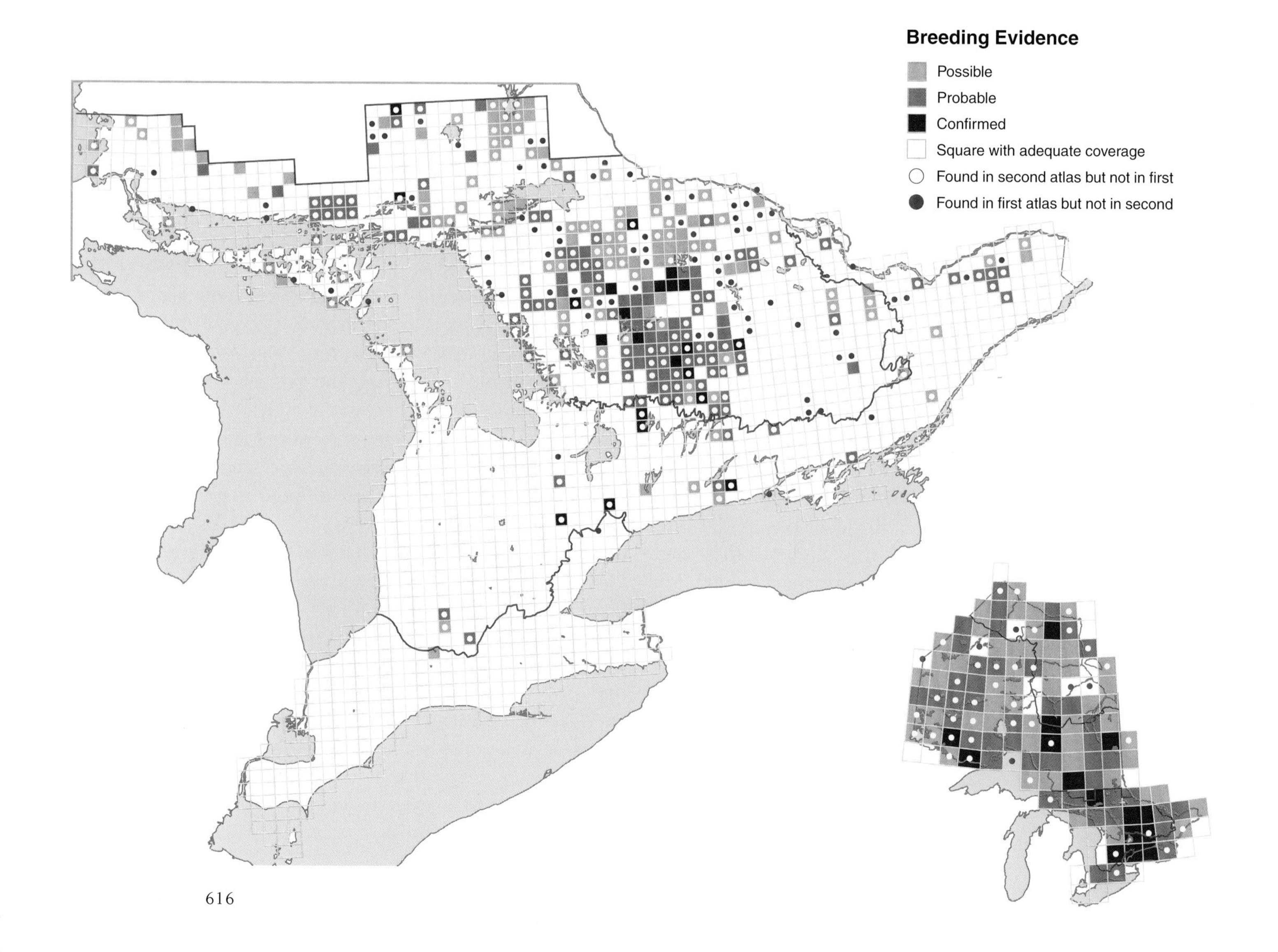

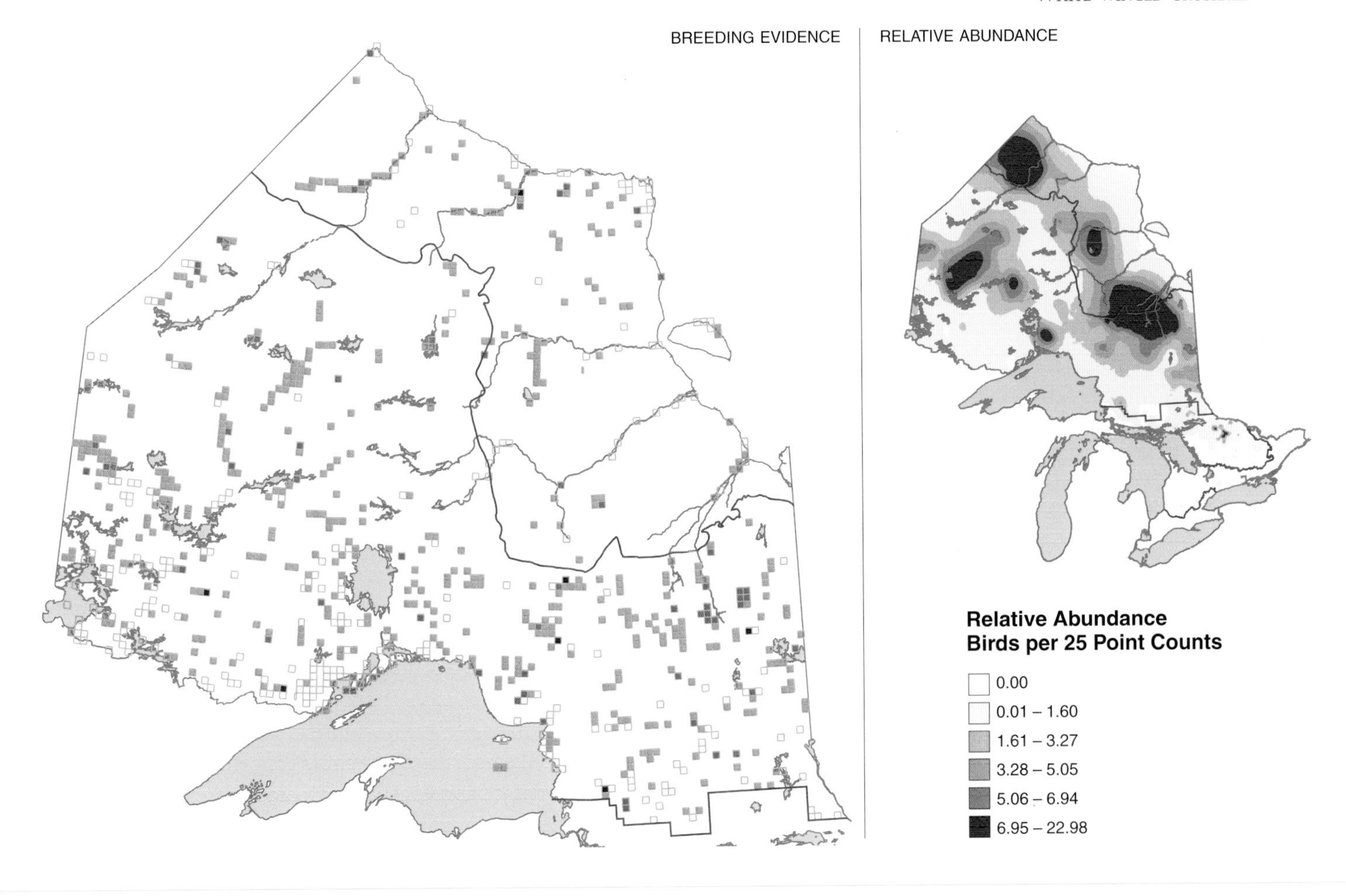

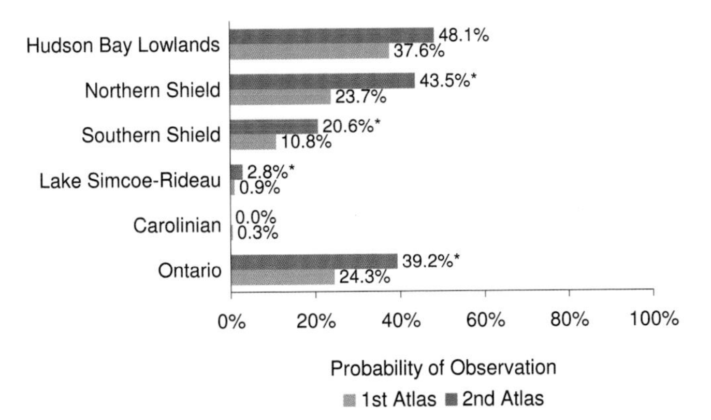

nearly doubled, with breeding evidence from a large number of new squares in northern Peterborough Co., the Haliburton Highlands, Muskoka Dist., and the North Channel and southern Temagami areas. In the Northern Shield, the probability of observation also nearly doubled with much of the increase in the area bounded by Lake-of-the-Woods and Lake Nipigon in the south and Red Lake and Pickle Lake in the north.

The distribution of the White-winged Crossbill changed very little in the interval between the atlases. Better observer knowledge of its breeding phenology and distribution, combined with more widespread and frequent irruptions into Ontario during the second atlas, explain the majority of the increase in breeding evidence.

Breeding biology: The White-winged Crossbill may nest in any month (Godfrey 1986), but the timing is determined by seed availability. Three discrete nesting periods are defined by the temporal and spatial availability of suitable cones: July to November, as crops mature on White Spruce and Tamarack; January and February, with large White Spruce crops; and March to June on Black Spruce. Double broods may occur in spring depending on the size of Black Spruce crop (Benkman 1985, 1989, 1990). Peak atlassing activity in June was poorly timed to maximize detection of this species and likely tended to underestimate its occurrence. At the beginning of the breeding cycle, males sing conspicuously from the tops of conifers and perform song flights for females, providing some of the easiest opportunities for detection. Nests are well concealed and only the females incubate. Adults carry food to the nest as a bolus in their crop and consume most fecal sacs at the nest. Nest detection is quite challenging, and only 12 nests have been reported to the ONRS (Peck and Peck 2006). The one nest found during the atlas was in northern Peel Region in 2001 (Coady 2001). Confirmation of breeding most often involved sightings of fledged young, but the proportion of confirmed records was very low at 4%.

Abundance: The abundance map reveals the highest abundance to be in spruce-dominated areas of the Hudson Bay Lowlands, the Northern Shield, and limited parts of Algonquin Prov. Park. Atlas point counts and BBS data must be cautiously interpreted due to this species' nomadic behaviour and propensity to breed outside the survey dates used by these projects. Accurate assessment of its changing abundance in Ontario will require specialized surveys optimized to the timing and spatial distribution of its occurrences. Future abundance of the nomadic White-winged Crossbill in Ontario will depend on the continent-wide health of the Boreal Forest as the climate continues to warm. – *Glenn Coady*

Common Redpoll

Sizerin flammé

Carduelis flammea

The Common Redpoll is most often observed in Ontario during its southerly winter irruptions. The extent of movement varies from winter to winter and is driven by the failure of seed production among high-latitude trees (primarily birch), which forces the species south in search of food.

This small finch is easily recognized by its conical yellow bill, dark face, and streaked flanks, and by the small red cap for which it is named. It is very similar to and perhaps conspecific with the Hoary Redpoll, as suggested by a recent molecular genetic study of the two (Kerr et al. 2007).

The Common Redpoll is circumpolar, found throughout the Arctic in North America, Europe, and Asia. In North America, it breeds from Alaska to Newfoundland, mainly south of the Arctic islands to the Boreal Forest (Knox and Lowther 2000a).

Distribution and population status: The Ontario breeding range of the Common Redpoll is largely restricted to the Hudson Bay Lowlands, where it is found throughout, from the Manitoba border south and east to the vicinity of Moosonee. There was no significant change in the probability of observation between atlases. During the second atlas, the species was documented in three new 100-km blocks; however, it was not reported in eight 100-km blocks in which it was reported during the first atlas. These latter 100-km blocks are all inland from the coast, suggesting that numbers are smaller inland and so birds are more easily overlooked. Reliable trend data are lacking because the remote nature of the species' breeding distribution precludes its detection on BBS surveys; its non-migratory nature means that it is not monitored through the CMMN; and the periodicity of its irruptions obscure patterns in CBC data (Knox and Lowther 2000a). The atlas data provide a distribution picture that agrees with the current literature (Godfrey 1986; Peck and James 1987; Knox and Lowther 2000a).

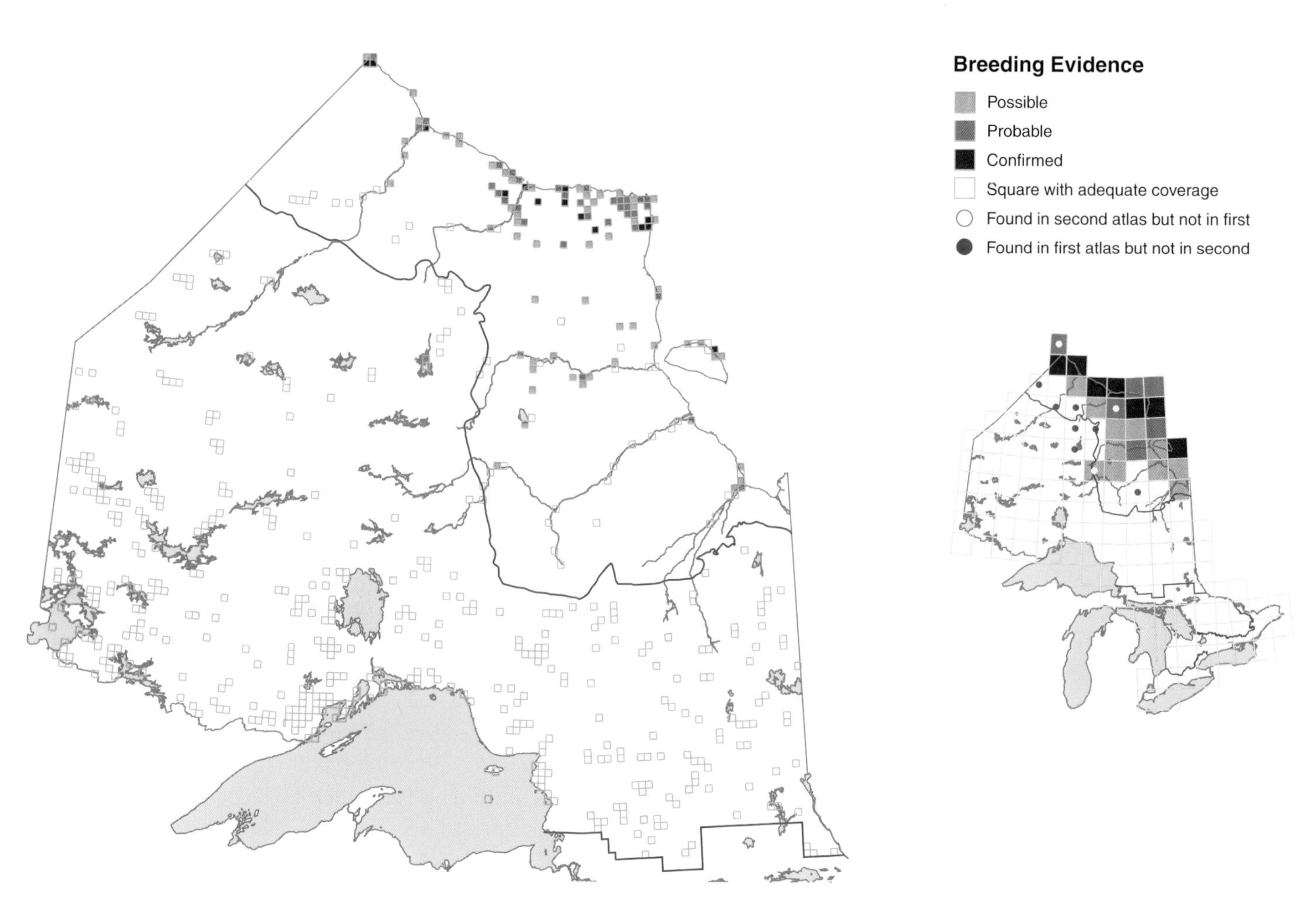

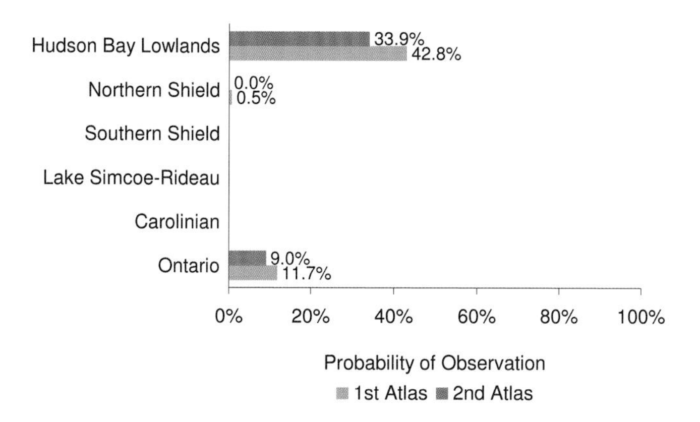

Breeding biology: The Common Redpoll generally nests between late May and mid-June, although second broods can be encountered as late as August (Knox and Lowther 2000a). Clues to nesting are provided by the easily observed courtship displays, which involve circling aerial display flights performed by the male in open country (Knox and Lowther 2000a). Nests, built primarily by the female, are constructed of loose twigs and grasses and lined with fine plant fibres and feathers. In Ontario, nests are almost always elevated in low willows (Peck and James 1987) but may be located in spruce in cold springs when leaf-out of deciduous shrubs is delayed. Incubation lasts about 12 days and is followed by a nestling period of 11-14 days (Baicich and Harrison 1997). Only the female incubates, but the male feeds her regularly during this period, helping the patient observer to locate the nest. The female does most of the feeding of the young, though the male may help directly or by passing food to the female. The species' diet is a mix of insects and seeds. Depending on the timing of successful first nests, second broods are common (Knox and Lowther 2000a), providing an opportunity to confirm nesting of the species on visits later in the summer.

It is likely that, due to the conspicuousness of the species and the open nature of its habitat, the distribution map provides a relatively accurate reflection of its range. Squares with confirmed breeding tend to predominate along the Hudson Bay and northern James Bay coasts, which may result from the ease in observing birds and locating nests in the sparse and stunted growth of the tundra.

Abundance: The sociable Common Redpoll tends to nest in loose colonies (Knox and Lowther 2000a). Accordingly, when present, it usually occurs in high numbers. Abundance data from the atlas indicate that the highest densities are along the Hudson Bay and northern James Bay shores and in the area of extensive tundra inland from Cape Henrietta Maria. Densities decline sharply inland from the coast and tundra areas, averaging 3.4 birds/25 point counts across the whole Hudson Bay Lowlands. Nesting may occur sporadically in the Northern Shield region as well (Peck and James 1987), but breeding evidence is more difficult to observe in the denser Boreal Forest, and numbers are low, with an average of only 0.01 birds/25 point counts in the region as a whole. – *Seabrooke Leckie and Ron Pittaway*

Nests are usually located in low willows, but in cold years in Ontario with delayed leaf emergence, they may be located exclusively in stunted spruce. Nests are frequently lined with Willow Ptarmigan feathers. *Photo: Mark Peck*

In Ontario, this species breeds in a variety of habitats from riparian willow thickets to dry lichen-heath tundra with scattered, stunted spruces. Near Oosteguanako Creek, south of West Pen Island, 5 July 2004.
Photo: Donald A. Sutherland

Hoary Redpoll

Sizerin blanchâtre

Carduelis hornemanni

Ron Ridout

The Hoary Redpoll, a bird of the arctic tundra, is most often observed in the winter in flocks of the more abundant Common Redpoll, whose irruptions to the south occur in roughly alternating years. Such irruptions are associated with food availability linked to seed crop failure in its northern range (Knox and Lowther 2000b). The Hoary Redpoll is well adapted to life in the far north, where few other bird species are able to remain throughout the year.

The range of the Hoary Redpoll is circumpolar, with breeding being restricted to the tundra and the tundra-taiga ecotone from the Subarctic to the high Arctic. Its North American breeding range extends across the continent from northern Labrador to Alaska and includes suitable high arctic islands (Godfrey 1986; Knox and Lowther 2000b). In Ontario, the species breeds in wet graminoid tundra, often within willow thickets surrounding ponds and small lakes, or on low gravel ridges with stunted spruces.

The subspecies of Hoary Redpoll that breeds in Ontario, *C.h. exilipes*, is very similar in appearance to the much more familiar Common Redpoll. The similarity between the two species has led to debate regarding their specific status. Although there is support for the view that the Hoary Redpoll is a distinct species (Sibley and Monroe 1990; Knox and Lowther 2000b), recent molecular genetic work suggests that the two are conspecific (Kerr et al. 2007).

Distribution and population status: The Hoary Redpoll appears to be a rare breeding species in Ontario, where it has only been documented at a few isolated locations along Hudson Bay. However, coverage of the Hudson Bay coast of Ontario has been uneven in both atlases. During the first atlas, the species was recorded in just three squares in two 100-km blocks along

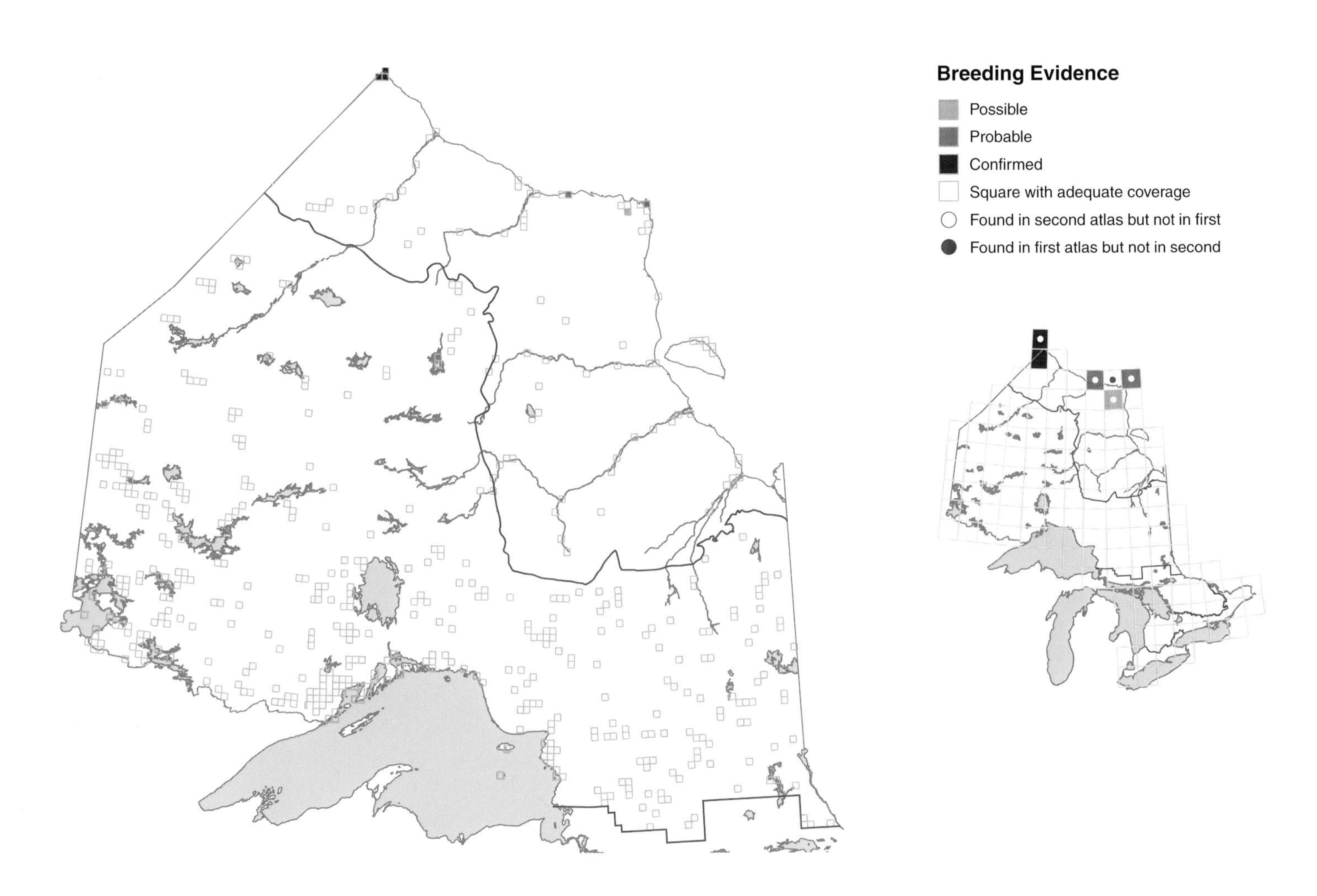

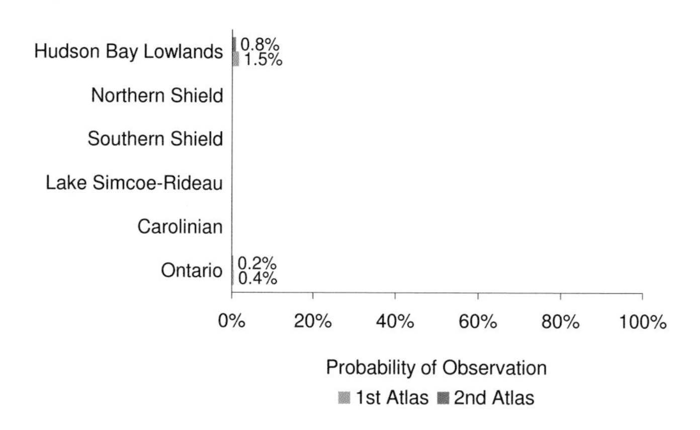

Hudson Bay, one west of Cape Henrietta Maria and the other along the Manitoba border. In the second atlas, it was recorded in six squares, representing five 100-km blocks. These squares were all located in the same general vicinity as in the first atlas. Breeding was confirmed in three squares, all along the Manitoba border, where nests were found with either eggs or young. These three nests are the first to be documented for the species in the province (Peck and Peck 2006).

The Hoary Redpoll is outnumbered by the Common Redpoll with which it frequently associates, and it consequently may be overlooked in some areas. Its population status likely varies greatly from year to year, as has been reported to be the case at Churchill, Manitoba (Jehl 2004). This has also been demonstrated at some locations in Ontario, such as near the Shagamu River mouth, where the species was observed on 31 May 1990 (Wilson and McRae 1993) but not during either atlas.

Breeding biology: The Hoary Redpoll has a short nesting season which begins in mid-May and ends in late July. Males deliver song throughout the breeding season, but the song is sufficiently similar to that of Common Redpoll that it is likely to have occasionally been overlooked. Nests are constructed entirely by the female. All three Ontario nests were located in White Spruce (Burke et al., in press). Nests have been found in spruce, Tamarack, willow, and birch at Churchill (Jehl 2004). All Ontario nests were lined with white ptarmigan feathers and Arctic Fox fur (Burke et al., in press). Clutches of four to five (range one to six) pale blue/green finely speckled eggs are common. The nestling period lasts for 12-15 days, during which the amount of brooding diminishes. Incubation and brooding, carried out entirely by the female, is tenacious. During incubation and brooding, the male feeds the female at the nest (Knox and Lowther 2000b). The species' diet consists mainly of small seeds from various trees, weeds, and grasses, supplemented with invertebrates in the summer, particularly when feeding nestlings. Evidence suggests that the reuse of a nest from a prior year may enable pairs to begin egg laying more quickly, making the most of the short breeding season (Knox and Lowther 2000b); however, breeding behaviour is poorly studied (Knox and Lowther 2000b).

Abundance: Point count data were obtained only from the Hudson Bay coast, reinforcing the view that the Hoary Redpoll is restricted to coastal tundra during summer. These data, particularly when compared to that for the Common Redpoll, suggest that the Hoary Redpoll is a rare breeder in Ontario. The breeding population in northern Ontario is the most southerly in the world. Hoary Redpolls may not breed in the province every year, similar to fluctuating populations in adjacent Manitoba. – *Seabrooke Leckie and Ron Pittaway*

Nests are constructed of coarse grass stems and in Ontario are lined with ptarmigan feathers and Arctic Fox fur. *Photo: George K. Peck*

All three Ontario nests have been located in stunted White Spruce. Near Oosteguanako Creek south of West Pen Island, 5 July 2004. *Photo: Colin D. Jones*

Pine Siskin

Tarin des pins

Carduelis pinus

Mark Peck

This dark, striped finch is sometimes mistaken for a sparrow. However, its yellow wing bar, yellow-edged flight feathers, slender bill, and husky calls make the Pine Siskin distinctive. Highly nomadic, it breeds in northern coniferous forests across North America and southward in mountains to Guatemala, occurring in flocks that break into loose groups and pairs for nesting. It may be a common breeder in an area one year and absent the next (Godfrey 1986). Though it shows a tendency for north-south migration, it is better considered an opportunistic nomad. Banding recoveries show that individuals will wander between Atlantic and Pacific coasts, probably in search of large coniferous seed crops. Periodic major irruptions occur when cone crops fail over vast areas (Dawson 1997).

Distribution and population status: The year-to-year breeding distribution and population in Ontario will always be difficult to determine because siskin movements and numbers are linked to conifer crops. Atlas data show changing population features that are characteristic of an irruptive species.

In the Carolinian region, where coniferous trees are uncommon, there were few squares with breeding evidence for the Pine Siskin. A comparison of the two atlases in the Lake Simcoe-Rideau region shows a fairly high turnover of occupied squares and a significant 23% decline in the probability of observation. In the Southern and Northern Shield regions, the breeding distribution appears similar in both atlases. However, in the Southern Shield, the probability of observation declined significantly by 31%. This decrease may reflect a shift in breeding distribution associated with the variable highs and lows of seed supplies. The effects of timber harvesting on siskin habitats have not been studied.

In the Hudson Bay Lowlands, the probability of observation declined significantly by 66% between atlases. The species was not recorded in 10 contiguous 100-km blocks in the northern part of

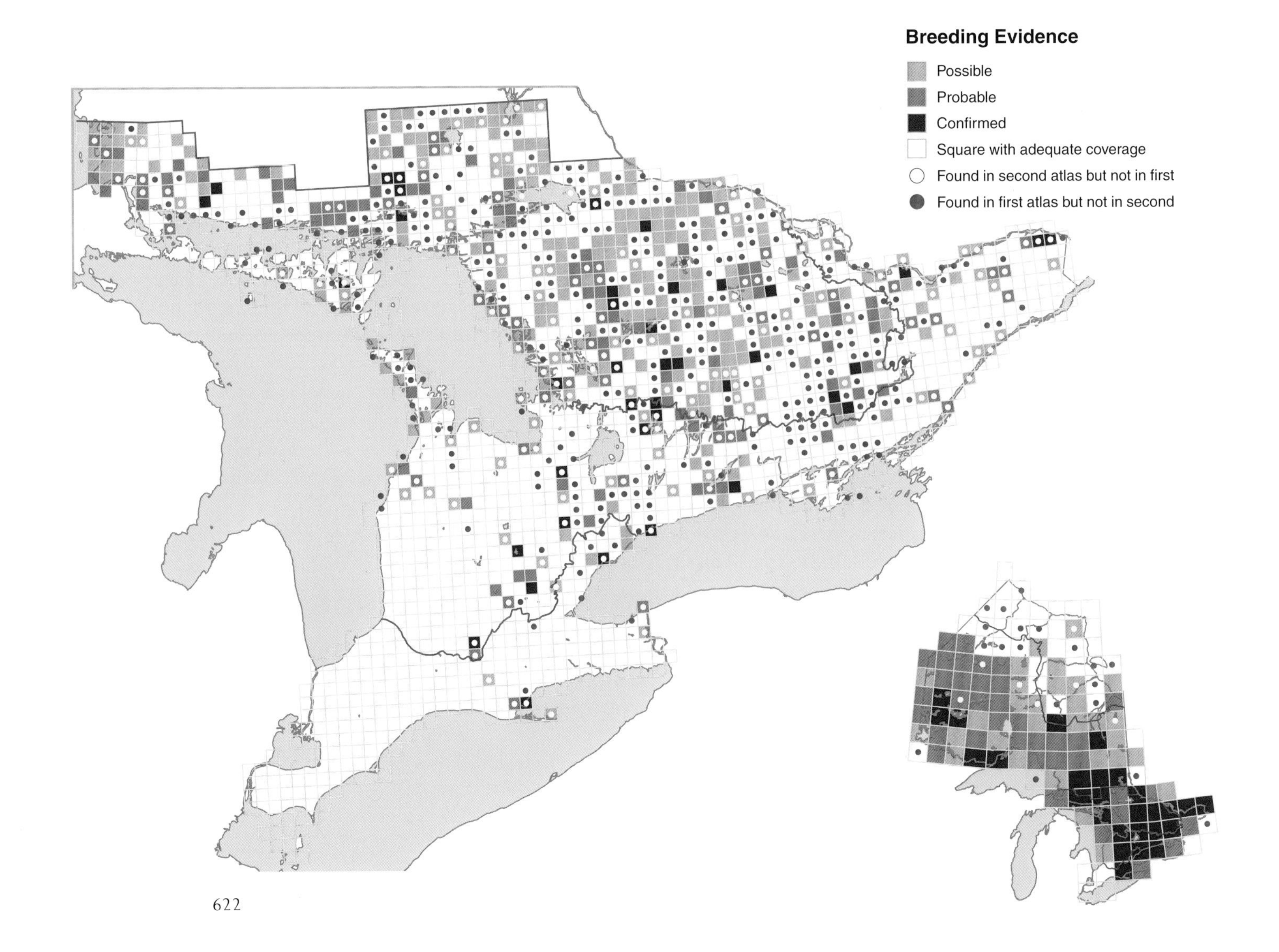

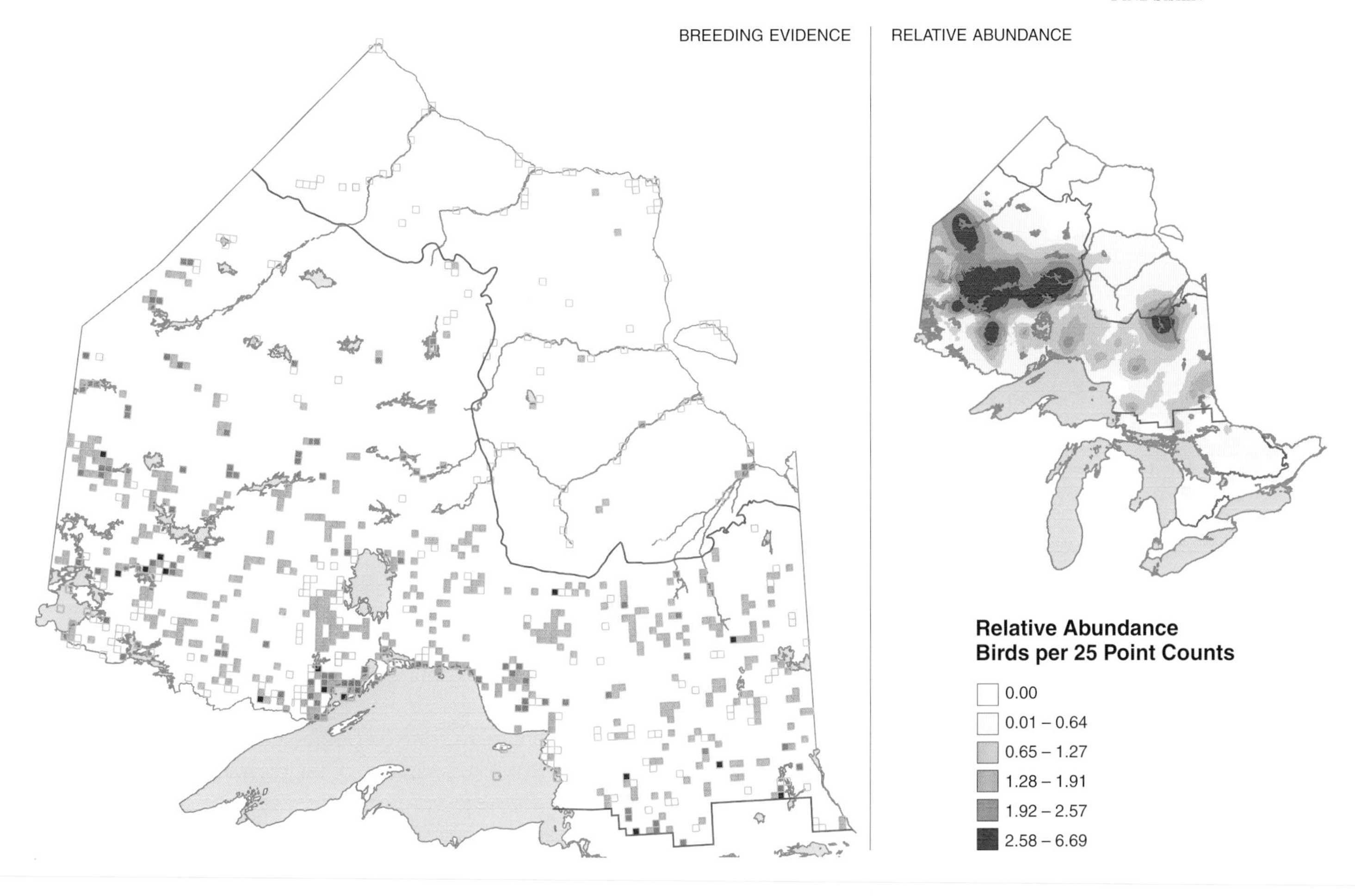

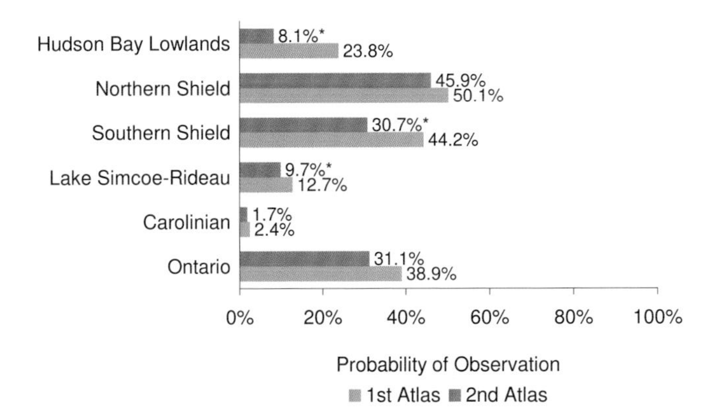

the region where it was reported during the first atlas; this may again reflect erratic movements to areas with better seed crops.

BBS data show a significant decline in Pine Siskin numbers across Canada (Downes et al. 2005). These data suggest that numbers peaked in the mid-1980s and have fluctuated widely at a lower level since then. It is unlikely that the changes are due to habitat loss, but the siskin's breeding requirements and irruptive movements may be involved.

Breeding biology: The Pine Siskin breeds between mid-February and late August (Dawson 1997). Early breeding and highest densities are associated with large crops of conifer seeds, particularly on White Spruce, White Cedar, and Eastern Hemlock. Breeding presence may be detected by its song of wheezy trills and twittering, often punctuated by a distinctive rising buzzy "*shreeEEEE*" call. Egg laying in Ontario fluctuates widely from March when snow often covers the ground to late July (Peck and James 1987). The species is usually single-brooded but may double-brood after an early nesting. Siskins sometimes move northward for the second brood (Dawson 1997).

Courtship flights begin in mid-February, with courtship feeding, copulation, and nest building occurring from late February and early March. However, the timing of these events varies by as much as two months. The Pine Siskin nests primarily in loose colonies in relatively open coniferous or mixed forest. Nests are built by the female alone and are usually in the outer needle-covered branches of conifers 1-15 m above ground, which makes nest-finding difficult. Only the female incubates and broods the young, but the male will feed the female on the nest. Initially only the male collects food for the young but is joined later by the female once the young no longer require brooding. Preferred foods fed to young are the small seeds of conifers and composite plants, and some insects (Dawson 1997).

Abundance: The breeding evidence and abundance maps illustrate a distribution that strongly correlates with areas of extensive coniferous forest. The siskin was essentially absent from the agricultural regions of the south and had a patchy distribution in the Lake Simcoe-Rideau region. Abundance gradually increased across the Southern Shield. The greatest abundance occurred in the western half of the Northern Shield, where presumably the conifer seed crop was heaviest during the atlas period, with areas of high density scattered throughout the rest of the region. Abundance declined northwards until siskins were almost absent from the Hudson Bay Lowlands, particularly in the northern part of the region. Given the nomadic movements of the species, future atlases may show abundance to be highest in different areas from those in this atlas, depending on where coniferous cone crops are abundant at the time. – *Ron Pittaway*

American Goldfinch

Chardonneret jaune

Carduelis tristis

George K. Peck

With its brilliant lemon-yellow breeding (alternate) plumage, the male goldfinch is sometimes known as the wild canary. The female, with more subdued plumage, is less easily recognized. The American Goldfinch has two body moults during the year and is the most seasonally and sexually dimorphic member of its *Carduelinae* subfamily (Middleton 1993). The species has a wide distribution that extends from the Atlantic to the Pacific oceans and from the Mexican border north to the Boreal Forest (Middleton 1993).

Distribution and population status: The American Goldfinch has adapted well to human-modified habitats where food such as the seeds of thistles and garden plants is abundant and nesting sites are available. Thus, the goldfinch has benefited from the impact of European settlement and is more widely distributed now than in historic times (McNicholl and Cranmer-Byng 1994). Both atlases recorded goldfinches in virtually every square in the agricultural and populated southern parts of the province south of the Shield. Most squares continue to show probable or confirmed breeding, and such status was recorded in the few squares from which the goldfinch was not reported in the first atlas. In the Southern Shield region, breeding evidence was limited in much of the Algonquin Prov. Park area and missing from a few coastal squares near the northern shores of Georgian Bay and Lake Huron, where much of the habitat is rocky and forested.

Between the first and second atlases, there was no significant difference in the probability of observation in the province as a whole, but there was a significant increase of 73% in the Northern Shield region. This resulted in several new 100-km blocks with breeding evidence and upgraded breeding status in others. These changes may be partly a result of increased forestry creating more successional habitat in the Boreal Forest. BBS data show no significant change in Ontario

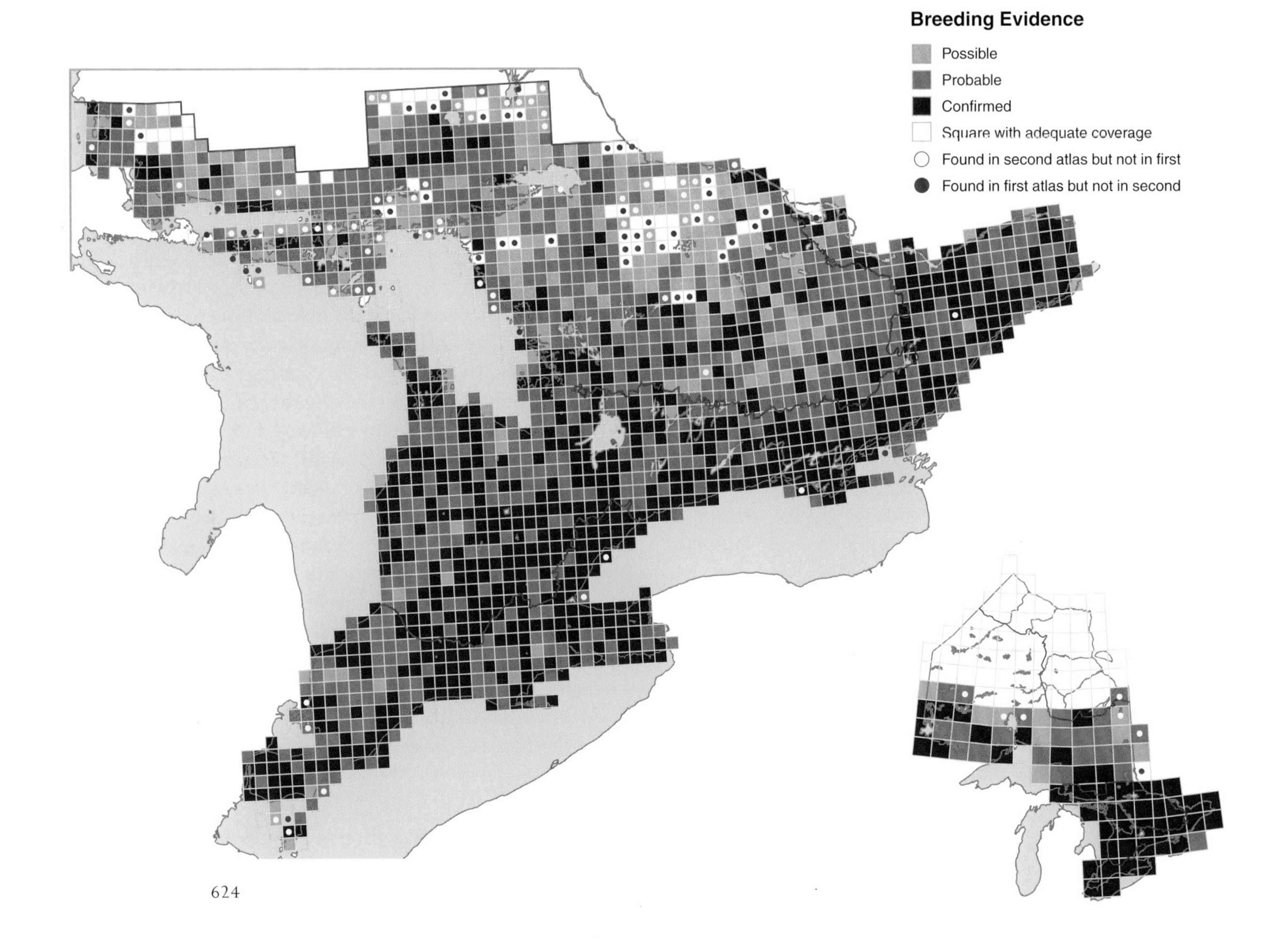

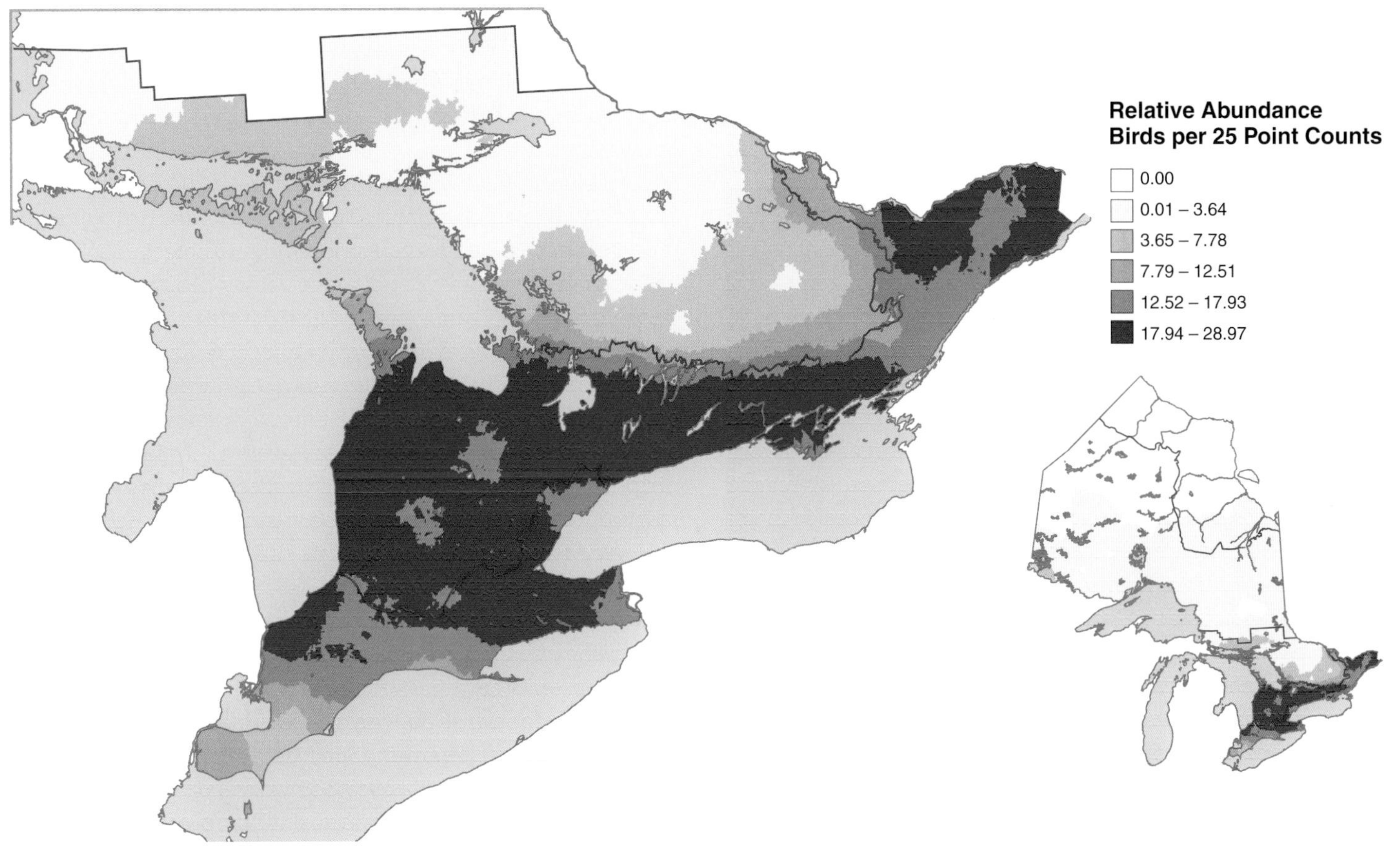

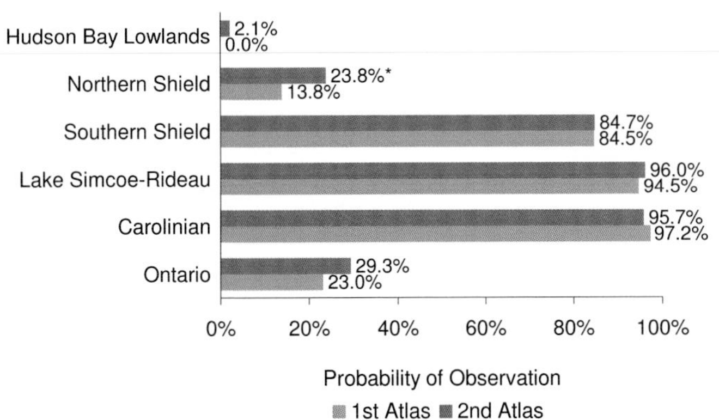

since 1968 (Downes et al. 2005), although northern Ontario is not well represented by BBS routes.

Breeding biology: The American Goldfinch prefers weedy fields, flood plains, and areas characteristic of early successional growth dominated by hawthorn, serviceberry, or other shrubs. It is a surprisingly late nester, probably an adaptation to the flowering of thistles and similar plants since the young are dependent on the seeds for food (Middleton 1993). Although breeding behaviour is apparent as early as April, nesting does not normally begin until late June, and the first eggs are not laid until July. Active nesting continues into September (Middleton 1993). Nests with eggs or young were reported from most 100-km blocks in southern Ontario, with confirmed breeding recorded in 33% of squares with breeding evidence. It is likely that the late nesting date meant that the easily detected nests were overlooked in many squares where atlassing had concluded by mid-summer. It is almost certain that the species breeds in most squares where it was recorded.

The nest, built by the female alone, is usually in the terminal forks of small deciduous trees and shrubs such as hawthorn, serviceberry, or dogwood, or in sapling deciduous trees such as maple, birch, or willow. Nests are compact, built of plant fibres, and lined with plant down, most commonly thistle. Nests usually survive after the birds have left and are frequently visible long after leaf fall (Middleton 1993).

Although the goldfinch is not territorial (only the immediate vicinity of the nest is defended), signs of nesting become clear when the males engage in their loose, circling song flights over the nesting areas. The species is not aggressive at the nest but, if disturbed, will show agitated behaviour accompanied by its distinctive alarm call. Incubation and the early stages of brooding are by the female alone, who sits tightly for long, unbroken spells (Middleton 1993).

Abundance: With its preference for old fields, flood plains and shrubby habitats, the American Goldfinch is patchily distributed in intensively farmed areas and largely absent from mature, undisturbed forests or open tundra. Predictably, as shown by the distribution map, it is most abundant in the Lake Simcoe-Rideau region and less so in the Carolinian region, particularly the extreme southwest, where intensive agriculture has left relatively little of the species' preferred habitat. Abundance drops markedly with increasing latitude and is low through much of the Southern and Northern Shield regions. The species is virtually absent as a breeder in the Hudson Bay Lowlands. Based on atlas point count data, the provincial population is estimated at 4,000,000 birds, with 2,500,000 of those in the Lake Simcoe-Rideau region. – *Seabrooke Leckie and Michael D. Cadman*

Evening Grosbeak

Gros-bec errant

Coccothraustes vespertinus

George K. Peck

The Evening Grosbeak is unmistakable in any plumage. Its impressively large bill easily cracks the stones of wild cherries, making loud "pops" during the northern summer. It formerly nested only in western North America before spreading eastward during historic times (Gillihan and Byers 2001). Logging and extensive fires that resulted in young forests with abundant wild cherries, a main summer food of the species, probably contributed to this range expansion (Brunton in McNicholl and Cranmer-Byng 1994). The first breeding records for Ontario were at Lake of the Woods in 1920, Muskoka in 1927 and Algonquin Prov. Park in 1932 (Godfrey 1986). It became a fairly common breeder in the province between 1940 and 1980 because of the increased food supply from large outbreaks of Spruce Budworm (Bolgiano 2004). After 1980, it declined as the budworm epidemics ended. The population is probably stable now but much lower than in the 1970s.

Distribution and population status: The Evening Grosbeak breeds across northern Ontario from Pickle Lake to Moosonee south to the southern edge of the Shield (Peck and James 1987). Data from the second atlas show a significant decline since the first atlas. The probability of observation for the province as a whole decreased by 30%. Declines were most pronounced in the Hudson Bay Lowlands and Northern Shield regions, where the probability of observation decreased by 82% and 26%, respectively. Significant declines of 21% and 10% occurred in the Southern Shield and Lake Simcoe-Rideau regions as well.

During outbreaks, Spruce Budworm larvae and pupae can account for as much as 80% of the diet of the Evening Grosbeak and for the species' population increase (Mitchell 1952). During the first atlas, the extent of areas affected by severe budworm outbreaks in Ontario ranged between 8,000,000 and 18,000,000 hectares annually. However, the extent of outbreaks in the province declined significantly between atlases. By 1997, the area of out-

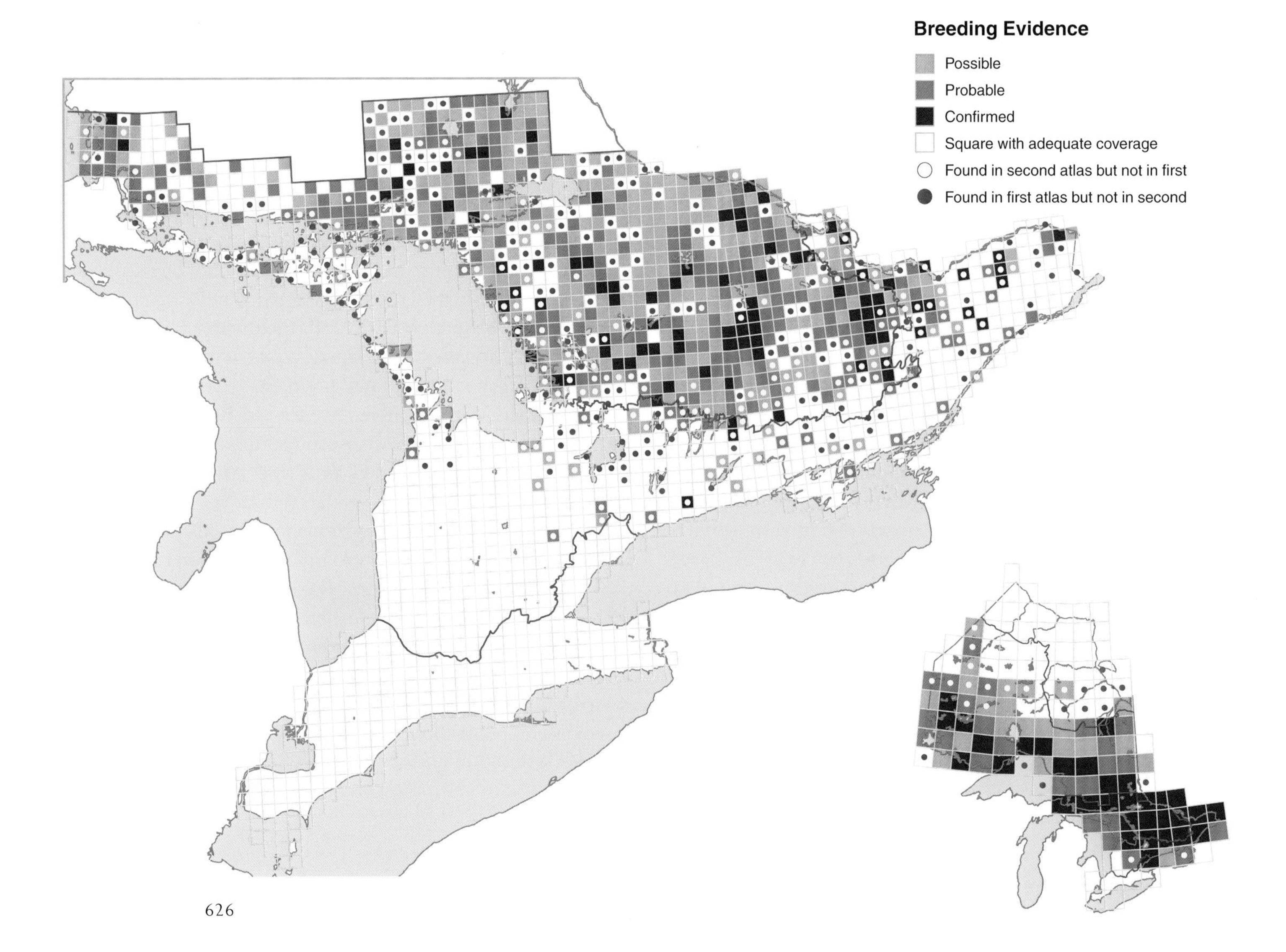

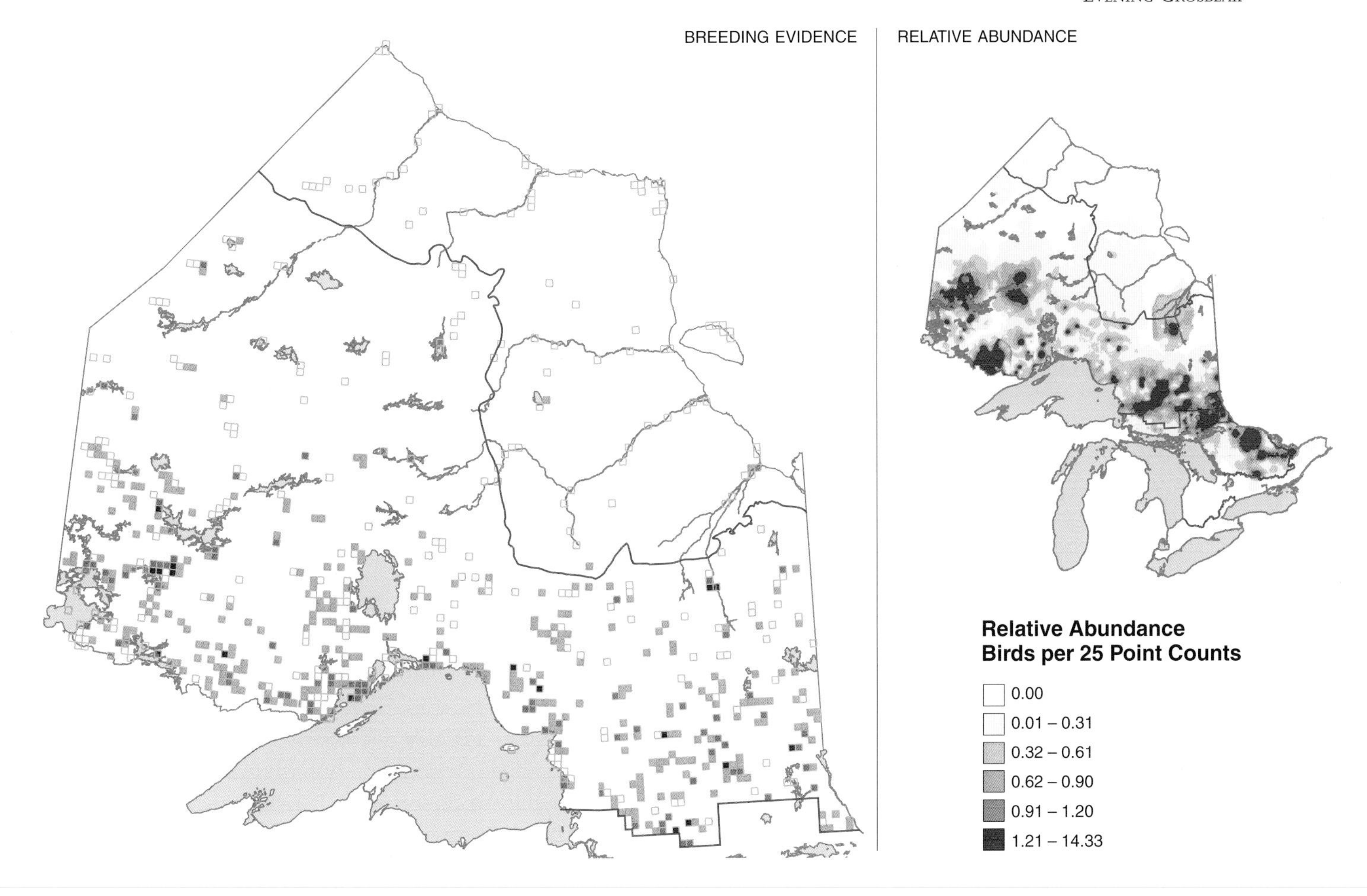

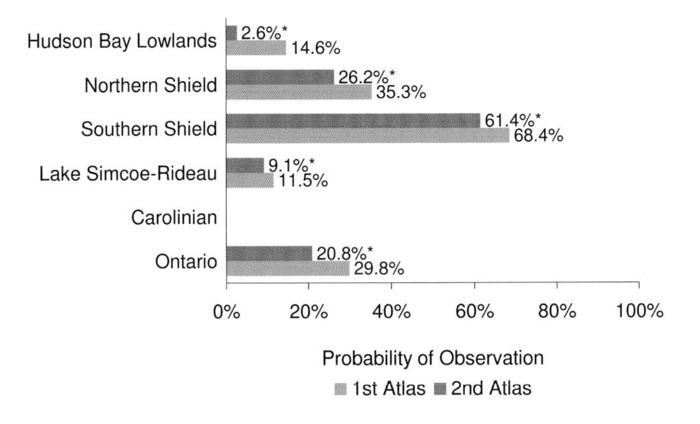

breaks had dropped to 53,000 hectares, and since then, annual outbreaks have ranged in extent between 81,000 and 337,000 hectares. Two moderate outbreaks of 200,000+ hectares occurred during this atlas period in 2003 and 2004 (National Forestry Database Program 2007).

BBS data suggest that Evening Grosbeak populations peaked in Ontario in the mid-1980s. As the size of annual Spruce Budworm outbreaks decreased dramatically, numbers of this grosbeak also declined. BBS data since 1981 show a significant annual decline of 11.9% in Ontario and 8.2% in Canada.

Breeding biology: In Ontario, the Evening Grosbeak breeds primarily in second growth and mature mixed forests (Peck and James 1987). It favours open forests, perhaps due to food sources in the deciduous understorey. Its selection of nesting areas is influenced more by food availability than habitat structure (Gillihan and Byers 2001). Pairs arrive at breeding areas as early as mid-April and soon begin nest construction (Gillihan and Byers 2001). Although normally vocal and conspicuous, birds are secretive around the nest site. Nests are rarely found, as they are constructed in dense foliage near or in the tops of trees. The height of nine nests in Ontario ranged between 7.5-16.8 m (Peck and James 1987) from the ground. The nest is a sparse structure usually placed in crotches against the main trunk or up to 3 m from the trunk (Peck and James 1987). Clutch sizes from five Ontario nests were either three or four eggs, with egg dates ranging from 13 June to 4 July (Peck and James 1987). Young leave the nest at 13-14 days old and stay near the nest tree for several days (Scott and Bekoff 1991). Confirmed breeding evidence in the second atlas accounted for only 10% of observations.

Abundance: The Evening Grosbeak has a widespread but uneven distribution across the province. Areas with the highest breeding densities were those having significant budworm outbreaks. The high abundance of the species in the Southern Shield region during the second atlas was likely a reflection of significant budworm outbreaks in the Sudbury-North Bay, Bancroft-Arnprior, and Petroglyphs Prov. Park areas (Howse and Scarr 2002). The Evening Grosbeak will move long distances to areas of food abundance and may be locally common some years and absent in others. It was fairly common during the first atlas with abundance estimates for most squares ranging from 11 to 100 pairs. During this atlas, it was an uncommon breeder in the absence of large budworm outbreaks. Ontario's population is currently probably stable, subject to the periodic fluctuations in Spruce Budworm. – *Tyler Hoar*

House Sparrow

Moineau domestique

Passer domesticus

Frank and Sandra Horvath

The House Sparrow is familiar to all Ontarians living in urban or agricultural areas. Widespread in Europe and parts of Asia and North Africa, it was successfully introduced to North America and many other parts of the world in the mid-1800s. Where introduced, it eventually came to be regarded as a pest because of its predation on crops and fouling of buildings with droppings and nests. Its numbers initially declined in both North America and Europe following the disappearance of horses as a primary means of transport, due to the dwindling supply of spilled grain and seeds in manure. Subsequent declines have been attributed to more efficient farming practices and increased use of pesticides (Lowther and Cink 2006).

Distribution and population status: The House Sparrow was introduced into Ontario around 1870 (Robbins 1973) and with subsequent introductions spread to the North Bay area by 1886. By 1969, it was a resident as far north as Dryden, Hearst, and Kapuskasing, with isolated records at Fort Severn and Attawapiskat. At the time of the first atlas, it was ubiquitous south of the Shield and established in urban and agricultural areas in both the Southern and Northern Shield regions.

The species' current distribution is generally the same as during the first atlas, but its probability of observation declined by a significant 20% between atlases in the province as a whole, and by a significant 6% and 49% in the Lake Simcoe-Rideau and Southern Shield regions, respectively. It differed from two other primarily urban species, the House Finch and the Rock Pigeon, which showed increases in these regions since the first atlas. However, the similarly ubiquitous European Starling has also decreased by a significant 13% in the Southern Shield, with a non-significant 2% decline in the Lake Simcoe-Rideau region. BBS data have shown significant declines for the House Sparrow in both Ontario and Canada

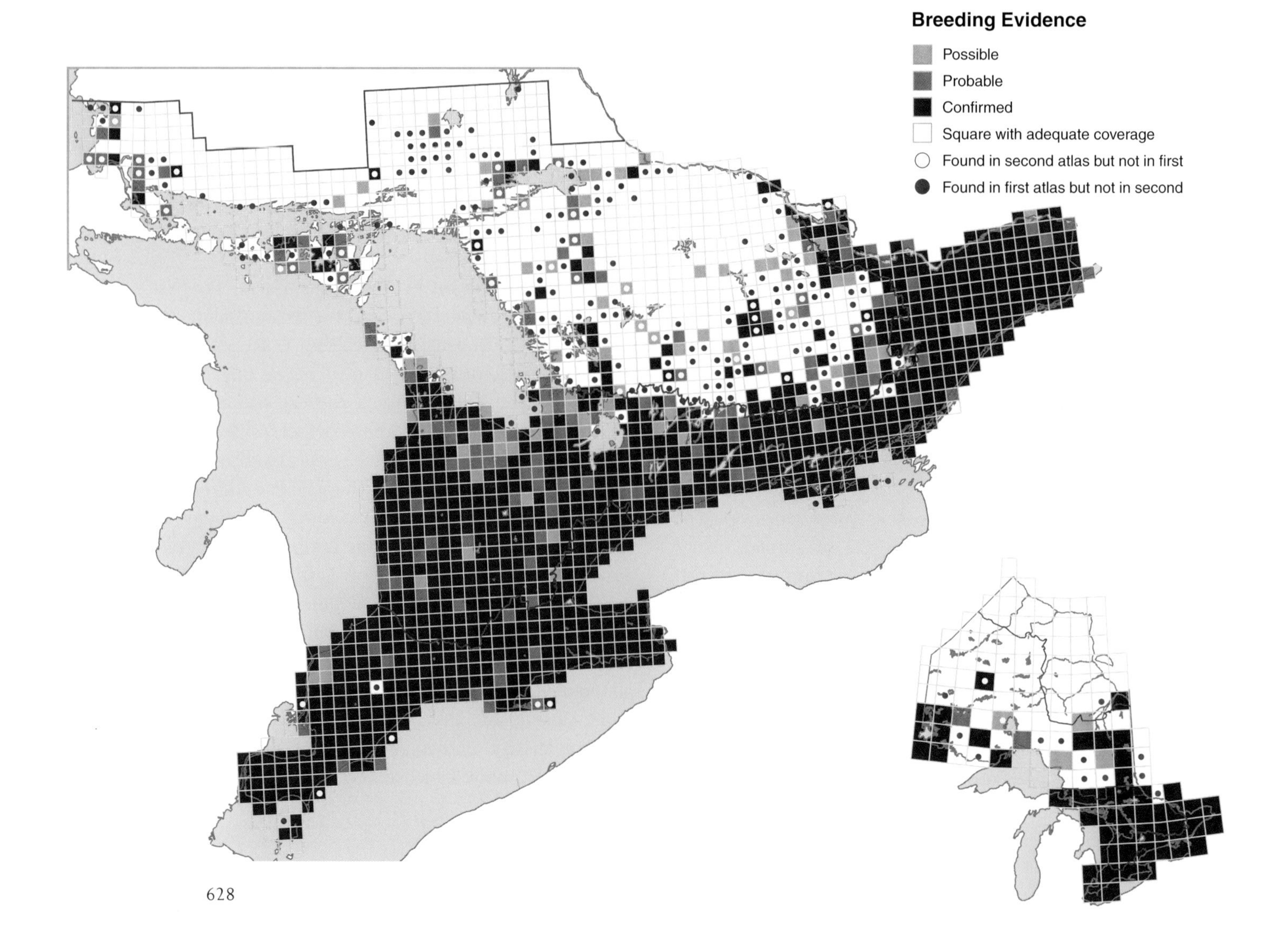

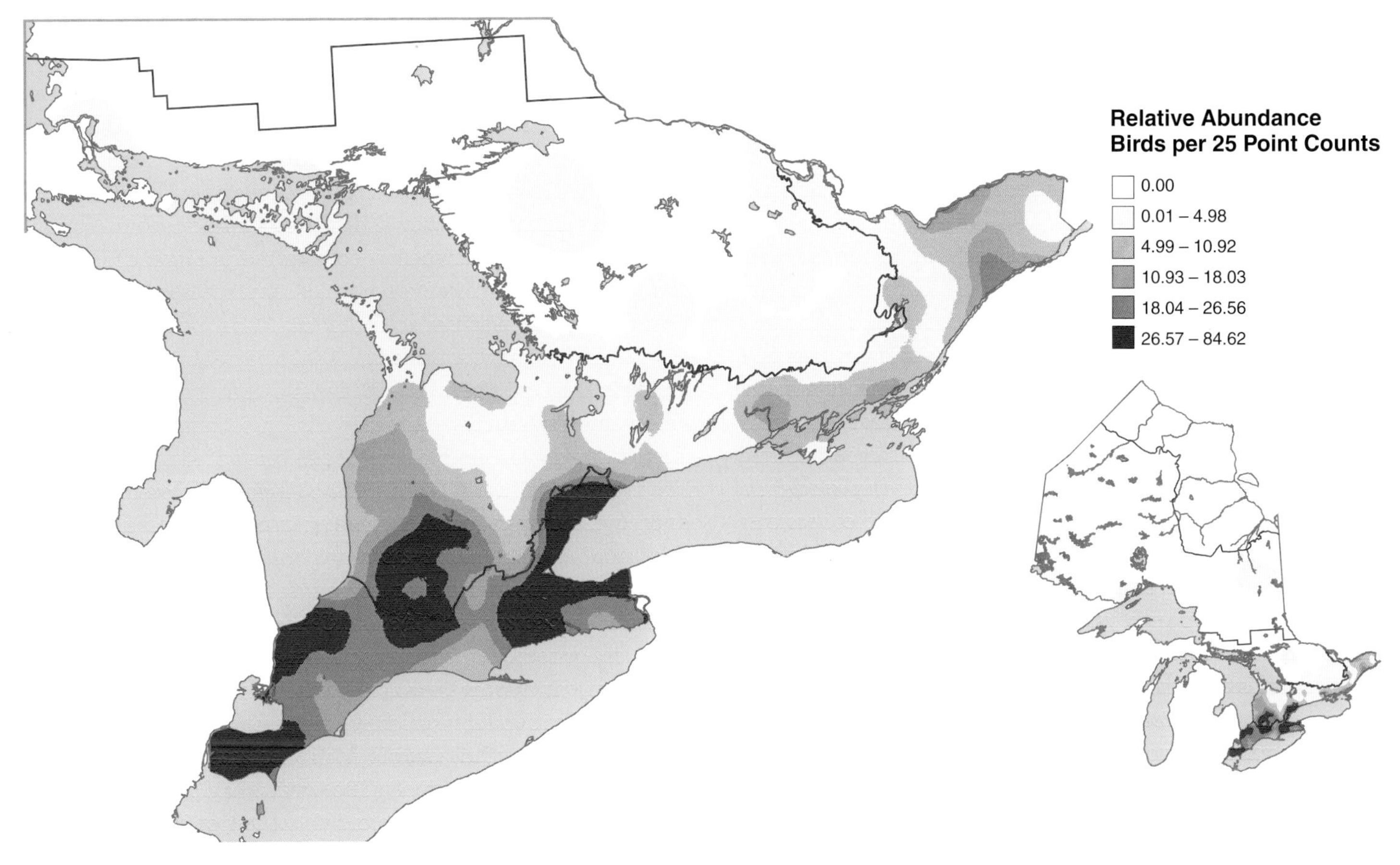

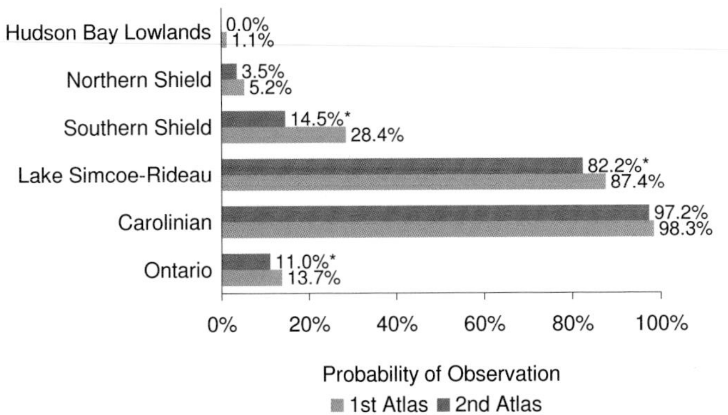

since surveys began in 1968. A similar trend is evident in CBC data (Holder 2003). In western Europe, significant declines have also been recorded (Summers-Smith 2003).

The decline does not seem to be related to increasing human population size in Ontario. It may instead be related to changes in land use, as most parts of the Southern Shield have lost farmland and gained forest cover through the retirement of marginal agricultural land. Although the decline is correlated with the expansion of the House Finch in eastern North America, there appears to be little competition between the two species (Bennett 1990; Holder 2003), and in Ontario the House Sparrow has disappeared primarily from areas that the House Finch has not yet colonized. Other proposed hypotheses include intensified farming practices, loss of nesting cavities due to changed building practices, increasing numbers of predators such as accipiters in urban areas, and increased mortality due to Salmonellosis infections at winter bird feeders (Cornelius 1969; Holder 2003; G. Coady, pers. comm.).

Breeding biology: Nests are placed in or on buildings and other structures, natural cavities, nest boxes, and old nests of other species. Cavities with active nests of other species are sometimes usurped. Males advertise their nest cavities loudly and, since they defend only their nest holes and not a larger territory, often nest in close proximity. This tendency to nest colonially also facilitates the noisy, communal courting of a female by several males. A pair reuses its nest site each year and remains nearby throughout the year, often roosting in the nest. Nesting occurs from April to August, and a pair often raises two broods in a season (Peck and James 1987). Fledglings remain with the male near the nest site for 7 to 10 days (Lowther and Cink 2006). These traits, as well as the species' preference for human habitats, combine to make it easily detected by atlassers.

In general, the distribution map accurately represents the House Sparrow's range. Gaps in the distribution on the Southern and Northern Shield regions and the Hudson Bay Lowlands reflect the species' absence from the vast areas of forest and wetlands in those regions.

Abundance: The results of the point counts reflect the House Sparrow's dependence on humans. It is common only south of the Shield but is most abundant in parts of the province with a high proportion of farmland or high human population density. These correspond to Ottawa-Carleton and farmlands to the southeast, the greater Toronto and Hamilton areas, the Niagara Peninsula, and the farmlands and urban centres in Perth, Waterloo, Wellington, Oxford, Lambton, and Essex Counties and Chatham-Kent. – *Anthony L. Lang*

Historical Breeders

The following species were not reported with breeding evidence during the second atlas but were reported with breeding evidence during the first atlas or have bred in the province at some point in the past.

Brant

Bernache cravant

Branta bernicla

The Atlantic Brant (the "light-bellied" subspecies *hrota*) is a low Arctic breeder, nesting in the Foxe Basin from northern Baffin Island south to Southampton Island and wintering principally along the mid-Atlantic coast of the US (Reed et al. 1998). A large proportion of the eastern breeding population stages in southern James Bay during migration. Individuals or small groups of summering, non-breeding birds are occasionally seen on the Hudson Bay coast of Ontario. No nest has been documented in Ontario (ONRS), but there are two reported instances of breeding in the province, both atypical of the species' range and habitat: 18 adults and five goslings are reported to have summered on Kelly Lake and Ramsey Lake, Sudbury Dist., in 1954, and an adult and a gosling were observed on islands in the St. Lawrence River near Cornwall, United Counties of Stormont, Dundas and Glengarry, in 1970 (Lumsden in Cadman et al.1987). – *Donald A. Sutherland*

Cinnamon Teal

Sarcelle cannelle

Anas cyanoptera

The Cinnamon Teal is a species of the western US and adjacent Canada, its breeding range extending east sparingly to the 100th meridian (Gammonley 1996). In Ontario, it is a rare vagrant and unexpected breeding species (James 1991). During the first atlas, breeding evidence was reported in four squares. A nest discovered at Amherstburg, Essex Co., on 24 June 1983 constitutes the first and only confirmation of breeding for the province. Until the death of the female, a pair present at Townsend, Haldimand Co., between 23 June and 9 July 1984, was probably nesting. An adult male present at Hillman Marsh, Essex Co., between 29 May and 11 June 1985, and another male observed at Sable Islands Provincial Nature Reserve, Rainy River Dist., on 1 July 1985 provided evidence of possible breeding. There has been no subsequent evidence of breeding in the province. – *Al Sandilands and Donald A. Sutherland*

King Eider

Eider à tête grise

Somateria spectabilis

Circumpolar in its distribution, the King Eider breeds in North America along the arctic and subarctic coasts south to southern Hudson Bay (Godfrey 1986). In Ontario, all breeding evidence has come from the Cape Henrietta Maria region. An adult with young established the first confirmation of breeding in Ontario on 23 August 1944 (Smith 1944). In 1947, broods of recently hatched young and flocks of both sexes were observed between Cape Henrietta Maria and Little Cape. There were no subsequent reports of breeding (Lumsden 1957; Peck 1972; Schueler et al. 1974) until the first atlas, when a female with a brood was observed at the Sutton River in July 1983. No further occurrences have been reported, either between atlases (cf. Wilson and McRae 1993) or during the second atlas, although the species' rarity and the restricted search effort in its remote historic breeding habitat make encounters a matter of chance. The King Eider appears to be a rare breeder on the Hudson Bay coast of Ontario. – *Donald A. Sutherland*

Greater Prairie-Chicken

Tétras des prairies

Tympanuchus cupido

The Greater Prairie-Chicken is considered extirpated in Canada, with the last documented sighting in Saskatchewan in 1992 (Houston 2002). In Ontario, it occurred historically in native prairie from Windsor to Lake Simcoe, and in agricultural lands on Manitoulin Island, in adjacent Algoma Dist., and in western Rainy River Dist. in northwestern Ontario. The population in southwestern Ontario persisted until 1923-24 on Walpole Island at the mouth of the St. Clair River (Lumsden 1966), while populations in western Rainy River Dist. and on Manitoulin Island disappeared in 1959 and 1966, respectively (Lumsden 2005). In Ontario, the Greater Prairie-Chicken declined due to the loss of native prairie remnants and extensive anthropogenic grasslands, and to introgression with the Sharp-tailed Grouse (Lumsden 2005). – *Harry G. Lumsden and Donald A. Sutherland*

Snowy Egret

Aigrette neigeuse

Egretta thula

This small heron occurs throughout the Americas, rarely but regularly as a vagrant north to southern Canada (Parsons and Master 2000). Although breeding on Bon Portage Island in Nova Scotia has been suspected since 1984 (Erskine 1992), the only instance of confirmed breeding of Snowy Egret in Canada occurred in 1986 when a nest with three young was found in a colony of Black-crowned Night-Herons at Hamilton Harbour, Ontario (Curry and Bryant 1987). It is possible that a pair nested undetected at this location prior to the first atlas, when six birds were observed throughout August 1980 (Curry 2006).

The Snowy Egret continues to be a rare but regular breeding season vagrant to the province (James 1991). During the second atlas, the Snowy Egret was reported in two squares, but without evidence of breeding. Occasional nesting could occur in the future at any established heronry in the province, but is most likely in the south. – *Bob Curry*

Cattle Egret

Héron garde-boeufs

Bubulcus ibis

Although the Cattle Egret was formerly an occasional, rare breeding species in Ontario (e.g., Luther Marsh, Wellington Co.; Presqu'ile Prov. Park, Northumberland Co.; Pigeon Is., Frontenac Co.; Amherst Is., Lennox and Addington Co.; Pelee Is. and East Sister Is., Essex Co.), no nests have been documented in the province since the mid-1970s (Blokpoel and Tessier 1991; James 1991; ONRS). During the first atlas, the species was reported from eight squares; however, in only a single square (Walpole Is. marshes) was it observed in habitat considered suitable for breeding (i.e., a mixed heronry). During the second atlas, non-breeding individuals were reported from three squares. Post-breeding adult and juvenile Cattle Egrets disperse widely from colonies in the species' extensive US breeding range (Telfair 2006), occurring nearly annually in Ontario, typically from late summer through fall. – *Donald A. Sutherland*

Yellow-crowned Night-Heron

Bihoreau violacé

Nyctanassa violacea

The Yellow-crowned Night-Heron breeds primarily in coastal regions from the American tropics to the southern US. Its breeding range underwent a significant northward expansion particularly between 1945 and 1955. In the Great Lakes region, it is a rare but local breeder in southwest Ohio, southern Wisconsin, and eastern Minnesota and a casual breeder in southern Michigan (Watts 1995). In Ontario, nesting has never been documented, although a single adult observed on 23 May 1954 in the heronry on East Sister Island, Essex Co., was suggestive of nesting (Peck and James 1983). Of two records during the first atlas, an adult observed in June 1982 carrying food in flight toward a small woodlot near Ojibway Park, Essex Co., was more suggestive of breeding, although a search for a nest was unsuccessful. Four spring and early summer reports (Crins 2003, 2005) during the second atlas period were presumed to be non-breeding vagrants. – *Donald A. Sutherland*

Purple Gallinule

Gallinule violacée

Talève violacée

Distributed throughout much of South America, north to the southern US, the Purple Gallinule is highly prone to vagrancy. The northern limit of its breeding range is obscured by the presence of overshoots, some of which occasionally breed (West and Hess 2002). Instances of extralimital breeding have been documented in the US north to Delaware, Illinois, and Ohio (West and Hess 2002). There has been no confirmation of breeding in Ontario. Occurrences of Purple Gallinule in the province typically involve vagrant hatch-year birds in autumn, but adults occasionally occur in spring. During the first atlas, one adult was observed in Point Pelee Nat. Park on 8 July 1981, and one adult was present in the marsh near Stoney Point, Lake St. Clair, from 3 May to 27 June 1984. There were no reports of Purple Gallinule during the second atlas. – *Donald A. Sutherland*

American Avocet

Avocette d'Amérique

Recurvirostra americana

A photograph of an adult American Avocet and one of three flightless young taken 6 July 1980 at Sable Islands Provincial Nature Reserve, Rainy River Dist. (Lamey 1981), constitutes the only documented evidence of breeding for Ontario. An apparent pair observed during a survey for the species on Sable Islands on 19 May 1981 was the only record during the first atlas. No breeding evidence was obtained during the second atlas. The American Avocet remains a rare but regular non-breeding transient in Ontario, with only a single record of breeding (James 1991). It nests on sparsely vegetated shores and islands in shallow lakes, primarily from the southern Prairie Provinces south through the Great Plains to northern Texas, but locally and irregularly east to western Minnesota, 160 km southwest of Lake of the Woods (Robinson et al. 1997). – *Donald A. Sutherland*

Purple Sandpiper

Bécasseau violet

Calidris maritima

The Purple Sandpiper has a holarctic breeding distribution. In North America, it breeds primarily in the Canadian Arctic archipelago, south in Hudson Bay to the Belcher Islands, where it is common (Manning 1976), reaching the southern limit of its range in James Bay on North Twin Island (Manning 1981). Nesting habitats include mossy tundra, heath-lichen gravel beaches and ridges, and poorly vegetated rocky plateaus along rivers and coasts (Payne and Pierce 2002).

The only evidence of breeding by the Purple Sandpiper in Ontario involves the brief observation of a single bird in suitable habitat at Cape Henrietta Maria on 6 July 1985. The species was not observed during the second atlas, despite considerable coverage of coastal areas of Hudson and northern James Bays in the vicinity of Cape Henrietta Maria. In view of the limited availability of suitable nesting habitat in the province, the probability of the Purple Sandpiper breeding in Ontario is low. – *Mark K. Peck*

California Gull

Goéland de Californie

Larus californicus

The California Gull breeds in large colonies from the southern Northwest Territories south through the Great Plains to Colorado, and in the arid west to central California (Winkler 1996). In Canada, it breeds regularly as far east as south-central Manitoba (Godfrey 1986). It is a rare but increasingly regular winter vagrant to eastern Canada, particularly the lower Great Lakes. During the first atlas, an apparently unmated adult California Gull attended nests with eggs in both 1981 and 1982 in a large Ring-billed Gull colony on the Leslie Street Spit, Toronto. Weseloh and Blokpoel (1983) and Blokpoel (in Cadman et al. 1987) provide additional details of these nesting attempts, which are thought to have involved the same young adult female, and which were both unsuccessful. There were no breeding season reports either in the period between the atlases or during the second atlas. – *Donald A. Sutherland*

Glaucous Gull

Goéland bourgmestre

Larus hyperboreus

The Glaucous Gull is a large, circumpolar-breeding, pale-winged gull seen in Ontario primarily during migration and wintering around the Great Lakes. Within North America, it breeds from Alaska throughout the Canadian Arctic east to the coast of Labrador and south in Hudson Bay to the Belcher Islands, 175 km north of Cape Henrietta Maria (Gilchrist and Robertson 1999; Gilchrist 2001). In the breeding season, it is a rare visitor to the Ontario coast of Hudson and James Bays. During the first atlas, there was a lone case of probable breeding by a suspected territorial pair at the mouth of the Sutton River. No breeding evidence was reported during the second atlas. However, there were eight sightings of birds along the Hudson Bay and northern James Bay coasts. Currently, this species is probably a non-breeding visitor to the province, with the chance of very rare, occasional breeding attempts. – *Tyler Hoar*

Black Guillemot

Guillemot à miroir

Cepphus grylle

The Black Guillemot is a mid-sized seabird that remains close to breeding areas year round, even in the high Arctic. It is common and widespread from Ellesmere Island and Greenland south to the Gulf of St. Lawrence and Maine. Nesting has been documented as far south as North Twin Island in James Bay (Manning 1981), but suitable rocky shoreline nesting habitat occurs mostly on the Québec side of Hudson and James Bays. In Ontario, occasional sightings have been made since the mid-1800s (Manning 1952; Todd 1963), but only one nesting event has been documented. In July 1957, about 80 birds were discovered at Manchuinagush Island west of Cape Henrietta Maria on Hudson Bay, with eggshells found at the site (Lumsden 1959). This and other islands have been searched unsuccessfully on a number of subsequent occasions, but the 1957 record remains the only provincial breeding record. The Black Guillemot is capable of nesting in very small colonies or singly (Butler and Buckley 2002), and it is possible that it could nest again within the limited available habitat in Ontario. – *Ross James*

Passenger Pigeon

Tourte voyageuse

Ectopistes migratorius

Accounts of the super-abundance of the Passenger Pigeon, now extinct for almost a century, are legendary. Formerly widespread and abundant in North America east of the Rocky Mountains, its principal breeding range included the southern Great Lakes states and southern Ontario, east through northern New England (Blockstein 2002). Lesser numbers bred in Ontario west to northern Lake of the Woods and north to Moose Factory (Mitchell 1935). Factors responsible for the species' decline included the clearing of forests, disturbance at colonies, and unrestricted harvest. A detailed history of the Passenger Pigeon in Ontario is provided in Mitchell (1935). Catastrophic declines occurred in the 1870s and 1880s. The last instance of breeding in Ontario occurred in Frontenac Co. in 1898 and the last authentic report of its occurrence in Simcoe Co. in 1902 (Mitchell 1935). – *Donald A. Sutherland*

Snowy Owl

Harfang des neiges

Bubo scandiacus

The Snowy Owl has a circumpolar distribution, breeding on arctic tundra generally north of 60° N (Parmelee 1992). In Canada, it breeds south to the Belcher Islands (Godfrey 1986) and irregularly to Churchill, Manitoba (Jehl 2004). Breeding has never been confirmed in Ontario, and breeding season occurrences are sporadic and apparently uncommon or rare: one bird at Cape Henrietta Maria, 20-22 July 1947 (Manning 1952); one or possibly two birds near Hook Point, James Bay, 2-3 July 1948; near the Brant River, 13 July 1968; and north of Hook Point, 29 July 1971 (Peck 1972). During the first atlas, one individual was observed 15 km southeast of Fort Severn, 18-21 July 1983. The only report during the second atlas involved two individuals observed on sand dunes 8 km north of Hook Point, 4 July 2002; these birds were not considered to be in suitable breeding habitat. – *Donald A. Sutherland*

Bewick's Wren

Troglodyte de Bewick

Thryomanes bewickii

The Bewick's Wren now breeds primarily in the south and west of North America, but during the 19th century, following forest clearing for agriculture, its range expanded as far north as Ontario (Kennedy and White 1997). The first Ontario record was in 1898 (Godfrey 1966), but the only nests in the province were found at Point Pelee Nat. Park in 1950, 1956, and 1957 (Peck and James 1987). Declines in the eastern and central North American populations of the species, first noted in the 1920s, continued through the 1970s; by the 1980s, much of the eastern population was gone (Kennedy and White 1997). Reasons for the decline are unclear, but interspecific competition with the expanding House Wren population has been suggested (Kennedy and White 1997). There was no breeding evidence documented for the Bewick's Wren during either atlas, and there have been no occurrences in the province since 2002 (A. Wormington, pers. comm.). – *David Brewer*

Mountain Bluebird

Merlebleu azuré

Sialia currucoides

The Mountain Bluebird is primarily a rare, non-breeding vagrant in Ontario and has only been documented breeding in the province on three occasions – near Port Stanley, Elgin Co., in 1985 and 1986, and near Rainy River in 1999. Each mating involved a male Mountain Bluebird with a female Eastern Bluebird. The breeding range of this western species has been expanding eastward since about 1900, and its continuous range currently extends east to south-central Manitoba (Power and Lombardo 1996). This species has not successfully established a breeding range in Ontario, and there were no records of the species in the second atlas. – *Cindy E.J. Cartwright*

Kirtland's Warbler

Paruline de Kirtland

Dendroica kirtlandii

Listed as Endangered in Michigan, the US, Ontario, Canada, and globally, the Kirtland's Warbler is a rare visitor to Ontario. There are 76 sight records of single birds in the province between 1900 and 2006 (Environment Canada 2006c). Just three of the sight records were females, and only 10 males were found in the species' preferred Jack Pine habitat. During the first atlas, one singing male was reported in Jack Pine forest north of Orillia in 1985. No breeding evidence was recorded for the species in the second atlas.

Currently, Michigan is the warbler's only known regular breeding area. The 1986 census of the species estimated 210 singing males all located in central Michigan. The 2006 census reported 1,457 singing males in central Michigan, 21 in northern Michigan, four in Wisconsin, and three near Petawawa, Ontario. The large increase in the last 20 years is attributed to a doubling of suitable Jack Pine habitat in Michigan resulting from increased reforestation and natural regeneration following a 10,000 ha forest fire in 1980, and control of local Brown-headed Cowbird populations. – *Paul Aird*

[*Editors' note:* In 2007, the first nest of the Kirtland's Warbler in Canada was discovered at Canadian Forces Base Petawawa, just east of Algonquin Prov. Park in Renfrew Co. Though nesting by the species on the base had been suspected as early as 1916, the nest with two eggs and two young found by researchers in June was the first confirmation of this fact. Two young were successfully fledged and the nest and two infertile eggs were later collected and deposited with the Royal Ontario Museum.]

Lark Sparrow

Bruant à joues marron

Chondestes grammacus

Widespread in the western half of the continent, the Lark Sparrow is a rare and irregular breeder east of Illinois (Martin and Parrish 2000). In Ontario, it formerly nested near London between 1878 and 1891 (Saunders and Dale 1933); at High Park, Toronto, between 1892 and 1898 (Baillie and Harrington 1937); at Point Pelee in 1884, 1905, and 1913 (Wormington 2006); and in the Long Point-Turkey Point vicinity between at least 1930 and 1976, when the last nest was reported near St. Williams (Hussell in Cadman et al. 1987). In 1973, an anomalous nesting occurred near Sudbury (Peck and James 1987). During the first atlas, there was a single record of probable breeding at Elbow Lake, 48 km northeast of Thunder Bay, where a pair was found on 9 June 1982. There have been no subsequent reports of breeding. During the second atlas, documentation was received for seven records, all involving apparent vagrants. – *Donald A. Sutherland*

Snow Bunting

Bruant des neiges

Plectrophenax nivalis

Circumpolar in its distribution, the Snow Bunting breeds on rocky tundra in both the nearctic and palearctic regions. In North America, it is principally a high arctic breeder, occurring south to western and southern Hudson Bay, where breeding occurs only sporadically (Lyon and Montgomerie 1995; Jehl 2004). Individuals and small flocks are present annually during summer along the Hudson Bay and upper James Bay coasts of Ontario, particularly in the vicinity of Cape Henrietta Maria (Manning 1952; Peck 1972; Schueler et al. 1974; Wilson and McRae 1993). Observations of the Snow Bunting during both atlases evidently involved primarily non-breeding individuals. The only instance of breeding reported in the province occurred during the first atlas and involved the observation of two adults and two or three newly fledged young on West Pen Island in July 1985 (Hussell in Cadman et al. 1987). – *Donald A. Sutherland*

Appendix 1

Ontario Breeding Bird Atlas: Data Processing, Review, and Validation

Denis Lepage

Overview

The final atlas database used in the production of this book included approximately 570,000 individual breeding evidence records, 592,000 point count records, and 22,000 significant species records. As the project progressed, it soon became clear that we needed to prioritize our efforts to ensure that we would minimize the risks of errors to the best extent possible. Atlas data were received mainly through three different processes: scannable data forms that used optical character recognition (OCR) technology (34% of all records), Internet data entry tools specially designed for this project (49%), and other large data sources provided by various institutions through standard data templates (17%). All data were subject to various degrees of pre-validation and added to a central database server hosted by Bird Studies Canada. The subsequent review processes were greatly facilitated by the development of Internet review and communication tools that provided atlassers, Regional Coordinators, and members of the Significant Species Committee remote access to the data. This also allowed them to review decisions and provide comments that were saved in the database alongside the data itself and that were available to other reviewers.

Scannable data forms

Scannable data forms were visually checked by several people. The Regional Coordinators (RCs) were instrumental in catching many of the most obvious errors through a customary scan of all data forms they received from atlassers. RCs were asked to check all forms for key pieces of information, such as the square number, the atlasser number, and the year, as well as to identify any problems or unusual records and interact with the atlassers to request additional information when needed. The same process was repeated by the atlas staff to ensure that forms were complete and free of obvious errors. Atlassers were approached individually for any missing information.

Scannable data forms were then processed by an OCR software system (Cardiff Teleform) that was "trained" to work with the atlas data. A human operator interacted with the software at all times and provided input in cases where the computer was not able to recognize some entries on the form or when invalid entries were detected. After the forms were scanned, the entries were verified against the original forms in order to detect any scanning errors (e.g., missed breeding evidence code, incorrect species entries).

Data entry and import processes

The online data entry tools provided a proficient way to control the flow of information into the database in several respects. Many types of invalid data (e.g., breeding codes or square numbers) entered by the atlassers simply generated online error messages and gave instructions that helped the atlassers remediate the problem right away. Those types of errors were also caught during the transfer of data from the scannable forms and the institutional datasets into the central database, and dealt with in various ways. For example, during the uploading of institutional data, records found to be invalid were temporarily stored in a separate table in the database until correct information was obtained from the source.

Institutional data

Many large datasets were provided by institutions conducting bird monitoring programs in Ontario, including three of the atlas partners, Bird Studies Canada, Environment Canada, and the Ontario Ministry of Natural Resources, as well as researchers, private industries, and other government agencies. The institutions were provided with a data template which they were required to complete and return to the atlas office. The institutional datasets were screened to ensure that valid codes were used (square numbers, species codes, breeding codes, etc.), and then transferred to the atlas database.

Data validation processes

Once the data were included in the central database, we used various additional mechanisms to detect errors or inconsistencies. All scannable and institutional data, once they were added to the database, were available online to the atlasser who submitted them. One of the simplest and most efficient ways to verify data was therefore to ask atlassers to go online and confirm that the data they had submitted matched what was stored in the database. Volunteers also came into the atlas office and checked random samples in paper form against the online database to ensure that the forms were scanned properly.

We also regularly ran a number of data queries to highlight various inconsistencies or problems in the data, often through cross-validations. For example, we were able to detect several problems by looking for breeding evidence records that lay outside of acceptable breeding dates, point counts conducted outside the prescribed survey date or time, or UTM coordinates that fell outside the square. Finding those inconsistencies allowed us to correct data entry errors, flag records that needed further attention, and flag those that could not be used because they did not adhere to the atlas protocols. In many cases, we were able to fix those problems through various investigative methods (e.g., by looking at other data forms submitted by the same atlasser); in other cases we contacted the atlassers for clarifications.

Significant species review

We put a great deal of emphasis upon verifying records of significant species. For the purpose of the atlas, "significant species" referred to provincially or regionally rare species and colonial species for which we were interested in gathering additional information, such as the date, precise location, and a description of the bird and its habitat and behaviour. The additional information, submitted through a

Rare/Colonial Species Form (a paper version or online), served mainly two purposes: to help evaluate the validity of unusual records, and to build a database that could be used for conservation purposes.

At the provincial level, "rare species" included all species considered Endangered, Threatened or of Special Concern by the Committee on the Status of Endangered Wildlife in Canada (COSEWIC) or the OMNR, as well as several other species that were very rare breeders in Ontario or had not been previously confirmed as breeding in the province, or for which there were very few nest records in the province. Atlassers were asked to provide documentation for all provincially rare species records with a breeding evidence level greater than "observed." In each of the 47 atlas administrative regions, species could also be identified as "regionally rare." Regionally rare species also required documentation through the same process as provincially rare birds. The list of regionally rare species was initially created using a simple rule (i.e., any species not reported in at least two squares in an atlas administrative region during the first atlas). This list was subsequently reviewed and, in some cases, modified by the RC and the atlas office to reflect changes that had occurred over the last 15-20 years. Documentation was also requested for confirmed breeding records of colonial species such as arctic-nesting geese, herons, cormorants, gulls, terns, and Cliff and Bank Swallows. For colonial species, we were primarily interested in obtaining the coordinates and information on colony size.

Atlassers were contacted (in some cases on numerous occasions), most often by email, to provide information on significant species records that were submitted without documentation, or that were incompletely documented. This was done initially by the RCs, and again by the atlas office if needed. Customized automated email reminders were sent at least once a year, and other specific requests were sent as needed throughout the data review process. At the end of the project, 92% of the significant species records had at least some additional information provided, and 65% had complete information available (including exact coordinates and date).

RCs were asked to review all records that had been flagged during any aspect of the review process, and to ensure that as many flagged records as possible were documented by the atlassers. RCs were also asked to look for unusual records that had not been flagged and to ensure that breeding codes were being used properly. Based on the information available for each record, and including their own expertise, the RCs could assign one of several possible decisions: to accept the record as is, to accept the record without documentation (either because the same bird had already been documented by someone else or the RC had every reason to believe that the record was valid), to request more information from the atlasser, to accept the record with a new breeding code (including "X," indicating "observed" but no breeding evidence), to reject the record, or to flag the record as needing further review by the atlas project's Significant Species Committee.

The Significant Species Committee, composed of 12 members, was formed to evaluate all atlas records and ensure that the atlas database would maintain the highest data quality standard possible. One of the main tasks of the committee was to review all 22,000 flagged records through an online review process. This process was initiated shortly after the first field season and completed in fall 2006. Members of the committee had access to all details provided by the atlassers, as well as review comments from RCs and other committee members. RCs were given several months following each field season to provide decisions on records from their region. After that date, records could potentially be reviewed by the committee without the input of the RC, although the best attempts were made to obtain all relevant information from the RCs (or the atlassers) in order to make an informed decision. Every flagged record was reviewed by two to three people (including the RCs). If all initial reviewers agreed on the decision, the record could be finalized. If there was any disagreement among the initial reviewers, or if they felt that more review was needed, the record was brought to the attention of the entire committee, which then reached most of its decisions by consensus.

When data collection was complete and most significant records had been documented, Rare/Colonial Species Forms were created from the database for flagged but undocumented records. These forms incorporated basic information extracted from breeding evidence forms: square, date, breeding evidence, and observer. Committee members reviewed each of these records individually and either accepted, rejected, or occasionally modified the breeding code, based on the available information and the decision and review comments of the RC.

Once a final decision was taken on any record, the atlasser and the RC were informed via email and given the opportunity to appeal the decision or to provide additional relevant information supporting or refuting the record.

Outliers and other invalid codes

While the mechanism used for assessing provincial and regionally rare species was an efficient way of highlighting unusual records and focusing our attention, we also realized that some potential outliers were not being evaluated properly. This mostly happened when a species was locally common at one end of an atlas administrative region but would not be expected to occur in other parts, based on the known range of the species or the absence of suitable habitat. We mostly dealt with those issues by visually inspecting the species distribution maps and the regional data summaries, highlighting potential records that needed further attention, and seeking additional information from the atlassers whenever needed. This inspection was done by members of the committee, by RCs, and by authors of the atlas species accounts.

In many cases, in the absence of any confirmed evidence of breeding, it was difficult to differentiate between local breeding birds and potential migrants or lingering birds observed during the breeding season. This was particularly true of many waterfowl species observed in southern Ontario. Decisions about whether to consider those birds as possible breeders were made largely on the basis of the date(s) of the record, suitability of the habitat at the site, and other elements provided by the atlasser (number of birds, behaviour, etc.). We also felt it was important to achieve some consistency by using the same approach for all species throughout the province, while also maintaining consistency with the approach taken by reviewers during the first atlas.

Finally, the committee conducted a review of the improper use of breeding codes for all species (e.g., "CF," or "carrying food," for a dabbling duck) using the committee expertise and available literature (such as the Birds of North America accounts). Codes determined to be invalid were then converted to the most appropriate code, or investigated further as needed.

Point counts

Atlassers doing point counts were instructed to record every bird detected during the five-minute sampling periods, and to report breeding evidence separately for the square on breeding evidence forms. Despite those instructions, at the end of the project, the database contained point count records that did not always have a matching breeding evidence code in the same square. This was either caused by atlassers failing to report the breeding evidence or, more often, by institutional datasets that only included point count data. After filtering out potential migrants and colonial birds, we converted the orphan point count records into the lowest level of breeding evidence possible (H). To filter out migrants and non-breeding birds from the analyses involving point counts, we flagged any point count record that did not have at least one possible breeding record in the same square during the entire project, as well as any point counts done outside the prescribed date or time. Point count maps were also examined for potential outliers.

Effort data

Effort data (total number of hours of atlas effort per square) were reported on breeding evidence forms. Atlassers doing point counts were asked also to report the breeding evidence and effort data using the breeding evidence form, but this was not consistently done by all atlassers, the result being that effort was sometimes underestimated. To partly correct for this, we looked at all cases where point counts were done in a square but where no effort information was reported at the same time (whether by the same atlasser who did the point counts or someone else). We then added 10 minutes of effort for each of those points, assuming that atlassers also reported breeding evidence in between each point. In the case of point counts provided by institutional datasets, however, we only added five minutes per point, as additional breeding evidence data were not always submitted.

We also checked overall effort data for outliers relative to the number of species found in a square, although raw effort ranged very widely among squares and was not strongly correlated with the number of species found ($r = 0.58, n = 4989$). Despite that, looking for outliers proved valuable for entering missing information or correcting other data entry errors.

The atlas technology at a glance

Database server: Microsoft SQL Server 2000

Web application: built using Java and JSP

OCR software: Cardiff Teleform

Appendix 2

Summary of Breeding Evidence Reported during the First and Second Atlas Projects

Species	Atlas	No. squares with breeding evidence: Possible	Probable	Confirmed	No. squares with breeding evidence by region: Ontario	Hudson Bay Lowlands	Northern Shield	Southern Shield	Lake Simcoe-Rideau	Carolinian
Acadian Flycatcher	1st	16	5	8	29				3	26
	2nd	18	12	20	50			1	5	44
Alder Flycatcher	1st	883	568	110	1561	86	300	599	478	98
	2nd	1599	732	169	2500	123	884	754	633	106
American Avocet	1st		1		1		1			
	2nd									
American Bittern	1st	589	356	135	1080	27	108	484	403	58
	2nd	705	405	90	1200	38	173	523	427	39
American Black Duck	1st	552	390	493	1435	84	334	550	372	95
	2nd	402	370	383	1155	97	259	463	278	58
American Coot	1st	71	55	64	190		4	16	115	55
	2nd	85	43	50	178	1	18	16	104	39
American Crow	1st	571	550	1083	2204	54	382	751	745	272
	2nd	977	465	1327	2769	60	899	784	753	273
American Golden-Plover	1st	4	1	1	6	6				
	2nd	4	5	2	11	11				
American Goldfinch	1st	349	1011	523	1883		182	700	729	272
	2nd	510	879	702	2091	3	336	735	738	279
American Kestrel	1st	526	465	738	1729	29	291	463	691	255
	2nd	712	496	625	1833	19	534	373	662	245
American Pipit	1st	4	2	9	15	15				
	2nd	11	10	9	30	30				
American Redstart	1st	628	816	525	1969	40	326	772	643	188
	2nd	1203	809	586	2598	46	821	810	715	206
American Robin	1st	334	311	1787	2432	82	537	788	746	279
	2nd	953	375	1817	3145	186	1120	809	748	282
American Three-toed Woodpecker	1st	33	5	9	47	15	30	1	1	
	2nd	73	15	17	105	20	79	6		
American Tree Sparrow	1st	2	9	14	25	25				
	2nd	26	11	13	50	50				
American White Pelican †	1st	1		1	2		2(1)			
	2nd		1	4	5	1	4(4)			
American Wigeon	1st	61	91	67	219	58	42	24	77	18
	2nd	103	115	44	262	66	65	32	87	12
American Woodcock	1st	503	506	415	1424	1	89	496	606	232
	2nd	688	586	303	1577	1	235	513	592	236
Arctic Tern †	1st	12	13	12	37	37(12)				
	2nd	58	67	20	145	142(20)	3			
Bald Eagle	1st	65	22	132	219	12	175	17	5	10
	2nd	562	122	304	988	123	630	110	75	50
Baltimore Oriole	1st	226	309	1025	1560		36	541	707	276
	2nd	240	212	930	1382		37	354	709	282
Bank Swallow	1st	269	77	1051	1397	55	110	400	597	235
	2nd	279	44	665	988	59	53	157	519	200
Barn Owl	1st	2		4	6				1	5
	2nd	3	2	2	7				1	6
Barn Swallow	1st	194	209	1616	2019	24	283	706	728	278
	2nd	214	171	1379	1764	14	203	554	712	281
Barred Owl	1st	284	220	59	563		46	387	126	4
	2nd	405	402	79	886	1	149	488	242	6
Bay-breasted Warbler	1st	258	101	67	426	44	204	166	12	
	2nd	645	71	40	756	24	576	146	10	
Belted Kingfisher	1st	601	526	1000	2127	71	368	738	700	250
	2nd	958	521	877	2356	85	597	743	690	241
Black Scoter	1st									
	2nd	6	9		15	15				
Black Tern	1st	94	91	160	345	10	20	48	228	39
	2nd	58	65	125	248	1	41	22	163	21
Black-and-white Warbler	1st	779	599	382	1760	66	319	758	581	36
	2nd	1354	669	397	2420	73	836	803	653	55
Black-backed Woodpecker	1st	206	62	70	338	19	122	192	5	
	2nd	341	66	75	482	30	229	217	6	
Black-billed Cuckoo	1st	605	320	206	1131	1	61	339	537	193
	2nd	698	387	237	1322		66	459	576	221
Black-billed Magpie	1st	4	1	1	6		6			
	2nd	13	6	20	39		39			
Blackburnian Warbler	1st	656	336	201	1193	10	256	668	241	18
	2nd	1131	398	176	1705	5	629	744	299	28

Species	Atlas	No. squares with breeding evidence			No. squares with breeding evidence by region					
		Possible	Probable	Confirmed	Ontario	Hudson Bay Lowlands	Northern Shield	Southern Shield	Lake Simcoe-Rideau	Carolinian
Black-capped Chickadee	1st	477	511	1205	2193	27	421	777	737	231
	2nd	859	466	1487	2812	26	965	815	747	259
Black-crowned Night-Heron †	1st	75	2	29	106			5(1)	58(16)	43(12)
	2nd	24	2	34	60			9(6)	32(17)	20(11)
Black-necked Stilt	1st									
	2nd			1	1					1
Blackpoll Warbler	1st	37	16	9	62	45	17			
	2nd	106	12	24	142	120	22			
Black-throated Blue Warbler	1st	433	255	124	812		103	600	109	
	2nd	772	438	156	1366		306	746	291	23
Black-throated Green Warbler	1st	712	362	187	1261	22	256	663	300	20
	2nd	1021	627	307	1955	11	538	792	570	44
Blue Jay	1st	483	599	934	2016		252	765	727	272
	2nd	914	509	1120	2543	3	707	808	750	275
Blue-gray Gnatcatcher	1st	73	87	88	248			14	105	129
	2nd	116	114	136	366			9	161	196
Blue-headed Vireo	1st	479	165	57	701	31	228	376	57	9
	2nd	1249	396	105	1750	79	738	686	231	16
Blue-winged Teal	1st	246	432	458	1136	22	114	268	564	168
	2nd	199	317	247	763	9	110	142	410	92
Blue-winged Warbler	1st	64	48	27	139			3	48	88
	2nd	113	76	51	240			17	109	114
Bobolink	1st	208	522	780	1510	2	67	476	709	256
	2nd	213	556	600	1369		45	362	706	256
Bohemian Waxwing	1st	3	4	4	11	11				
	2nd	9	5	2	16	12	4			
Bonaparte's Gull	1st	99	42	3	144	65	79			
	2nd	266	168	41	475	274	201			
Boreal Chickadee	1st	208	88	42	338	68	202	68		
	2nd	448	88	68	604	81	447	75	1	
Boreal Owl	1st	15	4	2	21	4	15	2		
	2nd	177	7	4	188	3	179	6		
Brewer's Blackbird	1st	29	35	65	129		40	63	24	2
	2nd	34	27	46	107		43	34	30	
Brewster's Warbler	1st	14	8	2	24			3	7	14
	2nd	24	12	11	47			8	26	13
Broad-winged Hawk	1st	612	428	298	1338	10	289	708	291	40
	2nd	988	470	332	1790	5	625	748	367	45
Brown Creeper	1st	592	240	186	1018	17	118	438	373	72
	2nd	1132	336	216	1684	55	524	568	457	80
Brown Thrasher	1st	369	469	684	1522	1	41	510	704	266
	2nd	419	460	536	1415	5	28	429	695	258
Brown-headed Cowbird	1st	287	584	893	1764	3	145	618	725	273
	2nd	318	492	659	1469	1	66	407	720	275
Bufflehead	1st	22	7	1	30	9	19	2		
	2nd	59	37	24	120	29	83	8		
Cackling Goose	1st									
	2nd	4			4	4				
California Gull	1st			1	1					1
	2nd									
Canada Goose	1st	207	136	589	932	183	57	81	430	181
	2nd	334	297	1682	2313	439	281	594	730	269
Canada Warbler	1st	593	421	203	1217	21	230	645	277	44
	2nd	954	343	127	1424	11	447	645	288	33
Canvasback	1st		3	4	7		1		1	5
	2nd	1	2	3	6		1		1	4
Cape May Warbler	1st	299	119	63	481	27	161	272	21	
	2nd	458	41	19	518	20	278	199	21	
Carolina Wren	1st	14	13	12	39			1	7	31
	2nd	68	76	88	232			3	65	164
Caspian Tern †	1st	38	4	20	62	3	1	28(8)	25(11)	5(1)
	2nd	12	2	20	34	2	5(2)	8(5)	15(10)	4(3)
Cattle Egret	1st	1			1					1
	2nd									
Cedar Waxwing	1st	483	1058	861	2402	79	525	786	738	274
	2nd	1062	996	798	2856	77	948	806	751	274
Cerulean Warbler	1st	57	40	11	108			27	35	46
	2nd	54	23	9	86			19	39	28
Chestnut-sided Warbler	1st	700	629	527	1856	22	389	784	546	115
	2nd	1237	683	602	2522	27	892	816	663	124
Chimney Swift	1st	477	608	235	1320		38	536	512	234
	2nd	408	302	128	838		29	265	345	199
Chipping Sparrow	1st	412	466	1401	2279	41	456	772	736	274
	2nd	908	477	1489	2874	49	1030	780	741	274
Chuck-will's-widow	1st	2	4		6				1	5
	2nd	3	1		4					4

Species	Atlas	No. squares with breeding evidence: Possible	Probable	Confirmed	No. squares with breeding evidence by region: Ontario	Hudson Bay Lowlands	Northern Shield	Southern Shield	Lake Simcoe-Rideau	Carolinian
Cinnamon Teal	1st	2	1	1	4		1			3
	2nd									
Clay-colored Sparrow	1st	70	66	36	172	10	36	23	96	7
	2nd	205	169	78	452	14	93	72	246	27
Cliff Swallow	1st	219	145	943	1307	6	162	459	562	118
	2nd	162	69	807	1038	6	116	178	538	200
Common Eider	1st	2		6	8	8				
	2nd	2	5	2	9	9				
Common Goldeneye	1st	296	90	244	630	74	440	89	27	
	2nd	407	224	414	1045	99	733	161	52	
Common Grackle	1st	291	311	1566	2168	18	374	761	733	282
	2nd	454	257	1683	2394	19	591	765	737	282
Common Loon	1st	664	572	603	1839	111	698	740	290	
	2nd	878	833	731	2442	252	1087	771	332	
Common Merganser	1st	516	242	540	1298	85	457	551	199	6
	2nd	589	438	575	1602	101	648	600	250	3
Common Moorhen	1st	94	84	150	328			49	216	63
	2nd	67	74	102	243			15	187	41
Common Nighthawk	1st	634	514	147	1295	46	241	484	394	130
	2nd	557	238	55	850	45	269	221	229	86
Common Raven	1st	684	425	393	1502	107	586	701	108	
	2nd	1285	465	819	2569	206	1152	795	415	1
Common Redpoll	1st	38	23	10	71	65	6			
	2nd	58	31	14	103	103				
Common Tern †	1st	160	66	117	343	15(4)	67(15)	95(34)	137(52)	29(12)
	2nd	159	100	127	386	16(3)	132(36)	83(39)	136(42)	19(7)
Common Yellowthroat	1st	467	770	971	2208	54	376	778	732	268
	2nd	932	843	989	2764	76	865	812	741	270
Connecticut Warbler	1st	44	7	3	54	4	46	4		
	2nd	144	15	5	164	10	151	2	1	
Cooper's Hawk	1st	204	63	78	345		16	170	133	26
	2nd	330	136	259	725		12	128	386	199
Dark-eyed Junco	1st	485	227	225	937	82	299	485	67	4
	2nd	1036	238	184	1458	164	739	475	77	3
Dickcissel	1st	1	1		2				1	1
	2nd	2	4	5	11				2	9
Double-crested Cormorant †	1st	114		53	167		43(18)	45(17)	66(11)	14(7)
	2nd	228	5	181	414	1(1)	128(48)	142(60)	114(56)	28(16)
Downy Woodpecker	1st	614	503	765	1882	10	220	682	701	269
	2nd	886	473	867	2226	5	479	750	717	275
Dunlin	1st	2	6	13	21	21				
	2nd	16	6	8	30	30				
Eared Grebe	1st									
	2nd		1	1	2		2			
Eastern Bluebird	1st	166	148	419	733		31	256	359	87
	2nd	175	202	858	1235		86	327	616	206
Eastern Kingbird	1st	228	579	1227	2034	15	225	779	738	277
	2nd	301	478	1101	1880	7	213	656	728	276
Eastern Meadowlark	1st	252	384	654	1290		8	320	707	255
	2nd	254	408	550	1212		7	271	693	241
Eastern Phoebe	1st	358	251	936	1545	1	101	584	669	190
	2nd	336	227	1234	1797	1	142	683	725	246
Eastern Screech-Owl	1st	223	262	132	617			33	369	215
	2nd	301	330	149	780			25	491	264
Eastern Towhee	1st	340	326	173	839		2	194	420	223
	2nd	319	358	152	829		6	156	448	219
Eastern Wood-Pewee	1st	646	697	357	1700		85	629	717	269
	2nd	736	729	314	1779	2	180	609	718	270
Eurasian Collared-Dove	1st									
	2nd	1	1		2				1	1
European Starling	1st	167	111	1531	1809	14	196	588	733	278
	2nd	180	68	1544	1792	15	226	542	729	280
Evening Grosbeak	1st	469	456	160	1085	25	327	613	120	
	2nd	652	333	114	1099	4	405	588	102	
Field Sparrow	1st	280	365	417	1062			253	556	253
	2nd	253	358	370	981		2	171	563	245
Forster's Tern †	1st	12	5	12	29		4		1	24(12)
	2nd	5	3	9	17		1		1(1)	15(8)
Fox Sparrow	1st	69	19	4	92	76	16			
	2nd	203	31	11	245	176	69			
Gadwall	1st	39	53	78	170	4	8	11	109	38
	2nd	34	71	65	170	3	7	21	107	32
Glaucous Gull	1st		1		1	1				
	2nd									
Golden Eagle	1st	2	1	1	4	3	1			
	2nd	16	2	11	29	27	2			

Species	Atlas	No. squares with breeding evidence			No. squares with breeding evidence by region					
		Possible	Probable	Confirmed	Ontario	Hudson Bay Lowlands	Northern Shield	Southern Shield	Lake Simcoe-Rideau	Carolinian
Golden-crowned Kinglet	1st	511	200	201	912	58	245	465	131	13
	2nd	1246	320	240	1806	65	931	575	215	20
Golden-winged Warbler	1st	207	157	105	469		2	258	146	63
	2nd	175	121	52	348		5	172	147	24
Grasshopper Sparrow	1st	166	164	112	442		2	19	325	96
	2nd	157	170	115	442		2	20	355	65
Gray Catbird	1st	300	539	864	1703	1	76	634	720	272
	2nd	369	469	765	1603	1	68	535	723	276
Gray Jay	1st	248	115	382	745	99	342	290	14	
	2nd	669	195	464	1328	161	817	333	17	
Gray Partridge	1st	33	27	52	112			3	77	32
	2nd	14	32	22	68			2	57	9
Gray-cheeked Thrush	1st	7	1		8	8				
	2nd	7	1		8	8				
Great Black-backed Gull †	1st	7	1	7	15			1	11(6)	3(1)
	2nd	10	5	23	38	3	2	8(6)	23(15)	2(2)
Great Blue Heron †	1st	1469	34	519	2022	13	400(81)	758(241)	660(161)	204(36)
	2nd	1190	22	461	1673	10(2)	298(37)	643(203)	543(177)	179(42)
Great Crested Flycatcher	1st	443	674	649	1766		42	733	729	262
	2nd	476	687	590	1753		56	700	734	263
Great Egret †	1st	12	1	6	19				5(1)	15(5)
	2nd	7	2	12	21				8(5)	13(7)
Great Gray Owl	1st	34	5	4	43	9	33	1		
	2nd	129	14	11	154	15	125	10	4	
Great Horned Owl	1st	395	359	432	1186	9	51	270	603	253
	2nd	473	252	359	1084	5	131	193	526	229
Greater Scaup	1st	6	5	6	17	15	2			
	2nd	3	29	2	34	32	2			
Greater Yellowlegs	1st	42	64	3	109	88	21			
	2nd	186	174	15	375	224	151			
Green Heron	1st	638	76	254	968		1	139	593	235
	2nd	349	294	239	882			102	556	224
Green-winged Teal	1st	221	169	125	515	75	99	121	185	35
	2nd	178	274	92	544	94	126	109	190	25
Hairy Woodpecker	1st	686	559	661	1906	33	255	710	682	226
	2nd	966	524	944	2434	48	652	786	715	233
Harris's Sparrow	1st			1	1	1				
	2nd	4			4	4				
Henslow's Sparrow	1st	12	23	3	38				36	2
	2nd	6	3		9				5	4
Hermit Thrush	1st	757	412	143	1312	62	327	719	198	6
	2nd	1484	552	255	2291	148	987	787	356	13
Herring Gull	1st	689	212	452	1353	123	393	579	208	50
	2nd	792	145	640	1577	180	657	538	167	35
Hoary Redpoll	1st	1	2		3	3				
	2nd	1	2	3	6	6				
Hooded Merganser	1st	345	171	243	759	10	184	407	137	21
	2nd	397	391	478	1266	25	300	554	322	65
Hooded Warbler	1st	11	6	4	21					21
	2nd	27	21	33	81			1	18	62
Horned Grebe	1st	2		1	3	1				2
	2nd	2	1	1	4		4			
Horned Lark	1st	211	357	376	944	34	8	51	591	260
	2nd	248	333	297	878	69	9	19	523	258
House Finch	1st	27	52	108	187			1	73	113
	2nd	184	279	467	930		7	53	597	273
House Sparrow	1st	130	123	1060	1313	4	76	280	681	272
	2nd	108	150	909	1167	1	75	154	662	275
House Wren	1st	224	250	754	1228	1	45	244	667	271
	2nd	273	276	790	1339	1	56	299	705	278
Hudsonian Godwit	1st	9	11	1	21	21				
	2nd	19	24	3	46	46				
Indigo Bunting	1st	402	717	443	1562	1	31	562	696	272
	2nd	455	688	510	1653		67	612	704	270
Kentucky Warbler	1st	7	2		9				3	6
	2nd	2	1		3					3
Killdeer	1st	241	337	1352	1930	47	244	627	737	275
	2nd	346	308	1133	1787	77	246	457	732	275
King Eider	1st			1	1	1				
	2nd									
King Rail	1st	9	7		16				5	11
	2nd	11	8		19				10	9
Kirtland's Warbler	1st		1		1				1	
	2nd									
Lapland Longspur	1st	3	6	9	18	18				
	2nd	7	13	3	23	23				

Species	Atlas	No. squares with breeding evidence			No. squares with breeding evidence by region					
		Possible	Probable	Confirmed	Ontario	Hudson Bay Lowlands	Northern Shield	Southern Shield	Lake Simcoe-Rideau	Carolinian
Lark Sparrow	1st		1		1		1			
	2nd									
Lawrence's Warbler	1st	3	1		4			2	1	1
	2nd	3	1	1	5				2	3
Le Conte's Sparrow	1st	17	17	4	38	11	25	1	1	
	2nd	82	29	11	122	25	70	23	4	
Least Bittern	1st	117	63	46	226		3	32	137	54
	2nd	110	69	31	210		3	29	147	31
Least Flycatcher	1st	973	846	303	2122	74	424	749	681	194
	2nd	1507	819	281	2607	77	887	763	690	190
Least Sandpiper	1st	8	17	17	42	41	1			
	2nd	24	21	24	69	69				
Lesser Scaup	1st	35	36	15	86	21	33	10	19	3
	2nd	43	92	10	145	66	38	20	19	2
Lesser Yellowlegs	1st	32	53	2	87	78	9			
	2nd	64	78	3	145	129	16			
Lincoln's Sparrow	1st	188	120	80	388	64	195	110	18	1
	2nd	648	171	126	945	155	566	187	36	1
Little Gull	1st	6	4	3	13	7		1	2	3
	2nd	1	1		2					2
Loggerhead Shrike	1st	60	28	57	145			23	120	2
	2nd	12	3	23	38		1	2	35	
Long-eared Owl	1st	92	57	27	176	2	5	25	112	32
	2nd	138	35	18	191	1	28	61	79	22
Long-tailed Duck	1st	4	4	4	12	12				
	2nd	7	14	4	25	25				
Louisiana Waterthrush	1st	17	11	12	40			4	10	26
	2nd	13	11	15	39			3	14	22
Magnolia Warbler	1st	725	379	284	1388	84	441	665	191	7
	2nd	1563	604	315	2482	143	1114	787	411	27
Mallard	1st	480	504	1132	2116	115	388	619	721	273
	2nd	401	651	1354	2406	156	577	662	743	268
Marbled Godwit	1st	5	10		15	14	1			
	2nd	14	8	4	26	22	4			
Marsh Wren	1st	142	167	118	427	2	9	61	279	76
	2nd	173	199	145	517		20	99	317	81
Merlin	1st	120	58	66	244	32	93	81	38	
	2nd	531	278	301	1110	75	361	459	210	5
Mountain Bluebird	1st			1	1					1
	2nd									
Mourning Dove	1st	288	439	687	1414	1	63	365	708	277
	2nd	242	500	823	1645	4	101	533	729	278
Mourning Warbler	1st	714	527	309	1550	30	286	634	500	100
	2nd	1199	564	270	2033	22	713	649	534	115
Mute Swan	1st	3	2	12	17				6	11
	2nd	25	29	81	135				71	64
Nashville Warbler	1st	708	514	462	1684	21	360	755	513	35
	2nd	1544	660	420	2624	48	1172	800	579	25
Nelson's Sharp-tailed Sparrow	1st	9	8	3	20	19	1			
	2nd	22	2	4	28	26	2			
Northern Bobwhite	1st	43	17	19	79				15	64
	2nd	23	7	4	34				10	24
Northern Cardinal	1st	144	269	358	771		2	29	465	275
	2nd	155	335	551	1041		6	95	660	280
Northern Flicker	1st	656	524	1245	2425	84	539	789	739	274
	2nd	1226	651	1156	3033	127	1086	804	740	276
Northern Goshawk	1st	213	45	100	358	7	52	179	118	2
	2nd	232	50	132	414	12	64	164	163	11
Northern Harrier	1st	574	463	296	1333	63	104	406	619	141
	2nd	845	437	250	1532	204	228	305	614	181
Northern Hawk Owl	1st	2	3	4	9	5	4			
	2nd	40	10	42	92	19	69	3	1	
Northern Mockingbird	1st	62	52	33	147		6	17	77	47
	2nd	138	82	109	329	3	3	37	153	133
Northern Parula	1st	165	69	11	245	1	93	105	42	4
	2nd	619	124	23	766	4	400	294	67	1
Northern Pintail	1st	54	78	84	216	50	14	19	118	15
	2nd	52	77	45	174	92	4	9	60	9
Northern Rough-winged Swallow	1st	224	266	644	1134		11	294	578	251
	2nd	232	217	505	954		12	150	537	255
Northern Saw-whet Owl	1st	266	179	25	470		8	261	192	9
	2nd	449	100	14	563		215	225	118	5
Northern Shoveler	1st	37	47	41	125	19	8	12	66	20
	2nd	61	82	49	192	42	23	19	88	20

Species	Atlas	No. squares with breeding evidence			No. squares with breeding evidence by region					
		Possible	Probable	Confirmed	Ontario	Hudson Bay Lowlands	Northern Shield	Southern Shield	Lake Simcoe-Rideau	Carolinian
Northern Shrike	1st	4		3	7	7				
	2nd	11	1	2	14	13	1			
Northern Waterthrush	1st	773	505	269	1547	103	298	583	496	67
	2nd	1244	599	216	2059	172	629	619	566	73
Northern Wheatear	1st	1			1	1				
	2nd		1		1	1				
Olive-sided Flycatcher	1st	563	232	68	863	32	199	546	86	
	2nd	706	136	32	874	60	345	419	50	
Orange-crowned Warbler	1st	55	11	8	74	38	36			
	2nd	149	14	12	175	117	58			
Orchard Oriole	1st	31	34	48	113			1	27	85
	2nd	94	74	121	289		2	1	93	193
Osprey	1st	436	137	364	937	90	237	409	199	2
	2nd	575	108	519	1202	108	309	418	353	14
Ovenbird	1st	788	949	477	2214	37	501	784	712	180
	2nd	1304	1012	488	2804	45	1054	812	722	171
Pacific Loon	1st	3	7	18	28	28				
	2nd	9	18	10	37	37				
Palm Warbler	1st	61	23	25	109	40	65	2	2	
	2nd	350	49	61	460	120	334	1	5	
Parasitic Jaeger	1st	5	10	2	17	17				
	2nd	14	3	2	19	19				
Pectoral Sandpiper	1st	1			1	1				
	2nd	2	1		3	3				
Peregrine Falcon	1st	2		1	3				3	
	2nd	12	16	68	96		49	19	8	20
Philadelphia Vireo	1st	239	106	47	392	30	181	161	20	
	2nd	553	97	23	673	58	375	209	31	
Pied-billed Grebe	1st	183	123	155	461	1	28	170	207	55
	2nd	319	157	255	731	2	60	258	342	69
Pileated Woodpecker	1st	768	430	236	1434	8	195	626	514	91
	2nd	1166	629	352	2147	15	585	762	655	130
Pine Grosbeak	1st	58	17	1	76	17	41	18		
	2nd	66	10	4	80	43	33	3	1	
Pine Siskin	1st	566	355	63	984	41	317	462	153	11
	2nd	754	209	55	1018	12	537	344	114	11
Pine Warbler	1st	324	184	112	620		12	388	178	42
	2nd	638	421	248	1307		102	643	459	103
Piping Plover	1st		2	1	3		2		1	
	2nd	1	2	2	5		2		2	1
Prairie Warbler	1st	16	16	14	46			30	10	6
	2nd	21	13	11	45			32	10	3
Prothonotary Warbler	1st	3	1	11	15				2	13
	2nd	4	3	10	17				2	15
Purple Finch	1st	667	642	254	1563	41	342	737	410	33
	2nd	948	555	340	1843	23	516	746	530	28
Purple Gallinule	1st	1	1		2					2
	2nd									
Purple Martin	1st	152	119	678	949		12	236	458	243
	2nd	128	57	417	602		7	52	330	213
Purple Sandpiper	1st	1			1	1				
	2nd									
Red Crossbill	1st	135	66	19	220	1	21	145	45	8
	2nd	108	22	10	140		50	75	15	
Red-bellied Woodpecker	1st	53	25	37	115				27	88
	2nd	135	143	163	441		1	3	194	243
Red-breasted Merganser	1st	105	107	111	323	60	106	66	88	3
	2nd	155	143	80	378	80	126	62	107	3
Red-breasted Nuthatch	1st	751	440	326	1517	15	352	710	383	57
	2nd	1320	581	546	2447	32	949	793	572	101
Red-eyed Virco	1st	835	954	636	2425	66	571	795	728	265
	2nd	1442	992	831	3265	76	1341	822	751	275
Redhead	1st	5	12	16	33		1	2	14	16
	2nd	6	24	7	37	2	4	3	14	14
Red-headed Woodpecker	1st	249	167	313	729		8	44	441	236
	2nd	131	66	133	330		10	21	164	135
Red-necked Grebe	1st		5	6	11	1	7	1	2	
	2nd	17	19	25	61		51	1	3	6
Red-necked Phalarope	1st	4	12	2	18	18				
	2nd	8	8	5	21	21				
Red-shouldered Hawk	1st	209	109	66	384		1	179	184	20
	2nd	248	159	111	518		3	269	227	19
Red-tailed Hawk	1st	497	423	618	1538	27	147	444	662	258
	2nd	793	418	633	1844	75	385	464	658	262

Species	Atlas	No. squares with breeding evidence: Possible	Probable	Confirmed	No. squares with breeding evidence by region: Ontario	Hudson Bay Lowlands	Northern Shield	Southern Shield	Lake Simcoe-Rideau	Carolinian
Red-throated Loon	1st	3	6	3	12	12				
	2nd	8	6	8	22	22				
Red-winged Blackbird	1st	223	416	1539	2178	17	362	775	741	283
	2nd	367	440	1432	2239	19	472	731	735	282
Ring-billed Gull †	1st	70	5	86	161	4(1)	23(11)	55(20)	63(39)	16(15)
	2nd	214	25	160	399	8	117(40)	118(49)	123(52)	31(19)
Ring-necked Duck	1st	314	174	108	596	28	290	221	57	
	2nd	199	507	173	879	32	410	342	95	
Ring-necked Pheasant	1st	135	104	92	331			3	165	163
	2nd	139	86	61	286			13	139	134
Rock Dove	1st	214	276	721	1211		49	256	646	260
	2nd	212	400	723	1335	1	68	327	676	263
Rose-breasted Grosbeak	1st	383	652	838	1873	2	171	745	717	238
	2nd	653	574	755	1982		281	728	714	259
Ross's Goose	1st			1	1	1				
	2nd			6	6	6				
Rough-legged Hawk	1st	2		1	3	3				
	2nd			2	2	2				
Ruby-crowned Kinglet	1st	641	281	136	1058	94	378	509	76	1
	2nd	1317	233	87	1637	177	996	428	36	
Ruby-throated Hummingbird	1st	770	648	304	1722		150	704	642	226
	2nd	775	751	477	2003		285	752	713	253
Ruddy Duck	1st	20	12	13	45		2	3	14	26
	2nd	26	51	18	95	4	13	1	47	30
Ruffed Grouse	1st	434	294	1086	1814	18	281	709	650	156
	2nd	873	370	1025	2268	20	718	758	672	100
Rusty Blackbird	1st	139	57	87	283	52	115	106	10	
	2nd	211	64	85	360	140	134	80	6	
Sandhill Crane	1st	93	71	32	196	81	42	49	22	2
	2nd	369	413	200	982	322	182	284	173	21
Savannah Sparrow	1st	338	491	832	1661	87	157	450	704	263
	2nd	480	472	885	1837	177	250	434	711	265
Scarlet Tanager	1st	677	548	178	1403	2	64	595	555	187
	2nd	813	559	172	1544		111	649	584	200
Sedge Wren	1st	138	99	28	265	1	22	86	130	26
	2nd	202	146	28	376	2	54	112	170	38
Semipalmated Plover	1st	4	7	23	34	34				
	2nd	22	10	21	53	53				
Semipalmated Sandpiper	1st	5	4	5	14	14				
	2nd	18	9	6	33	33				
Sharp-shinned Hawk	1st	537	114	127	778	20	89	329	302	38
	2nd	713	186	242	1141	24	171	339	462	145
Sharp-tailed Grouse	1st	18	11	26	55	6	32	10	7	
	2nd	85	27	32	144	55	57	17	15	
Short-billed Dowitcher	1st	4	3	1	8	8				
	2nd	15	13	3	31	31				
Short-eared Owl	1st	43	23	18	84	15	6	13	44	6
	2nd	106	31	21	158	66	21	17	46	8
Smith's Longspur	1st	2	5	12	19	19				
	2nd	8	20	9	37	37				
Snow Bunting	1st	2		1	3	3				
	2nd									
Snow Goose †	1st	2	2	39	43	43(39)				
	2nd	22	8	49	79	79(49)				
Snowy Owl	1st	1			1	1				
	2nd									
Solitary Sandpiper	1st	103	94	11	208	54	123	28	3	
	2nd	171	83	15	269	87	142	37	3	
Song Sparrow	1st	392	495	1454	2341	72	445	796	750	278
	2nd	865	459	1555	2879	112	924	810	754	279
Sora	1st	244	252	98	594	11	37	117	335	94
	2nd	350	291	100	741	17	87	145	384	108
Spotted Sandpiper	1st	583	813	803	2199	148	407	672	703	269
	2nd	863	822	605	2290	238	555	557	677	263
Sprague's Pipit	1st									
	2nd	1			1	1				
Spruce Grouse	1st	77	20	66	163	20	92	51		
	2nd	188	21	101	310	26	220	64		
Stilt Sandpiper	1st	3	5		8	8				
	2nd	2	8	3	13	13				
Summer Tanager	1st	1	1		2					2
	2nd	2	1		3					3
Surf Scoter	1st	1	1	1	3	3				
	2nd	6	13		19	19				

Species	Atlas	No. squares with breeding evidence			No. squares with breeding evidence by region					
		Possible	Probable	Confirmed	Ontario	Hudson Bay Lowlands	Northern Shield	Southern Shield	Lake Simcoe-Rideau	Carolinian
Swainson's Thrush	1st	751	308	136	1195	91	506	516	82	
	2nd	1502	333	92	1927	133	1134	567	93	
Swamp Sparrow	1st	673	676	616	1965	82	349	731	629	174
	2nd	1096	771	739	2606	113	851	781	672	189
Tennessee Warbler	1st	489	157	105	751	124	381	226	20	
	2nd	879	97	39	1015	149	682	172	12	
Tree Swallow	1st	401	381	1547	2329	92	436	785	742	274
	2nd	604	319	1424	2347	104	527	701	734	281
Trumpeter Swan	1st									
	2nd	21	30	58	109		13	21	66	9
Tufted Titmouse	1st	9	5	7	21				4	17
	2nd	37	26	36	99			1	7	91
Tundra Swan	1st	2	4	26	32	32				
	2nd	13	24	41	78	78				
Turkey Vulture	1st	599	491	109	1199		45	458	497	199
	2nd	1111	537	196	1844		314	635	650	245
Upland Sandpiper	1st	156	256	297	709		6	65	510	128
	2nd	157	177	151	485	2	6	48	361	68
Veery	1st	614	849	443	1906		230	785	708	183
	2nd	1052	900	349	2301	1	631	807	697	165
Vesper Sparrow	1st	441	418	408	1267		36	333	653	245
	2nd	455	394	210	1059		55	200	570	234
Virginia Rail	1st	225	253	158	636		12	180	355	89
	2nd	289	348	172	809		21	258	441	89
Warbling Vireo	1st	431	555	402	1388		28	427	668	265
	2nd	435	578	376	1389	4	34	394	683	274
Western Kingbird	1st	1			1		1			
	2nd			1	1		1			
Western Meadowlark	1st	39	33	8	80		11	2	48	19
	2nd	23	7	4	34		18	3	10	3
Whimbrel	1st	8	6	4	18	18				
	2nd	34	12	6	52	52				
Whip-poor-will	1st	409	431	44	884		30	455	341	58
	2nd	302	239	18	559		49	274	208	28
White-breasted Nuthatch	1st	490	404	473	1367		36	472	626	233
	2nd	538	444	598	1580		67	584	691	238
White-crowned Sparrow	1st	25	12	26	63	61	2			
	2nd	77	15	35	127	123	4			
White-eyed Vireo	1st	9	8	2	19				2	17
	2nd	7	4	4	15					15
White-throated Sparrow	1st	677	864	789	2330	158	694	790	660	28
	2nd	1345	1005	856	3206	250	1450	815	658	33
White-winged Crossbill	1st	200	77	17	294	42	103	133	14	2
	2nd	594	181	29	804	98	431	236	38	1
White-winged Scoter	1st	3	3		6	5	1			
	2nd	6	8		14	13	1			
Wild Turkey	1st	9		10	19				12	7
	2nd	254	163	494	911		3	162	542	204
Willow Flycatcher	1st	308	282	130	720		1	51	423	245
	2nd	362	350	147	859			93	508	258
Willow Ptarmigan	1st	10	7	5	22	22				
	2nd	77	36	14	127	127				
Wilson's Phalarope	1st	13	16	18	47	3	5	4	28	7
	2nd	5	15	10	30	2	4		17	7
Wilson's Snipe	1st	518	731	219	1468	72	176	508	604	108
	2nd	908	658	124	1690	152	435	455	571	77
Wilson's Warbler	1st	126	54	34	214	66	101	45	2	
	2nd	395	62	36	493	118	311	63	1	
Winter Wren	1st	996	435	123	1554	62	403	642	405	42
	2nd	1820	694	171	2685	132	1186	781	530	56
Wood Duck	1st	356	381	589	1326	1	76	518	530	201
	2nd	293	440	920	1653		147	623	639	244
Wood Thrush	1st	581	596	285	1462		19	548	643	252
	2nd	520	648	306	1474		24	514	676	260
Worm-eating Warbler	1st									
	2nd	2	1		3				1	2
Yellow Rail	1st	20	7	1	28	20	2		6	
	2nd	35	9	3	47	19	15	6	7	
Yellow Warbler	1st	452	592	1059	2103	126	268	699	739	271
	2nd	908	532	1001	2441	212	491	708	750	280
Yellow-bellied Flycatcher	1st	265	78	16	359	25	123	188	23	
	2nd	1046	122	27	1195	84	761	325	25	
Yellow-bellied Sapsucker	1st	528	344	681	1553	21	256	734	506	36
	2nd	968	378	828	2174	17	707	791	590	69

Species	Atlas	No. squares with breeding evidence			No. squares with breeding evidence by region					
		Possible	Probable	Confirmed	Ontario	Hudson Bay Lowlands	Northern Shield	Southern Shield	Lake Simcoe-Rideau	Carolinian
Yellow-billed Cuckoo	1st	197	115	40	352			33	166	153
	2nd	202	127	60	389		1	44	154	190
Yellow-breasted Chat	1st	19	22	4	45			1	8	36
	2nd	11	12	4	27				2	25
Yellow-crowned Night-Heron	1st	2			2				1	1
	2nd									
Yellow-headed Blackbird	1st	7	3	4	14		7		1	6
	2nd	9	4	6	19		13		1	5
Yellow-rumped Warbler	1st	673	521	542	1736	108	537	751	335	5
	2nd	1419	698	635	2752	194	1197	813	536	12
Yellow-throated Vireo	1st	218	155	79	452		1	138	175	138
	2nd	258	160	27	445		2	126	187	130

† indicates colonial species for which confirmed records alone were used to calculate change between atlases.
Results in parentheses show the number of squares with confirmed breeding evidence.

Appendix 3

Proportional Change between Atlases for Each Species by Region and Habitat Classification

The following table summarizes proportional change between atlases for each species by habitat classification for the province as a whole and each region. Results are ranked within each habitat grouping from the largest proportional increase to the largest proportional decrease between atlases in the province as a whole. Increases are shown in blue and decreases are shown in red. Unbolded values are based on relatively few squares where the species was present and are less reliable than bolded results. An asterisk (*) indicates statistical significance at p<0.1, and † indicates results are based on confirmed breeding records only. Proportional changes of over 200% are shown as >200%.

Habitat Association	Species	Ontario	Atlas Regions: Carolinian	Lake Simcoe-Rideau	Southern Shield	Northern Shield	Hudson Bay Lowlands
Woods and Forests	Wild Turkey	* >200%	* >200%	* >200%	* >200%		
	Hooded Warbler	* >200%	* >200%	* >200%	>200%		
	Tufted Titmouse	* >200%	* >200%	-25%			
	Red-bellied Woodpecker	* >200%	* 197%	* >200%	>200%		
	Orchard Oriole	* >200%	* 186%	* >200%	>200%		
	Northern Hawk Owl	* >200%		>200%	>200%	* >200%	* >200%
	Northern Parula	* 186%	-100%	* 50%	* 153%	* 197%	>200%
	Northern Saw-whet Owl	* 156%	-58%	* -54%	-10%	* >200%	
	Pine Warbler	* 151%	* 123%	* 187%	* 76%	* >200%	
	Merlin	* 134%	>200%	* >200%	* >200%	* 129%	* 83%
	Boreal Owl	118%			49%	* 155%	3%
	Brown Creeper	* 98%	-3%	12%	* 28%	* 99%	* 197%
	Blue-headed Vireo	* 85%	17%	* >200%	* 94%	* 72%	* 110%
	Barred Owl	* 69%	159%	* 71%	* 28%	* 106%	
	Black-throated Blue Warbler	* 63%	* >200%	* 154%	* 19%	* 93%	
	White-winged Crossbill	* 61%	-100%	* 198%	* 91%	* 83%	28%
	Nashville Warbler	* 50%	* -50%	1%	2%	* 45%	* >200%
	Pileated Woodpecker	* 48%	* 34%	* 42%	* 27%	* 55%	60%
	Golden-crowned Kinglet	* 47%	-10%	* 40%	* 17%	* 68%	8%
	Red-shouldered Hawk	44%	-19%	7%	* 83%	62%	
	Cooper's Hawk	44%	* >200%	* >200%	* -35%	-38%	
	Blackpoll Warbler	* 44%				30%	* 51%
	Long-eared Owl	41%	* -39%	* -36%	* 134%	* >200%	-100%
	Blue-gray Gnatcatcher	* 40%	* 48%	* 40%	-41%		
	Hermit Thrush	* 40%	85%	* 70%	* 11%	* 36%	* 59%
	Red-breasted Nuthatch	* 38%	* 81%	* 60%	* 12%	* 31%	* 141%
	Great Gray Owl	29%		>200%	* >200%	34%	-9%
	Winter Wren	* 28%	23%	* 21%	* 21%	* 23%	* 54%
	Blackburnian Warbler	* 27%	67%	4%	* 6%	* 35%	28%
	Pine Grosbeak	24%		>200%	* -73%	* -51%	* 174%
	Philadelphia Vireo	23%		13%	* 29%	21%	29%
	Magnolia Warbler	* 23%	* >200%	* 98%	* 13%	* 28%	10%
	Eastern Screech-Owl	* 23%	* 35%	* 18%	6%		
	Ruby-throated Hummingbird	* 21%	* 19%	* 19%	1%	* 39%	
	Black-and-white Warbler	* 21%	* 57%	* 11%	2%	* 28%	19%
	White-breasted Nuthatch	* 19%	-1%	* 7%	* 28%	66%	
	American Redstart	18%	-9%	* 8%	-1%	* 24%	35%
	Sharp-shinned Hawk	18%	* >200%	* 68%	-4%	22%	-13%
	Black-throated Green Warbler	* 17%	* 121%	* 94%	* 18%	* 23%	-45%
	Ruffed Grouse	16%	* -53%	* -14%	4%	* 27%	27%
	Chipping Sparrow	16%	-2%	0%	* -6%	* 21%	36%
	Gray Jay	* 16%		24%	3%	* 18%	* 13%
	Hairy Woodpecker	16%	-6%	0%	* 9%	* 16%	47%
	Ruby-crowned Kinglet	* 16%	-100%	* -59%	* -22%	* 18%	* 21%
	Broad-winged Hawk	14%	9%	6%	2%	16%	47%
	Yellow-rumped Warbler	* 11%	* 160%	* 46%	* 4%	* 8%	* 17%
	Red-eyed Vireo	* 10%	-1%	1%	* 2%	* 15%	5%

Habitat Association	Species	Ontario	Atlas Regions: Carolinian	Lake Simcoe-Rideau	Southern Shield	Northern Shield	Hudson Bay Lowlands
Woods and Forests (continued)	Eastern Wood-Pewee	9%	-6%	* -6%	* -15%	* 75%	>200%
	Veery	9%	* -27%	* -12%	0%	* 22%	>200%
	Common Raven	9%		* 199%	* 9%	2%	* 18%
	Yellow-bellied Sapsucker	8%	* 96%	* 14%	* 4%	13%	-24%
	Least Flycatcher	8%	* -23%	* -6%	-3%	6%	* 32%
	Northern Flicker	7%	* -7%	-2%	-1%	5%	* 27%
	Downy Woodpecker	7%	2%	-2%	5%	* 24%	* -71%
	Mourning Warbler	7%	5%	-6%	* -6%	* 19%	-34%
	Spruce Grouse	7%			38%	9%	-1%
	Boreal Chickadee	6%			18%	6%	8%
	American Three-toed Woodpecker	6%		-7%	187%	10%	-7%
	Swainson's Thrush	5%		4%	0%	* 5%	6%
	Ovenbird	5%	* -22%	-4%	* 2%	* 7%	5%
	Bay-breasted Warbler	4%		-40%	* -17%	* 22%	* -42%
	American Woodcock	1%	* -29%	* -21%	-2%	27%	-8%
	Scarlet Tanager	0%	-2%	-5%	2%	3%	-100%
	Tennessee Warbler	-1%		* -52%	* -27%	3%	-6%
	Black-backed Woodpecker	-4%		-17%	6%	-9%	13%
	Cape May Warbler	-4%		-1%	* -35%	-1%	2%
	Wood Thrush	-7%	-3%	-1%	* -15%	-2%	
	Olive-sided Flycatcher	-7%		* -44%	* -35%	-11%	23%
	Warbling Vireo	-8%	-4%	0%	* -15%	-17%	
	Great Crested Flycatcher	* -8%	-1%	* -7%	* -11%	-12%	
	Rose-breasted Grosbeak	* -8%	* 8%	* -6%	* -12%	-10%	
	Red Crossbill	-10%	* -100%	* -63%	* -51%	56%	-100%
	Yellow-throated Vireo	-10%	* -20%	-11%	-7%	>200%	
	Canada Warbler	-15%	* -36%	-3%	* -10%	-17%	-23%
	Purple Finch	* -18%	-36%	* 26%	* -6%	* -19%	* -38%
	Great Horned Owl	-19%	* -40%	* -37%	* -41%	32%	-36%
	Pine Siskin	-20%	-27%	* -23%	* -31%	-8%	* -66%
	Baltimore Oriole	* -20%	0%	* -4%	* -46%	-38%	
	Cerulean Warbler	-30%	* -47%	-3%	-33%		
	Evening Grosbeak	* -30%		* -21%	* -10%	* -26%	* -82%
	Northern Goshawk	-40%	* >200%	* 26%	-6%	* -54%	-25%
	Whip-poor-will	* -51%	* -54%	* -57%	* -57%	-38%	
	Red-headed Woodpecker	* -64%	* -62%	* -77%	* -55%	* -42%	
	Worm-eating Warbler	>200%		>200%			
	Black-billed Magpie	* >200%				* >200%	
	Golden Eagle	127%				>200%	99%
	Acadian Flycatcher	* 86%	* 88%	52%			
	Summer Tanager	59%	59%				
	Northern Shrike	1%					1%
	Bohemian Waxwing	-1%				>200%	-11%
	Louisiana Waterthrush	-25%	-15%	-29%	-51%		
	Gray-cheeked Thrush	-51%					-51%
	Chuck-will's-widow	-69%	-33%	-100%			
	Kentucky Warbler	-99%	-84%	-100%			
Grassland, Agricultural, Open	Peregrine Falcon	* >200%	* >200%	74%	* >200%	* >200%	
	Eastern Bluebird	* 121%	* >200%	* 134%	* 28%	* 177%	
	Short-eared Owl	* 106%	-16%	-13%	0%	60%	* 148%
	Red-tailed Hawk	32%	-2%	-5%	-2%	* 45%	65%
	Savannah Sparrow	12%	-5%	0%	-5%	-1%	* 40%
	Eastern Phoebe	* 9%	* 44%	* 17%	* 17%	-12%	
	American Kestrel	-3%	* -21%	* -15%	* -27%	15%	-39%
	Common Grackle	-6%	-1%	-1%	* -3%	-12%	40%
	Horned Lark	* -11%	* -16%	* -24%	* -68%	48%	17%
	Eastern Meadowlark	* -13%	* -16%	* -9%	* -17%	-39%	
	Killdeer	* -17%	* -11%	* -5%	* -39%	* -36%	* 70%
	Grasshopper Sparrow	-17%	* -48%	-5%	-18%	-30%	
	Tree Swallow	* -17%	6%	-2%	* -18%	* -28%	2%
	Eastern Kingbird	* -25%	* -8%	* -6%	* -27%	* -34%	-53%
	Bobolink	* -28%	* -10%	* -5%	* -28%	* -68%	-100%
	Vesper Sparrow	* -29%	* -16%	* -27%	* -53%	-8%	
	Northern Rough-winged Swallow	* -29%	* -11%	* -21%	* -52%	-47%	
	Brewer's Blackbird	-30%	-100%	8%	* -59%	-21%	
	Barn Swallow	* -35%	-3%	* -7%	* -32%	* -51%	-22%
	Brown-headed Cowbird	* -35%	1%	* -7%	* -48%	* -69%	>200%
	Upland Sandpiper	* -37%	* -52%	* -40%	* -41%	-25%	>200%
	Ring-necked Pheasant	* -39%	* -43%	* -38%	193%		

Habitat Association	Species	Ontario	Atlas Regions: Carolinian	Lake Simcoe-Rideau	Southern Shield	Northern Shield	Hudson Bay Lowlands
Grassland, Agricultural, Open (continued)	Common Nighthawk	* **-39%**	* **-59%**	* **-60%**	* **-67%**	* **-43%**	**-2%**
	Gray Partridge	* **-44%**	* -77%	* **-33%**	-35%		
	Bank Swallow	* **-45%**	* **-29%**	* **-31%**	* **-69%**	* **-65%**	-21%
	Purple Martin	* **-46%**	* **-21%**	* **-42%**	* **-80%**	-57%	
	Cliff Swallow	* **-50%**	* **58%**	* **-13%**	* **-67%**	* **-66%**	-30%
	Northern Bobwhite	* **-65%**	* **-67%**	-51%			
	Western Meadowlark	* **-77%**	* -89%	* -80%	51%	* -80%	
	Dickcissel	151%	>200%	100%			
	Western Kingbird	-21%				-21%	
	Barn Owl	-39%	-31%	-100%			
	Henslow's Sparrow	* -80%	0%	* -86%			
	Cattle Egret	-100%	-100%				
	Mountain Bluebird	-100%	-100%				
Shrub and Early Succession	Carolina Wren	* **>200%**	* **>200%**	* >200%	0%		
	Northern Mockingbird	* **190%**	* **>200%**	* **109%**	* 127%	187%	>200%
	Fox Sparrow	* **98%**				* **>200%**	* **60%**
	Clay-colored Sparrow	**80%**	* 149%	* **144%**	* **158%**	* **99%**	13%
	Blue-winged Warbler	* **74%**	* **23%**	* **193%**	* >200%		
	Northern Cardinal	**54%**	-1%	* **80%**	* **>200%**	>200%	
	Orange-crowned Warbler	* **48%**				**0%**	* **109%**
	Lincoln's Sparrow	* **46%**	2%	* 60%	* **51%**	* **37%**	* **60%**
	American Goldfinch	**27%**	-2%	**2%**	**0%**	* **73%**	>200%
	Black-billed Cuckoo	* **24%**	-1%	**5%**	* **56%**	**38%**	-100%
	Dark-eyed Junco	* **20%**	53%	-1%	* -15%	* **24%**	* **20%**
	Song Sparrow	**12%**	**1%**	-1%	* -2%	**10%**	* **37%**
	Chestnut-sided Warbler	**10%**	**9%**	* **14%**	**1%**	**6%**	* 101%
	Yellow Warbler	**8%**	**2%**	0%	-4%	**9%**	* **14%**
	Willow Flycatcher	**5%**	-8%	**6%**	* **79%**		
	White-throated Sparrow	**1%**	-21%	* -9%	-1%	0%	**6%**
	House Wren	-3%	-1%	**2%**	* **18%**	-25%	-100%
	Cedar Waxwing	-3%	-9%	* -3%	* -5%	**0%**	-12%
	Indigo Bunting	-4%	* -14%	* -11%	**1%**	**9%**	-100%
	Rusty Blackbird	-5%		-49%	* -30%	* -32%	* **37%**
	Yellow-billed Cuckoo	-5%	-2%	* -28%	* 89%	>200%	
	Eastern Towhee	-13%	* -17%	-4%	* -19%	-63%	
	Field Sparrow	* -15%	* -17%	-4%	* -33%		
	Gray Catbird	-15%	-3%	* -4%	* -26%	-24%	-100%
	Golden-winged Warbler	-19%	* -65%	-7%	* -27%	189%	
	Brown Thrasher	* -24%	* -32%	* -14%	* -29%	* -55%	>200%
	Loggerhead Shrike	* -63%	-100%	* -76%	* -95%	>200%	
	Brewster's Warbler	75%	0%	* >200%	162%		
	Harris's Sparrow	51%					51%
	Prairie Warbler	-3%	-49%	0%	2%		
	White-eyed Vireo	-29%	-29%				
	Yellow-breasted Chat	-55%	* -45%	* -86%	-100%		
	Lawrence's Warbler	-61%	>200%	-100%	-100%		
	Kirtland's Warbler	-100%		-100%			
Wetlands	Bald Eagle	* **>200%**	* >200%	* **>200%**	* **>200%**	* **>200%**	* **>200%**
	Trumpeter Swan	**>200%**	* >200%	* >200%	* >200%	>200%	
	Mute Swan	* **>200%**	* **>200%**	* >200%			
	Red-necked Grebe	**>200%**	>200%	-34%		* **>200%**	-100%
	Bufflehead	* **>200%**			>200%	* **189%**	* >200%
	Sandhill Crane	* **186%**	* >200%	* **>200%**	* **>200%**	* **>200%**	* **138%**
	Ruddy Duck	**175%**	21%	* **144%**	-100%	175%	>200%
	Le Conte's Sparrow	* **130%**		4%	* >200%	* **98%**	* >200%
	Yellow-bellied Flycatcher	* **124%**		-11%	* **54%**	* **113%**	* **>200%**
	Sharp-tailed Grouse	**118%**		60%	42%	**99%**	156%
	Canada Goose	* **109%**	* **109%**	* **121%**	* **>200%**	* **>200%**	* **22%**
	Double-crested Cormorant †	* **107%**	190%	* **>200%**	* **140%**	74%	
	Connecticut Warbler	* **94%**			-1%	* **50%**	* >200%
	Northern Shoveler	**88%**	-44%	**23%**	53%	* >200%	71%
	Hooded Merganser	* **80%**	* 183%	* **103%**	* **50%**	* **81%**	117%
	Greater Yellowlegs	* **78%**				* **>200%**	* **22%**
	American Coot	**78%**	* -31%	* -32%	-15%	* >200%	>200%
	Palm Warbler	* **74%**		>200%		* **76%**	* **73%**
	Virginia Rail	* **72%**	-14%	* **24%**	* **58%**	* >200%	
	Sora	**62%**	-14%	-2%	* **33%**	* **149%**	58%
	Pied-billed Grebe	**58%**	**25%**	* **35%**	* **42%**	**61%**	>200%
	Ring-necked Duck	* **58%**		* **45%**	* **70%**	* **61%**	25%

Habitat Association	Species	Ontario	Atlas Regions: Carolinian	Lake Simcoe-Rideau	Southern Shield	Northern Shield	Hudson Bay Lowlands
Wetlands (continued)	Wood Duck	* 53%	* 30%	* 29%	* 26%	* 122%	
	Wilson's Warbler	* 41%		-100%	17%	* 52%	* 30%
	Bonaparte's Gull	* 40%				* 53%	24%
	Ring-billed Gull †	33%	46%	3%	* 100%	27%	
	Alder Flycatcher	* 26%	-11%	* 38%	* 26%	* 25%	* 26%
	Sedge Wren	26%	-19%	0%	11%	37%	78%
	Gadwall	20%	-14%	-11%	* 160%	132%	7%
	Lesser Scaup	18%	-66%	-18%	97%	-22%	* 87%
	Swamp Sparrow	* 17%	-6%	3%	* 6%	* 21%	* 21%
	Northern Harrier	17%	16%	* -7%	* -27%	26%	* 37%
	Common Tern †	16%	-37%	* -41%	3%	19%	73%
	Mallard	15%	* -20%	1%	* 12%	* 20%	20%
	Common Yellowthroat	15%	-4%	1%	0%	* 17%	* 33%
	Northern Waterthrush	* 12%	12%	7%	* 6%	* 10%	* 19%
	American Bittern	11%	* -37%	-3%	9%	14%	25%
	Wilson's Snipe	9%	* -44%	* -12%	* -12%	10%	* 26%
	Lesser Yellowlegs	8%				3%	8%
	Common Goldeneye	7%		* 101%	* 73%	10%	-6%
	Black Tern	5%	* -41%	* -34%	* -52%	54%	-38%
	Osprey	4%	* >200%	* 94%	0%	4%	-3%
	Common Loon	1%		* 12%	3%	0%	3%
	Common Merganser	1%	-52%	* 17%	1%	10%	-21%
	Marsh Wren	1%	-14%	5%	* 68%	29%	-100%
	Green-winged Teal	-2%	-36%	-16%	-13%	0%	0%
	Belted Kingfisher	-8%	* -32%	* -12%	* -10%	* -11%	7%
	Spotted Sandpiper	-9%	* -18%	* -17%	* -30%	-7%	-2%
	Herring Gull	-11%	* -34%	* -14%	* -7%	-4%	* -25%
	Red-breasted Merganser	-16%	45%	16%	-14%	-4%	-26%
	Wilson's Phalarope	-21%	0%	* -48%	-100%	-65%	126%
	Red-winged Blackbird	* -22%	-1%	* -3%	* -10%	* -33%	9%
	American Black Duck	* -22%	* -59%	* -45%	* -22%	* -25%	-9%
	Northern Pintail	-23%	-36%	* -61%	-46%	* -82%	7%
	Great Blue Heron †	-23%	4%	-2%	* -22%	-42%	>200%
	American Wigeon	-24%	-44%	-13%	58%	-17%	-32%
	Green Heron	* -29%	* -26%	* -26%	* -43%	-100%	
	Least Bittern	-32%	* -44%	-7%	-33%	-60%	
	Common Moorhen	* -35%	* -38%	* -27%	* -78%		
	Blue-winged Teal	* -36%	* -63%	* -50%	* -53%	-20%	-67%
	Solitary Sandpiper	* -38%		-52%	27%	* -58%	-2%
	Black-necked Stilt	>200%	>200%				
	Great Black-backed Gull †	>200%	165%	148%	>200%		
	Great Egret †	>200%	0%	>200%			
	Canvasback	>200%	-50%	83%		>200%	
	Eared Grebe	>200%				>200%	
	Cackling Goose	>200%					>200%
	Surf Scoter	>200%					>200%
	Black Scoter	>200%					>200%
	Redhead	176%	-9%	-7%	>200%	84%	>200%
	Short-billed Dowitcher	131%					131%
	Nelson's Sharp-tailed Sparrow	41%				-15%	49%
	Semipalmated Plover	37%					37%
	Caspian Tern †	34%	>200%	-46%	104%		
	Black-crowned Night-Heron †	13%	-19%	11%	100%		
	Yellow-headed Blackbird	11%	-20%	1%		13%	
	Arctic Tern †	9%					9%
	Prothonotary Warbler	4%	-1%	124%			
	Marbled Godwit	-2%				>200%	-10%
	Red-throated Loon	-2%					-2%
	Forster's Tern †	-15%	-18%	>200%			
	Pacific Loon	-21%					-21%
	King Rail	-27%	-43%	28%			
	White-winged Scoter	-31%				55%	-44%
	Common Eider	-33%					-33%
	Yellow Rail	-33%		-33%	>200%	83%	* -52%
	Piping Plover	-49%	>200%	104%		-54%	
	Little Gull	-100%	137%	-100%			-100%
	Horned Grebe	-100%	-100%				
	Yellow-crowned Night-Heron	-100%	-100%	-100%			

Habitat Association	Species	Ontario	Carolinian	Lake Simcoe-Rideau	Southern Shield	Northern Shield	Hudson Bay Lowlands
			Atlas Regions				
Wetlands (continued)	Glaucous Gull	-100%					-100%
	King Eider	-100%					-100%
	Cinnamon Teal	-100%	-100%				
	American Avocet	-100%				-100%	
	California Gull	-100%	-100%				
	Purple Gallinule	-100%	-100%				
Tundra	White-crowned Sparrow	* **50%**				-61%	* **56%**
	Least Sandpiper	**15%**				-100%	**18%**
	Common Redpoll	**-23%**				-100%	**-21%**
	Ross's Goose	>200%					>200%
	Pectoral Sandpiper	>200%					>200%
	Semipalmated Sandpiper	* 76%					* 76%
	Tundra Swan	* 67%					* 67%
	Smith's Longspur	42%					42%
	Willow Ptarmigan	38%					38%
	American Tree Sparrow	38%					38%
	Whimbrel	18%					18%
	Lapland Longspur	4%					4%
	American Golden-Plover	4%					4%
	Long-tailed Duck	-5%					-5%
	Dunlin	-10%					-10%
	Greater Scaup	-18%				-100%	-15%
	Hudsonian Godwit	-19%					-19%
	American Pipit	-21%					-21%
	Rough-legged Hawk	-25%					-25%
	Stilt Sandpiper	-27%					-27%
	Snow Goose †	-35%					-35%
	Hoary Redpoll	-49%					-49%
	Parasitic Jaeger	* -55%					* -55%
	Red-necked Phalarope	-56%					-56%
	Purple Sandpiper	-100%					-100%
	Snow Bunting	-100%					-100%
	Snowy Owl	-100%					-100%
Urban and Suburban	House Finch	* **>200%**	* **>200%**	* **>200%**	* **>200%**	>200%	
	American Crow	* **28%**	**5%**	0%	**0%**	* **46%**	30%
	American Robin	**27%**	**0%**	-1%	-1%	* **19%**	* **93%**
	Mourning Dove	**24%**	-2%	**2%**	* **71%**	**24%**	>200%
	Blue Jay	**20%**	**2%**	-1%	**2%**	* **38%**	
	Rock Pigeon	**19%**	* -6%	* **5%**	* **34%**	* 92%	>200%
	Black-capped Chickadee	**14%**	* **11%**	-1%	**1%**	* **15%**	54%
	European Starling	**-10%**	**-3%**	**-2%**	* **-13%**	**-24%**	55%
	House Sparrow	* **-20%**	**-1%**	* **-6%**	* **-49%**	**-33%**	-100%
	Chimney Swift	* **-46%**	* **-32%**	* **-48%**	* **-58%**	-26%	
	Eurasian Collared-Dove	>200%	>200%	>200%			
Unassigned	Turkey Vulture	* **125%**	* **31%**	* **47%**	* **51%**	* **>200%**	

Unbolded results are less reliable. They indicate the change was based on relatively few squares where the species was present.
* indicates statistical significant change at p<0.1.
† indicates results are based on confirmed breeding records only.

Appendix 4

Abundance Data Collection and Mapping

Various methods for estimating relative abundance were investigated during the run-up to the atlas, and mapping techniques were explored after a few years of data collection. Here we provide a brief summary of the background studies conducted and the reasons why final methods were selected, along with some technical details about the analysis and mapping of the point count data not described in the main text which may prove useful to future atlas organizers.

Design of count and sampling protocols

An early decision was to make actual counts, as opposed to collecting presence/absence data alone. The latter is easy for observers unskilled in taking counts, and can be used to calculate frequency of detection, an index of relative abundance. However, for common species that are detected nearly everywhere, regional differences in abundance cannot be detected. Count data can later be converted to presence/absence if desired, but not vice versa.

To investigate count methods, a pilot study was done in the year prior to the atlas. About 70 volunteers collected data in designated squares at point counts located randomly at roadside and off-road locations, and did two-hour or four-hour area searches throughout 1-km^2 cells. All methods produced data that documented relative abundance, but point counts were overwhelmingly preferred, mainly for the following reasons:

- Analyses indicated that point counts provided equal precision to that of cell counts, but with about half the time commitment.
- Point counts are more readily standardized (cells were often incompletely covered), and so should be less biased and more repeatable in future.
- Trespass and land access issues were high with area searches.
- Point count locations were easy to find, whereas cell boundaries were not.
- Point counts produce data that are compatible with results of many other programs investigating bird abundance.

Limitations to point counts include somewhat unrepresentative sampling of habitats, issues of traffic safety, and inadequate coverage of certain avian groups such as waterfowl. These issues were addressed to the degree possible in designing the allocation of points, as described in the main text.

Details of the point count protocol were selected primarily for practical reasons. Five-minute counts were chosen to allow detection of more species than three-minute counts (particularly important in remote areas where considerable time may be spent simply reaching count sites), while still allowing more counts to be done in a day than would 10-minute counts. (The latter would also have been boring in bird-poor areas). Date and time of day restrictions on point counts, and recommended weather conditions, were based on those for the Breeding Bird Survey in Ontario.

Counts were recorded separately for individual birds detected within and beyond 100 m. Numbers detected within 100 m should be less affected by observer skill and hearing than unlimited distance counts, while still allowing the use of unlimited distance counts in analyses if desired. We selected 100 m so that numbers detected within the limit would be reasonably high. Precision estimates from the pilot season were based on counts within 100 m, which affected the final design for number and layout of count locations; thus our failure to do pilot work on other designs limited the final decision. Abundance maps were similar for both limited and unlimited distance counts, but the higher numbers recorded by the latter allowed a higher proportion of species to be mapped. We therefore used unlimited distance counts for abundance mapping.

Because a high proportion of species are not regularly detected on point counts, and many atlas participants were unlikely to do point counts in any case, we considered asking atlassers also to estimate abundance of all species in a square using an exponential scale (1, 2-10, 11-100, 101-1000, etc.). This was done in the first Ontario atlas, and while estimates of population size based on these estimates were not considered reliable enough to publish, the method probably gives a reasonable indication of relative abundance for some species not covered well by point counts. While comparison between atlases could have been valuable, it was felt that abundance estimates might differ systematically between observers who were doing point counts and those who were not, and that participants might feel they had a choice of count types and therefore might be dissuaded from doing point counts. It was ultimately decided not to collect these data, although in retrospect we think the value of such estimates might have outweighed the potential problems.

Using data from point counts in the pilot year, precision of mean abundance in a square was examined with respect to sample size. The target for counts/square was set at 25, as this number produced repeatable results with a good level of precision. While precision continued to improve with additional counts, the gain was relatively small, and the time needed to complete counts could start to interfere with collection of breeding evidence and sampling of additional squares.

A goal was set of covering two squares in every 100-km block north of the road system and five squares in every 100-km block in road-accessible parts of the Northern Shield region. Although it was expected that many of the same squares near northern communities would be covered again during the second atlas, sampling the same squares visited in the first atlas was not considered a priority; instead, the aim was to improve the representativeness of squares selected within 100-km blocks. However, due to the costs and difficulty of access, much of the atlassing in the far north was opportunity based, but with some effort made to maximize representativeness of the squares selected within blocks.

North of the road system, squares were selected with a goal of sampling each habitat in proportion to its occurrence in the 100-km block. Using a 14-class habitat/land-use classification developed from the provincial land-cover classification derived from LANDSAT (Spectranalysis 2004) (joining sparse vegetation and clearcuts into one category), we determined the proportion of each habitat in each 100-km block and computed an index of similarity for each square within every block. Accessible squares along rivers and lakeshores were identified, and from these the two squares with the greatest similarity were chosen. Atlassers were then directed to attempt to cover the two squares selected, but were given alternative squares with relatively high similarity to the 100-km block, should the original target squares prove to be unworkable (e.g., if a suitable camping site could not be found nearby).

Atlassers were given satellite maps of habitat (Figure 1.2b) and asked to sample the habitats in each square proportional to their occurrence in that square. The numbers of points to be run in various habitats were listed on a Square Summary Sheet for each square. (These sheets also summarized breeding evidence records from the first atlas and to date from the second atlas in each square.) Because of the difficulties of travelling on foot, several points were frequently clustered.

The method for laying out locations for point counts in southern Ontario is described in the main text. That same approach was used by volunteer atlassers in road-accessible parts of the north. However, a different strategy was employed by the field crews collecting data for BSC's Boreal Forest Bird Project (BFBP), who worked primarily within the southern portion of the Northern Shield region and provided 50% of the point count data from that part of the province. The following strategy was used to select sampling locations for the BFBP project, whose goal was to assess differences between bird communities in logged and burned landscapes

Squares were identified that were accessible by primary or secondary roads and by canoe. Squares were defined as recently cut or recently burned if more than 20% of the square had been cut or burned, respectively, within the last 20 years. Squares were classified as "old cut" or "old burned" if more than 20% of the square had been cut or burned, respectively, between 20 and 80 years ago. Squares with less than 20% of their area cut or burned within the last 80 years were defined as "mature forest." From the pool of the accessible squares in these categories, five were randomly selected without regard to category. Within each of these squares, 24 point counts were clustered into four groups of six points for ease of access and to minimize travel in roadless areas, so that one expert birder could cover two clusters in a day. In each cluster, one point count station was randomly selected on a road or waterway (i.e., lakeshore or river), and five others were selected in a roughly inverted U-shaped pattern such that each point was more than 250 m from the nearest one, and following the line of points brought the observer back to the road or waterway at the end of the cluster. Each point had to have a 100 m radius predominantly (i.e., more than 70%) within one habitat type. Cluster starting locations were at least 1.5 km apart on roads or waterways.

Because of this selection procedure, habitat in the squares selected for the BFBP was not always representative of the entire ecoregion, even though more than 80% of the sampled region was forested. Moreover, because the focus of the BFBP was forest landbirds, wetlands and water bodies were not sampled. Hence, very few waterbird species were detected during point counts. In contrast to southern Ontario, the majority of BFBP point counts (67%) conducted in road-accessible areas of northern Ontario were more than 250 m from the nearest road. Bird communities often differ between roadsides and off-road habitat, so BFBP counts probably over-represent forest interior and area-sensitive species and may under-represent early successional species that are common along roadsides. Because of these differences, BFBP breeding evidence data were not included in analysis of change since the first atlas. The BFBP point count data are included in abundance maps, and some species in that area may, as a result, appear more common than if point counts had been conducted by regular atlassers.

Mapping abundance

Data were screened and prepared for abundance mapping as described in the main text and in Appendix 1. As described previously, a decision was made early on to base interpolation on the mean abundance (log transformed) at square centroids, as maps based on individual point data showed a lot of local detail that was probably not biologically real and might have encouraged over-interpretation of maps. The pre-smoothing of data that resulted from use of centroid means gave results that fit better with the scale and intended use of the maps in this book. Researchers wishing to build spatial models at finer scales can still do so from the raw data.

Forest habitat was generally under-sampled throughout the province (even including off-road counts), but few squares had forest under-sampled by more than 20%. Trials that corrected for under-sampling did not much affect mean abundance for a square, so no adjustment was made to the mean counts in the final analyses. We removed from analysis the relatively few counts made outside the required limits for time of day and date, and did not further correct for time/date covariables, as investigation suggested the effect would be relatively slight. Effects of roadside and off-road sample locations were analyzed, and these (although significant in certain species) also had relatively small influence on abundance. We decided to use unadjusted counts for mapping, as atlassers are most likely to be interested in what was actually observed. Known and probable biases would instead be discussed in the species accounts.

Several interpolation approaches were considered for mapping abundance: inverse distance weighting, basic splining, and kriging (including ordinary, universal, and stratified kriging and co-kriging). All methods were tested on a sample of common and uncommon, widely and narrowly distributed species, using both point data or the average abundance for a square. The methods were compared quantitatively by creating the interpolated relative abundance maps using 80% of the data, and then comparing the correlation of predictions and actual values for the remaining 20% of the data points. These validation statistics, a visual assessment, and a cost-benefit analysis for each approach were all considered in the final choice of method. However, the decision ultimately was made on the way the maps looked and whether they depicted variation that was felt to be realistic. The aim was to depict broad-scale patterns, not to predict abundance at fine scales (where it is very easy to be proven wrong).

Ordinary kriging met the needs for the book as outlined here and was chosen as the final method. Ordinary kriging does not incorporate any large-scale trends in the level of spatial autocorrelation, which are quite likely in an area as large as Ontario. However, analyses after four years of data collection indicated that addition of co-variables through other approaches to kriging (see below) had relatively little effect on maps. Other approaches that we investigated are briefly described below.

Inverse distance weighting is less time consuming (and therefore less costly) than other methods, and was a good method for making preliminary maps. These were not at all realistic for northern Ontario, where sparse coverage resulted in the map showing strange plumes and bull's-eye patterns. Thin-plate smoothing splines were used to fit interpolation surfaces to the point count data using software called ANUSPLIN (Hutchinson 1987).

Spline procedures have the advantage of not requiring a subjective estimate of the spatial autocovariance function as well as using an objective criterion for assessing fit. Although the procedure produced smooth surfaces with fairly good fit, it was computationally time consuming and therefore expensive.

Universal kriging interpolates the residuals of trend surface analyses (e.g., with latitude or longitude), removing any such trends. However, universal kriging is more time consuming, and the resultant maps were not significantly improved in terms of validation statistics. Stratified kriging interpolates the data within different homogeneous areas or habitats that are expected to have different mean bird abundances or spatial structure in abundance variability. This method therefore potentially captures the balance between regional trends and local habitat effects. However, kriging in multiple strata is, again, time consuming, and assigning species to habitat classes based on LANDSAT categories was troublesome, as relatively poor correlation results were found between bird abundance and LANDSAT categories. Examples of habitat-stratified kriging maps were thought to show too much detail, much of it unlikely to represent actual abundance on the ground at each point.

Finally, we examined co-kriging. With this method, co-variables (e.g., percentage of forest cover in a square) must be preselected, which involves subjective decisions on what might affect bird abundance. In addition, co-kriging bases interpolation on the co-variate and the relationship between the co-variate and bird abundance, and this relationship was generally weak or unknown.

Using ordinary kriging, we interpolated abundance from the 24 nearest neighbours to each target cell. We used an "unlimited distance" approach for the interpolations so as to create smoother maps. This was particularly important in the north, where a limited distance approach would have left large areas of no estimation because of gaps in data collection. Because square centroids were used and these were relatively evenly spaced, prediction accuracy should be relatively constant across the resultant maps, particularly in the south. Partial squares were included (provided they contained at least 10 point counts) and given equal weight, so prediction variance will be higher in such areas. However, this difference in predictive accuracy is not apparent on resultant maps of relative mean bird abundance per square.

Appendix 5

Population Size Estimates for Ontario Birds, Based on Point Counts

Peter Blancher and Andrew R. Couturier

The 50,000 plus point counts conducted during the second atlas provide the best picture of relative abundance across Ontario that we have ever had for most bird species. Table C.1 shows the proportion of birds in each of the five atlas analysis regions, a simple result of combining relative abundance at point counts with region size. By making some assumptions about detection of birds on point counts, these data have also been used to calculate rough population sizes for 124 species frequently detected on point counts.

Population size estimates were calculated for each atlas region using methods developed for the Partners in Flight (PIF) landbird conservation program (Rich et al. 2004, Appendix B; Rosenberg and Blancher 2005; Blancher et al. 2007), described briefly here. The formula used was: Population Size = Count Average / Area per Count x Region Area x Detection Adjustments.

Count average was derived from the kriged maps of relative abundance presented in each species account, by averaging cell values within a region (cells in the abundance surface are 1 km x 1 km in size). This technique ensured that all parts of a region were given equal weight, regardless of distribution of counting effort.

Dividing the count average by area sampled per point count gives an approximate measure of density of birds. The area sampled depends on species-specific factors such as how far away a bird can be heard and how active birds are during five-minute counts on June mornings. Species were assigned to six detection distance categories ranging from 80 m for small, relatively quiet birds such as Brown Creepers and Golden-crowned Kinglets to 400 m for large, loud, and/or active flying birds such as the Common Raven, Pileated Woodpecker, and Chimney Swift, and 800 m for the Turkey Vulture. Distances assignments were taken from PIF but were adjusted if the proportion of birds within 100 m on atlas point counts indicated a species had been assigned to the wrong category. (Actual distances used and other details will be made available on the atlas web page.)

Region area provides the means for extrapolating density per point count to a regional total count. Area of open water was excluded from extrapolation.

Many birds within detection distance are not detected during five-minute counts. Two adjustments were used to account at least roughly for birds missed on June mornings. First, a species-specific "time of day" adjustment was used to increase the count average for birds that have a peak of activity during part of the morning and reduced detection at other times. For example, Wood Thrushes are detected 2.3 times more often at dawn as they are during the remainder of the morning, according to Breeding Bird Survey (BBS) data (Rosenberg and Blancher 2005), so the count average is multiplied by 2.3 to account for undetected birds later in the morning. A "pair" adjustment of 2 was also applied to all species on the assumption that on average each bird detected at the peak time of day (dawn for Wood Thrushes) represented one pair in the population, or two birds.

From the above, it should be clear that the estimates are useful as rough ballpark figures only, since atlas point counts do not collect data needed to estimate the proportion of birds present but not detected at various distances from the observer. Thogmartin et al. (2006) reviewed PIF population estimation methods and highlighted several limitations, some of which also apply to these atlas-based estimates. The most significant is uncertainty in detection distance, as population estimates vary inversely with the square of detection distance, so that the effect of halving detection distance is a population estimate four times as large. The proportion of birds within 100 m of atlas point counts was helpful in refining detection distances used by PIF, but only relative to other species. To the extent that there was habitat bias in the location of point counts, that bias will also be reflected in population estimates. Inclusion of off-road counts in habitats under-sampled by roadside counts means that atlas-based estimates are likely to be less biased than PIF estimates, which were based on BBS data. Atlas estimates are likely to be conservative for birds that are poorly detected in June relative to other seasons, for example, the Ruffed Grouse and some woodpeckers. There is also likely to be some unmeasured error associated with the "pair" and "time of day" detection adjustments.

For these reasons, all estimates in the table have been rounded off, in most cases to a single significant digit. As a result, sums across regions do not always add up to the same total as Ontario-wide estimates (rounding error). Nevertheless the estimates give a rough idea of the size of bird populations in Ontario. For most species, estimates presented here are likely to be conservative, as they produce total breeding bird densities that are about 50% of landbird densities calculated from Breeding Bird Census data (using data in Kennedy et al. 1999).

Atlas point count averages are highly correlated with BBS route averages for the 124 species treated here (r=0.89), so it is not surprising that population estimates are also highly correlated with those for Ontario in the PIF Landbird Population Estimates Database (http://www.rmbo.org/pif_db/laped/default.aspx; r=0.73, r=0.88 for log-scaled estimates). The largest differences between the two sets of estimates appear to be a result of three factors: higher roadside bias in BBS counts (e.g., lower atlas averages for the Eastern Phoebe and American Robin, higher for the Brown Creeper), poor BBS coverage in the north (e.g., higher atlas averages for the Palm Warbler and Yellow-bellied Flycatcher), and population declines since the 1990s data used by PIF (e.g., lower atlas estimates for the Chimney Swift, several swallows, and many grassland birds).

Species	Ontario	Hudson Bay Lowlands		Northern Shield		Southern Shield		Lake Simcoe-Rideau		Carolinian	
	Population Estimate	Population Estimate	% Provincial Population	Population Estimate	% Provincial Population	Population Estimate	% Provincial Population	Population Estimate	% Provincial Population	Population Estimate	% Provincial Population
Alder Flycatcher	3,000,000	700,000	21%	2,500,000	72%	150,000	5%	90,000	2%	2,000	0%
American Crow	1,000,000	60,000	6%	300,000	31%	150,000	16%	400,000	39%	100,000	9%
American Goldfinch	4,000,000	40,000	1%	400,000	10%	600,000	13%	2,500,000	58%	800,000	18%
American Redstart	3,000,000	400,000	10%	2,000,000	61%	700,000	21%	200,000	6%	25,000	1%
American Robin	10,000,000	2,000,000	19%	4,000,000	34%	1,000,000	9%	3,000,000	27%	1,200,000	11%
Baltimore Oriole	300,000			5,000	2%	20,000	7%	150,000	58%	100,000	33%
Barn Swallow	400,000	1,500	0%	15,000	3%	25,000	6%	250,000	60%	120,000	31%
Bay-breasted Warbler	5,000,000	500,000	10%	5,000,000	89%	60,000	1%	1,000	0%		
Belted Kingfisher	200,000	30,000	17%	120,000	59%	20,000	12%	20,000	11%	3,000	2%
Black-and-white Warbler	3,000,000	500,000	16%	2,000,000	60%	500,000	17%	200,000	7%	2,000	0%
Black-backed Woodpecker	500,000	120,000	29%	300,000	68%	10,000	2%				
Black-billed Cuckoo	40,000			10,000	23%	20,000	48%	10,000	25%	2,000	4%
Black-capped Chickadee	5,000,000	250,000	5%	2,500,000	49%	1,200,000	23%	1,000,000	21%	150,000	3%
Black-throated Blue Warbler	1,500,000			700,000	49%	700,000	49%	25,000	2%	375	0%
Black-throated Green Warbler	2,500,000	70,000	3%	1,200,000	52%	900,000	38%	200,000	7%	4,000	0%
Blackburnian Warbler	5,000,000	150,000	3%	4,000,000	74%	1,200,000	22%	60,000	1%	375	0%
Blackpoll Warbler	3,000,000	3,000,000	93%	200,000	7%						
Blue Jay	700,000			250,000	36%	200,000	27%	200,000	30%	50,000	7%
Blue-gray Gnatcatcher	30,000					1,500	5%	9,000	28%	20,000	67%
Blue-headed Vireo	2,500,000	500,000	19%	2,000,000	73%	200,000	8%	10,000	0%	375	0%
Bobolink	800,000			40,000	6%	70,000	10%	600,000	72%	100,000	13%
Boreal Chickadee	2,500,000	900,000	34%	1,500,000	65%	15,000	1%				
Broad-winged Hawk	200,000			150,000	77%	40,000	19%	6,000	3%	1,000	0%
Brown Creeper	5,000,000	800,000	17%	3,000,000	74%	300,000	7%	70,000	1%	7,000	0%
Brown Thrasher	100,000	1,000	1%	4,000	4%	15,000	18%	60,000	62%	15,000	15%
Brown-headed Cowbird	1,200,000			40,000	3%	60,000	5%	800,000	59%	400,000	33%
Canada Warbler	900,000	50,000	5%	600,000	71%	200,000	21%	20,000	2%	1,200	0%
Cape May Warbler	1,500,000	300,000	22%	1,200,000	75%	50,000	3%	1,000	0%		
Carolina Wren	4,000							375	7%	4,000	93%
Cedar Waxwing	4,000,000	300,000	8%	2,000,000	54%	600,000	14%	800,000	18%	250,000	6%
Chestnut-sided Warbler	5,000,000	150,000	3%	3,000,000	63%	1,500,000	31%	150,000	3%	8,000	0%
Chimney Swift	8,000			375	8%	2,000	25%	2,000	22%	4,000	46%
Chipping Sparrow	12,000,000	1,000,000	9%	7,000,000	63%	800,000	7%	1,500,000	15%	700,000	6%
Cliff Swallow	60,000	2,500	4%	12,000	20%	2,500	4%	30,000	50%	15,000	22%
Common Grackle	3,000,000	20,000	1%	250,000	7%	250,000	7%	1,500,000	51%	1,200,000	35%
Common Raven	600,000	150,000	26%	400,000	65%	50,000	8%	9,000	1%		
Common Yellowthroat	2,000,000	300,000	15%	1,200,000	53%	300,000	15%	300,000	15%	60,000	3%
Connecticut Warbler	250,000	50,000	20%	200,000	80%	375	0%				
Dark-eyed Junco	12,000,000	7,000,000	55%	5,000,000	44%	100,000	1%	4,000	0%		
Downy Woodpecker	800,000	30,000	4%	500,000	56%	120,000	14%	120,000	16%	90,000	10%
Eastern Bluebird	40,000			12,000	26%	5,000	11%	20,000	47%	7,000	15%
Eastern Kingbird	300,000			30,000	11%	30,000	12%	150,000	62%	40,000	14%
Eastern Meadowlark	150,000					12,000	9%	120,000	78%	20,000	13%
Eastern Phoebe	250,000			20,000	11%	100,000	38%	120,000	45%	15,000	6%
Eastern Towhee	40,000			375	4%	9,000	19%	25,000	54%	10,000	22%
Eastern Wood-Pewee	300,000	7,000	2%	40,000	14%	70,000	23%	150,000	46%	50,000	16%
European Starling	4,000,000	12,000	0%	100,000	2%	200,000	4%	2,500,000	55%	1,500,000	38%
Evening Grosbeak	250,000	12,000	5%	200,000	77%	40,000	18%	3,000	1%		
Field Sparrow	40,000			1,000	3%	4,000	12%	20,000	60%	9,000	25%
Fox Sparrow	300,000	250,000	78%	80,000	22%						
Golden-crowned Kinglet	12,000,000	1,500,000	11%	10,000,000	84%	500,000	4%	15,000	0%		
Golden-winged Warbler	25,000					15,000	65%	8,000	34%	375	1%
Grasshopper Sparrow	50,000					3,000	6%	40,000	86%	4,000	8%
Gray Catbird	700,000			30,000	5%	90,000	14%	300,000	51%	200,000	30%
Gray Jay	5,000,000	2,000,000	42%	3,000,000	57%	40,000	1%	375	0%		
Great Crested Flycatcher	400,000			20,000	5%	150,000	35%	200,000	49%	40,000	10%
Hairy Woodpecker	1,200,000	200,000	16%	800,000	60%	200,000	16%	90,000	7%	15,000	1%
Hermit Thrush	2,500,000	900,000	33%	1,500,000	60%	150,000	6%	15,000	1%	375	0%
Horned Lark	500,000	200,000	32%	375	0%	375	0%	150,000	30%	200,000	38%
House Finch	250,000			375	0%	1,200	1%	120,000	44%	150,000	56%
House Sparrow	2,000,000			30,000	1%	15,000	1%	900,000	42%	1,200,000	56%
House Wren	250,000			15,000	6%	15,000	6%	150,000	58%	80,000	30%
Indigo Bunting	300,000			20,000	7%	80,000	27%	120,000	42%	70,000	24%
Killdeer	500,000	40,000	7%	30,000	6%	8,000	2%	250,000	46%	200,000	39%
Least Flycatcher	5,000,000	800,000	17%	3,000,000	71%	400,000	8%	150,000	3%	12,000	0%

Species	Ontario	Hudson Bay Lowlands		Northern Shield		Southern Shield		Lake Simcoe-Rideau		Carolinian	
	Population Estimate	Population Estimate	% Provincial Population	Population Estimate	% Provincial Population	Population Estimate	% Provincial Population	Population Estimate	% Provincial Population	Population Estimate	% Provincial Population
Lincoln's Sparrow	3,000,000	2,000,000	56%	1,500,000	44%	10,000	0%	375	0%		
Magnolia Warbler	12,000,000	2,000,000	15%	9,000,000	78%	800,000	7%	40,000	0%	375	0%
Marsh Wren	100,000			375	1%	6,000	5%	70,000	67%	30,000	27%
Mourning Dove	1,200,000	3,000	0%	15,000	1%	70,000	6%	600,000	53%	500,000	39%
Mourning Warbler	1,500,000	60,000	4%	1,200,000	85%	120,000	8%	30,000	2%	3,000	0%
Nashville Warbler	15,000,000	1,200,000	8%	12,000,000	84%	1,200,000	7%	120,000	1%	1,000	0%
Northern Cardinal	500,000					4,000	1%	250,000	48%	250,000	51%
Northern Flicker	700,000	100,000	15%	400,000	67%	50,000	7%	50,000	8%	15,000	2%
Northern Mockingbird	9,000					375	1%	1,200	13%	7,000	86%
Northern Parula	500,000	6,000	1%	500,000	90%	40,000	8%	2,000	0%		
Northern Rough-winged Swallow	15,000					375	1%	7,000	43%	10,000	56%
Northern Waterthrush	2,000,000	1,000,000	49%	900,000	45%	70,000	3%	50,000	3%	3,000	0%
Olive-sided Flycatcher	100,000	25,000	23%	70,000	72%	5,000	5%	375	0%		
Orange-crowned Warbler	1,500,000	1,000,000	71%	400,000	29%						
Ovenbird	6,000,000	400,000	6%	4,000,000	66%	1,200,000	22%	300,000	6%	20,000	0%
Palm Warbler	7,000,000	4,000,000	58%	3,000,000	42%	375	0%	375	0%		
Philadelphia Vireo	900,000	250,000	26%	700,000	72%	20,000	2%	1,000	0%		
Pileated Woodpecker	150,000	9,000	6%	100,000	72%	20,000	15%	8,000	6%	1,000	1%
Pine Siskin	1,500,000	100,000	7%	1,200,000	90%	25,000	2%	1,500	0%	375	0%
Pine Warbler	300,000			60,000	19%	150,000	58%	60,000	20%	6,000	2%
Purple Finch	700,000	90,000	12%	400,000	61%	150,000	21%	40,000	6%	1,000	0%
Purple Martin	25,000			375	0%	375	2%	9,000	37%	15,000	61%
Red-bellied Woodpecker	20,000							5,000	25%	15,000	75%
Red-breasted Nuthatch	3,000,000	250,000	8%	2,500,000	76%	400,000	13%	70,000	2%	4,000	0%
Red-eyed Vireo	9,000,000	500,000	5%	6,000,000	68%	2,000,000	20%	500,000	6%	90,000	1%
Red-tailed Hawk	40,000	9,000	24%	15,000	39%	1,000	3%	8,000	21%	5,000	13%
Red-winged Blackbird	4,000,000	30,000	1%	200,000	5%	300,000	9%	2,000,000	58%	900,000	26%
Rock Pigeon	400,000			1,500	0%	15,000	4%	250,000	63%	120,000	33%
Rose-breasted Grosbeak	400,000			100,000	23%	150,000	35%	150,000	32%	40,000	9%
Ruby-crowned Kinglet	6,000,000	2,000,000	33%	4,000,000	67%	30,000	1%	375	0%		
Ruby-throated Hummingbird	500,000			150,000	43%	200,000	35%	100,000	17%	30,000	5%
Ruffed Grouse	250,000	20,000	8%	200,000	75%	30,000	13%	9,000	4%	375	0%
Rusty Blackbird	1,200,000	1,200,000	86%	200,000	14%	2,500	0%	1,500	0%		
Savannah Sparrow	4,000,000	2,500,000	67%	300,000	8%	70,000	2%	700,000	18%	200,000	6%
Scarlet Tanager	150,000			30,000	22%	70,000	46%	40,000	26%	9,000	6%
Song Sparrow	3,000,000	120,000	4%	700,000	24%	400,000	12%	1,200,000	43%	500,000	17%
Swainson's Thrush	8,000,000	2,000,000	24%	6,000,000	73%	200,000	3%	5,000	0%		
Swamp Sparrow	2,000,000	800,000	38%	900,000	45%	200,000	9%	150,000	7%	8,000	0%
Tennessee Warbler	5,000,000	2,000,000	34%	3,000,000	66%	20,000	0%	375	0%		
Tree Swallow	400,000	40,000	10%	60,000	17%	25,000	7%	200,000	51%	50,000	15%
Turkey Vulture	20,000			1,200	10%	2,500	14%	8,000	44%	6,000	32%
Upland Sandpiper	9,000			1,500	16%	375	5%	6,000	70%	1,000	9%
Veery	2,000,000	50,000	2%	1,000,000	50%	800,000	36%	250,000	11%	20,000	1%
Vesper Sparrow	80,000			15,000	22%	4,000	5%	30,000	40%	25,000	32%
Warbling Vireo	300,000			8,000	3%	30,000	11%	150,000	62%	70,000	24%
White-breasted Nuthatch	300,000			20,000	11%	120,000	36%	150,000	43%	30,000	10%
White-crowned Sparrow	500,000	500,000	94%	30,000	6%						
White-throated Sparrow	12,000,000	2,500,000	21%	10,000,000	73%	600,000	5%	120,000	1%	375	0%
White-winged Crossbill	5,000,000	2,000,000	42%	3,000,000	57%	60,000	1%	375	0%		
Willow Flycatcher	60,000					3,000	5%	30,000	48%	30,000	48%
Wilson's Snipe	500,000	400,000	73%	100,000	22%	9,000	2%	20,000	4%	375	0%
Wilson's Warbler	2,000,000	900,000	50%	900,000	49%	8,000	0%				
Winter Wren	6,000,000	1,200,000	18%	5,000,000	75%	400,000	6%	40,000	1%	1,000	0%
Wood Thrush	200,000			8,000	4%	50,000	27%	90,000	51%	30,000	18%
Yellow Warbler	4,000,000	1,200,000	35%	1,200,000	30%	250,000	7%	800,000	20%	250,000	7%
Yellow-bellied Flycatcher	6,000,000	1,200,000	23%	4,000,000	76%	100,000	2%	375	0%		
Yellow-bellied Sapsucker	1,200,000	100,000	8%	800,000	60%	400,000	28%	50,000	4%	2,000	0%
Yellow-rumped Warbler	12,000,000	3,000,000	24%	9,000,000	71%	600,000	5%	70,000	1%	375	0%
Yellow-throated Vireo	25,000			1,200	5%	8,000	31%	12,000	42%	6,000	22%

Appendix 6

Some Bird Conservation Initiatives in Ontario

In recent decades, concern for bird conservation has increased in importance provincially, nationally, and internationally. A number of major initiatives are underway to assess species' status to establish priorities for conservation action. This appendix summarizes two of those actions: designating species at risk and the North American Bird Conservation Initiative.

Designations for Species at Risk: Breeding Birds in Ontario

The Natural Heritage Information Centre (NHIC) was established in 1993. Originally a joint venture with OMNR, the Nature Conservancy of Canada, the Natural Heritage League, and The Nature Conservancy, the NHIC is now a unit of the Biodiversity Section within OMNR's Fish and Wildlife Branch. It is one of 74 conservation data centres in the NatureServe network operating in all US states, 11 provinces and territories in Canada, and many Latin American and Caribbean countries. The mission of the NHIC is to acquire, maintain, update, and make available to conservation partners data on Ontario's rare species, vegetation communities, and natural areas. The NHIC assigns conservation ranks to species based upon the number and estimated viability of occurrences in the province.

The Committee on the Status of Species at Risk in Ontario (COSSARO) is the provincial group that assesses and makes recommendations to the OMNR on the status of Ontario's species at risk. It uses NHIC data and rankings and other information in the assessments. The OMNR issues the Species at Risk in Ontario List (Ontario Ministry of Natural Resources 2006a). The provincial Endangered Species Act, 1971 (ESA) protects the species and habitat of regulated endangered species at risk. On 30 June 2008, a revised ESA (2007) will come into force, and additional endangered, threatened, and extirpated species will receive protection.

Criteria for assigning status to species (OMNR):

Extinct: A species that no longer exists anywhere.

Extirpated: A species that no longer exists in the wild in Ontario, but still occurs elsewhere.

Endangered – Regulated: A species facing imminent extinction or extirpation in Ontario which has been regulated under Ontario's Endangered Species Act.

Endangered – Not Regulated: A species facing imminent extinction or extirpation in Ontario which is a candidate for regulation under Ontario's Endangered Species Act.

Threatened: A species that is at risk of becoming endangered in Ontario if limiting factors are not reversed.

Special Concern: A species with characteristics that make it sensitive to human activities or natural events.

For a complete, up to date list of species at risk, visit the OMNR website. Table 6.1 lists the species at risk as of July 2007.

The Committee on the Status of Endangered Wildlife in Canada (COSEWIC) was created in 1977 to address the need for a single, official, scientifically sound, national classification of wildlife species at risk. COSEWIC uses a process based on both scientific and aboriginal or community knowledge to assess species at risk. Under the Species at Risk Act, the government of Canada will take COSEWIC's designations into consideration when establishing the legal list of species at risk.

Criteria for assigning status to species (COSEWIC):

Extinct: A wildlife species that no longer exists.

Extirpated: A wildlife species no longer existing in the wild in Canada, but occurring elsewhere.

Endangered: A wildlife species facing imminent extirpation or extinction.

Threatened: A wildlife species likely to become endangered if limiting factors are not reversed.

Special Concern: A wildlife species that may become a threatened or an endangered species because of a combination of biological characteristics and identified threats.

For a complete, up to date list of national species at risk, visit the COSEWIC website. Table 6.1 lists the species at risk as of July 2007.

The North American Bird Conservation Initiative

In recognition that many North American bird species were continuing to decline, and building on the success of the North American Waterfowl Management Plan and Migratory Bird Treaties, the North American Bird Conservation Initiative (NABCI) was launched in 1999 as a continental conservation initiative among agencies and organizations in Canada, the United States, and Mexico. Formed to facilitate coordination and communication among public and private organizations, initiatives, and individuals across the continent involved in conserving North American birds and their habitats, NABCI aims to maintain the diversity and abundance of all North American birds. NABCI established four bird groupings, called "pillars," for the purposes of conservation planning and implementation: waterfowl, waterbirds, shorebirds, and landbirds. In Canada and Ontario, NABCI implementation is dependent upon the following four partnerships and/or conservation initiatives (see websites for more information):

a) Partners in Flight – Canada is a national landbird conservation program that aims to ensure the long-term viability of populations of native landbirds and uses scoring criteria to assess species at the national level to highlight species of current or potential conservation concern. Scoring criteria are based upon relative abundance, extent of breeding range, regional stewardship responsibility, and threats in breeding and non-breeding ranges. Landbird conservation is guided by the

Table 6.1. Species of breeding birds at risk in Ontario, as listed by OMNR and COSEWIC (as of July 2007).

Species	OMNR Designation for Ontario	COSEWIC Designation for Canada
Passenger Pigeon	Extinct	Extinct
Greater Prairie-Chicken	Extirpated	Extirpated
Acadian Flycatcher	Endangered – Not Regulated	Endangered
American White Pelican	Endangered – Regulated	Not at Risk
Bald Eagle (southern Ontario)	Endangered – Regulated	Not at Risk
Barn Owl	Endangered – Not Regulated	Endangered
Eskimo Curlew	Endangered – Regulated	Endangered
Golden Eagle	Endangered – Regulated	Not at Risk
Henslow's Sparrow	Endangered – Regulated	Endangered
King Rail	Endangered – Regulated	Endangered
Kirtland's Warbler	Endangered – Regulated	Endangered
Loggerhead Shrike (subspecies *migrans*)	Endangered – Regulated	Endangered
Northern Bobwhite	Endangered – Not Regulated	Endangered
Piping Plover (subspecies *circumcinctus*)	Endangered – Regulated	Endangered
Prothonotary Warbler	Endangered – Regulated	Endangered
Hooded Warbler	Threatened	Threatened
Least Bittern	Threatened	Threatened
Peregrine Falcon (subspecies *anatum/tundrius*)	Threatened	Special Concern
Bald Eagle (northern Ontario)	Special Concern	Not at Risk
Black Tern	Special Concern	Not at Risk
Cerulean Warbler	Special Concern	Special Concern
Great Gray Owl	Special Concern	Not at Risk
Louisiana Waterthrush	Special Concern	Special Concern
Red-headed Woodpecker	Special Concern	Threatened
Red-shouldered Hawk	Special Concern	
Short-eared Owl	Special Concern	Special Concern
Yellow Rail	Special Concern	Special Concern
Yellow-breasted Chat (subspecies *virens*)	Special Concern	Special Concern
Chimney Swift		Threatened
Common Nighthawk		Threatened
Golden-winged Warbler		Threatened
Rusty Blackbird		Special Concern

Partners in Flight North American Landbird Conservation Plan (Rich et al. 2004) and by a series of Bird Conservation Region (BCR) Ontario Landbird Conservation Plans (Figure 6.1).

b) Canadian Shorebird Conservation Plan is a national plan intended to ensure that healthy shorebird populations and a diversity of habitats are distributed across their ranges within Canada and globally. Shorebirds are assigned conservation priority based upon occurrence and population trends. The Ontario Shorebird Conservation Plan (Ross et al. 2003) was developed to complement the Canadian plan, describe conservation priorities, and guide on-the-ground actions for species breeding in or migrating through Ontario.

c) North American Waterfowl Management Plan (NAWMP) is a continental plan first signed in 1986 to sustain abundant waterfowl populations by conserving wetlands and associated uplands through partnerships guided by sound science. NAWMP established regional partnerships called Joint Ventures throughout the continent to undertake conservation projects. Ontario is a partner in the Eastern Habitat Joint Venture (EHJV), a regional partnership established in 1989 covering the six eastern Canadian provinces. Recently, the EHJV has expanded its mission to include the conservation of all birds and the habitats that support them. In Ontario, conservation actions for waterfowl are guided by the Ontario Eastern Habitat Joint Venture Five-Year Implementation Plan 2006-2010, which includes population and habitat objectives and associated implementation actions for waterfowl in the province. Ontario is also a partner in the Black Duck Joint Venture and the Arctic Goose Joint Venture, which are aimed at improving knowledge about the respective species and their habitats for the purpose of conservation and management.

d) Wings Over Water – Canada's Waterbird Conservation Plan (Milko et al. 2003) is the Canadian component of the North American Waterbird Conservation Plan and aims to ensure that populations of waterbirds (i.e., seabirds, colonial waterbirds, marsh and other waterbird species) are sustained or restored throughout their historical range, in Canada and globally. Species are prioritized for conservation based upon population trends and size, threats to breeding and non-breeding distribution, and the percentage of the North American and global population within Canada. Efforts are currently underway to develop a waterbird conservation plan for Ontario.

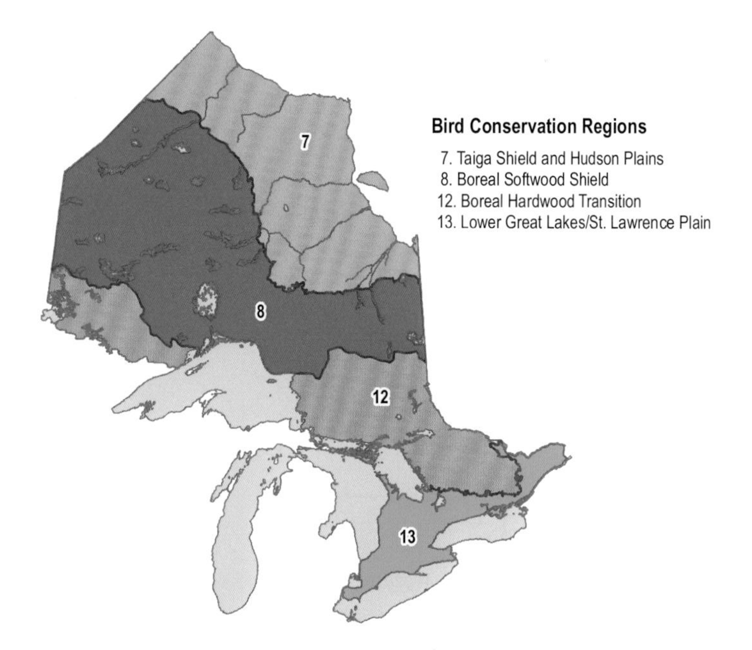

Figure 6.1. Bird Conservation Regions in Ontario.
Bird Conservation Regions are ecologically based units for addressing avian conservation needs within management units that are practical for landscape-oriented conservation action.

Appendix 7

Gazetteer of Ontario Place Names Used in the Text

Place name	Lat (N)	Long (W)
Acton	43° 37'	80° 02'
Agutua Moraine	52° 05'	92° 01'
Ajax	43° 51'	79° 02'
Akimiski Island, NU	53° 00'	81° 16'
Akimiski Strait, NU	53° 05'	82° 10'
Albany River	52° 17'	81° 33'
Alfred	45° 33'	74° 53'
Alfred Bog	45° 29'	74° 50'
Alfred Sewage Lagoon	45° 32'	74° 51'
Algoma Highlands	47° 11'	83° 42'
Algonquin Dome	Chapman & Putnam 1984	
Algonquin Highlands	Chapman & Putnam 1984	
Algonquin Prov. Park	45° 45'	78° 30'
Amherst Island	44° 09'	76° 42'
Amherstburg	42° 06'	83° 06'
Ancaster	43° 14'	79° 58'
Aquatuk Lake	54° 22'	84° 32'
Aquatuk River	54° 58'	84° 04'
Arab Lake	44° 31'	76° 32'
Armstrong	50° 18'	89° 02'
Arnprior	45° 26'	76° 21'
Atik Island	54° 43'	86° 30'
Atikokan	48° 45'	91° 37'
Attawapiskat	52° 55'	82° 25'
Attawapiskat River	52° 57'	82° 16'
Aurora	44° 00'	79° 28'
Ausable/Bayfield region	43° 33'	81° 41'
Awenda Prov. Park	44° 50'	79° 59'
Aylmer	42° 46'	80° 59'
Backus Woods	42° 39'	80° 29'
Baden	43° 24'	80° 40'
Badjeros	44° 16'	80° 17'
Baldwin	44° 15'	79° 20'
Bamberg	43° 29'	80° 41'
Bancroft	45° 03'	77° 51'
Barrie	44° 23'	79° 40'
Barrier Island	44° 58'	81° 04'
Bay of Quinte	44° 08'	77° 15'
Beachville	43° 05'	80° 49'
Bearskin Lake	53° 44'	91° 41'
Bearskin Lake First Nation	53° 55	90° 54'
Belleville	44° 09'	77° 22'
Berens Lake	51° 45'	93° 43'
Berens River	52° 01'	95° 10'
Bergin Island	45° 01'	74° 51'
Big Creek	42° 36'	80° 27'
Big Rideau lake	44° 43'	76° 12'
Big Sandy Bay	44° 06'	76° 27'
Big Trout Lake	53° 44'	89° 59'
Binbrook	43° 07'	79° 48'
Black Bay	48° 39'	88° 29'
Black Duck River	56° 50'	89° 01'
Blezard Valley	46° 41'	81° 02'
Bon Echo Prov. Park	44° 55'	77° 16'
Bowmanville	43° 54'	78° 41'
Bracebridge	45° 02'	79° 18'
Bradford	44° 06'	79° 33'
Bradley's Marsh	42° 19'	82° 25'
Brampton	43° 41'	79° 46'
Brant River	55° 04'	82° 50'
Brantford	43° 08'	80° 15'
Brighton	44° 02'	77° 44'
Brock Road	43° 52'	79° 05'
Brockville	44° 35'	75° 41'
Bronte Creek Prov. Park	43° 25'	79° 45'
Bronte Harbour	43° 23'	79° 42'
Bruce Peninsula	44° 52'	81° 15'
Burntpoint Creek	55° 15'	84° 07'
Burpee Township	48° 28'	88° 23'
Cache Bay	46° 22'	79° 59'
Caledon	43° 52'	79° 51'
Cambridge	43° 22'	80° 19'
Cameron Ranch	44° 37'	79° 03'
Campbellville	43° 29'	79° 59'
Canoe Lake	44° 35'	76° 32'
Cape Henrietta Maria	55° 08'	82° 20'
Carden Alvar	44° 39'	79° 00'
Carden Plain	Chapman & Putnam 1984	
Caribou Island	47° 22'	85° 49'
Cartier Moraine	46° 42'	81° 33'
Casselman	45° 18'	75° 05'
Cat Lake	51° 44'	91° 50'
Chantry Island	44° 29'	81° 24'
Chapleau	47° 50'	83° 24'
Chapleau Moraine	48° 24'	83° 38'
Chatham	42° 24'	82° 11'
Chelmsford	46° 35'	81° 12'
Clay Belt	McDermott 1961	
Clayton	45° 11'	76° 20'
Cobourg	43° 57'	78° 09'
Cochrane	49° 03'	81° 00'
Cook's Bay	44° 14'	79° 30'
Cornwall	45° 01'	74° 44'
Cranberry Marsh	43° 50'	78° 57'
Dealtown	42° 14'	82° 06'
Deep River	46° 03'	77° 25'
Detroit River	42° 20'	82° 55'
Dryden	49° 46'	92° 49'
Dryden Clay Plain	Hills and Morwick 1944	
Duck Islands	45° 42'	82° 55'
Dundalk Till Plain	Chapman & Putnam 1984	
Dundalk Uplands	Chapman & Putnam 1984	
Dundas Marsh	43° 16'	79° 55'
Dundas Valley	43° 14'	79° 59'
Dunnville	42° 54'	79° 36'
Ear Falls	50° 38'	93° 14'

East Pen Island 56° 45' 88° 38'
East Sister Island 41° 48' 82° 51'
Ekwan Point 53° 16' 82° 07'
Ekwan River 53° 12' 82° 14'
Elbow Lake 48° 48' 88° 44'
Emo 48° 37' 93° 50'
Englehart 47° 49' 79° 52'
English River 49° 13' 90° 57'
Erieau 42° 15' 81° 55'
Essex 42° 10' 82° 49'
False Duck Island 43° 56' 76° 48'
Fawn River 55° 21' 88° 19'
Fighting Island 42° 13' 83° 07'
Flagstaff Point 55° 16' 85° 00'
Flamborough Plain Chapman & Putnam 1984
Foleyet 48° 15' 82° 26'
Fort Albany 52° 12' 81° 41'
Fort Erie 42° 54' 78° 56'
Fort Frances 48° 36' 93° 23'
Fort Hope 51° 33' 87° 58'
Fort Severn 55° 59' 87° 37'
Fort William 48° 19' 89° 17'
Fraserdale 49° 50' 81° 36'
French River 45° 56' 80° 54'
Frontenac Axis Chapman & Putnam 1984
Frontenac Prov. Park 44° 32' 76° 30'
Galt Moraine Chapman & Putnam 1984
Gananoque 44° 19' 76° 09'
Georgetown 43° 38' 79° 54'
Geraldton 49° 43' 86° 56'
Glencoe 42° 45' 81° 43'
Goderich 43° 44' 81° 42'
Golden Horseshoe Barber 2001
Grand Bend 43° 18' 81° 45'
Grand River 42° 51' 79° 34'
Gravenhurst 44° 55' 79° 22
Great Clay Belt McDermott 1961
Greater Toronto Area (GTA) 43° 44' 79° 22'
Grimsby 43° 11' 79° 33'
Grundy Lake Prov. Park 45° 56' 80° 32'
Guelph 43° 32' 80° 15'
Gull Island 43° 59' 77° 44'
Gullery Island 52° 37' 80° 41'
Haldimand Clay Plain Chapman & Putnam 1984
Halfmoon Island 45° 26' 81° 28'
Haliburton 45° 03' 78° 31'
Haliburton Highlands Chapman & Putnam 1984
Halton Hills 43° 38' 79° 54'
Hamilton 43° 15' 79° 49'
Hamilton Bay 43° 17' 79° 53'
Hamilton Harbour 43° 17' 79° 49'
Harricanaw River 51° 10' 79° 45'
Harrow 42° 02' 82° 55'
Hawk Cliff 42° 40' 81° 10'
Hawley Lake 54° 30' 84° 37'
Hearst 49° 41' 83° 39'
High Bluff Island 43° 58' 77° 44'
High Park 43° 38' 79° 27'
Hillman Marsh 42° 02' 82° 30'
Holiday Beach
Conservation Area 42° 02' 83° 02'
Holland Marsh 44° 08' 79° 33'
Hook Point 54° 52' 82° 12'
Hope Bay 44° 54' 81° 09'
Horwood Lake 48° 00' 82° 20'
Hullett Marsh 43° 37' 81° 27'
Humber River 43° 38' 79° 28'
Huntsville 45° 19' 79° 13'
Indian Island 44° 04' 77° 34'
Iron Bridge 46° 16' 83° 13'
Iroquois Falls 48° 45' 80° 41'
Iroquois Plain Chapman & Putnam 1984
Ishpatina Ridge 48° 19' 80° 44'
Jarvis 42° 53' 80° 06'
Jarvis sewage lagoons 42° 52' 80° 06'
Jordain Lake 48° 58' 90° 00'
Junetown 44° 30' 75° 56'
Kapiskau Lake 52° 10' 85° 18'
Kapuskasing 49° 25' 82° 25'
Kashechewan 52° 18' 81° 37'
Kawartha Lakes 44° 28' 78° 25'
Kelly Lake 46° 26' 81° 03'
Kenogami River 51° 06' 84° 28'
Kenora 49° 46' 94° 29'
Kesagami Lake 50° 22' 80° 15'
Kettle Creek 42° 39' 81° 12'
Kettle Point 43° 11' 82° 01'
Killarney Prov. Park 46° 08' 81° 23'
Kingston 44° 18' 76° 24'
Kinushseo River 55° 13' 83° 38'
Kirkland Lake 48° 08' 80° 01'
Kiruna Lake 54° 30' 84° 54'
Kitchener 43° 26' 80° 30'
Kitchener-Waterloo 43° 27' 80° 29'
La Salle 42° 13' 83° 02'
Lac Seul 50° 19' 92° 38'
Lake Abitibi 48° 42' 79° 45'
Lake Algonquin 49° 18' 80° 59'
Lake Mindemoya 45° 45' 82° 13'
Lake Nipigon 49° 49' 88° 31'
Lake Nipissing 46° 16' 79° 42'
Lake of the Woods 49° 18' 94° 43'
Lake Opinicon 44° 32' 76° 22'
Lake River 54° 22' 82° 31'
Lake Rosseau 45° 10' 79° 35'
Lake Scugog 44° 10' 78° 51'
Lake Simcoe 44° 25' 79° 22'
Lake St. Clair 42° 26' 82° 42'
Lake St. Clair marshes 42° 22' 82° 24'
Lake St. Joseph 51° 04' 90° 35'
Lake St. Lawrence 45° 01' 74° 48'
Lake Superior Prov. Park 47° 39' 84° 52'

Lake Temagami	47° 01'	79° 52'
Lake Timiskaming	47° 29'	79° 32'
Lakitusaki River	54° 21'	82° 25'
LaRose Forest	45° 22'	75° 11'
Leslie Street Spit	43° 38'	79° 19'
Lillabelle Lake	49° 06'	81° 01'
Lindsay	44° 21'	78° 44'
Little Abitibi Lake	49° 22'	80° 32'
Little Abitibi River	50° 29'	81° 31'
Little Bear Island	55° 16'	82° 58'
Little Cape	55° 15'	83° 40'
Little Cataraqui Creek	44° 13'	76° 32'
Little Clay Belt	McDermott 1961	
Little Sachigo Lake	54° 08'	92° 14'
Little Shagamu River	55° 50'	86° 41'
Little Sturgeon Lake	49° 12'	88° 54'
London	42° 59'	81° 14'
Long Lake	44° 27'	78° 10'
Long Point	42° 34'	80° 23'
Long Point Bay	42° 37'	80° 23'
Long Point Prov. Park	42° 35'	80° 23'
Longlac	49° 46'	86° 32'
Longridge Point	51° 50'	80° 42'
Lower Beverley Lake	44° 35'	76° 08'
Lower Duck Islands	45° 28'	75° 35'
Luther Marsh	43° 56'	80° 25'
Mac Johnston Wildlife Area	44° 37'	75° 43'
Madawaska Highlands	Chapman & Putnam 1984	
Maitland River	43° 45'	81° 43'
Mammamattawa	50° 25'	84° 22'
Manchuinagush Island	55° 11'	82° 43'
Manitoulin Island	45° 46'	82° 17'
Marathon	48° 43'	86° 23'
Marysville	44° 14'	77° 06'
Massey	46° 12'	82° 04'
Matchedash Bay	44° 44'	79° 40'
Mattawa	46° 19'	78° 42'
Mattawa River	46° 19'	78° 42'
Mazinaw Lake	44° 52'	77° 10'
McGeachy's Pond	42° 16'	81° 56'
McNair Island	44° 35'	75° 39'
Mer Bleue	45° 24'	75° 30'
Mid Canada Line Radar Site 415	54° 44'	82° 24'
Mid Canada Line Radar Site 416	54° 45'	82° 22'
Middle Island	41° 41'	82° 40'
Middle Point Woods	41° 47'	82° 37'
Middle Sister Island	41° 50'	83° 00'
Midland	44° 45'	79° 53'
Minden	44° 55'	78° 43'
Minesing Swamp	44° 23'	79° 51'
Missinaibi River	50° 44'	81° 29'
Missisa Lake	52° 18'	85° 12'
Missisa River	53° 01'	84° 02'
Mississippi River	45° 26'	76° 17'
Mitchell's Bay	42° 28'	82° 24'
Mohawk Island	42° 50'	79° 31'
Mono Hills	44° 03'	80° 02'
Moose Bay	45° 04'	80° 03'
Moose Factory	51° 15'	80° 36'
Moose River	51° 20'	80° 23'
Moose River Crossing	50° 48'	81° 17'
Moosonee	51° 16'	80° 38'
Morrisburg	44° 54'	75° 10'
Muketei River	53° 08'	85° 17'
Mulmur Hills	44° 10'	80° 04'
Murdock River	46° 03'	80° 36'
Nabinamik	52° 45'	88° 32'
Nakina	50° 10'	86° 42'
Napanee	44° 14'	76° 57'
Napanee Plain	Chapman & Putnam 1984	
Nettichi River	52° 06'	81° 22'
New Liskeard	47° 30'	79° 40'
Niagara Escarpment	Chapman & Putnam 1984	
Niagara Falls	43° 06'	79° 04'
Niagara Peninsula	43° 01'	79° 21'
Niagara River	43° 15'	79° 04'
Niagara-on-the-Lake	43° 15'	79° 04'
Niblett Island	45° 03'	80° 03'
Nipigon Bay	48° 57'	88° 14'
Nipissing	46° 06'	79° 31'
Niskibi River	56° 30'	88° 08'
Noëlville	46° 07'	80° 25'
Norfolk Sand Plain	Chapman & Putnam 1984	
North Bay	46° 19'	79° 28'
North Channel	46° 05'	83° 05'
North Limestone Island	45° 24'	80° 32'
North Spirit Lake	52° 30'	93° 01'
North Washagami Lake	54° 30'	85° 03'
Northbluff Point	51° 30'	80° 27'
Nottawasaga Bay	44° 36'	80° 14'
Nottawasaga Island	44° 32'	80° 15'
Nowashe Creek	54° 06'	82° 19'
Oak Lake	50° 26'	93° 50'
Oak Ridges Moraine	Chapman & Putnam 1984	
Ojibway Park	42° 16'	83° 04'
Oliphant Beach	44° 44'	81° 16'
Onaman Lake	50° 00'	87° 26'
Oosteguanako Creek	56° 48'	88° 50'
Opapimiskan Lake	52° 37'	90° 24'
Opasquia Prov. Park	53° 31'	93° 00'
Opinnagau Lake	53° 55'	84° 22'
Orangeville	43° 55'	80° 06'
Orillia	44° 36'	79° 25'
Oshawa	43° 53'	78° 51'
Oshawa Second Marsh	43° 52'	78° 48'
Ottawa	45° 24'	75° 42'
Ottawa River	45° 34'	74° 25'
Ottawa Valley	45° 33'	74° 23'
Owen Sound	44° 40'	80° 54'
Paris Moraine	Chapman & Putnam 1984	

Parry Sound	45° 21'	80° 02'
Peawanuck	55° 01'	85° 25'
Pelee Island	41° 46'	82° 39'
Pembroke	45° 49'	77° 06'
Pen Islands	56° 45'	88° 38'
Perrault Falls	50° 20'	93° 08'
Perth	44° 54'	76° 15'
Perth Road	44° 28'	76° 29'
Petawawa	45° 54'	77° 16'
Peterborough	44° 18'	78° 19'
Petroglyphs Prov. Park	44° 37'	78° 03'
Pickering	43° 49'	79° 06'
Pickle Lake	51° 28'	90° 12'
Pigeon Island	44° 03'	76° 32'
Pikangikum	51° 48'	93° 59'
Pikangikum Lake	51° 48'	94° 00'
Pinery Prov. Park	43° 15'	81° 50'
Pinewood	48° 43'	94° 18'
Pitticow River	54° 53'	87° 46'
Pittock Lake	43° 08'	80° 46'
Pledger Lake	50° 53'	83° 42'
Point Pelee	41° 58'	82° 31'
Point Pelee Nat. Park	41° 57'	82° 31'
Pointe au Baril	45° 33'	80° 30'
Polar Bear Prov. Park	55° 06'	83° 51'
Port Alma	42° 11'	82° 15'
Port Arthur	48° 24'	89° 19'
Port Burwell	42° 39'	80° 49'
Port Colborne	42° 53'	79° 15'
Port Hope	43° 57'	78° 17'
Port Loring	45° 55'	79° 59'
Port Severn	44° 48'	79° 43'
Port Stanley	42° 39'	81° 13'
Portland	44° 41'	76° 11'
Presqu'ile Prov. Park	43° 59'	77° 42'
Prince Edward Point	43° 56'	76° 52'
Pukaskwa Nat. Park	48° 15'	85° 55'
Quetico Prov. Park	48° 28'	91° 30'
Rainy Lake	48° 38'	93° 01'
Rainy River (river)	48° 50'	94° 41'
Rainy River (town)	48° 43'	94° 33'
Rainy River Clay Plain	Hills and Morwick 1944	
Ramsey Lake	46° 28'	80° 56'
Red Lake	51° 01'	93° 50'
Rice Lake	44° 12'	78° 10'
Rideau Lakes	44° 43'	76° 12'
Rideau River	45° 26'	75° 41'
Rondeau Bay	42° 17'	81° 53'
Rondeau Prov. Park	42° 16'	81° 50'
Rossport	48° 50'	87° 31'
Royal Botanical Gardens	43° 17'	79° 52'
Ruthven	42° 03'	82° 40'
Sable Islands	48° 54'	94° 38'
Sable Islands Provincial Nature Reserve	48° 54'	94° 38'
Sachigo Lake	53° 47'	92° 05'
Sachigo River	55° 04'	88° 58'
Sandbanks Prov. Park	43° 55'	77° 16'
Sandy Lake	53° 00'	93° 00'
Sarnia	42° 58'	82° 23'
Saugeen River	44° 30'	81° 22'
Sault Ste. Marie	46° 31'	84° 18'
Scotch Bonnet Island	43° 53'	77° 32'
Selkirk Prov. Park	42° 49'	79° 57'
Severn River	56° 03'	87° 33'
Severn Sound	44° 48'	79° 49'
Shagamu River	55° 52'	86° 46'
Shamattawa River	55° 00'	85° 22'
Shegogau Creek	51° 35'	80° 32'
Shelburne	44° 04'	80° 12'
Shell Brook	55° 54'	86° 58'
Simcoe Island	44° 10'	76° 31'
Sioux Lookout	50° 05'	91° 55'
Skunk's Misery	42° 39'	81° 48'
Slate Falls	51° 09'	91° 34'
Smiths Falls	44° 53'	76° 00'
Smith's Falls Plain	Chapman & Putnam 1984	
Snake Island	44° 11'	76° 32'
South River	45° 50'	79° 23'
South Walsingham Forest	42° 37'	80° 33'
South Watcher Island	44° 57'	80° 04'
Southampton	44° 29'	81° 22'
Spooky Hollow	42° 43'	80° 19'
Squires Ridge	42° 34'	80° 15'
St. Clair Flats	42° 22'	82° 24'
St. Clair National Wildlife Area	42° 22'	82° 24'
St. Clair River	42° 36'	82° 31'
St. Joseph Island	46° 13'	83° 57'
St. Lawrence River	45° 12'	74° 20'
St. Lawrence Valley	45° 11'	74° 19'
St. Marys River	46° 15'	83° 46'
St. Thomas	42° 47'	81° 12'
St. Williams	42° 39'	80° 24'
St. Williams Forest	42° 42'	80° 27'
Stoney Point	42° 18'	82° 33'
Strachan Island	45° 01'	74° 48'
Stratford	43° 22'	80° 58'
Sturgeon Bay	44° 43'	79° 43'
Sturgeon River Valley	46° 19'	79° 58'
Sudbury	46° 29'	81° 00'
Sutton Lake	54° 15'	84° 44'
Sutton Narrows	54° 25'	84° 41'
Sutton Ridges	54° 29'	84° 50'
Sutton River	55° 12'	83° 41'
Swan River	53° 35'	82° 13'
Temagami	47° 03'	79° 47'
Temagami - Lake Timiskaming Area	47° 04'	79° 47'
Terrace Bay	48° 47'	87° 05'
Thames River	42° 19'	82° 27'
The Three Sisters	49° 22'	94° 08'

Thedford	43° 10'	81° 51'
Thousand Islands	44° 22'	75° 55'
Thousand Islands Nat. Park	44° 27'	75° 52'
Thunder Bay	48° 25'	89° 14'
Thunder Cape	48° 18'	88° 56'
Timmins	48° 29'	81° 22'
Toronto	43° 44'	79° 22'
Toronto Islands	43° 37'	79° 22'
Townsend	42° 53'	80° 09'
Townsend sewage lagoons	42° 54'	80° 10'
Tremblay Beach Conservation Area	42° 18'	82° 31'
Trenton	44° 06'	77° 34'
Trent-Severn Waterway	44° 32'	78° 32'
Trout Creek	45° 59'	79° 22'
Trout Lake Moraine	51° 07'	93° 22'
Turkey Point	42° 42'	80° 19'
Turkey Point Prov. Park	42° 40'	80° 20'
Upsala	49° 03'	90° 28'
Urfé Creek	43° 51'	79° 04'
Utica	44° 04'	79° 01'
Venison Creek	42° 39'	80° 33'
Vermillion Bay	49° 51'	93° 23'
Verner	46° 24'	80° 07'
Wabakimi Prov. Park	50° 35'	89° 35'
Wabuk Point	55° 20'	85° 05'
Wainfleet Bog	42° 55'	79° 18'
Wakami Lake	47° 29'	82° 51'
Wakami Lake Prov. Park	47° 29'	82° 49'
Wallaceburg	42° 35'	82° 23'
Walpole Island	42° 33'	82° 30'
Walpole Island First Nation	42° 34'	82° 30'
Walsingham	42° 43'	80° 35'
Warchesku River	54° 40'	84° 36'
Wasaga Beach Prov. Park	44° 30'	80° 01'
Waterloo	43° 28'	80° 31'
Waubaushene	44° 45'	79° 42'
Wawa	47° 59'	84° 46'
Weagamow Lake (lake)	52° 52'	91° 21'
Weagamow Lake (town)	52° 57'	91° 16'
Webbwood	46° 16'	81° 53'
Webequie	52° 59'	87° 21'
West Brother Island	45° 57'	81° 23'
West Pen Island	56° 50'	88° 48'
Westdale Ravine	43° 16'	79° 54'
Wheatley Prov. Park	42° 05'	82° 26'
Whitby Harbour	43° 52'	78° 56'
White River	48° 35'	85° 15'
Whitefish Lake	48° 13'	90° 00'
Wilson Creek	48° 48'	94° 41'
Wilson Tract	42° 38'	80° 33'
Windsor	42° 18'	83° 01'
Windy Point	48° 58'	94° 33'
Winisk	55° 15'	85° 12'
Winisk River	55° 16'	85° 05'
Winiskisis Channel	54° 02'	87° 05'
Wolfe Island	44° 09'	76° 25'
Wood Creek	55° 41'	86° 02'
Woodland Caribou Prov. Park	51° 00'	94° 43'

Appendix 8

Plant and Animal Names Used in the Text

Plant name used	Proper name
Alder	*Alnus* spp.
Green Alder	*A. viridis*
Speckled Alder	*A. incana*
Alfalfa	*Medicago sativa*
Apple	*Malus* spp.
Common Apple	*M. pumila*
Arrowheads	*Sagittaria* spp.
Ash	*Fraxinus* spp.
White Ash	*F. americana*
Aspen	*Populus* spp.
Trembling Aspen	*P. tremuloides*
Basswood	*Tilia americana*
Beech	*Fagus* spp.
American Beech	*F. grandifolia*
Birch	*Betula* spp.
Dwarf Birch	*B. glandulifera/B. glandulosa*
Mountain Birch	*B. occidentalis*
White Birch	*B. papyrifera*
Yellow Birch	*B. alleghaniensis*
Black Gum	*Nyssa sylvatica*
Blueberry	*Vaccinium* spp.
Bog Buckbean	*Menyanthes trifoliata*
Bulrush	*Scirpus and/or Schoenoplectus spp*
Burreed	*Sparganium* spp.
Butternut	*Juglans cinerea*
Cattail	*Typha* spp.
Cedar	*Thuja* spp.
Red Cedar	*Juniperus virginiana*
White Cedar	*T. occidentalis*
Cherry	*Prunus* spp.
Black Cherry	*P. serotina*
Chestnut	*Hippocastanum* spp.
American Chestnut	*Castanea dentata*
Common Dandelion	*Taraxacum officinale*
Composite Plants	Asteraceae (Family)
Conifers	Coniferophyta (Phylum)
Corn	*Zea mays*
Cottonwood	*Populus* spp.
Eastern Cottonwood	*P. deltoides*
Dogwood	*Cornus* spp.
Red-osier Dogwood	*C. sericea*
Eastern Bracken	*Pteridium aquilinum*
Elderberry	*Sambucus* spp.
Red Elderberry	*S. racemosa*
Elm	*Ulmus* spp.
White Elm	*U. americana*
Ericaceous Plants	Ericaceae (Family)
Fern	Polypodiales (Order)
Filamentous Green Algae	Chlorophyta: Spirogyra, Mougeotia and Cladophora.
Fir	*Abies* spp.
Balsam Fir	*A. balsamea*
Goldenrod	*Solidago* spp.
Grape	*Vitis* spp.
Grass	Poaceae (Family)
Hackberry	*Celtis* spp.
Common Hackberry	*C. occidentalis*
Hawthorn	*Crataegus* spp.
Hazel	*Corylus* spp.
American Hazel	*C. americana*
Hemlock	*Tsuga* spp.
Eastern Hemlock	*T. canadensis*
Hickory	*Carya* spp.
Bitternut Hickory	*C. cordiformis*
Shagbark Hickory	*C. ovata*
Hobblebush	*Viburnum lantanoides*
Horsetail	*Equisetum* spp.
Juniper	*Juniperus* spp.
Common Juniper	*J. communis*
Labrador Tea	*Ledum groenlandicum*
Lapland Rosebay	*Rhododendron lapponicum*
Leatherleaf	*Chamaedaphne calyculata*
Lichen	Lichenes (Division)
Tree Lichen	*Usnea* spp.
Maple	*Acer* spp.
Manitoba Maple	*A. negundo*
Red Maple	*A. rubrum*
Sugar Maple	*A. saccharum*
Moss	Musci (Class)
Beardmoss	*Usnea* spp.
Sphagnum	*Sphagnum* spp.
Mountain Ash	*Sorbus* spp.
Mountain Avens	*Dryas* spp.
Mountain Holly	*Nemopanthus mucronatus*
Mullein	*Verbascum* spp.
Great Mullein	*V. thapsus*
Oak	*Quercus* spp.
Bur Oak	*Q. macrocarpa*
Pin Oak	*Q. palustris*
Red Oak	*Q. rubra*
White Oak	*Q. alba*
Perennial Sow-thistle	*Sonchus arvensis*
Pine	*Pinus* spp.
Eastern White Pine	*P. strobus*
Jack Pine	*P. banksiana*
Red Pine	*P. resinosa*
Poison Ivy	*Rhus rydbergii*
Poison Sumac	*Toxicodendron vernix*
Pondweeds	Potamogetonaceae (Family)
Sago Pondweed	*Stuckenia pectinata*
Poplar	*Populus* spp.
Balsam Poplar	*P. balsamifera*
Raspberry	*Rubus* spp.
Reed	*Phragmites* spp.
Common Reed	*P. australis*
Rose	*Rosa* spp.

Rush	*Eleocharis* spp.	Sycamore	*Platanus occidentalis*
Rye	*Secale cereale*	Tamarack	*Larix laricina*
Sedge	Cyperaceae (Family)	Thistle	*Cirsium* spp., *Carduus* spp.
Serviceberry	*Amelanchier* spp.	Trailing Arbutus	*Epigaea repens*
Snowberry	*Symphoricarpos albus*	Tulip Tree	*Liriodendron tulipifera*
Soybean	*Glycine max*	Viburnum	*Viburnum* spp.
Spruce	*Picea* spp.	Northern Wild Raisin	*V. cassinoides*
Black Spruce	*P. mariana*	Wild Celery	*Vallisneria americana*
Red Spruce	*P. rubens*	Wild Rice	*Zizania* spp.
White Spruce	*P. glauca*	Willow	*Salix* spp.
Sumac	*Rhus* spp.	Arctic Willow	*S. arctica*
Fragrant Sumac	*R. aromatica*	Winter Wheat	*Triticum aestivum*
Sweet Gale	*Myrica gale*	Wolfberry	*Symphoricarpos occidentalis*

Animal name used	**Proper/English name**
Amphibians	Amphibia (Class)
Arctic Fox	*Vulpes lagopus*
Bark Beetles	Scolytidae (Family)
Beaver	American Beaver *Castor canadensis*
Bison	American Bison *Bos bison*
Cerambycidae	Long-horned Beetles
Crayfish	Decapoda (Order)
Crustaceans	Crustacea (Phylum or subphylum)
Deer Mouse	*Peromyscus maniculatus*
Dragonflies	Anisoptera (Suborder)
Earthworm	Annelida (Phylum), Haplotaxida (Order), Lumbricina (suborder)
Emerald Ash Borer	*Agrilus planipennis*
Fall Webworm	*Hyphantria cunea*
Forest Tent Caterpillar	*Malacosoma disstria*
Grey Squirrel	Eastern Grey Squirrel *Sciurus carolinensis*
Green Frog	*Rana clamitans*
Gypsy Moth	*Lymantria dispar*
Ips species	Ips (Genus)
Jack Pine Budworm	*Choristoneura pinus*
Lemming	Muridae (Family)
Mayfly	Ephemeroptera (Order)
Meadow Vole	*Microtus pennsylvanicus*
Mosquitoes	Culicidae (family)
Muskrat	Common Muskrat *Ondatra zibethicus*
Red Fox	*Vulpes vulpes*
Red Squirrel	*Tamiasciurus hudsonicus*
Red-backed Vole	Southern Red-backed Vole *Clethrionomys gapperi*
Rodents	Rodentia (Order)
Scolytidae	Bark Beetle (family)
Snails	Gastropoda (Class)
Snowshoe Hare	*Lepus americana*
Spiders	Araneae (Order) spp.
Spruce Budworm	*Choristoneura fumiferana*
Whitespotted Sawyer	*Monochamus scutellatus*
Wolf	*Canis* spp.
Wood Frog	*Rana sylvatica*
Wood-boring beetles	Cerambycidae
Worm	Annelida (Phylum)

Appendix 9

Glossary

Term	Definition
aerial insectivores	Those species (swallows, swifts, nightjars) that forage for insect prey in the air column.
aerie	The nest of a bird of prey on a cliff or a mountaintop. Alternatively spelled aery or eyrie.
agricultural ecumene	Areas of significant agricultural activity as indicated by the ratio of agricultural land to total land area, the ratio of total agricultural receipts to total land area, and total agricultural land (Statistics Canada 2003).
alvar	Areas of exposed limestone pavement or very shallow soils over limestone supporting distinct assemblages of plants and animals adapted to extreme variations in temperature and moisture.
arthropods	The largest phylum of animals, characterized by a segmented body, jointed appendages, an exoskeleton and bilateral symmetry. Insects and spiders are familiar arthropods.
Beech Bark Disease	A disease of the American Beech caused by fungi (*Nectria* spp.) transmitted by an insect, Beech Scale (*Cryptococcus fagisuga*). The disease can cause significant mortality in beech and is spreading rapidly in eastern North America.
brood parasite	An animal that lays its eggs in the nests of other species (interspecific brood parasite) or others of its own species (intraspecific brood parasite). Some brood parasites parasitize nests only occcasionally (hemi-parasites), while others such as cowbirds do so regularly (obligate brood parasites).
calidridine	The group of closely related sandpipers, primarily but not exclusively members of the genus Calidris.
chironomids	Members of the insect family Chironomidae (Order Diptera), primitive flies superficially resembling mosquitoes and commonly known as "non-biting midges." Both the larvae (often referred to as "blood worms") and the emerging adults are important food for a variety of bird species.
cloacal protuberance	A swelling of the cloaca in male birds, caused by the accumulation of sperm. The presence of a cloacal protuberance indicates both that the bird is a male and that it is in breeding condition.
congeners	Species belonging to the same genus.
conspecifics	Individuals of the same species.
cooperative breeding	Involves more than two birds of the same species providing care for nestlings from a single nest (e.g., American Crow, Gray Jay).
countersinging	Singing by one individual in direct response to singing by a neighbour so that the songs frequently overlap. In species in which both sexes sing (e.g., wrens), countersinging may occur between the male and female.
corvid	A bird of the Corvidae family of passerine birds that includes crows, ravens, jays, magpies, and nutcrackers.
crèches	An aggregation of young from different broods cared for by multiple parents, particularly colonial-nesting species, including geese.
crepuscular	Active during the hours of twilight at dawn and dusk.
DDT	Dichlorodiphenyltrichloroethane, a persistent organic pollutant that was heavily used to kill insects feeding on crops in the 1950s and 1960s until it was found to be harmful to other forms of life. DDT is banned in Canada.
diurnal	Active during the day.
dump nesting	The laying of eggs by one female in the nest of another, usually of the same species. Dump nesting is particularly common among a number of duck species.
extant	Term applied to taxa, species, genera, or families that are still in existence (i.e., not extinct).

extirpated	Extinct in a region or jurisdiction but still extant elsewhere.
floater	An adult or sub-adult excluded from reproduction but possibly in suitable breeding habitat.
graminoid	Literally, grass-like plants, particularly members of the plant families Poaceae (grasses), Cyperaceae (sedges), and Juncaceae (rushes).
gular pouch	A featherless, distensible pouch below the lower mandible, best developed in pelicans and their relatives, including cormorants.
Holarctic	A zoogeographic region that includes both the Nearctic and Palearctic regions of Eurasia and North America.
interspecific	Between different species, such as hybridization between different species of warblers.
intolerant-mixed woods	See tolerant hardwoods.
intraspecific	Between the same species, such as competition between members of the same species.
introgression	Infiltration of the genes of one species into the gene pool of another through repeated back-crossing of an interspecific hybrid with one of its parents.
isostatic rebound	Also known as post-glacial rebound. The rise of land masses that were depressed by the huge weight of ice sheets during the last ice age.
larid	Any member of the bird family Laridae (gulls and terns).
lek	A communal display ground or mating arena where males of a species display to attract females during the breeding season. Dominant males occupy the more central and conspicuous territories within the lek. Some grouse, shorebird and a few passerine species have lek-based breeding systems.
Lepidoptera	The insect order containing butterflies and moths.
macroinvertebrate	An invertebrate animal (without a backbone) large enough to be seen without magnification.
microtine	Of or relating to the subfamily Microtinae (sometimes Arvicolinae) within the rodent family Muridae, including voles, lemmings, and muskrats.
mimid	Member of the bird family Mimidae, including catbirds, thrashers, and mockingbirds.
monocot (monocotyledon)	Any member of the Monocotyledoneae, one of two major flowering plant divisions, which characteristically produce a single cotyledon (seed leaf) with parallel major veins.
monogamous	Having only one mate during a breeding season or during the breeding life of a pair.
monotypic	Referring to a taxonomic group with only one immediately subordinate taxon.
morphometric	Relating to measurements of the shape of an individual, such as body proportions.
muskeg	A bog of northern North America, commonly having sphagnum mosses, sedge, and sometimes stunted spruce and Tamarack trees. Much of the Hudson Bay Lowlands is muskeg.
Nearctic	A zoogeographic region encompassing Greenland and continental North America north of Mexico.
Newcastle Disease	A highly contagious viral infection of both domesticated and wild birds. Infections may result in acute respiratory distress and death, and can occasionally reach epidemic proportions.
nocturnal	Active at night.
nuptial	Relating to breeding.
oligotrophic	Refers to environments low in nutrients and with a limited capacity to sustain life. Oligotrophic lakes are low-nutrient lakes, whereas eutrophic lakes are those rich in nutrients.
Organochlorine	Any of various hydrocarbon chemicals that contain chlorine, e.g., DDT.
orographic precipitation	Rain or snow generated when a moisture-bearing air mass is forced to rise over a land surface, especially evident on the windward side of mountains.
Palearctic	A zoogeographic region encompassing Europe, Africa north of the tropic of Cancer, the northern part of the Arabian Peninsula, and Asia north of the Himalayas.
PCB	Any of a family of industrial compounds produced by chlorination of biphenyl, noted primarily as an environmental pollutant that accumulates in animal tissue with resultant pathogenic and teratogenic effects.

palsa	A landform feature of subarctic regions, consisting of a mound or ridge of peat created through frost heaving in the presence of a permanent ice lens. A palsa may be either unvegetated or sparsely vegetated with lichens, mosses, and heaths. In areas of wet, discontinuous permafrost, the development of palsas may result in palsa bogs. Palsas may develop in shallow lakes, creating palsa islands, or may coalesce to form palsa plateaus, raised areas supporting sparse spruce-lichen woodlands.
pelagic	Describes an animal relating to, living, or occurring primarily in open waters away from land.
philopatry	Tendency of a migrating animal to return to a specific location in order to breed or feed.
polyandrous	Mating pattern in which a female mates with more than one male in a single breeding season.
polygamous	Mating pattern in which individuals have more than one sexual partner.
polygynandry	Breeding system in which individuals have exclusive relationships with two or more partners (see Smith's Longspur).
polygyny	Mating system in which a male mates with two or several females.
polygynous	Mating pattern in which a male mates with more than one female in a single breeding season.
population ecumene	Inhabited land, defined by Statistics Canada as census blocks with a minimum population density of 0.4 persons per square kilometre (Statistics Canada 2002).
poults	The dependent young of gallinaceous species such as grouse, pheasant, quail, and turkey.
prebasic moult	The moult occurring just after the breeding season.
precocial	A newly hatched chick that is downy, open-eyed, mobile at hatching, and able to find its own food while following parents.
semi-parasitic	Only partially parasitic – a facultative parasite, laying its eggs in the nests of others but also in its own nest. Obligate parasites, such as cowbirds, lay their eggs only in the nests of other species.
semiprecocial	A newly hatched chick that is downy, open-eyed, and mobile at hatching but remains at or near the nest for the first two or three weeks.
sexually dimorphic	Systematically distinguished in form from different-sex individuals of the same species by characteristics such as size, proportions, and plumage colour and pattern.
subspecies	A category in biological classification that ranks immediately below a species and designates a population of a particular geographical region genetically distinguishable from other such populations of the same species and capable of interbreeding successfully with them where its range overlaps theirs.
supra-tidal	Areas occasionally inundated by exceptionally high tides.
sympatry	The occurrence of species together in the same area.
taiga	Northern portions of the Boreal Forest, often wet, and characterized by open, park-like lichen-woodlands dominated by spruce. Sometimes applied more generally to the whole Boreal Forest.
tolerant hardwood	Deciduous tree species such as maple, ash, and oak that are shade tolerant and gradually displace such shade intolerant species as aspen and birch in late-succession forests.
tribe	A taxonomic category placed between a subfamily and a genus or between a suborder and a family and usually containing several genera.
tundra polygons	Polygon-shaped patterning in areas of tundra resulting from repeated freezing and thawing.
Type E Botulism	A disease resulting from the ingestion of toxins produced by the bacterium Clostridium botulinum that produces Type E botulinum toxin. Fish-eating birds such as loons, grebes, waterfowl, gulls, and terns are particularly susceptible to the disease.
ungulate	Any of the hoofed mammals, including both domesticated and wild members of several familes (e.g., Cervidae – deer).

Literature Cited

ABRAHAM, K.F. 2002. Record roundup of Ross's Geese. OFO News 20:1.

ABRAHAM, K.F. 2005. The Cackling Goose: not new to Ontario. OFO News 23:2-6.

ABRAHAM, K.F., and G.H. FINNEY. 1986. Eiders of the eastern Canadian Arctic. Pp. 53-73 in Eider ducks in Canada (A. Reed, Ed.). Can.Wildl.Serv.Rep.Ser. No. 47.

ABRAHAM, K.F., and R.L. JEFFERIES. 1997. High goose populations: causes, impacts, and implications. Pp. 7-72 in Arctic ecosystems in peril: report of the Arctic Goose Habitat Working Group. Arctic Goose Venture Spec.Publ. (B.D.J Batt, Ed.). United States Fish and Wildlife Service, Washington, DC, and Canadian Wildlife Service, Ottawa.

ABRAHAM, K.F., and C.J. KEDDY. 2005. The Hudson Bay Lowland: a unique wetland legacy. Pp. 118-148 in The world's largest wetlands: ecology and conservation (L.H. Fraser and P.A. Keddy, Eds.). Cambridge University Press, Cambridge.

ABRAHAM, K.F., J.O. LEAFLOOR, and H.G. LUMSDEN. 1999. Establishment and growth of the Lesser Snow Goose nesting colony on Akimiski Island, James Bay, Northwest Territories. Can.Field-Nat. 113:245-250.

ABRAHAM, K.F., and N. WILSON. 1997. A collision of Oldsquaws. Ontario Birds 15:29-33.

ADKISSON, C.S. 1996. Red Crossbill (*Loxia curvirostra*). In The Birds of North America, No. 256 (A. Poole and F. Gill, Eds.). Academy of Natural Sciences, Philadelphia and American Ornithologists' Union, Washington, DC.

ADKISSON, C.S. 1999. Pine Grosbeak (*Pinicola enucleator*). In The Birds of North America, No. 456 (A. Poole and F. Gill, Eds.). The Birds of North America, Inc., Philadelphia.

AFTON, A.D. 1984. Influence of age and time on reproductive performance of female Lesser Scaup. Auk 101:255-265.

AHLERING, M.A., and J. FAABORG. 2006. Avian habitat management meets conspecific attraction: if you build it, will they come? Auk 123:301-312.

ALISAUSKAS, R.T., and T.W. ARNOLD. 1994. American Coot. Pp. 127-143 in Migratory shore and upland game bird management in North America (T.C. Tacha and C.E. Braun, Eds.). International Association of Fish and Wildlife Agencies, Washington, DC.

ALISON, R.M. 1975. Breeding biology and behavior of the Oldsquaw (*Clangula hyemalis* L.), Ornithol.Monogr. No.18. American Ornithologists' Union, Tampa.

ALISON, R.M. 1976. The history of the Wild Turkey in Ontario. Can.Field-Nat. 90:481-485.

ALLEN, A.W. 1984. Habitat suitability index models: Gray Partridge. Habitat Evaluation Procedures Group, Western Energy and Land Use Team, U.S. Fish and Wildlife Service.

ALTMAN, B., and R. SALLABANKS. 2000. Olive-sided Flycatcher (*Contopus cooperi*). In The Birds of North America, No. 502 (A. Poole and F. Gill, Eds.). The Birds of North America, Inc., Philadelphia.

ALVO, R., and M. ROBERT. 1999. COSEWIC status report on Yellow Rail (*Coturnicops noveboracensis*) in Canada. Committee on the Status of Endangered Wildlife in Canada, Ottawa.

ALVO, R., C. BLOMME, and D.V. WESELOH. 2002. Double-crested Cormorants, *Phalacrocorax auritus*, at inland lakes north of Lake Huron. Can.Field-Nat. 116:359-365.

AMERICAN ORNITHOLOGISTS' UNION. 1973. Thirty-second supplement to the American Ornithologists' Union Check-list of North American Birds. Auk 90:411-419.

AMERICAN ORNITHOLOGISTS' UNION. 1993. Thirty-ninth supplement to the American Ornithologists' Union Check-list of North American Birds. Auk 110:675-682.

AMERICAN ORNITHOLOGISTS' UNION. 1995. Fortieth supplement to the American Ornithologists' Union Check-list of North American Birds. Auk 112:819-830.

AMERICAN ORNITHOLOGISTS' UNION. 1998. Check-list of North American birds. 7th ed. American Ornithologists' Union, Washington, DC.

AMERICAN ORNITHOLOGISTS' UNION. 2000. Forty-second supplement to the American Ornithologists' Union Check-list of North American Birds. Auk 117:847-858.

AMERICAN ORNITHOLOGISTS' UNION. 2006. Check-list of North American Birds, 7th ed., including supplements 42 to 47. http://www.aou.org/checklist/index.php3.

AMMON, E.M. 1995. Lincoln's Sparrow (*Melospiza lincolnii*). In The Birds of North America, No. 191 (A. Poole and F. Gill, Eds.). Academy of Natural Sciences, Philadelphia and American Ornithologists' Union, Washington, DC.

AMMON, E.M., and W.M. GILBERT. 1999. Wilson's Warbler (*Wilsonia pusilla*). In The Birds of North America, No. 478 (A. Poole and F. Gill, Eds.). The Birds of North America, Inc., Philadelphia.

ANDERSEN, D.E., O.J. RONGSTAD, and W.R. MYTTON. 1989. Response of nesting Red-Railed Hawks to helicopter overflights. Condor 91:296-299.

ANDERSON, S.H., and H.H. SHUGART, JR. 1974. Habitat selection of breeding birds in an east Tennessee deciduous forest. Ecology 55:828-837.

ANDERSSON, M., and F. GÖTMARK. 1980. Social organization and foraging ecology in the Arctic Skua *Stercorarius parasiticus*: a test of the food defendability hypothesis. Oikos 35:63-71.

ANDRES, B.A. 1993. Foraging flights of Pacific, *Gavia pacifica*, and Red-throated, *G. stellata*, Loons on Alaska's coastal plain. Can.Field-Nat. 107:238-240.

ANDRLE, R.F., and J.R. CARROLL. 1988. The atlas of breeding birds in New York State. Cornell University Press, Ithaca.

ANGEHREN, P.A.M., H. BLOKPOEL, and P. COURTNEY. 1979. A review of the status of the Great Black-backed Gull in the Great Lakes area. Ont.Field Biol. 33:27-33.

ANKNEY, C.D., D.G. DENNIS, and R.C. BAILEY. 1987. Increasing Mallards, decreasing American Black Ducks: coincidence or cause and effect? J.Wildl.Manage. 51:523-529.

ANONYMOUS. 2003. White-winged Scoter (*Melanitta fusca*) in Sea Duck Information Series. Sea Duck Joint Venture. http://www.seaduckjv.org/infoseries/wwsc_sppfactsheet.pdf

ARCESE, P., M.K. SOGGE, A.B. MARR, and M.A. PATTEN. 2002. Song Sparrow (*Melospiza melodia*). In The Birds of North America, No. 704 (A. Poole and F. Gill, Eds.). The Birds of North America, Inc., Philadelphia.

ARMSTRONG, E.R. 1977. Reproductive biology and ecology of the Mourning Dove in southern Ontario. M.Sc. thesis, University of Guelph.

ARMSTRONG, E.R., and D. EULER. 1983. Habitat usage of two woodland *Buteo* species in central Ontario. Can.Field-Nat. 97:200-207.

ARMSTRONG, E.R., and D.L.G. NOAKES. 1983. Wintering biology of Mourning Doves, *Zenaida macroura*, in Ontario. Can.Field-Nat. 97:434-438.

ARNOLD, T.W., and R.G. CLARK. 1996.

Survival and philopatry of female dabbling ducks in southcentral Saskatchewan. J.Wildl.Manage. 60:560-568.

ASHKENAZIE, S., and U.N. SAFRIEL. 1979. Breeding cycle and behavior of the Semipalmated Sandpiper at Barrow, Alaska. Auk 96:56-67.

ASKINS, R.A. 2000. Restoring North America's birds: lessons from landscape ecology. Yale University Press, New Haven.

ASKINS, R.A. 2002. Restoring North America's birds: lessons from landscape ecology. 2nd ed. Yale University Press, New Haven.

ASSOCIATION of MUNICIPALITIES OF ONTARIO. 2007. Ontario municipal home pages. http://www.amp.on.ca/YLG/ylg/ontario.html Accessed 24 April 2007.

AUSTEN, M.J., H. BLOKPOEL, and G.D. TESSIER. 1996. Atlas of colonial waterbirds nesting on the Canadian Great Lakes 1989-1991. Part 4, Marsh-nesting terns on Lake Huron and the lower Great Lakes system in 1991. Canadian Wildlife Service, Ontario Region.

AUSTEN, M.J.W., M.D. CADMAN, and R.D. JAMES. 1994. Ontario birds at risk: status and conservation needs. Federation of Ontario Naturalists and Long Point Bird Observatory, Don Mills.

AUSTIN, J.E., A.D. AFTON, M.G. ANDERSON, R.G. CLARK, C.M. CUSTER, J.S. LAWRENCE, J.B. POLLARD, and J.K. RINGELMAN. 2000. Declining scaup populations: issues, hypotheses, and research needs. Wildl.Soc.Bull. 28:254-263.

AUSTIN, J.E., C.M. CUSTER, and A.D. AFTON. 1998. Lesser Scaup (*Aythya affinis*). *In* The Birds of North America, No. 338 (A. Poole and F. Gill, Eds.). The Birds of North America, Inc., Philadelphia.

AUSTIN, J.E., and M.R. MILLER. 1995. Northern Pintail (*Anas acuta*). *In* The Birds of North America, No. 163 (A. Poole and F. Gill, Eds.). Academy of Natural Sciences, Philadelphia, and American Ornithologists' Union, Washington, DC.

AVERY, M.L. 1995. Rusty Blackbird (*Euphagus carolinus*). *In* The Birds of North America, No. 200 (A. Poole and F. Gill, Eds.). Academy of Natural Sciences, Philadelphia, and American Ornithologists' Union, Washington, DC.

BAGG, A.M., and H.M. PARKER. 1951. The Turkey Vulture in New England and eastern Canada up to 1950. Auk 68:315-333.

BAICICH, P.J., and C.J.O. HARRISON. 1997. A guide to the nests, eggs, and nestlings of North American birds. Academic Press, San Diego.

BAILLIE, J.L., JR. 1925. The Hooded Warbler (*Wilsonia citrina*) in Ontario. Can.Field-Nat. 39:150-151.

BAILLIE, J.L., JR. 1939. Four additional breeding birds of Ontario. Can.Field-Nat. 53:130-131.

BAILLIE, J.L., JR. 1957. Recent additions to Ontario's bird list. Ont.Field Biol. 11:1-3.

BAILLIE, J.L., JR. 1960. New Ontario breeding birds. Ont.Field Biol. 14:14-23.

BAILLIE, J.L., JR. 1961. More new Ontario breeding birds. Ont.Field Biol. 15:1-9.

BAILLIE, J.L., JR. 1962. Fourteen additional Ontario breeding birds. Ont.Field Biol. 16:1-15.

BAILLIE, J.L., JR. 1963. The 13 most recent Ontario nesting birds. Ont.Field Biol. 17:15-26.

BAILLIE, J.L., JR., and P. HARRINGTON. 1936. The distribution of breeding birds in Ontario, part 1. Trans.R.Can.Inst. 21:1-150.

BAILLIE, J.L., JR., and P. HARRINGTON. 1937. The distribution of breeding birds in Ontario, part 2. Trans.R.Can.Inst. 21:199-283.

BAILLIE, J.L., JR., and C.E. HOPE. 1943. The summer birds of the northeast shore of Lake Superior, Ontario. R.Ont.Mus.Zool.Contrib. 23:1-27.

BAILLIE, J.L., JR., and C.E. HOPE. 1947. The summer birds of Sudbury District, Ontario. R.Ont.Mus.Zool.Contrib. 28:1-32.

BAIN, M. 1993. Ontario Bird Records Committee report for 1992. Ontario Birds 11:46-63.

BAKOWSKY W. 1999. Rare vegetation of Ontario: tallgrass prairie and savannah. Ontario Natural Heritage Information Centre Newsletter 5[1]. Ontario Ministry of Natural Resources.

BALDWIN, D.J.B., J.R. DESLOGES, and L.E. BAND. 2000. Physical geography of Ontario. Pp. 12-29 *in* Ecology of a managed terrestrial landscape: patterns and processes of forest landscapes in Ontario (A.H. Perera, D.L. Euler, and I.D. Thompson, Eds.). UBC Press, Vancouver.

BALTZ, M.E., and S.C. LATTA. 1998. Cape May Warbler (*Dendroica tigrina*). *In* The Birds of North America, No. 332 (A. Poole and F. Gill, Eds.). The Birds of North America, Inc., Philadelphia.

BANKS, R.C., C. CICERO, J.L. DUNN, A.W. KRATTER, P.C. RASMUSSEN, J.V. REMSEN, JR., J.D. RISING, and D.F. STOTZ. 2002. Forty-third supplement to the American Ornithologists' Union check-list of North American Birds. Auk 119:897-906.

BANKS, R.C., C. CICERO, J.L. DUNN, A.W. KRATTER, P.C. RASMUSSEN, J.V. REMSEN, JR., J.D. RISING, and D.F. STOTZ. 2003. Forty-fourth supplement to the American Ornithologists' Union check-list of North American Birds. Auk 120:923-931.

BANKS, R.C., C. CICERO, J.L. DUNN, A.W. KRATTER, P.C. RASMUSSEN, J.V. REMSEN, JR., J.D. RISING, and D.F. STOTZ. 2004. Forty-fifth supplement to the American Ornithologists' Union check-list of North American Birds. Auk 121:985-995.

BANKS, R.C., C. CICERO, J.L. DUNN, A.W. KRATTER, P.C. RASMUSSEN, J.V. REMSEN, JR., J.D. RISING, and D.F. STOTZ. 2006. Forty-seventh supplement to the American Ornithologists' Union check-list of North American Birds. Auk 123:926-936.

BANNOR, B.K., and E. KIVIAT. 2002. Common Moorhen (*Gallinula chloropus*). *In* The Birds of North America, No. 685 (A. Poole and F. Gill, Eds.). The Birds of North America, Inc., Philadelphia.

BARG, J.J., J. JONES, and R.J. ROBERTSON. 2005. Describing breeding territories of migratory passerines: suggestions for sampling, choice of estimator, and delineation of core areas. J. Anim. Ecol. 74:139-149.

BARNETT, P.J. 1992. Quaternary geology of Ontario. Pp. 1011-1088 *in* Geology of Ontario. Ontario Geological Survey, Spec.Vol. 4, part 2. (P.C. Thurston, H.R. Williams, R.H. Sutcliffe, and G.M. Scott, Eds.). Ontario Ministry of Northern Development and Mines, Toronto.

BARNETT, P.J., R.W. COWAN, and A.P. HENRY 1991. Quaternary Geology of Ontario, southern sheet. Ontario Geological Survey, Map 2556.

BARNETT, P.J., A.P. HENRY, and D. BABUIN 1991. Quaternary Geology of Ontario, west-central sheet. Ontario Geological Survey, Map 2554

BARNETT, P.J., A.P. HENRY, and D. BABUIN. 1991. Quaternary Geology of Ontario, east-central sheet. Ontario Geological Survey, Map 2555.

BARR, J.F. 1973. Feeding biology of the Common Loon (*Gavia immer*) in oligotrophic lakes of the pre-Cambrian shield. Ph.D. dissertation, University of Guelph.

BARR, J.F., C. EBERL, and J.W. MCINTYRE. 2000. Red-throated Loon (*Gavia stellata*). *In* The Birds of North America, No. 513 (A. Poole and F. Gill, Eds.). The Birds of North America, Inc., Philadelphia.

BART, J., R.A. STEHN, J.A. HERRICK, N.A. HEASLIP, T.A. BOOKHOUT, and J.R. STENZEL. 1984. Survey methods for breeding Yellow Rails. J.Wildl.Manage. 48:1382-1386.

BART, J., S. BROWN, B. HARRINGTON, and R.I.G. MORRISON. 2007. Survey trends of North American shorebirds: population declines or shifting distributions? J.Avian Biol. 38:73-82.

BAVRLIC, K., D.M. BURKE, E. NOL, and K. ELLIOT. In press. Nest cavity and tree reuse patterns of cavity-dependent vertebrates in partially harvested woodlots of southwestern Ontario. J.Wildl.Manage.

BEARDSLEE, C.S., and H.D. MITCHELL. 1965. Birds of the Niagara Frontier region. Bull.Buffalo Soc.Nat.Sci. 22:1-478.

BEASON, R.C. 1995. Horned Lark (*Eremophila alpestris*). *In* The Birds of North America, No. 195 (A. Poole and F. Gill, Eds.). Academy of Natural Sciences, Philadelphia, and American Ornithologists' Union, Washington, DC.

BECHARD, M.J., R.L. KNIGHT, D.G. SMITH, and R.E. FITZNER. 1990. Nest sites and habitats of sympatric hawks (*Buteo* spp.) in Washington. J.Field Ornithol. 61:159-170.

BECHARD, M.J., and T.R. SWEM. 2002. Rough-legged Hawk (*Buteo lagopus*). *In* The Birds of North America, No. 641 (A. Poole and F. Gill, Eds.).The Birds of North America, Inc., Philadelphia.

BELL, J.L., and R.C. WHITMORE. 1997. Eastern Towhee numbers increase following defoliation by Gypsy Moths. Auk 114:708-716.

BELLERBY, G., D.A. KIRK, and D.V.C. WESELOH. 2000. Staging Little Gulls, (*Larus minutus*), on the Niagara River, Ontario, 1987-1996. Can.Field-Nat. 114:584-590.

BELLROSE, F.C. 1980. Ducks, geese and swans of North America. 3rd ed. Stackpole Books, Harrisburg.

BELLROSE, F.C., and D.J. HOLM. 1994. Ecology and management of the Wood Duck. Wildlife Management Institute, Illinois. Natural History Survey and Stackpole Books, Mechanicsburg.

BELTHOFF, J.R., E.J. SPARKS, and G. RITCHISON. 1993. Home ranges of adult and juvenile Eastern Screech-Owls: size, seasonal variation and extent of overlap. J.Raptor Res. 27:8-15.

BENGTSON, S.A. 1970. Location of nest-sites of ducks in Lake M?vatn area, north-east Iceland. Oikos 21:218-229.

BENGTSON, S.A. 1971. Habitat selection of duck broods in Lake Myvatn area, north-east Iceland. Ornis Scand. 2:17-26.

BENKMAN, C.W. 1985. The foraging ecology of crossbills in eastern North America. Ph.D. dissertation, State University of New York, Albany.

BENKMAN, C.W. 1989. Breeding opportunities, foraging rates, and parental care in White-winged Crossbills. Auk 106:483-485.

BENKMAN, C.W. 1990. Foraging rates and timing of crossbill reproduction. Auk 107:376-386.

BENKMAN, C.W. 1992. White-winged Crossbill (*Loxia leucoptera*). *In* The Birds of North America, No. 27 (A. Poole and F. Gill, Eds.). Academy of Natural Sciences, Philadelphia, and American Ornithologists' Union, Washington, DC.

BENNETT, W.A. 1990. Scale of investigation and the detection of competition: an example from the House Sparrow and House Finch introductions in North America. Am.Nat. 135:725-747.

BENT, A.C. 1926. Life histories of North American marsh birds. Bull.U.S.Natl.Mus. No. 135.

BENT, A.C. 1929. Life histories of North American shorebirds, part 2. Bull.U.S.Natl.Mus. No. 146.

BENT, A.C. 1932. Life histories of North American gallinaceous birds. Bull.U.S.Natl.Mus. No. 162.

BENT, A.C. 1939. Life histories of North American woodpeckers. Bull.U.S.Natl.Mus. No. 174.

BENT, A.C. 1942. Life histories of North American flycatchers, larks, swallows, and allies. Bull.U.S.Natl.Mus. No. 179.

BENT, A.C. 1953. Life histories of North American wood warblers. Bull.U.S.Natl.Mus. No. 203.

BENT, A.C. 1958. Life histories of North American blackbirds, orioles, tanagers, and allies. Bull.U.S.Natl.Mus. No. 211.

BENT, A.C. 1989. Life histories of North American cuckoos, goatsuckers, hummingbirds, and their allies. Dover, Mineola.

BENTON, T.G., D.M. BRYANT, L. COLE, and H.Q.P. CRICK. 2002. Linking agricultural practice to insect and bird populations: a historical study over three decades. J.Appl.Ecol. 39:673-687.

BERGMAN, R.D., and D.V. DERKSEN. 1977. Observations on Arctic and Red-throated Loons at Storkersen Point, Alaska. Arctic 30:41-51.

BEVIER, L., A.F. POOLE , and W. MOSKOFF. 2004. Veery (*Catharus fuscescens*). The Birds of North America Online (A. Poole, Ed.). Cornell Laboratory of Ornithology. Retrieved from The Birds of North America Online Database, Ithaca. http://bna.birds.cornell.edu/BNA/account/Veery/.

BEYER, L.K. 1938. Nest life of the Bank Swallow. Wilson Bull. 50:122-137.

BILDSTEIN, K.L., and K. MEYER. 2000. Sharp-shinned Hawk (*Accipiter striatus*). *In* The Birds of North America, No. 482 (A. Poole and F. Gill, Eds.).The Birds of North America, Inc., Philadelphia.

BIRD, D.M., K.L. BILDSTEIN, D.R. ARDIA, K. STEENHOF, J.A. SMALLWOOD, J. MASON, M. MAURER, M.F. CAUSEY, D.H. MOSSOP, A. DIBERNARDO, R. LINDSAY, D. MCCARTNEY, and J. HENDRICKSON. 2004. Are American Kestrel populations in a state of decline in North America? *In* 2004 annual meeting of the Raptor Research Foundation, November 10-13, 2004. Raptor Research Foundation, Bakersfield.

BIRKHEAD, T.R. 1991. The magpies: the ecology and behaviour of Black-billed and Yellow-billed Magpies. T. & A.D. Poyser Ltd., London.

BLACKSHAW, S.H. 1988. Identifying the Eurasian Collared-Dove. Birding 20:311-312.

BLANCHER, P.J. 1978. Habitat distribution of the Eastern Kingbird (*Tyrannus tyrannus*). The influence of intraspecific competition. M.Sc. thesis, Dept. of Biology, Queen's University, Kingston.

BLANCHER, P.J. 2003. The importance of Canada's Boreal Forest to landbirds. Canadian Boreal Initiative, Boreal Songbird Initiative, Bird Studies Canada, Port Rowan.

BLANCHER, P.J., K.V. ROSENBER, A.O. PANJABI, B. ALTMAN, J. BART, C.J. BEARDMORE, G.S. BUTCHER, D. DEMAREST, R. DETTMERS, E.H. DUNN, W. EASTON, W.C. HUNTER, E.E. IÑIGO-ELIAS, D.N. PASHLEY, C.J. RALPH, T.D. RICH, C.M. RUSTAY, J.M. RUTH, and T.C. WILL. 2007. Guide to the Partners in Flight population estimates database. Version: North American Landbird Conservation Plan 2004. http://www.partnersinflight.org/pubs/ts/.

BLOCKSTEIN, D.E. 2002. Passenger Pigeon (*Ectopistes migratorius*). *In* The Birds of North America, No. 611 (A. Poole and F. Gill, Eds.).The Birds of North America, Inc., Philadelphia.

BLOKPOEL, H., and G.D. TESSIER. 1991. Distribution and abundance of colonial waterbirds nesting in the Canadian portions of the lower Great Lakes system in 1990. Canadian Wildlife Service.

BLOKPOEL, H., and G.D. TESSIER. 1993. Atlas of colonial waterbirds nesting on the Canadian Great Lakes, 1989-1991. Part 1, Cormorants, gulls and island-nesting terns on Lake Superior in 1989. Canadian Wildlife Service, Ontario Region.

BLOKPOEL, H., and G.D. TESSIER. 1996. Atlas of colonial waterbirds nesting on the Canadian Great Lakes, 1989-1991. Part 3, Cormorants, gulls and island-nesting terns on the lower Great Lakes system in 1990. Canadian Wildlife Service, Ontario Region.

BLOKPOEL, H., and G.D. TESSIER. 1997. Atlas of colonial waterbirds nesting on the Canadian Great Lakes, 1989-1991. Part 2, Cormorants, gulls and island-nesting terns on Lake Huron in 1989. Canadian Wildlife Service, Ontario Region.

BLOKPOEL, H., and G.D. TESSIER. 1998. Atlas of colonial waterbirds nesting on the Canadian Great Lakes, 1989-1991. Part 5, Herons and egrets in 1991. Canadian Wildlife Service, Nepean.

BOAG, D.A., and M.A. SCHROEDER. 1992. Spruce Grouse (*Falcipennis canadensis*). *In* The Birds of North America, No. 5 (A. Poole , A., P. Stettenheim, and F. Gill, Eds.). Academy of Natural Sciences, Philadelphia, and American Ornithologists' Union, Washington, DC.

BOARMAN, W.I., and B. HEINRICH. 1999. Common Raven (*Corvus corax*). *In* The Birds of North America, No. 476 (A. Poole and F. Gill, Eds.).The Birds of North America, Inc., Philadelphia.

BOCK, C.E., and L.W. LEPTHIEN. 1975. Distribution and abundance of the Black-billed Magpie (*Pica pica*) in North America. Great Basin Nat. 35:269-272.

BOLGIANO, N.C. 2004. Cause and effect: changes in boreal bird irruptions in Eastern North America relative to the 1970s Spruce Budworm infestation. Amer.Birds 58:26-33.

BOLLINGER, K.S. 2005. Waterfowl breeding population and habitat survey for Western Ontario, Statum 50. US Fish and Wildlife Service.

BOOKHOUT, T.A. 1995. Yellow Rail (*Coturnicops noveboracensis*). *In* The Birds of North America, No. 139 (A. Poole and F. Gill, Eds.).Academy of Natural Sciences, Philadelphia, and American Ornithologists' Union, Washington, DC.

BORDAGE, D., and J.L. SAVARD. 1995. Black Scoter (*Melanitta nigra*). *In* The Birds of North America, No. 177 (A. Poole and F. Gill, Eds.).Academy of Natural Sciences, Philadelphia, and American Ornithologists' Union, Washington, DC.

BOSAKOWSKI, T., R. KANE, and D.G. SMITH. 1989. Decline of the Long-eared Owl in New Jersey. Wilson Bull. 101:481-485.

BOSAKOWSKI, T., and D.G. SMITH. 1997. Distribution and species richness of a forest raptor community in relation to urbanization. J.Raptor Res. 31:26-33.

BOUSFIELD, M.A., I.R. KIRKHAM, and R.D. MCRAE. 1986. Breeding of Wilson's Phalarope, *Phalaropus tricolor*, at Churchill, Manitoba. Can.Field-Nat. 100:392-393.

BOUTIN, C., K.E. FREEMARK, and D.A. KIRK. 1999. Farmland birds in southern Ontario: field use, activity patterns and vulnerability to pesticide use. Agr.Ecosyst.Environ. 72:239-254.

BOUVIER, J.M. 1974. Breeding biology of the Hooded Merganser in southwestern Quebec, including interactions with Common Goldeneyes and Wood Ducks. Can.Field-Nat. 88:323-330.

BOWMAN, I., and J. SIDERIUS. 1984. Management guidelines for the protection of heronries in Ontario. Ontario Ministry of Natural Resources, Wildlife Branch, Toronto. http://ontarios-forests.mnr.gov.on.ca/guides.cfm.

BOYER, G.F., and O.E. DEVITT. 1961. A significant increase in the birds of Luther Marsh, Ontario, following freshwater impoundment. Can.Field-Nat. 75:225-237.

BRAUNE, B.M. 1989. Autumn migration and comments on the breeding range of Bonaparte's Gull, *Larus philadelphia*, in Eastern North America. Can.Field-Nat. 103:524-530.

BRAWN, J.D., and S.K. ROBINSON. 1996. Source-sink population dynamics may complicate the interpretation of long-term census data. Ecology 77:3-12.

BRENNAN, L.A. 1999. Northern Bobwhite (*Colinus virginianus*). *In* The Birds of North America, No. 397 (A. Poole and F. Gill, Eds.).The Birds of North America, Inc., Philadelphia.

BRENNAN, L.A., and W.P. KUVLESKY. 2005. North American grassland birds: an unfolding conservation crisis? J.Wildl.Manage. 69:1-13.

BREWER, D., A.W. DIAMOND, E.J. WOODSWORTH, B.T. COLLINS, and E.H. DUNN. 2000. Canadian atlas of bird banding, Vol. 1: Doves, cuckoos and hummingbirds through passerines, 1921-1995. Canadian Wildlife Service, Ottawa.

BREWER, D., and B.K. MACKAY. 2001. Wrens, dippers and thrashers: a guide to the wrens, dippers, and thrashers of the world. Yale University Press, New Haven.

BREWER, R., G.A. MCPEEK, and R.J. ADAMS, JR. 1991. The atlas of breeding birds of Michigan. Michigan State University Press, East Lansing.

BRISBIN, I.L., JR., and T.B. MOWBRAY. 2002. American Coot (*Fulica americana*) and Hawaiian Coot (*Fulica alai*). *In* The Birds of North America, No. 697 (A. Poole and F. Gill, Eds.).The Birds of North America, Inc., Philadelphia.

BRISKIE, J.V. 1993. Smith's Longspur (*Calcarius pictus*). *In* The Birds of North America, No. 34 (A. Poole, P. Stettenheim, and F. Gill, Eds.). Academy of Natural Sciences, Philadelphia, and American Ornithologists' Union, Washington, DC.

BRISKIE, J.V. 1994. Least Flycatcher (*Empidonax minimus*). *In* The Birds of North America, No. 99 (A. Poole and F. Gill, Eds.).Academy of Natural Sciences, Philadelphia, and American Ornithologists' Union, Washington, DC.

BROMMER, J.E. 2004. The range margins of northern birds shift polewards. Ann.Zool.Fennici 41:391-397.

BROOKS, R.P., and W.J. DAVIS. 1987. Habitat selection by breeding Belted Kingfishers (*Ceryle alcyon*). Amer.Midl.Nat. 117:63-70.

BROWN, C.R. 1997. Purple Martin (*Progne subis*). *In* The Birds of North America, No. 287 (A. Poole and F. Gill, Eds.). Academy of Natural Sciences, Philadelphia, and American Ornithologists' Union, Washington, DC.

BROWN, C.R., and M.B. BROWN. 1995. Cliff Swallow (*Petrochelidon pyrrhonota*). *In* The Birds of North America, No. 149 (A. Poole and F. Gill, Eds.). Academy of Natural Sciences, Philadelphia, and American Ornithologists' Union, Washington, DC.

BROWN, P.W., and L.H. FREDRICKSON. 1997. White-winged Scoter (*Melanitta fusca*). *In* The Birds of North America, No. 274 (A. Poole and F. Gill, Eds.). Academy of Natural Sciences, Philadelphia, and American Ornithologists' Union, Washington, DC.

BROWN S., C. DUNCAN, J. CHARDINE, and M. HOWE. 2005. Version 1.0. Red-necked Phalarope research, monitoring and conservation plan for the northeastern U.S. and Maritime Canada. http://www.whsrn.org/data/Unsorted/RNPHConservationPlanforNE-USandCanad0604-05-20519-1.pdf.

BRUA, R.B. 2001. Ruddy Duck (*Oxyura jamaicensis*). *In* The Birds of North America, No. 696 (A. Poole and F. Gill, Eds.). The Birds of North America, Inc., Philadelphia.

BRUGGINK, J.G., T.C. TACHA, J.C. DAVIES, and K.F. ABRAHAM. 1994. Nest and brood-rearing ecology of Mississippi Valley population Canada Geese. Wildlife Monogr. 126:5-39.

BRUNTON, D.F., and W.J. CRINS. 1975. Status and habitat preference of the Yellow-bellied Flycatcher in Algonquin Park, Ontario. Ont.Field Biol. 29:25-28.

BRYAN, S. 1991. Pelicans nesting on Lake Nipigon. Ontario Birds 9:58-63.

BUEHLER, D.A. 2000. Bald Eagle (*Haliaeetus leucocephalus*). *In* The Birds of North America, No. 506 (A. Poole and F. Gill, Eds.). The Birds of North America, Inc., Philadelphia.

BUFFINGTON, J.M., J.C. KILGO, R.A. SARGENT, K.V. MILLER, and B.R. CHAPMAN. 1997. Comparison of breeding bird communities in bottomland hardwood forests of different successional stages. Wilson Bull. 109:314-319.

BULL, E.L., and J.R. DUNCAN. 1993. Great Gray Owl (*Strix nebulosa*). In The Birds of North America, No. 41 (A. Poole and F. Gill, Eds.). Academy of Natural Sciences, Philadelphia, and American Ornithologists' Union, Washington, DC.

BULL, E.L., and M.G. HENJUM. 1990. Ecology of the Great Gray Owl. U.S. Department of Agriculture, Forest Service, Portland.

BULL, E.L., and J.E. JACKSON. 1995. Pileated Woodpecker (*Dryocopus pileatus*). In The Birds of North America, No. 148 (A. Poole and F. Gill, Eds.). Academy of Natural Sciences, Philadelphia, and American Ornithologists' Union, Washington, DC.

BURGER, J., and M. GOCHFELD. 2002. Bonaparte's Gull (*Larus philadelphia*). In The Birds of North America, No. 634 (A. Poole and F. Gill, Eds.). The Birds of North America, Inc., Philadelphia.

BURKE, D.M., and E. NOL. 1998. Influence of food abundance, nest-site habitat, and forest fragmentation on breeding Ovenbirds. Auk 115:96-104.

BURKE, P.S., J.D. MCCRACKEN, C.D. JONES, D.A. SUTHERLAND, R.C. RIDOUT, and M.E. OBBARD. 2007 (in press). First documented nests of Hoary Redpoll in Ontario. Ontario Birds.

BURKE, P.S., M.E. OBBARD, D.A. SUTHERLAND, C.D. JONES, J.D. MCCRACKEN, and R. RIDOUT. 2006. First documented nest of Stilt Sandpiper in Ontario. Ontario Birds 24:75-83.

BURNESS, G.P., R.D. MORRIS, and J.P. BRUCE. 1994. Seasonal and annual variation in brood attendance, prey type delivered to chicks, and foraging patterns of male Common Terns (*Sterna hirundo*). Can.J.Zool. 72:1243-1251.

BUSH, P.G. 2006. A multi-scale analysis of Northern Goshawk habitat in Ontario. Ph.D. dissertation, University of Western Ontario, London.

BUTCHER, G.S. and NIVEN, D.K. 2007. Combining data from the Christmas Bird Count and the Breeding Bird Survey to determine the continental status and trends of North America Birds. 34 pp. National Audobon Society, Ivyland. http://www.audubon.org/bird/stateofthebirds/CBID/content/Report.pdf.

BUTLER, R.G., and D.E. BUCKLEY. 2002. Black Guillemot (*Cepphus grylle*). In The Birds of North America, No. 675 (A. Poole and F. Gill, Eds.). The Birds of North America, Inc., Philadelphia.

BUTLER, R.W. 1992. Great Blue Heron (*Ardea herodias*). In The Birds of North America, No. 25 (A. Poole, P. Stettenheim, and F. Gill, Eds.). Academy of Natural Sciences, Philadelphia, and American Ornithologists' Union, Washington, DC.

BUTLER, R.W. 1997. The Great Blue Heron. UBC Press, Vancouver.

CABE, P.R. 1993. European Starling (*Sturnus vulgaris*). In The Birds of North America, No. 48 (A. Poole and F. Gill, Eds.). Academy of Natural Sciences, Philadelphia, and American Ornithologists' Union, Washington, DC.

CADE, T.J. 1967. Ecological and behavioral aspects of predation by the Northern Shrike. Living Bird 6:43-86.

CADE, T.J. 1982. The falcons of the world. Cornell University Press, Ithaca.

CADE, T.J., and E.C. ATKINSON. 2002. Northern Shrike (*Lanius excubitor*). In The Birds of North America, No. 671 (A. Poole and F. Gill, Eds.). The Birds of North America, Inc., Philadelphia.

CADE, T.J., and W.A. BURNHAM. 2003. Return of the Peregrine: a North American saga of tenacity and teamwork. The Peregrine Fund, Boise.

CADMAN, M.D. 1986. Status report on the Loggerhead Shrike (*Lanius ludovicianus*) in Canada. Committee on the Status of Endangered Wildlife in Canada, Ottawa.

CADMAN, M.D. 1993. Status report on the Northern Harrier *Circus cyaneus* in Canada. Committee on the Status of Endangered Wildlife in Canada.

CADMAN, M.D., P.F.J. EAGLES, and F.M. HELLEINER. 1987. Atlas of the breeding birds of Ontario. University of Waterloo Press, Waterloo.

CAFFREY, C. 1992. Female-biased delayed dispersal and helping in American Crows. Auk 109:609-619.

CAMPBELL, B.H. 1990. Factors affecting the nesting success of Dusky Canada Geese, *Branta canadensis occidentalis*, on the Copper River Delta, Alaska. Can.Field-Nat. 104:567-574.

CAMPBELL, C.A. 1975. Distribution and breeding success of the Loggerhead Shrike in southern Ontario. Can.Wildl.Serv.Rep. No. 6065.

CAMPBELL, R.S., F.C. COSBY, and C.J. WHITELAW. 1998. Nesting of the Northern Hawk Owl on Manitoulin Island in 1997. Ontario Birds 16:5-10.

CAMPBELL, R.W., N.K. DAWE, I. MCTAGGART-COWAN, J.M. COOPER, G.W. KAISER, and M.C.E. MCNALL. 1990. The birds of British Columbia, Vol. 1, Nonpasserines: introduction, loons through waterfowl. Royal British Columbia Museum, Victoria.

CAMPBELL, R.W., N.K. DAWE, I. MCTAGGART-COWAN, J.M. COOPER, G.W. KAISER, M.C.E. MCNALL, and G.E.J. SMITH. 1997. The birds of British Columbia, Vol. 3, Passerines: flycatchers through vireos. UBC Press, Vancouver.

CANADIAN COUNCIL OF FOREST MINISTERS. 1998. Compendium of Canadian forestry statistics. http://www.nfdp.ccfm.org.

CANADIAN WILDLIFE SERVICE WATERFOWL COMMITTEE. 2005. Population status of migratory game birds in Canada: November 2005. Canadian Wildlife Service.

CANADIAN WILDLIFE SERVICE WATERFOWL COMMITTEE. 2006. Population status of migratory game birds in Canada: November 2006. Canadian Wildlife Service.

CANNINGS, R.J. 1993. Northern Saw-whet Owl (*Aegolius acadicus*). In The Birds of North America, No. 42 (A. Poole and F. Gill, Eds.). Academy of Natural Sciences, Philadelphia, and American Ornithologists' Union, Washington, DC.

CARLETON, T.J. 2000. Vegetation responses to the managed forest landscape of central and northern Ontario. Pp. 178-197 in Ecology of a managed terrestrial landscape – patterns and processes of forest landscapes in Ontario (A.H. Perera, D. Euler, and I. Thompson, Eds.). UBC Press, Vancouver.

CAREY, M., D.E. BURHANS, and D.A. NELSON. 1994. Field Sparrow (*Spizella pusilla*). In The Birds of North America, No. 103 (A. Poole and F. Gill, Eds.). Academy of Natural Sciences, Philadelphia, and American Ornithologists' Union, Washington, DC.

CARNEY, M. 1999. What was found in the burn. Seasons 39:26-31.

CARPENTIER, A.G. 1989. Western Kingbird nesting in Rainy River District. Ontario Birds 7:33-34.

CARROLL, J.P. 1993. Gray Partridge (*Perdix perdix*). In The Birds of North America, No. 58 (A. Poole and F. Gill, Eds.). Academy of Natural Sciences, Philadelphia, and American Ornithologists' Union, Washington, DC.

CASTRALE, J.S., E.M. HOPKINS, and C.E. KELLER. 1998. Atlas of breeding birds of Indiana. Indiana Dep. Nat. Resour., Indianapolis.

CAVITT, J.F., and C.A. HAAS. 2000. Brown Thrasher (*Toxostoma rufum*). In The Birds of North America, No. 557 (A. Poole and F. Gill, Eds.). The Birds of North America, Inc., Philadelphia.

CHABOT, A., and C.M. FRANCIS. 1996. Are

marshes Areas of Concern? LPBO Newsletter 28:3-5.

CHABOT, A.A., D.M. BIRD, and R.D. TITMAN. 2001a. Breeding biology and nesting success of Loggerhead Shrikes in Ontario. Wilson Bull. 113:285-289.

CHABOT, A.A., R.D. TITMAN, and D.M. BIRD. 2001b. Habitat use by Loggerhead Shrikes in Ontario and Quebec. Can.Jour.Zool. 79:916-925.

CHAPMAN, F.M. 1968. The warblers of North America. Dover Publ., New York.

CHAPMAN, L.J., and D.F. PUTNAM. 1984. The physiography of southern Ontario. Ontario Geological Survey, Spec.Vol. 2, 3rd ed. Ontario Research Foundation, Ontario Geological Survey, Toronto.

CHESKEY, E.D. 1990. Red-breasted Nuthatch nesting in residential Waterloo. Ontario Birds 8:71-75.

CHEVEAU, M., P. DRAPEAU, L. IMBEAU, and Y. BERGERON. 2004. Owl winter irruptions as an indicator of small mammal population cycles in the boreal forest of eastern North America. Oikos 107:190-198.

CHILTON, G., M.C. BAKER, C.D. BARRENTINE, and M.A. CUNNINGHAM. 1995. White-crowned Sparrow (*Zonotrichia leucophrys*). In The Birds of North America, No. 183 (A. Poole and F. Gill, Eds.). Academy of Natural Sciences, Philadelphia, and American Ornithologists' Union, Washington, DC.

CIARANCA, M.A., C.C. ALLIN, and G.S. JONES. 1997. Mute Swan (*Cygnus olor*). In The Birds of North America, No. 273 (A. Poole and F. Gill, Eds.). Academy of Natural Sciences, Philadelphia, and American Ornithologists' Union, Washington, DC.

CIMPRICH, D.A., and F.R. MOORE. 1995. Gray Catbird (*Dumetella carolinensis*). In The Birds of North America, No. 167 (A. Poole and F. Gill, Eds.). Academy of Natural Sciences, Philadelphia, and American Ornithologists' Union, Washington, DC.

CINK, C.L. 2002. Whip-poor-will (*Caprimulgus vociferus*). In The Birds of North America, No. 620 (A. Poole and F. Gill, Eds.). The Birds of North America, Inc., Philadelphia.

CINK, C.L., and C.T. COLLINS. 2002. Chimney Swift (*Chaetura pelagica*). In The Birds of North America, No. 646 (A. Poole and F. Gill, Eds.). The Birds of North America, Inc., Philadelphia.

CITY OF TORONTO. 2007. Bird-friendly development guidelines. City of Toronto Green Development Standard. http://www.toronto.ca/lightsout/pdf/development_guidelines.pdf Accessed 11 September 2007.

CLARK, R.J. 1972. Observations of nesting Marsh Hawks in Manitoba. Blue Jay 30:43-48.

CLARK, R.J. 1975. A field study of the Short-eared Owl (*Asio flammeus*) Pontoppidan in North America. Wildlife Monogr. 47:1-67.

COADY, G. 2000. First nest records of Canvasback in Ontario. Ontario Birds 18:115-125.

COADY, G. 2001. First nest record of White-winged Crossbill in the Greater Toronto Area. Ontario Birds 19:101-111.

COADY, G., M.K. PECK, D.H. ELDER, and B. RATCLIFF. 2002. Breeding records of Eared Grebe in Ontario. Ontario Birds 20:106-119.

COADY, G., D.A. SUTHERLAND, C.D. JONES, M.K. PECK, and G. BINSFELD. 2007. First documented nest records of Ross's Goose in Ontario. Ontario Birds 25:16-25.

COHEN, J.B., J.S. BARCLAY, A.R. MAJOR, and J.P. FISHER. 2000. Wintering Greater Scaup as biomonitors of metal contamination in federal wildlife refuges in the Long Island region. Arch.Environ.Contam.Toxicol. 38:83-92.

COLEMAN, J.L., D.M. BIRD, and E.A. JACOBS. 2002. Habitat use and productivity of Sharp-shinned Hawks nesting in an urban area. Wilson Bull. 114:467-473.

COLLIER, B., K. GRAHAM, and D. RAGLIN. 1992 Unpubl. Ontario heronry inventory, 1990-1991; a catalogue of information on colony sites of Ontario's Great Blue Herons. Long Point Bird Observatory, Port Rowan.

COLLINS, B.T. 2005 Unpubl. analysis of Black Duck Breeding Ground Survey. Canadian Wildlife Service, Ottawa.

COLOMBO, S.J., D.W. MCKENNEY, K.M. LAWRENCE, and P.A. GRAY. 2007. Climate change projections for Ontario: practical information for policymakers and planners. Ontario Ministry of Natural Resources, Applied Research and Development Branch. Sault Ste. Marie.

COLWELL, M.A., and J.R. JEHL, JR. 1994. Wilson's Phalarope (*Phalaropus tricolor*). In The Birds of North America, No. 83 (A. Poole and F. Gill, Eds.). Academy of Natural Sciences, Philadelphia, and American Ornithologists' Union, Washington, DC.

COLWELL, M.A., and L.W. ORING. 1988. Breeding biology of Wilson's Phalarope in southcentral Saskatchewan. Wilson Bull. 100:567-582.

CONANT, B., and D.J. GROVES. 2001. Alaska-Yukon waterfowl breeding population survey. U.S. Fish and Wildlife Service, Juneau.

CONFER, J.L. 1992. Golden-winged Warbler (*Vermivora chrysoptera*). In The Birds of North America, No. 20 (Poole, A., P. Stettenheim, and F. Gill, Eds.). Academy of Natural Sciences, Philadelphia, and American Ornithologists' Union, Washington, DC.

CONNELLY, J.W., M.W. GRATSON, and K.P. REESE. 1998. Sharp-tailed Grouse (*Tympanuchus phasianellus*). In The Birds of North America, No. 354 (A. Poole and F. Gill, Eds.). The Birds of North America, Inc., Philadelphia.

CONWAY, C.J. 1995. Virginia Rail (*Rallus limicola*). In The Birds of North America, No. 173 (A. Poole and F. Gill, Eds.). Academy of Natural Sciences, Philadelphia, and American Ornithologists' Union, Washington, DC.

CONWAY, C.J. 1999. Canada Warbler (*Wilsonia canadensis*). In The Birds of North America, No. 421 (A. Poole and F. Gill, Eds.). The Birds of North America, Inc., Philadelphia.

CONWAY, C.J., and J.P. GIBBS. 2005. Effectiveness of call-broadcast surveys for monitoring marsh birds. Auk 122:26-35.

COOKE, F., R.K. ROSS, R.K. SCHMIDT, and A.J. PAKULAK. 1975. Birds of the tundra biome at Cape Churchill and La Perouse Bay. Can.Field-Nat. 89:413-422.

COOKE, F., R.F. ROCKWELL, and D.B. LANK. 1995. The Snow Geese of La Pérouse Bay: natural selection in the wild. Oxford University Press, New York..

COOPER, J.M. 1994. Least Sandpiper (*Calidris minutilla*). In The Birds of North America, No. 115 (A. Poole and F. Gill, Eds.). Academy of Natural Sciences, Philadelphia, and American Ornithologists' Union, Washington, DC.

CORNELIUS, L.W. 1969. Field notes on Salmonella infection in Greenfinches and House Sparrows. Bull.Wildlife Disease Assoc. 5:142-143.

COSEWIC. 2000. COSEWIC assessment and update status report on the Hooded Warbler *Wilsonia citrina* in Canada. Committee on the Status of Endangered Wildlife in Canada, Ottawa. www.sararegistry.gc.ca/status/status_e.cfm.

COSEWIC. 2003. COSEWIC assessment and update status report on the Cerulean Warbler *Dendroica cerulea* in Canada. Committee on the Status of Endangered Wildlife in Canada, Ottawa.

COSEWIC. 2005. Species Search: Warbler, Golden-winged. http://www.cosewic.gc.ca/eng/sct1/searchdetail_e.cfm?id=942&StartRow=1&boxStatus=All&boxTaxonomic=All&location=All&change=All&board=All&commonName=golden-winged%20warbler&scienceName=&returnFlag=0&Page=1

COSEWIC. 2006a. COSEWIC assessment and update status report on the Louisiana Waterthrush *Seiurus motacilla* in Canada. Committee on the Status of Endangered Wildlife in Canada, Ottawa.

COSEWIC. 2006b. COSEWIC assessment and update status report on the Red-shouldered Hawk *Buteo lineatus* in Canada. Committee on the Status of Endangered Wildlife in Canada, Ottawa.

COSEWIC. 2006c. COSEWIC assessment and status report on the Rusty Blackbird *Euphagus carolinus* in Canada. Committee on the Status of Endangered Wildlife in Canada, Ottawa. www.sararegistry.gc.ca/status/status_e.cfm.

COSEWIC. 2007a. Canadian Species at Risk, January 2007. Committee on the Status of Endangered Wildlife in Canada, Ottawa.

COSEWIC. 2007b. COSEWIC assessment and update status report on the Prothonotary Warbler *Protonotaria citrea* in Canada. Committee on the Status of Endangered Wildlife in Canada, Ottawa.

COUES, E. 1874. Birds of the northwest: a handbook of the ornithology of the region drained by the Missouri River and its tributaries. United States Department of the Interior, United States Geological Survey of the Territories, Washington, DC.

CRAIG, R.J. 1984. Comparative foraging ecology of Louisiana and Northern Waterthrushes. Wilson Bull. 96:173-183.

CRAIG, R.J. 1985. Comparative habitat use by Louisiana and Northern Waterthrushes. Wilson Bull. 97:347-355.

CRAMP, S. 1985. The birds of the western Palearctic. Oxford University Press, Oxford.

CRAMP, S. 1988. Handbook of the birds of Europe, the Middle East and North Africa: the birds of the western Palearctic, Vol. 5, Tyrant flycatchers to thrushes. Oxford University Press, Oxford.

CRAMP, S., and K.E.L. SIMMONS. 1977. Handbook of the birds of Europe, the Middle East, and North Africa: the birds of the western Palearctic, Vol. 1, Ostriches – ducks. Oxford University Press, Oxford.

CREWE, T.L. 2006. Trends in numbers of migrant birds at Long Point Bird Observatory (1961-2004) and Thunder Cape Bird Observatory (1995-2004). Bird Studies Canada, Port Rowan.

CREWE, T.L., and D.S. BADZINSKI. 2006a. Red-shouldered Hawk and Spring Woodpecker Survey. Bird Studies Canada, Port Rowan.

CREWE, T.L., and D.S. BADZINSKI. 2006b. Ontario Nocturnal Owl Survey: 2005 Final Report. Bird Studies Canada, Port Rowan.

CREWE, T.L., S. TIMMERMANS, and K. JONES. 2005. The Marsh Monitoring Program annual report, 1995-2003: annual indices and trends in bird abundance and amphibian occurrence in the Great Lakes Basin. Bird Studies Canada, Port Rowan.

CREWE, T.L., S. TIMMERMANS, and K. JONES. 2006. The Marsh Monitoring Program, 1995-2004. A decade of marsh monitoring in the Great Lakes Region. Bird Studies Canada in cooperation with Environment Canada, Port Rowan.

CRINS, W.J. 2003. Ontario Bird Records Committee report for 2002. Ontario Birds 21:54-75.

CRINS, W.J. 2004. Ontario Birds Records Committee report for 2003. Ontario Birds 22:54-74.

CRINS, W.J. 2005. Ontario Bird Records Committee report for 2004. Ontario Birds 23:54-75.

CRINS, W.J. 2006. Ontario Bird Records Committee report for 2005. Ontario Birds 24:54-74.

CRINS, W.J., P.A. GRAY, and P.W.C. UHLIG. 2007. The ecosystems of Ontario, part 1: ecozones and ecoregions [draft]. Ontario Ministry of Natural Resources, Sault Ste. Marie.

CROCOLL, S.T. 1994. Red-shouldered Hawk (*Buteo lineatus*). The Birds of North America Online (A. Poole, Ed.). Cornell Laboratory of Ornithology. Retrieved from The Birds of North America Online Database, Ithaca. http://bna.birds.cornell.edu/BNA/account/Red-shouldered_Hawk/

CUDDY, D. 1995. Protection and restoration of breeding habitat for the Loggerhead Shrike (*Lanius ludovicianus*) in Ontario, Canada. Pp. 283-286 *in* Shrikes (Laniidae) of the world: biology and conservation (R. Yosef and F.E. Lohrer, Eds.). Proceedings of the Western Foundation of Vertebrate Zoology.

CULLEN, S.A., J.R. JEHL, Jr., and G.L. NUECHTERLEIN. 1999. Eared Grebe (*Podiceps nigricollis*). *In* The Birds of North America, No. 433 (A. Poole and F. Gill, Eds.). The Birds of North America, Inc., Philadelphia.

CURRY, R. 1991. Ontario Bird Records Committee Report for 1990. Ontario Birds 9:18-44.

CURRY, R. 1994. Expanding Gadwall populations in Ontario. Pp. 221-228 *in* Ornithology in Ontario. Spec.Publ. No. 1 (M.K. McNicholl and J.L. Cranmer-Byng, Eds.). Ontario Field Ornithologists. Hawk Owl Publishing, Whitby.

CURRY, R. 2006. Birds of Hamilton and surrounding areas. Hamilton Naturalists' Club, Hamilton.

CURRY, R., and G.D. BRYANT. 1987. Snowy Egret: a new breeding species for Ontario and Canada. Ontario Birds 5: 64-67.

CURTIS, O.E., R.N. ROSENFIELD, and J. BIELEFELDT. 2006. Cooper's Hawk (*Accipiter cooperii*). The Birds of North America Online (A. Poole, Ed.). Cornell Laboratory of Ornithology. Retrieved from The Birds of North America Online Database, Ithaca. http://bna.birds.cornell.edu/BNA/account/Coopers_Hawk

CUTHBERT, F. 2006. Summary of Great Lakes Piping Plover reproductive success, 1984-2005. University of Minnesota Great Lakes Piping Plover Research Program.

CUTHBERT, F.J., J.E. MCKEARNAN, and A.R. JOSHI. 2001. Distribution and abundance of colonial waterbirds in the U.S. Great Lakes, 1997-1999. U.S. Fish and Wildlife Service.

CUTHBERT, F.J., and L.R. WIRES. 1999. Caspian Tern (*Sterna caspia*). *In* The Birds of North America, No. 403 (A. Poole and F. Gill, Eds.). The Birds of North America, Inc., Philadelphia.

CUTHBERT, F.J., L.R. WIRES, and J.E. MCKEARNAN. 2002. Potential impacts of nesting Double-crested Cormorants on Great Blue Herons and Black-crowned Night-Herons in the U.S. Great Lakes region. J.Great Lakes Res. 28:145-154.

CYR, A., and J. LARIVÉE. 1995. Atlas saisonnier des oiseaux du Québec. Les Presses de l'Université de Sherbrooke et Société de Loisir Ornithologique de l'Estrie, Sherbrooke, PQ.

DANCE, K.W. 1994. The Pileated Woodpecker in Ontario – then, now and tomorrow. Pp. 261-268 *in* Ornithology in Ontario. Spec.Publ. No. 1 (M.K. McNicholl and J.L. Cranmer-Byng, Eds.). Ontario Field Ornithologists. Hawk Owl Publishing, Whitby.

DAVIS, W.E., JR. 1993. Black-crowned Night-Heron (*Nycticorax nycticorax*). *In* The Birds of North America, No. 74 (A. Poole and F. Gill, Eds.). Academy of Natural Sciences, Philadelphia, and American Ornithologists' Union, Washington, DC.

DAVIS, W.E., JR., and J.A. KUSHLAN. 1994. Green Heron (*Butorides virescens*). *In* The Birds of North America, No. 129 (A. Poole and F. Gill, Eds.). Academy of Natural Sciences, Philadelphia, and American Ornithologists' Union, Washington, DC.

DAWSON, J.B., and N.D. PATRICK. 1960. The Hungarian Partridge in Ontario. Ontario Department of Lands and Forests, South Eastern Region Special Fish and Wildlife

Bulletin 1:1-35.

DAWSON, W.R. 1997. Pine Siskin (*Carduelis pinus*). *In* The Birds of North America, No. 280 (A. Poole and F. Gill, Eds.). Academy of Natural Sciences, Philadelphia, and American Ornithologists' Union, Washington, DC.

DE SMET, K.D. 1985. Status report on the Merlin (*Falco columbarius*) in North America. Committee on the Status of Endangered Wildlife in Canada, Ottawa.

DEAR, L.S. 1939. Bonaparte's Gull breeding in Ontario. Auk 56:186.

DEAR, L.S. 1940. Breeding birds of the region of Thunder Bay, Lake Superior, Ontario. Trans.R.Can.Inst. 23:119-143.

DECHANT, J.A., M.L. SONDREAL, D.H. JOHNSON, L.D. IGL, C.M. GOLDADE, A. ZIMMERMAN, and B.R. EULISS. 2003. Effects of management practices on grassland birds: Le Conte's Sparrow. Northern Prairie Wildlife Research Center, Jamestown. http://www.npwrc.usgs.gov/resource/literatr/grasbird/lcsp/lcsp.htm.

DEJONG, M.J. 1996. Northern Rough-winged Swallow (*Stelgidopteryx serripennis*). *In* The Birds of North America, No. 234 (A. Poole and F. Gill, Eds.). Academy of Natural Sciences, Philadelphia, and American Ornithologists' Union, Washington, DC.

DEKKER, D., R. LISTER, T.W. THORMIN, D.V. WESELOH, and L.M. WESELOH. 1979. Black-necked Stilts nesting near Edmonton, Alberta. Can.Field-Nat. 93:68-69.

DENNIS, D.G. 1974a. Breeding pair surveys of waterfowl in southern Ontario. Pp. 45-52 *in* Waterfowl studies in eastern Canada: 1969-1973 (H. Boyd, Ed.). Can.Wildl.Serv.Rep.Ser. No. 29.

DENNIS, D.G. 1974b. Waterfowl observations during the nesting season in Precambrian and Clay Belt areas of north-central Ontario. Pp. 53-56 *in* Waterfowl studies in eastern Canada: 1969-73 (H. Boyd, Ed.). Can.Wildl.Serv.Rep.Ser. No. 29.

DENNIS, D.G., and N.R. NORTH. 1984. Waterfowl densities in northwestern Ontario during the 1979 breeding season. Pp. 6-9 *in* Waterfowl studies in Ontario, 1973-1981 (S.G. Curtis, D.G. Dennis, and H. Boyd, Eds.). Can.Wildl.Serv. Occas. Pap. No. 54.

DENNIS, D.G., G.B. MCCULLOUGH, N.R. NORTH, and B. COLLINS. 1989. Surveys of breeding waterfowl in southern Ontario, 1971-87. Canadian Wildlife Service.

DERRICKSON, K.C., and R. BREITWISCH. 1992. Northern Mockingbird (*Mimus polyglottos*). *In* The Birds of North America, No. 7 (A. Poole, P. Stettenheim, and F. Gill, Eds.). Academy of Natural Sciences, Philadelphia, and American Ornithologists' Union, Washington, DC.

DEVITT, O.E. 1967. The birds of Simcoe County, Ontario. 2nd ed. Brereton Field Naturalist Club, Barrie.

DHONDT, A.A., D.L. TESSAGLIA, and R.L. SLOTHOWER. 1998. Epidemic mycoplasmal conjunctivitis in House Finches from eastern North America. J.Wildl.Dis. 34:265-280.

DICKERMAN, R.W. 1987. The "old north-eastern" subspecies of Red Crossbill. Amer.Birds 41:188-194.

DICKINSON, E.C. 2003. The Howard & Moore complete checklist of the birds of the world. 3rd ed. Princeton University Press, Princeton.

DICKSON, K.M. 2000. Towards conservation of the diversity of Canada Geese. Pp. 11-24 *in* Towards conservation of the diversity of Canada Geese (*Branta canadensis*). Can.Wildl.Serv. Occas. Pap. 103 (K.M. Dickson, Ed.). Canadian Wildlife Service, Ottawa.

DIXON, R.D., and V.A. SAAB. 2000. Black-backed Woodpecker (*Picoides arcticus*). *In* The Birds of North America, No. 509 (A. Poole and F. Gill, Eds.). The Birds of North America, Inc., Philadelphia.

DOBOS, R.Z. 1997. Ontario Bird Records Committee report for 1996. Ontario Birds 15:47-66.

DOBOS, R.Z. 1998. Ontario Bird Records Committee report for 1997. Ontario Birds 16:51-80.

DOBOS, R.Z. 1999. Ontario Bird Records Committee report for 1998. Ontario Birds 17:62-83.

DOBOS, R.Z., and R. EDMONDSTONE. 1998. Recent nestings of Red-necked Grebe on Lake Ontario. Ontario Birds 16:32-37.

DONALDSON, G.M., C. HYSLOP, R.I.G. MORRISON, H.L. DICKSON, and I. DAVIDSON. 2000. Canadian Shorebird Conservation Plan. Ministry of Environment, Canadian Wildlife Services, Ottawa.

DORE, W.G. 1969. Wild Rice. Canada Department of Agriculture, Ottawa.

DOWNES, C.M., and B.T. COLLINS. 2007. Canadian bird trends website Version 2.2. Canadian Wildlife Service, Environment Canada, Gatineau. http://www.cws-scf.ec.gc.ca/mgbc/trends/index.cfm?lang=e&go=home.page&CFID=10474683&CFTOKEN=97701949.

DOWNES, C.M., B.T. COLLINS, and M. DAMUS. 2005. Canadian bird trends website Version 2.1. Canadian Wildlife Service, Environment Canada, Gatineau. http://www.cws-scf.ec.gc.ca/mgbc/trends/default_e.cfm.

DRILLING, N., R. TITMAN, and F. MCKINNEY. 2002. Mallard (*Anas platyrhynchos*). *In* The Birds of North America, No. 658 (A. Poole and F. Gill, Eds.). The Birds of North America, Inc., Philadelphia.

DUBOWY, P.J. 1996. Northern Shoveler (*Anas clypeata*). *In* The Birds of North America, No. 217 (A. Poole and F. Gill, Eds.). Academy of Natural Sciences, Philadelphia, and American Ornithologists' Union, Washington, DC.

DUMONT, B. 2001. Hibou moyen-duc. 195 nichées et 519 juvéniles plus tard! Québec Oiseaux 2001:34-38.

DUNCAN, C.D. 1995. The migration of Red-necked Phalaropes: ecological mysteries and conservation concerns. Birding 28:482-488.

DUNCAN, C.D. 1996. Changes in the winter abundance of Sharp-shinned Hawks in New England. J.Field Ornithol. 67:254-262.

DUNCAN, J.R. 1987. Movement strategies, mortality, and behavior of radio-marked Great Gray Owls in southeastern Manitoba and northern Minnesota. Pp. 101-107 *in* Biology and conservation of northern forest owls: symposium proceedings, February 3-7, Winnipeg. Gen. Tech. Rep. RM–142 (R.W. Nero, R.J. Clark, R.J. Knapton, and R.H. Hamre, Eds.). USDA, Forest Service, Rocky Mountain Forest and Range Experiment Station, Fort Collins.

DUNCAN, J.R. 2003. Owls of the world: their lives, behavior and survival. Firefly Books, Richmond Hill.

DUNCAN, J.R., and P.A. DUNCAN. 1998. Northern Hawk Owl (*Surnia ulula*). *In* The Birds of North America, No. 356 (A. Poole and F. Gill, Eds.). The Birds of North America, Inc., Philadelphia.

DUNCAN, P., and D.A. KIRK. 1994. The status of the Northern Goshawk (*Accipiter gentiles*) in Canada. Committee on Status of Endangered Wildlife in Canada.

DUNN, E.H., and D.J. AGRO. 1995. Black Tern (*Chlidonias niger*). *In* The Birds of North America, No. 147 (A. Poole and F. Gill, Eds.). Academy of Natural Sciences, Philadelphia, and American Ornithologists' Union, Washington, DC.

DUNN, E.H., D.J.T. HUSSELL, and J. SIDERIUS. 1985. Status of the Great Blue Heron, *Ardea herodias*, in Ontario. Can.Field-Nat. 99:62-70.

EADIE, J. M., M.L. MALLORY, and H.G. LUMSDEN. 1995. Common Goldeneye (*Bucephala clangula*). The Birds of North America Online (A. Poole, Ed.). Cornell Laboratory of Ornithology. Retrieved from The Birds of North America Online

Database, Ithaca. http://bna.birds.cornell.edu/BNA/account/Common_Goldeneye/.

EATON, E.H. 1910. Birds of New York, part 1. State University of New York, Albany.

EATON, S.W. 1995. Northern Waterthrush (*Seiurus noveboracensis*). *In* The Birds of North America, No. 182 (A. Poole and F. Gill, Eds.). Academy of Natural Sciences, Philadelphia, and American Ornithologists' Union, Washington, DC.

ECKERLE, K.P., and C.F. THOMPSON. 2001. Yellow-breasted Chat (*Icteria virens*). *In* The Birds of North America, No. 575 (A. Poole and F. Gill, Eds.). The Birds of North America, Inc., Philadelphia.

ECOREGIONS WORKING GROUP. 1989. Ecoclimatic regions of Canada, first approximation. Ecol. Land Classif. Series No. 23. Environment Canada, Ottawa..

EHRLICH, P., D. DOBKIN, and D. WHEYE. 1988. The birders handbook: a field guide to the natural history of North American birds. Simon & Shuster, New York.

ELDER, D.H. 1991. Breeding habitat of the Connecticut Warbler in the Rainy River District. Ontario Birds 9:84-86.

ELDER, D.H. 1994. Marbled Godwit breeding record at Rainy River, Ontario. Birders Journal 3:154.

ELDER, D.H. 2004. Feeding strategies of American Three-toed and Black-backed Woodpeckers. Ontario Birds 22:75-78.

ELDER, D.H. 2006. The Black-billed Magpie in Ontario. Ontario Birds 24:6-12.

ELDER, D.H., and R.M. SIMMS. 1997. First Ontario breeding record for Eared Grebe. Ontario Birds 15:72-73.

ELLISON, W.G. 1992. Blue-gray Gnatcatcher (*Polioptila caerulea*). *In* The Birds of North America, No. 23 (A. Poole, P. Stettenheim, and F. Gill, Eds.). Academy of Natural Sciences, Philadelphia, and American Ornithologists' Union, Washington, DC.

ELPHICK, C.S., and J. KLIMA. 2002. Hudsonian Godwit (*Limosa haemastica*). *In* The Birds of North America, No. 629 (A. Poole and F. Gill, Eds.). The Birds of North America, Inc., Philadelphia.

ELPHICK, C.S., and T.L. TIBBITTS. 1998. Greater Yellowlegs (*Tringa melanoleuca*). *In* The Birds of North America, No. 355 (A. Poole and F. Gill, Eds.). The Birds of North America, Inc., Philadelphia.

ENGELMOER, M., and C.S. ROSELAAR. 1998. Geographical variation in waders. Kluwer Academic Publishers, Dordrecht, Netherlands.

ENGGIST-DUBLIN, P., and T.R. BIRKHEAD. 1992. Differences in the calls of European and North American Black-billed Magpies and Yellow-billed Magpies. Bioaccoustics 4:185-194.

ENVIRONMENT CANADA. 1999. Sustaining Canada's forests: timber harvesting. State of the Environment Reporting Program, Indicators and Assessment Office, Environment Canada, Ottawa.

ENVIRONMENT CANADA. 2005. Environment Canada climate trends and variation bulletin. http://www.msc-smc.ec.gc.ca/ccrm/bulletin/annual05/rtable_e.html?region=f&table=temperature&season=Annual&date=2005&rows=58.

ENVIRONMENT CANADA. 2006. Climate trends and variations bulletin for Canada. Meteorological Service of Canada, Climate Research Branch, Ottawa. http://www.msc-smc.ec.gc.ca/ccrm/bulletin/.

ENVIRONMENT CANADA. 2006a. Recovery strategy for the Henslow's Sparrow (*Ammodramus henslowii*) in Canada. *In* Species at Risk Act recovery strategy series, Environment Canada, Ottawa.

ENVIRONMENT CANADA. 2006b. Recovery strategy for the King Rail (*Rallus elegans*) [draft]. *In* Species At Risk Act recovery strategy series, Environment Canada, Ottawa.

ENVIRONMENT CANADA. 2006c. Recovery strategy for the Kirtland's Warbler (*Dendroica kirtlandii*) in Canada [proposed]. *In* Species at Risk Act recovery strategy series, Environment Canada, Ottawa.

EPP, A.E. 2000. Ontario forests and forest policy before the era of sustainable forestry. Pp. 237-275 *in* Ecology of a managed terrestrial landscape: patterns and processes of forest landscapes in Ontario (A.H. Perera, D.L. Euler, and I.D. Thompson, Eds.). UBC Press, Vancouver.

ERSKINE, A.J. 1977. Birds in boreal Canada: communities, densities and adaptations. Canadian Wildlife Service, Ottawa.

ERSKINE, A.J. 1992. Atlas of breeding birds of the Maritime Provinces. Nimbus Publishing and Nova Scotia Museum (Chelsea Green), Halifax.

ESCOTT, N.G. 1986. Thunder Bay's nesting Merlins. Ontario Birds 4:97-101.

ESCOTT, N.G. 2001. A concentration of Black-backed Woodpeckers in Thunder Bay District. Ontario Birds 19:119-129.

ESCOTT, N.G. 2002. An Influx of the Northern Hawk Owl in Thunder Bay District. Ontario Birds 20:75-86.

ESCOTT, N.G. 2003. The Sharp-tailed Grouse in Thunder Bay District. Ontario Birds 21:2-14.

EULER, D.L., and A.E. EPP. 2000. A new foundation for Ontario forest policy for the 21st century. Pp. 276-294 *in* Ecology of a managed terrestrial landscape: patterns and processes of forest landscapes in Ontario (A.H. Perera, D.L. Euler, and I.D. Thompson, Eds.). UBC Press, Vancouver.

EVANS, H.J., A.A. HOPKIN, and T.A. SCARR. 2005. Status of important forest pests in Ontario in 2005. Forest Pest Management Forum, Ottawa.

EVANS, K.E., and R.N. CONNER. 1979. Snag management. Pp. 214-225 *in* Proceedings of the workshop on management of northcentral and northeastern forests for nongame birds. General Technical Report NC-51 (R.M. Degraaf and K.E. Evans, Eds.). United States Department of Agriculture, Forest Service.

EVANS MACK, D., and W. YONG. 2000. Swainson's Thrush (*Catharus ustulatus*). *In* The Birds of North America, No. 540 (A. Poole and F. Gill, Eds.). The Birds of North America, Inc., Philadelphia.

EVANS OGDEN, L.J., and B.J. STUTCHBURY. 1994. Hooded Warbler (*Wilsonia citrina*). *In* The Birds of North America, No. 110 (A. Poole and F. Gill, Eds.). Academy of Natural Sciences, Philadelphia, and American Ornithologists' Union, Washington, DC.

EWINS, P.J. 1997. Osprey (*Pandion haliaetus*) populations in forested areas of North America: changes, their causes and management recommendations. J. Raptor Res. 31:138-150.

EWINS, P.J., and D.R. BAZELY. 1995. Phenology and breeding success of feral Rock Doves, *Columba livia*, in Toronto, Ontario. Can.Field-Nat. 109:426-432.

EWINS, P.J., D.V.C. WESELOH, R.J. NORSTROM, K. LEGIERSE, H.J. AUMAN, and J.P. LUDWIG. 1994. Caspian Terns on the Great Lakes: organochlorine contamination, reproduction, diet and population changes, 1972-1991. Canadian Wildlife Service, Ottawa.

EWINS, P.J., and D.V. WESELOH. 1999. Little Gull (*Larus minutus*). *In* The Birds of North America, No. 428 (A. Poole and F. Gill, Eds.). The Birds of North America, Inc., Philadelphia.

FALLS, J.B., and J.G. KOPACHENA. 1994. White-throated Sparrow (*Zonotrichia albicollis*). *In* The Birds of North America, No. 128 (A. Poole and F. Gill, Eds.). Academy of Natural Sciences, Philadelphia, and American Ornithologists' Union, Washington, DC.

FICKEN, M.S., M.A. MCLAREN, and J.P. HAILMAN. 1996. Boreal Chickadee (*Parus hudsonicus*). *In* The Birds of North America, No. 254 (A. Poole and F. Gill, Eds.). Academy of Natural Sciences, Philadelphia, and American Ornithologists' Union, Washington, DC.

FLAP. 2007. Fatal Light Awareness Program. http://www.flap.org/. Accessed 11 September 2007.

FLEMING, J.H. 1901. A list of the birds of the Districts of Parry Sound and Muskoka, Ontario. Auk 18:33-45.

FLEMING, J.H. 1906. Chuck-will's-widow and Mockingbird in Ontario. Auk 23:343-344.

FLEMING, J.H. 1907. Birds of Toronto, Canada, part 2. Auk 24:71-89.

FLYNN, L., E. NOL, and Y. ZHARIKOV. 1999. Philopatry, nest-site tenacity, and mate fidelity of Semipalmated Plovers. J. Avian Biol. 30:47-55.

FORBES, G. 1992. New breeding record for Great Gray Owl: most southerly in Canada. Ontario Birds 10:117-118.

FORSTER, J.R. 1772. An account of the birds sent from Hudson's Bay with observations relevant to their natural history and Latin descriptions of some of the most uncommon. Philos.T.Roy.Soc. 62:382-433.

FREDRICKSON, L.H. 1971. Common Gallinule breeding biology and development. Auk 88:914-919.

FREEMAN, M.M.R. 1970. Observations on the seasonal behavior of the Hudson Bay Eider (*Somateria mollissima sedentaria*). Can.Field-Nat. 84:145-153.

FREEMARK, K., and B. COLLINS. 1992. Landscape ecology of birds breeding in temperate forest fragments. Pp. 443-454 *in* Ecology and conservation of neotropical migrant landbirds (J.M. Hagan, III, and D.W. Johnston, Eds.). Smithson. Inst. Press, Washington, DC.

FRIESEN, L.E., M.D. CADMAN, and M.L. ALLEN. 2001. Triple brooding by southern Ontario Wood Thrushes. Wilson Bull. 113:237-239.

FRIESEN, L.E., M.D. CADMAN, and R.J. MACKAY. 1999a. Nesting success of neotropical migrant songbirds in a highly fragmented landscape. Conserv.Biol. 13:338-346.

FRIESEN, L.E., P.F.J. EAGLES, and R.J. MACKAY. 1995. Effects of residential development on forest-dwelling neotropical migrant songbirds. Conserv.Biol. 9:1408-1414.

FRIESEN, L.E., V.E. WYATT, and M.D. CADMAN. 1999b. Pairing success of Wood Thrushes in a fragmented agricultural landscape. Wilson Bull. 111:279-281.

FRONCZAK, D. 2006. Midwinter waterfowl survey, Mississippi Flyway. U.S. Fish and Wildlife Service, Columbia.

FYFE, R.W. 1976. Status of Canadian raptor populations. Can.Field-Nat. 90:370-375.

GAGE, S.H., C.A. MILLER, and L.J. MOOK. 1970. The feeding response of some forest birds to the Black-headed Budworm. Can.J.Zool. 48:359-366.

GAHBAUER, M.A. 2000. Birds of prey of the City of Toronto, Ontario, Canada. International Hawkwatcher 2:18-24.

GAMBLE, L.R., and T.M. BERGIN. 1996. Western Kingbird (*Tyrannus verticalis*). *In* The Birds of North America, No. 227 (A. Poole and F. Gill, Eds.). Academy of Natural Sciences, Philadelphia, and American Ornithologists' Union, Washington, DC.

GAMMONLEY, J.H. 1996. Cinnamon Teal (*Anas cyanoptera*). *In* The Birds of North America, No. 209 (A. Poole and F. Gill, Eds.). Academy of Natural Sciences, Philadelphia, and American Ornithologists' Union, Washington, DC.

GARDALI, T., and G. BALLARD. 2000. Warbling Vireo (*Vireo gilvus*). *In* The Birds of North America, No. 551 (A. Poole and F. Gill, Eds.). The Birds of North America, Inc., Philadelphia.

GARRISON, B.A. 1999. Bank Swallow (*Riparia riparia*). *In* The Birds of North America, No. 414 (A. Poole and F. Gill, Eds.). The Birds of North America, Inc., Philadelphia.

GAUTHIER, G. 1993. Bufflehead (*Bucephala albeola*). *In* The Birds of North America, No. 67 (A. Poole and F. Gill, Eds.). Academy of Natural Sciences, Philadelphia, and American Ornithologists' Union, Washington, DC.

GAUTHIER, J., and Y.E. AUBRY. 1996. The breeding birds of Québec: atlas of the breeding birds of Southern Québec. Association Québécoise des Groupes d'Ornithologues, Province of Quebec Society for the Protection of Birds, Canadian Wildlife Service, Environment Canada, Quebec Region, Montreal.

GAUTHIER, J., M. DIONNE, C. MAURICE, J. POTVIN, M.D. CADMAN, and D. BUSBY. 2007. Status of the Chimney Swift (*Chaetura pelagica*) in Canada. Canadian Wildlife Service, Environment Canada, Québec.

GEHLBACH, F.R. 1995. Eastern Screech-Owl (*Otus asio*). *In* The Birds of North America, No. 165 (A. Poole and F. Gill, Eds.). Academy of Natural Sciences, Philadelphia, and American Ornithologists' Union, Washington, DC.

GENDRON, M.H., and B.T. COLLINS, 2007. National harvest survey website, Version 1.2. Migratory Bird Populations Division, National Wildlife Research Centre, Canadian Wildlife Service, Ottawa.

GHALAMBOR, C.K., and T.E. MARTIN. 1999. Red-breasted Nuthatch (*Sitta canadensis*). *In* The Birds of North America, No. 459 (A. Poole and F. Gill, Eds.). The Birds of North America, Inc., Philadelphia.

GIBBS, J.P. 1991. Spatial relationships between nesting colonies and foraging areas of Great Blue Herons. Auk 108:764-770.

GIBBS, J.P., and S.M. MELVIN. 1993. Call-response surveys for monitoring breeding waterbirds. J.Wildl.Manage. 57:27-34.

GIBBS, J.P., S. MELVIN, and F.A. REID. 1992a. American Bittern (*Botaurus lentiginosus*). *In* The Birds of North America, No. 18 (A. Poole, P. Stettenheim, and F. Gill, Eds.). Academy of Natural Sciences, Philadelphia, and American Ornithologists' Union, Washington, DC.

GIBBS, J.P., F.A. REID, and S.M. MELVIN. 1992b. Least Bittern (*Ixobrychus exilis*). *In* The Birds of North America, No. 17 (A. Poole, P. Stettenheim, and F. Gill, Eds.). Academy of Natural Sciences, Philadelphia, and American Ornithologists' Union, Washington, DC.

GILCHRIST, H.G. 2001. Glaucous Gull (*Larus hyperboreus*). *In* The Birds of North America, No. 573 (A. Poole and F. Gill, Eds.). The Birds of North America, Inc., Philadelphia.

GILCHRIST, H.G., and G.J. ROBERTSON. 1998. Evidence of population declines among Common Eiders breeding in the Belcher Island, Northwest Territories. Arctic 51:378-385.

GILCHRIST, H.G., and G.J. ROBERTSON. 1999. Population trends of gulls and Arctic Terns nesting in the Belcher Islands, Nunavut. Arctic 52:325-331.

GILL, F.B. 1980. Historical aspects of hybridization between Blue-winged and Golden-winged Warblers. Auk 97:1-18.

GILL, F.B. 1987. Allozymes and genetic similarity of Blue-winged Warblers and Golden-winged Warblers. Auk 104:444-449.

GILL, F.B. 1997. Local cytonuclear extinction of the Golden-winged Warbler. Evolution 51:519-525.

GILL, F.B., R.A. CANTERBURY, and J.L. CONFER. 2001. Blue-winged Warbler (*Vermivora pinus*). *In* The Birds of North America, No. 584 (A. Poole and F. Gill, Eds.). The Birds of North America, Inc., Philadelphia.

GILLIHAN, S.W., and B. BYERS. 2001. Evening Grosbeak (*Coccothraustes verspertinus*). *In* The Birds of North America, No. 599 (A. Poole and F. Gill, Eds.). The Birds of North America, Inc., Philadelphia.

GILMORE, D., and C. MACDONALD. 1996. Northern forest owl survey: Red Lake. Ontario Birds 14:91-99.

GIUDICE, J.H., and J.T. RATTI. 2001. Ring-necked Pheasant (*Phasianus colchicus*). *In*

The Birds of North America, No. 572 (A. Poole and F. Gill, Eds.). The Birds of North America, Inc., Philadelphia.

GLASER, L.C., I.K. BARKER, D.V.C. WESELOH, J.P. LUDWIG, R.M. WINDINGSTAD, D.W. KEY, and T.K. BOLLINGER. 1999. The 1992 epizootic of Newcastle disease in Double-crested Cormorants in North America. J.Wildl.Dis. 35:319-330.

GLOVER, F.A. 1953. Nesting ecology of the Pied-billed Grebe in north-eastern Iowa. Wilson Bull. 65:32-39.

GODFREY, W.E. 1966. The birds of Canada. Bulletin No. 203. National Museum of Canada, Ottawa.

GODFREY, W.E. 1986. The birds of Canada. Rev. ed. National Museum of Canada, Ottawa.

GOGGANS, R, R.D. DIXON, and L.C. SEMINARA. 1988. Habitat use by Three-toed and Black-backed Woodpeckers. - Nongame Wildl. Prog. USDA Deschutes Natl. For. Tech. Rep. 87-3-02. Oregon Department of Fish and Wildlife.

GOGUEN, C.B., and N.E. MATHEWS. 2001. Brown-headed Cowbird behaviour and movements in relation to livestock grazing. Ecol.App. 11:1533-1544.

GOOD, T.P. 1998. Great Black-backed Gull (*Larus marinus*). In The Birds of North America, No. 330 (A. Poole and F. Gill, Eds.). The Birds of North America, Inc., Philadelphia.

GOODRICH, L.J., S.C. CROCOLL, and S.E. SENNER. 1996. Broad-winged Hawk (*Buteo platypterus*). In The Birds of North America, No. 218 (A. Poole and F. Gill, Eds.). Academy of Natural Sciences, Philadelphia, and American Ornithologists' Union, Washington, DC.

GOODWIN, C.E. 1980. The nesting season: Ontario region. Amer.Birds 34:890-892.

GOODWIN, C.E., and R.C. ROSCHE. 1974. The nesting season: Ontario–western New York region. Amer. Birds 28:896-900.

GOODWIN, D. 1976. Crows of the world. Cornell University Press, Ithaca.

GOUDIE, R.I., G.J. ROBERTSON, and A. REED. 2000. Common Eider (*Somateria mollissima*). In The Birds of North America, No. 546 (A. Poole and F. Gill, Eds.). The Birds of North America, Inc., Philadelphia.

GOWATY, P.A., and J.H. PLISSNER. 1998. Eastern Bluebird (*Sialia sialis*). In The Birds of North America, No. 381 (A. Poole and F. Gill, Eds.). The Birds of North America, Inc., Philadelphia.

GRABER, R.R., and J.W. GRABER. 1963. A comparative study of bird populations in Illinois, 1906-1909 and 1956-1958. Ill. Nat. Hist. Surv. Bull. 28:383-528.

GRAHAM, D., S.T.A. TIMMERMANS, and J. MCCRACKEN. 2002. A comparison of abundance of colonial marsh birds between 1991 and 2001 in the Canadian portions of Lakes Huron, St. Clair, Ontario and Erie. Bird Studies Canada, Port Rowan.

GRATTO-TREVOR, C.L. 1992. Semipalmated Sandpiper (*Calidris pusilla*). In The Birds of North America Online (A. Poole, Ed.). Cornell Laboratory of Ornithology. Retrieved from The Birds of North American Online Database, Ithaca. http://bna.birds.cornell.edu/BNA/demo/account/Semipalmated_Sandpiper/.

GRATTO-TREVOR, C.L. 1994. Monitoring shorebird populations in the Arctic. Bird Trends 3:10-12.

GRATTO-TREVOR, C.L. 2000. Marbled Godwit (*Limosa fedoa*). In The Birds of North America, No. 492 (A. Poole and F. Gill, Eds.). The Birds of North America, Inc., Philadelphia.

GREENBERG, R., and S. DROEGE. 1999. On the decline of the Rusty Blackbird and the use of ornithological literature to document long-term population trends. Conserv.Biol. 13:553-559.

GREENLAW, J.S. 1993. Behavioral and morphological diversification in Sharp-tailed Sparrows (*Ammodramus caudacutus*) of the Atlantic coast. Auk 110:286-303.

GREENLAW, J.S. 1996. Eastern Towhee (*Pipilo erythrophthalmus*). In The Birds of North America, No. 262 (A. Poole and F. Gill, Eds.). Academy of Natural Sciences, Philadelphia, and American Ornithologists' Union, Washington, DC.

GREENLAW, J.S., and J.D. RISING. 1994. Sharp-tailed Sparrow (*Ammodramus caudacutus*). In The Birds of North America, No. 112 (A. Poole and F. Gill, Eds.). Academy of Natural Sciences, Philadelphia, and American Ornithologists' Union, Washington, DC.

GRIER, J.W., T. ARMSTRONG, P. HUNTER, S. LOCKHART, and B. RANTA. 2003. Report on the status of Bald Eagles in Ontario. Ontario Ministry of Natural Resources, Thunder Bay.

GROSS, D.A., and P.E. LOWTHER. 2001. Yellow-bellied Flycatcher (*Empidonax flaviventris*). In The Birds of North America, No. 566 (A. Poole and F. Gill, Eds.). The Birds of North America, Inc., Philadelphia.

GROTH, J.G. 1993. Evolutionary differentiation in morphology, vocalizations, and allozymes among nomadic sibling species in the North American Red Crossbill (*Loxia curvirostra*) complex. University of California Press, Berkeley.

GROTH J.G. 1996. Crossbills audiovisual guide. Department of Ornithology, American Museum of Natural History, New York. http://research.amnh.org/ornithology/crossbills/.

GRUBB, T.C., JR., and V.V. PRAVOSUDOV. 1994. Tufted Titmouse (*Parus bicolor*). In The Birds of North America, No. 86 (A. Poole and F. Gill, Eds.). Academy of Natural Sciences, Philadelphia, and American Ornithologists' Union, Washington, DC.

GULLION, G.W. 1989. The Ruffed Grouse. NorthWord Press, Minocqua.

GUZY, M.J., and G. RITCHISON. 1999. Common Yellowthroat (*Geothlypis trichas*). In The Birds of North America, No. 448 (A. Poole and F. Gill, Eds.). The Birds of North America, Inc., Philadelphia.

HAGAN, J.M., III. 1993. Decline of the Rufous-sided Towhee in the Eastern United States. Auk 110:863-874.

HAGAR, J.A. 1966. Nesting of the Hudsonian Godwit at Churchill, Manitoba. Living Bird 5:5-43.

HAGGERTY, T.M., and E.S. MORTON. 1995. Carolina Wren (*Thryothorus ludovicianus*). In The Birds of North America, No. 188 (A. Poole and F. Gill, Eds.). Academy of Natural Sciences, Philadelphia, and American Ornithologists' Union, Washington, DC.

HALE, J.B., and L.E. GREGG. 1976. Woodcock use of clearcut aspen areas in Wisconsin. Wildl.Soc.Bull. 4:111-115.

HALKIN, S.L., and S.U. LINVILLE. 1999. Northern Cardinal (*Cardinalis cardinalis*). In The Birds of North America, No. 440 (A. Poole and F. Gill, Eds.). The Birds of North America, Inc., Philadelphia.

HALL, G.A. 1983. West Virginia birds. Carnegie Mus.Nat.Hist, Pittsburgh.

HALL, G.A. 1994. Magnolia Warbler (*Dendroica magnolia*). In The Birds of North America, No. 136 (A. Poole and F. Gill, Eds.). Academy of Natural Sciences, Philadelphia, and American Ornithologists' Union, Washington, DC.

HALL, J.A. 1988. Early chick mobility and brood movements in the Forster's Tern (*Sterna forsteri*). J. Field Ornithol. 59:247-251.

HALL, J.A. 1989. Aspects of Forster's tern (*Sterna forsteri*) reproduction on cobblestone islands in southcentral Washington. Northwest Science 63:90-95.

HAMAS, M.J. 1994. Belted Kingfisher (*Ceryle alcyon*). In The Birds of North America, No. 84 (A. Poole and F. Gill, Eds.). Academy of Natural Sciences, Philadelphia, and American Ornithologists' Union, Washington, DC.

HAMEL, P.B. 2000. Cerulean Warbler (*Dendroica cerulea*). In The Birds of North

America, No. 511 (A. Poole and F. Gill, Eds.). The Birds of North America, Inc., Philadelphia.

HAMERSTROM, F. 1979. Effect of prey on predator: voles and harriers. Auk 96:370-374.

HAMERSTROM, F. 1986. Harrier, hawk of the marshes. Smithsonian Institution Press, Washington, DC.

HAMES, R.S., K.V. ROSENBERG, J.D. LOWE, S.E. BARKER, and A.A. DHONDT. 2002. Adverse effects of acid rain on the distribution of the Wood Thrush *Hylocichla mustelina* in North America. Pp. 11235-11240 *in* Proc.Nat.Acad.Sci.U.S.A. No 99. Cornell Laboratory of Ornithology, Ithaca.

HAMPE, A., and R.J. PETITI. 2005. Conserving biodiversity under climate change: the rear edge matters. Ecol. Lett. 8: 461-467.

HANNERS, L.A., and S.R. PATTON. 1998. Worm-eating Warbler (*Helmitheros vermivorus*). *In* The Birds of North America, No. 367 (A. Poole and F. Gill, Eds.). The Birds of North America, Inc., Philadelphia.

HANNON, S.J., P.K. EASON, and K. MARTIN. 1998. Willow Ptarmigan (*Lagopus lagopus*). *In* The Birds of North America, No. 369 (A. Poole and F. Gill, Eds.). The Birds of North America, Inc., Philadelphia.

HANSON, H.C., H.G. LUMSDEN, J.J. LYNCH, and H.W. NORTON. 1972. Population characteristics of three mainland colonies of Blue and Lesser Snow Geese nesting in the southern Hudson Bay region. Research Report (Wildlife) No. 92. Ontario Ministry of Natural Resources.

HARRIS, C.G. 1998. Final report on the 1997 Prairie Warbler Survey along the southeastern shoreline of Georgian Bay, Ontario. Ontario Natural Heritage Information Centre, Ontario Ministry of Natural Resources, Peterborough.

HARRISON, H.H. 1975. A field guide to birds' nests. Houghton Mifflin, Boston.

HATCH, J.J. 2002. Arctic Tern (*Sterna paradisaea*). *In* The Birds of North America, No. 707 (A. Poole and F. Gill, Eds.). The Birds of North America, Inc., Philadelphia.

HATCH, J.J., and D.V. WESELOH. 1999. Double-crested Cormorant (*Phalacrocorax auritus*). *In* The Birds of North America, No. 441 (A. Poole and F. Gill, Eds.). The Birds of North America, Inc., Philadelphia.

HAUTALA, K. 2004. Evaluation of a spatial habitat suitability model for the Northern Goshawk (*Accipiter gentilis*) in west-central Alberta. M.Sc.F. thesis, Lakehead University, Thunder Bay.

HAWS, K.V. 2005. Piping Plover and Common Tern investigations, Lake of the Woods, 2003-2004. Minnesota Department of Natural Resources, Bemidji.

HAYWARD, G.D., and P.H. HAYWARD. 1993. Boreal Owl (*Aegolius funereus*). *In* The Birds of North America, No. 63 (A. Poole and F. Gill, Eds.). Academy of Natural Sciences, Philadelphia, and American Ornithologists' Union, Washington, DC.

HAYWORTH, A.M., and W.W. WEATHERS. 1984. Temperature regulation and climatic adaption in Black-billed and Yellow-billed Magpies. Condor 86:19-26.

HEAGY, A.E., and J.D. MCCRACKEN. 2004. Monitoring the state of Ontario's migratory landbirds. Bird Studies Canada. Port Rowan. http://www.bsc-eoc.org/download/StateofONbirds.pdf.

HEAGY, A.E., and J.D. MCCRACKEN. 2005. Ontario: State of the Region. N.Am.Birds 58:521.

HEALY, W.M. 1992. Behavior. Pp. 46-65 *in* The Wild Turkey: biology and management (J.G. Dickson, Ed.). National Wild Turkey Federation and the United States Department of Agriculture Forest Service, Harrisburg.

HEBERT, C.E., J. DUFFE, D.V.C. WESELOH, E.M.T. SENSESE, and G.D. HAFFNER. 2005. Unique island habitats may be threatened by Double-crested Cormorants. J.Wildl.Manage. 69:57-65.

HEJL, S.J., J.A. HOLMES, and D.E. KROODSMA. 2002. Winter Wren (*Troglodytes troglodytes*). *In* The Birds of North America, No. 623 (A. Poole and F. Gill, Eds.). The Birds of North America, Inc., Philadelphia.

HEJL, S.J., K.R. NEWLON, M.E. MCFADZEN, J.S. YOUNG, and C.K. GHALAMBOR. 2002. Brown Creeper (*Certhia americana*). *In* The Birds of North America, No. 669 (A. Poole and F. Gill, Eds.). The Birds of North America, Inc., Philadelphia.

HEPP, G.R., and F.C. BELLROSE. 1995. Wood Duck (*Aix sponsa*). *In* The Birds of North America, No. 169 (A. Poole and F. Gill, Eds.). Academy of Natural Sciences, Philadelphia, and American Ornithologists' Union, Washington, DC.

HERKERT, J.R., D.E. KROODSMA, and J.P. GIBBS. 2001. Sedge Wren (*Cistothorus platensis*). *In* The Birds of North America, No. 582 (A. Poole and F. Gill, Eds.). The Birds of North America, Inc., Philadelphia.

HERKERT, J.R., P.D. VICKERY, and D.E. KROODSMA. 2002. Henslow's Sparrow (*Ammodramus henslowii*). *In* The Birds of North America, No. 672 (A. Poole and F. Gill, Eds.). The Birds of North America, Inc., Philadelphia.

HEYDWEILLER, A.M. 1935. A comparison of winter and summer territories and seasonal variations of the Tree Sparrow (*Spizella arborea*). Bird-Banding 6:1-11.

HICKEY, J.J., and D.W. ANDERSON. 1969. The Peregrine Falcon: life history and population literature. pp. 3-42 *in* Peregrine Falcon populations, their biology and decline (J.J. Hickey, Ed.). University of Wisconsin Press, Madison.

HILL, G.E. 1993. House Finch (*Carpodacus mexicanus*). *In* The Birds of North America, No. 46 (A. Poole and F. Gill, Eds.). Academy of Natural Sciences, Philadelphia, and American Ornithologists' Union, Washington, DC.

HITCH, A.T., and P.L. LEBERG. 2007. Breeding distributions of North American bird species moving north as a result of climate change. Conserv.Biol. 21:534-539.

HOHMAN, W.L., and R.T. EBERHARDT. 1998. Ring-necked Duck (*Aythya collaris*). *In* The Birds of North America, No. 329 (A. Poole and F. Gill, Eds.). The Birds of North America, Inc., Philadelphia.

HOLDER, M. 2003. The decline of the House Sparrow. Birders Journal 12:61-66.

HOLLOWAY, G.L., B.J. NAYLOR, and W.R. WATT, 2004. Habitat relationships of wildlife in Ontario.

HOLMES, R.T. 1966. Breeding ecology and annual cycle adaptations in the Red-backed Sandpiper in northern Alaska. Condor 68:3-46.

HOLMES, R.T., and F.A. PITELKA. 1998. Pectoral Sandpiper (*Calidris melanotos*). *In* The Birds of North America, No. 348 (A. Poole and F. Gill, Eds.). The Birds of North America, Inc., Philadelphia.

HOLMES, R.T., N.L. RODENHOUSE, and T.S. SILLETT. 2005. Black-throated Blue Warbler (*Dendroica caerulescens*). The Birds of North America Online . (A. Poole, Ed.). Cornell Laboratory of Ornithology. Retrieved from The Birds of North America Online Database, Ithaca. http://bna.birds.cornell.edu/BNA/account/Black-throated Blue Warbler.

HOLMES, S.B. 1998. Reproduction and nest behaviour of Tennessee warblers *Vermivora peregrina* in forests treated with Lepidoptera-specific insecticides. J.Appl.Ecol. 35:185-194.

HOLROYD, G.L. 1983. Resource use by four avian species of aerial insect feeders. Ph.D. thesis, University of Toronto.

HOLROYD, G.L., and U. BANASCH. 1990. The reintroduction of the Peregrine Falcon, *Falco peregrinus anatum*, into southern Canada. Can.Field-Nat. 104:203-208.

HOPP, S.L., A. KIRBY, and C.A. BOONE. 1995. White-eyed Vireo (*Vireo griseus*). *In*

The Birds of North America, No. 168 (A. Poole and F. Gill, Eds.). Academy of Natural Sciences, Philadelphia, and American Ornithologists' Union, Washington, DC.

HOUSTON, C.S. 1977. Changing patterns of Corvidae on the prairies. Blue Jay 35:149-156.

HOUSTON, C.S. 1984. Arctic ordeal: the journal of John Richardson, surgeon-naturalist, with Franklin, 1819-1822. McGill-Queen's University Press, Montreal and Kingston.

HOUSTON, C.S. 2002. Spread and disappearance of the Greater Prairie-Chicken, *Tympanuchus cupido*, on the Canadian Prairies and adjacent areas. Can.Field-Nat. 116:1-21.

HOUSTON, C.S., and D.E. BOWEN, JR. 2001. Upland Sandpiper (*Bartramia longicauda*). In The Birds of North America, No. 580 (A. Poole and F. Gill, Eds.). The Birds of North America, Inc., Philadelphia.

HOUSTON, C.S., and B. LUTERBACH. 2004. Northward extension of Eurasian Collared-Dove in Saskatchewan. Blue Jay 62:28-30.

HOUSTON, C.S., D.G. SMITH, and C. ROHNER. 1998. Great Horned Owl (*Bubo virginianus*). In The Birds of North America, No. 372 (A. Poole and F. Gill, Eds.). The Birds of North America, Inc., Philadelphia.

HOWELL, J.C. 1973. Communicative behavior in the Cedar Waxwing (*Bombycilla cedrorum*) and the Bohemian Waxwing (*Bombycilla garrulus*). Ph.D. dissertation, University of Michigan, Ann Arbor.

HOWSE, G.M., and T. SCARR. 2001. Status of important forest pests in Ontario in 2001. Forest Pest Management Forum, Ottawa.

HOWSE, G.M., and T. SCARR. 2002. Status of important forest pests in Ontario 2002. Annual Forest Pest Management Forum, Ottawa, November 13–15 2002. Natural Resources Canada, Ottawa. http://www.glfc.cfs.nrcan.gc.ca/foresthealth/pdf/status_of_pests_in_ontario_2002.pdf

HOYT, J.S., and S.J. HANNON. 2002. Habitat associations of Black-backed and Three-toed Woodpeckers in the boreal forest of Alberta. Can.Jour.Forest Res. 32:1881-1888.

HUBBARD, M.W., D.L. GARNER, and E.E. KLAAS. 1999. Wild Turkey poult survival in southcentral Iowa. J.Wildl.Manage. 63:199-203.

HUDON, J. 2005. The official list of the birds of Alberta: now 400 species and counting. Nature Alberta 35:10-18.

HUGHES, J.M. 1999. Yellow-billed Cuckoo (*Coccyzus americanus*). In The Birds of North America, No. 418 (A. Poole and F. Gill, Eds.). The Birds of North America, Inc., Philadelphia.

HUGHES, J.M. 2001. Black-billed Cuckoo (*Coccyzus erythropthalmus*). In The Birds of North America, No. 587 (A. Poole and F. Gill, Eds.). The Birds of North America, Inc., Philadelphia.

HUNT, L.M., and M.A. GAHBAUER. 2004. Short-eared Owl (*Asio flammeus*) population monitoring in southern and eastern Ontario, summer 2003. The Migration Research Foundation, Ottawa

HUNT, P.D., and B.C. ELIASON. 1999. Blackpoll Warbler (*Dendroica striata*). In The Birds of North America, No. 431 (A. Poole and F. Gill, Eds.). The Birds of North America, Inc., Philadelphia.

HUNT, P.D., and D.J. FLASPOHLER. 1998. Yellow-rumped Warbler (*Dendroica coronata*). In The Birds of North America, No. 376 (A. Poole and F. Gill, Eds.). The Birds of North America, Inc., Philadelphia.

HUSSELL, D.J.T. 1981. Migrations of the Least Flycatcher in southern Ontario. J.Field Ornithol. 52:97-111.

HUSSELL, D.J.T. 1982. Migrations of the Yellow-bellied Flycatcher in southern Ontario. J.Field Ornithol. 53:223-234.

HUSSELL, D.J.T. 1991a. Spring migrations of Alder and Willow Flycatchers in southern Ontario. J.Field Ornithol. 62:69-77.

HUSSELL, D.J.T. 1991b. Fall migrations of Alder and Willow Flycatchers in southern Ontario. J.Field Ornithol. 62:260-270.

HUSSELL, D.J.T., and L. BROWN. 1992. Population changes in diurnally-migrating raptors at Duluth, Minnesota (1974-1989) and Grimsby, Ontario (1975-1990). Ontario Ministry of Natural Resources, Maple.

HUSSELL, D.J.T., M.H. MATHER, and P.H. SINCLAIR. 1992. Trends in numbers of tropical- and temperate-wintering migrant landbirds in migration at Long Point, Ontario, 1961-1988. Pp. 101-114 in Ecology and conservation of neotropical migrant landbirds (J.M. Hagan, III, and D.W. Johnston, Eds.). Smithson. Inst. Press, Washington, DC.

HUSSELL, D.J.T., and R. MONTGOMERIE. 2002. Lapland Longspur (*Calcarius lapponicus*). In The Birds of North America, No. 656 (A. Poole and F. Gill, Eds.). The Birds of North America, Inc., Philadelphia.

HUTCHINSON, M.F. 1987. Methods for generation of weather sequences. Pp. 149-157 in Agricultural environments: characterization, classification and mapping (A.H. Bunting, Ed.). CAB International, Wallingford.

HUTTO, R.L. 1995. Composition of bird communities following stand-replacement fires in northern Rocky Mountain (USA) conifer forests. Conserv.Biol. 9:1041-1058.

IGL, L.D., and D.H. JOHNSON. 1995. Dramatic increase of Le Conte's Sparrow in Conservation Reserve Program fields in the northern Great Plains. Prairie Nat. 27:89-94.

INGOLD, D. 1989. Nesting phenology and competition for nest sites among Red-headed and Red-bellied Woodpeckers and European Starlings. Auk 106:209-217.

INGOLD, J.L., and R. GALATI. 1997. Golden-crowned Kinglet (*Regulus satrapa*). In The Birds of North America, No. 301 (A. Poole and F. Gill, Eds.). Academy of Natural Sciences, Philadelphia, and American Ornithologists' Union, Washington, DC.

INGOLD, J.L., and G.E. WALLACE. 1994. Ruby-crowned Kinglet (*Regulus calendula*). In The Birds of North America, No. 119 (A. Poole and F. Gill, Eds.). Academy of Natural Sciences, Philadelphia, and American Ornithologists' Union, Washington, DC.

IPCC. 2007. Climate change 2007: the physical science basis: summary for policymakers. Report of the Intergovernmental Panel on Climate Change, Geneva.

IRON, J. 1998. Brewer's Blackbird: on hold? OFO News 16:10.

IRON, J., and R. PITTAWAY. 2002. 1905 bird checklist of Ontario birds: comparing 1905 and 2002. OFO News 20:6-17.

JACKSON, B.J.S., and J.A. JACKSON. 2000. Killdeer (*Charadrius vociferus*). In The Birds of North America, No. 517 (A. Poole and F. Gill, Eds.). The Birds of North America, Inc., Philadelphia.

JACKSON, J. 2005. Summary of Piping Plover survey results and management practices for Wasaga Beach Provincial Park.Ontario Ministry of Natural Resources, Ontario Parks.

JACKSON, J.A. 1983. Nesting phenology, nest site selection, and reproductive success of Black and Turkey Vultures. Pp. 245-270 in Vulture biology and management (S.R. Wilbur and J.A. Jackson, Eds.). University of California Press, Los Angeles.

JACKSON, J.A., and H.R. OUELLET. 2002. Downy Woodpecker (*Picoides pubescens*). In The Birds of North America, No. 613 (A. Poole and F. Gill, Eds.). The Birds of North America, Inc., Philadelphia.

JACKSON, J.A., H.R. OUELLET, and B.J.S. JACKSON. 2002. Hairy Woodpecker (*Picoides villosus*). In The Birds of North

America, No. 702 (A. Poole and F. Gill, Eds.). The Birds of North America, Inc., Philadelphia.

JAMES, D.A. 1960. The changing seasons. Audubon Field Notes 14:284-289.

JAMES, D.A. 1961. The changing seasons. Audubon Field Notes 15:304-308.

JAMES, R.D. 1978. Nesting of the House Finch (*Carpodacus mexicanus*) in Ontario. Ont.Field Biol. 32:30-32.

JAMES, R.D. 1981. Northern Shrike confirmed as a breeding species in Ontario. Ont.Field Biol. 35:93-94.

JAMES, R.D. 1984a. The breeding bird list for Ontario: additions and comments. Ontario Birds 2:24-29.

JAMES, R.D. 1984b. Habitat management guidelines for cavity-nesting birds in Ontario. Ontario Ministry of Natural Resources, Toronto.

JAMES, R.D. 1984c. Ontario Bird Records Committee report for 1983. Ontario Birds 2:53-65.

JAMES, R.D. 1991. Annotated checklist of the birds of Ontario. 2nd ed. Royal Ontario Museum Life Sciences Miscellaneous Publications, Toronto.

JAMES, R.D. 1998. Blue-headed Vireo (*Vireo solitarius*). *In* The Birds of North America, No. 379 (A. Poole and F. Gill, Eds.). The Birds of North America, Inc., Philadelphia.

JAMES, R.D. 1999. Update COSEWIC status report on Least Bittern (*Ixobrychus exilis*). Committee on the Status of Endangered Wildlife in Canada.

JAMES, R.D., and R. CANNINGS. 2003. Update COSEWIC status report on the Northern Bobwhite *Colinus virginianus* in Canada. Committee on the Status of Endangered Wildlife in Canada, Ottawa.

JAMES, R.D., and M.K. PECK. 1985. Bird and mammal observations in the Cape Henrietta Maria area – 1984. Ontario Ministry of Natural Resources, Toronto.

JAMES, R.D., and M.K. PECK. 1995. Breeding-bird populations in Jack Pine and mixed Jack Pine/deciduous stands in central Ontario. Royal Ontario Museum Life Sciences Contributions 158, Toronto.

JAMES, R.D., P.L. MCLAREN, and J.C. BARLOW. 1976. Annotated checklist of the birds of Ontario. Life Sci. Misc. Publ., R. Ont. Mus., Toronto.

JARVIE, S., H. BLOKPOEL, and T. CHIPPERFIELD. 1999. A geographic information system to monitor nest distributions of Double-crested Cormorants and Black-crowned Night-Herons at shared colony sites near Toronto, Canada. Pp. 121-129 *in* Symposium on Double-crested Cormorants: population status and management issues in the Midwest (M.E. Tobin, Ed.). United States Department of Agriculture, Milwaukee.

JEHL, J.R. JR. 1968. The breeding biology of Smith's Longspur. Wilson Bull. 80:123-149.

JEHL, J.R. JR. 2004. Birdlife of the Churchill Region: Status, History, Biology. Trafford Publishing, Victoria.

JEHL, J.R. JR., and W.L. LIN. 2001. Population status of shorebirds nesting at Churchill, Manitoba. Can.Field-Nat. 115:487-494.

JEHL, J.R. JR., J. KLIMA, and R.E. HARRIS. 2001. Short-billed Dowitcher (*Limnodromus griseus*). *In* The Birds of North America, No. 564 (A. Poole and F. Gill, Eds.). The Birds of North America, Inc., Philadelphia.

JERMYN, K. and D.V.C. WESELOH. 2002. Organochlorine contaminants and toxic equivalents in eggs of Forster's Terns (*Sterna forsteri*) from Lake St. Clair and Lake Simcoe, Ontario, 1999. Canadian Wildlife Service, Downsview.

JOBIN, B., J.-L. DESGRANGES, and C. BOUTIN. 1996. Population trends in selected species of farmland birds in relation to recent developments in agriculture in the St. Lawrence Valley. Agr.Ecosyst.Environ. 57:103-116.

JOHNSON, K. 1995. Green-winged Teal (*Anas crecca*). *In* The Birds of North America, No. 193 (A. Poole and F. Gill, Eds.). Academy of Natural Sciences, Philadelphia, and American Ornithologists' Union, Washington, DC.

JOHNSON, L.S. 1998. House Wren (*Troglodytes aedon*). *In* The Birds of North America, No. 380 (A. Poole and F. Gill, Eds.). The Birds of North America, Inc., Philadelphia.

JOHNSON, O.W., and P.G. CONNORS. 1996. American Golden-Plover (*Pluvialis dominica*), Pacific Golden-Plover (*Pluvialis fulva*). *In* The Birds of North America, No. 201-202 (A. Poole and F. Gill, Eds.). Academy of Natural Sciences, Philadelphia, and American Ornithologists' Union, Washington, DC.

JOHNSTON, R.F. 1992. Rock Dove (*Columba livia*). *In* The Birds of North America, No. 13 (A. Poole, P. Stettenheim, and F. Gill, Eds.). Academy of Natural Sciences, Philadelphia, and American Ornithologists' Union, Washington, DC.

JONES, C.D. 2005. The Ontario Great Gray Owl irruption of 2004-05: numbers, dates and distributions. Ontario Birds 23:106-121.

JONES, J., J.J. BARG, T.S. SILLETT, M.L. VEIT, and R.J. ROBERTSON. 2004. Minimum estimates of survival and population growth for Cerulean Warblers (*Dendroica cerulea*) breeding in Ontario, Canada. Auk 121:15-22.

JONES, P.W., and T.M. DONOVAN. 1996. Hermit Thrush (*Catharus guttatus*). *In* The Birds of North America, No. 261 (A. Poole and F. Gill, Eds.). Academy of Natural Sciences, Philadelphia, and American Ornithologists' Union, Washington, DC.

JONES, S.L., and J.E. CORNELY. 2002. Vesper Sparrow (*Pooecetes gramineus*). *In* The Birds of North America, No. 624 (A. Poole and F. Gill, Eds.). The Birds of North America, Inc., Philadelphia.

JOOS, R., D.V.C. WESELOH, and T. HOAR. 2005. Little Gull (*Larus minutus*) migration on the Great Lakes: do population numbers and behavioral patterns differentiate stopover from staging sites? Unpubl. manuscript.

KANTRUD, H.A., and K.F. HIGGINS. 1992. Nest and nest site characteristics of some ground-nesting, non-passerine birds of northern grasslands. Prairie Nat. 24:67-84.

KAUFMAN, K. 1996. Lives of North American Birds. Houghton Mifflin Co., Boston.

KAUFMANN, G.W. 1989. Breeding ecology of the Sora, *Porzana carolina*, and the Virginia Rail, *Rallus limicola*. Can.Field-Nat. 103:270-282.

KEAR, J. 2005. Ducks, geese and swans, Vol. 2. Oxford University Press, New York.

KELLEY, J.R., D.C. DUNCAN, and D.R. YPARRAGUIRRE. 2001. Distribution and abundance. Pp. 11-18 *in* The status of Ross's Geese (T.J. Moser, Ed.). Arctic Goose Joint Venture Spec.Publ. U.S. Fish and Wildlife Service, Washington DC and Canadian Wildlife Service, Ottawa.

KELLING, S. 2006. Dynamic dove expansions in North America. Bird Source. www.birdsource.org www.birdsource.org/features/doves/index.html.

KENDEIGH, S. C. 1947. Bird population studies in the coniferous forest biome during a spruce budworm outbreak. Ontario Department of Lands and Forest.

KENNAMER, J.E., M. KENNAMER, and R. BRENNEMAN. 1992. History. Pp. 6-17 *in* The Wild Turkey: biology and management (J.G. Dickson, Ed.). National Wild Turkey Federation and the United States Department of Agriculture Forest Service, Harrisburg.

KENNEDY, E.D., and D.W. WHITE. 1997. Bewick's Wren (*Thryomanes bewickii*). *In* The Birds of North America, No. 315 (A. Poole and F. Gill, Eds.). Academy of Natural Sciences, Philadelphia., and American Ornithologists' Union, Washington, DC.

KENNEDY, J.A., P. DILWORTH-CHRISTIE,

and A.J. ERSKINE. 1999. The Canadian breeding bird (mapping) census database. Technical Report Series No. 342. Can.Wildl.Tech.Rep.Ser. No. 342.

KENNEDY, P.L. 2003. Northern Goshawk (*Accipiter gentilis atricapillus*): a technical conservation assessment. USDA Forest Service, Rocky Mountain Region. http://www.fs.fed.us/r2/projects/scp/assessments/northerngoshawk.pdf

KEPPIE, D.M., and R.M. WHITING, JR. 1994. American Woodcock (*Scolopax minor*). *In* The Birds of North America, No. 100 (A. Poole and F. Gill, Eds.). Academy of Natural Sciences, Philadelphia, and American Ornithologists' Union, Washington, DC.

KERBES, R. H., K.M. MEERES, R.T ALISAUSKAS, F.D. CASWELL, K.F. ABRAHAM, AND R.K. ROSS. 2006. Surveys of nesting mid-continent Lesser Snow Geese and Ross's Geese in Eastern and Central Arctic Canada, 1997-1998. Canadian Wildlife Service, Prairie and Northern Region, Saskatoon.

KERR, K.C.R., M.Y. STOECKLE, C.J. DOVE, L.A. WEIGT, C.M. FRANCIS, and P.D.N. HEBERT. 2007. Comprehensive DNA barcode coverage of North American birds. Mol.Ecol.Notes (Online Early Articles) doi:10.1111/j.1471-8286.2006.01670.x.

KESSEL, B., D.A. ROCQUE, and J.S. BARCLAY. 2002. Greater Scaup (*Aythya marila*). *In* The Birds of North America, No. 650 (A. Poole and F. Gill, Eds.). The Birds of North America, Inc., Philadelphia.

KIFF, L.F. 1988. Commentary: changes in the status of the peregrine in North America, an overview. Pp. 123-139 *in* Peregrine Falcon populations: their management and recovery (T.J. Cade, J.H. Enderson, C.G. Thelander, and C.M. White, Eds.). The Peregrine Fund, Boise.

KILHAM, L. 1974. Early breeding season behavior of Downy Woodpeckers. Wilson Bull. 86:407-418.

KILHAM, L. 1983. Life history studies of woodpeckers of eastern North America. Publ.Nuttall Ornithol.Club No. 20.

KILHAM, L. 1989. The American Crow and the Common Raven. W.K. Moody, Jr. Natural History Series No. 10. Texas A&M University Press, College Station.

KIRK, D.A. 1995. Forest management and the Northern Goshawk (*Accipiter gentilis*): with special reference to Ontario. Ontario Ministry of Natural Resources, Central Region Science and Technology Unit, North Bay.

KIRK, D.A. 1996. Updated COSEWIC status report on the Cooper's Hawk (*Accipiter cooperii*) in Canada. Committee on the Status of Endangered Wildlife in Canada.

KIRK, D.A. 1997. Updated COSEWIC status report on Sharp-shinned Hawk (*Accipiter striatus*). Committee on the Status of Endangered Wildlife in Canada.

KIRK, D.A., and C. HYSLOP. 1998. Population status and recent trends in Canadian raptors: a review. Biol.Conserv. 83:91-118.

KIRK, D.A., and M.J. MOSSMAN. 1998. Turkey Vulture (*Cathartes aura*). *In* The Birds of North America, No. 339 (A. Poole and F. Gill, Eds.). The Birds of North America, Inc., Philadelphia.

KIRK, D.A., and B.J. NAYLOR. 1996. Habitat requirements of the Pileated Woodpecker (*Dryocopus pileatus*) with special reference to Ontario. Ontario Ministry of Natural Resources, North Bay.

KLIMA, J., and J.R. JEHL, JR. 1998. Stilt Sandpiper (*Calidris himantopus*). *In* The Birds of North America, No. 341 (A. Poole and F. Gill, Eds.). The Birds of North America, Inc., Philadelphia.

KNAPTON, R.W. 1979. Birds of the Gainsborough-Lyleton region (Saskatchewan and Manitoba). Saskatchewan Nat.Hist.Soc.

KNAPTON, R.W. 1984. The Henslow's Sparrow in Ontario: a historical perspective. Ontario Birds 2:70-74.

KNAPTON, R.W. 1994. Clay-colored Sparrow (*Spizella pallida*). *In* The Birds of North America, No. 120 (A. Poole and F. Gill, Eds.). Academy of Natural Sciences, Philadelphia, and American Ornithologists' Union, Washington, DC.

KNOPF, F.L. and R.M. EVANS. 2004. American White Pelican (*Pelecanus erythrorhynchos*). The Birds of North America Online (A. Poole, Ed.). Cornell Laboratory of Ornithology. Retrieved from The Birds of North America Online Database, Ithaca. http://bna.birds.cornell.edu/BNA/account/American_White_Pelican/.

KNOX, A.G., and P.E. LOWTHER. 2000a. Common Redpoll (*Carduelis flammea*). *In* The Birds of North America, No. 543(A. Poole and F. Gill, Eds.). The Birds of North America, Inc., Philadelphia.

KNOX, A.G., and P.E. LOWTHER. 2000b. Hoary Redpoll (*Carduelis hornemanni*). *In* The Birds of North America, No. 544 (A. Poole and F. Gill, Eds.). The Birds of North America, Inc., Philadelphia.

KOCHERT, M.N., K. STEENHOF, C.L. MCINTYRE, and E.H. CRAIG. 2002. Golden Eagle (*Aquila chrysaetos*). *In* The Birds of North America, No. 684 (A. Poole and F. Gill, Eds.). The Birds of North America, Inc., Philadelphia.

KORPIMAKI, E. 1986. Gradients in population fluctuations of Tengmalm's Owls *Aegolius funereus* in Europe. Oecologia 69:195-201.

KOZLOVIC, D. 1997 Unpubl. The King Rail field survey of Ontario marshes, 1997. Environment Canada, Canadian Wildlife Service, Guelph.

KRASNY, M.E., and M.C. WHITMORE. 1992. Gradual and sudden forest canopy gaps in Allegheny northern hardwood forests. Can.J.For.Res 22:139-143.

KREISEL, K.J., and S.J. STEIN. 1999. Bird use of burned and unburned coniferous forests during winter. Wilson Bull. 111:243-250.

KREN, J., and A.C. ZOERB. 1997. Northern Wheatear (*Oenanthe oenanthe*). *In* The Birds of North America, No. 316 (A. Poole and F. Gill, Eds.). Academy of Natural Sciences, Philadelphia, and American Ornithologists' Union, Washington, DC.

KRICHER, J.C. 1995. Black-and-white Warbler (*Mniotilta varia*). *In* The Birds of North America, No. 158 (A. Poole and F. Gill, Eds.). Academy of Natural Sciences, Philadelphia, and American Ornithologists' Union, Washington, DC.

KROODSMA, D.E., and J. VERNER. 1997. Marsh Wren (*Cistothorus palustris*). *In* The Birds of North America, No. 308 (A. Poole and F. Gill, Eds.). Academy of Natural Sciences, Philadelphia, and American Ornithologists' Union, Washington, DC.

KRUG, H. 1956. The Great Black-backed Gull nesting on Little Haystack Island, Lake Huron. Auk 73:559.

KUBIAK, T.J., H.J. HARRIS, L.M. SMITH, T.R. SCHWARTZ, D.L. STALLING, J.A. TRICK, L. SILEO, D.E. DOCHERTY, and T.C. ERDMAN. 1989. Microcontaminants and reproductive impairment of the Forster's Tern on Green Bay, Lake Michigan – 1983. Arch.Environ.Contam.Toxicol. 18:706-727.

LA SORTE, F.A., and F.R. THOMPSON, III. 2007. Poleward shifts in winter ranges of North American birds. Ecology 88:1803-1812.

LAING, D. 2006. Southern Ontario Bald Eagle monitoring program – 2005 final report. Bird Studies Canada, Port Rowan.

LAMBERT, A.B., and E. NOL. 1978. Status of the Piping Plover at Long Point. Long Point Bird Observatory.

LAMBERT, A.B., and R.B.H. SMITH. 1984. The status and distribution of the Prairie Warbler in Ontario. Ontario Birds 2:99-115.

LAMEY, J. 1981. Unusual records of birds for Ontario's Rainy River District. Ontario Bird Banding 14:38-42.

LANCASTER, H., C. LEYS, D. MARTIN, G. PRIEKSAITIS, and M. PRIEKSAITIS. 2004. Birds of Elgin County: a century of change. Naturalists of Elgin County, Aylmer.

LANG, A. 1991. Status report on the American Coot (*Fulica americana*). Committee on the Status of Endangered Wildlife in Canada.

LANG, A.L. 2000. The 1999 King Rail field survey of Ontario marshes. Environment Canada, Canadian Wildlife Service, Guelph.

LANGILLE, J.H. 1884. Our birds and their haunts. S.E. Cassino & Co., Boston.

LANTRY, B.F., T.H. ECKERT, and C.P. SCHNEIDER. 2002. The relationship between the abundance of Smallmouth Bass and Double-crested Cormorants in the Eastern Basin of Lake Ontario. J.Great Lakes Res. 28:193-201.

LANYON, W.E. 1994. Western Meadowlark (*Sturnella neglecta*). In The Birds of North America, No. 104 (A. Poole and F. Gill, Eds.). Academy of Natural Sciences, Philadelphia, and American Ornithologists' Union, Washington, DC.

LANYON, W.E. 1995. Eastern Meadowlark (*Sturnella magna*). In The Birds of North America, No. 160 (A. Poole and F. Gill, Eds.). Academy of Natural Sciences, Philadelphia, and American Ornithologists' Union, Washington, DC.

LANYON, W.E. 1997. Great Crested Flycatcher (*Myiarchus crinitus*). In The Birds of North America, No. 300 (A. Poole and F. Gill, Eds.). Academy of Natural Sciences, Philadelphia, and American Ornithologists' Union, Washington, DC.

LARSON, B.M., J.L. RILEY, E.A. SNELL, and H.G. GODSCHALK. 1999. The woodland heritage of southern Ontario: a study of ecological change, distribution and significance. Federation of Ontario Naturalists, Don Mills.

LAUGHLIN, S.B., J.R. CARROLL, and S.M. SUTCLIFFE. 1990. Standardized breeding criteria codes: recommendations for North American breeding bird atlas projects. In Handbook for atlassing American breeding birds (C.R. Smith, Ed.). Vermont Institute of Natural Science, Woodstock.

LAWRENCE, L.D. 1967. A comparative life-history study of four species of woodpeckers. American Ornithologists' Union, Washington, DC.

LAWRENCE, L.D.K. 1953. Nesting life and behavior of the Red-eyed Vireo. Can.Field-Nat. 67:47-77.

LEAHY, C.W. 2004. The birdwatcher's companion to North American birdlife. Princeton University Press, Princeton.

LEBLANC, J.P., S.S. BADZINSKI, and S.A. PETRIE. 2007. An assessment of wintering Mourning Dove abundance in Ontario: justification for an autumn harvest. Department of Biology, University of Western Ontario, London.

LEDERER, R.J., W.S. MAZEN, and P.J. METROPULOS. 1975. Population fluctuation in a Yellow-headed Blackbird marsh. Western Birds 6:1-6.

LEMIEUX, C.J., D.J. SCOTT, P.A. GRAY, and R. DAVIS. 2007. Climate change and Ontario's provincial parks: towards an adaptation strategy. Ontario Ministry of Natural Resources, Applied Research and Development Branch, Sault Ste. Marie.

LEMMON, C.R., G. BUGBEE, and G.R. STEPHENS. 1994. Tree damage by nesting Double-crested Cormorants in Connecticut. Connecticut Warbler 14:27-30.

LEMON, R.E. 1957. A study of nesting Cardinals (*Richmondena cardinalis*) at London, Canada. MA thesis, University of Western Ontario, London.

LEONARD, D.L., JR. 2001. Three-toed Woodpecker (*Picoides tridactylus*). In The Birds of North America, No. 588 (A. Poole and F. Gill, Eds.). The Birds of North America, Inc., Philadelphia.

LEONARD, M.L., and J. PICMAN. 1987. The adaptive significance of multiple nest building by male Marsh Wrens. Anim.Behav. 35:271-277.

LEPAGE, D., and C.M. FRANCIS. 2002. Do feeder counts reliably indicate bird population changes? 21 years of winter bird counts in Ontario, Canada. Condor 104:255-270.

LESCHACK, C.R., S.K. MCKNIGHT, and G.R. HEPP. 1997. Gadwall (*Anas strepera*). In The Birds of North America, No. 283 (A. Poole and F. Gill, Eds.). Academy of Natural Sciences, Philadelphia, and American Ornithologists' Union, Washington, DC.

LÉVESQUE, H., and R. McNEIL. 1986. Déplacements du Pigeon Biset (*Columba livia*) dans le vieux-port de Montréal. Nat.Can. 113:47-54.

LIMPERT, R.J., and S.L. EARNST. 1994. Tundra Swan (*Cygnus columbianus*). In The Birds of North America, No. 89 (A. Poole and F. Gill, Eds.). Academy of Natural Sciences, Philadelphia, and American Ornithologists' Union, Washington, DC.

LOCKHART, S., and V. MACINS. 2001. Status of the White Pelican breeding population on Lake of the Woods. Ontario Ministry of Natural Resources, Kenora.

LOFTIN, H. 1991. An annual cycle of pelagic birds in the Gulf of Panama. Ornithologia Neotropical 2:85-94.

LOKEMOEN, J.T., H.F. DUEBBERT, and D.E. SHARP. 1990. Homing and reproductive habits of Mallards, Gadwalls, and Blue-winged Teal. Wildlife Monogr. 106.

LONGCORE, J.R., D.G. MCAULEY, G.R. HEPP, and J.M. RHYMER. 2000. American Black Duck (*Anas rubripes*). In The Birds of North America, No. 481 (A. Poole and F. Gill, Eds.). The Birds of North America, Inc., Philadelphia.

LOWTHER, P.E. 1993. Brown-headed Cowbird (*Molothrus ater*). In The Birds of North America, No. 47 (A. Poole and F. Gill, Eds.). Academy of Natural Sciences, Philadelphia, and American Ornithologists' Union, Washington, DC.

LOWTHER, P.E. 1999. Alder Flycatcher (*Empidonax alnorum*). In The Birds of North America, No. 446 (A. Poole and F. Gill, Eds.). The Birds of North America, Inc., Philadelphia.

LOWTHER, P.E. 2005. Le Conte's Sparrow (*Ammodramus leconteii*). The Birds of North America Online . (A. Poole, Ed.). Cornell Laboratory of Ornithology. Retrieved from The Birds of North America Online Database, Ithaca. http://bna.birds.cornell.edu/BNA/account/Le_Contes_Sparrow/.

LOWTHER, P.E., and C.L. CINK. 2006. House Sparrow. (*Passer domesticus*). The Birds of North America Online (A. Poole, Ed.). Cornell Laboratory of Ornithology. Retrieved from The Birds of North America Online Database, Ithaca. http://bna.birds.cornell.edu/BNA/account/House_Sparrow/.

LOWTHER, P.E., C. CELADA, N.K. KLEIN, C.C. RIMMER, and D.A. SPECTOR. 1999. Yellow Warbler (*Dendroica petechia*). The Birds of North America Online (A. Poole, Ed.). Cornell Laboratory of Ornithology. Retrieved from The Birds of North America Online Database, Ithaca. http://bna.birds.cornell.edu/BNA/account/Yellow_Warbler/.

LOWTHER, P.E., C.C. RIMMER, B. KESSEL, S.L. JOHNSON, and W.G. ELLISON. 2001. Gray-cheeked Thrush (*Catharus minimus*). In The Birds of North America, No. 591 (A. Poole and F. Gill, Eds.). The Birds of North America, Inc., Philadelphia.

LUMSDEN, H.G. 1951. Breeding diving ducks on Lake St. Clair, Ontario. Can.Field-Nat. 65:31-32.

LUMSDEN, H.G. 1957. Notes on wildlife from the Cape Henrietta Maria region of Ontario. Ontario Department of Lands and Forests.

LUMSDEN, H.G. 1959. Mandt's Black Guillemot breeding on the Hudson Bay coast of Ontario. Can.Field-Nat. 73:54-55.

LUMSDEN, H.G. 1966. The Prairie Chicken in southwestern Ontario. Can.Field-Nat. 80:33-45.

LUMSDEN, H.G. 1971. The status of the Sandhill Crane in northern Ontario. Can.Field-Nat. 85:285-293.

LUMSDEN, H.G. 1976. The Whistling Swan in James Bay and the southern region of Hudson Bay. Arctic 28:194-200.

LUMSDEN, H.G. 1984a. The breeding status of Tundra Swans (*Cygnus columbianus*) in northern Ontario. Ont.Field Biol. 38:1-4.

LUMSDEN, H.G. 1984b. The pre-settlement breeding distribution of Trumpeter (*Cygnus buccinator*) and Tundra Swans (*C. columbianus*) in eastern Canada. Can.Field-Nat. 98:415-424.

LUMSDEN, H.G. 2005. "Prairie Grouse" *Tympanuchus cupido x phasianellus*, hybridization on Manitoulin Island, Ontario. Can.Field-Nat. 119:507-514.

LUMSDEN, H.G. 2005. The plumage and internal morphology of the "Prairie Grouse," *Tympanuchus cupido x phasianellus*, of Manitoulin Island, Ontario. Can.Field-Nat. 119:515-524.

LUMSDEN, H.G., and D.G. DENNIS. 1998. Giant Canada Geese in southern Ontario: a management experience. *In* Biology and Management of Canada Geese (D.H. Rusch, M.D. Samuel, D.D. Humburg, and B.D. Sullivan, Eds.). Proceedings of the International Canada Goose Symposium, Milwaukee.

LUNK, W.A. 1962. The Rough-winged Swallow, *Stelgidopteryx ruficollis* (Vieillot), a study based on its breeding biology in Michigan. Publ.Nuttall Ornithol.Club No. 4.

LYON, B., and R. MONTGOMERIE. 1995. Snow Bunting and McKay's Bunting (*Plectrophenax nivalis* and *Plectrophenax hyperboreus*). *In* The Birds of North America, No. 198-199 (A. Poole and F. Gill, Eds.). Academy of Natural Sciences, Philadelphia, and American Ornithologists' Union, Washington, DC.

MACFAYDEN, C.J. 1945. Breeding of *Tyrannus verticalis* in Ontario. Can.Field-Nat. 59:67.

MACINTYRE, K. 2002. A technical report outlining the status of Northern Bobwhite (*Colinus virginianus*) in the Aylmer District. Ontario Ministry of Natural Resources, Aylmer.

MACLULICH, D.A. 1938. Birds of Algonquin Provincial Park, Ontario. R.Ont.Mus.Zool.Contrib. 13:1-47.

MACOUN, J., and J.M. MACOUN. 1909. Catalogue of Canadian birds. Geol.Surv.Can., Dept. Mines.

MACWHIRTER, R.B., and K.L. BILDSTEIN. 1996. Northern Harrier (*Circus cyaneus*). *In* The Birds of North America, No. 210 (A. Poole and F. Gill, Eds.). Academy of Natural Sciences, Philadelphia, and American Ornithologists' Union, Washington, DC.

MAHER, W.J. 1974. Ecology of Pomarine, Parasitic, and Long-tailed Jaegers in northern Alaska. Pac.Coast Avifauna No. 37.

MALECKI, R.A., S. SHEAFFER, S., D.L. HOWELL, and T. STRANGE. 2006. Northern Pintails in Eastern North America: their seasonal distribution, movement patterns, and habitat affiliations. Atlantic Flyway Council Technical Section Final Report.

MALLORY, M., and K. METZ. 1999. Common Merganser (*Mergus merganser*). *In* The Birds of North America, No. 442 (A. Poole and F. Gill, Eds.). The Birds of North America, Inc., Philadelphia.

MALLORY, M.L., R.A. WALTON, and D.K. MCNICOL. 1999. Influence of intraspecific competition and habitat quality on diurnal activity budgets of breeding Common Goldeneyes. Écoscience 6:481-486.

MANITOBA AVIAN RESEARCH COMMITTEE. 2003. The birds of Manitoba. Manitoba Naturalists Society, Winnipeg.

MANNAN, R.W., and C.W. BOAL. 2000. Home range characteristics of male Cooper's Hawks in an urban environment. Wilson Bull. 112:21-27.

MANNING, T.H. 1952. Birds of the west James Bay and southern Hudson Bay coasts. Natl.Mus.Can.Bull. 125.

MANNING, T.H. 1976. Birds and mammals of the Belcher, Sleeper, Ottawa and King George Islands and Northwest Territories. Canadian Wildlife Service, Ottawa.

MANNING, T.H. 1981. Birds of the Twin Islands, James Bay, N.W.T., Canada. Syllogeus 30. Natl. Mus. Can, Ottawa.

MARKS, J.S., D.L. EVANS, and D.W. HOLT. 1994. Long-eared Owl (*Asio otus*). *In* The Birds of North America, No. 133 (A. Poole and F. Gill, Eds.). Academy of Natural Sciences, Philadelphia, and American Ornithologists' Union, Washington, DC.

MARTIN, J.W., and J.R. PARRISH. 2000. Lark Sparrow (*Chondestes grammacus*). *In* The Birds of North America, No. 488 (A. Poole and F. Gill, Eds.). The Birds of North America, Inc., Philadelphia.

MARTIN, M., and T.W. BARRY. 1978. Nesting behavior and food habits of Parasitic Jaegers at Anderson River Delta, Northwest Territories. Can.Field-Nat. 92:45-50.

MARTIN, S.G. 2002. Brewer's Blackbird (*Euphagus cyanocephalus*). *In* The Birds of North America, No. 616 (A. Poole and F. Gill, Eds.). The Birds of North America, Inc., Philadelphia.

MARTIN, S.G., and T.A. GAVIN. 1995. Bobolink (*Dolichonyx oryzivorus*). *In* The Birds of North America, No. 176 (A. Poole and F. Gill, Eds.). Academy of Natural Sciences, Philadelphia, and American Ornithologists' Union, Washington, DC.

MAZUR, K.M., P.C. JAMES, M.J. FITZSIMMONS, G. LANGEN, and R.H.M. ESPIE. 1997. Habitat associations of the Barred Owl in the boreal forest of Saskatchewan, Canada. J.Raptor Res. 31:253-259.

MAZUR, K.M., and P.C. JAMES. 2000. Barred Owl (*Strix varia*). *In* The Birds of North America, No. 508 (A. Poole and F. Gill, Eds.). The Birds of North America, Inc., Philadelphia.

MCALPINE, R.S. 1998. The impact of climate change on forest fires and forest fire management in Ontario. Pp. 21-24 *in* The impacts of climate change on Ontario's forests. Forest Research Information Paper No. 143. Ontario Forestry Research Institute, Ontario Ministry of Natural Resources, Sault Ste. Marie.

MCCABE, R.A. 1985. The loss of a large colony of Yellow-headed Blackbirds (*Xanthocephalus*) from southern Wisconsin. Proc.Int.Ornithol.Congr. 18:1034.

MCCARTY, J.P. 1996. Eastern Wood-Pewee (*Contopus virens*). *In* The Birds of North America, No. 245 (A. Poole and F. Gill, Eds.). Academy of Natural Sciences, Philadelphia, and American Ornithologists' Union, Washington, DC.

MCCRACKEN, J.D. 1987. Annotated checklist to the birds of Haldimand-Norfolk. *In* The natural areas inventory of the Regional Municipality of Haldimand-Norfolk, vol. 2. Annotated checklist, Norfolk Field Natur., Simcoe.

MCCRACKEN, J.D. 1988. An enigmatic case for the breeding of the Kentucky Warbler in Canada. Ontario Birds 6:101-105.

MCCRACKEN, J.D. 1994. Golden-winged and Blue-winged Warblers: their history and future in Ontario. Pp. 279-289 *in* Ornithology in Ontario. Spec.Publ. No. 1. (M.K. McNicholl and J.L. Cranmer-Byng, Eds.). Ontario Field Ornithologists. Hawk Owl Publishing, Whitby.

MCCRACKEN, J.D. 2005. Where the Bobolinks roam: the plight of North America's grassland birds. Biodiversity 6:20-29.

MCCRACKEN, J.D., M.S.W. BRADSTREET, and G.L. HOLROYD. 1981. Breeding birds of Long Point, Lake Erie: a study in community succession. Canadian Wildlife Service.

MCCRACKEN, J.D., R. WOOD, and P. PATEL. 2006. The 2005 Prothonotary Warbler recovery program in Canada: population surveys, nest box monitoring, habitat assessments, and colour banding. Bird Studies Canada, Port Rowan.

MCCRIMMON, D.A., Jr., J.C. OGDEN, and G.T. BANCROFT. 2001. Great Egret (*Ardea alba*). In The Birds of North America, No. 570 (A. Poole and F. Gill, Eds.). The Birds of North America, Inc., Philadelphia.

MCDERMOTT, G.L. 1961. Frontiers of settlement in the Great Clay Belt, Ontario and Quebec. Annals of the Association of American Geographers 51:261-273.

MCDONALD, M.V. 1998. Kentucky Warbler (*Oporornis formosus*). In The Birds of North America, No. 324 (A. Poole and F. Gill, Eds.). The Birds of North America, Inc., Philadelphia.

MCILHENNY, E.A. 1943. Major changes in the bird life of southern Louisiana during sixty years. Auk 60:541-549.

MCILWRAITH, T. 1886. The birds of Ontario. Lawson, Hamilton.

MCILWRAITH, T. 1894. The birds of Ontario. 2nd ed. William Briggs, Toronto.

MCINTYRE, J.W. 1988. The Common Loon: spirit of northern lakes. University of Minnesota Press, Minneapolis.

MCINTYRE, J.W., and J.F. BARR. 1997. Common Loon (*Gavia immer*). In The Birds of North America, No. 313 (A. Poole and F. Gill, Eds.). Academy of Natural Sciences, Philadelphia, and American Ornithologists' Union, Washington, DC.

MCKEANE, L., and D.V. WESELOH. 1993. Bringing the Bald Eagle back to Lake Erie. Environment Canada, State of the Environment Fact Sheet 93-3.

MCKENNEY, D.W., J.H. PEDLAR, P. PAPADOPOL, and M.F. HUTCHINSON. 2006. The development of 1901-2000 historical monthly climate models for Canada and the United States. Agriculture and Forest Meteorology 138:69-81.

MCLAREN, P.L., and M.A. MCLAREN. 1981a. Bird observations in northwestern Ontario, 1976-77. Ont.Field Biol. 35:1-6.

MCLAREN, M.A., and P.L. MCLAREN. 1981b. Relative abundances of birds in the boreal and subarctic habitats of northwestern Ontario and northeastern Manitoba. Can.Field-Nat. 95:418-427.

MCLAREN, M.A., N. DAWSON, G. HOLBURN, D. PHOENIX, and M. TWISS. 2006. Ontario Wildlife Assessment Program forest bird surveys, 2002-2004, with discussion of the survey protocol and potential application of distance sampling.

MCLAREN, P.L. 1975. Habitat selection and resource utilization in four species of wood warblers. Ph.D. dissertation, University of Toronto, Toronto.

MCNICHOLL, M.K., and J.L. CRANMER-BYNG. 1994. Ornithology in Ontario. Spec.Publ. No. 1, Ontario Field Ornithologists. Hawk Owl Publishing, Whitby.

MCNICHOLL, M.K., P.E. LOWTHER, and J.A. HALL. 2001. Forster's Tern (*Sterna forsteri*). In The Birds of North America, No. 595 (A. Poole and F. Gill, Eds.). The Birds of North America, Inc., Philadelphia.

MCNICOL, D.K., B.E. BENDELL, and R.K. ROSS. 1987. Studies of the effects of acidification on aquatic wildlife in Canada: waterfowl and trophic relationships in small lakes in northern Ontario. 74 pp. Canadian Wildlife Service.

MCNICOL, D.K., M.L. MALLORY, and C.H.R. WEDELES. 1995. Assessing biological recovery of acid-sensitive lakes in Ontario, Canada. Water, Air, and Soil Pollution 85:457-462.

MCRAE, R.D. 1984. First nesting of the Little Gull in Manitoba. Amer.Birds 38:368-369.

MEARNS, B., and R. MEARNS. 1992. Audubon to Xantus. Academic Press, San Diego.

MELCHER, C. P., A. Farmer, and G. FERNANDEZ. 2006. Conservation plan for the Marbled Godwit. Version 1.1. Manomet Center for Conservation Science. Manomet

MELLES, S.J. 2007. Effects of forest connectivity, habitat availability, and intraspecific biotic processes on range expansion: Hooded Warbler (*Wilsonia citrina*) as a model species. Ph.D. thesis, University of Toronto.

MELVIN, S.M., and J.P. GIBBS. 1996. Sora (*Porzana carolina*). In The Birds of North America, No. 250 (A. Poole and F. Gill, Eds.). Academy of Natural Sciences, Philadelphia, and American Ornithologists' Union, Washington, DC.

MENDALL, H.L. 1958. The Ring-necked Duck in the northeast. University of Maine Press, Orono.

MERENDINO, M.T., and C.D. ANKNEY. 1994. Habitat use by Mallards and American Black Ducks breeding in central Ontario. Condor 96:411-421.

MERENDINO, M.T., G.B. MCCULLOUGH, and N.R. NORTH. 1995. Wetland availability and use by breeding waterfowl in southern Ontario. J.Wildl.Manage. 59:527-532.

MIDDLETON, A.L.A. 1993. American Goldfinch (*Carduelis tristis*). In The Birds of North America, No. 80 (A. Poole and F. Gill, Eds.). Academy of Natural Sciences, Philadelphia, and American Ornithologists' Union, Washington, DC.

MIDDLETON, A.L.A. 1998. Chipping Sparrow (*Spizella passerina*). In The Birds of North America, No. 334 (A. Poole and F. Gill, Eds.). The Birds of North America, Inc., Philadelphia.

MIDDLETON, D.S. 1949. Close proximity of two nests of American Bitterns. Wilson Bull. 61:113.

MILKO, R., L. DICKSON, R. ELLIIOT, and G. Donaldson. 2003. Wings over water: Canada's Waterbird Conservation Plan. Canadian Wildlife Service, Environment Canada. http://www.cws-scf.ec.gc.ca/birds/wb_om_e.cfm.

MILLER, E.H. 1983. The structure of aerial displays in three species of Calidridinae (Scolopacidae). Auk 100:440-451.

MILLS, A. 1981. A cottager's guide to the birds of Muskoka and Parry Sound. Alex Mills, Guelph.

MILLS, A.M. 1986. The influence of moonlight on the behavior of goatsuckers (Caprimulgidae). Auk 103:370-378.

MINEAU, P. 2005. Direct losses of birds to pesticides: beginnings of a quantification. Pp. 1065-1070 in Bird conservation implementation and integration in the Americas: Third International Partners in Flight Conference 2002, Vol. 2 (C.J. Ralph and T.D. Rich, Eds.). U.S. Department of Agriculture, Albany.

MIRARCHI, R.E., and T.S. BASKETT. 1994. Mourning Dove (*Zenaida macroura*). In The Birds of North America, No. 117 (A. Poole and F. Gill, Eds.). Academy of Natural Sciences, Philadelphia, and American Ornithologists' Union, Washington, DC.

MITCHELL, M.H. 1935. The Passenger Pigeon in Ontario. R.Ont.Mus.Zool.Contrib. 7:1-181.

MITCHELL, R.T. 1952. Consumption of Spruce Budworms by birds in a Maine spruce-fir forest. J.Forestry 50:387-389.

MOFFATT, K.C., E.E. CRONE, K.D. HOLL, R.W. SCHLORFF, and B.A. GARRISON. 2005. Importance of hydrologic and landscape heterogeneity for restoring Bank Swallow (*Riparia riparia*) colonies along the Sacramento River, California. Restor.Ecol. 13:391-402.

MOLDENHAUER, R.R., and D.J. REGELSKI. 1996. Northern Parula (*Parula americana*). In The Birds of North America, No. 215 (A. Poole and F. Gill, Eds.). Academy of Natural Sciences, Philadelphia, and American Ornithologists' Union, Washington, DC.

MOORE, D.J. 2002. The provisioning tactics of parent Common Terns (*Sterna hirundo*) in relation to brood energy requirement. Ph.D. dissertation, Simon Fraser University, Burnaby.

MOORE, W.S. 1995. Northern Flicker (*Colaptes auratus*). In The Birds of North America, No. 166 (A. Poole and F. Gill, Eds.). Academy of Natural Sciences, Philadelphia, and American Ornithologists' Union, Washington, DC.

MORDEN, J.A., and W.E. SAUNDERS. 1882. List of the birds of western Ontario. Can.Sportsman Natur. 2:183-194.

MORNEAU, F., S. BRODEUR, R. DECARIE, S. CARRIERE, and D.M. BIRD. 1994. Abundance and distribution of nesting Golden Eagles in Hudson Bay, Québec. J.Raptor Res. 28:220-225.

MORRIER, A., L. LESAGE, A. REED, and J-P.L. SAVARD. 1997. Étude sur l'écologie de la Macreuse à Front Blanc au lac Malbaie, Réserve des Laurentides: 1994-1995. Canadian Wildlife Service, Québec Region, Québec

MORRIS, R.D., and R.A. HUNTER. 1976. Factors influencing desertion of colony sites by Common Terns (*Sterna hirundo*). Can.Field-Nat. 90:137-143.

MORRIS, R.D., H. BLOKPOEL, and G.D. TESSIER. 1992. Management efforts for the conservation of Common Tern colonies: two case histories. Biol.Conserv. 60:7-14.

MORRIS, R.D., D.V. WESELOH, and L. SHUTT. 2003. Distribution and abundance of nesting pairs of Herring Gulls (*Larus argentatus*) on the North American Great Lakes, 1976 to 2000. J.Great Lakes Res. 29:400-426.

MORRISON, R.I.G., R.W. BUTLER, H.L. DICKSON, A. BOURGET, P.W. HICKLIN, and J.P. GOOSSEN. 1991. Potential western hemisphere shorebird reserve network sites for migrant shorebirds in Canada. Environment Canada, Canadian Wildlife Service, Ottawa.

MORRISON, R.I.G., R.W. BUTLER, G.W. BEYERSBERGEN, H.L. DICKSON, A. BOURGET, P.W. HICKLIN, J.P. GOOSSEN, R.K. ROSS, and C.L. GRATTO-TREVOR. 1995. Potential Western Hemisphere Shorebird Reserve Network sites for shorebirds in Canada. 2nd ed. 1995.

MORRISON, R.I.G., R.E. GILL JR., B.A. HARRINGTON, S. SKAGEN, G.W. PAGE, C.L. GRATTO-TREVOR, and S.M. HAIG. 2001. Estimates of shorebird populations in North America. Canadian Wildlife Service, Ottawa.

MORRISON, M.L., and D.C. HAHN. 2002. Geographic variation in cowbird distribution, abundance, and parasitism. Studies in Avian Biology 25:65-72.

MORRISON, R.I.G., and T.H. MANNING. 1976. First breeding records of Wilson's Phalarope for James Bay, Ontario. Auk 93:656-657.

MORRISON, R.I.G., T.H. MANNING, and J.A. HAGAR. 1976. Breeding of the Marbled Godwit, *Limosa fedoa*, in James Bay. Can.Field-Nat. 90:487-490.

MORRISON, R.I.G., B.J. MCCAFFERY, R.E. GILL, Jr., S.K. SKAGEN, S.L. JONES, G.W. PAGE, C.L. GRATTO-TREVOR, and B.A. ANDRES. 2006. Population estimates of North American shorebirds. Wader Study Group Bulletin 111:67-85.

MORSE, D.H. 2004. Blackburnian Warbler (*Dendroica fusca*). *In* The Birds of North America Online (A. Poole, Ed.). Cornell Laboratory of Ornithology. Retrieved from The Birds of North America Online Database, Ithaca. http://bna.birds.cornell.edu/BNA/account/Blackburnian_Warbler/.

MORSE, D.H., and A. POOLE . 2005. Black-throated Green Warbler (*Dendroica virens*). The Birds of North America Online (A. Poole, Ed.). Cornell Laboratory of Ornithology. Retrieved from The Birds of North America Online databse, Ithaca. http://bna.birds.cornell.edu/BNA/account/Black-throated_Green_Warbler/.

MORSE, T.E., J.L. JAKABOSKY, and V.P. MCCROW. 1969. Some aspects of the breeding biology of the Hooded Merganser. J.Wildl.Manage. 33:596-604.

MOSER, T.J. 2006. The 2005 North American Trumpeter Swan survey. U.S. Fish and Wildlife Service, Division of Migratory Bird Management, Denver.

MOSKOFF, W., and S.K. ROBINSON. 1996. Philadelphia Vireo (*Vireo philadelphicus*). *In* The Birds of North America, No. 214 (A. Poole and F. Gill, Eds.). Academy of Natural Sciences, Philadelphia, and American Ornithologists' Union, Washington, DC.

MOSS, M.R. 1976. Forest regeneration in the rural-urban fringe: a study of succession in the Niagara Peninsula. Can.Geog. 20:141-157.

MOSS, M.R., and L.S. DAVIES. 1994. Measurement of spatial change in the forest component of the rural landscape of southern Ontario. Appl.Geogr. 14:214-231.

MOSSMAN, M.J., and R.M. HOFFMAN. 1989. Birds of southern Wisconsin upland forests. Passenger Pigeon 51:343-358.

MOWBRAY, T. 1999. American Wigeon (*Anas americana*). *In* The Birds of North America, No. 401 (A. Poole and F. Gill, Eds.). The Birds of North America, Inc., Philadelphia.

MOWBRAY, T.B. 1999. Scarlet Tanager (*Piranga olivacea*). *In* The Birds of North America, No. 479 (A. Poole and F. Gill, Eds.). The Birds of North America, Inc., Philadelphia.

MOWBRAY, T.B. 2002. Canvasback (*Aythya valisineria*). *In* The Birds of North America, No. 659 (A. Poole and F. Gill, Eds.). The Birds of North America, Inc., Philadelphia.

MOWBRAY, T.B., F. COOKE, and B. GANTER. 2000. Snow Goose (*Chen caerulescens*). *In* The Birds of North America, No. 514 (A. Poole and F. Gill, Eds.). The Birds of North America, Inc., Philadelphia.

MOWBRAY, T.B., C.R. ELY, J.S. SEDINGER, and R.E. TROST. 2002. Canada Goose (*Branta canadensis*). *In* The Birds of North America, No. 682 (A. Poole and F. Gill, Eds.). The Birds of North America, Inc., Philadelphia.

MUELLER, H. 1999. Common Snipe (*Gallinago gallinago*). *In* The Birds of North America, No. 417 (A. Poole and F. Gill, Eds.). The Birds of North America, Inc., Philadelphia.

MUELLER, H. 2005. Wilson's Snipe. (*Gallinago delicata*). The Birds of North America Online. (A. Poole, Ed.). Cornell Laboratory of Ornithology. Retrieved from The Birds of North America Online Database, Ithaca. http://bna.birds.cornell.edu/BNA/account/Wilsons_Snipe/.

MULLER, M.J., and R.W. STORER. 1999. Pied-billed Grebe (*Podilymbus podiceps*). *In* The Birds of North America, No. 410 (A. Poole and F. Gill, Eds.). The Birds of North America, Inc., Philadelphia.

MUNRO, J.A. 1949. Studies of waterfowl in British Columbia: Green-winged Teal. Can.J.Res. (D) 27:149-178.

MURPHY, E.C., and W.A. LEHNHAUSEN. 1998. Density and foraging ecology of woodpeckers following a stand-replacement fire. J.Wildl.Manage. 62:1359-1372.

MURPHY, M.T. 1996. Eastern Kingbird (*Tyrannus tyrannus*). *In* The Birds of North America, No. 253 (A. Poole and F. Gill, Eds.). Academy of Natural Sciences, Philadelphia, and American Ornithologists' Union, Washington, DC.

MURTON, R.K., R.J.P. THEARLE, B. LOFTS, and J. THOMPSON. 1972. Ecological studies of the feral pigeon *Columba livia* var. I. Population, breeding biology and methods of control. J.Appl.Ecol. 9:835-874.

NAKASHIMA, D.J., and D.J. Murray. 1988. The Common Eider (*Somateria mollissima sedentaria*) of eastern Hudson Bay: a survey of nest colonies and Inuit ecological knowledge. Environmental Studies Revolving Funds Report No. 102. Ottawa.

NASA. 2004. Land cover changes affect U.S. summer climate. http://www.nasa.gov/centers/goddard/news/topstory/2004/0223landsummer.html.

NASH, C.W. 1908. Checklist of the birds of Ontario. Pp. 7-82 in Manual of the vertebrates of Ontario. Department of Education, Toronto.

NASH, S.V., and J.A. DICK. 1981. First documentation of Greater Yellowlegs breeding in Ontario. Ont.Field Biol. 35:48.

NATIONAL AUDUBON SOCIETY. 2002. The Christmas Bird Count historical results. http://www.audubon.org/bird/cbc.

NATIONAL FORESTRY DATABASE PROGRAM. 2007. Area within which moderate to severe defoliation occurs, including area of beetle-killed trees by insects and province/territory, 1975-2004. Compendium of Canadian Forestry Statistics. http://nfdp.ccfm.org.

NATURAL RESOURCES AND VALUES INFORMATION SYSTEM. 2007. Ontario Ministry of Natural Resources Computer database application, Version 3.0.

NAUGLE, D.E., K.F. HIGGINS, and S.M. NUSSER. 1999. Effects of woody vegetation on prairie wetland birds. Can.Field-Nat. 113:487-492.

NAUGLER, C.T. 1993. American Tree Sparrow (*Spizella arborea*). *In* The Birds of North America, No. 37 (A. Poole, P. Stettenheim, and F. Gill, Eds.). Academy of Natural Sciences, Philadelphia, and American Ornithologists' Union, Washington, DC.

NAYLOR, B., D. KAMINSKI, P. BRIDGE, D. ELKIE, G. FERGUSON, G. LUCKING, and B. WATT. 1999. User's guide for OWHAM99 and OWHAM Tool, Version 4.0. Ontario Ministry of Natural Resources, Southern Science and Information Section.

NAYLOR, B.J. 1989. Adaptive significance of spring territories of female Spruce Grouse, *Dendragapus canadensis*. Ph.D. dissertation, University of Toronto.

NAYLOR B.J., J.A. BAKER, D.M. HOGG, J.G. MCNICHOL, and W.R. WATT. 1996. Forest management guidelines for the provision of Pileated Woodpecker habitat. Version 1.0. Queen's Printer for Ontario, Toronto. http://www.mnr.gov.on.ca/mnr/forests/forestdoc/guidelines/pdfs/pileated.pdf.

NAYLOR, B.J., J.A. BAKER, and K.J. SZUBA. 2004. Effects of forest management practices on Red-shouldered Hawks in Ontario. Forest.Chro. 80:54-60.

NAYLOR, B.J., and J.F. BENDELL. 1989. Clutch size and egg size of Spruce Grouse in relation to spring diet, food supply, and endogenous reserves. Can.J.Zool. 67:969-980.

NAYLOR, B.J., and K. SZUBA. 1998. Locating Red-shouldered Hawk nests. Pp. 139-163 *in* Selected wildlife and habitat features: inventory manual. Version 1.0 (W.B. Ranta, Ed.). OMNR, Queen's Printer for Ontario. http://www.mnr.gov.on.ca/mnr/forests/forestdoc/guidelines/wildlife/cover.pdf, Toronto.

NELMS, C.O., W.J. BLEIER, D.L. OTIS, and G.M. LINZ. 1994. Population estimates of breeding blackbirds in North Dakota, 1967, 1981-82, and 1990. Amer.Midl.Nat. 132:256-263.

NEW YORK STATE BREEDING BIRD ATLAS. 2000. 2000-2005. Release 1.0. New York State Department of Environmental Conservation [updated 11 June 2007, Albany. http://www.dec.ny.gov/animals/7312.html.

NGUYEN, L.P., J. HAMR, and G.H. PARKER. 2003. Survival and reproduction of Wild Turkey hens in central Ontario. Wilson Bull. 115:131-139.

NICHOLSON, J.C. 1981. The birds of Manitoulin Island and adjacent islands within Manitoulin District. 2nd ed. J.C. Nicholson, Sudbury.

NICOLL, F.I., and J.R. ZIMMERLING. 2006. The importance of wetlands to waterbirds in the boreal forest of Ontario. Ontario Birds 24:13-22.

NISBET, I.C.T. 2002. Common Tern (*Sterna hirundo*). *In* The Birds of North America, No. 618 (A. Poole and F. Gill, Eds.). The Birds of North America, Inc., Philadelphia.

NOL, E., and M.S. BLANKEN. 1999. Semipalmated Plover (*Charadrius semipalmatus*). *In* The Birds of North America, No. 444 (A. Poole and F. Gill, Eds.). The Birds of North America, Inc., Philadelphia.

NOL, E., C.M. FRANCIS, and D.M. BURKE. 2005. Using distance from putative source woodlots to predict occurrence of forest birds in putative sinks. Conserv.Biol. 19:836-844.

NOLAN, V., Jr., E.D. KETTERSON, and C.A. BUERKLE. 1999. Prairie Warbler (*Dendroica discolor*). *In* The Birds of North America, No. 455 (A. Poole and F. Gill, Eds.). The Birds of North America, Inc., Philadelphia.

NOLAN, V., Jr., E.D. KETTERSON, D.A. CRISTOL, C.M. ROGERS, E.D. CLOTFELTER, R.C. TITUS, S.J. SCHOECH, and E. SNAJDR. 2002. Dark-eyed Junco (*Junco hyemalis*). *In* The Birds of North America, No. 716 (A. Poole and F. Gill, Eds.). The Birds of North America, Inc., Philadelphia.

NOLAN, V., JR., and C.F. THOMPSON. 1975. The occurrence and significance of anomalous reproductive activities in two North American non-parasitic cuckoos *Coccyzus* spp. Ibis 117:496-503.

NOOKER, J.K., P.O. DUNN, and L.A. WHITTINGHAM. 2005. Effects of food abundance, weather, and female condition on reproduction in Tree Swallows (*Tachycineta bicolor*). Auk 122:1225-1238.

NORMENT, C.J., and S.A. SHACKLETON. 1993. Harris's Sparrow (*Zonotrichia querula*). *In* The Birds of North America, No. 64 (A. Poole and F. Gill, Eds.). Academy of Natural Sciences, Philadelphia, and American Ornithologists' Union, Washington, DC.

NORTHWATCH. 2001. Undermining Superior: a report on mining activities and impacts in the Lake Superior Basin. Northwatch, North Bay 11-9-2007. http://www.web.ca/~nwatch/mines/UnderMining_Superior.pdf.

NUECHTERLEIN, G.L., D. BUITRON, J.L. SACHS, and C.R. HUGHES. 2003. Red-necked Grebes become semicolonial when prime nesting substrate is available. Condor 105:80-94.

OBERTSON, G.J. 1995. Annual variation in Common Eider egg size: effects of temperature, clutch size, laying date, and laying sequence. Can.J.Zoo. 73:1579-1587.

OKINES, D., and J. MCCRACKEN. 2003. Loggerhead Shrike banding in Ontario: report on the 2003 field season. Ontario Region and Wildlife Preservation Trust. http://www.bsc-eoc.org/download/loshrpt2002.pdf.

OLSEN, K.M., and H. LARSSON. 2004. Gulls of North America, Europe, and Asia. Princeton University Press, Princeton.

ONTARIO MINISTRY OF AGRICULTURE, FOOD AND RURAL AFFAIRS. 2006. Grain corn: area and production, Ontario by county. 2005. http://www.omafra.gov.on.ca/english/stats/crops/ctygrcorn05.htm.

ONTARIO MINISTRY OF NATURAL RESOURCES. 1998. A silvicultural guide for the Great Lakes-St. Lawrence conifer forest in Ontario. Version 1.1. Queen's Printer for Ontario, Toronto. http://ontariosforests.mnr.gov.on.ca/guides.cfm.

ONTARIO MINISTRY OF NATURAL RESOURCES. 2000. Significant wildlife habitat: technical guide. Queen's Printer for Ontario, Peterborough.

ONTARIO MINISTRY OF NATURAL RESOURCES. 2001. Forest management guide for natural disturbance pattern emulation. Version 3.1. Ontario Ministry of Natural Resources, Queen's Printer for Ontario. http://ontariosforests.mnr.gov.on.ca/ontariosforests.cfm.

ONTARIO MINISTRY OF NATURAL RESOURCES. 2002. State of the Forest Report, 2001. Queen's Printer for Ontario. http://ontariosforests.mnr.gov.on.ca/publications.cfm#reports.

ONTARIO MINISTRY OF NATURAL

RESOURCES. 2004. Annual report on forest management. Ontario Ministry of Natural Resources, Queen's Printer for Ontario, Toronto.

ONTARIO MINISTRY OF NATURAL RESOURCES. 2006a. Species at Risk in Ontario list. Ontario Ministry of Natural Resources, Species at Risk Unit, Peterborough. http://www.mnr.gov.on.ca/mnr/speciesatrisk/status_list.html.

ONTARIO MINISTRY OF NATURAL RESOURCES. 2006b. State of the forest report, 2006. Queen's Printer for Ontario.

ONTARIO PARTNERS IN FLIGHT. 2006a. Ontario landbird conservation plan, Boreal Softwood Shield (North American Bird Conservation Region 8): priorities, objectives and recommended actions. Version 1. Environment Canada, Ontario Ministry of Natural Resources.

ONTARIO PARTNERS IN FLIGHT. 2006b. Ontario landbird conservation plan, Lower Great Lakes/St. Lawrence Plain (North American Bird Conservation Region 13): priorities, objectives and recommended actions. Environment Canada, Ontario Ministry of Natural Resources.

ORING, L.W. 1973. Solitary Sandpiper early reproductive behavior. Auk 90:652-663.

ORING, L.W., E.M. GRAY, and J.M. REED. 1997. Spotted Sandpiper (*Actitis macularia*). *In* The Birds of North America, No. 289 (A. Poole and F. Gill, Eds.). Academy of Natural Sciences, Philadelphia, and American Ornithologists' Union, Washington, DC.

PAGE, A.M. 1996. Status report on the Red-headed Woodpecker, *Melanerpes erythrocephalus*, in Canada. Committee on the Status of Endangered Wildlife in Canada, Ottawa.

PALA, S., P.J. BARNETT, and D. BABUIN. 1991. Quaternary geology of Ontario, northern sheet. Ontario Geological Survey, Map 2553.

PALMER, R.S. 1988. Handbook of North American birds, Vol. 5, Diurnal raptors. Yale University Press, New Haven and London.

PALMER, R.S., and W. TABER. 1946. Birds of the Mt. Katahdin region of Maine. Auk 63:299-314.

PARCHMAN, T.L., C.W. BENKMAN, and S.T. BRITCH. 2006. Patterns of genetic variation in the adaptive radiation of New World crossbills (Aves: *Loxia*). Mol.Ecol. 15:1873-1887.

PARKES, K.C. 1951. The genetics of the Golden-winged x Blue-winged Warbler complex. Wilson Bull. 63:5-15.

PARMELEE, D. 1992. Snowy Owl (*Bubo scandiacus*). *In* The Birds of North America, No. 10 (A. Poole, P. Stettenheim, and F. Gill, Eds.). Academy of Natural Sciences, Philadelphia, and American Ornithologists' Union, Washington, DC.

PARMELEE, D.F., H.A. STEPHENS, and R.H. SCHMIDT. 1967. The birds of southeastern Victoria Island and adjacent small islands. Natl.Mus.Can.Bull. No. 222.

PARSONS, K.C., and T.L. MASTER. 2000. Snowy Egret (*Egretta thula*). *In* The Birds of North America, No. 489 (A. Poole and F. Gill, Eds.). The Birds of North America, Inc., Philadelphia.

PARTNERS IN FLIGHT. 2004. Conservation objectives for Brown Thrasher in the Ontario portion of BCR 13. Partners in Flight Ontario Newsletter, September 2004, 2. www.bsc-eoc.org/PIF/PIFSept04Newsletter.pdf.

PARTNERS IN FLIGHT. 2005. Partners in Flight species assessment database. Rocky Mountain Bird Observatory, Fort Collins. http://www.rmbo.org/pif/pifdb.html.

PARTNERS IN FLIGHT. 2007. Partners in Flight landbird population estimates database. http://www.rmbo.org/pif_db/laped/default.aspx.

PAYNE, L.X., and E.P. PIERCE. 2002. Purple Sandpiper (*Calidris maritima*). *In* The Birds of North America, No. 706 (A. Poole and F. Gill, Eds.). The Birds of North America, Inc., Philadelphia.

PAYNE, R.B. 2006. Indigo Bunting (*Passerina cyanea*). The Birds of North America Online (A. Poole, Ed.). Cornell Laboratory of Ornithology. Retrieved from The Birds of North America Online Database, Ithaca. http://bna.birds.cornell.edu/BNA/account/Indigo_Bunting/.

PEAKALL, D.B. 1976. The Peregrine Falcon (*Falco peregrinus*) and pesticides. Can.Field-Nat. 90:301-307.

PECK, G.K. 1966. First published breeding record of Mute Swan for Ontario. Ont.Field Biol. 20:43.

PECK, G.K. 1972. Birds of the Cape Henrietta Maria region, Ontario. Can.Field-Nat. 86:333-348.

PECK, G.K. 1976. Recent revisions to the list of Ontario's breeding birds. Ont.Field Biol. 30:9-16.

PECK G.K. 2001. Ontario Nest Records Scheme thirty-second report (1956-2000). Royal Ontario Museum, Toronto.

PECK, G.K. 2002. Ontario Nest Records Scheme thirty-third report (1956-2001). Royal Ontario Museum, Toronto.

PECK, G.K. 2003a. Ontario Nest Record Scheme thirty-fourth report (1956 – 2002). Royal Ontario Museum, Toronto.

PECK, G.K. 2003b. Breeding status and nest site selection of Turkey Vulture in Ontario. Ontario Birds 21:129-136.

PECK, G.K. 2004. Ontario Nest Record Scheme thirty-fifth report (1956 – 2003). Royal Ontario Museum, Toronto.

PECK, G.K. 2005. Status and nest site selection of Common Raven in Ontario. Ontario Birds 23:76-86.

PECK, G.K., and R.D. JAMES. 1983. Breeding birds of Ontario: nidiology and distribution, Vol. 1: nonpasserines. Life Sci. Misc. Publ., R. Ont. Mus., Toronto.

PECK, G.K., and R.D. JAMES. 1987. Breeding Birds of Ontario: nidiology and distribution, Vol. 2: passerines. Life Sci. Misc. Publ., R. Ont. Mus., Toronto.

PECK, G.K., and R.D. JAMES. 1993a. Breeding birds of Ontario: nidiology and distribution, Vol. 1: nonpasserines (first revision, part A: loons to ducks). Ontario Birds 11:18-22.

PECK, G.K., and R.D. JAMES. 1993b. Breeding birds of Ontario: nidiology and distribution, Vol.1: nonpasserines (first revision, part B: vultures to phalaropes). Ontario Birds 11:83-91.

PECK, G.K., and R.D. JAMES. 1994. Breeding birds of Ontario: nidiology and distribution, Vol. 1: nonpasserines (first revision, part C: jaegers to woodpeckers). Ontario Birds 12:11-18.

PECK, G.K., and R.D. JAMES. 1997. Breeding birds of Ontario: nidiology and distribution, Vol. 2: passerines (first revision, part A: flycatchers to gnatcatchers). Ontario Birds 15:93-107.

PECK, G.K., and R.D. JAMES. 1999. Breeding birds of Ontario: nidology and distribution, Vol. 1: nonpasserines (additions and revisions). Ontario Birds 17:105-123.

PECK, G.K., and M.K. PECK. 2006. Ontario Nest Records Scheme thirty-seventh report (1956-2005). Royal Ontario Museum, Toronto.

PECK, M.K., G. COADY, G. BINSFELD, and K. KONZE. 2004a. First documented nesting of Pine Grosbeak in Ontario. Ontario Birds 22:2-8.

PECK, M.K., G. COADY, G. BINSFELD, and K.R. KONZE. 2004b. First documented nesting of Bohemian Waxwing in Ontario. Ontario Birds 22:9-14.

PECK, M.K., G. COADY, G. BINSFIELD, K.R. KONZE, P.C. HODGSON, and S. FURINO. 2004. Ontario Breeding Bird Atlas expeditions yield additional information on Solitary Sandpiper nests. Ontario Birds 22:120-124.

PECK, M.K., G. COADY, A.G. CARPENTIER, and B.S. CHERRIERE. 2004. First breeding and nest record of Black-necked Stilt in Ontario. Ontario Birds 22:106-119.

PECK, M.K., G. COADY, G. BINSFIELD, and K.R. KONZE. 2005 Unpubl. Survey of the upper Shamattawa River and the mouth of the Winisk River. The Second Ontario Breeding Bird Atlas (Squares 16FF07/08 and 16FG12/22), 10-22 June 2004.

PEDLAR, J.H., and R.K. ROSS. 1997. An update on the status of the Sandhill Crane in northern and central Ontario. Ontario Birds 15:4-13.

PEER, B.D., and E.K. BOLLINGER. 1997. Common Grackle (*Quiscalus quiscula*). *In* The Birds of North America, No. 271 (A. Poole and F. Gill, Eds.). Academy of Natural Sciences, Philadelphia, and American Ornithologists' Union, Washington, DC.

PEKARIK-KRESS, C. 2004. Organochlorine contaminants, immunocompetence and vitellogenin in Great Black-backed Gulls from Lake Ontario. M.Sc. thesis, University of Guelph, Guelph.

PENAK, B.L. 1986. Status Report on the Eastern Screech-Owl in Canada *Otus asio* (with an overview of status in North America). Committee on the Status of Endangered Wildlife in Canada, Ottawa.

PERRY, M.C., E.J.R. LOHNES, A.M. WELLS, P.C.OSENTON, and D.M.KIDWELLl. 2004. Atlantic Seaduck Project. USGS Patuxent Wildlife Research Center, Laurel. http://www.pwrc.usgs.gov/resshow/perry/scoters/.

PETERJOHN, B.G., and D.L. RICE. 1991. The Ohio breeding bird atlas. Ohio Dept.Nat.Res., Columbus.

PETERJOHN, B.G. 2001. The birds of Ohio: completely revised and updated with Ohio breeding bird atlas maps. Wooster Book Co., Wooster.

PETERJOHN, B.G., J.R. SAUER, and W.A. LINK. 1994. The 1992 and 1993 summary of the North American Breeding Bird Survey. Bird Populations 2:46-61.

PETERSEN, M.R. 1989. Nesting biology of Pacific Loons, *Gavia pacifica*, on the Yukon-Kuskokwim Delta, Alaska. Can.Field-Nat. 103:265-269.

PETERSON, R.T. 1980. Peterson Field Guide: eastern birds. Houghton Mifflin, Boston.

PETIT, L.J. 1999. Prothonotary Warbler (*Protonotaria citrea*). *In* The Birds of North America, No. 408 (A. Poole and F. Gill, Eds.). The Birds of North America, Inc., Philadelphia.

PETRIE, S.A., S.S. BADZINSKI, and K.G. DROUILLARD. 2007. Contaminants in Lesser and Greater Scaup staging on the lower Great Lakes. Arch.Environ.Contam.Toxicol. 52:580-589.

PETRIE, S.A., S.S. BADZINSKI, and K. WILCOX. 2002. Population trends and habitat use of Tundra Swans staging at Long Point, Lake Erie. Waterbirds 25 (Spec.Publ.1):143-149.

PETRIE, S.A., and C.M. FRANCIS. 2003. Rapid increase in the lower Great Lakes population of feral Mute Swans: a review and recommendation. Wildl.Soc.Bull. 31:407-416.

PETRIE, S.A., and K.L. WILCOX. 2003. Migration chronology of eastern-population Tundra Swans. Can.J.Zool. 81:861-870.

PICKWELL, G.B. 1931. The Prairie Horned Lark. Trans.Acad.Sci.St.Louis 27:1-153.

PICKWELL, G.B. 1942. *Otocoris alpestris praticola* Henshaw Prairie Horned Lark. Pp. 342-356 *in* Life histories of North American flycatchers, larks, swallows, and allies (A.C. Bent, Ed.). Bull. U.S. Natl. Mus. No. 179.

PIEROTTI, R.J., and T.P. GOOD. 1994. Herring Gull (*Larus argentatus*). *In* The Birds of North America, No. 124 (A. Poole and F. Gill, Eds.). Academy of Natural Sciences, Philadelphia, and American Ornithologists' Union, Washington, DC.

PITELKA, F.A. 1959. Numbers, breeding schedule, and territoriality in Pectoral Sandpipers of northern Alaska. Condor 61:233-264.

PITOCCHELLI, J. 1993. Mourning Warbler (*Oporornis philadelphia*). *In* The Birds of North America, No. 72 (A. Poole and F. Gill, Eds.). Academy of Natural Sciences, Philadelphia; American Ornithologists' Union, Washington, D.C.

PITOCCHELLI, J., J. BOUCHIE, and D. JONES. 1997. Connecticut Warbler (*Oporornis agilis*). *In* The Birds of North America, No. 320 (A. Poole and F. Gill, Eds.). Academy of Natural Sciences, Philadelphia, and American Ornithologists' Union, Washington, DC.

PITTAWAY, R. 1997. Magpie mystery. OFO News 15:1.

PITTAWAY, R. 1998. 500,000 Oldsquaws? OFO News 16:1.

POOLE, A.F. 1989. Ospreys: a natural and unnatural history. Cambridge University Press, Cambridge.

POOLE, A.F., L.R. BEVIER, C.A. MARANTZ, and B. MEANLEY. 2005. King Rail (*Rallus elegans*). The Birds of North American online (A. Poole, Ed.). Cornell Laboratory of Ornithology. Retrieved from The Birds of North American Online Database, Ithaca. http://bna.birds.cornell.edu/BNA/account/King_Rail/.

POOLE, A.F., R.O. BIERREGAARD, and M.S. MARTELL. 2002. Osprey (*Pandion haliaetus*). *In* The Birds of North America, No. 683 (A. Poole and F. Gill, Eds.). The Birds of North America, Inc., Philadelphia.

POON, W., and R.B.H. SMITH. 2005. Brown-headed Cowbird parasitism of Northern Mockingbirds in Ontario. Ontario Birds 23:2-14.

POPOTNIK, G.J., and W.M. GIULIANO. 2000. Response of birds to grazing of riparian zones. J.Wildl.Manage. 64:976-982.

PORTER, W.F. 1992. Habitat requirements. Pp. 202-213 *in* The Wild Turkey: biology and management. (J.G. Dickson, Ed.). Stackpole Books and National Wild Turkey Federation and United States Department of Agriculture Forest Service, Mechanicsburg.

PORTER, W.F., R.D. TANGEN, G.C. NELSON, and D.A. HAMILTON. 1980. Effects of corn food plots on Wild Turkeys in the upper Mississippi Valley. J.Wildl.Manage. 44:456-462.

POSTON, H. J. 1974. Home range and breeding biology of the Shoveler. Canadian Wildlife Service Report Series No. 25. Canadian Wildlife Service.

POULIN, R.G., S.D. GRINDAL, and R.M. BRIGHAM. 1996. Common Nighthawk (*Chordeiles minor*). *In* The Birds of North America, No. 213 (A. Poole and F. Gill, Eds.). Academy of Natural Sciences, Philadelphia, and American Ornithologists' Union, Washington, DC.

POWER, H.W., and M.P. LOMBARDO. 1996. Mountain Bluebird (*Sialia currucoides*). *In* The Birds of North America, No. 222 (A. Poole and F. Gill, Eds.). Academy of Natural Sciences, Philadelphia, and American Ornithologists' Union, Washington, DC.

PRAVOSUDOV, V.V., and T.C. GRUBB, JR. 1993. White-breasted Nuthatch (*Sitta carolinensis*). *In* The Birds of North America, No. 54 (A. Poole and F. Gill, Eds.). Academy of Natural Sciences, Philadelphia, and American Ornithologists' Union, Washington, DC.

PREBLE, N.A. 1957. Nesting habits of the Yellow-billed Cuckoo. Amer.Midl.Nat. 57:474-482.

PRESCOTT, K.W. 1965. The Scarlet Tanager (*Piranga olivacea*). New Jersey State Museum Investigations No. 2. Department of Education of New Jersey, Trenton.

PRESTON, C.R., and R.D. BEANE. 1993. Red-tailed Hawk (*Buteo jamaicensis*). *In* The Birds of North America, No. 52 (A. Poole and F. Gill, Eds.). Academy of Natural Sciences, Philadelphia, and American Ornithologists' Union, Washington, DC.

PREVETT, J.P., and F.C. JOHNSON. 1977. Continued eastern expansion of breeding range of Ross' Goose. Condor 79:121-123.

PRICE, J. 2004. Potential Impacts of climate change on the summer distributions of southern Ontario's passerine birds.

Ontario Birds 22:20-30.
PRICE, J., S. DROEGE, and A. PRICE. 1995. The summer atlas of North American birds. Academic Press, San Diego.
PROSSER, D.J., and R.P. BROOKS. 1998. A verified habitat suitability index for the Louisiana Waterthrush. J.Field Ornithol. 69:288-298.

QUILLIAM, H.R. 1973. History of the birds of Kingston, Ontario. 2nd ed. Kingston Field Naturalists, Kingston.

RATCLIFF, B. 2005. Update status report on American White Pelican (*Pelecanus Erythrorhynchos*) in Ontario. Committee on the Status of Species At Risk in Ontario (COSSARO), Ontario Ministry of Natural Resources.
RATCLIFF, B., and T. ARMSTRONG. 2002. The 2000 Ontario Peregrine Falcon survey. Ontario Birds 20:87-94.
RATCLIFF, B., and T. ARMSTRONG. 2006. The 2005 Ontario Peregrine Falcon survey: a summary report. Draft MS Report. Ontario Ministry of Natural Resources, Thunder Bay.
RAYNER, W.J. 1988. First nest record of White-eyed Vireo in Ontario. Ontario Birds 6:114-116.
READ, W.F., and R. ALVO 1996. Updated COSEWIC status report on the Eastern Bluebird in Canada. Committee on the Status of Endangered Wildlife in Canada, Ottawa.
REED, A., D.H. WARD, D.V. DERKSEN, and J.S. SEDINGER. 1998. Brant (*Branta bernicla*). *In* The Birds of North America, No. 337 (A. Poole and F. Gill, Eds.). The Birds of North America, Inc., Philadelphia.
REID, F.A. 1989. Differential habitat use by waterbirds in a managed wetland complex. Ph.D. dissertation. University of Missouri, Columbia.
REMPEL, R.S., K.F. ABRAHAM, T.R. GADAWSKI, S. GABOR, and R.K. ROSS. 1997. A simple wetland habitat classification for boreal forest waterfowl. J.Wildl.Manage. 61:746-757.
RICE, J.C. 1978a. Behavioral interactions of two interspecifically territorial vireos: song discrimination and natural interactions. Anim.Behav. 26:527-549.
RICE, J.C. 1978b. Ecological relationships of two interspecifically territorial vireos. Ecology 59:526-538.
RICH, T.D., C.J. BEARMORE, H. BERLANGA, P.J. BLANCHER, M.S.W. BRADSTREET, G.S. BUTHCER, D.W. DEMAREST, E.H. DUNN, W.C. HUNTER, E.E. IÑIGO-ELIAS, J.A. KENNEDY, A.M. MARTELL, A.O. PANJABI, D.N. PASHLEY, K.V. ROSENBERG, C.M. RUSTAY, J.S. WENDT, and T.C. WILL. 2004. Partners in Flight North American landbird conservation plan. Cornell Lab of Ornithology, Ithaca. http://www.partnersinflight.org/cont_plan/default.htm.
RICHARDS, J.M., and R.D. MCRAE. 1988. Observations on colonial waterbirds breeding at Presqu'ile Provincial Park. Ontario Birds 6:68-73.
RICHARDSON, M., and D.W. BRAUNING. 1995. Chestnut-sided Warbler (*Dendroica pensylvanica*). *In* The Birds of North America, No. 190 (A. Poole and F. Gill, Eds.). Academy of Natural Sciences, Philadelphia, and American Ornithologists' Union, Washington, DC.
RICKER, W.E., and C.H.D. CLARKE. 1939. Birds of the vicinity of Lake Nipissing, Ontario. No. 16. Contr. Roy. Ont. Mus. Zool.
RIDOUT, R. 1997a. Fall migration. Ontario Region. Field Notes 51:47-51.
RIDOUT, R. 1997b. Nesting season. Ontario Region. Field Notes 51:991-993.
RILEY, J.L. 1982. Habitats of Sandhill Cranes in the southern Hudson Bay Lowland, Ontario. Can.Field-Nat. 96:51-55.
RILEY, J.L. 2003. Flora of the Hudson Bay Lowland and its postglacial origins. NRC Press, Ottawa.
RIMMER, C.C., and K.P. MCFARLAND. 1998. Tennessee Warbler (*Vermivora peregrina*). *In* The Birds of North America, No. 350 (A. Poole and F. Gill, Eds.). The Birds of North America, Inc., Philadelphia.
RISING, J.D. 1996. A guide to the identification and natural history of the sparrows of the United States and Canada. Academic Press, New York.
RISING, J.D., and J.C. AVISE. 1993. Application of genealogical-concordance principles to the taxonomy and evolutionary history of the Sharp-tailed Sparrow (*Ammodramus caudacutus*). Auk 110:844-856.
RISING, J.D., and N.J. FLOOD. 1998. Baltimore Oriole (*Icterus galbula*). *In* The Birds of North America, No. 384 (A. Poole and F. Gill, Eds.). The Birds of North America, Inc., Philadelphia.
RISLEY, C.J. 1981. The status of the Eastern Bluebird (*Sialia sialis*) in Canada with particular reference to Ontario. Committee on the Status of Endangered Wildlife in Canada, Ottawa.
ROBBINS, C.S. 1973. Introduction, spread, and present abundance of the House Sparrow in North America. Ornithol.Monogr. 14:3-9.
ROBBINS, C.S., D. BYSTRAK, and P.H. GEISSLER. 1986. The breeding bird survey: its first fifteen years, 1965-1979. Patuxent Wildlife Research Center, Laurel.
ROBBINS, C.S., D.K. DAWSON, and B.A. DOWELL. 1989. Habitat area requirements of breeding forest birds of the middle Atlantic States. Wildlife Monogr. 103.
ROBBINS, M.B., and B.C. DALE. 1999. Sprague's Pipit (*Anthus spragueii*). *In* The Birds of North America, No. 439 (A. Poole and F. Gill, Eds.). The Birds of North America, Inc., Philadelphia.
ROBERT, M., B. JOBIN, F. SHAFFER, L. ROBILLARD, and B. GAGNON. 2004. Yellow Rail distribution and numbers in southern James Bay, Québec, Canada. Waterbirds 27:282-288.
ROBERTS, S.D., and W.F. PORTER. 1998. Influence of temperature and precipitation on survival of Wild Turkey poults. J.Wildl.Manage. 62:1499-1505.
ROBERTSON, G.J. 1995. Annual variation in Common Eider egg size: effects of temperature, clutch size, laying date, and laying sequence. Can.J.Zoo. 73:1579-1587.
ROBERTSON, G.J., and J.-P.L. SAVARD. 2002. Long-tailed Duck (*Clangula hyemalis*). *In* The Birds of North America, No. 651 (A. Poole and F. Gill, Eds.). The Birds of North America, Inc., Philadelphia.
ROBERTSON, R.J., B.J. STUTCHBURY, and R.R. COHEN. 1992. Tree Swallow (*Tachycineta bicolor*). *In* The Birds of North America, No. 11 (A. Poole, P. Stettenheim, and F. Gill, Eds.). Academy of Natural Sciences, Philadelphia, and American Ornithologists' Union, Washington, DC.
ROBINSON, J.A., L.W. ORING, J.P. SKORUPA, and R. BOETTCHER. 1997. American Avocet (*Recurvirostra americana*). *In* The Birds of North America, No. 275 (A. Poole and F. Gill, Eds.). Academy of Natural Sciences, Philadelphia, and American Ornithologists' Union, Washington, DC.
ROBINSON, J.A., J.M. REED, J.P. SKORUPA, and L.W. ORING. 1999. Black-necked Stilt (*Himantopus meicanus*). *In* The Birds of North America, No. 449 (A. Poole and F. Gill, Eds.). The Birds of North America Inc., Philadelphia.
ROBINSON, S.K. 1994. Use of bait and lures by Green-backed Herons in Amazonian Peru. Wilson Bull. 106:567-569.
ROBINSON, T.R., R.R. SARGENT, and M.B. SARGENT. 1996. Ruby-throated Hummingbird (*Archilochus colubris*). *In* The Birds of North America, No. 204 (A. Poole and F. Gill, Eds.). Academy of Natural Sciences, Philadelphia, and American Ornithologists' Union, Washington, DC.
ROBINSON, W.D. 1995. Louisiana Waterthrush (*Seiurus motacilla*). *In* The Birds of North America, No. 151 (A. Poole and F. Gill, Eds.). Academy of

Natural Sciences, Philadelphia, and American Ornithologists' Union, Washington, DC.

ROBINSON, W.D. 1996. Summer Tanager (*Piranga rubra*). In The Birds of North America, No. 248 (A. Poole and F. Gill, Eds.). Academy of Natural Sciences, Philadelphia, and American Ornithologists' Union, Washington, DC.

ROBINSON, W.L. 1980. Fool hen: the Spruce Grouse on the Yellow Dog Plains. University of Wisconsin Press, Madison.

ROCHE, E. 2007. Final Great Lakes Piping Plover call. University of Minnesota, St. Paul.

RODEWALD, P.G., and R.D. JAMES. 1996. Yellow-throated Vireo (*Vireo flavifrons*). In The Birds of North America, No. 247 (A. Poole and F. Gill, Eds.). Academy of Natural Sciences, Philadelphia, and American Ornithologists' Union, Washington, DC.

RODEWALD, P.G., J.H. WITHGOTT, and K.G. SMITH. 1999. Pine Warbler (*Dendroica pinus*). In The Birds of North America, No. 438 (A. Poole and F. Gill, Eds.). The Birds of North America, Inc., Philadelphia.

RODRIGUEZ, J. 2002. Range contraction in declining North American bird populations. Ecol.App. 12:238-248.

ROETKER, F., and B. FORTIER. 2005. Northern Manitoba and Northern Saskatchewan waterfowl breeding population survey. U.S. Fish and Wildlife Service.

ROHNER, C. 1996. The numerical response of Great Horned Owls to the snowshoe hare cycle: consequences of non-territorial "floaters" on demography. J.Anim.Ecol. 65:359-370.

ROHNER, C., and J.N.M. SMITH. 1996. Brood size manipulations in Great Horned Owls *Bubo virginianus*: are predators food limited at the peak of prey cycles? Ibis 138: 236-242.

ROHWER, F.C., W.P. JOHNSON, and E.R. LOOS. 2002. Blue-winged Teal (*Anas discors*). In The Birds of North America, No. 625 (A. Poole and F. Gill, Eds.). The Birds of North America, Inc., Philadelphia.

ROMAGOSA, C.M. 2002. Eurasian Collared-Dove (*Streptopelia decaocto*). In The Birds of North America, No. 630 (A. Poole and F. Gill, Eds.). The Birds of North America, Inc., Philadelphia.

ROMAGOSA, C.M., and T. MCENEANEY. 2000. Eurasian Collared-Dove in North America and the Caribbean. N.Am.Birds 53:348-353.

ROOT, T. 1988. Atlas of wintering North American birds: an analysis of Christmas Bird Count data. University of Chicago Press, Chicago.

ROSENBERG, K.V., and P.J. BLANCHER. 2005. Setting numerical population objectives for priority landbird species. Pp. 57-67 in Bird conservation and implementation in the Americas: proceedings of the Third International Partners in Flight Conference, Vol. 1 (C.J. Ralph and T.D. Rich, Eds.). United States Department of Agriculture, Forest Service, Pacific Southwest Research Station, General Technical Report PSW-GTR-191, Albany. http://www.fs.fed.us/psw/publications/documents/psw_gtr191/Asilomar/pdfs/57-67.pdf.

ROSENBERG, K.V., J.D. LOWE, and A.A. DHONDT. 1999. Effects of forest fragmentation on breeding tanagers: a continental perspective. Conserv.Biol. 13:568-583.

ROSENFIELD, R.N. 1984. Nesting biology of Broad-winged Hawks in Wisconsin. J.Raptor Res. 18:6-9.

ROSS, K., K. ABRAHAM, R. CLAY, B. COLLINS, J. IRON, R. JAMES, D. MCLACHLIN, and R. WEEBER. 2003. Ontario Shorebird Conservation Plan. Environment Canada, Downsview.

ROSS, R.K. 1987. Interim report on waterfowl breeding pair surveys in northern Ontario, 1980-83. Canadian Wildlfe Service.

ROSS, R.K. 1994. The Black Scoter in northern Ontario. Ontario Birds 12:1-7.

ROSS, R.K. 2004. Unpubl. Black Duck survey of Northeastern Ontario. Canadian Wildlife Service, Ottawa.

ROSS, R.K., K.F. ABRAHAM, T.R. GADAWSKI, R.S. REMPEL, T.S. GABOR, and R. MAHER. 2002. Abundance and distribution of breeding waterfowl in the Great Clay Belt of northern Ontario. Can.Field-Nat. 116:42-50.

ROSS, R.K. and FILLMAN, D. 1990. Distribution of American Black Duck and Mallard in northern Ontario. Canadian Wildlife Service.

ROSS, R.K., and N.R. NORTH. 1983. Breeding records of Northern Shoveler, *Anas clypeata*, along the northern coast of Ontario. Can.Field-Nat. 97:113.

ROTH, R.R., M.S. JOHNSON, and T.J. UNDERWOOD. 1996. Wood Thrush (*Hylocichla mustelina*). In The birds of North America, No. 246 (A. Poole and F. Gill, Eds.). Academy of Natural Sciences, Philadelphia, and American Ornithologists' Union, Washington, DC.

ROWE, J.S. 1972. Forest regions of Canada. Can.For.Serv.Publ. 1300, Ottawa.

ROWNTREE, A. 1979. Lowdown on wetlands. Ont.Fish Wildl.Rev. 18:11-18.

ROY, K.J. 2002. Ontario Bird Records Committee annual report for 2001. Ontario Birds 20:54-74.

RUBEGA, M.A., D. SCHAMEL, and D.M. TRACY. 2000. Red-necked Phalarope (*Phalaropus lobatus*). In The Birds of North America, No. 538 (A. Poole and F. Gill, Eds.). The Birds of North America, Inc., Philadelphia.

RUSCH, D.H., S. DESTEFANO, M.C. REYNOLDS, and D. LAUTEN. 2000. Ruffed Grouse (*Bonasa umbellus*). In The Birds of North America, No. 515 (A. Poole and F. Gill, Eds.). The Birds of North America, Inc., Philadelphia.

RUSSELL, R.P., JR. 1983. The Piping Plover in the Great Lakes region. Amer.Birds 37:951-955.

RUSSELL, R.W. 2002. Pacific Loon (*Gavia pacifica*) and Arctic Loon (*Gavia arctica*). In The Birds of North America, No. 657 (A. Poole and F. Gill, Eds.). The Birds of North America, Inc., Philadelphia.

RUTHERFORD, L.A. 1979. The decline of wetlands in southern Ontario. Faculty of Environmental Studies, University of Waterloo, Waterloo.

RYDER, J.P. 1993. Ring-billed Gull (*Larus delawarensis*). In The Birds of North America, No. 33 (A. Poole, P. Stettenheim, and F. Gill, Eds.). Academy of Natural Sciences, Philadelphia, and American Ornithologists' Union, Washington, DC.

RYDER, J.P., and R.T. ALISAUSKAS. 1995. Ross's Goose (*Chen rossii*). In The Birds of North America, No. 162 (A. Poole and F. Gill, Eds.). Academy of Natural Sciences, Philadelphia, and American Ornithologists' Union, Washington, DC.

RYSER, F.A. 1985. Birds of the Great Basin: a natural history. University of Nevada Press, Reno.

SADO, E.V., and B.F. CARSWELL. 1987. Surficial geology of Northern Ontario. Ontario Geological Survey, Map 2518.

SALISBURY, C.D.C., and L.D. SALISBURY. 1989. Successful breeding of Black-necked Stilts in Saskatchewan. Blue Jay 47:154-156.

SALLABANKS, R., and F.C. JAMES. 1999. American Robin (*Turdus migratorius*). In The Birds of North America, No. 462 (A. Poole and F. Gill, Eds.). The Birds of North America, Inc., Philadelphia.

SANDILANDS, A.P. 1984. Annotated checklist of the vascular plants and vertebrates of Luther Marsh, Ontario. Ont.Field Biol.Spec.Publ. No. 2. Ontario Field Biologist, Toronto.

SANDILANDS, A.P. 2005. Birds of Ontario: habitat requirements, limiting factors, and status – nonpasserines: waterfowl through cranes. UBC Press, Vancouver.

SARGENT, R.R. 1999. Ruby-throated Hummingbird. Stackpole Books,

Mechanicsburg.
SAUER, J.R., G.W. PENDLETON, and B.G. PETERJOHN. 1996. Evaluating causes of population change in North American insectivorous songbirds. Conserv.Biol. 10:465-478.
SAUER J.R., J.E. HINES, and J. FALLON. 2002. The North American Breeding Bird Survey, results and analysis, 1966-2001. Version 2002.1. USGS Patuxent Wildlife Research Center, Laurel. http://www.mbr-pwrc.usgs.gov/bbs/bbs2001.html.
SAUER J.R., J.E. HINES , and J. FALLON. 2005. The North American Breeding Bird Survey, results and analysis, 1966-2005. Version 6.2.2006. USGS Patuxent Wildlife Research Center, Laurel. http://www.mbr-pwrc.usgs.gov/bbs/bbs.html.
SAUER, J.R., J.E. HINES, and J. FALLON. 2005a. The North American Breeding Bird Survey, results and analysis, 1966-2004. Version 2005, 2nd ed. USGS Patuxent Wildlife Research Center, Laurel.
SAUER, J.R., J.E. HINES, and J. FALLON. 2007. The North American Breeding Bird Survey, results and analysis, 1966-2006. USGS Patuxent Wildlife Research Center, Laurel. http://www.mbr-pwrc.usgs.gov/bbs/bbs.html.
SAUNDERS W.E. 1930. Nature week by week column. London Advertiser, London.
SAUNDERS, W.E., and E.M.S. DALE. 1933. History and list of birds of Middlesex County, Ontario. Trans.R.Can.Inst. 19:161-250.
SAUROLA, P. 1997. Monitoring Finnish owls, 1982–1996: methods and results. Pp. 363-380 in Biology and Conservation of Owls of the Northern Hemisphere. Second International Symposium. February 5-9, 1997, Winnipeg, MB. General Technical Report NC-190 (J.R. Duncan, D.H. Johnson, and T.H. Nicholls, Eds.). US Dept.Agri., Forest Service, North Central Forest Experiment Station, St. Paul.
SAVARD, M. 2004. Small owls migration monitoring program at Tadoussac, Quebec: Boreal Owl (*Aegolius funereus*) capture frequency for 1996 to 2004. Unpublished report by Observatoire d'Oiseaux de Tadoussac.
SAVARD, J.-P.L., D. BORDAGE, and A. REED. 1998. Surf Scoter (*Melanitta perspicillata*). *In* The Birds of North America, No. 363 (A. Poole and F. Gill, Eds.). The Birds of North America, Inc., Philadelphia.
SAVARD, J.-P.L., and P. LAMOTHE. 1991. Distribution, abundance, and aspects of the breeding ecology of Black Scoters, *Melanitta nigra*, and Surf Scoters, *M. perspicillata*, in northern Quebec. Can.Field-Nat. 105:488-496.
SAWYER, M., and M.I. DYER. 1968. Yellow-headed Blackbird nesting in southern Ontario. Wilson Bull. 80:236-237.
SCHARF, W.C., and J. KREN. 1996. Orchard Oriole (*Icterus spurius*). *In* The Birds of North America, No. 255 (A. Poole and F. Gill, Eds.). Academy of Natural Sciences, Philadelphia, and American Ornithologists' Union, Washington, DC.
SCHIECK, J., and S.J. SONG. 2006. Changes in bird communities throughout succession following fire and harvest in boreal forests of western North America: literature review and meta-analysis. Can.J.For.Res. 36:1299-1318.
SCHMUTZ, J.K., R.J. ROBERTSON, and F. COOKE. 1983. Colonial nesting of the Hudson Bay Eider Duck. Can.J.Zool. 61:2424-2433.
SCHOLTEN, S.J., and R.D. MCRAE. 1994. Cliff nesting bird survey of the Sutton Ridges and Shamattawa River for 1994. Ontario Ministry of Natural Resources, Moosonee District.
SCHORGER, A.W. 1966. The Wild Turkey: its history and domestication. University of Oklahoma Press, Norman.
SCHUELER, F.W., D.H. BALDWIN, and J.D. RISING. 1974. The status of birds at selected sites in northern Ontario. Can.Field-Nat. 88:141-150.
SCOTT, A.C., and M. BEKOFF. 1991. Breeding behavior of Evening Grosbeaks. Condor 93:71-81.
SCOTT, G.A. 1963. First nesting of the Little Gull (*Larus minutus*) in Ontario and the New World. Auk 80:548-549.
SEDGWICK, J.A. 2000. Willow Flycatcher (*Empidonax traillii*). *In* The Birds of North America, No. 533 (A. Poole and F. Gill, Eds.). The Birds of North America, Inc., Philadelphia.
SEMPLE, J.B., and G.M. SUTTON. 1932. Nesting of Harris's Sparrow (*Zonotrichia querula*) at Churchill, Manitoba. Auk 49:166-183.
SETON, E.E.T. 1890. Manitoban notes. Auk 2:21-24.
SETTERINGTON, M.A., I.D. THOMPSON, and W.A. MONTEVECCHI. 2000. Woodpecker abundance and habitat use in mature balsam fir forests in Newfoundland. J.Wildl.Manage. 64:335-345.
SHACKELFORD, C.E., R.E. BROWN, and R.N. CONNER. 2000. Red-bellied Woodpecker (*Melanerpes carolinus*). *In* The Birds of North America, No. 500 (A. Poole and F. Gill, Eds.). The Birds of North America, Inc., Philadelphia.
SHARROCK, J.T.R. 1976. The atlas of the breeding birds in Britain and Ireland. T. & A.D. Poyser, Hertfordshire.
SHEPHERD, D. 1992. Monitoring Ontario's owl populations: a recommendation and report to Ontario Ministry of Natural Resources. Long Point Bird Observatory, Port Rowan.
SHEPPARD, R.W., W.E. HURLBURT, and G.H. DICKSON. 1936. A preliminary list of the birds of Lincoln and Welland counties, Ontario. Can.Field-Nat. 50:95-102.
SHERMAN, A.R. 1925. Down with the House Wren boxes. Wilson Bull. 37:5-13.
SHERRY, T.W., and R.T. HOLMES. 1997. American Redstart (*Setophaga ruticilla*). *In* The Birds of North America, No. 277 (A. Poole and F. Gill, Eds.). Academy of Natural Sciences, Philadelphia, and American Ornithologists' Union, Washington, DC.
SHORT, H.L., and R.J. COOPER. 1985. Habitat suitability index models: Great Blue Heron. U.S. Fish and Wildlife Service, Biological Report 82.
SIBLEY, D.A. 2000. The Sibley guide to birds. Alfred A. Knopf, New York.
SIBLEY, D.A. 2001. The Sibley guide to bird life and behavior. Alfred A. Knopf, New York.
SIBLEY, C.G., and B.L. MONROE, JR. 1990. Distribution and taxonomy of birds of the world. Yale University Press, New Haven.
SIEGFRIED, W.R., and P.G.H. FROST. 1975. Continuous breeding and associated behavior in the Moorhen *Gallinula chloropus*. Ibis 117:102-109.
SIMARD, J.H. 2001. Habitat selection, ecological energetics, and the effects of changes in White Pine forests on breeding Red Crossbills in Algonquin Provincial Park, Ontario. M.Sc. thesis, McGill University, Montreal.
SIMMONS, R., and P.C. SMITH. 1985. Do Northern Harriers (*Circus cyaneus*) choose nest sites adaptively? Can.J.Zool. 63:494-498.
SINCLAIR, P.H., W.A. NIXON, C.D. ECKERT, and N.L.E. HUGHES. 2003. Birds of the Yukon Territory. UBC Press, Vancouver.
SKEEL, M.A., and E.P. MALLORY. 1996. Whimbrel (*Numenius phaeopus*). *In The Birds of North* America, No. 219 (A. Poole and F. Gill, Eds.). Academy of Natural Sciences, Philadelphia, and American Ornithologists' Union, Washington, DC.
SMALLWOOD, J.A., and D.M. BIRD. 2002. American Kestrel (*Falco sparverius*). *In* The Birds of North America, No. 602 (A. Poole and F. Gill, Eds.). The Birds of North America, Inc., Philadelphia.
SMITH, A.R. 1996. Atlas of Saskatchewan birds. Spec.Publ. No. 22. Saskatchewan

Natural History Society, Regina.
SMITH, K.G., J.H. WITHGOTT, and P.G. RODEWALD. 2000. Red-headed Woodpecker (*Melanerpes erythrocephalus*). *In* The Birds of North America, No. 518 (A. Poole and F. Gill, Eds.). The Birds of North America, Inc., Philadelphia.
SMITH, P.W. 1987. The Eurasian Collared-Dove arrives in the Americas. Amer.Birds 41:1370-1379.
SMITH, P.W., and H.W. KALE, II. 1986. Eurasian Collared-Doves collected in Florida. Florida Field Naturalist 14:104-107.
SMITH, R.B.H., and W. POON. 2006. The changing status of the Northern Mockingbird in the Greater Toronto Area. Ontario Birds 24:106-159.
SMITH, R.H. 1944. An investigation of the waterfowl resources of the west coast of James Bay. Canadian Wildlife Service, Ottawa.
SMITH, S.M. 1993. Black-capped Chickadee (*Poecile atricapillus*). *In* The Birds of North America, No. 39 (A. Poole, P. Stettenheim, and F. Gill, Eds.). Academy of Natural Sciences, Philadelphia, and American Ornithologists' Union, Washington, DC.
SNELL, E.A. 1987. Wetland distribution and conversion in southern Ontario. Inland Waters and Lands Directorate, Environment Canada, Ottawa.
SNYDER, L.L. 1938. The summer birds of western Rainy River District, Ontario, part 1. Trans.R.Can.Inst. 22:121-153.
SNYDER, L.L. 1941. The birds of Prince Edward County, Ontario. Univ.Toronto Studies Biol.Ser. 48:25-92.
SNYDER, L.L. 1941. On the Hudson Bay eider. Occasional Papers of the Royal Ontario Museum of Zoology 6:1-7.
SNYDER, L.L. 1951. Ontario birds. Clarke, Irwin, Toronto.
SNYDER, L.L. 1953. On eastern Empidonaces with particular reference to variation in *E. traillii*. Contrib.R.Ont.Mus.Zool.Paleontol. 35:1-26.
SNYDER, L.L. 1957. Changes in the avifauna of Ontario. Pp. 26-42 *in* Changes in the fauna of Ontario (F.A. Urquhart, Ed.). University of Toronto Press, Toronto.
SNYDER, L.L. 1957a. Arctic birds of Canada. University of Toronto Press, Toronto.
SODHI, N.S., P.C. JAMES, I.G. WARKENTIN, and L.W. OLIPHANT. 1992. Breeding ecology of urban Merlins (*Falco columbarius*). Can.J.Zool. 70:1477-1483.
SOGGE, M.K., W.M. GILBERT, and C. VAN RIPER, III. 1994. Orange-crowned Warbler (*Vermivora celata*). *In* The Birds of North America, No. 101 (A. Poole and F. Gill, Eds.). Academy of Natural Sciences, Philadelphia, and American Ornithologists' Union, Washington, DC.
SOLYMÁR, B.D., and J.D. MCCRACKEN. 2002. Draft national recovery plan for the Barn Owl and its habitat. Ontario Barn Owl Recovery Team, Recovery of Nationally Endangered Wildlife Committee, Ottawa
SORENSON, M.D. 1991. The functional significance of parasitic egg laying and typical nesting in Redhead ducks: an analysis of individual behaviour. Anim.Behav. 42:771-796.
SOULLIERE, G.J. 1993. Short-billed Dowitcher nest found in Ontario. Ontario Birds 11:109-110.
SPECTROANALYSIS INC. 2004. Introduction to the Ontario Land Cover Data Base. 2nd ed. (2000). Report to the Inventory Monitoring and Assessment Section, Ontario Ministry of Natural Resources.
SPEIRS, J.M. 1985. Birds of Ontario, Vol. 2. Natural Heritage, Toronto.
SQUIRES, J.R., and R.T. REYNOLDS. 1997. Northern Goshawk (*Accipiter gentilis*). *In* The Birds of North America, No. 298 (A. Poole and F. Gill, Eds.). Academy of Natural Sciences, Philadelphia, and American Ornithologists' Union, Washington, DC.
STATISTICS CANADA. 2001. 2001 Census of agriculture. http://www.statcan.ca/english/agcensus2001/index.htm.
STATISTICS CANADA. 2002. GeoSuite, 2001 Census. CD-ROM Catalogue number 92F0150XCB.
STATISTICS CANADA. 2002a. Population Ecumene Census Division Boundary File 2001 Census Reference Guide. Catalogue No. 92F0159GIE. Minister of Industry Canada, Ottawa. http://www.statcan.ca/english/freepub/92F0175GIE/92F0175GIE2001000.pdf.
STATISTICS CANADA. 2003. Agricultural Ecumene Census Division Boundary File for the 2001 Census of Agriculture – Reference Guide. Catalogue No. 92F0175GIE. Minister of Industry Canada, Ottawa.
STATISTICS CANADA. 2006. Statistics Canada 2001 agricultural census custom tabulation.
STATISTICS CANADA. 2006. 2006 Census of agriculture. http://www40.statcan.ca/l01/cst01/agrc25g.htm.
STEDMAN, S.J. 2000. Horned Grebe (*Podiceps auritus*). *In* The Birds of North America, No. 505 (A. Poole and F. Gill, Eds.). The Birds of North America, Inc., Philadelphia.
STEELE, B.B. 1993. Selection of foraging and nesting sites by Black-throated Blue Warblers: their relative influence on habitat choice. Condor 95:568-579.
STEPNEY, P.H.R. 1979. Brewer's Blackbird breeding in the Northwest Territories. Can.Field-Nat. 93:76-77.
STEWART, D. B. and LOCKHART, W. L. 2005. An overview of the Hudson Bay marine ecosystem. Canadian Technical. Report, Fisheries and Aquatic Sciences, no. 2586. Department of Fisheries and Oceans.
STIRRETT, G.M. 1945. The Kentucky Warbler in Canada. Can.Field-Nat. 59:70.
STOUT, B.E., and G.L. NUECHTERLEIN. 1999. Red-necked Grebe (*Podiceps grisegena*). *In* The Birds of North America, No. 465 (A. Poole and F. Gill, Eds.). The Birds of North America, Inc., Philadelphia.
STOUT, W.E., R.K. ANDERSON, and J.M. PAPP. 1998. Urban, suburban and rural Red-tailed Hawk nesting habitat and populations in southeast Wisconsin. J.Raptor Res. 32:221-228.
STRAIGHT, C.A., and R.J. COOPER. 2000. Chuck-will's-widow (*Caprimulgus carolinensis*). *In* The Birds of North America, No. 499 (A. Poole and F. Gill, Eds.). The Birds of North America, Inc., Philadelphia.
STRICKLAND, D. 1991. Juvenile dispersal in Gray Jays: dominant brood member expels siblings from natal territory. Can.J.Zool. 69:2935-2945.
STRICKLAND, D. 1995. Birds of Algonquin Provincial Park. Ontario Ministry of Natural Resources and the Friends of Algonquin Park, Whitney.
STRICKLAND, D. 2006. The unloved and the unseen. Algonquin Provincial Park: The Raven 47:1-4.
STRICKLAND, D., and H. OUELLET. 1993. Gray Jay (*Perisoreus canadensis*). *In* The Birds of North America, No. 40 (A. Poole, P. Stettenheim, and F. Gill, Eds.). Academy of Natural Sciences, Philadelphia, and American Ornithologists' Union, Washington, DC.
STRICKLAND, D., and T.A. WAITE. 2001. Does initial suppression of allofeeding in small jays help to conceal their nests? Can.J.Zool. 79:2128-2146.
SULLIVAN, B.D., and J.J. DINSMORE. 1992. Home range and foraging habitat of American Crows, *Corvus brachyrhynchos*, in a waterfowl breeding area in Manitoba. Can.Field-Nat. 106:181-184.
SUMMERS-SMITH, J.D. 2003. The decline of the House Sparrow: a review. Brit.Birds 96:439-446.
SUTTON, G.M. 1932. The birds of Southampton Island. Mem.Carnegie Mus. 12:1-275.
SUTTON, G.M., and D.F. PARMELEE. 1954. Nesting of the Greenland Wheatear on

Baffin Island. Condor 56:295-306.
SZUBA, K.J. 1989. Comparative population dynamics of Hudsonian Spruce Grouse in Ontario. Ph.D. dissertation, University of Toronto, Toronto.
SZUBA, K.J., and J.F. BENDELL. 1983. Population densities and habitats of Spruce Grouse in Ontario. Pp. 199-213 *in* Resources and dynamics of the boreal zone (R.W. Wein, R.R. Riewe, and R. Methven, Eds.). Assoc. Can. Univ. North. Stud., Ottawa.
SZUBA, K.J., and B.J. NAYLOR. 1998. Forest raptors and their nests in central Ontario. Queen's Printer for Ontario, Toronto.

TACHA, T.C., S.A. NESBIT, and P.A. VOHS. 1992. Sandhill Crane (*Grus canadensis*). *In* The Birds of North America, No. 31 (A. Poole, P. Stettenheim, and F. Gill, Eds.). Academy of Natural Sciences, Philadelphia, and American Ornithologists' Union, Washington, DC.
TARVIN, K.A., and G.E. WOOLFENDEN. 1999. Blue Jay (*Cyanocitta cristata*). *In* The Birds of North America, No. 469 (A. Poole and F. Gill, Eds.). The Birds of North America, Inc., Philadelphia.
TATE, G.R. 1992. Short-eared Owl (*Asio flammeus*). Pp. 171-189 *in* Migratory nongame birds of management concern in the northeast (K.J. Schneider and D.M. Pence, Eds.). US Fish Wildl. Serv., Newton Corner.
TATE, J., JR. 1981. The Blue List for 1981: the first decade. Amer.Birds 35:3-10.
TATE, J., JR. 1986. The Blue List for 1986. Amer.Birds 40:227-236.
TATE, J., Jr., and D.J. TATE. 1982. The Blue List for 1982. Amer.Birds 36:126-135.
TAVERNER, P.A. 1922. Birds of eastern Canada, 2nd ed. Geol.Surv.Can., Mem. 104, Geol.Surv.Can.Biol. Ser. 3. Canada Dept. Mines, Ottawa.
TAVERNER, P.A. 1934. Birds of Canada. National Museum of Canada, Ottawa.
TAYLOR, P.S. 1974 Unpubl. Summer populations and food ecology of jaegers and Snowy Owls on Bathurst Island, N.W.T. University of Alberta, Edmonton.
TEBBEL, P.D., and C.D. ANKNEY. 1982. Status of Sandhill Cranes (*Grus canadensis*) in central Ontario. Can.Field-Nat. 96:163-166.
TELFAIR, R. C., II. 2006. Cattle Egret (*Bubulcus ibis*). The Birds of North America Online (Poole, A., Ed.).Cornell Laboratory of Ornithology. Retrieved from The Birds of North America Online Database, Ithaca. http://bna.birds.cornell.edu/BNA/account/Cattle_Egret/.
TEMPLE, S.A. 2002. Dickcissel (*Spiza americana*). *In* The Birds of North America, No. 703 (A. Poole and F. Gill, Eds.). The Birds of North America, Inc., Philadelphia.
TERRES, J.K. 1980. The Audubon encyclopedia of North American birds. Alfred A. Knopf, New York.
THALER, G.R., and R.C. PLOWRIGHT. 1973. An examination of the floristic zone concept with special reference to the northern limit of the Carolinian zone in southern Ontario. Can.J.Bot. 51:765-780.
THOGMARTIN, W.E., F.P. HOWE, F.C. JAMES, D.H. JOHNSON, E.T. REED, J.R. SAUER, and F.R. THOMPSON, III. 2006. A review of the population estimation approach of the North American landbird conservation plan. Auk 123:892-904.
THOMAS, C.D., and J.J. LENNON. 1999. Birds extend their ranges northwards. Nature 399:213.
THOMAS, V.G., and J.P. PREVETT. 1982. The roles of the James and Hudson Bay Lowland in the annual cycle of geese. Naturaliste Canadien 109:913-925.
THOMPSON, I.D. 2000. Forest vertebrates of Ontario: patterns of distribution. Pp. 54-73 *in* Ecology of a managed terrestrial landscape – patterns and processes of forest landscapes in Ontario (A.H. Perera, D. Euler, and I. Thompson, Eds.). Ontario Ministry of Natural Resources, Toronto, and UBC Press, Vancouver.
THOMPSON, I.D. 2000a. Factors influencing landscape ehange. Pp. 30-53 *in* Ecology of a managed terrestrial landscape:patterns and processes of forest landscapes in Ontario (A.H. Perera, D. Euler, and I. Thompson, Eds.). UBC Press, Vancouver.
THURSTON, P.C. 1991. Geology of Ontario: Introduction. Pp. 3-25 *in* Geology of Ontario. Ontario Geological Survey, Spec.Vol. 4, part 1 (P.C. Thurston, H.R. Williams, R.H. Sutcliffe, and G.M. Stott, Eds.). Ontario Ministry of Northern Development and Mines, Toronto.
TIBBITTS, T.L., and W. MOSKOFF. 1999. Lesser Yellowlegs (*Tringa flavipes*). *In* The Birds of North America, No. 427 (A. Poole and F. Gill, Eds.). The Birds of North America, Inc., Philadelphia.
TIMMERMANS, S.T.A. 2001. Temporal relations between marsh bird and amphibian population indices and Great lakes water levels: a case study from the Marsh Monitoring Program. Bird Studies Canada, Port Rowan.
TIMMERMANS, S.T.A., G.E. CRAIGIE, and K.E. JONES. 2004. Common Loon pairs rear four-chick broods. Wilson Bull. 116:97-101.
TIMMERMANS, S.T.A., T. CREWE, and K. JONES. 2006. 10 years in the marsh. Birdwatch Canada 34:8-12.
TISCHENDORF, L. 2003. The Prothonotary Warbler: population viability and critical habitat in southern Ontario, Canada. Interdepartmental Recovery Fund project. National Wildlife Research Centre, Canadian Wildlife Service. Environment Canada, Ottawa.
TITMAN, R.D. 1999. Red-breasted Merganser (*Mergus serrator*). *In* The Birds of North America, No. 443 (A. Poole and F. Gill, Eds.). The Birds of North America, Inc., Philadelphia.
TODD, W.E.C. 1943. The western element in James Bay avifauna. Can.Field-Nat. 57:79-80.
TODD, W.E.C. 1963. Birds of the Labrador Peninsula and adjacent areas. University of Toronto Press, Toronto.
TOOCHIN, R. 2006. Seasonal status of Vancouver birds (July 2006 ed.). Vancouver Natural History Society, Vancouver.
TOZER, D.C. 2003. Point count efficiency and nesting success in marsh-nesting birds. M.Sc. thesis, Trent University, Peterborough.
TOZER, D.C., K.F. ABRAHAM, and E. NOL. 2006. Improving the accuracy of counts of wetland breeding birds at the point scale. Wetlands 26:518-527.
TOZER, D.C., K.F. ABRAHAM, and E. NOL. 2007 In press. Observations of nesting Least Bitterns in response to short call-broadcasts. Northeastern Naturalist.
TOZER, R.G., and J.M. RICHARDS. 1974. Birds of the Oshawa–Lake Scugog region, Ontario. R.G. Tozer & J.M. Richards, Oshawa.
TROST, C.H. 1999. Black-billed Magpie (*Pica pica*). *In* The Birds of North America, No. 389 (A. Poole and F. Gill, Eds.). The Birds of North America, Inc., Philadelphia.
TUCK, L.M. 1968. Dowitcher breeding in Ontario. Ont.Field Biol. 21:39.
TUCK, L.M. 1972. The snipes: a study of the genus *Capella*. Can.Wildl.Serv.Monogr.Ser. No. 5.
TUFTS, R.W. 1986. Birds of Nova Scotia. 3rd ed. Nimbus Publ. and Nova Scotia Mus., Halifax.
TURISK, M. 2000. Breeding record of Great Gray Owl in Bruce County: southernmost in Canada. Ontario Birds 18:44-45.
TWEDT, D.J., and R.D. CRAWFORD. 1995. Yellow-headed Blackbird (*Xanthocephalus xanthocephalus*). *In* The Birds of North America, No. 192 (A. Poole and F. Gill, Eds.). Academy of Natural Sciences, Philadelphia, and American Ornithologists' Union, Washington, DC.

U.S. FISH AND WILDLIFE SERVICE. 2003. New York, eastern Ontario, and southern Quebec waterfowl breeding population survey 2003. U.S. Fish and Wildlife Service, Laurel. http://www.fws.gov/migratory-birds/reports/wps03/eont.pdf.

U.S. FISH AND WILDLIFE SERVICE. 2005. Waterfowl population status, 2005. U.S. Department of the Interior, Washington, DC.

U.S. FISH AND WILDLIFE SERVICE. 2006. Waterfowl Population Status, 2006. http://www.fws.gov/migratorybirds ed. U.S. Department of the Interior, Washington, DC.

VALLENDER, R., V.L. FRIESEN, R.J. ROBERTSON, and I.J. LOVETTE. 2007. Complex hybridization dynamics between Golden-winged and Blue-winged Warblers (*Vermivora chrysoptera* and *V. pinus*) revealed by AFLP, microsatellite, intron and mtDNA markers. Mol.Ecol. 16:2017-2029.

VAN DER VEEN, H.E. 1973. Some aspects of the breeding biology and demography of the Double-crested Cormorant (*Phalacrocorax auritus*) of Mandarte Island. Zoologisch Laboratorium der Rijksuniversiteit te Groningen, Groningen.

VAN SLEEUWEN, M. 2006. Natural Fire Regimes in Ontario. Ontario Ministry of Natural Resources, Ontario Parks, Peterborough.

VANA-MILLER, S. L. 1987. Habitat suitability index models: Osprey. 154 pp. U.S. Geological Survey.

VARRIN, R.J., J. BOWMAN, and P.A. GRAY. 2007. The known and potential effects of climate change on biodiversity in Ontario's terrestrial ecosystems: case studies and recommendations for adaptation. Climate Change Research Report No. 9. Applied Research and Development Branch, Ontario Ministry of Natural Resources, Sault Ste. Marie.

VERBEEK, N.A.M., and C. CAFFREY. 2002. American Crow (*Corvus brachyrhynchos*). In The Birds of North America, No. 647 (A. Poole and F. Gill, Eds.). The Birds of North America, Inc., Philadelphia.

VERBEEK, N.A.M., and P. HENDRICKS. 1994. American Pipit (*Anthus rubescens*). In The Birds of North America, No. 95 (A. Poole and F. Gill, Eds.). Academy of Natural Sciences, Philadelphia, and American Ornithologists' Union, Washington, DC.

VERNER, J. 1964. Evolution of polygamy in the Long-billed Marsh Wren. Evolution 18:252-261.

VICKERY, J.A., J.R. TALLOWIN, R.E. FEBER, E.J. ASTERAKI, P.W. ATKINSON, R.J. FULLER, and V.K. BROWN. 2001. The management of lowland neutral grasslands in Britain: effects of agricultural practices on birds and their food resources. J.Appl.Ecol. 38:647-664.

VICKERY, P.D. 1996. Grasshopper Sparrow (*Ammodramus savannarum*). In The Birds of North America, No. 239 (A. Poole and F. Gill, Eds.). Academy of Natural Sciences, Philadelphia, and American Ornithologists' Union, Washington, DC.

VILLARD, P. 1994. Foraging behaviour of Black-backed and Three-toed Woodpeckers during spring and summer in a Canadian boreal forest. Can.J.Zool. 72:1957-1959.

VON MORS, I., and Y. BÉGIN. 1993. Shoreline shrub population extension in response to recent isostatic rebound in eastern Hudson Bay, Quebec, Canada. Arct.Alp.Res 25:15-23.

VOROS S. 2006. Southern Ontario Land Resource Information System (SOLRIS): treed areas by upper tier. Ontario Ministry of Natural Resources Southern Region Planning Unit, Peterborough.

WAITE, T.A., and D. STRICKLAND. 1997. Cooperative breeding in Gray Jays: philopatric offspring provision juvenile siblings. Condor 99:523-525.

WAITE, T.A., and D. STRICKLAND. 2006. Climate change and the demographic demise of a hoarding bird living on the edge. Proc.R.Soc.B. 273:2809-2813.

WALK, J.W., and R.E. WARNER. 1999. Effects of habitat area on the occurrence of grassland birds in Illinois. Amer.Midl.Nat. 141:339-344.

WALKER, J. 2004. Third reported nest of Solitary Sandpiper in Ontario. Ontario Birds 22:31-33.

WALKINSHAW, L.H. 1968. *Passerherbulus caudacutus* (Latham). Le Conte's Sparrow. Pp. 765-776 in Life histories of North American cardinals, grosbeaks, buntings, towhees, finches, sparrows, and allies, part 2 (O.L Austin, Jr., Ed.). Bull. U.S. Natl. Mus. No. 237.

WALTERS, E.L., E.H. MILLER, and P.E. LOWTHER. 2002. Yellow-bellied Sapsucker (*Sphyrapicus varius*). In The Birds of North America, No. 662 (A. Poole and F. Gill, Eds.). The Birds of North America, Inc., Philadelphia.

WARKENTIN, I.G., and P.C. JAMES. 1988. Nest-site selection by urban Merlins. Condor 90:734-738.

WARKENTIN, I.G., N.S. SODHI, R.H.M. ESPIE, A.F. POOLE , L.W. OLIPHANT, and P.C. JAMES. 2005. Merlin (*Falco columbarius*). The Birds of North America Online (A. Poole, Ed.). Cornell Laboratory of Ornithology. Retrieved from The Birds of North America Online Database, Ithaca. http://bna.birds.cornell.edu/BNA/account/Merlin/.

WARNOCK, N.D., and R.E. GILL. 1996. Dunlin (*Calidris alpina*). In The Birds of North America, No. 203 (A. Poole and F. Gill, Eds.). Academy of Natural Sciences, Philadelphia, and American Ornithologists' Union, Washington, DC.

WATT, W., J. BAKER, D. HOGG, J.G. MCNICOL, and B. NAYLOR. 1996. Forest management guidelines for the provision of marten habitat. Version 1.0. Queen's Printer for Ontario. http://ontariosforests.mnr.gov.on.ca/ontariosforests.cfm.

WATTS, B.D. 1995. Yellow-crowned Night-Heron (*Nyctanassa violacea*). In The Birds of North America, No. 161 (A. Poole and F. Gill, Eds.). Academy of Natural Sciences, Philadelphia, and American Ornithologists' Union, Washington, DC.

WEATHERHEAD, P.J. 2005. Long-term decline in a Red-winged Blackbird population: ecological causes and sexual selection consequences. Proc.-R.Soc.Lond., Bio.Sci. 272:2313-2317.

WEAVER, J.E. 1989. On the ecology of Wild Turkeys reintroduced in southern Ontario. M.Sc. thesis, University of Western Ontario, London.

WECKSTEIN, J.D., D.E. KROODSMA, and R.C. FAUCETT. 2002. Fox Sparrow (*Passerella iliaca*). The Birds of North America Online (A. Poole, Ed.). Cornell Laboratory of Ornithology. Retrieved from The Birds of North America Online Database, Ithaca. http://bna.birds.cornell.edu/BNA/account/Fox_Sparrow/.

WEEKS, H.P., JR. 1994. Eastern Phoebe (*Sayornis phoebe*). The Birds of North America Online (A. Poole, Ed.). Cornell Laboratory of Ornithology. Retrieved from The Birds of North America Online Database, Ithaca. http://bna.birds.cornell.edu/BNA/account/Eastern_Phoebe/

WEIGAND, J.P. 1980. Ecology of the Hungarian Partridge in north-central Montana. Wildlife Monogr. 74.

WEIR, R.D. 1988. The nesting season. Ontario Region. Amer.Birds 42:1281-1286.

WEIR, R.D. 1989. Birds of the Kingston region. Kingston Field Naturalists, Kingston.

WELSH, D.A. 1971. Breeding and territoriality of the Palm Warbler in a Nova Scotia bog. Can.Field-Nat. 85:31-37.

WELSH, D.A., and D.R. FILLMAN. 1980. The impact of forest cutting on boreal bird populations. Amer.Birds 34:84-94.

WENINK, P.W. 1994. Mitochondrial DNA sequence evolution in shorebird populations. Ph.D. dissertation, Wageningen Agric. Univ., Wageningen, The Netherlands.

WESELOH, C., and H. BLOKPOEL. 1983.

Precautions for a rare visitor. Seasons 23:42-43.

WESELOH, D.V. 1984. Characteristics of a Greater Black-backed Gull colony on Lake Ontario, New York, 1981-1983. The Kingbird 34:91-95.

WESELOH, D.V., C. PEKARIK, R. JOOS, J. FARQUHAR, L. SHUTT, T. HAVELKA, I. MAZZOCCHI, G. BARRETT, R. MCCOLLOUGH, R.L. MILLER, and A. MATHERS. 2003. Monitoring Lake Ontario's waterbirds: contaminants in Herring Gull eggs and population changes in the Lake's nearly 1,000,000 colonial waterbirds. Pp. 597-631 *in* State of Lake Ontario (SOLO) – past, present and future (M. Munawa, Ed.). Ecovision World Monograph Series, 2003 Aquatic Ecosystem Health & Management Society Backhuys Publishers, Leiden, The Netherlands.

WESELOH, D.V., S.M. TEEPLE, and H. BLOKPOEL. 1988. The distribution and status of colonial waterbirds nesting in western Lake Erie. Pp. 134-144 *in* Biogeography of the island region of western Lake Erie. (J.F. Downhower, Ed.). Ohio State University Press, Columbus.

WESELOH, D.V.C. 1994. A history of the Little Gull (Larus minutus) in Ontario, 1930-1991. *In* Ornithology in Ontario. Spec.Publ. No. 1 (M.K. McNicholl, and J.L. Cranmer-Byng, Eds.). Ontario Field Ornithologists. Hawk Owl Publishing, Whitby.

WESELOH, D.V.C. 2004. The threat to Black-crowned Night-Heron colonies from nesting Double-crested Cormorants on the lower Great Lakes: a protocol and assessment. Canadian Wildlife Service, Downsview.

WESELOH, D.V.C. 2007. Discovery and nesting of the Little Gull on North Limestone Island, Georgian Bay, Lake Huron, 1979-1991. Ontario Birds 25:90-113.

WESELOH, D.V.C., P.J. EWINS, J. STRUGER, P. MINEAU, C.A. BISHOP, S. POSTUPALSKY, and J.P. LUDWIG. 1995. Double-crested Cormorants of the Great Lakes: changes in population size, breeding distribution and reproductive output between 1913 and 1991. Colon.Waterbirds 18, Spec.Pub. 1: The Double-crested Cormorant: biology, conservation and management: 48-59.

WESELOH, D.V.C., T. HAVELKA, F.J. CUTHBERT, and S. HANISH. 2006. The 2005 Great Lakes-wide census of nesting Double-crested Cormorants: Draft Report of Results. Canadian Wildlife Service, Downsview.

WESELOH, D.V.C., K.D. HUGHES, P.J. EWINS, D. BEST, T.J. KUBIAK, and M.C. SHIELDCASTLE. 2002. Herring Gulls and Great Black-backed Gulls as indicators of contaminants in Bald Eagles in Lake Ontario. Environ.Toxicol.Chem. 21:1015-1025.

WESELOH, D.V.C., C. PEKARIK, T. HAVELKA, G. BARRETT, and J. REID. 2002. Population trends and colony locations of Double-crested Cormorants in the Canadian Great Lakes and immediately adjacent areas, 1990-2000: a manager's guide. J.Great Lakes Res. 28:125-144.

WEST, R.L., and G.K. HESS. 2002. Purple Gallinule (*Porphyrula martinica*). *In* The Birds of North America, No. 626 (A. Poole and F. Gill, Eds.). The Birds of North America, Inc., Philadelphia.

WHEELWRIGHT, N.T., and J.D. RISING. 1993. Savannah Sparrow (*Passerculus sandwichensis*). *In* The Birds of North America, No. 45 (A. Poole and F. Gill, Eds.). Academy of Natural Sciences, Philadelphia, and American Ornithologists' Union, Washington, DC.

WHITAKER, D.M., W.A. MONTEVECCHI, and J.W. GOSSE. 1996. Breeding season irruptions of Rough-legged Hawks (*Buteo lagopus*) on insular Newfoundland. Arctic 49:306-310.

WHITE, A.W. 1986. Collared-Dove: the next new North American species? Birding 18:150-152.

WHITE, C.M., N.J. CLUM, T.J. CADE, and W.G. HUNT. 2002. Peregrine Falcon (*Falco peregrinus*). The Birds of North America Online (A. Poole, Ed.). Cornell Laboratory of Ornithology. Retrieved from The Birds of North America Online Database, Ithaca. http://bna.birds.cornell.edu/BNA/account/Peregrine_Falcon/.

WHITEHEAD, D.R., and T. TAYLOR. 2002. Acadian Flycatcher (*Empidonax virescens*). *In* The Birds of North America, No. 614 (A. Poole and F. Gill, Eds.). The Birds of North America, Inc., Philadelphia.

WHITELAW, C.J. 1998. Northern Owls in Sudbury and Manitoulin Districts: high numbers, out of season occurrences and breeding. Ontario Birds 16:1-4.

WIGGINS, D.A. 2004. Short-eared Owl (*Asio flammeus*): a technical conservation assessment. USDA Forest Service, Rocky Mountain Region.

WIGGINS, D.A., D.W. HOLT, and S.M. LEASURE. 2006. Short-eared Owl. (*Asio flammeus*). The Birds of North America Online (A. Poole, Ed.).Cornell Laboratory of Ornithology. Retreived from The Birds of North America Online Database, Ithaca. http://bna.birds.cornell.edu/BNA/account/Short-eared_Owl/.

WILBUR, S.R. 1983. The status of vultures in the western hemisphere. Pp. 113-123 *in* Vulture biology and management (S.R. Wilbur and J.A. Jackson, Eds.). University of California Press, Los Angeles.

WILEY, R.H., and D.S. LEE. 1999. Parasitic Jaeger (*Stercorarius parasiticus*). *In* The Birds of North America, No. 445 (A. Poole and F. Gill, Eds.). The Birds of North America, Inc., Philadelphia.

WILKINS, K.A., M.C. OTTO, and M.D. KONEFF. 2006. Trends in duck breeding populations, 1955-2006. U.S. Fish and Wildlife Service, Laurel. http://www.fws.gov/migratorybirds/reports/status06/final%20trend%20report%20bw.pdf.

WILLIAMS, J.M. 1996a. Nashville Warbler (*Vermivora ruficapilla*). *In* The Birds of North America, No. 205 (A. Poole and F. Gill, Eds.). Academy of Natural Sciences, Philadelphia, and American Ornithologists' Union, Washington, DC.

WILLIAMS, J.M. 1996b. Bay-breasted Warbler (*Dendroica castanea*). *In* The Birds of North America, No. 206 (A. Poole and F. Gill, Eds.). Academy of Natural Sciences, Philadelphia, and American Ornithologists' Union, Washington, DC.

WILSON, A. 1814. American ornithology; or, the natural history of the birds of the United States, vol. 9. Bradford and Inskeep, Philadelphia.

WILSON, N.C., and D. MCRAE. 1993 Unpubl. Seasonal and geographical distribution of birds for selected sites in Ontario's Hudson Bay Lowland. Ontario Ministry of Natural Resources, Toronto.

WILSON, W.H., JR. 1996. Palm Warbler (*Dendroica palmarum*). *In* The Birds of North America, No. 238 (A. Poole and F. Gill, Eds.). Academy of Natural Sciences, Philadelphia, and American Ornithologists' Union, Washington, DC.

WINKLER, D.W. 1996. California Gull (*Larus californicus*). *In* The Birds of North America, No. 259 (A. Poole and F. Gill, Eds.). Academy of Natural Sciences, Philadelphia, and American Ornithologists' Union, Washington, DC.

WINTER, L. and G.E. WALLACE. 2006. Impacts of feral and free-ranging cats on bird species of conservation concern: a five-state review of New York, New Jersey, Florida, California, and Hawaii. American Bird Conservancy, The Plains.

WINTER, M., J.A. SHAFFER, D.H. JOHNSON, T.M. DONOVAN, W.D. SVEDARSKI, P.W. JONES, and B.R. EULISS. 2005. Habitat and nesting of Le Conte's Sparrows in the northern tallgrass prairie. J.Field Ornithol. 76:61-71.

WINTERHALDER, K. 1995. Natural recovery of vascular plant communities on the industrial barrens of the Sudbury area. Pp. 93-102 *in* Restoration and recovery of an industrial region (J.M. Gunn, Ed.).

Springer-Verlag, New York.

WITMER, M.C. 2002. Bohemian Waxwing (*Bombycilla garrulus*). In The Birds of North America, No. 714 (A. Poole and F. Gill, Eds.). The Birds of North America, Inc., Philadelphia.

WITMER, M.C., D.J. MOUNTJOY, and L. ELLIOT. 1997. Cedar Waxwing (*Bombycilla cedrorum*). In The Birds of North America, No. 309 (A. Poole and F. Gill, Eds.). Academy of Natural Sciences, Philadelphia, and American Ornithologists' Union, Washington, DC.

WOOD, A.A. 1948 Unpubl. The birds of Kent County, Ontario.

WOODIN, M.C., and T.C. MICHOT. 2002. Redhead (*Aythya americana*). In The Birds of North America, No. 695 (A. Poole and F. Gill, Eds.). The Birds of North America, Inc., Philadelphia.

WOOTTON, J.T. 1996. Purple Finch (*Carpodacus purpureus*). In The Birds of North America, No. 208 (A. Poole and F. Gill, Eds.). Academy of Natural Sciences, Philadelphia, and American Ornithologists' Union, Washington, DC.

WORMINGTON, A. 2002. Chuck-will's-widow: a nest is found! Point Pelee Natural History News 2.

WORMINGTON, A. 2006. The breeding birds of Point Pelee National Park, with an emphasis on Species-at-Risk. Unpubl. report. Parks Canada, Leamington.

WOTTON, M., K. LOGAN, and R. MCALPINE. 2005. Climate change and the future fire environment in Ontario: fire occurrence and fire management impacts in Ontario under a changing climate. Ontario Ministry of Natural Resources, Sault Ste. Marie.

WRIGHT, H.W. 1921. The Mockingbird in the Boston Region and in New England and Canada. Auk 38:382-432.

WRIGHT, R.G., R.N. PAISLEY, and J.F. KUBISIAK. 1996. Survival of Wild Turkey hens in southwestern Wisconsin. J.Wildl.Manage. 60:313-320.

WYATT, V.E., and C.M. FRANCIS. 2002. Rose-breasted Grosbeak (*Pheucticus ludovicianus*). In The Birds of North America, No. 692 (A. Poole and F. Gill, Eds.). The Birds of North America, Inc., Philadelphia.

YEATTER, R.E. 1934. The Hungarian Partridge in the Great Lakes region. University of Michigan School of Forestry and Conservation Bulletin No. 5: 1-92.

YOSEF, R. 1994. The effects of fencelines on the reproductive success of Loggerhead Shrikes. Conserv.Biol. 8:281-285.

YOUNG, K.E. 1983. Seasonal and temporal patterning of Common Loon (*Gavia immer*) vocalizations. M.Sc. thesis, Syracuse University, Syracuse.

ZIMMERLING, J.R. 2005. Detectability of nonpasserines using "pishing" in eastern Ontario woodlands. Can.Field-Nat. 119:377-380.

ZIMMERLING, J.R. 2006. Why birds and birders flock to sewage lagoons. Birdwatch Canada 36:4-7.

ZIMMERLING, J.R., J.R. FISHER, C.D. ANKNEY, and C.A. DEBRUYNE. 2006. Mallard use of hen houses in eastern Ontario. Avian Conservation and Ecology 2:6.

ZINK, R.M., S. ROHWER, A.V. ANDREEV, and D.L. DITTMAN. 1995. Trans-Beringia comparisons of mitochondrial DNA differentiation in birds. Condor 97:639-649.

Index of English, French, and Scientific Names

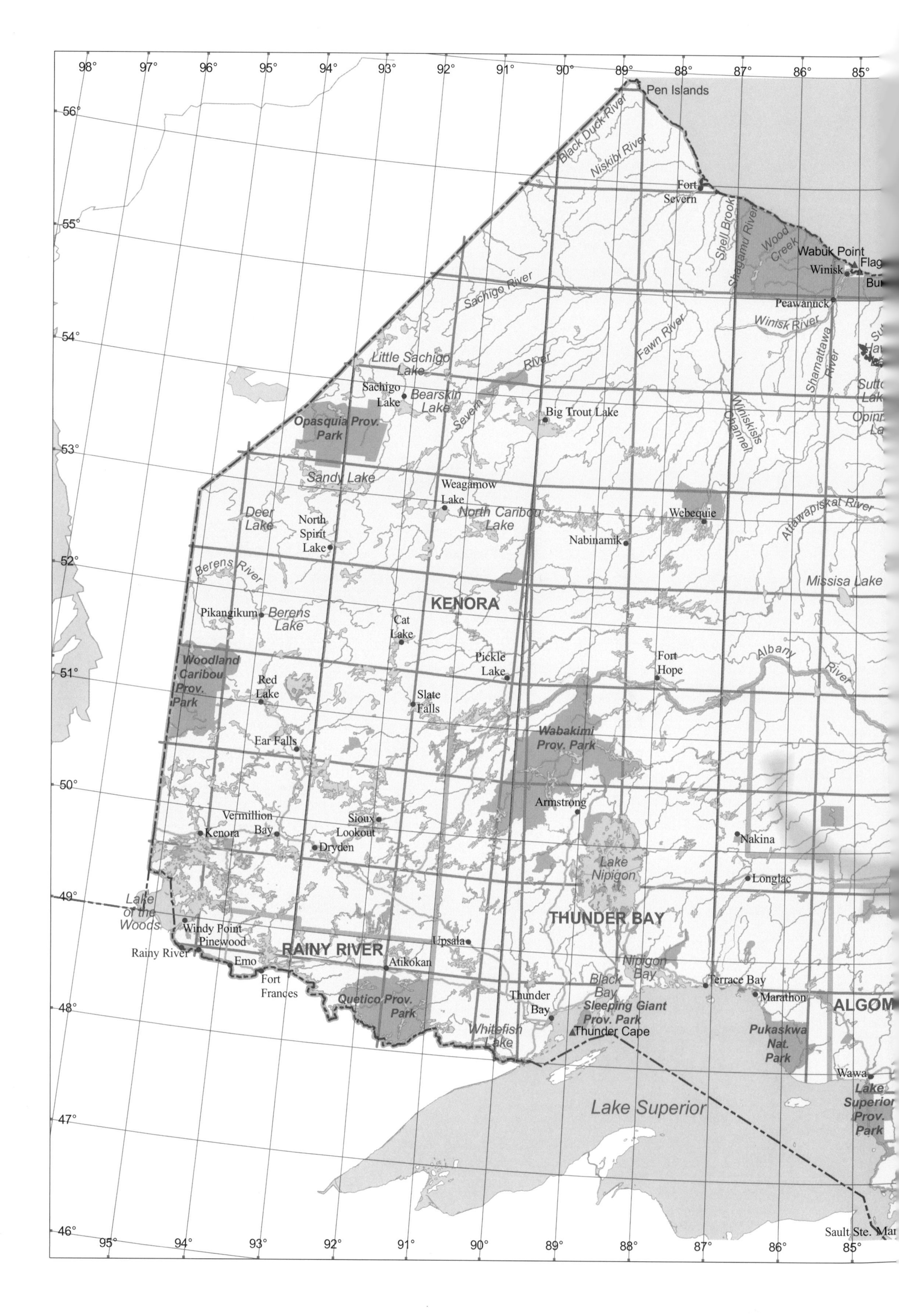

Pen Islands
Black Duck River
Niskibi River
Fort Severn
Shell Brook
Shagamu River
Wood Creek
Wabuk Point
Winisk
Peawanuck
Sachigo River
Winisk River
Fawn River
Shamattawa River
Little Sachigo Lake
Severn River
Sachigo Lake
Bearskin Lake
Big Trout Lake
Opasquia Prov. Park
Winiskisis Channel
Sandy Lake
Weagamow Lake
North Caribou Lake
Webequie
Attawapiskat River
Deer Lake
North Spirit Lake
Nabinamik
Berens River
Mississa Lake
KENORA
Pikangikum
Berens Lake
Cat Lake
Pickle Lake
Fort Hope
Albany River
Woodland Caribou Prov. Park
Red Lake
Slate Falls
Wabakimi Prov. Park
Ear Falls
Armstrong
Vermillion Bay
Sioux Lookout
Kenora
Dryden
Nakina
Lake Nipigon
Longlac
Lake of the Woods
Windy Point
Pinewood
Rainy River
THUNDER BAY
Upsala
RAINY RIVER
Emo
Atikokan
Nipigon Bay
Fort Frances
Black Bay
Terrace Bay
Marathon
Quetico Prov. Park
Thunder Bay
Sleeping Giant Prov. Park
Thunder Cape
Whitefish Lake
Pukaskwa Nat. Park
Wawa
Lake Superior
Lake Superior Prov. Park
Sault Ste. Mar